# THE COMPLETE WORKS OF
# GEOFFREY CHAUCER

OXFORD UNIVERSITY PRESS
AMEN HOUSE, E.C. 4
LONDON EDINBURGH GLASGOW
LEIPZIG NEW YORK TORONTO
MELBOURNE CAPETOWN BOMBAY
CALCUTTA MADRAS SHANGHAI
HUMPHREY MILFORD
PUBLISHER TO THE
UNIVERSITY

GEOFFREY CHAUCER

*From MS. Harl. 4866*

# THE COMPLETE WORKS OF
# GEOFFREY CHAUCER

Edited from numerous manuscripts by
## WALTER W. SKEAT

LONDON
OXFORD UNIVERSITY PRESS
HUMPHREY MILFORD
1933

821
C

PRINTED IN GREAT BRITAIN

O.S.A.

AMPLISSIMO PHILOSOPHORVM

ACADEMIAE FRIDERICIANAE HALENSIS

CVM VITEBERGENSI CONSOCIATAE ORDINI

CVIVS EX DECRETO

DIE III. M. AVGVSTI A. MDCCCXCIV

QVO DIE SACRA BISAECVLARIA VNIVERSITATIS

SOLEMNITER PERAGEBANTVR

AD GRADVM DOCTORIS HONORIS CAVSA

PROVECTVS SVM

HVNC LIBRVM GRATO ANIMO

DO DEDICO

# CONTENTS.

INTRODUCTION :—
                                                PAGE

LIFE OF CHAUCER . . . . . . . . . . . . . xii

WRITINGS OF CHAUCER AND EARLY EDITIONS . . . . . . . xvi

BRIEF ACCOUNT OF THE GRAMMAR, METRE, VERSIFICATION, AND PRONUN-
    CIATION . . . . . . . . . . . . xviii

ROMAUNT OF THE ROSE : Fragment A . . . . . . . . . 1

    ,,     ,,     Fragment B . . . . . . . . 18

    ,,     ,,     Fragment C . . . . . . . . 59

THE MINOR POEMS :—

    I. An A. B. C. . . . . . . . . . . 79

    II. The Compleynte unto Pite . . . . . . . 81

    III. The Book of the Duchesse . . . . . . . 83

    IV. The Compleynt of Mars . . . . . . . . 97

    V. The Parlement of Foules . . . . . . . 101

    VI. A Compleint to his Lady . . . . . . . 111

    VII. Anelida and Arcite . . . . . . . . . 113

    VIII. Chaucers Wordes unto Adam . . . . . . 118

    IX. The Former Age . . . . . . . . . 118

    X. Fortune . . . . . . . . . . . 119

    XI. Merciles Beaute . . . . . . . . . 121

    XII. To Rosemounde : A Balade . . . . . . 121

    XIII. Truth . . . . . . . . . . . 122

    XIV. Gentilesse . . . . . . . . . . 122

    XV. Lak of Stedfastnesse . . . . . . . . 123

    XVI. Lenvoy de Chaucer a Scogan . . . . . . 123

    XVII. Lenvoy de Chaucer a Bukton . . . . . 124

    XVIII. The Compleynt of Venus . . . . . . 125

    XIX. The Compleint of Chaucer to his Empty Purse . . . 126

    XX. Proverbs . . . . . . . . . . 126

    XXI. Against Women Unconstant . . . . . . 127

    XXII. An Amorous Compleint (Compleint Damours) . . . 127

    XXIII. A Balade of Compleynt . . . . . . . 129

    XXIV. Womanly Noblesse . . . . . . . . 129

# Contents.

|  |  | PAGE |
| --- | --- | --- |
| BOETHIUS DE CONSOLATIONE PHILOSOPHIE | . . . . . . . . | 130 |
| TROILUS AND CRISEYDE | . . . . . . . . . | 206 |
| THE HOUS OF FAME | . . . . . . . . . . | 326 |
| THE LEGEND OF GOOD WOMEN | . . . . . . . . | 349 |
| A TREATISE ON THE ASTROLABE | . . . . . . . | 396 |

THE CANTERBURY TALES :—

| GROUP A. | The Prologue . | . . . . . . . . . | 419 |
| | The Knightes Tale . | . . . . . . . . | 430 |
| | The Miller's Prologue | . . . . . . . . | 457 |
| | The Milleres Tale . | . . . . . . . . | 459 |
| | The Reeve's Prologue | . . . . . . . . | 467 |
| | The Reves Tale . | . . . . . . . . | 468 |
| | The Cook's Prologue | . . . . . . . . | 474 |
| | The Cokes Tale . | . . . . . . . . | 474 |

| GROUP B. | INTRODUCTION TO THE MAN OF LAW'S PROLOGUE . | . . . | 475 |
| | The Prologue of the Mannes Tale of Lawe . | . . . | 476 |
| | The Tale of the Man of Lawe | . . . . . | 477 |
| | The Shipman's Prologue | . . . . . . | 492 |
| | The Shipmannes Tale . | . . . . . . | 492 |
| | The Prioress's Prologue | . . . . . . | 498 |
| | The Prioresses Tale | . . . . . . . | 498 |
| | Prologue to Sir Thopas . | . . . . . . | 502 |
| | Sir Thopas . | . . . . . . . | 502 |
| | Prologue to Melibeus | . . . . . . . | 505 |
| | The Tale of Melibeus | . . . . . . . | 505 |
| | The Monk's Prologue | . . . . . . . | 530 |
| | The Monkes Tale : — Lucifer. Adam. Sampson. Hercules. Nabugodonosor. Balthasar. Cenobia. De Petro rege Ispannie. De Petro Rege de Cipro. De Barnabo de Lumbardia. De Hugelino. Nero. De Oloferno. De Rege Anthiocho. De Alexandro. De Iulio Cesare. Cresus | . | 531 |
| | The Prologue of the Nonne Prestes Tale | . . . | 542 |
| | The Nonne Preestes Tale | . . . . . | 543 |
| | Epilogue to the Nonne Preestes Tale | . . . . | 551 |

| GROUP C. | The Phisiciens Tale | . . . . . . . | 551 |
| | The Prologue of the Pardoneres Tale . | . . . . | 556 |
| | The Pardoneres Tale | . . . . . . | 558 |

# Contents.

PAGE

GROUP D. The Wife of Bath's Prologue . . . . . . . 565
The Tale of the Wyf of Bathe . . . . . . 576
The Friar's Prologue . . . . . . . . 581
The Freres Tale . . . . . . . . . 582
The Somnour's Prologue . . . . . . . 587
The Somnours Tale . . . . . . . . 588

GROUP E. The Clerk's Prologue . . . . . . . . 596
The Clerkes Tale . . . . . . . . . 597
The Merchant's Prologue . . . . . . . 612
The Marchantes Tale . . . . . . . . 613
Epilogue to the Marchantes Tale . . . . . . 627

GROUP F. The Squieres Tale . . . . . . . . . 628
The Wordes of the Franklin . . . . . . 636
The Franklin's Prologue . . . . . . . 637
The Frankeleyns Tale . . . . . . . . 637

GROUP G. The Seconde Nonnes Tale . . . . . . . 649
The Canon's Yeoman's Prologue . . . . . . 657
The Chanouns Yemannes Tale . . . . . . 659

GROUP H. The Manciple's Prologue . . . . . . . 669
The Maunciples Tale . . . . . . . . 670

GROUP I. The Parson's Prologue . . . . . . . . 674
The Persones Tale . . . . . . . . . 675

APPENDIX: VARIATIONS AND EMENDATIONS . . . . . . . 719

GLOSSARY TO CHAUCER'S WORKS . . . . . . . . . . 1

GLOSSARY TO FRAGMENTS B AND C OF THE ROMAUNT OF THE ROSE . . . 133

# INTRODUCTION.

## LIFE OF CHAUCER.

GEOFFREY CHAUCER was born in London, about 1340 (not 1328, as was formerly said). His father was John Chaucer, citizen and vintner of London, and his mother's name was Agnes. His grandfather was Robert Chaucer, of Ipswich and London, who married a widow named Maria Heyroun, with a son Thomas Heyroun. John Chaucer's house stood in Upper Thames Street, beside Walbrook, just where that street is now crossed by the South-Eastern Railway from Cannon-street Station. Here it was that the poet spent his earliest days, and in an interesting passage in his Pardoneres Tale (lines 549 572), he incidentally displays his knowledge of various wines and the ways of mixing them together.

John Chaucer, the poet's father, was in attendance on Edward III. in 1338, and this connexion with the court led to his son's employment there, some years after-wards, as a page in the household of Elizabeth, wife of Lionel, duke of Clarence, the third son of Edward III. In the household accounts of this princess, mention is made of various articles of clothing and other necessaries purchased for ' Geoffrey Chaucer' in April, May, and December, 1357, when he was about seventeen years old. In 1359, he joined the army of Edward III. when that king invaded France, and was there taken prisoner. In May, 1360, the peace of Bretigny (near Chartres) was concluded between the French and English kings. Chaucer had been set at liberty in March, when Edward paid 16l. towards his ransom.

**1367.** We can only conjecture the manner in which he spent his life from hints given us in his own works, and from various notices of him in official records. To consider the latter first, we find, from the Issue Rolls of the Exchequer, that a life-pension of 20 marks was granted by the king to Chaucer in 1367, in consideration of his services, as being one of the valets of the king's household. During 1368 and part of 1369 he was in London, and received his pension in person. In October, 1368, his patron, Prince Lionel, died, and it appears that Chaucer's services were consequently transferred to the next brother, John of Gaunt, duke of Lancaster.

**1369.** In the autumn of 1369, the year of the third great pestilence of Edward's reign, Blanche, the first wife of John of Gaunt, died at the early age of twenty-nine. Chaucer did honour to her memory in one of his earliest poems, entitled 'The Deth of Blaunche the Duchesse.'

**1370–1373.** From 1370 to 1386, Chaucer was attached to the court, and employed in frequent diplomatic services.

In December, 1372, being employed in the king's service, he left England for Genoa, Pisa, and Florence, and remained in Italy for nearly eleven months, but we again find him in London on November 22, 1373. This visit of his to Italy is of great importance, as it exercised a marked influence on his writings, and enables us to understand the development of his genius.

**1374.** His conduct during this mission to Italy met with the full approval of the king, who, on the celebration of the great festival at Windsor on St. George's day (April 23) in 1374, granted our poet a pitcher of wine daily, to be received from the king's butler. On May 10 of the same year, Chaucer took a lease of a house in Aldgate, for the term of his life, from the Corporation of London ; but he afterwards gave it up to a friend in October, 1386 ; and it is probable that he had ceased to reside in it for a year or more previously. On June 8, 1374, he was appointed to the important office of Comptroller of the Customs and Subsidy of Wools, Skins, and Leather, for the port of London ; and a few days later (June 13) received a life-pension of 10*l.* from the duke of Lancaster for the good service rendered by him and his wife Philippa to the said Duke, to his consort, and to his mother the Queen. This is the first mention of Philippa Chaucer as Geoffrey's wife, though a Philippa Chaucer is mentioned as one of the Ladies of the Chamber to Queen Philippa, on September 12, 1366, and subsequently. It has been conjectured that Chaucer was not married till 1374, and that he married a relative, or at least some one bearing the same name as himself ; but this supposition is needless and improbable ; there is no reason why the Philippa Chaucer mentioned in 1366 may not have been already married to the poet, who was then at least 26 years of age.

**1375.** In 1375 his income was increased by receiving from the Crown (November 8) the custody of the lands and person of one Edmond Staplegate, of Kent. This he retained for three years, during which he received 104*l.* ; together with some smaller sums from another source.

**1376.** On July 12, 1376, the king granted Chaucer the sum of 71*l.* 4*s.* 6*d.*, being the value of a fine paid by one John Kent for shipping wool without paying the duty thereon. Towards the end of this year, Sir John Burley and Geoffrey Chaucer were employed upon some secret service, for which the latter received 6*l.* 13*s.* 4*d.*

**1377.** In February, 1377, Chaucer was employed on a secret mission to Flanders, and received for it, in all, the sum of 30*l.* In April he was sent to France, to treat for peace with king Charles V. ; for this service he received, in all, the sum of 48*l.* 13*s.* 4*d.* On June 21, king Edward III. died, and was succeeded by his grandson, Richard II.

**1378.** In January, Chaucer seems to have been employed in France. Soon afterwards, he was again sent to Italy, from May 28 to September 19, being employed on a mission to Lombardy, to treat with Bernabo Visconti, duke of Milan ; to whose death (in 1385) the poet alludes in his Monkes Tale (ll. 3589–3596), where he describes him as—

> 'Of Melan grete Barnabo Viscounte,
> God of delyt, and scourge of Lumbardye.'

Before leaving England on this business, Chaucer appointed his friend John Gower, the poet, as one of his agents to represent him in his absence.

**1380.** By deed of May 1, 1380, one Cecilia Chaumpayne released Chaucer from a charge which she had brought against him, 'de raptu meo.' We have no means of ascertaining either the nature of the charge, or the circumstances of the case.

**1382.** We have seen that Chaucer had been appointed Comptroller of the Wool

Customs in 1374. Whilst still retaining this office, he was now also appointed Comptroller of the Petty Customs (May 8, 1382).

**1385.** In February, 1385, he was allowed the great privilege of nominating a permanent deputy to perform his duties as Comptroller. It is highly probable that he owed this favour to 'the good queen Anne,' first wife of king Richard II.; for, in the Prologue to the Legend of Good Women, probably written during this period of his newly-acquired freedom from irksome duties, he expresses himself most gratefully towards her.

If we may trust the description of his house and garden in the Prologue to the Legend of Good Women, probably composed in the spring of 1385, it would appear that he was then living in the country, and had already given up his house over the city gate at Aldgate to Richard Forster, who obtained a formal lease of it from the Corporation of London in October, 1386. We learn incidentally, from a note to the Envoy to Scogan, l. 45, that he was living at Greenwich at the time when he wrote that poem (probably in 1393). And it is highly probable that Chaucer's residence at Greenwich extended from 1385 to the end of 1399, when he took a new house at Westminster. This supposition agrees well with various hints that we obtain from other notices. Thus, in 1390, he was appointed (with five others) to superintend the repairing of the banks of the Thames between Woolwich and Greenwich. In the same year he was robbed at Hatcham (as we shall see below), which is near Deptford and Greenwich. And we find the singular reference in the Canterbury Tales (A 3907), where the Host suddenly exclaims—' Lo ! Grenewich, ther many a shrewe is inne'; which looks like a sly insinuation, on the Host's part, that Greenwich at that time contained many 'shrews' or rascals. Few places would serve better than Greenwich for frequent observation of Canterbury pilgrims.

**1386.** In this year Chaucer was elected a knight of the shire for Kent, in the Parliament held at Westminster. In August, his patron John of Gaunt went to Spain ; and during his absence, his brother Thomas, duke of Gloucester, contrived to deprive the king of all power, by appointing a regency of eleven persons, himself being at the head of them. As the duke of Gloucester was ill disposed towards his brother John, it is probable that we can thus account for the fact that, in December of this year, Chaucer was dismissed from both his offices, of Comptroller of Wool and Comptroller of Petty Customs, others being appointed in his place. This sudden and great loss reduced the poet from comparative wealth to poverty ; he was compelled to raise money upon his pensions, which were assigned to John Scalby on May 1, 1388.

In October of this year (1386), there was a famous trial between Richard Lord Scrope and Sir Thomas Grosvenor, during which Chaucer deposed that he was 'forty years of age and upwards, and had borne arms for twenty-seven years.' He was, in fact, about forty-six years old, having been born, as said above, about 1340. Moreover, it is probable that he first bore arms in 1359, when he went with the invading army to France. This exactly tallies with his own statement.

**1387.** In this year died Chaucer's wife, Philippa ; to this loss he alludes in his Envoy to Bukton. It must have been about this time that he was composing portions of his greatest poem, the Canterbury Tales.

**1389.** On May 3, Richard II. suddenly took the government into his own hands. John of Gaunt returned to England soon afterwards, and effected an outward reconciliation between the king and the duke of Gloucester. The Lancastrian party was now once more in power, and Chaucer was appointed Clerk of the King's Works at Westminster on July 12, at a salary of 2s. a day (more than 1l. of our present money, at the least).

**1390.** In this year, Chaucer was also appointed Clerk of the Works at St. George's Chapel at Windsor, and was put on a Commission to repair the banks of the Thames between Woolwich and Greenwich. In a writ, dated July 1 in this year, he was allowed the costs of putting up scaffolds in Smithfield for the King and Queen to view the tournament which had taken place there in May. This helps to explain the minute account of the method of conducting a tournament which we meet with in the Knight's Tale. In the preceding month he had been appointed, by the Earl of March, joint Forester (with Richard Brittle) of North Petherton Park in Somerset. In September, he was twice robbed of some of the king's money; once, at Westminster, of 10l. ; and again, near the 'foule ok' (foul oak) at Hatcham, Surrey, of 9l. 3s. 8d. ; but the repayment of these sums was forgiven him.

**1391.** This is the date given by Chaucer to his prose Treatise on the Astrolabe, which he compiled for the use of his 'little son' Lewis, of whom nothing more is known ; and it is supposed that he died at an early age. At this time, for some unknown reason, the poet unfortunately lost his appointment as Clerk of the Works.

**1394.** In February of this year, Chaucer received a grant from the king of 20l. a year for life ; nevertheless, he seems to have been in want of money, as we find him making applications for the advancement of money from his pension.

**1398.** In this year or the preceding, Chaucer was made sole Forester of North Petherton Park, instead of joint Forester, as in 1390. In the Easter Term, he was sued for a debt of 14l. 1s. 11d. In October, the king granted him a tun of wine yearly, for his life-time.

**1399.** On September 30, Henry IV. became king of England, and Chaucer addressed to him a complaint regarding his poverty, called a 'Compleynt to his Purs,' in response to which, only four days afterwards, Henry granted that the poet's pension of twenty marks (13l. 6s. 8d.) should be doubled, in addition to the 20l. a year which had been granted to him in 1394.

On Christmas eve of this year, Chaucer took a long lease of a house in the garden of the Chapel of St. Mary, Westminster ; this house stood near the spot now occupied by King Henry the Seventh's Chapel. The lease is in the Muniment Room of Westminster Abbey (Historical MSS. Commission, i. 95).

**1400.** The traditional date of Chaucer's death is October 25, 1400; in the second year of Henry IV. His death doubtless took place in his newly-acquired house at Westminster ; and he attained to the age of about sixty years. Of his family, nothing is known. His 'little son' Lewis probably died young ; and there is no evidence earlier than the reign of Henry VI. that the Thomas Chaucer whose great-grandson, John de la Pole, Earl of Lincoln, was declared heir to the throne by his uncle, Richard III., in 1484, was Chaucer's son. As Thomas Chaucer was a man of great wealth, and of some mark, we should have expected to find early and undoubted evidence as to his parentage. We find, however, that Thomas Gascoigne, who wrote a Theological Dictionary, and died in 1458, refers to the poet in these words :—'Fuit idem Chawserus pater Thomae Chawserus, armigeri, qui Thomas sepelitur in Nuhelm iuxta Oxoniam.' Gascoigne was in a position to know the truth, since he was Chancellor of Oxford, and Thomas Chaucer had held the manor of Ewelme, at no great distance, till his death in 1434. If this information be correct, it then becomes highly probable that Chaucer's wife Philippa was Philippa Roet, sister of the Katharine de Roet of Hainault, who married Sir John Swynford, and afterwards became the mistress, and in 1396 the third wife of John of Gaunt. This has been inferred from the fact that Thomas Chaucer's arms contain three wheels, supposed to represent the name of Roet; since the Old French *roet* means 'a little wheel.' Those who accept this inference see good reasons for explaining the favours extended to Chaucer both by John of Gaunt himself and his son King Henry IV.

## CHARACTER OF CHAUCER.

There is no space here for exhibiting fully the revelation of Chaucer's character as expressed by numerous passages in his works. We easily recognise in them a man of cheerful and genial nature, with great powers of originality, full of freshness and humour, a keen observer of men, and at the same time an enthusiastic and untiring student of books. He tells a story excellently and sets his characters before us with dramatic clearness; and he has also an exquisite ear for music and pays great attention to the melodious flow of his verse. Except in his prose tales, he frequently affects, in his Canterbury Tales, an air of simplicity which sits upon him gracefully enough. In his *Prologue to Sir Thopas*, he describes himself as a 'large,' i. e. a somewhat corpulent man, and no 'poppet' to embrace, that is, not slender in the waist; as having an 'elvish' or abstracted look, often staring on the ground 'as if he would find a hare,' and 'doing no dalliance' to any man, i. e. not entering briskly into casual conversation. His numerous references and quotations show that he was deeply read in all medieval learning, and well acquainted with Latin, French (both of England and of the continent), and Italian, besides being a master of the East-midland dialect of English. A passage in the *Reves Tale* imitates some of the peculiarities of the Northumbrian dialect with much fidelity. On the other hand, he occasionally introduces forms into his poems that are peculiarly Kentish; owing, as I am inclined to suggest, to his residence for some years at Greenwich. In his *Hous of Fame*, he tells us how he had 'set his wit to make books, songs, and ditties in rime,' and often 'made his head ache at night with writing in his study.' For, when he had done his official work for the day, and 'made his reckonings,' he used to go home and become wholly absorbed in his books, 'hearing neither this nor that'; and, 'in stead of rest and new things' (recreation), he used 'to sit at a book, as dumb as a stone, till his look was dased'; and thus did he 'live as a hermit, though (unlike a hermit) his abstinence was but little.' So great (as he tells us in the *Prologue to The Legend of Good Women*) was his love of nature, that, 'when the month of May is come, and I hear the birds sing, and see the flowers springing up, farewell then to my book and to my devotion' to reading. In many passages he insists on the value of the purity of womanhood and the nobility of manhood, taking the latter to be dependent upon good feeling and courtesy. As he says in *The Wife of Bath's Tale*, 'the man who is always the most virtuous, and most endeavours to be constant in the performance of gentle deeds, is to be taken to be the greatest gentleman. Christ desires that we should derive our gentleness from Him, and not from our ancestors, however rich.'

## WRITINGS OF CHAUCER.

Other notices of Chaucer must be gathered from his writings and from what we know about them. It is advisable to date his various works, where possible, as well as we can, and to consider the result.

Chaucer's works fall (as shewn by Ten Brink) into three periods. During the first of these, he imitated French models, particularly the famous and very long poem entitled *Le Roman de la Rose*, of which, as he himself tells us, he made a translation. It so happens that there exist what are apparently two, but are really three fragments of translations of two different parts of this poem; they are found in a MS. at Glasgow, written out about A. D. 1430-40, and in the early printed editions. These three fragments, marked A, B, C in the present volume, appear to be by different hands; and only the first of them can be reconciled with Chaucer's usual diction and grammar. We must regretfully infer that the major part of Chaucer's own translation is irrecoverably lost. The poems of this First Period were written before he set out on his Italian travels in 1372, and there is no trace in them of any Italian influence.

The poems of the Second Period (1373-1384) clearly shew the influence of Italian literature, especially of Dante's Divina Commedia, and of Boccaccio's poems entitled Il Teseide and Il Filostrato. Curiously enough, there is nothing to shew that Chaucer was acquainted, at first-hand, with Boccaccio's Decamerone.

The poems of the Third Period are chiefly remarkable for a larger share of originality, and are considered as beginning with the Legend of Good Women, the first poem in which the poet employed what is now known as the 'heroic' couplet, which he adapted from Guillaume de Machault.

The following list is arranged, *conjecturally*, in chronological order.

Origenes upon the Maudeleyne (*lost*).

Book of the Leoun (*lost*).

Ceys and Alcioun; afterwards (probably) partly preserved in the Book of the Duchesse.

The Romaunt of the Rose. (Fragment A (ll. 1-1705) is all that can fairly be claimed as Chaucer's work. Fragment B is written in a dialect approximating to that of Lincolnshire. The author of Fragment C, like that of B, remains unknown.)

A. B. C.—Minor Poems, I.

1369. Book of the Duchesse.—M. P. III.

Lyf of St. Cecyle (afterwards adapted to become the Second Nonnes Tale).

Monkes Tale (parts of); lines 3365-3652 clearly belong to a later period.

About 1372-3. Clerkes Tale; except E 995-1008, and the Envoy.

Palamon and Arcite; of which some scraps are preserved in other poems. It was also used as the basis of the Knightes Tale.

Compleint to his Lady.—M. P. VI.

An Amorous Compleint, made at Windsor.—M. P. XXII.

Womanly Noblesse.—M. P. XXIV.

Compleint unto Pitè.—M. P. II.

Anelida and Arcite (containing ten stanzas from Palamon).—M. P. VII.

The Tale of Melibeus (in its original form); partly translated from Albertano of Brescia.

The Persones Tale (in its original form); partly translated from Frère Lorens.

Of the Wretched Engendring of Mankind; mentioned in the Legend, Text A, l. 414; and partly preserved in scraps occurring in the Man of Lawes Tale, B 99–121, 421–7 771–7, 925–931, 1135–41.

Man of Lawes Tale (in its original form); partly translated from Nicholas Trivet. 1377–81. Translation of Boethius.

1379? Complaint of Mars.—M. P. IV.

1379–83. Troilus and Criseyde; (partly from Boccaccio's Il Filostrato and Guido delle Colonne's Historia Troiae; containing three stanzas from Palamon).

Wordes to Adam (concerning Boethius and Troilus).—M. P. VIII.

The Former Age; chiefly from Boethius, Book II. met. V.—M. P. IX.

Fortune; containing hints from Boethius.—M. P. X.

1382. Parlement of Foules (containing six stanzas from Palamon).—M. P. V.

1383–4. House of Fame; containing hints from Dante; *unfinished.*

1385–6. Legend of Good Women; *unfinished.*

1386. Canterbury Tales begun.

1387–8. Central period of the Canterbury Tales.

1389, &c. The Tales continued.

1391. Treatise on the Astrolabe; chiefly from Messahala; *unfinished.*

1393? Compleint of Venus.—M. P. XVIII.

1393. Lenvoy to Scogan.—M. P. XVI.

1396. Lenvoy to Bukton.—M. P. XVII.

1399. *Envoy to* Compleint to his Purse.—M. P. XIX.

The following occasional triple roundel and balades *may* have been composed between 1380 and 1396:—Merciless Beauté.—M. P. XI. Balade to Rosemounde.— M. P. XII. Against Women Unconstaunt.—M. P. XXI. Compleint to his Purse (except the Envoy).—M. P. XIX. Lak of Stedfastnesse.—M. P. XV. Gentilesse.— M. P. XIV. Truth.—M. P. XIII. Proverbes of Chaucer.—M. P. XX.

## EDITIONS OF CHAUCER.

Several of Chaucer's Poems were printed at various times by Caxton and others, but the first collected edition of his works was that edited by W. Thynne in 1532. This was reprinted, with the addition of the spurious *Plowman's Tale*, in 1542; and again, about 1550. Later editions appeared in 1561 (with large additions by John Stowe); in 1598 (re-edited by Thomas Speght), second edition, 1602, and reprinted in 1687. Still later editions were the very bad one by Urry, in 1721, and the excellent one by Tyrwhitt, of the Canterbury Tales *only*, in 1775–8. These editions, excepting Tyrwhitt's, have done much to confuse the public as to the genuine works of Chaucer, because in them a large number of poems, some known (even by the editors) to be by Lydgate, Gower, Hoccleve, and Scogan, together with others obviously spurious, were carelessly added to works by Chaucer himself; and many erroneous notions have been deduced from the study of this incongruous mixture.

It must suffice to say here that most of the later editions, since the publication of Tyrwhitt's remarks on the subject, reject many of these additional pieces, but still unadvisedly admit the poems entitled *The Court of Love, The Complaint of the Black Knight, Chaucer's Dream, The Flower and the Leaf,* and *The Cuckoo and the Nightingale.* Of these, *The Complaint of the Black Knight* is now known to be by Lydgate; *The Flower and the Leaf* cannot be earlier than 1450, and was probably written, as it purports to be, by a lady; whilst *The Court of Love* can hardly be earlier than 1500, and *Chaucer's Dream* (so called) is of still later date. Nothing but a complete ignorance of the history of the English language can connect these fifteenth-century and sixteenth-century poems with Chaucer. The only poem, in the above set, which can possibly be as old as the fourteenth century, is *The Cuckoo and the Nightingale.* There is no evidence of any kind to connect it with Chaucer; and Professor Lounsbury decisively rejects it, on the internal evidence. It admits a few rimes (see p. xxiv) such as Chaucer nowhere employs.

## GRAMMATICAL HINTS.

The following brief hints contain but a minimum of information, and include nothing that should not be extremely familiar to the student.

Observe that, in Chaucer's English, the final syllables *-e, -ed, -en, -es,* almost always form a distinct and separate syllable, so that a large number of words had then *a syllable more* than they have now. Unless this rule be observed, no progress in the study is possible. In particular, *always* sound this final *-e* (like the *a* in *China*) at the end of a line.

Final *-e* is elided, or slurred over, when the next word begins with a vowel, or is one of certain words beginning with *h*, viz. (1) a pronoun, as *he*; (2) part of the verb *have*; (3) the adverbs *heer, how*; (4) mute *h* in *honour, houre.* In a similar position, final *-er, -en, -el, -y*, are slurred over likewise ; thus *get-en* is really *get'n* in l. 291 [1].

Final *-e* is *sometimes* dropped in a few common words, such as *wĕre*, were, *hadde,* had, *wolde*, would.

Middle *-e-* is also sometimes dropped, as in *havenes*, pronounced (haavnez), l. 407. But *trew-e-ly* (481) is trisyllabic.

The reasons for sounding the final *-e, -en, -es,* as distinct syllables, are grammatical. These endings represent older inflexions, mostly Anglo-Saxon ; and were once, in fact, essential. But, in Chaucer's time, they were *beginning* to disappear, and many are now lost altogether.

Final **-e.** The various sources of the M. E. (i. e. Middle-English) final *-e* are, chiefly, these following.

1. The A.S. (Anglo-Saxon) sb. ended in a vowel. Thus A.S. *har-a*, a hare, became M.E. *har-e* (191).

2. The A.F. (Anglo-French) sb. ended in a vowel which was formerly sounded. Thus A.F. *mélodi-ë* (four syllables) is M.E. *melody-ë* (four syllables, 9).

3. The dative case often ends in *-e*, especially after the prepositions *at, by, for, in, of, on, to.* Thus *rŏt-e* (2) is the dative case of *root*, a root. We even find the form of an oblique case used as a nom. case, owing to confusion. Thus A.S. *hwelp*, a whelp, makes the dat. *hwelp-e* ; Chaucer has *whelp-e* as a nominative (257).

4. The forms *hell-e* (so in A.S.), *sonn-e* (A.S. *sunn-an*) are *genitives* ; see Book Duch. 171 ; A 1051. Similarly *-y* represents a genitive suffix in *lad-y*, 88, 695.

5. The *definite* form of the adjective (i. e. the form used when the def. art. *the* or a possessive or demonstrative pronoun precedes it) ends in *-e*. Ex. : *the yong-e*, 7.

6. The adj. pl. ends in *-e*; as *smal-e*, 9.

---

[1] The numbers refer to the lines of The Prologue to the Canterbury Tales ; see p. 419.

7. Even the adj. sing. may end in *-e*; as *swēt-e* (5), from A.S. *swēte*, sweet, in which the final *-e* is essential. So also *trewe*, from A.S. *trēowe*; 531.

8. Verbs: the infinitive and gerund (with *to*) end in *-en* or *-e*; as *biginn-e*, 42; *for to rȳs-e*, 33.

9. Strong verbs: the pp. (past participle) ends in *-en* or *-e*; as *y-ronn-e*, 8.

10. Weak verbs: the pt. t. (past tense) ends in *-ede, -de, -te, -e*; as *say-de*, 70. Sometimes in *-ed*, as *prov-ed*, 547. Observe *lakk-e-de*, 756; *lov'de*, 97; *wet-te*, 129; *went-e*, 78.

11. Verbs: various other inflexions in *-en* or *-e*. Thus *slēp-en*, 3 p. pr. pl., 10; *wēr-en*, 1 p. pt. pl., 29; *gæss-e*, 1 p. pr. s., 82; *smert-e*, 3 p. pr. s. subj., 230, &c.

12. Adverbs and prepositions may end in *-en* or *-e*; as *abov-en*, 53; *about-e*, prep. 158, adv. 488.

**Final -en.** The suffix *-en* usually denotes either (1) the pl. sb., as *hos-en*, 456; (2) the infin. or gerundial infin. of a verb, as *to wend-en*, 21; (3) the pp. of a strong verb, as *holp-en*, 18; (4) the pl. of any tense of a verb, as *wēr-en*, 1 p. pt. pl., 29; (5) a prep. or adverb, as *abov-en*, 53.

**Final -es.** The final *-es* denotes either (1) the gen. sing., as *lord-es*, 47; (2) the pl. sb., as *shour-es*, 1; or (3) an adverb, as *thrȳ-es*, 562. But the gen. of *lady* is *lady*; and of *fader*, is *fader*. And the plural may end in *-s*, as in *palmer-s*, 13.

The student should endeavour to make out, in every case, the reason for the use of final *-e, -en*, or *-es*. He will thus acquire the grammar. The above hints explain most cases that can arise.

**Further notes.** Some neuter sbs. do not change in the plural, as *hors*, pl. *hors*, 74. So also *neet, sheep, swȳn, yeer*.

Comparatives end in *-er*, as *grett-er*, adj., 197; or *-re*, as *fer-re*, adv., 48. Superlatives, in *-est*, occasional def. form *-est-e*, as *best-e*, 252. Pronouns: *tho*, those; *this*, pl. *thise*, these; *thilke*, that; *ilke*, same. *Atte*, for *at the*. *Ye*, nom.; *yow*, dat. and acc., you. *Hir*, their (also her); *hem*, them. *His*, his, its. *Whiche*, what sort of, 40; *what*, i.e. 'why,' 184; *That . . . he*, who, 44, 45; *whō sō*, whoever, 741. *Men*, one, with a sing. verb, as *men smoot*, one smote, 149.

**Verbs.** Verbs are distinguished as being *weak* or *strong*. In the former, the pp. ends in *-ed, -d*, or *-t*; in the latter, in *-en*, or *-e*.

A simple rule is this. In weak verbs, the pt. t. ends in *-ede* (rarely *-ed*), *-de, -te, -e*, so that the final *-e* is here extremely common, but it does not appear in the pp.; *conversely*, in strong verbs, it is the pp. that ends in *-en* or *-e*, which never appears in the first or third person *singular* of the past tense. Ex. *went-e*, 3 p. pt. s., 78, is a weak past tense; *cla-d*, 103, is a weak pp. Conversely, *y-ronn-e*, 8, is a strong pp.; *sleep*, 98, is a strong pt. t. The prefix *y-* (A.S. *ge-*) can be prefixed to *any* pp., and makes no difference.

Strong verbs usually shew vowel-change; thus *bigan* (44) is the pt. t. of *biginnen*. But note that this is not a sure guide; for *raugh-te* (136) is the pt. t. of *rech-en*, to reach, and is weak. *Slēp-en*, to sleep, pt. t. *sleep*, is strong.

In strong verbs, the vowel of the past tense is changed, sometimes, in the plural. Thus the pt. t. sing. of *rȳd-en*, to ride, is *rood*, 169; but the pl. is *rĭd-en*, 825. The pp. is also *rĭd-en*, 48.

The usual formulae for the conjugation of verbs are as follows.

**Present tense.** Sing. *-e, -est, -eth (-th)*; pl. *-en* or *-e*.

**Past tense; weak verbs.** Sing. *-ede (-de* or *-ed), -de, -te, -e* (in persons 1 and 3); *-edest, -dest, -test, -est* (2 person). Plural, *-eden, -ede, -de, -den -ten, -te, -e* (all persons).

**Past tense; strong verbs.** Sing. indic. *no suffix* (in persons 1 and 3); *-e*, occasionally (2 person). Sing. subj. *-e* (all persons). Plural of both moods : *-en, -e*.

**Imperative.** Sing. 2 person : *no suffix* (usually); *-e* (in some weak verbs). Plural, 2 person : *-eth, -th*; (sometimes *-e*).

**Infinitive :** *-en, -e*. The gerundial infinitive has *to* or *for to* prefixed, and often denotes purpose.

**Participles.** Present : *-ing*, often *-inge* at the end of a line. Pp. of weak verbs : *-ed, -d, -t*. Pp. of strong verbs : *-en, -e*.

N.B. We find the contracted form *bit*, for *biddeth*, in the 3 p. pr. s. indicative, 187. Similar contractions are common ; hence *hit* means 'hideth'; *rit* means ' rideth'; *sit*, 'sitteth '; *let*, 'leadeth,' B 1496; &c.

**Formation of Past Tenses.** The form of the pt. t. of a weak verb depends on the form of its stem. There are three classes of such verbs.

1. Infin. *-ien* ; pt. *-ede (-de)*, or *-ed*. Thus *lov-ien*, to love ; pt. t. *lov-ede ( pronounced* luv·də), or *lov-ed* (luv·ed). Compare *lakk-e-de*, 756 ; though the infin. is *lakk-en*.

2. Infin. *-en* ; pt. t. *-de, -te*, or sometimes (after *d* or *t*) *-e* ; without vowel-change, except such as is due to contraction. Ex. *hēr-en*, to hear, pt. t. *her-de* ; *kēp-en*, to keep, pt. t. *kep-te* ; *lēd-en*, to lead, pt. t. *lad-de* (short for *lēed-de*). Cf. *went-e*, went.

3. Infin. *-en*, with a modified vowel in the infinitive, the root-vowel appearing in the pt. t. and pp. Thus the root sôĸ (cf. Gothic *sōkjan*, to seek), appears in the A.S. pt. t. *sōh-te*, pp. *sōh-t*, M.E. *soght-e, sogh-t* ; but the ō becomes ē (as in A.S. *fōt*, foot, pl. *fēt*, feet) in the infin. *sēc-an*, M.E. *sēk-en*, E. *seek*. Cf. *tell-en*, pt. t. *tol-de* ; *tech-en*, pt. t. *taugh-te*.

N.B. The pp. of a weak verb results from the pt. t. by dropping *-e* (unless it has been dropped already); thus pt. t. *tol-de* gives pp. *tol-d*.

**Strong verbs.** The seven conjugations of strong verbs are given in my Principles of Etymology. I take as representative verbs the following : *fall, shake, bear, give, drink, drive, choose*. A more usual order (though it makes no real difference) is : 1. *drive*, 2. *choose*, 3. *drink*, 4. *bear*, 5. *give*, 6. *shake*, 7. *fall*.

The ' principal parts ' are : (a) the infinitive : (b) the past tense, singular ; (c) the pt. t. pl. ; (d) the pp.

1. 'Drive.' Here Chaucer has : (a) *rȳd-en*, to ride ; (b) *rood* ; (c) *rĭd-en* ; (d) *rĭd-en*. So also *byt-en*, bite, *rys-en*, rise, *shyn-en*, shine, *shryv-en*. shrive, *smyt-en*, smite, *wryt-en*, write [1]. I here write *y* to denote long *i*.

2. ' Choose.' As : (a) *sēth-en*, to seethe ; (b) *seeth* ; (c, d) *sod-en*.

3. 'Drink.' As : (a) *biginn-en* ; (b) *bigan* ; (c) *bigonnen* ; (d) *bigonnen*. So also *drinken, ginnen, rinnen*, to run, *singen, springen, swinken*, to toil, *winnen, delven, fighten* (pt. t. s. *faught*), *helpen, kerven, thresshen*.

4. 'Bear.' As : (a) *ber-en* ; (b) *bar* ; (c) *bēr-en* ; (d) *bor-en*. So also *breken, sheren, stelen*. Comen has : (b) *cōm* ; (c) *cōm-en* ; (d) *cŏm-en*.

5. ' Give.' As : (a) *yev-en, yiv-en* ; (b) *yaf* ; (c) *yēv-en* ; (d) *yiv-en*. So also *geten* (pp. *geten*); *speken* (pp. *spoken*).

6. ' Shake.' As : (a) *bak-en* ; (b) *book* ; (c) *bōk-en* ; (d) *bak-en*. So also *drawen, shaken, shaven, stonden* (pt. t. *stood*), *taken, sweren* (pp. *swor-e*).

7. ' Fall.' As : (a) *fall-en* ; (b) *fil* ; (c) *fill-en* ; (d) *fall-en*. So *holden*, pt. t. *hēld* ;

---

[1] Chaucer's Prologue does not contain specimens of *all* the parts of the verbs mentioned. Thus *sēthen* only occurs in the infinitive (383); however, the pl. t. *seeth* occurs elsewhere, viz. in the Clerkes Tale, E 227.

*lēt-en*, pt. t. *leet*; *slēp-en*, pt. t. *sleep*; *blōwen, grōwen, knōw-en*, pt. t. *blew*, &c.; *wēp-en*, pt. t. *weep*; *goon*, pp. *y-goon, y-go*, 286. Compare the complete list of strong M.E. verbs, in Specimens of English, ed. Morris and Skeat, pt. 1.

**Anomalous Verbs.** Among these note the following. *Been, ben*, are. Imper. pl. *beeth, beth*, be ye. Pp. *been, ben*, been.

*Can*, I know; pl. *connen*; pt. t. *coude*, knew, could : pp. *couth*, known. *Dar*, I dare; pt. t. *dorste*. *May*, I may; pl. *mowen*; subjunctive, *mowe*, pl. *mowen*. *Moot*, I must, I may, he must, he may; pl. *mōten, mōte*; pt. t. *mōste*. *Oghte*, ought. *Shal*, pl. *shullen, shul*; pt. t. *sholde*. *Witen*, to know; *woot, wōt*, I know, he knows; pl. *witen* (correctly; but Chaucer also has *ye woot*); pt. t. *wiste*, knew; pp. *wiṣt*. *Wil*, *wol, wole*, will; pl. *wolen, wilen*; pt. t. *wolde*. *Thar*, needs; pt. t. *thurte*.

**Negatives.** *Nam*, for *ne am*, am not; *nis*, for *ne is*, is not; *nas*, was not; *nēre*, were not; *nadde*, had not; *nil*, will not; *nolde*, would not; *noot*, I know not, he knows not; *niste*, knew not; *ne . . . ne*, neither . . . nor, 603. Double negatives, 70, 71, &c.

**Adverbs.** End in *-e*, as *dēp-e*, deeply; or *-ly*, as *subtil-ly*; or *-e-ly*, as *trew-e-ly*, truly; or *-en, -e*, as *bifor-en, bifor-e*; or in *-es*, as *thrȳ-es*, thrice. *Ther*, where, 547; *ther as*, where that, 34.

**Prepositions.** End in *-en, -e, -es*; &c. *Til*, for *to*, before a vowel. *With* adjoins its verb; 791.


## METRE.

Chaucer was our first great metrist, and enriched our literature with several forms of metre which had not been previously employed in English. These he borrowed chiefly from Guillaume de Machault, who made use of stanzas of seven, eight, and nine lines, and even wrote at least one Compleint in the 'heroic' couplet.

The metre of four accents, in rimed couplets, had been in use in English long before Chaucer's time; and he adopted it in translating Le Roman de la Rose (the original being in the same metre), in the Book of the Duchesse, and in the House of Fame.

The ballad-metre, as employed in the Tale of Sir Thopas, is also older than his time. In fact, this Tale is a burlesque imitation of some of the old Romances.

The four-line stanza, in the Proverbes, was likewise nothing new.

But he employed the following metres, in English, for the first time.

1. The 8-line stanza, with the rimes arranged in the order *ababbcbc*; i. e. with the first line (*a*) riming with the third (*a*), and so on. Exx. A.B.C. ; The Monkes Tale ; The Former Age ; Lenvoy to Bukton.

1 *b*. The same, thrice repeated, with a refrain. Ex. (part of) Fortune ; Compleint to Venus ; Balade to Rosemounde.

2. The 7-line stanza, with the rimes *ababbcc*; a favourite metre. Exx. Lyf of Seint Cecyle ; Clerkes Tale ; Palamon and Arcite ; (part of) Compleint to his Lady ; An Amorous Compleint ; Compleint to Pitè ; (part of) Anelida ; The Wretched Engendring of Mankind ; The Man of Lawes Tale ; (part of) The Compleint of Mars ; Troilus and Criseyde ; Wordes to Adam ; (part of) The Parlement of Foules ; (parts of) The Canterbury Tales ; Lenvoy to Scogan.

2 *b*. The same 7-line stanza, thrice repeated, with a refrain. Exx. Against Women

Unconstaunt; Compleint to his Purse; Lak of Stedfastnesse; Gentilesse; Truth. Also in the Legend of Good Women, 249-269.

2 c. The 7-line stanza, with the rimes *ababbab*. Ex. (part of) Fortune.

3. Terza Rima. Only a few lines; in the Compleint to his Lady.

4. The 10-line stanza, *aabaabcddc*. In the Compleint to his Lady.

5. The 9-line stanza, *aabaabbab*. Only in Anelida.

5 b. The same, with internal rimes. Only in Anelida.

5 c. The same as 5, but thrice repeated. Only in Womanly Noblesse.

6. Two stanzas of 16 lines each; with the rimes *aaabaaab · bbbabbba*. Only in Anelida.

7. The 9-line stanza, *aabaabbcc*. Only in the latter part of the Compleint of Mars.

8. The roundel. In the Parlement of Foules; and Merciless Beautè.

9. The heroic couplet. In the Legend of Good Women and parts of the Canterbury Tales.

10. A 6-line stanza, repeated six times; with the rimes *ababcb*. Only in the Envoy to the Clerkes Tale.

11. A 10-line stanza, *aabaabbaab*. Only in the Envoy to the Compleint of Venus.

12. A 6-line stanza, *ababaa*. Only in the Envoy to Womanly Noblesse.

13. A 5-line stanza, *aabba*. Only in the Envoy to Compleint to his Purse.

The following pieces are in prose. The Tale of Melibeus. The Persones Tale. The translation of Boethius, De Consolatione Philosophiae. The Treatise on the Astrolabe.

## VERSIFICATION.

Some lines drop the first syllable, and the first foot contains *one* syllable only; as: Ging | len in, &c. 170.

Many rimes are *double*, as *cloistre, oistre*, 181; *Rom-e, tó me*, 671; *non-es, noon is*, 523. *Always* sound final *-e* at the end of a line. Rimes may be treble, as *apothec-ár-i-es, letu-ár-i-es*, 425; so at ll. 207, 513, 709. Compare the Grammatical Hints.

**Caesura.** The caesura, or middle pause, allows extra syllables to be preserved. Thus, at l. 293, we have :—

> For him was léver—hav' át his béddes héed.

The pause gives time for the *-er* of *lēv-er*. Similarly, we may preserve the *-er* of *deliv-er*, 84; *-e* in *mor-e*, 98; *-e* in *curteisy-e*, 132; *-ie* (= *y*) in *car-ie*, 130. Compare also :—

> With-óut-e bak-e met-e—was nev'r his hous; 343.
> Thát | no dróp-e—ne fill' upon hir brest; 131.

The syllables *-er, -en, -el, -ed*, before a vowel, or *h* (in *he*, &c.), are light, and do not always count in scansion; see ll. 84, 291, 296, 334, &c. Cf. *ma | ny a breem* | ; 350. Read the lines *deliberately*, and remember the old pronunciation.

**Accent.** Variable, in some words; cf. *miller*, 545, with the archaic trisyllabic *mil-lér-e*, 541. Also, in French words, we have *hónour*, 582; but the archaic *honóur*, 46. Cf. *licóur*, 3; *vertú*, 4.

## PRONUNCIATION.

The M.E. pronunciation was widely different from the present, especially in the vowel-sounds. The sounds of the vowels were nearly as in French and Italian.

They can be denoted by phonetic *invariable* symbols, enclosed within marks of parenthesis. Convenient phonetic symbols are these following.

**Vowels.** (aa), as *a* in f*a*ther; (a) short, as *a* in *a*ha! (ae), open long *e*, as *a* in M*a*ry; (e), open short *e*, as *e* in b*e*d; (ee), close long *e*, as *e* in v*ei*l; (i) short, as F. *i* in f*i*n*i*, or (nearly) as E. *i* in *i*n; (ii), as *ee* in d*ee*p; (ao), open long *o*, as *aw* in s*aw*; (o) open short *o*, as *o* in n*o*t; (oo), close long *o*, as *o* in n*o*te, or *o* in German ' s*o* '; (u), as *u* in f*u*ll; (uu), as *oo* in f*oo*l; (ü), as F. *u* in F. ' *écu* '; (ü·), as long G. *ü* in G. ' gr*ü*n.' Also (ə), as final *a* in China.

**Diphthongs.** (ai), as *y* in fl*y*; (au), as *ow* in n*ow*; (ei), as *ei* in v*ei*l; (oi), as *oi* in b*oi*l.

**Consonants (special).** (k), as *c* in *c*at; (s), as *c* in *c*ity; (ch), as in *ch*ur*ch*; (tch), as in ca*tch*; (th), as *th* in *th*in; (dh), as *th* in *th*en. Also (h), when *not initial*, to denote a guttural sound, like G. *ch* in Na*ch*t, Li*ch*t, but weaker, and varying with the preceding vowel.

An accent is denoted by (·), as in M.E. *name* (naa·mə).

By help of these symbols, it is possible to explain the meaning of the M.E. symbols employed by the scribes in Chaucer's Tales. The following is a list of the sounds they denote. The letters *in thick type* are the letters *actually employed*; the letters within parenthesis denote the *sounds*, as above.

Observe that long ' ǫ,' also written ' ò,' means the same as (ao); and long ' ę,' also written ' è,' means the same as (ae).

**a** short, (a). Ex. *al* (al); *as* (az). N.B. The modern *a* in c*a*t (kæt) is denoted by (æ), and *does not occur* in Chaucer.

**a** long, (aa). (1) at the end of a syllable; as *age* (aa·jə); (2) before *s* or *ce*; as *cas* (kaas), *face* (faa·sə).

**ai, ay** (ei), originally perhaps (ai); but *ai* and *ei*, both being pronounced as (ei), had already been confused, and invariably rime together in Chaucer. Cf. E. *gay*, *prey*.

**au, aw** (au). Ex. *avaunt* (avau·nt); *awe* (au·ə).

**c**, as (k), except before *e* and *i*; as (s), before *e* and *i*.

**ch** (ch); **cch** (tch).

**e** short, (e). Ex. *fetheres* (fedh·rez); middle *e* dropped.

**e** final, (ə); and often dropped or elided or very lightly touched.

**e** long and open, (ae). Sometimes denoted by ' ę ' or ' ęę.' Ex. *clene* (klae·nə).

**e** long and close, (ee). Ex. *swete* (swee·tə); *weep* (weep).

**ei, ey** (ei). Ex. *streit* (streit); *wey* (wei).

**g** hard, i. e. (g), except before *e* and *i*; (j), before *e* and *i*. Ex. *go* (gao); *age* (aa·jə).

**gh** (h), G. *ch*. Ex. *light* (liiht). The vowel was at first short, then half-long (as probably in Chaucer), then wholly long, when the (h) dropped out. Later, (ii) became (ei), and is now (ai).

**gn** (n), with long preceding vowel; as *digne* (dii·nə).

**i** short, (i). As F. *i* in f*i*n*i*; but often as E. *i* in *i*n; the latter is near enough. So also **y**, when short, as in *many* (man·i).

**i, y** long, (ii). Ex. *I* (ii); *melodye* (mél·odii·ə).

**ie** (ee), the same as *ee*. Ex. *mischief* (mischeef).

**I** consonantal, (j). Ex. *Iay* (jei); *Iuge* (jü·jə). So in the MSS.; but here printed '**j**,' as in *jay* (jei).

**le**, often vocalic (l), as in E. *temple* (temp·l). But note *stables* (staa·blez).

**ng** (ngg); always as in E. *linger.* Ex. *thing* (thingg).

**o** short, (o), as in *of* (ov). But as (ǫu) before *gh.* And *note particularly*, that it is always (u), i. e. as *u* in *full*, wherever it has a sound like *u* in mod. E., as in *company*, *son*, *monk*, *cousin*, &c. Ex. *sonne* (sun·nə), *monk* (mungk), *moche* (muchə).

**o** long and open, (ao). Sometimes denoted by ' ǫ ' or ' ǫǫ.' Ex. *go* (gao); *stoon* (staon).

**o** long and close, (oo). Ex. *sote* (soo·tə); *hood* (hood).

**oi, oy** (oi).

**ou, ow** (uu); as in *flour* (fluur); *now* (nuu). Rarely (ǫu), as in *soule* (sǫulə).

**ogh** (ǫuh), with open *o*, as in E. *not*, followed by short (u).

**ough** (uuh); with *uu* as in E. *fool* (fuul); or as **ogh.**

**r** is always *strongly trilled.* **ssh** (shsh), as in *fresshe* (fresh·shə).

**u** short, (ü); French; as in *just* (jüst). Rarely (u), as in *cut* (kut); English.

**u** long, (ü·), as in *nature* (natü·rə); French.

**we** final, (wə), but often merely (u). Ex. *arwes* (ar·wez); *bowe* (baou·ə, bǫu·ə); *morwe* (moru); so *blew* (blee·u).

N.B. Open long *e* (ae) often arises from A.S. *ǣ, ēa*, or lengthening of *e.* Ex. *wẹre* (waerə), A.S. *wǣron*; *ẹẹk* (aek), A.S. *ēac*; *spẹken* (spaekən), A.S. *sprecan.* Open long *o* (ao) often arises from A.S. *ā*, or lengthening of *o.* Ex. *fǫ* (fao), A.S. *fā*; *ǫpen*, A.S. *open.* Chaucer refrains from riming open long *e* (ae), when arising from A.S. *ēa*, or lengthening of *e*, with the close *e* arising from A.S. *ē* or *ēo.* But there is some uncertainty about the quality of the *e* arising from A.S. *ǣ*, or from mutation.

The occurrence of rimes such as Chaucer *never* employs furnishes an easy test for poems which have been supposed to be his on insufficient grounds. Thus, in The Cuckoo and the Nightingale, stanza 13, *green* rimes with *been*; whereas the form *green* never occurs in Chaucer, who always employs *grēn-e* (gree·nə) as a dissyllable, in accordance with its etymology from A.S. *grēne.* In the same poem, *upon* rimes with *mon*, a man (stanza 17); but Chaucer knows nothing of such a form as *mon.*

Non-Chaucerian rimes occur in large numbers in Fragment B of the Romaunt of the Rose.

# THE ROMAUNT OF THE ROSE.

Words and syllables enclosed within square brackets are supplied by the Editor.
Readings marked with an obelus (†) are doubtful, and are accounted for in the
Appendix.

*[Only three Fragments of this translation have come down to us. Of these, Fragment A
is by Chaucer; Fragment B is by a Northerner, and has many corrupt readings; whilst
Fragment C is of doubtful origin, and I do not feel sure that it is Chaucer's.]*

## FRAGMENT A.

MANY men seyn that in sweveninges
Ther nis but fables and lesinges ;
But men may somme †swevenes seen,
Which hardely †ne false been,
But afterward ben apparaunte.   5
This may I drawe to waraunte
An authour, that hight Macrobes,
That halt not dremes false ne lees,
But undoth us the avisioun
That whylom mette king Cipioun.   10
  And who-so sayth, or weneth it be
A jape, or elles [a] nycetee
To wene that dremes after falle,
Let who-so liste a fool me calle.
For this trowe I, and say for me,   15
That dremes signifiaunce be
Of good and harme to many wightes,
That dremen in her slepe a-nightes
Ful many thinges covertly,
That fallen after al openly.   20

### The Dream.
Within my twenty yere of age,
Whan that Love taketh his corage
Of yonge folk, I wente sone
To bedde, as I was wont to done,
And fast I †sleep ; and in sleping,   25
Me mette swiche a swevening,

That lykede me wonders wel ;
But in that sweven is never a del
That it nis afterward befalle,
Right as this dreem wol telle us alle.   30
Now this dreem wol I ryme aright,
To make your hertes gaye and light ;
For Love it prayeth, and also
Commaundeth me that it be so.
And if ther any aske me,   35
Whether that it be he or she,
How [that] this book [the] which is here
Shall † hote, that I rede you here ;
It is the Romance of the Rose,
In which al the art of love I close.   40
  The mater fair is of to make ;
God graunte in gree that she it take
For whom that it begonnen is !
And that is she that hath, y-wis,
So mochel prys ; and ther-to she   45
So worthy is biloved be,
That she wel oughte, of prys and right,
Be cleped Rose of every wight.
  That it was May me thoughte tho,
It is fyve yere or more ago ;   50
That it was May, thus dremed me,
In tyme of love and jolitee,
That al thing ginneth waxen gay,

For ther is neither busk nor hay
In May, that it nil shrouded been,　55
And it with newe leves wreen.
These wodes eek recoveren grene,
That drye in winter been to sene ;
And th' erthe wexeth proud withalle,
For swote dewes that on it falle,　60
And [al] the pore estat forget
In which that winter hadde it set ;
And than bicometh the ground so proud
That it wol have a newe shroud,
And maketh so queynt his robe and fayr 65
That it †hath hewes an hundred payr
Of gras and floures, inde and pers,
And many hewes ful dyvers :
That is the robe I mene, y-wis,
Through which the ground to preisen is. 70
　The briddes, that han left hir song,
Whyl they han suffred cold so strong
In wedres grille, and derk to sighte,
Ben in May, for the sonne brighte,
So glade, that they shewe in singing,　75
That in hir herte is swich lyking,
That they mote singen and be light.
Than doth the nightingale hir might
To make noyse, and singen blythe.
Than is blisful, many a sythe,　80
The chelaundre and the papingay.
Than yonge folk entenden ay
For to ben gay and amorous,
The tyme is than so savorous.
Hard is his herte that loveth nought　85
In May, whan al this mirth is wrought ;
Whan he may on these braunches here
The smale briddes singen clere
Hir blisful swete song pitous ;
And in this sesoun delitous,　90
Whan love affrayeth alle thing,
Me thoughte a-night, in my sleping,
Right in my bed, ful redily,
That it was by the morowe erly,
And up I roos, and gan me clothe ;　95
Anoon I wissh myn hondes bothe ;
A sylvre nedle forth I drogh
Out of an aguiler queynt y-nogh,
And gan this nedle threde anon ;
For out of toun me list to gon　100
The sowne of briddes for to here,
That on thise †busshes singen clere.
And in the swete sesoun that leef is,
With a threde basting my slevis,

Aloon I wente in my playing,　105
The smale foules song harkning ;
That peyned hem ful many a payre
To singe on bowes blosmed fayre.
Jolif and gay, ful of gladnesse,
Toward a river †I gan me dresse,　110
That I herde renne faste by ;
For fairer playing non saugh I
Than playen me by that riveer,
For from an hille that stood ther neer
Cam doun the streem ful stif and bold.　115
Cleer was the water, and as cold
As any welle is, sooth to seyne ;
And somdel lasse it was than Seine,
But it was straighter wel away.
And never saugh I, er that day,　120
The water that so wel lyked me ;
And wonder glad was I to see
That lusty place, and that riveer ;
And with that water that ran so cleer
My face I wissh. Tho saugh I wel　125
The botme paved everydel
With gravel, ful of stones shene.
The medewe softe, swote, and grene,
Beet right on the water-syde.
Ful cleer was than the morow-tyde,　130
And ful attempre, out of drede.
Tho gan I walke through the mede,
Dounward ay in my pleying,
The river-syde costeying.

### The Garden.

　And whan I had a whyle goon,　135
I saugh a GARDIN right anoon,
Ful long and brood, and everydel
†Enclos it was, and walled wel,
With hye walles embatailled,
Portrayed without, and wel entailled 140
With many riche portraitures ;
And bothe images and peyntures
Gan I biholde bisily.
And I wol telle you, redily,
Of thilke images the semblaunce,　145
As fer as I have remembraunce.

### Hate.

　A-midde saugh I HATE stonde,
That for hir wrathe, ire, and onde,
Semed to been a †moveresse,
An angry wight, a chideresse ;　150
And ful of gyle, and fel corage,
By semblaunt was that ilke image.
And she was no-thing wel arrayed,

But lyk a wood womman afrayed;
Y-frounced foule was hir visage,    155
And grenning for dispitous rage;
Hir nose snorted up for tene.
Ful hidous was she for to sene,
Ful foul and rusty was she, this.
Hir heed y-writhen was, y-wis,    160
Ful grimly with a greet towayle.

### Felonye.

An image of another entayle,
A lift half, was hir faste by:
Hir name above hir heed saugh I,
And she was called FELONYE.    165

### Vilanye.

Another image, that VILANYE
Y-cleped was, saugh I and fond
Upon the walle on hir right hond.
Vilanye was lyk somdel
That other image; and, trusteth wel,    170
She semed a wikked creature.
By countenaunce, in portrayture,
She semed be ful despitous,
And eek ful proud and outrageous.
Wel coude he peynte, I undertake,    175
That swiche image coude make.
Ful foul and cherlish semed she,
And eek vilaynous for to be,
And litel coude of norture,
To worshipe any creature.    180

### Coveityse.

And next was peynted COVEITYSE,
That eggeth folk, in many gyse,
To take and yeve right nought ageyn,
And grete tresours up to leyn.
And that is she that for usure    185
Leneth to many a creature
The lasse for the more winning,
So coveitous is her brenning.
And that is she, for penyes fele,
That techeth for to robbe and stele    190
These theves, and these smale harlotes;
And that is routhe, for by hir throtes
Ful many oon hangeth at the laste.
She maketh folk compasse and caste
To taken other folkes thing,    195
Through robberie, or †miscounting.
And that is she that maketh trechoures;
And she [that] maketh false pledoures,
That with hir termes and hir domes
Doon maydens, children, and eek gromes
Hir heritage to forgo.    201

Ful croked were hir hondes two;
For Coveityse is ever wood
To grypen other folkes good.
Coveityse, for hir winning,    205
Ful leef hath other mennes thing.

### Avarice.

Another image set saugh I
Next Coveityse faste by,
And she was cleped AVARICE.
Ful foul in peynting was that vice;    210
Ful sad and caytif was she eek,
And al-so grene as any leek.
So yvel hewed was hir colour,
Hir semed have lived in langour.
She was lyk thing for hungre deed,    215
That ladde hir lyf only by breed
Kneden with eisel strong and egre;
And therto she was lene and megre.
And she was clad ful povrely,
Al in an old torn †courtepy,    220
As she were al with dogges torn;
And bothe bihinde and eek biforn
Clouted was she beggarly.
A mantel heng hir faste by,
Upon a perche, weyke and smalle;    225
A burnet cote heng therwithalle,
Furred with no menivere,
But with a furre rough of here,
Of lambe-skinnes hevy and blake;
It was ful old, I undertake.    230
For Avarice to clothe hir wel
Ne hasteth hir, never a del;
For certeynly it were hir loth
To weren ofte that ilke cloth;
And if it were forwered, she    235
Wolde have ful greet necessitee
Of clothing, er she boughte hir newe,
Al were it bad of wolle and hewe.
This Avarice held in hir hande
A purs, that heng [doun] by a bande;    240
And that she hidde and bond so stronge,
Men must abyde wonder longe
Out of that purs er ther come ought,
For that ne cometh not in hir thought;
It was not, certein, hir entente    245
That fro that purs a peny wente.

### Envye.

And by that image, nygh y-nough,
Was †peynt ENVYE, that never lough,
Nor never wel in herte ferde
But-if she outher saugh or herde    250

Som greet mischaunce, or greet disese.
No-thing may so moch hir plese
As mischef and misaventure ;
Or whan she seeth discomfiture
†On any worthy man [to] falle,        255
Than lyketh hir [ful] wel withalle.
She is ful glad in hir corage,
If she see any greet linage
Be brought to nought in shamful wyse.
And if a man in honour ryse,        260
Or by his witte, or by prowesse,
Of that hath she gret hevinesse ;
For, trusteth wel, she goth nigh wood
When any chaunce happeth good.
Envye is of swich crueltee,        265
That feith ne trouthe holdeth she
To freend ne felawe, bad or good.
Ne she hath kin noon of hir blood,
That she nis ful hir enemy ;
She nolde, I dar seyn hardely,        270
Hir owne fader ferde wel.
And sore abyeth she everydel
Hir malice, and hir maltalent :
For she is in so greet turment
And hath such [wo], whan folk doth
    good,        275
That nigh she melteth for pure wood ;
Hir herte kerveth and †to-breketh
That god the peple wel awreketh.
Envye, y-wis, shal never lette
Som blame upon the folk to sette.        280
I trowe that if Envye, y-wis,
Knewe the beste man that is
On this syde or biyond the see,
Yit somwhat lakken him wolde she.
And if he were so hende and wys,        285
That she ne mighte al abate his prys,
Yit wolde she blame his worthinesse,
Or by hir wordes make it lesse.
I saugh Envye, in that peynting,
Hadde a wonderful loking ;        290
For she ne loked but awry,
Or overthwart, al baggingly.
And she hadde [eek] a foul usage ;
She mighte loke in no visage
Of man or womman forth-right pleyn,        295
But shette oon yë for disdeyn ;
So for envye brenned she
Whan she mighte any man [y]-see,
That fair, or worthy were, or wys,
Or elles stood in folkes prys.        300

## Sorowe.

Sorowe was peynted next Envye
Upon that walle of masonrye.
But wel was seen in hir colour
That she hadde lived in langour ;
Hir semed havë the Jaunyce.        305
Nought half so pale was Avaryce,
Nor no-thing lyk, [as] of lenesse ;
For sorowe, thought, and greet distresse,
That she hadde suffred day and night
Made hir ful yelwe, and no-thing bright,
Ful fade, pale, and megre also.        311
Was never wight yit half so wo
As that hir semed for to be,
Nor so fulfilled of ire as she.
I trowe that no wight mighte hir plese,315
Nor do that thing that mighte hir ese ;
Nor she ne wolde hir sorowe slake,
Nor comfort noon unto hir take ;
So depe was hir wo bigonnen,
And eek hir herte in angre ronnen,        320
A sorowful thing wel semed she.
Nor she hadde no-thing slowe be
For to forcracchen al hir face,
And for to †rende in many place
Hir clothes, and for to tere hir swire,        325
As she that was fulfilled of ire ;
And al to-torn lay eek hir here
Aboute hir shuldres, here and there,
As she that hadde it al to-rent
For angre and for maltalent.        330
And eek I telle you certeynly
How that she weep ful tenderly.
In world nis wight so hard of herte
That hadde seen hir sorowes smerte,
That nolde have had of hir pitee,        335
So wo-bigoon a thing was she.
She al to-dasshte hir-self for wo,
And smoot togider hir handes two.
To sorwe was she ful ententyf,
That woful recchelees caityf ;        340
Hir roughte litel of pleying,
Or of clipping or [of] kissing ;
For who-so sorweful is in herte
Him liste not to pleye ne sterte,
Nor for to daunsen, ne to singe,        345
Ne may his herte in temper bringe
To make joye on even or morowe ;
For joye is contraire unto sorowe.

## Elde.

Elde was peynted after this,

That shorter was a foot, y-wis, 350
Than she was wont in her yonghede.
Unnethe hir-self she mighte fede ;
So feble and eek so old was she
That faded was al hir beautee.
Ful salowe was waxen hir colour, 355
Hir heed for-hoor was, whyt as flour.
Y-wis, gret qualm ne were it noon,
Ne sinne, although hir lyf were gon.
Al woxen was hir body unwelde,
And drye, and dwyned al for elde. 360
A foul forwelked thing was she
That whylom round and softe had be.
Hir eres shoken fast withalle,
As from her heed they wolde falle.
Hir face frounced and forpyned, 365
And bothe hir hondes lorn, fordwyned.
So old she was that she ne wente
A foot, but it were by potente.

### Time.

The TYME, that passeth night and day,
And restelees travayleth ay, 370
And steleth from us so prively,
That to us semeth sikerly
That it in oon point dwelleth ever,
And certes, it ne resteth never,
But goth so faste, and passeth ay, 375
That ther nis man that thinke may
What tyme that now present is :
Asketh at these clerkes this ;
For [er] men thinke it redily,
Three tymes been y-passed by. 380
The tyme, that may not sojourne,
But goth, and †never may retourne,
As water that doun renneth ay,
But never drope retourne may ;
Ther may no-thing as tyme endure, 385
Metal, nor erthely creature ;
For alle thing it fret, and shal :
The tyme eek, that chaungeth al,
And al doth waxe and fostred be,
And alle thing distroyeth he : 390
The tyme, that eldeth our auncessours
And eldeth kinges and emperours,
And that us alle shal overcomen
Er that deeth us shal have nomen :
The tyme, that hath al in welde 395
To elden folk, had maad hir elde
So inly, that, to my witing,
She mighte helpe hir-self no-thing,
But turned ageyn unto childhede ;

She had no-thing hir-self to lede, 400
Ne wit ne pith in[with] hir holde
More than a child of two yeer olde.
But natheles, I trowe that she
Was fair sumtyme, and fresh to see,
Whan she was in hir rightful age : 405
But she was past al that passage
And was a doted thing bicomen.
A furred cope on had she nomen ;
Wel had she clad hir-self and warm,
For cold mighte elles doon hir harm. 410
These olde folk have alwey colde,
Hir kind is swiche, whan they ben
      olde.

### Pope-holy.

Another thing was doon ther write,
That semede lyk an ipocrite,
And it was cleped POPE-HOLY. 415
That ilke is she that prively
Ne spareth never a wikked dede,
Whan men of hir taken non hede ;
And maketh hir outward precious,
With pale visage and pitous, 420
And semeth a simple creature ;
But ther nis no misaventure
That she ne thenketh in hir corage.
Ful lyk to hir was that image,
That maked was lyk hir semblaunce. 425
She was ful simple of countenance,
And she was clothed and eek shod,
As she were, for the love of god,
Yolden to religioun,
Swich semed hir devocioun. 430
A sauter held she faste in honde,
And bisily she gan to fonde
To make many a feynt prayere
To god, and to his seyntes dere.
Ne she was gay, fresh, ne jolyf, 435
But semed be ful ententyf
To gode werkes, and to faire,
And therto she had on an haire.
Ne certes, she was fat no-thing,
But semed wery for fasting ; 440
Of colour pale and deed was she.
From hir the gate †shal werned be
Of paradys, that blisful place ;
For swich folk maketh lene hir †face,
As Crist seith in his evangyle, 445
To gete hem prys in toun a whyle ;
And for a litel glorie veine
They lesen god and eek his reine.

### Povert.

And alderlast of everichoon,
Was peynted POVERT al aloon,          450
That not a peny hadde in wolde,
Al-though [that] she hir clothes solde,
And though she shulde anhonged be;
For naked as a worm was she.
And if the weder stormy were,          455
For colde she shulde have deyed there.
She nadde on but a streit old sak,
And many a clout on it ther stak ;
This was hir cote and hir mantel,
No more was there, never a del,          460
To clothe her with ; I undertake,
Gret leyser hadde she to quake.
And she was put, that I of talke,
Fer fro these other, up in an halke ;
There lurked and there coured she ;          465
For povre thing, wher-so it be,
Is shamfast, and despysed ay.
Acursed may wel be that day,
That povre man conceyved is ;
For god wot, al to selde, y-wis,          470
Is any povre man wel fed,
Or wel arayed or y-cled,
Or wel biloved, in swich wyse
In honour that he may aryse.

Alle these thinges, wel avysed,          475
As I have you er this devysed,
With gold and asure over alle
Depeynted were upon the walle.
Squar was the wal, and high somdel ;
Enclosed, and y-barred wel,          480
In stede of hegge, was that gardin ;
Com never shepherde therin.
Into that gardyn, wel [y-]wrought,
Who-so that me coude have brought,
By †laddre, or elles by degree,          485
It wolde wel have lyked me.
For swich solace, swich joye, and play,
I trowe that never man ne say,
As in that place delitous.
The gardin was not daungerous          490
To herberwe briddes many oon.
So riche a †yerd was never noon
Of briddes songe, and braunches grene.
Therin were briddes mo, I wene,
Than been in alle the rewme of Fraunce.
Ful blisful was the accordaunce          496
Of swete and pitous songe they made,
For al this world it onghte glade.

And I my-self so mery ferde,
Whan I hir blisful songes herde,          500
That for an hundred pound †nolde I,—
If that the passage openly
Hadde been unto me free—
That I nolde entren for to see
Thassemblee, god †it kepe and were !          505
Of briddes, whiche therinne were,
That songen, through hir mery throtes,
Daunces of love, and mery notes.

Whan I thus herde foules singe,
I fel faste in a weymentinge,          510
By which art, or by what engyn
I mighte come in that gardyn ;
But way I couthe finde noon
Into that gardin for to goon.
Ne nought wiste I if that ther were          515
Eyther hole or place [o]-where,
By which I mighte have entree ;
Ne ther was noon to teche me ;
For I was al aloon, y-wis,
†Ful wo and anguissous of this.          520
Til atte last bithoughte I me,
That by no weye ne mighte it be ;
That ther nas laddre or wey to passe,
Or hole, into so fair a place.

Tho gan I go a ful gret pas          525
Envyroning even in compas
The closing of the square wal,
Til that I fond a wiket smal
So shet, that I ne mighte in goon,
And other entree was ther noon.          530

### The Door.

Upon this dore I gan to smyte,
That was [so] fetys and so lyte ;
For other wey coude I not seke.
Ful long I shoof, and knokked eke,
And stood ful long and of[t] herkning 535
If that I herde †a wight coming ;
Til that the dore of thilke entree
A mayden curteys opened me.

### Ydelnesse.

Hir heer was as yelowe of hewe
As any basin scoured newe.          540
Hir flesh [as] tendre as is a chike,
With bente browes, smothe and slike;
And by mesure large were
The opening of hir yën clere.
Hir nose of good proporcioun,          545
Hir yën greye as a faucoun,
With swete breeth and wel savoured.

Hir face whyt and wel coloured,
With litel mouth, and round to see ;
A clove chin eek hadde she.                    550
Hir nekke was of good fasoun
In lengthe and gretnesse, by resoun,
Withoute bleyne, scabbe, or royne.
Fro Jerusalem unto Burgoyne
Ther nis a fairer nekke, y-wis,               555
To fele how smothe and softe it is.
Hir throte, al-so whyt of hewe
As snow on braunche snowed newe.
Of body ful wel wrought was she ;
Men neded not, in no cuntree,                 560
A fairer body for to seke.
And of fyn orfrays had she eke
A chapelet : so semly oon
Ne wered never mayde upon ;
And faire above that chapelet                 565
A rose gerland had she set.
She hadde [in honde] a gay mirour,
And with a riche gold tressour
Hir heed was tressed queyntely ;
Hir sleves sewed fetisly,                     570
And for to kepe hir hondes faire
Of gloves whyte she hadde a paire.
And she hadde on a cote of grene
Of cloth of Gaunt ; withouten wene,
Wel semed by hir apparayle                    575
She was not wont to greet travayle.
For whan she kempt was fetisly,
And wel arayed and richely,
Thanne had she doon al hir journee ;
For mery and wel bigoon was she.              580
She ladde a lusty lyf in May,
She hadde no thought, by night ne day,
Of no-thing, but it were oonly
To graythe hir wel and uncouthly.
  Whan that this dore hadde opened me
This †mayden, semely for to see,              586
I thanked hir as I best mighte,
And axede hir how that she highte,
And what she was, I axede eke.
And she to me was nought unmeke,              590
Ne of hir answer daungerous,
But faire answerde, and seide thus :—
' Lo, sir, my name is YDELNESSE ;
So clepe men me, more and lesse.
Ful mighty and ful riche am I,                595
And that of oon thing, namely ;
For I entende to no-thing
But to my joye, and my pleying,

And for to kembe and tresse me.
Aqueynted am I, and privee                    600
With Mirthe, lord of this gardyn,
That fro the lande †Alexandryn
Made the trees †be hider fet,
That in this gardin been y-set.               604
And when the trees were woxen on highte,
This wal, that stant here in thy sighte,
Dide Mirthe enclosen al aboute ;
And these images, al withoute,
He dide hem bothe entaile and peynte,
That neither ben jolyf ne queynte,           610
But they ben ful of sorowe and wo,
As thou hast seen a whyle ago.
  ' And ofte tyme, him to solace,
Sir Mirthe cometh into this place,
And eek with him cometh his meynee,
That liven in lust and jolitee.               616
And now is Mirthe therin, to here
The briddes, how they singen clere,
The mavis and the nightingale,
And other joly briddes smale.                 620
And thus he walketh to solace
Him and his folk ; for swetter place
To pleyen in he may not finde,
Although he soughte oon in-til Inde
The alther-fairest folk to see                625
That in this world may founde be
Hath Mirthe with him in his route,
That folowen him alwayes aboute.'
  When Ydelnesse had told al this,
And I hadde herkned wel, y-wis,               630
Than seide I to dame Ydelnesse,
' Now al-so wisly god me blesse,
Sith Mirthe, that is so fair and free,
Is in this yerde with his meynee,
Fro thilke assemblee, if I may,              635
Shal no man werne me to-day,
That I this night ne mote it see.
For, wel wene I, ther with him be
A fair and joly companye
Fulfilled of alle curtesye.'                  64c
And forth, without wordes mo,
In at the wiket wente I tho,
That Ydelnesse hadde opened me,
Into that gardin fair to see.

### The Garden.

  And whan I was [ther]in, y-wis,            645
Myn herte was ful glad of this.
For wel wende I ful sikerly
Have been in paradys erth[e]ly ;

So fair it was, that, trusteth wel,
It semed a place espirituel.    650
For certes, as at my devys,
Ther is no place in paradys
So good in for to dwelle or be
As in that GARDIN, thoughte me ;
For there was many a brid singing,    655
Throughout the yerde al thringing.
In many places were nightingales,
Alpes, finches, and wodewales,
That in her swete song delyten
In thilke †place as they habyten.    660
Ther mighte men see many flokkes
Of turtles and [of] laverokkes.
Chalaundres fele saw I there,
That wery, nigh forsongen were.
And thrustles, terins, and mavys,    665
That songen for to winne hem prys,
And eek to sormounte in hir song
†These other briddes hem among.
By note made fair servyse
These briddes, that I you devyse ;    670
They songe hir song as faire and wel
As angels doon espirituel.
And, trusteth wel, whan I hem herde,
Ful lustily and wel I ferde ;
For never yit swich melodye    675
Was herd of man that mighte dye.
Swich swete song was hem among,
That me thoughte it no briddes song,
But it was wonder lyk to be
Song of mermaydens of the see ;    680
That, for her singing is so clere,
Though we mermaydens clepe hem here
In English, as in our usaunce,
Men clepe[n] hem sereyns in Fraunce.
Ententif weren for to singe    685
These briddes that nought unkunninge
Were of hir craft, and apprentys,
But of [hir] song sotyl and wys.
And certes, whan I herde hir song,
And saw the grene place among,    690
In herte I wex so wonder gay,
That I was never erst, er that day,
So jolyf, nor so wel bigo,
Ne mery in herte, as I was tho.
And than wiste I, and saw ful wel,    695
That Ydelnesse me served wel,
That me putte in swich jolitee.
Hir freend wel oughte I for to be,
Sith she the dore of that gardyn

Hadde opened, and me leten in.    700
From hennesforth how that I wroughte,
I shal you tellen, as me thoughte.
First, whereof Mirthe served there,
And eek what folk ther with him were,
Without[e] fable I wol descryve.    705
And of that gardin eek as blyve
I wol you tellen after this.
The faire fasoun al, y-wis,
That wel [y-]wrought was for the nones,
I may not telle you al at ones :    710
But as I may and can, I shal
By ordre tellen you it al.
Ful fair servyse and eek ful swete
These briddes maden as they sete.
Layes of love, ful wel sowning    715
They songen in hir jargoning ;
Summe highe and summe eek lowe songe
Upon the braunches grene y-spronge.
The sweetnesse of hir melodye
Made al myn herte in †reverdye.    720
And whan that I hadde herd, I trowe,
These briddes singing on a rowe,
Than mighte I not withholde me
That I ne wente in for to see
Sir Mirthe ; for my desiring    725
Was him to seen, over alle thing,
His countenaunce and his manere :
That sighte was to me ful dere.

### Sir Mirthe.

Tho wente I forth on my right hond
Doun by a litel path I fond    730
Of mentes ful, and fenel grene ;
And faste by, withoute wene,
SIR MIRTHE I fond ; and right anoon
Unto sir Mirthe gan I goon,
Ther-as he was, him to solace.    735
And with him, in that lusty place,
So fair folk and so fresh hadde he,
That whan I saw, I wondred me
Fro whennes swich folk mighte come,
So faire they weren, alle and some ;    740
For they were lyk, as to my sighte,
To angels, that ben fethered brighte.

### Gladnesse.

This folk, of which I telle you so,
Upon a carole wenten tho.
A lady caroled hem, that highte    745
GLADNESSE, [the] blisful, the lighte ;
Wel coude she singe and lustily,
Non half so wel and semely.

And make in song swich refreininge,
It sat hir wonder wel to singe.          750
Hir vois ful cleer was and ful swete.
She was nought rude ne unmete,
But couthe y-now of swich doing
As longeth unto caroling :
For she was wont in every place          755
To singen first, folk to solace ;
For singing most she gaf hir to ;
No craft had she so leef to do.
    Tho mightest thou caroles seen,
And folk [ther] daunce and mery been, 760
And †make many a fair tourning
Upon the grene gras springing.
Ther mightest thou see these floutours,
Minstrales, and eek jogelours,
That wel to singe dide hir peyne.        765
Somme songe songes of Loreyne;
For in Loreyne hir notes be
Ful swetter than in this contree.
Ther was many a timbestere,
And saylours, that I dar wel swere       770
Couthe hir craft ful parfitly.
The timbres up ful sotilly
They caste, and hente[n hem] ful ofte
Upon a finger faire and softe,
That they [ne] fayled never-mo.          775
Ful fetis damiselles two,
Right yonge, and fulle of semlihede,
In kirtles, and non other wede,
And faire tressed every tresse,
Had Mirthe doon, for his noblesse,       780
Amidde the carole for to daunce ;
But her-of lyth no remembraunce,
How that they daunced queyntely.
That oon wolde come al prively
Agayn that other : and whan they were
Togidre almost, they threwe y-fere       786
Hir mouthes so, that through hir play
It semed as they kiste alway ;
To dauncen wel coude they the gyse ;
What shulde I more to you devyse ?       790
Ne †bede I never thennes go,
Whyles that I saw hem daunce so.

### Curtesye.

    Upon the carole wonder faste
I gan biholde ; til atte laste
A lady gan me for to espye,              795
And she was cleped CURTESYE,
The worshipful, the debonaire ;
I pray god ever falle hir faire !

Ful curteisly she called me,
' What do ye there, beau sire ?' quod
    she,                                800
' Come [neer], and if it lyke yow
To dauncen, daunceth with us now.'
And I, withoute tarying,
Wente into the caroling.
I was abasshed never a del,              805
But it me lykede right wel
That Curtesye me cleped so,
And bad me on the daunce go.
For if I hadde durst, certeyn
I wolde have caroled right fayn,         810
As man that was to daunce blythe.
Than gan I loken ofte sythe
The shap, the bodies, and the cheres,
The countenaunce and the maneres
Of alle the folk that daunced there,     815
And I shal telle what they were.

### Mirthe.

    Ful fair was Mirthe, ful long and high ;
A fairer man I never sigh.
As round as appel was his face,
Ful rody and whyt in every place.        820
Fetys he was and wel beseye,
With metely mouth and yën greye ;
His nose by mesure wrought ful right ;
Crisp was his heer, and eek ful bright.
His shuldres of a large brede,           825
And smalish in the girdilstede.
He semed lyk a portreiture,
So noble he was of his stature,
So fair, so joly, and so fetys,
With limes wrought at poynt devys,       830
Deliver, smert, and of gret might ;
Ne sawe thou never man so light.
Of berde unnethe hadde he no-thing,
For it was in the firste spring.
Ful yong he was, and mery of thought,
And in samyt, with briddes wrought  836
And with gold beten fetisly,
His body was clad ful richely.
Wrought was his robe in straunge gyse,
And al to-slitered for queyntyse        840
In many a place, lowe and hye.
And shod he was with greet maistrye,
With shoon decoped, and with laas.
By druerye, and by solas,
His leef a rosen chapelet               845
Had maad, and on his heed it set.
    And wite ye who was his leef?

### Gladnesse.

Dame GLADNES ther was him so leef,
That singeth so wel with glad corage,
That from she was twelve yeer of age, 850
She of hir love graunt him made.
Sir Mirthe hir by the finger hadde
[In] daunsing, and she him also ;
Gret love was atwixe hem two.
Bothe were they faire and brighte of hewe;
She semede lyk a rose newe     856
Of colour, and hir flesh so tendre,
That with a brere smale and slendre
Men mighte it cleve, I dar wel †sayn.
Hir forheed, frounceles al †playn.     860
Bente were hir browes two,
Hir yën greye, and gladde also,
That laughede ay in hir semblaunt,
First or the mouth, by covenaunt.
I †noot what of hir nose descryve ;     865
So fair hath no womman alyve . . . .
Hir heer was yelowe, and cleer shyning,
I wot no lady so lyking.
Of orfrays fresh was hir gerland ;
I, whiche seen have a thousand,     870
Saugh never, y-wis, no gerlond yit.
So wel [y]-wrought of silk as it.
And in an over-gilt samyt
Clad she was, by gret delyt.
Of which hir leef a robe werde,     875
The myrier she in herte ferde.

### Cupide.

And next hir wente, on hir other syde,
The god of Love, that can devyde
Love, †as him lyketh it [to] be.
But he can cherles daunten, he,     880
And maken folkes pryde fallen.
And he can wel these lordes thrallen,
And ladies putte at lowe degree,
Whan he may hem to proude see.
This God of Love of his fasoun     885
Was lyk no knave, ne quistroun ;
His beautee gretly was to pryse.
But of his robe to devyse
I drede encombred for to be.
For nought y-clad in silk was he,     890
But al in floures and flourettes,
Y-painted al with amorettes ;
And with losenges and scochouns,
With briddes, libardes, and lyouns,
And other beestes wrought ful wel.     895
His garnement was everydel

Y-portreyd and y-wrought with floures,
By dyvers medling of coloures.
Floures ther were of many gyse
Y-set by compas in assyse ;     900
Ther lakked no flour, to my dome,
Ne nought so muche as flour of brome,
Ne violete, no eek pervenke,
Ne flour non, that man can on thenke ;
And many a rose-leef ful long     905
Was entermedled ther-among :
And also on his heed was set
Of roses rede a chapelet.
But nightingales, a ful gret route,
That flyen over his heed aboute,     910
The leves felden as they flyen ;
And he was al with briddes wryen,
With popinjay, with nightingale,
With chalaundre, and with wodewale,
With finch,with lark,and with archaungel.
He semede as he were an aungel     916
That doun were comen fro hevene clere.

### Swete-Loking.

Love hadde with him a bachelere,
That he made alweyes with him be ;
SWETE-LOKING cleped was he.     920
This bachelere stood biholding
The daunce, and in his honde holding
†Turke bowes two hadde he.
That oon of hem was of a tree
That bereth a fruyt of savour wikke ; 925
Ful croked was that foule stikke,
And knotty here and there also,
And blak as bery, or any slo.
That other bowe was of a plante
Without wem, I dar warante,     930
Ful even, and by proporcioun
Tretys and long, of good fasoun.
And it was peynted wel and thwiten,
And over-al diapred and writen
With ladies and with bacheleres,     935
Ful lightsom and [ful] glad of cheres.
These bowes two held Swete-Loking,
That semed lyk no gadeling.
And ten brode arowes held he there,
Of which five in his right hond were. 940
But they were shaven wel and dight,
Nokked and fethered a-right ;
And al they were with gold bigoon,
And stronge poynted everichoon,
And sharpe for to kerven weel.     945
But iren was ther noon ne steel ;

For al was gold, men mighte it see,
Out-take the fetheres and the tree.

### Beautee.

The swiftest of these arowes fyve
Out of a bowe for to dryve,                   950
And best [y]-fethered for to flee,
And fairest eek, was cleped BEAUTEE.

### Simplesse.

That other arowe, that hurteth lesse,
Was cleped, as I trowe, SIMPLESSE.

### Fraunchyse.

The thridde cleped was FRAUNCHYSE;           955
That fethered was, in noble wyse,
With valour and with curtesye.

### Companye.

The fourthe was cleped COMPANYE,
That hevy for to †sheten is;
But who-so sheteth right, y-wis,             960
May therwith doon gret harm and wo.

### Fair-Semblaunt.

The fifte of these, and laste also,
FAIR-SEMBLAUNT men that arowe calle,
The leeste grevous of hem alle;
Yit can it make a ful gret wounde,           965
But he may hope his sores sounde,
That hurt is with that arowe, y-wis;
His wo the bet bistowed is.
For he may soner have gladnesse,
His langour oughte be the lesse.             970

Fyve arowes were of other gyse,
That been ful foule to devyse;
For shaft and ende, sooth to telle,
Were al-so blak as feend in helle.

### Pryde.

The first of hem is called PRYDE;            975

### Vilanye.

That other arowe next him bisyde,
It was [y]-cleped VILANYE;
That arowe was as with felonye
Envenimed, and with spitous blame.

### Shame.

The thridde of hem was cleped SHAME.  980

### Wanhope.

The fourthe, WANHOPE cleped is,

### Newe-Thought.

The fifte, the NEWE-THOUGHT, y-wis.

These arowes that I speke of here,
Were alle fyve †of oon manere,
And alle were they resemblable.              985
To hem was wel sitting and able
The foule croked bowe hidous,

That knotty was, and al roynous.
That bowe semede wel to shete
These arowes fyve, that been unmete,  990
Contrarie to that other fyve.
But though I telle not as blyve
Of hir power, ne of hir might,
Her-after shal I tellen right
The sothe, and eek signifiaunce,             995
As fer as I have remembraunce:
Al shal be seid, I undertake,
Er of this boke an ende I make.

Now come I to my tale ageyn.
But alderfirst, I wol you seyn             1000
The fasoun and the countenaunces
Of al the folk that on the daunce is.
The God of Love, jolyf and light,
Ladde on his honde a lady bright,
Of high prys, and of greet degree.         1005

### Beautee.

This lady called was BEAUTEE,
† As was an arowe, of which I tolde.
Ful wel [y]-thewed was she holde;
Ne she was derk ne broun, but bright,
And cleer as [is] the mone-light,          1010
Ageyn whom alle the sterres semen
But smale candels, as we demen.
Hir flesh was tendre as dewe of flour,
Hir chere was simple as byrde in bour;
As whyt as lilie or rose in rys            1015
Hir face, gentil and tretys.
Fetys she was, and smal to see;
No †windred browes hadde she,
Ne popped hir, for it neded nought
To windre hir, or to peynte hir ought.1020
Hir tresses yelowe and longe straughten,
Unto hir heles doun they raughten:
Hir nose, hir mouth, and eye and cheke
Wel wrought, and al the remenaunt eke.
A ful gret savour and a swote             1025
Me †thinketh in myn herte rote,
As helpe me god, whan I remembre
Of the fasoun of every membre!
In world is noon so fair a wight;
For yong she was, and hewed bright,         1030
†Wys, plesaunt, and fetys withalle,
Gente, and in hir middel smalle.

### Richesse.

Bisyde Beaute yede RICHESSE,
†An high lady of greet noblesse,
And greet of prys in every place.          1035
But who-so durste to hir trespace,

Or til hir folk, in †worde or dede,
He were ful hardy, out of drede ;
For bothe she helpe and hindre may :
And that is nought of yisterday　　1040
That riche folk have ful gret might
To helpe, and eek to greve a wight.
The beste and grettest of valour
Diden Richesse ful gret honour,
And besy weren hir to serve ;　　1045
For that they wolde hir love deserve,
They cleped hir ' Lady,' grete and smalle ;
This wyde world hir dredeth alle ;
This world is al in hir daungere.
Hir court hath many a losengere,　　1050
And many a traytour envious,
That been ful besy and curious
For to dispreisen, and to blame
That best deserven love and name
Bifore the folk, hem to bigylen,　　1055
These losengeres hem preyse, and smylen,
And thus the world with word anoynten ;
But afterward they †prikke and poynten
The folk right to the bare boon,
Bihinde her bak whan they ben goon,
And foule abate the folkes prys.　　1061
Ful many a worthy man and wys,
An hundred, have [they] don to dye,
These losengeres, through flaterye ;
And maketh folk ful straunge be,　　1065
Ther-as hem oughte be prive.
Wel yvel mote they thryve and thee,
And yvel aryved mote they be,
These losengeres, ful of envye !
No good man loveth hir companye.　　1070

Richesse a robe of purpre on hadde,
Ne trowe not that I lye or madde ;
For in this world is noon it liche,
Ne by a thousand deel so riche,
Ne noon so fair ; for it ful wel　　1075
With orfrays leyd was everydel,
And portrayed in the ribaninges
Of dukes stories, and of kinges.
And with a bend of gold tasseled,
And knoppes fyne of gold †ameled.　　1080
Aboute hir nekke of gentil entaile
Was shet the riche chevesaile,
In which ther was ful gret plentee
Of stones clere and bright to see.

Rychesse a girdel hadde upon,　　1085
The bokel of it was of a stoon
Of vertu grect, and mochel of might ;

For who-so bar the stoon so bright,
Of venim ††thurte him no-thing doute,
While he the stoon hadde him aboute.
That stoon was greetly for to love,　　1091
And til a riche mannes bihove
Worth al the gold in Rome and Fryse.
The mourdaunt, wought in noble wyse,
Was of a stoon ful precious,　　1095
That was so fyn and vertuous,
That hool a man it coude make
Of palasye, and of tooth-ake.
And yit the stoon hadde suche a grace,
That he was siker in every place,　　1100
Al thilke day, not blind to been,
That fasting mighte that stoon seen.
The barres were of gold ful fyne,
Upon a tissu of satyne,
Ful hevy, greet, and no-thing light,　　1105
In everich was a besaunt-wight.
Upon the tresses of Richesse
Was set a cercle, for noblesse,
Of brend gold, that ful lighte shoon ;
So fair, trowe I, was never noon.　　1110
But he were cunning, for the nones,
That coude devysen alle the stones
That in that cercle shewen clere ;
It is a wonder thing to here.
For no man coude preyse or gesse　　1115
Of hem the valewe or richesse.
Rubyes there were, saphyres, †jagounces,
And emeraudes, more than two ounces.
But al bifore, ful sotilly,
A fyn carboucle set saugh I.　　1120
The stoon so cleer was and so bright,
That, al-so sone as it was night,
Men mighte seen to go, for nede,
A myle or two, in lengthe and brede,
Swich light [tho] sprang out of the stoon,
That Richesse wonder brighte shoon, 1126
Bothe hir heed, and al hir face,
And eke aboute hir al the place.

Dame Richesse on hir hond gan lede
A yong man ful of semelihede,　　1130
That she best loved of any thing ;
His lust was muche in housholding.
In clothing was he ful fetys,
And lovede wel have hors of prys.
He wende to have reproved be　　1135
Of thefte or mordre, if that he
Hadde in his stable an hakeney.
And therfore he desyred ay

To been aqueynted with Richesse ;
For al his purpos, as I gesse, 1140
Was for to make greet dispense,
Withoute werning or defence.
And Richesse might it wel sustene,
And hir dispenses wel mayntene,
And him alwey swich plentee sende 1145
Of gold and silver for to spende
Withoute lakking or daungere,
As it were poured in a garnere.

### Largesse.

And after on the daunce wente
LARGESSE, that sette al hir entente 1150
For to be honourable and free ;
Of Alexandres kin was she ;
Hir moste joye was, y-wis,
Whan that she yaf, and seide 'have this.'
Not Avarice, the foule captyf, 1155
Was half to grype so ententyf,
As Largesse is to yeve and spende.
And god y-nough alwey hir sende,
So that the more she yaf awey,
The more, y-wis, she hadde alwey. 1160
Gret loos hath Largesse, and gret prys ;
For bothe wys folk and unwys
Were hoolly to hir baundon brought,
So wel with yiftes hath she wrought.
And if she hadde an enemy, 1165
I trowe, that she coude craftily
Make him ful sone hir freend to be,
So large of yift and free was she ;
Therfore she stood in love and grace
Of riche and povre in every place. 1170
A ful gret fool is he, y-wis,
That bothe riche and nigard is.
A lord may have no maner vice
That greveth more than avarice.
For nigard never with strengthe of hond
May winne him greet lordship or lond.
For freendes al to fewe hath he 1177
To doon his wil perfourmed be.
And who-so wol have freendes here,
He may not holde his tresour dere. 1180
For by ensample I telle this,
Right as an adamaunt, y-wis,
Can drawen to him sotilly
The yren, that is leyd thereby,
So draweth folkes hertes, y-wis, 1185
Silver and gold that yeven is.

Largesse hadde on a robe fresshe
Of riche purpur †Sarsinesshe.

Wel fourmed was hir face and clere,
And opened had she hir colere ; 1190
For she right there hadde in present
Unto a lady maad present
Of a gold broche, ful wel wrought.
And certes, it missat hir nought ;
For through hir smokke, wrought with
    silk, 1195
The flesh was seen, as whyt as milk.
Largesse, that worthy was and wys,
Held by the honde a knight of prys,
Was sib to Arthour of Bretaigne.
And that was he that bar the enseigne
Of worship, and the †gonfanoun. 1201
And yit he is of swich renoun,
That men of him seye faire thinges
Bifore barouns, erles, and kinges.
This knight was comen al newely 1205
Fro tourneyinge faste by ;
Ther hadde he doon gret chivalrye
Through his vertu and his maistrye ;
And for the love of his lemman
†Had cast doun many a doughty man. 1210

### Fraunchyse.

And next him daunced dame FRAUN-
    CHYSE,
Arrayed in ful noble gyse.
She was not broun ne dun of hewe,
But whyt as snowe y-fallen newe.
Hir nose was wrought at poynt devys,1215
For it was gentil and tretys ;
With eyen gladde, and browes bente ;
Hir heer doun to hir heles wente.
And she was simple as dowve on tree,
Ful debonaire of herte was she. 1220
She durste never seyn ne do
But that [thing] that hir longed to.
And if a man were in distresse,
And for hir love in hevinesse,
Hir herte wolde have ful greet pitee, 1225
She was so amiable and free.
For were a man for hir bistad,
She wolde ben right sore adrad
That she dide over greet outrage,
But she him holpe his harm to aswage ;
Hir thoughte it elles a vilanye. 1231
And she hadde on a sukkenye,
That not of †hempen herdes was ;
So fair was noon in alle Arras.
Lord, it was rideled fetysly ! 1235
Ther nas nat †oo poynt, trewely,

That it nas in his right assyse.
Ful wel y-clothed was Fraunchyse;
For ther is no cloth sitteth bet
On damiselle, than doth roket.     1240
A womman wel more fetys is
In roket than in cote, y-wis.
The whyte roket, rideled faire,
†Bitokened, that ful debonaire
And swete was she that it bere.     1245
    By hir daunced a bachelere ;
I can not telle you what he highte,
But fair he was, and of good highte,
Al hadde he be, I sey no more,
The lordes sone of Windesore.     1250

### Curtesye.

And next that daunced CURTESYE,
That preised was of lowe and hye,
For neither proud ne fool was she.
She for to daunce called me,
(I pray god yeve hir right good grace !) 1255
Whan I com first into the place.
She was not nyce, ne outrageous,
But wys and war, and vertuous,
Of faire speche, and faire answere ;
Was never wight misseid of here ;     1260
She bar no rancour to no wight.
Cleer broun she was, and therto bright
Of face, of body avenaunt ;
I wot no lady so plesaunt.
She were worthy for to bene     1265
An emperesse or crouned quene.
    And by hir wente a knight dauncing
That worthy was and wel speking,
And ful wel coude he doon honour.
The knight was fair and stif in stour, 1270
And in armure a semely man,
And wel biloved of his lemman.

### Ydelnesse.

Fair YDELNESSE than saugh I,
That alwey was me faste by.
Of hir have I, withouten fayle,     1275
Told yow the shap and aparayle ;
For (as I seide) lo, that was she
That dide me so great bountee,
That she the gate of the gardin
Undide, and leet me passen in.     1280

### Youthe.

And after daunced, as I gesse,
†YOUTHE, fulfild of lustinesse,
That nas not yit twelve yeer of age,
With herte wilde, and thought volage;

Nyce she was, but she ne mente     1285
Noon harm ne slight in hir entente,
But only lust and jolitee.
For yonge folk, wel witen ye,
Have litel thought but on hir play.
Hir lemman was bisyde alway,     1290
In swich a gyse, that he hir kiste
At alle tymes that him liste,
That al the daunce mighte it see ;
They make no force of privetee ;
For who spak of hem yvel or wel,     1295
They were ashamed never-a-del,
But men mighte seen hem kisse there,
As it two yonge douves were.
For yong was thilke bachelere,
Of beaute wot I noon his pere ;     1300
And he was right of swich an age
As Youthe his leef, and swich corage.
    The lusty folk †thus daunced there,
And also other that with hem were,
That weren alle of hir meynee ;     1305
Ful hende folk, and wys, and free,
And folk of fair port, trewely,
Ther weren alle comunly.
    Whan I hadde seen the countenaunces
Of hem that ladden thus these daunces,
Than hadde I wil to goon and see     1311
The gardin that so lyked me,
And loken on these faire †loreres,
On pyn-trees, cedres, and oliveres.
The daunces than †y-ended were ;     1315
For many of hem that daunced there
Were with hir loves went awey
Under the trees to have hir pley.
    A, lord ! they lived lustily !
A gret fool were he, sikerly,     1320
That nolde, his thankes, swich lyf lede !
For this dar I seyn, out of drede,
That who-so mighte so wel fare,
For better lyf †thurte him not care ;
For ther nis so good paradys     1325
As have a love at his devys.
    Out of that place wente I tho,
And in that gardin gan I go,
Pleying along ful merily.
The God of Love ful hastely     1330
Unto him Swete-Loking clepte,
No lenger wolde he that †he kepte
His bowe of golde, that shoon so bright.
He †bad him bende it anon-right ;
And he ful sone [it] sette †on ende,     1335

And at a braid he gan it bende,
And took him of his arowes fyve,
Ful sharpe and redy for to dryve.
Now god that sit in magestee
Fro deedly woundes kepe me,          1340
If so be that he †wol me shete ;
For if I with his arowe mete,
It †wol me greven sore, y-wis !
But I, that no-thing wiste of this,
Wente up and doun ful many a wey, 1345
And he me folwed faste alwey ;
But no-wher wolde I reste me,
Til I hadde al the †yerde in be.
    The gardin was, by mesuring,
Right even and squar in compassing ; 1350
It was as long as it was large.

### The Trees.

Of fruyt hadde every tree his charge,
But it were any hidous tree
Of which ther were two or three.
Ther were, and that wot I ful wel,   1355
Of pomgarnettes a ful gret del ;
That is a fruyt ful wel to lyke,
Namely to folk whan they ben syke.
And trees ther were, greet foisoun,
That baren notes in hir sesoun,      1360
Such as men notemigges calle,
That swote of savour been withalle.
And alemandres greet plentee,
Figes, and many a date-tree
Ther weren, if men hadde nede,       1365
Through the †yerd in length and brede.
Ther was eek wexing many a spyce,
As clow-gelofre, and licoryce,
Gingere, and greyn de †paradys,
Canelle, and setewale of prys,       1370
And many a spyce delitable,
To eten whan men ryse fro table.
And many hoomly trees ther were,
That peches, coynes, and apples bere,
Medlers, ploumes, peres, chesteynes, 1375
Cheryse, of whiche many on fayn is,
Notes, aleys, and bolas,
That for to seen it was solas ;
With many high lorer and pyn
Was renged clene al that gardyn ;    1380
With cipres, and with oliveres,
Of which that nigh no plente here is.
Ther were elmes grete and stronge,
Maples, asshe, ook, ash, planes longe,
Fyn ew, popler, and lindes faire,    1385

And othere trees ful many a payre.
    What sholde I telle you more of it ?
Ther were so many treës yit,
That I sholde al encombred be
Er I had rekened every tree.         1390
    These trees were set, that I devyse,
Oon from another, in assyse,
Five fadome or sixe, I trowe so,
But they were hye and grete also :
And for to kepe out wel the sonne,   1395
The croppes were so thikke y-ronne,
And every braunch in other †knet,
And ful of grene leves †set,
That sonne mighte noon descende,
Lest [it] the tendre grasses shende. 1400
Ther mighte men does and roes y-see,
And of squirels ful greet plentee,
From bough to bough alwey leping.
Conies ther were also playing,
That comen out of hir claperes       1405
Of sondry colours and maneres,
And maden many a turneying
Upon the fresshe gras springing.

### The Welles.

In places saw I WELLES there,
In whiche ther no frogges were,      1410
And fair in shadwe was every welle ;
But I ne can the nombre telle
Of stremes smale, that by devys
Mirthe had don come through condys,
Of which the water, in renning,      1415
Gan make a noyse ful lyking.
    About the brinkes of thise welles,
And by the stremes over-al elles
Sprang up the gras, as thikke y-set
And softe as any veluët,             1420
On which men mighte his lemman leye,
As on a fetherbed, to pleye,
For th'erthe was ful softe and swete.
Through moisture of the welle wete
Sprang up the sote grene gras,       1425
As fair, as thikke, as mister was.
But muche amended it the place,
That th'erthe was of swich a grace
That it of floures had plente,
That both in somer and winter be.    1430
    Ther sprang the violete al newe,
And fresshe pervinke, riche of hewe,
And floures yelowe, whyte, and rede ;
Swich plentee grew ther never in mede.
Ful gay was al the ground, and queynt,

And poudred, as men had it peynt,   1436
With many a fresh and sondry flour,
That casten up ful good savour.

    I wol not longe holde you in fable
Of al this gardin †delitable.   1440
I moot my tonge stinten nede,
For I ne may, withouten drede,
Naught tellen you the beautee al,
Ne half the bountee therewithal.

    I wente on right honde and on left 1445
Aboute the place ; it was not left,
Til I hadde al the †yerde in been,
In the †estres that men mighte seen.
And thus whyle I wente in my pley,
The God of Love me folowed ay,   1450
Right as an hunter can abyde
The beste, til he seeth his tyde
To †shete, at good mes, to the dere,
Whan that him nedeth go no nere.

    And so befil, I rested me   1455
Besyde a welle, under a tree,
Which tree in Fraunce men call a pyn.
But, sith the tyme of king Pepyn,
Ne grew ther tree in mannes sighte
So fair, ne so wel woxe in highte ;   1460
In al that yerde so high was noon.
And springing in a marble-stoon
Had nature set, the sothe to telle,
Under that pyn-tree a welle.
And on the border, al withoute,   1465
Was writen, in the stone aboute,
Lettres smale, that seyden thus,
'Here starf the faire Narcisus.'

### Narcisus.

NARCISUS was a bachelere,
That Love had caught in his daungere,
And in his net gan him so streyne,   1471
And dide him so to wepe and pleyne,
That nede him muste his lyf forgo.
For a fair lady, hight Echo,
Him loved over any creature,   1475
And gan for him swich peyne endure,
That on a tyme she him tolde,
That, if he hir loven nolde,
That hir behoved nedes dye,
Ther lay non other remedye.   1480
But natheles, for his beautee,
So fiers and daungerous was he,
That he nolde graunten hir asking,
For weping, ne for fair praying.
And whan she herde him werne hir so,

She hadde in herte so gret wo,   1486
And took it in so gret dispyt,
That she, withoute more respyt,
Was deed anoon. But, er she deyde,
Ful pitously to god she preyde,   1490
That proude-herted Narcisus,
That was in love so daungerous,
Mighte on a day ben hampred so
For love, and been so hoot for wo,
That never he mighte joye atteyne ; 1495
Than shulde he fele in every veyne
What sorowe trewe lovers maken,
That been so †vilaynsly forsaken.

    This prayer was but resonable,
Therfor god held it ferme and stable : 1500
For Narcisus, shortly to telle,
By aventure com to that welle
To reste him in that shadowing
A day, whan he com fro hunting.
This Narcisus had suffred paynes   1505
For renning alday in the playnes,
And was for thurst in greet distresse
Of hete, and of his werinesse
That hadde his breeth almost binomen.
Whan he was to that welle y-comen, 1510
That shadwed was with braunches grene,
He thoughte of thilke water shene
To drinke and fresshe him wel withalle ;
And doun on knees he gan to falle,
And forth his heed and nekke out-
     straughte   1515
To drinken of that welle a draughte.
And in the water anoon was sene
His nose, his mouth, his yën shene,
And he ther-of was al abasshed ;
His owne shadowe had him bitrasshed.
For wel wende he the forme see   1521
Of a child of greet beautee.
Wel couthe Love him wreke tho
Of daunger and of pryde also
That Narcisus somtyme him bere.   1525
He quitte him wel his guerdon there ;
For he †so musede in the welle,
That, shortly al the sothe to telle,
He lovede his owne shadowe so,
That atte laste he starf for wo.   1530
For whan he saugh that he his wille
Mighte in no maner wey fulfille,
And that he was so faste caught
That he him couthe comfort naught,
He loste his wit right in that place, 1535

And deyde within a litel space.
And thus his warisoun he took
For the lady that he forsook.

Ladyes, I preye ensample taketh,
Ye that ayeins your love mistaketh : 1540
For if hir deeth be yow to wyte,
God can ful wel your whyle quyte.

Whan that this lettre, of whiche I telle,
Had taught me that it was the welle
Of Narcisus in his beautee,          1545
I gan anoon withdrawe me,
Whan it fel in my remembraunce,
That him bitidde swich mischaunce.

**The Welle.**

But at the laste than thoughte I,
That scatheles, ful sikerly,         1550
I mighte unto THE WELLE go.
Wherof shulde I abasshen so ?
Unto the welle than wente I me,
And doun I louted for to see
The clere water in the stoon,        1555
And eek the gravel, which that shoon
Down in the botme, as silver fyn ;
For of the welle, this is the fyn,
In world is noon so cleer of hewe.
The water is ever fresh and newe     1560
That welmeth up in wawes brighte
The mountaunce of two finger highte.
Abouten it is gras springing,
For moiste so thikke and wel lyking,
That it ne may in winter dye,        1565
No more than may the see be drye.

Down at the botme set saw I
Two cristal stones craftely
In thilke fresshe and faire welle.
But o thing soothly dar I telle,     1570
That ye wol holde a greet mervayle
Whan it is told, withouten fayle.
For whan the sonne, cleer in sighte,
Cast in that welle his bemes brighte,
And that the heet descended is,      1575
Than taketh the cristal stoon, y-wis,
Agayn the sonne an hundred hewes,
Blewe, yelowe, and rede, that fresh and
    newe is.
Yit hath the merveilous cristal      1579
Swich strengthe, that the place overal,
Bothe fowl and tree, and leves grene,
And al the yerd in it is sene.
And for to doon you understonde,
To make ensample wol I fonde ;

Right as a mirour openly             1585
Sheweth al thing that stant therby,
As wel the colour as the figure,
Withouten any coverture ;
Right so the cristal stoon, shyning,
Withouten any disceyving,            1590
The †estres of the yerde accuseth
To him that in the water museth ;
For ever, in which half that †he be,
† He may wel half the gardin see ;
And if he turne, he may right wel    1595
Seen the remenaunt everydel.
For ther is noon so litel thing
So hid, ne closed with shitting,
That it ne is sene, as though it were
Peynted in the cristal there.        1600

This is the mirour perilous,
In which the proude Narcisus
Saw al his face fair and bright,
That made him sith to lye upright.
For who-so loke in that mirour,      1605
Ther may no-thing ben his socour
That he ne shal ther seen som thing
That shal him lede into †loving.
Ful many a worthy man hath it
Y-blent ; for folk of grettest wit   1610
Ben sone caught here and awayted ;
Withouten respyt been they bayted.
Heer comth to folk of-newe rage,
Heer chaungeth many wight corage ;
Heer lyth no reed ne wit therto ;    1615
For Venus sone, daun Cupido,
Hath sowen there of love the seed,
That help ne lyth ther noon, ne reed,
So cercleth it the welle aboute.
His ginnes hath he set withoute      1620
Right for to cacche in his panteres
These damoysels and bacheleres.
Love will noon other bridde cacche,
Though he sette either net or lacche. 1624
And for the seed that heer was sowen,
This welle is cleped, as wel is knowen,
The Welle of Love, of verray right,
Of which ther hath ful many a wight
Spoke in bokes dyversely.
But they shulle never so verily      1630
Descripcioun of the welle here,
No eek the sothe of this matere,
As ye shulle, whan I have undo
The craft that hir bilongeth to.

Alway me lyked for to dwelle,        1635

To seen the cristal in the welle,
That shewed me ful openly
A thousand thinges faste by.
But I may saye, in sory houre
Stood I to loken or to poure;　　　1640
For sithen [have] I sore †syked,
That mirour hath me now entryked.
But hadde I first knowen in my wit
The vertue and [the] †strengthe of it,
I nolde not have mused there;　　　1645
Me hadde bet ben elles-where;
For in the snare I fel anoon,
That hath †bitraisshed many oon.

### The Roser.

In thilke mirour saw I tho,
Among a thousand thinges mo,　　　1650
A roser charged ful of roses,
That with an hegge aboute enclos is.
Tho had I swich lust and envye,
That, for Parys ne for Pavye,
Nolde I have left to goon and see　　1655
Ther grettest hepe of roses be.
Whan I was with this rage hent,
That caught hath many a man and shent,
Toward the roser gan I go.
And whan I was not fer therfro,　　1660
The savour of the roses swote
Me smoot right to the herte rote,
As I hadde al embawmed †be.
And if I ne hadde endouted me
To have ben hated or assailed,　　　1665
My thankes, †wolde I not have failed
To pulle a rose of al that route
To bere[n] in myn honde aboute,
And smellen to it wher I wente;
But ever I dredde me to repente,　　1670

And lest it greved or for-thoughte
The lord that thilke gardyn wroughte.
Of roses were ther gret woon,
So faire †wexe never in roon.
Of knoppes clos, some saw I there,　1675
And some wel beter woxen were;
And some ther been of other meysoun,
That drowe nigh to hir sesoun,
And spedde hem faste for to sprede;
I love wel swiche roses rede;　　　1680
For brode roses, and open also,
Ben passed in a day or two;
But knoppes wilen fresshe be
Two dayes atte leest, or three.
The knoppes gretly lyked me,　　　1685
For fairer may ther no man see.
Who-so mighte have[n] oon of alle,
It oughte him been ful leef withalle.
Mighte I [a] gerlond of hem geten,
For no richesse I wolde it leten.　　1690

### The Knoppe.

Among the knoppes I chees oon
So fair, that of the remenaunt noon
Ne preyse I half so wel as it,
Whan I avyse it in my wit.
For it so wel was enlumyned　　　1695
With colour reed, as wel [y]-fyned
As nature couthe it make faire,
And it †had leves wel foure paire,
That Kinde had set through his knowing
About the rede †rose springing.　　1700
The stalke was as risshe right,
And theron stood the knoppe upright,
That it ne bowed upon no syde.
The swote smelle sprong so wyde
That it dide al the place aboute—　　1705

### FRAGMENT B.

*[Line 1705 is incomplete, as the sentence has no verb. Here the genuine portion ends.
Line 1706 gives a false rime, and is by another hand.]*

Whan I had smelled the savour swote,
No wille hadde I fro thens yit go,
But somdel neer it wente I tho
To take it; but myn hond, for drede,
Ne dorste I to the rose bede,　　　1710
For thistels sharpe, of many maneres,
Netles, thornes, and hoked breres;

†Ful muche they distourbled me,
For sore I dradde to harmed be.
The God of Love, with bowe bent,　1715
That al day set hadde his talent
To pursuen and to spyen me,
Was stonding by a fige-tree.
And whan he sawe how that I

Had chosen so ententifly     1720
The †botoun, more unto my pay
Than any other that I say,
He took an arowe ful sharply whet,
And in his bowe whan it was set,
He streight up to his ere drough     1725
The stronge bowe, that was so tough,
And shet at me so wonder smerte,
That through myn eye unto myn herte
The takel smoot, and depe it wente.
And ther-with-al such cold me hente,
That, under clothes warme and softe, 1731
†Sith that day I have chevered ofte.

   Whan I was hurt thus in [that] stounde,
I fel doun plat unto the grounde.
Myn herte failed and feynted ay,    1735
And long tyme [ther] a-swone I lay.
But whan I com out of swoning,
And hadde wit, and my feling,
I was al maat, and wende ful wel
Of blood have loren a ful gret del.    1740
But certes, the arowe that in me stood
Of me ne drew no drope of blood,
For-why I found my wounde al dreye.
Than took I with myn hondis tweye
The arowe, and ful fast out it plight, 1745
And in the pulling sore I sight.
So at the last the shaft of tree
I drough out, with the fethers three.
But yet the hoked heed, y-wis,
The whiche Beautee callid is,    1750
Gan so depe in myn herte passe,
That I it mighte nought arace ;
But in myn herte stille it stood,
Al bledde I not a drope of blood.
I was bothe anguissous and trouble   1755
For the peril that I saw double ;
I niste what to seye or do,
Ne gete a leche my woundis †to ;
For neithir thurgh gras ne rote,
Ne hadde I help of hope ne bote.    1760
But to the botoun ever-mo
Myn herte drew ; for al my wo,
My thought was in non other thing.
For hadde it been in my keping,
It wolde have brought my lyf agayn. 1765
For †certeinly, I dar wel seyn,
The sight only, and the savour,
Alegged muche of my langour.

   Than gan I for to drawe me
Toward the botoun fair to see ;    1770

And Love hadde gete him, in †a throwe,
Another arowe into his bowe,
And for to shete gan him dresse ;
The arowis name was Simplesse.
And whan that Love gan nyghe me nere,
He drow it up, withouten were,    1776
And shet at me with al his might,
So that this arowe anon-right
Thourghout [myn] eigh, as it was founde,
Into myn herte hath maad a wounde.
Thanne I anoon dide al my crafte   1781
For to drawen out the shafte,
And ther-with-al I sighed eft.
But in myn herte the heed was left,
Which ay encresid my desyre,    1785
Unto the botoun drawe nere ;
And ever, mo that me was wo,
The more desyr hadde I to go
Unto the roser, where that grew
The fresshe botoun so bright of hewe. 1790
Betir me were have leten be ;
But it bihoved nedes me
To don right as myn herte bad.
For ever the body must be lad
Aftir the herte ; in wele and wo,    1795
Of force togidre they must go.
But never this archer wolde fyne
To shete at me with all his pyne,
And for to make me to him mete.

   The thridde arowe he gan to shete 1800
Whan best his tyme he mighte espye,
The which was named Curtesye ;
Inte myn herte it dide avale.
A-swone I fel, bothe deed and pale ;
Long tyme I lay, and stired nought, 1805
Til I abraid out of my thought.
And faste than I avysed me
To drawe[n] out the shafte of tree ;
But ever the heed was left bihinde
For ought I couthe pulle or winde,   1810
So sore it stikid whan I was hit,
That by no craft I might it flit ;
But anguissous and ful of thought,
I †felte such wo, my wounde ay wrought,
That somoned me alway to go    1815
Toward the rose, that pleased me so ;
But I ne durste in no manere,
Bicause the archer was so nere.
For evermore gladly, as I rede,
Brent child of fyr hath muche drede. 1820
And, certis yit, for al my peyne,

Though that I sigh yit arwis reyne,
And grounde quarels sharpe of stele,
Ne for no payne that I might fele,
Yit might I not my-silf with-holde    1825
The faire roser to biholde ;
For Love me yaf sich hardement
For to fulfille his commaundement.
Upon my feet I roos up than
Feble, as a forwoundid man ;    1830
And forth to gon [my] might I sette,
And for the archer nolde I lette.
Toward the roser fast I drow ;
But thornes sharpe mo than y-now
Ther were, and also thistels thikke,    1835
And breres, brimme for to prikke,
That I ne mighte gete grace
The rowe thornes for to passe,
To sene the roses fresshe of hewe,
I must abide, though it me rewe,    1840
The hegge aboute so thikke was,
That closid the roses in compas.
But o thing lyked me right wele ;
I was so nygh, I mighte fele
Of the botoun the swote odour,    1845
And also see the fresshe colour ;
And that right gretly lyked me,
That I so neer †it mighte see.
Sich joye anoon therof hadde I,
That I forgat my malady.    1850
To sene †it hadde I sich delyt,
Of sorwe and angre I was al quit,
And of my woundes that I had †thar ;
For no-thing lyken me might †mar
Than dwellen by the roser ay,    1855
And thennes never to passe away.
But whan a whyle I had be thar,
The God of Love, which al to-shar
Myn herte with his arwis kene,
†Caste him to yeve me woundis grene.
He shet at me ful hastily    1861
An arwe named Company,
The whiche takel is ful able
To make these ladies merciable.
Than I anoon gan chaungen hewe    1865
For grevaunce of my wounde newe,
That I agayn fel in swoning,
And sighed sore in compleyning.
Sore I compleyned that my sore
On me gan greven more and more.    1870
I had non hope of allegeaunce ;
So nigh I drow to desperaunce,

I rought of dethe ne of lyf,
Whither that love wolde me dryf.
If me a martir wolde he make,    1875
I might his power nought forsake.
And whyl for anger thus I wook,
The God of Love an arowe took ;
Ful sharp it was and [ful] pugnaunt,
And it was callid Fair-Semblaunt,    1880
The which in no wys wol consente,
That any lover him repente
To serve his love with herte and alle,
For any peril that may bifalle.
But though this arwe was kene grounde
As any rasour that is founde,    1886
To cutte and kerve, at the poynt,
The God of Love it hadde anoynt
With a precious oynement,
Somdel to yeve aleggement    1890
Upon the woundes that he had
Through the body in my herte maad,
To helpe hir sores, and to cure,
And that they may the bet endure.
But yit this arwe, withoute more,    1895
Made in myn herte a large sore,
That in ful gret peyne I abood.
But ay the oynement wente abrood ;
Throughout my woundes large and wyde
It spredde aboute in every syde ;    1900
Through whos vertu and whos might
Myn herte joyful was and light.
I had been deed and al to-shent
But for the precious oynement.
The shaft I drow out of the arwe,    1905
Roking for wo right wondir narwe ;
But the heed which made me smerte,
Lefte bihinde in myn herte
With other foure, I dar well say,
That never wol be take away ;    1910
But the oynement halp me wele.
And yit sich sorwe dide I fele
†Of my woundes fresshe and newe,
That al-day I chaunged hewe,
As men might see in my visage.    1915
The arwis were so fulle of rage,
So variaunt of diversitee,
That men in everich mighte see
Both gret anoy and eek swetnesse,
And joye meynt with bittirnesse,    1920
Now were they esy, now where they wood,
In hem I felte both harm and good ;
Now sore without aleggement,

Now †softening with oynement ;
It softned here, and †prikked there, 1925
Thus ese and anger togider were.
  The God of Love deliverly
Com lepand to me hastily,
And seide to me, in gret rape,
' Yeld thee, for thou may not escape ! 1930
May no defence availe thee here ;
Therfore I rede mak no daungere.
If thou wolt yelde thee hastily,
Thou shalt [the] rather have mercy.
He is a fool in sikernesse, 1935
That with daunger or stoutnesse
Rebellith ther that he shulde plese ;
In such folye is litel ese.
Be meek, wher thou must nedis bowe ;
To stryve ageyn is nought thy prowe.
Come at ones, and have y-do, 1941
For I wol that it be so.
Than yeld thee here debonairly.'
And I answerid ful humbly,
' Gladly, sir ; at your bidding, 1945
I wol me yelde in alle thing.
To your servyse I wol me take ;
For god defende that I shulde make
Ageyn your bidding resistence ;
I wol not doon so gret offence ; 1950
For if I dide, it were no skile.
Ye may do with me what ye wile,
Save or spille, and also sloo ;
Fro you in no wyse may I go.
My lyf, my deth, is in your honde, 1955
I may not laste out of your bonde.
Pleyn at your list I yelde me,
Hoping in herte, that sumtyme ye
Comfort and ese shulle me sende ;
Or ellis shortly, this is the ende, 1960
Withouten helthe I moot ay dure,
But-if ye take me to your cure.
Comfort or helthe how shuld I have,
Sith ye me hurte, but ye me save ?
The helthe of †lovers moot be founde
Wher-as they token firste hir wounde.
And if ye list of me to make 1967
Your prisoner, I wol it take
Of herte and wil, fully at gree.
Hoolly and pleyn I yelde me, 1970
Withoute feyning or feyntyse,
To be governed by your empryse.
Of you I here so much prys,
I wol ben hool at your devys

For to fulfille your lyking 1975
And repente for no-thing,
Hoping to have yit in som tyde
Mercy, of that [that] I abyde.'
And with that covenaunt yeld I me,
Anoon doun kneling upon my knee, 1980
Profering for to kisse his feet ;
But for no-thing he wolde me lete,
And seide, ' I love thee bothe and preyse,
Sen that thyn answer doth me ese,
For thou answerid so curteisly. 1985
For now I wot wel uttirly,
That thou art gentil, by thy speche.
For though a man fer wolde seche,
He shulde not finden, in certeyn,
No sich answer of no vileyn ; 1990
For sich a word ne mighte nought
Isse out of a vilayns thought.
Thou shalt not lesen of thy speche,
For [to] thy helping wol I eche,
And eek encresen that I may. 1995
But first I wol that thou obay
Fully, for thyn avauntage,
Anon to do me here homage.
And sithe[n] kisse thou shalt my mouth,
Which to no vilayn was never couth 2000
For to aproche it, ne for to touche ;
For sauf †to cherlis I ne vouche
That they shulle never neigh it nere.
For curteys, and of fair manere,
Wel taught, and ful of gentilnesse 2005
He muste ben, that shal me kisse,
And also of ful high fraunchyse,
That shal atteyne to that empryse.
  ' And first of o thing warne I thee,
That peyne and gret adversitee 2010
He mot endure, and eek travaile,
That shal me serve, withoute faile.
But ther-ageyns, thee to comforte,
And with thy servise to desporte,
Thou mayst ful glad and joyful be 2015
So good a maister to have as me,
And lord of so high renoun.
I bere of Love the gonfanoun,
Of Curtesye the banere ;
For I am of the silf manere, 2020
Gentil, curteys, meek and free ;
That who [so] ever ententif be
Me to honoure, doute, and serve,
And also that he him observe
Fro trespas and fro vilanye, 2025

And him governe in curtesye
With wil and with entencioun ;
For whan he first in my prisoun
Is caught, than muste he uttirly,
Fro thennes-forth ful bisily,          2030
Caste him gentil for to be,
If he desyre helpe of me.'

Anoon withouten more delay,
Withouten daunger or affray,
I bicom his man anoon,          2035
And gave him thankes many a oon,
And kneled doun with hondis joynt,
And made it in my port ful †quoynt ;
The joye wente to myn herte rote.
Whan I had kissed his mouth so swote,
I had sich mirthe and sich lyking,          2041
It cured me of languisshing.
He askid of me than hostages :—
'I have,' he seide, ' †tan fele homages
Of oon and other, where I have been 2045
†Disceyved ofte, withouten wene.
These felouns, fulle of falsitee,
Have many sythes bigyled me,
And through falshede hir lust acheved,
Wherof I repente and am agreved.          2050
And I hem gete in my daungere,
Hir falshed shulle they bye ful dere.
But for I love thee, I seye thee pleyn,
I wol of thee be more certeyn ;
For thee so sore I wol now binde,          2055
That thou away ne shalt not winde
For to denyen the covenaunt,
Or doon that is not avenaunt.
That thou were fals it were greet reuthe,
Sith thou semest so ful of treuthe.'          2060

' Sire, if thee list to undirstande,
I merveile thee asking this demande.
For-why or wherfore shulde ye
Ostages or borwis aske of me,
Or any other sikirnesse,          2065
Sith ye wote, in sothfastnesse,
That ye have me †surprysed so,
And hool myn herte †tan me fro,
That it wol do for me no-thing
But-if it be at your bidding ?          2070
Myn herte is yours, and myn right nought,
As it bihoveth, in dede and thought,
Redy in alle to worche your wille,
Whether so [it] turne to good or ille.
So sore it lustith you to plese,          2075
No man therof may you †disseise.

Ye have theron set sich justise,
That it is werreyd in many wise.
And if ye doute it nolde obeye,
Ye may therof do make a keye,          2080
And holde it with you for ostage.'
' Now certis, this is noon outrage,'
Quoth Love, ' and fully I accord ;
For of the body he is ful lord
That hath the herte in his tresor ;          2085
Outrage it were to asken more.'

Than of his aumener he drough
A litel keye, fetys y-nough,
Which was of gold polisshed clere,
And seide to me, ' With this keye here
Thyn herte to me now wol I shette ;          2091
For al my jowellis loke and knette
I binde under this litel keye,
That no wight may carye aweye ;
This keye is ful of gret poeste.'          2095
With which anoon he touchid me
Undir the syde ful softely,
That he myn herte sodeynly
Without [al] anoy had spered,
That yit right nought it hath me dered.
Whan he had doon his wil al-out,          2101
And I had put him out of dout,
' Sire,' I seide, ' I have right gret wille
Your lust and plesaunce to fulfille.
Loke ye my servise take at gree,          2105
By thilke feith ye owe to me.
I seye nought for recreaundyse,
For I nought doute of your servyse.
But the servaunt traveileth in vayne,
That for to serven doth his payne          2110
Unto that lord, which in no wyse
Can him no thank for his servyse.'

Love seide, ' Dismaye thee nought,
Sin thou for sucour hast me sought,
In thank thy servise wol I take,          2115
And high of †gree I wol thee make,
If wikkidnesse ne hindre thee ;
But, as I hope, it shal nought be.
To worship no wight by aventure
May come, but-if he peyne endure.          2120
Abyde and suffre thy distresse ;
That hurtith now, it shal be lesse ;
I wot my-silf what may thee save,
What medicyne thou woldist have.
And if thy trouthe to me thou kepe, 2125
I shal unto thyn helping eke,
To cure thy woundes and make hem clene,

Wher-so they be olde or grene ;
Thou shalt be holpen, at wordis fewe.
For certeynly thou shalt wel shewe   2130
Wher that thou servest with good wille,
For to complisshen and fulfille
My comaundementis, day and night,
Whiche I to lovers yeve of right.'

  'Ah, sire, for goddis love,' said I,   2135
'Er ye passe hens, ententifly
Your comaundementis to me ye say,
And I shal kepe hem, if I may ;
For hem to kepen is al my thought.
And if so be I wot them nought,   2140
Than may I [sinne] unwitingly.
Wherfore I pray you enterely,
With al myn herte, me to lere,
That I trespasse in no manere.'

  The god of love than chargid me   2145
Anoon, as ye shal here and see,
Word by word, by right empryse,
So as the Romance shal devyse.

  The maister lesith his tyme to lere,
Whan the disciple wol not here.   2150
It is but veyn on him to swinke,
That on his lerning wol not thinke.
Who-so lust love, let him entende,
For now the Romance †ginneth amende.
Now is good to here, in fay,   2155
If any be that can it say,
And poynte it as the resoun is
Set ; for other-gate, y-wis,
It shal nought wel in alle thing
Be brought to good undirstonding ;   2160
For a reder that poyntith ille
A good sentence may ofte spille.
The book is good at the ending,
Maad of newe and lusty thing ;
For who-so wol the ending here,   2165
The crafte of love he shal now lere,
If that he wol so long abyde,
Til I this Romance may unhyde,
And undo the signifiaunce
Of this dreme into Romaunce.   2170
The sothfastnesse, that now is hid,
Without coverture shal be kid,
Whan I undon have this dreming,
Wherin no word is of lesing.

  'Vilany, at the beginning,   2175
I wol,' †sayd Love, ' over alle thing,
Thou leve, if thou wolt [not] be
Fals, and trespasse ageynes me.

I curse and blame generally
Alle hem that loven vilany ;   2180
For vilany makith vilayn,
And by his dedis a cherle is seyn.
Thise vilayns arn without pitee,
Frendshipe, love, and al bounte.
I nil receyve †to my servyse   2185
Hem that ben vilayns of empryse.

  ' But undirstonde in thyn entent,
That this is not myn entendement,
To clepe no wight in no ages
Only gentil for his linages.   2190
But who-so [that] is vertuous,
And in his port nought outrageous,
Whan sich oon thou seest thee biforn,
Though he be not gentil born,
Thou mayst wel seyn, this is †a soth, 2195
That he is gentil, bicause he doth
As longeth to a gentilman ;
Of hem non other deme I can.
For certeynly, withouten drede,
A cherle is demed by his dede,   2200
Of hye or lowe, as ye may see,
Or of what kinrede that he be.
Ne say nought, for noon yvel wille,
Thing that is to holden stille ;
It is no worship to misseye.   2205
Thou mayst ensample take of Keye,
That was somtyme, for misseying,
Hated bothe of olde and ying ;
As fer as Gaweyn, the worthy,
Was preysed for his curtesy,   2210
Keye was hated, for he was fel,
Of word dispitous and cruel.
Wherfore be wyse and aqueyntable,
Goodly of word, and resonable
Bothe to lesse and eek to mar.   2215
And whan thou comest ther men ar,
Loke that thou have in custom ay
First to salue hem, if thou may :
And if it falle, that of hem som
Salue thee first, be not dom,   2220
But quyte him curteisly anoon
Without abiding, er they goon.

  ' For no-thing eek thy tunge applye
To speke wordis of ribaudye.
To vilayn speche in no degree   2225
Lat never thy lippe unbounden be.
For I nought holde him, in good feith,
Curteys, that foule wordis seith.
And alle wimmen serve and preyse,

And to thy power hir honour reyse.　2230
And if that any missayere
Dispyse wimmen, that thou mayst here,
Blame him, and bidde him holde him stille.
And set thy might and al thy wille
Wimmen and ladies for to plese,　2235
And to do thing that may hem ese,
That they ever speke good of thee,
For so thou mayst best preysed be.

　' Loke fro pryde thou kepe thee wele ;
For thou mayst bothe perceyve and fele,
That pryde is bothe foly and sinne ;　2241
And he that pryde hath, him withinne,
Ne may his herte, in no wyse,
Meken ne souplen to servyse.
For pryde is founde, in every part,　2245
Contrarie unto Loves art.
And he that loveth trewely
Shulde him contene jolily,
Withouten pryde in sondry wyse,
And him disgysen in queyntyse.　2250
For queynt array, withouten drede,
Is no-thing proud, who takith hede ;
For fresh array, as men may see,
Withouten pryde may ofte be.

　' Mayntene thy-silf aftir thy rent,　2255
Of robe and eek of garnement ;
For many sythe fair clothing
A man amendith in mich thing.
And loke alwey that they be shape,
What garnement that thou shalt make,
Of him that can [hem] beste do,　2261
With al that perteyneth therto.
Poyntis and sleves be wel sittand,
Right and streight †upon the hand.
Of shoon and botes, newe and faire,　2265
Loke at the leest thou have a paire ;
And that they sitte so fetisly,
That these rude may uttirly
Merveyle, sith that they sitte so pleyn,
How they come on or of ageyn.　2270
Were streite gloves, with †aumenere
Of silk ; and alwey with good chere
Thou yeve, if thou have richesse ;
And if thou have nought, spend the lesse.
Alwey be merry, if thou may,　2275
But waste not thy good alway.
Have hat of floures fresh as May,
Chapelet of roses of Whitsonday ;
For sich array ne †cost but lyte.
Thyn hondis wash, thy teeth make whyte,

And let no filthe upon thee be.　2281
Thy nailes blak if thou mayst see,
Voide it awey deliverly,
And kembe thyn heed right jolily.
†Fard not thy visage in no wyse,　2285
For that of love is not th' empryse ;
For love doth haten, as I finde,
A beaute that cometh not of kinde.
Alwey in herte I rede thee
Glad and mery for to be,　2290
And be as joyful as thou can ;
Love hath no joye of sorowful man.
That yvel is ful of curtesye
That †lauhwith in his maladye ;
For ever of love the siknesse　2295
Is meynd with swete and bitternesse.
The sore of love is merveilous ;
For now the lover [is] joyous,
Now can he pleyne, now can he grone,
Now can he singen, now maken mone.
To-day he pleyneth for hevinesse,　2301
To-morowe he †pleyeth for jolynesse.
The lyf of love is ful contrarie,
Which stoundemele can ofte varie.
But if thou canst [som] mirthis make, 2305
That men in gree wole gladly take,
Do it goodly, I comaunde thee ;
For men sholde, wher-so-ever they be,
Do thing that hem [best] sitting is,
For therof cometh good loos and pris. 2310
Wher-of that thou be vertuous,
Ne be not straunge ne daungerous.
For if that thou good rider be,
Prike gladly, that men may se.
In armes also if thou conne,　2315
Pursue, til thou a name hast wonne.
And if thy voice be fair and clere,
Thou shalt maken no gret daungere
Whan to singe they goodly preye ;
It is thy worship for to obeye.　2320
Also to you it longith ay
To harpe and giterne, daunce and play ;
For if he can wel foote and daunce,
It may him greetly do avaunce.
Among eek, for thy lady sake,　2325
Songes and complayntes that thou make ;
For that wol †meve [hem] in hir herte,
Whan they reden of thy smerte.
Loke that no man for scarce thee holde,
For that may greve thee many-folde. 2330
Resoun wol that a lover be

In his yiftes more large and free
Than cherles that been not of loving,
For who ther-of can any thing,
He shal be leef ay for to yeve,          2335
In †Loves lore who so wolde leve;
For he that, through a sodeyn sight,
Or for a kissing, anon-right
Yaf hool his herte in wille and thought,
And to him-silf kepith right nought,     2340
Aftir †swich yift, is good resoun,
He yeve his good in abandoun.
  'Now wol I shortly here reherce,
Of that [that] I have seid in verse,
Al the sentence by and by,               2345
In wordis fewe compendiously,
That thou the bet mayst on hem thinke,
Whether-so it be thou wake or winke;
For [that] the wordis litel greve
A man to kepe, whanne it is breve.       2350
  'Who-so with Love wol goon or ryde
He mot be curteys, and void of pryde,
Mery and fulle of jolite,
And of largesse alosed be.
  'First I joyne thee, here in penaunce, 2355
That ever, withoute repentaunce,
Thou set thy thought in thy loving,
To laste withoute repenting;
And thenke upon thy mirthis swete,
That shal folowe aftir whan ye mete.     2360
  'And for thou trewe to love shalt be,
I wol, and [eek] comaunde thee,
That in oo place thou sette, al hool,
Thyn herte, withouten halfen dool,
For trecherie, †in sikernesse;           2365
For I lovede never doublenesse.
To many his herte that wol depart,
Everiche shal have but litel part.
But of him drede I me right nought,
That in oo place settith his thought.    2370
Therfore in oo place it sette,
And let it never thennes flette.
For if thou yevest it in lening,
I holde it but a wrecchid thing:
Therfore yeve it hool and quyte,         2375
And thou shalt have the more merite.
If it be lent, than aftir soon,
The bountee and the thank is doon;
But, in love, free yeven thing
Requyrith a gret guerdoning.             2380
Yeve it in yift al quit fully,
And make thy yift debonairly;

For men that yift [wol] holde more dere
That yeven is with gladsome chere.
That yift nought to preisen is           2385
That man yeveth, maugre his.
Whan thou hast yeven thyn herte, as I
Have seid thee here [al] openly,
Than aventures shulle thee falle,
Which harde and hevy been withalle.      2390
For ofte whan thou bithenkist thee
Of thy loving, wher-so thou be,
Fro folk thou must depart in hy,
That noon perceyve thy malady,
But hyde thyn harm thou must alone,      2395
And go forth sole, and make thy mone.
Thou shalt no whyl be in oo stat,
But whylom cold and whylom hat;
Now reed as rose, now yelowe and fade.
Such sorowe, I trowe, thou never hade;
Cotidien, ne [yit] quarteyne,            2401
It is nat so ful of peyne.
For ofte tymes it shal falle
In love, among thy peynes alle,
That thou thy-self, al hoolly,           2405
Foryeten shalt so utterly,
That many tymes thou shalt be
Stille as an image of tree,
Dom as a stoon, without stering
Of foot or hond, without speking;        2410
Than, sone after al thy peyne,
To memorie shalt thou come ageyn,
A[s] man abasshed wondre sore,
And after sighen more and more.
For wit thou wel, withouten wene,        2415
In swich astat ful oft have been
That have the yvel of love assayd,
Wher-through thou art so dismayd.
  'After, a thought shal take thee so,
That thy love is to fer thee fro:        2420
Thou shalt say, "God, what may this be,
That I ne may my lady see?
Myne herte aloon is to her go,
And I abyde al sole in wo,
Departed fro myn owne thought,           2425
And with myne eyen see right nought.
Alas, myn eyen †sende I ne may,
My careful herte to convay!
Myn hertes gyde but they be,
I praise no-thing what ever they see.    2430
Shul they abyde thanne? nay;
But goon †visyte without delay
That myn herte desyreth so.

For certeynly, but-if they go,
A fool my-self I may wel holde,     2435
Whan I ne see what myn herte wolde.
Wherfore I wol gon her to seen,
Or esed shal I never been,
But I have som tokening."
Then gost thou forth without dwelling ;
But ofte thou faylest of thy desyre,     2441
Er thou mayst come hir any nere,
And wastest in vayn thy passage.
Than fallest thou in a newe rage ;
For wante of sight thou ginnest morne,
And homward pensif dost retorne.     2446
In greet mischeef than shalt thou be,
For than agayn shal come to thee
Sighes and pleyntes, with newe wo,
That no icching prikketh so.     2450
Who wot it nought, he may go lere
Of hem that byen love so dere.

   ' No-thing thyn herte appesen may,
That oft thou wolt goon and assay,
If thou mayst seen, by aventure,     2455
Thy lyves joy, thyn hertis cure ;
So that, by grace if thou might
Atteyne of hir to have a sight,
Than shalt thou doon non other dede.
But with that sight thyn eyen fede. 2460
That faire fresh whan thou mayst see,
Thyn herte shal so ravisshed be,
That never thou woldest, thy thankis, lete,
Ne remove, for to see that swete.
The more thou seest in sothfastnesse, 2465
The more thou †coveytest of that swet-
    nesse ;
The more thyn herte brenneth in fyr,
The more thyn herte is in desyr.
For who considreth every del,
It may be lykned wondir wel,     2470
The peyne of love, unto a fere ;
For ever [the] more thou neighest nere
†Thought, or who-so that it be,
For verray sothe I telle it thee,
The hatter ever shal thou brenne,     2475
As experience shal thee kenne.
Wher-so [thou] comest in any cost,
Who is next fyr, he brenneth most.
And yit forsothe, for al thyn hete,
Though thou for love swelte and swete,
Ne for no-thing thou felen may,     2481
Thou shalt not willen to passe away.
And though thou go, yet must thee nede

Thenke al-day on hir fairhede,
Whom thou bihelde with so good wille ;
And holde thyself bigyled ille,     2486
That thou ne haddest non hardement
To shewe hir ought of thyn entent.
Thyn herte ful sore thou wolt dispyse,
And eek repreve of cowardyse,     2490
That thou, so dulle in every thing,
Were dom for drede, without speking,
Thou shalt eek thenke thou didest foly,
That thou wert hir so faste by,
And durst not auntre thee to say     2495
Som-thing, er thou cam away ;
For thou haddist no more wonne,
To speke of hir whan thou bigonne :
But †yif she wolde, for thy sake,
In armes goodly thee have take,     2500
It shulde have be more worth to thee
Than of tresour greet plentee.

   ' Thus shalt thou morne and eek com-
    pleyn,
And gete enchesoun to goon ageyn
Unto thy walk, or to thy place,     2505
Where thou biheld hir fleshly face.
And never, for fals suspeccioun,
Thou woldest finde occasioun
For to gon unto hir hous.
So art thou thanne desirous     2510
A sight of hir for to have,
If thou thine honour mightest save,
Or any erand mightist make
Thider, for thy loves sake ;
Ful fayn thou woldist, but for drede 2515
Thou gost not, lest that men take hede.
Wherfore I rede, in thy going,
And also in thyn ageyn-coming,
Thou be wel war that men ne wit ;
Feyne thee other cause than it     2520
To go that weye, or faste by ;
To hele wel is no folye.
And if so be it happe thee
That thou thy love ther mayst see,
In siker wyse thou hir salewe,     2525
Wherwith thy colour wol transmewe,
And eke thy blood shal al to-quake,
Thy hewe eek chaungen for hir sake.
But word and wit, with chere ful pale,
Shul wante for to telle thy tale.     2530
And if thou mayst so fer-forth winne,
That thou [thy] resoun durst biginne,
And woldist seyn three thingis or mo,

Thou shalt ful scarsly seyn the two.
Though thou bithenke thee never so wel,
Thou shalt foryete yit somdel,      2536
But-if thou dele with trecherye.
For fals lovers mowe al folye
Seyn, what hem lust, withouten drede,
They be so double in hir falshede ;    2540
For they in herte cunne thenke a thing
And seyn another, in hir spéking.
And whan thy speche is endid al,
Right thus to thee it shal bifal ;
If any word than come to minde,     2545
That thou to seye hast left bihinde,
Than thou shalt brenne in greet martyr ;
For thou shalt brenne as any fyr.
This is the stryf and eke the affray,
And the batail that lastith ay.      2550
This bargeyn ende may never take,
But-if that she thy pees wil make.
 ' And whan the night is comen, anon
A thousand angres shal come upon.
To bedde as fast thou wolt thee dight, 2555
Where thou shalt have but smal delyt ;
For whan thou wenest for to slepe,
So ful of peyne shalt thou crepe,
Sterte in thy bedde aboute ful wyde,
And turne ful ofte on every syde ;    2560
Now downward groffe, and now upright,
And walowe in wo the longe night ;
Thyne armis shalt thou sprede abrede,
As man in werre were †forwerreyd.
Than shal thee come a remembraunce
Of hir shape and hir semblaunce     2566
Wherto non other may be pere.
And wite thou wel, withoute were,
That thee shal †seme, somtyme that night,
That thou hast hir, that is so bright, 2570
Naked bitwene thyn armes there,
Al sothfastnesse as though it were.
Thou shalt make castels than in Spayne,
And dreme of joye, al but in vayne,
And thee delyten of right nought,    2575
Whyl thou so slomrest in that thought,
That is so swete and delitable,
The which, in soth, nis but a fable,
For it ne shal no whyle laste.
Than shalt thou sighe and wepe faste, 2580
And say, " Dere god, what thing is this ?
My dreme is turned al amis,
Which was ful swete and apparent,
But now I wake, it is al shent

Now yede this mery thought away !   2585
Twenty tymes upon a day
I wolde this thought wolde come ageyn,
For it alleggith wel my peyn.
It makith me ful of joyful thought,
It sleeth me, that it lastith noght.   2590
A, lord ! why nil ye me socoure,
The joye, I trowe, that I langoure ?
The deth I wolde me shulde slo
Whyl I lye in hir armes two.
Myn harm is hard, withouten wene, 2595
My greet unese ful ofte I mene.
But wolde Love do so I might
Have fully joye of hir so bright,
My peyne were quit me richely.
Allas, to greet a thing aske I !      2600
It is but foly, and wrong wening,
To aske so outrageous a thing.
And who-so askith folily,
He moot be warned hastily ;
And I ne wot what I may say,        2605
I am so fer out of the way ;
For I wolde have ful gret lyking
And ful gret joye of lasse thing.
For wolde she, of hir gentilnesse,
Withouten more, me onis kesse,      2610
It were to me a greet guerdoun,
Relees of al my passioun.
But it is hard to come therto ;
Al is but foly that I do,
So high I have myn herte set,       2615
Where I may no comfort get.
†I noot wher I sey wel or nought ;
But this I wot wel in my thought,
That it were †bet of hir aloon,
For to stinte my wo and moon,      2620
A loke on †me y-cast goodly,
†Than for to have, al utterly,
Of another al hool the pley.
A ! lord ! wher I shal byde the day
That ever she shal my lady be ?      2625
He is ful cured that may hir see.
A ! god ! whan shal the dawning spring?
To †ly thus is an angry thing ;
I have no joye thus here to ly
Whan that my love is not me by.    2630
A man to lyen hath gret disese,
Which may not slepe ne reste in ese.
I wolde it dawed, and were now day,
And that the night were went away ;
For were it day, I wolde upryse.     2635

A ! slowe sonne, shew thyn enpryse !
Speed thee to sprede thy bemis bright,
And chace the derknesse of the night,
To putte away the stoundes stronge,
Which in me lasten al to longe."　2640
　'The night shalt thou contene so,
Withoute rest, in peyne and wo ;
If ever thou knewe of love distresse,
Thou shalt mowe lerne in that siknesse.
And thus enduring shalt thou ly,　2645
And ryse on morwe up erly
Out of thy bedde, and harneys thee
Er ever dawning thou mayst see.
Al privily than shalt thou goon,
What †weder it be, thy-silf aloon,　2650
For reyn, or hayl, for snow, for slete,
Thider she dwellith that is so swete,
The which may falle aslepe be,
And thenkith but litel upon thee.
Than shalt thou goon, ful foule aferd ; 2655
Loke if the gate be unsperd,
And waite without in wo and peyn,
Ful yvel a-colde in winde and reyn.
Than shal thou go the dore bifore,
If thou maist fynde any score,　2660
Or hole, or reft, what ever it were ;
Than shalt thou stoupe, and lay to ere,
If they within a-slepe be ;
I mene, alle save thy lady free.
Whom waking if thou mayst aspye,　2665
Go put thy-silf in jupartye,
To aske grace, and thee bimene,
That she may wite, withouten wene,
That thou [a]night no rest hast had,
So sore for hir thou were bistad.　2670
Wommen wel ought pite to take
Of hem that sorwen for hir sake.
And loke, for love of that relyke,
That thou thenke non other lyke,
For †whom thou hast so greet annoy, 2675
†Shal kisse thee er thou go away,
And hold that in ful gret deyntee.
And, for that no man shal thee see
Bifore the hous, ne in the way,
Loke thou be goon ageyn er day.　2680
Suche coming, and such going,
Such hevinesse, and such walking,
Makith lovers, withouten wene,
Under hir clothes pale and lene,
For Love leveth colour ne cleernesse ; 2685
Who loveth trewe hath no fatnesse.

Thou shalt wel by thy-selfe see
That thou must nedis assayed be.
For men that shape hem other wey
Falsly her ladies to bitray,　2690
It is no wonder though they be fat ;
With false othes hir loves they gat ;
For oft I see suche losengeours
Fatter than abbatis or priours.
　'Yet with o thing I thee charge,　2695
That is to seye, that thou be large
Unto the mayd that hir doth serve,
So best hir thank thou shalt deserve.
Yeve hir yiftes, and get hir grace,
For so thou may [hir] thank purchace,2700
That she thee worthy holde and free,
Thy lady, and alle that may thee see.
Also hir servauntes worshipe ay,
And plese as muche as thou may ;
Gret good through hem may come to thee,
Bicause with hir they been prive.　2706
They shal hir telle how they thee fand
Curteis and wys, and wel doand,
And she shal preyse [thee] wel the †mare.
Loke out of londe thou be not †fare ; 2710
And if such cause thou have, that thee
Bihoveth †gon out of contree,
Leve hool thyn herte in hostage,
Til thou ageyn make thy passage.
Thenk long to see the swete thing　2715
That hath thyn herte in hir keping.
　'Now have I told thee, in what wyse
A lover shal do me servyse.
Do it than, if thou wolt have
The mede that thou aftir crave.'　2720
　Whan Love al this had boden me,
I seide him :—' Sire, how may it be
That lovers may in such manere
Endure the peyne ye have seid here ?
I merveyle me wonder faste,　2725
How any man may live or laste
In such peyne, and such brenning,
In sorwe and thought, and such sighing,
Ay unrelesed wo to make,
Whether so it be they slepe or wake. 2730
In such annoy continuely,
As helpe me god, this merveile I,
How man, but he were maad of stele,
Might live a month, such peynes to fele.'
　The God of Love than seide me,　2735
' Freend, by the feith I owe to thee,
May no man have good, but he it by.

A man loveth more tendirly
The thing that he hath bought most dere.
For wite thou wel, withouten were, 2740
In thank that thing is taken more,
For which a man hath suffred sore.
Certis, no wo ne may atteyne
Unto the sore of loves peyne.
Non yvel therto ne may amounte, 2745
No more than a man [may] counte
The dropes that of the water be.
For drye as wel the grete see
Thou mightist, as the harmes telle
Of hem that with Love dwelle 2750
In servyse ; for peyne hem sleeth,
And that ech man wolde flee the deeth,
And trowe they shulde never escape,
Nere that hope couthe hem make
Glad as man in prisoun set, 2755
And may not geten for to et
But barly-breed, and watir pure,
And lyeth in vermin and in ordure ;
With alle this, yit can he live,
Good hope such comfort hath him yive,
Which maketh wene that he shal be 2761
Delivered and come to liberte ;
In fortune is [his] fulle trust.
Though he lye in strawe or dust,
In hope is al his susteyning. 2765
And so for lovers, in hir wening,
Whiche Love hath shit in his prisoun ;
Good-Hope is hir salvacioun.
Good-Hope, how sore that they smerte,
Yeveth hem bothe wille and herte 2770
To profre hir body to martyre ;
For Hope so sore doth hem desyre
To suffre ech harm that men devyse,
For joye that †aftir shal aryse.

' Hope, in desire [to] cacche victorie ;
In Hope, of love is al the glorie, 2776
For Hope is al that love may yive ;
Nere Hope, ther shulde no lover live.
Blessid be Hope, which with desyre
Avaunceth lovers in such manere. 2780
Good-Hope is curteis for to plese,
To kepe lovers from al disese.
Hope kepith his lond, and wol abyde,
For any peril that may betyde ;
For Hope to lovers, as most cheef, 2785
Doth hem endure[n] al mischeef ;
Hope is her help, whan mister is.
And I shal yeve thee eek, y-wis,

Three other thingis, that greet solas
Doth to hem that be in my las. 2790
' The first[e] good that may be founde,
To hem that in my lace be bounde,
Is Swete-Thought, for to recorde
Thing wherwith thou canst accorde
Best in thyn herte, wher she be ; 2795
†Thought in absence is good to thee.
Whan any lover doth compleyne,
And liveth in distresse and peyne,
Than Swete-Thought shal come, as blyve,
Awey his angre for to dryve. 2800
It makith lovers have remembraunce
Of comfort, and of high plesaunce,
That Hope hath hight him for to winne
For Thought anoon than shal biginne,
As fer, god wot, as he can finde, 2805
To make a mirrour of his minde ;
For to biholde he wol not lette.
Hir person he shal afore him sette,
Hir laughing eyen, persaunt and clere,
Hir shape, hir fourme, hir goodly chere,
Hir mouth that is so gracious, 2811
So swete, and eek so saverous ;
Of alle hir fetures he shal take hede,
His eyen with alle hir limes fede.

' Thus Swete-Thenking shal aswage 2815
The peyne of lovers, and hir rage.
Thy joye shal double, withoute gesse,
Whan thou thenkist on hir semlinesse,
Or of hir laughing, or of hir chere,
That to thee made thy lady dere. 2820
This comfort wol I that thou take ;
And if the next thou wolt forsake
Which is not lesse saverous,
Thou shuldist †been to daungerous.

' The secounde shal be Swete-Speche,
That hath to many oon be leche, 2826
To bringe hem out of wo and were,
And helpe many a bachilere ;
And many a lady sent socoure,
That have loved par-amour, 2830
Through speking, whan they mighten
here
Of hir lovers, to hem so dere.
To †hem it voidith al hir smerte,
The which is closed in hir herte.
In herte it makith hem glad and light,
Speche, whan they mowe have sight. 2836
And therfore now it cometh to minde
In olde dawes, as I finde,

That clerkis writen that hir knewe,
Ther was a lady fresh of hewe,    2840
Which of hir love made a song,
On him for to remembre among,
In which she seide, " Whan that I here
Speken of him that is so dere,
To me it voidith al [my] smerte,    2845
Y-wis, he sit so nere myn herte.
To speke of him, at eve or morwe,
It cureth me of al my sorwe.
To me is noon so high plesaunce
As of his persone daliaunce."    2850
She wist ful wel that Swete-Speking
Comfortith in ful muche thing.
Hir love she had ful wel assayed,
Of him she was ful wel apayed ;
To speke of him hir joye was set.    2855
Therfore I rede thee that thou get
A felowe that can wel concele
And kepe thy counsel, and wel hele,
To whom go shewe hoolly thyn herte,
Bothe wele and wo, joye and smerte : 2860
To gete comfort to him thou go,
And privily, between yow two,
Ye shal speke of that goodly thing,
That hath thyn herte in hir keping ;
Of hir beaute and hir semblaunce,    2865
And of hir goodly countenaunce.
Of al thy state thou shalt him sey,
And aske him counseil how thou may
Do any thing that may hir plese ;
For it to thee shal do gret ese,    2870
That he may wite thou trust him so,
Bothe of thy wele and of thy wo.
And if his herte to love be set,
His companye is muche the bet,
For resoun wol, he shewe to thee    2875
Al uttirly his privite ;
And what she is he loveth so,
To thee pleynly he shal undo,
Withoute drede of any shame,
Bothe telle hir renoun and hir name. 2880
Than shal he forther, ferre and nere,
And namely to thy lady dere,
In siker wyse ; ye, every other
Shal helpen as his owne brother,
In trouthe withoute doublenesse,    2885
And kepen cloos in sikernesse.
For it is noble thing, in fay,
To have a man thou darst say
Thy prive counsel every del ;

For that wol comfort thee right wel, 2890
And thou shalt holde thee wel apayed,
Whan such a freend thou hast assayed.
   ' The thridde good of greet comfort
That yeveth to lovers most disport,
Comith of sight and biholding,    2895
That clepid is Swete-Loking,
The whiche may noon ese do,
Whan thou art fer thy lady fro ;
Wherfore thou prese alwey to be
In place, where thou mayst hir se.    2900
For it is thing most amerous,
Most delitable and saverous,
For to aswage a mannes sorowe,
To sene his lady by the morowe.
For it is a ful noble thinge    2905
Whan thyn eyen have meting
With that relyke precious,
Wherof they be so desirous.
But al day after, soth it is,
They have no drede to faren amis,    2910
They dreden neither wind ne reyn,
Ne [yit] non other maner peyn.
For whan thyn eyen were thus in blis,
Yit of hir curtesye, y-wis,
Aloon they can not have hir joye,    2915
But to the herte they [it] convoye ;
Part of hir blis to him †they sende,
Of al this harm to make an ende.
The eye is a good messangere,
Which can to the herte in such manere
Tidyngis sende, that [he] hath seen,    2921
To voide him of his peynes cleen.
Wherof the herte reioyseth so
That a gret party of his wo
Is voided, and put awey to flight.    2925
Right as the derknesse of the night
Is chased with clerenesse of the mone,
Right so is al his wo ful sone
Devoided clene, whan that the sight
Biholden may that fresshe wight    2930
That the herte desyreth so,
That al his derknesse is ago ;
For than the herte is al at ese,
Whan they seen that [that] may hem plese.
   ' Now have I †thee declared al-out, 2935
Of that thou were in drede and dout ;
For I have told thee feithfully
What thee may curen utterly,
And alle lovers that wole be
Feithful, and ful of stabilite.    2940

Good-Hope alwey kepe by thy syde,
And Swete-Thought make eek abyde,
Swete-Loking and Swete-Speche ;
Of alle harmes they shal be leche.
Of every thou shalt have greet plesaunce ;
If thou canst byde in sufferaunce,   2946
And serve wel withoute feyntyse,
Thou shalt be quit of thyn empryse,
With more guerdoun, if that thou live ;
But al this tyme this I thee yive.'   2950

The God of Love whan al the day
Had taught me, as ye have herd say,
And enfourmed compendiously,
He vanished awey al sodeynly,
And I alone lefte, al sole,   2955
So ful of compleynt and of dole,
For I saw no other man ther me by.
My woundes me greved wondirly ;
Me for to curen no-thing I knew,
Save the botoun bright of hew,   2960
Wheron was set hoolly my thought ;
Of other comfort knew I nought,
But it were through the God of Love ;
I knew nat elles to my bihove
That might me ese or comfort gete,   2965
But-if he wolde him entermete.

The roser was, withoute doute,
Closed with an hegge withoute,
As ye to-forn have herd me seyn ;
And fast I bisied, and wolde fayn   2970
Have passed the haye, if I might
Have geten in by any slight
Unto the botoun so fair to see.
But ever I dradde blamed to be,
If men wolde have suspeccioun   2975
That I wolde of entencioun
Have stole the roses that ther were ;
Therfore to entre I was in fere.
But at the last, as I bithought
Whether I sholde passe or nought,   2980
I saw com with a gladde chere
To me, a lusty bachelere,
Of good stature, and of good hight,
And Bialacoil forsothe he hight.
Sone he was to Curtesy,   2985
And he me graunted ful gladly
The passage of the outer hay,
And seide :—' Sir, how that ye may
Passe, if [it] your wille be,
The fresshe roser for to see,   2990
And ye the swete savour fele.

Your † warrant may [I be] right wele ;
So thou thee kepe fro folye,
Shal no man do thee vilanye.
If I may helpe you in ought,   2995
I shal not feyne, dredeth nought ;
For I am bounde to your servyse,
Fully devoide of feyntyse.'
Than unto Bialacoil saide I,
' I thank you, sir, ful hertely,   3000
And your biheest [I] take at gree,
That ye so goodly profer me ;
To you it cometh of greet fraunchyse,
That ye me profer your servyse.'
Than aftir, ful deliverly,   3005
Through the breres anoon wente I,
Wherof encombred was the hay.
I was wel plesed, the soth to say,
To see the botoun fair and swote,
So fresshe spronge out of the rote.   3010

And Bialacoil me served wel,
Whan I so nygh me mighte fele
Of the botoun the swete odour,
And so lusty hewed of colour.
But than a cherl (foule him bityde !)   3015
Bisyde the roses gan him hyde,
To kepe the roses of that roser,
Of whom the name was Daunger.
This cherl was hid there in the greves,
Covered with grasse and with leves,   3020
To spye and take whom that he fond
Unto that roser putte an hond.
He was not sole, for ther was mo ;
For with him were other two
Of wikked maners, and yvel fame.   3025
That oon was clepid, by his name,
Wikked-Tonge, god yeve him sorwe !
For neither at eve, ne at morwe,
He can of no man [no] good speke ,
On many a just man doth he wreke.   3030
Ther was a womman eek, that hight
Shame, that, who can reken right,
Trespas was hir fadir name,
Hir moder Resoun ; and thus was Shame
[On lyve] brought of these ilk two.   3035
And yet had Trespas never ado
With Resoun, ne never ley hir by,
He was so hidous and ugly,
I mene, this that Trespas hight ;
But Resoun conceyveth, of a sight,   3040
Shame, of that I spak aforn.
And whan that Shame was thus born,

It was ordeyned, that Chastitee
Shulde of the roser lady be,
Which, of the botouns more and las, 3045
With sondry folk assailed was,
That she ne wiste what to do.
For Venus hir assailith so,
That night and day from hir she stal
Botouns and roses over-al.    3050
To Resoun than prayeth Chastitee,
Whom Venus †flemed over the see,
That she hir doughter wolde hir lene,
To kepe the roser fresh and grene.
Anoon Resoun to Chastitee    3055
Is fully assented that it be,
And grauntid hir, at hir request,
That Shame, bicause she is honest,
Shal keper of the roser be.
And thus to kepe it ther were three, 3060
That noon shulde hardy be ne bold
(Were he yong, or were he old)
Ageyn hir wille awey to bere
Botouns ne roses, that ther were.
I had wel sped, had I not been    3065
Awayted with these three, and seen.
For Bialacoil, that was so fair,
So gracious and debonair,
Quitte him to me ful curteisly,
And, me to plese, bad that I    3070
Shuld drawe me to the botoun nere ;
Prese in, to touche the rosere
Which bar the roses, he yaf me leve ;
This graunt ne might but litel greve.
And for he saw it lyked me,    3075
Right nygh the botoun pullede he
A leef al grene, and yaf me that,
The which ful nygh the botoun sat ;
I made [me] of that leef ful queynt.
And whan I felte I was aqueynt    3080
With Bialacoil, and so prive,
I wende al at my wille had be.
Then wex I hardy for to tel
To Bialacoil how me bifel
Of Love, that took and wounded me, 3085
And seide : ' Sir, so mote I thee,
I may no joye have in no wyse,
Upon no syde, but it ryse ;
For sithe (if I shal not feyne)
In herte I have had so gret peyne, 3090
So gret annoy, and such affray,
That I ne wot what I shal say ;
I drede your wrath to disserve.

Lever me were, that knyves kerve
My body shulde in pecis smalle,    3095
Than in any wyse it shulde falle
That ye wratthed shulde been with me.'
' Sey boldely thy wille,' quod he,
' I nil be wroth, if that I may,    3099
For nought that thou shalt to me say.'
Thanne seide I, ' Sir, not you displese
To knowen of my greet unese,
In which only love hath me brought ;
For peynes greet, disese and thought,
Fro day to day he doth me drye ;    3105
Supposeth not, sir, that I lye.
In me fyve woundes dide he make,
The sore of whiche shal never slake
But ye the botoun graunte me,
Which is most passaunt of beautee, 3110
My lyf, my deth, and my martyre,
And tresour that I most desyre.'
Than Bialacoil, affrayed all,
Seyde, ' Sir, it may not fall ;
That ye desire, it may not †ryse.    3115
What ? wolde ye shende me in this wyse ?
A mochel foole than I were,
If I suffrid you awey to bere
The fresh botoun, so fair of sight.
For it were neither skile ne right    3120
Of the roser ye broke the rind,
Or take the rose aforn his kind ;
Ye ar not courteys to aske it.
Lat it stil on the roser sit,
And †growe til it amended be,    **3125**
And parfitly come to beaute.
I nolde not that it pulled wer
Fro the roser that it ber,
To me it is so leef and dere.'
With that sterte out anoon Daungere, 
Out of the place where he was hid.    3131
His malice in his chere was kid ;
Ful greet he was, and blak of hewe,
Sturdy and hidous, who-so him knewe ;
Like sharp urchouns his here was growe,
His eyes †rede as the fire-glow ;    3136
His nose frounced ful kirked stood,
He com criand as he were wood,
And seide, ' Bialacoil, tel me why
Thou bringest hider so boldly    3140
Him that so nygh [is] the roser ?
Thou worchist in a wrong maner ;
He thenkith to dishonour thee,
Thou art wel worthy to have maugree

To late him of the roser wit ;    3145
Who serveth a feloun is yvel quit.
Thou woldist have doon greet bountee,
And he with shame wolde quyte thee.
Flee hennes, felowe ! I rede thee go !
It wanteth litel †I wol thee slo ;    3150
For Bialacoil ne knew thee nought,
Whan thee to serve he sette his thought ;
For thou wolt shame him, if thou might,
Bothe ageyn resoun and right.
I wol no more in thee affye,    3155
That comest so slyghly for tespye ;
For it preveth wonder wel,
Thy slight and tresoun every del.'

   I durst no more ther make abode,
For the cherl, he was so wode ;    3160
So gan he threten and manace,
And thurgh the haye he did me chace.
For feer of him I tremblid and quook,
So cherlishly his heed he shook ;
And seide, if eft he might me take,    3165
I shulde not from his hondis scape.

   Than Bialacoil is fled and mate,
And I al sole, disconsolate,
Was left aloon in peyne and thought ;
For shame, to deth I was nygh brought.
Than thought I on myn high foly,    3171
How that my body, utterly,
Was yeve to peyne and to martyre ;
And therto hadde I so gret yre,
That I ne durst the hayes passe ;    3175
There nas non hope, there was no grace.
I trowe never man wiste of peyne,
But he were laced in Loves cheyne ;
Ne no man [wot], and sooth it is,
But-if he love, what anger is.    3180
Love holdith his heest to me right wele,
Whan peyne he seide I shulde fele.
Non herte may thenke, ne tunge seyne,
A quarter of my wo and peyne.
I might not with the anger laste ;    3185
Myn herte in poynt was for to braste,
Whan I thought on the rose, that so
Was through Daunger cast me fro.

   A long whyl stood I in that state,
Til that me saugh so mad and mate    3190
The lady of the highe ward,
Which from hir tour lokid thiderward.
Resoun men clepe that lady,
Which from hir tour deliverly
Come doun to me withouten more.    3195

But she was neither yong, ne hore,
Ne high ne low, ne fat ne lene,
But best, as it were in a mene.
Hir eyen two were cleer and light
As any candel that brenneth bright ;    3200
And on hir heed she hadde a crown.
Hir semede wel an high persoun ;
For rounde enviroun, hir crownet
Was ful of riche stonis fret.
Hir goodly semblaunt, by devys,    3205
I trowe were maad in paradys ;
†Nature had never such a grace,
To forge a werk of such compace.
For certeyn, †but the letter lye,
God him-silf, that is so high,    3210
Made hir aftir his image,
And yaf hir sith sich avauntage,
That she hath might and seignorye
To kepe men from al folye ;
Who-so wole trowe hir lore,    3215
Ne may offenden nevermore.

   And whyl I stood thus derk and pale,
Resoun bigan to me hir tale ;
She seide : ' Al hayl, my swete frend !
Foly and childhood wol thee shend,    3220
Which thee have put in greet affray ;
Thou hast bought dere the tyme of May,
That made thyn herte mery to be.
In yvel tyme thou wentist to see
The gardin, wherof Ydilnesse    3225
Bar the keye, and was maistresse
Whan thou yedest in the daunce
With hir, and hadde[st] aqueyntaunce :
Hir aqueyntaunce is perilous,
First softe, and aftir[ward] noyous ;    3230
She hath [thee] trasshed, withoute ween ;
The God of Love had thee not seen,
Ne hadde Ydilnesse thee conveyed
In the verger where Mirthe him pleyed.
If Foly have supprised thee,    3235
Do so that it recovered be ;
And be wel war to take no more
Counsel, that greveth aftir sore ;
He is wys that wol himsilf chastyse.
And though a young man in any wyse
Trespace among, and do foly,    3241
Lat him not tarye, but hastily
Lat him amende what so be mis.
And eek I counseile thee, y-wis,
The God of Love hoolly foryet,    3245
That hath thee in sich peyne set,

And thee in herte tormented so.
I can nat seen how thou mayst go
Other weyes to garisoun ;
For Daunger, that is so feloun,   3250
Felly purposith thee to werrey,
Which is ful cruel, the soth to sey.

  ' And yit of Daunger cometh no blame,
In reward of my doughter Shame,
Which hath the roses in hir warde,   3255
As she that may be no musarde.
And Wikked-Tunge is with these two,
That suffrith no man thider go ;
For er a thing be do, he shal,
Where that he cometh, over-al,   3260
In fourty places, if it be sought,
Seye thing that never was doon ne
    wrought ;
So moche tresoun is in his male,
Of falsnesse for to †feyne a tale.
Thou delest with angry folk, y-wis ;   3265
Wherfor to thee [it] bettir is
From these folk awey to fare,
For they wol make thee live in care.
This is the yvel that Love they calle,
Wherin ther is but foly alle,   3270
For love is foly everydel ;
Who loveth, in no wyse may do wel,
Ne sette his thought on no good werk.
His scole he lesith, if he †be clerk ;
Of other craft eek if he be,   3275
He shal not thryve therin ; for he
In love shal have more passioun
Than monke, hermyte, or chanoun.
The peyne is hard, out of mesure,
The joye may eek no whyl endure ;   3280
And in the possessioun
Is muche tribulacioun ;
The joye it is so short-lasting,
And but in happe is the geting ;
For I see ther many in travaille,   3285
That atte laste foule fayle.
I was no-thing thy counseler,
Whan thou were maad the homager
Of God of Love to hastily ;
Ther was no wisdom, but foly.   3290
Thyn herte was joly, but not sage,
Whan thou were brought in sich a rage,
To yelde thee so redily,
And to Love, of his gret maistry.

  ' I rede thee Love awey to dryve,   3295
That makith thee recche not of thy lyve.

The foly more fro day to day
Shal growe, but thou it putte away.
Take with thy teeth the bridel faste,
To daunte thyn herte ; and eek thee caste,
If that thou mayst, to gete †defence   3301
For to redresse thy first offence.
Who-so his herte alwey wol leve,
Shal finde among that shal him greve.'

  Whan I hir herd thus me chastyse,   3305
I answerd in ful angry wyse.
I prayed hir cessen of hir speche,
Outher to chastyse me or teche,
To bidde me my thought refreyne,
Which Love hath caught in his de-
    meyne :—   3310
' What ? wene ye Love wol consent,
That me assailith with bowe bent,
To draw myn herte out of his honde,
Which is so quikly in his bonde ?
That ye counsayle, may never be ;   3315
For whan he first arested me,
He took myn herte so hool him til,
That it is no-thing at my wil ;
He †taughte it so him for to obey,
That he it sparred with a key.   3320
I pray yow lat me be al stille.
For ye may wel, if that ye wille,
Your wordis waste in idilnesse ;
For utterly, withouten gesse,
Al that ye seyn is but in veyne.   3325
Me were lever dye in the peyne,
Than Love to me-ward shulde arette
Falsheed, or tresoun on me sette.
I wol me gete prys or blame,
And love trewe, to save my name ;   3330
†Who me chastysith, I him hate.'

  With that word Resoun wente hir gate,
Whan she saugh for no sermoning
She might me fro my foly bring.
Than dismayed, I lefte al sool,   3335
Forwery, forwandred as a fool,
For I ne knew no †chevisaunce.
Than fel into my remembraunce,
How Love bade me to purveye
A felowe, to whom I mighte seye   3340
My counsel and my privete,
For that shulde muche availe me.
With that bithought I me, that I
Hadde a felowe faste by,
Trewe and siker, curteys, and hend,   3345
And he was called by name a Freend ;

A trewer felowe was no-wher noon.
In haste to him I wente anoon,
And to him al my wo I tolde,
Fro him right nought I wold withholde.
I tolde him al withoute were,                    3351
And made my compleynt on Daungere,
How for to see he was hidous,
And to-me-ward contrarious ;
The whiche through his cruelte        3355
Was in poynt to have meygned me ;
With Bialacoil whan he me sey
Within the gardyn walke and pley,
Fro me he made him for to go,
And I bilefte aloon in wo ;            3360
I durst no lenger with him speke,
For Daunger seide he wolde be wreke,
Whan that he sawe how I wente
The fresshe botoun for to hente,
If I were hardy to come neer          3365
Bitwene the hay and the roser.

This Freend, whan he wiste of my
    thought,
He discomforted me right nought,
But seide, ' Felowe, be not so mad,
Ne so abaysshed nor bistad.           3370
My-silf I knowe ful wel Daungere,
And how he is feers of his chere,
At prime temps, Love to manace ;
Ful ofte I have ben in his caas.
A feloun first though that he be,     3375
Aftir thou shalt him souple see.
Of long passed I knew him wele ;
Ungoodly first though men him fele,
He wol meek aftir, in his bering,
Been, for service and obeysshing.     3380
I shal thee telle what thou shalt do :—
Mekely I rede thou go him to,
Of herte pray him specialy
Of thy trespace to have mercy,
And hote him wel,[him] here to plese, 3385
That thou shalt nevermore him displese.
Who can best serve of flatery,
Shal plese Daunger most uttirly.'

My Freend hath seid to me so wel,
That he me esid hath somdel,          3390
And eek allegged of my torment ;
For through him had I hardement
Agayn to Daunger for to go,
To preve if I might meke him so.

To Daunger cam I, al ashamèd,        3395
The which aforn me hadde blamed,

Desyring for to pese my wo ;
But over hegge durst I not go,
For he †forbad me the passage.
I fond him cruel in his rage,         3400
And in his hond a gret burdoun.
To him I knelid lowe adoun,
Ful meke of port, and simple of chere,
And seide, ' Sir, I am comen here
Only to aske of you mercy.            3405
That greveth me, [sir], ful gretly
That ever my lyf I wratthed you,
But for to amende I am come now,
With al my might, bothe loude and stille,
To doon right at your owne wille ;    3410
For Love made me for to do
That I have trespassed hidirto ;
Fro whom I ne may withdrawe myn
    herte ;
Yit shal I never, for joy ne smerte,
What so bifalle, good or ille,        3415
Offende more ageyn your wille.
Lever I have endure disese
Than do that shulde you displese.
  ' I you require and pray, that ye
Of me have mercy and pitee,           3420
To stinte your yre that greveth so,
That I wol swere for evermo
To be redressid at your lyking,
If I trespasse in any thing ;
Save that I pray thee graunte me      3425
A thing that may nat warned be,
That I may love, al only ;
Non other thing of you aske I.
I shal doon elles wel, y-wis,
If of your grace ye graunte me this.  3430
And ye [ne] may not letten me,
For wel wot ye that love is free,
And I shal loven, †sith that I wil,
Who-ever lyke it wel or il ;
And yit ne wold I, for al Fraunce,    3435
Do thing to do you displesaunce.'
  Than Daunger fil in his entent
For to foryeve his maltalent ;
But al his wratthe yit at laste
He hath relesed, I preyde so faste :  3440
Shortly he seide, ' Thy request
Is not to mochel dishonest ;
Ne I wol not werne it thee,
For yit no-thing engreveth me.
For though thou love thus evermore,   3445
To me is neither softe ne sore.

Love †wher thee list; what recchith me,
So [thou] fer fro my roses be ?
Trust not on me, for noon assay,
In any tyme to passe the hay.'    3450
Thus hath he graunted my prayere.

Than wente I forth, withouten were,
Unto my Freend, and tolde him al,
Which was right joyful of my tale.
He seide, 'Now goth wel thyn affaire, 3455
He shal to thee be debonaire.
Though he aforn was dispitous,
He shal heeraftir be gracious.
If he were touchid on som good veyne,
He shuld yit rewen on thy peyne.    3460
Suffre, I rede, and no boost make,
Til thou at good mes mayst him take.
By suffraunce, and [by] wordis softe,
A man may overcome[n] ofte
Him that aforn he hadde in drede,    3465
In bookis sothly as I rede.'

Thus hath my Freend with gret comfort
Avaunced me with high disport,
Which wolde me good as mich as I.
And thanne anoon ful sodeynly    3470
I took my leve, and streight I went
Unto the hay; for gret talent
I had to seen the fresh botoun,
Wherin lay my salvacioun ;
And Daunger took kepe, if that I    3475
Kepe him covenaunt trewly.
So sore I dradde his manasing,
I durst not breke[n] his bidding ;
For, lest that I were of him shent,
I brak not his comaundement,    3480
For to purchase his good wil.
It was [hard] for to come ther-til,
His mercy was to fer bihinde ;
I wepte, for I ne might it finde.
I compleyned and sighed sore,    3485
And languisshed evermore,
For I durst not over go
Unto the rose I loved so.
Thurghout my deming outerly,
†Than had he knowlege certeinly,    3490
†That Love me ladde in sich a wyse,
That in me ther was no feyntyse,
Falsheed, ne no trecherye.
And yit he, ful of vilanye,
Of disdeyne, and cruelte,    3495
On me ne wolde have pite,

His cruel wil for to refreyne,
Though I wepe alwey, and †compleyne.

And while I was in this torment,
Were come of grace, by god sent,    3500
Fraunchyse, and with hir Pite
Fulfild the botoun of bountee
They go to Daunger anon-right
To forther me with al hir might,
And helpe in worde and in dede,    3505
For wel they saugh that it was nede.
First, of hir grace, dame Fraunchyse
Hath taken [word] of this empryse :
She seide, 'Daunger, gret wrong ye do
To worche this man so muche wo,    3510
Or pynen him so angerly ;
It is to you gret vilany.
I can not see why, ne how,
That he hath trespassed ageyn you,
Save that he loveth ; wherfore ye shulde
The more in cherete of him holde.    3516
The force of love makith him do this ;
Who wolde him blame he dide amis ?
He leseth more than ye may do ;
His peyne is hard, ye may see, lo !    3520
And Love in no wyse wolde consente
That †he have power to repente ;
For though that quik ye wolde him sloo,
Fro Love his herte may not go.
Now, swete sir, †is it your ese    3525
Him for to angre or disese ?
Allas, what may it you avaunce
To doon to him so greet grevaunce ?
What worship is it agayn him take,
Or on your man a werre make,    3530
Sith he so lowly every wyse
Is redy, as ye lust devyse ?
If Love hath caught him in his lace,
You for t'obeye in every caas,
And been your suget at your wille,    3535
Shulde ye therfore willen him ille ?
Ye shulde him spare more, al-out,
Than him that is bothe proud and stout.
Curtesye wol that ye socour
Hem that ben meke undir your cure. 3540
His herte is hard, that wole not meke,
Whan men of mekenesse him biseke.'

'That is certeyn,' seide Pite ;
'We see ofte that humilitee
Bothe ire, and also felonye    3545
Venquissheth, and also melancolye ;
To stonde forth in such duresse,

This crueltee and wikkednesse.
Wherfore I pray you, sir Daungere,
For to mayntene no lenger here     3550
Such cruel werre agayn your man,
As hoolly youres as ever he can ;
Nor that ye worchen no more wo
†On this caytif that languisshith so,
Which wol no more to you trespasse, 3555
But put him hoolly in your grace.
His offense ne was but lyte ;
The God of Love it was to wyte,
That he your thral so gretly is,
And if ye harm him, ye doon amis ;  3560
For he hath had ful hard penaunce,
Sith that ye refte him th'aqueyntaunce
Of Bialacoil, his moste joye,
Which alle his peynes might acoye.
He was biforn anoyed sore,     3565
But than ye doubled him wel more ;
For he of blis hath ben ful bare,
Sith Bialacoil was fro him fare.
Love hath to him do greet distresse,
He hath no nede of more duresse.     3570
Voideth from him your ire, I rede ;
Ye may not winnen in this dede.
Maketh Bialacoil repeire ageyn,
And haveth pite upon his peyn ;
For Fraunchise wol, and I, Pite,     3575
That merciful to him ye be ;
And sith that she and I accorde,
Have upon him misericorde ;
For I you pray, and eek moneste,
Nought to refusen our requeste ;     3580
For he is hard and fel of thought,
That for us two wol do right nought.'
    Daunger ne might no more endure,
He meked him unto mesure.
    ' I wol in no wyse,' seith Daungere, 3585
' Denye that ye have asked here ;
It were to greet uncurtesye.
I wol ye have the companye
Of Bialacoil, as ye devyse ;
I wol him lette[n] in no wyse.'     3590
    To Bialacoil than wente in hy
Fraunchyse, and seide ful curteisly :—
' Ye have to longe be deignous
Unto this lover, and daungerous,
Fro him to withdrawe your presence, 3595
Which hath do to him grete offence,
That ye not wolde upon him see ;
Wherfore a sorowful man is he.

Shape ye to paye him, and to plese,
Of my love if ye wol have ese.     3600
Fulfil his wil, sith that ye knowe
Daungei is daunted and brought lowe
Thurgh help of me and of Pite ;
You †thar no more afered be.'
    ' I shal do right as ye wil,'     3605
Saith Bialacoil, ' for it is skil,
Sith Daunger wol that it so be.'
Than Fraunchise hath him sent to me.
    Bialacoil at the biginning
Salued me in his coming.     3610
No straungenes was in him seen,
No more than he ne had wrathed been.
As faire semblaunt than shewed he me,
And goodly, as aforn did he ;
And by the honde, withouten doute, 3615
Within the haye, right al aboute
He ladde me, with right good chere,
Al environ the vergere,
That Daunger had me chased fro.
Now have I leve over-al to go ;     3620
Now am I raised, at my devys,
Fro helle unto paradys.
Thus Bialacoil, of gentilnesse,
With alle his peyne and besinesse,
Hath shewed me, only of grace,     3625
The estres of the swote place.
    I saw the rose, whan I was nigh,
Was gretter woxen, and more high,
Fresh, rody, and fair of hewe,
Of colour ever yliche newe.     3630
And whan I had it longe seen,
I saugh that through the leves grene
The rose spredde to spanishing ;
To sene it was a goodly thing.
But it ne was so spred on brede,     3635
That men within might knowe the sede ;
For it covert was and [en]close
Bothe with the leves and with the rose.
The stalk was even and grene upright,
It was theron a goodly sight ;     3640
And wel the better, withouten wene,
For the seed was not [y]-sene.
Ful faire it spradde, †god it blesse !
For suche another, as I gesse,
Aforn ne was, ne more vermayle.     3645
I was abawed for merveyle,
For ever, the fairer that it was,
The more I am bounden in Loves laas.
Longe I abood there, soth to saye,

Til Bialacoil I gan to praye,            3650
Whan that I saw him in no wyse
To me warnen his servyse,
That he me wolde graunte a thing,
Which to remembre is wel sitting ;
This is to sayne, that of his grace      3655
He wolde me yeve leyser and space
To me that was so desirous
To have a kissing precious
Of the goodly freshe rose,
That †swetely smelleth in my nose ; 3660
' For if it you displesed nought,
I wolde gladly, as I have sought,
Have a cos therof freely
Of your yeft ; for certainly
I wol non have but by your leve,         3665
So loth me were you for to greve.'
    He sayde, ' Frend, so god me spede,
Of Chastite I have suche drede,
Thou shuldest not warned be for me,
But I dar not, for Chastite.             3670
Agayn hir dar I not misdo,
For alwey biddeth she me so
To yeve no lover leve to kisse ;
For who therto may winnen, y-wis,
He of the surplus of the pray           3675
May live in hope to get som day.
For who so kissing may attayne,
Of loves peyne hath, soth to sayne,
The beste and most avenaunt,
And ernest of the remenaunt.'           3680
    Of his answere I syghed sore ;
I durst assaye him tho no more,
I had such drede to greve him ay.
A man shulde not to muche assaye
To chafe his frend out of mesure,        3685
Nor put his lyf in aventure ;
For no man at the firste stroke
Ne may nat felle doun an oke ;
Nor of the reisins have the wyne,
Til grapes †rype and wel afyne          3690
Be sore empressid, I you ensure,
And drawen out of the pressure.
But I, forpeyned wonder stronge,
†Thought that I abood right longe
Aftir the kis, in peyne and wo,          3695
Sith I to kis desyred so :
Til that, †rewing on my distresse,
Ther †to me Venus the goddesse,
Which ay werreyeth Chastite,
Came of hir grace, to socoure me,        3700

Whos might is knowe fer and wyde,
For she is modir of Cupyde,
The God of Love, blinde as stoon,
That helpith lovers many oon.
This lady brought in hir right hond 3705
Of brenning fyr a blasing brond ;
Wherof the flawme and hote fyr
Hath many a lady in desyr
Of love brought, and sore het,
And in hir servise hir †hertes set.      3710
This lady was of good entayle,
Right wondirful of apparayle ;
By hir atyre so bright and shene,
Men might perceyve wel, and seen,
She was not of religioun.                3715
Nor I nil make mencioun
Nor of [hir] robe, nor of tresour,
Of broche, †nor of hir riche attour ;
Ne of hir girdil aboute hir syde,
For that I nil not long abyde.           3720
But knowith wel, that certeynly
She was arayed richely.
Devoyd of pryde certeyn she was ;
To Bialacoil she wente a pas,
And to him shortly, in a clause,         3725
She seide : ' Sir, what is the cause
Ye been of port so daungerous
Unto this lover, and deynous,
To graunte him no-thing but a kis ?
To werne it him ye doon amis ;           3730
Sith wel ye wote, how that he
Is Loves servaunt, as ye may see,
And hath beaute, wher-through [he] is
Worthy of love to have the blis.
How he is semely, biholde and see,       3735
How he is fair, how he is free,
How he is swote and debonair,
Of age yong, lusty, and fair.
Ther is no lady so hauteyne,
Duchesse, countesse, ne chasteleyne, 3740
That I nolde holde hir ungoodly
For to refuse him outerly.
His breeth is also good and swete,
And eke his lippis rody, and mete
Only to †pleyen, and to kisse.           3745
Graunte him a kis, of gentilnesse !
His teeth arn also whyte and clene ;
Me thinkith wrong, withouten wene,
If ye now werne him, trustith me,
To graunte that a kis have he ;          3750
The lasse †to helpe him that ye haste,

The more tyme shul ye waste.'
    Whan the flawme of the verry brond,
That Venus brought in hir right hond,
Had Bialacoil with hete smete,          3755
Anoon he †bad, withouten lette,
Graunte to me the rose kisse.
Than of my peyne I gan to lisse,
And to the rose anoon wente I,
And kissid it ful feithfully.           3760
Thar no man aske if I was blythe,
Whan the savour soft and lythe
Strook to myn herte withoute more,
And me alegged of my sore,
So was I ful of joye and blisse.        3765
It is fair sich a flour to kisse,
It was so swote and saverous.
I might not be so anguisshous,
That I mote glad and joly be,
Whan that I remembre me.                3770
Yit ever among, sothly to seyn,
I suffre noye and moche peyn.
    The see may never be so stil,
That with a litel winde it †nil
Overwhelme and turne also,              3775
As it were wood, in wawis go.
Aftir the calm the trouble sone
Mot folowe, and chaunge as the mone.
Right so fareth Love, that selde in oon
Holdith his anker ; for right anoon     3780
Whan they in ese wene best to live,
They been with tempest al fordrive.
Who serveth Love, can telle of wo ;
The stoundemele joye mot overgo.
Now he hurteth, and now he cureth,      3785
For selde in oo poynt Love endureth.
    Now is it right me to procede,
How Shame gan medle and take hede,
Thurgh whom felle angres I have had ;
And how the stronge wal was maad,       3790
And the castell of brede and lengthe,
That God of Love wan with his strengthe.
Al this in romance wil I sette,
And for no-thing ne wil I lette,
So that it lyking to hir be,            3795
That is the flour of beaute ;
For she may best my labour quyte,
That I for hir love shal endyte.
    Wikkid-Tunge, that the covyne
Of every lover can devyne               3800
Worst, and addith more somdel,
(For Wikkid-Tunge seith never wel),

To me-ward bar he right gret hate,
Espying me erly and late,
Til he hath seen the gret[e] chere      3805
Of Bialacoil and me y-fere.
He mighte not his tunge withstonde
Worse to reporte than he fonde,
He was so ful of cursed rage ;
It sat him wel of his linage,           3810
For him an Irish womman bar.
His tunge was fyled sharp, and squar,
Poignaunt and right kerving,
And wonder bitter in speking.
For whan that he me gan espye,          3815
He swoor, afferming sikirly,
Bitwene Bialacoil and me
Was yvel aquayntaunce and privee.
He spak therof so folily,
That he awakid Jelousy ;                3820
Which, al afrayed in his rysing,
Whan that he herde [him] jangling,
He ran anoon, as he were wood,
To Bialacoil ther that he stood ;
Which hadde lever in this caas         3825
Have been at Reynes or Amyas ;
For foot-hoot, in his felonye
To him thus seide Jelousye :—
' Why hast thou been so necligent,
To kepen, whan I was absent,            3830
This verger here left in thy ward ?
To me thou haddist no reward,
To truste (to thy confusioun)
Him thus, to whom suspeccioun
I have right greet, for it is nede ;    3835
It is wel shewed by the dede.
Greet faute in thee now have I founde ;
By god, anoon thou shalt be bounde,
And faste loken in a tour,
Withoute refuyt or socour.              3840
For Shame to long hath be thee fro ;
Over sone she was ago.
Whan thou hast lost bothe drede and fere,
It semed wel she was not here.
She was [not] bisy, in no wyse,         3845
To kepe thee and [to] chastyse,
And for to helpen Chastitee
To kepe the roser, as thinkith me.
For than this boy-knave so boldely
Ne sholde not have be hardy,            3850
[Ne] in this †verger had such game,
Which now me turneth to gret shame.'
    Bialacoil nist what to sey ;

Ful fayn he wolde have fled awey,
For fere han hid, nere than he 3855
Al sodeynly took him with me.
And whan I saugh he hadde so,
This Jelousye, take us two,
I was astoned, and knew no rede,
But fledde awey for verrey drede. 3860

Than Shame cam forth ful simply ;
She wende have trespaced ful gretly ;
Humble of hir port, and made it simple,
Wering a vayle in stede of wimple,
As nonnis doon in hir abbey. 3865
Bicause hir herte was in affray,
She gan to speke, within a throwe,
To Jelousye, right wonder lowe.
First of his grace she bisought,
And seide :—' Sire, ne leveth nought 3870
Wikkid-Tunge, that fals espye,
Which is so glad to feyne and lye.
He hath you maad, thurgh flatering,
On Bialacoil a fals lesing.
His falsnesse is not now anew, 3875
It is to long that he him knew.
This is not the firste day ;
For Wikkid-Tunge hath custom ay
Yongé folkis to bewreye,
And false lesinges on hem †leye. 3880
' Yit nevertheles I see among,
That the loigne it is so longe
Of Bialacoil, hertis to lure,
In Loves servise for to endure,
Drawing suche folk him to, 3885
That he had no-thing with to do ;
But in sothnesse I trowe nought,
That Bialacoil hadde ever in thought
To do trespace or vilanye ;
But, for his modir Curtesye 3890
Hath taught him ever [for] to be
Good of aqueyntaunce and privee ;
For he loveth non hevinesse,
But mirthe and pley, and al gladnesse ;
He hateth alle †trecherous, 3895
Soleyn folk and envious ;
For [wel] ye witen how that he
Wol ever glad and joyful be
Honestly with folk to pley.
I have be negligent, in good fey, 3900
To chastise him ; therfore now I
Of herte †crye hem mercy,
That I have been so recheles
To tamen him, withouten lees.

Of my foly I me repente ; 3905
Now wol I hool sette myn entente
To kepe, bothe †loude and stille,
Bialacoil to do your wille.'
' Shame, Shame,' seyde Jelousy,
' To be bitrasshed gret drede have I. 3910
Lecherye hath clombe so hye,
That almost blered is myn ye ;
No wonder is, if that drede have I.
Over-al regnith Lechery,
Whos might [yit] growith night and day.
Bothe in cloistre and in abbey 3916
Chastite is werreyed over-al.
Therfore I wol with siker wal
Close bothe roses and roser.
I have to longe in this maner 3920
Left hem unclosid wilfully ;
Wherfore I am right inwardly
Sorowful and repente me.
But now they shal no lenger be
Unclosid ; and yit I drede sore, 3925
I shal repente ferthermore,
For the game goth al amis.
Counsel I †mot [take] newe, y-wis.
I have to longe tristed thee,
But now it shal no lenger be ; 3930
For he may best, in every cost,
Disceyve, that men tristen most.
I see wel that I am nygh shent,
But-if I sette my ful entent
Remedye to purveye. 3935
Therfore close I shal the weye
Fro hem that wol the rose espye,
And come to wayte me vilanye,
For, in good feith and in trouthe,
I wol not lette, for no slouthe, 3940
To live the more in sikirnesse,
†To make anoon a forteresse,
†To enclose the roses of good savour.
In middis shal I make a tour
To putte Bialacoil in prisoun, 3945
For ever I drede me of tresoun.
I trowe I shal him kepe so,
That he shal have no might to go
Aboute to make companye
To hem that thenke of vilanye ; 3950
Ne to no such as hath ben here
Aforn, and founde in him good chere,
Which han assailed him to shende,
And with hir trowandyse to blende.
A fool is eyth [for] to bigyle ; 3955

But may I lyve a litel while,
He shal forthenke his fair semblaunt.'
    And with that word cam Drede avaunt,
Which was abasshed, and in gret fere,
Whan he wiste Jelousye was there.  3960
He was for drede in such affray,
That not a word durste he say,
But quaking stood ful stille aloon,
Til Jelousye his wey was goon,
Save Shame, that him not forsook ;  3965
Bothe Drede and she ful sore quook ;
[Til] that at laste Drede abreyde,
And to his cosin Shame seyde :
' Shame,' he seide, ' in sothfastnesse,
To me it is gret hevinesse,  3970
That the noyse so fer is go,
And the sclaundre of us two.
But sith that it is [so] bifalle,
We may it not ageyn [do] calle,
Whan onis sprongen is a fame.  3975
For many a yeer withouten blame
We han been, and many a day ;
For many an April and many a May
We han [y]-passed, not [a]shamed,
Til Jelousye hath us blamed  3980
Of mistrust and suspecioun
Causeles, withouten enchesoun.
Go we to Daunger hastily,
And late us shewe him openly,
That he hath not aright [y]-wrought, 3985
Whan that he sette nought his thought
To kepe better the purpryse ;
In his doing he is not wyse.
He hath to us [y]-do gret wrong,
That hath suffred now so long  3990
Bialacoil to have his wille,
Alle his lustes to fulfille.
He must amende it utterly,
Or ellis shal he †vilaynsly
Exyled be out of this londe ;  3995
For he the werre may not withstonde
Of Jelousye,.nor the greef,
Sith Bialacoil is at mischeef.'
    To Daunger, Shame and Drede anoon
The righte wey ben [bothe a]-goon.  4000
The cherl they founden hem aforn
Ligging undir an hawethorn.
Undir his heed no pilowe was,
But in the stede a trusse of gras.
He slombred, and a nappe he took,  4005
Til Shame pitously him shook,

And greet manace on him gan make.
'Why slepist thou whan thou shuld wake ?'
Quod Shame ; ' thou dost us vilanye !
Who tristith thee, he doth folye,  4010
To kepe roses or botouns,
Whan they ben faire in hir sesouns.
Thou art woxe to familiere
Where thou shulde be straunge of chere,
Stout of thy port, redy to greve.  4015
Thou dost gret foly for to leve
Bialacoil here-in, to calle
The yonder man to shenden us alle.
Though that thou slepe, we may here
Of Jelousie gret noyse here.  4020
Art thou now late ? ryse up †in hy,
And stoppe sone and deliverly
Alle the gappis of the hay ;
Do no favour, I thee pray.
It fallith no-thing to thy name  4025
†Make fair semblaunt, where thou maist
        blame.
    ' If Bialacoil be swete and free,
Dogged and fel thou shuldist be ;
Froward and outrageous, y-wis ;
A cherl chaungeth that curteis is.  4030
This have I herd ofte in seying,
That man [ne] may, for no daunting,
Make a sperhauke of a bosarde.
Alle men wole holde thee for musarde,
That debonair have founden thee ;  4035
It sit thee nought curteis to be ;
To do men plesaunce or servyse,
In thee it is recreaundyse.
Let thy werkis, fer and nere,
Be lyke thy name, which is Daungere.'
    Than, al abawid in shewing,  4041
Anoon spak Dreed, right thus seying,
And seide, ' Daunger, I drede me
That thou ne wolt [not] bisy be
To kepe that thou hast to kepe ;  4045
Whan thou shuldist wake, thou art aslepe.
Thou shalt be greved certeynly,
If thee aspye Jelousy,
Or if he finde thee in blame.
He hath to-day assailed Shame,  4050
And chased awey, with gret manace,
Bialacoil out of this place,
And swereth shortly that he shal
Enclose him in a sturdy wal ;
And al is for thy wikkednesse,  4055
For that thee faileth straungenesse.

Thyn herte, I trowe, be failed al ;
Thou shalt repente in special,
If Jelousye the sothe knewe ;
Thou shalt forthenke, and sore rewe.' 4060
    With that the cherl his clubbe gan shake,
Frouning his eyen gan to make,
And hidous chere ; as man in rage,
For ire he brente in his visage.
Whan that he herde him blamed so, 4065
He seide, ' Out of my wit I go ;
To be discomfit I have gret wrong.
Certis, I have now lived to long,
Sith I may not this closer kepe ;
Al quik I wolde be dolven depe,     4070
If any man shal more repeire
Into this garden, for foule or faire.
Myn herte for ire goth a-fere,
That I lete any entre here.
I have do foly, now I see,     4075
But now it shal amended be.
Who settith foot here any more,
Truly, he shal repente it sore ;
For no man mo into this place
Of me to entre shal have grace.     4080
Lever I hadde, with swerdis tweyne,
Thurgh-out myn herte, in every veyne
Perced to be, with many a wounde,
Than slouthe shulde in me be founde.
From hennesforth, by night or day, 4085
I shal defende it, if I may,
Withouten any excepcioun
Of ech maner condicioun ;
And if I †any man it graunte,
Holdeth me for recreaunte.'     4090
    Than Daunger on his feet gan stonde,
And hente a burdoun in his honde.
Wroth in his ire, ne lefte he nought,
But thurgh the verger he hath sought.
If he might finde hole or trace,     4095
Wher-thurgh that me[n] mot forth by pace,
Or any gappe, he dide it close,
That no man mighte touche a rose
Of the roser al aboute ;
He shitteth every man withoute.     4100
    Thus day by day Daunger is wers,
More wondirful and more divers,
And feller eek than ever he was ;
For him ful oft I singe ' allas ! '
For I ne may nought, thurgh his ire, 4105
Recover that I most desire.
Myn herte, allas, wol brest a-two,

For Bialacoil I wratthed so.
For certeynly, in every membre
I quake, whan I me remembre     4110
Of the botoun, which [that] I wolde
Fulle ofte a day seen and biholde.
And whan I thenke upon the kisse,
And how muche joye and blisse
I hadde thurgh the savour swete,     4115
For wante of it I grone and grete.
Me thenkith I fele yit in my nose
The swete savour of the rose.
And now I woot that I mot go
So fer the fresshe floures fro,     4120
To me ful welcome were the deeth ;
Absens therof, allas, me sleeth !
For whylom with this rose, allas,
I touched nose, mouth, and face ;
But now the deeth I must abyde.     4125
But Love consente, another tyde,
That onis I touche may and kisse,
I trowe my peyne shal never lisse.
Theron is al my coveityse,
Which brent myn herte in many wyse.
Now shal repaire agayn sighinge,     4131
Long wacche on nightis, and no slepinge;
Thought in wisshing, torment, and wo,
With many a turning to and fro,
That half my peyne I can not telle.     4135
For I am fallen into helle
From paradys and welthe, the more
My turment greveth ; more and more
Anoyeth now the bittirnesse,
That I toforn have felt swetnesse.     4140
And Wikkid-Tunge, thurgh his falshede,
Causeth al my wo and drede.
On me he leyeth a pitous charge,
Bicause his tunge was to large.
    Now it is tyme, shortly that I     4145
Telle you som-thing of Jelousy,
That was in gret suspecioun.
Aboute him lefte he no masoun,
That stoon coude leye, ne querrour ;
He hired hem to make a tour.     4150
And first, the roses for to kepe,
Aboute hem made he a diche depe,
Right wondir large, and also brood ;
Upon the whiche also stood
Of squared stoon a sturdy wal,     4155
Which on a cragge was founded al,
And right gret thikkenesse eek it bar.
Abouten, it was founded squar,

An hundred fadome on every syde,
It was al liche longe and wyde.      4160
Lest any tyme it were assayled,
Ful wel aboute it was batayled ;
And rounde enviroun eek were set
Ful many a riche and fair touret.
At every corner of this wal      4165
Was set a tour ful principal ;
And everich hadde, withoute fable,
A porte-colys defensable
To kepe of enemies, and to greve,
That there hir force wolde preve.      4170
And eek amidde this purpryse
Was maad a tour of gret maistryse ;
A fairer saugh no man with sight,
Large and wyde, and of gret might.
They [ne] dredde noon assaut      4175
Of ginne, gunne, nor skaffaut.
[For] the temprure of the mortere
Was maad of licour wonder dere ;
Of quikke lyme persant and egre,
The which was tempred with vinegre.
The stoon was hard †as ademant,      4181
Wherof they made the foundement.
The tour was rounde, maad in compas ;
In al this world no richer was,
Ne better ordeigned therwithal.      4185
Aboute the tour was maad a wal,
So that, bitwixt that and the tour,
†Rosers were set of swete savour,
With many roses that they bere.
And eek within the castel were      4190
Springoldes, gunnes, bows, archers ;
And eek above, atte corners,
Men seyn over the walle stonde
Grete engynes, †whiche were nigh honde ;
And in the kernels, here and there,      4195
Of arblasters gret plentee were.
Noon armure might hir stroke with-
      stonde,
It were foly to prece to honde.
Without the diche were listes made,
With walles batayled large and brade,4200
For men and hors shulde not atteyne
To neigh the diche over the pleyne.
Thus Jelousye hath enviroun
Set aboute his garnisoun
With walles rounde, and diche depe, 4205
Only the roser for to kepe.
And Daunger [eek], erly and late
The keyes kepte of the utter gate,

The which openeth toward the eest.
And he hadde with him atte leest      4210
Thritty servauntes, echon by name.
      That other gate kepte Shame,
Which openede, as it was couth,
Toward the parte of the south.
Sergeauntes assigned were hir to      4215
Ful many, hir wille for to do.
      Than Drede hadde in hir baillye
The keping of the conestablerye,
Toward the north, I undirstonde,
That opened upon the left honde,      4220
The which for no-thing may be sure,
But-if she do [hir] bisy cure
Erly on morowe and also late,
Strongly to shette and barre the gate.
Of every thing that she may see      4225
Drede is aferd, wher-so she be ;
For with a puff of litel winde
Drede is astonied in hir minde.
Therfore, for stelinge of the rose,
I rede hir nought the yate unclose.      4230
A foulis flight wol make hir flee,
And eek a shadowe, if she it see.
      Thanne Wikked-Tunge, ful of envye,
With soudiours of Normandye,
As he that causeth al the bate,      4235
Was keper of the fourthe gate,
And also to the tother three
He went ful ofte, for to see.
Whan his lot was to wake a-night,
His instrumentis wolde he dight,      4240
For to blowe and make soun,
Ofter than he hath enchesoun ;
And walken oft upon the wal,
Corners and wikettis over-al
Ful narwe serchen and espye ;      4245
Though he nought fond, yit wolde he lye.
Discordaunt ever fro armonye,
And distoned from melodye,
Controve he wolde, and foule fayle,
With hornpypes of Cornewayle.      4250
In floytes made he discordaunce,
And in his musik, with mischaunce,
He wolde seyn, with notes newe,
That he [ne] fond no womman trewe,
Ne that he saugh never, in his lyf,      4255
Unto hir husbonde a trewe wyf ;
Ne noon so ful of honestee,
That she nil laughe and mery be
Whan that she hereth, or may espye,

A man speken of lecherye.                    4260
Everich of hem hath somme vyce ;
Oon is dishonest, another is nyce ;
If oon be ful of vilanyĕ,
Another hath a likerous ye ;
If oon be ful of wantonesse,                 4265
Another is a chideresse.
  Thus Wikked-Tunge (god yeve him
      shame !)
Can putte hem everichone in blame
Withoute desert and causeles ;
He lyeth, though they been giltles.          4270
I have pite to seen the sorwe,
That †waketh bothe eve and morwe,
To innocents doth such grevaunce ;
I pray god yeve him evel chaunce,
That he ever so bisy is                       4275
Of any womman to seyn amis !
  Eek Jelousye god confounde,
That hath [y]-maad a tour so rounde,
And made aboute a garisoun
To sette Bialacoil in prisoun ;               4280
The which is shet there in the tour,
Ful longe to holde there sojour,
There for to live[n] in penaunce.
And for to do him more grevaunce,
†Ther hath ordeyned Jelousye                  4285
An olde vekke, for to espye
The maner of his governaunce ;
The whiche devel, in hir enfaunce,
Had lerned [muche] of Loves art,
And of his pleyes took hir part ;            4290
She was †expert in his servyse.
She knew ech wrenche and every gyse
Of love, and every [loveres] wyle,
It was [the] harder hir to gyle.
Of Bialacoil she took ay hede,               4295
That ever he liveth in wo and drede.
He kepte him coy and eek privee,
Lest in him she hadde see
Any foly countenaunce,
For she knew al the olde daunce.             4300
And aftir this, whan Jelousye
Had Bialacoil in his baillye,
And shette him up that was so free,
For seure of him he wolde be,
He trusteth sore in his castel ;             4305
The stronge werk him lyketh wel.
He dradde nat that no glotouns
Shulde stele his roses or botouns.
The roses weren assured alle,

Defenced with the stronge walle.             4310
Now Jelousye ful wel may be
Of drede devoid, in libertee,
Whether that he slepe or wake ;
For of his roses may noon be take.
  But I, allas, now morne shal ;             4315
Bicause I was without the wal,
Ful moche dole and mone I made.
Who hadde wist what wo I hadde,
I trowe he wolde have had pitee.
Love to deere had sold to me                 4320
The good that of his love hadde I.
I †wende a bought it al queyntly ;
But now, thurgh doubling of my peyn,
I see he wolde it selle ageyn,
And me a newe bargeyn lere,                  4325
The which al-out the more is dere,
For the solace that I have lorn,
Than I hadde it never aforn.
Certayn I am ful lyk, indeed,
To him that cast in erthe his seed ;         4330
And hath joie of the newe spring,
Whan it greneth in the ginning,
And is also fair and fresh of flour,
Lusty to seen, swote of odour ;
But er he it in sheves shere,                4335
May falle a weder that shal it dere,
And make[n] it to fade and falle,
The stalk, the greyn, and floures alle ;
That to the †tilier is fordone
The hope that he hadde to sone.              4340
I drede, certeyn, that so fare I ;
For hope and travaile sikerly
Ben me biraft al with a storm ;
The floure nil seden of my corn.
For Love hath so avaunced me,                4345
Whan I bigan my privitee
To Bialacoil al for to telle,
Whom I ne fond froward ne felle,
But took a-gree al hool my play.
But Love is of so hard assay,                4350
That al at onis he reved me,
Whan I †wend best aboven have be.
It is of Love, as of Fortune,
That chaungeth ofte, and nil contune ;
Which whylom wol on folke smyle,    4355
And gloumbe on hem another whyle ;
Now freend, now foo, [thou] shalt hir fele,
For [in] a twinkling tourneth hir wheel.
She can wrythe hir heed awey,
This is the concours of hir pley ;           4360

She can areyse that doth morne,
And whirle adown, and overturne
Who sittith hieghst, †al as hir †list ;
A fool is he that wol hir trist.
For it †am I that am com doun          4365
Thurgh †change and revolucioun !
Sith Bialacoil mot fro me twinne,
Shet in the prisoun yond withinne,
His absence at myn herte I fele ;
For al my joye and al myn hele        4370
Was in him and in the rose,
That but yon †wal, which him doth close,
Open, that I may him see,
Love nil not that I cured be
Of the peynes that I endure,           4375
Nor of my cruel aventure.
    A, Bialacoil, myn owne dere !
Though thou be now a prisonere,
Kepe atte leste thyn herte to me,
And suffre not that it daunted be ;    4380
Ne lat not Jelousye, in his rage,
Putten thyn herte in no servage.
Although he chastice thee withoute,
And make thy body unto him loute,
Have herte as hard as dyamaunt,        4385
Stedefast, and nought pliaunt ;
In prisoun though thy body be,
At large kepe thyn herte free.
A trewe herte wol not plye
For no manace that it may drye.        4390
If Jelousye doth thee payne,
Quyte him his whyle thus agayne,
To venge thee, atte leest in thought,
If other way thou mayest nought ;
And in this wyse sotilly               4395
Worche, and winne the maistry.
But yit I am in gret affray
Lest thou do not as I say ;
I drede thou canst me greet maugree,
That thou emprisoned art for me ;      4400
But that [is] not for my trespas,
For thurgh me never discovered was
Yit thing that oughte be secree.
Wel more anoy [ther] is in me,
Than is in thee, of this mischaunce ; 4405
For I endure more hard penaunce
Than any [man] can seyn or thinke,
That for the sorwe almost I sinke.
Whan I remembre me of my wo,
Ful nygh out of my wit I go.           4410
Inward myn herte I fele blede,

For comfortles the deeth I drede.
Ow I not wel to have distresse,
Whan false, thurgh hir wikkednesse,
And traitours, that arn envyous,       4415
To noyen me be so coragious ?
    A, Bialacoil ! ful wel I see,
That they hem shape to disceyve thee,
To make thee buxom to hir lawe,
And with hir corde thee to drawe       4420
Wher-so hem lust, right at hir wil ;
I drede they have thee brought thertil.
Withoute comfort, thought me sleeth ;
This game wol bringe me to my deeth.
For if your †gode wille I lese,        4425
I mote be deed ; I may not chese.
And if that thou foryete me,
Myn herte shal never in lyking be ;
Nor elles-where finde solace,
If I be put out of your grace,         4430
As it shal never been, I hope ;
Than shulde I falle[n] in wanhope.

    [*Here, at l.* 4070 *of the* French *text,*
    *ends the work of* G. de Lorris ; *and*
    *begins the work of* Jean de Meun.]

    Allas, in wanhope ?—nay, pardee !
For I wol never dispeired be.
If Hope me faile, than am I            4435
Ungracious and unworthy ;
In Hope I wol comforted be,
For Love, whan he bitaught hir me,
Seide, that Hope, wher-so I go,
Shulde ay be relees to my wo.          4440
    But what and she my balis bete,
And be to me curteis and swete ?
She is in no-thing ful certeyn.
Lovers she put in ful gret peyn,
And makith hem with wo to dele.        4445
Hir fair biheest disceyveth fele,
For she wol bihote, sikirly,
And failen aftir outrely.
A ! that is a ful noyous thing !
For many a lover, in loving,           4450
Hangeth upon hir, and trusteth fast,
Whiche lese hir travel at the last.
Of thing to comen she woot right nought ;
Therfore, if it be wysly sought,
Hir counseille, foly is to take.       4455
For many tymes, whan she wol make
A ful good silogisme, I drede

That aftirward ther shal in dede
Folwe an evel conclusioun ;
This put me in confusioun.     4460
For many tymes I have it seen,
That many have bigyled been,
For trust that they have set in Hope,
Which fel hem aftirward a-slope.

But natheles yit, gladly she wolde, 4465
That he, that wol him with hir holde,
Hadde alle tymes †his purpos clere,
Withoute deceyte, or any were.
That she desireth sikirly ;
Whan I hir blamed, I did foly.     4470
But what avayleth hir good wille,
Whan she ne may staunche my stounde
    ille ?
That helpith litel, that she may do,
Outake biheest unto my wo.
And heeste certeyn, in no wyse,     4475
Withoute yift, is not to †pryse.

Whan heest and deed a-sundir varie,
They doon [me have] a gret contrarie.
Thus am I possed up and doun
With dool, thought, and confusioun; 4480
Of my disese ther is no noumbre.
Daunger and Shame me encumbre,
Drede also, and Jelousye,
And Wikked-Tunge, ful of envye,
Of whiche the sharpe and cruel ire     4485
Ful oft me put in gret martire.
They han my joye fully let,
Sith Bialacoil they have bishet
Fro me in prisoun wikkidly,
Whom I love so entierly,     4490
That it wol my bane be,
But I the soner may him see.
And yit moreover, wurst of alle,
Ther is set to kepe, foule hir bifalle !
A rimpled vekke, fer ronne in age,     4495
Frowning and yelowe in hir visage,
Which in awayte lyth day and night,
That noon of hem may have a sight.
Now moot my sorwe enforced be ;
Ful soth it is, that Love yaf me     4500
Three wonder yiftes of his grace,
Which I have lorn now in this place,
Sith they ne may, withoute drede,
Helpen but litel, who taketh hede.
For here availeth no Swete-Thought, 4505
And Swete-Speche helpith right nought.
The thridde was called Swete-Loking,

That now is lorn, without lesing.
[The] yiftes were fair, but not forthy
They helpe me but simp[il]ly,     4510
But Bialacoil [may] loosed be,
To gon at large and to be free.
For him my lyf lyth al in dout,
But-if he come the rather ont.
Allas ! I trowe it wol not been !     4515
For how shuld I evermore him seen ?
He may not out, and that is wrong,
Bicause the tour is so strong.
How shulde he out ? by whos prowesse,
Out of so strong a forteresse ?     4520
By me, certeyn, it nil be do ;
God woot, I have no wit therto !
But wel I woot I was in rage,
Whan I to Love dide homage.
Who was in cause, in sothfastnesse, 4525
But hir-silf, dame Idelnesse,
Which me conveyed, thurgh fair prayere,
To entre into that fair vergere ?
She was to blame me to leve,
The which now doth me sore greve. 4530
A foolis word is nought to trowe,
Ne worth an appel for to lowe ;
Men shulde him snibbe bittirly,
At pryme temps of his foly.
I was a fool, and she me leved,     4535
Thurgh whom I am right nought releved.
She accomplisshed al my wil,
That now me greveth wondir il.
Resoun me seide what shulde falle.
A fool my-silf I may wel calle,     4540
That love asyde I had not leyde,
And trowed that dame Resoun seyde.
Resoun had bothe skile and right,
Whan she me blamed, with al hir might,
To medle of love, that hath me shent ;
But certeyn now I wol repent.     4546
' And shulde I repent ? Nay, parde !
A fals traitour than shulde I be.
The develles engins wolde me take,
If I my †lorde wolde forsake,     4550
Or Bialacoil falsly bitraye.
Shulde I at mischeef hate him ? nay,
Sith he now, for his curtesye,
Is in prisoun of Jelousye.
Curtesye certeyn dide he me,     4555
So †muche, it may not yolden be,
Whan he the hay passen me lete,
To kisse the rose, faire and swete :

Shulde I therfore cunne him maugree?
Nay, certeynly, it shal not be ;           4560
For Love shal never, †if god wil,
Here of me, thurgh word or wil,
Offence or complaynt, more or lesse,
Neither of Hope nor Idilnesse ;
For certis, it were wrong that I           4565
Hated hem for hir curtesye.
Ther is not ellis, but suffre and thinke,
And waken whan I shulde winke ;
Abyde in hope, til Love, thurgh chaunce,
Sende me socour or allegeaunce,           4570
Expectant ay til I may mete
To geten mercy of that swete.
    ' Whylom I thinke how Love to me
Seyde he wolde take[n] att[e] gree
My servise, if unpacience           4575
Caused me to doon offence.
He seyde, " In thank I shal it take,
And high maister eek thee make,
If wikkednesse ne reve it thee ;
But sone, I trowe, that shal not be." 4580
These were his wordis by and by ;
It semed he loved me trewly.
Now is ther not but serve him wele,
If that I thinke his thank to fele.
My good, myn harm, lyth hool in me ;
In Love may no defaute be ;           4586
For trewe Love †failid never man.
Sothly, the faute mot nedis than
(As God forbede !) be founde in me,
And how it cometh, I can not see.           4590
Now lat it goon as it may go ;
Whether Love wol socoure me or slo,
He may do hool on me his wil.
I am so sore bounde him til,
From his servyse I may not fleen ;           4595
For lyf and deth, withouten wene,
Is in his hand ; I may not chese ;
He may me do bothe winne and lese.
And sith so sore he doth me greve,
Yit, if my lust he wolde acheve           4600
To Bialacoil goodly to be,
I yeve no force what felle on me.
For though I dye, as I mot nede,
I praye Love, of his goodlihede,
To Bialacoil do gentilnesse,           4605
For whom I live in such distresse,
That I mote deyen for penaunce.
But first, withoute repentaunce,
I wol me confesse in good entent,

And make in haste my testament,           4610
As lovers doon that felen smerte :—
To Bialacoil leve I myn herte
Al hool, withoute departing,
Or doublenesse of repenting.'

### Coment Raisoun vient a L'amant.

    Thus as I made my passage           4615
In compleynt, and in cruel rage,
And I †nist wher to finde a leche
That couthe unto myn helping eche,
Sodeynly agayn comen doun
Out of hir tour I saugh Resoun,           4620
Discrete and wys, and ful plesaunt,
And of hir porte ful avenaunt.
The righte wey she took to me,
Which stood in greet perplexite,
That was posshed in every side,           4625
That I nist where I might abyde,
Til she, demurely sad of chere,
Seide to me as she com nere :—
    ' Myn owne freend, art thou yit greved?
How is this quarel yit acheved           4630
Of Loves syde ?  Anoon me telle ;
Hast thou not yit of love thy fille ?
Art thou not wery of thy servyse
That thee hath [pyned] in sich wyse ?
What joye hast thou in thy loving ? 4635
Is it swete or bitter thing ?
Canst thou yit chese, lat me see,
What best thy socour mighte be ?
    ' Thou servest a ful noble lord,
That maketh thee thral for thy reward,
Which ay renewith thy turment,           4641
With foly so he hath thee blent.
Thou felle in mischeef thilke day,
Whan thou didest, the sothe to say,
Obeysaunce and eek homage ;           4645
Thou wroughtest no-thing as the sage.
Whan thou bicam his liege man,
Thou didist a gret foly than ;
Thou wistest not what fel therto,
With what lord thou haddist to do. 4650
If thou haddist him wel knowe,
Thou haddist nought be brought so lowe ;
For if thou wistest what it were,
Thou noldist serve him half a yeer,
Not a weke, nor half a day,           4655
Ne yit an hour withoute delay,
Ne never †han loved paramours,

His lordship is so ful of shoures.
Knowest him ought?'
   *L'Amaunt.*     'Ye, dame, parde!'
   *Raisoun.*   'Nay, nay.'
   *L'Amaunt.*    'Yes, I.'
   *Raisoun.*      'Wherof, lat see?' 4660
   *L'Amaunt.*  'Of that he seyde I shulde
      be
Glad to have sich lord as he,
And maister of sich seignory.'
   *Raisoun.*  'Knowist him no more?'
   *L'Amaunt.*       'Nay, certis, I,
Save that he yaf me rewles there,    4665
And wente his wey, I niste where,
And I abood bounde in balaunce.'
   *Raisoun.* 'Lo, there a noble conisaunce!
But I wil that thou knowe him now
Ginning and ende, sith that thou    4670
Art so anguisshous and mate,
Disfigured out of astate;
Ther may no wrecche have more of wo,
Ne caitif noon enduren so.
It were to every man sitting     4675
Of his lord have knowleching.
For if thou knewe him, out of dout,
Lightly thou shulde escapen out
Of the prisoun that marreth thee.'
   *L'Amaunt.*  'Ye, dame! sith my lord
      is he,                4680
And I his man, maad with myn honde,
I wolde right fayn undirstonde
To knowe[n] of what kinde he be,
If any wolde enforme me.'
   *Raisoun.*  'I wolde,' seid Resoun, 'thee
      lere,               4685
Sith thou to lerne hast sich desire,
And shewe thee, withouten fable,
A thing that is not demonstrable.
Thou shalt [here lerne] without science,
And knowe, withoute experience,    4690
The thing that may not knowen be,
Ne wist ne shewid in no degree.
Thou mayst the sothe of it not witen,
Though in thee it were writen.
Thou shalt not knowe therof more    4695
Whyle thou art reuled by his lore;
But unto him that love wol flee,
The knotte may unclosed be,
Which hath to thee, as it is founde,
So long be knet and not unbounde.   4700
Now sette wel thyn entencioun,

To here of love discripcioun.
   'Love, it is an hateful pees,
A free acquitaunce, without relees,
†A trouthe, fret full of falshede,     4705
A sikernesse, al set in drede;
In herte is a dispeiring hope,
And fulle of hope, it is wanhope;
Wyse woodnesse, and wood resoun,
A swete peril, in to droune,        4710
An hevy birthen, light to bere,
A wikked wawe awey to were.
It is Caribdis perilous,
Disagreable and gracious.
It is discordaunce that can accorde,   4715
And accordaunce to discorde.
It is cunning withoute science,
Wisdom withoute sapience,
Wit withoute discrecioun,
Havoir, withoute possessioun.      4720
It is †sike hele and hool siknesse,
A †thrust drowned †in dronkenesse,
†An helthe ful of maladye,
And charitee ful of envye,
†An hunger ful of habundaunce,    4725
And a gredy suffisaunce;
Delyt right ful of hevinesse,
And dreri[h]ed ful of gladnesse;
Bitter swetnesse and swete errour,
Right evel savoured good savour;    4730
†Sinne that pardoun hath withinne,
And pardoun spotted without [with]
    sinne;
A peyne also it is, joyous,
And felonye right pitous;
Also pley that selde is stable,      4735
And stedefast [stat], right mevable;
A strengthe, weyked to stonde upright,
And feblenesse, ful of might;
Wit unavysed, sage folye,
And joye ful of turmentrye;       4740
A laughter it is, weping ay,
Rest, that traveyleth night and day;
Also a swete helle it is,
And a sorowful Paradys;
A plesaunt gayl and esy prisoun,    4745
And, ful of froste, somer sesoun;
Pryme temps, ful of frostes whyte,
And May, devoide of al delyte,
With seer braunches, blossoms ungrene;
And newe fruyt, fillid with winter tene.
It is a slowe, may not forbere     4751

Ragges, ribaned with gold, to were:
For al-so wel wol love be set
Under ragges as riche rochet ;
And eek as wel †be amourettes　　4755
In mourning blak, as bright burnettes.
For noon is of so mochel prys,
Ne no man founden [is] so wys,
Ne noon so high is of parage,
Ne no man founde of wit so sage,　　4760
No man so hardy ne so wight,
Ne no man of so mochel might,
Noon so fulfilled of bounte,
†But he with love may daunted be.
Al the world holdith this way ;　　4765
Love makith alle to goon miswey,
But it be they of yvel lyf,
Whom Genius cursith, man and wyf,
That wrongly werke ageyn nature.
Noon suche I love, ne have no cure　　4770
Of suche as Loves servaunts been,
And wol not by my counsel fleen.
For I ne preyse that loving,
Wher-thurgh man, at the laste ending,
Shal calle hem wrecchis fulle of wo,　　4775
Love greveth hem and shendith so.
But if thou wolt wel Love eschewe,
For to escape out of his mewe,
And make al hool thy sorwe to slake,
No bettir counsel mayst thou take,　　4780
Than thinke to fleen wel, y-wis ;
May nought helpe elles ; for wite thou
　　this :—
If thou flee it, it shal flee thee ;
Folowe it, and folowen shal it thee.'
　　L'Amaunt. Whan I hadde herd al
　　　　Resoun seyn,　　4785
Which hadde spilt hir speche in veyn :
'Dame,' seyde I, ' I dar wel sey
Of this avaunt me wel I may
That from your scole so deviaunt
I am, that never the more avaunt　　4790
Right nought am I, thurgh your doctryne;
I dulle under your disciplyne ;
I wot no more than [I] wist †er,
To me so contrarie and so fer
Is every thing that ye me lere ;　　4795
And yit I can it al †parcnere.
Myn herte foryetith therof right nought,
It is so writen in my thought ;
And depe †graven it is so tendir
That al by herte I can it rendre,　　4800

And rede it over comunely ;
But to my-silf lewedist am I.
　　' But sith ye love discreven so,
And lakke and preise it, bothe two,
Defyneth it into this letter,　　4805
That I may thenke on it the better
For I herde never †diffyne it ere,
And wilfully I wolde it lere.'
　　Raisoun. 'If love be serched wel and
　　　　sought,
It is a sykenesse of the thought　　4810
Annexed and †knet bitwixe tweyne,
†Which male and female, with oo cheyne,
So frely byndith, that they nil twinne,
Whether so therof they lese or winne,
The roote springith, thurgh hoot bren-
　　ning,　　4815
Into disordinat desiring
For to kissen and enbrace,
And at her lust them to solace.
Of other thing love recchith nought,
But setteth hir herte and al hir thought
More for delectacioun　　4821
Than any procreacioun
Of other fruyt by †engendring ;
Which love to god is not plesing ;
For of hir body fruyt to get　　4825
They yeve no force, they are so set
Upon delyt, to pley in-fere.
And somme have also this manere,
To feynen hem for love seke ;
Sich love I preise not at a leke.　　4830
For paramours they do but feyne ;
To love truly they disdeyne.
They falsen ladies traitoursly,
And sweren hem othes utterly,
With many a lesing, and many a fable,
And al they finden deceyvable.　　4836
And, whanne they †her lust han geten,
The hoote ernes they al foryeten.
Wimmen, the harm they byen ful sore ;
But men this thenken evermore,　　4840
That lasse harm is, so mote I thee,
Disceyve them, than disceyved be ;
And namely, wher they ne may
Finde non other mene wey.
For I wot wel, in sothfastnesse,　　4845
That †who doth now his bisynesse
With any womman for to dele,
For any lust that he may fele,
But-if it be for engendrure,

He doth trespasse, I you ensure.　4850
For he shulde setten al his wil
To geten a likly thing him til,
And to sustene[n], if he might,
And kepe forth, by kindes right,
His owne lyknesse and semblable,　4855
For bicause al is corumpable,
And faile shulde successioun,
Ne were †ther generacioun
Our sectis strene for to save.
Whan fader or moder arn in grave,　4860
Hir children shulde, whan they ben deede,
Ful diligent ben, in hir steede,
To use that werke on such a wyse,
That oon may thurgh another ryse.
Therfore set Kinde therin delyt,　4865
For men therin shulde hem delyte,
And of that dede be not erke,
But ofte sythes haunt that werke.
For noon wolde drawe therof a draught
Ne were delyt, which hath him caught.
This hadde sotil dame Nature ;　4871
For noon goth right, I thee ensure,
Ne hath entent hool ne parfyt ;
For hir desir is for delyt,
The which fortened crece and eke　4875
The pley of love for-ofte seke,
And thralle hem-silf, they be so nyce,
Unto the prince of every vyce.
For of ech sinne it is the rote,
Unlefulle lust, though it be sote,　4880
And of al yvel the racyne,
As Tullius can determyne,
Which in his tyme was ful sage,
In a boke he made of Age,
Wher that more he preyseth Elde,　4885
Though he be croked and unwelde,
And more of commendacioun,
Than Youthe in his discripcioun.
For Youthe set bothe man and wyf
In al perel of soule and lyf ;　4890
And perel is, but men have grace,
The †tyme of youthe for to pace,
Withoute any deth or distresse,
It is so ful of wildenesse ;
So ofte it doth shame or damage　4895
To him or to his linage.
It ledith man now up, now doun,
In mochel dissolucioun,
And makith him love yvel company,
And lede his lyf disrewlily,　4900

And halt him payed with noon estate.
Within him-silf is such debate,
He chaungith purpos and entent,
And yalt [him] into som covent,
To liven aftir her empryse,　4905
And lesith fredom and fraunchyse,
That Nature in him hadde set,
The which ageyn he may not get,
If he there make his mansioun
For to abyde professioun.　4910
Though for a tyme his herte absente,
It may not fayle, he shal repente,
And eke abyde thilke day
To leve his abit, and goon his way,
And lesith his worship and his name,
And dar not come ageyn for shame ; 4916
But al his lyf he doth so mourne,
Bicause he dar not hoom retourne.
Fredom of kinde so lost hath he
That never may recured be,　4920
†But-if that god him graunte grace
That he may, er he hennes pace,
Conteyne undir obedience
Thurgh the vertu of pacience.
For Youthe set man in al folye,　4925
In unthrift and in ribaudye,
In leccherye, and in outrage,
So ofte it chaungith of corage.
Youthe ginneth ofte sich bargeyn,
That may not ende withouten peyn. 4930
In gret perel is set youth-hede,
Delyt so doth his bridil lede.
Delyt †thus hangith, drede thee nought,
Bothe mannis body and his thought,
Only thurgh †Youthe, his chamberere,
That to don yvel is customere,　4936
And of nought elles taketh hede
But only folkes for to lede
Into disporte and wildenesse,
So is [she] froward from sadnesse.　4940
　‘ But Elde drawith hem therfro ;
Who wot it nought, he may wel go
†Demand of hem that now arn olde,
That whylom Youthe hadde in holde,
Which yit †remembre of tendir age, 4945
How it hem brought in many a rage,
And many a foly therin wrought.
But now that Elde hath †hem thurgh-
　　　sought,
They repente hem of her folye,
That Youthe hem putte in jupardye, 4950

In perel and in muche wo,
And made hem ofte amis to do,
And suen yvel companye,
Riot and avouterye.

'But Elde †can ageyn restreyne    4955
From suche foly, and refreyne,
And set men, by hir ordinaunce,
In good reule and in governaunce.
But yvel she spendith hir servyse,
For no man wol hir love, †ne pryse; 4960
She is hated, this wot I wele.
Hir acqueyntaunce wolde no man fele,
Ne han of Elde companye,
Men hate to be of hir alye.
For no man wolde bicomen olde,    4965
Ne dye, whan he is yong and bolde.
And Elde merveilith right gretly,
Whan they remembre hem inwardly
Of many a perelous empryse,
Whiche that they wrought in sondry
    wyse,    4970
How ever they might, withoute blame,
Escape awey withoute shame,
In youthe, withoute[n] damage
Or repreef of her linage,
Losse of membre, sheding of blode, 4975
Perel of deth, or losse of good.

'Wost thou nought where Youthe
    abit,
That men so preisen in her wit?
With Delyt she halt sojour,
For bothe they dwellen in oo tour.    4980
As longe as Youthe is in sesoun,
They dwellen in oon mansioun.
Delyt of Youthe wol have servyse
To do what so he wol devyse;
And Youthe is redy evermore    4985
For to obey, for smerte of sore,
Unto Delyt, and him to yive
Hir servise, whyl that she may live.

'Where Elde abit, I wol thee telle
Shortly, and no whyle dwelle,    4990
For thider bihoveth thee to go.
If Deth in youthe thee not slo,
Of this journey thou maist not faile.
With hir Labour and Travaile
Logged been, with Sorwe and Wo,    4995
That never out of hir courte go.
Peyne and Distresse, Syknesse and Ire,
And Malencoly, that angry sire,
Ben of hir paleys senatours;

Groning and Grucching, hir herber-
    geours,    5000
The day and night, hir to turment,
With cruel Deth they hir present,
And tellen hir, erliche and late,
That Deth †stant armed at hir gate.
Than bringe they to hir remembraunce
The foly dedis of hir infaunce,    5006
Which causen hir to mourne in wo
That Youthe hath hir bigiled so,
Which sodeynly awey is hasted.
She †wepeth the tyme that she hath
    wasted,    5010
Compleyning of the preterit,
And the present, that not abit,
And of hir olde vanitee,
That, but aforn hir she may see
In the future som socour,    5015
To leggen hir of hir dolour,
To graunt hir tyme of repentaunce,
For hir sinnes to do penaunce,
And at the laste so hir governe
To winne the joy that is eterne,    5020
Fro which go bakward Youthe †hir made,
In vanitee to droune and wade.
For present tyme abidith nought,
It is more swift than any thought;
So litel whyle it doth endure    5025
That ther nis compte ne mesure.

'But how that ever the game go,
Who list †have joye and mirth also
Of love, be it he or she,
High or lowe, who[so] it be,    5030
In fruyt they shulde hem delyte;
Her part they may not elles quyte,
To save hem-silf in honestee.
And yit ful many oon I see
Of wimmen, sothly for to seyne,    5035
That [ay] desire and wolde fayne
The pley of love, they be so wilde,
And not coveite to go with childe.
And if with child they be perchaunce,
They wole it holde a gret mischaunce;
But what-som-ever wo they fele,    5041
They wol not pleyne, but concele;
But-if it be any fool or nyce,
In whom that shame hath no justyce.
For to delyt echon they drawe,    5045
That haunte this werk, bothe high and
    lawe,
Save sich that ar[e]n worth right nought,

That for money wol be bought.
Such love I preise in no wyse,
Whan it is †given for coveitise.    5050
I preise no womman, though †she be wood,
That yeveth hir-silf for any good.
For litel shulde a man telle
Of hir, that wol hir body selle,
Be she mayde, be she wyf,    5055
That quik wol selle hir, by hir lyf.
How faire chere that ever she make,
He is a wrecche, I undirtake,
That †loveth such one, for swete or sour,
Though she him calle hir paramour, 5060
And laugheth on him, and makith him
     feeste.
For certeynly no suche [a] beeste
To be loved is not worthy,
Or bere the name of dru[e]ry.
Noon shulde hir please, but he were wood,
That wol dispoile him of his good.    5066
Yit nevertheles, I wol not sey
†But she, for solace and for pley,
May a jewel or other thing
Take of her loves free yeving ;    5070
But that she aske it in no wyse,
For drede of shame of coveityse.
And she of hirs may him, certeyn,
Withoute sclaundre, yeven ageyn,
And joyne her hertes togidre so    5075
In love, and take and yeve also.
Trowe not that I wolde hem twinne,
Whan in her love ther is no sinne ;
I wol that they togedre go,
And doon al that they han ado,    5080
As curteis shulde and debonaire,
And in her love beren hem faire,
Withoute vyce, bothe he and she ;
So that alwey, in honestee,
Fro foly love †they kepe hem clere    5085
That brenneth hertis with his fere ;
And that her love, in any wyse,
Be devoid of coveityse.
Good love shulde engendrid be
Of trewe herte, just, and secree,    5090
And not of such as sette her thought
To have her lust, and ellis nought,
So are they caught in Loves lace,
Truly, for bodily solace.
Fleshly delyt is so present    5095
With thee, that sette al thyn entent,
Withoute more (what shulde I glose ?)

For to gete and have the Rose ;
Which makith thee so mate and wood
That thou desirest noon other good. 5100
But thou art not an inche the nerre,
But ever abydest in sorwe and werre,
As in thy face it is sene ;
It makith thee bothe pale and lene ;
Thy might, thy vertu goth away.    5105
A sory gest, in goode fay,
Thou †herberedest than in thyn inne,
The God of Love whan thou let inne !
Wherfore I rede, thou shette him out,
Or he shal greve thee, out of doute ; 5110
For to thy profit it wol turne,
If he nomore with thee sojourne.
In gret mischeef and sorwe sonken
Ben hertis, that of love arn dronken,
As thou peraventure knowen shal,    5115
Whan thou hast lost †thy tyme al,
And spent †thy youthe in ydilnesse,
In waste, and woful lustinesse ;
If thou maist live the tyme to see
Of love for to delivered be,    5120
Thy tyme thou shalt biwepe sore
The whiche never thou maist restore.
(For tyme lost, as men may see,
For no-thing may recured be).
And if thou scape yit, atte laste,    5125
Fro Love, that hath thee so faste
Knit and bounden in his lace,
Certeyn, I holde it but a grace.
For many oon, as it is seyn,
Have lost, and spent also in veyn,    5130
In his servyse, withoute socour,
Body and soule, good, and tresour,
Wit, and strengthe, and eek richesse,
Of which they hadde never redresse.'
     Thus taught and preched hath Resoun,
But Love spilte hir sermoun,    5136
That was so imped in my thought,
That hir doctrine I sette at nought.
And yit ne seide she never a dele,
That I ne understode it wele,    5140
Word by word, the mater al.
But unto Love I was so thral,
Which callith over-al his pray,
He chasith so my thought †alway,
And holdith myn herte undir his sele, 
As trust and trew as any stele ;    5146
So that no devocioun
Ne hadde I in the sermoun

Of dame Resoun, ne of hir rede;
It toke no sojour in myn hede. 5150
For alle yede out at oon ere
That in that other she dide lere;
Fully on me she lost hir lore,
Hir speche me greved wondir sore.
   †Than unto hir for ire I seide, 5155
For anger, as I dide abraide :
'Dame, and is it youre wille algate,
That I not love, but that I hate
Alle men, as ye me teche?
For if I do aftir your speche, 5160
Sith that ye seyn love is not good,
Than must I nedis say with mood,
If I it leve, in hatrede ay
Liven, and voide love away
From me, [and been] a sinful wrecche,
Hated of all that [love that] tecche. 5166
I may not go noon other gate,
For either must I love or hate.
And if I hate men of-newe
More than love, it wol me rewe, 5170
As by your preching semeth me,
For Love no-thing ne preisith thee.
Ye yeve good counseil, sikirly,
That prechith me al-day, that I
Shulde not Loves lore alowe ; 5175
He were a fool, wolde you not trowe !
In speche also ye han me taught
Another love, that knowen is naught,
Which I have herd you not repreve,
To love ech other ; by your leve, 5180
If ye wolde diffyne it me,
I wolde gladly here, to see,
At the leest, if I may lere
Of sondry loves the manere.'
   *Raison.* 'Certis, freend, a fool art
      thou 5185
Whan that thou no-thing wolt allowe
That I [thee] for thy profit say.
Yit wol I sey thee more, in fay ;
For I am redy, at the leste,
To accomplisshe thy requeste, 5190
But I not wher it wol avayle ;
In veyne, perauntre, I shal travayle.
Love ther is in sondry wyse,
As I shal thee here devyse.
For som love leful is and good ; 5195
I mene not that which makith thee wood,
And bringith thee in many a fit,
And ravisshith fro thee al thy wit,

It is so merveilous and queynt;
With such love be no more aqueynt. 5200

### Comment Raisoun diffinist
### †Amistie.

'Love of Frendshipe also ther is,
Which makith no man doon amis,
Of wille knit bitwixe two,
That wol not breke for wele ne wo ;
Which long is lykly to contune, 5205
Whan wille and goodis ben in comune ;
Grounded by goddis ordinaunce,
Hool, withoute discordaunce ;
With hem holding comuntee
Of al her goode in charitee, 5210
That ther be noon excepcioun
Thurgh chaunging of entencioun ;
That ech helpe other at hir neede,
And wysly hele bothe word and dede ;
Trewe of mening, devoid of slouthe, 5215
For wit is nought withoute trouthe ;
So that the ton dar al his thought
Seyn to his freend, and spare nought,
As to him-silf, without dreding
To be discovered by wreying. 5220
For glad is that conjunccioun,
Whan ther is noon suspecioun
[Ne lak in hem], whom they wolde prove
That trew and parfit weren in love.
For no man may be amiable, 5225
But-if he be so ferme and stable,
That fortune chaunge him not, ne blinde,
But that his freend alwey him finde,
Bothe pore and riche, in oo[n] [e]state.
For if his freend, thurgh any gate, 5230
Wol compleyne of his povertee,
He shulde not byde so long, til he
Of his helping him requere ;
For good deed, don [but] thurgh prayere,
Is sold, and bought to dere, y-wis, 5235
To hert that of gret valour is.
For hert fulfilled of gentilnesse
Can yvel demene his distresse.
And man that worthy is of name
To asken often hath gret shame. 5240
· A good man brenneth in his thought
For shame, whan he axeth ought.
He hath gret thought, and dredith ay
For his disese, whan he shal pray
His freend, lest that he warned be, 5245

Til that he preve his stabiltee.
But whan that he hath founden oon
That trusty is and trew as stone,
And [hath] assayed him at al,
And found him stedefast as a wal,    5250
And of his freendship be certeyne,
He shal him shewe bothe joye and peyne,
And al that [he] dar thinke or sey,
Withoute shame, as he wel may.
For how shulde he ashamed be    5255
Of sich oon as I tolde thee?
For whan he woot his secree thought,
The thridde shal knowe ther-of right
    nought;
For tweyn in nombre is bet than three
In every counsel and secree.    5260
Repreve he dredeth never a del,
Who that biset his wordis wel;
For every wys man, out of drede,
Can kepe his tunge til he see nede;
And fooles can not holde hir tunge; 5265
A fooles belle is sone runge.
Yit shal a trewe freend do more
To helpe his felowe of his sore,
And socoure him, whan he hath nede,
In al that he may doon in dede;    5270
And gladder [be] that he him plesith
Than [is] his felowe that he esith.
And if he do not his requeste,
He shal as mochel him moleste
As his felow, for that he    5275
May not fulfille his voluntee
[As] fully as he hath requered.
If †bothe hertis Love hath fered,
Joy and wo they shul depart,
And take evenly ech his part.    5280
Half his anoy he shal have ay,
And comfort [him] what that he may;
And of †his blisse parte shal he,
If love wol departed be.

   'And whilom of this †amitee    5285
Spak Tullius in a ditee;
†" A man shulde maken his request
Unto his freend, that is honest;
And he goodly shulde it fulfille,
But it the more were out of skile,    5290
And otherwise not graunt therto,
Except only in †cases two:
If men his freend to deth wolde dryve,
Lat him be bisy to save his lyve.
Also if men wolen him assayle,    5295

Of his wurship to make him faile,
And hindren him of his renoun,
Lat him, with ful entencioun,
His dever doon in ech degree
That his freend ne shamed be,    5300
In this two †cases with his might,
Taking no kepe to skile nor right,
As ferre as love may him excuse;
This oughte no man to refuse."
This love that I have told to thee    5305
Is no-thing contrarie to me;
This wol I that thou folowe wel,
And leve the tother everydel.
This love to vertu al attendith,    5309
The tothir fooles blent and shendith.

   'Another love also there is,
That is contrarie unto this,
Which desyre is so constreyned
That [it] is but wille feyned;
Awey fro trouthe it doth so varie,    5315
That to good love it is contrarie;
For it maymeth, in many wyse,
Syke hertis with coveityse;
Al in winning and in profyt
Sich love settith his delyt.    5320
This love so hangeth in balaunce
That, if it lese his hope, perchaunce,
Of lucre, that he is set upon,
It wol faile, and quenche anon;
For no man may be amorous,    5325
Ne in his living vertuous,
But-[if] he love more, in mood,
Men for hem-silf than for hir good.
For love that profit doth abyde
Is fals, and bit not in no tyde.    5330
[This] love cometh of dame Fortune,
That litel whyle wol contune;
For it shal chaungen wonder sone,
And take eclips right as the mone,
Whan †she is from us [y]-let    5335
Thurgh erthe, that bitwixe is set
The sonne and hir, as it may falle,
Be it in party, or in alle;
The shadowe maketh her bemis merke,
And hir hornes to shewe derke,    5340
That part where she hath lost †the lyght
Of Phebus fully, and the sight;
Til, whan the shadowe is overpast,
She is enlumined ageyn as faste,    5344
†Thurgh brightnesse of the sonne bemes
That yeveth to hir ageyn hir lemes.

That love is right of sich nature ;
Now is [it] fair, and now obscure,
Now bright, now clipsy of manere,
And whylom dim, and whylom clere. 5350
As sone as Poverte ginneth take,
With mantel and [with] wedis blake
[It] hidith of Love the light awey,
That into night it turneth day ;
It may not see Richesse shyne      5355
Til the blakke shadowes fyne.
For, whan Richesse shyneth bright,
Love recovereth ageyn his light ;
And whan it failith, he wol flit,
And as she †groweth, so groweth it. 5360
  'Of this love, here what I sey :—
The riche men are loved ay,
And namely tho that sparand bene,
That wol not wasshe hir hertes clene
Of the filthe, nor of the vyce      5365
Of gredy brenning avaryce.
The riche man ful fond is, y-wis,
That weneth that he loved is.
If that his herte it undirstood,
It is not he, it is his good ;       5370
He may wel witen in his thought,
His good is loved, and he right nought.
For if he be a nigard eke,
Men wole not sette by him a leke,
But haten him ; this is the soth.   5375
Lo, what profit his catel doth !
Of every man that may him see,
It geteth him nought but enmitee.
But he amende †him of that vyce,
And knowe him-silf, he is not wys.  5380
  'Certis, he shulde ay freendly be,
To gete him love also ben free,
Or ellis he is not wyse ne sage
No more than is a gote ramage.
That he not loveth, his dede proveth,
Whan he his richesse so wel loveth, 5386
That he wol hyde it ay and spare,
His pore freendis seen forfare ;
To kepe †it ay is his purpose,
Til for drede his eyen close,        5390
And til a wikked deth him take ;
Him hadde lever asondre shake,
And late †his limes asondre ryve,
Than leve his richesse in his lyve.
He thenkith parte it with no man ;  5395
Certayn, no love is in him than.
How shulde love within him be,

Whan in his herte is no pite ?
That he trespasseth, wel I wat,
For ech man knowith his estat ;      5400
For wel him †oughte be reproved
That loveth nought, ne is not loved.
  'But sith we arn to Fortune comen,
And †han our sermoun of hir nomen,
A wondir wil I telle thee now,       5405
Thou herdist never sich oon, I trow.
I not wher thou me leven shal,
Though sothfastnesse it be †in al,
As it is writen, and is sooth,
That unto men more profit doth       5410
The froward Fortune and contraire,
Than the swote and debonaire :
And if thee thinke it is doutable,
It is thurgh argument provable.
For the debonaire and softe          5415
Falsith and bigylith ofte ;
For liche a moder she can cherishe
And milken as doth a norys ;
And of hir goode to †hem deles,
And yeveth †hem part of her joweles,
With grete richesse and dignitee ;   5421
And hem she hoteth stabilitee
In a state that is not stable,
But channging ay and variable ;
And fedith †hem with glorie veyne, 5425
And worldly blisse noncerteyne.
Whan she †hem settith on hir whele,
Than wene they to be right wele,
And in so stable state withalle,
That never they wene for to falle.   5430
And whan they set so high[e] be,
They wene to have in certeintee
Of hertly frendis †so gret noumbre,
That no-thing mighte her stat encombre ;
They truste hem so on every syde,    5435
Wening with †hem they wolde abyde
In every perel and mischaunce,
Withoute chaunge or variaunce,
Bothe of catel and of good ;
And also for to spende hir blood     5440
And alle hir membris for to spille,
Only to fulfille hir wille.
They maken it hole in many wyse,
And hoten hem hir ful servyse,
How sore that it do hem smerte,      5445
Into hir very naked sherte !
Herte and al, so hole they yeve,
For the tyme that they may live,

So that, with her flaterye,
They maken foolis glorifye     5450
Of hir wordis [greet] speking,
And han †there-of a rejoysing,
And trowe hem as the Evangyle ;
And it is al falsheed and gyle,
As they shal afterwarde[s] see,     5455
Whan they arn falle in povertee,
And been of good and catel bare ;
Than shulde they seen who freendis
    ware.
For of an hundred, certeynly,
Nor of a thousand ful scarsly,     5460
Ne shal they fynde unnethis oon,
Whan povertee is comen upon.
For †this Fortune that I of telle,
With men whan hir lust to dwelle,
Makith hem to lese hir conisaunce,     5465
And nourishith hem in ignoraunce.
'But froward Fortune and perverse,
Whan high estatis she doth reverse,
And maketh hem to tumble doun
Of hir whele, with sodeyn tourn,     5470
And from hir richesse doth hem flee,
And plongeth hem in povertee,
As a stepmoder envyous,
And leyeth a plastre dolorous
Unto her hertis, wounded egre,     5475
Which is not tempred with vinegre,
But with poverte and indigence,
†She sheweth, by experience,
That she is Fortune verely
In whom no man shulde affy,     5480
Nor in hir yeftis have fiaunce,
She is so ful of variaunce.
Thus can she maken high and lowe,
Whan they from richesse ar[e]n throwe,
Fully to knowen, withouten were,     5485
Freend of †effect, and freend of chere ;
And which in love weren trew and stable,
And whiche also weren variable,
After Fortune, hir goddesse,
In poverte, outher in richesse ;     5490
For al †she yeveth, out of drede,
Unhappe bereveth it in dede ;
For Infortune †lat not oon
Of freendis, whan Fortune is goon ;
I mene tho freendis that wol flee     5495
Anoon as entreth povertee.
And yit they wol not leve hem so,
But in ech place where they go

They calle hem " wrecche," scorne and
    blame,
And of hir mishappe hem diffame,     5500
And, namely, siche as in richesse
Pretendith most of stablenesse,
Whan that they sawe him set onlofte,
And weren of him socoured ofte,
And most y-holpe in al hir nede :     5505
But now they take no maner hede,
But seyn, in voice of flaterye,
That now apperith hir folye,
Over-al where-so they fare,
And singe, " Go, farewel feldefare."     5510
Alle suche freendis I beshrewe,
For of [the] trewe ther be to fewe ;
But sothfast freendis, what so bityde,
In every fortune wolen abyde ;
They han hir hertis in suche noblesse     5516
That they nil love for no richesse,
Nor, for that Fortune may hem sende,
They wolen hem socoure and defende ;
And chaunge for softe ne for sore,
For who is freend, loveth evermore.     5520
Though men drawe swerd his freend to slo,
He may not hewe hir love atwo.
But, in [the] case that I shal sey,
For pride and ire lese it he may,
And for reprove by nycetee,     5525
And discovering of privitee,
With tonge wounding, as feloun,
Thurgh venemous detraccioun.
Frend in this case wol gon his way,
For no-thing greve him more ne may ;
And for nought ellis wol he flee,     5531
If that he love in stabilitee.
And certeyn, he is wel bigoon
Among a thousand that fyndith oon.
For ther may be no richesse,     5535
Ageyns frendship, of worthinesse;
For it ne may so high atteigne
As may the valoure, sooth to seyne,
Of him that loveth trew and wel ;
Frendship is more than is catel.     5540
For freend in court ay better is
Than peny in [his] purs, certis ;
And Fortune, mishapping,
Whan upon men she is †falling,
Thurgh misturning of hir chaunce,     5545
And †casteth hem oute of balaunce,
She makith, thurgh hir adversitee,
Men ful cleerly for to see

Him that is freend in existence
From him that is by apparence.          5550
For Infortune makith anoon
To knowe thy freendis fro thy foon,
By experience, right as it is ;
The which is more to preyse, y-wis,
Than †is miche richesse and tresour ;
For more †doth profit and valour     5556
Poverte, and such adversitee,
Bifore than doth prosperitee ;
For the toon yeveth conisaunce,
And the tother ignoraunce.            5560
    ' And thus in poverte is in dede
Trouthe declared fro falsehede ;
For feynte frendis it wol declare,
And trewe also, what wey they fare.
For whan he was in his richesse,     5565
These freendis, ful of doublenesse,
Offrid him in many wyse
Hert and body, and servyse.
What wolde he than ha †yeve to ha
        bought
To knowen openly her thought,        5570
That he now hath so clerly seen ?
The lasse bigyled he sholde have been
And he hadde than perceyved it,
But richesse nold not late him wit.
Wel more avauntage doth him than, 5575
Sith that it makith him a wys man,
The greet mischeef that he †receyveth,
Than doth richesse that him deceyveth.
Richesse riche ne makith nought
Him that on tresour set his thought ;
For richesse stont in suffisaunce     5581
And no-thing in habundaunce ;
For suffisaunce al-only
Makith men to live richely.
For he that hath [but] miches tweyne,
Ne [more] value in his demeigne,     5586
Liveth more at ese, and more is riche,
Than doth he that is [so] chiche,
And in his bern hath, soth to seyn,
An hundred †muwis of whete greyn, 5590
Though he be chapman or marchaunt,
And have of golde many besaunt.
For in the geting he hath such wo,
And in the keping drede also,
And set evermore his bisynesse       5595
For to encrese, and not to lesse,
For to augment and multiply.
And though on hepis †it lye him by,

Yit never shal make his richesse
Asseth unto his gredinesse.          5600
But the povre that recchith nought,
Save of his lyflode, in his thought,
Which that he getith with his travaile,
He dredith nought that it shal faile,
Though he have lytel worldis good, 5605
Mete and drinke, and esy food,
Upon his travel and living,
And also suffisaunt clothing.
Or if in syknesse that he falle,
And lothe mete and drink withalle, 5610
Though he have nought, his mete to by,
He shal bithinke him hastely,
To putte him out of al daunger,
That he of mete hath no mister ;
Or that he may with litel eke        5615
Be founden, whyl that he is seke ;
Or that men shul him †bere in hast,
To live, til his syknesse be past,
To somme maysondewe bisyde ;         5619
He cast nought what shal him bityde.
He thenkith nought that ever he shal
Into any syknesse falle.
    ' And though it falle, as it may be,
That al betyme spare shal he
As mochel as shal to him suffyce,    5625
Whyl he is syke in any wyse,
He doth [it], for that he wol be
Content with his povertee
Withoute nede of any man.
So miche in litel have he can,       5630
He is apayed with his fortune ;
And for he nil be importune
Unto no wight, ne onerous,
Nor of hir goodes coveitous ;
Therfore he spareth, it may wel been,
His pore estat for to sustene.       5636
    ' Or if him lust not for to spare,
But suffrith forth, as nought ne ware,
Atte last it hapneth, as it may,
Right unto his laste day,            5640
And †taketh the world as it wolde be ;
For ever in herte thenkith he,
The soner that [the] deeth him slo,
To paradys the soner go
He shal, there for to live in blisse, 5645
Where that he shal no good misse.
Thider he hopith god shal him sende
Aftir his wrecchid lyves ende.
Pictagoras himsilf reherses,

In a book that the Golden Verses    5650
Is clepid, for the nobilitee
Of the honourable ditee :—
" Than, whan thou gost thy body fro,
Free in the eir thou shalt up go,
And leven al humanitee,     5655
And purely live in deitee."—
He is a fool, withouten were,
That trowith have his countre here.
" In erthe is not our countree,"
That may these clerkis seyn and see   5660
In Boece of Consolacioun,
Where it is maked mencioun
Of our countree pleyn at the eye,
By teching of philosophye,
Where lewid men might lere wit,    5665
Who-so that wolde translaten it.
If he be sich that can wel live
Aftir his rente may him yive,
And not desyreth more to have,
That may fro povertee him save :    5670
A wys man seide, as we may seen,
Is no man wrecched, but he it wene,
Be he king, knight, or ribaud.
And many a ribaud is mery and baud,
That swinkith, and berith, bothe day and
     night,     5675
Many a burthen of gret might,
The whiche doth him lasse offense,
For he suffrith in pacience.
They laugh and daunce, trippe and singe,
And ley not up for her living,     5680
But in the tavern al dispendith
The winning that god hem sendith.
Than goth he, fardels for to bere,
With as good chere as he dide ere ;
To swinke and traveile he not feynith,
For for to robben he disdeynith ;     5686
But right anoon, aftir his swinke,
He goth to tavern for to drinke.
Alle these ar riche in abundaunce,
That can thus have suffisaunce     5690
Wel more than can an usurere,
As god wel knowith, withoute were.
For an usurer, so god me see,
Shal never for richesse riche bee,
But evermore pore and indigent,     5695
Scarce, and gredy in his entent.
   ' For soth it is, whom it displese,
Ther may no marchaunt live at ese ;
His herte in sich a †were is set,

That it quik brenneth [more] to get,    5700
Ne never shal †enough have geten ;
Though he have gold in gerners yeten,
For to be nedy he dredith sore.
Wherfore to geten more and more
He set his herte and his desire ;     5705
So hote he brennith in the fire
Of coveitise, that makith him wood
To purchase other mennes good.
He undirfongith a gret peyne,
That undirtakith to drinke up Seyne ;
For the more he drinkith, ay     5711
The more he leveth, the soth to say.
†This is the thurst of fals geting,
That last ever in coveiting,
And the anguisshe and distresse     5715
With the fire of gredinesse.
She fighteth with him ay, and stryveth,
That his herte asondre ryveth ;
Such gredinesse him assaylith,
That whan he most hath, most he faylith.
   ' Phisiciens and advocates     5721
Gon right by the same yates ;
They selle hir science for winning,
And haunte hir crafte for greet geting.
Hir winning is of such swetnesse,    5725
That if a man falle in sikenesse,
They are ful glad, for hir encrese ;
For by hir wille, withoute lees,
Everiche man shulde be seke,     5729
And though they dye, they set not a leke.
After, whan they the gold have take,
Ful litel care for hem they make.
They wolde that fourty were seke at onis,
Ye, two hundred, in flesh and bonis,
And yit two thousand, as I gesse,    5735
For to encresen her richesse.
They wol not worchen, in no wyse,
But for lucre and coveityse ;
For fysyk ginneth first by *fy*,
The fysycien also sothely ;     5740
And sithen it goth fro *fy* to †*sy* ;
To truste on hem, it is foly ;
For they nil, in no maner gree,
Do right nought for charitee.
   ' Eke in the same secte are set     5745
Alle tho that prechen for to get
Worshipes, honour, and richesse.
Her hertis arn in greet distresse,
That folk [ne] live not holily.
But aboven al, specialy,     5750

Sich as prechen [for] veynglorie,
And toward god have no memorie,
But forth as ypocrites trace,
And to her soules deth purchace,
And outward †shewen holynesse,        5755
Though they be fulle of cursidnesse.
Not liche to the apostles twelve,
They deceyve other and hem-selve ;
Bigyled is the gyler than.
For preching of a cursed man,        5760
Though [it] to other may profyte,
Himsilf availeth not a myte ;
For oft good predicacioun
Cometh of evel entencioun.
To him not vailith his preching,        5765
Al helpe he other with his teching ;
For where they good ensaumple take,
There is he with veynglorie shake.
  ' But lat us leven these prechoures,
And speke of hem that in her toures 5770
Hepe up her gold, and faste shette,
And sore theron her herte sette.
They neither love god, ne drede
They kepe more than it is nede,
And in her bagges sore it binde,        5775
Out of the sonne, and of the winde ;
They putte up more than nede ware,
Whan they seen pore folk forfare,
For hunger dye, and for cold quake ;
God can wel vengeaunce therof take.        5780
†Three gret mischeves hem assailith,
And thus in gadring ay travaylith ;

With moche peyne they winne richesse ;
And drede hem holdith in distresse,
To kepe that they gadre faste ;        5785
With sorwe they leve it at the laste ;
With sorwe they bothe dye and live,
That †to richesse her hertis yive,
And in defaute of love it is,
As it shewith ful wel, y-wis.        5790
For if these gredy, the sothe to seyn,
Loveden, and were loved ageyn,
And good love regned over-alle,
Such wikkidnesse ne shulde falle ;
But he shulde yeve that most good had
To hem that weren in nede bistad,        5796
And live withoute fals usure,
For charitee ful clene and pure.
If they hem yeve to goodnesse,
Defending hem from ydelnesse,        5800
In al this world than pore noon
We shulde finde, I trowe, not oon.
But chaunged is this world unstable ;
For love is over-al vendable.
We see that no man loveth now        5805
But for winning and for prow ;
And love is thralled in servage
Whan it is sold for avauntage ;
Yit wommen wol hir bodies selle ;        5809
Suche soules goth to the devel of helle.'

[*Here ends* l. 5170 *of the* F. text. *A
great gap follows. The next line answers to* l. 10717 *of the same.*]

## FRAGMENT C.

Whan Love had told hem his entente,
The baronage to councel wente ;
In many sentences they fille,
And dyversly they seide hir wille :
But aftir discord they accorded,        5815
And hir accord to Love recorded.
' Sir,' seiden they, ' we been at oon,
By even accord of everichoon,
Out-take Richesse al-only,
That sworen hath ful hauteynly,        5820
That she the castel †nil assaile,
Ne smyte a stroke in this bataile,
With dart, ne mace, spere, ne knyf,

For man that speketh or bereth the lyf,
And blameth your empryse, y-wis,        5825
And from our hoost departed is,
(At leeste wey, as in this plyte,)
So hath she this man in dispyte ;
For she seith he ne loved hir never,
And therfor she wol hate him ever.        5830
For he wol gadre no tresore,
He hath hir wrath for evermore.
He agilte hir never in other caas,
Lo, here al hoolly his trespas !
She seith wel, that this other day        5835
He asked hir leve to goon the way

That is clepid To-moche-Yeving,
And spak ful faire in his praying ;
But whan he prayde hir, pore was he,
Therfore she warned him the entree. 5840
Ne yit is he not thriven so
That he hath geten a peny or two,
That quitly is his owne in hold.
Thus hath Richesse us alle told ;
And whan Richesse us this recorded, 5845
Withouten hir we been accorded.

    ' And we finde in our accordaunce,
That False-Semblant and Abstinaunce,
With alle the folk of hir bataile,
Shulle at the hinder gate assayle, 5850
That Wikkid-Tunge hath in keping,
With his Normans, fulle of jangling.
And with hem Curtesie and Largesse,
That shulle shewe hir hardinesse
To the olde wyf that †kepeth so harde
Fair-Welcoming within her warde. 5856
Than shal Delyte and Wel-Helinge
Fonde Shame adoun to bringe ;
With al hir hoost, erly and late,
They shulle assailen †thilke gate. 5860
Agaynes Drede shal Hardinesse
Assayle, and also Sikernesse,
With al the folk of hir leding,
That never wist what was fleing.

    ' Fraunchyse shal fighte, and eek Pitee,
With Daunger ful of crueltee. 5866
Thus is your hoost ordeyned wel ;
Doun shal the castel every del,
If everiche do his entente,
So that Venus be presente, 5870
Your moder, ful of vassalage,
That can y-nough of such usage ;
Withouten hir may no wight spede
This werk, neither for word ne dede.
Therfore is good ye for hir sende, 5875
For thurgh hir may this werk amende.'

      *Amour.* ' Lordinges, my moder, the
        goddesse,
That is my lady, and my maistresse,
Nis not [at] al at my willing,
Ne doth not al my desyring. 5880
Yit can she som-tyme doon labour,
Whan that hir lust, in my socour,
†Al my nedes for to acheve,
But now I thenke hir not to greve.
My moder is she, and of childhede 5885
I bothe worshipe hir, and eek drede ;

For who that dredeth sire ne dame
Shal it abye in body or name.
And, natheles, yit cunne we
Sende after hir, if nede be ; 5890
And were she nigh, she comen wolde,
I trowe that no-thing might hir holde.

    ' My moder is of greet prowesse ;
She hath tan many a forteresse,
That cost hath many a pound er this, 5895
Ther I nas not present, y-wis ;
And yit men seide it was my dede ;
But I come never in that stede ;
Ne me ne lyketh, so mote I thee,
Such †toures take withoute me. 5900
For-why me thenketh that, in no wyse,
It may ben cleped but marchandise.

    ' Go bye a courser, blak or whyte,
And pay therfor ; than art thou quyte.
The marchaunt oweth thee right nought,
Ne thou him, whan thou [hast] it bought.
I wol not selling clepe yeving, 5907
For selling axeth no guerdoning ;
Here lyth no thank, ne no meryte,
That oon goth from that other al quyte.
But this selling is not semblable ; 5911
For, whan his hors is in the stable,
He may it selle ageyn, pardee,
And winne on it, such hap may be ;
Al may the man not lese, y-wis, 5915
For at the leest the skin is his.
Or elles, if it so bityde
That he wol kepe his hors to ryde,
Yit is he lord ay of his hors.
But thilke chaffare is wel wors, 5920
There Venus entremeteth nought ;
For who-so such chaffare hath bought,
He shal not worchen so wysly,
That he ne shal lese al outerly
Bothe his money and his chaffare ; 5925
But the seller of the ware
The prys and profit have shal.
Certeyn, the byer shal lese al ;
For he ne can so dere it bye
To have lordship and ful maistrye, 5930
Ne have power to make letting
Neither for yift ne for preching,
That of his chaffare, maugre his,
Another shal have as moche, y-wis,
If he wol yeve as moche as he, 5935
Of what contrey so that he be ;
Or for right nought, so happe may,

If he can flater hir to hir pay.
Ben than suche marchaunts wyse?
No, but fooles in every wyse,　　5940
Whan they bye such thing wilfully,
Ther-as they lese her good †fully.
But natheles, this dar I saye,
My moder is not wont to paye,
For she is neither so fool ne nyce,　　5945
To entremete hir of sich vyce.
But truste wel, he shal paye al,
That repente of his bargeyn shal,
Whan Poverte put him in distresse,
Al were he scoler to Richesse,　　5950
That is for me in gret yerning,
Whan she assenteth to my willing.
' But, [by] my moder seint Venus,
And by hir fader Saturnus,
That hir engendrid by his lyf,　　5955
But not upon his wedded wyf!
Yit wol I more unto you swere,
To make this thing the sëurere;
Now by that feith, and that †leautee
†I owe to alle my brethren free,　　5960
Of which ther nis wight under heven
That can her fadres names neven,
So dyvers and so many ther be
That with my moder have be privee!
Yit wolde I swere, for sikernesse,　　5965
The pole of helle to my witnesse,
Now drinke I not this yeer clarree,
If that I lye, or forsworn be!
(For of the goddes the usage is,
That who-so him forswereth amis,　　5970
Shal that yeer drinke no clarree).
Now have I sworn y-nough, pardee;
If I forswere me, than am I lorn,
But I wol never be forsworn.
Sith Richesse hath me failed here,　　5975
She shal abye that trespas †dere,
At leeste wey, but [she] hir arme
With swerd, or sparth, or gisarme.
For certes, sith she loveth not me,
Fro thilke tyme that she may see　　5980
The castel and the tour to-shake,
In sory tyme she shal awake.
If I may grype a riche man,
I shal so pulle him, if I can,
That he shal, in a fewe stoundes,　　5985
Lese alle his markes and his poundes.
I shal him make his pens outslinge,
But-[if] they in his gerner springe;

Our maydens shal eek plukke him so,
That him shal neden fetheres mo,　　5990
And make him selle his lond to spende,
But he the bet cunne him defende.
' Pore men han maad hir lord of me;
Although they not so mighty be,
That they may fede me in delyt,　　5995
I wol not have hem in despyt.
No good man hateth hem, as I gesse;
For chinche and feloun is Richesse,
That so can chase hem and dispyse,
And hem defoule in sondry wyse.　　6000
They loven ful bet, so god me spede,
Than doth the riche, chinchy †gnede,
And been, in good feith, more stable
And trewer, and more serviable;
And therfore it suffyseth me　　6005
Hir goode herte, and hir †leautee.
They han on me set al hir thought,
And therfore I forgete hem nought.
I †wolde hem bringe in greet noblesse,
If that I were god of Richesse,　　6010
As I am god of Love, sothly,
Such routhe upon hir pleynt have I.
Therfore I must his socour be,
That peyneth him to serven me;
For if he deyde for love of this,　　6015
Than semeth in me no love ther is.'
' Sir,' seide they, ' sooth is, every del,
That ye reherce, and we wot wel
Thilk oth to holde is resonable;
For it is good and covenable,　　6020
That ye on riche men han sworn.
For, sir, this wot we wel biforn;
If riche men doon you homage,
That is as fooles doon outrage;
But ye shul not forsworen be,　　6025
Ne let therfore to drinke clarree,
Or piment maked fresh and newe.
Ladyes shulle hem such pepir brewe,
If that they falle into hir laas,
That they for wo mowe seyn ' Allas!'
Ladyes shuln ever so curteis be,　　6031
That they shal quyte your oth al free.
Ne seketh never other vicaire,
For they shal speke with hem so faire
That ye shal holde you payed ful wel,
Though ye you medle never a del.　　6036
Lat ladies worche with hir thinges,
They shal hem telle so fele tydinges,
And moeve hem eke so many requestis

By flatery, that not honest is,　　　6040
And therto yeve hem such thankinges,
What with kissing, and with talkinges,
That certes, if they trowed be,
Shal never leve hem lond ne fee
That it nil as the moeble fare,　　　6045
Of which they first delivered are.
Now may ye telle us al your wille,
And we your hestes shal fulfille.

　'But Fals-Semblant dar not, for drede
Of you, sir, medle him of this dede,　6050
For he seith that ye been his fo ;
He not, if ye wol worche him wo.
Wherfore we pray you alle, beau-sire,
That ye forgive him now your ire,
And that he may dwelle, as your man,
With Abstinence, his dere lemman ; 6056
This our accord and our wil now.'

　'Parfay,' seide Love, 'I graunte it yow ;
I wol wel holde him for my man ;　6059
Now lat him come :' and he forth ran.
'Fals-Semblant,' quod Love, 'in this wyse
I take thee here to my servyse,
That thou our freendis helpe alway,
And †hindre hem neither night ne day,
But do thy might hem to releve,　6065
And eek our enemies that thou greve.
Thyn be this might, I graunt it thee,
My king of harlotes shalt thou be ;
We wol that thou have such honour.
Certeyn, thou art a fals traitour,　6070
And eek a theef ; sith thou were born,
A thousand tyme thou art forsworn.
But, natheles, in our hering,
To putte our folk out of douting,
I bid thee teche hem, wostow how ? 6075
By somme general signe now,
In what place thou shalt founden be,
If that men had mister of thee ;
And how men shal thee best espye,
For thee to knowe is greet maistrye ; 6080
Tel in what place is thyn haunting.'

　*F. Sem.* 'Sir, I have fele dyvers woning,
That I kepe not rehersed be,
So that ye wolde respyten me.
For if that I telle you the sothe,　6085
I may have harm and shame bothe.
If that my felowes wisten it,
My tales shulden me be quit ;
For certeyn, they wolde hate me,
If ever I knewe hir cruelte ;　6090

For they wolde over-al holde hem stille
Of trouthe that is ageyn hir wille ;
Suche tales kepen they not here.
I might eftsone bye it ful dere,
If I seide of hem any thing,　　　6095
That ought displeseth to hir hering.
For what word that hem prikke or byteth,
In that word noon of hem delyteth,
Al were it gospel, the evangyle,
That wolde reprove hem of hir gyle, 6100
For they are cruel and hauteyn.
And this thing wot I wel, certeyn,
If I speke ought to peire hir loos,
Your court shal not so wel be cloos,
That they ne shal wite it atte last. 6105
Of good men am I nought agast,
For they wol taken on hem no-thing,
Whan that they knowe al my mening ;
But he that wol it on him take,
He wol himself suspecious make,　6110
That he his lyf let covertly,
In Gyle and in Ipocrisy,
That me engendred and yaf fostring.'

　'They made a ful good engendring,'
Quod Love, 'for who-so soothly telle, 6115
They engendred the devel of helle !

　'But nedely, how-so-ever it be,'
Quod Love, 'I wol and charge thee,
To telle anoon thy woning-places,
Hering ech wight that in this place is ;
And what lyf that thou livest also,　6121
Hyde it no lenger now ; wherto ?
Thou most discover al thy wurching,
How thou servest, and of what thing,
Though that thou shuldest for thy soth-
　　　sawe　　　　　　　　　6125
Ben al to-beten and to-drawe ;
And yit art thou not wont, pardee.
But natheles, though thou beten be,
Thou shalt not be the first, that so
Hath for soth-sawe suffred wo.'　6130

　*F. Sem.* 'Sir, sith that it may lyken
　　　you,
Though that I shulde be slayn right now,
I shal don your comaundement,
For therto have I gret talent.'　6134

　　Withouten wordes mo, right than,
Fals-Semblant his sermon bigan,
And seide hem thus in audience :—
'Barouns, tak hede of my sentence !
That wight that list to have knowing

Of Fals-Semblant, ful of flatering,    6140
He must in worldly folk him seke,
And, certes, in the cloistres eke ;
I wone no-where but in hem tweye ;
But not lyk even, sooth to seye ;
Shortly, I wol herberwe me        6145
There I hope best to hulstred be ;
And certeynly, sikerest hyding
Is underneth humblest clothing.
    ' Religious folk ben ful covert ;
Seculer folk ben more appert.      6150
But natheles, I wol not blame
Religious folk, ne hem diffame,
In what habit that ever they go :
Religioun humble, and trewe also,
Wol I not blame, ne dispyse,       6155
But I nil love it, in no wyse.
I mene of fals religious,
That stoute ben, and malicious ;
That wolen in an abit go,
And setten not hir herte therto.   6160
    ' Religious folk ben al pitous ;
Thou shalt not seen oon dispitous.
They loven no pryde, ne no stryf,
But humbly they wol lede hir lyf ;
With †swich folk wol I never be.   6165
And if I dwelle, I feyne me
I may wel in her abit go ;
But me were lever my nekke atwo,
Than †lete a purpose that I take,
What covenaunt that ever I make.   6170
I dwelle with hem that proude be,
And fulle of wyles and subtelte ;
That worship of this world coveyten,
And grete †nedes cunne espleyten ;  6174
And goon and gadren greet pitaunces,
And purchace hem the acqueyntaunces
Of men that mighty lyf may leden ;
And feyne hem pore, and hem-self feden
With gode morcels delicious,
And drinken good wyn precious,      6180
And preche us povert and distresse,
And fisshen hem-self greet richesse
With wyly nettis that they caste :
It wol come foul out at the laste.
They ben fro clene religioun went ;  6185
They make the world an argument
That hath a foul conclusioun.
" I have a robe of religioun,
Than am I al religious : "
This argument is al roignous ;      6190

It is not worth a croked brere ;
Habit ne maketh †monk ne frere,
But clene lyf and devocioun
Maketh gode men of religioun.
Nathelesse, ther can noon answere,  6195
How high that ever his heed he shere
With rasour whetted never so kene,
That Gyle in braunches cut thrittene ;
Ther can no wight distincte it so,
That he dar sey a word therto.      6200
    ' But what herberwe that ever I take,
Or what semblant that ever I make,
I mene but gyle, and folowe that ;
For right no mo than Gibbe our cat
[†Fro myce and rattes went his wyle],
Ne entende I [not] but to †begyle ;  6206
Ne no wight may, by my clothing,
Wite with what folk is my dwelling ,
Ne by my wordis yet, pardee,
So softe and so plesaunt they be.    6210
Bihold the dedes that I do ;
But thou be blind, thou oughtest so ;
For, varie hir wordis fro hir dede,
They thenke on gyle, without[en] drede,
What maner clothing that they were,
Or what estat that ever they bere,   6216
Lered or lewd, lord or lady,
Knight, squier, burgeis, or bayly.'
    Right thus whyl Fals-Semblant ser-
        moneth,
Eftsones Love him aresoneth,        6220
And brak his tale in the speking
As though he had him told lesing ;
And seide : ' What, devel, is that I here ?
What folk hast thou us nempned here ?
May men finde religioun            6225
In worldly habitacioun ? '
    F. Sem. ' Ye, sir ; it foloweth not that
        they
Shulde lede a wikked lyf, parfey,
Ne not therfore her soules lese,
That hem to worldly clothes chese ;  6230
For, certes, it were gret pitee.
Men may in seculer clothes see
Florisshen holy religioun.
Ful many a seynt in feeld and toun,
With many a virgin glorious,        6235
Devout, and ful religious,
Had deyed, that †comun clothe ay beren,
Yit seyntes never-the-les they weren.
I coude reken you many a ten ;

Ye, wel nigh alle these holy wimmen,
That men in chirches herie and seke, 6241
Bothe maydens, and these wyves eke,
That baren †many a fair child here,
Wered alwey clothis seculere,
And in the same dyden they, 6245
That seyntes weren, and been alwey.
The eleven thousand maydens dere,
That beren in heven hir cierges clere,
Of which men rede in chirche, and singe,
Were take in seculer clothing, 6250
Whan they resseyved martirdom,
And wonnen heven unto her hoom.
Good herte maketh the gode thought;
The clothing yeveth ne reveth nought.
The gode thought and the worching, 6255
That maketh †religioun flowring,
Ther lyth the good religioun
After the right entencioun.
 ' Who-so toke a wethers skin,
And wrapped a gredy wolf therin, 6260
For he shulde go with lambes whyte,
Wenest thou not he wolde hem byte?
Yis! never-the-las, as he were wood,
He wolde hem wery, and drinke the
    blood;
And wel the rather hem disceyve, 6265
For, sith they coude not perceyve
His treget and his crueltee,
They wolde him folowe, al wolde he flee.
 ' If ther be wolves of sich hewe
Amonges these apostlis newe, 6270
Thou, holy chirche, thou mayst be wayled!
Sith that thy citee is assayled
Thourgh knightes of thyn owne table,
God wot thy lordship is doutable!
If they enforce [hem] it to winne, 6275
That shulde defende it fro withinne,
Who might defence ayens hem make?
Without[en] stroke it mot be take
Of trepeget or mangonel;
Without displaying of pensel. 6280
And if god nil don it socour,
But lat [hem] renne in this colour,
Thou moost thyn heestes laten be.
Than is ther nought, but yelde thee,
Or yeve hem tribute, doutelees, 6285
And holde it of hem to have pees:
But gretter harm bityde thee,
That they al maister of it be.
Wel conne they scorne thee withal;

By day stuffen they the wal, 6290
And al the night they mynen there.
Nay, thou †most planten elleswhere
Thyn impes, if thou wolt fruyt have;
Abyd not there thy-self to save.
 ' But now pees! here I turne ageyn;
I wol no more of this thing †seyn, 6296
If I may passen me herby;
I mighte maken you wery.
But I wol heten you alway
To helpe your freendes what I may, 6300
So they wollen my company;
For they be shent al-outerly
But-if so falle, that I be
Oft with hem, and they with me.
And eek my lemman mot they serve, 6305
Or they shul not my love deserve.
Forsothe, I am a fals traitour;
God jugged me for a theef trichour;
Forsworn I am, but wel nygh non
Wot of my gyle, til it be don. 6310
 ' Thourgh me hath many oon deth
    resseyved,
That my treget never aperceyved;
And yit resseyveth, and shal resseyve,
That my falsnesse †never aperceyve:
But who-so doth, if he wys be, 6315
Him is right good be war of me.
But so sligh is the [†deceyving
That to hard is the] aperceyving.
For Protheus, that coude him chaunge
In every shap, hoomly and straunge, 6320
Coude never sich gyle ne tresoun
As I; for I com never in toun
Ther-as I mighte knowen be,
Though men me bothe might here and see.
Ful wel I can my clothes chaunge, 6325
Take oon, and make another straunge.
Now am I knight, now chasteleyn;
Now prelat, and now chapeleyn;
Now prest, now clerk, and now forstere;
Now am I maister, now scolere; 6330
Now monk, now chanoun, now baily;
What-ever mister man am I.
Now am I prince, now am I page,
And can by herte every langage.
Som-tyme am I hoor and old; 6335
Now am I yong, [and] stout, and bold;
Now am I Robert, now Robyn;
Now frere Menour, now Iacobyn;
And with me folweth my loteby,

To don me solas and company, 6340
That hight dame †Abstinence-Streyned,
In many a queynt array [y]-feyned.
Right as it cometh to hir lyking,
I fulfille al hir desiring.
Somtyme a wommans cloth take I ; 6345
Now am I mayde, now lady.
Somtyme I am religious ;
Now lyk an anker in an hous.
Somtyme am I prioresse,
And now a nonne, and now abbesse ; 6350
And go thurgh alle regiouns,
Seking alle religiouns.
But to what ordre that I am sworn,
I take the strawe, and †lete the corn ;
To †blynde folk [ther] I enhabite, 6355
I axe no-more but hir abite.
What wol ye more ? in every wyse,
Right as me list, I me disgyse.
Wel can I bere me under weed ;
Unlyk is my word to my deed. 6360
Thus make I in my trappes falle,
Thurgh my pryvileges, alle
That ben in Cristendom alyve.
I may assoile, and I may shryve,
That no prelat may lette me, 6365
Al folk, wher-ever they founde be :
I noot no prelat may don so,
But it the pope be, and no mo,
That made thilk establisshing.
Now is not this a propre thing ? 6370
But, were my sleightes aperceyved,
[†Ne shulde I more been receyved]
As I was wont ; and wostow why ?
For I dide hem a tregetry ;
But therof yeve I litel tale, 6375
I have the silver and the male ;
So have I preched and eek shriven,
So have I take, so have †me yiven,
Thurgh hir foly, husbond and wyf,
That I lede right a joly lyf, 6380
Thurgh simplesse of the prelacye ;
They know not al my tregetrye.
'But for as moche as man and wyf
Shuld shewe hir paroche-prest hir lyf
Ones a yeer, as seith the book, 6385
Er any wight his housel took,
Than have I pryvileges large,
That may of moche thing discharge ;
For he may seye right thus, pardee :—
"Sir Preest, in shrift I telle it thee, 6390

That he, to whom that I am shriven,
Hath me assoiled, and me yiven
Penaunce soothly, for my sinne,
Which that I fond me gilty inne ;
Ne I ne have never entencioun 6395
To make double confessioun,
Ne reherce eft my shrift to thee ;
O shrift is right y-nough to me.
This oughte thee suffyce wel,
Ne be not rebel never-a-del ; 6400
For certes, though thou haddest it sworn,
I wot no prest ne prelat born
That may to shrift eft me constreyne.
And if they don, I wol me pleyne ;
For I wot where to pleyne wel. 6405
Thou shalt not streyne me a del,
Ne enforce me, ne †yit me trouble,
To make my confessioun double.
Ne I have none affeccioun
To have double absolucioun. 6410
The firste is right y-nough to me ,
This latter assoiling quyte I thee.
I am unbounde ; what mayst thou finde
More of my sinnes me to unbinde ?
For he, that might hath in his hond, 6415
Of alle my sinnes me unbond.
And if thou wolt me thus constreyne,
That me mot nedis on thee pleyne,
There shal no jugge imperial,
Ne bisshop, ne official, 6420
Don jugement on me ; for I
Shal gon and pleyne me openly
Unto my shrift-fader newe,
(That hight not Frere Wolf untrewe !)
And he shal †chevise him for me, 6425
For I trowe he can hampre thee.
But, lord ! he wolde be wrooth withalle,
If men him wolde Frere Wolf calle !
For he wolde have no pacience,
But don al cruel vengeaunce ! 6430
He wolde his might don at the leest,
[Ne] no-thing spare for goddes heest.
And, god so wis be my socour,
But thou yeve me my Saviour
At Ester, whan it lyketh me, 6435
Withoute presing more on thee,
I wol forth, and to him goon,
And he shal housel me anoon,
For I am out of thy grucching ;
I kepe not dele with thee no-thing." 6440
Thus may he shryve him, that forsaketh

His paroche-prest, and to me taketh.
And if the prest wol him refuse,
I am ful redy him to accuse,
And him punisshe and hampre so,     6445
That he his chirche shal forgo.

    ' But who-so hath in his feling
The consequence of such shryving,
Shal seen that prest may never have might
To knowe the conscience aright     6450
Of him that is under his cure.
And this ageyns holy scripture,
That biddeth every herde honeste
Have verry knowing of his beste.
But pore folk that goon by strete,     6455
That have no gold, ne sommes grete,
Hem wolde I lete to hir prelates,
Or lete hir prestes knowe hir states,
For to me right nought yeve they.'

    *Amour.* ' And why †is it ? '
    *F. Sem.*     ' For they ne may.     6460
They ben so bare, I take no keep ;
But I wol have the fatte sheep ;—
Lat parish prestes have the lene,
I yeve not of hir harm a bene !
And if that prelats grucchen it,     6465
That oughten †wroth be in hir wit,
To lese her fatte bestes so,
I shal yeve hem a stroke or two,
That they shal lesen with [the] force,
Ye, bothe hir mytre and hir croce.     6470
Thus jape I hem, and have do longe,
My privileges been so stronge.'

    Fals-Semblant wolde have stinted here,
But Love ne made him no such chere
That he was wery of his sawe ;     6475
But for to make him glad and fawe,
He seide :—' Tel on more specialy,
How that thou servest untrewly.
Tel forth, and shame thee never a del ;
For as thyn abit shewith wel,     6480
Thou †semest an holy heremyte.'

    *F. Sem.* ' Soth is, but I am an ypocryte.'
    *Amour.* ' Thou gost and prechest pover-
       tee ? '
    *F. Sem.* ' Ye, sir ; but richesse hath
       poustee.'
    *Amour.* ' Thou prechest abstinence
       also ? '     6485
    *F. Sem.* ' Sir, I wol fillen, so mote I go,
My paunche of gode mete and wyne,
As shulde a maister of divyne ;

For how that I me pover feyne,
Yit alle pore folk I disdeyne.     6490
    ' I love †bet the acqueyntaunce
Ten tymes, of the king of Fraunce,
Than of †pore man of mylde mode,
Though that his soule be also gode.
For whan I see beggers quaking,     6495
Naked on mixens al stinking,
For hungre crye, and eek for care,
I entremete not of hir fare.
They been so pore, and ful of pyne,
They might not ones yeve me †dyne, 6500
For they have no-thing but hir lyf;
What shulde he yeve that likketh his
       knyf ?
It is but foly to entremete,
To seke in houndes nest fat mete.
Let bere hem to the spitel anoon,     6505
But, for me, comfort gete they noon.
But a riche sike usurere
Wolde I visyte and drawe nere ;
Him wol I comforte and rehete,
For I hope of his gold to gete.     6510
And if that wikked deth him have,
I wol go with him to his grave.
And if ther any reprove me,
Why that I lete the pore be,
Wostow how I †mot ascape ?     6515
I sey, and swerë him ful rape,
That riche men han more tecches
Of sinne, than han pore wrecches,
And han of counseil more mister ;
And therfore I wol drawe hem ner.     6520
But as gret hurt, it may so be,
Hath †soul in right gret poverte,
As soul in gret richesse, forsothe,
Al-be-it that they hurten bothe.
For richesse and mendicitees     6525
Ben cleped two extremitees ;
The mene is cleped suffisaunce,
Ther lyth of vertu the aboundaunce.
For Salamon, ful wel I woot,
In his Parables us wroot,     6530
As it is knowe of many a wight,
In his †thrittethe chapitre right :
" God, thou me kepe, for thy poustee,
Fro richesse and mendicitee ;
For if a riche man him dresse     6535
To thenke to moche on [his] richesse,
His herte on that so fer is set,
That he his creatour foryet ;

And him, that †begging wol ay greve,
How shulde I by his word him leve? 6540
Unnethe that he nis a micher,
Forsworn, or elles †god is lyer."
Thus seith Salamon[es] sawes;
Ne we finde writen in no lawes,
And namely in our Cristen lay— 6545
(Who seith ' ye,' I dar sey ' nay ')—
That Crist, ne his apostles dere,
Whyl that they walkede in erthe here,
Were never seen her bred begging,
For they nolde beggen for no-thing. 6550
And right thus were men wont to teche;
And in this wyse wolde it preche
The maistres of divinitee
Somtyme in Paris the citee.

  ' And if men wolde ther-geyn appose
The naked text, and lete the glose, 6556
It mighte sone assoiled be;
For men may wel the sothe see,
That, parde, they mighte axe a thing
Pleynly forth, without begging. 6560
For they weren goddes herdes dere,
And cure of soules hadden here,
They nolde no-thing begge hir fode;
For after Crist was don on rode,
With †hir propre hondes they wrought,
And with travel, and elles nought, 6566
They wonnen all hir sustenaunce,
And liveden forth in hir penaunce,
And the remenaunt †yeve away
To other pore †folk alwey. 6570
They neither bilden tour ne halle,
But †leye in houses smale withalle.
A mighty man, that can and may,
Shulde with his honde and body alway
Winne him his food in laboring, 6575
If he ne have rent or sich a thing,
Although he be religious,
And god to serven curious.
Thus mote he don, or do trespas,
But-if it be in certeyn cas, 6580
That I can reherce, if mister be,
Right wel, whan the tyme I see.
  ' Seke the book of Seynt Austin,
Be it in paper or perchemin, 6584
There-as he writ of these worchinges,
Thou shalt seen that non excusinges
A parfit man ne shulde seke
By wordes, ne by dedes eke,
Although he be religious,

And god to serven curious, 6590
That he ne shal, so mote I go,
With propre hondes and body also,
Gete his food in laboring,
If he ne have propretee of thing.
Yit shulde he selle al his substaunce, 6595
And with his swink have sustenaunce,
If he be parfit in bountee.
Thus han tho bookes tolde me:
For he that wol gon ydilly,
And useth it ay besily 6600
To haunten other mennes table,
He is a trechour, ful of fable;
Ne he ne may, by gode resoun,
Excuse him by his orisoun.
For men bihoveth, in som gyse, 6605
†Som-tyme leven goddes servyse
To gon and purchasen her nede.
Men mote eten, that is no drede,
And slepe, and eek do other thing;
So longe may they leve praying. 6610
So may they eek hir prayer blinne,
While that they werke, hir mete to winne.
Seynt Austin wol therto accorde,
In thilke book that I recorde.
Justinian eek, that made lawes, 6615
Hath thus forboden, by olde dawes,
" No man, up peyne to be deed,
Mighty of body, to begge his breed,
If he may swinke, it for to gete;
Men shulde him rather mayme or bete, 6621
Or doon of him apert justice,
Than suffren him in such malice."
They don not wel, so mote I go,
That taken such almesse so,
But if they have som privelege, 6625
That of the peyne hem wol allege.
But how that is, can I not see,
But-if the prince disseyved be;
Ne I ne wene not, sikerly,
That they may have it rightfully. 6630
But I wol not determyne
Of princes power, ne defyne,
Ne by my word comprende, y-wis,
If it so fer may strecche in this.
I wol not entremete a del; 6635
But I trowe that the book seith wel,
Who that taketh almesses, that be
Dewe to folk that men may see
Lame, feble, wery, and bare,
Pore, or in such maner care, 6640

(That conne winne hem nevermo,
For they have no power therto),
He eteth his owne dampning,
But-if he lye, that made al thing.
And if ye such a truaunt finde,　　6645
Chastise him wel, if ye be kinde.
But they wolde hate you, percas,
And, if ye fillen in hir laas,
They wolde eftsones do you scathe,
If that they mighte, late or rathe ;　6650
For they be not ful pacient,
That han the world thus foule blent.
And witeth wel, [wher] that god bad
The good man selle al that he had,
And folowe him, and to pore it yive, 6655
He wolde not therfore that he live
To serven him in mendience,
For it was never his sentence ;
But he bad wirken whan that nede is,
And folwe him in goode dedes.　　6660
Seynt Poule, that loved al holy chirche,
He bade th'apostles for to wirche,
And winnen hir lyflode in that wyse,
And hem defended truaundyse,　　6664
And seide, "Wirketh with your honden ; "
Thus shulde the thing be understonden.
He nolde, y-wis, †bidde hem begging,
Ne sellen gospel, ne preching,
Lest they berafte, with hir asking,
Folk of hir catel or of hir thing.　6670
For in this world is many a man
That yeveth his good, for he ne can
Werne it for shame, or elles he
**Wolde** of the asker delivered be ;
And, for he him encombreth so,　　6675
He yeveth him good to late him go :
But it can him no-thing profyte,
They lese the yift and the meryte.
The goode folk, that Poule to preched,
Profred him ofte, whan he hem teched,
Som of hir good in charite ;　　6681
But therof right no-thing took he ;
But of his hondwerk wolde he gete
Clothes to wryen him, and his mete.'
*Amour.* 'Tel me than how a man may
　　liven,　　　　　　　　　　　6685
That al his good to pore hath yiven,
And wol but only bidde his bedes,
And never with †hond laboure his nedes:
May he do so ?'
　　*F. Sem.*　　' Ye, sir.'

*Amour.*　　　' And how ?'
　　*F. Sem.* 'Sir, I wol gladly telle yow :—
Seynt Austin seith, a man may be　6691
In houses that han propretee,
As templers and hospitelers,
And as these chanouns regulers,
Or whyte monkes, or these blake—　6695
(I wole no mo ensamples make)—
And take therof his sustening,
For therinne lyth no begging ;
But other-weyes not, y-wis,
†Yif Austin gabbeth not of this.　　6700
And yit ful many a monk laboureth,
That god in holy chirche honoureth ;
For whan hir swinking is agoon,
They rede and singe in chirche anoon.
　　' And for ther hath ben greet discord,
As many a wight may bere record,　6706
Upon the estate of †mendience,
I wol shortly, in your presence,
Telle how a man may begge at nede,
That hath not wherwith him to fede, 6710
Maugre his felones jangelinges,
For sothfastnesse wol non hidinges ;
And yit, percas, I may abeye
That I to yow sothly thus seye.
　　' Lo, here the caas especial :　　6715
If a man be so bestial
That he of no craft hath science,
And nought desyreth ignorence,
Than may he go a-begging yerne,
Til he som maner craft can lerne,　6720
Thurgh which, without[e] truaunding,
He may in trouthe have his living.
Or if he may don no labour,
For elde, or syknesse, or langour,
Or for his tendre age also,　　　6725
Than may he yit a-begging go.
　　' Or if he have, peraventure,
Thurgh usage of his noriture,
Lived over deliciously,
Than oughten good folk comunly　6730
Han of his mischeef som pitee,
And suffren him also, that he
May gon aboute and begge his breed,
That he be not for hungur deed.
Or if he have of craft cunning,　　6735
And strengthe also, and desiring
To wirken, as he hadde what,
But he finde neither this ne that,
Than may he begge, til that he

Have geten his necessitee.  6740
  ' Or if his winning be so lyte,
That his labour wol not acquyte
Sufficiantly al his living,
Yit may he go his breed begging ;
Fro dore to dore he may go trace,  6745
Til he the remenaunt may purchace.
Or if a man wolde undertake
Any empryse for to make,
In the rescous of our lay,
And it defenden as he may,  6750
Be it with armes or lettrure,
Or other covenable cure,
If it be so he pore be,
Than may he begge, til that he
May finde in trouthe for to swinke,  6755
And gete him clothe[s], mete, and drinke.
Swinke he with hondes corporel,
And not with hondes espirituel.
  ' In al this[e] caas, and in semblables,
If that ther ben mo resonables,  6760
He may begge, as I telle you here,
And elles nought, in no manere ;
As William Seynt Amour wolde preche,
And ofte wolde dispute and teche
Of this matere alle openly  6765
At Paris ful solemp[ne]ly.
And al-so god my soule blesse,
As he had, in this stedfastnesse,
The accord of the universitee,
And of the puple, as semeth me.  6770
  ' No good man oughte it to refuse,
Ne oughte him therof to excuse,
Be wrooth or blythe who-so be ;
For I wol speke, and telle it thee,
Al shulde I dye, and be put doun,  6775
As was seynt Poul, in derk prisoun ;
Or be exiled in this caas
With wrong, as maister William was,
That my moder Ypocrisye
Banisshed for hir greet envye.  6780
  ' My moder flemed him, Seynt Amour :
This noble dide such labour
To susteyne ever the loyaltee,
That he to moche agilte me.
He made a book, and leet it wryte,  6785
Wherin his lyf he dide al wryte,
And wolde ich reneyed begging,
And lived by my traveyling,
If I ne had rent ne other good.
What ? wened he that I were wood ?  6790

For labour might me never plese,
I have more wil to been at ese ;
And have wel lever, sooth to sey,
Bifore the puple patre and prey,
And wrye me in my foxerye  6795
Under a cope of papelardye.'
  Quod Love, ' What devel is this I here?
What wordes tellest thou me here ? '
  F. Sem.  ' What, sir ? '
  Amour.      ' Falsnesse, that apert is ;
Than dredest thou not god ? '
  F. Sem.      No, certes :  6800
For selde in greet thing shal he spede
In this world, that god wol drede.
For folk that hem to vertu yiven,
And truly on her owne liven,
And hem in goodnesse ay contene,  6805
On hem is litel thrift y-sene ;
Such folk drinken gret misese ;
That lyf [ne] may me never plese.
But see what gold han usurers,
And silver eek in [hir] garners,  6810
Taylagiers, and these monyours,
Bailifs, bedels, provost, countours ;
These liven wel nygh by ravyne ;
The smale puple hem mote enclyne,
And they as wolves wol hem eten.  6815
Upon the pore folk they geten
Ful moche of that they spende or kepe ;
Nis none of hem that he nil strepe,
And †wryen him-self wel atte fulle ;
Without[e] scalding they hem pulle.  6820
The stronge the feble overgoth ;
But I, that were my simple cloth,
Robbe bothe †robbed and robbours,
And gyle †gyled and gylours.
By my treget, I gadre and threste  6825
The greet tresour into my cheste,
That lyth with me so faste bounde.
Myn highe paleys do I founde,
And my delytes I fulfille
With wyne at feestes at my wille,  6830
And tables fulle of entremees ;
I wol no lyf, but ese and pees,
And winne gold to spende also.
For whan the grete bagge is go,
It cometh right [eft] with my japes.  6835
Make I not wel tumble myn apes ?
To winne is alwey myn entent ;
My purchas is better than my rent ;
For though I shulde beten be,

Over-al I entremete me ;　　　　6840
Without[e] me may no wight dure.
I walke soules for to cure.
Of al the worlde cure have I
In brede and lengthe ; boldely
I wol bothe preche and eek counceilen ;
With hondes wille I not traveilen,　6846
For of the pope I have the bulle ;
I ne holde not my wittes dulle.
I wol not stinten, in my lyve,
These emperoures for to shryve,　　6850
Or kynges, dukes, and lordes grete ;
But pore folk al quyte I lete.
I love no such shryving, pardee,
But it for other cause be.
I rekke not of pore men,　　　　6855
Hir astate is not worth an hen.
Where fyndest thou a swinker of labour
Have me unto his confessour ?
But emperesses, and duchesses,
Thise quenes, and eek [thise] countesses,
Thise abbesses, and eek Bigyns,　　6861
These grete ladyes palasyns,
These joly knightes, and baillyves,
Thise nonnes, and thise burgeis wyves,
That riche been, and eek plesing,　6865
And thise maidens welfaring,
Wher-so they clad or naked be,
Uncounceiled goth ther noon fro me.
And, for her soules savetee,
At lord and lady, and hir meynee,　6870
I axe, whan they hem to me shryve,
The propretee of al hir lyve,
And make hem trowe, bothe meest and
　　leest,
Hir paroch-prest nis but a beest
Ayens me and my company,　　　6875
That shrewes been as greet as I ;
For whiche I wol not hyde in hold
No privetee that me is told,
That I by word or signe, y-wis,
†Nil make hem knowe what it is,　6880
And they wolen also tellen me ;
They hele fro me no privitee.
And for to make yow hem perceyven,
That usen folk thus to disceyven,
I wol you seyn, withouten drede,　6885
What men may in the gospel rede
Of Seynt Mathew, the gospelere,
That seith, as I shal you sey here.
　‘ Upon the chaire of Moyses—

Thus is it glosed, douteles :　　6890
That is the olde testament,
For therby is the chaire ment—
Sitte Scribes and Pharis[i]en ;—
That is to seyn, the cursed men
Whiche that we ypocrites calle—　6895
Doth that they preche, I rede you alle,
But doth not as they don a del,
That been not wery to seye wel,
But to do wel, no wille have they ;
And they wolde binde on folk alwey,
That ben to [be] begyled able,　　6901
†Burdens that ben importable ;
On folkes shuldres thinges they couchen
That they nil with her fingres touchen.’
　Amour. ‘ And why wol they not touche
　　　it ? ’
　F. Sem. 　　‘ Why ?　　　　6905
For hem ne list not, sikerly ;
For sadde †burdens that men taken
Make folkes shuldres aken.
And if they do ought that good be,
That is for folk it shulde see :　　6910
Her †borders larger maken they,
And make hir hemmes wyde alwey,
And loven setes at the table,
The firste and most honourable ;
And for to han the first chaieres　6915
In synagoges, to hem ful dere is ;
And willen that folk hem loute and grete,
Whan that they passen thurgh the strete,
And wolen be cleped ‘ Maister ’ also.
But they ne shulde not willen so ;　6920
The gospel is ther-ageyns, I gesse :
That sheweth wel hir wikkidnesse.
　‘ Another custom use we :—
Of hem that wol ayens us be,
We hate †hem deedly everichoon,　6925
And we wol werry †hem, as oon.
Him that oon hateth, hate we alle,
And conjecte how to doon him falle.
And if we seen him winne honour,
Richesse or preys, thurgh his valour, 6930
Provende, rent, or dignitee,
Ful fast, y-wis, compassen we
By what ladder he is clomben so ;
And for to maken him doun to go,
With traisoun we wole him defame, 6935
And doon him lese his gode name.
Thus from his ladder we him take,
And thus his freendes foes we make ;

But word ne wite shal he noon,
Til alle his freendes been his foon.      6940
For if we dide it openly,
We might have blame redily ;
For hadde he wist of our malyce,
He hadde him kept, but he were nyce.

'Another is this, that, if so falle      6945
That ther be oon among us alle
That doth a good turn, out of drede,
We seyn it is our alder dede.
Ye, sikerly, though he it feyned,
Or that him list, or that him deyned 6950
A man thurgh him avaunced be ;
Therof alle parceners be we,
And tellen folk, wher-so we go,
That man thurgh us is sprongen so.
And for to have of men preysing,      6955
We purchace, thurgh our flatering,
Of riche men, of gret poustee,
Lettres, to witnesse our bountee ;
So that man weneth, that may us see,
That alle vertu in us be.      6960
And alwey pore we us feyne ;
But how so that we begge or pleyne,
We ben the folk, without lesing,
That al thing have without having.
Thus be we dred of the puple, y-wis. 6965
And gladly my purpos is this :—
I dele with no wight, but he
Have gold and tresour gret plentee ;
Hir acqueyntaunce wel love I ;
This is moche my desyr, shortly.      6970
I entremete me of brocages,
I make pees and mariages,
I am gladly executour,
And many tymes procuratour ;
I am somtyme messager ;      6975
That falleth not to my mister.
And many tymes I make enquestes ;
For me that office not honest is ;
To dele with other mennes thing,
That is to me a gret lyking.      6980
And if that ye have ought to do
In place that I repeire to,
I shal it speden thurgh my wit,
As sone as ye have told me it.
So that ye serve me to pay,      6985
My servise shal be your alway.
But who-so wol chastyse me,
Anoon my love lost hath he ;
For I love no man in no gyse,

That wol me repreve or chastyse ;      6990
But I wolde al folk undertake,
And of no wight no teching take ;
For I, that other folk chastye,
Wol not be taught fro my folye.
'I love noon hermitage more ;      6995
Alle desertes, and holtes hore,
And grete wodes everichoon,
I lete hem to the Baptist Iohan.
I quethe him quyte, and him relesse
Of Egipt al the wildirnesse ;      7000
To fer were alle my mansiouns
Fro alle citees and goode tounes.
My paleis and myn hous make I
There men may renne in openly,
And sey that I the world forsake.      7005
But al amidde I bilde and make
My hous, and swimme and pley therinne
Bet than a fish doth with his finne.
'Of Antecristes men am I,
Of whiche that Crist seith openly,      7010
They have abit of holinesse,
And liven in such wikkednesse.
Outward, lambren semen we,
Fulle of goodnesse and of pitee,
And inward we, withouten fable,      7015
Ben gredy wolves ravisable.
We environe bothe londe and see ;
With al the world †werreyen we ;
We wol ordeyne of alle thing,
Of folkes good, and her living.      7020
'If ther be castel or citee
Wherin that any bougerons be,
Although that they of Milayne were,
For ther-of ben they blamed there :
Or if a wight, out of mesure,      7025
Wolde lene his gold, and take usure,
For that he is so coveitous :
Or if he be to leccherous,
Or †thefe, or haunte simonye ;
Or provost, ful of trecherye,      7030
Or prelat, living jolily,
Or prest that halt his quene him by ;
Or olde hores hostilers,
Or other bawdes or bordillers,
Or elles blamed of any vyce,      7035
Of whiche men shulden doon justyce :
By alle the seyntes that we pray,
But they defende †hem with lamprey,
With luce, with eles, with samouns,
With tendre gees, and with capouns, 7040

With tartes, or with †cheses fat,
With deynte flawnes, brode and flat,
With caleweys, or with pullaille,
With coninges, or with fyn vitaille,
That we, under our clothes wyde,      7045
Maken thurgh our golet glyde :
Or but he wol do come in haste
Roo-venisoun, [y]-bake in paste :
Whether so that he loure or groine,
He shal have of a corde a loigne,     7050
With whiche men shal him binde and
    lede,
To brenne him for his sinful dede,
That men shulle here him crye and rore
A myle-wey aboute, and more.
Or elles he shal in prisoun dye,      7055
But-if he wol [our] frendship bye,
Or smerten that that he hath do,
More than his gilt amounteth to.
But, and he couthe thurgh his sleight
Do maken up a tour of height,         7060
Nought roughte I whether of stone or tree,
Or erthe, or turves though it be,
Though it were of no vounde stone
Wrought with squyre and scantilone,
So that the tour were stuffed wel     7065
With alle richesse temporel ;
And thanne, that he wolde updresse
Engyns, bothe more and lesse,
To caste at us, by every syde—
To bere his goode name wyde—          7070
Such sleightes [as] I shal yow nevene,
Barelles of wyne, by sixe or sevene,
Or gold in sakkes gret plente.
He shulde sone delivered be.
And if he have noon sich pitaunces,   7075
Late him study in equipolences,
And lete lyes and fallaces,
If that he wolde deserve our graces ;
Or we shal bere him such witnesse
Of sinne, and of his wreechidnesse,   7080
And doon his loos so wyde renne,
That al quik we shulde him brenne,
Or elles yeve him suche penaunce,
That is wel wors than the pitaunce.
  ' For thou shalt never, for no-thing,
Con knowen aright by her clothing     7086
The traitours fulle of trecherye,
But thou her werkes can aspye.
And ne hadde the good keping be
Whylom of the universitee,            7090

That kepeth the key of Cristendome,
†They had been turmented, alle and some.
Suche been the stinking [fals] prophetis ;
Nis non of hem, that good prophete is ;
For they, thurgh wikked entencioun,   7095
The yeer of the incarnacioun
A thousand and two hundred yeer,
Fyve and fifty, ferther ne ner,
Broughten a book, with sory grace,
To yeven ensample in comune place,    7100
That seide thus, though it were fable :—
" This is the Gospel Perdurable,
That fro the Holy Goost is sent."
Wel were it worth to ben [y]-brent !
Entitled was in such manere           7105
This book, of which I telle here.
Ther nas no wight in al Parys,
Biforn Our Lady, at parvys,
†That [he] ne mighte bye the book,
†To copy, if him talent took.         7110
Ther might he see, by greet tresoun,
Ful many fals comparisoun :—
" As moche as, thurgh his grete might,
Be it of hete, or of light,
The sunne surmounteth the mone,       7115
That troubler is, and chaungeth sone,
And the note-kernel the shelle—
(I scorne nat that I yow telle)—
Right so, withouten any gyle,
Surmounteth this noble Evangyle       7120
The word of any evangelist."
And to her title they token Christ ;
And many such comparisoun,
Of which I make no mencioun,
Might men in that boke finde,         7125
Who-so coude of hem have minde.
  ' Th' universitee, that tho was aslepe,
Gan for to braide, and taken kepe ;
And at the noys the heed up-caste,
Ne never sithen slepte it faste,      7130
But up it sterte. and armes took
Ayens this fals horrible book,
Al redy batail for to make,
And to the juge the book to take.
But they that broughten the book there
Hente it anoon awey, for fere ;       7136
They nolde shewe it more a del,
But thenne it kepte, and kepen wil,
Til such a tyme that they may see
That they so stronge woxen be,        7140
That no wight may hem wel withstonde ;

For by that book they durst not stonde.
Away they gonne it for to bere,
For they ne durste not answere
By exposicioun †ne glose                    7145
To that that clerkes wole appose
Ayens the cursednesse, y-wis,
That in that boke writen is.
Now wot I not, ne I can not see
What maner ende that there shal be 7150
Of al this [boke] that they hyde ;
But yit algate they shal abyde
Til that they may it bet defende ;
This trowe I best, wol be hir ende.
  ' Thus Antecrist abyden we,         7155
For we ben alle of his meynee ;
And what man that wol not be so,
Right sone he shal his lyf forgo.
We wol a puple †on him areyse,
And thurgh our gyle doon him seise, 7160
And him on sharpe speres ryve,
Or other-weyes bringe him fro lyve,
But-if that he wol folowe, y-wis,
That in our boke writen is.
Thus moche wol our book signifye,   7165
That whyl [that] Peter hath maistrye,
May never Johan shewe wel his might.
  ' Now have I you declared right
The mening of the bark and rinde
That maketh the entenciouns blinde. 7170
But now at erst I wol biginne
To expowne you the pith withinne :—
[†And first, by Peter, as I wene,
The Pope himself we wolden mene,]
And [eek] the seculers comprehende, 7175
That Cristes lawe wol defende,
And shulde it kepen and mayntenen
Ayeines hem that al sustenen,
And falsly to the puple techen.
†And Johan bitokeneth hem †that pre-
    chen,                                          7180
That ther nis lawe covenable
But thilke Gospel Perdurable,
That fro the Holy Gost was sent
To turne folk that been miswent.
The strengthe of Johan they undirstonde
The grace in which, they seye, they
    stonde,                                         7186
That doth the sinful folk converte,
And hem to Jesus Crist reverte.
  ' Ful many another horriblete
May men in that boke see,              7190

That ben comaunded, douteles,
Ayens the lawe of Rome expres ;
And alle with Antecrist they holden,
As men may in the book biholden.
And than comaunden they to sleen   7193
Alle tho that with Peter been ;
But they shal nevere have that might,
And, god toforn, for stryf to fight,
That they ne shal y-nough [men] finde
That Peters lawe shal have in minde, 7200
And ever holde, and so mayntene,
That at the last it shal be sene,
That they shal alle come therto,
For ought that they can speke or do.
And thilke lawe shal not stonde,       7205
That they by Johan have undirstonde ;
But, maugre hem, it shal adoun,
And been brought to confusioun.
But I wol stinte of this matere,
For it is wonder long to here ;         7210
But hadde that ilke book endured,
Of better estate I were ensured ;
And freendes have I yit, pardee,
That han me set in greet degree.
  ' Of al this world is emperour        7215
Gyle my fader, the trechour,
And emp[e]resse my moder is,
Maugre the Holy Gost, y-wis.
Our mighty linage and our route
Regneth in every regne aboute ;       7220
And wel is †worth we maistres be,
For al this world governe we,
And can the folk so wel disceyve,
That noon our gyle can perceyve ;
And though they doon, they dar not
    saye ;                                            7225
The sothe dar no wight biwreye.
But he in Cristis wrath him ledeth,
That more than Crist my bretheren dre-
    deth.
He nis no ful good champioun,
That dredeth such similacioun ;        7230
Nor that for peyne wole refusen
Us to correcten and accusen.
He wol not entremete by right,
Ne have god in his eye-sight,
And therfore god shal him punyce ; 7235
But me ne rekketh of no vyce,
Sithen men us loven comunably,
And holden us for so worthy,
That we may folk repreve echoon,

And we nil have repref of noon.    7240
Whom shulden folk worshipen so
But us, that stinten never mo
To patren whyl that folk us see,
Though it not so bihinde hem be?
   'And where is more wood folye,    7245
Than to enhaunce chivalrye,
And love noble men and gay,
That joly clothes weren alway?
If they be sich folk as they semen,
So clene, as men her clothes demen,    7250
And that her wordes folowe her dede,
It is gret pite, out of drede,
For they wol be noon ypocrites!
Of hem, me thinketh [it] gret spite is;
I can not love hem on no syde.    7255
But Beggers with these hodes wyde,
With sleighe and pale faces lene,
And greye clothes not ful clene,
But fretted ful of tatarwagges,
And highe shoes, knopped with dagges,
That frouncen lyke a quaile-pype,    7261
Or botes riveling as a gype;
To such folk as I you devyse
Shulde princes and these lordes wyse
Take alle her londes and her thinges,    7265
Bothe werre and pees, in governinges;
To such folk shulde a prince him yive,
That wolde his lyf in honour live.
And if they be not as they seme,
That serven thus the world to queme,    7270
There wolde I dwelle, to disceyve
The folk, for they shal not perceyve.
   'But I ne speke in no such wyse,
That men shulde humble abit dispyse,
So that no pryde ther-under be.    7275
No man shulde hate, as thinketh me,
The pore man in sich clothing.
But god ne preiseth him no-thing,
That seith he hath the world forsake,
And hath to worldly glorie him take,    7280
And wol of siche delyces use;
Who may that Begger wel excuse?
That papelard, that him yeldeth so,
And wol to worldly ese go,
And seith that he the world hath left,
And gredily it grypeth eft,    7286
He is the hound, shame is to seyn,
That to his casting goth ageyn.
   'But unto you dar I not lye:
But mighte I felen or aspye    7290

That ye perceyved it no-thing,
Ye shulde[n] have a stark lesing
Right in your hond thus, to biginne,
I nolde it lette for no sinne.'
   The god lough at the wonder tho,    7295
And every wight gan laughe also,
And seide:—'Lo here a man aright
For to be trusty to every wight!'
   'Fals Semblant,' quod Love, 'sey to me,
Sith I thus have avaunced thee,    7300
That in my court is thy dwelling,
And of ribaudes shalt be my king,
Wolt thou wel holden my forwardes?'
   F. Sem.   'Ye, sir, from hennes fore-
        wardes;
Hadde never your fader here-biforn    7305
Servaunt so trewe, sith he was born.'
   Amour.   'That is ayeines al nature.'
   F. Sem.   'Sir, put you in that aven-
        ture;
For though ye borowes take of me,
The sikerer shal ye never be    7310
For ostages, ne sikirnesse,
Or chartres, for to bere witnesse.
I take your-self to record here,
That men ne may, in no manere,
Teren the wolf out of his hyde,    7315
Til he be †flayn, bak and syde,
Though men him bete and al defyle;
What? wene ye that I wole bigyle?
For I am clothed mekely,
Ther-under is al my trechery;    7320
Myn herte chaungeth never the mo
For noon abit, in which I go.
Though I have chere of simplenesse,
I am not wery of shrewednesse.
My lemman, Streyned-Abstinence,    7325
Hath mister of my purveaunce;
She hadde ful longe ago be deed,
Nere my councel and my reed;
Lete hir allone, and you and me.'
   And Love answerde, 'I truste thee    7330
Without[e] borowe, for I wol noon.'
And Fals-Semblant, the theef, anoon,
Right in that ilke same place,
That hadde of tresoun al his face    7334
Right blak withinne, and whyt withoute,
Thanketh him, gan on his knees loute.
   Than was ther nought, but 'Every man
Now to assaut, that sailen can,'
Quod Love, 'and that ful hardily.'

Than armed they hem communly   7340
Of sich armour as to hem fel.
Whan they were armed, fers and fel,
They wente hem forth, alle in a route,
And sette the castel al aboute ;
They wil nought away, for no drede, 7345
Til it so be that they ben dede,
Or til they have the castel take.
And foure batels they gan make,
And parted hem in foure anoon,
And toke her way, and forth they goon,
The foure gates for to assaile,   7351
Of whiche the kepers wol not faile ;
For they ben neither syke ne dede,
But hardy folk, and stronge in dede.

Now wole I seyn the countenaunce 7355
Of Fals-Semblant, and Abstinaunce,
That ben to Wikkid-Tonge went.
But first they helde her parlement,
Whether it to done were
To maken hem be knowen there,   7360
Or elles walken forth disgysed.
But at the laste they devysed,
That they wold goon in tapinage,
As it were in a pilgrimage,
Lyk good and holy folk unfeyned   7365
And Dame Abstinence-Streyned
Took on a robe of camelyne,
And gan hir †graithe as a Begyne.
A large coverchief of threde
She wrapped al aboute hir hede,   7370
But she forgat not hir sautere ;
A peire of bedes eek she bere
Upon a lace, al of whyt threde,
On which that she hir bedes bede ;
But she ne boughte hem never a del, 7375
For they were geven her, I wot wel,
God wot, of a ful holy frere,
That seide he was hir fader dere,
To whom she hadde ofter went
Than any frere of his covent.   7380
And he visyted hir also,
And many a sermoun seide hir to ;
He nolde lette, for man on lyve,
That he ne wolde hir ofte shryve.
And with so gret devocion   7385
They made[n] her confession,
That they had ofte, for the nones,
Two hedes in one hood at ones.

Of fair shape I †devyse her thee,
But pale of face somtyme was she ;   7390

That false traitouresse untrewe
Was lyk that salowe hors of hewe,
That in the Apocalips is shewed,
That signifyeth †tho folk beshrewed,
That been al ful of trecherye,   7395
And pale, thurgh hypocrisye ;
For on that hors no colour is,
But only deed and pale, y-wis.
Of suche a colour enlangoured
Was Abstinence, y-wis, coloured ;   7400
Of her estat she her repented,
As her visage represented.

She had a burdoun al of Thefte,
That Gyle had yeve her of his yefte ;
And a scrippe of Fainte Distresse,   7405
That ful was of elengenesse,
And forth she walked sobrely :
And False-Semblant saynt, *ie vous dy*,
†Had, as it were for such mistere,
Don on the cope of a frere,   7410
With chere simple, and ful pitous ;
His looking was not disdeinous,
Ne proud, but meke and ful pesible.
About his nekke he bar a bible,
And squierly forth gan he gon ;   7415
And, for to reste his limmes upon,
He had of Treson a potente ;
As he were feble, his way he wente.
But in his sleve he gan to thringe
A rasour sharp, and wel bytinge,   7420
That was forgèd in a forge,
Which that men clepen Coupe-gorge.

So longe forth hir way they nomen,
Til they to Wicked-Tonge comen,
That at his gate was sitting,   7425
And saw folk in the way passing.
The pilgrimes saw he faste by,
That beren hem ful mekely,
And †humblely they with him mette.
Dame Abstinence first him grette,   7430
And sith him False-Semblant salued,
And he hem : but he not †remued,
For he ne dredde hem not a-del.
For when he saw hir faces wel,
Alway in herte him thoughte so,   7435
He shulde knowe hem bothe two ;
For wel he knew Dame Abstinaunce,
But he ne knew not Constreynaunce.
He knew nat that she was constrayned,
Ne of her theves lyfe feyned,   7440
But wende she com of wil al free ;

But she com in another degree ;
And if of good wil she began,
That wil was failed her [as] than.
    And Fals-Semblant had he seyn als,
But he knew nat that he was fals.          7446
Yet fals was he, but his falsnesse
Ne coude he not espye, nor gesse ;
For Semblant was so slye wrought,
That falsnesse he ne espyed nought.     7450
But haddest thou knowen him beforn, ,
Thou woldest on a boke have sworn,
Whan thou him saugh in thilke aray
That he, that whylom was so gay,
And of the daunce Joly Robin,          7455
Was tho become a Jacobin.
But sothely, what so men him calle,
Frere[s] Prechours been good men alle ;
Hir order wickedly they beren,
Suche minstrelles if [that] they weren.
So been Augustins and Cordileres,     7461
And Carmes, and eek Sakked Freres,
And alle freres, shodde and bare,
(Though some of hem ben grete and
    square)
Ful holy men, as I hem deme ;          7465
Everich of hem wolde good man seme.
But shalt thou never of apparence
Seen conclude good consequence
In none argument, y-wis,
If existence al failed is.          7470
For men may finde alway sophyme
The consequence to envenyme,
Who-so that †hath the subteltee
The double sentence for to see.
    Whan the pilgrymes commen were     7475
To Wicked-Tonge, that dwelled there,
Hir harneis nigh hem was algate ;
By Wicked-Tonge adoun they sate,
That bad hem ner him for to come,
And of tydinges telle him some,          7480
And sayde hem :—' What cas maketh
    yow
To come into this place now ? '
' Sir,' seyde Strained-Abstinaunce,
' We, for to drye our penaunce,
With hertes pitous and devoute,          7485
Are commen, as pilgrimes gon aboute ;
Wel nigh on fote alway we go ;
Ful †dusty been our heles two ;
And thus bothe we ben sent
Thurghout this world that is miswent,

To yeve ensample, and preche also.     7491
To fisshen sinful men we go,
For other fisshing ne fisshe we.
And, sir, for that charitee,
As we be wont, herberwe we crave,     7495
Your lyf to amende ; Crist it save !
And, so it shulde you nat displese,
We wolden, if it were your ese,
A short sermoun unto you seyn.'
And Wikked-Tonge answerde ageyn,
' The hous,' quod he, ' such as ye see,     7501
Shal nat be warned you for me,
Sey what you list, and I wol here.'
' Graunt mercy, swete sire dere ! '
Quod alderfirst Dame Abstinence,     7505
And thus began she hir sentence :
    *Const. Abstinence.* ' Sir, the first vertue,
        certeyn,
The gretest, and most sovereyn
That may be founde in any man,
For having, or for wit he can,          7510
That is, his tonge to refreyne ;
Therto ought every wight him peyne.
For it is better stille be
Than for to speken harm, pardee !
And he that herkeneth it gladly,     7515
He is no good man, sikerly.
And, sir, aboven al other sinne,
In that art thou most gilty inne.
Thou spake a jape not long ago,
(And, sir, that was right yvel do)     7520
Of a yong man that here repaired,
And never yet this place apaired.
Thou seydest he awaited nothing
But to disceyve Fair-Welcoming.
Ye seyde nothing sooth of that ;     7525
But, sir, ye lye ; I tell you plat ;
He ne cometh no more, ne goth, pardee !
I trow ye shal him never see.
Fair-Welcoming in prison is,
That ofte hath pleyed with you, er this,
The fairest games that he coude,     7531
Withoute filthe, stille or loude ;
Now dar †he nat himself solace.
Ye han also the man do chace,
That he dar neither come ne go.     7535
What meveth you to hate him so
But properly your wikked thought,
That many a fals lesing hath thought ?
That meveth your foole eloquence,
That jangleth ever in audience,          7540

And on the folk areyseth blame,
And doth hem dishonour and shame,
For thing that may have no preving,
But lyklinesse, and contriving.
For I dar seyn, that Reson demeth,   7545
It is not al sooth thing that semeth
And it is sinne to controve
Thing that is [for] to reprove ;
This wot ye wel ; and, sir, therefore
Ye arn to blame [wel] the more.   7550
And, nathelesse, he rekketh lyte ;
He yeveth nat now thereof a myte ;
For if he thoughte harm, parfay,
He wolde come and gon al day ;
He coude him-selfe nat abstene.   7555
Now cometh he nat, and that is sene,
For he ne taketh of it no cure,
But-if it be through aventure,
And lasse than other folk, algate.
And thou here watchest at the gate,   7560
With spere in thyne arest alway ;
There muse, musard, al the day.
Thou wakest night and day for thought ;
Y-wis, thy traveyl is for nought.
And Jelousye, withouten faile,   7565
Shal never quyte thee thy travaile.
And scathe is, that Fair-Welcoming,
Without[en] any trespassing,
Shal wrongfully in prison be,
Ther wepeth and languissheth he.   7570
And though thou never yet, y-wis,
Agiltest man no more but this,
(Take not a-greef) it were worthy
To putte thee out of this baily,
And afterward in prison lye,   7575
And fettre thee til that thou dye ;
For thou shalt for this sinne dwelle
Right in the devils ers of helle,
But-if that thou repente thee.'   7579
    ' Ma fay, thou lyest falsly !' quod he.
'What ?  welcome with mischaunce now !
Have I therfor herbered you
To seye me shame, and eek reprove ?
With sory happe, to your bihove,
Am I to-day your herbergere !   7585
Go, herber you elleswhere than here,
That han a lyer called me !
Two tregetours art thou and he,
That in myn hous do me this shame,
And for my soth-sawe ye me blame.   7590
Is this the sermoun that ye make ?

To alle the develles I me take,
Or elles, god, thou me confounde :
But er men diden this castel founde,
It passeth not ten dayes or twelve,   7595
But it was told right to my-selve,
And as they seide, right so tolde I,
He kiste the Rose privily !
Thus seide I now, and have seid yore ;
I not wher he dide any more.   7600
Why shulde men sey me such a thing,
If it hadde been gabbing?
Right so seide I, and wol seye yit ;
I trowe, I lyed not of it ;
And with my bemes I wol blowe   7605
To alle neighboris a-rowe,
How he hath bothe comen and gon.'
    Tho spak Fals-Semblant right anon,
' Al is not gospel, out of doute,
That men seyn in the toune aboute ;   7610
Ley no deef ere to my speking ;
I swere yow, sir, it is gabbing !
I trowe ye wot wel certeynly,
That no man loveth him tenderly
That seith him harm, if he wot it,   7615
Al be he never so pore of wit.
And sooth is also sikerly,
(This knowe ye, sir, as wel as I),
That lovers gladly wol visyten
The places ther hir loves habyten.   7620
This man you loveth and eek honoureth ;
This man to serve you laboureth ;
And clepeth you his freend so dere,
And this man maketh you good chere,
And every-wher that [he] you meteth,
He you saleweth, and he you greteth. 7626
He preseth not so ofte, that ye
Ought of his come encombred be ;
Ther presen other folk on yow
Ful ofter than [that] he doth now.   7630
And if his herte him streyned so
Unto the Rose for to go,
Ye shulde him seen so ofte nede,
That ye shulde take him with the dede.
He coude his coming not forbere,   7635
Though ye him thrilled with a spere ;
It nere not thanne as it is now.
But trusteth wel, I swere it yow,
That it is clene out of his thought.
Sir, certes, he ne thenketh it nought ;
No more ne doth Fair-Welcoming,   7641
That sore abyeth al this thing.

And if they were of oon assent,
Ful sone were the Rose hent ;
The maugre youres wolde be.          7645
And sir, of o thing herkeneth me :—
Sith ye this man, that loveth yow,
Han seid such harm and shame now,
Witeth wel, if he gessed it,
Ye may wel demen in your wit,        7650
He nolde no-thing love you so,
Ne callen you his freend also,
But night and day he †wolde wake,
The castel to destroye and take,
If it were sooth as ye devyse ;      7655
Or som man in som maner wyse
Might it warne him everydel,
Or by him-self perceyven wel ;
For sith he might not come and gon
As he was whylom wont to don,       7660
He might it sone wite and see ;
But now al other-wyse †doth he.
Than have †ye, sir, al-outerly
Deserved helle, and jolyly
The deth of helle, douteles,         7665
That thrallen folk so gilteles.'

  Fals-Semblant proveth so this thing
That he can noon answering,
And seeth alwey such apparaunce,
That nygh he fel in repentaunce,     7670
And seide him :—' Sir, it may wel be.

Semblant, a good man semen ye ;
And, Abstinence, ful wyse ye seme ;
Of o talent you bothe I deme.        7674
What counceil wole ye to me yeven ?'
    *F. Sem.* 'Right here anoon thou shalt
       be shriven,
And sey thy sinne withoute more ;
Of this shalt thou repente sore ;
For I am preest, and have poustee
To shryve folk of most dignitee      7680
That been, as wyde as world may dure.
Of al this world I have the cure,
And that had never yit persoun,
No vicarie of no maner toun.
And, god wot, I have of thee         7685
A thousand tymes more pitee
Than hath thy preest parochial,
Though he thy freend be special.
I have avauntage, in o wyse,
That your prelates ben not so wyse   7690
Ne half so lettred as am I.
I am licenced boldely
In divinitee to rede,
And to confessen, out of drede.
If ye wol you now confesse,          7695
And leve your sinnes more and lesse,
Without abood, knele doun anon,
And you shal have absolucion.'       7698

**Explicit.**

# THE MINOR POEMS.

## I. AN A. B. C.

*Incipit carmen secundum ordinem literarum Alphabeti.*

ALMIGHTY and al merciable quene,
To whom that al this world fleeth for
    socour,
To have relees of sinne, sorwe and tene,
Glorious virgine, of alle floures flour,
To thee I flee, confounded in errour!  5
Help and releve, thou mighty debonaire,
Have mercy on my perilous langour!
Venquisshed m' hath my cruel adversaire.

Bountee so fix hath in thyn herte his
    tente,
That wel I wot thou wolt my socour be, 10
Thou canst not warne him that, with
    good entente,
Axeth thyn help. Thyn herte is ay so free,
Thou art largesse of pleyn felicitee,
Haven of refut, of quiete and of reste.
Lo, how that theves seven chasen me! 15
Help, lady bright, er that my ship to-
    breste!

Comfort is noon, but in yow, lady dere;
For lo, my sinne and my confusioun,
Which oughten not in thy presence ap-
    pere,
Han take on me a grevous accioun  20
Of verrey right and desperacioun;
And, as by right, they mighten wel sus-
    tene
That I were worthy my dampnacioun,
Nere mercy of you, blisful hevene quene.

Doute is ther noon, thou queen of miseri-
    corde,  25
That thou n'art cause of grace and mercy
    here;
God vouched sauf thurgh thee with us
    t'acorde.
For certes, Cristes blisful moder dere,
Were now the bowe bent in swich manere,
As it was first, of justice and of yre,  30
The rightful God nolde of no mercy here;
But thurgh thee han we grace, as we
    desyre.

Ever hath myn hope of refut been in thee,
For heer-biforn ful ofte, in many a wyse,
Hast thou to misericorde receyved me. 35
But mercy, lady, at the grete assyse,
Whan we shul come bifore the hye jus-
    tyse!
So litel fruit shal thanne in me be founde,
That, but thou er that day me †wel
    chastyse,
Of verrey right my werk me wol con-
    founde.  40

Fleeing, I flee for socour to thy tente
Me for to hyde from tempest ful of drede,
Biseching you that ye you not absente,
Though I be wikke. O help yit at this nede!
Al have I been a beste in wille and dede,
Yit, lady, thou me clothe with thy grace.
Thyn enemy and myn (lady, tak hede) 47
Un-to my deeth in poynt is me to chace.

Glorious mayde and moder, which that never

Were bitter, neither in erthe nor in see, 50

But ful of swetnesse and of mercy ever,

Help that my fader be not wroth with me!

Spek thou, for I ne dar not him y-see.

So have I doon in erthe, allas ther-whyle!

That certes, but-if thou my socour be, 55

To stink eterne he wol my gost exyle.

He vouched sauf, tel him, as was his wille,

Bicome a man, to have our alliaunce,

And with his precious blood he wroot the bille

Up-on the crois, as general acquitaunce,

To every penitent in ful creaunce ;    61

And therfor, lady bright, thou for us praye.

Than shalt thou bothe stinte al his grevaunce,

And make our foo to failen of his praye

I wot it wel, thou wolt ben our socour, 65

Thou art so ful of bountee, in certeyn.

For, whan a soule falleth in errour,

Thy pitee goth and haleth him ayeyn.

Than makest thou his pees with his sovereyn,

And bringest him out of the crooked strete.      70

Who-so thee loveth he shal not love in veyn,

That shal he finde, as he the lyf shal lete.

Kalenderes enlumined ben they

That in this world ben lighted with thy name,

And who-so goth to you the righte wey, 75

Him thar not drede in soule to be lame.

Now, queen of comfort, sith thou art that same

To whom I seche for my medicyne,

Lat not my foo no more my wounde entame,

Myn hele in-to thyn hand al I resigne. 80

Lady, thy sorwe can I not portreye

Under the cros, ne his grevous penaunce.

But, for your bothes peynes, I you preye,

Lat not our alder foo make his bobaunce,

That he hath in his listes of mischaunce 85

Convict that ye bothe have bought so dere.

As I seide erst, thou ground of our substaunce,

Continue on us thy pitous eyen clere !

Moises, that saugh the bush with flaumes rede

Brenninge, of which ther never a stikke brende,      90

Was signe of thyn unwemmed maidenhede.

Thou art the bush on which ther gan descende

The Holy Gost, the which that Moises wende

Had ben a-fyr ; and this was in figure.

Now lady, from the fyr thou us defende 95

Which that in helle eternally shal dure.

Noble princesse, that never haddest pere,

Certes, if any comfort in us be,

That cometh of thee, thou Cristes moder dere,

We han non other melodye or glee    100

Us to rejoyse in our adversitee,

N' advocat noon that wol and dar so preye

For us, and that for litel hyre as ye,

That helpen for an Ave-Marie or tweye.

O verrey light of eyen that ben blinde, 105

O verrey lust of labour and distresse,

O tresorere of bountee to mankinde,

Thee whom God chees to moder for humblesse !

From his ancille he made thee maistresse

Of hevene and erthe, our bille up for to bede.      110

This world awaiteth ever on thy goodnesse,

For thou ne failest never wight at nede.

Purpos I have sum tyme for t'enquere,

Wherfore and why the Holy Gost thee soughte,

Whan Gabrielles vois cam to thyn ere. 115

He not to werre us swich a wonder wroughte,

But for to save us that he sithen boughte.

Than nedeth us no wepen us for to save,

But only ther we did not, as us oughte,

Do penitence, and mercy axe and have. 120

Queen of comfort, yit whan I me bithink

That I agilt have bothe, him and thee,

And that my soule is worthy for to sinke,
Allas, I, caitif, whider may I flee?
Who shal un-to thy sone my mene be? 125
Who, but thy-self, that art of pitee welle?
Thou hast more reuthe on our adversitee
Than in this world mighte any tunge telle.

Redresse me, moder, and me chastyse,
For, certeynly, my fadres chastisinge 130
That dar I nought abyden in no wyse:
So hidous is his rightful rekeninge.
Moder, of whom our mercy gan to springe,
Beth ye my juge and eek my soules leche;
For ever in you is pitee haboundinge 135
To ech that wol of pitee you biseche.

Soth is, that God ne graunteth no pitee
With-oute thee; for God, of his goodnesse,
Foryiveth noon, but it lyke un-to thee.
He hath thee maked vicaire and mais-
tresse 140
Of al the world, and eek governeresse
Of hevene, and he represseth his justyse
After thy wille, and therefore in witnesse
He hath thee crouned in so ryal wyse.

Temple devout, ther god hath his won-
inge, 145
Fro which these misbileved pryved been,
To you my soule penitent I bringe.
Receyve me! I can no ferther fleen!
With thornes venimous, O hevene queen,
For which the erthe acursed was ful yore,
I am so wounded, as ye may wel seen, 151
That I am lost almost;—it smert so sore.

Virgine, that art so noble of apparaile,
And ledest us in-to the hye tour 154

Of Paradys, thou me wisse and counsaile,
How I may have thy grace and thy socour;
Al have I been in filthe and in errour.
Lady, un-to that court thou me ajourne
That cleped is thy bench, O fresshe flour!
Ther-as that mercy ever shal sojourne. 160

Xristus, thy sone, that in this world
alighte,
Up-on the cros to suffre his passioun,
And †eek, that Longius his herte pighte,
And made his herte blood to renne adoun;
And al was this for my salvacioun; 165
And I to him am fals and eek unkinde,
And yit he wol not my dampnacioun—
This thanke I you, socour of al mankinde.

Ysaac was figure of his deeth, certeyn,
That so fer-forth his fader wolde obeye 170
That him ne roughte no-thing to be slayn;
Right so thy sone list, as a lamb, to deye.
Now lady, ful of mercy, I you preye,
Sith he his mercy mesured so large,
Be ye not skant; for alle we singe and
seye 175
That ye ben from vengeaunce ay our targe.

Zacharie you clepeth the open welle
To wasshe sinful soule out of his gilt,
Therfore this lessoun oughte I wel to telle
That, nere thy tender herte, we weren
spilt. 180
Now lady brighte, sith thou canst and wilt
Ben to the seed of Adam merciable,
So bring us to that palais that is bilt
To penitents that ben to mercy able.
Amen. 184

*Explicit carmen.*

## II. THE COMPLEYNTE UNTO PITE.

Pite, that I have sought so yore ago,
With herte sore, and ful of besy peyne,
That in this world was never wight so wo
With-oute dethe; and, if I shal not feyne,
My purpos was, to Pite to compleyne 5
Upon the crueltee and tirannye
Of Love, that for my trouthe doth me dye.

And when that I, by lengthe of certeyn
yeres,
Had ever in oon a tyme sought to speke,
To Pite ran I, al bespreynt with teres, 10
To preyen hir on Crueltee m' awreke.
But, er I might with any worde out-
breke,

Or tellen any of my peynes smerte,
I fond hir deed, and buried in an herte.

Adoun I fel, when that I saugh the herse,
Deed as a stoon, whyl that the swogh me
　　laste ;　　　　　　　　　　　　16
But up I roos, with colour ful diverse,
And pitously on hir myn yën caste,
And ner the corps I gan to presen faste,
And for the soule I shoop me for to
　　preye ;　　　　　　　　　　　　20
I †nas but lorn ; ther †nas no more to
　　seye.

Thus am I slayn, sith that Pite is deed ;
Allas ! that day ! that ever hit shulde
　　falle !
What maner man dar now holde up his
　　heed ?
To whom shal any sorwful herte calle ? 25
Now Crueltee hath cast to sleen us alle,
In ydel hope, folk redelees of peyne—
Sith she is deed—to whom shul we com-
　　pleyne ?

But yet encreseth me this wonder newe,
That no wight woot that she is deed, but I ;
So many men as in hir tyme hir knewe,
And yet she dyed not so sodeynly ;　32
For I have sought hir ever ful besily
Sith first I hadde wit or mannes minde ;
But she was deed, er that I coude hir
　　finde.　　　　　　　　　　　　35

Aboute hir herse ther stoden lustily,
Withouten any wo, as thoughte me,
Bountee parfit, wel armed and richely,
And fresshe Beautee, Lust, and Jolitee,
Assured Maner, Youthe, and Honestee, 40
Wisdom, Estaat, [and] Dreed, and Go-
　　vernaunce,
Confedred bothe by bonde and alliaunce.

A compleynt hadde I, writen, in myn
　　hond,
For to have put to Pite as a bille,
But whan I al this companye ther fond,
That rather wolden al my cause spille 46
Than do me help, I held my pleynte stille ;
For to that folk, withouten any faile,
Withoute Pite may no bille availe.

Then leve I al thise virtues, sauf Pite, 50
Keping the corps, as ye have herd me seyn,

Confedred alle by bonde of Crueltee,
And been assented that I shal be sleyn.
And I have put my compleynt up ageyn ;
For to my foos my bille I dar not shewe,
Theffect of which seith thus, in wordes
　　fewe :—　　　　　　　　　　　　56

### The Bille.

¶ ' Humblest of herte, hyest of reverence,
Benigne flour, coroune of vertues alle,
Sheweth unto your rial excellence
Your servaunt, if I durste me so calle, 60
His mortal harm, in which he is y-falle,
And noght al only for his evel fare,
But for your renoun, as he shal declare.

' Hit stondeth thus : your contraire,
　　Crueltee,
Allyed is ageynst your regalye　　65
Under colour of womanly Beautee,
For men [ne] shuld not knowe hir
　　tirannye,
With Bountee, Gentilesse, and Curtesye,
And hath depryved you now of your place
That hight " Beautee, apertenant to
　　Grace."　　　　　　　　　　　70

' For kindly, by your heritage right,
Ye been annexed ever unto Bountee ;
And verrayly ye oughte do your might
To helpe Trouthe in his adversitee.
Ye been also the coroune of Beautee ; 75
And certes, if ye wanten in thise tweyne,
The world is lore ; ther †nis no more to
　　seyne.

¶ ' Eek what availeth Maner and Gen-
　　tilesse
Withoute you, benigne creature ?
Shal Crueltee be your governeresse ?　80
Allas ! what herte may hit longe endure ?
Wherfor, but ye the rather take cure
To breke that perilous alliaunce,
Ye sleen hem that ben in your obeisaunce.

' And further over, if ye suffre this,　85
Your renoun is fordo than in a throwe ;
Ther shal no man wite wel what Pite is.
Allas ! that your renoun shuld be so lowe !
Ye be than fro your heritage y-throwe
By Crueltee, that occupieth your place ; 90
And we despeired, that seken to your
　　grace

'Have mercy on me, thou Herenus quene,
That you have sought so tenderly and
   yore ;
Let som streem of your light on me be sene
That love and drede you, ay lenger the
   more.          95
For, sothly for to seyne, I bere the sore,
And, though I be not cunning for to
   pleyne,
For goddes love, have mercy on my peyne !

¶ ' My peyne is this, that what so I desire
That have I not, ne no-thing lyk therto ;
And ever set Desire myn herte on fire ;
Eek on that other syde, wher-so I go,  102
What maner thing that may encrese wo
That have I redy, unsoght, everywhere ;
Me [ne] lakketh but my deth, and than
   my bere.        105

' What nedeth to shewe parcel of my
   peyne ?
Sith every wo that herte may bethinke
I suffre, and yet I dar not to you pleyne ;
For wel I woot, al-though I wake or
   winke,
Ye rekke not whether I flete or sinke. 110
But natheles, my trouthe I shal sustene
Unto my deeth, and that shal wel be
   sene.

' This is to seyne, I wol be youres ever ;
Though ye me slee by Crueltee, your fo,
Algate my spirit shal never dissever  115
Fro your servyse, for any peyne or wo.
Sith ye be deed—allas ! that hit is so !—
Thus for your deth I may wel wepe and
   pleyne       118
With herte sore and ful of besy peyne.'

*Here endeth the exclamacion of the Deth of Pyte.*

---

# III. THE BOOK OF THE DUCHESSE.

*The Proem.*

I HAVE gret wonder, by this lighte,
How that I live, for day ne nighte
I may nat slepe wel nigh noght ;
I have so many an ydel thoght
Purely for defaute of slepe,     5
That, by my trouthe, I take †kepe
Of no-thing, how hit cometh or goth,
Ne me nis no-thing leef nor loth.
Al is y-liche good to me—
Joye or sorowe, wherso hit be—  10
For I have feling in no-thing,
But, as it were, a mased thing,
Alway in point to falle a-doun ;
For †sory imaginacioun
Is alway hoolly in my minde.  15
  And wel ye woot, agaynes kinde
Hit were to liven in this wyse ;
For nature wolde nat suffyse
To noon erthely creature
Not longe tyme to endure    20

Withoute slepe, and be[en] in sorwe ;
And I ne may, ne night ne morwe,
Slepe ; and †thus melancolye,
And dreed I have for to dye,
Defaute of slepe, and hevinesse  25
Hath sleyn my spirit of quiknesse,
That I have lost al lustihede.
Suche fantasyes ben in myn hede
So I not what is best to do.
  But men mighte axe me, why so  30
I may not slepe, and what me is ?
But natheles, who aske this
Leseth his asking trewely.
My-selven can not telle why
The sooth ; but trewely, as I gesse,  35
I holdë hit be a siknesse
That I have suffred this eight yere,
And yet my bote is never the nere ;
For ther is phisicien but oon,
That may me hele ; but that is doon.  40
Passe we over until eft ;
That wil not be, moot nede be left ;

Our first matere is good to kepe.
  So whan I saw I might not slepe,
Til now late, this other night,      45
Upon my bedde I sat upright,
And bad oon reche me a book,
A romaunce, and he hit me took
To rede and dryve the night away ;
For me thoghte it better play      50
Then playe[n] either at chesse or tables.
  And in this boke were writen fables
That clerkes hadde, in olde tyme,
And other poets, put in ryme
To rede, and for to be in minde      55
Whyl men loved the lawe of kinde.
This book ne spak but of such thinges,
Of quenes lyves, and of kinges,
And many othere thinges smale.
Amonge al this I fond a tale      60
That me thoughte a wonder thing.
  This was the tale : Ther was a king
That highte Seys, and hadde a wyf,
The beste that mighte bere lyf ;
And this quene highte Alcyone.      65
So hit befel, therafter sone,
This king wolde wenden over see.
To tellen shortly, whan that he
Was in the see, thus in this wyse,
Soche a tempest gan to ryse      70
That brak hir mast, and made it falle,
And clefte hir ship, and dreinte hem alle,
That never was founden, as it telles,
Bord ne man, ne nothing elles.
Right thus this king Seys loste his lyf. 75
  Now †for to speken of his wyf :—
This lady, that was left at home,
Hath wonder, that the king ne come
Hoom, for hit was a longe terme.
Anon her herte †gan to erme ;      80
And for that hir thoughte evermo
Hit was not wel †he dwelte so,
She longed so after the king
That certes, hit were a pitous thing
To telle hir hertely sorwful lyf      85
That †hadde, alas ! this noble wyf ;
For him she loved alderbest.
Anon she sente bothe eest and west
To seke him, but they founde nought.
  'Alas !' quoth she, 'that I was wrought !
And wher my lord, my love, be deed ? 91
Certes, I nil never ete breed,
I make a-vowe to my god here,

But I mowe of my lorde here !'
Such sorwe this lady to her took      95
That trewely I, which made this book,
Had swich pite and swich rowthe
To rede hir sorwe, that, by my trowthe,
I ferde the worse al the morwe
After, to thenken on her sorwe.      100
  So whan †she coude here no word
That no man mighte finde hir lord,
Ful oft she swouned, and seide 'alas !'
For sorwe ful nigh wood she was,
Ne she coude no reed but oon ;      105
But doun on knees she sat anoon,
And †weep, that pite was to here.
  'A ! mercy ! swete lady dere !'
Quod she to Juno, hir goddesse ;
'Help me out of this distresse,      110
And yeve me grace my lord to see
Sone, or wite wher-so he be,
Or how he fareth, or in what wyse,
And I shal make you sacrifyse,
And hoolly youres become I shal      115
With good wil, body, herte, and al ;
And but thou wilt this, lady swete,
Send me grace to slepe, and mete
In my slepe som certeyn sweven,
Wher-through that I may knowen even
Whether my lord be quik or deed.'    121
With that word she heng doun the heed,
And fil a-swown as cold as ston ;
Hir women caughte her up anon,
And broghten hir in bed al naked,      125
And she, forweped and forwaked,
Was wery, and thus the dede sleep
Fil on her, or she toke keep,
Through Juno, that had herd hir bone,
That made hir [for] to slepe sone ;      130
For as she prayde, †so was don,
In dede ; for Juno, right anon,
Called thus her messagere
To do her erande, and he com nere.
Whan he was come, she bad him thus : 135
'Go bet,' quod Juno, ' to Morpheus,
Thou knowest him wel, the god of sleep ;
Now understond wel, and tak keep.
Sey thus on my halfe, that he
Go faste into the grete see,      140
And bid him that, on alle thing,
He take up Seys body the king,
That lyth ful pale and no-thing rody.
Bid him crepe into the body,

And do it goon to Alcyone          145
The quene, ther she lyth alone,
And shewe hir shortly, hit is no nay,
How hit was dreynt this other day ;
And do the body speke †so
Right as hit was wont to do,          150
The whyles that hit was on lyve.
Go now faste, and hy thee blyve !'
   This messager took leve and wente
Upon his wey, and never ne stente
Til he com to the derke valeye          155
That stant bytwene roches tweye,
Ther never yet grew corn ne gras,
Ne tree, ne †nothing that ought was,
Beste, ne man, ne †nothing elles,
Save ther were a fewe welles          160
Came renning fro the cliffes adoun,
That made a deedly sleping soun,
And ronnen doun right by a cave
That was under a rokke y-grave
Amid the valey, wonder depe.          165
Ther thise goddes laye and slepe,
Morpheus, and Eclympasteyre,
That was the god of slepes heyre,
That slepe and did non other werk.
   This cave was also as derk          170
As helle pit over-al aboute ;
They had good leyser for to route
To envye, who might slepe beste ;
Some henge hir chin upon hir breste
And †slepe upright, hir heed y-hed,          175
And some lay[e] naked in hir bed,
And slepe whyles the dayes laste.
   This messager com flying faste,
And cryed, ' O ho ! awak anon !'          179
Hit was for noght ; ther herde him non.
' Awak !' quod he, ' who is, lyth there ?'
And blew his horn right in hir ere,
And cryed ' awaketh !' wonder hyë.
This god of slepe, with his oon yë
Cast up, †axed, ' who clepeth there ?'  185
' Hit am I,' quod this messagere ;
' Juno bad thou shuldest goon '—
And tolde him what he shulde doon
As I have told yow here-tofore ;
Hit is no need reherse hit more ;          190
And wente his wey, whan he had sayd.
   Anon this god of slepe a-brayd
Out of his slepe, and gan to goon,
And did as he had bede him doon ;
Took up the dreynte body sone,          195

And bar hit forth to Alcyone,
His wyf the quene, ther-as she lay,
Right even a quarter before day,
And stood right at hir beddes fete,
And called hir, right as she hete,          200
By name, and seyde, ' my swete wyf,
Awak ! let be your sorwful lyf !
For in your sorwe ther lyth no reed ;
For certes, swete, I †nam but deed ;
Ye shul me never on lyve y-see.          205
But good swete herte, [look] that ye
Bury my body, †at whiche a tyde
Ye mowe hit finde the see besyde ;
And far-wel, swete, my worldes blisse !
I praye god your sorwe lisse ;          210
To litel whyl our blisse lasteth !'
   With that hir eyen up she casteth,
And saw noght ; '†A !' quod she, ' for
    sorwe !'
And deyed within the thridde morwe.
But what she sayde more in that swow
I may not telle yow as now,          216
Hit were to longe for to dwelle ;
My first matere I wil yow telle,
Wherfor I have told this thing
Of Alcione and Seys the king.          220
   For thus moche dar I say[e] wel,
I had be dolven everydel,
And deed, right through defaute of sleep,
If I nad red and take[n] keep
Of this tale next before :          225
And I wol telle yow wherfore ;
For I ne might, for bote ne bale,
Slepe, or I had red this tale
Of this dreynte Seys the king,
And of the goddes of sleping.          230
Whan I had red this tale wel,
And over-loked hit everydel,
Me thoughte wonder if hit were so ;
For I had never herd speke, or tho,
Of no goddes that coude make          235
Men [for] to slepe, ne for to wake ;
For I ne knew never god but oon.
And in my game I sayde anoon—
And yet me list right evel to pleye—
' Rather then that I shulde deye          240
Through defaute of sleping thus,
I wolde yive thilke Morpheus,
Or his goddesse, dame Juno,
Or som wight elles, I ne roghte who—
To make me slepe and have som reste—

I wil yive him the alder-beste    246
Yift that ever he abood his lyve,
And here on warde, right now, as blyve ;
If he wol make me slepe a lyte,
Of downe of pure dowves whyte    250
I wil yive him a fether-bed,
Rayed with golde, and right wel cled
In fyn blak satin doutremere,
And many a pilow, and every bere
Of clothe of Reynes, to slepe softe ;    255
Him thar not nede to turnen ofte.
And I wol yive him al that falles
To a chambre ; and al his halles
I wol do peynte with pure golde,
And tapite hem ful many folde    260
Of oo sute ; this shal he have,
If I wiste wher were his cave,
If he can make me slepe sone,
As did the goddesse †Alcione.
And thus this ilke god, Morpheus,    265
May winne of me mo feës thus
Than ever he wan ; and to Juno,
That is his goddesse, I shal so do,
I trow that she shal holde her payd.'

   I hadde unneth that word y-sayd    270
Right thus as I have told yow,
That sodeynly, I niste how,
Swich a lust anoon me took
To slepe, that right upon my book
I fil aslepe, and therwith even    275
Me mette so inly swete a sweven,
So wonderful, that never yit
I trowe no man hadde the wit
To conne wel my sweven rede ;
No, not Joseph, withoute drede,    280
Of Egipte, he that redde so
The kinges meting Pharao,
No more than coude the leste of us ;
Ne nat scarsly Macrobeus,
(He that wroot al th'avisioun    285
That he mette, king Scipioun,
The noble man, the Affrican—
Swiche mervayles fortuned than)
I trowe, a-rede my dremes even.
Lo, thus hit was, this was my sweven. 290

### The Dream.

Me thoughte thus :—that hit was May,
And in the dawning ther I lay,
Me mette thus, in my bed al naked :—

†I loked forth, for I was waked
With smale foules a gret hepe,    295
That had affrayed me out of †slepe
Through noyse and swetnesse of hir song ;
And, as me mette, they sate among,
Upon my chambre-roof withoute,
Upon the tyles, †al a-boute,    300
And songen, everich in his wyse,
The moste solempne servyse
By note, that ever man, I trowe,
Had herd ; for som of hem song lowe,
Som hye, and al of oon acorde.    305
To telle shortly, at oo worde,
Was never y-herd so swete a steven,
But hit had be a thing of heven ;—
So mery a soun, so swete entunes,
That certes, for the toune of Tewnes, 310
I nolde but I had herd hem singe ;
For al my chambre gan to ringe
Through singing of hir armonye.
For instrument nor melodye
Was nowher herd yet half so swete,    315
Nor of acorde half so mete ;
For ther was noon of hem that feyned
To singe, for ech of hem him peyned
To finde out mery crafty notes ;
They ne spared not hir throtes.    320
And, sooth to seyn, my chambre was
Ful wel depeynted, and with glas
Were al the windowes wel y-glased,
Ful clere, and nat an hole y-crased,
That to beholde hit was gret joye.    325
For hoolly al the storie of Troye
Was in the glasing y-wroght thus,
Of Ector and †king Priamus,
Of Achilles and †Lamedon,
Of †Medea and of Jason,    330
Of Paris, Eleyne, and Lavyne.
And †alle the walles with colours fyne
Were peynted, bothe text and glose,
†Of al the Romaunce of the Rose.
My windowes weren shet echon,    335
And through the glas the sunne shon
Upon my bed with brighte bemes,
With many glade gilden stremes ;
And eek the welken was so fair,
Blew, bright, clere was the air,    340
And ful atempre, for sothe, hit was ;
For nother †cold nor hoot hit nas,
Ne in al the welken was a cloude.
   And as I lay thus, wonder loude

Me thoughte I herde an hunte blowe   345
T' assaye his horn, and for to knowe
Whether hit were clere or hors of soune.
†I herde goinge, up and doune,
Men, hors, houndes, and other thing ;
And al men speken of hunting,   350
How they wolde slee the hert with
    strengthe,
And how the hert had, upon lengthe,
So moche embosed, I not now what.
Anon-right, whan I herde that,
How that they wolde on hunting goon,
I was right glad, and up anoon ;   356
[I] took my hors, and forth I wente
Out of my chambre ; I never stente
Til I com to the feld withoute.
Ther overtook I a gret route   360
Of huntes and eek of foresteres,
With many relayes and lymeres,
And hyed hem to the forest faste,
And I with hem ;—so at the laste
I asked oon, ladde a lymere :—   365
' Say, felow, who shal hunte[n] here ?'
Quod I ; and he answerde ageyn,
' Sir, th'emperour Octovien,'
Quod he, ' and is heer faste by.'
' A goddes halfe, in good tyme,' quod I,
' Go we faste !' and gan to ryde.   371
Whan we came to the forest-syde,
Every man dide, right anoon,
As to hunting fil to doon.
·The mayster-hunte anoon, fot-hoot,   375
With a gret horne blew three moot
At the uncoupling of his houndes.
Within a whyl the hert [y]-founde is,
Y-halowed, and rechased faste
Longe tyme ; and †at the laste,   380
This hert rused and stal away
Fro alle the houndes a prevy way.
The houndes had overshote hem alle,
And were on a defaute y-falle ;
Therwith the hunte wonder faste   385
Blew a forloyn at the laste.

    I was go walked fro my tree,
And as I wente, ther cam by me
A whelp, that fauned me as I stood,
That hadde y-folowed, and coude no good.
Hit com and creep to me as lowe,   391
Right as hit hadde me y-knowe,
Hild doun his heed and joyned his eres,
And leyde al smothe doun his heres.

I wolde han caught hit, and anoon   395
Hit fledde, and was fro me goon ;
And I him folwed, and hit forth wente
Doun by a floury grene wente
Ful thikke of gras, ful softe and swete,
With floures fele, faire under fete,   400
And litel used, hit seemed thus ;
For bothe Flora and Zephirus,
They two that make floures growe,
Had mad hir dwelling ther, I trowe ;
For hit was, on to beholde,   405
As thogh the erthe envye wolde
To be gayer than the heven,
To have mo floures, swiche seven
As in the welken sterres be.
Hit had forgete the povertee   410
That winter, through his colde morwes,
Had mad hit suffre[n], and his sorwes ;
Al was forgeten, and that was sene.
For al the wode was waxen grene,
Swetnesse of dewe had mad it waxe.   415
  Hit is no need eek for to axe
Wher ther were many grene greves,
Or thikke of trees, so ful of leves ;
And every tree stood by him-selve
Fro other wel ten foot or twelve.   420
So grete trees, so huge of strengthe,
Of fourty or fifty fadme lengthe,
Clene withoute bough or stikke,
With croppes brode, and eek as thikke—
They were nat an inche a-sonder—   425
That hit was shadwe over-al under ;
And many an hert and many an hinde
Was both before me and bihinde.
Of founes, soures, bukkes, doës
Was ful the wode, and many roës,   430
And many squirelles, that sete
Ful hye upon the trees, and ete,
And in hir maner made festes.
Shortly, hit was so ful of bestes,
That thogh Argus, the noble countour,
Sete to rekene in his countour,   436
And rekene[d] with his figures ten—
For by tho figures mowe al ken,
If they be crafty, rekene and noumbre,
And telle of every thing the noumbre—
Yet shulde he fayle to rekene even   441
The wondres, me mette in my sweven.
  But forth they romed †wonder faste
Doun the wode ; so at the laste
I was war of a man in blak,   445

That sat and had y-turned his bak
To an oke, an huge tree.
'Lord,' thoghte I, 'who may that be?
What ayleth him to sitten here?'
Anoon-right I wente nere;　　　　　450
Than fond I sitte even upright
A wonder wel-faringe knight—
By the maner me thoughte so—
Of good mochel, and †yong therto,
Of the age of four and twenty yeer.　455
Upon his berde but litel heer,
And he was clothed al in blakke.
I stalked even unto his bakke,
And ther I stood as stille as ought,
That, sooth to saye, he saw me nought,
For-why he heng his heed adoune.　461
And with a deedly sorwful soune
He made of ryme ten vers or twelve,
Of a compleynt to him-selve,
The moste pite, the moste rowthe,　465
That ever I herde; for, by my trowthe,
Hit was gret wonder that nature
Might suffre[n] any creature
To have swich sorwe, and be not deed.
Ful pitous, pale, and nothing reed,　470
He sayde a lay, a maner song,
Withoute note, withoute song,
And hit was this; for †wel I can
Reherse hit; right thus hit began.—
¶'I have of sorwe so gret woon,　475
That joye gete I never noon,
　Now that I see my lady bright,
　Which I have loved with al my might,
Is fro me deed, and is a-goon.†　479
¶Allas, [o] deeth! what ayleth thee,　481
That thou noldest have taken me,
　Whan that thou toke my lady swete?
　That was so fayr, so fresh, so free,
So good, that men may wel [y]-see　485
Of al goodnesse she had no mete!'—
Whan he had mad thus his complaynte,
His sorowful herte gan faste faynte,
And his spirites wexen dede;
The blood was fled, for pure drede,　490
Doun to his herte, to make him warm—
For wel hit feled the herte had harm—
To wite eek why hit was a-drad
By kinde, and for to make hit glad;
·For hit is membre principal　495
Of the body; and that made al
His hewe chaunge and wexe grene

And pale, for †no blood was sene
In no maner lime of his.
　Anoon therwith whan I saw this,　500
He ferde thus evel ther he sete,
I wente and stood right at his fete,
And grette him, but he spak noght,
But argued with his owne thoght,
And in his witte disputed faste　505
Why and how his lyf might laste;
Him thoughte his sorwes were so smerte
And lay so colde upon his herte;
So, through his sorwe and hevy thoght,
Made him that he ne herde me noght;
For he had wel nigh lost his minde,　511
Thogh Pan, that men clepe god of kinde,
Were for his sorwes never so wrooth.
　But at the laste, to sayn right sooth,
He was war of me, how I stood　515
Before him, and dide of myn hood,
And †grette him, as I best coude.
Debonairly, and no-thing loude,
He sayde, 'I prey thee, be not wrooth,
I herde thee not, to sayn the sooth,　520
Ne I saw thee not, sir, trewely.'
　'A! goode sir, no fors,' quod I,
'I am right sory if I have ought
Destroubled yow out of your thought;
For-yive me if I have mis-take.'　525
　'Yis, th' amendes is light to make,'
Quod he, 'for ther lyth noon ther-to;
Ther is no-thing missayd nor do.'
　Lo! how goodly spak this knight,
As it had been another wight;　530
He made it nouther tough ne queynte.
And I saw that, and gan me aqueynte
With him, and fond him so tretable,
Right wonder skilful and resonable,
As me thoghte, for al his bale.　535
Anoon-right I gan finde a tale
To him, to loke wher I might ought
Have more knowing of his thought.
　'Sir,' quod I, 'this game is doon;
I holde that this hert be goon;　540
Thise huntes conne him nowher see.'
　'I do no fors therof,' quod he,
'My thought is ther-on never a del.'
　'By our lord,' quod I, 'I trow yow wel,
Right so me thinketh by your chere.　545
But, sir, oo thing wol ye here?
Me thinketh, in gret sorwe I yow see
But certes, [good] sir, yif that ye

Wolde ought discure me your wo,
I wolde, as wis god helpe me so,⠀⠀⠀550
Amende hit, yif I can or may;
Ye mowe preve hit by assay.
For, by my trouthe, to make yow hool,
I wol do al my power hool;
And telleth me of your sorwes smerte,
Paraventure hit may ese your herte,⠀556
That semeth ful seke under your syde.'
⠀⠀With that he loked on me asyde,
As who sayth, 'nay, that wol not be.'
'Graunt mercy, gode frend,' quod he,
'I thanke thee that thou woldest so,⠀561
But hit may never the rather be do.
No man may my sorwe glade,
That maketh my hewe to falle and
⠀⠀fade,
And hath myn understonding lorn,⠀565
That me is wo that I was born!
May noght make my sorwes slyde,
Nought the remedies of Ovyde;
Ne Orpheus, god of melodye,
Ne Dedalus, with †playes slye;⠀⠀570
Ne hele me may †phisicien,
Noght Ipocras, ne Galien;
Me is wo that I live houres twelve;
But who so wol assaye him-selve
Whether his herte can have pite⠀575
Of any sorwe, lat him see me.
I wrecche, that deeth hath mad al naked
Of alle blisse that was ever maked,
Y-worthe worste of alle wightes,
That hate my dayes and my nightes;⠀580
My lyf, my lustes be me lothe,
For al welfare and I be wrothe.
The pure deeth is so †my fo,
†Thogh I wolde deye, hit wolde not so;
For whan I folwe hit, hit wol flee;⠀585
I wolde have †hit, hit nil not me.
This is my peyne withoute reed,
Alway deying, and be not deed,
That †Sesiphus, that lyth in helle,
May not of more sorwe telle.⠀⠀⠀590
And who so wiste al, by my trouthe,
My sorwe, but he hadde routhe
And pite of my sorwes smerte,
That man hath a feendly herte.
For who so seeth me first on morwe⠀595
May seyn, he hath [y-]met with sorwe;
For I am sorwe and sorwe is I.
⠀⠀'Allas! and I wol telle the why;

My †song is turned to pleyning,
And al my laughter to weping,⠀⠀⠀600
My glade thoghtes to hevinesse,
In travaile is myn ydelnesse
And eek my reste; my wele is wo.
My good is harm, and ever-mo
In wrathe is turned my pleying,⠀⠀605
And my delyt in-to sorwing.
Myn hele is turned into seeknesse,
In drede is al my sikernesse.
To derke is turned al my light,
My wit is foly, my day is night,⠀⠀610
My love is hate, my sleep waking,
My mirthe and meles is fasting,
My countenaunce is nycete,
And al abaved wher-so I be,
My pees, in pleding and in werre;⠀615
Allas! how mighte I fare werre?
⠀⠀'My boldnesse is turned to shame,
For fals Fortune hath pleyd a game
Atte ches with me, allas! the whyle!
The trayteresse fals and ful of gyle,⠀620
That al behoteth and no-thing halt,
She goth upright and yet she halt,
That baggeth foule and loketh faire,
The dispitousë debonaire,
That scorneth many a creature!⠀⠀625
An ydole of fals portraiture
Is she, for she wil sone wryen;
She is the monstres heed y-wryen,
As filth over y-strawed with floures;
Hir moste worship and hir †flour is⠀630
To lyen, for that is hir nature;
Withoute feyth, lawe, or mesure
She is fals; and ever laughinge
With oon eye, and that other wepinge.
That is broght up, she set al doun.⠀635
I lykne hir to the scorpioun,
That is a fals flatering beste;
For with his hede he maketh feste,
But al amid his flateringe
With his tayle he wol stinge,⠀⠀⠀640
And envenyme; and so wol she.
She is th' envyous charite
That is ay fals, and semeth wele;
So turneth she hir false whele
Aboute, for it is no-thing stable,⠀645
Now by the fyre, now at table;
Ful many oon hath she thus y-blent.
She is pley of enchauntement,
That semeth oon and is nat so,

The false theef! what hath she do, 650
Trowest thou? by our lord, I wol thee
   seye.
Atte ches with me she gan to pleye:
With hir false draughtes divers
She stal on me, and took my fers
And whan I saw my fers aweye, 655
Alas! I couthe no lenger pleye,
But seyde, "farwel, swete, y-wis,
And farwel al that ever ther is!"
Therwith Fortune seyde "chek here!"
And "mate!" in †mid pointe of the
   chekkere 660
With a poune erraunt, allas!
Ful craftier to pley she was
Than Athalus, that made the game
First of the ches: so was his name.
But god wolde I had ones or twyes 665
Y-koud and knowe the jeupardyes
That coude the Grek Pithagores!
I shulde have pleyd the bet at ches,
And kept my fers the bet therby;
And thogh wherto? for trewely 670
I hold that wish nat worth a stree.
Hit had be never the bet for me.
For Fortune can so many a wyle,
Ther be but fewe can hir begyle,
And eek she is the las to blame; 675
My-self I wolde have do the same,
Before god, hadde I been as she;
She oghte the more excused be.
For this I say yet more therto,
Hadde I be god and mighte have do 680
My wille, whan †my fers she caughte,
I wolde have drawe the same draughte.
For, also wis god yive me reste,
I dar wel swere she took the beste!
   'But through that draughte I have
    lorn 685
My blisse; allas! that I was born!
For evermore, I trowe trewly,
For al my wil, my lust hoolly
Is turned; but yet, what to done?
By our lord, hit is to deye sone! 690
For no-thing I [ne] leve it noght,
But live and deye right in this thoght.
†Ther nis planete in firmament,
Ne in air, ne in erthe, noon element,
That they ne yive me a yift echoon 695
Of weping, whan I am aloon.
For whan that I avyse me wel,

And bethenke me every-del,
How that ther lyth in rekening,
In my sorwe, for no-thing; 700
And how ther leveth no gladnesse
May gladde me of my distresse,
And how I have lost suffisance,
And therto I have no plesance,
Than may I say, I have right noght. 705
And whan al this falleth in my thoght,
Allas! than am I overcome!
For that is doon is not to come!
I have more sorowe than Tantale.'
   And whan I herde him telle this tale
Thus pitously, as I yow telle, 711
Unnethe mighte I lenger dwelle,
Hit dide myn herte so moche wo.
   'A! good sir!' quod I, 'say not so!
Have som pite on your nature 715
That formed yow to creaturè;
Remembre yow of Socrates;
For he ne counted nat three strees
Of noght that Fortune coude do.'
   'No,' quod he, 'I can not so.' 720
   'Why so? good sir! †parde!' quod I;
'Ne say noght so, for trewely,
Thogh ye had lost the ferses twelve,
And ye for sorwe mordred your-selve,
Ye sholde be dampned in this cas 725
By as good right as Medea was,
That slow hir children for Jason;
And Phyllis †als for Demophon
Heng hir-self, so weylaway!
For he had broke his terme-day 730
To come to hir. Another rage
Had Dydo, †quene eek of Cartage,
That slow hir-self, for Eneas
Was fals; [a!] whiche a fool she was!
And Ecquo dyed for Narcisus 735
Nolde nat love hir; and right thus
Hath many another foly don.
And for Dalida dyed Sampson,
That slow him-self with a pilere.
But ther is †noon a-lyve here 740
Wolde for a fers make[n] this wo!'
   'Why so?' quod he; 'hit is nat so;
Thou wost ful litel what thou menest;
I have lost more than thou wenest.'
   'Lo, †sir, how may that be?' quod I; 745
'Good sir, tel me al hoolly
In what wyse, how, why, and wherfore
That ye have thus your blisse lore.'

'Blythly,' quod he, ' com sit adoun ;
I telle thee up condicioun            750
That thou †hoolly, with al thy wit,
Do thyn entent to herkene hit.'
' Yis, sir.'   ' Swere thy trouthe ther-to.'
' Gladly.'   ' Do than holde her-to !'
' I shal right blythly, so god me save,  755
Hoolly, with al the witte I have,
Here yow, as wel as I can.'
      ' A goddes half !' quod he, and began :—
' Sir,' quod he, ' sith first I couthe
Have any maner wit fro youthe,       760
Or kindely understonding
To comprehende, in any thing,
What love was, in myn owne wit,
Dredeles, I have ever yit
Be tributary, and yiven rente        765
To love hoolly with gode entente,
And through plesaunce become his thral,
With good wil, body, herte, and al.
Al this I putte in his servage,
As to my lorde, and dide homage ;    770
And ful devoutly †prayde him to,
He shulde besette myn herte so,
That it plesaunce to him were,
And worship to my lady dere.
      ' And this was longe, and many a yeer
Or that myn herte was set o-wher,    776
That I did thus, and niste why ;
I trowe hit cam me kindely.
Paraunter I was therto †able
As a whyt wal or a table ;           780
For hit is redy to cacche and take
Al that men wil therin make,
Wher-so men wol portreye or peynte,
Be the werkes never so queynte.
      ' And thilke tyme I ferde †so     785
I was able to have lerned tho,
And to have coud as wel or better,
Paraunter, other art or letter.
But for love cam first in my thought,
Therfore I forgat it nought.         790
I chees love to my firste craft,
Therfor hit is with me [y]-laft.
Forwhy I took hit of so yong age,
That malice hadde my corage
Nat that tyme turned to no-thing     795
Through to mochel knowleching.
For that tyme Youthe, my maistresse,
Governed me in ydelnesse ;
For hit was in my firste youthe,

And tho ful litel good I couthe ;    800
For al my werkes were flittinge,
†And al my thoghtes varyinge ;
Al were to me y-liche good,
That I knew tho ; but thus hit stood.
      ' Hit happed that I cam †a day    805
Into a place, ther †I say,
Trewly, the fayrest companyë
Of ladies, that ever man with yë
Had seen togedres in oo place.
Shal I clepe hit hap other grace     810
That broghte me ther ? nay, but Fortune,
That is to lyen ful comune,
The false trayteresse, pervers,
God wolde I coude clepe hir wers !
For now she worcheth me ful wo,      815
And I wol telle sone why so.
      ' Among thise ladies thus echoon,
Soth to seyn, I saw [ther] oon
That was lyk noon of [al] the route ;
For I dar swere, withoute doute,     820
That as the someres sonne bright
Is fairer, clerer, and hath more light
Than any †planete, [is] in heven,
The mone, or the sterres seven,
For al the worlde, so had she        825
Surmounted hem alle of beaute,
Of maner and of comlinesse,
Of stature and †wel set gladnesse,
Of goodlihede †so wel beseye—
Shortly, what shal I more seye ?     830
By god, and by his halwes twelve,
It was my swete, right as hir-selve !
She had so stedfast countenaunce,
So noble port and meyntenaunce.
And Love, that had herd my bone,     835
Had espyed me thus sone,
That she ful sone, in my thoght,
As helpe me god, so was y-caught
So sodenly, that I ne took
No maner †reed but at hir look       840
And at myn herte ; for-why hir eyen
So gladly, I trow, myn herte seyen,
That purely tho myn owne thoght
Seyde hit were †bet serve hir for noght
Than with another to be wel.         845
And hit was sooth, for, everydel,
I wil anoon-right telle thee why.
      ' I saw hir daunce so comlily,
Carole and singe so swetely,
Laughe and pleye so womanly,         850

3 1 0 1

And loke so debonairly,
So goodly speke and so frendly,
That certes, I trow, that evermore
Nas seyn so blisful a tresore.
For every heer [up]on hir hede,        855
Soth to seyn, hit was not rede,
Ne nouther yelw, ne broun hit nas ;
Me thoghte, most lyk gold hit was.
And whiche eyen my lady hadde !
Debonair, goode, glade, and sadde,        860
Simple, of good mochel, noght to wyde ;
Therto hir look nas not a-syde,
Ne overthwert, but beset so wel,
Hit drew and took up, everydel,
Alle that on hir gan beholde.        865
Hir eyen semed anoon she wolde
Have mercy ; fooles wenden so ;
But hit was never the rather do.
Hit nas no countrefeted thing,
It was hir owne pure loking,        870
That the goddesse, dame Nature,
Had made hem opene by mesure,
And close ; for, were she never so glad,
Hir loking was not foly sprad,
Ne wildely, thogh that she pleyde ;        875
But ever, me thoghte, hir eyen seyde,
" By god, my wrathe is al for-yive ! "
    ' Therwith hir liste so wel to live,
That dulnesse was of hir a-drad.
She nas to sobre ne to glad ;        880
In alle thinges more mesure
Had never, I trowe, creature.
But many oon with hir loke she herte,
And that sat hir ful lyte at herte,
For she knew no-thing of hir thoght ; 885
But whether she knew, or knew hit noght,
Algate she ne roghte of hem a stree !
To gete hir love no ner nas he
That woned at home, than he in Inde ;
The formest was alway behinde.        890
But gode folk, over al other,
She loved as man may do his brother ;
Of whiche love she was wonder large,
In skilful places that bere charge.
    ' †Which a visage had she ther-to ! 895
Allas ! myn herte is wonder wo
That I ne can discryven hit !
Me lakketh bothe English and wit
For to undo hit at the fulle ;
And eek my spirits be so dulle        900
So greet a thing for to devyse.

I have no wit that can suffyse
To comprehende[n] hir beaute ;
But thus moche dar I seyn, that she
Was †rody, fresh, and lyvely hewed ; 905
And every day hir beaute newed.
And negh hir face was alder-best ;
For certes, Nature had swich lest
To make that fair, that trewly she
Was hir cheef patron of beautee,        910
And cheef ensample of al hir werke,
And moustre ; for, be hit never so derke,
Me thinketh I see hir ever-mo.
And yet more-over, thogh alle tho
That ever lived were now a-lyve,        915
[They] ne sholde have founde to discryve
In al hir face a wikked signe ;
For hit was sad, simple, and benigne.
    ' And which a goodly softe speche
Had that swete, my lyves leche !        920
So frendly, and so wel y-grounded,
Up al resoun so wel y-founded,
And so tretable to alle gode,
That I dar swere †by the rode,
Of eloquence was never founde        925
So swete a sowninge facounde,
Ne trewer tonged, ne scorned lasse,
Ne bet coude hele ; that, by the masse
I durste swere, thogh the pope hit songe,
That ther was never †through hir tonge
Man ne woman gretly harmed ;        931
As for hir, [ther] was al harm hid ;
Ne lasse flatering in hir worde,
That purely, hir simple recorde
Was founde as trewe as any bonde,        935
Or trouthe of any mannes honde.
Ne chyde she coude never a del,
That knoweth al the world ful wel.
    ' But swich a fairnesse of a nekke
Had that swete, that boon nor brekke
Nas ther non sene, that mis-sat.        941
Hit was whyt, smothe, streght, and †flat,
Withouten hole ; †and canel-boon,
As by seming, had she noon.
Hir throte, as I have now memoire,        945
Semed a round tour of yvoire,
Of good gretnesse, and noght to grete.
    ' And gode faire WHYTE she hete,
That was my lady name right.
She was bothe fair and bright,        950
She hadde not hir name wrong.
Right faire shuldres, and body long

She hadde, and armes, every lith
Fattish, flesshy, not greet therwith;
Right whyte handes, and nayles rede, 955
Rounde brestes; and of good brede
Hir hippes were, a streight flat bak.
I knew on hir non other lak
That al hir limmes nere †sewing,
In as fer as I had knowing. 960
　'Therto she coude so wel pleye,
Whan that hir liste, that I dar seye,
That she was lyk to torche bright,
That every man may take of light
Ynogh, and hit hath never the lesse. 965
　'Of maner and of comlinesse
Right so ferde my lady dere;
For every wight of hir manere
Might cacche ynogh, if that he wolde,
If he had eyen hir to beholde. 970
For I dar †sweren, if that she
Had among ten thousand be,
She woldë have be, at the leste,
A cheef mirour of al the feste,
Thogh they had stonden in a rowe, 975
To mennes eyen that coude have knowe.
For wher-so men had pleyd or waked,
Me thoghte the felawship as naked
Withouten hir, that saw I ones,
As a coroune withoute stones. 980
Trewely she was, to myn yë,
The soleyn fenix of Arabye,
For ther liveth never but oon;
Ne swich as she ne knew I noon.
　'To speke of goodnesse; trewly she 985
Had as moche debonairte
As ever had Hester in the bible,
And more, if more were possible.
And, soth to seyne, therwith-al
She had a wit so general, 990
So hool enclyned to alle gode,
That al hir wit was set, by the rode,
Withoute malice, upon gladnesse;
†Therto I saw never yet a lesse
Harmful, than she was in doing. 995
I sey nat that she ne had knowing
What †was harm; or elles she
Had coud no good, so thinketh me.
　'And trewly, for to speke of trouthe,
But she had had, hit had be routhe. 1000
Therof she had so moche hir del—
And I dar seyn and swere hit wel—
That Trouthe him-self, over al and al,

Had chose his maner principal
In hir, that was his resting-place. 1005
Ther-to she hadde the moste grace,
To have stedfast perseveraunce,
And esy, atempre governaunce,
That ever I knew or wiste yit;
So pure suffraunt was hir wit. 1010
And reson gladly she understood,
Hit folowed wel she coude good.
She used gladly to do wel;
These were hir maners every-del.
　'Therwith she loved so wel right, 1015
She wrong do wolde to no wight;
No wight might do hir no shame,
She loved so wel hir owne name.
Hir luste to holde no wight in honde;
Ne, be thou siker, she †nolde fonde 1020
To holde no wight in balaunce,
By half word ne by countenaunce,
But-if men wolde upon hir lye;
Ne sende men in-to Walakye,
To Pruyse and in-to Tartarye, 1025
To Alisaundre, ne in-to Turkye,
And bidde him faste, anoon that he
Go hoodles †to the drye see,
And come hoom by the Carrenare;
And seye, "Sir, be now right ware 1030
That.I may of yow here seyn
Worship, or that ye come ageyn!"
She ne used no suche knakkes smale.
　'But wherfor that I telle my tale?
Right on this same, as I have seyd, 1035
Was hoolly al my love leyd;
For certes, she was, that swete wyf,
My suffisaunce, my lust, my lyf,
Myn hap, myn hele, and al my blisse,
My worldes welfare and my †lisse, 1040
And I hirs hoolly, everydel.'
　'By our lord,' quod I, 'I trowe yow wel!
Hardely, your love was wel beset,
I not how ye mighte have do bet.'
　'Bet? ne no wight so wel!' quod he. 1045
'I trowe hit, sir,' quod I, 'parde!'
'Nay, leve hit wel!' 'Sir, so do I;
I leve yow wel, that trewely
Yow thoghte, that she was the beste,
And to beholde the alderfaireste, 1050
Who so had loked †with your eyen.'
　'With myn? nay, alle that hir seyen
Seyde, and swore[n] hit was so.
And thogh they ne hadde, I wolde tho

Have loved best my lady fre, 1055
Thogh I had had al the beautep
That ever had Alcipyades,
And al the strengthe of Ercules,
And therto had the worthinesse
Of Alisaundre, and al the richesse 1060
That ever was in Babiloyne,
In Cartage, or in Macedoyne,
Or in Rome, or in Ninive;
And therto al-so hardy be
As was Ector, so have I joye, 1065
That Achilles slow at Troye—
And therfor was he slayn also
In a temple, for bothe two
Were slayn, he and †Antilogus,
And so seyth Dares Frigius, 1070
For love of [hir] Polixena—
Or been as wys as Minerva,
I wolde ever, withoute drede,
Have loved hir, for I moste nede!
"Nede!" nay, †I gabbe now, 1075
Noght "nede," and I wol telle how,
For of good wille myn herte hit wolde,
And eek to love hir I was holde
As for the fairest and the beste.
　'She was as good, so have I reste, 1080
As ever was Penelope of Grece,
Or as the noble wyf Lucrece,
That was the beste—he telleth thus,
The Romain Tytus Livius—
She was as good, and no-thing lyke, 1085
Thogh hir stories be autentyke;
Algate she was as trewe as she.
　'But wherfor that I telle thee
Whan I first my lady sey?
I was right yong, [the] sooth to sey, 1090
And ful gret need I hadde to lerne;
Whan my herte wolde yerne
To love, it was a greet empryse.
But as my wit coude best suffyse,
After my yonge childly wit, 1095
Withoute drede, I besette hit
To love hir in my beste wyse,
To do hir worship and servyse
That I †tho coude, by my trouthe,
Withoute feyning outher slouthe; 1100
For wonder fayn I wolde hir see.
So mochel hit amended me,
That, whan I saw hir first a-morwe,
I was warished of al my sorwe
Of al day after, til hit were eve; 1105

Me thoghte no-thing mighte me greve,
Were my sorwes never so smerte.
And yit she sit so in myn herte,
That, by my trouthe, I nolde noght,
For al this worlde, out of my thoght 1110
Leve my lady; no, trewly!'
　'Now, by my trouthe, sir,' quod I,
'Me thinketh ye have such a chaunce
As shrift withoute repentaunce.'
　'Repentaunce! nay fy,' quod he; 1115
'Shulde I now repente me
To love? nay, certes, than were I wel
Wers than was Achitofel,
Or Anthenor, so have I joye,
The traytour that betraysed Troye, 1120
Or the false Genelon,
He that purchased the treson
Of Rowland and of Olivere.
Nay, whyl I am a-lyve here
I nil foryete hir never-mo.' 1125
　'Now, gode sir,' quod I [right] tho,
'Ye han wel told me her-before.
It is no need reherse hit more
How ye sawe hir first, and where;
But wolde ye telle me the manere, 1130
To hir which was your firste speche—
Therof I wolde yow be-seche—
And how she knewë first your thoght,
Whether ye loved hir or noght,
And telleth me eek what ye have lore; 
I herde yow telle her-before.' 1136
　'Ye,' seyde he, 'thou nost what thou
　　menest;
I have lost more than thou wenest.'
　'What los is that, [sir]?' quod I tho;
'Nil she not love yow? is hit so? 1140
Or have ye oght [y-]doon amis,
That she hath left yow? is hit this?
For goddes love, tel me al.'
　'Before god,' quod he, 'and I shal.
I saye right as I have seyd, 1145
On hir was al my love leyd;
And yet she niste hit †never a del
Noght longe tyme, leve hit wel.
For be right siker, I durste noght 1149
For al this worlde telle hir my thoght,
Ne I wolde have wratthed hir, trewly.
For wostow why? she was lady
Of the body; she had the herte,
And who hath that, may not asterte.
　'But, for to kepe me fro ydelnesse, 1155

Trewly I did my besinesse
To make songes, as I best coude,
And ofte tyme I song hem loude ;
And made songes a gret del,
Al-thogh I coude not make so wel     1160
Songes, ne knowe the art al,
As coude Lamekes sone Tubal,
That fond out first the art of songe ;
For, as his brothers hamers ronge
Upon his anvelt up and doun,     1165
Therof he took the firste soun ;
But Grekes seyn, Pictagoras,
That he the firste finder was
Of the art ; Aurora telleth so,
But therof no fors, of hem two.     1170
Algates songes thus I made
Of my feling, myn herte to glade ;
And lo ! this was [the] alther-firste,
I not wher [that] hit were the werste.—
¶ "Lord, hit maketh myn herte light,
Whan I thenke on that swete wight  1176
   That is so semely on to see ;
   And wisshe to god hit might so be,
That she wolde holde me for hir knight,
My lady, that is so fair and bright ! "—
   'Now have I told thee, sooth to saye,
My firste song.   Upon a daye     1182
I bethoghte me what wo
And sorwe that I suffred tho
For hir, and yet she wiste hit noght, 1185
Ne telle hir durste I nat my thoght.
"Allas !" thoghte I, " I can no reed ;
And, but I telle hir, I †nam but deed ;
And if I telle hir, to seye †sooth,
I am a-dred she wol be wrooth ;     1190
Allas ! what shal I thanne do ?"
   'In this debat I was so wo,
Me thoghte myn herte braste a-tweyn !
So atte laste, soth to seyn,
I me bethoghte that nature     1195
Ne formed never in creature
So moche beaute, trewely,
And bounte, withouten mercy.
   'In hope of that, my tale I tolde
With sorwe, as that I never sholde,     1200
For nedes ; and, maugree my heed,
I moste have told hir or be deed.
I not wel how that I began,
Ful evel reherse[n] hit I can ;
And eek, as helpe me god with-al,     1205
I trowe hit was in the dismal,

That was the ten woundes of Egipte ;
For many a word I over-skipte
In my tale, for pure fere
Lest my wordes mis-set were.     1210
With sorweful herte, and woundes dede,
Softe and quaking for pure drede
And shame, and stinting in my tale
For ferde, and myn hewe al pale,
Ful ofte I wex bothe pale and reed ;  1215
Bowing to hir, I heng the heed ;
I durste nat ones loke hir on,
For wit, manere, and al was gon.
I seyde "mercy !" and no more ;
Hit nas no game, hit sat me sore     1220
   'So atte laste, sooth to seyn,
Whan that myn herte was come ageyn,
To telle shortly al my speche,
With hool herte I gan hir beseche
That she wolde be my lady swete ;     1225
And swor, and gan hir hertely hete
Ever to be stedfast and trewe,
And love hir alwey freshly newe,
And never other lady have,
And al hir worship for to save     1230
As I best coude ; I swor hir this—
" For youres is al that ever ther is
For evermore, myn herte swete !
And never †false yow, but I mete,
I nil, as wis god helpe me so ! "     1235
   'And whan I had my tale y-do,
God wot, she acounted nat a stree
Of al my tale, so thoghte me.
To telle shortly †as hit is,
Trewly hir answere, hit was this ;     1240
I can not now wel counterfete
Hir wordes, but this was the grete
Of hir answere ; she sayde, "nay"
Al-outerly.   Allas ! that day
The sorwe I suffred, and the wo !     1245
That trewly Cassandra, that so
Bewayled the destruccioun
Of Troye and of Ilioun,
Had never swich sorwe as I tho.
I durste no more say therto     1250
For pure fere, but stal away ;
And thus I lived ful many a day :
That trewely, I hadde no need
Ferther than my beddes heed
Never a day to seche sorwe ;     1255
I fond hit redy every morwe,
For-why I loved hir in no gere.

'So hit befel, another yere,
I thoughte ones I wolde fonde
To do hir knowe and understonde   1260
My wo ; and she wel understood
That I ne wilned thing but good,
And worship, and to kepe hir name
Over †al thing, and drede hir shame,
And was so besy hir to serve ;—  1265
And pite were I shulde sterve,
Sith that I wilned noon harm, y-wis.
So whan my lady knew al this,
My lady yaf me al hoolly
The noble yift of hir mercy,  1270
Saving hir worship, by al weyes ;
Dredles, I mene noon other weyes.
And therwith she yaf me a ring ;
I trowe hit was the firste thing ;
But if myn herte was y-waxe  1275
Glad, that is no need to axe !
As helpe me god, I was as blyve,
Reysed, as fro dethe to lyve,
Of alle happes the alder-beste,
The gladdest and the moste at reste.  1280
For trewely, that swete wight,
Whan I had wrong and she the right,
She wolde alwey so goodely
For-yeve me so debonairly.
In alle my youthe, in alle chaunce,  1285
She took me in hir governaunce.

  'Therwith she was alway so trewe,
Our joye was ever y-liche newe ;
Our hertes wern so even a payre,
That never nas that oon contrayre  1290
To that other, for no wo.
For sothe, y-liche they suffred tho
Oo blisse and eek oo sorwe bothe ;
Y-liche they were bothe gladde and
    wrothe ;
Al was us oon, withoute were.  1295
And thus we lived ful many a yere

So wel, I can nat telle how.'
  'Sir,' quod I, ' wher is she now?'
'Now !' quod he, and stinte anoon.
  Therwith he wex as deed as stoon,  1300
And seyde, ' allas ! that I was bore !
That was the los, that her-before
I tolde thee, that I had lorn.
Bethenk how I seyde her-beforn,  1304
"Thou wost ful litel what thou menest ;
I have lost more than thou wenest "—
God wot, allas ! right that was she !'
  ' Allas ! sir, how ? what may that be ?'
'She is deed !' ' Nay !' ' Yis, by my
    trouthe !'
' Is that your los ? by god, hit is routhe !'
  And with that worde, right anoon,  1311
They gan to strake forth ; al was doon,
For that tyme, the hert-hunting.
  With that, me thoghte, that this king
Gan [quikly] hoomward for to ryde  1315
Unto a place †ther besyde,
Which was from us but a lyte,
A long castel with walles whyte,
By seynt Johan ! on a riche hil,
As me mette ; but thus it fil.  1320
  Right thus me mette, as I yow telle,
That in the castel †was a belle,
As hit had smiten houres twelve.—

  Therwith I awook my-selve,
And fond me lying in my bed ;  1325
And the book that I had red,
Of Alcyone and Seys the king,
And of the goddes of sleping,
I fond it in myn honde ful even.
  Thoghte I, ' this is so queynt a sweven,
That I wol, by processe of tyme,  1331
Fonde to putte this sweven in ryme
As I can best ; and that anoon.'—
This was my sweven ; now hit is doon.  1334

**Explicit the Boke of the Duchesse.**

# IV. THE COMPLEYNT OF MARS.

### The Proem.

'GLADETH, ye foules, of the morow gray,
Lo! Venus risen among yon rowes rede!
And floures fresshe, honoureth ye this
   day ;
For when the sonne uprist, then wol ye
   sprede.
But ye lovers, that lye in any drede,    5
Fleëth, lest wikked tonges yow espye ;
Lo! yond the sonne, the candel of jelosye!

With teres blewe, and with a wounded
   herte
Taketh your leve ; and, with seynt John
   to borow,
Apeseth somwhat of your sorowes smerte,
Tyme cometh eft, that cese shal your
   sorow ;    11
The glade night is worth an hevy
   morow !'—
(Seynt Valentyne! a foul thus herde I
   singe
Upon thy day, er sonne gan up-springe).—

Yet sang this foul—'I rede yow al a-wake,
And ye, that han not chosen in humble
   wyse,    16
Without repenting cheseth yow your
   make.
And ye, that han ful chosen as I devyse,
Yet at the leste renoveleth your servyse ;
Confermeth it perpetuely to dure,    20
And paciently taketh your aventure.

And for the worship of this hye feste,
Yet wol I, in my briddes wyse, singe
The sentence of the compleynt, at the
   leste,
That woful Mars made atte departinge  25
Fro fresshe Venus in a morweninge,
Whan Phebus, with his fyry torches rede,
Ransaked every lover in his drede.

### The Story.

¶ Whylom the thridde hevenes lord
   above,
As wel by hevenish revolucioun    30

As by desert, hath wonne Venus his love,
And she hath take him in subjeccioun,
And as a maistresse taught him his
   lessoun,
Comaunding him that never, in hir ser-
   vyse,
He nere so bold no lover to despyse.    35

For she forbad him jelosye at alle,
And cruelte, and bost, and tirannye ;
She made him at hir lust so humble and
   talle,
That when hir deyned caste on him hir yë,
He took in pacience to live or dye ;    40
And thus she brydeleth him in hir man-
   ere,
With no-thing but with scourging of hir
   chere.

Who regneth now in blisse but Venus,
That hath this worthy knight in govern-
   aunce ?
Who singeth now but Mars, that serveth
   thus    45
The faire Venus, causer of plesaunce ?
He bynt him to perpetual obeisaunce,
And she bynt hir to loven him for ever,
But so be that his trespas hit dissever.

Thus be they knit, and regnen as in heven
By loking most ; til hit fil, on a tyde,   51
That by hir bothe assent was set a steven,
That Mars shal entre, as faste as he may
   glyde,
Into hir nexte paleys, to abyde,
Walking his cours til she had him a-take,
And he preyde hir to haste hir for his
   sake.    56

Then seyde he thus—"myn hertes lady
   swete,
Ye knowe wel my mischef in that place ;
For sikerly, til that I with yow mete,   59
My lyf stant ther in aventure and grace ;
But when I see the beaute of your face,
Ther is no dreed of deeth may do me
   smerte,
For al your lust is ese to myn herte."

E

She hath so gret compassion of hir knight,
That dwelleth in solitude til she come ; 65
For hit stood so, that ilke tyme, no wight
Counseyled him, ne seyde to him welcome,
That nigh hir wit for wo was overcome ;
Wherfore she spedde hir as faste in hir weye,
Almost in oon day, as he dide in tweye. 70

The grete joye that was betwix hem two,
Whan they be met, ther may no tunge telle,
Ther is no more, but unto bed they go,
And thus in joye and blisse I lete hem dwelle ;
This worthy Mars, that is of knighthod welle, 75
The flour of fairnes lappeth in his armes,
And Venus kisseth Mars, the god of armes.

Sojourned hath this Mars, of which I rede,
In chambre amid the paleys prively
A certeyn tyme, til him fel a drede, 80
Through Phebus, that was comen hastely
Within the paleys-yates sturdely,
With torche in honde, of which the stremes brighte
On Venus chambre knokkeden ful lighte.

The chambre, ther as lay this fresshe quene, 85
Depeynted was with whyte boles grete,
And by the light she knew, that shoon so shene,
That Phebus cam to brenne hem with his hete ;
This sely Venus, †dreynt in teres wete,
Enbraceth Mars, and seyde, "alas! I dye!
The torch is come, that al this world wol wrye." 91

Up sterte Mars, him liste not to slepe,
Whan he his lady herde so compleyne ;
But, for his nature was not for to wepe,
In stede of teres, fro his eyen tweyne 95
The fyry sparkes brosten out for peyne ;
And hente his hauberk, that lay him besyde ;
Flee wolde he not, ne mighte him-selven hyde.

He throweth on his helm of huge wighte,
And girt him with his swerde ; and in his honde 100

His mighty spere, as he was wont to fighte,
He shaketh so that almost it to-wonde ;
Ful hevy he was to walken over londe ;
He may not holde with Venus companye,
But bad hir fleen, lest Phebus hir espye.

O woful Mars! alas! what mayst thou seyn, 106
That in the paleys of thy disturbaunce
Art left behinde, in peril to be sleyn ?
And yet ther-to is double thy penaunce,
For she, that hath thyn herte in governaunce, 110
Is passed halfe the stremes of thyn yën ;
That thou nere swift, wel mayst thou wepe and cryen.

Now fleeth Venus un-to Cylenius tour,
With voide cours, for fere of Phebus light.
Alas ! and ther ne hath she no socour, 115
For she ne fond ne saw no maner wight ;
And eek as ther she had but litil might ;
Wher-for, hir-selven for to hyde and save,
Within the gate she fledde into a cave.

Derk was this cave, and smoking as the helle, 120
Not but two pas within the gate hit stood ;
A naturel day in derk I lete hir dwelle.
Now wol I speke of Mars, furious and wood ;
For sorow he wolde have seen his herte blood ;
Sith that he mighte †hir don no companye, 125
He ne roghte not a myte for to dye.

So feble he wex, for hete and for his wo,
That nigh he swelt, he mighte unnethe endure ;
He passeth but oo steyre in dayes two,
But ner the les, for al his hevy armure, 130
He foloweth hir that is his lyves cure ;
For whos departing he took gretter yre
Thanne for al his brenning in the fyre.

After he walketh softely a pas,
Compleyning, that hit pite was to here. 135
He seyde, "O lady bright, Venus ! alas !
That ever so wyde a compas is my spere !
Alas ! whan shal I mete yow, herte dere,
This twelfte day of April I endure,
Through jelous Phebus, this misaventure."

Now †helpe god sely Venus allone!  141
But, as god wolde, hit happed for to be,
That, whyl that Venus weping made hir
   mone,
Cylenius, ryding in his chevauchè,  144
Fro Venus valance mighte his paleys see,
And Venus he salueth, and maketh chere,
And hir receyveth as his frend ful dere.

Mars dwelleth forth in his adversitee,
Compleyning ever on hir departinge;
And what his compleynt was, remem-
   breth me;  150
And therfore, in this lusty morweninge,
As I best can, I wol hit seyn and singe,
And after that I wol my leve take;
And god yeve every wight joye of his
   make!

## The Compleynt of Mars.

### *The Proem of the Compleynt.*

¶ The ordre of compleynt requireth skil-
   fully,  155
That if a wight shal pleyne pitously,
  Ther mot be cause wherfor that men
   pleyne;
Or men may deme he pleyneth folily
And causeles; alas! that am not I!
  Wherfor the ground and cause of al
   my peyne,  160
  So as my troubled wit may hit ateyne,
I wol reherse; not for to have redresse,
But to declare my ground of hevinesse.

### *Devotion.*

¶ The firste tyme, alas! that I was wroght,
And for certeyn effectes hider broght 165
  By him that lordeth ech intelligence,
I yaf my trewe servise and my thoght,
For evermore—how dere I have hit
   boght!—
  To hir, that is of so gret excellence,
  That what wight that first sheweth his
   presence,  170
When she is wroth and taketh of him no
   cure,
He may not longe in joye of love endure.

This is no feyned mater that I telle;
My lady is the verrey sours and welle

Of beaute, lust, fredom, and gentil-
   nesse,  175
Of riche aray—how dere men hit selle!—
Of al disport in which men frendly dwelle,
  Of love and pley, and of benigne hum-
   blesse,
Of soune of instruments of al swetnesse;
And therto so wel fortuned and thewed,
That through the world hir goodnesse is
   y-shewed.  181

What wonder is then, thogh that I be-
   sette
My servise on suche oon, that may me
   knette
  To wele or wo, sith hit lyth in hir
   might?  184
Therfor my herte for ever I to hir hette;
Ne trewly, for my dethe, I shal not lette
  To ben hir trewest servaunt and hir
   knight.
  I flater noght, that may wite every
   wight;
For this day in hir servise shal I dye;
But grace be, I see hir never with yë.  190

### *A Lady in fear and woe.*

¶ To whom shal I than pleyne of my dis-
   tresse?
Who may me helpe, who may my harm
   redresse?
  Shal I compleyne unto my lady free?
Nay, certes! for she hath such hevinesse,
For fere and eek for wo, that, as I gesse,·
  In litil tyme hit wol hir bane be.  196
  But were she sauf, hit wer no fors of me.
Alas! that ever lovers mote endure,
For love, so many a perilous aventure!

For thogh so be that lovers be as trewe 200
As any metal that is forged newe,
  In many a cas hem tydeth ofte sorowe.
Somtyme hir ladies will not on hem rewe;
Somtyme, yif that jelosye hit knewe,
  They mighten lightly leye hir heed to
   borowe;  205
  Somtyme envyous folke with tunges
   horowe
Depraven hem; alas! whom may they
   plese?
But he be fals, no lover hath his ese.

But what availeth suche a long sermoun
Of aventures of lovë, up and doun ?    210
  I wol returne and speken of my peyne ;
The point is this of my destruccioun,
My righte lady, my salvacioun,
  Is in affray, and not to whom to pleyne.
O herte swete, O lady sovereyne !    215
For your disese, wel oghte I swoune and
  swelte,
Thogh I non other harm ne drede felte.

### Instability of Happiness.

¶ To what fyn made the god that sit so
  hye,
Benethen him, love other companye,
  And streyneth folk to love, malgre hir
  hede ?    220
And then hir joye, for oght I can espye,
Ne lasteth not the twinkeling of an yë,
  And somme han never joye til they be
  dede.
  What meneth this ? what is this misti-
  hede ?
Wherto constreyneth he his folk so faste
Thing to desyre, but hit shulde laste ?    226

And thogh he made a lover love a thing,
And maketh hit seme stedfast and during,
  Yet putteth he in hit such misaventure,
That reste nis ther noon in his yeving. 230
And that is wonder, that so just a king
  Doth such hardnesse to his creature.
  Thus, whether love breke or elles dure,
Algates he that hath with love to done
Hath ofter wo then changed is the mone.

Hit semeth he hath to lovers enmite,    236
And lyk a fissher, as men alday may see,
  Baiteth his angle-hook with som ples-
  aunce,
Til mony a fish is wood til that he be 239
Sesed ther-with ; and then at erst hath he
  Al his desyr, and ther-with al mis-
  chaunce ;
  And thogh the lyne breke, he hath
  penaunce ;
For with the hoke he wounded is so sore,
That he his wages hath for ever-more.

### The Brooch of Thebes.

¶ The broche of Thebes was of suche a
  kinde,    245
So ful of rubies and of stones Inde,

That every wight, that sette on hit an
  yë,
He wende anon to worthe out of his
  minde ;
So sore the beaute wolde his herte binde,
  Til he hit hadde, him thoghte he moste
  dye ;    250
  And whan that hit was his, than shulde
  he drye
Such wo for drede, ay whyl that he hit
  hadde,
That welnigh for the fere he shulde
  madde.

And whan hit was fro his possessioun,
Than had he double wo and passioun  255
  For he so fair a tresor had forgo ;
But yet this broche, as in conclusioun,
Was not the cause of this confusioun ;
  But he that wroghte hit enfortuned hit
  so,
  That every wight that had hit shuld
  have wo ;    •    260
And therfor in the worcher was the vyce,
And in the covetour that was so nyce.

So fareth hit by lovers and by me ;
For thogh my lady have so gret beautè,
  That I was mad til I had gete hir
  grace,    265
She was not cause of myn adversitee,
But he that wroghte hir, also mot I
  thee,
  That putte suche a beaute in hir face,
  That made me to covete and purchace
Myn owne deth ; him wyte I that I
  dye,    270
And myn unwit, that ever I clomb so
  hye

### An Appeal for Sympathy.

¶ But to yow, hardy knightes of renoun,
Sin that ye be of my divisioun,
  Al be I not worthy †so grete a name,
Yet, seyn these clerkes, I am your pa-
  troun ;    275
Ther-for ye oghte have som compassioun
  Of my disese, and take it noght a-game.
  The proudest of yow may be mad ful
  tame ;
Wherfor I prey yow, of your gentilesse,
That ye compleyne for myn hevinesse. 280

And ye, my ladies, that ben trewe and
    stable,
By way of kinde, ye oghten to be able
    To have pite of folk that be in peyne :
Now have ye cause to clothe yow in sable ;
Sith that your emperice, the honorable,
    Is desolat, wel oghte ye to pleyne ; 286
    Now shuld your holy teres falle and
    reyne.
Alas ! your honour and your emperice,
Nigh deed for drede, ne can hir not
    chevise.

Compleyneth eek, ye lovers, al in-fere, 290
For hir that, with unfeyned humble chere,
    Was ever redy to do yow socour ;
Compleyneth hir that ever hath had yow
    dere ;
Compleyneth beaute, fredom, and manere;
    Compleyneth hir that endeth your la-
    bour ;                 295
    Compleyneth thilke ensample of al
    honour,
That never dide but al gentilesse ;   297
Kytheth therfor on hir som kindenesse.'

# V. THE PARLEMENT OF FOULES.

### *The Proem.*

THE lyf so short, the craft so long to lerne,
Th'assay so hard, so sharp the conquering,
The dredful joye, that alwey slit so yerne,
Al this mene I by love, that my feling  4
Astonyeth with his wonderful worching
So sore y-wis, that whan I on him thinke,
Nat wot I wel wher that I wake or winke.

For al be that I knowe not love in dede,
Ne wot how that he quyteth folk hir hyre,
Yet happeth me ful ofte in bokes rede  10
Of his miracles, and his cruel yre ;  ·
Ther rede I wel he wol be lord and syre,
I dar not seyn, his strokes been so sore,
But god save swich a lord ! I can no
    more.

Of usage, what for luste what for lore,  15
On bokes rede I ofte, as I yow tolde.
But wherfor that I speke al this? not yore
Agon, hit happed me for to beholde
Upon a boke, was write with lettres olde ;
And ther-upon, a certeyn thing to lerne,20
The longe day ful faste I radde and yerne.

For out of olde feldes, as men seith,
Cometh al this newe corn fro yeer to yere ;
And out of olde bokes, in good feith,
Cometh al this newe science that men
    lere.                      25

But now to purpos as of this matere—
To rede forth hit gan me so delyte,
That al the day me thoughte but a lyte.

This book of which I make mencioun,
Entitled was al thus, as I shal telle,  30
' Tullius of the dreme of Scipioun ' ;
Chapitres seven hit hadde, of hevene and
    helle,
And erthe, and soules that therinne
    dwelle,
Of whiche, as shortly as I can hit trete, 34
Of his sentence I wol you seyn the grete.

First telleth hit, whan Scipioun was come
In Afrik, how he mette Massinisse,
That him for joye in armes hath y-nome.
Than telleth †hit hir speche and al the
    blisse
That was betwix hem, til the day gan
    misse ;                40
And how his auncestre, African so dere,
Gan in his slepe that night to him appere.

Than telleth hit that, fro a sterry place,
How African hath him Cartage shewed,
And warned him before of al his grace, 45
And seyde him, what man, lered other
    lewed,
That loveth comun profit, wel y-thewed,
He shal unto a blisful place wende,
Ther as joye is that last withouten ende.

Than asked he, if folk that heer be dede
Have lyf and dwelling in another place; 51
And African seyde, ' ye, withoute drede,'
And that our present worldes lyves space
Nis but a maner deth, what wey we trace,
And rightful folk shal go, after they dye,
To heven; and shewed him the galaxye. 56

Than shewed he him the litel erthe, that
heer is,
At regard of the hevenes quantite ;
And after shewed he him the nyne speres,
And after that the melodye herde he 60
That cometh of thilke speres thryes three,
That welle is of musyke and melodye
In this world heer, and cause of armonye.

Than bad he him, sin erthe was so lyte,
And ful of torment and of harde grace, 65
That he ne shulde him in the world
delyte.
Than tolde he him, in certeyn yeres space,
That every sterre shulde come into his
place
Ther hit was first ; and al shulde out of
minde 69
That in this worlde is don of al mankinde.

Than prayde him Scipioun to telle him al
The wey to come un-to that hevene blisse ;
And he seyde, ' know thy-self first im-
mortal,
And loke ay besily thou werke and wisse
To comun profit, and thou shalt nat misse
To comen swiftly to that place dere, 76
That ful of blisse is and of soules clere.

But brekers of the lawe, soth to seyne,
And lecherous folk, after that they be
dede, 79
Shul alwey whirle aboute th'erthe in peyne,
Til many a world be passed, out of drede,
And than, for-yeven alle hir wikked dede,
Than shul they come unto that blisful
place,
To which to comen god thee sende his
grace ! '—

The day gan failen, and the derke night,
That reveth bestes from hir besinesse, 86
Berafte me my book for lakke of light,
And to my bedde I gan me for to dresse,
Fulfild of thought and besy hevinesse ;

For bothe I hadde thing which that I
nolde, 90
And eek I ne hadde that thing that I
wolde.

But fynally my spirit, at the laste,
For-wery of my labour al the day,
Took rest, that made me to slepe faste,
And in my slepe I mette, as I lay, 95
How African, right in that selfe aray
That Scipioun him saw before that
tyde,
Was comen, and stood right at my beddes
syde.

The wery hunter, slepinge in his bed,
To wode ayein his minde goth anoon ; 100
The juge dremeth how his plees ben
sped ;
The carter dremeth how his cartes goon ;
The riche, of gold ; the knight fight with
his foon,
The seke met he drinketh of the tonne ;
The lover met he hath his lady wonne. 105

Can I nat seyn if that the cause were
For I had red of African beforn,
That made me to mete that he stood
there ;
But thus seyde he, ' thou hast thee so
wel born
In loking of myn olde book to-torn, 110
Of which Macrobie roghte nat a lyte,
That somdel of thy labour wolde I
quyte ! '—

Citherea ! thou blisful lady swete,
That with thy fyr-brand dauntest whom
thee lest,
And madest me this sweven for to mete,
Be thou my help in this, for thou mayst
best ; 116
As wisly as I saw thee north-north-west,
When I began my sweven for to wryte,
So yif me might to ryme hit and endyte !

### The Story.

This forseid African me hente anoon, 120
And forth with him unto a gate broghte
Right of a parke, walled with grene stoon;
And over the gate, with lettres large
y-wroghte,
Ther weren vers y-writen, as me thoghte,

On eyther halfe, of ful gret difference, 125
Of which I shal yow sey the pleyn sentence.

'Thorgh me men goon in-to that blisful
   place
Of hertes hele and dedly woundes cure ;
Thorgh me men goon unto the welle of
   Grace,
Ther grene and lusty May shal ever
   endure ;         130
This is the wey to al good aventure ;
Be glad, thou reder, and thy sorwe of-
   caste,
Al open am I ; passe in, and hy the
   faste !'

'Thorgh me men goon,' than spak that
   other syde,
'Unto the mortal strokes of the spere, 135
Of which Disdayn and Daunger is the
   gyde,
Ther tree shal never fruit ne leves bere.
This streem you ledeth to the sorwful
   were,
Ther as the fish in prison is al drye ;
Th'eschewing is only the remedye.'   140

Thise vers of gold and blak y-writen were,
The whiche I gan a stounde to beholde,
For with that oon encresed ay my fere,
And with that other gan myn herte bolde ;
That oon me hette, that other did me
   colde,         145
No wit had I, for errour, for to chese,
To entre or flee, or me to save or lese.

Right as, betwixen adamauntes two
Of even might, a pece of iren y-set,  149
That hath no might to meve to ne fro—
For what that on may hale, that other
   let—
Ferde I, that niste whether me was bet,
To entre or leve, til African my gyde
Me hente, and shoof in at the gates
   wyde,

And seyde, 'hit stondeth writen in thy
   face,         155
Thyn errour, though thou telle it not to
   me ;
But dred thee nat to come in-to this
   place,

For this wryting is no-thing ment by
   thee,
Ne by noon, but he Loves servant be ;
For thou of love hast lost thy tast, I
   gesse,         160
As seek man hath of swete and bitternesse.

But natheles, al-though that thou be
   dulle,
Yit that thou canst not do, yit mayst
   thou see ;
For many a man that may not stonde
   a pulle,
Yit lyketh him at the wrastling for
   to be,         165
And demeth yit wher he do bet or he ;
And if thou haddest cunning for t'endyte,
I shal thee shewen mater of to wryte.'

With that my hond in his he took anoon,
Of which I comfort caughte, and wente
   in faste ;         170
But lord ! so I was glad and wel begoon !
For over-al, wher that I myn eyen caste,
Were trees clad with leves that ay shal
   laste,
Eche in his kinde, of colour fresh and
   grene
As emeraude, that joye was to sene.  175

The bilder ook, and eek the hardy asshe ;
The piler elm, the cofre unto careyne ;
The boxtree piper ; holm to whippes
   lasshe ;
The sayling firr ; the cipres, deth to
   pleyne ;         179
The sheter ew, the asp for shaftes pleyne ;
The olyve of pees, and eek the drunken
   vyne,
The victor palm, the laurer to devyne.

A garden saw I, ful of blosmy bowes,
Upon a river, in a grene mede,    184
Ther as that swetnesse evermore y-now is,
With floures whyte, blewe, yelowe, and
   rede ;
And colde welle-stremes, no-thing dede,
That swommen ful of smale fisshes lighte,
With finnes rede and scales silver-brighte.

On every bough the briddes herde I singe,
With voys of aungel in hir armonye, 191

Som besyed hem hir briddes forth to
 bringe ;
The litel conyes to hir pley gunne hye,
And further al aboute I gan espye
The dredful roo, the buk, the hert and
 hinde, 195
Squerels, and bestes smale of gentil kinde.

Of instruments of strenges in acord
Herde I so pleye a ravisshing swetnesse,
That god, that maker is of al and lord,
Ne herde never better, as I gesse ; 200
Therwith a wind, unnethe hit might be
 lesse,
Made in the leves grene a noise softe
Acordant to the foules songe on-lofte.

The air of that place so attempre was
That never was grevaunce of hoot ne
 cold ; 205
Ther wex eek every holsom spyce and
 gras,
Ne no man may ther wexe seek ne old ;
Yet was ther joye more a thousand fold
Then man can telle ; ne never wolde it
 nighte,
But ay cleer day to any mannes sighte.

Under a tree, besyde a welle, I say 211
Cupyde our lord his arwes forge and fyle ;
And at his fete his bowe al redy lay,
And wel his doghter tempred al the whyle
The hedes in the welle, and with hir
 wyle 215
She couched hem after as they shulde
 serve,
Som for to slee, and som to wounde and
 kerve.

Tho was I war of Plesaunce anon-right,
And of Aray, and Lust, and Curtesye ;
And of the Craft that can and hath the
 might 220
To doon by force a wight to do folye—
Disfigurat was she, I nil not lye ;
And by him-self, under an oke, I gesse,
Sawe I Delyt, that stood with Gentil-
 nesse.

I saw Beautee, withouten any atyr, 225
And Youthe, ful of game and Iolyte,
Fool-hardinesse, Flatery, and Desyr,
Messagerye, and Mede, and other three—
Hir names shul noght here be told for me—

And upon pilers grete of jasper longe 230
I saw a temple of bras y-founded stronge.

Aboute the temple daunceden alway
Wommen y-nowe, of whiche somme ther
 were
Faire of hem-self, and somme of hem
 were gay ;
In kirtels, al disshevele, wente they
 there— 235
That was hir office alwey, yeer by yere—
And on the temple, of doves whyte and
 faire
Saw I sittinge many a hundred paire

Before the temple-dore ful soberly
Dame Pees sat, with a curteyn in hir
 hond : 240
And hir besyde, wonder discretly,
Dame Pacience sitting ther I fond
With face pale, upon an hille of sond ;
And alder-next, within and eek with-
 oute, 244
Behest and Art, and of hir folke a route.

Within the temple, of syghes hote as fyr
I herde a swogh that gan aboute renne ;
Which syghes were engendred with desyr,
That maden every auter for to brenne
Of newe flaume ; and wel aspyed I thenne
That al the cause of sorwes that they
 drye 251
Com of the bitter goddesse Jalousye.

The god Priapus saw I, as I wente,
Within the temple, in soverayn place
 stonde,
In swich aray as whan the asse him
 shente 255
With crye by night, and with his ceptre
 in honde ;
Ful besily men gunne assaye and fonde
Upon his hede to sette, of sondry hewe,
Garlondes ful of fresshe floures newe.

And in a privee corner, in disporte, 260
Fond I Venus and hir porter Richesse,
That was ful noble and hauteyn of hir
 porte ;
Derk was that place, but afterward light-
 nesse
I saw a lyte, unnethe hit might be lesse,
And on a bed of golde she lay to reste, 265
Til that the hote sonne gan to weste.

Hir gilte heres with a golden threde
Y-bounden were, untressed as she lay,
And naked fro the breste unto the hede
Men might hir see; and, sothly for to
    say, 270
The remenant wel kevered to my pay
Right with a subtil kerchef of Valence,
Ther was no thikker cloth of no de-
    fence.

The place yaf a thousand savours swote,
And Bachus, god of wyn, sat hir besyde,
And Ceres next, that doth of hunger
    bote; 276
And, as I seide, amiddes lay Cipryde,
To whom on knees two yonge folkes
    cryde
To ben hir help; but thus I leet hir lye,
And ferther in the temple I gan espye

That, in dispyte of Diane the chaste, 281
Ful many a bowe y-broke heng on the
    wal
Of maydens, suche as gunne hir tymes
    waste
In hir servyse; and peynted over al
Of many a story, of which I touche shal
A fewe, as of Calixte and Athalaunte, 286
And many a mayde, of which the name I
    wante;

Semyramus, Candace, and Ercules,
Biblis, Dido, Tisbe and Piramus,
Tristram, Isoude, Paris, and Achilles, 290
Eleyne, Cleopatre, and Troilus,
Silla, and eek the moder of Romulus—
Alle these were peynted on that other
    syde,
And al hir love, and in what plyte they
    dyde.

Whan I was come ayen into the place 295
That I of spak, that was so swote and
    grene,
Forth welk I tho, my-selven to solace.
Tho was I war wher that ther sat a
    quene
That, as of light the somer-sonne shene
Passeth the sterre, right so over mesure
She fairer was than any creature. 301

And in a launde, upon an hille of floures,
Was set this noble goddesse Nature;

Of braunches were hir halles and hir
    boures,
Y-wrought after hir craft and hir mesure;
Ne ther nas foul that cometh of en-
    gendrure, 306
That they ne were prest in hir presence,
To take hir doom and yeve hir audience.

For this was on seynt Valentynes day,
Whan every foul cometh ther to chese
    his make, 310
Of every kinde, that men thenke may;
And that so huge a noyse gan they
    make,
That erthe and see, and tree, and every
    lake
So ful was, that unnethe was ther space
For me to stonde, so ful was al the place.

And right as Aleyn, in the Pleynt of
    Kinde, 316
Devyseth Nature of aray and face,
In swich aray men mighte[n] hir ther
    finde.
This noble emperesse, ful of grace,
Bad every foul to take his owne place, 320
As they were wont alwey fro yeer to
    yere,
Seynt Valentynes day, to stonden there.

That is to sey, the foules of ravyne
Were hyest set; and than the foules
    smale,
That eten as hem nature wolde enclyne,
As worm, or thing of whiche I telle no
    tale; 326
But water-foul sat lowest in the dale;
And foul that liveth by seed sat on the
    grene,
And that so fele, that wonder was to
    sene.

Ther mighte men the royal egle finde,
That with his sharpe look perceth the
    sonne; 331
And other egles of a lower kinde,
Of which that clerkes wel devysen conne.
Ther was the tyraunt with his fethres
    donne
And greye, I mene the goshauk, that
    doth pyne 335
To briddes for his outrageous ravyne.

The gentil faucon, that with his feet distreyneth
The kinges hond ; the hardy sperhauk eke,
The quayles foo ; the merlion that peyneth
Him-self ful ofte, the larke for to seke ;
Ther was the douve, with hir eyen meke ;     341
The jalous swan, ayens his deth that singeth ;
The oule eek, that of dethe the bode bringeth ;

The crane the geaunt, with his trompes soune ;
The theef, the chogh ; and eek the jangling pye ;     345
The scorning jay ; the eles foo, the heroune ;
The false lapwing, ful of trecherye ;
The stare, that the counseyl can bewrye ;
The tame ruddok ; and the coward kyte ;
The cok, that orloge is of thorpes lyte ; 350

The sparow, Venus sone ; the nightingale,
That clepeth forth the fresshe leves newe ;
The swalow, mordrer of the flyës smale
That maken hony of floures fresshe of hewe ;
The wedded turtel, with hir herte trewe ;
The pecok, with his aungels fethres brighte ;     356
The fesaunt, scorner of the cok by nighte ;

The waker goos ; the cukkow ever unkinde ;
The popinjay, ful of delicasye ;
The drake, stroyer of his owne kinde ; 360
The stork, the wreker of avouterye ;
The hote cormeraunt of glotonye ;
The raven wys, the crow with vois of care ;
The throstel olde ; the frosty feldefare.

What shulde I seyn ? of foules every kinde     365
That in this worlde han fethres and stature,
Men mighten in that place assembled finde
Before the noble goddesse Nature.
And everich of hem did his besy cure

Benignely to chese or for to take,     370
By hir acord, his formel or his make.

But to the poynt—Nature held on hir honde
A formel egle, of shap the gentileste
That ever she among hir werkes fonde,
The most benigne and the goodlieste ;
In hir was every vertu at his reste,     376
So ferforth, that Nature hir-self had blisse
To loke on hir, and ofte hir bek to kisse.

Nature, the vicaire of th'almyghty lorde,
That hoot, cold, hevy, light, [and] moist and dreye     380
Hath knit by even noumbre of acorde,
In esy vois began to speke and seye,
' Foules, tak hede of my sentence, I preye,
And, for your ese, in furthering of your nede,     384
As faste as I may speke, I wol me spede.

Ye know wel how, seynt Valentynes day,
By my statut and through my governaunce,
Ye come for to chese—and flee your way—
Your makes, as I prik yow with plesaunce.
But natheles, my rightful ordenaunce 390
May I not lete, for al this world to winne,
That he that most is worthy shal beginne.

The tercel egle, as that ye knowen wel,
The foul royal above yow in degree,
The wyse and worthy, secree, trewe as stel,     395
The which I †formed have, as ye may see,
In every part as hit best lyketh me,
Hit nedeth noght his shap yow to devyse,
He shal first chese and speken in his gyse.

And after him, by order shul ye chese, 400
After your kinde, everich as yow lyketh,
And, as your hap is, shul ye winne or lese ;
But which of yow that love most entryketh,
God sende him hir that sorest for him syketh.'
And therwith-al the tercel gan she calle,
And seyde, ' my sone, the choys is to thee falle.     406

But natheles, in this condicioun
Mot be the choys of everich that is here,
That she agree to his eleccioun,   409
Who-so he be that shulde been hir fere ;
This is our usage alwey, fro yeer to yere ;
And who so may at this time have his
   grace,
In blisful tyme he com in-to this place.'

With hed enclyned and with ful humble
   chere
This royal tercel spak and taried nought ;
' Unto my sovereyn lady, and noght my
   fere,   416
I chese, and chese with wille and herte
   and thought,
The formel on your hond so wel y-
   wrought,
Whos I am al and ever wol hir serve,
Do what hir list, to do me live or sterve.

Beseching hir of mercy and of grace,   421
As she that is my lady sovereyne ;
Or let me dye present in this place.
For certes, long may I not live in peyne ;
For in myn herte is corven every veyne ;
Having reward [al] only to my trouthe, 426
My dere herte, have on my wo som
   routhe.

And if that I to hir be founde untrewe,
Disobeysaunt, or wilful negligent,
Avauntour, or in proces love a newe,   430
I pray to you this be my jugement,
That with these foules I be al to-rent,
That ilke day that ever she me finde
To hir untrewe, or in my gilte unkinde.

And sin that noon loveth hir so wel as I,
Al be she never of love me behette,   436
Than oghte she be myn thourgh hir
   mercy,
For other bond can I noon on hir knette.
For never, for no wo, ne shal I lette   439
To serven hir, how fer so that she wende ;
Sey what yow list, my tale is at an ende.'

Right as the fresshe, rede rose newe
Ayen the somer-sonne coloured is,
Right so for shame al wexen gan the
   hewe
Of this formel, whan she herde al this ;
She neyther answerde ' wel,' ne seyde
   amis.   446

So sore abasshed was she, til that Nature
Seyde, ' doghter, drede yow noght, I yow
   assure.'

Another tercel egle spak anoon
Of lower kinde, and seyde, ' that shal
   not be ;   450
I love hir bet than ye do, by seynt John,
Or atte leste I love hir as wel as ye ;
And lenger have served hir, in my degree,
And if she shulde have loved for long
   loving,   454
To me allone had been the guerdoning.

I dar eek seye, if she me finde fals,
Unkinde, jangler, or rebel any wyse,
Or jalous, do me hongen by the hals !
And but I bere me in hir servyse
As wel as that my wit can me suffyse, 460
Fro poynt to poynt, hir honour for to
   save,
Tak she my lyf, and al the good I have.'

The thridde tercel egle answerde tho,
' Now, sirs, ye seen the litel leyser here ;
For every foul cryeth out to been a-go 465
Forth with his make, or with his lady
   dere ;
And eek Nature hir-self ne wol nought
   here,
For tarying here, noght half that I wolde
   seye ;
And but I speke, I mot for sorwe deye.

Of long servyse avaunte I me no-thing,
But as possible is me to dye to-day   471
For wo, as he that hath ben languisshing
Thise twenty winter, and wel happen may
A man may serven bet and more to pay
In half a yere, al-though hit were no more,
Than som man doth that hath served ful
   yore.   476

I ne say not this by me, for I ne can
Do no servyse that may my lady plese ;
But I dar seyn, I am hir trewest man
As to my dome, and feynest wolde hir ese ;
At shorte wordes, til that deth me sese, 481
I wol ben hires, whether I wake or winke,
And trewe in al that herte may bethinke.'

Of al my lyf, sin that day I was born,
So gentil plee in love or other thing   485
Ne herde never no man me beforn,

E 5

Who-[so] that hadde leyser and cunning
For to reherse hir chere and hir speking;
And from the morwe gan this speche laste
Til dounward drow the sonne wonder faste.

The noyse of foules for to ben delivered 491
So loude rong, 'have doon and let us
　　wende!'
That wel wende I the wode had al to-
　　shivered.
'Come of!' they cryde, 'allas! ye wil us
　　shende!
Whan shal your cursed pleding have an
　　ende?　　　　　　　　　　　　495
How shulde a juge eyther party leve,
For yee or nay, with-outen any preve?'

The goos, the cokkow, and the doke also
So cryden 'kek, kek!' 'kukkow!' 'quek,
　　quek!' hye,
That thorgh myn eres the noyse wente tho.
The goos seyde, 'al this nis not worth a
　　flyo!　　　　　　　　　　　　501
But I can shape hereof a remedye,
And I wol sey my verdit faire and swythe
For water-foul, who-so be wrooth or
　　blythe.'

'And I for worm-foul,' seyde the fool
　　cukkow,　　　　　　　　　　　505
'For I wol, of myn owne auctoritè,
For comune spede, take the charge now,
For to delivere us is gret charitè.'
'Ye may abyde a whyle yet, parde!'
Seide the turtel, 'if hit be your wille 510
A wight may speke, him were as good be
　　stille.

I am a seed-foul, oon the unworthieste,
That wot I wel, and litel of kuninge;
But bet is that a wightes tonge reste
Than entremeten him of such doinge 515
Of which he neyther rede can nor singe.
And who-so doth, ful foule himself acloy-
　　eth,
For office uncommitted ofte anoyeth.'

Nature, which that alway had an ere
To murmour of the lewednes behinde, 520
With facound voys seide, 'hold your
　　tonges there!
And I shal sone, I hope, a counseyl finde
You to delivere, and fro this noyse un-
　　binde;

I juge, of every folk men shal oon calle
To seyn the verdit for you foules alle.' 525

Assented were to this conclusioun
The briddes alle; and foules of ravyne
Han chosen first, by pleyn eleccioun,
The tercelet of the faucon, to diffyne 529
Al hir sentence, and as him list, termyne;
And to Nature him gonnen to presente,
And she accepteth him with glad entente.

The tercelet seide than in this manere:
'Ful hard were hit to preve hit by resoun
Who loveth best this gentil formel here;
For everich hath swich replicacioun, 536
That noon by skilles may be broght
　　a-doun;
I can not seen that arguments avayle;
Than semeth hit ther moste be batayle.'

'Al redy!' quod these egles tercels tho.
'Nay, sirs!' quod he, 'if that I dorste it
　　seye,　　　　　　　　　　　　541
Ye doon me wrong, my tale is not y-do!
For sirs, ne taketh noght a-gref, I preye,
It may noght gon, as ye wolde, in this
　　weye;
Oure is the voys that han the charge in
　　honde,　　　　　　　　　　　545
And to the juges dome ye moten stonde;

And therfor pees! I seye, as to my wit,
Me wolde thinke how that the worthieste
Of knighthode, and lengest hath used hit,
Moste of estat, of blode the gentileste, 550
Were sittingest for hir, if that hir leste;
And of these three she wot hir-self, I trowe,
Which that he be, for hit is light to
　　knowe.'

The water-foules han her hedes leyd
Togeder, and of short avysement, 555
Whan everich had his large golee seyd,
They seyden sothly, al by oon assent,
How that 'the goos, with hir facounde
　　gent,
That so desyreth to pronounce our nede,
Shal telle our tale,' and preyde 'god hir
　　spede.'　　　　　　　　　　560

And for these water-foules tho began
The goos to speke, and in hir cakelinge
She seyde, 'pees! now tak kepe every
　　man,

And herkeneth which a reson I shal
    bringe ;
My wit is sharp, I love no taryinge ;   565
I seye, I rede him, though he were my
    brother,
But she wol love him, lat him love
    another !'

' Lo here ! a parfit reson of a goos !'
Quod the sperhauk ; 'never mot she thee !
Lo, swich hit is to have a tonge loos ! 570
Now parde, fool, yet were hit bet for
    thee
Have holde thy pees, than shewed thy
    nycete !
Hit lyth not in his wit nor in his wille,
But sooth is seyd, " a fool can noght be
    stille."'

The laughter aroos of gentil foules alle,
And right anoon the seed-foul chosen
    hadde    576
The turtel trewe, and gunne hir to hem
    calle,
And preyden hir to seye the sothe sadde
Of this matere, and asked what she radde ;
And she answerde, that pleynly hir en-
    tente    580
She wolde shewe, and sothly what she
    mente.

'Nay, god forbede a lover shulde chaunge !'
The turtel seyde, and wex for shame al
    reed ;
' Thogh that his lady ever-more be
    straunge,    584
Yet let him serve hir ever, til he be deed ;
For sothe, I preyse noght the gooses reed ;
For thogh she deyed, I wolde non other
    make,
I wol ben hires, til that the deth me take.'

' Wel bourded !' quod the doke, ' by my
    hat !    589
That men shulde alwey loven, causeles,
Who can a reson finde or wit in that ?
Daunceth he mury that is mirtheles ?
Who shulde recche of that is reccheles ?
Ye, quek !' yit quod the doke, ful wel and
    faire,
'There been mo sterres, god wot, than a
    paire !'    595

' Now fy, cherl !' quod the gentil tercelet,
' Out of the dunghil com that word ful
    right,
Thou canst noght see which thing is wel
    be-set :
Thou farest by love as oules doon by light,
The day hem blent, ful wel they see by
    night ;    600
Thy kind is of so lowe a wrechednesse,
That what love is, thou canst nat see ne
    gesse.'

Tho gan the cukkow putte him forth in
    prees
For foul that eteth worm, and seide blyve,
' So I,' quod he, ' may have my make in
    pees,    605
I recche not how longe that ye stryve ;
Lat ech of hem be soleyn al hir lyve,
This is my reed, sin they may not acorde ;
This shorte lesson nedeth noght recorde.'

' Ye ! have the glotoun fild ynogh his
    paunche,    610
Than are we wel !' seyde the merlioun ;
' Thou mordrer of the heysugge on the
    braunche
That broghte thee forth, thou †rewtheles
    glotoun !
Live thou soleyn, wormes corrupcioun !
For no fors is of lakke of thy nature ; 615
Go, lewed be thou, whyl the world may
    dure !'

' Now pees,' quod Nature, ' I comaunde
    here ;
For I have herd al your opinioun,
And in effect yet be we never the nere ;
But fynally, this is my conclusioun, 620
That she hir-self shal han the eleccioun
Of whom hir list, who-so be wrooth or
    blythe,
Him that she cheest, he shal hir have as
    swythe.

For sith hit may not here discussed be
Who loveth hir best, as seide the tercelet,
Than wol I doon hir this favour, that
    she    626
Shal have right him on whom hir herte
    is set,
And he hir that his herte hath on hir
    knet.

This juge I, Nature, for I may not lyë ;
To noon estat I have non other yë.    630

But as for counseyl for to chese a make,
If hit were reson, certes, than wolde I
Counseyle yow the royal tercel take,
As seide the tercelet ful skilfully,
As for the gentilest and most worthy,  635
Which I have wroght so wel to my ples-
    aunce ;
That to yow oghte been a suffisaunce.'

With dredful vois the formel hir an-
    swerde,
' My rightful lady, goddesse of Nature,
Soth is that I am ever under your yerde,
Lyk as is everiche other creature,    641
And moot be youres whyl my lyf may
    dure ;
And therfor graunteth me my firste bone,
And myn entente I wol yow sey right
    sone.'

' I graunte it you,' quod she; and right
    anoon    645
This formel egle spak in this degree,
' Almighty quene, unto this yeer be doon
I aske respit for to avysen me.
And after that to have my choys al
    free ;
This al and som, that I wolde speke and
    seye ;    650
Ye gete no more, al-though ye do me deye.

I wol noght serven Venus ne Cupyde
For sothe as yet, by no manere wey.'
' Now sin it may non other wyse betyde,'
Quod tho Nature, ' here is no more to
    sey ;    655
Than wolde I that these foules were a-wey
Ech with his make, for tarying lenger
    here '—
And seyde hem thus, as ye shul after here.

' To you speke I, ye tercelets,' quod
    Nature,
' Beth of good herte and serveth, alle
    three ;    660
A yeer is not so longe to endure,
And ech of yow peyne him, in his degree,
For to do wel ; for, god wot, quit is she

Fro yow this yeer; what after so befalle,
This entremes is dressed for you alle.'  665

And whan this werk al broght was to an
    ende,
To every foule Nature yaf his make
By even acorde, and on hir wey they
    wende.
A! lord! the blisse and joye that they
    make!    669
For ech of hem gan other in winges take,
And with hir nekkes ech gan other winde,
Thanking alwey the noble goddesse of
    kinde.

But first were chosen foules for to singe,
As yeer by yere was alwey hir usaunce
To singe a roundel at hir departinge,  675
To do Nature honour and plesaunce.
The note, I trowe, maked was in Fraunce ;
The wordes were swich as ye may heer
    finde,
The nexte vers, as I now have in minde.

        *Qui bien aime a tard oublie.*

' Now welcom somer, with thy sonne
    softe,    680
That hast this wintres weders over-shake,
And driven awey the longe nightes blake!
Seynt Valentyn, that art ful hy on-
    lofte ;—
Thus singen smale foules for thy sake—
    *Now welcom somer, with thy sonne softe,* 685
    *That hast this wintres weders over-shake.*

Wel han they cause for to gladen ofte,
Sith ech of hem recovered hath his make ;
Ful blisful may they singen whan they
    wake ;
    *Now welcom somer, with thy sonne softe,* 690
    *That hast this wintres weders over-shake,*
    *And driven awey the longe nightes blake.'*

And with the showting, whan hir song
    was do,
That foules maden at hir flight a-way,
I wook, and other bokes took me to  695
To rede upon, and yet I rede alway ;
I hope, y-wis, to rede so som day
That I shal mete som thing for to fare 698
The bet ; and thus to rede I nil not spare.

**Explicit tractatus de congregacione Volucrum die sancti Valentini.**

# VI.   A COMPLEINT TO HIS LADY.

### I.   (*In seven-line stanzas.*)

THE longe night, whan every creature
  Shulde have hir rest in somwhat, as by
    kinde,
Or elles ne may hir lyf nat long endure,
  Hit falleth most in-to my woful minde
  How I so fer have broght my-self be-
    hinde,                                          5
That, sauf the deeth, ther may no-thing
    me lisse,
So desespaired I am from alle blisse.

This same thoght me lasteth til the
    morwe,
  And from the morwe forth til hit be eve;
Ther nedeth me no care for to borwe,    10
  For bothe I have good leyser and good
    leve ;
  Ther is no wight that wol me wo bereve
To wepe y-nogh, and wailen al my fille ;
The sore spark of peyne †doth me spille.

### II.   (*In Terza Rima ; imperfect.*)

[†The sore spark of peyne doth me spille ;]
  This Love hath [eek] me set in swich a
    place                                           16
That my desyr [he] never wol fulfille ;
For neither pitee, mercy, neither grace
  Can I nat finde ; and †fro my sorwful
    herte,
  For to be deed, I can hit nat arace.    20
The more I love, the more she doth me
    smerte ;
  Through which I see, with-oute remedye,
  That from the deeth I may no wyse
    asterte ;
[†For this day in hir servise shal I dye].

### III.   (*In Terza Rima ; imperfect.*)

[†Thus am I slain, with sorwes ful dy-
    verse ;                                         25
  Ful longe agoon I oghte have taken
    hede]

Now sothly, what she hight I wol re-
    herse ;
Hir name is Bountee, set in womanhede,
  Sadnesse in youthe, and Beautee pryde-
    lees,
  And Plesaunce, under governaunce and
    drede ;                                         30
Hir surname eek is Faire Rewthelees,
  The Wyse, y-knit un-to Good Aventure,
  That, for I love hir, †sleeth me giltelees.
Hir love I best, and shal, whyl I may
    dure,
  Bet than my-self an hundred thousand
    deel,                                           35
  Than al this worldes richesse or crea-
    ture.
Now hath nat Love me bestowed weel
  To love, ther I never shal have part ?
  Allas ! right thus is turned me the wheel,
Thus am I slayn with loves fyry dart.   40
  I can but love hir best, my swete fo ;
  Love hath me taught no more of his art
But serve alwey, and stinte for no wo.

### IV.   (*In ten-line stanzas.*)

[With]-in my trewe careful herte ther is
So moche wo, and [eek] so litel blis,   45
  That wo is me that ever I was bore ;
For al that thing which I desyre I mis,
And al that ever I wolde nat, I-wis,
  That finde I redy to me evermore ;
And of al this I not to whom me pleyne. 50
  For she that mighte me out of this
    bringe
  Ne reccheth nat whether I wepe or
    singe ;
So litel rewthe hath she upon my peyne.

Allas ! whan sleping-time is, than I wake,
Whan I shulde daunce, for fere than I
    quake ;                                         55
  [†Yow rekketh never wher I flete or
    sinke ;]
This hevy lyf I lede for your sake,
Thogh ye ther-of in no wyse hede take,

[†For on my wo yow deyneth not to
    thinke.]           59
My hertes lady, and hool my lyves quene!
  For trewly dorste I seye, as that I fele,
  Me semeth that your swete herte of stele
Is whetted now ageynes me to kene.

My dere herte, and best beloved fo,
Why lyketh yow to do me al this wo,   65
  What have I doon that greveth yow, or
    sayd,
But for I serve and love yow and no mo?
And whylst I live, I wol †do ever so;
  And therfor, swete, ne beth nat evil
    apayd.
For so good and so fair as [that] ye be, 70
  Hit were [a] right gret wonder but ye
    hadde
Of alle servants, bothe goode and badde;
And leest worthy of alle hem, I am he.

But never-the-les, my righte lady swete,
Thogh that I be unconning and unmete 75
  To serve as I best coude ay your hy-
    nesse,
Yit is ther fayner noon, that wolde I hete,
Than I, to do †yow ese, or elles bete
  What-so I wiste were to †yow distresse.
And hadde I might as good as I have wille,
  Than shulde ye fele wher it wer so or
    noon;             81
  For †in this worlde living is ther noon
That fayner wolde your hertes wil fulfille.

For bothe I love, and eek dreed yow so
  sore,
And algates moot, and have doon yow,
  ful yore,            85
  That bet loved is noon, ne never shal;
And yit I wolde beseche yow of no more
But leveth wel, and be nat wrooth ther-
  fore,
  And lat me serve yow forth; lo! this
    is al.
For I am nat so hardy ne so wood    90
  For to desire that ye shulde love me;
  For wel I wot, allas! that may nat be;
I am so litel worthy, and ye so good.

For ye be oon the worthiest on-lyve,
And I the most unlykly for to thryve; 95
  Yit, for al this, [now] witeth ye right
    wele,

That ye ne shul me from your service
  dryve
That I nil ay, with alle my wittes fyve,
  Serve yow trewly, what wo so that I fele.
For I am set on yow in swich manere 100
  That, thogh ye never wil upon me rewe,
  I moste yow love, and †ever been as
    trewe
As any can or may on-lyve [here].

†The more that I love yow, goodly free,
The lasse finde I that ye loven me;   105
  Allas! whan shal that harde wit a-
    mende?
Wher is now al your wommanly pitee,
Your gentilesse and your debonairtee,
  Wil ye no thing ther-of upon me
    spende?
And so hool, swete, as I am youres al, 110
  And so gret wil as I have yow to serve,
  Now, certes, and ye lete me thus sterve,
Yit have ye wonne ther-on but a smal.

For, at my knowing, I do †no-thing
  why,
And this I wol beseche yow hertely,   115
  That, ther ever ye finde, whyl ye live,
A trewer servant to yow than am I,
Leveth [me] thanne, and sleeth me
  hardely,
  And I my deeth to you wol al forgive.
And if ye finde no trewer †man than me,
  [Why] will ye suffre than that I thus
    spille,             121
  And for no maner gilt but my good
    wille?
As good wer thanne untrewe as trewe
  to be.

But I, my lyf and deeth, to yow obeye,
And with right buxom herte hoolly I
  preye,            125
As [is] your moste plesure, so doth by me;
†Wel lever is me lyken yow and deye
Than for to any thing or thinke or seye
  That †mighte yow offende in any tyme.
And therfor, swete, rewe on my peynes
  smerte,           130
  And of your grace granteth me som
    drope;
For elles may me laste †blis ne hope,
Ne †dwellen in my trouble careful herte.

# VII. ANELIDA AND ARCITE.

### The Compleynt of feire Anelida and fals Arcite.

#### *Proem.*

THOU ferse god of armes, Mars the rede,
That in the frosty country called Trace,
Within thy grisly temple ful of drede
Honoured art, as patroun of that place !
With thy Bellona, Pallas, ful of grace,  5
Be present, and my song continue and
  gye ;
At my beginning thus to thee I crye.

For hit ful depe is sonken in my minde,
With pitous herte in English for t'endyte
This olde storie, in Latin which I finde,  10
Of quene Anelida and fals Arcite,
That elde, which that al can frete and
  byte,
As hit hath freten mony a noble storie,
Hath nigh devoured out of our memorie.

Be favorable eek, thou Polymnia,  15
On Parnaso that, with thy sustres glade,
By Elicon, not fer from Cirrea,
Singest with vois memorial in the shade,
Under the laurer which that may not
  fade,
And do that I my ship to haven winne ;  20
First folow I Stace, and after him
  Corinne.

#### *The Story.*

*Iamque domos patrias, &c.* ; Statii Thebais,
  xii. 519.

Whan Theseus, with werres longe and
  grete,
The aspre folk of Cithe had over-come,
With laurer crouned, in his char gold-
  bete,
Hoom to his contre-houses is y-come ;— 25
For which the peple blisful, al and somme,
So cryden, that unto the sterres hit wente,
And him to honouren dide al hir en-
  tente ;—

Beforn this duk, in signe of hy victorie,
The trompes come, and in his baner large
The image of Mars ; and, in token of
  glorie,  31
Men mighten seen of tresor many a
  charge,
Many a bright helm, and many a spere
  and targe,
Many a fresh knight, and many a blisful
  route,
On hors, on fote, in al the felde aboute. 35

Ipolita his wyf, the hardy quene
Of Cithia, that he conquered hadde,
With Emelye, hir yonge suster shene,
Faire in a char of golde he with him ladde,
That al the ground aboute hir char she
  spradde  40
With brightnesse of the beautee in hir
  face,
Fulfild of largesse and of alle grace.

With his triumphe and laurer-crouned
  thus,
In al the floure of fortunes yevinge,
Lete I this noble prince Theseus  45
Toward Athenes in his wey rydinge,
And founde I wol in shortly for to bringe
The slye wey of that I gan to wryte,
Of quene Anelida and fals Arcite.

Mars, which that through his furious
  course of yre,  50
The olde wrath of Juno to fulfille,
Hath set the peples hertes bothe on fyre
Of Thebes and Grece, everich other to
  kille
With blody speres, ne rested never stille,
But throng now her, now ther, among
  hem bothe,  55
That everich other slough, so wer they
  wrothe.

For whan Amphiorax and Tydeus,
Ipomedon, Parthonopee also
Were dede, and slayn [was] proud Cam-
  paneus,

And whan the wrecches Thebans, breth-
    eren two, 60
Were slayn, and king Adrastus hoom
    a-go,
So desolat stood Thebes and so bare,
That no wight coude remedie of his care.

And whan the olde Creon gan espye
How that the blood roial was broght
    adoun, 65
He held the cite by his tirannye,
And did the gentils of that regioun
To been his frendes, and dwellen in the
    toun.
So what for love of him, and what for awe,
The noble folk wer to the toune y-drawe.

Among al these, Anelida the quene 71
Of Ermony was in that toun dwellinge,
That fairer was then is the sonne shene ;
Through-out the world so gan hir name
    springe,
That hir to seen had every wight lykinge ;
For, as of trouthe, is ther noon hir liche, 76
Of al the women in this worlde riche.

Yong was this quene, of twenty yeer of
    elde,
Of midel stature, and of swich fairnesse,
That nature had a joye hir to behelde ; 80
And for to speken of hir stedfastnesse,
She passed hath Penelope and Lucresse,
And shortly, if she shal be comprehended,
In hir ne mighte no-thing been amended.

This Theban knight [Arcite] eek, sooth to
    seyn, 85
Was yong, and ther-with-al a lusty knight,
But he was double in love and no-thing
    pleyn,
And subtil in that crafte over any wight,
And with his cunning wan this lady
    bright ;
For so ferforth he gan hir trouthe assure,
That she him †trust over any creature. 91

What shuld I seyn ? she loved Arcite so,
That, whan that he was absent any throwe,
Anoon hir thoghte hir herte brast a-two ;
For in hir sight to hir he bar him lowe, 95
So that she wende have al his herte
    y-knowe ;
But he was fals ; it nas but feyned chere,
As nedeth not to men such craft to lere

But never-the-les ful mikel besinesse
Had he, er that he mighte his lady winne,
And swoor he wolde dyen for distresse, 101
Or from his wit he seyde he wolde twinne.
Alas, the whyle ! for hit was routhe and
    sinne,
That she upon his sorowes wolde rewe,
But no-thing thenketh the fals as doth
    the trewe. 105

Hir fredom fond Arcite in swich manere,
That al was his that she hath, moche or
    lyte,
Ne to no creature made she chere
Ferther than that hit lyked to Arcite ;
Ther was no lak with which he mighte
    hir wyte, 110
She was so ferforth yeven him to plese,
That al that lyked him, hit did hir ese.

Ther nas to hir no maner lettre y-sent
That touched love, from any maner
    wight,
That she ne shewed hit him, er hit was
    brent ; 115
So pleyn she was, and did hir fulle might,
That she nil hyden nothing from hir
    knight,
Lest he of any untrouthe hir upbreyde ;
Withouten bode his heste she obeyde.

And eek he made him jelous over here, 120
That, what that any man had to hir seyd,
Anoon he wolde preyen hir to swere
What was that word, or make him evel
    apayd ;
Than wende she out of hir wit have brayd ;
But al this nas but sleight and flaterye,
Withouten love he feyned jelosye. 126

And al this took she so debonerly,
That al his wille, hir thoghte hit skilful
    thing,
And ever the lenger †loved him tenderly,
And did him honour as he were a king. 130
Hir herte was wedded to him with a ring ;
So ferforth upon trouthe is hir entente,
That wher he goth, hir herte with him
    wente.

Whan she shal ete, on him is so hir
    thoght, 134
That wel unnethe of mete took she keep ;

And whan that she was to hir reste
  broght,
On him she thoghte alwey til that she
  sleep ;
Whan he was absent, prevely she weep ;
Thus liveth fair Anelida the quene   139
For fals Arcite, that did hir al this tene.

This fals Arcite, of his new-fangelnesse,
For she to him so lowly was and trewe,
Took lesse deyntee for hir stedfastnesse,
And saw another lady, proud and newe,
And right anon he cladde him in hir
  hewe—   145
Wot I not whether in whyte, rede, or
  grene—
And falsed fair Anelida the quene.

But never-the-les, gret wonder was hit
  noon
Thogh he wer fals, for hit is kinde of
  man,   149
Sith Lamek was, that is so longe agoon,
To been in love as fals as ever he can ;
He was the firste fader that began
To loven two, and was in bigamye ;
And he found tentes first, but-if men lye.

This fals Arcite sumwhat moste he feyne,
Whan he wex fals, to covere his trai-
  torye,   156
Right as an hors, that can both byte and
  pleyne ;
For he bar hir on honde of trecherye,
And swoor he coude hir doublenesse
  espye,
And al was falsnes that she to him mente ;
Thus swoor this theef, and forth his way
  he wente.   161

Alas ! what herte might enduren hit,
For routhe or wo, hir sorow for to telle ?
Or what man hath the cunning or the
  wit ?
Or what man might with-in the chambre
  dwelle,   165
If I to him rehersen shal the helle,
That suffreth fair Anelida the quene
For fals Arcite, that did hir al this tene ?

She wepeth, waileth, swowneth pitously,
To grounde deed she falleth as a stoon ;
Al crampissheth hir limes crokedly,   171
She speketh as hir wit were al agoon ;

Other colour then asshen hath she noon,
Noon other word ┤she speketh moche or
  lyte,
But ' mercy, cruel herte myn, Arcite !' 175

And thus endureth, til that she was so
  mate
That she ne hath foot on which she may
  sustene ;
But forth languisshing ever in this estate,
Of which Arcite hath nother routhe ne
  tene ;
His herte was elles-where, newe and
  grene,   180
That on hir wo ne deyneth him not to
  thinke,
Him rekketh never wher she flete or
  sinke.

His newe lady holdeth him so narowe
Up by the brydel, at the staves ende,
That every word, he dradde hit as an
  arowe ;   185
Hir daunger made him bothe bowe and
  bende,
And as hir liste, made him turne or
  wende ;
For she ne graunted him in hir livinge
No grace, why that he hath lust to singe;

But drof him forth, unnethe liste hir
  knowe   190
That he was servaunt †to hir ladyshippe,
But lest that he wer proude, she held
  him lowe ;
Thus serveth he, withouten fee or shipe,
She sent him now to londe, now to
  shippe ;   194
And for she yaf him daunger al his fille,
Therfor she had him at hir owne wille.

Ensample of this, ye thrifty wimmen alle,
Take here Anelida and fals Arcite,
That for hir liste him ' dere herte ' calle,
And was so meek, therfor he loved hir
  lyte ;   200
The kinde of mannes herte is to delyte
In thing that straunge is, also god me
  save !
For what he may not gete, that wolde he
  have.

Now turne we to Anelida ageyn,
That pyneth day by day in languisshing;

But whan she saw that hir ne gat no
   geyn,                                    206
Upon a day, ful sorowfully weping,
She caste hir for to make a compleyning,
And with hir owne honde she gan hit
   wryte ;
And sente hit to hir Theban knight
   Arcite.                                 210

## The Compleynt of Anelida the quene upon fals Arcite.

### Proem.

So thirleth with the poynt of remem-
   braunce,
The swerd of sorowe, y-whet with fals
   plesaunce,
   Myn herte, bare of blis and blak of
    hewe,
That turned is in quaking al my daunce,
My suretee in a-whaped countenaunce ; 215
   Sith hit availeth not for to ben trewe ;
   For who-so trewest is, hit shal hir
    rewe,
That serveth love and doth hir observ-
   aunce
   Alwey to oon, and chaungeth for no
    newe.

### (Strophe.)

#### 1.

I wot my-self as wel as any wight ;    220
For I loved oon with al my herte and
   might
   More then my-self, an hundred thou-
    sand sythe,
And called him my hertes lyf, my knight,
And was al his, as fer as hit was right ;
   And whan that he was glad, than was
    I blythe,                              225
   And his disese was my deeth as swythe ;
And he ayein his trouthe me had plight
For ever-more, his lady me to kythe.

#### 2.

Now is he fals, alas ! and causeles,
And of my wo he is so routheles,      230
   That with a worde him list not ones
   deyne
To bring ayein my sorowful herte in pees,
For he is caught up in a-nother lees.

Right as him list, he laugheth at my
   peyne,                                  234
And I ne can myn herte not restreyne,
That I ne love him alwey, never-the-les ;
   And of al this I not to whom me pleyne.

#### 3.

And shal I pleyne—alas ! the harde
   stounde—
Un-to my foo that yaf my herte a wounde,
   And yet desyreth that myn harm be
   more ?                                  240
Nay, certes ! ferther wol I never †founde
Non other help, my sores for to sounde.
   My destinee hath shapen it ful yore ;
   I wil non other medecyne ne lore ;
I wil ben ay ther I was ones bounde, 245
   That I have seid, be seid for ever-more !

#### 4.

Alas ! wher is become your gentilesse !
Your wordes fulle of plesaunce and hum-
   blesse ?
Your observaunces in so low manere,
And your awayting and your besinesse 250
Upon me, that ye calden your maistresse,
   Your sovereyn lady in this worlde here?
Alas ! and is ther nother word ne chere
Ye vouchesauf upon myn hevinesse ?
   Alas ! your love, I bye hit al to dere. 255

#### 5.

Now certes, swete, thogh that ye
   Thus causeles the cause be
   Of my dedly adversitee,
Your manly reson oghte it to respyte
   To slee your frend, and namely me, 260
   That never yet in no degree
   Offended yow, as wisly he,
That al wot, out of wo my soule quyte !

   ¶ But for I shewed yow, Arcite,
   Al that men wolde to me wryte,    265
   And was so besy, yow to delyte—
My honour save—meke, kinde, and free,
   Therfor ye putte on me the wyte,
   And of me recche not a myte,
   Thogh that the swerd of sorow byte 270
My woful herte through your crueltee.

#### 6.

My swete foo,  why do ye so,  for shame?
And thenke ye  that furthered be  your
   name,

To love a newe, and been untrewe?
  nay!
And putte yow  in sclaunder now  and
  blame,                                    275
And do to me  adversitee  and grame,
  That love yow most,    god, wel thou
  wost!  alway?
  Yet turn ayeyn,  and be al pleyn  som
  day,
And than shal this  that now is mis  be
  game,                                     279
  And al for-yive,  whyl that I live  may.

*(Antistrophe.)*

### 1.

Lo! herte myn, al this is for to seyne,
As whether shal I preye or elles pleyne?
  Whiche is the wey to doon yow to be
  trewe?
For either mot I have yow in my cheyne,
Or with the dethe ye mot departe us
  tweyne;                                   285
  Ther ben non other mene weyes newe;
  For god so wisly on my soule rewe,
As verily ye sleen me with the peyne;
  That may ye see unfeyned of myn hewe.

### 2.

For thus ferforth have I my deth [y]-
  soght,                                    290
My-self I mordre with my prevy thoght;
  For sorow and routhe of your unkinde-
  nesse
I wepe, I wake, I faste; al helpeth noght;
I weyve joye that is to speke of oght,
  I voyde companye, I flee gladnesse; 295
  Who may avaunte hir bet of hevinesse
Then I? and to this plyte have ye me
  broght,
  Withoute gilt; me nedeth no witnesse.

### 3.

And sholde I preye, and weyve woman-
  hede?
Nay! rather deth then do so foul a dede,
  And axe mercy gilteles! what nede? 301
And if I pleyne what lyf that I lede,
Yow rekketh not; that know I, out of
  drede;
  And if I unto yow myn othes bede

For myn excuse, a scorn shal be my
  mede;                                     305
Your chere floureth, but hit wol not sede;
  Ful longe agoon I oghte have take hede.

### 4.

For thogh I hadde yow to-morow ageyn,
I might as wel holde Averill fro reyn,
  As holde yow, to make yow stedfast. 310
Almighty god, of trouthe sovereyn,
Wher is the trouthe of man? who hath
  hit sleyn?
  Who that hem loveth shal hem fynde
  as fast
  As in a tempest is a roten mast.
Is that a tame best that is ay feyn    315
  To renne away, when he is leest agast?

### 5.

Now mercy, swete, if I misseye,
Have I seyd oght amis, I preye?
I not; my wit is al aweye.
I fare as doth the song of *Chaunte-pleure.*
  For now I pleyne, and now I pleye, 321
  I am so mased that I deye,
  Arcite hath born awey the keye
Of al my worlde, and my good aventure!

  ¶ For in this worlde nis creature    325
  Wakinge, in more discomfiture
  Then I, ne more sorow endure;
And if I slepe a furlong wey or tweye,
  Than thinketh me, that your figure
  Before me stant, clad in asure,     330
  To profren eft a newe assure
For to be trewe, and mercy me to preye.

### 6.

The longe night    this wonder sight    I
  drye,
And on the day  for this afray  I dye, 334
  And of al this  right noght, y-wis, ye
  recche.
Ne never mo  myn yën two  be drye,
And to your routhe  and to your trouthe
  I crye.
  But welawey! to fer be they to fecche;
  Thus holdeth me    my destinee  a
  wrecche.                               339
But me to rede  out of this drede  or gye
  Ne may my wit,  so weyk is hit,  not
  strecche.

*Conclusion.*

Than ende I thus, sith I may do no
　more,
I yeve hit up for now and ever-more ;
　For I shal never eft putten in balaunce
My sckernes, ne lerne of love the
　lore.　　　　　　　　　　　　345
But as the swan, I have herd seyd ful
　yore,
　　Ayeins his deth shal singe in his
　　penaunce,
　So singe I here my destiny or chaunce,

How that Arcite Anelida so sore
　Hath thirled with the poynt of remem-
　　braunce !　　　　　　　　　350

*The story continued.*

Whan that Anelida this woful quene
Hath of hir hande writen in this wyse,
With face deed, betwixe pale and grene,
She fel a-swowe ; and sith she gan to ryse,
And unto Mars avoweth sacrifyse　　355
With-in the temple, with a sorowful
　chere,
That shapen was as ye shal after here. 357

(*Unfinished.*)

# VIII. CHAUCERS WORDES UNTO ADAM, HIS OWNE SCRIVEYN.

ADAM scriveyn, if ever it thee bifalle
Boece or Troilus to wryten newe,
Under thy lokkes thou most have the
　scalle,
But after my making thou wryte trewe.

So ofte a daye I mot thy werk renewe,　5
Hit to correcte and eek to rubbe and
　scrape ;
And al is through thy negligence and
　rape.

# IX. THE FORMER AGE.

A BLISFUL lyf, a paisible and a swete
Ledden the peples in the former age ;
They helde hem payed †of fruites, that
　they ete,
Which that the feldes yave hem by usage ;
They ne were nat forpampred with out-
　rage ;　　　　　　　　　　　　5
Unknowen was the quern and eek the
　melle ;
They eten mast, hawes, and swich poun-
　age,
And dronken water of the colde welle.

Yit nas the ground nat wounded with
　the plough,
But corn up-sprong, unsowe of mannes
　hond,　　　　　　　　　　　　10
The which they †gniden, and eete nat
　half y-nough.
No man yit knew the forwes of his lond ;
No man the fyr out of the flint yit
　fond ;
Un-korven and un-grobbed lay the vyne ;
No man yit in the morter spyces grond 15
To clarre, ne to sause of galantyne.

No mader, welde, or wood no litestere
Ne knew; the flees was of his former
hewe;
No flesh ne wiste offence of egge or spere;
No coyn ne knew man which was fals or
trewe; 20
No ship yit karf the wawes grene and
blewe;
No marchaunt yit ne fette outlandish
ware;
No †trompes for the werres folk ne knewe,
No toures heye, and walles rounde or
square.

What sholde it han avayled to werreye? 25
Ther lay no profit, ther was no richesse,
But cursed was the tyme, I dar wel seye,
That men first dide hir swety bysinesse
To grobbe up metal, lurkinge in dark-
nesse,
And in the riveres first gemmes soghte. 30
Allas! than sprong up al the cursednesse
Of covetyse, that first our sorwe broghte!

Thise tyraunts putte hem gladly nat in
pres,
No †wildnesse, ne no busshes for to winne
Ther poverte is, as seith Diogenes, 35
Ther as vitaile is eek so skars and thinne
That noght but mast or apples is ther-
inne.
But, ther as bagges been and fat vitaile,
Ther wol they gon, and spare for no sinne
With al hir ost the cite for t'assaile. 40

Yit were no paleis-chaumbres, ne non
halles;
In caves and [in] wodes softe and swete
Slepten this blissed folk with-oute walles,
On gras or leves in parfit †quiete.
No doun of fetheres, ne no bleched
shete 45
Was kid to hem, but in seurtee they
slepte;
Hir hertes were al oon, with-oute galles,
Everich of hem his feith to other kepte.

Unforged was the hauberk and the plate;
The lambish peple, voyd of alle vyce, 50
Hadden no fantasye to debate,
But ech of hem wolde other wel cheryce;
No pryde, non envye, non avaryce,
No lord, no taylage by no tyrannye;
Humblesse and pees, good feith, the em-
perice, 55
[†Fulfilled erthe of olde curtesye.]

Yit was not Jupiter the likerous,
That first was fader of delicacye,
Come in this world; ne Nembrot, de-
sirous
To reynen, had nat maad his toures
hye. 60
Allas, allas! now may men wepe and
crye!
For in our dayes nis but covetyse
[And] doublenesse, and tresoun and envye,
Poysoun, manslauhtre, and mordre in
sondry wyse. 64

**Finit Etas prima. Chaucers.**

---

# X. FORTUNE.

*Balades de visage sanz peinture.*

### I. Le Pleintif countre Fortune.

This wrecched worldes transmutacioun,
As wele or wo, now povre and now
honour,
With-outen ordre or wys discrecioun
Governed is by Fortunes errour;
But natheles, the lak of hir favour 5

Ne may nat don me singen, though I dye
'*Iay tout perdu mon temps et mon labour:*'
For fynally, Fortune, I thee defye!

Yit is me left the light of my resoun,
To knowen frend fro fo in thy mirour. 10
So muche hath yit thy whirling up and
doun
Y-taught me for to knowen in an hour
But trewely, no force of thy reddour

To him that over him-self hath the mays-
    trye!
My suffisaunce shal be my socour :    15
For fynally, Fortune, I thee defye!

O Socrates, thou stedfast champioun,
She never mighte be thy tormentour ;
Thou never dreddest hir oppressioun,
Ne in hir chere tounde thou no savour. 20
Thou knewe wel deceit of hir colour,
And that hir moste worshipe is to lye.
I knowe hir eek a fals dissimulour :
For fynally, Fortune, I thee defye !

## II.  La respounse de Fortune au Pleintif.

No man is wrecched, but him-self hit
    wene,    25
And he that hath him-self hath suf-
    fisaunce.
Why seystow thanne I am to thee so
    kene,
That hast thy-self out of my governaunce?
Sey thus : 'Graunt mercy of thyn ha-
    boundaunce
That thou hast lent or this.' Why wolt
    thou stryve?    30
What wostow yit, how I thee wol
    avaunce?
And eek thou hast thy beste frend alyve!

I have thee taught divisioun bi-twene
Frend of effect, and frend of counten-
    aunce ;
Thee nedeth nat the galle of noon
    hyene,    35
That cureth eyen derke fro hir penaunce ;
Now seestow cleer, that were in ignor-
    aunce.
Yit halt thyn ancre, and yit thou mayst
    arryve
Ther bountee berth the keye of my sub-
    staunce :    39
And eek thou hast thy beste frend alyve.

How many have I refused to sustene,
Sin I thee fostred have in thy plesaunce!
Woltow than make a statut on thy quene
That I shal been ay at thyn ordinaunce?
Thou born art in my regne of variaunce,

Aboute the wheel with other most thou
    dryve.    46
My lore is bet than wikke is thy grev-
    aunce,
And eek thou hast thy beste frend alyve.

## III.  La respounse du Pleintif countre Fortune.

Thy lore I dampne, hit is adversitee.
My frend maystow nat reven, blind god-
    desse !    50
That I thy frendes knowe, I thanke hit
    thee.
Tak hem agayn, lat hem go lye on presse!
The negardye in keping hir richesse
Prenostik is thou wolt hir tour assayle ;
Wikke appetyt comth ay before seknesse :
In general, this reule may nat fayle.    56

## La respounse de Fortune countre le Pleintif.

Thou pinchest at my mutabilitee,
For I thee lente a drope of my richesse,
And now me lyketh to with-drawe me.
Why sholdestow my realtee oppresse ?    60
The see may ebbe and flowen more or lesse;
The welkne hath might to shyne, reyne,
    or hayle ;
Right so mot I kythen my brotelnesse.
In general, this reule may nat fayle.

Lo, th'execucion of the magestee    65
That al purveyeth of his rightwisnesse,
That same thing 'Fortune' clepen ye,
Ye blinde bestes, ful of lewednesse !
The hevene hath propretee of sikernesse,
This world hath ever resteles travayle ; 70
Thy laste day is ende of myn intresse :
In general, this reule may nat fayle.

## Lenvoy de Fortune.

Princes, I prey you of your gentilesse,
Lat nat this man on me thus crye and
    pleyne,
And I shal quyte you your bisinesse    75
At my requeste, as three of you or tweyne;
And, but you list releve him of his peyne,
Preyeth his beste frend, of his noblesse,
That to som beter estat he may atteyne. 79

*Explicit.*

# XI.  MERCILES BEAUTE : A TRIPLE ROUNDEL.

### I.  *Captivity.*

YOUR yën two wol slee me sodenly,
I may the beautè of hem not sustene,
So woundeth hit through-out my herte
    kene.

And but your word wol helen hastily
My hertes wounde, whyl that hit is grene,
    *Your yën two wol slee me sodenly,*　　6
    *I may the beautè of hem not sustene.*

Upon my trouthe I sey yow feithfully,
That ye ben of my lyf and deeth the quene ;
For with my deeth the trouthe shal be sene.
    *Your yën two wol slee me sodenly,*　　11
    *I may the beautè of hem not sustene,*
    *So woundeth hit through-out my herte kene.*

### II.  *Rejection.*

So hath your beautè fro your herte chaced
Pitee, that me ne availeth not to pleyne ;
For Daunger halt your mercy in his
    cheyne.　　16

Giltles my deeth thus han ye me pur-
    chaced ;
I sey yow sooth, me nedeth not to feyne ;

So hath your beautè fro your herte chaced
Pitee, that me ne availeth not to pleyne. 20

Allas! that nature hath in yow com-
    passed
So greet beautè, that no man may atteyne
To mercy, though he sterve for the peyne.
    *So hath your beautè fro your herte chaced*
    *Pitee, that me ne availeth not to pleyne ;* 25
    *For Daunger halt your mercy in his cheyne.*

### III.  *Escape.*

Sin I fro Love escaped am so fat,
I never thenk to ben in his prison lene ;
Sin I am free, I counte him not a bene.

He may answere, and seye this or that ; 30
I do no fors, I speke right as I mene.
    *Sin I fro Love escaped am so fat,*
    *I never thenk to ben in his prison lene.*

Love hath my name y-strike out of his
    sclat,
And he is strike out of my bokes clene 35
For ever-mo ; †ther is non other mene.
    *Sin I fro Love escaped am so fat,*
    *I never thenk to ben in his prison lene ;*
    *Sin I am free, I counte him not a bene.* 39

*Explicit.*

---

# XII.  TO ROSEMOUNDE.  A BALADE.

MADAME, ye ben of al beautè shryne
As fer as cercled is the mappemounde ;
For as the cristal glorious ye shyne,
And lyke ruby ben your chekes rounde.
Therwith ye ben so mery and so jocounde,
That at a revel whan that I see you
    daunce,　　6
It is an oynement unto my wounde,
Thogh ye to me ne do no daliaunce.

For thogh I wepe of teres ful a tyne,
Yet may that wo myn herte nat con-
    founde ;　　10
Your †seemly voys that ye so †smal out-
    twyne
Maketh my thoght in joye and blis
    habounde.
So curteisly I go, with lovè bounde,
That to my-self I sey, in my penaunce,

Suffyseth me to love you, Rosemounde, 15
Thogh ye to me ne do no daliaunce.

Nas never pyk walwed in galauntyne
As I in love am walwed and y-wounde ;
For which ful ofte I of my-self divyne

Tregentil.

That I am trewe Tristam the secounde. 20
My love may not refreyd be nor afounde ;
I brenne ay in an amorous plesaunce.
Do what you list, I wil your thral be
   founde,
Thogh ye to me ne do no daliaunce.    24

Chaucer.

---

# XIII.    TRUTH.

### Balade de bon conseyl.

FLEE fro the prees, and dwelle with soth-
   fastnesse,
Suffyce unto thy good, though hit be
   smal;
For hord hath hate, and climbing tikel-
   nesse,
Prees hath envye, and wele blent overal ;
Savour no more than thee bihove shal ; 5
Werk wel thy-self, that other folk canst
   rede :
And trouthe shal delivere, hit is no drede.

Tempest thee noght al croked to redresse,
In trust of hir that turneth as a bal :
Gret reste stant in litel besinesse ;    10
And eek be war to sporne ageyn an al ;
Stryve noght, as doth the crokke with
   the wal.
Daunte thy-self, that dauntest otheres
   dede ;
And trouthe shal delivere, hit is no drede.

That thee is sent, receyve in buxumnesse,
The wrastling for this worlde axeth a
   fal.    16
Her nis non hoom, her nis but wilder-
   nesse :
Forth, pilgrim, forth ! Forth, beste, out
   of thy stal !
Know thy contree, look up, thank God
   of al ;
Hold the hye wey, and lat thy gost thee
   lede :    20
And trouthe shal delivere, hit is no drede.

### Envoy.

Therfore, thou vache, leve thyn old
   wrecchednesse
Unto the worlde ; leve now to be thral ;
Crye him mercy, that of his hy goodnesse
Made thee of noght, and in especial    25
Draw unto him, and pray in general
For thee, and eek for other, hevenlich
   mede ;    27
And trouthe shal delivere, hit is no drede.

Explicit Le bon counseill de G. Chaucer.

---

# XIV.    GENTILESSE.

### Moral Balade of Chaucer.

THE firste stok, fader of gentilesse—
What man that claymeth gentil for to be,
Must folowe his trace, and alle his wittes
   dresse
Vertu to sewe, and vyces for to flee.
For unto vertu longeth dignitee,    5

And noght the revers, saufly dar I deme,
Al were he mytre, croune, or diademe.

This firste stok was ful of rightwisnesse,
Trewe of his word, sobre, pitous, and
   free,
Clene of his goste, and loved besinesse, 10
Ageinst the vyce of slouthe, in honestee ;

And, but his heir love vertu, as dide he,
He is noght gentil, thogh he riche seme,
Al were he mytre, croune, or diademe.

Vyce may wel be heir to old richesse;    15
But ther may no man, as men may wel see,

Bequethe his heir his vertuous noblesse
That is appropred unto no degree,
But to the firste fader in magestee,
That †maketh him his heir, that can him
    queme,    20
Al were he mytre, croune, or diademe.

---

## XV.  LAK OF STEDFASTNESSE.

### Balade.

Som tyme this world was so stedfast and
    stable,
That mannes word was obligacioun,
And now hit is so fals and deceivable,
That word and deed, as in conclusioun,
Ben no-thing lyk, for turned up so doun  5
Is al this world for mede and wilfulnesse,
That al is lost for lak of stedfastnesse.

What maketh this world to be so variable,
But lust that folk have in dissensioun?
Among us now a man is holde unable,  10
But-if he can, by som collusioun,
Don his neighbour wrong or oppressioun.
What causeth this, but wilful wrecched-
    nesse,
That al is lost, for lak of stedfastnesse?

Trouthe is put doun, resoun is holden
    fable;    15
Vertu hath now no dominacioun,
Pitee exyled, no man is merciable.
Through covetyse is blent discrecioun;
The world hath mad a permutacioun
Fro right to wrong, fro trouthe to fikel-
    nesse,    20
That al is lost, for lak of stedfastnesse.

### Lenvoy to King Richard.

O prince, desyre to be honourable,
Cherish thy folk and hate extorcioun!
Suffre no thing, that may be reprevable
To thyn estat, don in thy regioun.    25
Shew forth thy swerd of castigacioun,
Dred God, do law, love trouthe and worthi-
    nesse,    27
And wed thy folk agein to stedfastnesse.

*Explicit.*

---

## XVI.  LENVOY DE CHAUCER A SCOGAN.

To-broken been the statuts hye in hevene
That creat were eternally to dure,
Sith that I see the brighte goddes sevene
Mow wepe and wayle, and passioun en-
    dure,
As may in erthe a mortal creature.    5
Allas, fro whennes may this thing pro-
    cede?
Of whiche errour I deye almost for drede.

By worde eterne whylom was hit shape
That fro the fifte cercle, in no manere,
Ne mighte a drope of teres doun es-
    cape.    10
But now so wepeth Venus in hir spere,
That with hir teres she wol drenche us
    here.
Allas, Scogan! this is for thyn offence!
Thou causest this deluge of pestilence.

Hast thou not seyd, in blaspheme of this
   goddes,      15
Through pryde, or through thy grete
   rakelnesse,
Swich thing as in the lawe of love for-
   bode is?
That, for thy lady saw nat thy distresse,
Therfor thou yave hir up at Michelmesse!
Allas, Scogan! of olde folk ne yonge   20
Was never erst Scogan blamed for his
   tonge!

Thou drowe in scorn Cupyde eek to record
Of thilke rebel word that thou hast spoken,
For which he wol no lenger be thy lord.
And, Scogan, thogh his bowe be nat
   broken,      25
He wol nat with his arwes been y-wroken
On thee, ne me, ne noon of our figure;
We shul of him have neyther hurt ne cure.

Now certes, frend, I drede of thyn unhappe,
Lest for thy gilt the wreche of Love procede      30
On alle hem that ben hore and rounde of
   shape,

That ben so lykly folk in love to spede.
Than shul we for our labour han no mede;
But wel I wot, thou wilt answere and seye:
' Lo! olde Grisel list to ryme and pleye!'

Nay, Scogan, sey not so, for I m'excuse,   36
God help me so! in no rym, doutelees,
Ne thinke I never of slepe wak my muse,
That rusteth in my shethe stille in pees.
Whyl I was yong, I putte hir forth in
   prees,      40
But al shal passe that men prose or ryme;
Take every man his turn, as for his tyme.

### Envoy.

Scogan, that knelest at the stremes heed [1]
Of grace, of alle honour and worthinesse,
In th'ende of which streme [2] I am dul as
   deed,      45
Forgete in solitarie wildernesse;
Yet, Scogan, thenke on Tullius kinde-
   nesse,
Minne thy frend, ther it may fructifye!
Far-wel, and lok thou never eft Love
   defye!      49

[1] I. e. Windesore.    [2] I. e. Grenewich.

---

# XVII. LENVOY DE CHAUCER A BUKTON.

**The counseil of Chaucer touching
Mariage, which was sent to Bukton.**

My maister Bukton, whan of Criste our
   kinge
Was axed, what is trouthe or sothfast-
   nesse,
He nat a word answerde to that axinge,
As who saith: 'no man is al trewe,'
   I gesse.
And therfor, thogh I highte to expresse
The sorwe and wo that is in mariage,   6
I dar not wryte of hit no wikkednesse,
Lest I my-self falle eft in swich dotage.

I wol nat seyn, how that hit is the cheyne
Of Sathanas, on which he gnaweth ever,   10

But I dar seyn, were he out of his peyne,
As by his wille, he wolde be bounde
   never.
But thilke doted fool that eft hath lever
Y-cheyned be than out of prisoun crepe,
God lete him never fro his wo dissever,   15
Ne no man him bewayle, though he wepe.

But yit, lest thou do worse, tak a wyf;
Bet is to wedde, than brenne in worse
   wyse.
But thou shalt have sorwe on thy flesh,
   thy lyf,
And been thy wyves thral, as seyn these
   wyse;      20
And if that holy writ may nat suffyse,
Experience shal thee teche, so may happe,

That thee were lever to be take in Fryse
Than eft to falle of wedding in the trappe.

#### Envoy.

This litel writ, proverbes, or figure    25
I sende you, tak kepe of hit, I rede :

Unwys is he that can no wele endure.
If thou be siker, put thee nat in drede.
The Wyf of Bathe I pray you that ye rede
Of this matere that we have on honde. 30
God graunte you your lyf frely to lede
In fredom ; for ful hard is to be bonde.

*Explicit.*

---

# XVIII.  THE COMPLEYNT OF VENUS.

### I.  (*The Lover's worthiness.*)

Ther nis so hy comfort to my plesaunce,
Whan that I am in any hevinesse,
As for to have leyser of remembraunce
Upon the manhod and the worthinesse,
Upon the trouthe, and on the stedfastnesse
Of him whos I am al, whyl I may dure ;  6
Ther oghte blame me no creature,
For every wight preiseth his gentilesse.

In him is bountee, wisdom, governaunce
Wel more then any mannes wit can gesse ;
For grace hath wold so ferforth him
    avaunce      11
That of knighthode he is parfit richesse.
Honour honoureth him for his noblesse ;
Therto so wel hath formed him Nature,
That I am his for ever, I him assure,    15
For every wight preiseth his gentilesse.

And not-withstanding al his suffisaunce,
His gentil herte is of so greet humblesse
To me in worde, in werke, in contenaunce,
And me to serve is al his besinesse,    20
That I am set in verrey sikernesse.
Thus oghte I blesse wel myn aventure,
Sith that him list me serven and honoure ;
For every wight preiseth his gentilesse.

### II.  (*Disquietude caused by Jealousy.*)

Now certes, Love, hit is right covenable
That men ful dere bye thy noble thing, 26
As wake a-bedde, and fasten at the table,
Weping to laughe, and singe in com-
    pleyning,
And doun to caste visage and loking.

Often to chaungen hewe and contenaunce,
†Pleyne in sleping, and dremen at the
    daunce,      31
Al the revers of any glad feling.

Jalousye be hanged by a cable !
She wolde al knowe through hir espying ;
Ther doth no wight no-thing so resonable,
That al nis harm in hir imagening.    36
Thus dere abought is love, in yeving,
Which ofte he yiveth with-oute ordin-
    aunce,
As sorow ynogh, and litel of plesaunce,
Al the revers of any glad feling.    40

A litel tyme his yift is agreable,
But ful encomberous is the using ;
For sotel Jalousye, the deceyvable,
Ful often-tyme causeth destourbing.
Thus be we ever in drede and suffering,
In nouncerteyn we languisshe in pen-
    aunce,      46
And han ful often many an hard mes-
    chaunce,
Al the revers of any glad feling.

### III.  (*Satisfaction in Constancy.*)

But certes, Love, I sey nat in such wyse
That for t'escape out of your lace I mente ;
For I so longe have been in your servyse 51
That for to lete of wol I never assente ;
No force thogh Jalousye me tormente ;
Suffyceth me to see him whan I may,  54
And therfore certes, to myn ending-day
To love him best ne shal I never repente

And certes, Love, whan I me wel avyse
On any estat that man may represente,

Than have ye maked me, through your
    franchyse,
Chese the best that ever on erthe wente.
Now love wel, herte, and look thou never
    stente ;                61
And let the jelous putte hit in assay
That, for no peyne wol I nat sey nay ;
To love him best ne shal I never repente.

Herte, to thee hit oghte y-nogh suffyse   65
That Love so hy a grace to thee sente,
To chese the worthiest in alle wyse
And most agreable unto myn entente.
Seche no ferther, neyther wey ne wente,
Sith I have suffisaunce unto my pay.    70
Thus wol I ende this compleynt or lay ;
To love him best ne shal I never repente.

### Lenvoy.

Princess, receyveth this compleynt in
    gree,
Unto your excellent benignitee
    Direct after my litel suffisaunce.     75
For eld, that in my spirit dulleth me,
Hath of endyting al the soteltee
    Wel ny bereft out of my remem-
      braunce ;
    And eek to me hit is a greet pen-
      aunce,
Sith rym in English hath swich scarsitee,
To folowe word by word the curiositee   81
    Of Graunson, flour of hem that make
      in Fraunce.

## XIX. THE COMPLEINT OF CHAUCER TO HIS EMPTY PURSE.

To you, my purse, and to non other wight
Compleyne I, for ye be my lady dere !
I am so sory, now that ye be light ;
For certes, but ye make me hevy chere,
Me were as leef be leyd up-on my bere ;   5
For whiche un-to your mercy thus I crye :
Beth hevy ageyn, or elles mot I dye !

Now voucheth sauf this day, or hit be
    night,
That I of you the blisful soun may here,
Or see your colour lyk the sonne bright,
That of yelownesse hadde never pere.    11
Ye be my lyf, ye be myn hertes stere,
Quene of comfort and of good companye :
Beth hevy ageyn, or elles mot I dye !

Now purs, that be to me my lyves light,   15
And saveour, as doun in this worlde here,
Out of this toune help me through your
    might,
Sin that ye wole nat been my tresorere ;
For I am shave as nye as any frere.
But yit I pray un-to your curtesye :     20
Beth hevy ageyn, or elles mot I dye !

### Lenvoy de Chaucer.

O conquerour of Brutes Albioun !
Which that by lyne and free eleccioun
Ben verray king, this song to you I sende;
And ye, that mowen al our harm amende,
Have minde up-on my supplicacioun !   26

## XX. PROVERBS.

### Proverbe of Chaucer.

#### I.

WHAT shul thise clothes †many-fold,
    Lo ! this hote somers day ?—
After greet heet cometh cold ;
    No man caste his pilche away.      4

#### II.

Of al this world the wyde compas
    Hit wol not in myn armes tweyne.—
Who-so mochel wol embrace
    Litel therof he shal distreyne.

# APPENDIX.

*[The following Poems are also probably genuine; but are placed here for lack of external evidence.]*

## XXI. AGAINST WOMEN UNCONSTANT.

### Balade.

MADAME, for your newe-fangelnesse,
Many a servaunt have ye put out of grace,
I take my leve of your unstedfastnesse,
For wel I wot, whyl ye have lyves space,
Ye can not love ful half yeer in a place ; 5
To newe thing your lust is ever kene ;
In stede of blew, thus may ye were al
    grene.

Right as a mirour nothing may enpresse,
But, lightly as it cometh, so mot it pace,
So fareth your love, your werkes bereth
    witnesse.                                    10
Ther is no feith that may your herte en-
    brace ;

But, as a wedercok, that turneth his face
With every wind, ye fare, and that is
    sene ;
In stede of blew, thus may ye were al
    grene.

Ye might be shryned, for your brotelnesse,
Bet than Dalyda, Creseide or Candace ; 16
For ever in chaunging †stant your siker-
    nesse,
That tache may no wight fro your herte
    arace ;
If ye lese oon, ye can wel tweyn purchace ;
Al light for somer, ye woot wel what I
    mene,                                         20
In stede of blew, thus may ye were al
    grene.

*Explicit.*

## XXII. AN AMOROUS COMPLEINT. (COMPLEINT DAMOURS.)

### An amorous Compleint, made at Windsor.

I, WHICH that am the sorwefulleste
    man
That in this world was ever yit livinge,
And leest recoverer of him-selven can,
Beginne †thus my deedly compleininge
On hir, that may to lyf and deeth me
    bringe,                                       5

Which hath on me no mercy ne no rewthe
That love hir best, but sleeth me for my
    trewthe.

Can I noght doon ne seye that may yow
    lyke,
†For certes, now, allas ! allas ! the whyle !
Your plesaunce is to laughen whan I
    syke,                                         10
And thus ye me from al my blisse exyle.

Ye han me cast in thilke spitous yle
Ther never man on lyve mighte asterte ;
This have I for I lovĕ you, swete herte !

Sooth is, that wel I woot, by lyklinesse,
If that it were thing possible to do        16
T'acompte youre beutee and goodnesse,
I have no wonder thogh ye do me wo ;
Sith I, th'unworthiest that may ryde or go,
Durste ever thinken in so hy a place,        20
What wonder is, thogh ye do me no grace?

Allas ! thus is my lyf brought to an ende,
My deeth, I see, is my conclusioun ;
I may wel singe, 'in sory tyme I spende
My lyf ;' that song may have confusioun !
For mercy, pitee, and deep affeccioun,        26
I sey for me, for al my deedly chere,
Alle thise diden, in that, me love yow dere.

And in this wyse and in dispayre I live
In lovĕ ; nay, but in dispayre I dye !        30
But shal I thus [to] yow my deeth for-give,
That causeles doth me this sorow drye ?
Ye, certes, I ! For she of my folye
Hath nought to done, although she do me
        sterve ;
Hit is nat with hir wil that I hir serve!  35

Than sith I am of my sorowe the cause
And sith that I have this, withoute hir
        reed,
Than may I seyn, right shortly in a clause,
It is no blame unto hir womanheed
Though swich a wrecche as I be for hir
        deed ;        40
[And] yet alwey two thinges doon me dyĕ,
That is to seyn, hir beutee and myn yĕ.

So that, algates, she is the verray rote
Of my disese, and of my dethe also ;
For with oon word she mighte be my bote,
If that she vouched sauf for to do so.  46
But [why] than is hir gladnesse at my wo ?
It is hir wone plesaunce for to take,
To seen hir servaunts dyen for hir sake !

But certes, than is al my wonderinge,  50
Sithen she is the fayrest creature
As to my dome, that ever was livinge,
The benignest and beste eek that nature
Hath wrought or shal, whyl that the
        world may dure,

Why that she lefte pite so behinde ?    55
It was, y-wis, a greet defaute in kinde.

Yit is al this no lak to hir, pardee,
But god or nature sore wolde I blame ;
For, though she shewe no pite unto me,
Sithen that she doth othere men the same,
I ne oughte to despyse my ladies game ; 61
It is hir pley to laughen whan men syketh,
And I assente, al that hir list and lyketh !

Yit wolde I, as I dar, with sorweful herte
Biseche un-to your meke womanhede  65
That I now dorste my sharpe sorwes
        smerte
Shewe by worde, that ye wolde ones rede
The pleynte of me, the which ful sore
        drede
That I have seid here, through myn un-
        conninge,
In any worde to your displesinge.        70

Lothest of anything that ever was loth
Were me, as wisly god my soule save !
To seyn a thing through which ye might
        be wroth ;
And, to that day that I be leyd in grave,
A trewer servaunt shulle ye never have ;
And, though that I on yow have pleyned
        here,        76
Forgiveth it me, myn owne lady dere !

Ever have I been, and shal, how-so I
        wende,
Outher to live or dye, your humble trewe ;
Ye been to me my ginning and myn ende,
Sonne of the sterre bright and clere of
        hewe,        81
Alwey in oon to love yow freshly newe,
By god and by my trouthe, is myn entente;
To live or dye, I wol it never repente !

This compleynt on seint Valentynes day,
Whan every foul [ther] chesen shal his
        make,        86
To hir, whos I am hool, and shal alwey,
This woful song and this compleynt I
        make,
That never yit wolde me to mercy take ;
And yit wol I [for] evermore her serve  90
And love hir best, although she do me
        sterve.

*Explicit.*

## XXIII.  A BALADE OF COMPLEYNT.

*[This is added as being a good example of a* Compleynt *in* Chaucer's *style.]*

COMPLEYNE ne coude, ne might myn herte
    never
My peynes halve, ne what torment I have,
Though that I sholde in your presence
    ben ever,
My hertes lady, as wisly he me save
That bountee made, and beutee list to
    grave       5
In your persone, and bad hem bothe infere
Ever t'awayte, and ay be wher ye were.

As wisly he gye alle my joyes here
As I am youres, and to yow sad and trewe,
And ye, my lyf and cause of my good
    chere,       10

And deeth also, whan ye my peynes newe,
My worldes joye, whom I wol serve and
    sewe,
My heven hool, and al my suffisaunce,
Whom for to serve is set al my plesaunce.

Beseching yow in my most humble wyse
T'accepte in worth this litel povre dyte,  16
And for my trouthe my service nat de-
    spyse,
Myn observaunce eek have nat in despyte,
Ne yit to long to suffren in this plyte;
I yow beseche, myn hertes lady, here,  20
Sith I yow serve, and so wil yeer by
    yere.

---

## XXIV.  WOMANLY NOBLESSE.

*[This genuine poem was first printed in* June, 1894.]*

### Balade that Chaucier made.

So hath my herte caught in rémembraunce
Your beautè hool, and stedfast govern-
    aunce,
    Your vertues allè, and your hy noblesse,
That you to serve is set al my plesaunce ;
So wel me lykth your womanly conten-
    aunce,       5
    Your fresshe fetures and your com-
      linesse,
    That, whyl I live, my herte to his
      maistresse,
You hath ful chose, in trew perséveraunce,
    Never to chaunge, for no maner dis-
      tresse.

And sith I [you] shal do this ob-
    servaunce       10
Al my lyf, withouten displesaunce,
    You for to serve with al my besinesse,
[Taketh me, lady, in your obeisaunce]
And have me somwhat in your souven-
    aunce.
    My woful herte suffreth greet duresse ; 15
    And [loke] how humbl[el]y, with al
      simplesse,

My wil I cónforme to your ordenaunce,
    As you best list, my peynes † to redresse.

Considring eek how I hange in balaunce
In your servycè ; swich, lo ! is my
    chaunce,       20
    Abyding grace, whan that your gentil-
      nesse
Of my gret wo list doon allegeaunce,
And with your pitè me som wyse avaunce,
    In ful rebating of my hevinesse ;
    And think †resóun, that wommanly
      noblesse       25
Shuld nat desyre † for to doon outrance
Ther-asshe findeth noon unbuxumnesse.

### Lenvoye.

Auctour of norture, lady of plesaunce,
    Soveraine of beautè, flour of womman-
      hede,
Take ye non hede unto myn ignoraunce, 30
    But this receyveth of your goodlihede,
Thinking that I have caught in re-
    membraunce
Your beautè hool, your stedfast govern-
    aunce.

F

# BOETHIUS DE CONSOLATIONE PHILOSOPHIE.

---

## BOOK I.

METRE I. *Carmina qui quondam studio florente peregi.*

ALLAS! I, weping, am constreined to biginnen vers of sorowful matere, that whylom in florisching studie made delitable ditees. For lo! rendinge Muses of 5 poetes endyten to me thinges to be writen; and drery vers of wrecchednesse weten my face with verray teres. At the leeste, no drede ne mighte overcomen tho Muses, that they ne weren 10 felawes, and folweden my wey, *that is to seyn, whan I was exyled*; they that weren glorie of my youthe, whylom weleful and grene, comforten now the sorowful werdes of me, olde man. For elde 15 is comen unwarly upon me, hasted by the harmes that I have, and sorow hath comaunded his age to be in me. Heres hore ben shad overtymeliche upon myn heved, and the slake skin trembleth upon 20 myn empted body. Thilke deeth of men is weleful that ne cometh not in yeres that ben swete, but cometh to wrecches, often y-cleped. Allas! allas! with how deef an ere deeth, cruel, torneth awey 25 fro wrecches, and naiteth to closen wepinge eyen! Whyl Fortune, unfeithful, favorede me with lighte goodes, the sorowful houre, *that is to seyn, the deeth*, hadde almost dreynt myn heved. But 30 now, for Fortune cloudy hath chaunged hir deceyvable chere to me-ward, myn unpitous lyf draweth a-long unagreable dwellinges *in me*. O ye, my frendes, what or whertoavauntede ye me to ben weleful? for he that hath fallen stood nat in 35 stedefast degree.

PROSE I. *Hec dum mecum tacitus ipse reputarem.*

Whyle that I stille recordede thise thinges with my-self, and markede my weeply compleynte with office of pointel, I saw, stondinge aboven the heighte of myn heved, a woman of ful greet re- 5 verence by semblaunt, hir eyen brenninge and cleer-seinge over the comune might of men; with a lyfly colour, and with swich vigour and strengthe that it ne mighte nat ben empted; al were it 10 so that she was ful of so greet age, that men ne wolde nat trowen, in no manere, that she were of oure elde. The stature of hir was of a doutous jugement; for som-tyme she constreinede and shronk 15 hir-selven lyk to the comune mesure of men, and sum-tyme it semede that she touchede the hevene with the heighte of hir heved; and whan she heef hir heved hyer, she percede the selve hevene, so 20 that the sighte of men looking was in ydel. Hir clothes weren maked of right delye thredes and subtil crafte, of perdurable matere; the whiche clothes she

25 hadde woven with hir owene hondes, as
I knew wel after by hir-self, declaringe
and shewinge to me the beautee; the
whiche clothes a derknesse of a forleten
and dispysed elde hadde dusked and
30 derked, as it is wont to derken bi-
smokede images.    In the nethereste
hem or bordure of thise clothes men
redden, y-woven in, a Grekissh P, *that
signifyeth the lyf Actif*; and aboven that
35 lettre, in the heyeste bordure, a Grekissh
T, *that signifyeth the lyf Contemplatif.*
And bi-twixen these two lettres ther
weren seyn degrees, nobly y-wroght in
manere of laddres; by whiche degrees
40 men mighten climben fro the nethereste
lettre to the uppereste. Natheles, handes
of some men hadde corven that cloth
by violence and by strengthe; and
everiche man of hem hadde born awey
45 swiche peces as he mighte geten. And
forsothe, this forseide woman bar smale
bokes in hir right hand, and in hir left
hand she bar a ceptre.    And whan she
say thise poetical Muses aprochen aboute
50 my bed, and endytinge wordes to my
wepinges, she was a litel amoved, and
glowede with cruel eyen. 'Who,' quod
she, 'hath suffred aprochen to this syke
man thise comune strompetes of swich
55 a place that men clepen the theatre?
The whiche nat only ne asswagen nat
hise sorwes with none remedies, but they
wolden feden and norisshen hem with
swete venim. Forsothe, thise ben tho
60 that with thornes and prikkinges of
talents or affecciouns, whiche that ne
ben no-thing fructefyinge nor profitable,
destroyen the corn plentevous of fruites
of resoun; for they holden the hertes
65 of men in usage, but they ne delivere
nat folk fro maladye. But if ye Muses
hadden withdrawen fro me, with your
flateryes, any uncunninge and unprofitable man, as men ben wont to finde
70 comunly amonges the poeple, I wolde
wene suffre the lasse grevously; for-why,
in swiche an unprofitable man, myn
ententes ne weren no-thing endamaged.
But ye withdrawen †from me this man,
75 that hath be norisshed in the studies or

scoles of Eleaticis and of Achademicis *in
Grece.* But goth now rather awey, ye
mermaidenes, whiche that ben swete til
it be at the laste, and suffreth this man
to be cured and heled by myne Muses,' 80
*that is to seyn, by noteful sciences.* And
thus this companye of Muses y-blamed
casten wrothly the chere dounward to
the erthe; and, shewinge by reednesse
hir shame, they passeden sorowfully the 85
threshfold.    And I, of whom the sighte,
plounged in teres, was derked so that
I ne mighte not knowen what that
womman was, of so imperial auctoritee,
I wex al abaisshed and astoned, and caste 90
my sighte doun to the erthe, and bigan
stille for to abyde what she wolde don
afterward. Tho com she ner, and sette
hir doun up-on the uttereste corner of
my bed; and she, biholdinge my chere, 95
that was cast to the erthe, hevy and
grevous of wepinge, compleinede, with
thise wordes that I shal seyen, the perturbacioun of my thought.

METRE II.    *Heu quam precipiti mersa
profundo.*

'Allas! how the thought of man, dreint
in over-throwinge deepnesse, dulleth, and
forleteth his propre cleernesse, mintinge
to goon in-to foreine derknesses, as ofte
as his anoyous bisinesse wexeth with- 5
oute mesure, that is driven to and fro
with worldly windes! This man, that
whylom was free, to whom the hevene
was open and knowen, and was wont
to goon in heveneliche pathes, and saugh 10
the lightnesse of the rede sonne, and
saugh the sterres of the colde mone, and
whiche sterre in hevene useth wandering
recourses, y-flit by dyverse speres—this
man, overcomer, hadde comprehended 15
al this by noumbre *of acountinge in astronomye.* And over this, he was wont to
seken the causes whennes the souning
windes moeven and bisien the smothe
water of the see; and what spirit torneth 20
the stable hevene; and why the sterre
aryseth out of the rede eest, to fallen in
the westrene wawes; and what atempreth

the lusty houres of the firste somer
25 sesoun, that highteth and apparaileth
the erthe with rosene flowres; and who
maketh that plentevouse autompne, in
fulle yeres, fleteth with hevy grapes.
And eek this man was wont to telle the
30 dyverse causes of nature that weren
y-hidde. Allas! now lyeth he empted of
light of his thought; and his nekke is
pressed with hevy cheynes; and bereth
his chere enclyned adoun for the grete
35 weighte, and is constreined to looken on
the fool erthe!

## PROSE II. *Set medicine, inquit, tempus est.*

But tyme is now,' quod she, ' of medicine more than of compleinte.' Forsothe
than she, entendinge to me-ward with
alle the lookinge of hir eyen, seide :—'Art
5 nat thou he,' quod she, ' that whylom
y-norisshed with my milk, and fostered
with myne metes, were escaped and
comen to corage of a parfit man? Certes,
I yaf thee swiche armures that, yif thou
10 thy-self ne haddest first cast hem a-wey,
they shulden han defended thee in sikernesse that may nat ben over-comen.
Knowest thou me nat? Why art thou
stille? Is it for shame or for astoninge?
15 It were me lever that it were for shame;
but it semeth me that astoninge hath
oppressed thee.' And whan she say me
nat only stille, but with-outen office of
tunge and al doumb, she leide hir hand
20 softely upon my brest, and seide : 'Here
nis no peril,' quod she ; ' he is fallen into
a litargie, whiche that is a comune
sykenes to hertes that ben deceived. He
hath a litel foryeten him-self, but certes
25 he shal lightly remembren him-self, yif
so be that he hath knowen me or now;
and that he may so don, I wil wypen
a litel his eyen, that ben derked by the
cloude of mortal thinges.' Thise wordes
30 seide she, and with the lappe of hir garment, y-plyted in a frounce, she dryede
myn eyen, that weren fulle of the wawes
of my wepinges.

## METRE III. *Tunc me discussa liquerunt nocte tenebre.*

Thus, whan that night was discussed
and chased a-wey, derknesses forleften
me, and to myn eyen repeirede ayein hir
firste strengthe. And, right by ensaumple
as the sonne is hid whan the sterres ben 5
clustred (*that is to seyn, whan sterres ben
covered with cloudes*) by a swifte winde
that highte Chorus, and that the firmament stant derked by wete ploungy
cloudes, and that the sterres nat apperen 10
up-on hevene, so that the night semeth
sprad up-on erthe : yif thanne the wind
that highte Borias, y-sent out of the caves
of the contree of Trace, beteth this night
(*that is to seyn, chaseth it a-wey*), and 15
descovereth the closed day : than shyneth
Phebus y-shaken with sodein light, and
smyteth with his bemes in mervelinge
eyen.

## PROSE III. *Haud aliter tristicie nebulis dissolutis.*

Right so, and non other wyse, the
cloudes of sorwe dissolved and don a-wey,
I took hevene, and receivede minde to
knowen the face of my fysicien ; so that
I sette myn eyen on hir, and fastnede my 5
lookinge. I beholde my norice Philosophie, in whos houses I hadde conversed
and haunted fro my youthe ; and I seide
thus. ' O thou maistresse of alle vertues,
descended from the soverein sete, why 10
artow comen in-to this solitarie place of
myn exil? Artow comen for thou art
maked coupable with me of false blames?'
*Phil.* ' O,' quod she, ' my norry, sholde
I forsaken thee now, and sholde I nat 15
parten with thee, by comune travaile, the
charge that thou hast suffred for envie of
my name? Certes, it nere not leveful ne
sittinge thing to Philosophie, to leten
with-outen companye the wey of him that 20
is innocent. Sholde I thanne redoute my
blame, and agrysen as though ther were
bifallen a newe thing? *quasi diceret, non.*
For trowestow that Philosophie be now
alderfirst assailed in perils by folk of 25
wikkede maneres? Have I nat striven

with ful greet stryf, in olde tyme, bifore the age of my Plato, ayeines the foolhardinesse of folye? And eek, the same Plato 30 livinge, his maister Socrates deservede victorie of unrightful deeth in my presence. The heritage of which Socrates— *the heritage is to seyn the doctrine of the whiche Socrates in his opinioun of Felicitee,* 35 *that I clepe welefulnesse*—whan that the poeple of Epicuriens and Stoiciens and many othre enforceden hem to go ravisshe everich man for his part—*that is to seyn, that everich of hem wolde drawen to the* 40 *defence of his opinioun the wordes of Socrates*—they, as in partie of hir preye, to-drowen me, cryinge and debatinge ther-ayeins, and corven and to-renten my clothes that I hadde woven with myn 45 handes; and with tho cloutes that they hadden araced out of my clothes they wenten awey, weninge that I hadde gon with hem everydel. In whiche *Epicuriens and Stoiciens,* for as moche as ther 50 semede some traces or steppes of myn habite, the folye of men, weninge tho *Epicuriens and Stoiciens* my famuleres, perverted (*sc. persequendo*) some through the errour of the wikkede or uncunninge 55 multitude of hem. *This is to seyn that, for they semede philosophres, they weren pursued to the deeth and slayn.* So yif thou hast nat knowen the exilinge of Anaxogore, ne the enpoysoninge of Socrates, ne 60 the tourments of Zeno, for they weren straungeres: yit mightestow han knowen the Senecciens and the Canios and the †Soranos, of whiche folk the renoun is neither over-olde ne unsolempne. The 65 whiche men, no-thing elles ne broughte hem to the deeth but only for they weren enfourmed of myne maneres, and semeden most unlyke to the studies of wikkede folk. And forthy thou oughtest nat 70 to wondren though that I, in the bittre see of this lyf, be fordriven with tempestes blowinge aboute, in the whiche tempestes this is my most purpos, *that is to seyn,* to displesen to wikkede men. Of 75 whiche shrewes, al be the ost never so greet, it is to dispyse; for it nis governed with no leder of resoun, but it is ravisshed

only by fletinge errour folyly and lightly. And if they som-tyme, makinge an ost ayeins us, assaile us as strenger, our leder 80 draweth to-gidere hise richesses in-to his tour, and they ben ententif aboute sarpulers or sachels unprofitable for to taken. But we that ben heye aboven, siker fro alle tumulte and wode noise, warnestored 85 and enclosed in swich a palis, whider as that chateringe or anoyinge folye ne may nat atayne, we scorne swiche ravineres and henteres of fouleste thinges.

METRE IV. *Quisquis composito serenus euo.*

Who-so it be that is cleer of vertu, sad, and wel ordinat of livinge, that hath put under foot the proude werdes and looketh upright up-on either fortune, he may holde his chere undiscomfited. The rage 5 ne the manaces of the see, commoevinge or chasinge upward hete fro the botme, ne shal not moeve that man; ne the unstable mountaigne that highte Vesevus, that wrytheth out through his brokene 10 chiminees smokinge fyres. Ne the wey of †thonder-leyt, that is wont to smyten heye toures, ne shal nat moeve that man. Wher-to thanne, o wrecches, drede ye tirauntes that ben wode and felonous 15 with-oute any strengthe? Hope after no-thing, ne drede nat; and so shaltow desarmen the ire of thilke unmighty tiraunt. But who-so that, quakinge, dredeth or desireth thing that nis nat 20 stable of his right, that man that so doth hath cast awey his sheld and is remoeved fro his place, and enlaceth him in the cheyne with the which he may ben drawen. 25

PROSE IV. *Sentisne, inquit, hec.*

Felestow,' quod she, 'thise thinges, and entren they aught in thy corage? Artow lyke an asse to the harpe? Why wepestow, why spillestow teres? Yif thou abydest after help of thy leche, thee 5 bihoveth discovere thy wounde.' Tho I, that hadde gadered strengthe in my corage, answerede and seide: 'And nedeth it yit,' quod I, 'of rehersinge or of amonicioun; and sheweth it nat 10

y-nough by him-self the sharpnesse of
Fortune, that wexeth wood ayeins me?
Ne moeveth it nat thee to seen the face
or the manere of this place (*i. prisoun*)?
15 Is this the librarie whiche that thou
haddest chosen for a right certein sete to
thee in myn hous, ther-as thou desputedest
ofte with me of the sciences of thinges
touchinge divinitee and touchinge man-
20 kinde? Was thanne myn habite swich
as it is now? Was than my face or my
chere swiche as now (*quasi diceret, non*),
whan I soughte with thee secrets of
nature, whan thou enformedest my ma-
25 neres and the resoun of alle my lyf to the
ensaumple of the ordre of hevene? Is nat
this the guerdoun that I referre to thee,
to whom I have be obeisaunt? Certes,
thou confermedest, by the mouth of Plato,
30 this sentence, *that is to seyn*, that comune
thinges or comunalitees weren blisful, yif
they that hadden studied al fully to wisdom governeden thilke thinges, or elles
yif it so bifille that the governoures of
35 comunalitees studieden to geten wisdom.
Thou seidest eek, by the mouth of the
same Plato, that it was a necessarie
cause, wyse men to taken and desire the
governaunce of comune thinges, for that
40 the governements of citees, y-left in the
handes of felonous tormentours citizenes,
ne sholde nat bringe in pestilence and
destruccioun to gode folk. And therfor
I, folwinge thilke auctoritee (*sc. Platonis*),
45 desired to putten forth in execucioun and
in acte of comune administracioun thilke
thinges that I hadde lerned of thee among
my secree resting-whyles. Thou, and god
that putte thee in the thoughtes of wyse
50 folk, ben knowinge with me, that no-
thing ne broughte me to maistrie or
dignitee, but the comune studie of alle
goodnesse. And ther-of comth it that
bi-twixen wikked folk and me han ben
55 grevous discordes, that ne mighten ben
relesed by preyeres; for this libertee hath
the freedom of conscience, that the wrath he
of more mighty folk hath alwey ben despysed of me for savacioun of right. How
60 ofte have I resisted and withstonde thilke
man that highte Conigaste, that made

alwey assautes ayeins the prospre fortunes
of pore feble folk? How ofte eek have
I put of or cast out him, Trigwille, provost of the kinges hous, bothe of the 65
wronges that he hadde bigunne to don,
and eek fully performed? How ofte have
I covered and defended by the auctoritee
of me, put ayeins perils—*that is to seyn,
put myn auctoritee in peril for*—the 70
wrecched pore folk, that the covetyse of
straungeres unpunished tourmenteden
alwey with miseyses and grevaunces out
of noumbre? Never man ne drow me yit
fro right to wronge. Whan I say the 75
fortunes and the richesses of the poeple
of the provinces ben harmed or amenused,
outher by privee ravynes or by comune
tributes or cariages, as sory was I as they
that suffreden the harm. —— **Glossa.** 80
*Whan that Theodoric, the king of Gothes,
in a dere yere, hadde hise gerneres ful of
corn, and comaundede that no man ne sholde
byen no corn til his corn were sold, and that
at a grevous dere prys, Boece withstood that* 85
*ordinaunce, and over-com it, knowinge al
this the king him-self.*——**Textus.** Whan
it was in the soure hungry tyme, ther
was establisshed or cryed grevous and
inplitable coempcioun, that men sayen 90
wel it sholde greetly turmenten and endamagen al the province of Campaigne,
I took stryf ayeins the provost of the
pretorie for comune profit. And, the king
knowinge of it, I overcom it, so that the 95
coempcioun ne was not axed ne took
effect.——[**Glossa.**] †*Coempcioun, that is to
seyn, comune achat or bying to-gidere, that
were establisshed up-on the poeple by swiche
a manere imposicioun, as who-so boughte* 100
*a busshel corn, he moste yeve the king the
fifte part.*——[**Textus.**] Paulin, a counseiller of Rome, the richesses of the
whiche Paulin the houndes of the palays,
*that is to seyn, the officeres,* wolden han 105
devoured by hope and covetise, yit drow
I him out of the jowes (*sc. faucibus*) of hem
that gapeden. And for as moche as the
peyne of the accusacioun ajuged biforn ne
sholde nat sodeinly henten ne punisshen 110
wrongfully Albin, a counseiller of Rome,
I putte me ayeins the hates and indig-

naciouns of the accusor Ciprian. Is it nat thanne y-nough y-seyn, that I have pur-
15 chased grete discordes ayeins my-self? But I oughte be the more assured ayeins alle othre folk (s. Romayns), that for the love of rightwisnesse I ne reserved never no-thing to my-self to hemward of the
20 kinges halle, sc. officers, by the whiche I were the more siker. But thorugh tho same accusors accusinge, I am con-dempned. Of the noumbir of the whiche accusors oon Basilius, that whylom was
25 chased out of the kinges service, is now compelled in accusinge of my name, for nede of foreine moneye. Also Opilion and Gaudencius han accused me, al be it so that the justice regal hadde whylom
30 demed hem bothe to go in-to exil for hir trecheryes and fraudes withoute noumbir. To whiche jugement they nolden nat obeye, but defendeden hem by the siker-nesse of holy houses, that is to seyn, fledden
35 into seintuaries; and whan this was aper-ceived to the king, he comaundede, that but they voidede the citee of Ravenne by certein day assigned, that men sholde merken hem on the forheved with an hoot
40 yren and chasen hem out of the toune. Now what thing, semeth thee, mighte ben lykned to this crueltee? For certes, thilke same day was received the accusinge of my name by thilke same accusors. What
45 may ben seid her-to? (quasi diceret, nichil). Hath my studie and my cunninge de-served thus; or elles the forseide damp-nacioun of me, made that hem rightful accusors or no? (quasi diceret, non). Was
50 not Fortune ashamed of this? Certes, al hadde nat Fortune ben ashamed that innocence was accused, yit oughte she han had shame of the filthe of myne accusours.

55 But, axestow in somme, of what gilt I am accused, men seyn that I wolde save the companye of the senatours. And desirest thou to heren in what manere? I am accused that I sholde han des-
60 tourbed the accusor to beren lettres, by whiche he sholde han maked the sena-toures gilty ayeins the kinges real ma-jestee. O maistresse, what demestow of

this? Shal I forsake this blame, that I ne be no shame to thee? (quasi diceret, non). 165 Certes, I have wold it, that is to seyn, the savacioun of the senat, ne I shal never leten to wilne it, and that I confesse and am aknowe; but the entente of the accusor to be destourbed shal cese. For 170 shal I clepe it thanne a felonie or a sinne that I have desired the savacioun of the ordre of the senat? (quasi diceret, dubito quid). And certes yit hadde thilke same senat don by me, thorugh hir decrets and 175 hir jugements, as though it were a sinne or a felonie; that is to seyn, to wilne the savacioun of hem (sc. senatus). But folye, that lyeth alwey to him-self, may not chaunge the merite of thinges. Ne I trowe 180 nat, by the jugement of Socrates, that it were leveful to me to hyde the sothe, ne assente to lesinges. But certes, how so ever it be of this, I putte it to gessen or preisen to the jugement of thee and of 185 wyse folk. Of whiche thing al the ordi-naunce and the sothe, for as moche as folk that ben to comen after our dayes shullen knowen it, I have put it in scrip-ture and in remembraunce. For touching 190 the lettres falsly maked, by whiche lettres I am accused to han hoped the fredom of Rome, what aperteneth me to speke ther-of? Of whiche lettres the fraude hadde ben shewed apertly, yif I hadde had 195 libertee for to han used and been at the confessioun of myne accusours, the whiche thing in alle nedes hath greet strengthe. For what other fredom may men hopen? Certes, I wolde that som 200 other fredom mighte ben hoped. I wolde thanne han answered by the wordes of a man that highte Canius; for whan he was accused by Gaius Cesar, Ger-meynes sone, that he (Canius) was know- 205 inge and consentinge uf a conjuracioun y-maked ayeins him (sc. Gaius), this Canius answerede thus: "Yif I hadde wist it, thou haddest nat wist it." In which thing sorwe hath nat so dulled my 210 wit, that I pleyne only that shrewede folk aparailen felonies ayeins vertu; but I wondre greetly how that they may per-forme thinges that they hadde hoped for to

215 don. For-why, to wilne shrewednesse,
that comth peraventure of oure defaute;
but it is lyk a monstre and a mervaille,
how that, in the present sighte of god,
may ben acheved and performed swiche
220 thinges as every felonous man hath conceived in his thought ayeins innocents.
For which thing oon of thy famileres nat
unskilfully axed thus : " Yif god is,
whennes comen wikkede thinges ? And
225 yif god ne is, whennes comen gode
thinges ? " But al hadde it ben leveful
that felonous folk, that now desiren the
blood and the deeth of alle gode men and
eek of alle the senat, han wilned to gon
230 destroyen me, whom they han seyen
alwey batailen and defenden gode men
and eek al the senat, yit had I nat
desserved of the faderes, *that is to seyn, of
the senatoures*, that they sholden wilne my
235 destruccioun.

Thou remembrest wel, as I gesse, that
whan I wolde doon or seyen any thing,
thou thyself, alwey present, rewledest me.
At the city of Verone, whan that the
240 king, gredy of comune slaughter, caste
him to transporten up al the ordre of the
senat the gilt of his real majestee, of the
whiche gilt that Albin was accused, with
how gret sikernesse of peril to me de-
245 fendede I al the senat ! Thou wost wel
that I seye sooth, ne I ne avauntede me
never in preysinge of my-self. For alwey,
whan any wight receiveth precious renoun
in avauntinge him-self of his werkes, he
250 amenuseth the secree of his conscience.
But now thou mayst wel seen to what
ende I am comen for myne innocence;
I receive peyne of fals felonye for guerdon
of verray vertu. And what open con-
255 fessioun of felonye hadde ever juges so
acordaunt in crueltee, *that is to seyn, as
myn accusinge hath*, that either errour of
mannes wit or elles condicioun of Fortune, that is uncertain to alle mortal
260 folk, ne submittede some of hem, *that is
to seyn, that it ne enclynede som juge to han
pitee or compassioun?* For al-thogh I
hadde ben accused that I wolde brenne
holy houses, and strangle preestes with
265 wikkede swerde, or that I hadde greythed

deeth to al gode men, algates the sentence
sholde han punisshed me, present, confessed, or convict. But now I am remewed
fro the citee *of Rome* almost fyve hundred
thousand pas, I am with-oute defence 270
dampned to proscripcioun and to the
deeth, for the studie and bountees that
I have doon to the senat. But O, wel ben
they worthy of merite (*as who seith, nay*),
ther mighte never yit non of hem be 275
convict of swiche a blame as myne is ! Of
whiche trespas, myne accusours sayen ful
wel the dignitee; the whiche dignitee,
for they wolden derken it with medeling
of som felonye, they baren me on hand, 280
and lyeden, that I hadde polut and defouled my conscience with sacrilege, for
coveitise of dignitee. And certes, thou thy-
self, that art plaunted in me, chacedest
out of the sege of my corage al coveitise of 285
mortal thinges; ne sacrilege hadde no
leve to han a place in me biforn thyne
eyen. For thou droppedest every day in
myne eres and in my thought thilke
comaundement of Pictagoras, *that is to* 290
*seyn*, men shal serve to godde, *and not to*
*goddes*. Ne it was nat convenient, *ne no*
*nede*, to taken help of the foulest spirites;
I, that thou hast ordeined and set in
swiche excellence that thou makedest me 295
lyk to god. And over this, the right clene
secree chaumbre of myne hous, *that is to*
*seyn, my wyf*, and the companye of myn
honest freendes, and my wyves fader, as
wel holy as worthy to ben reverenced 300
thorugh his owne dedes, defenden me
from alle suspecioun of swich blame. But
O malice ! For they that accusen me
taken of thee, *Philosophie*, feith of so gret
blame ! For they trowen that I have had 305
affinitee to malefice *or enchauntement*,
by-cause that I am replenisshed and
fulfilled with thy techinges, and enformed
of thy maneres. And thus it suffiseth not
only, that thy reverence ne availe me not, 310
but-yif that thou, of thy free wille, rather
be blemished with myn offencioun. But
certes, to the harmes that I have, ther
bitydeth yit this encrees of harm, that
the gessinge and the jugement of moche 315
folk ne looken no-thing to the desertes of

thinges, but only to the aventure of fortune; and jugen that only swiche thinges ben purveyed of god, whiche that
20 temporel welefulnesse commendeth.——
Glose. *As thus: that, yif a wight have prosperitee, he is a good man and worthy to han that prosperitee; and who-so hath adversitee, he is a wikked man, and god*
25 *hath forsake him, and he is worthy to han that adversitee. This is the opinioun of some folk.*——And ther-of comth that good gessinge, first of alle thing, forsaketh wrecches: certes, it greveth me to thinke
30 right now the dyverse sentences that the poeple seith of me. And thus moche I seye, that the laste charge of contrarious fortune is this: that, whan that any blame is leyd upon a caitif, men wenen
35 that he hath deserved that he suffreth. And I, that am put awey fro gode men, and despoiled of dignitees, and defouled of my name by gessinge, have suffred torment for my gode dedes. Certes, me
40 semeth that I see the felonous covines of wikked men habounden in joye and in gladnesse. And I see that every lorel shapeth him to finde out newe fraudes for to accuse gode folk. And I see that gode
45 men beth overthrowen for drede of my peril; and every luxurious tourmentour dar doon alle felonye unpunisshed and ben excited therto by yiftes; and inno-cents ne ben not only despoiled of siker-
50 nesse but of defence; and therfore me list to cryen *to god* in this wyse :—

METRE V. *O stelliferi conditor orbis.*

O thou maker of the whele that bereth the sterres, which that art y-fastned to thy perdurable chayer, and tornest the hevene with a ravisshing sweigh, and
5 constreinest the sterres to suffren thy lawe; so that the mone som-tyme shyning with hir ful hornes, meting with alle the bemes of the sonne hir brother, hydeth the sterres that ben lesse; and somtyme,
10 whan the mone, pale with hir derke hornes, approcheth the sonne, leseth hir lightes; and that the eve-sterre Hesperus, whiche that in the firste tyme of the night

bringeth forth hir colde arysinges, cometh
15 eft ayein hir used cours, and is pale *by the morwe* at the rysing of the sonne, and is thanne cleped Lucifer. Thou restreinest the day by shorter dwelling, in the tyme of colde winter that maketh the leves to
20 falle. Thou dividest the swifte tydes of the night, whan the hote somer is comen. Thy might atempreth the variaunts sesons of the yere; so that Zephirus the deboneir wind bringeth ayein, *in the first*
25 *somer sesoun,* the leves that the wind that highte Boreas hath reft awey *in autumpne, that is to seyn, in the laste ende of somer*; and the sedes that the sterre that highte Arcturus saw, ben waxen heye cornes
30 whan the sterre Sirius eschaufeth hem. Ther nis no-thing unbounde from his olde lawe, ne forleteth the werke of his propre estat. O thou governour, governinge alle thinges by certein ende, why re-
35 fusestow only to governe the werkes of men by dewe manere? Why suffrest thou that slydinge fortune torneth so grete entrechaunginges of thinges, so that anoyous peyne, that sholde dewely
40 punisshe felouns, punissheth innocents? And folk of wikkede maneres sitten in heye chayres, and anoyinge folk treden, and that unrightfully, on the nekkes of holy men? And vertu, cler-shyninge
45 naturelly, is hid in derke derkenesses, and the rightful man bereth the blame and the peyne of the feloun. Ne forsweringe ne the fraude, covered and kembd with a fals colour, ne anoyeth nat to shrewes;
50 the whiche shrewes, whan hem list to usen hir strengthe, they rejoysen hem to putten under hem the sovereyne kinges, whiche that poeple with-outen noumbre dreden. O thou, what so ever thou
55 be that knittest alle bondes of thinges, loke on thise wrecchede erthes; we men that ben nat a foule party, but a fayr party of so grete a werk, we ben tormented in this see of fortune. Thou governour,
60 withdraw and restreyne the ravisshinge flodes, and fastne and ferme thise erthes stable with thilke bonde, with whiche thou governest the hevene that is so large.'

PROSE V. *Hic ubi continuato dolore delatraui.*

Whan I hadde, with a continuel sorwe, sobbed or borken out thise thinges, she with hir chere pesible, and no-thing amoeved with my compleintes, seide thus:
5 'Whan I say thee,' quod she, 'sorweful and wepinge, I wiste anon that thou were a wrecche and exiled ; but I wiste never how fer thyne exile was, yif thy tale ne hadde shewed it to me. But certes, al be
10 thou fer fro thy contree, thou nart nat put out of it ; but thou hast failed of thy weye and gon amis. And yif thou hast lever for to wene that thou be put out of thy contree, than hast thou put out thy-
15 self rather than any other wight hath. For no wight but thy-self ne mighte never han don that to thee. For yif thou remembre of what contree thou art born, it nis nat governed by emperours, ne by
20 governement of multitude, as weren the contrees of hem of Athenes ; but oo lord and oo king, *and that is god, that is lord of thy contree,* whiche that rejoyseth him of the dwelling of hise citezenes, and nat
25 for to putte hem in exil ; of the whiche lorde it is a soverayne fredom to be governed by the brydel of him and obeye to his justice. Hastow foryeten thilke right olde lawe of thy citee, in the whiche
30 citee it is ordeined and establisshed, that for what wight that hath lever founden ther-in his sete or his hous than elles-wher, he may nat be exiled by no right from that place? For who-so that is
35 contened in-with the palis and the clos of thilke citee, ther nis no drede that he may deserve to ben exiled. But who-so that leteth the wil for to enhabite there, he forleteth also to deserve to ben citezein
40 of thilke citee. So that I sey, that the face of this place ne moveth me nat so mochel as thyne owne face. Ne I axe nat rather the walles of thy librarie, apar-ayled and wrought with yvory and with
45 glas, than after the sete of thy thought. In whiche I putte nat whylom bokes, but I putte that that maketh bokes worthy of prys or precious, that is to seyn, the

sentence of my bokes. And certeinly of thy desertes, bistowed in comune good, 50 thou hast seid sooth, but after the multi-tude of thy gode dedes, thou hast seid fewe ; and of the honestee or of the fals-nesse of thinges that ben aposed ayeins thee, thou hast remembred thinges that 55 ben knowen to alle folk. And of the felonyes and fraudes of thyne accusours, it semeth thee have y-touched it forsothe rightfully and shortly, al mighten tho same thinges betere and more plenti- 60 vously ben couth in the mouthe of the poeple that knoweth al this. Thou hast eek blamed gretly and compleined of the wrongful dede of the senat. And thou hast sorwed for my blame, and thou hast 65 wopen for the damage of thy renoun that is apayred; and thy laste sorwe eschaufede ayeins fortune, and compleinest that guerdouns ne ben nat evenliche yolden to the desertes of folk. And in the latere 70 ende of thy wode Muse, thou preyedest that thilke pees that governeth the hevene sholde governe the erthe. But for that manye tribulaciouns of affecciouns han assailed thee, and sorwe and ire and 75 wepinge to-drawen thee dyversely ; as thou art now feble of thought, mightier remedies ne shullen nat yit touchen thee, for whiche we wol usen somdel lighter medicines : so that thilke passiouns that 80 ben woxen harde in swellinge, by pertur-baciouns flowing in-to thy thought, mowen wexen esy and softe, to receiven the strengthe of a more mighty and more egre medicine, by an esier touchinge. 85

## METRE VI.

*Cum Phebi radiis graue
Cancri sidus inestuat.*

Whan that the hevy sterre of the Cancre eschaufeth by the bemes of Phe-bus, *that is to seyn, whan that Phebus the sonne is in the signe of the Cancre,* who-so yeveth thanne largely hise sedes to the 5 feldes that refusen to receiven hem, lat him gon, bigyled of trust that he hadde to his corn, to acorns of okes. Yif thou wolt gadre violettes, ne go thou not to

10 the purpur wode whan the feld, chirkinge, agryseth of colde by the felnesse of
the winde that highte Aquilon. Yif thou
desirest or wolt usen grapes, ne seke thou
nat, with a glotonous hond, to streyne
15 and presse the stalkes of the vine in the
ferst somer sesoun ; for Bachus, the god
of wyne, hath rather yeven hise yiftes to
autumpne, *the later ende of somer.* God
tokneth and assigneth the tymes, ablinge
20 hem to hir propres offices ; ne he ne
suffreth nat the stoundes whiche that
him-self hath devyded and constreyned
to ben y-medled to-gidere. And forthy
he that forleteth certein ordinaunce of
25 doinge by over-throwinge wey, he ne hath
no glade issue or ende of his werkes.

PROSE VI. *Primum igitur pæerisne me
pauculis rogacionibus.*

First woltow suffre me to touche and
assaye the estat of thy thought by a fewe
demaundes, so that I may understonde
what be the manere of thy curacioun ? '
5 *Boece.* ' Axe me,' quod I, ' at thy wille,
what thou wolt, and I shal answere.'

Tho seide she thus : ' Whether wenestow,' quod she, ' that this world be
governed by foolish happes and for-
10 tunous, or elles that there be in it any
governement of resoun ? ' ' Certes,'
quod I, ' I ne trowe nat in no manere,
that so certein thinges sholde be moeved
by fortunous fortune ; but I wot wel that
15 god, maker and mayster, is governour of
his werk. Ne never nas yit day that
mighte putte me out of the sothnesse of
that sentence.'

' So is it,' quod she ; ' for the same
20 thing songe thou a litel her-biforn, and
biweyledest and biweptest, that only men
weren put out of the cure of god. For of
alle other thinges thou ne doutedest nat
that they nere governed by resoun. But
25 owh ! (*i. pape* !) I wondre gretly, certes,
why that thou art syk, sin that thou art
put in so holsom a sentence. But lat us
seken depper ; I conjecte that ther lakketh I not nere what. But sey me this :
30 sin that thou ne doutest nat that this

world be governed by god, with whiche
governailes takestow hede that it is
governed ? ' ' Unnethe,' quod I, ' knowe
I the sentence of thy questioun ; so that
I ne may nat yit answeren to thy de- 35
maundes.'

' I nas nat deceived,' quod she, ' that
ther ne faileth somwhat, by whiche the
maladye of thy perturbacioun is crept
in-to thy thought, so as the strengthe of 40
the palis chyning is open. But sey me
this : remembrest thou what is the ende
of thinges, and whider that the entencioun of alle kinde tendeth ? ' ' I have
herd it told som-tyme,' quod I ; ' but 45
drerinesse hath dulled my memorie.'

' Certes,' quod she, ' thou wost wel
whennes that alle thinges ben comen and
procedeth ? ' ' I wot wel,' quod I, and
answerede, that ' god is beginning of al.' 50
' And how may this be,' quod she, ' that,
sin thou knowest the beginning of
thinges, that thou ne knowest nat what
is the ende of thinges ? But swiche ben
the customes of perturbaciouns, and this 55
power they han, that they may moeve
a man out of his place, *that is to seyn, fro
the stablenes and perfeccioun of his knowinge;* but, certes, they may nat al arace
him, ne aliene him in al. But I wolde 60
that thou woldest answere to this :
remembrestow that thou art a man ? '
' Why sholde I nat remembre that ? '
quod I.

' Maystow nat telle me thanne,' quod 65
she, ' what thing is a man ? ' ' Axestow
me nat,' quod I, ' whether that I be
a resonable mortal beest ? I woot wel, and
I confesse wel that I am it.'

' Wistestow never yit that thou were 70
any other thing ? ' quod she. ' No,'
quod I.

' Now woot I,' quod she, ' other cause of
thy maladye, and that right grete. Thou
hast left for to knowen thy-self, what 75
thou art ; thorugh whiche I have pleynly
founden the cause of thy maladye, or elles
the entree of recoveringe of thyn hele.
For-why, for thou art confounded with
foryeting of thy-self, for-thy sorwestow 80
that thou art exiled of thy propre goodes.

And for thou ne wost what is the ende of thinges, for-thy demestow that felonous and wikked men ben mighty and weleful.
85 And for thou hast foryeten by whiche governements the world is governed, for-thy wenestow that thise mutaciouns of fortune fleten with-oute governour. Thise ben grete causes not only to maladye,
90 but, certes, grete causes to deeth. But I thanke the auctor and the maker of hele, that nature hath not al forleten thee. I have grete norisshinges of thyn hele, and that is, the sothe sentence of
95 governaunce of the worlde; that thou bilevest that the governinge of it nis nat subject ne underput to the folie of thise happes aventurous, but to the resoun of god. And ther-for doute thee no-thing;
100 for of this litel spark thyn hete of lyf shal shyne.    But for as moche as it is nat tyme yit of faster remedies, and the nature of thoughtes deceived is this, that as ofte as they casten awey sothe
105 opiniouns, they clothen hem in false opiniouns, of which false opiniouns the derkenesse of perturbacioun wexeth up, that confoundeth the verray insighte: and that derkenesse shal I assaye som-
110 what to maken thinne and wayk by lighte and meneliche remedies; so that,

after that the derkenesse of deceivinge desiringes is don awey, thou mowe knowe the shyninge of verray light.

## Metre VII. *Nubibus atris.*

The sterres, covered with blake cloudes, ne mowen yeten a-doun no light. Yif the trouble wind that hight Auster, turning and walwinge the see, medleth the hete, *that is to seyn, the boyling up from the* 5 *botme;* the wawes, that whylom weren clere as glas and lyke to the faire clere dayes, withstande anon the sightes of men by the filthe and ordure that is resolved. And the fletinge streem, that royleth 10 doun dyversly fro heye mountaignes, is arested and resisted ofte tyme by the encountringe of a stoon that is departed and fallen from som roche.    And for-thy, yif thou wolt loken and demen 15 sooth with cleer light, and holden the wey with a right path, weyve thou joye, dryf fro thee drede, fleme thou hope, ne lat no sorwe aproche; *that is to seyn, lat non of thise four passiouns over-comen thee* 20 *or blende thee.* For cloudy and derke is thilke thought, and bounde with brydles, where-as thise thinges regnen.'

**Explicit Liber Primus.**

# BOOK II.

## Prose I. *Postea paulisper conticuit.*

After this she stinte a litel; and, after that she hadde gadered by atempre stillenesse myn attencioun, she seide thus: (*As who mighte seyn thus: After thise*
5 *thinges she stinte a litel; and whan she aperceived by atempre stillenesse that I was ententif to herkene hir, she bigan to speke in this wyse*): ' Yif I,' quod she, ' have understonden and knowen outrely the causes
10 and the habit of thy maladye, thou languissest and art defeted for desyr and talent of thy rather fortune. She, that

ilke Fortune only, that is chaunged, as thou feynest, to thee-ward, hath perverted the cleernesse and the estat of thy corage. 15 I understonde the fele-folde colours and deceites of thilke merveilous monstre Fortune, and how she useth ful flateringe familaritee with hem that she enforceth to bigyle; so longe, til that she confounde 20 with unsufferable sorwe hem that she hath left in despeyr unpurveyed. And yif thou remembrest wel the kinde, the maneres, and the desert of thilke Fortune, thou shalt wel knowe that, as in hir, 25 thou never ne haddest ne hast y-lost any fair thing. But, as I trowe, I shal nat

gretly travailen to do thee remembren on
thise thinges. For thou were wont to
30 hurtelen and despysen hir, with manly
wordes, whan she was blaundissinge and
present, and pursewedest hir with sentences that were drawen out of myn
entree, *that is to seyn, out of myn informa-*
35 *cioun.* But no sodein mutacioun ne
bitydeth nat with-oute a manere chaunginge of corages ; and so is it befallen that
thou art a litel departed fro the pees of
thy thought.
40 But now is tyme that thou drinke and
ataste some softe and delitable thinges ;
so that, whan they ben entred with-in
thee, it mowe maken wey to strengere
drinkes of medicynes. Com now forth
45 therfore the suasioun of swetenesse rethorien, whiche that goth only the right
wey, whyl she forsaketh nat myne
estatuts. And with Rhetorice com forth
Musice, a damisel of our hous, that
50 singeth now lighter moedes *or prolaciouns,*
now hevyer. What eyleth thee, man ?
What is it that hath cast thee in-to
morninge and in-to wepinge ? I trowe
that thou hast seyn som newe thing and
55 uncouth. Thou wenest that Fortune be
chaunged ayein thee ; but thou wenest
wrong, yif thou that wene. Alwey tho
ben hir maneres ; she hath rather kept,
as to thee-ward, hir propre stablenesse in
60 the chaunginge of hir-self. Right swich
was she whan she flatered thee, and
deceived thee with unleveful lykinges of
fals welefulnesse. Thou hast now knowen
and ataynt the doutous or double visage
65 of thilke blinde goddesse Fortune. She,
that yit covereth hir and wimpleth hir
to other folk, hath shewed hir everydel to thee. Yif thou aprovest hir and
thenkest that she is good, use hir maneres
70 and pleyne thee nat. And yif thou
agrysest hir false trecherye, despyse and
cast awey hir that pleyeth so harmfully ;
for she, that is now cause of so muche
sorwe to thee, sholde ben cause to thee of
75 pees and of joye. She hath forsaken thee,
forsothe ; the whiche that never man
may ben siker that she ne shal forsake
him.——Glose. *But natheles, some bokes*

*han the text thus :* For sothe, she hath
forsaken thee, ne ther nis no man siker 80
that she ne hath nat forsaken.——

Holdestow than thilke welefulnesse
precious to thee that shal passen ? And
is present Fortune dereworthe to thee,
which that nis nat feithful for to dwelle ; 85
and, whan she goth awey, that she
bringeth a wight in sorwe ? For sin she
may nat ben with-holden at a mannes
wille, she maketh him a wrecche whan
she departeth fro him. What other thing 90
is flittinge Fortune but a maner she vinge
of wrecchednesse that is to comen ? Na
it ne suffyseth nat only to loken on thinge
that is present biforn the eyen of a man.
But wisdom loketh and amesureth the 95
ende of thinges ; and the same chaunginge from oon in-to an-other, *that is to*
*seyn, from adversitee in-to prosperitee,*
maketh that the manaces of Fortune ne
ben nat for to dreden, ne the flateringes 100
of hir to ben desired. Thus, at the laste,
it bihoveth thee to suffren with evene
wille in pacience al that is don in-with the
floor of Fortune, *that is to seyn, in this*
*world,* sin thou hast ones put thy nekke 105
under the yok of hir. For yif thou wolt
wryten a lawe of wendinge and of dwellinge to Fortune, whiche that thou hast
chosen frely to ben thy lady, artow nat
wrongful in that, and makest Fortune 110
wroth and aspere by thyn inpatience,
and yit thou mayst nat chaunge hir ?
Yif thou committest and bitakest thy
sailes to the winde, thou shalt be shoven,
not thider that thou woldest, but whider 115
that the wind shoveth thee. Yif thou
castest thy sedes in-to the feldes, thou
sholdest han in minde that the yeres ben,
amonges, other-whyle plentevous and
other-whyle bareyne. Thou hast bitaken 120
thy-self to the governaunce of Fortune,
and for-thy it bihoveth thee to ben
obeisaunt to the maneres of thy lady.
Enforcest thou thee to aresten or with-
holden the swiftnesse and the sweigh of 125
hir turninge whele ? O thou fool of alle
mortal fooles, if Fortune bigan to dwelle
stable, she cesede thanne to ben Fortune !

METRE I.  *Hec cum superba uerterit uices dextra.*

Whan Fortune with a proud right hand hath torned hir chaunginge stoundes, she fareth lyk the maneres of the boilinge Eurype.——**Glosa.** *Eurype*
5 *is an arm of the see that ebbeth and floweth; and som-tyme the streem is on o syde, and som-tyme on the other.——*
**Text.** She, cruel Fortune, casteth adoun kinges that whylom weren y-drad; and
10 she, deceivable, enhaunseth up the humble chere of him that is discomfited. Ne she neither hereth ne rekketh of wrecchede wepinges; and she is so hard that she laugheth and scorneth the wep-
15 inges of hem, the whiche she hath maked wepe with hir free wille. Thus she pleyeth, and thus she proeveth hir strengthes; and sheweth a greet wonder to alle hir servauntes, yif that a wight
20 is seyn weleful, and overthrowe in an houre.

PROSE II.  *Vellem autem pauca tecum.*

Certes, I wolde pleten with thee a fewe thinges, usinge the wordes of Fortune; tak hede now thy-self, yif that she axeth right. "O thou man, wher-fore makest
5 thou me gilty by thyne every-dayes pleyn-inges? What wrong have I don thee? What goodes have I bireft thee that weren thyne? Stryf or plete with me, bifore what juge that thou wolt, of the
10 possessioun of richesses or of dignitees. And yif thou mayst shewen me that ever any mortal man hath received any of tho thinges to ben hise in propre, than wol I graunte frely that alle thilke thinges
15 weren thyne whiche that thou axest. Whan that nature broughte thee forth out of thy moder wombe, I receyved thee naked and nedy of alle thinges, and I norisshede thee with my richesses,
20 and was redy and ententif through my favour to susteyne thee; and that maketh thee now inpacient ayeins me; and I envirounde thee with alle the aboun-

dance and shyninge of alle goodes that ben in my right. Now it lyketh me to 25 with-drawen my hand; thou hast had grace as he that hath used of foreine goodes; thou hast no right to pleyne thee, as though thou haddest outrely for-lorn alle thy thinges. Why pleynest thou 30 thanne? I have done thee no wrong. Richesses, honours, and swiche other thinges ben of my right. My servauntes knowen me for hir lady; they comen with me, and departen whan I wende. 35 I dar wel affermen hardily, that yif tho thinges, of which thou pleynest that thou hast forlorn, hadde ben thyne, thou ne haddest not lorn hem. Shal I thanne only ben defended to usen my right? 40 Certes, it is leveful to the hevene to make clere dayes, and, after that, to coveren tho same dayes with derke nightes. The yeer hath eek leve to apparailen the visage of the erthe, now with floures and 45 now with fruit, and to confounden hem som-tyme with reynes and with coldes. The see hath eek his right to ben som-tyme calme and blaundishing with smothe water, and som-tyme to ben hor- 50 rible with wawes and with tempestes. But the covetise of men, that may nat ben stanched, shal it binde me to ben stedefast, sin that stedefastnesse is un-couth to my maneres? Swich is my 55 strengthe, and this pley I pleye con-tinuely. I torne the whirlinge wheel with the torninge cercle; I am glad to chaungen the lowest to the heyest, and the heyest to the lowest. Worth up, if 60 thou wolt, so it be by this lawe, that thou ne holde nat that I do thee wronge thogh thou descende adoun, whan the resoun of my pley axeth it. Wistest thou nat how Cresus, the king of Lydiens, of 65 whiche king Cyrus was ful sore agast a litel biforn, that this rewliche Cresus was caught of Cyrus and lad to the fyr to ben brent, but that a rayn descendede doun fro hevene that rescowede him? 70 And is it out of thy minde how that Paulus, consul of Rome, whan he hadde taken the king of Perciens, weep pitously for the captivitee of the self kinge?

75 What other thing biwailen the cryinges
of tragedies but only the dedes of Fortune,
that with an unwar stroke overtorneth
realmes of grete nobley?——**Glose.** *Tra-*
*gedie is to seyn, a ditee of a prosperitee for*
80 *a tyme, that endeth in wrecchednesse.*——
Lernedest nat thou *in Greke,* whan thou
were yonge, that in the entree, *or in the*
*çelere,* of Jupiter, ther ben couched two
tonnes; that on is ful of good, that other
85 is ful of harm? What right hast thou to
pleyne, yif thou hast taken more plentevously of the gode syde, *that is to seyn, of*
*my richesses and prosperites;* and what
eek if I ne be nat al departed fro thee?
90 What eek yif my mutabilitee yiveth thee
rightful cause of hope to han yit beter
thinges? Natheles dismaye thee nat in
thy thought; and thou that art put in
the comune realme of alle, ne desyre nat
95 to liven by thyn only propre right.

### METRE II. *Si quantas rapidis flatibus*
*incitus.*

Though Plentee, *that is goddesse of*
*richesses,* hielde adoun with ful horn, and
withdraweth nat hir hand, as many
richesses as the see torneth upward
5 sandes whan it is moeved with ravisshinge blastes, or elles as many richesses
as ther shynen brighte sterres on hevene
on the sterry nightes; yit, for al that,
mankinde nolde not cese to wepe wrecch-
10 ede pleyntes. And al be it so that god
receyveth gladly hir preyers, and yiveth
them (as fool-large) moche gold, and
aparaileth coveitous men with noble or
clere honours: yit semeth hem haven
15 y-geten no-thing, but alwey hir cruel
ravyne, devouringe al that they han
geten, sheweth other gapinges; *that is to*
*seyn, gapen and desyren yit after mo rich-*
*esses.* What brydles mighten withholden,
20 to any certein ende, the desordenee covetise of men, whan, ever the rather that it
fleteth in large yiftes, the more ay brenneth in hem the thurst of havinge?
Certes he that, quakinge and dredful,
25 weneth him-selven nedy, he ne liveth
never-more riche."

PROSE III. *Hiis igitur si pro se tecum*
*Fortuna loqueretur.*

Therfor, yif that Fortune spake with
thee for hir-self in this manere, for-sothe
thou ne haddest nat what thou mightest
answere. And, if thou hast any-thing
wherwith thou mayest rightfully de- 5
fenden thy compleint, it behoveth thee
to shewen it; and I wol yeven thee space
to tellen it.'    *Boece.* 'Certeynly,' quod
I thanne, 'thise beth faire thinges,
and enointed with hony swetenesse of 10
rethorike and musike; and only whyl
they ben herd they ben delicious. But to
wrecches is a depper felinge of harm;
*this is to seyn, that wrecches felen the*
*harmes that they suffren more grevously* 15
*than the remedies or the delites of thise*
*wordes mowen gladen or comforten hem;* so
that, whan thise thinges stinten for to
soune in eres, the sorwe that is inset
greveth the thought.'                20

*Phil.* 'Right so is it,' quod she.  'For
thise ne ben yit none remedies of thy
maladye; but they ben a maner norisshinges of thy sorwe, yit rebel ayein thy
curacioun. For whan that tyme is, I 25
shal moeve swiche thinges that percen
hem-self depe. But natheles, that thou
shalt not wilne to leten thy-self a wrecche,
hast thou foryeten the noumber and the
manere of thy welefulnesse? I holde me 30
stille, how that the soverayne men of the
citee token thee in cure and kepinge,
whan thou were orphelin of fader and
moder, and were chosen in affinitee of
princes of the citee; and thou bigunne 35
rather to be leef and dere than forto ben
a neighbour; the whiche thing is the
most precious kinde of any propinquitee
or alyaunce that may ben. Who is it
that ne seide tho that thou were right 40
weleful, with so grete a nobleye of thy
fadres-in-lawe, and with the chastitee of
thy wyf, and with the oportunitee and
noblesse of thy masculin children, *that is*
*to seyn, thy sones?* And over al this—me 45
list to passen the comune thinges—how
thou haddest in thy youthe dignitees that

weren werned to olde men. But it delyteth me to comen now to the singuler
50 uphepinge of thy welefulnesse. Yif any
fruit of mortal thinges may han any
weighte or prys of welefulnesse, mightest
thou ever foryeten, for any charge of
harm that mighte bifalle, the remem-
55 braunce of thilke day that thou saye thy
two sones maked conseileres, and y-lad
to-gedere fro thyn house under so greet
assemblee of senatoures and under the
blythenesse of poeple ; and whan thou
60 saye hem set in the court in here chayeres
of dignitees? Thou, rethorien or pro-
nouncere of kinges preysinges, deservedest
glorie of wit and of eloquence, whan
thou, sittinge bitwene thy two sones, con-
65 seileres, in the place that highte Circo,
†fulfuldest the abydinge of the multitude of poeple that was sprad abouten
thee, with so large preysinge and laude,
as men singen in victories. Tho yave
70 thou wordes to Fortune, as I trowe,
*that is to seyn, tho feffedest thou Fortune
with glosinge wordes and deceivedest hir,*
whan she acoyede thee and norisshede
thee as hir owne delyces. Thou bere
75 away of Fortune a yifte, *that is to seyn,*
*swiche guerdoun,* that she never yaf to
privee man. Wilt thou therfor leye
a rekeninge with Fortune? She hath
now twinkled first upon thee with a wik-
80 kede eye. Yif thou considere the noumbre and the manere of thy blisses and of
thy sorwes, thou mayst nat forsaken that
thou art yit blisful. For if thou therfor
wenest thy-self nat weleful, for thinges
85 that tho semeden joyful ben passed, ther
nis nat why thou sholdest wene thy-self
a wrecche ; for thinges that semen now
sorye passen also. Art thou now comen
first, a sodein gest, in-to the shadwe or
90 tabernacle of this lyf; or trowest thou
that any stedefastnesse be in mannes
thinges, whan ofte a swift houre dissolveth the same man ; *that is to seyn,*
*whan the soule departeth fro the body ?*
95 For, al-though that selde is ther any feith
that fortunous thinges wolen dwellen, yit
natheles the laste day of a mannes lyf is
a manere deeth to Fortune, and also to

thilke that hath dwelt. And therfor,
what, wenestow, thar [thee] recche, yif 100
thou forlete hir in deyinge, or elles that
she, *Fortune,* forlete thee in fleeinge
awey ?

### Metre III.   *Cum polo Phebus*
*roseis quadrigis.*

Whan Phebus, the sonne, biginneth to
spreden his cleernesse with rosene chari-
ettes, thanne the sterre, y-dimmed, paleth
hir whyte cheres, by the flambes of the
sonne that overcometh the sterre-light. 5
*This is to seyn, whan the sonne is risen,*
*the dey-sterre wexeth pale, and leseth hir*
*light for the grete brightnesse of the sonne.*
Whan the wode wexeth rody of rosene
floures, in the first somer sesoun, thorugh 10
the brethe of the winde Zephirus that
wexeth warm, yif the cloudy wind Auster
blowe felliche, than goth awey the faire-
nesse of thornes.   Ofte the see is cleer
and calm withoute moevinge flodes ; and 15
ofte the horrible wind Aquilon moeveth
boilinge tempestes and over-whelveth the
see.   Yif the forme of this worlde is so
selde stable, and yif it turneth by so
many entrechaunginges, wolt thou thanne 20
trusten in the tomblinge fortunes of
men ?   Wolt thou trowen on flittinge
goodes ? It is certein and establisshed
by lawe perdurable, that no-thing that is
engendred nis stedefast ne stable.' 25

### Prose IV.   *Tunc ego, uera,*
*inquam, commemoras.*

Thanne seide I thus : ' O norice of alle
vertues, thou seist ful sooth ; ne I ne may
nat forsake the right swifte cours of my
prosperitee ; *that is to seyn, that prosperitee*
*ne be comen to me wonder swiftly and sone.* 5
But this is a thing that greetly smerteth
me whan it remembreth me. For in alle
adversitee of fortune, the most unsely
kinde of contrarious fortune is to han
ben weleful.' 10

*Phil.* ' But that thou,' quod she, ' abyest
thus the torment of thy false opinioun,
that mayst thou nat rightfully blamen
ne aretten to thinges : *as who seith, for*

15 *thou hast yit many habundaunces of thinges.*
——Text. For al be it so that the ydel
name of aventurous welefulnesse moeveth
thee now, it is leveful that thou rekne
with me of how manye grete thinges
20 thou hast yit plentee. And therfor, yif
that thilke thing that thou haddest for
most precious in al thy richesse of fortune be kept to thee yit, by the grace of
god, unwemmed and undefouled, mayst
25 thou thanne pleyne rightfully upon the
meschef of Fortune, sin thou hast yit thy
beste thinges ? · Certes, yit liveth in good
point thilke precious honour of mankinde, Symacus, thy wyves fader, which
30 that is a man maked alle of sapience and
of vertu ; the whiche man thou woldest
byen redely with the prys of thyn owne
lyf. He biwayleth the wronges that men
don to thee, and nat for him-self ; for he
35 liveth in sikernesse of any sentences put
ayeins him. And yit liveth thy wyf,
that is atempre of wit, and passinge other
wimmen in clennesse of chastetee ; and
for I wol closen shortely hir bountees, she
40 is lyk to hir fader. I telle thee wel, that
she liveth looth of this lyf, and kepeth to
thee only hir goost ; and is al maat and
overcomen by wepinge and sorwe for
desyr of thee, in the whiche thing only
45 I moot graunten that thy welefulnesse is
amenused. What shal I seyn eek of thy
two sones, conseilours, of whiche, as of
children of hir age, ther shyneth the
lyknesse of the wit of hir fader or of hir
50 elder fader ? And sin the sovereyn cure
of alle mortel folk is to saven hir owen
lyves, O how weleful art thou, yif thou
knowe thy goodes ! For yit ben ther
thinges dwelled to thee-ward, that no
55 man douteth that they ne ben more
dereworthe to thee than thyn owen lyf.
And for-thy drye thy teres, for yit nis
nat everich fortune al hateful to thee-
ward, ne over greet tempest hath nat yit
60 fallen upon thee, whan that thyn ancres
cleven faste, that neither wolen suffren
the counfort of this tyme present ne the
hope of tyme cominge to passen ne to
faylen.' *Boece.* 'And I preye,' quod I,
65 'that faste moten they halden ; for

whyles that they halden, how-so-ever that
thinges ben, I shal wel fleten forth and
escapen ; but thou mayst wel seen how
grete aparayles and aray that me lakketh, that ben passed away fro me.' 70
*Phil.* 'I have som-what avaunsed and
forthered thee,' quod she, 'yif that thou
anoye nat or forthinke nat of al thy
fortune : *as who seith, I have som-what*
*comforted thee, so that thou tempest thee* 75
*nat thus with al thy fortune, sin thou hast*
*yit thy beste thinges.* But I may nat suffren
thy delices, that pleynest so wepinge and
anguissous, for that ther lakketh som-
what to thy welefulnesse. For what man 80
is so sad or of so parfit welefulnesse, that
he ne stryveth and pleyneth on som halve
ayen the qualitee of his estat ? For-why
ful anguissous thing is the condicioun of
mannes goodes ; for either it cometh nat 85
al-togider to a wight, or elles it last nat
perpetuel. For sum man hath grete
richesses, but he is ashamed of his un-
gentel linage ; and som is renowned of
noblesse of kinrede, but he is enclosed in 90
so grete anguisshe of nede of thinges, that
him were lever that he were unknowe.
And som man haboundeth both in richesse and noblesse, but yit he bewaileth
his chaste lyf, for he ne hath no wyf. 95
And som man is wel and selily y-maried,
but he hath no children, and norisseth
his richesses to the eyres of strange
folkes. And som man is gladed with
children, but he wepeth ful sory for the 100
trespas of his sone or of his doughter.
And for this ther ne acordeth no wight
lightly to the condicioun of his fortune ;
for alwey to every man ther is in som-
what that, unassayed, he ne wot nat ; or 105
elles he dredeth that he hath assayed.
And adde this also, that every weleful
man hath a ful delicat felinge ; so that,
but-yif alle thinges bifalle at his owne
wil, for he is impacient, or is nat used to 110
han non adversitee, anon he is throwen
adoun for every litel thing. And ful litel
thinges ben tho that withdrawen the
somme or the perfeccioun of blisfulnesse
fro hem that ben most fortunat. How 115
many men, trowest thou, wolden demen

hem-self to ben almost in hevene, yif
they mighten atayne to the leest party of
the remnaunt of thy fortune? This same
120 place that thou clepest exil, is contree to
hem that enhabiten heer, and forthy
nothing [is] wrecched but whan thou
wenest it : *as who seith, thou thy-self, ne
no wight elles, nis a wrecche, but whan he*
125 *weneth him-self a wrecche by reputacioun of
his corage.* And ayeinward, alle fortune
is blisful to a man by the agreabletee or
by the egalitee of him that suffreth it.
What man is that, that is so weleful,
130 that nolde changen his estat whan he
hath lost pacience? The swetnesse of
mannes welefulnesse is sprayned with
many biternesses ; the whiche welefulnesse, al-though it seme swete and joyful
135 to hem that useth it, yit may it nat ben
with-holden that it ne goth away whan it
wole. Thanne is it wel sene, how wrecched
is the blisfulnesse of mortal thinges, that
neither it dureth perpetuel with hem
140 that every fortune receiven agreablely or
egaly, ne it delyteth nat in al to hem
that ben anguissous. O ye mortal folk,
what seke ye thanne blisfulnesse out of
your-self, whiche that is put in your-self?
145 Errour and folye confoundeth yow.

I shal shewe thee shortely the poynt
of sovereyne blisfulnesse. Is ther any-
thing more precious to thee than thy-
self? Thou wolt answere, "nay." Thanne,
150 yif it so be that thou art mighty over
thy-self, *that is to seyn, by tranquillitee of
thy sowle,* than hast thou thing in thy
power that thou noldest never lesen, ne
Fortune ne may nat beneme it thee.
155 And that thou mayst knowe that blisfulnesse ne may nat standen in thinges that
ben fortunous and temporel, now understonde and gader it to-gidere thus : Yif
blisfulnesse be the sovereyn good of nature
160 that liveth by resoun, ne thilke thing nis
nat sovereyn good that may be taken
awey in any wyse, (for more worthy
thing and more digne is thilke thing that
may nat ben taken awey); than sheweth
165 it wel, that the unstablenesse of fortune
may nat atayne to receiven verray blisfulnesse. And yit more-over : what man

that this toumbling welefulnesse ledeth,
either he woot that it is chaungeable, or
elles he woot it nat. And yif he woot 170
it nat, what blisful fortune may ther be
in the blindnesse of ignorance? And yif
he woot that it is chaungeable, he moot
alwey ben adrad that he ne lese that
thing that he ne doubteth nat but that 175
he may lesen it ; *as who seith, he mot ben
alwey agast, lest he lese that he wot wel he
may lese it.* For which, the continuel
dreed that he hath ne suffreth him nat
to ben weleful. Or yif he lese it, he 180
weneth to be dispysed and forleten.
Certes eek, that is a ful litel good that
is born with evene herte whan it is lost ;
*that is to seyn, that men do no more fors of
the lost than of the havinge.* And for as 185
moche as thou thy-self art he, to whom it
hath ben shewed and proved by ful
manye demonstraciouns, as I wot wel,
that the sowles of men ne mowe nat
deyen in no wyse ; and eek sin it is cleer 190
and certein, that fortunous welefulnesse
endeth by the deeth of the body ; it may
nat ben douted that, yif that deeth may
take awey blisfulnesse, that alle the kinde
of mortal thinges ne descendeth in-to 195
wrecchednesse by the ende of the deeth.
And sin we knowen wel, that many a
man hath sought the fruit of blisfulnesse
nat only with suffringe of deeth, but eek
with suffringe of peynes and tormentes ; 200
how mighte than this present lyf maken
men blisful, sin that, whan thilke selve
lyf is ended, it ne maketh folk no
wrecches?

MÉTRE IV.   *Quisquis uolet perennem.*

What maner man, stable and war, that
wole founden him a perdurable sete, and
ne wole nat ben cast down with the loude
blastes of the wind Eurus ; and wole
despyse the see, manasinge with flodes ; 5
lat him eschewen to bilde on the cop
of the mountaigne or in the moiste sandes.
For the felle wind Auster tormenteth the
cop of the mountaigne with all his
strengthes ; and the lause sandes refusen 10
to beren the hevy wighte.   And forthy,

if thou wolt fleen the perilous aventure,
*that is to seyn, of the worlde*; have minde
certeinly to ficchen thyn hous of a merye
15 site in a lowe stoon. For al-though the
wind, troubling the see, thondre with
over-throwinges, thou that art put in
quiete, and weleful by strengthe of thy
palis, shalt leden a cleer age, scorninge
20 the woodnesses and the ires of the eyr.

PROSE V. *Set cum rationum iam in te.*

But for as moche as the norisshinges
of my resouns descenden now in-to thee,
I trowe it were tyme to usen a litel
strenger medicynes. Now understond
5 heer, al were it so that the yiftes of
Fortune ne were nat brutel ne transitorie,
what is ther in hem that may be thyn
in any tyme, or elles that it nis foul, yif
that it be considered and loked perfitly?
10 Richesses, ben they precious by the nature
of hem-self, or elles by the nature of
thee? What is most worth of richesses?
Is it nat gold or might of moneye
assembled? Certes, thilke gold and
15 thilke moneye shyneth and yeveth betere
renoun to hem that despenden it thanne
to thilke folk that mokeren it; for avarice maketh alwey mokereres to ben hated,
and largesse maketh folk cleer of renoun.
20 For sin that swich thing as is transferred
fram o man to another ne may nat
dwellen with no man; certes, thanne is
thilke moneye precious whan it is translated into other folk and stenteth to ben
25 had, by usage of large yevinge *of him
that hath yeven it.* And also: yif that al
the moneye that is over-al in the worlde
were gadered toward o man, it sholde
maken alle other men to ben nedy as of
30 that. And certes a voys al hool, *that
is to seyn, with-oute amenusinge,* fulfilleth
to-gidere the hering of moche folk; but
certes, youre richesses ne mowen nat
passen in-to moche folke with-oute amen-
35 usinge. And whan they ben apassed,
nedes they maken hem pore that for-gon
the richesses. O! streite and nedy clepe
I this richesse, sin that many folk ne
may nat han it al, ne al may it nat

comen to o man with-outen povertee of 40
alle other folk! And the shyninge of
gemmes, *that I clepe precious stones,*
draweth it nat the eyen of folk to hemward, *that is to seyn, for the beautee?* But
certes, yif ther were beautee or bountee 45
in the shyninge of stones, thilke cleernesse is of the stones hem-self, and nat
of men; for whiche I wondre gretly that
men mervailen on swiche thinges. For-
why, what thing is it, that yif it wanteth 50
moeving and joynture of sowle and body,
that by right mighte semen a fair creature to him that hath a sowle of resoun?
For al be it so that gemmes drawen to
hem-self a litel of the laste beautee of the 55
world, through the entente of hir creatour
and through the distinccioun of hem-self;
yit, for as mochel as they ben put under
youre excellence, theyne han nat deserved
by no wey that ye sholden mervailen on 60
hem. And the beautee of feldes, delyteth
it nat mochel un-to yow?'

*Boece.* 'Why sholde it nat delyten us,
sin that it is a right fair porcioun of the
right faire werke, *that is to seyn, of this* 65
*world?* And right so ben we gladed som-
tyme of the face of the see whan it is
cleer; and also mervailen we on the
hevene and on the sterres, and on the
sonne and on the mone.'                      70

*Philosophye.* 'Aperteneth,' quod she,
'any of thilke thinges to thee? Why
darst thou glorifyen thee in the shyninge
of any swiche thinges? Art thou distingwed and embelised by the springinge 75
floures of the first somer sesoun, or
swelleth thy plentee in the fruites of
somer? Why art thou ravisshed with
ydel joyes? Why embracest thou straunge
goodes as they weren thyne? Fortune ne 80
shal never maken that swiche thinges
ben thyne, that nature of thinges hath
maked foreine fro thee. Sooth is that,
with-outen doute, the frutes of the erthe
owen to ben to the norissinge of bestes. 85
And yif thou wolt fulfille thy nede after
that it suffyseth to nature, than is it no
nede that thou seke after the superfluitee
of fortune. For with ful fewe things
and with ful litel thinges nature halt hir 90

apayed; and yif thou wolt achoken the
fulfillinge of nature with superfluitees,
certes, thilke thinges that thou wolt
thresten or pouren in-to nature shullen
95 ben unjoyful to thee, or elles anoyous.
Wenest thou eek that it be a fair thing
to shyne with dyvorse clothinge? Of
whiche clothinge yif the beautee be
agreeable to loken up-on, I wol mervailen
100 on the nature of the matere of thilke
clothes, or elles on the werkman that
wroughte hem. But also a long route of
meynee, maketh that a blisful man? The
whiche servants, yif they ben vicious of
105 condiciouns, it is a great charge and a
distruccioun to the hous, and a greet
enemy to the lord him-self. And yif they
ben goode men, how shal straunge or
foreine goodnesse ben put in the noumbre
110 of thy richesse? So that, by all these
forseide thinges, it is clearly y-shewed,
that never oon of thilke thinges that
thou acountedest for thyne goodes nas
nat thy good. In the whiche thinges,
115 yif ther be no beautee to ben desyred,
why sholdest thou ben sory yif thou lese
hem, or why sholdest thou rejoysen thee
to holden hem? For yif they ben faire
of hir owne kinde, what aperteneth that
120 to thee? For al so wel sholden they han
ben faire by hem-selve, though they weren
departed fram alle thyne richesses. For-
why faire ne precious ne weren they nat,
for that they comen among thy richesses;
125 but, for they semeden faire and precious,
ther-for thou haddest lever rekne hem
amonges thy richesses. But what desirest thou of Fortune with so grete a
noise, and with so grete a fare? I trowe
130 thou seke to dryve awey nede with habundaunce of thinges; but certes, it
torneth to you al in the contrarie.
Forwhy certes, it nedeth of ful manye
helpinges to kepen the diversitee of
135 precious ostelments. And sooth it is,
that of manye thinges han they nede
that manye thinges han; and ayeinward,
of litel nedeth hem that mesuren hir fille
after the nede of kinde, and nat after
140 the outrage of coveityse. Is it thanne so,
that ye men ne han no proper good

y-set in you, for which ye moten seken
outward youre goodes in foreine and
subgit thinges? So is thanne the condicioun of thinges torned up-so-down, 145
that a man, that is a devyne beest by
merite of his resoun, thinketh that him-
self nis neither faire ne noble, but-yif
it be thorugh possessioun of ostelments
that ne han no sowles. And certes, al 150
other thinges ben apayed of hir owne
beautee; but ye men, that ben semblable
to god by your resonable thought, desiren
to aparailen your excellent kinde of the
lowest thinges; ne ye understonden nat 155
how greet a wrong ye don to your
creatour. For he wolde that mankinde
were most worthy and noble of any othre
erthely thinges; and ye threste adoun
your dignitees benethe the lowest thinges. 160
For yif that al the good of every thinge
be more precious than is thilke thing
whos that the good is: sin ye demen
that the fouleste thinges ben youre
goodes, thanne submitten ye and putten 165
your-selven under tho fouleste thinges
by your estimacioun; and certes, this
tydeth nat with-oute youre desertes. For
certes, swiche is the condicioun of alle
mankinde, that only whan it hath know- 170
inge of it-selve, than passeth it in
noblesse alle other thinges; and whan
it forleteth the knowinge of it-self, than
is it brought binethen alle beestes. For-
why al other livinge beestes han of kinde 175
to knowe nat hem-self; but whan that
men leten the knowinge of hemself, it
cometh hem of vice. But how brode
sheweth the errour and the folye of yow
men, that wenen that any thing may 180
ben aparailed with straunge aparailements! But for sothe that may nat ben
doon. For yif a wight shyneth with
thinges that ben put to him, *as thus, if
thilke thinges shynen with which a man is* 185
*aparailed*, certes, thilke thinges ben
comended and preysed with which he is
aparailed; but natheles, the thing that
is covered and wrapped under that
dwelleth in his filthe. And I denye 190
that thilke thing be good that anoyeth
him that hath it. Gabbe I of this?

Thou wolt seye "nay." Certes, richesses han anoyed ful ofte hem that han tho 195 richesses; sin that every wikked shrewe, (and for his wikkednesse the more gredy after other folkes richesses, wher-so ever it be in any place, be it gold or precious stones), weneth him only most worthy 200 that hath hem. Thou thanne, that so bisy dredest now the swerd and now the spere, yif thou haddest entred in the path of this lyf a voide wayferinge man, than woldest thou singe beforn the theef; 210 *as who seith, a pore man, that berth no richesse on him by the weye, may boldely singe biforn theves, for he hath nat wherof to ben robbed.* O precious and right cleer is the blisfulnesse of mortal richesses, 215 that, whan thou hast geten it, than hast thou lorn thy sikernesse!

### METRE V. *Felix nimium prior etas.*

Blisful was the first age of men! They helden hem apayed with the metes that the trewe feldes broughten forth. They ne distroyede nor deceivede nat hem-self 5 with outrage. They weren wont lightly to slaken hir hunger at even with acornes of okes. They ne coude nat medly the yifte of Bachus to the cleer hony; *that is to seyn, they coude make no piment nor* 10 *clarree*; ne they coude nat medle the brighte fleeses of the contree of Seriens with the venim of Tyrie; *this is to seyn, they coude nat deyen whyte fleeses of Serien contree with the blode of a maner shelfisshe* 15 *that men finden in Tyrie, with whiche blood men deyen purpur.* They slepen hoolsom slepes up-on the gras, and dronken of the renninge wateres; and layen under the shadwes of the heye pyn-trees. Ne no 20 gest ne straungere ne carf yit the heye see with ores or with shippes; ne they ne hadde seyn yit none newe strondes, to leden marchaundyse in-to dyverse contrees. Tho weren the cruel clariouns 25 ful hust and ful stille, ne blood y-shad by egre hate ne hadde nat deyed yit armures. For wher-to or which wood- nesse of enemys wolde first moeven armes, whan they seyen cruel woundes, ne none

medes be of blood y-shad? I wolde 30 that oure tymes sholde torne ayein to the olde maneres! But the anguissous love of havinge brenneth in folk more cruely than the fyr of the mountaigne Ethna, *that ay brenneth.* Allas! what 35 was he that first dalf up the gobetes or the weightes of gold covered under erthe, and the precious stones that wolden han ben hid? He dalf up precious perils. *That is to seyn, that he that hem first up* 40 *dalf, he dalf up a precious peril; for-why for the preciousnesse of swiche thinge, hath many man ben in peril.*

### PROSE VI. *Quid autem de dignitatibus.*

But what shal I seye of dignitees and of powers, the whiche ye men, that neither knowen verray dignitee ne verray power, areysen hem as heye as the hevene? The whiche dignitees and 5 powers, yif they comen to any wikked man, they don as grete damages and destrucciouns as doth the flaumbe of the mountaigne Ethna, whan the flaumbe walweth up; ne no deluge ne doth so 10 cruel harmes. Certes, thee remembreth wel, as I trowe, that thilke dignitee that men clepen the imperie of consulers, the whiche that whylom was biginninge of fredom, youre eldres coveiteden to han 15 don away that dignitee, for the pryde of the consulers. And right for the same pryde your eldres, biforn that tyme, hadden don awey, out of the citee of Rome, the kinges name; *that is to seyn,* 20 *they nolde han no lenger no king.* But now, yif so be that dignitees and powers be yeven to goode men, the whiche thing is ful selde, what agreable thing is ther in tho dignitees or powers but only the 25 goodnesse of folkes that usen hem? And therfor it is thus, that honour ne comth nat to vertu for cause of dignitee, but ayeinward honour comth to dignitee for cause of vertu. But whiche is thilke 30 youre dereworthe power, that is so cleer and so requerable? O ye ertheliche bestes, considere ye nat over which thinge that it semeth that ye han power?

35 Now yif thou saye a mous amonges other
mys, that chalaunged to him-self-ward
right and power over alle other mys,
how greet scorn woldest thou han of it !
*Glosa. So fareth it by men ; the body hath*
40 *power over the body.* For yif thou loke
wel up-on the body of a wight, what
thing shalt thou finde more freele than is
mankinde ; the whiche men wel ofte ben
slayn with bytinge of smale flyes, or elles
45 with the entringe of crepinge wormes
in-to the privetees of mannes body? But
wher shal man finden any man that may
exercen or haunten any right up-on
another man, but only up-on his body,
50 or elles up-on thinges that ben lowere
than the body, the whiche I clepe fortunous possessiouns? Mayst thou ever
have any comaundement over a free
corage? Mayst thou remuen fro the estat
55 of his propre reste a thought that is
clyvinge to-gidere in him-self by stedefast resoun? As whylom a tyraunt
wende to confounde a free man of corage,
and wende to constreyne him by torment,
60 to maken him discoveren and acusen folk
that wisten of a coniuracioun, *which I
clepe a confederacie,* that was cast ayeins
this tyraunt ; but this free man boot of
his owne tonge and caste it in the visage
65 of thilke wode tyraunt ; so that the torments that this tyraunt wende to han
maked matere of crueltee, this wyse man
maked it matere of vertu.

But what thing is it that a man may
70 don to another man, that he ne may
receyven the same thing of othre folk
in him-self : *or thus, what may a man don
to folk, that folk ne may don him the same?*
I have herd told of Busirides, that was
75 wont to sleen his gestes that herberweden
in his hous ; and he was sleyn him-self
of Ercules that was his gest. Regulus
hadde taken in bataile many men of
Affrike and cast hem in-to feteres ; but
80 sone after he moste yeve his handes to
ben bounde with the cheynes of hem that
he hadde whylom overcomen. Wenest
thou thanne that he be mighty, that
hath no power to don a thing, that othre
85 ne may don in him that he doth in othre?

And yit more-over, yif it so were that
thise dignitees or poweres hadden any
propre or natural goodnesse in hem-self,
never nolden they comen to shrewes.
For contrarious thinges ne ben nat wont 90
to ben y-felawshiped to-gidere. Nature
refuseth that contrarious thinges ben
y-joigned. And so, as I am in certein
that right wikked folk han dignitees ofte
tyme, than sheweth it wel that dignitees 95
and powers ne ben nat goode of hir owne
kinde ; sin that they suffren hem-self to
cleven or joinen hem to shrewes. And
certes, the same thing may I most
digneliche jugen and seyn of alle the 100
yiftes of fortune that most plentevously
comen to shrewes ; of the whiche yiftes,
I trowe that it oughte ben considered,
that no man douteth that he nis strong
in whom he seeth strengthe ; and in 105
whom that swiftnesse is, sooth it is that
he is swift. Also musike maketh mu-
siciens, and phisike maketh phisiciens,
and rethorike rethoriens. For-why the
nature of every thing maketh his pro- 110
pretee, ne it is nat entremedled with the
effects of the contrarious thinges ; and,
as of wil, it chaseth out thinges that ben
to it contrarie. But certes, richesse may
not restreyne avarice unstaunched ; ne 115
power ne maketh nat a man mighty
over him-self, whiche that vicious lustes
holden destreyned with cheynes that ne
mowen nat be unbounden. And dignitees that ben yeven to shrewede folk nat 120
only ne maketh hem nat digne, but it
sheweth rather al openly that they ben
unworthy and undigne. And why is it
thus? Certes, for ye han joye to clepen
thinges with false names that beren hem 125
alle in the contrarie ; the whiche names
ben ful ofte reproeved by the effecte of
the same thinges ; so that thise ilke
richesses ne oughten nat by right to ben
cleped richesses ; ne swich power ne 130
oughte nat ben cleped power ; ne swich
dignitee ne oughte nat ben cleped dignitee. And at the laste, I may conclude the same thing of alle the yiftes
of Fortune, in which ther nis nothing 135
to ben desired, ne that hath in him-self

naturel bountee, as it is ful wel y-sene.
For neither they ne joignen hem nat
alwey to goode men, ne maken hem
140 alwey goode to whom that they ben
y-joigned.

### METRE VI. *Nouimus quantas dederit ruinas.*

We han wel knowen how many grete
harmes and destrucciouns weren don *by
the emperor Nero.* He leet brenne the
citee of Rome, and made sleen the
5 senatoures. And he, cruel, whylom slew
his brother; and he was maked moist
with the blood of his moder; *that is to
seyn, he leet sleen and slitten the body of
his moder, to seen wher he was conceived*;
10 and he loked on every halve up-on her
colde dede body, ne no tere ne wette his
face, but *he was so hard-herted that* he
mighte ben domes-man or juge of hir
dede beautee. And natheles, yit govern-
15 ede this *Nero* by ceptre alle the poeples
that Phebus the sonne may seen, cominge from his outereste arysinge til he
hyde his bemes under the wawes; *that
is to seyn, he governed alle the poeples by*
20 *ceptre imperial that the sonne goth aboute,
from est to west.* And eek *this Nero
governed by ceptre* alle the poeples that
ben under the colde sterres that highten
" septem triones"; *this is to seyn, he gover-*
25 *nede alle the poeples that ben under the
party of the north.* And eek *Nero governed*
alle the poeples that the violent wind
Nothus scorkleth, and baketh the brenning sandes by his drye hete; *that is to
30 seyn, alle the poeples in the south.* But yit
ne mighte nat al his hye power torne the
woodnesse of this wikked Nero. Allas !
it is a grevous fortune, as ofte as wikked
swerd is joigned to cruel venim; *that is*
35 *to seyn, venimous crueltee to lordshippe.'*

### PROSE VII. *Tum ego, scis, inquam.*

Thanne seyde I thus : ' Thou wost wel
thy-self that the coveitise of mortal
thinges ne hadde never lordshipe of me ;
but I have wel desired matere of thinges
5 to done, *as who seith, I desire to han*

matere *of governaunce over comunalitees,*
for vertu, stille, ne sholde nat elden ;'
*that is to seyn, that* [*him*] *leste that, or he
wex olde, his vertu, that lay now ful stille,
ne should nat perisshe unexercised in govern-* 10
*aunce of comune ; for which men mighten
speken or wryten of his goode governement.*

*Philosophye.* 'For sothe,' quod she,
'and that is a thing that may drawen 15
to governaunce swiche hertes as ben
worthy and noble of hir nature; but
natheles, it may nat drawen or tollen
swiche hertes as ben y-brought to the
fulle perfeccioun of vertu, that is to seyn, 20
coveitise of glorie and renoun to han wel
administred the comune thinges or don
gode desertes to profit of the comune.
For see now and considere, how litel and
how voide of alle prys is thilke glorie. 25
Certein thing is, as thou hast lerned by
the demonstracioun of astronomye, that
al the environinge of the erthe aboute
ne halt nat but the resoun of a prikke
at regard of the greetnesse of hevene ; 30
that is to seyn, that yif ther were maked
comparisoun of the erthe to the greetnesse of hevene, men wolden jugen in al,
that the erthe ne helde no space. Of the
whiche litel regioun of this worlde, the 35
ferthe partye is enhabited with livinge
bestes that we knowen, as thou thyself
hast y-lerned by Tholomee that proveth
it. And yif thou haddest with-drawen
and abated in thy thought fro thilke 40
ferthe partye as moche space as the see
and the mareys contenen and over-goon,
and as moche space as the regioun of
droughte over-streccheth, *that is to seyn,
sandes and desertes,* wel unnethe sholde 45
ther dwellen a right streit place to the
habitacioun of men. And ye thanne,
that ben environed and closed with-in
the leste prikke of thilke prikke, thinken
ye to manifesten your renoun and don 50
youre name to ben born forth ? But
your glorie, that is so narwe and so
streite y-throngen in-to so litel boundes,
how mochel coveiteth it in largesse and
in greet doinge ? And also sette this 55
there-to : that many a nacioun, dyverse

of tonge and of maneres and eek of resoun of hir livinge, ben enhabited in the clos of thilke litel habitacle; to the 60 whiche naciouns, what for difficultee of weyes and what for dyversitee of langages, and what for defaute of unusage and entrecomuninge of marchaundise, nat only the names of singuler men ne 65 may nat strecchen, but eek the fame of citees ne may nat strecchen. At the laste, certes, in the tyme of Marcus Tullius, as him-self writ in his book, that the renoun of the comune of Rome ne 70 hadde nat yit passed ne cloumben over the mountaigne that highte Caucasus; and yit was, thilke tyme, Rome wel waxen and greetly redouted of the Parthes and eek of other folk enhabitinge aboute. 75 Seestow nat thanne how streit and how compressed is thilke glorie that ye travailen aboute to shewe and to multiplye? May thanne the glorie of a singuler Romaine strecchen thider as the fame 80 of the name of Rome may nat climben ne passen? And eek, seestow nat that the maneres of dyverse folk and eek hir lawes ben discordaunt among hem-self; so that thilke thing that som men jugen 85 worthy of preysinge, other folk jugen that it is worthy of torment? And therof comth it that, though a man delyte him in preysinge of his renoun, he may nat in no wyse bringen forth ne spreden 90 his name to many maner poeples. Therefor every man oughte to ben apayed of his glorie that is publisshed among his owne neighbours; and thilke noble renoun shal ben restreyned within the 95 boundes of o manere folke. But how many a man, that was ful noble in his tyme, hath the wrecched and nedy foryetinge of wryteres put out of minde and don awey! Al be it so that, certes, 100 thilke wrytinges profiten litel; the whiche wrytinges long and derk elde doth awey, bothe hem and eek hir autours. But ye men semen to geten yow a perdurabletee, whan ye thenken that, in tyme to- 105 cominge, your fame shal lasten. But natheles, yif thou wolt maken comparisoun to the endeles spaces of eternitee,

what thing hast thou by whiche thou mayst rejoysen thee of long lastinge of thy name? For yif ther were maked 110 comparisoun of the abydinge of a moment to ten thousand winter, for as mochel as bothe the spaces ben ended, yit hath the moment som porcioun of it, al-though it litel be. But natheles, thilke selve noum- 115 bre of yeres, and eek as many yeres as ther-to may be multiplyed, ne may nat, certes, ben comparisoned to the perdurabletee that is endeles; for of thinges that han ende may be maked comparisoun, 120 but of thinges that ben with-outen ende, to thinges that han ende, may be maked no comparisoun. And forthy is it that, al-though renoun, of as long tyme as ever thee list to thinken, were thought to the 125 regard of eternitee, that is unstaunchable and infinit, it ne sholde nat only semen litel, but pleynliche right naught. But ye men, certes, ne conne don nothing a-right, but-yif it be for the audience 130 of poeple and for ydel rumours; and ye forsaken the grete worthinesse of conscience and of vertu, and ye seken your guerdouns of the smale wordes of straunge folk. Have now heer and 135 understonde, in the lightnesse of swich pryde and veine glorie, how a man scornede festivaly and merily swich vanitee. Whylom ther was a man that hadde assayed with stryvinge wordes 140 another man, the whiche, nat for usage of verray vertu but for proud veine glorie, had taken up-on him falsly the name of a philosophre. This rather man *that I spak of* thoughte he wolde assaye, 145 wher he, thilke, were a philosophre or no; that is to seyn, yif that he wolde han suffred lightly in pacience the wronges that weren don un-to him. This feynede philosophre took pacience a litel 150 whyle, and, whan he hadde received wordes of outrage, he, as in stryvinge ayein and rejoysinge of him-self, seyde at the laste right thus: "understondest thou nat that I am a philosophre?" That 155 other man answerde ayein ful bytingly, and seyde: "I hadde wel understonden it, yif thou haddest holden thy tonge

stille." But what is it to thise noble
160 worthy men (for, certes, of swiche folke
speke I) that seken glorie with vertu?
What is it?' quod she; 'what atteyneth
fame to swiche folk, whan the body is
resolved by the deeth at the laste? For
165 yif it so be that men dyen in al, *that
is to seyn, body and sowle,* the whiche
thing our resoun defendeth us to bileven,
thanne is ther no glorie in no wyse. *For
what sholde thilke glorie ben,* whan he,
170 of whom thilke glorie is seyd to be, nis
right naught in no wyse? And yif the
sowle, whiche that hath in it-self science
of goode werkes, unbounden fro the
prison of the erthe, wendeth frely to the
175 hevene, despyseth it nat thanne alle
erthely occupacioun; and, being in
hevene, rejoyseth that it is exempt fro
alle erthely thinges? *As who seith, thanne
rekketh the sowle of no glorie of renoun
180 of this world.*

### Metre VII. *Quicunque solam mente
praecipiti petit.*

Who-so that, with overthrowinge
thought, only seketh glorie of fame,
and weneth that it be soverceyn good :
lat him loken up-on the brode shewinge
5 contrees of hevene, and up-on the streite
site of this erthe; and he shal ben
ashamed of the encrees of his name, that
may nat fulfille the litel compas *of the
erthe.* O! what coveiten proude folk to
10 liften up hir nekkes in ydel in the dedly
yok *of this worlde?* For al-though that
renoun y-sprad, passinge to ferne poeples,
goth by dyverse tonges; and al-though
that grete houses or kinredes shynen
15 with clere titles of honours; yit, natheles,
deeth despyseth alle heye glorie of fame :
and deeth wrappeth to-gidere the heye
hevedes and the lowe, and maketh egal
and evene the heyeste to the loweste.
20 Wher wonen now the bones of trewe
Fabricius? What is now Brutus, or
stierne Catoun? The thinne fame, yit
lastinge, of hir ydel names, is marked
with a fewe lettres; but al-though that
25 we han knowen the faire wordes of the

fames of hem, it is nat yeven to knowe
hem that ben dede and consumpte. Liggeth thanne stille, al outrely unknow-
able; ne fame ne maketh yow nat knowe.
And yif ye wene to liven the longer for 30
winde of your mortal name, whan o
cruel day shal ravisshe yow, thanne is
the seconde deeth dwellinge un-to yow.'
**Glose.** *The first deeth he clepeth heer the
departinge of the body and the sowle; and* 35
*the seconde deeth he clepeth, as heer, the
stintinge of the renoun of fame.*

### Prose VIII. *Set ne me inexorabile contra
fortunam.*

'But for as mochel as thou shalt nat
wenen,' quod she, 'that I bere untretable
bataile ayeins fortune, yit som-tyme it
bifalleth that she, deceyvable, deserveth
to han right good thank of men; and 5
that is, whan she hir-self opneth, and
whan she descovereth hir frount, and
sheweth hir maneres. Peraventure yit
understondest thou nat that I shal seye.
It is a wonder that I desire to telle, and 10
forthy unnethe may I unpleyten my
sentence with wordes; for I deme that
contrarious Fortune profiteth more to
men than Fortune debonaire. For alwey, whan Fortune semeth debonaire, 15
than she lyeth falsly in bihetinge the
hope of welefulnesse; but forsothe contrarious Fortune is alwey soothfast, whan
she sheweth hir-self unstable thorugh
hir chaunginge. The amiable Fortune 20
deceyveth folk; the contrarie Fortune
techeth. The amiable Fortune bindeth
with the beautee of false goodes the
hertes of folk that usen hem; the contrarie Fortune unbindeth hem by the 25
knowinge of freele welefulnesse. The
amiable Fortune mayst thou seen alwey
† windy and flowinge, and ever misknowinge of hir-self; the contrarie Fortune is atempre and restreyned, and wys 30
thorugh exercise of hir adversitee. At
the laste, amiable Fortune with hir
flateringes draweth miswandringe men
fro the sovereyne good; the contrarious
Fortune ledeth ofte folk ayein to sooth- 35

fast goodes, and haleth hem ayein as with an hooke. Wenest thou thanne that thou oughtest to leten this a litel thing, that this aspre and horrible
40 Fortune hath discovered to thee the thoughtes of thy trewe freendes? For-why this ilke Fortune hath departed and uncovered to thee bothe the certein visages and eek the doutous visages of
45 thy felawes. Whan she departed awey fro thee, she took awey hir freendes, and lafte thee thyne freendes. Now whan thou were riche and weleful, as thee semede, with how mochel woldest thou
50 han bought the fulle knowinge of this, *that is to seyn, the knowinge of thy verray freendes?* Now pleyne thee nat thanne of richesse y-lorn, sin thou hast founden the moste precious kinde of richesses,
55 that is to seyn, thy verray freendes.

METRE VIII. *Quod mundus stabili fide.*

That the world with stable feith varieth acordable chaunginges; that the con-trarious qualitee of elements holden among hem-self aliaunce perdurable; that Phebus the sonne with his goldene chariet 5 bringeth forth the rosene day; that the mone hath commaundement over the nightes, which nightes Hesperus the eve-sterre hath brought; that the see, greedy to flowen, constreyneth with a certein 10 ende hise flodes, so that it is nat leveful to strecche hise brode termes or boundes up-on the erthes, *that is to seyn, to covere al the erthe:*—al this acordaunce of thinges is bounden with Love, that 15 governeth erthe and see, and hath also commaundements to the hevenes. And yif this Love slakede the brydeles, alle thinges that now loven hem to-gederes wolden maken a bataile continuely, and 20 stryven to fordoon the fasoun of this worlde, the whiche they now leden in acordable feith by faire moevinges. This Love halt to-gideres poeples joigned with an holy bond, and knitteth sacrement 25 of mariages of chaste loves; and Love endyteth lawes to trewe felawes. O! weleful were mankinde, yif thilke Love that governeth hevene governed youre corages!' 30

Explicit Liber secundus.

# BOOK III.

### PROSE I. *Iam cantum illa finierat.*

By this she hadde ended hir song, whan the sweetnesse of hir ditee hadde thorugh-perced me that was desirous of herkninge, and I astoned hadde yit
5 streighte myn eres, *that is to seyn, to herkne the bet what she wolde seye*; so that a litel here-after I seyde thus: 'O thou that art sovereyn comfort of an-guissous corages, so thou hast remounted
10 and norisshed me with the weighte of thy sentences and with delyt of thy singinge; so that I trowe nat now that I be unparigal to the strokes of Fortune: *as who seyth, I dar wel now suffren al the*
15 *assautes of Fortune, and wel defende me* *fro hir.* And tho remedies whiche that thou seydest her-biforn weren right sharpe, nat only that I am nat a-grisen of hem now, but I, desirous of heringe, axe gretely to heren the remedies.' Than 20 seyde she thus: 'That felede I ful wel,' quod she, 'whan that thou, ententif and stille, ravisshedest my wordes; and I abood til that thou haddest swich habite of thy thought as thou hast now; or elles 25 til that I my-self hadde maked to thee the same habit, which that is a more verray thing. And certes, the remenaunt of thinges that ben yit to seye ben swiche, that first whan men tasten hem they ben 30 bytinge, but whan they ben receyved withinne a wight, than ben they swete.

But for thou seyst that thou art so
desirous to herkne hem, with how gret
35 brenninge woldest thou glowen, yif thou
wistest whider I wol leden thee!'
'Whider is that?' quod I.

'To thilke verray welefulnesse,' quod
she, 'of whiche thyn herte dremeth;
40 but for as moche as thy sighte is ocupied
and distorbed by imaginacioun *of erthely
thinges*, thou mayst nat yit seen thilke
selve welefulnesse.'    'Do,' quod I, 'and
shewe me what is thilke verray weleful-
45 nesse, I preye thee, with-oute taryinge.'

'That wole I gladly don,' quod she,
'for the cause of thee; but I wol first
marken thee by wordes and I wol enforcen me to enformen thee thilke *false*
50 cause *of blisfulnesse* that thou more knowest; so that, whan thou hast fully biholden thilke false goodes, and torned
thyn eyen to that other syde, thou mowe
knowe the cleernesse of verray blisful-
55 nesse.

METRE I.    *Qui serere ingenuum uolet
agrum.*

Who-so wole sowe a feeld plentivous,
lat him first delivere it fro thornes, and
kerve asunder with his hook the busshes
and the fern, so that the corn may comen
5 hevy of eres and of greynes. Hony is
the more swete, yif mouthes han first
tasted savoures that ben wikkid. The
sterres shynen more agreably whan the
wind Nothus leteth his ploungy blastes;
10 and after that Lucifer the day-sterre
hath chased awey the derke night, the
day the fairere ledeth the rosene hors
*of the sonne*. And right so thou, biholdinge first the false goodes, bigin to
15 with-drawen thy nekke fro the yok *of
erthely affecciouns*; and after-ward the
verray goodes shollen entren in-to thy
corage.'

PROSE II.    *Tunc defixo paullulum uisu.*

Tho fastnede she a litel the sighte of
hir eyen, and with-drow hir right as it
were in-to the streite sete of hir thought;

and bigan to speke right thus : 'Alle the
cures,' quod she, 'of mortal folk, whiche 5
that travaylen hem in many maner
studies, goon certes by diverse weyes,
but natheles they enforcen hem alle to
comen only to oon ende of blisfulnesse.
And blisfulnesse is swiche a good, that 10
who-so that hath geten it, he ne may,
over that, no-thing more desyre. And
this thing is forsothe the sovereyn good
that conteyneth in him-self alle maner
goodes; to the whiche good yif ther 15
failede any thing, it mighte nat ben
cleped sovereyn good : for thanne were
ther som good, out of this ilke sovereyn
good, that mighte ben desired. Now is
it cleer and certein thanne, that blisful- 20
nesse is a parfit estat by the congregacioun of alle goodes; the whiche
blisfulnesse, as I have seyd, alle mortal
folk enforcen hem to geten by diverse
weyes. For-why the coveitise of verray 25
good is naturelly y-plaunted in the hertes
of men; but the miswandringe errour
mis-ledeth hem in-to false goodes. Of
the whiche men, som of hem wenen that
sovereyn good be to liven with-oute nede 30
of any thing, and travaylen hem to be
haboundaunt of richesses. And som
other men demen that sovereyn good
be, for to ben right digne of reverence ;
and enforcen hem to ben reverenced 35
among hir neighbours by the honours
that they han y-geten. And som folk
ther ben that holden, that right heigh
power be sovereyn good, and enforcen
hem for to regnen, or elles to joignen 40
hem to hem that regnen. And it semeth
to some other folk, that noblesse of renoun be the sovereyn good; and hasten
hem to geten glorious name by the arts
of werre and of pees. And many folk 45
mesuren and gessen that sovereyn good
be joye and gladnesse, and wenen that
it be right blisful thing to ploungen hem
in voluptuous delyt. And ther ben folk
that entrechaungen the causes and the 50
endes of thise forseyde goodes, as they
that desiren richesses to han power and
delytes; or elles they desiren power for
to han moneye, or for cause of renoun.

55 In thise thinges, and in swiche othre
thinges, is torned alle the entencioun of
desiringes and of werkes of men; as
thus: noblesse and favour of people,
whiche that yeveth to men, as it semeth
60 hem, a maner cleernesse of renoun; and
wyf and children, that men desiren for
cause of delyt and of merinesse. But
forsothe, frendes ne sholden nat be
rekned a-mong the godes of fortune, but
65 of vertu; for it is a ful holy maner thing.
Alle thise othre thinges, forsothe, ben
taken for cause of power or elles for
cause of delyt.    Certes, now am I redy
to referren the goodes of the body to thise
70 forseide thinges aboven; for it semeth
that strengthe and gretnesse of body
yeven power and worthinesse, and that
beautee and swiftnesse yeven noblesses
and glorie of renoun; and hele of body
75 semeth yeven delyt. In alle thise thinges
it semeth only that blisfulnesse is desired.
For-why thilke thing that every man
desireth most over alle thinges, he
demeth that it be the sovereyn good;
80 but I have defyned that blisfulnesse is
the sovereyn good; for which every wight
demeth, that thilke estat that he desireth
over alle thinges, that it be blisfulnesse.
Now hast thou thanne biforn thyn eyen
85 almest al the purposed forme of the welefulnesse of man-kinde, that is to seyn,
richesses, honours, power, and glorie, and
delyts. The whiche delyt only considerede
Epicurus, and juged and establisshed that
90 delyt is the sovereyn good; for as moche
as alle othre thinges, as him thoughte,
bi-refte awey joye and mirthe fram the
herte.  But I retorne ayein to the studies
of men, of whiche men the corage alwey
95 reherseth and seketh the sovereyn good,
al be it so that it be with a derked
memorie; but he not by whiche path,
right as a dronken man not nat by
whiche path he may retorne him to his
100 hous.  Semeth it thanne that folk folyen
and erren that enforcen hem to have
nede of nothing? Certes, ther nis non
other thing that may so wel performe
blisfulnesse, as an estat plentivous of alle
105 goodes, that ne hath nede of non other

thing, but that is suffisaunt of himself
unto him-self.  And folyen swiche folk
thanne, that wenen that thilke thing
that is right good, that it be eek right
worthy of honour and of reverence? 110
Certes, nay.  For that thing nis neither
foul ne worthy to ben despised, that wel
neigh al the entencioun of mortal folk
travaylen for to geten it.  And power,
oughte nat that eek to ben rekened 115
amonges goodes?  What elles?  For it
is nat to wene that thilke thing, that is
most worthy of alle thinges, be feble and
with-oute strengthe.  And cleernesse of
renoun, oughte that to ben despised? 120
Certes, ther may no man forsake, that al
thing that is right excellent and noble,
that it ne semeth to ben right cleer and
renomed.  For certes, it nedeth nat to
seye, that blisfulnesse be [nat] anguissous 125
ne drery, ne subgit to grevaunces ne to
sorwes, sin that in right litel thinges
folk seken to have and to usen that may
delyten hem.    Certes, thise ben the
thinges that men wolen and desiren to 130
geten. And for this cause desiren they
richesses, dignitees, regnes, glorie, and
delices. For therby wenen they to han
suffisaunce, honour, power, renoun, and
gladnesse.  Than is it good, that men 135
seken thus by so many diverse studies.
In whiche desyr it may lightly ben
shewed how gret is the strengthe of
nature; for how so that men han diverse
sentences and discordinge, algates men 140
acorden alle in lovinge the ende of good.

## Metre II.  *Quantas rerum flectat habenas.*

It lyketh me to shewe, by subtil song,
with slakke and delitable soun of strenges,
how that Nature, mighty, enclineth and
flitteth the governements of thinges, and
by whiche lawes she, purveyable, kepeth 5
the grete world; and how she, bindinge,
restreyneth alle thinges by a bonde that
may nat ben unbounde.  Al be it so that
the lyouns of the contre of Pene beren
the faire chaynes, and taken metes of 10
the handes of folk that yeven it hem,
and dreden hir sturdy maystres of whiche

they ben wont to suffren betinges : yif
that hir horrible mouthes ben be-bled,
15 *that is to seyn, of bestes devoured,* hir
corage of time passed, that hath ben ydel
and rested, repeyreth ayein ; and they
roren grevously and remembren on hir
nature, and slaken hir nekkes fram hir
20 chaynes unbounde ; and hir mayster, first
to-torn with blody tooth, assayeth the
wode wrathes of hem ; *this is to seyn,
they freten hir mayster.* And the jange-
linge brid that singeth on the heye
25 braunches, *that is to seyn, in the wode,*
and after is enclosed in a streyt cage :
al-though that the pleyinge bisinesse of
men yeveth hem honiede drinkes and
large metes with swete studie, yit nathe-
30 les, yif thilke brid, skippinge out of hir
streyte cage, seeth the agreables shadewes
of the wodes, she defouleth with hir feet
hir metes y-shad, and seketh mourninge
only the wode ; and twitereth, desiringe
35 the wode, with hir swete vois. The yerde
of a tree, that is haled a-doun by mighty
strengthe, boweth redily the crop a-doun :
but yif that the hand of him that it bente
lat it gon ayein, anon the crop loketh
40 up-right to hevene. The sonne Phebus,
that falleth at even in the westrene
wawes, retorneth ayein eftsones his carte,
by privee path, ther-as it is wont aryse.
Alle thinges seken ayein to hir propre
45 cours, and alle thinges rejoysen hem of
hir retorninge ayein to hir nature. Ne
non ordinaunce nis bitaken to thinges,
but that that hath joyned the endinge
to the beginninge, and hath maked the
50 cours of it-self stable, *that it chaungeth
nat from his propre kinde.*

PROSE III. *Vos quoque, o terrena animalia.*

Certes also ye men, that ben ertheliche
beestes, dremen alwey youre beginninge,
al-though it be with a thinne imaginacioun ; and by a maner thoughte, al be
5 it nat cleerly ne parfitly, ye loken fram
a-fer to thilke verray fyn of blisfulnesse ;
and ther-fore naturel entencioun ledeth
you to thilke verray good, but many
maner errours mis-torneth you ther-fro.

Consider now yif that by thilke thinges, 10
by whiche a man weneth to geten him
blisfulnesse, yif that he may comen to
thilke ende that he weneth to come by
nature. For yif that moneye or honours,
or thise other forseyde thinges bringen 15
to men swich a thing that no good ne
fayle hem ne semeth fayle, certes than
wole I graunte that they ben maked
blisful by thilke thinges that they han
geten. But yif so be that thilke thinges 20
ne mowen nat performen that they biheten, and that ther be defaute of manye
goodes, sheweth it nat thanne cleerly
that fals beautee of blisfulnesse is knowen
and ateint in thilke thinges ? First and 25
forward thou thy-self, that haddest habundaunces of richesses nat long agon,
I axe yif that, in the habundaunce of alle
thilke richesses, thou were never anguissous or sory in thy corage of any 30
wrong or grevaunce that bi-tidde thee on
any syde ? ' 'Certes,' quod I, 'it ne remembreth me nat that evere I was so
free of my thought that I ne was alwey
in anguissh of som-what.' 35
'And was nat that,' quod she, ' for that
thee lakked som-what that thou noldest
nat han lakked, or elles thou haddest
that thou noldest nat han had ?' 'Right
so is it,' quod I. 40
'Thanne desiredest thou the presence
of that oon and the absence of that
other ?' 'I graunte wel,' quod I.
'Forsothe,' quod she, 'than nedeth
ther som-what that every man desireth ?' 45
' Ye, ther nedeth,' quod I.
' Certes,' quod she, 'and he that hath
lakke or nede of aught nis nat in every
wey suffisaunt to himself?' 'No,'
quod I. 50
' And thou,' quod she, ' in al the plentee
of thy richesses haddest thilke lakke of
suffisaunse ?' ' What elles ?' quod I.
' Thanne may nat richesses maken that
a man nis nedy, ne that he be suffisaunt 55
to him-self ; and that was it that they
bi-highten, as it semeth. And eek certes
I trowe, that this be gretly to considere,
that moneye ne hath nat in his owne
kinde that it ne may ben bi-nomen of 60

hem that han it, maugre hem?'    'I bi-knowe it wel,' quod I.

'Why sholdest thou nat bi-knowen it,' quod she, 'whan every day the strenger 65 folk bi-nemen it fro the febler, maugre hem? For whennes comen elles alle thise foreyne compleyntes or quereles of plet-inges, but for that men axen ayein here moneye that hath ben bi-nomen hem by 70 force or by gyle, and alwey maugre hem?'    'Right so is it,' quod I.

'Than,' quod she, 'hath a man nede to seken him foreyne helpe by whiche he may defende his moneye?'    'Who may 75 sey nay?' quod I.

'Certes,' quod she; 'and him nedede non help, yif he ne hadde no moneye that he mighte lese?'    'That is douteles,' quod I.

80 'Than is this thinge torned in-to the contrarye,' quod she.    'For richesses, that men wenen sholde make suffisaunce, they maken a man rather han nede of foreyne help! Which is the manere or 85 the gyse,' quod she, 'that richesse may dryve awey nede? Riche folk, may they neither han hunger ne thurst? Thise riche men, may they fele no cold on hir limes on winter? But thou wolt answeren, 90 that riche men han y-now wher-with they may staunchen hir hunger, slaken hir thurst, and don a-wey cold. In this wyse may nede be counforted by richesses; but certes, nede ne may nat al outrely 95 ben don a-wey. For though this nede, that is alwey gapinge and gredy, be ful-fild with richesses, and axe any thing, yit dwelleth thanne a nede that mighte be fulfild. I holde me stille, and telle 100 nat how that litel thing suffiseth to nature; but certes to avarice y-nough ne suffiseth no-thing. For sin that rich-esses ne may nat al don awey nede, but richesses maken nede, what may it thanne 105 be, that ye wenen that richesses mowen yeven you suffisaunce?

### Metre III.    *Quamvis fluente diues auri gurgite.*

Al were it so that a riche coveytous man hadde a river fletinge al of gold, yit

sholde it never staunchen his coveitise; and though he hadde his nekke y-charged with precious stones of the rede 5 see, and though he do ere his feldes plen-tivous with an hundred oxen, never ne shal his bytinge bisinesse for-leten him whyl he liveth, ne the lighte richesses ne sholle nat beren him companye whan he 10 is deed.

### Prose IV.    *Set dignitates.*

But dignitees, to whom they ben comen, maken they him honorable and reverent? Han they nat so gret strengthe, that they may putte vertues in the hertes of folk that usen the lordshipes of hem?   Or 5 elles may they don a-wey the vyces? Certes, they ne be nat wont to don awey wikkednesse, but they ben wont rather to shewen wikkednesse.   And ther-of comth it that I have right grete desdeyn, 10 that dignitees ben yeven ofte to wikked men; for which thing Catullus cleped *a consul of Rome, that highte* Nonius, "postum" or "boch"; *as who seyth, he cleped him a congregacioun of vyces in his* 15 *brest, as a postum is ful of corupcioun,* al were this Nonius set in a chayre of dignitee.   Seest thou nat thanne how gret vilenye dignitees don to wikked men? Certes, unworthinesse of wikked 20 men sholde be the lasse y-sene, yif they nere renomed of none honours. Certes, thou thyself ne mightest nat ben brought with as manye perils as thou mightest suffren that thou woldest beren the 25 magistrat with Decorat; *that is to seyn, that for no peril that mighte befallen thee by offence of the king Theodorike, thou noldest nat be felawe in governaunce with Decorat*; whan thou saye that he hadde 30 wikked corage of a likerous shrewe and of an accusor. Ne I ne may nat, for swiche honours, jugen hem worthy of reverence, that I deme and holde un-worthy to han thilke same honours. Now 35 yif thou saye a man that were fulfild of wisdom, certes, thou ne mightest nat deme that he were unworthy to the honour, or elles to the wisdom of which

40 he is fulfild?'—'No,' quod I.—'Certes, dignitees,' quod she, 'apertienen proprely to vertu; and vertu transporteth dignitee anon to thilke man to which she hir-self is conjoigned. And for as moche as 45 honours of poeple ne may nat maken folk digne of honour, it is wel seyn cleerly that they ne han no propre beautee of dignitee. And yit men oughten taken more heed in this. For yif it so be that 50 a wikked wight be so mochel the foulere and the more out-cast, that he is despysed of most folk, so as dignitee ne may nat maken shrewes digne of reverence, the which shrewes dignitee sheweth to moche 55 folk, thanne maketh dignitee shrewes rather so moche more despysed than preysed; and forsothe nat unpunisshed: *that is for to seyn, that shrewes revengen hem ayeinward up-on dignitees*; for they 60 yilden ayein to dignitees as gret guerdoun, whan they bi-spotten and defoulen dignitees with hir vilenye. And for as mochel as thou mowe knowe that thilke verray reverence ne may nat comen by 65 thise shadewy transitorie dignitees, undirstond now thus : yif that a man hadde used and had many maner dignitees of consules, and were comen peraventure amonge straunge naciouns, sholde thilke 70 honour maken him worshipful and redouted of straunge folk? Certes, yif that honour of poeple were a naturel yift to dignitees, it ne mighte never cesen nowher amonges no maner folk to 75 don his office, right as fyr in every contree ne stinteth nat to eschaufen and to ben hoot. But for as moche as for to ben holden honourable or reverent ne cometh nat to folk of hir propre 80 strengthe of nature, but only of the false opinioun of folk, *that is to seyn, that wenen that dignitees maken folk digne of honour*; anon therfore whan that they comen ther-as folk ne knowen nat thilke digni-85 tees, hir honours vanisshen awey, and that anon. But that is amonges straunge folk, mayst thou seyn ; but amonges hem ther they weren born, ne duren nat thilke dignitees alwey? Certes, the dig-90 nitee of the provostrie of Rome was

whylom a gret power; now is it nothing but an ydel name, and the rente of the senatorie a gret charge. And yif a wight whylom hadde the office to taken hede to the vitailes of the poeple, as of corn and 95 other thinges, he was holden amonges grete; but what thing is now more outcast thanne thilke provostrie? And, as I have seyd a litel her-biforn, that thilke thing that hath no propre beautee of 100 him-self receiveth som-tyme prys and shyninge, and som-tyme leseth it by the opinioun of usaunces. Now yif that dignitees thanne ne mowen nat maken folk digne of reverence, and yif that dignitees 105 wexen foule of hir wille by the filthe of shrewes, and yif that dignitees lesen hir shyninge by chaunginge of tymes, and yif they wexen foule by estimacioun of poeple : what is it that they han in hem-110 self of beautee that oughte ben desired? *as who seyth, non* ; thanne ne mowen they yeven no beautee of dignitee to non other.

## METRE IV. *Quamvis se, Tyrio superbus ostro.*

Al be it so that the proude Nero, with alle his wode luxurie, kembde him and aparailede him with faire purpres of Tirie, and with whyte perles, algates yit throf he hateful to alle folk : *this is to* 5 *seyn, that al was he behated of alle folk.* Yit this wikked *Nero hadde gret lordshìp, and* yaf whylom to the reverents senatours the unworshipful setes of dignitees. *Unworshipful setes he clepeth here, for that* 10 *Nero, that was so wikked, yaf tho dignitees.* Who-so wolde thanne resonably wenen, that blisfulnesse were in swiche honours as ben yeven by vicious shrewes?

## PROSE V. *An uero regna regumque familiaritas.*

But regnes and familiaritees of kinges, may they maken a man to ben mighty? How elles, whan hir blisfulnesse dureth perpetuely ? But certes, the olde age of tyme passed, and eek of present tyme 5 now, is ful of ensaumples how that

kinges ben chaunged in-to wrecchednesse
out of hir welefulnesse. O ! a noble thing
and a cleer thing is power, that is nat
10 founden mighty to kepen it-self! And
yif that power of reaumes be auctour and
maker of blisfulnesse, yif thilke power
lakketh on any syde, amenuseth it nat
thilke blisfulnesse and bringeth in
15 wrecchednesse? But yit, al be it so
that the reaumes of mankinde strecchen
brode, yit mot ther nede ben moche folk,
over whiche that every king ne hath no
lordshipe ne comaundement. And certes,
20 up-on thilke syde that power faileth,
which that maketh folk blisful, right
on that same syde noun-power entreth
under-nethe, that maketh hem wrecches ;
in this manere thanne moten kinges han
25 more porcioun of wrecchednesse than of
welefulnesse. A tyraunt, *that was king
of Sisile*, that hadde assayed the peril
of his estat, shewede by similitude the
dredes of reaumes by gastnesse of a swerd
30 that heng over the heved *of his familier*.
What thing is thanne this power, that
may nat don awey the bytinges of bisinesse, ne eschewe the prikkes of drede ?
And certes, yit wolden they liven in
35 sikernesse, but they may nat ; and yit
they glorifye hem in hir power. Holdest
thou thanne that thilke man be mighty,
that thou seest that he wolde don that
he may nat don ? And holdest thou
40 thanne him a mighty man, that hath
envirownede his sydes with men of armes
or serjaunts, and dredeth more hem that
he maketh agast than they dreden him,
and that is put in the handes of his
45 servaunts for he sholde seme mighty ?
But of familieres or servaunts of kinges
what sholde I telle thee anything, sin
that I myself have shewed thee that
reaumes hem-self ben ful of gret feblesse ?
50 The whiche familieres, certes, the ryal
power of kinges, in hool estat and in
estat abated, ful ofte throweth adown.
Nero constreynede Senek, his familier
and his mayster, to chesen on what deeth
55 he wolde deyen. Antonius comaundede
that knightes slowen with hir swerdes
Papinian *his familier*, which Papinian

hadde ben longe tyme ful mighty
amonges hem of the court. And yit,
certes, they wolden bothe han renounced 60
hir power ; of whiche two Senek enforcede him to yeven to Nero his richesses, and also to han gon in-to solitarie
exil. But whan the grete weighte, *that
is to seyn, of lordes power or of fortune*, 65
draweth hem that shullen falle, neither
of hem ne mighte do that he wolde.
What thing is thanne thilke power, that
though men han it, yit they ben agast ;
and whanne thou woldest han it, thou 70
nart nat siker ; and yif thou woldest
forleten it, thou mayst nat eschuen it ?
But whether swiche men ben frendes
at nede, as ben conseyled by fortune and
nat by vertu ? Certes, swiche folk as 75
weleful fortune maketh freendes, contrarious fortune maketh hem enemys.
And what pestilence is more mighty for
to anoye a wight than a familier enemy ?

## METRE V.    *Qui se uolet esse potentem.*

Who-so wol be mighty, he mot daunten
his cruel corage, ne putte nat his nekke,
overcomen, under the foule reynes of
lecherye. For al-be-it so that thy lordshipe strecche so fer, that the contree 5
of Inde quaketh at thy comaundements
or at thy lawes, and that the last *ile in
the see, that hight* Tyle, be thral to thee,
yit, yif thou mayst nat putten awey thy
foule derke desyrs, and dryven out fro 10
thee wrecched complaintes, certes, it nis
no power that thou hast.

## PROSE VI.    *Gloria uero quam fallax saepe.*

But glorie, how deceivable and how
foul is it ofte ! For which thing nat
unskilfully a tragedien, *that is to seyn,
a maker of ditees that highten tragedies*,
cryde and seide : " O glorie, glorie," quod 5
he, " thou art nothing elles to thousandes
of folkes but a greet sweller of eres ! "
For manye han had ful greet renoun by
the false opinioun of the poeple, and what
thing may ben thought fouler than swiche 10
preysinge ? For thilke folk that ben
preysed falsly, they moten nedes han

shame of hir preysinges. And yif that folk han geten hem thonk or preysinge 15 by hir desertes, what thing hath thilke prys eched or encresed to the conscience of wyse folk, that mesuren hir good, nat by the rumour of the poeple, but by the soothfastnesse of conscience? And 20 yif it seme a fair thing, a man to han encresed and spred his name, than folweth it that it is demed to ben a foul thing, yif it ne be y-sprad and encresed. But, as I seyde a litel her-biforn that, sin 25 ther mot nedes ben many folk, to whiche folk the renoun of a man ne may nat comen, it befalleth that he, that thou wenest be glorious and renomed, semeth in the nexte partie of the erthes to ben 30 with-oute glorie and with-oute renoun.

And certes, amonges thise thinges I ne trowe nat that the prys and grace of the poeple nis neither worthy to ben remembred, ne cometh of wyse jugement, 35 ne is ferme perdurably. But now, of this name of gentilesse, what man is it that ne may wel seen how veyn and how flittinge a thing it is? For yif the name of gentilesse be referred to renoun and 40 cleernesse of linage, thanne is gentil name but a foreine thing, *that is to seyn, to hem that glorifyen hem of hir linage.* For it semeth that gentilesse be a maner preysinge that comth of the deserte of an-45 cestres. And yif preysinge maketh gentilesse, thanne moten they nedes be gentil that ben preysed. For which thing it folweth, that yif thou ne have no gentilesse of thy-self, *that is to seyn, preyse* 50 *that comth of thy deserte,* foreine gentilesse ne maketh thee nat gentil. But certes, yif ther be any good in gentilesse, I trowe it be al-only this, that it semeth as that a maner necessitee be imposed to gentil 55 men, for that they ne sholden nat outrayen or forliven fro the virtues of hir noble kinrede.

### METRE VI. *Omne hominum genus in terris.*

Al the linage of men that ben in erthe ben of semblable birthe. On allone is fader of thinges. On allone ministreth

alle thinges. He yaf to the sonne hise bemes; he yaf to the mone hir hornes. 5 He yaf the men to the erthe; he yaf the sterres to the hevene. He encloseth with membres the soules that comen fro his hye sete. Thanne comen alle mortal folk of noble sede; why noisen ye or bosten of 10 youre eldres? For yif thou loke your biginninge, and god your auctor and your maker, thanne nis ther no forlived wight, but-yif he norisshe his corage un-to vyces, and forlete his propre burthe. 15

### PROSE VII. *Quid autem de corporis uoluptatibus.*

But what shal I seye of delices of body, of whiche delices the desiringes ben ful of anguissh, and the fulfillinges of hem ben ful of penaunce? How greet syknesse and how grete sorwes unsufferable, 5 right as a maner fruit of wikkednesse, ben thilke delices wont to bringen to the bodies of folk that usen hem! Of whiche delices I not what joye may ben had of hir moevinge. But this wot I wel, that 10 who-so-ever wole remembren him of hise luxures, he shal wel understonde that the issues of delices ben sorwful and sorye. And yif thilke delices mowen maken folk blisful, than by the same 15 cause moten thise bestes ben cleped blisful; of whiche bestes al the entencioun hasteth to fulfille hir bodily jolitee. And the gladnesse of wyf and children were an honest thing, but it hath ben seyd 20 that it is over muchel ayeins kinde, that children han ben founden tormentours to hir fadres, I not how manye: of whiche children how bytinge is every condicioun, it nedeth nat to tellen it thee, that hast 25 or this tyme assayed it, and art yit now anguissous. In this approve I the sentence of my disciple Euripidis, that seyde, that " he that hath no children is weleful by infortune." 30

### METRE VII. *Habet omnis hoc uoluptas.*

Every delyt hath this, that it anguissheth hem with prikkes that usen it. It resembleth to thise flyinge flyes that we

clepen been, that, after that he hath shad
5 hise agreable honies, he fleeth awey, and
stingeth the hertes, of hem that ben
y-smite, with bytinge overlonge holdinge.

## Prose VIII. *Nihil igitur dubium est.*

Now is it no doute thanne that thise
weyes ne ben a maner misledinges to
blisfulnesse, ne that they ne mowe nat
leden folk thider as they biheten to leden
5 hem. But with how grete harmes thise
forseyde weyes ben enlaced, I shal shewe
thee shortly. For-why yif thou enforcest
thee to asemble moneye, thou most bireven him his moneye that hath it. And
10 yif thou wolt shynen with dignitees, thou
most bisechen and supplien hem that
yeven tho dignitees. And yif thou covei-
test by honour to gon biforn other folk,
thou shalt defoule thy-self thorugh hum-
15 blesse of axinge. Yif thou desirest power,
thou shalt by awaytes of thy subgits
anoyously ben cast under manye periles.
Axest thou glorie? Thou shalt ben so
destrat by aspre thinges that thou shalt
20 forgoon sikernesse. And yif thou wolt
leden thy lyf in delices, every wight shal
despisen thee and forleten thee, as thou
that art thral to thing that is right foul
and brotel ; that is to seyn, servaunt to
25 thy body. Now is it thanne wel seen,
how litel and how brotel possessioun they
coveiten, that putten the goodes of the
body aboven hir owne resoun. For mayst
thou sormounten thise olifaunts in gret-
30 nesse or weight of body ? Or mayst thou
ben stronger than the bole ? Mayst thou
ben swifter than the tygre ? Bihold the
spaces and the stablenesse and the swifte
cours of the hevene, and stint som-tyme
35 to wondren on foule thinges ; the which
hevene, certes, nis nat rather for thise
thinges to ben wondred up-on, than for
the resoun by which it is governed. But
the shyning of thy forme, *that is to seyn,*
40 *the beautee of thy body,* how swiftly passinge is it, and how transitorie ; certes, it
is more flittinge than the mutabilitee of
flowers of the somer-sesoun. For so Aristotle telleth, that yif that men hadden

eyen of a beest that highte lynx, so that 45
the lokinge of folk mighte percen thorugh
the thinges that with-stonden it, who-so
loked thanne in the entrailes of the body
of Alcibiades, that was ful fayr in the
superfice with-oute, it shold seme right 50
foul. And forthy, yif thou semest fayr,
thy nature maketh nat that, but the
desceivaunce of the feblesse of the eyen
that loken. But preyse the goodes of the
body as mochel as ever thee list ; so that 55
thou knowe algates that, what-so it be,
*that is to seyn, of the goodes of thy body,*
which that thou wondrest up-on, may
ben destroyed or dissolved by the hete of
a fevere of three dayes. Of alle whiche 60
forseyde thinges I may reducen this
shortly in a somme, that thise worldly
goodes, whiche that ne mowen nat yeven
that they biheten, ne ben nat parfit by
the congregacioun of alle goodes ; that 65
they ne ben nat weyes ne pathes that
bringen men to blisfulnesse, ne maken
men to ben blisful.

## Metre VIII. *Eheu ! quae miseros tramite deuios.*

Allas ! which folye and which ignoraunce misledeth wandringe wrecches
fro the path of verray goode !    Certes,
ye ne seken no gold in grene trees, ne ye
ne gaderen nat precious stones in the 5
vynes, ne ye ne hyden nat your ginnes
in the hye mountaignes to cacchen fish
of whiche ye may maken riche festes.
And yif yow lyketh to hunte to roes, ye
ne gon nat to the fordes of the water that 10
highte Tyrene. And over this, men
knowen wel the crykes and the cavernes
of the see y-hid in the flodes, and knowen
eek which water is most plentivous of
whyte perles, and knowen which water 15
haboundeth most of rede purpre, *that is to
seyn, of a maner shelle-fish with which men
dyen purpre ;* and knowen which strondes
habounden most with tendre fisshes, or of
sharpe fisshes that highten echines. But 20
folk suffren hem-self to ben so blinde,
that hem ne reccheth nat to knowe where
thilke goodes ben y-hid whiche that they

coveiten, but ploungen hem in erthe and
25 seken there thilke good that sormounteth
the hevene that bereth the sterres. What
preyere may I maken that be digne to
the nyce thoughtes of men? But I preye
that they coveiten richesse and honours,
30 so that, whan they han geten tho false
goodes with greet travaile, that ther-by
they mowe knowen the verray goodes.

PROSE IX. *Hactenus mendacis formam.*

It suffyseth that I have shewed hider-to
the forme of false welefulnesse, so that,
yif thou loke now cleerly, the order of
myn entencioun requireth from hennes-
5 forth to shewen thee the verray welefulnesse.' 'For sothe,' quod I, 'I see wel
now that suffisaunce may nat comen by
richesses, ne power by reames, ne reverence by dignitees, ne gentilesse by glorie,
10 ne joye by delices.'

'And hast thou wel knowen the causes,'
quod she, 'why it is?' 'Certes, me
semeth,' quod I, 'that I see hem right as
though it were thorugh a litel clifte; but
15 me were lever knowen hem more openly
of thee.'

'Certes,' quod she, 'the resoun is al
redy. For thilke thing that simply is
o thing, with-outen any devisioun, the
20 errour and folye of mankinde departeth
and devydeth it, and misledeth it and
transporteth from verray and parfit good
to goodes that ben false and unparfit.
But sey me this. Wenest thou that he,
25 that hath nede of power, that him ne
lakketh no-thing?' 'Nay,' quod I.

'Certes,' quod she, 'thou seyst a-right.
For yif so be that ther is a thing, that in
any partye be febler of power, certes, as
30 in that, it mot nedes ben nedy of foreine
help.' 'Right so is it,' quod I.

'Suffisaunce and power ben thanne of
o kinde?' 'So semeth it,' quod I.

'And demest thou,' quod she, 'that
35 a thing that is of this manere, *that is to
seyn, suffisaunt and mighty*, oughte ben
despysed, or elles that it be right digne of
reverence aboven alle thinges?' 'Certes,'

quod I, 'it nis no doute, that it is right
worthy to ben reverenced.' 40

'Lat us,' quod she, 'adden thanne
reverence to suffisaunce and to power, so
that we demen that thise three thinges
ben al o thing.' 'Certes,' quod I, 'lat us
adden it, yif we wolen graunten the sothe.' 45

'What demest thou thanne?' quod
she; 'is that a derk thing and nat noble,
*that is suffisaunt, reverent, and mighty*, or
elles that it is right noble and right
cleer by celebritee of renoun? Consider 50
thanne,' quod she, 'as we han graunted
her-biforn, that he that ne hath nede of
no-thing, and is most mighty and most
digne of honour, yif him nedeth any
cleernesse of renoun, which cleernesse he 55
mighte nat graunten of him-self, so that,
for lakke of thilke cleernesse, he mighte
seme the febeler on any syde or the more
out-cast?' Glose. *This is to seyn, nay;
for who-so that is suffisaunt, mighty, and* 60
*reverent, cleernesse of renoun folweth of the
forseyde thinges; he hath it al redy of his
suffisaunce.* Boece. 'I may nat,' quod
I, 'denye it; but I mot graunte as it is,
that this thing be right celebrable by 65
cleernesse of renoun and noblesse.'

'Thanne folweth it,' quod she, 'that we
adden cleernesse of renoun to the three
forseyde thinges, so that ther ne be
amonges hem no difference?' 'This is 70
a consequence,' quod I.

'This thing thanne,' quod she, 'that ne
hath nede of no foreine thing, and that
may don alle thinges by hise strengthes,
and that is noble and honourable, nis nat 75
that a mery thing and a joyful?' 'But
whennes,' quod I, 'that any sorwe mighte
comen to this thing that is swiche, certes,
I may nat thinke.'

'Thanne moten we graunte,' quod she, 80
'that this thing be ful of gladnesse, yif
the forseyde thinges ben sothe; and
certes, also mote we graunten that suffisaunce, power, noblesse, reverence, and
gladnesse ben only dyverse by names, but 85
hir substaunce hath no diversitee.' 'It
mot needly been so,' quod I.

'Thilke thing thanne,' quod she, 'that
is oon and simple in his nature, the

90 wikkednesse of men departeth it and
devydeth it; and whan they enforcen
hem to geten partye of a thing that ne
hath no part, they ne geten hem neither
thilke partye that nis non, ne the thing
95 al hool that they ne desire nat.'    'In
which manere?' quod I.

'Thilke man,' quod she, 'that secheth
richesses to fleen povertee, he ne travaileth him nat for to gete power; for he
100 hath lever ben derk and vyl; and eek
withdraweth from him-self many naturel
delyts, for he nolde lese the moneye that
he hath assembled. But certes, in this
manere he ne geteth him nat suffisaunce
105 that power forleteth, and that molestie
prikketh, and that filthe maketh out-cast,
and that derkenesse hydeth. And certes,
he that desireth only power, he wasteth
and scatereth richesse, and despyseth
110 delyts, and eek honour that is with-oute
power, ne he ne preyseth glorie no-thing.
Certes, thus seest thou wel, that manye
thinges faylen to him; for he hath som-
tyme defaute of many necessitees, and
115 many anguisshes byten him; and whan
he ne may nat don tho defautes a-wey, he
forleteth to ben mighty, and that is the
thing that he most desireth. And right
thus may I maken semblable resouns of
120 honours, and of glorie, and of delyts.
For so as every of thise forseyde thinges
is the same that thise other thinges ben,
*that is to seyn, al oon thing,* who-so that
ever seketh to geten that oon of thise,
125 and nat that other, he ne geteth nat that
he desireth.'    *Boece.* 'What seyst thou
thanne, yif that a man coveiteth to geten
alle thise thinges to-gider?'

*Philosophie.* 'Certes,' quod she, 'I
130 wolde seye, that he wolde geten him
sovereyn blisfulnesse; but that shal he
nat finde in tho thinges that I have
shewed, that ne mowen nat yeven that
they beheten.'    'Certes, no,' quod I.

135 'Thanne,' quod she, 'ne sholden men
nat by no wey seken blisfulnesse in swiche
thinges as men wene that they ne mowen
yeven but o thing senglely of alle that
men seken.'    'I graunte wel,' quod I;
140 'ne no sother thing ne may ben sayd.'

'Now hast thou thanne,' quod she, 'the
forme and the causes of false welefulnesse. Now torne and flitte the eyen
of thy thought; for ther shalt thou
seen anon thilke verray blisfulnesse that 14
I have bihight thee.'    'Certes,' quod I,
'it is cleer and open, thogh it were to
a blinde man; and that shewedest thou
me ful wel a litel her-biforn, whan thou
enforcedest thee to shewe me the causes 15
of the false blisfulnesse. For but-yif I
be bigyled, thanne is thilke the verray
blisfulnesse parfit, that parfitly maketh
a man suffisaunt, mighty, honourable,
noble, and ful of gladnesse. And, for 15
thou shalt wel knowe that I have wel
understonden thise thinges with-in my
herte, I knowe wel that thilke blisfulnesse, that may verrayly yeven oon of
the forseyde thinges, sin they ben al oon, 16
I knowe, douteles, that thilke thing is
the fulle blisfulnesse.'

'O my norie,' quod she, 'by this
opinioun I seye that thou art blisful, yif
thou putte this ther-to that I shal seyn.' 16
'What is that?' quod I.

'Trowest thou that ther be any thing
in thise erthely mortal toumbling thinges
that may bringen this estat?'    'Certes,'
quod I, 'I trowe it naught; and thou 17
hast shewed me wel that over thilke good
ther nis no-thing more to ben desired.'

'Thise thinges thanne,' quod she, '*that
is to sey, erthely suffisaunce and power and
swiche thinges,* either they semen lyke- 17
nesses of verray good, or elles it semeth
that they yeve to mortal folk a maner of
goodes that ne ben nat parfit; but thilke
good that is verray and parfit, that may
they nat yeven.'    'I acorde me wel,' 18
quod I.

'Thanne,' quod she, 'for as mochel as
thou hast knowen which is thilke verray
blisfulnesse, and eek whiche thilke
thinges ben that lyen falsly blisfulnesse, 18
*that is to seyn, that by deceite semen verray
goodes,* now behoveth thee to knowe
whennes and where thou mowe seke
thilke verray blisfulnesse.'    'Certes,'
quod I, 'that desire I greetly, and have 19
abiden longe tyme to herknen it.'

'But for as moche,' quod she, 'as it lyketh to my disciple Plato, in his book of "in Timeo," that in right litel thinges men sholden bischen the help of god, what jugest thou that be now to done, so that we may deserve to finde the sete of thilke verray good?' 'Certes,' quod I, 'I deme that we shollen clepen the fader of alle goodes; for with-outen him nis ther no-thing founden a-right.'

'Thou seyst a-right,' quod she; and bigan anon to singen right thus :—

METRE IX.  *O qui perpetua mundum ratione gubernas.*

'O thou fader, creator of hevene and of erthes, that governest this world by per-durable resoun, that comaundest the tymes to gon from sin that age hadde
5 beginninge; thou that dwellest thy-self ay stedefast and stable, and yevest alle othre thinges to ben moeved ; ne foreine causes necesseden thee never to compoune werk of floteringe matere, but only the
10 forme of soverein good y-set with-in thee with-oute envye, *that moevede thee freely.* Thou that art alder-fayrest, beringe the faire world in thy thought, formedest this world to the lyknesse semblable of
15 that faire world in thy thought. Thou drawest al thing of thy soverein en-saumpler, and comaundest that this world, parfitliche y-maked, have freely and absolut his parfit parties. Thou
20 bindest the elements by noumbres pro-porcionables, that the colde thinges mowen acorden with the hote thinges, and the drye thinges with the moiste thinges ; that the fyr, that is purest, ne
25 flee nat over hye, ne that the hevinesse ne drawe nat adoun over-lowe the erthes that ben plounged in the wateres. Thou knittest to-gider the mene sowle of treble kinde, moevinge alle thinges, and de-
30 vydest it by membres acordinge ; and whan it is thus devyded, it hath asembled a moevinge in-to two roundes ; it goth to torne ayein to him-self, and environeth a ful deep thought, and torneth the

hevene by semblable image. Thou by 35 evene-lyke causes enhansest the sowles and the lasse lyves, and, ablinge hem heye by lighte cartes, thou sowest hem in-to hevene and in-to erthe ; and whan they ben converted to thee by thy be- 40 nigne lawe, thou makest hem retorne ayein to thee by ayein-ledinge fyr. O fader, yive thou to the thought to styen up in-to thy streite sete, and graunte him to environue the welle of good ; and, the 45 lighte y-founde, graunte him to fichen the clere sightes of his corage in thee. And scater thou and to-breke thou the weightes and the cloudes of erthely hevinesse, and shyne thou by thy brightnesse. For thou 50 art cleernesse ; thou art peysible reste to debonaire folk ; thou thy-self art bigin-ninge, berer, leder, path, and terme ; to loke on thee, that is our ende.

PROSE X.  *Quoniam igitur quae sit imperfecti.*

For as moche thanne as thou hast seyn, which is the forme of good that nis nat parfit, and which is the forme of good that is parfit, now trowe I that it were good to shewe in what this perfeccioun of blisful- 5 nesse is set. And in this thing, I trowe that we sholden first enquere for to witen, yif that any swiche maner good as thilke good that thou hast diffinisshed a litel heer-biforn, *that is to seyn, soverein good,* 10 may ben founde in the nature of thinges ; for that veyn imaginacioun of thought ne deceyve us nat, and putte us out of the sothfastnesse of thilke thing that is sum-mitted unto us. But it may nat ben 15 deneyed that thilke good ne is, and that it nis right as welle of alle goodes. For al thing that is cleped inparfit is proeved inparfit by the amenusinge of perfeccioun or of thing that is parfit. And ther-of 20 comth it, that in every thing general, yif that men seen any-thing that is inparfit, certes, in thilke general ther mot ben som-thing that is parfit ; for yif so be that perfeccioun is don awey, men may nat 25 thinke ne seye fro whennes thilke thing is that is cleped inparfit. For the nature of thinges ne took nat hir beginninge of thinges amenused and inparfit, but it

30 procedeth of thinges that ben al hoole and absolut, and descendeth so doun in-to outterest thinges, and in-to thinges empty and with-outen frut. But, as I have y-shewed a litel her-biforn, that yif ther

35 be a blisfulnesse that be freele and veyn and inparfit, ther may no man doute that ther nis som blisfulnesse that is sad, stedefast, and parfit.' *Boece.* 'This is concluded,' quod I, 'fermely and soth-

40 fastly.'

*Philosophie.* 'But considere also,' quod she, 'in wham this blisfulnesse en-habiteth. The comune acordaunce and conceite of the corages of men proeveth

45 and graunteth, that god, prince of alle thinges, is good. For, so as nothing ne may ben thought bettre than god, it may nat ben douted thanne that he, that nothing nis bettre, that he nis good.

50 Certes, resoun sheweth that god is so good, that it proveth by verray force that parfit good is in him. For yif god ne is swich, he ne may nat ben prince of alle thinges ; for certes som-thing possessing

55 in it-self parfit good, sholde ben more worthy than god, and it sholde semen that thilke thing were first, and elder than god. For we han shewed apertly that alle thinges that ben parfit ben first or

60 thinges that ben unparfit ; and for-thy, for as moche as that my resoun or my proces ne go nat a-wey with-oute an ende, we owen to graunten that the soverein god is right ful of soverein parfit good.

65 And we han establisshed that the soverein good is verray blisfulnesse : thanne mot it nedes be, that verray blisfulnesse is set in soverein god.' 'This take I wel,' quod I, 'ne this ne may nat ben withseid in no

70 manere.'

'But I preye,' quod she, 'see now how thou mayst proeven, holily and with-oute corupcioun, this that I have seyd, that the soverein god is right ful of soverein

75 good.' 'In which manere ?' quod I.

'Wenest thou aught,' quod she, 'that this prince of alle thinges have y-take thilke soverein good any-wher out of him-

self, of which soverein good men proveth that he is ful, right as thou mightest 80 thinken that god, that hath blisfulnesse in him-self, and thilke blisfulnesse that is in him, weren dyvers in substaunce ? For yif thou wene that god have received thilke good out of him-self, thou mayst 85 wene that he that yaf thilke good to god be more worthy than is god. But I am bi-knowen and confesse, and that right dignely, that god is right worthy aboven alle thinges ; and, yif so be that this good 90 be in him by nature, but that it is dyvers fro him by weninge resoun, sin we speke of god prince of alle thinges : feigne who-so feigne may, who was he that hath conjoigned thise dyverse thinges to-gider ? 95 And eek, at the laste, see wel that a thing that is dyvers from any thing, that thilke thing nis nat that same thing fro which it is understonden to ben dyvers. Thanne folweth it, that thilke thing that by his 100 nature is dyvers fro soverein good, that that thing nis nat soverein good ; but certes, that were a felonous corsednesse to thinken that of him that nothing nis more worth. For alwey, of alle thinges, 105 the nature of hem ne may nat ben bettre than his biginning ; for which I may concluden, by right verray resoun, that thilke that is biginning of alle thinges, thilke same thing is soverein good in his 110 substaunce.' 'Thou hast seyd right-fully,' quod I

'But we han graunted,' quod she, 'that the soverein good is blisfulnesse.' 'And that is sooth,' quod I. 115

'Thanne,' quod she, 'moten we nedes graunten and confessen that thilke same soverein good be god.' 'Certes,' quod I, 'I ne may nat denye ne withstonde the resouns purposed ; and I see wel that 120 it folweth by strengthe of the premisses.'

'Loke now,' quod she, 'yif this be proved yit more fermely thus : that ther ne mowen nat ben two soverein goodes that ben dyverse amonge hem-self. For 125 certes, the goodes that ben dyverse amonges hem-self, that oon nis nat that that other is ; thanne ne may neither of hem ben parfit, so as either of hem lak-

30 keth to other. But that that nis nat
parfit, men may seen apertly that it nis
nat soverein. The thinges, thanne, that
ben sovereinly goode, ne mowen by no
wey ben dyverse. But I have wel con-
35 cluded that blisfulnesse and god ben the
soverein good; for whiche it mot nedes
ben, that soverein blisfulnesse is soverein
divinitee.' 'Nothing,' quod I, 'nis
more soothfast than this, ne more ferme
40 by resoun; ne a more worthy thing than
god may nat ben concluded.'

'Up-on thise thinges thanne,' quod she,
'right as thise geometriens, whan they
han shewed hir proposiciouns, ben wont
45 to bringen in thinges that they clepen
porismes, *or declaraciouns of forseide
thinges*, right so wole I yeve thee heer as
a corollarie, *or a mede of coroune*. For-
why, for as moche as by the getinge of
50 blisfulnesse men ben maked blisful, and
blisfulnesse is divinitee : thanne is it
manifest and open, that by the getinge of
divinitee men ben maked blisful. Right
as by the getinge of justice [they ben
55 maked just], and by the getinge of sapience they ben maked wyse : right so,
nedes, by the semblable resoun, whan
they han geten divinitee, they ben maked
goddes. Thanne is every blisful man
60 god ; but certes, by nature, ther nis but
o god ; but, by the participacioun of
divinitee, ther ne let ne desturbeth
nothing that ther ne ben manye goddes.'
'This is,' quod I, 'a fair thing and
65 a precious, clepe it as thou wolt; be it
porisme or corollarie,' *or mede of coroune
or declaringes*.

'Certes,' quod she, 'nothing nis fayrer
than is the thing that by resoun sholde
70 ben added to thise forseide thinges.'
'What thing?' quod I.

'So,' quod she, 'as it semeth that blisfulnesse conteneth many thinges, it were
for to witen whether that alle thise
75 thinges maken or conjoignen as a maner
body of blisfulnesse, by dyversitee of
parties or of membres ; or elles, yif that
any of alle thilke thinges be swich that it
acomplisshe by him-self the substaunce of
80 blisfulnesse, so that alle thise othre thinges

ben referred and brought to blisfulnesse,'
*that is to seyn, as to the cheef of hem.*
'I wolde,' quod I, 'that thou makedest
me cleerly to understonde what thou
85 seyst, and that thou recordedest me the
forseyde thinges.'

'Have I nat juged,' quod she, 'that
blisfulnesse is good ?' 'Yis, forsothe,'
quod I ; 'and that soverein good.'

90 'Adde thanne,' quod she, 'thilke good,
*that is maked blisfulnesse*, to alle the forseide thinges ; for thilke same blisfulnesse that is demed to ben soverein
suffisaunce, thilke selve is soverein power,
95 soverein reverence, soverein cleernesse *or
noblesse*, and soverein delyt. **Conclusio.**
What seyst thou thanne of alle thise
thinges, that is to seyn, suffisaunce,
power, and this othre thinges; ben they
200 thanne as membres of blisfulnesse, or ben
they referred and brought to soverein
good, right as alle thinges that ben
brought to the chief of hem ?' 'I understonde wel ;' quod I, 'what thou pur-
205 posest to seke ; but I desire for to herkne
that thou shewe it me.'

'Tak now thus the discrecioun of this
question,' quod she. 'Yif alle thise
thinges,' quod she, 'weren membres to
210 felicitee, than weren they dyverse that
oon from that other ; and swich is the
nature of parties or of membres, that
dyverse membres compounen a body.'
'Certes,' quod I, 'it hath wel ben shewed
215 heer-biforn, that alle thise thinges ben
alle o thing.'

'Thanne ben they none membres,' quod
she ; 'for elles it sholde seme that blisfulnesse were conioigned al of on mem-
220 bre allone ; but that is a thing that may
nat be don.' 'This thing,' quod I, 'nis
nat doutous ; but I abyde to herknen the
remnaunt of thy questioun.'

'This is open and cleer,' quod she,
225 'that alle othre thinges ben referred and
brought to good. For therefore is suffisaunce requered, for it is demed to ben
good ; and forthy is power requered, for
men trowen also that it be good ; and this
230 same thing mowen we thinken and con-
jecten of reverence, and of noblesse, and

of delyt. Thanne is soverein good the somme and the cause of al that aughte ben desired ; for-why thilke thing that
235 with-holdeth no good in it-self, ne semblaunce of good, it ne may nat wel in no manere be desired ne requered. And the contrarie : for thogh that thinges by hir nature ne ben nat goode, algates, yif men
240 wene that ben goode, yit ben they desired as though that they weren verrayliche goode. And therfor is it that men oughten to wene by right, that bountee be the sovereign fyn, and the cause of alle
245 the thinges that ben to requeren. But certes, thilke that is cause for which men requeren any thing, it semeth that thilke same thing be most desired. As thus : yif that a wight wolde ryden for cause of
250 hele, he ne desireth nat so mochel the moevinge to ryden, as the effect of his hele. Now thanne, sin that alle thinges ben requered for the grace of good, they ne ben nat desired of alle folk more
255 thanne the same good. But we han graunted that blisfulnesse is that thing, for whiche that alle thise othre thinges ben desired ; thanne is it thus : that, certes, only blisfulnesse is requered and
260 desired. By whiche thing it sheweth cleerly, that of good and of blisfulnesse is al oon and the same substaunce.' 'I see nat,' quod I, 'wherfore that men mighten discorden in this.'
265 'And we han shewed that god and verray blisfulnesse is al oo thing.' 'That is sooth,' quod I.

'Thanne mowen we conclude sikerly, that the substaunce of god is set in thilke
270 same good, and in non other place.

METRE X. *Huc omnes pariter uenite capti.*

O cometh alle to-gider now, ye that ben y-caught and y-bounde with wikkede cheynes, by the deceivable delyt of erthely thinges enhabitinge in your thought !
5 Heer shal ben the reste of your labours, heer is the havene stable in peysible quiete ; this allone is the open refut to wrecches. **Glosa.** *This is to seyn, that ye that ben combred and deceived with*

*worldely affecciouns, cometh now to this* 10 *soverein good, that is god, that is refut to hem that wolen comen to him.* **Textus.** Alle the thinges that the river Tagus yeveth yow with his goldene gravailes, or elles alle the thinges that the river 15 Hermus yeveth with his rede brinke, or that Indus yeveth, that is next the hote party of the world, that medleth the grene stones with the whyte, ne sholde nat cleeren the lookinge of your thought, 20 but hyden rather your blinde corages with-in hir derknesse. Al that lyketh yow heer, and excyteth and moeveth your thoughtes, the erthe hath norisshed it in hise lowe caves. But the shyninge, by 25 whiche the hevene is governed and whennes he hath his strengthe, that eschueth the derke overthrowinge of the sowle ; and who-so may knowen thilke light of blisfulnesse, he shal wel seyn, 30 that the whyte bemes of the sonne ne ben nat cleer.'

PROSE XI. *Assentior, inquam.*

*Boece.* 'I assente me,' quod I ; 'for alle thise thinges ben strongly bounden with right ferme resouns.'

*Philosophie.* 'How mochel wilt thou preysen it,' quod she, 'yif that thou 5 knowe what thilke good is ? ' 'I wol preyse it,' quod I, 'by prys with-outen ende, yif it shal bityde me to knowe also to-gider god that is good.'

'Certes,' quod she, 'that shal I do thee 10 by verray resoun, yif that tho thinges that I have concluded a litel her-biforn dwellen only in hir first graunting.' 'They dwellen graunted to thee,' quod I ; *this is to seyn, as who seith : I graunte thy* 15 *forseide conclusiouns.*

'Have I nat shewed thee,' quod she, 'that the thinges that ben requered of many folkes ne ben nat verray goodes ne parfite, for they ben dyverse that oon fro 20 that othre ; and so as ech of hem is lakkinge to other, they ne han no power to bringen a good that is ful and absolut ? But thanne at erst ben they verray good, whanne they ben gadered to-gider alle 25

in-to o forme and in-to oon wirkinge, so
that thilke thing that is suffisaunce,
thilke same be power, and reverence, and
noblesse, and mirthe ; and forsothe, but-
30 yif alle thise thinges ben alle oon same
thing, they ne han nat wherby that they
mowen ben put in the noumber of thinges
that oughten ben requered or desired.'
' It is shewed,' quod I ; ' ne her-of may
35 ther no man douten.'

' The thinges thanne,' quod she, ' that
ne ben no goodes whanne they ben dyverse, and whan they beginnen to ben
alle oon thing thanne ben they goodes,
40 ne comth it hem nat thanne by the
getinge of unitee, that they ben maked
goodes ? ' ' So it semeth,' quod I.

' But al thing that is good,' quod she,
' grauntest thou that it be good by the
45 participacioun of good, or no ? ' ' I
graunte it,' quod I.

' Thanne most thou graunten,' quod
she, ' by semblable resoun, that oon and
good be oo same thing. For of thinges,
50 of whiche that the effect nis nat naturelly
diverse, nedes the substaunce mot be oo
same thing.' ' I ne may nat denye
that,' quod I.

' Hast thou nat knowen wel,' quod she,
55 ' that al thing is hath so longe his
dwellinge and his substaunce as longe as
it is oon ; but whan it forleteth to ben
oon, it mot nedes dyen and corumpe to-
gider ? ' ' In which manere ? ' quod I.
60 ' Right as in bestes,' quod she, ' whan
the sowle and the body ben conjoigned
in oon and dwellen to-gider, it is cleped
a beest. And whan hir unitee is destroyed
by the disseveraunce of that oon from
65 that other, than sheweth it wel that it is
a ded thing, and that it nis no lenger
no beest. And the body of a wight, whyl
it dwelleth in oo forme by conjunccioun
of membres, it is wel seyn that it is
70 a figure of man-kinde. And yif the
parties of the body ben so devyded and
dissevered, *that oon fro that other,* that
they destroyen unitee, the body forleteth
to ben that it was biforn. And, who-so
75 wolde renne in the same manere by alle
thinges, he sholde seen that, with-oute

doute, every thing is in his substaunce as
longe as it is oon ; and whan it forleteth
to ben oon, it dyeth and perissheth.'
' Whan I considere,' quod I, ' manye 80
thinges, I see non other.'

' Is ther any-thing thanne,' quod she,
' that, in as moche as it liveth naturelly,
that forleteth the talent or appetyt of his
beinge, and desireth to come to deeth and 85
to corupcioun ? ' ' Yif I considere,'
quod I, ' the beestes that han any maner
nature of wilninge and of nillinge, I ne
finde no beest, but-yif it be constreined
fro with-oute forth, that forleteth or 90
despyseth the entencioun to liven and
to duren, or that wole, his thankes,
hasten him to dyen. For every beest
travaileth him to deffende and kepe the
savacioun of his lyf, and eschueth deeth 95
and destruccioun. But certes, I doute
me of herbes and of trees, *that is to seyn,
that I am in a doute of swiche thinges as
herbes or trees,* that ne han no felinge
sowles, *ne no naturel wirkinges servinge to* 100
*appetytes as bestes han, whether they han*
*appetyt to dwellen and to duren.*'

' Certes,' quod she, ' ne ther-of thar
thee nat doute. Now loke up-on thise
herbes and thise trees ; they wexen first 105
in swiche places as ben covenable to hem,
in whiche places they ne mowen nat sone
dyen ne dryen, as longe as hir nature
may deffenden hem. For som of hem
waxen in feeldes, and som in moun- 110
taignes, and othre waxen in mareys, and
othre cleven on roches, and somme waxen
plentivous in sondes ; and yif that any
wight enforce him to beren hem in-to
othre places, they wexen drye. For 115
nature yeveth to every thing that that
is convenient to him, and travaileth that
they ne dye nat, as longe as they han
power to dwellen and to liven. What
woltow seyn of this, that they drawen 120
alle hir norisshinges by hir rotes, right
as they hadden hir mouthes y-plounged
with-in the erthes, and sheden by hir
maryes hir wode and hir bark ? And
what woltow seyn of this, that thilke 125
thing that is right softe, as the marye is,
that is alwey hid in the sete, al with-

inne, and that is defended fro with-oute
by the stedefastnesse of wode; and that
130 the uttereste bark is put ayeins the destemperaunce of the hevene, as a defendour
mighty to suffren harm? And thus,
certes, maystow wel seen how greet is
the diligence of nature; for alle thinges
135 renovelen and puplisshen hem with seed
y-multiplyed; ne ther nis no man that ne
wot wel that they ne ben right as
a foundement and edifice, for to duren
nat only for a tyme, but right as for
140 to duren perdurably by generacioun. And
the thinges eek that men wenen ne haven
none sowles, ne desire they nat ech of
hem by semblable resoun to kepen that
is hirs, *that is to seyn, that is acordinge to*
145 *hir nature in conservacioun of hir beinge
and enduringe?* For wher-for elles bereth
lightnesse the flaumbes up, and the
weighte presseth the erthe a-doun, but
for as moche as thilke places and thilke
150 moevinges ben covenable to everich of
hem? And forsothe every thing kepeth
thilke that is acordinge and propre to
him, right as thinges that ben contraries
and enemys corompen hem. And yit the
155 harde thinges, as stones, clyven and
holden hir parties to-gider right faste and
harde, and deffenden hem in withstondinge that they ne departe nat lightly
a-twinne. And the thinges that ben
160 softe and fletinge, as is water and eyr,
they departen lightly, and yeven place
to hem that breken or devyden hem;
but natheles, they retornen sone ayein
in-to the same thinges fro whennes they
165 ben arraced. But fyr fleeth and refuseth
al devisioun. Ne I ne trete nat heer
now of wilful moevinges of the sowle
that is knowinge, but of the naturel
entencioun of thinges, as thus: right as
170 we swolwe the mete that we receiven and
no thinke nat on it, and as we drawen
our breeth in slepinge that we wite it
nat whyle we slepen. For certes, in the
beestes, the love of hir livinges ne of hir
175 beinges ne comth nat of the wilninges
of the sowle, but of the biginninges of
nature. For certes, thorugh constreininge causes, wil desireth and embraceth

ful ofte tyme the deeth that nature
dredeth; *that is to seyn as thus: that* 180
*a man may ben constreyned so, by som
cause, that his wil desireth and taketh the
deeth which that nature hateth and dredeth ful sore.* And somtyme we seeth
the contrarye, as thus: that the wil of 185
a wight destorbeth and constreyneth that
that nature desireth and requereth alwey, *that is to seyn,* the werk of generacioun, by the whiche generacioun only
dwelleth and is sustened the long dura- 190
bletee of mortal thinges. And thus this
charitee and this love, that every thing
hath to him-self, ne comth nat of the
moevinge of the sowle, but of the entencioun of nature. For the purviaunce 195
of god hath yeven to thinges that ben
creat of him this, that is a ful gret cause
to liven and to duren; for which they
desiren naturelly hir lyf as longe as ever
they mowen. For which thou mayst nat 200
drede, by no manere, that alle the
thinges that ben anywhere, that they ne
requeren naturelly the ferme stablenesse
of perdurable dwellinge, and eek the
eschuinge of destruccioun.' 'Now con- 205
fesse I wel,' quod I, 'that I see now wel
certeinly, with-oute doutes, the thinges
that whylom semeden uncertain to me.'

'But,' quod she, 'thilke thing that
desireth to be and to dwellen perdurably, 210
he desireth to ben oon; for yif that that
oon were destroyed, certes, beinge ne
shulde ther non dwellen to no wight.'
'That is sooth,' quod I.

'Thanne,' quod she, 'desiren alle 215
thinges oon?' 'I assente,' quod I.

'And I have shewed,' quod she, 'that
thilke same oon is thilke that is good?'
'Ye, for sothe,' quod I.

'Alle thinges thanne,' quod she, 're- 220
quiren good; and thilke good thanne
mayst thou descryven right thus: good
is thilke thing that every wight desireth.'
'Ther ne may be thought,' quod I, 'no
more verray thing. For either alle 225
thinges ben referred and brought to
nought, and floteren with-oute governour,
despoiled of oon as of hir propre heved;
or elles, yif ther be any thing to which

30 that alle thinges tenden and hyen, that thing moste ben the soverein good of alle goodes.'

Thanne seyde she thus : ' O my nory,' quod she, ' I have gret gladnesse of thee ;
35 for thou hast ficched in thyn herte the middel soothfastnesse, *that is to seyn*, the prikke ; but this thing hath ben descovered to thee, in that thou seydest that thou wistest nat a litel her-biforn.'
40 ' What was that ?' quod I.

' That thou ne wistest nat,' quod she, ' which was the ende of thinges ; and certes, that is the thing that every wight desireth ; and for as mochel as we han
45 gadered and comprehended that good is thilke thing that is desired of alle, thanne moten we nedes confessen, that good is the fyn of alle thinges.

### Metre XI. *Quisquis profunda mente uestigat uerum.*

Who-so that seketh sooth by a deep thoght, and coveiteth nat to ben deceived by no mis-weyes, lat him rollen and trenden with-inne him-self the light of
5 his inward sighte ; and lat him gadere ayein, enclyninge in-to a compas, the longe moevinges *of his thoughtes* ; and lat him techen his corage that he hath enclosed and hid in his tresors, al that
10 he compasseth or seketh fro with-oute. And thanne thilke thinge, that the blake cloude of errour whylom hadde y-covered, shal lighten more cleerly thanne Phebus him-self ne shyneth. Glosa. *Who-so*
15 *wole seken the deep grounde of sooth in his thought, and wol nat be deceived by false proposiciouns that goon amis fro the trouthe, lat him wel examine and rolle with-inne himself the nature and the propretees of the*
20 *thing ; and lat him yit eftsones examine and rollen his thoughtes by good deliberacioun, or that he deme ; and lat him techen his sowle that it hath, by natural principles kindeliche y-hid with-in it-self, alle the*
25 *trouthe the whiche he imagineth to ben in thinges with-oute. And thanne alle the derknesse of his misknowinge shal seme more evidently to sighte of his understondinge*

*thanne the sonne ne semeth to sighte with-*
30 *oute-forth.* For certes the body, bringinge the weighte of foryetinge, ne hath nat chased out of your thoughte al the cleernesse *of your knowinge* ; for certeinly the seed of sooth haldeth and clyveth
35 with-in your corage, and it is awaked and excyted by the winde and by the blastes of doctrine. For wherfor elles demen ye of your owne wil the rightes, whan ye ben axed, but-yif so were that
40 the norisshinge *of resoun* ne livede y-plounged in the depthe of your herte ? *this is to seyn, how sholden men demen the sooth of any thing that were axed, yif ther ner̃ a rote of soothfastnesse that were y-*
45 *plounged and hid in naturel principles, the whiche soothfastnesse lived with-in the deepnesse of the thought.* And yif so be that the Muse and the doctrine of Plato singeth sooth, al that every wight lerneth,
50 he ne doth no-thing elles thanne but recordeth, as men recorden thinges that ben foryeten.'

### Prose XII. *Tum ego, Platoni, inquam.*

Thanne seide I thus : ' I acorde me gretly to Plato, for thou remembrest and recordest me thise thinges yit the secounde tyme ; *that is to seyn*, first whan
5 I loste my memorie by the contagious conjunccioun of the body with the sowle ; and eftsones afterward, whan I loste it, confounded by the charge and by the burdene of my sorwe.'

10 And thanne seide she thus : ' yif thou loke,' quod she, ' first the thinges that thou hast graunted, it ne shal nat ben right fer that thou ne shalt remembren thilke thing that thou seydest that thou
15 nistest nat.' ' What thing ?' quod I.

' By whiche governement,' quod she, ' that this world is governed.' ' Me remembreth it wel,' quod I ; ' and I confesse wel that I ne wiste it naught. But
20 al-be-it so that I see now from a-fer what thou purposest, algates, I desire yit to herkene it of thee more pleynly.'

' Thou ne wendest nat,' quod she, ' a litel her-biforn, that men sholden

25 doute that this world nis governed by
god.' ' Certes,' quod I, ' ne yit ne doute
I it naught, ne I nel never wene that
it were to doute ; as who seith, but I wot
wel that god governeth this world ; and
30 I shal shortly answeren thee by what
resouns I am brought to this. This
world,' quod I, ' of so manye dyverse and
contrarious parties, ne mighte never han
ben assembled in o forme, but-yif ther
35 nere oon that conjoignede so manye dyverse thinges ; and the same dyversitee
of hir natures, that so discorden that
oon fro that other, moste departen and
unjoignen the thinges that ben con-
40 joigned, yif ther ne were oon that con-
tenede that he hath conjoined and y-
bounde. Ne the certein ordre of nature
ne sholde nat bringe forth so ordenee
moevinges, by places, by tymes, by
45 doinges, by spaces, by qualitees, yif ther
ne were oon that were ay stedefast
dwellinge, that ordeynede and disponede
thise dyversitees of moevinges. And
thilke thing, what-so-ever it be, by which
50 that alle thinges ben y-maked and y-lad,
I clepe him " god "; that is a word that
is used to alle folk.'

Thanne seyde she : ' sin thou felest
thus thise thinges,' quod she, ' I trowe
55 that I have litel more to done that thou,
mighty of welefulnesse, hool and sounde,
ne see eftsones thy contree. But lat us
loken the thinges that we han purposed
her-biforn. Have I nat noumbred and
60 seyd,' quod she, ' that suffisaunce is in
blisfulnesse, and we han acorded that
god is thilke same blisfulnesse ?' ' Yis,
forsothe,' quod I.

' And that, to governe this world,'
65 quod she, ' ne shal he never han nede
of non help fro with-oute ? For elles,
yif he hadde nede of any help, he ne
sholde nat have any ful suffisaunce ? '
' Yis, thus it mot nedes be,' quod I.

70 ' Thanne ordeineth he by him-self alone alle thinges ?' quod she. ' That
may nat be deneyed,' quod I.

' And I have shewed that god is the
same good ? ' ' It remembreth me wel,'
75 quod I.

' Thanne ordeineth he alle thinges by
thilke good,' quod she ; ' sin he, which
that we han acorded to be good, governeth
alle thinges by him-self; and he is as
a keye and a stere by which that the 80
edifice of this world is y-kept stable
and with-oute coroumpinge.' ' I acorde
me greetly,' quod I ; ' and I aperceivede
a litel her-biforn that thou woldest seye
thus ; al-be-it so that it were by a thinne 85
suspecioun.'

' I trowe it wel,' quod she ; ' for, as
I trowe, thou ledest now more ententifly
thyne eyen to loken the verray goodes.
But natheles the thing that I shal telle 90
thee yit ne sheweth nat lasse to loken.'
' What is that ?' quod I.

' So as men trowen,' quod she, ' and
that rightfully, that god governeth alle
thinges by the keye of his goodnesse, 95
and alle thise same thinges, as I have
taught thee, hasten hem by naturel entencioun to comen to good : ther may no
man douten that they ne be governed
voluntariely, and that they ne converten 100
hem of hir owne wil to the wil of hir
ordenour, as they that ben acordinge and
enclyninge to hir governour and hir
king.' ' It mot nedes be so,' quod I ;
' for the reaume ne sholde nat semen 105
blisful yif ther were a yok of misdrawinges in dyverse parties ; ne the
savinge of obedient thinges ne sholde nat
be.'

' Thanne is ther nothing,' quod she, 110
' that kepeth his nature, that enforceth
him to goon ayein god ? ' ' No,' quod I.

' And yif that any-thing enforcede him
to with-stonde god, mighte it availen at
the laste ayeins him, that we han 115
graunted to ben almighty by the right
of blisfulnesse ?' ' Certes,' quod I, ' al-
outrely it ne mighte nat availen him.'

' Thanne is ther no-thing,' quod she,
' that either wole or may with-stonden 120
to this soverein good ?' ' I trowe nat,'
quod I.

' Thanne is thilke the soverein good,'
quod she, ' that alle thinges governeth
strongly, and ordeyneth hem softely.' 125
Thanne seyde I thus : ' I delyte me,'

quod I, ' nat only in the endes or in the somme of the resouns that thou hast concluded and proeved, but thilke wordes
130 that thou usest delyten me moche more ; so, at the laste, fooles that sumtyme renden grete thinges oughten ben a-shamed of hem-self ;' *that is to seyn, that we fooles that reprehenden wikkedly the*
135 *thinges that touchen goddes governaunce, we oughten ben ashamed of our-self : as I, that seyde that god refuseth only the werkes of men, and ne entremeteth nat of hem.*

140 ' Thou hast wel herd,' quod she, ' the fables of the poetes, how the giaunts assaileden the hevene *with the goddes* ; but forsothe, the debonair force *of god* deposede hem, as it was worthy; *that is*
145 *to seyn, destroyede the giaunts, as it was worthy.* But wilt thou that we joignen to-gider thilke same resouns ? For per-aventure, of swich conjuncioun may sterten up som fair sparkle of sooth.'
150 ' Do,' quod I, ' as thee liste.'
' Wenest thou,' quod she, ' that god ne be almighty ? No man is in doute of it.'
' Certes,' quod I, ' no wight ne douteth it, yif he be in his minde.'
155 ' But he,' quod she, ' that is almighty, ther nis nothing that he ne may?'
' That is sooth,' quod I.
' May god don yvel ?' quod she. ' Nay, forsothe,' quod I.
160 ' Thanne is yvel nothing,' quod she, ' sin that he ne may nat don yvel that may don alle thinges.' ' Scornest thou me?' quod I; ' *or elles pleyest thou or deceivest thou me,* that hast so woven me
165 with thy resouns the hous of Dedalus, so entrelaced that it is unable to be un-laced ; thou that other-whyle entrest ther thou issest, and other-whyle issest ther thou entrest, ne foldest thou nat
170 to-gider, *by replicacioun of wordes,* a maner wonderful cercle or environinge of the simplicitee devyne? For certes, a litel her-biforn, whan thou bigunne at blisful-nesse, thou seydest that it is soverein
175 good ; and seydest that it is set in soverein god ; and seydest that god him-self is soverein good ; and that god is the fulle

blisfulnesse ; for which thou yave me as a covenable yift, *that is to seyn,* that no wight nis blisful but-yif he be god also 180 ther-with. And seidest eek, that the forme of good is the substaunce of god and of blisfulnesse ; and seidest, that thilke same oon is thilke same good, that is requered and desired of alle the 185 kinde of thinges. And thou proevedest, in disputinge, that god governeth all the thinges of the world by the governementes of bountee, *and seydest,* that alle thinges wolen obeyen to him ; and *seydest,* that 190 the nature of yvel nis no-thing. And thise thinges ne shewedest thou nat with none resouns y-taken fro with-oute, but by proeves *in cercles and* hoomlich knowen ; the whiche proeves drawen to hem-self 195 hir feith and hir acord, everich of hem of other.'

Thanne seyde she thus : ' I ne scorne thee nat, *ne pleye, ne deceive thee* ; but I have shewed thee the thing that is 200 grettest over alle thinges by the yift of god, that we whylom preyeden. For this is the forme of the devyne substaunce, that is swich that it ne slydeth nat in-to outterest foreine thinges, ne ne receiveth 205 no straunge thinges in him ; but right as Parmenides seyde *in Greek* of thilke devyne substaunce ; he seyde thus : that " thilke devyne substaunce torneth the world and the moevable cercle of thinges, 210 whyl thilke devyne substaunce kepeth it-self with-oute moevinge ;" *that is to seyn, that it ne moeveth never-mo, and yit it moeveth alle othre thinges.* But natheles, yif I have stired resouns that ne ben nat 215 taken fro with-oute the compas of thing of which we treten, but resouns that ben bistowed with-in that compas, ther nis nat why that thou sholdest merveilen ; sin thou hast lerned by the sentence of 220 Plato, that " nedes the wordes moten be cosines to the thinges of which they speken."

## Metre XII. *Felix, qui potuit boni.*

Blisful is that man that may seen the clere welle of good ; blisful is he that

may unbinden him fro the bondes of the hevy erthe. The poete of Trace, *Orpheus,*
5 that whylom hadde right greet sorwe for the deeth of his wyf, after that he hadde maked, by his weeply songes, the wodes, moevable, to rennen; and hadde maked the riveres to stonden stille; and
10 hadde maked the hertes and the hindes to joignen, dredeles, hir sydes to cruel lyouns, *for to herknen his songe*; and hadde maked that the hare was nat agast of the hounde, which that was plesed by
15 his songe: so, whan the moste ardaunt love of his wif brende the entrailes of his brest, ne the songes that hadden overcomen alle thinges ne mighten nat asswagen hir lord *Orpheus,* he pleynede
20 him of the hevene goddes that weren cruel to him; he wente him to the houses of helle. And there he temprede hise blaundisshinge songes by resowninge strenges, and spak and song in wepinge
25 al that ever he hadde received and laved out of the noble welles of his moder *Calliope* the goddesse; and he song with as mochel as he mighte of wepinge, and with as moche as love, that doublede his
30 sorwe, mighte yeve him and techen him; and he commoevede the helle, and requerede and bisoughte by swete preyere the lordes of sowles in helle, of relesinge; *that is to seyn, to yilden him his wyf.*
35    *Cerberus,* the porter of helle, with his three hevedes, was caught and al abayst for the newe song; and the three goddesses, *Furies,* and vengeresses of felonyes, that tormenten and agasten the sowles
40 by anoy, woxen sorwful and sory, and

wepen teres for pitee. Tho ne was nat the heved of Ixion y-tormented by the overthrowinge wheel; and Tantalus, that was destroyed by the woodnesse of longe thurst, despyseth the flodes to drinke; 45 the fowl that highte voltor, that eteth the stomak or the giser of Tityus, is so fulfild of his song that it nil eten ne tyren no more. At the laste the lord and juge of sowles was moeved to miseri- 50 cordes and cryde, "we ben overcomen," quod he; "yive we to Orpheus his wyf to bere him companye; he hath wel ybought hir by his song and his ditee; but we wol putte a lawe in this, and 55 covenaunt in the yifte: *that is to seyn,* that, til he be out of helle, yif he loke behinde him, that his wyf shal comen ayein unto us." But what is he that may yive a lawe to loveres? Love is 60 a gretter lawe and a strenger to him-self *than any lawe that men may yeven.* Allas! whan Orpheus and his wyf weren almest at the termes of the night, *that is to seyn, at the laste boundes of helle,* Orpheus 65 lokede abakward on Eurydice his wyf, and loste hir, and was deed.

This fable aperteineth to yow alle, whoso-ever desireth or seketh to lede his thought in-to the soverein day, *that is to* 70 *seyn, to cleernesse of soverein good.* For who-so that ever be so overcomen that he ficche his eyen into the putte of helle, *that is to seyn, who-so sette his thoughtes in erthely thinges,* al that ever he hath 75 drawen of the noble good celestial, he leseth it whan he loketh the helles,' *that is to seyn, in-to lowe thinges of the erthe*

Explicit Liber tercius.

# BOOK IV.

PROSE I. *Hec cum Philosophia, dignitate uultus.*

WHAN Philosophye hadde songen softely and delitably the forseide thinges, kepinge the dignitee of hir chere and the weighte of hir wordes, I thanne, that ne hadde

nat al-outerly foryeten the wepinge and 5 the mourninge that was set in myn herte, forbrak the entencioun of hir that entendede yit to seyn some othre thinges. 'O,' quod I, 'thou that art gyderesse of verrey light; the thinges that thou hast 10 seid me hider-to ben so clere to me and

so shewinge by the devyne lookinge of hem, and by thy resouns, that they ne mowen ben overcomen. And thilke
15 thinges that thou toldest me, al-be-it so that I hadde whylom foryeten hem, for the sorwe of the wrong that hath ben don to me, yit natheles they ne weren nat al-outrely unknowen to me. But this
20 same is, namely, a right greet cause of my sorwe, so as the governour of thinges is good, yif that yveles mowen ben by any weyes ; or elles yif that yveles passen with-oute punisshinge. The whiche thing
25 only, how worthy it is to ben wondred up-on, thou considerest it wel thy-self certeinly. But yit to this thing ther is yit another thing y-joigned, more to ben wondred up-on. For felonye is emperesse,
30 and floureth *ful of richesses* ; and vertu nis nat al-only with-oute medes, but it is cast under and fortroden under the feet of felonous folk ; and it abyeth the torments in stede of wikkede felounes.
35 Of alle whiche thinges ther nis no wight that may merveylen y-nough, ne com-pleine, that swiche thinges ben doon in the regne of god, that alle thinges woot and alle thinges may, and ne wole nat
40 but only gode thinges.'

Thanne seyde she thus : ' Certes,' quod she, ' that were a greet merveyle, and an enbasshinge with-outen ende, and wel more horrible than alle monstres, yif it
45 were as thou wenest; *that is to seyn*, that in the right ordenee hous of so mochel a fader and an ordenour of meynee, that the vesseles that ben foule and vyle sholden ben honoured and heried, and
50 the precious vesseles sholden ben de-fouled and vyle ; but it nis nat so. For yif tho thinges that I have concluded a litel her-biforn ben kept hole and un-raced, thou shalt wel knowe by the
55 autoritee of god, of the whos regne I speke, that certes the gode folk ben alwey mighty, and shrewes ben alwey out-cast and feble ; ne the vyces ne ben never-mo with-oute peyne, ne the vertues
60 ne ben nat with-oute mede ; and that blisfulnesses comen alwey to goode folk, and infortune comth alwey to wikked

folk. And thou shalt wel knowe many thinges of this kinde, that shollen cesen
65 thy pleintes, and strengthen thee with stedefast sadnesse. And for thou hast seyn the forme of the verray blisfulnesse by me, that have whylom shewed it thee, and thou hast knowen in whom blisful-
70 nesse is y-set, alle thinges y-treted that I trowe ben necessarie to putten forth, I shal shewe thee the wey that shal bringen thee ayein un-to thyn hous. And I shal ficchen fetheres in thy thought,
75 by whiche it may arysen in heighte, so that, alle tribulacioun y-don awey, thou, by my gydinge and by my path and by my sledes, shalt mowe retorne hool and sound in-to thy contree.

### METRE I. *Sunt etenim pennae uolucres mihi.*

I have, forsothe, swifte fetheres that surmounten the heighte of hevene. Whan the swifte thought hath clothed it-self in tho fetheres, it despyseth the hateful
5 erthes, and surmounteth the roundnesse of the grete ayr ; and it seeth the cloudes behinde his bak ; and passeth the heighte of the region of the fyr, that eschaufeth by the swifte moevinge of the firmament,
10 til that he areyseth him in-to the houses that beren the sterres, and joyneth his weyes with the sonne Phebus, and felaw-shipeth the wey of the olde colde Satur-nus ; and he y-maked a knight of the
15 clere sterre ; *that is to seyn, that the thought is maked goddes knight by the sekinge of trouthe to comen to the verray knowleche of god*. And thilke thoght renneth by the cercle of the sterres, in
20 alle places ther-as the shyninge night is peinted ; *that is to seyn, the night that is cloudeles ; for on nightes that ben cloudeles it semeth as the hevene were peinted with dyverse images of sterres*. And whanne
25 he hath y-doon ther y-nough, he shal forleten the laste hevene, and he shal pressen and wenden on the bak of the swifte firmament, and he shal ben maked parfit of the worshipful light *of god*.
30 Ther halt the lord of kinges the ceptre

of his might, and atempreth the governements of the world, and the shyninge
juge of thinges, stable in him-self, governeth the swifte cart or wayn, *that is to*
35 *seyn, the circuler moevinge of the sonne.*
And yif thy wey ledeth thee ayein so
that thou be brought thider, thanne
wolt thou seye now that that is the
contree that thou requerest, of which
40 thou ne haddest no minde : " but now it
remembreth me wel, heer was I born,
heer wol I fastne my degree, heer wole
I dwelle." But yif thee lyketh thanne
to loken on the derknesse of the erthe
45 that thou hast forleten, thanne shalt
thou seen that thise felonous tyraunts,
that the wrecchede peple dredeth, now
shollen ben exyled fro thilke fayre contree.'

PROSE II. *Tum ego, Papae, inquam.*

Than seyde I thus : ' owh ! I wondre me
that thou bihetest me so grete thinges ;
ne I ne doute nat that thou ne mayst
wel performe that thou bihetest. But
5 I preye thee only this, that thou ne
tarye nat to telle me thilke thinges that
thou hast moeved.'

' First,' quod she, ' thou most nedes
knowen, that goode folk ben alwey
10 stronge and mighty, and the shrewes
ben feble and desert and naked of alle
strengthes. And of thise thinges, certes,
everich of hem is declared and shewed
by other. For so as good and yvel ben
15 two contraries, yif so be that good be
stedefast, than sheweth the feblesse of
yvel al openly ; and yif thou knowe
cleerly the frelenesse of yvel, the stedefastnesse of good is knowen. But for as
20 moche as the fey of my sentence shal
be the more ferme and haboundaunt,
I will gon by that oo wey and by that
other ; and I wole conferme the thinges
that ben purposed, now on this syde and
25 now on that syde. Two thinges ther ben
in whiche the effect of alle the dedes of
mankinde standeth, that is to seyn, wil
and power ; and yif that oon of thise two
fayleth, ther nis nothing that may be

don. For yif that wil lakketh, ther nis 30
no wight that undertaketh to don that
he wol nat don ; and yif power fayleth,
the wil nis but in ydel and stant for
naught. And ther-of cometh it, that yif
thou see a wight that wolde geten that 35
he may nat geten, thou mayst nat douten
that power ne fayleth him to haven that
he wolde.' ' This is open and cleer,'
quod I ; ' ne it may nat ben deneyed in
no manere.'
40
' And yif thou see a wight,' quod she,
' that hath doon that he wolde doon,
thou nilt nat douten that he ne hath
had power to don it ? ' ' No,' quod I.

' And in that that every wight may, 45
in that men may holden him mighty ;
*as who seyth, in so moche as man is mighty*
*to don a thing, in so mochel men halt him*
*mighty ;* and in that that he ne may, in
that men demen him to be feble.' ' I 50
confesse it wel,' quod I.

' Remembreth thee,' quod she, ' that
I have gadered and shewed by forseyde
resouns that al the entencioun of the wil
of mankinde, which that is lad by dyverse 55
studies, hasteth to comen to blisfulnesse ? '
' It remembreth me wel,' quod I, ' that it
hath ben shewed.'

' And recordeth thee nat thanne,' quod
she, ' that blisfulnesse is thilke same good 60
that men requeren ; so that, whan that
blisfulnesse is requered of alle, that good
also is requered and desired of alle ? '
' It ne recordeth me nat,' quod I ; ' for
I have it gretly alwey ficched in my 65
memorie.'

' Alle folk thanne,' quod she, ' goode
and eek badde, enforcen hem with-oute
difference of entencioun to comen to
good ? ' ' This is a verray conse- 70
quence,' quod I.

' And certein is,' quod she, ' that by the
getinge of good ben men y-maked goode?'
' This is certein,' quod I.

' Thanne geten goode men that they 75
desiren ? ' ' So semeth it,' quod I.

' But wikkede folk,' quod she, ' yif they
geten the good that they desiren, they ne
mowe nat be wikkede ? ' ' So is it,'
quod I.
80

'Thanne, so as that oon and that other,' quod she, 'desiren good; and the goode folk geten good, and nat the wikke folk; thanne nis it no doute that the
85 goode folk ne ben mighty and the wikkede folk ben feble?' 'Who-so that ever,' quod I, 'douteth of this, he ne may nat considere the nature of thinges ne the consequence of resouns.'
90 And over this quod she, 'Yif that ther be two thinges that han oo same purpose by kinde, and that oon of hem pursueth and parformeth thilke same thing by naturel office, and that other ne may nat
95 doon thilke naturel office, but folweth, by other manere thanne is convenable to nature, him that acomplissheth his purpos kindely, and yit he ne acomplissheth nat his owne purpos: whether of thise
100 two demestow for more mighty?' 'Yif that I conjecte,' quod I, 'that thou wolt seye, algates yit I desire to herkne it more pleynly of thee.'

'Thou wilt nat thanne deneye,' quod
105 she, 'that the moevement of goinge nis in men by kinde?' 'No, forsothe,' quod I. 'Ne thou ne doutest nat,' quod she, 'that thilke naturel office of goinge ne be the office of feet?' 'I ne doute it
110 nat,' quod I.

'Thanne,' quod she, 'yif that a wight be mighty to moeve and goth upon his feet, and another, to whom thilke naturel office of feet lakketh, enforceth him to
115 gon crepinge up-on his handes: whiche of thise two oughte to ben holden the more mighty by right?' 'Knit forth the remenaunt,' quod I; 'for no wight ne douteth that he that may gon by naturel
120 office of feet ne be more mighty than he that ne may nat.'

'But the soverein good,' quod she, 'that is eveneliche purposed to the gode folk and to badde, the gode folk seken it
125 by naturel office of vertues, and the shrewes enforcen hem to geten it by dyverse coveityse *of erthely thinges*, which that nis no naturel office to geten thilke same soverein good. Trowestow that it
130 be any other wyse?' 'Nay,' quod I; 'for the consequence is open and shew-

inge of thinges that I have graunted; that nedes gode folk moten ben mighty, and shrewes feeble and unmighty.'

'Thou rennest a-right biforn me,' quod 135 she, 'and this is the jugement; *that is to seyn, I juge of thee* right as thise leches ben wont to hopen *of syke folk, whan they aperceyven* that nature is redressed and withstondeth to the maladye. But, 140 for I see thee now al redy to the understondinge, I shal shewe thee more thikke and continuel resouns. For loke now how greetly sheweth the feblesse and infirmitee of wikkede folk, that ne mowen 145 nat comen to that hir naturel entencioun ledeth hem, and yit almost thilke naturel entencioun constreineth hem. And what *were to demen thanne of shrewes,* yif thilke naturel help hadde forleten hem, the 150 which *naturel help of intencioun* goth awey biforn hem, and is so greet that unnethe it may ben overcome? Consider thanne how greet defaute of power and how greet feblesse ther is in wikkede 155 felonous folk; *as who seyth, the gretter thing that is coveited and the desire nat acomplisshed, of the lasse might is he that coveiteth it and may nat acomplisshe. And forthy Philosophie seyth thus by soverein* 160 *good:* Ne shrewes ne requeren nat lighte medes ne veyne games, whiche they ne may folwen ne holden; but they failen of thilke somme and of the heighte of thinges, *that is to seyn, soverein good*; ne 165 thise wrecches ne comen nat to the effect *of soverein good,* the which they enforcen hem only to geten, by nightes and by dayes; in the getinge of which good the strengthe of good folk is ful wel y-sene. 170 For right so as thou mightest demen him mighty of goinge, that gooth on his feet til he mighte come to thilke place, fro the whiche place ther ne laye no wey forther to ben gon; right so most thou nedes 175 demen him for right mighty, that geteth and ateyneth to the ende of alle thinges that ben to desire, biyonde the whiche ende ther nis nothing to desire. Of the which *power of good folk* men may conclude, that 180 the wikked men semen to be bareine and naked of alle strengthe. For-why for-

leten they vertues and folwen vyces?
Nis it nat for that they ne knowen nat
185 the goodes? But what thing is more feble
and more caitif thanne is the blindnesse
of ignoraunce? Or elles they knowen ful
wel whicho thinges that they oughten
folwe, but lecherye and coveityse over-
190 throweth hem mistorned; and certes, so
doth distemperaunce to feble men, that
ne mowen nat wrastlen ayeins the vyces.
Ne knowen they nat thanne wel that they
forleten the good wilfully, and tornen
195 hem wilfully to vyces? And in this wyse
they ne forleten nat only to ben mighty,
but they forleten al-outrely in any wyse
for to ben. For they that forleten the
comune fyn of alle thinges that ben, they
200 forleten also therwith-al for to ben. And
per-aventure it sholde semen to som folk
that this were a merveile to seyen: that
shrewes, whiche that contienen the more
partye of men, ne ben nat ne han no
205 beinge; but natheles, it is so, and thus
stant this thing. For they that ben
shrewes, I deneye nat that they ben
shrewes; but I deneye, and seye simplely
and pleinly, that they ne ben nat, ne han
210 no beinge. For right as thou mightest
seyen of the carayne of a man, that it
were a deed man, but thou ne mightest
nat simplely callen it a man; so graunte
I wel forsothe, that vicious folk ben wik-
215 ked, but I ne may nat graunten absolutly
and simplely that they ben. For thilke
thing that with-holdeth ordre and kepeth
nature, thilke thing is and hath beinge;
but what thing that faileth of that, *that
220 is to seyn, that he forleteth naturel ordre,*
he forleteth thilke thing that is set in his
nature. But thou wolt seyn, that shrewes
mowen. Certes, that ne deneye I nat;
but certes, hir power ne descendeth nat
225 of strengthe, but of feblesse. For they
mowen don wikkednesses; the whiche
they ne mighte nat don, yif they mighten
dwellen in the forme and in the doinge of
good folk. And thilke power sheweth ful
230 evidently that they ne mowen right
naught. For so as I have gadered and
proeved a litel her-biforn, that yvel is
naught; and so as shrewes mowen only

but shrewednesses, this conclusioun is
al cleer, that shrewes ne mowen right 23.
naught, ne han no power. And for as
moche as thou understonde which is the
strengthe of this power of shrewes, I have
definisshed a litel her-biforn, that nothing
is so mighty as soverein good.' 'That 24
is sooth,' quod I.
'And thilke same soverein good may
don non yvel?' 'Certes, no,' quod I.
'Is ther any wight thanne,' quod she,
'that weneth that men mowen doon alle 24.
thinges?' 'No man,' quod I, 'but-yif
he be out of his witte.'
'But, certes, shrewes mowen don yvel,'
quod she. 'Ye, wolde god,' quod I,
'that they mighten don non!' 25
'Thanne,' quod she, 'so as he that is
mighty to doon only but goode thinges
may don alle thinges; and they that ben
mighty to don yvele thinges ne mowen
nat alle thinges: thanne is it open thing 25
and manifest, that they that mowen don
yvel ben of lasse power. And yit, *to proeve
this conclusioun,* ther helpeth me this, that
I have y-shewed her-biforn, that alle
power is to be noumbred among thinges 26
that men oughten requere. And I have
shewed that alle thinges, that oughten
ben desired, ben referred to good, right as
to a maner heighte of hir nature. But for
to mowen don yvel and felonye ne may 26
nat ben referred to good. Thanne nis nat
yvel of the noumbir of thinges that
oughte ben desired. But alle power
oughte ben desired and requered. Than
is it open and cleer that the power ne the 27
mowinge of shrewes nis no power; and of
alle thise thinges it sheweth wel, that the
goode folke ben certeinly mighty, and the
shrewes douteles ben unmighty. And it
is cleer and open that thilke opinioun of 27.
Plato is verray and sooth, that seith, that
only wyse men may doon that they
desiren; and shrewes mowen haunten
that hem lyketh, but that they desiren,
*that is to seyn, to comen to sovereign good,* 28
they ne han no power to acomplisshen
that. For shrewes don that hem list,
whan, by tho thinges in which they
delyten, they wenen to ateine to thilke

285 good that they desiren ; but they ne geten
ne ateinen nat ther-to, for vyces ne comen
nat to blisfulnesse.

### Metre II. *Quos uides sedere celsos.*

Who-so that the covertoures of hir
veyne aparailes mighte strepen of thise
proude kinges, that thou seest sitten on
heigh in hir chaires gliteringe in shyninge
5 purpre, environued with sorwful armures,
manasinge with cruel mouth, blowinge
by woodnesse of herte, he shulde seen
thanne that thilke lordes beren with-inne
hir corages ful streite cheines. For
10 lecherye tormenteth hem in that oon
syde with gredy venims ; and troublable
ire, that araiseth in him the flodes *of
troublinges*, tormenteth up-on that other
syde hir thought ; or sorwe halt hem wery
15 and y-caught ; or slydinge and deceivinge
hope tormenteth hem. And therfore, sen
thou seest oon heed, *that is to seyn, oon
tyraunt*, beren so manye tyrannyes,
thanne ne doth thilke tyraunt nat that
20 he desireth, sin he is cast doun with so
manye wikkede lordes ; *that is to seyn,
with so manye vyces, that han so wikkedly
lordshipes over him.*

### Prose III. *Videsne igitur quanto in coeno.*

Seestow nat thanne in how grete filthe
thise shrewes ben y-wrapped, and with
which cleernesse thise good folk shynen ?
In this sheweth it wel, that to goode folk
5 ne lakketh never-mo hir medes, ne
shrewes lakken never-mo torments. For
of alle thinges that ben y-doon, thilke
thing, for which any-thing is don, it
semeth as by right that thilke thing be
10 the mede of that ; as thus : yif a man
renneth in the stadie, *or in the forlong*,
for the corone, thanne lyth the mede in
the corone for which he renneth. And
I have shewed that blisfulnesse is thilke
15 same good for which that alle thinges
ben doon. Thanne is thilke same good
purposed to the workes of mankinde
right as a comune mede ; which mede ne
may ben dissevered fro good folk. For no

wight as by right, fro thennes-forth that 20
him lakketh goodnesse, ne shal ben
eleped good. For which thing, folk of
goode maneres, hir medes ne forsaken hem
never-mo. For al-be-it so that shrewes
wexen as wode as hem list *ayeins goode* 25
*folk*, yit never-the-lesse the corone of
wyse men shal nat fallen ne faden. For
foreine shrewednesse ne binimeth nat fro
the corages of goode folk hir propre
honour. But yif that any wight rejoyse 30
him of goodnesse that he hadde take fro
with-oute *(as who seith, yif that any wight
hadde his goodnesse of any other man than
of him-self)*, certes, he that yaf him thilke
goodnesse, or elles som other wight, 35
mighte binime it him. But for as moche
as to every wight his owne propre bountee
yeveth him his mede, thanne at erst shal
he failen of mede whan he forleteth to
ben good. And at the laste, so as alle 40
medes ben requered for men wenen that
they ben goode, who is he that wolde
deme, that he that is right mighty of good
were part-les of mede ? And of what
mede shal he be guerdoned ? Certes, of 45
right faire mede and right grete aboven
alle medes. Remembre thee of thilke
noble corolarie that I yaf thee a litel
her-biforn ; and gader it to-gider in this
manere :—so as good him-self is blisful- 50
nesse, thanne is it cleer and certein, that
alle good folk ben maked blisful for they
ben goode ; and thilke folk that ben blisful, it acordeth and is covenable to ben
goddes. Thanne is the mede of goode 55
folk swich that no day shal enpeiren it,
ne no wikkednesse ne shal derken it, ne
power of no wight ne shal nat amenusen
it, *that is to seyn*, to ben maked goddes.
And sin it is thus, *that goode men ne failen* 60
*never-mo of hir mede*, certes, no wys man
ne may doute of undepartable peyne of
the shrewes ; *that is to seyn, that the peyne
of shrewes ne departeth nat from hem-self
never-mo*. For so as goode and yvel, and 65
peyne and medes ben contrarye, it mot
nedes ben, that right as we seen bityden
in guerdoun of goode, that also mot the
peyne of yvel answery, by the contrarye
party, to shrewes. Now thanne, so as 70

bountee and prowesse ben the mede to
goode folk, al-so is shrewednesse it-self
torment to shrewes. Thanne, who-so that
ever is entecched and defouled with
75 peyne, he ne douteth nat, that he is
entecched and defouled with yvel. Yif
shrewes thanne wolen preysen hem-self,
may it semen to hem that they ben with-
outen party of torment, sin they ben
80 swiche that the uttereste wikkednesse
(*that is to seyn, wikkede thewes, which that
is the uttereste and the worste kinde of
shrewednesse*) ne defouleth ne enteccheth
nat hem only, but infecteth and en-
85 venimeth hem gretly? And also look on
shrewes, that ben the contrarie party of
goode men, how greet peyne felawshipeth
and folweth hem! For thou hast lerned
a litel her-biforn, that al thing that is
90 and hath beinge is oon, and thilke same
oon is good; thanne is this the consequence, that it semeth wel, that al that is
and hath beinge is good; *this is to seyn,
as who seyth, that beinge and unitee and
95 goodnesse is al oon.* And in this manere
it folweth thanne, that al thing that
faileth to ben good, it stinteth for to be
and for to han any beinge: wherfore it
is, that shrewes stinten for to ben that
100 they weren. But thilke other forme of
mankinde, that is to seyn, the forme of
the body with-oute, sheweth yit that thise
shrewes weren whylom men; wher-for,
whan they ben perverted and torned in-to
105 malice, certes, than han they forlorn the
nature of mankinde. But so as only
bountee and prowesse may enhaunsen
every man over other men; thanne mot
it nedes be that shrewes, which that
110 shrewednesse hath cast out of the condicioun of mankinde, ben put under the
merite and the desert of men. Thanne
bitydeth it, that yif thou seest a wight
that be transformed into vyces, thou ne
115 mayst nat wene that he be a man. For
yif he be ardaunt in avaryce, and that he
be a ravinour by violence of foreine
richesse, thou shalt seyn that he is lyke
to the wolf. And yif he be felonous and
120 with-oute reste, and exercyse his tonge
to chydinges, thou shalt lykne him to the

hound. And yif he be a prevey awaitour
y-hid, and rejoyseth him to ravisshe by
wyles, thou shalt seyn him lyke to the
fox-whelpes. And yif he be distempre 125
and quaketh for ire, men shal wene that
he bereth the corage of a lyoun. And yif
he be dredful and fleinge, and dredeth
thinges that ne oughten nat to ben dred,
men shal holden him lyk to the hert. 130
And yif he be slow and astoned and
lache, he liveth as an asse. And yif he
be light and unstedefast of corage, and
chaungeth ay his studies, he is lykned to
briddes. And if he be plounged in foule 135
and unclene luxuries, he is with-holden
in the foule delyces of the foule sowe.
Thanne folweth it, that he that forleteth
bountee and prowesse, he forleteth to ben
a man; sin he may nat passen in-to the 140
condicioun of god, he is torned in-to
a beest.

## METRE III.    *Vela Neritii dulcis.*

Eurus *the wind* aryvede the sailes of
*Ulixes*, duk of the contree of Narice, and
his wandringe shippes by the see, in-to
the ile ther-as *Circes*, the faire goddesse,
doughter of the sonne, dwelleth; that 5
medleth to hir newe gestes drinkes that
ben touched and maked with enchauntements. And after that hir hand, mighty
over the herbes, hadde chaunged hir
gestes in-to dyverse maneres; that oon of 10
hem, is covered his face with forme of
a boor; that other is chaunged in-to
a lyoun of the contree of Marmorike, and
his nayles and his teeth wexen; that
other of hem is neweliche chaunged in-to 15
a wolf, and howleth whan he wolde wepe;
that other goth debonairely in the hous
as a tygre of Inde. But al-be-it so that
the godhed of *Mercurie, that is cleped* the
brid of Arcadie, hath had mercy of the 20
duke *Ulixes*, biseged with dyverse yveles,
and hath unbounden him fro the pestilence of his ostesse, algates the roweres
and the marineres hadden by this y-
drawen in-to hir mouthes and dronken 25
the wikkede drinkes. They that weren
woxen swyn hadden by this y-chaunged

hir mete of breed, for to eten akornes of okes. Non of hir limes ne dwelleth with hem hole, but they han lost the voice and the body; only hir thought dwelleth with hem stable, that wepeth and biweileth the monstruous chaunginge that they suffren. O overlight hand (*as who seyth, O! feble and light is the hand of Circes the enchaunteresse, that chaungeth the bodyes of folkes in-to bestes, to regard and to comparisoun of mutacioun that is maked by vyces*); ne the herbes *of Circes* ne ben nat mighty. For al-be-it so that they may chaungen the limes of the body, algates yit they may nat chaunge the hertes; for with-inne is y-hid the strengthe and vigor of men, in the secree tour *of hir hertes; that is to seyn, the strengthe of resoun.* But thilke venims *of vyces* to-drawen a man to hem more mightily *than the venim of Circes;* for vyces ben so cruel that they percen and thorugh-passen the corage with-inne; and, thogh they ne anoye nat the body, yit vyces wooden *to destroye men by wounde of thought.*'

Prose IV.  *Tum ego, Fateor, inquam.*

Than seyde I thus: 'I confesse and am a-knowe it,' quod I; 'ne I ne see nat that men may sayn, as by right, that shrewes ne ben chaunged in-to bestes by the qualitee of hir soules, al-be-it so that they kepen yit the forme of the body of mankinde. But I nolde nat of shrewes, of which the thought cruel woodeth al-wey in-to destruccioun of goode men, that it were leveful to hem to don that.'

'Certes,' quod she, 'ne is nis nat leveful to hem, as I shal wel shewe thee in covenable place; but natheles, yif so were that thilke that men wenen be leveful to shrewes were binomen hem, *so that they ne mighte nat anoyen or doon harm to goode men*, certes, a greet partye of the peyne to shrewes sholde ben allegged and releved. For al-be-it so that this ne seme nat credible thing, per-aventure, to some folk, yit moot it nedes be, that shrewes ben more wrecches and unsely whan they may doon and performe that they co-

veiten, than yif they mighte nat complisshen that they coveiten. For yif so be that it be wrecchednesse to wilne to don yvel, than is more wrecchednesse to mowen don yvel; with-oute whiche mowinge the wrecched wil sholde languisshe with-oute effect. Than, sin that everiche of thise thinges hath his wrecchednesse, *that is to seyn, wil to don yvel and mowinge to don yvel*, it moot nedes be that they ben constreyned by three unselinesses, that wolen and mowen and performen felonyes and shrewednesses.' 'I acorde me,' quod I; 'but I desire gretly that shrewes losten sone thilke unselinesse, *that is to seyn*, that shrewes weren despoyled of mowinge to don yvel.'

'So shullen they,' quod she, 'soner, per-aventure, than thou woldest; or soner than they hem-self wene to lakken *mowinge to don yvel.* For ther nis no-thing so late in so shorte boundes of this lyf, that is long to abyde, nameliche, to a corage inmortel; of whiche shrewes the grete hope, and the hye compassinges of shrewednesses, is ofte destroyed by a sodeyn ende, or they ben war; and that thing estableth to shrewes the ende of hir shrewednesse. For yif that shrewednesse maketh wrecches, than mot he nedes ben most wrecched that lengest is a shrewe; the whiche wikked shrewes wolde I demen aldermost unsely and caitifs, yif that hir shrewednesse ne were finisshed, at the leste wey, by the outtereste deeth. For yif I have concluded sooth of the unselinesse of shrewednesse, than sheweth it cleerly that thilke wrecchednesse is withouten ende, the whiche is certein to ben perdurable.' 'Certes,' quod I, 'this conclusioun is hard and wonderful to graunte; but I knowe wel that it acordeth moche to the thinges that I have graunted her-biforn.'

'Thou hast,' quod she, 'the right estimacioun of this; but who-so-ever wene that it be a hard thing to acorde him to a conclusioun, it is right that he shewe that some of the premisses ben false; or elles he moot shewe that the collacioun of proposiciouns nis nat speedful to a

75 necessarie conclusioun. And yif it be nat
so, but that the premisses ben y-graunted,
ther is not why he sholde blame the
argument.    For this thing that I shal
telle thee now ne shal nat seme lasse
80 wonderful; but of the thinges that ben
taken also it is necessarie;' *as who seyth,
it folweth of that which that is purposed
biforn.*    'What is that?' quod I.

'Certes,' quod she, 'that is, that thise
85 wikked shrewes ben more blisful, *or elles
lasse wrecches*, that abyen the torments
that they han deserved, than yif no peyne
of justice ne chastysede hem.  Ne this ne
seye I nat now, for that any man mighte
90 thenke, that the maners of shrewes ben
coriged and chastysed by veniaunce, and
that they ben brought to the right wey by
the drede of the torment, ne for that they
yeven to other folk ensaumple to fleen
95 fro vyces; but I understande yit in
another manere, that shrewes ben more
unsely whan they ne ben nat punisshed,
al-be-it so that ther ne be had no resoun
or lawe of correccioun, ne non ensaumple
100 of lokinge.'    'And what manere shal
that ben,' quod I, ' other than hath be
told her-biforn?'

'Have we nat thanne graunted,' quod
she, 'that goode folk ben blisful, and
105 shrewes ben wrecches?'    'Yis,' quod I.

'Thanne,' quod she, 'yif that any good
were added to the wreechednesse of any
wight, nis he nat more weleful than he
that ne hath no medlinge of good in his
110 solitarie wreechednesse?'   'So semeth it,'
quod I.

'And what seystow thanne,' quod she,
'of thilke wrecche that lakketh alle
goodes, *so that no good nis medled in his
115 wreechednesse*, and yit, over al his wikkednesse for which he is a wrecche, that ther
be yit another yvel anexed and knit to
him, shal nat men demen him more
unsely than thilke wrecche of whiche the
120 unselinesse is releved by the participacioun of som good?'    'Why sholde he
nat?' quod I.

'Thanne, certes,' quod she, 'han
shrewes, whan they ben punisshed, som-
125 what of good anexed to hir wreeched-

nesse, that is to seyn, the same peyne
that they suffren, which that is good by
the resoun of justice; and whan thilke
same shrewes ascapen with-oute torment,
than han they som-what more of yvel yit 130
over the wikkednesse that they han don,
*that is to seyn*, defaute of peyne; which
defaute of peyne, thou hast graunted, is
yvel for the deserte of felonye.'  'I ne may
nat denye it,' quod I.                              135

'Moche more thanne,' quod she, 'ben
shrewes unsely, whan they ben wrongfully delivered fro peyne, than whan
they ben punisshed by rightful venjaunce. But this is open thing and cleer, 140
that it is right that shrewes ben punisshed, and it is wikkednesse and wrong
that they escapen unpunisshed.'   'Who
mighte deneye that?' quod I.

'But,' quod she, 'may any man denye 145
that al that is right nis good; and also
the contrarie, that al that is wrong is
wikke?'    'Certes,' quod I, 'these
thinges ben clere y-nough; and that we
han concluded a litel her-biforn.  But 150
I praye thee that thou telle me, yif thou
acordest to leten no torment to sowles,
after that the body is ended by the
deeth;' *this is to seyn, understandestow
aught that sowles han any torment after the 155
deeth of the body?*

'Certes,' quod she, 'ye; and that right
greet; of which sowles,' quod she, ' I
trowe that some ben tormented by asprenesse of peyne; and some sowles, I trowe, 160
ben exercised by a purginge mekenesse.
But my conseil nis nat to determinye of
thise peynes. But I have travailed and
told yit hiderto, for thou sholdest knowe
that the mowinge of shrewes, which 165
mowinge thee semeth to ben unworthy,
nis no mowinge : and eek of shrewes, of
which thou pleinedest that they ne were
nat punisshed, that thou woldest seen
that they ne weren never-mo with-outen 170
the torments of hir wikkednesse : and of
the licence *of the mowinge to don yvel*, that
thou preydest that it mighte sone ben
ended, and that thou woldest fayn lernen
that it ne sholde nat longe dure : and 175
that shrewes ben more unsely yif they

were of lenger duringe, and most unsely
yif they weren perdurable. And after
this, I have shewed thee that more unsely
180 ben shrewes, whan they escapen with-
oute hir rightful peyne, than whan they
ben punisshed by rightful venjaunce.
And of this sentence folweth it, that
thanne ben shrewes constreined at the
185 laste with most grevous torment, whan
men wene that they ne be nat punisshed.'
'Whan I consider thy resouns,' quod I,
'I ne trowe nat that men seyn any-thing
more verayly. And yif I torne ayein to
190 the studies of men, who is he to whom it
sholde seme that he ne sholde nat only
leven thise thinges, but eek gladly herkne
hem ?'
'Certes,' quod she, 'so it is; but men
195 may nat. For they han hir eyen so wont
to the derknesse *of erthely thinges*, that
they ne may nat liften hem up to the
light of cleer sothfastnesse ; but they ben
lyke to briddes, of which the night light-
200 neth hir lokinge, and the day blindeth
hem. For whan men loken nat the ordre
of thinges, but hir lustes and talents, they
wene that either the leve or the mowinge
to don wikkednesse, or elles the scapinge
205 with-oute peyne, be weleful. But consider the jugement of the perdurable lawe.
For yif thou conferme thy corage to the
beste thinges, thou ne hast no nede of no
juge to yeven thee prys or mede ; for
210 thou hast joyned thy-self to the most
excellent thing. And yif thou have enclyned thy studies to the wikked thinges,
ne seek no foreyne wreker out of thy-
self ; for thou thy-self hast thrist thy-self
215 in-to wikke thinges : right as thou
mightest loken by dyverse tymes the
foule erthe and the hevene, and that alle
other thinges stinten fro with-oute, *so
that thou nere neither in hevene ne in erthe,
220 ne saye no-thing more;* than it sholde
semen to thee, as by only resoun of
lokinge, that thou were now in the sterres
and now in the erthe. But the poeple ne
loketh nat on thise thinges. What
225 thanne? Shal we thanne aprochen us to
hem that I have shewed that they ben lyk
to bestes? And what woltow seyn of

this : yif that a man hadde al forlorn his
sighte and hadde foryeten that he ever
saugh, and wende that no-thing ne fayl- 230
ede him of perfeccioun of mankinde, now
we that mighten seen the same thinges,
wolde we nat wene that he were blinde?
Ne also ne acordeth nat the poeple to
that I shal seyn, the which thing is sus- 235
tened by a stronge foundement of resouns,
*that is to seyn*, that more unsely ben they
that don wrong to othre folk than they
that the wrong suffren.' 'I wolde
heren thilke same resouns,' quod I. 240
'Denyestow,' quod she, 'that alle
shrewes ne ben worthy to han torment?'
'Nay,' quod I.
'But,' quod she, 'I am certein, by
many resouns, that shrewes ben unsely.' 245
'It acordeth,' quod I.
'Thanne ne doutestow nat,' quod she,
'that thilke folk that ben worthy of torment, that they ne ben wrecches?' 'It
acordeth wel,' quod I. 250
'Yif thou were thanne,' quod she,
'y-set a juge or a knower of thinges,
whether, trowestow, that men sholden
tormenten him that hath don the wrong,
or elles him that hath suffred the wrong?' 255
'I ne doute nat,' quod I, 'that I nolde
don suffisaunt satisfaccioun to him that
hadde suffred the wrong by the sorwe of
him that hadde don the wrong.'
'Thanne semeth it,' quod she, 'that the 260
doere of wrong is more wrecche than he
that suffred wrong?' 'That folweth
wel,' quod I.
'Than,' quod she, 'by these causes and
by othre causes that ben enforced by the 265
same rote, filthe or sinne, by the propre
nature of it, maketh men wrecches ; and
it sheweth wel, that the wrong that men
don nis nat the wrecchednesse of him
that receyveth the wrong, but the 270
wrecchednesse of him that doth the
wrong. But certes,' quod she, 'thise
oratours or advocats don al the contrarye : for they enforcen hem to commoeve the juges to han pitee of hem that 275
han suffred and receyved the thinges that
ben grevous and aspre, and yit men
sholden more rightfully han pitee of hem

that don the grevaunces and the wronges; 280 the whiche shrewes, it were a more covenable thing, that the accusours or advocats, nat wroth but pitous and debonair, ledden tho shrewes that han don wrong to the jugement, right as men 285 leden syke folk to the leche, for that they sholde seken out the maladyes of sinne by torment. And by this covenaunt, either the entente of deffendours or advocats sholde faylen and cesen in al, or 290 elles, yif the office of advocats wolde bettre profiten to men, it sholde ben torned in-to the habite of accusacioun ; *that is to seyn, they sholden accuse shrewes, and nat excuse hem.* And eek the shrewes 295 hem-self, yif hit were leveful to hem to seen at any clifte the vertu that they han forleten, and sawen that they sholden putten adoun the filthes of hir vyces by the torments of peynes, they ne oughte 300 nat, right for the recompensacioun for to geten hem bountee and prowesse which that they han lost, demen ne holden that thilke peynes weren torments to hem ; and eek they wolden refuse the attend- 305 aunce of hir advocats, and taken hem-self to hir juges and to hir accusors. For which it bitydeth that, as to the wyse folk, ther nis no place y-leten to hate ; *that is to seyn, that ne hate hath no place* 310 *amonges wyse men.* For no wight nil haten goode men, but-yif he were overmochel a fool ; and for to haten shrewes, it nis no resoun. For right so as languissinge is maladye of body, right so ben 315 vyces and sinne maladye of corage. And so as we ne deme nat, that they that ben syke of hir body ben worthy to ben hated, but rather worthy of pitee : wel more worthy, nat to ben hated, but for to ben 320 had in pitee, ben they of whiche the thoughtes ben constreined by felonous wikkednesse, that is more cruel than any languissinge of body.

METRE IV.　*Quid tantos iuuat excitare motus.*

What delyteth you to excyten so grete moevinges *of hateredes*, and to hasten and

bisien the fatal disposicioun of your deeth with your propre handes ? *that is to seyn, by batailes or by contek.* For yif ye axen 5 the deeth, it hasteth him of his owne wil ; ne deeth ne tarieth nat his swifte hors. And the men that the serpent and the lyoun and the tygre and the bere and the boor seken to sleen with hir teeth, yit 10 thilke same men seken to sleen everich of hem other with swerd. Lo ! for hir maneres ben dyverse and descordaunt, they moeven unrightful ostes and cruel batailes, and wilnen to perisshe by entre- 15 chaunginge of dartes. But the resoun of crueltee nis nat y-nough rightful. Wiltow thanne yelden a covenable guerdoun to the desertes of men ? Love rightfully goode folk, and have pitee on shrewes.' 20

PROSE V.　*Hic ego uideo inquam.*

'Thus see I wel,' quod I, 'either what blisfulnesse or elles what unselinesse is establisshed in the desertes of goode men and of shrewes. But in this ilke fortune of poeple I see somwhat of good and som- 5 what of yvel. For no wyse man hath lever ben exyled, poore and nedy, and nameles, than for to dwellen in his citee and flouren of richesses, and be redoutable by honour, and strong of power. For in 10 this wyse more cleerly and more witnesfully is the office of wyse men y-treted, whan the blisfulnesse and the poustee of governours is, as it were, y-shad amonges poeples that be neighebours *and subgits*; 15 sin that, namely, prisoun, lawe, and thise othre torments of lawful peynes ben rather owed to felonous citezeins, for the whiche felonous citezeins tho peynes ben establisshed, *than for good folk.* Thanne 20 I mervaile me greetly,' quod I, 'why that the thinges ben so mis entrechaunged, that torments of felonyes pressen and confounden goode folk, and shrewes ravisshen medes of vertu, *and ben in* 25 *honours and in gret estats.* And I desyre eek for to witen of thee, what semeth thee to ben the resoun of this so wrongful a conclusioun ? For I wolde wondre wel the lasse, yif I trowede that al thise 30 thinges weren medled by fortunous happe; but now hepeth and encreseth myn astonyinge god, governour of thinges, that, so as god yeveth ofte tymes to gode men 35 godes and mirthes, and to shrewes yveles and aspre thinges; and yeveth ayeinward to gode folk hardnesses, and to shrewes he graunteth hem hir wil and that they desyren: what difference thanne 40 may ther be bitwixen that that god doth, and the happe of fortune, yif men ne knowe nat the cause why that it is?'

'Ne it nis no mervaile,' quod she, 'though that men wenen that ther be 45 somewhat folissh and confuse, whan the resoun of the ordre is unknowe. But al-though that thou ne knowe nat the cause of so greet a disposicioun, natheles, for as moche as god, the gode governour, 50 atempreth and governeth the world, ne doute thee nat that alle thinges ben doon a-right.

### METRE V. *Si quis Arcturi sidera nescit.*

Who-so that ne knowe nat the sterres of Arcture, y-torned neigh to the soverein contree or point, *that is to seyn, y-torned neigh to the soverein pool of the firmament,* 5 and wot nat why *the sterre* Bootes passeth or gadereth his weynes, and drencheth his late flambes in the see, and why that Bootes *the sterre* unfoldeth his over-swifte arysinges, thanne shal he wondren of the 10 lawe of the heye eyr. *And eek, yif that he ne knowe nat why that* the hornes of the fulle mone wexen pale and infect by the boundes of the derke night; and *how* the mone, derk and confuse, discovereth the 15 sterres that she hadde y-covered by hir clere visage. The comune errour moeveth folk, and maketh wery hir basins of bras by thikke strokes; *that is to seyn, that ther is a maner of poeple that highte Cori-* 20 *bantes, that wenen that, whan the mone is in the eclipse, that it be enchaunted; and ther-fore, for to rescowe the mone, they beten hir basins with thikke strokes.* Ne no man ne wondreth whan the blastes of the 25 wind Chorus beten the strondes of the see by quakinge flodes; ne no man ne

wondreth whan the weighte of the snowe, y-harded by the colde, is resolved by the brenninge hete of Phebus the sonne; for heer seen men redely the causes. But 30 the causes y-hid, *that is to seyn, in hevene,* troublen the brestes of men; the moevable poeple is astoned of alle thinges that comen selde and sodeinly in our age. But yif the troubly errour of our igno- 35 raunce departede fro us, *so that we wisten the causes why that swiche thinges bi-tyden,* certes, they sholden cese to seme wondres.

### PROSE VI. *Ita est, inquam.*

'Thus is it,' quod I. 'But so as thou hast yeven or bi-hight me to unwrappen the hid causes of thinges, and to dis-covere me the resouns covered with derk-nesses, I prey thee that thou devyse and 5 juge me of this matere, and that thou do me to understonden it; for this miracle or this wonder troubleth me right gretly.'

And thanne she, a litel what smylinge, seyde: 'thou clepest me,' quod she, 'to 10 telle thing that is grettest of alle thinges that mowen ben axed, and to the whiche questioun unnethes is ther aught y-nough to laven it; *as who seyth, unnethes is ther suffisauntly anything to answere parfitly to* 15 *thy questioun.* For the matere of it is swich, that whan o doute is determined and cut awey, ther wexen other doutes with-oute number; right as the hevedes wexen of Ydre, *the serpent that Ercules* 20 *slowh.* Ne ther ne were no manere ne non ende, but-yif that a wight con-streinede tho doutes by a right lyfly and quik fyr of thought; *that is to seyn, by vigour and strengthe of wit.* For in this 25 manere men weren wont to maken ques-tions of the simplicitee of the purviaunce of god, and of the order of destinee, and of sodein happe, and of the knowinge and predestinacioun divyne, and of the libertee 30 of free wille; the whiche thinges thou thy-self aperceyvest wel, of what weight they ben. But for as mochel as the knowinge of thise thinges is a maner porcioun of the medicine of thee, al-be-it 35

so that I have litel tyme to don it, yit
natheles I wol enforcen me to shewe
somwhat of it. But al-thogh the norisshinges of ditee of musike delyteth
40 thee, thou most suffren and forberen
a litel of thilke delyte, whyle that I weve
to thee resouns y-knit by ordre.'     'As
it lyketh to thee,' quod I, ' so do.'

Tho spak she right as by another
45 biginninge, and seyde thus. 'The engendringe of alle thinges,' quod she, 'and
alle the progressiouns of muable nature,
and al that moeveth in any manere,
taketh his causes, his ordre, and his
50 formes, of the stablenesse of the divyne
thoght ; and thilke divyne thought, that
is y-set and put in the tour, *that is to seyn*,
*in the heighte*, of the simplicitee of god,
stablissheth many maner gyses to thinges
55 that ben to done; the whiche maner,
whan that men loken it in thilke pure
clennesse of the divyne intelligence, it is
y-cleped purviaunce ; but whan thilke
maner is referred by men to thinges that
60 it moeveth and disponeth, thanne of olde
men it was cleped destinee. The whiche
thinges, yif that any wight loketh wel in
his thought the strengthe of that oon and
of that other, he shal lightly mowen seen,
65 that thise two thinges ben dyverse. For
purviaunce is thilke divyne reson that is
establisshed in the soverein prince of
thinges ; the whiche purviaunce disponeth alle thinges. But destinee is the
70 disposicioun and ordinaunce clyvinge to
moevable thinges, by the whiche disposicioun the purviaunce knitteth alle
thinges in hir ordres ; for purviaunce
embraceth alle thinges to-hepe, al-thogh
75 that they ben dyverse, and al-thogh they
ben infinite ; but destinee departeth and
ordeineth alle thinges singulerly, and
divyded in moevinges, in places, in
formes, in tymes, as thus : lat the un-
80 foldinge of temporel ordinaunce, assembled and ooned in the lokinge of the
divyne thought, be cleped purviaunce ;
and thilke same assemblinge and oon-
inge, divyded and unfolden by tymes, lat
85 that ben called destinee. And al-be-it so
that thise thinges ben dyverse, yit nathe-

les hangeth that oon on that other; for-
why the order destinal procedeth of the
simplicitee of purviaunce. For right as
a werkman, that aperceyveth in his 90
thoght the forme of the thing that he
wol make, and moeveth the effect of the
werk, and ledeth that he hadde loked
biforn in his thoght simply and presently, by temporel ordinaunce : certes, 95
right so god disponeth in his purviaunce,
singulerly and stably, the thinges that
ben to done, but he aministreth in many
maneres and in dyverse tymes, by destinee, thilke same thinges that he hath 100
disponed.     Thanne, whether that destinee be exercysed outher by some divyne
spirits, servaunts to the divyne purviaunce, or elles by som sowle, or elles by
alle nature servinge to god, or elles by 105
the celestial moevinges of sterres, or elles
by the vertu of angeles, or elles by the
dyverse subtilitee of develes, or elles by
any of hem, or elles by hem alle, the
destinal ordinaunce is y-woven and acom- 110
plisshed. Certes, it is open thing, that
the purviaunce is an unmoevable and
simple forme of thinges to done ; and the
moveable bond and the temporel ordinaunce of thinges, whiche that the 115
divyne simplicitee of purviaunce hath
ordeyned to done, that is destinee. For
which it is, that alle thinges that ben
put under destinee ben, certes, subgits to
purviaunce, to whiche purviaunce des- 120
tinee itself is subgit and under. But
some thinges ben put under purviaunce,
that surmounten the ordinaunce of destinee ; and tho ben thilke that stably ben
y-ficched negh to the firste godhed : they 125
surmounten the ordre of destinal moevabletee.     For right as of cercles that
tornen a-boute a same centre or a-boute
a poynt, thilke cercle that is innerest or
most with-inne joyneth to the simplesse 130
of the middel, and is, as it were, a centre
or a poynt to that other cercles that
tornen a-bouten him ; and thilke that is
outterest, compassed by larger envyron-
ninge, is unfolden by larger spaces, in so 135
moche as it is forthest fro the middel
simplicitee of the poynt ; and yif ther be

any-thing that knitteth and felawship-
peth him-self to thilke middel poynt, it
140 is constreined in-to simplicitee, *that is to
seyn, in-to unmoevabletee,* and it ceseth to
be shad and to fleten dyversely : right so,
by semblable resoun, thilke thing that
departeth forthest fro the first thoght of
145 god, it is unfolden and summitted to
gretter bondes of destinee : and in so
moche is the thing more free and laus
fro destinee, as it axeth and holdeth him
ner to thilke centre of thinges, *that is to
150 seyn, god* And yif the thing clyveth to
the stedefastnesse of the thoght of god,
and be with-oute moevinge, certes, it sormounteth the necessitee of destinee.
Thanne right swich comparisoun as it is
155 of skilinge to understondinge, and of
thing that is engendred to thing that is,
and of tyme to eternitee, and of the cercle
to the centre, right so is the ordre of
moevable destinee to the stable sim-
160 plicitee of purviaunce. Thilke ordinaunce moeveth the hevene and the
sterres, and atempreth the elements to-
gider amonges hem-self, and transformeth
hem by entrechaungeable mutacioun ;
165 and thilke same ordre neweth ayein alle
thinges growinge and fallinge a-doun, by
semblable progressiouns of sedes and of
sexes, *that is to seyn, male and femele.*
And this ilke ordre constreineth the for-
170 tunes and the dedes of men by a bond of
causes, nat able to ben unbounde ; the
whiche destinal causes, whan they passen
out fro the biginninges of the unmoevable
purviaunce, it mot nedes be that they ne
175 be nat mutable. And thus ben the
thinges ful wel y-governed, yif that the
simplicitee dwellinge in the divyne thoght
sheweth forth the ordre of causes, unable
to ben y-bowed ; and this ordre con-
180 streineth by his propre stabletee the
moevable thinges, or elles they sholden
fleten folily. For which it is, that alle
thinges semen to ben confus and trouble
to us men, for we ne mowen nat considere
185 thilke ordinaunce ; natheles, the propre
maner of every thinge, dressinge hem to
goode, disponeth hem alle.

For ther nis no-thing don for cause of

yvel ; ne thilke thing that is don by wikkede folk *nis nat don for yvel.* The whiche 190
shrewes, as I have shewed ful plenti-
vously, seken good, but wikked errour
mistorneth hem, ne the ordre cominge
fro the poynt of soverein good ne declyneth nat fro his biginninge. But thou 195
mayst seyn, what unreste may ben a
worse confusioun than that gode men han
somtyme adversitee and somtyme prosperitee, and shrewes also now han
thinges that they desiren, and now 200
thinges that they haten ? Whether men
liven now in swich hoolnesse of thoght,
(*as who seyth, ben men now so wyse*), that
swiche folk as they demen to ben gode
folk or shrewes, that it moste nedes ben 205
that folk ben swiche as they wenen ?
But in this manere the domes of men
discorden, that thilke men that some
folk demen worthy of mede, other folk
demen hem worthy of torment. But lat 210
us graunte, I pose that som man may wel
demen or knowen the gode folk and the
badde ; may he thanne knowen and seen
thilke innereste atempraunce of corages,
as it hath ben wont to be seyd of bodies ; 215
*as who seyth, may a man speken and deter-
minen of atempraunces in corages, as men
were wont to demen or speken of complexiouns and atempraunces of bodies?* Ne
it ne is nat an unlyk miracle, to hem 220
that ne knowen it nat, (*as who seith, but
it is lyke a merveil or a miracle to hem that
ne knowen it nat*), why that swete thinges
ben covenable to some bodies that ben
hole, and to some bodies bittere thinges 225
ben covenable ; and also, why that some
syke folk ben holpen with lighte medicynes, and some folk ben holpen with
sharpe medicynes. But natheles, the
leche that knoweth the manere and the 230
atempraunce of hele and of maladye, ne
merveileth of it no-thing. But what
other thing semeth hele of corages but
bountee and prowesse ? And what other
thing sèmeth maladye *of corages* but 235
vyces ? Who is elles kepere of good or
dryver awey of yvel, but god, governour
and lecher of thoughtes ? The whiche god,
whan he hath biholden from the heye

240 tour of his purveaunce, he knoweth what
is covenable to every wight, and leneth
hem that he wot that is covenable to
hem. Lo, her-of comth and her-of is don
this noble miracle of the ordre destinal,
245 whan god, that al knoweth, doth swiche
thing, of which thing that unknowinge
folk ben astoned. But for to constreine,
*as who seyth, but for to comprehende and
telle* a fewe thinges of the divyne deep-
250 nesse, the whiche that mannes resoun
may understonde, thilke man that thou
wenest to ben right juste and right kepinge of equitee, the contrarie of that
semeth to the divyne purveaunce, that al
255 wot. And Lucan, my familer, telleth
that " the victorious cause lykede to the
goddes, and the cause overcomen lykede
to Catoun." Thanne, what-so-ever thou
mayst seen that is don in this werld
260 unhoped or unwened, certes, it is the
right ordre of thinges ; but, as to thy
wikkede opinioun, it is a confusioun. But
I suppose that som man be so wel
y-thewed, that the divyne jugement and
265 the jugement of mankinde acorden hem
to-gider of him ; but he is so unstedefast
of corage, that, yif any adversitee come
to him, he wol forleten, par-aventure, to
continue innocence, by the whiche he ne
270 may nat with-holden fortune. Thanne
the wyse dispensacioun of god spareth
him, the whiche man adversitee mighte
enpeyren ; for that god wol nat suffren
him to travaile, to whom that travaile
275 nis nat covenable. Another man is parfit
in alle vertues, and is an holy man, and
negh to god, so that the purviaunce of
god wolde demen, that it were a felonye
that he were touched with any adver-
280 sitees ; so that he wol nat suffre that
swich a man be moeved with any bodily
maladye. But so as seyde a philosophre,
the more excellent by me : *he seyde in
Grek*, that " vertues han edified the body
285 of the holy man." And ofte tyme it
bitydeth, that the somme of thinges that
ben to done is taken to governe to gode
folk, for that the malice haboundant of
shrewes sholde ben abated. And god
290 yeveth and departeth to othre folk pros-

peritees and adversitees y-medled to-
hepe, after the qualitee of hir corages, and
remordeth som folk *by adversitee*, for they
ne sholde nat wexen proude by longe
welefulnesse. And other folk he suffreth 295
to ben travailed with harde thinges, for
that they sholden conffermen the vertues
of corage by the usage and exercitacioun
of pacience. And other folk dreden more
than they oughten †that whiche they 300
mighten wel beren ; and somme dispyse
that they mowe nat beren ; and thilke
folk god ledeth in-to experience of him-
self by aspre and sorwful thinges. And
many othre folk han bought honourable 305
renoun of this world by the prys of
glorious deeth. And som men, that ne
mowen nat ben overcomen by torments,
have yeven ensaumple to othre folk, that
vertu may nat ben overcomen by adver- 310
sitees ; and of alle thinges ther nis no
doute, that they ne ben don rightfully
and ordenely, to the profit of hem to
whom we seen thise thinges bityde. For
certes, that adversitee comth somtyme 315
to shrewes, and somtyme that that they
desiren, it comth of thise forseide causes.
And of sorwful thinges *that bityden to
shrewes*, certes, no man ne wondreth ; for
alle men wenen that they han wel de- 320
served it, and that they ben of wikkede
merite ; of whiche shrewes the torment
somtyme agasteth othre to don felonyes,
and somtyme it amendeth hem that
suffren the torments. And the pros- 325
peritee *that is yeven to shrewes* sheweth
a greet argument to gode folk, what thing
they sholde demen of thilke welefulnesse,
the whiche prosperitee men seen ofte
serven to shrewes. In the which thing 330
I trowe that god dispenseth ; for, per-
aventure, the nature of som man is so
overthrowinge *to yvel*, and so uncovenable, that the nedy povertee of his
houshold mighte rather egren him to don 335
felonyes. And to the maladye of him god
putteth remedie, to yeven him richesses.
And som other man biholdeth his conscience defouled with sinnes, and maketh
comparisoun of his fortune and of him- 340
self ; and dredeth, per-aventure, that his

blisfulnesse, of which the usage is joyeful
to him, that the lesinge of thilke blisfulnesse ne be nat sorwful to him ; and
345 therfor he wol chaunge his maneres, and,
for he dredeth to lese his fortune, he forleteth his wikkednesse. To othre folk is
welefulnesse y-yeven unworthily, the
whiche overthroweth hem in-to distruc-
350 cioun that they han deserved. And to som
othre folk is yeven power to punisshen,
for that it shal be cause of *continua-
cioun and* exercysinge to gode folk and
cause of torment to shrewes. For so as
355 ther nis non alyaunce by-twixe gode folk
and shrewes, ne shrewes ne mowen nat
acorden amonges hem-self. And why
nat? For shrewes discorden of hem-self
by hir vyces, the whiche vyces al to-
360 renden hir consciences ; and don ofte
tyme thinges, the whiche thinges, whan
they han don hem, they demen that tho
thinges ne sholden nat han ben don. For
which thing thilke soverein purveaunce
365 hath maked ofte tyme fair miracle ; so
that shrewes han maked shrewes to ben
gode men. For whan that som shrewes
seen that they suffren wrongfully felonyes
of othre shrewes, they wexen eschaufed
370 in-to hate of hem that anoyeden hem, and
retornen to the frut of vertu, whan they
studien to ben unlyk to hem that they
han hated. Certes, only this is the divyne
might, to the whiche might yveles ben
375 thanne gode, whan it useth tho yveles
covenably, and draweth out the effect of
any gode; *as who seyth, that yvel is good
only to the might of god, for the might of god
ordeyneth thilke yvel to good.* For oon
380 ordre embraseth alle thinges, so that
what wight that departeth fro the resoun
of thilke ordre which that is assigned to
him, algates yit he slydeth in-to another
ordre, so that no-thing nis leveful to folye
385 in the reame of the divyne purviaunce ;
*as who seyth, nothing nis with-outen ordi-
naunce in the reame of the divyne purviaunce ;* sin that the right stronge god
governeth alle thinges in this world. For
390 it nis nat leveful to man to comprehenden by wit, ne unfolden by word, alle
the subtil ordinaunces and disposiciouns

of the divyne entente. For only it oughte
suffise to han loked, that god him-self,
maker of alle natures, ordeineth and 395
dresseth alle thinges to gode ; whyl that
he hasteth to with-holden the thinges
that he hath maked in-to his semblaunce,
*that is to seyn, for to with-holden thinges
in-to good, for he him-self is good,* he 400
chaseth out al yvel fro the boundes of his
comunalitee by the ordre of necessitee
destinable. For which it folweth, that
yif thou loke the purviaunce ordeininge
the thinges that men wenen ben out- 405
rageous or haboundant in erthes, thou ne
shalt not seen in no place no-thing of
yvel. But I see now that thou art
charged with the weighte of the questioun, and wery with the lengthe of my 410
resoun ; and that thou abydest som sweetnesse of songe. Tak thanne this draught ;
and whan thou art wel refresshed and
refect, thou shal be more stedefast to stye
in-to heyere questiouns. 415

METRE VI. *Si uis celsi iura tonantis.*

If thou, wys, wilt demen in thy pure
thought the rightes or the lawes of the
heye thonderer, *that is to seyn, of god,* loke
thou and bihold the heightes of the
soverein hevene. There kepen the sterres, 5
by rightful alliaunce of thinges, hir olde
pees. The sonne, y-moeved by his rody
fyr, ne distorbeth nat the colde cercle of
the mone. Ne the sterre y-cleped 'the
Bere,' that enclyneth his ravisshinge 10
courses abouten the soverein heighte of
the worlde, ne the same sterre Ursa nis
never-mo wasshen in the depe westrene
see, ne coveiteth nat to deyen his flaumbes
in the see of the occian, al-thogh he see 15
othre sterres y-plounged in the see. And
Hesperus *the sterre* bodeth and telleth
alwey the late nightes ; and Lucifer *the
sterre* bringeth ayein the clere day. And
thus maketh Love entrechaungeable the 20
perdurable courses ; and thus is discordable bataile y-put out of the contree of
the sterres. This acordaunce atempreth
by evenelyk maneres the elements, that
the moiste thinges, stryvinge with the 25

drye thinges, yeven place by stoundes;
and the colde thinges joynen hem by
feyth to the hote thinges; and that the
lighte fyr aryseth in-to heighte; and the
30 hevy erthes avalen by hir weightes. By
thise same causes the floury yeer yildeth
swote smelles in the firste somer-sesoun
warminge; and the hote somer dryeth
the cornes; and autumpne comth ayein,
35 hevy of apples; and the fletinge reyn
bideweth the winter. This atempraunce
norissheth and bringeth forth al thing
that †bretheth lyf in this world; and
thilke same atempraunce, ravisshinge,
40 hydeth and binimeth, and drencheth
under the laste deeth, alle thinges y-born.
Amonges thise thinges sitteth the heye
maker, king and lord, welle and beginninge, lawe and wys juge, to don equitee;
45 and governeth and enclyneth the brydles
of thinges. And tho thinges that he
stereth to gon by moevinge, he withdraweth and aresteth; and affermeth the
moevable or wandringe thinges. For yif
50 that he ne clepede ayein the right goinge
of thinges, and yif that he ne con-
streinede hem nat eft-sones in-to roundnesses enclynede, the thinges that ben
now ꝑontinued by stable ordinaunce, they
55 sholden departen from hir welle, *that is to
seyn, from hir biginninge*, and faylen, *that
is to seyn, torne in-to nought*.　This is
the comune Love to alle thinges ; and alle
thinges axen to ben holden by the fyn of
60 good. For elles ne mighten they nat
lasten ; yif they ne come nat eft-sones
ayein, by Love retorned, to the cause that
hath yeven hem beinge, *that is to seyn, to
god*.

## Prose VII. *Iamne igitur uides.*

Seestow nat thanne what thing folweth
alle the thinges that I have seyd? '
*Boece*. 'What thing?' quod I.

'Certes,' quod she, 'al-outrely, that alle
5 fortune is good.'　　　'And how may that
be?' quod I.

'Now understand,' quod she, 'so as alle
fortune, whether so it be joyeful fortune
or aspre fortune, is yeven either by cause

of guerdoning or elles of exercysinge of 10
good folk, or elles by cause to punisshen
or elles chastysen shrewes ; thanne is alle
fortune good, the whiche fortune is certein that it be either rightful or elles
profitable.'　　'Forsothe, this is a ful 15
verray resoun,' quod I; 'and yif I consider the purviaunce and the destinee
that thou taughtest me a litel her-biforn,
this sentence is sustened by stedefast
resouns. But yif it lyke unto thee, lat us 20
noumbren hem amonges thilke thinges,
of whiche thou seydest a litel her-biforn,
that they ne were nat able to ben wened
to the poeple.'

'Why so?' quod she.　　'For that the 25
comune word of men,' quod I, 'misuseth
this *maner speche of fortune*, and seyn ofte
tymes that the fortune of som wight is
wikkede.'

'Wiltow thanne,' quod she, 'that I 30
aproche a litel to the wordes of the poeple,
so that it seme nat to hem that I be over-
moche departed as fro the usage of mankinde?'　　'As thou wolt,' quod I.

'Demestow nat,' quod she, 'that al 35
thing that profiteth is good?'　　'Yis,'
quod I.

'And certes, thilke thing that exer-
cyseth or corigeth, profiteth?'　　'I confesse it wel,' quod I.　　　　　　　　　40

'Thanne is it good?' quod she.　'Why
nat?' quod I.

'But this is the fortune,' quod she, 'of
hem that either ben put in vertu and
batailen ayeins aspre thinges, or elles of 45
hem that eschuen and declynen fro vyces
and taken the wey of vertu.'　　'This ne
may I nat denye,' quod I.

'But what seystow of the mery fortune
that is yeven to good folk in guerdoun ? 50
Demeth aught the poeple that it is wikked?'　　'Nay, forsothe,' quod I; 'but
they demen, as it sooth is, that it is right
good.'

'And what seystow of that other for- 55
tune,' quod she, 'that, al-thogh that it be
aspre, and restreineth the shrewes by
rightful torment, weneth aught the
poeple that it be good?'　　'Nay,' quod
I, 'but the poeple demeth that it is most 60

wrecched of alle thinges that may ben thought.'

'War now, and loke wel,' quod she, 'lest that we, in folwinge the opinioun of 65 the poeple, have confessed and concluded thing that is unable to be wened *to the poeple.*' 'What is that,' quod I.

'Certes,' quod she, 'it folweth or comth of thinges that ben graunted, that alle 70 fortune, what-so-ever it be, of hem that ben either in possessioun of vertu, or in the encres of vertu, or elles in the purchasinge of vertu, that thilke fortune is good ; and that alle fortune is right wik- 75 kede to hem that dwellen in shrewednesse ;' *as who seyth, and thus weneth nat the poeple.* 'That is sooth,' quod I, 'albe-it so that no man dar confesse it ne biknowen it.'

80 'Why so?' quod she ; 'for right as the stronge man ne semeth nat to abaissen or disdaignen as ofte tyme as he hereth the noise of the bataile, ne also it ne semeth nat, to the wyse man, to beren it gre- 85 vously, as ofte as he is lad in-to the stryf of fortune. For bothe to that oon man and eek to that other thilke difficultee is the matere ; to that oon man, of encres of his glorious renoun, and to that 90 other man, to confirme his sapience, *that is to seyn, to the aspresnesse of his estat.* For therfore is it called "vertu," for that it susteneth and enforseth, by hise strengthes, that it nis nat overcomen by 95 adversitees. Ne certes, thou that art put in the encres or in the heighte of vertu, ne hast nat comen to fleten with delices, and for to welken in bodily luste ; thou sowest or plauntest a ful egre bataile *in* 100 *thy corage* ayeins every fortune : for that the sorwful fortune ne confounde thee nat, ne that the merye fortune ne corumpe thee nat, occupye the mene by stedefast strengthes. For al that ever is 105 under the mene, or elles al that overpasseth the mene, despyseth welefulnesse (*as who seyth, it is vicious*), and ne hath no mede of his travaile. For it is set in your hand (*as who seyth, it lyth in your power*) 110 what fortune yow is levest, *that is to seyn, good or yvel.* For alle fortune that semeth

sharp or aspre, yif it ne exercyse nat *the gode folk*, ne chastyseth *the wikked folk*, it punissheth.

## METRE VII. *Bella bis quinis operatus annis.*

The wreker Attrides, *that is to seyn, Agamenon,* that wroughte and continuede the batailes by ten yeer, recovered and purgede *in wrekinge,* by the destruccioun of Troye, the loste chaumbres of mariage 5 of his brother ; *this is to seyn, that he, Agamenon, wan ayein Eleyne, that was Menelaus wyf his brother.* In the mene whyle that thilke *Agamenon* desirede to yeven sayles to the Grekissh navye, and 10 boughte ayein the windes by blood, he unclothede him of pitee of fader; and the sory preest yiveth in sacrifyinge the wrecched cuttinge of throte of the doughter ; *that is to seyn, that Agamenon let* 15 *cutten the throte of his doughter by the preest, to maken allyaunce with his goddes, and for to han wind with whiche he mighte wenden to Troye.* Itacus, *that is to seyn, Ulixes,* biwepte his felawes y-lorn, the 20 whiche felawes the ferse Poliphemus, ligginge in his grete cave, hadde freten and dreynt in his empty wombe. But natheles Poliphemus, wood for his blinde visage, yald to Ulixes joye by his sorwful teres ; 25 *that is to seyn, that Ulixes smoot out the eye of Poliphemus that stood in his forehed, for which Ulixes hadde joye, whan he say Poliphemus wepinge and blinde.* Hercules is celebrable for his harde travailes ; 30 he dauntede the proude Centaures, *half hors, half man;* and he birafte the dispoylinge fro the cruel lyoun, *that is to seyn, he slowh the lyoun and rafte him his skin.* He smoot the briddes *that highten* 35 *Arpyes* with certein arwes. He ravisshede apples fro the wakinge dragoun, and his hand was the more hevy for the goldene metal. He drow Cerberus, *the hound of helle,* by his treble cheyne. He, over- 40 comer, as it is seyd, hath put an unmeke lord foddre to his cruel hors ; *this is to seyn, that Hercules slowh Diomedes, and made his hors to freten him.* And he,

45 Hercules, slowh Ydra *the serpent*, and
brende the venim. And Achelous the
flood, defouled in his forhed, dreynte his
shamefast visage in his strondes; *this is
to seyn, that Achelous coude transfigure*
50 *him-self in-to dyverse lyknesses ; and, as he
faught with Hercules, at the laste he tornede
him in-to a bole ; and Hercules brak of oon
of his hornes, and he, for shame, hidde him
in his river.* And he, Hercules, caste
55 adoun Antheus the gyaunt in the
strondes of Libie ; and Cacus apaysede
the wratthes of Evander ; *this is to seyn,
that Hercules slowh the monstre Cacus, and
apaysede with that deeth the wratthe of
60 Evander.* And the bristlede boor markede
with scomes the shuldres of Hercules, the

whiche shuldres the heye cercle of hevene
sholde thriste. And the laste of his labours was, that he sustened the hevene
up-on his nekke unbowed ; and he de-.65
servede eft-sones the hevene, to ben the
prys of his laste travaile.    Goth now
thanne, ye stronge men, ther-as the heye
wey of the grete ensaumple ledeth yow.
O nyce men, why nake ye youre bakkes ? 70
*As who seyth : O ye slowe and delicat men,
why flee ye adversitees, and ne fighten nat
ayeins hem by vertu, to winnen the mede of
the hevene ?* For the erthe, overcomen,
yeveth the sterres' ; *this is to seyn, that,* 75
*whan that erthely lust is overcomen, a man
is maked worthy to the hevene.*

## BOOK V.

### PROSE I. *Dixerat, orationisque
cursum.*

She hadde seyd, and torned the cours
of hir resoun to some othre thinges to ben
treted and to ben y-sped. Thanne seyde
I, 'Certes, rightful is thyn amonestinge
5 and ful digne by auctoritee. But that
thou seidest whylom, that the questioun
of the divyne purviaunce is enlaced with
many other questiouns, I understonde
wel and proeve it by the same thing. But
10 I axe yif that thou wenest that hap be
any thing in any weys ; and, yif thou
wenest that hap be anything, what is
it ?'

Thanne quod she, 'I haste me to yilden
15 and assoilen to thee the dette of my
bihest, and to shewen and opnen the wey,
by which wey thou mayst come ayein to
thy contree. But al-be-it so that the
thinges which that thou axest ben right
20 profitable to knowe, yit ben they diverse
somwhat fro the path of my purpos ; and
it is to douten that thou ne be maked
wery by mis-weyes, so that thou ne mayst
nat suffyce to mesuren the right wey.'
25 'Ne doute thee ther-of nothing,' quod I.

'For, for to knowen thilke thinges to-
gedere, in the whiche thinges I delyte me
greetly, that shal ben to me in stede of
reste ; sin it is nat to douten of the
thinges folwinge, whan every syde of thy 30
disputacioun shal han be stedefast to me
by undoutous feith.'

Thanne seyde she, 'That manere wol
I don thee '; and bigan to speken right
thus.   'Certes,' quod she, 'yif any wight 35
diffinisshe hap in this manere, that is to
seyn, that "hap is bitydinge y-brought
forth by foolish moevinge and by no
knettinge of causes," I conferme that hap
nis right naught in no wyse ; and I deme 40
al-outrely that hap nis, ne dwelleth but
a voice, *as who seith, but an ydel word*,
with-outen any significacioun of thing
submitted to that vois.  For what place
mighte ben left, or dwellinge, to folye 45
and to disordenaunce, sin that god ledeth
and constreineth alle thinges by ordre ?
For this sentence is verray and sooth,
that "nothing ne hath his beinge of
naught" ; to the whiche sentence none 50
of thise olde folk ne withseyde never ;
al-be-it so that they ne understoden ne
meneden it naught by god, prince and

beginnere of werkinge, but they casten
55 [it] as a manere foundement of subject
material, that is to seyn, of the nature of
alle resoun. And yif that any thing is
woxen or comen of no causes, than shal it
seme that thilke thing is comen or woxen
60 of naught; but yif this ne may nat ben
don, thanne is it nat possible, that hap
be any swich thing as I have diffinisshed
a litel heer-biforn.'    'How shal it
thanne be?' quod I.    'Nis ther thanne
65 no-thing that by right may be cleped
either "hap" or elles "aventure of fortune"; or is ther aught, al-be-it so that
it is hid fro the peple, to which these
wordes ben covenable?'

70    'Myn Aristotulis,' quod she, 'in the
book of his Phisik, diffinissheth this thing
by short resoun, and neigh to the sothe.'
'In which manere?' quod I.

'As ofte,' quod she, 'as men doon any
75 thing for grace of any other thing, and
an-other thing than thilke thing that
men entenden to don bitydeth by some
causes, it is cleped "hap." Right as
a man dalf the erthe by cause of tilyinge
80 of the feeld, and founde ther a gobet of
gold bidolven, thanne wenen folk that it
is bifalle by fortunous bitydinge. But,
for sothe, it nis nat of naught, for it hath
his propre causes; of whiche causes the
85 cours unforeseyn and unwar semeth to
han maked hap. For yif the tilyere of
the feld ne dolve nat in the erthe, and yif
the hyder of the gold ne hadde hid the
gold in thilke place, the gold ne hadde
90 nat been founde. Thise ben thanne the
causes of the abregginge of fortuit hap,
the which abregginge of fortuit hap
comth of causes encountringe and flowinge to-gidere to hem-self, and nat by the
95 entencioun of the doer. For neither the
hyder of the gold ne the delver of the
feeld ne understoden nat that the gold
sholde han ben founde; but, as I sayde,
it bitidde and ran to-gidere that he dalf
00 ther-as that other hadde hid the gold.
Now may I thus diffinisshe "hap." Hap
is an unwar bitydinge of causes assembled in thinges that ben don for som
other thing. But thilke ordre, procedinge

by an uneschuable bindinge to-gidere, 105
which that descendeth fro the welle of
purviaunce that ordeineth alle thinges in
hir places and in hir tymes, maketh that
the causes rennen and assemblen to-
gidere.                                      110

METRE I. *Rupis Achemenie scopulis,
ubi uersa sequentum.*

Tigris and Eufrates resolven and
springen of oo welle, in the cragges of the
roche of the contree of Achemenie, ther-as
the fleinge bataile ficcheth hir dartes,
retorned in the brestes of hem that fol- 5
wen hem. And sone after tho same
riveres, Tigris and Eufrates, unjoinen and
departen hir wateres. And yif they
comen to-gideres, and ben assembled and
cleped to-gidere into o cours, thanne 10
moten thilke thinges fleten to-gidere
which that the water of the entre-
chaunginge flood bringeth. The shippes
and the stokkes arraced with the flood
moten assemblen; and the wateres y- 15
medled wrappeth or implyeth many fortunel happes or maneres; the whiche
wandringe happes, natheles, thilke declyninge lownesse of the erthe and the
flowinge ordre of the slydinge water 20
governeth. Right so Fortune, that semeth
as that it fleteth with slaked or un-
governede brydles, it suffereth brydles,
*that is to seyn, to be governed,* and passeth
by thilke lawe, *that is to seyn, by thilke* 25
*divyne ordenaunce.'*

PROSE II. *Animaduerto, inquam.*

'This understonde I wel,' quod I, 'and
I acorde wel that it is right as thou
seyst. But I axe yif ther be any libertee
of free wil in this ordre of causes that
clyven thus to-gidere in hem-self; or 5
elles I wolde witen yif that the destinal
cheyne constreineth the movinges of the
corages of men?'

'Yis,' quod she; 'ther is libertee of
free wil. Ne ther ne was nevere no 10
nature of resoun that it ne hadde libertee

of free wil. For every thing that may
naturely usen resoun, it hath doom by
which it decerneth and demeth every
15 thing; thanne knoweth it, by it-self,
thinges that ben to fleen and thinges
that ben to desiren. And thilke thing
that any wight demeth to ben desired,
that axeth or desireth he; and fleeth
20 thilke thing that he troweth ben to fleen.
Wherfore in alle thinges that resoun is,
in hem also is libertee of willinge and of
nillinge. But I ne ordeyne nat, *as who
seyth, I ne graunte nat*, that this libertee
25 be evene-lyk in alle thinges. Forwhy in
the sovereines devynes substaunces, *that
is to seyn, in spirits*, jugement is more
cleer, and wil nat y-corumped, and might
redy to speden thinges that ben desired.
30 But the soules of men moten nedes be
more free whan they loken hem in the
speculacioun or lokinge of the devyne
thought, and lasse free whan they slyden
in-to the bodies; and yit lasse free whan
35 they ben gadered to-gidere and comprehended in erthely membres. But the
laste servage is whan that they ben yeven
to vyces, and han y-falle from the possessioun of hir propre resoun. For after
40 that they han cast awey hir eyen fro the
light of the sovereyn soothfastnesse to
lowe thinges and derke, anon they derken
by the cloude of ignoraunce and ben
troubled by felonous talents; to the
45 whiche talents whan they aprochen and
asenten, they hepen and encresen the
servage which they han joyned to hem-
self; and in this manere they ben caitifs
fro hir propre libertee. The whiche
50 thinges, nathelesse, the lokinge of the
devyne purviaunce seeth, that alle thinges
biholdeth and seeth fro eterne, and ordeineth hem everich in hir merites as
they ben predestinat : *and it is seyd in
55 Greek, that* "alle thinges he seeth and
alle thinges he hereth."

METRE II. *Puro clarum lumine Phebum.*

Homer with the hony mouth, *that is to
seyn, Homer with the swete ditees*, singeth,
that the sonne is cleer by pure light;

natheles yit ne may it nat, by the infirme
light of his bemes, breken or percen the 5
inwarde entrailes of the erthe, or elles of
the see. So ne seeth nat *god*, maker of
the grete world : to him, that loketh alle
thinges from an heigh, ne withstondeth
nat no thinges by hevinesse of erthe ; ne 10
the night ne withstondeth nat to him by
the blake cloudes. *Thilke god* seeth, in
oo strok of thought, alle thinges that ben,
or weren, or sholle comen ; and *thilke
god*, for he loketh and seeth alle thinges 15
alone, thou mayst seyn that he is the
verray sonne.'

PROSE III. *Tum ego, en, inquam.*

Thanne seyde I, ' now am I confounded
by a more hard doute than I was.'

' What doute is that ? ' quod she. ' For
certes, I conjecte now by whiche thinges
thou art troubled.'                           5

' It semeth,' quod I, ' to repugnen and
to contrarien greetly, that god knoweth
biforn alle thinges, and that ther is any
freedom of libertee. For yif so be that
god loketh alle thinges biforn, ne god ne 10
may nat ben desseived in no manere,
than mot it nedes been, that alle thinges
bityden the whiche that the purviaunce
of god hath seyn biforn to comen. For
which, yif that god knoweth biforn nat 15
only the werkes of men, but also hir
conseiles and hir willes, thanne ne shal
ther be no libertee of arbitre ; ne, certes,
ther ne may be noon other dede, ne no
wil, but thilke which that the divyne 20
purviaunce, that may nat ben desseived,
hath feled biforn. For yif that they
mighten wrythen awey in othre manere
than they ben purveyed, than sholde ther
be no stedefast prescience of thing to 25
comen, but rather an uncertein opinioun ;
the whiche thing to trowen of god, I deme
it felonye and unleveful. Ne I ne proeve
nat thilke same resoun, *as who seyth, I ne
alowe nat, or I ne preyse nat, thilke same* 30
*resoun*, by which that som men wenen
that they mowen assoilen and unknitten
the knotte of this questioun. For, certes,

they seyn that thing nis nat to comen
35 for that the purviaunce of god hath seyn
it biforn that is to comen, but rather the
contrarye, *and that is this* : that, for that
the thing is to comen, therfore ne may it
nat ben hid fro the purviaunce of god ;
40 and in this manere this necessitee slydeth
ayein in-to the contrarye partye : ne it
ne bihoveth nat, nedes, that thinges bityden that ben purvyed, but it bihoveth,
nedes, that thinges that ben to comen
45 ben y-porveyed : but as it were y-travailed,
*as who seyth, that thilke answere procedeth*
*right as thogh men travaileden, or weren*
*bisy to enqueren,* the whiche thing is cause
of the whiche thing :—as, whether the
50 prescience is cause of the necessitee of
thinges to comen, or elles that the
necessitee of thinges to comen is cause
of the purviaunce. But I ne enforce me
nat now to shewen it, that the bitydinge
55 of thinges y-wist biforn is necessarie, how
so or in what manere that the ordre of
causes hath it-self ; al-thogh that it ne
seme nat that the prescience bringe in
necessitee of bitydinge to thinges to
60 comen. For certes, yif that any wight
sitteth, it bihoveth by necessitee that the
opinioun be sooth of him that conjecteth
that he sitteth ; and ayeinward also is it
of the contrarye : yif the opinioun be
65 sooth of any wight for that he sitteth,
it bihoveth by necessitee that he sitte.
Thanne is heer necessitee in that oon
and in that other : for in that oon is
necessitee of sittinge, and, certes, in that
70 other is necessitee of sooth. But therfore
ne sitteth nat a wight, for that the
opinioun of the sittinge is sooth ; but the
opinioun is rather sooth, for that a wight
sitteth biforn. And thus, al-thogh that
75 the cause of the sooth cometh of that
other syde (*as who seyth, that al-thogh the*
*cause of sooth comth of the sitting, and nat*
*of the trewe opinioun*), algates yit is ther
comune necessitee in that oon and in
80 that other. Thus sheweth it, that I may
make semblable skiles of the purviaunce
of god and of thinges to comen. For
althogh that, for that thinges ben to
comen, ther-fore ben they purveyed, nat,

certes, for that they ben purveyed, ther- 85
fore ne bityde they nat. Yit natheles,
bihoveth it by necessitee, that either the
thinges to comen ben y-purveyed of god,
or elles that the thinges that ben purveyed of god bityden. And this thing 90
only suffiseth y-nough to destroyen the
freedom of oure arbitre, *that is to seyn, of*
*oure free wil.* But now, certes, *sheweth it*
*wel, how fer fro the sothe and* how up-so-
doun is this thing that we seyn, that the 95
bitydinge of temporel thinges is cause of
the eterne prescience. But for to wenen
that god purvyeth the thinges to comen
for they ben to comen, what other thing
is it but for to wene that thilke thinges 100
that bitidden whylom ben causes of thilke
soverein purvyaunce *that is in god?* And
her-to *I adde yit this thing* : that, right
as whan that I wot that a thing is, it
bihoveth by necessitee that thilke selve 105
thing be ; and eek, whan I have knowe
that any thing shal bityden, so byhoveth
it by necessitee that thilke thing bityde :
—so folweth it thanne, that the bitydinge
of the thing y-wist biforn ne may nat 110
ben eschued. And at the laste, yif that
any wight wene a thing to ben other
weyes thanne it is, it is nat only unscience, but it is deceivable opinioun ful
diverse and fer fro the sothe of science. 115
Wherfore, yif any thing be so to comen,
that the bitydinge of hit ne be nat certein ne necessarie, who may weten biforn
that thilke thing is to comen ? For right
as science ne may nat ben medled with 120
falsnesse (*as who seyth, that yif I wot*
*a thing, it ne may nat be false that I ne wot*
*it*), right so thilke thing that is conceived
by science ne may nat ben non other
weys than as it is conceived. For that is 125
the cause why that science wanteth lesing
(*as who seyth, why that witinge ne receiveth*
*nat lesinge of that it wot*) ; for it bihoveth,
by necessitee, that every thing be right
as science comprehendeth it to be. What 130
shal I thanne seyn ? In whiche manere
knoweth god biforn the thinges to comen,
yif they ne be nat certein ? For yif that
he deme that they ben to comen uneschewably, and so may be that it is 135

possible that they ne shollen nat comen,
god is deceived. But nat only to trowen
that god is deceived, but for to speke it
with mouth, it is a felonous sinne. But
140 yif that god wot that, right so as thinges
ben *to comen*, so shullen they comen—so
that he wite egaly, *as who seyth, indifferently*, that thinges mowen ben doon or
elles nat y-doon—what is thilke prescience
145 that ne comprehendeth no certein thing
ne stable? Or elles what difference is
ther bitwixe the prescience and thilke
jape-worthy divyninge of Tiresie the
divynour, *that seyde* : "Al that I seye,"
150 quod he, "either it shal be, or elles it
ne shal nat be ?" Or elles how mochel
is worth the devyne prescience more
than the opinioun of mankinde, yif so be
that it demeth the thinges uncertein, as
155 men doon ; of the whiche domes of men
the bitydinge nis nat certein? But yif
so be that non uncertein thing ne may
ben in him that is right certein welle
of alle thinges, thanne is the bitydinge
160 certein of thilke thinges whiche he hath
wist biforn fermely to comen. For which
it folweth, that the freedom of the conseiles and of the werkes of mankind nis
non, sin that the thoght of god, that
165 seeth alle thinges without errour of falsnesse, bindeth and constreineth hem to
a bitydinge *by necessitee*. And yif this
thing be ones y-graunted and received,
*that is to seyn, that ther nis no free wille*,
170 than sheweth it wel, how greet destruccioun and how grete damages ther folwen
of thinges of mankinde. For in ydel ben
ther thanne purposed and bihight medes
to gode folk, and peynes to badde folk,
175 sin that no moevinge of free corage
voluntarie ne hath nat deserved hem,
*that is to seyn, neither mede ne peyne* ; and
it sholde seme thanne, that thilke thing
is alderworst, which that is now demed
180 for aldermost just and most rightful, *that
is to seyn*, that shrewes ben punisshed, or
elles that gode folk ben y-gerdoned : the
whiche folk, sin that hir propre wil ne
sent hem nat to that oon ne to that
185 other, *that is to seyn, neither to gode ne
to harm*, but constreineth hem certein

necessitee of thinges to comen : thanne
ne shollen ther nevere ben, ne nevere
weren, vyce ne vertu, but it sholde rather
ben confusioun of alle desertes medled 190
with-outen discrecioun. And yit *ther folweth an-other inconvenient*, †than whiche
ther ne may ben thoght no more felonous
ne more wikke ; *and that is this*: that, so
as the ordre of thinges is y-led and comth 195
of the purviaunce of god, ne that no-thing
nis leveful to the conseiles of mankinde
(*as who seyth, that men han no power to
doon no-thing, ne wilne no-thing*), than folweth it, that oure vyces ben referred to 200
the maker of alle good (*as who seyth, than
folweth it, that god oughte han the blame of
oure vyces, sin he constreineth us by necessitee to doon vyces*). Thanne is ther no
resoun to hopen *in god*, ne for to preyen 205
*to god* ; for what sholde any wight hopen
*to god*, or why sholde he preyen *to god*,
sin that the ordenaunce of destinee, which
that ne may nat ben inclyned, knitteth
and streineth alle thinges that men may 210
desiren ? Thanne sholde ther be doon
awey thilke only allyaunce bitwixen god
and men, that is to seyn, to hopen and to
preyen. But by the prys of rightwisnesse
and of verray mekenesse we deserven the 215
gerdoun of the divyne grace, which that
is inestimable, *that is to seyn, that it is so
greet, that it ne may nat ben ful y-preysed*.
And this is only the manere, *that is to
seyn, hope and preyeres*, for which it 220
semeth that men mowen speke with god,
and by resoun of supplicacioun be conjoined to thilke cleernesse, that nis nat
aproched no rather or that men beseken
it and impetren it. And yif men wene 225
nat that hope ne preyeres ne han no
strengthes, by the necessitee of thinges
to comen y-received, what thing is ther
thanne by whiche we mowen ben conjoined and clyven to thilke soverein 230
prince of thinges ? For which it bihoveth,
by necessitee, that the linage of mankinde, as thou songe a litel her-biforn,
be departed and unjoined from his welle,
and failen *of his biginninge, that is to* 235
*seyn*, god.

METRE III.  *Quenam discors federa rerum.*

What discordable cause hath to-rent
and unjoined the bindinge, *or the alliaunce,*
of thinges, *that is to seyn, the conjunccioun
of god and man?* Whiche god hath
5 establisshed so greet bataile bitwixen
thise two soothfast or verray thinges,
*that is to seyn, bitwixen the purviaunce of
god and free wil,* that they ben singuler
and devyded, ne that they ne wolen nat
10 be medeled ne coupled to-gidere ? But
ther nis no discord to the verray thinges,
but they clyven, certein, alwey to hem-
self. But the thought of man, confounded
and overthrowen by the dirke membres
15 of the body, ne may nat, by fyr of his
derked looking, *that is to seyn, by the
vigour of his insighte, whyl the soule is in
the body,* knowe the thinne subtil knittinges of thinges. But wherfore enchaufeth
20 it so, by so greet love, to finden thilke
notes of sooth y-covered ; *that is to seyn,
wherfore enchaufeth the thoght of man by
so greet desyr to knowen thilke notificacions
that ben y-hid under the covertoures of
25 sooth ?* Wot it aught thilke thing that it,
anguissous, desireth to knowe ? *As who
seith, nay ; for no man travaileth for to
witen thinges that he wot. And therfore
the texte seith thus :* but who travaileth to
30 witen thinges y-knowe ? And yif that he
ne knoweth hem nat, what seketh thilke
blinde thoght ? What is he that desireth
any thing of which he wot right naught?
*As who seith, who so desireth any thing,*
35 *nedes, somwhat he knoweth of it ; or elles,
he ne coude nat desire it.* Or who may
folwen thinges that ne ben nat y-wist?
*And thogh that he seke tho thinges,* wher
shal he finde hem ? What wight, that is
40 al unconninge and ignoraunt, may
knowen the forme that is y-founde ? But
whan the soule biholdeth and seeth the
heye thoght, *that is to seyn, god,* than
knoweth it to-gidere the somme and the
45 singularitees, *that is to seyn, the principles
and everich by him-self.* But now, whyl
the soule is hid in the cloude and in the
derkenesse of the membres of the body,
it ne hath nat al for-yeten it-self, but

it with-holdeth the somme of thinges, 50
and leseth the singularitees. Thanne,
who-so that seeketh soothnesse, he nis in
neither nother habite ; for he noot nat al,
ne he ne hath nat al foryeten : but yit
him remembreth the somme of thinges 55
that he with-holdeth, and axeth conseil,
and retreteth deepliche thinges y-seyn
biforn, *that is to seyn, the grete somme in
his minde :* so that he mowe adden the
parties that he hath for-yeten to thilke 60
that he hath with-holden.'

PROSE IV.  *Tum illa : Vetus, inquit, hec est.*

Thanne seide she : ' this is,' quod she,
' the olde question of the purviaunce of
god ; and Marcus Tullius, whan he devyded the divynaciouns, *that is to seyn, in
his book that he wroot of divynaciouns,* he 5
moevede gretly this questioun ; and thou
thy-self has y-sought it mochel, and
outrely, and longe ; but yit ne hath it
nat ben determined ne y-sped fermely
and diligently of any of yow. And the 10
cause of this derkenesse and of this difficultee is, for that the moevinge of the
resoun of mankinde ne may nat moeven
to (*that is to seyn, applyen or joinen to*) the
simplicitee of the devyne prescience ; the 15
whiche *simplicitee of the devyne prescience,*
yif that men mighten thinken it in any
maner, *that is to seyn, that yif men mighten
thinken and comprehenden the thinges as
god seeth hem,* thanne ne sholde ther 20
dwellen outrely no doute : the whiche
*resoun and cause of difficultee* I shal assaye
at the laste to shewe and to speden,
whan I have first y-spended and answered
to tho resouns by which thou art y- 25
moeved. For I axe why thou wenest that
thilke resouns of hem that assoilen this
questioun ne ben nat speedful y-nough
ne sufficient : the whiche *solucioun, or
the whiche resoun,* for that it demeth that 30
the prescience nis nat cause of necessitee
to thinges to comen, than ne weneth it
nat that freedom of wil be destorbed or
y-let by prescience. For ne drawestow
nat arguments from elles-where of the 35
necessitee of thinges to-comen (*as who*

seith, *any other wey than thus*) but that
thilke thinges that the prescience wot
biforn ne mowen nat unbityde? *That is*
40 *to seyn, that they moten bityde.* But
thanne, yif that prescience ne putteth
no necessitee to thinges to comen, as
thou thy-self hast confessed it and bi-
knowen a litel her-biforn, what cause or
45 what is it (*as who seith, ther may no cause
be*) by which that the endes voluntarie of
thinges mighten be constreined to certein
bitydinge? For by grace of positioun, so
that thou mowe the betere understonde
50 this that folweth, I pose, *per impossibile,*
that ther be no prescience. Thanne axe
I,' quod she, ' in as mochel as apertineth
to that, sholden thanne thinges that
comen of free wil ben constreined to bi-
55 tyden by necessitee?'    *Boece.* 'Nay,'
quod I.

'Thanne ayeinward,' quod she, 'I suppose that ther be prescience, but that it
ne putteth no necessitee to thinges;
60 thanne trowe I, that thilke selve freedom
of wil shal dwellen al hool and absolut
and unbounden. But thou wolt seyn
that, al-be-it so that prescience nis nat
cause of the necessitee of bitydinge to
65 thinges to comen, algates yit it is a signe
that the thinges ben to bityden by
necessitee. By this manere thanne, al-
thogh the prescience ne hadde never
y-ben, yit *algate or at the leeste weye* it
70 is certein thing, that the endes and
bitydinges of thinges to comen sholden
ben necessarie. For every signe sheweth
and signifyeth only what the thing is,
but it ne maketh nat the thing that it
75 signifyeth. For which it bihoveth first
to shewen, that no-thing ne bitydeth
that it ne bitydeth by necessitee, so that
it may appere that the prescience is signe
of this necessitee ; or elles, yif ther nere
80 no necessitee, certes, thilke prescience
ne mighte nat be signe of thing that nis
nat. But certes, it is now certein that
the proeve of this, y-sustened by stidefast
resoun, ne shal nat ben lad ne proeved
85 by signes ne by arguments y-taken fro
with-oute, but by causes covenable and
necessarie. But *thou mayst seyn,* how

may it be that the thinges ne bityden
nat that ben y-purveyed to comen? But,
90 certes, right as we trowen that tho
thinges which that the purviance wot
biforn to comen ne ben nat to bityden ;
but that ne sholden we nat demen ; but
rather, al-thogh that they shal bityden,
95 yit ne have they no necessitee of hir
kinde to bityden. And this maystow
lightly aperceiven by this that I shal
seyn. For we seen many thinges whan
they ben don biforn oure eyen, right as
100 men seen the cartere worken in the
torninge or atempringe or adressinge of
hise cartes or charietes. And by this
manere (*as who seith, maystow understonde*)
of alle othere *workmen.* Is ther thanne
105 any necessitee, *as who seith, in oure
lokinge,* that constreineth or compelleth
any of thilke thinges to ben don so?'
*Boece.* 'Nay,' quod I ; 'for in ydel and
in veyn were al the effect of craft, yif
110 that alle thinges weren moeved by constreininge ;' *that is to seyn, by constreininge
of oure eyen or of oure sight.*

'The thinges thanne,' quod she, ' that,
whan men doon hem, ne han no neces-
115 sitee that men doon hem, eek tho same
thinges, first or they ben doon, they ben
to comen with-oute necessitee. For-why
ther ben somme thinges to bityden, of
which the endes and the bitydinges of
120 hem ben absolut and quit of alle necessitee. For certes, I ne trowe nat that
any man wolde seyn this : that tho
thinges that men doon now, that they
ne weren to bityden first or they weren
125 y-doon ; and thilke same thinges, al-
thogh that men had y-wist hem biforn,
yit they han free bitydinges. For right
as science of thinges present ne bringeth
in no necessitee to thinges that men
130 doon, right so the prescience of thinges
to comen ne bringeth in no necessitee to
thinges to bityden. But thou mayst seyn,
that of thilke same it is y-douted, as
whether that of thilke thinges that ne
135 han non issues and bitydinges necessaries,
yif ther-of may ben any prescience ; for
certes, they semen to discorden. For
thou wenest that, yif that thinges ben

y-seyn biforn, that necessitee folweth 140 hem; and yif necessitee faileth hem, they ne mighten nat ben wist biforn, and that no-thing ne may ben comprehended by science but certein; and yif tho thinges that ne han no certein bi- 145 tydinges ben purveyed as certein, it sholde ben dirknesse of opinioun, nat soothfastnesse of science. And thou wenest that it be diverse fro the hoolnesse of science that any man sholde 150 deme a thing to ben other-weys thanne it is it-self. And the cause of this erroure is, that of alle the thinges that every wight hath y-knowe, they wenen that tho thinges been y-knowe al-oonly by the 155 strengthe and by the nature of the thinges that ben y-wist or y-knowe; and it is al the contrarie. For al that ever is y-knowe, it is rather comprehended and knowen, nat after his strengthe and 160 his nature, but after the facultee, *that is to seyn, the power and the nature,* of hem that knowen. And, for that this thing shal mowen shewen by a short ensaumple: the same roundnesse of a body, other- 165 weys the sighte of the eye knoweth it, and other-weyes the touchinge. The lokinge, by castinge of his bemes, waiteth and seeth from afer al the body to-gidere, with-oute moevinge of it-self; but the 170 touchinge clyveth and conjoineth to the rounde body, and moeveth aboute the environinge, and comprehendeth by parties the roundnesse. And the man him-self, other-weys wit biholdeth him, 175 and other-weys imaginacioun, and otherweys resoun, and other-weys intelligence. For the wit comprehendeth withouteforth the figure of the body of the man that is establissed in the matere subject; 180 but the imaginacioun comprehendeth only the figure withoute the matere. Resoun surmounteth imaginacioun, and comprehendeth by universal lokinge the comune spece that is in the singuler 185 peces. But the eye of intelligence is heyere; for it surmounteth the environinge of the universitee, and looketh, over that, by pure subtilitee of thoght, thilke same simple forme *of man that is per-*

*durably in the divyne thoght.* In whiche 190 this oughte greetly to ben considered, that the heyeste strengthe to comprehenden thinges enbraseth and contieneth the lowere strengthe; but the lowere strengthe ne aryseth nat in no manere 195 to heyere strengthe. For wit ne may no-thing comprehende out of matere, ne the imaginacioun ne loketh nat the universels speces, ne resoun taketh nat the simple forme *so as intelligence taketh it*; 200 but intelligence, that looketh al aboven, whan it hath comprehended the forme, it knoweth and demeth alle the thinges that ben under that forme. But *she knoweth hem* in thilke manere in the 205 whiche it comprehendeth thilke same simple forme that ne may never ben knowen to none of that other; *that is to seyn, to none of tho three forseide thinges of the sowle.* For it knoweth the univer- 210 sitee of resoun, and the figure of the imaginacioun, and the sensible material *conceived by wit*; ne it ne useth nat nor of resoun ne of imaginacioun ne of wit withoute-forth; but it biholdeth alle 215 thinges, so as I shal seye, by a strok of thought formely, *withoute discours or collacioun.* Certes resoun, whan it looketh any-thing universel, it ne useth nat of imaginacioun, nor of witte, and algates 220 yit it comprehendeth the thinges imaginable and sensible; for resoun is she that diffinisseth the universel of hir conseyte right thus :—man is a resonable twofoted beest. And how so that this 225 knowinge is universel, yet nis ther no wight that ne woot wel that a man is a thing imaginable and sensible; and this same considereth wel resoun; but that nis nat by imaginacioun nor by wit, 230 but it looketh it by a resonable concepcioun. Also imaginacioun, al-be-it so that it taketh of wit the beginninges to seen and to formen the figures, algates, althogh that wit ne were nat present, yit 235 it environeth and comprehendeth alle thinges sensible; nat by resoun sensible of deminge, but by resoun imaginatif. Seestow nat thanne that alle the thinges, in knowinge, usen more of hir facultee 240

or of hir power than *they doon of the faculteee or power* of thinges that ben y-knowe? Ne that nis nat wrong; for so as every jugement is the dede or doinge
245 of him that demeth, it bihoveth that every wight performe the werk and his entencioun, nat of foreine power, but of his propre power.

## METRE IV. *Quondam porticus attulit.*

The Porche, *that is to seyn, a gate of the town of Athenes ther-as philosophres hadden hir congregacioun to desputen,* thilke Porche broughte som-tyme olde
5 men, ful derke in hir sentences, *that is to seyn, philosophres that highten Stoiciens,* that wenden that images and sensibilitees, *that is to seyn, sensible imaginaciouns, or elles imaginaciouns of sensible*
10 *thinges,* weren empreinted in-to sowles fro bodies withoute-forth; *as who seith, that thilke Stoiciens wenden that the sowle hadde ben naked of it-self, as a mirour or a clene parchemin, so that alle figures*
15 *mosten first comen fro thinges fro withoute-forth in-to sowles, and ben empreinted in-to sowles* : Text : right as we ben wont som-tyme, by a swifte pointel, to ficchen lettres empreinted in the smothenesse or
20 in the pleinnesse of the table of wex *or in parchemin* that ne hath no figure ne note in it. **Glose.** *But now argueth Boece ayeins that opinioun, and seith thus* : But yif the thryvinge sowle ne un-
25 pleyteth no-thing, *that is to seyn, ne doth no-thing,* by his propre moevinges, but suffreth and lyth subgit to tho figures and to tho notes of bodies withoute-forth, and yildeth images ydel and veyn in the
30 manere of a mirour, whennes thryveth thanne or whennes comth thilke knowinge in our sowle, that discerneth and biholdeth alle thinges? And whennes is thilke strengthe that biholdeth the singu-
35 ler thinges; or whennes is the strengthe that devydeth thinges y-knowe; and thilke strengthe that gadereth to-gidere the thinges devyded; and the strengthe that cheseth his entrechaunged wey?

For som-tyme it heveth up the heved, 40 *that is to seyn, that it heveth up the entencioun to right heye thinges* ; and som-tyme it descendeth in-to right lowe thinges. And whan it retorneth in-to him-self, it reproeveth and destroyeth the false 45 thinges by the trewe thinges. Certes, this strengthe is cause more efficient, and mochel more mighty *to seen and to knowe thinges,* than thilke cause that suffreth and receiveth the notes and the 50 figures impressed in maner of matere. Algates the passioun, *that is to seyn, the suffraunce or the wit,* in the quike body, goth biforn, excitinge and moevinge the strengthes of the thought. Right so as 55 whan that cleernesse smyteth the eyen *and moeveth hem to seen,* or right so as vois or soun hurteleth to the eres *and commoeveth hem to herkne,* than is the strengthe of the thought y-moeved and 60 excited, and clepeth forth, to semblable moevinges, the speces that it halt with-inne it-self; and addeth tho speces to the notes and to the thinges withoute-forth, and medleth the images of thinges 65 withoute-forth to tho formes y-hidde with-inne him-self.

## PROSE V. *Quod si in corporibus sentiendis.*

But what yif that in bodies to ben feled, *that is to seyn, in the takinge of knowelechinge of bodily thinges,* and al-be-it so that the qualitees of bodies, that ben objecte fro withoute-forth, moeven 5 and entalenten the instruments of the wittes; and al-be-it so that the passioun of the body, *that is to seyn, the wit or the suffraunce,* goth to-forn the strengthe of the workinge corage, the which passioun 10 or suffraunce clepeth forth the dede of the thoght in him-self, and moeveth and exciteth in this mene whyle the formes that resten withinne-forth; and yif that, in sensible bodies, as I have seyd, our 15 corage nis nat y-taught or empreinted by passioun *to knowe thise thinges,* but demeth and knoweth, of his owne strengthe, the passioun or suffraunce

subject to the body : moche more thanne
tho thinges that ben absolut and quite
fro alle talents or affecciouns of bodies,
*as god or his aungeles,* ne folwen nat in
discerninge thinges object fro withoute-
forth, but they accomplisshen and speden
the dede of hir thoght. By this resoun
thanne ther comen many maner knowinges to dyverse and differinge substaunces. For the wit of the body, the
whiche wit is naked and despoiled of
alle other knowinges, thilke wit comth
to beestes that ne mowen nat moeven
hem-self her and ther, as *oystres and
muscules, and other swiche* shelle-fish of
the see, that clyven and ben norisshed
to roches. But the imaginacioun comth
to remuable beestes, that semen to han
talent to fleen or to desiren any thing.
But resoun is al-only to the linage of
mankinde, right as intelligence is only
[to] the devyne nature : of which it folweth, that thilke knowinge is more worth
than thise othre, sin it knoweth by his
propre nature nat only his subject, *as
who seith, it ne knoweth nat al-only that
apertieneth properly to his knowinge,* but
it knoweth the subjects of alle other
knowinges. But how shal it thanne be,
yif that wit and imaginacioun stryven
ayein resoninge, and seyn, that of thilke
universel thing that resoun weneth to
seen, that it nis right naught? *For wit
and imaginacioun seyn that* that, that is
sensible or imaginable, it ne may nat be
universel. Thanne is either the jugement of resoun sooth, ne that ther nis
nothing sensible ; or elles, for that resoun
wot wel that many thinges ben subject
to wit and to imaginacioun, thanne is
the concepcioun of resoun veyn and false,
which that loketh and comprehendeth
that that is sensible and singuler as
universel. And yif that resoun wolde
answeren ayein to thise two, *that is to
seyn, to witte and to imaginacioun,* and
seyn, that soothly she hir-self, *that is to
seyn, resoun,* loketh and comprehendeth,
by resoun of universalitee, bothe that
that is sensible and that that is imaginable ; and that thilke two, *that is to seyn.*

*wit and imaginacioun,* ne mowen nat
strecchen ne enhansen hem-self to the
knowinge of universalitee, for that the
knowinge of hem ne may exceden ne
surmounte the bodily figures : certes, of
the knowinge of thinges, men oughten
rather yeven credence to the more stedefast and to the more parfit jugement.
In this maner stryvinge thanne, we
that han strengthe of resoninge and of
imagininge and of wit, *that is to seyn,
by resoun and by imaginacioun and by wit,*
we sholde rather preyse the cause of
resoun ; *as who seith, than the cause of
wit and of imaginacioun.*

Semblable thing is it, that the resoun
of mankinde ne weneth nat that the
devyne intelligence bi-holdeth or knoweth thinges to comen, but right as the
resoun of mankinde knoweth hem. For
thou arguest and seyst thus : that yif
it ne seme nat to men that some thinges
han certein and necessarie bitydinges,
they ne mowen nat ben wist biforn certeinly to bityden. And thanne nis ther
no prescience of thilke thinges ; and yif
we trowe that prescience be in thise
thinges, thanne is ther no-thing that it
ne bitydeth by necessitee. But certes,
yif we mighten han the jugement of the
devyne thoght, as we ben parsoneres of
resoun, right so as we han demed that
it behoveth that imaginacioun and wit
be binethe resoun, right so wolde we
demen that it were rightful thing, that
mannes resoun oughte to submitten it-
self and to ben binethe the divyne
thoght. For which, yif that we mowen,
*as who seith, that, yif that we mowen,*
*I counseyle, that* we enhanse us in-to the
heighte of thilke sovereyn intelligence ;
for ther shal resoun wel seen that, that
it ne may nat biholden in it-self. And
certes that is this, in what maner the
prescience of god seeth alle thinges certeins and diffinisshed, al-thogh they ne
han no certein issues or bitydinges ; ne
this is non opinioun, but it is rather the
simplicitee of the sovereyn science, that
nis nat enclosed nor y-shet within none
boundes.

METRE V. *Quam uariis terris animalia permeant figuris.*

The beestes passen by the erthes by ful diverse figures. For som of hem han hir bodies straught and crepen in the dust, and drawen after hem a tras or a foruh
5 y-continued ; *that is to seyn, as nadres or snakes.* And other beestes, by the wandringe lightnesse of hir winges, beten the windes, and over-swimmen the spaces of the longe eyr by moist fleeinge. And other
10 beestes gladen hem-self to diggen hir tras or hir steppes in the erthe with hir goings or with hir feet, and to goon either by the grene feldes, or elles to walken under the wodes. And al-be-it so that thou
15 seest that they alle discorden by diverse formes, algates hir faces, enclined, hevieth hir dulle wittes. Only the linage of man heveth heyeste his heye heved, and stondeth light with his up-right body,
20 and biholdeth the erthes under him. And, but-yif thou, erthely man, wexest yvel out of thy wit, this figure amonesteth thee, that axest the hevene with thy righte visage, and hast areysed thy fore-
25 heved, to beren up a-heigh thy corage ; so that thy thoght ne be nat y-hevied ne put lowe under fote, sin that thy body is so heye areysed.

PROSE VI. *Quoniam igitur, uti paullo ante.*

Therfor thanne, as I have shewed a litel her-biforn, that al thing that is y-wist nis nat knowen by his nature propre, but by the nature of hem that
5 comprehenden it, lat us loke now, in as mochel as it is leveful to us, *as who seith, lat us loke now as we mowen,* which that the estat is of the devyne substaunce ; so that we mowen eek knowen what his
10 science is. The commune jugement of alle creatures resonables thanne is this: that god is eterne. Lat us considere thanne what is eternitee ; for certes that shal shewen us to-gidere the devyne
15 nature and the devyne science. Eternitee, thanne, is parfit possessioun and al-

togidere of lyf interminable ; and that sheweth more cleerly by the comparisoun or the collacioun of temporel thinges. For al thing that liveth in tyme it is present, and procedeth fro preterits in-to 2 futures, *that is to seyn, fro tyme passed in-to tyme cominge ;* ne ther nis no-thing establisshed in tyme that may embracen to-gider al the space of his lyf. For certes, yit ne hath it taken the tyme of 2 to-morwe, and it hath lost the tyme of yisterday. And certes, in the lyf of this day, ye ne liven no more but right as in the moevable and transitorie moment. Thanne thilke thing that suffreth tem- 3 porel condicioun, al-thogh that it never bigan to be, ne thogh it never cese for to be, as Aristotle demed of the world, and al-thogh that the lyf of it be strecched with infinitee of tyme, yit algates nis 3 it no swich thing that men mighten trowen by right that it is eterne. For al-thogh that it comprehende and embrace the space of lyf infinit, yit algates ne embraceth it nat the space of the lyf 4 al-togider ; for it ne hath nat the futures that ne ben nat yit, *ne it ne hath no lenger the preterits that ben y-doon or y-passed.* But thilke thing thanne, that hath and comprehendeth to-gider al the plentee of 4 the lyf interminable, to whom ther ne faileth naught of the future, and to whom ther nis naught of the preterit escaped nor y-passed, thilke same is y-witnessed and y-proeved by right to ben eterne. And 5 it bihoveth by necessitee that thilke thing be al-wey present to him-self, and compotent ; *as who seith, al-wey present to him-self, and so mighty that al be right at his plesaunce ;* and that he have al present 5 the infinitee of the moevable tyme. Wher-for som men trowen wrongfully that, whan they heren that it semede to Plato that this world ne hadde never beginninge of tyme, ne that it never 6 shal han failinge, they wenen in this maner that this world be maked coeterne with his maker ; *as who seith, they wene that this world and god ben maked togider eterne, and that is a wrongful weninge.* 6 For other thing is it to ben y-lad by lyf interminable, as Plato graunted to the world, and other thing is it to embrace to-gider al the present of the lyf interminable, the whiche thing it is cleer and manifest that it is propre to the devyne thoght.

Ne it ne sholde nat semen to us, that god is elder thanne thinges that ben y-maked by quantitee of tyme, but rather by the propretee of his simple nature. For this ilke infinit moevinge of temporel thinges folweth this presentarie estat of lyf unmoevable ; and so as it ne may nat countrefeten it ne feynen it ne be evenlyke to it for the inmoevabletee, *that is to seyn, that is in the eternitee of god*, it faileth and falleth in-to moevinge fro the simplicitee of the presence *of god*, and disencreseth in-to the infinit quantitee of future and of preterit : and so as it ne may nat han to-gider al the plentee of the lyf, algates yit, for as moche as it ne ceseth never for to ben in som maner, it semeth som-del to us, that it folweth and resembleth thilke thing that it ne may nat atayne to ne fulfillen, and bindeth it-self to som maner presence of this litel and swifte moment : the which *presence of this litel and swifte moment*, for that it bereth a maner image or lyknesse of the ay-dwellinge presence *of god*, it graunteth, to swiche maner thinges as it bitydeth to, that it semeth hem as thise thinges *han y-ben, and* ben.

And, for that *the presence of swich litel moment* ne may nat dwelle, ther-for it ravisshed and took the infinit wey of tyme, *that is to seyn, by successioun* ; and by this maner is it y-doon, for that it sholde continue the lyf in goinge, of the whiche lyf it ne mighte nat enbrace the plentee in dwellinge. And for-thy, yif we wollen putten worthy names to thinges, and folwen Plato, lat us seye thanne soothly, that god is eterne, and the world is perpetuel. Thanne, sin that every jugement knoweth and comprehendeth by his owne nature thinges that ben subject un-to him, ther is soothly to god, al-weys, an eterne and presentarie estat ; and the science of him, that over-passeth

al temporel moevement, dwelleth in the simplicitee of his presence, and embraceth and considereth alle the infinit spaces of 120 tymes, preterits and futures, and loketh, in his simple knowinge, alle thinges *of preterit* right as they weren y-doon presently right now. Yif thou wolt thanne thenken and avyse the prescience, by 125 which it knoweth alle thinges, thou ne shal nat demen it as prescience of thinges to comen, but thou shalt demen it more rightfully that it is science of presence or of instaunce, that never ne faileth. For 130 which it nis nat y-cleped "previdence," but it sholde rather ben cleped "purviaunce," that is establisshed ful fer fro right lowe thinges, and biholdeth from a-fer alle thinges, right as it were fro the 135 heye heighte of thinges. Why axestow thanne, or why desputestow thanne, that thilke thinges ben doon by necessitee whiche that ben y-seyn and knowen by the devyne sighte, sin that, forsothe, men 140 ne maken nat thilke thinges necessarie which that they seen ben y-doon in hir sighte ? For addeth thy biholdinge any necessitee to thilke thinges that thou biholdest presente ? ' 'Nay,' quod I. 145

*Philosophie.* 'Certes, thanne, if men mighte maken any digne comparisoun or collacioun of the presence devyne and of the presence of mankinde, right so as ye seen some thinges in this temporel pre- 150 sent, right so seeth god alle thinges by his eterne present. Wher-fore this devyne prescience ne chaungeth nat the nature ne the propretee of thinges, but biholdeth swiche thinges present to him- 155 ward as they shullen bityde to yow-ward in tyme to comen. Ne it confoundeth nat the jugement of thinges ; but by o sighte of his thought, he knoweth the thinges to comen, as wel necessarie as nat 160 necessarie. Right so as whan ye seen to-gider a man walken on the erthe and the sonne arysen in the hevene, al-be-it so that ye seen and biholden that oon and that other to-gider, yit natheles ye demen 165 and discernen that that oon is voluntarie and that other necessarie. Right so thanne the devyne lookinge, biholdinge

alle thinges under him, ne troubleth nat
170 the qualitee of thinges that ben certeinly
present to him-ward ; but, as to the condicioun of tyme, forsothe, they ben
future. For which it folweth, that this
nis noon opinioun, but rather a stedefast
175 knowinge, y-strengthed by soothnesse,
that, whanne that god knoweth anything
to be, he ne unwot nat that thilke thing
wanteth necessitee to be ; *this is to seyn,
that, whan that god knoweth any thing to
180 bityde, he wot wel that it ne hath no necessitee to bityde.* And yif thou seyst heer,
that thilke thing that god seeth to
bityde, it ne may nat unbityde (*as who
seith, it mot bityde*), and thilke thing that
185 ne may nat unbityde it mot bityde by
necessitee, and that thou streyne me by
this name of necessitee : certes, I wol wel
confessen and biknowe a thing of ful sad
trouthe, but unnethe shal ther any wight
190 mowe *seen it or* come ther-to, but-yif that
he be biholder of the devyne thoght. For
I wol answeren thee thus : that thilke
thing that is future, whan it is referred
to the devyne knowinge, thanne is it
195 necessarie ; but certes, whan it is understonden in his owne kinde, men seen
it is outrely free, and absolut *fro alle
necessitee.*

For certes, ther ben two maneres of
200 necessitee. That oon necessitee is simple,
as thus : that it bihoveth by necessitee,
that alle men be mortal *or deedly.*
Another necessitee is conditionel, as thus :
yif thou wost that a man walketh, it
205 bihoveth by necessitee that he walke.
Thilke thing thanne that any wight hath
y-knowe to be, it ne may ben non other
weyes thanne he knoweth it to be. But
this condicioun ne draweth nat with hir
210 thilke necessitee simple. For certes, this
necessitee *conditionel,* the propre nature
of it ne maketh it nat, but the adjeccioun
of the condicioun *maketh it.* For no necessitee ne constreyneth a man to gon,
215 that goth by his propre wil; al-be-it so
that, whan he goth, that it is necessarie
that he goth. Right on this same maner
thanne, yif that the purviaunce of god
seeth any thing present, than mot thilke

thing ben by necessitee, al-thogh that it
ne have no necessitee of his owne nature.
But certes, the futures that bityden by freedom of arbitre, god seeth hem alle to-gider
present. Thise thinges thanne, yif they
ben referred to the devyne sighte, thanne
ben they maked necessarie by the condicioun of the devyne knowinge. But
certes, yif thilke thinges be considered by
hem-self, they ben absolut *of necessitee,*
and ne forleten nat ne cesen nat of the
libertee of hir owne nature. Thanne,
certes, with-oute doute, alle the thinges
shollen ben doon which that god wot
biforn that they ben to comen. But som
of hem comen and bityden of free arbitre
*or of free wille,* that, al-be-it so that they
bityden, yit algates ne lese they nat hir
propre nature in beinge; by the which
first, or that they weren y-doon, they
hadden power nat to han bitid.' *Boece.*
'What is this to seyn thanne,' quod I,
'that thinges ne ben nat necessarie *by hir
propre nature,* so as they comen in alle
maneres in the lyknesse of necessitee by
the condicioun of the devyne science ?'

'This is the difference,' quod she ; 'that
tho thinges that I purposede thee a litel
heer-biforn, that is to seyn, the sonne
arysinge and the man walkinge, that,
ther-whyles that thilke thinges been y-
doon, they ne mighte nat ben undoon ;
natheles, that oon of hem, or it was
y-doon, it bihoved by necessitee that it
was y-doon, but nat that other. Right so
*is it here,* that the thinges that god hath
present, with-oute doute they shollen
been. But som of hem descendeth of the
nature of thinges, *as the sonne arysinge ;*
and som descendeth of the power of the
doeres, *as the man walkinge.* Thanne
seide I no wrong, that yif these thinges
ben referred to the devyne knowinge,
thanne ben they necessarie ; and yif they
ben considered by hem-self, thanne ben
they absolut fro the bond of necessitee.
Right so as alle thinges that apereth or
sheweth to the wittes, yif thou referre it
to resoun, it is universel ; and yif thou
referre it or loke it to it-self, than is it
singuler. But now, yif thou seyst thus,

that yif it be in my power to chaunge my purpos, than shal I voide the purviaunce of god, whan that, peraventure, I shal han chaunged the thinges that he knoweth biforn, thanne shal I answere thee thus. Certes, thou mayst wel chaunge thy purpos; but, for as mochel as the present soothnesse of the devyne purviaunce biholdeth that thou mayst chaunge thy purpos, and whether thou wolt chaunge it or no, and whiderward that thou torne it, thou ne mayst nat eschuen the devyne prescience; right as thou ne mayst nat fleen the sighte of the presente eye, al-though that thou torne thy-self by thy free wil in-to dyverse acciouns. But thou mayst seyn ayein: "How shal it thanne be? Shal nat the devyne science be chaunged by my disposicioun, whan that I wol o thing now, and now another? And thilke prescience, ne semeth it nat to entrechaunge stoundes of knowinge;"' *as who seith, ne shal it nat seme to us, that the devyne prescience entrechaungeth hise dyverse stoundes of knowinge, so that it knowe sum-tyme o thing and sum-tyme the contrarie of that thing?* 'No, forsothe,' *quod I.*

*Philosophie.* 'For the devyne sighte renneth to-forn and seeth alle futures, and clepeth hem ayein, and retorneth hem to the presence of his propre knowinge; ne he ne entrechaungeth nat, so as thou wenest, the stoundes of forknowinge, as now this, now that; but he aydwellinge comth biforn, and embraceth at o strook alle thy mutaciouns. And this presence to comprehenden and to seen alle thinges, god ne hath nat taken it of the bitydinge of thinges to come, but of his propre simplicitee. And her-by is assoiled thilke thing that thou puttest a litel her-biforn, *that is to seyn,* that it is unworthy thing to seyn, that our futures yeven cause of the science of god. For 315 certes, this strengthe of the devyne science, which that embraceth alle thinges by his presentarie knowinge, establissheth maner to alle thinges, and it ne oweth naught to latter thinges; and 320 sin that these thinges ben thus, *that is to seyn, sin that necessitee nis nat in thinges by the devyne prescience,* than is ther freedom of arbitre, that dwelleth hool and unwemmed to mortal men. Ne the lawes ne 325 purposen nat wikkedly medes and peynes to the willinges of men that ben unbounden and quite of alle necessitee. And god, biholder and for-witer of alle thinges, dwelleth above; and the present eternitee 330 of his sighte renneth alwey with the dyverse qualitee of oure dedes, dispensinge and ordeyninge medes to goode men, and torments to wikked men. Ne in ydel ne in veyn ne ben ther nat put in god 335 hope and preyeres, that ne mowen nat ben unspeedful ne with-oute effect, whan they ben rightful. Withstond thanne and eschue thou vyces; worshipe and love thou virtues; areys thy corage to right- 340 ful hopes; yilde thou humble preyeres a-heigh. Gret necessitee of prowesse and vertu is encharged and commaunded to yow, yif ye nil nat dissimulen; sin that ye worken and doon, *that is to seyn,* 345 *your dedes or your workes,* biforn the eyen of the juge that seeth *and demeth* alle thinges.' *To whom be glorye and worshipe by infinit tymes.* AMEN.

# TROILUS AND CRISEYDE.

## BOOK I.

1. THE double sorwe of Troilus to tellen,
That was the king Priamus sone of
    Troye,
In lovinge, how his aventures fellen
Fro wo to wele, and after out of joye,
My purpos is, er that I parte fro ye.      5
Thesiphone, thou help me for t'endyte
Thise woful vers, that wepen as I wryte !

2. To thee clepe I, thou goddesse of tor-
    ment,
Thou cruel Furie, sorwing ever in peyne ;
Help me, that am the sorwful instrument
That helpeth lovers, as I can, to pleyne !
For wel sit it, the sothe for to seyne,     12
A woful wight to han a drery fere,
And, to a sorwful tale, a sory chere.

3. For I, that god of Loves servaunts serve,
Ne dar to Love, for myn unlyklinesse,    16
Preyen for speed, al sholde I therfor
    sterve,
So fer am I fro his help in derknesse ;
But nathelees, if this may doon gladnesse
To any lover, and his cause avayle,       20
Have he my thank, and myn be this tra-
    vayle !

4. But ye loveres, that bathen in glad-
    nesse,
If any drope of pitee in yow be,
Remembreth yow on passed hevinesse
That ye han felt, and on the adversitee   25
Of othere folk, and thenketh how that ye
Han felt that Love dorste yow displese ;
Or ye han wonne him with to greet an ese.

5. And preyeth for hem that ben in the cas
Of Troilus, as ye may after here,         30
That love hem bringe in hevene to solas,
And eek for me preyeth to god so dere,
That I have might to shewe, in som
    manere,
Swich peyne and wo as Loves folk endure,
In Troilus unsely aventure.               35

6. And biddeth eek for hem that been
    despeyred
In love, that never nil recovered be,
And eek for hem that falsly been apeyred
Thorugh wikked tonges, be it he or she ;
Thus biddeth god, for his benignitee,     40
To graunte hem sone out of this world to
    pace,
That been despeyred out of Loves grace.

7. And biddeth eek for hem that been at
    ese,
That god hem graunte ay good perseve-
    raunce,
And sende hem might hir ladies so to
    plese,                                 45
That it to Love be worship and plesaunce.
For so hope I my soule best avaunce,
To preye for hem that Loves servaunts be,
And wryte hir wo, and live in charitee.

8. And for to have of hem compassioun 50
As though I were hir owene brother dere.
Now herkeneth with a gode entencioun,
For now wol I gon streight to my matere,
In whiche ye may the double sorwes here

Of Troilus, in loving of Criseyde,    55
And how that she forsook him er she
    deyde.

—◦◦—

9. It is wel wist, how that the Grekes
    stronge
In armes with a thousand shippes wente
To Troye-wardes, and the citee longe
Assegeden neigh ten yeer er they stente, 60
And, in diverse wyse and oon entente,
The ravisshing to wreken of Eleyne,
By Paris doon, they wroughten al hir
    peyne.

10. Now fil it so, that in the toun ther was
Dwellinge a lord of greet auctoritee,    65
A gret devyn that cleped was Calkas,
That in science so expert was, that he
Knew wel that Troye sholde destroyed be,
By answere of his god, that highte thus,
Daun Phebus or Apollo Delphicus.    70

11. So whan this Calkas knew by calcu-
    linge,
And eek by answere of this Appollo,
That Grekes sholden swich a peple bringe,
Thorugh which that Troye moste been
    for-do,
He caste anoon out of the toun to go ;  75
For wel wiste he, by sort, that Troye
    sholde
Destroyed been, ye, wolde who-so nolde.

12. For which, for to departen softely
Took purpos ful this forknowinge wyse,
And to the Grekes ost ful prively    80
He stal anoon ; and they, in curteys wyse,
Him deden bothe worship and servyse,
In trust that he hath conning hem to rede
In every peril which that is to drede

13. The noyse up roos, whan it was first
    aspyed,    85
Thorugh al the toun, and generally was
    spoken,
That Calkas traytor fled was, and allyed
With hem of Grece ; and casten to ben
    wroken
On him that falsly hadde his feith so
    broken ;
And seyden, he and al his kin at ones  90
Ben worthy for to brennen, fel and bones.

14. Now hadde Calkas left, in this mes-
    chaunce,
Al unwist of this false and wikked dede,
His doughter, which that was in gret
    penaunce,
For of hir lyf she was ful sore in drede,  95
As she that niste what was best to rede ;
For bothe a widowe was she, and allone
Of any freend, to whom she dorste hir
    mone.

15. Criseyde was this lady name a-right ;
As to my dome, in al Troyes citee    100
Nas noon so fair, for passing every wight
So aungellyk was hir natyf beautee,
That lyk a thing inmortal semed she,
As doth an hevenish parfit creature,
That doun were sent in scorning of
    nature.    105

16. This lady, which that al-day herde at
    ere
Hir fadres shame, his falsnesse and
    tresoun,
Wel nigh out of hir wit for sorwe and fere,
In widewes habit large of samit broun,
On knees she fil biforn Ector a-doun ;  110
With pitous voys, and tendrely wepinge,
His mercy bad, hir-selven excusinge.

17. Now was this Ector pitous of nature,
And saw that she was sorwfully bigoon,
And that she was so fair a creature ;  115
Of his goodnesse he gladed hir anoon,
And seyde, 'lat your fadres treson goon
Forth with mischaunce, and ye your-self,
    in joye,
Dwelleth with us, whyl you good list, in
    Troye.

18. And al th'onour that men may doon
    yow have,    120
As ferforth as your fader dwelled here,
Ye shul han, and your body shal men save,
As fer as I may ought enquere or here.'
And she him thonked with ful humble
    chere,
And ofter wolde, and it hadde ben his
    wille,    125
And took hir leve, and hoom, and held
    hir stille.

19. And in hir hous she abood with swich
  meynee
As to hir honour nede was to holde ;
And whyl she was dwellinge in that citee,
Kepte hir estat, and bothe of yonge and
  olde         130
Ful wel beloved, and wel men of hir tolde.
But whether that she children hadde or
  noon,
I rede it nought ; therfore I lete it goon.

20. The thinges fellen, as they doon of
  werre,
Bitwixen hem of Troye and Grekes
  ofte ;         135
For som day boughten they of Troye it
  derre,
And eft the Grekes founden no thing softe
The folk of Troye ; and thus fortune on-
  lofte,
And under eft, gan hem to wheelen bothe
After hir cours, ay whyl they were wrothe.

21. But how this toun com to destruc-
  cioun         141
Ne falleth nought to purpos me to telle ;
For it were here a long disgressioun
Fro my matere, and yow to longe dwelle.
But the Troyane gestes, as they felle,  145
In Omer, or in Dares, or in Dyte,
Who-so that can, may rede hem as they
  wryte.

22. But though that Grekes hem of Troye
  shetten,
And hir citee bisegede al a-boute,
Hir olde usage wolde they not letten,  150
As for to honoure hir goddes ful devoute ;
But aldermost in honour, out of doute,
They hadde a relik hight Palladion,
That was hir trist a-boven everichon.

23. And so bifel, whan comen was the
  tyme         155
Of Aperil, whan clothed is the mede
With newe grene, of lusty Ver the pryme,
And swote smellen floures whyte and rede,
In sondry wyses shewed, as I rede,
The folk of Troye hir observaunces olde,
Palladiones feste for to holde.   161

24. And to the temple, in al hir beste wyse,
In general, ther wente many a wight,

To herknen of Palladion the servyse ;
And namely, so many a lusty knight,  165
So many a lady fresh and mayden bright,
Ful wel arayed, bothe moste and leste,
Ye, bothe for the seson and the feste.

25. Among thise othere folk was Criseyde,
In widewes habite blak ; but natheless,
Right as our firste lettre is now an A,  171
In beautee first so stood she, makeless ;
Hir godly looking gladede al the prees.
Nas never seyn thing to ben preysed derre,
Nor under cloude blak so bright a sterre

26. As was Criseyde, as folk seyde everich-
  oon         176
That hir bihelden in hir blake wede ;
And yet she stood ful lowe and stille
  alloon,
Bihinden othere folk, in litel brede,
And neigh the dore, ay under shames
  drede,         180
Simple of a-tyr, and debonaire of chere,
With ful assured loking and manere.

27. This Troilus, as he was wont to gyde
His yonge knightes, ladde hem up and
  doun
In thilke large temple on every syde,  185
Biholding ay the ladyes of the toun,
Now here, now there, for no devocioun
Hadde he to noon, to reven him his reste,
But gan to preyse and lakken whom him
  leste.

28. And in his walk ful fast he gan to
  wayten         190
If knight or squyer of his companye
Gan for to syke, or lete his eyen bayten
On any woman that he coude aspye ;
He wolde smyle, and holden it folye,
And seye him thus, ' god wot, she slepeth
  softe         195
For love of thee, whan thou tornest ful
  ofte !

29. ' I have herd told, pardieux, of your
  livinge,
Ye lovers, and your lewede observaunces,
And which a labour folk han in winninge
Of love, and, in the keping, which dou-
  taunces ;        200

And whan your preye is lost, wo and
    penaunces ;
O verrey foles ! nyce and blinde be ye ;
Ther nis not oon can war by other be.'

30. And with that word he gan cast up
    the browe,
Ascaunces, 'lo ! is this nought wysly
    spoken ? '              205
At which the god of love gan loken rowe
Right for despyt, and shoop for to ben
    wroken ;
He kidde anoon his bowe nas not broken ;
For sodeynly he hit him at the fulle ;
And yet as proud a pekok can he pulle. 210

31. O blinde world, O blinde entencioun !
How ofte falleth al th'effect contraire
Of surquidrye and foul presumpcioun ;
For caught is proud, and caught is de-
    bonaire.
This Troilus is clomben on the staire, 215
And litel weneth that he moot descenden.
But al-day fayleth thing that foles
    wenden.

32. As proude Bayard ginneth for to
    skippe
Out of the wey, so priketh him his corn,
Til he a lash have of the longe whippe, 220
Than thenketh he, 'though I praunce al
    biforn
First in the trays, ful fat and newe shorn,
Yet am I but an hors, and horses lawe
I moot endure, and with my feres drawe.'

33. So ferde it by this fers and proude
    knight ;            225
Though he a worthy kinges sone were,
And wende no-thing hadde had swiche
    might
Ayens his wil that sholde his herte stere,
Yet with a look his herte wex a-fere,
That he, that now was most in pryde
    above,            230
Wex sodeynly most subget un-to love.

34. For-thy ensample taketh of this man,
Ye wyse, proude, and worthy folkes alle,
To scornen Love, which that so sone can
The freedom of your hertes to him thralle;
For ever it was, and ever it shal bifalle,

That Love is he that alle thing may
    binde ;
For may no man for-do the lawe of kinde.

35. That this be sooth, hath preved and
    doth yit ;         239
For this trowe I ye knowen, alle or some,
Men reden not that folk han gretter wit
Than they that han be most with love
    y-nome ;
And strengest folk ben therwith overcome,
The worthiest and grettest of degree; 244
This was, and is, and yet men shal it see.

36. And trewelich it sit wel to be so ;
For alderwysest han ther-with ben plesed;
And they that han ben aldermost in wo,
With love han been conforted most and
    esed ;         249
And ofte it hath the cruel herte apesed,
And worthy folk maad worthier of name,
And causeth most to dreden vyce and
    shame.

37. Now sith it may not goodly be with-
    stonde,
And is a thing so vertuous in kinde,
Refuseth not to Love for to be bonde, 255
Sin, as him-selven list, he may yow binde.
The yerde is bet that bowen wole and
    winde
Than that that brest ; and therfor I yow
    rede
To folwen him that so wel can yow lede.

38. But for to tellen forth in special  260
As of this kinges sone of which I tolde,
And leten other thing collateral,
Of him thenke I my tale for to holde,
Bothe of his joye, and of his cares colde ;
And al his werk, as touching this matere,
For I it gan, I wil ther-to refere.    266

39. With-inne the temple he wente him
    forth pleyinge,
This Troilus, of every wight aboute,
On this lady and now on that lokinge,
Wher-so she were of toune, or of with-
    oute :         270
And up-on cas bifel, that thorugh a route
His eye perced, and so depe it wente,
Til on Criseyde it smoot, and ther it
    stente.

40. And sodeynly he wex ther-with
   astoned,
And gan hire bet biholde in thrifty wyse :
'O mercy, god!' thoughte he, 'wher
   hastow woned,          276
That art so fair and goodly to devyse?'
Ther-with his herte gan to sprede and
   ryse,
And softe sighed, lest men mighte him
   here,
And caughte a-yein his firste pleyinge
   chere.                   280

41. She nas not with the leste of hir
   stature,
But alle hir limes so wel answeringe
Weren to womanhode, that creature
Was never lasse mannish in seminge. 284
And eek the pure wyse of here meninge
Shewede wel, that men might in hir gesse
Honour, estat, and wommanly noblesse.

42. To Troilus right wonder wel with-alle
Gan for to lyke hir mening and hir
   chere,
Which somdel deynous was, for she leet
   falle                    290
Hir look a lite a-side, in swich manere,
Ascaunces, 'what! may I not stonden
   here?'
And after that hir loking gan she lighte,
That never thoughte him seen so good
   a sighte.

43. And of hir look in him ther gan to
   quiken                   295
So greet desir, and swich affeccioun,
That in his hertes botme gan to stiken
Of hir his fixe and depe impressioun :
And though he erst hadde poured up
   and doun,                299
He was tho glad his hornes in to shrinke ;
Unnethes wiste he how to loke or winke.

44. Lo, he that leet him-selven so kon-
   ninge,
And scorned hem that loves peynes dryen,
Was ful unwar that love hadde his
   dwellinge
With-inne the subtile stremes of hir yën ;
That sodeynly him thoughte he felte
   dyen,                    306

Right with hir look, the spirit in his
   herte ;
Blessed be love, that thus can folk converte !

45. She, this in blak, lykinge to Troilus,
Over alle thing he stood for to biholde ;
Ne his desir, ne wherfor he stood thus,
He neither chere made, ne worde tolde ;
But from a-fer, his maner for to holde,
On other thing his look som-tyme he caste,
And eft on hir, whyl that servyse laste. 315

46. And after this, not fulliche al a-
   whaped,
Out of the temple al esiliche he wente,
Repentinge him that he hadde ever y-
   japed
Of loves folk, lest fully the descente
Of scorn fille on him-self ; but, what he
   mente,                  320
Lest it were wist on any maner syde,
His wo he gan dissimulen and hyde.

47. Whan he was fro the temple thus
   departed,
He streyght anoon un-to his paleys torneth,
Right with hir look thurgh-shoten and
   thurgh-darted,          325
Al feyneth he in lust that he sojorneth ;
And al his chere and speche also he
   borneth ;
And ay, of loves servants every whyle,
Him-self to wrye, at hem he gan to smyle.

48. And seyde, 'lord, so ye live al in lest,
Ye loveres ! for the conningest of yow, 331
That serveth most ententiflich and best,
Him tit as often harm ther-of as prow ;
Your hyre is quit ayein, ye, god wot how !
Nought wel for wel, but scorn for good
   servyse ;               335
In feith, your ordre is ruled in good wyse !

49. In noun-certeyn ben alle your ob-
   servaunces,
But it a sely fewe poyntes be ;
Ne no-thing asketh so grete attendaunces
As doth your lay, and that knowe alle ye ;
But that is not the worste, as mote I thee ;
But, tolde I yow the worste poynt, I leve,
Al seyde I sooth, ye wolden at me greve !

50. But tak this, that ye loveres ofte
  eschuwe,
Or elles doon of good entencioun,  345
Ful ofte thy lady wole it misconstrue,
And deme it harm in hir opinioun ;
And yet if she, for other enchesoun,
Be wrooth, than shalt thou han a groyn
  anoon :
Lord! wel is him that may be of yow oon !'

51. But for al this, whan that he say his
  tyme,  351
He held his pees, non other bote him
  gayned ;
For love bigan his fetheres so to lyme,
That wel unnethe un-to his folk he feyned
That othere besye nedes him destrayned ;
For wo was him, that what to doon he
  niste,  356
But bad his folk to goon wher that hem
  liste.

52. And whan that he in chaumbre was
  allone,
He doun up-on his beddes feet him sette,
And first he gan to syke, and eft to
  grone,  360
And thoughte ay on hir so, with-outen
  lette,
That, as he sat and wook, his spirit mette
That he hir saw a temple, and al the wyse
Right of hir loke, and gan it newe avyse.

53. Thus gan he make a mirour of his
  minde,  365
In which he saugh al hoolly hir figure ;
And that he wel coude in his herte finde,
It was to him a right good aventure
To love swich oon, and if he dide his cure
To serven hir, yet mighte he falle in
  grace,  370
Or elles, for oon of hir servaunts pace.

54. Imagininge that travaille nor grame
Ne mighte, for so goodly oon, be lorn
As she, ne him for his desir ne shame,
Al were it wist, but in prys and up-born
Of alle lovers wel more than biforn ;  376
Thus argumented he in his ginninge,
Ful unavysed of his wo cominge.

55. Thus took he purpos loves craft to
  suwe,
And thoughte he wolde werken prively,

First, to hyden his desir in muwe  381
From every wight y-born, al-outrely,
But he mighte ought recovered be therby ;
Remembring him, that love to wyde y-
  blowe
Yelt bittre fruyt, though swete seed be
  sowe.  385

56. And over al this, yet muchel more he
  thoughte
What for to speke, and what to holden
  inne,
And what to arten hir to love he soughte,
And on a song anoon-right to biginne, 389
And gan loude on his sorwe for to winne ;
For with good hope he gan fully assente
Criseyde for to love, and nought repente.

57. And of his song nought only the
  sentence,
As writ myn autour called Lollius,
But pleynly, save our tonges difference,
I dar wel sayn, in al that Troilus  396
Seyde in his song ; lo ! every word right
  thus
As I shal seyn ; and who-so list it here,
Lo ! next this vers, he may it finden here.

### Cantus Troili.

58. 'If no love is, O god, what fele I so ?
And if love is, what thing and whiche
  is he ?  401
If love be good, from whennes comth my
  wo ?
If it be wikke, a wonder thinketh me,
When every torment and adversitee
That cometh of him, may to me savory
  thinke ;  405
For ay thurst I, the more that I it drinke.

59. And if that at myn owene lust I
  brenne,
Fro whennes cometh my wailing and my
  pleynte ?
If harme agree me, wher-to pleyne I
  thenne ?
I noot, ne why unwery that I feynte. 410
O quike deeth, o swete harm so queynte,
How may of thee in me swich quantitee,
But-if that I consente that it be ?

60. And if that I consente, I wrongfully
Compleyne, y-wis ; thus possed to and fro,

Al stereelees with-inne a boot am I      416
A-mid the see, by-twixen windes two,
That in contrarie stonden ever-mo.
Allas! what is this wonder maladye?  419
For hete of cold, for cold of hete, I dye.'

61. And to the god of love thus seyde he
With pitous voys, ' O lord, now youres is
My spirit, which that oughte youres be.
Yow thanke I, lord, that han me brought
   to this ;
But whether goddesse or womman, y-wis,
She be, I noot, which that ye do me
   serve ;                                    426
But as hir man I wole ay live and sterve.

62. Ye stonden in hire eyen mightily,
As in a place un-to your vertu digne ;
Wherfore, lord, if my servyse or I      430
May lyke yow, so beth to me benigne ;
For myn estat royal here I resigne
In-to hir hond, and with ful humble chere
Bicome hir man, as to my lady dere.'  434

63. In him ne deyned sparen blood royal
The fyr of love, wher-fro god me blesse,
Ne him forbar in no degree, for al
His vertu or his excellent prowesse ;
But held him as his thral lowe in distresse,
And brende him so in sondry wyse ay
   newe,                                      440
That sixty tyme a day he loste his hewe.

64. So muche, day by day, his owene
   thought,
For lust to hir, gan quiken and encrese,
That every other charge he sette at nought ;
For-thy ful ofte, his hote fyr to cese,  445
To seen hir goodly look he gan to prese ;
For ther-by to ben esed wel he wende,
And ay the neer he was, the more he
   brende.

65. For ay the neer the fyr, the hotter is,
This, trowe I, knoweth al this companye.
But were he fer or neer, I dar seye this,
By night or day, for wysdom or folye, 452
His herte, which that is his brestes yë,
Was ay on hir, that fairer was to sene
Than ever was Eleyne or Polixene.    455

66. Eek of the day ther passed nought an
   houre
That to him-self a thousand tyme he seyde,

' Good goodly, to whom serve I and la-
   boure,                                     458
As I best can, now wolde god, Criseyde,
Ye wolden on me rewe er that I deyde !
My dere herte, allas ! myn hele and hewe
And lyf is lost, but ye wole on me rewe.'

67. Alle othere dredes weren from him
   fledde,
Bothe of th'assege and his savacioun ;
Ne in him desyr noon othere fownes
   bredde                                     465
But arguments to this conclusioun,
That she on him wolde han compassioun,
And he to be hir man, whyl he may dure;
Lo, here his lyf, and from the deeth his
   cure !                                     469

68. The sharpe shoures felle of armes preve,
That Ector or his othere bretheren diden,
Ne made him only ther-fore ones meve ;
And yet was he, wher-so men wente or
   riden,
Founde oon the best, and lengest tyme
   abiden                                     474
Ther peril was, and dide eek such travayle
In armes, that to thenke it was mervayle.

69. But for non hate he to the Grekes
   hadde,
Ne also for the rescous of the toun,
Ne made him thus in armes for to madde,
But only, lo, for this conclusioun,      480
To lyken hir the bet for his renoun ;
Fro day to day in armes so he spedde,
That alle the Grekes as the deeth him
   dredde.

70. And fro this forth tho refte him love
   his sleep,
And made his mete his foo ; and eek his
   sorwe                                      485
Gan multiplye, that, who-so toke keep,
It shewed in his hewe, bothe eve and
   morwe ;
Therfor a title he gan him for to borwe
Of other syknesse, lest of him men wende
That the hote fyr of love him brende. 490

71. And seyde, he hadde a fever and ferde
   amis ;
But how it was, certayn, can I not seye,

If that his lady understood not this,
Or feyned hir she niste, oon of the tweye;
But wel I rede that, by no maner weye,
Ne semed it [as] that she of him roughte,
Nor of his peyne, or what-so-ever he
    thoughte.

72. But than fel to this Troylus such wo,
That he was wel neigh wood; for ay his
    drede                                        499
Was this, that she som wight had loved so,
That never of him she wolde have taken
    hede;
For whiche him thoughte he felte his
    herte blede.
Ne of his wo ne dorste he not biginne
To tellen it, for al this world to winne.

73. But whanne he hadde a space fro his
    care,                                        505
Thus to him-self ful ofte he gan to pleyne;
He sayde, ' O fool, now art thou in the
    snare,
That whilom japedest at loves peyne;
Now artow hent, now gnaw thyn owene
    cheyne;
Thou were ay wont eche lovere reprehende
Of thing fro which thou canst thee nat
    defende.                                     511

74. What wole now every lover seyn of
    thee,
If this be wist, but ever in thyn absence
Laughen in scorn, and seyn, " lo, ther
    gooth he,
That is the man of so gret sapience,     515
That held us loveres leest in reverence!
Now, thonked be god, he may goon in the
    daunce
Of hem that Love list febly for to avaunce!

75. But, O thou woful Troilus, god wolde,
Sin thow most loven thurgh thy destinee,
That thow beset were on swich oon that
    sholde                                       521
Knowe al thy wo, al lakkede hir pitee:
But al so cold in love, towardes thee,
Thy lady is, as frost in winter mone,    524
And thou fordoon, as snow in fyr is sone."

76. God wolde I were aryved in the port
Of deeth, to which my sorwe wil me lede!

A, lord, to me it were a greet comfort;
Then were I quit of languisshing in drede.
For by myn hidde sorwe y-blowe on brede
I shal bi-japed been a thousand tyme  531
More than that fool of whos folye men
    ryme.

77. But now help god, and ye, swete, for
    whom
I pleyne, y-caught, ye, never wight so
    faste!                                       534
O mercy, dere herte, and help me from
The deeth, for I, whyl that my lyf may
    laste,
More than my-self wol love yow to my
    laste.
And with som freendly look gladeth me,
    swete,
Though never more thing ye me bi-hete!'

78. This wordes and ful manye an-other to
He spak, and called ever in his com-
    pleynte                                      541
Hir name, for to tellen hir his wo,
Til neigh that he in salte teres dreynte.
Al was for nought, she herde nought his
    pleynte;
And whan that he bithoughte on that
    folye,                                       545
A thousand fold his wo gan multiplye.

79. Bi-wayling in his chambre thus allone,
A freend of his, that called was Pandare,
Com ones in unwar, and herde him grone,
And sey his freend in swich distresse and
    care:                                        550
' Allas !' quod he, ' who causeth al this
    fare?
O mercy, god ! what unhap may this
    mene?
Han now thus sone Grekes maad yow
    lene?

80. Or hastow som remors of conscience,
And art now falle in som devocioun,   555
And waylest for thy sinne and thyn
    offence,
And hast for ferde caught attricioun?
God save hem that bi-seged han our toun,
And so can leye our jolytee on presse,
And bring our lusty folk to holinesse!'

81. These wordes seyde he for the nones
　　alle,　　　　　　　　　　　　561
That with swich thing he mighte him
　　angry maken,
And with an angre don his sorwe falle,
As for the tyme, and his corage awaken ;
But wel he wiste, as fer as tonges spaken,
Ther nas a man of gretter hardinesse 566
Than he, ne more desired worthinesse.

82. 'What cas,' quod Troilus, 'or what
　　aventure
Hath gyded thee to see my languisshinge,
That am refus of every creature?　　570
But for the love of god, at my preyinge,
Go henne a-way, for certes, my deyinge
Wol thee disese, and I mot nedes deye ;
Ther-for go wey, ther is no more to seye.

83. But if thou wene I be thus syk for
　　drede,　　　　　　　　　　　575
It is not so, and ther-for scorne nought ;
Ther is a-nother thing I take of hede
Wel more than ought the Grekes han
　　y-wrought,
Which cause is of my deeth, for sorwe
　　and thought.
But though that I now telle thee it ne
　　leste,　　　　　　　　　　　580
Be thou nought wrooth, I hyde it for the
　　beste.'

84. This Pandare, that neigh malt for wo
　　and routhe,
Ful often seyde, 'allas ! what may this be?
Now freend,' quod he, 'if ever love or
　　trouthe
Hath been, or is, bi-twixen thee and me,
Ne do thou never swiche a crueltee　586
To hyde fro thy freend so greet a care ;
Wostow nought wel that it am I, Pandare?

85. I wole parten with thee al thy peyne,
If it be so I do thee no comfort,　　590
As it is freendes right, sooth for to seyne,
To entreparten wo, as glad desport.
I have, and shal, for trewe or fals report,
In wrong and right y-loved thee al my
　　lyve ;　　　　　　　　　　　594
Hyd not thy wo fro me, but telle it blyve.'

86. Then gan this sorwful Troilus to syke,
And seyde him thus, 'god leve it be my
　　beste

To telle it thee ; for, sith it may thee
　　lyke,
Yet wole I telle it, though myn herte
　　breste ;　　　　　　　　　　599
And wel wot I thou mayst do me no reste.
But lest thow deme I truste not to thee,
Now herkne, freend, for thus it stant with
　　me.

87. Love, a-yeins the which who-so de-
　　fendeth
Him-selven most, him alder-lest avayleth,
With desespeir so sorwfully me offendeth,
That streyght un-to the deeth myn herte
　　sayleth.　　　　　　　　　　606
Ther-to desyr so brenningly me assaylleth,
That to ben slayn it were a gretter joye
To me than king of Grece been and Troye !

88. Suffiseth this, my fulle freend Pandare,
That I have seyd, for now wostow my wo ;
And for the love of god, my colde care 612
So hyd it wel, I telle it never to mo ;
For harmes mighte folwen, mo than two,
If it were wist ; but be thou in gladnesse,
And lat me sterve, unknowe, of my dis-
　　tresse.'　　　　　　　　　　616

89. 'How hastow thus unkindely and
　　longe
Hid this fro me, thou fool?' quod Pan-
　　darus ;
'Paraunter thou might after swich oon
　　longe,
That myn avys anoon may helpen us.' 620
'This were a wonder thing,' quod Troilus,
'Thou coudest never in love thy-selven
　　wisse ;
How devel maystow bringen me to blisse?'

90. 'Ye, Troilus, now herke,' quod Pan-
　　dare,
'Though I be nyce ; it happeth ofte so, 625
That oon that exces doth ful yvele fare
By good counseyl can kepe his freend
　　ther-fro.
I have my-self eek seyn a blind man go
Ther-as he fel that coude loke wyde ;
A fool may eek a wys man ofte gyde. 630

91. A whetston is no kerving instrument,
And yet it maketh sharpe kerving-tolis.

And ther thow woost that I have ought
   miswent,
Eschewe thou that, for swich thing to
   thee scole is ;
Thus ofte wyse men ben war by folis. 635
If thou do so, thy wit is wel biwared ;
By his contrarie is every thing declared.

92. For how might ever sweetnesse have
   be knowe
To him that never tasted bitternesse ?
Ne no man may be inly glad, I trowe, 640
That never was in sorwe or som distresse ;
Eek whyt by blak, by shame eek worthi-
   nesse,
Ech set by other, more for other semeth ;
As men may see ; and so the wyse it
   demeth.

93. Sith thus of two contraries is a lore,
I, that have in love so ofte assayed  646
Grevaunces, oughte conne, and wel the
   more
Counsayllen thee of that thou art amayed.
Eek thee ne oughte nat ben yvel apayed,
Though I desyre with thee for to bere 650
Thyn hevy charge ; it shal the lasse dere.

94. I woot wel that it fareth thus by me
As to thy brother Parys an herdesse,
Which that y-cleped was Oënone,  654
Wroot in a compleynt of hir hevinesse :
Ye sey the lettre that she wroot, y gesse?'
' Nay, never yet, y-wis,' quod Troilus.
' Now,' quod Pandare, ' herkneth ; it was
   thus.—

95. " Phebus, that first fond art of medi-
   cyne,"
Quod she, "and coude in every wightes
   care  660
Remede and reed, by herbes he knew fyne,
Yet to him-self his conninge was ful bare ;
For love hadde him so bounden in a snare,
Al for the doughter of the kinge Admete,
That al his craft ne coude his sorwe
   bete."—  665

96. Right so fare I, unhappily for me ;
I love oon best, and that me smerteth sore ;
And yet, paraunter, can I rede thee,
And not my-self ; repreve me no more. 669
I have no cause, I woot wel, for to sore

As doth an hauk that listeth for to
   pleye,
But to thyn help yet somwhat can I seye.

97. And of o thing right siker maystow be,
That certayn, for to deyen in the peyne,
That I shal never-mo discoveren thee ; 675
Ne, by my trouthe, I kepe nat restreyne
Thee fro thy love, thogh that it were
   Eleyne,
That is thy brotheres wyf, if ich it wiste;
Be what she be, and love hir as thee liste.

98. Therfore, as freend fullich in me
   assure,  680
And tel me plat what is thyn enchesoun,
And final cause of wo that ye endure ;
For douteth no-thing, myn entencioun
Nis nought to yow of reprehencioun
To speke as now, for no wight may
   bireve  685
A man to love, til that him list to leve.

99. And witeth wel, that bothe two ben
   vyces,
Mistrusten alle, or elles alle leve ;
But wel I woot, the mene of it no vyce is,
For for to trusten sum wight is a preve 690
Of trouthe, and for-thy wolde I fayn re-
   meve
Thy wrong conceyte, and do thee som
   wight triste,
Thy wo to telle ; and tel me, if thee liste.

100. The wyse seyth, " wo him that is
   allone,
For, and he falle, he hath noon help to
   ryse ;"  695
And sith thou hast a felawe, tel thy mone;
For this nis not, certeyn, the nexte wyse
To winnen love, as techen us the wyse,
To walwe and wepe as Niobe the quene,
Whos teres yet in marbel been y-sene. 700

101. Lat be thy weping and thy drerinesse,
And lat us lissen wo with other speche ;
So may thy woful tyme seme lesse.
Delyte not in wo thy wo to seche,  704
As doon thise foles that hir sorwes eche
With sorwe, whan they han misaventure,
And listen nought to seche hem other
   cure.

102. Men seyn, "to wrecche is conso-
    lacioun
To have an-other felawe in his peyne ;"
That oughte wel ben our opinioun,    710
For, bothe thou and I, of love we pleyne ;
So ful of sorwe am I, soth for to seyne,
That certeynly no more harde grace
May sitte on me, for-why ther is no
    space.

103. If god wole thou art not agast of me,
Lest J wolde of thy lady thee bigyle,   716
Thow wost thy-self whom that I love,
    pardee,
As I best can, gon sithen longe whyle.
And sith thou wost I do it for no wyle, 719
And sith I am he that thou tristest most,
Tel me sumwhat, sin al my wo thou wost.'

104. Yet Troilus, for al this, no word
    seyde,
But longe he lay as stille as he ded were ;
And after this with sykinge he abreyde,
And to Pandarus voys he lente his ere, 725
And up his eyen caste he, that in fere
Was Pandarus, lest that in frenesye
He sholde falle, or elles sone dye :

105. And cryde ' a-wake ' ful wonderly
    and sharpe ;
' What ? slombrestow as in a lytargye ?
Or artow lyk an asse to the harpe,   731
That hereth soun, whan men the strenges
    plye,
But in his minde of that no melodye
May sinken, him to glade, for that he
So dul is of his bestialitee ?'     735

106. And with that Pandare of his wordes
    stente ;
But Troilus yet him no word answerde,
For-why to telle nas not his entente
To never no man, for whom that he so
    ferde.     739
For it is seyd, ' man maketh ofte a yerde
With which the maker is him-self y-beten
In sondry maner,' as thise wyse treten,

107. And namely, in his counseyl tellinge
That toucheth love that oughte be secree ;
For of him-self it wolde y-nough out-
    springe,     745

But-if that it the bet governed be.
Eek som-tyme it is craft to seme flee
Fro thing which in effect men hunte faste ;
Al this gan Troilus in his herte caste.

108. But nathelees, whan he had herd
    him crye     750
' Awake !' he gan to syke wonder sore,
And seyde, ' freend, though that I stille
    lye,
I am not deef ; now pees, and cry no more ;
For I have herd thy wordes and thy lore ;
But suffre me my mischef to biwayle, 755
For thy proverbes may me nought avayle.

109. Nor other cure canstow noon for me.
Eek I nil not be cured, I wol deye ;
What knowe I of the quene Niobe ?
Lat be thyne olde ensaumples, I thee
    preye ;     760
' No,' quod tho Pandarus, 'therfore I seye,
Swich is delyt of foles to biwepe
Hir wo, but seken bote they ne kepe.

110. Now knowe I that ther reson in thee
    fayleth.
But tel me, if I wiste what she were   765
For whom that thee al this misaunter
    ayleth,
Dorstestow that I tolde hir in hir ere
Thy wo, sith thou darst not thy-self for
    fere,
And hir bisoughte on thee to han som
    routhe ?'
' Why, nay,' quod he, ' by god and by my
    trouthe !'     770

111. ' What ? not as bisily,' quod Pandarus,
' As though myn owene lyf lay on this
    nede ?'
' No, certes, brother,' quod this Troilus.
' And why ?'—' For that thou sholdest
    never spede.'
' Wostow that wel ?'—' Ye, that is out of
    drede,'     775
Quod Troilus, 'for al that ever ye conne,
She nil to noon swich wrecche as I be
    wonne.'

112. Quod Pandarus, ' allas ! what may
    this be,
That thou despeyred art thus causelees ?

What? liveth not thy lady? *benedicite !* 780
How wostow so that thou art gracelees?
Swich yvel is not alwey botelees.
Why, put not impossible thus thy cure,
Sin thing to come is ofte in aventure.

113. I graunte wel that thou endurest wo
As sharp as doth he, Ticius, in helle,  786
Whos stomak foules tyren ever-mo
That highte volturis, as bokes telle.
But I may not endure that thou dwelle
In so unskilful an opinioun          790
That of thy wo is no curacioun.

114. But ones niltow, for thy coward
    herte,
And for thyn ire and folish wilfulnesse,
For wantrust, tellen of thy sorwes smerte,
Ne to thyn owene help do bisinesse    795
As muche as speke a resoun more or lesse,
But lyest as he that list of no-thing recche.
What womman coude love swich a
    wrecche?

115. What may she demen other of thy
    deeth,
If thou thus deye, and she not why it is, 800
But that for fere is yolden up thy breeth,
For Grekes han biseged us, y-wis?
Lord, which a thank than shaltow han of
    this!
Thus wol she seyn, and al the toun at
    ones,
"The wrecche is deed, the devel have his
    bones!"                         805

116. Thou mayst allone here wepe and
    crye and knele;
But, love a woman that she woot it
    nought,
And she wol quyte that thou shalt not
    fele;
Unknowe, unkist, and lost that is un-
    sought.
What! many a man hath love ful dere
    y-bought                       810
Twenty winter that his lady wiste,
That never yet his lady mouth he kiste.

117. What? shulde he therfor fallen in
    despeyr,
Or be recreaunt for his owene tene,

Or sleen him-self, al be his lady fayr? 815
Nay, nay, but ever in oon be fresh and
    grene
To serve and love his dere hertes quene,
And thenke it is a guerdoun hir to serve
A thousand-fold more than he can deserve.'

118. And of that word took hede Troilus,
And thoughte anoon what folye he was
    inne,                         821
And how that sooth him seyde Pandarus,
That for to sleen him-self mighte he not
    winne,
But bothe doon unmanhod and a sinne, 824
And of his deeth his lady nought to wyte;
For of his wo, god woot, she knew ful lyte.

119. And with that thought he gan ful
    sore syke,
And seyde, 'allas! what is me best to do?'
To whom Pandare answerde, 'if thee lyke,
The best is that thou telle me thy wo;  830
And have my trouthe, and thou it finde so,
I be thy bote, or that it be ful longe,
To peces do me drawe, and sithen honge!'

120. ' Ye, so thou seyst,' quod Troilus tho,
    ' allas !
But, god wot, it is not the rather so ;  835
Ful hard were it to helpen in this cas,
For wel finde I that Fortune is my fo,
Ne alle the men that ryden conne or go
May of hir cruel wheel the harm with-
    stonde ;
For, as hir list, she pleyeth with free and
    bonde.'                        840

121. Quod Pandarus, ' than blamestow
    Fortune
For thou art wrooth, ye, now at erst I see ;
Wostow nat wel that Fortune is commune
To every maner wight in som degree? 844
And yet thou hast this comfort, lo, pardee!
That, as hir joyes moten over-goon,
So mote hir sorwes passen everichoon.

122. For if hir wheel stinte any-thing to
    torne,
Than cessed she Fortune anoon to be :
Now, sith hir wheel by no wey may
    sojorne,                       850
What wostow if hir mutabilitee
Right as thy-selven list, wol doon by thee,

Or that she be not fer fro thyn helpinge?
Paraunter, thou hast cause for to singe!

123. And therfor wostow what I thee
    beseche?              855
Lat be thy wo and turning to the grounde;
For who-so list have helping of his leche,
To him bihoveth first unwrye his wounde.
To Cerberus in helle ay be I bounde,
Were it for my suster, al thy sorwe,   860
By my wil, she sholde al be thyn to-morwe.

124. Loke up, I seye, and tel me what she is
Anoon, that I may goon aboute thy nede;
Knowe ich hir ought? for my love, tel me
    this;              864
Than wolde I hopen rather for to spede.'
Tho gan the veyne of Troilus to blede,
For he was hit, and wex al reed for shame;
'A ha!' quod Pandare, 'here biginneth
    game!'

125. And with that word he gan him for
    to shake,
And seyde, 'theef, thou shalt hir name
    telle.'              870
But tho gan sely Troilus for to quake
As though men sholde han lad him in-to
    helle,
And seyde, 'allas! of al my wo the welle,
Than is my swete fo called Criseyde!'
And wel nigh with the word for fere he
    deyde.             875

126. And whan that Pandare herde hir
    name nevene,
Lord, he was glad, and seyde, 'freend so
    dere,
Now fare a-right, for Joves name in hevene,
Love hath biset thee wel, be of good chere;
For of good name and wysdom and
    manere           880
She hath y-nough, and eek of gentilesse;
If she be fayr, thow wost thy-self, I gesse.

127. Ne I never saw a more bountevous
Of hir estat, ne a gladder, ne of speche
A freendlier, ne a more gracious    885
For to do wel, ne lasse hadde nede to
    seche
What for to doon; and al this bet to eche,
In honour, to as fer as she may strecche,
A kinges herte semeth by hires a wrecche.

128. And for-thy loke of good comfort
    thou be;           890
For certeinly, the firste poynt is this
Of noble corage and wel ordeyne,
A man to have pees with him-self, y-wis;
So oughtest thou, for nought but good it is
To loven wel, and in a worthy place;  895
Thee oughte not to clepe it hap, but grace.

129. And also thenk, and ther-with glade
    thee,
That sith thy lady vertuous is al,
So folweth it that ther is som pitee
Amonges alle thise othere in general;  900
And for-thy see that thou, in special,
Requere nought that is ayein hir name;
For vertue streccheth not him-self to
    shame.

130. But wel is me that ever I was born,
That thou biset art in so good a place;  905
For by my trouthe, in love I dorste have
    sworn,
Thee sholde never han tid thus fayr a
    grace;
And wostow why? for thou were wont to
    chace
At love in scorn, and for despyt him
    calle
"Seynt Idiot, lord of thise foles alle."  910

131. How often hastow maad thy nyce
    japes,
And seyd, that loves servants everichone
Of nycetee ben verray goddes apes;
And some wolde monche hir mete alone,
Ligging a-bedde, and make hem for to
    grone;           915
And som, thou seydest, hadde a blaunche
    fevere,
And preydest god he sholde never kevere!

132. And some of hem toke on hem, for
    the colde,
More than y-nough, so seydestow ful ofte;
And some han feyned ofte tyme, and tolde
How that they wake, whan they slepen
    softe;           921
And thus they wolde han brought hem-
    self a-lofte,
And nathelees were under at the laste;
Thus seydestow, and japedest ful faste.

133. Yet seydestow, that, for the more part,     925
These loveres wolden speke in general,
And thoughten that it was a siker art,
For fayling, for to assayen over-al.
Now may I jape of thee, if that I shal!
But nathelees, though that I sholde deye,
That thou art noon of tho, that dorste I seye.     931

134. Now beet thy brest, and sey to god of love,
" Thy grace, lord! for now I me repente
If I mis spak, for now my-self I love :"
Thus sey with al thyn herte in good en-
    tente.'     935
Quod Troilus, ' a ! lord ! I me consente,
And pray to thee my japes thou foryive,
And I shal never-more whyl I live.'

135. 'Thow seyst wel,' quod Pandare, 'and now I hope
That thou the goddes wratthe hast al
    apesed ;     940
And sithen thou hast wepen many a drope,
And seyd swich thing wher-with thy god is plesed,
Now wolde never god but thou were esed ;
And think wel, she of whom rist al thy wo
Here-after may thy comfort been al-so. 945

136. For thilke ground, that bereth the wedes wikke,
Bereth eek thise holsom herbes, as ful ofte
Next the foule netle, rough and thikke,
The rose waxeth swote and smothe and softe ;
And next the valey is the hil a-lofte ; 950
And next the derke night the glade morwe ;
And also joye is next the fyn of sorwe.

137. Now loke that atempre be thy brydel,
And, for the beste, ay suffre to the tyde,
Or elles al our labour is on ydel ;     955
He hasteth wel that wysly can abyde ;
Be diligent, and trewe, and ay wel hyde.
Be lusty, free, persevere in thy servyse,
And al is wel, if thou werke in this wyse.

138. But he that parted is in every place     960
Is no-wher hool, as writen clerkes wyse ;

What wonder is, though swich oon have no grace ?
Eek wostow how it fareth of som servyse ?
As plaunte a tre or herbe, in sondry wyse,
And on the morwe pulle it up as blyve, 965
No wonder is, though it may never thryve.

139. And sith that god of love hath thee bistowed
In place digne un-to thy worthinesse,
Stond faste, for to good port hastow rowed ;
And of thy-self, for any hevinesse,     970
Hope alwey wel ; for, but-if drerinesse
Or over-haste our bothe labour shende,
I hope of this to maken a good ende.

140. And wostow why I am the lasse a-
    fered
Of this matere with my nece trete ?     975
For this have I herd seyd of wyse y-lered,
" Was never man ne woman yet bigete
That was unapt to suffren loves hete
Celestial, or elles love of kinde ;"     979
For-thy som grace I hope in hir to finde.

141. And for to speke of hir in special,
Hir beautee to bithinken and hir youthe,
It sit hir nought to be celestial
As yet, though that hir liste bothe and couthe ;     984
But trewely, it sete hir wel right nouthe
A worthy knight to loven and cheryce,
And but she do, I holde it for a vyce.

142. Wherfore I am, and wol be, ay redy
To peyne me to do yow this servyse ;
For bothe yow to plese thus hope I     990
Her-afterward ; for ye beth bothe wyse,
And conne it counseyl kepe in swich a wyse,
That no man shal the wyser of it be ;
And so we may be gladed alle three.

143. And, by my trouthe, I have right now of thee     995
A good conceyt in my wit, as I gesse,
And what it is, I wol now that thou see.
I thenke, sith that love, of his goodnesse,
Hath thee converted out of wikkednesse,
That thou shalt be the beste post, I leve,     1000
Of al his lay, and most his foos to-greve.

144. Ensample why, see now these wyse
    clerkes,
That erren aldermost a-yein a lawe,
And ben converted from hir wikked
    werkes
Thorugh grace of god, that list hem to
    him drawe,      1005
Than arn they folk that han most god in
    awe,
And strengest-feythed been, I under-
    stonde,
And conne an errour alder-best with-
    stonde.'

145. Whan Troilus had herd Pandare
    assented
To been his help in loving of Criseyde, 1010
Wex of his wo, as who seyth, untormented,
But hotter wex his love, and thus he seyde,
With sobre chere, al-though his herte
    pleyde,
'Now blisful Venus helpe, er that I sterve,
Of thee, Pandare, I may som thank de-
    serve.      1015

146. But, dere frend, how shal myn wo
    ben lesse
Til this be doon? and goode, eek tel me
    this,
How wiltow seyn of me and my destresse?
Lest she be wrooth, this drede I most,
    y-wis,
Or nil not here or trowen how it is. 1020
Al this drede I, and eek for the manere
Of thee, hir eem, she nil no swich thing
    here.'

147. Quod Pandarus, 'thou hast a ful
    gret care
Lest that the cherl may falle out of the
    mone!      1024
Why, lord! I hate of thee thy nyce fare!
Why, entremete of that thou hast to done!
For goddes love, I bidde thee a bone,
So lat me alone, and it shal be thy beste.'—
'Why, freend,' quod he, 'now do right as
    thee leste.

148. But herke, Pandare, o word, for I
    nolde      1030
That thou in me wendest so greet folye,
That to my lady I desiren sholde

That toucheth harm or any vilenye;
For dredelees, me were lever dye      1034
Than she of me ought elles understode
But that, that mighte sounen in-to gode.'

149. Tho lough this Pandare, and anoon
    answerde,
'And I thy borw? fy! no wight dooth
    but so;
I roughte nought though that she stode
    and herde      1039
How that thou seyst; but fare-wel, I wol go.
A-dieu! be glad! god spede us bothe two!
Yif me this labour and this besinesse,
And of my speed be thyn al that swetnesse.'

150. Tho Troilus gan doun on knees to
    falle,      1044
And Pandare in his armes hente faste,
And seyde, 'now, fy on the Grekes alle!
Yet, pardee, god shal helpe us at the laste;
And dredelees, if that my lyf may laste,
And god to-forn, lo, som of hem shal
    smerte;
And yet me athinketh that this avaunt
    me asterte!      1050

151. Now, Pandare, I can no more seye,
But thou wys, thou wost, thou mayst,
    thou art al!
My lyf, my deeth, hool in thyn honde
    I leye;
Help now,' quod he. 'Yis, by my trouthe,
    I shal.'
'God yelde thee, freend, and this in
    special,'      1055
Quod Troilus, 'that thou me recomaunde
To hir that to the deeth me may
    comaunde.'

152. This Pandarus tho, desirous to serve
His fulle freend, than seyde in this manere,
'Far-wel, and thenk I wol thy thank
    deserve;      1060
Have here my trouthe, and that thou
    shalt wel here.'—
And wente his wey, thenking on this
    matere,
And how he best mighte hir beseche of
    grace,
And finde a tyme ther-to, and a place.

153. For every wight that hath an hous
 to founde                                    1065
Ne renneth nought the werk for to bi-
 ginne
With rakel hond, but he wol byde a
 stounde,
And sende his hertes lyne out fro with-inne
Alderfirst his purpos for to winne.    1069
Al this Pandare in his herte thoughte,
And caste his werk ful wysly, or he
 wroughte.

154. But Troilus lay tho no lenger doun,
But up anoon up-on his stede bay,
And in the feld he pleyde tho leoun ;
Wo was that Greek that with him mette
 that day.                                    1075
And in the toun his maner tho forth ay
So goodly was, and gat him so in grace,
That ech him lovede that loked on his face.

155. For he bicom the frendlyeste wight,
The gentileste, and eek the moste free,   1080
The thriftieste and oon the beste knight,
That in his tyme was, or mighte be.
Dede were his japes and his crueltee,
His heighe port and his manere
 estraunge,
And ech of tho gan for a vertu chaunge.

156. Now lat us stinte of Troilus a
 stounde,                                      1086
That fareth lyk a man that hurt is
 sore,
And is somdel of akinge of his wounde
Y-lissed wel, but heled no del more :
And, as an esy pacient, the lore        1090
Abit of him that gooth aboute his cure ;
And thus he dryveth forth his aventure.

**Explicit Liber Primus.**

# BOOK II.

## Incipit prohemium Secundi Libri.

1. Out of these blake wawes for to sayle,
O wind, O wind, the weder ginneth clere ;
For in this see the boot hath swich tra-
 vayle,
Of my conning that unnethe I it stere :
This see clepe I the tempestous matere   5
Of desespeyr that Troilus was inne :
But now of hope the calendes biginne.

2. O lady myn, that called art Cleo,
Thou be my speed fro this forth, and my
 muse,
To ryme wel this book, til I have do ;   10
Me nedeth here noon other art to use.
For-why to every lovere I me excuse,
That of no sentement I this endyte,
But out of Latin in my tonge it wryte.

3. Wherfore I nil have neither thank ne
 blame                                         15
Of al this werk, but pray yow mekely,
Disblameth me, if any word be lame,
For as myn auctor seyde, so seye I.
Eek though I speke of love unfelingly,

No wonder is, for it no-thing of newe is ; 20
A blind man can nat juggen wel in hewis.

4. Ye knowe eek, that in forme of speche
 is chaunge
With-inne a thousand yeer, and wordes
 tho
That hadden prys, now wonder nyce and
 straunge
Us thinketh hem ; and yet they spake
 hem so,                                        25
And spedde as wel in love as men now do ;
Eek for to winne love in sondry ages,
In sondry londes, sondry been usages.

5. And for-thy if it happe in any wyse,
That here be any lovere in this place   30
That herkeneth, as the story wol devyse,
How Troilus com to his lady grace,
And thenketh, so nolde I nat love pur-
 chace,
Or wondreth on his speche and his doinge,
I noot ; but it is me no wonderinge ;   35

6. For every wight which that to Rome
 went,
Halt nat o path, or alwey o manere ;

Eek in som lond were al the gamen shent,
If that they ferde in love as men don here,
As thus, in open doing or in chere,　40
In visitinge, in forme, or seyde hir sawes ;
For-thy men seyn, ech contree hath his
　　lawes.

7. Eek scarsly been ther in this place three
That han in love seyd lyk and doon in al ;
For to thy purpos this may lyken thee, 45
And thee right nought, yet al is seyd or
　　shal ;
Eek som men grave in tree, som in stoon
　　wal,
As it bitit ; but sin I have begonne,
Myn auctor shal I folwen, if I conne.

**Explicit prohemium Secundi Libri.**

**Incipit Liber Secundus.**

8. In May, that moder is of monthes glade,
That fresshe floures, blewe, and whyte,
　　and rede,　　　　　　　　　　51
Ben quike agayn, that winter dede made,
And ful of bawme is fletinge every mede ;
Whan Phebus doth his brighte bemes
　　sprede
Right in the whyte Bole, it so bitidde　55
As I shal singe, on Mayes day the thridde,

9. That Pandarus, for al his wyse speche,
Felte eek his part of loves shottes kene,
That, coude he never so wel of loving
　　preche,
It made his hewe a-day ful ofte grene ; 60
So shoop it, that him fil that day a tene
In love, for which in wo to bedde he wente,
And made, er it was day, ful many a wente.

10. The swalwe Proignè, with a sorwful lay,
Whan morwe com, gan make hir wey-
　　mentinge,　　　　　　　　　65
Why she forshapen was ; and ever lay
Pandare a-bedde, half in a slomeringe,
Til she so neigh him made hir chiteringe
How Tereus gan forth hir suster take,
That with the noyse of hir he gan a-wake ;

11. And gan to calle, and dresse him up
　　to ryse,　　　　　　　　　　71
Remembringe him his erand was to done
From Troilus, and eek his greet empryse ;

And caste and knew in good plyt was the
　　mone
To doon viage, and took his wey ful sone
Un-to his neces paleys ther bi-syde ;　76
Now Janus, god of entree, thou him gyde !

12. Whan he was come un-to his neces
　　place,
' Wher is my lady ?' to hir folk seyde he ;
And they him tolde ; and he forth in gan
　　pace,　　　　　　　　　　　80
And fond, two othere ladyes sete and she
With-inne a paved parlour ; and they three
Herden a mayden reden hem the geste
Of the Sege of Thebes, whyl hem leste. 84

13. Quod Pandarus, 'ma dame, god yow see,
With al your book and al the companye !'
' Ey, uncle myn, welcome y-wis,' quod she,
And up she roos, and by the hond in hye
She took him faste, and seyde, ' this night
　　thrye,
To goode mote it turne, of yow I mette !'
And with that word she doun on bench
　　him sette.　　　　　　　　　　91

14. ' Ye, nece, ye shal fare wel the bet,
If god wole, al this yeer,' quod Pandarus ;
' But I am sory that I have yow let　94
To herknen of your book ye preysen thus ;
For goddes love, what seith it ? tel it us.
Is it of love ? O, som good ye me lere !'
'Uncle,' quod she, 'your maistresse is not
　　here !'

15. With that they gonnen laughe, and
　　tho she seyde,　　　　　　　99
'This romaunce is of Thebes, that we rede ;
And we han herd how that king Laius
　　deyde
Thurgh Edippus his sone, and al that dede ;
And here we stenten at these lettres rede,
How the bisshop, as the book can telle,
Amphiorax, fil thurgh the ground to helle.'

16. Quod Pandarus, ' al this knowe I my-
　　selve,　　　　　　　　　　106
And al th'assege of Thebes and the care ;
For her-of been ther maked bokes twelve :—
But lat be this, and tel me how ye fare ;
Do wey your barbe, and shew your face
　　bare ;　　　　　　　　　　110

Do wey your book, rys up, and lat us
daunce,
And lat us don to May som observaunce.'

17. 'A! god forbede!' quod she, 'be ye
mad?
Is that a widewes lyf, so god you save?
By god, ye maken me right sore a-drad, 115
Ye ben so wilde, it semeth as ye rave!
It sete me wel bet ay in a cave
To bidde, and rede on holy seyntes lyves:
Lat maydens gon to daunce, and yonge
wyves.'

18. 'As ever thryve I,' quod this Pandarus,
'Yet coude I telle a thing to doon you
pleye.'                                        121
'Now uncle dere,' quod she, 'tel it us
For goddes love; is than th'assege aweye?
I am of Grekes so ferd that I deye.'
'Nay, nay,' quod he, 'as ever mote I
thryve!                                        125
It is a thing wel bet than swiche fyve.'

19. 'Ye, holy god!' quod she, 'what thing
is that?
What? bet than swiche fyve? ey, nay,
y-wis!
For al this world ne can I reden what
It sholde been; som jape, I trowe, is this;
And but your-selven telle us what it is, 131
My wit is for to arede it al to lene;
As help me god, I noot nat what ye mene.'

20. 'And I your borow, ne never shal,
for me,
This thing be told to yow, as mote I
thryve!                                        135
'And why so, uncle myn? why so?' quod
she.
'By god,' quod he, 'that wole I telle as
blyve;
For prouder womman were ther noon on-
lyve,
And ye it wiste, in al the toun of Troye;
I jape nought, as ever have I joye!' 140

21. Tho gan she wondren more than bi-
forn
A thousand fold, and doun hir eyen caste;
For never, sith the tyme that she was born,
To knowe thing desired she so faste; 144

And with a syk she seyde him at the laste,
'Now, uncle myn, I nil yow nought dis-
plese,
Nor axen more, that may do yow disese.'

22. So after this, with many wordes glade,
And freendly tales, and with mery chere,
Of this and that they pleyde, and gunnen
wade                                           150
In many an unkouth glad and deep
matere,
As freendes doon, whan they ben met
y-fere;
Til she gan axen him how Ector ferde,
That was the tounes wal and Grekes yerde.

23. 'Ful wel, I thanke it god,' quod Pan-
darus,                                         155
'Save in his arm he hath a litel wounde;
And eek his fresshe brother Troilus,
The wyse worthy Ector the secounde,
In whom that every vertu list abounde,
As alle trouthe and alle gentillesse, 160
Wysdom, honour, fredom, and worthi-
nesse.'

24. 'In good feith, eem,' quod she, 'that
lykoth me;
They faren wel, god save hem bothe two!
For trewely I holde it greet deyntee
A kinges sone in armes wel to do, 165
And been of good condiciouns ther-to;
For greet power and moral vertu here
Is selde y-seye in o persone y-fere.'

25. 'In good feith, that is sooth,' quod
Pandarus;
'But, by my trouthe, the king hath sones
tweye,                                         170
That is to mene, Ector and Troilus,
That certainly, though that I sholde deye,
They been as voyde of vyces, dar I seye,
As any men that liveth under the sonne,
Hir might is wyde y-knowe, and what
they conne.                                    175

26. Of Ector nedeth it nought for to telle;
In al this world ther nis a bettre knight
Than he, that is of worthinesse welle;
And he wel more vertu hath than might.
This knoweth many a wys and worthy
wight.                                         180

The same prys of Troilus I seye,
God help me so, I knowe not swiche
  tweye.'

27. 'By god,' quod she, 'of Ector that is
  sooth ;
Of Troilus the same thing trowe I ;
For dredelees, men tellen that he dooth
In armes day by day so worthily,   186
And bereth him here at hoom so gentilly
To every wight, that al the prys hath he
Of hem that me were levest preysed be.'

28. 'Ye sey right sooth, y-wis,' quod Pan-
  darus ;   190
'For yesterday, who-so hadde with him
  been,
He might have wondred up-on Troilus ;
For never yet so thikke a swarm of been
Ne fleigh, as Grekes fro him gonne fleen ;
And thorugh the feld, in every wightes
  ere,   195
Ther nas no cry but "Troilus is there!"

29. Now here, now there, he hunted hem
  so faste,
Ther nas but Grekes blood ; and Troilus,
Now hem he hurte, and hem alle doun he
  caste ;
Ay where he wente it was arayed thus : 200
He was hir deeth, and sheld and lyf for us ;
That as that day ther dorste noon with-
  stonde,
Whyl that he held his blody swerd in
  honde.

30. Therto he is the freendlieste man
Of grete estat, that ever I saw my lyve ;
And wher him list, best felawshipe can 206
To suche as him thinketh able for to
  thryve.'
And with that word tho Pandarus, as
  blyve,
He took his leve, and seyde, 'I wol go
  henne :'
'Nay, blame have I, myn uncle,' quod she
  thenne.   210

31. 'What eyleth yow to be thus wery
  sone,
And namelich of wommen ? wol ye so ?
Nay, sitteth down ; by god, I have to done

With yow, to speke of wisdom er ye go.'
And every wight that was a-boute hem
  tho,   215
That herde that, gan fer a-wey to stonde,
Whyl they two hadde al that hem liste
  in honde.

32. Whan that hir tale al brought was to
  an ende
Of hire estat and of hir governaunce, 219
Quod Pandarus, 'now is it tyme I wende ;
But yet, I seye, aryseth, lat us daunce,
And cast your widwes habit to mis-
  chaunce :
What list yow thus your-self to disfigure,
Sith yow is tid thus fair an aventure ?'

33. 'A ! wel bithought ! for love of god,'
  quod she,   225
'Shal I not witen what ye mene of this ?'
'No, this thing axeth layser,' tho quod he,
'And eek me wolde muche greve, y-wis,
If I it tolde, and ye it toke amis.
Yet were it bet my tonge for to stille 230
Than seye a sooth that were ayeins your
  wille.

34. For, nece, by the goddesse Minerve,
And Juppiter, that maketh the thonder
  ringe,
And by the blisful Venus that I serve,
Ye been the womman in this world
  livinge,   235
With-oute paramours, to my witinge,
That I best love, and lothest am to greve,
And that ye witen wel your-self, I leve.'

35. 'Y-wis, myn uncle,' quod she, 'grant
  mercy ;
Your freendship have I founden ever yit ;
I am to no man holden trewely   241
So muche as yow, and have so litel
  quit ;
And, with the grace of god, emforth my
  wit,
As in my gilt I shal you never offende ;
And if I have er this, I wol amende. 245

36. But, for the love of god, I yow be-
  seche,
As ye ben he that I most love and triste,
Lat be to me your fremde maner speche,

And sey to me, your nece, what yow liste :'
And with that word hir uncle anoon hir
　　kiste,　　　　　　　　　　　　　　250
And seyde, ' gladly, leve nece dere,
Tak it for good that I shal seye yow here.'

37. With that she gan hir eyen doun to
　　caste,
And Pandarus to coghe gan a lyte,　254
And seyde, ' nece, alwey, lo ! to the laste,
How-so it be that som men hem delyte
With subtil art hir tales for to endyte,
Yet for al that, in hir entencioun,
Hir tale is al for som conclusioun.

38. And sithen th'ende is every tales
　　strengthe,　　　　　　　　　　　260
And this matere is so bihovely,
What sholde I peynte or drawen it on
　　lengthe
To yow, that been my freend so feithfully ?'
And with that word he gan right inwardly
Biholden hir, and loken on hir face,　265
And seyde, ' on suche a mirour goode
　　grace !'

39. Than thoughte he thus, ' if I my tale
　　endyte
Ought hard, or make a proces any whyle,
She shal no savour han ther-in but lyte,
And trowe I wolde hir in my wil bigyle.
For tendre wittes wenen al be wyle　271
Ther-as they can nat pleynly understonde;
For-thy hir wit to serven wol I fonde '—

40. And loked on hir in a besy wyse,　274
And she was war that he byheld hir so,
And seyde, 'lord! so faste ye me avyse !
Sey ye me never er now? what sey ye, no?'
'Yes, yes,' quod he, ' and bet wole er I go ;
But, by my trouthe, I thoughte now
　　if ye
Be fortunat, for now men shal it see.　280

41. For to every wight som goodly aven-
　　ture
Som tyme is shape, if he it can receyven ;
And if that he wol take of it no cure,
Whan that it cometh, but wilfully it
　　weyven,
Lo, neither cas nor fortune him deceyven,

But right his verray slouthe and wrecched-
　　nesse ;　　　　　　　　　　　　　286
And swich a wight is for to blame, I gesse.

42. Good aventure, O bele nece, have ye
Ful lightly founden, and ye conne it take;
And, for the love of god, and eek of me,
Cacche it anoon, lest aventure slake.　291
What sholde I lenger proces of it make ?
Yif me your hond, for in this world is
　　noon,
If that you list, a wight so wel begoon.　294

43. And sith I speke of good entencioun,
As I to yow have told wel here-biforn,
And love as wel your honour and renoun
As creature in al this world y-born ;
By alle the othes that I have yow sworn,
And ye be wrooth therfore, or wene I lye,
Ne shal I never seen yow eft with yë.　301

44. Beth nought agast, ne quaketh nat ;
　　wher-to ?
Ne chaungeth nat for fere so your hewe;
For hardely, the werste of this is do ;
And though my tale as now be to yow
　　newe,　　　　　　　　　　　　　305
Yet trist alwey, ye shal me finde trewe ;
And were it thing that me thoughte
　　unsittinge,
To yow nolde I no swiche tales bringe.'

45. ' Now, my good eem, for goddes love,
　　I preye,'　　　　　　　　　　　　309
Quod she, ' com of, and tel me what it is;
For bothe I am agast what ye wol seye,
And eek me longeth it to wite, y-wis.
For whether it be wel or be amis,
Sey on, lat me not in this fere dwelle :'
' So wol I doon, now herkneth, I shal
　　telle :　　　　　　　　　　　　　315

46. Now, nece myn, the kinges dere sone,
The goode, wyse, worthy, fresshe, and free,
Which alwey for to do wel is his wone,
The noble Troilus, so loveth thee,
That, bot ye helpe, it wol his bane be.　320
Lo, here is al, what sholde I more seye ?
Doth what yow list, to make him live or
　　deye.

47. But if ye lete him deye, I wol sterve ;
Have her my trouthe, nece, I nil not lyen;

Al sholde I with this knyf my throte
 kerve'—       325
With that the teres braste out of his yën,
And seyde, 'if that ye doon us bothe
 dyen,
Thus giltelees, than have ye fisshed faire;
What mende ye, though that we bothe
 apeyre?

48. Allas! he which that is my lord so
 dere,        330
That trewe man, that noble gentil knight,
That nought desireth but your freendly
 chere,
I see him deye, ther he goth up-right,
And hasteth him, with al his fulle might,
For to be slayn, if fortune wol assente; 335
Allas! that god yow swich a beautee
 sente!

49. If it be so that ye so cruel be,
That of his deeth yow liste nought to
 recche,
That is so trewe and worthy, as ye see,
No more than of a japere or a wrecche, 340
If ye be swich, your beautee may not
 strecche
To make amendes of so cruel a dede;
Avysement is good bifore the nede.

50. Wo worth the faire gemme vertulees!
Wo worth that herbe also that dooth no
 bote!        345
Wo worth that beautee that is routhelees!
Wo worth that wight that tret ech under
 fote!
And ye, that been of beautee crop and
 rote,
If therwith-al in you ther be no routhe,
Than is it harm ye liven, by my trouthe!

51. And also thenk wel, that this is no
 gaude;        351
For me were lever, thou and I and he
Were hanged, than I sholde been his
 baude,
As heye, as men mighte on us alle y-see:
I am thyn eem, the shame were to me, 355
As wel as thee, if that I sholde assente,
Thorugh myn abet, that he thyn honour
 shente.

52. Now understond, for I yow nought
 requere
To binde yow to him thorugh no beheste,
But only that ye make him bettre chere 360
Than ye han doon er this, and more feste,
So that his lyf be saved, at the leste.
This al and som, and playnly our entente;
God helpe me so, I never other mente. 364

53. Lo, this request is not but skile, y-wis,
Ne doute of reson, pardee, is ther noon.
I sette the worste that ye dredden this,
Men wolden wondren seen him come or
 goon:
Ther-ayeins answere I thus a-noon, 369
That every wight, but he be fool of kinde,
Wol deme it love of freendship in his
 minde.

54. What? who wol deme, though he see
 a man
To temple go, that he the images eteth?
Thenk eek how wel and wysly that he can
Governe him-self, that he no-thing for-
 yeteth,       375
That, wher he cometh, he prys and thank
 him geteth;
And eek ther-to, he shal come here so
 selde,
What fors were it though al the toun
 behelde?

55. Swich love of freendes regneth al this
 toun;
And wrye yow in that mantel ever-mo;
And, god so wis be my savacioun, 381
As I have seyd, your beste is to do so.
But alwey, goode nece, to stinte his wo,
So lat your daunger sucred ben a lyte,
That of his deeth ye be nought for to
 wyte.'       385

56. Criseyde, which that herde him in
 this wyse,
Thoughte, 'I shal fele what he meneth,
 y-wis.'
'Now, eem,' quod she, 'what wolde ye
 devyse,
What is your reed I sholde doon of this?'
'That is wel seyd,' quod he, 'certayn,
 best is      390

That ye him love ayein for his lovinge,
As love for love is skilful guerdoninge.

57. Thenk eek, how elde wasteth every
    houre
In eche of yow a party of beautee ;
And therfore, er that age thee devoure, 395
Go love, for, olde, ther wol no wight of
    thee.
Lat this proverbe a lore un-to yow be ;
    To late y-war, quod Beautee, whan it
        paste ;''
And elde daunteth daunger at the laste.

58. The kinges fool is woned to cryen
    loude,                                   400
Whan that him thinketh a womman
    bereth hir hyë,
" So longe mote ye live, and alle proude,
Til crowes feet be growe under your yë,
And sende yow thanne a mirour in to
    pryë                                      404
In whiche ye may see your face a-morwe !''
Nece, I bid wisshe yow no more sorwe.'

59. With this he stente, and caste adoun
    the heed,
And she bigan to breste a-wepe anoon.
And seyde, 'allas, for wo ! why nere I
    deed ?
For of this world the feith is al agoon ! 410
Allas ! what sholden straunge to me doon,
When he, that for my beste freend I
    wende,
Ret me to love, and sholde it me defende ?

60. Allas ! I wolde han trusted, doutelees,
That if that I, thurgh my disaventure, 415
Had loved other him or Achilles,
Ector, or any mannes creature,
Ye nolde han had no mercy ne mesure
On me, but alwey had me in repreve ;
This false world, allas ! who may it leve ?

61. What ? is this al the joye and al the
    feste ?                                  421
Is this your reed, is this my blisful cas ?
Is this the verray mede of youre beheste ?
Is al this peynted proces seyd, allas ! 424
Right for this fyn ? O lady myn, Pallas !
Thou in this dredful cas for me purveye ;
For so astonied am I that I deye !'

62. With that she gan ful sorwfully to
    syke ;
' A ! may it be no bet ?' quod Pandarus ;
' By god, I shal no-more come here this
    wyke,                                    430
And god to-forn, that am mistrusted thus ;
I see ful wel that ye sette lyte of us,
Or of our deeth ! Allas ! I woful wrecche !
Mighte he yet live, of me is nought to
    recche.

63. O cruel god, O dispitouse Marte,   435
O Furies three of helle, on yow I crye !
So lat me never out of this hous departe,
If that I mente harm or vilanye !
But sith I see my lord mot nedes dye,
And I with him, here I me shryve, and
    seye                                     440
That wikkedly ye doon us bothe deye.

64. But sith it lyketh yow that I be
    deed,
By Neptunus, that god is of the see,
Fro this forth shal I never eten breed
Til I myn owene herte blood may see ; 445
For certayn, I wole deye as sone as he '—
And up he sterte, and on his wey he
    raughte,
Til she agayn him by the lappe caughte.

65. Criseyde, which that wel neigh starf
    for fere,
So as she was the ferfulleste wight   450
That mighte be, and herde eek with hir
    ere,
And saw the sorwful ernest of the knight,
And in his preyere eek saw noon unright,
And for the harm that mighte eek fallen
    more,
She gan to rewe, and dradde hir wonder
    sore ;                                   455

66. And thoughte thus, ' unhappes fallen
    thikke
Alday for love, and in swich maner cas,
As men ben cruel in hem-self and wikke ;
And if this man slee here him-self, allas !
In my presence, it wol be no solas.    460
What men wolde of hit deme I can nat
    seye ;
It nedeth me ful sleyly for to pleye.'

67. And with a sorwful syk she seyde
　　thrye,
'A! lord! what me is tid a sory chaunce!
For myn estat now lyth in jupartye, 465
And eek myn emes lyf lyth in balaunce;
But nathelees, with goddes governaunce,
I shal so doon, myn honour shal I kepe,
And eek his lyf;' and stinte for to wepe.

68. 'Of harmes two, the lesse is for to
　　chese;　　　　　　　　　　　　470
Yet have I lever maken him good chere
In honour, than myn emes lyf to lese;
Ye seyn, ye no-thing elles me requere?'
'No, wis,'quod he, 'myn owene nece dere.'
'Now wel,'quod she, 'and I wol doon my
　　peyne;　　　　　　　　　　　　475
I shal myn herte ayeins my lust con-
　　streyne,

69. But that I nil not holden him in
　　honde,
Ne love a man, ne can I not, ne may
Ayeins my wil; but elles wol I fonde,
Myn honour sauf, plese him fro day to
　　day;　　　　　　　　　　　　　480
Ther-to nolde I nought ones have seyd nay,
But that I dredde, as in my fantasye;
But cesse cause, ay cesseth maladye.

70. And here I make a protestacioun,
That in this proces if ye depper go, 485
That certaynly, for no savacioun
Of yow, though that ye sterve bothe two,
Though al the world on o day be my fo,
Ne shal I never on him han other
　　routhe.'—
'I graunte wel,' quod Pandare, 'by my
　　trouthe.　　　　　　　　　　　490

71. But may I truste wel ther-to,' quod he,
'That, of this thing that ye han hight me
　　here,
Ye wol it holden trewly un-to me?'
'Ye, doutelees,' quod she, 'myn uncle
　　dere.'
'Ne that I shal han cause in this matere,'
Quod he, 'to pleyne, or after yow to
　　preche?'　　　　　　　　　　　496
'Why, no, pardee; what nedeth more
　　speche?'

72. Tho fillen they in othere tales glade,
Til at the laste, 'O good eem,' quod she
　　tho,
'For love of god, which that us bothe
　　made,　　　　　　　　　　　　500
Tel me how first ye wisten of his wo:
Wot noon of hit but ye?' He seyde,
　　'no.'
'Can he wel speke of love?' quod she,
　　'I preye,
Tel me, for I the bet me shal purveye.'

73. Tho Pandarus a litel gan to smyle,
And seyde, 'by my trouthe, I shal yow
　　telle.　　　　　　　　　　　　506
This other day, nought gon ful longe
　　whyle,
In-with the paleys-gardyn, by a welle,
Gan he and I wel half a day to dwelle,
Right for to speken of an ordenaunce, 510
How we the Grekes mighte disavaunce.

74. Sone after that bigonne we to lepe,
And casten with our dartes to and fro,
Til at the laste he seyde, he wolde slepe,
And on the gres a-doun he leyde him tho;
And I after gan rome to and fro　　516
Til that I herde, as that I welk allone,
How he bigan ful wofully to grone.

75. Tho gan I stalke him softely bihinde,
And sikerly, the sothe for to seyne,　520
As I can clepe ayein now to my minde,
Right thus to Love he gan him for to
　　pleyne;
He seyde, "lord! have routhe up-on my
　　peyne,
Al have I been rebel in myn entente;
Now, mea culpa, lord! I me repente. 525

76. O god, that at thy disposicioun
Ledest the fyn, by juste purveyaunce,
Of every wight, my lowe confessioun
Accepte in gree, and send me swich
　　penaunce　　　　　　　　　　529
As lyketh thee, but from desesperaunce,
That may my goost departe awey fro thee,
Thou be my sheld, for thy benignitee.

77. For certes, lord, so sore hath she me
　　wounded
That stod in blak, with loking of hir yën,

That to myn hertes botme it is y-sounded,
Thorugh which I woot that I mot nedes
　　dyen ;　　　　　　　　　　　　536
This is the worste, I dar me not bi-wryen ;
And wel the hotter been the gledes rede,
That men hem wryen with asshen pale
　　and dede."

78. With that he smoot his heed adoun
　　anoon,　　　　　　　　　　　540
And gan to motre, I noot what, trewely.
And I with that gan stille awey to goon,
And leet ther-of as no-thing wist hadde I,
And come ayein anoon and stood him by,
And seyde, "a-wake, ye slepen al to
　　longe ;　　　　　　　　　　　545
It semeth nat that love dooth yow longe,

79. That slepen so that no man may yow
　　wake.
Who sey ever or this so dul a man ?"
"Ye, freend," quod he, "do ye your hedes
　　ake
For love, and lat me liven as I can." 550
But though that he for wo was pale and
　　wan,
Yet made he tho as fresh a contenaunce
As though he shulde have led the newe
　　daunce.

80. This passed forth, til now, this other
　　day,
It fel that I com roming al allone　　555
Into his chaumbre, and fond how that he
　　lay
Up-on his bed ; but man so sore grone
Ne herde I never, and what that was his
　　mone,
Ne wiste I nought ; for, as I was cominge,
Al sodeynly he lefte his compleyninge. 560

81. Of which I took somwhat suspecioun,
And neer I com, and fond he wepte sore ;
And god so wis be my savacioun,
As never of thing hadde I no routhe more.
For neither with engyn, ne with no lore,
Unethes mighte I fro the deeth him
　　kepe ;　　　　　　　　　　　566
That yet fele I myn herte for him wepe.

82. And god wot, never, sith that I was
　　born,
Was I so bisy no man for to preche,

Ne never was to wight so depe y-sworn,
Or he me tolde who mighte been his
　　leche.　　　　　　　　　　　571
But now to yow rehersen al his speche,
Or alle his woful wordes for to soune,
Ne bid me not, but ye wol see me swowne.

83. But for to save his lyf, and elles
　　nought,　　　　　　　　　　575
And to non harm of yow, thus am I
　　driven ;
And for the love of god that us hath
　　wrought,
Swich chere him dooth, that he and I
　　may liven.
Now have I plat to yow myn herte
　　schriven ;　　　　　　　　　　579
And sin ye woot that myn entente is clene,
Tak hede ther-of, for I non yvel mene.

84. And right good thrift, I pray to god,
　　have ye,
That han swich oon y-caught with-oute
　　net ;
And be ye wys, as ye ben fair to see,
Wel in the ring than is the ruby set. 585
Ther were never two so wel y-met,
Whan ye ben his al hool, as he is youre :
Ther mighty god yet graunte us see that
　　houre !'

85. 'Nay, therof spak I not, a, ha !' quod
　　she,
'As helpe me god, ye shenden every deel !'
'O mercy, dere nece,' anoon quod he, 591
'What-so I spak, I mente nought but
　　weel,
By Mars the god, that helmed is of steel ;
Now beth nought wrooth, my blood, my
　　nece dere.'
'Now wel,' quod she, 'foryeven be it here !'

86. With this he took his leve, and hoom
　　he wente ;　　　　　　　　　　596
And lord, how he was glad and wel bi-
　　goon !
Criseyde aroos, no lenger she ne stente,
But straught in-to hir closet wente anoon,
And sette here doun as stille as any stoon,
And every word gan up and doun to
　　winde,　　　　　　　　　　601
That he hadde seyd, as it com hir to
　　minde ;

87. And wex somdel astonied in hir
    thought,
Right for the newe cas; but whan that
    she
Was ful avysed, tho fond she right nought
Of peril, why she oughte afered be.   606
For man may love, of possibilitee,
A womman so, his herte may to-breste,
And she nought love ayein, but-if hir leste.

88. But as she sat allone and thoughte
    thus,         610
Th'ascry aroos at skarmish al with-oute,
And men cryde in the strete, ' see, Troilus
Hath right now put to flight the Grekes
    route !'
With that gan al hir meynee for to shoute,
'A ! go we see, caste up the latis wyde ;
For thurgh this strete he moot to palays
    ryde ;         616

89. For other wey is fro the yate noon
Of Dardanus, ther open is the cheyne.'
With that com he and al his folk anoon
An esy pas rydinge, in routes tweyne,  620
Right as his happy day was, sooth to seyne,
For which, men say, may nought dis-
    turbed be
That shal bityden of necessitee.

90. This Troilus sat on his baye stede,
Al armed, save his heed, ful richely,  625
And wounded was his hors, and gan to
    blede,
On whiche he rood a pas, ful softely;
But swich a knightly sighte, trewely,
As was on him, was nought, with-outen
    faile,         629
To loke on Mars, that god is of batayle.

91. So lyk a man of armes and a knight
He was to seen, fulfild of heigh prowesse;
For bothe he hadde a body and a might
To doon that thing, as wel as hardinesse;
And eek to seen him in his gere him
    dresse,         635
So fresh, so yong, so weldy semed he,
It was an heven up-on him for to see.

92. His helm to-hewen was in twenty
    places,
That by a tissew heng, his bak bihinde,

His sheld to-dasshed was with swerdes
    and maces,         640
In which men mighte many an arwe
    finde
That thirled hadde horn and nerf and
    rinde ;
And ay the peple cryde, ' here cometh our
    joye,
And, next his brother, holdere up of
    Troye !'

93. For which he wex a litel reed for
    shame,         645
Whan he the peple up-on him herde
    cryen,
That to biholde it was a noble game,
How sobreliche he caste doun his yën.
Cryseyda gan al his chere aspyen,
And leet so softe it in hir herte sinke,  650
That to hir-self she seyde, ' who yaf me
    drinke ?'

94. For of hir owene thought she wex al
    reed,
Remembringe hir right thus, ' lo, this is
    he
Which that myn uncle swereth he moot
    be deed,
But I on him have mercy and pitee ;'  655
And with that thought, for pure a-shamed,
    she
Gan in hir heed to pulle, and that as
    faste,
Whyl he and al the peple for-by paste,

95. And gan to caste and rollen up and
    doun
With-inne hir thought his excellent
    prowesse,         660
And his estat, and also his renoun,
His wit, his shap, and eek his gentilesse;
But most hir favour was, for his distresse
Was al for hir, and thoughte it was a
    routhe
To sleen swich oon, if that he mente
    trouthe.         665

96. Now mighte som envyous jangle thus,
'This was a sodeyn love, how mighte it be
That she so lightly lovede Troilus
Right for the firste sighte; ye, pardee ?'

Now who-so seyth so, mote he never
　　thee !　　　　　　　　　　　670
For every thing, a ginning hath it nede
Er al be wrought, with-outen any drede.

97. For I sey nought that she so sodeynly
Yaf him hir love, but that she gan enclyne
To lyke him first, and I have told yow
　　why;　　　　　　　　　　　675
And after that, his manhod and his pyne
Made love with-inne hir for to myne,
For which, by proces and by good servyse,
He gat hir love, and in no sodeyn wyse.

98. And also blisful Venus, wel arayed, 680
Sat in hir seventhe hous of hevene tho,
Disposed wel, and with aspectes payed,
To helpen sely Troilus of his wo.
And, sooth to seyn, she nas nat al a fo
To Troilus in his nativitee ;　　　　685
God woot that wel the soner spedde he.

99. Now lat us stinte of Troilus a throwe,
That rydeth forth, and lat us tourne faste
Un-to Criseyde, that heng hir heed ful
　　lowe,
Ther-as she sat allone, and gan to caste 690
Wher-on she wolde apoynte hir at the
　　laste,
If it so were hir eem ne wolde cesse,
For Troilus, up-on hir for to presse.

100. And, lord ! so she gan in hir thought
　　argue
In this matere of which I have yow
　　told,　　　　　　　　　　695
And what to doon best were, and what
　　eschue,
That plyted she ful ofte in many fold.
Now was hir herte warm, now was it cold,
And what she thoughte somwhat shal I
　　wryte,
As to myn auctor listeth for to endyte. 700

101. She thoughte wel, that Troilus per-
　　sone
She knew by sighte and eek his gentil-
　　lesse,
And thus she seyde, ‘ al were it nought to
　　done,
To graunte him love, yet, for his worthi-
　　nesse,

It were honour, with pley and with glad-
　　nesse,　　　　　　　　　　705
In honestee, with swich a lord to dele,
For myn estat, and also for his hele.

102. Eek, wel wot I my kinges sone is he;
And sith he hath to see me swich delyt,
If I wolde utterly his sighte flee,　　710
Paraunter he mighte have me in dispyt,
Thurgh which I mighte stonde in worse
　　plyt;
Now were I wys, me hate to purchace,
With-outen nede, ther I may stonde in
　　grace ?

103. In every thing, I woot, ther lyth
　　mesure.　　　　　　　　　　715
For though a man forbede dronkenesse,
He nought for-bet that every creature
Be drinkelees for alwey, as I gesse ;
Eek sith I woot for me is his distresse,
I ne oughte not for that thing him des-
　　pyse,　　　　　　　　　　720
Sith it is so, he meneth in good wyse.

104. And eek I knowe, of longe tyme
　　agoon,
His thewes goode, and that he is not nyce.
Ne avauntour, seyth men, certein, is he
　　noon ;
To wys is he to do so gret a vyce ;　725
Ne als I nel him never so cheryce,
That he may make avaunt, by juste cause;
He shal me never binde in swiche a clause.

105. Now set a cas, the hardest is, y-wis,
Men mighten deme that he loveth me : 730
What dishonour were it un-to me, this ?
May I him lette of that ? why nay, pardee !
I knowe also, and alday here and see,
Men loven wommen al this toun aboute ;
Be they the wers ? why, nay, with-outen
　　doute.　　　　　　　　　　735

106. I thenk eek how he able is for to
　　have
Of al this noble toun the thriftieste,
To been his love, so she hir honour save;
For out and out he is the worthieste, 739
Save only Ector, which that is the beste,
And yet his lyf al lyth now in my cure,
But swich is love, and eek myn aventure,

107. Ne me to love, a wonder is it nought ;
For wel wot I my-self, so god me spede,
Al wolde I that noon wistĕ of this thought,
I am oon the fayreste, out of drede,    746
And goodlieste, who-so taketh hede ;
And so men seyn in al the toun of Troye.
What wonder is it though he of me have
     joye ?

108. I am myn owene woman, wel at ese,
I thanke it god, as after myn estat ;    751
Right yong, and stonde unteyd in lusty
     lese,
With-outen jalousye or swich debat ;
Shal noon housbonde seyn to me "chek-
     mat !"
For either they ben ful of jalousye,    755
Or maisterful, or loven novelrye.

109. What shal I doon ? to what fyn live
     I thus ?
Shal I nat loven, in cas if that me leste ?
What, *par dieux* ! I am nought religious !
And though that I myn herte sette at
     reste    760
Upon this knight, that is the worthieste,
And kepe alwey myn honour and my
     name,
By alle right, it may do me no shame.'

110. But right as whan the sonne shyneth
     brighte,
In March, that chaungeth ofte tyme his
     face,    765
And that a cloud is put with wind to
     flighte
Which over-sprat the sonne as for a space,
A cloudy thought gan thorugh hir soule
     pace,
That over-spradde hir brighte thoughtes
     alle,
So that for fere almost she gan to falle. 770

111. That thought was this, 'allas ! sin
     I am free,
Sholde I now love, and putte in jupartye
My sikernesse, and thrallen libertee ?
Allas ! how dorste I thenken that folye ?
May I nought wel in other folk aspye    775
Hir dredful joye, hir constreynt, and hir
     peyne ?
Ther loveth noon, that she nath why to
     pleyne.

112. For love is yet the moste stormy lyf,
Right of him-self, that ever was bigonne ;
For ever som mistrust, or nyce stryf,    780
Ther is in love, som cloud is over the
     sonne :
Ther-to we wrecched wommen no-thing
     conne,
Whan us is wo, but wepe and sitte and
     thinke ;
Our wreche is this, our owene wo to
     drinke.

113. Also these wikked tonges been so
     prest    785
To speke us harm, eek men be so untrewe,
That, right anoon as cessed is hir lest,
So cesseth love, and forth to love a newe :
But harm y-doon, is doon, who-so it rewe.
For though these men for love hem first
     to-rende,    790
Ful sharp biginning breketh ofte at ende.

114. How ofte tyme hath it y-knowen be,
The treson, that to womman hath be do ?
To what fyn is swich love, I can nat see,
Or wher bicomth it, whan it is ago ;    795
Ther is no wight that woot, I trowe so,
Wher it bycomth ; lo, no wight on it
     sporneth ;
That erst was no-thing, in-to nought it
     torneth.

115. How bisy, if I love, eek moste I be
To plesen hem that jangle of love, and
     demen,    800
And coye hem, that they sey non harm of
     me ?
For though ther be no cause, yet hem
     semen
Al be for harm that folk hir freendes
     quemen ;
And who may stoppen every wikked tonge,
Or soun of belles whyl that they be
     ronge ?'    805

116. And after that, hir thought bigan to
     clere,
And seyde, 'he which that no-thing
     under-taketh,
No-thing ne acheveth, be him looth or
     dere·'

And with an other thought hir herte
  quaketh;
Than slepeth hope, and after dreed
  awaketh;        810
Now hoot, now cold; but thus, bi-twixen
  tweye,
She rist hir up, and went hir for to pleye.

117. Adoun the steyre anoon-right tho
  she wente
In-to the gardin, with hir neces three,
And up and doun ther made many a
  wente,        815
Flexippe, she, Tharbe, and Antigone,
To pleyen, that it joye was to see;
And othere of hir wommen, a gret route,
Hir folwede in the gardin al aboute.

118. This yerd was large, and rayled alle
  the aleyes,        820
And shadwed wel with blosmy bowes
  grene,
And benched newe, and sonded alle the
  weyes,
In which she walketh arm in arm bi-
  twene;
Til at the laste Antigone the shene
Gan on a Trojan song to singe clere,  825
That it an heven was hir voys to here.—

119. She seyde, 'O love, to whom I have
  and shal
Ben humble subgit, trewe in myn entente,
As I best can, to yow, lord, yeve ich al
For ever-more, myn hertes lust to rente. 830
For never yet thy grace no wight sente
So blisful cause as me, my lyf to lede
In alle joye and seurtee, out of drede.

120. Ye, blisful god, han me so wel beset
In love, y-wis, that al that bereth lyf 835
Imaginen ne cowde how to ben bet;
For, lord, with-outen jalousye or stryf,
I love oon which that is most ententyf
To serven wel, unwery or unfeyned,
That ever was, and leest with harm dis-
  treyned.        840

121. As he that is the welle of worthinesse,
Of trouthe ground, mirour of goodliheed,
Of wit Appollo, stoon of sikernesse,
Of vertu rote, of lust findere and heed,

Thurgh which is alle sorwe fro me deed, 845
Y-wis, I love him best, so doth he me;
Now good thrift have he, wher-so that he
  be!

122. Whom sholde I thanke but yow, god
  of love,
Of al this blisse, in which to bathe I
  ginne?
And thanked be ye, lord, for that I love! 850
This is the righte lyf that I am inne,
To flemen alle manere vyce and sinne:
This doth me so to vertu for to entende,
That day by day I in my wil amende.

123. And who-so seyth that for to love is
  vyce,        855
Or thraldom, though he fele in it dis-
  tresse,
He outher is envyous, or right nyce,
Or is unmighty, for his shrewednesse,
To loven; for swich maner folk, I gesse,
Defamen love, as no-thing of him knowe;
They speken, but they bente never his
  bowe.        861

124. What is the sonne wers, of kinde
  righte,
Though that a man, for feblesse of his
  yën,
May nought endure on it to see for
  brighte?
Or love the wers, though wrecches on it
  cryen?        865
No wele is worth, that may no sorwe
  dryen.
And for-thy, who that hath an heed of
  verre,
Fro cast of stones war him in the werre!

125. But I with al myn herte and al my
  might,        869
As I have seyd, wol love, un-to my laste,
My dere herte, and al myn owene knight,
In which myn herte growen is so faste,
And his in me, that it shal ever laste.
Al dredde I first to love him to biginne,
Now woot I wel, ther is no peril inne.' 875

126. And of hir song right with that word
  she stente,
And therwith-al, 'now, nece,' quod Criseyde,

I 3

'Who made this song with so good en-
　　tente?'
Antigone answerde anoon, and seyde,
'Ma dame, y-wis, the goodlieste mayde 880
Of greet estat in al the toun of Troye;
And let hir lyf in most honour and joye.'

127. 'Forsothe, so it semeth by hir song,'
Quod tho Criseyde, and gan ther-with to
　　syke,
And seyde, 'lord, is there swich blisse
　　among　　　　　　　　　　　　　885
These lovers, as they conne faire endyte?'
'Ye, wis,' quod fresh Antigone the whyte,
'For alle the folk that han or been on lyve
Ne conne wel the blisse of love discryve.

128. But wene ye that every wrecche
　　woot　　　　　　　　　　　　　890
The parfit blisse of love? why, nay, y-wis;
They wenen al be love, if oon be hoot;
Do wey, do wey, they woot no-thing of
　　this!
Men mosten axe at seyntes if it is
Aught fair in hevene; why? for they
　　conne telle;　　　　　　　　　　895
And axen fendes, is it foul in helle.'

129. Criseyde un-to that purpos nought
　　answerde,
But seyde, 'y-wis, it wol be night as
　　faste.'
But every word which that she of hir
　　herde,
She gan to prenten in hir herte faste; 900
And ay gan love hir lasse for to agaste
Than it dide erst, and sinken in hir herte,
That she wex somwhat able to converte.

130. The dayes honour, and the hevenes yë,
The nightes fo, al this clepe I the sonne, 905
Gan westren faste, and dounward for to
　　wrye,
As he that hadde his dayes cours y-ronne;
And whyte thinges wexen dimme and
　　donne
For lak of light, and sterres for to appere,
That she and al hir folk in wente y-fere.

131. So whan it lyked hir to goon to reste,
And voyded weren they that voyden
　　oughte,　　　　　　　　　　　912

She seyde, that to slepe wel hir leste.
Hir wommen sone til hir bed hir broughte.
Whan al was hust, than lay she stille, and
　　thoughte　　　　　　　　　　915
Of al this thing the manere and the wyse.
Reherce it nedeth nought, for ye ben wyse.

132. A nightingale, upon a cedre grene,
Under the chambre-wal ther as she lay,
Ful loude sang ayein the mone shene, 920
Paraunter, in his briddes wyse, a lay
Of love, that made hir herte fresh and gay.
That herkned she so longe in good entente,
Til at the laste the dede sleep hir hente.

133. And, as she sleep, anoon-right tho
　　hir mette,　　　　　　　　　　925
How that an egle, fethered whyt as boon,
Under hir brest his longe clawes sette,
And out hir herte he rente, and that
　　a-noon,
And dide his herte in-to hir brest to goon,
Of which she nought agroos ne no-thing
　　smerte,　　　　　　　　　　930
And forth he fleigh, with herte left for
　　herte.

134. Now lat hir slepe, and we our tales
　　holde
Of Troilus, that is to paleys riden,
Fro the scarmuch, of the whiche I tolde,
And in his chambre sit, and hath abiden
Til two or three of his messages yeden 936
For Pandarus, and soughten him ful faste,
Til they him founde, and broughte him at
　　the laste.

135. This Pandarus com leping in at ones
And seide thus, 'who hath ben wel y-bete
To-day with swerdes, and with slinge-
　　stones,　　　　　　　　　　941
But Troilus, that hath caught him an
　　hete?'
And gan to jape, and seyde, 'lord, so ye
　　swete!
But rys, and lat us soupe and go to reste;'
And he answerde him, 'do we as thee
　　leste.'　　　　　　　　　　　945

136. With al the haste goodly that they
　　mighte,
They spedde hem fro the souper un-to
　　bedde;

And every wight out at the dore him
   dighte,
And wher him list upon his wey he
   spedde ;
But Troilus, that thoughte his herte
   bledde          950
For wo, til that he herde som tydinge,
He seyde, 'freend, shal I now wepe or
   singe ? '

137. Quod Pandarus, 'ly stille, and lat me
   slepe,
And don thyn hood, thy nedes spedde be ;
And chese, if thou wolt singe or daunce or
   lepe ;         955
At shorte wordes, thow shalt trowe me.—
Sire, my nece wol do wel by thee,
And love thee best, by god and by my
   trouthe,
But lak of pursuit make it in thy slouthe.

138. For thus ferforth I have thy work
   bigonne,         960
Fro day to day, til this day, by the morwe,
Hir love of freendship have I to thee
   wonne,
And also hath she leyd hir feyth to borwe.
Algate a foot is hameled of thy sorwe.'
What sholde I lenger sermon of it holde?
As ye han herd bifore, al he him tolde. 966

139. But right as floures, thorugh the
   colde of night
Y-closed, stoupen on hir stalkes lowe,
Redressen hem a-yein the sonne bright,
And spreden on hir kinde cours by rowe ;
Right so gan tho his eyen up to throwe 971
This Troilus, and seyde, ' O Venus dere,
Thy might, thy grace, y-heried be it here ! '

140. And to Pandare he held up bothe his
   hondes,
And seyde, 'lord, al thyn be that I have ; 975
For I am hool, al brosten been my bondes ;
A thousand Troians who so that me yave,
Eche after other, god so wis me save,
Ne mighte me so gladen ; lo, myn herte,
It spredeth so for joye, it wol to-sterte ! 980

141. But lord, how shal I doon, how shal
   I liven ?
Whan shal I next my dere herte see ?

How shal this longe tyme a-wey be driven,
Til that thou be ayein at hir fro me ?
Thou mayst answere, "a-byd, a-byd," but
   he         985
That hangeth by the nekke, sooth to seyne,
In grete disese abydeth for the peyne.'

142. 'Al esily, now, for the love of Marte,'
Quod Pandarus, ' for every thing hath
   tyme ;         989
So longe abyd til that the night departe ;
For al so siker as thow lyst here by me,
And god toforn, I wol be there at pryme,
And for thy werk somwhat as I shal seye,
Or on som other wight this charge leye.

143. For pardee, god wot, I have ever
   yit         995
Ben redy thee to serve, and to this night
Have I nought fayned, but emforth my
   wit
Don al thy lust, and shal with al my
   might.
Do now as I shal seye, and fare a-right ;
And if thou nilt, wyte al thy-self thy care,
On me is nought along thyn yvel fare. 1001

144. I woot wel that thow wyser art than I
A thousand fold, but if I were as thou,
God helpe me so, as I wolde outrely,
Right of myn owene hond, wryte hir
   right now         1005
A lettre, in which I wolde hir tellen how
I ferde amis, and hir beseche of routhe ;
Now help thy-self, and leve it not for
   slouthe.

145. And I my-self shal ther-with to hir
   goon ;
And whan thou wost that I am with hir
   there,         1010
Worth thou up-on a courser right anoon,
Ye, hardily, right in thy beste gere,
And ryd forth by the place, as nought ne
   were,
And thou shalt finde us, if I may, sittinge
At som windowe, in-to the strete lokinge.

146. And if thee list, than maystow us
   saluwe,         1016
And up-on me makë thy contenaunce ;

But, by thy lyf, be war and faste eschuwe
To tarien ought, god shilde us fro mis-
    chaunce !
Ryd forth thy wey, and hold thy govern-
    aunce ;                              1020
And we shal speke of thee som-what, I
    trowe,
Whan thou art goon, to do thyne eres
    glowe !

147. Touching thy lettre, thou art wys
    y-nough,                            1023
I woot thow nilt it digneliche endyte ;
As make it with thise argumentes tough ;
Ne scrivenish or craftily thou it wryte;
Beblotte it with thy teres eek a lyte ;
And if thou wryte a goodly word al softe,
Though it be good, reherce it not to ofte.

148. For though the beste harpour upon
    lyve                                1030
Wolde on the beste souned joly harpe
That ever was, with alle his fingres fyve,
Touche ay o streng, or ay o werbul harpe,
Were his nayles poynted never so sharpe,
It shulde maken every wight to dulle, 1035
To here his glee, and of his strokes fulle.

149. Ne jompre eek no discordaunt thing
    y-fere,
As thus, to usen termes of phisyk ;
In loves termes, hold of thy matere
The forme alwey, and do that it be
    lyk ;                               1040
For if a peyntour wolde peynte a pyk
With asses feet, and hede it as an ape,
It cordeth nought; so nere it but a jape.'

150. This counseyl lyked wel to Troilus;
But, as a dreedful lover, he seyde this :—
'Allas, my dere brother Pandarus,    1046
I am ashamed for to wryte, y-wis,
Lest of myn innocence I seyde a-mis,
Or that she nolde it for despyt receyve;
Thanne were I deed, ther mighte it no-
    thing weyve.'                       1050

151. To that Pandare answerde, ' if thee
    lest,
Do that I seye, and lat me therwith goon ;
For by that lord that formed est and west,
I hope of it to bringe answere anoon

Right of hir hond, and if that thou nilt
    noon,                               1055
Lat be ; and sory mote he been his lyve,
Ayeins thy lust that helpeth thee to
    thryve.'

152. Quod Troilus, ' *Depardieux*, I assente;
Sin that thee list, I will aryse and wryte;
And blisful god preye ich, with good
    entente,                            1060
The vyage, and the lettre I shal endyte,
So spede it; and thou, Minerva, the whyte,
Yif thou me wit my lettre to devyse :'
And sette him doun, and wroot right in
    this wyse.—

153. First he gan hir his righte lady
    calle,                              1065
His hertes lyf, his lust, his sorwes leche,
His blisse, and eek this othere termes
    alle,
That in swich cas these loveres alle seche;
And in ful humble wyse, as in his speche,
He gan him recomaunde un-to hir grace;
To telle al how, it axeth muchel space. 1071

154. And after this, ful lowly he hir
    prayde
To be nought wrooth, though he, of his
    folye,
So hardy was to hir to wryte, and seyde,
That love it made, or elles moste he dye,
And pitously gan mercy for to crye ; 1076
And after that he seyde, and ley ful loude,
Him-self was litel worth, and lesse he
    coude ;

155. And that she sholde han his conning
    excused,
That litel was, and eek he dredde hir so,
And his unworthinesse he ay acused ; 1081
And after that, than gan he telle his wo;
But that was endeles, with-outen ho
And seyde, he wolde in trouthe alwey him
    holde ;—
And radde it over, and gan the lettre
    folde.                              1085

156. And with his salte teres gan he bathe
The ruby in his signet, and it sette
Upon the wex deliverliche and rathe ;
Ther-with a thousand tymes, er he lette,

He kiste tho the lettre that he shette, 1090
And seyde, 'lettre, a blisful destenee
Thee shapen is, my lady shal thee see.'

157. This Pandare took the lettre, and
    that by tyme
A-morwe, and to his neces paleys sterte,
And faste he swoor, that it was passed
    pryme,                1095
And gan to jape, and seyde, ' y-wis, myn
    herte,
So fresh it is, al-though it sore smerte,
I may not slepe never a Mayes morwe ;
I have a joly wo, a lusty sorwe.'

158. Criseyde, whan that she hir uncle
    herde,               1100
With dreedful herte, and desirous to here
The cause of his cominge, thus answerde,
'Now by your feyth, myn uncle,' quod
    she, ' dere,
What maner windes gydeth yow now
    here ?            1104
Tel us your joly wo and your penaunce,
How ferforth be ye put in loves daunce.'

159. 'By god,' quod he, ' I hoppe alwey
    bihinde !'
And she to-laugh, it thoughte hir herte
    breste.
Quod Pandarus, ' loke alwey that ye finde
Game in myn hood, but herkneth, if yow
    leste ;           1110
Ther is right now come in-to toune a geste,
A Greek espye, and telleth newe thinges,
For which come I to telle yow tydinges.

160. Into the gardin go we, and we shal
    here,
Al prevely, of this a long sermoun.'   1115
With that they wenten arm in arm y-fere
In-to the gardin from the chaumbre doun.
And whan that he so fer was that the
    soun
Of that he speke, no man here mighte,
He seyde hir thus, and out the lettre
    plighte,           1120

161. ' Lo, he that is al hoolly youres free
Him recomaundeth lowly to your grace,
And sent to you this lettre here by me ;
Avyseth you on it, whan ye han space,

And of som goodly answere yow purchace;
Or, helpe me god, so pleynly for to seyne,
He may not longe liven for his peyne.'

162. Ful dredfully tho gan she stonde
    stille,
And took it nought, but al hir humble
    chere
Gan for to chaunge, and seyde, ' scrit ne
    bille,           1130
For love of god, that toucheth swich
    matere,
Ne bring me noon; and also, uncle
    dere,
To myn estat have more reward, I preye,
Than to his lust ; what sholde I more
    seye ?

163. And loketh now if this be reson-
    able,           1135
And letteth nought, for favour ne for
    slouthe,
To seyn a sooth ; now were it covenable
To myn estat, by god, and by your trouthe,
To taken it, or to han of him routhe,
In harming of my-self or in repreve ?  1140
Ber it a-yein, for him that ye on leve !'

164. This Pandarus gan on hir for to
    stare,
And seyde, ' now is this the grettest
    wonder
That ever I sey ! lat be this nyce fare !
To deethe mote I smiten be with thonder,
If, for the citee which that stondeth
    yonder,           1146
Wolde I a lettre un-to yow bringe or take
To harm of yow; what list yow thus it
    make ?

165. But thus ye faren, wel neigh alle and
    some,           1149
That he that most desireth yow to serve,
Of him ye recche leest wher he bicome,
And whether that he live or elles sterve.
But for al that that ever I may deserve,
Refuse it nought,' quod he, and hente hir
    faste,
And in hir bosom the lettre doun he
    thraste,           1155

166. And seyde hir, 'now cast it away anoon,
That folk may seen and gauren on us tweye.'
Quod she, 'I can abyde til they be goon,'
And gan to smyle, and seyde him, 'eem, I preye,
Swich answere as yow list your-self pur-veye,               1160
For trewely I nil no lettre wryte.'
'No? than wol I,' quod he, 'so ye endyte.'

167. Therwith she lough, and seyde, 'go we dyne.'
And he gan at him-self to jape faste, 1164
And seyde, 'nece, I have so greet a pyne
For love, that every other day I faste'—
And gan his beste japes forth to caste;
And made hir so to laughe at his folye,
That she for laughter wende for to dye.

168. And whan that she was comen in-to halle,                   1170
'Now, eem,' quod she, 'we wol go dyne anoon;'
And gan some of hir women to hir calle,
And streyght in-to hir chaumbre gan she goon;
But of hir besinesses, this was oon
A-monges othere thinges, out of drede,
Ful prively this lettre for to rede;      1176

169. Avysed word by word in every lyne,
And fond no lak, she thoughte he coude good;
And up it putte, and went hir in to dyne.
And Pandarus, that in a study stood, 1180
Er he was war, she took him by the hood,
And seyde, 'ye were caught er that ye wiste;'
'I vouche sauf,' quod he, 'do what yow liste.'

170. Tho wesshen they, and sette hem doun and ete;
And after noon ful sleyly Pandarus 1185
Gan drawe him to the window next the strete,
And seyde, 'nece, who hath arayed thus
The yonder hous, that stant afor-yeyn us?'

'Which hous?' quod she, and gan for to biholde,
And knew it wel, and whos it was him tolde,                     1190

171. And fillen forth in speche of thinges smale,
And seten in the window bothe tweye.
Whan Pandarus saw tyme un-to his tale,
And saw wel that hir folk were alle aweye,
'Now, nece myn, tel on,' quod he, 'I seye,                      1195
How lyketh yow the lettre that ye woot?
Can he ther-on? for, by my trouthe, I noot.'

172. Therwith al rosy hewed tho wex she,
And gan to humme, and seyde, 'so I trowe.'
'Aquyte him wel, for goddes love,' quod he;                     1200
'My-self to medes wol the lettre sowe,'
And held his hondes up, and sat on knowe,
'Now, goode nece, be it never so lyte,
Yif me the labour, it to sowe and plyte.'

173. 'Ye, for I can so wryte,' quod she tho;                    1205
'And eek I noot what I sholde to him seye.'
'Nay, nece,' quod Pandare, 'sey not so;
Yet at the leste thanketh him, I preye,
Of his good wil, and doth him not to deye.
Now for the love of me, my nece dere, 1210
Refuseth not at this tyme my preyere.'

174. 'Depar-dieux,' quod she, 'god leve al be wel!
God helpe me so, this is the firste lettre
That ever I wroot, ye, al or any del.'
And in-to a closet, for to avyse hir bettre,
She wente allone, and gan hir herte un-fettre                   1216
Out of disdaynes prison but a lyte;
And sette hir doun, and gan a lettre wryte,

175. Of which to telle in short is myn entente                 1219
Th'effect, as fer as I can understonde:—
She thonked him of al that he wel mente

Towardes hir, but holden him in honde
She nolde nought, ne make hir-selven
    bonde
In love, but as his suster, him to plese,
She wolde fayn, to doon his herte an ese.

176. She shette it, and to Pandarus gan
    goon,    1226
There as he sat and loked in-to strete,
And doun she sette hir by him on a stoon
Of jaspre, up-on a quisshin gold y-bete,
And seyde, 'as wisly helpe me god the
    grete,    1230
I never dide a thing with more peyne
Than wryte this, to which ye me con-
    streyne;'

177. And took it him : he thonked hir
    and seyde,
'God woot, of thing ful ofte looth bigonne
Cometh ende good; and nece myn, Cri-
    seyde,    1235
That ye to him of hard now ben y-wonne
Oughte he be glad, by god and yonder
    sonne!
For-why men seyth, "impressioun[e]s
    lighte
Ful lightly been ay redy to the flighte."

178. But ye han pleyed tyraunt neigh to
    longe,    1240
And hard was it your herte for to grave;
Now stint, that ye no longer on it honge,
Al wolde ye the forme of daunger save.
But hasteth yow to doon him joye have;
For trusteth wel, to longe y-doon hard-
    nesse    1245
Causeth despyt ful often, for distresse.'

179. And right as they declamed this
    matere,
Lo, Troilus, right at the stretes ende,
Com ryding with his tenthe some y-fere,
Al softely, and thiderward gan bende  1250
Ther-as they sete, as was his wey to wende
To paleys-ward ; and Pandare him aspyde,
And seyde, 'nece, y-see who cometh here
    ryde!

180. O flee not in, he seeth us, I suppose;
Lest he may thinke that ye him eschuwe.'

'Nay, nay,' quod she, and wex as reed as
    rose.    1256
With that he gan hir humbly to saluwe,
With dreedful chere, and ofte his hewes
    muwe ;
And up his look debonairly he caste,
And bekked on Pandare, and forth he
    paste.    1260

181. God woot if he sat on his hors a-right,
Or goodly was beseyn, that ilke day!
God woot wher he was lyk a manly
    knight!
What sholde I drecche, or telle of his
    aray?
Criseyde, which that alle these thinges
    say,    1265
To telle in short, hir lyked al y-fere,
His persone, his aray, his look, his chere,

182. His goodly manere and his gentil-
    lesse,
So wel, that never, sith that she was born,
Ne hadde she swich routhe of his dis-
    tresse ;    1270
And how-so she hath hard ben her-biforn,
To god hope I, she hath now caught a
    thorn.
She shal not pulle it out this nexte wyke ;
God sende mo swich thornes on to pyke!

183. Pandare, which that stood hir faste
    by,    1275
Felte iren hoot, and he bigan to smyte,
And seyde, 'nece, I pray yow hertely,
Tel me that I shal axen yow a lyte.
A womman, that were of his deeth to
    wyte,
With-outen his gilt, but for hir lakked
    routhe,    1280
Were it wel doon?' Quod she, 'nay, by
    my trouthe !'

184. 'God helpe me so,' quod he, 'ye sey
    me sooth.
Ye felen wel your-self that I not lye ;
Lo, yond he rit !' Quod she, 'ye, so he
    dooth.'
'Wel,' quod Pandare, 'as I have told yow
    thrye,    1285
Lat be your nyce shame and your folye,
And spek with him in esing of his herte ;
Lat nycetee not do yow bothe smerte.'

185. But ther-on was to heven and to
   done ;
Considered al thing, it may not be ;   1290
And why, for shame ; and it were eek to
   sone
To graunten him so greet a libertee.
' For playnly hir entente,' as seyde she,
Was for to love him unwist, if she mighte,
And guerdon him with no-thing but with
   sighte.'          1295

186. But Pandarus thoughte, ' it shal not
   be so,
If that I may ; this nyce opinioun
Shal not be holden fully yeres two.'
What sholde I make of this a long ser-
   moun ?
He moste assente on that conclusioun 1300
As for the tyme ; and whan that it was eve,
And al was wel, he roos and took his leve.

187. And on his wey ful faste homward he
   spedde,
And right for joye he felte his herte
   daunce ;
And Troilus he fond alone a-bedde, 1305
That lay as dooth these loveres, in a
   traunce,
Bitwixen hope and derk desesperaunce.
But Pandarus, right at his in-cominge,
He song, as who seyth, ' lo ! sumwhat
   I bringe.'

188. And seyde, ' who is in his bed so
   sone            1310
Y-buried thus ? ' ' It am I, freend,' quod
   he.
' Who, Troilus ? nay helpe me so the
   mone,'
Quod Pandarus, ' thou shalt aryse and see
A charme that was sent right now to thee,
The which can helen thee of thyn ac-
   cesse,           1315
If thou do forth-with al thy besinesse.'

189. ' Ye, through the might of god ! '
   quod Troilus.
And Pandarus gan him the lettre take,
And seyde, ' pardee, god hath holpen us ;
Have here a light, and loke on al this
   blake.'           1320
But ofte gan the herte glade and quake

Of Troilus, whyl that he gan it rede,
So as the wordes yave him hope or drede,

190. But fynally, he took al for the beste
That she him wroot, for sumwhat he bi-
   held           1325
On which, him thoughte, he mighte his
   herte reste,
Al covered she the wordes under sheld.
Thus to the more worthy part he held,
That, what for hope and Pandarus bi-
   heste,
His grete wo for-yede he at the leste. 1330

191. But as we may alday our-selven see,
Through more wode or col, the more fyr ;
Right so encrees of hope, of what it be,
Therwith ful ofte encreseth eek desyr ;
Or, as an ook cometh of a litel spyr,   1335
So through this lettre, which that she
   him sente,
Encresen gan desyr, of which he brente.

192. Wherfore I seye alwey, that day and
   night
This Troilus gan to desiren more
Than he dide erst, thurgh hope, and dide
   his might         1340
To pressen on, as by Pandarus lore,
And wryten to hir of his sorwes sore
Fro day to day ; he leet it not refreyde,
That by Pandare he wroot somwhat or
   seyde ;

193. And dide also his othere obser-
   vaunces          1345
That to a lovere longeth in this cas ;
And, after that these dees turnede on
   chaunces,
So was he outher glad or seyde ' allas ! '
And held after his gestes ay his pas ;
And aftir swiche answeres as he hadde,
So were his dayes sory outher gladde. 1351

194. But to Pandare alwey was his recours,
And pitously gan ay til him to pleyne,
And him bisoughte of rede and som
   socours ;
And Pandarus, that sey his wode peyne,
Wex wel neigh deed for routhe, sooth to
   seyne,          1356

And bisily with al his herte caste
Som of his wo to sleen, and that as faste ;

195. And seyde, 'lord, and freend, and
     brother dere,
God woot that thy disese doth me wo. 1360
But woltow stinten al this woful chere,
And, by my trouthe, or it be dayes two,
And god to-forn, yet shal I shape it so,
That thou shalt come in-to a certayn
     place,
Ther-as thou mayst thy-self hir preye of
     grace,            1365

196. And certainly, I noot if thou it wost,
But tho that been expert in love it seye,
It is oon of the thinges that furthereth
     most,
A man to have a leyser for to preye,
And siker place his wo for to biwreye; 1370
For in good herte it moot som routhe
     impresse,
To here and see the giltles in distresse.

197. Paraunter thenkestow : though it
     be so
That kinde wolde doon hir to biginne
To han a maner routhe up-on my wo, 1375
Seyth Daunger, "Nay, thou shalt me
     never winne;
So reuleth hir hir hertes goost with-inne,
That, though she bende, yet she stant on
     rote;
What in effect is this un-to my bote?"

198. Thenk here-ayeins, whan that the
     sturdy ook,            1380
On which men hakketh ofte, for the
     nones,
Receyved hath the happy falling strook,
The grete sweigh doth it come al at ones,
As doon these rokkes or these milne-stones.
For swifter cours cometh thing that is of
     wighte,            1385
Whan it descendeth, than don thinges
     lighte.

199. And reed that boweth doun for every
     blast,
Ful lightly, cesse wind, it wol aryse ;
But so nil not an ook whan it is cast ;
It nedeth me nought thee longe to forbyse.

Men shal rejoysen of a greet empryse 1391
Acheved wel, and stant with-outen doute,
Al han men been the lenger ther-aboute.

200. But, Troilus, yet tel me, if thee lest,
A thing now which that I shal axen
     thee;            1395
Which is thy brother that thou lovest
     best
As in thy verray hertes privetee?'
'Y-wis, my brother Deiphebus,' quod he.
'Now,' quod Pandare, 'er houres twyes
     twelve,
He shal thee ese, unwist of it him-selve.

201. Now lat me allone, and werken as
     I may,'            1401
Quod he; and to Deiphebus wente he tho
Which hadde his lord and grete freend
     ben ay;
Save Troilus, no man he lovede so.
To telle in short, with-outen wordes mo,
Quod Pandarus, 'I pray yow that ye be
Freend to a cause which that toucheth
     me.'            1407

202. 'Yis, pardee,' quod Deiphebus, 'wel
     thow wost,
In al that ever I may, and god to-fore,
Al nere it but for man I love most,    1410
My brother Troilus; but sey wherfore
It is; for sith that day that I was bore,
I nas, ne never-mo to been I thinke,
Ayeins a thing that mighte thee for-
     thinke.'

203. Pandare gan him thonke, and to
     him seyde,            1415
'Lo, sire, I have a lady in this toun,
That is my nece, and called is Criseyde,
Which som men wolden doon oppressioun,
And wrongfully have hir possessioun :
Wherfor I of your lordship yow biseche
To been our freend, with-oute more
     speche.'            1421

204. Deiphebus him answerde, 'O, is not
     this,
That thow spekest of to me thus
     straungely,
Crisëyda, my freend?' He seyde, 'Yis.'
'Than nedeth,' quod Deiphebus hardely,

Na-more to speke, for trusteth wel, that I
Wol be hir champioun with spore and
    yerde;        1427
I roughte nought though alle hir foos it
    herde.

205. But tel me, thou that woost al this
    matere,
How I might best avaylen ? now lat see.'
Quod Pandarus, 'if ye, my lord so dere,
Wolden as now don this honour to me,
To prayen hir to-morwe, lo, that she
Com un-to yow hir pleyntes to devyse,
Hir adversaries wolde of hit agryse.    1435

206. And if I more dorste preye as now,
And chargen yow to have so greet tra-
    vayle,
To han som of your bretheren here with
    yow,
That mighten to hir cause bet avayle,
Than, woot I wel, she mighte never fayle
For to be holpen, what at your instaunce,
What with hir othere freendes govern-
    aunce.'    1442

207. Deiphebus, which that comen was,
    of kinde,
To al honour and bountee to consente,
Answerde, 'it shal be doon ; and I can
    finde    1445
Yet gretter help to this in myn entente.
What wolt thow seyn, if I for Eleyne
    sente
To speke of this? I trow it be the beste ;
For she may leden Paris as hir leste.

208. Of Ector, which that is my lord, my
    brother,    1450
It nedeth nought to preye him freend
    to be ;
For I have herd him, o tyme and eek other,
Speke of Criseyde swich honour, that he
May seyn no bet, swich hap to him hath
    she.
It nedeth nought his helpes for to
    crave ;    1455
He shal be swich, right as we wole him
    have.

209. Spek thou thy-self also to Troilus
On my bihalve, and pray him with us
    dyne.'

'Sire, al this shal be doon,' quod Pan-
    darus ;
And took his leve, and never gan to
    fyne,    1460
But to his neces hous, as streght as lyne,
He com; and fond hir fro the mete aryse ;
And sette him doun, and spak right in
    this wyse.

210. He seyde, 'O veray god, so have
    I ronne !
Lo, nece myn, see ye nought how I swete?
I noot whether ye the more thank me
    conne.    1466
Be ye nought war how that fals Poliphete
Is now aboute eft-sones for to plete,
And bringe on yow advocacyës newe ?'
'I ? no,' quod she, and chaunged al hir
    hewe.    1470

211. 'What is he more aboute, me to
    drecche
And doon me wrong? what shal I do,
    allas ?
Yet of him-self no-thing ne wolde I recche,
Nere it for Antenor and Eneas,
That been his freendes in swich maner
    cas ;    1475
But, for the love of god, myn uncle dere,
No fors of that, lat him have al y-fere ;

212 With-outen that, I have ynough for
    us.'
'Nay,' quod Pandare, 'it shal no-thing
    be so.    1479
For I have been right now at Deiphebus,
And Ector, and myne othere lordes mo,
And shortly maked eche of hem his fo ;
That, by my thrift, he shal it never winne
For ought he can, whan that so he bi-
    ginne.'

213. And as they casten what was best to
    done,    1485
Deiphebus, of his owene curtasye,
Com hir to preye, in his propre persone,
To holde him on the morwe companye
At diner, which she nolde not denye,
But goodly gan to his preyere obeye.    1490
He thonked hir, and wente up-on his
    weye.

214. Whanne this was doon, this Pandare
     up a-noon,
To telle in short, and forth gan for to
     wende
To Troilus, as stille as any stoon,
And al this thing he tolde him, word and
     ende ;         1495
And how that he Deiphebus gan to blende ;
And seyde him, 'now is tyme, if that thou
     conne,
To bere thee wel to-morwe, and al is
     wonne.

215. Now spek, now prey, now pitously
     compleyne ;
Lat not for nyce shame, or drede, or
     slouthe ;        1500
Som-tyme a man mot telle his owene
     peyne ;
Bileve it, and she shal han on thee routhe ;
Thou shalt be saved by thy feyth, in
     trouthe.
But wel wot I, thou art now in a drede ;
And what it is, I leye, I can arede.    1505

216. Thow thinkest now, "how sholde
     I doon al this?
For by my cheres mosten folk aspye,
That for hir love is that I fare a-mis ;
Yet hadde I lever unwist for sorwe dye."
Now thenk not so, for thou dost greet
     folye.        1510
For right now have I founden o manere
Of sleighte, for to coveren al thy chere.

217. Thow shalt gon over night, and that
     as blyve,
Un-to Deiphebus hous, as thee to pleye,
Thy maladye a-wey the bet to dryve,    1515
For-why thou semest syk, soth for to seye.
Sone after that, doun in thy bed thee leye,
And sey, thow mayst no lenger up endure,
And lye right there, and byde thyn aven-
     ture.

218. Sey that thy fever is wont thee for
     to take        1520
The same tyme, and lasten til a-morwe ;
And lat see now how wel thou canst
     it make,
For, par-dee, syk is he that is in sorwe.

Go now, farewel ! and, Venus here to
     borwe,        1524
I hope, and thou this purpos holde ferme,
Thy grace she shal fully ther conferme.'

219. Quod Troilus, 'y-wis, thou nedelees
Counseylest me, that sykliche I me feyne !
For I am syk in ernest, doutelees,
So that wel neigh I sterve for the peyne.'
Quod Pandarus, 'thou shalt the bettre
     pleyne,       1531
And hast the lasse nede to countrefete ;
For him men demen hoot that men seen
     swete.

220. Lo, holde thee at thy triste cloos,
     and I
Shal wel the deer un-to thy bowe dryve.'
Therwith he took his leve al softely,    1536
And Troilus to paleys wente blyve.
So glad ne was he never in al his lyve ;
And to Pandarus reed gan al assente,
And to Deiphebus hous at night he
     wente.       1540

221. What nedeth yow to tellen al the
     chere
That Deiphebus un-to his brother made,
Or his accesse, or his syklich manere,
How men gan him with clothes for to
     lade,
Whan he was leyd, and how men wolde
     him glade ?      1545
But al for nought, he held forth ay the
     wyse
That ye han herd Pandare er this devyse.

222. But certeyn is, er Troilus him leyde,
Deiphebus had him prayed, over night,
To been a freend and helping to Criseyde.
God woot, that he it grauntede anon-
     right,       1551
To been hir fulle freend with al his might.
But swich a nede was to preye him
     thenne,
As for to bidde a wood man for to renne.

223. The morwen com, and neighen gan
     the tyme     1555
Of meel-tyd, that the faire quene Eleyne
Shoop hir to been, an houre after the
     pryme,

With Deiphebus, to whom she nolde
   feyne ;
But as his suster, hoomly, sooth to seyne,
She com to diner in hir playn entente. 1560
But god and Pandare wiste al what this
   mente.

224. Come eek Criseyde, al innocent of
   this,
Antigone, hir sister Tarbe also ;
But flee we now prolixitee best is,
For love of god, and lat us faste go   1565
Right to the effect, with-oute tales mo,
Why al this folk assembled in this place ;
And lat us of hir saluinges pace.

225. Gret honour dide hem Deiphebus,
   certeyn,
And fedde hem wel with al that mighte
   lyke.    1570
But ever-more, 'allas !' was his refreyn,
'My goode brother Troilus, the syke,
Lyth yet'—and therwith-al he gan to
   syke ;
And after that, he peyned him to glade
Hem as he mighte, and chere good he
   made.    1575

226. Compleyned eek Eleyne of his syk-
   nesse
So feithfully, that pitee was to here,
And every wight gan waxen for accesse
A leche anoon, and seyde, 'in this manere
Men curen folk ; this charme I wol yow
   lere.'    1580
But there sat oon, al list hir nought to
   teche,
That thoughte, best coude I yet been his
   leche.

227. After compleynt, him gonnen they
   to preyse,
As folk don yet, whan som wight hath
   bigonne
To preyse a man, and up with prys him
   reyse    1585
A thousand fold yet hyer than the sonne :—
'He is, he can, that fewe lordes conne.'
And Pandarus, of that they wolde afferme,
He not for-gat hir preysing to conferme.

228. Herde al this thing Criseyde wel
   y-nough,    1590
And every word gan for to notifye ;
For which with sobre chere hir herte
   lough ;
For who is that ne wolde hir glorifye,
To mowen swich a knight don live or
   dye ?
But al passe I, lest ye to longe dwelle ; 1595
For for o fyn is al that ever I telle.

229. The tyme com, fro diner for to ryse,
And, as hem oughte, arisen everychoon,
And gonne a whyl of this and that devyse.
But Pandarus brak al this speche anoon,
And seyde to Deiphebus, 'wole ye goon,
If youre wille be, as I yow preyde,   1602
To speke here of the nedes of Criseyde ? '

230. Eleyne, which that by the hond hir
   held,
Took first the tale, and seyde, 'go we
   blyve ;'    1605
And goodly on Criseyde she biheld,
And seyde, ' Joves lat him never thryve,
That dooth yow harm, and bringe him
   sone of lyve !
And yeve me sorwe, but he shal it rewe,
If that I may, and alle folk be trewe.' 1610

231. 'Tel thou thy neces cas,' quod Dei-
   phebus
To Pandarus, 'for thou canst best it
   telle.'—
' My lordes and my ladyes, it stant thus ;
What sholde I lenger,' quod he, ' do yow
   dwelle ? '
He rong hem out a proces lyk a belle, 1615
Up-on hir fo, that highte Poliphete,
So heynous, that men mighte on it spete.

232. Answerde of this ech worse of hem
   than other,
And Poliphete they gonnen thus to
   warien,
'An-honged be swich oon, were he my
   brother ;    1620
And so he shal, for it ne may not varien.'
What sholde I lenger in this tale tarien ?
Pleynly, alle at ones, they hir highten,
To been hir helpe in al that ever they
   mighten.

233. Spak than Eleyne, and seyde, ' Pan-
　　darus,　　　　　　　　　　　1625
Woot ought my lord, my brother, this
　　matere,
I mene, Ector? or woot it Troilus?'
He seyde, ' ye, but wole ye now me here ?
Me thinketh this, sith Troilus is here,
It were good, if that ye wolde assente, 1630
She tolde hir-self him al this, er she wente.

234. For he wole have the more hir grief
　　at herte,
By cause, lo, that she a lady is ;
And, by your leve, I wol but right in
　　sterte,
And do yow wite, and that anoon, y-
　　wis,　　　　　　　　　　　　1635
If that he slepe, or wole ought here of
　　this.'
And in he lepte, and seyde him in his
　　ere,
'God have thy soule, y-brought have I
　　thy bere !'

235. To smylen of this gan tho Troilus,
And Pandarus, with-oute rekeninge, 1640
Out wente anoon t' Eleyne and Deiphebus,
And seyde hem, ' so there be no taryinge,
Ne more pres, he wol wel that ye bringe
Criseyda, my lady, that is here ;
And as he may enduren, he wole here. 1645

236. But wel ye woot, the chaumbre is
　　but lyte,
And fewe folk may lightly make it warm ;
Now loketh ye, (for I wol have no wyte,
To bringe in prees that mighte doon him
　　harm
Or him disesen, for my bettre arm), 1650
Wher it be bet she byde til eft-sones ;
Now loketh ye, that knowen what to
　　doon is.

237. I sey for me, best is, as I can knowe,
That no wight in ne wente but ye tweye,
But it were I, for I can, in a throwe, 1655
Reherce hir cas, unlyk that she can seye ;
And after this, she may him ones preye
To ben good lord, in short, and take hir
　　leve ;
This may not muchel of his ese him reve.

238. And eek, for she is straunge, he wol
　　forbere　　　　　　　　　　1660
His ese, which that him thar nought for
　　yow ;
Eek other thing, that toucheth not to
　　here,
He wol me telle, I woot it wel right now,
That secret is, and for the tounes prow.'
And they, that no-thing knewe of this
　　entente,　　　　　　　　　1665
With-oute more, to Troilus in they wente.

239. Eleyne in al hir goodly softe wyse,
Gan him saluwe, and womanly to pleye,
And seyde, ' ywis, ye moste alweyes aryse !
Now fayre brother, beth al hool, I preye !'
And gan hir arm right over his sholder
　　leye,　　　　　　　　　　　1671
And him with al hir wit to recomforte ;
As she best coude, she gan him to dis-
　　porte.

240. So after this quod she, ' we yow
　　biseke,
My dere brother, Deiphebus, and I, 1675
For love of god, and so doth Pandare eke,
To been good lord and freend, right
　　hertely,
Un-to Criseyde, which that certeinly
Receyveth wrong, as woot wel here Pan-
　　dare,
That can hir cas wel bet than I declare.'

241. This Pandarus gan newe his tunge
　　affyle,　　　　　　　　　　1681
And al hir cas reherce, and that anoon ;
Whan it was seyd, sone after, in a whyle,
Quod Troilus, ' as sone as I may goon,
I wol right fayn with al my might ben
　　oon,　　　　　　　　　　　1685
Have god my trouthe, hir cause to sustene.'
' Good thrift have ye,' quod Eleyne the
　　quene.

242. Quod Pandarus, ' and it your wille be,
That she may take hir leve, er that she
　　go ?'
' Or elles god for-bede,' tho quod he, 1690
' If that she vouche sauf for to do so.'
And with that word quod Troilus, ' ye two.
Deiphebus, and my suster leef and dere,
To yow have I to speke of o matere,

243. To been avysed by your reed the
     bettre':—      1695
And fond, as hap was, at his beddes heed,
The copie of a tretis and a lettre,
That Ector hadde him sent to axen reed,
If swich a man was worthy to ben deed,
Woot I nought who ; but in a grisly wyse
He preyede hem anoon on it avyse.    1701

244. Deiphebus gan this lettre to unfolde
In ernest greet ; so dide Eleyne the quene ;
And rominge outward, fast it gan biholde,
Downward a steyre, in-to an herber
     grene.      1705
This ilke thing they redden hem bi-twene ;
And largely, the mountaunce of an houre,
They gonne on it to reden and to poure.

245. Now lat hem rede, and turne we
     anoon
To Pandarus, that gan ful faste prye 1710
That al was wel, and out he gan to goon
In-to the grete chambre, and that in hye,
And seyde, ' god save al this companye !
Com, nece myn ; my lady quene Eleyne
Abydeth yow, and eek my lordes tweyne.

246. Rys, take with yow your nece An-
     tigone,      1716
Or whom yow list, or no fors, hardily ;
The lasse prees, the bet ; com forth with
     me,
And loke that ye thonke humblely    1719
Hem alle three, and, whan ye may goodly
Your tyme y-see, taketh of hem your leve,
Lest we to longe his restes him bireve.'

247. Al innocent of Pandarus entente,
Quod tho Criseyde, ' go we, uncle dere ';
And arm in arm inward with him she
     wente,      1725
Avysed wel hir wordes and hir chere ;
And Pandarus, in ernestful manere,
Seyde, ' alle folk, for goddes love, I preye,
Stinteth right here, and softely yow pleye.

248. Aviseth yow what folk ben here
     with-inne,      1730
And in what plyt oon is, god him a-
     mende !
And inward thus ful softely biginne ;
Nece, I conjure and heighly yow defende,
On his half, which that sowle us alle
     sende,
And in the vertue of corounes tweyne,
Slee nought this man, that hath for yow
     this peyne !      1736

249. Fy on the devel ! thenk which oon
     he is,
And in what plyt he lyth ; com of anoon ;
Thenk al swich taried tyd, but lost it nis !
That wol ye bothe seyn, whan ye ben oon.
Secoundelich, ther yet devyneth noon 1741
Up-on yow two ; com of now, if ye conne ;
Whyl folk is blent, lo, al the tyme is
     wonne !

250. In titering, and pursuite, and de-
     layes,
The folk devyne at wagginge of a stree ;
And though ye wolde han after merye
     dayes,      1746
Than dar ye nought, and why ? for she,
     and she
Spak swich a word ; thus loked he, and he ;
Lest tyme I loste, I dar not with yow dele ;
Com of therfore, and bringeth him to hele.'

251. But now to yow, ye lovers that ben
     here,      1751
Was Troilus nought in a cankedort,
That lay, and mighte whispringe of hem
     here,
And thoughte, 'O lord, right now renneth
     my sort
Fully to dye, or han anoon comfort '; 1755
And was the firste tyme he shulde hir
     preye
Of love ; O mighty god, what shal he seye?

**Explicit Secundus Liber.**

# BOOK III.

### Incipit Prohemium Tercii Libri.

1. O BLISFUL light, of whiche the bemes
clere
Adorneth al the thridde hevene faire !
O sonnes leef, O Joves doughter dere,
Plesaunce of love, O goodly debonaire.
In gentil hertes ay redy to repaire !    5
O verray cause of hele and of gladnesse,
Y-heried be thy might and thy goodnesse !

2. In hevene and helle, in erthe and
salte see
Is felt thy might, if that I wel descerne ;
As man, brid, best, fish, herbe and grene
tree    10
Thee fele in tymes with vapour eterne.
God loveth, and to love wol nought werne ;
And in this world no lyves creature,
With-outen love, is worth, or may endure.

3. Ye Joves first to thilke effectes glade, 15
Thorugh which that thinges liven alle
and be,
Comeveden, and amorous †him made
On mortal thing, and as yow list, ay ye
Yeve him in love ese or adversitee ;
And in a thousand formes doun him sente
For love in erthe, and whom yow liste,
he hente.    21

4. Ye fierse Mars apeysen of his ire,
And, as yow list, ye maken hertes digne ;
Algates, hem that ye wol sette a-fyre,
They dreden shame, and vices they re-
signe ;    25
Ye do hem corteys be, fresshe and benigne,
And hye or lowe, after a wight entendeth ;
The joyes that he hath, your might him
sendeth.

5. Ye holden regne and hous in unitee ;
Ye soothfast cause of frendship been also ;
Ye knowe al thilke covered qualitee    31
Of thinges which that folk on wondren so,

Whan they can not construe how it may jo,
She loveth him, or why he loveth here ;
As why this fish, and nought that, cometh
to were.    35

6. Ye folk a lawe han set in universe,
And this knowe I by hem that loveres be,
That who-so stryveth with yow hath the
werse .
Now, lady bright, for thy benignitee,
At reverence of hem that serven thee,    40
Whos clerk I am, so techeth me devyse
Som joye of that is felt in thy servyse.

7. Ye in my naked herte sentement
Inhelde, and do me shewe of thy swet-
nesse.—
Caliope, thy vois be now present,    45
For now is nede ; sestow not my destresse,
How I mot telle anon-right the gladnesse
Of Troilus, to Venus heryinge ?
To which gladnes, who nede hath, god
him bringe !

### Explicit prohemium Tercii Libri.

### Incipit Liber Tercius.

8. LAY al this mene whyle Troilus,    50
Recordinge his lessoun in this manere,
' Ma fey !' thought he, 'thus wole I seye
and thus ;
Thus wole I pleyne un-to my lady dere ;
That word is good, and this shal be my
chere ;
This nil I not foryeten in no wyse.'    55
God leve him werken as he gan devyse.

9. And lord, so that his herte gan to
quappe,
Heringe hir come, and shorte for to syke !
And Pandarus, that ladde hir by the
lappe,
Com neer, and gan in at the curtin pyke,
And seyde, ' god do bote on alle syke !    61
See, who is here yow comen to visyte ;
Lo, here is she that is your deeth to wyte.'

10. Ther-with it semed as he wepte al-
      most ;
' A ha,' quod Troilus so rewfully,     65
' Wher me be wo, O mighty god, thou
      wost !
Who is al there ? I see nought trewely.'
'Sire,' quod Criseyde, 'it is Pandare and I.'
' Ye, swete herte? allas, I may nought ryse
To knele, and do yow honour in som
      wyse.'                70

11. And dressede him upward, and she
      right tho
Gan bothe here hondes softe upon him
      leye,
' O, for the love of god, do ye not so
To me,' quod she, ' ey ! what is this to
      seye ?
Sire, come am I to yow for causes tweye ;
First, yow to thonke, and of your lord-
      shipe eke            76
Continuaunce I wolde yow biseke.'

12. This Troilus, that herde his lady
      preye
Of lordship him, wex neither quik ne
      deed,
Ne mighte a word for shame to it seye, 80
Al-though men sholde smyten of his heed.
But lord, so he wex sodeinliche reed,
And sire, his lesson, that he wende conne,
To preyen hir, is thurgh his wit y-ronne.

13. Criseyde al this aspyede wel **y-nough,**
For she was wys, and lovede him **never-**
      **the-lasse,**       86
Al nere he malapert, or made it tough,
Or was to bold, to singe a fool a masse.
But whan his shame gan somwhat to
      passe,
His resons, as I may my rymes holde,   90
I yow wol telle, as techen bokes olde.

14. In chaunged vois, right for his verrey
      drede,
Which vois eek quook, and ther-to his
      manere
Goodly abayst, and now his hewes rede,
Now pale, un-to Criseyde, his lady dere, 95
With look doun cast and humble yolden
      chere,

Lo, th'alderfirste word that him asterte
Was, twyes, 'mercy, mercy, swete herte!'

15. And stinte a whyl, and whan he
      mighte out-bringe,       99
The nexte word was, 'god wot, for I have,
As feythfully as I have had konninge,
Ben youres, also god my sowle save ;
And shal, til that I, woful wight, be
      grave.
And though I dar ne can un-to yow
      pleyne,
Y-wis, I suffre nought the lasse peyne. 105

16. Thus muche as now, O wommanliche
      wyf,
I may out-bringe, and if this yow displese,
That shal I wreke upon myn owne lyf
Right sone, I trowe, and doon your herte
      an ese,       109
If with my deeth your herte I may apese.
But sin that ye han herd me som-what
      seye,
Now recche I never how sone that I deye.'

17 Ther-with his manly sorwe to biholde,
It mighte han maad an herte of stoon to
      rewe ;       114
And Pandare weep as he to watre wolde,
And poked ever his nece newe and newe,
And seyde, ' wo bigon ben hertes trewe !
For love of god, make of this thing an
      ende,
Or slee us bothe at ones, er that ye wende.'

18. 'I ? what ?' quod she, ' by god and by
      my trouthe,       120
I noot nought what ye wilne that I seye.'
' I ? what ?' quod he, ' that ye han on him
      routhe,
For goddes love, and doth him nought to
      deye.'
' Now thanne thus,' quod she, ' I wolde
      him preye
To telle me the fyn of his entente ;   125
Yet wiste I never wel what that he mente.'

19. ' What that I mene, O swete herte
      dere ?'
Quod Troilus, ' O goodly fresshe free !
That, with the stremes of your eyen clere,
Ye wolde som-tyme freendly on me see, 130

And thanne agreën that I may ben he,
With-oute braunche of vyce in any wyse,
In trouthe alwey to doon yow my servyse

20.  As to my lady right and chief resort,
With al my wit and al my diligence,   135
And I to han, right as yow list, comfort,
Under your yerde, egal to myn offence,
As deeth, if that I breke your defence ;
And that ye deigne me so muche honoure,
Me to comaunden ought in any houre. 140

21.  And I to been your verray humble
    trewe,
Secret, and in my paynes pacient,
And ever-mo desire freshly newe,
To serven, and been †y-lyke ay diligent,
And, with good herte, al holly your
    talent    145
Receyven wel, how sore that me smerte,
Lo, this mene I, myn owene swete herte.'

22.  Quod Pandarus, 'lo, here an hard
    request,
And resonable, a lady for to werne !
Now, nece myn, by natal Joves fest,   150
Were I a god, ye sholde sterve as yerne,
That heren wel, this man wol no-thing
    yerne
But your honour, and seen him almost
    sterve,
And been so looth to suffren him yow
    serve.'

23  With that she gan hir eyen on him
    caste    155
Ful esily, and ful debonairly,
Avysing hir, and hyed not to faste
With never a word, but seyde him softely,
' Myn honour sauf, I wol wel trewely,
And in swich forme as he can now
    devyse,    160
Receyven him fully to my servyse,

24.  Biseching him, for goddes love, that
    he
Wolde, in honour of trouthe and gentil-
    esse,
As I wel mene, eek mene wel to me,   164
And myn honour, with wit and besinesse,
Ay kepe ; and if I may don him gladnesse,

From hennes-forth, y-wis, I nil not feyne :
Now beeth al hool, no lenger ye ne pleyne.

25  But nathelees, this warne I yow,'
    quod she,
' A kinges sone al-though ye be, y-wis, 170
Ye shul na-more have soverainetee
Of me in love, than right in that cas is ;
Ne I nil forbere, if that ye doon a-mis,
To wrathen yow ; and whyl that ye me
    serve,
Cherycen yow right after ye deserve.   175

26.  And shortly, derë herte and al my
    knight,
Beth glad, and draweth yow to lustinesse,
And I shal trewely, with al my might,
Your bittre tornen al in-to swetnesse ; 179
If I be she that may yow do gladnesse,
For every wo ye shal recovere a blisse ';
And him in armes took, and gan him
    kisse.

27  Fil Pandarus on knees, and up his
    yën
To hevene threw, and held his hondes
    hye,
' Immortal god !' quod he, ' that mayst
    nought dyen,    185
Cupide I mene, of this mayst glorifye ;
And Venus, thou mayst make melodye ;
With-outen hond, me semeth that in
    towne,
For this merveyle, I here ech belle sowne.

28.  But ho ! no more as now of this
    matere,    190
For-why this folk wol comen up anoon,
That han the lettre red : lo, I hem here.
But I conjure thee, Criseyde, and oon,
And two, thou Troilus, whan thow mayst
    goon,
That at myn hous ye been at my warn-
    inge,    195
For I ful wel shal shape your cominge ;

29  And eseth ther your hertes right
    y-nough ;
And lat see which of yow shal bere the
    belle
To speke of love a-right!' ther-with he
    lough.

' For ther have ye a layser for to telle.' 200
Quod Troilus, ' how longe shal I dwelle
Er this be doon ?' Quod he, ' whan thou
    mayst ryse,
This thing shal be right as I yow devyse.'

30. With that Eleyne and also Deiphebus
Tho comen upward, right at the steyres
    ende ;     205
And lord, so than gan grone Troilus,
His brother and his suster for to blende.
Quod Pandarus, ' it tyme is that we
    wende ;
Tak, nece myn, your leve at alle three,
And lat hem speke, and cometh forth
    with me.'     210

31. She took hir leve at hem ful thriftily,
As she wel coude, and they hir reverence
Un-to the fulle diden hardely,
And speken wonder wel, in hir absence,
Of hir, in preysing of hir excellence,     215
Hir governaunce, hir wit ; and hir man-
    ere
Commendeden, it joye was to here.

32. Now lat hir wende un-to hir owne
    place,
And torne we to Troilus a-yein,     219
That gan ful lightly of the lettre passe
That Deiphebus hadde in the gardin seyn.
And of Eleyne and him he wolde fayn
Delivered been, and seyde, that him leste
To slepe, and after tales have reste.

33. Eleyne him kiste, and took hir leve
    blyve,     225
Deiphebus eek, and hoom wente every
    wight ;
And Pandarus, as faste as he may dryve,
To Troilus tho com, as lyne right ;
And on a paillet, al that glade night,
By Troilus he lay, with mery chere,     230
To tale ; and wel was hem they were
    y-fere.

34. Whan every wight was voided but
    they two,
And alle the dores were faste y-shette,
To telle in short, with-oute wordes mo,
This Pandarus, with-outen any lette,     235
Up roos, and on his beddes syde him sette,

And gan to speken in a sobre wyse
To Troilus, as I shal yow devyse.

35. ' Myn alderlevest lord, and brother
    dere,
God woot, and thou, that it sat me so
    sore,     240
When I thee saw so languisshing to-yere,
For love, of which thy wo wex alwey
    more ;
That I, with al my might and al my lore,
Hath ever sithen doon my bisinesse
To bringe thee to joye out of distresse ;

36. And have it brought to swich plyt as
    thou wost,     246
So that, thorugh me, thow stondest now
    in weye
To fare wel, I seye it for no bost,
And wostow why ? for shame it is to seye,
For thee have I bigonne a gamen pleye
Which that I never doon shal eft for
    other,     251
Al-though he were a thousand fold my
    brother.

37. That is to seye, for thee am I bicomen,
Bitwixen game and ernest, swich a mene
As maken wommen un-to men to comen ;
Al sey I nought, thou wost wel what I
    mene.     256
For thee have I my nece, of vyces clene,
So fully maad thy gentilesse triste,
That al shal been right as thy-selve liste.

38. But god, that al wot, take I to wit-
    nesse,     260
That never I this for coveityse wroughte,
But only for to abregge that distresse,
For which wel nygh thou deydest, as me
    thoughte.
But gode brother, do now as thee oughte,
For goddes love, and keep hir out of
    blame,     265
Sin thou art wys, and save alwey hir
    name.

39. For wel thou wost, the name as yet
    of here
Among the peple, as who seyth, halwed is;
For that man is unbore, I dar wel swere,
That ever wiste that she dide amis.     270

But wo is me, that I, that cause al this,
May thenken that she is my nece dere,
And I hir eem, and traytor eek y-fere!

40. And were it wist that I, through myn
        engyn,
Hadde in my nece y-put this fantasye, 275
To do thy lust, and hoolly to be thyn,
Why, al the world up-on it wolde crye,
And seye, that I the worste trecherye
Dide in this cas, that ever was bigonne,
And she for-lost, and thou right nought
        y-wonne.                            280

41. Wher-fore, er I wol ferther goon a
        pas,
Yet eft I thee biseche and fully seye,
That privetee go with us in this cas,
That is to seye, that thou us never wreye;
And be nought wrooth, though I thee
        ofte preye                          285
To holden secree swich an heigh matere;
For skilful is, thow wost wel, my preyere.

42. And thenk what wo ther hath bitid
        er this,
For makinge of avauntes, as men rede ;
And what mischaunce in this world yet
        ther is,                            290
Fro day to day, right for that wikked
        dede ;
For which these wyse clerkes that ben
        dede
Han ever yet proverbed to us yonge,
That "firste vertu is to kepe tonge."

43. And, nere it that I wilne as now
        t'abregge                           295
Diffusioun of speche, I coude almost
A thousand olde stories thee alegge
Of wommen lost, thorugh fals and foles
        bost ;
Proverbes canst thy-self y-nowe, and wost,
Ayeins that vyce, for to been a labbe, 300
Al seyde men sooth as often as they gabbe.

44. O tonge, allas! so often here-biforn
Hastow made many a lady bright of hewe
Seyd, "welawey! the day that I was born!"
And many a maydes sorwes for to newe ;
And, for the more part, al is untrewe 306

That men of yelpe, and it were brought
        to preve ;
Of kinde non avauntour is to leve.

45. Avauntour and a lyere, al is on ;  309
As thus: I pose, a womman graunte me
Hir love, and seyth that other wol she non,
And I am sworn to holden it secree,
And after I go telle it two or three ;
Y-wis, I am avauntour at the leste,
And lyere, for I breke my biheste.      315

46. Now loke thanne, if they be nought
        to blame,
Swich maner folk ; what shal I clepe
        hem, what,
That hem avaunte of wommen, and by
        name,
That never yet bihighte hem this ne that,
Ne knewe hem more than myn olde hat?
No wonder is, so god me sende hele,    321
Though wommen drede with us men to
        dele.

47. I sey not this for no mistrust of yow,
Ne for no wys man, but for foles nyce,
And for the harm that in the world is
        now,                                325
As wel for foly ofte as for malyce ;
For wel wot I, in wyse folk, that vyce
No womman drat, if she be wel avysed ;
For wyse ben by foles harm chastysed.

48. But now to purpos ; leve brother dere,
Have al this thing that I have seyd in
        minde,                              331
And keep thee clos, and be now of good
        chere,
For at thy day thou shalt me trewe finde.
I shal thy proces sette in swich a kinde,
And god to-forn, that it shall thee suffyse,
For it shal been right as thou wolt de-
        vyse.                               336

49. For wel I woot, thou menest wel,
        parde ;
Therfore I dar this fully undertake.
Thou wost eek what thy lady graunted
        thee,
And day is set, the chartres up to make.
Have now good night, I may no lenger
        wake ;                              341

And bid for me, sin thou art now in blisse,
That god me sende deeth or sone lisse.'

50. Who mighte telle half the joye or feste
Which that the sowle of Troilus tho felte,
Heringe th'effect of Pandarus biheste? 346
His olde wo, that made his herte swelte,
Gan tho for joye wasten and to-melte,
And al the richesse of his sykes sore
At ones fledde, he felte of hem no more.

51. But right so as these holtes and these
hayes,     351
That han in winter dede been and dreye,
Revesten hem in grene, whan that May is,
Whan every lusty lyketh best to pleye :
Right in that selve wyse, sooth to seye, 355
Wex sodeynliche his herte ful of joye,
That gladder was ther never man in Troye.

52. And gan his look on Pandarus up
caste
Ful sobrely, and frendly for to see,     359
And seyde, 'freend, in Aprille the laste,
As wel thou wost, if it remembre thee,
How neigh the deeth for wo thou founde
me ;
And how thou didest al thy bisinesse
To knowe of me the cause of my distresse.

53. Thou wost how longe I it for-bar to
seye     365
To thee, that art the man that I best
triste ;
And peril was it noon to thee by-wreye,
That wiste I wel ; but tel me, if thee liste,
Sith I so looth was that thy-self it wiste,
How dorste I mo tellen of this matere, 370
That quake now, and no wight may us
here ?

54. But natheles, by that god I thee swere,
That, as him list, may al this world
governe,
And, if I lye, Achilles with his spere
Myn herte cleve, al were my lyf eterne,
As I am mortal, if I late or yerne     376
Wolde it biwreye, or dorste, or sholde
conne,
For al the good that god made under
sonne ;

55. That rather deye I wolde, and de-
termyne,
As thinketh me, now stokked in presoun,
In wrecchednesse, in filthe, and in ver-
myne,     381
Caytif to cruel king Agamenoun ;
And this, in alle the temples of this
toun,
Upon the goddes alle, I wol thee swere,
To-morwe day, if that thee lyketh here. 385

56. And that thou hast so muche y-doon
for me,
That I ne may it never-more deserve,
This knowe I wel, al mighte I now for
thee
A thousand tymes on a morwen sterve,
I can no more, but that I wol thee serve
Right as thy sclave, whider-so thou
wende,     391
For ever-more, un-to my lyves ende !

57. But here, with al myn herte, I thee
biseche,
That never in me thou deme swich folye
As I shal seyn ; me thoughte, by thy
speche,     395
That this, which thou me dost for com-
panye,
I sholde wene it were a bauderye ;
I am nought wood, al-if I lewed be ;
It is not so, that woot I wel, pardee.

58. But he that goth, for gold or for
richesse,     400
On swich message, calle him what thee
list ;
And this that thou dost, calle it gentilesse,
Compassioun, and felawship, and trist ;
Departe it so, for wyde-where is wist
How that there is dyversitee requered 405
Bitwixen thinges lyke, as I have lered.

59. And, that thou knowe I thenke
nought ne wene
That this servyse a shame be or jape,
I have my faire suster Polixene,
Cassandre, Eleyne, or any of the frape ;
Be she never so faire or wel y-shape, 411
Tel me, which thou wilt of everichone,
To han for thyn, and lat me thanne allone.

60. But sin that thou hast don me this
　　　servyse,　　　　　　　　　　414
My lyf to save, and for noon hope of mede,
So, for the love of god, this grete empryse
Parforme it out; for now is moste nede.
For high and low, with-outen any drede,
I wol alwey thyne hestes alle kepe;
Have now good night, and lat us bothe
　　　slepe.'　　　　　　　　　　420

61. Thus held him ech with other wel
　　　apayed,
That al the world ne mighte it bet
　　　amende;
And, on the morwe, whan they were
　　　arayed,
Ech to his owene nedes gan entende.
But Troilus, though as the fyr he brende
For sharp desyr of hope and of plesaunce,
He not for-gat his gode governaunce. 427

62. But in him-self with manhod gan
　　　restreyne
Ech rakel dede and ech unbrydled chere,
That alle tho that liven, sooth to seyne,
Ne sholde han wist, by word or by manere,
What that he mente, as touching this
　　　matere.　　　　　　　　　　432
From every wight as fer as is the cloude
He was, so wel dissimulen he coude.

63. And al the whyl which that I yow
　　　devyse,　　　　　　　　　　435
This was his lyf; with al his fulle might,
By day he was in Martes high servyse,
This is to seyn, in armes as a knight;
And for the more part, the longe night
He lay, and thoughte how that he mighte
　　　serve　　　　　　　　　　440
His lady best, hir thank for to deserve.

64. Nil I nought swerë, al-though he lay
　　　softe,
That in his thought he nas sumwhat
　　　disesed,
Ne that he tornede on his pilwes ofte,
And wolde of that him missed han ben
　　　sesed;　　　　　　　　　　445
But in swich cas man is nought alwey
　　　plesed,
For ought I wot, no more than was he;
That can I deme of possibilitee.

65. But certeyn is, to purpos for to go,
That in this whyle, as writen is in
　　　geste,　　　　　　　　　　450
He say his lady som-tyme; and also
She with him spak, whan that she dorste
　　　or leste,
And by hir bothe avys, as was the beste,
Apoynteden ful warly in this nede,
So as they dorste, how they wolde pro-
　　　cede.　　　　　　　　　　455

66. But it was spoken in so short a wyse,
In swich awayt alwey, and in swich fere,
Lest any wyght divynen or devyse
Wolde of hem two, or to it leye an ere,
That al this world so leef to hem ne
　　　were　　　　　　　　　　460
As that Cupido wolde hem grace sende
To maken of hir speche aright an ende.

67. But thilke litel that they speke or
　　　wroughte,
His wyse goost took ay of al swich hede,
It semed hir, he wiste that she thoughte
With-outen word, so that it was no nede
To bidde him ought to done, or ought
　　　forbede;　　　　　　　　　　467
For which she thoughte that love, al
　　　come it late,
Of alle joye hadde opned hir the yate.

68. And shortly of this proces for to
　　　pace,　　　　　　　　　　470
So wel his werk and wordes he bisette,
That he so ful stood in his lady grace,
That twenty thousand tymes, or she lette,
She thonked god she ever with him
　　　mette;
So coude he him governe in swich ser-
　　　vyse,　　　　　　　　　　475
That al the world ne mighte it bet
　　　devyse.

69. For-why she fond him so discreet in al,
So secret, and of swich obëisaunce,
That wel she felte he was to hir a wal
Of steel, and sheld from every disple-
　　　saunce;　　　　　　　　　　480
That, to ben in his gode governaunce,
So wys he was, she was no more afered,
I mene, as fer as oughte ben requered.

70. And Pandarus, to quike alwey the fyr,
Was ever y-lyke prest and diligent ;    485
To ese his frend was set al his desyr.
He shoof ay on, he to and fro was sent ;
He lettres bar whan Troilus was absent.
That never man, as in his freendes nede,
Ne bar him bet than he, with-outen
    drede.    490

71. But now, paraunter, som man wayten
    wolde
That every word, or sonde, or look, or
    chere
Of Troilus that I rehersen sholde,
In al this whyle, un-to his lady dere ;
I trowe it were a long thing for to
    here ;    495
Or of what wight that stant in swich dis-
    joynte,
His wordes alle, or every look, to poynte.

72. For sothe, I have not herd it doon er
    this,
In storye noon, ne no man here, I wene ;
And though I wolde I coude not, y-wis ;
For ther was som epistel hem bitwene, 501
That wolde, as seyth myn auctor, wel
    contene
Neigh half this book, of which him list
    not wryte ;
How sholde I thanne a lyne of it endyte ?

73. But to the grete effect : than sey I
    thus,    505
That stonding in concord and in quiete
Thise ilke two, Criseyde and Troilus,
As I have told, and in this tyme swete,
Save only often mighte they not mete,
Ne layser have hir speches to fulfelle,  510
That it befel right as I shal yow telle,

74. That Pandarus, that ever dide his
    might
Right for the fyn that I shal speke of
    here,
As for to bringe to his hous som night
His faire nece, and Troilus y-fere,    515
Wher-as at leyser al this heigh matere,
Touching hir love, were at the fulle up-
    bounde,
Hadde out of doute a tyme to it founde.

75. For he with greet deliberacioun
Hadde every thing that her-to mighte
    avayle    520
Forn-cast, and put in execucioun,
And neither laft for cost ne for travayle ;
Come if hem lest, hem sholde no-thing
    fayle ;
And for to been in ought espyed there,
That, wiste he wel, an inpossible were.

76. Dredelees, it cleer was in the wind
Of every pye and every lette-game ;    527
Now al is wel, for al the world is blind
In this matere, bothe fremed and tame.
This timber is al redy up to frame ;   530
Us lakketh nought but that we witen
    wolde
A certein houre, in whiche she comen
    sholde.

77. And Troilus, that al this purveyaunce
Knew at the fulle, and waytede on it ay,
Hadde here-up-on eek made gret orde-
    naunce,    535
And founde his cause, and ther-to his
    aray,
If that he were missed, night or day,
Ther-whyle he was aboute this servyse,
That he was goon to doon his sacrifyse,

78. And moste at swich a temple alone
    wake,    540
Answered of Appollo for to be ;
And first, to seen the holy laurer quake,
Er that Apollo spak out of the tree,
To telle him next whan Grekes sholden
    flee ;
And forthy lette him no man, god for-
    bede,    545
But preye Apollo helpen in this nede.

79. Now is ther litel more for to done,
But Pandare up, and shortly for to seyne,
Right sone upon the chaunging of the
    mone,
Whan lightles is the world a night or
    tweyne,    550
And that the welken shoop him for to
    reyne,
He streight a-morwe un-to his nece
    wente ;
Ye han wel herd the fyn of his entente.

80. Whan he was come, he gan anoon to
        pleye
As he was wont, and of him-self to jape ;
And fynally, he swor and gan hir seye, 556
By this and that, she sholde him not
        escape,
Ne lenger doon him after hir to gape :
But certeynly she moste, by hir leve,
Come soupen in his hous with him at
        eve.                                    560

81. At whiche she lough, and gan hir
        faste excuse,
And seyde, ' it rayneth ; lo, how sholde
        I goon ? '
' Lat be,' quod he, ' ne stond not thus to
        muse ;
This moot be doon, ye shal be ther anoon.'
So at the laste her-of they felle at oon, 565
Or elles, softe he swor hir in hir ere,
He nolde never come ther she were.

82. Sone after this, to him she gan to
        rowne,
And asked him if Troilus were there ?
He swor hir, ' nay, for he was out of
        towne,'                                570
And seyde, ' nece, I pose that he were,
Yow †thurfte never have the more fere.
For rather than men mighte him ther
        aspye,
Me were lever a thousand-fold to dye.'

83 Nought list myn auctor fully to
        declare                                575
What that she thoughte whan he seyde
        so,
That Troilus was out of town y-fare,
As if he seyde ther-of sooth or no ;
But that, with-oute awayt, with him to go,
She graunted him, sith he hir that bi-
        soughte,                               580
And, as his nece, obeyed as hir oughte

84. But nathelees, yet gan she him bi-
        seche,
Al-though with him to goon it was no fere,
For to be war of goosish peples speche,
That dremen thinges whiche that never
        were,                                  585
And wel avyse him whom he broughte
        there ;

And seyde him, ' eem, sin I mot on yow
        triste,
Loke al be wel, and do now as yow liste.'

85. He swor hir, ' yis, by stokkes and by
        stones,
And by the goddes that in hevene dwelle,
Or elles were him lever, soule and bones,
With Pluto king as depe been in helle 592
As Tantalus ! ' What sholde I more telle ?
Whan al was wel, he roos and took his
        leve,
And she to souper com, whan it was eve,

86. With a certayn of hir owene men, 596
And with hir faire nece Antigone,
And othere of hir wommen nyne or ten ;
But who was glad now, who, as trowe ye,
But Troilus, that stood and mighte it
        see                                    600
Thurgh-out a litel windowe in a stewe,
Ther he bishet, sin midnight, was in
        mewe,

87. Unwist of every wight but of Pandare?
But to the poynt ; now whan she was
        y-come
With alle joye, and alle frendes fare,   605
Hir eem anoon in armes hath hir nome,
And after to the souper, alle and some,
Whan tyme was, ful softe they hem sette ;
God wot, ther was no deyntee for to fette.

88. And after souper gonnen they to
        ryse,                                  610
At ese wel, with hertes fresshe and glade,
And wel was him that coude best devyse
To lyken hir, or that hir laughen made.
He song ; she pleyde ; he tolde tale of
        Wade.
But at the laste, as every thing hath
        ende,                                  615
She took hir leve, and nedes wolde wende.

89. But O, Fortune, executrice of wierdes,
O influences of thise hevenes hye !
Soth is, that, under god, ye ben our
        hierdes,
Though to us bestes been the causes
        wrye,                                  620
This mene I now, for she gan hoomward
        hye,

But execut was al bisyde hir leve,
At the goddes wil ; for which she moste
    bleve.

90. The bente mone with hir hornes pale,
Saturne, and Jove, in Cancro joyned
    were,     625
That swich a rayn from hevene gan avale,
That every maner womman that was there
Hadde of that smoky reyn a verray fere ;
At which Pandare tho lough, and seyde
    thenne,
' Now were it tyme a lady to go henne ! 630

91. But goode nece, if I mighte ever plese
Yow any-thing, than prey I yow,' quod he,
' To doon myn herte as now so greet an
    ese
As for to dwelle here al this night with me,
For-why this is your owene hous, pardee.
For, by my trouthe, I sey it nought a-
    game,     636
To wende as now, it were to me a shame.'

92. Criseyde, whiche that coude as muche
    good
As half a world, tok hede of his preyere ;
And sin it ron, and al was on a flood, 640
She thoughte, as good chep may I dwellen
    here,
And graunte it gladly with a freendes
    chere,
And have a thank, as grucche and thanne
    abyde ;
For hoom to goon it may nought wel
    bityde.

93. ' I wol,' quod she, ' myn uncle leef
    and dere,     645
Sin that yow list, it skile is to be so ;
I am right glad with yow to dwellen here ;
I seyde but a-game, I wolde go.'
' Y-wis, graunt mercy, nece !' quod he
    tho ;     649
' Were it a game or no, soth for to telle,
Now am I glad, sin that yow list to dwelle.'

94. Thus al is wel ; but tho bigan aright
The newe joye, and al the feste agayn ;
But Pandarus, if goodly hadde he might,
He wolde han hyed hir to bedde fayn, 655
And seyde, ' lord, this is an huge rayn !

This were a weder for to slepen inne ;
And that I rede us sone to biginne.

95. And nece, woot ye wher I wol yow
    leye,     659
For that we shul not liggen fer asonder,
And for ye neither shullen, dar I seye,
Heren noise of reynes nor of thonder ?
By god, right in my lyte closet yonder.
And I wol in that outer hous allone
Be wardeyn of your wommen everichone.

96. And in this middel chaumbre that ye
    see     666
Shul youre wommen slepen wel and softe;
And ther I seyde shal your-selve be ;
And if ye liggen wel to-night, com ofte,
And careth not what weder is on-lofte. 670
The wyn anon, and whan so that yow
    leste,
So go we slepe, I trowe it be the beste.'

97. Ther nis no more, but here-after sone,
The voydè dronke, and travers drawe
    anon,
Gan every wight, that hadde nought to
    done     675
More in that place, out of the chaumber
    gon.
And ever-mo so sternelich it ron,
And blew ther-with so wonderliche loude,
That wel neigh no man heren other coude.

98. Tho Pandarus, hir eem, right as him
    oughte,     680
With women swiche as were hir most
    aboute,
Ful glad un-to hir beddes syde hir
    broughte,
And took his leve, and gan ful lowe loute,
And seyde, ' here at this closet-dore with-
    oute,
Right over-thwart, your wommen liggen
    alle,     685
That, whom yow liste of hem, ye may
    here calle.'

99. So whan that she was in the closet
    leyd,
And alle hir wommen forth by orde-
    naunce
A-bedde weren, ther as I have seyd,

There was no more to skippen nor to
　　traunce,　　　　　　　　　　690
But boden go to bedde, with mischaunce,
If any wight was steringe any-where,
And late hem slepe that a-bedde were.

100. But Pandarus, that wel coude eche
　　a del
The olde daunce, and every poynt ther-
　　inne,　　　　　　　　　　　695
Whan that he sey that alle thing was wel,
He thoughte he wolde up-on his werk
　　biginne,
And gan the stewe-dore al softe un-pinne,
And stille as stoon, with-outen lenger
　　lette,
By Troilus a-doun right he him sette. 700

101. And, shortly to the poynt right for
　　to gon,
Of al this werk he tolde him word and
　　ende,
And seyde, 'make thee redy right anon,
For thou shalt in-to hevene blisse wende.'
'Now blisful Venus, thou me grace
　　sende,'　　　　　　　　　　705
Quod Troilus, 'for never yet no nede
Hadde I er now, ne halvendel the drede.'

102. Quod Pandarus, 'ne drede thee never
　　a del,
For it shal been right as thou wilt desyre;
So thryve I, this night shal I make it
　　wel,　　　　　　　　　　　710
Or casten al the gruwel in the fyre.'
'Yit blisful Venus, this night thou me
　　enspyre,'
Quod Troilus, 'as wis as I thee serve,
And ever bet and bet shal, til I sterve.

103. And if I hadde, O Venus ful of
　　mirthe,　　　　　　　　　　715
Aspectes badde of Mars or of Saturne,
Or thou combust or let were in my birthe,
Thy fader pray al thilke harm disturne
Of grace, and that I glad ayein may
　　turne,
For love of him thou lovedest in the
　　shawe,　　　　　　　　　　720
I mene Adoon, that with the boor was
　　slawe.

104. O Jove eek, for the love of faire
　　Europe,
The whiche in forme of bole away thou
　　fette;
Now help, O Mars, thou with thy blody
　　cope,
For love of Cipris, thou me nought ne
　　lette;　　　　　　　　　　725
O Phebus, thenk whan Dane hir-selven
　　shette
Under the bark, and laurer wex for drede,
Yet for hir love, O help now at this nede!

105. Mercurie, for the love of Hiersè eke,
For which Pallas was with Aglauros
　　wrooth,　　　　　　　　　　730
Now help, and eek Diane, I thee biseke,
That this viage be not to thee looth.
O fatal sustren, which, er any clooth
Me shapen was, my destenè me sponne,
So helpeth to this werk that is bi-gonne!'

106. Quod Pandarus, 'thou wrecched
　　mouses herte,　　　　　　　736
Art thou agast so that she wol thee byte?
Why, don this furred cloke up-on thy
　　sherte,
And folowe me, for I wol han the wyte;
But byd, and lat me go bifore a lyte.' 740
And with that word he gan un-do a
　　trappe,
And Troilus he broughte in by the lappe.

107. The sterne wind so loude gan to
　　route
That no wight other noyse mighte here;
And they that layen at the dore with-
　　oute,　　　　　　　　　　745
Ful sikerly they slepten alle y-fere;
And Pandarus, with a ful sobre chere,
Goth to the dore anon with-outen lette,
Ther-as they laye, and softely it shette.

108. And as he com ayeinward prively,
His nece awook, and asked 'who goth
　　there?'　　　　　　　　　　751
'My dere nece,' quod he, 'it am I;
Ne wondreth not, ne have of it no fere;'
And ner he com, and seyde hir in hir ere,
'No word, for love of god I yow biseche;
Lat no wight ryse and heren of our
　　speche.'　　　　　　　　　　756

109. 'What! which wey be ye comen,
   *benedicite?*'
Quod she, 'and how thus unwist of hem
   alle?'
'Here at this secree trappe-dore,' quod he.
Quod tho Criseyde, 'lat me som wight
   calle.'             760
'Ey! god forbede that it sholde falle,'
Quod Pandarus, 'that ye swich foly
   wroughte!
They mighte deme thing they never er
   thoughte!

110. It is nought good a sleping hound to
   wake,
Ne yeve a wight a cause to devyne;   765
Your wommen slepen alle, I under-take,
So that, for hem, the hous men mighte
   myne;
And slepen wolen til the sonne shyne.
And whan my tale al brought is to an
   ende,
Unwist, right as I com, so wol I wende.

111. Now nece myn, ye shul wel under-
   stonde,'            771
Quod he, 'so as ye wommen demen alle,
That for to holde in love a man in honde,
And him hir "leef" and "dere herte"
   calle,
And maken him an howve above a calle,
I mene, as love an other in this whyle,   776
She doth hir-self a shame, and him a gyle.

112. Now wherby that I telle yow al this?
Ye woot your-self, as wel as any wight,
How that your love al fully graunted is
To Troilus, the worthieste knight,   781
Oon of this world, and ther-to trouthe
   plyght,
That, but it were on him along, ye nolde
Him never falsen, whyl ye liven sholde.

113. Now stant it thus, that sith I fro
   yow wente,         785
This Troilus, right platly for to seyn,
Is thurgh a goter, by a privé wente,
In-to my chaumbre come in al this reyn,
Unwist of every maner wight, certeyn,
Save of my-self, as wisly have I joye,   790
And by that feith I shal Pryam of Troye!

114. And he is come in swich peyne and
   distresse
That, but he be al fully wood by this,
He sodeynly mot falle in-to wodnesse,
But-if god helpe; and cause why this is,
He seyth him told is, of a freend of his,
How that ye sholde love oon that hatte
   Horaste,         797
For sorwe of which this night shalt been
   his laste.'

115. Criseyde, which that al this wonder
   herde,
Gan sodeynly aboute hir herte colde,   800
And with a syk she sorwfully answerde,
'Allas! I wende, who-so tales tolde,
My dere herte wolde me not holde
So lightly fals! allas! conceytes wronge,
What harm they doon, for now live I to
   longe!         805

116. Horaste! allas! and falsen Troilus?
I knowe him not, god helpe me so,' quod
   she;
'Allas! what wikked spirit tolde him
   thus?
Now certes, eem, to-morwe, and I him see,
I shal ther-of as ful excusen me    810
As ever dide womman, if him lyke';
And with that word she gan ful sore syke.

117. 'O god!' quod she, 'so worldly seli-
   nesse,
Which clerkes callen fals felicitee,
Y-medled is with many a bitternesse!   815
Ful anguisshous than is, god woot,' quod
   she,
'Condicioun of veyn prosperitee;
For either joyes comen nought y-fere,
Or elles no wight hath hem alwey here.

118. O brotel wele of mannes joye un-
   stable!         820
With what wight so thou be, or how thou
   pleye,
Either he woot that thou, joye, art mu-
   able,
Or woot it not, it moot ben oon of tweye;
Now if he woot it not, how may he seye
That he hath verray joye and selinesse,   825
That is of ignoraunce ay in derknesse?

119. Now if he woot that joye is transi-
      torie,
As every joye of worldly thing mot flee,
Than every tyme he that hath in me-
      morie,
The drede of lesing maketh him that he
May in no parfit selinesse be.        831
And if to lese his joye he set a myte,
Than semeth it that joye is worth ful
      lyte.

120. Wherfore I wol deffyne in this
      matere,
That trewely, for ought I can espye,  835
Ther is no verray wele in this world here.
But O, thou wikked serpent Jalousye,
Thou misbeleved and envious folye,
Why hastow Troilus me mad untriste,
That never yet agilte him, that I wiste?'

121. Quod Pandarus, 'thus fallen is this
      cas.'                             841
' Why, uncle myn,' quod she, ' who tolde
      him this?
Why doth my dere herte thus, allas?'
' Ye woot, ye nece myn,' quod he, ' what is ;
I hope al shal be wel that is amis.   845
For ye may quenche al this, if that yow
      leste,
And doth right so, for I holde it the
      beste.'

122. ' So shal I do to-morwe, y-wis,' quod
      she,
' And god to-forn, so that it shal suffyse.'
' To-morwe? allas, that were a fayr,' quod
      he,                               850
' Nay, nay, it may not stonden in this
      wyse ;
For, nece myn, thus wryten clerkes wyse,
That peril is with dreeching in y-drawe ;
Nay, swich abodes been nought worth an
      hawe.

123. Nece, al thing hath tyme, I dar
      avowe ;                           855
For whan a chaumber a-fyr is, or an halle,
Wel more nede is, it sodeynly rescowe
Than to dispute, and axe amonges alle
How is this candel in the straw y-falle ?
A ! *benedicite!* for al among that fare  860
The harm is doon, and fare-wel feldefare !

124. And, nece myn, ne take it not a-
      greef,
If that ye suffre him al night in this wo,
God help me so, ye hadde him never leef,
That dar I seyn, now there is but we
      two ;                             865
But wel I woot, that ye wol not do so ;
Ye been to wys to do so gret folye,
To putte his lyf al night in jupartye.'

125. ' Hadde I him never leef ? By god,
      I wene
Ye hadde never thing so leef,' quod she.
' Now by my thrift,' quod he, ' that shal
      be sene ;                         871
For, sin ye make this ensample of me,
If I al night wolde him in sorwe see
For al the tresour in the toun of Troye,
I bidde god, I never mote have joye !  875

126. Now loke thanne, if ye, that been
      his love,
Shul putte al night his lyf in jupartye
For thing of nought ! Now, by that god
      above,
Nought only this delay comth of folye,
But of malyce, if that I shal nought lye.
What, platly, and ye suffre him in dis-
      tresse,                           881
Ye neither bountee doon ne gentilesse !'

127. Quod tho Criseyde, ' wole ye doon
      o thing,
And ye therwith shal stinte al his disese ;
Have here, and bereth him this blewe
      ring,                             885
For ther is no-thing mighte him bettre
      plese,
Save I my-self, ne more his herte apese ;
And sey my dere herte, that his sorwe
Is causeles, that shal be seen to-morwe.'

128. ' A ring ? ' quod he, ' ye, hasel-wodes
      shaken !                         890
Ye, nece myn, that ring moste han a stoon
That mighte dede men alyve maken ;
And swich a ring, trowe I that ye have
      noon.
Discrecioun out of your heed is goon ;
That fele I now,' quod he, ' and that is
      routhe ;                         895
O tyme y-lost, wel maystow cursen
      slouthe !

**K 2**

129. Wot ye not wel that noble and heigh
    corage
Ne sorweth not, ne stinteth eek for lyte?
But if a fool were in a jalous rage,
I nolde setten at his sorwe a myte,      900
But feffe him with a fewe wordes whyte
Another day, whan that I mighte him
    finde :
But this thing stont al in another kinde.

130. This is so gentil and so tendre of
    herte,
That with his deeth he wol his sorwes
    wreke;                               905
For trusteth wel, how sore that him
    smerte,
He wol to yow no jalouse wordes speke.
And for-thy, nece, er that his herte breke,
So spek your-self to him of this matere;
For with o word ye may his herte stere.

131. Now have I told what peril he is
    inne,                               911
And his coming unwist is t' every wight;
Ne, pardee, harm may ther be noon ne
    sinne;
I wol my-self be with yow al this night.
Ye knowe eek how it is your owne knight,
And that, by right, ye moste upon him
    triste,                            916
And I al prest to fecche him whan yow
    liste.'

132. This accident so pitous was to here,
And eek so lyk a sooth, at pryme face,
And Troilus hir knight to hir so dere, 920
His privè coming, and the siker place,
That, though that she dide him as
    thanne a grace,
Considered alle thinges as they stode,
No wonder is, sin she dide al for gode.

133. Cryseyde answerde, 'as wisly god at
    reste                              925
My sowle bringe, as me is for him wo!
And eem, y-wis, fayn wolde I doon the
    beste,
If that I hadde grace to do so.
But whether that ye dwelle or for him go,
I am, til god me bettre minde sende, 930
At dulcarnon, right at my wittes ende.'

134. Quod Pandarus, 'ye, nece, wol ye
    here?
Dulcarnon called is "fleminge of
    wrecches";
It semeth hard, for wrecches wol not lere
For verray slouthe or othere wilful
    tecches;                           935
This seyd by hem that be not worth two
    fecches.
But ye ben wys, and that we han on
    honde
Nis neither hard, ne skilful to withstonde.'

135. 'Thanne, eem,' quod she, 'doth her-
    of as yow list;
But er he come I wil up first aryse; 940
And, for the love of god, sin al my trist
Is on yow two, and ye ben bothe wyse,
So wircheth now in so discreet a wyse,
That I honour may have, and he ples-
    aunce;
For I am here al in your governaunce.'

136. 'That is wel seyd,' quod he, 'my
    nece dere,                         946
Ther good thrift on that wyse gentil
    herte!
But liggeth stille, and taketh him right
    here,
It nedeth not no ferther for him sterte;
And ech of yow ese otheres sorwes smerte,
For love of god; and, Venus, I thee
    herie;                             951
For sone hope I we shulle ben alle merie.'

137. This Troilus ful sone on knees him
    sette
Ful sobrely, right by hir beddes heed,
And in his beste wyse his lady grette; 955
But lord, so she wex sodeynliche reed!
Ne, though men sholden smyten of hir
    heed,
She coude nought a word a-right out-
    bringe
So sodeynly, for his sodeyn cominge.

138. But Pandarus, that so wel coude fele
In every thing, to pleye anoon bigan, 961
And seyde, 'nece, see how this lord can
    knele!
Now, for your trouthe, seeth this gentil
    man !'

And with that word he for a quisshen
   ran,
And seyde, 'kneleth now, whyl that yow
   leste, 965
Ther god your hertes bringe sone at
   reste!'

139. Can I not seyn, for she bad him not
   ryse,
If sorwe it putte out of hir remembraunce,
Or elles if she toke it in the wyse
Of duëtee, as for his observaunce; 970
But wel finde I she dide him this
   plesaunce,
That she him kiste, al-though she syked
   sore;
And bad him sitte a-dounwith-outen more.

140. Quod Pandarus, 'now wol ye wel
   biginne;
Now doth him sitte, gode nece dere, 975
Upon your beddes syde al there with-
   inne,
That ech of yow the bet may other here.'
And with that word he drow him to the
   fere,
And took a light, and fond his conten-
   aunce
As for to loke up-on an old romaunce. 980

141. Criseyde, that was Troilus lady right,
And cleer stood on a ground of sikernesse,
Al thoughte she, hir servaunt and hir
   knight
Ne sholde of right non untrouthe in hir
   gesse, 984
Yet nathelees, considered his distresse,
And that love is in cause of swich folye,
Thus to him spak she of his jelousye:

142. 'Lo, herte myn, as wolde the excel-
   lence
Of love, ayeins the which that no man
   may,
Ne oughte eek goodly maken resistence;
And eek bycause I felte wel and say 991
Your grete trouthe, and servyse every day;
And that your herte al myn was, sooth to
   seyne,
This droof me for to rewe up-on your
   peyne.

143. And your goodnesse have I founde
   alwey yit, 995
Of whiche, my dere herte and al my
   knight,
I thonke it yow, as fer as I have wit,
Al can I nought as muche as it were right;
And I, emforth my conninge and my
   might,
Have and ay shal, how sore that me
   smerte, 1000
Ben to yow trewe and hool, with al myn
   herte;

144. And dredelees, that shal be founde
   at preve.—
But, herte myn, what al this is to seyne
Shal wel be told, so that ye noght yow
   greve,
Though I to yow right on your-self com-
   pleyne. 1005
For ther-with mene I fynally the peyne,
That halt your herte and myn in hevi-
   nesse,
Fully to sleen, and every wrong redresse.

145. My goode, myn, not I for-why ne
   how
That Jalousye, allas! that wikked wivere,
Thus causelees is cropen in-to yow; 1011
The harm of which I wolde fayn delivere!
Allas! that he, al hool, or of him slivere,
Shuld have his refut in so digne a place,
Ther Jove him sone out of your herte
   arace! 1015

146. But O, thou Jove, O auctor of nature,
Is this an honour to thy deitee,
That folk ungiltif suffren here injure,
And who that giltif is, al quit goth he?
O were it leful for to pleyne on thee, 1020
That undeserved suffrest jalousye,
And that I wolde up-on thee pleyne and
   crye!

147. Eek al my wo is this, that folk now
   usen
To seyn right thus, "ye, Jalousye is
   Love!" 1024
And wolde a busshel venim al excusen,
For that o greyn of love is on it shove!
But that wot heighe god that sit above,

If it be lyker love, or hate, or grame ;
And after that, it oughte bere his name.

148. But certeyn is, som maner jalousye
Is excusable more than som, y-wis.    1031
As whan cause is, and som swich fantasye
With pietee so wel repressed is,
That it unnethe dooth or seyth amis,
But goodly drinketh up al his distresse ;
And that excuse I, for the gentilesse. 1036

149. And som so ful of furie is and despyt,
That it sourmounteth his repressioun ;
But herte myn, ye be not in that plyt,
That thanke I god, for whiche your
     passioun      1040
I wol not calle it but illusioun,
Of habundaunce of love and bisy cure,
That dooth your herte this disese endure.

150. Of which I am right sory, but not
     wrooth ;      1044
But, for my devoir and your hertes reste,
Wher-so yow list, by ordal or by ooth,
By sort, or in what wyse so yow leste,
For love of god, lat preve it for the beste !
And if that I be giltif, do me deye,    1049
Allas ! what mighte I more doon or seye ?'

151. With that a fewe brighte teres newe
Out of hir eyen fille, and thus she seyde,
'Now god, thou wost, in thought ne dede
     untrewe
To Troilus was never yet Criseyde.'
With that hir heed doun in the bed she
     leyde,      1055
And with the shete it wreigh, and syghed
     sore,
And held hir pees ; not o word spak she
     more.

152. But now help god to quenchen al
     this sorwe,
So hope I that he shal, for he best may ;
For I have seyn, of a ful misty morwe 1060
Folwen ful ofte a mery someres day ;
And after winter folweth grene May.
Men seen alday, and reden eek in stories,
That after sharpe shoures been victories.

153. This Troilus, whan he hir wordes
     herde,      1065
Have ye no care, him liste not to slepe ;

For it thoughte him no strokes of a yerde
To here or seen Criseyde his lady wepe ;
But wel he felte aboute his herte crepe,
For every teer which that Criseyde a-
     sterte,      1070
The crampe of deeth, to streyne him by
     the herte.

154. And in his minde he gan the tyme
     acurse
That he cam there, and that he was born ;
For now is wikke y-turned in-to worse,
And al that labour he hath doon biforn,
He wende it lost, he thoughte he nas but
     lorn.      1076
'O Pandarus,' thoughte he, 'allas ! thy
     wyle
Serveth of nought, so weylawey the
     whyle !'

155. And therwithal he heng a-doun the
     heed,
And fil on knees, and sorwfully he sighte ;
What mighte he seyn ? he felte he nas
     but deed,      1081
For wrooth was she that shulde his sorwes
     lighte.
But nathelees, whan that he speken
     mighte,
Than seyde he thus, ' god woot, that of
     this game,
Whan al is wist, than am I not to blame !'

156. Ther-with the sorwe so his herte
     shette,      1086
That from his eyen fil ther not a tere,
And every spirit his vigour in-knette,
So they astoned and oppressed were.
The feling of his sorwe, or of his fere, 1090
Or of ought elles, fled was out of towne ;
And doun he fel al sodeynly a-swowne.

157. This was no litel sorwe for to see ;
But al was hust, and Pandare up as faste,
'O nece, pees, or we be lost,'quod he, 1095
'Beth nought agast ;' but certeyn, at the
     laste,
For this or that, he in-to bedde him caste,
And seyde, 'O theef, is this a mannes
     herte ?'
And of he rente al to his bare sherte ;

158. And seyde, 'nece, but ye helpe us
      now,                                    1100
Allas, your owne Troilus is lorn !'
'Y-wis, so wolde I, and I wiste how,
Ful fayn,' quod she ; 'allas ! that I was
      born !'
'Ye, nece, wol ye pullen out the thorn
That stiketh in his herte ?' quod Pandare ;
'Sey "al foryeve," and stint is al this
      fare !'                                  1106

159. 'Ye, that to me,' quod she, 'ful
      lever were
Than al the good the sonne aboute gooth';
And therwith-al she swoor him in his ere,
'Y-wis, my dere herte, I am nought
      wrooth,                                  1110
Have here my trouthe and many another
      ooth ;
Now speek to me, for it am I, Criseyde !'
But al for nought ; yet mighte he not
      a-breyde.

160. Therwith his pous and pawmes of
      his hondes
They gan to frote, and wete his temples
      tweyne,                                  1115
And, to deliveren him from bittre bondes,
She ofte him kiste ; and, shortly for to
      seyne,
Him to revoken she dide al hir peyne.
And at the laste, he gan his breeth to
      drawe,
And of his swough sone after that adawe,

161. And gan bet minde and reson to him
      take,                                    1121
But wonder sore he was abayst, y-wis.
And with a syk, whan he gan bet a-wake,
He seyde, 'O mercy, god, what thing is
      this ?'
'Why do ye with your-selven thus amis ?'
Quod tho Criseyde, 'is this a mannes
      game ?                                   1126
What, Troilus ! wol ye do thus, for
      shame ?'

162. And therwith-al hir arm over him
      she leyde,
And al foryaf, and ofte tyme him keste.
He thonked hir, and to hir spak, and
      seyde                                    1130

As fil to purpos for his herte reste.
And she to that answerde him as hir
      leste ;
And with hir goodly wordes him disporte
She gan, and ofte his sorwes to comforte.

163. Quod Pandarus, 'for ought I can
      espyen,                                  1135
This light nor I ne serven here of nought;
Light is not good for syke folkes yën.
But for the love of god, sin ye be brought
In thus good plyt, lat now non hevy
      thought
Ben hanginge in the hertes of yow
      tweye :'                                  1140
And bar the candel to the chimeneye.

164. Sone after this, though it no nede
      were,
Whan she swich othes as hir list devyse
Hadde of him take, hir thoughte tho no
      fere,
Ne cause eek non, to bidde him thennes
      ryse.                                     1145
Yet lesse thing than othes may suffyse
In many a cas ; for every wight, I gesse,
That loveth wel meneth but gentilesse.

165. But in effect she wolde wite anoon
Of what man, and eek where, and also
      why                                      1150
He jelous was, sin ther was cause noon ;
And eek the signe, that he took it by,
She bad him that to telle hir bisily,
Or elles, certeyn, she bar him on honde,
That this was doon of malis, hir to fonde.

166. With-outen more, shortly for to
      seyne,                                   1156
He moste obeye un-to his lady heste ;
And for the lasse harm, he moste feyne.
He seyde hir, whan she was at swiche
      a feste
She mighte on him han loked at the
      leste ;                                   1160
Not I not what, al dere y-nough a risshe,
As he that nedes moste a cause fisshe.

167. And she answerde, 'swete, al were
      it so,
What harm was that, sin I non yvel
      mene ?

For, by that god that boughte us bothe
    two,                1165
In alle thinge is myn entente clene.
Swich arguments ne been not worth a
    bene ;
Wol ye the childish jalous contrefete ?
Now were it worthy that ye were y-bete.'

168. Tho Troilus gan sorwfully to syke,
Lest she be wrooth, him thoughte his
    herte deyde ;            1171
And seyde, ' allas ! upon my sorwes syke
Have mercy, swete herte myn, Criseyde!
And if that, in tho wordes that I seyde,
Be any wrong, I wol no more trespace ;
Do what yow list, I am al in your grace.'

169. And she answerde, ' of gilt miseri-
    corde !
That is to seyn, that I foryeve al this ;
And ever-more on this night yow recorde,
And beth wel war ye do no more amis.'1180
' Nay, dere herte myn,' quod he, ' y-wis.'
' And now,' quod she, ' that I have do
    yow smerte,
Foryeve it me, myn owene swete herte.'

170. This Troilus, with blisse of that sup-
    prysed,            1184
Put al in goddes hond, as he that mente
No-thing but wel ; and, sodeynly avysed,
He hir in armes faste to him hente.
And Pandarus, with a ful good entente,
Leyde him to slepe, and seyde, ' if ye ben
    wyse,
Swowneth not now, lest more folk aryse.'

171. What mighte or may the sely larke
    seye,            1191
Whan that the sparhauk hath it in his
    foot ?
I can no more, but of thise ilke tweye,
To whom this tale sucre be or soot,
Though that I tarie a yeer, som-tyme
    I moot,            1195
After myn auctor, tellen hir gladnesse,
As wel as I have told hir hevinesse.

172. Criseyde, which that felte hir thus
    y-take,
As writen clerkes in hir bokes olde,

Right as an aspes leef she gan to quake,
Whan she him felte hir in his armes
    folde.            1201
But Troilus, al hool of cares colde,
Gan thanken tho the blisful goddes
    sevene ;
Thus sondry peynes bringen folk to
    hevene.

173. This Troilus in armes gan hir
    streyne,            1205
And seyde, ' O swete, as ever mote I goon,
Now be ye caught, now is ther but we
    tweyne ;
Now yeldeth yow, for other boot is noon.'
To that Criseyde answerde thus anoon,
' Ne hadde I er now, my swete herte
    dere,            1210
Ben yolde, y-wis, I were now not here !'

174. O ! sooth is seyd, that heled for to be
As of a fevre or othere greet syknesse,
Men moste drinke, as men may often see,
Ful bittre drink ; and for to han glad-
    nesse,            1215
Men drinken often peyne and greet dis-
    tresse ;
I mene it here, as for this aventure,
That thourgh a peyne hath founden al
    his cure.

175. And now swetnesse semeth more
    swete,
That bitternesse assayed was biforn ; 1220
For out of wo in blisse now they flete.
Non swich they felten, sith they were
    born ;
Now is this bet, than bothe two be lorn !
For love of god, take every womman
    hede
To werken thus, if it comth to the nede.

176. Criseyde, al quit from every drede
    and tene,            1226
As she that juste cause hadde him to triste,
Made him swich feste, it joye was to sene,
Whan she his trouthe and clene entente
    wiste.            1229
And as aboute a tree, with many a twiste,
Bitrent and wryth the sote wode-binde,
Gan eche of hem in armes other winde.

177. And as the newe abaysshed nightin-
    gale,
That stinteth first whan she biginneth
    singe,
Whan that she hereth any herde tale, 1235
Or in the hegges any wight steringe,
And after siker dooth hir voys out-ringe;
Right so Criseyde, whan hir drede stente,
Opned hir herte, and tolde him hir entente.

178. And right as he that seeth his deeth
    y-shapen,                            1240
And deye moot, in ought that he may
    gesse,
And sodeynly rescous doth him escapen,
And from his deeth is brought in siker-
    nesse,
For al this world, in swich present glad-
    nesse                               1244
Was Troilus, and hath his lady swete ;
With worse hap god lat us never mete !

179. Hir armes smale, hir streyghte bak
    and softe,
Hir sydes longe, fleshly, smothe, and
    whyte
He gan to stroke, and good thrift bad ful
    ofte
Hir snowish throte, hir brestes rounde and
    lyte ;                              1250
Thus in this hevene he gan him to delyte,
And ther-with-al a thousand tyme hir
    kiste ;
That, what to done, for joye unnethe he
    wiste.

180. Than seyde he thus, ' O, Love, O,
    Charitee,
Thy moder eek, Citherea the swete,  1255
After thy-self next heried be she,
Venus mene I, the wel-willy planete ;
And next that, Imenëus, I thee grete ;
For never man was to yow goddes holde
As I, which ye han brought fro cares
    colde.                              1260

181. Benigne Love, thou holy bond of
    thinges,
Who-so wol grace, and list thee nought
    honouren,
Lo, his desyr wol flee with-outen winges.

For, noldestow of bountee hem socouren
That serven best and most alwey labouren,
Yet were al lost, that dar I wel seyn,
    certes,                            1266
But-if thy grace passed our desertes.

182. And for thou me, that coude leest
    deserve
Of hem that nombred been un-to thy
    grace,
Hast holpen, ther I lykly was to sterve,
And me bistowed in so heygh a place 1271
That thilke boundes may no blisse pace,
I can no more, but laude and reverence
Be to thy bounte and thyn excellence !'

183. And therwith-al Criseyde anoon he
    kiste,                             1275
Of which, certeyn, she felte no disese.
And thus seyde he, ' now wolde god I
    wiste,
Myn herte swete, how I yow mighte plese !
What man,' quod he, ' was ever thus at ese
As I, on whiche the faireste and the
    beste                              1280
That ever I say, deyneth hir herte reste.

184. Here may men seen that mercy
    passeth right ;
The experience of that is felt in me,
That am unworthy to so swete a wight.
But herte myn, of your benignitee,  1285
So thenketh, though that I unworthy be,
Yet mot I nede amenden in som wyse,
Right thourgh the vertu of your heyghe
    servyse.

185. And for the love of god, my lady
    dere,
Sin god hath wrought me for I shal yow
    serve,                             1290
As thus I mene, that ye wol be my stere,
To do me live, if that yow liste, or sterve,
So techeth me how that I may deserve
Your thank, so that I, thurgh myn
    ignoraunce,                        1294
Ne do no-thing that yow be displesaunce.

186. For certes, fresshe wommanliche wyf,
This dar I seye, that trouthe and dili-
    gence,
That shal ye finden in me al my lyf,

Ne I wol not, certeyn, breken your de-
　fence ;
And if I do, present or in absence,　1300
For love of god, lat slee me with the dede,
If that it lyke un-to your womanhede.'

187. ' Y-wis,' quod she, ' myn owne hertes
　　list,
My ground of ese, and al myn herte dere,
Graunt mercy, for on that is al my
　trist ;　　　　　　　　　　　　　1305
But late us falle awey fro this matere ;
For it suffyseth, this that seyd is here.
And at o word, with-outen repentaunce,
Wel-come, my knight, my pees, my
　suffisaunce !'

188. Of hir delyt, or joyes oon the leste
Were impossible to my wit to seye ;　1311
But juggeth, ye that han ben at the feste
Of swich gladnesse, if that hem liste pleye !
I can no more, but thus thise ilke tweye
That night, be-twixen dreed and siker-
　nesse,　　　　　　　　　　　　　1315
Felten in love the grete worthinesse.

189. O blisful night, of hem so longe
　　y-sought,
How blithe un-to hem bothe two thou
　were !
Why ne hadde I swich on with my soule
　y-bought,
Ye, or the leeste joye that was there ?　1320
A-wey, thou foule daunger and thou fere,
And lat hem in this hevene blisse dwelle,
That is so heygh, that al ne can I telle !

190. But sooth is, though I can not tellen al,
As can myn auctor, of his excellence,　1325
Yet have I seyd, and, god to-forn, I shal
In every thing al hoolly his sentence.
And if that I, at loves reverence,
Have any word in eched for the beste,
Doth therwith-al right as your-selven
　leste.　　　　　　　　　　　　　1330

191. For myne wordes, here and every
　　part,
I speke hem alle under correccioun
Of yow, that feling han in loves art,
And putte it al in your discrecioun
T' encrese or maken diminucioun　1335

Of my langage, and that I yow bi-seche ;
But now to purpos of my rather speche.

192. Thise ilke two, that ben in armes
　　laft,
So looth to hem a-sonder goon it were,
That ech from other wende been biraft,
Or elles, lo, this was hir moste fere,　1341
That al this thing but nyce dremes were ;
For which ful ofte ech of hem seyde, ' O
　swete,
Clippe ich yow thus, or elles I it mete ?'

193. And, lord ! so he gan goodly on hir
　　see,　　　　　　　　　　　　　1345
That never his look ne bleynte from hir
　face,
And seyde, ' O dere herte, may it be
That it be sooth, that ye ben in this
　place ?'
' Ye, herte myn, god thank I of his grace !'
Quod tho Criseyde, and therwith-al him
　kiste,　　　　　　　　　　　　　1350
That where his spirit was, for joye he niste.

194. This Troilus ful ofte hir eyen two
Gan for to kisse, and seyde, ' O eyen clere,
It were ye that wroughte me swich wo,
Ye humble nettes of my lady dere !　1355
Though ther be mercy writen in your
　chere,
God wot, the text ful hard is, sooth, to
　finde,
How coude ye with-outen bond me binde ?'

195. Therwith he gan hir faste in armes
　　take,　　　　　　　　　　　　　1359
And wel an hundred tymes gan he syke,
Nought swiche sorwful sykes as men make
For wo, or elles whan that folk ben syke,
But esy sykes, swiche as been to lyke,
That shewed his affeccioun with-inne ;
Of swiche sykes coude he nought bilinne.

196. Sone after this they speke of sondry
　　thinges,　　　　　　　　　　　1366
As fil to purpos of this aventure,
And pleyinge entrechaungeden hir ringes,
Of which I can nought tellen no scripture ;
But wel I woot a broche, gold and asure,
In whiche a ruby set was lyk an herte,　1371
Criseyde him yaf, and stak it on his
　sherte.

197. Lord! trowe ye, a coveitous, a wrecche,
That blameth love and holt of it despyt,
That, of tho pens that he can mokre and
    kecche,                                    1375
Was ever yet y-yeve him swich delyt,
As is in love, in oo poynt, in som plyt?
Nay, doutelees, for also god me save,
So parfit joye may no nigard have!

198. They wol sey 'yis,' but lord! so
    that they lye,                             1380
Tho bisy wrecches, ful of wo and drede!
They callen love a woodnesse or folye,
But it shal falle hem as I shal yow rede;
They shul forgo the whyte and eke the
    rede,
And live in wo, ther god yeve hem mis-
    chaunce,                                   1385
And every lover in his trouthe avaunce!

199. As wolde god, tho wrecches, that
    dispyse
Servyse of love, hadde eres al-so longe
As hadde Myda, ful of coveityse;
And ther-to dronken hadde as hoot and
    stronge                                    1390
As Crassus dide for his affectis wronge,
To techen hem that they ben in the vyce,
And loveres nought, al-though they holde
    hem nyce!

200. Thise ilke two, of whom that I yow
    seye,                                      1394
Whan that hir hertes wel assured were,
Tho gonne they to speken and to pleye,
And eek rehercen how, and whanne, and
    where,
They knewe hem first, and every wo and
    fere
That passed was; but al swich hevinesse,
I thanke it god, was tourned to gladnesse.

201. And ever-mo, whan that hem fel to
    speke                                      1401
Of any thing of swich a tyme agoon,
With kissing al that tale sholde breke,
And fallen in a newe joye anoon,
And diden al hir might, sin they were
    oon,                                       1405
For to recoveren blisse and been at ese,
And passed wo with joye countrepeyse.

202. Reson wil not that I speke of sleep,
For it accordeth nought to my matere;
God woot, they toke of that ful litel keep,
But lest this night, that was to hem so
    dere,                                      1411
Ne sholde in veyn escape in no manere,
It was biset in joye and bisinesse
Of al that souneth in-to gentilnesse.   1414

203. But whan the cok, comune astrologer,
Gan on his brest to bete, and after crowe,
And Lucifer, the dayes messager,
Gan for to ryse, and out hir bemes
    throwe;
And estward roos, to him that coude it
    knowe,                                     1419
*Fortuna maior,* †than anoon Criseyde,
With herte sore, to Troilus thus seyde:—

204. 'Myn hertes lyf, my trist and my
    plesaunce,
That I was born, allas! what me is wo,
That day of us mot make desseveraunce!
For tyme it is to ryse, and hennes go, 1425
Or elles I am lost for evermo!
O night, allas! why niltow over us hove,
As longe as whanne Almena lay by Jove?

205. O blake night, as folk in bokes rede,
That shapen art by god this world to
    hyde                                       1430
At certeyn tymes with thy derke wede,
That under that men mighte in reste
    abyde,
Wel oughte bestes pleyne, and folk thee
    chyde,
That there-as day with labour wolde us
    breste,
That thou thus fleest, and deynest us
    nought reste!                              1435

206. Thou dost, allas! to shortly thyn
    offyce,
Thou rakel night, ther god, makere of
    kinde,
Thee, for thyn hast and thyn unkinde
    vyce,
So faste ay to our hemi-spere binde,
That never-more under the ground thou
    winde!                                     1440
For now, for thou so hyest out of Troye,
Have I forgon thus hastily my joye!'

207. This Troilus, that with tho wordes
felte,
As thoughte him tho, for piëtous distresse,
The blody teres from his herte melte, 1445
As he that never yet swich hevinesse
Assayed hadde, out of so greet gladnesse,
Gan therwith-al Criseyde his lady dere
In armes streyne, and seyde in this
manere:—

208. ' O cruel day, accusour of the joye
That night and love han stole and faste
y-wryen, 1451
A-cursed be thy coming in-to Troye,
For every bore hath oon of thy bright yën!
Envyous day, what list thee so to spyen?
What hastow lost, why sekestow this
place, 1455
Ther god thy lyght so quenche, for his
grace?

209. Allas! what han thise loveres thee
agilt,
Dispitous day? thyn be the pyne of helle!
For many a lovere hastow shent, and
wilt;
Thy pouring in wol no-wher lete hem
dwelle. 1460
What proferestow thy light here for to
selle?
Go selle it hem that smale seles graven,
We wol thee nought, us nedeth no day
haven.'

210. And eek the sonne Tytan gan he
chyde,
And seyde, ' O fool, wel may men thee
dispyse, 1465
That hast the Dawing al night by thy
syde,
And suffrest hir so sone up fro thee ryse,
For to disesen loveres in this wyse.
What! hold your bed ther, thou, and eek
thy Morwe!
I bidde god, so yeve yow bothe sorwe!'

211. Therwith ful sore he sighte, and
thus he seyde, 1471
' My lady right, and of my wele or wo
The welle and rote, O goodly myn, Criseyde,
And shal I ryse, allas! and shal I go?
Now fele I that myn herte moot a-two! 1475

For how sholde I my lyf an houre save,
Sin that with yow is al the lyf I have?

212. What shal I doon, for certes, I not
how,
Ne whanne, allas! I shal the tyme see,
That in this plyt I may be eft with yow;
And of my lyf, god woot how that shal
be, 1481
Sin that desyr right now so byteth me,
That I am deed anoon, but I retourne.
How sholde I longe, allas! fro yow so-
journe?

213. But nathelees, myn owene lady
bright, 1485
Yit were it so that I wiste outrely,
That I, your humble servaunt and your
knight,
Were in your herte set so fermely
As ye in myn, the which thing, trewely,
Me lever were than thise worldes tweyne,
Yet sholde I bet enduren al my peyne.'

214. To that Criseyde answerde right
anoon, 1492
And with a syk she seyde, ' O herte dere,
The game, y-wis, so ferforth now is goon,
That first shal Phebus falle fro his spere,
And every egle been the dowves fere, 1496
And every roche out of his place sterte,
Er Troilus out of Criseydes herte!

215. Ye be so depe in-with myn herte
grave,
That, though I wolde it turne out of my
thought, 1500
As wisly verray god my soule save,
To dyen in the peyne, I coude nought!
And, for the love of god that us hath
wrought,
Lat in your brayn non other fantasye
So crepe, that it cause me to dye! 1505

216. And that ye me wolde han as faste
in minde
As I have yow, that wolde I yow bi-seche;
And, if I wiste soothly that to finde,
God mighte not a poynt my joyes eche!
But, herte myn, with-oute more speche,
Beth to me trewe, or elles were it routhe;
For I am thyn, by god and by my trouthe!

217. Beth glad for-thy, and live in siker-
    nesse ;
Thus seyde I never er this, ne shal to
    mo ;                                        1514
And if to yow it were a gret gladnesse
To turne ayein, soone after that ye go,
As fayn wolde I as ye, it were so,
As wisly god myn herte bringe at reste !'
And him in armes took, and ofte keste.

218. Agayns his wil, sin it mot nedes be,
This Troilus up roos, and faste him
    cledde,                                     1521
And in his armes took his lady free
An hundred tyme, and on his wey him
    spedde,
And with swich wordes as his herte
    bledde,
He seyde, ' farewel, my dere herte swete,
Ther god us graunte sounde and sone to
    mete !'                                     1526

219. To which no word for sorwe she
    answerde,
So sore gan his parting hir destreyne ;
And Troilus un-to his palays ferde,
As woo bigon as she was, sooth to seyne ;
So hard him wrong of sharp desyr the
    peyne                                       1531
For to ben eft there he was in plesaunce,
That it may never out of his remem-
    braunce.

220. Retorned to his real palais, sone 1534
He softe in-to his bed gan for to slinke,
To slepe longe, as he was wont to done,
But al for nought ; he may wel ligge and
    winke,
But sleep ne may ther in his herte
    sinke ;
Thenkinge how she, for whom desyr him
    brende,
A thousand-fold was worth more than he
    wende.                                      1540

221. And in his thought gan up and doun
    to winde
Hir wordes alle, and every contenaunce,
And fermely impressen in his minde
The leste poynt that to him was plesaunce ;
And verrayliche, of thilke remembraunce,

Desyr al newe him brende, and lust to
    brede                                       1546
Gan more than erst, and yet took he non
    hede.

222. Criseyde also, right in the same wyse,
Of Troilus gan in hir herte shette        1549
His worthinesse, his lust, his dedes wyse,
His gentilesse, and how she with him
    mette,
Thonkinge love he so wel hir bisette ;
Desyring eft to have hir herte dere
In swich a plyt, she dorste make him
    chere.

223. Pandare, a-morwe which that comen
    was                                         1555
Un-to his nece, and gan hir fayre grete,
Seyde, ' al this night so reyned it, allas !
That al my drede is that ye, nece swete,
Han litel layser had to slepe and mete ;
Al night,' quod he, ' hath reyn so do me
    wake,                                       1560
That som of us, I trowe, hir hedes ake.'

224. And ner he com, and seyde, ' how
    stont it now
This mery morwe, nece, how can ye fare ?'
Criseyde answerde, 'never the bet for yow,
Fox that ye been, god yeve your herte
    care !                                      1565
God helpe me so, ye caused al this fare,
Trow I,' quod she, ' for alle your wordes
    whyte ;
O ! who-so seeth yow knoweth yow ful
    lyte !'

225. With that she gan hir face for to
    wrye
With the shete, and wex for shame al
    reed ;                                      1570
And Pandarus gan under for to prye,
And seyde, ' nece, if that I shal ben deed,
Have here a swerd, and smyteth of myn
    heed.'
With that his arm al sodeynly he thriste
Under hir nekke, and at the laste hir
    kiste.                                      1575

226. I passe al that which chargeth
    nought to seye,
What ! God foryaf his deeth, and she
    al-so

Foryaf, and with hir uncle gan to pleye,
For other cause was ther noon than so.
But of this thing right to the effect to go,
Whan tyme was, hom til hir hous she
    wente,      1581
And Pandarus hath fully his entente.

227. Now torne we ayein to Troilus,
That restelees ful longe a-bedde lay,
And prevely sente after Pandarus,    1585
To him to come in al the haste he may.
He com anoon, nought ones seyde he
    ' nay,'
And Troilus ful sobrely he grette,
And doun upon his beddes syde him
    sette.      1589

228. This Troilus, with al the affeccioun
Of frendes love that herte may devyse,
To Pandarus on knees fil adoun,
And er that he wolde of the place aryse,
He gan him thonken in his beste wyse ;
A hondred sythe he gan the tyme blesse,
That he was born to bringe him fro
    distresse.      1596

229. He seyde, ' O frend, of frendes th'
    alderbeste
That ever was, the sothe for to telle,
Thou hast in hevene y-brought my soule
    at reste
Fro Flegiton, the fery flood of helle ; 1600
That, though I mighte a thousand tymes
    selle,
Upon a day, my lyf in thy servyse,
It mighte nought a mote in that suffyse.

230. The sonne, which that al the world
    may see,
Saw never yet, my lyf, that dar I leye,
So inly fair and goodly as is she,     1606
Whos I am al, and shal, til that I deye ;
And, that I thus am hires, dar I seye,
That thanked be the heighe worthinesse
Of love, and eek thy kinde bisinesse. 1610

231. Thus hastow me no litel thing y-yive,
Fo which to thee obliged be for ay
My lyf, and why? for thorugh thyn help
    I live ;
For elles deed hadde I be many a day.'

And with that word doun in his bed he
    lay,      1615
And Pandarus ful sobrely him herde
Til al was seyd, and thanne he him
    answerde :

232. ' My dere frend, if I have doon for
    thee
In any cas, god wot, it is me leef ;
And am as glad as man may of it be, 1620
God help me so ; but tak now not a-greef
That I shal seyn, be war of this myscheef,
That, there-as thou now brought art in-to
    blisse,
That thou thy-self ne cause it nought to
    misse.

233. For of fortunes sharp adversitee 1625
The worst kinde of infortune is this,
A man to have ben in prosperitee,
And it remembren, whan it passed is.
Thou art wys y-nough, for-thy do nought
    amis ;
Be not to rakel, though thou sitte
    warme,      1630
For if thou be, certeyn, it wol thee
    harme.

234. Thou art at ese, and hold thee wel
    ther-inne.
For also seur as reed is every fyr,
As greet a craft is kepe wel as winne ;
Brydle alwey wel thy speche and thy
    desyr.      1635
For worldly joye halt not but by a wyr ;
That preveth wel, it brest alday so ofte ;
For-thy nede is to werke with it softe.'

235. Quod Troilus, ' I hope, and god to-
    forn,
My dere frend, that I shal so me bere,
That in my gilt ther shal no thing be
    lorn,      1641
N' I nil not rakle as for to greven here ;
It nedeth not this matere ofte tere ;
For wistestow myn herte wel, Pandare,
God woot, of this thou woldest litel care.'

236. Tho gan he telle him of his glade
    night.      1646
And wher-of first his herte dredde, and
    how,

And seyde, 'freend, as I am trewe knight,
And by that feyth I shal to god and yow,
I hadde it never half so hote as now; 1650
And ay the more that desyr me byteth
To love hir best, the more it me delyteth.

237. I noot my-self not wisly what it is;
But now I fele a newe qualitee,
Ye, al another than I dide er this.' 1655
Pandare answerde, and seyde thus, that he
That ones may in hevene blisse be,
He feleth other weyes, dar I leye,
Than thilke tyme he first herde of it seye.

238. This is o word for al; this Troilus
Was never ful, to speke of this matere,
And for to preysen un-to Pandarus 1662
The bountee of his righte lady dere,
And Pandarus to thanke and maken
   chere.
This tale ay was span-newe to biginne 1665
Til that the night departed hem a-twinne.

239. Sone after this, for that fortune it
   wolde,
I-comen was the blisful tyme swete,
That Troilus was warned that he sholde,
Ther he was erst, Criseyde his lady
   mete;              1670
For which he felte his herte in joye
   flete;
And feythfully gan alle the goddes herie;
And lat see now if that he can be merie.

240. And holden was the forme and al
   the wyse,
Of hir cominge, and eek of his also, 1675
As it was erst, which nedeth nought
   devyse.
But playnly to the effect right for to go,
In joye and seurte Pandarus hem two
A-bedde broughte, whan hem bothe leste,
And thus they ben in quiete and in
   reste.              1680

241. Nought nedeth it to yow, sin they
   ben met,
To aske at me if that they blythe were;
For if it erst was wel, tho was it bet
A thousand-fold, this nedeth not enquere.
A-gon was every sorwe and every fere;

And bothe, y-wis, they hadde, and so
   they wende,           1686
As muche joye as herte may comprende.

242. This is no litel thing of for to seye,
This passeth every wit for to devyse; 1689
For eche of hem gan otheres lust obeye;
Felicitee, which that thise clerkes wyse
Commenden so, ne may not here suffyse.
This joye may not writen been with inke,
This passeth al that herte may bithinke.

243. But cruel day, so wel-awey the
   stounde!           1695
Gan for to aproche, as they by signes
   knewe,
For whiche hem thoughte felen dethes
   wounde;
So wo was hem, that changen gan hir
   hewe,            1698
And day they gonnen to dispyse al newe,
Calling it traytour, envyous, and worse,
And bitterly the dayes light they curse.

244. Quod Troilus, 'allas! now am I war
That Pirous and tho swifte stedes three,
Whiche that drawen forth the sonnes
   char,
Han goon som by-path in despyt of me;
That maketh it so sone day to be; 1706
And, for the sonne him hasteth thus to
   ryse,
Ne shal I never doon him sacrifyse!'

245. But nedes day departe moste hem
   sone,
And whanne hir speche doon was and hir
   chere,           1710
They twinne anoon as they were wont to
   done,
And setten tyme of meting eft y-fere;
And many a night they wroughte in this
   manere.
And thus Fortune a tyme ladde in joye
Criseyde, and eek this kinges sone of
   Troye.           1715

246. In suffisaunce, in blisse, and in sing-
   inges,
This Troilus gan al his lyf to lede;
He spendeth, justeth, maketh †festey-
   inges;

He yeveth frely ofte, and chaungeth
    wede,      1719
And held aboute him alwey, out of drede,
A world of folk, as cam him wel of kinde,
The fressheste and the beste he coude
    finde ;

247. That swich a voys was of him and
    a stevene
Thorugh-out the world, of honour and
    largesse,      1724
That it up rong un-to the yate of hevene.
And, as in love, he was in swich gladnesse,
That in his herte he demede, as I gesse,
That there nis lovere in this world at ese
So wel as he, and thus gan love him
    plese.

248. The godlihede or beautee which that
    kinde      1730
In any other lady hadde y-set
Can not the mountaunce of a knot un-
    binde,
A-boute his herte, of al Criseydes net.
He was so narwe y-masked and y-knet,
That it undoon on any manere syde, 1735
That nil not been, for ought that may
    betyde.

249. And by the hond ful ofte he wolde
    take
This Pandarus, and in-to gardin lede,
And swich a feste and swich a proces
    make      1739
Him of Criseyde, and of hir womanhede,
And of hir beautee, that, with-outen drede,
It was an hevene his wordes for to here ;
And thanne he wolde singe in this
    manere

250. ' Love, that of erthe and see hath
    governaunce,
Love, that his hestes hath in hevene hye,
Love, that with an holsom alliaunce 1746
Halt peples joyned, as him list hem gye,
Love, that knetteth lawe of companye,
And couples doth in vertu for to dwelle,
Bind this acord, that I have told and
    telle ;      1750

251. That that the world with feyth,
    which that is stable,
Dyverseth so his stoundes concordinge,

That elements that been so discordable
Holden a bond perpetuely duringe,
That Phebus mote his rosy day forth
    bringe,      1755
And that the mone hath lordship over
    the nightes,
Al this doth Love ; ay heried be his
    mightes !

252. That that the see, that gredy is to
    flowen,
Constreyneth to a certeyn ende so 1759
His flodes, that so fersly they ne growen
To drenchen erthe and al for ever-mo ;
And if that Love ought lete his brydel go,
Al that now loveth a-sonder sholde lepe,
And lost were al, that Love halt now to-
    hepe.

253. So wolde god, that auctor is of
    kinde,      1765
That, with his bond, Love of his vertu
    liste
To cerclen hertes alle, and faste binde,
That from his bond no wight the wey out
    wiste.
And hertes colde, hem wolde I that he
    twiste
To make hem love, and that hem leste ay
    rewe      1770
On hertes sore, and kepe hem that ben
    trewe.'

254. In alle nedes, for the tounes werre,
He was, and ay the firste in armes dight ;
And certeynly, but-if that bokes erre, 1774
Save Ector, most y-drad of any wight ;
And this encrees of hardinesse and might
Cam him of love, his ladies thank to
    winne,
That altered his spirit so with-inne.

255. In tyme of trewe, on haukinge wolde
    he ryde,
Or elles hunten boor, bere, or lyoun ; 1780
The smale bestes leet he gon bi-syde.
And whan that he com rydinge in-to
    toun,
Ful ofte his lady, from hir window doun,
As fresh as faucon comen out of muwe,
Ful redy was, him goodly to saluwe. 1785

256. And most of love and vertu was his
     speche,
And in despyt hadde alle wrecchednesse;
And doutelees, no nede was him biseche
To honouren hem that hadde worthi-
     nesse,                            1789
And esen hem that weren in distresse.
And glad was he if any wight wel ferde,
That lover was, whan he it wiste or herde.

257. For sooth to seyn, he lost held every
     wight
But-if he were in loves heigh servyse,
I mene folk that oughte it been of right.
And over al this, so wel coude he de-
     vyse                             1796
Of sentement, and in so unkouth wyse
Al his array, that every lover thoughte,
That al was wel, what-so he seyde or
     wroughte.

258. And though that he be come of
     blood royal,                     1800
Him liste of pryde at no wight for to
     chase;
Benigne he was to ech in general,

For which he gat him thank in every
     place.
Thus wolde Love, y-heried be his grace,
That Pryde, Envye, Ire, and Avaryce 1805
He gan to flee, and every other vyce.

259. Thou lady bright, the doughter to
     Dione,
Thy blinde and winged sone eek, daun
     Cupyde;
Ye sustren nyne eek, that by Elicone
In hil Parnaso listen for to abyde,    1810
That ye thus fer han deyned me to gyde,
I can no more, but sin that ye wol wende,
Ye heried been for ay, with-outen ende!

260. Thourgh yow have I seyd fully in
     my song
Th'effect and joye of Troilus servyse, 1815
Al be that ther was som disese among,
As to myn auctor listeth to devyse.
My thridde book now ende ich in this
     wyse;
And Troilus in luste and in quiete   1819
Is with Criseyde, his owne herte swete.

**Explicit Liber Tercius.**

# BOOK IV.

### [Prohemium.]

1. But al to litel, weylawey the whyle,
Lasteth swich joye, y-thonked be For-
     tune!
That semeth trewest, whan she wol
     bygyle,
And can to foles so hir song entune,
That she hem hent and blent, traytour
     comune;                             5
And whan a wight is from hir wheel
     y-throwe,
Than laugheth she, and maketh him the
     mowe.

2. From Troilus she gan hir brighte face
Awey to wrythe, and took of him non
     hede,

But caste him clene oute of his lady
     grace,                             10
And on hir wheel she sette up Diomede;
For which right now myn herte ginneth
     blede,
And now my penne, allas! with which
     I wryte,
Quaketh for drede of that I moot endyte.

3. For how Criseyde Troilus forsook,   15
Or at the leste, how that she was un-
     kinde,
Mot hennes-forth ben matere of my
     book,
As wryten folk thorugh which it is in
     minde.
Allas! that they shulde ever cause
     finde

To speke hir harm ; and if they on hir
    lye,             20
Y-wis, hem-self sholde han the vilanye.

4. O ye Herines, Nightes doughtren three,
That endelees compleynen ever in pyne,
Megera, Alete, and eek Thesiphone ;
Thou cruel Mars eek, fader to Quiryne, 25
This ilke ferthe book me helpeth fyne,
So that the los of lyf and love y-fere
Of Troilus be fully shewed here.

### Explicit † prohemium. Incipit Quartus Liber.

5. Ligginge in ost, as I have seyd er this,
The Grekes stronge, aboute Troye toun, 30
Bifel that, whan that Phebus shyning is
Up-on the brest of Hercules Lyoun,
That Ector, with ful many a bold baroun,
Caste on a day with Grekes for to fighte,
As he was wont to greve hem what he
    mighte.         35

6. Not I how longe or short it was bi-
    twene
This purpos and that day they fighte
    mente ;
But on a day wel armed, bright and
    shene,
Ector, and many a worthy wight out
    wente,
With spere in hond and bigge bowes
    bente ;         40
And in the berd, with-oute lenger lette,
Hir fomen in the feld anoon hem mette.

7. The longe day, with speres sharpe
    y-grounde,
With arwes, dartes, swerdes, maces felle,
They fighte and bringen hors and man
    to grounde,     45
And with hir axes out the braynes quelle.
But in the laste shour, sooth for to telle,
The folk of Troye hem-selven so mis-
    ledden,
That with the worse at night homward
    they fledden.

8. At whiche day was taken Antenor, 50
Maugre Polydamas or Monesteo,
Santippe, Sarpedon, Polynestor,

Polyte, or eek the Trojan daun Ripheo,
And othere lasse folk, as Phebuseo.
So that, for harm, that day the folk of
    Troye     55
Dredden to lese a greet part of hir joye.

9. Of Pryamus was yeve, at Greek re-
    queste,
A tyme of trewe, and tho they gonnen
    trete,
Hir prisoneres to chaungen, moste and
    leste,     59
And for the surplus yeven sommes grete.
This thing anoon was couth in every
    strete,
Bothe in th'assege, in toune, and every-
    where,
And with the firste it cam to Calkas ere.

10. Whan Calkas knew this tretis sholde
    holde,
In consistorie, among the Grekes, sone 65
He gan in thringe forth, with lordes olde,
And sette him there-as he was wont to
    done ;
And with a chaunged face hem bad a
    bone,
For love of god, to don that reverence,
To stinte noyse, and yeve him audience.

11. Thanne seyde he thus, 'lo ! lordes
    myne, I was     71
Trojan, as it is knowen out of drede ;
And if that yow remembre, I am Calkas,
That alderfirst yaf comfort to your nede,
And tolde yow how that ye sholden spede.
For dredelees, thorugh yow, shal, in a
    stounde,     76
Ben Troye y-brend, and beten doun to
    grounde.

12. And in what forme, or in what maner
    wyse
This town to shende, and al your lust to
    acheve,
Ye han er this wel herd it me devyse; 80
This knowe ye, my lordes, as I leve.
And for the Grekes weren me so leve,
I com my-self in my propre persone,
To teche in this how yow was best to
    done ;

13. Havinge un-to my tresour ne my
rente                                    85
Right no resport, to respect of your ese.
Thus al my good I loste and to yow
wente,
Wening in this you, lordes, for to plese.
But al that los ne doth me no disese.
I vouche-sauf, as wisly have I joye,    90
For you to lese al that I have in Troye,

14. Save of a doughter, that I lafte, allas!
Slepinge at hoom, whanne out of Troye
I sterte.
O sterne, O cruel fader that I was!
How mighte I have in that so hard an
herte?                                   95
Allas! I ne hadde y-brought hir in hir
sherte!
For sorwe of which I wol not live to
morwe,
But-if ye lordes rewe up-on my sorwe.

15. For, by that cause I say no tyme er
now
Hir to delivere, I holden have my pees;
But now or never, if that it lyke yow, 101
I may hir have right sone, doutelees.
O help and grace! amonges al this prees,
Rewe on this olde caitif in destresse,
Sin I through yow have al this hevinesse!

16. Ye have now caught and fetered in
prisoun                                 106
Trojans y-nowe; and if your willes be,
My child with oon may have redempcioun.
Now for the love of god and of bountee,
Oon of so fele, allas! so yeve him me. 110
What nede were it this preyere for to
werne,
Sin ye shul bothe han folk and toun as
yerne?

17. On peril of my lyf, I shal not lye,
Appollo hath me told it feithfully;
I have eek founde it by astronomye,    115
By sort, and by augurie eek trewely,
And dar wel seye, the tyme is faste by,
That fyr and flaumbe on al the toun shal
sprede;
And thus shal Troye turne in asshen
dede.

18. For certeyn, Phebus and Neptunus
bothe,                                  120
That makeden the walles of the toun,
Ben with the folk of Troye alwey so
wrothe,
That thei wol bringe it to confusioun,
Right in despyt of king Lameadoun.    124
By-cause he nolde payen hem hir hyre,
The toun of Troye shal ben set on-fyre.'

19. Telling his tale alwey, this olde greye,
Humble in speche, and in his lokinge eke,
The salte teres from his eyën tweye    129
Ful faste ronnen doun by eythér cheke.
So longe he gan of socour hem by-seke
That, for to hele him of his sorwes sore,
They yave him Antenor, with-oute more.

20. But who was glad y-nough but Calkas
tho?
And of this thing ful sone his nedes
leyde                                   135
On hem that sholden for the tretis go,
And hem for Antenor ful ofte preyde
To bringen hoom king Toas and Criseyde;
And whan Pryam his save-garde sente,
Th'embassadours to Troye streyght they
wente.                                  140

21. The cause y-told of hir cominge, the
olde
Pryam the king ful sone in general
Let here-upon his parlement to holde,
Of which the effect rehersen yow I shal.
Th'embassadours ben answered for fynal,
Th'eschaunge of prisoners and al this
nede                                    146
Hem lyketh wel, and forth in they pro-
cede.

22. This Troilus was present in the place,
Whan axed was for Antenor Criseyde,
For which ful sone chaungen gan his face,
As he that with tho wordes wel neigh
deyde.                                  151
But nathelees, he no word to it seyde,
Lest men sholde his affeccioun espye;
With mannes herte he gan his sorwes
drye.

23. And ful of anguish and of grisly
drede                                   155
Abood what lordes wolde un-to it seye;

And if they wolde graunte, as god for-
    bede,
Th'eschaunge of hir, than thoughte he
    thinges tweye,
First, how to save hir honour, and what
    weye
He mighte best th'eschaunge of hir with-
    stonde ;          160
Ful faste he caste how al this mighte
    stonde.

24. Love him made al prest to doon hir
    byde,
And rather dye than she sholde go;
But resoun seyde him, on that other syde,
'With-oute assent of hir ne do not so, 165
Lest for thy werk she wolde be thy fo,
And seyn, that thorugh thy medling is
    y-blowe
Your bother love, there it was erst un-
    knowe.'

25. For which he gan deliberen, for the
    beste,
That though the lordes wolde that she
    wente,          170
He wolde late hem graunte what hem
    leste,
And telle his lady first what that they
    mente.
And whan that she had seyd him hir
    entente,
Ther-after wolde he werken also blyve,
Though al the world ayein it wolde
    stryve.          175

26. Ector, which that wel the Grekes
    herde,
For Antenor how they wolde han Cri-
    seyde,
Gan it withstonde, and sobrely an-
    swerde :—
'Sires, she nis no prisoner,' he seyde ;
'I noot on yow who that this charge
    leyde,          180
But, on my part, ye may eft-sone him
    telle,
We usen here no wommen for to selle.'

27. The noyse of peple up-stirte thanne
    at ones,
As breme as blase of straw y-set on fyre ;

For infortune it wolde, for the nones, 185
They sholden hir confusioun desyre.
' Ector,' quod they, ' what goost may yow
    enspyre,
This womman thus to shilde and doon us
    lese
Daun Antenor?—a wrong wey now ye
    chese—

28. That is so wys, and eek so bold baroun,
And we han nede of folk, as men may
    see ;          191
He is eek oon, the grettest of this toun ;
O Ector, lat tho fantasyës be !
O king Pryam,' quod they, ' thus seggen
    we,          194
That al our voys is to for-gon Criseyde;'
And to deliveren Antenor they preyde.

29. O Juvenal, lord ! trewe is thy sen-
    tence,
That litel witen folk what is to yerne
That they ne finde in hir desyr offence ;
For cloud of errour lat hem not descerne
What beste is ; and lo, here ensample as
    yerne.          201
This folk desiren now deliveraunce
Of Antenor, that broughte hem to mis-
    chaunce !

30. For he was after traytour to the toun
Of Troye ; allas ! they quitte him out to
    rathe ;          205
O nyce world, lo, thy discrecioun !
Criseyde, which that never dide hem
    skathe,
Shal now no lenger in hir blisse bathe ;
But Antenor, he shal com hoom to toune,
And she shal out : thus seyden here and
    howne.          210

31. For which delibered was by parle-
    ment,
For Antenor to yelden up Criseyde,
And it pronounced by the president,
Al-theigh that Ector 'nay' ful ofte
    preyde.
And fynaly, what wight that it with-
    seyde,          215
It was for nought ; it moste been, and
    sholde ;
For substaunce of the parlement it wolde.

32. Departed out of parlement echone,
This Troilus, with-oute wordes mo,
Un-to his chaumbre spedde him faste
   alloue,        220
But-if it were a man of his or two,
The whiche he bad out faste for to go,
By-cause he wolde slepen, as he seyde,
And hastely up-on his bed him·leyde.

33. And as in winter leves been biraft, 225
Eche after other, til the tree be bare,
So that ther nis but bark and braunche
   y-laft,
Lyth Troilus, biraft of ech wel-fare,
Y-bounden in the blake bark of care,
Disposed wood out of his wit to breyde,
So sore him sat the chaunginge of Cri-
   seyde.        231

34. He rist him up, and every dore he
   shette
And windowe eek, and tho this sorweful
   man
Up-on his beddes syde a-doun him sette,
Ful lyk a deed image pale and wan; 235
And in his brest the heped wo bigan
Out-breste, and he to werken in this
   wyse
In his woodnesse, as I shal yow devyse.

35. Right as the wilde bole biginneth
   springe
Now here, now there, y-darted to the
   herte,        240
And of his deeth roreth in compleyninge,
Right so gan he aboute the chaumbre
   sterte,
Smyting his brest ay with his festes
   smerte ;
His heed to the wal, his body to the
   grounde
Ful ofte he swapte, him-selven to confounde.       245

36. His eyen two, for pitee of his herte,
Out stremeden as swifte welles tweye ;
The heighe sobbes of his sorwes smerte
His speche him rafte, unnethes mighte
   he seye,       249
' O deeth, allas ! why niltow do me deye?
A-cursed be the day which that nature
Shoop me to ben a lyves creature !'

37. But after, whan the furie and the
   rage
Which that his herte twiste and faste
   threste,       254
By lengthe of tyme somwhat gan asswage,
Up-on his bed he leyde him doun to reste ;
But tho bigonne his teres more out-breste,
That wonder is, the body may suffyse
To half this wo, which that I yow devyse.

38. Than seyde he thus, ' Fortune ! allas
   the whyle !       260
What have I doon, what have I thus
   a-gilt ?
How mightestow for reuthe me bigyle?
Is ther no grace, and shal I thus be spilt ?
Shal thus Criseyde awey, for that thou
   wilt ?       264
Allas ! how maystow in thyn herte finde
To been to me thus cruel and unkinde?

39. Have I thee nought honoured al my
   lyve,
As thou wel wost, above the goddes alle ?
Why wiltow me fro joye thus depryve ?
O Troilus, what may men now thee calle
But wrecche of wrecches, out of honour
   falle       271
In-to miserie, in which I wol biwayle
Criseyde, allas ! til that the breeth me
   fayle ?

40. Allas, Fortune ! if that my lyf in joye
Displesed hadde un-to thy foule envye,
Why ne haddestow my fader, king of
   Troye,       276
By-raft the lyf, or doon my bretheren dye,
Or slayn my-self, that thus compleyne
   and crye,
I, combre-world, that may of no-thing
   serve,
But ever dye, and never fully sterve? 280

41. If that Criseyde allone were me laft,
Nought roughte I whider thou woldest
   me stere ;
And hir, allas ! than hastow me biraft.
But ever-more, lo ! this is thy manere,
To reve a wight that most is to him dere,
To preve in that thy gerful violence. 286
Thus am I lost, ther helpeth no defence.

42. O verray lord of love, O god, allas !
That knowest best myn herte and al my
    thought,
What shal my sorwful lyf don in this cas
If I for-go that I so dere have bought? 291
Sin ye Cryseyde and me han fully brought
In-to your grace, and bothe our hertes
    seled,
How may ye suffre, allas ! it be repeled ?

43. What I may doon, I shal, whyl I may
    dure                                    295
On lyve in torment and in cruel peyne,
This infortune or this disaventure,
Allone as I was born, y-wis, compleyne ;
Ne never wil I seen it shyne or reyne ;
But ende I wil, as Edippe, in derknesse
My sorwful lyf, and dyen in distresse. 301

44. O wery goost, that errest to and fro,
Why niltow fleen out of the wofulleste
Body, that ever mighte on grounde go ?
O soule, lurkinge in this wo, unneste, 305
Flee forth out of myn herte, and lat it
    breste,
And folwe alwey Criseyde, thy lady dere ;
Thy righte place is now no lenger here !

45. O wofulle eyen two, sin your disport
Was al to seen Criseydes eyen brighte,
What shal ye doon but, for my discom-
    fort,                                    311
Stonden for nought, and wepen out your
    sighte?
Sin she is queynt, that wont was yow to
    lighte,
In veyn fro-this-forth have I eyen tweye
Y-formed, sin your vertue is a-weye.   315

46. O my Criseyde, O lady sovereyne
Of thilke woful soule that thus cryeth,
Who shal now yeven comfort to my peyne?
Allas, no wight ; but when myn herte
    dyeth,
My spirit, which that so un-to yow hyeth,
Receyve in gree, for that shal ay yow
    serve ;                                 321
For-thy no fors is, though the body sterve.

47. O ye loveres, that heighe upon the
    wheel
Ben set of Fortune, in good aventure,

God leve that ye finde ay love of steel, 325
And longe mot your lyf in joye endure !
But whan ye comen by my sepulture,
Remembreth that your felawe resteth
    there ;
For I lovede eek, though I unworthy
    were.                                   329

48. O olde unholsom and mislyved man,
Calkas I mene, allas ! what eyleth thee
To been a Greek, sin thou art born
    Trojan ?
O Calkas, which that wilt my bane be,
In cursed tyme was thou born for me !
As wolde blisful Jove, for his joye,   335
That I thee hadde, where I wolde, in
    Troye !'

49. A thousand sykes, hottere than the
    glede,
Out of his brest ech after other wente,
Medled with pleyntes newe, his wo to
    fede,                                   339
For which his woful teres never stente ;
And shortly, so his peynes him to-rente,
And wex so mat, that joye nor penaunce
He feleth noon, but lyth forth in a traunce.

50. Pandare, which that in the parlement
Hadde herd what every lord and burgeys
    seyde,                                  345
And how ful graunted was, by oon assent,
For Antenor to yelden so Criseyde,
Gan wel neigh wood out of his wit to
    breyde,
So that, for wo, he niste what he mente ;
But in a rees to Troilus he wente.     350

51. A certeyn knight, that for the tyme
    kepte
The chaumbre-dore, un-dide it him anoon ;
And Pandare, that ful tendreliche wepte,
In-to the derke chaumbre, as stille as
    stoon,
Toward the bed gan softely to goon,   355
So confus, that he niste what to seye ;
For verray wo his wit was neigh aweye.

52. And with his chere and loking al
    to-torn,
For sorwe of this, and with his armes
    folden,

He stood this woful Troilus biforn,     360
And on his pitous face he gan biholden;
But lord, so often gan his herte colden,
Seing his freend in wo, whos hevinesse
His herte slow, as thoughte him, for dis-
    tresse.

53. This woful wight, this Troilus, that
    felte                                365
His freend Pandare y-comen him to see,
Gan as the snow ayein the sonne melte,
For which this sorwful Pandare, of pitee,
Gan for to wepe as tendreliche as he;
And specheles thus been thise ilke tweye,
That neyther mighte o word for sorwe
    seye.                                371

54. But at the laste this woful Troilus,
Ney deed for smert, gan bresten out to
    rore,
And with a sorwful noyse he seyde thus,
Among his sobbes and his sykes sore, 375
'Lo! Pandare, I am deed, with-outen
    more.
Hastow nought herd at parlement,' he
    seyde,
' For Antenor how lost is my Criseyde?'

55. This Pandarus, ful deed and pale of
    hewe,
Ful pitously answerde and seyde, ' yis!
As wisly were it fals as it is trewe,   381
That I have herd, and wot al how it is.
O mercy, god, who wolde have trowed
    this?
Who wolde have wend that, in so litel
    a throwe,                           384
Fortune our joye wolde han over-throwe?

56. For in this world ther is no creature,
As to my doom, that ever saw ruyne
Straungere than this, thorugh cas or
    aventure.
But who may al eschewe or al devyne?
Swich is this world; for-thy I thus de-
    fyne,                               390
†Ne truste no wight finden in Fortune
Ay propretee; hir yeftes been comune.

57. But tel me this, why thou art now so
    mad
To sorwen thus? Why lystow in this
    wyse,

Sin thy desyr al holly hastow had,     395
So that, by right, it oughte y-now suffyse?
But I, that never felte in my servyse
A frendly chere or loking of an yë,
Lat me thus wepe and wayle, til I dye.

58. And over al this, as thou wel wost
    thy-selve,                          400
This town is ful of ladies al aboute;
And, to my doom, fairer than swiche
    twelve
As ever she was, shal I finde, in som
    route,
Ye, oon or two, with-outen any doute. 404
For-thy be glad, myn owene dere brother,
If she be lost, we shul recovere another.

59. What, god for-bede alwey that ech
    plesaunce
In o thing were, and in non other wight!
If oon can singe, another can wel daunce;
If this be goodly, she is glad and light;
And this is fayr, and that can good
    a-right.                            411
Ech for his vertu holden is for dere,
Bothe heroner and faucon for rivere.

60. And eek, as writ Zanzis, that was ful
    wys,
" The newe love out chaceth ofte the
    olde;"                              415
And up-on newe cas lyth newe avys.
Thenk eek, thy-self to saven artow holde;
Swich fyr, by proces, shal of kinde colde.
For sin it is but casuel plesaunce,
Som cas shal putte it out of remem-
    braunce.                            420

61. For al-so seur as day cometh after
    night,
The newe love, labour or other wo,
Or elles selde seinge of a wight,
Don olde affecciouns alle over-go.
And, for thy part, thou shalt have oon of
    tho                                425
To abrigge with thy bittre peynes smerte;
Absence of hir shal dryve hir out of herte.'

62. Thise wordes seyde he for the nones
    alle,
To helpe his freend, lest he for sorwe
    deyde.

For doutelees, to doon his wo to falle, 430
He roughte not what unthrift that he
    seyde.
But Troilus, that neigh for sorwe deyde,
Tok litel hede of al that ever he mente ;
Oon ere it herde, at the other out it
    wente :—

63. But at the laste answerde and seyde,
    ' freend,             435
This lechecraft, or heled thus to be,
Were wel sitting, if that I were a feend,
To traysen hir that trewe is unto me !
I pray god, lat this consayl never y-thee ;
But do me rather sterve anon-right
    here             440
Er I thus do as thou me woldest lere.

64. She that I serve, y-wis, what so thou
    seye,
To whom myn herte enhabit is by right,
Shal han me holly hires til that I deye.
For, Pandarus, sin I have trouthe hir
    hight,          445
I wol not been untrewe for no wight ;
But as hir man I wol ay live and sterve,
And never other creature serve.

65. And ther thou seyst, thou shalt as
    faire finde
As she, lat be, make no comparisoun 450
To creature y-formed here by kinde.
O leve Pandare, in conclusioun,
I wol not be of thyn opinioun,
Touching al this ; for whiche I thee bi-
    seche,
So hold thy pees ; thou sleest me with
    thy speche.        455

66. Thow biddest me I sholde love an-
    other
Al freshly newe, and lat Criseyde go !
It lyth not in my power, leve brother.
And though I mighte, I wolde not do so.
But canstow pleyen raket, to and fro, 460
Netle in, dokke out, now this, now that,
    Pandare ?
Now foule falle hir, for thy wo that care !

67. Thow farest eek by me, thou Pan-
    darus,
As he, that whan a wight is wo bi-goon,

He cometh to him a pas, and seyth right
    thus,        465
"Thenk not on smert, and thou shalt fele
    noon."
Thou most me first transmuwen in a
    stoon,
And reve me my passiounes alle,
Er thou so lightly do my wo to falle.

68. The deeth may wel out of my brest
    departe       470
The lyf, so longe may this sorwe myne ;
But fro my soule shal Criseydes darte
Out never-mo; but doun with Proserpyne,
Whan I am deed, I wol go wone in pyne ;
And ther I wol eternally compleyne  475
My wo, and how that twinned be we
    tweyne.

69. Thow hast here maad an argument,
    for fyn,
How that it sholde lasse peyne be
Criseyde to for-goon, for she was myn,
And live in ese and in felicitee.    480
Why gabbestow, that seydest thus to me
That "him is wors that is fro wele y-
    throwe,
Than he hadde erst non of that wele
    y-knowe ? "

70. But tel me now, sin that thee thinketh
    so light
To chaungen so in love, ay to and fro, 485
Why hastow not don bisily thy might
To chaungen hir that doth thee al thy wo?
Why niltow lete hir fro thyn herte go ?
Why niltow love an-other lady swete,
That may thyn herte setten in quiete ?

71. If thou hast had in love ay yet mis-
    chaunce,       491
And canst it not out of thyn herte dryve,
I, that livede in lust and in plesaunce
With hir as muche as creature on-lyve,
How sholde I that foryete, and that so
    blyve ?       495
O where hastow ben hid so longe in muwe,
That canst so wel and formely arguwe ?

72. Nay, nay, god wot, nought worth is al
    thy reed,
For which, for what that ever may bifalle,

With-outen wordes mo, I wol be deed. 500
O deeth, that endere art of sorwes alle,
Com now, sin I so ofte after thee calle;
For sely is that deeth, soth for to seyne,
That, ofte y-cleped, cometh and endeth
		peyne.

73. Wel wot I, wnyl my lyf was in quiete,
Er thou me slowe, I wolde have yeven
		hyre;	506
But now thy cominge is to me so swete,
That in this world I no-thing so desyre.
O deeth, sin with this sorwe I am a-fyre,
Thou outher do me anoon in teres drenche,
Or with thy colde strook myn hete
		quenche!	511

74. Sin that thou sleest so fele in sondry
		wyse
Ayens hir wil, unpreyed, day and night,
Do me, at my requeste, this servyse,
Delivere now the world, so dostow right,
Of me, that am the wofulleste wight	516
That ever was; for tyme is that I sterve,
Sin in this world of right nought may
		I serve.'

75. This Troilus in teres gan distille,
As licour out of alambyk ful faste;	520
And Pandarus gan holde his tunge stille,
And to the ground his eyen doun he
		caste.
But nathelees, thus thoughte he at the
		laste,
'What, parde, rather than my felawe
		deye,
Yet shal I som-what more un-to him seye:'

76. And seyde, 'freend, sin thou hast
		swich distresse,	526
And sin thee list myn arguments to blame,
Why nilt thy-selven helpen doon redresse,
And with thy manhod letten al this
		grame?
Go ravisshe hir ne canstow not for shame!
And outher lat hir out of toune fare,	531
Or hold hir stille, and leve thy nyce fare.

77. Artow in Troye, and hast non hardi-
		ment
To take a womman which that loveth
		thee,

And wolde hir-selven been of thyn assent?
Now is not this a nyce vanitee?	536
Rys up anoon, and lat this weping be,
And kyth thou art a man, for in this
		houre
I wil be deed, or she shal bleven oure.'

78. To this answerde him Troilus ful
		softe,	540
And seyde, 'parde, leve brother dere,
Al this have I my-self yet thought ful ofte,
And more thing than thou devysest here.
But why this thing is laft, thou shalt wel
		here;	544
And whan thou me hast yeve an audience,
Ther-after mayst thou telle al thy sen-
		tence.

79. First, sin thou wost this toun hath al
		this werre
For ravisshing of wommen so by might,
It sholde not be suffred me to erre,	549
As it stant now, ne doon so gret unright.
I sholde han also blame of every wight,
My fadres graunt if that I so withstode,
Sin she is chaunged for the tounes goode.

80. I have eek thought, so it were hir
		assent,
To aske hir at my fader, of his grace; 555
Than thenke I, this were hir accusement,
Sin wel I woot I may hir not purchace.
For sin my fader, in so heigh a place
As parlement, hath hir eschaunge enseled,
He nil for me his lettre be repeled.	560

81. Yet drede I most hir herte to per-
		tourbe
With violence, if I do swich a game;
For if I wolde it openly distourbe,
It moste been disclaundre to hir name.
And me were lever deed than hir defame,
As nolde god but-if I sholde have	566
Hir honour lever than my lyf to save!

82. Thus am I lost, for ought that I can
		see;
For certeyn is, sin that I am hir knight,
I moste hir honour lever han than me
In every cas, as lovere oughte of right. 571
Thus am I with desyr and reson twight;

Desyr for to distourben hir me redeth,
And reson nil not, so myn herte dredeth.'

83. Thus wepinge that he coude never
cesse,    575
He seyde, 'allas! how shal I, wrecche,
fare?
For wel fele I alwey my love encresse,
And hope is lasse and lasse alwey, Pan-
dare!
Encressen eek the causes of my care;
So wel-a-wey, why nil myn herte breste?
For, as in love, ther is but litel reste.' 581

84. Pandare answerde, 'freend, thou
mayst, for me,
Don as thee list; but hadde ich it so hote,
And thyn estat, she sholde go with me;
Though al this toun cryede on this thing
by note,    585
I nolde sette at al that noyse a grote.
For when men han wel cryed, than wol
they roune;
A wonder last but nyne night never in
toune.

85. Devyne not in reson ay so depe
Ne curteysly, but help thy-self anoon; 590
Bet is that othere than thy-selven wepe,
And namely, sin ye two been al oon.
Rys up, for by myn heed, she shal not
goon;
And rather be in blame a lyte y-founde
Than sterve here as a gnat, with-oute
wounde.    595

86. It is no shame un-to yow, ne no vyce
Hir to with-holden, that ye loveth most.
Paraunter, she mighte holden thee for
nyce
To lete hir go thus to the Grekes ost.
Thenk eek Fortune, as wel thy-selven
wost,    600
Helpeth hardy man to his empryse,
And weyveth wrecches, for hir cowardyse.

87. And though thy lady wolde a litel hir
greve,
Thou shalt thy pees ful wel here-after
make,
But as for me, certayn, I can not leve 605
That she wolde it as now for yvel take.

Why sholde than for ferd thyn herte
quake?
Thenk eek how Paris hath, that is thy
brother,
A love; and why shaltow not have
another?

88. And Troilus, o thing I dar thee
swere,    610
That if Criseyde, whiche that is thy leef,
Now loveth thee as wel as thou dost here,
God helpe me so, she nil not take a-greef,
Though thou do bote a-noon in this
mischeef.
And if she wilneth fro thee for to passe,
Thanne is she fals; so love hir wel the
lasse.    616

89. For-thy tak herte, and thenk, right as
a knight,
Thourgh love is broken alday every lawe.
Kyth now sumwhat thy corage and thy
might,
Have mercy on thy-self, for any awe. 620
Lat not this wrecched wo thin herte
gnawe,
But manly set the world on sixe and
sevene;
And, if thou deye a martir, go to hevene.

90. I wol my-self be with thee at this
dede,
Though ich and al my kin, up-on a
stounde,    625
Shulle in a strete as dogges liggen dede,
Thourgh-girt with many a wyd and blody
wounde.
In every cas I wol a freend be founde.
And if thee list here sterven as a wrecche,
A-dieu, the devel spede him that it
recche!'    630

91. This Troilus gan with tho wordes
quiken,
And seyde, 'freend, graunt mercy, ich
assente;
But certaynly thou mayst not me so
priken,
Ne peyne noon ne may me so tormente,
That, for no cas, it is not myn entente,
At shorte wordes, though I dyen sholde,
To ravisshe hir, but-if hir-self it wolde.' 637

92. 'Why, so mene I,' quod Pandarus, 'al
　　this day.
But tel me than, hastow hir wel assayed,
That sorwest thus?' And he answerde,
　　'nay.'　　　　　　　　　　　640
'Wher-of artow,' quod Pandare, 'than
　　a-mayed,
That nost not that she wol ben yvel
　　apayed
To ravisshe hir, sin thou hast not ben
　　there,
But-if that Jove tolde it in thyn ere?

93. For-thy rys up, as nought ne were,
　　anoon,　　　　　　　　　　　645
And wash thy face, and to the king thou
　　wende,
Or he may wondren whider thou art goon.
Thou most with wisdom him and othere
　　blende ;
Or, up-on cas, he may after thee sende
Er thou be war ; and shortly, brother
　　dere,　　　　　　　　　　　650
Be glad, and lat me werke in this matere.

94. For I shal shape it so, that sikerly
Thou shalt this night som tyme, in som
　　manere,
Com speke with thy lady prevely,
And by hir wordes eek, and by hir chere,
Thou shalt ful sone aparceyve and wel
　　here　　　　　　　　　　　656
Al hir entente, and in this cas the beste ;
And fare now wel, for in this point I
　　reste.'

95. The swifte Fame, whiche that false
　　thinges
Egal reporteth lyk the thinges trewe, 660
Was thorugh-out Troye y-fled with preste
　　winges
Fro man to man, and made this tale al
　　newe,
How Calkas doughter, with hir brighte
　　hewe,
At parlement, with-oute wordes more,
I-graunted was in chaunge of Antenore. 665

96. The whiche tale anoon-right as Cri-
　　seyde
Had herd, she which that of hir fader
　　roughte,

As in this cas, right nought, ne whanne
　　he deyde,
Ful bisily to Juppiter bisoughte
Yeve him mischaunce that this tretis
　　broughte.　　　　　　　　　　670
But shortly, lest thise tales sothe were,
She dorste at no wight asken it, for fere ;

97. As she that hadde hir herte and al hir
　　minde
On Troilus y-set so wonder faste,
That al this world ne mighte hir love
　　unbinde,　　　　　　　　　　675
Ne Troilus out of hir herte caste ;
She wol ben his, whyl that hir lyf may
　　laste.
And thus she brenneth bothe in love and
　　drede,
So that she niste what was best to rede.

98. But as men seen in toune, and al
　　aboute,　　　　　　　　　　680
That wommen usen frendes to visyte,
So to Criseyde of wommen com a route
For pitous joye, and wenden hir delyte ;
And with hir tales, dere y-nough a myte,
These wommen, whiche that in the cite
　　dwelle,　　　　　　　　　　685
They sette hem doun, and seyde as I shal
　　telle.

99. Quod first that oon, 'I am glad,
　　trewely,
By-cause of yow, that shal your fader see.'
A-nother seyde, ' y-wis, so nam not I ;
For al to litel hath she with us be.' 690
Quod tho the thridde, 'I hope, y-wis,
　　that she
Shal bringen us the pees on every syde,
That, whan she gooth, almighty god hir
　　gyde !'

100. Tho wordes and tho wommannisshe
　　thinges,
She herde hem right as though she
　　thennes were ;　　　　　　　　695
For, god it wot, hir herte on other thing
　　is,
Although the body sat among hem there.
Hir advertence is alwey elles-where ;
For Troilus ful faste hir soule soughte ;
With-outen word, alwey on him she
　　thoughte.　　　　　　　　　　700

101. Thise wommen, that thus wenden
    hir to plese,
Aboute nought gonne alle hir tales
    spende ;
Swich vanitee ne can don hir non ese,
As she that, al this mene whyle, brende
Of other passioun than that they wende,
So that she felte almost hir herte dye 706
For wo, and wery of that companye.

102. For which no lenger mighte she
    restreyne
Hir teres, so they gonnen up to welle,
That yeven signes of the bitter peyne 710
In whiche hir spirit was, and moste
    dwelle ;
Remembring hir, fro heven unto which
    helle
She fallen was, sith she forgoth the
    sighte
Of Troilus, and sorowfully she sighte. 714

103. And thilke foles sitting hir aboute
Wenden, that she wepte and syked sore
By-cause that she sholde out of that route
Departe, and never pleye with hem more.
And they that hadde y-knowen hir of yore
Seye hir so wepe, and thoughte it kinde-
    nesse,      720
And eche of hem wepte eek for hir dis-
    tresse ;

104. And bisily they gonnen hir conforten
Of thing, god wot, on which she litel
    thoughte ;
And with hir tales wenden hir disporten,
And to be glad they often hir bisoughte.
But swich an ese ther-with they hir
    wroughte      726
Right as a man is esed for to fele,
For ache of heed, to clawen him on his
    hele !

105. But after al this nyce vanitee
They took hir leve, and hoom they wenten
    alle.      730
Criseyde, ful of sorweful pitee,
In-to hir chaumbre up wente out of the
    halle,
And on hir bed she gan for deed to falle,
In purpos never thennes for to ryse ;
And thus she wroughte, as I shal yow
    devyse.      735

106. Hir ounded heer, that sonnish was
    of hewe,
She rente, and eek hir fingres longe and
    smale
She wrong ful ofte, and bad god on hir
    rewe,
And with the deeth to doon bote on hir
    bale.
Hir hewe, whylom bright, that tho was
    pale,      740
Bar witnes of hir wo and hir constreynte ;
And thus she spak, sobbinge, in hir com-
    pleynte :

107. 'Alas !' quod she, 'out of this
    regioun
I, woful wrecche and infortuned wight,
And born in corsed constellacioun,      745
Mot goon, and thus departen fro my
    knight ;
Wo worth, allas ! that ilke dayes light
On which I saw him first with eyen
    tweyne,
That causeth me, and I him, al this
    peyne !'

108. Therwith the teres from hir eyen
    two      750
Doun fille, as shour in Aperill, ful swythe;
Hir whyte brest she bet, and for the wo
After the deeth she cryed a thousand
    sythe,
Sin he that wont hir wo was for to lythe,
She mot for-goon ; for which disaventure
She held hir-self a forlost creature.      756

109. She seyde, 'how shal he doon, and
    I also ?
How sholde I live, if that I from him
    twinne ?
O dere herte eek, that I love so,
Who shal that sorwe sleen that ye ben
    inne ?      760
O Calkas, fader, thyn be al this sinne !
O moder myn, that cleped were Argyve,
Wo worth that day that thou me bere on
    lyve !

110. To what fyn sholde I live and sorwen
    thus ?
How sholde a fish with-oute water dure?
What is Criseyde worth, from Troilus? 766

How sholde a plaunte or lyves creature
Live, with-oute his kinde noriture ?
For which ful oft a by-word here I seye,
That, " rotelees, mot grene sone deye." 770

111. I shal don thus, sin neither swerd ne
    darte
Dar I non handle, for the crueltee,
That ilke day that I from yow departe,
If sorwe of that nil not my bane be,
Than shal no mete or drinke come in
    me    775
Til I my soule out of my breste unshethe ;
And thus my-selven wol I do to dethe.

112. And, Troilus, my clothes everichoon
Shul blake been, in tokeninge, herte
    swete,
That I am as out of this world agoon, 780
That wont was yow to setten in quiete ;
And of myn ordre, ay til deeth me mete,
The observaunce ever, in your absence,
Shal sorwe been, compleynte, and absti-
    nence.

113. Myn herte and eek the woful goost
    ther-inne    785
Biquethe I, with your spirit to compleyne
Eternally, for they shul never twinne.
For though in erthe y-twinned be we
    tweyne,
Yet in the feld of pitee, out of peyne,
That hight Elysos, shul we been y-fere, 790
As Orpheus and Erudice his fere.

114. Thus herte myn, for Antenor, allas !
I sone shal be chaunged, as I wene.
But how shul ye don in this sorwful
    cas,
How shal your tendre herte this sustene?
But herte myn, for-yet this sorwe and
    tene,    796
And me also ; for, soothly for to seye,
So ye wel fare, I recche not to deye.'

115. How mighte it ever y-red ben or
    y-songe,
The pleynte that she made in hir dis-
    tresse ?    800
I noot ; but, as for me, my litel tonge,
If I discreven wolde hir hevinesse,
It sholde make hir sorwe seme lesse

Than that it was, and childishly deface
Hir heigh compleynte, and therfore I it
    pace.    805

116. Pandare, which that sent from
    Troilus
Was to Criseyde, as ye han herd devyse,
That for the beste it was accorded thus,
And he ful glad to doon him that servyse,
Un-to Criseyde, in a ful secree wyse, 810
Ther-as she lay in torment and in rage,
Com hir to telle al hoolly his message.

117. And fond that she hir-selven gan to
    trete
Ful pitously ; for with hir salte teres
Hir brest, hir face y-bathed was ful
    wete ;    815
The mighty tresses of hir sonnish heres,
Unbroyden, hangen al aboute hir eres ;
Which yaf him verray signal of martyre
Of deeth, which that hir herte gan
    desyre.

118. Whan she him saw, she gan for sorwe
    anoon    820
Hir tery face a-twixe hir armes hyde,
For which this Pandare is so wo bi-goon,
That in the hous he mighte unnethe
    abyde,
As he that pitee felte on every syde.
For if Criseyde hadde erst compleyned
    sore,    825
Tho gan she pleyne a thousand tymes
    more.

119. And in hir aspre pleynte than she
    seyde,
' Pandare first of joyes mo than two
Was cause causinge un-to me, Criseyde,
That now transmuwed been in cruel
    wo.    830
Wher shal I seye to yow " wel come " or
    no,
That alderfirst me broughte in-to servyse
Of love, allas ! that endeth in swich wyse?

120. Endeth than love in wo ? Ye, or men
    lyeth !    834
And alle worldly blisse, as thinketh me,
The ende of blisse ay sorwe it occupyeth ;
And who-so troweth not that it so be,

Lat him upon me, woful wrecche, y-see,
That my-self hate, and ay my birthe
    acorse,
Felinge alwey, fro wikke I go to worse.

121. Who-so me seeth, he seeth sorwe al
    at ones,      841
Peyne, torment, pleynte, wo, distresse.
Out of my woful body harm ther noon is,
As anguish, langour, cruel bitternesse,
A-noy, smert, drede, fury, and eek sik-
    nesse.      845
I trowe, y-wis, from hevene teres reyne,
For pitee of myn aspre and cruel peyne!'

122. 'And thou, my suster, ful of dis-
    comfort,'      848
Quod Pandarus, 'what thenkestow to do?
Why ne hastow to thy-selven som resport,
Why woltow thus thy-selve, allas, for-do?
Leef al this werk and tak now hede to
That I shal seyn, and herkne, of good
    entente,
This, which by me thy Troilus thee
    sente.'

123. Torned hir tho Criseyde, a wo
    makinge      855
So greet that it a deeth was for to see :—
'Allas!' quod she, 'what wordes may ye
    bringe?
What wol my dere herte seyn to me,
Which that I drede never-mo to see? 859
Wol he have pleynte or teres, er I wende?
I have y-nowe, if he ther-after sende!'

124. She was right swich to seen in hir
    visage
As is that wight that men on bere binde ;
Hir face, lyk of Paradys the image,
Was al y-chaunged in another kinde. 865
The pleye, the laughtre men was wont to
    finde
In hir, and eek hir joyes everychone,
Ben fled, and thus lyth now Criseyde
    allone.

125. Aboute hir eyen two a purpre ring
Bi-trent, in sothfast tokninge of hir
    peyne,      870
That to biholde it was a dedly thing,
For which Pandare mighte not restreyne

The teres from his eyen for to reyne.
But nathelees, as he best mighte, he seyde
From Troilus thise wordes to Criseyde. 875

126. 'Lo, nece, I trowe ye han herd al
    how
The king, with othere lordes, for the
    beste,
Hath mad eschaunge of Antenor and
    yow,
That cause is of this sorwe and this
    unreste.
But how this cas doth Troilus moleste, 880
That may non erthely mannes tonge
    seye ;
For verray wo his wit is al aweye.

127. For which we han so sorwed, he
    and I,
That in-to litel bothe it hadde us slawe ;
But thurgh my conseil this day, fynally,
He somwhat is fro weping now with-
    drawe.      886
And semeth me that he desyreth fawe
With yow to been al night, for to devyse
Remede in this, if ther were any wyse.

128. This, short and pleyne, th'effect of
    my message,      890
As ferforth as my wit can comprehende.
For ye, that been of torment in swich rage,
May to no long prologe as now entende ;
And her-upon ye may answere him sende.
And, for the love of god, my nece dere,
So leef this wo er Troilus be here.'      896

129. ' Gret is my wo,' quod she, and sighte
    sore,
As she that feleth dedly sharp distresse ;
' But yet to me his sorwe is muchel more,
That love him bet than he him-self,
    I gesse.      900
Allas! for me hath he swich hevinesse ?
Can he for me so pitously compleyne ?
Y-wis, this sorwe doubleth al my peyne.

130. Grevous to me, god wot, is for to
    twinne,'
Quod she, ' but yet it hardere is to me 905
To seen that sorwe which that he is inne ;
For wel wot I, it wol my bane be ;
And deye I wol in certayn,' tho quod she ;

'But bidde him come, er deeth, that thus
　　me threteth,
Dryve out that goost, which in myn herte
　　beteth.'　　　　　　　　　　910

131. Thise wordes seyd, she on hir armes
　　two
Fil gruf, and gan to wepe pitously.
Quod Pandarus, 'allas! why do ye so,
Syn wel ye wot the tyme is faste by,
That he shal come? Arys up hastely,　915
That he yow nat biwopen thus ne finde,
But ye wol han him wood out of his
　　minde!

132. For wiste he that ye ferde in this
　　manere,
He wolde him-selve slee; and if I wende
To han this fare, he sholde not come
　　here　　　　　　　　　　　　920
For al the good that Pryam may despende.
For to what fyn he wolde anoon pretende,
That knowe I wel; and for-thy yet I seye,
So leef this sorwe, or platly he wol deye.

133. And shapeth yow his sorwe for to
　　abregge,　　　　　　　　　　925
And nought encresse, leve nece swete;
Beth rather to him cause of flat than
　　egge,
And with som wysdom ye his sorwes bete.
What helpeth it to wepen ful a strete,
Or though ye bothe in salte teres dreynte?
Bet is a tyme of cure ay than of pleynte. 931

134. I mene thus; whan I him hider
　　bringe,
Sin ye ben wyse, and bothe of oon assent,
So shapeth how distourbe your goinge,
Or come ayen, sone after ye be went.　935
Wommen ben wyse in short avysement;
And lat sen how your wit shal now
　　avayle;
And what that I may helpe, it shal not
　　fayle.'

135. 'Go,' quod Criseyde, 'and uncle,
　　trewely,
I shal don al my might, me to restreyne
From weping in his sight, and bisily,　941
Him for to glade, I shal don al my peyne,
And in myn herte seken every veyne;

If to this soor ther may be founden salve,
It shal not lakken, certain, on myn
　　halve.'　　　　　　　　　　945

136. Goth Pandarus, and Troilus he
　　soughte,
Til in a temple he fond him allone,
As he that of his lyf no lenger roughte;
But to the pitouse goddes everichone
Ful tendrely he preyde, and made his
　　mone,　　　　　　　　　　950
To doon him sone out of this world to
　　pace;
For wel he thoughte ther was non other
　　grace.

137. And shortly, al the sothe for to seye,
He was so fallen in despeyr that day,
That outrely he shoop him for to deye. 955
For right thus was his argument alwey:
He seyde, he nas but loren, waylawey!
'For al that comth, comth by necessitee;
Thus to be lorn, it is my destinee.

138. For certaynly, this wot I wel,' he
　　seyde,　　　　　　　　　　960
'That for-sight of divyne purveyaunce
Hath seyn alwey me to for-gon Criseyde,
Sin god seeth every thing, out of dout-
　　aunce,
And hem desponeth, thourgh his orde-
　　naunce,
In hir merytes sothly for to be,　　965
As they shul comen by predestinee.

139. But nathelees, allas! whom shal I
　　leve?
For ther ben grete clerkes many oon,
That destinee thorugh argumentes preve;
And som men seyn that nedely ther is
　　noon;　　　　　　　　　　970
But that free chois is yeven us everichoon.
O, welaway! so sleye arn clerkes olde,
That I not whos opinion I may holde.

140. For som men seyn, if god seth al
　　biforn,
Ne god may not deceyved ben, pardee, 975
Than moot it fallen, though men hadde it
　　sworn,
That purveyaunce hath seyn bifore to be.
Wherfor I seye, that from eterne if he

Hath wist biforn our thought eek as our
   dede,
We have no free chois, as these clerkes
   rede.         980

141. For other thought nor other dede
   also
Might never be, but swich as purveyaunce,
Which may not ben deceyved never-mo,
Hath feled biforn, with-outen ignoraunce.
For if ther mighte been a variaunce  985
To wrythen out fro goddes purveyinge,
Ther nere no prescience of thing cominge;

142. But it were rather an opinioun
Uncerteyn, and no stedfast forseinge;
And certes, that were an abusioun,   990
That god shuld han no parfit cleer witinge
More than we men that han doutous
   weninge.
But swich an errour up-on god to gesse
Were fals and foul, and wikked corsed-
   nesse.

143. Eek this is an opinioun of somme 995
That han hir top ful heighe and smothe
   y-shore;
They seyn right thus, that thing is not to
   come
For that the prescience hath seyn bifore
That it shal come; but they seyn, that
   therfore
That it shal come, therfore the purvey-
   aunce      1000
Wot it biforn with-outen ignoraunce;

144. And in this manere this necessitee
Retorneth in his part contrarie agayn.
For needfully bihoveth it not to be
That thilke thinges fallen in certayn 1005
That ben purveyed; but nedely, as they
   seyn,
Bihoveth it that thinges, whiche that
   falle,
That they in certayn ben purveyed alle.

145. I mene as though I laboured me in
   this,
To enqueren which thing cause of which
   thing be;      1010
As whether that the prescience of god is
The certayn cause of the necessitee

Of thinges that to comen been, pardee;
Or if necessitee of thing cominge
Be cause certeyn of the purveyinge.  1015

146. But now ne enforce I me nat in
   shewinge
How the ordre of causes stant; but wel
   wot I,
That it bihoveth that the bifallinge
Of thinges wist biforen certeynly
Be necessarie, al seme it not ther-by 1020
That prescience put falling necessaire
To thing to come, al falle it foule or
   faire.

147. For if ther sit a man yond on a see,
Than by necessitee bihoveth it
That, certes, thyn opinioun soth be,  1025
That wenest or conjectest that he sit;
And ferther-over now ayenward yit,
Lo, right so it is of the part contrarie,
As thus; (now herkne, for I wol not
   tarie):

148. I seye, that if the opinioun of thee
Be sooth, for that he sit, than seye I
   this,      1031
That he mot sitten by necessitee;
And thus necessitee in either is.
For in him nede of sitting is, y-wis,
And in thee nede of sooth; and thus, for-
   sothe,      1035
Ther moot necessitee ben in yow bothe.

149. But thou mayst seyn, the man sit
   not therfore,
That thyn opinion of sitting soth is;
But rather, for the man sit ther bifore,
Therfore is thyn opinion sooth, y-wis. 1040
And I seye, though the cause of sooth of
   this
Comth of his sitting, yet necessitee
Is entrechaunged, bothe in him and thee.

150. Thus on this same wyse, out of
   doutaunce,
I may wel maken, as it semeth me,  1045
My resoninge of goddes purveyaunce,
And of the thinges that to comen be;
By whiche reson men may wel y-see,
That thilke thinges that in erthe falle,
That by necessitee they comen alle.  1050

151. For al-though that, for thing shal
    come, y-wis,
Therfore is it purveyed, certaynly,
Nat that it comth for it purveyed is :
Yet nathelees, bihoveth it nedfully,
That thing to come be purveyed, trewely;
Or elles, thinges that purveyed be,   1056
That they bityden by necessitee.

152. And this suffyseth right y-now,
    certeyn,
For to destroye our free chois every del.—
But now is this abusion to seyn,   1060
That fallinge of the thinges temporel
Is cause of goddes prescience eternel.
Now trewely, that is a fals sentence,
That thing to come sholde cause his
    prescience.

153. What mighte I wene, and I hadde
    swich a thought,   1065
But that god purveyth thing that is to
    come
For that it is to come, and elles nought ?
So mighte I wene that thinges alle and
    some,
That whylom been bifalle and over-come,
Ben cause of thilke sovereyn purvey-
    aunce,   1070
That for-wot al with-outen ignoraunce.

154. And over al this, yet seye I more
    herto,
That right as whan I woot ther is a
    thing,
Y-wis, that thing mot nedefully be so ;
Eek right so, whan I woot a thing
    coming,   1075
So mot it come ; and thus the bifalling
Of thinges that ben wist bifore the tyde,
They mowe not been eschewed on no
    syde.'

155. Than seyde he thus, 'almighty Jove
    in trone,
That wost of al this thing the soothfast-
    nesse,   1080
Rewe on my sorwe, or do me deye sone,
Or bring Criseyde and me fro this dis-
    tresse.'
And whyl he was in al this hevinesse,

Disputinge with him-self in this matere,   ·
Com Pandare in, and seyde as ye may
    here.   1085

156. 'O mighty god,' quod Pandarus, 'in
    trone,
Ey ! who seigh ever a wys man faren so ?
Why, Troilus, what thenkestow to done ?
Hastow swich lust to been thyn owene fo ?
What, parde, yet is not Criseyde a-go ! 1090
Why lust thee so thy-self for-doon for
    drede,
That in thyn heed thyn eyen semen dede ?

157. Hastow not lived many a yeer bi-
    forn
With-outen hir, and ferd ful wel at ese ?
Artow for hir and for non other born ?
Hath kind thee wroughte al-only hir to
    plese ?   1096
Lat be, and thenk right thus in thy disese :
That, in the dees right as ther fallen
    chaunces,
Right so in love, ther come and goon
    plesaunces.

158. And yet this is a wonder most of alle,
Why thou thus sorwest, sin thou nost
    not yit,    ·   1101
Touching hir goinge, how that it shal
    falle,
Ne if she can hir-self distorben it.
Thou hast not yet assayed al hir wit.
A man may al by tyme his nekke bede 1105
Whan it shal of, and sorwen at the nede.

159. For-thy take hede of that that I shal
    seye ;
I have with hir y-spoke and longe y-be,
So as accorded was bitwixe us tweye.
And ever-mo me thinketh thus, that she
Hath som-what in hir hertes prevetee,
Wher-with she can, if I shal right arede,
Distorbe al this, of which thou art in
    drede.   1113

160. For which my counseil is, whan it is
    night,
Thou to hir go, and make of this an
    ende ;
And blisful Juno, thourgh hir grete
    mighte,   1116

L

Shal, as I hope, hir grace un-to us sende.
Myn herte seyth, " certeyn, she shal not
    wende ; "
And for-thy put thyn herte a whyle in
    reste ;                 1119
And hold this purpos, for it is the beste.'

161. This Troilus answerde, and sighte
    sore,
'Thou seyst right wel, and I wil do right
    so ;'
And what him liste, he seyde un-to it
    more.
And whan that it was tyme for to go,
Ful prevely him-self, with-outen mo, 1125
Un-to hir com, as he was wont to done ;
And how they wroughte, I shal yow telle
    sone.

162. Soth is, that whan they gonne first
    to mete,             1128
So gan the peyne hir hertes for to twiste,
That neither of hem other mighte grete,
But hem in armes toke and after kiste.
The lasse wofulle of hem bothe niste
Wher that he was, ne mighte o word
    out-bringe,
As I seyde erst, for wo and for sobbinge.

163. Tho woful teres that they leten
    falle               1135
As bittre weren, out of teres kinde,
For peyne, as is ligne-aloës or galle.
So bittre teres weep nought, as I finde,
The woful Myrra through the bark and
    rinde.
That in this world ther nis so hard an
    herte,             1140
That nolde han rewed on hir peynes
    smerte.

164. But whan hir woful wery gostes
    tweyne
Retorned been ther-as hem oughte dwelle,
And that som-what to wayken gan the
    peyne
By lengthe of pleynte, and ebben gan the
    welle             1145
Of hire teres, and the herte unswelle,
With broken voys, al hoors for-shright,
    Criseyde
To Troilus thise ilke wordes seyde :

165. ' O Jove, I deye, and mercy I be-
    seche !
Help, Troilus !' and ther-with-al hir face
Upon his brest she leyde, and loste
    speche ;            1151
Hir woful spirit from his propre place,
Right with the word, alwey up poynt to
    pace.
And thus she lyth with hewes pale and
    grene,
That whylom fresh and fairest was to
    sene.            1155

166. This Troilus, that on hir gan biholde,
Clepinge hir name, (and she lay as for
    deed,
With-oute answere, and felte hir limes
    colde,
Hir eyen throwen upward to hir heed),
This sorwful man can now noon other
    reed,            1160
But ofte tyme hir colde mouth he kiste ;
Wher him was wo, god and him-self it
    wiste !

167. He rist him up, and long streight he
    hir leyde ;
For signe of lyf, for ought he can or
    may,
Can he noon finde in no-thing on Cri-
    seyde,            1165
For which his song ful ofte is 'weylaway !'
But whan he saugh that specheles she
    lay,
With sorwful voys, and herte of blisse al
    bare,
He seyde how she was fro this world
    y-fare !

168. So after that he longe hadde hir
    compleyned,            1170
His hondes wronge, and seyd that was to
    seye,
And with his teres salte hir brest bi-
    reyned,
He gan tho teres wypen of ful dreye,
And pitously gan for the soule preye,
And seyde, ' O lord, that set art in thy
    trone,            1175
Rewe eek on me, for I shal folwe hir
    sone !'

169. She cold was and with-outen sente-
    ment,
For aught he woot, for breeth ne felte he
    noon ;
And this was him a preignant argument
That she was forth out of this world
    agoon ;        1180
And whan he seigh ther was non other
    woon,
He gan hir limes dresse in swich manere
As men don hem that shul be leyd on bere.

170. And after this, with sterne and cruel
    herte,
His swerd a-noon out of his shethe he
    twighte,        1185
Him-self to sleen, how sore that him
    smerte,
So that his sowle hir sowle folwen mighte,
Ther-as the doom of Mynos wolde it dighte ;
Sin love and cruel Fortune it ne wolde,
That in this world he lenger liven sholde.

171. Thanne seyde he thus, fulfild of
    heigh desdayn,        1191
' O cruel Jove, and thou, Fortune adverse,
This al and som, that falsly have ye
    slayn
Criseyde, and sin ye may do me no werse,
Fy on your might and werkes so di-
    verse !        1195
Thus cowardly ye shul me never winne ;
Ther shal no deeth me fro my lady twinne.

172. For I this world, sin ye han slayn hir
    thus,
Wol lete, and folowe hir spirit lowe or hye;
Shal never lover seyn that Troilus    1200
Dar not, for fere, with his lady dye ;
For certeyn, I wol bere hir companye.
But sin ye wol not suffre us liven here,
Yet suffreth that our soules ben y-fere.

173. And thou, citee, whiche that I leve
    in wo,        1205
And thou, Pryam, and bretheren al y-fere,
And thou, my moder, farewel ! for I go ;
And Attropos, make redy thou my bere !
And thou, Criseyde, o swete herte dere,
Receyve now my spirit !' wolde he seye,
With swerd at herte, al redy for to deye.

174. But as god wolde, of swough ther-
    with she abreyde,      1212
And gan to syke, and ' Troilus ' she cryde;
And he answerde, ' lady myn Criseyde,
Live ye yet ?' and leet his swerd doun
    glyde.        1215
' Ye, herte myn, that thanked be Cupyde !'
Quod she, and ther-with-al she sore sighte;
And he bigan to glade hir as he mighte ;

175. Took hir in armes two, and kiste hir
    ofte,
And hir to glade he dide al his entente ;
For which hir goost, that flikered ay
    on-lofte,        1221
In-to hir woful herte ayein it wente.
But at the laste, as that hir eyen glente
A-syde, anoon she gan his swerd aspye,
As it lay bare, and gan for fere crye,  1225

176. And asked him, why he it hadde
    out-drawe ?
And Troilus anoon the cause hir tolde,
And how himself ther-with he wolde
    have slawe.
For which Criseyde up-on him gan bi-
    holde,
And gan him in hir armes faste folde,  1230
And seyde, ' O mercy, god, lo, which a
    dede !
Allas ! how neigh we were bothe dede !

177. Thanne if I ne hadde spoken, as
    grace was,
Ye wolde han slayn your-self anoon ?'
    quod she.
' Ye, douteless ;' and she answerde, 'allas!
For, by that ilke lord that made me,  1236
I nolde a forlong wey on-lyve han be,
After your deeth, to han be crowned quene
Of al the lond the sonne on shyneth shene.

178. But with this selve swerd, which
    that here is,      1240
My-selve I wolde have slayn !'—quod she
    tho ;
' But ho, for we han right y-now of this,
And late us ryse and streight to bedde go,
And there lat vs speken of our wo.
For, by the morter which that I see
    brenne,        1245
Knowe I ful wel that day is not fer henne.'

179. Whan they were in hir bedde, in
        armes folde,
Nought was it lyk tho nightes here-biforn ;
For pitously ech other gan biholde,    1249
As they that hadden al hir blisse y-lorn,
Biwaylinge ay the day that they were born.
Til at the last this sorwful wight Criseyde
To Troilus these ilke wordes seyde :—

180. 'Lo, herte myn, wel wot ye this,'
        quod she,                        1254
'That if a wight alwey his wo compleyne,
And seketh nought how holpen for to be,
It nis but folye and encrees of peyne ;
And sin that here assembled be we tweyne
To finde bote of wo that we ben inne,
It were al tyme sone to biginne.        1260

181. I am a womman, as ful wel ye woot,
And as I am avysed sodeynly,
So wol I telle yow, whyl it is hoot.
Me thinketh thus, that neither ye nor I
Oughte half this wo to make skilfully. 1265
For there is art y-now for to redresse
That yet is mis, and sleen this hevinesse.

182. Sooth is, the wo, the whiche that we
        ben inne,
For ought I woot, for no-thing elles is
But for the cause that we sholden twinne.
Considered al, ther nis no-more amis. 1271
But what is thanne a remede un-to this,
But that we shape us sone for to mete ?
This al and som, my dere herte swete.

183. Now that I shal wel bringen it
        aboute                           1275
To come ayein, sone after that I go,
Ther-of am I no maner thing in doute.
For dredeles, with-inne a wouke or two,
I shal ben here ; and, that it may be so
By alle right, and in a wordes fewe,   1280
I shal yow wel an heep of weyes shewe.

184. For which I wol not make long
        sermoun,
For tyme y-lost may not recovered be ;
But I wol gon to my conclusioun,       1284
And to the beste, in ought that I can see.
And, for the love of god, for-yeve it me
If I speke ought ayein your hertes reste ;
For trewely, I speke it for the beste ;

185. Makinge alwey a protestacioun,
That now these wordes, whiche that I shal
        seye,                           1290
Nis but to shewe yow my mocioun,
To finde un-to our helpe the beste weye ;
And taketh it non other wyse, I preye.
For in effect what-so ye me comaunde,
That wol I doon, for that is no demaunde.

186. Now herkeneth this, ye han wel
        understonde,                     1296
My going graunted is by parlement
So ferforth, that it may not be with-stonde
For al this world, as by my jugement.
And sin ther helpeth noon avysement 1300
To letten it, lat it passe out of minde ;
And lat us shape a bettre wey to finde.

187. The sothe is, that the twinninge of
        us tweyne
Wol us disese and cruelliche anoye.
But him bihoveth som-tyme han a peyne,
That serveth love, if that he wol have
        joye.                           1306
And sin I shal no ferthere out of Troye
Than I may ryde ayein on half a morwe,
It oughte lasse causen us to sorwe :

188. So as I shal not so ben hid in muwe,
That day by day, myn owene herte dere,
Sin wel ye woot that it is now a truwe,
Ye shul ful wel al myn estat y-here. 1313
And er that truwe is doon, I shal ben here,
And thanne have ye bothe Antenor y-
        wonne
And me also ; beth glad now, if ye conne ;

189. And thenk right thus, " Criseyde is
        now agoon,                       1317
But what ! she shal come hastely ayeyn ;"
And whanne, allas ? by god, lo, right
        anoon,
Er dayes ten, this dar I saufly seyn. 1320
And thanne at erste shul we been so fayn,
So as we shulle to-gederes ever dwelle,
That al this world ne mighte our blisse
        telle.

190. I see that ofte, ther-as we ben now,
That for the beste, our conseil for to hyde,
Ye speke not with me, nor I with yow 1326
In fourtenight ; ne see yow go ne ryde.

May ye not ten dayes thanne abyde,
For myn honour, in swich an aventure?
Y-wis, ye mowen elles lyte endure!    1330

191. Ye knowe eek how that al my kin is
    here,
But-if that onliche it my fader be;
And eek myn othere thinges alle y-fere,
And nameliche, my dere herte, ye,
Whom that I nolde leven for to see    1335
For al this world, as wyd as it hath space;
Or elles, see ich never Joves face!

192. Why trowe ye my fader in this wyse
Coveiteth so to see me, but for drede    1339
Lest in this toun that folkes me dispyse
By-cause of him, for his unhappy dede?
What woot my fader what lyf that I lede?
For if he wiste in Troye how wel I fare,
Us neded for my wending nought to care.

193. Ye seen that every day eek, more
    and more,    1345
Men trete of pees; and it supposed is,
That men the quene Eleyne shal restore,
And Grekes us restore that is mis.
So though ther nere comfort noon but
    this,    1349
That men purposen pees on every syde,
Ye may the bettre at ese of herte abyde.

194. For if that it be pees, myn herte
    dere,
The nature of the pees mot nedes dryve
That men moste entrecomunen y-fere,
And to and fro eek ryde and gon as blyve
Alday as thikke as been flen from an
    hyve;    1356
And every wight han libertee to bleve
Wher-as him list the bet, with-outen leve.

195. And though so be that pees ther may
    be noon,
Yet hider, though ther never pees ne
    were,    1360
I moste come; for whider sholde I goon,
Or how mischaunce sholde I dwelle there
Among tho men of armes ever in fere?
For which, as wisly god my soule rede,
I can not seen wher-of ye sholden drede.

196. Have here another wey, if it so be
That al this thing ne may yow not suffyse.

My fader, as ye knowen wel, pardee,
Is old, and elde is ful of coveityse.
And I right now have founden al the
    gyse,    1370
With-oute net, wher-with I shal him
    hente;
And herkeneth how, if that ye wole
    assente.

197. Lo, Troilus, men seyn that hard it is
The wolf ful, and the wether hool to have;
This is to seyn, that men ful ofte, y-wis,
Mot spenden part, the remenaunt for to
    save.    1376
For ay with gold men may the herte
    grave
Of him that set is up-on coveityse;
And how I mene, I shal it yow devyse.

198. The moeble which that I have in
    this toun    1380
Un-to my fader shal I take, and seye,
That right for trust and for savacioun
It sent is from a freend of his or tweye,
The whiche freendes ferventliche him
    preye
To senden after more, and that in hye,
Whyl that this toun stant thus in ju-
    partye.    1386

199. And that shal been an huge
    quantitee,
Thus shal I seyn, but, lest it folk aspyde,
This may be sent by no wight but by me;
I shal eek shewen him, if pees bityde, 1390
What frendes that ich have on every syde
Toward the court, to doon the wrathe
    pace
Of Priamus, and doon him stonde in
    grace.

200. So, what for o thing and for other,
    swete,
I shal him so enchaunten with my sawes,
That right in hevene his sowle is, shal he
    mete;    1396
For al Appollo, or his clerkes lawes,
Or calculinge avayleth nought three
    hawes;
Desyr of gold shal so his sowle blende,
That, as me lyst, I shal wel make an
    ende.    1400

201. And if he wolde ought by his sort it
        preve
If that I lye, in certayn I shal fonde
Distorben him, and plukke him by the
        sleve,
Makinge his sort, and beren him on
        honde,
He hath not wel the goddes understonde.
For goddes speken in amphibologyes, 1406
And, for a sooth, they tellen twenty lyes.

202. Eek drede fond first goddes, I sup-
        pose,
Thus shal I seyn, and that his coward
        herte
Made him amis the goddes text to glose,
Whan he for ferde out of his Delphos
        sterte.                                    1411
And but I make him sone to converte,
And doon my reed with-inne a day or
        tweye,
I wol to yow oblige me to deye.'

203. And treweliche, as writen wel I finde,
That al this thing was seyd of good en-
        tente ;                                    1416
And that hir herte trewe was and kinde
Towardes him, and spak right as she
        mente,
And that she starf for wo neigh, whan
        she wente,
And was in purpos ever to be trewe ; 1420
Thus writen they that of hir werkes
        knewe.

204. This Troilus, with herte and eres
        spradde,
Herde al this thing devysen to and fro ;
And verraylich him semed that he hadde
The selve wit ; but yet to lete hir go 1425
His herte misforyaf him ever-mo.
But fynally, he gan his herte wreste
To trusten hir, and took it for the beste.

205. For which the grete furie of his
        penaunce
Was queynt with hope, and ther-with
        hem bitwene                               1430
Bigan for joye the amorouse daunce.
And as the briddes, whan the sonne is
        shene,
Delyten in hir song in leves grene,

Right so the wordes that they spake
        y-fere
Delyted hem, and made hir hertes clere.

206. But natheles, the wending of Cri-
        seyde,                                    1436
For al this world, may nought out of his
        minde ;
For which ful ofte he pitously hir preyde,
That of hir heste he might hir trewe
        finde.                                    1439
And seyde hir, 'certes, if ye be unkinde,
And but ye come at day set in-to Troye,
Ne shal I never have hele, honour, ne
        joye.

207. For al-so sooth as sonne up-rist on
        morwe,
And, god ! so wisly thou me, woful
        wrecche,                                  1444
To reste bringe out of this cruel sorwe,
I wol my-selven slee if that ye drecche,
But of my deeth though litel be to recche,
Yet, er that ye me cause so to smerte,
Dwel rather here, myn owene swete herte !

208. For trewely, myn owene lady dere,
Tho sleightes yet that I have herd yow
        stere                                     1451
Ful shaply been to failen alle y-fere.
For thus men seyn, " that oon thenketh
        the bere,
But al another thenketh his ledere."
Your sire is wys, and seyd is, out of drede,
" Men may the wyse at-renne, and not at-
        rede."                                    1456

209. It is ful hard to halten unespyed
Bifore a crepul, for he can the craft ;
Your fader is in sleighte as Argus yëd ;
For al be that his moeble is him biraft,
His olde sleighte is yet so with him laft,
Ye shal not blende him for your woman-
        hede,                                     1462
Ne feyne a-right, and that is al my drede.

210. I noot if pees shal ever-mo bityde ;
But, pees or no, for ernest ne for game,
I woot, sin Calkas on the Grekes syde
Hath ones been, and lost so foule his
        name,                                     1467

He dar no more come here ayein for
    shame ;
For which that weye, for ought I can
    espye,
To trusten on, nis but a fantasye.    1470

211. Ye shal eek seen, your fader shal
    yow glose
To been a wyf, and as he can wel preche,
He shal som Greek so preyse and wel
    alose,
That ravisshen he shal yow with his
    speche,          1474
Or do yow doon by force as he shal teche.
And Troilus, of whom ye nil han routhe,
Shal causeles so sterven in his trouthe !

212. And over al this, your fader shal
    despyse
Us alle, and seyn this citee nis but lorn ;
And that th'assege never shal aryse, 1480
For-why the Grekes han it alle sworn
Til we be slayn, and doun our walles torn.
And thus he shal you with his wordes
    fere,
That ay drede I, that ye wol bleve there.

213. Ye shul eek seen so many a lusty
    knight          1485
A-mong the Grekes, ful of worthinesse,
And eche of hem with herte, wit, and
    might
To plesen yow don al his besinesse,
That ye shul dullen of the rudenesse
Of us sely Trojanes, but-if routhe   1490
Remorde yow, or vertue of your trouthe.

214. And this to me so grevous is to
    thinke,
That fro my brest it wol my soule rende ;
Ne dredeles, in me ther may not sinke
A good opinioun, if that ye wende ;  1495
For-why your faderes sleighte wol us
    shende.
And if ye goon, as I have told yow yore,
So thenk I nam but deed, with-oute more.

215. For which, with humble, trewe, and
    pitous herte,       1499
A thousand tymes mercy I yow preye ;
So reweth on myn aspre peynes smerte,

And doth somwhat, as that I shal yow
    seye,
And lat us stele away bitwixe us tweye ;
And thenk that folye is, whan man may
    chese,         1504
For accident his substaunce ay to lese.

216. I mene this, that sin we mowe er
    day
Wel stele away, and been to-gider so,
What wit were it to putten in assay,
In cas ye sholden to your fader go,
If that ye mighte come ayein or no ? 1510
Thus mene I, that it were a gret folye
To putte that sikernesse in jupartye.

217. And vulgarly to speken of substaunce
Of tresour, may we bothe with us lede
Y-nough to live in honour and plesaunce,
Til in-to tyme that we shul ben dede ;
And thus we may eschewen al this
    drede.
For everich other wey ye can recorde,
Myn herte, y-wis, may not ther-with
    acorde.         1519

218. And hardily, ne dredeth no poverte,
For I have kin and freendes elles-where
That, though we comen in our bare sherte,
Us sholde neither lakke gold ne gere,
But been honoured whyl we dwelten
    there.         1524
And go we anoon, for, as in myn entente,
This is the beste, if that ye wole assente.'

219. Criseyde, with a syk, right in this
    wyse         1527
Answerde, ' y-wis, my dere herte trewe,
We may wel stele away, as ye devyse,
And finde swiche unthrifty weyes newe ;
But afterward, ful sore it wol us rewe.
And help me god so at my moste nede
As causeles ye suffren al this drede !

220. For thilke day that I for cherisshinge
Or drede of fader, or of other wight, 1535
Or for estat, delyt, or for weddinge
Be fals to yow, my Troilus, my knight,
Saturnes doughter, Juno, thorugh hir
    might,
As wood as Athamante do me dwelle
Eternaly in Stix, the put of helle !   1540

221. And this on every god celestial
I swere it yow, and eek on eche goddesse,
On every Nymphe and deite infernal,
On Satiry and Fauny more and lesse,
That halve goddes been of wildernesse ;
And Attropos my threed of lyf to-breste
If I be fals ; now trowe me if thow leste !

222. And thou, Simoys, that as an arwe
     clere      1548
Thorugh Troye rennest ay downward to
     the see,
Ber witnesse of this word that seyd is
     here,      1550
That thilke day that ich untrewe be
To Troilus, myn owene herte free,
That thou retorne bakwarde to thy welle,
And I with body and soule sinke in helle!

223. But that ye speke, awey thus for
     to go      1555
And leten alle your freendes, god for-
     bede,
For any womman, that ye sholden so,
And namely, sin Troye hath now swich
     nede
Of help ; and eek of o thing taketh hede,
If this were wist, my lif laye in balaunce,
And your honour ; god shilde us fro mis-
     chaunce !      1561

224. And if so be that pees her-after take,
As alday happeth, after anger, game,
Why, lord ! the sorwe and wo ye wolden
     make,      1564
That ye ne dorste come ayein for shame !
And er that ye juparten so your name,
Beth nought to hasty in this hote fare ;
For hasty man ne wanteth never care.

225. What trowe ye the peple eek al
     aboute      1569
Wolde of it seye ? It is ful light to arede.
They wolden seye, and swere it, out of
     doute,
That love ne droof yow nought to doon
     this dede,
But lust voluptuous and coward drede.
Thus were al lost, y-wis, myn herte dere,
Your honour, which that now shyneth so
     clere.      1575

226. And also thenketh on myn honestee,
That floureth yet, how foule I sholde it
     shende,
And with what filthe it spotted sholde be,
If in this forme I sholde with yow wende.
Ne though I livede un-to the worldes
     ende,      1580
My name sholde I never ayeinward
     winne ;
Thus were I lost, and that were routhe
     and sinne.

227. And for-thy slee with reson al this
     hete ;
Men seyn, "the suffraunt overcometh,"
     pardee ;
Eek " who-so wol han leef, he leef mot
     lete ; "      1585
Thus maketh vertue of necessitee
By pacience, and thenk that lord is he
Of fortune ay, that nought wol of hir
     recche ;
And she ne daunteth no wight but a
     wrecche.

228. And trusteth this, that certes, herte
     swete,      1590
Er Phebus suster, Lucina the shene,
The Leoun passe out of this Ariete,
I wol ben here, with-outen any wene.
I mene, as helpe me Juno, hevenes quene,
The tenthe day, but-if that deeth me
     assayle,      1595
I wol yow seen, with-outen any fayle.'

229. 'And now, so this be sooth,' quod
     Troilus,
' I shal wel suffre un-to the tenthe day,
Sin that I see that nede it moot be thus.
But, for the love of god, if it be may, 1600
So lat us stele prively away ;
For ever in oon, as for to live in reste,
Myn herte seyth that it wol been the
     beste.'

230. ' O mercy, god, what lyf is this?'
     quod she ;      1604
' Allas, ye slee me thus for verray tene !
I see wel now that ye mistrusten me ;
For by your wordes it is wel y-sene.
Now, for the love of Cynthia the shene,

Mistrust me not thus causeles, for routhe;
Sin to be trewe I have yow plight my
 trouthe.                                    1610

231. And thenketh wel, that som tyme it
 is wit
To spende a tyme, a tyme for to winne;
Ne, pardee, lorn am I nought fro yow yit,
Though that we been a day or two
 a-twinne.
Dryf out the fantasyes yow with-inne; 1615
And trusteth me, and leveth eek your
 sorwe,
Or here my trouthe, I wol not live til
 morwe.

232. For if ye wiste how sore it doth me
 smerte,
Ye wolde cesse of this; for god, thou
 wost,
The pure spirit wepeth in myn herte, 1620
To see yow wepen that I love most,
And that I moot gon to the Grekes ost.
Ye, nere it that I wiste remedye
To come ayein, right here I wolde dye!

233. But certes, I am not so nyce a wight
That I ne can imaginen a way      1626
To come ayein that day that I have hight.
For who may holde thing that wol a-way?
My fader nought, for al his queynte pley.
And by my thrift, my wending out of
 Troye                               1630
Another day shal torne us alle to joye.

234. For-thy, with al myn herte I yow
 beseke,
If that yow list don ought for my preyere,
And for the love which that I love yow
 eke,
That er that I departe fro yow here,  1635
That of so good a comfort and a chere
I may you seen, that ye may bringe at
 reste
Myn herte, which that is at point to
 breste.

235. And over al this, I pray yow,' quod
 she tho,                             1639
'Myn owene hertes soothfast suffisaunce,
Sin I am thyn al hool, with-outen mo,
That whyl that I am absent, no plesaunce

Of othere do me fro your remembraunce.
For I am ever a-gast, for-why men rede,
That "love is thing ay ful of bisy drede."

236. For in this world ther liveth lady
 noon,                               1646
If that ye were untrewe, as god defende!
That so bitraysed were or wo bigoon
As I, that alle trouthe in yow entende.
And douteles, if that ich other wende,
I nere but deed; and er ye cause finde,
For goddes love, so beth me not un-
 kinde.'

237. To this answerde Troilus and seyde,
'Now god, to whom ther nis no cause
 y-wrye,                             1654
Me glade, as wis I never un-to Criseyde,
Sin thilke day I saw hir first with yë,
Was fals, ne never shal til that I dye.
At shorte wordes, wel ye may me leve;
I can no more, it shal be founde at preve.'

238. 'Graunt mercy, goode myn, y-wis,'
 quod she,                           1660
'And blisful Venus lat me never sterve
Er I may stonde of plesaunce in degree
To quyte him wel, that so wel can deserve;
And whyl that god my wit wol me con-
 serve,
I shal so doon, so trewe I have yow
 founde,                             1665
That ay honour to me-ward shal rebounde.

239. For trusteth wel, that your estat
 royal
Ne veyn delyt, nor only worthinesse
Of yow in werre, or torney marcial, 1669
Ne pompe, array, nobley, or eek richesse,
Ne made me to rewe on your distresse;
But moral vertue, grounded upon trouthe,
That was the cause I first hadde on yow
 routhe!

240. Eek gentil herte and manhod that ye
 hadde,
And that ye hadde, as me thoughte, in
 despyt                              1675
Every thing that souned in-to badde,
As rudenesse and poeplish appetyt;
And that your reson brydled your delyt,

L 3

This made, aboven every creature,
That I was your, and shal, whyl I may
   dure.     1680

241. And this may lengthe of yeres not
   for-do,
Ne remuable fortune deface ;
But Juppiter, that of his might may do
The sorwful to be glad, so yeve us grace,
Er nightes ten, to meten in this place,
So that it may your herte and myn suf-
   fyse ;     1686
And fareth now wel, for tyme is that ye
   ryse.'

242. And after that they longe y-pleyned
   hadde,
And ofte y-kist and streite in armes folde,
The day gan ryse, and Troilus him
   cladde,     1690

And rewfulliche his lady gan biholde,
As he that felte dethes cares colde.
And to hir grace he gan him recomaunde ;
Wher him was wo, this holde I no de-
   maunde.     1694

243. For mannes heed imaginen ne can,
Ne entendement considere, ne tonge
   telle
The cruel peynes of this sorwful man,
That passen every torment doun in
   helle.     1698
For whan he saugh that she ne mighte
   dwelle,
Which that his soule out of his herte
   rente,
With-outen more, out of the chaumbre
   he wente.     1701

**Explicit Liber Quartus.**

# BOOK V.

### Incipit Liber Quintus.

1. Aprochen gan the fatal destinee
That Joves hath in disposicioun,
And to yow, angry Parcas, sustren three,
Committeth, to don execucioun ;
For which Criseyde moste out of the
   toun,     5
And Troilus shal dwelle forth in pyne
Til Lachesis his threed no lenger twyne.—

2. The golden-tressed Phebus heighe on-
   lofte
Thryës hadde alle with his bemes shene
The snowes molte, and Zephirus as ofte 10
Y-brought ayein the tendre leves grene,
Sin that the sone of Ecuba the quene
Bigan to love hir first, for whom his sorwe
Was al, that she departe sholde a-morwe.

3. Ful redy was at pryme Dyomede,     15
Criseyde un-to the Grekes ost to lede,
For sorwe of which she felte hir herte
   blede,
As she that niste what was best to rede.
And trewely, as men in bokes rede,

Men wiste never womman han the care, 20
Ne was so looth out of a toun to fare.

4. This Troilus, with-outen reed or lore,
As man that hath his joyes eek forlore,
Was waytinge on his lady ever-more
As she that was the soothfast crop and
   more     25
Of al his lust, or joyes here-tofore.
But Troilus, now farewel al thy joye,
For shaltow never seen hir eft in
   Troye !

5. Soth is, that whyl he bood in this
   manere,
He gan his wo ful manly for to hyde,     30
That wel unnethe it seen was in his
   chere ;
But at the yate ther she sholde oute
   ryde
With certeyn folk, he hoved hir t'abyde,
So wo bigoon, al wolde he nought him
   pleyne,
That on his hors unnethe he sat for
   peyne.     35

6. For ire he quook, so gan his herte
    gnawe,
Whan Diomede on horse gan him dresse,
And seyde un-to him-self this ilke sawe,
'Allas,' quod he, 'thus foul a wrecched-
    nesse
Why suffre ich it, why nil ich it re-
    dresse?                               40
Were it not bet at ones for to dye
Than ever-more in langour thus to drye?

7. Why nil I make at ones riche and
    pore
To have y-nough to done, er that she go?
Why nil I bringe al Troye upon a rore? 45
Why nil I sleen this Diomede also?
Why nil I rather with a man or two
Stele hir a-way?  Why wol I this endure?
Why nil I helpen to myn owene cure?'

8. But why he nolde doon so fel a dede,
That shal I seyn, and why him liste it
    spare:                               51
He hadde in herte alwey a maner drede,
Lest that Criseyde, in rumour of this fare,
Sholde han ben slayn; lo, this was al his
    care.
And elles, certeyn, as I seyde yore,   55
He hadde it doon, with-outen wordes
    more.

9. Criseyde, whan she redy was to ryde,
Ful sorwfully she sighte, and seyde
    'allas!'
But forth she moot, for ought that may
    bityde,
And forth she rit ful sorwfully a pas.  60
Ther nis non other remedie in this cas.
What wonder is though that hir sore
    smerte,
Whan she forgoth hir owene swete herte?

10. This Troilus, in wyse of curteisye,
With hauke on hond, and with an huge
    route                                 65
Of knightes, rood and dide hir companye,
Passinge al the valey fer with-oute.
And ferther wolde han riden, out of
    doute,
Ful fayn, and wo was him to goon so
    sone;
But torne he moste, and it was eek to
    done.                                 70

11. And right with that was Antenor
    y-come
Out of the Grekes ost, and every wight
Was of it glad, and seyde he was wel-
    come.
And Troilus, al nere his herte light,
He peyned him with al his fulle might 75
Him to with-holde of wepinge at the
    leste,
And Antenor he kiste, and made feste.

12. And ther-with-al he moste his leve
    take,
And caste his eye upon hir pitously,
And neer he rood, his cause for to make,
To take hir by the honde al sobrely.   81
And lord! so she gan wepen tendrely!
And he ful softe and sleighly gan hir
    seye,
'Now hold your day, and dooth me not to
    deye.'

13. With that his courser torned he
    a-boute                               85
With face pale, and un-to Diomede
No word he spak, ne noon of al his route;
Of which the sone of Tydeus took hede,
As he that coude more than the crede
In swich a craft, and by the reyne hir
    hente;                                90
And Troilus to Troye homwarde he wente.

14. This Diomede, that ladde hir by the
    brydel,
Whan that he saw the folk of Troye
    aweye,
Thoughte, 'al my labour shal not been
    on ydel,
If that I may, for somwhat shal I seye. 95
For at the worste it may yet shorte our
    weye.
I have herd seyd, eek tymes twyës twelve,
"He is a fool that wol for-yete him-
    selve."'

15. But natheles this thoughte he wel
    ynough,
'That certaynly I am aboute nought  100
If that I speke of love, or make it tough;
For douteles, if she have in hir thought
Him that I gesse, he may not been
    y-brought

So sone awey ; but I shal finde a mene,
That she not wite as yet shal what I
   mene.'     105

16. This Diomede, as he that coude his
   good,
Whan this was doon, gan fallen forth in
   speche
Of this and that, and asked why she
   stood
In swich disese, and gan hir eek biseche,
That if that he encrese mighte or eche 110
With any thing hir ese, that she sholde
Comaunde it him, and seyde he doon it
   wolde.

17. For trewely he swoor hir, as a knight,
That ther nas thing with whiche he
   mighte hir plese,
That he nolde doon his peyne and al his
   might     115
To doon it, for to doon hir herte an ese.
And preyede hir, she wolde hir sorwe
   apese,
And seyde, 'y-wis, we Grekes con have
   joye
To honouren yow, as wel as folk of Troye.'

18. He seyde eek thus, 'I woot, yow
   thinketh straunge,     120
No wonder is, for it is to yow newe,
Th'aqueintaunce of these Trojanes to
   chaunge,
For folk of Grece, that ye never knewe.
But wolde never god but-if as trewe
A Greek ye shulde among us alle finde 125
As any Trojan is, and eek as kinde.

19. And by the cause I swoor yow right,
   lo, now,
To been your freend, and helply, to my
   might,
And for that more acqueintaunce eek of
   yow
Have ich had than another straunger
   wight,     130
So fro this forth I pray yow, day and
   night,
Comaundeth me, how sore that me smerte,
To doon al that may lyke un-to your
   herte ;

20. And that ye me wolde as your brother
   trete,
And taketh not my frendship in despyt ;
And though your sorwes be for thinges
   grete,     136
Noot I not why, but out of more respyt,
Myn herte hath for to amende it greet
   delyt.
And if I may your harmes not redresse,
I am right sory for your hevinesse.     140

21. And though ye Trojans with us
   Grekes wrothe
Han many a day be, alwey yet, pardee,
O god of love in sooth we serven bothe.
And, for the love of god, my lady free,
Whom so ye hate, as beth not wroth with
   me.     145
For trewely, ther can no wight yow
   serve,
That half so looth your wraththe wolde
   deserve.

22. And nere it that we been so neigh the
   tente
Of Calkas, which that seen us bothe
   may,
I wolde of this yow telle al myn entente ;
But this enseled til another day.     151
Yeve me your hond, I am, and shal ben
   ay,
God help me so, whyl that my lyf may
   dure,
Your owene aboven every creature.

23. Thus seyde I never er now to womman
   born ;     155
For god myn herte as wisly glade so,
I lovede never womman here-biforn
As paramours, ne never shal no mo.
And, for the love of god, beth not my fo ;
Al can I not to yow, my lady dere,     160
Compleyne aright, for I am yet to lere.

24. And wondreth not, myn owene lady
   bright,
Though that I speke of love to you thus
   blyve ;
For I have herd or this of many a wight,
Hath loved thing he never saugh his
   lyve.     165
Eek I am not of power for to stryve

Ayens the god of love, but him obeye
I wol alwey, and mercy I yow preye.

25. Ther been so worthy knightes in this
    place,                                    169
And ye so fair, that everich of hem alle
Wol peynen him to stonden in your grace.
But mighte me so fair a grace falle,
That ye me for your servaunt wolde calle,
So lowly ne so trewely you serve
Nil noon of hem, as I shal, til I sterve.' 175

26. Criseide un-to that purpos lyte an-
    swerde,
As she that was with sorwe oppressed so
That, in effect, she nought his tales herde,
But here and there, now here a word or
    two.
Hir thoughte hir sorwful herte brast
    a-two.                                     180
For whan she gan hir fader fer aspye,
Wel neigh doun of hir hors she gan to
    sye.

27. But natheles she thonked Diomede
Of al his travaile, and his goode chere,
And that him liste his friendship hir to
    bede;                                     185
And she accepteth it in good manere,
And wolde do fayn that is him leef and
    dere;
And trusten him she wolde, and wel she
    mighte,
As seyde she, and from hir hors she
    alighte.

28. Hir fader hath hir in his armes nome,
And tweynty tyme he kiste his doughter
    swete,                                    ·191
And seyde, ' O dere doughter myn, wel-
    come !'
She seyde eek, she was fayn with him to
    mete,
And stood forth mewet, mildë, and man-
    suete.
But here I leve hir with hir fader dwelle,
And forth I wol of Troilus yow telle.  196

29. To Troye is come this woful Troilus,
In sorwe aboven alle sorwes smerte,
With felon look, and face dispitous.

Tho sodeinly doun from his hors he
    sterte,                                   200
And thorugh his paleys, with a swollen
    herte,
To chambre he wente ; of no-thing took
    he hede,
Ne noon to him dar speke a word for
    drede.

30. And there his sorwes that he spared
    hadde
He yaf an issue large, and ' deeth !' he
    cryde ;                                   205
And in his throwes frenetyk and madde
He cursed Jove, Appollo, and eek Cupyde,
He cursed Ceres, Bacus, and Cipryde,
His burthe, him-self, his fate, and eek
    nature,
And, save his lady, every creature.    210

31. To bedde he goth, and weyleth there
    and torneth
In furie, as dooth he, Ixion, in helle;
And in this wyse he neigh til day so-
    jorneth.
But tho bigan his herte a lyte unswelle
Thorugh teres which that gonnen up to
    welle ;                                   215
And pitously he cryde up-on Criseyde,
And to him-self right thus he spak, and
    seyde :—

32. ' Wher is myn owene lady lief and
    dere,
Wher is hir whyte brest, wher is it,
    where ?
Wher been hir armes and hir eyen clere,
That yesternight this tyme with me
    were ?                                     221
Now may I wepe allone many a tere,
And graspe aboute I may, but in this
    place,
Save a pilowe, I finde nought t'enbrace.

33. How shal I do ?  Whan shal she com
    ayeyn ?                                   225
I noot, allas ! why leet ich hir to go ?
As wolde god, ich hadde as tho be sleyn !
O herte myn, Criseyde, O swete fo !
O lady myn, that I love and no mo !  229
To whom for ever-mo myn herte I dowe;
See how I deye, ye nil me not rescowe !

34. Who seeth yow now, my righte lode-
      sterre?
Who sit right now or stant in your
      presence?
Who can conforten now your hertes
      werre?
Now I am gon, whom yeve ye audience?
Who speketh for me right now in myn
      absence?            236
Allas, no wight; and that is al my care;
For wel wot I, as yvel as I ye fare.

35. How shulde I thus ten dayes ful
      endure,
Whan I the firste night have al this
      tene?            240
How shal she doon eek, sorwful creature?
For tendernesse, how shal she this sus-
      tene,
Swich wo for me? O pitous, pale, and
      grene
Shal been your fresshe wommanliche face
For langour, er ye torne un-to this
      place.'          245

36. And whan he fil in any slomeringes,
Anoon biginne he sholde for to grone,
And dremen of the dredfulleste thinges
That mighte been; as, mete he were
      allone
In place horrible, makinge ay his mone,
Or meten that he was amonges alle   251
His enemys, and in hir hondes falle.

37. And ther-with-al his body sholde
      sterte,
And with the stert al sodeinliche awake,
And swich a tremour fele aboute his
      herte,          255
That of the feer his body sholde quake;
And there-with-al he sholde a noyse
      make,
And seme as though he sholde falle depe
From heighe a-lofte; and than he wolde
      wepe,

38. And rewen on him-self so pitously, 260
That wonder was to here his fantasye.
Another tyme he sholde mightily
Conforte him-self, and seyn it was folye,
So causeles swich drede for to drye,

And eft biginne his aspre sorwes newe,
That every man mighte on his sorwes
      rewe.         266

39. Who coude telle aright or ful dis-
      cryve
His wo, his pleynte, his langour, and his
      pyne?
Nought al the men that han or been on-
      lyve.
Thou, redere, mayst thy-self ful wel
      devyne      270
That swich a wo my wit can not defyne.
On ydel for to wryte it sholde I swinke,
Whan that my wit is wery it to thinke.

40. On hevene yet the sterres were sene,
Al-though ful pale y-waxen was the
      mone;      275
And whyten gan the orisonte shene
Al estward, as it woned is to done.
And Phebus with his rosy carte sone
Gan after that to dresse him up to fare,
Whan Troilus hath sent after Pandare.

41. This Pandare, that of al the day
      biforn      281
Ne mighte have comen Troilus to see,
Al-though he on his heed it hadde y-sworn,
For with the king Pryam alday was he,
So that it lay not in his libertee   285
No-wher to gon, but on the morwe he
      wente
To Troilus, whan that he for him sente.

42. For in his herte he coude wel devyne,
That Troilus al night for sorwe wook;
And that he wolde telle him of his pyne,
This knew he wel y-nough, with-oute
      book.      291
For which to chaumbre streight the wey
      he took,
And Troilus tho sobreliche he grette,
And on the bed ful sone he gan him sette.

43. 'My Pandarus,' quod Troilus, 'the
      sorwe      295
Which that I drye, I may not longe
      endure.
I trowe I shal not liven til to-morwe;
For whiche I wolde alwey, on aventure,
To thee devysen of my sepulture

The forme, and of my moeble thou dispone                                    300
Right as thee semeth best is for to done.

44. But of the fyr and flaumbe funeral
In whiche my body brenne shal to glede,
And of the feste and pleyes palestral   304
At my vigile, I pray thee take good hede
That al be wel ; and offre Mars my stede,
My swerd, myn helm, and, leve brother
dere,
My sheld to Pallas yef, that shyneth
clere.

45. The poudre in which myn herte y-
brend shal torne,
That preye I thee thou take and it con-
serve                                   310
In a vessel, that men clepeth an urne,
Of gold, and to my lady that I serve,
For love of whom thus pitously I sterve,
So yeve it hir, and do me this plesaunce,
To preye hir kepe it for a remembraunce.

46. For wel I fele, by my maladye,    316
And by my dremes now and yore ago,
Al certeinly, that I mot nedes dye.
The owle eek, which that hight Ascaphilo,
Hath after me shright alle thise nightes
two.                                    320
And, god Mercurie ! of me now, woful
wrecche,
The soule gyde, and, whan thee list, it
fecche ! '

47. Pandare answerde, and seyde, 'Troilus,
My dere freend, as I have told thee yore,
That it is folye for to sorwen thus,   325
And causeles, for whiche I can no-more.
But who-so wol not trowen reed ne lore,
I can not seen in him no remedye,
But lete him worthen with his fantasye.

48. But Troilus, I pray thee tel me now,
If that thou trowe, er this, that any
wight                                   331
Hath loved paramours as wel as thou?
Ye, god wot, and fro many a worthy
knight
Hath his lady goon a fourtenight,
And he not yet made halvendel the
fare.                                   335
What nede is thee to maken al this care ?

49. Sin day by day thou mayst thy-selven
see
That from his love, or elles from his wyf,
A man mot twinnen of necessitee,
Ye, though he love hir as his owene lyf; 340
Yet nil he with him-self thus maken
stryf.
For wel thow wost, my leve brother dere,
That alwey freendes may nought been
y-fere.

50. How doon this folk that seen hir loves
wedded
By freendes might, as it bi-tit ful ofte, 345
And seen hem in hir spouses bed y-bedded ?
God woot, they take it wysly, faire and
softe.
For-why good hope halt up hir herte on-
lofte,
And for they can a tyme of sorwe endure ;
As tyme hem hurt, a tyme doth hem
cure.                                   350

51. So sholdestow endure, and late slyde
The tyme, and fonde to ben glad and
light.
Ten dayes nis so long not t' abyde.
And sin she thee to comen hath bihight,
She nil hir hestes breken for no wight. 355
For dred thee not that she nil finden weye
To come ayein, my lyf that dorste I leye.

52. Thy swevenes eek and al swich fan-
tasye
Dryf out, and lat hem faren to mis-
chaunce ;
For they procede of thy malencolye,   360
That doth thee fele in sleep al this pen-
aunce.
A straw for alle swevenes signifiaunce !
God helpe me so, I counte hem not a
bene,
Ther woot no man aright what dremes
mene.

53. For prestes of the temple tellen this,
That dremes been the revelaciouns    366
Of goddes, and as wel they telle, y-wis,
That they ben infernals illusiouns ;
And leches seyn, that of complexiouns
Proceden they, or fast, or glotonye.   370
Who woot in sooth thus what they
signifye ?

54. Eek othere seyn that thorugh im-
    pressiouns,
As if a wight hath faste a thing in minde,
That ther-of cometh swiche avisiouns ;
And othere seyn, as they in bokes finde,
That, after tymes of the yeer by kinde,
Men dreme, and that th'effect goth by the
    mone ;                   377
But leve no dreem, for it is nought to
    done.

55. Wel worth of dremes ay thise olde
    wyves,
And treweliche eek augurie of thise
    foules ;                  380
For fere of which men wenen lese her
    lyves,
As ravenes qualm, or shryking of thise
    oules.
To trowen on it bothe fals and foul is.
Allas, allas, so noble a creature
As is a man, shal drede swich ordure ! 385

56. For which with al myn herte I thee
    beseche,
Un-to thy-self that al this thou foryive ;
And rys up now with-oute more speche,
And lat us caste how forth may best be
    drive
This tyme, and eek how freshly we may
    live                    390
Whan that she cometh, the which shal
    be right sone ;
God help me so, the beste is thus to done.

57. Rys, lat us speke of lusty lyf in Troye
That we han lad, and forth the tyme
    dryve ;
And eek of tyme cominge us rejoye,    395
That bringen shal our blisse now so blyve;
And langour of these twyes dayes fyve
We shal ther-with so foryete or oppresse,
That wel unnethe it doon shal us duresse.

58. This toun is ful of lordes al aboute,
And trewes lasten al this mene whyle.
Go we pleye us in som lusty route    402
To Sarpedon, not hennes but a myle.
And thus thou shalt the tyme wel bigyle,
And dryve it forth un-to that blisful
    morwe,                   405
That thou hir see, that cause is of thy
    sorwe.

59. Now rys, my dere brother Troilus ;
For certes, it noon honour is to thee
To wepe, and in thy bed to jouken thus.
For trewely, of o thing trust to me,    410
If thou thus ligge a day, or two, or three,
The folk wol wene that thou, for
    cowardyse,
Thee feynest syk, and that thou darst
    not ryse.'

60. This Troilus answerde, ' O brother
    dere,
This knowen folk that han y-suffred
    peyne,                  415
That though he wepe and make sorwful
    chere,
That feleth harm and smert in every
    veyne,
No wonder is ; and though I ever pleyne,
Or alwey wepe, I am no-thing to blame,
Sin I have lost the cause of al my game.

61. But sin of fyne force I moot aryse,
I shal aryse, as sone as ever I may ;    422
And god, to whom myn herte I sacrifyse,
So sende us hastely the tenthe day !
For was ther never fowl so fayn of May,
As I shal been, whan that she cometh in
    Troye,                  426
That cause is of my torment and my joye.

62. But whider is thy reed,' quod Troilus,
' That we may pleye us best in al this
    toun ? '
' By god, my conseil is,' quod Pandarus,
' To ryde and pleye us with king Sarpe-
    doun.'                  431
So longe of this they speken up and doun,
Til Troilus gan at the laste assente
To ryse, and forth to Sarpedoun they
    wente.

63. This Sarpedoun, as he that honourable
Was ever his lyve, and ful of heigh
    prowesse,                436
With al that mighte y-served been on
    table,
That deyntee was, al coste it greet
    richesse,
He fedde hem day by day, that swich
    noblesse,

As seyden bothe the moste and eek the
leste,                                         440
Was never er that day wist at any feste.

64. Nor in this world ther is non instru-
ment
Delicious, through wind, or touche, or
corde,
As fer as any wight hath ever y-went,
That tonge telle or herte may recorde, 445
That at that feste it nas wel herd acorde;
Ne of ladies eek so fayr a companye
On daunce, er tho, was never y-seyn with
yë.

65. But what avayleth this to Troilus,
That for his sorwe no-thing of it roughte?
For ever in oon his herte piëtous       451
Ful bisily Criseyde his lady soughte.
On hir was ever al that his herte thoughte.
Now this, now that, so faste imagininge,
That glade, y-wis, can him no festeyinge.

66. These ladies eek that at this feste
been,                                          456
Sin that he saw his lady was a-weye,
It was his sorwe upon hem for to seen,
Or for to here on instrumentz so pleye.
For she, that of his herte berth the keye,
Was absent, lo, this was his fantasye, 461
That no wight sholde make melodye.

67. Nor ther nas houre in al the day or
night,
Whan he was ther-as no wight mighte
him here,
That he ne seyde, ' O lufsom lady bright,
How have ye faren, sin that ye were
here?                                          466
Wel-come, y-wis, myn owene lady dere.'
But welaway, al this nas but a mase ;
Fortune his howve entended bet to glase.

68. The lettres eek, that she of olde tyme
Hadde him y-sent, he wolde allone rede,
An hundred sythe, a-twixen noon and
pryme ;                                        472
Refiguringe hir shap, hir womanhede,
With-inne his herte, and every word and
dede
That passed was, and thus he droof to an
ende                                           475
The ferthe day, and seyde, he wolde
wende.

69. And seyde, ' leve brother Pandarus,
Intendestow that we shul herë bleve
Til Sarpedoun wol forth congeyen us ?
Yet were it fairer that we toke our leve.
For goddes love, lat us now sone at eve
Our leve take, and homward lat us torne;
For trewely, I nil not thus sojorne.' 483

70. Pandare answerde, ' be we comen
hider
To fecchen fyr, and rennen hoom ayeyn?
God helpe me so, I can not tellen whider
We mighten goon, if I shal soothly seyn,
Ther any wight is of us more fayn
Than Sarpedoun ; and if we hennes hye
Thus sodeinly, I holde it vilanye,     490

71. Sin that we seyden that we wolde
bleve
With him a wouke ; and now, thus
sodeinly,
The ferthe day to take of him our leve,
He wolde wondren on it, trewely !     494
Lat us holde forth our purpos fermely ;
And sin that ye bihighten him to byde,
Hold forward now, and after lat us ryde.'

72. Thus Pandarus, with alle peyne and
wo,
Made him to dwelle ; and at the woukes
ende,
Of Sarpedoun they toke hir leve tho, 500
And on hir wey they spedden hem to
wende.
Quod Troilus, ' now god me grace sende,
That I may finden, at myn hom-cominge.
Criseyde comen !' and ther-with gan he
singe.

73. ' Ye, hasel-wode !' thoughte this Pan-
dare,                                          505
And to him-self ful softely he seyde,
' God woot, refreyden may this hote fare
Er Calkas sende Troilus Criseyde !'
But natheles, he japed thus, and seyde,
And swor, y-wis, his herte him wel
bihighte,                                      510
She wolde come as sone as ever she
mighte.

74. Whan they un-to the paleys were
y-comen
Of Troilus, they doun of hors alighte,

And to the chambre hir wey than han
  they nomen.
And in-to tyme that it gan to nighte, 515
They spaken of Crisëyde the brighte.
And after this, whan that hem bothe
  leste,
They spedde hem fro the soper un-to
  reste.

75. On morwe, as sone as day bigan to
  clere,
This Troilus gan of his sleep t'abreyde, 520
And to Pandare, his owene brother dere,
'For love of god,' ful pitously he seyde,
'As go we seen the paleys of Criseyde ;
For sin we yet may have namore feste,
So lat us seen hir paleys at the leste.' 525

76. And ther-with-al, his meynee for to
  blende,
A cause he fond in toune for to go,
And to Criseydes hous they gonnen wende.
But lord ! this sely Troilus was wo !
Him thoughte his sorweful herte braste
  a-two. 530
For whan he saugh hir dores sperred alle,
Wel neigh for sorwe a-doun he gan to
  falle.

77. Therwith whan he was war and gan
  biholde
How shet was every windowe of the place,
As frost, him thoughte, his herte gan to
  colde ; 535
For which with chaunged deedlich pale
  face,
With-outen word, he forth bigan to pace ;
And, as god wolde, he gan so faste ryde,
That no wight of his contenaunce aspyde.

78. Than seyde he thus, 'O paleys desolat,
O hous, of houses whylom best y-hight,
O paleys empty and disconsolat, 542
O thou lanterne, of which queynt is the
  light,
O paleys, whylom day, that now art night,
Wel oughtestow to falle, and I to dye, 545
Sin she is went that wont was us to gye !

79. O paleys, whylom croune of houses alle,
Enlumined with sonne of alle blisse !

O ring, fro which the ruby is out-falle,
O cause of wo, that cause hast been of
  lisse ! 550
Yet, sin I may no bet, fayn wolde I kisse
Thy colde dores, dorste I for this route ;
And fare-wel shryne, of which the seynt
  is oute !'

80. Ther-with he caste on Pandarus his yë
With chaunged face, and pitous to biholde;
And whan he mighte his tyme aright
  aspye, 556
Ay as he rood, to Pandarus he tolde
His newe sorwe, and eek his joyes olde,
So pitously and with so dede an hewe,
That every wight mighte on his sorwe rewe.

81. Fro thennesforth he rydeth up and
  doun, 561
And every thing com him to remem-
  braunce
As he rood forth by places of the toun
In whiche he whylom hadde al his ples-
  aunce. 564
'Lo, yond saugh I myn owene lady daunce;
And in that temple, with hir eyen clere,
Me caughte first my righte lady dere.

82. And yonder have I herd ful lustily
My dere herte laughe, and yonder pleye
Saugh I hir ones eek ful blisfully. 570
And yonder ones to me gan she seye,
"Now goode swete, love me wel, I preye."
And yond so goodly gan she me biholde,
That to the deeth myn herte is to hir holde.

83. And at that corner, in the yonder hous,
Herde I myn alderlevest lady dere 576
So wommanly, with voys melodious,
Singen so wel, so goodly, and so clere,
That in my soule yet me thinketh I here
The blisful soun ; and, in that yonder
  place, 580
My lady first me took un-to hir grace.'

84. Thanne thoughte he thus, 'O blisful
  lord Cupyde,
Whanne I the proces have in my memorie,
How thou me hast werreyed on every syde,
Men mighte a book make of it, lyk a storie.
What nede is thee to seke on me victorie,

Sin I am thyn, and hoolly at thy wille?
What joye hastow thyn owene folk to
   spille?     588

85. Wel hastow, lord, y-wroke on me thyn
   ire,
Thou mighty god, and dredful for to greve!
Now mercy, lord, thou wost wel I desire
Thy grace most, of alle lustes leve.     592
And live and deye I wol in thy bileve;
For which I n'axe in guerdon but a bone,
That thou Criseyde ayein me sende sone.

86. Distreyne hir herte as faste to retorne
As thou dost myn to longen hir to see;
Than woot I wel, that she nil not sojorne.
Now, blisful lord, so cruel thou ne be
Un-to the blood of Troye, I preye thee, 600
As Juno was un-to the blood Thebane,
For which the folk of Thebes caughte hir
   bane.'

87. And after this he to the yates wente
Ther-as Criseyde out-rood a ful good paas,
And up and doun ther made he many
   a wente,     605
And to him-self ful ofte he seyde 'allas!
From hennes rood my blisse and my solas!
As wolde blisful god now, for his joye,
I mighte hir seen ayein come in-to Troye.

88. And to the yonder hille I gan hir gyde,
Allas! and there I took of hir my leve!
And yond I saugh hir to hir fader ryde,
For sorwe of which myn herte shal to-
   cleve.     613
And hider hoom I com whan it was eve;
And here I dwelle out-cast from alle joye,
And shal, til I may seen hir eft in Troye.'

89. And of him-self imagined he ofte
To ben defet, and pale, and waxen lesse
Than he was wont, and that men seyde
   softe,
'What may it be? who can the sothe
   gesse     620
Why Troilus hath al this hevinesse?'
And al this nas but his malencolye,
That he hadde of him-self swich fantasye.

90. Another tyme imaginen he wolde
That every wight that wente by the weye

Had of him routhe, and that they seyen
   sholde,     626
'I am right sory Troilus wol deye.'
And thus he droof a day yet forth or tweye.
As ye have herd, swich lyf right gan he lede,
As he that stood bitwixen hope and drede.

91. For which him lyked in his songes
   shewe     631
Th'encheson of his wo, as he best mighte,
And make a song of wordes but a fewe,
Somwhat his woful herte for to lighte.
And whan he was from every mannes
   sighte,     635
With softe voys he, of his lady dere,
That was absent, gan singe as ye may here.

92. 'O sterre, of which I lost have al the
   light,
With herte soor wel oughte I to bewayle,
That ever derk in torment, night by night,
Toward my deeth with wind in stere I
   sayle;     641
For which the tenthe night if that I fayle
The gyding of thy bemes brighte an houre,
My ship and me Caribdis wol devoure.'

93. This song whan he thus songen hadde,
   sone     645
He fil ayein in-to his sykes olde;
And every night, as was his wone to done,
He stood the brighte mone to beholde,
And al his sorwe he to the mone tolde;
And seyde, 'y-wis, whan thou art horned
   newe,     650
I shal be glad, if al the world be trewe!

94. I saugh thyn hornes olde eek by the
   morwe,
Whan hennes rood my righte lady dere,
That cause is of my torment and my sorwe;
For whiche, O brighte Lucina the clere, 655
For love of god, ren faste aboute thy spere!
For whan thyn hornes newe ginne springe,
Than shal she come, that may my blisse
   bringe!'

95. The day is more, and lenger every
   night,
Than they be wont to be, him thoughte
   tho;     660

And that the sonne wente his course
    unright
By lenger wey than it was wont to go ;
And seyde, ' y-wis, me dredeth ever-mo,
The sonnes sone, Pheton, be on-lyve,
And that his fadres cart amis he dryve.' 665

96. Upon the walles faste eek wolde he
    walke,
And on the Grekes ost he wolde see,
And to him-self right thus he wolde talke,
' Lo, yonder is myn owene lady free,
Or elles yonder, ther tho tentes be !   670
And thennes comth this eyr, that is so
    sote,
That in my soule I fele it doth me bote.

97. And hardely this wind, that more and
    more
Thus stoundemele encreseth in my face,
Is of my ladyes depe sykes sore.     675
I preve it thus, for in non othere place
Of al this toun, save onliche in this space,
Fele I no wind that souneth so lyk peyne ;
It seyth, " allas ! why twinned be we
    tweyne ? " '

98. This longe tyme he dryveth forth right
    thus,     680
Til fully passed was the nynthe night ;
And ay bi-syde him was this Pandarus,
That bisily dide alle his fulle might
Him to comforte, and make his herte light ;
Yevinge him hope alwey, the tenthe morwe
That she shal come, and stinten al his
    sorwe.     686

99. Up-on that other syde eek was Cri-
    seyde,
With wommen fewe, among the Grekes
    stronge ;
For which ful ofte a day 'allas !' she seyde,
' That I was born ! Wel may myn herte
    longe     690
After my deeth ; for now live I to longe !
Allas ! and I ne may it not amende ;
For now is wors than ever yet I wende.

100. My fader nil for no-thing do me grace
To goon ayein, for nought I can him
    queme ;     695
And if so be that I my terme passe,

My Troilus shal in his herte deme     697
That I am fals, and so it may wel seme.
Thus shal I have unthank on every syde ;
That I was born, so weylawey the tyde !

101. And if that I me putte in jupartye,
To stele awey by nighte, and it bifalle
That I be caught, I shal be holde a spye ;
Or elles, lo, this drede I most of alle,
If in the hondes of som wrecche I falle,
I am but lost, al be myn herte trewe ; 706
Now mighty god, thou on my sorwe rewe !'

102. Ful pale y-waxen was hir brighte face,
Hir limes lene, as she that al the day
Stood whan she dorste, and loked on the
    place     710
Ther she was born, and ther she dwelt
    hadde ay.
And al the night wepinge, allas ! she lay.
And thus despeired, out of alle cure,
She ladde hir lyf, this woful creature.

103. Ful ofte a day she sighte eek for
    destresse,     715
And in hir-self she wente ay portrayinge
Of Troilus the grete worthinesse,
And alle his goodly wordes recordinge
Sin first that day hir love bigan to springe.
And thus she sette hir woful herte a-fyre
Thorugh remembraunce of that she gan
    desyre.     721

104. In al this world ther nis so cruel
    herte
That hir hadde herd compleynen in hir
    sorwe,
That nolde han wopen for hir peynes
    smerte,
So tendrely she weep, bothe eve and morwe.
Hir nedede no teres for to borwe.     726
And this was yet the worste of al hir peyne,
Ther was no wight to whom she dorste hir
    pleyne.

105. Ful rewfully she loked up-on Troye,
Biheld the toures heighe and eek the
    halles ;     730
' Allas !' quod she, 'the plesaunce and the
    joye
The whiche that now al torned in-to
    galle is,

Have I had ofte with-inne yonder walles!
O Troilus, what dostow now,' she seyde ;
' Lord ! whether yet thou thenke up-on
　　Criseyde ?　　　　　　　　　　735

106. Allas! I ne hadde trowed on your lore,
And went with yow, as ye me radde er this !
Thanne hadde I now not syked half so sore.
Who mighte have seyd, that I had doon
　　a-mis
To stele awey with swich on as he is ? 740
But al to late cometh the letuarie,
Whan men the cors un-to the grave carie.

107. To late is now to speke of this matere ;
Prudence, allas ! oon of thyn eyen three
Me lakked alwey, er that I cam here ; 745
On tyme y-passed, wel remembred me ;
And present tyme eek coude I wel y-see.
But futur tyme, er I was in the snare,
Coude I not seen ; that causeth now my
　　care.　　　　　　　　　　　　749

108. But natheles, bityde what bityde,
I shal to-morwe at night, by est or weste,
Out of this ost stele on som maner syde,
And go with Troilus wher-as him leste.
This purpos wol I holde, and this is beste.
No fors of wikked tonges janglerye,　755
For ever on love han wrecches had envye.

109. For who-so wole of every word take
　　hede,
Or rewlen him by every wightes wit,
Ne shal he never thryven, out of drede.
For that that som men blamen ever yit,
Lo, other maner folk commenden it.　761
And as for me, for al swich variaunce,
Felicitee clepe I my suffisaunce.

110. For which, with-outen any wordes mo,
To Troye I wol, as for conclusioun.'　765
But god it wot, er fully monthes two,
She was ful fer fro that entencioun.
For bothe Troilus and Troye toun
Shal knotteles through-out hir herte
　　slyde ;
For she wol take a purpos for t'abyde. 770

111. This Diomede, of whom yow telle
　　I gan,
Goth now, with-inne him-self ay arguinge

With al the sleighte and al that ever he
　　can,
How he may best, with shortest taryinge,
In-to his net Criseydes herte bringe.　775
To this entente he coude never fyne ;
To fisshen hir, he leyde out hook and lyne.

112. But natheles, wel in his herte he
　　thoughte,
That she nas nat with-oute a love in Troye.
For never, sithen he hir thennes broughte,
Ne coude he seen her laughe or make
　　joye.　　　　　　　　　　　　781
He niste how best hir herte for t'acoye.
' But for t'assaye,' he seyde, ' it nought
　　ne greveth ;
For he that nought n'assayeth, nought
　　n'acheveth.'

113. Yet seide he to him-self upon a night,
' Now am I not a fool, that woot wel how
Hir wo for love is of another wight,
And here-up-on to goon assaye hir now ?
I may wel wite, it nil not been my prow.
For wyse folk in bokes it expresse,　790
" Men shal not wowe a wight in hevinesse."

114. But who-so mighte winnen swich
　　a flour
From him, for whom she morneth night
　　and day,
He mighte seyn, he were a conquerour.'
And right anoon, as he that bold was ay,
Thoughte in his herte, ' happe, how happe
　　may,　　　　　　　　　　　　796
Al sholde I deye, I wole hir herte seche ;
I shal no more lesen but my speche.'

115. This Diomede, as bokes us declare,
Was in his nedes prest and corageous ;
With sterne voys and mighty limes square,
Hardy, testif, strong, and chevalrous
Of dedes, lyk his fader Tideus.
And som men seyn, he was of tunge large ;
And heir he was of Calidoine and Arge. 805

116. Criseyde mene was of hir stature,
Ther-to of shap, of face, and eek of chere,
Ther mighte been no fairer creature.
And ofte tyme this was hir manere,
To gon y-tressed with hir heres clere 810

Doun by hir coler at hir bak bihinde,
Which with a threde of gold she wolde
   binde.

117. And, save hir browes joyneden y-fere,
Ther nas no lak, in ought I can espyen ;
But for to speken of hir eyen clere,    815
Lo, trewely, they writen that hir syen,
That Paradys stood formed in hir yën.
And with hir riche beautee ever-more
Strof love in hir, ay which of hem was
   more.

118. She sobre was, eek simple, and wys
   with-al,                820
The beste y-norisshed eek that mighte be,
And goodly of hir speche in general,
Charitable, estatliche, lusty, and free ;
Ne never-mo ne lakkede hir pitee ;
Tendre-herted, slydinge of corage ;    825
But trewely, I can not telle hir age.

119. And Troilus wel waxen was in highte,
And complet formed by proporcioun
So wel, that kinde it not amenden mighte ;
Yong, fresshe, strong, and hardy as lyoun ;
Trewe as steel in ech condicioun ;    831
On of the beste enteched creature,
That is, or shal, whyl that the world may
   dure.

120. And certainly in storie it is y-founde,
That Troilus was never un-to no wight, 835
As in his tyme, in no degree secounde
In durring don that longeth to a knight.
Al mighte a geaunt passen him of might,
His herte ay with the firste and with the
   beste                839
Stod paregal, to durre don that him leste.

121. But for to tellen forth of Diomede :—
It fil that after, on the tenthe day,
Sin that Criseyde out of the citee yede,
This Diomede, as fresshe as braunche in
   May,
Com to the tente ther-as Calkas lay,    845
And feyned him with Calkas han to done ;
But what he mente, I shal yow telle sone.

122. Criseyde, at shorte wordes for to telle,
Welcomed him, and doun by hir him sette ;
And he was ethe y-nough to maken dwelle.

And after this, with-outen longe lette, 851
The spyces and the wyn men forth hem
   fette ;
And forth they speke of this and that
   y-fere,
As freendes doon, of which som shal ye
   here.

123. He gan first fallen of the werre in
   speche              855
Bitwixe hem and the folk of Troye toun ;
And of th'assege he gan hir eek byseche,
To telle him what was hir opinioun.
Fro that demaunde he so descendeth doun
To asken hir, if that hir straunge thoughte
The Grekes gyse, and werkes that they
   wroughte ?          861

124. And why hir fader tarieth so longe
To wedden hir un-to som worthy wight ?
Criseyde, that was in hir peynes stronge
For love of Troilus, hir owene knight, 865
As fer-forth as she conning hadde or
   might,
Answerde him tho ; but, as of his entente,
It semed not she wiste what he mente.

125. But natheles, this ilke Diomede
Gan in him-self assure, and thus he seyde,
' If ich aright have taken of yow hede, 871
Me thinketh thus, O lady myn, Criseyde,
That sin I first hond on your brydel
   leyde,
Whan ye out come of Troye by the morwe,
Ne coude I never seen yow but in sorwe.

126. Can I not seyn what may the cause
   be                876
But-if for love of som Troyan it were,
The which right sore wolde athinken me
That ye, for any wight that dwelleth
   there,
Sholden spille a quarter of a tere,    880
Or pitously your-selven so bigyle ;
For dredelees, it is nought worth the
   whyle.

127. The folk of Troye, as who seyth, alle
   and some
In preson been, as ye your-selven see ;
For thennes shal not oon on-lyve come 885

For al the gold bitwixen sonne and see,
Trusteth wel, and understondeth me,
Ther shal not oon to mercy goon on-lyve,
Al were he lord of worldes twyës fyve!

128. Swich wreche on hem, for fecching
of Eleyne,                                    890
Ther shal be take, er that we hennes
wende,
That Manes, which that goddes ben of
peyne,
Shal been agast that Grekes wol hem
shende.
And men shul drede, un-to the worldes
ende,                                          894
From hennes-forth to ravisshe any quene,
So cruel shal our wreche on hem be sene.

129. And but-if Calkas lede us with am-
bages,
That is to seyn, with double wordes slye,
Swich as men clepe a "word with two
visages,"
Ye shul wel knowen that I nought ne
lye,                                           900
And al this thing right seen it with your
yë,
And that anoon; ye nil not trowe how
sone;
Now taketh heed, for it is for to done.

130. What wene ye your wyse fader
wolde
Han yeven Antenor for yow anoon,     905
If he ne wiste that the citee sholde
Destroyed been? Why, nay, so mote
I goon!
He knew ful wel ther shal not scapen oon
That Troyan is; and for the grete fere,
He dorste not, ye dwelte lenger there. 910

131. What wole ye more, lufsom lady
dere?
Lat Troye and Troyan fro your herte
pace!
Dryf out that bittre hope, and make good
chere,
And clepe ayein the beautee of your face,
That ye with salte teres so deface.      915
For Troye is brought in swich a jupartye,
That, it to save, is now no remedye.

132. And thenketh wel, ye shal in Grekes
finde
A more parfit love, er it be night,
Than any Troyan is, and more kinde,  920
And bet to serven yow wol doon his
might.
And if ye vouche sauf, my lady bright,
I wol ben he to serven yow my-selve,
Ye, lever than be lord of Greces twelve!'

133. And with that word he gan to waxen
reed,                                         925
And in his speche a litel wight he quook,
And caste a-syde a litel wight his heed,
And stinte a whyle; and afterward awook,
And sobreliche on hir he threw his look,
And seyde, 'I am, al be it yow no joye,
As gentil man as any wight in Troye. 931

134. For if my fader Tydeus,' he seyde,
'Y-lived hadde, I hadde been, er this,
Of Calidoine and Arge a king, Criseyde!
And so hope I that I shal yet, y-wis. 935
But he was slayn, allas! the more harm
is,
Unhappily at Thebes al to rathe,
Polymites and many a man to scathe.

135. But herte myn, sin that I am your
man,
And been the ferste of whom I seche
grace,                                        940
To serven you as hertely as I can,
And ever shal, whyl I to live have space,
So, er that I departe out of this place,
Ye wol me graunte, that I may to-morwe,
At bettre leyser, telle yow my sorwe.' 945

136. What shold I telle his wordes that he
seyde?
He spak y-now, for o day at the meste;
It preveth wel, he spak so that Criseyde
Graunted, on the morwe, at his requeste,
For to speken with him at the leste,   950
So that he nolde speke of swich matere;
And thus to him she seyde, as ye may
here:

137. As she that hadde hir herte on
Troilus
So faste, that ther may it noon arace;
And straungely she spak, and seyde thus

'O Diomede, I love that ilke place    956
Ther I was born; and Joves, for his
    grace,
Delivere it sone of al that doth it care !
God, for thy might, so leve it wel to fare !

138. That Grekes wolde hir wraththe on
    Troye wreke,     960
If that they mighte, I knowe it wel,
    y-wis.
But it shal not bifallen as ye speke ;
And god to-forn, and ferther over this,
I wot my fader wys and redy is ;
And that he me hath bought, as ye me
    tolde,     965
So dere, I am the more un-to him holde.

139. That Grekes been of heigh con-
    dicioun,
I woot eek wel ; but certein, men shal
    finde
As worthy folk with-inne Troye toun,
As conning, and as parfit and as kinde,
As been bitwixen Orcades and Inde.   971
And that ye coude wel your lady serve,
I trowe eek wel, hir thank for to deserve.

140. But as to speke of love, y-wis,' she
    seyde,
'I hadde a lord, to whom I wedded was,
The whos myn herte al was, til that he
    deyde ;     976
And other love, as helpe me now Pallas,
Ther in myn herte nis, ne never was.
And that ye been of noble and heigh
    kinrede,
I have wel herd it tellen, out of drede. 980

141. And that doth me to han so gret a
    wonder,
That ye wol scornen any womman so.
Eek, god wot, love and I be fer a-sonder;
I am disposed bet, so mote I go,
Un-to my deeth, to pleyne and maken
    wo.     985
What I shal after doon, I can not seye ;
But trewely, as yet me list not pleye.

142. Myn herte is now in tribulacioun,
And ye in armes bisy, day by day.
Here-after, whan ye wonnen han the
    toun,     990

Paraunter, thanne so it happen may,
That whan I see that I never er say,
Than wole I werke that I never wroughte !
This word to yow y-nough suffysen
    oughte.

143. To-morwe eek wol I speke with yow
    fayn,     995
So that ye touchen nought of this matere.
And whan yow list, ye may come here
    ayeyn ;
And, er ye gon, thus muche I seye yow
    here :
As helpe me Pallas with hir heres clere,
If that I sholde of any Greek han routhe,
It sholde be your-selven, by my trouthe !

144. I sey not therfore that I wol yow
    love,     1002
Ne I sey not nay, but in conclusioun,
I mene wel, by god that sit above :'—
And ther-with-al she caste hir eyen
    doun,
And gan to syke, and seyde, 'O Troye
    toun,     1006
Yet bidde I god, in quiete and in reste
I may yow seen, or do myn herte breste.'

145. But in effect, and shortly for to seye,
This Diomede al freshly newe ayeyn 1010
Gan pressen on, and faste hir mercy
    preye ;     1011
And after this, the sothe for to seyn,
Hir glove he took, of which he was ful
    fayn.
And fynally, whan it was waxen eve,
And al was wel, he roos and took his
    leve.     1015

146. The brighte Venus folwede and ay
    taughte
The wey, ther brode Phebus doun alighte ;
And Cynthea hir char-hors over-raughte
To whirle out of the Lyon, if she mighte;
And Signifer his candeles shewed brighte,
Whan that Criseyde un-to hir bedde
    wente     1021
In-with hir fadres faire brighte tente.

147. Retorning in hir soule ay up and
    doun
The wordes of this sodein Diomede,

His greet estat, and peril of the toun, 1025
And that she was allone and hadde nede
Of freendes help; and thus bigan to
    brede
The cause why, the sothe for to telle,
That she tok fully purpos for to dwelle.

148. The morwe com, and goostly for to
    speke,                                1030
This Diomede is come un-to Criseyde,
And shortly, lest that ye my tale breke,
So wel he for him-selve spak and seyde,
That alle hir sykes sore adoun he leyde.
And fynally, the sothe for to seyne,   1035
He refte hir of the grete of al hir peyne.

149. And after this the story telleth us,
That she him yaf the faire baye stede,
The which he ones wan of Troilus;
And eek a broche (and that was litel
    nede)                                1040
That Troilus was, she yaf this Diomede.
And eek, the bet from sorwe him to
    releve,
She made him were a pencel of hir sleve.

150. I finde eek in the stories elles-where,
Whan through the body hurt was Dio-
    mede                                 1045
Of Troilus, tho weep she many a tere,
Whan that she saugh his wyde woundes
    blede ;
And that she took to kepen him good
    hede,
And for to hele him of his sorwes smerte.
Men seyn, I not, that she yaf him hir
    herte.                               1050

151. But trewely, the story telleth us,
Ther made never womman more wo
Than she, whan that she falsed Troilus.
She seyde, ' allas ! for now is clene a-go
My name of trouthe in love, for ever-mo !
For I have falsed oon, the gentileste
That ever was, and oon the worthieste !  .

152. Allas, of me, un-to the worldes ende,
Shal neither been y-writen nor y-songe
No good word, for thise bokes wol me
    shende,                              1060
O, rolled shal I been on many a tonge !

Through-out the world my belle shal be
    ronge ;
And wommen most wol hate me of alle.
Allas, that swich a cas me sholde falle !

153. They wol seyn, in as muche as in
    me is,                               1065
I have hem doon dishonour, weylawey !
Al be I not the firste that dide amis,
What helpeth that to do my blame awey ?
But sin I see there is no bettre way,
And that to late is now for me to rewe,
To Diomede algate I wol be trewe.     1071

154. But Troilus, sin I no better may,
And sin that thus departen ye and I,
Yet preye I god, so yeve yow right good
    day
As for the gentileste, trewely,        1075
That ever I say, to serven feithfully,
And best can ay his lady honour kepe :'—
And with that word she brast anon to
    wepe.

155. ' And certes, yow ne haten shal I
    never,
And freendes love, that shal ye han of
    me,                                  1080
And my good word, al mighte I liven ever.
And, trewely, I wolde sory be
For to seen yow in adversitee.
And giltelees, I woot wel, I yow leve ;
But al shal passe ; and thus take I my
    leve.'                               1085

156. But trewely, how longe it was bi-
    twene,
That she for-sook him for this Diomede,
Ther is non auctor telleth it, I wene.
Take every man now to his bokes hede ;
He shal no terme finden, out of drede.
For though that he bigan to wowe hir
    sone,                                1091
Er he hir wan, yet was ther more to done.

157. Ne me ne list this sely womman
    chyde
Ferther than the story wol devyse.
Hir name, allas ! is publisshed so wyde,
That for hir gilt it oughte y-now suffyse.
And if I mighte excuse hir any wyse,

For she so sory was for hir untrouthe,
Y-wis, I wolde excuse hir yet for routhe.

158. This Troilus, as I biforn have told,
Thus dryveth forth, as wel as he hath
might. 1101
But often was his herte hoot and cold,
And namely, that ilke nynthe night,
Which on the morwe she hadde him
byhight
To come ayein : god wot, ful litel reste
Hadde he that night ; no-thing to slepe
him leste. 1106

159. The laurer-crouned Phebus, with his
hete,
Gan, in his course ay upward as he wente,
To warmen of †th' est see the wawes wete ;
And Nisus doughter song with fresh en-
tente, 1110
Whan Troilus his Pandare after sente ;
And on the walles of the toun they
pleyde,
To loke if they can seen ought of Criseyde.

160. Til it was noon, they stoden for to
see
Who that ther come ; and every maner
wight, 1115
That cam fro fer, they seyden it was she,
Til that they coude knowen him a-right,
Now was his herte dul, now was it light ;
And thus by-japed stonden for to stare
Aboute nought, this Troilus and Pandare.

161. To Pandarus this Troilus tho seyde,
'For ought I wot, bi-for noon, sikerly,
In-to this toun ne comth nought here
Criseyde.
She hath y-now to done, hardily, 1124
To winnen from hir fader, so trowe I ;
Hir olde fader wol yet make hir dyne
Er that she go ; god yeve his herte pyne !'

162. Pandare answerde, 'it may wel be,
certeyn ;
And for-thy lat us dyne, I thee biseche ;
And after noon than mayst thou come
ayeyn.' 1130
And hoom they go, with-oute more
speche ;

And comen ayein, but longe may they
seche
Er that they finde that they after cape ;
Fortune hem bothe thenketh for to jape.

163. Quod Troilus, 'I see wel now, that
she 1135
Is taried with hir olde fader so,
That er she come, it wol neigh even be.
Com forth, I wol un-to the yate go.
Thise portours been unkonninge ever-mo ;
And I wol doon hem holden up the yate
As nought ne were, al-though she come
late.' 1141

164. The day goth faste, and after that
comth eve,
And yet com nought to Troilus Criseyde.
He loketh forth by hegge, by tree, by
greve,
And fer his heed over the wal he leyde.
And at the laste he torned him, and
seyde, 1146
' By god, I woot hir mening now, Pandare !
Al-most, y-wis, al newe was my care.

165. Now douteles, this lady can hir
good ;
I woot, she meneth ryden prively. 1150
I comende hir wysdom, by myn hood !
She wol not maken peple nycely
Gaure on hir, whan she comth ; but
softely
By nighte in-to the toun she thenketh
ryde.
And, dere brother, thenk not longe t'
abyde. 1155

166. We han nought elles for to doon,
y-wis.
And Pandarus, now woltow trowen me ?
Have here my trouthe, I see hir ! yond
she is.
Heve up thyn eyen, man ! maystow not
see ? '
Pandare answerde, 'nay, so mote I thee !
Al wrong, by god ; what seystow, man,
wher art ? 1161
That I see yond nis but a fare-cart.'

167. 'Allas, thou seist right sooth,' quod
Troilus ;
' But hardely, it is not al for nought 1164

That in myn herte I now rejoyse thus.
It is ayein som good I have a thought.
Noot I not how, but sin that I was
   wrought,
Ne felte I swich a confort, dar I seye ;
She comth to-night, my lyf, that dorste
   I leye !'

168. Pandare answerde, 'it may be wel,
   y-nough' ;              1170
And held with him of al that ever he
   seyde ;
But in his herte he thoughte, and softe
   lough,
And to him-self ful sobrely he seyde :
'From hasel-wode, ther Joly Robin pleyde,
Shal come al that that thou abydest
   here ;               1175
Ye, fare-wel al the snow of ferne yere !'

169. The wardein of the yates gan to calle
The folk which that with-oute the yates
   were,
And bad hem dryven in hir bestes alle,
Or al the night they moste bleven there.
And fer with-in the night, with many
   a tere,              1181
This Troilus gan hoomward for to ryde ;
For wel he seeth it helpeth nought t'a-
   byde.

170. But natheles, he gladded him in this ;
He thoughte he misacounted hadde his
   day,               1185
And seyde, 'I understonde have al a-mis.
For thilke night I last Criseyde say,
She seyde, "I shal ben here, if that I
   may,
Er that the mone, O dere herte swete !
The Lyon passe, out of this Ariete."   1190

171. For which she may yet holde al hir
   biheste.'
And on the morwe un-to the yate he
   wente,
And up and down, by west and eek by
   este,
Up-on the walles made he many a wente.
But al for nought ; his hope alwey him
   blente ;            1195

For which at night, in sorwe and sykes
   sore
He wente him hoom, with-outen any
   more.

172. This hope al clene out of his herte
   fledde,
He nath wher-on now lenger for to honge ;
But for the peyne him thoughte his herte
   bledde,            1200
So were his throwes sharpe and wonder
   stronge.
For when he saugh that she abood so
   longe,
He niste what he juggen of it mighte,
Sin she hath broken that she him bi-
   highte.

173. The thridde, ferthe, fifte, sixte day
After tho dayes ten, of which I tolde,
Bitwixen hope and drede his herte lay,
Yet som-what trustinge on hir hestes olde.
But whan he saugh she nolde hir terme
   holde,
He can now seen non other remedye, 1210
But for to shape him sone for to dye.

174. Ther-with the wikked spirit, god us
   blesse,
Which that men clepeth wode jalousye,
Gan in him crepe, in al this hevinesse ;
For which, by-cause he wolde sone dye,
He ne eet ne dronk, for his malencolye,
And eek from every companye he fledde ;
This was the lyf that al the tyme he
   ledde.

175. He so defet was, that no maner man
Unnethe mighte him knowe ther he
   wente ;            1220
So was he lene, and ther-to pale and wan,
And feble, that he walketh by potente ;
And with his ire he thus him-selven
   shente.
And who-so axed him wher-of him smerte,
He seyde, his harm was al aboute his
   herte.            1225

176. Pryam ful ofte, and eek his moder
   dere,
His bretheren and his sustren gonne him
   freyne

Why he so sorwful was in al his chere,
And what thing was the cause of al his
    peyne?
But al for nought; he nolde his cause
    pleyne,    1230
But seyde, he felte a grevous maladye
A-boute his herte, and fayn he wolde dye.

177 So on a day he leyde him doun to
    slepe,
And so bifel that in his sleep him
    thoughte,
That in a forest faste he welk to wepe 1235
For love of hir that him these peynes
    wroughte;
And up and doun as he the forest soughte,
He mette he saugh a boor with tuskes
    grete,
That sleep ayein the bright sonnes hete.

178. And by this boor, faste in his armes
    folde,    1240
Lay kissing ay his lady bright Criseyde:
For sorwe of which, whan he it gan
    biholde,
And for despyt, out of his slepe he breyde,
And loude he cryde on Pandarus, and
    seyde,
'O Pandarus, now knowe I crop and
    rote!    1245
I nam but deed, ther nis non other bote!

179. My lady bright Criseyde hath me
    bitrayed,
In whom I trusted most of any wight,
She elles-where hath now hir herte
    apayed;
The blisful goddes, through hir grete
    might,    1250
Han in my dreem y-shewed it ful right.
Thus in my dreem Criseyde I have
    biholde'—
And al this thing to Pandarus he tolde.

180. 'O my Criseyde, allas! what subtil-
    tee,
What newe lust, what beautee, what
    science,    1255
What wratthe of juste cause have ye to
    me?
What gilt of me, what fel experience
Hath fro me raft, allas! thyn advertence?

O trust, O feyth, O depe asëuraunce,
Who hath me reft Criseyde, al my ple-
    saunce?    1260

181. Allas! why leet I you from hennes
    go,
For which wel neigh out of my wit I
    breyde?
Who shal now trowe on any othes mo?
God wot I wende, O lady bright, Criseyde,
That every word was gospel that ye seyde!
But who may bet bigylen, if him liste, 1266
Than he on whom men weneth best to
    triste?

182. What shal I doon, my Pandarus,
    allas!
I fele now so sharpe a newe peyne,
Sin that ther is no remedie in this cas,
That bet were it I with myn hondes
    tweyne    1271
My-selven slow, than alwey thus to pleyne.
For through my deeth my wo sholde han
    an ende,
Ther every day with lyf my-self I shende.'

183. Pandare answerde and seyde, 'allas
    the whyle    1275
That I was born; have I not seyd er this,
That dremes many a maner man bigyle?
And why? for folk expounden hem a-mis.
How darstow seyn that fals thy lady is,
For any dreem, right for thyn owene
    drede?    1280
Lat be this thought, thou canst no dremes
    rede.

184. Paraunter, ther thou dremest of this
    boor,
It may so be that it may signifye
Hir fader, which that old is and eek hoor,
Ayein the sonne lyth, on poynt to dye, 1285
And she for sorwe ginneth wepe and crye,
And kisseth him, ther he lyth on the
    grounde;
Thus shuldestow thy dreem a-right ex-
    pounde.'

185. 'How mighte I thanne do?' quod
    Troilus,
'To knowe of this, ye, were it never so
    lyte?'    1290

' Now seystow wysly,' quod this Pandarus,
' My reed is this, sin thou canst wel
        endyte,
That hastely a lettre thou hir wryte,
Thorugh which thou shalt wel bringen it
        aboute,
To knowe a sooth of that thou art in
        doute.                           1295

186. And see now why ; for this I dar wel
        seyn,
That if so is that she untrewe be,
I can not trowe that she wol wryte ayeyn.
And if she wryte, thou shalt ful sone see,
As whether she hath any libertee     1300
To come ayein, or elles in som clause,
If she be let, she wol assigne a cause.

187. Thou hast not writen hir sin that
        she wente,
Nor she to thee, and this I dorste leye,
Ther may swich cause been in hir en-
        tente,                          1305
That hardely thou wolt thy-selven seye,
That hir a-bood the beste is for yow tweye.
Now wryte hir thanne, and thou shalt
        fele sone
A sothe of al; ther is no more to done.'

188. Acorded been to this conclusioun, 1310
And that anoon, these ilke lordes two ;
And hastely sit Troilus adoun,
And rolleth in his herte to and fro,
How he may best discryven hir his wo.
And to Criseyde, his owene lady dere, 1315
He wroot right thus, and seyde as ye may
        here.

189. ' Right fresshe flour, whos I have
        been and shal,
With-outen part of elles-where servyse,
With herte, body, lyf, lust, thought, and
        al ;
I, woful wight, in every humble wyse 1320
That tonge telle or herte may devyse,
As ofte as matere occupyeth place,
Me recomaunde un-to your noble grace.

190. Lyketh it yow to witen, swete herte,
As ye wel knowe how longe tyme agoon
That ye me lafte in aspre peynes smerte,

Whan that ye wente, of which yet bote
        noon                            1327
Have I non had, but ever wers bigoon
Fro day to day am I, and so mot dwelle,
While it yow list, of wele and wo my
        welle !                         1330

191. For which to yow, with dredful
        herte trewe,
I wryte, as he that sorwe dryfth to wryte,
My wo, that every houre encreseth newe,
Compleyninge as I dar or can endyte.
And that defaced is, that may ye wyte 1335
The teres, which that fro myn eyen reyne,
That wolde speke, if that they coude, and
        pleyne.

192. Yow first bischeche I, that your eyen
        clere
To look on this defouled ye not holde ;
And over al this, that ye, my lady dere,
Wol vouche-sauf this lettre to biholde. 1341
And by the cause eek of my cares colde,
That sleeth my wit, if ought amis me
        asterte,
For-yeve it me, myn owene swete herte.

193. If any servant dorste or oughte of
        right                           1345
Up-on his lady pitously compleyne,
Than wene I, that ich oughte be that
        wight,
Considered this, that ye these monthes
        tweyne
Han taried, ther ye seyden, sooth to
        seyne,
But dayes ten ye nolde in ost sojourne, 1350
But in two monthes yet ye not retourne.

194. But for-as-muche as me mot nedes
        lyke
Al that yow list, I dar not pleyne more,
But humblely with sorwful sykes syke ;
Yow wryte ich myn unresty sorwes sore,
Fro day to day desyring ever-more   1356
To knowen fully, if your wil it were,
How ye han ferd and doon, whyl ye be
        there.

195. The whos wel-fare and hele eek god
        encresse                        1359
In honour swich, that upward in degree

It growe alwey, so that it never cesse;
Right as your herte ay can, my lady free,
Devyse, I prey to god so mote it be.
And graunte it that ye sone up-on me
　　rewe
As wisly as in al I am yow trewe.　1365

196. And if yow lyketh knowen of the fare
Of me, whos wo ther may no wight dis-
　　cryve,
I can no more but, cheste of every care,
At wrytinge of this lettre I was on-lyve,
Al redy out my woful gost to dryve; 1370
Which I delaye, and holde him yet in
　　honde,
Upon the sight of matere of your sonde.

197. Myn eyen two, in veyn with which
　　I see,
Of sorweful teres salte arn waxen welles;
My song, in pleynte of myn adversitee;
My good in harm; myn ese eek waxen
　　helle is.　　　　　　　　　　1376
My joye, in wo; I can sey yow nought
　　elles,
But turned is, for which my lyf I warie,
Everich joye or ese in his contrarie.

198. Which with your cominge hoom
　　ayein to Troye　　　　　　1380
Ye may redresse, and, more a thousand
　　sythe
Than ever ich hadde, encresen in me joye.
For was ther never herte yet so blythe
To han his lyf, as I shal been as swythe
As I yow see; and, though no maner
　　routhe　　　　　　　　　　1385
Commeve yow, yet thinketh on your
　　trouthe.

199. And if so be my gilt hath deeth
　　deserved,
Or if you list no more up-on me see,
In guerdon yet of that I have you served,
Biseche I yow, myn hertes lady free, 1390
That here-upon ye wolden wryte me,
For love of god, my righte lode-sterre,
Ther deeth may make an ende of al my
　　werre.

200. If other cause aught doth yow for to
　　dwelle,　　　　　　　　　　1394
That with your lettre ye me recomforte;

For though to me your absence is an helle,
With pacience I wol my wo comporte,
And with your lettre of hope I wol
　　desporte.
Now wryteth, swete, and lat me thus not
　　pleyne;
With hope, or deeth, delivereth me fro
　　peyne.　　　　　　　　　　1400

201. Y-wis, myn owene dere herte trewe,
I woot that, whan ye next up-on me see,
So lost have I myn hele and eek myn hewe,
Criseyde shal nought conne knowe me!
Y-wis, myn hertes day, my lady free, 1405
So thursteth ay myn herte to biholde
Your beautee, that my lyf unnethe I holde.

202. I sey no more, al have I for to seye
To you wel more than I telle may; 1409
But whether that ye do me live or deye,
Yet pray I god, so yeve yow right good day.
And fareth wel, goodly fayre fresshe may,
As ye that lyf or deeth me may comaunde;
And to your trouthe ay I me recomaunde

203. With hele swich that, but ye yeven
　　me　　　　　　　　　　　　1415
The same hele, I shal noon hele have.
In you lyth, whan yow list that it so be,
The day in which me clothen shal my
　　grave.
In yow my lyf, in yow might for to save
Me from disese of alle peynes smerte; 1420
And fare now wel, myn owene swete herte!
　　　　　　　　　Le vostre T.'

204. This lettre forth was sent un-to
　　Criseyde,
Of which hir answere in effect was this;
Ful pitously she wroot ayein, and seyde,
That al-so sone as that she might, y-wis,
She wolde come, and mende al that was
　　mis.　　　　　　　　　　　1426
And fynally she wroot and seyde him
　　thanne,
She wolde come, ye, but she niste whanne.

205. But in hir lettre made she swich
　　festes,
That wonder was, and swereth she loveth
　　him best,　　　　　　　　　1430
Of which he fond but botmelees bihestes.

But Troilus, thou mayst now, est or west,
Pype in an ivy leef, if that thee lest ;
Thus gooth the world ; god shilde us fro
    mischaunce,
And every wight that meneth trouthe
    avaunce !              1435

206. Encresen gan the wo fro day to night
Of Troilus, for taryinge of Criseyde ;
And lessen gan his hope and eek his
    might,
For which al doun he in his bed him
    leyde ;
He ne eet, ne dronk, ne sleep, ne word he
    seyde,              1440
Imagininge ay that she was unkinde ;
For which wel neigh he wex out of his
    minde.

207. This dreem, of which I told have eek
    biforn,
May never come out of his remembraunce ;
He thoughte ay wel he hadde his lady
    lorn,              1445
And that Joves, of his purveyaunce,
Him shewed hadde in sleep the signifi-
    aunce
Of hir untrouthe and his disaventure,
And that the boor was shewed him in
    figure.

208. For which he for Sibille his suster
    sente,              1450
That called was Cassandre eek al aboute ;
And al his dreem he tolde hir er he stente,
And hir bisoughte assoilen him the doute
Of the stronge boor, with tuskes stoute ;
And fynally, with-inne a litel stounde,
Cassandre him gan right thus his dreem
    expounde.         1456

209. She gan first smyle, and seyde, ' O
    brother dere,
If thou a sooth of this desyrest knowe,
Thou most a fewe of olde stories here,
To purpos, how that fortune over-throwe
Hath lordes olde ; through which, with-
    inne a throwe,        1461
Thou wel this boor shalt knowe, and of
    what kinde
He comen is, as men in bokes finde.

210. Diane, which that wrooth was and in
    ire
For Grekes nolde doon hir sacrifyse,  1465
Ne encens up-on hir auter sette a-fyre,
She, for that Grekes gonne hir so dispyse,
Wrak hir in a wonder cruel wyse.
For with a boor as greet as oxe in stalle
She made up frete hir corn and vynes alle.

211. To slee this boor was al the contree
    reysed,          1471
A-monges which ther com, this boor to see,
A mayde, oon of this world the best
    y-preysed ;
And Meleagre, lord of that contree,
He lovede so this fresshe mayden free  1475
That with his manhod, er he wolde stente,
This boor he slow, and hir the heed he
    sente ;

212. Of which, as olde bokes tellen us,
Ther roos a contek and a greet envye ;
And of this lord descended Tydeus    1480
By ligne, or elles olde bokes lye ;
But how this Meleagre gan to dye
Thorugh his moder, wol I yow not telle,
For al to long it were for to dwelle.'

[*Argument of the 12 Books of* Statius'
Thebais.]

Associat profugum Tideo *primus* Polimi-
    tem ;
Tidea legatum docet insidiasque *secundus*;
*Tercius* Hemoniden canit et vates lati-
    tantes ;
*Quartus* habet reges ineuntes prelia sep-
    tem ;                 4
Mox furie Lenne *quinto* narratur et anguis;
Archimori bustum *sexto* ludique leguntur;
Dat Graios Thebes et vatem *septimus*
    vmbris ;
*Octauo* cecidit Tideus, spes, vita Pelasgis;
Ypomedon *nono* moritur cum Partho-
    nopeo ;            9
Fulmine percussus, *decimo* Capaneus
    superatur ;
*Vndecimo* sese perimunt per vulnera
    fratres ;
Argiuam flentem narrat *duodenus* et
    ignem.             12

213. She tolde eek how Tydeus, er she
    stente,              1485
Un-to the stronge citee of Thebes,
To cleyme kingdom of the citee, wente,
For his felawe, daun Polymites,
Of which the brother, daun Ethyocles,
Ful wrongfully of Thebes held the
    strengthe ;         1490
This tolde she by proces, al by lengthe.

214. She tolde eek how Hemonides asterte,
Whan Tydeus slough fifty knightes stoute.
She tolde eek al the prophesyes by herte,
And how that sevene kinges, with hir
    route,         1495
Bisegeden the citee al aboute ;
And of the holy serpent, and the welle,
And of the furies, al she gan him telle.

215. Of Archimoris buryinge and the
    pleyes,
And how Amphiorax fil through the
    grounde,        1500
How Tydeus was slayn, lord of Argeyes,
And how Ypomedoun in litel stounde
Was dreynt, and deed Parthonope of
    wounde ;
And also how Cappanëus the proude
With thonder-dint was slayn, that cryde
    loude.        1505

216. She gan eek telle him how that
    either brother,
Ethyocles and Polimyte also,
At a scarmyche, eche of hem slough other,
And of Argyves wepinge and hir wo ;
And how the town was brent she tolde
    eek tho.        1510
And so descendeth doun from gestes olde
To Diomede, and thus she spak and tolde.

217. 'This ilke boor bitokneth Diomede,
Tydeus sone, that doun descended is
Fro Meleagre, that made the boor to
    blede.        1515
And thy lady, wher-so she be, y-wis,
This Diomede hir herte hath, and she his.
Weep if thou wolt, or leef ; for, out of
    doute,
This Diomede is inne, and thou art oute.'

218. 'Thou seyst nat sooth,' quod he,
    'thou sorceresse,
With al thy false goost of prophesye ! 1521
Thou wenest been a greet devyneresse ;
Now seestow not this fool of fantasye
Peyneth hir on ladyes for to lye?
Awey,' quod he, 'ther Joves yeve thee
    sorwe !        1525
Thou shalt be fals, paraunter, yet to-
    morwe !

219. As wel thou mightest lyen on Alceste,
That was of creatures, but men lye,
That ever weren, kindest and the beste.
For whanne hir housbonde was in ju-
    partye        1530
To dye him-self, but-if she wolde dye,
She chees for him to dye and go to
    helle,
And starf anoon, as us the bokes telle.'

220. Cassandre goth, and he with cruel
    herte        1534
For-yat his wo, for angre of hir speche ;
And from his bed al sodeinly he sterte,
As though al hool him hadde y-mad a
    leche.        1537
And day by day he gan enquere and seche
A sooth of this, with al his fulle cure ;
And thus he dryeth forth his aventure.

221. Fortune, whiche that permutacioun
Of thinges hath, as it is hir committed
Through purveyaunce and disposicioun
Of heighe Jove, as regnes shal ben flitted
Fro folk in folk, or whan they shal ben
    smitted,        1545
Gan pulle awey the fetheres brighte of
    Troye
Fro day to day, til they ben bare of joye.

222. Among al this, the fyn of the parodie
Of Ector gan approchen wonder blyve ;
The fate wolde his soule sholde unbodie,
And shapen hadde a mene it out to dryve ;
Ayeins which fate him helpeth not to
    stryve ;        1552
But on a day to fighten gan he wende,
At which, allas ! he caughte his lyves
    ende.

223. For which me thinketh every maner
    wight                 1555
That haunteth armes oughte to biwayle
The deeth of him that was so noble
    a knight;
For as he drough a king by th'aventayle,
Unwar of this, Achilles through the mayle
And through the body gan him for to
    ryve;                 1560
And thus this worthy knight was brought
    of lyve.

224. For whom, as olde bokes tellen us,
Was maad swich wo, that tonge it may
    not telle;
And namely, the sorwe of Troilus,   1564
That next him was of worthinesse welle.
And in this wo gan Troilus to dwelle,
That, what for sorwe, and love, and for
    unreste,
Ful ofte a day he bad his herte breste.

225. But natheles, though he gan him
    dispeyre,             1569
And dradde ay that his lady was untrewe,
Yet ay on hir his herte gan repeyre.
And as these loveres doon, he soughte ay
    newe
To gete ayein Criseyde, bright of hewe.
And in his herte he wente hir excusinge,
That Calkas causede al hir taryinge. 1575

226. And ofte tyme he was in purpos
    grete
Him-selven lyk a pilgrim to disgyse,
To seen hir; but he may not contrefete
To been unknowen of folk that weren
    wyse,              1579
Ne finde excuse aright that may suffyse,
If he among the Grekes knowen were;
For which he weep ful ofte many a tere.

227. To hir he wroot yet ofte tyme al
    newe
Ful pitously, he lefte it nought for slouthe,
Biseching hir that, sin that he was trewe,
†She wolde come ayein and holde hir
    trouthe.           1586
For which Criseyde up-on a day, for
    routhe,
I take it so, touching al this matere,
Wrot him ayein, and seyde as ye may
    here.

228. 'Cupydes sone, ensample of goodli-
    hede,             1590
O swerd of knighthod, sours of gentilesse!
How mighte a wight in torment and in
    drede
And helelees, yow sende as yet gladnesse?
I hertelees, I syke, I in distresse;   1594
Sin ye with me, nor I with yow may dele,
Yow neither sende ich herte may nor hele.

229. Your lettres ful, the papir al y-
    pleynted,
Conseyved hath myn hertes pietee;
I have eek seyn with teres al depeynted
Your lettre, and how that ye requeren me
To come ayein, which yet ne may not be.
But why, lest that this lettre founden
    were,             1602
No mencioun ne make I now, for fere.

230. Grevous to me, god woot, is your
    unreste,
Your haste, and that, the goddes or-
    denaunce,          1605
It semeth not ye take it for the beste.
Nor other thing nis in your remem-
    braunce,
As thinketh me, but only your plesaunce.
But beth not wrooth, and that I yow
    biseche;           1609
For that I tarie, is al for wikked speche.

231. For I have herd wel more than I
    wende,
Touching us two, how thinges han y-
    stonde;
Which I shal with dissimulinge amende.
And beth nought wrooth, I have eek
    understonde,        1614
How ye ne doon but holden me in honde.
But now no fors, I can not in yow gesse
But alle trouthe and alle gentilesse.

232. Comen I wol, but yet in swich dis-
    joynte
I stonde as now, that what yeer or what
    day
That this shal be, that can I not apoynte.
But in effect, I prey yow, as I may,  1621
Of your good word and of your frendship
    ay.

M

For trewely, whyl that my lyf may dure,
As for a freend, ye may in me assure.

233. Yet preye I yow on yvel ye ne take,
That it is short which that I to yow
wryte ; 1626
I dar not, ther I am, wel lettres make.
Ne never yet ne coude I wel endyte.
Eek greet effect men wryte in place lyte.
Th'entente is al, and nought the lettres
space ; 1630
And fareth now wel, god have you in his
grace !

#### La vostre C.'

234. This Troilus this lettre thoughte al
straunge,
Whan he it saugh, and sorwefully he
sighte ;
Him thoughte it lyk a kalendes of
chaunge ;
But fynally, he ful ne trowen mighte 1635
That she ne wolde him holden that she
highte ;
For with ful yvel wil list him to leve
That loveth wel, in swich cas, though
him greve.

235. But natheles, men seyn that, at the
laste, 1639
For any thing, men shal the sothe see ;
And swich a cas bitidde, and that as faste,
That Troilus wel understood that she
Nas not so kinde as that hir oughte be.
And fynally, he woot now, out of doute,
That al is lost that he hath been aboute.

236. Stood on a day in his malencolye 1646
This Troilus, and in suspecioun
Of hir for whom he wende for to dye.
And so bifel, that through-out Troye toun,
As was the gyse, y-bore was up and doun
A maner cote-armure, as seyth the storie,
Biforn Deiphebe, in signe of his victorie,

237. The whiche cote, as telleth Lollius,
Deiphebe it hadde y-rent from Diomede
The same day ; and whan this Troilus 1655
It saugh, he gan to taken of it hede,
Avysing of the lengthe and of the brede,
And al the werk ; but as he gan biholde,
Ful sodeinly his herte gan to colde.

238. As he that on the coler fond with-
inne 1660
A broche, that he Criseyde yaf that morwe
That she from Troye moste nedes twinne,
In remembraunce of him and of his sorwe :
And she him leyde ayein hir feyth to
borwe 1664
To kepe it ay ; but now, ful wel he wiste,
His lady nas no lenger on to triste.

239. He gooth him hoom, and gan ful
sone sende
For Pandarus ; and al this newe chaunce,
And of this broche, he tolde him word
and ende, 1669
Compleyninge of hir hertes variaunce,
His longe love, his trouthe, and his pen-
aunce ;
And after deeth, with-outen wordes more,
Ful faste he cryde, his reste him to restore.

240. Than spak he thus, 'O lady myn
Criseyde,
Wher is your feyth, and wher is your
biheste ? 1675
Wher is your love, wher is your trouthe ?'
he seyde ;
' Of Diomede have ye now al this feste !
Allas, I wolde have trowed at the leste,
That, sin ye nolde in trouthe to me stonde,
That ye thus nolde han holden me in
honde ! 1680

241. Who shal now trowe on any othes
mo ?
Allas, I never wolde han wend, er this,
That ye, Criseyde, coude han chaunged so ;
Ne, but I hadde a-gilt and doon amis, 1684
So cruel wende I not your herte, y-wis,
To slee me thus ; allas, your name of
trouthe
Is now for-doon, and that is al my routhe.

242. Was ther non other broche yow liste
lete
To feffe with your newe love,'quod he, 1689
' But thilke broche that I, with teres wete,
Yow yaf, as for a remembraunce of me ?
Non other cause, allas, ne hadde ye
But for despyt, and eek for that ye mente
Al-outrely to shewen your entente !

243. Through which I see that clene out
 of your minde     1695
Ye han me cast, and I ne can nor may,
For al this world, with-in myn herte finde
T' unloven yow a quarter of a day!
In cursed tyme I born was, weylaway!
That ye, that doon me al this wo endure,
Yet love I best of any creature.  1701

244. Now god,' quod he, ' me sende yet
 the grace
That I may meten with this Diomede!
And trewely, if I have might and space,
Yet shal I make, I hope, his sydes blede.
O god,' quod he, ' that oughtest taken hede
To fortheren trouthe, and wronges to
 punyce,     1707
Why niltow doon a vengeaunce on this
 vyce?

245. O Pandare, that in dremes for to
 triste
Me blamed hast, and wont art ofte up-
 breyde,     1710
Now maystow see thy-selve, if that thee
 liste,
How trewe is now thy nece, bright Cri-
 seyde!
In sondry formes, god it woot,' he seyde,
' The goddes shewen bothe joye and tene
In slepe, and by my dreme it is now sene.

246. And certaynly, with-oute more
 speche,     1716
From hennes-forth, as ferforth as I may,
Myn owene deeth in armes wol I seche;
I recche not how sone be the day!
But trewely, Criseyde, swete may, 1720
Whom I have ay with al my might y-
 served,
That ye thus doon, I have it nought
 deserved.'

247. This Pandarus, that alle these thinges
 herde,
And wiste wel he seyde a sooth of this,
He nought a word ayein to him answerde;
For sory of his frendes sorwe he is, 1726
And shamed, for his nece hath doon a-mis;
And stant, astoned of these causes tweye,
As stille as stoon; a word ne coude he
 seye.

248. But at the laste thus he spak, and
 seyde,     1730
' My brother dere, I may thee do no-more.
What shulde I seyn? I hate, y-wis,
 Criseyde!
And god wot, I wol hate hir evermore!
And that thou me bisoughtest doon of
 yore,     1734
Havinge un-to myn honour ne my reste
Right no reward, I dide al that thee leste.

249. If I dide ought that mighte lyken
 thee,
It is me leef; and of this treson now,
God woot, that it a sorwe is un-to me!
And dredelees, for hertes ese of yow, 1740
Right fayn wolde I amende it, wiste I how.
And fro this world, almighty god I preye,
Delivere hir sone; I can no-more seye.'

250. Gret was the sorwe and pleynt of
 Troilus;
But forth hir cours fortune ay gan to
 holde.     1745
Criseyde loveth the sone of Tydeus,
And Troilus mot wepe in cares colde.
Swich is this world; who-so it can bi-
 holde,
In eche estat is litel hertes reste; 1749
God leve us for to take it for the beste!

251. In many cruel batayle, out of drede,
Of Troilus, this ilke noble knight,
As men may in these olde bokes rede,
Was sene his knighthod and his grete
 might.
And dredelees, his ire, day and night, 1755
Ful cruelly the Grekes ay aboughte;
And alwey most this Diomede he soughte.

252. And ofte tyme, I finde that they
 mette     1758
With blody strokes and with wordes grete,
Assayinge how hir speres weren whette;
And god it woot, with many a cruel hete
Gan Troilus upon his helm to-bete.
But natheles, fortune it nought ne wolde,
Of otheres hond that either deyen sholde.—

253. And if I hadde y-taken for to wryte
The armes of this ilke worthy man, 1766

Than wolde I of his batailles endyte.
But for that I to wryte first bigan
Of his love, I have seyd as that I can. 1769
His worthy dedes, who-so list hem here,
Reed Dares, he can telle hem alle y-fere.

254. Bisechinge every lady bright of hewe,
And every gentil womman, what she be,
That al be that Criseyde was untrewe,
That for that gilt she be not wrooth with
　　me.　　　　　　　　　　　　　　1775
Ye may hir gilt in othere bokes see;
And gladlier I wol wryten, if yow leste,
Penelopeës trouthe and good Alceste.

255. Ne I sey not this al-only for these
　　men,
But most for wommen that bitraysed be
Through false folk; god yeve hem sorwe,
　　amen!　　　　　　　　　　　　　1781
That with hir grete wit and subtiltee
Bitrayse yow! and this commeveth me
To speke, and in effect yow alle I preye,
Beth war of men, and herkeneth what
　　I seye!—　　　　　　　　　　　1785

256. Go, litel book, go litel myn tregedie,
Ther god thy maker yet, er that he dye,
So sende might to make in som comedie!
But litel book, no making thou n'envye,
But subgit be to alle poesye;　　　　1790
And kis the steppes, wher-as thou seest
　　pace
Virgile, Ovyde, Omer, Lucan, and Stace.

257. And for ther is so greet diversitee
In English and in wryting of our tonge,
So preye I god that noon miswryte thee,
Ne thee mismetre for defaute of tonge. 1796
And red wher-so thou be, or elles songe,
That thou be understonde I god beseche!
But yet to purpos of my rather speche.—

258. The wraththe, as I began yow for to
　　seye,　　　　　　　　　　　　　1800
Of Troilus, the Grekes boughten dere;
For thousandes his hondes maden deye,
As he that was with-outen any pere,
Save Ector, in his tyme, as I can here.
But weylaway, save only goddes wille, 1805
Dispitously him slough the fiers Achille.

259. And whan that he was slayn in this
　　manere,
His lighte goost ful blisfully is went
Up to the holownesse of the seventh spere,
In convers letinge every element;　1810
And ther he saugh, with ful avysement,
The erratik sterres, herkeninge armonye
With sownes fulle of hevenish melodye.

260. And doun from thennes faste he gan
　　avyse　　　　　　　　　　　　　1814
This litel spot of erthe, that with the see
Enbraced is, and fully gan despyse
This wrecched world, and held al vanitee
To respect of the pleyn felicitee
That is in hevene above; and at the laste,
Ther he was slayn, his loking doun he
　　caste;　　　　　　　　　　　　1820

261. And in him-self he lough right at
　　the wo
Of hem that wepten for his deeth so faste;
And dampned al our werk that folweth so
The blinde lust, the which that may not
　　laste,　　　　　　　　　　　　1824
And sholden al our herte on hevene caste.
And forth he wente, shortly for to telle,
Ther as Mercurie sorted him to dwelle.—

262. Swich fyn hath, lo, this Troilus for
　　love,
Swich fyn hath al his grete worthinesse;
Swich fyn hath his estat real above, 1830
Swich fyn his lust, swich fyn hath his
　　noblesse;
Swich fyn hath false worldes brotelnesse.
And thus bigan his lovinge of Criseyde,
As I have told, and in this wyse he deyde.

263. O yonge fresshe folkes, he or she, 1835
In which that love up groweth with your
　　age,
Repeyreth hoom from worldly vanitee,
And of your herte up-casteth the visage
To thilke god that after his image
Yow made, and thinketh al nis but
　　a fayre　　　　　　　　　　　　1840
This world, that passeth sone as floures
　　fayre.

264. And loveth him, the which that
　　right for love
Upon a cros, our soules for to beye,

First starf, and roos, and sit in hevene
  a-bove ;
For he nil falsen no wight, dar I seye,  1845
That wol his herte al hoolly on him leye.
And sin he best to love is, and most meke,
What nedeth feyned loves for to seke ?

265. Lo here, of Payens corsed olde rytes,
Lo here, what alle hir goddes may availle ;
Lo here, these wrecched worldes appe-
       tytes ;           -           1851
Lo here, the fyn and guerdon for travaille
Of Jove, Appollo, of Mars, of swich
       rascaille !
Lo here, the forme of olde clerkes speche
In poetrye, if ye hir bokes seche.—  1855

266. O moral Gower, this book I directe
To thee, and to the philosophical Strode,
To vouchen sauf, ther nede is, to corecte,

Of your benignitees and zeles gode.
And to that sothfast Crist, that starf on
  rode,                              1860
With al myn herte of mercy ever I preye ;
And to the lord right thus I speke and
  seye :

267. Thou oon, and two, and three, eterne
  on-lyve,
That regnest ay in three and two and
  oon,
Uncircumscript, and al mayst circum-
  scryve,                           1865
Us from visible and invisible foon
Defende ; and to thy mercy, everychoon,
So make us, Jesus, for thy grace, digne,
For love of mayde and moder thyn
  benigne !  Amen.

**Explicit Liber Troili et Criseydis.**

# THE HOUS OF FAME.

## BOOK I.

God turne us every dreem to gode !
For hit is wonder, by the rode,
To my wit, what causeth swevenes
Either on morwes, or on evenes ;
And why th'effect folweth of somme,     5
And of somme hit shal never come ;
Why that is an avisioun,
And †this a revelacioun ;
Why this a dreem, why that a sweven,
And nat to every man liche even ;     10
Why this a fantom, †these oracles,
I noot; but who-so of these miracles
The causes knoweth bet than I,
Devyne he ; for I certeinly
Ne can hem noght, ne never thinke     15
To besily my wit to swinke,
To knowe of hir signifiaunce
The gendres, neither the distaunce
Of tymes of hem, ne the causes
For-why this †more than that cause is;     20
As if folkes complexiouns
Make hem dreme of reflexiouns ;
Or elles thus, as other sayn,
For to greet feblenesse of †brayn,
By abstinence, or by seeknesse,     25
Prison, stewe, or greet distresse ;
Or elles by disordinaunce
Of naturel acustomaunce,
That som man is to curious
In studie, or melancolious,     30
Or thus, so inly ful of drede,

That no man may him bote bede ;
Or elles, that devocioun
Of somme, and contemplacioun
Causeth swiche dremes ofte ;     35
Or that the cruel lyf unsofte
Which these ilke lovers leden
That hopen over muche or dreden,
That purely hir impressiouns
Causeth hem avisiouns;     40
Or if that spirits have the might
To make folk to dreme a-night ;
Or if the soule, of propre kinde,
Be so parfit, as men finde,
That hit forwot that is to come,     45
And that hit warneth alle and somme
Of everiche of hir aventures
By avisiouns, or by figures,
But that our flesh ne hath no might
To understonden hit aright,     50
For hit is warned to derkly;—
But why the cause is, noght wot I.
Wel worthe, of this thing, grete clerkes,
That trete of this and other werkes ;
For I of noon opinioun     55
Nil as now make mencioun,
But only that the holy rode
Turne us every dreem to gode !
For never, sith that I was born,
Ne no man elles, me biforn,     60
Mette, I trowe stedfastly,
So wonderful a dreem as I

The tenthe day [dide] of Decembre,
The which, as I can now remembre,
I wol yow tellen every del.     65

### The Invocation.

But at my ginning, trusteth wel,
I wol make invocacioun,
With special devocioun,
Unto the god of slepe anoon,
That dwelleth in a cave of stoon     70
Upon a streem that comth fro Lete,
That is a flood of helle unswete ;
Besyde a folk men clepe Cimerie,
Ther slepeth ay this god unmerie
With his slepy thousand sones     75
That alway for to slepe hir wone is—
And to this god, that I of rede,
Preye I, that he wol me spede
My sweven for to telle aright,
If every dreem stonde in his might.     80
And he, that mover is of al
That is and was, and ever shal,
So yive hem joye that hit here
Of alle that they dreme to-yere,
And for to stonden alle in grace     85
Of hir loves, or in what place
That hem wer levest for to stonde,
And shelde hem fro †povert and shonde,
And fro unhappe and ech disese,
And sende hem al that may hem plese,     90
That take hit wel, and scorne hit noght,
Ne hit misdemen in her thoght
Through malicious entencioun.
And who-so, through presumpcioun,
Or hate or scorne, or through envye,     95
Dispyt, or jape, or vilanye,
Misdeme hit, preye I Jesus god
That (dreme he barfoot, dreme he shod),
That every harm that any man
Hath had, sith [that] the world began,     100
Befalle him therof, or he sterve,
And graunte he mote hit ful deserve,
Lo ! with swich a conclusioun
As had of his avisioun
Cresus, that was king of Lyde,     105
That high upon a gebet dyde !
This prayer shal he have of me;
I am no bet in charite !
    Now herkneth, as I have you seyd,
What that I mette, or I abreyd.     110

### The Dream.

Of Decembre the tenthe day,
Whan hit was night, to slepe I lay
Right ther as I was wont to done,
And fil on slepe wonder sone,
As he that wery was for-go     115
On pilgrimage myles two
To the corseynt Leonard,
To make lythe of that was hard.
    But as I †sleep, me mette I was
Within a temple y-mad of glas ;     120
In whiche ther were mo images
Of gold, stondinge in sondry stages,
And mo riche tabernacles,
And with perree mo pinacles,
And mo curious portreytures,     125
And queynte maner of figures
Of olde werke, then I saw ever.
For certeynly, I niste never
Wher that I was, but wel wiste I,
Hit was of Venus redely,     130
The temple ; for, in portreyture,
I saw anoon-right hir figure
Naked fletinge in a see.
And also on hir heed, pardee,
Hir rose-garlond whyt and reed,     135
And hir comb to kembe hir heed,
Hir dowves, and daun Cupido,
Hir blinde sone, and Vulcano,
That in his face was ful broun.
    But as I romed up and doun,     140
I fond that on a wal ther was
Thus writen, on a table of bras :
' I wol now singe, if that I can,
The armes, and al-so the man,
That first cam, through his destinee,     145
Fugitif of Troye contree,
In Itaile, with ful moche pyne,
Unto the strondes of Lavyne.'
And tho began the story anoon,
As I shal telle yow echoon.     150
    First saw I the destruccioun
Of Troye, through the Greek Sinoun,
[That] with his false forsweringe,
And his chere and his lesinge
Made the hors broght into Troye,     155
Thorgh which Troyens loste al hir joye.
And after this was grave, allas !
How Ilioun assailed was
And wonne, and king Priam y-slayn,

And Polites his sone, certayn,　　160
Dispitously, of dan Pirrus.
　　And next that saw I how Venus,
Whan that she saw the castel brende,
Doun fro the hevene gan descende,
And bad hir sone Eneas flee ;　　165
And how he fledde, and how that he
Escaped was from al the pres,
And took his fader, Anchises,
And bar him on his bakke away,
Cryinge, 'Allas, and welaway!'　　170
The whiche Anchises in his honde
Bar the goddes of the londe,
Thilke that unbrende were.
　　And I saw next, in alle this fere,
How Creusa, dann Eneas wyf,　　175
Which that he lovede as his lyf,
And hir yonge sone Iulo,
And eek Ascanius also,
Fledden eek with drery chere,
That hit was pitee for to here ;　　180
And in a forest, as they wente,
At a turninge of a wente,
How Creusa was y-lost, allas!
That deed, [but] noot I how, she was ;
How he hir soughte, and how hir gost　185
Bad him to flee the Grekes ost,
And seyde, he moste unto Itaile,
As was his destinee, sauns faille ;
That hit was pitee for to here,
Whan hir spirit gan appere,　　190
The wordes that she to him seyde,
And for to kepe hir sone him preyde.
Ther saw I graven eek how he,
His fader eek, and his meynee,
With his shippes gan to sayle　　195
Toward the contree of Itaile,
As streight as that they mighte go.
　　Ther saw I thee, cruel Juno,
That art daun Jupiteres wyf,
That hast y-hated, al thy lyf,　　200
Al the Troyanisshe blood,
Renne and crye, as thou were wood,
On Eolus, the god of windes,
To blowen out, of alle kindes,
So loude, that he shulde drenche　　205
Lord and lady, grome and wenche
Of al the Troyan nacioun,
Withoute any savacioun.
　　Ther saw I swich tempeste aryse,
That every herte mighte agryse,　　210

To see hit peynted on the walle.
　　Ther saw I graven eek withalle,
Venus, how ye, my lady dere,
Wepinge with ful woful chere,
Prayen Jupiter an hye　　215
To save and kepe that navye
Of the Troyan Eneas,
Sith that he hir sone was.
　　Ther saw I Joves Venus kisse,
And graunted of the tempest lisse.　　220
Ther saw I how the tempest stente,
And how with alle pyne he wente,
And prevely took arrivage
In the contree of Cartage ;
And on the morwe, how that he　　225
And a knight, hight Achatee,
Metten with Venus that day,
Goinge in a queynt array,
As she had ben an hunteresse,
With wind blowinge upon hir tresse;　230
How Eneas gan him to pleyne,
Whan that he knew hir, of his peyne ;
And how his shippes dreynte were,
Or elles lost, he niste where ;
How she gan him comforte tho,　　235
And bad him to Cartage go,
And ther he shuldë his folk finde,
That in the see were left behinde.
　　And, shortly of this thing to pace,
She made Eneas so in grace　　240
Of Dido, quene of that contree,
That, shortly for to tellen, she
Becam his love, and leet him do
That that wedding longeth to.
What shulde I speke more queynte,　245
Or peyne me my wordes peynte,
To speke of love? hit wol not be ;
I can not of that facultee.
And eek to telle the manere
How they aqueynteden in-fere,　　250
Hit were a long proces to telle,
And over long for yow to dwelle.
　　Ther saw I grave, how Eneas
Tolde Dido every cas,
That him was tid upon the see.　　255
　　And after grave was, how she
Made of him, shortly, at oo word,
Hir lyf, hir love, hir lust, hir lord :
And dide him al the reverence,
And leyde on him al the dispence.　260
That any woman mighte do,

Weninge hit had al be so,
As he hir swoor; and her-by demed
That he was good, for he swich semed.
Allas! what harm doth apparence,    265
Whan hit is fals in existence!
For he to hir a traitour was;
Wherfor she slow hir-self, allas!
    Lo, how a woman doth amis,
To love him that unknowen is!    270
For, by Crist, lo! thus hit fareth;
'Hit is not al gold, that glareth.'
For, al-so brouke I wel myn heed,
Ther may be under goodliheed
Kevered many a shrewed vyce;    275
Therfor be no wight so nyce,
To take a love only for chere,
For speche, or for frendly manere;
For this shal every woman finde
That som man, of his pure kinde,    280
Wol shewen outward the faireste,
Til he have caught that what him leste;
And thanne wol he causes finde,
And swere how that she is unkinde,
Or fals, or prevy, or double was.    285
Al this seye I by Eneas
And Dido, and hir nyce lest,
That lovede al to sone a gest;
Therfor I wol seye a proverbe,
That 'he that fully knoweth th'erbe    290
May saufly leye hit to his yë';
Withoute dreed, this is no lye.
    But let us speke of Eneas,
How he betrayed hir, allas!
And lefte hir ful unkindely.    295
So whan she saw al-utterly,
That he wolde hir of trouthe faile,
And wende fro hir to Itaile,
She gan to wringe hir hondes two.
    'Allas!' quod she, 'what me is wo! 300
Allas! is every man thus trewe,
That every yere wolde have a newe,
If hit so longe tyme dure,
Or elles three, peraventure?
As thus: of oon he wolde have fame    305
In magnifying of his name;
Another for frendship, seith he;
And yet ther shal the thridde be,
That shal be taken for delyt,
Lo, or for singular profyt.'    310
    In swiche wordes gan to pleyne
Dido of hir grete peyne,

As me mette redely;
Non other auctour alegge I.
'Allas!' quod she, 'my swete herte,    315
Have pitee on my sorwes smerte,
And slee me not! go noght away!
O woful Dido, wel away!'
Quod she to hir-selve tho.
'O Eneas! what wil ye do?    320
O, that your love, ne your bonde,
That ye han sworn with your right honde,
Ne my cruel deeth,' quod she,
'May holde yow still heer with me!
O, haveth of my deeth pitee!    325
Y-wis, my dere herte, ye
Knowen ful wel that never yit,
As fer-forth as I hadde wit,
Agilte [I] yow in thoght ne deed.
O, have ye men swich goodliheed    330
In speche, and never a deel of trouthe?
Allas, that ever hadde routhe
Any woman on any man!
Now see I wel, and telle can,
We wrecched wimmen conne non art; 335
For certeyn, for the more part,
Thus we be served everichone.
How sore that ye men conne grone,
Anoon, as we have yow receyved,
Certeinly we ben deceyved;    340
For, though your love laste a sesoun,
Wayte upon the conclusioun,
And eek how that ye determynen,
And for the more part diffynen.
    'O, welawey that I was born!    345
For through yow is my name lorn,
And alle myn actes red and songe
Over al this lond, on every tonge.
O wikke Fame! for ther nis
Nothing so swift, lo, as she is!    350
O, sooth is, every thing is wist,
Though hit be kevered with the mist.
Eek, thogh I mighte duren ever,
That I have doon, rekever I never,
That I ne shal be seyd, allas,    355
Y-shamed be through Eneas,
And that I shal thus juged be—
"Lo, right as she hath doon, now she
Wol do eftsones, hardily;"
Thus seyth the peple prevely.'—    360
But that is doon, nis not to done;
†Al hir compleynt ne al hir mone,
Certeyn, availeth hir not a stree.

And whan she wiste sothly he
Was forth unto his shippes goon,    365
She †in hir chambre wente anoon,
And called on hir suster Anne,
And gan hir to compleyne thanne;
And seyde, that she cause was
That she first lovede †Eneas,    370
And thus counseilled hir therto.
But what! when this was seyd and do,
She roof hir-selve to the herte,
And deyde through the wounde smerte.
But al the maner how she deyde,    375
And al the wordes that she seyde,
Who-so to knowe hit hath purpos,
Reed Virgile in Eneidos
Or the Epistle of Ovyde,
What that she wroot or that she dyde: 380
And nere hit to long to endyte,
By god, I woldë hit here wryte.

But, welaway! the harm, the routhe,
That hath betid for swich untrouthe,
As men may ofte in bokes rede,    385
And al day seen hit yet in dede,
That for to thenken hit, a tene is.
Lo, Demophon, duk of Athenis,
How he forswor him ful falsly
And trayed Phillis wikkedly,    390
The kinges doghter was of Trace,
And falsly gan his terme pace;
And when she wiste that he was fals,
She heng hir-self right by the hals,
For he had do hir swich untrouthe;    395
Lo! was not this a wo and routhe?
Eek lo! how fals and reccheles
Was to Briseida Achilles,
And Paris to †Oënone;
And Jason to Isiphile;    400
And eft Jason to Medea;
And Ercules to Dyanira;
For he lefte hir for Iöle,
That made him cacche his deeth, pardee.

How fals eek was he, Theseus;    405
That, as the story telleth us,
How he betrayed Adriane;
The devel be his soules bane!
For had he laughed, had he loured,
He mostë have be al devoured,    410
If Adriane ne had y-be!
And, for she had of him pitee,
She made him fro the dethe escape,
And he made hir a ful fals jape;

For after this, within a whyle    415
He lefte hir slepinge in an yle,
Deserte alone, right in the see,
And stal away, and leet hir be;
And took hir suster Phedra tho
With him, and gan to shippe go.    420
And yet he had y-sworn to here,
On al that ever he mighte swere,
That, so she saved him his lyf,
He wolde have take hir to his wyf;
For she desired nothing elles,    425
In certein, as the book us telles.

But to excusen Eneas
Fulliche of al his greet trespas,
The book seyth, Mercurie, sauns faile,
Bad him go into Itaile,    430
And leve Auffrykes regioun,
And Dido and hir faire toun.

Tho saw I grave, how to Itaile
Daun Eneas is go to saile;
And how the tempest al began,    435
And how he loste his steresman,
Which that the stere, or he took keep,
Smot over-bord, lo! as he sleep.
And also saw I how Sibyle
And Eneas, besyde an yle,    440
To helle wente, for to see
His fader, Anchises the free.
How he ther fond Palinurus,
And Dido, and eek Deiphebus;
And every tourment eek in helle    445
Saw he, which is long to telle.
Which who-so willeth for to knowe,
He moste rede many a rowe
On Virgile or on Claudian,
Or Daunte, that hit telle can.    450
Tho saw I grave al th'arivaile
That Eneas had in Itaile;
And with king Latine his tretee,
And alle the batailles that he
Was at him-self, and eek his knightes, 455
Or he had al y-wonne his rightes;
And how he Turnus refte his lyf,
And wan Lavyna to his wyf;
And al the mervelous signals
Of the goddes celestials;    460
How, maugre Juno, Eneas,
For al hir sleighte and hir compas,
Acheved al his aventure;
For Jupiter took of him cure
At the prayere of Venus    465

The whiche I preye alway save us,
And us ay of our sorwes lighte !
   Whan I had seyen al this sighte
In this noble temple thus,
'A, Lord !' thoughte I, 'that madest us,
Yet saw I never swich noblesse          471
Of images, ne swich richesse,
As I saw graven in this chirche ;
But not woot I who dide hem wirche,
Ne wher I am, ne in what contree.          475
But now wol I go out and see,
Right at the wiket, if I can
See o-wher stering any man,
That may me telle wher I am.'
   When I out at the dores cam,          480
I faste aboute me beheld.
Then saw I but a large feld,
As fer as that I mighte see,
Withouten toun, or hous, or tree,
Or bush, or gras, or ered lond ;          485
For al the feld nas but of sond
As smal as man may see yet lye

In the desert of Libye ;
Ne I no maner creature,
That is y-formed by nature,          490
Ne saw, me [for] to rede or wisse.
' O Crist,' thoughte I, ' that art in blisse,
Fro fantom and illusioun
Me save !' and with devocioun
Myn yën to the heven I caste.          495
   Tho was I war, lo ! at the laste,
That faste by the sonne, as hyë
As kenne mighte I with myn yë,
Me thoughte I saw an egle sore,
But that hit semed moche more          500
Then I had any egle seyn.
But this as sooth as deeth, certeyn,
Hit was of golde, and shoon so brighte,
That never saw men such a sighte,
But-if the heven hadde y-wonne          505
Al newe of golde another sonne ;
So shoon the egles fethres brighte,
And somwhat dounward gan hit lighte.

**Explicit liber primus.**

## BOOK II.

### Incipit liber secundus.

#### Proem.

   Now herkneth, every maner man
That English understonde can,          510
And listeth of my dreem to lere ;
For now at erste shul ye here
So †selly an avisioun,
That Isaye, ne Scipioun,
Ne king Nabugodonosor,          515
Pharo, Turnus, ne Elcanor,
Ne mette swich a dreem as this !
Now faire blisful, O Cipris,          (10)
So be my favour at this tyme !
And ye, me to endyte and ryme          520
Helpeth, that on Parnaso dwelle
By Elicon the clere welle.

   O Thought, that wroot al that I mette,
And in the tresorie hit shette
Of my brayn ! now shal men see          525
If any vertu in thee be,
To tellen al my dreem aright ;
Now kythe thyn engyn and might !          (20)

#### The Dream.

   This egle, of which I have yow told,
That shoon with fethres as of gold,          530
Which that so hyë gan to sore,
I gan beholde more and more,
To see hir beautee and the wonder ;
But never was ther dint of thonder,
Ne that thing that men calle foudre,          535
That smoot somtyme a tour to poudre,
And in his swifte coming brende,
That so swythe gan descende,          (30)
As this foul, whan hit behelde
That I a-roume was in the felde ;          540
And with his grimme pawes stronge,
Within his sharpe nayles longe,
Me, fleinge, at a swappe he hente,
And with his sours agayn up wente,
Me caryinge in his clawes starke          545
As lightly as I were a larke,
How high, I can not telle yow,
For I cam up, I niste how.          (40)
For so astonied and a-sweved

Was every vertu in my heved,     550
What with his sours and with my drede,
That al my feling gan to dede ;
For-why hit was to greet affray.
    Thus I longe in his clawes lay,
Til at the laste he to me spak     555
In mannes vois, and seyde, ' Awak !
And be not †so a-gast, for shame !'
And called me tho by my name.     (50)
And, for I sholde the bet abreyde—
Me mette—' Awak,' to me he seyde,     560
Right in the same vois and stevene
That useth oon I coude nevene ;
And with that vois, soth for to sayn,
My minde cam to me agayn ;
For hit was goodly seyd to me,     565
So nas hit never wont to be.
    And herwithal I gan to stere,
And he me in his feet to bere,     (60)
Til that he felte that I had hete,
And felte eek tho myn herte bete.     570
And tho gan he me to disporte,
And with wordes to comforte,
And sayde twyës, ' Seynte Marie !
Thou art noyous for to carie,
And nothing nedeth hit, pardee !     575
For al-so wis god helpe me
As thou non harm shalt have of this ;
And this cas, that betid thee is,     (70)
Is for thy lore and for thy prow ;—
Let see ! darst thou yet loke now ?     580
Be ful assured, boldely,
I am thy frend.' And therwith I
Gan for to wondren in my minde.
' O god,' thoughte I, ' that madest kinde,
Shal I non other weyes dye ?     585
Wher Joves wol me stellifye,
Or what thing may this signifye ?
I neither am Enok, ne Elye,     (80)
Ne Romulus, ne Ganymede
That was y-bore up, as men rede,     590
To hevene with dan Jupiter,
And maad the goddes boteler.'
    Lo ! this was tho my fantasye !
But he that bar me gan espye
That I so thoghte, and seyde this :—     595
' Thou demest of thy-self amis ;
For Joves is not ther-aboute—
I dar wel putte thee out of doute—     (90)
To make of thee as yet a sterre.
But er I bere thee moche ferre,     600

I wol thee telle what I am,
And whider thou shalt, and why I cam
To †done this, so that thou take
Good herte, and not for fere quake.'
' Gladly,' quod I. ' Now wel,' quod he :—
' First I, that in my feet have thee,     606
Of which thou hast a feer and wonder,
Am dwelling with the god of thonder,
Which that men callen Jupiter,     (101)
That dooth me flee ful ofte fer     610
To do al his comaundement.
And for this cause he hath me sent
To thee : now †herkne, by thy trouthe !
Certeyn, he hath of thee routhe,
That thou so longe trewely     615
Hast served so ententifly
His blinde nevew Cupido,
And fair Venus [goddesse] also,     (110)
Withoute guerdoun ever yit,
And nevertheles hast set thy wit—     620
Although that in thy hede ful †lyte is—
To make bokes, songes, dytees,
In ryme, or elles in cadence,
As thou best canst, in reverence
Of Love, and of his servants eke,     625
That have his servise soght, and seke ;
And peynest thee to preyse his art,
Althogh thou haddest never part ;     (120)
Wherfor, al-so god me blesse,
Joves halt hit greet humblesse     630
And vertu eek, that thou wolt make
A-night ful ofte thyn heed to ake,
In thy studie so thou wrytest,
And ever-mo of love endytest,
In honour of him and preysinges,     635
And in his folkes furtheringes,
And in hir matere al devysest,     (129)
And noght him nor his folk despysest,
Although thou mayst go in the daunce
Of hem that him list not avaunce.     640
    ' Wherfor, as I seyde, y-wis,
Jupiter considereth this,
And also, beau sir, other thinges ;
That is, that thou hast no tydinges
Of Loves folk, if they be glade,     645
Ne of noght elles that god made ;
And noght only fro fer contree
That ther no tyding comth to thee,     (140)
But of thy verray neyghebores,
That dwellen almost at thy dores,     650
Thou herest neither that ne this ;

For whan thy labour doon al is,
And hast y-maad thy rekeninges,
In stede of reste and newe thinges,
Thou gost hoom to thy hous anoon ;      655
And, also domb as any stoon,
Thou sittest at another boke,
Til fully daswed is thy loke,          (150)
And livest thus as an hermyte,
Although thyn abstinence is lyte.      660
    'And therfor Joves, through his grace,
Wol that I bere thee to a place,
Which that hight THE HOUS OF FAME,
To do thee som disport and game,
In som recompensacioun                 665
Of labour and devocioun
That thou hast had, lo ! causeles,
To Cupido, the reccheles !             (160)
And thus this god, thorgh his meryte,
Wol with som maner thing thee quyte,
So that thou wolt be of good chere.    671
For truste wel, that thou shalt here,
When we be comen ther I seye,
Mo wonder thinges, dar I leye,
Of Loves folke mo tydinges,            675
Bothe soth-sawes and lesinges ;
And mo loves newe begonne,
And longe y-served loves wonne,        (170)
And mo loves casuelly
That been betid, no man wot why,       680
But as a blind man stert an hare ;
And more jolytee and fare,
Whyl that they finde love of stele,
As thinketh hem, and over-al wele ;
Mo discords, and mo jelousyes,         685
Mo murmurs, and mo novelryes,
And mo dissimulaciouns,
And feyned reparaciouns ;              (180)
And mo berdes in two houres
Withoute rasour or sisoures            690
Y-maad, then greynes be of sondes ;
And eke mo holdinge in hondes,
And also mo renovelaunces
Of olde forleten aqueyntaunces ;
Mo love-dayes and acordes              695
Then on instruments ben cordes ;
And eke of loves mo eschaunges
Than ever cornes were in graunges ;   (190)
Unethe maistow trowen this ?'—         699
Quod he.  ' No, helpe me god so wis !'—
Quod I.  ' No ?  why ?' quod he.  ' For hit
Were impossible, to my wit,

Though that Fame hadde al the pyes
In al a realme, and al the spyes,
How that yet she shulde here al this,  705
Or they espye hit.'  ' O yis, yis !'
Quod he to me, ' that can I preve
By resoun, worthy for to leve,         (200)
So that thou yeve thyn advertence
To understonde my sentence.            710
    ' First shalt thou heren wher she dwell-
              eth,
And so thyn owne book hit telleth ;
Hir paleys stant, as I shal seye,
Right even in middes of the weye
Betwixen hevene, erthe, and see ;      715
That, what-so-ever in al these three
Is spoken, in privee or aperte,
The wey therto is so overte,           (210)
And stant eek in so juste a place,
That every soun mot to hit pace,       720
Or what so comth fro any tonge,
Be hit rouned, red, or songe,
Or spoke in seurtee or drede,
Certein, hit moste thider nede.
    ' Now herkne wel ; for-why I wille  725
Tellen thee a propre skile,
And †worthy demonstracioun
In myn imagynacioun.                   (220)
    ' Geffrey, thou wost right wel this,
That every kindly thing that is,       730
Hath a kindly stede ther he
May best in hit conserved be ;
Unto which place every thing,
Through his kindly enclyning,
Moveth for to come to,                 735
Whan that hit is awey therfro ;
As thus ; lo, thou mayst al day see
That any thing that hevy be,           (230)
As stoon or leed, or thing of wighte,
And ber hit never so hye on highte,    740
Lat go thyn hand, hit falleth doun.
    ' Right so seye I by fyre or soun,
Or smoke, or other thinges lighte,
Alwey they seke upward on highte ;
Whyl ech of hem is at his large,       745
Light thing up, and dounward charge.
    ' And for this cause mayst thou see,
That every river to the see           (240)
Enclyned is to go, by kinde.
And by these skilles, as I finde,      750
Hath fish dwellinge in floode and see,
And trees eek in erthe be.

Thus every thing, by this resoun,
Hath his propre mansioun,
To which hit seketh to repaire,    755
As ther hit shulde not apaire.
Lo, this sentence is knowen couthe
Of every philosophres mouthe,    (250)
As Aristotle and dan Platon,
And other clerkes many oon ;    760
And to confirme my resoun,
Thou wost wel this, that speche is soun,
Or elles no man mighte hit here ;
Now †herkne what I wol thee lere.

   'Soun is noght but air y-broken,    765
And every speche that is spoken,
Loud or privee, foul or fair,
In his substaunce is but air ;    (260)
For as flaumbe is but lighted smoke,
Right so soun is air y-broke.    770
But this may be in many wyse,
Of which I wil thee two devyse,
As soun that comth of pype or harpe.
For whan a pype is blowen sharpe,
The air is twist with violence,    775
And rent ; lo, this is my sentence ;
Eek, whan men harpe-stringes smyte,
Whether hit be moche or lyte,    (270)
Lo, with the strook the air to-breketh ; 779
Right so hit breketh whan men speketh.
Thus wost thou wel what thing is speche.

   'Now hennesforth I wol thee teche,
How every speche, or noise, or soun,
Through his multiplicacioun,
Thogh hit were pyped of a mouse,    785
Moot nede come to Fames House.
I preve hit thus—tak hede now—
By experience ; for if that thou    (280)
Throwe on water now a stoon,
Wel wost thou, hit wol make anoon    790
A litel roundel as a cercle,
Paraventure brood as a covercle ;
And right anoon thou shalt see weel,
That wheel wol cause another wheel,
And that the thridde, and so forth,
     brother,    795
Every cercle causing other,
Wyder than himselve was ;
And thus, fro roundel to compas,    (290)
Ech aboute other goinge,
Caused of otheres steringe,    800
And multiplying ever-mo,
Til that hit be so fer y-go

That hit at bothe brinkes be.
Al-thogh thou mowe hit not y-see
Above, hit goth yet alway under,    805
Although thou thenke hit a gret wonder.
And who-so seith of trouthe I varie,
Bid him proven the contrarie.    (300)
And right thus every word, y-wis,
That loude or privee spoken is,    810
Moveth first an air aboute,
And of this moving, out of doute,
Another air anoon is meved,
As I have of the water preved,
That every cercle causeth other.    815
Right so of air, my leve brother ;
Everich air in other stereth    (309)
More and more, and speche up bereth,
Or vois, or noise, or word, or soun,
Ay through multiplicacioun,    820
Til hit be atte House of Fame ;—
Tak hit in ernest or in game.

   'Now have I told, if thou have minde,
How speche or soun, of pure kinde,
Enclyned is upward to meve ;    825
This, mayst thou fele, wel I preve.
And that †the mansioun, y-wis,
That every thing enclyned to is,    (320)
Hath his kindeliche stede :
†Than sheweth hit, withouten drede, 830
That kindely the mansioun
Of every speche, of every soun,
Be hit either foul or fair,
Hath his kinde place in air.
And sin that every thing, that is    835
Out of his kinde place, y-wis,
Moveth thider for to go
If hit a-weye be therfro,    (330)
As I before have preved thee,
Hit seweth, every soun, pardee,    840
Moveth kindely to pace
Al up into his kindely place.
And this place of which I telle,
Ther as Fame list to dwelle,
Is set amiddes of these three,    845
Heven, erthe, and eek the see,
As most conservatif the soun.
Than is this the conclusioun,    (340)
That every speche of every man
As I thee telle first began,    850
Moveth up on high to pace
Kindely to Fames place.

   'Telle me this feithfully,

Have I not preved thus simply,
Withouten any subtiltee                        855
Of speche, or gret prolixitee
Of termes of philosophye,
Of figures of poetrye,                    (350)
Or colours of rethoryke?
Pardee, hit oghte thee to lyke;           860
For hard langage and hard matere
Is encombrous for to here
At ones; wost thou not wel this?'
And I answerde, and seyde, 'Yis.'
  'A ha!' quod he, 'lo, so I can          865
Lewedly to a lewed man
Speke, and shewe him swiche skiles,
That he may shake hem by the biles, (360)
So palpable they shulden be.
But tel me this, now pray I thee,         870
How thinkth thee my conclusioun?'
[Quod he].  'A good persuasioun,'
Quod I, 'hit is; and lyk to be
Right so as thou hast preved me.'
  'By god,' quod he, 'and as I leve,      875
Thou shalt have yit, or hit be eve,
Of every word of this sentence
A preve, by experience;                   (370)
And with thyn eres heren wel
Top and tail, and everydel,               880
That every word that spoken is
Comth into Fames Hous, y-wis,
As I have seyd; what wilt thou more?'
And with this word upper to sore
He gan, and seyde, 'By Seynt Jame!  885
Now wil we speken al of game.'—
  'How farest thou?' quod he to me.
'Wel,' quod I.  'Now see,' quod he, (380)
'By thy trouthe, yond adoun,
Wher that thou knowest any toun,          890
Or hous, or any other thing.
And whan thou hast of ought knowing,
Loke that thou warne me,
And I anoon shal telle thee
How fer that thou art now therfro.'       895
  And I adoun †gan loken tho,
And beheld feldes and plaines,            (389)
And now hilles, and now mountaines,
Now valeys, and now forestes,
And now, unethes, grete bestes;           900
Now riveres, now citees,
Now tounes, and now grete trees,
Now shippes sailinge in the see.
  But thus sone in a whyle he

Was flowen fro the grounde so hyë,        905
That al the world, as to myn yë,
No more semed than a prikke;
Or elles was the air so thikke           (400)
That I ne mighte not discerne.
With that he spak to me as yerne,         910
And seyde: 'Seestow any toun
Or ought thou knowest yonder doun?'
  I seyde, 'Nay.'  'No wonder nis,'
Quod he, 'for half so high as this
Nas Alexander Macedo;                     915
Ne the king, dan Scipio,
That saw in-dreme, at point devys,
Helle and erthe, and paradys;            (410)
Ne eek the wrecche Dedalus,
Ne his child, nyce Icarus,                920
That fleigh so highe that the hete
His winges malt, and he fel wete
In-mid the see, and ther he dreynte,
For whom was maked moch compleynte.
  'Now turn upward,' quod he, 'thy face,
And behold this large place,              926
This air; but loke thou ne be
Adrad of hem that thou shalt see; (420)
For in this regioun, certein,
Dwelleth many a citezein,                 930
Of which that speketh dan Plato.
These ben the cyrish bestes, lo!'
And so saw I al that meynee
Bothe goon and also flee.
  'Now,' quod he tho, 'cast up thyn yë; 935
See yonder, lo, the Galaxyë,
Which men clepeth the Milky Wey,
For hit is whyt: and somme, parfey, (430)
Callen hit Watlinge Strete:
That ones was y-brent with hete,          940
Whan the sonnes sone, the rede,
That highte Pheton, wolde lede
Algate his fader cart, and gye.
The cart-hors gonne wel espye
That he ne coude no governaunce,          945
And gonne for to lepe and launce,
And beren him now up, now doun,
Til that he saw the Scorpioun,           (440)
Which that in heven a signe is yit.
And he, for ferde, loste his wit,         950
Of that, and leet the reynes goon
Of his hors; and they anoon
Gonne up to mounte, and doun descende
Til bothe the eyr and erthe brende;
Til Jupiter, lo, atte laste,              955

Him slow, and fro tne carte caste.
Lo, is it not a greet mischaunce,
To lete a fole han governaunce    (450)
Of thing that he can not demeine ?'
    And with this word, soth for to seyne,
He gan alway upper to sore,    961
And gladded me ay more and more,
So feithfully to me spak he.
    Tho gan I loken under me,
And beheld the eyrish bestes,    965
Cloudes, mistes, and tempestes,
Snowes, hailes, reines, windes,
And th'engendring in hir kindes,    (460)
And al the wey through whiche I cam ;
'O god,' quod I, 'that made Adam,    970
Moche is thy might and thy noblesse !'
    And tho thoughte I upon Boëce,
That writ, 'a thought may flee so hyë,
With fetheres of Philosophye,
To passen everich element ;    975
And whan he hath so fer y-went,
Than may be seen, behind his bak,
Cloud, and al that I of spak.'    (470)
    Tho gan I wexen in a were,
And seyde, 'I woot wel I am here ;    980
But wher in body or in gost
I noot, y-wis ; but god, thou wost !'
For more cleer entendement
Nadde he me never yit y-sent.
And than thoughte I on Marcian,    985
And eek on Anteclaudian,
That sooth was hir descripcioun
Of al the hevenes regioun,    (480)
As fer as that I saw the preve ;
Therfor I can him now beleve.    990
    With that this egle gan to crye :
'Lat be,' quod he, ' thy fantasye ;
Wilt thou lere of sterres aught ?'
'Nay, certeinly,' quod I, 'right naught ;
And why ? for I am now to old.'    995
'Elles I wolde thee have told,'
Quod he, 'the sterres names, lo,
And al the hevenes signes to,    (490)
And which they been.' 'No fors,' quod I.
'Yis, pardee,' quod he; 'wostow why ?   1000
For whan thou redest poetrye,
How goddes gonne stellifye
Brid, fish, beste, or him or here,
As the Raven, or either Bere,
Or Ariones harpe fyn,    1005
Castor, Pollux, or Delphyn,

Or †Atlantes doughtres sevene,
How alle these arn set in hevene ;    (500)
For though thou have hem ofte on honde,
Yet nostow not wher that they stonde.'
'No fors,' quod I, 'hit is no nede :    1011
I leve as wel, so god me spede,
Hem that wryte of this matere,
As though I knew hir places here ;
And eek they shynen here so brighte,
Hit shulde shenden al my sighte,    1016
To loke on hem.' 'That may wel be,'
Quod he. And so forth bar he me    (510)
A whyl, and than he gan to crye,
That never herde I thing so hye,    1020
'Now up the heed ; for al is wel ;
Seynt Julyan, lo, bon hostel !
See here the House of Fame, lo !
Maistow not heren that I do ?'
'What ?' quod I. 'The grete soun,'   1025
Quod he, 'that rumbleth up and doun
In Fames Hous, ful of tydinges,
Bothe of fair speche and chydinges,  (520)
And of fals and soth compouned.
Herkne wel ; hit is not rouned.    1030
Herestow not the grete swogh ?'
'Yis, pardee,' quod I, ' wel y-nogh.'
'And what soun is it lyk ?' quod he.
'Peter ! lyk beting of the see,'
Quod I, 'again the roches holowe,    1035
Whan tempest doth the shippes swalowe;
And lat a man stonde, out of doute,
A myle thens, and here hit route;    (530)
Or elles lyk the last humblinge
After the clappe of a thundringe,    1040
When Joves hath the air y-bete ;
But hit doth me for fere swete.'
'Nay, dred thee not therof,' quod he,
'Hit is nothing wil byten thee ;
Thou shalt non harm have, trewely.' 1045
    And with this word bothe he and I
As nigh the place arryved were
As men may casten with a spere.    (540)
I nistë how, but in a strete
He sette me faire on my fete,    1050
And seyde, 'Walke forth a pas,
And tak thyn aventure or cas,
That thou shalt finde in Fames place.'
    'Now,' quod I, 'whyl we han space
To speke, or that I go fro thee,    1055
For the love of god, tel me,
In sooth that wil I of thee lere,

If this noise that I here                    (550)
Be, as I have herd thee tellen,
Of folk that doun in erthe dwellen,    1060
And comth here in the same wyse
As I thee herde or this devyse ;
And that ther lyves body nis
In al that hous that yonder is,
That maketh al this loude fare ?'    1065
'No,' quod he, 'by Seynte Clare,
And also wis god rede me !
But o thinge I wil warne thee        (560)
Of the which thou wolt have wonder.
Lo, to the House of Fame yonder    1070
Thou wost how cometh every speche,
Hit nedeth noght thee eft to teche.
But understond now right wel this ;
Whan any speche y-comen is

Up to the paleys, anon-right         1075
Hit wexeth lyk the same wight
Which that the word in erthe spak,
Be hit clothed reed or blak ;        (570)
And hath so verray his lyknesse
That spak the word, that thou wilt gesse
That hit the same body be,           1081
Man or woman, he or she.
And is not this a wonder thing ?'
'Yis,' quod I tho, 'by hevene king !'
And with this worde, 'Farwel,' quod he,
'And here I wol abyden thee ;        1086
And god of hevene sende thee grace,
Som good to lernen in this place.'   (580)
And I of him took leve anoon,
And gan forth to the paleys goon.    1090

**Explicit liber secundus.**

# BOOK III.

### Incipit liber tercius.

#### Invocation.

O god of science and of light,
Apollo, through thy grete might,
This litel laste book thou gye !
Nat that I wilne, for maistrye,
Here art poetical be shewed ;        1095
But, for the rym is light and lewed,
Yit make hit sumwhat agreable,
Though som vers faile in a sillable ;
And that I do no diligence
To shewe craft, but o sentence.   (10) 1100
And if, divyne vertu, thou
Wilt helpe me to shewe now
That in myn hede y-marked is—
Lo, that is for to menen this,
The Hous of Fame to descryve—       1105
Thou shalt see me go, as blyve,
Unto the nexte laure I see,
And kisse hit, for hit is thy tree ;
Now entreth in my breste anoon !—

#### The Dream.

Whan I was fro this egle goon,   (20) 1110
I gan beholde upon this place.

And certein, or I ferther pace,
I wol yow al the shap devyse
Of hous and †site ; and al the wyse
How I gan to this place aproche      1115
That stood upon so high a roche,
Hyer stant ther noon in Spaine.
But up I clomb with alle paine,
And though to climbe hit greved me,
Yit I ententif was to see,      (30) 1120
And for to pouren wonder lowe,
If I coude any weyes knowe
What maner stoon this roche was ;
For hit was lyk a thing of glas,
But that hit shoon ful more clere ;  1125
But of what congeled matere
Hit was, I niste redely.
    But at the laste espyed I,
And found that hit was, every deel,
A roche of yse, and not of steel.  (40) 1130
Thoughte I, 'By Seynt Thomas of Kent !
This were a feble foundement
To bilden on a place hye ;
He oughte him litel glorifye
That her-on bilt, god so me save !'  1135
    Tho saw I al the half y-grave
With famous folkes names fele,
That had y-been in mochel wele,

And hir fames wyde y-blowe.
But wel unethes coude I knowe  (50) 1140
Any lettres for to rede
Hir names by ; for, out of drede,
They were almost of-thowed so,
That of the lettres oon or two
Was molte away of every name,          1145
So unfamous was wexe hir fame ;
But men seyn, ' What may ever laste? '

Tho gan I in myn herte caste,
That they were molte awey with hete,
And not awey with stormes bete. (60) 1150
For on that other syde I sey
Of this hille, that northward lay,
How hit was writen ful of names
Of folk that hadden grete fames
Of olde tyme, and yit they were          1155
As fresshe as men had writen hem
          there
The selve day right, or that houre
That I upon hem gan to poure.
But wel I wiste what hit made ;
Hit was conserved with the shade—  (70)
Al this wrytinge that I sy—          1161
Of a castel, that stood on hy,
And stood eek on so cold a place,
That hete mighte hit not deface.

Tho gan I up the hille to goon,          1165
And fond upon the coppe a woon,
That alle the men that ben on lyve
Ne han the cunning to descryve
The beautee of that ilke place,
Ne coude casten no compace     (80) 1170
Swich another for to make,
That mighte of beautee be his make,
Ne [be] so wonderliche y-wrought ;
That hit astonieth yit my thought,
And maketh al my wit to swinke          1175
On this castel to bethinke.
So that the grete †craft, beautee,
The cast, the curiositee
Ne can I not to yow devyse,
My wit ne may me not suffyse.  (90) 1180

But natheles al the substance
I have yit in my remembrance ;
For-why me thoughte, by Seynt Gyle !
Al was of stone of beryle,
Bothe castel and the tour,          1185
And eek the halle, and every bour,
Withouten peces or joininges.
But many subtil compassinges,

†Babewinnes and pinacles,
Imageries and tabernacles,     (100) 1190
I saw ; and ful eek of windowes,
As flakes falle in grete snowes.
And eek in ech of the pinacles
Weren sondry habitacles,
In whiche stoden, al withoute—          1195
Ful the castel, al aboute—
Of alle maner of minstrales,
And gestiours, that tellen tales
Bothe of weping and of game,
Of al that longeth unto Fame.  (110) 1200

Ther herde I pleyen on an harpe
That souned bothe wel and sharpe,
Orpheus ful craftely,
And on his syde, faste by,
Sat the harper Orion,          1205
And Eacides Chiron,
And other harpers many oon,
And the Bret Glascurion ;
And smale harpers with her glees
†Seten under hem in sees,     (120) 1210
And gonne on hem upward to gape,
And countrefete hem as an ape,
Or as craft countrefeteth kinde.

Tho saugh I stonden hem behinde,
A-fer fro hem, al by hemselve,          1215
Many thousand tymes twelve,
That maden loude menstralcyes
In cornemuse, and shalmyes,
And many other maner pype,
That craftely begunne pype     (130) 1220
Bothe in doucet and in rede,
That ben at festes with the brede ;
And many floute and lilting-horne,
And pypes made of grene corne,
As han thise litel herde-gromes,          1225
That kepen bestes in the bromes.

Ther saugh I than Atiteris,
And of Athenes dan Pseustis,
And Marcia that lost her skin,
Bothe in face, body, and chin,  (140) 1230
For that she wolde envyen, lo !
To pypen bet then Apollo.
Ther saugh I famous, olde and yonge,
Pypers of the Duche tonge,
To lerne love-daunces, springes,          1235
Reyes, and these straunge thinges.

Tho saugh I in another place
Stonden in a large space,
Of hem that maken blody soun

In trumpe, beme, and clarioun ; (150) 1240
For in fight and blood-shedinge
Is used gladly clarioninge.
　　Ther herde I trumpen Messenus,
Of whom that speketh Virgilius.
Ther herde I Joab trumpe also,　　1245
Theodomas, and other mo ;
And alle that used clarion
In Cataloigne and Aragon,
That in hir tyme famous were
To lerne, saugh I trumpe there. (160) 1250
　　Ther saugh I sitte in other seës,
Pleyinge upon sondry gleës,
Whiche that I cannot nevene,
Mo then sterres been in hevene,
Of whiche I nil as now not ryme,　　1255
For ese of yow, and losse of tyme :
For tyme y-lost, this knowen ye,
By no way may recovered be.
　　Ther saugh I †pleyen jogelours,
Magiciens and tregetours,　　(170) 1260
And phitonesses, charmeresses,
Olde wicches, sorceresses,
That use exorsisaciouns
And eek thise fumigaciouns ;
And clerkes eek, which conne wel　　1265
Al this magyke naturel,
That craftely don hir ententes,
To make, in certeyn ascendentes,
Images, lo, through which magyk
To make a man ben hool or syk. (180) 1270
Ther saugh I †thee, queen Medea,
And Circes eke, and Calipsa ;
Ther saugh I Hermes Ballenus,
Lymote, and eek Simon Magus.　　1274
Ther saugh I, and knew hem by name,
That by such art don men han fame.
Ther saugh I Colle tregetour
Upon a table of sicamour
Pleye an uncouthe thing to telle ;
I saugh him carien a wind-melle (190) 1280
Under a walsh-note shale.
　　What shuld I make lenger tale
Of al the peple that I say,
Fro hennes in-to domesday ?
　　Whan I had al this folk beholde, 1285
And fond me lous, and noght y-holde,
And eft y-mused longe whyle
Upon these walles of beryle,
That shoon ful lighter than a glas,
And made wel more than hit was　(200)

To semen, every thing, y-wis,　　1291
As kinde thing of fames is ;
I gan forth romen til I fond
The castel-yate on my right hond,
Which that so wel corven was　　1295
That never swich another nas ;
And yit hit was by aventure
Y-wrought, as often as by cure.
　　Hit nedeth noght yow for to tellen,
To make yow to longe dwellen, (210) 1300
Of this yates florisshinges,
Ne of compasses, ne of kervinges,
Ne how they †hatte in masoneries,
As, corbets fulle of imageries.
But, lord ! so fair hit was to shewe, 1305
For hit was al with gold behewe.
But in I wente, and that anoon ;
Ther mette I crying many oon,—
‘ A larges, larges, hold up wel !
God save the lady of this pel, (220) 1310
Our owne gentil lady Fame,
And hem that wilnen to have name
Of us !’ Thus herde I cryen alle,
And faste comen out of halle,
And shoken nobles and sterlinges.　1315
And somme crouned were as kinges,
With crounes wroght ful of losenges ;
And many riban, and many frenges
Were on hir clothes trewely.
　　Tho atte laste aspyed I　　(230) 1320
That pursevauntes and heraudes,
That cryen riche folkes laudes,
Hit weren alle ; and every man
Of hem, as I yow tellen can,
Had on him throwen a vesture,　　1325
Which that men clepe a cote-armure,
Enbrowded wonderliche riche,
Al-though they nere nought y-liche.
But noght nil I, so mote I thryve,
Been aboute to discryve　　(240) 1330
Al these armes that ther weren,
That they thus on hir cotes beren,
For hit to me were impossible ;
Men mighte make of hem a bible
Twenty foot thikke, as I trowe.　　1335
For certeyn, who-so coude y-knowe
Mighte ther alle the armes seen
Of famous folk that han y-been
In Auffrike, Europe, and Asye,
Sith first began the chevalrye. (250) 1340
　　Lo ! how shulde I now telle al this ?

Ne of the halle eek what nede is
To tellen yow, that every wal
Of hit, and floor, and roof and al
Was plated half a fote thikke     1345
Of gold, and that nas no-thing wikke,
But, for to prove in alle wyse,
As fyn as ducat in Venyse,
Of whiche to lyte al in my pouche is?
And they wer set as thikke of nouchis (260)
Fulle of the fynest stones faire,     1351
That men rede in the Lapidaire,
As greses growen in a mede;
But hit were al to longe to rede
The names; and therfore I pace.     1355

But in this riche lusty place,
That Fames halle called was,
Ful moche prees of folk ther nas,
Ne crouding, for to mochil prees.
But al on hye, above a dees,     (270) 1360
†Sitte in a see imperial,
That maad was of a rubee al,
Which that a carbuncle is y-called,
I saugh, perpetually y-stalled,
A feminyne creature;     1365
That never formed by nature
Nas swich another thing y-seye.
For altherfirst, soth for to seye,
Me thoughte that she was so lyte,
That the lengthe of a cubyte     (280) 1370
Was lenger than she semed be;
But thus sone, in a whyle, she
Hir tho so †wonderliche streighte,
That with hir feet she th'erthe reighte,
And with hir heed she touched hevene,
Ther as shynen sterres sevene.     1376
And ther-to eek, as to my wit,
I saugh a gretter wonder yit,
Upon hir eyen to beholde;
But certeyn I hem never tolde; (290) 1380
For as fele eyen hadde she
As fetheres upon foules be,
Or weren on the bestes foure,
That goddes trone gunne honoure,
As John writ in th'apocalips.     1385
Hir heer, that oundy was and crips,
As burned gold hit shoon so see.
And sooth to tellen, also she
Had also fele up-stonding eres
And tonges, as on bestes heres; (300) 1390
And on hir feet wexen saugh I
Partriches winges redely

But, lord! the perrie and the richesse
I saugh sitting on this goddesse!
And, lord! the hevenish melodye     1395
Of songes, ful of armonye,
I herde aboute her trone y-songe,
That al the paleys-walles ronge!
So song the mighty Muse, she
That cleped is Caliopee,     (310) 1400
And hir eighte sustren eke,
That in hir face semen meke;
And evermo, eternally,
They songe of Fame, as tho herde I:—
'Heried be thou and thy name,     1405
Goddesse of renoun and of fame!'
Tho was I war, lo, atte laste,
As I myn eyen gan up caste,
That this ilke noble quene
On hir shuldres gan sustene     (320) 1410
Bothe th'armes and the name
Of tho that hadde large fame;
Alexander, and Hercules
That with a sherte his lyf lees!
†Thus fond I sitting this goddesse,     1415
In nobley, honour, and richesse;
Of which I stinte a whyle now,
Other thing to tellen yow.
Tho saugh I stonde on either syde,
Streight doun to the dores wyde, (330) 1420
Fro the dees, many a pileer
Of metal, that shoon not ful cleer;
But though they nere of no richesse,
Yet they were maad for greet noblesse,
And in hem greet [and hy] sentence; 1425
And folk of digne reverence,
Of whiche I wol yow telle fonde,
Upon the piler saugh I stonde.
Alderfirst, lo, ther I sigh,
Upon a piler stonde on high,     (340) 1430
That was of lede and yren fyn,
Him of secte Saturnyn,
Th' Ebrayk Josephus, the olde,
That of Jewes gestes tolde;
And bar upon his shuldres hye     1435
The fame up of the Jewerye.
And by him stoden other sevene,
Wyse and worthy for to nevene,
To helpen him bere up the charge,
Hit was so hevy and so large.     (350) 1440
And for they writen of batailes,
As wel as other olde mervailes,
Therfor was, lo, this pileer,

Of which that I yow telle heer,
Of lede and yren bothe, y-wis.　　1445
For yren Martes metal is,
Which that god is of bataile ;
And the leed, withouten faile,
Is, lo, the metal of Saturne,
That hath ful large wheel to turne.　(360)
Tho stoden forth, on every rowe,　1451
Of hem which that I coude knowe,
Thogh I hem noght by ordre telle,
To make yow to long to dwelle.

These, of whiche I ginne rede,　1455
Ther saugh I stonden, out of drede :
Upon an yren piler strong,
That peynted was, al endelong,
With tygres blode in every place,
The Tholosan that highte Stace, (370) 1460
That bar of Thebes up the fame
Upon his shuldres, and the name
Also of cruel Achilles.
And by him stood, withouten lees,
Ful wonder hye on a pileer　　1465
Of yren, he, the gret Omeer ;
And with him Dares and Tytus
Before, and eek he, Lollius,
And Guido eek de Columpnis,
And English Gaufride eek, y-wis ; (380) 1470
And ech of these, as have I joye,
Was besy for to bere up Troye.
So hevy ther-of was the fame,
That for to bere hit was no game.
But yit I gan ful wel espye,　　1475
Betwix hem was a litel envye.
Oon seyde, Omere made lyes,
Feyninge in his poetryes,
And was to Grekes favorable ;
Therfor held he hit but fable.　(390) 1480

Tho saugh I stonde on a pileer,
That was of tinned yren cleer,
That Latin poete, [dan] Virgyle,
That bore hath up a longe whyle
The fame of Pius Eneas.　　1485

And next him on a piler was,
Of coper, Venus clerk, Ovyde,
That hath y-sowen wonder wyde
The grete god of Loves name.
And ther he bar up wel his fame,　(400)
Upon this piler, also hye　　1491
As I might see hit with myn yë :
For-why this halle, of whiche I rede
Was woxe on †highte, lengthe and brede,

Wel more, by a thousand del,　　1495
Than hit was erst, that saugh I wel.
Tho saugh I, on a piler by,
Of yren wroght ful sternely,
The grete poete, daun Lucan,
And on his shuldres bar up than,　(410)
As highe as that I mighte see,　　1501
The fame of Julius and Pompee.
And by him stoden alle these clerkes,
That writen of Romes mighty werkes,
That, if I wolde hir names telle,　1505
Al to longe moste I dwelle.

And next him on a piler stood
Of soulfre, lyk as he were wood,
Dan Claudian, the soth to telle,
That bar up al the fame of helle, (420) 1510
Of Pluto, and of Proserpyne,
That quene is of the derke pyne.
What shulde I more telle of this ?
The halle was al ful, y-wis,
Of hem that writen olde gestes,　　1515
As ben on treës rokes nestes ;
But hit a ful confus matere
Were al the gestes for to here,
That they of write, and how they
　　　highte.
But whyl that I beheld this sighte, (430)
I herde a noise aprochen blyve,　1521
That ferde as been don in an hyve,
Agen her tyme of out-fleyinge ;
Right swiche a maner murmuringe,
For al the world, hit semed me.　1525

Tho gan I loke aboute and see,
That ther com entring †in the halle
A right gret company with-alle,
And that of sondry regiouns,
Of alleskinnes condiciouns,　　(440) 1530
That dwelle in erthe under the mone,
Pore and ryche.　And also sone
As they were come into the halle,
They gonne doun on kneës falle
Before this ilke noble quene,　　1535
And seyde, ' Graunte us, lady shene,
Ech of us, of thy grace, a bone !'
And somme of hem she graunted
　　　sone,
And somme she werned wel and faire ;
And somme she graunted the contraire
Of hir axing utterly.　　　(451) 1541
But thus I seye yow trewely,
What hir cause was, I niste.

For this folk, ful wel I wiste,
They hadde good fame ech deserved, 1545
Althogh they were diversly served ;
Right as hir suster, dame Fortune,
Is wont to serven in comune.

Now herkne how she gan to paye
That gonne hir of hir grace praye ;   (460)
And yit, lo, al this companye     1551
Seyden sooth, and noght a lye.

'Madame,' seyden they, 'we be
Folk that heer besechen thee,
That thou graunte us now good fame, 1555
And lete our werkes han that name ;
In ful recompensacioun
Of good werk, give us good renoun.'
'I werne yow hit,' quod she anoon,
'Ye gete of me good fame noon, (470) 1560
By god ! and therfor go your wey.'

'Alas,' quod they, 'and welaway !
Telle us, what may your cause be ?'

'For me list hit noght,' quod she ;
'No wight shal speke of yow, y-wis, 1565
Good ne harm, ne that ne this.'
And with that word she gan to calle
Hir messanger, that was in halle,
And bad that he shulde faste goon,
†Up peyne to be blind anoon,   (480) 1570
For Eolus, the god of winde ;—
'In Trace ther ye shul him finde,
And bid him bringe his clarioun,
That is ful dyvers of his soun,
And hit is cleped Clere Laude,     1575
With which he wont is to heraude
Hem that me list y-preised be :
And also bid him how that he
Bringe his other clarioun,
That highte Sclaundre in every toun, (490)
With which he wont is to diffame   1581
Hem that me list, and do hem shame.'

This messanger gan faste goon,
And found wher, in a cave of stoon,
In a contree that highte Trace,     1585
This Eolus, with harde grace,
Held the windes in distresse,
And gan hem under him to presse,
That they gonne as beres rore,
He bond and pressed hem so sore.   (500)
This messanger gan faste crye,   1591
'Rys up,' quod he, 'and faste hye,
Til that thou at my lady be ;
And tak thy clarions eek with thee,

And speed thee forth.' And he anon 1595
Took to a man, that hight Triton,
His clariouns to bere tho,
And leet a certeyn wind to go,
That blew so hidously and hye,
That hit ne lefte not a skye   (510) 1600
In al the welken longe and brood.

This Eolus no-wher abood
Til he was come at Fames feet,
And eek the man that Triton heet ;
And ther he stood, as still as stoon.  1605
And her-withal ther com anoon
Another huge companye
Of gode folk, and gunne crye,
'Lady, graunte us now good fame,
And lat our werkes han that name  (520)
Now, in honour of gentilesse,     1611
And also god your soule blesse !
For we han wel deserved hit,
Therfor is right that we ben quit.'

'As thryve I,' quod she, 'ye shal
faile,
Good werkes shal yow noght availe  1616
To have of me good fame as now.
But wite ye what ? I graunte yow,
That ye shal have a shrewed fame  1619
And wikked loos, and worse name,  (530)
Though ye good loos have wel deserved.
Now go your wey, for ye be served ;
And thou, dan Eolus, let see !
Tak forth thy trumpe anon,' quod she,
'That is y-cleped Sclaunder light,   1625
And blow hir loos, that every wight
Speke of hem harm and shrewednesse,
In stede of good and worthinesse.
For thou shalt trumpe al the contraire
Of that they han don wel or faire.'  1630
'Alas,' thoughte I, 'what aventures
Han these sory creatures !     (542)
For they, amonges al the pres,
Shul thus be shamed gilteles !
But what ! hit moste nedes be.'   1635

What did this Eolus, but he
Tok out his blakke trumpe of bras,
That fouler than the devil was,
And gan this trumpe for to blowe,
As al the world shulde overthrowe ; (550)
That through-out every regioun   1641
Wente this foule trumpes soun,
As swift as pelet out of gonne,
Whan fyr is in the poudre ronne.

And swiche a smoke gan out-wende  1645
Out of his foule trumpes ende,
Blak, blo, grenish, swartish reed,
As doth wher that men melte leed,
Lo, al on high fro the tuel !
And therto oo thing saugh I wel, (560) 1650
That, the ferther that hit ran,
The gretter wexen hit began,
As doth the river from a welle,
And hit stank as the pit of helle.
Alas, thus was hir shame y-ronge,  1655
And giltelees, on every tonge.

Tho com the thridde companye,
And gunne up to the dees to hye,
And doun on knees they fille anon,
And seyde, 'We ben everichon  (570) 1660
Folk that han ful trewely
Deserved fame rightfully,
And praye yow, hit mot be knowe,
Right as hit is, and forth y-blowe.'
' I graunte,' quod she, ' for me list  1665
That now your gode †werk be wist ;
And yit ye shul han better loos,
Right in dispyt of alle your foos,
Than worthy is ; and that anoon :
Lat now,' quod she, 'thy trumpe goon, (580)
Thou Eolus, that is so blak ;  1671
And out thyn other trumpe tak
That highte Laude, and blow hit so
That through the world hir fame go
Al esely, and not to faste,  1675
That hit be knowen atte laste.'

' Ful gladly, lady myn,' he seyde ;
And out his trumpe of golde he brayde
Anon, and sette hit to his mouthe,
And blew hit est, and west, and southe,(590)
And north, as loude as any thunder,  1681
That every wight hadde of hit wonder,
So brode hit ran, or than hit stente.
And, certes, al the breeth that wente
Out of his trumpes mouthe smelde  1685
As men a pot-ful †bawme helde
Among a basket ful of roses ;
This favour dide he til hir loses.

And right with this I gan aspye,
Ther com the ferthe companye— (600) 1690
But certeyn they were wonder fewe—
And gonne stonden in a rewe,
And seyden, ' Certes, lady brighte,
We han don wel with al our mighte ;
But we ne kepen have no fame.  1695

Hyd our werkes and our name,
For goddes love ! for certes we
Han certeyn doon hit for bountee,
And for no maner other thing.'
' I graunte yow al your asking,'  (610) 1700
Quod she ; ' let your †werk be deed.'

With that aboute I clew myn heed,
And saugh anoon the fifte route
That to this lady gonne loute,
And doun on knees anoon to falle ;  1705
And to hir tho besoughten alle
To hyde hir gode werkes eek,
And seyde, they yeven noght a leek
For fame, ne for swich renoun ;
For they, for contemplacioun  (620) 1710
And goddes love, hadde y-wrought ;
Ne of fame wolde they nought.
' What ?' quod she, ' and be ye wood ?
And wene ye for to do good,
And for to have of that no fame ?  1715
Have ye dispyt to have my name ?
Nay, ye shul liven everichoon !
Blow thy trumpe and that anoon,'
Quod she, ' thou Eolus, I hote,
And ring this folkes †werk by note, (630)
That al the world may of hit here.'  1721
And he gan blowe hir loos so clere
In his golden clarioun,
That through the world wente the soun,
†So kenely, and eek so softe ;  1725
But atte laste hit was on-lofte.

Thoo com the sexte companye,
And gonne faste on Fame crye.
Right verraily, in this manere
They seyden : 'Mercy, lady dere ! (640) 1730
To telle certein, as hit is,
We han don neither that ne this,
But ydel al our lyf y-be.
But, natheles, yit preye we,
That we mowe han so good a fame,  1735
And greet renoun and knowen name,
As they that han don noble gestes,
And acheved alle hir lestes,
As wel of love as other thing ;
Al was us never broche ne ring, (650) 1740
Ne elles nought, from wimmen sent,
Ne ones in hir herte y-ment
To make us only frendly chere,
But mighte temen us on bere ;
Yit lat us to the peple seme  1745
Swiche as the world may of us deme,

That wimmen loven us for wood,
Hit shal don us as moche good,
And to our herte as moche availe
To countrepeise ese and travaile, (660) 1750
As we had wonne hit with labour;
For that is dere boght honour
At regard of our grete ese.
And yit thou most us more plese;
Let us be holden eek, therto,            1755
Worthy, wyse, and gode also,
And riche, and happy unto love.
For goddes love, that sit above,
Though we may not the body have
Of wimmen, yet, so god yow save! (670) 1760
Let men glewe on us the name;
Suffyceth that we han the fame.'

    'I graunte,' quod she, 'by my trouthe!
Now, Eolus, with-outen slouthe,
Tak out thy trumpe of gold, †let see, 1765
And blow as they han axed me,
That every man wene hem at ese,
Though they gon in ful badde lese.'
This Eolus gan hit so blowe,    (679) 1769
That through the world hit was y-
        knowe.

    Tho com the seventh route anoon,
And fel on kneës everichoon,
And seyde, 'Lady, graunte us sone
The same thing, the same bone,
That [ye] this nexte folk han doon.' 1775
'Fy on yow,' quod she, 'everichoon!
Ye masty swyn, ye ydel wrecches,
Ful of roten slowe tecches!
What? false theves! wher ye wolde
Be famous good, and no-thing nolde (690)
Deserve why, ne never roughte?     1781
Men rather yow to-hangen oughte!
For ye be lyk the sweynte cat,
That wolde have fish; but wostow what?
He wolde no-thing wete his clowes.   1785
Yvel thrift come on your jowes,
And eek on myn, if I hit graunte,
Or do yow favour, yow to avaunte!
Thou Eolus, thou king of Trace!
Go, blow this folk a sory grace,' (700) 1790
Quod she, 'anoon; and wostow how?
As I shal telle thee right now;
Sey: "These ben they that wolde honour
Have, and do noskinnes labour,
Ne do no good, and yit han laude;   1795
And that men wende that bele Isaude

Ne coude hem noght of love werne;
And yit she that grint at a querne
Is al to good to ese hir herte."'
    This Eolus anon up sterte,    (710) 1800
And with his blakke clarioun
He gan to blasen out a soun,
As loude as belweth wind in helle.
And eek therwith, [the] sooth to telle,
This soun was [al] so ful of japes,    1805
As ever mowes were in apes.
And that wente al the world aboute,
That every wight gan on hem shoute,
And for to laughe as they were wode;
Such game fonde they in hir hode.   (720)
    Tho com another companye,    1811
That had y-doon the traiterye,
The harm, the †gretest wikkednesse
That any herte couthe gesse;
And preyed hir to han good fame,    1815
And that she nolde hem doon no
        shame,
But yeve hem loos and good renoun,
And do hit blowe in clarioun.
'Nay, wis!' quod she, 'hit were a
        vyce;
Al be ther in me no justyce,    (730) 1820
Me listeth not to do hit now,
Ne this nil I not graunte you.'
    Tho come ther lepinge in a route,
And gonne choppen al aboute
Every man upon the croune,    1825
That al the halle gan to soune,
And seyden: 'Lady, lefe and dere,
We ben swich folk as ye mowe here.
To tellen al the tale aright,
We ben shrewes, every wight, (740) 1830
And han delyt in wikkednesse,
As gode folk han in goodnesse;
And joye to be knowen shrewes,
And fulle of vyce and wikked thewes;
Wherfor we preyen yow, a-rowe,    1835
That our fame swich be knowe
In alle thing right as hit is.'

    'I graunte hit yow,' quod she, 'y-wis.
But what art thou that seyst this tale,
That werest on thy hose a pale, (750) 1840
And on thy tipet swiche a belle!'
'Madame,' quod he, 'sooth to telle,
I am that ilke shrewe, y-wis,
That brende the temple of Isidis
In Athenes, lo, that citee.'    1845

'And wherfor didest thou so?' quod
   she.
'By my thrift,' quod he, 'madame,
I wolde fayn han had a fame,
As other folk hadde in the toun,
Al-thogh they were of greet renoun    (760)
For hir vertu and for hir thewes ;    1851
Thoughte I, as greet a fame han shrewes,
Thogh hit be †but for shrewednesse,
As gode folk han for goodnesse ;
And sith I may not have that oon,    1855
That other nil I noght for-goon.
And for to gette of Fames hyre,
The temple sette I al a-fyre.
Now do our loos be blowen swythe,
As wisly be thou ever blythe.'    (770) 1860
'Gladly,' quod she ; 'thou Eolus,
Herestow not what they preyen us?'
'Madame, yis, ful wel,' quod he,
'And I wil trumpen hit, parde !'
And tok his blakke trumpe faste,    1865
And gan to puffen and to blaste,
Til hit was at the worldes ende.
  With that I gan aboute wende ;
For oon that stood right at my bak,
Me thoughte, goodly to me spak, (780) 1870
And seyde : 'Frend, what is thy name ?
Artow come hider to han fame ? '
'Nay, for-sothe, frend !' quod I ;
'I cam noght hider, graunt mercy !
For no swich cause, by my heed !    1875
Suffyceth me, as I were deed,
That no wight have my name in
  honde.
I woot my-self best how I stonde ;
For what I drye or what I thinke,
I wol my-selven al hit drinke,    (790) 1880
Certeyn, for the more part,
As ferforth as I can myn art.'
'But what dost thou here than ?' quod he.
Quod I, 'that wol I tellen thee,
The cause why I stonde here :—    1885
Som newe tydings for to lere:—
Som newe †thinges, I not what,
Tydinges, other this or that,
Of love, or swiche thinges glade,
For certeynly, he that me made    (800) 1890
To comen hider, seyde me,
I shulde bothe here and see,
In this place, wonder thinges ;
But these be no swiche tydinges

As I mene of.' 'No ?' quod he.    1895
And I answerde, 'No, pardee !
For wel I †wiste, ever yit,
Sith that first I hadde wit,
That som folk han desyred fame
Dyversly, and loos, and name ;    (810) 1900
But certeynly, I niste how
Ne wher that Fame †dwelte, er now ;
Ne eek of hir descripcioun,
Ne also hir condicioun,
Ne the ordre of hir dome,    1905
Unto the tyme I hider come.'
'†Whiche be, lo, these tydinges,
That thou now [thus] hider bringes,
That thou hast herd ?' quod he to me ;
'But now, no fors ; for wel I see (820) 1910
What thou desyrest for to here.
Com forth, and stond no longer here,
And I wol thee, with-outen drede,
In swich another place lede,
Ther thou shalt here many oon.'    1915
  Tho gan I forth with him to goon
Out of the castel, soth to seye.
Tho saugh I stonde in a valeye,
Under the castel, faste by,
An hous, that *domus Dedali*,    (830) 1920
That *Laborintus* cleped is,
Nas maad so wonderliche, y-wis,
Ne half so queynteliche y-wrought.
And evermo, so swift as thought,
This queynte hous aboute wente,    1925
That never-mo hit stille stente.
And ther-out com so greet a noise,
That, had hit stonden upon Oise,
Men mighte hit han herd esely
To Rome, I trowe sikerly.    (840) 1930
And the noyse which that I herde,
For al the world right so hit ferde,
As doth the routing of the stoon
That from th'engyn is leten goon.
  And al this hous, of whiche I rede, 1935
Was made of twigges, falwe, rede,
And grene eek, and som weren whyte,
Swiche as men to these cages thwyte,
Or maken of these paniers,
Or elles †hottes or dossers ;    (850) 1940
That, for the swough and for the
  twigges,
This hous was also ful of gigges,
And also ful eek of chirkinges,
And of many other werkinges :

And eek this hous hath of entrees    1945
As fele as leves been on trees
In somer, whan they grene been ;
And on the roof men may yit seen
A thousand holes, and wel mo,
To leten wel the soun out go.    (860) 1950
   And by day, in every tyde,
Ben al the dores open wyde,
And by night, echoon, unshette ;
Ne porter ther is non to lette
No maner tydings in to pace ;    1955
Ne never reste is in that place,
That hit nis fild ful of tydinges,
Other loude, or of whispringes ;
And, over alle the houses angles,
Is ful of rouninges and of jangles (870) 1960
Of †werre, of pees, of mariages,
Of †reste, of labour of viages,
Of abood, of deeth, of lyfe,
Of love, of hate, acorde, of stryfe,
Of loos, of lore, and of winnings,    1965
Of hele, of sekenesse, of bildinges,
Of faire windes, †of tempestes,
Of qualme of folk, and eek of bestes ;
Of dyvers transmutaciouns
Of estats, and eek of regiouns;    (880) 1970
Of trust, of drede, of jelousye,
Of wit, of winninge, of folye ;
Of plentee, and of greet famyne,
Of chepe, of derth, and of ruyne ;
Of good or †mis governement,    1975
Of fyr, of dyvers accident.
   And lo, this hous, of whiche I wryte,
Siker be ye, hit nas not lyte ;
For hit was sixty myle of lengthe ;
Al was the timber of no strengthe,    (890)
Yet hit is founded to endure    1981
Whyl that it list to Aventure,
That is the moder of tydinges,
As the see of welles and springes,—
And hit was shapen lyk a cage.    1985
   ' Certes,' quod I, ' in al myn age,
Ne saugh I swich a hous as this.'
And as I wondred me, y-wis,
Upon this hous, tho war was I
How that myn egle, faste by,    (900) 1990
Was perched hye upon a stoon ;
And I gan streighte to him goon
And seyde thus : ' I preye thee
That thou a whyl abyde me
For goddes love. and let me seen    1995

What wondres in this place been ;
For yit, paraventure, I may lere
Som good ther-on, or sumwhat here
That leef me were, or that I wente.'
   ' Peter ! that is myn entente,'    (910) 2000
Quod he to me ; ' therfor I dwelle ;
But certein, oon thing I thee telle,
That, but I bringe thee ther-inne,
Ne shalt thou never cunne ginne
To come in-to hit, out of doute,    2005
So faste hit whirleth, lo, aboute.
But sith that Joves, of his grace,
As I have seyd, wol thee solace
Fynally with †swiche thinges,
Uncouthe sightes and tydinges,    (920) 2010
To passe with thyn hevinesse ;
Suche routhe hath he of thy distresse,
That thou suffrest debonairly—
And wost thy-selven utterly
Disesperat of alle blis,    2015
Sith that Fortune hath maad a-mis
The †fruit of al thyn hertes reste
Languisshe and eek in point to breste—
That he, through his mighty meryte,
Wol do thee ese, al be hit lyte,    (930) 2020
And †yaf expres commaundement,
To whiche I am obedient,
To furthre thee with al my might,
And wisse and teche thee aright
Wher thou maist most tydinges here ;    2025
Shaltow †anoon heer many oon lere.'
   With this worde he, right anoon,
Hente me up bitwene his toon,
And at a windowe in me broghte,    2029
That in this hous was, as me thoghte—(940)
And ther-withal, me thoghte hit stente,
And no-thing hit aboute wente—
And me sette in the flore adoun.
But which a congregacioun
Of folk, as I saugh rome aboute,    2035
Some within and some withoute,
Nas never seen, ne shal ben eft ;
That, certes, in the world nis left
So many formed by Nature,
Ne deed so many a creature ;    (950) 2040
That wel unethe, in that place,
Hadde I oon foot-brede of space ;
And every wight that I saugh there
Rouned ech in otheres ere
A newe tyding prevely,    2045
Or elles tolde al openly

Right thus, and seyde : ' Nost not
    thou
That is betid, lo, late or now ? '
   ' No,' quod †the other, 'tel me what ;'—
And than he tolde him this and that, (960)
And swoor ther-to that hit was sooth—
'Thus hath he seyd'—and 'Thus he
    dooth '—  2052
'†Thus shal hit be'—'†Thus herde I
    seye '—
'That shal be found' — 'That dar I
    leye :'—
That al the folk that is a-lyve  2055
Ne han the cunning to discryve
The thinges that I herde there,
What aloude, and what in ere.
But al the wonder-most was this :—
Whan oon had herd a thing, y-wis, (970)
He com †forth to another wight, 2061
And gan him tellen, anoon-right,
The same that to him was told,
Or hit a furlong-way was old,
But gan somwhat for to eche  2065
To this tyding in this speche
More than hit ever was.
And nat so sone departed nas
That he fro him, that he ne mette
With the thridde; and, or he lette (980)
Any stounde, he tolde him als ;  2071
Were the tyding sooth or fals,
Yit wolde he telle hit nathelees,
And evermo with more encrees
Than hit was erst.  Thus north and
    southe  2075
Went every †word fro mouth to mouthe,
And that encresing ever-mo,
As fyr is wont to quikke and go
From a sparke spronge amis,
Til al a citee brent up is. (990) 2080
   And, whan that was ful y-spronge,
And woxen more on every tonge
Than ever hit was, †hit wente anoon
Up to a windowe, out to goon ;
Or, but hit mighte out ther pace, 2085
Hit gan out crepe at som crevace,
And fleigh forth faste for the nones.
   And somtyme saugh I tho, at ones,
A lesing and a sad soth-sawe,
That gonne of aventure drawe (1000) 2090
Out at a windowe for to pace ;
And, when they metten in that place,

They were a-chekked bothe two,
And neither of hem moste out go ;
For other so they gonne croude, 2095
Til eche of hem gan cryen loude,
' Lat me go first !'  ' Nay, but lat me !
And here I wol ensuren thee
With the nones that thou wolt do so,
That I shal never fro thee go, (1010) 2100
But be thyn owne sworen brother !
We wil medle us ech with other,
That no man, be he never so wrothe,
Shal han †that oon of two, but bothe
At ones, al beside his leve,  2105
Come we a-morwe or on eve,
Be we cryed or stille y-rouned.'
Thus saugh I fals and sooth com-
    pouned
Togeder flee for oo tydinge.
   Thus out at holes gonne wringe (1020)
Every tyding streight to Fame ;  2111
And she gan yeven eche his name,
After hir disposicioun,
And yaf hem eek duracioun,
Some to wexe and wane sone,  2115
As dooth the faire whyte mone,
And leet hem gon.  Ther mighte I
    seen
Wenged wondres faste fleen,
Twenty thousand in a route,
As Eolus hem blew aboute. (1030) 2120
   And, lord !  this hous, in alle tymes,
Was ful of shipmen and pilgrymes,
With scrippes bret-ful of lesinges,
Entremedled with tydinges,
And eek alone by hem-selve.  2125
O, many a thousand tymes twelve
Saugh I eek of these pardoneres,
Currours, and eek messangeres,
With boistes crammed ful of lyes
As ever vessel was with lyes. (1040) 2130
And as I alther-fastest wente
Aboute, and dide al myn entente
Me for to pleye and for to lere,
And eek a tyding for to here,
That I had herd of som contree  2135
That shal not now be told for me ;—
For hit no nede is, redely ;
Folk can singe hit bet than I ;
For al mot out, other late or rathe,
Alle the sheves in the lathe ;— (1050) 2140
I herde a gret noise withalle

In a corner of the halle,
Ther men of love tydings tolde,
And I gan thiderward beholde;
For I saugh renninge every wight,　2145
As faste as that they hadden might;
And everich cryed, 'What thing is
　　that?'
And som seyde I not never what.
And whan they were alle on an hepe,
Tho behinde gonne up lepe,　(1060) 2150

And clamben up on othere faste,
And up the †nose on hye caste,
And troden faste on othere heles
And stampe, as men don after eles.
　Atte laste I saugh a man,　2155
Which that I [nevene] naught ne can;
But he semed for to be
A man of greet auctoritee . . .　(1068) 2158

(*Unfinished.*)

# THE LEGEND OF GOOD WOMEN.

TEXT A (*Earlier Version*).

*The prologe of .ix. goode Wimmen.*

A THOUSAND sythes have I herd men
telle,
That ther is joye in heven, and peyne in
helle ;
And I acorde wel that hit be so ;
But natheles, this wot I wel also,
That ther nis noon that dwelleth in this
contree,                                    5
That either hath in helle or heven y-be,
Ne may of hit non other weyes witen,
But as he hath herd seyd, or founde hit
writen ;
For by assay ther may no man hit preve.
But goddes forbode, but men shulde leve
Wel more thing then men han seen with
yë !                                        11
Men shal nat wenen every-thing a lyë
For that he seigh it nat of yore ago.
God wot, a thing is never the lesse so

Thogh every wight ne may hit nat y-see.
Bernard the monk ne saugh nat al, parde !
    Than mote we to bokes that we finde,
Through which that olde thinges been in
minde,
And to the doctrine of these olde wyse,
Yeven credence, in every skilful wyse,   20
And trowen on these olde aproved stories
Of holinesse, of regnes, of victories,
Of love, of hate, of other sundry thinges,
Of whiche I may not maken rehersinges.
And if that olde bokes were a-weye,      25
Y-loren were of remembraunce the keye.
Wel oghte us than on olde bokes leve,

TEXT B (*Later Version*).

*The prologe of .ix. goode Wimmen.*

A THOUSAND tymes have I herd men
telle,
That ther is joye in heven, and peyne in
helle ;
And I acorde wel that hit is so ;
But natheles, yit wot I wel also,
That ther nis noon dwelling in this
contree,                                    5
That either hath in heven or helle y-be,
Ne may of hit non other weyes witen,
But as he hath herd seyd, or founde hit
writen ;
For by assay ther may no man hit preve.
But god forbede but men shulde leve   10
Wel more thing then men han seen with
yë !
Men shal nat wenen every-thing a lyë
But-if him-self hit seeth, or elles dooth ;
For, god wot, thing is never the lasse
sooth,                                      14
Thogh every wight ne may hit nat y-see.
Bernard the monk ne saugh nat al, parde !
    Than mote we to bokes that we finde,
Through which that olde thinges been in
minde,
And to the doctrine of these olde wyse,
Yeve credence, in every skilful wyse,   20
That tellen of these olde appreved stories,
Of holinesse, of regnes, of victories,
Of love, of hate, of other sundry thinges,
Of whiche I may not maken rehersinges.
And if that olde bokes were a-weye,      25
Y-loren were of remembraunce the keye.
Wel oghte us than honouren and beleve

Ther-as ther is non other assay by preve.
   And, as for me, though that my wit be
      lyte,
On bokes for to rede I me delyte,    30
And in myn herte have hem in reverence;

And to hem yeve swich lust and swich
      credence,
That ther is wel unethe game noon
That from my bokes make me to goon,
But hit be other up-on the haly-day,   35
Or elles in the joly tyme of May;

Whan that I here the smale foules singe,

And that the floures ginne for to springe,
Farwel my studie, as lasting that sesoun!
   Now have I therto this condicioun   40
That, of alle the floures in the mede,
Than love I most these floures whyte and
      rede,
Swiche as men callen daysies in our toun.
To hem have I so greet affeccioun,   44
As I seyde erst, whan comen is the May,
That in my bed ther daweth me no day
That I nam up, and walking in the mede
To seen these floures agein the sonne
      sprede,
Whan it up-riseth by the morwe shene, 49
The longe day, thus walking in the grene.
And whan the sonne ginneth for to weste,
Than closeth hit, and draweth hit to reste.
So sore hit is afered of the night,
Til on the morwe, that hit is dayes light.
This dayesye, of alle floures flour,   55
Fulfild of vertu and of alle honour,
And ever y-lyke fair and fresh of hewe,
As wel in winter as in somer newe,

[Cf. ll. 51-3, above.]

These bokes, ther we han non other preve.
   And as for me, thogh that I can but
      lyte,
On bokes for to rede I me delyte,    30
And to hem yeve I feyth and ful
      credence,
And in myn herte have hem in reverence

So hertely, that ther is game noon
That fro my bokes maketh me to goon,
But hit be seldom, on the holyday;   35
Save, certeynly, whan that the month of
      May
Is comen, and that I here the foules
      singe,
And that the floures ginnen for to springe,
Farwel my book and my devocioun!
   Now have I than swich a condicioun,
That, of alle the floures in the mede,   41
Than love I most these floures whyte and
      rede,
Swiche as men callen daysies in our toun.
To hem have I so greet affeccioun,   44
As I seyde erst, whan comen is the May,
That in my bed ther daweth me no day
That I nam up, and walking in the mede
To seen this flour agein the sonne sprede,

Whan hit upryseth erly by the morwe;
That blisful sighte softneth al my sorwe,
So glad am I whan that I have presence
Of hit, to doon al maner reverence,   52

As she, that is of alle floures flour,
Fulfilled of al vertu and honour,   54
And ever y-lyke fair, and fresh of hewe;
And I love hit, and ever y-lyke newe,
And ever shal, til that myn herte dye;
Al swere I nat, of this I wol nat lye,
Ther loved no wight hotter in his lyve.
   And whan that hit is eve, I renne
      blyve,   60
As sone as ever the sonne ginneth weste,
To seen this flour, how it wol go to reste,
For fere of night, so hateth she derknesse!
Hir chere is pleynly sprad in the bright-
      nesse
Of the sonne, for ther hit wol unclose. 65
Allas! that I ne had English, ryme or
      prose,

Fain wolde I preisen, if I coude aright; 59
But wo is me, hit lyth nat in my might!

For wel I wot, that folk han her-beforn
Of making ropen, and lad a-wey the corn;
And I come after, glening here and
there,
And am ful glad if I may finde an ere
Of any goodly word that they han left. 65
And, if hit happe me rehersen eft
That they han in her fresshe songes sayd,
I hope that they wil nat ben evel apayd,
Sith hit is seid in forthering and honour
Of hem that either serven leef or flour. 70

[Cf. p. 354, col. 2, ll. 188-196.]
For trusteth wel, I ne have nat under-
take
As of the leef, ageyn the flour, to make;
Ne of the flour to make, ageyn the leef,
No more than of the corn ageyn the
sheef.
For, as to me, is leefer noon ne lother; 75
I am with-holde yit with never nother.
I not who serveth leef, ne who the flour;
That nis nothing the entent of my labour.
For this werk is al of another tunne, 79
Of olde story, er swich stryf was begunne.
But wherfor that I spak, to yeve cre-
dence
To bokes olde and doon hem reverence,
Is for men shulde autoritees beleve,
Ther as ther lyth non other assay by
preve.
For myn entent is, or I fro yow fare, 85
The naked text in English to declare
Of many a story, or elles of many a geste,
As autours seyn; leveth hem if yow leste!

Suffisant this flour to preyse aright!
But helpeth, ye that han conning and
might,
Ye lovers, that can make of sentement;
In this cas oghte ye be diligent 70
To forthren me somwhat in my labour,
Whether ye ben with the leef or with the
flour.
For wel I wot, that ye han her-biforn
Of making ropen, and lad awey the corn;
And I come after, glening here and
there, 75
And am ful glad if I may finde an ere
Of any goodly word that ye han left.
And thogh it happen me rehercen eft
That ye han in your fresshe songes sayd,
For-bereth me, and beth nat evel apayd,
Sin that ye see I do hit in the honour 81
Of love, and eek in service of the flour,
Whom that I serve as I have wit or
might.
She is the clernesse and the verray light,
That in this derke worlde me wynt and
ledeth, 85
The herte in-with my sorowful brest yow
dredeth,
And loveth so sore, that ye ben verrayly
The maistresse of my wit, and nothing I.
My word, my werk, is knit so in your
bonde,
That, as an harpe obeyeth to the honde 90
And maketh hit soune after his finger-
inge,
Right so mowe ye out of myn herte
bringe
Swich vois, right as yow list, to laughe
or pleyne.
Be ye my gyde and lady sovereyne;
As to myn erthly god, to yow I calle, 95
Bothe in this werke and in my sorwes
alle.
But wherfor that I spak, to give cre-
dence
To olde stories, and doon hem reverence,
And that men mosten more thing beleve
Then men may seen at eye or elles preve?
That shal I seyn, whan that I see my
tyme; 101
I may not al at ones speke in ryme.
My besy gost, that thrusteth alwey newe

Whan passed was almost the month of
    May,
And I had romed, al the someres day,   90
The grene medew, of which that I yow
    tolde,
Upon the fresshe daysy to beholde,
And that the sonne out of the south gan
    weste,
And closed was the flour and goon to
    reste
For derknesse of the night, of which she
    dredde,                                95
Hoom to myn hous ful swiftly I me
    spedde ;
And, in a litel erber that I have,
Y-benched newe with turves fresshe y-
    grave,
I bad men shulde me my couche make ;
For deyntee of the newe someres sake,  100
I bad hem strowe floures on my bed.
Whan I was layd, and had myn eyen hed,
I fel a-slepe with-in an houre or two.
Me mette how I was in the medew tho,
And that I romed in that same gyse,   105
To seen that flour, as ye han herd devyse.
Fair was this medew, as thoughte me
    overal ;
With floures swote enbrowded was it al ;

As for to speke of gomme, or erbe, or
    tree,
Comparisoun may noon y-maked be.    110
For hit surmounted pleynly alle odoures,
And eek of riche beaute alle floures.
Forgeten had the erthe his pore estat
Of winter, that him naked made and mat,
And with his swerd of cold so sore had
    greved.                               115
Now had the atempre sonne al that re-
    leved,
And clothed him in grene al newe agayn.
The smale foules, of the seson fayn,
That from the panter and the net ben
    scaped,                               119
Upon the fouler, that hem made a-whaped
In winter, and distroyed had hir brood,

To seen this flour so yong, so fresh of
    hewe,
Constreyned me with so gledy desyr,   105
That in my herte I fele yit the fyr,
That made me to ryse er hit wer day—
And this was now the firste morwe of
    May—
With dredful herte and glad devocioun,
For to ben at the resureccioun        110
Of this flour, whan that it shuld unclose
Agayn the sonne, that roos as rede as
    rose,
That in the brest was of the beste that
    day,
That Agenores doghter ladde away.    114
    [Cf. p. 354, col. 2, ll. 197-210.]

And doun on knees anon-right I me sette,
And, as I coude, this fresshe flour I grette ;
Kneling alwey, til hit unclosed was,
Upon the smale softe swote gras,
That was with floures swote enbrouded al,

Of swich swetnesse and swich odour
    over-al,                             120
That, for to speke of gomme, or herbe, or
    tree,
Comparisoun may noon y-maked be ;
For hit surmounteth pleynly alle odoures,
And eek of riche beautee alle floures.
Forgeten had the erthe his pore estat 125
Of winter, that him naked made and mat,
And with his swerd of cold so sore greved ;

Now hath the atempre sonne al that re-
    leved
That naked was, and clad hit new agayn.
The smale foules, of the seson fayn,   130
That from the panter and the net ben
    scaped,
Upon the fouler, that hem made a-whaped
In winter, and distroyed had hir brood,

In his despyt, hem thoughte hit did hem
   good
To singe of him, and in hir song despyse
The foule cherl that, for his covetyse, 124
Had hem betrayed with his sophistrye.
This was hir song—' the fouler we defye!'
Somme songen [layes] on the braunches
   clere
Of love and [May], that joye hit was to
   here,
In worship and in preysing of hir make,
And of the newe blisful someres sake, 130

That songen, ' blissed be seynt Valentyn !
[For] at his day I chees yow to be myn,
With-oute repenting, myn herte swete !'
And therwith-al hir bekes gonnen mete.
†They dide honour and humble obei-
   saunces,      135
And after diden other observaunces

Right [plesing] un-to love and to nature ;
So ech of hem [doth wel] to creature.
This song to herkne I dide al myn
   entente,      139
For-why I mette I wiste what they mente.

In his despyt, hem thoughte hit did hem
   good      134
To singe of him, and in hir song despyse
The foule cherl that, for his covetyse,
Had hem betrayed with his sophistrye.
This was hir song—' the fouler we defye,
And al his craft !' And somme songen
   clere      139
Layes of love, that joye hit was to here,

In worshipinge and preisinge of hir make.
And, for the newe blisful somers sake,
Upon the braunches ful of blosmes softe,
In hir delyt, they turned hem ful ofte, 144
And songen, ' blessed be seynt Valentyn !
For on his day I chees yow to be myn,
Withouten repenting, myn herte swete !'
And therwith-al hir bekes gonnen mete,
Yelding honour and humble obeisaunces

To love, and diden hir other obser-
   vaunces      150
That longeth unto love and to nature ;
Construeth that as yow list, I do no cure.
   And tho that hadde doon unkinde-
   nesse—
As dooth the tydif, for new-fangelnesse—
Besoghto mercy of hir trespassinge,  155
And humblely songen hir repentinge,
And sworen on the blosmes to be trewe,
So that hir makes wolde upon hem rewe,
And at the laste maden hir acord.
Al founde they Daunger for a tyme a
   lord,      160
Yet Pitee, through his stronge gentil
   might,
Forgaf, and made Mercy passen Right,
Through innocence and ruled curtesye.
But I ne clepe nat innocence folye,
Ne fals pitee, for ' vertu is the mene,' 165
As Etik saith, in swich manere I mene.
And thus thise foules, voide of al malyce,
Acordeden to love, and laften vyce
Of hate, and songen alle of oon acord,
' Welcome, somer, our governour and
   lord !'      170
   And Zephirus and Flora gentilly
Yaf to the floures, softe and tenderly,
Hir swote breth, and made hem for to
   sprede,
As god and goddesse of the floury mede ;

N

In which me thoghte I mighte, day by
    day,        175
Dwellen alwey, the joly month of May,
Withouten sleep, withouten mete or
    drinke.
A-doun ful softely I gan to sinke;
And, leninge on myn elbowe and my
    syde,        179
The longe day I shoop me for to abyde
For nothing elles, and I shal nat lye,
But for to loke upon the dayesye,
That wel by reson men hit calle may
The ' dayesye ' or elles the ' ye of day,'
The emperice and flour of floures alle. 185
I pray to god that faire mot she falle,
And alle that loven floures, for hir sake!

[Cf. p. 351, col. 1, ll. 71–80.]

But natheles, ne wene nat that I make
In preysing of the flour agayn the leef,
No more than of the corn agayn the
    sheef :        190
For, as to me, nis lever noon ne lother;
I nam with-holden yit with never nother.
Ne I not who serveth leef, ne who the
    flour ;
Wel brouken they hir service or labour;
For this thing is al of another tonne, 195
Of olde story, er swich thing was be-
    gonne.

[Cf. p. 352, col. 1, ll. 93–106.]

  Whan that the sonne out of the south
    gan weste,
And that this flour gan close and goon to
    reste
For derknesse of the night, the which she
    dredde,
Hoom to myn hous ful swiftly I me
    spedde        200
To goon to reste, and erly for to ryse,
To seen this flour to sprede, as I devyse.
And, in a litel herber that I have,
That benched was on turves fresshe y-
    grave,        204
I bad men sholde me my couche make;
For deyntee of the newe someres sake,
I bad hem strawen floures on my bed.
Whan I was leyd, and had myn eyen
    hed,

Til at the laste a larke song above :   141
' I see,' quod she, 'the mighty god of love!
Lo ! yond he cometh, I see his winges
    sprede!'
Tho gan I loken endelong the mede,

I fel on slepe in-with an houre or two;
Me mette how I lay in the medew tho, 210
To seen this flour that I so love and drede.

And from a-fer com walking in the mede

And saw him come, and in his hond a
    quene, 145
Clothed in ryal abite al of grene.
A fret of gold she hadde next hir heer,
And up-on that a whyt coroun she beer
With many floures, and I shal nat lye ;
For al the world, right as the dayesye 150
I-coroned is with whyte leves lyte,
Swich were the floures of hir coroun
    whyte.
For of o perle fyn and oriental
Hir whyte coroun was y-maked al ;
For which the whyte coroun, above the
    grene, 155
Made hir lyk a daysie for to sene,
Considered eek the fret of gold above.
    Y-clothed was this mighty god of love
Of silk, y-brouded ful of grene greves ;
A garlond on his heed of rose-leves 160
Steked al with lilie floures newe ;
But of his face I can nat seyn the hewe.


For sekirly his face shoon so brighte,

That with the gleem a-stoned was the
    sighte ; 164
A furlong-wey I mighte him nat beholde.
But at the laste in hande I saw him
    holde
Two fyry dartes, as the gledes rede ;
And aungellich his wenges gan he sprede.


And al be that men seyn that blind is he,
Al-gate me thoughte he mighte wel y-see ;
For sternely on me he gan biholde, 171
So that his loking doth myn herte colde.
And by the hande he held the noble
    quene,
Corouned with whyte, and clothed al in
    grene,
So womanly, so benigne, and so meke, 175
That in this world, thogh that men wolde
    seke,
Half hir beautee shulde men nat finde
In creature that formed is by kinde,
Hir name was Alceste the debonayre ;
I prey to god that ever falle she fayre ! 180
For ne hadde confort been of hir pre-
    sence,
I had be deed, withouten any defence,

The god of love, and in his hande a
    quene ;
And she was clad in real habit grene.
A fret of gold she hadde next hir heer, 215
And upon that a whyt coroun she beer
With florouns smale, and I shal nat lye ;
For al the world, ryght as a dayesye
Y-corouned is with whyte leves lyte, 219
So were the florouns of hir coroun
    whyte.
For of o perle fyne, oriental,
Hir whyte coroun was y-maked al ;
For which the whyte coroun, above the
    grene,
Made hir lyk a daysie for to sene,
Considered eek hir fret of gold above. 225
    Y-clothed was this mighty god of love
In silke, enbrouded ful of grene greves,
In-with a fret of rede rose-leves,
The fresshest sin the world was first
    bigonne. 229
His gilte heer was corouned with a sonne,
In-stede of gold, for hevinesse and wighte ;
Therwith me thoughte his face shoon so
    brighte

That wel unnethes mighte I him beholde ;
And in his hande me thoughte I saugh
    him holde
Two fyry dartes, as the gledes rede ; 235
And aungellyke his winges saugh I
    sprede.

And al be that men seyn that blind is he,
Al-gate me thoughte that he mighte see ;
For sternely on me he gan biholde,
So that his loking doth myn herte colde.
And by the hande he held this noble
    quene, 241
Corouned with whyte, and clothed al in
    grene,
So womanly, so benigne, and so meke,
That in this world, thogh that men wolde
    seke,
Half hir beautee shulde men nat finde 245
In creature that formed is by kinde.
    [Cf. p. 357, col. 2, ll. 276-9.]

For drede of Loves wordes and his chere,
As, whan tyme is, her-after ye shal here.
Byhind this god of love, up-on this grene,
I saw cominge of ladyës nyntene　　186
In ryal abite, a ful esy pas,
And after hem com of wemen swich a tras
That, sin that god Adam made of erthe,
The thredde part of wemen, ne the ferthe,
Ne wende I nat by possibilitee　　191
Hadden ever in this world-y-be;
And trewe of love thise wemen were
　　echoon.
　　Now whether was that a wonder thing
　　　　or noon,
That, right anoon as that they gonne
　　espye　　　　　　　　195
This flour, which that I clepe the dayesye,
Ful sodeinly they stinten alle at-ones,
And kneled adoun, as it were for the
　　nones.
And after that they wenten in compas,
Daunsinge aboute this flour an esy pas, 200
And songen, as it were in carole-wyse,
This balade, which that I shal yow devyse.

[Cf. p. 357, col. 2, ll. 280-296.]

And therfor may I seyn, as thinketh me,
This song, in preysing of this lady fre.

### Balade.

Hyd, Absolon, thy gilte tresses clere;
Ester, ley thou thy meknesse al a-doun;
Hyd, Jonathas, al thy frendly manere; 205
Penalopee, and Marcia Catoun,
Mak of your wyfhod no comparisoun;
Hyde ye your beautes, Isoude and Eleyne,
Alceste is here, that al that may desteyne.

Thy faire bodye, lat hit nat appere,　210
Lavyne; and thou, Lucresse of Rome
　　toun,
And Polixene, that boghte love so dere,
Eek Cleopatre, with al thy passioun,
Hyde ye your trouthe in love and your
　　renoun;
And thou, Tisbe, that hast for love swich
　　peyne:　　　　　　　215
Alceste is here, that al that may desteyne.

Herro, Dido, Laudomia, alle in-fere,
Eek Phyllis, hanging for thy Demophoun,
And Canace, espyed by thy chere,
Ysiphile, betrayed with Jasoun,　　220

### Balade.

Hyd, Absolon, thy gilte tresses clere; 249
Ester, ley thou thy meknesse al a-doun;
Hyd, Jonathas, al thy frendly manere;
Penalopee, and Marcia Catoun,
Mak of your wyfhod no comparisoun;
Hyde ye your beautes, Isoude and Eleyne,
My lady cometh, that al this may dis-
　　teyne.
　　　　　　　　　　255

Thy faire body, lat hit nat appere,
Lavyne; and thou, Lucresse of Rome
　　toun,
And Polixene, that boghten love so dere,
And Cleopatre, with al thy passioun,
Hyde ye your trouthe of love and your
　　renoun;　　　　　　260
And thou, Tisbe, that hast of love swich
　　peyne;
My lady cometh, that al this may dis-
　　teyne.

Herro, Dido, Laudomia, alle y-fere,
And Phyllis, hanging for thy Demophoun,
And Canace, espyed by thy chere, 265
Ysiphile, betraysed with Jasoun,

Mak of your trouthe in love no bost ne
  soun ;
Nor Ypermistre or Adriane, ne pleyne ;
Alceste is here, that al that may desteyne.


Whan that this balade al y-songen was,



[Cf. pp. 355-6, col. 1, ll. 179-198.]

Maketh of your trouthe neyther boost ne
  soun ;
Nor Ypermistre or Adriane, ye tweyne ;
My lady cometh, that al this may disteyne.

  This balade may ful wel y-songen be, 270
As I have seyd erst, by my lady free ;
For certeynly, alle these mow nat suffyse
To apperen with my lady in no wyse.
For as the sonne wol the fyr disteyne,
So passeth al my lady sovereyne,      275
That is so good, so fair, so debonaire ;
I prey to god that ever falle hir faire !
For, nadde comfort been of hir presence,
I had ben deed, withouten any defence,
For drede of Loves wordes and his chere;
As, when tyme is, her-after ye shal here.
  Behind this god of love, upon the grene,
I saugh cominge of ladyës nyntene
In real habit, a ful esy paas ;
And after hem com of women swich a
  traas,                              285
That, sin that god Adam had maad of
  erthe,
The thridde part of mankynd, or the
  ferthe,
Ne wende I nat by possibilitee,
Had ever in this wyde worlde y-be ;
And trewe of love thise women were
  echoon.                             290
  Now whether was that a wonder thing
  or noon,
That, right anoon as that they gonne
  espye
This flour, which that I clepe the dayesye,
Ful sodeinly they stinten alle at ones,
And kneled doun, as it were for the
  nones,                              295
And songen with o vois, ' Hele and honour
To trouthe of womanhede, and to this flour
That berth our alder prys in figuringe !
Hir whyte coroun berth the witnessinge !'
  And with that word, a-compas en-
  viroun,                             300
They setten hem ful softely adoun.
First sat the god of love, and sith his
  quene
With the whyte coroun, clad in grene ;
And sithen al the remenant by and by,
As they were of estaat, ful curteisly ; 305

Upon the softe and swote grene gras, 225
They setten hem ful softely adoun,
By ordre alle in compas, alle enveroun.
First sat the god of love, and than this
  quene
With the whyte coroun, clad in grene ;
And sithen al the remenant by and by,
As they were of degree, ful curteisly ; 231

Ne nat a word was spoken in the place
The mountance of a furlong-wey of space.
  I, lening faste by under a bente,
Abood, to knowen what this peple mente,
As stille as any stoon ; til at the laste,   236
The god of love on me his eye caste,
And seyde, ' who resteth ther ? ' and I
      answerde
Un-to his axing, whan that I him herde,
And seyde, ' sir, hit am I ' ; and cam him
      neer,                                  240
And salued him.   Quod he, ' what dostow
      heer
In my presence, and that so boldely ?
For it were better worthy, trewely,
A werm to comen in my sight than
      thou.'
' And why, sir,' quod I, ' and hit lyke
      yow ? '                                245
' For thou,' quod he, ' art ther-to nothing
      able.
My servaunts been alle wyse and honour-
      able.
Thou art my mortal fo, and me warreyest,

And of myne olde servaunts thou mis-
      seyest,
And hinderest hem, with thy translacioun,
And lettest folk to han devocioun       251
To serven me, and haldest hit folye
To troste on me.   Thou mayst hit nat
      denye ;
For in pleyn text, hit nedeth nat to
      glose,
Thou hast translated the Romauns of the
      Rose,                                  255
That is an heresye ageyns my lawe,
And makest wyse folk fro me withdrawe.
And thinkest in thy wit, that is ful cool,
That he nis but a verray propre fool
That loveth paramours, to harde and
      hote.                                   260
Wel wot I ther-by thou beginnest dote
As olde foles, whan hir spirit fayleth ;
Than blame they folk, and wite nat what
      hem ayleth.
Hast thou nat mad in English eek the
      book
How that Crisseyde Troilus forsook,    265
In shewinge how that wemen han don
      mis ?

Ne nat a word was spoken in the place
The mountance of a furlong-wey of space.
  I kneling by this flour, in good entente
Abood, to knowen what this peple mente,
As stille as any stoon ; til at the laste, 310
This god of love on me his eyen caste,
And seyde, ' who kneleth ther ? ' and I
      answerde
Unto his asking, whan that I hit herde,
And seyde, ' sir, hit am I ' ; and com him
      neer,
And salued him.   Quod he, ' what dostow
      heer                                   315
So nigh myn owne flour, so boldely ?
For it were better worthy, trewely,
A worm to neghen neer my flour than
      thou.'
'And why, sir,' quod I, ' and hit lyke
      yow ? '
' For thou,' quod he, ' art ther-to nothing
      able.                                  320
Hit is my relik, digne and delytable,

And thou my fo, and al my folk wer-
      reyest,
And of myn olde servaunts thou mis-
      seyest,
And hindrest hem, with thy translacioun,
And lettest folk from hir devocioun    325
To serve me, and holdest hit folye
To serve Love.   Thou mayst hit nat denye;

For in pleyn text, with-outen nede of
      glose,
Thou hast translated the Romaunce of
      the Rose,
That is an heresye ageyns my lawe,    330
And makest wyse folk fro me withdrawe.

And of Criseyde thou hast seyd as thee
      liste,
That maketh men to wommen lasse triste,
That ben as trewe as ever was any steel.

But natheles, answere me now to this,
Why noldest thou as wel han seyd good-
  nesse
Of wemen, as thou hast seyd wikkednesse?
Was ther no good matere in thy minde,
Ne in alle thy bokes coudest thou nat
  finde                                    271
Sum story of wemen that were goode and
  trewe?
Yis! god wot, sixty bokes olde and newe
Hast thou thy-self, alle fulle of stories
  grete,
That bothe Romains and eek Grekes
  trete                                    275
Of sundry wemen, which lyf that they
  ladde,
And ever an hundred gode ageyn oon
  badde.
This knoweth god, and alle clerkes eke,
That usen swiche materes for to seke. 279
What seith Valerie, Titus, or Claudian?
What seith Jerome ageyns Jovinian?
How clene maydens, and how trewe
  wyves,                                   282
How stedfast widwes during al hir lyves,
Telleth Jerome; and that nat of a fewe,
But, I dar seyn, an hundred on a rewe;
That hit is pitee for to rede, and routhe,
The wo that they enduren for hir trouthe.
For to hir love were they so trewe,
That, rather than they wolde take a
  newe,
They chosen to be dede in sundry wyse,
And deyden, as the story wol devyse; 291
And some were brend, and some were cut
  the hals,
And some dreynt, for they wolden nat be
  fals.
For alle keped they hir maydenhed,
Or elles wedlok, or hir widwehed.       295
And this thing was nat kept for holi-
  nesse,
But al for verray vertu and clennesse,
And for men shulde sette on hem no lak;
And yit they weren hethen, al the pak,
That were so sore adrad of alle shame. 300
These olde wemen kepte so hir name,
That in this world I trow men shal nat
  finde
A man that coude be so trewe and kinde,
As was the leste woman in that tyde.

Of thyn answere avyse thee right weel.

What seith also the epistels of Ovyde 305
Of trewe wyves, and of hir labour?
What Vincent, in his Storial Mirour?
Eek al the world of autours maystow
    here,
Cristen and hethen, trete of swich matere;
It nedeth nat alday thus for t'endyte. 310
But yit I sey, what eyleth thee to wryte
The draf of stories, and forgo the corn?
By seint Venus, of whom that I was born,
Although [that] thou reneyed hast my
    lay,
As othere olde foles many a day,   315

Thou shalt repente hit, that hit shal be
    sene!'
  Than spak Alceste, the worthieste
    quene,
And seyde, 'god, right of your curtesye,
Ye moten herknen if he can replye
Ageyns these points that ye han to him
    meved;     320
A god ne sholde nat be thus agreved,
But of his deitee he shal be stable,
And therto rightful and eek merciable.
He shal nat rightfully his yre wreke 324
Or he have herd the tother party speke.
Al ne is nat gospel that is to yow pleyned;
The god of love herth many a tale
    y-feyned.
For in your court is many a losengeour,
And many a queynte totelere accusour,
That tabouren in your eres many a thing
For hate, or for jelous imagining,  331
And for to han with yow som daliaunce.
Envye (I prey to god yeve hir mischaunce!)

Is lavender in the grete court alway.
For she ne parteth, neither night ne day,
Out of the hous of Cesar; thus seith
    Dante;     336
Who-so that goth, alwey she moot [nat]
    wante.
This man to yow may wrongly been
    accused,
Ther as by right him oghte been excused.
Or elles, sir, for that this man is nyce, 340
He may translate a thing in no malyce,
But for he useth bokes for to make,

For, thogh that thou reneyed hast my
    lay,     336
As other wrecches han doon many a day,
By seynt Venus, that my moder is,
If that thou live, thou shalt repenten
    this
So cruelly, that hit shal wel be sene!' 340

  Tho spak this lady, clothed al in grene,

And seyde, 'god, right of your curtesye,
Ye moten herknen if he can replye
Agayns al this that ye han to him
    meved;
A god ne sholde nat be thus agreved, 345
But of his deitee he shal be stable,
And therto gracious and merciable.
And if ye nere a god, that knowen al,
Than mighte hit be, as I yow tellen shal;
This man to you may falsly been ac-
    cused,     350
Ther as by right him oghte been excused.
For in your court is many a losengeour,
And many a queynte totelere accusour,
That tabouren in your eres many a soun,
Right after hir imaginacioun,   355
To have your daliance, and for envye;
These been the causes, and I shall nat
    lye.
Envye is lavender of the court alway;
For she ne parteth, neither night ne day,
Out of the hous of Cesar; thus seith
    Dante;     360
Who-so that goth, algate she wol nat
    wante.
    [Cf. ll. 350-1 above.]

And eek, paraunter, for this man is nyce,
He mighte doon hit, gessing no malyce,
But for he useth thinges for to make;

And takth non heed of what matere he take;

Therfor he wroot the Rose and eek Crisseyde

Of innocence, and niste what he seyde;

Or him was boden make thilke tweye 346

Of som persone, and durste hit nat with-seye;

For he hath writen many a book er this.

He ne hath nat doon so grevously amis

To translaten that olde clerkes wryten, 350

As thogh that he of malice wolde endyten

Despyt of love, and hadde him-self y-wroght.

This shulde a rightwys lord han in his thoght,

And nat be lyk tiraunts of Lumbardye,

That usen wilfulhed and tirannye, 355

For he that king or lord is naturel,

Him oghte nat be tiraunt ne cruel,

As is a fermour, to doon the harm he can.

He moste thinke hit is his lige man,

And that him oweth, of verray duetee, 360

Shewen his peple pleyn benignitee,

And wel to here hir excusaciouns,

And hir compleyntes and peticiouns,

In duewe tyme, whan they shal hit profre.

This is the sentence of the philosophre:

A king to kepe his liges in justyce; 366

With-outen doute, that is his offyce.

And therto is a king ful depe y-sworn,

Ful many an hundred winter heer-biforn;

And for to kepe his lordes hir degree, 370

As hit is right and skilful that they be

Enhaunced and honoured, and most dere—

For they ben half-goddes in this world here—

This shal he doon, bothe to pore [and] riche,

Al be that her estat be nat a-liche, 375

And han of pore folk compassioun.

For lo, the gentil kind of the lioun!

For whan a flye offendeth him or byteth,

He with his tayl awey the flye smyteth

Al esily; for, of his genterye, 380

Him deyneth nat to wreke him on a flye,

As doth a curre or elles another beste.

In noble corage oghte been areste,

And weyen every thing by equitee,

And ever han reward to his owen degree.

---

Him rekketh noght of what matere he take; 365

Or him was boden maken thilke tweye

Of som persone, and durste hit nat with-seye;

Or him repenteth utterly of this.

He ne hath nat doon so grevously amis

To translaten that olde clerkes wryten, 370

As thogh that he of malice wolde endyten

Despyt of love, and had him-self hit wroght.

This shulde a rightwys lord have in his thoght,

And nat be lyk tiraunts of Lumbardye,

Than han no reward but at tirannye. 375

For he that king or lord is naturel,

Him oghte nat be tiraunt ne cruel,

As is a fermour, to doon the harm he can.

He moste thinke hit is his lige man,

And is his tresour, and his gold in cofre.

This is the sentence of the philosophre: 381

A king to kepe his liges in justyce;

With-outen doute, that is his offyce.

Al wol he kepe his lordes hir degree,

As hit is right and skilful that they be 385

Enhaunced and honoured, and most dere—

For they ben half-goddes in this world here—

Yit mot he doon bothe right, to pore and riche,

Al be that hir estat be nat y-liche,

And han of pore folk compassioun. 390

For lo, the gentil kynd of the leoun!

For whan a flye offendeth him or byteth,

He with his tayl awey the flye smyteth

Al esily; for, of his genterye, 394

Him deyneth nat to wreke him on a flye,

As doth a curre or elles another beste.

In noble corage oghte been areste,

And weyen every thing by equitee,

And ever han reward to his owen degree.

For, sir, hit is no maystrie for a lord  386
To dampne a man with-oute answere or word;
And, for a lord, that is ful foul to use.
And if so be he may him nat excuse,
[But] axeth mercy with a sorweful herte,
And profreth him, right in his bare sherte,  391
To been right at your owne jugement,
Than oghte a god, by short avysement,
Considre his owne honour and his trespas.
For sith no cause of deeth lyth in this cas,  395
Yow oghte been the lighter merciable;
Leteth your yre, and beth somwhat tretable!
The man hath served yow of his conning,
And forthered your lawe with his making.
Whyl he was yong, he kepte your estat;
I not wher he be now a renegat.  401
But wel I wot, with that he can endyte,
He hath maked lewed folk delyte
To serve you, in preysing of your name.
He made the book that hight the Hous of Fame,  405
And eek the Deeth of Blaunche the Duchesse,
And the Parlement of Foules, as I gesse,
And al the love of Palamon and Arcyte
Of Thebes, thogh the story is knowen lyte;
And many an ympne for your halydayes,
That highten Balades, Roundels, Virelayes;  411
And for to speke of other besinesse,
He hath in prose translated Boëce;
And of the Wreched Engendring of Mankinde,
As man may in pope Innocent y-finde;  415
And mad the Lyf also of seynt Cecyle;
He made also, goon sithen a greet whyl,
Origenes upon the Maudeleyne;
Him oghte now to have the lesse peyne;
He hath mad many a lay and many a thing.  420
　　Now as ye been a god, and eek a king,
I, your Alceste, whylom quene of Trace,
I axe yow this man, right of your grace,
That ye him never hurte in al his lyve;
And he shal sweren yow, and that as blyve,  425
He shal no more agilten in this wyse;

For, sir, hit is no maystrie for a lord  400
To dampne a man with-oute answere of word;
And, for a lord, that is ful foul to use.
And if so be he may him nat excuse,
But asketh mercy with a dredful herte,
And profreth him, right in his bare sherte,  405
To been right at your owne jugement,
Than oghte a god, by short avysement,
Considre his owne honour and his trespas.
For sith no cause of deeth lyth in this cas,
Yow oghte been the lighter merciable; 410
Leteth your yre, and beth somwhat tretable!
The man hath served yow of his conning,
And forthred wel your lawe in his making.

Al be hit that he can nat wel endyte,
Yet hath he maked lewed folk delyte 415
To serve you, in preysing of your name.
He made the book that hight the Hous of Fame,
And eek the Deeth of Blaunche the Duchesse,
And the Parlement of Foules, as I gesse,
And al the love of Palamon and Arcyte 420
Of Thebes, thogh the story is knowen lyte;
And many an ympne for your halydayes,
That highten Balades, Roundels, Virelayes;
And, for to speke of other holynesse,
He hath in prose translated Boëce,  425

And mad the Lyf also of seynt Cecyle;
He made also, goon sithen a greet whyl,
Origenes upon the Maudeleyne;
Him oghte now to have the lesse peyne;
He hath mad many a lay and many a thing.  430
　　'Now as ye been a god, and eek a king,
I, your Alceste, whylom quene of Trace,
I aske yow this man, right of your grace,
That ye him never hurte in al his lyve;
And he shal sweren yow, and that as blyve,  435
He shal no more agilten in this wyse;

But he shal maken, as ye wil devyse,
Of wemen trewe in lovinge al hir lyve,
Wher-so ye wil, of maiden or of wyve,
And forthren yow, as muche as he mis-
    seyde    430
Or in the Rose or elles in Criseyde.'
    The god of love answerde hir thus
    anoon,
' Madame,' quod he, ' hit is so long agoon
That I yow knew so charitable and trewe,
That never yit, sith that the world was
    newe,    435
To me ne fond I better noon than ye.
That, if that I wol save my degree,
I may ne wol nat warne your requeste ;
Al lyth in yow, doth with him what yow
    leste,    439
And al foryeve, with-outen lenger space ;
For who-so yeveth a yift, or doth a grace,
Do hit by tyme, his thank is wel the
    more ;
And demeth ye what he shal do therfore.
Go thanke now my lady heer,' quod he.
    I roos, and doun I sette me on my
    knee,    445
And seyde thus : ' Madame, the god above
Foryelde yow, that ye the god of love
Han maked me his wrathe to foryive ;
And yeve me grace so long for to live,
That I may knowe soothly what ye be, 450
That han me holpen, and put in swich
    degree.
But trewely I wende, as in this cas,
Naught have agilt, ne doon to love
    trespas.
Forwhy a trewe man, with-outen drede,
Hath nat to parten with a theves dede ;
Ne a trewe lover oghte me nat blame, 456
Thogh that I speke a fals lover som shame.
They oghte rather with me for to holde,
For that I of Creseyde wroot or tolde,
Or of the Rose ; what-so myn auctour
    mente,    460
Algate, god wot, hit was myn entente
To forthren trouthe in love and hit
    cheryce ;
And to be war fro falsnesse and fro vyce
By swich ensample ; this was my men-
    inge.'
    And she answerde, ' lat be thyn argu-
    inge ;    465

But he shal maken, as ye wil devyse,
Of wommen trewe in lovinge al hir lyve,
Wher-so ye wil, of maiden or of wyve,
And forthren yow, as muche as he mis-
    seyde    440
Or in the Rose or elles in Creseyde.'
    The god of love answerde hir thus
    anoon,
' Madame,' quod he, ' hit is so long agoon
That I yow knew so charitable and trewe,
That never yit, sith that the world was
    newe,    445
To me ne fond I better noon than ye.
If that I wolde save my degree,
I may ne wol nat werne your requeste ;
Al lyth in yow, doth with him as yow
    leste.
I al foryeve, with-outen lenger space ; 450
For who-so yeveth a yift, or doth a grace,
Do hit by tyme, his thank is wel the
    more ;
And demeth ye what he shal do therfore.
Go thanke now my lady heer,' quod he.
    I roos, and doun I sette me on my
    knee,    455
And seyde thus : ' Madame, the god above
Foryelde yow, that ye the god of love
Han maked me his wrathe to foryive ;
And yeve me grace so long for to live,
That I may knowe soothly what ye be, 460
That han me holpe and put in this
    degree.
But trewely I wende, as in this cas,
Naught have agilt, ne doon to love
    trespas.
Forwhy a trewe man, with-outen drede,
Hath nat to parten with a theves dede ;
Ne a trewe lover oghte me nat blame,
Thogh that I speke a fals lover som shame.
They oghte rather with me for to holde,
For that I of Creseyde wroot or tolde,
Or of the Rose ; what-so myn auctour
    mente,    470
Algate, god wot, hit was myn entente
To forthren trouthe in love and hit
    cheryce ;
And to be war fro falsnesse and fro vyce
By swich ensample ; this was my men-
    inge.'
    And she answerde, ' lat be thyn argu-
    inge ;    475

For Love ne wol nat countrepleted be
In right ne wrong ; and lerne this at me !
Thou hast thy grace, and hold thee right
 ther-to.
Now wol I seyn what penance thou shalt
 do
For thy trespas, and understond hit here :
Thou shalt, whyl that thou livest, yeer by
 yere,   471
The moste party of thy lyve spende
In making of a glorious Legende
Of Gode Wemen, maidenes and wyves, 474
That were trewe in lovinge al hir lyves ;
And telle of false men that hem bitrayen,
That al hir lyf ne doon nat but assayen
How many wemen they may doon a
 shame ;
For in your world that is now holden
 game.
And thogh thee lesteth nat a lover be, 480
Spek wel of love ; this penance yeve
 I thee.
And to the god of love I shal so preye,
That he shal charge his servants, by any
 weye,
To forthren thee, and wel thy labour
 quyte ;
Go now thy wey, thy penance is but lyte.'

The god of love gan smyle, and than he
 seyde,   486
' Wostow,' quod he, ' wher this be wyf or
 mayde,
Or quene, or countesse, or of what degree,
That hath so litel penance yeven thee,
That hast deserved sorer for to smerte ?
But pitee renneth sone in gentil herte ;
That mayst thou seen, she kytheth what
 she is.'
And I answerde, ' nay, sir, so have I blis,
No more but that I see wel she is good.'
 ' That is a trewe tale, by myn hood,' 495
Quod Love, ' and that thou knowest wel,
 pardee,
If hit be so that thou avyse thee.
Hastow nat in a book, lyth in thy cheste,
The gret goodnesse of the quene Alceste,
That turned was into a dayesye :   500
She that for hir husbonde chees to dye,

For Love ne wol nat countrepleted be
In right ne wrong ; and lerne that of me !
Thou hast thy grace, and hold thee right
 ther-to.
Now wol I seyn what penance thou shalt
 do
For thy trespas, and understond hit here:
Thou shalt, whyl that thou livest, yeer
 by yere,   481
The moste party of thy tyme spende
In making of a glorious Legende
Of Gode Wommen, maidenes and wyves,
That weren trewe in lovinge al hir lyves;
And telle of false men that hem bitrayen,
That al hir lyf ne doon nat but assayen
How many wommen they may doon a
 shame ;
For in your world that is now holde a
 game.
And thogh thee lyke nat a lover be,   490
Spek wel of love ; this penance yive I
 thee.
And to the god of love I shal so preye,
That he shal charge his servants, by any
 weye,
To forthren thee, and wel thy labour
 quyte ;
Go now thy wey, this penance is but lyte.
And whan this book is maad, yive hit the
 quene   496
On my behalfe, at Eltham, or at Shene.'
 The god of love gan smyle, and than he
 seyde,
' Wostow,' quod he, ' wher this be wyf or
. mayde,
Or quene, or countesse, or of what degree,
That hath so litel penance yiven thee, 501
That hast deserved sorer for to smerte ?
But pitee renneth sone in gentil herte ;
That maystow seen, she kytheth what
 she is.'   504
And I answerde, ' nay, sir, so have I blis,
No more but that I see wel she is good.'
 ' That is a trewe tale, by myn hood,'
Quod Love, ' and that thou knowest wel,
 pardee,
If hit be so that thou avyse thee.   509
Hastow nat in a book, lyth in thy cheste,
The grete goodnesse of the quene Alceste,
That turned was into a dayesye :
She that for hir husbonde chees to dye,

And eek to goon to helle, rather than he,
And Ercules rescued hir, pardee,
And broghte hir out of helle agayn to
   blis?' 504
   And I answerde ageyn, and seyde, 'yis,
Now knowe I hir! And is this good
   Alceste,
The dayesye, and myn owne hertes reste?
Now fele I wel the goodnesse of this wyf,
That bothe after hir deeth, and in hir lyf,
Hir grete bountee doubleth hir renoun!
Wel hath she quit me myn affeccioun
That I have to hir flour, the dayesye!
No wonder is thogh Jove hir stellifye,
As telleth Agaton, for hir goodnesse!
Hir whyte coroun berth of hit witnesse;
For also many vertues hadde she, 516
As smale floures in hir coroun be.
In remembraunce of hir and in honour,
Cibella made the dayesy and the flour 519
Y-coroned al with whyt, as men may see;
And Mars yaf to hir coroun reed, pardee,
In stede of rubies, set among the whyte.'
   Therwith this quene wex reed for shame
   a lyte, 523
Whan she was preysed so in hir presence.
Than seyde Love, 'a ful gret negligence
Was hit to thee, to write unstedfastnesse
Of women, sith thou knowest hir good-
   nesse
By preef, and eek by stories heer-biforn;
Let be the chaf, and wryt wel of the corn.
Why noldest thou han writen of Alceste,
And leten Criseide been a-slepe and
   reste? 531
For of Alceste shulde thy wryting be,
Sin that thou wost that kalender is she
Of goodnesse, for she taughte of fyn
   lovinge,
And namely of wyfhood the livinge, 535
And alle the boundes that she oghte kepe;
Thy litel wit was thilke tyme a-slepe.
But now I charge thee, upon thy lyf,
That in thy Legend thou make of this
   wyf,
Whan thou hast othere smale maad be-
   fore; 540
And fare now wel, I charge thee no more.

And eek to goon to helle, rather than he,
And Ercules rescowed hir, pardee, 515
And broghte hir out of helle agayn to
   blis?'
   And I answerde ageyn, and seyde, 'yis,
Now knowe I hir! And is this good
   Alceste, 518
The dayesye, and myn owne hertes reste?
Now fele I wel the goodnesse of this wyf,
That bothe after hir deeth, and in hir lyf,
Hir grete bountee doubleth hir renoun!
Wel hath she quit me myn affeccioun
That I have to hir flour, the dayesye!
No wonder is thogh Jove hir stellifye, 525
As telleth Agaton, for hir goodnesse!
Hir whyte coroun berth of hit witnesse;
For also many vertues hadde she,
As smale floures in hir coroun be. 529
In remembraunce of hir and in honour,
Cibella made the dayesy and the flour
Y-coroned al with whyt, as men may see;
And Mars yaf to hir coroun reed, pardee,
In stede of rubies, set among the whyte.'
   Therwith this quene wex reed for shame
   a lyte, 535
Whan she was preysed so in hir presence.
Than seyde Love, 'a ful gret negligence
Was hit to thee, that ilke tyme thou
   made 538
"Hyd, Absolon, thy tresses," in balade;
That thou forgete hir in thy song to sette,
Sin that thou art so gretly in hir dette,

And wost so wel, that kalender is she
To any woman that wol lover be
For she taughte al the craft of fyn
   lovinge,
And namely of wyfhood the livinge, 545
And alle the boundes that she oghte kepe;
Thy litel wit was thilke tyme a-slepe.
But now I charge thee, upon thy lyf,
That in thy Legend thou make of this
   wyf,
Whan thou hast other smale y-maad be-
   fore; 550
And fare now wel, I charge thee no more.
   But er I go, thus muche I wol thee
   telle,
Ne shal no trewe lover come in helle.

Thise other ladies sittinge here arowe
Ben in thy balade, if thou canst hem
    knowe, 555
And in thy bokes alle thou shalt hem
    finde;
Have hem now in thy Legend alle in
    minde,
I mene of hem that been in thy knowinge.
For heer ben twenty thousand mo sittinge
Than thou knowest, that been good
    wommen alle 560
And trewe of love, for aught that may
    befalle;
Make the metres of hem as the leste.
I mot gon hoom, the sonne draweth weste,
To Paradys, with al this companye;
And serve alwey the fresshe dayesye. 565
   At Cleopatre I wol that thou beginne;
And so forth; and my love so shalt thou
    winne.

For lat see now what man that lover be,
Wol doon so strong a peyne for love as
    she.
I wot wel that thou mayst nat al hit
    ryme, 570
That swiche lovers diden in hir tyme;
It were to long to reden and to here;
Suffyceth me, thou make in this manere,
That thou reherce of al hir lyf the grete,
After thise olde auctours listen to trete.
For who-so shal so many a storie telle, 576
Sey shortly, or he shal to longe dwelle.'

*At Cleopatre I wol that thou beginne;*
*And so forth; and my love so shalt thou*
   *winne.'* 543

And with that word of sleep I gan a-awake,
And right thus on my Legend gan I make.

And with that word my bokes gan I take.
And right thus on my Legend gan I make.

Explicit prohemium.

# I. THE LEGEND OF CLEOPATRA.

*Incipit Legenda Cleopatrie, Martiris,*
*Egipti regine.*

AFTER the deeth of Tholomee the king, 580
That al Egipte hadde in his governing,
Regned his quene Cleopataras;
Til on a tyme befel ther swiche a cas,
That out of Rome was sent a senatour,
For to conqueren regnes and honour 585
Unto the toun of Rome, as was usaunce,
To have the world unto her obeisaunce;

And, sooth to seye, Antonius was his
    name.
So fil hit, as Fortune him oghte a
    shame (10)
Whan he was fallen in prosperitee, 590
Rebel unto the toun of Rome is he.
And over al this, the suster of Cesar,
He lafte hir falsly, er that she was war,
And wolde algates han another wyf;
For whiche he took with Rome and Cesar
    stryf. 595

Natheles, for-sooth, this ilke senatour
Was a ful worthy gentil werreyour,
And of his deeth hit was ful greet damage.
But love had broght this man in swiche
   a rage, (20)
And him so narwe bounden in his las,
Al for the love of Cleopataras, 601
That al the world he sette at no value.
Him thoughte, nas to him no thing so
   due
As Cleopatras for to love and serve ; 604
Him roghte nat in armes for to sterve
In the defence of hir, and of hir right.

  This noble quene eek lovede so this
   knight,
Through his desert, and for his chivalrye;
As certeinly, but-if that bokes lye, (30)
He was, of persone and of gentilesse, 610
And of discrecioun and hardinesse,
Worthy to any wight that liven may.
And she was fair as is the rose in May.
And, for to maken shortly is the beste,
She wex his wyf, and hadde him as hir
   leste. 615

  The wedding and the feste to devyse,
To me, that have y-take swiche empryse
Of so many a storie for to make, (39)
Hit were to long, lest that I sholde slake
Of thing that bereth more effect and
   charge ; 620
For men may overlade a ship or barge ;
And forthy to th'effect than wol I skippe,
And al the remenant, I wol lete hit
   slippe.

  Octovian, that wood was of this dede,
Shoop him an ost on Antony to lede 625
Al-outerly for his destruccioun,
With stoute Romains, cruel as leoun ;
To ship they wente, and thus I let hem
   saile.

  Antonius was war, and wol nat faile (50)
To meten with thise Romains, if he
   may ; 630
Took eek his reed, and bothe, upon
   a day,
His wyf and he, and al his ost, forth
   wente
To shippe anoon, no lenger they ne stente ;
And in the see hit happed hem to mete—
Up goth the trompe—and for to shoute
   and shete, 635

And peynen hem to sette on with the
   sonne.
With grisly soun out goth the grete
   gonne,
And heterly they hurtlen al at ones,
And fro the top doun cometh the grete
   stones. (60)
In goth the grapenel so ful of crokes 640
Among the ropes, and the shering-hokes.
In with the polax presseth he and he ;
Behind the mast beginneth he to flee,
And out agayn, and dryveth him over-
   borde ; 644
He stingeth him upon his speres orde ;
He rent the sail with hokes lyke a sythe ;
He bringeth the cuppe, and biddeth hem
   be blythe ;
He poureth pesen upon the hacches slider ;
With pottes ful of lym they goon to-
   gider ; (70)
And thus the longe day in fight they
   spende 650
Til, at the laste, as every thing hath ende,
Antony is shent, and put him to the
   flighte,
And al his folk to-go, that best go mighte.
  Fleeth eek the queen, with al her
   purpre sail,
For strokes, which that wente as thikke
   as hail ; 655
No wonder was, she mighte hit nat endure.
And whan that Antony saw that aven-
   ture,
' Allas !' quod he, ' the day that I was
   born !
My worshipe in this day thus have I
   lorn !' (80)
And for dispeyr out of his witte he sterte,
And roof him-self anoon through-out the
   herte 661
Er that he ferther wente out of the
   place.
His wyf, that coude of Cesar have no
   grace,
To Egipte is fled, for drede and for dis-
   tresse ;
But herkneth, ye that speke of kinde-
   nesse. 665
  Ye men, that falsly sweren many an ooth
That ye wol dye, if that your love be
   wrooth,

Heer may ye seen of women whiche a
  trouthe!
This woful Cleopatre hath mad swich
  routhe                               (90)
That ther nis tonge noon that may hit
  telle.                              670
But on the morwe she wol no lenger
  dwelle,
But made hir subtil werkmen make a
  shryne
Of alle the rubies and the stones fyne
In al Egipte that she coude espye;
And putte ful the shryne of spycerye, 675
And leet the cors embaume; and forth
  she fette
This dede cors, and in the shryne hit
  shette.
And next the shryne a pit than doth she
  grave;
And alle the serpents that she mighte
  have,                              (100)
She putte hem in that grave, and thus
  she seyde:                         680
'Now love, to whom my sorweful herte
  obeyde
So forforthly that, fro that blisful houre
That I yow swor to been al frely youre,
I mene yow, Antonius my knight!    684
That never waking, in the day or night.

Ye nere out of myn hertes remembraunce
For wele or wo, for carole or for daunce;
And in my-self this covenant made I
  tho,                               (109)
That, right swich as ye felten, wele or wo,
As ferforth as hit in my power lay,  690
Unreprovable unto my wyfhood ay,
The same wolde I felen, lyf or deeth.
And thilke covenant, whyl me lasteth
  breeth,
I wol fulfille, and that shal wel be sene;
Was never unto hir love a trewer quene.'
And with that word, naked, with ful
  good herte,                        696
Among the serpents in the pit she sterte,
And ther she chees to han hir buryinge.
Anoon the neddres gonne hir for to
  stinge,                            (120)
And she hir deeth receyveth, with good
  chere,                             700
For love of Antony, that was hir so dere:—
And this is storial sooth, hit is no fable.
  Now, er I finde a man thus trewe and
  stable,
And wol for love his deeth so freely
  take,
I pray god lat our hedes never ake!  705

*Explicit Legenda Cleopatrie. Martiris.*

## II. THE LEGEND OF THISBE OF BABYLON.

*Incipit Legenda Tesbe Babilonie, Martiris.*

At Babiloine whylom fil it thus,
The whiche toun the queen Semiramus
Leet dichen al about, and walles make
Ful hye, of harde tyles wel y-bake.
Ther weren dwellinge in this noble toun
Two lordes, which that were of greet
  renoun,                            711
And woneden so nigh, upon a grene,
That ther nas but a stoon-wal hem bi-
  twene,
As ofte in grete tounes is the wone.
And sooth to seyn, that o man hadde
  a sone,                            715
Of al that londe oon of the lustieste. (11)
That other hadde a doghter, the faireste,

That estward in the world was tho dwel-
  lingo.
The name of everich gan to other springe.
By wommen, that were neighebores
  aboute.                            720
For in that contree yit, withouten doute,
Maidens been y-kept, for jelosye,
Ful streite, lest they diden som folye.
  This yonge man was cleped Piramus,
And Tisbe hight the maid, Naso seith
  thus;                              725
And thus by report was hir name y-shove
That, as they wexe in age, wex hir
  love;                              (22)
And certein, as by reson of hir age,
Ther mighte have been bitwix hem
  mariage,                           729

But that hir fadres nolde hit nat assente;
And bothe in love y-lyke sore they brente,
That noon of alle hir frendes mighte hit
  lette
But prively somtyme yit they mette
By sleighte, and speken som of hir desyr;
As, wry the gleed, and hotter is the fyr;
Forbede a love, and it is ten so wood. 736
  This wal, which that bitwix hem bothe
    stood,                              (32)
Was cloven a-two, right fro the toppe
  adoun,
Of olde tyme of his fundacioun;
But yit this clifte was so narwe and
  lyte,                                  740
It nas nat sene, dere y-nogh a myte.
But what is that, that love can nat espye?
Ye lovers two, if that I shal nat lye,
Ye founden first this litel narwe clifte;
And, with a soun as softe as any shrifte,
They lete hir wordes through the clifte
  pace,                            (41) 746
And tolden, whyl that they stode in the
  place,
Al hir compleynt of love, and al hir wo,
At every tyme whan they dorste so.
  Upon that o syde of the wal stood he,
And on that other syde stood Tisbe,   751
The swote soun of other to receyve,
And thus hir wardeins wolde they de-
  ceyve.
And every day this wal they wolde threte,
And wisshe to god, that it were doun
  y-bete.                          (50) 755
Thus wolde they seyn—'allas! thou
  wikked wal,
Through thyn envye thou us lettest al!
Why nilt thou cleve, or fallen al a-two?
Or, at the leste, but thou woldest so,
Yit woldestow but ones lete us mete, 760
Or ones that we mighte kissen swete,
Than were we covered of our cares colde.
But natheles, yit be we to thee holde
In as muche as thou suffrest for to goon
Our wordes through thy lyme and eek
  thy stoon.                       (60) 765
Yit oghte we with thee ben wel apayd.'
  And whan thise ydel wordes weren sayd,
The colde wal they wolden kisse of stoon,
And take hir leve, and forth they wolden
  goon.

And this was gladly in the even-tyde 770
Or wonder erly, lest men hit espyde;
And longe tyme they wroghte in this
  manere
Til on a day, whan Phebus gan to clere,
Aurora with the stremes of hir hete
Had dryed up the dew of herbes wete; 775
Unto this clifte, as it was wont to be, (71)
Com Pyramus, and after com Tisbe,
And plighten trouthe fully in hir fey
That ilke same night to stele awey,
And to begyle hir wardeins everichoon, 780
And forth out of the citee for to goon;
And, for the feldes been so brode and
  wyde,
For to mete in o place at o tyde,
They sette mark hir meting sholde be
Ther king Ninus was graven, under a
  tree;                            (80) 785
For olde payens that ydoles heried
Useden tho in feldes to ben beried;
And faste by this grave was a welle.
And, shortly of this tale for to telle,
This covenant was affermed wonder
  faste;                                790
And longe hem thoughte that the sonne
  laste,
That hit nere goon under the see adoun.
  This Tisbe hath so greet affeccioun
And so greet lyking Piramus to see,
That, whan she seigh her tyme mighte
  be,                              (90) 795
At night she stal awey ful prively
With her face y-wimpled subtilly;
For alle her frendes—for to save her
  trouthe—
She hath for-sake; allas! and that is
  routhe
That ever woman wolde be so trewe 800
To trusten man, but she the bet him
  knewe!
And to the tree she goth a ful good pas,
For love made her so hardy in this cas;
And by the welle adoun she gan her
  dresse.                              804
Allas! than comth a wilde leonesse (100)
Out of the wode, withouten more areste,
With blody mouthe, of strangling of a
  beste,
To drinken of the welle, ther as she sat;
And, whan that Tisbe had espyed that,

She rist her up, with a ful drery herte, 810
And in a cave with dredful foot she sterte,
For by the mone she seigh hit wel with-
　　alle.　　　　　　　　　　　　812
And, as she ran, her wimpel leet she falle,
And took noon heed, so sore she was
　　a-whaped.　　　　　　　　　(109)
And eek so glad of that she was escaped ;
And thus she sit, and darketh wonder
　　stille.　　　　　　　　　　　816
Whan that this leonesse hath dronke her
　　fille,
Aboute the welle gan she for to winde,
And right anoon the wimpel gan she
　　finde,
And with her blody mouth hit al to-
　　rente.　　　　　　　　　　　820
Whan this was doon, no lenger she ne
　　stente,
But to the wode her wey than hath she
　　nome.
　　And, at the laste, this Piramus is come,
But al to longe, allas ! at hoom was he.
The mone shoon, men mighte wel y-see, 825
And in his weye, as that he com ful
　　faste,　　　　　　　　　　　(121)
His eyen to the grounde adoun he caste,
And in the sonde, as he beheld adoun,
He seigh the steppes brode of a leoun,
And in his herte he sodeinly agroos, 830
And pale he wex, therwith his heer
　　aroos,
And neer he com, and fond the wimpel
　　torn.
'Allas !' quod he, 'the day that I was
　　born !
This o night wol us lovers bothe slee !
How sholde I axen mercy of Tisbe 835
Whan I am he that have yow slain, allas !
My bidding hath yow slain, as in this
　　cas.　　　　　　　　　　　(132)
Allas ! to bidde a woman goon by nighte
In place ther as peril fallen mighte,
And I so slow ! allas, I ne hadde be 840
Here in this place a furlong-wey or ye !
Now what leoun that be in this foreste,
My body mote he †trenden, or what beste
That wilde is, gnawen mote he now myn
　　herte !'
And with that worde he to the wimpel
　　sterte,　　　　　　　　(140) 845

And kiste hit ofte, and weep on hit ful
　　sore,
And seide, ' wimpel, allas ! ther nis no
　　more
But thou shalt fele as wel the blood
　　of me
As thou hast felt the bleding of Tisbe !'
And with that worde he smoot him to the
　　herte.　　　　　　　　　　850
The blood out of the wounde as brode
　　sterte
As water, whan the conduit broken is.
　　Now Tisbe, which that wiste nat of
　　this,
But sitting in her drede, she thoghte thus,
' If hit so falle that my Piramus 855
Be comen hider, and may me nat y-finde,
He may me holden fals and eek unkinde.'
And out she comth, and after him gan
　　espyen　　　　　　　　　(153)
Bothe with her herte and with her yën,
And thoghte, ' I wol him tellen of my
　　drede　　　　　　　　　　860
Bothe of the leonesse and al my dede.'
And at the laste her love than hath she
　　founde
Beting with his heles on the grounde,
Al blody, and therwith-al a-bak she sterte,
And lyke the wawes quappe gan her
　　herte,　　　　　　　　(160) 865
And pale as box she wex, and in a throwe
Avysed her, and gan him wel to knowe,
That hit was Piramus, her herte dere.
Who coude wryte whiche a deedly chere
Hath Tisbe now, and how her heer she
　　rente,　　　　　　　　　　870
And how she gan her-selve to turmente,
And how she lyth and swowneth on the
　　grounde,
And how she weep of teres ful his wounde,
How medeleth she his blood with her
　　compleynte,
And with his blood her-selven gan she
　　peynte ;　　　　　　　　(170) 875
How clippeth she the dede cors, allas !
How doth this woful Tisbe in this cas !
How kisseth she his frosty mouth so cold !
' Who hath doon this, and who hath
　　been so bold 879
To sleen my leef ?　O spek, my Piramus !
I am thy Tisbe, that thee calleth thus !'

And therwith-al she lifteth up his heed.
This woful man, that was nat fully
    deed,
Whan that he herde the name of Tisbe
    cryen,
On her he caste his hevy deedly yën    885
And doun again, and yeldeth up the
    gost.                               (181)
Tisbe rist up, withouten noise or bost,
And seigh her wimpel and his empty
    shethe,
And eek his swerd, that him hath doon
    to dethe ;
Than spak she thus : ' My woful hand,'
    quod she,                          890
' Is strong y-nogh in swiche a werk to
    me ;
For love shal yive me strengthe and
    hardinesse
To make my wounde large y-nogh, I gesse.
I wol thee folwen deed, and I wol be
Felawe and cause eek of thy deeth,' quod
    she.                         (190) 895
' And thogh that nothing save the deeth
    only
Mighte thee fro me departe trewely,
Thou shalt no more departe now fro
    me
Than fro the deeth, for I wol go with
    thee !

' And now, ye wrecched jelous fadres
    oure,                              900
We, that weren whylom children youre,
We prayen yow, withouten more envye,
That in o grave y-fere we moten lye,
Sin love hath brought us to this pitous
    ende !                             (199)
And rightwis god to every lover sende, 905
That loveth trewely, more prosperitee
Than ever hadde Piramus and Tisbe !
And lat no gentil woman her assure
To putten her in swiche an aventure.
But god forbede but a woman can      910
Been as trewe and loving as a man !
And, for my part, I shal anoon it kythe !'
And, with that worde, his swerd she took
    as swythe,
That warm was of her loves blood and
    hoot,                             (209)
And to the herte she her-selven smoot. 915
    And thus ar Tisbe and Piramus ago.
Of trewe men I finde but fewe mo
In alle my bokes, save this Piramus,
And therfor have I spoken of him thus.
For hit is deyntee to us men to finde  920
A man that can in love be trewe and
    kinde.
Heer may ye seen, what lover so he be,
A woman dar and can as wel as he.
                *Explicit legenda Tesbe.*

# III. THE LEGEND OF DIDO, QUEEN OF CARTHAGE.

*Incipit Legenda Didonis Martiris,*
        *Cartaginis regine.*

GLORY and honour, Virgil Mantuan,
Be to thy name ! and I shal, as I can, 925
Folow thy lantern, as thou gost biforn,
How Eneas to Dido was forsworn.
In thyn Eneïd and Naso wol I take
The tenour, and the grete effectes
    make.
    Whan Troye broght was to destruc-
        cioun                         930
By Grekes sleighte, and namely by
    Sinoun,
Feyning the hors y-offred to Minerve,
Through which that many a Troyan
    moste sterve ;                     (10)

And Ector had, after his deeth, appered,
And fyr so wood, it mighte nat be
    stered,                           935
In al the noble tour of Ilioun,
That of the citee was the cheef dungeoun ;
And al the contree was so lowe y-broght,
And Priamus the king fordoon and
    noght ;
And Eneas was charged by Venus     940
To fleen awey, he took Ascanius,
That was his sone, in his right hand, and
    fledde ;
And on his bakke he bar and with him
    ledde                             (20)
His olde fader, cleped Anchises,
And by the weye his wyf Creusa he
    lees.                              945

And mochel sorwe hadde he in his minde
Er that he coude his felawshippe finde.
But, at the laste, whan he had hem
founde,                                   948
He made him redy in a certein stounde,
And to the see ful faste he gan him hye,
And saileth forth with al his companye
Toward Itaile, as wolde destinee.
But of his aventures in the see        (30)
Nis nat to purpos for to speke of here,
For hit acordeth nat to my matere.    955
But, as I seide, of him and of Dido
Shal be my tale, til that I have do.

So longe he sailed in the salte see
Til in Libye unnethe aryved he,
With shippes seven and with no more
navye ;                                960
And glad was he to londe for to hye,
So was he with the tempest al to-shake.
And whan that he the haven had y-
take,                                   (40)
He had a knight, was called Achates ; 964
And him of al his felawshippe he chees
To goon with him, the contre for tespye ;
He took with him no more companye.
But forth they goon, and lafte his shippes
ryde,
His fere and he, with-outen any gyde. 969
So longe he walketh in this wildernesse
Til, at the laste, he mette an hunteresse.
A bowe in honde and arwes hadde she,
Her clothes cutted were unto the knee ; (50)
But she was yit the fairest creature
That ever was y-formed by nature ;    975
And Eneas and Achates she grette,
And thus she to hem spak, whan she hem
mette.
'Sawe ye,' quod she, ' as ye han walked
wyde,
Any of my sustren walke yow besyde,
With any wilde boor or other beste    980
That they han hunted to, in this foreste,
Y-tukked up, with arwes in her cas ? ' (59)

'Nay, soothly, lady,' quod this Eneas;
'But, by thy beaute, as hit thinketh me,
Thou mightest never erthely womman be,
But Phebus suster artow, as I gesse.  986
And, if so be that thou be a goddesse,
Have mercy on our labour and our wo.'
'I nam no goddes, soothly,' quod she
tho ;

' For maidens walken in this contree here,
With arwes and with bowe, in this
manere.                                991
This is the regne of Libie, ther ye been,
Of which that Dido lady is and queen '—
And shortly tolde him al the occasioun (71)
Why Dido com into that regioun,       995
Of which as now me lusteth nat to ryme ;
Hit nedeth nat ; hit nere but los of tyme.
For this is al and som, it was Venus,
His owne moder, that spak with him thus ;
And to Cartage she bad he sholde him
dighte,                               1000
And vanished anoon out of his sighte.
I coude folwe, word for word, Virgyle,
But it wolde lasten al to longe a whyle. (80)

This noble queen, that cleped was Dido,
That whylom was the wyf of Sitheo, 1005
That fairer was then is the brighte sonne,
This noble toun of Cartage hath begonne ;
In which she regneth in so greet honour,
That she was holde of alle quenes flour,
Of gentilesse, of freedom, of beautee ; 1010
That wel was him that mighte her ones
see ;
Of kinges and of lordes so desyred,   (89)
That al the world her beaute hadde y-
fyred ;
She stood so wel in every wightes grace.
Whan Eneas was come un-to that
place,                                1015
Unto the maister-temple of al the toun
Ther Dido was in her devocioun,
Ful prively his wey than hath he nome.
Whan he was in the large temple come,
I can nat seyn if that hit be possible, 1020
But Venus hadde him maked invisible—
Thus seith the book, with-outen any lees.
And whan this Eneas and Achates   (100)
Hadden in this temple been over-al,
Than founde they, depeynted on a wal,
How Troye and al the lond destroyed was.
'Allas ! that I was born,' quod Eneas, 1027
' Through-out the world our shame is kid
so wyde,
Now it is peynted upon every syde !
We, that weren in prosperitee,       1030
Be now disslaundred, and in swich degree,
No lenger for to liven I ne kepe ! '
And, with that worde, he brast out for to
wepe                                 (110)

So tendrely, that routhe hit was to sene.

This fresshe lady, of the citee quene, 1035
Stood in the temple, in her estat royal,
So richely, and eek so fair with-al,
So yong, so lusty, with her eyen glade,
That, if that god, that heven and erthe made,
Wolde han a love, for beaute and goodnesse, 1040
And womanhod, and trouthe, and seemlinesse,
Whom sholde he loven but this lady swete?
There nis no womman to him half so mete. (120)

Fortune, that hath the world in governaunce,
Hath sodeinly broght in so newe a chaunce, 1045
That never was ther yit so fremd a cas.
For al the companye of Eneas,
Which that he wende han loren in the see,
Aryved is, nat fer fro that citee;
For which, the grettest of his lordes some
By aventure ben to the citee come, 1051
Unto that same temple, for to seke
The quene, and of her socour her beseke;
Swich renoun was ther spronge of her goodnesse. (131)
And, whan they hadden told al hir distresse, 1055
And al hir tempest and hir harde cas,
Unto the quene appered Eneas,
And openly beknew that hit was he.
Who hadde joye than but his meynee,
That hadden founde hir lord, hir governour? 1060
The quene saw they dide him swich honour,
And had herd ofte of Eneas, er tho,
And in her herte she hadde routhe and wo (140)
That ever swich a noble man as he
Shal been disherited in swich degree; 1065
And saw the man, that he was lyk a knight,
And suffisaunt of persone and of might,
And lyk to been a veray gentil man;
And wel his wordes he besette can,

And had a noble visage for the nones, 1070
And formed wel of braunes and of bones.
For, after Venus, hadde he swich fairnesse,
That no man might be half so fair, I gesse. (150)
And wel a lord he semed for to be.
And, for he was a straunger, somwhat she 1075
Lyked him the bet, as, god do bote,
To som folk ofte newe thing is swote.
Anoon her herte hath pitee of his wo,
And, with that pitee, love com in also;
And thus, for pitee and for gentilesse, 1080
Refresshed moste he been of his distresse.
She seide, certes, that she sory was
That he hath had swich peril and swich cas; (160)
And, in her frendly speche, in this manere
She to him spak, and seide as ye may here. 1085
' Be ye nat Venus sone and Anchises?
In good feith, al the worship and encrees
That I may goodly doon yow, ye shul have.
Your shippes and your meynee shal I save;'
And many a gentil word she spak him to;
And comaunded her messageres go 1091
The same day, with-outen any faile,
His shippes for to seke, and hem vitaile.
She many a beste to the shippes sente, (171)
And with the wyn she gan hem to presente; 1095
And to her royal paleys she her spedde,
And Eneas alwey with her she ledde.
What nedeth yow the feste to descryve?
He never beter at ese was his lyve.
Ful was the feste of deyntees and richesse, 1100
Of instruments, of song, and of gladnesse,
And many an amorous loking and devys.
This Eneas is come to Paradys (180)
Out of the swolow of helle, and thus in joye 1104
Remembreth him of his estat in Troye.
To dauncing-chambres ful of parements,
Of riche beddes, and of ornaments,
This Eneas is lad, after the mete.
And with the quene whan that he had sete,

And spyces parted, and the wyn agoon,
Unto his chambres was he lad anoon    1111
To take his ese and for to have his reste,
With al his folk, to doon what so hem
    leste.                                    (190)
    Ther nas coursere wel y-brydled noon,
Ne stede, for the justing wel to goon,  1115
Ne large palfrey, esy for the nones,
Ne juwel, fretted ful of riche stones,
Ne sakkes ful of gold, of large wighte,
Ne ruby noon, that shynede by nighte,
Ne gentil hautein faucon heronere,    1120
Ne hound, for hert or wilde boor or
    dere,
Ne coupe of gold, with florins newe y-bete,
That in the lond of Libie may be gete,
That Dido ne hath hit Eneas y-sent; (201)
And al is payed, what that he hath spent.
    Thus can this †noble quene her gestes
    calle,                                    1126
As she that can in freedom passen alle.
    Eneas sothly eek, with-outen lees,
Hath sent un-to his shippe, by Achates,
After his sone, and after riche thinges,
Both ceptre, clothes, broches, and eek
    ringes,                                   1131
Som for to were, and som for to presente
To her, that al thise noble thinges him
    sente ;                                   (210)
And bad his sone, how that he sholde
    make
The presenting, and to the quene hit
    take.                                     1135
    Repaired is this Achates again,
And Eneas ful blisful is and fain
To seen his yonge sone Ascanius.
But natheles, our autour telleth us,
That Cupido, that is the god of love,   1140
At preyere of his moder, hye above,
Hadde the lyknes of the child y-take,
This noble quene enamoured to make (220)
On Eneas ; but, as of that scripture,
Be as be may, I make of hit no cure.  1145
But sooth is this, the quene hath mad
    swich chere
Un-to this child, that wonder is to here ;
And of the present that his fader sente
She thanked him ful ofte, in good entente.
    Thus is this quene in plesaunce and in
    joye,                                     1150
With al this newe lusty folk of Troye.

And of the dedes hath she more en-
    quered
Of Eneas, and al the story lered      (230)
Of Troye ; and al the longe day they
    tweye
Entendeden to speken and to pleye ;   1155
Of which ther gan to breden swich a fyr,
That sely Dido hath now swich desyr
With Eneas, her newe gest, to dele,
That she hath lost her hewe, and eek her
    hele.
Now to th'effect, now to the fruit of al, 1160
Why I have told this story, and tellen
    shal.
    Thus I beginne ; hit fil, upon a night,
When that the mone up-reysed had her
    light,                                    (240)
This noble quene un-to her reste wente ;
She syketh sore, and gan her-self tur-
    mente.                                    1165
She waketh, walweth, maketh many a
    brayd,
As doon thise loveres, as I have herd sayd.
And at the laste, unto her suster Anne
She made her moon, and right thus spak
    she thanne.
    'Now, dere suster myn, what may hit
    be                                        1170
That me agasteth in my dreme?' quod
    she.
'This ilke Troyan is so in my thoght,
For that me thinketh he is so wel
    y-wroght,                                 (250)
And eek so lykly for to be a man,
And therwithal so mikel good he can, 1175
That al my love and lyf lyth in his cure.
Have ye not herd him telle his aventure?
Now certes, Anne, if that ye rede hit me,
I wolde fain to him y-wedded be ;    1179
This is th'effect ; what sholde I more seye?
In him lyth al, to do me live or deye.'
    Her suster Anne, as she that coude her
    good,
Seide as her thoughte, and somdel hit
    with-stood.                               (260)
But her-of was so long a sermoning,
Hit were to long to make rehersing; 1185
But fynally, hit may not been with-
    stonde ;
Love wol love—for no wight wol hit
    wonde.

The dawening up-rist out of the see ;
This amorous quene chargeth her meynee
The nettes dresse, and speres brode and
    kene ; 1190
An hunting wol this lusty fresshe quene ;
So priketh her this newe joly wo.
To hors is al her lusty folk y-go ; (270)
Un-to the court the houndes been y-broght,
And up-on coursers, swift as any thoght,
Her yonge knightes hoven al aboute, 1196
And of her wommen eek an huge route.
Up-on a thikke palfrey, paper-whyt,
With sadel rede, enbrouded with delyt,
Of gold the barres up-enbossed hye, 1200
Sit Dido, al in gold and perre wrye ;
And she is fair, as is the brighte morwe,
That heleth seke folk of nightes sorwe. (280)
  Up-on a courser, startling as the fyr,
Men mighte turne him with a litel wyr,
Sit Eneas, lyk Phebus to devyse ; 1206
So was he fresshe arayed in his wyse.
The fomy brydel with the bit of gold
Governeth he, right as him-self hath
    wold.
And forth this noble quene thus lat I
    ryde 1210
An hunting, with this Troyan by her syde.
The herd of hertes founden is anoon,
With 'hey ! go bet ! prik thou ! lat goon,
    lat goon ! (290)
Why nil the leoun comen or the bere,
That I mighte ones mete him with this
    spere ? ' 1215
Thus seyn thise yonge folk, and up they
    kille
These † hertes wilde, and han hem at hir
    wille.
  Among al this to-romblen gan the
    heven,
The thunder rored with a grisly steven ;
Doun com the rain, with hail and sleet
    so faste, 1220
With hevenes fyr, that hit so sore agaste
This noble quene, and also her meynee,
That ech of hem was glad a-wey to flee. (300)
And shortly, fro the tempest her to save,
She fledde her-self into a litel cave, 1225
And with her wente this Eneas al-so ;
I noot, with hem if ther wente any mo ;
The autour maketh of hit no mencioun.
And heer began the depe affeccioun

Betwix hem two ; this was the firste
    morwe 1230
Of her gladnesse, and ginning of her
    sorwe.
For ther hath Eneas y-kneled so, (309)
And told her al his herte, and al his wo,
And sworn so depe, to her to be trewe,
For wele or wo, and chaunge for no
    newe, 1235
And as a fals lover so wel can pleyne,
That sely Dido rewed on his peyne,
And took him for husband, †to been his
    wyf
For ever-mo, whyl that hem laste lyf.
And after this, whan that the tempest
    stente, 1240
With mirth out as they comen, hoom
    they wente.
  The wikked fame up roos, and that
    anon, (319)
How Eneas hath with the quene y-gon
In-to the cave ; and demed as hem liste ;
And whan the king, that Yarbas hight,
    hit wiste, 1245
As he that had her loved ever his lyf,
And wowed her, to have her to his wyf,
Swich sorwe as he hath maked, and swich
    chere,
Hit is a routhe and pitee for to here.
But, as in love, al-day hit happeth so, 1250
That oon shal laughen at anothers wo ;
Now laugheth Eneas, and is in joye
And more richesse than ever he was in
    Troye. (330)
  O sely womman, ful of innocence, 1254
Ful of pitee, of trouthe, and conscience,
What maked yow to men to trusten so ?
Have ye swich routhe upon hir feined wo,
And han swich olde ensamples yow
    beforn ?
See ye nat alle, how they been for-sworn ?
Wher see ye oon, that he ne hath laft his
    leef, 1260
Or been unkinde, or doon hir som mis-
    cheef,
Or pilled her, or bosted of his dede ? (339)
Ye may as wel hit seen, as ye may rede ;
Tak heed now of this grete gentil-man,
This Troyan, that so wel her plesen can,
That feineth him so trewe and obeising,
So gentil and so privy of his doing, 1267

And can so wel doon alle his obeisaunces,
And waiten her at festes and at daunces,
And when she goth to temple and hoom
   ageyn,            1270
And fasten til he hath his lady seyn,
And bere in his devyses, for her sake,
Noot I nat what; and songes wolde he
   make,           (350)
Justen, and doon of armes many thinges,
Sende her lettres, tokens, broches, ringes—
Now herkneth, how he shal his lady
   serve !           1276
Ther-as he was in peril for to sterve
For hunger, and for mischeef in the
   see,
And desolat, and fled from his contree,
And al his folk with tempest al to-driven,
She hath her body and eek her reame
   yiven           1281
In-to his hond, ther-as she mighte have
   been
Of other lond than of Cartage a queen,
And lived in joye y-nogh ; what wolde ye
   more ?           (361)
   This Eneas, that hath so depe y-swore,
Is wery of his craft with-in a throwe; 1286
The hote ernest is al over-blowe.
And prively he doth his shippes dighte,
And shapeth him to stele a-wey by nighte.
   This Dido hath suspecioun of this, 1290
And thoughte wel, that hit was al a-mis;
For in his bedde he lyth a-night and
   syketh ;
She asketh him anoon, what him mis-
   lyketh—        (370)
'My dere herte, which that I love most ?'
  'Certes,' quod he, 'this night my fadres
   gost           1295
Hath in my sleep so sore me tormented,
And eek Mercurie his message hath pre-
   sented,
That nedes to the conquest of Itaile
My destinee is sone for to saile ;
For which, me thinketh, brosten is myn
   herte !'        1300
Ther-with his false teres out they sterte;
And taketh her with-in his armes two.
   'Is that in ernest,' quod she ; 'wil ye
   so ?         (380)
Have ye nat sworn to wyve me to take,
Alas ! what womman wil ye of me make ?

I am a gentil-woman and a queen, 1306
Ye wil nat fro your wyf thus foule fleen ?
That I was born ! allas ! what shal I do ?'
   To telle in short, this noble queen Dido,
She seketh halwes, and doth sacrifyse ;
She kneleth, cryeth, that routhe is to
   devyse ;        1311
Conjureth him, and profreth him to be
His thral, his servant in the leste gree ;
She falleth him to fote, and swowneth
   there         (391)
Dischevele, with her brighte gilte here,
And seith, 'have mercy ! let me with
   yow ryde !       1316
Thise lordes, which that wonen me besyde
Wil me destroyen only for your sake.
And, so ye wil me now to wyve take,
As ye han sworn, than wol I yive yow
   leve         1320
To sleen me with your swerd now sone at
   eve !
For than yit shal I dyen as your wyf.
I am with childe, and yive my child his
   lyf.         (400)
Mercy, lord ! have pite in your thoght !'
But al this thing availeth her right noght ;
For on a night, slepinge, he let her lye,
And stal a-wey un-to his companye, 1327
And, as a traitour, forth he gan to saile
Toward the large contree of Itaile.
Thus hath he laft Dido in wo and pyne ;
And wedded ther a lady hight Lavyne.
   A cloth he lafte, and eek his swerd
   stonding,    (409) 1332
Whan he fro Dido stal in her sleping,
Right at her beddes heed, so gan he hye
Whan that he stal a-wey to his navye ;
Which cloth, whan sely Dido gan awake,
She hath hit kist ful ofte for his sake ;
And seide, 'O cloth, whyl Jupiter hit
   leste,
Tak now my soule, unbind me of this
   unreste !       1339
I have fulfild of fortune al the cours.'
And thus, allas ! with-outen his socours,
Twenty tyme y-swowned hath she thanne.
And, whan that she un-to her suster
   Anne         (420)
Compleyned had, of which I may nat
   wryte—        1344
So greet a routhe I have hit for t'endyte—

And bad her norice and her suster goon
To fecchen fyr and other thing anoon,
And seide, that she wolde sacrifye.
And, whan she mighte her tyme wel
espye,
Up-on the fyr of sacrifys she sterte, 1350
And with his swerd she roof her to the
herte.

But, as myn autour seith, right thus
she seyde;                          (429)
Or she was hurt, before that she deyde,
She wroot a lettre anoon, that thus be-
gan :—
'Right so,' quod she, ' as that the whyte
swan                                1355
Ayeins his deeth beginneth for to singe,
Right so to yow make I my compleyninge.

Nat that I trowe to geten yow again,
For wel I woot that it is al in vain,
Sin that the goddes been contraire to me.
But sin my name is lost through yow,'
quod she,                           1361
' I may wel lese a word on yow, or letter,
Al-be-it that I shal be never the better ;
For thilke wind that blew your ship
a-wey,                              (441)
The same wind hath blowe a-wey your
fey.'—                              1365
But who wol al this letter have in
minde,
Rede Ovide, and in him he shal hit finde.

*Explicit Legenda Didonis Martiris,*
*Cartaginis regine.*

# IV. THE LEGEND OF HYPSIPYLE AND MEDEA.

*Incipit Legenda Ysiphile et Medee,*
*Martirum.*

### PART I. THE LEGEND OF HYPSIPYLE.

THOU rote of false lovers, duk Jasoun !
Thou sly devourer and confusioun
Of gentil-wommen, tender creatures, 1370
Thou madest thy reclaiming and thy
lures
To ladies of thy statly apparaunce,
And of thy wordes, farced with plesaunce,
And of thy feyned trouthe and thy
manere,
With thyn obeisaunce and thy humble
chere,                               (8) 1375
And with thy counterfeted peyne and wo.
Ther other falsen oon, thou falsest two !
O ! ofte swore thou that thou woldest dye
For love, whan thou ne feltest maladye
Save foul delyt, which that thou callest
love !                              1380
If that I live, thy name shal be shove
In English, that thy sleighte shal be
knowe !
Have at thee, Jasoun ! now thyn horn is
blowe !
But certes, hit is bothe routhe and wo
That love with false loveres werketh so ;

For they shul have wel better love and
chere                               1386
Than he that hath aboght his love ful
dere,                               (20)
Or had in armes many a blody box.
For ever as tendre a capoun et the fox,
Thogh he be fals and hath the foul be-
trayed,                             1390
As shal the good-man that ther-for hath
payed ;
Al have he to the capoun skille and
right,
The false fox wol have his part at night.
On Jasoun this ensample is wel y-sene
By Isiphile and Medea the quene.    1395
In Tessalye, as Guido telleth us,
Ther was a king that highte Pelleus, (30)
That had a brother, which that highte
Eson ;
And, whan for age he mighte unnethes
gon,
He yaf to Pelleus the governing    1400
Of al his regne, and made him lord and
king.
Of which Eson this Jasoun geten was,
That, in his tyme, in al that lond, ther nas
Nat swich a famous knight of gentilesse,
Of freedom, and of strengthe and lusti-
nesse.                              1405

After his fader deeth, he bar him so   (39)
That ther nas noon that liste been his fo,
But dide him al honour and companye ;
Of which this Pelleus hath greet envye,
Imagining that Jasoun mighte be   1410
Enhaunsed so, and put in swich degree
With love of lordes of his regioun,
That from his regne he may be put adoun.
And in his wit, a-night, compassed he
How Jasoun mighte best destroyed be 1415
Withoute slaunder of his compasment.
And at the laste he took avisement   (50)
To senden him in-to som fer contree
Ther as this Jasoun may destroyed be.
This was his wit ; al made he to Jasoun
Gret chere of love and of affeccioun, 1421
For drede lest his lordes hit espyde.
So fil hit so, as fame renneth wyde,
Ther was swich tyding over-al and swich
    los,
That in an yle that called was Colcos, 1425
Beyonde Troye, estward in the see,
That ther-in was a ram, that men mighte
    see,   (60)
That had a flees of gold, that shoon so
    brighte,
That no-wher was ther swich an-other
    sighte ;   1429
But hit was kept alway with a dragoun,
And many othere merveils, up and doun,
And with two boles, maked al of bras,
That spitten fyr, and moche thing ther
    was.
But this was eek the tale, nathelees,
That who-so wolde winne thilke flees, 1435
He moste bothe, or he hit winne mighte,
With the boles and the dragoun fighte ;
And king Oëtes lord was of that yle.   (71)
    This Pelleus bethoghte upon this wyle ;
That he his nevew Jasoun wolde enhorte
To sailen to that lond, him to disporte,
And seide, ' Nevew, if hit mighte be
That swich a worship mighte fallen thee,
That thou this famous tresor mightest
    winne,   1444
And bringen hit my regioun with-inne,
Hit were to me gret plesaunce and honour ;
Than were I holde to quyte thy labour. (80)
And al the cost I wol my-selven make ;
And chees what folk that thou wilt with
    thee take ;   1449

Lat see now, darstow taken this viage ?'
Jasoun was yong, and lusty of corage,
And under-took to doon this ilke em-
    pryse.
    Anoon Argus his shippes gan devyse ;
With Jasoun wente the stronge Ercules,
And many an-other that he with him
    chees.   1455
But who-so axeth who is with him gon,
Lat him go reden Argonauticon,   (90)
For he wol telle a tale long y-now.
Philotetes anoon the sail up-drow,
Whan that the wind was good, and gan
    him hye   1460
Out of his contree called Tessalye.
So long he sailed in the salte see
Til in the yle † Lemnoun aryved he—
Al be this nat rehersed of Guido,
Yet seith Ovyde in his Epistles so—   1465
And of this yle lady was and quene
The faire yonge Isiphilee, the shene, (100)
That whylom Thoas doghter was, the
    king.
Isiphilee was goon in her playing ; 1469
And, roming on the clyves by the see,
Under a banke anoon espyed she
Wher that the ship of Jasoun gan aryve.
Of her goodnesse adoun she sendeth blyve
To witen yif that any straunge wight 1474
With tempest thider were y-blowe a-night,
To doon him socour ; as was her usaunce
To forthren every wight, and doon ple-
    saunce   (110)
Of veray bountee and of curtesye.
    This messagere adoun him gan to hye,
And fond Jasoun, and Ercules also, 1480
That in a cogge to londe were y-go
Hem to refresshen and to take the eyr.
The morwening atempre was and fair ;
And in his wey the messagere hem mette.
Ful cunningly thise lordes two he grette,
And dide his message, axing hem anoon
Yif they were broken, or oght wo begoon,
Or hadde nede of lodesmen or vitaile ; (121)
For of socour they shulde no-thing faile,
For hit was utterly the quenes wille. 1490
    Jasoun answerde, mekely and stille,
' My lady,' quod he, ' thanke I hertely
Of hir goodnesse ; us nedeth, trewely,
No-thing as now, but that we wery be,
And come for to pleye, out of the see, 1495

Til that the wind be better in our weye.'
This lady rometh by the clif to pleye, (130)
With her meynee, endelong the stronde,
And fynt this Jasoun and this other
   stonde, 1499
In spekinge of this thing, as I yow tolde.
This Ercules and Jasoun gan beholde
How that the quene hit was, and faire
   her grette
Anon-right as they with this lady mette ;
And she took heed, and knew, by hir
   manere,
By hir aray, by wordes and by chere, 1505
That hit were gentil-men, of greet degree.
And to the castel with her ledeth she
Thise straunge folk, and doth hem greet
   honour, (141)
And axeth hem of travail and labour
That they han suffred in the salte see ; 1510
So that, within a day, or two, or three,
She knew, by folk that in his shippes be,
That hit was Jasoun, ful of renomee,
And Ercules, that had the grete los, 1514
That soghten the aventures of Colcos ;
And dide hem honour more then before,
And with hem deled ever lenger the
   more, (150)
For they ben worthy folk, with-outen lees.
And namely, most she spak with Ercules ;
To him her herte bar, he sholde be 1520
Sad, wys, and trewe, of wordes avisee,
With-outen any other affeccioun
Of love, or evil imaginacioun.
   This Ercules hath so this Jasoun preysed,
That to the sonne he hath him up
   areysed, 1525
That half so trewe a man ther nas of love
Under the cope of heven that is above ;
And he was wys, hardy, secree, and
   riche.— (161)
Of thise three pointes ther nas noon him
   liche ;
Of freedom passed he, and lustihede, 1530
Alle tho that liven or ben dede ;
Ther-to so greet a gentil-man was he,
And of Tessalie lykly king to be.
Ther nas no lak, but that he was agast
To love, and for to speke shamefast. 1535
He hadde lever him-self to mordre, and
   dye (169)
Than that men shulde a lover him espye :—

' As wolde almighty god that I had yive
My blood and flesh, so that I mighte live,
With the nones that he hadde o-wher
   a wyf 1540
For his estat ; for swich a lusty lyf
She sholde lede with this lusty knight !'
   And al this was compassed on the
   night
Betwixe him Jasoun and this Ercules.
Of thise two heer was mad a shrewed lees
To come to hous upon an innocent ; 1546
For to be-dote this queen was hir assent.
And Jasoun is as coy as is a maide, (181)
He loketh pitously, but noght he saide,
But frely yaf he to her conseileres 1550
Yiftes grete, and to her officeres.
As wolde god I leiser hadde, and tyme,
By proces al his wowing for to ryme.
But in this hous if any fals lover be,
Right as him-self now doth, right so dide
   he, 1555
With feyning and with every sotil dede.
Ye gete no more of me, but ye wil rede
Th'original, that telleth al the cas. (191)
   The somme is this, that Jasoun wedded
   was
Unto this quene, and took of her sub-
   staunce 1560
What-so him liste, unto his purveyaunce ;
And upon her begat he children two,
And drow his sail, and saw her never-mo.
   A lettre sente she to him certein,
Which were to long to wryten and to
   sein, 1565
And him repreveth of his grete untrouthe,
And preyeth him on her to have som
   routhe. (200)
And of his children two, she seide him
   this,
That they be lyke, of alle thing, y-wis,
To Jasoun, save they coude nat begyle ;
And preyed god, or hit were longe whyle,
That she, that had his herte y-raft her fro,
Moste finden him to her untrewe al-so,
And that she moste bothe her children
   spille, 1574
And alle tho that suffreth him his wille.
And trew to Jasoun was she al her lyf,
And ever kepte her chast, as for his wyf ;
Ne never had she joye at her herte, (211)
But dyed, for his love, of sorwes smerte.

Part II. The Legend of Medea.

To Colcos comen is this duk Jasoun,
That is of love devourer and dragoun. 1581
As matere appetyteth forme al-wey,
And from forme in-to forme hit passen
    may,
Or as a welle that were botomlees,
Right so can fals Jasoun have no pees.
For, to desyren, through his appetyt, 1586
To doon with gentil wommen his delyt,
This is his lust and his felicitee.    (221)

Jasoun is romed forth to the citee,
That whylom cleped was Jaconitos, 1590
That was the maister-toun of al Colcos,
And hath y-told the cause of his coming
Un-to Oëtes, of that contre king,
Preying him that he moste doon his
    assay     1594
To gete the flees of gold, if that he may;
Of which the king assenteth to his bone,
And doth him honour, as hit is to done,
So ferforth, that his doghter and his eyr,
Medea, which that was so wys and fair
That fairer saw ther never man with yë,
He made her doon to Jasoun companye
At mete, and sitte by him in the halle.

Now was Jasoun a semely man with-
    alle,     (236)
And lyk a lord, and had a greet renoun,
And of his loke as real as leoun,    1605
And goodly of his speche, and famulere,
And coude of love al craft and art plenere
With-oute boke, with everich observaunce.
And, as fortune her oghte a foul mes-
    chaunce,
She wex enamoured upon this man. 1610
'Jasoun,' quod she, 'for ought I see or
    can,
As of this thing the which ye been aboute,
Ye han your-self y-put in moche doute.
For, who-so wol this aventure acheve,
He may nat wel asterten, as I leve, 1615
With-outen deeth, but I his helpe be. (249)
But natheles, hit is my wille,' quod she,
'To forthren yow, so that ye shal nat dye,
But turnen, sound, hoom to your Tessalye.'

'My righte lady,' quod this Jasoun tho,
'That ye han of my dethe or of my wo
Any reward, and doon me this honour,
I wot wel that my might ne my labour

May nat deserve hit in my lyves day; 1624
God thanke yow, ther I ne can ne may.
Your man am I, and lowly you beseche,
To been my help, with-oute more speche;
But certes, for my deeth shal I nat
    spare.'     (261)
Tho gan this Medea to him declare
The peril of this cas, fro point to point,
And of his batail, and in what disjoint
He mote stande, of which no creature,
Save only she, ne mighte his lyf assure.
And shortly, to the point right for to go,
They been accorded ful, betwix hem two,
That Jasoun shal her wedde, as trewe
    knight ;     1636
And term y-set, to come sone at night (270)
Unto her chambre, and make ther his
    ooth,
Upon the goddes, that he, for leef ne
    looth,     1639
Ne sholde her never falsen, night ne day,
To been her husbond, whyl he liven may,
As she that from his deeth him saved
    here.
And her-upon, at night they mette y-fere,
And doth his ooth, and goth with her to
    bedde.     1644
And on the morwe, upward he him spedde;
For she hath taught him how he shal
    nat faile     (279)
The flees to winne, and stinten his bataile;
And saved him his lyf and his honour ;
And gat him greet name as a conquerour
Right through the sleight of her en-
    chantement.     1650
Now hath Jasoun the flees, and hoom
    is went
With Medea, and tresor ful gret woon.
But unwist of her fader is she goon
To Tessaly, with duk Jasoun her leef,
That afterward hath broght her to mes-
    cheef.     1655
For as a traitour he is from her go,
And with her lafte his yonge children
    two,     (290)
And falsly hath betrayed her, allas !
And ever in love a cheef traitour he was ;
And wedded yit the thridde wyf anon, 1660
That was the doghter of the king Creon.

This is the meed of loving and guerdoun
That Medea received of Jasoun

Right for her trouthe and for her kinde-
    nesse,
That loved him better than her-self, I
    gesse, 1665
And lafte her fader and her heritage.
And of Jasoun this is the vassalage, (300)
That, in his dayes, nas ther noon y-founde
So fals a lover going on the grounde.
And therfor in her lettre thus she
    seyde 1670
First, whan she of his falsnesse him um-
    breyde,
'Why lyked me thy yelow heer to see
More then the boundes of myn honestee,

Why lyked me thy youthe and thy fair-
    nesse,
And of thy tonge the infinit gracious-
    nesse? 1675
O, haddest thou in thy conquest deed
    y-be,
Ful mikel untrouthe had ther dyed with
    thee!' (310)
    Wel can Ovyde her lettre in vers endyte,
Which were as now to long for me to
    wryte.

*Explicit Legenda Ysiphile et Medee,*
*Martirum.*

# V. THE LEGEND OF LUCRETIA.

*Incipit Legenda Lucrecie Rome, Martiris.*

Now moot I seyn the exiling of kinges
Of Rome, for hir horrible doinges, 1681
And of the laste king Tarquinius,
As saith Ovyde and Titus Livius.
But for that cause telle I nat this storie,
But for to preise and drawen to memorie
The verray wyf, the verray trewe Lucresse,
That, for her wyfhood and her stedfast-
    nesse, 1687
Nat only that thise payens her comende,
But he, that cleped is in our legende (10)
The grete Austin, hath greet compas-
    sioun 1690
Of this Lucresse, that starf at Rome toun;
And in what wyse, I wol but shortly trete,
And of this thing I touche but the grete.
    Whan Ardea beseged was aboute
With Romains, that ful sterne were and
    stoute, 1695
Ful longe lay the sege, and litel wroghte,
So that they were half ydel, as hem
    thoghte; (18)
And in his pley Tarquinius the yonge
Gan for to jape, for he was light of tonge,
And seyde, that 'it was an ydel lyf; 1700
No man did ther no more than his wyf;
And lat us speke of wyves, that is best;
Praise every man his owne, as him lest,
And with our speche lat us ese our herte.'
    A knight, that highte Colatyne, up
    sterte, 1705

And seyde thus, 'nay, for hit is no nede
To trowen on the word, but on the
    dede.
I have a wyf,' quod he, 'that, as I trowe,
Is holden good of alle that ever her
    knowe; (30)
Go we to-night to Rome, and we shul
    see.' 1710
    Tarquinius answerde, 'that lyketh me.'
To Rome be they come, and faste hem
    dighte
To Colatynes hous, and doun they lighte,
Tarquinius, and eek this Colatyne.
The husbond knew the estres wel and
    fyne, 1715
And prively into the hous they goon;
Nor at the gate porter was ther noon;
And at the chambre-dore they abyde. (39)
This noble wyf sat by her beddes syde
Dischevele, for no malice she ne thoghte;
And softe wolle our book seith that she
    wroghte 1721
To kepen her fro slouthe and ydelnesse;
And bad her servants doon hir businesse,
And axeth hem, 'what tydings heren ye?
How seith men of the sege, how shal hit
    be? 1725
God wolde the walles weren falle adoun;
Myn husbond is so longe out of this toun,
For which the dreed doth me so sore
    smerte,
Right as a swerd hit stingeth to myn
    herte (50)

Whan I think on the sege or of that place ;
God save my lord, I preye him for his
    grace :'—             1731
And ther-with-al ful tenderly she weep,
And of her werk she took no more keep,
But mekely she leet her eyen falle ;
And thilke semblant sat her wel with-alle.
And eek her teres, ful of honestee,   1736
Embelisshed her wyfly chastitee ;
Her countenaunce is to her herte digne,
For they acordeden in dede and signe. (60)
And with that word her husbond Colatyn,
Or she of him was war, com sterting in,
And seide, 'dreed thee noght, for I am
    here !'              1742
And she anoon up roos, with blisful chere,
And kiste him, as of wyves is the wone.

Tarquinius, this proude kinges sone,
Conceived hath her beautee and her
    chere,              1746
Her yelow heer, her shap, and her manere,
Her hew, her wordes that she hath com-
    pleyned,
And by no crafte her beautee nas nat
    feyned ;           (70)
And caughte to this lady swich desyr,
That in his herte brende as any fyr   1751
So woodly, that his wit was al forgeten.
For wel, thoghte he, she sholde nat be
    geten ;
And ay the more that he was in dispair,
The more he coveteth and thoghte her
    fair.             1755
His blinde lust was al his covetinge.

A-morwe, whan the brid began to singe,
Unto the sege he comth ful privily,
And by himself he walketh sobrely,  (80)
Th'image of her recording alwey newe ;
' Thus lay her heer, and thus fresh was
    her hewe ;         1761
Thus sat, thus spak, thus span ; this was
    her chere,
Thus fair she was, and this was her
    manere.'
Al this conceit his herte hath now y-take.
And, as the see, with tempest al to-shake,
That, after whan the storm is al ago, 1766
Yet wol the water quappe a day or two,
Right so, thogh that her forme wer
    absent,        (89)
The plesaunce of her forme was present ;

But natheles, nat plesaunce, but delyt,
Or an unrightful talent with despyt ; 1771
' For, maugre her, she shal my lemman
    be ;
Hap helpeth hardy man alday,' quod he ;
' What ende that I make, hit shal be so ;'
And girt him with his swerde, and gan
    to go ;          1775
And forth he rit til he to Rome is come,
And al aloon his wey than hath he nome
Unto the house of Colatyn ful right.
Doun was the sonne, and day hath lost
    his light ;        (100)
And in he com un-to a privy halke,  1780
And in the night ful theefly gan he stalke,
Whan every night was to his reste broght,
Ne no wight had of tresoun swich a
    thoght.
Were hit by window or by other gin, 1784
With swerde y-drawe, shortly he comth in
Ther as she lay, this noble wyf Lucresse.
And, as she wook, her bed she felte presse.
' What beste is that,' quod she, ' that
    weyeth thus ?'
' I am the kinges sone, Tarquinius,' (110)
Quod he, ' but and thou crye, or noise
    make,          1790
Or if thou any creature awake,
By thilke god that formed man on lyve,
This swerd through-out thyn herte shal
    I ryve.'
And ther-withal unto her throte he sterte,
And sette the point al sharp upon her
    herte.          1795
No word she spak, she hath no might
    therto.
What shal she sayn ? her wit is al ago.
Right as a wolf that fynt a lomb aloon,
To whom shal she compleyne, or make
    moon ?        (120)
What ! shal she fighte with an hardy
    knight ?         1800
Wel wot men that a woman hath no
    might.
What ! shal she crye, or how shal she
    asterte
That hath her by the throte, with swerde
    at herte ?
She axeth grace, and seith al that she can.
' Ne wolt thou nat,' quod he, this cruel
    man,         1805

'As wisly Jupiter my soule save,
As I shal in the stable slee thy knave,
And leye him in thy bed, and loude crye,
That I thee finde in suche avouterye ; (130)
And thus thou shalt be deed, and also
   lese               1810
Thy name, for thou shalt non other chese.'
   Thise Romain wyves loveden so hir
      name
At thilke tyme, and dredden so the shame,
That, what for fere of slaundre and drede
   of deeth,           1814
She loste bothe at-ones wit and breeth,
And in a swough she lay and wex so
   deed,
Men mighte smyten of her arm or heed ;
She feleth no-thing, neither foul ne fair.
   Tarquinius, that art a kinges eyr, (140)
And sholdest, as by linage and by right,
Doon as a lord and as a verray knight,
Why hastow doon dispyt to chivalrye ?
Why hastow doon this lady vilanye ?
Allas ! of thee this was a vileins dede !
   But now to purpos ; in the story I rede,
Whan he was goon, al this mischaunce is
   falle.          1826
This lady sente after her frendes alle,
Fader, moder, husbond, al y-fere ; (149)
And al dischevele, with her heres clere,
In habit swich as women used tho  1830
Unto the burying of her frendes go,
She sit in halle with a sorweful sighte.
Her frendes axen what her aylen mighte,
And who was deed? And she sit ay
   wepinge,
A word for shame ne may she forth out-
   bringe,        1835
Ne upon hem she dorste nat beholde.
But atte laste of Tarquiny she hem tolde,
This rewful cas, and al this thing horrible.
The wo to tellen hit were impossible, (160)
That she and alle her frendes made
   atones.        1840
Al hadde folkes hertes been of stones,
Hit mighte have maked hem upon her
   rewe,
Her herte was so wyfly and so trewe.
She seide, that, for her gilt ne for her
   blame,
Her husbond sholde nat have the foule
   name,        1845

That wolde she nat suffre, by no wey.
And they answerden alle, upon hir fey,
That they foryeve hit her, for hit was
   right ;        (169)
Hit was no gilt, hit lay nat in her might ;
And seiden her ensamples many oon. 1850
But al for noght; for thus she seide
   anoon,
'Be as be may,' quod she, 'of forgiving,
I wol nat have no forgift for no-thing.'
But prively she caughte forth a knyf, 1854
And therwith-al she rafte her-self her lyf;
And as she fel adoun, she caste her look,
And of her clothes yit she hede took ;
For in her falling yit she hadde care
Lest that her feet or swiche thing lay
   bare ;        (180)
So wel she loved clennesse and eek trouthe.
   Of her had al the toun of Rome routhe,
And Brutus by her chaste blode hath
   swore        1862
That Tarquin sholde y-banisht be ther-fore,
And al his kin ; and let the peple calle,
And openly the tale he tolde hem alle,
And openly let carie her on a bere  1866
Through al the toun, that men may see
   and here
The horrible deed of her oppressioun.
Ne never was ther king in Rome toun (190)
Sin thilke day ; and she was holden there
A seint, and ever her day y-halwed dere
As in hir lawe : and thus endeth Lucresse,
The noble wyf, as Titus bereth witnesse.
   I tell hit, for she was of love so trewe,
Ne in her wille she chaunged for no newe.
And for the stable herte, sad and kinde,
That in these women men may alday
   finde ;        1877
Ther as they caste hir herte, ther hit
   dwelleth.
For wel I wot, that Crist †him-selve
   telleth,        (200)
That in Israel, as wyd as is the lond, 1880
That so gret feith in al the lond he ne
   fond
As in a woman ; and this is no lye.
And as of men, loketh which tirannye
They doon alday ; assay hem who so liste,
The trewest is ful brotel for to triste. 1885

*Explicit Legenda Lucrecie Rome, Martiris.*

## VI. THE LEGEND OF ARIADNE.

*Incipit Legenda Adriane de Athenes.*

Juge infernal, Minos, of Crete king,
Now cometh thy lot, now comestow on
    the ring ;
Nat for thy sake only wryte I this storie,
But for to clepe agein unto memorie 1889
Of Theseus the grete untrouthe of love ;
For which the goddes of the heven above
Ben wrothe, and wreche han take for thy
    sinne.
Be reed for shame ! now I thy lyf beginne.
    Minos, that was the mighty king of
    Crete,
That hadde an hundred citees stronge
    and grete,                    (10) 1895
To scole hath sent his sone Androgeus,
To Athenes ; of the whiche hit happed
    thus,
That he was slayn, lerning philosophye,
Right in that citee, nat but for envye.
    The grete Minos, of the whiche I speke,
His sones deeth is comen for to wreke ;
Alcathoe he bisegeth harde and longe.
But natheles the walles be so stronge,
And Nisus, that was king of that citee,
So chivalrous, that litel dredeth he ; 1905
Of Minos or his ost took he no cure,  (21)
Til on a day befel an aventure,
That Nisus doghter stood upon the wal,
And of the sege saw the maner al.   1909
So happed hit, that, at a scarmishing,
She caste her herte upon Minos the king,
For his beautee and for his chivalrye,
So sore, that she wende for to dye.
And, shortly of this proces for to pace,
She made Minos winnen thilke place, 1915
So that the citee was al at his wille,  (31)
To saven whom him list, or elles spille ;
But wikkedly he quitte her kindenesse,
And let her drenche in sorowe and dis-
    tresse,                            1919
Nere that the goddes hadde of her pite ;
But that tale were to long as now for me.
    Athenes wan this king Minos also,
And Alcathoe and other tounes mo ;

And this th'effect, that Minos hath so
    driven
Hem of Athenes, that they mote him
    yiven                         (40) 1925
Fro yere to yere her owne children dere
For to be slayn, as ye shul after here.
    This Minos hath a monstre, a wikked
    beste,
That was so cruel that, without areste,
Whan that a man was broght in his
    presence,                          1930
He wolde him ete, ther helpeth no de-
    fence.
And every thridde yeer, with-outen doute,
They casten lot, and, as hit com aboute
On riche, on pore, he moste his sone
    take,                          (49) 1934
And of his child he moste present make
Unto Minos, to save him or to spille,
Or lete his beste devoure him at his
    wille.
And this hath Minos don, right in despyt ;
To wreke his sone was set al his delyt,
And maken hem of Athenes his thral 1940
Fro yere to yere, whyl that he liven shal ;
And hoom he saileth whan this toun is
    wonne.
This wikked custom is so longe y-ronne
Til that of Athenes king Egeus
Mot sende his owne sone, Theseus,   1945
Sith that the lot is fallen him upon,  (61)
To be devoured, for grace is ther non.
And forth is lad this woful yonge knight
Unto the court of king Minos ful right,
And in a prison, fetered, cast is he  1950
Til thilke tyme he sholde y-freten be.
    Wel maystow wepe, O woful Theseus,
That art a kinges sone, and dampned
    thus.
Me thinketh this, that thou were depe
    y-holde                           1954
To whom that saved thee fro cares colde !
And now, if any woman helpe thee,  (71)
Wel oughtestow her servant for to be,
And been her trewe lover yeer by yere !
But now to come ageyn to my matere.

The tour, ther as this Theseus is throwe
Doun in the botom derke and wonder
   lowe, 1961
Was joyning in the walle to a foreyne ;
And hit was longing to the doghtren
   tweyne
Of king Minos, that in hir chambres grete
Dwelten above, toward the maister-
   strete, (80) 1965
In mochel mirthe, in joye and in solas.
Not I nat how, hit happed ther, per cas,
As Theseus compleyned him by nighte,
The kinges doghter, Adrian that highte,
And eek her suster Phedra, herden al 1970
His compleyning, as they stode on the wal
And lokeden upon the brighte mone ;
Hem leste nat to go to bedde sone.
And of his wo they had compassioun ;
A kinges sone to ben in swich prisoun
And be devoured, thoughte hem gret
   pitee. (91) 1976
   Than Adrian spak to her suster free,
And seyde, ' Phedra, leve suster dere,
This woful lordes sone may ye nat here,
How pitously compleyneth he his kin,
And eek his pore estat that he is in, 1981
And gilteless ? now certes, hit is routhe !
And if ye wol assenten, by my trouthe,
He shal be holpen, how so that we do !'
   Phedra answerde, ' y-wis, me is as wo
For him as ever I was for any man ; 1986
And, to his help, the beste reed I can (102)
Is that we doon the gayler prively
To come, and speke with us hastily,
And doon this woful man with him to
   come. 1990
For if he may this monstre overcome,
Than were he quit ; ther is noon other
   bote.
Lat us wel taste him at his herte-rote,
That, if so be that he a wepen have,
Wher that he dar, his lyf to kepe and
   save, (110) 1995
Fighten with this fend, and him defende.
For, in the prison, ther he shal descende,
Ye wite wel, that the beste is in a place
That nis nat derk, and hath roum eek
   and space
To welde an ax or swerd or staf or knyf,
So that, me thinketh, he sholde save his
   lyf ; 2001

If that he be a man, he shal do so.
And we shul make him balles eek also
Of wexe and towe, that, whan he gapeth
   faste, 2004
Into the bestes throte he shal hem caste
To slake his hunger and encombre his
   teeth ; (121)
And right anon, whan that Theseus seeth
The beste achoked, he shal on him lepe
To sleen him, or they comen more to-hepe.
This wepen shal the gayler, or that tyde,
Ful privily within the prison hyde ; 2011
And, for the hous is crinkled to and fro,
And hath so queinte weyes for to go—
For hit is shapen as the mase is wroght—
Therto have I a remedie in my thoght,
That, by a clewe of twyne, as he hath
   goon, (131) 2016
The same wey he may returne anoon,
Folwing alwey the threed, as he hath
   come.
And, whan that he this beste hath over-
   come,
Then may he fleen awey out of this drede,
And eek the gayler may he with him
   lede, 2021
And him avaunce at hoom in his contree,
Sin that so greet a lordes sone is he.
This is my reed, if that he dar hit take.'
   What sholde I lenger sermoun of hit
   make ? 2025
The gayler cometh, and with him Theseus.
And whan thise thinges been acorded
   thus, (142)
Adoun sit Theseus upon his knee :—
' The righte lady of my lyf,' quod he,
' I, sorweful man, y-dampned to the deeth,
Fro yow, whyl that me lasteth lyf or
   breeth, 2031
I wol nat twinne, after this aventure,
But in your servise thus I wol endure,
That, as a wrecche unknowe, I wol yow
   serve 2034
For ever-mo, til that myn herte sterve.
Forsake I wol at hoom myn heritage, (151)
And, as I seide, ben of your court a page,
If that ye vouche-sauf that, in this place,
Ye graunte me to han so gret a grace
That I may han nat but my mete and
   drinke ; 2040
And for my sustenance yit wol I swinke,

Right as yow list, that Minos ne no
    wight—
Sin that he saw me never with eyen
    sight—
Ne no man elles, shal me conne espye ;
So slyly and so wel I shal me gye,    2045
And me so wel disfigure and so lowe, (161)
That in this world ther shal no man me
    knowe,
To han my lyf, and for to han presence
Of yow, that doon to me this excellence.
And to my fader shal I senden here    2050
This worthy man, that is now your gay-
    lere,
And, him to guerdon, that he shal wel be
Oon of the grettest men of my contree.
And yif I dorste seyn, my lady bright,
I am a kinges sone, and eek a knight ;
As wolde god, yif that hit mighte be (171)
Ye weren in my contree, alle three,
And I with yow, to bere yow companye,
Than shulde ye seen yif that I ther-of lye !
And, if I profre yow in low manere    2060
To ben your page and serven yow right
    here,
But I yow serve as lowly in that place,
I prey to Mars to yive me swiche a grace
That shames deeth on me ther mote
    falle,
And deeth and povert to my frendes
    alle ;    2065
And that my spirit by nighte mote go (181)
After my deeth, and walke to and fro ;
That I mote of a traitour have a name,
For which my spirit go, to do me shame !
And yif I ever claime other degree,    2070
But-if ye vouche-sauf to yive hit me,
As I have seid, of shames deeth I deye !
And mercy, lady ! I can nat elles seye !'
    A seemly knight was Theseus to see,
And yong, but of a twenty yeer and
    three ;    2075
But who-so hadde y-seyn his counten-
    aunce,    (191)
He wolde have wept, for routhe of his
    penaunce ;
For which this Adriane in this manere
Answerde to his profre and to his chere.
    'A kinges sone, and eek a knight,'
    quod she,    2080
'To been my servant in so low degree,

God shilde hit, for the shame of women
    alle !
And leve me never swich a cas befalle !
But sende yow grace and sleighte of
    herte also,
Yow to defende and knightly sleen your
    fo,    2085
And leve herafter that I may yow finde
To me and to my suster here so kinde,
That I repente nat to give yow lyf ! (203)
Yit were hit better that I were your
    wyf,
Sin that ye been as gentil born as I, 2090
And have a reaume, nat but faste by,
Then that I suffred giltles yow to sterve,
Or that I let yow as a page serve ;
Hit is not profit, as unto your kinrede ;
But what is that that man nil do for
    drede ?    2095
And to my suster, sin that hit is so (211)
That she mot goon with me, if that I go,
Or elles suffre deeth as wel as I,
That ye unto your sone as trewely    2099
Doon her be wedded at your hoom-coming.
This is the fynal ende of al this thing ;
Ye swere hit heer, on al that may be
    sworn.'
    'Ye, lady myn,' quod he, ' or elles torn
Mote I be with the Minotaur to-morwe !
And haveth her-of my herte-blood to
    borwe,    (220) 2105
Yif that ye wile ; if I had knyf or spere,
I wolde hit leten out, and ther-on swere,
For than at erst I wot ye wil me leve.
By Mars, that is the cheef of my bileve,
So that I mighte liven and nat faile 2110
To-morwe for t'acheve my bataile,
I nolde never fro this place flee,
Til that ye shuld the verray preve see.
For now, if that the sooth I shal yow say,
I have y-loved yow ful many a day,    2115
Thogh ye ne wiste hit nat, in my contree.
And aldermost desyred yow to see (232)
Of any erthly living creature ;    2118
Upon my trouthe I swere, and yow assure,
Thise seven yeer I have your servant be ;
Now have I yow, and also have ye me,
My dere herte, of Athenes duchesse !'
    This lady smyleth at his stedfastnesse,
And at his hertly wordes, and his chere,
And to her suster seide in this manere,

Al softely, 'now, suster myn,' quod she,
'Now be we duchesses, bothe I and ye,
And sikered to the regals of Athenes, (243)
And bothe her-after lykly to be quenes,
And saved fro his deeth a kinges sone,
As ever of gentil women is the wone 2131
To save a gentil man, emforth hir might,
In honest cause, and namely in his right.
Me thinketh no wight oghte her-of us
    blame,
Ne beren us ther-for an evel name.' 2135
    And shortly of this matere for to make,
This Theseus of her hath leve y-take, (252)
And every point †performed was in dede
As ye have in this covenant herd me rede.
His wepen, his clew, his thing that I have
    said,                                   2140
Was by the gayler in the hous y-laid
Ther as this Minotaur hath his dwelling,
Right faste by the dore, at his entring.
And Theseus is lad unto his deeth,   2144
And forth un-to this Minotaur he geeth,
And by the teching of this Adriane (261)
He overcom this beste, and was his bane;
And out he cometh by the clewe again
Ful prevely, whan he this beste hath
    slain ;                                 2149
And by the gayler geten hath a barge,
And of his wyves tresor gan hit charge,
And took his wyf, and eek her suster free,
And eek the gayler, and with hem alle
    three
Is stole awey out of the lond by nighte,
And to the contre of Ennopye him
    dighte                                  2155
Ther as he had a frend of his knowinge.
Ther festen they, ther dauncen they and
    singe ;                                (272)
And in his armes hath this Adriane,
That of the beste hath kept him from his
    bane ;                                  2159
And gat him ther a newe barge anoon,
And of his contree-folk a ful gret woon,
And taketh his leve, and hoomward sail-
    eth he.
And in an yle, amid the wilde see,
Ther as ther dwelte creature noon
Save wilde bestes, and that ful many
    oon,                                    2165
He made his ship a-londe for to sette ;
And in that yle half a day he lette, (282)

And seide, that on the lond he moste him
    reste.
His mariners han doon right as him
    leste ;
And, for to tellen shortly in this cas, 2170
Whan Adriane his wyf a-slepe was,
For that her suster fairer was than she,
He taketh her in his hond, and forth
    goth he
To shippe, and as a traitour stal his way
Whyl that this Adriane a-slepe lay, 2175
And to his contree-ward he saileth
    blyve—                                 (291)
A twenty devil way the wind him
    dryve !—
And fond his fader drenched in the see.
    Me list no more to speke of him, parde ;
Thise false lovers, poison be hir bane !
But I wol turne again to Adriane    2181
That is with slepe for werinesse atake.
Ful sorwefully her herte may awake.
Allas ! for thee my herte hath now
    pite !
Right in the dawening awaketh she, 2185
And gropeth in the bedde, and fond right
    noght.                                 (301)
'Allas !' quod she, 'that ever I was
    wroght !
I am betrayed !' and her heer to-rente,
And to the stronde bar-fot faste she
    wente,
And cryed, 'Theseus ! myn herte swete !
Wher be ye, that I may nat with yow
    mete,                                   2191
And mighte thus with bestes been y-
    slain ? '
    The holwe rokkes answerde her again ;
No man she saw, and yit shyned the
    mone,                                   2194
And hye upon a rokke she wente sone,
And saw his barge sailing in the see. (311)
Cold wex her herte, and right thus seide
    she.
'Meker than ye finde I the bestes wilde !'
Hadde he nat sinne, that her thus be-
    gylde ?
She cryed, 'O turne again, for routhe and
    sinne !                                2200
Thy barge hath nat al his meiny inne ! '
Her kerchef on a pole up stikked she,
Ascaunce that he sholde hit wel y-see,

And him remembre that she was behinde,
And turne again, and on the stronde her
　　finde ;　　　　　　　　　(320) 2205
But al for noght ; his wey he is y-goon.
And doun she fil a-swown upon a stoon ;
And up she rist, and kiste, in al her care,
The steppes of his feet, ther he hath fare,
And to her bedde right thus she speketh
　　tho :—　　　　　　　　　　2210
'Thou bed,' quod she, 'that hast receyved
　　two,
Thou shalt answere of two, and nat of
　　oon !
Wher is thy gretter part away y-goon ?
Allas ! wher shal I, wrecched wight, be-
　　come !
For, thogh so be that ship or boot heer
　　come,　　　　　　　　　　2215

Hoom to my contree dar I nat for
　　drede ;　　　　　　　　　　(331)
I can my-selven in this cas nat rede !'
　　What shal I telle more her compleyn-
　　　　ing ?
Hit is so long, hit were an hevy thing.
In her epistle Naso telleth al ;　　2220
But shortly to the ende I telle shal.
The goddes have her holpen, for pitee ;
And, in the signe of Taurus, men may
　　see
The stones of her coroun shyne clere.—
I wol no more speke of this matere ;
But thus this false lover can begyle 2226
His trewe love.  The devil †him quyte
　　his whyle !　　　　　　　　(342)

*Explicit Legenda Adriane de Athenes.*


# VII. THE LEGEND OF PHILOMELA.

*Incipit Legenda Philomene.*

*Deus dator formarum.*

Thou yiver of the formes, that hast
　　wroght
The faire world, and bare hit in thy
　　thoght
Eternally, or thou thy werk began,　2230
Why madest thou, unto the slaundre of
　　man,
Or—al be that hit was not thy doing,
As for that fyn to make swiche a
　　thing—
Why suffrest thou that Tereus was bore,
That is in love so fals and so forswore,
That, fro this world up to the firste
　　hevene,　　　　　　　　　2236
Corrumpeth, whan that folk his name
　　nevene ?　　　　　　　　　(10)
And, as to me, so grisly was his dede,
That, whan that I his foule story rede,
Myn eyen wexen foule and sore also ; 2240
Yit last the venim of so longe ago,
That hit enfecteth him that wol beholde
The story of Tereus, of which I tolde.
　　Of Trace was he lord, and kin to Marte,
The cruel god that stant with blody
　　darte ;　　　　　　　　　2245

And wedded had he, with a blisful chere,
King Pandiones faire doghter dere,　(20)
That highte Progne, flour of her contree,
Thogh Juno list nat at the feste be,
Ne Ymeneus, that god of wedding is ;
But at the feste redy been, y-wis,　　2251
The furies three, with alle hir mortel
　　brond.
The owle al night aboute the balkes wond,
That prophet is of wo and of mischaunce.
This revel, ful of songe and ful of daunce,
Lasteth a fourtenight, or litel lasse.　2256
But, shortly of this story for to passe, (30)
For I am wery of him for to telle,
Five yeer his wyf and he togeder dwelle,
Til on a day she gan so sore longe　2260
To seen her suster, that she saw nat longe,
That for desyr she niste what to seye.
But to her husband gan she for to preye,
For goddes love, that she moste ones
　　goon　　　　　　　　　　2264
Her suster for to seen, and come anoon,
Or elles, but she moste to her wende,
She preyde him, that he wolde after her
　　sende ;　　　　　　　　　(40)
And this was, day by day, al her prayere
With al humblesse of wyfhood, word, and
　　chere.　　　　　　　　　2269

This Tereus let make his shippes yare,
And into Grece him-self is forth y-fare
Unto his fader in lawe, and gan him
    preye
To vouche-sauf that, for a month or
    tweye,
That Philomene, his wyves suster, mighte
On Progne his wyf but ones have a
    sighte—                                2275
'And she shal come to yow again anoon.
Myself with her wol bothe come and
    goon,                                   (50)
And as myn hertes lyf I wol her kepe.'
    This olde Pandion, this king, gan
    wepe
For tendernesse of herte, for to leve  2280
His doghter goon, and for to yive her
    leve;
Of al this world he lovede no-thing so;
But at the laste leve hath she to go.
For Philomene, with salte teres eke,
Gan of her fader grace to beseke      2285
To seen her suster, that her longeth so;
And him embraceth with her armes two.
And therwith-al so yong and fair was she
That, whan that Tereus saw her beautee,
And of array that ther was noon her
    liche,                            (63) 2290
And yit of bountee was she two so riche,
He caste his fyry herte upon her so
That he wol have her, how so that hit go,
And with his wyles kneled and so preyde,
Til at the laste Pandion thus seyde :—
    'Now, sone,' quod he, 'that art to me
    so dere,                              2296
I thee betake my yonge doghter here,  (70)
That bereth the key of al my hertes lyf.
And grete wel my doghter and thy wyf,
And yive her leve somtyme for to pleye,
That she may seen me ones er I deye.'
And soothly, he hath mad him riche
    feste,                                2302
And to his folk, the moste and eek the
    leste,
That with him com; and yaf him yiftes
    grete,
And him conveyeth through the maister-
    strete                               2305
Of Athenes, and to the see him broghte,
And turneth hoom; no malice he ne
    thoghte.                              (80)

The ores pulleth forth the vessel faste,
And into Trace arriveth at the laste,
And up into a forest he her ledde,    2310
And to a cave privily him spedde ;
And, in this derke cave, yif her leste,
Or leste noght, he bad her for to reste ;
Of whiche her herte agroos, and seyde
    thus,
' Wher is my suster, brother Tereus?' 2315
And therwith-al she wepte tenderly,
And quook for fere, pale and pitously,
Right as the lamb that of the wolf is
    biten ;
Or as the colver, that of the egle is
    smiten,
And is out of his clawes forth escaped, 2320
Yet hit is afered and awhaped
Lest hit be hent eft-sones, so sat she
But utterly hit may non other be.
By force hath he, this traitour, doon that
    dede,
That he hath reft her of her mayden-
    hede,                                 2325
Maugree her heed, by strengthe and by
    his might.                           (99)
Lo ! here a dede of men, and that a right !
She cryeth 'suster !' with ful loud
    stevene,
And 'fader dere !' and 'help me, god in
    hevene !'                            2329
Al helpeth nat ; and yet this false theef
Hath doon this lady yet a more mischeef,
For fere lest she sholde his shame crye,
And doon him openly a vilanye,
And with his swerd her tong of kerveth
    he,
And in a castel made her for to be   2335
Ful privily in prison evermore,
And kepte her to his usage and his
    store,                               (110)
So that she mighte him nevermore asterte.
O sely Philomene ! wo is thyn herte;
God wreke thee, and sende thee thy
    bone !                               2340
Now is hit tyme I make an ende sone.
    This Tereus is to his wyf y-come,
And in his armes hath his wyf y-nome,
And pitously he weep, and shook his
    heed,
And swor her that he fond her suster
    deed ;                               2345

For which this sely Progne hath swich
    wo,                                (119) 2346
That ny her sorweful herte brak a-two ;
And thus in teres lete I Progne dwelle,
And of her suster forth I wol yow telle.

    This woful lady lerned had in youthe
So that she werken and enbrouden couthe,
And weven in her stole the radevore
As hit of women hath be woned yore.
And, shortly for to seyn, she hath her
    fille
Of mete and drink, and clothing at her
    wille,                                2355
And coude eek rede, and wel y-nogh
    endyte,
But with a penne coude she nat wryte ;
But lettres can she weven to and fro,  (131)
So that, by that the yeer was al a-go,
She had y-woven in a stamin large    2360
How she was broght from Athenes in a
    barge,
And in a cave how that she was broght ;
And al the thing that Tereus hath wroght,
She waf hit wel, and wroot the story
    above,
How she was served for her suster love ;
And to a knave a ring she yaf anoon,  2366
And prayed him, by signes, for to goon (140)
Unto the quene, and beren her that clooth,
And by signes swor him many an ooth,
She sholde him yeve what she geten
    mighte.                              2370
    This knave anoon unto the quene him
    dighte,

And took hit her, and al the maner tolde.
And, whan that Progne hath this thing
    beholde,
No word she spak, for sorwe and eek for
    rage ;
But feyned her to goon on pilgrimage 2375
To Bachus temple ; and, in a litel
    stounde,
Her dombe suster sitting hath she founde,
Weping in the castel her aloon.     (151)
Allas ! the wo, the compleint, and the
    moon
That Progne upon her dombe suster
    maketh !                            2380
In armes everich of hem other taketh,
And thus I lete hem in hir sorwe dwelle.
    The remenant is no charge for to
    telle,
For this is al and som, thus was she
    served,
That never harm a-gilte ne deserved 2385
Unto this cruel man, that she of wiste.
Ye may be war of men, yif that yow
    liste.                            (160)
For, al be that he wol nat, for his shame,
Doon so as Tereus, to lese his name,
Ne serve yow as a mordrour or a knave,
Ful litel whyle shul ye trewe him have,
That wol I seyn, al were he now my
    brother,                            2392
But hit so be that he may have non
    other.                             (166)

*Explicit Legenda Philomene.*

## VIII. THE LEGEND OF PHYLLIS.

*Incipit Legenda Phillis.*

By preve as wel as by auctoritee,
That wikked fruit cometh of a wikked
    tree,                               2395
That may ye finde, if that it lyketh
    yow.
But for this ende I speke this as now,
To telle you of false Demophon.
In love a falser herde I never non,
But-if hit were his fader Theseus.    2400

'God, for his grace, fro swich oon kepe
    us ! '
Thus may thise women prayen that hit
    here.                                 (9)
Now to th'effect turne I of my matere.
    Destroyed is of Troye the citee ;   2404
This Demophon com sailing in the see
Toward Athenes, to his paleys large ;
With him com many a ship and many a
    barge

Ful of his folk, of which ful many oon
Is wounded sore, and seek, and wo be-
    goon.                                    2409
And they han at the sege longe y-lain.
Behinde him com a wind and eek a rain
That shoof so sore, his sail ne mighte
    stonde,                                  (19)
Him were lever than al the world a-londe,
So hunteth him the tempest so and fro.
So derk hit was, he coude nowher go ; 2415
And with a wawe brosten was his stere.
His ship was rent so lowe, in swich
    manere,
That carpenter ne coude hit nat amende.
The see, by nighte, as any torche brende
For wood, and posseth him now up now
    doun,                                    2420
Til Neptune hath of him compassioun,
And Thetis, Chorus, Triton, and they
    alle,
And maden him upon a lond to falle,    (30)
Wher-of that Phillis lady was and quene,
Ligurgus doghter, fairer on to sene    2425
Than is the flour again the brighte sonne.
Unnethe is Demophon to londe y-wonne,
Wayk and eek wery, and his folk for-
    pyned
Of werinesse, and also enfamyned ;     2429
And to the deeth he almost was y-driven.
His wyse folk to conseil han him yiven
To seken help and socour of the queen,
And loken what his grace mighte been, (40)
And maken in that lond som chevisaunce,
To kepen him fro wo and fro mischaunce.
For seek was he, and almost at the deeth ;
Unnethe mighte he speke or drawe his
    breeth,                                  2437
And lyth in Rodopeya him for to reste.
Whan he may walke, him thoughte hit
    was the beste
Unto the court to seken for socour.    2440
Men knewe him wel, and diden him
    honour ;
For at Athenes duk and lord was he,
As Theseus his fader hadde y-be,       (50)
That in his tyme was of greet renoun,
No man so greet in al his regioun ;    2445
And lyk his fader of face and of stature,
And fals of love ; hit com him of nature ;
As doth the fox Renard, the foxes sone,
Of kinde he coude his olde faders wone

Withoute lore, as can a drake swimme,
Whan hit is caught and caried to the
    brimme.                                  2451
This honourable Phillis doth him chere,
Her lyketh wel his port and his manere.
But for I am agroted heer-biforn        (61)
To wryte of hem that been in love for-
    sworn,                                   2455
And eek to haste me in my legende,
Which to performe god me grace sende,
Therfor I passe shortly in this wyse ;
Ye han wel herd of Theseus devyse
In the betraising of fair Adriane,      2460
That of her pite kepte him from his
    bane.
At shorte wordes, right so Demophon
The same wey, the same path hath gon (70)
That dide his false fader Theseus.
For unto Phillis hath he sworen thus, 2465
To wedden her, and her his trouthe
    plighte,
And piked of her al the good he mighte,
Whan he was hool and sound and hadde
    his reste ;
And doth with Phillis what so that him
    leste.
And wel coude I, yif that me leste so, 2470
Tellen al his doing to and fro.
  He seide, unto his contree moste he
    saile,
For ther he wolde her wedding apparaile
As fil to her honour and his also.      (81)
And openly he took his leve tho,       2475
And hath her sworn, he wolde nat sojorne,
But in a month he wolde again retorne.
And in that lond let make his ordinaunce
As verray lord, and took the obeisaunce
Wel and hoomly, and let his shippes
    dighte,                                  2480
And hoom he goth the nexte wey he
    mighte ;
For unto Phillis yit ne com he noght.
And that hath she so harde and sore
    aboght,                                  (90)
Allas ! that, as the stories us recorde,
She was her owne deeth, right with a
    corde,                                   2485
Whan that she saw that Demophon her
    trayed.
  But to him first she wroot and faste
    him prayed

He wolde come, and her deliver of peyne,
As I reherse shal a word or tweyne.
Me list nat vouche-sauf on him to swinke,
Ne spende on him a penne ful of inke, 2491
For fals in love was he, right as his syre;
The devil sette hir soules bothe a-fyre!
But of the lettre of Phillis wol I wryte
A word or tweyne, al-thogh hit be but
     lyte.      (102) 2495

'Thyn hostesse,' quod she, 'O Demophon,
Thy Phillis, which that is so wo begon,
Of Rodopeye, upon yow moot compleyne,
Over the terme set betwix us tweyne,
That ye ne holden forward, as ye seyde;
Your anker, which ye in our haven
     leyde,      2501
Highte us, that ye wolde comen, out of
     doute,
Or that the mone ones wente aboute. (110)
But tymes foure the mone hath hid her
     face
Sin thilke day ye wente fro this place, 2505
And foure tymes light the world again.
But for al that, yif I shal soothly sain,
Yit hath the streem of Sitho nat y-broght
From Athenes the ship; yit comth hit
     noght.
And, yif that ye the terme rekne wolde,
As I or other trewe lovers sholde,    2511
I pleyne not, god wot, beforn my day.'—

But al her lettre wryten I ne may (120)
By ordre, for hit were to me a charge;
Her lettre was right long and ther-to
     large;      2515
But here and there in ryme I have hit
     laid,
Ther as me thoughte that she wel hath
     said.—

She seide, 'thy sailes comen nat again,
Ne to thy word ther nis no fey certein;
But I wot why ye come nat,' quod she;
'For I was of my love to you so free.    2521
And of the goddes that ye han forswore,
Yif that hir vengeance falle on yow ther-
     fore,      (130)
Ye be nat suffisaunt to bere the peyne.
To moche trusted I, wel may I pleyne, 2525

Upon your linage and your faire tonge,
And on your teres falsly out y-wronge.
How coude ye wepe so by craft?' quod
     she;
'May ther swiche teres feyned be?
Now certes, yif ye wolde have in memorie,
Hit oghte be to yow but litel glorie    2531
To have a sely mayde thus betrayed!
To god,' quod she, 'preye I, and ofte have
     prayed,      (140)
That hit be now the grettest prys of alle,
And moste honour that ever yow shal
     befalle!      2535
And whan thyn olde auncestres peynted
     be,
In which men may hir worthinesse see,
Than, preye I god, thou peynted be also,
That folk may reden, for-by as they go,
"Lo! this is he, that with his flaterye 2540
Betrayed hath and doon her vilanye·
That was his trewe love in thoghte and
     dede!"

But sothly, of oo point yit may they rede,
That ye ben lyk your fader as in this; (151)
For he begyled Adriane, y-wis,      2545
With swiche an art and swiche sotelte
As thou thy-selven hast begyled me.
As in that point, al-thogh hit be nat fayr,
Thou folwest him, certein, and art his eyr.
But sin thus sinfully ye me begyle,    2550
My body mote ye seen, within a whyle,
Right in the haven of Athenes fletinge,
With-outen sepulture and buryinge; (160)
Thogh ye ben harder then is any stoon.'

And, whan this lettre was forth sent
     anoon,      2555
And knew how brotel and how fals he
     was,
She for dispeyr for-dide herself, allas!
Swich sorwe hath she, for she besette her
     so.
Be war, ye women, of your sotil fo,    2559
Sin yit this day men may ensample see;
And trusteth, as in love, no man but
     me.      (168)

*Explicit Legenda Phillis.*

# IX. THE LEGEND OF HYPERMNESTRA.

*Incipit Legenda Ypermistre.*

In Grece whylom weren brethren two,
Of whiche that oon was called Danao,
That many a sone hath of his body wonne,
As swiche false lovers ofte conne.    2565
Among his sones alle ther was oon
That aldermost he lovede of everichoon.
And whan this child was born, this Danao
Shoop him a name, and called him
    Lino.
That other brother called was Egiste,    2570
That was of love as fals as ever him
    liste,    (10)
And many a doghter gat he in his lyve;
Of which he gat upon his righte wyve
A doghter dere, and dide her for to calle
Ypermistra, yongest of hem alle;    2575
The whiche child, of her nativitee,
To alle gode thewes born was she,
As lyked to the goddes, or she was born,
That of the shefe she sholde be the
    corn;    (18)
The Wirdes, that we clepen Destinee,    2580
Hath shapen her that she mot nedes be
Pitouse, sadde, wyse, and trewe as steel;
And to this woman hit accordeth weel.
For, though that Venus yaf her greet
    beautee,
With Jupiter compouned so was she    2585
That conscience, trouthe, and dreed of
    shame,
And of her wyfhood for to kepe her name,
This, thoughte her, was felicitee as here.
And rede Mars was, that tyme of the
    yere,
So feble, that his malice is him raft,    2590
Repressed hath Venus his cruel craft;    (30)
†What with Venus and other oppressioun
Of houses, Mars his venim is adoun,
That Ypermistra dar nat handle a knyf
In malice, thogh she sholde lese her lyf.
But natheles, as heven gan tho turne,    2596
To badde aspectes hath she of Saturne,

That made her for to deyen in prisoun,
As I shal after make mencioun.
    To Danao and Egistes also—    2600
Al-thogh so be that they were brethren
    two,    (40)
For thilke tyme nas spared no linage—
Hit lyked hem to maken mariage
Betwix Ypermistra and him Lino,
And casten swiche a day hit shal be so; 2605
And ful acorded was hit witterly;
The array is wroght, the tyme is faste by.
And thus Lino hath of his fadres brother
The doghter wedded, and eche of hem
    hath other.
    The torches brennen and the lampes
    brighte,    2610
The sacrifices been ful redy dighte;    (50)
Th'encens out of the fyre reketh sote,
The flour, the leef is rent up by the
    rote
To maken garlands and corounes hye;
Ful is the place of soun of minstralcye,
Of songes amorous of mariage,    2616
As thilke tyme was the pleyn usage.
And this was in the paleys of Egiste,
That in his hous was lord, right as him
    liste;
And thus the day they dryven to an
    ende;    2620
The frendes taken leve, and hoom they
    wende.    (60)
The night is come, the bryd shal go to
    bedde;
Egiste to his chambre faste him spedde,
And privily he let his doghter calle.
Whan that the hous was voided of hem
    alle,    2625
He loked on his doghter with glad
    chere,
And to her spak, as ye shul after here.
    'My righte doghter, tresor of myn
    herte!
Sin first that day that shapen was my
    sherte,

Or by the fatal sustren had my dom, 2630
So ny myn herte never thing me com (70)
As thou, myn Ypermistra, doghter
　　dere !
Tak heed what I thy fader sey thee
　　here,
And werk after thy wyser ever-mo.
For alderfirste, doghter, I love thee so 2635
That al the world to me nis half so leef ;
Ne I nolde rede thee to thy mischeef
For al the gode under the colde mone ;
And what I mene, hit shal be seid right
　　sone,
With protestacioun, as in this wyse, 2640
That, but thou do as I shal thee devyse,
Thou shalt be deed, by him that al hath
　　wroght !　　　　　　　　　　(81)
At shorte wordes, thou n'escapest noght
Out of my paleys, or that thou be deed,
But thou consente and werke after my
　　reed ;　　　　　　　　　　2645
Tak this to thee for ful conclusioun.'
　　This Ypermistra caste her eyen doun,
And quook as dooth the leef of aspe
　　grene ;
Deed wex her hewe, and lyk as ash to
　　sene,　　　　　　　　　　2649
And seyde, 'lord and fader, al your wille,
After my might, god wot, I shal fulfille,
So hit to me be no confusioun.'　　(91)
　　'I nil,' quod he, 'have noon excepcioun';
And out he caughte a knyf, as rasour kene ;
'Hyd this,' quod he, 'that hit be nat y-
　　sene ;　　　　　　　　　　2655
And, whan thyn husbond is to bedde y-go,
Why! that he slepeth, cut his throte a-two.
For in my dremes hit is warned me
How that my nevew shal my bane be,
But whiche I noot, wherfor I wol be
　　siker.　　　　　　　　　　2660
Yif thou sey nay, we two shul have a
　　biker　　　　　　　　　　(100)
As I have seyd, by him that I have
　　sworn.'
　　This Ypermistra hath ny her wit forlon ;
And, for to passen harmles of that place,
She graunted him ; ther was non other
　　grace.　　　　　　　　　　2665
And therwith-al a costrel taketh he,
And seyde, 'herof a draught, or two or
　　three ;

Yif him to drinke, whan he goth to
　　reste,
And he shal slepe as longe as ever thee
　　leste,
The narcotiks and opies been so stronge :
And go thy wey, lest that him thinke
　　longe.'　　　　　　　　　(110) 2671
　　Out comth the bryd, and with ful sober
　　chere,
As is of maidens ofte the manere,
To chambre is broght with revel and with
　　songe,
And shortly, lest this tale be to longe, 2675
This Lino and she ben sone broght to
　　bedde ;
And every wight out at the dore him
　　spedde.
　　The night is wasted, and he fel a-slepe ;
Ful tenderly beginneth she to wepe.
She rist her up, and dredfully she
　　quaketh,　　　　　　　　2680
As doth the braunche that Zephirus
　　shaketh,　　　　　　　　(120)
And husht were alle in Argon that citee.
As cold as any frost now wexeth she ;
For pite by the herte her streyneth so,
And dreed of deeth doth her so moche wo,
That thryes doun she fil in swiche a
　　were.　　　　　　　　　　2686
She rist her up, and stakereth heer and
　　there,
And on her handes faste loketh she.
'Allas ! and shul my handes blody be ?
I am a maid, and, as by my nature, 2690
And by my semblant and by my vesture,
Myn handes been nat shapen for a knyf,
As for to reve no man fro his lyf.　　(132)
What devil have I with the knyf to do ?
And shal I have my throte corve a-two ?
Then shal I blede, allas ! and me be-
　　shende ;　　　　　　　　2696
And nedes cost this thing mot have an
　　ende ;
Or he or I mot nedes lese our lyf.
Now certes,' quod she, ' sin I am his wyf,
And hath my feith, yit is it bet for me
For to be deed in wyfly honestee (140) 2701
Than be a traitour living in my shame.
Be as be may, for ernest or for game,
He shal awake, and ryse and go his way
Out at this goter, or that hit be day !'—

And weep ful tenderly upon his face,  2706
And in her armes gan him to embrace,
And him she roggeth and awaketh softe ;
And at the window leep he fro the
    lofte
Whan she hath warned him, and doon
    him bote.                         2710
    This Lino swifte was, and light of fote,
And from his wyf he ran a ful good pas.
This sely woman is so wayk, allas !  (152)
And helples so, that, or that she fer
    wente,
Her cruel fader dide her for to hente. 2715

Allas ! Lino ! why art thou so unkinde ?
Why ne haddest thou remembred in thy
    minde
To taken her, and lad her forth with
    thee ?
For, whan she saw that goon awey was he,
And that she mighte nat so faste go,  2720
Ne folwen him, she sette her doun right
    tho,                             (160)
Til she was caught and fetered in prisoun.
    This tale is seid for this conclusioun. . .

⟨*Unfinished.*⟩

# A TREATISE ON THE ASTROLABE.

—◆—

## PROLOGUS.

Litel Lowis my sone, I have perceived wel by certeyne evidences thyn abilite to lerne sciencez touchinge noumbres and proporciouns; and as wel considere I thy
5 bisy preyere in special to lerne the Tretis of the Astrolabie. Than, for as mechel as a philosofre seith, 'he wrappeth him in his frend, that condescendeth to the rightful preyers of his frend,' ther-for
10 have I geven thee a suffisaunt Astrolabie as for oure orizonte, compowned after the latitude of Oxenford; up-on which, by mediacion of this litel tretis, I purpose to teche thee a certein nombre of conclu-
15 sions apertening to the same instrument. I seye a certein of conclusiouns, for three causes. The furste cause is this : truste wel that alle the conclusiouns that han ben founde, or elles possibly mighten be
20 founde in so noble an instrument as an Astrolabie, ben un-knowe perfitly to any mortal man in this regioun, as I suppose. A-nother cause is this; that sothly, in any tretis of the Astrolabie that I have seyn,
25 there ben some conclusions that wole nat in alle thinges performen hir bihestes ; and some of hem ben to harde to thy tendre age of ten yeer to conseyve. This tretis, divided in fyve parties, wole I shewe
30 thee under ful lighte rewles and naked wordes in English; for Latin ne canstow

yit but smal, my lyte sone. But natheles, suffyse to thee thise trewe conclusiouns in English, as wel as suffyseth to thise noble clerkes Grekes thise same conclusiouns in 35 Greek, and to Arabiens in Arabik, and to Jewes in Ebrew, and to the Latin folk in Latin ; whiche Latin folk han hem furst out of othre diverse langages, and writen in hir owne tonge, that is to sein, in 40 Latin. And god wot, that in alle thise langages, and in many mo, han thise conclusiouns ben suffisantly lerned and taught, and yit by diverse rewles, right as diverse pathes leden diverse folk the 45 righte wey to Rome. Now wol I prey meekly every discreet persone that redeth or hereth this litel tretis, to have my rewde endyting for excused, and my superfluite of wordes, for two causes. The 50 firste cause is, for that curious endyting and hard sentence is ful hevy atones for swich a child to lerne. And the seconde cause is this, that sothly me semeth betre to wryten un-to a child twyes a good 55 sentence, than he forgete it ones. And Lowis, yif so be that I shewe thee in my lighte English as trewe conclusiouns touching this matere, and naught only as trewe but as many and as subtil con- 60 clusiouns as ben shewed in Latin in any commune tretis of the Astrolabie, con me

the more thank; and preye god save the king, that is lord of this langage, and alle
65 that him feyth bereth and obeyeth, ever-ech in his degre, the more and the lasse. But considere wel, that I ne usurpe nat to have founde this werk of my labour or of myn engyn. I nam but a lewd com-
70 pilatour of the labour of olde Astro-logiens, and have hit translated in myn English only for thy doctrine ; and with this swerd shal I sleen envye.

I. The firste partie of this tretis shal
75 reherse the figures and the membres of thyn Astrolabie, bi-cause that thou shalt han the grettre knowing of thyn owne instrument.

II. The second partie shal teche thee
80 werken the verrey practik of the forseide conclusiouns, as ferforth and as narwe as may be shewed in so smal an instru-ment portatif aboute. For wel wot every astrologien that smalest fraccions ne wol
85 nat ben shewed in so smal an instrument, as in subtil tables calculed for a cause.

III. The thridde partie shal contienen diverse tables of longitudes and latitudes of sterres fixe for the Astrolabie, and
90 tables of declinacions of the sonne, and tables of longitudes of citeez and of townes ; and as wel for the governance

of a clokke as for to finde the altitude meridian ; and many another notable conclusioun, after the kalendres of the 95 reverent clerkes, frere I. Somer and frere N. Lenne.

IV. The ferthe partie shal ben a theorik to declare the moevinge of the celestial bodies with the causes. The whiche 100 ferthe partie in special shal shewen a table of the verray moeving of the mone from houre to houre, every day and in every signe, after thyn almenak ; upon which table ther folwith a canon, suffi- 105 sant to teche as wel the maner of the wyrking of that same conclusioun, as to knowe in oure orizonte with which de-gree of the zodiac that the mone ariseth in any latitude ; and the arising of any 110 planete after his latitude fro the ecliptik lyne.

V. The fifte partie shal ben an intro-ductorie after the statutz of oure doctours, in which thou maist lerne a gret part of 115 the general rewles of theorik in astrologie. In which fifte partie shaltow finde tables of equacions of houses aftur the latitude of Oxenford ; and tables of dignetes of planetes, and other noteful thinges, yif 120 god wol vouche-sauf and his modur the mayde. mo than I behete. &c.

# PART I.

HERE BIGINNETH THE DESCRIPCION OF THE ASTROLABIE.

1. Thyn Astrolabie hath a ring to putten on the thoumbe of thy right hand in taking the heighte of thinges. And tak keep, for from hennes-forthward,
5 I wol clepe the heighte of any thing that is taken by thy rewle, the altitude, with-oute mo wordes.

2. This ring renneth in a maner turet, fast to the moder of thyn Astrolabie, in so rowm a space that hit desturbeth nat the instrument to hangen after his righte
5 centre.

3. The Moder of thyn Astrolabie is the thikkeste plate, perced with a large hole, that resseyveth in hir wombe the thinne plates compowned for diverse clymatz, and thy riet shapen in manere of a net or 5 of a webbe of a loppe ; and for the more declaracioun, lo here the figure.

4. This moder is devyded on the bak-half with a lyne, that cometh dessend-inge fro the ring down to the nethereste bordure. The whiche lyne, fro the for-seide ring un-to the centre of the large 5 hole amidde, is cleped the south lyne, or elles the lyne meridional. And the remenant of this lyne downe to the bor-

dure is cleped the north lyne, or elles the
10 lyne of midnight. And for the more
declaracioun, lo here the figure.

5. Over-thwart this for-seide longe
lyne, ther crosseth him another lyne of
the same lengthe from est to west. Of
the whiche lyne, from a litel croys + in
5 the bordure un-to the centre of the large
hole, is cleped the Est lyne, or elles the
lyne Orientale; and the remenant of this
lyne fro the forseide + un-to the bordure,
is cleped the West lyne, or the lyne Occi-
10 dentale. Now hastow here the foure
quarters of thin astrolabie, devyded after
the foure principals plages or quarters of
the firmament. And for the more declaracioun, lo here thy figure.

6. The est side of thyn Astrolabie is
cleped the right side, and the west side
is cleped the left side. Forget nat this,
litel Lowis. Put the ring of thyn Astro-
5 labie upon the thoumbe of thy right
hand, and thanne wole his right syde be
toward thy left syde, and his left syde
wol be toward thy right syde; tak this
rewle general, as wel on the bak as on
10 the wombe-side. Upon the ende of this
est lyne, as I first seide, is marked a litel
+, wher-as evere-mo generaly is considered the entring of the first degree in
which the sonne aryseth. And for the
15 more declaracioun, lo here the figure.

7. Fro this litel + up to the ende of
the lyne meridional, under the ring,
shaltow finden the bordure devyded with
90 degrees ; and by that same proporcioun
5 is every quarter of thin Astrolabie devyded. Over the whiche degrees ther
ben noumbres of augrim, that devyden
thilke same degrees fro fyve to fyve, as
sheweth by longe strykes by-twene. Of
10 whiche longe strykes the space by-twene
contienith a mile-wey. And every degree
of the bordure contieneth foure minutes,
that is to seyn, minutes of an houre.
And for more declaracioun, lo here the
15 figure.

8. Under the compas of thilke degrees
ben writen the names of the Twelve
Signes, as Aries, Taurus, Gemini, Cancer,
Leo, Virgo, Libra, Scorpio, Sagittarius,
Capricornus, Aquarius, Pisces ; and the 5
nombres of the degrees of tho signes ben
writen in augrim above, and with longe
devisiouns, fro fyve to fyve ; devyded fro
tyme that the signe entreth un-to the
laste ende. But understond wel, that 10
thise degrees of signes ben everich of hem
considered of 60 minutes, and every
minute of 60 secondes, and so forth in-to
smale fraccions infinit, as seith Alka-
bucius. And ther-for, know wel, that 15
a degree of the bordure contieneth foure
minutes, and a degree of a signe contieneth 60 minutes, and have this in
minde. And for the more declaracioun,
lo here thy figure.       20

9. Next this folweth the Cercle of the
Dayes, that ben figured in maner of
degrees, that contienen in noumbre 365 ;
divyded also with longe strykes fro fyve
to fyve, and the nombres in augrim 5
writen under that cercle. And for more
declaracioun, lo here thy figure.

10. Next the Cercle of the Dayes, folweth the Cercle of the names of the
Monthes ; that is to seyen, Januare,
Februare, Marcius, Aprile, Mayus, Juin,
Julius, Augustus, Septembre, October, 5
Novembre, Decembre. The names of
thise monthes were cleped in Arabiens,
somme for hir propretees, and some by
statutz of lordes, some by other lordes of
Rome. Eek of thise monthes, as lyked 10
to Julius Cesar and to Cesar Augustus,
some were compowned of diverse nombres of dayes, as Juil and August. Thanne
hath Januare 31 dayes, Februare 28,
March 31, Aprille 30, May 31, Junius 30, 15
Julius 31, Augustus 31, September 30,
Octobre 31, Novembre 30, December 31.
Natheles, al-though that Julius Cesar
took 2 dayes out of Feverer and put hem
in his moneth of Juille, and Augustus 20
Cesar cleped the moneth of August after
his name, and ordeyned it of 31 dayes,
yit truste wel, that the sonne dwelleth
ther-for nevere the more ne lesse in oon
signe than in another.       25

11. Than folwen the names of the
Halidayes in the Kalender, and next
hem the lettres of the Abc. on which

they fallen. And for the more declara-
5 cioun, lo here thy figure.

12. Next the forseide Cercle of the
Abc., under the cros-lyne, is marked the
scale, in maner of two squyres, or elles in
manere of laddres, that serveth by hise
5 12 poyntes and his devisiouns of ful
many a subtil conclusioun. Of this forseide scale, fro the croos-lyne un-to the
verre angle, is cleped †umbra versa, and
the nether partie is cleped the †umbra
10 recta, or elles umbra extensa. And for
the more declaracioun, lo here the figure.

13. Thanne hastow a brood Rewle,
that hath on either ende a square plate
perced with a certein holes, some more
and some lesse, to resseyven the stremes
5 of the sonne by day, and eek by mediacioun of thyn eye, to knowe the altitude
of sterres by nighte. And for the more
declaracioun, lo here thy figure.

14. Thanne is ther a large Pyn, in
maner of an extree, that goth thorow
the hole, that halt the tables of the
clymates and the riet in the wombe of
5 the Moder, thorw which Pyn ther goth
a litel wegge which that is cleped 'the
hors,' that streyneth alle thise parties to-
hepe; this forseide grete Pyn, in maner
of an extree, is imagined to be the Pol
10 Artik in thyn Astrolabie. And for the
more declaracioun, lo here the figure.

15. The wombe-side of thyn Astrolabie
is also devyded with a longe croys in
foure quarters from est to west, fro south
to north, fro right syde to left syde, as is
5 the bak-syde. And for the more declaracioun, lo here thy figure.

16. The bordure of which wombe-side
is devyded fro the poynt of the est lyne
un-to the poynt of the south lyne under
the ring, in 90 degres; and by that same
5 proporcioun is every quarter devyded as
is the bak-syde, that amonteth 360 degrees. And understond wel, that degrees
of this bordure ben answering and consentrik to the degrees of the Equinoxial,
10 that is devyded in the same nombre as
every othere cercle is in the heye hevene.
This same bordure is devyded also with
23 lettres capitals and a smal croys +

above the south lyne, that sheweth the
24 houres equals of the clokke; and, as 15
I have said, 5 of thise degrees maken
a mile-wey, and 3 mile-wey maken an
houre. And every degree of this bordure
conteneth 4 minutes, and every minut
60 secoundes; now have I told thee twye. 20
And for the more declaracioun, lo here
the figure.

17. The plate under thy riet is des-
cryved with 3 principal cercles; of whiche
the leste is cleped the cercle of Cancer,
by-cause that the heved of Cancer turneth
evermor consentrik up-on the same 5
cercle. In this heved of Cancer is the
grettest declinacioun northward of the
sonne. And ther-for is he cleped the
Solsticioun of Somer; whiche declinacioun, aftur Ptholome, is 23 degrees 10
and 50 minutes, as wel in Cancer as in
Capricorne. This signe of Cancer is
cleped the Tropik of Somer, of tropos,
that is to seyn 'agaynward;' for thanne
by-ginneth the sonne to passe fro us- 15
ward. And for the more declaracioun,
lo here the figure.

The middel cercle in wydnesse, of thise
3, is cleped the Cercle Equinoxial; up-on
whiche turneth evermo the hedes of 20
Aries and Libra. And understond wel,
that evermo this Cercle Equinoxial turneth justly fro verrey est to verrey west;
as I have shewed thee in the spere solide.
This same cercle is cleped also the Weyere, 25
equator, of the day; for whan the sonne
is in the hevedes of Aries and Libra,
than ben the dayes and the nightes ilyke
of lengthe in al the world. And therfore ben thise two signes called the 30
Equinoxies. And alle that moeveth with-
in the hevedes of thise Aries and Libra,
his moeving is cleped north-ward; and
alle that moeveth with-oute thise hevedes,
his moeving is cleped south-ward as fro 35
the equinoxial. Tak keep of thise latitudes north and sowth, and forget it nat.
By this Cercle Equinoxial ben considered
the 24 houres of the clokke; for everemo
the arysing of 15 degrees of the equinoxial 40
maketh an houre equal of the clokke.
This equinoxial is cleped the girdel of

the firste moeving, or elles of the *angulus primi motus vel primi mobilis.* And *nota,*
45 that firste moeving is cleped 'moeving' of the firste moevable of the 8 spere, whiche moeving is fro est to west, and eft agayn in-to est; also it is clepid 'girdel' of the first moeving, for it
50 departeth the firste moevable, that is to seyn, the spere, in two ilyke parties, evene-distantz fro the poles of this world.

The wydeste of thise three principal cercles is cleped the Cercle of Capricorne,
55 by-cause that the heved of Capricorne turneth evermo consentrik up-on the same cercle. In the heved of this forseide Capricorne is the grettest declinacioun southward of the sonne, and ther-
60 for is it cleped the Solsticioun of Winter. This signe of Capricorne is also cleped the Tropik of Winter, for thanne byginneth the sonne to come agayn to us-ward. And for the more declaracioun, lo here
65 thy figure.

18. Upon this forseide plate ben compassed certein cercles that highten Almicanteras, of which som of hem semen perfit cercles, and somme semen inperfit.
5 The centre that standith a-middes the narwest cercle is cleped the Senith ; and the netherest cercle, or the firste cercle, is clepid the Orisonte, that is to seyn, the cercle that devydeth the two emi-
10 speries, that is, the partie of the hevene a-bove the erthe and the partie be-nethe. Thise Almicanteras ben compowned by two and two, al-be-it so that on divers Astrolabies some Almicanteras ben de-
15 vyded by oon, and some by two, and somme by three, after the quantite of the Astrolabie. This forseide senith is imagened to ben the verrey point over the crowne of thyn heved ; and also this
20 senith is the verrey pool of the orisonte in every regioun. And for the more declaracioun, lo here thy figure.

19. From this senith, as it semeth, ther come a maner crokede strykes lyke to the clawes of a loppe, or elles like to the werk of a womanes calle, in kerving over-
5 thwart the Almikanteras. And thise same strykes or divisiouns ben cleped

Azimuthz. And they devyden the orisonte of thyn Astrolabie in four and twenty devisiouns. And thise Azimutz
10 serven to knowe the costes of the firmament, and to othre conclusiouns, as for to knowe the cenith of the sonne and of every sterre. And for more declaracioun, lo here thy figure.

20. Next thise azimutz, under the Cercle of Cancer, ben ther twelve devisiouns embelif, moche like to the shap of the azimutes, that shewen the spaces of the houres of planetes ; and for more
5 declaracioun, lo here thy figure.

21. The Riet of thyn Astrolabie with thy zodiak, shapen in maner of a net or of a loppe-webbe after the olde descripcioun, which thow mayst tornen up
5 and doun as thy-self lyketh, conteneth certein nombre of sterres fixes, with hir longitudes and latitudes determinat ; yif so be that the makere have nat erred. The names of the sterres ben writen in the margin of the riet ther as they sitte ;
10 of whiche sterres the smale poynt is cleped the Centre. And understond also that alle sterres sittinge with-in the zodiak of thyn Astrolabie ben cleped 'sterres of the north,' for they arysen
15 by northe the est lyne. And alle the remenant fixed, out of the zodiak, ben cleped 'sterres of the south;' but I sey nat that they arysen alle by southe the est lyne ; witnesse on Aldeberan and
20 Algomeysa. Generally understond this rewle, that thilke sterres that ben cleped sterres of the north arysen rather than the degree of hir longitude, and alle the sterres of the south arysen after the
25 degree of hir longitude ; this is to seyn, sterres fixed in thyn Astrolabie. The mesure of this longitude of sterres is taken in the lyne ecliptik of hevene, under which lyne, whan that the sonne
30 and the mone ben lyne-right or elles in the superfice of this lyne, than is the eclips of the sonne or of the mone ; as I shal declare, and eek the cause why. But sothly the Ecliptik Lyne of thy
35 zodiak is the outtereste bordure of thy zodiak, ther the degrees ben marked.

Thy Zodiak of thyn Astrolabie is shapen as a compas which that conteneth a large brede, as after the quantite of thyn Astrolabie ; in ensample that the zodiak in hevene is imagened to ben a superfice contening a latitude of twelve degrees, wheras al the remenant of cercles in the hevene ben imagined verrey lynes withoute eny latitude. Amiddes this celestial zodiak ys imagined a lyne, which that is cleped the Ecliptik Lyne, under which lyne is evermo the wey of the sonne. Thus ben ther six degrees of the zodiak on that oon side of the lyne, and six degrees on that other. This zodiak is devided in twelve principal devisiouns, that departen the twelve signes. And, for the streitnes of thin Astrolabie, than is every smal devisioun in a signe departid by two degrees and two ; I mene degrees contening sixty minutes. And this forseide hevenissh zodiak is cleped the Cercle of the Signes, or the Cercle of the Bestes ; for *zodia* in langage of Greek sowneth 'bestes' in Latin tonge ; and in the zodiak ben the twelve signes that han names of bestes ; or elles, for whan the sonne entreth in any of the signes, he taketh the propretee of swich bestes ; or elles, for that the sterres that ben there fixed ben disposed in signes of bestes, or shape like bestes ; or elles, whan the planetes ben under thilke signes, they causen us by hir influence operaciouns and effectes lyk to the operaciouns of bestes. And understonde also, that whan an hot planete cometh in-to an hot signe, than encresseth his hete ;

and yif a planete be cold, thanne amenuseth his coldnesse, by-cause of the hote signe. And by this conclusioun maystow take ensample in alle the signes, be they moist or drye, or moeble or fix ; rekening the qualitee of the planete as I first seide. And everich of thise twelve signes hath respecte to a certein parcelle of the body of a man and hath it in governance ; as Aries hath thyn heved, and Taurus thy nekke and thy throte, Gemini thyn armholes and thyn armes, and so forth ; as shal be shewed more pleyn in the fifte partie of this tretis. This zodiak, which that is part of the eighte spere, overkerveth the equinoxial ; and he overkerveth him again in evene parties ; and that on half declineth southward, and that other northward, as pleynly declareth the tretis of the spere. And for more declaracioun, lo here thy figure.

22. Thanne hastow a label, that is schapen lyk a rewle, save that it is streit and hath no plates on either ende with holes ; but, with the smale point of the forseide label, shaltow calcule thyne equaciouns in the bordure of thin Astrolabie, as by thyn almury. And for the more declaracioun, lo here thy figure.

23. Thyn Almury is cleped the Denticle of Capricorne, or elles the Calculer. This same Almury sit fix in the heed of Capricorne, and it serveth of many a necessarie conclusioun in equaciouns of thinges, as shal be shewed ; and for the more declaracioun, lo here thy figure.

*Here endeth the descripcion of the Astrolabie.*

# PART II.

HERE BYGINNEN THE CONCLUSIONS OF THE ASTROLABIE.

**1.** *To fynde the degree in which the sonne is day by day, after hir cours a-boute.*

Rekene and knowe which is the day of thy monthe ; and ley thy rewle up that same day ; and thanne wol the verray point of thy rewle sitten in the

bordure, up-on the degree of thy sonne. Ensample as thus ; the yeer of oure lord 1391, the 12 day of March at midday, I wolde knowe the degree of the sonne. I soughte in the bak-half of myn Astrolabie, and fond the cercle of the dayes, the which I knowe by the names of the monthes writen under the same cercle. Tho leide I my rewle over this forseide

day, and fond the point of my rewle in
15 the bordure up-on the firste degree of
Aries, a litel with-in the degree; and
thus knowe I this conclusioun. Another
day, I wolde knowe the degree of my
sonne, and this was at midday in the
20 13 day of Decembre; I fond the day of
the monthe in maner as I seide; tho
leide I my rewle up-on this forseide 13
day, and fond the point of my rewle in
the bordure up-on the first degree of
25 Capricorne, a lite with-in the degree;
and than hadde I of this conclusioun the
ful experience. And for the more declaracioun, lo here thy figure.

## 2. To knowe the altitude of the sonne, or of othre celestial bodies.

Put the ring of thyn Astrolabie up-on
thy right thoumbe, and turne thy lift
syde agayn the light of the sonne. And
remeve thy rewle up and doun, til that
5 the stremes of the sonne shyne thorgh
bothe holes of thy rewle. Loke thanne
how many degrees thy rewle is areised
fro the litel crois up-on thyn est line, and
tak ther the altitude of thy sonne. And
10 in this same wyse maistow knowe by
nighte the altitude of the mone, or of
brighte sterres. This chapitre is so general
ever in oon, that ther nedith no more
declaracion; but forget it nat. And for
15 the more declaracioun, lo here the figure.

## 3. To knowe every tyme of the day by light of the sonne, and every tyme of the night by the sterres fixe, and eke to knowe by night or by day the degree of any signe that assendeth on the Est Orisonte, which that is cleped communly the Assendent, or elles Oruscupum.

Tak the altitude of the sonne whan
thee list, as I have said; and set the
degree of the sonne, in cas that it be
by-forn the middel of the day, among
5 thyn almikanteras on the est side of thyn
Astrolabie; and yif it be after the middel
of the day, set the degree of thy sonne
up-on the west side; tak this manere of
setting for a general rewle, ones for
10 evere. And whan thou hast set the

degree of thy sonne up as many almikanteras of heyghte as was the altitude
of the sonne taken by thy rewle, ley over
thy label, up-on the degree of the sonne;
and thanne wol the point of thy label 1
sitten in the bordure, up-on the verrey
tyd of the day. Ensample as thus: the
yeer of oure lord 1391, the 12 day of
March, I wold knowe the tyd of the day.
I took the altitude of my sonne, and 2
fond that it was 25 degrees and 30 of
minutes of heyghte in the bordure on the
bak-syde. Tho turnede I myn Astrolabie, and by-cause that it was by-forn
midday, I turnede my riet, and sette the 2
degree of the sonne, that is to seyn, the
1 degree of Aries, on the right syde of
myn Astrolabie, up-on that 25 degrees
and 30 of minutes of heyghte among myn
almikanteras; tho leide I my label up-on 3
the degree of my sonne, and fond the
poynte of my label in the bordure, up-on
a capital lettre that is cleped an X; tho
rekened I alle the capitalles lettres fro
the lyne of midnight un-to this forseide 3
lettre X, and fond that it was 9 of the
clokke of the day. Tho loked I down
up-on the est orisonte, and fond there
the 20 degree of Geminis assending;
which that I tok for myn assendent. 4
And in this wyse hadde I the experience
for ever-mo in which maner I sholde
knowe the tyd of the day, and eek myn
assendent. Tho wolde I wite the same
night folwing the hour of the night, and 4
wroughte in this wyse. Among an heep
of sterris fixe, it lyked me for to take the
altitude of the feire white sterre that is
cleped Alhabor; and fond hir sitting on
the west side of the lyne of midday, 5
†18 degres of heighte taken by my rewle
on the bak-syde. Tho sette I the centre
of this Alhabor up-on †18 degrees among
myn almikanteras, up-on the west syde;
by-cause that she was founden on the 5
west syde. Tho leide I my label over
the degree of the sonne that was descended under the weste orisonte, and
rikened alle the lettres capitals fro the
lyne of midday un-to the point of my 6
label in the bordure; and fond that it

was passed †8 of the clokke the space of †2 degrees. Tho loked I doun up-on myn est orisonte, and fond ther †23 degrees of
5 Libra assending, whom I tok for myn assendent ; and thus lerned I to knowe ones for ever in which manere I shuld come to the houre of the night and to myn assendent ; as verreyly as may be
10 taken by so smal an instrument. But natheles, in general, wolde I warne thee for evere, ne mak thee nevere bold to have take a just ascendent by thyn Astrolabie, or elles to have set justly
15 a clokke, whan any celestial body by which thow wenest governe thilke thinges ben ney the south lyne ; for trust wel, whan that the sonne is ney the meridional lyne, the degree of the sonne
20 renneth so longe consentrik up-on the almikanteras, that sothly thou shalt erre fro the just assendent. The same conclusioun sey I by the centre of any sterre fix by night ; and more-over, by experi-
25 ence, I wot wel that in oure orisonte, from 11 of the clokke un-to oon of the clokke, in taking of a just assendent in a portatif Astrolabie, hit is to hard to knowe. I mene, from 11 of the clokke
30 biforn the houre of noon til oon of the clokke next folwing. And for the more declaracion, lo here thy figure.

### 4. *Special declaracion of the assendent.*

The assendent sothly, as wel in alle nativitez as in questiouns and elecciouns of tymes, is a thing which that thise astrologiens gretly observen ; wher-fore
5 me semeth convenient, sin that I speke of the assendent, to make of it special declaracioun. The assendent sothly, to take it at the largeste, is thilke degree that assendeth at any of thise forseide
10 tymes upon the est orisonte ; and therefor, yif that any planet assende at that same tyme in thilke for-seide †degree of his longitude, men seyn that thilke planete is *in horoscopo.* But sothly, the
15 hous of the assendent, that is to seyn, the firste hous or the est angle, is a thing more brood and large. For after the statutz of astrologiens, what celestial body

that is 5 degres above thilk degree that assendeth, or with-in that noumbre, that 20 is to seyn, nere the degree that assendeth, yit rikne they thilke planet in the assendent. And what planete that is under thilke degree that assendith the space of †25 degrees, yit seyn they that thilke 25 planete is lyk to him that is in the hous of the assendent ; but sothly, yif he passe the bondes of thise forseide spaces, above or bynethe, they seyn that the planete is failling fro the assendent. Yit sein thise 30 astrologiens, that the assendent, and eke the lord of the assendent, may be shapen for to be fortunat or infortunat, as thus : a fortunat assendent clepen they whan that no wikkid planete, as Saturne or 35 Mars, or elles the Tail of the Dragoun, is in the hous of the assendent, ne that no wikked planete have non aspecte of enemite up-on the assendent ; but they wol caste that they have a fortunat 40 planete in hir assendent and yit in his felicitee, and than sey they that it is wel. Forther-over, they seyn that the infortuning of an assendent is the contrarie of thise forseide thinges The lord of 45 the assendent, sey they, that he is fortunat, whan he is in good place fro the assendent as in angle ; or in a succedent, where-as he is in his dignitee and conforted with frendly aspectes of planetes 50 and wel resceived, and eek that he may seen the assendent, and that he be nat retrograd ne combust, ne joigned with no shrewe in the same signe ; ne that he be nat in his descencioun. ne joigned with 55 no planete in his discencioun, ne have up-on him non aspecte infortunat ; and than sey they that he is wel. Natheles, thise ben observauncez of judicial matiere and rytes of payens, in which my spirit 60 ne hath no feith, ne no knowing of hir *horoscopum* ; for they seyn that every signe is departed in 3 evene parties by 10 degrees, and thilke porcioun they clepe a Face. And al-thogh that a planete 65 have a latitude fro the ecliptik, yit sey some folk, so that the planete aryse in that same signe with any degree of the forseide face in which his longitude is

70 rekned, that yit is the planete *in horo-scopo*, be it in nativite or in eleccioun, &c. And for the more declaracioun, lo here the figure.

5. *To knowe the verrey equacioun of the degree of the sonne, yif so be that it falle by-twixe thyn Almikanteras.*

For as moche as the almikanteras in thyn Astrolabie been compouned by two and two, where-as some almikanteras in sondry Astrolabies ben compouned by
5 oon and oon, or elles by two and two, it is necessarie to thy lerning to teche thee first to knowe and worke with thyn owne instrument. Wher-for, whan that the degree of thy sonne falleth by-twixe
10 two almikanteras, or elles yif thyn almi-kanteras ben graven with over gret a point of a compas, (for bothe thise thinges may causen errour as wel in knowing of the tyd of the day as of the
15 verrey assendent), thou most werken in this wyse. Set the degree of thy sonne up-on the heyer almikanteras of bothe, and waite wel wher as thin almury toucheth the bordure, and set
20 ther a prikke of inke. Set doun agayn the degree of thy sonne up-on the nethere almikanteras of bothe, and set ther another prikke. Remewe thanne thyn almury in the bordure evene amid-
25 des bothe prikkes, and this wol lede justly the degree of thy sonne to sitte by-twixe bothe almikanteras in his right place. Ley thanne thy label over the degree of thy sonne; and find in the
30 bordure the verrey tyde of the day or of the night. And as verreyly shaltow finde up-on thyn est orisonte thyn assen-dent. And for more declaracioun, lo here thy figure.

6. *To knowe the spring of the dawing and the ende of the evening, the which ben called the two crepusculis:*

Set the nadir of thy sonne up-on 18 degrees of heighte among thyn almikan-teras on the west syde, and ley thy label on the degree of thy sonne, and thanne
5 shal the poynt of thy label schewe the spring of day. Also set the nadir of thy

sonne up-on 18 degrees of heighte a-mong thyn almikanteras on the est side, and ley over thy label up-on the degree of the sonne, and with the point of thy label find in the bordure the ende of the evening, that is, verrey night. The nadir of the sonne is thilke degree that is opposit to the degree of the sonne, in the seventhe signe, as thus: every degree of Aries by ordre is nadir to every degree of Libra by ordre; and Taurus to Scor-pion; Gemini to Sagittare; Cancer to Capricorne; Leo to Aquarie; Virgo to Pisces; and yif any degree in thy zodiak be dirk, his nadir shal declare him. And for the more declaracioun, lo here thy figure.

7. *To knowe the arch of the day, that some folk callen the day artificial, from the sonne arysing til hit go to reste.*

Set the degree of thy sonne up-on thyn est orisonte, and ley thy label on the degree of the sonne, and at the poynt of thy label in the bordure set a prikke. Turn thanne thy riet aboute til the 5 degree of the sonne sit up-on the west orisonte, and ley thy label up-on the same degree of the sonne, and at the point of thy label set a-nother prikke. Rekne thanne the quantitee of tyme in 10 the bordure by-twixe bothe prikkes, and tak ther thyn ark of the day. The reme-nant of the bordure under the orisonte is the ark of the night. Thus maistow rekne bothe arches, or every porcion, 15 of whether that thee lyketh. And by this manere of wyrking maistow see how longe that any sterre fix dwelleth a-bove the erthe, fro tyme that he ryseth til he go to reste. But the day natural, that 20 is to seyn 24 houres, is the revolucioun of the equinoxial with as moche partie of the zodiak as the sonne of his propre moevinge passeth in the mene whyle. And for the more declaracioun, lo here 25 thy figure.

8. *To turn the houres in-equales in houres equales.*

Knowe the nombre of the degrees in the houres in-equales, and departe hem

by 15, and tak ther thyn houres equales.
And for the more declaracioun, lo here
thy figure.

9. *To knowe the quantitee of the day vul-*
*gare, that is to seyen, from spring of the*
*day un-to verrey night.*

Know the quantitee of thy crepusculis,
as I have taught in the chapitre bi-forn,
and adde hem to the arch of thy day
artificial ; and tak ther the space of alle
the hole day vulgar, un-to verrey night.
The same manere maystow worke, to
knowe the quantitee of the vulgar night.
And for the more declaracioun, lo here
the figure.

10. *To knowe the quantite of houres*
*inequales by day.*

Understond wel, that thise houres in-
equales ben cleped houres of planetes,
and understond wel that som-tyme ben
they lengere by day than by night, and
som-tyme the contrarie. But understond
wel, that evermo, generaly, the houre inequal of the day with the houre in-equal
of the night contenen 30 degrees of the
bordure, whiche bordure is ever-mo
answering to the degrees of the equinoxial ; wher-for departe the arch of the
day artificial in 12, and tak ther the
quantitee of the houre in-equal by day.
And yif thow abate the quantitee of the
houre in-equal by daye out of 30, than
shal the remenant that leveth performe
the houre inequal by night. And for
the more declaracioun, lo here the figure.

11. *To knowe the quantite of houres equales.*

The quantitee of houres equales, that
is to seyn, the houres of the clokke, ben
departed by 15 degrees al-redy in the
bordure of thyn Astrolabie, as wel by
night as by day, generaly for evere.
What nedeth more declaracioun ? Wherfor, whan thee list to know how manye
houres of the clokke ben passed, or any
part of any of thise houres that ben
passed, or elles how many houres or
partie of houres ben to come, fro swich
a tyme to swich a tyme, by day or by
nighte, knowe the degree of thy sonne,

and ley thy label on it ; turne thy riet
aboute joyntly with thy label, and with
the point of it rekne in the bordure fro
the sonne aryse un-to the same place
ther thou desirest, by day as by nighte.
This conclusioun wol I declare in the
laste chapitre of the 4 partie of this tretis
so openly, that ther shal lakke no worde
that nedeth to the declaracioun. And
for the more declaracioun, lo here the
figure.

12. *Special declaracioun of the houres*
*of planetes.*

Understond wel, that evere-mo, fro the
arysing of the sonne til it go to reste, the
nadir of the sonne shal shewe the houre
of the planete, and fro that tyme forward
al the night til the sonne aryse ; than
shal the verrey degree of the sonne shewe
the houre of the planete. Ensample as
thus. The 13 day of March fil up-on a
Saterday per aventure, and, at the arising of the sonne, I fond the secounde
degree of Aries sitting up-on myn est
orisonte, al-be-it that it was but lite ;
than fond I the ♎ degree of Libra, nadir
of my sonne, dessending on my west
orisonte, up-on which west orisonte every
day generally, at the sonne ariste, entreth
the houre of any planete, after which
planete the day bereth his name ; and
endeth in the nexte stryk of the plate
under the forseide west orisonte ; and
evere, as the sonne climbeth uppere and
uppere, so goth his nadir dounere and
dounere, teching by swich strykes the
houres of planetes by ordre as they sitten
in the hevene. The first houre inequal
of every Satterday is to Saturne ; and
the secounde, to Jupiter ; the 3, to Mars ;
the 4, to the Sonne ; the 5, to Venus ; the
6, to Mercurius ; the 7, to the Mone ; and
thanne agayn, the 8 is to Saturne ; the 9,
to Jupiter ; the 10, to Mars ; the 11, to
the Sonne ; the 12, to Venus ; and now
is my sonne gon to reste as for that
Setterday. Thanne sheweth the verrey
degree of the sonne the houre of Mercurie
entring under my west orisonte at eve ;
and next him succedeth the Mone ; and so

forth by ordre, planete after planete, in houre after houre, al the night longe til the
40 sonne aryse. Now ryseth the sonne that Sonday by the morwe; and the nadir of the sonne, up-on the west orizonte, sheweth me the entring of the houre of the forseide sonne. And in this maner
45 succedeth planete under planete, fro Saturne un-to the Mone, and fro the Mone up a-gayn to Saturne, houre after houre generaly. And thus knowe I this conclusioun. And for the more declara-
50 cioun, lo here the figure.

### 13. To knowe the altitude of the sonne in middes of the day, that is cleped the altitude meridian.

Set the degree of the sonne up-on the lyne meridional, and rikene how many degrees of almikanteras ben by-twixe thyn est orisonte and the degree of the
5 sonne. And tak ther thyn altitude meridian; this is to seyne, the heyest of the sonne as for that day. So maystow knowe in the same lyne, the heyest cours that any sterre fix climbeth by
10 night; this is to seyn, that whan any sterre fix is passed the lyne meridional, than by-ginneth it to descende, and so doth the sonne. And for the more declaracioun, lo here thy figure.

### 14. To knowe the degree of the sonne by thy riet, for a maner curiositee, &c.

Sek bysily with thy rewle the heyest of the sonne in midde of the day; turne thanne thyn Astrolabie, and with a prikke of ink marke the nombre of that
5 same altitude in the lyne meridional. Turne thanne thy riet aboute til thou fynde a degree of thy zodiak acording with the prikke, this is to seyn, sittinge on the prikke; and in sooth, thou shalt
10 finde but two degrees in al the zodiak of that condicioun; and yit thilke two degrees ben in diverse signes; than maistow lightly by the sesoun of the yere knowe the signe in whiche that is the
15 sonne. And for the more declaracioun, lo here thy figure.

### 15. To know which day is lyk to which day as of lengthe, &c.

Loke whiche degrees ben y-lyke fer fro the hevedes of Cancer and Capricorn; and lok, whan the sonne is in any of thilke degrees, than ben the dayes y-lyke
5 of lengthe. This is to seyn, that as long is that day in that monthe, as was swich a day in swich a month; ther varieth but lite. Also, yif thou take two dayes naturaly in the yeer y-lyke fer fro eyther
10 pointe of the equinoxial in the opposit parties, than as long is the day artificial of that on day as is the night of that othere, and the contrarie. And for the more declaracioun, lo here thy figure.

### 16. This chapitre is a maner declaracioun to conclusiouns that folwen.

Understond wel that thy zodiak is departid in two halfe cercles, as fro the heved of Capricorne un-to the heved of Cancer; and agaynward fro the heved of
5 Cancer un-to the heved of Capricorne. The heved of Capricorne is the lowest point, wher-as the sonne goth in winter; and the heved of Cancer is the heyest point, in whiche the sonne goth in somer.
10 And ther-for understond wel, that any two degrees that ben y-lyke fer fro any of thise two hevedes, truste wel that thilke two degrees ben of y-lyke declinacioun, be it southward or northward;
15 and the dayes of hem ben y-lyke of lengthe, and the nightes also; and the shadwes y-lyke, and the altitudes y-lyke at midday for evere. And for more declaracioun, lo here thy figure.

### 17. To knowe the verrey degree of any maner sterre straunge or unstraunge after his longitude, though he be indeterminat in thyn Astrolabie ; sothly to the trowthe, thus he shal be knowe.

Tak the altitude of this sterre whan he is on the est side of the lyne meridional, as ney as thou mayst gesse; and tak an assendent a-non right by som maner sterre fix which that thou knowest; and
5 for-get nat the altitude of the firste sterre, ne thyn assendent. And whan that this is don, espye diligently whan this same

firste sterre passeth any-thing the south westward, and hath him a-non right in the same noumbre of altitude on the west side of this lyne meridional as he was caught on the est side; and tak a newe assendent a-non right by som maner sterre fixe which that thou knowest; and for-get nat this secounde assendent. And whan that this is don, rikne thanne how manye degrees ben by-twixe the firste assendent and the seconde assendent, and rikne wel the middel degree by-twene bothe assendentes, and set thilke middel degree up-on thin est orisonte; and waite thanne what degree that sit up-on the lyne meridional, and tak ther the verrey degree of the ecliptik in which the sterre stondeth for the tyme. For in the ecliptik is the longitude of a celestial body rekened, evene fro the heved of Aries un-to the ende of Pisces. And his latitude is rikned after the quantitee of his declinacion, north or south to-warde the poles of this world; as thus. Yif it be of the sonne or of any fix sterre, rekene his latitude or his declinacioun fro the equinoxial cercle; and yif it be of a planete, rekne than the quantitee of his latitude fro the ecliptik lyne. Al-be-it so that fro the equinoxial may the declinacion or the latitude of any body celestial be rikned, after the site north or south, and after the quantitee of his declinacion. And right so may the latitude or the declinacion of any body celestial, save only of the sonne, after his site north or south, and after the quantitee of his declinacioun, be rekned fro the ecliptik lyne; fro which lyne alle planetes som tyme declynen north or south, save only the for-seide sonne. And for the more declaracioun, lo here thy figure.

18. *To knowe the degrees of the longitudes of fixe sterres after that they ben determinat in thin Astrolabie, yif so be that they ben trewly set.*

Set the centre of the sterre up-on the lyne meridional, and tak keep of thy zodiak, and loke what degree of any signe

that sit on the same lyne meridional at that same tyme, and tak the degree in 5 which the sterre standeth; and with that same degree comth that same sterre un-to that same lyne fro the orisonte. And for more declaracioun, lo here thy figure. 10

19. *To knowe with which degree of the zodiak any sterre fixe in thyn Astrolabie aryseth up-on the est orisonte, al-thogh his dwelling be in a-nother signe.*

Set the centre of the sterre up-on the est orisonte, and loke what degree of any signe that sit up-on the same orisonte at that same tyme. And understond wel, that with that same degree aryseth that 5 same sterre; and this merveyllous arysing with a strange degree in another signe is by-cause that the latitude of the sterre fix is either north or south fro the equinoxial. But sothly, the latitudes of 10 planetes ben comunly rekned fro the ecliptik, bi-cause that non of hem declineth but fewe degrees out fro the brede of the zodiak. And tak good keep of this chapitre of arysing of the celestial 15 bodies; for truste wel, that neyther mone ne sterre as in oure embelif orisonte aryseth with that same degree of his longitude, save in oo cas; and that is, whan they have no latitude fro the 20 ecliptik lyne. But natheles, som tyme is everiche of thise planetes under the same lyne. And for more declaracioun, lo here thy figure.

20. *To knowe the declinacioun of any degree in the zodiak fro the equinoxial cercle, &c.*

Set the degree of any signe up-on the lyne meridional, and rikne his altitude in almikanteras fro the est orisonte up to the same degree set in the forseide lyne, and set ther a prikke. Turne up 5 thanne thy riet, and set the heved of Aries or Libra in the same meridional lyne, and set ther a-nother prikke. And whan that this is don, considere the altitudes of hem bothe; for sothly the 10 difference of thilke altitudes is the declinacion of thilke degree fro the equinoxial. And yif so be that thilke degree be north-

ward fro the equinoxial, than is his
15 declinacion north ; yif it be southward,
than is it south. And for the more
declaracioun, lo here thy figure.

21. *To knowe for what latitude in any*
*regioun the almikanteras of any table*
*ben compouned.*

Rikne how manye degrees of almikanteras, in the meridional lyne, be fro the
cercle equinoxial un-to the senith ; or
elles fro the pool artik un-to the north
5 orisonte ; and for so gret a latitude or for
so smal a latitude is the table compouned.
And for more declaracion, lo here thy
figure.

22. *To knowe in special the latitude of*
*oure countray, I mene after the latitude*
*of Oxenford, and the heighte of oure pol.*

Understond wel, that as fer is the heved
of Aries or Libra in the equinoxial from
oure orisonte as is the senith from the pole
artik ; and as hey is the pol artik fro the
5 orisonte, as the equinoxial is fer fro the
senith. I prove it thus by the latitude
of Oxenford. Understond wel, that the
heyghte of oure pool artik fro oure north
orisonte is 51 degrees and 50 minutes ;
10 than is the senith from oure pool artik
38 degrees and 10 minutes ; than is the
equinoxial from oure senith 51 degrees
and 50 minutes ; than is oure south
orisonte from oure equinoxial 38 degrees
15 and 10 minutes. Understond wel this
rekning. Also for-get nat that the senith
is 90 degrees of heyghte fro the orisonte,
and oure equinoxial is 90 degrees from
oure pool artik. Also this shorte rewle
20 is soth, that the latitude of any place in
a regioun is the distance fro the senith
unto the equinoxial. And for more
declaracioun, lo here thy figure.

23. *To prove evidently the latitude of any*
*place in a regioun, by the preve of the*
*heyghte of the pol artik in that same*
*place.*

In some winters night, whan the firmament is clere and thikke-sterred, waite
a tyme til that any sterre fix sit lyne-right
perpendiculer over the pol artik, and
5 clepe that sterre A. And wayte a-nother

sterre that sit lyne-right under A, and
under the pol, and clepe that sterre F.
And understond wel, that F is nat considered but only to declare that A sit
evene overe the pool. Tak thanne a-non
right the altitude of A from the orisonte,
and forget it nat. Lat A and F go farwel
til agayns the dawening a gret whyle ;
and come thanne agayn, and abyd til
that A is evene under the pol and under
F ; for sothly, than wol F sitte over the
pool, and A wol sitte under the pool.
Tak than eft-sones the altitude of A from
the orisonte, and note as wel his secounde
altitude as his firste altitude ; and whan
that this is don, rikne how manye degrees
that the firste altitude of A excedeth
his seconde altitude, and tak half thilke
porcioun that is exceded, and adde it to
his seconde altitude ; and tak ther the
elevacioun of thy pool, and eke the
latitude of thy regioun. For thise two
ben of a nombre ; this is to seyn, as
many degrees as thy pool is elevat, so
michel is the latitude of the regioun.
Ensample as thus : par aventure, the
altitude of A in the evening is 56 degrees
of heyghte. Than wol his seconde altitude
or the dawing be 48 ; that is 8 lasse than
56, that was his firste altitude at even.
Take thanne the half of 8, and adde it to
48, that was his seconde altitude, and
than hastow 52. Now hastow the heyghte
of thy pol, and the latitude of the regioun.
But understond wel, that to prove this
conclusioun and many a-nother fair conclusioun, thou most have a plomet hanging on a lyne heyer than thin heved
on a perche ; and thilke lyne mot
hange evene perpendiculer by-twixe the
pool and thyn eye ; and thanne shaltow
seen yif A sitte evene over the pool and
over F at evene ; and also yif F sitte
evene over the pool and over A or day.
And for more declaracion, lo here thy
figure.

24. *Another conclusioun to prove the heyghte*
*of the pool artik fro the orisonte.*

Tak any sterre fixe that nevere dis-
sendeth under the orisonte in thilke

regioun, and considere his heyest altitude and his lowest altitude fro the orisonte ; and make a nombre of bothe thise altitudes. Tak thanne and abate half that nombre, and tak ther the elevacioun of the pol artik in that same regioun. And for more declaracioun, lo here thy figure.

## 25. *A-nother conclusioun to prove the latitude of the regioun, &c.*

Understond wel that the latitude of any place in a regioun is verreyly the space by-twixe the senith of hem that dwellen there and the equinoxial cerkle, north or southe, taking the mesure in the meridional lyne, as sheweth in the almikanteras of thyn Astrolabie. And thilke space is as moche as the pool artik is hey in the same place fro the orisonte. And than is the depressioun of the pol antartik, that is to seyn, than is the pol antartik by-nethe the orisonte, the same quantite of space, neither more ne lasse. Thanne, yif thow desire to knowe this latitude of the regioun, tak the altitude of the sonne in the middel of the day, whan the sonne is in the hevedes of Aries or of Libra ; (for thanne moeveth the sonne in the lyne equinoxial); and abate the nombre of that same sonnes altitude out of 90, and thanne is the remenaunt of the noumbre that leveth the latitude of the regioun. As thus : I suppose that the sonne is thilke day at noon 38 degrees and 10 minutes of heyghte. Abate thanne thise degrees and minutes out of 90; so leveth there 51 degrees and 50 minutes, the latitude. I sey nat this but for ensample ; for wel I wot the latitude of Oxenforde is certein minutes lasse, as I mighte prove. Now yif so be that thee semeth to long a taryinge, to abyde til that the sonne be in the hevedes of Aries or of Libra, thanne waite whan the sonne is in any other degree of the zodiak, and considere the degree of his declinacion fro the equinoxial lyne ; and yif it so be that the sonnes declinacion be northward fro the equinoxial, abate thanne fro the sonnes altitude at noon the nombre of his de-

clinacion, and thanne hastow the heyghte of the hevedes of Aries and Libra. As thus : my sonne is, par aventure, in the †firste degree of Leoun, †58 degrees and 10 minutes of heyghte at noon and his declinacion is almost †20 degrees northward fro the equinoxial ; abate thanne thilke †20 degrees of declinacion out of the altitude at noon, than leveth thee 38 degrees and odde minutes ; lo ther the heved of Aries or Libra, and thyn equinoxial in that regioun. Also yif so be that the sonnes declinacioun be southward fro the equinoxial, adde thanne thilke declinacion to the altitude of the sonne at noon ; and tak ther the hevedes of Aries and Libra, and thyn equinoxial. Abate thanne the heyghte of the equinoxial out of 90 degrees, and thanne leveth there the distans of the pole, 51 degrees and 50 minutes, of that regioun fro the equinoxial. Or elles, yif thee lest, take the heyest altitude fro the equinoxial of any sterre fix that thou knowest, and tak his nethere elongacioun lengthing fro the same equinoxial lyne, and wirke in the maner forseid. And for more declaracion, lo here thy figure.

## 26. *Declaracioun of the assensioun of signes, &c.*

The excellence of the spere solide, amonges other noble conclusiouns, sheweth manifeste the diverse assenciouns of signes in diverse places, as wel in the righte cercle as in the embelif cercle. Thise auctours wryten that thilke signe is cleped of right ascensioun, with which more part of the cercle equinoxial and lasse part of the zodiak ascendeth ; and thilke signe assendeth embelif, with whiche lasse part of the equinoxial and more part of the zodiak assendeth. Ferther-over they seyn, that in thilke cuntrey where as the senith of hem that dwellen there is in the equinoxial lyne, and her orisonte passing by the poles of this worlde, thilke folke han this right cercle and the right orisonte ; and everemo the arch of the day and the arch of the night is ther y-like long, and the sonne twyes every yeer passinge thorow the senith of her heved; and two someres and two winteres in a yeer han this forseide poeple. And the almikanteras 25 in her Astrolabies ben streighte as a lyne, so as sheweth in this figure. The utilite to knowe the assenciouns in the righte cercle is this: truste wel that by mediaciouh of thilke assenciouns thise astro30 logiens, by hir tables and hir instrumentz, knowen verreyly the assencioun of every degree and minut in al the zodiak, as shal be shewed. And nota, that this forseid righte orisonte, that is cleped 35 orison rectum, divydeth the equinoxial in-to right angles; and the embelif orisonte, wher-as the pol is enhaused up-on the orisonte, overkerveth the equinoxial in embelif angles, as sheweth in the figure. 40 And for the more declaracioun, lo here the figure.

27. *This is the conclusioun to knowe the assenciouns of signes in the right cercle, that is, circulus directus, &c.*

Set the heved of what signe thee liste to knowe his assending in the right cercle up-on the lyne meridional; and waite wher thyn almury toucheth the bordure, 5 and set ther a prikke. Turne thanne thy riet westward til that the ende of the forseide signe sitte up-on the meridional lyne; and eft-sones waite wher thyn almury toucheth the bordure, and set 10 ther another prikke. Rikne thanne the nombre of degrees in the bordure bytwixe bothe prikkes, and tak the assencioun of the signe in the right cercle. And thus maystow wyrke with every 15 porcioun of thy zodiak, &c. And for the more declaracioun, lo here thy figure.

28. *To knowe the assencions of signes in the embelif cercle in every regioun, I mene, in circulo obliquo.*

Set the heved of the signe which as thee list to knowe his ascensioun up-on the est orisonte, and waite wher thyn almury toucheth the bordure, and set 5 ther a prikke. Turne thanne thy riet upward til that the ende of the same

signe sitte up-on the est orisonte, and waite eft-sones wher as thyn almury toucheth the bordure, and set ther a-nother prikke. Rikne thanne the 10 noumbre of degrees in the bordure bytwixe bothe prikkes, and tak ther the assencioun of the signe in the embelif cercle. And understond wel, that alle signes in thy zodiak, fro the heved of 15 Aries unto the ende of Virgo, ben cleped signes of the north fro the equinoxial; and these signes arysen by-twixe the verrey est and the verrey north in oure orisonte generaly for evere. And alle 20 signes fro the heved of Libra un-to the ende of Pisces ben cleped signes of the south fro the equinoxial; and thise signes arysen ever-mo by-twixe the verrey est and the verrey south in oure orisonte. 25 Also every signe by-twixe the heved of Capricorne un-to the ende of Geminis aryseth on oure orisonte in lasse than two houres equales; and thise same signes, fro the heved of Capricorne un-to the 30 ende of Geminis, ben cleped 'tortuos signes' or 'croked signes,' for they arisen embelif on oure orisonte; and thise crokede signes ben obedient to the signes that ben of right assencioun. The signes 35 of right assencioun ben fro the heved of Cancer to the †ende of Sagittare; and thise signes arysen more upright, and they ben called eke sovereyn signes; and everich of hem aryseth in more space 40 than in two houres. Of which signes, Gemini obeyeth to Cancer; and Taurus to Leo; Aries to Virgo; Pisces to Libra; Aquarius to Scorpioun; and Capricorne to Sagittare. And thus ever-mo two 45 signes, that ben y-lyke fer fro the heved of Capricorne, obeyen everich of hem til other. And for more declaracioun, lo here the figure.

29. *To knowe justly the foure quarters of the world, as est, west, north, and sowth.*

Take the altitude of thy sonne whan thee list, and note wel the quarter of the world in which the sonne is for the tyme by the azimutz. Turne thanne thyn Astrolabie, and set the degree of the 5

sonne in the almikanteras of his altitude, on thilke side that the sonne stant, as is the manere in taking of houres ; and ley thy label on the degree of the sonne, and
o rikene how many degrees of the bordure ben by-twixe the lyne meridional and the point of thy label ; and note wel that noumbre. Turne thanne a-gayn thyn Astrolabie, and set the point of thy gret
15 rewle, ther thou takest thyne altitudes, up-on as many degrees in his bordure fro his meridional as was the point of thy label fro the lyne meridional on the wombe-syde. Tak thanne thyn Astro-
20 labie with bothe handes sadly and slely, and lat the sonne shyne thorow bothe holes of thy rewle ; and sleyly, in thilke shyninge, lat thyn Astrolabie couch adoun evene up-on a smothe grond, and thanne
25 wol the verrey lyne meridional of thyn Astrolabie lye evene south, and the est lyne wole lye est, and the west lyne west, and north lyne north, so that thou werke softly and avisely in the couching ; and
30 thus hastow the 4 quarters of the firmament. And for the more declaracioun, lo here the figure.

30. *To knowe the altitude of planetes fro the wey of the sonne, whether so they be north or south fro the forseide wey.*

Lok whan that a planete is in the lyne meridional, yif that hir altitude be of the same heyghte that is the degree of the sonne for that day, and than is the planete
5 in the verrey wey of the sonne, and hath no latitude. And yif the altitude of the planete be heyere than the degree of the sonne, than is the planete north fro the wey of the sonne swich a quantite of lati-
10 tude as sheweth by thyn almikanteras. And yif the altitude of the planete be lasse than the degree of the sonne, thanne is the planete south fro the wey of the sonne swich a quantite of latitude as sheweth
15 by thyn almikanteras. This is to seyn, fro the wey wher-as the sonne wente thilke day, but nat from the wey of the sonne in every place of the zodiak. And for the more declaracioun, lo here the
20 figure.

31. *To knowe the senith of the arysing of the sonne, this is to seyn, the partie of the orisonte in which that the sonne aryseth.*

Thou most first considere that the sonne aryseth nat al-wey verrey est, but some tyme by north the est, and som tyme by southe the est. Sothly, the sonne aryseth never-mo verrey est in oure ori- 5 sonte, but he be in the heved of Aries or Libra. Now is thyn orisonte departed in 24 parties by thy azimutz, in significacion of 24 partiez of the world ; al-be-it so that shipmen rikne thilke partiez in 32. 10 Thanne is ther no more but waite in which azimut that thy sonne entreth at his arysing ; and take ther the senith of the arysing of the sonne. The manere of the devisioun of thyn Astrolabie is this ; 15 I mene, as in this cas. First is it devided in 4 plages principals with the lyne that goth from est to west, and than with a-nother lyne that goth fro south to north. Than is it devided in smale partiez of 20 azimutz, as est, and est by southe, whereas is the firste azimut above the est lyne ; and so forth, fro partie to partie, til that thou come agayn un-to the est lyne. Thus maistow understond also the senith of 25 any sterre, in which partie he ryseth, &c. And for the more declaracion, lo here the figure.

32. *To knowe in which partie of the firmament is the conjunccioun.*

Considere the tyme of the conjunccion by thy kalender, as thus ; lok how many houres thilke conjunccion is fro the mid-day of the day precedent, as sheweth by the canoun of thy kalender. Rikne 5 thanne thilke nombre of houres in the bordure of thyn Astrolabie, as thou art wont to do in knowing of the houres of the day or of the night ; and ley thy label over the degree of the sonne ; and thanne 10 wol the point of thy label sitte up-on the hour of the conjunccion. Loke thanne in which azimut the degree of thy sonne sitteth, and in that partie of the firmament is the conjunccioun. And for the 15 more declaracioun, lo here thy figure.

33. *To knowe the senith of the altitude of the sonne, &c.*

This is no more to seyn but any tyme of the day tak the altitude of the sonne ; and by the azimut in which he stondeth, maystou seen in which partie of the fir-
5 mament he is. And in the same wyse maystou seen, by the night, of any sterre, whether the sterre sitte est or west or north, or any partie by-twene, after the name of the azimut in which is the sterre.
10 And for the more declaracioun, lo here the figure.

34. *To knowe sothly the degree of the longitude of the mone, or of any planete that hath no latitude for the tyme fro the ecliptik lyne.*

Tak the altitude of the mone, and rikne thyn altitude up among thyne al-mikanteras on which syde that the mone stande ; and set there a prikke. Tak
5 thenne anon-right, up-on the mones syde, the altitude of any sterre fix which that thou knowest, and set his centre up-on his altitude among thyn almikanteras ther the sterre is founde. Waite thanne
10 which degree of the zodiak toucheth the prikke of the altitude of the mone, and tak ther the degree in which the mone standeth. This conclusioun is verrey sooth, yif the sterres in thyn Astrolabie
15 stonden after the trowthe ; of comune, tretis of Astrolabie ne make non excep-cioun whether the mone have latitude, or non ; ne on whether syde of the mone the altitude of the sterre fix be taken. And
20 *nota*, that yif the mone shewe himself by light of day, than maystow wyrke this same conclusioun by the sonne, as wel as by the fix sterre. And for the more de-claracioun, lo here thy figure.

35. *This is the workinge of the conclusioun, to knowe yif that any planete be directe or retrograde.*

Tak the altitude of any sterre that is cleped a planete, and note it wel. And tak eek anon the altitude of any sterre fix that thou knowest, and note it wel
5 also. Come thanne agayn the thridde or

the ferthe night next folwing ; for thanne shaltow aperceyve wel the moeving of a planete, whether so he moeve forthward or bakward. Awaite wel thanne whan that thy sterre fix is in the same altitude 10 that she was whan thou toke hir firste altitude ; and tak than eftsones the alti-tude of the forseide planete, and note it wel. For trust wel, yif so be that the planete be on the right syde of the meri- 15 dional lyne, so that his seconde altitude be lasse than his firste altitude was, thanne is the planete directe. And yif he be on the west syde in that condicion, thanne is he retrograd. And yif so be 20 that this planete be up-on the est syde whan his altitude is taken, so that his secounde altitude be more than his firste altitude, thanne is he retrograde, and yif he be on the west syde, than is he directe. 25 But the contrarie of thise parties is of the cours of the mone ; for sothly, the mone moeveth the contrarie from othere plan-etes as in hir episicle, but in non other manere. And for the more declaracioun, 30 lo here thy figure.

36. *The conclusiouns of equaciouns of houses, after the Astrolabie, &c.*

Set the by-ginning of the degree that assendeth up-on the ende of the 8 houre inequal ; thanne wol the by-ginning of the 2 hous sitte up-on the lyne of mid-night. Remeve thanne the degree that 5 assendeth, and set him on the ende of the 10 hour inequal ; and thanne wol the byginning of the 3 hous sitte up-on the midnight lyne. Bring up agayn the same degree that assendeth first, and set him 10 up-on the orisonte ; and thanne wol the beginning of the 4 hous sitte up-on the lyne of midnight. Tak thanne the nadir of the degree that first assendeth, and set him on the ende of the 2 houre 15 inequal ; and thanne wol the beginning of the 5 hous sitte up-on the lyne of mid-night.; set thanne the nadir of the assen-dent on the ende of the 4 houre, than wol the beginning of the 6 house sitte on the 20 midnight lyne. The beginning of the 7 hous is nadir of the assendent, and the beginning of the 8 hous is nadir of the 2 ; and the beginning of the 9 hous is 5 nadir of the 3 ; and the beginning of the 10 hous is the nadir of the 4 ; and the beginning of the 11 hous is nadir of the 5 ; and the beginning of the 12 hous is nadir of the 6. And for the more declaracion, 10 lo here the figure.

### 37. A-nother manere of equaciouns of houses by the Astrolabie.

Tak thyn assendent, and thanne hastow thy 4 angles ; for wel thou wost that the opposit of thyn assendent, that is to seyn, thy beginning of the 7 hous, sit up-on the 5 west orizonte ; and the beginning of the 10 hous sit up-on the lyne meridional ; and his opposit up-on the lyne of mid-night. Thanne ley thy label over the degree that assendeth, and rekne fro the 10 point of thy label alle the degrees in the bordure, til thou come to the meridional lyne ; and departe alle thilke degrees in 3 evene parties, and take the evene equacion of 3 ; for ley thy label over 15 everich of 3 parties, and than maistow see by thy label in which degree of the zodiak [is] the beginning of everich of thise same houses fro the assendent : that is to seyn, the beginning of the 20 12 house next above thyn assendent ; and thanne the beginning of the 11 house ; and thanne the 10, up-on the meridional lyne ; as I first seide. The same wyse wirke thou fro the assendent doun to the 25 lyne of midnight ; and thanne thus hastow other 3 houses, that is to seyn, the beginning of the 2, and the 3, and the 4 houses ; thanne is the nadir of thise 3 houses the beginning of the 3 houses 30 that folwen. And for the more declara-cioun, lo here thy figure.

### 38. To finde the lyne merydional to dwelle fix in any certein place.

Tak a rond plate of metal ; for warping, the brodere the bettre ; and make ther-upon a just compas, a lite with-in the bordure ; and ley this ronde plate up-on 5 an evene grond, or on an evene ston, or on an evene stok fix in the gronde ; and

ley it even by a level. And in centre of the compas stike an evene pin or a wyr upright ; the smallere the betere. Set thy pin by a plom-rewle evene upright ; 10 and let this pin be no lengere than a quarter of the diametre of thy compas, fro the centre. And waite bisily aboute 10 or 11 of the clokke ; and whan the sonne shyneth, whan the shadwe of the 15 pin entreth any-thing with-in the cercle of thy plate an heer-mele, and mark ther a prikke with inke. Abyde thanne stille waiting on the sonne after 1 of the clokke, til that the schadwe of the wyr or of the 20 pin passe ony-thing out of the cercle of the compas, be it never so lyte ; and set ther a-nother prikke of inke. Take than a compas, and mesure evene the middel by-twixe bothe prikkes ; and set ther a 25 prikke. Take thanne a rewle, and draw a stryke, evene a-lyne fro the pin un-to the middel prikke ; and tak ther thy lyne meridional for evere-mo, as in that same place. And yif thow drawe a cros-lyne 30 over-thwart the compas, justly over the lyne meridional, than hastow est and west and south ; and, par consequence, than the nadir of the south lyne is the north lyne. And for more declaracioun, 35 lo here thy figure.

### 39. Descripcion of the meridional lyne, of longitudes, and latitudes of citees and townes from on to a-nother of clymatz.

This lyne meridional is but a maner descripcion of lyne imagined, that passeth upon the poles of this world and by the senith of oure heved. And hit is y-cleped the lyne meridional ; for in what place 5 that any maner man is at any tyme of the yeer, whan that the sonne by moeving of the firmament cometh to his verrey meridian place, than is hit verrey midday, that we clepen oure noon, as to thilke 10 man ; and therfore is it cleped the lyne of midday. And nota, for evermo, of 2 citees or of 2 tounes, of whiche that o toun aprocheth more toward the est than doth that other toun, truste wel that 15 thilke tounes han diverse meridians. Nota also, that the arch of the equinoxial,

that is conteyned or bounded by-twixe the 2 meridians, is cleped the longitude of
20 the toun. And yif so be that two tounes have y-lyke meridian, or oon meridian, than is the distance of hem bothe y-lyke fer fro the est ; and the contrarie. And in this manere they chaunge nat her
25 meridian, but sothly they chaungen her almikanteras ; for the enhausing of the pool and the distance of the sonne. The longitude of a clymat is a lyne imagined fro est to west, y-lyke distant by-twene
30 them alle. The latitude of a clymat is a lyne imagined from north to south the space of the erthe, fro the byginning of the firste clymat unto the verrey ende of the same climat, evene directe agayns
35 the pole artik. Thus seyn some auctours; and somme of hem seyn that yif men clepen the latitude, thay mene the arch meridian that is contiened or intercept by-twixe the senith and the equinoxial.
40 Thanne sey they that the distaunce fro the equinoxial unto the ende of a clymat, evene agayns the pole artyk, is the latitude of a clymat for sothe. And for more declaracioun, lo here thy figure.

40. *To knowe with which degree of the zodiak that any planete assendith on the orisonte, whether so that his latitude be north or south.*

Knowe by thyn almenak the degree of the ecliptik of any signe in which that the planete is rekned for to be, and that is cleped the degree of his longitude; and
5 knowe also the degree of his latitude fro the ecliptik, north or south. And by thise samples folwinge in special, maystow wirke † for sothe in every signe of the zodiak. The degree of the longitude,
10 par aventure, of Venus or of another planete, was 6 of Capricorne, and the latitude of him was northward 2 degrees fro the ecliptik lyne. I tok a subtil compas, and cleped that oon poynt of my
15 compas A, and that other poynt F. Than tok I the point of A, and set it in the ecliptik lyne evene in my zodiak, in the degree of the longitude of Venus, that is to seyn, in the 6 degree of Capricorne;

and thanne sette I the point of F upward 20 in the same signe, bycause that the latitude was north, up-on the latitude of Venus, that is to seyn, in the 6 degree fro the heved of Capricorne ; and thus have I 2 degrees by-twixe my two prikkes. 25 Than leide I doun softely my compas, and sette the degree of the longitude up-on the orisonte ; tho tok I and wexede my label in maner of a peyre tables to resceyve distinctly the prikkes of my 30 compas. Tho tok I this forseide label, and leide it fix over the degree of my longitude ; tho tok I up my compas, and sette the point of A in the wex on my label, as evene as I coude gesse over the 35 ecliptik lyne, in the ende of the longitude ; and sette the point of F endlang in my label up-on the space of the latitude, inwarde and over the zodiak, that is to seyn, north-ward fro the ecliptik. 40 Than leide I doun my compas, and lokede wel in the wey upon the prikke of A and of F ; tho turned I my riet til that the prikke of F sat up-on the orisonte ; than saw I wel that the body of Venus, in hir 45 latitude of 2 degrees septentrionalis, assended, in the ende of the 6 degree, in the heved of Capricorne. And *nota*, that in the same maner maistow wirke with any latitude septentrional in alle 50 signes ; but sothly the latitude meridional of a planete in Capricorne may not be take, by-cause of the litel space by-twixe the ecliptik and the bordure of the Astrolabie ; but sothly, in alle other signes it 55 may.

Also the degree, par aventure, of Jupiter or of a-nother planete, was in the first degree of Pisces in longitude, and his latitude was 3 degrees meridional ; 60 tho tok I the point of A, and sette it in the firste degree of Pisces on the ecliptik, and thanne sette I the point of F dounward in the same signe, by-cause that the latitude was south 3 degrees, that is to 65 seyn, fro the heved of Pisces ; and thus have I 3 degrees by-twixe bothe prikkes ; thanne sette I the degree of the longitude up-on the orisonte. Tho tok I my label, and leide it fix upon the degree of the 70 longitude; tho sette I the point of A on my label, evene over the ecliptik lyne, in the ende evene of the degree of the longitude, and sette the point of F endlang in 5 my label the space †of 3 degrees of the latitude fro the zodiak, this is to seyn, southward fro the ecliptik, toward the bordure; and turned my riet til the prikke of F sat up-on the orisonte; 0 thanne saw I wel that the body of Jupiter, in his latitude of 3 degrees meridional, ascended with 14 degrees of Pisces *in horoscopo*. And in this maner maistow wirke with any latitude meri- 5 dional, as I first seide, save in Capricorne. And yif thou wolt pleye this craft with

the arysing of the mone, loke thou rekne wel hir cours houre by houre; for she ne dwelleth nat in a degree of hir longitude but a litel whyle, as thou wel knowest; 90 but natheles, yif thou rekne hir verreye moeving by thy tables houre after houre, †thou shalt do wel y-now.

*Explicit tractatus de Conclusionibus Astro-labii, compilatus per Galfridum Chau-ciers ad Filium suum Lodewicum, scolarem tunc temporis Oxonie, ac sub tutela illius nobilissimi philosophi Ma-gistri N. Strode, etc.*

\*   \*   \*   \*   \*   \*   \*

# SUPPLEMENTARY PROPOSITIONS.

### 41. *Umbra Recta.*

Yif it so be that thou wilt werke by *umbra recta*, and thou may come to the bas of the toure, in this maner thou schalt werke. Tak the altitude of the 5 tour by bothe holes, so that thy rewle ligge even in a poynt. Ensample as thus : I see him thorw at the poynt of 4 ; than mete I the space be-tween me and the tour, and I finde it 20 feet ; than 0 be-holde I how 4 is to 12, right so is the space betwixe thee and the tour to the altitude of the tour. For 4 is the thridde part of 12, so is the space be-tween thee and the tour the thridde part of the 5 altitude of the tour ; than thryes 20 feet is the heyghte of the tour, with adding of thyn owne persone to thyn eye. And this rewle is so general in *umbra recta*, fro the poynt of oon to 12. And yif thy 0 rewle falle upon 5, than is 5 12-partyes of the heyght the space be-tween thee and the toure; with adding of thyn owne heyght.

### 42. *Umbra Versa.*

Another maner of werkinge, by *vmbra versa*. Yif so be that thou may nat come

to the bas of the tour, I see him thorw the nombre of 1 ; I sette ther a prikke at my fote ; than go I neer to the tour, and 5 I see him thorw at the poynt of 2, and there I sette a-nother prikke; and I beholde how 1 hath him to 12, and ther finde I that it hath him twelfe sythes; than beholde I how 2 hath him to 12, and 10 thou shalt finde it sexe sythes; than thou shalt finde that as 12 above 6 is the numbre of 6, right so is the space between thy two prikkes the space of 6 tymes thyn altitude. And note, that at 15 the ferste altitude of 1, thou settest a prikke ; and afterward, whan thou seest him at 2, ther thou settest an-other prikke ; than thou findest between two prikkys 60 feet; than thou shalt finde 20 that 10 is the 6-party of 60. And then is 10 feet the altitude of the tour. For other poyntis, yif it fille in *umbra versa*, as thus : I sette caas it fill upon †2, and at the secunde upon †3 ; than schalt thou 25 finde that 2 is 6 partyes of 12 ; and 3 is 4 partyes of 12 ; than passeth 6 4, by nombre of 2 ; so is the space between two prikkes twyes the heyghte of the tour. And yif the differens were thryes, than 30

shulde it be three tymes ; and thus mayst
thou werke fro 2 to 12 ; and yif it be 4, 4
tymes ; or 5, 5 tymes ; *et sic de ceteris.*

### 43. *Umbra Recta.*

An-other maner of wyrking be *umbra
recta.* Yif it so be that thou mayst nat
come to the baas of the tour, in this
maner thou schalt werke. Sette thy rewle
5 upon 1 till thou see the altitude, and
sette at thy foot a prikke. Than sette
thy rewle upon 2, and beholde what is
the differense be-tween 1 and 2, and thou
shalt finde that it is 1. Than mete the
10 space be-tween two prikkes, and that is
the 12 partie of the altitude of the tour.
And yif ther were 2, it were the 6 partye ;
and yif ther were 3, the 4 partye ; *et sic
deinceps.* And note, yif it were 5, it were
15 the 5 party of 12 ; and 7, 7 party of 12 ;
and note, at the altitude of thy conclusioun, adde the stature of thyn heyghte
to thyn eye.

\*   \*   \*   \*   \*   \*

44. *Another maner conclusion, to knowe the
mene mote and the argumentis of any
planete. To know the mene mote and
the argumentis of every planete fro yere
to yere, from day to day, from houre
to houre, and from smale fraccionis
infinite.*

In this maner shalt thou worche :
consider thy rote first, the whiche is
made the beginning of the tables fro the
yere of oure lord 1397, and entere hit in-to
5 thy slate for the laste meridie of December ; and than consider the yere of oure
lord, what is the date, and be-hold
whether thy date be more or lasse than
the yere 1397. And yf hit so be that hit
10 be more, loke how many yeres hit passeth,
and with so many entere into thy tables
in the first lyne ther-as is writen *anni
collecti et expansi.* And loke where the
same planet is writen in the hede of thy
15 table, and than loke what thou findest in
directe of the same yere of oure lord
whiche is passid, be hit 8, or 9, or 10, or

what nombre that evere it be, til the
tyme that thou come to 20, or 40, or 60.
And that thou findest in directe †wryte
in thy slate under thy rote, and adde hit
to-geder, and that is thy mene mote, for
the laste meridian of the December, for
the same yere whiche that thou hast
purposed. And if hit so be that hit passe
20, consider wel that fro 1 to 20 ben *anni
expansi,* and fro 20 to 3000 ben *anni collecti ;*
and if thy nombere passe 20, than take
that thou findest in directe of 20, and if
hit be more, as 6 or 18, than take that
thou findest in directe there-of, that is to
sayen, signes, degrees, minutes, and secoundes, and adde to-gedere un-to thy
rote ; and thus to make rotes. And note,
that if hit so be that the yere of oure lord
be †lasse than the rote, which is the yere
of oure lord 1397, than shalt thou wryte
in the same wyse furst thy rote in thy
slate, and after entere in-to thy table in
the same yere that be lasse, as I taught
be-fore ; and than consider how many
signes, degrees, minutes, and secoundes
thyn entringe conteyneth. And so be
that ther be 2 entrees, than adde hem
togeder, and after with-drawe hem from
the rote, the yere of oure lord 1397 ; and
the residue that leveth is thy mene mote
fro the laste meridie of December, the
whiche thou hast purposed ; and if hit so
be that thou wolt weten thy mene mote
for any day, or for any fraccioun of day,
in this maner thou shalt worche. Make
thy rote fro the laste day of Decembere in
the maner as I have taught, and afterward behold how many monethes, dayes,
and houres ben passid from the meridie
of Decembere, and with that entere with
the laste moneth that is ful passed, and
take that thou findest in directe of him,
and wryte hit in thy slate ; and entere
with as mony dayes as be more, and wryte
that thou findest in directe of the same
planete that thou worchest for ; and in
the same wyse in the table of houres, for
houres that ben passed, and adde alle
these to thy rote ; and the residue is the
mene mote for the same day and the
same houre.

### 45. *Another manere to knowe the mene mote.*

Whan thou wolt make the mene mote of eny planete to be by Arsechieles tables, take thy rote, the whiche is for the yere of oure lord 1397; and if so be that thy yere be passid the date, wryte that date, and than wryte the nombere of the yeres. Than with-drawe the yeres out of the yeres that ben passed that rote. En-sampul as thus : the yere of oure lord 1400, †I wolde witen, precise, my rote ; than wroot I furst 1400. And under that nombere I wrote a 1397 ; than withdrow I the laste nombere out of that, and than fond I the residue was 3 yere ; I wiste that 3 yere was passed fro the rote, the whiche was writen in my tables. Than after-ward soghte I in my tables the *annis collectis et expansis*, and amonge myn expanse yeres fond I 3 yeer. Than tok I alle the signes, degrees, and minutes, that I fond directe under the same planete that I wroghte for, and wroot so many signes, degrees, and minutes in my slate, and after-ward added I to signes, degrees, minutes, and secoundes, the whiche I fond in my rote the yere of oure lord 1397; and kepte the residue; and than had I the mene mote for the laste day of Decembere. And if thou woldest wete the mene mote of any planete in March, Aprile, or May, other in any other tyme or moneth of the yere, loke how many monethes and dayes ben passed from the laste day of Decembere, the yere of oure lord 1400 ; and so with monethes and dayes entere in-to thy table ther thou findest thy mene mote y-writen in monethes and dayes, and take alle the signes, degrees, minutes, and secoundes that thou findest y-write in directe of thy monethes, and adde to signes, degrees, minutes, and secoundes that thou findest with thy rote the yere of oure lord 1400, and the residue that leveth is the mene mote for that same day. And note, if hit so be that thou woldest wete the mene mote in any yere that is lasse than thy rote, with-drawe the nombere of so many yeres as hit is lasse than the yere of oure lord a 1397, and kepe the residue ; and so many yeres, monethes, and dayes entere in-to thy tabelis of thy mene mote. And take alle the signes, degrees, and minutes, and secoundes, that thou findest in directe of alle the yeres, monethes, and dayes, and wryte hem in thy slate ; and above thilke nombere wryte the signes, degrees, minutes, and secoundes, the whiche thou findest with thy rote the yere of oure lord a 1397; and with-drawe alle the nethere signes and degrees fro the signes and degrees, minutes, and secoundes of other signes with thy rote ; and thy residue that leveth is thy mene mote for that day.

### 46. *For to knowe at what houre of the day, or of the night, shal be flode or ebbe*.

First wite thou certeinly, how that haven stondeth, that thou list to werke for ; that is to say in whiche place of the firmament the mone being, maketh fulle see. Than awayte thou redily in what degree of the zodiak that the mone at that tyme is inne. Bringe furth than the labelle, and set the point therof in that same cost that the mone maketh flode, and set thou there the degree of the mone according with the egge of the label. Than afterward awayte where is than the degree of the sonne, at that tyme. Remeve thou than the label fro the mone, and bringe and sette it justly upon the degree of the sonne. And the point of the label shal than declare to thee, at what houre of the day or of the night shal be flode. And there also maist thou wite by the same point of the label, whether it be, at that same tyme, flode or ebbe, or half flode, or quarter flode, or ebbe, or half or quarter ebbe ; or ellis at what houre it was last, or shal be next by night or by day, thou than shalt esely knowe, &c. Furthermore, if it so be that thou happe to worke for this matere aboute the tyme of the conjunccioun, bringe furthe the degree of the

---

* Perhaps not genuine.

30 mone with the labelle to that coste as it
is before seyd. But than thou shalt
understonde that thou may not bringe
furthe the label fro the degree of the
mone as thou dide before; for-why the
35 sonne is than in the same degree with
the mone. And so thou may at that
tyme by the point of the labelle unremeved knowe the houre of the flode or
of the ebbe, as it is before seyd, &c. And
40 evermore as thou findest the mone passe

fro the sonne, so remeve thou the labelle
than fro the degree of the mone, and
bringe it to the degree of the sonne.
And worke thou than as thou dide before,
&c. Or elles knowe thou what houre it 45
is that thou art inne, by thyn instrument. Than bringe thou furth fro
thennes the labelle and ley it upon the
degree of the mone, and therby may
thou wite also whan it was flode, or whan 50
it wol be next, be it night or day; &c.

# THE CANTERBURY TALES.

—◆—

## GROUP A.  THE PROLOGUE.

**Here biginneth the Book of the Tales of Caunterbury.**

Whan that Aprille with his shoures sote
The droghte of Marche hath perced to
    the rote,
And bathed every veyne in swich licour,
Of which vertu engendred is the flour ;
Whan Zephirus eek with his swete breeth 5
Inspired hath in every holt and heeth
The tendre croppes, and the yonge sonne
Hath in the Ram his halfe cours y-ronne,
And smale fowles maken melodye,
That slepen al the night with open yë, 10
(So priketh hem nature in hir corages) :
Than longen folk to goon on pilgrimages
(And palmers for to seken straunge
    strondes)
To ferne halwes, couthe in sondry londes ;
And specially, from every shires ende 15
Of Engelond, to Caunterbury they wende,
The holy blisful martir for to seke,
That hem hath holpen, whan that they
    were seke.
    Bifel that, in that seson on a day,
In Southwerk at the Tabard as I lay   20
Redy to wenden on my pilgrimage
To Caunterbury with ful devout corage,
At night was come in-to that hostelrye
Wel nyne and twenty in a companye,
Of sondry folk, by aventure y-falle   25
In felawshipe, and pilgrims were they alle,
That toward Caunterbury wolden ryde ;
The chambres and the stables weren wyde,
And wel we weren esed atte beste.
And shortly, whan the sonne was to reste,

So hadde I spoken with hem everichon, 31
That I was of hir felawshipe anon,
And made forward erly for to ryse,
To take our wey, ther as I yow devyse.
    But natheles, whyl I have tyme and
    space,   35
Er that I ferther in this tale pace,
Me thinketh it acordaunt to resoun,
To telle yow al the condicioun
Of ech of hem, so as it semed me,
And whiche they weren, and of what
    degree ;   40
And eek in what array that they were
    inne :
And at a knight than wol I first biginne.
    A Knight ther was, and that a worthy
    man,      **Knight.**
That fro the tyme that he first bigan
To ryden out, he loved chivalrye,   45
Trouthe and honour, fredom and cur-
    teisye.
Ful worthy was he in his lordes werre,
And therto hadde he riden (no man
    ferre)
As wel in Cristendom as hethenesse,
And ever honoured for his worthinesse. 50
    At Alisaundre he was, whan it was
    wonne ;
Ful ofte tyme he hadde the bord bigonne
Aboven alle naciouns in Pruce.
In Lettow hadde he reysed and in Ruce,
No Cristen man so ofte of his degree.   55
In Gernade at the sege eek hadde he be

Of Algezir, and riden in Belmarye.
At Lyeys was he, and at Satalye,
Whan they were wonne; and in the
    Grete See
At many a noble aryve hadde he be.      60
At mortal batailles hadde he been fiftene,
And foughten for our feith at Tramissene
In listes thryes, and ay slayn his fo.
This ilke worthy knight had been also
Somtyme with the lord of Palatye,      65
Ageyn another hethen in Turkye :
And evermore he hadde a sovereyn prys.
And though that he were worthy, he was
    wys,
And of his port as meke as is a mayde.
He never yet no vileinye ne sayde      70
In al his lyf, un-to no maner wight.
He was a verray parfit gentil knight.
But for to tellen yow of his array,
His hors were gode, but he was nat gay.
Of fustian he wered a gipoun      75
Al bismotered with his habergeoun ;
For he was late y-come from his viage,
And wente for to doon his pilgrimage.

    With him ther was his sone, a yong
        SQUYER,                **Squyer.**
A lovyere, and a lusty bacheler,      80
With lokkes crulle, as they were leyd in
    presse.
Of twenty yeer of age he was, I gesse.
Of his stature he was of evene lengthe,
And wonderly deliver, and greet of
    strengthe.
And he had been somtyme in chivachye, 85
In Flaundres, in Artoys, and Picardye,
And born him wel, as of so litel space,
In hope to stonden in his lady grace.
Embrouded was he, as it were a mede
Al ful of fresshe floures, whyte and rede. 90
Singinge he was, or floytinge, al the day ;
He was as fresh as is the month of May.
Short was his goune, with sleves longe
    and wyde.
Wel coude he sitte on hors, and faire ryde.
He coude songes make and wel endyte,  95
Juste and eek daunce, and wel purtreye
    and wryte.
So hote he lovede, that by nightertale
He sleep namore than dooth a nightingale.
Curteys he was, lowly, and servisable,
And carf biforn his fader at the table. 100

A YEMAN hadde he, and servaunts namo
At that tyme, for him liste ryde so ;
And he was clad in cote and hood of
    grene ;                **Yeman.**
A sheef of pecok-arwes brighte and
    kene
Under his belt he bar ful thriftily ;   105
(Wel coude he dresse his takel yemanly :
His arwes drouped noght with fetheres
    lowe),
And in his hand he bar a mighty bowe.
A not-heed hadde he, with a broun visage.
Of wode-craft wel coude he al the usage. 110
Upon his arm he bar a gay bracer,
And by his syde a swerd and a bokeler,
And on that other syde a gay daggere,
Harneised wel, and sharp as point of
    spere ;
A Cristofre on his brest of silver shene. 115
An horn he bar, the bawdrik was of
    grene ;
A forster was he, soothly, as I gesse.

    Ther was also a Nonne, a PRIORESSE,
That of hir smyling was ful simple and
    coy ;                **Prioresse.**
Hir gretteste ooth was but by sëynt
    Loy ;                120
And she was cleped madame Eglentyne.
Ful wel she song the service divyne,
Entuned in hir nose ful semely ;
And Frensh she spak ful faire and fetisly,
After the scole of Stratford atte Bowe, 125
For Frensh of Paris was to hir unknowe.
At mete wel y-taught was she with-alle ;
She leet no morsel from hir lippes falle,
Ne wette hir fingres in hir sauce depe.
Wel coude she carie a morsel, and wel
    kepe,                130
That no drope ne fille up-on hir brest.
In curteisye was set ful muche hir lest.
Hir over lippe wyped she so clene,
That in hir coppe was no ferthing sene
Of grece, whan she dronken hadde hir
    draughte.                135
Ful semely after hir mete she raughte,
And sikerly she was of greet disport,
And ful plesaunt, and amiable of port,
And peyned hir to countrefete chere
Of court, and been estatlich of manere, 140
And to ben holden digne of reverence.
But, for to speken of hir conscience,

She was so charitable and so pitous,
She wolde wepe, if that she sawe a mous
Caught in a trappe, if it were deed or
   bledde.  145
Of smale houndes had she, that she fedde
With rosted flesh, or milk and wastel-
   breed.
But sore weep she if oon of hem were
   deed,
Or if men smoot it with a yerde smerte :
And al was conscience and tendre herte.
Ful semely hir wimpel pinched was ;  151
Hir nose tretys ; hir eyen greye as glas ;
Hir mouth ful smal, and ther-to softe and
   reed ;
But sikerly she hadde a fair forheed ;
It was almost a spanne brood, I trowe ;  155
For, hardily, she was nat undergrowe.
Ful fetis was hir cloke, as I was war.
Of smal coral aboute hir arm she bar
A peire of bedes, gauded al with grene ;
And ther-on heng a broche of gold ful
   shene,  160
On which ther was first write a crowned A,
And after, *Amor vincit omnia.*  **Nonne.**
Another NONNE with hir hadde she,
That was hir chapeleyne, and PREESTES
   THREE.  **3 Preestes.**

A MONK ther was, a fair for the maistrye,
An out-rydere, that lovede venerye ;  166
A manly man, to been an abbot able.
Ful many a deyntee hors hadde he in
   stable :  **Monk.**
And, whan he rood, men mighte his
   brydel here
Ginglen in a whistling wind as clere,  170
And eek as loude as dooth the chapel-
   belle
Ther as this lord was keper of the celle.
The reule of seint Maure or of seint
   Beneit,
By-cause that it was old and som-del
   streit,
This ilke monk leet olde thinges pace,  175
And held after the newe world the
   space.
He yaf nat of that text a pulled hen,
That seith, that hunters been nat holy
   men ;
Ne that a monk, whan he is cloisterlees,
Is lykned til a fish that is waterlees ;  180

This is to seyn, a monk out of his cloistre.
But thilke text held he nat worth an
   oistre ;
And I seyde, his opinioun was good.
What sholde he studie, and make him-
   selven wood,
Upon a book in cloistre alwey to poure,  185
Or swinken with his handes, and laboure,
As Austin bit ? How shal the world be
   served ?
Lat Austin have his swink to him reserved.
Therfore he was a pricasour aright ;
Grehoundes he hadde, as swifte as fowel
   in flight ;  190
Of priking and of hunting for the hare
Was al his lust, for no cost wolde he
   spare.
I seigh his sleves purfiled at the hond
With grys, and that the fyneste of a lond ;
And, for to festne his hood under his
   chin,  195
He hadde of gold y-wroght a curious pin :
A love-knotte in the gretter ende ther was.
His heed was balled, that shoon as any
   glas,
And eek his face, as he had been anoint.
He was a lord ful fat and in good point ; 200
His eyen stepe, and rollinge in his heed,
That stemed as a forneys of a leed ;
His botes souple, his hors in greet estat.
Now certeinly he was a fair prelat ;
He was nat pale as a for-pyned goost,  205
A fat swan loved he best of any roost.
His palfrey was as broun as is a berye.

A FRERE ther was, a wantown and a
   merye,  **Frere.**
A limitour, a ful solempne man.  209
In alle the ordres foure is noon that can
So muche of daliaunce and fair langage.
He hadde maad ful many a mariage
Of yonge wommen, at his owne cost.
Un-to his ordre he was a noble post.
Ful wel biloved and famulier was he  215
With frankeleyns over-al in his contree,
And eek with worthy wommen of the
   toun :
For he had power of confessioun,
As seyde him-self, more than a curat,
For of his ordre he was licentiat.  220
Ful swetely herde he confessioun,
And plesaunt was his absolucioun ;

He was an esy man to yeve penaunce
Ther as he wiste to han a good pitaunce ;
For unto a povre ordre for to yive    225
Is signe that a man is wel y-shrive.
For if he yaf, he dorste make avaunt,
He wiste that a man was repentaunt.
For many a man so hard is of his herte,
He may nat wepe al-thogh him sore
    smerte.    230
Therfore, in stede of weping and preyeres,
Men moot yeve silver to the povre freres.
His tipet was ay farsed ful of knyves
And pinnes, for to yeven faire wyves.
And certeinly he hadde a mery note ; 235
Wel coude he singe and pleyen on a rote.
Of yeddinges he bar utterly the prys.
His nekke whyt was as the flour-de-lys ;
Ther-to he strong was as a champioun.
He knew the tavernes wel in every toun,
And everich hostiler and tappestere  241
Bet than a lazar or a beggestere ;
For un-to swich a worthy man as he
Acorded nat, as by his facultee,    244
To have with seke lazars aqueyntaunce.
It is nat honest, it may nat avaunce
For to delen with no swich poraille,
But al with riche and sellers of vitaille.
And over-al, ther as profit sholde aryse,
Curteys he was, and lowly of servyse.  250
Ther nas no man no-wher so vertuous.
He was the beste beggere in his hous ;
†And  yaf  a  certeyn  ferme  for  the
    graunt ;              252 b
†Noon of his bretheren cam ther in his
    haunt ;              252 c
For thogh a widwe hadde noght a sho,
So plesaunt was his ' *In principio*,'
Yet  wolde  he  have  a  ferthing,  er  he
    wente.              255
His purchas was wel bettre than his rente.
And rage he coude, as it were right a
    whelpe.
In love-dayes ther coude he muchel
    helpe.              (260)
For there he was nat lyk a cloisterer,
With a thredbar cope, as is a povre
    scoler,              260
But he was lyk a maister or a pope.
Of double worsted was his semi-cope,
That rounded as a belle out of the presse.
Somwhat he lipsed, for his wantownesse,

To make his English swete up-on his
    tonge ;              265
And in his harping, whan that he had
    songe,
His eyen twinkled in his heed aright,
As  doon  the  sterres  in  the  frosty
    night.              (270)
This worthy limitour was cleped Huberd.
A MARCHANT was ther with a forked
    berd,              **Marchant.**
In mottelee, and hye on horse he sat, 271
Up-on his heed a Flaundrish bever hat ;
His botes clasped faire and fetisly.
His resons he spak ful solempnely,    274
Souninge alway th'encrees of his winning.
He wolde the see were kept for any thing
Bitwixe Middelburgh and Orewelle.
Wel  coude  he  in  eschaunge  sheeldes
    selle.              (280)
This worthy man ful wel his wit bisette ;
Ther wiste no wight that he was in dette,
So estatly was he of his governaunce, 281
With his bargaynes, and with his chevi-
    saunce.
For sothe he was a worthy man with-alle,
But sooth to seyn, I noot how men him
    calle.              **Clerk.**
A CLERK ther was of Oxenford also,
That un-to logik hadde longe y-go.    286
As lene was his hors as is a rake,
And he nas nat right fat, I undertake ; (290)
But loked holwe, and ther-to soberly.
Ful thredbar was his overest courtepy ; 290
For he had geten him yet no benefyce,
Ne was so worldly for to have offyce.
For him was lever have at his beddes
    heed
Twenty bokes, clad in blak or reed,
Of Aristotle and his philosophye,    295
Than robes riche, or fithele, or gay sautrye.
But al be that he was a philosophre,
Yet hadde he but litel gold in cofre ; (300)
But al that he mighte of his freendes
    hente,
On bokes and on lerninge he it spente, 300
And bisily gan for the soules preye
Of hem that yaf him wher-with to scoleye.
Of studie took he most cure and most
    hede.
Noght o word spak he more than was
    nede,

And that was seyd in forme and rever-
  ence,                                     305
And short and quik, and ful of hy
  sentence.
Souninge in moral vertu was his speche,
And gladly wolde he lerne, and gladly
  teche.             **Man of Lawe.** (310)
  A SERGEANT OF THE LAWE, war and wys,
That often hadde been at the parvys, 310
Ther was also, ful riche of excellence.
Discreet he was, and of greet reverence :
He semed swich, his wordes weren so
  wyse.
Justyce he was ful often in assyse,     314
By patente, and by pleyn commissioun ;
For his science, and for his heigh re-
  noun
Of fees and robes hadde he many oon.
So greet a purchasour was no-wher
  noon.                                    (320)
Al was fee simple to him in effect,
His purchasing mighte nat been infect. 320
No-wher so bisy a man as he ther nas,
And yet he semed bisier than he was.
In termes hadde he caas and domes alle,
That from the tyme of king William were
  falle.
Therto he coude endyte, and make a
  thing,                                    325
Ther coude no wight pinche at his
  wryting ;
And every statut coude he pleyn by rote.
He rood but hoomly in a medlee cote (330)
Girt with a ceint of silk, with barres
  smale ;
Of his array telle I no lenger tale.      330
  A FRANKELEYN was in his companye ;
Whyt was his berd, as is the dayesye.
Of his complexioun he was sangwyn.
Wel loved he by the morwe a sop in
  wyn.                      **Frankeleyn.**
To liven in delyt was ever his wone,   335
For he was Epicurus owne sone,
That heeld opinioun, that pleyn delyt
Was verraily felicitee parfyt.            (340)
An housholdere, and that a greet, was he ;
Seint Julian he was in his contree.       340
His breed, his ale, was alwey after oon ;
A bettre envyned man was no-wher noon.
With-oute bake mete was never his hous,
Of fish and flesh, and that so plentevous,

It snewed in his hous of mete and
  drinke,                                   345
Of alle deyntees that men coude thinke.
After the sondry sesons of the yeer,   (349)
So chaunged he his mete and his soper.
Ful many a fat partrich hadde he in
  mewe,
And many a breem and many a luce in
  stewe.                                    350
Wo was his cook, but-if his sauce were
Poynaunt and sharp, and redy al his gere.
His table dormant in his halle alway
Stood redy covered al the longe day.
At sessiouns ther was he lord and sire ; 355
Ful ofte tyme he was knight of the shire.
An anlas and a gipser al of silk       (359)
Heng at his girdel, whyt as morne milk.
A shirreve hadde he been, and a countour;
Was no-wher such a worthy vavasour. 360
  An HABERDASSHER and a CARPENTER,
             **Haberdassher.  Carpenter.**
A WEBBE, a DYERE, and a TAPICER,
             **Webbe.  Dyere.  Tapicer.**
Were with us eek, clothed in o liveree,
Of a solempne and greet fraternitee.    364
Ful fresh and newe hir gere apyked was ;
Hir knyves were y-chaped noght with
  bras,
But al with silver, wroght ful clene and
  weel,                                    (369)
Hir girdles and hir pouches every-deel.
Wel semed ech of hem a fair burgeys,
To sitten in a yeldhalle on a deys.      370
Everich, for the wisdom that he can,
Was shaply for to been an alderman.
For catel hadde they y-nogh and rente,
And eek hir wyves wolde it wel assente ;
And elles certein were they to blame.  375
It is ful fair to been y-clept ' ma dame,'
And goon to vigilyes al bifore,
And have a mantel royalliche y-bore. (380)
  A COOK they hadde with hem for the
  nones,                           **Cook**
To boille the chiknes with the mary-
  bones,                                    380
And poudre-marchant tart, and galingale.
Wel coude he knowe a draughte of
  London ale.
He coude roste, and sethe, and broille,
  and frye,
Maken mortreux, and wel bake a pye.

But greet harm was it, as it thoughte
me,                                      385
That on his shine a mormal hadde he;
For blankmanger, that made he with the
beste.                                   (389)
 A SHIPMAN was ther, woning fer by
weste:     **Shipman.**
For aught I woot, he was of Dertemouthe.
He rood up-on a rouncy, as he couthe, 390
In a gowne of falding to the knee.
A daggere hanging on a laas hadde he
Aboute his nekke under his arm adoun.
The hote somer had maad his hewe al
broun;
And, certeinly, he was a good felawe. 395
Ful many a draughte of wyn had he
y-drawe
From Burdeux-ward, whyl that the chap-
man sleep.
Of nyce conscience took he no keep. (400)
If that he faught, and hadde the hyer
hond,
By water he sente hem hoom to every
lond.                                    400
But of his craft to rekene wel his tydes,
His stremes and his daungers him bisydes,
His herberwe and his mone, his lode-
menage,
Ther nas noon swich from Hulle to
Cartage.
Hardy he was, and wys to undertake; 405
With many a tempest hadde his berd
been shake.
He knew wel alle the havenes, as they
were,                                    (409)
From Gootlond to the cape of Finistere,
And every cryke in Britayne and in
Spayne;                                  409
His barge y-cleped was the Maudelayne.
 With us ther was a DOCTOUR OF PHISYK,
In al this world ne was ther noon him
lyk      **Doctour.**
To speke of phisik and of surgerye;
For he was grounded in astronomye.
He kepte his pacient a ful greet del 415
In houres, by his magik naturel.
Wel coude he fortunen the ascendent
Of his images for his pacient.  (420)
He knew the cause of everich maladye,
Were it of hoot or cold, or moiste, or
drye,                                    420

And where engendred, and of what
humour;
He was a verrey parfit practisour.
The cause y-knowe, and of his harm the
rote,
Anon he yaf the seke man his bote.
Ful redy hadde he his apothecaries, 425
To sende him drogges and his letuaries,
For ech of hem made other for to
winne;
Hir frendschipe nas nat newe to biginne.
Wel knew he th'olde Esculapius, (431)
And Deiscorides, and eek Rufus, 430
Old Ypocras, Haly, and Galien;
Serapion, Razis, and Avicen;
Averrois, Damascien, and Constantyn;
Bernard, and Gatesden, and Gilbertyn.
Of his diete mesurable was he, 435
For it was of no superfluitee,
But of greet norissing and digestible.
His studie was but litel on the bible. (440)
In sangwin and in pers he clad was al,
Lyned with taffata and with sendal; 440
And yet he was but esy of dispence;
He kepte that he wan in pestilence.
For gold in phisik is a cordial,
Therfore he lovede gold in special. 444
 A good WYF was ther of bisyde BATHE,
But she was som-del deef, and that was
scathe.     **Wyf of Bathe.**
Of clooth-making she hadde swiche an
haunt,                                   (459)
She passed hem of Ypres and of Gaunt.
In al the parisshe wyf ne was ther
noon
That to th' offring bifore hir sholde
goon;                                    450
And if ther dide, certeyn, so wrooth was
she,
That she was out of alle charitee.
Hir coverchiefs ful fyne were of ground;
I dorste swere they weyeden ten pound
That on a Sonday were upon hir heed. 455
Hir hosen weren of fyn scarlet reed,
Ful streite y-teyd, and shoos ful moiste
and newe.
Bold was hir face, and fair, and reed of
hewe.                                    (460)
She was a worthy womman al hir lyve,
Housbondes at chirche-dore she hadde
fyve,                                    460

Withouten other companye in youthe ;
But therof nedeth nat to speke as nouthe.
And thryes hadde she been at Jerusalem ;
She hadde passed many a straunge
   streem ;        464
At Rome she hadde been, and at Boloigne,
In Galice at seint Jame, and at Coloigne.
She coude muche of wandring by the
   weye :
Gat-tothed was she, soothly for to seye.
Up-on an amblere esily she sat,   (471)
Y-wimpled wel, and on hir heed an hat
As brood as is a bokeler or a targe ;  471
A foot-mantel aboute hir hipes large,
And on hir feet a paire of spores sharpe.
In felawschip wel coude she laughe and
   carpe.
Of remedyes of love she knew per-
   chaunce,       475
For she coude of that art the olde daunce.
                    **Persoun.**

   A good man was ther of religioun,
And was a povre PERSOUN of a toun ; (480)
But riche he was of holy thoght and werk.
He was also a lerned man, a clerk,  480
That Cristes gospel trewely wolde preche;
His parisshens devoutly wolde he teche.
Benigne he was, and wonder diligent,
And in adversitee ful pacient ;
And swich he was y-preved ofte sythes.
Ful looth were him to cursen for his
   tythes,       486
But rather wolde he yeven, out of doute,
Un-to his povre parisshens aboute  (490)
Of his offring, and eek of his substaunce.
He coude in litel thing han suffisaunce.
Wyd was his parisshe, and houses fer
   a-sonder,      491
But he ne lafte nat, for reyn ne thonder,
In siknes nor in meschief, to visyte
The ferreste in his parisshe, muche and
   lyte,
Up-on his feet, and in his hand a staf. 495
This noble ensample to his sheep he yaf,
That first he wroghte, and afterward he
   taughte ;
Out of the gospel he tho wordes caughte ;
And this figure he added eek ther-to, (501)
That if gold ruste, what shal iren do ? 500
For if a preest be foul, on whom we truste,
No wonder is a lewed man to ruste ;

And shame it is, if a preest take keep,
A shiten shepherde and a clene sheep.
Wel oghte a preest ensample for to yive,
By his clennesse, how that his sheep
   shold live.      506
He sette nat his benefice to hyre,
And leet his sheep encombred in the
   myre,      (510)
And ran to London, un-to sëynt Poules,
To seken him a chaunterie for soules, 510
Or with a bretherhed to been withholde ;
But dwelte at hoom, and kepte wel his
   folde,
So that the wolf ne made it nat miscarie ;
He was a shepherde and no mercenarie.
And though he holy were, and vertuous,
He was to sinful man nat despitous,  516
Ne of his speche daungerous ne digne,
But in his teching discreet and benigne.
To drawen folk to heven by fairnesse (521)
By good ensample, was his bisinesse : 520
But it were any persone obstinat,
What-so he were, of heigh or lowe estat,
Him wolde he snibben sharply for the
   nones.
A bettre preest, I trowe that nowher
   noon is.
He wayted after no pompe and reverence,
Ne maked him a spyced conscience,  526
But Cristes lore, and his apostles twelve,
He taughte, and first he folwed it him-
   selve.      (530)
   With him ther was a PLOWMAN, was his
   brother,      **Plowman.**
That hadde y-lad of dong ful many a
   fother,      530
A trewe swinker and a good was he,
Livinge in pees and parfit charitee.
God loved he best with al his hole herte
At alle tymes, thogh him gamed or
   smerte,
And thanne his neighebour right as him-
   selve.      535
He wolde thresshe, and ther-to dyke and
   delve,
For Cristes sake, for every povre wight,
Withouten hyre, if it lay in his might.
His tythes payed he ful faire and wel, (541)
Bothe of his propre swink and his catel.
In a tabard he rood upon a mere.  541
   Ther was also a Reve and a Millere,

A Somnour and a Pardoner also,
A Maunciple, and my-self; ther were
  namo.
  The MILLER was a stout carl, for the
    nones, **Miller.**
Ful big he was of braun, and eek of
  bones; 546
That proved wel, for over-al ther he cam,
At wrastling he wolde have alwey the
  ram. (550)
He was short-sholdred, brood, a thikke
  knarre,
Ther nas no dore that he nolde heve of
  harre, 550
Or breke it, at a renning, with his heed.
His berd as any sowe or fox was reed,
And ther-to brood, as though it were
  a spade.
Up-on the cop right of his nose he hade
A werte, and ther-on stood a tuft of heres,
Reed as the bristles of a sowes eres; 556
His nose-thirles blake were and wyde.
A swerd and bokeler bar he by his syde;
His mouth as greet was as a greet forneys.
He was a janglere and a goliardeys, 560
And that was most of sinne and har-
  lotryes. (563)
Wel coude he stelen corn, and tollen
  thryes;
And yet he hadde a thombe of gold,
  pardee.
A whyt cote and a blew hood wered he.
A baggepype wel coude he blowe and
  sowne, 565
And ther-with-al he broghte us out of
  towne. **Maunciple.**
  A gentil MAUNCIPLE was ther of a temple,
Of which achatours mighte take exemple
For to be wyse in bying of vitaille (571)
For whether that he payde, or took by
  taille, 570
Algate he wayted so in his achat,
That he was ay biforn and in good stat.
Now is nat that of God a ful fair grace,
That swich a lewed mannes wit shal pace
The wisdom of an heep of lerned men? 575
Of maistres hadde he mo than thryes
  ten,
That were of lawe expert and curious;
Of which ther were a doseyn in that
  hous

Worthy to been stiwardes of rente and
  lond (581)
Of any lord that is in Engelond, 580
To make him live by his propre good,
In honour dettelees, but he were wood,
Or live as scarsly as him list desire;
And able for to helpen al a shire
In any cas that mighte falle or happe; 585
And yit this maunciple sette hir aller
  cappe. **Reve.**
  The REVE was a sclendre colerik man,
His berd was shave as ny as ever he
  can. (590)
His heer was by his eres round y-shorn.
His top was dokked lyk a preest biforn.
Ful longe were his legges, and ful lene,
Y-lyk a staf, ther was no calf y-sene.
Wel coude he kepe a gerner and a binne;
Ther was noon auditour coude on him
  winne.
Wel wiste he, by the droghte, and by the
  reyn, 595
The yelding of his seed, and of his
  greyn.
His lordes sheep, his neet, his dayerye,
His swyn, his hors, his stoor, and his
  pultrye, (600)
Was hoolly in this reves governing, 599
And by his covenaunt yaf the rekening,
Sin that his lord was twenty yeer of age;
Ther coude no man bringe him in
  arrerage.
Ther nas baillif, ne herde, ne other hyne,
That he ne knew his sleighte and his
  covyne; 604
They were adrad of him, as of the deeth.
His woning was ful fair up-on an heeth,
With grene treës shadwed was his place.
He coude bettre than his lord purchace.
Ful riche he was astored prively, (611)
His lord wel coude he plesen subtilly, 610
To yeve and lene him of his owne good,
And have a thank, and yet a cote and
  hood.
In youthe he lerned hadde a good mister;
He was a wel good wrighte, a carpenter.
This reve sat up-on a ful good stot, 615
That was al pomely grey, and highte
  Scot.
A long surcote of pers up-on he hade,
And by his syde he bar a rusty blade. (620)

Of Northfolk was this reve, of which I
telle, 619
Bisyde a toun men clepen Baldeswelle.
Tukked he was, as is a frere, aboute,
And ever he rood the hindreste of our
route.

A SOMNOUR was ther with us in that
place, **Somnour.**
That hadde a fyr-reed cherubinnes face,
For sawcefleem he was, with eyen narwe.
As hoot he was, and lecherous, as a
sparwe; 626
With scalled browes blake, and piled berd;
Of his visage children were aferd. (630)
Ther nas quik-silver, litarge, ne brim-
stoon,
Boras, ceruce, ne oille of tartre noon, 630
Ne oynement that wolde clense and
byte,
That him mighte helpen of his whelkes
whyte,
Nor of the knobbes sittinge on his chekes.
Wel loved he garleek, oynons, and eek
lekes,
And for to drinken strong wyn, reed as
blood. 635
Than wolde he speke, and crye as he
were wood.
And whan that he wel dronken hadde the
wyn, (639)
Than wolde he speke no word but Latyn.
A fewe termes hadde he, two or three,
That he had lerned out of som decree; 640
No wonder is, he herde it al the day;
And eek ye knowen wel, how that a jay
Can clepen 'Watte,' as well as can the
pope.
But who-so coude in other thing him
grope, 644
Thanne hadde he spent al his philosophye;
Ay ' *Questio quid iuris* ' wolde he crye.
He was a gentil harlot and a kinde; (649)
A bettre felawe sholde men noght finde.
He wolde suffre, for a quart of wyn,
A good felawe to have his concubyn 650
A twelf-month, and excuse him atte fulle:
Ful prively a finch eek coude he pulle.
And if he fond o-wher a good felawe,
He wolde techen him to have non awe,
In swich cas, of the erchedeknes curs, 655
But-if a mannes soule were in his purs;

For in his purs he sholde y-punisshed be.
' Purs is the erchedeknes helle,' seyde
he. (660)
But wel I woot he lyed right in dede;
Of cursing oghte ech gilty man him
drede— 660
For curs wol slee, right as assoilling
saveth—
And also war him of a *significavit.*
In daunger hadde he at his owne gyse
The yonge girles of the diocyse,
And knew hir counseil, and was al hir
reed. 665
A gerland hadde he set up-on his heed,
As greet as it were for an ale-stake;
A bokeler hadde he maad him of a cake.

With him ther rood a gentil PARDONER
Of Rouncival, his freend and his compeer,
That streight was comen fro the court of
Rome. **Pardoner.**
Ful loude he song, ' Com hider, love, to
me.' (670) 672
This somnour bar to him a stif burdoun,
Was never trompe of half so greet a soun.
This pardoner hadde heer as yelow as
wex, 675
But smothe it heng, as dooth a strike of
flex;
By ounces henge his lokkes that he hadde,
And ther-with he his shuldres over-
spradde; (680)
But thinne it lay, by colpons oon and
oon;
But hood, for jolitee, ne wered he noon,
For it was trussed up in his walet. 681
Him thoughte, he rood al of the newe jet;
Dischevele, save his cappe, he rood al
bare.
Swiche glaringe eyen hadde he as an
hare.
A vernicle hadde he sowed on his cappe.
His walet lay biforn him in his lappe, 686
Bret-ful of pardoun come from Rome al
hoot. (689)
A voys he hadde as smal as hath a goot.
No berd hadde he, ne never sholde have,
As smothe it was as it were late y-shave;
I trowe he were a gelding or a mare. 691
But of his craft, fro Berwik into Ware,
Ne was ther swich another pardoner.
For in his male he hadde a pilwe-beer,

Which that, he seyde, was our lady
veyl :      695
He seyde, he hadde a gobet of the seyl
That seynt Peter hadde, whan that he
wente      (699)
Up-on the see, til Jesu Crist him hente.
He hadde a croys of latoun, ful of stones,
And in a glas he hadde pigges bones. 700
But with thise relikes, whan that he
fond
A povre person dwelling up-on lond,
Up-on a day he gat him more moneye
Than that the person gat in monthes
tweye.
And thus, with feyned flaterye and japes,
He made the person and the peple his
apes.      706
But trewely to tellen, atte laste,      (709)
He was in chirche a noble ecclesiaste.
Wel coude he rede a lessoun or a storie,
But alderbest he song an offertorie ;    710
For wel he wiste, whan that song was
songe,
He moste preche, and wel affyle his
tonge,
To winne silver, as he ful wel coude ;
Therefore he song so meriely and loude.
    Now have I told you shortly, in a clause,
Th'estat, th'array, the nombre, and eek the
cause      716
Why that assembled was this companye
In Southwerk, at this gentil hostelrye,
That highte the Tabard, faste by the
Belle.      (721)
But now is tyme to yow for to telle     720
How that we baren us that ilke night,
Whan we were in that hostelrye alight.
And after wol I telle of our viage,
And al the remenaunt of our pilgrimage.
But first I pray yow, of your curteisye, 725
That ye n'arette it nat my vileinye,
Thogh that I pleynly speke in this
matere,      (729)
To telle yow hir wordes and hir chere ;
Ne thogh I speke hir wordes properly.
For this ye knowen al-so wel as I,     730
Who-so shal telle a tale after a man,
He moot reherce, as ny as ever he can,
Everich a word, if it be in his charge,
Al speke he never so rudeliche and
large;

Or elles he moot telle his tale untrewe, 735
Or feyne thing, or finde wordes newe.
He may nat spare, al-thogh he were his
brother ;      (739)
He moot as wel seye o word as another.
Crist spak him-self ful brode in holy
writ,
And wel ye woot, no vileinye is it.     740
Eek Plato seith, who-so that can him
rede,
The wordes mote be cosin to the dede.
Also I prey yow to foryeve it me,
Al have I nat set folk in hir degree
Here in this tale, as that they sholde
stonde ;      745
My wit is short, ye may wel understonde.
    Greet chere made our hoste us everichon,
And to the soper sette us anon ;     (750)
And served us with vitaille at the beste.
Strong was the wyn, and wel to drinke
us leste.      750
A semely man our hoste was with-alle
For to han been a marshal in an halle ;
A large man he was with eyen stepe,
A fairer burgeys is ther noon in Chepe :
Bold of his speche, and wys, and wel
y-taught,      755
And of manhod him lakkede right naught.
Eek therto he was right a mery man,
And after soper pleyen he bigan,     (760)
And spak of mirthe amonges othere
thinges,
Whan that we hadde maad our reken-
inges ;      760
And seyde thus : ' Now, lordinges, trewely,
Ye been to me right welcome hertely :
For by my trouthe, if that I shal nat
lye,
I ne saugh this yeer so mery a companye
At ones in this herberwe as is now.    765
Fayn wolde I doon yow mirthe, wiste
I how.
And of a mirthe I am right now bithoght,
To doon yow ese, and it shal coste
noght.      (770)
  Ye goon to Caunterbury ; God yow
spede,
The blisful martir quyte yow your
mede.      770
And wel I woot, as ye goon by the weye,
Ye shapen yow to talen and to pleye ;

For trewely, confort ne mirthe is noon
To ryde by the weye doumb as a stoon ;
And therfore wol I maken yow disport,
As I seyde erst, and doon yow som con-
        fort.                              776
And if yow lyketh alle, by oon assent,
Now for to stonden at my jugement, (780)
And for to werken as I shal yow seye,
To-morwe, whan ye ryden by the weye,
Now, by my fader soule, that is deed, 781
But ye be merye, I wol yeve yow myn
        heed.
Hold up your hond, withouten more
        speche.'
    Our counseil was nat longe for to
        seche ;
Us thoughte it was noght worth to make
        it wys,                            785
And graunted him withouten more
        avys,
And bad him seye his verdit, as him
        leste.
'Lordinges,' quod he, 'now herkneth
        for the beste ;                    (790)
But tak it not, I prey yow, in desdeyn ;
This is the poynt, to speken short and
        pleyn,                             790
That ech of yow, to shorte with your
        weye,
In this viage, shal telle tales tweye,
To Caunterbury-ward, I mene it so,
And hom-ward he shal tellen othere
        two,
Of aventures that whylom han bifalle. 795
And which of yow that bereth him best
        of alle,
That is to seyn, that telleth in this cas
Tales of best sentence and most solas, (800)
Shal have a soper at our aller cost
Here in this place, sitting by this post,
Whan that we come agayn fro Caunter-
        bury.                              801
And for to make yow the more mery,
I wol my-selven gladly with yow ryde,
Right at myn owne cost, and be your
        gyde.
And who-so wol my jugement withseye
Shal paye al that we spenden by the
        weye.                              806
And if ye vouche-sauf that it be so,
Tel me anon, with-outen wordes mo, (810)

And I wol erly shape me therfore.'
    This thing was graunted, and our othes
        swore                             810
With ful glad herte, and preyden him
        also
That he wold vouche-sauf for to do so,
And that he wolde been our governour,
And of our tales juge and reportour,
And sette a soper at a certeyn prys ;  815
And we wold reuled been at his devys,
In heigh and lowe ; and thus, by oon
        assent,
We been acorded to his jugement.   (820)
And ther-up-on the wyn was fet anon ;
We dronken, and to reste wente echon,
With-outen any lenger taryinge.       821
    A-morwe, whan that day bigan to springe,
Up roos our host, and was our aller
        cok,
And gadrede us togidre, alle in a flok,
And forth we riden, a litel more than
        pas,                              825
Un-to the watering of seint Thomas.
And there our host bigan his hors areste,
And seyde ; 'Lordinges, herkneth, if yow
        leste.                            (830)
Ye woot your forward, and I it yow re-
        corde.
If even-song and morwe-song acorde, 830
Lat see now who shal telle the firste
        tale.
As ever mote I drinke wyn or ale,
Who-so be rebel to my jugement
Shal paye for al that by the weye is
        spent.
Now draweth cut, er that we ferrer
        twinne ;                          835
He which that hath the shortest shal
        biginne.
Sire knight,' quod he, 'my maister and
        my lord,                          (839)
Now draweth cut, for that is myn acord.
Cometh neer,' quod he, 'my lady prior-
        esse ;
And ye, sir clerk, lat be your shamfast-
        nesse,                            840
Ne studieth noght ; ley hond to, every
        man.'
    Anon to drawen every wight bigan,
And shortly for to tellen, as it was,
Were it by aventure, or sort, or cas,

The sothe is this, the cut fil to the knight,
Of which ful blythe and glad was every
          wight ;                               846
And telle he moste his tale, as was resoun,
By forward and by composicioun,      (850)
As ye han herd ; what nedeth wordes mo?
And whan this gode man saugh it
          was so,                               850
As he that wys was and obedient
To kepe his forward by his free assent,

He seyde : ' Sin I shal beginne the
          game,
What, welcome be the cut, a Goddes
          name !
Now lat us ryde, and herkneth what I
          seye.'                               855
   And with that word we riden forth our
          weye ;                              (858)
And he bigan with right a mery chere
His tale anon, and seyde in this manere.

Here endeth the prolog of this book; and here biginneth the first tale,
which is the Knightes Tale.

# THE  KNIGHTES  TALE.

*Iamque domos patrias, Scithice post aspera gentis*
*Prelia, laurigero, &c.*      [Statius, *Theb.* xii. 519.]

WHYLOM, as olde stories tellen us,
Ther was a duk that highte Theseus ; 860
Of Athenes he was lord and governour,
And in his tyme swich a conquerour,
That gretter was ther noon under the
          sonne.
Ful many a riche contree hadde he
          wonne ;                              864
What with his wisdom and his chivalrye,
He conquered al the regne of Femenye,
That whylom was y-cleped Scithia ;
And weddede the quene Ipolita,      (10)
And broghte hir hoom with him in his
          contree                               869
With muchel glorie and greet solempnitee,
And eek hir yonge suster Emelye.
And thus with victorie and with melodye

Lete I this noble duk to Athenes
          ryde,
And al his hoost, in armes, him bisyde.
   And certes, if it nere to long to here, 875
I wolde han told yow fully the manere,
How wonnen was the regne of Femenye
By Theseus, and by his chivalrye ;      (20)
And of the grete bataille for the nones
Bitwixen Athenës and Amazones;      880
And how asseged was Ipolita,
The faire hardy quene of Scithia ;
And of the feste that was at hir weddinge,
And of the tempest at hir hoom-cominge;
But al that thing I moot as now forbere.
I have, God woot, a large feeld to ere, 886
And wayke been the oxen in my plough.
The remenant of the tale is long y-nough.

I wol nat letten eek noon of this route ;
Lat every felawe telle his tale aboute,    890
And lat see now who shal the soper
    winne ;    (33)
And ther I lefte, I wol ageyn biginne.

This duk, of whom I make mencioun,
When he was come almost unto the
    toun,
In al his wele and in his moste pryde, 895
He was war, as he caste his eye asyde,
Wher that ther kneled in the hye weye
A companye of ladies, tweye and tweye,
Ech after other, clad in clothes blake ; (41)
But swich a cry and swich a wo they
    make,    900
That in this world nis creature livinge,
That herde swich another weymentinge ;
And of this cry they nolde never stenten,
Til they the reynes of his brydel henten.
' What folk ben ye, that at myn hoom-
    cominge    905
Perturben so my feste with cryinge ? '
Quod Theseus, ' have ye so greet envye
Of myn honour, that thus compleyne and
    crye ?    (50)
Or who hath yow misboden, or offended ?
And telleth me if it may been amended ;
And why that ye ben clothed thus in
    blak ? '    911
    The eldest lady of hem alle spak,
When she hadde swowned with a deedly
    chere,
That it was routhe for to seen and here,
And seyde : ' Lord, to whom Fortune hath
    yiven    915
Victorie, and as a conquerour to liven,
Noght greveth us your glorie and your
    honour;
But we biseken mercy and socour.    (60)
Have mercy on our wo and our distresse.
Som drope of pitee, thurgh thy gentil-
    esse,    920
Up-on us wrecched wommen lat thou falle.
For certes, lord, ther nis noon of us alle,
That she nath been a duchesse or a quene;
Now be we caitifs, as it is wel sene :
Thanked be Fortune, and hir false wheel,
That noon estat assureth to be weel.    926
And certes, lord, t'abyden your presence,
Here in the temple of the goddesse
    Clemence    (70)

We han ben waytinge al this fourtenight ;
Now help us, lord, sith it is in thy might.
    I wrecche, which that wepe and waille
    thus,    931
Was whylom wyf to king Capaneus,
That starf at Thebes, cursed be that day !
And alle we, that been in this array,
And maken al this lamentacioun,    935
We losten alle our housbondes at that
    toun,
Whyl that the sege ther-aboute lay.
And yet now th'olde Creon, weylaway !
The lord is now of Thebes the citee,    (81)
Fulfild of ire and of iniquitee,    940
He, for despyt, and for his tirannye,
To do the dede bodyes vileinye,
Of alle our lordes, whiche that ben slawe,
Hath alle the bodyes on an heep y-drawe,
And wol nat suffren hem, by noon assent,
Neither to been y-buried nor y-brent,    946
But maketh houndes ete hem in despyt.'
And with that word, with-outen more
    respyt,    (90)
They fillen gruf, and cryden pitously,
' Have on us wrecched wommen som
    mercy,    950
And lat our sorwe sinken in thyn herte.'
    This gentil duk doun from his courser
    sterte
With herte pitous, whan he herde hem
    speke.
Him thoughte that his herte wolde breke,
Whan he saugh hem so pitous and so
    mat,    955
That whylom weren of so greet estat.
And in his armes he hem alle up hente,
And hem conforteth in ful good entente ;
And swoor his ooth, as he was trewe
    knight,    (101)
He wolde doon so ferforthly his might
Up-on the tyraunt Creon hem to wreke,
That al the peple of Grece sholde speke
How Creon was of Theseus y-served,
As he that hadde his deeth ful wel de-
    served.    964
And right anoon, with-outen more abood,
His baner he desplayeth, and forth rood
To Thebes-ward, and al his host bisyde ;
No neer Athenës wolde he go ne ryde,
Ne take his ese fully half a day,    (111)
But onward on his wey that night he lay;

And sente anoon Ipolita the quene,    971
And Emelye hir yonge suster shene,
Un-to the toun of Athenës to dwelle;
And forth he rit; ther nis namore to
      telle.
    The rede statue of Mars, with spere
      and targe,    975
So shyneth in his whyte baner large,
That alle the feeldes gliteren up and doun;
And by his baner born is his penoun (120)
Of gold ful riche, in which ther was
      y-bete
The Minotaur, which that he slough in
      Crete.    980
Thus rit this duk, thus rit this conquerour,
And in his host of chivalrye the flour,
Til that he cam to Thebes, and alighte
Faire in a feeld, ther as he thoghte fighte.
But shortly for to speken of this thing, 985
With Creon, which that was of Thebes
      king,
He faught, and slough him manly as
      a knight
In pleyn bataille, and putte the folk to
      flight;    (130)
And by assaut he wan the citee after,
And rente adoun bothe wal, and sparre,
      and rafter;    990
And to the ladyes he restored agayn
The bones of hir housbondes that were
      slayn,
To doon obséquies, as was tho the gyse.
But it were al to long for to devyse    994
The grete clamour and the waymentinge
That the ladyes made at the brenninge
Of the bodyes, and the grete honour
That Theseus, the noble conquerour, (140)
Doth to the ladyes, whan they from him
      wente;    999
But shortly for to telle is myn entente.
Whan that this worthy duk, this Theseus,
Hath Creon slayn, and wonne Thebes
      thus,
Stille in that feeld he took al night his
      reste,
And dide with al the contree as him
      leste.    1004
    To ransake in the tas of bodyes dede,
Hem for to strepe of harneys and of wede,
The pilours diden bisinesse and cure,
After the bataille and disconfiture.    (150)

And so bifel, that in the tas they founde,
Thurgh-girt with many a grevous blody
      wounde,    1010
Two yonge knightes ligging by and by,
Bothe in oon armes, wroght ful richely,
Of whiche two, Arcita hight that oon,
And that other knight hight Palamon.
Nat fully quike, ne fully dede they were,
But by hir cote-armures, and by hir gere,
The heraudes knewe hem best in special,
As they that weren of the blood royal (160)
Of Thebes, and of sustren two y-born.
Out of the tas the pilours han hem torn,
And han hem caried softe un-to the
      tente    1021
Of Theseus, and he ful sone hem sente
To Athenës, to dwellen in prisoun
Perpetuelly, he nolde no raunsoun.
And whan this worthy duk hath thus
      y-don,    1025
He took his host, and hoom he rood anon
With laurer crowned as a conquerour;
And there he liveth, in joye and in
      honour,    (170)
Terme of his lyf; what nedeth wordes
      mo?
And in a tour, in angwish and in wo, 1030
Dwellen this Palamoun and eek Arcite,
For evermore, ther may no gold hem
      quyte.
    This passeth yeer by yeer, and day by
      day,
Til it fil ones, in a morwe of May,
That Emelye, that fairer was to sene 1035
Than is the lilie upon his stalke grene,
And fressher than the May with floures
      newe—    (179)
For with the rose colour stroof hir hewe,
I noot which was the fairer of hem two—
Er it were day, as was hir wone to do,
She was arisen, and al redy dight;    1041
For May wol have no slogardye a-night.
The sesoun priketh every gentil herte,
And maketh him out of his sleep to sterte,
And seith, 'Arys, and do thyn obser-
      vaunce.'    (187) 1045
This maked Emelye have remembraunce
To doon honour to May, and for to ryse.
Y-clothed was she fresh, for to devyse;
Hir yelow heer was broyded in a tresse,
Bihinde hir bak, a yerde long, I gesse.

And in the gardin, at the sonne up-riste,
She walketh up and doun, and as hir
　　liste
She gadereth floures, party whyte and
　　rede,
To make a sotil gerland for hir hede,
And as an aungel hevenly she song. 1055
The grete tour, that was so thikke and
　　strong,
Which of the castel was the chief don-
　　geoun,　　　　　　　　　　　　(199)
(Ther-as the knightes weren in prisoun,
Of whiche I tolde yow, and tellen shal)
Was evene joynant to the gardin-wal, 1060
Ther as this Emelye hadde hir pleyinge.
Bright was the sonne, and cleer that
　　morweninge,
And Palamon, this woful prisoner,
As was his wone, by leve of his gayler,
Was risen, and romed in a chambre on
　　heigh,　　　　　　　　　　　　1065
In which he al the noble citee seigh,
And eek the gardin, ful of braunches
　　grene,　　　　　　　　　　　　(209)
Ther-as this fresshe Emelye the shene
Was in hir walk, and romed up and
　　doun.　　　　　　　　　　　　1069
This sorweful prisoner, this Palamoun,
Goth in the chambre, roming to and fro,
And to him-self compleyning of his wo ;
That he was born, ful ofte he seyde, 'alas !'
And so bifel, by aventure or cas,
That thurgh a window, thikke of many
　　a barre　　　　　　　　　　　1075
Of yren greet, and square as any sparre,
He caste his eye upon Emelya,
And ther-with-al he bleynte, and cryde
　　' a !'　　　　　　　　　　　　(220)
As though he stongen were un-to the
　　herte.　　　　　　　　　　　1079
And with that cry Arcite anon up-sterte,
And seyde, 'Cosin myn, what eyleth
　　thee,
That art so pale and deedly on to see ?
Why crydestow ? who hath thee doon
　　offence ?
For Goddes love, tak al in pacience 1084
Our prisoun, for it may non other be ;
Fortune hath yeven us this adversitee.
Som wikke aspect or disposicioun
Of Saturne, by sum constellacioun, (230)

Hath yeven us this, al-though we hadde
　　it sworn ;
So stood the heven whan that we were
　　born ;　　　　　　　　　　　1090
We moste endure it : this is the short and
　　pleyn.'
　This Palamon answerde, and seyde
　　ageyn,
' Cosyn, for sothe, of this opinioun
Thou hast a veyn imaginacioun.
This prison caused me nat for to crye. 1095
But I was hurt right now thurgh-out
　　myn yë
In-to myn herte, that wol my bane be.
The fairnesse of that lady that I see (240)
Yond in the gardin romen to and fro,
Is cause of al my crying and my wo. 1100
I noot wher she be womman or goddesse ;
But Venus is it, soothly, as I gesse.'
And ther-with-al on kneës doun he fil,
And seyde : ' Venus, if it be thy wil
Yow in this gardin thus to transfigure 1105
Bifore me, sorweful wrecche creature,
Out of this prisoun help that we may
　　scapen.
And if so be my destinee be shapen (250)
By eterne word to dyen in prisoun,
Of our linage have som compassioun, 1110
That is so lowe y-broght by tirannye.'
And with that word Arcite gan espye
Wher-as this lady romed to and fro.
And with that sighte hir beautee hurte
　　him so,　　　　　　　　　　1114
That, if that Palamon was wounded sore,
Arcite is hurt as muche as he, or more.
And with a sigh he seyde pitously : (259)
' The fresshe beautee sleeth me sodeynly
Of hir that rometh in the yonder place ;
And, but I have hir mercy and hir grace,
That I may seen hir atte leeste weye, 1121
I nam but deed ; ther nis namore to seye.'
　This Palamon, whan he tho wordes
　　herde,
Dispitously he loked, and answerde :
' Whether seistow this in ernest or in
　　pley ? '　　　　　　　　　　1125
　'Nay,' quod Arcite, 'in ernest, by my
　　fey !
God help me so, me list ful yvele pleye.'
　This Palamon gan knitte his browes
　　tweye :　　　　　　　　　　(270)

'It nere,' quod he, 'to thee no greet
　　honour
For to be fals, ne for to be traytour　1130
To me, that am thy cosin and thy brother
Y-sworn ful depe, and ech of us til other,
That never, for to dyen in the peyne,
Til that the deeth departe shal us tweyne,
Neither of us in love to hindren other, 1135
Ne in non other cas, my leve brother ;
But that thou sholdest trewely forthren me
In every cas, and I shal forthren thee. (280)
This was thyn ooth, and myn also, certeyn ;
I wot right wel, thou darst it nat withseyn.
Thus artow of my counseil, out of doute.
And now thou woldest falsly been aboute
To love my lady, whom I love and serve,
And ever shal, til that myn herte sterve.
Now certes, fals Arcite, thou shalt nat so.
I loved hir first, and tolde thee my wo 1146
As to my counseil, and my brother sworn
To forthre me, as I have told biforn. (290)
For which thou art y-bounden as a knight
To helpen me, if it lay in thy might, 1150
Or elles artow fals, I dar wel seyn.'

　　This Arcite ful proudly spak ageyn,
'Thou shalt,' quod he, 'be rather fals
　　than I ;
But thou art fals, I telle thee utterly ;
For *par amour* I loved hir first er thow. 1155
What wiltow seyn ? thou wistest nat yet
　　now
Whether she be a womman or goddesse !
Thyn is affeccioun of holinesse, 　(300)
And myn is love, as to a creature ;
For which I tolde thee myn aventure 1160
As to my cosin, and my brother sworn.
I pose, that thou lovedest hir biforn ;
Wostow nat wel the olde clerkes sawe,
That "who shal yeve a lover any lawe ?"
Love is a gretter lawe, by my pan, 　1165
Than may be yeve to any erthly man.
And therefore positif lawe and swich
　　decree
Is broke al-day for love, in ech degree. (310)
A man moot nedes love, maugree his heed.
He may nat fleen it, thogh he sholde be
　　deed, 　1170
Al be she mayde, or widwe, or elles wyf.
And eek it is nat lykly, al thy lyf,
To stonden in hir grace ; namore shal I ;
For wel thou woost thy-selven, verraily,

That thou and I be dampned to prisoun
Perpetuelly ; us gayneth no raunsoun.
We stryve as dide the houndes for the
　　boon, 　1177
They foughte al day, and yet hir part was
　　noon ; 　(320)
Ther cam a kyte, whyl that they were
　　wrothe,
And bar awey the boon bitwixe hem
　　bothe. 　1180
And therfore, at the kinges court, my
　　brother,
Ech man for him-self, ther is non other.
Love if thee list ; for I love and ay shal ;
And soothly, leve brother, this is al.
Here in this prisoun mote we endure, 1185
And everich of us take his aventure.'

　　Greet was the stryf and long bitwixe
　　hem tweye,
If that I hadde leyser for to seye ; 　(330)
But to th'effect. It happed on a day,
(To telle it yow as shortly as I may) 1190
A worthy duk that highte Perotheus,
That felawe was un-to duk Theseus
Sin thilke day that they were children
　　lyte,
Was come to Athenes, his felawe to visyte,
And for to pleye, as he was wont to do,
For in this world he loved no man so : 1196
And he loved him as tendrely ageyn.
So wel they loved, as olde bokes seyn, (340)
That whan that oon was deed, sothly to
　　telle,
His felawe wente and soghte him doun in
　　helle ; 　1200
But of that story list me nat to wryte.
Duk Perotheus loved wel Arcite,
And hadde him knowe at Thebes yeer by
　　yere ;
And fynally, at requeste and preyere 1204
Of Perotheus, with-oute any raunsoun,
Duk Theseus him leet out of prisoun,
Freely to goon, wher that him liste over-al,
In swich a gyse, as I you tellen shal. (350)
　　This was the forward, pleynly for t'en-
　　dyte,
Bitwixen Theseus and him Arcite : 　1210
That if so were, that Arcite were y-founde
Ever in his lyf, by day or night or stounde
In any contree of this Theseus,
And he were caught, it was acorded thus,

That with a swerd he sholde lese his
heed;　1215
Ther nas non other remedye ne reed,
But taketh his leve, and homward he him
spedde;　(359)
Let him be war, his nekke lyth to wedde!
How greet a sorwe suffreth now Arcite!
The deeth he feleth thurgh his herte
smyte;　1220
He wepeth, wayleth, cryeth pitously;
To sleen him-self he wayteth prively.
He seyde, 'Allas that day that I was born!
Now is my prison worse than biforn;
Now is me shape eternally to dwelle　1225
Noght in purgatorie, but in helle.
Allas! that ever knew I Perotheus!
For elles hadde I dwelled with Theseus
Y-fetered in his prisoun ever-mo.　(371)
Than hadde I been in blisse, and nat in wo.
Only the sighte of hir, whom that I serve,
Though that I never hir grace may deserve,
Wolde han suffised right y-nough for me.
O dere cosin Palamon,' quod he,
'Thyn is the victorie of this aventure, 1235
Ful blisfully in prison maistow dure;
In prison? certes nay, but in paradys!
Wel hath fortune y-turned thee the dys,
That hast the sighte of hir, and I th'ab-
sence.　(381) 1239
For possible is, sin thou hast hir presence,
And art a knight, a worthy and an able,
That by som cas, sin fortune is chaunge-
able,
Thou mayst to thy desyr som-tyme atteyne.
But I, that am exyled, and bareyne
Of alle grace, and in so greet despeir, 1245
That ther nis erthe, water, fyr, ne eir,
Ne creature, that of hem maked is,
That may me helpe or doon confort in this:
Wel oughte I sterve in wanhope and dis-
tresse;　(391)
Farwel my lyf, my lust, and my gladnesse!
Allas, why pleynen folk so in commune
Of purveyaunce of God, or of fortune,
That yeveth hem ful ofte in many a gyse
Wel bettre than they can hem-self devyse?
Som man desyreth for to han richesse, 1255
That cause is of his mordre or greet sik-
nesse.
And som man wolde out of his prison fayn,
That in his hous is of his meynee slayn.

Infinite harmes been in this matere; (401)
We witen nat what thing we preyen here.
We faren as he that dronke is as a
mous;　1261
A dronke man wot wel he hath an hous,
But he noot which the righte wey is thider;
And to a dronke man the wey is slider.
And certes, in this world so faren we;
We seken faste after felicitee,　1266
But we goon wrong ful often, trewely.
Thus may we seyen alle, and namely I, (410)
That wende and hadde a greet opinioun,
That, if I mighte escapen from prisoun,
Than hadde I been in joye and perfit
hele,　1271
Ther now I am exyled fro my wele.
Sin that I may nat seen yow, Emelye,
I nam but deed; ther nis no remedye.'
Up-on that other syde Palamon,　1275
Whan that he wiste Arcite was agon,
Swich sorwe he maketh, that the grete
tour
Resouneth of his youling and clamour.
The pure fettres on his shines grete (421)
Weren of his bittre salte teres wete. 1280
'Allas!' quod he, 'Arcita, cosin myn,
Of al our stryf, God woot, the fruyt is thyn.
Thow walkest now in Thebes at thy large,
And of my wo thou yevest litel charge.
Thou mayst, sin thou hast wisdom and
manhede,　1285
Assemblen alle the folk of our kinrede,
And make a werre so sharp on this citee,
That by som aventure, or som tretee,
Thou mayst have hir to lady and to wyf,
For whom that I †mot nedes lese my lyf.
For, as by wey of possibilitee,　(433) 1291
Sith thou art at thy large, of prison free,
And art a lord, greet is thyn avauntage,
More than is myn, that sterve here in a
cage.　1294
For I mot wepe and wayle, whyl I live,
With al the wo that prison may me yive,
And eek with peyne that love me yiveth
also,　(439)
That doubleth al my torment and my wo.'
Ther-with the fyr of jelousye up-sterte
With-inne his brest, and hente him by
the herte　1300
So woodly, that he lyk was to biholde
The box-tree, or the asshen dede and colde.

Tho seyde he; 'O cruel goddes, that governe
This world with binding of your word eterne,
And wryten in the table of athamaunt 1305
Your parlement, and your eterne graunt,
What is mankinde more un-to yow holde
Than is the sheep, that rouketh in the folde?    (450)
For slayn is man right as another beste,
And dwelleth eek in prison and areste,
And hath siknesse, and greet adversitee,
And ofte tymes giltelees, pardee !    1312
    What governaunce is in this prescience,
That giltelees tormenteth innocence?
And yet encreseth this al my penaunce,
That man is bounden to his observaunce,
For Goddes sake, to letten of his wille,
Ther as a beest may al his lust fulfille. (460)
And whan a beest is deed, he hath no peyne ;
But man after his deeth moot wepe and pleyne,    1320
Though in this world he have care and wo:
With-outen doute it may stonden so.
Th' answere of this I lete to divynis,
But wel I woot, that in this world gret pyne is.
Allas! I see a serpent or a theef,    1325
That many a trewe man hath doon mescheef,
Goon at his large, and wher him list may turne.    (469)
But I mot been in prison thurgh Saturne,
And eek thurgh Juno, jalous and eek wood,
That hath destroyed wel ny al the blood
Of Thebes, with his waste walles wyde.
And Venus sleeth me on that other syde
For jelousye, and fere of him Arcite.'
    Now wol I stinte of Palamon a lyte,
And lete him in his prison stille dwelle,
And of Arcita forth I wol yow telle.  1336
    The somer passeth, and the nightes longe    (479)
Encresen double wyse the peynes stronge
Bothe of the lovere and the prisoner.
I noot which hath the wofullere mester.
For shortly for to seyn, this Palamoun
Perpetuelly is dampned to prisoun,  1342
In cheynes and in fettres to ben deed ;
And Arcite is exyled upon his heed

For ever-mo as out of that contree,    1345
Ne never-mo he shal his lady see.
    Yow loveres axe I now this questioun,
Who hath the worse, Arcite or Palamoun?
That oon may seen his lady day by day,
But in prison he moot dwelle alway.  1350
That other wher him list may ryde or go,
But seen his lady shal he never-mo. (494)
Now demeth as yow liste, ye that can,
For I wol telle forth as I bigan.

### Explicit prima Pars.

### Sequitur pars secunda.

Whan that Arcite to Thebes comen was,
Ful ofte a day he swelte and seyde 'allas,'
For seen his lady shal he never-mo.  1357
And shortly to concluden al his wo, (500)
So muche sorwe had never creature
That is, or shal, whyl that the world may dure.    1360
His sleep, his mete, his drink is him biraft,
That lene he wex, and drye as is a shaft.
His eyen holwe, and grisly to biholde ;
His hewe falwe, and pale as asshen colde,
And solitarie he was, and ever allone,  1365
And wailling al the night, making his mone.
And if he herde song or instrument,
Then wolde he wepe, he mighte nat be stent ;    (510)
So feble eek were his spirits, and so lowe,    1369
And chaunged so, that no man coude knowe
His speche nor his vois, though men it herde.
And in his gere, for al the world he ferde
Nat oonly lyk the loveres maladye
Of Hereos, but rather lyk manye
Engendred of humour malencolyk,  1375
Biforen, in his celle fantastyk.
And shortly, turned was al up-so-doun
Bothe habit and eek disposicioun (520)
Of him, this woful lovere daun Arcite.
    What sholde I al-day of his wo endyte?
Whan he endured hadde a yeer or two
This cruel torment, and this peyne and wo,
At Thebes, in his contree, as I seyde,
Up-on a night, in sleep as he him leyde,
Him thoughte how that the winged god Mercurie    1385
Biforn him stood, and bad him to be murye.

His slepy yerde in hond he bar uprighte ;
An hat he werede up-on his heres brighte.
Arrayed was this god (as he took keep)
As he was whan that Argus took his sleep ;
And seyde him thus : ' T' Athénes shaltou
    wende ;        (533) 1391
Ther is thee shapen of thy wo an ende.'
And with that word Arcite wook and sterte.
' Now trewely, how sore that me smerte,'
Quod he, 't' Athénes right now wol I fare ;
Ne for the drede of deeth shal I nat spare
To see my lady, that I love and serve ;
In hir presence I recche nat to sterve.' (540)
    And with that word he caughte a greet
    mirour,        1399
And saugh that chaunged was al his colour,
And saugh his visage al in another kinde.
And right anoon it ran him in his minde,
That, sith his face was so disfigured
Of maladye, the which he hadde endured,
He mighte wel, if that he bar him lowe,
Live in Athénes ever-more unknowe, 1406
And seen his lady wel ny day by day.
And right anon he chaunged his array,
And cladde him as a povre laborer,  (551)
And al allone, save oonly a squyer,  1410
That knew his privetee and al his cas,
Which was disgysed povrely, as he was,
T' Athénes is he goon the nexte way.
And to the court he wente up-on a day,
And at the gate he profreth his servyse,
To drugge and drawe, what so men wol
    devyse.        1416
And shortly of this matere for to seyn,
He fil in office with a chamberleyn, (560)
The which that dwelling was with Emelye ;
For he was wys, and coude soon aspye 1420
Of every servaunt, which that serveth
    here.
Wel coude he hewen wode, and water bere,
For he was yong and mighty for the nones,
And ther-to he was strong and big of bones
To doon that any wight can him devyse.
A yeer or two he was in this servyse,
Page of the chambre of Emelye the brighte ;
And ' Philostrate ' he seide that he highte.
But half so wel biloved a man as he (571)
Ne was ther never in court, of his degree;
He was so gentil of condicioun,  1431
That thurghout al the court was his re-
    noun.

They seyden, that it were a charitee
That Theseus wolde enhauncen his degree,
And putten him in worshipful servyse,
Ther as he mighte his vertu excercyse.
And thus, with-inne a whyle, his name is
    spronge        1437
Bothe of his dedes, and his goode tonge,
That Theseus hath taken him so neer (581)
That of his chambre he made him a squyer,
And yaf him gold to mayntene his degree ;
And eek men broghte him out of his
    contree
From yeer to yeer, ful prively, his rente ;
But honestly and slyly he it spente,
That no man wondred how that he it
    hadde.        1445
And three yeer in this wyse his lyf he
    ladde,
And bar him so in pees and eek in werre,
Ther nas no man that Theseus hath derre.
And in this blisse lete I now Arcite, (591)
And speke I wol of Palamon a lyte.  1450
    In derknesse and horrible and strong
    prisoun
This seven yeer hath seten Palamoun,
Forpyned, what for wo and for distresse ;
Who feleth double soor and hevinesse
But Palamon ? that love destreyneth so,
That wood out of his wit he gooth for wo ;
And eek therto he is a prisoner  1457
Perpetuelly, noght oonly for a yeer.  (600)
Who coude ryme in English proprely
His martirdom ? for sothe, it am nat I ;
Therefore I passe as lightly as I may.
    It fel that in the seventhe yeer, in May,
The thridde night, (as olde bokes seyn,
That al this storie tellen more pleyn,)
Were it by aventure or destinee,  1465
(As, whan a thing is shapen, it shal be,)
That, sone after the midnight, Palamoun,
By helping of a freend, brak his prisoun,
And fleeth the citee, faste as he may go ;
For he had yive his gayler drinke so 1470
Of a clarree, maad of a certeyn wyn, (613)
With nercotikes and opie of Thebes fyn,
That al that night, thogh that men wolde
    him shake,
The gayler sleep, he mighte nat awake ;
And thus he fleeth as faste as ever he
    may.        1475
The night was short, and faste by the day,

That nedes-cost he moste him-selven hyde,
And til a grove, faste ther besyde,    (620)
With dredful foot than stalketh Pala-
moun.

For shortly, this was his opinioun,    1480
That in that grove he wolde him hyde al
day,
And in the night than wolde he take his
way
To Thebes-ward, his freendes for to preye
On Theseus to helpe him to werreye ;
And shortly, outher he wolde lese his lyf,
Or winnen Emelye un-to his wyf ;    1486
This is th'effect and his entente pleyn.

Now wol I torne un-to Arcite ageyn,(630)
That litel wiste how ny that was his
care,
Til that fortune had broght him in the
snare.    1490

The bisy larke, messager of day,
Saluëth in hir song the morwe gray ;
And fyry Phebus ryseth up so brighte,
That al the orient laugheth of the lighte,
And with his stremes dryeth in the greves
The silver dropes, hanging on the leves.
And Arcite, that is in the court royal
With Theseus, his squyer principal,    (640)
Is risen, and loketh on the myrie day.
And, for to doon his observaunce to May,
Remembring on the poynt of his desyr,
He on a courser, sterting as the fyr,    1502
Is riden in-to the feeldes, him to pleye,
Out of the court, were it a myle or tweye ;
And to the grove, of which that I yow
tolde,    1505
By aventure, his wey he gan to holde,
To maken him a gerland of the greves,
Were it of wodebinde or hawethorn-leves,
And loude he song ageyn the sonne shene :
' May, with alle thy floures and thy grene,
Wel-come be thou, faire fresshe May, 1511
I hope that I som grene gete may.'    (654)
And from his courser, with a lusty herte,
In-to the grove ful hastily he sterte,
And in a path he rometh up and doun,
Ther-as, by aventure, this Palamoun 1516
Was in a bush, that no man mighte him
see,
For sore afered of his deeth was he.    (660)
No-thing ne knew he that it was Arcite :
God wot he wolde have trowed it ful lyte.

But sooth is seyd, gon sithen many yeres,
That ' feeld hath eyen, and the wode hath
eres.'    1522
It is ful fair a man to bere him evene,
For al-day meteth men at unset stevene.
Ful litel woot Arcite of his felawe,    1525
That was so ny to herknen al his sawe,
For in the bush he sitteth now ful stille.

Whan that Arcite had romed al his fille,
And songen al the roundel lustily,    (671)
In-to a studie he fil sodeynly,    1530
As doon thise loveres in hir queynte geres,
Now in the croppe, now doun in the breres,
Now up, now doun, as boket in a welle.
Right as the Friday, soothly for to telle,
Now it shyneth, now it reyneth faste, 1535
Right so can gery Venus overcaste
The hertes of hir folk ; right as hir day
Is gerful, right so chaungeth she array.
Selde is the Friday al the wyke y-lyke.

Whan that Arcite had songe, he gan to
syke,    (682) 1540
And sette him doun with-outen any more :
' Alas !' quod he, ' that day that I was bore !
How longe, Juno, thurgh thy crueltee,
Woltow werreyen Thebes the citee ?
Allas ! y-broght is to confusioun    1545
The blood royal of Cadme and Amphioun ;
Of Cadmus, which that was the firste
man    (689)
That Thebes bulte, or first the toun bigan,
And of the citee first was crouned king,
Of his linage am I, and his of-spring 1550
By verray ligne, as of the stok royal :
And now I am so caitif and so thral,
That he, that is my mortal enemy,
I serve him as his squyer povrely.    1554
And yet doth Juno me wel more shame,
For I dar noght biknowe myn owne name ;
But ther-as I was wont to highte Arcite,
Now highte I Philostrate, noght worth a
myte.    (700)
Allas ! thou felle Mars, allas ! Juno, 1559
Thus hath your ire our kinrede al fordo,
Save only me, and wrecched Palamoun,
That Theseus martyreth in prisoun.
And over al this, to sleen me utterly,
Love hath his fyry dart so brenningly
Y-stiked thurgh my trewe careful herte,
That shapen was my deeth erst than my
sherte.    1566

Ye sleen me with your eyen, Emelye ;
Ye been the cause wherfor that I dye. (710)
Of al the remenant of myn other care
Ne sette I nat the mountaunce of a tare,
So that I coude don aught to your ple-
   saunce !'  1571
And with that word he fil doun in a
   traunce
A longe tyme ; and after he up-sterte.
   This Palamoun, that thoughte that
   thurgh his herte  (716) 1574
He felte a cold swerd sodeynliche glyde,
For ire he quook, no lenger wolde he byde.
And whan that he had herd Arcites tale,
As he were wood, with face deed and pale,
He sterte him up out of the buskes thikke,
And seyde : 'Arcite, false traitour wikke,
Now artow hent, that lovest my lady so,
For whom that I have al this peyne and
   wo,  1582
And art my blood, and to my counseil
   sworn,
As I ful ofte have told thee heer-biforn,
And hast by-japed here duk Theseus, 1585
And falsly chaunged hast thy name thus ;
I wol be deed, or elles thou shalt dye.
Thou shalt nat love my lady Emelye, (730)
But I wol love hir only, and namo ;
For I am Palamoun, thy mortal fo.  1590
And though that I no wepne have in this
   place,
But out of prison am astert by grace,
I drede noght that outher thou shalt dye,
Or thou ne shalt nat loven Emelye.
Chees which thou wilt, for thou shalt nat
   asterte.'  1595
   This Arcite, with ful despitous herte,
Whan he him knew, and hadde his tale
   herd,
As fiers as leoun, pulled out a swerd, (740)
And seyde thus : 'by God that sit above,
Nere it that thou art sik, and wood for love,
And eek that thou no wepne hast in this
   place,  1601
Thou sholdest never out of this grove pace,
That thou ne sholdest dyen of myn hond.
For I defye the seurtee and the bond
Which that thou seyst that I have maad
   to thee.  1605
What, verray fool, think wel that love is
   free,  (748)

And I wol love hir, maugre al thy might !
But, for as muche thou art a worthy knight,
And wilnest to darreyne hir by batayle,
Have heer my trouthe, to-morwe I wol
   nat fayle,  1610
With-outen witing of any other wight,
That here I wol be founden as a knight,
And bringen harneys right y-nough for
   thee ;
And chees the beste, and leve the worste
   for me.
And mete and drinke this night wol I
   bringe  1615
Y-nough for thee, and clothes for thy
   beddinge.  (758)
And, if so be that thou my lady winne,
And slee me in this wode ther I am inne,
Thou mayst wel have thy lady, as for me.'
This Palamon answerde : 'I graunte it
   thee.'  1620
And thus they been departed til a-morwe,
When ech of hem had leyd his feith to
   borwe.
   O Cupide, out of alle charitee !
O regne, that wolt no felawe have with
   thee !
Ful sooth is seyd, that love ne lordshipe
Wol noght, his thankes, have no felawe-
   shipe ;  1626
Wel finden that Arcite and Palamoun.
Arcite is riden anon un-to the toun, (770)
And on the morwe, er it were dayes
   light,
Ful prively two harneys hath he dight, 1630
Bothe suffisaunt and mete to darreyne
The bataille in the feeld bitwix hem
   tweyne.
And on his hors, allone as he was born,
He carieth al this harneys him biforn ;
And in the grove, at tyme and place y-set,
This Arcite and this Palamon ben met.
Tho chaungen gan the colour in hir face ;
Right as the hunter in the regne of Trace,
That stondeth at the gappe with a spere,
Whan hunted is the leoun or the bere,
And hereth him come russhing in the
   greves,  (783) 1641
And breketh bothe bowes and the leves,
And thinketh, 'heer cometh my mortel
   enemy,
With-oute faile, he moot be deed, or I ;

For outher I mot sleen him at the gappe,
Or he mot sleen me, if that me mishappe:'
So ferden they, in chaunging of hir
    hewe,                                  1647
As fer as everich of hem other knewe. (790)
Ther nas no good day, ne no saluing;
But streight, with-outen word or rehersing,
Everich of hem halp for to armen other,
As freendly as he were his owne brother;
And after that, with sharpe speres stronge
They foynen ech at other wonder longe.
Thou mightest wene that this Palamoun
In his fighting were a wood leoun,    1656
And as a cruel tygre was Arcite:
As wilde bores gonne they to smyte, (800)
That frothen whyte as foom for ire
    wood.
Up to the ancle foghte they in hir blood.
And in this wyse I lete hem fighting dwelle;
And forth I wol of Theseus yow telle
    The destinee, ministre general,
That executeth in the world over-al
The purveyaunce, that God hath seyn
    biforn,                              1665
So strong it is, that, though the world
    had sworn
The contrarie of a thing, by ye or nay,
Yet somtyme it shal fallen on a day  (810)
That falleth nat eft with-inne a thousand
    yere.
For certeinly, our appetytes here,    1670
Be it of werre, or pees, or hate, or love,
Al is this reuled by the sighte above.
This mene I now by mighty Theseus,
That for to honten is so desirous,
And namely at the grete hert in May, 1675
That in his bed ther daweth him no
    day,
That he nis clad, and redy for to ryde
With hunte and horn, and houndes him
    bisyde.                             (820)
For in his hunting hath he swich delyt,
That it is al his joye and appetyt    1680
To been him-self the grete hertes bane:
For after Mars he serveth now Diane.

    Cleer was the day, as I have told er this,
And Theseus, with alle joye and blis,
With his Ipolita, the fayre quene,    1685
And Emelye, clothed al in grene,
On hunting be they riden royally.
And to the grove, that stood ful faste by,

In which ther was an hert, as men him
    tolde,                              (831)
Duk Theseus the streighte wey hath
    holde.                              1690
And to the launde he rydeth him ful right,
For thider was the hert wont have his
    flight,
And over a brook, and so forth on his weye.
This duk wol han a cours at him, or tweye,
With houndes, swiche as that him list
    comaunde.                          1695
    And whan this duk was come un-to the
    launde,
Under the sonne he loketh, and anon
He was war of Arcite and Palamon,    (840)
That foughten breme, as it were bores two;
The brighte swerdes wenten to and fro 1700
So hidously, that with the leeste strook
It seemed as it wolde felle an ook;
But what they were, no-thing he ne woot.
This duk his courser with his spores
    smoot,
And at a stert he was bitwix hem two, 1705
And pulled out a swerd and cryed, 'ho!
Namore, up peyne of lesing your heed.
By mighty Mars, he shal anon be deed, (850)
That smyteth any strook, that I may seen!
But telleth me what mister men ye been,
That been so hardy for to fighten here 1711
With-outen juge or other officere,
As it were in a listes royally?'
    This Palamon answerde hastily
And seyde: 'sire, what nedeth wordes
    mo?                                 1715
We have the deeth deserved bothe two.
Two woful wrecches been we, two cay-
    tyves,                             (859)
That been encombred of our owne lyves;
And as thou art a rightful lord and juge,
Ne yeve us neither mercy ne refuge, 1720
But slee me first, for seynte charitee;
But slee my felawe eek as wel as me.
Or slee him first; for, though thou knowe
    it lyte,
This is thy mortal fo, this is Arcite, 1724
That fro thy lond is banished on his heed,
For which he hath deserved to be deed.
For this is he that cam un-to thy gate,
And seyde, that he highte Philostrate. (870)
Thus hath he japed thee ful many a yeer,
And thou has maked him thy chief squyer:

And this is he that loveth Emelye. 1731
For sith the day is come that I shal dye,
I make pleynly my confessioun,
That I am thilke woful Palamoun,
That hath thy prison broken wikkedly.
I am thy mortal fo, and it am I 1736
That loveth so hote Emelye the brighte,
That I wol dye present in hir sighte. (880)
Therfore I axe deeth and my juwyse;
But slee my felawe in the same wyse, 1740
For bothe han we deserved to be slayn.'

　This worthy duk answerde anon agayn,
And seyde, 'This is a short conclusioun :
Youre owne mouth, by your confessioun,
Hath dampned you, and I wol it recorde,
It nedeth noght to pyne yow with the
　　corde. 1746
Ye shul be deed, by mighty Mars the
　rede !'
　The quene anon, for verray womman-
　　hede, (890)
Gan for to wepe, and so dide Emelye,
And alle the ladies in the companye. 1750
Gret pitee was it, as it thoughte hem alle,
That ever swich a chaunce sholde falle;
For gentil men they were, of greet estat,
And no-thing but for love was this debat;
And sawe hir blody woundes wyde and
　　sore; 1755
And alle cryden, bothe lasse and more,
'Have mercy, lord, up-on us wommen
　alle !'
And on hir bare knees adoun they falle,
And wolde have kist his feet ther-as he
　stood, (901)
Til at the laste aslaked was his mood; 1760
For pitee renneth sone in gentil herte.
And though he first for ire quook and
　sterte,
He hath considered shortly, in a clause,
The trespas of hem bothe, and eek the
　cause :
And al-though that his ire hir gilt
　accused, (907) 1765
Yet in his reson he hem bothe excused ;
As thus : he thoghte wel, that every man
Wol helpe him-self in love, if that he can,
And eek delivere him-self out of prisoun ;
And eek his herte had compassioun 1770
Of wommen, for they wepen ever in oon;
And in his gentil herte he thoghte anoon,

And softe un-to himself he seyde : 'fy
Up-on a lord that wol have no mercy,
But been a leoun, bothe in word and
　dede, 1775
To hem that been in repentaunce and
　drede
As wel as to a proud despitous man (919)
That wol maynteyne that he first bigan !
That lord hath litel of discrecioun,
That in swich cas can no divisioun, 1780
But weyeth pryde and humblesse after
　oon.'
And shortly, whan his ire is thus agoon,
He gan to loken up with eyen lighte,
And spak thise same wordes al on
　highte :—
'The god of love, a ! benedicite, 1785
How mighty and how greet a lord is he !
Ayeins his might ther gayneth none
　obstacles,
He may be cleped a god for his miracles ;
For he can maken at his owne gyse (931)
Of everich herte, as that him list devyse.
Lo heer, this Arcite and this Palamoun,
That quitly weren out of my prisoun, 1792
And mighte han lived in Thebes royally,
And witen I am hir mortal enemy,
And that hir deeth lyth in my might
　also ; 1795
And yet hath love, maugree hir eyen two,
Y-broght hem hider bothe for to dye !
Now loketh, is nat that an heigh folye ?
Who may been a fool, but-if he love ? (941)
Bihold, for Goddes sake that sit above, 1800
Se how they blede ! be they noght wel
　arrayed ?
Thus hath hir lord, the god of love,
　y-payed
Hir wages and hir fees for hir servyse !
And yet they wenen for to been ful wyse
That serven love, for aught that may
　bifalle ! 1805
But this is yet the beste game of alle,
That she, for whom they han this jolitee,
Can hem ther-for as muche thank as me ;
She woot namore of al this hote fare, (951)
By God, than woot a cokkow or an hare !
But al mot been assayed, hoot and cold ;
A man mot been a fool, or yong or old ;
I woot it by my-self ful yore agoon : 1813
For in my tyme a servant was I oon.

And therfore, sin I knowe of loves peyne,
And woot how sore it can a man distreyne,
As he that hath ben caught ofte in his las,
I yow foryeve al hoolly this trespas,   (960)
At requeste of the quene that kneleth here,
And eek of Emelye, my suster dere.   1820
And ye shul bothe anon un-to me swere,
That never-mo ye shul my contree dere,
Ne make werre up-on me night ne day,
But been my freendes in al that ye may;
I yow foryeve this trespas every del.'   1825
And they him swore his axing fayre and
     wel,
And him of lordshipe and of mercy preyde,
And he hem graunteth grace, and thus he
     seyde:   (970)
  'To speke of royal linage and richesse,
Though that she were a quene or a prin-
     cesse,   1830
Ech of yow bothe is worthy, doutelees,
To wedden whan tyme is, but nathelees
I speke as for my suster Emelye,
For whom ye have this stryf and jelousye;
Ye woot your-self, she may not wedden two
At ones, though ye fighten ever-mo:   1836
That oon of yow, al be him looth or leef,
He moot go pypen in an ivy-leef;   (980)
This is to seyn, she may nat now han
     bothe,
Al be ye never so jelous, ne so wrothe.   1840
And for-thy I yow putte in this degree,
That ech of yow shal have his destinee
As him is shape; and herkneth in what
     wyse;
Lo, heer your ende of that I shal devyse.
  My wil is this, for plat conclusioun,   1845
With-outen any replicacioun,
If that yow lyketh, tak it for the beste,
That everich of yow shal gon wher him
     leste   (990)
Frely, with-outen raunson or daunger;
And this day fifty wykes, fer ne ner,   1850
Everich of yow shal bringe an hundred
     knightes,
Armed for listes up at alle rightes,
Al redy to darreyne hir by bataille.
And this bihote I yow, with-outen faille,
Up-on my trouthe, and as I am a knight,
That whether of yow bothe that hath
     might,   (998) 1856
This is to seyn, that whether he or thou

May with his hundred, as I spak of now,
Sleen his contrarie, or out of listes dryve,
Him shal I yeve Emelya to wyve,   1860
To whom that fortune yeveth so fair a
     grace.
The listes shal I maken in this place,
And God so wisly on my soule rewe,
As I shal even juge been and trewe.   1864
Ye shul non other ende with me maken,
That oon of yow ne shal be deed or taken.
And if yow thinketh this is wel y-sayd,
Seyeth your avys, and holdeth yow apayd.
This is your ende and your conclusioun.'
  Who loketh lightly now but Palamoun?
Who springeth up for joye but Arcite?   1871
Who couthe telle, or who couthe it endyte,
The joye that is maked in the place
Whan Theseus hath doon so fair a grace?
But doun on knees wente every maner
     wight,   1875
And thanked him with al her herte and
     might,
And namely the Thebans ofte sythe.
And thus with good hope and with herte
     blythe   (1020)
They take hir leve, and hom-ward gonne
     they ryde
To Thebes, with his olde walles wyde.   1880

**Explicit secunda pars.**

**Sequitur pars tercia.**

I trowe men wolde deme it necligence,
If I foryete to tellen the dispence
Of Theseus, that goth so bisily
To maken up the listes royally;
That swich a noble theatre as it was,   1885
I dar wel seyn that in this world ther
     nas.
The circuit a myle was aboute,   (1029)
Walled of stoon, and diched al with-oute.
Round was the shap, in maner of compas,
Ful of degrees, the heighte of sixty pas,   1890
That, whan a man was set on o degree,
He letted nat his felawe for to see.
  Est-ward ther stood a gate of marbel
     whyt,
West-ward, right swich another in the
     opposit.   1894
And shortly to concluden, swich a place
Was noon in erthe, as in so litel space;
For in the lond ther nas no crafty man,
That geometrie or ars-metrik can,   (1040)

Ne purtreyour, ne kerver of images,
That Theseus ne yaf him mete and wages
The theatre for to maken and devyse. 1901
And for to doon his ryte and sacrifyse,
He est-ward hath, up-on the gate above,
In worship of Venus, goddesse of love,
Don make an auter and an oratorie ; 1905
And west-ward, in the minde and in
    memorie
Of Mars, he maked hath right swich
    another,
That coste largely of gold a fother. (1050)
And north-ward, in a touret on the wal,
Of alabastre whyt and reed coral    1910
An oratorie riche for to see,
In worship of Dyane of chastitee,
Hath Theseus don wroght in noble wyse.
    But yet hadde I foryeten to devyse
The noble kerving, and the portreitures,
The shap, the countenaunce, and the
    figures,    1916
That weren in thise oratories three.
    First in the temple of Venus maystow
        see    (1060)
Wroght on the wal, ful pitous to biholde,
The broken slepes, and the sykes colde ;
The sacred teres, and the waymenting ;
The fyry strokes of the desiring,    1922
That loves servaunts in this lyf enduren ;
The othes, that hir covenants assuren ;
Plesaunce and hope, desyr, fool-hardi-
    nesse,    1925
Beautee and youthe, bauderie, richesse,
Charmes and force, lesinges, flaterye,
Dispense, bisynesse, and jelousye,    (1070)
That wered of yelwe goldes a gerland,
And a cokkow sitting on hir hand ;    1930
Festes, instruments, caroles, daunces,
Lust and array, and alle the circum-
    staunces
Of love, whiche that I rekne and rekne
    shal,
By ordre weren peynted on the wal, 1934
And mo than I can make of mencioun.
For soothly, al the mount of Citheroun,
Ther Venus hath hir principal dwelling,
Was shewed on the wal in portreying,
With al the gardin, and the lustinesse.
Nat was foryeten the porter Ydelnesse,
Ne Narcisus the faire of yore agon,    1941
Ne yet the folye of king Salamon,    (1084)

Ne yet the grete strengthe of Hercules—
Th'enchauntements of Medea and Circes—
Ne of Turnus, with the hardy fiers corage,
The riche Cresus, caytif in servage.    1946
Thus may ye seen that wisdom ne
    richesse,
Beautee ne sleighte, strengthe, ne hardi-
    nesse,    (1090)
Ne may with Venus holde champartye ;
For as hir list the world than may she
    gye.    1950
Lo, alle thise folk so caught were in
    hir las,
Til they for wo ful ofte seyde 'allas !'
Suffyceth heer ensamples oon or two,
And though I coude rekne a thousand mo.
    The statue of Venus, glorious for to see,
Was naked fleting in the large see,    1956
And fro the navele doun all covered
    was
With wawes grene, and brighte as any
    glas.    (1100)
A citole in hir right hand hadde she,
And on hir heed, ful semely for to see, 1960
A rose gerland, fresh and wel smellinge ;
Above hir heed hir dowves flikeringe.
Biforn hir stood hir sone Cupido,
Up-on his shuldres winges hadde he two ;
And blind he was, as it is ofte sene ; 1965
A bowe he bar and arwes brighte and
    kene.
    Why sholde I noght as wel eek telle
        yow al
The portreiture, that was up-on the wal
With-inne the temple of mighty Mars the
    rede ?    (1111)
Al peynted was the wal, in lengthe and
    brede,    1970
Lyk to the estres of the grisly place,
That highte the grete temple of Mars in
    Trace,
In thilke colde frosty regioun,
Ther-as Mars hath his sovereyn mansioun.
    First on the wal was peynted a foreste,
In which ther dwelleth neither man ne
    beste,    1976
With knotty knarry bareyn treës olde
Of stubbes sharpe and hidous to biholde ;
In which ther ran a rumbel and a swough,
As though a storm sholde bresten every
    bough :    1980

And downward from an hille, under a
  bente,          (1123) 1981
Ther stood the temple of Mars armi-
  potente,
Wroght al of burned steel, of which
  thentree
Was long and stroit, and gastly for to see.
And ther-out cam a rage and such a vese,
That it made al the gates for to rese. 1986
The northren light in at the dores shoon,
For windowe on the wal ne was ther noon,
Thurgh which men mighten any light
  discerne.          (1131)
The dores were alle of adamant eterne,
Y-clenched overthwart and endelong 1991
With iren tough ; and, for to make it
  strong,
Every piler, the temple to sustene,
Was tonne-greet, of iren bright and shene.
    Ther saugh I first the derke imagining
Of felonye, and al the compassing ;  1996
The cruel ire, reed as any glede ;  (1139)
The pykepurs, and eek the pale drede ;
The smyler with the knyf under the cloke ;
The shepne brenning with the blake
  smoke ;          2000
The treson of the mordring in the bedde ;
The open werre, with woundes al bi-
  bledde ;
Contek, with blody knyf and sharp
  manace ;
Al ful of chirking was that sory place.
The sleere of him-self yet saugh I ther, 2005
His herte-blood hath bathed al his heer ;
The nayl y-driven in the shode a-night ;
The colde deeth, with mouth gaping up-
  right.          (1150)
Amiddes of the temple sat meschaunce,
With disconfort and sory contenaunce.
Yet saugh I woodnesse laughing in his
  rage ;          2011
Armed compleint, out-hees, and fiers
  outrage.
The careyne in the bush, with throte
  y-corve :
A thousand slayn, and nat of qualm
  y-storve ;          2014
The tiraunt, with the prey by force y-raft ;
The toun destroyed, ther was no-thing laft.
Yet saugh I brent the shippes hoppesteres ;
The hunte strangled with the wilde beres :

The sowe freten the child right in the
  cradel ;          (1161)
The cook y-scalded, for al his longe ladel.
Noght was foryeten by th' infortune of
  Marte ;          2021
The carter over-riden with his carte,
Under the wheel ful lowe he lay adoun.
Ther were also, of Martes divisioun,
The barbour, and the bocher, and the
  smith          2025
That forgeth sharpe swerdes on his stith.
And al above, depeynted in a tour, (1169)
Saw I conquest sittinge in greet honour,
With the sharpe swerde over his heed
Hanginge by a sotil twynes threed.  2030
Depeynted was the slaughtre of Julius,
Of grete Nero, and of Antonius ;
Al be that thilke tyme they were unborn,
Yet was hir deeth depeynted ther-biforn,
By manasinge of Mars, right by figure ;
So was it shewed in that portreiture
As is depeynted in the sterres above, (1179)
Who shal be slayn or elles deed for love.
Suffyceth oon ensample in stories olde,
I may not rekne hem alle, thogh I wolde.
    The statue of Mars up-on a carte stood,
Armed, and loked grim as he were wood ;
And over his heed ther shynen two figures
Of sterres, that been cleped in scriptures,
That oon Puella, that other Rubeus. 2045
This god of armes was arrayed thus :—
A wolf ther stood biforn him at his feet
With eyen rede, and of a man he eet ; (1190)
With sotil pencel was depeynt this storie,
In redoutinge of Mars and of his glorie.
    Now to the temple of Diane the chaste
As shortly as I can I wol me haste,  2052
To telle yow al the descripcioun.
Depeynted been the walles up and doun
Of hunting and of shamfast chastitee. 2055
Ther saugh I how woful Calistopee, (1198)
Whan that Diane agreved was with here,
Was turned from a womman til a bere,
And after was she maad the lode-sterre ;
Thus was it peynt, I can say yow no
  ferre ;          2060
Hir sone is eek a sterre, as men may see.
Ther saugh I Dane, y-turned til a tree,
I mene nat the goddesse Diane,
But Penneus doughter, which that highte
  Dane.          2064

Ther saugh I Attheon an hert y-maked,
For vengeaunce that he saugh Diane al
   naked;
I saugh how that his houndes have him
   caught,
And freten him, for that they knewe him
   naught.   (1210)
Yet peynted was a litel forther-moor,
How Atthalante hunted the wilde boor,
And Meleagre, and many another mo, 2071
For which Diane wroghte him care and wo.
Ther saugh I many another wonder storie,
The whiche me list nat drawen to
   memorie.   2074
This goddesse on an hert ful hye seet,
With smale houndes al aboute hir feet;
And undernethe hir feet she hadde a
   mone,   (1219)
Wexing it was, and sholde wanie sone.
In gaude grene hir statue clothed was,
With bowe in honde, and arwes in a cas.
Hir eyen caste she ful lowe adoun,   2081
Ther Pluto hath his derke regioun.
A womman travailinge was hir biforn,
But, for hir child so longe was unborn,
Ful pitously Lucyna gan she calle,   2085
And seyde, 'help, for thou mayst best of
   alle.'
Wel couthe he peynten lyfly that it
   wroghte,   (1229)
With many a florin he the hewes boghte.
   Now been thise listes maad, and
   Theseus,
That at his grete cost arrayed thus   2090
The temples and the theatre every del,
Whan it was doon, him lyked wonder
   wel.
But stinte I wol of Theseus a lyte,
And speke of Palamon and of Arcite.

   The day approcheth of hir retourninge,
That everich sholde an hundred knightes
   bringe,   2096
The bataille to darreyne, as I yow tolde;
And til Athénes, hir covenant for to holde,
Hath everich of hem broght an hundred
   knightes   (1241)
Wel armed for the werre at alle rightes.
And sikerly, ther trowed many a man 2101
That never, sithen that the world bigan,
As for to speke of knighthod of hir hond,
As fer as God hath maked see or lond,

Nas, of so fewe, so noble a companye. 2105
For every wight that lovede chivalrye,
And wolde, his thankes, han a passant
   name,
Hath preyed that he mighte ben of that
   game;   (1250)
And wel was him, that ther-to chosen was.
For if ther fille to-morwe swich a cas, 2110
Ye knowen wel, that every lusty knight,
That loveth paramours, and hath his
   might,
Were it in Engelond, or elles-where,
They wolde, hir thankes, wilnen to be
   there.
To fighte for a lady, *ben'cite!*   2115
It were a lusty sighte for to see.
   And right so ferden they with Palamon.
With him ther wenten knightes many
   oon;   (1260)
Som wol ben armed in an habergeoun,
In a brest-plat and in a light gipoun; 2120
And somme woln have a peyre plates
   large;
And somme woln have a Pruce sheld, or a
   targe;
Somme woln ben armed on hir legges weel,
And have an ax, and somme a mace of
   steel.   2124
Ther nis no newe gyse, that it nas old.
Armed were they, as I have you told,
Everich after his opinioun.
   Ther maistow seen coming with Pala-
   moun   (1270)
Ligurge him-self, the grete king of Trace;
Blak was his berd, and manly was his
   face.
The cercles of his eyen in his heed,   2131
They gloweden bitwixe yelow and reed:
And lyk a griffon loked he aboute,
With kempe heres on his browes stoute;
His limes grete, his braunes harde and
   stronge,   2135
His shuldres brode, his armes rounde and
   longe.
And as the gyse was in his contree,
Ful hye up-on a char of gold stood he,
With foure whyte boles in the trays. (1281)
In-stede of cote-armure over his harnays,
With nayles yelwe and brighte as any
   gold,   2141
He hadde a beres skin, col-blak, for-old.

His longe heer was kembd bihinde his bak,
As any ravenes fether it shoon for-blak :
A wrethe of gold arm-greet, of huge
     wighte,      2145
Upon his heed, set ful of stones brighte,
Of fyne rubies and of dyamaunts.
Aboute his char ther wenten whyte
     alaunts,      (1290)
Twenty and mo, as grete as any steer,
To hunten at the leoun or the deer,    2150
And folwed him, with mosel faste
     y-bounde,
Colers of gold, and torets fyled rounde.
An hundred lordes hadde he in his route
Armed ful wel, with hertes sterne and
     stoute.

With Arcita, in stories as men finde, 2155
The grete Emetreus, the king of Inde,
Up-on a stede bay, trapped in steel,
Covered in cloth of gold diapred weel, (1300)
Cam ryding lyk the god of armes, Mars.
His cote-armure was of cloth of Tars, 2160
Couched with perles whyte and rounde
     and grete.
His sadel was of brend gold newe y-bete ;
A mantelet upon his shuldre hanginge
Bret-ful of rubies rede, as fyr sparklinge.
His crispe heer lyk ringes was y-ronne, 2165
And that was yelow, and glitered as the
     sonne.
His nose was heigh, his eyen bright citryn,
His lippes rounde, his colour was sangwyn,
A fewe fraknes in his face y-spreynd, (1311)
Betwixen yelow and somdel blak y-meynd,
And as a leoun he his loking caste.    2171
Of fyve and twenty yeer his age I caste.
His berd was wel bigonne for to springe ;
His voys was as a trompe thunderinge.
Up-on his heed he wered of laurer grene
A gerland fresh and lusty for to sene. 2176
Up-on his hand he bar, for his deduyt,
An egle tame, as eny lilie whyt.      (1320)
An hundred lordes hadde he with him
     there,
Al armed, sauf hir heddes, in al hir gere,
Ful richely in alle maner thinges.    2181
For trusteth wel, that dukes, erles, kinges,
Were gadered in this noble companye,
For love and for encrees of chivalrye.
Aboute this king ther ran on every part
Ful many a tame leoun and lepart. 2186

And in this wyse thise lordes, alle and
     some,
Ben on the Sonday to the citee come (1330)
Aboute pryme, and in the toun alight.
   This Theseus, this duk, this worthy
     knight,      2190
Whan he had broght hem in-to his citee,
And inned hem, everich in his degree,
He festeth hem, and dooth so greet labour
To esen hem, and doon hem al honour,
That yet men weneth that no mannes wit
Of noon estat ne coude amenden it. 2196
The minstralcye, the service at the feste,
The grete yiftes to the moste and leste,
The riche array of Theseus paleys, (1341)
Ne who sat first ne last up-on the deys,
What ladies fairest been or best daunsinge,
Or which of hem can dauncen best and
     singe,      2202
Ne who most felingly speketh of love :
What haukes sitten on the perche above,
What houndes liggen on the floor adoun :
Of al this make I now no mencioun ; 2206
But al th'effect, that thinketh me the
     beste ;
Now comth the poynt, and herkneth if
     yow leste.      (1350)
   The Sonday night, er day bigan to
     springe,
When Palamon the larke herde singe, 2210
Although it nere nat day by houres two,
Yet song the larke, and Palamon also.
With holy herte, and with an heigh corage
He roos, to wenden on his pilgrimage
Un-to the blisful Citherea benigne,    2215
I mene Venus, honurable and digne.
And in hir houre he walketh forth a pas
Un-to the listes, ther hir temple was, (1360)
And doun he kneleth, and with humble
     chere      2219
And herte soor, he seyde as ye shul here.
   Faireste of faire, o lady myn, Venus,
Doughter to Jove and spouse of Vulcanus,
Thou glader of the mount of Citheroun,
For thilke love thou haddest to Adoun,
Have pitee of my bittre teres smerte, 2225
And tak myn humble preyer at thyn herte.
Allas ! I ne have no langage to telle (1369)
Th'effectes ne the torments of myn helle ;
Myn herte may myne harmes nat biwreye ;
I am so confus, that I can noght seye. 2230

But mercy, lady bright, that knowest weel
My thought, and seest what harmes that
    I feel,
Considere al this, and rewe up-on my
    sore,
As wisly as I shal for evermore,   2234
Emforth my might, thy trewe servant be,
And holden werre alwey with chastitee ;
That make I myn avow, so ye me helpe.
I kepe noght of armes for to yelpe, (1380)
Ne I ne axe nat to-morwe to have victorie,
Ne renoun in this cas, ne veyne glorie 2240
Of pris of armes blowen up and doun,
But I wolde have fully possessioun
Of Emelye, and dye in thy servyse ;
Find thou the maner how, and in what
    wyse.
I recche nat, but it may bettre be,   2245
To have victorie of hem, or they of me,
So that I have my lady in myne armes.
For though so be that Mars is god of
    armes,    (1390)
Your vertu is so greet in hevene above,
That, if yow list, I shal wel have my love.
Thy temple wol I worshipe evermo,  2251
And on thyn auter, wher I ryde or go,
I wol don sacrifice, and fyres bete.
And if ye wol nat so, my lady swete,  2254
Than preye I thee, to-morwe with a spere
That Arcita me thurgh the herte bere.
Thanne rekke I noght, whan I have lost
    my lyf,    (1399)
Though that Arcita winne hir to his wyf.
This is th'effect and ende of my preyere,
Yif me my love, thou blisful lady dere.'

When th'orisoun was doon of Palamon,
His sacrifice he dide, and that anon  2262
Ful pitously, with alle circumstaunces,
Al telle I noght as now his observaunces.
But atte laste the statue of Venus shook,
And made a signe, wher-by that he took
That his preyere accepted was that day.
For thogh the signe shewed a delay, (1410)
Yet wiste he wel that graunted was his
    bone ;
And with glad herte he wente him hoom
    ful sone.    2270

The thridde houre inequal that Palamon
Bigan to Venus temple for to goon,
Up roos the sonne, and up roos Emelye,
And to the temple of Diane gan hye.

Hir maydens, that she thider with hir
    ladde,    2275
Ful redily with hem the fyr they hadde,
Th'encens, the clothes, and the remenant
    al
That to the sacrifyce longen shal ;  (1420)
The hornes fulle of meth, as was the gyse ;
Ther lakked noght to doon hir sacrifyse.
Smoking the temple, ful of clothes faire,
This Emelye, with herte debonaire,  2282
Hir body wessh with water of a welle ;
But how she dide hir ryte I dar nat telle,
But it be any thing in general ;   2285
And yet it were a game to heren al ;
To him that meneth wel, it were no
    charge :
But it is good a man ben at his large. (1430)
Hir brighte heer was kempt, untressed al ;
A coroune of a grene ook cerial   2290
Up-on hir heed was set ful fair and mete.
Two fyres on the auter gan she bete,
And dide hir thinges, as men may biholde
In Stace of Thebes, and thise bokes olde.
Whan kindled was the fyr, with pitous
    chere    2295
Un-to Diane she spak, as ye may here.
  ' O chaste goddesse of the wodes grene,
To whom bothe heven and erthe and see
    is sene,    (1440)
Quene of the regne of Pluto derk and
    lowe,
Goddesse of maydens, that myn herte hast
    knowe    2300
Ful many a yeer, and woost what I desire,
As keep me fro thy vengeaunce and thyn
    ire,
That Attheon aboughte cruelly.
Chaste goddesse, wel wostow that I
Desire to been a mayden al my lyf,  2305
Ne never wol I be no love ne wyf.
I am, thou woost, yet of thy companye,
A mayde, and love hunting and venerye,
And for to walken in the wodes wilde,
And noght to been a wyf, and be with
    childe.    (1452) 2310
Noght wol I knowe companye of man.
Now help me, lady, sith ye may and can,
For tho thre formes that thou hast in thee.
And Palamon, that hath swich love to me,
And eek Arcite, that loveth me so sore,
This grace I preye thee with-oute more,

As sende love and pees bitwixe hem two ;
And fro me turne awey hir hertes so, (1460)
That al hir hote love, and hir desyr,
And al hir bisy torment, and hir fyr 2320
Be queynt, or turned in another place ;
And if so be thou wolt not do me grace,
Or if my destinee be shapen so,
That I shal nedes have oon of hem two,
As sende me him that most desireth me.
Bihold, goddesse of clene chastitee, 2326
The bittre teres that on my chekes falle.
Sin thou are mayde, and keper of us alle,
My maydenhede thou kepe and wel
     conserve, (1471)
And whyl I live a mayde, I wol thee
     serve.' 2330
The fyres brenne up-on the auter clere,
Whyl Emelye was thus in hir preyere ;
But sodeinly she saugh a sighte queynte,
For right anon oon of the fyres queynte,
And quiked agayn, and after that anon
That other fyr was queynt, and al agon ;
And as it queynte, it made a whistelinge,
As doon thise wete brondes in hir bren-
     ninge, (1480)
And at the brondes ende out-ran anoon
As it were blody dropes many oon ; 2340
For which so sore agast was Emelye,
That she was wel ny mad, and gan to crye,
For she ne wiste what it signifyed ;
But only for the fere thus hath she cryed,
And weep, that it was pitee for to here.
And ther-with-al Diane gan appere, 2346
With bowe in hond, right as an hunter-
     esse,
And seyde : 'Doghter, stint thyn hevi-
     nesse. (1490)
Among the goddes hye it is affermed,
And by eterne word write and confermed,
Thou shalt ben wedded un-to oon of tho
That han for thee so muchel care and wo ;
But un-to which of hem I may nat telle.
Farwel, for I ne may no lenger dwelle.
The fyres which that on myn auter
     brenne 2355
Shul thee declaren, er that thou go henne,
Thyn aventure of love, as in this cas.'
And with that word, the arwes in the cas
Of the goddesse clateren faste and ringe,
And forth she wente, and made a vanissh-
     inge ; (1502) 2360

For which this Emelye astoned was,
And seyde, ' What amounteth this, allas !
I putte me in thy proteccioun,
Diane, and in thy disposicioun.'
And hoom she gooth anon the nexte
     weye. 2365
This is th'effect, ther is namore to seye.

The nexte houre of Mars folwinge this,
Arcite un-to the temple walked is (1510)
Of fierse Mars, to doon his sacrifyse,
With alle the rytes of his payen wyse. 2370
With pitous herte and heigh devocioun,
Right thus to Mars he seyde his orisoun :
' O stronge god, that in the regnes colde
Of Trace honoured art, and lord y-holde,
And hast in every regne and every lond
Of armes al the brydel in thyn hond, 2376
And hem fortunest as thee list devyse,
Accept of me my pitous sacrifyse. (1520)
If so be that my youthe may deserve,
And that my might be worthy for to
     serve 2380
Thy godhede, that I may been oon of
     thyne,
Than preye I thee to rewe up-on my pyne.
For thilke peyne, and thilke hote fyr,
In which thou whylom brendest for desyr,
Whan that thou usedest the grete beautee
Of fayre yonge fresshe Venus free, 2386
And haddest hir in armes at thy wille,
Al-though thee ones on a tyme misfille
Whan Vulcanus had caught thee in his
     las, (1531)
And fond thee ligging by his wyf, allas !
For thilke sorwe that was in thyn herte,
Have routhe as wel up-on my peynes
     smerte. 2392
I am yong and unkonning, as thou wost,
And, as I trowe, with love offended
     most,
That ever was any lyves creature ; 2395
For she, that dooth me al this wo endure,
Ne reccheth never wher I sinke or flete.
And wel I woot, er she me mercy hete,
I moot with strengthe winne hir in the
     place ; (1541)
And wel I woot, withouten help or grace
Of thee, ne may my strengthe noght
     availle. 2401
Than help me, lord, to-morwe in my
     bataille,

For thilke fyr that whylom brente thee,
As wel as thilke fyr now brenneth me ;
And do that I to-morwe have victorie. 2405
Myn be the travaille, and thyn be the
glorie !
Thy soverein temple wol I most honouren
Of any place, and alwey most labouren
In thy plesaunce and in thy craftes
stronge,                                    (1551)
And in thy temple I wol my baner honge,
And alle the armes of my companye ; 2411
And evere-mo, un-to that day I dye,
Eterne fyr I wol biforn thee finde.
And eek to this avow I wol me binde :
My berd, myn heer that hongeth long
adoun,                                      2415
That never yet ne felte offensioun
Of rasour nor of shere, I wol thee yive,
And been thy trewe servant whyl I live.
Now lord, have routhe up-on my sorwes
sore,                                       (1561)
Yif me †victorie, I aske thee namore.' 2420

The preyere stinte of Arcita the stronge,
The ringes on the temple-dore that honge,
And eek the dores, clatereden ful faste,
Of which Arcita som-what him agaste.
The fyres brende up-on the auter brighte,
That it gan al the temple for to lighte ;
And swete smel the ground anon up-yaf,
And Arcita anon his hand up-haf,    (1570)
And more encens in-to the fyr he caste,
With othere rytes mo ; and atte laste 2430
The statue of Mars bigan his hauberk
ringe.
And with that soun he herde a murmur-
inge
Ful lowe and dim, that sayde thus,
' Victorie ' :
For which he yaf to Mars honour and
glorie.
And thus with joye, and hope wel to fare,
Arcite anon un-to his inne is fare,  2436
As fayn as fowel is of the brighte sonne.

And right anon swich stryf ther is bi-
gonne                                       (1580)
For thilke graunting, in the hevene above,
Bitwixe Venus, the goddesse of love, 2440
And Mars, the sterne god armipotente,
That Jupiter was bisy it to stente ;
Til that the pale Saturnus the colde,
That knew so manye of aventures olde,

Fond in his olde experience an art,  2445
That he ful sone hath plesed every part.
As sooth is sayd, elde hath greet avantage ;
In elde is bothe wisdom and usage ; (1590)
Men may the olde at-renne, and noght
at-rede.
Saturne anon, to stinten stryf and drede,
Al be it that it is agayn his kynde,  2451
Of al this stryf he gan remedie fynde.

' My dere doghter Venus,' quod Saturne,
' My cours, that hath so wyde for to turne,
Hath more power than wot any man. 2455
Myn is the drenching in the see so wan ;
Myn is the prison in the derke cote ;
Myn is the strangling and hanging by the
throte ;                                    (1600)
The murmure, and the cherles rebelling,
The groyning, and the pryvee empoyson-
ing :                                       2460
I do vengeance and pleyn correccioun
Whyl I dwelle in the signe of the Leoun.
Myn is the ruine of the hye halles,
The falling of the toures and of the walles
Up-on the mynour or the carpenter. 2465
I slow Sampsoun in shaking the piler ;
And myne be the maladyes colde,
The derke tresons, and the castes olde ;
My loking is the fader of pestilence. (1611)
Now weep namore, I shal doon diligence
That Palamon, that is thyn owne knight,
Shal have his lady, as thou hast him hight.
Though Mars shal helpe his knight, yet
nathelees
Bitwixe yow ther moot be som tyme pees,
Al be ye noght of o complexioun,     2475
That causeth al day swich divisioun.
I am thin ayel, redy at thy wille ;
Weep thou namore, I wol thy lust ful-
fille.'                                     (1620)
Now wol I stinten of the goddes above,
Of Mars, and of Venus, goddesse of love,
And telle yow, as pleynly as I can,   2481
The grete effect, for which that I bigan.

### Explicit tercia pars.
### Sequitur pars quarta.

Greet was the feste in Athenes that day,
And eek the lusty seson of that May
Made every wight to been in swich
plesaunce,                                  2485
That al that Monday justen they and
daunce,

Q

And spenden it in Venus heigh servyse.
But by the cause that they sholde ryse
Erly, for to seen the grete fight,    (1631)
Unto hir reste wente they at night.    2490
And on the morwe, whan that day gan
    springe,
Of hors and harneys, noyse and clateringe
Ther was in hostelryes al aboute ;
And to the paleys rood ther many a
    route
Of lordes, up-on stedes and palfreys. 2495
Ther maystow seen devysing of herneys
So uncouth and so riche, and wroght so
    weel
Of goldsmithrie, of browding, and of
    steel ;    (1640)
The sheeldes brighte, testers, and trap-
    pures ;
Gold-hewen helmes, hauberks, cote-ar-
    mures ;    2500
Lordes in paraments on hir courseres,
Knightes of retenue, and eek squyeres
Nailinge the speres, and helmes bokelinge,
Gigginge of sheeldes, with layneres la-
    cinge ;
Ther as need is, they weren no-thing ydel ;
The fomy stedes on the golden brydel 2506
Gnawinge, and faste the armurers also
With fyle and hamer prikinge to and
    fro ;    (1650)
Yemen on fote, and communes many oon
With shorte staves, thikke as they may
    goon ;    2510
Pypes, trompes, nakers, clariounes,
That in the bataille blowen blody sounes ;
The paleys ful of peples up and doun,
Heer three, ther ten, holding hir ques-
    tioun,
Divyninge of thise Theban knightes two.
Somme seyden thus, somme seyde it shal
    be so ;    2516
Somme helden with him with the blake
    berd,
Somme with the balled, somme with the
    thikke-herd ;    (1660)
Somme sayde, he loked grim and he
    wolde fighte ;
He hath a sparth of twenty pound of
    wighte.    2520
Thus was the halle ful of divyninge,
Longe after that the sonne gan to springe.

The grete Theseus, that of his sleep
    awaked
With minstralcye and noyse that was
    maked,
Held yet the chambre of his paleys riche,
Til that the Thebane knightes, bothe y-
    liche    2526
Honoured, were into the paleys fet.
Duk Theseus was at a window set,    (1670)
Arrayed right as he were a god in trone.
The peple preesseth thider-ward ful sone
Him for to seen, and doon heigh reverence,
And eek to herkne his hest and his
    sentence.
An heraud on a scaffold made an ho,
Til al the noyse of peple was y-do ;
And whan he saugh the peple of noyse al
    stille,    2535
Tho showed he the mighty dukes wille.
'The lord hath of his heigh discrecioun
Considered, that it were destruccioun (1680)
To gentil blood, to fighten in the gyse
Of mortal bataille now in this empryse ;
Wherfore, to shapen that they shul not
    dye,    2541
He wol his firste purpos modifye.
No man therfor, up peyne of los of lyf,
No maner shot, ne pollax, ne short knyf
Into the listes sende, or thider bringe ; 2545
Ne short swerd for to stoke, with poynt
    bytinge,
No man ne drawe, ne bere it by his syde.
Ne no man shal un-to his felawe ryde (1690)
But o cours, with a sharp y-grounde spere ;
Foyne, if him list, on fote, him-self to
    were.    2550
And he that is at meschief, shal be take,
And noght slayn, but be broght un-to the
    stake
That shal ben ordeyned on either syde ;
But thider he shal by force, and ther
    abyde.
And if so falle, the chieftayn be take 2555
On either syde, or elles slee his make,
No lenger shal the turneyinge laste.
God spede yow ; goth forth, and ley on
    faste.    (1700)
With long swerd and with maces fight
    your fille.
Goth now your wey ; this is the lordes
    wille.'    2560

The voys of peple touchede the hevene,
So loude cryden they with mery stevene :
'God save swich a lord, that is so good,
He wilneth no destruccioun of blood !'
Up goon the trompes and the melodye. 2565
And to the listes rit the companye
By ordinaunce, thurgh-out the citee large,
Hanged with cloth of gold, and nat with
   sarge.   (1710)
Ful lyk a lord this noble duk gan ryde,
Thise two Thebanes up-on either syde ; 2570
And after rood the quene, and Emelye,
And after that another companye
Of oon and other, after hir degree.
And thus they passen thurgh-out the
   citee,
And to the listes come they by tyme. 2575
It nas not of the day yet fully pryme,
Whan set was Theseus ful riche and hye,
Ipolita the quene and Emelye,   (1720)
And other ladies in degrees aboute.
Un-to the seetes preesseth al the route. 2580
And west-ward, thurgh the gates under
   Marte,
Arcite, and eek the hundred of his parte,
With baner reed is entred right anon ;
And in that selve moment Palamon
Is under Venus, est-ward in the place, 2585
With baner whyt, and hardy chere and
   face.
In al the world, to seken up and doun,
So even with-outen variacioun,   (1730)
Ther nere swiche companyes tweye.
For ther nas noon so wys that coude
   seye,   2590
That any hadde of other avauntage
Of worthinesse, ne of estaat, ne age,
So even were they chosen, for to gesse.
And in two renges faire they hem dresse.
Whan that hir names rad were everi-
   choon,   2595
That in hir nombre gyle were ther noon,
Tho were the gates shet, and cryed was
   loude :
'Do now your devoir, yonge knightes
   proude !'   (1740)
   The heraudes lefte hir priking up and
   doun ;   2599
Now ringen trompes loude and clarioun ;
Ther is namore to seyn, but west and est
In goon the speres ful sadly in arest ;

In goth the sharpe spore in-to the syde.
Ther seen men who can juste, and who
   can ryde ;
Ther shiveren shaftes up-on sheeldes
   thikke ;   2605
He feleth thurgh the herte-spoon the
   prikke.
Up springen speres twenty foot on highte ;
Out goon the swerdes as the silver
   brighte.   (1750)
The helmes they to-hewen and to-shrede ;
Out brest the blood, with sterne stremes
   rede.   2610
With mighty maces the bones they to-
   breste.
He thurgh the thikkeste of the throng
   gan threste.
Ther stomblen stedes stronge, and doun
   goth al.
He rolleth under foot as dooth a bal. 2614
He foyneth on his feet with his tronchoun,
And he him hurtleth with his hors adoun.
He thurgh the body is hurt, and sithen
   y-take,
Maugree his heed, and broght un-to the
   stake,   (1760)
As forward was, right ther he moste
   abyde ;
Another lad is on that other syde.   2620
And som tyme dooth hem Theseus to reste,
Hem to refresshe, and drinken if hem
   leste.
Ful ofte a-day han thise Thebanes two
Togidre y-met, and wroght his felawe wo ;
Unhorsed hath ech other of hem tweye.
Ther nas no tygre in the vale of Galgo-
   pheye,   2626
Whan that hir whelp is stole, whan it is
   lyte,
So cruel on the hunte, as is Arcite (1770)
For jelous herte upon this Palamoun :
Ne in Belmarye ther nis so fel leoun, 2630
That hunted is, or for his hunger wood,
Ne of his praye desireth so the blood,
As Palamon to sleen his fo Arcite.
The jelous strokes on hir helmes byte ;
Out renneth blood on both hir sydes
   rede.   2635
   Som tyme an ende ther is of every dede ;
For er the sonne un-to the reste wente,
The stronge king Emetreus gan hente

This Palamon, as he faught with Arcite,
And made his swerd depe in his flesh to
   byte ;    (1782) 2640
And by the force of twenty is he take
Unyolden, and y-drawe unto the stake.
And in the rescous of this Palamoun
The stronge king Ligurge is born adoun ;
And king Emetreus, for al his strengthe,
Is born out of his sadel a swerdes lengthe,
So hitte him Palamon er he were take ;
But al for noght, he was broght to the
   stake.    (1790)
His hardy herte mighte him helpe naught ;
He moste abyde, whan that he was caught
By force, and eek by composicioun.   2651

Who sorweth now but woful Palamoun,
That moot namore goon agayn to fighte ?
And whan that Theseus had seyn this
   sighte,    2654
Un-to the folk that foghten thus echoon
He cryde, ' Ho ! namore, for it is doon !
I wol be trewe juge, and no partye.
Arcite of Thebes shal have Emelye, (1800)
That by his fortune hath hir faire y-
   wonne.'

Anon ther is a noyse of peple bigonne 2660
For joye of this, so loude and heigh with-
   alle,
It semed that the listes sholde falle.

What can now faire Venus doon above ?
What seith she now ? what dooth this
   quene of love ?
But wepeth so, for wanting of hir wille,
Til that hir teres in the listes fille ;   2666
She seyde : ' I am ashamed, doutelees.'
Saturnus seyde : ' Doghter, hold thy pees.
Mars hath his wille, his knight hath al
   his bone,    (1811)
And, by myn heed, thou shalt ben esed
   sone.'    2670
The trompes, with the loude minstral-
   cye,
The heraudes, that ful loude yolle and
   crye,
Been in hir wele for joye of daun Arcite.
But herkneth me, and stinteth now a
   lyte,
Which a miracle ther bifel anon.   2675

This fierse Arcite hath of his helm y-don,
And on a courser, for to shewe his face,
He priketh endelong the large place, (1820)

Loking upward up-on this Emelye ;   2679
And she agayn him caste a freendlich yë,
(For wommen, as to speken in comune,
They folwen al the favour of fortune);
And she was al his chere, as in his herte.
Out of the ground a furie infernal sterte,
From Pluto sent, at requeste of Saturne,
For which his hors for fere gan to turne,
And leep asyde, and foundred as he leep ;
And, er that Arcite may taken keep, (1830)
He pighte him on the pomel of his heed,
That in the place he lay as he were
   deed,    2690
His brest to-brosten with his sadel-bowe.
As blak he lay as any cole or crowe,
So was the blood y-ronnen in his face.
Anon he was y-born out of the place
With herte soor, to Theseus paleys.   2695
Tho was he corven out of his harneys,
And in a bed y-brought ful faire and
   blyve,
For he was yet in memorie and alyve, (1840)
And alway crying after Emelye.

Duk Theseus, with al his companye, 2700
Is comen hoom to Athenes his citee,
With alle blisse and greet solempnitee.
Al be it that this aventure was falle,
He nolde noght disconforten hem alle.
Men seyde eek, that Arcite shal nat dye ;
He shal ben heled of his maladye.   2706
And of another thing they were as fayn,
That of hem alle was ther noon y-slayn,
Al were they sore y-hurt, and namely oon,
That with a spere was thirled his brest-
   boon.    (1852) 2710
To othere woundes, and to broken armes,
Some hadden salves, and some hadden
   charmes ;
Fermacies of herbes, and eek save
They dronken, for they wolde hir limes
   have.
For which this noble duk, as he wel can,
Conforteth and honoureth every man, 2716
And made revel al the longe night,
Un-to the straunge lordes, as was right.
Ne ther was holden no disconfitinge, (1861)
But as a justes or a tourneyinge ;   2720
For soothly ther was no disconfiture,
For falling nis nat but an aventure ;
Ne to be lad with fors un-to the stake
Unyolden, and with twenty knightes take.

O persone allone, with-outen mo,  2725
And haried forth by arme, foot, and to,
And eek his stede driven forth with staves,
With footmen, bothe yemen and eek
    knaves,  (1870)
It nas aretted him no vileinye,  2729
Ther may no man clepen it cowardye.

For which anon duk Theseus leet crye,
To stinten alle rancour and envye,
The gree as wel of o syde as of other,
And either syde y-lyk, as otheres brother;
And yaf hem yiftes after hir degree,  2735
And fully heeld a feste dayes three;
And conveyed the kinges worthily
Out of his toun a journee largely.  (1880)
And hoom wente every man the righte
    way.
Ther was namore, but 'far wel, have good
    day!'  2740
Of this bataille I wol namore endyte,
But speke of Palamon and of Arcite.

Swelleth the brest of Arcite, and the
    sore
Encreesseth at his herte more and more.
The clothered blood, for any lechecraft,
Corrupteth, and is in his bouk y-laft, 2746
That neither veyne-blood, ne ventusinge,
Ne drinke of herbes may ben his helpinge.
The vertu expulsif, or animal,  (1891)
Fro thilke vertu cleped natural  2750
Ne may the venim voyden, ne expelle.
The pypes of his longes gonne to swelle,
And every lacerte in his brest adoun
Is shent with venim and corrupcioun.
Him gayneth neither, for to gete his lyf,
Vomyt upward, ne dounward laxatif; 2756
Al is to-brosten thilke regioun,
Nature hath now no dominacioun.  (1900)
And certeinly, ther nature wol nat wirche,
Far-wel, phisyk! go ber the man to
    chirche!  2760
This al and som, that Arcita mot dye,
For which he sendeth after Emelye,
And Palamon, that was his cosin dere;
Than seyde he thus, as ye shul after
    here.

'Naught may the woful spirit in myn
    herte  2765
Declare o poynt of alle my sorwes smerte
To yow, my lady, that I love most;
But I biquethe the service of my gost (1910)

To yow aboven every creature,
Sin that my lyf may no lenger dure.  2770
Allas, the wo! allas, the peynes stronge,
That I for yow have suffred, and so longe!
Allas, the deeth! allas, myn Emelye!
Allas, departing of our companye!  2774
Allas, myn hertes quene! allas, my wyf!
Myn hertes lady, endere of my lyf!
What is this world? what asketh men to
    have?
Now with his love, now in his colde grave
Allone, with-outen any companye.  (1921)
Far-wel, my swete fo! myn Emelye! 2780
And softe tak me in your armes tweye,
For love of God, and herkneth what I seye.
    I have heer with my cosin Palamon
Had stryf and rancour, many a day a-gon,
For love of yow, and for my jelousye. 2785
And Jupiter so wis my soule gye,
To speken of a servant proprely,
With alle circumstaunces trewely,  (1930)
That is to seyn, trouthe, honour, and
    knighthede,
Wisdom, humblesse, estaat, and heigh
    kinrede,  2790
Fredom, and al that longeth to that art,
So Jupiter have of my soule part,
As in this world right now ne knowe I non
So worthy to ben loved as Palamon, 2794
That serveth yow, and wol don al his lyf.
And if that ever ye shul been a wyf,
Foryet nat Palamon, the gentil man.'(1939)
And with that word his speche faille gan,
For from his feet up to his brest was come
The cold of deeth, that hadde him over-
    come.  2800
And yet more-over, in his armes two
The vital strengthe is lost, and al ago.
Only the intellect, with-outen more,
That dwelled in his herte syk and sore,
Gan faillen, when the herte felte deeth,
Dusked his eyen two, and failled breeth.
But on his lady yet caste he his yë; (1949)
His laste word was, 'mercy, Emelye!'
His spirit chaunged hous, and wente ther,
As I cam never, I can nat tellen wher. 2810
Therfor I stinte, I nam no divinistre;
Of soules finde I nat in this registre,
Ne me ne list thilke opiniouns to telle
Of hem, though that they wryten wher
    they dwelle.

Arcite is cold, ther Mars his soule gye ;
Now wol I speken forth of Emelye.   2816

Shrighte Emelye, and howleth Palamon,
And Theseus his suster took anon   (1960)
Swowninge, and bar hir fro the corps away.
What helpeth it to tarien forth the day,
To tellen how she weep, bothe eve and
  morwe ?                              2821
For in swich cas wommen have swich
  sorwe,
Whan that hir housbonds been from hem
  ago,
That for the more part they sorwen so,
Or elles fallen in swich maladye,   2825
That at the laste certeinly they dye.

Infinite been the sorwes and the teres
Of olde folk, and folk of tendre yeres, (1970)
In al the toun, for deeth of this Theban ;
For him ther wepeth bothe child and
  man ;                                2830
So greet a weping was ther noon, certayn,
Whan Ector was y-broght, al fresh y-slayn,
To Troye ; allas ! the pitee that was ther,
Cracching of chekes, rending eek of heer.
' Why woldestow be deed,' thise wommen
  crye,                                2835
' And haddest gold y-nough, and Emelye ?'
No man mighte gladen Theseus,
Savinge his olde fader Egeus,       (1980)
That knew this worldes transmutacioun,
As he had seyn it chaungen up and doun,
Joye after wo, and wo after gladnesse :
And shewed hem ensamples and lyknesse.
' Right as ther deyed never man,' quod
  he,                                  2843
' That he ne livede in erthe in som degree,
Right so ther livede never man,' he seyde,
' In al this world, that som tyme he ne
  deyde.                       (1988) 2846
This world nis but a thurghfare ful of wo,
And we ben pilgrimes, passinge to and fro ;
Deeth is an ende of every worldly sore.'
And over al this yet seyde he muchel more
To this effect, ful wysly to enhorte   2851
The peple, that they sholde hem reconforte.

Duk Theseus, with al his bisy cure,
Caste now wher that the sepulture
Of good Arcite may best y-maked be,   2855
And eek most honurable in his degree.
And at the laste he took conclusioun,   (1999)
That ther as first Arcite and Palamoun

Hadden for love the bataille hem bitwene,
That in that selve grove, swote and grene,
Ther as he hadde his amorous desires,   2861
His compleynt, and for love his hote fires,
He wolde make a fyr, in which th'office
Funeral he mighte al accomplice ;
And leet comaunde anon to hakke and
  hewe                         (2007) 2865
The okes olde, and leye hem on a rewe
In colpons wel arrayed for to brenne ;
His officers with swifte feet they renne
And ryde anon at his comaundement.
And after this, Theseus hath y-sent   2870
After a bere, and it al over-spradde
With cloth of gold, the richest that he
  hadde.
And of the same suyte he cladde Arcite ;
Upon his hondes hadde he gloves whyte ;
Eek on his heed a croune of laurer
  grene,                               2875
And in his hond a swerd ful bright and
  kene.                               (2018)
He leyde him bare the visage on the bere,
Therwith he weep that pitee was to here.
And for the peple sholde seen him alle,
Whan it was day, he broghte him to the
  halle,                               2880
That roreth of the crying and the soun.

Tho cam this woful Theban Palamoun,
With flotery berd, and ruggy asshy heres,
In clothes blake, y-dropped al with teres ;
And, passing othere of weping, Emelye,
The rewfulleste of al the companye.   2886
In as muche as the service sholde be
The more noble and riche in his degree,
Duk Theseus leet forth three stedes bringe,
That trapped were in steel al gliteringe,
And covered with the armes of daun
  Arcite.                      (2033) 2891
Up-on thise stedes, that weren grete and
  whyte,
Ther seten folk, of which oon bar his sheeld,
Another his spere up in his hondes heeld ;
The thridde bar with him his bowe Tur-
  keys,                                2895
Of brend gold was the cas, and eek the
  harneys ;                           (2038)
And riden forth a pas with sorweful chere
Toward the grove, as ye shul after here.
The nobleste of the Grekes that ther were
Upon hir shuldres carieden the bere,   2900

With slakke pas, and eyen rede and wete,
Thurgh-out the citee, by the maister-strete,
That sprad was al with blak, and wonder
    hye
Right of the same is al the strete y-wrye.
Up-on the right hond wente old Egeus, 2905
And on that other syde duk Theseus,
With vessels in hir hand of gold ful fyn,
Al ful of hony, milk, and blood, and wyn;
Eek Palamon, with ful greet companye;
And after that cam woful Emelye,    2910
With fyr in honde, as was that tyme the
    gyse, .                       (2053)
To do th'office of funeral servyse.

  Heigh labour, and ful greet apparaillinge
Was at the service and the fyr-makinge,
That with his grene top the heven raughte,
And twenty fadme of brede the armes
    straughte;                    2916
This is to seyn, the bowes were so brode.
Of stree first ther was leyd ful many a
    lode.                        (2060)
But how the fyr was maked up on highte,
And eek the names how the trees highte,
As ook, firre, birch, asp, alder, holm,
    popler,                      2921
Wilow, elm, plane, ash, box, chasteyn,
    lind, laurer,
Mapul, thorn, beech, hasel, ew, whippel-
    tree,
How they weren feld, shal nat be told for
    me;
Ne how the goddes ronnen up and doun,
Disherited of hir habitacioun,      2926
In which they woneden in reste and pees,
Nymphes, Faunes, and Amadrides; (2070)
Ne how the bestes and the briddes alle
Fledden for fere, whan the wode was falle;
Ne how the ground agast was of the light,
That was nat wont to seen the sonne bright;
Ne how the fyr was couched first with stree,
And than with drye stokkes cloven a three,
And than with grene wode and spycerye,
And than with cloth of gold and with
    perrye,                      2936
And gerlandes hanging with ful many
    a flour,
The mirre, th'encens, with al so greet
    odour;
Ne how Arcite lay among al this,   (2081)
Ne what richesse aboute his body is; 2940

Ne how that Emelye, as was the gyse,
Putte in the fyr of funeral servyse;
Ne how she swowned whan men made the
    fyr,
Ne what she spak, ne what was hir desyr;
Ne what jeweles men in the fyr tho caste,
Whan that the fyr was greet and brente
    faste;                        2946
Ne how som caste hir sheeld, and som hir
    spere,
And of hir vestiments, whiche that they
    were,                        (2090)
And cuppes ful of wyn, and milk, and
    blood,
Into the fyr, that brente as it were wood;
Ne how the Grekes with an huge route
Thryës riden al the fyr aboute     2952
Up-on the left hand, with a loud shoutinge,
And thryës with hir speres clateringe;
And thryës how the ladies gonne crye; 2955
Ne how that lad was hom-ward Emelye;
Ne how Arcite is brent to asshen colde;
Ne how that liche-wake was y-holde (2100)
Al thilke night, ne how the Grekes pleye
The wake-pleyes, ne kepe I nat to seye; 2960
Who wrastleth best naked, with oille
    enoynt,
Ne who that bar him best, in no disjoynt.
I wol nat tellen eek how that they goon
Hoom til Athenes, whan the pley is doon;
But shortly to the poynt than wol I wende,
And maken of my longe tale an ende. 2966
  By processe and by lengthe of certeyn
    yeres
Al stinted is the moorning and the teres.
Of Grekes, by oon general assent,  (2111)
Than semed me ther was a parlement 2970
At Athenes, up-on certeyn poynts and cas;
Among the whiche poynts y-spoken was
To have with certeyn contrees alliaunce,
And have fully of Thebans obeisaunce.
For which this noble Theseus anon  2975
Leet senden after gentil Palamon,
Unwist of him what was the cause and
    why;
But in his blake clothes sorwefully (2120)
He cam at his comaundemente in hye.
Tho sente Theseus for Emelye.      2980
Whan they were set, and hust was al the
    place,
And Theseus abiden hadde a space

Er any word cam from his wyse brest,
His eyen sette he ther as was his lest,
And with a sad visage he syked stille,   2985
And after that right thus he seyde his wille.
  ' The firste moevere of the cause above,
Whan he first made the faire cheyne of
     love,                                    (2130)
Greet was th'effect, and heigh was his
     entente ;
Wel wiste he why, and what ther-of he
     mente ;                                  2990
For with that faire cheyne of love he bond
The fyr, the eyr, the water, and the
     lond
In certeyn boundes, that they may nat flee ;
That same prince and that moevere,' quod
     he,
' Hath stablissed, in this wrecched world
     adoun,                                   2995
Certeyne dayes and duracioun
To al that is engendred in this place,  (2139)
Over the whiche day they may nat pace,
Al mowe they yet tho dayes wel abregge ;
Ther needeth non auctoritee allegge,    3000
For it is preved by experience,
But that me list declaren my sentence.
Than may men by this ordre wel discerne,
That thilke moevere stable is and eterne.
Wel may men knowe, but it be a fool,    3005
That every part deryveth from his hool.
For nature hath nat take his beginning
Of no party ne cantel of a thing,      (2150)
But of a thing that parfit is and stable,
Descending so, til it be corrumpable.   3010
And therfore, of his wyse purveyaunce,
He hath so wel biset his ordinaunce,
That speces of thinges and progressiouns
Shullen enduren by successiouns,
And nat eterne be, with-oute lyë :     3015
This maistow understonde and seen at yë.
  ' Lo the ook, that hath so long a noris-
     shinge
From tyme that it first biginneth springe,
And hath so long a lyf, as we may see,  (2161)
Yet at the laste wasted is the tree.    3020
  ' Considereth eek, how that the harde
     stoon
Under our feet, on which we trede and
     goon,
Yit wasteth it, as it lyth by the weye.
The brode river somtyme wexeth dreye.

The grete tounes see we wane and wende.
Than may ye see that al this thing hath
     ende.                                    3026
  ' Of man and womman seen we wel also,
That nedeth, in oon of thise termes two,
This is to seyn, in youthe or elles age, (2171)
He moot ben deed, the king as shal a
     page ;                                   3030
Som in his bed, som in the depe see,
Som in the large feeld, as men may se ;
Ther helpeth noght, al goth that ilke weye.
Thanne may I seyn that al this thing moot
     deye.                                    3034
What maketh this but Jupiter the king ?
The which is prince and cause of alle thing,
Converting al un-to his propre welle,
From which it is deryved, sooth to telle.
And here-agayns no creature on lyve (2181)
Of no degree availleth for to stryve.  3040
  ' Thanne is it wisdom, as it thinketh me,
To maken vertu of necessitee,
And take it wel, that we may nat eschue,
And namely that to us alle is due.
And who-so gruccheth ought, he dooth
     folye,                                   3045
And rebel is to him that al may gye.
And certeinly a man hath most honour
To dyen in his excellence and flour,  (2190)
Whan he is siker of his gode name ;
Than hath he doon his freend, ne him, no
     shame.                                   3050
And gladder oghte his freend ben of his
     deeth,
Whan with honour up-yolden is his breeth,
Than whan his name apalled is for age ;
For al forgeten is his vasselage.
Than is it best, as for a worthy fame, 3055
To dyen whan that he is best of name.
The contrarie of al this is wilfulnesse.
Why gruccben we ? why have we hevi-
     nesse,                                   (2200)
That good Arcite, of chivalrye flour
Departed is, with duetee and honour,  3060
Out of this foule prison of this lyf ?
Why gruccben heer his cosin and his wyf
Of his wel-fare that loved hem so weel ?
Can he hem thank ? nay, God wot, never
     a deel,
That bothe his soule and eek hem-self
     offende,                                 3065
And yet they mowe hir lustes nat amende.

'What may I conclude of this longe serie,
But, after wo, I rede us to be merie,  (2210)
And thanken Jupiter of al his grace?
And, er that we departen from this
    place,  3070
I rede that we make, of sorwes two,
O parfyt joye, lasting ever-mo;
And loketh now, wher most sorwe is her-
    inne,
Ther wol we first amenden and biginne.
  'Suster,' quod he, 'this is my fulle assent,
With al th'avys heer of my parlement,  3076
That gentil Palamon, your owne knight,
That serveth yow with wille, herte, and
    might,  (2220)
And ever hath doon, sin that ye first him
    knewe,  3079
That ye shul, of your grace, up-on him rewe,
And taken him for housbonde and for
    lord:
Leen me your hond, for this is our acord.
Lat see now of your wommanly pitee.
He is a kinges brother sone, pardee;
And, though he were a povre bacheler, 3085
Sin he hath served yow so many a yeer,

And had for yow so greet adversitee,
It moste been considered, leveth me; (2230)
For gentil mercy oghte to passen right.'
  Than seyde he thus to Palamon ful right;
'I trowe ther nedeth litel sermoning 3091
To make yow assente to this thing.
Com neer, and tak your lady by the hond.'
Bitwixen hem was maad anon the bond,
That highte matrimoine or mariage, 3095
By al the counseil and the baronage.
And thus with alle blisse and melodye
Hath Palamon y-wedded Emelye.  (2240)
And God, that al this wyde world hath
    wroght,
Sende him his love, that hath it dere
    a-boght.  3100
For now is Palamon in alle wele,
Living in blisse, in richesse, and in hele;
And Emelye him loveth so tendrely,
And he hir serveth al-so gentilly,
That never was ther no word hem bitwene
Of jelousye, or any other tene.  3106
Thus endeth Palamon and Emelye;
And God save al this faire companye!—
    Amen.  (2250)

Here is ended the Knightes Tale.

# THE MILLER'S PROLOGUE.

### Here folwen the wordes bitwene the Host and the Millere.

WHAN that the Knight had thus his tale
    y-told,
In al the route nas ther yong ne old  3110
That he ne seyde it was a noble storie,
And worthy for to drawen to memorie;
And namely the gentils everichoon.
Our Hoste lough and swoor, 'so moot I goon,
This gooth aright; unbokeled is the male;
Lat see now who shal telle another tale:
For trewely, the game is wel bigonne.  3117
Now telleth ye, sir Monk, if that ye conne,

Sumwhat, to quyte with the Knightes
    tale.'  (11)
The Miller, that for-dronken was al
    pale,  3120
So that unnethe up-on his hors he sat,
He nolde avalen neither hood ne hat,
Ne abyde no man for his curteisye,
But in Pilates vois he gan to crye,
And swoor by armes and by blood and
    bones,  3125
'I can a noble tale for the nones,

With which I wol now quyte the Knightes
tale.'
Our Hoste saugh that he was dronke of
ale,                                                 (20)
And seyde : 'abyd, Robin, my leve brother,
Som bettre man shal telle us first another :
Abyd, and lat us werken thriftily.'      3131
  'By goddes soul,' quod he, 'that wol
  nat I ;
For I wol speke, or elles go my wey.'
Our Hoste answerde : 'tel on, a devel
wey !
Thou art a fool, thy wit is overcome.' 3135
  'Now herkneth,' quod the Miller, 'alle
  and some !
But first I make a protestacioun
That I am dronke, I knowe it by my
soun ;                                               (30)
And therfore, if that I misspeke or seye,
Wyte it the ale of Southwerk, I yow
preye;                                               3140
For I wol telle a legende and a lyf
Bothe of a Carpenter, and of his wyf,
How that a clerk hath set the wrightes
cappe.'
  The Reve answerde and seyde, 'stint thy
  clappe,
Lat be thy lewed dronken harlotrye. 3145
It is a sinne and eek a greet folye
To apeiren any man, or him diffame,
And eek to bringen wyves in swich
fame.                                                (40)
Thou mayst y-nogh of othere thinges
seyn.'
  This dronken Miller spak ful sone ageyn,
And seyde, 'leve brother Osewold,    3151
Who hath no wyf, he is no cokewold.
But I sey nat therfore that thou art oon ;
Ther been ful gode wyves many oon,

†And ever a thousand gode ayeyns oon
badde,                                               3155
†That knowestow wel thy-self, but-if thou
madde.
Why artow angry with my tale now ?
I have a wyf, pardee, as well as thou, (50)
Yet nolde I, for the oxen in my plogh,
Taken up-on me more than y-nogh,    3160
As demen of my-self that I were oon ;
I wol beleve wel that I am noon.
An housbond shal nat been inquisitif
Of goddes privetee, nor of his wyf.
So he may finde goddes foyson there, 3165
Of the remenant nedeth nat enquere.'
  What sholde I more seyn, but this
  Millere
He nolde his wordes for no man forbere, (60)
But tolde his cherles tale in his manere ;
Me thinketh that I shal reherce it here. 3170
And ther-fore every gentil wight I
preye,
For goddes love, demeth nat that I seye
Of evel entente, but that I moot reherce
Hir tales alle, be they bettre or werse,
Or elles falsen som of my matere.     3175
And therfore, who-so list it nat y-here,
Turne over the leef, and chese another
tale;                                                (69)
For he shal finde y-nowe, grete and smale,
Of storial thing that toucheth gentillesse,
And eek moralitee and holinesse ;    3180
Blameth nat me if that ye chese amis.
The Miller is a cherl, ye knowe wel
this ;
So was the Reve, and othere many mo,
And harlotrye they tolden bothe two.
Avyseth yow and putte me out of blame;
And eek men shal nat make ernest of
game.                                         (78) 3186

Here endeth the prologe.

# THE MILLERES TALE.

### Here biginneth the Millere his tale.

WHYLOM ther was dwellinge at Oxenford
A riche gnof, that gestes heeld to bord,
And of his craft he was a Carpenter.
With him ther was dwellinge a povre
    scoler,     3190
Had lerned art, but al his fantasye
Was turned for to lerne astrologye,
And coude a certeyn of conclusiouns
To demen by interrogaciouns,
If that men axed him in certein houres, 3195
Whan that men sholde have droghte or
    elles shoures,     (10)
Or if men axed him what sholde bifalle
Of every thing, I may nat rekene hem alle.

  This clerk was cleped hende Nicholas;
Of derne love he coude and of solas; 3200
And ther-to he was sleigh and ful privee,
And lyk a mayden meke for to see.
A chambre hadde he in that hostelrye
Allone, with-outen any companye,
Ful fetisly y-dight with herbes swote; 3205
And he him-self as swete as is the rote (20)
Of licorys, or any cetewale.
His Almageste and bokes grete and smale,
His astrelabie, longinge for his art,
His augrim-stones layen faire a-part 3210
On shelves couched at his beddes heed:
His presse y-covered with a falding reed.
And al above ther lay a gay sautrye,
On which he made a nightes melodye
So swetely, that al the chambre rong; 3215
And *Angelus ad virginem* he song;   (30)
And after that he song the kinges note;
Ful often blessed was his mery throte.
And thus this swete clerk his tyme spente
After his freendes finding and his rente.

  This Carpenter had wedded newe a wyf
Which that he lovede more than his lyf;
Of eightetene yeer she was of age.
Jalous he was, and heeld hir narwe in cage,

For she was wilde and yong, and he was
    old,     (39) 3225
And demed him-self ben lyk a cokewold.
He knew nat Catoun, for his wit was rude,
That bad man sholde wedde his similitude.
Men sholde wedden after hir estaat,
For youthe and elde is often at debaat. 3230
But sith that he was fallen in the snare,
He moste endure, as other folk, his care.

  Fair was this yonge wyf, and ther-with-al
As any wesele hir body gent and smal.
A ceynt she werede barred al of silk, 3235
A barmcloth eek as whyt as morne milk
Up-on hir lendes, ful of many a gore. (51)
Whyt was hir smok and brouded al bifore
And eek bihinde, on hir coler aboute,
Of col-blak silk, with-inne and eek with-
    oute.     3240
The tapes of hir whyte voluper
Were of the same suyte of hir coler;
Hir filet brood of silk, and set ful hye:
And sikerly she hadde a likerous yë. 3244
Ful smale y-pulled were hir browes two,
And tho were bent, and blake as any
    sloo.     (60)
She was ful more blisful on to see
Than is the newe pere-jonette tree;   3248
And softer than the wolle is of a wether.
And by hir girdel heeng a purs of lether
Tasseld with silk, and perled with latoun.
In al this world, to seken up and doun,
There nis no man so wys, that coude
    thenche
So gay a popelote, or swich a wenche. 3254
Ful brighter was the shyning of hir hewe
Than in the tour the noble y-forged newe.
But of hir song, it was as loude and yerne
As any swalwe sittinge on a berne.   (72)
Ther-to she coude skippe and make game,
As any kide or calf folwinge his dame. 3260

Hir mouth was swete as bragot or the
    meeth,
Or hord of apples leyd in hey or heeth.
Winsinge she was, as is a joly colt,
Long as a mast, and upright as a bolt.
A brooch she baar up-on hir lowe coler, 3265
As brood as is the bos of a bocler.    (80)
Hir shoes were laced on hir legges hye ;
She was a prymerole, a pigges-nye
For any lord to leggen in his bedde,
Or yet for any good yeman to wedde. 3270

    Now sire, and eft sire, so bifel the cas,
That on a day this hende Nicholas
Fil with this yonge wyf to rage and pleye,
Whyl that hir housbond was at Oseneye,
As clerkes ben ful subtile and ful queynte ;
And prively he caughte hir by the queynte,
And seyde, 'y-wis, but if ich have my
    wille,          (91) 3277
For derne love of thee, lemman, I spille.'
And heeld hir harde by the haunche-bones,
And seyde, 'lemman, love me al at-ones,
Or I wol dyen, also god me save !'     3281
And she sprong as a colt doth in the trave,
And with hir heed she wryed faste awey,
And seyde, 'I wol nat kisse thee, by my fey,
Why, lat be,' quod she, 'lat be, Nicholas,
Or I wol crye out "harrow" and "allas."
Do wey your handes for your curteisye !'

    This Nicholas gan mercy for to crye,
And spak so faire, and profred hir so faste,
That she hir love him graunted atte
    laste,          (104) 3290
And swoor hir ooth, by seint Thomas of
    Kent,
That she wol been at his comandement,
Whan that she may hir leyser wel espye.
'Myn housbond is so ful of jalousye,
That but ye wayte wel and been privee, 3295
I woot right wel I nam but deed,' quod she.
'Ye moste been ful derne, as in this cas.'
    'Nay ther-of care thee noght,' quod
    Nicholas,          (112)
'A clerk had litherly biset his whyle,
But-if he coude a carpenter bigyle.'    3300
And thus they been acorded and y-sworn
To wayte a tyme, as I have told biforn.
Whan Nicholas had doon thus everydeel,
And thakked hir aboute the lendes weel,
He kist hir swete, and taketh his sautrye,
And pleyeth faste, and maketh melodye.

    Than fil it thus, that to the parish-
    chirche,          (121)
Cristes owne werkes for to wirche,
This gode wyf wente on an haliday ;
Hir forheed shoon as bright as any day, 3310
So was it wasshen whan she leet hir werk.
    Now was ther of that chirche a parish-
    clerk,
The which that was y-cleped Absolon.
Crul was his heer, and as the gold it shoon,
And strouted as a fanne large and brode ;
Ful streight and even lay his joly shode.
His rode was reed, his eyen greye as goos ;
With Powles window corven on his shoos,
In hoses rede he wente fetisly.        (133)
Y-clad he was ful smal and propisely, 3320
Al in a kirtel of a light wachet ;
Ful faire and thikke been the poyntes set,
And ther-up-on he hadde a gay surplys
As whyt as is the blosme up-on the rys.
A mery child he was, so god me save, 3325
Wel coude he laten blood and clippe and
    shave,          (140)
And make a chartre of lond or acquitaunce.
In twenty manere coude he trippe and
    daunce
After the scole of Oxenforde tho,
And with his legges casten to and fro, 3330
And pleyen songes on a small rubible ;
Ther-to he song som-tyme a loud quinible ;
And as wel coude he pleye on his giterne.
In al the toun nas brewhous ne taverne
That he ne visited with his solas,     3335
Ther any gaylard tappestere was.     (150)
But sooth to seyn, he was somdel squaymous
Of farting, and of speche daungerous.

    This Absolon, that jolif was and gay,
Gooth with a sencer on the haliday, 3340
Sensinge the wyves of the parish faste ;
And many a lovely look on hem he caste,
And namely on this carpenteres wyf.
To loke on hir him thoughte a mery lyf,
She was so propre and swete and likerous.
I dar wel seyn, if she had been a mous, (160)
And he a cat, he wolde hir hente anon.
    This parish-clerk, this joly Absolon,
Hath in his herte swich a love-longinge,
That of no wyf ne took he noon offringe ;
For curteisye, he seyde, he wolde noon.
The mone, whan it was night, ful brighte
    shoon,          3352

And Absolon his giterne hath y-take,
For paramours, he thoghte for to wake.
And forth he gooth, jolif and amorous, 3355
Til he cam to the carpenteres hous   (170)
A litel after cokkes hadde y-crowe ;
And dressed him up by a shot-windowe
That was up-on the carpenteres wal.
He singeth in his vois gentil and smal,
' Now, dere lady, if thy wille be,    3361
I preye yow that ye wol rewe on me,'
Ful wel acordaunt to his giterninge.
This carpenter awook, and herde him
      singe,
And spak un-to his wyf, and seyde
      anon,                       3365
'What ! Alison ! herestow nat Absolon
That chaunteth thus under our boures
      wal ?'                       (181)
And she answerde hir housbond ther-
      with-al,
' Yis, god wot, John, I here it every-del.'
   This passeth forth ; what wol ye bet
      than wel ?                   3370
Fro day to day this joly Absolon
So woweth hir, that him is wo bigon.
He waketh al the night and al the day ;
He kempte hise lokkes brode, and made
      him gay ;                    3374
He woweth hir by menes and brocage,
And swoor he wolde been hir owne
      page ;                        (190)
He singeth, brokkinge as a nightingale ;
He sente hir piment, meeth, and spyced
      ale,
And wafres, pyping hote out of the glede ;
And for she was of toune, he profred
      mede.                        3380
For som folk wol ben wonnen for richesse,
And som for strokes, and som for gentil-
      lesse.
   Somtyme, to shewe his lightnesse and
      maistrye,
He pleyeth Herodes on a scaffold hye.
But what availleth him as in this cas ? 3385
She loveth so this hende Nicholas,   (200)
That Absolon may blowe the bukkes horn ;
He ne hadde for his labour but a scorn :
And thus she maketh Absolon hir ape,
And al his ernest turneth til a jape.  3390
Ful sooth is this proverbe, it is no lye,
Men seyn right thus, ' alwey the nye slye

Maketh the ferre leve to be looth.'
For though that Absolon be wood   or
      wrooth,                       3394
By-cause that he fer was from hir sighte,
This nye Nicholas stood in his lighte. (210)
   Now bere thee wel, thou hende Nicho-
      las !
For Absolon may waille and singe ' allas.'
And so bifel it on a Saterday,
This carpenter was goon til Osenay ; 3400
And hende Nicholas and Alisoun
Acorded been to this conclusioun,
That Nicholas shal shapen him a wyle
This sely jalous housbond to bigyle ;
And if so be the game wente aright, 3405
She sholde slepen in his arm al night,
For this was his desyr and hir also.  (221)
And right anon, with-outen wordes mo,
This Nicholas no lenger wolde tarie,
But doth ful softe un-to his chambre
      carie                          3410
Bothe mete and drinke for a day or
      tweye,
And to hir housbonde bad hir for to seye,
If that he axed after Nicholas,
She sholde seye she niste where he was,
Of al that day she saugh him nat with yë ;
She trowed that he was in maladye, (230)
For, for no cry, hir mayde coude him
      calle ;                        3417
He nolde answere, for no-thing that
      mighte falle.
   This passeth forth al thilke Saterday,
That Nicholas stille in his chambre lay,
And eet and sleep, or dide what him
      leste,                         3421
Til Sonday, that the sonne gooth to reste.
   This sely carpenter hath greet merveyle
Of Nicholas, or what thing mighte him
      eyle,                          3424
And seyde, ' I am adrad, by seint Thomas,
It stondeth nat aright with Nicholas. (240)
God shilde that he deyde sodeynly !
This world is now ful tikel, sikerly ;
I saugh to-day a cors y-born to chirche
That now, on Monday last, I saugh him
      wirche.                        3430
   Go up,' quod he un-to his knave anoon,
' Clepe at his dore, or knokke with a stoon,
Loke how it is, and tel me boldely.'
   This knave gooth him up ful sturdily,

And at the chambre-dore, whyl that he
   stood,       3435
He cryde and knokked as that he were
   wood :—       (250)
'What! how! what do ye, maister
   Nicholay?
How may ye slepen al the longe day?'
   But al for noght, he herde nat a word ;
An hole he fond, ful lowe up-on a bord,
Ther as the cat was wont in for to
   crepe ;      3441
And at that hole he looked in ful depe,
And at the laste he hadde of him a sighte.
This Nicholas sat gaping ever up-righte,
As he had kyked on the newe mone. 3445
Adoun he gooth, and tolde his maister
   sone      (260)
In what array he saugh this ilke man.

   This carpenter to blessen him bigan,
And seyde, 'help us, seinte Frideswyde !
A man woot litel what him shal bityde.
This man is falle, with his astromye, 3451
In som woodnesse or in som agonye ;
I thoghte ay wel how that it sholde be !
Men sholde nat knowe of goddes privetee.
Ye, blessed be alwey a lewed man, 3455
That noght but only his bileve can ! (270)
So ferde another clerk with astromye ;
He walked in the feeldes for to prye
Up-on the sterres, what ther sholde bifalle,
Til he was in a marle-pit y-falle ; 3460
He saugh nat that. But yet, by seint
   Thomas,
Me reweth sore of hende Nicholas.
He shal be rated of his studying,
If that I may, by Jesus, hevene king !
Get me a staf, that I may underspore,
Whyl that thou, Robin, hevest up the
   dore.    (280) 3466
He shal out of his studying, as I gesse '—
And to the chambre-dore he gan him
   dresse.
His knave was a strong carl for the nones,
And by the haspe he haf it up atones ;
In-to the floor the dore fil anon. 3471
This Nicholas sat ay as stille as stoon,
And ever gaped upward in-to the eir.
This carpenter wende he were in despeir,
And hente him by the sholdres mightily,
And shook him harde, and cryde spit-
   ously,    (290) 3476

'What! Nicholay! what, how! what!
   loke adoun !
Awake, and thenk on Cristes passioun ;
I crouche thee from elves and fro wightes !'
Ther-with the night-spel seyde he anon-
   rightes    3480
On foure halves of the hous aboute,
And on the threshfold of the dore with-
   oute :—
   'Jesu Crist, and seynt Benedight,
   Blesse this hous from every wikked
      wight,
   For nightes verye, the white pater-
      noster !—    3485
   Where wentestow, seynt Petres soster?'
And atte laste this hende Nicholas (301)
Gan for to syke sore, and seyde, 'allas !
Shal al the world be lost eftsones now?'
   This carpenter answerde, 'what
   seystow?    3490
What ! thenk on god, as we don, men
   that swinke.'
   This Nicholas answerde, 'fecche me
   drinke ;
And after wol I speke in privetee
Of certeyn thing that toucheth me and
   thee ;    3494
I wol telle it non other man, certeyn.'
   This carpenter goth doun, and comth
   ageyn,    (310)
And broghte of mighty ale a large quart ;
And whan that ech of hem had dronke
   his part,
This Nicholas his dore faste shette, 3499
And doun the carpenter by him he sette.
He seyde, 'John, myn hoste lief and
   dere,
Thou shalt up-on thy trouthe swere me
   here,
That to no wight thou shalt this conseil
   wreye ;
For it is Cristes conseil that I seye, 3504
And if thou telle it man, thou are forlore ;
For this vengaunce thou shalt han ther-
   fore,    (320)
That if thou wreye me, thou shalt be
   wood !'
   'Nay, Crist forbede it, for his holy blood !'
Quod tho this sely man, 'I nam no labbe,
Ne, though I seye, I nam nat lief to
   gabbe.    3510

Sey what thou wolt, I shal it never telle
To child ne wyf, by him that harwed
   helle !'
   ' Now John,' quod Nicholas, ' I wol nat
   lye ;
I have y-founde in myn astrologye,
As I have loked in the mone bright,  3515
That now, a Monday next, at quarter-
   night,      (330)
Shal falle a reyn and that so wilde and
   wood,
That half so greet was never Noës flood.
This world,' he seyde, ' in lasse than in
   an hour
Shal al be dreynt, so hidous is the shour;
Thus shal mankynde drenche and lese
   hir lyf.'      3521
   This carpenter answerde, ' allas, my wyf!
And shal she drenche? allas! myn Ali-
   soun ! '
For sorwe of this he fil almost adoun,
And seyde, ' is ther no remedie in this
   cas ?'      3525
   ' Why, yis, for gode,' quod hende
   Nicholas,      (340)
' If thou wolt werken after lore and reed;
Thou mayst nat werken after thyn owene
   heed.
For thus seith Salomon, that was ful
   trewe,
" Werk al by conseil, and thou shalt nat
   rewe."      3530
And if thou werken wolt by good conseil,
I undertake, with-outen mast and seyl,
Yet shal I saven hir and thee and me.
Hastow nat herd how saved was Noë,
Whan that our lord had warned him
   biforn      3535
That al the world with water sholde be
   lorn ?'      (350)
   ' Yis,' quod this carpenter, ' ful yore
   ago.'
   ' Hastow nat herd,' quod Nicholas, ' also
The sorwe of Noë with his felawshipe, 3539
Er that he mighte gete his wyf to shipe ?
Him had be lever, I dar wel undertake,
At thilke tyme, than alle hise wetheres
   blake,
That she hadde had a ship hir-self allone.
And ther-fore. wostou what is best to
   done ?      3544

This asketh haste, and of an hastif thing
Men may nat preche or maken tarying.
   Anon go gete us faste in-to this in  (361)
A kneding-trogh, or elles a kimelin,
For ech of us, but loke that they be
   large,
In whiche we mowe swimme as in a barge,
And han ther-inne vitaille suffisant  3551
But for a day ; fy on the remenant !
The water shal aslake and goon away
Aboute pryme up-on the nexte day.
But Robin may nat wite of this, thy
   knave,      (369) 3555
Ne eek thy mayde Gille I may nat save ;
Axe nat why, for though thou aske me,
I wol nat tellen goddes privetee.
Suffiseth thee, but if thy wittes madde,
To han as greet a grace as Noë hadde. 3560
Thy wyf shal I wel saven, out of doute,
Go now thy wey, and speed thee heer-
   aboute.
   But whan thou hast, for hir and thee
   and me,
Y-geten us thise kneding-tubbes three,
Than shaltow hange hem in the roof ful
   hye,      3565
That no man of our purveyaunce spye.
And whan thou thus hast doon as I have
   seyd,      (381)
And hast our vitaille faire in hem y-leyd,
And eek an ax, to smyte the corde atwo
When that the water comth, that we
   may go,      3570
And broke an hole an heigh, up-on the
   gable,
Unto the gardin-ward, over the stable,
That we may frely passen forth our way
Whan that the grete shour is goon away—
Than shaltow swimme as myrie, I under-
   take,      3575
As doth the whyte doke after hir drake.
Than wol I clepe, " how! Alison! how!
   John !      (391)
Be myrie, for the flood wol passe anon."
And thou wolt seyn, " hayl, maister
   Nicholay !
Good morwe, I se thee wel, for it is day."
And than shul we be lordes al our lyf 3581
Of al the world, as Noë and his wyf.
   But of o thyng I warne thee ful right,
Be wel avysed, on that ilke night  3584

That we ben entred in-to shippes bord,
That noon of us ne speke nat a word, (400)
Ne clepe, ne crye, but been in his preyere;
For it is goddes owne heste dere.
     Thy wyf and thou mote hange fer
       a-twinne,
For that bitwixe yow shal be no sinne
No more in looking than ther shal in
     dede;            3591
This ordinance is seyd, go, god thee spede!
Tomorwe at night, whan men ben alle
     aslepe,
In-to our kneding-tubbes wol we crepe,
And sitten ther, abyding goddes grace.
Go now thy wey, I have no lenger space
To make of this no lenger sermoning. (411)
Men seyn thus, "send the wyse, and sey
     no-thing;"         3598
Thou art so wys, it nedeth thee nat teche;
Go, save our lyf, and that I thee biseche.'
     This sely carpenter goth forth his wey.
Ful ofte he seith 'allas' and 'weylawey,'
And to his wyf he tolde his privetee;
And she was war, and knew it bet than
     he,             (418) 3604
What al this queynte cast was for to seye.
But nathelees she ferde as she wolde deye,
And seyde, 'allas! go forth thy wey anon,
Help us to scape, or we ben lost echon;
I am thy trewe verray wedded wyf;
Go, dere spouse, and help to save our
     lyf.'           3610
Lo! which a greet thyng is affeccioun!
Men may dye of imaginacioun,
So depe may impressioun be take.
This sely carpenter biginneth quake; 3614
Him thinketh verraily that he may see
Noës flood come walwing as the see (430)
To drenchen Alisoun, his hony dere.
He wepeth, weyleth, maketh sory chere,
He syketh with ful many a sory swogh.
He gooth and geteth him a kneding-trogh,
And after that a tubbe and a kimelin, 3621
And prively he sente hem to his in,
And heng hem in the roof in privetee.
His owne hand he made laddres three,
To climben by the ronges and the stalkes
Un-to the tubbes hanginge in the balkes,
And hem vitailled, bothe trogh and tubbe,
With breed and chese, and good ale in
     a jubbe,         (442) 3628

Suffysinge right y-nogh as for a day.
But er that he had maad al this array,
He sente his knave, and eek his wenche
     also,           3631
Up-on his nede to London for to go.
And on the Monday, whan it drow to
     night,
He shette his dore with-oute candel-light,
And dressed al thing as it sholde be. 3635
And shortly, up they clomben alle three;
They sitten stille wel a furlong-way. (451)
     'Now, *Pater-noster*, clom!' seyde Nicho-
       lay,
And 'clom,' quod John, and 'clom,' seyde
     Alisoun.
This carpenter seyde his devocioun, 3640
And stille he sit, and biddeth his preyere,
Awaytinge on the reyn, if he it here.
     The dede sleep, for wery bisinesse,
Fil on this carpenter right, as I gesse,
Aboute corfew-tyme, or litel more; 3645
For travail of his goost he groneth
     sore,           (460)
And eft he routeth, for his heed mislay.
Doun of the laddre stalketh Nicholay,
And Alisoun, ful softe adoun she spedde;
With-outen wordes mo, they goon to
     bedde          3650
Ther-as the carpenter is wont to lye.
Ther was the revel and the melodye;
And thus lyth Alison and Nicholas,
In bisinesse of mirthe and of solas, 3654
Til that the belle of laudes gan to ringe,
And freres in the chauncel gonne singe.
     This parish-clerk, this amorous Ab-
     solon,          (471)
That is for love alwey so wo bigon,
Up-on the Monday was at Oseneye
With companye, him to disporte and
     pleye,          3660
And axed up-on cas a cloisterer
Ful prively after John the carpenter;
And he drough him a-part out of the
     chirche,
And seyde, 'I noot, I saugh him here nat
     wirche
Sin Saterday; I trow that he be went 3665
For timber, ther our abbot hath him
     sent;          (480)
For he is wont for timber for to go,
And dwellen at the grange a day or two;

Or elles he is at his hous, certeyn ;  3669
Wher that he be, I can nat sothly seyn.'
  This Absolon ful joly was and light,
And thoghte, 'now is tyme wake al night ;
For sikirly I saugh him nat stiringe  3673
Aboute his dore sin day bigan to springe.
So moot I thryve, I shal, at cokkes crowe,
Ful prively knokken at his windowe (490)
That stant ful lowe up-on his boures wal.
To Alison now wol I tellen al
My love-longing, for yet I shal nat
    misse
That at the leste wey I shal hir kisse. 3680
Som maner confort shal I have, parfay,
My mouth hath icched al this longe
    day ;
That is a signe of kissing atte leste.
Al night me mette eek, I was at a feste.
Therfor I wol gon slepe an houre or
    tweye,  3685
And al the night than wol I wake and
    pleye.'  (500)
  Whan that the firste cok hath crowe,
    anon
Up rist this joly lover Absolon,
And him arrayeth gay, at point-devys.
But first he cheweth greyn and lycorys,
To smellen swete, er he had kembd his
    heer.  3691
Under his tonge a trewe love he beer,
For ther-by wende he to ben gracious.
He rometh to the carpenteres hous,
And stille he stant under the shot-
    windowe ;  (509) 3695
Un-to his brest it raughte, it was so lowe ;
And softe he cogheth with a semi-soun—
'What do ye, hony-comb, swete Alisoun ?
My faire brid, my swete cinamome,
Awaketh, lemman myn, and speketh to
    me !  3700
Wel litel thenken ye up-on my wo,
That for your love I swete ther I go.
No wonder is thogh that I swelte and
    swete ;
I moorne as doth a lamb after the tete.
Y-wis, lemman, I have swich love-long-
    inge,  3705
That lyk a turtel trewe is my moorninge ;
I may nat ete na more than a mayde.' (521)
  'Go fro the window, Jakke fool,' she
    sayde,

'As help me god, it wol nat be "com ba
    me,"  3709
I love another, and elles I were to blame,
Wel bet than thee, by Jesu, Absolon !
Go forth thy wey, or I wol caste a ston,
And lat me slepe, a twenty devel wey !'
  'Allas,' quod Absolon, 'and weylawey !
That trewe love was ever so yvel biset !
Than kisse me, sin it may be no bet, (530)
For Jesus love and for the love of me.'
  'Wiltow than go thy wey ther-with ?'
    quod she.
  'Ye, certes, lemman,' quod this Ab-
    solon.
  'Thanne make thee redy,' quod she,
    'I come anon ;'  3720
†And un-to Nicholas she seyde stille,
†'Now hust, and thou shalt laughen al
    thy fille.'
  This Absolon doun sette him on his
    knees,
And seyde, 'I am a lord at alle degrees ;
For after this I hope ther cometh more !
Lemman, thy grace, and swete brid, thyn
    ore !'  (540) 3726
  The window she undoth, and that in
    haste,
'Have do,' quod she, 'com of, and speed
    thee faste,
Lest that our neighebores thee espye.'
  This Absolon gan wype his mouth ful
    drye ;  3730
Derk was the night as pich, or as the cole,
And at the window out she putte hir hole,
And Absolon, him fil no bet ne wers,
But with his mouth he kiste hir naked
    ers
Ful savourly, er he was war of this.  3735
  Abak he sterte, and thoghte it was
    amis,  (550)
For wel he wiste a womman hath no
    berd ;
He felte a thing al rough and long y-herd,
And seyde, 'fy ! allas ! what have I do ?'
  'Tehee !' quod she, and clapte the
    window to ;  3740
And Absolon goth forth a sory pas.
  'A berd, a berd !' quod hende Nicholas,
'By goddes corpus, this goth faire and
    weel !'
  This sely Absolon herde every deel, 3744

And on his lippe he gan for anger byte ;
And to him-self he seyde, ' I shal thee
    quyte !'    (560)
  Who rubbeth now, who froteth now his
    lippes
With dust, with sond, with straw, with
    clooth, with chippes,
But Absolon, that seith ful ofte, ' allas !
My soule bitake I un-to Sathanas,    3750
But me wer lever than al this toun,'
    quod he,
' Of this despyt awroken for to be !
Allas !' quod he, ' allas ! I ne hadde y-
    bleynt !'
His hote love was cold and al y-queynt ;
For fro that tyme that he had kiste hir
    ers,    3755
Of paramours he sette nat a kers,    (570)
For he was heled of his maladye ;
Ful ofte paramours he gan deffye,
And weep as dooth a child that is y-bete.
A softe paas he wente over the strete 3760
Un-til a smith men cleped daun Gerveys,
That in his forge smithed plough-harneys ;
He sharpeth shaar and culter bisily.
This Absolon knokketh al esily,
And seyde, ' undo, Gerveys, and that
    anon.'    3765
  ' What, who artow ?' ' It am I, Ab-
    solon.'    (580)
' What, Absolon ! for Cristes swete tree,
Why ryse ye so rathe, ey, ben'cite !
What eyleth yow ? som gay gerl, god it
    woot,    3669
Hath broght yow thus up-on the viritoot ;
By seynt Note, ye woot wel what I mene.'
  This Absolon ne roghte nat a bene
Of al his pley, no word agayn he yaf ;
He hadde more tow on his distaf
Than Gerveys knew, and seyde, ' freend
    so dere,    (589) 3775
That hote culter in the chimenee here,
As lene it me, I have ther-with to done,
And I wol bringe it thee agayn ful sone.'
  Gerveys answerde, ' certes, were it gold,
Or in a poke nobles alle untold,    3780
Thou sholdest have, as I am trewe smith ;
Ey, Cristes foo ! what wol ye do ther-
    with ?'
  ' Ther-of,' quod Absolon, ' be as be may ;
I shal wel telle it thee to-morwe day '—

And caughte the culter by the colde
    stele.    3785
Ful softe out at the dore he gan to stele,
And wente un-to the carpenteres wal. (601)
He cogheth first, and knokketh ther-
    with-al
Upon the windowe, right as he dide er.
  This Alison answerde, ' Who is ther 3790
That knokketh so ? I warante it a theef.'
  ' Why, nay,' quod he, ' god woot, my
    swete leef,
I am thyn Absolon, my dereling !
Of gold,' quod he, ' I have thee broght
    a ring ;
My moder yaf it me, so god me save, 3795
Ful fyn it is, and ther-to wel y-grave ; (610)
This wol I yeve thee, if thou me kisse !'
  This Nicholas was risen for to pisse,
And thoghte he wolde amenden al the
    jape,    3799
He sholde kisse his ers er that he scape.
And up the windowe dide he hastily,
And out his ers he putteth prively
Over the buttok, to the haunche-bon ;
And ther-with spak this clerk, this
    Absolon,
' Spek, swete brid, I noot nat wher thou
    art.'    3805
  This Nicholas anon leet flee a fart, (620)
As greet as it had been a thonder-dent,
That with the strook he was almost
    y-blent ;
And he was redy with his iren hoot,
And Nicholas amidde the ers he smoot.
  Of gooth the skin an hande-brede
    aboute,    3811
The hote culter brende so his toute,
And for the smert he wende for to dye.
As he were wood, for wo he gan to crye—
' Help ! water ! water ! help, for goddes
    herte !'    3815
  This carpenter out of his slomber sterte,
And herde oon cryen ' water ' as he were
    wood,    (631)
And thoghte, ' Allas ! now comth Nowélis
    flood !'
He sit him up with-outen wordes mo, 3819
And with his ax he smoot the corde a-two,
And doun goth al ; he fond neither to
    selle,
Ne breed ne ale, til he cam to the selle

Up-on the floor ; and ther aswowne he lay.
Up sterte hir Alison, and Nicholay,
And cryden 'out' and 'harrow' in the
strete.                                    (639) 3825
The neighebores, bothe smale and grete,
In ronnen, for to gauren on this man,
That yet aswowne he lay, bothe pale and
wan ;
For with the fal he brosten hadde his
arm ;
But stonde he moste un-to his owne
harm.                                           3830
For whan he spak, he was anon bore
doun
With hende Nicholas and Alisoun.
They tolden every man that he was
wood,
He was agast so of ' Nowélis flood'
Thurgh fantasye, that of his vanitee 3835
He hadde y-boght him kneding-tubbes
three,                                       (650)

And hadde hem hanged in the roof above;
And that he preyed hem, for goddes love,
To sitten in the roof, par companye.   3839
The folk gan laughen at his fantasye ;
In-to the roof they kyken and they gape,
And turned al his harm un-to a jape.
For what so that this carpenter answerde,
It was for noght, no man his reson herde ;
With othes grete he was so sworn adoun,
That he was holden wood in al the toun ;
For every clerk anon-right heeld with
other.                                    (661) 3847
They seyde, 'the man is wood, my leve
brother ;'
And every wight gan laughen of this stryf.
Thus swyved was the carpenteres wyf,
For al his keping and his jalousye ;   3851
And Absolon hath kist hir nether yë ;
And Nicholas is scalded in the toute.
This tale is doon, and god save al the
route !                                    (668) 3854

**Here endeth the Millere his tale**

# THE REEVE'S PROLOGUE.

### The prologe of the Reves tale.

WHAN folk had laughen at this nyce cas
Of Absolon and hende Nicholas,        3856
Diverse folk diversely they seyde ;
But, for the more part, they loughe and
pleyde,
Ne at this tale I saugh no man him greve,
But it were only Osewold the Reve,    3860
By-cause he was of carpenteres craft.
A litel ire is in his herte y-laft,
He gan to grucche and blamed it a lyte.
  'So thee'k,' quod he, 'ful wel coude
I yow quyte                                (10)
With blering of a proud milleres yë,  3865
If that me liste speke of ribaudye.
But ik am old, me list not pley for age ;
Gras-tyme is doon, my fodder is now
forage,

This whyte top wryteth myne olde yeres,
Myn herte is al-so mowled as myne heres,
But-if I fare as dooth an open-ers ;    3871
That ilke fruit is ever leng the wers,
Til it be roten in mullok or in stree.
We olde men, I drede, so fare we ;      (20)
Til we be roten, can we nat be rype ;  3875
We hoppen ay, whyl that the world wol
pype.
For in oure wil ther stiketh ever a nayl,
To have an hoor heed and a grene tayl,
As hath a leek ; for thogh our might be
goon,
Our wil desireth folie ever in oon.    3880
For whan we may nat doon, than wol we
speke ;
Yet in our asshen olde is fyr y-reke.

Foure gledes han we, whiche I shal
devyse,
Avaunting, lying, anger, coveityse ; (30)
Thise foure sparkles longen un-to elde.
Our olde lemes mowe wel been unwelde,
But wil ne shal nat faillen, that is sooth.
And yet ik have alwey a coltes tooth, 3888
As many a yeer as it is passed henne
Sin that my tappe of lyf bigan to renne.
For sikerly, whan I was bore, anon 3891
Deeth drogh the tappe of lyf and leet it
gon ;
And ever sith hath so the tappe y-ronne,
Til that almost al empty is the tonne. (40)
The streem of lyf now droppeth on the
chimbe ; 3895
The sely tonge may wel ringe and chimbe
Of wrecchednesse that passed is ful yore ;
With olde folk, save dotage, is namore.'
  Whan that our host hadde herd this
  sermoning,
He gan to speke as lordly as a king ; 3900

He seide, 'what amounteth al this wit ?
What shul we speke alday of holy writ ?
The devel made a reve for to preche,
And of a souter a shipman or a leche. (50)
Sey forth thy tale, and tarie nat the tyme,
Lo, Depeford ! and it is half-way pryme.
Lo, Grenewich, ther many a shrewe is
inne ; 3907
It were al tyme thy tale to biginne.'
  'Now, sires,' quod this Osewold the Reve,
'I pray yow alle that ye nat yow greve,
Thogh I answere and somdel sette his
howve ; 3911
For leveful is with force force of-showve.
  This dronke millere hath y-told us heer,
How that bigyled was a carpenteer, (60)
Peraventure in scorn, for I am oon. 3915
And, by your leve, I shal him quyte anoon ;
Right in his cherles termes wol I speke.
I pray to god his nekke mote breke ;
He can wel in myn yë seen a stalke, 3919
But in his owne he can nat seen a balke.

# THE REVES TALE.

### Here biginneth the Reves tale.

At Trumpington, nat fer fro Cantebrigge,
Ther goth a brook and over that a brigge,
Up-on the whiche brook ther stant a melle ;
And this is verray soth that I yow telle.
A Miller was ther dwelling many a day ;
As eny pecok he was proud and gay. 3926
Pypen he coude and fisshe, and nettes
bete,
And turne coppes, and wel wrastle and
shete ;
And by his belt he baar a long panade,
And of a swerd ful trenchant was the
blade. 3930
A joly popper baar he in his pouche ; (11)
Ther was no man for peril dorste him
touche.

A Sheffeld thwitel baar he in his hose ;
Round was his face, and camuse was his
nose.
As piled as an ape was his skulle. 3935
He was a market-beter atte fulle.
Ther dorste no wight hand up-on him
legge,
That he ne swoor he sholde anon abegge.
A theef he was for sothe of corn and mele,
And that a sly, and usaunt for to stele.
His name was hoten dëynous Simkin. (21)
A wyf he hadde, y-comen of noble kin ;
The person of the toun hir fader was.
With hir he yaf ful many a panne of bras,
For that Simkin sholde in his blood allye.
She was y-fostred in a nonnerye ; 3946

For Simkin wolde no wyf, as he sayde,
But she were wel y-norissed and a mayde,
To saven his estaat of yomanrye.    3949
And she was proud, and pert as is a pye.
A ful fair sighte was it on hem two ;    (31)
On haly-dayes biforn hir wolde he go
With his tipet bounden about his heed,
And she cam after in a gyte of reed ;
And Simkin hadde hosen of the same.
Ther dorste no wight clepen hir but
    'dame.'    3956
Was noon so hardy that wente by the
    weye
That with hir dorste rage or ones pleye,
But-if he wolde be slayn of Simkin    3959
With panade, or with knyf, or boydekin.
For jalous folk ben perilous evermo,    (41)
Algate they wolde hir wyves wenden so.
And eek, for she was somdel smoterlich,
She was as digne as water in a dich ;
And ful of hoker and of bisemare.    3965
Hir thoughte that a lady sholde hir
    spare,
What for hir kinrede and hir nortelrye
That she had lerned in the nonnerye.

A doghter hadde they bitwixe hem two
Of twenty yeer, with-outen any mo,    3970
Savinge a child that was of half-yeer age ;
In cradel it lay and was a propre page.
This wenche thikke and wel y-growen
    was,    (53)
With camuse nose and yën greye as glas ;
With buttokes brode and brestes rounde
    and hye,    3975
But right fair was hir heer, I wol nat lye.
The person of the toun, for she was feir,
In purpos was to maken hir his heir
Bothe of his catel and his messuage, 3979
And straunge he made it of hir mariage.
His purpos was for to bistowe hir hye (61)
In-to som worthy blood of auncetrye ;
For holy chirches good moot been de-
    spended
On holy chirches blood, that is descended.
Therfore he wolde his holy blood honoure,
Though that he holy chirche sholde de-
    voure.    3986
    Gret soken hath this miller, out of doute,
With whete and malt of al the land aboute ;
And nameliche ther was a greet collegge,
Men clepen the Soler-halle at Cantebregge,

Ther was hir whete and eek hir malt
    y-grounde.    (71) 3991
And on a day it happed, in a stounde,
Sik lay the maunciple on a maladye ;
Men wenden wisly that he sholde dye.
For which this miller stal bothe mele and
    corn    3995
An hundred tyme more than biforn ;
For ther-biforn he stal but curteisly,
But now he was a theef outrageously,
For which the wardeyn chidde and made
    fare.    (79)
But ther-of sette the miller nat a tare ; 4000
He craketh boost, and swoor it was nat so.

    Than were ther yonge povre clerkes two,
That dwelten in this halle, of which I seye.
Testif they were, and lusty for to pleye,
And, only for hir mirthe and revelrye,
Up-on the wardeyn bisily they crye, 4006
To yeve hem leve but a litel stounde
To goon to mille and seen hir corn y-
    grounde ;
And hardily, they dorste leye hir nekke,
The miller shold nat stele hem half a
    pekke    (90) 4010
Of corn by sleighte, ne by force hem reve ;
And at the laste the wardeyn yaf hem leve.
John hight that oon, and Aleyn hight
    that other ;
Of o toun were they born, that highte
    Strother,    4014
Fer in the north, I can nat telle where.
    This Aleyn maketh redy al his gere,
And on an hors the sak he caste anon.
Forth goth Aleyn the clerk, and also John,
With good swerd and with bokeler by hir
    syde.    (99) 4019
John knew the wey, hem nedede no gyde,
And at the mille the sak adoun he layth.
Aleyn spak first, 'al hayl, Symond, y-fayth ;
How fares thy faire doghter and thy wyf ?'
    'Aleyn ! welcome,' quod Simkin, 'by my
    lyf,
And John also, how now, what do ye heer ?'
    'Symond,' quod John, 'by god, nede
    has na peer ;    4026
Him boës serve him-selve that has na
    swayn,
Or elles he is a fool, as clerkes sayn.
Our manciple, I hope he wil be deed, 4029
Swa werkes ay the wanges in his heed.

And forthy is I come, and eek Alayn, (111)
To grinde our corn and carie it ham agayn;
I pray yow spede us hethen that ye
    may.'
    'It shal be doon,' quod Simkin, 'by my
    fay;                                    4034
What wol ye doon whyl that it is in hande?'
    'By god, right by the hoper wil I stande,'
Quod John, 'and se how that the corn
    gas in ;
Yet saugh I never, by my fader kin, 4038
How that the hoper wagges til and fra.'
    Aleyn answerde, 'John, and wiltow swa,
Than wil I be bynethe, by my croun, (121)
And se how that the mele falles doun
In-to the trough ; that sal be my disport.
For John, in faith, I may been of your
    sort ;
I is as ille a miller as are ye.'       4045
    This miller smyled of hir nycetee,
And thoghte, 'al this nis doon but for a
    wyle ;
They wene that no man may hem bigyle ;
But, by my thrift, yet shal I blere hir yë
For al the sleighte in hir philosophye. 4050
The more queynte crekes that they make,
The more wol I stele whan I take.   (132)
In stede of flour, yet wol I yeve hem
    bren.
"The gretteste clerkes been noght the
    wysest men,"
As whylom to the wolf thus spak the
    mare ;                                  4055
Of al hir art I counte noght a tare.'
    Out at the dore he gooth ful prively,
Whan that he saugh his tyme, softely ;
He loketh up and doun til he hath founde
The clerkes hors, ther as it stood y-bounde
Bihinde the mille, under a levesel;  4061
And to the hors he gooth him faire and
    wel ;                                  (142)
He strepeth of the brydel right anon.
And whan the hors was loos, he ginneth
    gon
Toward the fen, ther wilde mares renne,
Forth with wehee, thurgh thikke and
    thurgh thenne.                         4066
    This miller gooth agayn, no word he
    seyde,
But dooth his note, and with the clerkes
    pleyde,

Til that hir corn was faire and wel y-
    grounde.
And whan the mele is sakked and y-
    bounde,                            (150) 4070
This John goth out and fynt his hors away,
And gan to crye ' harrow ' and 'weylaway !
Our hors is lorn ! Alayn, for goddes banes,
Step on thy feet, com out, man, al at anes !
Allas, our wardeyn has his palfrey lorn.'
This Aleyn al forgat, bothe mele and corn,
Al was out of his mynde his housbondrye.
' What ? whilk way is he geen?' he gan
    to crye.
    The wyf cam leping inward with a ren,
She seyde, 'allas ! your hors goth to the
    fen                                (160) 4080
With wilde mares, as faste as he may go.
Unthank come on his hand that bond
    him so,
And he that bettre sholde han knit the
    reyne.'
    'Allas,' quod John, 'Aleyn, for Cristes
    peyne,
Lay doun thy swerd, and I wil myn alswa;
I is ful wight, god waat, as is a raa ; 4086
By goddes herte he sal nat scape us bathe.
Why nadstow pit the capul in the lathe?
Il-hayl, by god, Aleyn, thou is a fonne !'
    This sely clerkes han ful faste y-ronne
To-ward the fen, bothe Aleyn and eek
    John.                               (171) 4091
    And whan the miller saugh that they
    were gon,
He half a busshel of hir flour hath take,
And bad his wyf go knede it in a cake.
He seyde, ' I trowe the clerkes were aferd ;
Yet can a miller make a clerkes berd 4096
For al his art; now lat hem goon hir weye.
Lo wher they goon, ye, lat the children
    pleye ;
They gete him nat so lightly, by my croun !'
    Thise sely clerkes rennen up and doun
With 'keep, keep, stand, stand, jossa,
    warderere,                         (181) 4101
Ga whistle thou, and I shal kepe him
    here !'
But shortly, til that it was verray night,
They coude nat, though they do al hir
    might,                                 4104
Hir capul cacche, he ran alwey so faste,
Til in a dich they caughte him atte laste.

Wery and weet, as beste is in the reyn,
Comth sely John, and with him comth
　　Aleyn.
'Allas,' quod John, 'the day that I was
　　born!
Now are we drive til hething and til
　　scorn.　　　　　　　　　　(190) 4110
Our corn is stole, men wil us foles calle,
Bathe the wardeyn and our felawes alle,
And namely the miller; weylaway!'
　　Thus pleyneth John as he goth by the
　　　　way
Toward the mille, and Bayard in his hond.
The miller sitting by the fyr he fond, 4116
For it was night, and forther mighte they
　　noght;
But, for the love of god, they him bisoght
Of herberwe and of ese, as for hir peny.
　　The miller seyde agayn, 'if ther be eny,
Swich as it is, yet shal ye have your part.
Myn hous is streit, but ye han lerned art;
Ye conne by argumentes make a place
A myle brood of twenty foot of space. (204)
Lat see now if this place may suffyse, 4125
Or make it roum with speche, as is youre
　　gyse.'
　　'Now, Symond,' seyde John, 'by seint
　　　　Cutberd,
Ay is thou mery, and this is faire answerd.
I have herd seyd, man sal taa of twa
　　thinges　　　　　　　　　　　4129
Slyk as he fyndes, or taa slyk as he bringes.
But specially, I pray thee, hoste dere, (211)
Get us som mete and drinke, and make
　　us chere,
And we wil payen trewely atte fulle.
With empty hand men may na haukes
　　tulle,
Lo here our silver, redy for to spende.' 4135
　　This miller in-to toun his doghter sende
For ale and breed, and rosted hem a goos,
And bond hir hors, it sholde nat gon loos;
And in his owne chambre hem made a
　　bed　　　　　　　　　　　(219) 4139
With shetes and with chalons faire y-spred,
Noght from his owne bed ten foot or twelve.
His doghter hadde a bed, al by hir-selve,
Right in the same chambre, by and by;
It mighte be no bet, and cause why, 4144
Ther was no roumer herberwe in the place.
They soupen and they speke, hem to solace,

And drinken ever strong ale atte beste.
Aboute midnight wente they to reste.
　　Wel hath this miller vernisshed his
　　　heed;
Ful pale he was for-dronken, and nat
　　reed.　　　　　　　　　　　4150
He yexeth, and he speketh thurgh the
　　nose　　　　　　　　　　　(231)
As he were on the quakke, or on the
　　pose.
To bedde he gooth, and with him goth
　　his wyf.
As any jay she light was and jolyf,
So was hir joly whistle wel y-wet.　4155
The cradel at hir beddes feet is set,
To rokken, and to yeve the child to souke.
And whan that dronken al was in the
　　crouke,
To bedde went the doghter right anon;
To bedde gooth Aleyn and also John; 4160
Ther nas na more, hem nedede no dwale.
This miller hath so wisly bibbed ale, (242)
That as an hors he snorteth in his sleep,
Ne of his tayl bihinde he took no keep.
His wyf bar him a burdon, a ful strong,
Men mighte hir routing here two furlong;
The wenche routeth eek *par companye.*
　　Aleyn the clerk, that herd this melodye,
He poked John, and seyde, 'slepestow?
Herdestow ever slyk a sang er now? 4170
Lo, whilk a compline is y-mel hem alle!
A wilde fyr up-on thair bodyes falle! (252)
Wha herkned ever slyk a ferly thing?
Ye, they sal have the flour of il ending.
This lange night ther tydes me na reste;
But yet, na fors; al sal be for the beste.
For John,' seyde he, 'als ever moot I
　　thryve,
If that I may, yon wenche wil I swyve.
Som esement has lawe y-shapen us; 4179
For John, ther is a lawe that says thus,
That gif a man in a point be y-greved, (261)
That in another he sal be releved.
Our corn is stoln, shortly, it is na nay,
And we han had an il fit al this day.
And sin I sal have neen amendement, 4185
Agayn my los I wil have esement.
By goddes saule, it sal neen other be!'
　　This John answerde, 'Alayn, avyse thee,
The miller is a perilous man,' he seyde,
'And gif that he out of his sleep abreyde

He mighte doon us bathe a vileinye.' (271)
　　Aleyn answerde, ' I count him nat a
　　flye ;' 4192
And up he rist, and by the wenche he
　　crepte.

This wenche lay upright, and faste slepte,
Til he so ny was, er she mighte espye, 4195
That it had been to late for to crye,
And shortly for to seyn, they were at on ;
Now pley, Aleyn ! for I wol speke of John.

　　This John lyth stille a furlong-wey or
　　two,
And to him-self he maketh routhe and
　　wo : (280) 4200
' Allas !' quod he, ' this is a wikked jape ;
Now may I seyn that I is but an ape.
Yet has my felawe som-what for his harm ;
He has the milleris doghter in his arm.
He auntred him, and has his nedes sped,
And I lye as a draf-sek in my bed ; 4206
And when this jape is tald another day,
I sal been halde a daf, a cokenay !
I wil aryse, and auntre it, by my fayth !
" Unhardy is unsely," thus men sayth.'
And up he roos and softely he wente (291)
Un-to the cradel, and in his hand it hente,
And baar it softe un-to his beddes feet.

　　Sone after this the wyf hir routing leet,
And gan awake, and wente hir out to
　　pisse, 4215
And cam agayn, and gan hir cradel misse,
And groped heer and ther, but she fond
　　noon.
' Allas !' quod she, ' I hadde almost mis-
　　goon ;
I hadde almost gon to the clerkes bed.
Ey, ben'cite ! thanne hadde I foule y-sped :'
And forth she gooth til she the cradel
　　fond. (301) 4221
She gropeth alwey forther with hir hond,
And fond the bed, and thoghte noght but
　　good,
By-cause that the cradel by it stood, 4224
And niste wher she was, for it was derk ;
But faire and wel she creep in to the clerk,
And lyth ful stille, and wolde han caught
　　a sleep.

With-inne a whyl this John the clerk up
　　leep, 4228
And on this gode wyf he leyth on sore.
So mery a fit ne hadde she nat ful yore ;

He priketh harde and depe as he were
　　mad. (311)
This joly lyf han thise two clerkes lad
Til that the thridde cok bigan to singe.

　　Aleyn wex wery in the daweninge, 4234
For he had swonken al the longe night ;
And seyde, ' far wel, Malin, swete wight !
The day is come, I may no lenger byde ;
But evermo, wher so I go or ryde,
I is thyn awen clerk, swa have I seel !'
　　' Now dere lemman,' quod she, ' go, far
　　weel ! (320) 4240
But er thou go, o thing I wol thee telle,
Whan that thou wendest homward by
　　the melle,
Right at the entree of the dore bihinde,
Thou shalt a cake of half a busshel finde
That was y-maked of thyn owne mele,
Which that I heelp my fader for to stele.
And, gode lemman, god thee save and
　　kepe !' 4247
And with that word almost she gan to
　　wepe.

　　Aleyn up-rist, and thoughte, ' er that
　　it dawe,
I wol go crepen in by my felawe ; 4250
And fond the cradel with his hand anon,
' By god,' thoghte he, ' al wrang I have
　　misgon ; (332)
Myn heed is toty of my swink to-night,
That maketh me that I go nat aright. 4254
I woot wel by the cradel, I have misgo,
Heer lyth the miller and his wyf also.'
And forth he goth, a twenty devel way,
Un-to the bed ther-as the miller lay.
He wende have cropen by his felawe John ;
And by the miller in he creep anon, 4260
And caughte hym by the nekke, and softe
　　he spak : (341)
He seyde, ' thou, John, thou swynes-heed,
　　awak
For Cristes saule, and heer a noble game.
For by that lord that called is seint
　　Jame,
As I have thryes, in this shorte night, 4265
Swyved the milleres doghter bolt-upright,
Whyl thow hast as a coward been agast.'
　　' Ye, false harlot,' quod the miller,
　　' hast ?
A ! false traitour ! false clerk !' quod he,
' Thou shalt be deed, by goddes dignitee !'

Who dorste be so bold to disparage     (351)
My doghter, that is come of swich linage?'
And by the throte-bolle he caughte Alayn.
And he hente hym despitously agayn,
And on the nose he smoot him with his
 fest.     4275
Doun ran the blody streem up-on his brest;
And in the floor, with nose and mouth
 to-broke,
They walwe as doon two pigges in a poke.
And up they goon, and doun agayn anon,
Til that the miller sporned at a stoon, 4280
And doun he fil bakward up-on his wyf,
That wiste no-thing of this nyce stryf;
For she was falle aslepe a lyte wight (363)
With John the clerk, that waked hadde
 al night.
And with the fal, out of hir sleep she
 breyde—     4285
'Help, holy croys of Bromeholm,' she
 seyde,
'*In manus tuas!* lord, to thee I calle!
Awak, Symond! the feend is on us falle,
Myn herte is broken, help, I nam but
 deed;
There lyth oon up my wombe and up
 myn heed;     4290
Help, Simkin, for the false clerkes fighte.'
 This John sterte up as faste as ever he
 mighte,     (372)
And graspeth by the walles to and fro,
To finde a staf; and she sterte up also,
And knew the estres bet than dide this
 John,     4295
And by the wal a staf she fond anon,

And saugh a litel shimering of a light,
For at an hole in shoon the mone bright;
And by that light she saugh hem bothe
 two,
But sikerly she niste who was who, 4300
But as she saugh a whyt thing in hir yë.
And whan she gan the whyte thing espye,
She wende the clerk hadde wered a volu-
 peer.     (383)
And with the staf she drough ay neer and
 neer,     4304
And wende han hit this Aleyn at the fulle,
And smoot the miller on the pyled skulle,
That doun he gooth and cryde, 'harrow!
 I dye!'
Thise clerkes bete him weel and lete him
 lye;
And greythen hem, and toke hir hors anon,
And eek hir mele, and on hir wey they
 gon.     (390) 4310
And at the mille yet they toke hir cake
Of half a busshel flour, ful wel y-bake.
 Thus is the proude miller wel y-bete,
And hath y-lost the grinding of the whete,
And payed for the soper every-deel 4315
Of Aleyn and of John, that bette him weel.
His wyf is swyved, and his doghter als;
Lo, swich it is a miller to be fals!
And therfore this proverbe is seyd ful
 sooth,     4319
'Him thar nat wene wel that yvel dooth;
A gylour shal him-self bigyled be.'     (401)
And God, that sitteth heighe in magestee,
Save al this companye grete and smale!
Thus have I quit the miller in my tale.

Here is ended the Reves tale.

# THE COOK'S PROLOGUE.

### The prologe of the Cokes tale.

THE Cook of London, whyl the Reve spak,
For joye, him thoughte, he clawed him
    on the bak,                    4326
'Ha! ha!' quod he, 'for Cristes passioun,
This miller hadde a sharp conclusioun
Upon his argument of herbergage!
Wel seyde Salomon in his langage,    4330
"Ne bringe nat every man in-to thyn
    hous;"
For herberwing by nighte is perilous.
Wel oghte a man avysed for to be    (9)
Whom that he broghte in-to his privetee.
I pray to god, so yeve me sorwe and care,
If ever, sith I highte Hogge of Ware,    4336
Herde I a miller bettre y-set a-werk.
He hadde a jape of malice in the derk.
But god forbede that we stinten here;
And therfore, if ye vouche-sauf to here
A tale of me, that am a povre man,    4341
I wol yow telle as wel as ever I can
A litel jape that fil in our citee.'

  Our host answerde, and seide, 'I graunte
      it thee;                    (20) 4344

Now telle on, Roger, loke that it be good;
For many a pastee hastow laten blood,
And many a Jakke of Dover hastow sold
That hath been twyes hoot and twyes cold.
Of many a pilgrim hastow Cristes curs,
For of thy persly yet they fare the wors,
That they han eten with thy stubbel-goos;
For in thy shoppe is many a flye loos. (28)
Now telle on, gentil Roger, by thy name.
But yet I pray thee, be nat wrooth for game,
A man may seye ful sooth in game and
    pley.'                        4355
  'Thou seist ful sooth,' quod Roger, 'by
      my fey,
But "sooth pley, quaad pley," as the Flem-
      ing seith;                  (33)
And ther-fore, Herry Bailly, by thy feith,
Be thou nat wrooth, er we departen heer,
Though that my tale be of an hostileer.
But nathelees I wol nat telle it yit,    4361
But er we parte, y-wis, thou shalt be quit.'
And ther-with-al he lough and made chere,
And seyde his tale, as ye shul after here.

### Thus endeth the Prologe of the Cokes tale.

# THE COKES TALE.

### Heer bigynneth the Cokes tale.

A PRENTIS whylom dwelled in our citee,
And of a craft of vitaillers was he;    4366
Gaillard he was as goldfinch in the shawe,
Broun as a berie, a propre short felawe,
With lokkes blake, y-kempt ful fetisly.
Dauncen he coude so wel and jolily,    4370
That he was cleped Perkin Revelour.
He was as ful of love and paramour

As is the hyve ful of hony swete;
Wel was the wenche with him mighte
    mete.                          (10)
At every brydale wolde he singe and
    hoppe,
He loved bet the tavern than the shoppe.    4375
  For whan ther any ryding was in Chepe,
Out of the shoppe thider wolde he lepe.

Til that he hadde al the sighte y-seyn,
And daunced wel, he wolde nat come
ageyn. 4380
And gadered him a meinee of his sort
To hoppe and singe, and maken swich
disport.
And ther they setten steven for to mete
To pleyen at the dys in swich a strete. (20)
For in the toune nas ther no prentys, 4385
That fairer coude caste a paire of dys
Than Perkin coude, and ther-to he was free
Of his dispense, in place of privetee.
That fond his maister wel in his chaffare ;
For often tyme he fond his box ful bare.
For sikerly a prentis revelour, 4391
That haunteth dys, riot, or paramour,
His maister shal it in his shoppe abye,
Al have he no part of the minstralcye ; (30)
For thefte and riot, they ben convertible,
Al conne he pleye on giterne or ribible.
Revel and trouthe, as in a low degree,
They been ful wrothe al day, as men may
see.
   This joly prentis with his maister bood,
Til he were ny out of his prentishood, 4400
Al were he snibbed bothe erly and late,
And somtyme lad with revel to Newgate ;
But atte laste his maister him bithoghte,

Up-on a day, whan he his paper soghte, (40)
Of a proverbe that seith this same word,
' Wel bet is roten appel out of hord 4406
Than that it rotie al the remenaunt.'
So fareth it by a riotous servaunt ;
It is wel lasse harm to lete him pace,
Than he shende alle the servants in the
place. 4410
Therfore his maister yaf him acquitance,
And bad him go with sorwe and with
meschance ;
And thus this joly prentis hadde his
leve.
Now lat him riote al the night or leve. (50)
   And for ther is no theef with-oute a
louke, 4415
That helpeth him to wasten and to souke
Of that he brybe can or borwe may,
Anon he sente his bed and his array
Un-to a compeer of his owne sort,
That lovede dys and revel and disport, 4420
And hadde a wyf that heeld for count-
enance (57)
A shoppe, and swyved for hir sustenance.

\*   \*   \*   \*   \*   \*

**Of this Cokes tale maked Chaucer
na more.**

---

# GROUP B.

# INTRODUCTION TO THE MAN OF LAW'S PROLOGUE.

### The wordes of the Hoost to the companye.

Our Hoste sey wel that the brighte sonne
Th'ark of his artificial day had ronne
The fourthe part, and half an houre, and
more ;
And though he were not depe expert in
lore,
He wiste it was the eightetethe day 5
Of April, that is messager to May ;

And sey wel that the shadwe of every tree
Was as in lengthe the same quantitee
That was the body erect that caused it.
And therfor by the shadwe he took his wit
That Phebus, which that shoon so clere
and brighte, 11
Degrees was fyve and fourty clombe on
highte ;

And for that day, as in that latitude,
It was ten of the clokke, he gan conclude,
And sodeynly he plighte his hors aboute.
  'Lordinges,' quod he, 'I warne yow, al
    this route,        16
The fourthe party of this day is goon ;
Now, for the love of god and of seint
  John,
Leseth no tyme, as ferforth as ye may ;
Lordinges, the tyme wasteth night and
  day,        20
And steleth from us, what prively slepinge,
And what thurgh necligence in our
  wakinge,
As dooth the streem, that turneth never
  agayn,
Descending fro the montaigne in-to playn.
Wel can Senek, and many a philosophre 25
Biwailen tyme, more than gold in cofre.
" For los of catel may recovered be,
But los of tyme shendeth us," quod he.
It wol nat come agayn, with-outen drede,
Na more than wol Malkins maydenhede,
Whan she hath lost it in hir wantownesse ;
Lat us nat moulen thus in ydelnesse.  32
Sir man of lawe,' quod he, 'so have ye
  blis,
Tel us a tale anon, as forward is ;
Ye been submitted thurgh your free
  assent        35
To stonde in this cas at my jugement.
Acquiteth yow, and holdeth your biheste,
Than have ye doon your devoir atte leste.'
  'Hoste,' quod he, '*depardieux* ich as-
  sente,
To breke forward is not myn entente.  40
Biheste is dette, and I wol holde fayn
Al my biheste ; I can no better seyn.
For swich lawe as man yeveth another
  wight,
He sholde him-selven usen it by right ; 44
Thus wol our text ; but natheles certeyn
I can right now no thrifty tale seyn,
†But Chaucer, though he can but lewedly
On metres and on ryming craftily,
Hath seyd hem in swich English as he can
Of olde tyme, as knoweth many a man. 50
And if he have not seyd hem, leve brother,
In o book, he hath seyd hem in another.
For he hath told of loveres up and doun
Mo than Ovyde made of mencioun

In his Epistelles, that been ful olde.  55
What sholde I tellen hem, sin they ben
  tolde ?
In youthe he made of Ceys and Alcion,
And sithen hath he spoke of everichon,
Thise noble wyves and thise loveres eke.
Who-so that wol his large volume seke 60
Cleped the Seintes Legende of Cupyde,
Ther may he seen the large woundes wyde
Of Lucresse, and of Babilan Tisbee ;
The swerd of Dido for the false Enee ;
The tree of Phillis for hir Demophon ; 65
The pleinte of Dianire and Hermion,
Of Adriane and of Isiphilee ;
The bareyne yle stonding in the see ;
The dreynte Leander for his Erro ;
The teres of Eleyne, and eek the wo  70
Of Brixseyde, and of thee, Ladomëa ;
The crueltee of thee, queen Medëa,
Thy litel children hanging by the hals
For thy Jason, that was of love so fals !
O Ypermistra, Penelopee, Alceste,  75
Your wyfhod he comendeth with the beste !
  But certeinly no word ne wryteth he
Of thilke wikke ensample of Canacee,
That lovede hir owne brother sinfully ;
Of swiche cursed stories I sey " fy " ;  80
Or elles of Tyro Apollonius,
How that the cursed king Antiochus
Birafte his doghter of hir maydenhede,
That is so horrible a tale for to rede,
Whan he hir threw up-on the pavement.
And therfor he, of ful avysement,  86
Nolde never wryte in none of his sermouns
Of swiche unkinde abhominaciouns,
Ne I wol noon reherse, if that I may.
  But of **my** tale how shal I doon this day ?
Me were looth be lykned, doutelees,  91
To Muses that men clepe Pierides—
*Metamorphoseos* wot what I mene :—
But nathelees, I recche noght a bene  94
Though I come after him with hawe-bake ;
I speke in prose, and lat him rymes make.'
And with that word he, with a sobre chere,
Bigan his tale, as ye shal after here.

### The Prologe of the Mannes Tale of Lawe.

O hateful harm ! condicion of poverte !
With thurst, with cold, with hunger so
  confounded !        100

To asken help thee shameth in thyn
  herte ;
If thou noon aske, with nede artow so
  wounded,
That verray nede unwrappeth al thy
  wounde hid !
Maugree thyn heed, thou most for indigence           104
Or stele, or begge, or borwe thy despence !

Thou blamest Crist, and seyst ful bitterly,
He misdeparteth richesse temporal ;
Thy neighebour thou wytest sinfully, (10)
And seyst thou hast to lyte, and he hath al.
'Parfay,' seistow, 'somtyme he rekne shal,
Whan that his tayl shal brennen in the
  glede,           111
For he noght helpeth needfulle in hir
  nede.'

Herkne what is the sentence of the
  wyse :—
' Bet is to dyën than have indigence ;'  114
'Thy selve neighebour wol thee despyse ;'

If thou be povre, farwel thy reverence !
Yet of the wyse man tak this sentence :—
'Alle the dayes of povre men ben wikke ;'
Be war therfor, er thou come in that
  prikke !          (21)

'If thou be povre, thy brother hateth
  thee,          120
And alle thy freendes fleen fro thee, alas !'
O riche marchaunts, ful of wele ben ye,
O noble, o prudent folk, as in this cas !
Your bagges been nat filled with *ambes as*,
But with *sis cink*, that renneth for your
  chaunce ;      125
At Cristemasse merie may ye daunce !

Ye seken lond and see for your winninges,
As wyse folk ye knowen al th'estaat  (30)
Of regnes ; ye ben fadres of tydinges
And tales, bothe of pees and of debat. 130
I were right now of tales desolat,
Nere that a marchaunt, goon is many a
  yere,
Me taughte a tale, which that ye shal here.

---

# THE TALE OF THE MAN OF LAWE.

### Here beginneth the Man of Lawe his Tale.

In Surrie whylom dwelte a companye
Of chapmen riche, and therto sadde and
  trewe,        135
That wyde-wher senten her spycerye,
Clothes of gold, and satins riche of hewe ;
Her chaffar was so thrifty and so newe, (40)
That every wight hath deyntee to chaffare
With hem, and eek to sellen hem hir
  ware.        140

Now fel it, that the maistres of that sort
Han shapen hem to Rome for to wende ;
Were it for chapmanhode or for disport,
Non other message wolde they thider
  sende,

But comen hem-self to Rome, this is the
  ende ;        145
And in swich place, as thoughte hem
  avantage
For her entente, they take her herbergage.

Sojourned han thise marchants in that
  toun        (50)
A certein tyme, as fel to hir plesance.
And so bifel, that th'excellent renoun 150
Of th'emperoures doghter, dame Custance,
Reported was, with every circumstance,
Un-to thise Surrien marchants in swich
  wyse,
Fro day to day, as I shal yow devyse.

This was the commune vois of every
    man—                                155
'Our Emperour of Rome, god him see,
A doghter hath that, sin the world bigan,
To rekne as wel hir goodnesse as beautee,
Nas never swich another as is she ;    (61)
I prey to god in honour hir sustene,   160
And wolde she were of al Europe the
    quene.

In hir is heigh beautee, with-oute pryde,
Yowthe, with-oute grenehede or folye ;
To alle hir werkes vertu is hir gyde,
Humblesse hath slayn in hir al tirannye.
She is mirour of alle curteisye ;    (68) 166
Hir herte is verray chambre of holinesse,
Hir hand, ministre of fredom for almesse.'

And al this vois was soth, as god is trewe,
But now to purpos lat us turne agayn; 170
Thise marchants han doon fraught hir
    shippes newe,
And, whan they han this blisful mayden
    seyn,
Hoom to Surrye been they went ful fayn,
And doon her nedes as they han don yore,
And liven in wele; I can sey yow no more.

Now fel it, that thise marchants stode in
    grace                              176
Of him, that was the sowdan of Surrye ;
For whan they came from any strange
    place,                             (80)
He wolde, of his benigne curteisye,
Make hem good chere, and bisily espye 180
Tydings of sondry regnes, for to lere
The wondres that they mighte seen or here.

Amonges othere thinges, specially
Thise marchants han him told of dame
    Custance,
So gret noblesse in ernest, ceriously,  185
That this sowdan hath caught so gret
    plesance
To han hir figure in his remembrance,
That al his lust and al his bisy cure  (90)
Was for to love hir whyl his lyf may dure.

Paraventure in thilke large book     190
Which that men clepe the heven, y-writen
    was

With sterres, whan that he his birthe took,
That he for love shulde han his deeth, allas !
For in the sterres, clerer than is glas,
Is writen, god wot, who-so coude it rede, 195
The deeth of every man, withouten drede.

In sterres, many a winter ther biforn,
Was writen the deeth of Ector, Achilles,
Of Pompey, Julius, er they were born; (101)
The stryf of Thebes ; and of Ercules,  200
Of Sampson, Turnus, and of Socrates
The deeth ; but mennes wittes been so
    dulle,
That no wight can wel rede it atte fulle.

This sowdan for his privee conseil sente,
And, shortly of this mater for to pace, 205
He hath to hem declared his entente,
And seyde hem certein, ' but he mighte
    have grace                        (109)
To han Custance with-inne a litel space,
He nas but deed ;' and charged hem, in
    hye,
To shapen for his lyf som remedye.     210

Diverse men diverse thinges seyden ;
They argumenten, casten up and doun
Many a subtil resoun forth they leyden,
They speken of magik and abusioun ;
But finally, as in conclusioun,        215
They can not seen in that non avantage,
Ne in non other wey, save mariage.   (119)

Than sawe they ther-in swich difficultee
By wey of resoun, for to speke al playn,
By-cause that ther was swich diversitee 220
Bitwene hir bothe lawes, that they sayn,
They trowe ' that no cristen prince wolde
    fayn
Wedden his child under oure lawes swete
That us were taught by Mahoun our
    prophete.'

And he answerde, ' rather than I lese 225
Custance, I wol be cristned doutelees ;
I mot ben hires, I may non other chese.
I prey yow holde your arguments in
    pees ;                             (130)
Saveth my lyf, and beeth noght recchelees
To geten hir that hath my lyf in cure ; 230
For in this wo I may not longe endure.'

What nedeth gretter dilatacioun?
I seye, by tretis and embassadrye,
And by the popes mediacioun,
And al the chirche, and al the chivalrye,
That, in destruccioun of Maumetrye, 236
And in encrees of Cristes lawe dere,
They ben acorded, so as ye shal here ; (140)

How that the sowdan and his baronage
And alle his liges shulde y-cristned be, 240
And he shal han Custance in mariage,
And certein gold, I noot what quantitee,
And her-to founden suffisant seurtee ;
This same acord was sworn on eyther syde ;
Now, faire Custance, almighty god thee
gyde !                                         245

Now wolde som men waiten, as I gesse,
That I shulde tellen al the purveyance
That th'emperour, of his grete noblesse,
Hath shapen for his doghter dame Cus-
tance.                                         (151)
Wel may men knowe that so gret ordin-
ance                                          250
May no man tellen in a litel clause
As was arrayed for so heigh a cause.

Bisshopes ben shapen with hir for to
wende,
Lordes, ladyes, knightes of renoun,
And other folk y-nowe, this is the ende ;
And notified is thurgh-out the toun   256
That every wight, with gret devocioun,
Shulde preyen Crist that he this mariage
Receyve in gree, and spede this viage. (160)

The day is comen of hir departinge,
I sey, the woful day fatal is come,
That ther may be no lenger taryinge,
But forthward they hem dressen, alle and
some ;
Custance, that was with sorwe al over-
come,                                      264
Ful pale arist, and dresseth hir to wende ;
For wel she seeth ther is non other ende.

Allas ! what wonder is it though she wepte,
That shal be sent to strange nacioun (170)
Fro freendes, that so tendrely hir kepte,
And to be bounden under subieccioun 270
Of oon, she knoweth not his condicioun.

Housbondes been alle gode, and han ben
yore,
That knowen wyves, I dar say yow no more.

'Fader,' she sayde, 'thy wrecched child
Custance,
Thy yonge doghter, fostred up so softe, 275
And ye, my moder, my soverayn plesance
Over alle thing, out-taken Crist on-lofte,
Custance, your child, hir recomandeth
ofte                                        (180)
Un-to your grace, for I shal to Surryë,
Ne shal I never seen yow more with yë. 280

Allas ! un-to the Barbre nacioun
I moste anon, sin that it is your wille ;
But Crist, that starf for our redempcioun,
So yeve me grace, his hestes to fulfille ;
I, wrecche womman, no fors though I
spille.                                      285
Wommen are born to thraldom and
penance,
And to ben under mannes governance.'

I trowe at Troye, whan Pirrus brak the
wal                                         (190)
Or Ylion brende, at Thebes the citee, 289
N'at Rome, for the harm thurgh Hanibal
That Romayns hath venquisshed tymes
three,
Nas herd swich tendre weping for pitee
As in the chambre was for hir departinge ;
Bot forth she moot, wher-so she wepe or
singe.

O firste moeving cruel firmament,    295
With thy diurnal sweigh that crowdest ay
And hurlest al from Est til Occident, (199)
That naturelly wolde holde another way,
Thy crowding set the heven in swich array
At the beginning of this fiers viage,   300
That cruel Mars hath slayn this mariage.

Infortunat ascendent tortuous,
Of which the lord is helples falle, allas !
Out of his angle in-to the derkest hous.
O Mars, O Atazir, as in this cas !     305
O feble mone, unhappy been thy pas !
Thou knittest thee ther thou art nat
receyved,
Ther thou were weel, fro thennes artow
weyved.                                     (210)

Imprudent emperour of Rome, allas !  309
Was ther no philosophre in al thy toun ?
Is no tyme bet than other in swich cas ?
Of viage is ther noon eleccioun,
Namely to folk of heigh condicioun,
Nat whan a rote is of a birthe y-knowe ?
Allas !  we ben to lewed or to slowe.  315

To shippe is brought this woful faire mayde
Solempnely, with every circumstance.
'Now Jesu Crist be with yow alle,' she
    sayde ;  (220)
Ther nis namore but ' farewel !  faire
    Custance ! '  319
She peyneth hir to make good countenance,
And forth I lete hir sayle in this manere,
And turne I wol agayn to my matere.

The moder of the sowdan, welle of vyces,
Espyëd hath hir sones pleyn entente,
How he wol lete his olde sacrifyces,  325
And right anon she for hir conseil sente ;
And they ben come, to knowen what she
    mente.
And when assembled was this folk y-fere,
She sette hir doun, and sayde as ye shal
    here.  (231)

'Lordes,' quod she, 'ye knowen everichon,
How that my sone in point is for to lete 331
The holy lawes of our Alkaron,
Yeven by goddes message Makomete.
But oon avow to grete god I hete,  334
The lyf shal rather out of my body sterte
Than Makometes lawe out of myn herte !

What shulde us tyden of this newe lawe
But thraldom to our bodies and penance ?
And afterward in helle to be drawe  (241)
For we reneyed Mahoun our creance ? 340
But, lordes, wol ye maken assurance,
As I shal seyn, assenting to my lore,
And I shall make us sauf for evermore ? '

They sworen and assenten, every man, 344
To live with hir and dye, and by hir stonde ;
And everich, in the beste wyse he can,
To strengthen hir shal alle his freendes
    fonde ;
And she hath this empryse y-take on
    honde,  (250)

Which ye shal heren that I shal devyse,
And to hem alle she spak right in this
    wyse.  350

'We shul first feyne us cristendom to take,
Cold water shal not greve us but a lyte ;
And I shal swich a feste and revel make,
That, as I trowe, I shal the sowdan quyte.
For though his wyf be cristned never so
    whyte,  355
She shal have nede to wasshe awey the
    rede,
Thogh she a font-ful water with hir lede.'

O sowdanesse, rote of iniquitee,  (260)
Virago, thou Semyram the secounde,
O serpent under femininitee,  360
Lyk to the serpent depe in helle y-bounde,
O feyned womman, al that may confounde
Vertu and innocence, thurgh thy malyce,
Is bred in thee, as nest of every vyce !

O Satan, envious sin thilke day  365
That thou were chased from our heritage,
Wel knowestow to wommen the olde way !
Thou madest Eva bringe us in servage. (270)
Thou wolt fordoon this cristen mariage.
Thyn instrument so, weylawey the whyle !
Makestow of wommen, whan thou wolt
    begyle.  371

This sowdanesse, whom I thus blame and
    warie,
Leet prively hir conseil goon hir way.
What sholde I in this tale lenger tarie ?
He rydeth to the sowdan on a day,  375
And seyde him, that she wolde reneye
    hir lay,
And cristendom of preestes handes fonge,
Repenting hir she hethen was so longe,(280)

Biseching him to doon hir that honour,
That she moste han the cristen men to
    feste ;  380
'To plesen hem I wol do my labour.'
The sowdan seith, 'I wol don at your heste,'
And kneling thanketh hir of that requeste.
So glad he was, he niste what to seye ;
She kiste hir sone, and hoom she gooth
    hir weye.  385

**Explicit prima pars.     Sequitur
    pars secunda.**

Arryved ben this Cristen folk to londe,
In Surrie, with a greet solempne route,
And hastily this sowdan sente his sonde,
First to his moder, and al the regne
aboute,                                        (291)
And seyde, his wyf was comen, out of
doute,                                              390
And preyde hir for to ryde agayn the
quene,
The honour of his regne to sustene.

Gret was the prees, and riche was th'array
Of Surriens and Romayns met y-fere;
The moder of the sowdan, riche and gay,
Receyveth hir with al-so glad a chere 396
As any moder mighte hir doghter dere,
And to the nexte citee ther bisyde    (300)
A softe pas solempnely they ryde.

Noght trowe I the triumphe of Julius, 400
Of which that Lucan maketh swich a bost,
Was royaller, ne more curious
Than was th'assemblee of this blisful host.
But this scorpioun, this wikked gost,
The sowdanesse, for al hir flateringe, 405
Caste under this ful mortally to stinge.

The sowdan comth him-self sone after this
So royally, that wonder is to telle,    (310)
And welcometh hir with alle joye and blis.
And thus in merthe and joye I lete hem
dwelle.                                            410
The fruyt of this matere is that I telle.
Whan tyme cam, men thoughte it for the
beste
That revel stinte, and men goon to hir
reste.

The tyme cam, this olde sowdanesse   414
Ordeyned hath this feste of which I tolde,
And to the feste Cristen folk hem dresse
In general, ye! bothe yonge and olde. (319)
Here may men feste and royaltee biholde,
And deyntees mo than I can yow devyse,
But al to dere they boughte it er they ryse.

O sodeyn wo! that ever art successour 421
To worldly blisse, spreynd with bitter-
nesse;
Th' ende of the joye of our worldly labour;
Wo occupieth the fyn of our gladnesse.
Herke this conseil for thy sikernesse, 425

Up-on thy glade day have in thy minde
The unwar wo or harm that comth bihinde.

For shortly for to tellen at o word,  (330)
The sowdan and the Cristen everichone
Ben al to-hewe and stiked at the bord, 430
But it were only dame Custance allone.
This olde sowdanesse, cursed crone,
Hath with hir frendes doon this cursed
dede,
For she hir-self wolde al the contree lede.

Ne ther was Surrien noon that was con-
verted                                              435
That of the conseil of the sowdan woot,
That he nas al to-hewe er he asterted.
And Custance han they take anon, foot-
hoot,                                               (340)
And in a shippe al sterelees, god woot,
They han hir set, and bidde hir lerne
sayle                                                 440
Out of Surrye agaynward to Itayle.

A certein tresor that she thider ladde,
And, sooth to sayn, vitaille gret plentee
They han hir yeven, and clothes eek she
hadde,
And forth she sayleth in the salte see. 445
O my Custance, ful of benignitee,
O emperoures yonge doghter dere,   (349)
He that is lord of fortune be thy stere!

She blesseth hir, and with ful pitous voys
Un-to the croys of Crist thus seyde she,
' O clere, o welful auter,' holy croys,   451
Reed of the lambes blood full of pitee,
That wesh the world fro the olde iniquitee,
Me fro the feend, and fro his clawes kepe,
That day that I shal drenchen in the
depe.                                                455

Victorious tree, proteccioun of trewe,
That only worthy were for to bere   (359)
The king of heven with his woundes newe,
The whyte lamb, that hurt was with the
spere,                                              459
Flemer of feendes out of him and here
On which thy limes feithfully extenden,
Me keep, and yif me might my lyf t'amen-
den.'

Yeres and dayes fleet this creature
Thurghout the see of Grece un-to the
    strayte
Of Marrok, as it was hir aventure ;    465
On many a sory meel now may she bayte ;
After her deeth ful often may she wayte,
Er that the wilde wawes wol hir dryve
Un-to the placë, ther she shal arryve. (371)

Men mighten asken why she was not
    slayn ?    470
Eek at the feste who mighte hir body save?
And I answere to that demaunde agayn,
Who saved Daniel in the horrible cave,
Ther every wight save he, maister and
    knave,    474
Was with the leoun frete er he asterte ?
No wight but god, that he bar in his herte.

God liste to shewe his wonderful miracle
In hir, for we sholde seen his mighty
    werkes ;    (380)
Crist, which that is to every harm triacle,
By certein menes ofte, as knowen clerkes,
Doth thing for certein ende that ful
    derk is    481
To mannes wit, that for our ignorance
Ne conne not knowe his prudent pur-
    veyance.

Now, sith she was not at the feste y-slawe,
Who kepte hir fro the drenching in the
    see ?    485
Who kepte Jonas in the fisshes mawe
Til he was spouted up at Ninivee ?
Wel may men knowe it was no wight
    but he    (390)
That kepte peple Ebraik fro hir drench-
    inge,
With drye feet thurgh-out the see pass-
    inge.    490

Who bad the foure spirits of tempest,
That power han t'anoyen land and see,
'Bothe north and south, and also west
    and est,
Anoyeth neither see, ne land, ne tree ?'
Sothly, the comaundour of that was he,
That fro the tempest ay this womman
    kepte    496
As wel whan [that] she wook as whan she
    slepte.

Wher mighte this womman mete and
    drinke have ?    (400)
Three yeer and more how lasteth hir
    vitaille ?    499
Who fedde the Egipcien Marie in the cave,
Or in desert ? no wight but Crist, sans
    faille.
Fyve thousand folk it was as gret mer-
    vaille
With loves fyve and fisshes two to fede.
God sente his foison at hir grete nede.

She dryveth forth in-to our occean    505
Thurgh-out our wilde see, til, atte laste,
Under an hold that nempnen I ne can,
Fer in Northumberlond the wawe hir
    caste,    (410)
And in the sond hir ship stiked so faste,
That thennes wolde it noght of al a tyde,
The wille of Crist was that she shulde
    abyde.    511

The constable of the castel doun is fare
To seen this wrak, and al the ship he
    soghte,
And fond this wery womman ful of care ;
He fond also the tresor that she broghte.
In hir langage mercy she bisoghte    516
The lyf out of hir body for to twinne, (419)
Hir to delivere of wo that she was inne.

A maner Latin corrupt was hir speche,
But algates ther-by was she understonde;
The constable, whan him list no lenger
    seche,    521
This woful womman broghte he to the
    londe ;
She kneleth doun, and thanketh goddes
    sonde.
But what she was, she wolde no man seye,
For foul ne fair, thogh that she shulde
    deye.    525

She seyde, she was so mased in the see
That she forgat hir minde, by hir trouthe;
The constable hath of hir so greet pitee,
And eek his wyf, that they wepen for
    routhe,    (431) 529
She was so diligent, with-outen slouthe,
To serve and plesen everich in that place,
That alle hir loven that loken on hir face.

This constable and dame Hermengild his
   wyf
Were payens, and that contree every-
   where ;
But Hermengild lovede hir right as hir
   lyf,   535
And Custance hath so longe sojourned
   there,
In orisons, with many a bitter tere,
Til Jesu hath converted thurgh his grace
Dame Hermengild, constablesse of that
   place.   (441) 539

In al that lond no Cristen durste route,
Alle Cristen folk ben fled fro that contree
Thurgh payens, that conquereden al
   aboute
The plages of the North, by land and see ;
To Walis fled the Cristianitee
Of olde Britons, dwellinge in this yle ; 545
Ther was hir refut for the mene whyle.

But yet nere Cristen Britons so exyled (449)
That ther nere somme that in hir privetee
Honoured Crist, and hethen folk bigyled ;
And ny the castel swiche ther dwelten
   three.   550
That oon of hem was blind, and mighte
   nat see
But it were with thilke yën of his minde,
With whiche men seen, after that they
   ben blinde.

Bright was the sonne as in that someres
   day,   554
For which the constable and his wyf also
And Custance han y-take the righte way
Toward the see, a furlong wey or two,
To pleyen and to romen to and fro ; (460)
And in hir walk this blinde man they
   mette   559
Croked and old, with yën faste y-shette.

'In name of Crist,' cryde this blinde
   Britoun,
'Dame Hermengild, yif me my sighte
   agayn.'
This lady wex affrayed of the soun,
Lest that hir housbond, shortly for to
   sayn,
Wolde hir for Jesu Cristes love han slayn,

Til Custance made hir bold, and bad hir
   werche   566
The wil of Crist, as doghter of his chirche.

The constable wex abasshed of that sight,
And seyde, ' what amounteth al this fare ?'
Custance answerde, 'sire, it is Cristes
   might,   (472) 570
That helpeth folk out of the feendes snare.'
And so ferforth she gan our lay declare,
That she the constable, er that it were eve,
Converted, and on Crist made him bileve.

This constable was no-thing lord of this
   place   (477) 575
Of which I speke, ther he Custance fond,
But kepte it strongly, many wintres space,
Under Alla, king of al Northumberlond,
That was ful wys, and worthy of his hond
Agayn the Scottes, as men may wel here,
But turne I wol agayn to my matere. 581

Sathan, that ever us waiteth to bigyle,
Saugh of Custance al hir perfeccioun,
And caste anon how he mighte qnyte hir
   whyle,
And made a yong knight, that dwelte in
   that toun,   585
Love hir so hote, of foul affeccioun,
That verraily him thoughte he shulde
   spille   (489)
But he of hir mighte ones have his wille.

He woweth hir, but it availleth noght,
She wolde do no sinne, by no weye ; 590
And, for despyt, he compassed in his
   thoght
To maken hir on shamful deth to deye.
He wayteth whan the constable was aweye,
And prively, up-on a night, he crepte 594
In Hermengildes chambre whyl she slepte.

Wery, for-waked in her orisouns,
Slepeth Custance, and Hermengild also.
This knight, thurgh Sathanas tempta-
   ciouns,   (500)
Al softely is to the bed y-go,
And kitte the throte of Hermengild a-two,
And leyde the blody knyf by dame
   Custance,   601
And wente his wey, ther god yeve him
   meschance !

Sone after comth this constable hoom
    agayn,
And eek Alla, that king was of that lond,
And saugh his wyf despitously y-slayn, 605
For which ful ofte he weep and wrong his
    hond,
And in the bed the blody knyf he fond
By dame Custance ; allas ! what mighte
    she seye ?    (510)
For verray wo hir wit was al aweye.

To king Alla was told al this meschance,
And eek the tyme, and where, and in
    what wyse    611
That in a ship was founden dame Custance,
As heer-biforn that ye han herd devyse.
The kinges herte of pitee gan agryse,
Whan he saugh so benigne a creature 615
Falle in disese and in misaventure.

For as the lomb toward his deeth is broght,
So stant this innocent bifore the king ;
This false knight that hath this tresoun
    wroght    (521)
Berth hir on hond that she hath doon
    this thing.    620
†But nathelees, ther was [ful] greet
    moorning
Among the peple, and seyn, ' they can not
    gesse
That she hath doon so greet a wikked-
    nesse.    623

For they han seyn hir ever so vertuous,
And loving Hermengild right as her lyf.'
Of this bar witnesse everich in that hous
Save he that Hermengild slow with his
    knyf.
This gentil king hath caught a gret motyf
Of this witnesse, and thoghte he wolde
    enquere    (531)
Depper in this, a trouthe for to lere.   630

Allas ! Custance ! thou hast no champioun,
Ne fighte canstow nought, so weylawey !
But he, that starf for our redempcioun
And bond Sathan (and yit lyth ther he
    lay)
So be thy stronge champioun this day ! 635
For, but-if Crist open miracle kythe,
Withouten gilt thou shalt be slayn as
    swythe.

She sette her doun on knees, and thus
    she sayde,    (540)
' Immortal god, that savedest Susanne
Fro false blame, and thou, merciful
    mayde,    640
Mary I mene, doghter to Seint Anne,
Bifore whos child aungeles singe Osanne,
If I be giltlees of this felonye,
My socour be, for elles I shal dye ! '   644

Have ye nat seyn som tyme a pale face,
Among a prees, of him that hath be lad
Toward his deeth, wher-as him gat no
    grace,
And swich a colour in his face hath had,
Men mighte knowe his face, that was
    bistad,    (551)
Amonges alle the faces in that route : 650
So stant Custance, and loketh hir aboute.

O quenes, livinge in prosperitee,
Duchesses, and ye ladies everichone,
Haveth som routhe on hir adversitee ;
An emperoures doghter stant allone ; 655
She hath no wight to whom to make hir
    mone.
O blood royal, that stondest in this drede,
Fer ben thy freendes at thy grete nede !

This Alla king hath swich compassioun,
As gentil herte is fulfild of pitee, (562) 660
That from his yën ran the water doun.
' Now hastily do fecche a book,' quod he,
' And if this knight wol sweren how that
    she
This womman slow, yet wole we us avyse
Whom that we wole that shal ben our
    justyse.'    665

A Briton book, writen with Evangyles,
Was fet, and on this book he swoor anoon
She giltyy was, and in the mene whyles
A hand him smoot upon the nekke-boon,
That doun he fil atones as a stoon, (572) 670
And bothe his yën broste out of his face
In sight of every body in that place.

A vois was herd in general audience,
And seyde, ' thou hast desclaundred
    giltelees
The doghter of holy chirche in hey
    presence ;    675

Thus hastou doon, and yet holde I my
 pees.'
Of this mervaille agast was al the prees ;
As mased folk they stoden everichone, (580)
For drede of wreche, save Custance allone.

Greet was the drede and eek the repent-
 ance      680
Of hem that hadden wrong suspeccioun
Upon this sely innocent Custance ;
And, for this miracle, in conclusioun,
And by Custances mediacioun,
The king, and many another in that
 place,      685
Converted was, thanked be Cristes grace!

This false knight was slayn for his un-
 trouthe
By jugement of Alla hastifly ; (590)
And yet Custance hadde of his deeth gret
 routhe.
And after this Jesus, of his mercy, 690
Made Alla wedden ful solempnely
This holy mayden, that is so bright and
 shene,
And thus hath Crist y-maad Custance
 a quene.

But who was woful, if I shal nat lye,
Of this wedding but Donegild, and na mo,
The kinges moder, ful of tirannye? 696
Hir thoughte hir cursed herte brast a-two ;
She wolde noght hir sone had do so ; (600)
Hir thoughte a despit, that he sholde take
So strange a creature un-to his make. 700

Me list nat of the chaf nor of the stree
Maken so long a tale, as of the corn.
What sholde I tellen of the royaltee
At mariage, or which cours gooth biforn,
Who bloweth in a trompe or in an horn ?
The fruit of every tale is for to seye ; 706
They ete, and drinke, and daunce, and
 singe, and pleye.

They goon to bedde, as it was skile and
 right ;      (610)
For, thogh that wyves been ful holy
 thinges,
They moste take in pacience at night 710
Swich maner necessaries as been plesinges
To folk that han y-wedded hem with
 ringes,

And leye a lyte hir holinesse asyde
As for the tyme ; it may no bet bityde.

On hir he gat a knave-child anoon, 715
And to a bishop and his constable eke
He took his wyf to kepe, whan he is goon
To Scotland-ward, his fo-men for to seke ;
Now faire Custance, that is so humble
 and meke,     (621)
So longe is goon with childe, til that stille
She halt hir chambre, abyding Cristes
 wille.      721

The tyme is come, a knave-child she ber ;
Mauricius at the font-stoon they him calle ;
This constable dooth forth come a mes-
 sager,
And wroot un-to his king, that cleped
 was Alle,     725
How that this blisful tyding is bifalle,
And othere tydings speedful for to seye ;
He tak'th the lettre, and forth he gooth
 his weye.     (630)

This messager, to doon his avantage, 729
Un-to the kinges moder rydeth swythe,
And salueth hir ful faire in his langage,
' Madame,' quod he, ' ye may be glad and
 blythe,
And thanke god an hundred thousand
 sythe ;
My lady quene hath child, with-outen
 doute,     734
To joye and blisse of al this regne aboute.

Lo, heer the lettres seled of this thing,
That I mot bere with al the haste I may ;
If ye wol aught un-to your sone the king,
I am your servant, bothe night and day.'
Donegild answerde, ' as now at this tyme,
 nay ;     (642) 740
But heer al night I wol thou take thy
 reste,
Tomorwe wol I seye thee what me leste.'

This messager drank sadly ale and wyn,
And stolen were his lettres prively
Out of his box, whyl he sleep as a swyn :
And countrefeted was ful subtilly 746
Another lettre, wroght ful sinfully,
Un-to the king direct of this matere (650)
Fro his constable, as ye shul after here.

The lettre spak, 'the queen delivered was
Of so horrible a feendly creature,    751
That in the castel noon so hardy was
That any whyle dorste ther endure.
The moder was an elf, by aventure
Y-come, by charmes or by sorcerye,    755
And every wight hateth hir companye.'

Wo was this king whan he this lettre
      had seyn,    (659)
But to no wighte he tolde his sorwes sore,
But of his owene honde he wroot ageyn,
'Welcome the sonde of Crist for evermore
To me, that am now lerned in his lore; 761
Lord, welcome be thy lust and thy
      plesaunce,
My lust I putte al in thyn ordinaunce!

Kepeth this child, al be it foul or fair,
And eek my wyf, un-to myn hoom-
      cominge;    765
Crist, whan him list, may sende me an
      heir
More agreable than this to my lykinge.'
This lettre he seleth, prively wepinge, (670)
Which to the messager was take sone,
And forth he gooth; ther is na more to
      done.    770

O messager, fulfild of dronkenesse,
Strong is thy breeth, thy limes faltren ay,
And thou biwreyest alle secreenesse.
Thy mind is lorn, thou janglest as a jay,
Thy face is turned in a newe array!    775
Ther dronkenesse regneth in any route,
Ther is no conseil hid, with-outen doute.

O Donegild, I ne have noon English digne
Un-to thy malice and thy tirannye!    (681)
And therfor to the feend I thee resigne,
Let him endyten of thy traitorye!    781
Fy, mannish, fy! o nay, by god, I lye,
Fy, *feendly* spirit, for I dar wel telle,
Though thou heer walke, thy spirit is in
      helle!    784

This messager comth fro the king agayn,
And at the kinges modres court he lighte,
And she was of this messager ful fayn,
And plesed him in al that ever she
      mighte.    (690)
He drank, and wel his girdel under-
      pighte.

He slepeth, and he snoreth in his gyse 790
Al night, †un-til the sonne gan aryse.

Eft were his lettres stolen everichon
And countrefeted lettres in this wyse;
'The king comandeth his constable anon,
Up peyne of hanging, and on heigh juÿse,
That he ne sholde suffren in no wyse  796
Custance in-with his regne for t'abyde
Thre dayes and a quarter of a tyde; (700)

But in the same ship as he hir fond,
Hir and hir yonge sone, and al hir gere,
He sholde putte, and croude hir fro the
      lond,    801
And charge hir that she never eft come
      there.'
O my Custance, wel may thy goost have
      fere
And sleping in thy dreem been in penance,
When Donegild caste al this ordinance!

This messager on morwe, whan he wook,
Un-to the castel halt the nexte wey, (709)
And to the constable he the lettre took;
And whan that he this pitous lettre sey,
Ful ofte he seyde 'allas!' and 'wey-
      lawey!'    810
'Lord Crist,' quod he, 'how may this
      world endure?
So ful of sinne is many a creature!

O mighty god, if that it be thy wille,
Sith thou art rightful juge, how may it be
That thou wolt suffren innocents to spille,
And wikked folk regne in prosperitee? 816
O good Custance, allas! so wo is me
That I moot be thy tormentour, or deye
On shames deeth; ther is noon other
      weye!'    (721)

Wepen bothe yonge and olde in al that
      place,    820
Whan that the king this cursed lettre
      sente,
And Custance, with a deedly pale face,
The ferthe day toward hir ship she wente.
But natheles she taketh in good entente
The wille of Crist, and, kneling on the
      stronde,    825
She seyde, 'lord! ay wel-com be thy
      sonde!

He that me kepte fro the false blame
Whyl I was on the londe amonges yow,
He can me kepe from harme and eek fro
  shame          (731)
In salte see, al-thogh I see nat how.   830
As strong as ever he was, he is yet now.
In him triste I, and in his moder dere,
That is to me my seyl and eek my stere.'

Hir litel child lay weping in hir arm, 834
And kneling, pitously to him she seyde,
'Pees, litel sone, I wol do thee non
  harm.'
With that hir kerchef of hir heed she
  breyde,
And over his litel yën she it leyde ;  (740)
And in hir arm she lulleth it ful faste,
And in-to heven hir yën up she caste. 840

'Moder,' quod she, 'and mayde bright,
  Marye,
Sooth is that thurgh wommannes egge-
  ment
Mankind was lorn and damned ay to dye,
For which thy child was on a croys y-
  rent ;
Thy blisful yën sawe al his torment ; 845
Than is ther no comparisoun bitwene
Thy wo and any wo man may sustene.

Thou sawe thy child y-slayn bifor thyn
  yën,         (750)
And yet now liveth my litel child, parfay !
Now, lady bright, to whom alle woful
  cryën,         850
Thou glorie of wommanhede, thou faire
  may,
Thou haven of refut, brighte sterre of day,
Rewe on my child, that of thy gentillesse
Rewest on every rewful in distresse !

O litel child, allas ! what is thy gilt,  855
That never wroughtest sinne as yet,
  pardee,
Why wil thyn harde fader han thee spilt?
O mercy, dere constable !' quod she ; (760)
'As lat my litel child dwelle heer with
  thee ;
And if thou darst not saven him, for
  blame,        860
So kis him ones in his fadres name !'

Ther-with she loketh bakward to the
  londe,
And seyde, 'far-wel, housbond routhelees !'
And up she rist, and walketh doun the
  stronde
Toward the ship ; hir folweth al the prees,
And ever she preyeth hir child to holde
  his pees ;        866
And taketh hir leve, and with an holy
  entente
She blesseth hir ; and in-to ship she
  wente.        (770)

Vitailled was the ship, it is no drede,
Habundantly for hir, ful longe space, 870
And other necessaries that sholde nede
She hadde y-nogh, heried be goddes grace!
For wind and weder almighty god pur-
  chace,
And bringe hir hoom ! I can no bettre
  seye ;        874
But in the see she dryveth forth hir weye.

Explicit secunda pars.
Sequitur pars tercia.

Alla the king comth hoom, sone after this,
Unto his castel of the which I tolde, (779)
And axeth wher his wyf and his child is.
The constable gan aboute his herte colde,
And pleynly al the maner he him tolde 880
As ye han herd, I can telle it no bettre,
And sheweth the king his seel and [eek]
  his lettre,

And seyde, 'lord, as ye comaunded me
Up peyne of deeth, so have I doon, certein.'
This messager tormented was til he  885
Moste biknowe and tellen, plat and plein,
Fro night to night, in what place he had
  leyn.
And thus, by wit and subtil enqueringe,
Ymagined was by whom this harm gan
  springe.        (791)

The hand was knowe that the lettre wroot,
And al the venim of this cursed dede, 891
But in what wyse, certeinly I noot.
Th'effect is this, that Alla, out of drede,
His moder slow, that men may pleinly
  rede,

For that she traitour was to hir ligeaunce.
Thus endeth olde Donegild with meschaunce.                                    896

The sorwe that this Alla, night and day,
Maketh for his wyf and for his child also,
Ther is no tonge that it telle may.    (801)
But now wol I un-to Custance go,       900
That fleteth in the see, in peyne and wo,
Fyve yeer and more, as lyked Cristes
sonde,
Er that hir ship approched un-to londe.

Under an hethen castel, atte laste,
Of which the name in my text noght
I finde,                               905
Custance and eek hir child the see up-
caste.
Almighty god, that saveth al mankinde,
Have on Custance and on hir child som
minde,                                (810)
That fallen is in hethen land eft-sone, 909
In point to spille, as I shal telle yow sone.

Doun from the castel comth ther many
a wight
To gauren on this ship and on Custance.
But shortly, from the castel, on a night,
The lordes styward—god yeve him mes-
chaunce !—                            914
A theef, that had reneyed our creaunce,
Com in-to ship allone, and seyde he sholde
Hir lemman be, wher-so she wolde or
nolde.                                (819)

Wo was this wrecched womman tho bigon,
Hir child cryde, and she cryde pitously ;
But blisful Marie heelp hir right anon ;
For with hir strugling wel and mightily
The theef fil over bord al sodeinly,   922
And in the see he dreynte for vengeance ;
And thus hath Crist unwemmed kept
Custance.

**Auctor.**

O foule lust of luxurie ! lo, thyn ende !
Nat only that thou feyntest mannes
minde,                                926
But verraily thou wolt his body shende ;
Th'ende of thy werk or of thy lustes
blinde                                (830)
Is compleyning, how many-oon may men
finde

That noght for werk som-tyme, but for
th'entente                            930
To doon this sinne, ben outher sleyn or
shente !

How may this wayke womman han this
strengthe
Hir to defende agayn this renegat ?
O Golias, unmesurable of lengthe,
How mighte David make thee so mat, 935
So yong and of armure so desolat ?
How dorste he loke up-on thy dredful face?
Wel may men seen, it nas but goddes
grace !                               (840)

Who yaf Judith corage or hardinesse
To sleen him, Olofernus, in his tente, 940
And to deliveren out of wrecchednesse
The peple of god ? I seye, for this entente,
That, right as god spirit of vigour sente
To him, and saved hem out of meschance,
So sente he might and vigour to Custance.

Forth goth hir ship thurgh-out the narwe
mouth                                946
Of Jubaltar and Septe, dryving ay,
Som-tyme West, som-tyme North and
South,                                (850)
And som-tyme Est, ful many a wery
day,
Til Cristes moder (blessed be she ay !) 950
Hath shapen, thurgh hir endelees good-
nesse,
To make an ende of al hir hevinesse.

Now lat us stinte of Custance but a throwe,
And speke we of the Romain Emperour,
That out of Surrie hath by lettres knowe
The slaughtre of Cristen folk, and dis-
honour                               956
Don to his doghter by a fals traitour,
I mene the cursed wikked sowdanesse,
That at the feste leet sleen both more and
lesse.                                (861)

For which this emperour hath sent anoon
His senatour, with royal ordinance,   961
And othere lordes, got wot, many oon,
On Surriens to taken heigh vengeance.
They brennen, sleen, and bringe hem to
meschance

Ful many a day; but shortly, this is
  the ende,                                965
Homward to Rome they shapen hem to
  wende.

This senatour repaireth with victorie
To Rome-ward, sayling ful royally,  (870)
And mette the ship dryving, as seith the
  storie,
In which Custance sit ful pitously.    970
No-thing ne knew he what she was, ne
  why
She was in swich array; ne she nil seye
Of hir estaat, althogh she sholde deye.

He bringeth hir to Rome, and to his wyf
He yaf hir, and hir yonge sone also;  975
And with the senatour she ladde her lyf.
Thus can our lady bringen out of wo (879)
Woful Custance, and many another mo.
And longe tyme dwelled she in that place,
In holy werkes ever, as was hir grace. 980

The senatoures wyf hir aunte was,
But for al that she knew hir never the
  more;
I wol no lenger tarien in this cas,
But to king Alla, which I spak of yore,
That for his wyf wepeth and syketh
  sore,                                  985
I wol retourne, and lete I wol Custance
Under the senatoures governance.

King Alla, which that hadde his moder
  slayn,                                (890)
Upon a day fil in swich repentance,
That, if I shortly tellen shal and plain, 990
To Rome he comth, to receyven his
  penance;
And putte him in the popes ordinance
In heigh and low, and Jesu Crist bisoghte
Foryeve his wikked werkes that he
  wroghte.                               994

The fame anon thurgh Rome toun is born,
How Alla king shal come in pilgrimage,
By herbergeours that wenten him biforn;
For which the senatour, as was usage, (900)
Rood him ageyn, and many of his linage,
As wel to shewen his heighe magnificence
As to don any king a reverence.        1001

Greet chere dooth this noble senatour
To king Alla, and he to him also;
Everich of hem doth other greet honour;
And so bifel that, in a day or two,   1005
This senatour is to king Alla go
To feste, and shortly, if I shal nat lye,
Custances sone wente in his companye.

Som men wolde seyn, at requeste of
  Custance,                             (911)
This senatour hath lad this child to feste;
I may nat tellen every circumstance, 1011
Be as be may, ther was he at the leste.
But soth is this, that, at his modres heste,
Biforn Alla, during the metes space,
The child stood, loking in the kinges face.

This Alla king hath of this child greet
  wonder,                               1016
And to the senatour he seyde anon,
'Whos is that faire child that stondeth
  yonder?'                              (920)
'I noot,' quod he, 'by god, and by seint
  John!                                 1019
A moder he hath, but fader hath he non
That I of woot'—but shortly, in a stounde,
He tolde Alla how that this child was
  founde.

'But god wot,' quod this senatour also,
'So vertuous a livere in my lyf,      1024
Ne saugh I never as she, ne herde of mo
Of worldly wommen, mayden, nor of wyf;
I dar wel seyn hir hadde lever a knyf
Thurgh-out her breste, than been a wom-
  man wikke;                            (930)
Ther is no man coude bringe hir to that
  prikke.'

Now was this child as lyk un-to Custance
As possible is a creature to be.      1031
This Alla hath the face in remembrance
Of dame Custance, and ther-on mused he
If that the childes moder were aught she
That was his wyf, and prively he sighte,
And spedde him fro the table that he
  mighte.                               1036

'Parfay,' thoghte he, 'fantome is in myn
  heed!
I oghte deme, of skilful jugement,  (940)

That in the salte see my wyf is deed.'
And afterward he made his argument—
'What woot I, if that Crist have hider
   y-sent                                        1041
My wyf by see, as wel as he hir sente
To my contree fro thennes that she
   wente?'

And, after noon, hoom with the senatour
Goth Alla, for to seen this wonder chaunce.
This senatour dooth Alla greet honour,
And hastifly he sente after Custaunce.
But trusteth weel, hir liste nat to daunce
Whan that she wiste wherefor was that
   sonde.                                (951) 1049
Unnethe up-on hir feet she mighte stonde.

When Alla saugh his wyf, faire he hir
   grette,
And weep, that it was routhe for to see.
For at the firste look he on hir sette
He knew wel verraily that it was she.
And she for sorwe as domb stant as a tree;
So was hir herte shet in hir distresse  1056
Whan she remembred his unkindenesse.

Twyës she swowned in his owne sighte;
He weep, and him excuseth pitously:—
'Now god,' quod he, 'and alle his halwes
   brighte                                (962) 1060
So wisly on my soule as have mercy,
That of your harm as giltelees am I
As is Maurice my sone so lyk your face;
Elles the feend me fecche out of this place!'

Long was the sobbing and the bitter peyne
Er that hir woful hertes mighte cesse;
Greet was the pitee for to here hem pleyne,
Thurgh whiche pleintes gan hir wo en-
   cresse.                                        (970)
I prey yow al my labour to relesse;
I may nat telle hir wo un-til tomorwe, 1070
I am so wery for to speke of sorwe.

But fynally, when that the sooth is wist
That Alla giltelees was of hir wo,
I trowe an hundred tymes been they kist,
And swich a blisse is ther bitwix hem two
That, save the joye that lasteth evermo,
Ther is non lyk, that any creature    1077
Hath seyn or shal, whyl that the world
   may dure.                                    (980)

Tho preyde she hir housbond mekely,
In relief of hir longe pitous pyne,  1080
That he wold preye hir fader specially
That, of his magestee, he wolde enclyne
To vouche-sauf som day with him to dyne;
She preyde him eek, he sholde by no weye
Un-to hir fader no word of hir seye. 1085

Som men wold seyn, how that the child
   Maurice
Doth this message un-to this emperour;
But, as I gesse, Alla was nat so nyce (990)
To him, that was of so sovereyn honour
As he that is of Cristen folk the flour, 1090
Sente any child, but it is bet to deme
He wente him-self, and so it may wel seme.

This emperour hath graunted gentilly
To come to diner, as he him bisoghte;
And wel rede I, he loked bisily    1095
Up-on this child, and on his doghter
   thoghte.
Alla goth to his in, and, as him oghte,
Arrayed for this feste in every wyse (1000)
As ferforth as his conning may suffyse.

The morwe cam, and Alla gan him dresse,
And eek his wyf, this emperour to mete;
And forth they ryde in joye and in glad-
   nesse.                                        1102
And whan she saugh hir fader in the strete,
She lighte doun, and falleth him to fete.
'Fader,' quod she, 'your yonge child
   Custance                                    1105
Is now ful clene out of your remembrance.

I am your doghter Cústancë,' quod she,
'That whylom ye han sent un-to Surrye.
It am I, fader, that in the salte see (1011)
Was put allone and dampned for to dye.
Now, gode fader, mercy I yow crye,  1111
Send me namore un-to non hethenesse,
But thonketh my lord heer of his kinde-
   nesse.'

Who can the pitous joye tellen al
Bitwix hem three, sin they ben thus
   y-mette?                                    1115
But of my tale make an ende I shal;
The day goth faste, I wol no lenger lette.
This glade folk to diner they hem sette;

In joye and blisse at mete I lete hem
    dwelle        (1021) 1119
A thousand fold wel more than I can telle.

This child Maurice was sithen emperour
Maad by the pope, and lived Cristenly.
To Cristes chirche he dide greet honour;
But I lete al his storie passen by,
Of Custance is my tale specially.    1125
In olde Romayn gestes may men finde
Maurices lyf; I bere it noght in minde.

This king Alla, whan he his tyme sey, (1030)
With his Custance, his holy wyf so swete,
To Engelond been they come the righte
    wey,        1130
Wher-as they live in joye and in quiete.
But litel whyl it lasteth, I yow hete,
Joye of this world, for tyme wol nat
    abyde;
Fro day to night it changeth as the tyde.

Who lived ever in swich delyt o day 1135
That him ne moeved outher conscience,
Or ire, or talent, or som kin affray, (1039)
Envye, or pryde, or passion, or offence?
I ne seye but for this ende this sentence,
That litel whyl in joye or in plesance 1140
Lasteth the blisse of Alla with Custance.

For deeth, that taketh of heigh and low
    his rente,
When passed was a yeer, even as I gesse,
Out of this world this king Alla he hente,
For whom Custance hath ful gret hevi-
    nesse.        1145
Now lat us preyen god his soule blesse!
And dame Custance, fynally to seye,
Towards the toun of Rome gooth hir weye.

To Rome is come this holy creature, (1051)
And fyndeth ther hir frendes hole and
    sounde:        1150
Now is she scaped al hir aventure;
And whan that she hir fader hath y-founde,
Doun on hir kneës falleth she to grounde;
Weping for tendrenesse in herte blythe,
She herieth god an hundred thousand
    sythe.        1155

In vertu and in holy almes-dede   (1058)
They liven alle, and never a-sonder wende;
Til deeth departed hem, this lyf they lede.
And fareth now weel, my tale is at an ende.
Now Jesu Crist, that of his might may
    sende        1160
Joye after wo, governe us in his grace,
And kepe us alle that ben in this place!
    Amen.

Here endeth the Tale of the Man of Lawe; and next folweth the
Shipmannes Prolog.

\*\*\* For l. 5583 in Tyrwhitt's Text, see Group D, l. 1.

# THE SHIPMAN'S PROLOGUE.

Here biginneth the Shipmannes Prolog.

\*\*\* *In* Tyrwhitt's text, *ll.* 12903-12924.

Our hoste up-on his stiropes stood
anon,
And seyde, 'good men, herkneth everich
on ;
This was a thrifty tale for the nones ! 1165
Sir parish prest,' quod he, 'for goddes
bones,
Tel us a tale, as was thy forward yore.
I see wel that ye lerned men in lore
Can moche good, by goddes dignitee !'
The Persone him answerde, '*ben'cite*! 1170
What eyleth the man, so sinfully to
swere?'
Our hoste answerde, 'O Jankin, be ye
there ?                               (10)
I smelle a loller in the wind,' quod he.
'How ! good men,' quod our hoste, 'herk-
neth me ;

Abydeth, for goddes digne passioun, 1175
For we shal han a predicacioun ;
This loller heer wil prechen us som-what.'
    'Nay, by my fader soule ! that shal be
    nat,'
Seyde the Shipman ; 'heer he shal nat
    preche,
He shal no gospel glosen heer ne teche. 1180
We leve alle in the grete god,' quod he,
' He wolde sowen som difficultee,      (20)
Or springen cokkel in our clene corn ;
And therfor, hoste, I warne thee biforn,
My joly body shal a tale telle,       1185
And I shal clinken yow so mery a belle,
That I shal waken al this companye ;
But it shal nat ben of philosophye,
Ne †*physices*, ne termes queinte of lawe ;
Ther is but litel Latin in my mawe.' 1190

Here endeth the Shipman his Prolog.

---

# THE SHIPMANNES TALE.

Here biginneth the Shipmannes Tale.

A Marchant whylom dwelled at Seint
Denys,
That riche was, for which men helde him
wys ;
A wyf he hadde of excellent beautee,
And compaignable and revelous was she,
Which is a thing that causeth more
dispence                               1195
Than worth is al the chere and reverence
That men hem doon at festes and at
daunces ;
Swiche salutaciouns and contenaunces
Passen as dooth a shadwe up-on the wal.

But wo is him that payen moot for al ; 1200
The sely housbond, algate he mot paye ;
He moot us clothe, and he moot us
arraye,                               (12)
Al for his owene worship richely,
In which array we daunce jolily.      1204
And if that he noght may, par-aventure,
Or elles, list no swich dispence endure,
But thinketh it is wasted and y-lost,
Than moot another payen for our cost,
Or lene us gold, and that is perilous.
    This noble Marchant heeld a worthy
    hous,                            (20) 1210

For which he hadde alday so greet repair
For his largesse, and for his wyf was fair,
That wonder is ; but herkneth to my tale.
Amonges alle his gestes, grete and smale,
Ther was a monk, a fair man and a bold,
I trowe of thritty winter he was old, 1216
That ever in oon was drawing to that place.
This yonge monk, that was so fair of face,
Aqueinted was so with the gode man,
Sith that hir firste knoweliche bigan, 1220
That in his hous as famulier was he   (31)
As it possible is any freend to be.

  And for as muchel as this gode man
And eek this monk, of which that I bigan,
Were bothe two y-born in o village, 1225
The monk him claimeth as for cosinage ;
And he again, he seith nat ones nay,
But was as glad ther-of as fowel of day ;
For to his herte it was a greet plesaunce.
Thus been they knit with eterne alliaunce,
And ech of hem gan other for t'assure 1231
Of bretherhede, whyl that hir lyf may
  dure.   (42)
  Free was daun John, and namely of
  dispence,
As in that hous ; and ful of diligence 1234
To doon plesaunce, and also greet costage.
He noght forgat to yeve the leeste page
In al that hous ; but, after hir degree,
He yaf the lord, and sitthe al his meynee,
When that he cam, som maner honest
  thing ;   1239
For which they were as glad of his coming
As fowel is fayn, whan that the sonne
  up-ryseth.   (51)
Na more of this as now, for it suffyseth.

  But so bifel, this marchant on a day
Shoop him to make redy his array
Toward the toun of Brugges for to fare, 1245
To byen ther a porcioun of ware ;
For which he hath to Paris sent anon
A messager, and preyed hath daun John
That he sholde come to Seint Denys to
  pleye   1249
With him and with his wyf a day or tweye,
Er he to Brugges wente, in alle wyse.   (61)
  This noble monk, of which I yow devyse,
Hath of his abbot, as him list, licence,
By-cause he was a man of heigh prudence,
And eek an officer, out for to ryde, 1255
To seen hir graunges and hir bernes wyde ;

And un-to Seint Denys he comth anon.
Who was so welcome as my lord daun
  John,
Our dere cosin, ful of curteisye ?   1259
With him broghte he a jubbe of Malvesye,
And eek another, ful of fyn Vernage, (71)
And volatyl, as ay was his usage.
And thus I lete hem ete and drinke and
  pleye,
This marchant and this monk, a day or
  tweye.

  The thridde day, this marchant up
  aryseth,   1265
And on his nedes sadly him avyseth,
And up in-to his countour-hous goth he
To rekene with him-self, as wel may be,
Of thilke yeer, how that it with him stood,
And how that he despended hadde his
  good ;   1270
And if that he encressed were or noon. (81)
His bokes and his bagges many oon
He leith biforn him on his counting-bord ;
Ful riche was his tresor and his hord,
For which ful faste his countour-dore he
  shette ;   1275
And eek he nolde that no man sholde him
  lette
Of his accountes, for the mene tyme ;
And thus he sit til it was passed pryme.

  Daun John was risen in the morwe also,
And in the gardin walketh to and fro, 1280
And hath his thinges seyd ful curteisly.
  This gode wyf cam walking prively (92)
In-to the gardin, ther he walketh softe,
And him saleweth, as she hath don ofte.
A mayde child cam in hir companye, 1285
Which as hir list she may governe and gye,
For yet under the yerde was the mayde.
' O dere cosin myn, daun John,' she sayde,
' What eyleth yow so rathe for to ryse ? '
' Nece,' quod he, ' it oghte y-nough suffyse
Fyve houres for to slepe up-on a night, (101)
But it were for an old appalled wight,
As been thise wedded men, that lye and
  dare
As in a forme sit a wery hare,
Were al for-straught with houndes grete
  and smale.   1295
But dere nece, why be ye so pale ?
I trowe certes that our gode man   (107)
Hath yow laboured sith the night bigan,

That yow were nede to resten hastily ? '  1299
And with that word he lough ful merily,
And of his owene thought he wex al reed.

This faire wyf gan for to shake hir heed,
And seyde thus, ' ye, god wot al,' quod she ;
' Nay, cosin myn, it stant nat so with me.
For, by that god that yaf me soule and lyf,
In al the reme of France is ther no wyf 1306
That lasse lust hath to that sory pley.
For I may singe " allas " and " weylawey,
That I was born," but to no wight,' quod she,
' Dar I nat telle how that it stant with me.
Wherfore I thinke out of this land to
wende,                              (121) 1311
Or elles of my-self to make an ende,
So ful am I of drede and eek of care.'

This monk bigan up-on this wyf to stare,
And seyde, ' allas, my nece, god forbede
That ye, for any sorwe or any drede, 1316
Fordo your-self ; but telleth me your grief ;
Paraventure I may, in your meschief,
Conseille or helpe, and therfore telleth me
Al your anoy, for it shal been secree ; 1320
For on my porthors here I make an ooth,
That never in my lyf, for lief ne looth, (132)
Ne shal I of no conseil yow biwreye.'

' The same agayn to yow,' quod she,
' I seye ;                              1324
By god and by this porthors, I yow swere,
Though men me wolde al in-to peces tere,
Ne shal I never, for to goon to helle,
Biwreye a word of thing that ye me telle,
Nat for no cosinage ne alliance,
But verraily, for love and affiance.'  1330
Thus been they sworn, and heer-upon they
kiste,                              (141)
And ech of hem tolde other what hem liste.
' Cosin,' quod she, ' if that I hadde
a space,
As I have noon, and namely in this place,
Than wolde I telle a legende of my lyf, 1335
What I have suffred sith I was a wyf
With myn housbonde, al be he your cosyn.'
' Nay,' quod this monk, ' by god and seint
Martyn,
He is na more cosin un-to me    1339
Than is this leef that hangeth on the tree !
I clepe him so, by Seint Denys of Fraunce,
To have the more cause of aqueintaunce
Of yow, which I have loved specially (153)
Aboven alle wommen sikerly ;

This swere I yow on my professioun. 1345
Telleth your grief, lest that he come adoun,
And hasteth yow, and gooth your wey
anon.'

' My dere love,' quod she, ' o my daun
John,                              (158)
Ful lief were me this conseil for to hyde,
But out it moot, I may namore abyde. 1350
Myn housbond is to me the worste man
That ever was, sith that the world bigan.
But sith I am a wyf, it sit nat me
To tellen no wight of our privetee,  1354
Neither a-bedde, ne in non other place ;
God shilde I sholde it tellen, for his grace !
A wyf ne shal nat seyn of hir housbonde
But al honour, as I can understonde ;
Save un-to yow thus muche I tellen
shal ;
As help me god, he is noght worth at al 1360
In no degree the value of a flye.    (171)
But yet me greveth most his nigardye ;
And wel ye woot that wommen naturelly
Desyren thinges sixe, as wel as I.  1364
They wolde that hir housbondes sholde be
Hardy, and wyse, and riche, and ther-to
free,
And buxom to his wyf, and fresh a-bedde.
But, by that ilke lord that for us bledde,
For his honour, my-self for to arraye,
A Sonday next, I moste nedes paye  1370
An hundred frankes, or elles am I lorn.
Yet were me lever that I were unborn (182)
Than me were doon a sclaundre or vil-
einye ;
And if myn housbond eek it mighte espye,
I nere but lost, and therfore I yow preye
Lene me this somme, or elles moot I
deye.                              1376
Daun John, I seye, lene me thise hundred
frankes ;
Pardee, I wol nat faille yow my thankes,
If that yow list to doon that I yow praye.
For at a certein day I wol yow paye, 1380
And doon to yow what plesance and
servyce                              (191)
That I may doon, right as yow list devyse.
And but I do, god take on me vengeance
As foul as ever had Geniloun of France !'
This gentil monk answerde in this
manere ;                              1385
' Now, trewely, myn owene lady dere,

I have,' quod he, 'on yow so greet a routhe,
That I yow swere and plighte yow my
trouthe,
That whan your housbond is to Flaundres
fare,
I wol delivere yow out of this care; 1390
For I wol bringe yow an hundred frankes.'
And with that word he caughte hir by the
flankes, (202)
And hir embraceth harde, and kiste hir
ofte.
'Goth now your wey,' quod he, 'al stille
and softe,
And lat us dyne as sone as that ye may;
For by my chilindre it is pryme of day. 1396
Goth now, and beeth as trewe as I shal be.'
'Now, elles god forbede, sire,' quod she,
And forth she gooth, as jolif as a pye,
And bad the cokes that they sholde hem
hye, 1400
So that men mighte dyne, and that anon.
Up to hir housbonde is this wyf y-gon, (212)
And knokketh at his countour boldely.
'Qui la?' quod he. 'Peter! it am I,'
Quod she, 'what, sire, how longe wol ye
faste? 1405
How longe tyme wol ye rekene and caste
Your sommes, and your bokes, and your
thinges?
The devel have part of alle swiche reken-
inges!
Ye have y-nough, pardee, of goddes sonde;
Com doun to-day, and lat your bagges
stonde. 1410
Ne be ye nat ashamed that daun John (221)
Shal fasting al this day elenge goon?
What! lat us here a messe, and go we
dyne.'
'Wyf,' quod this man, 'litel canstow
devyne
The curious bisinesse that we have. 1415
For of us chapmen, al-so god me save,
And by that lord that cleped is Seint
Yve,
Scarsly amonges twelve ten shul thryve,
Continuelly, lastinge un-to our age. 1419
We may wel make chere and good visage,
And dryve forth the world as it may be,
And kepen our estaat in privetee, (232)
Til we be deed, or elles that we pleye
A pilgrimage, or goon out of the weye.

And therfor have I greet necessitee 1425
Up-on this queinte world t'avyse me;
For evermore we mote stonde in drede
Of hap and fortune in our chapmanhede.
To Flaundres wol I go to-morwe at day,
And come agayn, as sone as ever I may.
For which, my dere wyf, I thee biseke, (241)
As be to every wight buxom and meke,
And for to kepe our good be curious,
And honestly governe wel our hous. 1434
Thou hast y-nough, in every maner wyse,
That to a thrifty houshold may suffyse.
Thee lakketh noon array ne no vitaille,
Of silver in thy purs shaltow nat faille.'
And with that word his countour-dore he
shette,
And doun he gooth, no lenger wolde he
lette, 1440
But hastily a messe was ther seyd, (251)
And spedily the tables were y-leyd,
And to the diner faste they hem spedde;
And richely this monk the chapman fedde.
At-after diner daun John sobrely 1445
This chapman took a-part, and prively
He seyde him thus, 'cosyn, it standeth so,
That wel I see to Brugges wol ye go.
God and seint Austin spede yow and gyde!
I prey yow, cosin, wysly that ye ryde; 1450
Governeth yow also of your diete (261)
Atemprely, and namely in this hete.
Bitwix us two nedeth no strange fare;
Fare-wel, cosyn; god shilde yow fro
care.
If any thing ther be by day or night, 1455
If it lye in my power and my might,
That ye me wol comande in any wyse,
It shal be doon, right as ye wol devyse.
O thing, er that ye goon, if it may be,
I wolde prey yow; for to lene me 1460
An hundred frankes, for a wyke or tweye,
For certein beestes that I moste beye, (272)
To store with a place that is oures.
God help me so, I wolde it were youres!
I shal nat faille surely of my day, 1465
Nat for a thousand frankes, a myle-way.
But lat this thing be secree, I yow preye,
For yet to-night thise beestes moot I beye;
And fare-now wel, myn owene cosin
dere,
Graunt mercy of your cost and of your
chere.' (280) 1470

This noble marchant gentilly anon
Answerde, and seyde, 'o cosin myn, daun
John,
Now sikerly this is a smal requeste ;
My gold is youres, whan that it yow leste.
And nat only my gold, but my chaffare ;
Take what yow list, god shilde that ye
spare.                                     1476
But o thing is, ye knowe it wel y-nogh,
Of chapmen, that hir moneye is hir plogh.
We may creaunce whyl we have a name,
But goldlees for to be, it is no game. 1480
Paye it agayn whan it lyth in your ese ;
After my might ful fayn wolde I yow
plese.'                                      (292)
  Thise hundred frankes he fette forth
anon,
And prively he took hem to daun John.
No wight in al this world wiste of this
lone,                                        1485
Savinge this marchant and daun John
allone.
They drinke, and speke, and rome a whyle
and pleye,
Til that daun John rydeth to his abbeye.
  The morwe cam, and forth this mar-
chant rydeth
To Flaundres-ward ; his prentis wel him
gydeth,                                      1490
Til he cam in-to Brugges merily.    (301)
Now gooth this marchant faste and bisily
Aboute his nede, and byeth and creaun-
ceth.
He neither pleyeth at the dees ne daun-
ceth ;
But as a marchant, shortly for to telle, 1495
He let his lyf, and there I lete him dwelle.
  The Sonday next this Marchant was
agon,
To Seint Denys y-comen is daun John,
With crowne and berd all fresh and newe
y-shave.
In al the hous ther nas so litel a knave, 1500
Ne no wight elles, that he nas ful fayn, (311)
For that my lord daun John was come
agayn.
And shortly to the point right for to gon,
This faire wyf accorded with daun John,
That for thise hundred frankes he sholde
al night                                     1505
Have hir in his armes bolt-upright ;

And this acord parfourned was in dede.
In mirthe al night a bisy lyf they lede
Til it was day, that daun John wente his
way,
And bad the meynee ' fare-wel, have good
day !'                              (320) 1510
For noon of hem, ne no wight in the toun,
Hath of daun John right no suspecioun.
And forth he rydeth hoom to his abbeye,
Or where him list ; namore of him I seye.
  This marchant, whan that ended was
the faire,                                  1515
To Seint Denys he gan for to repaire,
And with his wyf he maketh feste and
chere,
And telleth hir that chaffare is so dere,
That nedes moste he make a chevisaunce.
For he was bounde in a reconissaunce 1520
To paye twenty thousand sheeld anon. (331)
For which this marchant is to Paris gon,
To borwe of certein frendes that he hadde
A certein frankes ; and somme with him
he ladde.
And whan that he was come in-to the toun,
For greet chertee and greet affeccioun, 1526
Un-to daun John he gooth him first, to
pleye ;
Nat for to axe or borwe of him moneye,
But for to wite and seen of his welfare,
And for to tellen him of his chaffare, 1530
As freendes doon whan they ben met
y-fere.                                      (341)
Daun John him maketh feste and mery
chere ;
And he him tolde agayn ful specially,
How he hadde wel y-boght and graciously,
Thanked be god, al hool his marchandyse.
Save that he moste, in alle maner wyse, 1536
Maken a chevisaunce, as for his beste,
And thanne he sholde been in joye and
reste.
  Daun John answerde, 'certes, I am fayn
That ye in hele ar comen hoom agayn. 1540
And if that I were riche, as have I blisse,
Of twenty thousand sheeld sholde ye nat
misse,                                       (352)
For ye so kindely this other day
Lente me gold ; and as I can and may,
I thanke yow, by god and by seint Jame!
But nathelees I took un-to our dame, 1546
Your wyf at hoom, the same gold ageyn

Upon your bench; she woot it wel, certeyn,
By certein tokenes that I can hir telle.
Now, by your leve, I may no lenger dwelle,
Our abbot wol out of this toun anon ;   (361)
And in his companye moot I gon.   1552
Grete wel our dame, myn owene nece swete,
And fare-wel, dere cosin, til we mete :'
     This Marchant, which that was ful war
          and wys,   1555
Creaunced hath, and payd eek in Parys,
To certeyn Lumbardes, redy in hir hond,
The somme of gold, and gat of hem his bond ;
And hoom he gooth, mery as a papejay.
For wel he knew he stood in swich array,
That nedes moste he winne in that viage   (371)
A thousand frankes above al his costage.
     His wyf ful redy mette him atte gate,
As she was wont of old usage algate,   1564
And al that night in mirthe they bisette ;
For he was riche and cleerly out of dette.
Whan it was day, this marchant gan embrace
His wyf al newe, and kiste hir on hir face,
And up he gooth and maketh it ful tough.
     'Namore,' quod she, 'by god, ye have
          y-nough !'   1570
And wantounly agayn with him she pleyde ;   (381)
Til, atte laste, that this Marchant seyde,
'By god,' quod he, 'I am a litel wrooth
With yow, my wyf, al-thogh it be me looth.
And woot ye why? by god, as that I gesse,   1575
That ye han maad a maner straungenesse
Bitwixen me and my cosyn daun John.
Ye sholde han warned me, er I had gon,
That he yow hadde an hundred frankes payed
By redy tokene ; and heeld him yvel apayed,   1580
For that I to him spak of chevisaunce,
Me semed so, as by his contenaunce. (392)
But nathelees, by god our hevene king,
I thoghte nat to axe of him no-thing.

I prey thee, wyf, ne do namore so ;   1585
Tel me alwey, er that I fro thee go,
If any dettour hath in myn absence
Y-payëd thee ; lest, thurgh thy necligence,
I mighte him axe a thing that he hath payed.'   (399) 1589
     This wyf was nat afered nor affrayed,
But boldely she seyde, and that anon :
' Marie, I defye the false monk, daun John !
I kepe nat of hise tokenes never a deel ;
He took me certein gold, that woot I weel !
What ! yvel thedom on his monkes snoute !
For, god it woot, I wende, withouten doute,
That he had yeve it me bycause of yow,
To doon ther-with myn honour and my prow,
For cosinage, and eek for bele chere
That he hath had ful ofte tymes here. 1600
But sith I see I stonde in this disjoint, (411)
I wol answere yow shortly, to the point.
Ye han mo slakker dettours than am I !
For I wol paye yow wel and redily
Fro day to day ; and, if so be I faille, 1605
I am your wyf ; score it up-on my taille,
And I shal paye, as sone as ever I may.
For, by my trouthe, I have on myn array,
And nat on wast, bistowed every deel.
And for I have bistowed it so weel   1610
For your honour, for goddes sake, I seye,
As be nat wrooth, but lat us laughe and pleye.   (422)
Ye shal my joly body have to wedde ;
By god, I wol nat paye yow but a-bedde.
Forgive it me, myn owene spouse dere ;
Turne hiderward and maketh bettre chere.'   1616
     This marchant saugh ther was no remedye,
And, for to chyde, it nere but greet folye,
Sith that the thing may nat amended be.
' Now, wyf,' he seyde, ' and I foryeve it thee ;   1620
But, by thy lyf, ne be namore so large ;
Keep bet our good, this yeve I thee in charge.'   (432)
     Thus endeth now my tale, and god us sende
Taling y-nough, un-to our lyves ende.
     Amen.

**Here endeth the Shipmannes Tale.**

# THE PRIORESS'S PROLOGUE.

**Bihold the mery wordes of the Host to the Shipman and to the lady Prioresse.**

'WEL seyd, by *corpus dominus*,' quod our hoste,    1625
'Now longe moot thou sayle by the coste,
Sir gentil maister, gentil marineer!
God yeve this monk a thousand last quad yeer!
A ha! felawes! beth ware of swiche a jape!
The monk putte in the mannes hood an ape,    1630
And in his wyves eek, by seint Austin!
Draweth no monkes more un-to your in.
But now passe over, and lat us seke aboute,

Who shal now telle first, of al this route,    (10)
Another tale;' and with that word he sayde,    1635
As curteisly as it had been a mayde,
'My lady Prioresse, by your leve,
So that I wiste I sholde yow nat greve,
I wolde demen that ye tellen sholde
A tale next, if so were that ye wolde.    1640
Now wol ye vouche-sauf, my lady dere?'
    'Gladly,' quod she, and seyde as ye shal here.    (18)

*Explicit.*

---

# THE PRIORESSES TALE.

**The Prologe of the Prioresses Tale.**

*Domine, dominus noster.*

O LORD our lord, thy name how merveillous
Is in this large worlde y-sprad—quod she :—
For noght only thy laude precious    1645
Parfourned is by men of dignitee,
But by the mouth of children thy bountee
Parfourned is, for on the brest soukinge
Som tyme shewen they thyn heryinge.

Wherfor in laude, as I best can or may,
Of thee, and of the whyte lily flour    1651
Which that thee bar, and is a mayde alway,    (10)

To telle a storie I wol do my labour;
Not that I may encresen hir honour;
For she hir-self is honour, and the rote
Of bountee, next hir sone, and soules bote.—    1656

O moder mayde! o mayde moder free!
O bush unbrent, brenninge in Moyses sighte,
That ravisedest doun fro the deitee,
Thurgh thyn humblesse, the goost that in th'alighte,    1660
Of whos vertu, whan he thyn herte lighte,
Conceived was the fadres sapience,    (20)
Help me to telle it in thy reverence!

Lady! thy bountee, thy magnificence,
Thy vertu, and thy grete humilitee   1665
Ther may no tonge expresse in no science;
For som-tyme, lady, er men praye to thee,
Thou goost biforn of thy benignitee,
And getest us the light, thurgh thy preyere,
To gyden us un-to thy sone so dere.   1670

My conning is so wayk, o blisful quene,
For to declare thy grete worthinesse,   (30)
That I ne may the weighte nat sustene,
But as a child of twelf monthe old, or
   lesse,   1674
That can unnethes any word expresse,
Right so fare I, and therfor I yow preye,
Gydeth my song that I shal of yow seye.

*Explicit.*

### Here biginneth the Prioresses Tale.

Ther was in Asie, in a greet citee,
Amonges Cristen folk, a Jewerye,
Sustened by a lord of that contree   1680
For foule usure and lucre of vilanye,
Hateful to Crist and to his companye;
And thurgh the strete men mighte ryde
   or wende,   (41)
For it was free, and open at either ende.

A litel scole of Cristen folk ther stood
Doun at the ferther ende, in which ther
   were   1686
Children an heep, y-comen of Cristen
   blood,
That lerned in that scole yeer by yere
Swich maner doctrine as men used there,
This is to seyn, to singen and to rede,   1690
As smale children doon in hir childhede.

Among thise children was a widwes sone,
A litel clergeon, seven yeer of age,   (51)
That day by day to scole was his wone,
And eek also, wher-as he saugh th'image
Of Cristes moder, hadde he in usage,
As him was taught, to knele adoun and
   seye
His *Ave Marie*, as he goth by the weye.

Thus hath this widwe hir litel sone y-
   taught
Our blisful lady, Cristes moder dere,   1700
To worshipe ay, and he forgat it naught,

For sely child wol alday sone lere;   (60)
But ay, whan I remembre on this matere,
Seint Nicholas stant ever in my presence,
For he so yong to Crist did reverence.   1705

This litel child, his litel book lerninge,
As he sat in the scole at his prymer,
He *Alma redemptoris* herde singe,
As children lerned hir antiphoner;
And, as he dorste, he drough him ner and
   ner,   1710
And herkned ay the wordes and the note,
Til he the firste vers coude al by rote.   (70)

Noght wiste he what this Latin was to
   seye,
For he so yong and tendre was of age;
But on a day his felaw gan he preye   1715
T'expounden him this song in his langage,
Or telle him why this song was in usage;
This preyde he him to construe and de-
   clare
Ful ofte tyme upon his knowes bare.

His felaw, which that elder was than he,
Answerde him thus: 'this song, I have
   herd seye,
Was maked of our blisful lady free,   (80)
Hir to salue, and eek hir for to preye
To been our help and socour whan we
   deye.   1724
I can no more expounde in this matere;
I lerne song, I can but smal grammere.'

'And is this song maked in reverence
Of Cristes moder?' seyde this innocent;
'Now certes, I wol do my diligence   1729
To conne it al, er Cristemasse is went;
Though that I for my prymer shal be
   shent,
And shal be beten thryës in an houre, (90)
I wol it conne, our lady for to honoure.'

His felaw taughte him homward prively,
Fro day to day, til he coude it by rote,
And than he song it wel and boldely
Fro word to word, acording with the note;
Twyës a day it passed thurgh his throte,
To scoleward and homward whan he
   wente;   1739
On Cristes moder set was his entente.

As I have seyd, thurgh-out the Jewerye
This litel child, as he cam to and fro, (100)
Ful merily than wolde he singe, and crye
O *Alma redemptoris* ever-mo.
The swetnes hath his herte perced so 1745
Of Cristes moder, that, to hir to preye,
He can nat stinte of singing by the weye.

Our firste fo, the serpent Sathanas,
That hath in Jewes herte his waspes nest,
Up swal, and seide, ' O Hebraik peple,
    allas !       1750
Is this to yow a thing that is honest,
That swich a boy shal walken as him lest
In your despyt, and singe of swich sen-
    tence,       (111)
Which is agayn your lawes reverence ? '

Fro thennes forth the Jewes han con-
    spyred       1755
This innocent out of this world to chace ;
An homicyde ther-to han they hyred,
That in an aley hadde a privee place ;
And as the child gan for-by for to pace,
This cursed Jew him hente and heeld
    him faste,       1760
And kitte his throte, and in a pit him
    caste.

I seye that in a wardrobe they him threwe
Wher-as these Jewes purgen hir entraille.
O cursed folk of Herodes al newe,    (122)
What may your yvel entente yow availle ?
Mordre wol out, certein, it wol nat faille,
And namely ther th'onour of god shal
    sprede,
The blood out cryeth on your cursed dede.

' O martir, souded to virginitee,     1769
Now maystou singen, folwing ever in oon
The whyte lamb celestial,' quod she,
' Of which the grete evangelist, seint John,
In Pathmos wroot, which seith that they
    that goon       (131)
Biforn this lamb, and singe a song al newe,
That never, fleshly, wommen they ne
    knewe.'       1775

This povre widwe awaiteth al that night
After hir litel child, but he cam noght ;
For which, as sone as it was dayes light,

With face pale of drede and bisy thoght,
Sho hath at scole and elles-wher him soght,
Til finally she gan so fer espye     1781
That he last seyn was in the Jewerye. (140)

With modres pitee in hir brest enclosed,
She gooth, as she were half out of hir
    minde,
To every place wher she hath supposed
By lyklihede hir litel child to finde ; 1786
And ever on Cristes moder meke and
    kinde
She cryde, and atte laste thus she wroghte,
Among the cursed Jewes she him soghte.

She frayneth and she preyeth pitously
To every Jew that dwelte in thilke place,
To telle hir, if hir child wente oght for-by.
They seyde, ' nay '; but Jesu, of his grace,
Yaf in hir thought, inwith a litel space,
That in that place after hir sone she cryde,
Wher he was casten in a pit bisyde. 1796

O grete god, that parfournest thy laude
By mouth of innocents, lo heer thy might !
This gemme of chastitee, this emeraude,
And eek of martirdom the ruby bright,
Ther he with throte y-corven lay upright,
He ' *Alma redemptoris* ' gan to singe (160)
So loude, that al the place gan to ringe.

The Cristen folk, that thurgh the strete
    wente,       1804
In coomen, for to wondre up-on this thing,
And hastily they for the provost sente ;
He cam anon with-outen tarying,
And herieth Crist that is of heven king,
And eek his moder, honour of mankinde,
And after that, the Jewes leet he binde.

This child with pitous lamentacioun 1811
Up-taken was, singing his song alway ;
And with honour of greet processioun
They carien him un-to the nexte abbay.
His moder swowning by the bere lay ;
Unnethe might the peple that was there
This newe Rachel bringe fro his bere.

With torment and with shamful deth
    echon       (176)
This provost dooth thise Jewes for to
    sterve       1819

That of this mordre wiste, and that anon ;
He nolde no swich cursednesse observe.
Yvel shal have, that yvel wol deserve.
Therfor with wilde hors he dide hem
    drawe,           (181)
And after that he heng hem by the lawe.

Up-on his bere ay lyth this innocent 1825
Biforn the chief auter, whyl masse laste,
And after that, the abbot with his covent
Han sped hem for to burien him ful faste ;
And whan they holy water on him
    caste,
Yet spak this child, whan spreynd was
    holy water,          1830
And song—'O Alma redemptoris mater !'

This abbot, which that was an holy man
As monkes been, or elles oghten be, (191)
This yonge child to conjure he bigan,
And seyde, 'o dere child, I halse thee,
In vertu of the holy Trinitee,     1836
Tel me what is thy cause for to singe,
Sith that thy throte is cut, to my sem-
    inge ?'

'My throte is cut un-to my nekke-boon,'
Seyde this child, ' and, as by wey of kinde,
I sholde have deyed, ye, longe tyme agoon,
But Jesu Crist, as ye in bokes finde, (200)
Wil that his glorie laste and be in minde ;
And, for the worship of his moder dere,
Yet may I singe "O Alma" loude and
    clere.           1845

This welle of mercy, Cristes moder swete,
I lovede alwey, as after my conninge ;
And whan that I my lyf sholde forlete,
To me she cam, and bad me for to singe
This antem verraily in my deyinge, 1850

As ye han herd, and, whan that I had
    songe,
Me thoughte, she leyde a greyn up-on my
    tonge.          (210)

Wherfor I singe, and singe I moot certeyn
In honour of that blisful mayden free,
Til fro my tonge of-taken is the greyn ;
And afterward thus seyde she to me,
"My litel child, now wol I fecche thee
Whan that the greyn is fro thy tonge
    y-take ;          1858
Be nat agast, I wol thee nat forsake."'

This holy monk, this abbot, him mene I,
Him tonge out-caughte, and took a-wey
    the greyn,
And he yaf up the goost ful softely. (220)
And whan this abbot had this wonder
    seyn,
His salte teres trikled doun as reyn, 1864
And gruf he fil al plat up-on the grounde,
And stille he lay as he had been y-bounde.

The covent eek lay on the pavement
Weping, and herien Cristes moder dere,
And after that they ryse, and forth ben
    went,          1869
And toke awey this martir fro his bere,
And in a tombe of marbul-stones clere
Enclosen they his litel body swete ; (230)
Ther he is now, god leve us for to mete.

O yonge Hugh of Lincoln, slayn also
With cursed Jewes, as it is notable, 1875
For it nis but a litel whyle ago ;
Preye eek for us, we sinful folk unstable,
That, of his mercy, god so merciable
On us his grete mercy multiplye, (237)
For reverence of his moder Marye. Amen.

Here is ended the Prioresses Tale.

# PROLOGUE TO SIR THOPAS.

**Bihold the murye wordes of the Host to Chaucer.**

WHAN seyd was al this miracle, every man
As sobre was, that wonder was to see,
Til that our hoste japen tho bigan,
And than at erst he loked up-on me,
And seyde thus, ' what man artow? ' quod
    he ;                1885
'Thou lokest as thou woldest finde an
    hare,
For ever up-on the ground I see thee stare.

Approche neer, and loke up merily.
Now war yow, sirs, and lat this man have
    place ;
He in the waast is shape as wel as I ; 1890
This were a popet in an arm t'enbrace (11)

For any womman, smal and fair of face.
He semeth elvish by his contenaunce,
For un-to no wight dooth he daliaunce.

Sey now somwhat, sin other folk han
    sayd ;               1895
Tel us a tale of mirthe, and that anoon ;'—
' Hoste,' quod I, ' ne beth nat yvel apayd,
For other tale certes can I noon,
But of a ryme I lerned longe agoon.'
' Ye, that is good,' quod he ; ' now shul
    we here         1900
Som deyntee thing, me thinketh by his
    chere.'         (21)

*Explicit.*

# SIR THOPAS.

**Here biginneth Chaucers Tale of Thopas.**

LISTETH, lordes, in good entent,
And I wol telle verrayment
    Of mirthe and of solas ;
Al of a knyght was fair and gent    1905
In bataille and in tourneyment,
    His name was sir Thopas.

Y-born he was in fer contree,
In Flaundres, al biyonde the see,
    At Popering, in the place ;    1910
His fader was a man ful free,    (10)
And lord he was of that contree,
    As it was goddes grace.

Sir Thopas wex a doghty swayn,
Whyt was his face as payndemayn,  1915
    His lippes rede as rose ;

His rode is lyk scarlet in grayn,
And I yow telle in good certayn,
    He hadde a semely nose.

His heer, his berd was lyk saffroun,  1920
That to his girdel raughte adoun ;  (20)
    His shoon of Cordewane.
Of Brugges were his hosen broun,
His robe was of ciclatoun,
    That coste many a jane.    1925

He coude hunte at wilde deer,
And ryde an hauking for riveer,
    With grey goshauk on honde ;
Ther-to he was a good archeer,
Of wrastling was ther noon his peer, 1930
    Ther any ram shal stonde.    (30)

Ful many a mayde, bright in bour,
They moorne for him, paramour,
  Whan hem were bet to slepe ;
But he was chast and no lechour,   1935
And sweet as is the bremble-flour
  That bereth the rede hepe.

And so bifel up-on a day,
For sothe, as I yow telle may,
  Sir Thopas wolde out ryde ;   1940
He worth upon his stede gray,   (40)
And in his honde a launcegay,
  A long swerd by his syde.

He priketh thurgh a fair forest,
Ther-inne is many a wilde best,   1945
  Ye, bothe bukke and hare ;
And, as he priketh north and est,
I telle it yow, him hadde almest
  Bitid a sory care.   1949

Ther springen herbes grete and smale,
The lycorys and cetewale,   (50)
  And many a clowe-gilofre ;
And notemuge to putte in ale,
Whether it be moyste or stale,
  Or for to leye in cofre.   1955

The briddes singe, it is no nay,
The sparhauk and the papejay,
  That joye it was to here ;
The thrustelcok made eek his lay,
The wodedowve upon the spray   1960
  She sang ful loude and clere.   (60)

Sir Thopas fil in love-longinge
Al whan he herde the thrustel singe,
  And priked as he were wood :
His faire stede in his prikinge   1965
So swatte that men mighte him wringe,
  His sydes were al blood.

Sir Thopas eek so wery was
For prikinge on the softe gras,
  So fiers was his corage,   1970
That doun he leyde him in that plas   (70)
  To make his stede som solas,
  And yaf him good forage.

' O seinte Marie, ben'cite !
What eyleth this love at me   1975
  To binde me so sore ?

Me dremed al this night, pardee,
An elf-queen shal my lemman be,
  And slepe under my gore.

An elf-queen wol I love, y-wis,   1980
For in this world no womman is   (80)
  Worthy to be my make   [T. 13722
     In toune ;   [T. 13722
Alle othere wommen I forsake,   [T. 13723
And to an elf-queen I me take   1985
  By dale and eek by doune ! '

In-to his sadel he clamb anoon,
And priketh over style and stoon
  An elf-queen for t'espye,
Til he so longe had riden and goon   1990
That he fond, in a privee woon,   (90)
  The contree of Fairye   [T. 13731
     So wilde ;   [T. 13734
For in that contree was ther noon
†That to him dorste ryde or goon,   1995
  Neither wyf ne childe.

Til that ther cam a greet geaunt,
His name was sir Olifaunt,
  A perilous man of dede ;
He seyde, ' child, by Termagaunt,   2000
But-if thou prike out of myn haunt,   (100)
  Anon I slee thy stede   [T. 13743
     With mace.   [T. 13743
Heer is the queen of Fayërye,
With harpe and pype and simphonye   2005
  Dwelling in this place.'

The child seyde, ' al-so mote I thee,
Tomorwe wol I mete thee
  Whan I have myn armoure ;
And yet I hope, par ma fay,   2010
That thou shalt with this launcegay   (110)
  Abyen it ful soure ;   [T. 13752
     Thy mawe   [T. 13752
Shal I percen, if I may,
Er it be fully pryme of day,   2015
  For heer thou shalt be slawe.'

Sir Thopas drow abak ful faste ;
This geaunt at him stones caste
  Out of a fel staf-slinge ;
But faire escapeth child Thopas,   2020
And al it was thurgh goddes gras,   (120)
  And thurgh his fair beringe.

Yet listeth, lordes, to my tale
Merier than the nightingale,
　　For now I wol yow roune　　　2025
How sir Thopas with sydes smale,
Priking over hil and dale,
　　Is come agayn to toune.

His merie men comanded he
To make him bothe game and glee,　2030
　　For nedes moste he fighte　　(130)
With a geaunt with hevedes three,
For paramour and jolitee
　　Of oon that shoon ful brighte.

'Do come,' he seyde, 'my minstrales, 2035
And gestours, for to tellen tales
　　Anon in myn arminge;
Of romances that been royales,
Of popes and of cardinales,
　　And eek of love-lykinge.'　　　2040

They fette him first the swete wyn, (140)
And mede eek in a maselyn,
　　And royal spicerye
Of gingebreed that was ful fyn,
And lycorys, and eek comyn,　　　2045
　　With sugre that is so trye.

He dide next his whyte lere
Of clooth of lake fyn and clere
　　A breech and eek a sherte;
And next his sherte an aketoun,　　2050
And over that an habergeoun　　(150)
　　For percinge of his herte;

And over that a fyn hauberk,
Was al y-wroght of Jewes werk,
　　Ful strong it was of plate;　　2055
And over that his cote-armour
As whyt as is a lily-flour,
　　In which he wol debate.

His sheeld was al of gold so reed,
And ther-in was a bores heed,　　2060
　　A charbocle bisyde;　　　　(160)
And there he swoor, on ale and breed,
How that 'the geaunt shal be deed,
　　Bityde what bityde!'

His jambeux were of quirboilly,　2065
His swerdes shethe of yvory,
　　His helm of laton bright;

His sadel was of rewel-boon,
His brydel as the sonne shoon,
　　Or as the mone light.　　　　2070

His spere was of fyn ciprees,　　(170)
That bodeth werre, and no-thing pees,
　　The heed ful sharpe y-grounde;
His stede was al dappel-gray,
It gooth an ambel in the way　　2075
　　Ful softely and rounde　　[T. 13815
　　　　　　　In londe.　[T. 13815
Lo, lordes myne, heer is a fit!
If ye wol any more of it,
　　To telle it wol I fonde.　　　2080


[*The Second Fit.*]

Now hold your mouth, *par charitee*, (180)
Bothe knight and lady free,
　　And herkneth to my spelle;
Of bataille and of chivalry,
And of ladyes love-drury　　　2085
　　Anon I wol yow telle.

Men speke of romances of prys,
Of Horn child and of Ypotys,
　　Of Bevis and sir Gy,
Of sir Libeux and Pleyn-damour;　2090
But sir Thopas, he bereth the flour　(190)
　　Of royal chivalry.

His gode stede al he bistrood,
And forth upon his wey he glood
　　As sparkle out of the bronde;　2095
Up-on his crest he bar a tour,
And ther-in stiked a lily-flour,
　　God shilde his cors fro shonde!

And for he was a knight auntrous,
He nolde slepen in non hous,　　2100
　　But liggen in his hode;　　(200)
His brighte helm was his wonger,
And by him baiteth his dextrer
　　Of herbes fyne and gode.

Him-self drank water of the wel,　2105
As did the knight sir Percivel,
　　So worthy under wede,
Til on a day——　　　　　　(207)

**Here the Host stinteth Chaucer of his Tale of Thopas.**

# PROLOGUE TO MELIBEUS.

'No more of this, for goddes dignitee,'
Quod oure hoste, 'for thou makest me 2110
So wery of thy verray lewednesse
That, also wisly god my soule blesse,
Myn eres aken of thy drasty speche;
Now swiche a rym the devel I biteche!
This may wel be rym dogerel,' quod he.
   'Why so?' quod I, 'why wiltow lette me
More of my tale than another man,
Sin that it is the beste rym I can?'   (10)
   'By god,' quod he, 'for pleynly, at
      a word,
Thy drasty ryming is nat worth a tord;
Thou doost nought elles but despendest
      tyme,                                    2121
Sir, at o word, thou shalt no lenger
      ryme.
Lat see wher thou canst tellen aught in
      geste,
Or telle in prose somwhat at the leste
In which ther be som mirthe or som
      doctryne.'                               2125
   'Gladly,' quod I, 'by goddes swete pyne,
I wol yow telle a litel thing in prose,
That oghte lyken yow, as I suppose,   (20)
Or elles, certes, ye been to daungerous.
It is a moral tale vertuous,                   2130
Al be it told som-tyme in sondry wyse
Of sondry folk, as I shal yow devyse.

As thus; ye woot that every evangelist,
That telleth us the peyne of Jesu Crist,
Ne saith nat al thing as his felaw dooth,
But natheles, hir sentence is al sooth, 2136
And alle acorden as in hir sentence,
Al be ther in hir telling difference.   (30)
For somme of hem seyn more, and somme
      lesse,
Whan they his pitous passioun expresse;
I mene of Mark [and] Mathew, Luk and
      John;                              2141
But doutelees hir sentence is al oon.
Therfor, lordinges alle, I yow biseche,
If that ye thinke I varie as in my speche,
As thus, thogh that I telle som-what more
Of proverbes, than ye han herd bifore,
Comprehended in this litel tretis here,
To enforce with the th'effect of my matere,
And thogh I nat the same wordes seye (41)
As ye han herd, yet to yow alle I preye,
Blameth me nat; for, as in my sentence,
Ye shul not fynden moche difference
Fro the sentence of this tretis lyte
After the which this mery tale I wryte.
And therfor herkneth what that I shal
      seye,                               2155
And lat me tellen al my tale, I preye.' (48)

                    *Explicit.*

---

# THE TALE OF MELIBEUS.

### Here biginneth Chaucers Tale of Melibee.

§ 1. A yong man called Melibeus,
mighty and riche, bigat up-on his wyf
that called was Prudence, a doghter
which that called was Sophie. /
   § 2. Upon a day bifel, that he for his
desport is went in-to the feeldes him to
pleye. / His wyf and eek his doghter

hath he left inwith his hous, of which the
dores weren fast y-shette. / Three of his
olde foos han it espyed, and setten laddres
to the walles of his hous, and by the
windowes been entred, / and betten his 2160
wyf, and wounded his doghter with fyve
mortal woundes in fyve sondry places; /

this is to seyn, in hir feet, in hir handes, in hir eres, in hir nose, and in hir mouth; and leften hir for deed, and wenten awey. /

§ 3. Whan Melibeus retourned was into his hous, and saugh al this meschief, he, lyk a mad man, rendinge his clothes, gan to wepe and crye. /

§ 4. Prudence his wyf, as ferforth as she dorste, bisoghte him of his weping for to stinte; / but nat for-thy he gan to 2165 crye and wepen ever lenger the more. /

§ 5. This noble wyf Prudence remembered hir upon the sentence of Ovide, in his book that cleped is The Remedie of Love, wher-as he seith; / 'he is a fool that destourbeth the moder to wepen in the deeth of hir child, til she have wept hir fille, as for a certein tyme; / and thanne shal man doon his diligence with amiable wordes hir to reconforte, and preyen hir of hir weping for to stinte.' / For which resoun this noble wyf Prudence suffred hir housbond for to wepe and crye as for a certein space; / and whan she saugh hir tyme, she seyde him in this wyse. 'Allas, my lord,' quod she, 'why 2170 make ye your-self for to be lyk a fool? / For sothe, it aperteneth nat to a wys man, to maken swiche a sorwe. / Your doghter, with the grace of god, shal warisshe and escape. / And al were it so that she right now were deed, ye ne oghte nat as for hir deeth your-self to destroye. / Senek seith: "the wise man shal nat take to greet disconfort for the deeth of his children, / but certes he sholde suffren it in pacience, as wel as he abydeth the 2175 deeth of his owene propre persone."' /

§ 6. This Melibeus answerde anon and seyde, 'What man,' quod he, 'sholde of his weping stinte, that hath so greet a cause for to wepe? / Jesu Crist, our lord, him-self wepte for the deeth of Lazarus his freend.'/ Prudence answerde, 'Certes, wel I woot, attempree weping is no-thing defended to him that sorweful is, amonges folk in sorwe, but it is rather graunted him to wepe. / The Apostle Paul un-to the Romayns wryteth, "man shal rejoyse with hem that maken joye,

and wepen with swich folk as wepen." / But thogh attempree weping be y-graunted, outrageous weping certes is defended. / Mesure of weping sholde be 2180 considered, after the lore that techeth us Senek. / "Whan that thy freend is deed," quod he, "lat nat thyne eyen to moyste been of teres, ne to muche drye; althogh the teres come to thyne eyen, lat hem nat falle." / And whan thou hast for-goon thy freend, do diligence to gete another freend; and this is more wysdom than for to wepe for thy freend which that thou hast lorn; for ther-inne is no bote. / And therfore, if ye governe yow by sapience, put awey sorwe out of your herte. / Remembre yow that Jesus Syrak seith: "a man that is joyous and glad in herte, it him conserveth florisshing in his age; but soothly sorweful herte maketh his bones drye." / He seith eek thus: 2185 "that sorwe in herte sleeth ful many a man." / Salomon seith: "that, right as motthes in the shepes flees anoyeth to the clothes, and the smale wormes to the tree, right so anoyeth sorwe to the herte." / Wherfore us oghte, as wel in the deeth of our children as in the losse of our goodes temporels, have pacience. /

§ 7. Remembre yow up-on the pacient Job, whan he hadde lost his children and his temporel substance, and in his body endured and receyved ful many a grevous tribulacioun; yet seyde he thus: / "our lord hath yeven it me, our lord hath biraft it me; right as our lord hath wold, right so it is doon; blessed be the name of our lord."' / To thise foreseide thinges 2190 answerde Melibeus un-to his wyf Prudence: 'Alle thy wordes,' quod he, 'been sothe, and ther-to profitable; but trewely myn herte is troubled with this sorwe so grevously, that I noot what to done.' / 'Lat calle,' quod Prudence, 'thy trewe freendes alle, and thy linage whiche that been wyse; telleth your cas, and herkneth what they seye in conseiling, and yow governe after hir sentence. / Salomon seith: "werk alle thy thinges by conseil, and thou shalt never repente."' /

§ 8. Thanne, by the conseil of his wyf

Prudence, this Melibeus leet callen a greet congregacioun of folk; / as surgiens, phisiciens, olde folk and yonge, and somme of hise olde enemys reconsiled as by hir semblaunt to his love and in-to his
195 grace; / and ther-with-al ther comen somme of hise neighebores that diden him reverence more for drede than for love, as it happeth ofte. / Ther comen also ful many subtile flatereres, and wyse advocats lerned in the lawe. /

§ 9. And whan this folk togidre assembled weren, this Melibeus in sorweful wyse shewed hem his cas; / and by the manere of his speche it semed that in herte he bar a cruel ire, redy to doon vengeaunce up-on hise foos, and sodeynly desired that the werre sholde biginne; /
but nathelees yet axed he hir conseil upon
200 this matere. / A surgien, by licence and assent of swiche as weren wyse, up roos and un-to Melibeus seyde as ye may here. /

§ 10. 'Sir,' quod he, 'as to us surgiens aperteneth, that we do to every wight the beste that we can, wher-as we been withholde, and to our pacients that we do no damage; / wherfore it happeth, many tyme and ofte, that whan twey men han everich wounded other, oon same surgien heleth hem bothe; / wherefore un-to our art it is nat pertinent to norice werre, ne parties to supporte. / But certes, as to the warisshinge of your doghter, al-be-it so that she perilously be wounded, we shullen do so ententif bisinesse fro day to night, that with the grace of god she shal be hool and sound as sone as is
205 possible.' / Almost right in the same wyse the phisiciens answerden, save that they seyden a fewe wordes more: / 'That, right as maladyes been cured by hir contraries, right so shul men warisshe werre by vengeaunce.' / His neighebores, ful of envye, his feyned freendes that semeden reconsiled, and his flatereres, / maden semblant of weping, and empeireden and agreggeden muchel of this matere, in preising greetly Melibee of might, of power, of richesse, and of freendes, despysinge the power of his

adversaries, / and seiden outrely that he anon sholde wreken him on his foos and biginne werre. / 2210

§ 11. Up roos thanne an advocat that was wys, by leve and by conseil of othere that were wyse, and seyde: / 'Lordinges, the nede for which we been assembled in this place is a ful hevy thing and an heigh matere, / by-cause of the wrong and of the wikkednesse that hath be doon, and eek by resoun of the grete damages that in tyme cominge been possible to fallen for this same cause; / and eek by resoun of the grete richesse and power of the parties bothe; / for the whiche resouns it were a ful greet peril to erren in this matere. / Wherfore, 2215 Melibeus, this is our sentence: we conseille yow aboven alle thing, that right anon thou do thy diligence in kepinge of thy propre persone, in swich a wyse that thou ne wante noon espye ne wacche, thy body for to save. / And after that we conseille, that in thyn hous thou sette suffisant garnisoun, so that they may as wel thy body as thyn hous defende. / But certes, for to moeve werre, or sodeynly for to doon vengeaunce, we may nat demen in so litel tyme that it were profitable. / Wherfore we axen leyser and espace to have deliberacioun in this cas to deme. / For the commune proverbe seith thus: "he that sone demeth, sone shal repente." / And eek men seyn that 2220 thilke juge is wys, that sone understondeth a matere and juggeth by leyser. / For al-be-it so that alle tarying be anoyful, algates it is nat to repreve in yevinge of jugement, ne in vengeance-taking, whan it is suffisant and resonable. / And that shewed our lord Jesu Crist by ensample; for whan that the womman that was taken in avoutrie was broght in his presence, to knowen what sholde be doon with hir persone, al-be-it so that he wiste wel him-self what that he wolde answere, yet ne wolde he nat answere sodeynly, but he wolde have deliberacioun, and in the ground he wroot twyes. / And by thise causes we axen deliberacioun, and we shal thanne, by the grace of god, conseille thee thing that shal be profitable.'/

§ 12. Up stirten thanne the yonge folk at-ones, and the moste partie of that companye han scorned the olde wyse men, and bigonnen to make noyse, and
2225 seyden : that, / right so as whyl that iren is hoot, men sholden smyte, right so, men sholde wreken hir wronges whyle that they been fresshe and newe; and with loud voys they cryden, 'werre! werre!'/

Up roos tho oon of thise olde wyse, and with his hand made contenaunce that men sholde holden hem stille and yeven him audience. / 'Lordinges,' quod he, 'ther is ful many a man that cryeth "werre! werre!" that woot ful litel what werre amounteth. / Werre at his biginning hath so greet an entree and so large, that every wight may entre whan him lyketh, and lightly finde werre. / But, certes, what ende that shal ther-of
2230 bifalle, it is nat light to knowe. / For sothly, whan that werre is ones bigonne, ther is ful many a child unborn of his moder, that shal sterve yong by-cause of that ilke werre, or elles live in sorwe and dye in wrecchednesse. / And ther-fore, er that any werre biginne, men moste have greet conseil and greet deliberacioun.'/ And whan this olde man wende to enforcen his tale by resons, wel ny alle at-ones bigonne they to ryse for to breken his tale, and beden him ful ofte his wordes for to abregge. / For soothly, he that precheth to hem that listen nat heren his wordes, his sermon hem anoyeth. / For Jesus Syrak seith : that 'musik in wepinge is anoyous thing'; this is to seyn : as muche availleth to speken bifore folk to whiche his speche anoyeth, as dooth to singe
2235 biforn him that wepeth. / And whan this wyse man saugh that him wanted audience, al shamefast he sette him doun agayn. / For Salomon seith : 'ther-as thou ne mayst have noon audience, enforce thee nat to speke.'/ 'I see wel,' quod this wyse man, 'that the commune proverbe is sooth; that "good conseil wanteth whan it is most nede."'/

§ 13. Yet hadde this Melibeus in his conseil many folk, that prively in his ere conseilled him certeyn thing, and conseilled him the contrarie in general audience. /

Whan Melibeus hadde herd that the gretteste partie of his conseil weren accorded that he sholde maken werre, anoon he consented to hir conseilling, and fully affermed hir sentence. / Thanne 2240 dame Prudence, whan that she saugh how that hir housbonde shoop him for to wreken him on his foos, and to biginne werre, she in ful humble wyse, when she saugh hir tyme, seide him thise wordes :/ 'My lord,' quod she, 'I yow biseche as hertely as I dar and can, ne haste yow nat to faste, and for alle guerdons as yeveth me audience. / For Piers Alfonce seith : "who-so that dooth to that other good or harm, haste thee nat to quyten it; for in this wyse thy freend wol abyde, and thyn enemy shal the lenger live in drede." / The proverbe seith : "he hasteth wel that wysely can abyde"; and in wikked haste is no profit.'/

§ 14. This Melibee answerde un-to his wyf Prudence : 'I purpose nat,' quod he, 'to werke by thy conseil, for many causes and resouns. For certes every wight wolde holde me thanne a fool; / this is 2245 to seyn, if I, for thy conseilling, wolde chaungen thinges that been ordeyned and affermed by so manye wyse. / Secoundly I seye, that alle wommen been wikke and noon good of hem alle. For "of a thousand men," seith Salomon, "I fond a good man : but certes, of alle wommen, good womman fond I never."/ And also certes, if I governed me by thy conseil, it sholde seme that I hadde yeve to thee over me the maistrie; and god forbede that it so were. / For Jesus Syrak seith; "that if the wyf have maistrie, she is contrarious to hir housbonde." / And Salomon seith : "never in thy lyf, to thy wyf, ne to thy child, ne to thy freend, ne yeve no power over thy-self. For bettre it were that thy children aske of thy persone thinges that hem nedeth, than thou see thy-self in the

50 handes of thy children."/ And also, if
I wolde werke by thy conseilling, certes
my conseilling moste som tyme be secree,
til it were tyme that it moste be knowe ;
and this ne may noght be. / [†For it is
writen, that "the janglerie of wommen
can hyden thinges that they witen
noght." / Furthermore, the philosophre
seith, "in wikked conseil wommen venquisshe men " ; and for thise resouns I ne
ow nat usen thy conseil.']/

§ 15. Whanne dame Prudence, ful
debonairly and with greet pacience,
hadde herd al that hir housbonde lyked
for to seye, thanne axed she of him
licence for to speke, and seyde in this
wyse. / 'My lord,' quod she, 'as to your
firste resoun, certes it may lightly ben
answered. For I seye, that it is no folie
to chaunge conseil whan the thing is
chaunged ; or elles whan the thing
255 semeth otherweyes than it was biforn. /
And more-over I seye, that though ye han
sworn and bihight to perfourne your
emprise, and nathelees ye weyve to perfourne thilke same emprise by juste
cause, men sholde nat seyn therefore that
ye were a lyer ne forsworn. / For the
book seith, that "the wyse man maketh
no lesing whan he turneth his corage to
the bettre." / And al-be-it so that your
emprise be establissed and ordeyned by
greet multitude of folk, yet thar ye nat
accomplice thilke same ordinaunce but
yow lyke. / For the trouthe of thinges
and the profit been rather founden in
fewe folk that been wyse and ful of
resoun, than by greet multitude of folk,
ther every man cryeth and clatereth what
that him lyketh. Soothly swich multitude is nat honeste. / As to the seconde
resoun, where-as ye seyn that "alle
wommen been wikke," save your grace,
certes ye despysen alle wommen in this
wyse ; and "he that alle despyseth alle
260 displeseth," as seith the book. / And
Senek seith that "who-so wole have
sapience, shal no man dispreise ; but he
shal gladly techen the science that he
can, with-outen presumpcioun or pryde. /
And swiche thinges as he nought ne can,

he shal nat been ashamed to lerne hem
and enquere of lasse folk than him-self."/
And sir, that ther hath been many
a good womman, may lightly be preved./
For certes, sir, our lord Jesu Crist wolde
never have descended to be born of
a womman, if alle wommen hadden ben
wikke. / And after that, for the grete
bountee that is in wommen, our lord Jesu
Crist, whan he was risen fro deeth to
lyve, appeered rather to a womman than
to his apostles. / And though that 2265
Salomon seith, that "he ne fond never
womman good," it folweth nat therfore
that alle wommen ben wikke. / For
though that he ne fond no good womman,
certes, ful many another man hath
founden many a womman ful good and
trewe. / Or elles per-aventure the entente of Salomon was this ; that, as in
sovereyn bountee, he fond no womman ; /
this is to seyn, that ther is no wight that
hath sovereyn bountee save god allone ;
as he him-self recordeth in his Evaun-
gelie. / For ther nis no creature so good
that him ne wanteth somwhat of the
perfeccioun of god, that is his maker. / 2270
Your thridde resoun is this : ye seyn that
"if ye governe yow by my conseil, it
sholde seme that ye hadde yeve me the
maistrie and the lordshipe over your
persone."/ Sir, save your grace, it is nat
so. For if it were so, that no man sholde
be conseilled but only of hem that hadden
lordshipe and maistrie of his persone, men
wolden nat be conseilled so ofte. / For
soothly, thilke man that asketh conseil of
a purpos, yet hath he free chois, wheither
he wole werke by that conseil or noon. /
And as to your fourthe resoun, ther ye
seyn that "the janglerie of wommen hath
hid thinges that they woot noght," as
who seith, that "a womman can nat hyde
that she woot " ; / sir, thise wordes been
understonde of wommen that been jan-
gleresses and wikked ; / of whiche wom- 2275
men, men seyn that "three thinges
dryven a man out of his hous ; that is to
seyn, smoke, dropping of reyn, and
wikked wyves" ; / and of swiche wommen
seith Salomon, that "it were bettre

dwelle in desert, than with a womman
that is riotous." / And sir, by your leve,
that am nat I; / for ye han ful ofte
assayed my grete silence and my gret
pacience; and eek how wel that I can
hyde and hele thinges that men oghte
secreely to hyde. / And soothly, as to
your fifthe resoun, wher-as ye seyn, that
"in wikked conseil wommen venquisshe
men"; god woot, thilke resoun stant
2280 here in no stede. / For understond now,
ye asken conseil to do wikkednesse; / and
if ye wole werken wikkednesse, and your
wyf restreyneth thilke wikked purpos,
and overcometh yow by resoun and by
good conseil; / certes, your wyf oghte
rather to be preised than y-blamed. /
Thus sholde ye understonde the philosophre that seith, "in wikked conseil
wommen venquisshen hir housbondes." /
And ther-as ye blamen alle wommen and
hir resouns, I shal shewe yow by manye
ensamples that many a womman hath
ben ful good, and yet been; and hir
2285 conseils ful hoolsome and profitable. /
Eek som men han seyd, that "the conseillinge of wommen is outher to dere, or
elles to litel of prys." / But al-be-it so,
that ful many a womman is badde, and
hir conseil vile and noght worth, yet han
men founde ful many a good womman,
and ful discrete and wise in conseillinge. /
Lo, Jacob, by good conseil of his moder
Rebekka, wan the benisoun of Ysaak his
fader, and the lordshipe over alle his
bretheren. / Judith, by hir good conseil,
delivered the citee of Bethulie, in which
she dwelled, out of the handes of Olofernus, that hadde it biseged and wolde
have al destroyed it. / Abigail delivered
Nabal hir housbonde fro David the king,
that wolde have slayn him, and apaysed
the ire of the king by hir wit and by hir
2290 good conseilling. / Hester by hir good
conseil enhaunced greetly the peple of
god in the regne of Assuerus the king. /
And the same bountee in good conseilling
of many a good womman may men telle. /
And moreover, whan our lord hadde creat
Adam our forme-fader, he seyde in this
wyse: / "it is nat good to been a man

allone; make we to him an help semblable to himself." / Here may ye se that,
if that wommen were nat goode, and hir
conseils goode and profitable, / our lord 2295
god of hevene wolde never han wroght
hem, ne called hem help of man, but
rather confusioun of man. / And ther
seyde ones a clerk in two vers: "what is
bettre than gold? Jaspre. What is bettre
than jaspre? Wisdom. / And what is
bettre than wisdom? Womman. And
what is bettre than a good womman?
No-thing." / And sir, by manye of othre
resons may ye seen, that manye wommen
been goode, and hir conseils goode and
profitable. / And therfore sir, if ye wol
triste to my conseil, I shal restore yow
your doghter hool and sound. / And eek 2300
I wol do to yow so muche, that ye shul
have honour in this cause.' /

§ 16. Whan Melibee hadde herd the
wordes of his wyf Prudence, he seyde
thus: / 'I see wel that the word of
Salomon is sooth; he seith, that "wordes
that been spoken discreetly by ordinaunce,
been honycombes; for they yeven swetnesse to the soule, and hoolsomnesse to
the body." / And wyf, by-cause of thy
swete wordes, and eek for I have assayed
and preved thy grete sapience and thy
grete trouthe, I wol governe me by thy
conseil in alle thing.' /

§ 17. 'Now sir,' quod dame Prudence,
'and sin ye vouche-sauf to been governed
by my conseil, I wol enforme yow how ye
shul governe your-self in chesinge of your
conseillours. / Ye shul first, in alle your 2305
werkes, mekely biseken to the heighe god
that he wol be your conseillour; / and
shapeth yow to swich entente, that he
yeve yow conseil and confort, as taughte
Thobie his sone: / "at alle tymes thou
shalt blesse god, and praye him to dresse
thy weyes"; and looke that alle thy
conseils been in him for evermore. / Seint
Jame eek seith: "if any of yow have
nede of sapience, axe it of god." / And
afterward thanne shul ye taken conseil
in your-self, and examine wel your
thoghtes, of swich thing as yow thinketh
that is best for your profit. / And thanne 2310

shul ye dryve fro your herte three thinges that been contrariouse to good conseil, / that is to seyn, ire, coveitise, and hastifnesse. /

§ 18. First, he that axeth conseil of him-self, certes he moste been with-outen ire, for manye causes. / The firste is this : he that hath greet ire and wratthe in him-self, he weneth alwey that he may do thing that he may nat do. / And secoundely, he that is irous and wroth, he ne may nat wel deme ; / and he that may nat wel deme, may nat wel conseille. / The thridde is this ; that "he that is irous and wrooth," as seith Senek, "ne may nat speke but he blame thinges"; / and with his viciouse wordes he stireth other folk to angre and to ire. / And eek sir, ye moste dryve coveitise out of your herte. / For the apostle seith, that "coveitise is rote of alle harmes." / And trust wel that a coveitous man ne can noght deme ne thinke, but only to fulfille the ende of his coveitise ; / and certes, that ne may never been accompliced ; for ever the more habundaunce that he hath of richesse, the more he desyreth. / And sir, ye moste also dryve out of your herte hastifnesse ; for certes, / ye ne may nat deme for the beste a sodeyn thought that falleth in youre herte, but ye moste avyse yow on it ful ofte. / For as ye herde biforn, the commune proverbe is this, that "he that sone demeth, sone repenteth." /

§ 19. Sir, ye ne be nat alwey in lyke disposicioun ; / for certes, som thing that somtyme semeth to yow that it is good for to do, another tyme it semeth to yow the contrarie. /

§ 20. Whan ye han taken conseil in your-self, and han demed by good deliberacion swich thing as you semeth best, / thanne rede I yow, that ye kepe it secree. / Biwrey nat your conseil to no persone, but-if so be that ye wenen sikerly that, thurgh your biwreying, your condicioun shal be to yow the more profitable. / For Jesus Syrak seith : "neither to thy foo ne to thy freend discovere nat thy secree ne thy folie ; /

for they wol yeve yow audience and loking and supportacioun in thy presence, and scorne thee in thyn absence." / Another clerk seith, that "scarsly shaltou finden any persone that may kepe conseil secreely." / The book seith : "whyl that thou kepest thy conseil in thyn herte, thou kepest it in thy prisoun : / and whan thou biwreyest thy conseil to any wight, he holdeth thee in his snare." / And therefore yow is bettre 2335 to hyde your conseil in your herte, than praye him, to whom ye han biwreyed your conseil, that he wole kepen it cloos and stille. / For Seneca seith : "if so be that thou ne mayst nat thyn owene conseil hyde, how darstou prayen any other wight thy conseil secreely to kepe ?" / But nathelees, if thou wene sikerly that the biwreying of thy conseil to a persone wol make thy condicioun to stonden in the bettre plyt, thanne shaltou tellen him thy conseil in this wyse. / First, thou shalt make no semblant whether thee were lever pees or werre, or this or that, ne shewe him nat thy wille and thyn entente ; / for trust wel, that comunly thise conseillours been flatereres, / namely the conseillours of grete 2340 lordes ; / for they enforcen hem alwey rather to speken plesante wordes, enclyninge to the lordes lust, than wordes that been trewe or profitable. / And therfore men seyn, that "the riche man hath seld good conseil but-if he have it of him-self." / And after that, thou shalt considere thy freendes and thyne enemys. / And as touchinge thy freendes, thou shalt considere whiche of hem been most feithful and most wyse, and eldest and most approved in conseilling. / And of 2345 hem shalt thou aske thy conseil, as the caas requireth. /

§ 21. I seye that first ye shul clepe to your conseil your freendes that been trewe. / For Salomon seith : that "right as the herte of a man delyteth in savour that is sote, right so the conseil of trewe freendes yeveth swetenesse to the soule." / He seith also : "ther may no-thing be lykned to the trewe freend." / For

certes, gold ne silver beth nat so muche
2350 worth as the gode wil of a trewe freend. /
And eek he seith, that "a trewe freend
is a strong deffense; who-so that it
findeth, certes he findeth a greet tresour." / Thanne shul ye eek considere,
if that your trewe freendes been discrete and wyse. For the book seith:
"axe alwey thy conseil of hem that been
wyse." / And by this same resoun shul
ye clepen to your conseil, of your freendes
that been of age, swiche as han seyn and
been expert in manye thinges, and been
approved in conseillinges. / For the
book seith, that "in olde men is the
sapience and in longe tyme the prudence." / And Tullius seith : that "grete
thinges ne been nat ay accompliced by
strengthe, ne by delivernesse of body,
but by good conseil, by auctoritee of persones, and by science; the whiche three
thinges ne been nat feble by age, but
certes they enforcen and encreesen day
2355 by day." / And thanne shul ye kepe
this for a general reule. First shul ye
clepen to your conseil a fewe of your
freendes that been especiale ; / for Salomon seith : "manye freendes have thou;
but among a thousand chese thee oon to
be thy conseillour." / For al-be-it so
that thou first ne telle thy conseil but
to a fewe, thou mayst afterward telle it
to mo folk, if it be nede. / But loke
alwey that thy conseillours have thilke
three condiciouns that I have seyd bifore ;
that is to seyn, that they be trewe, wyse,
and of old experience. / And werke nat
alwey in every nede by oon counseillour
allone ; for somtyme bihoveth it to been
2360 conseilled by manye. / For Salomon
seith : "salvacioun of thinges is wher-as
ther been manye conseillours." /

§ 22. Now sith that I have told yow
of which folk ye sholde been counseilled,
now wol I teche yow which conseil ye
oghte to eschewe. / First ye shul eschewe
the conseiling of foles ; for Salomon seith :
"taak no conseil of a fool, for he ne can
noght conseille but after his owene lust
and his affeccioun." / The book seith :
that "the propretee of a fool is this ; he

troweth lightly harm of every wight,
and lightly troweth alle bountee in him-
self." / Thou shalt eek eschewe the conseilling of alle flatereres, swiche as enforcen hem rather to preise your persone
by flaterye than for to telle yow the
sothfastnesse of thinges. /                    230

§ 23. Wherfore Tullius seith : "amonges
alle the pestilences that been in freendshipe, the gretteste is flaterye." And therfore is it more nede that thou eschewe and
drede flatereres than any other peple. /
The book seith : "thou shalt rather drede
and flee fro the swete wordes of flateringe
preiseres, than fro the egre wordes of thy
freend that seith thee thy sothes." /
Salomon seith, that "the wordes of a
flaterere is a snare to cacche with innocents." / He seith also, that "he that
speketh to his freend wordes of swetnesse
and of plesaunce, setteth a net biforn
his feet to cacche him." / And therfore
seith Tullius : "enclyne nat thyne eres to
flatereres, ne taketh no conseil of wordes
of flaterye." / And Caton seith : "avyse 237
thee wel, and eschewe the wordes of
swetnesse and of plesaunce." / And eek
thou shalt eschewe the conseilling of
thyne olde enemys that been reconsiled. /
The book seith : that "no wight retourneth saufly in-to the grace of his
olde enemy." / And Isope seith : "ne
trust nat to hem to whiche thou hast
had som-tyme werre or enmitee, ne telle
hem nat thy conseil." / And Seneca
telleth the cause why. "It may nat be,"
seith he, "that, where greet fyr hath
longe tyme endured, that ther ne dwelleth som vapour of warmnesse." / And 237
therfore seith Salomon : "in thyn olde
foo trust never." / For sikerly, though
thyn enemy be reconsiled and maketh
thee chere of humilitee, and louteth to
thee with his heed, ne trust him never. /
For certes, he maketh thilke feyned humilitee more for his profit than for any
love of thy persone ; by-cause that he
demeth to have victorie over thy persone
by swich feyned contenance, the which
victorie he mighte nat have by stryf or
werre. / And Peter Alfonce seith : "make

no felawshipe with thyne olde enemys; for if thou do hem bountee, they wol perverten it in-to wikkednesse." / And eek thou most eschewe the conseilling of hem that been thy servants, and beren thee greet reverence; for peraventure they 380 seyn it more for drede than for love. / And therfore seith a philosophre in this wyse : " ther is no wight parfitly trewe to him that he to sore dredeth." / And Tullius seith : " ther nis no might so greet of any emperour, that longe may endure, but-if he have more love of the peple than drede." / Thou shalt also eschewe the conseiling of folk that been dronkelewe; for they ne can no conseil hyde. / For Salomon seith : " ther is no privetee ther-as regneth dronkenesse." / Ye shul also han in suspect the conseilling of swich folk as conseille yow a thing prively, and conseille yow 385 the contrarie openly. / For Cassidorie seith : that " it is a maner sleighte to hindre, whan he sheweth to doon a thing openly and werketh prively the contrarie." / Thou shalt also have in suspect the conseilling of wikked folk. For the book seith : " the conseilling of wikked folk is alwey ful of fraude : " / And David seith : " blisful is that man that hath nat folwed the conseilling of shrewes." / Thou shalt also eschewe the conseilling of yong folk; for hir conseil is nat rype. /

§ 24. Now sir, sith I have shewed yow of which folk ye shul take your conseil, and of which folk ye shul folwe the 390 conseil, / now wol I teche yow how ye shal examine your conseil, after the doctrine of Tullius. / In the examininge thanne of your conseillour, ye shul considere manye thinges. / Alderfirst thou shalt considere, that in thilke thing that thou purposest, and upon what thing thou wolt have conseil, that verray trouthe be seyd and conserved; this is to seyn, telle trewely thy tale. / For he that seith fals may nat wel be conseilled, in that cas of which he lyeth. / And after this, thou shalt considere the thinges that acorden to that thou purposest for to do by thy conseillours, if resoun

accorde therto; / and eek, if thy might 2395 may atteine ther-to; and if the more part and the bettre part of thy conseillours acorde ther-to, or no. / Thanne shaltou considere what thing shal folwe of that conseilling; as hate, pees, werre, grace, profit, or damage; and manye othere thinges. / And in alle thise thinges thou shalt chese the beste, and weyve alle othere thinges. / Thanne shaltow considere of what rote is engendred the matere of thy conseil, and what fruit it may conceyve and engendre. / Thou shalt eek considere alle thise causes, fro whennes they been sprongen. / And 2400 whan ye han examined your conseil as I have seyd, and which partie is the bettre and more profitable, and hast approved it by manye wyse folk and olde ; / thanne shaltou considere, if thou mayst parfourne it and maken of it a good ende. / For certes, resoun wol nat that any man sholde biginne a thing, but-if he mighte parfourne it as him oghte. / Ne no wight sholde take up-on hym so hevy a charge that he mighte nat bere it. / For the proverbe seith : " he that to muche embraceth, distreyneth litel." / And Catoun seith : " assay 2405 to do swich thing as thou hast power to doon, lest that the charge oppresse thee so sore, that thee bihoveth to weyve thing that thou hast bigonne." / And if so be that thou be in doute, whether thou mayst parfourne a thing or noon, chese rather to suffre than biginne. / And Piers Alphonce seith : " if thou hast might to doon a thing of which thou most repente thee, it is bettre ' nay' than ' ye ' ; " / this is to seyn, that thee is bettre holde thy tonge stille, than for to speke. / Thanne may ye understonde by strenger resons, ·that if thou hast power to parfourne a werk of which thou shalt repente, thanne is it bettre that thou suffre than biginne. / Wel seyn 2410 they, that defenden every wight to assaye any thing of which he is in doute, whether he may parfourne it or no. / And after, whan ye han examined your conseil as I have seyd biforn, and knowen

wel that ye may parfourne youre emprise, conferme it thanne sadly til it be
at an ende. /

§ 25. Now is it resoun and tyme that
I shewe yow, whanne, and wherfore, that
ye may chaunge your conseil with-outen
your repreve. / Soothly, a man may
chaungen his purpos and his conseil if
the cause cesseth, or whan a newe caas
bitydeth. / For the lawe seith: that
"upon thinges that newely bityden
2415 bihoveth newe conseil."/ And Senek
seith: "if thy conseil is comen to the
eres of thyn enemy, chaunge thy conseil." / Thou mayst also chaunge thy
conseil if so be that thou finde that, by
errour or by other cause, harm or damage
may bityde. / Also, if thy conseil be
dishonest, or elles cometh of dishoneste
cause, chaunge thy conseil. / For the
lawes seyn : that "alle bihestes that been
dishoneste been of no value."/ And
eek, if it so be that it be inpossible, or
2420 may nat goodly be parfourned or kept. /

§ 26. And take this for a general reule,
that every conseil that is affermed so
strongly that it may nat be chaunged,
for no condicioun that may bityde, I
seye that thilke conseil is wikked.' /

§ 27. This Melibeus, whanne he hadde
herd the doctrine of his wyf dame Prudence, answerde in this wyse. / 'Dame,'
quod he, 'as yet in-to this tyme ye han
wel and covenably taught me as in
general, how I shal governe me in the
chesinge and in the withholdinge of
my conseillours. / But now wolde I
fayn that ye wolde condescende in
especial, / and telle me how lyketh
yow, or what semeth yow, by our
conseillours that we han chosen in our
2425 present nede.' /

§ 28. 'My lord,' quod she, 'I biseke
yow in al humblesse, that ye wol nat
wilfully replye agayn my resouns, ne
distempre your herte thogh I speke
thing that yow displese. / For god wot
that, as in myn entente, I speke it for
your beste, for your honour and for your
profite eke. / And soothly, I hope that
your benignitee wol taken it in pacience./

Trusteth me wel,' quod she, 'that your
conseil as in this caas ne sholde nat,
as to speke properly, be called a conseilling, but a mocioun or a moevyng of
folye ; / in which conseil ye han erred in
many a sondry wyse. /                     243

§ 29. First and forward, ye han erred
in th'assemblinge of your conseillours. /
For ye sholde first have cleped a fewe
folk to your conseil, and after ye mighte
han shewed it to mo folk, if it hadde
been nede. / But certes, ye han sodeynly
cleped to your conseil a greet multitude
of peple, ful chargeant and ful anoyous
for to here. / Also ye han erred, for
there-as ye sholden only have cleped to
your conseil your trewe freendes olde and
wyse, / ye han y-cleped straunge folk,
and yong folk, false flatereres, and enemys
reconsiled, and folk that doon yow
reverence withouten love. / And eek 243
also ye have erred, for ye han broght
with yow to your conseil ire, covetise,
and hastifnesse; / the whiche three
thinges been contrariouse to every conseil
honeste and profitable; / the whiche
three thinges ye han nat anientissed or
destroyed hem, neither in your-self ne
in your conseillours, as yow oghte. / Ye
han erred also, for ye han shewed to
your conseillours your talent, and your
affeccioun to make werre anon and for
to do vengeance; / they han espyed by
your wordes to what thing ye been
enclyned. / And therfore han they 244
rather conseilled yow to your talent than
to your profit. / Ye han erred also, for
it semeth that yow suffyseth to han been
conseilled by thise conseillours only, and
with litel avys; / wher-as, in so greet
and so heigh a nede, it hadde been
necessarie mo conseillours, and more
deliberacioun to parfourne your emprise./
Ye han erred also, for ye han nat
examined your conseil in the forseyde
manere, ne in due manere as the caas
requireth. / Ye han erred also, for ye
han maked no divisioun bitwixe your
conseillours; this is to seyn, bitwixen
your trewe freendes and your feyned
conseillours ; / ne ye han nat knowe 2445

the wil of your trewe freendes olde and wyse; / but ye han cast alle hir wordes in an hochepot, and enclyned your herte to the more part and to the gretter nombre; and ther been ye condescended. / And sith ye wot wel that men shal alwey finde a gretter nombre of foles than of wyse men, / and therfore the conseils that been at congregaciouns and multitudes of folk, ther-as men take more reward to the nombre than to the sapience of persones, / ye see wel that in swiche conseillinges foles han the mais-2450 trie.' / Melibeus answerde agayn, and seyde: ' I graunte wel that I have erred ; / but ther-as thou hast told me heer-biforn, that he nis nat to blame that chaungeth hise conseillours in certein caas, and for certeine juste causes, / I am al redy to chaunge my conseillours, right as thou wolt devyse. / The proverbe seith : that "for to do sinne is mannish, but certes for to persevere longe in sinne is werk of the devel."' /

§ 30. To this sentence answerde anon 2455 dame Prudence, and seyde : / 'Examineth,' quod she, 'your conseil, and lat us see the whiche of hem han spoken most resonably, and taught yow best conseil. / And for-as-muche as that the examin-acioun is necessarie, lat us biginne at the surgiens and at the phisiciens, that first speken in this matere. / I sey yow, that the surgiens and phisiciens han seyd yow in your conseil discreetly, as hem oughte ; / and in hir speche seyden ful wysly, that to the office of hem aper-teneth to doon to every wight honour and profit, and no wight for to anoye ; / and, after hir craft, to doon greet dili-gence un-to the cure of hem whiche that 2460 they han in hir governaunce. / And sir, right as they han answered wysly and discreetly, / right so rede I that they been heighly and sovereynly guer-doned for hir noble speche ; / and eek for they sholde do the more ententif bisinesse in the curacioun of your doghter dere. / For al-be-it so that they been your freendes, therfore shal ye nat suffren that they serve yow for noght ; /

but ye oghte the rather guerdone hem and shewe hem your largesse. / And as 2465 touchinge the proposicioun which that the phisiciens entreteden in this caas, this is to seyn, / that, in maladyes, that oon contrarie is warisshed by another con-trarie, / I wolde fayn knowe how ye understonde thilke text, and what is your sentence.' / 'Certes,' quod Melibeus, ' I understonde it in this wyse : / that, right as they han doon me a contrarie, right so sholde I doon hem another. / 2470 For right as they han venged hem on me and doon me wrong, right so shal I venge me upon hem and doon hem wrong ; / and thanne have I cured oon contrarie by another.' /

§ 31. ' Lo, lo ! ' quod dame Prudence, ' how lightly is every man enclyned to his owene desyr and to his owene ple-saunce ! / Certes,' quod she, ' the wordes of the phisiciens ne sholde nat han been understonden in this wyse. / For certes, wikkednesse is nat contrarie to wikked-nesse, ne vengeaunce to vengeaunce, ne wrong to wrong ; but they been sembla-ble. / And therfore, o vengeaunce is nat 2475 warisshed by another vengeaunce, ne o wrong by another wrong ; / but everich of hem encreesceth and aggreggeth other. / But certes, the wordes of the phisiciens sholde been understonden in this wyse : / for good and wikkednesse been two contraries, and pees and werre, vengeaunce and suffraunce, discord and accord, and manye othere thinges. / But certes, wikkednesse shal be warisshed by goodnesse, discord by accord, werre by pees, and so forth of othere thinges. / 2480 And heer-to accordeth Seint Paul the apostle in manye places. / He seith : "ne yeldeth nat harm for harm, ne wikked speche for wikked speche ; / but do wel to him that dooth thee harm, and blesse him that seith to thee harm." / And in manye othere places he amones-teth pees and accord. / But now wol I speke to yow of the conseil which that was yeven to yow by the men of lawe and the wyse folk, / that seyden alle by oon 2485 accord as ye han herd bifore ; / that, over

alle thynges, ye sholde doon your diligence to kepen your persone and to
warnestore your hous. / And seyden
also, that in this caas ye oghten for to
werken ful avysely and with greet deliberacioun. / And sir, as to the firste
point, that toucheth to the keping of
your persone; / ye shul understonde that
he that hath werre shal evermore mekely
2490 and devoutly preyen biforn alle thinges, /
that Jesus Crist of his grete mercy wol
han him in his proteccioun, and been his
sovereyn helping at his nede. / For
certes, in this world ther is no wight that
may be conseilled ne kept suffisantly
withouten the keping of our lord Jesu
Crist. / To this sentence accordeth the
prophete David, that seith : / "if god ne
kepe the citee, in ydel waketh he that it
kepeth." / Now sir, thanne shul ye com-
mitte the keping of your persone to your
trewe freendes that been approved and
2495 y-knowe; / and of hem shul ye axen help
your persone for to kepe.  For Catoun
seith : "if thou hast nede of help, axe it
of thy freendes; / for ther nis noon so
good a phisicien as thy trewe freend." /
And after this, thanne shul ye kepe yow
fro alle straunge folk, and fro lyeres, and
have alwey in suspect hir companye. /
For Piers Alfonce seith: "ne tak no
companye by the weye of a straunge man,
but-if so be that thou have knowe him of
a lenger tyme. / And if so be that he
falle in-to thy companye paraventure
2500 withouten thyn assent, / enquere thanne,
as subtilly as thou mayst, of his conversacioun and of his lyf bifore, and feyne thy
wey; seye that thou goost thider as thou
wolt nat go; / and if he bereth a spere,
hold thee on the right syde, and if he
bere a swerd, hold thee on the lift syde." /
And after this, thanne shul ye kepe yow
wysely from alle swich manere peple as I
have seyd bifore, and hem and hir conseil
eschewe. / And after this, thanne shul
ye kepe yow in swich manere, / that for
any presumpcioun of your strengthe, that
ye ne dispyse nat ne acounte nat the might
of your adversarie so litel, that ye lete
the keping of your persone for your pre-

sumpcioun; / for every wys man dredeth 250
his enemy. / And Salomon seith : "weleful
is he that of alle hath drede; / for certes,
he that thurgh the hardinesse of his herte
and thurgh the hardinesse of him-self
hath to greet presumpcioun, him shal
yvel bityde." / Thanne shul ye evermore
countrewayte embusshements and alle
espiaille. / For Senek seith : that "the
wyse man that dredeth harmes escheweth
harmes; / ne he ne falleth in-to perils,
that perils escheweth." / And al-be-it so 2510
that it seme that thou art in siker place,
yet shaltow alwey do thy diligence in
kepinge of thy persone; / this is to seyn,
ne be nat necligent to kepe thy persone,
nat only fro thy gretteste enemys but fro
thy leeste enemy. / Senek seith : "a
man that is wel avysed, he dredeth his
leste enemy." / Ovide seith : that "the
litel wesele wol slee the grete bole and the
wilde hert." / And the book seith : "a 2515
litel thorn may prikke a greet king ful
sore; and an hound wol holde the wilde
boor." / But nathelees, I sey nat thou
shalt be so coward that thou doute
ther wher-as is no drede. / The book
seith : that " somme folk han greet
lust to deceyve, but yet they dreden
hem to be deceyved." / Yet shaltou
drede to been empoisoned, and kepe
yow from the companye of scorneres. /
For the book seith : "with scorneres
make no companye, but flee hir wordes
as venim." /                                              2520
    § 32. Now as to the seconde point,
wher-as your wyse conseillours conseilled
yow to warnestore your hous with gret
diligence, / I wolde fayn knowe, how that
ye understonde thilke wordes, and what
is your sentence.' /
    § 33. Melibeus answerde and seyde,
' Certes I understande it in this wise;
that I shal warnestore myn hous with
toures, swiche as han castelles and
othere manere edifices, and armure
and artelleries, / by whiche thinges I
may my persone and myn hous so
kepen and defenden, that myne enemys
shul been in drede myn hous for to
approche.' /

§ 34. To this sentence answerde anon Prudence; 'warnestoring,' quod she, 'of heighe toures and of grete edifices apper-²⁵²⁵ teneth som-tyme to pryde; / and eek men make heighe toures and grete edifices with grete costages and with greet tra-vaille; and whan that they been accom-pliced, yet be they nat worth a stree, but-if they be defended by trewe freendes that been olde and wyse. / And understond wel, that the gretteste and strongeste garnison that a riche man may have, as wel to kepen his persone as hise goodes, is / that he be biloved amonges his sub-gets and with hise neighebores. / For thus seith Tullius : that "ther is a maner garnison that no man may venquisse ne disconfite, and that is, / a lord to be biloved of hise citezeins and of his ³⁰peple." /

§ 35. Now sir, as to the thridde point; wher-as your olde and wise conseillours seyden, that yow ne oghte nat sodeynly ne hastily proceden in this nede, / but that yow oghte purveyen and apparaillen yow in this caas with greet diligence and greet deliberacioun; / trewely, I trowe that they seyden right wysly and right sooth. / For Tullius seith, "in every nede, er thou biginne it, apparaille thee with greet diligence." / Thanne seye I, that in vengeance-taking, in werre, in ³⁵bataille, and in warnestoring, / er thow biginne, I rede that thou apparaille thee ther-to, and do it with greet delibera-cioun. / For Tullius seith : that "long apparailling biforn the bataille maketh short victorie." / And Cassidorus seith : "the garnison is stronger whan it is longe tyme avysed." /

§ 36. But now lat us speken of the conseil that was accorded by your neighe-bores, swiche as doon yow reverence withouten love, / your olde enemys recon-⁵⁴⁰siled, your flatereres / that conseilled yow certeyne thinges prively, and openly con-seilleden yow the contrarie; / the yonge folk also, that conseilleden yow to venge yow and make werre anon. / And certes, sir, as I have seyd biforn, ye han greetly erred to han cleped swich maner folk to

your conseil; / which conseillours been y-nogh repreved by the resouns afore-seyd. / But nathelees, lat us now de-scende to the special. Ye shuln first procede after the doctrine of Tullius. / ²⁵⁴⁵ Certes, the trouthe of this matere or of this conseil nedeth nat diligently en-quere; / for it is wel wist whiche they been that han doon to yow this trespas and vileinye, / and how manye trespas-sours, and in what manere they han to yow doon al this wrong and al this vileinye. / And after this, thanne shul ye examine the seconde condicioun, which that the same Tullius addeth in this matere. / For Tullius put a thing, which that he clepeth "consentinge," this is to seyn; / who been they and how manye, ²⁵⁵⁰ and whiche been they, that consenteden to thy conseil, in thy wilfulnesse to doon hastif vengeance. / And lat us considere also who been they, and how manye been they, and whiche been they, that con-senteden to your adversaries. / And certes, as to the firste poynt, it is wel knowen whiche folk been they that con-senteden to your hastif wilfulnesse; / for trewely, alle tho that conseilleden yow to maken sodeyn werre ne been nat your freendes. / Lat us now considere whiche been they, that ye holde so greetly your freendes as to your persone. / For ²⁵⁵⁵ al-be-it so that ye be mighty and riche, certes ye ne been nat but allone. / For certes, ye ne han no child but a doghter; / ne ye ne han bretheren ne cosins ger-mayns, ne noon other neigh kinrede, / wherfore that your enemys, for drede, sholde stinte to plede with yow or to destroye your persone. / Ye knowen also, that your richesses moten been dis-pended in diverse parties; / and whan ²⁵⁶⁰ that every wight hath his part, they ne wollen taken but litel reward to venge thy deeth. / But thyne enemys been three, and they han manie children, bretheren, cosins, and other ny kinrede; / and, though so were that thou haddest slayn of hem two or three, yet dwellen ther y-nowe to wreken hir deeth and to slee thy persone. / And though so be

that your kinrede be more siker and
stedefast than the kin of your adversarie, / yet nathelees your kinrede nis
but a fer kinrede ; they been but litel sib
2565 to yow, / and the kin of your enemys
been ny sib to hem. And certes, as in
that, hir condicioun is bet than youres. /
Thanne lat us considere also if the conseilling of hem that conseilleden yow to
taken sodeyn vengeaunce, whether it
accorde to resoun ? / And certes, ye
knowe wel "nay." / For as by right and
resoun, ther may no man taken vengeance
on no wight, but the juge that hath the
jurisdiccioun of it, / whan it is graunted
him to take thilke vengeance, hastily or
2570 attemprely, as the lawe requireth. / And
yet more-over, of thilke word that Tullius
clepeth "consentinge," / thou shalt considere if thy might and thy power may
consenten and suffyse to thy wilfulnesse
and to thy conseillours. / And certes,
thou mayst wel seyn that "nay." / For
sikerly, as for to speke proprely, we may
do no-thing but only swich thing as we
may doon rightfully. / And certes, rightfully ne mowe ye take no vengeance as of
2575 your propre auctoritee. / Thanne mowe
ye seen, that your power ne consenteth
nat ne accordeth nat with your wilfulnesse. / Lat us now examine the thridde
point that Tullius clepeth "consequent." /
Thou shalt understonde that the vengeance that thou purposest for to take
is the consequent. / And ther-of folweth
another vengeaunce, peril, and werre ;
and othere damages with-oute nombre, of
whiche we be nat war as at this tyme. /
And as touchinge the fourthe point, that
2580 Tullius clepeth "engendringe," / thou
shalt considere, that this wrong which
that is doon to thee is engendred of the
hate of thyne enemys ; / and of the
vengeance-takinge upon that wolde engendre another vengeance, and muchel
sorwe and wastinge of richesses, as I
seyde. /

§ 37. Now sir, as to the point that
Tullius clepeth "causes," which that is
the laste point, / thou shalt understonde
that the wrong that thou hast receyved

hath certeine causes, / whiche that
clerkes clepen *Oriens* and *Efficiens*, and
*Causa longinqua* and *Causa propinqua* ;
this is to seyn, the fer cause and the ny
cause. / The fer cause is almighty god, 2585
that is cause of alle thinges. / The neer
cause is thy three enemys. / The cause
accidental was hate. / The cause material
been the fyve woundes of thy doghter. /
The cause formal is the manere of hir
werkinge, that broghten laddres and
cloumben in at thy windowes. / The 2590
cause final was for to slee thy doghter ;
it letted nat in as muche as in hem was. /
But for to speken of the fer cause, as to
what ende they shul come, or what shal
finally bityde of hem in this caas, ne can
I nat deme but by conjectinge and by
supposinge. / For we shul suppose that
they shul come to a wikked ende, / by-
cause that the Book of Decrees seith :
"selden or with greet peyne been causes
y-broght to good ende whanne they been
baddely bigonne." /

§ 38. Now sir, if men wolde axe me,
why that god suffred men to do yow this
vileinye, certes, I can nat wel answere as
for no sothfastnesse. / For th'apostle 2595
seith, that "the sciences and the jugge-
mentz of our lord god almighty been ful
depe ; / ther may no man comprehende
ne serchen hem suffisantly." / Nathelees, by certeyne presumpcions and conjectinges, I holde and bileve / that god,
which that is ful of justice and of rightwisnesse, hath suffred this bityde by
juste cause resonable. /

§ 39. Thy name is Melibee, this is to
seyn, "a man that drinketh hony." / 2600
Thou hast y-dronke so muchel hony of
swete temporel richesses and delices
and honours of this world, / that thou
art dronken ; and hast forgeten Jesu
Crist thy creatour ; / thou ne hast nat
doon to him swich honour and reverence
as thee oughte. / Ne thou ne hast nat
wel y-taken kepe to the wordes of Ovide,
that seith : / "under the hony of the
godes of the body is hid the venim that
sleeth the soule." / And Salomon seith, 2605
"if thou hast founden hony, ete of it that

suffyseth ; / for if thou ete of it out of
mesure, thou shalt spewe," and be nedy
and povre. / And peraventure Crist hath
thee in despit, and hath turned awey fro
thee his face and hise eres of misericorde ; / and also he hath suffred that
thou hast been punisshed in the manere
that thow hast y-trespassed. / Thou hast
510 doon sinne agayn our lord Crist ; / for
certes, the three enemys of mankinde,
that is to seyn, the flessh, the feend, and
the world, / thou hast suffred hem entre
in-to thyn herte wilfully by the windowes
of thy body, / and hast nat defended thy-
self suffisantly agayns hir assautes and
hir temptaciouns, so that they han
wounded thy soule in fyve places ; / this
is to seyn, the deedly sinnes that been
entred in-to thyn herte by thy fyve
wittes. / And in the same manere our
lord Crist hath wold and suffred, that thy
three enemys been entred in-to thyn hous
615 by the windowes, / and han y-wounded
thy doghter in the fore-seyde manere.' /

§ 40. 'Certes,' quod Melibee, 'I see wel
that ye enforce yow muchel by wordes to
overcome me in swich manere, that I shal
nat venge me of myne enemys ; / shewinge me the perils and the yveles that
mighten falle of this vengeance. / But
who-so wolde considere in alle vengeances
the perils and yveles that mighte sewe of
vengeance-takinge, / a man wolde never
2620 take vengeance, and that were harm ; /
for by the vengeance-takinge been the
wikked men dissevered fro the gode
men. / And they that han wil to do
wikkednesse restreyne hir wikked purpos,
whan they seen the punissinge and chastysinge of the trespassours.' / [†And to
this answerde dame Prudence : 'Certes,'
seyde she, 'I graunte wel that of vengeaunce cometh muchel yvel and muchel
good ; / but vengeaunce-taking aperteneth
nat unto everichoon, but only unto juges
and unto hem that han jurisdiccioun
upon the trespassours.] / And yet seye I
more, that right as a singuler persone
sinneth in takinge vengeance of another
2625 man, / right so sinneth the juge if he do
no vengeance of hem that it han de-

served. / For Senek seith thus : "that
maister," he seith, " is good that proveth
shrewes." / And as Cassidore seith : " A
man dredeth to do outrages, whan he
woot and knoweth that it displeseth to
the juges and sovereyns." / And another
seith : "the juge that dredeth to do right,
maketh men shrewes." / And Seint Paule
the apostle seith in his epistle, whan he
wryteth un-to the Romayns : that " the
juges beren nat the spere with-outen
cause ; " / but they beren it to punisse 2630
the shrewes and misdoeres, and for to
defende the gode men. / If ye wol thanne
take vengeance of your enemys, ye shul
retourne or have your recours to the juge
that hath the jurisdiccion up-on hem ; /
and he shal punisse hem as the lawe
axeth and requyreth.' /

§ 41. 'A !' quod Melibee, 'this vengeance lyketh me no-thing. / I bithenke
me now and take hede, how fortune hath
norissed me fro my childhede, and hath
holpen me to passe many a strong pas. / 2635
Now wol I assayen hir, trowinge, with
goddes help, that she shal helpe me my
shame for to venge.' /

§ 42. 'Certes,' quod Prudence, 'if ye
wol werke by my conseil, ye shul nat
assaye fortune by no wey ; / ne ye shul
nat lene or bowe unto hir, after the word
of Senek : / for " thinges that been folily
doon, and that been in hope of fortune,
shullen never come to good ende." / And
as the same Senek seith : " the more cleer
and the more shyning that fortune is, the
more brotil and the sonner broken she
is." / Trusteth nat in hir, for she nis 2640
nat stidefast ne stable ; / for whan thow
trowest to be most seur or siker of hir
help, she wol faille thee and deceyve
thee. / And wheras ye seyn that fortune
hath norissed yow fro your childhede, /
I seye, that in so muchel shul ye the
lasse truste in hir and in hir wit. / For
Senek seith : " what man that is norissed
by fortune, she maketh him a greet
fool." / Now thanne, sin ye desyre and 2645
axe vengeance, and the vengeance that is
doon after the lawe and bifore the juge
ne lyketh yow nat, / and the vengeance

that is doon in hope of fortune is perilous and uncertein, / thanne have ye
noon other remedie but for to have your
recours unto the sovereyn juge that
vengeth alle vileinyes and wronges ; /
and he shal venge yow after that him-self
witnesseth, wher-as he seith : / " leveth
2650 the vengeance to me, and I shal do it." ' /

§ 43. Melibee answerde, ' if I ne venge
me nat of the vileinye that men han
doon to me, / I sompne or warne hem
that han doon to me that vileinye and
alle othere, to do me another vileinye. /
For it is writen : " if thou take no vengeance of an old vileinye, thou sompnest
thyne adversaries to do thee a newe
vileinye." / And also, for my suffrance,
men wolden do to me so muchel vileinye,
that I mighte neither bere it ne sustene ; /
and so sholde I been put and holden over
2655 lowe. / For men seyn : " in muchel
suffringe shul manye thinges falle un-to
thee whiche thou shalt nat mowe
suffre." ' /

§ 44. ' Certes,' quod Prudence, ' I
graunte yow that over muchel suffraunce
nis nat good ; / but yet ne folweth it nat
ther-of, that every persone to whom men
doon vileinye take of it vengeance ; / for
that aperteneth and longeth al only to
the juges, for they shul venge the vileinyes
and iniuries. / And ther-fore tho two
auctoritees that ye han seyd above, been
2660 only understonden in the juges ; / for
whan they suffren over muchel the
wronges and the vileinyes to be doon
withouten punisshinge, / they sompne
nat a man al only for to do newe wronges,
but they comanden it. / Also a wys man
seith : that " the juge that correcteth nat
the sinnere comandeth and biddeth him
do sinne." / And the juges and sovereyns
mighten in hir land so muchel suffre of
the shrewes and misdoeres, / that they
sholden by swich suffrance, by proces of
tyme, wexen of swich power and might,
that they sholden putte out the juges
2665 and the sovereyns from hir places, / and
atte laste maken hem lesen hir lordshipes. /

§ 45. But lat us now putte, that ye

have leve to venge yow. / I seye ye been
nat of might and power as now to venge
yow. / For if ye wole maken comparisoun
un-to the might of your adversaries, ye
shul finde in manye thinges, that I have
shewed yow er this, that hir condicioun
is bettre than youres. / And therfore
seye I, that it is good as now that ye
suffre and be pacient. /

§ 46. Forther-more, ye knowen wel that,
after the comune sawe, " it is a woodnesse
a man to stryve with a strenger or a more
mighty man than he is him-self ; / and
for to stryve with a man of evene strengthe,
that is to seyn, with as strong a man as
he, it is peril ; / and for to stryve with a
weyker man, it is folie." / And therfore
sholde a man flee stryvinge as muchel as
he mighte. / For Salomon seith : " it is
a greet worship to a man to kepen him
fro noyse and stryf." / And if it so
bifalle or happe that a man of gretter
might and strengthe than thou art do
thee grevaunce, / studie and bisie thee
rather to stille the same grevaunce, than
for to venge thee. / For Senek seith :
that " he putteth him in greet peril that
stryveth with a gretter man than he is
him-self." / And Catoun seith : " if a
man of hyer estaat or degree, or more
mighty than thou, do thee anoy or grevaunce, suffre him ; / for he that ones
hath greved thee may another tyme
releve thee and helpe." / Yet sette I
caas, ye have bothe might and licence for
to venge yow. / I seye, that ther be ful
manye thinges that shul restreyne yow
of vengeance-takinge, / and make yow
for to enclyne to suffre, and for to han
pacience in the thinges that han been
doon to yow. / First and foreward, if ye
wole considere the defautes that been in
your owene persone, / for whiche defautes
god hath suffred yow have this tribulacioun, as I have seyd yow heer-biforn. /
For the poete seith, that " we oghte
paciently taken the tribulacions that
comen to us, whan we thinken and consideren that we han deserved to have
hem." / And Seint Gregorie seith : that
" whan a man considereth wel the nombre

of hise defautes and of his sinnes, / the
peynes and the tribulaciouns that he
suffreth semen the lesse un-to hym; /
and in-as-muche as him thinketh hise
sinnes more hevy and grevous, / in-so-
muche semeth his peyne the lighter and
90 the esier un-to him." / Also ye owen to
enclyne and bowe your herte to take the
pacience of our lord Jesu Crist, as seith
seint Peter in hise epistles : / "Jesu
Crist," he seith, "hath suffred for us,
and yeven ensample to every man to
folwe and sewe him ; / for he dide never
sinne, ne never cam ther a vileinous
word out of his mouth : / whan men
cursed him, he cursed hem noght; and
whan men betten him, he manaced hem
noght." / Also the grete pacience, which
the seintes that been in paradys han had
in tribulaciouns that they han y-suffred,
95 with-outen hir desert or gilt, / oghte
muchel stiren yow to pacience. / Furthermore, ye sholde enforce yow to have
pacience, / consideringe that the tribulaciouns of this world but litel whyle
endure, and sone passed been and
goon. / And the joye that a man
seketh to have by pacience in tribulaciouns is perdurable, after that the
apostle seith in his epistle : / "the joye
of god," he seith, " is perdurable," that is
00 to seyn, everlastinge. / Also troweth
and bileveth stedefastly, that he nis nat
wel y-norissed ne wel y-taught, that can
nat have pacience or wol nat receyve
pacience. / For Salomon seith : that "the
doctrine and the wit of a man is knowen
by pacience." / And in another place he
seith : that " he that is pacient governeth
him by greet prudence." / And the same
Salomon seith : " the angry and wrathful
man maketh noyses, and the pacient man
atempreth hem and stilleth." / He seith
05 also : "it is more worth to be pacient
than for to be right strong ; / and he that
may have the lordshipe of his owene
herte is more to preyse, than he that
by his force or strengthe taketh grete
citees." / And therfore seith seint Jame
in his epistle : that "pacience is a greet
vertu of perfeccioun." ' /

§ 47. 'Certes,' quod Melibee, 'I graunte
yow, dame Prudence, that pacience is
a greet vertu of perfeccioun ;/ but every
man may nat have the perfeccioun that
ye seken ; / ne I nam nat of the nombre
of right parfite men, / for myn herte may 2710
never been in pees un-to the tyme it be
venged./ And al-be-it so that it was
greet peril to myne enemys, to do me
a vileinye in takinge vengeance up-on
me, / yet token they noon hede of the
peril, but fulfilleden hir wikked wil and
hir corage. / And therfore, me thinketh
men oghten nat repreve me, though I
putte me in a litel peril for to venge me, /
and though I do a greet excesse, that is
to seyn, that I venge oon outrage by
another.' /                                    2715

§ 48. 'A !' quod dame Prudence, 'ye
seyn your wil and as yow lyketh ; / but
in no caas of the world a man sholde nat
doon outrage ne excesse for to vengen
him. / For Cassidore seith : that "as
yvel doth he that vengeth him by outrage,
as he that doth the outrage." / And
therfore ye shul venge yow after the
ordre of right, that is to seyn by the lawe,
and noght by excesse ne by outrage. /
And also, if ye wol venge yow of the outrage of your adversaries in other maner
than right comandeth, ye sinnen ; / and 2720
therfore seith Senek : that "a man shal
never vengen shrewednesse by shrewednesse." / And if ye seye, that right axeth
a man to defenden violence by violence,
and fighting by fighting, / certes ye seye
sooth, whan the defense is doon anon
with-outen intervalle or with-outen tarying or delay, / for to defenden him and
nat for to vengen him. / And it bihoveth
that a man putte swich attemperance
in his defence, / that men have no 2725
cause ne matere to repreven him that
defendeth him of excesse and outrage ;
for elles were it agayn resoun. / Pardee,
ye knowen wel, that ye maken no defence as now for to defende yow, but for
to venge yow ; / and so seweth it that ye
han no wil to do your dede attemprely. /
And therfore, me thinketh that pacience
is good. For Salomon seith : that " he

that is nat pacient shal have greet harm." /

§ 49. 'Certes,' quod Melibee, 'I graunte yow, that whan a man is inpacient and wroth, of that that toucheth him noght and that aperteneth nat un-to him, though
2730 it harme him, it is no wonder. / For the lawe seith : that "he is coupable that entremetteth or medleth with swich thyng as aperteneth nat un-to him." / And Salomon seith : that "he that entremetteth him of the noyse or stryf of another man, is lyk to him that taketh an hound by the eres." / For right as he that taketh a straunge hound by the eres is outherwhyle biten with the hound, / right in the same wyse is it resoun that he have harm, that by his inpacience medleth him of the noyse of another man, wher-as it aperteneth nat un-to him. / But ye knowen wel that this dede, that is to seyn, my grief and my disese, toucheth
2735 me right ny. / And therfore, though I be wroth and inpacient, it is no merveille. / And savinge your grace, I can nat seen that it mighte greetly harme me though I toke vengeaunce ; / for I am richer and more mighty than myne enemys been. / And wel knowen ye, that by moneye and by havinge grete possessions been all the thinges of this world governed. / And Salomon seith : that
2740 "alle thinges obeyen to moneye." ' /

§ 50. Whan Prudence hadde herd hir housbonde avanten him of his richesse and of his moneye, dispreisinge the power of hise adversaries, she spak, and seyde in this wyse : / 'certes, dere sir, I graunte yow that ye been rich and mighty, / and that the richesses been goode to hem that han wel y-geten hem and wel conne usen hem. / For right as the body of a man may nat liven with-oute the soule, namore may it live with-outen temporel goodes. / And by richesses
2745 may a man gete him grete freendes. / And therfore seith Pamphilles : " if a net-herdes doghter," seith he, " be riche, she may chesen of a thousand men which she wol take to hir housbonde ; / for, of a thousand men, oon wol nat forsaken

hir ne refusen hir." / And this Pamphilles seith also : " if thou be right happy, that is to seyn, if thou be right riche, thou shalt find a greet nombre of felawes and freendes. / And if thy fortune change that thou wexe povre, farewel freendshipe and felaweshipe ; / for thou shalt be allone with-outen any companye, but-if it be the companye of povre
2750 folk." / And yet seith this Pamphilles
moreover : that "they that been thralle and bonde of linage shullen been maad worthy and noble by the richesses." / And right so as by richesses ther comen manye goodes, right so by poverte come ther manye harmes and yveles. / For greet poverte constreyneth a man to do manye yveles. / And therfore clepeth Cassidore poverte "the moder of ruine," / that is to seyn, the moder of over-throwinge or fallinge doun. / And ther-
2755 fore seith Piers Alfonce : " oon of the
gretteste adversitees of this world is / whan a free man, by kinde or by burthe, is constreyned by poverte to eten the almesse of his enemy." / And the same seith Innocent in oon of hise bokes ; he seith : that " sorweful and mishappy is the condicioun of a povre begger ; / for if he axe nat his mete, he dyeth for hunger ; / and if he axe, he dyeth for shame ; and algates necessitee constreyn-eth him to axe." / And therfore seith 2760 Salomon : that " bet it is to dye than for to have swich poverte." / And as the same Salomon seith : " bettre it is to dye of bitter deeth than for to liven in swich wyse." / By thise resons that I have seid un-to yow, and by manye othere resons that I coude seye, / I graunte yow that richesses been goode to hem that geten hem wel, and to hem that wel usen tho richesses. / And therfore wol I shewe yow how ye shul have yow, and how ye shul bere yow in gaderinge of richesses, and in what manere ye shul usen hem. / 2765

§ 51. First, ye shul geten hem with-outen greet desyr, by good leyser sokingly, and nat over hastily. / For a man that is to desyringe to gete richesses abaun-doneth him first to thefte and to alle

•

other yveles. / And therfore seith Salomon : " he that hasteth him to bisily to wexe riche shal be noon innocent." / He seith also : that " the richesse that hastily cometh to a man, sone and lightly gooth and passeth fro a man ; / but that richesse that cometh litel and litel wexeth alwey 2770 and multiplyeth." / And sir, ye shul geten richesses by your wit and by your travaille un-to your profit ; / and that with-outen wrong or harm-doinge to any other persone. / For the lawe seith : that " ther maketh no man himselven riche, if he do harm to another wight " ; / this is to seyn, that nature defendeth and forbedeth by right, that no man make himself· riche un-to the harm of another persone. / And Tullius seith : that " no sorwe ne no drede of deeth, ne no-thing 2775 that may falle un-to a man / is so muchel agayns nature, as a man to encressen his owene profit to the harm of another man. / And though the grete men and the mighty men geten richesses more lightly than thou, / yet shaltou nat been ydel ne slow to do thy profit ; for thou shalt in alle wyse flee ydelnesse." / For Salomon seith : that " ydelnesse techeth a man to do manye yveles." / And the same Salomon seith : that " he that travailleth and bisieth him to tilien his land, shal eten 2780 breed ; / but he that is ydel and casteth him to no bisinesse ne occupacioun, shal falle in-to poverte, and dye for hunger." / And he that is ydel and slow can never finde covenable tyme for to doon his profit. / For ther is a versifiour seith : that " the ydel man excuseth hym in winter, by cause of the grete cold ; and in somer, by enchesoun of the hete." / For thise causes seith Caton : " waketh and enclyneth nat yow over muchel for to slepe ; for over muchel reste norisseth and causeth manye vices." / And therfore seith seint Jerome : " doth somme gode dedes, that the devel which is our 2785 enemy ne finde yow nat unoccupied." / For the devel ne taketh nat lightly un-to his werkinge swiche as he findeth occupied in gode werkes." /

§ 52. Thanne thus, in getinge richesses, ye mosten flee ydelnesse. / And afterward, ye shul use the richesses, whiche ye have geten by your wit and by your travaille, / in swich a manere, that men holde nat yow to scars, ne to sparinge, ne to fool-large, that is to seyn, over-large a spender. / For right as men blamen an avaricious man by-cause of his scarsetee and chincherye, / in the same wyse is he 2790 to blame that spendeth over largely. / And therfore seith Caton : " use," he seith, " thy richesses that thou hast geten / in swich a manere, that men have no matere ne cause to calle thee neither wrecche ne chinche ; for it is a greet shame to a man to have a povere herte and a riche purs." / He seith also : " the goodes that thou hast y-geten, use hem by mesure," that is to seyn, spende hem mesurably ; / for they 2795 that folily wasten and despenden the goodes that they han, / whan they han namore propre of hir owene, they shapen hem to take the goodes of another man. / I seye thanne, that ye shul fleen avarice ; / usinge your richesses in swich manere, that men seye nat that your richesses been y-buried, / but that ye have hem in your might and in your weeldinge. / For 2800 a wys man repreveth the avaricious man, and seith thus, in two vers : / " wherto and why burieth a man hise goodes by his grete avarice, and knoweth wel that nedes moste he dye ; / for deeth is the ende of every man as in this present lyf." / And for what cause or enchesoun joyneth he him or knitteth he him so faste un-to hise goodes, / that alle his wittes mowen nat disseveren him or departen him from hise goodes ; / and knoweth wel, or oghte 2805 knowe, that whan he is deed, he shal nothing bere with him out of this world ? / And ther-fore seith seint Augustin : that " the avaricious man is likned un-to helle ; / that the more it swelweth, the more desyr it hath to swelwe and devoure." / And as wel as ye wolde eschewe to be called an avaricious man or chinche, / as wel sholde ye kepe yow and governe yow in swich a wyse that men calle yow nat fool-large. / Therfore seith Tullius : 2810 " the goodes," he seith, " of thyn hous ne sholde nat been hid, ne kept so cloos but that they mighte been opened by pitee and debonairetee"; / that is to seyn, to yeven part to hem that han greet nede; / "ne thy goodes shullen nat been so opene, to been every mannes goodes." / Afterward, in getinge of your richesses and in usinge hem, ye shul alwey have three thinges in your herte; / that is to seyn, our lord god, conscience, and good 2815 name. / First, ye shul have god in your herte; / and for no richesse ye shullen do no-thing, which may in any manere displese god, that is your creatour and maker. / For after the word of Salomon: "it is bettre to have a litel good with the love of god, / than to have muchel good and tresour, and lese the love of his lord god." / And the prophete seith : that "bettre it is to been a good man and have litel good 2820 and tresour, / than to been holden a shrewe and have grete richesses." / And yet seye I ferthermore, that ye sholde alwey doon your bisinesse to gete yow richesses, / so that ye gete hem with good conscience. / And th'apostle seith : that "ther nis thing in this world, of which we sholden have so greet joye as whan our • conscience bereth us good witnesse." / And the wyse man seith : "the substance of a man is ful good, whan sinne is nat 2825 in mannes conscience." / Afterward, in getinge of your richesses, and in usinge of hem, / yow moste have greet bisinesse and greet diligence, that your goode name be alwey kept and conserved. / For Salomon seith : that "bettre it is and more it availleth a man to have a good name, than for to have grete richesses." / And therfore he seith in another place : "do greet diligence," seith Salomon, "in keping of thy freend and of thy gode name; / for it shal lenger abide with thee 2830 than any tresour, be it never so precious." / And certes he sholde nat be called a gentil man, that after god and good conscience, alle thinges left, ne dooth his diligence and bisinesse to kepen his good name. / And Cassidore seith : that "it is signe of a gentil herte, whan a man loveth and desyreth to han a good name." / And

therfore seith seint Augustin : that "ther been two thinges that arn necessarie and nedefulle, / and that is good conscience and good loos; / that is to seyn, good conscience to thyn owene persone inward, and good loos for thy neighebore outward." / And he that trusteth him so 283 muchel in his gode conscience, / that he displeseth and setteth at noght his gode name or loos, and rekketh noght though he kepe nat his gode name, nis but a cruel cherl. /

§ 53. Sire, now have I shewed yow how ye shul do in getinge richesses, and how ye shullen usen hem; / and I see wel, that for the trust that ye han in youre richesses, ye wole moeve werre and bataille. / I conseille yow, that ye biginne no werre in trust of your richesses; for they ne suffysen noght werres to mayntene. / And therfore seith a philosophre : 284 "that man that desyreth and wole algates han werre, shal never have suffisaunce ; / for the richer that he is, the gretter despenses moste he make, if he wole have worship and victorie." / And Salomon seith : that "the gretter richesses that a man hath, the mo despendours he hath." / And dere sire, al-be-it so that for your richesses ye mowe have muchel folk, / yet bihoveth it nat, ne it is nat good, to biginne werre, where-as ye mowe in other manere have pees, un-to your worship and profit. / For the victories 284 of batailles that been in this world, lyen nat in greet nombre or multitude of the peple ne in the vertu of man ; / but it lyth in the wil and in the hand of our lord god almighty. / And therfore Judas Machabeus, which was goddes knight, / whan he sholde fighte agayn his adversarie that hadde a greet nombre, and a gretter multitude of folk and strenger than was this peple of Machabee, / yet he reconforted his litel companye, and seyde right in this wyse : / "als lightly," 2850 quod he, "may our lord god almighty yeve victorie to a fewe folk as to many folk ; / for the victorie of bataile cometh nat by the grete nombre of peple, / but it cometh from our lord god of hevene." /

And dere sir, for as muchel as there is no man certein, if he be worthy that god yeve him victorie, [† namore than he is certein whether he be worthy of the love of god] or naught, after that Salomon seith, / therfore every man sholde greetly 355 drede werres to biginne. / And by-cause that in batailles fallen manye perils, / and happeth outher-while, that as sone is the grete man sleyn as the litel man ; / and, as it is written in the seconde book of Kinges, "the dedes of batailles been aventurouse and nothing certeyne ; / for as lightly is oon hurt with a spere as another." / And for ther is gret peril in werre, therfore .sholde a man flee and eschewe werre, in as muchel as a 360 man may goodly. / For Salomon seith : "he that loveth peril shal falle in peril."' /

§ 54. After that Dame Prudence hadde spoken in this manere, Melibee answerde and seyde, / 'I see wel, dame Prudence, that by your faire wordes and by your resons that ye han shewed me, that the werre lyketh yow no-thing ; / but I have nat yet herd your conseil, how I shal do in this nede.' /

§ 55. 'Certes,' quod she, 'I conseille yow that ye accorde with youre adver-365 saries, and that ye have pees with hem. / For seint Jame seith in hise epistles : that "by concord and pees the smale richesses wexen grete, / and by debaat and discord the grete richesses fallen doun." / And ye knowen wel that oon of the gretteste and most sovereyn thing, that is in this world, is unitee and pees. / And ther-fore seyde oure lord Jesu Crist to hise apostles in this wyse : / "wel happy and blessed been they that loven and pur-chacen pees ; for they been called children 370 of god."' / 'A !' quod Melibee, 'now see I wel that ye loven nat myn honour ne my worshipe. / Ye knowen wel that myne adversaries han bigonnen this debaat and brige by hir outrage ; / and ye see wel that they ne requeren ne preyen me nat of pees, ne they asken nat to be reconsiled. / Wol ye thanne that I go and meke me and obeye me to hem,

and crye hem mercy ? / For sothe, that were nat my worship. / For right as men 2875 seyn, that "over-greet homlinesse en-gendreth dispreysinge," so fareth it by to greet humylitee or mekenesse.' /

§ 56. Thanne bigan dame Prudence to maken semblant of wratthe, and seyde, / 'certes, sir, sauf your grace, I love your honour and your profit as I do myn owene, and ever have doon ; / ne ye ne noon other syen never the contrarie. / And yit, if I hadde seyd that ye sholde han purchaced the pees and the recon-siliacioun, I ne hadde nat muchel mis-taken me, ne seyd amis. / For the wyse 2880 man seith : " the dissensioun biginneth by another man, and the reconsiling bi-ginneth by thy-self." / And the prophete seith : " flee shrewednesse and do good-nesse ; / seke pees and folwe it, as muchel as in thee is." / Yet seye I nat that ye shul rather pursue to your adversaries for pees than they shuln to yow ; / for I knowe wel that ye been so hard-herted, that ye wol do no-thing for me. / And 2885 Salomon seith : "he that hath over-hard an herte, atte laste he shal mishappe and mistyde."' /

§ 57. Whanne Melibee hadde herd dame Prudence maken semblant of wratthe, he seyde in this wyse, / 'dame, I prey yow that ye be nat displesed of thinges that I seye ; / for ye knowe wel that I am angry and wrooth, and that is no wonder ; / and they that been wrothe witen nat wel what they doon, ne what they seyn. / 2890 Therfore the prophete seith : that "trou-bled eyen han no cleer sighte." / But seyeth and conseileth me as yow lyketh ; for I am redy to do right as ye wol desyre ; / and if ye repreve me of my folye, I am the more holden to love yow and to preyse yow. / For Salomon seith : that "he that repreveth him that doth folye, / he shal finde gretter grace than he that deceyveth him by swete wordes."' / 2895

§ 58. Thanne seide dame Prudence, 'I make no semblant of wratthe ne anger but for your grote profit. / For Salomon seith : " he is more worth, that repreveth or chydeth a fool for his folye, shewinge

him semblant of wratthe, / than he that
supporteth him and preyseth him in his
misdoinge, and laugheth at his folye." /
And this same Salomon seith afterward :
that "by the sorweful visage of a man,"
that is to seyn, by the sory and hevy
countenaunce of a man, / "the fool cor-
2900 recteth and amendeth him-self." ' /

§ 59. Thanne seyde Melibee, 'I shal
nat conne answere to so manye faire
resouns as ye putten to me and shewen. /
Seyeth shortly your wil and your conseil,
and I am al ready to fulfille and parfourne it.' /

§ 60. Thanne dame Prudence discovered
al hir wil to him, and seyde, / ' I conseille
yow,' quod she, ' aboven alle thinges, that
ye make pees bitwene god and yow ; /
and beth reconsiled un-to him and to his
2905 grace. / For as I have seyd yow heer-
biforn, god hath suffred yow to have this
tribulacioun and disese for your sinnes. /
And if ye do as I sey yow, god wol sende
your adversaries un-to yow, / and maken
hem fallen at your feet, redy to do your
wil and your comandements. / For
Salomon seith : "whan the condicioun
of man is plesaunt and likinge to god, / he
chaungeth the hertes of the mannes adversaries, and constreyneth hem to biseken
2910 him of pees and of grace." / And I prey
yow, lat me speke with your adversaries
in privee place ; / for they shul nat knowe
that it be of your wil or your assent. /
And thanne, whan I knowe hir wil and
hir entente, I may conseille yow the more
seurly.' /

§ 61. ' Dame,' quod Melibee, ' dooth
your wil and your lykinge, / for I putte
me hoolly in your disposicioun and or-
2915 dinaunce.' /

§ 62. Thanne Dame Prudence, whan
she saugh the gode wil of her housbonde,
delibered and took avys in hir-self, /
thinkinge how she mighte bringe this
nede un-to a good conclusioun and to
a good ende. / And whan she saugh hir
tyme, she sente for thise adversaries to
come un-to hir in-to a privee place, / and
shewed wysly un-to hem the grete goodes
that comen of pees, / and the grete

harmes and perils that been in werre ; / 2920
and seyde to hem in a goodly manere,
how that hem oughte have greet repentaunce / of the injurie and wrong that
they hadden doon to Melibee hir lord, and
to hir, and to hir doghter. /

§ 63. And whan they herden the good-
liche wordes of dame Prudence, / they
weren so surprised and ravisshed, and
hadden so greet joye of hir, that wonder
was to telle. / ' A ! lady !' quod they,
' ye han shewed un-to us " the blessinge
of swetnesse," after the sawe of David the
prophete ; / for the reconsilinge which 2925
we been nat worthy to have in no manere, /
but we oghte requeren it with greet contricioun and humilitee, / ye of your grete
goodnesse have presented unto us. / Now
see we wel that the science and the conninge of Salomon is ful trewe ; / for he
seith : that "swete wordes multiplyen
and encresen freendes, and maken shrewes
to be debonaire and meke." / 2930

§ 64. Certes,' quod they, ' we putten
our dede and al our matere and cause al
hoolly in your goode wil ; / and been redy
to obeye to the speche and comandement
of my lord Melibee. / And therfore, dere
and benigne lady, we preyen yow and
biseke yow as mekely as we conne and
mowen, / that it lyke un-to your grete
goodnesse to fulfillen in dede your good-
liche wordes ; / for we consideren and
knowlichen that we han offended and
greved my lord Melibee out of mesure ; / 2935
so forforth, that we be nat of power to
maken hise amendes. / And therfore
we oblige and binden us and our freendes
to doon al his wil and hise comandements. / But peraventure he hath swich
hevinesse and swich wratthe to us-ward,
by-cause of our offence, / that he wole
enjoyne us swich a peyne as we mowe nat
bere ne sustene. / And therfore, noble
lady, we biseke to your wommanly pitee, / 2940
to taken swich avysement in this nede,
that we, ne our freendes, be nat desherited
ne destroyed thurgh our folye.' /

§ 65. ' Certes,' quod Prudence, ' it is an
hard thing and right perilous, / that
a man putte him al outrely in the arbi-

tracioun and juggement, and in the might and power of hise enemys. / For Salomon seith : "leveth me, and yeveth credence to that I shal seyn ; I seye," quod he, "ye peple, folk, and governours of holy chirche, / to thy sone, to thy wyf, to thy freend, ne to thy brother / ne yeve thou never might ne maistrie of thy body, whyl thou livest." / Now sithen he defendeth, that man shal nat yeven to his brother ne to his freend the might of his body, / by a strenger resoun he defendeth and forbedeth a man to yeven him-self to his enemy. / And nathelees I conseille you, that ye mistruste nat my lord. / For I woot wel and knowe verraily, that he is debonaire and meke, large, curteys, / and nothing desyrous ne coveitous of good ne richesse. / For ther nis no-thing in this world that he desyreth, save only worship and honour. / Forther-more I knowe wel, and am right seur, that he shal no-thing doon in this nede with-outen my conseil. / And I shal so werken in this cause, that, by grace of our lord god, ye shul been reconsiled un-to us.' /

§ 66. Thanne seyden they with o vois, 'worshipful lady, we putten us and our goodes al fully in your wil and disposicioun ; / and been redy to comen, what day that it lyke un-to your noblesse to limite us or assigne us, / for to maken our obligacioun and bond as strong as it lyketh un-to your goodnesse ; / that we mowe fulfille the wille of yow and of my lord Melibee.' /

§ 67. Whan dame Prudence hadde herd the answeres of thise men, she bad hem goon agayn prively ; / and she retourned to hir lord Melibee, and tolde him how she fond hise adversaries ful repentant, / knowlechinge ful lowely hir sinnes and trespas, and how they were redy to suffren al peyne, / requiringe and preyinge him of mercy and pitee. /

§ 68. Thanne seyde Melibee, 'he is wel worthy to have pardoun and foryifnesse of his sinne, that excuseth nat his sinne, / but knowlecheth it and repenteth him, axinge indulgence. / For Senek seith : "ther is the remissioun and foryifnesse,

whereas confessioun is" ; / for confession is neighebore to innocence. / And he seith in another place : "he that hath shame for his sinne and knowlecheth it, is worthy remissioun." And therfore I assente and conferme me to have pees ; / but it is good that we do it nat with-outen the assent and wil of our freendes.' /

§ 69. Thanne was Prudence right glad and joyeful, and seyde, / 'Certes, sir,' quod she, 'ye han wel and goodly answered. / For right as by the conseil, assent, and help of your freendes, ye han been stired to venge yow and maken werre, / right so with-outen hir conseil shul ye nat accorden yow, ne have pees with your adversaries. / For the lawe seith : "ther nis no-thing so good by wey of kinde, as a thing to been unbounde by him that it was y-bounde." ' /

§ 70. And thanne dame Prudence, with-outen delay or taryinge, sente anon hir messages for hir kin, and for hir olde freendes whiche that were trewe and wyse, / and tolde hem by ordre, in the presence of Melibee, al this matere as it is aboven expressed and declared ; / and preyden hem that they wolde yeven hir avys and conseil, what best were to doon in this nede. / And whan Melibees freendes hadde taken hir avys and deliberacioun of the forseide matere, / and hadden examined it by greet bisinesse and greet diligence, / they yave ful conseil for to have pees and reste ; / and that Melibee sholde receyve with good herte hise adversaries to foryifnesse and mercy. /

§ 71. And whan dame Prudence hadde herd the assent of hir lord Melibee, and the conseil of hise freendes, / accorde with hir wille and hir entencioun, / she was wonderly glad in hir herte, and seyde : / 'ther is an old proverbe,' quod she, 'seith : that "the goodnesse that thou mayst do this day, do it ; / and abyde nat ne delaye it nat til to-morwe." / And therfore I conseille that ye sende your messages, swiche as been discrete and wyse, / un-to your adversaries ; tellinge hem, on your bihalve, / that if they wole trete of pees and of accord, / that they shape hem, with-outen delay or tarying, to comen un-to us.' / Which *1990* thing parfourned was in dede. / And whanne thise trespassours and repentinge folk of hir folies, that is to seyn, the adversaries of Melibee, / hadden herd what thise messagers seyden un-to hem, / they weren right glad and joyeful, and answereden ful mekely and benignely, / yeldinge graces and thankinges to hir lord Melibee and to al his companye ; / and shopen hem, with-outen delay, to go with the messagers, and obeye to the *2995* comandement of hir lord Melibee. /

§ 72. And right anon they token hir wey to the court of Melibee, / and token with hem somme of hir trewe freendes, to maken feith for hem and for to been hir borwes. / And whan they were comen to the presence of Melibee, he seyde hem thise wordes : / ' it standeth thus,' quod Melibee, ' and sooth it is, that ye, / causeless, and with-outen skile and *3000* resoun, / han doon grete injuries and wronges to me and to my wyf Prudence, and to my doghter also. / For ye han entred in-to myn hous by violence, / and have doon swich outrage, that alle men knowen wel that ye have deserved the deeth ; / and therfore wol I knowe and wite of yow, / whether ye wol putte the punissement and the chastysinge and the vengeance of this outrage in the wil of me and of my wyf Prudence ; or ye wol *3005* nat ? ' /

§ 73. Thanne the wyseste of hem three answerde for hem alle, and seyde : / ' sire,' quod he, ' we knowen wel, that we been unworthy to comen un-to the court of so greet a lord and so worthy as ye been. / For we han so greetly mistaken us, and han offended and agilt in swich a wyse agayn your heigh lordshipe, / that trewely we han deserved the deeth. / But yet, for the grete goodnesse and debonairetee that all the world witnesseth *3010* of your persone, / we submitten us to the excellence and benignitee of your gracious lordshipe, / and been redy to obeie to alle your comandements ; / bisekinge yow, that of your merciable pitee ye wol con-

sidere our grete repentaunce and lowe submissioun, / and graunten us foryevenesse of our outrageous trespas and offence. / For wel we knowe, that your liberal grace and mercy strecchen hem ferther in-to goodnesse, than doon our outrageouse giltes and trespas in-to wikkednesse ; / al-be-it that cursedly and *30* dampnably we han agilt agayn your heigh lordshipe.' /

§ 74. Thanne Melibee took hem up fro the ground ful benignely, / and receyved hir obligaciouns and hir bondes by hir othes up-on hir plegges and borwes, / and assigned hem a certeyn day to retourne un-to his court, / for to accepte and receyve the sentence and jugement that Melibee wolde comande to be doon on hem by the causes afore-seyd ; / whiche *30.* thinges ordeyned, every man retourned to his hous. /

§ 75. And whan that dame Prudence saugh hir tyme, she freyned and axed hir lord Melibee, / what vengeance he thoughte to taken of hise adversaries ? /

§ 76. To which Melibee answerde and seyde, ' certes,' quod he, ' I thinke and purpose me fully / to desherite hem of al that ever they han, and for to putte hem in exil for ever.' /                                                    *30.*

§ 77. ' Certes,' quod dame Prudence, ' this were a cruel sentence, and muchel agayn resoun. / For ye been riche y-nough, and han no nede of other mennes good ; / and ye mighte lightly in this wyse gete yow a coveitous name, / which is a vicious thing, and oghte been eschewed of every good man. / For after the sawe of the word of the apostle : " coveitise is rote of alle harmes." / And *30.* therfore, it were bettre for yow to lese so muchel good of your owene, than for to taken of hir good in this manere. / For bettre it is to lesen good with worshipe, than it is to winne good with vileinye and shame. / And every man oghte to doon his diligence and his bisinesse to geten him a good name. / And yet shal he nat only bisie him in kepinge of his good name, / but he shal also enforcen him alwey to do som-thing by which he

35 may renovelle his good name; / for it is
written, that "the olde good loos or good
name of a man is sone goon and passed,
whan it is nat newed ne renovelled." /
And as touchinge that ye seyn, ye wole
exile your adversaries, / that thinketh
me muchel agayn resoun and out of
mesure, / considered the power that they
han yeve yow up-on hem-self. / And it
is writen, that "he is worthy to lesen his
privilege that misuseth the might and
40 the power that is yeven him." / And I
sette cas ye mighte enjoyne hem that
peyne by right and by lawe, / which I
trowe ye mowe nat do, / I seye, ye mighte
nat putten it to execucioun per-aventure, / and thanne were it lykly to retourne to the werre as it was biforn. /
And therfore, if ye wole that men do yow
obeisance, ye moste demen more cur-
45 teisly ; / this is to seyn, ye moste yeven
more esy sentences and jugements. /
For it is writen, that "he that most
curteisly comandeth, to him men most
obeyen." / And therfore, I prey yow
that in this necessitee and in this nede,
ye caste yow to overcome your herte. /
For Senek seith : that "he that overcometh his herte, overcometh twyes." /
And Tullius seith : "ther is no-thing
50 so comendable in a greet lord / as whan
he is debonaire and meke, and appeseth
him lightly." / And I prey yow that ye
wole forbere now to do vengeance, / in
swich a manere, that your goode name
may be kept and conserved ; / and that
men mowe have cause and matere to
preyse yow of pitee and of mercy ; / and
that ye have no cause to repente yow of
55 thing that ye doon. / For Senek seith :
"he overcometh in an yvel manere, that
repenteth him of his victorie." / Wherfore I pray yow, lat mercy been in your
minde and in your herte, / to th'effect

and entente that god almighty have
mercy on yow in his laste jugement. /
For seint Jame seith in his epistle :
"jugement withouten mercy shal be
doon to him, that hath no mercy of
another wight." ' /

§ 78. Whanne Melibee hadde herd the
grete skiles and resouns of dame Prudence, and hir wise informaciouns and
techinges, / his herte gan enclyne to the 3060
wil of his wyf, consideringe hir trewe
entente ; / and conformed him anon,
and assented fully to werken after hir
conseil ; / and thonked god, of whom
procedeth al vertu and alle goodnesse,
that him sente a wyf of so greet discrecioun. / And whan the day cam that
hise adversaries sholde apperen in his
presence, / he spak unto hem ful goodly,
and seyde in this wyse : / 'al-be-it so that 3065
of your pryde and presumpcioun and
folie, and of your necligence and unconninge, / ye have misborn yow and
trespassed un-to me ; / yet, for as much
as I see and biholde your grete humilitee, /
and that ye been sory and repentant of
your giltes, / it constreyneth me to doon
yow grace and mercy. / Therfore I re- 3070
ceyve yow to my grace, / and foryeve
yow outrely alle the offences, injuries,
and wronges, that ye have doon agayn
me and myne ; / to this effect and to this
ende, that god of his endelees mercy /
wole at the tyme of our dyinge foryeven
us our giltes that we han trespassed to
him in this wrecched world. / For doutelees, if we be sory and repentant of the
sinnes and giltes whiche we han trespassed in the sighte of our lord god, / he 3075
is so free and so merciable, / that he
wole foryeven us our giltes, / and bringen
us to his blisse that never hath ende.
Amen.' /                                    3078

Here is ended Chaucers Tale of Melibee and of Dame Prudence.

# THE MONK'S PROLOGUE.

[T. 13895-13956.]

### The mery wordes of the Host to the Monk.

WHAN ended was my tale of Melibee,
And of Prudence and hir benignitee, 3080
Our hoste seyde, 'as I am faithful man,
And by the precious *corpus Madrian*,
I hadde lever than a barel ale
That goode lief my wyf hadde herd this
tale !
For she nis no-thing of swich pacience
As was this Melibeus wyf Prudence. 3086
By goddes bones ! whan I bete my knaves,
She bringth me forth the grete clobbed
staves, (10)
And cryeth, "slee the dogges everichoon,
And brek hem, bothe bak and every boon."
And if that any neighebor of myne 3091
Wol nat in chirche to my wyf enclyne,
Or be so hardy to hir to trespace,
Whan she comth hoom, she rampeth in
my face, 3094
And cryeth, "false coward, wreek thy wyf!
By *corpus* bones ! I wol have thy knyf,
And thou shalt have my distaf and go
spinne !"
Fro day to night right thus she wol bi-
ginne ;— (20)
"Allas!" she seith, "that ever I was shape
To wedde a milksop or a coward ape, 3100
That wol be overlad with every wight !
Thou darst nat stonden by thy wyves
right !"
This is my lyf, but-if that I wol fighte ;
And out at dore anon I moot me dighte,
Or elles I am but lost, but-if that I 3105
Be lyk a wilde leoun fool-hardy.
I woot wel she wol do me slee som day
Som neighebor, and thanne go my wey. (30)

For I am perilous with knyf in honde,
Al be it that I dar nat hir withstonde, 3110
For she is big in armes, by my feith,
That shal he finde, that hir misdooth or
seith.
But lat us passe awey fro this matere.
My lord the Monk,' quod he, ' be mery
of chere ;
For ye shul telle a tale trewely. 3115
Lo ! Rouchestre stant heer faste by !
Ryd forth, myn owene lord, brek nat our
game, (39)
But, by my trouthe, I knowe nat your name,
Wher shal I calle yow my lord dan John,
Or dan Thomas, or elles dan Albon? 3120
Of what hous be ye, by your fader kin ?
I vow to god, thou hast a ful fair skin,
It is a gentil pasture ther thou goost ;
Thou art nat lyk a penaunt or a goost.
Upon my feith, thou art som officer, 3125
Some worthy sexteyn, or som celerer,
For by my fader soule, as to my doom,
Thou art a maister whan thou art at hoom ;
No povre cloisterer, ne no novys, (51)
But a governour, wyly and wys. 3130
And therwithal of brawnes and of bones
A wel-faring persone for the nones.
I pray to god, yeve him confusioun
That first thee broghte un-to religioun ;
Thou woldest han been a trede-foul aright.
Haddestow as greet a leve, as thou hast
might 3136
To parfourne al thy lust in engendrure,
Thou haddest bigeten many a creature.
Alas ! why werestow so wyd a cope? (61)
God yeve me sorwe ! but, and I were a pope,

Not only thou, but every mighty man, 3141
Thogh he were shorn ful hye upon his pan,
Sholde have a wyf; for al the world is lorn !
Religioun hath take up al the corn   3144
Of treding, and we borel men ben shrimpes !
Of feble trees ther comen wrecched impes.
This maketh that our heires been so
    sclendre                              (69)
And feble, that they may nat wel engendre.
This maketh that our wyves wol assaye
Religious folk, for ye may bettre paye 3150
Of Venus payements than mowe we ;
God woot, no lussheburghes payen ye !
But be nat wrooth, my lord, for that I
    pleye ;
Ful ofte in game a sooth I have herd seye.'
    This worthy monk took al in pacience,
And seyde, ' I wol doon al my diligence,
As fer as souneth in-to honestee,   3157
To telle yow a tale, or two, or three.   (80)
And if yow list to herkne hiderward,
I wol yow seyn the lyf of seint Edward ;

Or elles first Tragedies wol I telle   3161
Of whiche I have an hundred in my celle.
Tragedie is to seyn a certeyn storie,
As olde bokes maken us memorie,
Of him that stood in greet prosperitee 3165
And is y-fallen out of heigh degree
Into miserie, and endeth wrecchedly.
And they ben versifyed comunly   (90)
Of six feet, which men clepe *exametron.*
In prose eek been endyted many oon, 3170
And eek in metre, in many a sondry wyse.
Lo ! this declaring oughte y-nough suffise.
    Now herkneth, if yow lyketh for to here ;
But first I yow biseke in this matere, 3174
Though I by ordre telle nat thise thinges,
Be it of popes, emperours, or kinges,
After hir ages, as men writen finde,   (99)
But telle hem som bifore and som bihinde,
As it now comth un-to my remembraunce ;
Have me excused of myn ignoraunce.' 3180

*Explicit.*

# THE MONKES TALE.

### Here biginneth the Monkes Tale, de Casibus Virorum Illustrium.

I wol biwayle in maner of Tragedie
The harm of hem that stode in heigh de-
    gree,
And fillen so that ther nas no remedie
To bringe hem out of hir adversitee ; 3184
For certein, whan that fortune list to flee,
Ther may no man the cours of hir with-
    holde ;
Lat no man truste on blind prosperitee ;
Be war by thise ensamples trewe and olde.

### LUCIFER.

At Lucifer, though he an angel were,
And nat a man, at him I wol biginne ; 3190
For, thogh fortune may non angel dere, (11)

From heigh degree yet fel he for his sinne
Doun in-to helle, wher he yet is inne.
O Lucifer ! brightest of angels alle,
Now artow Sathanas, that maist nat
    twinne                                3195
Out of miserie, in which that thou art falle.

### ADAM.

Lo Adam, in the feld of Damassene,
With goddes owene finger wroght was he,
And nat bigeten of mannes sperme un-
    clene,
And welte al Paradys, saving o tree.   3200
Had never worldly man so heigh degree
As Adam, til he for misgovernaunce   (22)

Was drive out of his hye prosperitee
To labour, and to helle, and to meschaunce.

### SAMPSON.

Lo Sampson, which that was annunciat
By th'angel, longe er his nativitee,          3206
And was to god almighty consecrat,
And stood in noblesse, whyl he mighte see.
Was never swich another as was he,
To speke of strengthe, and therwith hardi-
nesse;          3210
But to his wyves tolde he his secree,          (31)
Through which he slow him-self, for
wrecchednesse.

Sampson, this noble almighty champioun,
Withouten wepen save his hondes tweye,
He slow and al to-rente the leoun,          3215
Toward his wedding walking by the weye.
His false wyf coude him so plese and
preye
Til she his conseil knew, and she untrewe
Un-to his foos his conseil gan biwreye,          3219
And him forsook, and took another newe.

Three hundred foxes took Sampson for ire,
And alle hir tayles he togider bond,          (42)
And sette the foxes tayles alle on fire,
For he on every tayl had knit a brond;
And they brende alle the cornes in that
lond,          3225
And alle hir oliveres and vynes eek.
A thousand men he slow eek with his hond,
And had no wepen but an asses cheek.

Whan they were slayn, so thursted him
that he          3229
Was wel ny lorn, for which he gan to preye
That god wolde on his peyne han som
pitee,          (51)
And sende him drinke, or elles moste he
deye;
And of this asses cheke, that was dreye,
Out of a wang-tooth sprang anon a welle,
Of which he drank y-nogh, shortly to seye,
Thus heelp him god, as *Judicum* can telle.

By verray force, at Gazan, on a night,          3237
Maugree Philistiens of that citee,
The gates of the toun he hath up-plight,
And on his bak y-caried hem hath he          3240

Hye on an hille, that men mighte hem
see.          (61)
O noble almighty Sampson, leef and dere,
Had thou nat told to wommen thy secree,
In al this worlde ne hadde been thy pere!

This Sampson never sicer drank ne wyn,
Ne on his heed cam rasour noon ne shere,
By precept of the messager divyn,          3247
For alle his strengthes in his heres were;
And fully twenty winter, yeer by yere,
He hadde of Israel the governaunce.          3250
But sone shal he wepen many a tere,          (71)
For wommen shal him bringen to mes-
chaunce!

Un-to his lemman Dalida he tolde
That in his heres al his strengthe lay,
And falsly to his fo-men she him solde.
And sleping in hir barme up-on a day          3256
She made to clippe or shere his heer awey,
And made his fo-men al his craft espyen;
And whan that they him fonde in this
array,
They bounde him faste, and putten out his
yën.          3260

But er his heer were clipped or y-shave,          (81)
Ther was no bond with which men might
him binde;
But now is he in prisoun in a cave,
Wher-as they made him at the querne
grinde.          3264
O noble Sampson, strongest of mankinde,
O whylom juge in glorie and in richesse,
Now maystow wepen with thyn yën blinde,
Sith thou fro wele art falle in wrecched-
nesse.

Th'ende of this caytif was as I shal seye;
His fo-men made a feste upon a day,          3270
And made him as hir fool bifore hem pleye,
And this was in a temple of greet array.          (92)
But atte last he made a foul affray;
For he two pilers shook, and made hem
falle,          3274
And doun fil temple and al, and ther it lay,
And slow him-self, and eek his fo-men alle.

This is to seyn, the princes everichoon,
And eek three thousand bodies wer ther
slayn          (98)

With falling of the grete temple of stoon.
Of Sampson now wol I na-more seyn. 3280
Beth war by this ensample old and playn
That no men telle hir conseil til hir wyves
Of swich thing as they wolde han secree
   fayn,
If that it touche hir limmes or hir lyves.

### HERCULES.

Of Hercules the sovereyn conquerour 3285
Singen his workes laude and heigh renoun;
For in his tyme of strengthe he was the
   flour.
He slow, and rafte the skin of the leoun;
He of Centauros leyde the boost adoun;
He Arpies slow, the cruel briddes felle; 3290
He golden apples rafte of the dragoun; (111)
He drow out Cerberus, the hound of helle :

He slow the cruel tyrant Busirus,
And made his hors to frete him, flesh and
   boon;
He slow the firy serpent venimous; 3295
Of Achelois two hornes, he brak oon;
And he slow Cacus in a cave of stoon;
He slow the geaunt Antheus the stronge;
He slow the grisly boor, and that anoon,
And bar the heven on his nekke longe. 3300

Was never wight, sith that the world
   bigan, (121)
That slow so many monstres as dide he.
Thurgh-out this wyde world his name ran,
What for his strengthe, and for his heigh
   bountee, 3304
And every reaume wente he for to see.
He was so strong that no man mighte him
   lette;
At bothe the worldes endes, seith Trophee,
In stede of boundes, he a piler sette.

A lemman hadde this noble champioun,
That highte Dianira, fresh as May; 3310
And, as this clerkes maken mencioun, (131)
She hath him sent a sherte fresh and gay.
Allas! this sherte, allas and weylaway!
Envenimed was so subtilly with-alle, 3314
That, er that he had wered it half a day,
It made his flesh al from his bones falle.

But nathelees somme clerkes hir excusen
By oon that highte Nessus, that it maked;

Be as be may, I wol hir noght accusen;
But on his bak this sherte he wered al
   naked, 3320
Til that his flesh was for the venim blaked.
And whan he sey noon other remedye, (142)
In hote coles he hath him-selven raked,
For with no venim deyned him to dye.

Thus starf this worthy mighty Hercules;
Lo, who may truste on fortune any
   throwe? 3326
For him that folweth al this world of prees,
Er he be war, is ofte y-leyd ful lowe.
Ful wys is he that can him-selven knowe.
Beth war, for whan that fortune list to
   glose, 3330
Than wayteth she hir man to overthrowe
By swich a wey as he wolde leest sup-
   pose. (152)

### NABUGODONOSOR (NEBUCHADNEZZAR).

The mighty trone, the precious tresor,
The glorious ceptre and royal magestee
That hadde the king Nabugodonosor, 3335
With tonge unnethe may discryved be.
He twyës wan Jerusalem the citee;
The vessel of the temple he with him ladde.
At Babiloyne was his sovereyn see, 3339
In which his glorie and his delyt he hadde.

The fairest children of the blood royal (161)
Of Israel he leet do gelde anoon,
And maked ech of hem to been his thral.
Amonges othere Daniel was oon, 3344
That was the wysest child of everichoon;
For he the dremes of the king expouned,
Wher-as in Chaldey clerk ne was ther noon
That wiste to what fyn his dremes souned.

This proude king leet make a statue of
   golde, 3349
Sixty cubytes long, and seven in brede,
To which image bothe yonge and olde (171)
Comaunded he to loute, and have in drede;
Or in a fourneys ful of flambes rede
He shal be brent, that wolde noght obeye.
But never wolde assente to that dede 3355
Daniel, ne his yonge felawes tweye.

This king of kinges proud was and elaat,
He wende that god, that sit in magestee,

Ne mighte him nat bireve of his estaat :
But sodeynly he loste his dignitee,    3360
And lyk a beste him semed for to be,    (181)
And eet hay as an oxe, and lay ther-oute ;
In reyn with wilde bestes walked he,
Til certein tyme was y-come aboute.

And lyk an egles fetheres wexe his heres,
His nayles lyk a briddes clawes were ;    3366
Til god relessed him a certein yeres,
And yaf him wit ; and than with many a
    tere
He thanked god, and ever his lyf in fere
Was he to doon amis, or more trespace, 3370
And, til that tyme he leyd was on his
    bere,
He knew that god was ful of might and
    grace.    (192)

### BALTHASAR (BELSHAZZAR).

His sone, which that highte Balthasar,
That heeld the regne after his fader day,
He by his fader coude nought be war,    3375
For proud he was of herte and of array ;
And eek an ydolastre was he ay.
His hye estaat assured him in pryde.
But fortune caste him doun, and ther he
    lay,
And sodeynly his regne gan divyde.    3380

A feste he made un-to his lordes alle    (201)
Up-on a tyme, and bad hem blythe be,
And than his officeres gan he calle—
' Goth, bringeth forth the vessels,' [tho]
    quod he,    3384
'Which that my fader, in his prosperitee,
Out of the temple of Jerusalem birafte,
And to our hye goddes thanke we
Of honour, that our eldres with us lafte.'

His wyf, his lordes, and his concubynes
Ay dronken, whyl hir appetytes laste, 3390
Out of thise noble vessels sundry wynes ;
And on a wal this king his yën caste,    (212)
And sey an hond armlees, that wroot ful
    faste,
For fere of which he quook and syked
    sore.    3394
This hond, that Balthasar so sore agaste,
Wroot *Mane, techel, phares*, and na-more.

In al that lond magicien was noon
That coude expoune what this lettre
    mente ;
But Daniel expouned it anoon,    3399
And seyde, ' king, god to thy fader lente
Glorie and honour, regne, tresour, rente
And he was proud, and no-thing god ne
    dradde,    (222)
And therfor god gret wreche up-on him
    sente,
And him birafte the regne that he hadde.

He was out cast of mannes companye,
With asses was his habitacioun,    3406
And eet hey as a beste in weet and drye,
Til that he knew, by grace and by resoun,
That god of heven hath dominacioun
Over every regne and every creature ; 3410
And thanne had god of him compassioun,
And him restored his regne and his
    figure.    (232)

Eek thou, that art his sone, art proud also,
And knowest alle thise thinges verraily,
And art rebel to god, and art his fo.    3415
Thou drank eek of his vessels boldely ;
Thy wyf eek and thy wenches sinfully
Dronke of the same vessels sondry wynes,
And heriest false goddes cursedly ;    3419
Therfor to thee y-shapen ful gret pyne is.

This hand was sent from god, that on the
    walle    (241)
Wroot *mane, techel, phares*, truste me ;
Thy regne is doon, thou weyest noght at
    alle ;
Divyded is thy regne, and it shal be 3424
To Medes and to Perses yeven,' quod he.
And thilke same night this king was
    slawe,
And Darius occupyeth his degree,
Thogh he therto had neither right ne
    lawe.

Lordinges, ensample heer-by may ye take
How that in lordshipe is no siker-
    nesse ;    3430
For whan fortune wol a man forsake, (251)
She bereth awey his regne and his richesse,
And eek his freendes, bothe more and
    lesse ;

For what man that hath freendes thurgh
   fortune,    3434
Mishap wol make hem enemys, I gesse :
This proverbe is ful sooth and ful commune.

### CENOBIA (ZENOBIA).

Cenobia, of Palimerie quene,
As writen Persiens of hir noblesse,
So worthy was in armes and so kene,    3439
That no wight passed hir in hardinesse,
Ne in linage, ne in other gentillesse. (261)
Of kinges blode of Perse is she descended ;
I seye nat that she hadde most fairnesse,
But of hir shape she mighte nat been
   amended.    3444

From hir childhede I finde that she fledde
Office of wommen, and to wode she wente ;
And many a wilde hertes blood she shedde
With arwes brode that she to hem sente.
She was so swift that she anon hem hente,
And whan that she was elder, she wolde
   kille    3450
Leouns, lepardes, and beres al to-rente, (271)
And in hir armes welde hem at hir wille.

She dorste wilde beestes dennes seke,
And rennen in the montaignes al the
   night,
And slepen under a bush, and she coude
   eke    3455
Wrastlen by verray force and verray might
With any yong man, were he never so
   wight ;
Ther mighte no-thing in hir armes stonde.
She kepte hir maydenhod from every
   wight,
To no man deigned hir for to be bonde. 3460

But atte laste hir frendes han hir maried
To Odenake, a prince of that contree, (282)
Al were it so that she hem longe taried ;
And ye shul understonde how that he
Hadde swiche fantasyes as hadde she. 3465
But nathelees, whan they were knit in-
   fere,
They lived in joye and in felicitee ;
For ech of hem hadde other leef and dere.

Save o thing, that she never wolde assente
By no wey, that he sholde by hir lye    3470

But ones, for it was hir pleyn entente (291)
To have a child, the world to multiplye ;
And al-so sone as that she mighte espye
That she was nat with childe with that
   dede,
Than wolde she suffre him doon his fan-
   tasye    3475
Eft-sone, and nat but ones, out of drede.

And if she were with childe at thilke cast,
Na-more sholde he pleyen thilke game
Til fully fourty dayes weren past ;
Than wolde she ones suffre him do the
   same.    3480
Al were this Odenake wilde or tame, (301)
He gat na-more of hir, for thus she seyde,
' It was to wyves lecherye and shame
In other cas, if that men with hem
   pleyde.'    3484

Two sones by this Odenake hadde she,
The whiche she kepte in vertu and let-
   trure ;
But now un-to our tale turne we.
I seye, so worshipful a creature,
And wys therwith, and large with mesure,
So penible in the werre, and curteis
   eke,    3490
Ne more labour mighte in werre endure,
Was noon, thogh al this world men sholde
   seke.    (312)

Hir riche array ne mighte nat be told
As wel in vessel as in hir clothing ;
She was al clad in perree and in gold, 3495
And eek she lafte noght, for noon hunting,
To have of sondry tonges ful knowing,
Whan that she leyser hadde, and for to
   entende
To lernen bokes was al hir lyking,    3499
How she in vertu mighte hir lyf dispende.

And, shortly of this storie for to trete, (321)
So doughty was hir housbonde and eek
   she,
That they conquered many regnes grete
In th'orient, with many a fair citee,
Apertenaunt un-to the magestee    3505
Of Rome, and with strong hond helde
   hem ful faste ;
Ne never mighte hir fo-men doon hem flee,
Ay whyl that Odenakes dayes laste.

Hir batailes, who-so list hem for to rede,
Agayn Sapor the king and othere mo, 3510
And how that al this proces fil in dede,(331)
Why she conquered and what title had
　　therto,
And after of hir meschief and hir wo,
How that she was biseged and y-take,
Let him un-to my maister Petrark go, 3515
That writ y-nough of this, I undertake.

When Odenake was deed, she mightily
The regnes heeld, and with hir propre
　　honde
Agayn hir foos she faught so cruelly,
That ther nas king ne prince in al that
　　londe　　　　　　　　(340) 3520
That he nas glad, if that he grace fonde,
That she ne wolde up-on his lond werreye ;
With hir they made alliaunce by bonde
To been in pees, and lete hir ryde and
　　pleye.

The emperour of Rome, Claudius, 3525
Ne him bifore, the Romayn Galien,
Ne dorste never been so corageous,
Ne noon Ermyn, ne noon Egipcien,
Ne Surrien, ne noon Arabien,
Within the feld that dorste with hir fighte
Lest that she wolde hem with hir hondes
　　slen　　　　　　　　(351) 3531
Or with hir meynee putten hem to flighte.

In kinges habit wente hir sones two,
As heires of hir fadres regnes alle,
And Hermanno, and Thymalaö　3535
Her names were, as Persiens hem calle.
But ay fortune hath in hir hony galle ;
This mighty quene may no whyl endure.
Fortune out of hir regne made hir falle
To wrecchednesse and to misaventure. 3540

Aurelian, whan that the governaunce (361)
Of Rome cam in-to his hondes tweye,
He shoop up-on this queen to do ven-
　　geaunce,
And with his legiouns he took his weye
Toward Cenobie, and, shortly for to seye,
He made hir flee, and atte laste hir
　　hente,　　　　　　　　　　3546
And fettred hir, and eek hir children
　　tweye,
And wan the lond, and hoom to Rome he
　　wente.

Amonges othere thinges that he wan,
Hir char, that was with gold wrought and
　　perree,　　　　　　　(370) 3550
This grete Romayn, this Aurelian,
Hath with him lad, for that men sholde
　　it see.
Biforen his triumphe walketh she
With gilte cheynes on hir nekke hanging ;
Corouned was she, as after hir degree, 3555
And ful of perree charged hir clothing.

Allas, fortune ! she that whylom was
Dredful to kinges and to emperoures,
Now gaureth al the peple on hir, allas !
And she that helmed was in starke
　　stoures,　　　　　　　(380) 3560
And wan by force tounes stronge and
　　toures,
Shal on hir heed now were a vitremyte ;
And she that bar the ceptre ful of
　　floures
Shal bere a distaf, hir cost for to quyte.
　　　　　　　　　　　[T. 14380

(Nero *follows in* T. ; *see* p. 537.)

## De Petro Rege Ispannie.

O noble, o worthy Petro, glorie of
　　Spayne,　　　　　　　[T. 14685
Whom fortune heeld so hy in magestee,
Wel oughten men thy pitous deeth com-
　　playne !　　　　　　　　3567
Out of thy lond thy brother made thee flee;
And after, at a sege, by subtiltee,
Thou were bitrayed, and lad un-to his
　　tente,　　　　　　　　(390) 3570
Wher-as he with his owene hond slow thee,
Succeding in thy regne and in thy rente.

The feeld of snow, with th'egle of blak
　　ther-inne,　　　　　　[T. 14693.
Caught with the lymrod, coloured as the
　　glede,　　　　　　　　　3574
He brew this cursednes and al this sinne.
The 'wikked nest' was werker of this nede;
Noght Charles Oliver, that ay took hede
Of trouthe and honour, but of Armorike
Genilon Oliver, corrupt for mede, 3579
Broghte this worthy king in swich a brike.

## De Petro Rege de Cipro.

O worthy Petro, king of Cypre, also, (401)
That Alisaundre wan by heigh maistrye,

Ful many a hethen wroghtestow ful wo,
Of which thyn owene liges hadde envye,
And, for no thing but for thy chivalrye,
They in thy bedde han slayn thee by the
   morwe.            3586
Thus can fortune hir wheel governe and
   gye,          [T. 14707.
And out of joye bringe men to sorwe.

### De Barnabo de Lumbardia.

Of Melan grete Barnabo Viscounte, 3589
God of delyt, and scourge of Lumbardye,
Why sholde I nat thyn infortune acounte,
Sith in estaat thou clombe were so hye?
Thy brother sone, that was thy double
   allye,          (413)
For he thy nevew was, and sone-in-lawe,
With-inne his prisoun made thee to dye;
But why, ne how, noot I that thou were
   slawe.          3596

### De Hugelino, Comite de Pize.

Of the erl Hugelyn of Pyse the langour
Ther may no tonge telle for pitee;
But litel out of Pyse stant a tour,
In whiche tour in prisoun put was he, 3600
And with him been his litel children
   three.          (421)
The eldeste scarsly fyf yeer was of age.
Allas, fortune! it was greet crueltee
Swiche briddes for to putte in swiche a
   cage!          3604

Dampned was he to deye in that prisoun,
For Roger, which that bisshop was of Pyse,
Hadde on him maad a fals suggestioun,
Thurgh which the peple gan upon him
   ryse,          (428)
And putten him to prisoun in swich wyse
As ye han herd, and mete and drink he
   hadde          3610
So smal, that wel unnethe it may suffyse,
And therwith-al it was ful povre and
   badde.

And on a day bifil that, in that hour,
Whan that his mete wont was to be broght,
The gayler shette the dores of the tour.
He herde it wel,—but he spak right noght,
And in his herte anon ther fil a thoght,
That they for hunger wolde doon him dyen.

'Allas!' quod he, 'allas! that I was
   wroght!'      (439) 3619
Therwith the teres fillen from his yën.

His yonge sone, that three yeer was of age,
Un-to him seyde, 'fader, why do ye wepe?
Whan wol the gayler bringen our potage,
Is ther no morsel breed that ye do kepe?
I am so hungry that I may nat slepe. 3625
Now wolde god that I mighte slepen ever!
Than sholde nat hunger in my wombe
   crepe;
Ther is no thing, save breed, that me
   were lever.'

Thus day by day this child bigan to crye,
Til in his fadres barme adoun it lay, 3630
And seyde, 'far-wel, fader, I moot dye,'
And kiste his fader, and deyde the same
   day.          (452)
And whan the woful fader deed it sey,
For wo his armes two he gan to byte,
And seyde, 'allas, fortune! and weylaway!
Thy false wheel my wo al may I wyte!'

His children wende that it for hunger was
That he his armes gnow, and nat for wo,
And seyde, 'fader, do nat so, allas!
But rather eet the flesh upon us two; 3640
Our flesh thou yaf us, tak our flesh us fro
And eet y-nough:' right thus they to him
   seyde,      (462)
And after that, with-in a day or two,
They leyde hem in his lappe adoun, and
   deyde.          3644

Him-self, despeired, eek for hunger starf;
Thus ended is this mighty Erl of Pyse;
From heigh estaat fortune awey him carf.
Of this Tragedie it oghte y-nough suffyse.
Who-so wol here it in a lenger wyse, (469)
Redeth the grete poete of Itaille, 3650
That highte Dant, for he can al devyse
Fro point to point, nat o word wol he faille.
            [T. 14772.

(For T. 14773, see p. 542; for T. 14380,
   see p. 536).

### Nero.

           [T. 14381.
Al-though that Nero were as vicious
As any feend that lyth ful lowe adoun,

Yet he, as telleth us Swetonius,　　3655
This wyde world hadde in subjeccioun,
Both Est and West, †South and Septem-
　　trioun;
Of rubies, saphires, and of perles whyte
Were alle his clothes brouded up and doun;
For he in gemmes greetly gan delyte. 3660

More delicat, more pompous of array, (481)
More proud was never emperour than he;
That ilke cloth, that he had wered o day,
After that tyme he nolde it never see.
Nettes of gold-thred hadde he gret plentee
To fisshe in Tybre, whan him liste pleye.
His lustes were al lawe in his decree,
For fortune as his freend him wolde obeye.

He Rome brende for his delicacye;
The senatours he slow up-on a day,　3670
To here how men wolde wepe and crye;
And slow his brother, and by his sister
　　lay.　　　　　　　　　　　　　　(492)
His moder made he in pitous array;
For he hir wombe slitte, to biholde
Wher he conceyved was; so weilawey!
That he so litel of his moder tolde!　3676

No tere out of his yën for that sighte
Ne cam, but seyde, 'a fair womman was
　she.'
Gret wonder is, how that he coude or
　　mighte　　　　　　　　　　　(499)
Be domesman of hir dede beautee.　3680
The wyn to bringen him comaunded he,
And drank anon; non other wo he made.
Whan might is joyned un-to crueltee,
Allas! to depe wol the venim wade!　3684

In youthe a maister hadde this emperour,
To teche him letterure and curteisye,
For of moralitee he was the flour,
As in his tyme, but-if bokes lye;
And whyl this maister hadde of him
　　maistrye,　　　　　　　　　　　3689
He maked him so conning and so souple
That longe tyme it was er tirannye　(511)
Or any vyce dorste on him uncouple.

This Seneca, of which that I devyse,
By-cause Nero hadde of him swich drede,
For he fro vyces wolde him ay chastyse
Discreetly as by worde and nat by dede;—

'Sir,' wolde he seyn, 'an emperour moot
　nede　　　　　　　　　　　　　3697
Be vertuous, and hate tirannye'—
For which he in a bath made him to blede
On bothe his armes, til he moste dye.

This Nero hadde eek of acustumaunce
In youthe ageyn his maister for to ryse,
Which afterward him thoughte a greet
　　grevaunce;　　　　　　　　　(523)
Therfor he made him deyen in this wyse.
But natheles this Seneca the wyse　3705
Chees in a bath to deye in this manere
Rather than han another tormentyse;
And thus hath Nero slayn his maister dere.

Now fil it so that fortune list no lenger
The hye pryde of Nero to cheryce;　3710
For though that he were strong, yet was
　　she strenger;　　　　　　　　(531)
She thoughte thus, 'by god, I am to nyce
To sette a man that is fulfild of vyce
In heigh degree, and emperour him calle.
By god, out of his sete I wol him tryce;
When he leest weneth, sonest shal he
　　falle.'　　　　　　　　　　　3716

The peple roos up-on him on a night
For his defaute, and whan he it espyed,
Out of his dores anon he hath him dight
Alone, and, ther he wende han ben allyed,
He knokked faste, and ay, the more he
　　cryed,　　　　　　　　　　(541) 3721
The faster shette they the dores alle;
Tho wiste he wel he hadde him-self mis-
　　gyed,
And wente his wey, no lenger dorste he
　　calle.

The peple cryde and rombled up and doun,
That with his eres herde he how they
　　seyde,　　　　　　　　　　　3726
'Wher is this false tyraunt, this Neroun?'
For fere almost out of his wit he breyde,
And to his goddes pitously he preyde
For socour, but it mighte nat bityde. 3730
For drede of this, him thoughte that he
　　deyde,　　　　　　　　　　　(551)
And ran in-to a gardin, him to hyde.

And in this gardin fond he cherles tweye
That seten by a fyr ful greet and reed,

And to thise cherles two he gan to preye
To sleen him, and to girden of his heed,
That to his body, whan that he were deed,
Were no despyt y-doon, for his defame.
Him-self he slow, he coude no better reed,
Of which fortune lough, and hadde a
    game. 3740

### DE OLOFERNO (HOLOFERNES).

Was never capitayn under a king (561)
That regnes mo putte in subjeccioun,
Ne strenger was in feeld of alle thing,
As in his tyme, ne gretter of renoun, 3744
Ne more pompous in heigh presumpcioun
Than Oloferne, which fortune ay kiste
So likerously, and ladde him up and doun
Til that his heed was of, er that he wiste.

Nat only that this world hadde him in
    awe
For lesinge of richesse or libertee, 3750
But he made every man reneye his lawe.
'Nabugodonosor was god,' seyde he, (572)
'Noon other god sholde adoured be.'
Ageyns his heste no wight dar trespace
Save in Bethulia, a strong citee, 3755
Wher Eliachim a prest was of that place.

But tak kepe of the deeth of Olofern ;
Amidde his host he dronke lay a night,
With-inne his tente, large as is a bern,
And yit, for al his pompe and al his
    might, 3760
Judith, a womman, as he lay upright,
Sleping, his heed of smoot, and from his
    tente (582)
Ful prively she stal from every wight,
And with his heed unto hir toun she
    wente.

### DE REGE ANTHIOCHO ILLUSTRI.

What nedeth it of King Anthiochus 3765
To telle his hye royal magestee,
His hye pryde, his werkes venimous ?
For swich another was ther noon as he.
Rede which that he was in Machabee,
And rede the proude wordes that he seyde,
And why he fil fro heigh prosperitee, (591)
And in an hil how wrechedly he deyde.

Fortune him hadde enhaunced so in pryde
That verraily he wende he mighte attayne
Unto the sterres, upon every syde, 3775
And in balance weyen ech montayne,
And alle the flodes of the see restrayne.
And goddes peple hadde he most in hate,
Hem wolde he sleen in torment and in
    payne,
Wening that god ne mighte his pryde
    abate. (600) 3780

And for that Nichanor and Thimothee
Of Jewes weren venquisshed mightily,
Unto the Jewes swich an hate hadde he
That he bad greithe his char ful hastily,
And swoor, and seyde, ful despitously,
Unto Jerusalem he wolde eft-sone, 3786
To wreken his ire on it ful cruelly ;
But of his purpos he was let ful sone.

God for his manace him so sore smoot
With invisible wounde, ay incurable, 3790
That in his guttes carf it so and boot (611)
That his peynes weren importable.
And certeinly, the wreche was resonable,
For many a mannes guttes dide he peyne ;
But from his purpos cursed and damp-
    nable 3795
For al his smert he wolde him nat re-
    streyne ;

But bad anon apparaillen his host,
And sodeynly, er he of it was war,
God daunted al his pryde and al his bost.
For he so sore fil out of his char, 3800
That it his limes and his skin to-tar, (621)
So that he neither mighte go ne ryde,
But in a chayer men aboute him bar,
Al for-brused, bothe bak and syde. 3804

The wreche of god him smoot so cruelly
That thurgh his body wikked wormes
    crepte ;
And ther-with-al he stank so horribly,
That noon of al his meynee that him
    kepte,
Whether so he wook or elles slepte, 3809
Ne mighte noght for stink of him endure.
In this meschief he wayled and eek wepte,
And knew god lord of every creature.

To al his host and to him-self also (633)
Ful wlatsom was the stink of his careyne ;

No man ne mighte him bere to ne fro.
And in this stink and this horrible
　peyne　3816
He starf ful wrecchedly in a monteyne.
Thus hath this robbour and this homicyde,
That many a man made to wepe and
　pleyne,　3819
Swich guerdon as bilongeth unto pryde.

## De Alexandro.

The storie of Alisaundre is so comune,
That every wight that hath discrecioun
Hath herd somwhat or al of his fortune.
This wyde world, as in conclusioun, (644)
He wan by strengthe, or for his hye
　renoun　3825
They weren glad for pees un-to him sende.
The pryde of man and beste he leyde
　adoun,
Wher-so he cam, un-to the worldes ende.

Comparisoun might never yit be maked
Bitwixe him and another conquerour;
For al this world for drede of him hath
　quaked,　(651) 3831
He was of knighthode and of fredom flour;
Fortune him made the heir of hir honour;
Save wyn and wommen, no-thing mighte
　aswage
His hye entente in armes and labour;
So was he ful of leonyn corage.　3836

What preys were it to him, though I yow
　tolde
Of Darius, and an hundred thousand mo,
Of kinges, princes, erles, dukes bolde,
Whiche he conquered, and broghte hem
　in-to wo?　3840
I seye, as fer as man may ryde or go, (661)
The world was his, what sholde I more
　devyse?
For though I write or tolde you evermo
Of his knighthode, it mighte nat suffyse.

Twelf yeer he regned, as seith Machabee;
Philippes sone of Macedoyne he was, 3846
That first was king in Grece the contree.
O worthy gentil Alisaundre, allas!
That ever sholde fallen swich a cas! 3849
Empoisoned of thyn owene folk thou were;

Thy *sys* fortune hath turned into *as*, (671)
And yit for thee ne weep she never a tere!

Who shal me yeven teres to compleyne
The deeth of gentillesse and of fraunchyse,
That al the world welded in his demeyne,
And yit him thoughte it mighte nat
　suffyse?　3856
So ful was his corage of heigh empryse.
Allas! who shal me helpe to endyte
False fortune, and poison to despyse,
The whiche two of al this wo I wyte? 3860

## De Julio Cesare.

By wisdom, manhede, and by greet labour
Fro humble bed to royal magestee, (682)
Up roos he, Julius the conquerour,
That wan al th'occident by lond and see,
By strengthe of hond, or elles by tretee,
And un-to Rome made hem tributarie;
And sitthe of Rome the emperour was he,
Til that fortune wex his adversarie.

O mighty Cesar, that in Thessalye
Ageyn Pompeius, fader thyn in lawe, 3870
That of th'orient hadde al the chivalrye
As fer as that the day biginneth dawe,
Thou thurgh thy knighthode hast hem
　take and slawe,　(693)
Save fewe folk that with Pompeius fledde,
Thurgh which thou puttest al th'orient
　in awe.　3875
Thanke fortune, that so wel thee spedde!

But now a litel whyl I wol biwaille
This Pompeius, this noble governour
Of Rome, which that fleigh at this bataille;
I seye, oon of his men, a fals traitour, (700)
His heed of smoot, to winnen him favour
Of Julius, and him the heed he broghte.
Allas, Pompey, of th'orient conquerour,
That fortune unto swich a fyn thee
　broghte!

To Rome ageyn repaireth Julius　3885
With his triumphe, laureat ful hye,
But on a tyme Brutus Cassius,
That ever hadde of his hye estaat envye,
Ful prively hath maad conspiracye
Ageins this Julius, in subtil wyse,　3890

And cast the place, in whiche he sholde
    dye         (711)
With boydekins, as I shal yow devyse.

This Julius to the Capitolie wente
Upon a day, as he was wont to goon,
And in the Capitolie anon him hente 3895
This false Brutus, and his othere foon,
And stikede him with boydekins anoon
With many a wounde, and thus they lete
    him lye;
But never gronte he at no strook but oon,
Or elles at two, but-if his storie lye. 3900

So manly was this Julius at herte    (721)
And so wel lovede estaatly honestee,
That, though his deedly woundes sore
    smerte,
His mantel over his hippes casteth he,
For no man sholde seen his privitee. 3905
And, as he lay on deying in a traunce,
And wiste verraily that deed was he,
Of honestee yit hadde he remembraunce.

Lucan, to thee this storie I recomende,
And to Sweton, and to †Valerie also, 3910
That of this storie wryten word and
    ende,        (731)
How that to thise grete conqueroures two
Fortune was first freend, and sithen fo.
No man ne truste up-on hir favour longe,
But have hir in awayt for ever-mo. 3915
Witnesse on alle thise conqueroures
    stronge.

### Cresus.

This riche Cresus, whylom king of Lyde,
Of whiche Cresus Cyrus sore him dradde,
Yit was he caught amiddes al his pryde,
And to be brent men to the fyr him ladde.
But swich a reyn doun fro the welkne
    shadde        (741) 3921
That slow the fyr, and made him to escape;
But to be war no grace yet he hadde,
Til fortune on the galwes made him gape.

Whan he escaped was, he can nat stente
For to biginne a newe werre agayn. 3926

He wende wel, for that fortune him sente
Swich hap, that he escaped thurgh the
    rayn,        (748)
That of his foos he mighte nat be slayn;
And eek a sweven up-on a night he mette,
Of which he was so proud and eek so fayn,
That in vengeaunce he al his herte sette.

Up-on a tree he was, as that him thoughte,
Ther Juppiter him wesh, bothe bak and
    syde,        (754)
And Phebus eek a fair towaille him
    broughte        3935
To drye him with, and ther-for wex his
    pryde;
And to his doghter, that stood him bisyde,
Which that he knew in heigh science
    habounde,
He bad hir telle him what it signifyde,
And she his dreem bigan right thus ex-
    pounde.        3940

'The tree,' quod she, 'the galwes is to
    mene,        (761)
And Juppiter bitokneth snow and reyn,
And Phebus, with his towaille so clene,
Tho ben the sonne stremes for to seyn;
Thou shalt anhanged be, fader, certeyn;
Reyn shal thee wasshe, and sonne shal
    thee drye;'        3946
Thus warned she him ful plat and ful
    pleyn,
His doughter, which that called was
    Phanye.

Anhanged was Cresus, the proude king,
His royal trone mighte him nat availle.—
Tragedie is noon other maner thing, (771)
Ne can in singing crye ne biwaille, 3952
But for that fortune alwey wol assaille
With unwar strook the regnes that ben
    proude;
For when men trusteth hir, than wol she
    faille,        3955
And covere hir brighte face with a cloude.
[See l. 3565 on p. 536.
*Explicit Tragedia.*

**Here stinteth the Knight the Monk of his Tale.**

# THE PROLOGUE OF THE NONNE PRESTES TALE.

**The prologue of the Nonne Preestes Tale.**

'Ho!' quod the knight, 'good sir, na-
    more of this,                            3957
That ye han seyd is right y-nough, y-wis,
And mochel more ; for litel hevinesse
Is right y-nough to mochel folk, I gesse.
I seye for me, it is a greet disese     3961
Wher-as men han ben in greet welthe
    and ese,
To heren of hir sodeyn fal, allas !
And the contrarie is joie and greet
    solas,                                  3964
As whan a man hath been in povre estaat,
And clymbeth up, and wexeth fortunat,
And ther abydeth in prosperitee,     (11)
Swich thing is gladsom, as it thinketh me,
And of swich thing were goodly for to
    telle.'
'Ye,' quod our hoste, 'by seint Poules
    belle,                                  3970
Ye seye right sooth ; this monk, he
    clappeth loude,
He spak how "fortune covered with a
    cloude"
I noot never what, and als of a "Tragedie"
Right now ye herde, and parde ! no
    remedie
It is for to biwaille, ne compleyne     3975
That that is doon, and als it is a peyne,
As ye han seyd, to here of hevinesse.   (21)
Sir monk, na-more of this, so god yow
    blesse !
Your tale anoyeth al this companye ;
Swich talking is nat worth a boterflye ;
For ther-in is ther no desport ne game.
Wherfor, sir Monk, or dan Piers by your
    name,                                  3982

I preye yow hertely, telle us somwhat elles,
For sikerly, nere clinking of your belles,
That on your brydel hange on every syde
By heven king, that for us alle dyde,  (30)
I sholde er this han fallen doun for slepe
Although the slough had never been so
    depe ;                                 3988
Than had your tale al be told in vayn.
For certeinly, as that thise clerkes seyn,
"Wher-as a man may have noon audience
Noght helpeth it to tellen his sentence."
And wel I woot the substance is in me,
If any thing shal wel reported be.      3994
Sir, sey somwhat of hunting, I yow preye.
'Nay,' quod this monk, 'I have no lus
    to pleye ;                             (40)
Now let another telle, as I have told.'
Than spak our host, with rude spech
    and bold,
And seyde un-to the Nonnes Preest anon
'Com neer, thou preest, com hider, thou
    sir John,                             4000
Tel us swich thing as may our herte
    glade,
Be blythe, though thou ryde up-on a jade
What though thyn hors be bothe foul
    and lene,                             (47)
If he wol serve thee, rekke nat a bene ;
Look that thyn herte be mery evermo.'
'Yis, sir,' quod he, 'yis, host, so mote I go
But I be mery, y-wis, I wol be blamed :'—
And right anon his tale he hath attamed
And thus he seyde un-to us everichon,
This swete preest, this goodly man, si
    John.            *Explicit.*          4010

# THE NONNE PREESTES TALE.

## Here biginneth the Nonne Preestes Tale of the Cok and Hen, Chauntecleer and Pertelote.

A POVRE widwe, somdel stape in age,
Was whylom dwelling in a narwe cotage,
Bisyde a grove, stonding in a dale.
This widwe, of which I telle yow my tale,
Sin thilke day that she was last a wyf,
In pacience ladde a ful simple lyf,    4016
For litel was hir catel and hir rente ;
By housbondrye, of such as God hir sente,
She fond hir-self, and eek hir doghtren
    two.
Three large sowes hadde she, and namo,
Three kyn, and eek a sheep that highte
    Malle,                    (11) 4021
Ful sooty was hir bour, and eek hir halle,
In which she eet ful many a selendre
    meel.
Of poynaunt sauce hir neded never a deel.
No deyntee morsel passed thurgh hir
    throte ;                     4025
Hir dyete was accordant to hir cote.
Repleccioun ne made hir never syk ;
Attempree dyete was al hir phisyk,
And exercyse, and hertes suffisaunce. 4029
The goute lette hir no-thing for to daunce,
N'apoplexye shente nat hir heed ;     (21)
No wyn ne drank she, neither whyt ne
    reed ;
Hir bord was served most with whyt and
    blak,
Milk and broun breed, in which she fond
    no lak,
Seynd bacoun, and somtyme an ey or
    tweye,                    4035
For she was as it were a maner deye.
    A yerd she hadde, enclosed al aboute
With stikkes, and a drye dich with-oute,
In which she hadde a cok, hight Chaun-
    tecleer,                    4039
In al the land of crowing nas his peer. (30)
His vois was merier than the mery orgon
On messe-dayes that in the chirche gon ;

Wel sikerer was his crowing in his logge,
Than is a clokke, or an abbey orlogge.
By nature knew he ech ascencioun    4045
Of equinoxial in thilke toun ;
For whan degrees fiftene were ascended,
Thanne crew he, that it mighte nat ben
    amended.                     (38)
His comb was redder than the fyn coral,
And batailed, as it were a castel-wal. 4050
His bile was blak, and as the jeet it shoon ;
Lyk asur were his legges, and his toon ;
His nayles whytter than the lilie flour,
And lyk the burned gold was his colour.
This gentil cok hadde in his governaunce
Sevene hennes, for to doon al his plesaunce,
Whiche were his sustres and his para-
    mours,                    4057
And wonder lyk to him, as of colours.
Of whiche the faireste hewed on hir throte
Was cleped faire damoysele Pertelote.
Curteys she was, discreet, and debonaire,
And compaignable, and bar hir-self so
    faire,                     (52)
Sin thilke day that she was seven night
    old,
That trewely she hath the herte in hold
Of Chauntecleer loken in every lith ; 4065
He loved hir so, that wel was him ther-
    with.
But such a joye was it to here hem singe,
Whan that the brighte sonne gan to
    springe,                    4068
In swete accord, 'my lief is faren in londe.'
For thilke tyme, as I have understonde,
Bestes and briddes coude speke and singe.
    And so bifel, that in a daweninge,   (62)
As Chauntecleer among his wyves alle
Sat on his perche, that was in the halle,
And next him sat this faire Pertelote, 4075
This Chauntecleer gan gronen in his
    throte,

As man that in his dreem is drecched sore.
And whan that Pertelote thus herde him
    rore,                                    4078
She was agast, and seyde, ' O herte dere,
What eyleth yow, to grone in this manere?
Ye been a verray sleper, fy for shame !' (71)
And  he  answerde  and  seyde  thus,
    ' madame,
I pray yow, that ye take it nat a-grief :
By god, me mette I was in swich meschief
Right now, that yet myn herte is sore
    afright.                                 4085
Now god,' quod he, ' my swevene recche
    aright,
And keep my body out of foul prisoun !
Me mette, how that I romed up and doun
Withinne our yerde, wher-as I saugh
    a beste,
Was lyk an hound, and wolde han maad
    areste                                   4090
Upon my body, and wolde han had me
    deed.                                    (81)
His colour was bitwixe yelwe and reed ;
And tipped was his tail, and bothe his eres,
With blak, unlyk the remenant of his
    heres ;
His snowte smal, with glowinge eyen
    tweye.                                   4095
Yet of his look for fere almost I deye ;
This caused me my groning, doutelees.'
    ' Avoy !' quod she, ' fy on yow, herte-
    lees !
Allas !' quod she, ' for, by that god above,
Now han ye lost myn herte and al my
    love ;                                   4100
I can nat love a coward, by my feith. (91)
For certes, what so any womman seith,
We alle desyren, if it mighte be,
To han housbondes hardy, wyse, and free,
And secree, and no nigard, ne no fool, 4105
Ne him that is agast of every tool,
Ne noon avauntour, by that god above !
How dorste ye seyn for shame unto your
    love,
That any thing mighte make yow aferd ?
Have ye no mannes herte, and han a berd ?
Allas ! and conne ye been agast of swe-
    venis ?                         (101)  4111
No-thing, god wot, but vanitee, in sweven
    is.
Swevenes engendren of replecciouns,

And ofte of fume, and of complecciouns,
Whan humours been to habundant in a
    wight.                                   4115
Certes this dreem, which ye han met
    to-night,
Cometh of the grete superfluitee
Of youre rede colera, pardee,
Which causeth folk to dreden in here
    dremes                          (109)
Of arwes, and of fyr with rede lemes, 4120
Of grete bestes, that they wol hem byte,
Of contek, and of whelpes grete and lyte ;
Right as the humour of malencolye
Causeth ful many a man, in sleep, to crye,
For fere of blake beres, or boles blake, 4125
Or elles, blake develes wole hem take.
Of othere humours coude I telle also,
That werken many a man in sleep ful wo ;
But I wol passe as lightly as I can.
    Lo Catoun, which that was so wys
    a man,                                  4130
Seyde he nat thus, ne do no fors of
    dremes ?                        (121)
Now, sire,' quod she, ' whan we flee fro
    the bemes,
For Goddes love, as tak som laxatyf ;
Up peril of my soule, and of my lyf, 4134
I counseille yow the beste, I wol nat lye,
That bothe of colere and of malencolye
Ye purge yow ; and for ye shul nat tarie,
Though in this toun is noon apotecarie,
I shal my-self to herbes techen yow,
That shul ben for your hele, and for your
    prow ;                                  4140
And in our yerd tho herbes shal I finde,
The whiche han of hir propretee, by
    kinde,                          (132)
To purgen yow binethe, and eek above.
Forget not this, for goddes owene love !
Ye been ful colerik of compleccioun. 4145
Ware the sonne in his ascencioun
Ne fynde yow nat repleet of humours
    hote ;
And if it do, I dar wel leye a grote,
That ye shul have a fevere terciane,
Or an agu, that may be youre bane. 4150
A day or two ye shul have digestyves (141)
Of wormes, er ye take your laxatyves,
Of lauriol, centaure, and fumetere,
Or elles of ellebor, that groweth there,
Of catapuce, or of gaytres beryis,    4155

Of erbe yve, growing in our yerd, that
   mery is;
Pekke hem up right as they growe, and
   ete hem in.
Be mery, housbond, for your fader kin!
Dredeth no dreem; I can say yow na-
   more.'                                      (149)
  'Madame,' quod he, '*graunt mercy* of
   your lore.                                    4160
But nathelees, as touching daun Catoun,
That hath of wisdom such a greet renoun,
Though that he bad no dremes for to
   drede,
By god, men may in olde bokes rede
Of many a man, more of auctoritee  4165
Than ever Catoun was, so mote I thee,
That al the revers seyn of his sentence,
And han wel founden by experience,
That dremes ben significaciouns,
As wel of joye as tribulaciouns       4170
That folk enduren in this lyf present. (161)
Ther nedeth make of this noon argument;
The verray preve sheweth it in dede.

  Oon of the gretteste auctours that men
   rede
Seith thus, that whylom two felawes
   wente                                         4175
On pilgrimage, in a ful good entente;
And happed so, thay come into a toun,
Wher-as ther was swich congregacioun
Of peple, and eek so streit of herbergage
That they ne founde as muche as o cotage
In which they bothe mighte y-logged be.
Wherfor thay mosten, of necessitee,  (172)
As for that night, departen compaignye;
And ech of hem goth to his hostelrye,
And took his logging as it wolde falle. 4185
That oon of hem was logged in a stalle,
Fer in a yerd, with oxen of the plough;
That other man was logged wel y-nough,
As was his aventure, or his fortune,  4189
That us governeth alle as in commune.

  And so bifel, that, longe er it were day,
This man mette in his bed, ther-as he lay,
How that his felawe gan up-on him
   calle,                                        (183)
And seyde, "allas! for in an oxes stalle
This night I shal be mordred ther I lye.
Now help me, dere brother, er I dye; 4196
In alle haste com to me," he sayde.
This man out of his sleep for fere abrayde;

But whan that he was wakned of his sleep,
He turned him, and took of this no keep;
Him thoughte his dreem nas but a vanitee.
Thus twyës in his sleping dremed he.  (192)
And atte thridde tyme yet his felawe
Cam, as him thoughte, and seide, " I am
   now slawe;
Bihold my blody woundes, depe and wyde!
Arys up erly in the morwe-tyde,      4206
And at the west gate of the toun,"quod he,
" A carte ful of dong ther shaltow see,
In which my body is hid ful prively;
Do thilke carte aresten boldely.      4210
My gold caused my mordre, sooth to
   sayn;"                                        (201)
And tolde him every poynt how he was
   slayn,
With a ful pitous face, pale of hewe.
And truste wel, his dreem he fond ful
   trewe;
For on the morwe, as sone as it was day,
To his felawes in he took the way;   4216
And whan that he cam to this oxes stalle,
After his felawe he bigan to calle.

  The hostiler answered him anon,
And seyde, " sire, your felawe is agon, 4220
As sone as day he wente out of the toun."
This man gan fallen in suspecioun,   (212)
Remembring on his dremes that he mette,
And forth he goth, no lenger wolde he
   lette,                                         4224
Unto the west gate of the toun, and fond
A dong-carte, as it were to donge lond,
That was arrayed in the same wyse
As ye han herd the dede man devyse;
And with an hardy herte he gan to crye
Vengeaunce and justice of this felonye:—
" My felawe mordred is this same night,
And in this carte he lyth gapinge upright.
I crye out on the ministres," quod he, (223)
" That sholden kepe and reulen this citee;
Harrow! allas! her lyth my felawe
   slayn!"                                        4235
What sholde I more un-to this tale sayn?
The peple out-sterte, and caste the cart to
   grounde,
And in the middel of the dong they
   founde
The dede man, that mordred was al newe.
  O blisful god, that art so just and
   trewe!
                         4240

Lo, how that thou biwreyest mordre
    alway !                                    (231)
Mordre wol out, that see we day by day.
Mordre is so wlatsom and abhominable
To god, that is so just and resonable,
That he ne wol nat suffre it heled be; 4245
Though it abyde a yeer, or two, or three,
Mordre wol out, this my conclusioun.
And right anoon, ministres of that toun
Han hent the carter, and so sore him
    pyned,                                     (239)
And eek the hostiler so sore engyned, 4250
That thay biknewe hir wikkednesse anoon,
And were an-hanged by the nekke-boon.
    Here may men seen that dremes been
        to drede.
And certes, in the same book I rede,
Right in the nexte chapitre after this,
(I gabbe nat, so have I joye or blis,)   4256
Two men that wolde han passed over see,
For certeyn cause, in-to a fer contree,
If that the wind ne hadde been contrarie,
That made hem in a citee for to tarie, 4260
That stood ful mery upon an haven-
    syde.                                      (251)
But on a day, agayn the even-tyde,
The wind gan chaunge, and blew right
    as hem leste.
Jolif and glad they wente un-to hir reste,
And casten hem ful erly for to saille ; 4265
But †to that oo man fil a greet mervaille.
That oon of hem, in sleping as he lay,
Him mette a wonder dreem, agayn the
    day ;
Him thoughte a man stood by his beddes
    syde,
And him comaunded, that he sholde
    abyde,                                     4270
And seyde him thus, "if thou to-morwe
    wende,                                     (261)
Thou shalt be dreynt; my tale is at an
    ende."
He wook, and tolde his felawe what he
    mette,
And preyde him his viage for to lette ;
As for that day, he preyde him to abyde.
His felawe, that lay by his beddes syde,
Gan for to laughe, and scorned him ful
    faste.
" No dreem,"quod he, " may so myn herte
    agaste,

That I wol lette for to do my thinges.
I sette not a straw by thy dreminges, 4280
For swevenes been but vanitees and japes.
Men dreme al-day of owles or of apes, (272)
And eke of many a mase therwithal ;
Men dreme of thing that never was ne
    shal.                                      4284
But sith I see that thou wolt heer abyde,
And thus for-sleuthen wilfully thy tyde,
God wot it reweth me; and have good
    day."
And thus he took his leve, and wente his
    way.
But er that he hadde halfe his cours
    y-seyled,
Noot I nat why, ne what mischaunce it
    eyled,                                     4290
But casuelly the shippes botme rente, (281)
And ship and man under the water wente
In sighte of othere shippes it byside,
That with hem seyled at the same tyde.
And therfor, faire Pertelote so dere, 4295
By swiche ensamples olde maistow lere,
That no man sholde been to recchelees
Of dremes, for I sey thee, doutelees,
That many a dreem ful sore is for to
    drede.                                     4299
    Lo, in the lyf of seint Kenelm, I rede,
That was Kenulphus sone, the noble king
Of Mercenrike, how Kenelm mette a
    thing ;                                    (292)
A lyte er he was mordred, on a day,
His mordre in his avisioun he say.
His norice him expouned every del   4305
His sweven, and bad him for to kepe him
    wel
For traisoun ; but he nas but seven yeer
    old,
And therfore litel tale hath he told
Of any dreem, so holy was his herte.
By god, I hadde lever than my sherte 4310
That ye had rad his legende, as have I.
Dame Pertelote, I sey yow trewely,   (302)
Macrobeus, that writ th'avisioun
In Affrike of the worthy Cipioun,
Affermeth dremes, and seith that they
    been                                       4315
Warning of thinges that men after seen.
    And forther-more, I pray yow loketh
        wel
In th'olde testament, of Daniel,

If he held dremes any vanitee. 4319
Reed eek of Joseph, and ther shul ye see
Wher dremes ben somtyme (I sey nat alle)
Warning of thinges that shul after falle.
Loke of Egipt the king, daun Pharao, (313)
His bakere and his boteler also, 4324
Wher they ne felte noon effect in dremes.
Who-so wol seken actes of sondry remes,
May rede of dremes many a wonder thing.

Lo Cresus, which that was of Lyde king,
Mette he nat that he sat upon a tree, 4329
Which signified he sholde anhanged be?
Lo heer Andromacha, Ectores wyf, (321)
That day that Ector sholde·lese his lyf,
She dremed on the same night biforn,
How that the lyf of Ector sholde be lorn,
If thilke day he wente in-to bataille; 4335
She warned him. but it mighte nat
    availle;
He wente for to fighte nathelees,
But he was slayn anoon of Achilles.
But thilke tale is al to long·to telle, 4339
And eek it is ny day, I may nat dwelle.
Shortly I seye, as for conclusioun, (331)
That I shal han of this avisioun
Adversitee; and I seye forther-more,
That I ne telle of laxatyves no store,
For they ben venimous, I woot it wel; 4345
I hem defye, I love hem never a del.

Now let us speke of mirthe, and stinte
    al this;
Madame Pertelote, so have I blis,
Of o thing god hath sent me large grace;
For whan I see the beautee of your face,
Ye ben so scarlet-reed about your yën,
It maketh al my drede for to dyen; (342)
For, also siker as *In principio*,
*Mulier est hominis confusio;* 4354
Madame, the sentence of this Latin is—
Womman is mannes joye and al his blis.
For whan I fele a-night your softe syde,
Al-be-it that I may nat on yow ryde,
For that our perche is maad so narwe,
    alas!
I am so ful of joye and of solas 4360
That I defye bothe sweven and dreem.'
And with that word he fley doun fro the
    beem, (352)
For it was day, and eek his hennes alle;
And with a chuk he gan hem for to calle,
For he had founde a corn, lay in the yerd.

Royal he was, he was namore aferd; 4366
He fethered Pertelote twenty tyme,
And trad as ofte, er that it was pryme.
He loketh as it were a grim leoun; 4369
And on his toos he rometh up and doun,
Him deyned not to sette his foot to
    grounde. (361)
He chukketh, whan he hath a 'corn
    y-founde,
And to him rennen thanne his wyves
    alle.
Thus royal, as a prince is in his halle,
Leve I this Chauntecleer in his pasture;
And after wol I telle his aventure. 4376
    Whan that the month in which the
        world bigan,
That highte March, whan god first maked
    man,
Was complet, and [y]-passed were also,
Sin March bigan, thritty dayes and two,
Bifel that Chauntecleer, in al his pryde,
His seven wyves walking by his syde, (372)
Caste up his eyen to the brighte sonne,
That in the signe of Taurus hadde
    y-ronne
Twenty degrees and oon, and somwhat
    more; 4385
And knew by kynde, and by noon other
    lore,
That it was pryme, and crew with blisful
    stevene.
'The sonne,' he sayde, ' is clomben up on
    hevene
Fourty degrees and oon, and more, y-wis.
Madame Pertelote, my worldes blis, 4390
Herkneth thise blisful briddes how they
    singe, (381)
And see the fresshe floures how they
    springe;
Ful is myn herte of revel and solas.'
But sodeinly him fil a sorweful cas;
For ever the latter ende of joye is wo. 4395
God woot that worldly joye is sone ago;
And if a rethor coude faire endyte,
He in a cronique saufly mighte it wryte,
As for a sovereyn notabilitee. 4399
Now every wys man, lat him herkne me;
This storie is al-so trewe, I undertake, (391)
As is the book of Launcelot de Lake,
That wommen holde in ful gret reverence.
Now wol I torne agayn to my sentence.

A col-fox, ful of sly iniquitee,    4405
That in the grove hadde woned yeres
    three,
By heigh imaginacioun forn-cast,
The same night thurgh-out the hegges
    brast
Into the yerd, ther Chauntecleer the faire
Was wont, and eek his wyves, to repaire;
And in a bed of wortes stille he lay,   (401)
Til it was passed undern of the day,
Wayting his tyme on Chauntecleer to
    falle,
As gladly doon thise homicydes alle,
That in awayt liggen to mordre men. 4415
O false mordrer, lurking in thy den!
O newe Scariot, newe Genilon!
False dissimilour, O Greek Sinon,
That broghtest Troye al outrely to sorwe!
O Chauntecleer, acursed be that morwe,
That thou into that yerd flough fro the
    bemes!          (411) 4421
Thou were ful wel y-warned by thy
    dremes,
That thilke day was perilous to thee.
But what that god forwoot mot nedes be,
After the opinioun of certeyn clerkis. 4425
Witnesse on him, that any perfit clerk is,
That in scole is gret altercacioun
In this matere, and greet disputisoun,
And hath ben of an hundred thousand
    men.
But I ne can not bulte it to the bren, 4430
As can the holy doctour Augustyn,   (421)
Or Boëce, or the bishop Bradwardyn,
Whether that goddes worthy forwiting
Streyneth me nedely for to doon a thing,
(Nedely clepe I simple necessitee);   4435
Or elles, if free choys be graunted me
To do that same thing, or do it noght,
Though god forwoot it, er that it was
    wroght;
Or if his witing streyneth nevere a del
But by necessitee condicionel.        4440
I wol not han to do of swich matere;(431)
My tale is of a cok, as ye may here,
That took his counseil of his wyf, with
    sorwe,
To walken in the yerd upon that morwe
That he had met the dreem, that I yow
    tolde.                          4445
Wommennes counseils been ful ofte colde;

Wommannes counseil broghte us first to
    wo,
And made Adam fro paradys to go,
Ther-as he was ful mery, and wel at ese.—
But for I noot, to whom it mighte
    displese,                       4450
If I counseil of wommen wolde blame,(441)
Passe over, for I seyde it in my game.
Rede auctours, wher they trete of swich
    matere,
And what thay seyn of wommen ye may
    here.
Thise been the cokkes wordes, and nat
    myne;                          4455
I can noon harm of no womman divyne.—
Faire in the sond, to bathe hir merily,
Lyth Pertelote, and alle hir sustres by,
Agayn the sonne; and Chauntecleer so
    free
Song merier than the mermayde in the
    see;                           4460
For Phisiologus seith sikerly,       (451)
How that they singen wel and merily.
And so bifel that, as he caste his yë,
Among the wortes, on a boterflye,    4464
He was war of this fox that lay ful lowe.
No-thing ne liste him thanne for to crowe,
But cryde anon, 'cok, cok,' and up he
    sterte,
As man that was affrayed in his herte.
For naturelly a beest desyreth flee
Fro his contrarie, if he may it see,   4470
Though he never erst had seyn it with
    his yë.                        (461)
    This Chauntecleer, whan he gan him
    espye,
He wolde han fled, but that the fox anon
Seyde, 'Gentil sire, allas! wher wol ye
    gon?
Be ye affrayed of me that am your
    freend?                        4475
Now certes, I were worse than a feend,
If I to yow wolde harm or vileinye.
I am nat come your counseil for t'espye;
But trewely, the cause of my cominge
Was only for to herkne how that ye
    singe.                   (470) 4480
For trewely ye have as mery a stevene
As eny aungel hath, that is in hevene;
Therwith ye han in musik more felinge
Than hadde Boëce, or any that can singe.

My lord your fader (god his soule blesse!)
And eek your moder, of hir gentilesse,
Han in myn hous y-been, to my gret ese;
And certes, sire, ful fayn wolde I yow
 plese.      4488
But for men speke of singing, I wol saye,
So mote I brouke wel myn eyen tweye,
Save yow, I herde never man so singe,
As dide your fader in the morweninge;
Certes, it was of herte, al that he song.
And for to make his voys the more strong,
He wolde so peyne him, that with bothe
 his yën      4495
He moste winke, so loude he wolde cryen,
And stonden on his tiptoon ther-with-al,
And strecche forth his nekke long and
 smal.
And eek he was of swich discrecioun,
That ther nas no man in no regioun 4500
That him in song or wisdom mighte
 passe.      (491)
I have wel rad in daun Burnel the Asse,
Among his vers, how that ther was a cok,
For that a preestes sone yaf him a knok
Upon his leg, whyl he was yong and
 nyce,      4505
He made him for to lese his benefyce.
But certeyn, ther nis no comparisoun
Bitwix the wisdom and discrecioun
Of youre fader, and of his subtiltee. (499)
Now singeth, sire, for seinte Charitee, 4510
Let see, conne ye your fader countrefete?'
This Chauntecleer his winges gan to bete,
As man that coude his tresoun nat espye,
So was he ravisshed with his flaterye.

 Allas! ye lordes, many a fals flatour
Is in your courtes, and many a losengeour,
That plesen yow wel more, by my feith,
Than he that soothfastnesse unto yow
 seith.
Redeth Ecclesiaste of flaterye;
Beth war, ye lordes, of hir trecherye. 4520
 This Chauntecleer stood hye up-on his
 toos,      (511)
Strecching his nekke, and heeld his eyen
 cloos,
And gan to crowe loude for the nones;
And daun Russel the fox sterte up at
 ones,      4524
And by the gargat hente Chauntecleer,
And on his bak toward the wode him beer,

For yet ne was ther no man that him
 sewed.
O destinee, that mayst nat been eschewed!
Allas, that Chauntecleer fleigh fro the
 bemes!      4529
Allas, his wyf ne roghte nat of dremes!
And on a Friday fil al this meschaunce. (521)
O Venus, that art goddesse of plesaunce,
Sin that thy servant was this Chaunte-
 cleer,
And in thy service dide al his poweer,
More for delyt, than world to multiplye,
Why woldestow suffre him on thy day to
 dye?      4536
O Gaufred, dere mayster soverayn,
That, whan thy worthy king Richard
 was slayn
With shot, compleynedest his deth so
 sore,
Why ne hadde I now thy sentence and
 thy lore,      4540
The Friday for to chyde, as diden ye? (531)
(For on a Friday soothly slayn was he.)
Than wolde I shewe yow how that I coude
 pleyne
For Chauntecleres drede, and for his
 peyne.
 Certes, swich cry ne lamentacioun 4545
Was never of ladies maad, whan Ilioun
Was wonne, and Pirrus with his streite
 swerd,
Whan he hadde hent king Priam by the
 berd,
And slayn him (as saith us *Eneydos*),
As maden alle the hennes in the clos, 4550
Whan they had seyn of Chauntecleer the
 sighte.      (541)
But sovereynly dame Pertelote shrighte,
Ful louder than dide Hasdrubales wyf,
Whan that hir housbond hadde lost his lyf,
And that the Romayns hadde brend
 Cartage;      4555
She was so ful of torment and of rage,
That wilfully into the fyr she sterte,
And brende hir-selven with a stedfast
 herte.
O woful hennes, right so cryden ye,
As, whan that Nero brende the citee 4560
Of Rome, cryden senatoures wyves, (551)
For that hir housbondes losten alle hir
 lyves;

Withouten gilt this Nero hath hem slayn.
Now wol I torne to my tale agayn :—
  This sely widwe, and eek hir doghtres
    two,        4565
Herden thise hennes crye and maken wo,
And out at dores sterten they anoon,
And syen the fox toward the grove goon,
And bar upon his bak the cok away ;
And cryden, ' Out ! harrow ! and weyla-
    way !        4570
Ha, ha, the fox !' and after him they
    ran,        (561)
And eek with staves many another man ;
Ran Colle our dogge, and Talbot, and
    Gerland,
And Malkin, with a distaf in hir hand ;
Ran cow and calf, and eek the verray
    hogges        4575
So were they fered for berking of the
    dogges
And shouting of the men and wimmen
    eke,
They ronne so, hem thoughte hir herte
    breke.
They yelleden as feendes doon in helle ;
The dokes cryden as men wolde hem
    quelle ;      (571) 4580
The gees for fere flowen over the trees ;
Out of the hyve cam the swarm of bees ;
So hidous was the noyse, a ! *benedicite !*
Certes, he Jakke Straw, and his meynee,
Ne made never shoutes half so shrille, 4585
Whan that they wolden any Fleming
    kille,
As thilke day was maad upon the fox.
Of bras thay broghten bemes, and of box,
Of horn, of boon, in whiche they blewe
    and pouped,
And therwithal thay shryked and they
    houped ;      4590
It semed as that heven sholde falle. (581)
Now, gode men, I pray yow herkneth alle !
  Lo, how fortune turneth sodeinly
The hope and pryde eek of hir enemy !
This cok, that lay upon the foxes bak, 4595
In al his drede, un-to the fox he spak,
And seyde, ' sire, if that I were as ye,
Yet sholde I seyn (as wis god helpe me),
Turneth agayn, ye proude cherles alle !

A verray pestilence up-on yow falle ! 4600
Now am I come un-to this wodes syde,
Maugree your heed, the cok shal heer
    abyde ;      (592)
I wol him ete in feith, and that anon.'—
The fox answerde, ' in feith, it shal be
    don,'—
And as he spak that word, al sodeinly 4605
This cok brak from his mouth deliverly,
And heighe up-on a tree he fleigh anon.
And whan the fox saugh that he was
    y-gon,
' Allas !' quod he, ' O Chauntecleer, allas !
I have to yow,' quod he, ' y-doon trespas,
In-as-muche as I maked yow aferd, (601)
Whan I yow hente, and broghte out of
    the yerd ;
But, sire, I dide it in no wikke entente ;
Com doun, and I shal telle yow what
    I mente.
I shal seye sooth to yow, god help me so.'
' Nay than,' quod he, ' I shrewe us bothe
    two,        4616
And first I shrewe my-self, bothe blood
    and bones,
If thou bigyle me ofter than ones.
Thou shalt na-more, thurgh thy flaterye,
Do me to singe and winke with myn yë.
For he that winketh, whan he sholde see,
Al wilfully, god lat him never thee !' (612)
' Nay,' quod the fox, ' but god yeve him
    meschaunce,
That is so undiscreet of governaunce,
That jangleth whan he sholde holde his
    pees.'      4625
  Lo, swich it is for to be recchelees,
And necligent, and truste on flaterye.
But ye that holden this tale a folye,
As of a fox, or of a cok and hen,
Taketh the moralitee, good men.    4630
For seint Paul seith, that al that writen
    is,      (621)
To our doctryne it is y-write, y-wis.
Taketh the fruyt, and lat the chaf be
    stille.
  Now, gode god, if that it be thy wille,
As seith my lord, so make us alle good
    men ;      4635
And bringe us to his heighe blisse. Amen.

**Here is ended the Nonne Preestes Tale.**

# EPILOGUE TO THE NONNE
# PREESTES TALE.

'Sir Nonnes Preest,' our hoste seyde anoon,
'Y-blessed be thy breche, and every stoon!
This was a mery tale of Chauntecleer.
But, by my trouthe, if thou were seculer,
Thou woldest been a trede-foul a-right. 4641
For, if thou have corage as thou hast
    might,
Thee were nede of hennes, as I wene,
Ya, mo than seven tymes seventene.

See, whiche braunes hath this gentil
    Preest,                          4645
So greet a nekke, and swich a large breest!
He loketh as a sperhauk with his yën ; (11)
Him nedeth nat his colour for to dyen
With brasil, ne with greyn of Portingale.
Now sire, faire falle yow for youre tale!'
    And after that he, with ful mery chere,
Seide to another, as ye shullen here. 4652

*\** B. 4652 = T. 15468 ; C. 1 = T. 11935.

# GROUP C.

# THE PHISICIENS TALE.

### Here folweth the Phisiciens Tale.

Ther was, as telleth Titus Livius,
A knight that called was Virginius,
Fulfild of honour and of worthinesse,
And strong of freendes and of greet
    richesse.                       [T. 11938
    This knight a doghter hadde by his wyf,
No children hadde he mo in al his lyf.  6
Fair was this mayde in excellent beautee
Aboven every wight that man may see ;
For nature hath with sovereyn diligence
Y-formed hir in so greet excellence,   10
As though she wolde seyn, 'lo! I, Nature,
Thus can I forme and peynte a creature,
Whan that me list ; who can me countre-
    fete ?
Pigmalion noght, though he ay forge and
    bete,

Or grave, or peynte ; for I dar wel seyn, 15
Apelles, Zanzis, sholde werche in veyn,
Outher to grave or peynte or forge or bete,
If they presumed me to countrefete.
For he that is the former principal
Hath maked me his vicaire general,   20
To forme and peynten erthely creaturis
Right as me list, and ech thing in my
    cure is
Under the mone, that may wane and waxe,
And for my werk right no-thing wol I axe ;
My lord and I ben ful of oon accord ;  25
I made hir to the worship of my lord.
So do I alle myne othere creatures,
What colour that they han, or what
    figures.'—
Thus semeth me that Nature wolde seye.

This mayde of age twelf yeer was and
tweye,                                    30
In which that Nature hadde swich delyt.
For right as she can peynte a lilie whyt
And reed a rose, right with swich peynture
She peynted hath this noble creature
Er she were born, up-on hir limes free, 35
Wher-as by right swiche colours sholde be;
And Phebus dyed hath hir tresses grete
Lyk to the stremes of his burned hete.
And if that excellent was hir beautee,
A thousand-fold more vertuous was she. 40
In hir ne lakked no condicioun,
That is to preyse, as by discrecioun.
As wel in goost as body chast was she;
For which she floured in virginitee
With alle humilitee and abstinence,    45
With alle attemperaunce and pacience,
With mesure eek of bering and array.
Discreet she was in answering alway ;
Though she were wys as Pallas, dar I seyn,
Hir facound eek ful wommanly and pleyn,
No countrefeted termes hadde she    51
To seme wys ; but after hir degree
She spak, and alle hir wordes more and
lesse
Souninge in vertu and in gentillesse.
Shamfast she was in maydens shamfast-
nesse,                                    55
Constant in herte, and ever in bisinesse
To dryve hir out of ydel slogardye.
Bacus hadde of hir mouth right no
maistrye ;
For wyn and youthe doon Venus encrece,
As men in fyr wol casten oile or grece. 60
And of hir owene vertu, unconstreyned,
She hath ful ofte tyme syk hir feyned,
For that she wolde fleen the companye
Wher lykly was to treten of folye,
As is at festes, revels, and at daunces. 65
That been occasions of daliaunces
Swich thinges maken children for to be
To sone rype and bold, as men may see,
Which is ful perilous, and hath ben yore.
For al to sone may she lerne lore    70
Of boldnesse, whan she woxen is a wyf.

And ye maistresses in your olde lyf,
That lordes doghtres han in governaunce,
Ne taketh of my wordes no displesaunce ;
Thenketh that ye ben set in governinges 75
Of lordes doghtres, only for two thinges ;

Outher for ye han kept your honestee,
Or elles ye han falle in freletee,
And knowen wel y-nough the olde daunce,
And han forsaken fully swich meschaunce
For evermo ; therfore, for Cristes sake, 81
To teche hem vertu loke that ye ne slake.
A theef of venisoun, that hath forlaft
His likerousnesse, and al his olde craft,
Can kepe a forest best of any man.    85
Now kepeth hem wel, for if ye wol, ye can ;
Loke wel that ye un-to no vice assente,
Lest ye be dampned for your wikke en-
tente ;
For who-so doth, a traitour is certeyn.
And taketh kepe of that that I shal
seyn ;                                    90
Of alle tresons sovereyn pestilence
Is whan a wight bitrayseth innocence.

Ye fadres and ye modres eek also,
Though ye han children, be it oon or two,
Your is the charge of al hir surveyaunce, 95
Whyl that they been under your govern-
aunce.
Beth war that by ensample of your livinge,
Or by your necligence in chastisinge,
That they ne perisse ; for I dar wel seye,
If that they doon, ye shul it dere abeye. 100
Under a shepherde softe and necligent
The wolf hath many a sheep and lamb
to-rent.
Suffyseth oon ensample now as here,
For I mot turne agayn to my matere.
This mayde, of which I wol this tale
expresse,                                105
So kepte hir-self, hir neded no maistresse ;
For in hir living maydens mighten rede,
As in a book, every good word or dede,
That longeth to a mayden vertuous;
She was so prudent and so bountevous. 110
For which the fame out-sprong on every
syde
Bothe of hir beautee and hir bountee wyde;
That thurgh that land they preysed hir
echone,
That loved vertu, save envye allone,
That sory is of other mennes wele,    115
And glad is of his sorwe and his unhele ;
(The doctour maketh this descripcioun).
This mayde up-on a day wente in the toun
Toward a temple, with hir moder dere,
As is of yonge maydens the manere.    120

Now was ther thanne a justice in that
  toun,
That governour was of that regioun.
And so bifel, this juge his eyen caste
Up-on this mayde, avysinge him ful faste,
As she cam forby ther this juge stood. 125
Anon his herte chaunged and his mood,
So was he caught with beautee of this
  mayde ;
And to him-self ful prively he sayde,
'This mayde shal be myn, for any man.'
  Anon the feend in-to his herte ran, 130
And taughte him sodeynly, that he by
  slighte
The mayden to his purpos winne mighte.
For certes, by no force, ne by no mede,
Him thoughte, he was nat able for to spede ;
For she was strong of freendes, and eek she
Confermed was in swich soverayn bountee,
That wel he wiste he mighte hir never
  winne               137
As for to make hir with hir body sinne.
For which, by greet deliberacioun,
He sente after a cherl, was in the toun, 140
Which that he knew for subtil and for
  bold.
This juge un-to this cherl his tale hath told
In secree wyse, and made him to ensure,
He sholde telle it to no creature,
And if he dide, he sholde lese his heed. 145
Whan that assented was this cursed reed,
Glad was this juge and maked him greet
  chere,
And yaf him yiftes preciouse and dere.
  Whan shapen was al hir conspiracye
Fro point to point, how that his lecherye
Parfourned sholde been ful subtilly, 151
As ye shul here it after openly,
Hoom gooth the cherl, that highte Clau-
  dius.
This false juge that highte Apius,
So was his name, (for this is no fable, 155
But knowen for historial thing notable,
The sentence of it sooth is, out of doute),
This false juge gooth now faste aboute
To hasten his delyt al that he may.
And so bifel sone after, on a day, 160
This false juge, as telleth us the storie,
As he was wont, sat in his consistorie,
And yaf his domes up-on sondry cas.
This false cherl cam forth a ful greet pas,

And seyde, 'lord, if that it be your wille, 165
As dooth me right up-on this pitous bille,
In which I pleyne up-on Virginius.
And if that he wol seyn it is nat thus,
I wol it preve, and finde good witnesse,
That sooth is that my bille wol expresse.'
  The juge answerde, 'of this, in his
    absence,                 171
I may nat yeve diffinitif sentence.
Lat do him calle, and I wol gladly here ;
Thou shalt have al right, and no wrong
  here.'              174
  Virginius cam, to wite the juges wille,
And right anon was rad this cursed bille ;
The sentence of it was as ye shul here.
  'To yow, my lord, sire Apius so dere,
Sheweth your povre servant Claudius,
How that a knight, called Virginius, 180
Agayns the lawe, agayn al equitee,
Holdeth, expres agayn the wil of me,
My servant, which that is my thral by
  right,
Which fro myn hous was stole up-on
  a night,
Whyl that she was ful yong ; this wol
  I preve             185
By witnesse, lord, so that it nat yow greve.
She nis his doghter nat, what so he seye ;
Wherfore to yow, my lord the juge, I preye,
Yeld me my thral, if that it be your wille.'
Lo ! this was al the sentence of his bille.
  Virginius gan up-on the cherl biholde,
But hastily, er he his tale tolde,    192
And wolde have preved it, as sholde
  a knight,
And eek by witnessing of many a wight,
That it was fals that seyde his adversarie,
This cursed juge wolde no-thing tarie, 196
Ne here a word more of Virginius,
But yaf his jugement, and seyde thus :—
  'I deme anon this cherl his servant have ;
Thou shalt no lenger in thyn hous hir
  save.             200
Go bring hir forth, and put hir in our
  warde,
The cherl shal have his thral, this I
  awarde.'
  And whan this worthy knight Virginius,
Thurgh sentence of this justice Apius,
Moste by force his dere doghter yiven 205
Un-to the juge, in lecherye to liven,

He gooth him hoom, and sette him in his
     halle,
And leet anon his dere doghter calle,
And, with a face deed as asshen colde,
Upon hir humble face he gan biholde, 210
With fadres pitee stiking thurgh his herte,
Al wolde he from his purpos nat converte.
    'Doghter,' quod he, 'Virginia, by thy
     name,
Ther been two weyes, outher deeth or
     shame,
That thou most suffre ; allas ! that I was
     bore !              215
For never thou deservedest wherfore
To dyen with a swerd or with a knyf.
O dere doghter, ender of my lyf,
Which I have fostred up with swich
     plesaunce,
That thou were never out of my remem-
     braunce !          220
O doghter, which that art my laste wo,
And in my lyf my laste joye also,
O gemme of chastitee, in pacience
Take thou thy deeth, for this is my sen-
     tence.
For love and nat for hate, thou most be
     deed ;            225
My pitous hand mot smyten of thyn heed.
Allas ! that ever Apius thee say !
Thus hath he falsly juged thee to-day'—
And tolde hir al the cas, as ye bifore   229
Han herd ; nat nedeth for to telle it more.
    'O mercy, dere fader,' quod this mayde,
And with that word she both hir armes
     layde
About his nekke, as she was wont to do :
The teres broste out of hir eyen two,
And seyde, 'gode fader, shal I dye ?   235
Is ther no grace ? is ther no remedye ?'
    'No, certes, dere doghter myn,' quod he.
    'Thanne yif me leyser, fader myn,' quod
     she,
' My deeth for to compleyne a litel space ;
For pardee, Jepte yaf his doghter grace 240
For to compleyne, er he hir slow, allas !
And god it woot, no-thing was hir trespas,
But for she ran hir fader first to see,
To welcome him with greet solempnitee.'
And with that word she fil aswowne anon,
And after, whan hir swowning is agon, 246

She ryseth up, and to hir fader sayde,
' Blessed be god, that I shal dye a mayde.
Yif me my deeth, er that I have a shame ;
Doth with your child your wil, a goddes
     name !'            250
    And with that word she preyed him ful
     ofte,
That with his swerd he wolde smyte softe,
And with that word aswowne doun she fil.
Hir fader, with ful sorweful herte and wil,
Hir heed of smoot, and by the top it
     hente,            255
And to the juge he gan it to presente,
As he sat yet in doom in consistorie.
And whan the juge it saugh, as seith the
     storie,
He bad to take him and anhange him
     faste.            259
But right anon a thousand peple in thraste,
To save the knight, for routhe and for
     pitee,
For knowen was the false iniquitee.
The peple anon hath suspect of this thing,
By manere of the cherles chalanging,
That it was by th'assent of Apius ;    265
They wisten wel that he was lecherous.
For which un-to this Apius they gon,
And caste him in a prison right anon,
Wher-as he slow him-self ; and Claudius,
That servant was un-to this Apius,    270
Was demed for to hange upon a tree ;
But that Virginius, of his pitee,
So preyde for him that he was exyled ;
And elles, certes, he had been bigyled.
The remenant were anhanged, more and
     lesse,            275
That were consentant of this cursed-
     nesse.—
    Heer men may seen how sinne hath his
     meryte !
Beth war, for no man woot whom god
     wol smyte
In no degree, ne in which maner wyse
The worm of conscience may agryse   280
Of wikked lyf, though it so privee be,
That no man woot ther-of but god and he.
For be he lewed man, or elles lered,
He noot how sone that he shal been afered.
Therfore I rede yow this conseil take, 285
Forsaketh sinne, er sinne yow forsake.

**Here endeth the Phisiciens Tale.**

# WORDS OF THE HOST.

**The wordes of the Host to the Phisicien and the Pardoner.**

OUR Hoste gan to swere as he were wood,
'Harrow!' quod he, 'by nayles and by blood!
This was a fals cherl and a fals justyse!
As shamful deeth as herte may devyse 290
Come to thise juges and hir advocats!
Algate this sely mayde is slayn, allas!
Allas! to dere boghte she beautee!     .
Wherfore I seye al day, as men may see,
That yiftes of fortune or of nature     295
Ben cause of deeth to many a creature. (10)
Hir beautee was hir deeth, I dar wel sayn;
Allas! so pitously as she was slayn!
Of bothe yiftes that I speke of now
Men han ful ofte more harm than prow.
But trewely, myn owene mayster dere, 301
This is a pitous tale for to here.
But natheles, passe over, is no fors;
I prey to god, so save thy gentil cors, 304
And eek thyne urinals and thy jordanes,
Thyn Ypocras, and eek thy Galianes, (20)
And every boist ful of thy letuarie;
God blesse hem, and our lady seinte Marie!
So mot I theen, thou art a propre man,
And lyk a prelat, by seint Ronyan! 310

Seyde I nat wel? I can nat speke in terme;
But wel I woot, thou doost my herte to erme,
That I almost have caught a cardiacle.
By corpus bones! but I have triacle, 314
Or elles a draught of moyste and corny ale,
Or but I here anon a mery tale,     (30)
Myn herte is lost for pitee of this mayde.
Thou bel amy, thou Pardoner,' he seyde,
'Tel us som mirthe or japes right anon.'
'It shall be doon,' quod he, 'by seint Ronyon!     320
But first,' quod he, 'heer at this ale-stake
I wol both drinke, and eten of a cake.'
But right anon thise gentils gonne to crye,
'Nay! lat him telle us of no ribaudye;
Tel us som moral thing, that we may lere     325
Som wit, and thanne wol we gladly here.'     (40)
'I graunte, y-wis,' quod he, 'but I mot thinke
Up-on som honest thing, whyl that I drinke.'

# THE PROLOGUE OF THE PARDONERS TALE.

### Here folweth the Prologe of the Pardoners Tale.

*Radix malorum est Cupiditas: Ad Thimotheum, sexto.*

'LORDINGS,' quod he, ' in chirches whan I
    preche,
I peyne me to han an hauteyn speche, 330
And ringe it out as round as gooth a belle,
For I can al by rote that I telle.
My theme is alwey oon, and ever was—
" *Radix malorum est Cupiditas.*"

First I pronounce whennes that I come,
And than my bulles shewe I, alle and
    somme.                                    336
Our lige lordes seel on my patente,
That shewe I first, my body to warente, (10)
That no man be so bold, ne preest ne clerk,
Me to destourbe of Cristes holy werk; 340
And after that than telle I forth my tales,
Bulles of popes and of cardinales,
Of patriarkes, and bishoppes I shewe ;
And in Latyn I speke a wordes fewe,
To saffron with my predicacioun,      345
And for to stire men to devocioun.      (18)
Than shewe I forth my longe cristal stones,
Y-crammed ful of cloutes and of bones ;
Reliks been they, as wenen they echoon.
Than have I in latoun a sholder-boon 350
Which that was of an holy Jewes shepe.
" Good men," seye I, " tak of my wordes
    kepe ;
If that this boon be wasshe in any welle,
If cow, or calf, or sheep, or oxe swelle
That any worm hath ete, or worm y-
    stonge,                                   355
Tak water of that welle, and wash his
    tonge,
And it is hool anon ; and forthermore,
Of pokkes and of scabbe, and every sore (30)

Shal every sheep be hool, that of this welle
Drinketh a draughte ; tak kepe eek what
    I telle.                                  360
If that the good-man, that the bestes oweth,
Wol every wike, er that the cok him
    croweth,
Fastinge, drinken of this welle a draughte,
As thilke holy Jewe our eldres taughte,
His bestes and his stoor shal multiplye. 365
And, sirs, also it heleth jalousye ;
For, though a man be falle in jalous rage,
Let maken with this water his potage, (40)
And never shal he more his wyf mistriste,
Though he the sooth of hir defaute wiste ;
Al had she taken preestes two or three. 371
    Heer is a miteyn eek, that ye may see.
He that his hond wol putte in this miteyn,
He shal have multiplying of his greyn,
Whan he hath sowen, be it whete or otes,
So that he offre pens, or elles grotes.   376
    Good men and wommen, o thing warne
    I yow,
If any wight be in this chirche now,    (50)
That hath doon sinne horrible, that he
Dar nat, for shame, of it y-shriven be, 380
Or any womman, be she yong or old,
That hath y-maad hir housbond cokewold,
Swich folk shul have no power ne no grace
To offren to my reliks in this place.
And who-so findeth him out of swich
    blame,                                     385
He wol com up and offre in goddes name,
And I assoille him by the auctoritee
Which that by bulle y-graunted was to
    me."                                       (60)

By this gaude have I wonne, yeer by
    yeer,
An hundred mark sith I was Pardoner.
I stonde lyk a clerk in my pulpet,   391
And whan the lewed peple is doun y-set,
I preche, so as ye han herd bifore,
And telle an hundred false japes more.
Than peyne I me to strecche forth the
    nekke,   395
And est and west upon the peple I bekke,
As doth a dowve sitting on a berne. (69)
Myn hondes and my tonge goon so yerne,
That it is joye to see my bisinesse.
Of avaryce and of swich cursednesse  400
Is al my preching, for to make hem free
To yeve her pens, and namely un-to me.
For my entente is nat but for to winne,
And no-thing for correccioun of sinne. 404
I rekke never, whan that they ben beried,
Though that her soules goon a-blake-
    beried !
For certes, many a predicacioun
Comth ofte tyme of yvel entencioun ; (80)
Som for plesaunce of folk and flaterye,
To been avaunced by ipocrisye,   410
And som for veyne glorie, and som for hate.
For, whan I dar non other weyes debate,
Than wol I stinge him with my tonge
    smerte
In preching, so that he shal nat asterte
To been defamed falsly, if that he   415
Hath trespased to my brethren or to me.
For, though I telle noght his propre name,
Men shal wel knowe that it is the same (90)
By signes and by othere circumstances.
Thus quyte I folk that doon us dis-
    plesances ;   420
Thus spitte I out my venim under hewe
Of holynesse, to seme holy and trewe.

    But shortly myn entente I wol devyse ;
I preche of no-thing but for coveityse.
Therfor my theme is yet, and ever was—

" *Radix malorum est cupiditas.*"   426
Thus can I preche agayn that same vyce
Which that I use, and that is avaryce. (100)
But, though my-self be gilty in that sinne,
Yet can I maken other folk to twinne 430
From avaryce, and sore to repente.
But that is nat my principal entente.
I preche no-thing but for coveityse ;
Of this matere it oughte y-nogh suffyse.
    Than telle I hem ensamples many oon
Of olde stories, longe tyme agoon :   436
For lewed peple loven tales olde ;
Swich thinges can they wel reporte and
    holde.   (110)
What? trowe ye, the whyles I may preche,
And winne gold and silver for I teche, 440
That I wol live in povert wilfully ?
Nay, nay, I thoghte it never trewely !
For I wol preche and begge in sondry
    londes ;
I wol not do no labour with myn hondes,
Ne make baskettes, and live therby,  445
Because I wol nat beggen ydelly.
I wol non of the apostles counterfete ;
I wol have money, wolle, chese, and whete,
Al were it yeven of the povrest page, (121)
Or of the povrest widwe in a village,  450
Al sholde hir children sterve for famyne.
Nay ! I wol drinke licour of the vyne,
And have a joly wenche in every toun.
But herkneth, lordings, in conclusioun ;
Your lyking is that I shal telle a tale. 455
Now, have I dronke a draughte of corny
    ale,
By god, I hope I shal yow telle a thing
That shal, by resoun, been at your lyking.
For, though myself be a ful vicious
    man,
A moral tale yet I yow telle can, (132) 460
Which I am wont to preche, for to winne.
Now holde your pees, my tale I wol
    beginne.'

# THE PARDONERS TALE.

### Here biginneth the Pardoners Tale.

In Flaundres whylom was a companye
Of yonge folk, that haunteden folye,
As ryot, hasard, stewes, and tavernes, 465
Wher-as, with harpes, lutes, and giternes,
They daunce and pleye at dees bothe day
    and night,    (139)
And ete also and drinken over hir might,
Thurgh which they doon the devel sacri-
    fyse
With-in that develes temple, in cursed
    wyse,    470
By superfluitee abhominable ;
Hir othes been so grete and so dampnable,
That it is grisly for to here hem swere ;
Our blissed lordes body they to-tere ;
Hem thoughte Jewes rente him noght
    y-nough ;    475
And ech of hem at otheres sinne lough.
And right anon than comen tombesteres
Fetys and smale, and yonge fruytes-
    teres,    (150)
Singers with harpes, baudes, wafereres,
Whiche been the verray develes officeres
To kindle and blowe the fyr of lecherye,
That is annexed un-to glotonye ;    482
The holy writ take I to my witnesse,
That luxurie is in wyn and dronkenesse.

  Lo, how that dronken Loth, unkindely,
Lay by his doghtres two, unwitingly ; 486
So dronke he was, he niste what he
    wroghte.    (159)
  Herodes, (who-so wel the stories soghte),
Whan he of wyn was replet at his feste,
Right at his owene table he yaf his heste
To sleen the Baptist John ful giltelees. 491
  Senek seith eek a good word douteles ;
He seith, he can no difference finde
Bitwix a man that is out of his minde

And a man which that is dronkelewe, 495
But that woodnesse, y-fallen in a shrewe,
Persevereth lenger than doth dronkenesse.
O glotonye, ful of cursednesse,    (170)
O cause first of our confusioun,
O original of our dampnacioun,    500
Til Crist had boght us with his blood
    agayn !
Lo, how dere, shortly for to sayn,
Aboght was thilke cursed vileinye ;
Corrupt was al this world for glotonye !
  Adam our fader, and his wyf also, 505
Fro Paradys to labour and to wo
Were driven for that vyce, it is no drede ;
For whyl that Adam fasted, as I rede, (180)
He was in Paradys ; and whan that he
Eet of the fruyt defended on the tree, 510
Anon he was out-cast to wo and peyne.
O glotonye, on thee wel oghte us pleyne!
O, wiste a man how many maladyes
Folwen of excesse and of glotonyes,
He wolde been the more mesurable    515
Of his diete, sittinge at his table.
Allas ! the shorte throte, the tendre
    mouth,
Maketh that, Est and West, and North
    and South,    (190)
In erthe, in eir, in water men to-swinke
To gete a glotoun deyntee mete and
    drinke !    520
Of this matere, o Paul, wel canstow trete,
' Mete un-to wombe, and wombe eek un-to
    mete,
Shal god destroyen bothe,' as Paulus seith.
Allas ! a foul thing is it, by my feith, 524
To seye this word, and fouler is the dede,
Whan man so drinketh of the whyte and
    rede,

That of his throte he maketh his privee,
Thurgh thilke cursed superfluitee.    (200)
    The apostel weping seith ful pitously,
'Ther walken many of whiche yow told
    have I,                                    530
I seye it now weping with pitous voys,
[That] they been enemys of Cristes croys,
Of whiche the ende is deeth, wombe is
    her god.'
O wombe ! O bely ! O stinking cod,
Fulfild of donge and of corrupcioun !   535
At either ende of thee foul is the soun.
How greet labour and cost is thee to
    finde !
Thise cokes, how they stampe, and streyne,
    and grinde,                               (210)
And turnen substaunce in-to accident,
To fulfille al thy likerous talent !    540
Out of the harde bones knokke they
The mary, for they caste noght a-wey
That may go thurgh the golet softe and
    swote ;
Of spicerye, of loof, and bark, and rote
Shal been his sauce y-maked by delyt, 545
To make him yet a newer appetyt.
But certes, he that haunteth swich delyces
Is deed, whyl that he liveth in tho vyces.
    A lecherous thing is wyn, and dronke-
        nesse                                 (221) 549
Is ful of stryving and of wrecchednesse.
O dronke man, disfigured is thy face,
Sour is thy breeth, foul artow to embrace,
And thurgh thy dronke nose semeth the
    soun
As though thou seydest ay 'Sampsoun,
    Sampsoun ';
And yet, god wot, Sampsoun drank never
    no wyn.                                   555
Thou fallest, as it were a stiked swyn ;
Thy tonge is lost, and al thyn honest cure ;
For dronkenesse is verray sepulture (230)
Of mannes wit and his discrecioun.      559
In whom that drinke hath dominacioun,
He can no conseil kepe, it is no drede.
Now kepe yow fro the whyte and fro the
    rede,
And namely fro the whyte wyn of Lepe,
That is to selle in Fish-strete or in Chepe.
This wyn of Spayne crepeth subtilly    565
In othere wynes, growing faste by,
Of which ther ryseth swich fumositee,

That whan a man hath dronken draughtes
    three,                                    (240)
And weneth that he be at hoom in
    Chepe,
He is in Spayne, right at the toune of
    Lepe,                                     570
Nat at the Rochel, ne at Burdeux toun ;
And thanne wol he seye, 'Sampsoun,
    Sampsoun.'
    But herkneth, lordings, o word, I yow
    preye,
That alle the sovereyn actes, dar I seye,
Of victories in th'olde testament,      575
Thurgh verray god, that is omnipotent,
Were doon in abstinence and in preyere ;
Loketh the Bible, and ther ye may it
    lere.                                     (250)
Loke, Attila, the grete conquerour,
Deyde in his sleep, with shame and dis-
    honour,                                   580
Bledinge ay at his nose in dronkenesse ;
A capitayn shoulde live in sobrenesse.
And over al this, avyseth yow right wel
What was comaunded un-to Lamuel—
Nat Samuel, but Lamuel, seye I—         585
Redeth the Bible, and finde it expresly
Of wyn-yeving to hem that han justyse.
Na-more of this, for it may wel suffyse. (260)
    And now that I have spoke of glotonye,
Now wol I yow defenden hasardrye.   590
Hasard is verray moder of lesinges,
And of deceite, and cursed forsweringes,
Blaspheme of Crist, manslaughtre, and
    wast also
Of catel and of tyme ; and forthermo,
It is repreve and contrarie of honour  595
For to ben holde a commune hasardour.
And ever the hyër he is of estaat,
The more is he holden desolaat.        (270)
If that a prince useth hasardrye,
In alle governaunce and policye        600
He is, as by commune opinioun,
Y-holde the lasse in reputacioun.
    Stilbon, that was a wys embassadour,
Was sent to Corinthe, in ful greet honour,
Fro Lacidomie, to make hir alliaunce. 605
And whan he cam, him happede, par
    chaunce,
That alle the grettest that were of that
    lond,
Pleyinge atte hasard he hem fond.    (280)

For which, as sone as it mighte be,    609
He stal him hoom agayn to his contree,
And seyde, 'ther wol I nat lese my name ;
N' I wol nat take on me so greet defame,
Yow for to allye un-to none hasardours.
Sendeth othere wyse embassadours ;    614
For, by my trouthe, me were lever dye,
Than I yow sholde to hasardours allye.
For ye that been so glorious in honours
Shul nat allyen yow with hasardours (290)
As by my wil, ne as by my tretee.'
This wyse philosophre thus seyde he.    620
  Loke eek that, to the king Demetrius
The king of Parthes, as the book seith us,
Sente him a paire of dees of gold in scorn,
For he hadde used hasard ther-biforn ;
For which he heeld his glorie or his
    renoun    625
At no value or reputacioun.
Lordes may finden other maner pley
Honeste y-nough to dryve the day awey.
  Now wol I speke of othes false and
    grete    (301)
A word or two, as olde bokes trete.    630
Gret swering is a thing abhominable,
And false swering is yet more reprevable.
The heighe god forbad swering at al,
Witnesse on Mathew ; but in special
Of swering seith the holy Jeremye,    635
'Thou shalt seye sooth thyn othes, and
    nat lye,
And swere in dome, and eek in rightwis-
    nesse ;'
But ydel swering is a cursednesse.    (310)
Bihold and see, that in the firste table
Of heighe goddes hestes honurable,    640
How that the seconde heste of him is this—
'Tak nat my name in ydel or amis.'
Lo, rather he forbedeth swich swering
Than homicyde or many a cursed thing ;
I seye that, as by ordre, thus it stondeth ;
This knowen, that his hestes under-
    stondeth,    646
How that the second heste of god is
    that.
And forther over, I wol thee telle al plat,
That vengeance shal nat parten from his
    hous,    (321)
That of his othes is to outrageous.    650
'By goddes precious herte, and by his
    nayles,

And by the blode of Crist, that it is in
    Hayles,
Seven is my chaunce, and thyn is cink
    and treye ;
By goddes armes, if thou falsly pleye,
This dagger shal thurgh-out thyn herte
    go '—    655
This fruyt cometh of the bicched bones two,
Forswering, ire, falsnesse, homicyde.    (329)
Now, for the love of Crist that for us dyde,
Leveth your othes, bothe grete and smale ;
But, sirs, now wol I telle forth my tale.    660

  THISE ryotoures three, of whiche I telle,
Longe erst er pryme rong of any belle,
Were set hem in a taverne for to drinke ;
And as they satte, they herde a belle clinke
Biforn a cors, was caried to his grave ; 665
That oon of hem gan callen to his knave,
'Go bet,' quod he, 'and axe redily,    (339)
What cors is this that passeth heer forby ;
And look that thou reporte his name wel.'
  'Sir,' quod this boy, 'it nedeth never-
    a-del.    670
It was me told, er ye cam heer, two houres ;
He was, pardee, an old felawe of youres ;
And sodeynly he was y-slayn to-night,
For-dronke, as he sat on his bench up-
    right ;
Ther cam a privee theef, men clepeth
    Deeth,    675
That in this contree al the peple sleeth,
And with his spere he smoot his herte
    a-two,    (349)
And wente his wey with-outen wordes mo.
He hath a thousand slayn this pestilence :
And, maister, er ye come in his presence,
Me thinketh that it were necessarie    681
For to be war of swich an adversarie :
Beth redy for to mete him evermore.
Thus taughte me my dame, I sey na-more.'
'By seinte Marie,' seyde this taverner, 685
'The child seith sooth, for he hath slayn
    this yeer,
Henne over a myle, with-in a greet village,
Both man and womman, child and hyne,
    and page.    (360)
I trowe his habitacioun be there ;
To been avysed greet wisdom it were, 690
Er that he dide a man a dishonour.'
'Ye, goddes armes,' quod this ryotour,

' Is it swich peril with him for to mete?
I shal him seke by wey and eek by strete,
I make avow to goddes digne bones!  695
Herkneth, felawes, we three been al ones;
Lat ech of us holde up his hond til other,
And ech of us bicomen otheres brother, (370)
And we wol sleen this false traytour Deeth;
He shal be slayn, which that so many
    sleeth,                                 700
By goddes dignitee, er it be night.'
    Togidres han thise three her trouthes
        plight,
To live and dyen ech of hem for other,
As though he were his owene y-boren
    brother.
And up they sterte al dronken, in this
    rage,                                   705
And forth they goon towardes that village,
Of which the taverner had spoke biforn,
And many a grisly ooth than han they
    sworn,                                  (380)
And Cristes blessed body they to-rente—
' Deeth shal be deed, if that they may him
    hente.'                                 710
    Whan they han goon nat fully half a
        myle,
Right as they wolde han troden over a
    style,
An old man and a povre with hem mette.
This olde man ful mekely hem grette,
And seyde thus, ' now, lordes, god yow
    see!'                                   715
The proudest of thise ryotoures three
Answerde agayn, ' what? carl, with sory
    grace,                                  (389)
Why artow al forwrapped save thy face?
Why livestow so longe in so greet age?'
    This olde man gan loke in his visage, 720
And seyde thus, ' for I ne can nat finde
A man, though that I walked in-to Inde,
Neither in citee nor in no village,
That wolde chaunge his youthe for myn
    age;
And therfore moot I han myn age stille,
As longe time as it is goddes wille.   726
    Ne deeth, allas! ne wol nat han my lyf;
Thus walke I, lyk a restelees caityf, (400)
And on the ground, which is my modres
    gate,
Iknokke with my staf, bothe erly and late,
And seye, " leve moder, leet me in!   731

Lo, how I vanish, flesh, and blood, and
    skin!
Allas! whan shul my bones been at reste?
Moder, with yow wolde I chaunge my
    cheste,                                 734
That in my chambre longe tyme hath be,
Ye! for an heyre clout to wrappe me!"
But yet to me she wol nat do that grace,
For which ful pale and welked is my face.
    But, sirs, to yow it is no curteisye (411)
To speken to an old man vileinye,   740
But he trespasse in worde, or elles in dede.
In holy writ ye may your-self wel rede,
" Agayns an old man, hoor upon his heed,
Ye sholde aryse;" wherfor I yeve yow
    reed,
Ne dooth un-to an old man noon harm
    now,                                    745
Na-more than ye wolde men dide to yow
In age, if that ye so longe abyde;
And god be with yow, wher ye go or ryde.
I moot go thider as I have to go.'   (421)
    ' Nay, olde cherl, by god, thou shalt nat
        so,'                               750
Seyde this other hasardour anon;
' Thou partest nat so lightly, by seint John!
Thou spak right now of thilke traitour
    Deeth,
That in this contree alle our frendes
    sleeth.
Have heer my trouthe, as thou art his
    aspye,                                  755
Tel wher he is, or thou shalt it abye,
By god, and by the holy sacrament!
For soothly thou art oon of his assent, (430)
To sleen us yonge folk, thou false theef!'
    ' Now, sirs,' quod he, ' if that yow be so
        leef                               760
To finde Deeth, turne up this croked
    wey,
For in that grove I lafte him, by my fey,
Under a tree, and ther he wol abyde;
Nat for your boost he wol him no-thing
    hyde.
See ye that ook? right ther ye shul him
    finde.                                 765
God save yow, that boghte agayn man-
    kinde,
And yow amende!'—thus seyde this olde
    man.
And everich of thise ryotoures ran,  (440)

Til he cam to that tree, and ther they
  founde
Of florins fyne of golde y-coyned rounde
Wel ny an eighte busshels, as hem
  thoughte.　　　　　　　　　771
No lenger thanne after Deeth they soughte,
But ech of hem so glad was of that sighte,
For that the florins been so faire and
  brighte,
That doun they sette hem by this precious
  hord.　　　　　　　　　775
The worste of hem he spake the firste word.
  'Brethren,' quod he, 'tak kepe what I
  seye ;
My wit is greet, though that I bourde and
  pleye.　　　　　　　　　(450)
This tresor hath fortune un-to us yiven,
In mirthe and jolitee our lyf to liven, 780
And lightly as it comth, so wol we spende.
Ey ! goddes precious dignitee ! who wende
To-day, that we sholde han so fair a grace?
But mighte this gold be caried fro this
  place　　　　　　　　　784
Hoom to myn hous, or elles un-to youres—
For wel ye woot that al this gold is oures—
Than were we in heigh felicitee.
But trewely, by daye it may nat be ; (460)
Men wolde seyn that we were theves
  stronge,　　　　　　　　　789
And for our owene tresor doon us honge.
This tresor moste y-caried be by nighte
As wysly and as slyly as it mighte.
Wherfore I rede that cut among us alle
Be drawe, and lat see wher the cut wol
  falle ;
And he that hath the cut with herte blythe
Shal renne to the toune, and that ful
  swythe,　　　　　　　　　796
And bringe us breed and wyn ful prively.
And two of us shul kepen subtilly　(470)
This tresor wel ; and, if he wol nat tarie,
Whan it is night, we wol this tresor
  carie　　　　　　　　　800
By oon assent, wher-as us thinketh best.'
That oon of hem the cut broughte in his
  fest,
And bad hem drawe, and loke wher it wol
  falle ;
And it fil on the yongeste of hem alle ;
And forth toward the toun he wente anon.
And al-so sone as that he was gon,　806

That oon of hem spak thus un-to that
  other,
'Thou knowest wel thou art my sworne
  brother,　　　　　　　　　(480)
Thy profit wol I telle thee anon.
Thou woost wel that our felawe is agon ;
And heer is gold, and that ful greet
  plentee,　　　　　　　　　811
That shal departed been among us three.
But natheles, if I can shape it so
That it departed were among us two,
Hadde I nat doon a freendes torn to thee?'
  That other answerde, 'I noot how that
  may be ;　　　　　　　　　816
He woot how that the gold is with us
  tweye,
What shal we doon, what shal we to him
  seye ?'　　　　　　　　　(490)
  'Shal it be conseil ?' seyde the firste
  shrewe,
'And I shal tellen thee, in wordes fewe,
What we shal doon, and bringe it wel
  aboute.'　　　　　　　　　821
  'I graunte,' quod that other, 'out of
  doute,
That, by my trouthe, I wol thee nat bi-
  wreye.'
  'Now,' quod the firste, 'thou woost wel
  we be tweye,　　　　　　　　824
And two of us shul strenger be than oon.
Look whan that he is set, and right anoon
Arys, as though thou woldest with him
  pleye ;
And I shal ryve him thurgh the sydes
  tweye　　　　　　　　　(500)
Whyl that thou strogelest with him as in
  game,
And with thy dagger look thou do the
  same ;　　　　　　　　　830
And than shal al this gold departed be,
My dere freend, bitwixen me and thee ;
Than may we bothe our lustes al fulfille,
And pleye at dees right at our owene
  wille.'
And thus acorded been thise shrewes
  tweye　　　　　　　　　835
To sleen the thridde, as ye han herd me
  seye.
  This yongest, which that wente un-to
  the toun,
Ful ofte in herte he rolleth up and doun

The beautee of thise florins newe and
brighte.                                    (511)
'O lord!' quod he, 'if so were that I
mighte                                          840
Have al this tresor to my-self allone,
Ther is no man that liveth under the trone
Of god, that sholde live so mery as I!'
And atte laste the feend, our enemy,
Putte in his thought that he shold poyson
beye,                                            845
With which he mighte sleen his felawes
tweye;
For-why the feend fond him in swich
lyvinge,                                        (519)
That he had leve him to sorwe bringe,
For this was outrely his fulle entente
To sleen hem bothe, and never to repente.
And forth he gooth, no lenger wolde he
tarie,                                          851
Into the toun, un-to a pothecarie,
And preyed him, that he him wolde
selle
Som poyson, that he mighte his rattes
quelle;
And eek ther was a polcat in his hawe,
That, as he seyde, his capouns hadde
y-slawe,                                        856
And fayn he wolde wreke him, if he
mighte,
On vermin, that destroyed him by nighte.
The pothecarie answerde, 'and thou
shalt have                                     (531)
A thing that, al-so god my soule save,   860
In al this world ther nis no creature,
That ete or dronke hath of this confiture
Noght but the mountance of a corn of
whete,
That he ne shal his lyf anon forlete;
Ye, sterve he shal, and that in lasse whyle
Than thou wolt goon a paas nat but a
myle;                                            866
This poyson is so strong and violent.'
  This cursed man hath in his hond
y-hent                                          (540)
This poyson in a box, and sith he ran
In-to the nexte strete, un-to a man,    870
And borwed [of] him large botels three;
And in the two his poyson poured he;
The thridde he kepte clene for his drinke.
For al the night he shoop him for to
swinke                                          874

In carynge of the gold out of that place.
And whan this ryotour, with sory grace,
Had filled with wyn his grete botels three,
To his felawes agayn repaireth he.    (550)
  What nedeth it to sermone of it more?
For right as they had cast his deeth bifore,
Right so they han him slayn, and that
anon.                                            881
And whan that this was doon, thus spak
that oon,
'Now lat us sitte and drinke, and make
us merie,
And afterward we wol his body berie.'
And with that word it happed him, par
cas,                                             885
To take the botel ther the poyson was,
And drank, and yaf his felawe drinke also,
For which anon they storven bothe two.
  But, certes, I suppose that Avicen   (561)
Wroot never in no canon, ne in no fen,
Mo wonder signes of empoisoning      891
Than hadde thise wrecches two, or hir
ending.
Thus ended been thise homicydes two,
And eek the false empoysoner also.

  O cursed sinne, ful of cursednesse!  895
O traytours homicyde, o wikkednesse!
O glotonye, luxurie, and hasardrye!  (569)
Thou blasphemour of Crist with vileinye
And othes grete, of usage and of pryde!
Allas! mankinde, how may it bityde, 900
That to thy creatour which that thee
wroghte,
And with his precious herte-blood thee
boghte,
Thou art so fals and so unkinde, allas!
  Now, goode men, god forgeve yow your
trespas,                                         904
And ware yow fro the sinne of avaryce.
Myn holy pardoun may yow alle waryce,
So that ye offre nobles or sterlinges,
Or elles silver broches, spones, ringes. (580)
Boweth your heed under this holy bulle!
Cometh up, ye wyves, offreth of your
wolle!                                           910
Your name I entre heer in my rolle anon;
In-to the blisse of hevene shul ye gon;
I yow assoile, by myn heigh power,
Yow that wol offre, as clene and eek as
cleer

As ye were born; and, lo, sirs, thus I
   preche.     915
And Jesu Crist, that is our soules leche,
So graunte yow his pardon to receyve ;
For that is best ; I wol yow nat deceyve.
  But sirs, o word forgat I in my tale, (591)
I have relikes and pardon in my male, 920
As faire as any man in Engelond,
Whiche were me yeven by the popes hond,
If any of yow wol, of devocioun,
Offren, and han myn absolucioun,
Cometh forth anon, and kneleth heer
   adoun,     925
And mekely receyveth my pardoun :
Or elles, taketh pardon as ye wende, (599)
Al newe and fresh, at every tounes ende,
So that ye offren alwey newe and newe
Nobles and pens, which that be gode and
   trewe.     930
It is an honour to everich that is heer,
That ye mowe have a suffisant pardoneer
T'assoille yow, in contree as ye ryde,
For aventures which that may bityde.
Peraventure ther may falle oon or two 935
Doun of his hors, and breke his nekke
   atwo.
Look which a seuretee is it to yow alle
That I am in your felaweship y-falle, (610)
That may assoille yow, bothe more and
   lasse,
Whan that the soule shal fro the body
   passe.     940
I rede that our hoste heer shal biginne,
For he is most envoluped in sinne.
Com forth, sir hoste, and offre first anon,
And thou shalt kisse the reliks everichon,

Ye, for a grote ! unbokel anon thy purs.'
  ' Nay, nay,' quod he, 'than have I
   Cristes curs !     946
Lat be,' quod he, 'it shal nat be, so
   thee'ch !
Thou woldest make me kisse thyn old
   breech,     (620)
And swere it were a relik of a seint,
Thogh it were with thy fundement de-
   peint !     950
But by the croys which that seint Eleyne
   fond,
I wolde I hadde thy coillons in myn hond
In stede of relikes or of seintuarie ;
Lat cutte hem of, I wol thee helpe hem
   carie ;
They shul be shryned in an hogges tord.'
  This pardoner answerde nat a word ; 956
So wrooth he was, no word ne wolde he
   seye.
  ' Now,' quod our host, ' I wol no lenger
   pleye     (630)
With thee, ne with noon other angry man.'
But right anon the worthy Knight bigan,
Whan that he saugh that al the peple
   lough,     961
' Na-more of this, for it is right y-nough ;
Sir Pardoner, be glad and mery of chere ;
And ye, sir host, that been to me so dere,
I prey yow that ye kisse the Pardoner. 965
And Pardoner, I prey thee, drawe thee
   neer,
And, as we diden, lat us laughe and
   pleye.'     (639)
Anon they kiste, and riden forth **hir**
   weye.     [T. 12902

**Here is ended the Pardoners Tale.**

(*For* T. 12903, *see* p. 492).

# GROUP D.

# THE WIFE OF BATH'S PROLOGUE.

**The Prologe of the Wyves Tale of Bathe.**

'Experience, though noon auctoritee
Were in this world, were right y-nough
  to me
To speke of wo that is in mariage;
For, lordinges, sith I twelf yeer was of age,
Thonked be god that is eterne on lyve,  5
Housbondes at chirche-dore I have had
  fyve;
For I so ofte have y-wedded be;
And alle were worthy men in hir degree.
But me was told certeyn, nat longe agon is,
That sith that Crist ne wente never but
  onis  10
To wedding in the Cane of Galilee,
That by the same ensample taughte he me
That I ne sholde wedded be but ones.
Herke eek, lo! which a sharp word for
  the nones
Besyde a welle Jesus, god and man,  15
Spak in repreve of the Samaritan:
"Thou hast y-had fyve housbondes," quod
  he,
"And thilke man, the which that hath
  now thee,
Is noght thyn housbond;" thus seyde he
  certeyn;
What that he mente ther-by, I can nat
  seyn;  20
But that I axe, why that the fifthe man
Was noon housbond to the Samaritan?
How manye mighte she have in mariage?
Yet herde I never tellen in myn age
Upon this nombre diffinicioun;  25
Men may devyne and glosen up and doun.
But wel I woot expres, with-oute lye,
God bad us for to wexe and multiplye;
That gentil text can I wel understonde.
Eek wel I woot he seyde, myn housbonde

Sholde lete fader and moder, and take
  me;  31
But of no nombre mencioun made he,
Of bigamye or of octogamye;
Why sholde men speke of it vileinye?
  Lo, here the wyse king, dan Salomon; 35
I trowe he hadde wyves mo than oon;
As, wolde god, it leveful were to me
To be refresshed half so ofte as he!
Which yifte of god hadde he for alle his
  wyvis!
No man hath swich, that in this world
  alyve is.  40
God woot, this noble king, as to my wit,
The firste night had many a mery fit
With ech of hem, so wel was him on lyve!
Blessed be god that I have wedded fyve!*
Welcome the sixte, whan that ever he
  shal.  45
For sothe, I wol nat kepe me chast in al;
Whan myn housbond is fro the world
  y-gon,
Som Cristen man shal wedde me anon;
For thanne th'apostle seith, that I am
  free
To wedde, a godd's half, wher it lyketh
  me.  50
He seith that to be wedded is no sinne;
Bet is to be wedded than to brinne.
What rekketh me, thogh folk seye vileinye
Of shrewed Lameth and his bigamye?

---

\* *Here some MSS. insert the following genuine
(but rejected) lines :—*
  Of whiche I have y-piked out the beste
  Bothe of hir nether purs and of hir cheste.
  Diverse scoles maken parfit clerkes,
  Divers praktik, in many sondry werkes,
  Maketh the werkman parfit sekirly.
  Of fyve husbondes scolering am I.

I woot wel Abraham was an holy man, 55
And Jacob eek, as ferforth as I can ;
And ech of hem hadde wyves mo than
 two ;
And many another holy man also.
Whan saugh ye ever, in any maner age,
That hye god defended mariage    60
By expres-word ? I pray you, telleth me ;
Or wher comanded he virginitee ?
I woot as wel as ye, it is no drede,
Th'apostel, whan he speketh of mayden-
 hede;
He seyde, that precept ther-of hadde he
 noon.    65
Men may conseille a womman to been oon,
But conseilling is no comandement ;
He putte it in our owene jugement
For hadde god comanded maydenhede,
Thanne hadde he dampned wedding with
 the dede ;    70
And certes, if ther were no seed y-sowe,
Virginitee, wher-of than sholde it growe?
Poul dorste nat comanden atte leste
A thing of which his maister yaf noon
 heste.
The dart is set up for virginitee ;    75
Cacche who so may, who renneth best lat
 see.
But this word is nat take of every wight,
But ther as god list give it of his might.
I woot wel, that th'apostel was a mayde ;
But natheless, thogh that he wroot and
 sayde,    80
He wolde that every wight were swich as
 he,
Al nis but conseil to virginitee ;
And for to been a wyf, he yaf me leve
Of indulgence ; so it is no repreve
To wedde me, if that my make dye,    85
With-oute excepcioun of bigamye.
Al were it good no womman for to touche,
He mente as in his bed or in his couche ;
For peril is bothe fyr and tow t'assemble;
Ye knowe what this ensample may
 resemble.    90
This is al and som, he heeld virginitee
More parfit than wedding in freletee.
Freeltee clepe I, but-if that he and she
Wolde leden al hir lyf in chastitee.
 I graunte it wel, I have noon envye, 95
Thogh maydenhede preferre bigamye ;

Hem lyketh to be clene, body and goost,
Of myn estaat I nil nat make no boost.
For wel ye knowe, a lord in his houshold,
He hath nat every vessel al of gold ;    100
Somme been of tree, and doon hir lord
 servyse.
God clepeth folk to him in sondry wyse,
And everich hath of god a propre yifte,
Som this, som that,—as him lyketh shifte.
 Virginitee is greet perfeccioun,    105
And continence eek with devocioun.
But Crist, that of perfeccioun is welle,
Bad nat every wight he sholde go selle
All that he hadde, and give it to the pore,
And in swich wyse folwe him and his
 fore.    110
He spak to hem that wolde live parfitly ;
And lordinges, by your leve, that am nat I.
I wol bistowe the flour of al myn age
In th' actes and in fruit of mariage.
 Telle me also, to what conclusioun 115
Were membres maad of generacioun,
And for what profit was a wight
 y-wroght ?
Trusteth right wel, they wer nat maad
 for noght.
Glose who-so wole, and seye bothe up and
 doun,
That they were maked for purgacioun 120
Of urine, and our bothe thinges smale
Were eek to knowe a femele from a
 male,
And for noon other cause : sey ye no ?
The experience woot wel it is noght so ;
So that the clerkes be nat with me
 wrothe,    125
I sey this, that they maked been for bothe,
This is to seye, for office, and for ese
Of engendrure, ther we nat god displese.
Why sholde men elles in hir bokes sette,
That man shal yelde to his wyf hir
 dette?    130
Now wher-with sholde he make his
 payement,
If he ne used his sely instrument ?
Than were they maad up-on a creature,
To purge uryne, and eek for engendrure.
 But I seye noght that every wight is
 holde,    135
That hath swich harneys as I to yow
 tolde,

To goon and usen hem in engendrure;
Than sholde men take of chastitee no
    cure.
Crist was a mayde, and shapen as a man,
And many a seint, sith that the world
    bigan,          140
Yet lived they ever in parfit chastitee.
I nil envye no virginitee;
Lat hem be breed of pured whete-seed,
And lat us wyves hoten barly-breed;
And yet with barly-breed, Mark telle can,
Our lord Jesu refresshed many a man. 146
In swich estaat as god hath cleped us
I wol persevere, I nam nat precious.
In wyfhode I wol use myn instrument
As frely as my maker hath it sent.    150
If I be daungerous, god yeve me sorwe!
Myn housbond shal it have bothe eve and
    morwe,
Whan that him list com forth and paye
    his dette.
An housbonde I wol have, I nil nat lette,
Which shal be bothe my dettour and my
    thral,         155
And have his tribulacioun with-al
Up-on his flessh, whyl that I am his wyf.
I have the power duringe al my lyf
Up-on his propre body, and noght he.
Right thus th'apostel tolde it un-to me;
And bad our housbondes for to love us
    weel.         161
Al this sentence me lyketh every-deel'—
Up sterte the Pardoner, and that anon,
'Now dame,' quod he, 'by god and by
    seint John,
Ye been a noble prechour in this cas! 165
I was aboute to wedde a wyf; allas!
What sholde I bye it on my flesh so dere?
Yet hadde I lever wedde no wyf to-yere!'
    'Abyde!' quod she, 'my tale is nat
    bigonne;
Nay, thou shalt drinken of another tonne
Er that I go, shal savoure wors than ale.
And whan that I have told thee forth
    my tale
Of tribulacioun in mariage,
Of which I am expert in al myn age,
This to seyn, my-self have been the
    whippe;—    175
Than maystow chese whether thou wolt
    sippe

Of thilke tonne that I shal abroche.
Be war of it, er thou to ny approche;
For I shal telle ensamples mo than ten.
Who-so that nil be war by othere men, 180
By him shul othere men corrected be.
The same wordes wryteth Ptholomee;
Rede in his Almageste, and take it there.'
    'Dame, I wolde praye yow, if your wil
    it were,'
Seyde this Pardoner, 'as ye bigan, 185
Telle forth your tale, spareth for no man,
And teche us yonge men of your praktike.'
    'Gladly,' quod she, 'sith it may yow
    lyke.
But yet I praye to al this companye,
If that I speke after my fantasye,    190
As taketh not a-grief of that I seye;
For myn entente nis but for to pleye.
    Now sires, now wol I telle forth my
    tale.—
As ever mote I drinken wyn or ale,
I shal seye sooth, tho housbondes that
    I hadde,         195
As three of hem were gode and two were
    badde.
The three men were gode, and riche, and
    olde;
Unnethe mighte they the statut holde
In which that they were bounden un-to
    me.         199
Ye woot wel what I mene of this, pardee!
As help me god, I laughe whan I thinke
How pitously a-night I made hem swinke;
And by my fey, I tolde of it no stoor.
They had me yeven hir gold and hir
    tresoor;
Me neded nat do lenger diligence    205
To winne hir love, or doon hem reverence.
They loved me so wel, by god above,
That I ne tolde no deyntee of hir love!
A wys womman wol sette hir ever in oon
To gete hir love, ther as she hath noon. 210
But sith I hadde hem hoolly in myn hond,
And sith they hadde me yeven all hir
    lond,
What sholde I taken hede hem for to
    plese,
But it were for my profit and myn ese?
I sette hem so a-werke, by my fey,    215
That many a night they songen "wei-
    lawey!"

The bacoun was nat fet for hem, I trowe,
That som men han in Essex at Dunmowe.
I governed hem so wel, after my lawe,
That ech of hem ful blisful was and fawe
To bringe me gaye thinges fro the fayre. 221
They were ful glad whan I spak to hem
     fayre ;
For god it woot, I chidde hem spitously.

     Now herkneth, how I bar me proprely,
Ye wyse wyves, that can understonde. 225
     Thus shul ye speke and bere hem wrong
       on honde ;
For half so boldely can ther no man
Swere and lyen as a womman can.
I sey nat this by wyves that ben wyse,
But-if it be whan they hem misavyse. 230
A wys wyf, if that she can hir good,
Shal beren him on hond the cow is wood,
And take witnesse of hir owene mayde
Of hir assent ; but herkneth how I sayde.

     "Sir olde kaynard, is this thyn array ?
Why is my neighebores wyf so gay ? 236
She is honoured over-al ther she goth ;
I sitte at hoom, I have no thrifty cloth.
What dostow at my neighebores hous ?
Is she so fair ? artow so amorous ? 240
What rowne ye with our mayde? ben'-
     cite !
Sir olde lechour, lat thy japes be !
And if I have a gossib or a freend,
With-outen gilt, thou chydest as a feend,
If that I walke or pleye un-to his hous ! 245
Thou comest hoom as dronken as a mous,
And prechest on thy bench, with yvel
     preef !
Thou seist to me, it is a greet meschief
To wedde a povre womman, for costage ;
And if that she be riche, of heigh parage,
Than seistow that it is a tormentrye 251
To suffre hir pryde and hir malencolye.
And if that she be fair, thou verray knave,
Thou seyst that every holour wol hir have ;
She may no whyle in chastitee abyde, 255
That is assailled up-on ech a syde.

     Thou seyst, som folk desyre us for
     richesse,
Som for our shap, and som for our fair-
     nesse ;
And som, for she can outher singe or
     daunce, 259
And som, for gentilesse and daliaunce ;

Som, for hir handes and hir armes smale ;
Thus goth al to the devel by thy tale.
Thou seyst, men may nat kepe a castel-
     wal ;
It may so longe assailled been over-al.

     And if that she be foul, thou seist that
     she 265
Coveiteth every man that she may see ;
For as a spaynel she wol on him lepe,
Til that she finde som man hir to chepe ;
Ne noon so grey goos goth ther in the
     lake, 269
As, seistow, that wol been with-oute make.
And seyst, it is an hard thing for to welde
A thing that no man wol, his thankes,
     helde.
Thus seistow, lorel, whan thow goost to
     bedde ;
And that no wys man nedeth for to
     wedde, 274
Ne no man that entendeth un-to hevene.
With wilde thonder-dint and firy levene
Mote thy welked nekke be to-broke !

     Thow seyst that dropping houses, and
     eek smoke,
And chyding wyves, maken men to flee
Out of hir owene hous ; a ! ben'cite ! 280
What eyleth swich an old man for to
     chyde ?

     Thow seyst, we wyves wol our vyces
     hyde
Til we be fast, and than we wol hem
     shewe ;
Wel may that be a proverbe of a shrewe !
     Thou seist, that oxen, asses, hors, and
     houndes, 285
They been assayed at diverse stoundes ;
Bacins, lavours, er that men hem bye,
Spones and stoles, and al swich hous-
     bondrye,
And so been pottes, clothes, and array ;
But folk of wyves maken noon assay 290
Til they be wedded ; olde dotard shrewe !
And than, seistow, we wol oure vices
     shewe.

     Thou seist also, that it displeseth me
But-if that thou wolt preyse my beautee,
And but thou poure alwey up-on my
     face, 295
And clepe me 'faire dame' in every
     place ;

And but thou make a feste on thilke
    day
That I was born, and make me fresh and
    gay,
And but thou do to my norice honour,
And to my chamberere with-inne my
    bour,        300
And to my fadres folk and his allyes ;—
Thus seistow, olde barel ful of lyes !
  And yet of our apprentice Janekyn.
For his crisp heer, shyninge as gold so fyn,
And for he squiereth me bothe up and
    doun,        305
Yet hastow caught a fals suspecioun ;
I wol hym noght, thogh thou were deed
    to-morwe.
  But tel me this, why hydestow, with
    sorwe,
The keyes of thy cheste awey fro me?
It is my good as wel as thyn, pardee.  310
What wenestow make an idiot of our
    dame ?
Now by that lord, that called is seint
    Jame,
Thou shalt nat bothe, thogh that thou
    were wood,
Be maister of my body and of my good ;
That oon thou shalt forgo, maugree thyne
    yën ;        315
What nedeth thee of me to enquere or
    spyën ?
I trowe, thou woldest loke me in thy
    cheste !
Thou sholdest seye, 'wyf, go wher thee
    leste,
Tak your disport, I wol nat leve no talis ;
I knowe yow for a trewe wyf, dame Alis.'
We love no man that taketh kepe or
    charge        321
Wher that we goon, we wol ben at our
    large.
  Of alle men y-blessed moot he be,
The wyse astrologien Dan Ptholome,  324
That seith this proverbe in his Almageste,
'Of alle men his wisdom is the hyeste,
That rekketh never who hath the world
    in honde.'
By this proverbe thou shalt understonde,
Have thou y-nogh, what thar thee recche
    or care
How merily that othere folkes fare?  330

For certeyn, olde dotard, by your leve,
Ye shul have queynte right y-nough at eve.
He is to greet a nigard that wol werne
A man to lighte his candle at his lanterne ;
He shal have never the lasse light,
    pardee ;        335
Have thou y-nough, thee thar nat pleyne
    thee.
  Thou seyst also, that if we make us gay
With clothing and with precious array.
That it is peril of our chastitee ;
And yet, with sorwe, thou most enforce
    thee,        340
And seye thise wordes in the apostles
    name,
'In habit, maad with chastitee and
    shame,
Ye wommen shul apparaille yow,' quod
    he,
'And noght in tressed heer and gay
    perree,
As perles, ne with gold, ne clothes riche;'
After thy text, ne after thy rubriche  346
I wol nat wirche as muchel as a gnat.
Thou seydest this, that I was lyk a cat;
For who-so wolde senge a cattes skin,
Thanne wolde the cat wel dwellen in
    his in ;        350
And if the cattes skin be slyk and gay,
She wol nat dwelle in house half a day,
But forth she wole, er any day be dawed,
To shewe hir skin, and goon a-cater-
    wawed ;
This is to seye, if I be gay, sir shrewe,  355
I wol renne out, my borel for to shewe.
  Sire olde fool, what eyleth thee to
    spyën ?
Thogh thou preye Argus, with his
    hundred yën,
To be my warde-cors, as he can best,
In feith, he shal nat kepe me but me
    lest ;        360
Yet coude I make his berd, so moot
    I thee.
  Thou seydest eek, that ther ben thinges
    three,
The whiche thinges troublen al this erthe,
And that no wight ne may endure the
    ferthe :
O leve sir shrewe, Jesu shorte thy lyf! 365
Yet prechestow, and seyst, an hateful wyf

Y-rekened is for oon of thise meschances.
Been ther none othere maner resem-
   blances
That ye may lykne your parables to,
But-if a sely wyf be oon of tho ?     370
   Thou lykenest wommanes love to helle,
To bareyne lond, ther water may not
   dwelle.
Thou lyknest it also to wilde fyr ;
The more it brenneth, the more it hath
   desyr
To consume every thing that brent
   wol be.     375
Thou seyst, that right as wormes shende
   a tree,
Right so a wyf destroyeth hir housbonde ;
This knowe they that been to wyves
   bonde."
   Lordinges, right thus, as ye have
   understonde,
Bar I stifly myne olde housbondes on
   honde,     380
That thus they seyden in hir dronkenesse ;
And al was fals, but that I took witnesse
On Janekin and on my nece also.
O lord, the peyne I dide hem and the wo,
Ful giltelees, by goddes swete pyne !   385
For as an hors I coude byte and whyne.
I coude pleyne, thogh I were in the
   gilt,
Or elles often tyme hadde I ben spilt.
Who-so that first to mille comth, first
   grint ;
I pleyned first, so was our werre y-stint.
They were ful glad t'excusen hem ful
   blyve     391
Of thing of which they never agilte hir
   lyve.
   Of wenches wolde I beren him on
   honde,
Whan that for syk unnethes mighte he
   stonde.
Yet tikled it his herte, for that he     395
Wende that I hadde of him so greet
   chiertee.
I swoor that al my walkinge out by nighte
Was for t'espye wenches that he dighte ;
Under that colour hadde I many a mirthe.
For al swich wit is yeven us in our birthe ;
Deceite, weping, spinning god hath yive
To wommen kindely, whyl they may live.

And thus of o thing I avaunte me,     403
Atte ende I hadde the bettre in ech
   degree,
By sleighte, or force, or by som maner
   thing,     405
As by continuel murmur or grucching ;
Namely a-bedde hadden they meschaunce,
Ther wolde I chyde and do hem no
   plesaunce ;
I wolde no lenger in the bed abyde,
If that I felte his arm over my syde,   410
Til he had maad his raunson un-to me ;
Than wolde I suffre him do his nycetee.
And ther-fore every man this tale I telle,
Winne who-so may, for al is for to selle.
With empty hand men may none haukes
   lure ;     415
For winning wolde I al his lust endure,
And make me a feyned appetyt ;
And yet in bacon hadde I never delyt ;
That made me that ever I wolde hem
   chyde.     419
For thogh the pope had seten hem bisyde,
I wolde nat spare hem at hir owene bord.
For by my trouthe, I quitte hem word
   for word.
As help me verray god omnipotent,
Thogh I right now sholde make my
   testament,
I ne owe hem nat a word that it nis quit
I broghte it so aboute by my wit,     426
That they moste yeve it up, as for the
   beste ;
Or elles hadde we never been in reste.
For thogh he loked as a wood leoun,
Yet sholde he faille of his conclusioun. 430
   Thanne wolde I seye, " gode lief, tak
   keep
How mekely loketh Wilkin oure sheep ;
Com neer, my spouse, lat me ba thy
   cheke !
Ye sholde been al pacient and meke,
And han a swete spyced conscience,   435
Sith ye so preche of Jobes pacience.
Suffreth alwey, sin ye so wel can preche ;
And but ye do, certein we shal yow
   teche
That it is fair to have a wyf in pees.
Oon of us two moste bowen, doutelees ; 440
And sith a man is more resonable
Than womman is, ye moste been suffrable.

What eyleth yow to grucche thus and
 grone?
Is it for ye wolde have my queynte allone?
Why taak it al, lo, have it every-deel; 445
Peter! I shrewe yow but ye love it weel!
For if I wolde selle my *bele chose*,
I coude walke as fresh as is a rose ;
But I wol kepe it for your owene tooth.
Ye be to blame, by god, I sey yow sooth.''
 Swiche maner wordes hadde we on
 honde.         451
Now wol I speken of my fourthe hous-
 bonde.
 My fourthe housbonde was a revelour,
This is to seyn, he hadde a paramour ;
And I was yong and ful of ragerye,  455
Stiborn and strong, and joly as a pye.
Wel coude I daunce to an harpe smale,
And singe, y-wis, as any nightingale,
Whan I had dronke a draughte of swete
 wyn.
Metellius, the foule cherl, the swyn,  460
That with a staf birafte his wyf hir lyf,
For she drank wyn, thogh I hadde been
 his wyf,
He sholde nat han daunted me fro drinke ;
And, after wyn, on Venus moste I thinke :
For al so siker as cold engendreth hayl,
A likerous mouth moste han a likerous
 tayl.         466
In womman vinolent is no defence,
This knowen lechours by experience.
 But, lord Crist! whan that it remem-
 breth me
Up-on my yowthe, and on my jolitee, 470
It tikleth me aboute myn herte rote.
Unto this day it dooth myn herte bote
That I have had my world as in my tyme.
But age, allas! that al wol envenyme, 474
Hath me biraft my beautee and my pith ;
Lat go, fare-wel, the devel go therwith !
The flour is goon, ther is na-more to telle,
The bren, as I best can, now moste I selle ;
But yet to be right mery wol I fonde.
Now wol I tellen of my fourthe hous-
 bonde.         480
 I seye, I hadde in herte greet despyt
That he of any other had delyt.
But he was quit, by god and by seint
 Joce !
I made him of the same wode a croce ;

Nat of my body in no foul manere,  485
But certeinly, I made folk swich chere,
That in his owene grece I made him frye
For angre, and for verray jalousye.
By god, in erthe I was his purgatorie, 489
For which I hope his soule be in glorie.
For god it woot, he sat ful ofte and song
Whan that his shoo ful bitterly him
 wrong.
Ther was no wight, save god and he, that
 wiste,
In many wyse, how sore I him twiste.
He deyde whan I cam fro Jerusalem, 495
And lyth y-grave under the rode-beem,
Al is his tombe noght so curious
As was the sepulcre of him, Darius,
Which that Appelles wroghte subtilly ;
It nis but wast to burie him preciously. 500
Lat him fare-wel, god yeve his soule reste,
He is now in the grave and in his cheste.
 Now of my fifthe housbond wol I telle.
God lete his soule never come in helle !
And yet was he to me the moste shrewe ;
That fele I on my ribbes al by rewe,  506
And ever shal, un-to myn ending-day.
But in our bed he was so fresh and gay,
And ther-with-al so wel coude he me glose,
Whan that he wolde han my *bele chose*, 510
That thogh he hadde me bet on every
 boon,
He coude winne agayn my love anoon.
I trowe I loved him beste, for that he
Was of his love daungerous to me.
We wommen han, if that I shal nat lye,
In this matere a queynte fantasye ;  516
Wayte what thing we may nat lightly
 have,
Ther-after wol we crye al-day and crave.
Forbede us thing, and that desyren we ;
Prees on us faste, and thanne wol we flee.
With daunger oute we al our chaffare ; 521
Greet prees at market maketh dere ware,
And to greet cheep is holde at litel prys ;
This knoweth every womman that is wys.
 My fifthe housbonde, god his soule
 blesse !         525
Which that I took for love and no
 richesse,
He som-tyme was a clerk of Oxenford,
And had left scole, and wente at hoom to
 bord

With my gossib, dwellinge in oure toun,
God have hir soule! hir name was
    Alisoun.     530
She knew myn herte and eek my privetee
Bet than our parisshe-preest, so moot
    I thee!
To hir biwreyed I my conseil al.
For had myn housbonde pissed on a wal,
Or doon a thing that sholde han cost his
    lyf,     535
To hir, and to another worthy wyf,
And to my nece, which that I loved
    weel,
I wolde han told his conseil every-deel.
And so I dide ful often, god it woot,
That made his face ful often reed and
    hoot     540
For verray shame, and blamed him-self
    for he
Had told to me so greet a privetee

    And so bifel that ones, in a Lente,
(So often tymes I to my gossib wente,
For ever yet I lovede to be gay,     545
And for to walke, in March, Averille, and
    May,
Fro hous to hous, to here sondry talis),
That Jankin clerk, and my gossib dame
    Alis,
And I my-self, in-to the feldes wente.
Myn housbond was at London al that
    Lente;     550
I hadde the bettre leyser for to pleye,
And for to see, and eek for to be seye
Of lusty folk; what wiste I wher my grace
Was shapen for to be, or in what place?
Therefore I made my visitaciouns,     555
To vigilies and to processiouns,
To preching eek and to thise pilgrimages,
To pleyes of miracles and mariages,
And wered upon my gaye scarlet gytes.
Thise wormes, ne thise motthes, ne thise
    mytes,     560
Upon my peril, frete hem never a deel;
And wostow why? for they were used
    weel.

    Now wol I tellen forth what happed me.
I seye, that in the feeldes walked we,
Til trewely we hadde swich daliance,     565
This clerk and I, that of my purveyance
I spak to him, and seyde him, how that he,
If I were widwe, sholde wedde me.

For certeinly, I sey for no bobance,
Yet was I never with-outen purveyance
Of mariage, n'of othere thinges eek.     571
I holde a mouses herte nat worth a leek,
That hath but oon hole for to sterte to,
And if that faille, thanne is al y-do.

    I bar him on honde, he hadde en-
    chanted me;     575
My dame taughte me that soutiltee.
And eek I seyde, I mette of him al night;
He wolde han slayn me as I lay up-right,
And al my bed was ful of verray blood,
But yet I hope that he shal do me
    good;     580
For blood bitokeneth gold, as me was
    taught.
And al was fals, I dremed of it right
    naught,
But as I folwed ay my dames lore,
As wel of this as of other thinges more.

    But now sir, lat me see, what I shal
    seyn?     585
A! ha! by god, I have my tale ageyn.

    Whan that my fourthe housbond was
    on bere,
I weep algate, and made sory chere,
As wyves moten, for it is usage,
And with my coverchief covered my
    visage;     590
But for that I was purveyed of a make,
I weep but smal, and that I undertake.

    To chirche was myn housbond born
    a-morwe
With neighebores, that for him maden
    sorwe;
And Jankin oure clerk was oon of tho. 595
As help me god, whan that I saugh
    him go
After the bere, me thoughte he hadde a
    paire
Of legges and of feet so clene and faire,
That al myn herte I yaf un-to his hold.
He was, I trowe, a twenty winter old, 600
And I was fourty, if I shal seye sooth;
But yet I hadde alwey a coltes tooth.
Gat-tothed I was, and that bicam me
    weel;
I hadde the prente of sëynt Venus seel.
As help me god, I was a lusty oon,     605
And faire and riche, and yong, and wel
    bigoon;

And trewely, as myne housbondes tolde
  me,
I had the beste *quoniam* mighte be.
For certes, I am al Venerien  609
In felinge, and myn herte is Marcien.
Venus me yaf my lust, my likerousnesse,
And Mars yaf me my sturdy hardinesse.
Myn ascendent was Taur, and Mars ther-
  inne.
Allas! allas! that ever love was sinne!
I folwed ay myn inclinacioun  615
By vertu of my constellacioun;
That made me I coude noght withdrawe
My chambre of Venus from a good felawe.
Yet have I Martes mark up-on my face,
And also in another privee place.  620
For, god so wis be my savacioun,
I ne loved never by no discrecioun,
But ever folwede myn appetyt,
Al were he short or long, or blak or
  whyt;
I took no kepe, so that he lyked me,  625
How pore he was, ne eek of what degree.
  What sholde I seye, but, at the monthes
  ende,
This joly clerk Jankin, that was so hende,
Hath wedded me with greet solempnitee,
And to him yaf I al the lond and fee  630
That ever was me yeven ther-bifore;
But afterward repented me ful sore.
He nolde suffre nothing of my list.
By god, he smoot me ones on the list,
For that I rente out of his book a leef, 635
That of the strook myn ere wex al deef.
Stiborn I was as is a leonesse,
And of my tonge a verray jangleresse,
And walke I wolde, as I had doon biforn,
From hous to hous, al-though he had it
  sworn.  640
For which he often tymes wolde preche,
And me of olde Romayn gestes teche,
How he, Simplicius Gallus, lefte his wyf,
And hir forsook for terme of al his lyf,
Noght but for open-heeded he hir say 645
Lokinge out at his dore upon a day.
  Another Romayn tolde he me by name,
That, for his wyf was at a someres game
With-oute his witing, he forsook hir eke.
And than wolde he up-on his Bible seke
That ilke proverbe of Ecclesiaste,  651
Wher he comandeth and forbedeth faste,

Man shal nat suffre his wyf go roule
  aboute;
Than wolde he seye right thus, with-
  outen doute,
"Who-so that buildeth his hous al of
  salwes,  655
And priketh his blinde hors over the
  falwes,
And suffreth his wyf to go seken halwes,
Is worthy to been hanged on the gal-
  wes!"
But al for noght, I sette noght an hawe
Of his proverbes n'of his olde sawe,  660
Ne I wolde nat of him corrected be.
I hate him that my vices telleth me,
And so do mo, god woot! of us than I.
This made him with me wood al outrely;
I nolde noght forbere him in no cas.  665
  Now wol I seye yow sooth, by seint
  Thomas,
Why that I rente out of his book a leef,
For which he smoot me so that I was
  deef.
He hadde a book that gladly, night and
  day,
For his desport he wolde rede alway.  670
He cleped it Valerie and Theofraste,
At whiche book he lough alwey ful faste.
And eek ther was som-tyme a clerk at
  Rome,
A cardinal, that highte Seint Jerome,
That made a book agayn Jovinian;  675
In whiche book eek ther was Tertulan,
Crisippus, Trotula, and Helowys,
That was abbesse nat fer fro Parys;
And eek the Parables of Salomon,
Ovydes Art, and bokes many on,  680
And alle thise wer bounden in o volume.
And every night and day was his custume,
Whan he had leyser and vacacioun
From other worldly occupacioun,  684
To reden on this book of wikked wyves.
He knew of hem mo legendes and lyves
Than been of gode wyves in the Bible.
For trusteth wel, it is an impossible
That any clerk wol speke good of wyves,
But-if it be of holy seintes lyves,  690
Ne of noon other womman never the mo.
Who peyntede the leoun, tel me who?
By god, if wommen hadde writen stories,
As clerkes han with-inne hir oratories,

They wolde han writen of men more
wikkednesse    695
Than all the mark of Adam may redresse.
The children of Mercurie and of Venus
Been in hir wirking ful contrarious;
Mercurie loveth wisdom and science,
And Venus loveth ryot and dispence. 700
And, for hir diverse disposicioun,
Ech falleth in otheres exaltacioun;
And thus, god woot! Mercurie is desolat
In Pisces, wher Venus is exaltat;
And Venus falleth ther Mercurie is
reysed;    705
Therfore no womman of no clerk is preysed.
The clerk, whan he is old, and may noght
do
Of Venus werkes worth his olde sho,
Than sit he doun, and writ in his dotage
That wommen can nat kepe hir mariage!
But now to purpos, why I tolde thee
That I was beten for a book, pardee. 712
Up-on a night Jankin, that was our
syre,
Redde on his book, as he sat by the fyre,
Of Eva first, that, for hir wikkednesse,
Was al mankinde broght to wrecched-
nesse,    716
For which that Jesu Crist him-self was
slayn,
That boghte us with his herte-blood agayn.
Lo, here expres of womman may ye finde,
That womman was the los of al mankinde.
   Tho redde he me how Sampson loste
his heres,    721
Slepinge, his lemman kitte hem with hir
sheres;
Thurgh whiche tresoun loste he bothe
his yën.
   Tho redde he me, if that I shal nat lyen,
Of Hercules and of his Dianyre,    725
That caused him to sette himself a-fyre.
   No-thing forgat he the penaunce and
wo
That Socrates had with hise wyves two;
How Xantippa caste pisse up-on his heed;
This sely man sat stille, as he were deed;
He wyped his heed, namore dorste he seyn
But "er that thonder stinte, comth a
reyn."    732
   Of Phasipha, that was the quene of
Crete,

For shrewednesse, him thoughte the tale
swete;
Fy! spek na-more—it is a grisly thing—
Of hir horrible lust and hir lyking.    736
   Of Clitemistra, for hir lecherye,
That falsly made hir housbond for to dye,
He redde it with ful good devocioun.
   He tolde me eek for what occasioun 740
Amphiorax at Thebes loste his lyf;
Myn housbond hadde a legende of his wyf,
Eriphilem, that for an ouche of gold
Hath prively un-to the Grekes told
Wher that hir housbonde hidde him in a
place,    745
For which he hadde at Thebes sory grace.
   Of Lyma tolde he me, and of Lucye,
They bothe made hir housbondes for to
dye;
That oon for love, that other was for
hate;
Lyma hir housbond, on an even late, 750
Empoysoned hath, for that she was his fo.
Lucya, likerous, loved hir housbond so,
That, for he sholde alwey up-on hir thinke,
She yaf him swich a maner love-drinke,
That he was deed, er it were by the
morwe;    755
And thus algates housbondes han sorwe.
   Than tolde he me, how oon Latumius
Compleyned to his felawe Arrius,
That in his gardin growed swich a tree,
On which, he seyde, how that his wyves
three    760
Hanged hem-self for herte despitous.
"O leve brother," quod this Arrius,
"Yif me a plante of thilke blissed tree,
And in my gardin planted shal it be!"
   Of latter date, of wyves hath he red,
That somme han slayn hir housbondes in
hir bed,    766
And lete hir lechour dighte hir al the
night
Whyl that the corps lay in the floor up-
right.
And somme han drive nayles in hir brayn
Whyl that they slepte, and thus they han
hem slayn.    770
Somme han hem yeve poysoun in hir
drinke.
He spak more harm than herte may
bithinke.

And ther-with-al, he knew of mo pro-
verbes
Than in this world ther growen gras or
herbes.
" Bet is," quod he, " thyn habitacioun 775
Be with a leoun or a foul dragoun,
Than with a womman usinge for to chyde.
Bet is," quod he, " hye in the roof abyde
Than with an angry wyf doun in the
hous ;
They been so wikked and contrarious ; 780
They haten that hir housbondes loveth
ay."
He seyde, " a womman cast hir shame
away,
Whan she cast of hir smok ;" and forther-
mo,
" A fair womman, but she be chaast also,
Is lyk a gold ring in a sowes nose." 785
Who wolde wenen, or who wolde suppose
The wo that in myn herte was, and pyne ?
And whan I saugh he wolde never fyne
To reden on this cursed book al night,
Al sodeynly three leves have I plight 790
Out of his book, right as he radde, and
eke,
I with my fist so took him on the cheke,
That in our fyr he fil bakward adoun.
And he up-stirte as dooth a wood leoun,
And with his fist he smoot me on the
heed, 795
That in the floor I lay as I were deed.
And when he saugh how stille that I lay,
He was agast, and wolde han fled his
way,
Til atte laste out of my swogh I breyde :
" O ! hastow slayn me, false theef ?" I
seyde, 800
" And for my land thus hastow mordred
me ?
Er I be deed, yet wol I kisse thee."
And neer he cam, and kneled faire
adoun,
And seyde, " dere suster Alisoun, 804
As help me god, I shal thee never smyte ;
That I have doon, it is thy-self to wyte.
Foryeve it me, and that I thee biseke "—
And yet eft-sones I hitte him on the cheke,
And seyde, " theef, thus muchel am I
wreke ;
Now wol I dye, I may no lenger speke." 809

But atte laste, with muchel care and wo,
We fille acorded, by us selven two.
He yaf me al the brydel in myn hond
To han the governance of hous and lond,
And of his tonge and of his hond also, 815
And made him brenne his book anon
right tho.
And whan that I hadde geten un-to me,
By maistrie, al the soveraynetee,
And that he seyde, " myn owene trewe
wyf,
Do as thee lust the terme of al thy lyf,
Keep thyn honour, and keep eek myn
estaat "— 821
After that day we hadden never debaat.
God help me so, I was to him as kinde
As any wyf from Denmark un-to Inde,
And also trewe, and so was he to me. 825
I prey to god that sit in magestee,
So blesse his soule, for his mercy dere !
Now wol I seye my tale, if ye wol here.'

## Biholde the wordes bitween the Somonour and the Frere.

THE Frere lough, whan he hadde herd
al this,
' Now, dame,' quod he, ' so have I joye or
blis, 830
This is a long preamble of a tale !'
And whan the Somnour herde the Frere
gale,
' Lo !' quod the Somnour, ' goddes armes
two !
A frere wol entremette him ever-mo.
Lo, gode men, a flye and eek a frere 835
Wol falle in every dish and eek matere.
What spekestow of preambulacioun ?
What ! amble, or trotte, or pees, or go
sit doun ;
Thou lettest our disport in this manere.'
' Ye, woltow so, sir Somnour ?' quod
the Frere, 840
' Now, by my feith, I shal, er that I go,
Telle of a Somnour swich a tale or two,
That alle the folk shal laughen in this
place.'
' Now elles, Frere, I bishrewe thy
face,'
Quod this Somnour, ' and I bishrewe me,
But-if I telle tales two or three 846

Of freres er I come to Sidingborne,
That I shal make thyn herte for to morne;
For wel I woot thy pacience is goon.'
  Our hoste cryde ' pees ! and that anoon !'
And seyde, 'lat the womman telle hir
      tale.                          851
Ye fare as folk that dronken been of ale.

Do, dame, tel forth your tale, and that
      is best.'
  ' Al redy, sir,' quod she, ' right as yow
      lest,
If I have licence of this worthy Frere.'
  ' Yis, dame,' quod he, ' tel forth, and
      I wol here.'                   856

### Here endeth the Wyf of Bathe hir Prologe.

# THE TALE OF THE WYF OF BATHE.

### Here biginneth the Tale of the Wyf of Bathe.

In th'olde dayes of the king Arthour,
Of which that Britons speken greet
      honour,
Al was this land fulfild of fayerye.    859
The elf-queen, with hir joly companye,
Daunced ful ofte in many a grene mede ;
This was the olde opinion, as I rede.
I speke of manye hundred yeres ago ;
But now can no man see none elves mo.
For now the grete charitee and prayeres
Of limitours and othere holy freres,   (10)
That serchen every lond and every streem,
As thikke as motes in the sonne-beem,
Blessinge halles, chambres, kichenes,
      boures,
Citees, burghes, castels, hye toures,   870
Thropes, bernes, shipnes, dayeryes,
This maketh that ther been no fayeryes.
For ther as wont to walken was an elf,
Ther walketh now the limitour him-
      self
In undermeles and in morweninges,     875
And seyth his matins and his holy thinges
As he goth in his limitacioun.         (21)
Wommen may go saufly up and doun,
In every bush, or under every tree ;
Ther is noon other incubus but he,     880
And he ne wol doon hem but dishonour.
  And so bifel it, that this king Arthour
Hadde in his hous a lusty bacheler,

That on a day cam rydinge fro river ;
And happed that, allone as she was
      born,                     (29) 885
He saugh a mayde walkinge him biforn,
Of whiche mayde anon, maugree hir heed,
By verray force he rafte hir maydenheed ;
For which oppressioun was swich clamour
And swich pursute un-to the king Ar-
      thour,                         890
That dampned was this knight for to be
      deed
By cours of lawe, and sholde han lost his
      heed
Paraventure, swich was the statut tho ;
But that the quene and othere ladies mo
So longe preyeden the king of grace,   895
Til he his lyf him graunted in the place,
And yaf him to the quene al at hir
      wille,                         (41)
To chese, whether she wolde him save or
      spille.
  The quene thanketh the king with al
      hir might,                    899
And after this thus spak she to the knight,
Whan that she saugh hir tyme, up-on a
      day :
' Thou standest yet,' quod she, ' in swich
      array,
That of thy lyf yet hastow no suretee.
I grante thee lyf, if thou canst tellen me

What thing is it that wommen most
   desyren?          905
Be war, and keep thy nekke-boon from
   yren.          (50)
And if thou canst nat tellen it anon,
Yet wol I yeve thee leve for to gon
A twelf-month and a day, to seche and
   lere
An answere suffisant in this matere.   910
And suretee wol I han, er that thou pace,
Thy body for to yelden in this place.'
   Wo was this knight and sorwefully he
   syketh ;
But what ! he may nat do al as him lyketh.
And at the laste, he chees him for to
   wende,         915
And come agayn, right at the yeres ende,
With swich answere as god wolde him
   purveye ;         (61)
And taketh his leve, and wendeth forth
   his weye.
He seketh every hous and every place,
Wher-as he hopeth for to finde grace, 920
To lerne, what thing wommen loven
   most ;
But he ne coude arryven in no cost,
Wher-as he mighte finde in this matere
Two creatures accordinge in-fere.
   Somme seyde, wommen loven best
   richesse,         925
Somme seyde, honour, somme seyde, joly-
   nesse ;         (70)
Somme, riche array, somme seyden, lust
   abedde,
And ofte tyme to be widwe and wedde.
   Somme seyde, that our hertes been
   most esed,
Whan that we been y-flatered and y-
   plesed.         930
He gooth ful ny the sothe, I wol nat lye ;
A man shal winne us best with flaterye ;
And with attendance, and with bisinesse,
Been we y-lymed, bothe more and lesse.
   And somme seyn, how that we loven
   best
For to be free, and do right as us lest, (80)
And that no man repreve us of our vyce,
But seye that we be wyse, and no-thing
   nyce.
For trewely, ther is noon of us alle,   939
If any wight wol clawe us on the galle,

That we nil kike, for he seith us sooth ;
Assay, and he shal finde it that so dooth.
For be we never so vicious with-inne,
We wol been holden wyse, and clene of
   sinne.
   And somme seyn, that greet delyt han
   we         (89) 945
For to ben holden stable and eek secree,
And in o purpos stedefastly to dwelle,
And nat biwreye thing that men us telle.
But that tale is nat worth a rake-stele ;
Pardee, we wommen conne no-thing hele ;
Witnesse on Myda ; wol ye here the tale ?
   Ovyde, amonges othere thinges smale,
Seyde, Myda hadde, under his longe heres,
Growinge up-on his heed two asses eres,
The whiche vyce he hidde, as he best
   mighte,         955
Ful subtilly from every mannes sighte,
That, save his wyf, ther wiste of it na-
   mo.         (101)
He loved hir most, and trusted hir also ;
He preyede hir, that to no creature
She sholde tellen of his disfigure.   960
   She swoor him 'nay, for al this world
   to winne,
She nolde do that vileinye or sinne,
To make hir housbond han so foul a name ;
She nolde nat telle it for hir owene shame.'
But nathelees, hir thoughte that she dyde,
That she so longe sholde a conseil hyde ;
Hir thoughte it swal so sore aboute hir
   herte,         (111)
That nedely som word hir moste asterte ;
And sith she dorste telle it to no man,
Doun to a mareys faste by she ran ;   970
Til she came there, hir herte was a-fyre,
And, as a bitore bombleth in the myre,
She leyde hir mouth un-to the water doun :
' Biwreye me nat, thou water, with thy
   soun,'        (118) 974
Quod she, ' to thee I telle it, and namo ;
Myn housbond hath longe asses eres two !
Now is myn herte all hool, now is it oute ;
I mighte no lenger kepe it, out of doute.'
Heer may ye se, thogh we a tyme abyde,
Yet out it moot, we can no conseil hyde ;
The remenant of the tale if ye wol here,
Redeth Ovyde, and ther ye may it lere.
   This knight, of which my tale is spe-
   cially,         983

U

Whan that he saugh he mighte nat come
　　therby,
This is to seye, what wommen loven moost,
With-inne his brest ful sorweful was the
　　goost ;　　　　　　　　(130) 986
But hoom he gooth, he mighte nat
　　sojourne.
The day was come, that hoomward moste
　　he tourne,
And in his wey it happed him to ryde,
In al this care, under a forest-syde,　990
Wher-as he saugh up-on a daunce go
Of ladies foure and twenty, and yet mo ;
Toward the whiche daunce he drow ful
　　yerne,
In hope that som wisdom sholde he lerne.
But certeinly, er he came fully there, 995
Vanisshed was this daunce, he niste where.
No creature saugh he that bar lyf,　(141)
Save on the grene he saugh sittinge a wyf;
A fouler wight ther may no man devyse.
Agayn the knight this olde wyf gan ryse,
And seyde, ' sir knight, heer-forth ne lyth
　　no wey.　　　　　　　　　1001
Tel me, what that ye seken, by your fey ?
Paraventure it may the bettre be ;
Thise olde folk can muchel thing,' quod
　　she.
　　' My leve mooder,' quod this knight
　　certeyn,　　　　　　　　1005
' I nam but deed, but-if that I can seyn
What thing it is that wommen most
　　desyre ;　　　　　　　　(151)
Coude ye me wisse, I wolde wel quyte
　　your hyre.'
　　' Plight me thy trouthe, heer in myn
　　hand,' quod she,
' The nexte thing that I requere thee, 1010
Thou shalt it do, if it lye in thy might ;
And I wol telle it yow er it be night.'
' Have heer my trouthe,' quod the knight,
　　' I grante.'
　　' Thanne,' quod she, ' I dar me wel
　　avante,　　　　　　　　1014
Thy lyf is sauf, for I wol stonde therby,
Up-on my lyf, the queen wol seye as I.
Lat see which is the proudeste of hem
　　alle,　　　　　　　　　(161)
That wereth on a coverchief or a calle,
That dar seye nay, of that I shal thee
　　teche ;

Lat us go forth with-outen lenger speche.'
Tho rouned she a pistel in his ere,　1021
And bad him to be glad, and have no
　　fere.
　　Whan they be comen to the court, this
　　knight
Seyde, ' he had holde his day, as he
　　hadde hight,
And redy was his answere,' as he sayde.
Ful many a noble wyf, and many a
　　mayde,　　　　　　　　(170) 1026
And many a widwe, for that they ben
　　wyse,
The quene hir-self sittinge as a justyse,
Assembled been, his answere for to here ;
And afterward this knight was bode
　　appere.　　　　　　　　　1030
　　To every wight comanded was silence,
And that the knight sholde telle in
　　audience,
What thing that worldly wommen loven
　　best.
This knight ne stood nat stille as doth
　　a best,
But to his questioun anon answerde 1035
With manly voys, that al the court it
　　herde :　　　　　　　　　(180)
　　' My lige lady, generally,' quod he,
' Wommen desyren to have sovereyntee
As wel over hir housbond as hir love,
And for to been in maistrie him above ;
This is your moste desyr, thogh ye me
　　kille,　　　　　　　　　1041
Doth as yow list, I am heer at your wille.'
　　In al the court ne was ther wyf ne
　　mayde,
Ne widwe, that contraried that he sayde,
But seyden, ' he was worthy han his
　　lyf.'　　　　　　　　　1045
　　And with that word up stirte the olde
　　wyf,　　　　　　　　　(190)
Which that the knight saugh sittinge in
　　the grene :
' Mercy,' quod she, ' my sovereyn lady
　　quene !
Er that your court departe, do me right.
I taughte this answere un-to the knight ;
For which he plighte me his trouthe
　　there,　　　　　　　　　1051
The firste thing I wolde of him requere,
He wolde it do, if it lay in his might.

Bifore the court than preye I thee, sir
   knight,'
Quod she, 'that thou me take un-to thy
   wyf ;                1055
For wel thou wost that I have kept thy
   lyf.               (200)
If I sey fals, sey nay, up-on thy fey !'
  This knight answerde, 'allas ! and
   weylawey !
I woot right wel that swich was my
   biheste.           1059
For goddes love, as chees a newe requeste ;
Tak al my good, and lat my body go.'
  'Nay than,' quod she, 'I shrewe us
   bothe two !
For thogh that I be foul, and old, and
   pore,
I nolde for al the metal, ne for ore,
That under erthe is grave, or lyth above,
But-if thy wyf I were, and eek thy
   love.'        (210) 1066
  'My love?' quod he ; 'nay, my damp-
   nacioun !
Allas ! that any of my nacioun
Sholde ever so foule disparaged be !'
But al for noght, the ende is this, that he
Constreyned was, he nedes moste hir
   wedde ;         1071
And taketh his olde wyf, and gooth to
   bedde.
  Now wolden som men seye, paraventure,
That, for my necligence, I do no cure
To tellen yow the joye and al th'array
That at the feste was that ilke day. (220)
To whiche thing shortly answere I shal ;
I seye, ther nas no joye ne feste at al,
Ther nas but hevinesse and muche sorwe ;
For prively he wedded hir on a morwe,
And al day after hidde him as an oule ;
So wo was him, his wyf looked so foule.
  Greet was the wo the knight hadde in
   his thoght,
Whan he was with his wyf a-bedde y-
   broght ;       1084
He walweth, and he turneth to and fro.
His olde wyf lay smylinge evermo,  (230)
And seyde, 'o dere housbond, *ben'cite !*
Fareth every knight thus with his wyf
   as ye ?
Is this the lawe of king Arthures hous ?
Is every knight of his so dangerous ? 1090

I am your owene love and eek your wyf ;
I am she, which that saved hath your lyf ;
And certes, yet dide I yow never unright ;
Why fare ye thus with me this firste night ?
Ye faren lyk a man had lost his wit ; 1095
What is my gilt ? for godd's love, tel
   me it,        (240)
And it shal been amended, if I may.'
  'Amended ?' quod this knight, 'allas !
   nay, nay !
It wol nat been amended never mo !
Thou art so loothly, and so old also, 1100
And ther-to comen of so lowe a kinde,
That litel wonder is, thogh I walwe and
   winde.
So wolde god myn herte wolde breste !'
  'Is this,' quod she, 'the cause of your
   unreste ?'       1104
  'Ye, certainly,' quod he, 'no wonder is.'
  'Now, sire,' quod she, 'I coude amende
   al this,        (250)
If that me liste, er it were dayes three,
So wel ye mighte bere yow un-to me.
  But for ye speken of swich gentillesse
As is descended out of old richesse, 1110
That therfore sholden ye be gentil men,
Swich arrogance is nat worth an hen.
Loke who that is most vertuous alway,
Privee and apert, and most entendeth ay
To do the gentil dedes that he can, 1115
And tak him for the grettest gentil
   man.        (260)
Crist wol, we clayme of him our gentil-
   lesse,
Nat of our eldres for hir old richesse.
For thogh they yeve us al hir heritage,
For which we clayme to been of heigh
   parage,        1120
Yet may they nat biquethe, for no-thing,
To noon of us hir vertuous living,
That made hem gentil men y-called be ;
And bad us folwen hem in swich degree.
  Wel can the wyse poete of Florence,
That highte Dant, speken in this sentence ;
Lo in swich maner rym is Dantes tale :
"Ful selde up ryseth by his branches
   smale      (272) 1128
Prowesse of man ; for god, of his good-
   nesse,
Wol that of him we clayme our gentil-
   lesse ;"       1130

For of our eldres may we no-thing
   clayme            1131
But temporel thing, that man may hurte
   and mayme.
Eek every wight wot this as wel as I,
If gentillesse were planted naturelly
Un-to a certeyn linage, doun the lyne,
Privee ne apert, than wolde they never
   fyne            (280) 1136
To doon of gentillesse the faire offyce ;
They mighte do no vileinye or vyce.

   Tak fyr, and ber it in the derkeste hous
Bitwix this and the mount of Caucasus,
And lat men shette the dores and go
   thenne ;           1141
Yet wol the fyr as faire lye and brenne,
As twenty thousand men mighte it biholde ;
His office naturel ay wol it holde,
Up peril of my lyf, til that it dye.    1145

   Heer may ye see wel, how that genterye
Is nat annexed to possessioun,     (291)
Sith folk ne doon hir operacioun
Alwey, as dooth the fyr, lo ! in his kinde.
For, god it woot, men may wel often finde
A lordes sone do shame and vileinye ; 1151
And he that wol han prys of his gentrye
For he was boren of a gentil hous,
And hadde hise eldres noble and vertuous,
And nil him-selven do no gentil dedis, 1155
Ne folwe his gentil auncestre that deed is,
He nis nat gentil, be he duk or erl ; (301)
For vileyns sinful dedes make a cherl.
For gentillesse nis but renomee     1159
Of thyne auncestres, for hir heigh bountee,
Which is a strange thing to thy persone.
Thy gentillesse cometh fro god allone ;
Than comth our verray gentillesse of grace,
It was no-thing biquethe us with our place.

   Thenketh how noble, as seith Valerius,
Was thilke Tullius Hostilius,    (310) 1166
That out of povert roos to heigh noblesse.
Redeth Senek, and redeth eek Boëce,
Ther shul ye seen expres that it no drede is,
That he is gentil that doth gentil dedis ;
And therfore, leve housbond, I thus con-
   clude,           1171
Al were it that myne auncestres were rude,
Yet may the hye god, and so hope I,
Grante me grace to liven vertuously. 1174
Thanne am I gentil, whan that I biginne
To liven vertuously and weyve sinne. (320)

And ther-as ye of povert me repreve,
The hye god, on whom that we bileve,
In wilful povert chees to live his lyf. 1179
And certes every man, mayden, or wyf,
May understonde that Jesus, hevene king,
Ne wolde nat chese a vicious living.
Glad povert is an honest thing, certeyn ;
This wol Senek and othere clerkes seyn.
Who-so that halt him payd of his poverte,
I holde him riche, al hadde he nat a
   sherte.           (330) 1186
He that coveyteth is a povre wight,
For he wolde han that is nat in his might.
But he that noght hath, ne coveyteth have,
Is riche, al-though ye holde him but a
   knave.           1190

   Verray povert, it singeth proprely ;
Juvenal seith of povert merily :
"The povre man, whan he goth by the
   weye,
Bifore the theves he may singe and pleye."
Povert is hateful good, and, as I gesse, 1195
A ful greet bringer out of bisinesse ; (340)
A greet amender eek of sapience
To him that taketh it in pacience.
Povert is this, al-though it seme elenge :
Possessioun, that no wight wol chalenge.
Povert ful ofte, whan a man is lowe, 1201
Maketh his god and eek him-self to knowe.
Povert a spectacle is, as thinketh me,
Thurgh which he may his verray frendes
   see.
And therfore, sire, sin that I noght yow
   greve,           1205
Of my povert na-more ye me repreve. (350)
   Now, sire, of elde ye repreve me ;
And certes, sire, thogh noon auctoritee
Were in no book, ye gentils of honour
Seyn that men sholde an old wight doon
   favour,           1210
And clepe him fader, for your gentillesse ;
And auctours shal I finden, as I gesse.

   Now ther ye seye, that I am foul and old,
Than drede you noght to been a cokewold ;
For filthe and elde, al-so mote I thee, 1215
Been grete wardeyns up-on chastitee. (360)
But nathelees, sin I knowe your delyt,
I shal fulfille your worldly appetyt.
   Chees now,' quod she, 'oon of thise
   thinges tweye,         1219
To han me foul and old til that I deye,

And be to yow a trewe humble wyf,
And never yow displese in al my lyf,
Or elles ye wol han me yong and fair,
And take your aventure of the repair 1224
That shal be to your hous, by-cause of me,
Or in som other place, may wel be. (370)
Now chees your-selven, whether that yow
　　lyketh.'
　This knight avyseth him and sore
　　syketh,
But atte laste he seyde in this manere,
'My lady and my love, and wyf so dere,
I put me in your wyse governance ; 1231
Cheseth your-self, which may be most
　　plesance,
And most honour to yow and me also.
I do no fors the whether of the two ;
For as yow lyketh, it suffiseth me.' 1235
　'Thanne have I gete of yow maistrye,'
　　quod she, (380)
'Sin I may chese, and governe as me lest?'
　'Ye, certes, wyf,' quod he, 'I holde it
　　best.'
　'Kis me,' quod she, 'we be no lenger
　　wrothe ; 1239
For, by my trouthe, I wol be to yow bothe,
This is to seyn, ye, bothe fair and good.
I prey to god that I mot sterven wood,

But I to yow be al-so good and trewe
As ever was wyf, sin that the world was
　　newe.
And, but I be to-morn as fair to sene 1245
As any lady, emperyce, or quene, (390)
That is bitwixe the est and eke the west,
Doth with my lyf and deeth right as yow
　　lest.
Cast up the curtin, loke how that it is.'
　And whan the knight saugh verraily al
　　this, 1250
That she so fair was, and so yong ther-to,
For joye he hente hir in his armes two,
His herte bathed in a bath of blisse ;
A thousand tyme a-rewe he gan hir
　　kisse.
And she obeyed him in every thing 1255
That mighte doon him plesance or lyking.
　And thus they live, un-to hir lyves
　　ende, (401)
In parfit joye ; and Jesu Crist us sende
Housbondes meke, yonge, and fresshe a-
　　bedde, 1259
And grace t'overbyde hem that we wedde.
And eek I preye Jesu shorte hir lyves
That wol nat be governed by hir wyves ;
And olde and angry nigardes of dispence,
God sende hem sone verray pestilence.

**Here endeth the Wyves Tale of Bathe.**

---

# THE FRIAR'S PROLOGUE.

### The Prologe of the Freres tale.

This worthy limitour, this noble Frere, 1265
He made alwey a maner louring chere
Upon the Somnour, but for honestee
No vileyns word as yet to him spak he.
But atte laste he seyde un-to the Wyf,
'Dame,' quod he, 'god yeve yow right
　　good lyf ! 1270
Ye han heer touched, al-so mote I thee,
In scole-matere greet difficultee ;

Ye han seyd muchel thing right wel, I
　　seye ; (9)
But dame, here as we ryden by the weye,
Us nedeth nat to speken but of game, 1275
And lete auctoritees, on goddos name,
To preching and to scole eek of clergye.
But if it lyke to this companye,
I wol yow of a somnour telle a game. 1279
Pardee, ye may wel knowe by the name,

That of a somnour may no good be
　　sayd ;
I praye that noon of you be yvel apayd.
A somnour is a renner up and doun
With mandementes for fornicacioun, (20)
And is y-bet at every tounes ende.' 1285
　　Our host tho spak, 'a! sire, ye sholde
　　　　be hende
And curteys, as a man of your estaat ;
In companye we wol have no debaat.
Telleth your tale, and lat the Somnour
　　be.'

'Nay,' quod the Somnour, 'lat him
　　seye to me　　　　　　　　　　1290
What so him list ; whan it comth to my lot,
By god, I shal him quyten every grot.
I shal him tellen which a greet honour (29)
It is to be a flateringe limitour ;　[T. 6876
And his offyce I shal him telle, y-wis.'
　　　　　　　　　　　　　　　　　[T. 6879
　　Our host answerde, 'pees, na-more of
　　　　this.'　　　　　　　　　　1296
And after this he seyde un-to the Frere,
'Tel forth your tale, leve maister deere.'

**Here endeth the Prologe of the Frere.**

# THE FRERES TALE.

**Here biginneth the Freres tale.**

Whilom ther was dwellinge in my contree
An erchedeken, a man of heigh degree,
That boldely dide execucioun　　　1301
In punisshinge of fornicacioun,
Of wicchecraft, and eek of bauderye,
Of diffamacioun, and avoutrye,
Of chirche-reves, and of testaments, 1305
Of contractes, and of lakke of sacraments,
And eek of many another maner cryme
　　　　　　　　　　　　　　　　　[T. om.
Which nedeth nat rehercen at this tyme ;
　　　　　　　　　　　　　　　　　[T. om.
Of usure, and of symonye also.　　(11)
But certes, lechours dide he grettest wo ;
They sholde singen, if that they were
　　hent ;　　　　　　　　　　　　1311
And smale tytheres weren foule y-shent.
If any persone wolde up-on hem pleyne,
Ther mighte asterte him no pecunial
　　peyne.
For smale tythes and for smal offringe 1315
He made the peple pitously to singe.
For er the bisshop caughte hem with his
　　hook,

They weren in the erchedeknes book. (20)
Thanne hadde he, thurgh his jurisdic-
　　cioun,
Power to doon on hem correccioun.　1320
He hadde a Somnour redy to his hond,
A slyer boy was noon in Engelond ;
For subtilly he hadde his espiaille,
That taughte him, wher that him mighte
　　availle.　　　　　　　　　　　1324
He coude spare of lechours oon or two,
To techen him to foure and twenty mo.
For thogh this Somnour wood were as an
　　hare,
To telle his harlotrye I wol nat spare ; (30)
For we been out of his correccioun ;
They han of us no jurisdiccioun,　　1330
Ne never shullen, terme of alle hir lyves.
　'Peter ! so been the wommen of the
　　styves,'
Quod the Somnour, 'y-put out of my cure !'
　'Pees, with mischance and with mis-
　　aventure,'
Thus seyde our host, 'and lat him telle
　　his tale.　　　　　　　　　　1335

Now telleth forth, thogh that the Som-
nour gale,
Ne spareth nat, myn owene maister dere.'
  This false theef, this Somnour, quod
    the Frere, (40)
Hadde alwey baudes redy to his hond,
As any hauk to lure in Engelond, 1340
That tolde him al the secree that they
  knewe ;
For hir acqueyntance was nat come of-
newe.
They weren hise approwours prively ;
He took him-self a greet profit therby ;
His maister knew nat alwey what he wan.
With-outen mandement, a lewed man 1346
He coude somne, on peyne of Cristes curs,
And they were gladde for to fille his
  purs, (50)
And make him grete festes atte nale.
And right as Judas hadde purses smale,
And was a theef, right swich a theef was
  he ; 1351
His maister hadde but half his duëtee.
He was, if I shal yeven him his laude,
A theef, and eek a Somnour, and a baude.
He hadde eek wenches at his retenue, 1355
That, whether that sir Robert or sir Huwe,
Or Jakke, or Rauf, or who-so that it were,
That lay by hem, they tolde it in his ere;
Thus was the wenche and he of oon as-
  sent. (61)
And he wolde fecche a feyned mande-
  ment, 1360
And somne hem to the chapitre bothe two,
And pile the man, and lete the wenche go.
Thanne wolde he seye, ' frend, I shal for
  thy sake 1363
Do stryken hir out of our lettres blake ;
Thee thar na-more as in this cas travaille ;
I am thy freend, ther I thee may availle.'
Certeyn he knew of bryberyes mo
Than possible is to telle in yeres two. (70)
For in this world nis dogge for the bowe,
That can an hurt deer from an hool
  y-knowe, 1370
Bet than this Somnour knew a sly lechour,
Or an avouter, or a paramour.
And, for that was the fruit of al his rente,
Therfore on it he sette al his entente.
  And so bifel, that ones on a day 1375
This Somnour, ever waiting on his pray,

Rood for to somne a widwe, an old ribybe,
Feyninge a cause, for he wolde brybe. (80)
And happed that he saugh bifore him ryde
A gay yeman, under a forest-syde. 1380
A bowe he bar, and arwes brighte and
  kene ;
He hadde up-on a courtepy of grene ;
An hat up-on his heed with frenges blake.
  'Sir,' quod this Somnour, 'hayl! and
  wel a-take ! '
'Wel-come,' quod he, 'and every good
  felawe ! 1385
Wher rydestow under this grene shawe ? '
Seyde this yeman, ' wiltow fer to day ? '
  This Somnour him answerde, and seyde,
  'nay ; (90)
Heer faste by,' quod he, ' is myn entente
To ryden, for to reysen up a rente 1390
That longeth to my lordes duëtee.'
  'Artow thanne a bailly ? ' ' Ye ! ' quod
  he.
He dorste nat, for verray filthe and shame,
Seye that he was a somnour, for the
  name.
  'Depardieux,' quod this yeman, 'dere
  brother, 1395
Thou art a bailly, and I am another.
I am unknowen as in this contree ; (99)
Of thyn aqueyntance I wolde praye thee,
And eek of brotherhede, if that yow leste.
I have gold and silver in my cheste ; 1400
If that thee happe to comen in our shyre,
Al shal be thyn, right as thou wolt desyre.'
  'Grantmercy,' quod this Somnour, ' by
  my feith ! '
Everich in otheres hand his trouthe leith,
For to be sworne bretheren til they deye.
In daliance they ryden forth hir weye. 1406
  This Somnour, which that was as ful
  of jangles,
As ful of venim been thise wariangles, (110)
And ever enquering up-on every thing,
  'Brother,' quod he, 'where is now your
  dwelling, 1410
Another day if that I sholde yow seche ? '
  This yeman him answerde in softe
  speche,
'Brother,' quod he, ' fer in the north
  contree,
Wher, as I hope, som-tyme I shal thee see.
Er we departe, I shal thee so wel wisse,

That of myn hous ne shaltow never
　　misse.'　　　　　　　　　　1416
　'Now, brother,' quod this Somnour, 'I
　　yow preye,
Teche me, whyl that we ryden by the
　　weye,　　　　　　　　　　(120)
Sin that ye been a baillif as am I,
Som subtiltee, and tel me feithfully　1420
In myn offyce how I may most winne ;
And spareth nat for conscience ne sinne,
But as my brother tel me, how do ye ?'
　　'Now, by my trouthe, brother dere,'
　　seyde he,
'As I shal tellen thee a feithful tale,　1425
My wages been ful streite and ful smale.
My lord is hard to me and daungerous,
And myn offyce is ful laborous ;　　(130)
And therfore by extorcions I live.
For sothe, I take al that men wol me
　　yive ;　　　　　　　　　　1430
Algate, by sleyghte or by violence,
Fro yeer to yeer I winne al my dispence.
I can no bettre telle feithfully.'
　　'Now, certes,' quod this Somnour, 'so
　　fare I ;
I spare nat to taken, god it woot,　　1435
But-if it be to hevy or to hoot.
What I may gete in conseil prively,
No maner conscience of that have I ; (140)
Nere myn extorcioun, I mighte nat liven,
Ne of swiche japes wol I nat be shriven.
Stomak ne conscience ne knowe I noon ;
I shrewe thise shrifte-fadres everichoon.
Wel be we met, by god and by seint
　　Jame !
But, leve brother, tel me than thy name,'
Quod this Somnour ; and in this mene
　　whyle,　　　　　　　　　　1445
This yeman gan a litel for to smyle.
　'Brother,' quod he, 'wiltow that I thee
　　telle ?
I am a feend, my dwelling is in helle. (150)
And here I ryde about my purchasing,
To wite wher men wolde yeve me any
　　thing.　　　　　　　　　　1450
My purchas is th'effect of al my rente.
Loke how thou rydest for the same en-
　　tente,
To winne good, thou rekkest never how ;
Right so fare I, for ryde wolde I now
Un-to the worldes ende for a preye.' 1455

　'A,' quod this Somnour, 'ben'cite, what
　　sey ye ?
I wende ye were a yeman trewely.
Ye han a mannes shap as wel as I ; (160)
Han ye figure than determinat
In helle, ther ye been in your estat ?' 1460
　'Nay, certeinly,' quod he, 'ther have
　　we noon ;
But whan us lyketh, we can take us oon,
Or elles make yow seme we ben shape
Som-tyme lyk a man, or lyk an ape ;
Or lyk an angel can I ryde or go.　1465
It is no wonder thing thogh it be so ;
A lousy jogelour can deceyve thee,
And pardee, yet can I more craft than
　　he.'　　　　　　　　　　(170)
　'Why,' quod the Somnour, 'ryde ye
　　thanne or goon　　　　　　1469
In sondry shap, and nat alwey in oon ?'
　'For we,' quod he, 'wol us swich formes
　　make
As most able is our preyes for to take.'
　　'What maketh yow to han al this
　　labour ?'
　'Ful many a cause, leve sir Somnour,'
Seyde this feend, 'but alle thing hath
　　tyme.　　　　　　　　　　1475
The day is short, and it is passed pryme,
And yet ne wan I no-thing in this day.
I wol entende to winnen, if I may,　(180)
And nat entende our wittes to declare.
For, brother myn, thy wit is al to bare 1480
To understonde, al-thogh I tolde hem thee.
But, for thou axest why labouren we ;
For, som-tyme, we ben goddes instru-
　　ments,
And menes to don his comandements,
Whan that him list, up-on his creatures,
In divers art and in divers figures.　1486
With-outen him we have no might, cer-
　　tayn,　　　　　　　　　　(189)
If that him list to stonden ther-agayn.
And som-tyme, at our prayere, han we leve
Only the body and nat the soule greve ;
Witnesse on Job, whom that we diden
　　wo.　　　　　　　　　　1491
And som-tyme han we might of bothe two,
This is to seyn, of soule and body eke.
And somtyme be we suffred for to seke
Up-on a man, and doon his soule unreste,
And nat his body, and al is for the beste.

Whan he withstandeth our temptacioun,
It is a cause of his savacioun ;          (200)
Al-be-it that it was nat our entente
He sholde be sauf, but that we wolde
    him hente.                    1500
And som-tyme be we servant un-to man,
As to the erchebisshop Seint Dunstan
And to the apostles servant eek was I.'
    'Yet tel me,' quod the Somnour, 'feith-
    fully,
Make ye yow newe bodies thus alway 1505
Of elements?' the feend answerde, 'nay ;
Som-tyme we feyne, and som-tyme we
    aryse
With dede bodies in ful sondry wyse, (210)
And speke as renably and faire and wel
As to the Phitonissa dide Samuel.     1510
And yet wol som men seye it was nat he ;
I do no fors of your divinitee.
But o thing warne I thee, I wol nat jape,
Thou wolt algates wite how we ben shape ;
Thou shalt her-afterward, my brother
    dere,                           1515
Com ther thee nedeth nat of me to lere.
For thou shalt by thyn owene experience
Conne in a chayer rede of this sentence
Bet than Virgyle, whyl he was on lyve,
Or Dant also ; now lat us ryde blyve. 1520
For I wol holde companye with thee (223)
Til it be so, that thou forsake me.'
    'Nay,' quod this Somnour, 'that shal
    nat bityde ;
I am a yeman, knowen is ful wyde ;
My trouthe wol I holde as in this cas. 1525
For though thou were the devel Sathanas,
My trouthe wol I holde to my brother,
As I am sworn, and ech of us til other (230)
For to be trewe brother in this cas ;
And bothe we goon abouten our purchas.
Tak thou thy part, what that men wol
    thee yive,                        1531
And I shal myn ; thus may we bothe live.
And if that any of us have more than
    other,
Lat him be trewe, and parte it with his
    brother.'
    'I graunte,' quod the devel, 'by my fey.'
And with that word they ryden forth hir
    wey.                            1536
And right at the entring of the tounes
    ende,

To which this Somnour shoop him for to
    wende,                          (240)
They saugh a cart, that charged was with
    hey,
Which that a carter droof forth in his wey.
Deep was the wey, for which the carte
    stood.                          1541
The carter smoot, and cryde, as he were
    wood,
'Hayt, Brok ! hayt, Scot ! what spare ye
    for the stones?
The feend,' quod he, 'yow fecche body
    and bones,
As ferforthly as ever were ye foled ! 1545
So muche wo as I have with yow tholed !
The devel have al, bothe hors and cart
    and hey !'
    This Somnour seyde, 'heer shal we
    have a pley ;'                   (250)
And neer the feend he drough, as noght
    ne were,
Ful prively, and rouned in his ere : 1550
'Herkne, my brother, herkne, by thy
    feith ;
Herestow nat how that the carter seith ?
Hent it anon, for he hath yeve it thee,
Bothe hey and cart, and eek hise caples
    three.'
    'Nay,' quod the devel, 'god wot, never
    a deel ;                        1555
It is nat his entente, trust me weel.
Axe him thy-self, if thou nat trowest me,
Or elles stint a while, and thou shalt
    see.'                           (260)
    This carter thakketh his hors upon the
    croupe,
And they bigonne drawen and to-stoupe ;
'Heyt, now !' quod he, 'ther Jesu Crist
    yow blesse,                     1561
And al his handwerk, bothe more and
    lesse !
That was wel twight, myn owene lyard
    boy !
I pray god save thee and seynt Loy !
Now is my cart out of the slow, pardee !'
    'Lo ! brother,' quod the feend, 'what
    tolde I thee?                   1566
Heer may ye see, myn owene dere brother,
The carl spak oo thing, but he thoghte
    another.                        (270)
Lat us go forth abouten our viage ;

Heer winne I no-thing up-on cariage.'
　Whan that they comen som-what out
　　of toune,　　　　　　　　　1571
This Somnour to his brother gan to roune,
'Brother,' quod he, 'heer woneth an old
　rebekke,
That hadde almost as lief to lese hir nekke
As for to yeve a peny of hir good.　1575
I wol han twelf pens, though that she be
　wood,
Or I wol sompne hir un-to our offyce;
And yet, god woot, of hir knowe I no
　vyce.　　　　　　　　　　　(280)
But for thou canst nat, as in this contree,
Winne thy cost, tak heer ensample of
　me.'　　　　　　　　　　　1580
　This Somnour clappeth at the widwes
　　gate.
'Com out,' quod he, 'thou olde viritrate!
I trowe thou hast som frere or preest
　with thee!'
　'Who clappeth?' seyde this widwe,
　'ben'cite!
God save you, sire, what is your swete
　wille?'　　　　　　　　　　1585
　'I have,' quod he, 'of somonce here
　　a bille;
Up peyne of cursing, loke that thou be
To-morn bifore the erchedeknes knee (290)
T'answere to the court of certeyn thinges.'
　'Now, lord,' quod she, 'Crist Jesu, king
　　of kinges,　　　　　　　　1590
So wisly helpe me, as I ne may.
I have been syk, and that ful many a day.
I may nat go so fer,' quod she, 'ne ryde,
But I be deed, so priketh it in my syde.
May I nat axe a libel, sir Somnour,　1595
And answere there, by my procutour,
To swich thing as men wol opposen me?'
　'Yis,' quod this Somnour, 'pay anon,
　　lat se,　　　　　　　　　(300)
Twelf pens to me, and I wol thee acquyte.
I shall no profit han ther-by but lyte;　1600
My maister hath the profit, and nat I.
Com of, and lat me ryden hastily;
Yif me twelf pens, I may no lenger tarie.'
　'Twelf pens,' quod she, 'now lady
　　Seinte Marie
So wisly help me out of care and sinne,
This wyde world thogh that I sholde
　winne,　　　　　　　　　　1606

Ne have I nat twelf pens with-inne myn
　hold.　　　　　　　　　　(309)
Ye knowen wel that I am povre and old;
Kythe your almesse on me povre wrecche.'
　'Nay than,' quod he, 'the foule feend
　　me fecche　　　　　　　　1610
If I th'excuse, though thou shul be spilt!'
　'Alas,' quod she, 'god woot, I have no
　　gilt.'
　'Pay me,' quod he, 'or by the swete
　　seinte Anne,
As I wol bere awey thy newe panne
For dette, which that thou owest me of
　old,　　　　　　　　　　1615
Whan that thou madest thyn housbond
　cokewold,
I payde at hoom for thy correccioun.'
　'Thou lixt,' quod she, 'by my sava-
　　cioun!　　　　　　　　　(320)
Ne was I never er now, widwe ne wyf,
Somoned un-to your court in al my lyf;
Ne never I nas but of my body trewe!　1621
Un-to the devel blak and rough of hewe
Yeve I thy body and my panne also!'
　And whan the devel herde hir cursen so
Up-on hir knees, he seyde in this manere,
'Now Mabely, myn owene moder dere,　1626
Is this your wil in ernest, that ye seye?'
　'The devel,' quod she, 'so fecche him
　　er he deye,　　　　　　　(330)
And panne and al, but he wol him re-
　pente!'　　　　　　　　　1629
　'Nay, olde stot, that is nat myn entente,'
Quod this Somnour, 'for to repente me,
For any thing that I have had of thee;
I wolde I hadde thy smok and every
　clooth!'
　'Now, brother,' quod the devel, 'be nat
　　wrooth;
Thy body and this panne ben myne by
　right.　　　　　　　　　1635
Thou shalt with me to helle yet to-night,
Where thou shalt knowen of our privetee
More than a maister of divinitee:'　(340)
And with that word this foule feend him
　hente;　　　　　　　　　1639
Body and soule, he with the devel wente
Wher-as that somnours han hir heritage.
And god, that maked after his image
Mankinde, save and gyde us alle and
　some;

And leve this Somnour good man to
 bicome !
Lordinges, I coude han told yow, quod
 this Frere,        1645
Hadde I had leyser for this Somnour here,
After the text of Crist [and] Poul and John,
And of our othere doctours many oon,
Swiche peynes, that your hertes mighte
 agryse,         (351)
Al-be-it so, no tonge may devyse,   1650
Thogh that I mighte a thousand winter
 telle,
The peyne of thilke cursed hous of helle.
But, for to kepe us fro that cursed place,
Waketh, and preyeth Jesu for his grace

So kepe us fro the temptour Sathanas. 1655
Herketh this word, beth war as in this
 cas;
The leoun sit in his await alway
To slee the innocent, if that he may. (360)
Disposeth ay your hertes to withstonde
The feend, that yow wolde make thral
 and bonde.        1660
He may nat tempten yow over your might ;
For Crist wol be your champion and
 knight.
And prayeth that thise Somnours hem
 repente
Of hir misdedes, er that the feend hem
 hente.

**Here endeth the Freres tale.**

---

# THE SOMNOUR'S PROLOGUE.

### The prologe of the Somnours Tale.

THIS Somnour in his stiropes hye stood ;
Up-on this Frere his herte was so wood,
That lyk an aspen leef he quook for yre.
 'Lordinges,' quod he, 'but o thing I
 desyre ;
I yow biseke that, of your curteisye,
Sin ye han herd this false Frere lye, 1670
As suffereth me I may my tale telle !
This Frere bosteth that he knoweth helle,
And god it woot, that it is litel wonder ;
Freres and feendes been but lyte a-sonder.
For pardee, ye han ofte tyme herd telle,
How that a frere ravisshed was to helle
In spirit ones by a visioun ;   (13) 1677
And as an angel ladde him up and doun,
To shewen him the peynes that ther were,
In al the place saugh he nat a frere ; 1680
Of other folk he saugh y-nowe in wo.
Un-to this angel spak the frere tho :

" Now, sir," quod he, " han freres swich
 a grace         (19)
That noon of hem shal come to this place?"
" Yis," quod this angel, " many a mil-
 lioun ! "         1685
And un-to Sathanas he ladde him doun.
" And now hath Sathanas," seith he,
 " a tayl
Brodder than of a carrik is the sayl.
Hold up thy tayl, thou Sathanas ! " quod
 he,         1689
" Shewe forth thyn ers, and lat the frere see
Wher is the nest of freres in this place ! "
And, er that half a furlong-wey of space,
Right so as bees out swarmen from an
 hyve,
Out of the develes ers ther gonne dryve (30)
Twenty thousand freres in a route,   1695
And thurgh-out helle swarmeden aboute

And comen agayn, as faste as they may
    gon,
And in his ers they crepten everichon.
He clapte his tayl agayn, and lay ful stille.
This frere, whan he loked hadde his fille
Upon the torments of this sory place, 1701
His spirit god restored of his grace

Un-to his body agayn, and he awook ;
But natheles, for fere yet he quook, (40)
So was the develes ers ay in his minde,
That is his heritage of verray kinde. 1706
God save yow alle, save this cursed
    Frere ;
My prologe wol I ende in this manere.'

Here endeth the Prologe of the Somnours Tale.

# THE SOMNOURS TALE.

Here biginneth the Somonour his Tale.

LORDINGES, ther is in Yorkshire, as I
    gesse,
A mersshy contree called Holdernesse,
In which ther wente a limitour aboute, 1711
To preche, and eek to begge, it is no doute.
And so bifel, that on a day this frere
Had preched at a chirche in his manere,
And specially, aboven every thing, 1715
Excited he the peple in his preching
To trentals, and to yeve, for goddes sake,
Wher-with men mighten holy houses
    make, (10)
Ther as divyne service is honoured,
Nat ther as it is wasted and devoured, 1720
Ne ther it nedeth nat for to be yive,
As to possessioners, that mowen live,
Thanked be god, in wele and habundaunce.
'Trentals,' seyde he, 'deliveren fro pen-
    aunce 1724
Hir freendes soules, as wel olde as yonge,
Ye, whan that they been hastily y-songe ;
Nat for to holde a preest joly and gay,
He singeth nat but o masse in a day ; (20)
Delivereth out,' quod he, 'anon the soules;
Ful hard it is with fleshhook or with oules
To been y-clawed, or to brenne or bake ;
Now spede yow hastily, for Cristes sake.'
And whan this frere had seyd al his
    entente,
With *qui cum patre* forth his wey he wente.

Whan folk in chirche had yeve him
    what hem leste, 1735
He wente his wey, no lenger wolde he
    reste,
With scrippe and tipped staf, y-tukked
    hye ; (29)
In every hous he gan to poure and prye,
And beggeth mele, and chese, or elles corn.
His felawe hadde a staf tipped with horn,
A peyre of tables al of yvory, 1741
And a poyntel polisshed fetisly,
And wroot the names alwey, as he stood,
Of alle folk that yaf him any good, 1744
Ascaunces that he wolde for hem preye.
' Yeve us a busshel whete, malt, or reye,
A goddes kechil, or a trip of chese,
Or elles what yow list, we may nat chese ;
A goddes halfpeny or a masse-peny, (41)
Or yeve us of your brawn, if ye have eny ;
A dagon of your blanket, leve dame, 1751
Our suster dere, lo ! here I write your name;
Bacon or beef, or swich thing as ye finde.'
A sturdy harlot wente ay hem bihinde,
That was hir hostes man, and bar a sak,
And what men yaf hem, leyde it on his
    bak. 1756
And whan that he was out at dore anon,
He planed awey the names everichon (50)
That he biforn had writen in his tables ;
He served hem with nyfles and with fables.

'Nay, ther thou lixt, thou Somnour,'
    quod the Frere.                    1761
'Pees,' quod our Host, 'for Cristes
    moder dere ;
Tel forth thy tale and spare it nat at al.'
So thryve I, quod this Somnour, so I shal.—
    So longe he wente hous by hous, til he
Cam til an hous ther he was wont to be
Refresshed more than in an hundred
    placis.                            1767
Sik lay the gode man, whos that the place
    is ;                                (60)
Bedrede up-on a couche lowe he lay.
'Deus hic,' quod he, 'O Thomas, freend,
    good day,'                         1770
Seyde this frere curteisly and softe.
'Thomas,' quod he, 'god yelde yow ! ful
    ofte
Have I up-on this bench faren ful weel.
Here have I eten many a mery meel ; '
And fro the bench he droof awey the cat,
And leyde adoun his potente and his hat,
And eek his scrippe, and sette him softe
    adoun.                             1777
His felawe was go walked in-to toun, (70)
Forth with his knave, in-to that hostelrye
Wher-as he shoop him thilke night to lye.
'O dere maister,' quod this syke man,
'How han ye fare sith that March bigan ?
I saugh yow noght this fourtenight or
    more.'
'God woot,' quod he, 'laboured have I ful
    sore ;
And specially, for thy savacioun      1785
Have I seyd many a precious orisoun,
And for our othere frendes, god hem
    blesse !
I have to-day been at your chirche at
    messe,                              (80)
And seyd a sermon after my simple wit,
Nat al after the text of holy writ ;   1790
For it is hard to yow, as I suppose,
And therfore wol I teche yow al the glose.
Glosinge is a glorious thing, certeyn,
For lettre sleeth, so as we clerkes seyn.
Ther have I taught hem to be charitable,
And spende hir good ther it is resonable,
And ther I saugh our dame ; a ! wher
    is she ?'                           (89) 1797
'Yond in the yerd I trowe that she be,'
Seyde this man, 'and she wol come anon.'

'Ey, maister ! wel-come be ye, by seint
    John !'                            1800
Seyde this wyf, 'how fare ye hertely ?'
    The frere aryseth up ful curteisly,
And hir embraceth in his armes narwe,
And kiste hir swete, and chirketh as
    a sparwe
With his lippes : 'dame,' quod he, 'right
    weel,                              1805
As he that is your servant every deel.
Thanked be god, that yow yaf soule and lyf,
Yet saugh I nat this day so fair a wyf (100)
In al the chirche, god so save me !'
'Ye, god amende defautes, sir,' quod she,
'Algates wel-come be ye, by my fey !' 1811
'Graunt mercy, dame, this have I founde
    alwey.
But of your grete goodnesse, by your
    leve,
I wolde prey yow that ye nat yow greve,
I wol with Thomas speke a litel throwe.
Thise curats been ful necligent and slowe
To grope tendrely a conscience. (109) 1817
In shrift, in preching is my diligence,
And studie in Petres wordes, and in Poules.
I walke, and fisshe Cristen mennes soules,
To yelden Jesu Crist his propre rente ; 1821
To sprede his word is set al myn en-
    tente.'
'Now, by your leve, o dere sir,' quod she,
'Chydeth him weel, for seinte Trinitee.
He is as angry as a pissemyre,       1825
Though that he have al that he can
    desyre.
Though I him wrye a-night and make
    him warm,                          (119)
And on hym leye my leg outher myn arm,
He groneth lyk our boor, lyth in our sty.
Other desport right noon of him have I ;
I may nat plese him in no maner cas.'
'O Thomas ! Je vous dy, Thomas !
    Thomas !
This maketh the feend, this moste ben
    amended.
Ire is a thing that hye god defended, 1834
And ther-of wol I speke a word or two.'
'Now maister,' quod the wyf, 'er that
    I go,
What wol ye dyne ? I wol go ther-aboute.'
'Now dame,' quod he, 'Je vous dy sanz
    doute,                            (130)

Have I nat of a capon but the livere,
And of your softe breed nat but a shivere,
And after that a rosted pigges heed, 1841
(But that I nolde no beest for me were
   deed),
Thanne hadde I with yow hoomly suffi-
   saunce.
I am a man of litel sustenaunce.
My spirit hath his fostring in the Bible.
The body is ay so redy and penyble 1846
To wake, that my stomak is destroyed.
I prey yow, dame, ye be nat anoyed, (140)
Though I so freendly yow my conseil
   shewe ;              1849
By god, I wolde nat telle it but a fewe.'
   'Now, sir,' quod she, 'but o word er I go;
My child is deed with-inne thise wykes
   two,
Sone after that ye wente out of this toun.'
   'His deeth saugh I by revelacioun,' 1854
Seith this frere, ' at hoom in our dortour.
I dar wel seyn that, er that half an hour
After his deeth, I saugh him born to blisse
In myn avisioun, so god me wisse !  (150)
So dide our sexteyn and our fermerer,
That han been trewe freres fifty yeer ;
They may now, god be thanked of his
   lone,                  1861
Maken hir jubilee and walke allone.
And up I roos, and al our covent eke,
With many a tere trikling on my cheke,
Withouten noyse or clateringe of belles ;
*Te deum* was our song and no-thing elles,
Save that to Crist I seyde an orisoun,
Thankinge him of his revelacioun.  (160)
For sir and dame, trusteth me right weel,
Our orisons been more effectueel,    1870
And more we seen of Cristes secree thinges
Than burel folk, al-though they weren
   kinges.
We live in povert and in abstinence,
And burel folk in richesse and despence
Of mete and drinke, and in hir foul delyt.
We han this worldes lust al in despyt.
Lazar and Dives liveden diversly,    1877
And diverse guerdon hadden they ther-by.
Who-so wol preye, he moot faste and be
   clene,              (171) 1879
And fatte his soule and make his body lene.
We fare as seith th'apostle; cloth and fode
Suffysen us, though they be nat ful gode.

The clennesse and the fastinge of us freres
Maketh that Crist accepteth our preyeres.
   Lo, Moyses fourty dayes and fourty
   night                  1885
Fasted, er that the heighe god of might
Spak with him in the mountain of Sinay.
With empty wombe, fastinge many a day,
Receyved he the lawe that was writen (181)
With goddes finger ; and Elie, wel ye
   witen,                 1890
In mount Oreb, er he hadde any speche
With hye god, that is our lyves leche,
He fasted longe and was in contemplaunce.
   Aaron, that hadde the temple in govern-
   aunce,                 1894
And eek the othere preestes everichon,
In-to the temple whan they sholde gon
To preye for the peple, and do servyse,
They nolden drinken, in no maner wyse,
No drinke, which that mighte hem dronke
   make,              (191) 1899
But there in abstinence preye and wake,
Lest that they deyden ; tak heed what
   I seye.
But they be sobre that for the peple preye,
War that I seye ; namore ! for it suffyseth.
Our lord Jesu, as holy writ devyseth, 1904
Yaf us ensample of fastinge and preyeres.
Therfor we mendinants, we sely freres,
Been wedded to poverte and continence,
To charitee, humblesse, and abstinence,
To persecucion for rightwisnesse, (201) 1909
To wepinge, misericorde, and clennesse.
And therfor may ye see that our preyeres—
I speke of us, we mendinants, we freres—
Ben to the hye god more acceptable
Than youres, with your festes at the table.
Fro Paradys first, if I shal nat lye,   1915
Was man out chaced for his glotonye ;
And chaast was man in Paradys, certeyn.
   But herkne now, Thomas, what I shal
   seyn.                (210)
I ne have no text of it, as I suppose,
But I shall finde it in a maner glose, 1920
That specially our swete lord Jesus
Spak this by freres, whan he seyde thus :
" Blessed be they that povre in spirit
   been."
And so forth al the gospel may ye seen,
Wher it be lyker our professioun,   1925
Or hirs that swimmen in possessioun.

Fy on hir pompe and on hir glotonye !
And for hir lewednesse I hem diffye. (220)
  Me thinketh they ben lyk Jovinian,
Fat as a whale, and walkinge as a swan ;
Al vinolent as botel in the spence.   1931
Hir preyer is of ful gret reverence ;
Whan they for soules seye the psalm of
    Davit,
Lo, " buf ! " they seye, " *cor meum eruc-
    tavit !* "
Who folweth Cristes gospel and his fore,
But we that humble been and chast and
    pore,               1936
Werkers of goddes word, not auditours ?
Therfore, right as an hauk up, at a
    sours,         (230)
Up springeth in-to their, right so prayeres
Of charitable and chaste bisy freres 1940
Maken hir sours to goddes eres two.
Thomas ! Thomas ! so mote I ryde or go,
And by that lord that clepid is seint Yve,
Nere thou our brother, sholdestou nat
    thryve !         1944
In our chapitre praye we day and night
To Crist, that he thee sende hele and
    might,
Thy body for to welden hastily.'
  ' God woot,' quod he, ' no-thing ther-of
    fele I ;       (240)
As help me Crist, as I, in fewe yeres, 1949
Han spended, up-on dyvers maner freres,
Ful many a pound ; yet fare I never the
    bet.
Certeyn, my good have I almost biset.
Farwel, my gold ! for it is al ago ! '
  The frere answerde, ' O Thomas, dostow
    so ?       1954
What nedeth yow diverse freres seche ?
What nedeth him that hath a parfit leche
To sechen othere leches in the toun ?
Your inconstance is your confusioun. (250)
Holde ye than me, or elles our covent,
To praye for yow ben insufficient ?  1960
Thomas, that jape nis nat worth a myte ;
Your maladye is for we han to lyte.
" A ! yif that covent half a quarter otes ! "
" A ! yif that covent four and twenty
    grotes ! "
" A ! yif that frere a peny, and lat him
    go ! "      1965
Nay, nay, Thomas ! it may no-thing be so.

What is a ferthing worth parted in twelve ?
Lo, ech thing that is oned in him-selve
Is more strong than whan it is to-
    scatered.    (261)
Thomas, of me thou shalt nat been y-
    flatered ;      1970
Thou woldest han our labour al for noght.
The hye god, that al this world hath
    wroght,
Seith that the werkman worthy is his
    hyre.
Thomas ! noght of your tresor I desyre
As for my-self, but that al our covent 1975
To preye for yow is ay so diligent,
And for to builden Cristes owene chirche.
Thomas ! if ye wol lernen for to wirche,
Of buildinge up of chirches may ye
    finde      (271)
If it be good, in Thomas lyf of Inde. 1980
Ye lye heer, ful of anger and of yre,
With which the devel set your herte
    a-fyre,
And chyden heer this sely innocent,
Your wyf, that is so meke and pacient.
And therfor, Thomas, trowe me if thee
    leste,      1985
Ne stryve nat with thy wyf, as for thy
    beste ;
And ber this word awey now, by thy feith,
Touchinge this thing, lo, what the wyse
    seith :    (280)
" With-in thyn hous ne be thou no leoun ;
To thy subgits do noon oppressioun ; 1990
Ne make thyne aqueyntances nat to flee."
And Thomas, yet eft-sones I charge thee,
Be war from hir that in thy bosom slepeth ;
War fro the serpent that so slyly crepeth
Under the gras, and stingeth subtilly. 1995
Be war, my sone, and herkne paciently,
That twenty thousand men han lost hir
    lyves,
For stryving with hir lemmans and hir
    wyves.    (290)
Now sith ye han so holy and meke a wyf,
What nedeth yow, Thomas, to maken
    stryf ?      2000
Ther nis, y-wis, no serpent so cruel,
Whan man tret on his tayl, ne half so fel,
As womman is, whan she hath caught
    an ire ;
Vengeance is thanne al that they desyre.

Ire is a sinne, oon of the grete of sevene,
Abhominable un-to the god of hevene ;
And to him-self it is destruccion.
This every lewed viker or person    (300)
Can seye, how Ire engendreth homicyde.
Ire is, in sooth, executour of pryde.   2010
I coude of Ire seye so muche sorwe,
My tale sholde laste til to-morwe.
And therfor preye I god bothe day and
    night,                     2013
An irous man, god sende him litel might !
It is greet harm and, certes, gret pitee,
To sette an irous man in heigh degree.
    Whilom ther was an irous potestat,
As seith Senek, that, duringe his estaat,
Up-on a day out riden knightes two, (311)
And as fortune wolde that it were so, 2020
That oon of hem cam hoom, that other
    noght.
Anon the knight bifore the juge is broght,
That seyde thus, " thou hast thy felawe
    slayn,
For which I deme thee to the deeth, cer-
    tayn."
And to another knight comanded he, 2025
" Go lede him to the deeth, I charge thee."
And happed, as they wente by the weye
Toward the place ther he sholde deye,
The knight cam, which men wenden had
    be deed.                  (321)
Thanne thoughte they, it was the beste
    reed,                  2030
To lede hem bothe to the juge agayn.
They seiden, " lord. the knight ne hath
    nat slayn
His felawe ; here he standeth hool alyve."
" Ye shul be deed," quod he, " so moot I
    thryve !
That is to seyn, bothe oon, and two, and
    three ! "                2035
And to the firste knight right thus spak he,
" I dampned thee, thou most algate be
    deed.
And thou also most nedes lese thyn heed,
For thou art cause why thy felawe deyth."
And to the thridde knight right thus he
    seyth,           (332) 2040
" Thou hast nat doon that I comanded
    thee."
And thus he dide don sleen hem alle three.
    Irous Cambyses was eek dronkelewe,

And ay delyted him to been a shrewe.
And so bifel, a lord of his meynee,   2045
That lovede vertuous moralitee,
Seyde on a day bitwix hem two right thus :
" A lord is lost, if he be vicious ;    (340)
And dronkenesse is eek a foul record
Of any man, and namely in a lord.   2050
Ther is ful many an eye and many an ere
Awaiting on a lord, and he noot where.
For goddes love, drink more attemprely ;
Wyn maketh man to lesen wrecchedly
His minde, and eek his limes everichon."
    "The revers shaltou se," quod he, " anon ;
And preve it, by thyn owene experience,
That wyn ne dooth to folk no swich
    offence.             (350) 2058
Ther is no wyn bireveth me my might
Of hand ne foot, ne of myn eyen sight "—
And, for despyt, he drank ful muchel more
An hondred part than he had doon bifore ;
And right anon, this irous cursed wrecche
Leet this knightes sone bifore him feeche,
Comandinge him he sholde bifore him
    stonde.               2065
And sodeynly he took his bowe in honde,
And up the streng he pulled to his ere,
And with an arwe he slow the child right
    there :               (360)
" Now whether have I a siker hand or
    noon ? "
Quod he, " is al my might and minde
    agoon?              2070
Hath wyn bireved me myn eyen sight ? "
    What sholde I telle th'answere of the
    knight ?
His sone was slayn, ther is na-more to seye.
Beth war therfor with lordes how ye pleye.
Singeth Placebo, and I shal, if I can, 2075
But-if it be un-to a povre man.
To a povre man men sholde hise vyces telle,
But nat to a lord, thogh he sholde go to
    helle.              (370)
    Lo irous Cirus, thilke Percien,
How he destroyed the river of Gysen, 2080
For that an hors of his was dreynt ther-
    inne,
Whan that he wente Babiloigne to winne.
He made that the river was so smal,
That wommen mighte wade it over-al.
Lo, what seyde he, that so wel teche can?
" Ne be no felawe to an irous man,   2086

Ne with no wood man walke by the weye,
Lest thee repente ; " ther is na-more to
   seye. (380)
  Now Thomas, leve brother, lef thyn ire ;
Thou shalt me finde as just as is a squire.
Hold nat the develes knyf ay at thyn herte ;
Thyn angre dooth thee al to sore smerte ;
But shewe to me al thy confessioun.'
  ' Nay,' quod the syke man, ' by Seint
   Simoun ! 2094
I have be shriven this day at my curat ;
I have him told al hoolly myn estat ;
Nedeth na-more to speke of it,' seith he,
' But if me list of myn humilitee.' (390)
  ' Yif me thanne of thy gold, to make
   our cloistre,'
Quod he, ' for many a muscle and many
   an oistre, 2100
Whan other men han ben ful wel at eyse,
Hath been our fode, our cloistre for to reyse.
And yet, god woot, unnethe the fundement
Parfourned is, ne of our pavement 2104
Nis nat a tyle yet with-inne our wones ;
By god, we owen fourty pound for stones !
Now help, Thomas, for him that harwed
   helle !
For elles moste we our bokes selle. (400)
And if ye lakke our predicacioun, 2109
Than gooth the world al to destruccioun.
For who-so wolde us fro this world bireve,
So god me save, Thomas, by your leve,
He wolde bireve out of this world the sonne.
For who can teche and werchen as we
   conne ? 2114
And that is nat of litel tyme,' quod he ;
' But sith that Elie was, or Elisee,
Han freres been, that finde I of record,
In charitee, y-thanked be our lord. (410)
Now Thomas, help, for seinte Charitee !'
And doun anon he sette him on his knee.
  This syke man wex wel ny wood for ire ;
He wolde that the frere had been on-fire
With his false dissimulacioun.
' Swich thing as is in my possessioun,'
Quod he, ' that may I yeven, and non
   other. 2125
Ye sey me thus, how that I am your
   brother ? '
  ' Ye, certes,' quod the frere, ' trusteth
   weel ;
I took our dame our lettre with our seel.'

' Now wel,' quod he, ' and som-what
   shal I yive (421)
Un-to your holy covent whyl I live, 2130
And in thyn hand thou shalt it have
   anoon ;
On this condicioun, and other noon,
That thou departe it so, my dere brother,
That every frere have also muche as other.
This shaltou swere on thy professioun,
With-outen fraude or cavillacioun.' 2136
  ' I swere it,' quod this frere, ' upon my
   feith ! '
And ther-with-al his hand in his he leith :
' Lo, heer my feith ! in me shal be no lak.'
  ' Now thanne, put thyn hand doun by
   my bak,' (432) 2140
Seyde this man, ' and grope wel bihinde ;
Bynethe my buttok ther shaltow finde
A thing that I have hid in privetee.'
  ' A ! ' thoghte this frere, ' this shal go
   with me ! '
And doun his hand he launcheth to the
   clifte, 2145
In hope for to finde ther a yifte. (438)
And whan this syke man felte this frere
Aboute his tuwel grope there and here,
Amidde his hand he leet the frere a fart.
Ther nis no capul, drawinge in a cart, 2150
That mighte have lete a fart of swich
   a soun.
  The frere up stirte as doth a wood
   leoun :
' A ! false cherl,' quod he, ' for goddes
   bones,
This hastow for despyt doon, for the
   nones !
Thou shalt abye this fart, if that I may !'
  His meynee, whiche that herden this
   affray, 2156
Cam lepinge in, and chaced out the frere ;
And forth he gooth, with a ful angry
   chere, (450)
And fette his felawe, ther-as lay his stoor.
He looked as it were a wilde boor ; 2160
He grinte with his teeth, so was he wrooth.
A sturdy pas doun to the court he gooth,
Wher-as ther woned a man of greet
   honour,
To whom that he was alwey confessour ;
This worthy man was lord of that village.
This frere cam, as he were in a rage, 2166

Wher-as this lord sat eting at his bord.
Unnethes mighte the frere speke a word,
Til atte laste he seyde : 'god yow see!' (461)
    This lord gan loke, and seide, 'ben'-
        cite!    2170
What, frere John, what maner world is
    this?
I see wel that som thing ther is amis.
Ye loken as the wode were ful of thevis,
Sit doun anon, and tel me what your
    greef is,
And it shal been amended, if I may.' 2175
    'I have,' quod he, 'had a despyt this day,
God yelde yow! adoun in your village,
That in this world is noon so povre a page,
That he nolde have abhominacioun (471)
Of that I have receyved in your toun. 2180
And yet ne greveth me no-thing so sore,
As that this olde cherl, with lokkes hore,
Blasphemed hath our holy covent eke.'
    'Now, maister,' quod this lord, 'I yow
        biseke.'
    'No maister, sire,' quod he, 'but servi-
        tour,    2185
Thogh I have had in scole swich honour.
God lyketh nat that "Raby" men us calle,
Neither in market ne in your large halle.'
    'No fors,' quod he, 'but tel me al your
        grief.'    (481)
    'Sire,' quod this frere, 'an odious mes-
        chief    2190
This day bitid is to myn ordre and me,
And so *per consequens* to ech degree
Of holy chirche, god amende it sone !'
    'Sir,' quod the lord, 'ye woot what is
        to done.
Distempre yow noght, ye be my con-
        fessour;    2195
Ye been the salt of the erthe and the
    savour.
For goddes love your pacience ye holde ;
Tel me your grief :' and he anon him
    tolde,    (490)
As ye han herd biforn, ye woot wel what.
    The lady of the hous ay stille sat,   2200
Til she had herd al what the frere sayde :
'Ey, goddes moder,' quod she, 'blisful
    mayde !
Is ther oght elles? telle me feithfully.'
    'Madame,' quod he, 'how thinketh yow
        her-by?'

    'How that me thinketh?' quod she;
      'so god me speede,    2205
I seye, a cherl hath doon a cherles dede.
What shold I seye? god lat him never
    thee !
His syke heed is ful of vanitee,    (500)
I hold him in a maner frenesye.'
    'Madame,' quod he, 'by god I shal nat
      lye ;    2210
But I on other weyes may be wreke,
I shal diffame him over-al ther I speke,
This false blasphemour, that charged me
To parte that wol nat departed be,
To every man y-liche, with meschaunce !'
    The lord sat stille as he were in a
      traunce,    2216
And in his herte he rolled up and doun,
'How hadde this cherl imaginacioun (510)
To shewe swich a probleme to the frere?
Never erst er now herde I of swich matere ;
I trowe the devel putte it in his minde.
In ars-metryke shal ther no man finde,
Biforn this day, of swich a questioun.
Who sholde make a demonstracioun,
That every man sholde have y-liche his
      part    2225
As of the soun or savour of a fart? (518)
O nyce proude cherl, I shrewe his face !
Lo, sires,' quod the lord, with harde grace,
'Who ever herde of swich a thing er now?
To every man y-lyke? tel me how.   2230
It is an inpossible, it may nat be !
Ey, nyce cherl, god lete him never thee !
The rumblinge of a fart, and every soun,
Nis but of eir reverberacioun,    2234
And ever it wasteth lyte and lyte awey.
Ther is no man can demen, by my fey,
If that it were departed equally.   (529)
What, lo, my cherl, lo, yet how shrewedly
Un-to my confessour to-day he spak !
I holde him certeyn a demoniak !   2240
Now ete your mete, and lat the cherl go
    pleye,
Lat him go honge himself, a devel weye !'
    Now stood the lordes squyer at the bord,
That carf his mete, and herde, word by
    word,    2244
Of alle thinges of which I have yow sayd.
'My lord,' quod he, 'be ye nat yvel apayd ;
I coude telle, for a goune-clooth,
To yow, sir frere, so ye be nat wrooth, (540)

How that this fart sholde even deled be
Among your covent, if it lyked me.'　2250
　'Tel,' quod the lord, 'and thou shalt
　　have anon
A goune-cloth, by god and by Seint John!'
　'My lord,' quod he, 'whan that the
　　weder is fair,
With-outen wind or perturbinge of air,
Lat bringe a cartwheel here in-to this
　　halle,　2255
But loke that it have his spokes alle.
Twelf spokes hath a cartwheel comunly.
And bring me than twelf freres, woot ye
　　why?　(550)
For thrittene is a covent, as I gesse.
The confessour heer, for his worthinesse,
Shal parfourne up the nombre of his
　　covent.　2261
Than shal they knele doun, by oon assent,
And to every spokes ende, in this manere,
Ful sadly leye his nose shal a frere.
Your noble confessour, ther god him save,
Shal holde his nose upright, under the
　　nave.　2266
Than shal this cherl, with bely stif and
　　toght
As any tabour, hider been y-broght；(560)
And sette him on the wheel right of this
　　cart,　2269
Upon the nave, and make him lete a fart.

And ye shul seen, up peril of my lyf,
By preve which that is demonstratif,
That equally the soun of it wol wende,
And eek the stink, un-to the spokes
　　ende；
Save that this worthy man, your con-
　　fessour,　2275
By-cause he is a man of greet honour,
Shal have the firste fruit, as reson is；
The noble usage of freres yet is this, (570)
The worthy men of hem shul first be
　　served；　2279
And certeinly, he hath it weel deserved.
He hath to-day taught us so muchel good
With preching in the pulpit ther he stood,
That I may vouche-sauf, I sey for me,
He hadde the firste smel of fartes three,
And so wolde al his covent hardily；　2285
He bereth him so faire and holily.'
　The lord, the lady, and ech man, save
　　the frere,　(579)
Seyde that Jankin spak, in this matere,
As wel as Euclide or [as] Ptholomee.
Touchinge this cherl, they seyde, subtiltee
And heigh wit made him speken as he
　　spak；　2291
He nis no fool, ne no demoniak.
And Jankin hath y-wonne a newe goune.—
My tale is doon　we been almost at
　　toune.　2294

**Here endeth the Somnours Tale.**

# GROUP E.

# THE CLERK'S PROLOGUE.

### Here folweth the Prologe of the Clerkes Tale of Oxenford.

'Sir clerk of Oxenford,' our hoste sayde,
'Ye ryde as coy and stille as dooth a
    mayde,
Were newe spoused, sitting at the bord ;
This day ne herde I of your tonge a word.
I trowe ye studie aboute som sophyme, 5
But Salomon seith, "every thing hath
    tyme."
    For goddes sake, as beth of bettre chere,
It is no tyme for to studien here.
Telle us som mery tale, by your fey ;
For what man that is entred in a pley, 10
He nedes moot unto the pley assente.
But precheth nat, as freres doon in Lente,
To make us for our olde sinnes wepe,
Ne that thy tale make us nat to slepe.
    Telle us som mery thing of aventures ;—
Your termes, your colours, and your
    figures,            16
Kepe hem in stoor til so be ye endyte
Heigh style, as whan that men to kinges
    wryte.
Speketh so pleyn at this tyme, I yow preye,
That we may understonde what ye seye.'
    This worthy clerk benignely answerde,
'Hoste,' quod he, 'I am under your yerde ;
Ye han of us as now the governaunce,
And therfor wol I do yow obeisaunce,
As fer as reson axeth, hardily.     25
I wol yow telle a tale which that I
Lerned at Padowe of a worthy clerk,
As preved by his wordes and his werk.

He is now deed and nayled in his cheste,
I prey to god so yeve his soule reste !   30
    Fraunceys Petrark, the laureat poete,
Highte this clerk, whos rethoryke sweete
Enlumined al Itaille of poetrye,
As Linian dide of philosophye
Or lawe, or other art particuler ;     35
But deeth, that wol nat suffre us dwellen
    heer
But as it were a twinkling of an yë,
Hem bothe hath slayn, and alle shul we
    dyë.
    But forth to tellen of this worthy man,
That taughte me this tale, as I bigan, 40
I seye that first with heigh style he
    endyteth,
Er he the body of his tale wryteth,
A proheme, in the which discryveth he
Pemond, and of Saluces the contree,   44
And speketh of Apennyn, the hilles hye,
That been the boundes of West Lum-
    bardye,
And of Mount Vesulus in special,
Where as the Poo, out of a welle smal,
Taketh his firste springing and his sours,
That estward ay encresseth in his cours 50
To Emelward, to Ferrare, and Venyse :
The which a long thing were to devyse.
And trewely, as to my jugement,
Me thinketh it a thing impertinent,
Save that he wol conveyen his matere : 55
But this his tale, which that ye may here.'

# THE CLERKES TALE.

### Here biginneth the Tale of the Clerk of Oxenford.

Ther is, at the west syde of Itaille,
Doun at the rote of Vesulus the colde,
A lusty playne, habundant of vitaille,
Wher many a tour and toun thou mayst
 biholde,      60
That founded were in tyme of fadres olde,
And many another delitable sighte,
And Saluces this noble contree highte.

A markis whylom lord was of that londe,
As were his worthy eldres him bifore ; 65
And obeisant and redy to his honde  (10)
Were alle his liges, bothe lasse and more.
Thus in delyt he liveth, and hath don yore,
Biloved and drad, thurgh favour of for-
 tune,      69
Bothe of his lordes and of his commune.

Therwith he was, to speke as of linage,
The gentilleste y-born of Lumbardye,
A fair persone, and strong, and yong of
 age,
And ful of honour and of curteisye ;
Discreet y-nogh his contree for to gye, 75
Save in somme thinges that he was to
 blame,      (20)
And Walter was this yonge lordes name.

I blame him thus, that he considereth
 noght      78
In tyme cominge what mighte him bityde,
But on his lust present was al his thoght,
As for to hauke and hunte on every syde ;
Wel ny alle othere cures leet he slyde,
And eek he nolde, and that was worst of
 alle,      (27)
Wedde no wyf, for noght that may bifalle.

Only that point his peple bar so sore,  85
That flokmele on a day they to him wente,
And oon of hem, that wysest was of lore,
Or elles that the lord best wolde assente

That he sholde telle him what his peple
 mente,      89
Or elles coude he shewe wel swich matere,
He to the markis seyde as ye shul here.

' O noble markis, your humanitee
Assureth us and yeveth us hardinesse,
As ofte as tyme is of necessitee  94
That we to yow mowe telle our hevinesse
Accepteth, lord, now for your gentillesse.
That wo with pitous herte un-to yow
 pleyne,      (41)
And lete your eres nat my voys disdeyne.

Al have I noght to done in this matere
More than another man hath in this place,
Yet for as muche as ye, my lord so
 dere,      101
Han alwey shewed me favour and grace,
I dar the better aske of yow a space
Of audience, to shewen our requeste,
And ye, my lord, to doon right as yow
 leste.      105

For certes, lord, so wel us lyketh yow (50)
And al your werk and ever han doon,
 that we
Ne coude nat us self devysen how
We mighte liven in more felicitee,
Save o thing, lord, if it your wille be, 110
That for to been a wedded man yow leste,
Than were your peple in sovereyn hertes
 reste.

Boweth your nekke under that blisful yok
Of soveraynetee, noght of servyse,
Which that men clepeth spousaille or
 wedlok ;      115
And thenketh, lord, among your thoghtes
 wyse,      (60)
How that our dayes passe in sondry wyse ;

For though we slepe or wake, or rome, or
    ryde,
Ay fleeth the tyme, it nil no man abyde.

And though your grene youthe floure as
    yit,    120
In crepeth age alwey, as stille as stoon,
And deeth manaceth every age, and smit
In ech estaat, for ther escapeth noon :
And al so certein as we knowe echoon
That we shul deye, as uncerteyn we alle
Been of that day whan deeth shal on us
    falle.    (70) 126

Accepteth than of us the trewe entente,
That never yet refuseden your heste,
And we wol, lord, if that ye wol assente,
Chese yow a wyf in short tyme, atte leste,
Born of the gentilleste and of the meste
Of al this lond, so that it oghte seme
Honour to god and yow, as we can deme.

Deliver us out of al this bisy drede,
And tak a wyf, for hye goddes sake ;  135
For if it so bifelle, as god forbede,    (80)
That thurgh your deeth your linage
    sholde slake,
And that a straunge successour sholde
    take
Your heritage, o ! wo were us alyve !
Wherfor we pray you hastily to wyve.' 140

Hir meke preyere and hir pitous chere
Made the markis herte han pitee.
' Ye wol,' quod he, ' myn owene peple
    dere,
To that I never erst thoghte streyne me.
I me rejoysed of my libertee,    145
That selde tyme is founde in mariage ; (90)
Ther I was free, I moot been in servage.

But nathelees I see your trewe entente,
And truste upon your wit, and have don ay ;
Wherfor of my free wil I wol assente  150
To wedde me, as sone as ever I may.
But ther-as ye han profred me to-day
To chese me a wyf, I yow relesse
That choys, and prey yow of that profre
    cesse.    154

For god it woot, that children ofte been
Unlyk her worthy eldres hem bifore ; (100)

Bountee comth al of god, nat of the streen
Of which they been engendred and y-bore ;
I truste in goddes bountee, and therfore
My mariage and myn estaat and reste 160
I him bitake ; he may don as him leste.

Lat me alone in chesinge of my wyf,
That charge up-on my bak I wol endure ;
But I yow preye, and charge up-on your lyf,
That what wyf that I take, ye me assure
To worshipe hir, whyl that hir lyf may
    dure,    (110) 166
In word and werk, bothe here and every-
    where,
As she an emperoures doghter were.

And forthermore, this shal ye swere, that
    ye
Agayn my choys shul neither grucche ne
    stryve ;    170
For sith I shal forgoon my libertee
At your requeste, as ever moot I thryve,
Ther as myn herte is set, ther wol I wyve ;
And but ye wole assente in swich manere,
I prey yow, speketh na-more of this
    matere.'    (119) 175

With hertly wil they sworen, and assenten
To al this thing, ther seyde no wight nay ;
Bisekinge him of grace, er that they
    wenten,
That he wolde graunten hem a certein day
Of his spousaille, as sone as ever he may ;
For yet alwey the peple som-what dredde
Lest that this markis no wyf wolde wedde.

He graunted hem a day, swich as him
    leste,
On which he wolde be wedded sikerly, 184
And seyde, he dide al this at hir requeste ;
And they, with humble entente, buxomly,
Knelinge up-on her knees ful reverently
Him thanken alle, and thus they han an
    ende    (132)
Of hir entente, and hoom agayn they
    wende.

And heer-up-on he to his officeres    190
Comaundeth for the feste to purveye,
And to his privee knightes and squyeres
Swich charge yaf, as him liste on hem leye :

And they to his comandement obeye,
And ech of hem doth al his diligence　195
To doon un-to the feste reverence.　(140)

### Explicit prima pars.

### Incipit secunda pars.

Noght fer fro thilke paleys honurable
Ther-as this markis shoop his mariage,
Ther stood a throp, of site delitable,
In which that povre folk of that village 200
Hadden hir bestes and hir herbergage,
And of hir labour took hir sustenance
After that th'erthe yaf hem habundance.

Amonges thise povre folk ther dwelte
　　a man
Which that was holden povrest of hem
　　alle;　　　　　　　　　　　　　　205
But hye god som tyme senden can　(150)
His grace in-to a litel oxes stalle :
Janicula men of that throp him calle.
A doghter hadde he, fair y-nogh to sighte,
And Grisildis this yonge mayden highte.

But for to speke of vertuous beautee,　211
Than was she oon the faireste under
　　sonne ;
For povreliche y-fostred up was she,
No likerous lust was thurgh hir herte
　　y-ronne ;　　　　　　　　　　(158) 214
Wel ofter of the welle than of the tonne
She drank, and for she wolde vertu plese,
She knew wel labour, but non ydel ese.

But thogh this mayde tendre were of age,
Yet in the brest of hir virginitee
Ther was enclosed rype and sad corage ;
And in greet reverence and charitee　221
Hir olde povre fader fostred she ;
A fewe sheep spinning on feeld she kepte,
She wolde noght been ydel til she slepte.

And whan she hoomward cam, she wolde
　　bringe　　　　　　　　　　　　225
Wortes or othere herbes tymes ofte,　(170)
The whiche she shredde and seeth for hir
　　livinge,
And made hir bed ful harde and no-thing
　　softe ;
And ay she kepte hir fadres lyf on-lofte
With everich obeisaunce and diligence 230
That child may doon to fadres reverence.

Up-on Grisilde, this povre creature,
Ful ofte sythe this markis sette his yë
As he on hunting rood paraventure ;　234
And whan it fil that he mighte hir espye,
He noght with wantoun loking of folye
His yën caste on hir, but in sad wyse (181)
Up-on hir chere he wolde him ofte avyse,

Commending in his herte hir womman-
　　hede,
And eek hir vertu, passing any wight 240
Of so yong age, as wel in chere as dede.
For thogh the peple have no greet insight
In vertu, he considered ful right
Hir bountee, and disposed that he wolde
Wedde hir only, if ever he wedde sholde.

The day of wedding cam, but no wight
　　can　　　　　　　　　　　　(190) 246
Telle what womman that it sholde be ;
For which merveille wondred many a man,
And seyden, whan they were in privetee,
' Wol nat our lord yet leve his vanitee ? 250
Wol he nat wedde ? allas, allas the whyle !
Why wol he thus him-self and us bigyle ? '

But natheles this markis hath don make
Of gemmes, set in gold and in asure,
Broches and ringes, for Grisildis sake, 255
And of hir clothing took he the mesure
By a mayde, lyk to hir stature,　　(201)
And eek of othere ornamentes alle
That un-to swich a wedding sholde falle.

The tyme of undern of the same day　260
Approcheth, that this wedding sholde be ;
And al the paleys put was in array,
Bothe halle and chambres, ech in his
　　degree ;
Houses of office stuffed with plentee　264
Ther maystow seen of deyntevous vitaille,
That may be founde, as fer as last Itaille.

This royal markis, richely arrayed,　(211)
Lordes and ladyes in his companye,
The whiche unto the feste were y-prayed,
And of his retenue the bachelrye,　270
With many a soun of sondry melodye,
Un-to the village, of the which I tolde,
In this array the righte wey han holde.

Grisilde of this, god woot, ful innocent,
That for hir shapen was al this array, 275

To fecchen water at a welle is went, (220)
And cometh hoom as sone as ever she may.
For wel she hadde herd seyd, that thilke
    day
The markis sholde wedde, and, if she
    mighte,
She wolde fayn han seyn som of that
    sighte.      280

She thoghte, ' I wol with othere maydens
    stonde,
That been my felawes, in our dore, and see
The markisesse, and therfor wol I fonde
To doon at hoom, as sone as it may be,
The labour which that longeth un-to me ;
And than I may at leyser hir biholde, 286
If she this wey un-to the castel holde.' (231)

And as she wolde over hir threshfold goon,
The markis cam and gan hir for to calle ;
And she set doun hir water-pot anoon 290
Bisyde the threshfold, in an oxes stalle,
And doun up-on hir knees she gan to falle,
And with sad contenance kneleth stille
Til she had herd what was the lordes wille.

This thoghtful markis spak un-to this
    mayde      (239) 295
Ful sobrely, and seyde in this manere,
' Wher is your fader, Grisildis ? ' he sayde,
And she with reverence, in humble chere,
Answerde, ' lord, he is al redy here.'
And in she gooth with-outen lenger lette,
And to the markis she hir fader fette. 301

He by the hond than took this olde man,
And seyde thus, whan he him hadde
    asyde,
' Janicula, I neither may ne can      304
Lenger the plesance of myn herte hyde.
If that thou vouche-sauf, what-so bityde,
Thy doghter wol I take, er that I wende,
As for my wyf, un-to hir lyves ende. (252)

Thou lovest me, I woot it wel, certeyn,
And art my feithful lige man y-bore ; 310
And al that lyketh me, I dar wel seyn
It lyketh thee, and specially therfore
Tel me that poynt that I have seyd bifore,
If that thou wolt un-to that purpos drawe,
To take me as for thy sone-in-lawe ? ' 315

This sodeyn cas this man astoned so, (260)
That reed he wex, abayst, and al quaking
He stood ; unnethes seyde he wordes mo,
But only thus : ' lord,' quod he, ' my wil-
    ling
Is as ye wole, ne ayeines your lyking 320
I wol no-thing ; ye be my lord so dere ;
Right as yow lust governeth this matere.'

' Yet wol I,' quod this markis softely,
' That in thy chambre I and thou and she
Have a collacion, and wostow why ?      325
For I wol axe if it hir wille be      (270)
To be my wyf, and reule hir after me ;
And al this shal be doon in thy presence,
I wol noght speke out of thyn audience.'

And in the chambre whyl they were
    aboute      330
Hir tretis, which as ye shal after here,
The peple cam un-to the hous with-oute,
And wondred hem in how honest manere
And tentifly she kepte hir fader dere. (278)
But outerly Grisildis wondre mighte, 335
For never erst ne saugh she swich a sighte.

No wonder is thogh that she were astoned
To seen so greet a gest come in that place ;
She never was to swiche gestes woned,
For which she loked with ful pale face.
But shortly forth this tale for to chace,
Thise arn the wordes that the markis
    sayde      342
To this benigne verray feithful mayde.

' Grisilde,' he seyde, ' ye shul wel under-
    stonde
It lyketh to your fader and to me      345
That I yow wedde, and eek it may so
    stonde,      (290)
As I suppose, ye wol that it so be.
But thise demandes axe I first,' quod he,
' That, sith it shal be doon in hastif wyse,
Wol ye assente, or elles yow avyse ?      350

I seye this, be ye redy with good herte
To al my lust, and that I frely may,
As me best thinketh, do yow laughe or
    smerte,
And never ye to grucche it, night ne day ?
And eek whan I sey "ye," ne sey nat
    "nay,"      355

Neither by word ne frowning contenance ;
Swer this, and here I swere our alliance.'

Wondring upon this word, quaking for
   drede,       (302)
She seyde, 'lord, undigne and unworthy
Am I to thilke honour that ye me bede ; 360
But as ye wol your-self, right so wol I.
And heer I swere that never willingly
In werk ne thoght I nil yow disobeye,
For to be deed, though me were looth to
   deye.'       (308) 364

' This is y-nogh, Grisilde myn ! ' quod he.
And forth he gooth with a ful sobre chere
Out at the dore, and after that cam she,
And to the peple he seyde in this manere,
' This is my wyf,' quod he, ' that standeth
  • here.       369
Honoureth hir, and loveth hir, I preye,
Who-so me loveth ; ther is na-more to
   seye.'

And for that no-thing of hir olde gere
She sholde bringe in-to his hous, he bad
That wommen sholde dispoilen hir right
   there ;       (318) 374
Of which thise ladyes were nat right glad
To handle hir clothes wher-in she was clad.
But natheles this mayde bright of hewe
Fro foot to heed they clothed han al newe.

Hir heres han they kembd, that lay un-
   tressed
Ful rudely, and with hir fingres smale 380
A corone on hir heed they han y-dressed,
And sette hir ful of nowches grete and
   smale ;
Of hir array what sholde I make a tale ?
Unnethe the peple hir knew for hir fair-
   nesse,
Whan she translated was in swich rich-
   esse.       385

This markis hath hir spoused with a ring
Broght for the same cause, and than hir
   sette       (331)
Up-on an hors, snow-whyt and wel am-
   bling,
And to his paleys, er he lenger lette,
With joyful peple that hir ladde and
   mette,       390

Conveyed hir, and thus the day they
   spende
In revel, til the sonne gan descende.

And shortly forth this tale for to chace,
I seye that to this newe markisesse
God hath swich favour sent hir of his
   grace,       395
That it ne semed nat by lyklinesse  (340)
That she was born and fed in rudenesse,
As in a cote or in an oxe-stalle,
But norished in an emperoures halle.

To every wight she woxen is so dere  400
And worshipful, that folk ther she was
   bore
And from hir birthe knewe hir yeer by
   yere,
Unnethe trowed they, but dorste han
   swore
That to Janicle, of which I spak bifore,
She doghter nas, for, as by conjecture, 405
Hem thoughte she was another creature.

For thogh that ever vertuous was she, (351)
She was encressed in swich excellence
Of thewes gode, y-set in heigh bountee,
And so discreet and fair of eloquence, 410
So benigne and so digne of reverence,
And coude so the peples herte embrace,
That ech hir lovede that loked on hir face.

Noght only of Saluces in the toun
Publiced was the bountee of hir name, 415
But eek bisyde in many a regioun,  (360)
If oon seyde wel, another seyde the same ;
So spradde of hir heigh bountee the fame,
That men and wommen, as wel yonge as
   olde,
Gon to Saluce, upon hir to biholde.  420

Thus Walter lowly, nay but royally,
Wedded with fortunat honestetee,
In goddes pees liveth ful esily
At hoom, and outward grace y-nogh had
   he ;       (368) 424
And for he saugh that under low degree
Was ofte vertu hid, the peple him helde
A prudent man, and that is seyn ful selde.

Nat only this Grisildis thurgh hir wit
Coude al the feet of wyfly hoomlinesse,

But eek, whan that the cas requyred it,
The commune profit coude she redresse.
Ther nas discord, rancour, ne hevinesse
In al that lond, that she ne coude apese,
And wysly bringe hem alle in reste and
     ese.

Though that hir housbonde absent were
     anoon,      435
If gentil men, or othere of hir contree
Were wrothe, she wolde bringen hem
     atoon ;      (381)
So wyse and rype wordes hadde she,
And jugements of so greet equitee,
That she from heven sent was, as men
     wende,      440
Peple to save and every wrong t'amende.

Nat longe tyme after that this Grisild
Was wedded, she a doughter hath y-bore,
Al had hir lever have born a knave child.
Glad was this markis and the folk ther-
     fore ;      445
For though a mayde child come al bifore,
She may unto a knave child atteyne (391)
By lyklihed, sin she nis nat bareyne.

### Explicit secunda pars.

### Incipit tercia pars.

Ther fil, as it bifalleth tymes mo,
Whan that this child had souked but
     a throwe,      450
This markis in his herte longeth so
To tempte his wyf, hir sadnesse for to
     knowe,
That he ne mighte out of his herte throwe
This merveillous desyr, his wyf t'assaye,
Needless, god woot, he thoughte hir for
     t'affraye.      455

He hadde assayed hir y-nogh bifore, (400)
And fond hir ever good ; what neded it
Hir for to tempte and alwey more and
     more ?
Though som men preise it for a subtil wit,
But as for me, I seye that yvel it sit    460
T'assaye a wyf whan that it is no nede,
And putten her in anguish and in drede.

For which this markis wroghte in this
     manere ;
He cam alone a-night, ther as she lay,

With sterne face and with ful trouble
     chere,      465
And seyde thus, ' Grisild,' quod he, ' that
     day      (410)
That I yow took out of your povre array,
And putte yow in estaat of heigh noblesse,
Ye have nat that forgeten, as I gesse.

I seye, Grisild, this present dignitee, 470
In which that I have put yow, as I trowe,
Maketh yow nat foryetful for to be
That I yow took in povre estaat ful lowe
For any wele ye moot your-selven knowe.
Tak hede of every word that I yow seye,
Ther is no wight that hereth it but we
     tweye.      (420) 476

Ye woot your-self wel, how that ye cam
     here
In-to this hous, it is nat longe ago,
And though to me that ye be lief and
     dere,
Un-to my gentils ye be no-thing so ;    480
They seyn, to hem it is greet shame and
     wo
For to be subgets and ben in servage
To thee, that born art of a smal village.

And namely, sith thy doghter was y-bore,
Thise wordes han they spoken doutelees ;
But I desyre, as I have doon bifore,  (430)
To live my lyf with hem in reste and
     pees ;
I may nat in this caas be recchelees.
I moot don with thy doghter for the
     beste,
Nat as I wolde, but as my peple leste. 490

And yet, god wot, this is ful looth to me ;
But nathelees with-oute your witing
I wol nat doon, but this wol I,' quod he,
' That ye to me assente as in this thing.
Shewe now your pacience in your werking
That ye me highte and swore in your
     village      (440) 496
That day that maked was our mariage.'

Whan she had herd al this, she noght
     ameved
Neither in word, or chere, or counten-
     aunce ;
For, as it semed, she was nat agreved : 500

She seyde, 'lord, al lyth in your ples-
    aunce,
My child and I with hertly obeisaunce
Ben youres al, and ye mowe save or spille
Your owene thing; werketh after your
    wille.                                        504

Ther may no-thing, god so my soule save,
Lyken to yow that may displese me; (450)
Ne I desyre no-thing for to have,
Ne drede for to lese, save only ye;
This wil is in myn herte and ay shal be.
No lengthe of tyme or deeth may this
    deface,                                       510
Ne chaunge my corage to another place.'

Glad was this markis of hir answering,
But yet he feyned as he were nat so;
Al drery was his chere and his loking
Whan that he sholde out of the chambre
    go.                                           515
Sone after this, a furlong wey or two, (460)
He prively hath told al his entente
Un-to a man, and to his wyf him sente.

A maner sergeant was this privee man,
The which that feithful ofte he founden
    hadde                                         520
In thinges grete, and eek swich folk wel
    can
Don execucioun on thinges badde.
The lord knew wel that he him loved and
    dradde;
And whan this sergeant wiste his lordes
    wille,
In-to the chambre he stalked him ful
    stille.                                        525

'Madame,' he seyde, 'ye mote foryeve it
    me,                                           (470)
Thogh I do thing to which I am con-
    streyned;
Ye ben so wys that ful wel knowe ye
That lordes hestes mowe nat been y-
    feyned;
They mowe wel been biwailled or com-
    pleyned,                                       530
But men mot nede un-to her lust obeye,
And so wol I; ther is na-more to seye.

This child I am comanded for to take'—
And spak na-more, but out the child he
    hente

Despitously, and gan a chere make       535
As though he wolde han slayn it er he
    wente.                                        (480)
Grisildis mot al suffren and consente;
And as a lamb she sitteth meke and stille,
And leet this cruel sergeant doon his wille.

Suspecious was the diffame of this man,
Suspect his face, suspect his word also; 541
Suspect the tyme in which he this bigan.
Allas! hir doghter that she lovede so
She wende he wolde han slawen it right
    tho.                                          544
But natheles she neither weep ne syked,
Consenting hir to that the markis lyked.

But atte laste speken she bigan,     (491)
And mekely she to the sergeant preyde,
So as he was a worthy gentil man,
That she moste kisse hir child er that it
    deyde;                                        550
And in her barm this litel child she leyde
With ful sad face, and gan the child to kisse
And lulled it, and after gan it blisse.

And thus she seyde in hir benigne voys,
' Far weel, my child; I shal thee never
    see;                                          555
But, sith I thee have marked with the
    croys,                                        (500)
Of thilke fader blessed mote thou be,
That for us deyde up-on a croys of tree.
Thy soule, litel child, I him bitake,
For this night shaltow dyen for my sake.'

I trowe that to a norice in this cas    561
It had ben hard this rewthe for to se;
Wel mighte a mooder than han cryed
    'allas!'
But nathelees so sad stedfast was she,
That she endured all adversitee,        565
And to the sergeant mekely she sayde, (510)
' Have heer agayn your litel yonge mayde.

Goth now,' quod she, 'and dooth my
    lordes heste,
But o thing wol I preye yow of your grace,
That, but my lord forbad yow, atte leste
Burieth this litel body in som place    571
That bestes ne no briddes it to-race.'
But he no word wol to that purpos seye,
But took the child and wente upon his
    weye.

This sergeant cam un-to his lord ageyn, 575
And of Grisildis wordes and hir chere (520)
He tolde him point for point, in short and
playn,
And him presenteth with his doghter
dere.

Somwhat this lord hath rewthe in his
manere ;
But nathelees his purpos heeld he stille,
As lordes doon, whan they wol han hir
wille ;                              581

And bad his sergeant that he prively
Sholde this child ful softe winde and
wrappe
With alle circumstances tendrely,
And carie it in a cofre or in a lappe ; 585
But, up-on peyne his heed of for to
swappe,                             (530)
That no man sholde knowe of his entente,
Ne whenne he cam, ne whider that he
wente ;

But at Boloigne to his suster dere,
That thilke tyme of Panik was countesse,
He sholde it take, and shewe hir this
matere,                             591
Bisekinge hir to don hir bisinesse
This child to fostre in alle gentilesse ;
And whos child that it was he bad hir
hyde
From every wight, for oght that may
bityde.                             595

The sergeant gooth, and hath fulfild this
thing ;                             (540)
But to this markis now retourne we ;
For now goth he ful faste imagining
If by his wyves chere he mighte see,
Or by hir word aperceyve that she 600
Were chaunged ; but he never hir coude
finde
But ever in oon y-lyke sad and kinde.

As glad, as humble, as bisy in servyse,
And eek in love as she was wont to be,
Was she to him in every maner wyse ; 605
Ne of hir doghter noght a word spak she.
Non accident for noon adversitee (551)
Was seyn in hir, ne never hir doghter
name
Ne nempned she, in ernest nor in game.
**Explicit tercia pars.**

## Sequitur pars quarta.

In this estaat ther passed been foure
yeer
Er she with childe was ; but, as god wolde,
A knave child she bar by this Walter,
Ful gracious and fair for to biholde.
And whan that folk it to his fader tolde,
Nat only he, but al his contree, merie 615
Was for this child, and god they thanke
and herie.                          (560)

Whan it was two yeer old, and fro the
brest
Departed of his norice, on a day
This markis caughte yet another lest
To tempte his wyf yet ofter, if he may. 620
O needles was she tempted in assay !
But wedded men ne knowe no mesure,
Whan that they finde a pacient creature.

'Wyf,' quod this markis, 'ye han herd er
this,
My peple sikly berth our mariage,     625
And namely, sith my sone y-boren is, (570)
Now is it worse than ever in al our age.
The murmur sleeth myn herte and my
corage ;
For to myne eres comth the voys so
smerte,
That it wel ny destroyed hath myn herte.

Now sey they thus, "whan Walter is
agoon,                              631
Then shal the blood of Janicle succede
And been our lord, for other have we
noon ; "
Swiche wordes seith my peple, out of
drede.
Wel oughte I of swich murmur taken
hede ;                              635
For certeinly I drede swich sentence, (580)
Though they nat pleyn speke in myn
audience.

I wolde live in pees, if that I mighte ;
Wherfor I am disposed outerly,
As I his suster servede by nighte,    640
Right so thenke I to serve him prively ;
This warne I yow, that ye nat sodeynly
Out of your-self for no wo sholde outraye ;
Beth pacient, and ther-of I yow preye.'

'I have,' quod she, 'seyd thus, and ever
shal,    (589) 645
I wol no thing, ne nil no thing, certayn,
But as yow list; noght greveth me at al,
Thogh that my doghter and my sone be
slayn,
At your comandement, this is to sayn.
I have noght had no part of children
tweyne    650
But first siknesse, and after wo and peyne.

Ye been our lord, doth with your owene
thing
Right as yow list; axeth no reed at me.
For, as I lefte at hoom al my clothing,
Whan I first cam to yow, right so,' quod
she,    655
'Lefte I my wil and al my libertee, (600)
And took your clothing; wherfor I yow
preye,
Doth your plesaunce, I wol your lust
obeye.

And certes, if I hadde prescience
Your wil to knowe er ye your lust me
tolde,    660
I wolde it doon with-outen necligence;
But now I woot your lust and what ye
wolde,
Al your plesaunce ferme and stable
I holde;
For wiste I that my deeth wolde do yow
ese,    664
Right gladly wolde I dyen, yow to plese.

Deth may noght make no comparisoun
Un-to your love:' and, whan this markis
sey    (611)
The constance of his wyf, he caste adoun
His yën two, and wondreth that she may
In pacience suffre al this array.    670
And forth he gooth with drery conten-
aunce,
But to his herte it was ful greet plesaunce.

This ugly sergeant, in the same wyse
That he hir doghter caughte, right so he,
Or worse, if men worse can devyse,    675
Hath hent hir sone, that ful was of
beautee.    (620)
And ever in oon so pacient was she,
That she no chere made of hevinesse,
But kiste hir sone, and after gan it blesse;

Save this; she preyed him that, if he
mighte,    680
Hir litel sone he wolde in erthe grave,
His tendre limes, delicat to sighte,
Fro foules and fro bestes for to save.
But she non answer of him mighte have.
He wente his wey, as him no-thing ne
roghte;    685
But to Boloigne he tendrely it broghte.

This markis wondreth ever lenger the
more    (631)
Up-on hir pacience, and if that he
Ne hadde soothly knowen ther-bifore,
That parfitly hir children lovede she, 690
He wolde have wend that of som subtiltee,
And of malice or for cruel corage,
That she had suffred this with sad visage.

But wel he knew that next him-self,
certayn,    694
She loved hir children best in every wyse.
But now of wommen wolde I axen fayn,
If thise assayes mighte nat suffyse? (641)
What coude a sturdy housbond more
devyse
To preve hir wyfhod and hir stedfast-
nesse,    699
And he continuing ever in sturdinesse?

But ther ben folk of swich condicioun,
That, whan they have a certein purpos
take,
They can nat stinte of hir entencioun,
But, right as they were bounden to
a stake,
They wol nat of that firste purpos slake.
Right so this markis fulliche hath pur-
posed    (650) 706
To tempte his wyf, as he was first disposed.

He waiteth, if by word or contenance
That she to him was changed of corage;
But never coude he finde variance;    710
She was ay oon in herte and in visage;
And ay the forther that she was in age,
The more trewe, if that it were possible,
She was to him in love, and more penible.

For which it semed thus, that of hem two
Ther nas but o wil; for, as Walter leste,
The same lust was hir plesance also, (661)

And, god be thanked, al fil for the beste.
She shewed wel, for no worldly unreste
A wyf, as of hir-self, no-thing ne sholde
Wille in effect, but as hir housbond wolde.

The sclaundre of Walter ofte and wyde
    spradde,     722
That of a cruel herte he wikkedly,
For he a povre womman wedded hadde,
Hath mordred bothe his children prively.
Swich murmur was among hem comunly.
No wonder is, for to the peples ere   (671)
Ther cam no word but that they mordred
    were.

For which, wher-as his peple ther-bifore
Had loved him wel, the sclaundre of his
    diffame     730
Made hem that they him hatede therfore;
To been a mordrer is an hateful name.
But natheles, for ernest ne for game
He of his cruel purpos nolde stente ;    734
To tempte his wyf was set al his entente.

Whan that his doghter twelf yeer was of
    age,     (680)
He to the court of Rome, in subtil wyse
Enformed of his wil, sente his message,
Comaunding hem swiche bulles to devyse
As to his cruel purpos may suffyse,    740
How that the pope, as for his peples reste,
Bad him to wedde another, if him leste.

I seye, he bad they sholde countrefete
The popes bulles, making mencioun
That he hath leve his firste wyf to lete, 745
As by the popes dispensacioun,    (690)
To stinte rancour and dissencioun
Bitwixe his peple and him ; thus seyde
    the bulle,
The which they han publiced atte fulle.

The rude peple, as it no wonder is,    750
Wenden ful wel that it had been right so ;
But whan thise tydinges cam to Grisildis,
I deme that hir herte was ful wo.
But she, y-lyke sad for evermo,
Disposed was, this humble creature,    755
Th'adversitee of fortune al t'endure. (700)

Abyding ever his lust and his plesaunce,
To whom that she was yeven, herte and al,
As to hir verray worldly suffisaunce ;

But shortly if this storie I tellen shal, 760
This markis writen hath in special
A lettre in which he sheweth his entente,
And secrely he to Boloigne it sente.

To th'erl of Panik, which that hadde tho
Wedded his suster, preyde he specially 765
To bringen hoom agayn his children two
In honurable estaat al openly.    (711)
But o thing he him preyede outerly,
That he to no wight, though men wolde
    enquere,
Sholde nat telle, whos children that they
    were,     770

But seye, the mayden sholde y-wedded be
Un-to the markis of Saluce anon.
And as this erl was preyed, so dide he ;
For at day set he on his wey is goon
Toward Saluce, and lordes many oon, 775
In riche array, this mayden for to gyde ;
Hir yonge brother ryding hir bisyde. (721)

Arrayed was toward hir mariage
This fresshe mayde, ful of gemmes clere ;
Hir brother, which that seven yeer was of
    age,     780
Arrayed eek ful fresh in his manere.
And thus in greet noblesse and with glad
    chere,
Toward Saluces shaping hir journey,
Fro day to day they ryden in hir wey.

**Explicit quarta pars.**

**Sequitur quinta pars.**

Among al this, after his wikke usage, 785
This markis, yet his wyf to tempte more
To the uttereste preve of hir corage, (731)
Fully to han experience and lore
If that she were as stedfast as bifore,
He on a day in open audience     790
Ful boistously hath seyd hir this sentence:

'Certes, Grisilde, I hadde y-nough ples-
    aunce
To han yow to my wyf for your goodnesse,
As for your trouthe and for your obeis-
    aunce,
Nought for your linage ne for your
    richesse ;     795
But now knowe I in verray soothfast-
    nesse     (740)

That in gret lordshipe, if I wel avyse,
Ther is gret servitute in sondry wyse.

I may nat don as every plowman may ;
My peple me constreyneth for to take   800
Another wyf, and cryen day by day ;
And eek the pope, rancour for to slake,
Consenteth it, that dar I undertake ;
And treweliche thus muche I wol yow
    seye,
My newe wyf is coming by the weye.   805

Be strong of herte, and voyde anon hir
    place,                              (750)
And thilke dower that ye broghten me
Tak it agayn, I graunte it of my grace ;
Retourneth to your fadres hous,' quod he ;
'No man may alwey han prosperitee ;   810
With evene herte I rede yow t'endure
The strook of fortune or of aventure.'

And she answerde agayn in pacience,
'My lord,' quod she, 'I woot, and wiste
    alway
How that bitwixen your magnificence   815
And my poverte no wight can ne may   (760)
Maken comparison ; it is no nay.
I ne heeld me never digne in no manere
To be your wyf, no, ne your chamberere.

And in this hous, ther ye me lady made—
The heighe god take I for my witnesse,   821
And also wisly he my soule glade—
I never heeld me lady ne maistresse,
But humble servant to your worthinesse,
And ever shal, whyl that my lyf may
    dure,                              825
Aboven every worldly creature.       (770)

That ye so longe of your benignitee
Han holden me in honour and nobleye,
Wher-as I was noght worthy for to be,
That thonke I god and yow, to whom
    I preye                            830
Foryelde it yow ; there is na-more to seye.
Un-to my fader gladly wol I wende,
And with him dwelle un-to my lyves ende.

Ther I was fostred of a child ful smal,
Til I be deed, my lyf ther wol I lede   835
A widwe clene, in body, herte, and al. (780)
For sith I yaf to yow my maydenhede,
And am your trewe wyf, it is no drede,

God shilde swich a lordes wyf to take
Another man to housbonde or to make. 840

And of your newe wyf, god of his grace
So graunte yow wele and prosperitee :
For I wol gladly yelden hir my place,
In which that I was blisful wont to be,
For sith it lyketh yow, my lord,' quod
    she,                               845
'That whylom weren al myn hertes reste,
That I shal goon, I wol gon whan yow
    leste.                            (791)

But ther-as ye me profre swich dowaire
As I first broghte, it is wel in my minde
It were my wrecched clothes, no-thing
    faire,                            850
The which to me were hard now for to
    finde.
O gode god ! how gentil and how kinde
Ye semed by your speche and your visage
The day that maked was our mariage !

But sooth is seyd, algate I finde it trewe—
For in effect it preved is on me— (800) 856
Love is noght old as whan that it is newe.
But certes, lord, for noon adversitee,
To dyen in the cas, it shal nat be     859
That ever in word or werk I shal repente
That I yow yaf myn herte in hool entente.

My lord, ye woot that, in my fadres place,
Ye dede me strepe out of my povre wede,
And richely me cladden, of your grace.
To yow broghte I noght elles, out of drede,
But feyth and nakednesse and mayden-
    hede.                         (810) 866
And here agayn my clothing I restore,
And eek my wedding-ring, for evermore.

The remenant of your jewels redy be   869
In-with your chambre, dar I saufly sayn ;
Naked out of my fadres hous,' quod she,
'I cam, and naked moot I turne agayn.
Al your plesaunce wol I folwen fayn ;
But yet I hope it be nat your entente   874
That I smoklees out of your paleys wente.

Ye coude nat doon so dishoneste a thing,
That thilke wombe in which your children
    leye                             (821)
Sholde, biforn the peple, in my walking,

Be seyn al bare ; wherfor I yow preye,
Lat me nat lyk a worm go by the weye. 880
Remembre yow, myn owene lord so dere,
I was your wyf, thogh I unworthy were.

Wherfor, in guerdon of my maydenhede,
Which that I broghte, and noght agayn
I bere,                                            884
As voucheth sauf to yeve me, to my mede,
But swich a smok as I was wont to were,
That I therwith may wrye the wombe of
here                                             (831)
That was your wyf ; and heer take I my
leve
Of yow, myn owene lord, lest I yow greve.'

'The smok,' quod he, 'that thou hast on
thy bak,                                         890
Lat it be stille, and ber it forth with thee.'
But wel unnethes thilke word he spak,
But wente his wey for rewthe and for
pitee.
Biforn the folk hir-selven strepeth she,
And in hir smok, with heed and foot al
bare,                                       (839) 895
Toward hir fader hous forth is she fare.

The folk hir folwe wepinge in hir weye,
And fortune ay they cursen as they goon ;
But she fro weping kepte hir yën dreye,
Ne in this tyme word ne spak she noon. 900
Hir fader, that this tyding herde anoon,
Curseth the day and tyme that nature
Shoop him to been a lyves creature.

For out of doute this olde povre man
Was ever in suspect of hir mariage ;    905
For ever he demed, sith that it bigan,(850)
That whan the lord fulfild had his corage,
Him wolde thinke it were a disparage
To his estaat so lowe for t'alighte,
And voyden hir as sone as ever he mighte.

Agayns his doghter hastilich goth he,  911
For he by noyse of folk knew hir cominge,
And with hir olde cote, as it mighte be,
He covered hir, ful sorwefully wepinge ;
But on hir body mighte he it nat bringe.
For rude was the cloth, and more of age
By dayes fele than at hir mariage.   (861)

Thus with hir fader, for a certeyn space,
Dwelleth this flour of wyfly pacience,

That neither by hir wordes ne hir face 920
Biforn the folk, ne eek in hir absence,
Ne shewed she that hir was doon offence ;
Ne of hir heigh estaat no remembraunce
Ne hadde she, as by hir countenaunce.

No wonder is, for in hir grete estaat   925
Hir goost was ever in pleyn humylitee ;
No tendre mouth, non herte delicaat, (871)
No pompe, no semblant of royaltee,
But ful of pacient benignitee,
Discreet and prydeles, ay honurable,   930
And to hir housbonde ever meke and
stable.

Men speke of Job and most for his hum-
blesse,
As clerkes, whan hem list, can wel endyte,
Namely of men, but as in soothfastnesse,
Thogh clerkes preyse wommen but a
lyte,                                           935
Ther can no man in humblesse him ac-
quyte                                          (880)
As womman can, ne can ben half so trewe
As wommen been, but it be falle of-newe.

### [Pars Sexta.]

Fro Boloigne is this erl of Panik come,
Of which the fame up-sprang to more and
lesse,                                          940
And in the peples eres alle and some
Was couth eek, that a newe markisesse
He with him broghte, in swich pompe and
richesse,
That never was ther seyn with mannes yë
So noble array in al West Lumbardye. 945

The markis, which that shoop and knew
al this,                                        (890)
Er that this erl was come, sente his message
For thilke sely povre Grisildis ;
And she with humble herte and glad
visage,                                         949
Nat with no swollen thoght in hir corage,
Cam at his heste, and on hir knees hir
sette,
And reverently and wysly she him grette.

'Grisild,' quod he, 'my wille is outerly,
This mayden, that shal wedded been to me,
Receyved be to-morwe as royally        955

As it possible is in myn hous to be. (900)
And eek that every wight in his degree
Have his estaat in sitting and servyse
And heigh plesaunce, as I can best devyse.

I have no wommen suffisaunt certayn 960
The chambres for t'arraye in ordinaunce
After my lust, and therfor wolde I fayn
That thyn were al swich maner govern-
aunce ;
Thou knowest eek of old al my plesaunce ;
Though thyn array be badde and yvel
biseye, 965
Do thou thy devoir at the leeste weye.' (910)

'Nat only, lord, that I am glad,' quod she,
' To doon your lust, but I desyre also
Yow for to serve and plese in my degree
With-outen feynting, and shal evermo. 970
Ne never, for no wele ne no wo,
Ne shal the gost with-in myn herte stente
To love yow best with al my trewe entente.'

And with that word she gan the hous to
dighte,
And tables for to sette and beddes make ;
And peyned hir to doon al that she
mighte, (920) 976
Preying the chambereres, for goddes sake,
To hasten hem, and faste swepe and shake ;
And she, the moste servisable of alle,
Hath every chambre arrayed and his halle.

Abouten undern gan this erl alighte, 981
That with him broghte thise noble child-
ren tweye,
For which the peple ran to seen the sighte
Of hir array, so richely biseye ;
And than at erst amonges hem they seye,
That Walter was no fool, thogh that him
leste (930) 986
To chaunge his wyf, for it was for the beste.

For she is fairer, as they demen alle,
Than is Grisild, and more tendre of age,
And fairer fruit bitwene hem sholde
falle, 990
And more plesant, for hir heigh linage ;
Hir brother eek so fair was of visage,
That hem to seen the peple hath caught
plesaunce,
Commending now the markis govern-
aunce.—

*Auctor.* ' O stormy peple ! unsad and ever
untrewe ! (939) 995
Ay undiscreet and chaunging as a vane,
Delyting ever in rumbel that is newe,
For lyk the mone ay wexe ye and wane ;
Ay ful of clapping, dere y-nogh a jane ;
Your doom is fals, your constance yvel
preveth, 1000
A ful greet fool is he that on yow leveth !'

Thus seyden sadde folk in that citee, ·
Whan that the peple gazed up and doun,
For they were glad, right for the noveltee,
To han a newe lady of hir toun. 1005
Na-more of this make I now mencioun ;
But to Grisilde agayn wol I me dresse, (951)
And telle hir constance and hir bisinesse.—

Ful bisy was Grisilde in every thing
That to the feste was apertinent ; 1010
Right noght was she abayst of hir clothing,
Though it were rude and somdel eek to-
rent.
But with glad chere to the yate is went,
With other folk, to grete the markisesse,
And after that doth forth hir bisinesse. 1015

With so glad chere his gestes she receyveth,
And conningly, everich in his degree, (961)
That no defaute no man aperceyveth ;
But ay they wondren what she mighte be
That in so povre array was for to see, 1020
And coude swich honour and reverence ;
And worthily they preisen hir prudence.

In al this mene whyle she ne stente
This mayde and eek hir brother to com-
mende
With al hir herte, in ful benigne entente,
So wel, that no man coude hir prys
amende. (970) 1026
But atte laste, whan that thise lordes
wende
To sitten doun to mete, he gan to calle
Grisilde, as she was bisy in his halle.

' Grisilde,' quod he, as it were in his
pley, 1030
' How lyketh thee my wyf and hir beautee?'
' Right wel,' quod she, 'my lord ; for, in
good fey,
A fairer say I never noon than she.
I prey to god yeve hir prosperitee ; 1034

X

And so hope I that he wol to yow sende
Plesance y-nogh un-to your lyves ende.

O thing biseke I yow and warne also, (981)
That ye ne prikke with no tormentinge
This tendre mayden, as ye han don mo;
For she is fostred in hir norishinge    1040
More tendrely, and, to my supposinge,
She coude nat adversitee endure
As coude a povre fostred creature.'

And whan this Walter say hir pacience,
Hir glade chere and no malice at al,   1045
And he so ofte had doon to hir offence,(990)
And she ay sad and constant as a wal,
Continuing ever hir innocence overal,
This sturdy markis gan his herte dresse
To rewen up-on hir wyfly stedfastnesse.1050

'This is y-nogh, Grisilde myn,' quod he,
'Be now na-more agast ne yvel apayed ;
I have thy feith and thy benignitee,
As wel as ever womman was, assayed,
In greet estaat, and povreliche arrayed.1055
Now knowe I, dere wyf, thy stedfast-
nesse,'—           (1000)
And hir in armes took and gan hir kesse.

And she for wonder took of it no keep ;
She herde nat what thing he to hir seyde;
She ferde as she had stert out of a sleep,
Til she out of hir masednesse abreyde. 1061
'Grisilde,' quod he, 'by god that for us
deyde,
Thou art my wyf, ne noon other I have,
Ne never hadde, as god my soule save !

This is thy doghter which thou hast sup-
posed            1065
To be my wyf; that other feithfully (1010)
Shal be myn heir, as I have ay purposed ;
Thou bare him in thy body trewely.
At Boloigne have I kept hem prively ; 1069
Tak hem agayn, for now maystow nat
seye
That thou hast lorn non of thy children
tweye.

And folk that otherweyes han seyd of me,
I warne hem wel that I have doon this
dede
For no malice ne for no crueltee,    1074

But for t'assaye in thee thy wommanhede,
And nat to sleen my children, god for-
bede !            (1020)
But for to kepe hem prively and stille,
Til I thy purpos knewe and al thy wille.'

Whan she this herde, aswowne doun she
falleth            1079
For pitous joye, and after hir swowninge
She bothe hir yonge children un-to hir
calleth,
And in hir armes, pitously wepinge,
Embraceth hem, and tendrely kissinge
Ful lyk a mooder, with hir salte teres 1084
She batheth bothe hir visage and hir heres.

O, which a pitous thing it was to see (1030)
Hir swowning, and hir humble voys to
here !
'Grauntmercy, lord, that thanke I yow,'
quod she,
'That ye han saved me my children dere!
Now rekke I never to ben deed right
here ;            1090
Sith I stonde in your love and in your grace,
No fors of deeth, ne whan my spirit pace!

O tendre, o dere, o yonge children myne,
Your woful mooder wende stedfastly 1094
That cruel houndes or som foul vermyne
Hadde eten yow ; but god, of his mercy,
And your benigne fader tendrely    (1041)
Hath doon yow kept ;' and in that same
stounde
Al sodeynly she swapte adoun to grounde.

And in her swough so sadly holdeth she
Hir children two, whan she gan hem
t'embrace,           1101
That with greet sleighte and greet diffi-
cultee
The children from hir arm they gonne
arace.            (1047)
O many a teer on many a pitous face 1104
Doun ran of hem that stoden hir bisyde ;
Unnethe abouten hir mighte they abyde.

Walter hir gladeth, and hir sorwe slaketh;
She ryseth up, abaysed, from hir traunce,
And every wight hir joye and feste maketh,
Til she hath caught agayn hir conten-
aunce.            1110

Walter hir dooth so feithfully plesaunce,
That it was deyntee for to seen the chere
Bitwixe hem two, now they ben met y-fere.

Thise ladyes, whan that they hir tyme say,
Han taken hir, and in-to chambre goon,
And strepen hir out of hir rude array,(1060)
And in a cloth of gold that brighte shoon,
With a coroune of many a riche stoon
Up-on hir heed, they in-to halle hir
broghte,                                    1119
And ther she was honoured as hir oghte.

Thus hath this pitous day a blisful ende,
For every man and womman dooth his
might
This day in murthe and revel to dispende
Til on the welkne shoon the sterres light.
For more solempne in every mannes sight
This feste was, and gretter of costage, 1126
Than was the revel of hir mariage. (1071)

Ful many a yeer in heigh prosperitee
Liven thise two in concord and in reste,
And richely his doghter maried he    1130
Un-to a lord, oon of the worthieste
Of al Itaille ; and than in pees and reste
His wyves fader in his court he kepeth,
Til that the soule out of his body crepeth.

His sone succedeth in his heritage    1135
In reste and pees, after his fader day; (1080)
And fortunat was eek in mariage,
Al putte he nat his wyf in greet assay.
This world is nat so strong, it is no nay,
As it hath been in olde tymes yore,    1140
And herkneth what this auctour seith
therfore.

This storie is seyd, nat for that wyves
sholde
Folwen Grisilde as in humilitee,
For it were importable, though they wolde;
But for that every wight, in his degree,1145
Sholde be constant in adversitee    (1090)
As was Grisilde; therfor Petrark wryteth
This storie, which with heigh style he
endyteth.

For, sith a womman was so pacient    1149
Un-to a mortal man, wel more us oghte
Receyven al in gree that god us sent ;

For greet skile is, he preve that he wroghte.
But he ne tempteth no man that he boghte,
As seith seint Jame, if ye his pistel rede ;
He preveth folk al day, it is no drede,  1155

And suffreth us, as for our excercyse,(1100)
With sharpe scourges of adversitee
Ful ofte to be bete in sondry wyse ;
Nat for to knowe our wil, for certes he,
Er we were born, knew al our freletee;1160
And for our beste is al his governaunce ;
Lat us than live in vertuous suffraunce.*

But o word, lordinges, herkneth er I go:—
It were ful hard to finde now a dayes (1108)
In al a toun Grisildes three or two ;  1165
For, if that they were put to swiche assayes,
The gold of hem hath now so badde alayes
With bras, that thogh the coyne be fair
at yë,
It wolde rather breste a-two than plye.

For which heer, for the wyves love of
Bathe,                                    1170
Whos lyf and al hir secte god mayntene
In heigh maistrye, and elles were it scathe,
I wol with lusty herte fresshe and grene
Seyn yow a song to glade yow, I wene,
And lat us stinte of ernestful matere :—
Herkneth my song, that seith in this
manere.                          (1120) 1176

### Lenvoy de Chaucer.

Grisilde is deed, and eek hir pacience,
And bothe atones buried in Itaille ;
For which I crye in open audience,
No wedded man so hardy be t'assaille 1180
His wyves pacience, in hope to finde
Grisildes, for in certein he shall faille !

---

* It seems to have been Chaucer's intention,
in the first instance, to end this Tale here. Hence,
we find, in MSS. E. Hn. Cm. Dd., the following
genuine, but rejected stanza, suitable for insertion
at this point :—

**Bihold the merye wordes of the Hoste.**

This worthy Clerk, whan ended was his tale,
Our hoste seyde, and swoor by goddes bones,
' Me were lever than a barel ale
My wyf at hoom had herd this legende ones ;
This is a gentil tale for the nones,
As to my purpos, wiste ye my wille ;
But thing that wol nat be, lat it be stille.'

**Here endeth the Tale of the Clerk
of Oxenford.**

O noble wyves, ful of heigh prudence,
Lat noon humilitee your tonge naille, 1184
Ne lat no clerk have cause or diligence
To wryte of yow a storie of swich mervaille
As of Grisildis pacient and kinde ; (1131)
Lest Chichevache yow swelwe in hir en-
    traille !

Folweth Ekko, that holdeth no silence,
But evere answereth at the countretaille ;
Beth nat bidaffed for your innocence, 1191
But sharply tak on yow the governaille.
Emprinteth wel this lesson in your minde
For commune profit, sith it may availle.

Ye archewyves, stondeth at defence, 1195
Sin ye be stronge as is a greet camaille;(1140)
Ne suffreth nat that men yow doon offence.
And sclendre wyves, feble as in bataille,

Beth egre as is a tygre yond in Inde ;
Ay clappeth as a mille, I yow consaille.1200

Ne dreed hem nat, do hem no reverence ;
For though thyn housbonde armed be in
    maille,
The arwes of thy crabbed eloquence
Shal perce his brest, and eek his aventaille;
In jalousye I rede eek thou him binde, 1205
And thou shalt make him couche as dooth
    a quaille.     (1150)

If thou be fair, ther folk ben in presence
Shew thou thy visage and thyn apparaille ;
If thou be foul, be free of thy dispence,1209
To gete thee freendes ay do thy travaille ;
Be ay of chere as light as leef on linde,
And lat him care, and wepe, and wringe,
    and waille !     (1156)

**Here endeth the Clerk of Oxonford his Tale.**

---

# THE MERCHANT'S PROLOGUE.

### The Prologe of the Marchantes Tale.

'Weping and wayling, care, and other
    sorwe
I know y-nogh, on even and a-morwe,'
Quod the Marchaunt, ' and so don othere
    mo     1215
That wedded been, I trowe that it be so.
For, wel I woot, it fareth so with me.
I have a wyf, the worste that may be ;
For thogh the feend to hir y-coupled were,
She wolde him overmacche, I dar wel
    swere.     1220
What sholde I yow reherce in special
Hir hye malice? she is a shrewe at al. (10)
Ther is a long and large difference
Bitwix Grisildis grete pacience
And of my wyf the passing crueltee. 1225
Were I unbounden, al-so moot I thee !
I wolde never eft comen in the snare.
We wedded men live in sorwe and care ;

Assaye who-so wol, and he shal finde
I seye sooth, by seint Thomas of Inde, 1230
As for the more part, I sey nat alle.
God shilde that it sholde so bifalle !  (20)
A ! good sir hoost ! I have y-wedded be
Thise monthes two, and more nat, pardee;
And yet, I trowe, he that all his lyve 1235
Wyflees hath been, though that men wolde
    him ryve
Un-to the herte, ne coude in no manere
Tellen so muchel sorwe, as I now here
Coude tellen of my wyves cursednesse ! '
    ' Now,' quod our hoost, ' Marchaunt, so
      god yow blesse,     1240
Sin ye so muchel knowen of that art,
Ful hertely I pray yow telle us part.' (30)
    ' Gladly,' quod he, ' but of myn owene
    sore,
For sory herte, I telle may na-more.' 1244

# THE MARCHANTES TALE.

### Here biginneth the Marchantes Tale.

Whylom ther was dwellinge in Lumbardye
A worthy knight, that born was of Pavye,
In which he lived in greet prosperitee ;
And sixty yeer a wyf lees man was he,
And folwed ay his bodily delyt
On wommen, ther-as was his appetyt,  1250
As doon thise foles that ben seculeer.
And whan that he was passed sixty yeer,
Were it for holinesse or for dotage,
I can nat seye, but swich a greet corage, (10)
Hadde this knight to been a wedded man,
That day and night he dooth al that he can
T'espyen where he mighte wedded be ;
Preyinge our lord to granten him, that he
Mighte ones knowe of thilke blisful lyf
That is bitwixe an housbond and his wyf ;
And for to live under that holy bond  1261
With which that first god man and
    womman bond.

'Non other lyf,' seyde he, 'is worth a bene ;
For wedlok is so esy and so clene,   (20)
That in this world it is a paradys.'   1265
Thus seyde this olde knight, that was so
    wys.

And certeinly, as sooth as god is king,
To take a wyf, it is a glorious thing,
And namely whan a man is old and hoor ;
Thanne is a wyf the fruit of his tresor. 1270
Than sholde he take a yong wyf and a feir,
On which he mighte engendren him an
    heir,
And lede his lyf in joye and in solas,
Wher-as thise bacheleres singe 'allas,' (30)
Whan that they finden any adversitee 1275
In love, which nis but childish vanitee.
And trewely it sit wel to be so,
That bacheleres have often peyne and wo ;
On brotel ground they builde, and brotel-
    nesse          1279
They finde, whan they wene sikernesse.

They live but as a brid or as a beste,
In libertee, and under non areste,
Ther-as a wedded man in his estaat
Liveth a lyf blisful and ordinaat,   (40)
Under the yok of mariage y-bounde ;  1285
Wel may his herte in joye and blisse
    habounde.
For who can be so buxom as a wyf ?
Who is so trewe, and eek so ententyf
To kepe him, syk and hool, as is his make ?
For wele or wo, she wol him nat forsake.
She nis nat wery him to love and serve,
Thogh that he lye bedrede til he sterve.
And yet somme clerkes seyn, it nis nat so,
Of whiche he, Theofraste, is oon of tho. (50)
What force though Theofraste liste lye? 1295
'Ne take no wyf,' quod he, 'for hous-
    bondrye,
As for to spare in houshold thy dispence ;
A trewe servant dooth more diligence,
Thy good to kepe, than thyn owene wyf.
For she wol clayme half part al hir lyf ; 1300
And if that thou be syk, so god me save,
Thy verray frendes or a trewe knave
Wol kepe thee bet than she that waiteth ay
After thy good, and hath don many a day.'
And if thou take a wyf un-to thyn
    hold,          (61) [T. om.
Ful lightly maystow been a coke-
    wold.          1306 [T. om.
This sentence, and an hundred thinges
    worse,
Wryteth this man, ther god his bones
    corse !
But take no kepe of al swich vanitee ;
Deffye Theofraste and herke me.    1310
    A wyf is goddes yifte verraily ;
Alle other maner yiftes hardily,
As londes, rentes, pasture, or commune,
Or moebles, alle ben yiftes of fortune, (70)

That passen as a shadwe upon a wal. 1315
But dredelees, if pleynly speke I shal,
A wyf wol laste, and in thyn hous endure,
Wel lenger than thee list, paraventure.
   Mariage is a ful gret sacrement ;
He which that hath no wyf, I holde him
   shent ;     1320
He liveth helplees and al desolat,
I speke of folk in seculer estaat.
And herke why, I sey nat this for noght,(79)
That womman is for mannes help y-wroght.
The hye god, whan he hadde Adam maked,
And saugh him al allone, bely-naked, 1326
God of his grete goodnesse seyde than,
'Lat us now make an help un-to this man
Lyk to him-self ;' and thanne he made
   him Eve.     1329
Heer may ye se, and heer-by may ye preve,
That wyf is mannes help and his confort,
His paradys terrestre and his disport
So buxom and so vertuous is she,
They moste nedes live in unitee. (90) 1334
O flesh they been, and o flesh, as I gesse,
Hath but on herte, in wele and in distresse.
   A wyf ! a ! Seinte Marie, ben'cite !
How mighte a man han any adversitee
That hath a wyf ? certes, I can nat seye.1339
The blisse which that is bitwixe hem tweye
Ther may no tonge telle, or herte thinke.
If he be povre, she helpeth him to swinke ;
She kepeth his good, and wasteth never
   a deel ;
Al that hir housbonde lust, hir lyketh
   weel ;     (100)
She seith not ones 'nay,' when he seith
   'ye.'     1345
'Do this,' seith he ; 'al redy, sir,' seith she.
O blisful ordre of wedlok precious,
Thou art so mery, and eek so vertuous,
And so commended and appreved eek,
That every man that halt him worth a
   leek,     1350
Up-on his bare knees oghte al his lyf
Thanken his god that him hath sent a
   wyf ;
Or elles preye to god him for to sende
A wyf, to laste un-to his lyves ende. (110)
For thanne his lyf is set in sikernesse ; 1355
He may nat be deceyved, as I gesse,
So that he werke after his wyves reed ;
Than may he boldly beren up his heed,

They been so trewe and ther-with-al so
   wyse ;
For which, if thou wolt werken as the
   wyse,     1360
Do alwey so as wommen wol thee rede.
   Lo, how that Jacob, as thise clerkes
   rede,
By good conseil of his moder Rebekke,
Bond the kides skin aboute his nekke ; (120)
Thurgh which his fadres benisoun he wan.
   Lo, Judith, as the storie eek telle can,
By wys conseil she goddes peple kepte,
And slow him, Olofernus, whyl he slepte.
   Lo Abigayl, by good conseil how she 1369
Saved hir housbond Nabal, whan that he
Sholde han be slayn ; and loke, Ester also
By good conseil delivered out of wo
The peple of god, and made him, Mar-
   dochee,
Of Assuere enhaunced for to be. (130)
   Ther nis no-thing in gree superlatyf,1375
As seith Senek, above an humble wyf.
   Suffre thy wyves tonge, as Caton bit ;
She shal comande, and thou shalt suffren
   it ;
And yet she wol obeye of curteisye.
A wyf is keper of thyn housbondrye ; 1380
Wel may the syke man biwaille and wepe,
Ther-as ther nis no wyf the hous to kepe.
I warne thee, if wysly thou wolt wirche,
Love wel thy wyf, as Crist loveth his
   chirche.     (140) 1384
If thou lovest thy-self, thou lovest thy wyf ;
No man hateth his flesh, but in his lyf
He fostreth it, and therfore bidde I thee,
Cherisse thy wyf, or thou shalt never thee.
Housbond and wyf, what so men jape or
   pleye,
Of worldly folk holden the siker weye ;1390
They been so knit, ther may noon harm
   bityde :
And namely, up-on the wyves syde.
For which this Januarie, of whom I tolde,
Considered hath, in with his dayes olde,(150)
The lusty lyf, the vertuous quiete,     1395
That is in mariage hony-swete ;
And for his freendes on a day he sente,
To tellen hem th'effect of his entente.
   With face sad, his tale he hath hem
   told ;     1399
He seyde, 'freendes, I am hoor and old,

And almost, god wot, on my pittes brinke ;
Up-on my soule somwhat moste I thinke.
I have my body folily despended ;     (159)
Blessed be god, that it shal been amended !
For I wol be, certeyn, a wedded man, 1405
And that anoon in al the haste I can,
Un-to som mayde fair and tendre of age.
I prey yow, shapeth for my mariage
Al sodeynly, for I wol nat abyde ;
And I wol fonde t'espyen, on my syde, 1410
To whom I may be wedded hastily.
But for-as-muche as ye ben mo than I,
Ye shullen rather swich a thing espyen
Than I, and wher me best were to allyen.
    But o thing warne I yow, my freendes
    dere,           (171) 1415
I wol non old wyf han in no manere.
She shal nat passe twenty yeer, certayn ;
Old fish and yong flesh wolde I have ful
    fayn.
Bet is,' quod he, ' a pyk than a pikerel ;
And bet than old boef is the tendre veel,
I wol no womman thritty yeer of age, 1421
It is but bene-straw and greet forage.
And eek thise olde widwes, god it woot,
They conne so muchel craft on Wades
    boot,          (180)
So muchel broken harm, whan that hem
    leste,          1425
That with hem sholde I never live in reste.
For sondry scoles maken sotil clerkis ;
Womman of manye scoles half a clerk is.
But certeynly, a yong thing may men gye,
Right as men may warm wex with handes
    plye.          1430
Wherfore I sey yow pleynly, in a clause,
I wol non old wyf han right for this
    cause.          (188)
For if so were, I hadde swich mischaunce,
That I in hir ne coude han no plesaunce,
Thanne sholde I lede my lyf in avoutrye,
And go streight to the devel, whan I dye.
Ne children sholde I none up-on hir geten;
Yet were me lever houndes had me eten,
Than that myn heritage sholde falle 1439
In straunge hand, and this I tell yow alle.
I dote nat, I woot the cause why
Men sholde wedde, and forthermore wot I,
Ther speketh many a man of mariage,
That woot na-more of it than woot my
    page,          (200) 1444

For whiche causes man sholde take a wyf.
If he ne may nat liven chast his lyf,
Take him a wyf with greet devocioun,
By-cause of leveful procreacioun
Of children, to th'onour of god above,
And nat only for paramour or love ; 1450
And for they sholde lecherye eschue,
And yelde hir dettes whan that they ben
    due ;
Or for that ech of hem sholde helpen
    other          (209)
In meschief, as a suster shal the brother;
And live in chastitee ful holily.     1455
But sires, by your leve, that am nat I.
For god be thanked, I dar make avaunt,
I fele my limes stark and suffisaunt
To do al that a man bilongeth to ;
I woot my-selven best what I may do. 1460
Though I be hoor, I fare as dooth a tree
That blosmeth er that fruyt y-woxen be;
A blosmy tree nis neither drye ne deed.
I fele me nowher hoor but on myn heed ;
Myn herte and alle my limes been as
    grene          (221) 1465
As laurer thurgh the yeer is for to sene.
And sin that ye han herd al myn entente,
I prey yow to my wil ye wole assente.'
    Diverse men diversely him tolde
Of mariage manye ensamples olde.   1470
Somme blamed it, somme preysed it,
    certeyn ;
But atte laste, shortly for to seyn,
As al day falleth altercacioun     1473
Bitwixen freendes in disputisoun,     (230)
Ther fil a stryf bitwixe his bretheren two,
Of whiche that oon was cleped Placebo,
Justinus soothly called was that other.
    Placebo seyde, ' o Januarie, brother,
Ful litel nede had ye, my lord so dere,
Conseil to axe of any that is here ;   1480
But that ye been so ful of sapience,
That yow ne lyketh, for your heighe
    prudence,
To weyven fro the word of Salomon.
This word seyde he un-to us everichon :
" Wirk alle thing by conseil," thus seyde
    he,          (241) 1485
" And thanne shaltow nat repente thee."
But though that Salomon spak swich
    a word,
Myn owene dere brother and my lord,

So wisly god my soule bringe at reste,
I hold your owene conseil is the beste. 1490
For brother myn, of me tak this motyf,
I have now been a court-man al my lyf.
And god it woot, though I unworthy be,
I have stonden in ful greet degree    (250)
Abouten lordes of ful heigh estaat ;    1495
Yet hadde I never with noon of hem
    debaat.
I never hem contraried, trewely ;
I woot wel that my lord can more than I.
What that he seith, I holde it ferme and
    stable ;
I seye the same, or elles thing semblable.
A ful gret fool is any conseillour,    1501
That serveth any lord of heigh honour,
That dar presume, or elles thenken it,
That his conseil sholde passe his lordes
    wit.    (260)
Nay, lordes been no foles, by my fay ; 1505
Ye han your-selven shewed heer to-day
So heigh sentence, so holily and weel,
That I consente and conferme every-deel
Your wordes alle, and your opinioun. 1509
By god, ther nis no man in al this toun
N'in al Itaille, that coude bet han sayd ;
Crist halt him of this conseil wel apayd.
And trewely, it is an heigh corage
Of any man, that stapen is in age,    (270)
To take a yong wyf ; by my fader kin,
Your herte hangeth on a joly pin.    1516
Doth now in this matere right as yow
    leste,
For finally I holde it for the beste.'

    Justinus, that ay stille sat and herde,
Right in this wyse to Placebo answerde :
' Now brother myn, be pacient, I preye,
Sin ye han seyd, and herkneth what I
    seye.    1522
Senek among his othere wordes wyse
Seith, that a man oghte him right wel
    avyse,    (280)
To whom he yeveth his lond or his
    catel.    1525
And sin I oghte avyse me right wel
To whom I yeve my good awey fro me,
Wel muchel more I oghte avysed be
To whom I yeve my body ; for alwey
I warne yow wel, it is no childes pley 1530
To take a wyf with-oute avysement.
Men moste enquere, this is myn assent,

Wher she be wys, or sobre, or dronke-
    lewe,    (289)
Or proud, or elles other-weys a shrewe ;
A chydester, or wastour of thy good, 1535
Or riche, or poore, or elles mannish wood.
Al-be-it so that no man finden shal
Noon in this world that trotteth hool
    in al,
Ne man ne beest, swich as men coude
    devyse ;
But nathelees, it oghte y-nough suffise 1540
With any wyf, if so were that she hadde
Mo gode thewes than hir vyces badde ;
And al this axeth leyser for t'enquere.
For god it woot, I have wept many a tere
Ful prively, sin I have had a wyf. (301) 1545
Preyse who-so wole a wedded mannes lyf,
Certein, I finde in it but cost and care,
And observances, of alle blisses bare. 1548
And yet, god woot, my neighebores aboute,
And namely of wommen many a route,
Seyn that I have the moste stedefast wyf,
And eek the mekeste oon that bereth lyf.
But I wot best wher wringeth me my
    sho.    (309)
Ye mowe, for me, right as yow lyketh do ;
Avyseth yow, ye been a man of age,    1555
How that ye entren in-to mariage,
And namely with a yong wyf and a fair.
By him that made water, erthe, and air,
The yongest man that is in al this route
Is bisy y-nogh to bringen it aboute    1560
To han his wyf allone, trusteth me.
Ye shul nat plese hir fully yeres three,
This is to seyn, to doon hir ful plesaunce.
A wyf axeth ful many an observaunce. (320)
I prey yow that ye be nat yvel apayd.'
    ' Wel,' quod this Januarie, ' and hastow
    sayd ?    1566
Straw for thy Senek, and for thy pro-
    verbes,
I counte nat a panier ful of herbes
Of scole-termes ; wyser men than thow,
As thou hast herd, assenteden right now
To my purpos ; Placebo, what sey ye ?'
    ' I seye, it is a cursed man,' quod he,
' That letteth matrimoine, sikerly.'    (329)
And with that word they rysen sodeynly,
And been assented fully, that he sholde
Be wedded whanne him list and wher he
    wolde.    1576

Heigh fantasye and curious bisinesse
Fro day to day gan in the soule impresse
Of Januarie aboute his mariage.
Many fair shap, and many a fair visage
Ther passeth thurgh his herte, night by
night.                                    (337) 1581
As who-so toke a mirour polished bright,
And sette it in a commune market-place,
Than sholde he see many a figure pace
By his mirour; and, in the same wyse,
Gan Januarie inwith his thoght devyse
Of maydens, whiche that dwelten him
bisyde.                                       1587
He wiste nat wher that he mighte abyde.
For if that oon have beautee in hir face,
Another stant so in the peples grace   1590
For hir sadnesse, and hir benignitee,
That of the peple grettest voys hath she.
And somme were riche, and hadden badde
name.                                     (349)
But nathelees, bitwixe ernest and game,
He atte laste apoynted him on oon,   1595
And leet alle othere from his herte
goon,
And chees hir of his owene auctoritee;
For love is blind al day, and may nat see.
And whan that he was in his bed y-
broght,
He purtreyed, in his herte and in his
thoght,                                     1600
Hir fresshe beautee and hir age tendre,
Hir myddel smal, hir armes longe and
sclendre,
Hir wyse governaunce, hir gentillesse,
Hir wommanly beringe and hir sadnesse.
And whan that he on hir was con-
descended,                              (361) 1605
Him thoughte his chois mighte nat ben
amended.
For whan that he him-self concluded
hadde,
Him thoughte ech other mannes wit so
badde,
That inpossible it were to replye
Agayn his chois, this was his fantasye. 1610
His freendes sente he to at his instaunce,
And preyed hem to doon him that ples-
aunce,
That hastily they wolden to him come;
He wolde abregge hir labour, alle and
some.                                     (370) 1614

Nedeth na-more for him to go ne ryde,
He was apoynted ther he wolde abyde.
Placebo cam, and eek his freendes sone,
And alderfirst he bad hem alle a bone,
That noon of hem none argumentes make
Agayn the purpos which that he hath
take;                                        1620
'Which purpos was plesant to god,' seyde
he,
'And verray ground of his prosperitee.'
He seyde, ther was a mayden in the
toun,
Which that of beautee hadde greet re-
noun,                                        (380)
Al were it so she were of smal degree; 1625
Suffyseth him hir youthe and hir beautee.
Which mayde, he seyde, he wolde han to
his wyf,
To lede in ese and holinesse his lyf.
And thanked god, that he mighte han
hire al,                                     1629
That no wight of his blisse parten shal.
And preyde hem to labouren in this
nede,
And shapen that he faille nat to spede;
For thanne, he seyde, his spirit was at ese.
'Thanne is,' quod he, 'no-thing may me
displese,                               (390) 1634
Save o thing priketh in my conscience,
The which I wol reherce in your presence.
  I have,' quod he, 'herd seyd, ful yore
ago,
Ther may no man han parfite blisses two,
This is to seye, in erthe and eek in
hevene.
For though he kepe him fro the sinnes
sevene,                                      1640
And eek from every branche of thilke
tree,
Yet is ther so parfit felicitee,
And so greet ese and lust in mariage, (399)
That ever I am agast, now in myn age,
That I shal lede now so mery a lyf,   1645
So delicat, with-outen wo and stryf,
That I shal have myn hevene in erthe
here.
For sith that verray hevene is boght so
dere,
With tribulacioun and greet penaunce,
How sholde I thanne, that live in swich
plesaunce                                    1650

As alle wedded men don with hir wyvis,
Come to the blisse ther Crist eterne on
          lyve is?
This is my drede, and ye, my bretheren
          tweye,                              (409)
Assoilleth me this questioun, I preye.'
  Justinus, which that hated his folye, 1655
Answerde anon, right in his japerye;
And for he wolde his longe tale abregge,
He wolde noon auctoritee allegge,     1658
But seyde, 'sire, so ther be noon obstacle
Other than this, god of his hye miracle
And of his mercy may so for yow wirche,
That, er ye have your right of holy
          chirche,                            (418)
Ye may repente of wedded mannes lyf,
In which ye seyn ther is no wo ne stryf.
And elles, god forbede but he sente   1665
A wedded man him grace to repente
Wel ofte rather than a sengle man!
And therfore, sire, the beste reed I can,
Dispeire yow noght, but have in your
          memorie,                            1669
Paraunter she may be your purgatorie!
She may be goddes mene, and goddes
          whippe;
Than shal your soule up to hevene skippe
Swifter than dooth an arwe out of the
          bowe!                               (429)
I hope to god, her-after shul ye knowe,
That their nis no so greet felicitee   1675
In mariage, ne never-mo shal be,
That yow shal lette of your savacioun,
So that ye use, as skile is and resoun,
The lustes of your wyf attemprely,    1679
And that ye plese hir nat to amorously,
And that ye kepe yow eek from other
          sinne.
My tale is doon:—for my wit is thinne.
Beth nat agast her-of, my brother dere.'—
(But lat us waden out of this matere. (440)
The Wyf of Bathe, if ye han understonde,
Of mariage, which we have on honde, 1686
Declared hath ful wel in litel space).—
  'Fareth now wel, god have yow in his
          grace.'
  And with this word this Justin and his
          brother
Han take hir leve, and ech of hem of
          other.                             1690
For whan they sawe it moste nedes be,

They wroghten so, by sly and wys trotee,
That she, this mayden, which that Mains
          highte,
As hastily as ever that she mighte,   (450)
Shal wedded be un-to this Januarie.   1695
I trowe it were to longe yow to tarie,
If I yow tolde of every scrit and bond,
By which that she was feffed in his lond;
Or for to herknen of hir riche array.
But finally y-comen is the day        1700
That to the chirche bothe be they went
For to receyve the holy sacrement.
Forth comth the preest, with stole aboute
          his nekke,                         (459)
And bad hir be lyk Sarra and Rebekke,
In wisdom and in trouthe of mariage;
And seyde his orisons, as is usage,   1706
And crouched hem, and bad god sholde
          hem blesse,
And made al siker y-nogh with holinesse.
  Thus been they wedded with solemp-
          nitee,
And at the feste sitteth he and she   1710
With other worthy folk up-on the deys.
Al ful of joye and blisse is the paleys,
And ful of instruments and of vitaille,
The moste deyntevous of al Itaille.   (470)
Biforn hem stoode swiche instruments of
          soun,                              1715
That Orpheus, ne of Thebes Amphioun,
Ne maden never swich a melodye.
  At every cours than cam loud minstral-
          cye,
That never tromped Joab, for to here,
Nor he, Theodomas, yet half so clere, 1720
At Thebes, whan the citee was in doute.
Bacus the wyn hem skinketh al aboute,
And Venus laugheth up-on every wight.
For Januarie was bicome hir knight, (480)
And wolde bothe assayen his corage  1725
In libertee, and eek in mariage;
And with hir fyrbrond in hir hand aboute
Daunceth biforn the bryde and al the
          route.
And certeinly, I dar right wel seyn this,
Ymeneüs, that god of wedding is,     1730
Saugh never his lyf so mery a wedded
          man.
Hold thou thy pees, thou poete Marcian,
That wrytest us that ilke wedding murie
Of hir, Philologye, and him, Mercurie,

And of the songes that the Muses songe.
To smal is bothe thy penne, and eek thy
　　tonge,　　　　　　　　　　(492) 1736
For to descryven of this mariage.
Whan tendre youthe hath wedded stoup-
　　ing age,
Ther is swich mirthe that it may nat be
　　writen;
Assayeth it your-self, than may ye witen
If that I lye or noon in this matere. 1741
　Maius, that sit with so benigne a chere,
Hir to biholde it semed fayërÿe;　　(499)
Quene Ester loked never with swich an yë
On Assuer, so meke a look hath she. 1745
I may yow nat devyse al hir beautee;
But thus muche of hir beautee telle I
　　may,
That she was lyk the brighte morwe of
　　May,
Fulfild of alle beautee and plesaunce.

　This Januarie is ravisshed in a traunce
At every time he loked on hir face; 1751
But in his herte he gan hir to manace,
That he that night in armes wolde hir
　　streyne
Harder than ever Paris dide Eleyne. (510)
But nathelees, yet hadde he greet pitee,
That thilke night offenden hir moste he;
And thoughte, 'allas! o tendre creature!
Now wolde god ye mighte wel endure
Al my corage, it is so sharp and kene;
I am agast ye shul it nat sustene.　　1760
But god forbede that I dide al my might!
Now wolde god that it were woxen night,
And that the night wolde lasten evermo.
I wolde that al this peple were ago.' (520)
And finally, he doth al his labour,　1765
As he best mighte, savinge his honour,
To haste hem fro the mete in subtil
　　wyse.

　The tyme cam that reson was to ryse;
And after that, men daunce and drinken
　　faste,　　　　　　　　　　　　　1769
And spyces al aboute the hous they caste;
And ful of joye and blisse is every man;
All but a squyer, highte Damian,
Which carf biforn the knight ful many
　　a day.
He was so ravisshed on his lady May, (530)
That for the verray peyne he was ny
　　wood;　　　　　　　　　　　　　1775

Almost he swelte and swowned ther he
　　stood.
So sore hath Venus hurt him with hir
　　brond,
As that she bar it daunsinge in hir
　　hond.
And to his bed he wente him hastily;
Na-more of him as at this tyme speke I.
But ther I lete him wepe y-nough and
　　pleyne,　　　　　　　　　(537) 1781
Til fresshe May wol rewen on his peyne.
　O perilous fyr, that in the bedstraw
　　bredeth!　　　　　　　　　　**Auctor.**
O famulier foo, that his servyce bedeth!
O servant traitour, false hoomly hewe, 1785
Lyk to the naddre in bosom sly untrewe,
God shilde us alle from your aqueynt-
　　aunce!
O Januarie, dronken in plesaunce
Of mariage, see how thy Damian,
Thyn owene squyer and thy borne man,
Entendeth for to do thee vileinye.　1791
God graunte thee thyn hoomly fo t'espye.
For in this world nis worse pestilence (549)
Than hoomly foo al day in thy presence.

　Parfourned hath the sonne his ark
　　diurne,　　　　　　　　　　　1795
No lenger may the body of him sojurne
On th'orisonte, as in that latitude.
Night with his mantel, that is derk and
　　rude,
Gan oversprede the hemisperie aboute;
For which departed is this lusty route
Fro Januarie, with thank on every syde.
Hom to hir houses lustily they ryde, 1802
Wher-as they doon hir thinges as hem
　　leste,
And whan they sye hir tyme, goon to
　　reste.　　　　　　　　　　　　　(560)
Sone after that, this hastif Januarie 1805
Wolde go to bedde, he wolde no lenger
　　tarie.
He drinketh ipocras, clarree, and vernage
Of spyces hote, t'encresen his corage;
And many a letuarie hadde he ful fyn,
Swiche as the cursed monk dan Con-
　　stantyn　　　　　　　　　　　1810
Hath writen in his book *de Coitu*;　(567)
To eten hem alle, he nas no-thing eschu.
And to his privee freendes thus seyde he:
'For goddes love, as sone as it may be,

Lat voyden al this hous in curteys wyse.'
And they han doon right as he wol
   devyse.      1816
Men drinken, and the travers drawe anon ;
The bryde was broght a-bedde as stille as
   stoon ;
And whan the bed was with the preest
   y-blessed,
Out of·the chambre hath every wight
   him dressed.      1820
And Januarie hath faste in armes take
His fresshe May, his paradys, his make.
He lulleth hir, he kisseth hir ful ofte
With thikke bristles of his berd unsofte,
Lyk to the skin of houndfish, sharp as
   brere,      (581) 1825
For he was shave al newe in his manere.
He rubbeth hir aboute hir tendre face,
And seyde thus, ' allas ! I moot trespace
To yow, my spouse, and yow gretly offende,
Er tyme come that I wil doun descende.
But nathelees, considereth this,' quod he,
'Ther nis no werkman, what-so-ever he be,
That may bothe werke wel and hastily ;
This wol be doon at leyser parfitly.  (590)
It is no fors how longe that we pleye ; 1835
In trewe wedlok wedded be we tweye ;
And blessed be the yok that we been
   inne,
For in our actes we mowe do no sinne.
A man may do no sinne with his wyf,
Ne hurte him-selven with his owene knyf;
For we han leve to pleye us by the
   lawe.'      1841
Thus laboureth he til that the day gan
   dawe ;
And than he taketh a sop in fyn clarree,
And upright in his bed than sitteth he,
And after that he sang ful loude and
   clere,      (601) 1845
And kiste his wyf, and made wantoun
   chere.
He was al coltish, ful of ragerye,
And ful of jargon as a flekked pye.
The slakke skin aboute his nekke shaketh,
Whyl that he sang ; so chaunteth he and
   craketh.      1850
But god wot what that May thoughte in
   hir herte,
Whan she him saugh up sittinge in his
   sherte,

In his night-cappe, and with his nekke
   lene ;
She preyseth nat his pleying worth a
   bene.      (610) 1854
Than seide he thus, ' my reste wol I take ;
Now day is come, I may no lenger wake.'
And doun he leyde his heed, and sleep
   til pryme.
And afterward, whan that he saugh his
   tyme,
Up ryseth Januarie ; but fresshe May
Holdeth hir chambre un-to the fourthe
   day,      1860
As usage is of wyves for the beste.
For every labour som-tyme moot han
   reste,
Or elles longe may he nat endure ;
This is to seyn, no lyves creature,  (620)
Be it of fish, or brid, or beest, or man. 1865
                         Auctor.
  Now wol I speke of woful Damian,
That languissheth for love, as ye shul
   here ;
Therfore I speke to him in this manere :
I seye, ' O sely Damian, allas !
Answere to my demaunde, as in this cas,
How shaltow to thy lady fresshe May 1871
Telle thy wo ? She wole alwey seye "nay";
Eek if thou speke, she wol thy wo bi-
   wreye ;      (629)
God be thyn help, I can no bettre seye.
  This syke Damian in Venus fyr  1875
So brenneth, that he dyeth for desyr ;
For which he putte his lyf in aventure,
No lenger mighte he in this wyse endure ;
But prively a penner gan he borwe,
And in a lettre wroot he al his sorwe, 1880
In manere of a compleynt or a lay,
Un-to his faire fresshe lady May.
And in a purs of silk, heng on his sherte,
He hath it put, and leyde it at his
   herte.      (640) 1884
  The mone that, at noon, was, thilke day
That Januarie hath wedded fresshe May,
In two of Taur, was in-to Cancre gliden ;
So longe hath Maius in hir chambre
   biden,
As custume is un-to thise nobles alle.
A bryde shal nat eten in the halle,  1890
Til dayes foure or three dayes atte leste
Y-passed been ; than lat hir go to feste.

The fourthe day compleet fro noon to
　　noon,　　　　　　　　　　　　　(649)
Whan that the heighe masse was y-doon,
In halle sit this Januarie, and May　1895
As fresh as is the brighte someres day.
And so bifel, how that this gode man
Remembred him upon this Damian,
And seyde, ' Seinte Marie ! how may this be,
That Damian entendeth nat to me ?　1900
Is he ay syk, or how may this bityde ? '
His squyeres, whiche that stoden ther
　　bisyde,　　　　　　　　　　　　(658)
Excused him by-cause of his siknesse,
Which letted him to doon his bisinesse ;
Noon other cause mighte make him tarie.
　' That me forthinketh,' quod this Jan-
　　uarie,　　　　　　　　　　　　　1906
' He is a gentil squyer, by my trouthe !
If that he deyde, it were harm and routhe ;
He is as wys, discreet, and as secree
As any man I woot of his degree ;　1910
And ther-to manly and eek servisable,
And for to been a thrifty man right able.
But after mete, as sone as ever I may,
I wol my-self visyte him and eek May,
To doon him al the confort that I can.'
And for that word him blessed every man,
That, of his bountee and his gentillesse,
He wolde so conforten in siknesse　(674)
His squyer, for it was a gentil dede.
' Dame,' quod this Januarie, ' tak good
　　hede,　　　　　　　　　　　　　1920
At-after mete ye, with your wommen alle,
Whan ye han been in chambre out of
　　this halle,
That alle ye go see this Damian ;
Doth him disport, he is a gentil man ; (680)
And telleth him that I wol him visyte,
Have I no-thing but rested me a lyte ;
And spede yow faste, for I wole abyde
Til that ye slepe faste by my syde.'
And with that word he gan to him to calle
A squyer, that was marchal of his halle,
And tolde him certeyn thinges, what he
　　wolde.　　　　　　　　　　　　1931
　This fresshe May hath streight hir wey
　　y-holde,
With alle hir wommen, un-to Damian.
Doun by his beddes syde sit she than, (690)
Confortinge him as goodly as she may.
This Damian, whan that his tyme he say,

In secree wise his purs, and eek his bille,
In which that he y-writen hadde his
　　wille,　　　　　　　　　　　　　1938
Hath put in-to hir hand, with-outen more,
Save that he syketh wonder depe and sore,
And softely to hir right thus seyde he :
' Mercy ! and that ye nat discovere me ;
For I am deed, if that this thing be kid.'
This purs hath she inwith hir bosom hid,
And wente hir wey ; ye gete namore of me.
But un-to Januarie y-comen is she,　1946
That on his beddes syde sit ful softe. (703)
He taketh hir, and kisseth hir ful ofte,
And leyde him doun to slepe, and that
　　anon.
She feyned hir as that she moste gon　1950
Ther-as ye woot that every wight mot
　　nede.
And whan she of this bille hath taken
　　hede,
She rente it al to cloutes atte laste,
And in the privee softely it caste.　(710)
Who studieth now but faire fresshe
　　May ?　　　　　　　　　　　　　1955
Adoun by olde Januarie she lay,
That sleep, til that the coughe hath him
　　awaked ;
Anon he preyde hir strepen hir al naked ;
He wolde of hir, he seyde, han som ple-
　　saunce,
And seyde, hir clothes dide him encom-
　　braunce,　　　　　　　　　　　1960
And she obeyeth, be hir lief or looth.
But lest that precious folk be with me
　　wrooth,
How that he wroghte, I dar nat to yow
　　telle ;
Or whether hir thoughte it paradys or
　　helle ;　　　　　　　　　　　　(720)
But here I lete hem werken in hir wyse
Til evensong rong, and that they moste
　　aryse.　　　　　　　　　　　　1966
　Were it by destinee or aventure,
Were it by influence or by nature,
Or constellacion, that in swich estat
The hevene stood, that tyme fortunat 1970
Was for to putte a bille of Venus werkes
(For alle thing hath tyme, as seyn thise
　　clerkes)
To any womman, for to gete hir love,
I can nat seye ; but grete god above, (730)

That knoweth that non act is causelees,
He deme of al, for I wol holde my pees.
But sooth is this, how that this fresshe
   May     1977
Hath take swich impression that day,
For pitee of this syke Damian,
That from hir herte she ne dryve can 1980
The remembraunce for to doon him ese.
'Certeyn,' thoghte she, 'whom that this
   thing displese,
I rekke noght, for here I him assure,
To love him best of any creature,     (740)
Though he na-more hadde than his sherte.'
Lo, pitee renneth sone in gentil herte.

Heer may ye se how excellent franchyse
In wommen is, whan they hem narwe
   avyse.     1988
Som tyrant is, as ther be many oon,
That hath an herte as hard as any stoon,
Which wolde han lete him sterven in
   the place     1991
Wel rather than han graunted him hir
   grace ;
And hem rejoysen in hir cruel pryde,
And rekke nat to been an homicyde. (750)
This gentil May, fulfilled of pitee, 1995
Right of hir hande a lettre made she,
In which she graunteth him hir verray
   grace ;
Ther lakketh noght but only day and
   place,
Wher that she mighte un-to his lust
   suffyse :
For it shal be right as he wol devyse. 2000
And whan she saugh hir time, up-on a day,
To visite this Damian goth May,
And sotilly this lettre doun she threste
Under his pilwe, rede it if him leste. (760)
She taketh him by the hand, and harde
   him twiste     2005
So secrely, that no wight of it wiste,
And bad him been al hool, and forth she
   wente
To Januarie, whan that he for hir sente.
Up ryseth Damian the nexte morwe,
Al passed was his siknesse and his sorwe.
He kembeth him, he proyneth him and
   pyketh,     2011
He dooth al that his lady lust and lyketh ;
And eek to Januarie he gooth as lowe
As ever dide a dogge for the bowe.     (770)

He is so plesant un-to every man,     2015
(For craft is al, who-so that do it can)
That every wight is fayn to speke him
   good ;
And fully in his lady grace he stood.
Thus lete I Damian aboute his nede,
And in my tale forth I wol procede. 2020
   Somme clerkes holden that felicitee
Stant in delyt, and therefor certeyn he,
This noble Januarie, with al his might,
In honest wyse, as longeth to a knight,
Shoop him to live ful deliciously. (781) 2025
His housinge, his array, as honestly
To his degree was maked as a kinges.
Amonges othere of his honest thinges,
He made a gardin, walled al with stoon ;
So fair a gardin woot I nowher noon. 2030
For out of doute, I verraily suppose,
That he that wroot the Romance of the
   Rose
Ne coude of it the beautee wel devyse ;
Ne Priapus ne mighte nat suffyse,     (790)
Though he be god of gardins, for to
   telle     2035
The beautee of the gardin and the welle,
That stood under a laurer alwey grene.
Ful ofte tyme he, Pluto, and his quene,
Proserpina, and al hir fayërye
Disporten hem and maken melodye 2040
Aboute that welle, and daunced, as men
   tolde.
This noble knight, this Januarie the olde,
Swich deintee hath in it to walke and
   pleye,     (799)
That he wol no wight suffren bere the keye
Save he him-self ; for of the smale wiket
He bar alwey of silver a smal cliket, 2046
With which, whan that him leste, he it
   unshette.
And whan he wolde paye his wyf hir dette
In somer seson, thider wolde he go,
And May his wyf, and no wight but they
   two ;     2050
And thinges whiche that were nat doon
   a-bedde,
He in the gardin parfourned hem and
   spedde.
And in this wyse, many a mery day,
Lived this Januarie and fresshe May. (810)
But worldly joye may nat alwey dure 2055
To Januarie, ne to no creature.

Auctor.

O sodeyn hap, o thou fortune instable,
Lyk to the scorpioun so deceivable,
That flaterest with thyn heed when thou
　wolt stinge ;
Thy tayl is deeth, thurgh thyn enveni-
　minge.　　　　　　　　　　　2060
O brotil joye ! o swete venim queynte !
O monstre, that so subtilly canst peynte
Thy yiftes, under hewe of stedfastnesse,
That thou deceyvest bothe more and lesse !
Why hastow Januarie thus deceyved, (821)
That haddest him for thy ful frend re-
　ceyved ?　　　　　　　　　　2066
And now thou hast biraft him bothe hise
　yën,
For sorwe of which desyreth he to dyen.

　Allas ! this noble Januarie free,
Amidde his lust and his prosperitee, 2070
Is woxen blind, and that al sodeynly.
He wepeth and he wayleth pitously ;
And ther-with-al the fyr of jalousye, (829)
Lest that his wyf sholde falle in som folye,
So brente his herte, that he wolde fayn 2075
That som man bothe him and hir had
　slayn.
For neither after his deeth, nor in his lyf,
Ne wolde he that she were love ne wyf,
But ever live as widwe in clothes blake,
Soul as the turtle that lost hath hir make.
But atte laste, after a monthe or tweye,
His sorwe gan aswage, sooth to seye ; 2082
For whan he wiste it may noon other be,
He paciently took his adversitee ;　(840)
Save, out of doute, he may nat forgoon
That he nas jalous evermore in oon ;
Which jalousye it was so outrageous,
That neither in halle, n'in noon other hous,
Ne in noon other place, never-the-mo,
He nolde suffre hir for to ryde or go, 2090
But-if that he had hand on hir alway ;
For which ful ofte wepeth fresshe May,
That loveth Damian so benignely,
That she mot outher dyen sodeynly, (850)
Or elles she mot han him as hir leste ; 2095
She wayteth whan hir herte wolde breste.

　Up-on that other syde Damian
Bicomen is the sorwefulleste man
That ever was ; for neither night ne day
Ne mighte he speke a word to fresshe
　May,　　　　　　　　　　　2100

As to his purpos, of no swich matere,
But-if that Januarie moste it here,
That hadde an hand up-on hir evermo.
But nathelees, by wryting to and fro (860)
And privee signes, wiste he what she
　mente ;　　　　　　　　　　2105
And she knew eek the fyn of his entente.

Auctor.

O Januarie, what mighte it thee availle,
Thou mightest see as fer as shippes saille ?
For also good is blind deceyved be,
As be deceyved whan a man may see. 2110
Lo, Argus, which that hadde an hondred
　yën,
For al that ever he coude poure or pryen,
Yet was he blent ; and, god wot, so ben
　mo,
That wenen wisly that it be nat so.　(870)
Passe over is an ese, I sey na-more.　2115

　This fresshe May, that I spak of so
　yore,
In warme wex hath emprented the cliket,
That Januarie bar of the smale wiket,
By which in-to his gardin ofte he wente.
And Damian, that knew al hir entente,
The cliket countrefeted prively ;　　2121
Ther nis na-more to seye, but hastily
Som wonder by this cliket shal bityde,
Which ye shul heren, if ye wole abyde.

　O noble Ovyde, ful sooth seystou, god
　woot !　　　　　　　　　　Auctor.
What sleighte is it, thogh it be long and
　hoot,　　　　　　　　　(882) 2126
That he nil finde it out in som manere ?
By Piramus and Tesbee may men lere ;
Thogh they were kept ful longe streite
　overal,
They been accorded, rouninge thurgh a
　wal,　　　　　　　　　　　2130
Ther no wight coude han founde out
　swich a sleighte.　　　　　　(887)

　But now to purpos ; er that dayes eighte
Were passed, er the monthe of Juil, bifil
That Januarie hath caught so greet a wil,
Thurgh egging of his wyf, him for to pleye
In his gardin, and no wight but they tweye,
That in a morwe un-to this May seith he :
' Rys up, my wyf, my love, my lady free ;
The turtles vois is herd, my douve swete ;
The winter is goon, with alle his reynes
　wete ;　　　　　　　　　　2140

Com forth now, with thyn eyën columbyn !
How fairer been thy brestes than is wyn !
The gardin is enclosed al aboute ;
Com forth, my whyte spouse ; out of
     doute,               (900)
Thou hast me wounded in myn herte,
     o wyf!                2145
No spot of thee ne knew I al my lyf.
Com forth, and lat us taken our disport ;
I chees thee for my wyf and my confort.'
   Swiche olde lewed wordes used he ;
On Damian a signe made she,      2150
That he sholde go biforen with his cliket :
This Damian thanne hath opened the
     wiket,
And in he stirte, and that in swich manere,
That no wight mighte it see neither
     y-here ;               (910)
And stille he sit under a bush anoon. 2155
   This Januarie, as blind as is a stoon,
With Maius in his hand, and no wight mo,
In-to his fresshe gardin is ago,
And clapte to the wiket sodeynly.
   ' Now, wyf,' quod he, ' heer nis but thou
     and I,               2160
That art the creature that I best love.
For, by that lord that sit in heven above,
Lever ich hadde dyen on a knyf,
Than thee offende, trewe dere wyf ! (920)
For goddes sake, thenk how I thee chees,
Noght for no coveityse, doutelees,    2166
But only for the love I had to thee.
And though that I be old, and may nat see,
Beth to me trewe, and I shal telle yow why.
Three thinges, certes, shul ye winne ther-
     by ;               2170
First, love of Crist, and to your-self honour,
And al myn heritage, toun and tour ;
I yeve it yow, maketh chartres as yow
     leste ;               (929)
This shal be doon to-morwe er sonne reste.
So wisly god my soule bringe in blisse, 2175
I prey yow first, in covenant ye me kisse.
And thogh that I be jalous, wyte me noght.
Ye been so depe enprented in my thoght,
That, whan that I considere your beautee,
And ther-with-al the unlykly elde of me
I may nat, certes, thogh I sholde dye,
Forbere to been out of your companye
For verray love ; this is with-outen doute.
Now kis me, wyf, and lat us rome aboute.'

This fresshe May, whan she thise wordes
     herde,          (941) 2185
Benignely to Januarie answerde.
But first and forward she bigan to wepe,
' I have,' quod she, ' a soule for to kepe
As wel as ye, and also myn honour,
And of my wyfhod thilke tendre flour, 2190
Which that I have assured in your hond,
Whan that the preest to yow my body
     bond ;
Wherfore I wole answere in this manere
By the leve of yow, my lord so dere : (950)
I prey to god, that never dawe the day 2195
That I ne sterve, as foule as womman may,
If ever I do un-to my kin that shame,
Or elles I empeyre so my name,
That I be fals ; and if I do that lakke,
Do strepe me and put me in a sakke, 2200
And in the nexte river do me drenche.
I am a gentil womman and no wenche.
Why speke ye thus ? but men ben ever
     untrewe,            (959)
And wommen have repreve of yow ay newe.
Ye han non other contenance, I leve, 2205
But speke to us of untrust and repreve.'
   And with that word she saugh wher
     Damian
Sat in the bush, and coughen she bigan,
And with hir finger signes made she,
That Damian sholde climbe up-on a tree,
That charged was with fruit, and up he
     wente ;           2211
For verraily he knew al hir entente,
And every signe that she coude make
Wel bet than Januarie, hir owene make.
For in a lettre she had told him al    2215
Of this matere, how he werchen shal. (972)
And thus I lete him sitte up-on the pyrie,
And Januarie and May rominge myrie.
   Bright was the day, and blew the firma-
     ment.
Phebus of gold his stremes doun hath
     sent,              2220
To gladen every flour with his warmnesse.
He was that tyme *in Geminis*, as I gesse,
But litel fro his declinacioun
Of Cancer, Jovis exaltacioun.      (980)
And so bifel, that brighte morwe-tyde, 2225
That in that gardin, in the ferther syde,
Pluto, that is the king of fayërye,
And many a lady in his companye,

Folwinge his wyf, the quene Proserpyne,
Ech after other, right as any lyne— 2230
Whyl that she gadered floures in the mede,
In Claudian ye may the story rede,
How in his grisly carte he hir fette :—
This king of fairye thanne adoun him
      sette       (990) 2234
Up-on a bench of turves, fresh and grene,
And right anon thus seyde he to his quene.
' My wyf,' quod he, ' ther may no wight
      sey nay ;
Th'experience so preveth every day
The treson whiche that wommen doon to
      man.       2239
Ten hondred thousand [stories] telle I can
Notable of your untrouthe and brotilnesse.
O Salomon, wys, richest of richesse, 2242
Fulfild of sapience and of worldly glorie,
Ful worthy been thy wordes to memorie
To every wight that wit and reson can.
Thus preiseth he yet the bountee of man :
"Amonges a thousand men yet fond I oon,
But of wommen alle fond I noon." (1004)
   Thus seith the king that knoweth your
      wikkednesse ;
And Jesus *filius Syrak*, as I gesse, 2250
Ne speketh of yow but selde reverence.
A wilde fyr and corrupt pestilence
So falle up-on your bodies yet to-night!
Ne see ye nat this honurable knight, (1010)
By-cause, allas! that he is blind and old,
His owene man shal make him cokewold ;
Lo heer he sit, the lechour, in the tree. 2257
Now wol I graunten, of my magestee,
Un-to this olde blinde worthy knight
That he shal have a yeyn his eyen sight, 2260
Whan that his wyf wold doon him vileinye ;
Than shal he knowen al hir harlotrye
Both in repreve of hir and othere mo.'

   ' Ye shal,' quod Proserpyne, ' wol ye so ;
Now, by my modres sires soule I swere,
That I shal yeven hir suffisant answere,
And alle wommen after, for hir sake ;
That, though they be in any gilt y-take,
With face bold they shulle hem-self
      excuse,
And bere hem doun that wolden hem
      accuse.      2270
For lakke of answer, noon of hem shal dyen.
Al hadde man seyn a thing with bothe his
      yën,      (1028)

Yit shul we wommen visage it hardily,
And wepe, and swere, and chyde subtilly,
So that ye men shul been as lewed as gees.
What rekketh me of your auctoritees ?
   I woot wel that this Jew, this Salomon,
Fond of us wommen foles many oon.
But though that he ne fond no good
      womman,      2279
Yet hath ther founde many another man
Wommen ful trewe, ful gode, and ver-
      tuous.
Witnesse on hem that dwelle in Cristes
      hous,
With martirdom they preved hir con-
      stance.      (1039)
The Romayn gestes maken remembrance
Of many a verray trewe wyf also. 2285
But sire, ne be nat wrooth, al-be-it so,
Though that he seyde he fond no good
      womman,
I prey yow take the sentence of the man ;
He mente thus, that in sovereyn bontee
Nis noon but god, that sit in Trinitee. 2290
   Ey ! for verray god, that nis but oon,
What make ye so muche of Salomon ?
What though he made a temple, goddes
      hous ?      (1049)
What though he were riche and glorious ?
So made he eek a temple of false goddis,
How mighte he do a thing that more for-
      bode is ?      2296
Pardee, as faire as ye his name emplastre,
He was a lechour and an ydolastre ;
And in his elde he verray god forsook.
And if that god ne hadde, as seith the book,
Y-spared him for his fadres sake, he sholde
Have lost his regne rather than he wolde.
I sette noght of al the vileinye, (1059)
That ye of wommen wryte, a boterflye.
I am a womman, nedes moot I speke, 2305
Or elles swelle til myn herte breke.
For sithen he seyde that we ben jan-
      gleresses,
As ever hool I mote brouke my tresses,
I shal nat spare, for no curteisye, 2309
To speke him harm that wolde us vileinye.'
   ' Dame,' quod this Pluto, ' be no lenger
      wrooth ;
I yeve it up ; but sith I swoor myn ooth
That I wolde graunten him his sighte
      ageyn,      (1069)

My word shal stonde, I warne yow, certeyn.
I am a king, it sit me noght to lye.'   2315
  'And I,' quod she, 'a queene of fayërye.
Hir answere shal she have, I undertake ;
Lat us na-more wordes heer-of make.
For sothe, I wol no lenger yow contrarie.'
  Now lat us turne agayn to Januarie, 2320
That in the gardin with his faire May
Singeth, ful merier than the papejay,
'Yow love I best, and shal, and other
     noon.'
So longe aboute the aleyes is he goon, (1080)
Til he was come agaynes thilke pyrie, 2325
Wher-as this Damian sitteth ful myrie
An heigh, among the fresshe leves grene.
   This fresshe May, that is so bright and
     shene,
Gan for to syke, and seyde, 'allas, my
     syde !
Now sir,' quod she, 'for aught that may
     bityde,                2330
I moste han of the peres that I see,
Or I mot dye, so sore longeth me
To eten of the smale peres grene.   (1089)
Help, for hir love that is of hevene quene !
I telle yow wel, a womman in my
     plyt                  2335
May han to fruit so greet an appetyt,
That she may dyen, but she of it have.'
  'Allas !' quod he, 'that I ne had heer
     a knave
That coude climbe; allas! allas!' quod he,
'That I am blind.'   'Ye, sir, no fors,'
     quod she :              2340
'But wolde ye vouche-sauf, for goddes
     sake,
The pyrie in with your armes for to take,
(For wel I woot that ye mistruste me)
Thanne sholde I climbe wel y-nogh,' quod
     she,              (1100)
'So I my foot mighte sette upon your bak.'
  'Certes,' quod he, 'ther-on shal be no
     lak,               2346
Mighte I yow helpen with myn herte
     blood.'
He stoupeth doun, and on his bak she stood,
And caughte hir by a twiste, and up she
     gooth.
Ladies, I prey yow that ye be nat wrooth ;
I can nat glose, I am a rude man.   2351
And sodeynly anon this Damian

Gan pullen up the smok, and in he throng.
  And whan that Pluto saugh this grete
     wrong,            (1110)
To Januarie he gaf agayn his sighte, 2355
And made him see, as wel as ever he
     mighte.
And whan that he hadde caught his
     sighte agayn,
Ne was ther never man of thing so fayn.
But on his wyf his thoght was evermo ;
Up to the tree he caste his eyen two, 2360
And saugh that Damian his wyf had
     dressed
In swich manere, it may nat ben ex-
     pressed
But if I wolde speke uncurteisly :
And up he yaf a roring and a cry   (1120)
As doth the moder whan the child shal
     dye :             2365
'Out ! help ! allas ! harrow !' he gan to crye,
'O stronge lady store, what dostow ?'
   And she answerde, 'sir, what eyleth
     yow ?
Have pacience, and reson in your minde,
I have yow holpe on bothe your eyen
     blinde.           2370
Up peril of my soule, I shal nat lyen,
As me was taught, to hele with your yën,
Was no-thing bet to make yow to see
Than strugle with a man up-on a tree. (1130)
God woot, I dide it in ful good entente.'
  'Strugle !' quod he, 'ye, algate in it
     wente !           2376
God yeve yow bothe on shames deeth to
     dyen!
He swyved thee, I saugh it with myne yën,
And elles be I hanged by the hals !'
  'Thanne is,' quod she, 'my medicyne
     al fals ;           2380
For certeinly, if that ye mighte see,
Ye wolde nat seyn thise wordes un-to me ;
Ye han som glimsing and no parfit sighte.'
  'I see,' quod he, 'as wel as ever I
     mighte,           (1140)
Thonked be god ! with bothe myne eyen
     two,            2385
And by my trouthe, me thoughte he dide
     thee so.'
  'Ye maze, maze, gode sire,' quod she,
'This thank have I for I have maad yow
     see ;

Allas!' quod she, 'that ever I was so
    kinde !'
  'Now, dame,' quod he, 'lat al passe out
    of minde.           2390
Com doun, my lief, and if I have missayd,
God help me so, as I am yvel apayd.
But, by my fader soule, I wende han seyn,
How that this Damian had by thee leyn,
And that thy smok had leyn up-on his
    brest.'         (1151) 2395
  'Ye, sire,' quod she, 'ye may wene as
    yow lest ;
But, sire, a man that waketh out of his
    sleep,
He may nat sodeynly wel taken keep
Up-on a thing, ne seen it parfitly,
Til that he be adawed verraily ;   2400
Right so a man, that longe hath blind y-be,
Ne may nat sodeynly so wel y-see,

First whan his sighte is newe come ageyn,
As he that hath a day or two y-seyn. (1160)
Til that your sighte y-satled be a whyle,
Ther may ful many a sighte yow bigyle.
Beth war, I prey yow; for, by hevene
    king,         2407
Ful many a man weneth to seen a thing,
And it is al another than it semeth.
He that misconceyveth, he misdemeth.'
And with that word she leep doun fro the
    tree.         2411
  This Januarie, who is glad but he ?
He kisseth hir, and clippeth hir ful ofte,
And on hir wombe he stroketh hir ful
    softe,        (1170)
And to his palays hoom he hath hir lad.
Now, gode men, I pray yow to be glad. 2416
Thus endeth heer my tale of Januarie ;
God blesse us and his moder Seinte Marie !

**Here is ended the Marchantes Tale of Januarie.**

# EPILOGUE TO THE MARCHANTES
# TALE.

' Ey ! goddes mercy !' seyde our Hoste tho,
' Now swich a wyf I pray god kepe me fro !
Lo, whiche sleightes and subtilitees  2421
In wommen been ! for ay as bisy as bees
Ben they, us sely men for to deceyve,
And from a sothe ever wol they weyve ;
By this Marchauntes Tale it preveth weel.
But doutelees, as trewe as any steel  2426
I have a wyf, though that she povre be ;
But of hir tonge a labbing shrewe is she,
And yet she hath an heep of vyces mo ; (11)
Ther-of no fors, lat alle swiche thinges go.

But, wite ye what ? in conseil be it seyd,
Me reweth sore I am un-to hir teyd.  2432
For, and I sholde rekenen every vyce
Which that she hath, y-wis, I were to
    nyce,
And cause why ; it sholde reported be 2435
And told to hir of somme of this meynee ;
Of whom, it nedeth nat for to declare,
Sin wommen connen outen swich chaf-
    fare ;        (20)
And eek my wit suffyseth nat ther-to
To tellen al ; wherfor my tale is do.' 2440

## GROUP F.

# THE SQUIERES TALE.

### The Squire's Prologue.

'Squier, com neer, if it your wille be,
And sey somwhat of love ; for, certes, ye
Connen ther-on as muche as any man.'
'Nay, sir,' quod he, ' but I wol seye as I can
With hertly wille ; for I wol nat rebelle 5
Agayn your lust ; a tale wol I telle.
Have me excused if I speke amis,
My wil is good ; and lo, my tale is this.'

### Here biginneth the Squieres Tale.

At Sarray, in the land of Tartarye,    (1)
Ther dwelte a king, that werreyed Russye,
Thurgh which ther deyde many a doughty
     man.      11
This noble king was cleped Cambinskan,
Which in his tyme was of so greet renoun
That ther nas no-wher in no regioun
So excellent a lord in alle thing ;    15
Him lakked noght that longeth to a king.
As of the secte of which that he was born
He kepte his lay, to which that he was
     sworn ;      (10)
And ther-to he was hardy, wys, and riche,
And †piëtous and just, alwey y-liche ; 20
Sooth of his word, benigne and honurable,
Of his corage as any centre stable ;
Yong, fresh, and strong, in armes desirous
As any bacheler of al his hous.
A fair persone he was and fortunat,    25
And kepte alwey so wel royal estat,
That ther was nowher swich another man.
This noble king, this Tartre Cambinskan
Hadde two sones on Elpheta his wyf, (21)
Of whiche th'eldeste highte Algarsyf, 30
That other sone was cleped Cambalo.
A doghter hadde this worthy king also,
That yongest was, and highte Canacee.
But for to telle yow al hir beautee,

It lyth nat in my tonge, n'in my conning ;
I dar nat undertake so heigh a thing. 36
Myn English eek is insufficient ;
It moste been a rethor excellent,    (30)
That coude his colours longing for that art,
If he sholde hir discryven every part. 40
I am non swich, I moot speke as I can.

And so bifel that, whan this Cambinskan
Hath twenty winter born his diademe,
As he was wont fro yeer to yeer, I deme,
He leet the feste of his nativitee    45
Don cryen thurghout Sarray his citee,
The last Idus of March, after the yeer.
Phebus the sonne ful joly was and cleer ;
For he was neigh his exaltacioun    (41)
In Martes face, and in his mansioun    50
In Aries, the colerik hote signe.
Ful lusty was the weder and benigne,
For which the foules, agayn the sonne
     shene,
What for the seson and the yonge grene,
Ful loude songen hir affecciouns ;    55
Hem semed han geten hem protecciouns
Agayn the swerd of winter kene and cold.
This Cambinskan, of which I have yow
     told,      (50)
In royal vestiment sit on his deys,
With diademe, ful heighe in his paleys,
And halt his feste, so solempne and so
     riche      61
That in this world ne was ther noon it
     liche.
Of which if I shal tellen al th'array,
Than wolde it occupye a someres day ;
And eek it nedeth nat for to devyse    65
At every cours the ordre of hir servyse.
I wol nat tellen of hir strange sewes, (59)
Ne of hir swannes, ne of hir heronsewes.
Eek in that lond, as tellen knightes olde,
Ther is som mete that is ful deyntee holde,

That in this lond men recche of it but
　smal ;　71
Ther nis no man that may reporten al.
I wol nat tarien yow, for it is pryme,
And for it is no fruit but los of tyme ;
Un-to my firste I wol have my recours. 75
　And so bifel that, after the thridde cours,
Why that this king sit thus in his nobleye,
Herkninge his minstralles hir thinges
　pleye　(70)
Biforn him at the bord deliciously,
In at the halle-dore al sodeynly　80
Ther cam a knight up-on a stede of bras,
And in his hand a brood mirour of glas.
Upon his thombe he hadde of gold a
　ring,
And by his syde a naked swerd hanging ;
And up he rydeth to the heighe bord. 85
In al the halle ne was ther spoke a word
For merveille of this knight ; him to bi-
　holde
Ful bisily ther wayten yonge and olde.
　This strange knight, that cam thus
　sodeynly,　(81)
Al armed save his heed ful richely,　90
Saluëth king and queen, and lordes alle,
By ordre, as they seten in the halle,
With so heigh reverence and obeisaunce
As wel in speche as in contenaunce,
That Gawain, with his olde curteisye, 95
Though he were come ageyn out of Fairye,
Ne coude him nat amende with a word.
And after this, biforn the heighe bord, (90)
He with a manly voys seith his message,
After the forme used in his langage, 100
With-outen vyce of sillable or of lettre ;
And, for his tale sholde seme the bettre,
Accordant to his wordes was his chere,
As techeth art of speche hem that it
　lere ;
Al-be-it that I can nat soune his style, 105
Ne can nat climben over so heigh a style,
Yet seye I this, as to commune entente,
Thus muche amounteth al that ever he
　mente,　(100)
If it so be that I have it in minde.
　He seyde, ' the king of Arabie and of
　Inde,　110
My lige lord, on this solempne day
Saluëth yow as he best can and may,
And sendeth yow, in honour of your feste,

By me, that am al redy at your heste,
This stede of bras, that esily and wel　115
Can, in the space of o day naturel,
This is to seyn, in foure and twenty houres,
Wher-so yow list, in droghte or elles
　shoures,　(110)
Beren your body in-to every place
To which your herte wilneth for to pace
With-outen wem of yow, thurgh foul or
　fair ;　121
Or, if yow list to fleen as hye in the air
As doth an egle, whan him list to sore,
This same stede shal bere yow ever-more
With-outen harm, til ye be ther yow
　leste,　125
Though that ye slepen on his bak or reste ;
And turne ayeyn, with wrything of a pin.
He that it wroghte coude ful many a gin ;
He wayted many a constellacioun　(121)
Er he had doon this operacioun ;　130
And knew ful many a seel and many
　a bond.
　This mirour eek, that I have in myn
　hond,
Hath swich a might, that men may in it
　see
Whan ther shal fallen any adversitee
Un-to your regne or to your-self also ; 135
And openly who is your freend or foo.
And over al this, if any lady bright
Hath set hir herte on any maner wight,
If he be fals, she shal his treson see, (131)
His newe love and al his subtiltee　140
So openly, that ther shal no-thing hyde.
Wherfor, ageyn this lusty someres tyde,
This mirour and this ring, that ye may see,
He hath sent to my lady Canacee,
Your excellente doghter that is here. 145
　The vertu of the ring, if ye wol here,
Is this ; that, if hir lust it for to were (139)
Up-on hir thombe, or in hir purs it bere,
Ther is no foul that fleeth under the
　hevene
That she ne shal wel understonde his
　stevene,　150
And knowe his mening openly and pleyn,
And answere him in his langage ageyn.
And every gras that groweth up-on rote
She shal eek knowe, and whom it wol do
　bote,
Al be his woundes never so depe and wyde.

This naked swerd, that hangeth by my
    syde, 156
Swich vertu hath, that what man so ye
    smyte,
Thurgh-out his armure it wol kerve and
    byte, (150)
Were it as thikke as is a branched ook ;
And what man that is wounded with the
    strook 160
Shal never be hool til that yow list, of
    grace,
To stroke him with the platte in thilke
    place
Ther he is hurt : this is as muche to seyn
Ye mote with the platte swerd ageyn
Stroke him in the wounde, and it wol
    close ; 165
This is a verray sooth, with-outen glose,
It failleth nat whyl it is in your hold.'
    And whan this knight hath thus his
        tale told, (160)
He rydeth out of halle, and doun he lighte.
His stede, which that shoon as sonne
    brighte, 170
Stant in the court, as stille as any stoon.
This knight is to his chambre lad anon,
And is unarmed and to mete y-set.
    The presents been ful royally y-fet,
This is to seyn, the swerd and the mirour,
And born anon in-to the heighe tour 176
With certeine officers ordeyned therfore ;
And un-to Canacee this ring was bore (170)
Solempnely, ther she sit at the table.
But sikerly, with-outen any fable, 180
The hors of bras, that may nat be remewed,
It stant as it were to the ground y-glewed.
Ther may no man out of the place it dryve
For noon engyn of windas or polyve ; 184
And cause why, for they can nat the craft.
And therefore in the place they han it
    laft
Til that the knight hath taught hem the
    manere
To voyden him, as ye shal after here. (180)
    Greet was the prees, that swarmeth to
        and fro, 189
To gauren on this hors that stondeth so ;
For it so heigh was, and so brood and long,
So wel proporcioned for to ben strong,
Right as it were a stede of Lumbardye ;
Ther-with so horsly, and so quik of yë

As it a gentil Poileys courser were. 195
For certes, fro his tayl un-to his ere,
Nature ne art ne coude him nat amende
In no degree, as al the peple wende. (190)
But evermore hir moste wonder was,
How that it coude goon, and was of
    bras ; 200
It was of Fairye, as the peple semed.
Diverse folk diversely they demed ;
As many hedes, as many wittes ther been.
They murmureden as dooth a swarm of
    been,
And maden skiles after hir fantasyes, 205
Rehersinge of thise olde poetryes,
And seyden, it was lyk the Pegasee,
The hors that hadde winges for to flee ; (200)
Or elles it was the Grekes hors Synon,
That broghte Troye to destruccion, 210
As men may in thise olde gestes rede.
'Myn herte,' quod oon, 'is evermore in
    drede ;
I trowe som men of armes been ther-inne,
That shapen hem this citee for to winne.
It were right good that al swich thing
    were knowe.' 215
Another rowned to his felawe lowe,
And seyde, 'he lyeth, it is rather lyk
An apparence y-maad by som magyk, (210)
As jogelours pleyen at thise festes grete.'
Of sondry doutes thus they jangle and
    trete, 220
As lewed peple demeth comunly
Of thinges that ben maad more subtilly
Than they can in her lewednes compre-
    hende ;
They demen gladly to the badder ende.
    And somme of hem wondred on the
        mirour, 225
That born was up in-to the maister-tour,
How men mighte in it swiche thinges see.
Another answerde, and seyde it mighte
    wel be (220)
Naturelly, by composiciouns
Of angles and of slye reflexiouns, 230
And seyden, that in Rome was swich oon.
They speken of Alocen and Vitulon,
And Aristotle, that writen in hir lyves
Of queynte mirours and of prospectyves,
As knowen they that han hir bokes herd.
    And othere folk han wondred on the
        swerd 236

That wolde percen thurgh-out every-thing;
And fille in speche of Thelophus the king,
And of Achilles with his queynte spere,
For he coude with it bothe hele and dere,
Right in swich wyse as men may with the
    swerd                 (233) 241
Of which right now ye han your-selven
    herd.
They speken of sondry harding of metal,
And speke of medicynes ther-with-al,
And how, and whanne, it sholde y-harded
    be;                       245
Which is unknowe algates unto me.
  Tho speke they of Canaceës ring,
And seyden alle, that swich a wonder
    thing                (240)
Of craft of ringes herde they never non,
Save that he, Moyses, and king Salomon
Hadde a name of konning in swich art. 251
Thus seyn the peple, and drawen hem
    apart.
But nathelees, somme seyden that it was
Wonder to maken of fern-asshen glas,
And yet nis glas nat lyk asshen of fern;
But for they han y-knowen it so fern, 256
Therfore cesseth her jangling and her
    wonder.
As sore wondren somme on cause of
    thonder,              (250)
On ebbe, on flood, on gossomer, and on
    mist,                  259
And alle thing, til that the cause is wist.
Thus jangle they and demen and devyse,
Til that the king gan fro the bord aryse.
  Phebus hath laft the angle meridional,
And yet ascending was the beest royal,
The gentil Leon, with his Aldiran,   265
Whan that this Tartre king, this Cam-
    binskan,          (258)
Roos fro his bord, ther that he sat ful hye.
Toforn him gooth the loude minstralcye,
Til he cam to his chambre of parements,
Ther as they sownen diverse instruments,
That it is lyk an heven for to here.   271
Now daunsen lusty Venus children dere,
For in the Fish hir lady sat ful hye,
And loketh on hem with a freendly yë.
  This noble king is set up in his trone. 275
This strange knight is fet to him ful sone,
And on the daunce he gooth with Canacee.
Heer is the revel and the jolitee   (270)

That is nat able a dul man to devyse. 279
He moste han knowen love and his servyse,
And been a festlich man as fresh as
    May,
That sholde yow devysen swich array.
  Who coude telle yow the forme of
    daunces,
So uncouthe and so fresshe contenaunces,
Swich subtil loking and dissimulinges 285
For drede of jalouse mennes aperceyvinges?
No man but Launcelot, and he is deed.
Therfor I passe of al this lustiheed; (280)
I seye na-more, but in this jolynesse
I lete hem, til men to the soper dresse. 290
  The styward bit the spyces for to hye,
And eek the wyn, in al this melodye.
The usshers and the squyers ben y-goon;
The spyces and the wyn is come anoon.
They ete and drinke; and whan this hadde
    an ende,            295
Un-to the temple, as reson was, they
    wende.
  The service doon, they soupen al by day.
What nedeth yow rehercen hir array? (290)
Ech man wot wel, that at a kinges feeste
Hath plentee, to the moste and to the
    leeste,            300
And deyntees **mo** than been in my
    knowing.
At-after soper gooth this noble king
To seen this hors of bras, with al the route
Of lordes and of ladyes him aboute.
  Swich wondring was ther on this hors
    of bras          305
That, sin the grete sege of Troye was,
Ther-as men wondreden on an hors also,
Ne was ther swich a wondring as was tho.
But fynally the king axeth this knight (301)
The vertu of this courser and the might,
And preyede him to telle his governaunce.
  This hors anoon bigan to trippe and
    daunce,          312
Whan that this knight leyde hand up-on
    his reyne,
And seyde, 'sir, ther is na-more to seyne,
But, whan yow list to ryden any-where, 315
Ye moten trille a pin, stant in his ere,
Which I shall telle yow bitwix vs two. (309)
Ye mote nempne him to what place also
Or to what contree that yow list to ryde. 319
And whan ye come ther as yow list abyde,

Bidde him descende, and trille another pin,
For ther-in lyth the effect of al the gin,
And he wol doun descende and doon your
   wille ;
And in that place he wol abyde stille,
Though al the world the contrarie hadde
   y-swore ;     325
He shal nat thennes ben y-drawe n'y-
   bore.
Or, if yow liste bidde him thennes goon,
Trille this pin, and he wol vanishe anoon
Out of the sighte of every maner wight,(321)
And come agayn, be it by day or night, 330
When that yow list to clepen him ageyn
In swich a gyse as I shal to yow seyn
Bitwixe yow and me, and that ful sone.
Ryde whan yow list, ther is na-more to
   done.'
   Enformed whan the king was of that
     knight,     335
And hath conceyved in his wit aright
The maner and the forme of al this thing,
Thus glad and blythe, this noble doughty
   king     (330)
Repeireth to his revel as biforn.
The brydel is un-to the tour y-born,    340
And kept among his jewels leve and
   dere.
The hors vanisshed, I noot in what manere,
Out of hir sighte ; ye gete na-more of me.
But thus I lete in lust and Iolitee
This Cambynskan his lordes festeyinge,345
Til wel ny the day bigan to springe.

### Explicit prima pars.

### Sequitur pars secunda.

The norice of digestioun, the slepe,
Gan on hem winke, and bad hem taken
   kepe,     (340)
That muchel drink and labour wolde han
   reste ;
And with a galping mouth hem alle he
   keste,     350
And seyde, ' it was tyme to lye adoun,
For blood was in his dominacioun ;
Cherissheth blood, natures freend,' quod
   he.
They thanken him galpinge, by two, by
   three,
And every wight gan drawe him to his
   reste,     355

As slepe hem bad ; they toke it for the
   beste.
Hir dremes shul nat been y-told for me ;
Ful were hir hedes of fumositee,     (350)
That causeth dreem, of which ther nis no
   charge.     359
They slepen til that it was pryme large,
The moste part, but it were Canacee ;
She was ful mesurable, as wommen be.
For of hir fader hadde she take leve
To gon to reste, sone after it was eve ;
Hir liste nat appalled for to be,     365
Nor on the morwe unfestlich for to see ;
And slepte hir firste sleep, and thanne
   awook.     (359)
For swich a joye she in hir herte took
Both of hir queynte ring and hir mirour,
That twenty tyme she changed hir colour ;
And in hir slepe, right for impressioun 371
Of hir mirour, she hadde a visioun.
Wherfore, er that the sonne gan up glyde,
She cleped on hir maistresse hir bisyde,
And seyde, that hir liste for to ryse.    375
   Thise olde wommen that been gladly
     wyse,
As is hir maistresse, answerde hir anoon,
And seyde, ' madame, whider wil ye
   goon     (370)
Thus erly ? for the folk ben alle on reste.'
' I wol,' quod she, ' aryse, for me leste 380
No lenger for to slepe, and walke aboute.'
   Hir maistresse clepeth wommen a gret
   route,
And up they rysen, wel a ten or twelve ;
Up ryseth fresshe Canacee hir-selve,
As rody and bright as dooth the yonge
   sonne,     385
That in the Ram is four degrees up-ronne ;
Noon hyer was he, whan she redy was ;
And forth she walketh esily a pas,    (380)
Arrayed after the lusty seson sote     389
Lightly, for to pleye and walke on fote ;
Nat but with fyve or six of hir meynee ;
And in a trench, forth in the park, goth
   she.
The vapour, which that fro the erthe glood,
Made the sonne to seme rody and brood ;
But nathelees, it was so fair a sighte    395
That it made alle hir hertes for to lighte,
What for the seson and the morweninge,
And for the foules that she herde singe ;

For right anon she wiste what they mente
Right by hir song, and knew al hir entente.
　The knotte, why that every tale is told,
If it be taried til that lust be cold
Of hem that han it after herkned yore,
The savour passeth ever lenger the more,
For fulsomnesse of his prolixitee.　405
And by the same reson thinketh me,
I sholde to the knotte condescende,
And maken of hir walking sone an
　　ende.　(400)
　Amidde a tree fordrye, as whyt as chalk,
As Canacee was pleying in hir walk,　410
Ther sat a faucon over hir heed ful hye,
That with a pitous voys so gan to crye
That all the wode resouned of hir cry.
Y-beten hath she hir-self so pitously　414
With bothe hir winges, til the rede blood
Ran endelong the tree ther-as she stood.
And ever in oon she cryde alwey and
　　shrighte,
And with hir beek hir-selven so she
　　prighte,　(410)
That ther nis tygre, ne noon so cruel
　　beste,
That dwelleth either in wode or in foreste
That nolde han wept, if that he wepe
　　coude,　421
For sorwe of hir, she shrighte alwey so
　　loude.
For ther nas never yet no man on lyve—
If that I coude a faucon wel discryve—
That herde of swich another of fairnesse,
As wel of plumage as of gentillesse　426
Of shap, and al that mighte y-rekened be.
A faucon peregryn than semed she　(420)
Of fremde land; and evermore, as she
　　stood,
She swowneth now and now for lakke of
　　blood,　430
Til wel neigh is she fallen fro the tree.
　This faire kinges doghter, Canacee,
That on hir finger bar the queynte ring,
Thurgh which she understood wel every
　　thing
That any foul may in his ledene seyn, 435
And coude answere him in his ledene
　　ageyn,
Hath understonde what this faucon seyde,
And wel neigh for the rewthe almost she
　　deyde.　(430)

And to the tree she gooth ful hastily,
And on this faucon loketh pitously,　440
And heeld hir lappe abrood, for wel she
　　wiste
The faucon moste fallen fro the twiste,
When that it swowned next, for lakke of
　　blood.
A longe while to wayten hir she stood
Till atte laste she spak in this manere 445
Un-to the hauk, as ye shul after here.
　'What is the cause, if it be for to telle,
That ye be in this furial pyne of helle?'
Quod Canacee un-to this hauk above. (441)
'Is this for sorwe of deeth or los of love?
For, as I trowe, thise ben causes two　451
That causen moost a gentil herte wo;
Of other harm it nedeth nat to speke.
For ye your-self upon your-self yow wreke,
Which proveth wel, that either love or
　　drede　455
Mot been encheson of your cruel dede,
Sin that I see non other wight yow chace.
For love of god, as dooth your-selven grace
Or what may ben your help; for west nor
　　eest　(451)
Ne sey I never er now no brid ne beest
That ferde with him-self so pitously. 461
Ye slee me with your sorwe, verraily;
I have of yow so gret compassioun.
For goddes love, com fro the tree adoun;
And, as I am a kinges doghter trewe, 465
If that I verraily the cause knewe
Of your disese, if it lay in my might,
I wolde amende it, er that it were night,
As wisly helpe me gret god of kinde! (461)
And herbes shal I right y-nowe y-finde
To hele with your hurtes hastily.'　471
　Tho shrighte this faucon more pitously
Than ever she dide, and fil to grounde
　　anoon,
And lyth aswowne, deed, and lyk a stoon,
Til Canacee hath in hir lappe hir take 475
Un-to the tyme she gan of swough awake.
And, after that she of hir swough gan
　　breyde,
Right in hir haukes ledene thus she
　　seyde:—　(470)
'That pitee renneth sone in gentil herte,
Feling his similitude in peynes smerte, 480
Is preved al-day, as men may it see,
As wel by werk as by auctoritee;

For gentil herte kytheth gentillesse.
I see wel, that ye han of my distresse
Compassioun, my faire Canacee,     485
Of verray wommanly benignitee
That nature in your principles hath set.
But for non hope for to fare the bet, (480)
But for to obeye un-to your herte free,
And for to maken other be war by me,
As by the whelp chasted is the leoun, 491
Right for that cause and that conclusioun,
Whyl that I have a leyser and a space,
Myn harm I wol confessen, er I pace.'
And ever, whyl that oon hir sorwe tolde,
That other weep, as she to water wolde,
Til that the faucon bad hir to be stille ;
And, with a syk, right thus she seyde hir
     wille.        (490) 498
   'Ther I was bred (allas ! that harde
     day !)
And fostred in a roche of marbul gray
So tendrely, that nothing eyled me,    501
I niste nat what was adversitee,
Til I coude flee ful hye under the sky.
Tho dwelte a tercelet me faste by,
That semed welle of alle gentillesse ; 505
Al were he ful of treson and falsnesse,
It was so wrapped under humble chere,
And under hewe of trouthe in swich
     manere,          (500)
Under plesance, and under bisy peyne,
That no wight coude han wend he coude
     feyne,          510
So depe in greyn he dyed his coloures.
Right as a serpent hit him under floures
Til he may seen his tyme for to byte,
Right so this god of love, this ypocryte,
Doth so his cerimonies and obeisaunces,
And kepeth in semblant alle his obser-
     vances          516
That sowneth in-to gentillesse of love.
As in a toumbe is al the faire above, (510)
And under is the corps, swich as ye woot,
Swich was this ypocryte, bothe cold and
     hoot,          520
And in this wyse he served his entente,
That (save the feend) non wiste what he
     mente.
Til he so longe had wopen and com-
     pleyned,
And many a yeer his service to me feyned,
Til that myn herte, to pitous and to nyce,

Al innocent of his crouned malice,    526
For-fered of his deeth, as thoughte me,
Upon his othes and his seuretee,     (520)
Graunted him love, on this condicioun,
That evermore myn honour and renoun
Were saved, bothe privee and apert ; 531
This is to seyn, that, after his desert,
I yaf him al myn herte and al my
     thoght—
God woot and he, that otherwyse noght—
And took his herte in chaunge for myn
     for ay.          535
But sooth is seyd, gon sithen many a day,
" A trew wight and a theef thenken nat
     oon."
And, whan he saugh the thing so fer
     y-goon,          (530)
That I had graunted him fully my love,
In swich a gyse as I have seyd above, 540
And yeven him my trewe herte, as free
As he swoor he his herte yaf to me ;
Anon this tygre, ful of doublenesse,
Fil on his knees with so devout hum-
     blesse,
With so heigh reverence, and, as by his
     chere,          545
So lyk a gentil lovere of manere,
So ravisshed, as it semed, for the joye,
That never Jason, ne Parys of Troye, (540)
Jason ? certes, ne non other man,
Sin Lameth was, that alderfirst bigan 550
To loven two, as writen folk biforn,
Ne never, sin the firste man was born,
Ne coude man, by twenty thousand part,
Countrefete the sophimes of his art ;
Ne were worthy unbokele his galoche, 555
Ther doublenesse or feyning sholde ap-
     proche,
Ne so coude thanke a wight as he did me !
His maner was an heven for to see    (550)
Til any womman, were she never so
     wys ;
So peynted he and kembde at point-devys
As wel his wordes as his contenaunce. 561
And I so loved him for his obeisaunce,
And for the trouthe I demed in his herte,
That, if so were that any thing him
     smerte,
Al were it never so lyte, and I it wiste, 565
Me thoughte, I felte deeth myn herte
     twiste.

And shortly, so ferforth this thing is
    went,                                        (559)
That my wil was his willes instrument ;
This is to seyn, my wil obeyed his wil
In alle thing, as fer as reson fil,        570
Keping the boundes of my worship ever.
Ne never hadde I thing so leef, ne lever,
As him, god woot ! ne never shal na-mo.
    This lasteth lenger than a yeer or two,
That I supposed of him noght but good.
But fynally, thus atte laste it stood,   576
That fortune wolde that he moste twinne
Out of that place which that I was inne.
Wher me was wo, that is no questioun ;
I can nat make of it discripcioun ;      580
For o thing dar I tellen boldely,         (573)
I knowe what is the peyne of deth ther-by ;
Swich harm I felte for he ne mighte
    bileve.
So on a day of me he took his leve,
So sorwefully eek, that I wende verraily
That he had felt as muche harm as I,   586
Whan that I herde him speke, and saugh
    his hewe.                                    (579)
But nathelees, I thoughte he was so trewe,
And eek that he repaire sholde ageyn
With-inne a litel whyle, sooth to seyn ; 590
And reson wolde eek that he moste go
For his honour, as ofte it happeth so,
That I made vertu of necessitee,
And took it wel, sin that it moste be.
As I best mighte, I hidde fro him my
    sorwe,                                       595
And took him by the hond, seint John to
    borwe,
And seyde him thus : " lo, I am youres al ;
Beth swich as I to yow have been, and
    shal."                                       (590)
What he answerde, it nede'th noght re-
    herce,
Who can sey bet than he, who can do
    werse?                                       600
Whan he hath al wel seyd, thanne hath
    he doon.
" Therfor bihoveth him a ful long spoon
That shal ete with a feend," thus herde
    I seye.
So atte laste he moste forth his weye,
And forth he fleeth, til he cam ther him
    leste.                                       605
Whan it cam him to purpos for to reste,

I trowe he hadde thilke text in minde,
That " alle thing, repeiring to his kinde,
Gladeth him-self " ; thus seyn men, as I
    gesse ;                                      (601)
Men loven of propre kinde newfangel-
    nesse,                                       610
As briddes doon that men in cages fede.
For though thou night and day take of
    hem hede,
And strawe hir cage faire and softe as
    silk,
And yeve hem sugre, hony, breed and
    milk,
Yet right anon, as that his dore is uppe,
He with his feet wol spurne adoun his
    cuppe,                                       616
And to the wode he wol and wormes ete ;
So newefangel been they of hir mete, (610)
And loven novelryes of propre kinde ;
No gentillesse of blood [ne] may hem
    binde.                                       620
So ferde this tercelet, allas the day !
Though he were gentil born, and fresh
    and gay,
And goodly for to seen, and humble and
    free,
He saugh up-on a tyme a kyte flee,
And sodeynly he loved this kyte so,    625
That al his love is clene fro me ago,
And hath his trouthe falsed in this wyse ;
Thus hath the kyte my love in hir ser-
    vyse,                                        (620)
And I am lorn with-outen remedye !'
And with that word this faucon gan to
    crye,                                        630
And swowned eft in Canaceës barme.
    Greet was the sorwe, for the haukes
    harme,
That Canacee and alle hir wommen made ;
They niste how they mighte the faucon
    glade.                                       634
But Canacee hom bereth hir in hir lappe,
And softely in plastres gan hir wrappe,
Ther as she with hir beek had hurt hir-
    selve.                                       (629)
Now can nat Canacee but herbes delve
Out of the grounde, and make salves
    newe
Of herbes precious, and fyne of hewe, 640
To helen with this hauk ; fro day to night
She dooth hir bisinesse and al hir might.

And by hir beddes heed she made a mewe,
And covered it with veluëttes blewe,
In signe of trouthe that is in wommen
　　sene.　　　　　　　　　　　　　　645
And al with-oute, the mewe is peynted
　　grene,
In which were peynted alle thise false
　　foules,　　　　　　　　　　　　(639)
As beth thise tidifs, tercelets, and oules,
Right for despyt were peynted hem bisyde,
And pyes, on hem for to crye and chyde.

　　Thus lete I Canacee hir hauk keping;
I wol na-more as now speke of hir ring,
Til it come eft to purpos for to seyn
How that this faucon gat hir love ageyn
Repentant, as the storie telleth us,　655
By mediacioun of Cambalus,
The kinges sone, of whiche I yow tolde.
But hennes-forth I wol my proces holde
To speke of aventures and of batailles,
That never yet was herd so grete mer-
　　vailles.　　　　　　　　　　(652) 660

　　First wol I telle yow of Cambinskan,
That in his tyme many a citee wan;
And after wol I speke of Algarsyf,
How that he wan Theodora to his wyf,
For whom ful ofte in greet peril he was,
Ne hadde he ben holpen by the stede of
　　bras;　　　　　　　　　　　　666
And after wol I speke of Cambalo,
That faught in listes with the bretheren
　　two　　　　　　　　　　　　(660)
For Canacee, er that he mighte hir winne.
And ther I lefte I wol ageyn biginne. 670

　　　　　Explicit secunda pars.

　　　　　Incipit pars tercia.

Appollo whirleth up his char so hye,
　　　　　　　　　　　　　　[T. om.
Til that the god Mercurius hous the
　　slye—　　　　　　　　　　[T. om.
　　　　　　(Unfinished.)

Here folwen the wordes of the Frankelin
　　to the Squier, and the wordes of the
　　Host to the Frankelin.

'In feith, Squier, thou hast thee wel
　　y-quit,

And gentilly I preise wel thy wit,'
Quod the Frankeleyn, 'considering thy
　　youthe,　　　　　　　　　　　675
So feelingly thou spekest, sir, I allow
　　the!
As to my doom, there is non that is
　　here
Of eloquence that shal be thy pere,
If that thou live; god yeve thee good
　　chaunce,　　　　　　　　　　679
And in vertu sende thee continuaunce!
For of thy speche I have greet deyntee.
I have a sone, and, by the Trinitee,　(10)
I hadde lever than twenty pound worth
　　lond,
Though it right now were fallen in myn
　　hond,
He were a man of swich discrecioun　685
As that ye been! fy on possessioun
But-if a man be vertuous with-al.
I have my sone snibbed, and yet shal,
For he to vertu listeth nat entende;
But for to pleye at dees, and to despende,
And lese al that he hath, is his usage. 691
And he hath lever talken with a page(20)
Than to comune with any gentil wight
Ther he mighte lerne gentilesse aright.'
　　'Straw for your gentilesse,' quod our
　　host;　　　　　　　　　　　695
' What, frankeleyn? pardee, sir, wel thou
　　wost
That eche of yow mot tellen atte leste
A tale or two, or breken his biheste.'
　　'That knowe I wel, sir,' quod the
　　frankeleyn;
' I prey yow, haveth me nat in desdeyn
Though to this man I speke a word or
　　two.'　　　　　　　　　　　701
　　'Telle on thy tale with-outen wordes
　　mo.'　　　　　　　　　　　(30)
' Gladly, sir host,' quod he, ' I wol obeye
Un-to your wil; now herkneth what
　　I seye.
I wol yow nat contrarien in no wyse　705
As fer as that my wittes wol suffyse;
I prey to god that it may plesen yow,
Than woot I wel that it is good y-now.'

# THE FRANKLIN'S PROLOGUE.

### The Prologe of the Frankeleyns Tale.

Thise olde gentil Britons in hir dayes
Of diverse aventures maden layes,        710
Rymeyed in hir firste Briton tonge ;
Which layes with hir instruments they
    songe,                            (40)
Or elles redden hem for hir plesaunce ;
And oon of hem have I in remembraunce,
Which I shal seyn with good wil as I
    can.                              715
  But, sires, by-cause I am a burel man,
At my biginning first I yow biseche
Have me excused of my rude speche ;

I lerned never rethoryk certeyn ;
Thing that I speke, it moot be bare and
    pleyn.                            720
I sleep never on the mount of Pernaso,
Ne lerned Marcus Tullius Cithero.     (50)
Colours ne knowe I none, with-outen
    drede,
But swiche colours as growen in the mede,
Or elles swiche as men dye or peynte. 725
Colours of rethoryk ben me to queynte ;
My spirit feleth noght of swich matere.
But if yow list, my tale shul ye here.

# THE FRANKELEYNS TALE.

### Here biginneth the Frankeleyns Tale.

In Armorik, that called is Britayne,
Ther was a knight that loved and dide
    his payne                         730
To serve a lady in his beste wyse ;
And many a labour, many a greet empryse
He for his lady wroghte, er she were
    wonne.
For she was oon, the faireste under sonne,
And eek therto come of so heigh kinrede,
That wel unnethes dorste this knight, for
    drede,                             736
Telle hir his wo, his peyne, and his
    distresse.
But atte laste, she, for his worthinesse, (10)
And namely for his meke obeysaunce,
Hath swich a pitee caught of his pen-
    unce,                             740

That prively she fil of his accord
To take him for hir housbonde and hir
    lord,
Of swich lordshipe as men han over hir
    wyves ;
And for to lede the more in blisse hir
    lyves,                            744
Of his free wil he swoor hir as a knight,
That never in al his lyf he, day ne
    night,
Ne sholde up-on him take no maistrye
Agayn hir wil, ne kythe hir jalousye, (20)
But hir obeye, and folwe hir wil in al
As any lovere to his lady shal ;         750
Save that the name of soveraynetee,
That wolde he have for shame of his
    degree.

She thanked him, and with ful greet
    humblesse
She seyde, 'sire, sith of your gentillesse
Ye profre me to have so large a reyne, 755
Ne wolde never god bitwixe us tweyne,
As in my gilt, were outher werre or stryf.
Sir, I wol be your humble trewe wyf, (30)
Have heer my trouthe, til that myn herte
    breste.'
Thus been they bothe in quiete and in
    reste.     760
   For o thing, sires, saufly dar I seye,
That frendes everich other moot obeye,
If they wol longe holden companye.
Love wol nat ben constreyned by mais-
    trye;
Whan maistrie comth, the god of love
    anon     765
Beteth hise winges, and farewel! he is
    gon!
Love is a thing as any spirit free;
Wommen of kinde desiren libertee,   (40)
And nat to ben constreyned as a thral;
And so don men, if I soth seyen shal. 770
Loke who that is most pacient in love,
He is at his avantage al above.
Pacience is an heigh vertu certeyn;
For it venquisseth, as thise clerkes seyn,
Thinges that rigour sholde never atteyne.
For every word men may nat chyde or
    pleyne.     776
Lerneth to suffre, or elles, so moot I goon,
Ye shul it lerne, wher-so ye wole or noon.
For in this world, certein, ther no wight
    is,     (51)
That he ne dooth or seith som-tyme amis.
Ire, siknesse, or constellacioun,     781
Wyn, wo, or chaunginge of complexioun
Causeth ful ofte to doon amis or speken.
On every wrong a man may nat be wreken;
After the tyme, moste be temperaunce 785
To every wight that can on governaunce.
And therfore hath this wyse worthy
    knight,
To live in ese, suffrance hir bihight,  (60)
And she to him ful wisly gan to swere
That never sholde ther be defaute in here.
   Heer may men seen an humble wys
    accord;     791
Thus hath she take hir servant and hir
    lord,

Servant in love, and lord in mariage;
Than was he bothe in lordship and
    servage;
Servage? nay, but in lordshipe above, 795
Sith he hath bothe his lady and his love;
His lady, certes, and his wyf also,
The which that lawe of love acordeth to.
And whan he was in this prosperitee, (71)
Hoom with his wyf he gooth to his
    contree,     800
Nat fer fro Penmark, ther his dwelling
    was,
Wher-as he liveth in blisse and in solas.
   Who coude telle, but he had wedded be,
The joye, the ese, and the prosperitee
That is bitwixe an housbonde and his wyf?
A yeer and more lasted this blisful lyf, 806
Til that the knight of which I speke of
    thus,
That of Kayrrud was cleped Arveragus, (80)
Shoop him to goon, and dwelle a yeer or
    tweyne
In Engelond, that cleped was eek Briteyne,
To seke in armes worship and honour; 811
For al his lust he sette in swich labour;
And dwelled ther two yeer, the book seith
    thus.
   Now wol I stinte of this Arveragus,
And speken I wole of Dorigene his wyf, 815
That loveth hir housbonde as hir hertes
    lyf.
For his absence wepeth she and syketh,
As doon thise noble wyves whan hem
    lyketh.     (90)
She moorneth, waketh, wayleth, fasteth,
    pleyneth;     819
Desyr of his presence hir so distreyneth,
That al this wyde world she sette at noght.
Hir frendes, whiche that knewe hir hevy
    thoght,
Conforten hir in al that ever they may;
They prechen hir, they telle hir night
    and day,
That causelees she sleeth hir-self, allas! 825
And every confort possible in this cas
They doon to hir with al hir bisinesse,
Al for to make hir leve hir hevinesse. (100)
   By proces, as ye knowen everichoon,
Men may so longe graven in a stoon,  830
Til som figure ther-inne emprented be.
So longe han they conforted hir, til she

Receyved hath, by hope and by resoun,
Th'emprenting of hir consolacioun,      834
Thurgh which hir grete sorwe gan aswage;
She may nat alwey duren in swich rage.

And eek Arveragus, in al this care,
Hath sent hir lettres hoom of his welfare,
And that he wol come hastily agayn ; (111)
Or elles hadde this sorwe hir herte slayn.

Hir freendes sawe hir sorwe gan to
    slake,      841
And preyede hir on knees, for goddes
    sake,
To come and romen hir in companye,
Awey to dryve hir derke fantasye.
And finally, she graunted that requeste ;
For wel she saugh that it was for the
    beste.      (118) 846

Now stood hir castel faste by the see,
And often with hir freendes walketh she
Hir to disporte up-on the bank an heigh,
Wher-as she many a ship and barge seigh
Seilinge hir cours, wher-as hem liste go ;
But than was that a parcel of hir wo.
For to hir-self ful ofte 'allas !' seith she,
'Is ther no ship, of so manye as I see,
Wol bringen hom my lord ? than were
    myn herte      855
Al warisshed of his bittre peynes smerte.'

Another tyme ther wolde she sitte and
    thinke,
And caste hir eyen dounward fro the
    brinke.      (130)
But whan she saugh the grisly rokkes
    blake,
For verray fere so wolde hir herte quake,
That on hir feet she mighte hir noght
    sustene.      861
Than wolde she sitte adoun upon the
    grene,
And pitously in-to the see biholde,
And seyn right thus, with sorweful sykes
    colde :

'Eterne god, that thurgh thy purvey-
    aunce      865
Ledest the world by certein governaunce,
In ydel, as men seyn, ye no-thing make ;
But, lord, thise grisly feendly rokkes
    blake,      (140)
That semen rather a foul confusioun
Of werk than any fair creacioun      870
Of swich a parfit wys god and a stable,

Why han ye wroght this werk unreson-
    able ?
For by this werk, south, north, ne west,
    ne eest,
Ther nis y-fostred man, ne brid, ne beest ;
It dooth no good, to my wit, but anoyeth.
See ye nat, lord, how mankinde it
    destroyeth ?      876
An hundred thousand bodies of mankinde
Han rokkes slayn, al be they nat in minde,
Which mankinde is so fair part of thy
    werk      (151)
That thou it madest lyk to thyn owene
    merk.      880
Than semed it ye hadde a greet chiertee
Toward mankinde ; but how than may
    it be
That ye swiche menes make it to de-
    stroyen,
Whiche menes do no good, but ever
    anoyen ?
I woot wel clerkes wol seyn, as hem
    leste,      885
By arguments, that al is for the beste,
Though I ne can the causes nat y-knowe.
But thilke god, that made wind to blowe,
As kepe my lord ! this my conclusioun ;
To clerkes lete I al disputisoun. (162) 890
But wolde god that alle thise rokkes blake
Were sonken in-to helle for his sake !
Thise rokkes sleen myn herte for the fere.'
Thus wolde she seyn, with many a pitous
    tere.

Hir freendes sawe that it was no disport
To romen by the see, but disconfort ; 896
And shopen for to pleyen somwher elles.
They leden hir by riveres and by welles,
And eek in othere places delitables ; (171)
They dauncen, and they pleyen at ches
    and tables.      900

So on a day, right in the morwe-tyde,
Un-to a gardin that was ther bisyde,
In which that they had maad hir ordin-
    aunce
Of vitaille and of other purveyaunce,
They goon and pleye hem al the longe
    day.      905
And this was on the sixte morwe of May,
Which May had peynted with his softe
    shoures
This gardin ful of leves and of floures ; (180)

And craft of mannes hand so curiously
Arrayed hadde this gardin, trewely, 910
That never was ther gardin of swich prys,
But-if it were the verray paradys.
Th' odour of floures and the fresshe sighte
Wolde han maad any herte for to lighte
That ever was born, but-if to gret sik-
nesse, 915
Or to gret sorwe helde it in distresse;
So ful it was of beautee with plesaunce.
At-after diner gonne they to daunce, (190)
And singe also, save Dorigen allone,
Which made alwey hir compleint and hir
mone; 920
For she ne saugh him on the daunce go,
That was hir housbonde and hir love also.
But nathelees she moste a tyme abyde,
And with good hope lete hir sorwe slyde.

Up-on this daunce, amonges othere men,
Daunced a squyer biforen Dorigen, 926
That fressher was and jolyer of array,
As to my doom, than is the monthe of
May. (200)
He singeth, daunceth, passinge any man
That is, or was, sith that the world bigan.
Ther-with he was, if men sholde him
discryve, 931
Oon of the beste faringe man on-lyve;
Yong, strong, right vertuous, and riche
and wys,
And wel biloved, and holden in gret prys.
And shortly, if the sothe I tellen shal, 935
Unwiting of this Dorigen at al,
This lusty squyer, servant to Venus,
Which that y-cleped was Aurelius, (210)
Had loved hir best of any creature
Two yeer and more, as was his aventure,
But never dorste he telle hir his gre-
vaunce; 941
With-outen coppe he drank al his pen-
aunce.
He was despeyred, no-thing dorste he seye,
Save in his songes somwhat wolde he wreye
His wo, as in a general compleyning; 945
He seyde he lovede, and was biloved no-
thing. (218)
Of swich matere made he manye layes,
Songes, compleintes, roundels, virelayes,
How that he dorste nat his sorwe telle,
But languissheth, as a furie dooth in helle;
And dye he moste, he seyde, as dide Ekko

For Narcisus, that dorste nat telle hir wo.
In other manere than ye here me seye,
Ne dorste he nat to hir his wo biwreye;
Save that, paraventure, som-tyme at
daunces, 955
Ther yonge folk kepen hir observaunces,
It may wel be he loked on hir face
In swich a wyse, as man that asketh grace;
But no-thing wiste she of his entente. (231)
Nathelees, it happed, er they thennes
wente, 960
By-cause that he was hir neighebour,
And was a man of worship and honour,
And hadde y-knowen him of tyme yore,
They fille in speche; and forth more and
more
Un-to his purpos drough Aurelius, 965
And whan he saugh his tyme, he seyde
thus:
'Madame,' quod he, 'by god that this
world made,
So that I wiste it mighte your herte
glade, (240)
I wolde, that day that your Arveragus
Wente over the see, that I, Aurelius, 970
Had went ther never I sholde have come
agayn;
For wel I woot my service is in vayn.
My guerdon is but bresting of myn herte;
Madame, reweth upon my peynes smerte;
For with a word ye may me sleen or save,
Heer at your feet god wolde that I were
grave! 976
I ne have as now no leyser more to
seye;
Have mercy, swete, or ye wol do me deye!'
She gan to loke up-on Aurelius: (251)
'Is this your wil,' quod she, 'and sey ye
thus? 980
Never erst,' quod she, 'ne wiste I what
ye mente.
But now, Aurelie, I knowe your entente,
By thilke god that yaf me soule and lyf,
Ne shal I never been untrewe wyf 984
In word ne werk, as fer as I have wit:
I wol ben his to whom that I am knit;
Tak this for fynal answer as of me.'
But after that in pley thus seyde she: (260)
'Aurelie,' quod she, 'by heighe god
above, 989
Yet wolde I graunte yow to been your love,

Sin I yow see so pitously complayne ;
Loke what day that, endelong Britayne,
Ye remoeve alle the rokkes, stoon by stoon,
That they ne lette ship ne boot to goon—
I seye, whan ye han maad the coost so
    clene               995
Of rokkes, that ther nis no stoon y-sene,
Than wol I love yow best of any man ;
Have heer my trouthe in al that ever I
    can.'            (270)
'Is ther non other grace in yow?' quod he.
'No, by that lord,' quod she, 'that maked
    me !            1000
For wel I woot that it shal never bityde.
Lat swiche folies out of your herte slyde.
What deyntee sholde a man han in his lyf
For to go love another mannes wyf,
That hath hir body whan so that him
    lyketh ?'         1005
Aurelius ful ofte sore syketh ;
Wo was Aurelie, whan that he this herde,
And with a sorweful herte he thus an-
    swerde :       (280)
'Madame,' quod he, 'this were an in-
    possible !      1009
Than moot I dye of sodein deth horrible.'
And with that word he turned him anoon.
Tho come hir othere freendes many oon,
And in the aleyes romeden up and doun,
And no-thing wiste of this conclusioun,
But sodeinly bigonne revel newe   1015
Til that the brighte sonne loste his hewe ;
For th'orisonte hath reft the sonne his
    light ;        (289)
This is as muche to seye as it was night.
And hoom they goon in joye and in solas,
Save only wrecche Aurelius, allas !   1020
He to his hous is goon with sorweful herte ;
He seeth he may nat fro his deeth asterte.
Him semed that he felte his herte colde ;
Up to the hevene his handes he gan holde,
And on his knowes bare he sette him doun,
And in his raving seyde his orisoun.  1026
For verray wo out of his wit he breyde.
He niste what he spak, but thus he seyde ;
With pitous herte his pleynt hath he
    bigonne       (301)
Un-to the goddes, and first un-to the
    sonne :        1030
  He seyde, 'Appollo, god and governour
Of every plaunte, herbe, tree and flour,

That yevest, after thy declinacioun,
To ech of hem his tyme and his sesoun,
As thyn herberwe chaungeth lowe or hye,
Lord Phebus, cast thy merciable yë  1036
On wrecche Aurelie, which that am but
    lorn.        (309)
Lo, lord ! my lady hath my deeth y-sworn
With-oute gilt, but thy benignitee  1039
Upon my dedly herte have som pitee !
For wel I woot, lord Phebus, if yow lest,
Ye may me helpen, save my lady, best.
Now voucheth sauf that I may yow devyse
How that I may been holpe and in what
    wyse.       1044
  Your blisful suster, Lucina the shene,
That of the see is chief goddesse and quene,
Though Neptunus have deitee in the see,
Yet emperesse aboven him is she :  (320)
Ye knowen wel, lord, that right as hir
    desyr       1049
Is to be quiked and lightned of your fyr,
For which she folweth yow ful bisily,
Right so the see desyreth naturelly
To folwen hir, as she that is goddesse
Bothe in the see and riveres more and
    lesse.
Wherfore, lord Phebus, this is my re-
    queste—      1055
Do this miracle, or do myn herte breste—
That now, next at this opposicioun,  (329)
Which in the signe shal be of the Leoun,
As preyeth hir so greet a flood to bringe,
That fyve fadme at the leeste it overspringe
The hyeste rokke in Armorik Briteyne ;
And lat this flood endure yeres tweyne ;
Than certes to my lady may I seye :
"Holdeth your heste, the rokkes been
    aweye."      1064
  Lord Phebus, dooth this miracle for me ;
Preye hir she go no faster cours than ye ;
I seye, preyeth your suster that she go
No faster cours than ye thise yeres two.
Than shal she been evene atte fulle alway,
And spring-flood laste bothe night and
    day.      (342) 1070
And, but she vouche-sauf in swiche manere
To graunte me my sovereyn lady dere,
Prey hir to sinken every rok adoun
In-to hir owene derke regioun
Under the ground, ther Pluto dwelleth
    inne,      1075

Y

Or never-mo shal I my lady winne.
Thy temple in Delphos wol I barefoot seke;
Lord Phebus, see the teres on my cheke,
And of my peyne have som compassioun.'
And with that word in swowne he fil
          adoun,                      (352) 1080
And longe tyme he lay forth in a traunce.
  His brother, which that knew of his
          penaunce,
Up caughte him and to bedde he hath
          him broght.
Dispeyred in this torment and this thoght
Lete I this woful creature lye;        1085
Chese he, for me, whether he wol live or
          dye.

  Arveragus, with hele and greet honour,
As he that was of chivalrye the flour, (360)
Is comen hoom, and othere worthy men.
O blisful artow now, thou Dorigen, 1090
That hast thy lusty housbonde in thyne
          armes,
The fresshe knight, the worthy man of
          armes,
That loveth thee, as his owene hertes lyf.
No-thing list him to been imaginatyf
If any wight had spoke, whyl he was
          oute,                         1095
To hire of love; he hadde of it no doute.
He noght entendeth to no swich matere,
But daunceth, justeth, maketh hir good
          chere;                        (370)
And thus in joye and blisse I lete hem
          dwelle,
And of the syke Aurelius wol I telle. 1100

  In langour and in torment furious
Two yeer and more lay wrecche Aurelius,
Er any foot he mighte on erthe goon;
Ne confort in this tyme hadde he noon,
Save of his brother, which that was a clerk;
He knew of al this wo and al this werk.
For to non other creature certeyn   1107
Of this matere he dorste no word seyn.
Under his brest he bar it more secree (381)
Than ever dide Pamphilus for Galathee.
His brest was hool, with-oute for to sene,
But in his herte ay was the arwe kene.
And wel ye knowe that of a sursanure
In surgerye is perilous the cure,
But men mighte touche the arwe, or come
          therby.                       1115
His brother weep and wayled prively,

Til atte laste him fil in remembraunce,
That whyl he was at Orliens in Fraunce,
As yonge clerkes, that been likerous (391)
To reden artes that been curious,    1120
Seken in every halke and every herne
Particuler sciences for to lerne,
He him remembred that, upon a day,
At Orliens in studie a book he say
Of magik naturel, which his felawe, 1125
That was that tyme a bacheler of lawe,
Al were he ther to lerne another craft,
Had prively upon his desk y-laft;    (400)
Which book spak muchel of the opera-
          ciouns,
Touchinge the eighte and twenty man-
          siouns                       1130
That longen to the mone, and swich folye,
As in our dayes is nat worth a flye;
For holy chirches feith in our bileve
Ne suffreth noon illusion us to greve.
And whan this book was in his remem-
          braunce,                      1135
Anon for joye his herte gan to daunce,
And to him-self he seyde prively :
' My brother shal be warisshed hastily;
For I am siker that ther be sciences, (411)
By whiche men make diverse apparences
Swiche as thise subtile tregetoures pleye.
For ofte at festes have I wel herd seye,
That tregetours, with-inne an halle large,
Have maad come in a water and a barge,
And in the halle rowen up and doun. 1145
Somtyme hath semed come a grim leoun;
And somtyme floures springe as in a mede;
Somtyme a vyne, and grapes whyte and
          rede;                         (420)
Somtyme a castel, al of lym and stoon;
And whan hem lyked, voyded it anoon.
Thus semed it to every mannes sighte.

  Now than conclude I thus, that if I
          mighte                        1152
At Orliens som old felawe y-finde,
That hadde this mones mansions in minde,
Or other magik naturel above,       1155
He sholde wel make my brother han his
          love.
For with an apparence a clerk may
          make
To mannes sighte, that alle the rokkes
          blake                         (430)
Of Britaigne weren y-voyded everichon,

And shippes by the brinke comen and
  gon,                                    1160
And in swich forme endure a day or two ;
Than were my brother warisshed of his
  wo.
Than moste she nedes holden hir biheste,
Or elles he shal shame hir atte leste.'
  What sholde I make a lenger tale of
  this?                                   1165
Un-to his brotheres bed he comen is,
And swich confort he yaf him for to gon
To Orliens, that he up stirte anon,   (440)
And on his wey forthward thanne is he
  fare,
In hope for to ben lissed of his care. 1170
  Whan they were come almost to that
  citee,
But-if it were a two furlong or three,
A yong clerk rominge by him-self they
  mette,
Which that in Latin thriftily hem grette,
And after that he seyde a wonder thing :
'I knowe,' quod he, 'the cause of your
  coming';                               1176
And er they ferther any fote wente, (449)
He tolde hem al that was in hir entente.
  This Briton clerk him asked of felawes
The whiche that he had knowe in olde
  dawes ;                                1180
And he answerde him that they dede were,
For which he weep ful ofte many a tere.
  Doun of his hors Aurelius lighte anon,
And forth with this magicien is he gon
Hoom to his hous, and made hem wel at
  ese.                                   1185
Hem lakked no vitaille that mighte hem
  plese ;
So wel arrayed hous as ther was oon
Aurelius in his lyf saugh never noon. (460)
  He shewed him, er he wente to sopeer,
Forestes, parkes ful of wilde deer;   1190
Ther saugh he hertes with hir hornes
  hye,
The gretteste that ever were seyn with yë.
He saugh of hem an hondred slayn with
  houndes,
And somme with arwes blede of bittre
  woundes.
He saugh, whan voided were thise wilde
  deer,                                  1195
Thise fauconers upon a fair river,

That with hir haukes han the heron
  slayn.
Tho saugh he knightes justing in a playn ;
And after this, he dide him swich ple-
  saunce,                                (471)
That he him shewed his lady on a daunce
On which him-self he daunced, as him
  thoughte.                              1201
And whan this maister, that this magik
  wroughte,
Saugh it was tyme, he clapte his handes
  two,
And farewel ! al our revel was ago.
And yet remoeved they never out of the
  hous,                                  1205
Why l they saugh al this sighte merveillous,
But in his studie, ther-as his bookes be,
They seten stille, and no wight but they
  three.                                 (480)
  To him this maister called his squyer,
And seyde him thus : 'is redy our soper?
Almost an houre it is, I undertake,  1211
Sith I yow bad our soper for to make,
Whan that thise worthy men wenten
  with me
In-to my studie, ther-as my bookes be.'
  'Sire,' quod this squyer, 'whan it lyketh
  yow,                                   1215
It is al redy, though ye wol right now.'
  'Go we than soupe,' quod he, 'as for the
  beste ;
This amorous folk som-tyme mote han
  reste.'                                (490)
  At-after soper fille they in tretee,
What somme sholde this maistres guer-
  don be,                                1220
To remoeven alle the rokkes of Britayne,
And eek from Gerounde to the mouth of
  Sayne.
  He made it straunge, and swoor, so god
  him save,
Lasse than a thousand pound he wolde
  nat have,
Ne gladly for that somme he wolde nat
  goon.                                  1225
  Aurelius, with blisful herte anoon,
Answerde thus, 'fy on a thousand pound !
This wyde world, which that men seye is
  round,                                 (500)
I wolde it yeve, if I were lord of it.   1229
This bargayn is ful drive, for we ben knit.

Ye shal be payed trewely, by my trouthe !
But loketh now, for no necligence or
　　slouthe,
Ye tarie us heer no lenger than to-morwe.'
' Nay,' quod this clerk, ' have heer my
　　feith to borwe.'
　　To bedde is goon Aurelius whan him
　　leste,　　　　　　　　　　　　　　1235
And wel ny al that night he hadde his
　　reste ;　　　　　　　　　　　　　　(508)
What for his labour and his hope of blisse,
His woful herte of penaunce hadde a lisse.
　　Upon the morwe, whan that it was day,
To Britaigne toke they the righte way, 1240
Aurelius, and this magicien bisyde,
And been descended ther they wolde
　　abyde ;
And this was, as the bokes me remembre,
The colde frosty seson of Decembre.
　　Phebus wex old, and hewed lyk latoun,
That in his hote declinacioun　　　1246
Shoon as the burned gold with stremes
　　brighte ;　　　　　　　　　　　　(519)
But now in Capricorn adoun he lighte,
Wher-as he shoon ful pale, I dar wel seyn.
The bittre frostes, with the sleet and reyn,
Destroyed hath the grene in every yerd.
Janus sit by the fyr, with double berd,
And drinketh of his bugle-horn the wyn.
Biforn him stant braun of the tusked
　　swyn,　　　　　　　　　　　　　1254
And ' Nowel' cryeth every lusty man.
　　Aurelius, in al that ever he can,
Doth to his maister chere and reverence,
And preyeth him to doon his diligence
To bringen him out of his peynes smerte,
Or with a swerd that he wolde slitte his
　　herte.　　　　　　　　　　　(532) 1260
　　This subtil clerk swich routhe had of
　　this man,
That night and day he spedde him that
　　he can,
To wayte a tyme of his conclusioun ;
This is to seye, to make illusioun,
By swich an apparence or jogelrye,　1265
I ne can no termes of astrologye,
That she and every wight sholde wene
　　and seye,　　　　　　　　　　　(539)
That of Britaigne the rokkes were aweye,
Or elles they were sonken under grounde.
So atte laste he hath his tyme y-founde

To maken his japes and his wrecched-
　　nesse　　　　　　　　　　　　　1271
Of swich a supersticious cursednesse.
His tables Toletanes forth he broght,
Ful wel corrected, ne ther lakked noght,
Neither his collect ne his expans yeres,
Ne his rotes ne his othere geres,　　1276
As been his centres and his arguments,
And his proporcionels convenients　(550)
For his equacions in every thing.
And, by his eighte spere in his wirking,
He knew ful wel how fer Alnath was
　　shove　　　　　　　　　　　　1281
Fro the heed of thilke fixe Aries above
That in the ninthe speere considered is ;
Ful subtilly he calculed al this.
　　Whan he had founde his firste man-
　　sioun,　　　　　　　　　　　　　1285
He knew the remenant by proporcioun ;
And knew the arysing of his mone
　　weel,
And in whos face, and terme, and every-
　　deel ;　　　　　　　　　　　　(560)
And knew ful weel the mones mansioun
Acordaunt to his operacioun,　　　1290
And knew also his othere observaunces
For swiche illusiouns and swiche mes-
　　chaunces
As hethen folk used in thilke dayes ;
For which no lenger maked he delayes,
But thurgh his magik, for a wyke or
　　tweye,　　　　　　　　　　　　1295
It semed that alle the rokkes were aweye.
　　Aurelius, which that yet despeired is
Wher he shal han his love or fare amis,
Awaiteth night and day on this miracle ;
And whan he knew that ther was noon
　　obstacle,　　　　　　　　　　(572) 1300
That voided were thise rokkes everichon,
Doun to his maistres feet he fil anon,
And seyde, ' I woful wrecche, Aurelius,
Thanke yow, lord, and lady myn Venus,
That me han holpen fro my cares colde :'
And to the temple his wey forth hath he
　　holde,　　　　　　　　　　　　1306
Wher-as he knew he sholde his lady see.
And whan he saugh his tyme, anon-right
　　he,　　　　　　　　　　　　　(580)
With dredful herte and with ful humble
　　chere,
Salewed hath his sovereyn lady dere : 1310

'My righte lady,' quod this woful man,
'Whom I most drede and love as I best
    can,
And lothest were of al this world displese,
Nere it that I for yow have swich disese,
That I moste dyen heer at your foot
    anon, 1315
Noght wolde I telle how me is wo bigon;
But certes outher moste I dye or pleyne;
Ye slee me giltelees for verray peyne. (590)
But of my deeth, thogh that ye have no
    routhe,
Avyseth yow, er that ye breke your
    trouthe. 1320
Repenteth yow, for thilke god above,
Er ye me sleen by-cause that I yow love.
For, madame, wel ye woot what ye han
    hight;
Nat that I chalange any thing of right
Of yow my sovereyn lady, but your grace;
But in a gardin yond, at swich a place,
Ye woot right wel what ye bihighten me;
And in myn hand your trouthe plighten
    ye (600)
To love me best, god woot, ye seyde so,
Al be that I unworthy be therto. 1330
Madame, I speke it for the honour of yow,
More than to save myn hertes lyf right
    now;
I have do so as ye comanded me;
And if ye vouche-sauf, ye may go see.
Doth as yow list, have your biheste in
    minde, 1335
For quik or deed, right ther ye shul me
    finde;
In yow lyth al, to do me live or deye;—
But wel I woot the rokkes been aweye!'
  He taketh his leve, and she astonied
    stood, (611)
In al hir face nas a drope of blood; 1340
She wende never han come in swich a
    trappe:
'Allas!' quod she, 'that ever this sholde
    happe!
For wende I never, by possibilitee,
That swich a monstre or merveille mighte
    be!
It is agayns the proces of nature:' 1345
And hoom she gooth a sorweful creature.
For verray fere unnethe may she go,
She wepeth, wailleth, al a day or two, (620)

And swowneth, that it routhe was to see;
But why it was, to no wight tolde she; 1350
For out of toune was goon Arveragus.
But to hir-self she spak, and seyde thus,
With face pale and with ful sorweful
    chere,
In hir compleynt, as ye shul after here:
'Allas,' quod she, 'on thee, Fortune,
    I pleyne, 1355
That unwar wrapped hast me in thy
    cheyne;
For which, t'escape, woot I no socour
Save only deeth or elles dishonour; (630)
Oon of thise two bihoveth me to chese.
But nathelees, yet have I lever lese 1360
My lyf than of my body have a shame,
Or knowe my-selven fals, or lese my name,
And with my deth I may be quit, y-wis.
Hath ther nat many a noble wyf, er
    this, 1364
And many a mayde y-slayn hir-self, allas!
Rather than with hir body doon trespas?
  Yis, certes, lo, thise stories beren wit-
    nesse;
Whan thretty tyraunts, ful of cursed-
    nesse, (640)
Had slayn Phidoun in Athenes, atte feste,
They comanded his doghtres for t'areste,
And bringen hem biforn hem in despyt
Al naked, to fulfille hir foul delyt, 1372
And in hir fadres blood they made hem
    daunce
Upon the pavement, god yeve hem mis-
    chaunce!
For which thise woful maydens, ful of
    drede, 1375
Rather than they wolde lese hir mayden-
    hede,
They prively ben stirt in-to a welle,
And dreynte hem-selven, as the bokes
    telle. (650)
  They of Messene lete enquere and seke
Of Lacedomie fifty maydens eke, 1380
On whiche they wolden doon hir lecherye;
But was ther noon of al that companye
That she nas slayn, and with a good
    entente
Chees rather for to dye than assente
To been oppressed of hir maydenhede. 1385
Why sholde I thanne to dye been in
    drede?

Lo, eek, the tiraunt Aristoclides    (659)
That loved a mayden, heet Stimphalides,
Whan that hir fader slayn was on a night,
Un-to Dianes temple goth she right, 1390
And hente the image in hir handes two,
Fro which image wolde she never go.
No wight ne mighte hir handes of it arace,
Til she was slayn right in the selve place.
Now sith that maydens hadden swich
despyt    1395
To been defouled with mannes foul delyt,
Wel oghte a wyf rather hir-selven slee
Than be defouled, as it thinketh me. (670)
What shal I seyn of Hasdrubales wyf,
That at Cartage birafte hir-self hir lyf?
For whan she saugh that Romayns wan
the toun,    1401
She took hir children alle, and skipte
adoun
In-to the fyr, and chees rather to dye
Than any Romayn dide hir vileinye.
Hath nat Lucresse y-slayn hir-self,
allas!    1405
At Rome, whanne she oppressed was
Of Tarquin, for hir thoughte it was
a shame
To liven whan she hadde lost hir name?
The sevene maydens of Milesie also (681)
Han slayn hem-self, for verray drede and
wo,    1410
Rather than folk of Gaule hem sholde
oppresse.
Mo than a thousand stories, as I gesse,
Coude I now telle as touchinge this
matere.
Whan Habradate was slayn, his wyf so
dere
Hirselven slow, and leet hir blood to
glyde    1415
In Habradates woundes depe and wyde,
And seyde, "my body, at the leeste way,
Ther shal no wight defoulen, if I may."
What sholde I mo ensamples heer-of
sayn,    (691) 1419
Sith that so manye han hem-selven slayn
Wel rather than they wolde defouled be?
I wol conclude, that it is bet for me
To sleen my-self, than been defouled thus.
I wol be trewe un-to Arveragus,
Or rather sleen my-self in som manere,
As dide Demociones doghter dere,    1426

By-cause that she wolde nat defouled be.
O Cedasus! it is ful greet pitee,    (700)
To reden how thy doghtren deyde, allas!
That slowe hem-selven for swich maner
cas.    1430
As greet a pitee was it, or wel more,
The Theban mayden, that for Nichanore
Hir-selven slow, right for swich maner
wo.
Another Theban mayden dide right so;
For oon of Macedoine hadde hir oppressed,
She with hir deeth hir maydenhede re-
dressed.    1436
What shal I seye of Nicerates wyf,
That for swich cas birafte hir-self hir lyf?
How trewe eek was to Alcebiades    (711)
His love, that rather for to dyen chees 1440
Than for to suffre his body unburied be!
Lo which a wyf was Alcestè,' quod she.
' What seith Omer of gode Penalopee?
Al Grece knoweth of hir chastitee.
Pardee, of Laodomya is writen thus, 1445
That whan at Troye was slayn Prothe-
selaus,
No lenger wolde she live after his day.
The same of noble Porcia telle I may;
With-oute Brutus coude she nat live, (721)
To whom she hadde al hool hir herte
yive.    1450
The parfit wyfhod of Arthemesye
Honoured is thurgh al the Barbarye.
O Teuta, queen! thy wyfly chastitee
To alle wyves may a mirour be.    1454
The same thing I seye of Bilia,    [T. *om.*
Of Rodogone, and eek Valeria.'    [T. *om.*
Thus pleyned Dorigene a day or tweye,
Purposinge ever that she wolde deye. (730)
But nathelees, upon the thridde night,
Hom cam Arveragus, this worthy knight,
And asked hir, why that she weep so
sore?    1461
And she gan wepen ever lenger the more.
' Allas!' quod she, 'that ever was
I born! ·
Thus have I seyd,' quod she, 'thus have
I sworn '—
And told him al as ye han herd bifore; 1465
It nedeth nat reherce it yow na-more.
This housbond with glad chere, in
freendly wyse,
Answerde and seyde as I shal yow devyse:

'Is ther oght elles, Dorigen, but this?' (741)
'Nay, nay,' quod she, 'god help me so,
    as wis ;                                    1470
This is to muche, and it were goddes wille.'
'Ye, wyf,' quod he, 'lat slepen that is
    stille ;
It may be wel, paraventure, yet to-day.
Ye shul your trouthe holden, by my fay !
For god so wisly have mercy on me,   1475
I hadde wel lever y-stiked for to be,
For verray love which that I to yow have,
But-if ye sholde your trouthe kepe and
    save.                                       (750)
Trouthe is the hyeste thing that man
    may kepe :'—
But with that word he brast anon to
    wepe,                                        1480
And seyde, 'I yow forbede, up peyne of
    deeth,
That never, whyl thee lasteth lyf ne
    breeth,
To no wight tel thou of this aventure.
As I may best, I wol my wo endure,
Ne make no contenance of hevinesse, 1485
That folk of yow may demen harm or
    gesse.'
    And forth he cleped a squyer and
    a mayde :
'Goth forth anon with Dorigen,' he
    sayde,                                       (760)
'And bringeth hir to swich a place
    anon.'
They take hir leve, and on hir wey they
    gon ;                                        1490
But they ne wiste why she thider wente.
He nolde no wight tellen his entente. (764)
    Paraventure an heep of yow, y-wis,
                                    [T. om.
Wol holden him a lewed man in this,
                                    [T. om.
That he wol putte his wyf in jupartye ;
                                    [T. om.
Herkneth the tale, er ye up-on hir crye.
                                    [T. om.
She may have bettre fortune than yow
    semeth ;                        [T. om.
And whan that ye han herd the tale,
    demeth.                         [T. om.
    This squyer, which that highte Aurelius,
On Dorigen that was so amorous, (772) 1500
Of aventure happed hir to mete

Amidde the toun, right in the quikkest
    strete,
As she was boun to goon the wey forth-
    right
Toward the gardin ther-as she had hight.
And he was to the gardinward also ; 1505
For wel he spyed, whan she wolde go
Out of hir hous to any maner place.
But thus they mette, of aventure or
    grace ;                                      (780)
And he saleweth hir with glad entente,
And asked of hir whiderward she wente?
    And she answerde, half as she were mad,
'Un-to the gardin, as myn housbond bad,
My trouthe for to holde, allas ! allas !'
    Aurelius gan wondren on this cas,
And in his herte had greet compassioun
Of hir and of hir lamentacioun,     1516
And of Arveragus, the worthy knight,
That bad hir holden al that she had
    hight,                                       (790)
So looth him was his wyf sholde breke
    hir trouthe ;
And in his herte he caughte of this greet
    routhe,                                      1520
Consideringe the beste on every syde,
That fro his lust yet were him lever abyde
Than doon so heigh a cherlish wrecched-
    nesse
Agayns franchyse and alle gentillesse ;
For which in fewe wordes seyde he thus :
    'Madame, seyth to your lord Arveragus,
That sith I see his grete gentillesse (800)
To yow, and eek I see wel your distresse,
That him were lever han shame (and that
    were routhe)
Than ye to me sholde breke thus your
    trouthe,                                     1530
I have wel lever ever to suffre wo
Than I departe the love bitwix yow two.
I yow relesse, madame, in-to your hond
Quit every surement and every bond, 1534
That ye han maad to me as heer-biforn,
Sith thilke tyme which that ye were born.
My trouthe I plighte, I shal yow never
    repreve
Of no biheste, and here I take my leve,
As of the treweste and the beste wyf (811)
That ever yet I knew in al my lyf.   1540
But every wyf be-war of hir biheste,
On Dorigene remembreth atte leste.

Thus can a squyer doon a gentil dede,
As well as can a knight, with-outen drede.'
  She thonketh him up-on hir knees al
    bare,      1545
And hoom un-to hir housbond is she fare,
And tolde him al as ye han herd me sayd;
And be ye siker, he was so weel apayd, (820)
That it were inpossible me to wryte;
What sholde I lenger of this cas endyte?
  Arveragus and Dorigene his wyf   1551
In sovereyn blisse leden forth hir lyf.
Never eft ne was ther angre hem bitwene;
He cherisseth hir as though she were
  a quene;      1554
And she was to him trewe for evermore.
Of thise two folk ye gete of me na-more.
  Aurelius, that his cost hath al forlorn,
Curseth the tyme that ever he was born:
'Allas,' quod he, 'allas! that I bihighte
Of pured gold a thousand pound of
  wighte      (832) 1560
Un-to this philosophre! how shal I do?
I see na-more but that I am fordo.
Myn heritage moot I nedes selle,
And been a begger; heer may I nat
  dwelle,
And shamen al my kinrede in this place,
But I of him may gete bettre grace. 1566
But nathelees, I wol of him assaye, (839)
At certeyn dayes, yeer by yeer, to paye;
And thanke him of his grete curteisye;
My trouthe wol I kepe, I wol nat lye.' 1570
· With herte soor he gooth un-to his cofre,
And broghte gold un-to this philosophre,
The value of fyve hundred pound, I gesse,
And him bisecheth, of his gentillesse,
To graunte him dayes of the remenaunt,
And seyde, 'maister, I dar wel make
  avaunt,      1576
I failled never of my trouthe as yit;
For sikerly my dette shal be quit   (850)
Towardes yow, how-ever that I fare
To goon a-begged in my kirtle bare. 1580
But wolde ye vouche-sauf, up-on seurtee,
Two yeer or three for to respyten me,
Than were I wel; for elles moot I selle
Myn heritage; ther is na-more to telle.'
  This philosophre sobrely answerde, 1585

And seyde thus, whan he thise wordes
  herde:      (858)
'Have I nat holden covenant un-to thee?'
'Yes, certes, wel and trewely,' quod he.
'Hastow nat had thy lady as thee lyketh?'
'No, no,' quod he, and sorwefully he
  syketh.      1590
'What was the cause? tel me if thou can.'
Aurelius his tale anon bigan,
And tolde him al, as ye han herd bifore;
It nedeth nat to yow reherce it more.
  He seide, 'Arveragus, of gentillesse, 1595
Had lever dye in sorwe and in distresse
Than that his wyf were of hir trouthe
  fals.'      (869)
The sorwe of Dorigen he tolde him als,
How looth hir was to been a wikked wyf,
And that she lever had lost that day hir
  lyf,      1600
And that hir trouthe she swoor. thurgh
  innocence:
'She never erst herde speke of apparence;
That made me han of hir so greet pitee.
And right as frely as he sente hir me,
As frely sente I hir to him ageyn.   1605
This al and som, ther is na-more to seyn.'
  This philosophre answerde, 'leve
    brother,
Everich of yow dide gentilly til other. (880)
Thou art a squyer, and he is a knight;
But god forbede, for his blisful might, 1610
But-if a clerk coude doon a gentil dede
As wel as any of yow, it is no drede!
  Sire, I relesse thee thy thousand pound,
As thou right now were cropen out of the
  ground,      1614
Ne never er now ne haddest knowen me.
For sire, I wol nat take a peny of thee
For al my craft, ne noght for my travaille.
Thou hast y-payed wel for my vitaille; (890)
It is y-nogh, and farewel, have good day:'
And took his hors, and forth he gooth
  his way.      1620
  Lordinges, this question wolde I aske
    now,
Which was the moste free, as thinketh yow?
Now telleth me, er that ye ferther wende.
I can na-more, my tale is at an ende. (896)

### Here is ended the Frankeleyns Tale.

\*\*\* *The six lines, numbered* 11929-34 *in* Tyrwhitt's text, *are spurious; for his* ll. 11935-12902, *see* pp. 551-564; *for* ll. 12903-15468, *see* pp. 492-551.

## GROUP G.

# THE SECONDE NONNES TALE.

### The Prologe of the Seconde Nonnes Tale.

THE ministre and the norice un-to vyces,
Which that men clepe in English ydel-
nesse,
That porter of the gate is of delyces,
T'eschue, and by hir contrarie hir op-
presse,
That is to seyn, by leveful bisinesse,  5
Wel oghten we to doon al our entente,
Lest that the feend thurgh ydelnesse us
hente.

For he, that with his thousand cordes slye
Continuelly us waiteth to biclappe,
Whan he may man in ydelnesse espye, 10
He can so lightly cacche him in his trappe,
Til that a man be hent right by the lappe,
He nis nat war the feend hath him in
honde;
Wel oughte us werche, and ydelnes with-
stonde.

And though men dradden never for to dye,
Yet seen men wel by reson doutelees,  16
That ydelnesse is roten slogardye,
Of which ther never comth no good
encrees;
And seen, that slouthe hir holdeth in
a lees
Only to slepe, and for to ete and drinke,
And to devouren al that othere swinke. 21

And for to putte us fro swich ydelnesse,
That cause is of so greet confusioun,
I have heer doon my feithful bisinesse,
After the legende, in translacioun  25
Right of thy glorious lyf and passioun,
Thou with thy gerland wroght of rose
and lilie;
Thee mene I, mayde and martir, seint
Cecilie!

### *Inuocacio ad Mariam.*

AND thou that flour of virgines art alle,
Of whom that Bernard list so wel to
wryte,  30
To thee at my biginning first I calle;
Thou comfort of us wrecches, do me
endyte
Thy maydens deeth, than wan thurgh hir
meryte
The eternal lyf, and of the feend victorie,
As man may after reden in hir storie. 35

Thou mayde and mooder, doghter of thy
sone,
Thou welle of mercy, sinful soules cure,
In whom that god, for bountee, chees to
wone,
Thou humble, and heigh over every
creature,
Thou nobledest so ferforth our nature, 40
That no desdeyn the maker hadde of
kinde,
His sone in blode and flesh to clothe and
winde.

Withinne the cloistre blisful of thy sydes
Took mannes shap the eternal love and
pees,
That of the tryne compas lord and gyde
is,  45
Whom erthe and see and heven, out of
relees,
Ay herien; and thou, virgin wemmelees,
Bar of thy body, and dweltest mayden
pure,
The creatour of every creature.

Assembled is in thee magnificence  50
With mercy, goodnesse, and with swich
pitee

That thou, that art the sonne of excel-
   lence,
Nat only helpest hem that preyen thee,
But ofte tyme, of thy benignitee,     54
Ful frely, er that men thyn help biseche,
Thou goost biforn, and art hir lyves leche.

Now help, thou meke and blisful fayre
   mayde,
Me, flemed wrecche, in this desert of galle ;
Think on the womman Cananee, that
   sayde
That whelpes eten somme of the crommes
   alle     60
That from hir lordes table been y-falle ;
And though that I, unworthy sone of Eve,
Be sinful, yet accepte my bileve.

And, for that feith is deed with-outen
   werkes,
So for to werken yif me wit and space, 65
That I be quit fro thennes that most derk
   is !
O thou, that art so fayr and ful of grace,
Be myn advocat in that heighe place
Ther-as withouten ende is songe 'Osanne,'
Thou Cristes mooder, doghter dere of
   Anne !     70

And of thy light my soule in prison lighte,
That troubled is by the contagioun
Of my body, and also by the wighte
Of erthly luste and fals affeccioun ;
O haven of refut, o salvacioun     75
Of hem that been in sorwe and in dis-
   tresse,
Now help, for to my werk I wol me dresse.

Yet preye I yow that reden that I wryte,
Foryeve me, that I do no diligence
This ilke storie subtilly to endyte ;     80
For both have I the wordes and sentence
Of him that at the seintes reverence
The storie wroot, and folwe hir legende,
And prey yow, that ye wol my werk
   amende.

*Interpretacio nominis Cecilie, quam ponit
frater Iacobus Ianuensis in Legenda
Aurea.*

FIRST wolde I yow the name of seint
   Cecilie     85
Expoune, as men may in hir storie see,

It is to seye in English 'hevenes lilie,'
For pure chastnesse of virginitee ;
Or, for she whytnesse hadde of honestee,
And grene of conscience, and of good
   fame     90
The sote savour, 'lilie' was hir name.

Or Cecile is to seye 'the wey to blinde,'
For she ensample was by good techinge ;
Or elles Cecile, as I writen finde,
Is joyned, by a maner conjoininge     95
Of 'hevene' and 'Lia'; and heer, in
   figuringe,
The 'heven' is set for thoght of holinesse,
And 'Lia' for hir lasting bisinesse.

Cecile may eek be seyd in this manere,
'Wanting of blindnesse,' for hir grete
   light     100
Of sapience, and for hir thewes clere ;
Or elles, lo ! this maydens name bright
Of 'hevene' and 'leos' comth, for which
   by right
Men mighte hir wel 'the heven of peple'
   calle,     104
Ensample of gode and wyse werkes alle.

For 'leos' 'peple' in English is to seye,
And right as men may in the hevene see
The sonne and mone and sterres every
   weye,
Right so men gostly, in this mayden free,
Seyen of feith the magnanimitee,     110
And eek the cleernesse hool of sapience,
And sondry werkes, brighte of excellence.

And right so as thise philosophres wryte
That heven is swift and round and eek
   brenninge,
Right so was fayre Cecilie the whyte     115
Ful swift and bisy ever in good werkinge,
And round and hool in good perseveringe,
And brenning ever in charitee ful brighte ;
Now have I yow declared what she highte.

*Explicit.*

**Here biginneth the Seconde Nonnes
Tale, of the lyf of Seinte Cecile.**

THIS mayden bright Cecilie, as hir lyf
   seith,     120
Was comen of Romayns, and of noble
   kinde,

And from hir cradel up fostred in the
feith
Of Crist, and bar his gospel in hir minde;
She never cessed, as I writen finde,
Of hir preyere, and god to love and drede,
Biseking him to kepe hir maydenhede. 126

And when this mayden sholde unto a man
Y-wedded be, that was ful yong of age,
Which that y-cleped was Valerian,
And day was comen of hir mariage,   130
She, ful devout and humble in hir corage,
Under hir robe of gold, that sat ful fayre,
Had next hir flesh y-clad hir in an heyre.

And whyl the organs maden melodye,
To god alone in herte thus sang she ;   135
' O lord, my soule and eek my body gye
Unwemmed, lest that I confounded be :'
And, for his love that deyde upon a tree,
Every seconde or thridde day she faste,
Ay biddinge in hir orisons ful faste.   140

The night cam, and to bedde moste she
gon
With hir housbonde, as ofte is the manere,
And prively to him she seyde anon,
' O swete and wel biloved spouse dere,
Ther is a conseil, and ye wolde it here,
Which that right fain I wolde unto yow
seye,   146
So that ye swere ye shul me nat biwreye.'

Valerian gan faste unto hir swere,
That for no cas, ne thing that mighte be,
He sholde never-mo biwreyen here ;   150
And thanne at erst to him thus seyde she,
' I have an angel which that loveth me,
That with greet love, wher-so I wake or
slepe,
Is redy ay my body for to kepe.   154

And if that he may felen, out of drede,
That ye me touche or love in vileinye,
He right anon wol slee yow with the dede,
And in your yowthe thus ye shulden dye;
And if that ye in clene love me gye,
He wol yow loven as me, for your clen-
nesse,   160
And shewen yow his joye and his bright-
nesse.'

Valerian, corrected as god wolde,
Answerde agayn, ' if I shal trusten thee,
Lat me that angel see, and him biholde ;
And if that it a verray angel be,   165
Than wol I doon as thou hast preyed me ;
And if thou love another man, for sothe
Right with this swerd than wol I slee yow
bothe.'

Cecile answerde anon right in this wyse,
' If that yow list, the angel shul ye see, 170
So that ye trowe on Crist and yow bap-
tyse.
Goth forth to Via Apia,' quod she,
' That fro this toun ne stant but myles
three,
And, to the povre folkes that ther dwelle,
Sey hem right thus, as that I shal yow
telle.   175

Telle hem that I, Cecile, yow to hem sente,
To shewen yow the gode Urban the olde,
For secree nedes and for good entente.
And whan that ye seint Urban han bi-
holde,
Telle him the wordes whiche I to yow
tolde;   180
And whan that he hath purged yow fro
sinne,
Thanne shul ye see that angel, er ye
twinne.'

Valerian is to the place y-gon,
And right as him was taught by his
leringe,
He fond this holy olde Urban anon   185
Among the seintes buriels lotinge.
And he anon, with-outen taryinge,
Dide his message ; and whan that he it
tolde,
Urban for joye his hondes gan up holde.

The teres from his yën leet he falle— 190
' Almighty lord, O Jesu Crist,' quod he,
' Sower of chast conseil, herde of us alle,
The fruit of thilke seed of chastitee
That thou hast sowe in Cecile, tak to thee!
Lo, lyk a bisy bee, with-outen gyle,   195
Thee serveth ay thyn owene thral Cecile !

For thilke spouse, that she took but now
Ful lyk a fiers leoun, she sendeth here,

As meke as ever was any lamb, to yow !'
And with that worde, anon ther gan
   appere                                     200
An old man, clad in whyte clothes clere,
That hadde a book with lettre of golde in
   honde,
And gan biforn Valerian to stonde.

Valerian as deed fil doun for drede
Whan he him saugh, and he up hente
   him tho,                                   205
And on his book right thus he gan to
   rede—
'Oo Lord, oo feith, oo god with-outen mo,
Oo Cristendom, and fader of alle also,
Aboven alle and over al everywhere'—
Thise wordes al with gold y-writen were.

Whan this was rad, than seyde this olde
   man,                                       211
'Levestow this thing or no? sey ye or
   nay.'
'I leve al this thing,' quod Valerian,
'For other thing than this, I dar wel say,
Under the hevene no wight thinke may.'
Tho vanisshed th'olde man, he niste
   where,                                     216
And pope Urban him cristened right
   there.

Valerian goth hoom, and fint Cecilie
With-inne his chambre with an angel
   stonde ;
This angel hadde of roses and of lilie   220
Corones two, the which he bar in honde ;
And first to Cecile, as I understonde,
He yaf that oon, and after gan he take
That other to Valerian, hir make.

'With body clene and with unwemmed
   thoght                                     225
Kepeth ay wel thise corones,' quod he ;
'Fro Paradys to yow have I hem broght,
Ne never-mo ne shal they roten be,
Ne lese her sote savour, trusteth me ;
Ne never wight shal seen hem with his yë,
But he be chaast and hate vileinyë.      231

And thou, Valerian, for thou so sone
Assentedest to good conseil also,
Sey what thee list, and thou shalt han
   thy bone.'

'I have a brother,' quod Valerian tho, 235
'That in this world I love no man so.
I pray yow that my brother may han
   grace
To knowe the trouthe, as I do in this
   place.'

The angel seyde, 'god lyketh thy requeste,
And bothe, with the palm of martirdom,
Ye shullen come unto his blisful feste.'
And with that word Tiburce his brother
   com.
And whan that he the savour undernom
Which that the roses and the lilies caste,
With-inne his herte he gan to wondre
   faste,                                     245

And seyde, 'I wondre, this tyme of the
   yeer,
Whennes that sote savour cometh so
Of rose and lilies that I smelle heer.
For though I hadde hem in myn hondes
   two,                                       249
The savour mighte in me no depper go.
The sote smel that in myn herte I finde
Hath chaunged me al in another kinde.'

Valerian seyde, 'two corones han we,
Snow-whyte and rose-reed, that shynen
   clere,
Whiche that thyn yën han no might to
   see ;                                       255
And as thou smellest hem thurgh my
   preyere,
So shaltow seen hem, leve brother dere,
If it so be thou wolt, withouten slouthe,
Bileve aright and knowen verray trouthe.'

Tiburce answerde, 'seistow this to me 260
In soothnesse, or in dreem I herkne this?'
'In dremes,' quod Valerian, 'han we be
Unto this tyme, brother myn, y-wis.
But now at erst in trouthe our dwelling is.'
'How woostow this,' quod Tiburce, 'in
   what wyse ?'                               265
Quod Valerian, 'that shal I thee devyse.

The angel of god hath me the trouthe
   y-taught
Which thou shalt seen, if that thou wolt
   reneye

The ydoles and be clene, and elles
 naught.'—                        269
And of the miracle of thise corones tweye
Seint Ambrose in his preface list to seye ;
Solempnely this noble doctour dere
Commendeth it, and seith in this manere:

The palm of martirdom for to receyve,
Seinte Cecile, fulfild of goddes yifte,  275
The world and eek hir chambre gan she
 weyve ;
Witnes Tyburces and †Valerians shrifte,
To whiche god of his bountee wolde
 shifte
Corones two of floures wel smellinge,
And made his angel hem the corones
 bringe :                        280

The mayde hath broght thise men to
 blisse above ;
The world hath wist what it is worth,
 certeyn,
Devocioun of chastitee to love.—
Tho shewede him Cecile al open and pleyn
That alle ydoles nis but a thing in veyn ;
For they been dombe, and therto they
 been deve,                      286
And charged him his ydoles for to leve.

'Who so that troweth nat this, a beste
 he is,'
Quod tho Tiburce, 'if that I shal nat lye.'
And she gan kisse his brest, that herde
 this,                           290
And was ful glad he coude trouthe espye.
'This day I take thee for myn allye,'
Seyde this blisful fayre mayde dere ;
And after that she seyde as ye may here :

'Lo, right so as the love of Crist,' quod
 she,                            295
'Made me thy brotheres wyf, right in
 that wyse
Anon for myn allye heer take I thee,
Sin that thou wolt thyn ydoles despyse.
Go with thy brother now, and thee bap-
 tyse,
And make thee clene ; so that thou mowe
 biholde                         300
The angels face of which thy brother
 tolde.'

Tiburce answerde and seyde, 'brother
 dere,
First tel me whider I shal, and to what
 man ?'
'To whom ?' quod he, 'com forth with
 right good chere,
I wol thee lede unto the pope Urban.'  305
' Til Urban ? brother myn Valerian,'
Quod tho Tiburce, 'woltow me thider lede ?
Me thinketh that it were a wonder dede.

Ne menestow nat Urban,' quod he tho,
' That is so ofte dampned to be deed,  310
And woneth in halkes alwey to and fro,
And dar nat ones putte forth his heed ?
Men sholde him brennen in a fyr so reed
If he were founde, or that men mighte him
 spye ;
And we also, to bere him companye—  315

And whyl we seken thilke divinitee
That is y-hid in hevene prively,
Algate y-brend in this world shul we be ?'
To whom Cecile answerde boldely,    319
' Men mighten dreden wel and skilfully
This lyf to lese, myn owene dere brother,
If this were livinge only and non other.

But ther is better lyf in other place,
That never shal be lost, ne drede thee
 noght,
Which goddes sone us tolde thurgh his
 grace ;                         325
That fadres sone hath alle thinges wroght ;
And al that wroght is with a skilful thoght,
The goost, that fro the fader gan procede,
Hath sowled hem, withouten any drede.

By word and by miracle goddes sone,  330
Whan he was in this world, declared here
That ther was other lyf ther men may
 wone.'
To whom answerde Tiburce, 'O suster dere,
Ne seydestow right now in this manere,
Ther nis but o god, lord in soothfastnesse ;
And now of three how maystow bere
 witnesse ?'                      336

' That shal I telle,' quod she, ' er I go.
Right as a man hath sapiences three,
Memorie, engyn, and intellect also,
So, in o being of divinitee,         340

Three persones may ther right wel be.'
Tho gan she him ful bisily to preche
Of Cristes come and of his peynes teche,

And many pointes of his passioun ;
How goddes sone in this world was with-
   holde,     345
To doon mankinde pleyn remissioun,
That was y-bounde in sinne and cares
   colde :
Al this thing she unto Tiburce tolde.
And after this Tiburce, in good entente,
With Valerian to pope Urban he wente,

That thanked god ; and with glad herte
   and light     351
He cristned him, and made him in that
   place
Parfit in his lerninge, goddes knight.
And after this Tiburce gat swich grace,
That every day he saugh, in tyme and
   space,     355
The angel of god ; and every maner bone
That he god axed, it was sped ful sone.

It were ful hard by ordre for to seyn
How many wondres Jesus for hem
   wroghte ;
But atte laste, to tellen short and pleyn,
The sergeants of the toun of Rome hem
   soghte,     361
And hem biforn Almache the prefect
   broghte,
Which hem apposed, and knew al hir
   entente,
And to the image of Jupiter hem sente,

And seyde, ' who so wol nat sacrifyse, 365
Swap of his heed, this is my sentence
   here.'
Anon thise martirs that I yow devyse,
Oon Maximus, that was an officere
Of the prefectes and his corniculere,
Hem hente ; and whan he forth the
   seintes ladde,     370
Him-self he weep, for pitee that he hadde.

Whan Maximus had herd the seintes lore,
He gat him of the tormentoures leve,
And ladde hem to his hous withoute
   more ;     374
And with hir preching, er that it were eve,

They gonnen fro the tormentours to reve,
And fro Maxime, and fro his folk echone
The false feith, to trowe in god allone.

Cecilie cam, whan it was woxen night,
With preestes that hem cristned alle
   y-fere ;     380
And afterward, whan day was woxen
   light,
Cecile hem seyde with a ful sobre chere,
' Now, Cristes owene knightes leve and
   dere,
Caste alle awey the werkes of derknesse,
And armeth yow in armure of bright-
   nesse.     385

Ye han for sothe y-doon a greet bataille,
Your cours is doon, your feith han ye
   conserved,
Goth to the corone of lyf that may nat
   faille ;
The rightful juge, which that ye han
   served,     389
Shall yeve it yow, as ye han it deserved.'
And whan this thing was seyd as I devyse,
Men ladde hem forth to doon the sacrifyse.

But whan they weren to the place broght,
To tellen shortly the conclusioun,
They nolde encense ne sacrifice right
   noght,     395
But on hir knees they setten hem adoun
With humble herte and sad devocioun,
And losten bothe hir hedes in the place.
Hir soules wenten to the king of grace.

This Maximus, that saugh this thing
   bityde,     400
With pitous teres tolde it anon-right,
That he hir soules saugh to heven glyde
With angels ful of cleernesse and of light,
And with his word converted many a
   wight ;
For which Almachius dide him so to-bete
With whippe of leed, til he his lyf gan
   lete.     406

Cecile him took and buried him anoon
By Tiburce and Valerian softely,
Withinne hir burying-place, under the
   stoon.
And after this Almachius hastily     410

Bad his ministres fecchen openly
Cecile, so that she mighte in his presence
Doon sacrifyce, and Jupiter encense.

But they, converted at hir wyse lore,
Wepten ful sore, and yaven ful credence
Unto hir word, and cryden more and
  more,    416
'Crist, goddes sone withouten difference,
Is verray god, this is al our sentence,
That hath so good a servant him to serve;
This with o voys we trowen, thogh we
  sterve!'    420

Almachius, that herde of this doinge,
Bad fecchen Cecile, that he might hir see,
And alderfirst, lo! this was his axinge,
'What maner womman artow?' tho quod
  he.    424
'I am a gentil womman born,' quod she.
'I axe thee,' quod he, 'thogh it thee greve,
Of thy religioun and of thy bileve.'

'Ye han bigonne your question folily,'
Quod she, 'that wolden two answeres
  conclude
In oo demande; ye axed lewedly.'    430
Almache answerde unto that similitude,
'Of whennes comth thyn answering so
  rude?'
'Of whennes?' quod she, whan that she
  was freyned,
'Of conscience and of good feith un-
  feyned.'    434

Almachius seyde, 'ne takestow non hede
Of my power?' and she answerde him
  this—
'Your might,' quod she, 'ful litel is to
  drede;
For every mortal mannes power nis
But lyk a bladdre, ful of wind, y-wis. 439
For with a nedles poynt, whan it is blowe,
May al the boost of it be leyd ful lowe.'

'Ful wrongfully bigonne thou,' quod he,
'And yet in wrong is thy perseveraunce;
Wostow nat how our mighty princes free
Han thus comanded and maad ordin-
  aunce,    445
That every Cristen wight shal han pen-
  aunce

But-if that he his Cristendom withseye,
And goon al quit, if he wol it reneye?'

'Your princes erren, as your nobley dooth,'
Quod tho Cecile, 'and with a wood
  sentence    450
Ye make us gilty, and it is nat sooth;
For ye, that knowen wel our innocence,
For as muche as we doon a reverence
To Crist, and for we bere a Cristen name,
Ye putte on us a cryme, and eek a blame.

But we that knowen thilke name so  456
For vertuous, we may it nat withseye.'
Almache answerde, 'chees oon of thise
  two,
Do sacrifyce, or Cristendom reneye,
That thou mowe now escapen by that
  weye.'    460
At which the holy blisful fayre mayde
Gan for to laughe, and to the juge seyde,

'O juge, confus in thy nycetee,
Woltow that I reneye innocence,    464
To make me a wikked wight?' quod she;
'Lo! he dissimuleth here in audience,
He stareth and woodeth in his advertence!'
To whom Almachius, 'unsely wrecche,
Ne woostow nat how far my might may
  strecche?

Han noght our mighty princes to me
  yeven,    470
Ye, bothe power and auctoritee
To maken folk to dyen or to liven?
Why spekestow so proudly than to me?'
'I speke noght but stedfastly,' quod she,
'Nat proudly, for I seye, as for my syde,
We haten deedly thilke vyce of pryde.

And if thou drede nat a sooth to here,
Than wol I shewe al openly, by right,
That thou hast maad a ful gret lesing here.
Thou seyst, thy princes han thee yeven
  might    480
Bothe for to sleen and for to quiken a
  wight;
Thou, that ne mayst but only lyf bireve,
Thou hast non other power ne no leve!

But thou mayst seyn, thy princes han
  thee maked    484
Ministre of deeth; for if thou speke of mo,

Thou lyest, for thy power is ful naked.'
'Do wey thy boldnes,' seyde Almachius
  tho,
'And sacrifyce to our goddes, er thou go;
I recche nat what wrong that thou me
  profre,
For I can suffre it as a philosophre;    490

But thilke wronges may I nat endure
That thou spekest of our goddes here,'
  quod he.
Cecile answerede, 'O nyce creature,
Thou seydest no word sin thou spak to me
That I ne knew therwith thy nycetee; 495
And that thou were, in every maner
  wyse,
A lewed officer and a veyn justyse.

Ther lakketh no-thing to thyn utter yën
That thou nart blind, for thing that we
  seen alle    499
That it is stoon, that men may wel espyen,
That ilke stoon a god thou wolt it calle.
I rede thee, lat thyn hand upon it falle,
And taste it wel, and stoon thou shalt it
  finde,
Sin that thou seest nat with thyn yën
  blinde.

It is a shame that the peple shal    505
So scorne thee, and laughe at thy folye;
For comunly men woot it wel overal,
That mighty god is in his hevenes hye,
And thise images, wel thou mayst espye,
To thee ne to hem-self mowe nought
  profyte,    510
For in effect they been nat worth a myte.'

Thise wordes and swiche othere seyde she,
And he weex wroth, and bad men sholde
  hir lede
Hom til hir hous, 'and in hir hous,' quod
  he,
'Brenne hir right in a bath of flambes
  rede.'    515
And as he bad, right so was doon in dede;
For in a bath they gonne hir faste shetten,
And night and day greet fyr they under
  betten.

The longe night and eek a day also,
For al the fyr and eek the bathes hete,
She sat al cold, and felede no wo,    521
It made hir nat a drope for to swete.
But in that bath hir lyf she moste lete;
For he, Almachius, with ful wikke entente
To sleen hir in the bath his sonde sente.

Three strokes in the nekke he smoot hir
  tho,    526
The tormentour, but for no maner chaunce
He mighte noght smyte al hir nekke
  a-two;
And for ther was that tyme an ordin-
  aunce,
That no man sholde doon man swich
  penaunce    530
The ferthe strook to smyten, softe or sore,
This tormentour ne dorste do na-more.

But half-deed, with hir nekke y-corven
  there,
He lefte hir lye, and on his wey is went.
The Cristen folk, which that aboute hir
  were,    535
With shetes han the blood ful faire y-hent.
Three dayes lived she in this torment,
And never cessed hem the feith to teche;
That she hadde fostred, hem she gan to
  preche;

And hem she yaf hir moebles and hir
  thing,    540
And to the pope Urban bitook hem tho,
And seyde, 'I axed this at hevene king,
To han respyt three dayes and na-mo,
To recomende to yow, er that I go,
Thise soules, lo! and that I mighte do
  werche    545
Here of myn hous perpetuelly a cherche.'

Seint Urban, with his deknes, prively
The body fette, and buried it by nighte
Among his othere seintes honestly.
Hir hous the chirche of seint Cecilie
  highte;    550
Seint Urban halwed it, as he wel mighte;
In which, into this day, in noble wyse,
Men doon to Crist and to his seint servyse.

**Here is ended the Seconde Nonnes Tale.**

# THE CANON'S YEOMAN'S PROLOGUE.

### The prologe of the Chanons Yemannes Tale.

WHAN ended was the lyf of seint Cecyle,
Er we had riden fully fyve myle,            555
At Boghton under Blee us gan atake
A man, that clothed was in clothes blake,
And undernethe he hadde a whyt surplys.
His hakeney, that was al pomely grys,
So swatte, that it wonder was to see ;      560
It semed he had priked myles three.
The hors eek that his yeman rood upon
So swatte, that unnethe mighte it gon. (10)
Aboute the peytrel stood the foom ful hye,
He was of fome al flekked as a pye.         565
A male tweyfold on his croper lay,
It semed that he caried lyte array.
Al light for somer rood this worthy man,
And in myn herte wondren I bigan
What that he was, til that I understood
How that his cloke was sowed to his
    hood ;                                   571
For which, when I had longe avysed me,
I demed him som chanon for to be.     (20)
His hat heng at his bak doun by a laas,
For he had riden more than trot or paas ;
He had ay priked lyk as he were wood.
A clote-leef he hadde under his hood    577
For swoot, and for to kepe his heed from
    hete.
But it was joye for to seen him swete !
His forheed dropped as a stillatorie,       580
Were ful of plantain and of paritorie.
And whan that he was come, he gan to
    crye,
'God save,' quod he, 'this joly companye !
Faste have I priked,' quod he, 'for your
    sake,                                    (31)
By-cause that I wolde yow atake,            585
To ryden in this mery companye.'
His yeman eek was ful of curteisye,
And seyde, ' sires, now in the morwe-tyde
Out of your hostelrye I saugh you ryde,

And warned heer my lord and my
    soverayn,                                590
Which that to ryden with yow is ful fayn,
For his desport ; he loveth daliaunce.'
    ' Freend, for thy warning god yeve thee
    good chaunce,'                          (40)
Than seyde our host, ' for certes, it wolde
    seme
Thy lord were wys, and so I may wel
    deme ;                                   595
He is ful jocund also, dar I leye.
Can he oght telle a mery tale or tweye,
With which he glade may this companye ?'
    ' Who, sire ? my lord ? ye, ye, withouten
    lye,
He can of murthe, and eek of jolitee   600
Nat but ynough ; also sir, trusteth me,
And ye him knewe as wel as do I,
Ye wolde wondre how wel and craftily (50)
He coude werke, and that in sondry wyse.
He hath take on him many a greet
    empryse,                                605
Which were ful hard for any that is
    here
To bringe aboute, but they of him lere.
As homely as he rit amonges yow,
If ye him knewe, it wolde be for your
    prow ;                                  609
Ye wolde nat forgoon his aqueyntaunce
For mochel good, I dar leye in balaunce
Al that I have in my possessioun.
He is a man of heigh discrecioun,      (60)
I warne you wel, he is a passing man.'
    ' Wel,' quod our host, ' I pray thee, tel
    me than,                               615
Is he a clerk, or noon ? tel what he is.'
    'Nay, he is gretter than a clerk, y-wis,'
Seyde this yeman, ' and in wordes fewe,
Host, of his craft som-what I wol yow
    shewe.                                  619

I seye, my lord can swich subtilitee—
(But al his craft ye may nat wite at me;
And som-what helpe I yet to his werking)—
That al this ground on which we been
     ryding,    (70)
Til that we come to Caunterbury toun,
He coude al clene turne it up-so-doun,   625
And pave it al of silver and of gold.'

And whan this yeman hadde thus y-told
Unto our host, he seyde, 'ben'cite!
This thing is wonder merveillous to me,
Sin that thy lord is of so heigh prudence,
By-cause of which men sholde him rever-
     ence,    631
That of his worship rekketh he so lyte;
His oversloppe nis nat worth a myte, (80)
As in effect, to him, so mote I go!
It is al baudy and to-tore also.   635
Why is thy lord so sluttish, I thee preye,
And is of power better cloth to beye,
If that his dede accorde with thy speche?
Telle me that, and that I thee biseche.'

'Why?' quod this yeman, 'wherto axe
     ye me?    640
God help me so, for he shal never thee!
(But I wol nat avowe that I seye,
And therfor kepe it secree, I yow preye).
He is to wys, in feith, as I bileve;   (91)
That that is overdoon, it wol nat preve 645
Aright, as clerkes seyn, it is a vyce.
Wherfor in that I holde him lewed and
     nyce.
For whan a man hath over-greet a wit,
Ful oft him happeth to misusen it;
So dooth my lord, and that me greveth
     sore.    650
God it amende, I can sey yow na-more.'

'Ther-of no fors, good yeman,' quod our
     host;
'Sin of the conning of thy lord thou
     wost,    (100)
Tel how he dooth, I pray thee hertely,
Sin that he is so crafty and so sly.   655
Wher dwellen ye, if it to telle be?'

'In the suburbes of a toun,' quod he,
'Lurkinge in hernes and in lanes blinde,
Wher-as thise robbours and thise theves
     by kinde
Holden hir privee fereful residence,   660
As they that dar nat shewen hir presence;
So faren we, if I shal seye the sothe.'

'Now,' quod our host, 'yit lat me talke
     to the;    (110)
Why artow so discoloured of thy face?'

'Peter!' quod he, 'god yeve it harde
     grace,    665
I am so used in the fyr to blowe,
That it hath chaunged my colour, I trowe.
I am nat wont in no mirour to prye,
But swinke sore and lerne multiplye.
We blondren ever and pouren in the fyr,
And for al that we fayle of our desyr,   671
For ever we lakken our conclusioun.
To mochel folk we doon illusioun,   (120)
And borwe gold, be it a pound or two,
Or ten, or twelve, or many sommes mo, 675
And make hem wenen, at the leeste weye,
That of a pound we coude make tweye!
Yet is it fals, but ay we han good hope
It for to doon, and after it we grope.
But that science is so fer us biforn,   680
We mowen nat, al-though we hadde it
     sworn,
It overtake, it slit awey so faste;
It wol us maken beggers atte laste.' (130)
     Whyl this yeman was thus in his
     talking,
This chanoun drough him neer, and herde
     al thing    685
Which this yeman spak, for suspecioun
Of mennes speche ever hadde this cha-
     noun.
For Catoun seith, that he that gilty is
Demeth al thing be spoke of him, y-wis.
That was the cause he gan so ny him drawe
To his yeman, to herknen al his sawe. 691
And thus he seyde un-to his yeman tho,
'Hold thou thy pees, and spek no wordes
     mo,    (140)
For if thou do, thou shalt it dere abye;
Thou sclaundrest me heer in this com-
     panye,    695
And eek discoverest that thou sholdest
     hyde.'

'Ye,' quod our host, 'telle on, what so
     bityde;
Of al his threting rekke nat a myte!'

'In feith,' quod he, 'namore I do but lyte.'
And whan this chanon saugh it wolde
     nat be,    700
But his yeman wolde telle his privetee,
He fledde awey for verray sorwe and shame.

'A!' quod the yeman, 'heer shal aryse
game,                                              (150)
Al that I can anon now wol I telle.        704
Sin he is goon, the foule feend him quelle !
For never her-after wol I with him mete
For peny ne for pound, I yow bihete !
He that me broghte first unto that game,
Er that he dye, sorwe have he and shame !
For it is ernest to me, by my feith ;     710
That fele I wel, what so any man seith.

And yet, for al my smerte and al my
grief,
For al my sorwe, labour, and meschief,
I coude never leve it in no wyse.         (161)
Now wolde god my wit mighte suffyse 715
To tellen al that longeth to that art !
But natheles yow wol I tellen part ;
Sin that my lord is gon, I wol nat spare ;
Swich thing as that I knowe, I wol de-
clare.'—                                        719

Here endeth the Prologe of the Chanouns Yemannes Tale.

---

# THE CHANOUNS YEMANNES TALE.

### Here biginneth the Chanouns Yeman his Tale.

*[Prima Pars.]*

WITH this chanoun I dwelt have seven
yeer,                                              720
And of his science am I never the neer.
Al that I hadde, I have y-lost ther-by ;
And god wot, so hath many mo than I. (170)
Ther I was wont to be right fresh and gay
Of clothing and of other good array,    725
Now may I were an hose upon myn heed ;
And wher my colour was bothe fresh and
reed,
Now is it wan and of a leden hewe ;
Who-so it useth, sore shal he rewe.
And of my swink yet blered is myn yë, 730
Lo ! which avantage is to multiplye !
That slyding science hath me maad so bare,
That I have no good, wher that ever I fare ;
And yet I am endetted so ther-by     (181)
Of gold that I have borwed, trewely,    735
That whyl I live, I shal it quyte never.
Lat every man be war by me for ever !
What maner man that casteth him ther-to,
If he continue, I holde his thrift y-do.
So helpe me god, ther-by shal he nat winne,
But empte his purs, and make his wittes
thinne.                                            (188) 741
And whan he, thurgh his madnes and folye,

Hath lost his owene good thurgh jupartye,
Thanne he excyteth other folk ther-to,
To lese hir good as he him-self hath do. 745
For unto shrewes joye it is and ese
To have hir felawes in peyne and disese ;
Thus was I ones lerned of a clerk.
Of that no charge, I wol speke of our werk.
Whan we been ther as we shul exercyse
Our elvish craft, we semen wonder wyse,
Our termes been so clergial and so
queynte.                                          (199) 752
I blowe the fyr til that myn herte feynte.

What sholde I tellen ech proporcioun
Of thinges whiche that we werche upon,
As on fyve or sixe ounces, may wel be, 756
Of silver or som other quantitee,
And bisie me to telle yow the names
Of orpiment, brent bones, yren squames,
That into poudre grounden been ful smal ?
And in an erthen potte how put is al,    761
And salt y-put in, and also papeer,     (209)
Biforn thise poudres that I speke of heer,
And wel y-covered with a lampe of glas,
And mochel other thing which that ther
was ?                                              765
And of the pot and glasses enluting,
That of the eyre mighte passe out no-thing ?

And of the esy fyr and smart also,
Which that was maad, and of the care
    and wo            769
That we hadde in our matires sublyming,
And in amalgaming and calcening
Of quik-silver, y-clept Mercurie crude?
For alle our sleightes we can nat con-
    clude.            (220)
Our orpiment and sublymed Mercurie,
Our grounden litarge eek on the porphurie,
Of ech of thise of ounces a certeyn     776
Nought helpeth us, our labour is in veyn.
Ne eek our spirites ascencioun,
Ne our materes that lyen al fixe adoun,
Mowe in our werking no-thing us avayle.
For lost is al our labour and travayle,    781
And al the cost, a twenty devel weye,
Is lost also, which we upon it leye.    (230)

    Ther is also ful many another thing
That is unto our craft apertening;     785
Though I by ordre hem nat reherce can,
By-cause that I am a lewed man,
Yet wol I telle hem as they come to minde,
Though I ne can nat sette hem in hir
    kinde;
As bole armoniak, verdegrees, boras,    790
And sondry vessels maad of erthe and glas,
Our urinales and our descensories,
Violes, croslets, and sublymatories,    (240)
Cucurbites, and alembykes eek,
And othere swiche, dere y-nough a leek.
Nat nedeth it for to reherce hem alle,    796
Watres rubifying and boles galle,
Arsenik, sal armoniak, and brimstoon;
And herbes coude I telle eek many oon,
As egremoine, valerian, and lunarie,    800
And othere swiche, if that me liste tarie.
Our lampes brenning bothe night and day,
To bringe aboute our craft, if that we
    may.            (250)
Our fourneys eek of calcinacioun,
And of watres albificacioun,        805
Unslekked lym, chalk, and gleyre of an ey,
Poudres diverse, asshes, dong, pisse, and
    cley,
Cered pokets, sal peter, vitriole;
And divers fyres maad of wode and cole;
Sal tartre, alkaly, and sal preparat,    810
And combust materes and coagulat,
Cley maad with hors or mannes heer, and
    oile

Of tartre, alum, glas, berm, wort, and
    argoile,            (260)
Resalgar, and our materes enbibing;
And eek of our materes encorporing,    815
And of our silver citrinacioun,
Our cementing and fermentacioun,
Our ingottes, testes, and many mo.

    I wol yow telle, as was me taught also,
The foure spirites and the bodies sevene,
By ordre, as ofte I herde my lord hem
    nevene.            821
The firste spirit quik-silver called is, (269)
The second orpiment, the thridde, y-wis,
Sal armoniak, and the ferthe brimstoon.
The bodies sevene eek, lo! hem heer anoon:
Sol gold is, and Luna silver we threpe, 826
Mars yren, Mercurie quik-silver we clepe,
Saturnus leed, and Jupiter is tin,
And Venus coper, by my fader kin!    829

    This cursed craft who-so wol exercyse,
He shal no good han that him may suffyse;
For al the good he spendeth ther-aboute,
He lese shal, ther-of have I no doute. (280)
Who-so that listeth outen his folye,    834
Lat him come forth, and lerne multiplye;
And every man that oght hath in his cofre,
Lat him appere, and wexe a philosofre.
Ascaunce that craft is so light to lere?
Nay, nay, god woot, al be he monk or
    frere,
Preest or chanoun, or any other wight, 840
Though he sitte at his book bothe day and
    night,
In lernyng of this elvish nyce lore,
Al is in veyn, and parde, mochel more!
To lerne a lewed man this subtiltee, (291)
Fy! spek nat ther-of, for it wol nat be; 845
Al conne he letterure, or conne he noon,
As in effect, he shal finde it al oon.
For bothe two, by my savacioun,
Concluden, in multiplicacioun,
Y-lyke wel, whan they han al y-do;    850
This is to seyn, they faylen bothe two.

    Yet forgat I to maken rehersaille
Of watres corosif and of limaille,    (300)
And of bodyes mollificacioun,
And also of hir induracioun,        855
Oiles, ablucions, and metal fusible,
To tellen al wolde passen any bible
That o-wher is; wherfor, as for the beste,
Of alle thise names now wol I me reste.

For, as I trowe, I have yow told y-nowe 860
To reyse a feend, al loke he never so rowe.

A! nay! lat be; the philosophres stoon,
Elixir clept, we sechen faste echoon; (310)
For hadde we him, than were we siker
y-now.

But, unto god of heven I make avow, 865
For al our craft, whan we han al y-do,
And al our sleighte, he wol nat come us to.
He hath y-maad us spenden mochel good,
For sorwe of which almost we wexen wood,
But that good hope crepeth in our herte,
Supposinge ever, though we sore smerte,
To be releved by him afterward; 872
Swich supposing and hope is sharp and
hard; (320)
I warne yow wel, it is to seken ever;
That futur temps hath maad men to dis-
sever, 875
In trust ther-of, from al that ever they
hadde.
Yet of that art they can nat wexen sadde,
For unto hem it is a bitter swete;
So semeth it; for nadde they but a shete
Which that they mighte wrappe hem inne
a-night, 880
And a bak to walken inne by day-light,
They wolde hem selle and spenden on this
craft; (329)
They can nat stinte til no-thing be laft.
And evermore, wher that ever they goon,
Men may hem knowe by smel of brim-
stoon; 885
For al the world, they stinken as a goot;
Her savour is so rammish and so hoot,
That, though a man from hem a myle be,
The savour wol infecte him, trusteth me;
Lo, thus by smelling and threedbare array,
If that men liste, this folk they knowe may.
And if a man wol aske hem prively, 892
Why they been clothed so unthriftily, (340)
They right anon wol rownen in his ere,
And seyn, that if that they espyed were,
Men wolde hem slee, by-cause of hir
science; 896
Lo, thus this folk bitrayen innocence!

Passe over this; I go my tale un-to.
Er than the pot be on the fyr y-do,
Of metals with a certein quantitee, 900
My lord hem trempeth, and no man but
he—

Now he is goon, I dar seyn boldely—
For, as men seyn, he can don craftily; (350)
Algate I woot wel he hath swich a name,
And yet ful ofte he renneth in a blame; 905
And wite ye how? ful ofte it happeth so,
The pot to-breketh, and farewel! al is go!
Thise metals been of so greet violence,
Our walles mowe nat make hem resistence,
But if they weren wroght of lym and stoon;
They percen so, and thurgh the wal they
goon, 911
And somme of hem sinken in-to the
ground— (359)
Thus han we lost by tymes many a pound—
And somme are scatered al the floor aboute,
Somme lepe in-to the roof; with-outen
doute, 915
Though that the feend noght in our sighte
him shewe,
I trowe he with us be, that ilke shrewe!
In helle wher that he is lord and sire,
Nis ther more wo, ne more rancour ne ire.
Whan that our pot is broke, as I have
sayd, 920
Every man chit, and halt him yvel apayd.
Som seyde, it was long on the fyr-
making, (369)
Som seyde, nay! it was on the blowing;
(Than was I fered, for that was myn office);
'Straw!' quod the thridde, 'ye been lewed
and nyce, 925
It was nat tempred as it oghte be.'
'Nay!' quod the ferthe, 'stint, and herkne
me;
By-cause our fyr ne was nat maad of beech,
That is the cause, and other noon, so
theech!'
I can nat telle wher-on it was long, 930
But wel I wot greet stryf is us among.
'What!' quod my lord, 'ther is na-more
to done,
Of thise perils I wol be war eft-sone; (380)
I am right siker that the pot was crased.
Be as be may, be ye no-thing amased; 935
As usage is, lat swepe the floor as swythe,
Plukke up your hertes, and beth gladde
and blythe.'
The mullok on an hepe y-sweped was,
And on the floor y-cast a canevas,
And al this mullok in a sive y-throwe, 940
And sifted, and y-piked many a throwe.

'Pardee,' quod oon, 'somwhat of our metal
Yet is ther heer, though that we han nat al.
Al-though this thing mishapped have as now,    (391)
Another tyme it may be wel y-now,   945
Us moste putte our good in aventure ;
A marchant, parde ! may nat ay endure
Trusteth me wel, in his prosperitee ;
Somtyme his good is drenched in the see,
And somtym comth it sauf un-to the londe.'    950
    'Pees ! ' quod my lord, 'the next tyme I wol fonde    (398)
To bringe our craft al in another plyte ;
And but I do, sirs, lat me han the wyte ;
Ther was defaute in som-what, wel I woot.'
    Another seyde, the fyr was over hoot :—
But, be it hoot or cold, I dar seye this, 956
That we concluden evermore amis.
We fayle of that which that we wolden have,
And in our madnesse evermore we rave.
And whan we been togidres everichoon,
Every man semeth a Salomon.    961
But al thing which that shyneth as the gold    (409)
Nis nat gold, as that I have herd it told ;
Ne every appel that is fair at yë
Ne is nat good, what-so men clappe or crye.    965
Right so, lo ! fareth it amonges us ;
He that semeth the wysest, by Jesus !
Is most fool, whan it cometh to the preef ;
And he that semeth trewest is a theef ;
That shul ye knowe, er that I fro yow wende,    970
By that I of my tale have maad an ende.

*Explicit prima pars.*

*Et sequitur pars secunda.*

Ther is a chanoun of religioun
Amonges us, wolde infecte al a toun, (420)
Though it as greet were as was Ninivee,
Rome, Alisaundre, Troye, and othere three.
His sleightes and his infinit falsnesse   976
Ther coude no man wryten, as I gesse,
Thogh that he mighte liven a thousand yeer.
In al this world of falshede nis his peer ;
For in his termes so he wolde him winde,

And speke his wordes in so sly a kinde, 981
Whan he commune shal with any wight,
That he wol make him doten anon right,
But it a feend be, as him-selven is.    (431)
Ful many a man hath he bigyled er this,
And wol, if that he live may a whyle ;   986
And yet men ryde and goon ful many a myle
Him for to seke and have his aqueyntaunce,
Noght knowinge of his false governaunce.
And if yow list to yeve me audience,   990
I wol it tellen heer in your presence.
    But worshipful chanouns religious,
Ne demeth nat that I sclaundre your hous,
Al-though my tale of a chanoun be.   (441)
Of every ordre som shrewe is, parde,   995
And god forbede that al a companye
Sholde rewe a singuler mannes folye.
To sclaundre yow is no-thing myn entente,
But to correcten that is mis I mente.
This tale was nat only told for yow,   1000
But eek for othere mo ; ye woot wel how
That, among Cristes apostelles twelve,
Ther nas no traytour but Judas him-selve.
Than why sholde al the remenant have blame    (451)
That giltlees were ? by yow I seye the same.
Save only this, if ye wol herkne me,   1006
If any Judas in your covent be,
Remeveth him bitymes, I yow rede,
If shame or los may causen any drede. 1009
And beth no-thing displesed, I yow preye,
But in this cas herkneth what I shal seye.

In London was a preest, an annueleer,
That therin dwelled hadde many a yeer,
Which was so plesaunt and so servisable
Unto the wyf, wher-as he was at table, (462)
That she wolde suffre him no-thing for to paye    1016
For bord ne clothing, wente he never so gaye ;
And spending-silver hadde he right y-now.
Therof no fors ; I wol procede as now, 1019
And telle forth my tale of the chanoun,
That broghte this preest to confusioun.
    This false chanoun cam up-on a day
Unto this preestes chambre, wher he lay,
Biseching him to lene him a certeyn (471)
Of gold, and he wolde quyte it him ageyn.

'Lene me a mark,' quod he, 'but dayes
three, 1026
And at my day I wol it quyten thee.
And if so be that thou me finde fals,
Another day do hange me by the hals!'
 This preest him took a mark, and that
as swythe, 1030
And this chanoun him thanked ofte sythe,
And took his leve, and wente forth his
weye, (479)
And at the thridde day broghte his moneye,
And to the preest he took his gold agayn,
Wherof this preest was wonder glad and
fayn. 1035
 'Certes,' quod he, 'no-thing anoyeth me
To lene a man a noble, or two or three,
Or what thing were in my possessioun,
Whan he so trewe is of condicioun,
That in no wyse he breke wol his day; 1040
To swich a man I can never seye nay.'
 'What!' quod this chanoun, 'sholde I
be untrewe? (489)
Nay, that were thing y-fallen al of-newe.
Trouthe is a thing that I wol ever kepe
Un-to that day in which that I shal crepe
In-to my grave, and elles god forbede; 1046
Bileveth this as siker as is your crede.
God thanke I, and in good tyme be it sayd,
That ther was never man yet yvel apayd
For gold ne silver that he to me lente, 1050
Ne never falshede in myn herte I mente.
And sir,' quod he, 'now of my privetee,
Sin ye so goodlich han been un-to me, (500)
And kythed to me so greet gentillesse, 1054
Somwhat to quyte with your kindenesse,
I wol yow shewe, and, if yow list to lere,
I wol yow teche pleynly the manere,
How I can werken in philosophye.
Taketh good heed, ye shul wel seen at yë,
That I wol doon a maistrie er I go.' 1060
 'Ye,' quod the preest, 'ye, sir, and wol
ye so?
Marie! ther-of I pray yow hertely!' (509)
 'At your comandement, sir, trewely,'
Quod the chanoun, 'and elles god forbede!'
 Lo, how this theef coude his servyse
bede! 1065
Ful sooth it is, that swich profred servyse
Stinketh, as witnessen thise olde wyse;
And that ful sone I wol it verifye
In this chanoun, rote of al trecherye, 1069

That ever-more delyt hath and gladnesse—
Swich feendly thoughtes in his herte im-
presse—
How Cristes peple he may to meschief
bringe; (519)
God kepe us from his fals dissimulinge!
 Noght wiste this preest with whom that
he delte,
Ne of his harm cominge he no-thing felte.
O sely preest! O sely innocent! 1076
With coveityse anon thou shalt be blent!
O gracelees, ful blind is thy conceit,
No-thing ne artow war of the deceit
Which that this fox y-shapen hath to thee!
His wyly wrenches thou ne mayst nat flee.
Wherfor, to go to the conclusioun 1082
That refereth to thy confusioun, (530)
Unhappy man! anon I wol me hye
To tellen thyn unwit and thy folye, 1085
And eek the falsnesse of that other
wrecche,
As ferforth as that my conning may
strecche.
 This chanoun was my lord, ye wolden
wene?
Sir host, in feith, and by the hevenes
quene,
It was another chanoun, and nat he, 1090
That can an hundred fold more subtiltee!
He hath bitrayed folkes many tyme;
Of his falshede it dulleth me to ryme. (540)
Ever whan that I speke of his falshede,
For shame of him my chekes wexen rede;
Algates, they biginnen for to glowe, 1096
For reednesse have I noon, right wel I
knowe,
In my visage; for fumes dyverse
Of metals, which ye han herd me reherce,
Consumed and wasted han my reednesse.
Now tak heed of this chanouns cursed-
nesse! 1101
 'Sir,' quod he to the preest, 'lat your
man gon (549)
For quik-silver, that we it hadde anon;
And lat him bringen ounces two or three;
And whan he comth, as faste shul ye see
A wonder thing, which ye saugh never er
this.' 1106
 'Sir,' quod the preest, 'it shal be doon,
y-wis.'
He bad his servant fecchen him this thing,

And he al redy was at his bidding,
And wente him forth, and cam anon
    agayn     1110
With this quik-silver, soothly for to sayn,
And took thise ounces three to the cha-
    noun ;     (559)
And he hem leyde fayre and wel adoun,
And bad the servant coles for to bringe,
That he anon mighte go to his werkinge.

    The coles right anon weren y-fet,     1116
And this chanoun took out a crosselet
Of his bosom, and shewed it the preest.
'This instrument,' quod he, 'which that
    thou seest,
Tak in thyn hand, and put thy-self ther-
    inne     1120
Of this quik-silver an ounce, and heer bi-
    ginne,
In the name of Crist, to wexe a philosofre.
Ther been ful fewe, whiche that I wolde
    profre     (570)
To shewen hem thus muche of my science.
For ye shul seen heer, by experience,     1125
That this quik-silver wol I mortifye
Right in your sighte anon, withouten lye,
And make it as good silver and as fyn
As ther is any in your purs or myn,
Or elleswher, and make it malliable ;     1130
And elles, holdeth me fals and unable
Amonges folk for ever to appere !     (579)
I have a poudre heer, that coste me dere,
Shal make al good, for it is cause of al
My conning, which that I yow shewen
    shal.     1135
Voydeth your man, and lat him be ther-
    oute,
And shet the dore, whyls we been aboute
Our privetee, that no man us espye
Whyls that we werke in this philosophye.'
Al as he bad, fulfilled was in dede,     1140
This ilke servant anon-right out yede,
And his maister shette the dore anon,
And to hir labour speedily they gon. (59c)
    This preest, at this cursed chanouns
    bidding,
Up-on the fyr anon sette this thing,     1145
And blew the fyr, and bisied him ful faste;
And this chanoun in-to the croslet caste
A poudre, noot I wher-of that it was
Y-maad, other of chalk, other of glas,
Or som-what elles, was nat worth a flye

To blynde with the preest ; and bad him
    hye     1151
The coles for to couchen al above     (599)
The croslet ; 'for, in tokening I thee
    love,'
Quod this chanoun, 'thyn owene hondes
    two
Shul werche al thing which that shal heer
    be do.'     1155
    'Graunt mercy,' quod the preest, and
    was ful glad,
And couched coles as the chanoun bad.
And whyle he bisy was, this feendly
    wrecche,
This fals chanoun, the foule feend him
    fecche !
Out of his bosom took a bechen cole,     1160
In which ful subtilly was maad an hole,
And ther-in put was of silver lymaille
An ounce, and stopped was, with-outen
    fayle,     (610)
The hole with wex, to kepe the lymail in.
And understondeth, that this false gin
Was nat maad ther, but it was maad
    bifore ;     1166
And othere thinges I shal telle more
Herafterward, which that he with him
    broghte ;
Er he cam ther, him to bigyle he thoghte,
And so he dide, er that they wente
    a-twinne ;     1170
Til he had terved him, coude he not blinne.
It dulleth me whan that I of him speke,
On his falshede fayn wolde I me wreke,
If I wiste how ; but he is heer and ther :
He is so variaunt, he abit no-wher.     1175
    But taketh heed now, sirs, for goddes
    love !     (623)
He took his cole of which I spak above,
And in his hond he baar it prively.
And whyls the preest couchede busily
The coles, as I tolde yow er this,     1180
This chanoun seyde, 'freend, ye doon amis;
This is nat couched as it oghte be ;
But sone I shal amenden it,' quod he. (630)
' Now lat me medle therwith but a whyle,
For of yow have I pitee, by seint Gyle ! 1185
Ye been right hoot, I see wel how ye swete,
Have heer a cloth, and wype awey the
    wete.'
And whyles that the preest wyped his face,

This chanoun took his cole with harde
grace,                                          1189
And leyde it above, up-on the middeward
Of the croslet, and blew wel afterward,
Til that the coles gonne faste brenne.
'Now yeve us drinke,' quod the chanoun
thenne,                                        (640)
'As swythe al shal be wel, I undertake ;
Sitte we doun, and lat us mery make.'  1195
And whan that this chanounes bechen
cole
Was brent, al the lymaille, out of the hole,
Into the croslet fil anon adoun ;
And so it moste nedes, by resoun,
Sin it so even aboven couched was ;    1200
But ther-of wiste the preest no-thing, alas!
He demed alle the coles y-liche good,
For of the sleighte he no-thing under-
stood.                                         (650)
And whan this alkamistre saugh his tyme,
'Rys up,' quod he, 'sir preest, and stondeth
by me ;                                        1205
And for I woot wel ingot have ye noon,
Goth, walketh forth, and bring us a chalk-
stoon ;
For I wol make oon of the same shap
That is an ingot, if I may han hap.
And bringeth eek with yow a bolle or
a panne,                                       1210
Ful of water, and ye shul see wel thanne
How that our bisinesse shal thryve and
preve.
And yet, for ye shul han no misbileve (660)
Ne wrong conceit of me in your absence,
I ne wol nat been out of your presence, 1215
But go with yow, and come with yow
ageyn.'
The chambre-dore, shortly for to seyn,
They opened and shette, and wente hir
weye.
And forth with hem they carieden the
keye,                                          1219
And come agayn with-outen any delay.
What sholde I tarien al the longe day ?
He took the chalk, and shoop it in the
wyse
Of an ingot, as I shal yow devyse.      (670)
I seye, he took out of his owene sleve
A teyne of silver (yvele mote he cheve !)
Which that ne was nat but an ounce of
weighte ;                                      1225

And taketh heed now of his cursed
sleighte !
He shoop his ingot, in lengthe and eek
in brede,
Of this teyne, with-outen any drede,
So slyly, that the preest it nat espyde ; 1230
And in his sleve agayn he gan it hyde ;
And fro the fyr he took up his matere,
And in th'ingot putte it with mery chere,
And in the water-vessel he it caste    (681)
Whan that him luste, and bad the preest
as faste,                                      1235
'Look what ther is, put in thyn hand and
grope,
Thow finde shalt ther silver, as I hope ;
What, devel of helle ! sholde it elles be ?
Shaving of silver silver is, pardee ! '
He putte his hond in, and took up a teyne
Of silver fyn, and glad in every veyne 1241
Was this preest, whan he saugh that it
was so.
'Goddes blessing, and his modres also, (690)
And alle halwes have ye, sir chanoun,'
Seyde this preest, 'and I hir malisoun, 1245
But, and ye vouche-sauf to techen me
This noble craft and this subtilitee,
I wol be youre, in al that ever I may ! '
Quod the chanoun, 'yet wol I make assay
The second tyme, that ye may taken hede
And been expert of this, and in your nede
Another day assaye in myn absence  1252
This disciplyne and this crafty science.
Lat take another ounce,' quod he tho, (701)
'Of quik-silver, with-outen wordes mo, 1255
And do ther-with as ye han doon er this
With that other, which that now silver is.'
This preest him bisieth in al that he can
To doon as this chanoun, this cursed man,
Comanded him, and faste he blew the fyr,
For to come to th'effect of his desyr.  1261
And this chanoun, right in the mene
whyle,
Al redy was, the preest eft to bigyle, (710)
And, for a countenance, in his hande he bar
An holwe stikke (tak keep and be war !)
In the ende of which an ounce, and
na-more,                                       1266
Of silver lymail put was, as bifore
Was in his cole, and stopped with wex
weel
For to kepe in his lymail every deel.

And whyl this preest was in his bisinesse,
This chanoun with his stikke gan him
dresse 1271
To him anon, and his pouder caste in (719)
As he did er ; (the devel out of his skin
Him terve, I pray to god, for his falshede ;
For he was ever fals in thoght and dede) ;
And with this stikke, above the croslet,
That was ordeyned with that false get,
He stired the coles, til relente gan
The wex agayn the fyr, as every man,
But it a fool be, woot wel it mot nede, 1280
And al that in the stikke was out yede,
And in the croslet hastily it fel. (729)
Now gode sirs, what wol ye bet than wel ?
Whan that this preest thus was bigyled
ageyn, 1284
Supposing noght but trouthe, soth to seyn,
He was so glad, that I can nat expresse
In no manere his mirthe and his glad-
nesse ;
And to the chanoun he profred eftsone
Body and good ; 'ye,' quod the chanoun
sone,
' Though povre I be, crafty thou shalt me
finde ; 1290
I warne thee, yet is ther more bihinde.
Is ther any coper her-inne ? ' seyde he.
' Ye,' quod the preest, 'sir, I trowe wel
ther be.' (740)
' Elles go bye us som, and that as swythe,
Now, gode sir, go forth thy wey and
hy the.'
He wente his wey, and with the coper
cam, 1296
And this chanoun it in his handes nam,
And of that coper weyed out but an ounce.
Al to simple is my tonge to pronounce,
As ministre of my wit, the doublenesse
Of this chanoun, rote of al cursednesse. 1301
He semed freendly to hem that knewe
him noght,
But he was feendly bothe in herte and
thoght. (750)
It werieth me to telle of his falsnesse,
And nathelees yet wol I it expresse, 1305
To th'entente that men may be war therby,
And for noon other cause, trewely.
He putte his ounce of coper in the
croslet,
And on the fyr as swythe he hath it set,

And caste in poudre, and made the preest
to blowe, 1310
And in his werking for to stoupe lowe,
As he dide er, and al nas but a jape ;
Right as him liste, the preest he made
his ape ; (760)
And afterward in th'ingot he it caste,
And in the panne putte it at the laste 1315
Of water, and in he putte his owene hond.
And in his sleve (as ye biforn-hond
Herde me telle) he hadde a silver teyne.
He slyly took it out, this cursed heyne—
Unwiting this preest of his false craft—
And in the pannes botme he hath it laft ;
And in the water rombled to and fro,
And wonder prively took up also (770)
The coper teyne, noght knowing this
preest,
And hidde it, and him hente by the breest,
And to him spak, and thus seyde in his
game, 1326
' Stoupeth adoun, by god, ye be to blame,
Helpeth me now, as I dide yow whyl-er,
Putte in your hand, and loketh what is
ther.' 1329
This preest took up this silver teyne anon,
And thanne seyde the chanoun, ' lat us
gon
With thise three teynes, which that we
han wroght,
To som goldsmith, and wite if they been
oght. (780)
For, by my feith, I nolde, for myn hood,
But-if that they were silver, fyn and
good, 1335
And that as swythe preved shal it be.'
Un-to the goldsmith with thise teynes
three
They wente, and putte thise teynes in assay
To fyr and hamer ; mighte no man sey nay,
But that they weren as hem oghte be.
This sotted preest, who was gladder
than he ? 1341
Was never brid gladder agayn the day,
Ne nightingale, in the sesoun of May, (790)
Nas never noon that luste bet to singe ;
Ne lady lustier in carolinge 1345
Or for to speke of love and wommanhede,
Ne knight in armes to doon an hardy dede
To stonde in grace of his lady dere,
Than had this preest this sory craft to lere;

And to the chanoun thus he spak and
    seyde, 1350
'For love of god, that for us alle deyde,
And as I may deserve it un-to yow,
What shal this receit coste? telleth now!'
  'By our lady,' quod this chanoun, 'it is
    dere, (801)
I warne yow wel; for, save I and a frere,
In Engelond ther can no man it make.'
  'No fors,' quod he, 'now, sir, for goddes
    sake, 1357
What shal I paye? telleth me, I preye.'
  'Y-wis,' quod he, 'it is ful dere, I seye;
Sir, at o word, if that thee list it have,
Ye shul paye fourty pound, so god me
    save! 1361
And, nere the freendship that ye dide er
    this
To me, ye sholde paye more, y-wis.' (810)
  This preest the somme of fourty pound
    anon
Of nobles fette, and took hem everichon
To this chanoun, for this ilke receit; 1366
Al his werking nas but fraude and deceit.
  'Sir preest,' he seyde, 'I kepe han no loos
Of my craft, for I wolde it kept were cloos;
And as ye love me, kepeth it secree; 1370
For, and men knewe al my subtilitee,
By god, they wolden han so greet envye
To me, by-cause of my philosophye, (820)
I sholde be deed, ther were non other
    weye.'
  'God it forbede!' quod the preest,
  'what sey ye?' 1375
Yet hadde I lever spenden al the good
Which that I have (and elles wexe I wood!)
Than that ye sholden falle in swich mes-
    cheef.'
  'For your good wil, sir, have ye right
    good preef,'
Quod the chanoun, 'and far-wel, grant
    mercy!' 1380
He wente his wey and never the preest
    him sy
After that day; and whan that this preest
    sholde (829)
Maken assay, at swich tyme as he wolde,
Of this receit, far-wel! it wolde nat be!
Lo, thus byjaped and bigyled was he! 1385
Thus maketh he his introduccioun
To bringe folk to hir destruccioun.—

Considereth, sirs, how that, in ech
    estaat,
Bitwixe men and gold ther is debaat
So ferforth, that unnethes is ther noon.
This multiplying blent so many oon, 1391
That in good feith I trowe that it be
The cause grettest of swich scarsetee. (840)
Philosophres speken so mistily
In this craft, that men can nat come
    therby, 1395
For any wit that men han now a-dayes.
They mowe wel chiteren, as doon thise
    jayes,
And in her termes sette hir lust and peyne,
But to hir purpos shul they never atteyne.
A man may lightly lerne, if he have aught,
To multiplye, and bringe his good to
    naught! (848) 1401
  Lo! swich a lucre is in this lusty game,
A mannes mirthe it wol torne un-to grame,
And empten also grete and hevy purses,
And maken folk for to purchasen curses
Of hem, that han hir good therto y-lent.
O! fy! for shame! they that han been
    brent, 1407
Allas! can they nat flee the fyres hete?
Ye that it use, I rede ye it lete,
Lest ye lese al; for bet than never is
    late. 1410
Never to thryve were to long a date.
Though ye prolle ay, ye shul it never
    finde; (859)
Ye been as bolde as is Bayard the blinde,
That blundreth forth, and peril casteth
    noon;
He is as bold to renne agayn a stoon 1415
As for to goon besydes in the weye.
So faren ye that multiplye, I seye.
If that your yën can nat seen aright,
Loke that your minde lakke nought his
    sight. (866)
For, though ye loke never so brode, and
    stare, 1420
Ye shul nat winne a myte on that chaffare,
But wasten al that ye may rape and renne.
Withdrawe the fyr, lest it to faste brenne;
Medleth na-more with that art, I mene,
For, if ye doon, your thrift is goon ful
    clene. 1425
And right as swythe I wol yow tellen here,
What philosophres seyn in this matere.

Lo, thus seith Arnold of the Newe Toun,
As his Rosarie maketh mencioun ;
He seith right thus, with-outen any lye,
'Ther may no man Mercurie mortifye, 1431
But it be with his brother knowleching.
How that he, which that first seyde this
    thing,     (880)
Of philosophres fader was, Hermes;
He seith, how that the dragoun, doutelees,
Ne deyeth nat, but-if that he be slayn 1436
With his brother ; and that is for to sayn,
By the dragoun, Mercurie and noon other
He understood ; and brimstoon by his
    brother,
That out of *sol* and *luna* were y-drawe.
And therfor,' seyde he, ' tak heed to my
    sawe,     1441
Let no man bisy him this art for to seche,
But-if that he th'entencioun and speche
Of philosophres understonde can ;   (891)
And if he do, he is a lewed man.     1445
For this science and this conning,' quod he,
' Is of the secree of secrees, parde.'
    Also ther was a disciple of Plato,
That on a tyme seyde his maister to,
As his book Senior wol bere witnesse, 1450
And this was his demande in soothfast-
    nesse :
· Tel me the name of the privy stoon ? '
    And Plato answerde unto him anoon,
'Tak the stoon that Titanos men name.'
    ' Which is that ?' quod he.   ' Magnesia
    is the same,'     (902) 1455

Seyde Plato.   ' Ye, sir, and is it thus ?
This is *ignotum per ignotius.*
What is Magnesia, good sir, I yow preye?'
    ' It is a water that is maad, I seye,
Of elementes foure,' quod Plato.     1460
    ' Tel me the rote, good sir,' quod he tho,
' Of that water, if that it be your wille ? '
    ' Nay, nay,' quod Plato, ' certein, that
    I nille.     (910)
The philosophres sworn were everichoon,
That they sholden discovere it un-to
    noon,     1465
Ne in no book it wryte in no manere ;
For un-to Crist it is so leef and dere
That he wol nat that it discovered be,
But wher it lyketh to his deitee
Man for t'enspyre, and eek for to defende
Whom that him lyketh ; lo, this is the
    ende.'     1471
    Thanne conclude I thus ; sith god of
    hevene
Ne wol nat that the philosophres nevene
How that a man shal come un-to this
    stoon,     (921)
I rede, as for the beste, lete it goon.   1475
For who-so maketh god his adversarie,
As for to werken any thing in contrarie
Of his wil, certes, never shal he thryve,
Thogh that he multiplye terme of his
    lyve.
And ther a poynt ; for ended is my tale ;
God sende every trewe man bote of his
    bale !—Amen.     (928) 1481

**Here is ended the Chanouns Yemannes Tale.**

# GROUP H.

# THE MANCIPLE'S PROLOGUE.

### Here folweth the Prologe of the Maunciples Tale.

WITE ye nat wher ther stant a litel toun
Which that y-cleped is Bob-up-and-doun,
Under the Blee, in Caunterbury weye?
Ther gan our hoste for to jape and pleye,
And seyde, 'sirs, what! Dun is in the
  myre!  5
Is ther no man, for preyere ne for hyre,
That wol awake our felawe heer bihinde?
A theef mighte him ful lightly robbe and
  binde.
See how he nappeth! see, for cokkes bones,
As he wol falle from his hors at ones.  10
Is that a cook of Londoun, with mes-
  chaunce?
Do him come forth, he knoweth his pen-
  aunce,
For he shal telle a tale, by my fey!
Al-though it be nat worth a botel hey.
Awake, thou cook,' quod he, 'god yeve
  thee sorwe,  15
What eyleth thee to slepe by the morwe?
Hastow had fleen al night, or artow
  dronke,
Or hastow with som quene al night y-
  swonke,
So that thou mayst nat holden up thyn
  heed?'
  This cook, that was ful pale and no-
  thing reed,  20
Seyde to our host, 'so god my soule blesse,
As ther is falle on me swich hevinesse,
Noot I nat why, that me were lever slepe
Than the beste galoun wyn in Chepe.'
  'Wel,' quod the maunciple, 'if it may
  doon ese  25
To thee, sir cook, and to no wight displese
Which that heer rydeth in this companye,
And that our host wol, of his curteisye,
I wol as now excuse thee of thy tale;
For, in good feith, thy visage is ful pale,

Thyn yën daswen eek, as that me
  thinketh,  31
And wel I woot, thy breeth ful soure
  stinketh,
That sheweth wel thou art not wel dis-
  posed;
Of me, certein, thou shalt nat been
  y-glosed.
Se how he ganeth, lo, this dronken wight,
As though he wolde us swolwe anon-right.
Hold cloos thy mouth, man, by thy fader
  kin!  37
The devel of helle sette his foot ther-in!
Thy cursed breeth infecte wol us alle;
Fy, stinking swyn, fy! foule moot thee
  falle!  40
A! taketh heed, sirs, of this lusty man.
Now, swete sir, wol ye justen atte fan?
Ther-to me thinketh ye been wel y-shape!
I trowe that ye dronken han wyn ape,
And that is whan men pleyen with a
  straw.'  45
And with this speche the cook wex wrooth
  and wraw,
And on the maunciple he gan nodde faste
For lakke of speche, and doun the hors
  him caste,
Wher as he lay, til that men up him took;
This was a fayr chivachee of a cook!  50
Allas! he nadde holde him by his ladel!
And, er that he agayn were in his sadel,
Ther was greet showving bothe to and fro,
To lifte him up, and muchel care and wo,
So unweldy was this sory palled gost.  55
And to the maunciple thanne spak our
  host,
'By-cause drink hath dominacioun
Upon this man, by my savacioun
I trowe he lewedly wolde telle his tale.
For, were it wyn, or old or moysty ale, 60

That he hath dronke, he speketh in his
   nose,
And fneseth faste, and eek he hath the
   pose.
He hath also to do more than y-nough
To kepe him and his capel out of slough ;
And, if he falle from his capel eft-sone, 65
Than shul we alle have y-nough to done,
In lifting up his hevy dronken cors.
Telle on thy tale, of him make I no fors.
   But yet, maunciple, in feith thou art to
   nyce,
Thus openly repreve him of his vyce.   70
Another day he wol, peraventure,
Reclayme thee, and bringe thee to lure ;
I mene, he speke wol of smale thinges,
As for to pinchen at thy rekeninges,
That wer not honeste, if it cam to preef.'
   ' No,' quod the maunciple, 'that were
     a greet mescheef !           76
So mighte he lightly bringe me in the
   snare.
Yet hadde I lever payen for the mare
Which he rit on, than he sholde with me
   stryve ;                   79
I wol nat wratthe him, al-so mote I thryve !
That that I spak, I seyde it in my bourde ;
And wite ye what ? I have heer, in
   a gourde,

A draught of wyn, ye, of a rype grape,
And right anon ye shul seen a good jape.
This cook shal drinke ther-of, if I may ; 85
Up peyne of deeth, he wol nat seye me nay !'
   And certeinly, to tellen as it was,
Of this vessel the cook drank faste, allas !
What neded him ? he drank y-nough
   biforn.
And whan he hadde pouped in this horn,
To the maunciple he took the gourde
   agayn ;                   91
And of that drinke the cook was wonder
   fayn,
And thanked him in swich wyse as he
   coude.
   Than gan our host to laughen wonder
   loude,
And seyde, ' I see wel, it is necessarie, 95
Wher that we goon, good drink we with
   us carie ;
For that wol turne rancour and disese
T'acord and love, and many a wrong apese.
O thou Bachus, y-blessed be thy name,
That so canst turnen ernest in-to game !
Worship and thank be to thy deitee ! 101
Of that matere ye gete na-more of me.
Tel on thy tale, maunciple, I thee preye.'
   ' Wel, sir,' quod he, 'now herkneth
   what I seye.'

**Thus endeth the Prologe of the Manciple.**

# THE MAUNCIPLES TALE.

### Here biginneth the Maunciples Tale of the Crowe.

Whan Phebus dwelled here in this erthe
   adoun,                  105
As olde bokes maken mencioun,
He was the moste lusty bachiler
In al this world, and eek the beste archer ;
He slow Phitoun, the serpent, as he lay
Slepinge agayn the sonne upon a day; 110

And many another noble worthy dede
He with his bowe wroghte, as men may
   rede.
   Pleyen he coude on every minstralcye,
And singen, that it was a melodye,    (10)
To heren of his clere vois the soun.    115
Certes the king of Thebes, Amphioun,

That with his singing walled that citee,
Coude never singen half so wel as he.
Therto he was the semelieste man    119
That is or was, sith that the world bigan.
What nedeth it his fetures to discryve ?
For in this world was noon so fair on lyve.
He was ther-with fulfild of gentillesse,
Of honour, and of parfit worthinesse. (20)

This Phebus, that was flour of bachelrye,
As wel in fredom as in chivalrye,    126
For his desport, in signe eek of victorie
Of Phitoun, so as telleth us the storie,
Was wont to beren in his hand a bowe.

Now had this Phebus in his hous a crowe,
Which in a cage he fostred many a day,
And taughte it speken, as men teche a jay.
Whyt was this crowe, as is a snow-whyt
   swan,    (29)
And countrefete the speche of every man
He coude, whan he sholde telle a tale. 135
Ther-with in al this world no nightingale
Ne coude, by an hondred thousand deel,
Singen so wonder merily and weel.

Now had this Phebus in his hous a wyf,
Which that he lovede more than his lyf,
And night and day dide ever his diligence
Hir for to plese, and doon hir reverence,
Save only, if the sothe that I shal sayn,
Jalous he was, and wolde have kept hir
   fayn ;    (40)
For him were looth by-japed for to be. 145
And so is every wight in swich degree ;
But al in ydel, for it availleth noght.
A good wyf, that is clene of werk and
   thoght,
Sholde nat been kept in noon await,
   certayn ;
And trewely, the labour is in vayn    150
To kepe a shrewe, for it wol nat be.
This holde I for a verray nycetee,
To spille labour, for to kepe wyves ;
Thus writen olde clerkes in hir lyves. (50)

But now to purpos, as I first bigan : 155
This worthy Phebus dooth all that he can
To plesen hir, weninge by swich plesaunce,
And for his manhede and his governaunce,
That no man sholde han put him from
   hir grace.
But god it woot, ther may no man embrace
As to destreyne a thing, which that nature
Hath naturelly set in a creature.    162

Tak any brid, and put it in a cage,
And do al thyn entente and thy corage (60)
To fostre it tendrely with mete and
   drinke,    165
Of alle deyntees that thou canst bithinke,
And keep it al-so clenly as thou may ;
Al-though his cage of gold be never so gay,
Yet hath this brid, by twenty thousand
   fold,
Lever in a forest, that is rude and cold, 170
Gon ete wormes and swich wrecchednesse.
For ever this brid wol doon his bisinesse
To escape out of his cage, if he may ;
His libertee this brid desireth ay.    (70)

Lat take a cat, and fostre him wel with
   milk,    175
And tendre flesh, and make his couche
   of silk,
And lat him seen a mous go by the wal ;
Anon he weyveth milk, and flesh, and al,
And every deyntee that is in that hous,
Swich appetyt hath he to ete a mous. 180
Lo, here hath lust his dominacioun,
And appetyt flemeth discrecioun.

A she-wolf hath also a vileins kinde ;
The lewedeste wolf that she may finde, (80)
Or leest of reputacion wol she take,    185
In tyme whan hir lust to han a make.

Alle thise ensamples speke I by thise
   men
That been untrewe, and no-thing by wom-
   men.
For men han ever a likerous appetyt
On lower thing to parfourne hir delyt 190
Than on hir wyves, be they never so faire,
Ne never so trewe, ne so debonaire.
Flesh is so newefangel, with meschaunce,
That we ne conne in no-thing han ple-
   saunce    (90)
That souneth in-to vertu any whyle.    195

This Phebus, which that thoghte upon
   no gyle,
Deceyved was, for al his jolitee ;
For under him another hadde she,
A man of litel reputacioun,    199
Noght worth to Phebus in comparisoun.
The more harm is ; it happeth ofte so,
Of which ther cometh muchel harm and
   wo.

And so bifel, whan Phebus was absent,
His wyf anon hath for hir lemman sent ;

Hir lemman? certes, this is a knavish
    speche!                          (101) 205
Foryeveth it me, and that I yow biseche.
The wyse Plato seith, as ye may rede,
The word mot nede accorde with the
    dede.
If men shal telle proprely a thing,
The word mot cosin be to the werking. 210
I am a boistous man, right thus seye I,
Ther nis no difference, trewely,
Bitwixe a wyf that is of heigh degree,
If of hir body dishonest she be,     (110)
And a povre wenche, other than this—
If it so be, they werke bothe amis—  216
But that the gentile, in estaat above,
She shal be cleped his lady, as in love ;
And for that other is a povre womman,
She shal be cleped his wenche, or his
    lemman.                          220
And, god it woot, myn owene dere brother,
Men leyn that oon as lowe as lyth that
    other.
Right so, bitwixe a titlelees tiraunt
And an outlawe, or a theef erraunt, (120)
The same I seye, ther is no difference. 225
To Alisaundre told was this sentence ;
That, for the tyrant is of gretter might,
By force of meynee for to sleen doun-right,
And brennen hous and hoom, and make
    al plain,
Lo! therfor is he cleped a capitain ;  230
And, for the outlawe hath but smal mey-
    nee,
And may nat doon so greet an harm as he,
Ne bringe a contree to so greet mescheef,
Men clepen him an outlawe or a theef.
But, for I am a man noght textuel,    235
I wol noght telle of textes never a del ;
I wol go to my tale, as I bigan.       (133)
    Whan Phebus wyf had sent for hir lem-
        man,
Anon they wroghten al hir lust volage.
    The whyte crowe, that heng ay in the
        cage,                         240
Biheld hir werk, and seyde never a word.
And whan that hoom was come Phebus,
    the lord,
This crowe sang 'cokkow! cokkow!
    cokkow!'
    'What, brid?' quod Phebus, 'what
        song singestow?                (140)

Ne were thow wont so merily to singe 245
That to myn herte it was a rejoisinge
To here thy vois? allas! what song is this?'
    'By god,' quod he, 'I singe nat amis ;
Phebus,' quod he, 'for al thy worthinesse,
For al thy beautee and thy gentilesse, 250
For al thy song and al thy minstralcye,
For al thy waiting, blered is thyn yë
With oon of litel reputacioun,         (149)
Noght worth to thee, as in comparisoun,
The mountance of a gnat ; so mote I thryve !
For on thy bed thy wyf I saugh him swyve.'
    What wol ye more? the crowe anon
        him tolde,                      257
By sadde tokenes and by wordes bolde,
How that his wyf had doon hir lecherye,
Him to gret shame and to gret vileinye ;
And tolde him ofte, he saugh it with his
    yën.                              261
This Phebus gan aweyward for to wryen,
Him thoughte his sorweful herte brast
    a-two ;
His bowe he bente, and sette ther-inne
    a flo,                           (160)
And in his ire his wyf thanne hath he
    slayn.                            265
This is th'effect, ther is na-more to sayn ;
For sorwe of which he brak his min-
    stralcye,
Bothe harpe, and lute, and giterne, and
    sautrye ;
And eek he brak his arwes and his
    bowe.
And after that, thus spak he to the crowe :
    'Traitour,' quod he, 'with tonge of
        scorpioun,                     271
Thou hast me broght to my confusioun !
Allas! that I was wroght! why nere I
    deed?
O dere wyf, O gemme of lustiheed,   (170)
That were to me so sad and eek so trewe,
Now lystow deed, with face pale of hewe,
Ful giltelees, that dorste I swere, y-wis !
O rakel hand, to doon so foule amis !
O trouble wit, O ire recchelees,
That unavysed smytest giltelees !      280
O wantrust, ful of fals suspecioun,
Where was thy wit and thy discrecioun?
O every man, be-war of rakelnesse,
Ne trowe no-thing with-outen strong wit-
    nesse ;                           (180)

Smyt nat to sone, er that ye witen why,
And beeth avysed wel and sobrely      286
Er ye doon any execucioun,
Up-on your ire, for suspecioun.
Allas! a thousand folk hath raket ire 289
Fully fordoon, and broght hem in the mire.
Allas! for sorwe I wol my-selven slee!'
    And to the crowe, 'O false theef!'
       seyde he,                    (188)
'I wol thee quyte anon thy false tale!
Thou songe whylom lyk a nightingale;
Now shaltow, false theef, thy song forgon,
And eek thy whyte fetheres everichon,
Ne never in al thy lyf ne shaltou speke.
Thus shal men on a traitour been awreke;
Thou and thyn of-spring ever shul be blake,
Ne never swete noise shul ye make,    300
But ever crye agayn tempest and rayn,
In tokeninge that thurgh thee my wyf is
       slayn.'
And to the crowe he stirte, and that anon,
And pulled his whyte fetheres everichon,
And made him blak, and refte him al his
       song,                         (201) 305
And eek his speche, and out at dore him
       slong
Un-to the devel, which I him bitake
And for this caas ben alle crowes blake.—
    Lordings, by this ensample I yow preye,
Beth war, and taketh kepe what I seye:
Ne telleth never no man in your lyf   311
How that another man hath dight his wyf;
He wol yow haten mortally, certeyn.
Daun Salomon, as wyse clerkes seyn, (210)
Techeth a man to kepe his tonge wel; 315
But as I seyde, I am noght textuel.
But nathelees, thus taughte me my dame:
'My sone, thenk on the crowe, a goddes
       name;
My sone, keep wel thy tonge and keep
       thy freend.
A wikked tonge is worse than a feend. 320
My sone, from a feend men may hem
       blesse;
My sone, god of his endelees goodnesse
Walled a tonge with teeth and lippes eke,
For man sholde him avyse what he speke.
My sone, ful ofte, for to muche speche,

Hath many a man ben spilt, as clerkes
       teche;                        (222) 326
But for a litel speche avysely
Is no men shent, to speke generally.
My sone, thy tonge sholdestow restreyne
At alle tyme, but whan thou doost thy
       peyne                          330
To speke of god, in honour and preyere.
The firste vertu, sone, if thou wolt lere,
Is to restreyne and kepe wel thy tonge.—
Thus lerne children whan that they ben
       yonge.—                       (230) 334
My sone, of muchel speking yvel-avysed,
Ther lasse speking hadde y-nough suffysed,
Comth muchel harm, thus was me told
       and taught.
In muchel speche sinne wanteth naught.
Wostow wher-of a rakel tonge serveth?
Right as a swerd forcutteth and forkerveth
An arm a-two, my dere sone, right so 341
A tonge cutteth frendship al a-two.
A jangler is to god abhominable;     (239)
Reed Salomon, so wys and honurable;
Reed David in his psalmes, reed Senekke.
My sone, spek nat, but with thyn heed
       thou bekke.                    346
Dissimule as thou were deef, if that thou
       here
A jangler speke of perilous matere.
The Fleming seith, and lerne it, if thee
       leste,                         349
That litel jangling causeth muchel reste.
My sone, if thou no wikked word hast seyd,
Thee thar nat drede for to be biwreyd;
But he that hath misseyd, I dar wel sayn,
He may by no wey clepe his word agayn.
Thing that is seyd, is seyd; and forth it
       gooth,                        (251) 355
Though him repente, or be him leef or
       looth.
He is his thral to whom that he hath sayd
A tale, of which he is now yvel apayd.
My sone, be war, and be non auctour newe
Of tydinges, whether they ben false or
       trewe.                         360
Wher-so thou come, amonges hye or lowe,
Kepe wel thy tonge, and thenk up-on the
       crowe.'

**Here is ended the Maunciples Tale of the Crowe.**

## GROUP I.

# THE PARSON'S PROLOGUE.

### Here folweth the Prologe of the Persones Tale.

By that the maunciple hadde his tale al
   ended,
The sonne fro the south lyne was de-
   scended
So lowe, that he nas nat, to my sighte,
Degreës nyne and twenty as in highte. 4
Foure of the clokke it was tho, as I gesse:
For eleven foot, or litel more or lesse,
My shadwe was at thilke tyme, as there,
Of swich feet as my lengthe parted were
In six feet equal of proporcioun.
Ther-with the mones exaltacioun,   10
I mene Libra, alwey gan ascende,
As we were entringe at a thropes ende;
For which our host, as he was wont to gye,
As in this caas, our joly companye,
Seyde in this wyse, 'lordings everichoon,
Now lakketh us no tales mo than oon. 16
Fulfild is my sentence and my decree;
I trowe that we han herd of ech degree.
Almost fulfild is al myn ordinaunce;
I prey to god, so yeve him right good
   chaunce,   20
That telleth this tale to us lustily.
Sir preest,' quod he, 'artow a vicary?
Or art a person? sey sooth, by thy fey!
Be what thou be, ne breke thou nat our
   pley;
For every man, save thou, hath told his
   tale,   25
Unbokel, and shewe us what is in thy male;
For trewely, me thinketh, by thy chere,
Thou sholdest knitte up wel a greet matere.
Tel us a tale anon, for cokkes bones!'
   This Persone him answerde, al at ones,
'Thou getest fable noon y-told for me; 31
For Paul, that wryteth unto Timothee,
Repreveth hem that weyven soothfast-
   nesse,
And tellen fables and swich wrecched-
   nesse.   34
Why sholde I sowen draf out of my fest,
Whan I may sowen whete, if that me lest?

For which I seye, if that yow list to here
Moralitee and vertuous matere,
And thanne that ye wol yeve me audience,
I wol ful fayn, at Cristes reverence,   40
Do yow plesaunce leefful, as I can.
But trusteth wel, I am a Southren man,
I can nat geste—rum, ram, ruf—by lettre,
Ne, god wot, rym holde I but litel bettre;
And therfor, if yow list, I wol nat glose.
I wol yow telle a mery tale in prose   46
To knitte up al this feeste, and make an
   ende.
And Jesu, for his grace, wit me sende
To shewe yow the wey, in this viage,
Of thilke parfit glorious pilgrimage   50
That highte Jerusalem celestial.
And, if ye vouche-sauf, anon I shal
Biginne upon my tale, for whiche I preye
Telle your avys, I can no bettre seye.
But nathelees, this meditacioun   55
I putte it ay under correccioun
Of clerkes, for I am nat textuel;
I take but the sentens, trusteth wel.
Therfor I make protestacioun
That I wol stonde to correccioun.'   60
   Up-on this word we han assented sone,
For, as us semed, it was for to done,
To enden in som vertuous sentence,
And for to yeve him space and audience;
And bede our host he sholde to him
   seye,   65
That alle we to telle his tale him preye.
   Our host hadde the wordes for us alle:—
'Sir preest,' quod he, 'now fayre yow
   bifalle!
Sey what yow list, and we wol gladly
   here'—
And with that word he seyde in this
   manere—   70
'Telleth,' quod he, 'your meditacioun.
But hasteth yow, the sonne wol adoun;
Beth fructuous, and that in litel space,
And to do wel god sende yow his grace!'

Explicit prohemium.

# THE PERSONES TALE.

### Here biginneth the Persones Tale.

*Jer. 6°. State super vias et videte et inter-
rogate de viis antiquis, que sit via bona ;
et ambulate in ea, et inuenietis refrigerium
animabus vestris, &c.*

§ 1. Our swete lord god of hevene, that
no man wol perisse, but wole that we
comen alle to the knoweleche of him,
and to the blisful lyf that is perdurable, /
amonesteth us by the prophete Jeremie,
that seith in this wyse : / 'stondeth upon
the weyes, and seeth and axeth of olde
pathes (that is to seyn, of olde sentences)
which is the goode wey ; / and walketh
in that wey, and ye shul finde refresshinge for your soules,' &c. / Manye been
the weyes espirituels that leden folk to
oure Lord Jesu Crist, and to the regne of
glorie. / Of whiche weyes, ther is a ful
noble wey and a ful covenable, which
may nat faile to man ne to womman,
that thurgh sinne hath misgoon fro the
righte wey of Jerusalem celestial ; / and
this wey is cleped Penitence, of which
man sholde gladly herknen and enquere
with al his herte ; / to witen what is
Penitence, and whennes it is cleped Penitence, and in how manye maneres been
the accions or werkinges of Penitence, /
and how manye spyces ther been of Penitence, and whiche thinges apertenen and
bihoven to Penitence, and whiche thinges
destourben Penitence. /

§ 2. Seint Ambrose seith, that 'Penitence is the pleyninge of man for the
gilt that he hath doon, and na-more to
do any thing for which him oghte to
pleyne.' / And som doctour seith : 'Penitence is the waymentinge of man, that
sorweth for his sinne and pyneth him-
self for he hath misdoon.' / Penitence,
with certeyne circumstances, is verray
repentance of a man that halt him-self

in sorwe and other peyne for hise giltes. /
And for he shal be verray penitent, he
shal first biwailen the sinnes that he
hath doon, and stidefastly purposen in
his herte to have shrift of mouthe, and
to doon satisfaccioun, / and never to doon
thing for which him oghte more to biwayle
or to compleyne, and to continue in goode
werkes : or elles his repentance may nat
availle. / For as seith seint Isidre : 'he is
a japer and a gabber, and no verray repentant, that eftsoone dooth thing, for which
him oghte repente.' / Wepinge, and nat for
to stinte to doon sinne, may nat avaylle. / 90
But natheless, men shal hope that every
tyme that man falleth, be it never so
ofte, that he may arise thurgh Penitence,
if he have grace : but certeinly it is greet
doute. / For as seith Seint Gregorie : 'unnethe aryseth he out of sinne, that is
charged with the charge of yvel usage.' /
And therfore repentant folk, that stinte
for to sinne, and forlete sinne er that
sinne forlete hem, holy chirche holdeth
hem siker of hir savacioun. / And he
that sinneth, and verraily repenteth him
in his laste ende, holy chirche yet hopeth
his savacioun, by the grete mercy of oure
lord Jesu Crist, for his repentaunce ; but
tak the siker wey. /                    (20)

§ 3. And now, sith I have declared
yow what thing is Penitence, now shul
ye understonde that ther been three
accions of Penitence. / The firste accion 95
of Penitence is, that a man be baptized
after that he hath sinned. / Seint Augustin seith : 'but he be penitent for his
olde sinful lyf, he may nat biginne the
newe clene lif.' / For certes, if he be
baptized withouten penitence of his olde
gilt, he receiveth the mark of baptisme,
but nat the grace ne the remission of his
sinnes, til he have repentance verray. /

Another defaute is this, that men doon deedly sinne after that they han received baptisme. / The thridde defaute is, that men fallen in venial sinnes after hir
100 baptisme, fro day to day. / Ther-of seith Seint Augustin, that 'penitence of goode and humble folk is the penitence of every day.' /

§ 4. The spyces of Penitence been three. That oon of hem is solempne, another is commune, and the thridde is privee. / Thilke penance that is solempne, is in two maneres; as to be put out of holy chirche in lente, for slaughtre of children, and swich maner thing. / Another is, whan a man hath sinned openly, of which sinne the fame is openly spoken in the contree; and thanne holy chirche by jugement destreineth him for to do open
(30) penaunce. / Commune penaunce is that preestes enjoinen men comunly in certeyn caas; as for to goon, peraventure, naked
105 in pilgrimages, or bare-foot. / Privee penaunce is thilke that men doon alday for privee sinnes, of whiche we shryve us prively and receyve privee penaunce. /

§ 5. Now shaltow understande what is bihovely and necessarie to verray parfit Penitence. And this stant on three thinges; / Contricioun of herte, Confessioun of Mouth, and Satisfaccioun. / For which seith Seint John Crisostom : 'Penitence destreyneth a man to accepte benignely every peyne that him is enjoyned, with contricion of herte, and shrift of mouth, with satisfaccion; and in werkinge of alle maner humilitee.' / And this is fruitful Penitence agayn three thinges in whiche we wratthe oure
110 lord Jesu Crist : / this is to seyn, by delyt in thinkinge, by recchelesnesse in spekinge, and by wikked sinful werkinge. / And agayns thise wikkede giltes is Penitence, that may be lykned un-to a tree. /

§ 6. The rote of this tree is Contricion, that hydeth him in the herte of him that is verray repentant, right as the rote of a tree hydeth him in the erthe. / Of the rote of Contricion springeth a stalke, that bereth braunches and leves of Con-
(40) fession, and fruit of Satisfaccion. / For

which Crist seith in his gospel : 'dooth digne fruit of Penitence'; for by this fruit may men knowe this tree, and nat by the rote that is hid in the herte of man, ne by the braunches ne by the leves of Confession. / And therefore oure Lord Jesu Crist seith thus : 'by the fruit of hem ye shul knowen hem.'/ Of this rote eek springeth a seed of grace, the which seed is moder of sikernesse, and this seed is egre and hoot. / The grace of this seed springeth of god, thurgh remembrance of the day of dome and on the peynes of helle. / Of this matere seith Salomon, that 'in the drede of god man forleteth his sinne.' / The hete of this seed is the love of god, and the desiring of the joye perdurable. / This hete draweth the herte of a man to god, and dooth him haten his sinne. / For soothly, ther is no-thing that savoureth so wel to a child as the milk of his norice, ne no-thing is to him more abhominable than thilke milk whan it is medled with other mete. / Right so the sinful man that loveth his sinne, him semeth that it is to him most swete of any-thing; / but fro that tyme that he loveth sadly our lord Jesu Crist, and desireth the lif perdurable, ther nis to him no-thing more abhominable. / For soothly, the lawe of god is the love of god; for which David the prophete seith : 'I have loved thy lawe and hated wikkednesse and hate'; he that loveth god kepeth his lawe and his word. / This tree saugh the prophete Daniel in spirit, up-on the avision of the king Nabugodonosor, whan he conseiled him to do penitence. / Penaunce is the tree of lyf to hem that it receiven, and he that holdeth him in verray penitence is blessed; after the sentence of Salomon. /

§ 7. In this Penitence or Contricion man shal understonde foure thinges, that is to seyn, what is Contricion : and whiche been the causes that moeven a man to Contricion : and how he sholde be contrit : and what Contricion availleth to the soule. / Thanne is it thus : that Contricion is the verray sorwe that a man receiveth in his herte for his sinnes, with sad purpos to shryve him, and to do penaunce, and nevermore to do sinne./ And this sorwe shal been in this manere, as seith seint Bernard: 'it shal been hevy and grevous, and ful sharpe and poinant in herte.'/ First, for man hath agilt his lord and his creatour; and more sharpe and poinant, for he hath agilt his fader celestial;/ and yet more sharpe and poinant, for he hath wrathed and agilt him that boghte him; which with his precious blood hath delivered us fro the bondes of sinne, and fro the crueltee of the devel and fro the peynes of helle./

§ 8. The causes that oghte moeve a man to Contricion been six. First, a man shal remembre him of his sinnes;/ but loke he that thilke remembrance ne be to him no delyt by no wey, but greet shame and sorwe for his gilt. For Job seith: 'sinful men doon werkes worthy of Confession.'/ And therfore seith Ezechie: 'I wol remembre me alle the yeres of my lyf, in bitternesse of myn herte.'/ And god seith in the Apocalips: 'remembreth yow fro whennes that ye been falle'; for biforn that tyme that ye sinned, ye were the children of god, and limes of the regne of god;/ but for your sinne ye been woxen thral and foul, and membres of the feend, hate of aungels, sclaundre of holy chirche, and fode of the false serpent; perpetuel matere of the fyr of helle./ And yet more foul and abhominable, for ye trespassen so ofte tyme, as doth the hound that retourneth to eten his spewing./ And yet be ye fouler for your longe continuing in sinne and your sinful usage, for which ye be roten in your sinne, as a beest in his dong./ Swiche manere of thoghtes maken a man to have shame of his sinne, and no delyt, as god seith by the prophete Ezechiel:/ 'ye shal remembre yow of youre weyes, and they shuln displese yow.' Sothly, sinnes been the weyes that leden folk to helle./

§ 9. The seconde cause that oghte make a man to have desdeyn of sinne is this:

that, as seith seint Peter, 'who-so that doth sinne is thral of sinne'; and sinne put a man in greet thraldom./ And therfore seith the prophete Ezechiel: 'I wente sorweful in desdayn of my-self.' And certes, wel oghte a man have desdayn of sinne, and withdrawe him from that thraldom and vileinye./ And lo, what seith Seneca in this matere. He seith thus: 'though I wiste that neither god ne man ne sholde nevere knowe it, yet wolde I have desdayn for to do sinne.'/ (70) And the same Seneca also seith: 'I am born to gretter thinges than to be thral to my body, or than for to maken of my body a thral.'/ Ne a fouler thral may 145 no man ne womman maken of his body, than for to yeven his body to sinne./ Al were it the fouleste cherl, or the fouleste womman that liveth, and leest of value, yet is he thanne more foule and more in servitute./ Evere fro the hyer degree that man falleth, the more is he thral, and more to god and to the world vile and abhominable./ O gode god, wel oghte man have desdayn of sinne; sith that, thurgh sinne, ther he was free, now is he maked bonde./ And therfore seyth Seint Augustin: 'if thou hast desdayn of thy servant, if he agilte or sinne, have thou thanne desdayn that thou thy-self sholdest do sinne.'/ Take reward 150 of thy value, that thou ne be to foul to thy-self./ Allas! wel oghten they thanne have desdayn to been servauntz and thralles to sinne, and sore been ashamed of hem-self,/ that god of his endelees goodnesse hath set hem in heigh estaat, or yeven hem wit, strengthe of body, hele, beautee, prosperitee,/ and boghte hem fro the deeth with his herte blood, that they so unkindely, agayns his gentilesse, quyten him so vileinsly, to slaughtre of hir owene soules./ O gode god, ye (80) wommen that been of so greet beautee, remembreth yow of the proverbe of Salomon, that seith:/ 'he lykneth a 155 fair womman, that is a fool of hir body, lyk to a ring of gold that were in the groyn of a sowe.'/ For right as a sowe wroteth in everich ordure, so wroteth she hir beautee in the stinkinge ordure of sinne. /

§ 10. The thridde cause that oghte moeve a man to Contricion, is drede of the day of dome, and of the horrible peynes of helle. / For as seint Jerome seith : 'at every tyme that me remembreth of the day of dome, I quake ; / for whan I ete or drinke, or what-so that I do, evere semeth me that the trompe 160 sowneth in myn ere : / riseth up, ye that been dede, and cometh to the jugement.'/ O gode god, muchel oghte a man to drede swich a jugement, 'ther-as we shullen been alle,' as seint Poul seith, 'biforn the sete of oure lord Jesu Crist'; / wher-as he shal make a general congregacion, wher-as no man may been absent. / For certes, there availleth noon essoyne ne (90) excusacion. / And nat only that oure defautes shullen be juged, but eek that 165 alle oure werkes shullen openly be knowe./ And as seith Seint Bernard : 'ther ne shal no pledinge availle, ne no sleighte ; we shullen yeven rekeninge of everich ydel word.'/ Ther shul we han a juge that may nat been deceived ne corrupt. And why? For, certes, alle our thoghtes been discovered as to him ; ne for preyere ne for mede he shal nat been corrupt. / And therfore seith Salomon : 'the wratthe of god ne wol nat spare no wight, for preyere ne for yifte'; and therfore, at the day of doom, ther nis noon hope to escape. / Wherfore, as seith Seint Anselm : 'ful greet angwissh shul the sinful folk have at that tyme ; / ther shal the sterne and wrothe juge sitte above, and under him the horrible put of helle open to destroyen him that moot biknowen hise sinnes, whiche sinnes openly been shewed biforn god and bi- 170 forn every creature. / And on the left syde, mo develes than herte may bithinke, for to harie and drawe the sinful soules to the pyne of helle. / And with-inne the hertes of folk shal be the bytinge conscience, and with-oute-forth shal be the world al brenninge. / Whider shal thanne the wrecched sinful man flee to hyden him ? Certes, he may nat hyden

him ; he moste come forth and shewen him.'/ For certes, as seith seint Jerome: 'the erthe shal casten him out of him, and the see also ; and the eyr also, that shal be ful of thonder-clappes and light-ninges.' / Now sothly, who-so wel re- ( membreth him of thise thinges, I gesse that his sinne shal nat turne him in-to delyt, but to greet sorwe, for drede of the peyne of helle. / And therfore seith Job 1 to god : 'suffre, lord, that I may a whyle biwaille and wepe, er I go with-oute returning to the derke lond, covered with the derknesse of deeth ; / to the lond of misese and of derknesse, where-as is the shadwe of deeth ; where-as ther is noon ordre or ordinance, but grisly drede that evere shal laste.' / Lo, here may ye seen that Job preyde respyt a whyle, to biwepe and waille his trespas ; for soothly oon day of respyt is bettre than al the tresor of the world. / And for-as-muche as a man may acquiten him-self biforn god by penitence in this world, and nat by tresor, therfore sholde he preye to god to yeve him respyt a whyle, to biwepe and biwaillen his trespas. / For certes, al the sorwe that a man mighte make fro the beginning of the world, nis but a litel thing at regard of the sorwe of helle. / The cause why that Job clepeth 1 helle 'the lond of derknesse'; / understondeth that he clepeth it 'londe' or erthe, for it is stable, and nevere shal faille ; 'derk,' for he that is in helle hath defaute of light material. / For certes, the derke light, that shal come out of the fyr that evere shal brenne, shal turne him al to peyne that is in helle ; for it sheweth him to the horrible develes that him tormenten. / 'Covered with the derknesse of deeth': that is to seyn, that he that is in helle shal have defaute of the sighte of god ; for certes, the sighte of god is the lyf perdurable. / 'The (1 derknesse of deeth' been the sinnes that the wrecched man hath doon, whiche that destourben him to see the face of god ; right as doth a derk cloude bitwixe us and the sonne. / 'Lond of misese': / 18 by-cause that ther been three maneres of defautes, agayn three thinges that folk of this world han in this present lyf, that is to seyn, honours, delyces, and richesses. / Agayns honour, have they in helle shame and confusion. / For wel ye woot that men clepen 'honour' the reverence that man doth to man ; but in helle is noon honour ne reverence. For certes, na-more reverence shal be doon there to a king than to a knave. / For which god seith by the prophete Jeremye : 'thilke folk that me despysen shul been in despyt.' / 'Honour' is eek cleped greet lordshipe ; ther shal no man serven other but of harm and torment. 'Honour' is eek cleped greet dignitee and heigh-nesse ; but in helle shul they been al fortroden of develes. / And god seith : 'the horrible develes shulle goon and comen up-on the hevedes of the dampned folk.' And this is for-as-muche as, the hyer that they were in this present lyf, the more shulle they been abated and defouled in helle. / Agayns the richesses of this world, shul they han misese of poverte ; and this poverte shal been in foure thinges : / in defaute of tresor, of which that David seith ; 'the riche folk, that embraceden and oneden al hir herte to tresor of this world, shul slepe in the slepinge of deeth ; and no-thing ne shul they finden in hir handes of al hir tresor.' / And more-over, the miseise of helle shal been in defaute of mete and drinke. / For god seith thus by Moyses ; 'they shul been wasted with hunger, and the briddes of helle shul devouren hem with bitter deeth, and the galle of the dragon shal been hir drinke, and the venim of the dragon hir morsels.' / And forther-over, hir miseise shal been in defaute of clothing : for they shulle be naked in body as of clothing, save the fyr in which they brenne and othere filthes ; / and naked shul they been of soule, of alle manere vertues, which that is the cloth-ing of the soule. Where been thanne the gaye robes and the softe shetes and the smale shertes ? / Lo, what seith god of hem by the prophete Isaye : 'that under hem shul been strawed motthes, and hir

covertures shulle been of wormes of helle.' / And forther-over, hir miseise shal been in defaute of freendes ; for he nis nat povre that hath goode freendes, but there is no freend ; / for neither god ne no creature shal been freend to hem, and everich of hem shal haten other with deedly hate. / 'The sones and the doghtren shullen rebellen agayns fader and mooder, and kinrede agayns kinrede, and chyden and despysen everich of hem other,' bothe day and night, as god seith by the prophete Michias. / And the lovinge children, that whylom loveden so fleshly everich other, wolden everich of hem eten other if they mighte. / For how sholden they love hem togidre in the peyne of helle, whan they hated ech of hem other in the prosperitee of this lyf ? / For truste wel, hir fleshly love was deedly hate ; as seith the prophete David : 'who-so that loveth wikkednesse he hateth his soule.' / And who-so hateth his owene soule, certes, he may love noon other wight in no manere. / And therefore, in helle is no solas ne no frendshipe, but evere the more fleshly kinredes that been in helle, the more cursinges, the more chydinges, and the more deedly hate ther is among hem. / And forther-over, they shul have defaute of alle manere delyces ; for certes, delyces been after the appe-tytes of the fyve wittes, as sighte, heringe, smellinge, savoringe, and touchinge. / But in helle hir sighte shal be ful of derknesse and of smoke, and therfore ful of teres ; and hir heringe, ful of way-mentinge and of grintinge of teeth, as seith Jesu Crist ; / hir nosethirles shullen be ful of stinkinge stink. And as seith Isaye the prophete : 'hir savoring shal be ful of bitter galle.' / And touchinge of al hir body, y-covered with 'fyr that nevere shal quenche, and with wormes that nevere shul dyen,' as god seith by the mouth of Isaye. / And for-as-muche as they shul nat wene that they may dyen for peyne, and by hir deeth flee fro peyne, that may they understonden by the word of Job, that seith : 'ther-as is the shadwe of deeth.' / Certes, a

shadwe hath the lyknesse of the thing
of which it is shadwe, but shadwe is nat
the same thing of which it is shadwe. /
Right so fareth the peyne of helle; it is
lyk deeth for the horrible anguissh, and
why? For it peyneth hem evere, as
though they sholde dye anon; but certes
they shal nat dye. / For as seith Seint
Gregorie: 'to wrecche caytives shal be
deeth with-oute deeth, and ende with-
outen ende, and defaute with-oute fail-
(140) inge. / For hir deeth shal alwey liven,
and hir ende shal everemo biginne, and
215 hir defaute shal nat faille.' / And therfore seith Seint John the Evangelist:
'they shullen folwe deeth, and they shul
nat finde him; and they shul desyren
to dye, and deeth shal flee fro hem.' /
And eek Job seith: that 'in helle is
noon ordre of rule.' / And al-be-it so
that god hath creat alle thinges in right
ordre, and no-thing with-outen ordre,
but alle thinges been ordeyned and nombred; yet nathelees they that been
dampned been no-thing in ordre, ne
holden noon ordre. / For the erthe ne
shal bere hem no fruit. / For, as the
prophete David seith: 'god shal destroye
the fruit of the erthe as fro hem'; ne
water ne shal yeve hem no moisture; ne
220 the eyr no refresshing, ne fyr no light. /
For as seith seint Basilie: 'the brenninge
of the fyr of this world shal god yeven in
helle to hem that been dampned; / but
the light and the cleernesse shal be yeven
in hevene to hise children'; right as the
gode man yeveth flesh to hise children,
and bones to his houndes. / And for
they shullen have noon hope to escape,
seith seint Job atte laste: that 'ther
shal horrour and grisly drede dwellen
with-outen ende.' / Horrour is alwey
drede of harm that is to come, and this
drede shal evere dwelle in the hertes of
hem that been dampned. And therefore
han they lorn al hir hope, for sevene
(150) causes. / First, for god that is hir juge
shal be with-outen mercy to hem; ne
they may nat plese him, ne noon of hise
halwes; ne they ne may yeve no-thing
225 for hir raunson; / ne they have no vois

to speke to him; ne they may nat flee
fro peyne; ne they have no goodnesse in
hem, that they mowe shewe to delivere
hem fro peyne. / And therfore seith
Salomon: 'the wikked man dyeth; and
whan he is deed, he shal have noon hope
to escape fro peyne.' / Who-so thanne
wolde wel understande these peynes, and
bithinke him weel that he hath deserved
thilke peynes for his sinnes, certes, he
sholde have more talent to syken and to
wepe than for to singen and to pleye. /
For as that seith Salomon: 'who-so that
hadde the science to knowe the peynes
that been establissed and ordeyned for
sinne, he wolde make sorwe.' / 'Thilke
science,' as seith seint Augustin, 'maketh
a man to waymenten in his herte.' /          2

§ 11. The fourthe point, that oghte
maken a man to have contricion, is the
sorweful remembrance of the good that
he hath left to doon here in erthe; and
eek the good that he hath lorn. / Soothly,
the gode werkes that he hath left, outher
they been the gode werkes that he
wroghte er he fel in-to deedly sinne, or
elles the gode werkes that he wroghte
while he lay in sinne. / Soothly, the
gode werkes, that he dide biforn that he
fil in sinne, been al mortified and astoned
and dulled by the ofte sinning. / The
othere gode werkes, that he wroghte
whyl he lay in deedly sinne, they been
outrely dede as to the lyf perdurable in
hevene. / Thanne thilke gode werkes (∗
that been mortified by ofte sinning,
whiche gode werkes he dide whyl he was
in charitee, ne mowe nevere quiken agayn
with-outen verray penitence. / And ther-    2
of seith god, by the mouth of Ezechiel:
that, 'if the rightful man returne agayn
from his rightwisnesse and werke wikkednesse, shal he live?' / Nay; for alle the
gode werkes that he hath wroght ne shul
nevere been in remembrance; for he shal
dyen in his sinne. / And up-on thilke
chapitre seith seint Gregorie thus: 'that
we shulle understonde this principally; /
that whan we doon deedly sinne, it is
for noght thanne to rehercen or drawen
in-to memorie the gode werkes that we

han wroght biforn.' / For certes, in the werkinge of the deedly sinne, ther is no trust to no good werk that we han doon biforn ; that is to seyn, as for to have therby the lyf perdurable in hevene. / But nathelees, the gode werkes quiken agayn, and comen agayn, and helpen, and availlen to have the lyf perdurable in hevene, whan we han contricion. / But soothly, the gode werkes that men doon whyl they been in deedly sinne, for-as-muche as they were doon in deedly sinne, they may nevere quiken agayn. / For certes, thing that nevere hadde lyf may nevere quikene ; and nathelees, albe-it that they ne availle noght to han the lyf perdurable, yet availlen they to abregge of the peyne of helle, or elles to geten temporal richesse, / or elles that god wole the rather enlumine and lightne the herte of the sinful man to have repentance ; / and eek they availlen for to usen a man to doon gode werkes, that the feend have the lasse power of his soule. / And thus the curteis lord Jesu Crist wole that no good werk be lost ; for in somwhat it shal availle. / But for-as-muche as the gode werkes that men doon whyl they been in good lyf, been al mortified by sinne folwinge ; and eek, sith that alle the gode werkes that men doon whyl they been in deedly synne, been outrely dede as for to have the lyf perdurable ; / wel may that man, that no good werke ne dooth, singe thilke newe Frenshe song : ' Jay tout perdu mon temps et mon labour.' / For certes, sinne bireveth a man bothe goodnesse of nature and eek the goodnesse of grace. / For soothly, the grace of the holy goost fareth lyk fyr, that may nat been ydel ; for fyr faileth anoon as it forleteth his wirkinge, and right so grace fayleth anoon as it forleteth his werkinge. / Than leseth the sinful man the goodnesse of glorie, that only is bihight to gode men that labouren and werken. / Wel may he be sory thanne, that oweth al his lif to god as longe as he hath lived, and eek as longe as he shal live, that no goodnesse ne hath to paye with his dette

to god, to whom he oweth al his lyf. / For trust wel, ' he shal yeven acountes,' as seith seint Bernard, ' of alle the godes that han be yeven him in this present lyf, and how he hath hem despended ; / in so muche that ther shal nat perisse an heer of his heed, ne a moment of an houre ne shal nat perisse of his tyme, that he ne shal yeve of it a rekening.' /   (180)

§ 12. The fifthe thing that oghte moeve a man to contricion, is remembrance of the passion that oure lord Jesu Crist suffred for oure sinnes. / For, as seith 255 seint Bernard : ' whyl that I live, I shal have remembrance of the travailles that oure lord Crist suffred in preching ; / his werinesse in travailling, hise temptacions whan he fasted, hise longe wakinges whan he preyde, hise teres whan that he weep for pitee of good peple ; / the wo and the shame and the filthe that men seyden to him ; of the foule spitting that men spitte in his face, of the buffettes that men yaven him, of the foule mowes, and of the repreves that men to him seyden ; / of the nayles with whiche he was nailed to the croys, and of al the remenant of his passion that he suffred for my sinnes, and no-thing for his gilt.' / And ye shul understonde, that in mannes sinne is every manere of ordre or ordinance turned up-so-doun. / 260 For it is sooth, that god, and reson, and sensualitee, and the body of man been so ordeyned, that everich of thise foure thinges sholde have lordshipe over that other ; / as thus : god sholde have lordshipe over reson, and reson over sensualitee, and sensualitee over the body of man. / But sothly, whan man sinneth, al this ordre or ordinance is turned up-so-doun. / And therfore thanne, for-as-muche as the reson of man ne wol nat be subget ne obeisant to god, that is his lord by right, therfore leseth it the lordshipe that it sholde have over sensualitee, and eek over the body of man. / And (190) why ? For sensualitee rebelleth thanne agayns reson ; and by that wey leseth reson the lordshipe over sensualitee and over the body. / For right as reson is 265

rebel to god, right so is bothe sensualitee rebel to reson and the body also. / And certes, this disordinance and this rebellion oure lord Jesu Crist aboghte up-on his precious body ful dere, and herkneth in which wyse. / For-as-muche thanne as reson is rebel to god, therfore is man worthy to have sorwe and to be deed. / This suffred oure lord Jesu Crist for man, after that he hadde be bitraysed of his disciple, and distreyned and bounde, 'so that his blood brast out at every nail of hise handes,' as seith seint Augustin. / And forther-over, for-as-muchel as reson of man ne wol nat daunte sensualitee whan it may, therfore is man worthy to have shame; and this suffred oure lord Jesu Crist for man,
270 whan they spetten in his visage. / And forther-over, for-as-muchel thanne as the caitif body of man is rebel bothe to reson and to sensualitee, therfore is it worthy the deeth. / And this suffred oure lord Jesu Crist for man up-on the croys, where-as ther was no part of his body free, with-outen greet peyne and bitter passion. / And al this suffred Jesu Crist, that nevere forfeted. And therfore resonably may be seyd of Jesu in this manere : 'to muchel am I peyned for the thinges that I nevere deserved, and to muche defouled for shendshipe that man is worthy to have.' / And therfore may the sinful man wel seye, as seith seint Bernard : 'acursed be the bitternesse of my sinne, for which ther moste
(200) be suffred so muchel bitternesse.' / For certes, after the diverse discordances of oure wikkednesses, was the passion of
275 Jesu Crist ordeyned in diverse thinges, / as thus. Certes, sinful mannes soule is bitraysed of the devel by coveitise of temporel prosperitee, and scorned by deceite whan he cheseth fleshly delyces ; and yet is it tormented by inpacience of adversitee, and bispet by servage and subjeccion of sinne ; and atte laste it is slayn fynally. / For this disordinaunce of sinful man was Jesu Crist first bitraysed, and after that was he bounde, that cam for to unbynden us of sinne

and peyne. / Thanne was he biscorned, that only sholde han been honoured in alle thinges and of alle thinges. / Thanne was his visage, that oghte be desired to be seyn of al man-kinde, in which visage aungels desyren to looke, vileynsly bispet. / Thanne was he scourged that no-thing hadde agilt; and fynally, thanne was he crucified and slayn. / Thanne 28 was acompliced the word of Isaye : 'he was wounded for oure misdedes, and defouled for oure felonies.' / Now sith that Jesu Crist took up-on him-self the peyne of alle oure wikkednesses, muchel oghte sinful man wepen and biwayle, that for hise sinnes goddes sone of hevene sholde al this peyne endure. /

§ 13. The sixte thing that oghte moeve a man to contricion, is the hope of three thynges ; that is to seyn, foryifnesse of sinne, and the yifte of grace wel for to do, and the glorie of hevene, with which god shal guerdone a man for hise gode dedes. / And for-as-muche as Jesu Crist yeveth us thise yiftes of his largesse and of his sovereyn bountee, therfore is he cleped *Jesus Nazarenus rex Judeorum.* / (2 Jesus is to seyn 'saveour' or 'salvacion,' on whom men shul hope to have foryifnesse of sinnes, which that is proprely salvacion of sinnes. / And therfore seyde 28 the aungel to Joseph : 'thou shalt clepen his name Jesus, that shal saven his peple of hir sinnes.' / And heer-of seith seint Peter : 'ther is noon other name under hevene that is yeve to any man, by which a man may be saved, but only Jesus.' / *Nazarenus* is as muche for to seye as 'florisshinge,' in which a man shal hope, that he that yeveth him remission of sinnes shal yeve him eek grace wel for to do. For in the flour is hope of fruit in tyme cominge ; and in foryifnesse of sinnes hope of grace wel for to do. / 'I was atte dore of thyn herte,' seith Jesus, 'and cleped for to entre ; he that openeth to me shal have foryifnesse of sinne. / I wol entre in-to him by my grace, and soupe with him,' by the goode werkes that he shal doon ; whiche werkes been the foode of god ; 'and he shal soupe with me,' by the grete joye that I shal yeven him. / Thus shal man hope, for hise werkes of penaunce, that god shall yeven him his regne; as he bihoteth him in the gospel. /

§ 14. Now shal a man understonde, in which manere shal been his contricion. I seye, that it shal been universal and total; this is to seyn, a man shal be verray repentant for alle hise sinnes that he hath doon in delyt of his thoght; for delyt is ful perilous. / For ther been two manere of consentinges; that oon of hem is cleped consentinge of affeccion, whan a man is moeved to do sinne, and delyteth him longe for to thinke on that sinne; / and his reson aperceyveth it wel, that it is sinne agayns the lawe of god, and yet his reson refreyneth nat his foul delyt or talent, though he see wel apertly that it is agayns the reverence of god; al-though his reson ne consente noght to doon that sinne in dede, / yet seyn somme doctours that swich delyt that dwelleth longe, it is ful perilous, al be it nevere so lite. / And also a man sholde sorwe, namely, for al that evere he hath desired agayn the lawe of god with perfit consentinge of his reson; for ther-of is no doute, that it is deedly sinne in consentinge. / For certes, ther is no deedly sinne, that it nas first in mannes thought, and after that in his delyt; and so forth in-to consentinge and in-to dede. / Wherfore I seye, that many men ne re-penten hem nevere of swiche thoghtes and delytes, ne nevere shryven hem of it, but only of the dede of grete sinnes outward. / Wherfore I seye, that swiche wikked delytes and wikked thoghtes been subtile bigyleres of hem that shullen be dampned. / More-over, man oghte to sorwe for hise wikkede wordes as wel as for hise wikkede dedes; for certes, the repentance of a singuler sinne, and nat repente of alle hise othere sinnes, or elles repenten him of alle hise othere sinnes, and nat of a singuler sinne, may nat availle. / For certes, god almighty is al good; and ther-fore he foryeveth al, or elles right noght. / And heer-of seith

seint Augustin: 'I woot certeinly / that god is enemy to everich sinnere'; and how thanne? He that observeth o sinne, shal he have foryifnesse of the reme-naunt of hise othere sinnes? Nay. / And forther-over, contricion sholde be wonder sorweful and anguissous, and therfore yeveth him god pleynly his mercy; and therfore, whan my soule was anguissous with-inne me, I hadde remembrance of god that my preyere mighte come to him. / Forther-over, (230) contricion moste be continuel, and that man have stedefast purpos to shryven him, and for to amenden him of his lyf. / 305 For soothly, whyl contricion lasteth, man may evere have hope of foryifnesse; and of this comth hate of sinne, that destroy-eth sinne bothe in himself, and eek in other folk, at his power. / For which seith David: 'ye that loven god hateth wikkednesse.' For trusteth wel, to love god is for to love that he loveth, and hate that he hateth. /

§ 15. The laste thing that man shal understonde in contricion is this; wher-of avayleth contricion. I seye, that som tyme contricion delivereth a man fro sinne; / of which that David seith: 'I seye,' quod David, that is to seyn, 'I purposed fermely to shryve me; and thow, Lord, relesedest my sinne.' / And right so as contricion availleth noght, with-outen sad purpos of shrifte, if man have oportunitee, right so litel worth is shrifte or satisfaccion with-outen con-tricion. / And more-over, contricion 310 destroyeth the prison of helle, and maketh wayk and feble alle the strengthes of the develes, and restoreth the yiftes of the holy goost and of alle gode vertues;/ and it clenseth the soule of sinne, and delivereth the soule fro the peyne of helle, and fro the companye of the devel, and fro the servage of sinne, and restoreth it to alle godes espirituels, and to the companye and communion of holy chirche. / And forther-over, it maketh him that whylom was sone of ire to be sone of grace; and alle thise thinges been preved by holy writ. / And therfore, he that wolde sette his entente to thise thinges, he were ful wys; for soothly, he ne sholde nat thanne in al his lyf have corage to sinne, but yeven his body and al his herte to the service of Jesu Crist, (240) and ther-of doon him hommage. / For soothly, oure swete lord Jesu Crist hath spared us so debonairly in our folies, that if he ne hadde pitee of mannes soule, 315 a sory song we mighten alle singe. /

### Explicit prima pars Penitentie; et sequitur secunda pars eiusdem.

§ 16. The seconde partie of Penitence is Confession, that is signe of contricion. / Now shul ye understonde what is Confession, and whether it oghte nedes be doon or noon, and whiche thinges been covenable to verray Confession. /

§ 17. First shaltow understonde that Confession is verray shewinge of sinnes to the preest ; / this is to seyn 'verray,' for he moste confessen him of alle the condiciouns that bilongen to his sinne, as ferforth as he can. / Al moot be seyd, and no thing excused ne hid ne forwrapped, and noght avaunte him of his 320 gode werkes. / And forther over, it is necessarie to understonde whennes that sinnes springen, and how they encresen, and whiche they been. /

§ 18. Of the springinge of sinnes seith seint Paul in this wise : that 'right as by a man sinne entred first in-to this world, and thurgh that sinne deeth, right so thilke deeth entred in-to alle men that sinneden.'/ And this man was Adam, by whom sinne entred in-to this world whan he brak the comaundement of god. / And therfore, he that first was so mighty that he sholde not have dyed, bicam swich oon that he moste nedes dye, whether he wolde or noon ; and all his progenie in this world that in thilke man (250) sinneden. / Loke that in th'estaat of innocence, when Adam and Eve naked weren in paradys, and no-thing ne hadden 325 shame of hir nakednesse, / how that the serpent, that was most wyly of alle othere bestes that god hadde maked, seyde to

the womman : 'why comaunded god to yow, ye sholde nat eten of every tree in paradys?' / The womman answerde : 'of the fruit,' quod she, 'of the trees in paradys we feden us ; but soothly, of the fruit of the tree that is in the middel of paradys, god forbad us for to ete, ne nat touchen it, lest per-aventure we should dyen.' / The serpent seyde to the womman : 'nay, nay, ye shul nat dyen of deeth ; for sothe, god woot, that what day that ye eten ther-of, youre eyen shul opene, and ye shul been as goddes, knowinge good and harm. '/ The womman thanne saugh that the tree was good to feding, and fair to the eyen, and delytable to the sighte ; she tok of the fruit of the tree, and eet it, and yaf to hir housbonde, and he eet ; and anoon the eyen of hem bothe openeden. / And whan that they knewe that they were naked, they sowed of fige-leves a manere of breches to hiden hir membres. / There may ye seen that deedly sinne hath first suggestion of the feend, as sheweth here by the naddre ; and afterward, the delyt of the flesh, as sheweth here by Eve ; and after that, the consentinge of resoun, as sheweth here by Adam. / For trust wel, thogh so were that the feend tempted Eve, that is to seyn the flesh, and the flesh hadde delyt in the beautee of the fruit defended, yet certes, til that resoun, that is to seyn, Adam, consented to the etinge of the fruit, yet stood he in th'estaat of innocence. / Of thilke Adam toke we thilke sinne original ; for of him fleshly descended be we alle, and engendred of vile and corrupt matere. / And whan the soule is put in our body, right anon is contract original sinne ; and that, that was erst but only peyne of concupiscence, is afterward bothe peyne and sinne. / And therfore be we alle born sones of wratthe and of dampnacion perdurable, if it nere baptesme that we receyven, which binimeth us the culpe ; but for sothe, the peyne dwelleth with us, as to temptacion, which peyne highte concupiscence. / Whan it is wrongfully disposed or ordeyned in man, it maketh him coveite,

by coveitise of flesh, fleshly sinne, by
sighte of hise eyen as to erthely thinges,
and coveitise of hynesse by pryde of
herte. /

§ 19. Now as for to speken of the firste
coveitise, that is, concupiscence after the
lawe of oure membres, that weren lawe-
fulliche y-maked and by rightful jugement of god; / I seye, for-as-muche as
man is nat obeisaunt to god, that is his
lord, therfore is the flesh to him dis-
obeisaunt thurgh concupiscence, which
yet is cleped norissinge of sinne and
occasion of sinne. / Therfore, al the
whyle that a man hath in him the peyne of
concupiscence, it is impossible but he be
tempted somtyme, and moeved in his
flesh to sinne. / And this thing may nat
faille as longe as he liveth; it may wel
wexe feble and faille, by vertu of baptesme
and by the grace of god thurgh penitence; / but fully ne shal it nevere
quenche, that he ne shal som tyme be
moeved in him-self, but-if he were al
refreyded by siknesse, or by malefice of
sorcerie or colde drinkes. / For lo, what
seith seint Paul: 'the flesh coveiteth
agayn the spirit, and the spirit agayn the
flesh; they been so contrarie and so
stryven, that a man may nat alwey doon
as he wolde.' / The same seint Paul,
after his grete penaunce in water and in
lond (in water by night and by day, in
greet peril and in greet peyne, in lond,
in famine, in thurst, in cold and clothlees, and ones stoned almost to the
deeth) / yet seyde he: 'allas! I, caytif
man, who shal delivere me fro the
prisoun of my caytif body?' / And seint
Jerome, whan he longe tyme hadde woned
in desert, where-as he hadde no companye but of wilde bestes, where-as he ne
hadde no mete but herbes and water to
his drinke, ne no bed but the naked erthe,
for which his flesh was blak as an
Ethiopen for hete and ny destroyed for
cold, / yet seyde he: that 'the brenninge of
lecherie boiled in al his body.' / Wherfore
I woot wel sikerly, that they been
deceyved that seyn, that they ne be nat
tempted in hir body. / Witnesse on

Seint Jame the Apostel, that seith: that
'every wight is tempted in his owen concupiscence;' that is to seyn, that everich
of us hath matere and occasion to be
tempted of the norissinge of sinne that
is in his body. / And therfore seith
Seint John the Evaungelist: 'if that
we seyn that we beth with-oute sinne,
we deceyve us-selve, and trouthe is nat
in us.' /

§ 20. Now shal ye understonde in what
manere that sinne wexeth or encreseth
in man. The firste thing is thilke norissinge of sinne, of which I spak biforn,
thilke fleshly concupiscence. / And after
that comth the subjeccion of the devel,
this is to seyn, the develes bely, with
which he bloweth in man the fyr of
fleshly concupiscence. / And after that,
a man bithinketh him whether he wol
doon, or no, thilke thing to which he is
tempted. / And thanne, if that a man
withstonde and weyve the firste entysinge
of his flesh and of the feend, thanne is it
no sinne; and if it so be that he do nat
so, thanne feleth he anon flambe of
delyt. / And thanne is it good to be
war, and kepen him wel, or elles he wol
falle anon in-to consentinge of sinne;
and thanne wol he do it, if he may have
tyme and place. / And of this matere
seith Moyses by the devel in this manere:
'the feend seith, I wole chace and pursue
the man by wikked suggestion, and I wole
hente him by moevynge or stiringe of
sinne. I wol departe my pryse or my
praye by deliberacion, and my lust shal
been accompliced in delyt; I wol drawe
my swerd in consentinge:' / for certes,
right as a swerd departeth a thing in two
peces, right so consentinge departeth god
fro man: 'and thanne wol I sleen him
with myn hand in dede of sinne'; thus
seith the feend. / For certes, thanne is
a man al deed in soule. And thus is
sinne accompliced by temptacion, by
delyt, and by consentinge; and thanne is
the sin cleped actuel. /

§ 21. For sothe, sinne is in two
maneres; outher it is venial, or deedly
sinne. Soothly, whan man loveth any

350

(280)

355

0

0)

45

creature more than Jesu Crist oure
creatour, thanne is it deedly sinne. And
venial synne is it, if man love Jesu Crist
lasse than him oghte. / For sothe, the
dede of this venial sinne is ful perilous;
for it amenuseth the love that men
sholde han to god more and more. / And
therfore, if a man charge him-self with
manye swiche venial sinnes, certes, but-if
so be that he som tyme descharge him of
hem by shrifte, they mowe ful lightly
amenuse in him al the love that he hath
360 to Jesu Crist; / and in this wise skippeth
venial in-to deedly sinne. For certes, the
more that a man chargeth his soule with
venial sinnes, the more is he enclyned to
fallen in-to deedly sinne. / And therfore,
lat us nat be necligent to deschargen us
of venial sinnes. For the proverbe seith:
that manye smale maken a greet. / And
herkne this ensample. A greet wawe of
the see comth som-tyme with so greet
a violence that it drencheth the ship.
And the same harm doth som-tyme
the smale dropes of water, that entren
thurgh a litel crevace in-to the thurrok,
and in-to the botme of the ship, if men
be so necligent that they ne descharge
hem nat by tyme. / And therfore, al-
thogh ther be a difference bitwixe thise
two causes of drenchinge, algates the
(290) ship is dreynt. / Right so fareth it som-
tyme of deedly sinne, and of anoyouse
veniale sinnes, whan they multiplye in
a man so greetly, that thilke worldly
thinges that he loveth, thurgh whiche he
sinneth venially, is as greet in his herte
365 as the love of god, or more. / And therfore, the love of every thing, that is nat
biset in god ne doon principally for
goddes sake, al-though that a man love it
lasse than god, yet is it venial sinne; /
and deedly sinne, whan the love of any
thing weyeth in the herte of man as
muchel as the love of god, or more. /
'Deedly sinne,' as seith seint Augustin,
'is, whan a man turneth his herte fro
god, which that is verray sovereyn
bountee, that may nat chaunge, and
yeveth his herte to thing that may
chaunge and flitte'; / and certes, that is

every thing, save god of hevene. For
sooth is, that if a man yeve his love, the
which that he oweth al to god with al his
herte, un-to a creature, certes, as muche
of his love as he yeveth to thilke creature,
so muche he bireveth fro god; / and
therfore doth he sinne. For he, that is
dettour to god, ne yeldeth nat to god al
his dette, that is to seyn, al the love of
his herte. /               3

§ 22. Now sith man understondeth
generally, which is venial sinne, thanne
is it covenable to tellen specially of sinnes
whiche that many a man per-aventure ne
demeth hem nat sinnes, and ne shryveth
him nat of the same thinges; and yet
nathelees they been sinnes. / Soothly,
as thise clerkes wryten, this is to seyn,
that at every tyme that a man eteth or
drinketh more than suffyseth to the
sustenaunce of his body, in certein he
dooth sinne. / And eek whan he speketh
more than nedeth, it is sinne. Eke whan
he herkneth nat benignely the compleint
of the povre. / Eke whan he is in hele
of body and wol nat faste, whan othere
folk faste, with-outen cause resonable.
Eke whan he slepeth more than nedeth,
or whan he comth by thilke enchesoun
to late to chirche, or to othere werkes of
charite. / Eke whan he useth his wyf, (3
with-outen sovereyn desyr of engendrure,
to the honour of god, or for the entente
to yelde to his wyf the dette of his body./ 37
Eke whan he wol nat visite the sike and
the prisoner, if he may. Eke if he love
wyf or child, or other worldly thing,
more than resoun requyreth. Eke if he
flatere or blandishe more than him oghte
for any necessitee. / Eke if he amenuse
or withdrawe the almesse of the povre.
Eke if he apparailleth his mete more
deliciously than nede is, or ete it to
hastily by likerousnesse. / Eke if he tale
vanitees at chirche or at goddes service,
or that he be a talker of ydel wordes of
folye or of vileinye; for he shal yelden
acountes of it at the day of dome. / Eke
whan he biheteth or assureth to do thinges
that he may nat perfourne. Eke whan
that he, by lightnesse or folie, misseyeth

or scorneth his neighebore. / Eke whan he hath any wikked suspecion of thing, so ther he ne woot of it no soothfastnesse. / Thise thinges and mo with-oute nombre been sinnes, as seith seint Augustin. /

Now shal men understonde, that al-be-it so that noon erthely man may eschue alle venial sinnes, yet may he refreyne him by the brenninge love that he hath to oure lord Jesu Crist, and by preyeres and confession and othere gode werkes, so that it shal but litel greve. / For, as seith seint Augustin : ' if a man love god in swiche manere, that al that evere he doth is in the love of god, and for the love of god verraily, for he brenneth in the love of god : / loke, how muche that a drope of water that falleth in a fourneys ful of fyr anoyeth or greveth, so muche anoyeth a venial sinne un-to a man that is parfit in the love of Jesu Crist.' / Men may also refreyne venial sinne by receyvinge worthily of the precious body of Jesu Crist ; / by receyving eek of holy water ; by almesdede ; by general confession of Confiteor at masse and at complin ; and by blessinge of bisshopes and of preestes, and by othere gode werkes. /

Explicit secunda pars Penitentie.

Sequitur de Septem Peccatis Mortalibus et eorum dependenciis circumstanciis et speciebus.

§ 23. Now is it bihovely thing to telle whiche been the deedly sinnes, this is to seyn, chieftaines of sinnes ; alle they renne in o lees, but in diverse maneres. Now been they cleped chieftaines for-as-muche as they been chief, and †springers of alle othere sinnes. / Of the roote of thise sevene sinnes thanne is Pryde, the general rote of alle harmes ; for of this rote springen certein braunches, as Ire, Envye, Accidie or Slewthe, Avarice or Coveitise (to commune understondinge), Glotonye, and Lecherye. / And everich of thise chief sinnes hath hise braunches and hise twigges, as shal be declared in hir chapitres folwinge. /

## De Superbia.

§ 24. And thogh so be that no man can outrely telle the nombre of the twigges and of the harmes that cometh of Pryde, yet wol I shewe a partie of hem, as ye shul understonde. / Ther is Inobedience, Avauntinge, Ipocrisie, Despyt, Arrogance, Impudence, Swellinge of herte, Insolence, Elacion, Impacience, Strif, Contumacie, Presumpcion, Irreverence, Pertinacie, Veyne Glorie ; and many another twig that I can nat declare. / Inobedient, is he that disobeyeth for despyt to the comandements of god and to hise sovereyns, and to his goostly fader. / Avauntour, is he that bosteth of the harm or of the bountee that he hath doon. / Ipocrite, is he that hydeth to shewe him swiche as he is, and sheweth him swiche as he noght is. / Despitous, is he that hath desdeyn of his neighebore, that is to seyn, of his evene-cristene, or hath despyt to doon that him oghte to do. / Arrogant, is he that thinketh that ho hath thilke bountees in him that he hath noght, or weneth that he sholde have hem by hise desertes ; or elles he demeth that he be that he nis nat. / Impudent, is he that for his pride hath no shame of hise sinnes. / Swellinge of herte, is whan a man rejoyseth him of harm that he hath doon. / Insolent, is he that despyseth in his jugement alle othere folk as to regard of his value, and of his conning, and of his speking, and of his bering. / Elacion, is whan he ne may neither suffre to have maister ne felawe. / Impacient, is he that wol nat been y-taught ne undernome of his vyce, and by stryf werreyeth trouthe witingly, and deffendeth his folye. / Contumax, is he that thurgh his indignacion is agayns everich auctoritee or power of hem that been hise sovereyns. / Presumpcion, is whan a man undertaketh an empryse that him oghte nat do, or elles that he may nat do ; and that is called Surquidrie. Irreverence, is whan men do nat honour thereas hem oghte to doon, and waiten to be reverenced. / Pertinacie

390

(320)

395

400

is whan man deffendeth his folye, and
(330) trusteth to muchel in his owene wit. /
Veyne glorie, is for to have pompe and
delyt in his temporel hynesse, and
405 glorifie him in this worldly estaat. /
Janglinge, is whan men speken to muche
biforn folk, and clappen as a mille, and
taken no kepe what they seye. /

§ 25. And yet is ther a privee spece of
Pryde, that waiteth first to be salewed er
he wole salewe, al be he lasse worth than
that other is, per-aventure ; and eek he
waiteth or desyreth to sitte, or elles to
goon above him in the wey, or kisse pax,
or been encensed, or goon to offring biforn
his neighebore, / and swiche semblable
thinges ; agayns his duetee, per-aventure,
but that he hath his herte and his
entente in swich a proud desyr to be
magnifyed and honoured biforn the
peple. /

§ 26. Now been ther two maneres of
Pryde ; that oon of hem is with-inne the
herte of man, and that other is with-
oute. / Of whiche soothly thise forseyde
thinges, and mo than I have seyd, apertenen to pryde that is in the herte of
man ; and that othere speces of pryde
410 been with-oute. / But natheles that oon
of thise speces of pryde is signe of that
other, right as the gaye leefsel atte taverne
is signe of the wyn that is in the celer. /
And this is in manye thinges : as in speche
and contenaunce, and in outrageous array
of clothing ; / for certes, if ther ne hadde
be no sinne in clothing, Crist wolde nat
have noted and spoken of the clothing of
thilke riche man in the gospel. / And, as
seith Seint Gregorie, that precious clothing
is coupable for the derthe of it, and for
his softenesse, and for his strangenesse
and degysinesse, and for the superfluitee,
(340) or for the inordinat scantnesse of it. /
Allas ! may men nat seen, as in oure
dayes, the sinful costlewe array of clothinge, and namely in to muche superfluitee,
415 or elles in to desordinat scantnesse ? /

§ 27. As to the firste sinne, that is in
superfluitee of clothinge, which that
maketh it so dere, to harm of the peple ; /
nat only the cost of embroudinge, the

degyse endentinge or barringe, oundinge,
palinge, windinge, or bendinge, and
semblable wast of clooth in vanitee ; /
but ther is also costlewe furringe in hir
gounes, so muche pounsoninge of chisels
to maken holes, so muche dagginge of
sheres ; / forth - with the superfluitee in
lengthe of the forseide gounes, trailinge
in the dong and in the myre, on horse
and eek on fote, as wel of man as of
womman, that al thilke trailing is verraily
as in effect wasted, consumed, thredbare,
and roten with donge, rather than it is
yeven to the povre ; to greet damage of
the forseyde povre folk. / And that in
sondry wyse : this is to seyn, that the
more that clooth is wasted, the more it
costeth to the peple for the scantnesse ; / 4
and forther-over, if so be that they wolde
yeven swich pounsoned and dagged clothing to the povre folk, it is nat convenient
to were for hir estaat, ne suffisant to bete
hir necessitee, to kepe hem fro the dis-
temperance of the firmament. / Upon
that other syde, to speken of the horrible
disordinat scantnesse of clothing, as been
thise cutted sloppes or hainselins, that
thurgh hir shortnesse ne covere nat the
shameful membres of man, to wikked
entente. / Allas ! somme of hem shewen
the boce of hir shap, and the horrible
swollen membres, that semeth lyk the
maladie of hirnia, in the wrappinge of hir
hoses ; / and eek the buttokes of hem
faren as it were the hindre part of a she-
ape in the fulle of the mone. / And (3
more-over, the wrecched swollen membres that they shewe thurgh the degysinge, in departinge of hir hoses in whyt
and reed, semeth that half hir shameful
privee membres weren flayn. / And if 42
so be that they departen hire hoses in
othere colours, as is whyt and blak, or
whyt and blew, or blak and reed, and so
forth ; / thanne semeth it, as by variance
of colour, that half the partie of hir
privee membres were corrupt by the fyr
of seint Antony, or by cancre, or by other
swich meschaunce. / Of the hindre part
of hir buttokes, it is ful horrible for to
see. For certes, in that partie of hir

body ther-as they purgen hir stinkinge ordure, / that foule partie shewe they to the peple proudly in despyt of honestetee, the which honestetee that Jesu Crist and hise freendes observede to shewen in hir lyve. / Now as of the outrageous array of wommen, god woot, that though the visages of somme of hem seme ful chaast and debonaire, yet notifie they in hir array of atyr likerousnesse and ᴵ30 pryde. / I sey nat that honestetee in clothinge of man or womman is uncovenable, but certes the superfluitee or disordinat scantitee of clothinge is reprevable. / Also the sinne of aornement or of apparaille is in thinges that apertenen to rydinge, as in to manye delicat horses that been holden for delyt, that been so faire, fatte, and costlewe ; / and also to many a vicious knave that is sustened by cause of hem ; in to curious harneys, as in sadeles, in crouperes, peytrels, and brydles covered with precious clothing and riche, barres and plates of gold and of silver. / For which god seith by Zakarie the prophete, 'I wol confounde ₆60) the ryderes of swiche horses.' / This folk taken litel reward of the rydinge of goddes sone of hevene, and of his harneys whan he rood up-on the asse, and ne hadde noon other harneys but the povre clothes of hise disciples; ne we ne rede ᴵ435 nat that evere he rood on other beest. / I speke this for the sinne of superfluitee, and nat for reasonable honestetee, whan reson it requyreth. / And further, certes pryde is greetly notified in holdinge of greet meinee, whan they be of litel profit or of right no profit. / And namely, whan that meinee is felonous and damageous to the peple, by hardinesse of heigh lordshipe or by wey of offices. / For certes, swiche lordes sellen thanne hir lordshipe to the devel of helle, whanne they sustenen the wikkednesse of hir meinee. / Or elles whan this folk of lowe degree, as thilke that holden hostelries, sustenen the thefte of hir hostilers, ᴵ440 and that is in many manere of deceites. / Thilke manere of folk been the flyes that folwen the hony, or elles the houndes

that folwen the careyne. Swiche forseyde folk stranglen spiritually hir lordshipes ; / for which thus seith David the prophete, 'wikked deeth mote come up-on thilke lordshipes, and god yeve that they mote descenden in-to helle al doun ; for in hir houses been iniquitees and shrewednesses,' and nat god of hevene. / And certes, but-if they doon amendement, right as god yaf his benison to †Laban by the service of Jacob, and to †Pharao by the service of Joseph, right so god wol yeve his malison to swiche lordshipes as sustenen the wikkednesse of hir servaunts, but-if they come to amendement./ Pryde of the table appereth eek ful ofte ; for certes, riche men been cleped to festes, and povre folk been put awey and rebuked. / Also in excesse of diverse (370) metes and drinkes ; and namely, swiche manere bake metes and dish-metes, brenninge of wilde fyr, and peynted and castelled with papir, and semblable wast; so that it is abusion for to thinke. / And 445 eek in to greet preciousnesse of vessel and curiositee of minstralcie, by whiche a man is stired the more to delyces of luxurie, / if so be that he sette his herte the lasse up-on oure lord Jesu Crist, certein it is a sinne ; and certeinly the delyces mighte been so grete in this caas, that man mighte lightly falle by hem in-to deedly sinne. / The especes that sourden of Pryde, soothly whan they sourden of malice ymagined, avysed, and forncast, or elles of usage, been deedly synnes, it is no doute. / And whan they sourden by freletee unavysed sodeinly, and sodeinly withdrawen ayein, al been they grevouse sinnes, I gesse that they ne been nat deedly. / Now mighte men axe wher-of that Pryde sourdeth and springeth, and I seye : somtyme it springeth of the goodes of nature, and som-tyme of the goodes of fortune, and som-tyme of the goodes of grace. / Certes, 450 the goodes of nature stonden outher in goodes of body or in goodes of soule. / Certes, goodes of body been hele of body, as strengthe, delivernesse, beautee, gentrye, franchise. / Goodes of nature of the soule been good wit, sharp understondynge, subtil engin, vertu naturel, good memorie. / Goodes of fortune been richesses, highe degrees of lordshipes, (380) preisinges of the peple. / Goodes of grace been science, power to suffre spirituel travaille, benignitee, vertuous contemplacion, withstondinge of temptacion, 455 and semblable thinges. / Of whiche forseyde goodes, certes it is a ful greet folye a man to pryden him in any of hem alle. / Now as for to speken of goodes of nature, god woot that som-tyme we han hem in nature as muche to oure damage as to oure profit. / As, for to speken of hele of body; certes it passeth ful lightly, and eek it is ful ofte encheson of the siknesse of oure soule ; for god woot, the flesh is a ful greet enemy to the soule : and therfore, the more that the body is hool, the more be we in peril to falle. / Eke for to pryde him in his strengthe of body, it is an heigh folye ; for certes, the flesh coveiteth agayn the spirit, and ay the more strong that the flesh is, the sorier may the soule be : / and, over al this, strengthe of body and worldly hardinesse causeth ful ofte many 460 a man to peril and meschaunce. / Eek for to pryde him of his gentrye is ful greet folye ; for ofte tyme the gentrye of the body binimeth the gentrye of the soule ; and eek we ben alle of o fader and of o moder ; and alle we been of o nature roten and corrupt, both riche and povre. / For sothe, oo manere gentrye is for to preise, that apparailleth mannes corage with vertues and moralitees, and maketh him Cristes child. / For truste wel, that over what man sinne hath maistrie, he is a verray cherl to sinne. /

§ 28. Now been ther generale signes of gentilesse ; as eschewinge of vyce and ribaudye and servage of sinne, in word, (390) in werk, and contenance ; / and usinge vertu, curteisye, and clennesse, and to be liberal, that is to seyn, large by mesure ; for thilke that passeth mesure is folye 465 and sinne. / Another is, to remembre him of bountee that he of other folk hath receyved. / Another is, to be benigne to hise goode subgetis ; wherfore, as seith

Senek, 'ther is no-thing more covenable to a man of heigh estaat than debonairetee and pitee. / And therfore thise flyes that men clepeth bees, whan they maken hir king, they chesen oon that hath no prikke wherwith he may stinge.' / Another is, a man to have a noble herte and a diligent, to attayne to heighe vertuouse thinges. / Now certes, a man to pryde him in the goodes of grace is eek an outrageous folye ; for thilke yiftes of grace that sholde have turned him to goodnesse and to medicine, turneth him to venim and to confusion, as seith seint Gregorie. / 470 Certes also, who-so prydeth him in the goodes of fortune, he is a ful greet fool ; for som-tyme is a man a greet lord by the morwe, that is a caitif and a wrecche er it be night : / and somtyme the richesse of a man is cause of his deeth ; somtyme the delyces of a man is cause of the grevous maladye thurgh which he dyeth. / Certes, the commendacion of the peple is somtyme ful fals and ful brotel for to triste ; this day they preyse, tomorwe they blame. / God woot, desyr to have commendacion of the peple hath caused deeth to many a bisy man. (40

### Remedium contra peccatum Superbie.

§ 29. Now sith that so is, that ye han understonde what is pryde, and whiche been the speces of it, and whennes pride sourdeth and springeth ; / now shul ye 475 understonde which is the remedie agayns the sinne of pryde, and that is, humilitee or mekenesse. / That is a vertu, thurgh which a man hath verray knoweleche of him-self, and holdeth of him-self no prys ne deyntee as in regard of hise desertes, consideringe evere his freletee. / Now been ther three maneres of humilitee ; as humilitee in herte, and another humilitee in his mouth ; the thridde in hise werkes. / The humilitee in herte is in foure maneres : that oon is, whan a man holdeth him-self as noght worth biforn god of hevene. Another is, whan he ne despyseth noon other man. / The thridde is, whan he rekketh nat thogh men holde him noght worth. The ferthe is, whan he nis nat

80 sory of his humiliacion. / Also, the humilitee of mouth is in foure thinges : in
attempree speche, and in humblesse of
speche, and whan he biknoweth with his
owene mouth that he is swich as him
thinketh that he is in his herte. Another
is, whan he preiseth the bountee of
another man, and nothing ther-of amenuseth. / Humilitee eek in werkes is in
foure maneres : the firste is, whan he
putteth othere men biforn him. The
seconde is, to chese the lowest place
over-al. The thridde is, gladly to assente
to good conseil. / The ferthe is, to stonde
gladly to the award of hise sovereyns, or
of him that is in hyer degree ; certein,
this is a greet werk of humilitee. /

### Sequitur de Inuidia.

§ 30. After Pryde wol I speken of the
foule sinne of Envye, which is, as by the
word of the philosophre, sorwe of other
mannes prosperitee ; and after the word
of seint Augustin, it is sorwe of other
mannes wele, and joye of othere mennes
10) harm. / This foule sinne is platly agayns
the holy goost. Al-be-it so that every
sinne is agayns the holy goost, yet nathelees, for as muche as bountee aperteneth
proprely to the holy goost, and Envye
comth proprely of malice, therfore it is
proprely agayn the bountee of the holy
485 goost. / Now hath malice two speces,
that is to seyn, hardnesse of herte in
wikkednesse, or elles the flesh of man is
so blind, that he considereth nat that he
is in sinne, or rekketh nat that he is in
sinne; which is the hardnesse of the
devel. / That other spece of malice is,
whan a man werreyeth trouthe, whan he
woot that it is trouthe. And eek, whan
he werreyeth the grace that god hath
yeve to his neighebore; and al this is by
Envye. / Certes, thanne is Envye the
worste sinne that is. For soothly, alle
othere sinnes been som-tyme only agayns
o special vertu; / but certes, Envye is
agayns alle vertues and agayns alle good-
nesses ; for it is sory of alle the bountees
of his neighebore ; and in this manere it
is divers from alle othere sinnes. / For

wel unnethe is ther any sinne that it ne
hath som delyt in itself, save only Envye,
that evere hath in itself anguish and
sorwe. / The speces of Envye been thise : 490
ther is first, sorwe of other mannes goodnesse and of his prosperitee; and prosperitee is kindely matere of joye; thanne
is Envye a sinne agayns kinde. / The
seconde spece of Envye is joye of other
mannes harm ; and that is proprely lyk
to the devel, that evere rejoyseth him of
mannes harm. / Of thise two speces
comth bakbyting ; and this sinne of bakbyting or detraccion hath certeine speces,
as thus. Som man preiseth his neighebore by a wikke entente ; / for he maketh
alwey a wikked knotte atte laste ende.
Alwey he maketh a ' but ' atte laste ende,
that is digne of more blame, than worth
is al the preisinge. / The seconde spece (420)
is, that if a man be good and dooth or
seith a thing to good entente, the bakbyter
wol turne all thilke goodnesse up-so-doun
to his shrewed entente. / The thridde 495
is, to amenuse the bountee of his neighebore. / The fourthe spece of bakbyting
is this; that if men speke goodnesse of
a man, thanne wol the bakbyter seyn,
' parfey, swich a man is yet bet than he ';
in dispreisinge of him that men preise. /
The fifte spece is this; for to consente
gladly and herkne gladly to the harm
that men speke of other folk. This sinne
is ful greet, and ay encreseth after the
wikked entente of the bakbyter. / After
bakbyting cometh grucching or murmuracion ; and somtyme it springeth of
inpacience agayns god, and somtyme
agayns man. / Agayns god it is, whan
a man gruccheth agayn the peynes of
helle, or agayns poverte, or los of catel,
or agayn reyn or tempest ; or elles gruccheth that shrewes han prosperitee, or
elles for that goode men han adversitee. / 500
And alle thise thinges sholde men suffre
paciently, for they comen by the rightful
jugement and ordinance of god. / Som-
tyme comth grucching of avarice ; as
Judas grucched agayns the Magdaleyne, whan she enoynte the heved of
oure lord Jesu Crist with hir precious

oynement. / This maner murmure is swich as whan man gruccheth of goodnesse that him-self dooth, or that other folk doon of hir owene catel. / Somtyme comth murmure of Pryde ; as whan Simon the Pharisee grucched agayn the Magdaleyne, whan she approched to Jesu (430) Crist, and weep at his feet for hir sinnes. / And somtyme grucching sourdeth of Envye ; whan men discovereth a mannes harm that was privee, or bereth him on 505 hond thing that is fals. / Murmure eek is ofte amonges servaunts, that grucchen whan hir sovereyns bidden hem doon leveful thinges ; / and, for-as-muche as they dar nat openly withseye the comaundements of hir sovereyns, yet wol they seyn harm, and grucche, and murmure prively for verray despyt ; / whiche wordes men clepen the develes *Paternoster*, though so be that the devel ne hadde nevere *Pater-noster*, but that lewed folk yeven it swich a name. / Som tyme grucching comth of ire or prive hate, that norisseth rancour in herte, as afterward I shal declare. / Thanne cometh eek bitternesse of herte ; thurgh which bitternesse every good dede of his neighe- 510 bor semeth to him bitter and unsavory. / Thanne cometh discord, that unbindeth alle manere of frendshipe. Thanne comth scorninge, as whan a man seketh occasioun to anoyen his neighebor, al do he never so weel. / Thanne comth accusinge, as whan man seketh occasion to anoyen his neighebor, which that is lyk to the craft of the devel, that waiteth bothe night and day to accusen us alle. / Thanne comth malignitee, thurgh which a man anoyeth his neighebor prively if he may ; / and if he noght may, algate his wikked wil ne shal nat wante, as for to brennen his hous prively, or empoysone or sleen hise bestes, and semblable (440) thinges. /

### Remedium contra peccatum Inuidie.

§ 31. Now wol I speke of the remedie agayns this foule sinne of Envye. First, is the love of god principal, and loving of his neighebor as him-self ; for soothly,

that oon ne may nat been withoute that other. / And truste wel, that in the 515 name of thy neighebore thou shalt understonde the name of thy brother ; for certes alle we have o fader fleshly, and o moder, that is to seyn, Adam and Eve ; and eek o fader espirituel, and that is god of hevene./ Thy neighebore artow holden for to love, and wilne him alle goodnesse ; and therfore seith god, 'love thy neighebore as thyselve,' that is to seyn, to salvacion bothe of lyf and of soule. / And more-over, thou shalt love him in word, and in benigne amonestinge, and chastysinge ; and conforten him in hise anoyes, and preye for him with al thyn herte. / And in dede thou shalt love him in swich wyse, that thou shalt doon to him in charitee as thou woldest that it were doon to thyn owene persone. / And therfore, thou ne shalt doon him no damage in wikked word, ne harm in his body, ne in his catel, ne in his soule, by entysing of wikked ensample. / Thou 520 shalt nat desyren his wyf, ne none of hise thinges. Understond eek, that in the name of neighebor is comprehended his enemy. / Certes man shal loven his enemy by the comandement of god ; and soothly thy frend shaltow love in God. / I seye, thyn enemy shaltow love for goddes sake, by his comandement. For if it were reson that a man sholde haten his enemy, for sothe god nolde nat receiven us to his love that been hise enemys. / Agayns three manere of wronges that his enemy dooth to hym, he shal doon three thinges, as thus. / Agayns hate (450) and rancour of herte, he shal love him in herte. Agayns chyding and wikkede wordes, he shal preye for his enemy. And agayn the wikked dede of his enemy, he shal doon him bountee. / For Crist 525 seith, 'loveth youre enemys, and preyeth for hem that speke yow harm ; and eek for hem that yow chacen and pursewen, and doth bountee to hem that yow haten.' Lo, thus comaundeth us oure lord Jesu Crist, to do to oure enemys. / For soothly, nature dryveth us to loven oure freendes, and parfey, oure enemys han more nede

to love than our freendes ; and they that
more nede have, certes, to hem shal men
doon goodnesse ; / and certes, in thilke
dede have we remembrance of the love
of Jesu Crist, that deyde for hise enemys. /
And in-as-muche as thilke love is the
more grevous to perfourne, in-so-muche
is the more gretter the merite ; and therfore the lovinge of oure enemy hath confounded the venim of the devel. / For
right as the devel is disconfited by humilitee, right so is he wounded to the deeth
530 by love of oure enemy. / Certes, thanne
is love the medicine that casteth out the
venim of Envye fro mannes herte. / The
speces of this pas shullen be more largely
in hir chapitres folwinge declared. /

### Sequitur de Ira.

§ 32. After Envye wol I discryven the
sinne of Ire. For soothly, who-so hath
envye upon his neighebor, anon he wole
comunly finde him a matere of wratthe,
in word or in dede, agayns him to whom
he hath envye. / And as wel comth Ire
of Pryde, as of Envye ; for soothly, he
that is proude or envious is lightly
460) wrooth. /

§ 33. This sinne of Ire, after the dis-
cryving of seint Augustin, is wikked wil
535 to been avenged by word or by dede. /
Ire, after the philosophre, is the fervent
blood of man y-quiked in his herte, thurgh
which he wole harm to him that he hateth. /
For certes the herte of man, by eschaufinge
and moevinge of his blood, wexeth so
trouble, that he is out of alle jugement of
resoun. / But ye shal understonde that
Ire is in two maneres ; that oon of hem
is good, and that other is wikked. / The
gode Ire is by jalousye of goodnesse, thurgh
which a man is wrooth with wikkednesse
and agayns wikkednesse ; and therfore
seith a wys man, that ‘Ire is bet than
pley.’ / This Ire is with debonairetee,
and it is wrooth withouten bitternesse ;
nat wrooth agayns the man, but wrooth
with the misdede of the man ; as seith the
prophete David, *Irascimini et nolite pec-*
540 *care.* / Now understondeth, that wikked
Ire is in two maneres, that is to seyn,

sodeyn Ire or hastif Ire, withouten avisement and consentinge of resoun. / The
mening and the sens of this is, that the
resoun of man ne consente nat to thilke
sodeyn Ire ; and thanne it is venial. /
Another Ire is ful wikked, that comth of
felonye of herte avysed and cast biforn ;
with wikked wil to do vengeance, and
therto his resoun consenteth ; and soothly
this is deedly sinne. / This Ire is so displesant to god, that it troubleth his hous
and chaceth the holy goost out of mannes
soule, and wasteth and destroyeth the
lyknesse of god, that is to seyn, the vertu
that is in mannes soule ; / and put in (470)
him the lyknesse of the devel, and
binimeth the man fro god that is his
rightful lord. / This Ire is a ful greet 545
plesaunce to the devel ; for it is the
develes fourneys, that is eschaufed with
the fyr of helle. / For certes, right so as
fyr is more mighty to destroyen erthely
thinges than any other element, right so
Ire is mighty to destroyen alle spirituel
thinges. / Loke how that fyr of smale
gledes, that been almost dede under
asshen, wollen quike agayn whan they
been touched with brimstoon ; right so
Ire wol everemo quiken agayn, whan it
is touched by the pryde that is covered in
mannes herte. / For certes fyr ne may
nat comen out of no-thing, but-if it were
first in the same thing naturelly ; as fyr
is drawen out of flintes with steel. / And
right so as pryde is ofte tyme matere of
Ire, right so is rancour norice and keper
of Ire. / Ther is a maner tree, as seith 550
seint Isidre, that whan men maken fyr
of thilke tree, and covere the coles of it
with asshen, soothly the fyr of it wol
lasten al a yeer or more. / And right so
fareth it of rancour ; whan it is ones conceyved in the hertes of som men, certein,
it wol lasten peraventure from oon Estre-
day unto another Estre-day, and more. /
But certes, thilke man is ful fer fro the
mercy of god al thilke whilc. /

§ 34. In this forseyde develes fourneys
ther forgen three shrewes : Pryde, that
ay bloweth and encreseth the fyr by chydinge and wikked wordes. / Thanne stant (480)

Envye, and holdeth the hote iren upon
the herte of man with a peire of longe
555 tonges of long rancour. / And thanne
stant the sinne of contumelie or stryf and
cheeste, and batereth and forgeth by
vileyns reprevinges. / Certes, this cursed
sinne anoyeth bothe to the man him-self
and eek to his neighebor. For soothly,
almost al the harm that any man dooth
to his neighebore comth of wratthe. /
For certes, outrageous wratthe doth al
that evere the devel him comaundeth ;
for he ne spareth neither Crist, ne his
swete mooder. / And in his outrageous
anger and Ire, allas ! allas ! ful many oon
at that tyme feleth in his herte ful wikkedly, bothe of Crist and of alle hise
halwes. / Is nat this a cursed vice ? Yis,
certes. Allas ! it binimeth from man his
wit and his resoun, and al his debonaire
560 lyf espirituel that sholde kepen his soule. /
Certes, it binimeth eek goddes due lordshipe, and that is mannes soule, and the
love of hise neighebores. It stryveth eek
alday agayn trouthe. It reveth him the
quiete of his herte, and subverteth his
soule. /

§ 35. Of Ire comen thise stinkinge
engendrures : first hate, that is old
wratthe ; discord, thurgh which a man
forsaketh his olde freend that he hath
loved ful longe. / And thanne cometh
werre, and every manere of wrong that
man dooth to his neighebore, in body or
in catel. / Of this cursed sinne of Ire
cometh eek manslaughtre. And understonde wel, that homicyde, that is manslaughtre, is in dyverse wyse. Som manere
(490) of homicyde is spirituel, and som is bodily. /
Spirituel manslaughtre is in six thinges.
First, by hate ; as seint John seith, 'he
565 that hateth his brother is homicyde.' /
Homicyde is eek by bakbytinge ; of whiche
bakbyteres seith Salomon, that 'they han
two swerdes with whiche they sleen hir
neighebores.' For soothly, as wikke is to
binime his good name as his lyf. / Homicyde is eek, in yevinge of wikked conseil
by fraude ; as for to yeven conseil to
areysen wrongful custumes and taillages. /
Of whiche seith Salomon, ' Leon rorynge

and bere hongry been lyke to the cruel
lordshipes,' in withholdinge or abregginge
of the shepe (or the hyre), or of the wages
of servaunts, or elles in usure or in with-
drawinge of the almesse of povre folk. /
For which the wyse man seith, ' fedeth
him that almost dyeth for honger ' ; for
soothly, but-if thou fede him, thou sleest
him ; and alle thise been deedly sinnes. /
Bodily manslaughtre is, whan thow sleest
him with thy tonge in other manere ; as
whan thou comandest to sleen a man, or
elles yevest him conseil to sleen a man. / 570
Manslaughtre in dede is in foure maneres.
That oon is by lawe ; right as a justice
dampneth him that is coupable to the
deeth. But lat the justice be war that he
do it rightfully, and that he do it nat for
delyt to spille blood, but for kepinge of
rightwisenesse. / Another homicyde is,
that is doon for necessitee, as whan o man
sleeth another in his defendaunt, and
that he ne may noon otherwise escape
from his owene deeth. / But certeinly,
if he may escape withouten manslaughtre
of his adversarie, and sleeth him, he doth
sinne, and he shal bere penance as for
deedly sinne. / Eek if a man, by caas or
aventure, shete an arwe or caste a stoon
with which he sleeth a man, he is homicyde. / Eek if a womman by necligence (500)
overlyeth hir child in hir sleping, it is
homicyde and deedly sinne. / Eek whan 575
man destourbeth concepcion of a child,
and maketh a womman outher bareyne
by drinkinge venemouse herbes, thurgh
which she may nat conceyve, or sleeth
a child by drinkes wilfully, or elles putteth certeine material thinges in hir
secree places to slee the child ; / or elles
doth unkindely sinne, by which man or
womman shedeth hir nature in manere
or in place ther-as a child may nat be
conceived ; or elles, if a womman have
conceyved and hurt hir-self, and sleeth
the child, yet is it homicyde. / What
seye we eek of wommen that mordren hir
children for drede of worldly shame ?
Certes, an horrible homicyde. / Homicyde is eek if a man approcheth to a
womman by desir of lecherye, thurgh

which the child is perissed, or elles
smyteth a womman witingly, thurgh
which she leseth hir child. Alle thise
been homicydes and horrible deedly
sinnes. / Yet comen ther of Ire manye
mo sinnes, as wel in word as in thoght
and in dede ; as he that arretteth upon
god, or blameth god, of thing of which he
is him-self gilty ; or despyseth god and
alle hise halwes, as doon thise cursede
80 hasardours in diverse contrees. / This
cursed sinne doon they, whan they felen
in hir hertes ful wikkedly of god and of
hise halwes. / Also, whan they treten
unreverently the sacrement of the auter,
thilke sinne is so greet, that unnethe
may it been relesed, but that the mercy
of god passeth alle hise werkes ; it is so
greet and he so benigne. / Thanne comth
of Ire attry angre ; whan a man is sharply
amonested in his shrifte to forleten his
sinne, / than wole he be angry and
answeren hokerly and angrily, and deffenden or excusen his sinne by unstedefast-
nesse of his flesh ; or elles he dide it for
to holde companye with hise felawes, or
10 elles, he seith, the fend entyced him ; /
or elles he dide it for his youthe, or elles
his complexioun is so corageous, that he
may nat forbere ; or elles it is his destinee,
as he seith, unto a certein age ; or elles,
he seith, it cometh him of gentillesse of
585 hise auncestres ; and semblable thinges. /
Alle this manere of folk so wrappen hem
in hir sinnes, that they ne wol nat delivere hem-self. For soothly, no wight that
excuseth him wilfully of his sinne may
nat been delivered of his sinne, til that
he mekely biknoweth his sinne. / After
this, thanne cometh swering, that is
expres agayn the comandement of god ;
and this bifalleth ofte of anger and of
Ire. / God seith : 'thou shalt nat take
the name of thy lord god in veyn or in
ydel.' Also oure lord Jesu Crist seith by
the word of seint Mathew : ' *Nolite iurare
omnino :* / ne wol ye nat swere in alle
manere ; neither by hevene, for it is
goddes trone ; ne by erthe, for it is the
bench of his feet ; ne by Jerusalem, for it
is the citee of a greet king ; ne by thyn

heed, for thou mayst nat make an heer
whyt ne blak. / But seyeth by youre
word, " ye, ye," and " nay, nay " ; and
what that is more, it is of yvel,' seith
Crist. / For Cristes sake, ne swereth nat 590
so sinfully, in dismembringe of Crist by
soule, herte, bones, and body. For certes,
it seemeth that ye thinke that the cursede
Jewes ne dismembred nat y-nough the
preciouse persone of Crist, but ye dis-
membre him more. / And if so be that
the lawe compelle yow to swere, thanne
rule yow after the lawe of god in youre
swering, as seith Jeremye *quarto capitulo,*
' *Iurabis in veritate, in iudicio et in iusticia :*
thou shalt kepe three condicions ; thou
shalt swere in trouthe, in doom, and in
rightwisnesse.' / This is to seyn, thou
shalt swere sooth ; for every lesinge is
agayns Crist. For Crist is verray trouthe.
And think wel this, that every greet
swerere, nat compelled lawefully to swere,
the wounde shal nat departe from his
hous whyl he useth swich unleveful
swering. / Thou shalt sweren eek in
doom, whan thou art constreyned by thy
domesman to witnessen the trouthe. / (520)
Eek thou shalt nat swere for envye ne for
favour, ne for mede, but for rightwisnesse ; for declaracioun of it to the worship of god and helping of thyne evene-
cristene. / And therfore, every man that 595
taketh goddes name in ydel, or falsly
swereth with his mouth, or elles taketh
on him the name of Crist, to be called a
Cristene man, and liveth agayns Cristes
livinge and his techinge, alle they taken
goddes name in ydel. / Loke eek what
seint Peter seith, *Actuum quarto capitulo,*
' *Non est aliud nomen sub celo,*' &c. ' Ther
nis noon other name,' seith seint Peter,
' under hevene, yeven to men, in which
they mowe be saved ;' that is to seyn, but
the name of Jesu Crist. / Take kepe eek
how that the precious name of Crist, as
seith seint Paul *ad Philipenses secundo,*
' *In nomine Jesu,* &c. : that in the name of
Jesu every knee of hevenely creatures, or
erthely, or of helle sholden bowe ' ; for it
is so heigh and so worshipful, that the
cursede feend in helle sholde tremblen to

heren it y-nempned. / Thanne semeth it, that men that sweren so horribly by his blessed name, that they despyse him more boldely than dide the cursede Jewes, or elles the devel, that trembleth whan he hereth his name. /

§ 36. Now certes, sith that swering, but-if it be lawefully doon, is so heighly deffended, muche worse is forswering 600 falsly, and yet nedelees. /

§ 37. What seye we eek of hem that delyten hem in swering, and holden it a gentrie or a manly dede to swere grete othes? And what of hem that, of verray usage, ne cesse nat to swere grete othes, al be the cause nat worth a straw? Certes, this is horrible sinne. / Sweringe sodeynly with-oute avysement is eek a sinne. / But lat us go now to thilke horrible swering of adjuracioun and conjuracioun, as doon thise false enchauntours or nigromanciens in bacins ful of water, or in a bright swerd, in a cercle, or in a fyr, or in a shulder-boon of a sheep. / I can nat seye but that they doon cursedly and damnably, agayns 530 Crist and al the feith of holy chirche. /

§ 38. What seye we of hem that bileven in divynailes, as by flight or by noyse of briddes, or of bestes, or by sort, by geomancie, by dremes, by chirkinge of dores, or crakkinge of houses, by gnawynge of 605 rattes, and swich manere wrecchednesse? / Certes, al this thing is deffended by god and by al holy chirche. For which they been acursed, til they come to amendement, that on swich filthe setten hir bileve. / Charmes for woundes or maladye of men, or of bestes, if they taken any effect, it may be peraventure that god suffreth it, for folk sholden yeve the more feith and reverence to his name. /

§ 39. Now wol I speken of lesinges, which generally is fals significacioun of word, in entente to deceyven his evenecristene. / Som lesinge is of which ther comth noon avantage to no wight : and som lesinge turneth to the ese or profit of o man, and to disese and damage of another man. / Another lesinge is for to saven his lyf or his catel. Another

lesinge comth of delyt for to lye, in which delyt they wol forge a long tale, and peynten it with alle circumstaunces, where al the ground of the tale is fals. / 610 Som lesinge comth, for he wole sustene his word ; and som lesinge comth of recchelesnesse, with-outen avysement ; and semblable thinges. /

§ 40. Lat us now touche the vyce of flateringe, which ne comth nat gladly but for drede or for coveitise. / Flaterye is generally wrongful preisinge. Flatereres been the develes norices, that norissen hise children with milk of losengerie. / For sothe, Salomon seith, that ' flaterie is wors than detraccioun.' For som-tyme detraccion maketh an hautein man be the more humble, for he dredeth detraccion ; but certes flaterye, that maketh a man to enhauncen his herte and his contenaunce. / Flatereres been the de- 540 veles enchauntours ; for they make a man to wene of him-self be lyk that he nis nat lyk. / They been lyk to Judas 615 that bitraysed [god ; and thise flatereres bitraysen] a man to sellen him to his enemy, that is, to the devel. / Flatereres been the develes chapelleyns, that singen evere *Placebo*. / I rekene flaterye in the vyces of Ire ; for ofte tyme, if o man be wrooth with another, thanne wol he flatere som wight to sustene him in his querele. /

§ 41. Speke we now of swich cursinge as comth of irous herte. Malisoun generally may be seyd every maner power of harm. Swich cursinge bireveth man fro the regne of god, as seith seint Paul. / And ofte tyme swich cursinge wrongfully retorneth agayn to him that curseth, as a brid that retorneth agayn to his owene nest. / And over alle thing men oghten 620 eschewe to cursen hir children, and yeven to the devel hir engendrure, as ferforth as in hem is ; certes, it is greet peril and greet sinne. /

§ 42. Lat us thanne speken of chydinge and reproche, whiche been ful grete woundes in mannes herte ; for they unsowen the semes of frendshipe in mannes herte. / For certes, unnethes may a man pleynly been accorded with him that hath him openly revyled and repreved in disclaundre. This is a ful grisly sinne, as Crist seith in the gospel. / And tak kepe now, that he that repreveth his neighebor, outher he repreveth him by som harm of peyne that he hath on his body, as 'mesel,' 'croked harlot,' or by

50) som sinne that he dooth. / Now if he repreve him by harm of peyne, thanne turneth the repreve to Jesu Crist; for peyne is sent by the rightwys sonde of god, and by his suffraunce, be it meselrie,

25 or maheym, or maladye. / And if he repreve him uncharitably of sinne, as, 'thou holour,' 'thou dronkelewe harlot,' and so forth; thanne aperteneth that to the rejoysinge of the devel, that evere hath joye that men doon sinne. / And certes, chydinge may nat come but out of a vileyns herte. For after the habundance of the herte speketh the mouth ful ofte. / And ye shul understonde that loke, by any wey, whan any man shal chastyse another, that he be war from chydinge or reprevinge. For trewely, but he be war, he may ful lightly quiken the fyr of angre and of wratthe, which that he sholde quenche, and per-aventure sleeth him which that he mighte chastyse with benignitee. / For as seith Salomon, 'the amiable tonge is the tree of lyf,' that is to seyn, of lyf espirituel : and sothly, a deslavee tonge sleeth the spirites of him that repreveth, and eek of him that is repreved. / Lo, what seith seint Augustin : 'ther is no-thing so lyk the develes child as he that ofte chydeth.' Seint Paul seith eek : 'I, servant of god, bihove nat

630 to chyde.' / And how that chydinge be a vileyns thing bitwixe alle manere folk, yet it is certes most uncovenable bitwixe a man and his wyf ; for there is nevere reste. And therfore seith Salomon, 'an hous that is uncovered and droppinge, and a chydinge wyf, been lyke.' / A man that is in a droppinge hous in many places, though he eschewe the droppinge in o place, it droppeth on him in another place ; so fareth it by a chydinge wyf. But she chyde him in o place, she wol

chyde him in another. / And therfore, 'bettre is a morsel of breed with joye than an hous ful of delyces, with chydinge,' seith Salomon. / Seint Paul seith : 'O ye wommen, be ye subgetes to youre housbondes as bihoveth in god ; and ye men, loveth youre wyves.' *Ad Colossenses, tertio.* /     (56o)

§ 43. Afterward speke we of scorninge, which is a wikked sinne; and namely, whan he scorneth a man for hise gode werkes. / For certes, swiche scorneres 635 faren lyk the foule tode, that may nat endure to smelle the sote savour of the vyne whanne it florissheth. / Thise scorneres been parting felawes with the devel; for they han joye whan the devel winneth, and sorwe whan he leseth. / They been adversaries of Jesu Crist; for they haten that he loveth, that is to seyn, salvacion of soule. /

§ 44. Speke we now of wikked conseil; for he that wikked conseil yeveth is a traytour. For he deceyveth him that trusteth in him, *ut Achitofel ad Absolonem.* But natholees, yet is his wikked conseil first agayn him-self. / For, as seith the wyse man, every fals livinge hath this propertee in him-self, that he that wole anoye another man, he anoyeth first him-self. / And men shul understonde, 640 that man shal nat taken his conseil of fals folk, ne of angry folk, or grevous folk, ne of folk that loven specially to muchel hir owene profit, ne to muche worldly folk, namely, in conseilinge of soules. /

§ 45. Now comth the sinne of hem that sowen and maken discord amonges folk, which is a sinne that Crist hateth outrely; and no wonder is. For he deyde for to make concord. / And more shame do they to Crist, than dide they that him crucifyede; for god loveth bettre, that frendshipe be amonges folk, than he dide his owene body, the which that he yaf for unitee. Therfore been they lykned to the devel, that evere been aboute to maken discord. /

§ 46. Now comth the sinne of double tonge; swiche as speken faire biforn folk, and wikkedly bihinde; or elles they maken semblant as though they speke of good entencioun, or elles in game and pley, and yet they speke of wikked (570) entente. /

§ 47. Now comth biwreying of conseil, thurgh which a man is defamed; certes, 645 unnethe may he restore the damage. /

Now comth manace, that is an open folye; for he that ofte manaceth, he threteth more than he may perfourne ful ofte tyme. /

Now cometh ydel wordes, that is with-outen profit of him that speketh tho wordes, and eek of him that herkneth tho wordes. Or elles ydel wordes been tho that been nedelees, or with-outen entente of naturel profit. / And al-be-it that ydel wordes been som tyme venial sinne, yet sholde men douten hem; for we shul yeve rekeninge of hem bifore god. /

Now comth janglinge, that may nat been withoute sinne. And, as seith Salomon, 'it is a sinne of apert folye.' / And therfore a philosophre seyde, whan men axed him how that men sholde plese the peple; and he answerde, 'do many 650 gode werkes, and spek fewe jangles.' /

After this comth the sinne of japeres, that been the develes apes; for they maken folk to laughe at hir japerie, as folk doon at the gaudes of an ape. Swiche japeres deffendeth seint Paul. / Loke how that vertuouse wordes and holy conforten hem that travaillen in the service of Crist; right so conforten the vileyns wordes and knakkes of japeris hem that travaillen in the service of the devel. / Thise been the sinnes that comen of the tonge, that comen of Ire and of othere sinnes mo. /

Sequitur remedium contra peccatum Ire.

§ 48. The remedye agayns Ire is a vertu that men clepen Mansuetude, that is Debonairetee; and eek another vertu, (580) that men callen Pacience or Suffrance. /

§ 49. Debonairetee withdraweth and refreyneth the stiringes and the moe-vynges of mannes corage in his herte, in

swich manere that they ne skippe nat out by angre ne by Ire. / Suffrance 65 suffreth swetely alle the anoyaunces and the wronges that men doon to man out-ward. / Seint Jerome seith thus of debonairetee, that 'it doth noon harm to no wight, ne seith; ne for noon harm that men doon or seyn, he ne eschaufeth nat agayns his resoun.' / This vertu som-tyme comth of nature; for, as seith the philosophre, 'a man is a quik thing, by nature debonaire and tretable to goodnesse; but whan debonairetee is enformed of grace, thanne is it the more worth.' /

§ 50. Pacience, that is another remedye agayns Ire, is a vertu that suffreth swetely every mannes goodnesse, and is nat wrooth for noon harm that is doon to him. / The philosophre seith, that 'pacience is thilke vertu that suffreth debonairely alle the outrages of adver-sitee and every wikked word.' / This 66 vertu maketh a man lyk to god, and maketh him goddes owene dere child, as seith Crist. This vertu disconfiteth thyn enemy. And therfore seith the wyse man, 'if thou wolt venquisse thyn enemy, lerne to suffre.' / And thou shalt under-stonde, that man suffreth foure manere of grevances in outward thinges, agayns the whiche foure he moot have foure manere of paciences. /

§ 51. The firste grevance is of wikkede wordes; thilke suffrede Jesu Crist with-outen grucching, ful paciently, whan the Jewes despysed and repreved him ful ofte. / Suffre thou therfore paciently; for the wyse man seith: 'if thou stryve with a fool, though the fool be wrooth or though he laughe, algate thou shalt have no reste.' / That other grevance outward (59 is to have damage of thy catel. Ther-agayns suffred Crist ful paciently, whan he was despoyled of al that he hadde in this lyf, and that nas but hise clothes. / 66 The thridde grevance is a man to have harm in his body. That suffred Crist ful paciently in al his passioun. / The fourthe grevance is in outrageous labour in werkes. Wherfore I seye, that folk that maken hir servants to travaillen to grevously, or out of tyme, as on halydayes, soothly they do greet sinne. / Heer-agayns suffred Crist ful paciently, and taughte us pacience, whan he bar up-on his blissed shulder the croys, up-on which he sholde suffren despitous deeth. / Heer may men lerne to be pacient; for certes, noght only Cristen men been pacient for love of Jesu Crist, and for guerdoun of the blisful lyf that is perdurable; but certes, the olde payens, that nevere were Cristene, commendeden and useden the vertu of pacience. /

§ 52. A philosophre up-on a tyme, that wolde have beten his disciple for his grete trespas, for which he was greetly amoeved, 570 and broghte a yerde to scourge the child; / and whan this child saugh the yerde, he seyde to his maister, 'what thenke ye to do?' 'I wol bete thee,' quod the maister, 'for thy correccion.' / 'For sothe,' quod the child, 'ye oghten first correcte youre-self, that han lost al youre pacience for the gilt of a child.' / 'For sothe,' quod the maister al wopinge, 'thou seyst sooth; have thou the yerde, my dere sone, and correcte me for myn inpacience.' / Of Pacience comth Obe-dience, thurgh which a man is obedient to Crist and to alle hem to whiche he 500) oghte to been obedient in Crist. / And understond wel that obedience is parfit, whan that a man doth gladly and hastily, with good herte entierly, al that he 675 sholde do. / Obedience generally, is to perfourne the doctrine of god and of his sovereyns, to whiche him oghte to ben obeisaunt in alle rightwysnesse. /

### Sequitur de Accidia.

§ 53. After the sinnes of Envie and of Ire, now wol I speken of the sinne of Accidie. For Envye blindeth the herte of a man, and Ire troubleth a man; and Accidie maketh him hevy, thoghtful, and wrawe. / Envye and Ire maken bitter-nesse in herte; which bitternesse is moder of Accidie, and binimeth him the love of alle goodnesse. Thanne is Accidie the anguissh of a trouble herte; and seint

Augustin seith : 'it is anoy of goodnesse and joye of harm.' / Certes, this is a dampnable sinne; for it doth wrong to Jesu Crist, in-as-muche as it binimeth the service that men oghte doon to Crist with alle diligence, as seith Salomon. / But Accidie dooth no swich diligence; he dooth alle thing with anoy, and with wrawnesse, slaknesse, and excusacioun, and with ydelnesse and unlust, for which the book seith : 'acursed be he that doth the service of god necligently.' / Thanne 680 is Accidie enemy to everich estaat of man; for certes, the estaat of man is in three maneres. / Outher it is th'estaat of inno-cence, as was th'estaat of Adam biforn that he fil into sinne; in which estaat he was holden to wirche, as in heryinge and adouringe of god. / Another estaat is the estaat of sinful men, in which estaat men been holden to laboure in preyinge to god for amendement of hir sinnes, and that he wole graunte hem to arysen out of hir sinnes. / Another estaat is th'estaat of grace, in which estaat he is holden to werkes of penitence; and certes, to alle thise thinges is Accidie enemy and contrarie. For he loveth no bisinesse at al. / Now certes, this foule (610) sinne Accidie is eek a ful greet enemy to the lyflode of the body; for it ne hath no purveaunce agayn temporel necessitee; for it forsleweth and forsluggeth, and destroyeth alle goodes temporeles by reccheleesnesse. / 685

§ 54. The fourthe thinge is, that Accidie is lyk to hem that been in the peyne of helle, by-cause of hir slouthe and of hir hevinesse; for they that been dampned been so bounde, that they ne may neither wel do ne wel thinke. / Of Accidie comth first, that a man is anoyed and encombred for to doon any goodnesse, and maketh that god hath abhominacion of swich Accidie, as seith seint Johan. /

§ 55. Now comth Slouthe, that wol nat suffre noon hardnesse ne no penaunce. For soothly, Slouthe is so tendre, and so delicat, as seith Salomon, that he wol nat suffre noon hardnesse ne penaunce, and therfore he shendeth al that he dooth. / Agayns this roten-herted sinne of Accidie and Slouthe sholde men exercise hem-self to doon gode werkes, and manly and vertuously cacchen corage wel to doon ; thinkinge that oure lord Jesu Crist quyteth every good dede, be it never so lyte. / Usage of labour is a greet thing ; for it maketh, as seith seint Bernard, the laborer to have stronge armes and harde sinwes ; and Slouthe maketh 690 hem feble and tendre. / Thanne comth drede to biginne to werke any gode werkes ; for certes, he that is enclyned to sinne, him thinketh it is so greet an empryse for to undertake to doon werkes of goodnesse, / and casteth in his herte that the circumstaunces of goodnesse been so grevouse and so chargeaunt for to suffre, that he dar nat undertake to do werkes of goodnesse, as seith seint Gregorie. /

§ 56. Now comth wanhope, that is despeir of the mercy of god, that comth somtyme of to muche outrageous sorwe, and somtyme of to muche drede : imagininge that he hath doon so muche sinne, that it wol nat availlen him, though he wolde repenten him and forsake sinne : / thurgh which despeir or drede he abaundoneth al his herte to every maner sinne, (620) as seith seint Augustin. / Which dampnable sinne, if that it continue un-to his 695 ende, it is cleped sinning in the holy gost. / This horrible sinne is so perilous, that he that is despeired, ther nis no felonye ne no sinne that he douteth for to do ; as shewed wel by Judas. / Certes, aboven alle sinnes thanne is this sinne most displesant to Crist, and most adversarie. / Soothly, he that despeireth him is lyk the coward champioun recreant, that seith creant withoute nede. Allas ! allas ! nedeles is he recreant and nedeles despeired. / Certes, the mercy of god is evere redy to every penitent, and is aboven alle hise werkes. / Allas ! can nat a man bithinke him on the gospel of seint Luk, 15., where-as Crist seith that 'as wel shal ther be joye in hevene upon a sinful man that doth penitence, as up-on nynety and nyne rightful men

that neden no penitence ?' / Loke forther, 70. in the same gospel, the joye and the feste of the gode man that hadde lost his sone, whan his sone with repentaunce was retourned to his fader. / Can they nat remembren hem eek, that, as seith seint Luk xxiii° capitulo, how that the theef that was hanged bisyde Jesu Crist, seyde : 'Lord, remembre of me, whan thou comest in-to thy regne ?' / 'For sothe,' seyde Crist, 'I seye to thee, to-day shaltow been with me in Paradys.' / Certes, ther is noon so horrible sinne of man, that it ne may, in his lyf, be destroyed by penitence, thurgh vertu of the passion and of the deeth of Crist. / (63 Allas ! what nedeth man thanne to been despeired, sith that his mercy so redy is and large ? Axe and have. / Thanne comth 705 Sompnolence, that is, sluggy slombringe, which maketh a man be hevy and dul, in body and in soule ; and this sinne comth of Slouthe. / And certes, the tyme that, by wey of resoun, men sholde nat slepe, that is by the morwe ; but-if ther were cause resonable. / For soothly, the morwetyde is most covenable, a man to seye his preyeres, and for to thinken on god, and for to honoure god, and to yeven almesse to the povre, that first cometh in the name of Crist. / Lo ! what seith Salomon : 'who-so wolde by the morwe awaken and seke me, he shal finde.' / Thanne comth Necligence, or recchelesnesse, that rekketh of no-thing. And how that ignoraunce be moder of alle harm, certes, Necligence is the norice. / Necligence 710 ne doth no fors, whan he shal doon a thing, whether he do it weel or baddely. /

§ 57. Of the remedie of thise two sinnes, as seith the wyse man, that 'he that dredeth god, he spareth nat to doon that him oghte doon.' / And he that loveth god, he wol doon diligence to plese god by his werkes, and abaundone him-self, with al his might, wel for to doon. / Thanne comth ydelnesse, that is the yate of alle harmes. An ydel man is lyk to a place that hath no walles ; the develes may entre on every syde and sheten at him at discovert, by temptacion on every

40) syde. / This ydelnesse is the thurrok of alle wikked and vileyns thoghtes, and of
715 alle jangles, trufles, and of alle ordure. / Certes, the hevene is yeven to hem that wol labouren, and nat to ydel folk. Eek David seith : that 'they ne been nat in the labour of men, ne they shul nat been whipped with men,' that is to seyn, in purgatorie. / Certes, thanne semeth it, they shul be tormented with the devel in helle, but-if they doon penitence. /

§ 58. Thanne comth the sinne that men clepen *Tarditas*, as whan a man is to latrede or taryinge, er he wole turne to god ; and certes, that is a greet folye. He is lyk to him that falleth in the dich, and wol nat aryse. / And this vyce comth of a fals hope, that he thinketh that he shal live longe ; but that hope faileth ful ofte. /

§ 59. Thanne comth Lachesse ; that is he, that whan he biginneth any good werk, anon he shal forleten it and stinten ;
as doon they that han any wight to governe, and ne taken of him na-more kepe, anon as they finden any contrarie
720 or any anoy. / Thise been the newe shepherdes, that leten hir sheep witingly go renne to the wolf that is in the breres, or do no fors of hir owene governaunce. / Of this comth poverte and destruccioun, bothe of spirituel and temporel thinges. Thanne comth a manere coldnesse, that freseth al the herte of man. / Thanne comth undevocioun, thurgh which a man is so blent, as seith seint Bernard, and hath swiche langour in soule, that he may neither rede ne singe in holy chirche, ne here ne thinke of no devocioun, ne travaille with hise handes in no good werk, that it nis him unsavory and al apalled. / Thanne wexeth he slow and slombry, and sone wol be wrooth, and
650) sone is enclyned to hate and to envye. / Thanne comth the sinne of worldly sorwe, swich as is cleped *tristicia*, that sleeth
725 man, as seint Paul seith. / For certes, swich sorwe werketh to the deeth of the soule and of the body also ; for ther-of comth, that a man is anoyed of his owene lyf. / Wherfore swich sorwe short-

eth ful ofte the lyf of a man, er that his tyme be come by wey of kinde. /

## Remedium contra peccatum Accidie.

§ 60. Agayns this horrible sinne of Accidie, and the branches of the same, ther is a vertu that is called *Fortitudo* or Strengthe ; that is, an affeccioun thurgh which a man despyseth anoyous thinges. / This vertu is so mighty and so vigorous, that it dar withstonde mightily and wysely kepen him-self fro perils that been wikked, and wrastle agayn the assautes of the devel. / For it enhaunceth and enforceth the soule, right as Accidie abateth it and maketh it feble. For this *Fortitudo* may endure by long suffraunce the travailles that been covenable. / 730

§ 61. This vertu hath manye speces ; and the firste is cleped Magnanimitee, that is to seyn, greet corage. For certes, ther bihoveth greet corage agains Accidie, lest that it ne swolwe the soule by the sinne of sorwe, or destroye it by wan-hope. / This vertu maketh folk to under-take harde thinges and grevouse thinges, by hir owene wil, wysely and resonably. / And for as muchel as the devel fighteth agayns a man more by queyntise and by sleighte than by strengthe, therfore men shal withstonden him by wit and by resoun and by discrecioun. / Thanne arn ther the vertues of feith, and hope in god and in hise seintes, to acheve and acomplice the gode werkes in the whiche he purposeth fermely to continue. / (660) Thanne comth seuretee or sikernesse ; and that is, whan a man ne douteth no travaille in tyme cominge of the gode werkes that a man hath bigonne. / 735 Thanne comth Magnificence, that is to seyn, whan a man dooth and perfourneth grete werkes of goodnesse that he hath bigonne ; and that is the ende why that men sholde do gode werkes ; for in the acomplissinge of grete goode werkes lyth the grete guerdoun. / Thanne is ther Constaunce, that is, stablenesse of corage ; and this sholde been in herte by stedefast feith, and in mouth, and in beringe, and in chere and in dede. / Eke ther been mo speciale remedies agains Accidie, in diverse werkes, and in consideracioun of the peynes of helle, and of the joyes of hevene, and in trust of the grace of the holy goost, that wole yeve him might to perfourne his gode entente. /

### Sequitur de Auaricia.

§ 62. After Accidie wol I speke of Avarice and of Coveitise, of which sinne seith seint Paule, that ' the rote of alle harmes is Coveitise': *Ad Timotheum, sexto capitulo*. / For soothly, whan the herte of a man is confounded in it-self and troubled, and that the soule hath lost the confort of god, thanne seketh he an ydel 740 solas of worldly thinges. /

§ 63. Avarice, after the descripcion of seint Augustin, is likerousnesse in herte to have erthely thinges. / Som other folk seyn, that Avarice is, for to pur-chacen manye erthely thinges, and no-thing yeve to hem that han nede. / And understond, that Avarice ne stant nat only in lond ne catel, but somtyme in science and in glorie, and in every manere of outrageous thing is Avarice and Coveitise. / And the difference bitwixe Avarice and Coveitise is this. Coveitise is for to coveite swiche thinges as thou hast nat; and Avarice is for to withholde and kepe swiche thinges as thou hast, (670) with-oute rightful nede. / Soothly, this Avarice is a sinne that is ful dampnable; for al holy writ curseth it, and speketh agayns that vyce; for it dooth wrong to 745 Jesu Crist. / For it bireveth him the love that men to him owen, and turneth it bakward agayns alle resoun; / and maketh that the avaricious man hath more hope in his catel than in Jesu Crist, and dooth more observance in kepinge of his tresor than he dooth to service of Jesu Crist. / And therfore seith seint Paul *ad Ephesios, quinto*, that ' an avaricious man is in the thraldom of ydolatrie.' /

§ 64. What difference is bitwixe an ydolastre and an avaricious man, but that an ydolastre, per aventure, ne hath

but o mawmet or two, and the avaricious man hath manye? For certes, every florin in his cofre is his mawmet. / And certes, the sinne of Mawmetrye is the firste thing that God deffended in the ten comaundments, as bereth witnesse *Exodi, capitulo xx°* : / ' Thou shalt have no false 750 goddes bifore me, ne thou shalt make to thee no grave thing.' Thus is an avaricious man, that loveth his tresor biforn god, an ydolastre, / thurgh this cursed sinne of Avarice. Of Coveitise comen thise harde lordshipes, thurgh whiche men been distreyned by tailages, custumes, and cariages, more than hir duetee or resoun is. And eek they taken of hir bonde-men amerciments, whiche mighten more resonably ben cleped extorcions than amerciments. / Of whiche amerciments and raunsoninge of bonde-men, somme lordes stywardes seyn, that it is rightful; for-as-muche as a cherl hath no temporel thing that it ne is his lordes, as they seyn. / But certes, thise lordshipes doon wrong, that bireven hir bonde-folk thinges that they nevere yave hem : *Augustinus de Civitate, libro nono*. / (68 Sooth is, that the condicioun of thraldom and the firste cause of thraldom is for sinne; *Genesis, quinto*. / 755

§ 65. Thus may ye seen that the gilt disserveth thraldom, but nat nature. / Wherfore thise lordes ne sholde nat muche glorifyen hem in hir lordshipes, sith that by naturel condicion they been nat lordes of thralles; but for that thraldom comth first by the desert of sinne. / And forther-over, ther-as the lawe seith, that temporel godes of bonde-folk been the godes of hir lordshipes, ye, that is for to understonde, the godes of the emperour, to deffenden hem in hir right, but nat for to robben hem ne reven hem. / And therfore seith Seneca : ' thy prudence sholde live benignely with thy thralles.' / Thilke that thou clepest thy thralles been goddes peple; for humble folk been Cristes freendes; they been contubernial with the lord. / 760

§ 66. Think eek, that of swich seed as cherles springeth, of swich seed springen

lordes. As wel may the cherl be saved as the lord. / The same deeth that taketh the cherl, swich deeth taketh the lord. Wherfore I rede, do right so with thy cherl, as thou woldest that thy lord dide with thee, if thou were in his plyt. / Every sinful man is a cherl to sinne. I rede thee, certes, that thou, lord, werke in swiche wyse with thy cherles, that they rather love thee than drede. / I woot wel ther is degree above degree, as reson is; and skile it is, that men do hir devoir ther-as it is due; but certes, extorcious and despit of youre underlinges is damp-
o) nable. /

§ 67. And forther-over understond wel, that thise conquerours or tiraunts maken ful ofte thralles of hem, that been born of as royal blood as been they that hem
55 conqueren. / This name of thraldom was nevere erst couth, til that Noe seyde, that his sone Canaan sholde be thral to hise bretheren for his sinne. / What seye we thanne of hem that pilen and doon extorcions to holy chirche? Certes, the swerd, that men yeven first to a knight whan he is newe dubbed, signi-fyeth that he sholde deffenden holy chirche, and nat robben it ne pilen it; and who so dooth, is traitour to Crist. / And, as seith seint Augustin, 'they been the develes wolves, that stranglen the sheep of Jesu Crist'; and doon worse than wolves. / For soothly, whan the wolf hath ful his wombe, he stinteth to strangle sheep. But soothly, the pilours and destroyours of goddes holy chirche ne do nat so; for they ne stinte nevere to pile. / Now, as I have seyd, sith so is that sinne was first cause of thraldom, thanne is it thus; that thilke tyme that al this world was in sinne, thanne was al
770 this world in thraldom and subjeccioun. / But certes, sith the tyme of grace cam, god ordeyned that som folk sholde be more heigh in estaat and in degree, and som folk more lowe, and that everich sholde be served in his estaat and in his degree. / And therfore, in somme con-trees ther they byen thralles, whan they han turned hem to the feith, they maken

hir thralles free out of thraldom. And therfore, certes, the lord oweth to his man that the man oweth to his lord. / The Pope calleth him-self servant of the servaunts of god; but for-as-muche as the estaat of holy chirche ne mighte nat han be, ne the commune profit mighte nat han be kept, ne pees and reste in erthe, but-if god hadde ordeyned that som men hadde hyer degree and som men lower : / therfore was sovereyntee ordeyned to kepe and mayntene and deffenden hir underlinges or hir subgets in resoun, as ferforth as it lyth in hir power; and nat to destroyen hem ne confounde. / Wherfore I seye, that thilke (700) lordes that been lyk wolves, that devouren the possessiouns or the catel of povre folk wrongfully, with-outen mercy or mesure, / 775 they shul receyven by the same mesure that they han mesured to povre folk the mercy of Jesu Crist, but-if it be amended. / Now comth deceite bitwixe marchant and marchant. And thow shalt understonde, that marchandyse is in two maneres; that oon is bodily, and that other is goostly. That oon is honeste and leveful, and that other is deshoneste and unleve-ful. / Of thilke bodily marchandyse, that is leveful and honeste, is this; that, there-as god hath ordeyned that a regne or a contree is suffisaunt to him-self, thanne is it honeste and leveful, that of habun-daunce of this contree, that men helpe another contree that is more nedy. / And therfore, ther mote been marchants to bringen fro that o contree to that other hire marchandyses. / That other mar-chandise, that men haunten with fraude and trecherie and deceite, with lesinges and false othes, is cursed and dampnable. / 780 Espirituel marchandyse is proprely Sy-monye, that is, ententif desyr to byen thing espirituel, that is, thing that aperteneth to the seintuarie of god and to cure of the soule. / This desyr, if so be that a man do his diligence to parfournen it, al-be-it that his desyr ne take noon effect, yet is it to him a deedly sinne ; and if he be ordred, he is irreguler. / Certes, Symonye is cleped of Symon

Magus, that wolde han boght, for temporel catel, the yifte that god hadde
yeven, by the holy goost, to seint Peter
and to the apostles. / And therfore
understond, that bothe he that selleth
and he that byeth thinges espirituels,
been cleped Symonials ; be it by catel, be
it by procuringe, or by fleshly preyere
of hise freendes, fleshly freendes, or
(710) espirituel freendes. / Fleshly, in two
maneres ; as by kinrede or othere freendes.
Soothly, if they praye for him that is nat
worthy and able, it is Symonye if he take
the benefice ; and if he be worthy and
785 able, ther nis noon. / That other manere
is, whan a man or womman preyen for
folk to avauncen hem, only for wikked
fleshly affeccioun that they have un-to
the persone ; and that is foul Symonye. /
But certes, in service, for which men
yeven thinges espirituels un-to hir
servants, it moot been understonde that
the service moot been honeste, and elles
nat ; and eek that it be with-outen bar-
gayninge, and that the persone be able. /
For, as seith seint Damasie, 'alle the
sinnes of the world, at regard of this
sinne, arn as thing of noght' ; for it is
the gretteste sinne that may be, after the
sinne of Lucifer and Antecrist. / For,
by this sinne, god forleseth the chirche,
and the soule that he boghte with his
precious blood, by hem that yeven
chirches to hem that been nat digne. /
For they putten in theves, that stelen the
soules of Jesu Christ and destroyen his
790 patrimoine. / By swiche undigne preestes
and curates han lewed men the lasse
reverence of the sacraments of holy
chirche ; and swiche yeveres of chirches
putten out the children of Crist, and
putten in-to the chirche the develes owene
sone. / They sellen the soules that
lambes sholde kepen to the wolf that
strangleth hem. And therfore shul they
nevere han part of the pasture of lambes,
that is, the blisse of hevene. / Now
comth hasardrye with hise apurtenaunces,
as tables and rafles ; of which comth
deceite, false othes, chydinges, and alle
ravines, blaspheminge and reneyinge of
god, and hate of hise neighebores, wast of
godes, misspendinge of tyme, and som-
tyme manslaughtre. / Certes, hasardours
ne mowe nat been with-outen greet sinne
whyles they haunte that craft. / Of (7-
avarice comen eek lesinges, thefte, fals
witnesse, and false othes. And ye shul
understonde that thise been grete sinnes,
and expres agayn the comaundements of
god, as I have seyd. / Fals witnesse is in 79
word and eek in dede. In word, as for to
bireve thy neighebores goode name by
thy fals witnessing, or bireven him his
catel or his heritage by thy fals witnessing ; whan thou, for ire or for mede, or
for envye, berest fals witnesse, or accusest
him or excusest him by thy fals witnesse,
or elles excusest thy-self falsly. / Ware
yow, questemongeres and notaries ! Certes,
for fals witnessing was Susanna in ful
gret sorwe and peyne, and many another
mo. / The sinne of thefte is eek expres
agayns goddes heste, and that in two
maneres, corporel and espirituel. / Corporel, as for to take thy neighebores catel
agayn his wil, be it by force or by sleighte,
be it by met or by mesure. / By steling
eek of false enditements upon him, and
in borwinge of thy neighebores catel, in
entente nevere to payen it agayn, and
semblable thinges. / Espirituel thefte is 80
Sacrilege, that is to seyn, hurtinge of holy
thinges, or of thinges sacred to Crist, in
two maneres ; by reson of the holy place,
as chirches or chirche-hawes, / for which
every vileyns sinne that men doon in
swiche places may be cleped sacrilege, or
every violence in the semblable places.
Also, they that withdrawen falsly the
rightes that longen to holy chirche. /
And pleynly and generally, sacrilege is to
reven holy thing fro holy place, or unholy thing out of holy place, or holy thing
out of unholy place. /

### Relevacio contra peccatum Avaricie.

§ 68. Now shul ye understonde, that
the relevinge of Avarice is misericorde,
and pitee largely taken. And men
mighten axe, why that misericorde and
pitee is relevinge of Avarice ? / Certes, (73

the avaricious man sheweth no pitee ne misericorde to the nedeful man; for he delyteth him in the kepinge of his tresor, and nat in the rescowinge ne relevinge of his evene-cristene. And therfore speke 5 I first of misericorde. / Thanne is misericorde, as seith the philosophre, a vertu, by which the corage of man is stired by the misese of him that is misesed. / Up-on which misericorde folweth pitee, in parfourninge of charitable werkes of misericorde. / And certes, thise thinges moeven a man to misericorde of Jesu Crist, that he yaf him-self for oure gilt, and suffred deeth for misericorde, and forgaf us oure originale sinnes; / and therby relessed us fro the peynes of helle, and amenused the peynes of purgatorie by penitence, and yeveth grace wel to do, and atte laste the blisse of hevene. / The speces of misericorde been, as for to lene and for to yeve and to foryeven and relesse, and for to han pitee in herte, and compassioun of the meschief of his evene-cristene, and eek to chastyse there as 10 nede is. / Another manere of remedie agayns Avarice is resonable largesse; but soothly, here bihoveth the consideracioun of the grace of Jesu Crist, and of hise temporel goodes, and eek of the godes perdurables that Crist yaf to us; / and to han remembrance of the deeth that he shal receyve, he noot whanne, where, ne how; and eek that he shal forgon al that he hath, save only that he hath despended in gode werkes. /

§ 69. But for-as-muche as som folk been unmesurable, men oghten eschue foollargesse, that men clepen wast. / Certes, he that is fool-large ne yeveth nat his catel, but he leseth his catel. Soothly, what thing that he yeveth for veyne glorie, as to minstrals and to folk, for to beren his renoun in the world, he hath 20 sinne ther-of and noon almesse. / Certes, he leseth foule his good, that ne seketh with the yifte of his good no-thing but 25 sinne. / He is lyk to an hors that seketh rather to drinken drovy or trouble water than for to drinken water of the clere welle. / And for-as-muchel as they yeven

ther as they sholde nat yeven, to hem aperteneth thilke malisoun that Crist shal yeven at the day of dome to hem that shullen been dampned. /

### Sequitur de Gula.

§ 70. After Avarice comth Glotonye, which is expres eek agayn the comandement of god. Glotonye is unmesurable appetyt to ete or to drinke, or elles to doon y-nogh to the unmesurable appetyt and desordeynee coveityse to eten or to drinke. / This sinne corrumped al this world, as is wel shewed in the sinne of Adam and of Eve. Loke eek, what seith seint Paul of Glotonye. / 'Manye,' seith seint Paul, 'goon, of whiche I have ofte seyd to yow, and now I seye it wepinge, that they been the enemys of the croys of Crist; of whiche the ende is deeth, and of whiche hir wombe is hir god, and hir glorie in confusioun of hem that so saveren erthely thinges.' / He that is 820 usaunt to this sinne of Glotonye, he ne may no sinne withstonde. He moot been in servage of alle vyces, for it is the develes hord ther he hydeth him and resteth. / This sinne hath manye speces. The firste is dronkenesse, that is the horrible sepulture of mannes resoun; and therfore, whan a man is dronken, he hath lost his resoun; and this is deedly sinne. / But soothly, whan that a man is nat wont to strong drinke, and peraventure ne knoweth nat the strengthe of the drinke, or hath feblesse in his heed, or hath travailed, thurgh which he drinketh the more, al be he sodeynly caught with drinke, it is no deedly sinne, but venial. / The seconde spece of Glotonye is, that the spirit of a man wexeth al trouble; for dronkenesse bireveth him the discrecioun of his wit. / The thridde spece of (750] Glotonye is, whan a man devoureth his mete, and hath no rightful manere of etinge. / The fourthe is whan, thurgh 825 the grete habundaunce of his mete, the humours in his body been destempred. / The fifthe is, foryetelnesse by to muchel drinkinge; for which somtyme a man foryeteth er the morwe what he dide at even or on the night biforn. /

§ 71. In other manere been distinct the speces of Glotonye, after seint Gregorie. Tho firste is, for to ete biforn tyme to ete. The seconde is, whan a man get him to delicat mete or drinke. / The thridde is, whan men taken to muche over mesure. The fourthe is curiositee, with greet entente to maken and apparaillen his mete. The fifthe is, for to eten to gredily. / Thise been the fyve fingres of the develes hand, by whiche he draweth 830 folk to sinne. /

### Remedium contra peccatum Gule.

§ 72. Agayns Glotonye is the remedie Abstinence, as seith Galien ; but that holde I nat meritorie, if he do it only for the hele of his body. Seint Augustin wole, that Abstinence be doon for vertu and with pacience. / Abstinence, he seith, is litel worth, but-if a man have good wil ther-to, and but it be enforced by pacience and by charitee, and that men doon it for godes sake, and in hope to have the blisse of hevene. /

§ 73. The felawes of Abstinence been Attemperaunce, that holdeth the mene in alle thinges : eek Shame, that eschueth alle deshonestee : Suffisance, that seketh no riche metes ne drinkes, ne dooth no fors of to outrageous apparailinge of mete. / Mesure also, that restreyneth by resoun the deslavee appetyt of etinge : Sobrenesse also, that restreyneth the (760) outrage of drinke : / Sparinge also, that restreyneth the delicat ese to sitte longe at his mete and softely ; wherfore som folk stonden of hir owene wil, to eten at 835 the lasse leyser. /

### Sequitur de Luxuria.

§ 74. After Glotonye, thanne comth Lecherie ; for thise two sinnes been so ny cosins, that ofte tyme they wol nat departe. / God woot, this sinne is ful displesaunt thing to god ; for he seyde himself, ' do no lecherie.' And therfore he putte grete peynes agayns this sinne in the olde lawe. / If womman thral were

taken in this sinne, she sholde be beten with staves to the deeth. And if she were a gentil womman, she sholde be slayn with stones. And if she were a bisshoppes doghter, she sholde been brent, by goddes comandement. / Forther over, by the sinne of Lecherie, god dreynte al the world at the diluge. And after that, he brente fyve citees with thonder-leyt, and sank hem in-to helle. /

§ 75. Now lat us speke thanne of thilke stinkinge sinne of Lecherie that men clepe Avoutrie of wedded folk, that is to seyn, if that oon of hem be wedded, or elles bothe. / Seint John seith, that 84 avoutiers shullen been in helle in a stank brenninge of fyr and of brimston ; in fyr, for the lecherie ; in brimston, for the stink of hir ordure. / Certes, the brekinge of this sacrement is an horrible thing ; it was maked of god him-self in paradys, and confermed by Jesu Crist, as witnesseth seint Mathew in the gospel : ' A man shal lete fader and moder, and taken him to his wyf, and they shullen be two in o flesh.' / This sacrement bitokneth the knittinge togidre of Crist and of holy chirche. / And nat only that god forbad avoutrie in dede, but eek he comanded that thou sholdest nat coveite thy neighebores wyf. / In this (7 heeste, seith seint Augustin, is forboden alle manere coveitise to doon lecherie. Lo what seith seint Mathew in the gospel : that ' who-so seeth a womman to coveitise of his lust, he hath doon lecherie with hir in his herte.' / Here may ye seen that 84 nat only the dede of this sinne is forboden, but eek the desyr to doon that sinne. / This cursed sinne anoyeth grevousliche hem that it haunten. And first, to hir soule ; for he oblygeth it to sinne and to peyne of deeth that is perdurable. / Un-to the body anoyeth it grevously also, for it dreyeth him, and wasteth, and shent him, and of his blood he maketh sacrifyce to the feend of helle ; it wasteth his catel and his substaunce. / And certes, if it be a foul thing, a man to waste his catel on wommen, yet is it a fouler thing whan that, for swich ordure, wommen dispenden up-on men hir catel and substaunce. / This sinne, as seith the prophete, bireveth man and womman hir gode fame, and al hir honour ; and it is ful pleasaunt to the devel ; for ther-by winneth he the moste partie of this ⊃ world. / And right as a marchant de- lyteth him most in chaffare that he hath most avantage of, right so delyteth the feend in this ordure. /

§ 76. This is that other hand of the devel, with fyve fingres, to cacche the peple to his vileinye. / The firste finger is the fool lookinge of the fool womman and of the fool man, that sleeth, right as the basilicok sleeth folk by the venim of his sighte ; for the coveitise of eyen fol- weth the coveitise of the herte. / The seconde finger is the vileyns touchinge in wikkede manere ; and ther-fore seith Salomon, that who-so toucheth and hand- leth a womman, he fareth lyk him that handleth the scorpioun that stingeth and sodeynly sleeth thurgh his enveniminge ; as who-so toucheth warm pich, it shent ◦) his fingres. / The thridde, is foule wordes, that fareth lyk fyr, that right anon bren- 5 neth the herte. / The fourthe finger is the kissinge ; and trewely he were a greet fool that wolde kisse the mouth of a bren- ninge ovene or of a fourneys. / And more fooles been they that kissen in vileinye ; for that mouth is the mouth of helle : and namely, thise olde dotardes holours, yet wol they kisse, though they may nat do, and smatre hem. / Certes, they been lyk to houndes ; for an hound, whan he comth by the roser or by othere †busshes, though he may nat pisse, yet wole he heve up his leg and make a con- tenaunce to pisse. / And for that many man weneth that he may nat sinne, for no likerousnesse that he doth with his wyf ; certes, that opinion is fals. God woot, a man may sleen him-self with his owene knyf, and make him-selven dronken of his owene tonne. / Certes, be it wyf, be it child, or any worldly thing that he loveth biforn god, it is his maumet, and ◦ he is an ydolastre. / Man sholde loven his wyf by discrecioun, paciently and

atemprely ; and thanne is she as though it were his suster. / The fifthe finger of the develes hand is the stinkinge dede of Lecherie. / Certes, the fyve fingres of Glotonie the feend put in the wombe of a man, and with hise fyve fyngres of Lecherie he gripeth him by the reynes, for to throwen him in-to the fourneys of helle ; / ther-as they shul han the fyr and the wormes that evere shul lasten, and wepinge and wailinge, sharp hunger and thurst, and grimnesse of develes that shullen al to-trede hem, with-outen respit and with-outen ende. / Of Lecherie, as (790) I seyde, sourden diverse speces ; as forni- cacioun, that is bitwixe man and womman that been nat maried ; and this is deedly sinne and agayns nature. / Al that is 865 enemy and destruccioun to nature is agayns nature. / Parfay, the resoun of a man telleth eek him wel that it is deedly sinne, for-as-muche as god forbad Lecherie. And seint Paul yeveth hem the regne, that nis dewe to no wight but to hem that doon deedly sinne. / Another sinne of Lecherie is to bireve a mayden of hir maydenhede ; for he that so dooth, certes, he casteth a mayden out of the hyeste degree that is in this present lyf, / and bireveth hir thilke precious fruit that the book clepeth ' the hundred fruit.' I ne can seye it noon other weyes in Eng- lish, but in Latin it highte Centesimus fructus. Certes, he that so dooth is cause of manye damages and vileinyes, mo than any man can rekene ; right as he som- tyme is cause of alle damages that bestes don in the feeld, that breketh the hegge or the closure ; thurgh which he de- stroyeth that may nat been restored. / 870 For certes, na-more may maydenhede be restored than an arm that is smiten fro the body may retourne agayn to wexe. / She may have mercy, this woot I wel, if she do penitence ; but nevere shal it be that she nas corrupt. / And al-be-it so that I have spoken somwhat of Avoutrie, it is good to shewen mo perils that longen to Avoutrie, for to eschue that foule sinne. / Avoutrie in Latin is for to seyn, approchinge of other mannes bed, thurgh

which tho that whylom weren o flessh
(800) abaundone hir bodyes to othere persones. /
Of this sinne, as seith the wyse man,
folwen manye harmes. First, brekinge
of feith ; and certes, in feith is the keye
875 of Cristendom. / And whan that feith is
broken and lorn, soothly Cristendom stant
veyn and with-outen fruit. / This sinne
is eek a thefte ; for thefte generally is for
to reve a wight his thing agayns his
wille. / Certes, this is the fouleste thefte
that may be, whan a womman steleth hir
body from hir housbonde and yeveth it
to hire holour to defoulen hir ; and steleth
hir soule fro Crist, and yeveth it to the
devel. / This is a fouler thefte, than for
to breke a chirche and stele the chalice ;
for thise avoutiers breken the temple of
god spiritually, and stelen the vessel of
grace, that is, the body and the soule, for
which Crist shal destroyen hem, as seith
seint Paul. / Soothly of this thefte
douted gretly Joseph, whan that his
lordes wyf preyed him of vileinye, whan
he seyde, 'lo, my lady, how my lord hath
take to me under my warde al that he
hath in this world ; ne no-thing of hise
thinges is out of my power, but only ye
880 that been his wyf. / And how sholde
I thanne do this wikkednesse, and sinne
so horribly agayns god, and agayns my
lord ? God it forbede.' Allas ! al to litel
is swich trouthe now y-founde ! / The
thridde harm is the filthe thurgh which
they breken the comandement of god, and
defoulen the auctour of matrimoine, that
is Crist. / For certes, in-so-muche as the
sacrement of mariage is so noble and so
digne, so muche is it gretter sinne for to
breken it ; for god made mariage in
paradys, in the estaat of innocence, to
multiplye man-kinde to the service of
god. / And therfore is the brekinge
ther-of more grevous. Of which brekinge
comen false heires ofte tyme, that wrongfully occupyen folkes heritages. And
therfore wol Crist putte hem out of the
regne of hevene, that is heritage to gode
(810) folk. / Of this brekinge comth eek ofte
tyme, that folk unwar wedden or sinnen
with hir owene kinrede ; and namely

thilke harlottes that haunten bordels of
thise fool wommen, that mowe be lykned
to a commune gonge, where-as men purgen
hir ordure. / What seye we eek of putours 88
that liven by the horrible sinne of puterie,
and constreyne wommen to yelden to
hem a certeyn rente of hir bodily puterie,
ye, somtyme of his owene wyf or his
child ; as doon this baudes ? Certes,
thise been cursede sinnes. / Understond
eek, that avoutrie is set gladly in the ten
comandements bitwixe thefte and manslaughtre ; for it is the gretteste thefte
that may be ; for it is thefte of body and
of soule. / And it is lyk to homicyde ;
for it kerveth a-two and breketh a-two
hem that first were maked o flesh, and
therfore, by the olde lawe of god, they
sholde be slayn. / But nathelees, by the
lawe of Jesu Crist, that is lawe of pitee,
whan he seyde to the womman that was
founden in avoutrie, and sholde han been
slayn with stones, after the wil of the
Jewes, as was hir lawe : ' Go,' quod Jesu
Crist, ' and have na-more wil to sinne ' ;
or, ' wille na-more to do sinne.' / Soothly,
the vengeaunce of avoutrie is awarded to
the peynes of helle, but-if so be that it be
destourbed by penitence. / Yet been ther 8
mo speces of this cursed sinne ; as whan
that oon of hem is religious, or elles
bothe ; or of folk that been entred in-to
ordre, as subdekne or dekne, or preest, or
hospitaliers. And evere the hyer that
he is in ordre, the gretter is the sinne. /
The thinges that gretly agreggen hir
sinne is the brekinge of hir avow of
chastitee, whan they receyved the ordre. /
And forther-over, sooth is, that holy
ordre is chief of al the tresorie of god,
and his especial signe and mark of chastitee ; to shewe that they been joyned to
chastitee, which that is most precious
lyf that is. / And thise ordred folk been
specially tytled to god, and of the special
meynee of god ; for which, whan they
doon deedly sinne, they been the special
traytours of god and of his peple ; for they
liven of the peple, to preye for the peple,
and whyle they been suche traitours, hir
preyers availen nat to the peple. / Preestes (8

been aungeles, as by the dignitee of hir misterye; but for sothe, seint Paul seith, that 'Sathanas transformeth him in an aungel of light.' / Soothly, the preest that haunteth deedly sinne, he may be lykned to the aungel of derknesse transformed in the aungel of light; he semeth aungel of light, but for sothe he is aungel of derknesse. / Swiche preestes been the sones of Helie, as sheweth in the book of Kinges, that they weren the sones of Belial, that is, the devel. / Belial is to seyn 'with-outen juge'; and so faren they; hem thinketh they been free, and han no juge, na-more than hath a free bole that taketh which cow that him lyketh in the toun. / So faren they by wommen. For right as a free bole is y-nough for al a toun, right so is a wikked preest corrupcioun y-nough for al a parisshe, or for al a contree. / Thise preestes, as seith the book, ne conne nat the misterie of preesthode to the peple, ne god ne knowe they nat; they ne helde hem nat apayd, as seith the book, of soden flesh that was to hem offred, but they toke by force the flesh that is rawe. / Certes, so thise shrewes ne holden hem nat apayed of rosted flesh and sode flesh, with which the peple fedden hem in greet reverence, but they wole have raw flesh of folkes wyves and hir doghtres. / And certes, thise wommen that consenten to hir harlotrie doon greet wrong to Crist and to holy chirche and alle halwes, and to alle soules; for they bireven alle thise him that sholde worshipe Crist and holy chirche, and preye for Cristene soules. / And therfore han swiche preestes, and hir lemmanes eek that consenten to hir lecherie, the malisoun of al the court Cristen, til they come to amendement. / The thridde spece of avoutrie is som-tyme bitwixe a man and his wyf; and that is whan they take no reward in hir assemblinge, but only to hire fleshly delyt, as seith seint Jerome; / and ne rekken of no-thing but that they been assembled; by-cause that they been maried, al is good y-nough, as thinketh to hem. / But in swich folk hath the devel power,

as seyde the aungel Raphael to Thobie; for in hir assemblinge they putten Jesu Crist out of hir herte, and yeven hem-self to alle ordure. / The fourthe spece is, the assemblee of hem that been of hire kinrede, or of hem that been of oon affinitee, or elles with hem with whiche hir fadres or hir kinrede han deled in the sinne of lecherie; this sinne maketh hem lyk to houndes, that taken no kepe to kinrede. / And certes, parentele is in two maneres, outher goostly or fleshly; goostly, as for to delen with hise godsibbes. / For right so as he that engendreth a child is his fleshly fader, right so is his godfader his fader espirituel. For which a womman may in no lasse sinne assemblen with hir godsib than with hir owene fleshly brother. / The fifthe spece is thilke abhominable sinne, of which that no man unnethe oghte speke ne wryte, nathelees it is openly rehersed in holy writ. / This cursednesse doon men and wommen in diverse entente and in diverse manere; but though that holy writ speke of horrible sinne, certes, holy writ may nat been defouled, na-more than the sonne that shyneth on the mixen. / Another sinne aperteneth to lecherie, that comth in slepinge; and this sinne cometh ofte to hem that been maydenes, and eek to hem that been corrupt; and this sinne men clepen pollucioun, that comth in foure maneres. / Somtyme, of languissinge of body; for the humours been to ranke and habundaunt in the body of man. Somtyme of infermetee; for the feblesse of the vertu retentif, as phisik maketh mencioun. Somtyme, for surfeet of mete and drinke. / And somtyme of vileyns thoghtes, that been enclosed in mannes minde whan he goth to slepe; which may nat been with-oute sinne. For which men moste kepen hem wysely, or elles may men sinnen ful grevously. /

(840)

### Remedium contra peccatum Luxurie.

§ 77. Now comth the remedie agayns Lecherie, and that is, generally, Chastitee and Continence, that restreyneth alle the

desordeynee moevinges that comen of
915 fleshly talentes. / And evere the gretter
merite shal he han, that most restreyneth
the wikkede eschaufinges of the ordure
of this sinne. And this is in two maneres,
that is to seyn, chastitee in mariage, and
chastitee in widwehode. / Now shaltow
understonde, that matrimoine is leefful
assemblinge of man and of womman, that
receyven by vertu of the sacrement the
bond, thurgh which they may nat be
departed in al hir lyf, that is to seyn,
whyl that they liven bothe. / This, as
seith the book, is a ful greet sacrement.
God maked it, as I have seyd, in paradys,
and wolde him-self be born in mariage. /
And for to halwen mariage, he was at
a weddinge, where-as he turned water
in-to wyn; which was the firste miracle
that he wroghte in erthe biforn hise disciples. / Trewe effect of mariage clenseth
fornicacioun and replenisseth holy chirche
of good linage; for that is the ende of
mariage; and it chaungeth deedly sinne
in-to venial sinne bitwixe hem that been
y-wedded, and maketh the hertes al oon
of hem that been y-wedded, as wel as the
920 bodies. / This is verray mariage, that
was establissed by god er that sinne bigan,
whan naturel lawe was in his right point
in paradys; and it was ordeyned that o
man sholde have but o womman, and
o womman but o man, as seith seint
Augustin, by manye resouns. /

§ 78. First, for mariage is figured bitwixe Crist and holy chirche. And that
other is, for a man is heved of a womman;
algate, by ordinaunce it sholde be so. /
For if a womman had mo men than oon,
thanne sholde she have mo hevedes than
oon, and that were an horrible thing
biforn god; and eek a womman ne mighte
nat plese to many folk at ones. And also
ther ne sholde nevere be pees ne reste
amonges hem; for everich wolde axen
his owene thing. / And forther-over, no
man ne sholde knowe his owene engendrure, ne who sholde have his heritage;
and the womman sholde been the lasse
biloved, fro the time that she were con-
(850) joynt to many men. /

§ 79. Now comth, how that a man
sholde bere him with his wyf; and
namely, in two thinges, that is to seyn in
suffraunce and reverence, as shewed Crist
whan he made first womman. / For he
ne made hir nat of the heved of Adam,
for she sholde nat clayme to greet lordshipe. / For ther-as the womman hath
the maistrie, she maketh to muche
desray; ther neden none ensamples of
this. The experience of day by day oghte
suffyse. / Also certes, god ne made nat
womman of the foot of Adam, for she ne
sholde nat been holden to lowe; for she
can nat paciently suffre: but god made
womman of the rib of Adam, for womman
sholde be felawe un-to man. / Man sholde
bere him to his wyf in feith, in trouthe,
and in love, as seith seint Paul: that
'a man sholde loven his wyf as Crist
loved holy chirche, that loved it so wel
that he deyde for it.' So sholde a man
for his wyf, if it were nede. /

§ 80. Now how that a womman sholde
be subget to hir housbonde, that telleth
seint Peter. First, in obedience. / And
eek, as seith the decree, a womman that
is a wyf, as longe as she is a wyf, she hath
noon auctoritee to swere ne bere witnesse
with-oute leve of hir housbonde, that is
hir lord; algate, he sholde be so by
resoun. / She sholde eek serven him in
alle honestee, and been attempree of hir
array. I wot wel that they sholde setten
hir entente to plesen hir housbondes, but
nat by hir queyntise of array. / Seint
Jerome seith, that wyves that been ap-
parailled in silk and in precious purpre
ne mowe nat clothen hem in Jesu Crist.
What seith seint John eek in this matere? /
Seint Gregorie eek seith, that no wight
seketh precious array but only for veyne
glorie, to been honoured the more biforn
the peple. / It is a greet folye, a womman
to have a fair array outward and in hir-
self be foul inward. / A wyf sholde eek
be mesurable in lokinge and in beringe
and in laughinge, and discreet in alle hir
wordes and hir dedes. / And aboven alle
worldly thing she sholde loven hir housbonde with al hir herte, and to him be

trewe of hir body ; / so sholde an housbonde eek be to his wyf.  For sith that al
the body is the housbondes, so sholde hir
herte been, or elles ther is bitwixe hem
two, as in that, no parfit mariage. /
Thanne shal men understonde that for
three thinges a man and his wyf fleshly
mowen assemble.  The firste is in entente
of engendrure of children to the service
of god, for certes that is the cause fynal
of matrimoine. /  Another cause is, to
yelden everich of hem to other the dette
of hir bodies, for neither of hem hath
power over his owene body.  The thridde
is, for to eschewe lecherye and vileinye.
₁₀ The ferthe is for sothe deedly sinne. /
As to the firste, it is meritorie ; the
seconde also ; for, as seith the decree, that
she hath merite of chastitee that yeldeth
to hir housbonde the dette of hir body,
ye, though it be agayn hir lykinge and
the lust of hir herte. /  The thridde
manere is venial sinne, and trewely scarsly
may ther any of thise be with-oute venial
sinne, for the corrupcion and for the
delyt. /  The fourthe manere is for to
understonde, if they assemble only for
amorous love and for noon of the forseyde causes, but for to accomplice thilke
brenninge delyt, they rekke nevere how
ofte, sothly it is deedly sinne ; and yet,
with sorwe, somme folk wol peynen hem
more to doon than to hir appetyt suffyseth. /

§ 81. The seconde manere of chastitee
is for to been a clene widewe, and eschue
the embracinges of man, and desyren the
₅₀ embracinge of Jesu Crist. /  Thise been
tho that han been wyves and han forgoon
hir housbondes, and eek wommen that
han doon lecherie and been releeved by
₅ Penitence. /  And certes, if that a wyf
coude kepen hir al chaast by licence of
hir housbonde, so that she yeve nevere
noon occasion that he agilte, it were to
hire a greet merite. /  Thise manere
wommen that observen chastitee moste
be clene in herte as well as in body and
in thoght, and mesurable in clothinge
and in contenaunce ; and been abstinent
in etinge and drinkinge, in spekinge, and

in dede.  They been the vessel or the
boyste of the blissed Magdalene, that
fulfilleth holy chirche of good odour. /
The thridde manere of chastitee is virginitee, and it bihoveth that she be holy
in herte and clene of body ; thanne is
she spouse to Jesu Crist, and she is the
lyf of angeles. /  She is the preisinge of
this world, and she is as thise martirs in
egalitee ; she hath in hir that tonge may
nat telle ne herte thinke.  Virginitee baar
oure lord Jesu Crist, and virgine was
him-selve. /                                    950

§ 82. Another remedie agayns Lecherie
is, specially to withdrawen swiche thinges
as yeve occasion to thilke vileinye ; as
ese, etinge and drinkinge ; for certes,
whan the pot boyleth strongly, the beste
remedie is to withdrawe the fyr. /  Slepinge longe in greet quiete is eek a greet
norice to Lecherie. /

§ 83. Another remedie agayns Lecherie
is, that a man or a womman eschue the
companye of hem by whiche he douteth
to be tempted ; for al-be-it so that the
dede is withstonden, yet is ther greet
temptacioun. /  Soothly a whyt wal, al-
though it ne brenne noght fully by
stikinge of a candele, yet is the wal blak
of the leyt. /  Ful ofte tyme I rede, that (880)
no man truste in his owene perfeccioun,
but he be stronger than Sampson, and
holier than † David, and wyser than
Salomon. /                                    955

§ 84. Now after that I have declared
yow, as I can, the sevene deedly sinnes,
and somme of hir braunches and hir remedies, soothly, if I coude, I wolde telle
yow the ten comandements. /  But so
heigh a doctrine I lete to divines.  Nathelees, I hope to god they been touched in
this tretice, everich of hem alle. /

### De Confessione.

§ 85. Now for-as-muche as the second
partie of Penitence stant in Confessioun
of mouth, as I bigan in the firste chapitre,
I seye, seint Augustin seith : / sinne is
every word and every dede, and al that
men coveiten agayn the lawe of Jesu

Crist; and this is for to sinne in herte, in mouth, and in dede, by thy fyve wittes, that been sighte, heringe, smellinge, tastinge or savouringe, and felinge. / Now is it good to understonde that that 960 agreggeth muchel every sinne. / Thou shalt considere what thou art that doost the sinne, whether thou be male or femele, yong or old, gentil or thral, free or servant, hool or syk, wedded or sengle, ordred or unordred, wys or fool, clerk or seculer ; / if she be of thy kinrede, bodily or goostly, or noon ; if any of thy kinrede have sinned with hir or noon, and manye mo thinges. /

§ 86. Another circumstaunce is this; whether it be doon in fornicacioun, or in avoutrie, or noon ; incest, or noon ; mayden, or noon ; in manere of homicyde, or noon ; horrible grete sinnes, or smale ; and how longe thou hast continued in sinne. / The thridde circumstaunce is the place ther thou hast do sinne; whether in other mennes hous or in thyn owene ; in feeld or in chirche, or in chirche-hawe; (890) in chirche dedicat, or noon. / For if the chirche be halwed, and man or womman spille his kinde in-with that place by wey of sinne, or by wikked temptacion, the chirche is entredited til it be reconciled 965 by the bishop ; / and the preest that dide swich a vileinye, to terme of al his lyf, he sholde na-more singe masse ; and if he dide, he sholde doon deedly sinne at every tyme that he so songe masse. / The fourthe circumstaunce is, by whiche mediatours or by whiche messagers, as for entycement, or for consentement to bere companye with felaweshipe ; for many a wrecche, for to bere companye, wil go to the devel of helle. / Wher-fore they that eggen or consenten to the sinne been parteners of the sinne, and of the dampnacioun of the sinner. / The fifthe circumstaunce is, how manye tymes that he hath sinned, if it be in his minde, and how ofte that he hath falle. / For he that ofte falleth in sinne, he despiseth the mercy of god, and encreesseth his sinne, and is unkinde to Crist; and he wexeth the more feble to withstonde

sinne, and sinneth the more lightly, / 97 and the latter aryseth, and is the more eschew for to shryven him, namely, to him that is his confessour. / For which that folk, whan they falle agayn in hir olde folies, outher they forleten hir olde confessours al outrely, or elles they departen hir shrift in diverse places ; but soothly, swich departed shrift deserveth no mercy of god of hise sinnes. / The sixte circumstaunce is, why that a man sinneth, as by whiche temptacioun ; and if him-self procure thilke temptacioun, or by the excytinge of other folk ; or if he sinne with a womman by force, or by hir owene assent ; / or if the womman, maugree hir heed, hath been afforced, or noon ; this shal she telle ; for coveitise, or for poverte, and if it was hir procuringe, or noon ; and swiche manere harneys. / (9 The seventhe circumstaunce is, in what manere he hath doon his sinne, or how that she hath suffred that folk han doon to hir. / And the same shal the man 97 telle pleynly, with alle circumstaunces ; and whether he hath sinned with comune bordel-wommen, or noon ; / or doon his sinne in holy tymes, or noon ; in fastingtymes, or noon ; or biforn his shrifte, or after his latter shrifte ; / and hath, peraventure, broken ther-fore his penance enjoyned ; by whos help and whos conseil ; by sorcerie or craft ; al moste be told. / Alle thise thinges, after that they been grete or smale, engreggen the conscience of man. And eek the preest that is thy juge, may the bettre been avysed of his jugement in yevinge of thy penaunce, and that is after thy contricioun. / For understond wel, that after tyme that a man hath defouled his baptesme by sinne, if he wole come to salvacioun, ther is noon other wey but by penitence and shrifte and satisfaccioun ; / and namely 9 by the two, if ther be a confessour to which he may shryven him ; and the thridde. if he have lyf to parfournen it. /

§ 87. Thanne shal man looke and considere, that if he wole maken a trewe and a profitable confessioun, ther moste be foure condiciouns. / First, it moot been in sorweful bitternesse of herte, as seyde the king Ezekias to god : 'I wol remembre me alle the yeres of my lyf in bitternesse of myn herte.' / This condicioun of bitternesse hath fyve signes. The firste is, that confessioun moste be shamefast, nat for to covere ne hyden his sinne, for he hath agilt his god and defouled his (10) soule. / And her-of seith seint Augustin : 'the herte travailleth for shame of his sinne'; and for he hath greet shamefastnesse, he is digne to have greet mercy of (85) god. / Swich was the confession of the publican, that wolde nat heven up hise eyen to hevene, for he hadde offended god of hevene ; for which shamefastnesse he hadde anon the mercy of god. / And ther-of seith seint Augustin, that swich shamefast folk been next foryevenesse and remissioun. / Another signe is humilitee in confessioun ; of which seith seint Peter, 'Humbleth yow under the might of god.' The hond of god is mighty in confessioun, for ther-by god foryeveth thee thy sinnes ; for he allone hath the power. / And this humilitee shal been in herte, and in signe outward ; for right as he hath humilitee to god in his herte, right so sholde he humble his body outward to the preest that sit in goddes place. / For which in no manere, sith that Crist is sovereyn and the preest mene and mediatour bitwixe Crist and the sinnere, and the (990) sinnere is the laste by wey of resoun, / thanne sholde nat the sinnere sitte as heighe as his confessour, but knele biforn him or at his feet, but-if maladie destourbe it. For he shal nat taken kepe who sit there, but in whos place that he sitteth. / A man that hath trespased to a lord, and comth for to axe mercy and maken his accord, and set him doun anon by the lord, men wolde holden him outrageous, and nat worthy so sone for to have remissioun ne mercy. / The thridde signe is, how that thy shrift sholde be ful of teres, if man may ; and if man may nat wepe with hise bodily eyen, lat him wepe in herte. / Swich was the confession of seint Peter ; for after that he hadde

forsake Jesu Crist, he wente out and weep ful bitterly. / The fourthe signe is, (920) that he ne lette nat for shame to shewen his confessioun. / Swich was the con- (995) fessioun of the Magdelene, that ne spared, for no shame of hem that weren atte feste, for to go to oure lord Jesu Crist and biknowe to him hir sinnes. / The fifthe signe is, that a man or a womman be obeisant to receyven the penaunce that him is enjoyned for hise sinnes ; for certes Jesu Crist, for the giltes of a man, was obedient to the deeth. /

§ 88. The seconde condicion of verray confession is, that it be hastily doon ; for certes, if a man hadde a deedly wounde, evere the lenger that he taried to warisshe him-self, the more wolde it corrupte and haste him to his deeth ; and eek the wounde wolde be the wors for to hele. / And right so fareth sinne, that longe tyme is in a man unshewed. / Certes, a man oghte hastily shewen hise sinnes for manye causes ; as for drede of deeth, that cometh ofte sodenly, and is in no certeyn what tyme it shal be, ne in what place ; and eek the drecchinge of o synne draweth in another ; / and eek the lenger that he (1000) tarieth, the ferther he is fro Crist. And if he abyde to his laste day, scarsly may he shryven him or remembre him of hise sinnes, or repenten him, for the grevous maladie of his deeth. / And for-as-muche as he ne hath nat in his lyf herkned Jesu Crist, whanne he hath spoken, he shal crye to Jesu Crist at his laste day, and scarsly wol he herkne him. / And understond that this condicioun moste han foure thinges. Thy shrift moste be purveyed bifore and avysed ; for wikked haste doth no profit ; and that a man conne shryve him of hise sinnes, be it of pryde, or of envye, and so forth of the speces and circumstances ; / and that he have comprehended in his minde the nombre and the greetnesse of hise sinnes, and how longe that he hath leyn in sinne ; / and eek that he be contrit of (930) hise sinnes, and in stedefast purpos, by the grace of god, nevere eft to falle in sinne ; and eek that he drede and countre-

waite him-self, that he flee the occasiouns
1005 of sinne to whiche he is enclyned. / Also
thou shalt shryve thee of alle thy sinnes
to o man, and nat a parcel to o man and
a parcel to another ; that is to understonde, in entente to departe thy confessioun as for shame or drede ; for it nis but
stranglinge of thy soule. / For certes,
Jesu Crist is entierly al good ; in him nis
noon inperfeccioun ; and therfore outher
he foryeveth al parfitly or never a deel. /
I seye nat that if thou be assigned to the
penitauncer for certein sinne, that thou
art bounde to shewen him al the remenaunt of thy sinnes, of whiche thou hast
be shriven to thy curat, but-if it lyke to
thee of thyn humilitee ; this is no departinge of shrifte. / Ne I seye nat,
ther-as I speke of divisioun of confessioun,
that if thou have lycence for to shryve
thee to a discreet and an honeste preest,
where thee lyketh, and by lycence of thy
curat, that thou ne mayst wel shryve
thee to him of alle thy sinnes. / But lat
no blotte be bihinde ; lat no sinne been
untold, as fer as thou hast remem-
1010 braunce. / And whan thou shalt be
shriven to thy curat, telle him eek alle
the sinnes that thou hast doon sin thou
were last y-shriven ; this is no wikked
entente of divisioun of shrifte. /

§ 89. Also the verray shrifte axeth
certeine condiciouns. First, that thou
shryve thee by thy free wil, noght constreyned, ne for shame of folk, ne for
maladie, ne swiche thinges ; for it is
resoun that he that trespasseth by his
free wil, that by his free wil he confesse
his trespas ; / and that noon other man
telle his sinne but he him-self, ne he shal
nat nayte ne denye his sinne, ne wratthe
him agayn the preest for his amonestinge
to leve sinne. / The seconde condicioun
is, that thy shrift be laweful ; that is to
seyn, that thou that shryvest thee, and
eek the preest that hereth thy confessioun,
(940) been verraily in the feith of holy chirche ; /
and that a man ne be nat despeired of the
1015 mercy of Jesu Crist, as Caym or Judas. /
And eek a man moot accusen him-self of
his owene trespas, and nat another ; but

he shal blame and wyten him-self and
his owene malice of his sinne, and noon
other ; / but nathelees, if that another
man be occasioun or entycer of his sinne,
or the estaat of a persone be swich thurgh
which his sinne is agregged, or elles that
he may nat pleynly shryven him but he
telle the persone with which he hath
sinned ; thanne may he telle ; / so that
his entente ne be nat to bakbyte the
persone, but only to declaren his confessioun. /

§ 90. Thou ne shalt nat eek make no
lesinges in thy confessioun ; for humilitee,
per-aventure, to seyn that thou hast doon
sinnes of whiche that thou were nevere
gilty. / For seint Augustin seith : if
thou, by cause of thyn humilitee, makest
lesinges on thy-self, though thou ne were
nat in sinne biforn, yet artow thanne in
sinne thurgh thy lesinges. / Thou most 1020
eek shewe thy sinne by thyn owene propre
mouth, but thou be wexe doumb, and nat
by no lettre ; for thou that hast doon the
sinne, thou shalt have the shame therfore. /
Thou shalt nat eek peynte thy confessioun
by faire subtile wordes, to covere the more
thy sinne ; for thanne bigylestow thy-self
and nat the preest ; thou most tellen it
pleynly, be it nevere so foul ne so horrible. / Thou shalt eek shryve thee to a
preest that is discreet to conseille thee,
and eek thou shalt nat shryve thee for
veyne glorie, ne for ypocrisye, ne for no
cause, but only for the doute of Jesu Crist
and the hele of thy soule. / Thou shalt
nat eek renne to the preest sodeynly, to
tellen him lightly thy sinne, as who-so
telleth a jape or a tale, but avysely and
with greet devocioun. / And generally, (950)
shryve thee ofte. If thou ofte falle, ofte
thou aryse by confessioun. / And thogh 1025
thou shryve thee ofter than ones of sinne,
of which thou hast be shriven, it is the
more merite. And, as seith seint Augustin, thou shalt have the more lightly
relesing and grace of god, bothe of sinne
and of peyne. / And certes, ones a yere
atte leeste wey it is laweful for to been
housled ; for certes ones a yere alle thinges
renovellen. /

**Explicit secunda pars Penitencie; et sequitur tercia pars eiusdem, de Satisfaccione.**

§ 91. Now have I told you of verray Confessioun, that is the seconde partie of Penitence. /

The thridde partie of Penitence is Satisfaccioun; and that stant most generally in almesse and in bodily peyne. / Now been ther three manere of almesses; contricion of herte, where a man offreth himself to god; another is, to han pitee of defaute of hise neighebores; and the thridde is, in yevinge of good conseil goostly and bodily, where men han nede, and namely in sustenaunce of mannes fode. / And tak keep, that a man hath need of thise thinges generally; he hath need of fode, he hath nede of clothing, and herberwe, he hath nede of charitable conseil, and visitinge in prisone and in maladie, and sepulture of his dede body. / And if thou mayst nat visite the nedeful with thy persone, visite him by thy message and by thy yiftes. / Thise been generally almesses or werkes of charitee of hem that han temporel richesses or discrecioun in conseilinge. Of thise werkes shaltow heren at the day of dome. /

§ 92. Thise almesses shaltow doon of thyne owene propre thinges, and hastily, and prively if thou mayst; / but nathelees, if thou mayst nat doon it prively, thou shalt nat forbere to doon almesse though men seen it; so that it be nat doon for thank of the world, but only for thank of Jesu Crist. / For as witnesseth seint Mathew, *capitulo quinto*, 'A citee may nat been hid that is set on a montayne; ne men lighte nat a lanterne and put it under a busshel; but men sette it on a candle-stikke, to yeve light to the men in the hous. / Right so shal youre light lighten bifore men, that they may seen youre gode werkes, and glorifie youre fader that is in hevene.' /

§ 93. Now as to spoken of bodily peyne, it stant in preyeres, in wakinges, in fastinges, in vertuouse techinges of orisouns. / And ye shul understonde, that orisouns or preyeres is for to seyn a pitous wil of herte, that redresseth it in god and expresseth it by word outward, to remoeven harmes and to han thinges espirituel and durable, and somtyme temporel thinges; of whiche orisouns, certes, in the orisoun of the *Pater-noster*, hath Jesu Crist enclosed most thinges. / Certes, it is privileged of three thinges in his dignitee, for which it is more digne than any other preyere; for that Jesu Crist him-self maked it; / and it is short, for it sholde be coud the more lightly, and for to withholden it the more esily in herte, and helpen him-self the ofter with the orisoun; / and for a man sholde be the lasse wery to seyen it, and for a man may nat excusen him to lerne it, it is so short and so esy; and for it comprehendeth in it-self alle gode preyeres. / The exposicioun of this holy preyere, that is so excellent and digne, I bitake to thise maistres of theologie; save thus muchel wol I seyn: that, whan thou prayest that god sholde foryeve thee thy giltes as thou foryevest hem that agilten to thee, be ful wel war that thou be nat out of charitee. / This holy orisoun amenuseth eek venial sinne; and therfore it aperteneth specially to penitence. /

§ 94. This preyere moste be trewely seyd and in verray feith, and that men preye to god ordinatly and discreetly and devoutly; and alwey a man shal putten his wil to be subget to the wille of god. / This orisoun moste eek been seyd with greet humblesse and ful pure; honestly, and nat to the anoyaunce of any man or womman. It moste eek been continued with the werkes of charitee. / It avayleth eek agayn the vyces of the soule; for, as seith seint Jerome, 'By fastinge been saved the vyces of the flesh, and by preyere the vyces of the soule.' /

§ 95. After this, thou shalt understonde, that bodily peyne stant in wakinge; for Jesu Crist seith, 'waketh, and preyeth that ye ne entre in wikked temptacioun.' / Ye shul understanden also, that fastinge stant in three thinges; in forberinge of bodily mete and drinke, and in forberinge

(970)

1040

1045

30

50

53

A a 5

of worldly jolitee, and in forberinge of deedly sinne; this is to seyn, that a man shal kepen him fro deedly sinne with al his might. /

§ 96. And thou shalt understanden eek, that god ordeyned fastinge; and to fastinge 1050 appertenen foure thinges. / Largenesse to povre folk, gladnesse of herte espirituel, nat to been angry ne anoyed, ne grucche for he fasteth; and also resonable houre for to ete by mesure; that is for to seyn, a man shal nat ete in untyme, ne sitte the lenger at his table to ete for he fasteth. /

§ 97. Thanne shaltow understonde, that bodily peyne stant in disciplyne or techinge, by word or by wrytinge, or in ensample. Also in weringe of heyres or of stamin, or of haubergeons on hir naked flesh, for Cristes sake, and swiche manere penances. / But war thee wel that swiche manere penances on thy flesh ne make nat thyn herte bitter or angry or anoyed of thy-self; for bettre is to caste awey thyn heyre, than for to caste away the sikernesse of Jesu Crist. / And therfore seith seint Paul: 'Clothe yow, as they that been chosen of god, in herte of misericorde, debonairetee, suffraunce, and swich manere of clothinge'; of whiche Jesu Crist is more apayed than of heyres, (980) or haubergeons, or hauberkes. /

§ 98. Thanne is disciplyne eek in knokkinge of thy brest, in scourginge with 1055 yerdes, in knelinges, in tribulacions; / in suffringe paciently wronges that been doon to thee, and eek in pacient suffraunce of maladies, or lesinge of worldly catel, or of wyf, or of child, or othere freendes. /

§ 99. Thanne shaltow understonde, whiche thinges destourben penaunce; and this is in foure maneres, that is, drede, shame, hope, and wanhope, that is, desperacion. / And for to speke first of drede; for which he weneth that he may suffre no penaunce; / ther-agayns is remedie for to thinke, that bodily penaunce is but short and litel at regard of the peyne of helle, that is so cruel and so long, that it lasteth with-outen ende. /

§ 100. Now again the shame that a man hath to shryven him, and namely, thise

ypocrites that wolden been holden so parfite that they han no nede to shryven hem; / agayns that shame, sholde a man 106 thinke that, by wey of resoun, that he that hath nat been ashamed to doon foule thinges, certes him oghte nat been ashamed to do faire thinges, and that is confessiouns. / A man sholde eek thinke, that god seeth and woot alle hise thoghtes and alle hise werkes; to him may no thing been hid ne covered. / Men sholden eek remembren hem of the shame that is to come at the day of dome, to hem that been nat penitent and shriven in this present lyf. / For alle the creatures in erthe and in helle shullen seen apertly al that they hyden in this world. /    (99

§ 101. Now for to speken of the hope of hem that been necligent and slowe to shryven hem, that stant in two maneres. / 106 That oon is, that he hopeth for to live longe and for to purchacen muche richesse for his delyt, and thanne he wol shryven him; and, as he seith, him semeth thanne tymely y-nough to come to shrifte. / Another is, surquidrie that he hath in Cristes mercy. / Agayns the firste vyce, he shal thinke, that oure lyf is in no sikernesse; and eek that alle the richesses in this world ben in aventure, and passen as a shadwe on the wal. / And, as seith seint Gregorie, that it aperteneth to the grete rightwisnesse of god, that nevere shal the peyne stinte of hem that nevere wolde withdrawen hem fro sinne, hir thankes, but ay continue in sinne; for thilke perpetuel wil to do sinne shul they han perpetuel peyne. /

§ 102. Wanhope is in two maneres: the firste wanhope is in the mercy of Crist; that other is that they thinken, that they ne mighte nat longe persevere in goodnesse. / The firste wanhope comth 107 of that he demeth that he hath sinned so greetly and so ofte, and so longe leyn in sinne, that he shal nat be saved. / Certes, agayns that cursed wanhope sholde he thinke, that the passion of Jesu Crist is more strong for to unbinde than sinne is strong for to binde. / Agayns the seconde wanhope, he shal thinke, that as ofte as

he falleth he may aryse agayn by penitence. And thogh he never so longe
have leyn in sinne, the mercy of Crist is
alwey redy to receiven him to mercy. /
Agayns the wanhope, that he demeth
that he sholde nat longe persevere in
goodnesse, he shal thinke, that the
feblesse of the devel may no-thing doon
1000) but-if men wol suffren him ; / and eek
he shal han strengthe of the help of god,
1075 and of al holy chirche, and of the proteccioun of aungels, if him list. /

§ 103. Thanne shal men understonde
what is the fruit of penaunce ; and, after
the word of Jesu Crist, it is the endelees
blisse of hevene, / ther joye hath no contrarioustee of wo ne grevaunce, ther alle
harmes been passed of this present lyf;
ther-as is the sikernesse fro the peyne of
helle ; ther-as is the blisful companye
that rejoysen hem everemo, everich of
otheres joye ; / ther-as the body of man,
that whylom was foul and derk, is more
cleer than the sonne ; ther-as the body,
that whylom was syk, freele, and feble,
and mortal, is inmortal, and so strong
and so hool that ther may no-thing
apeyren it ; / ther-as ne is neither hunger,
thurst, ne cold, but every soule replenissed
with the sighte of the parfit knowinge of
god. / This blisful regne may men purchace by poverte espirituel, and the glorie
by lowenesse ; the plentee of joye by
hunger and thurst, and the reste by
travaille ; and the lyf by deeth and
1080 mortificacion of sinne. /

### Here taketh the makere of this book
### his leve.

§ 104. Now preye I to hem alle that
herkne this litel tretis or rede, that if
ther be any thing in it that lyketh hem,
that ther-of they thanken oure lord Jesu
Crist, of whom procedeth al wit and al
goodnesse. / And if ther be any thing
that displese hem, I preye hem also that
they arrette it to the defaute of myn
unconninge, and nat to my wil, that
wolde ful fayn have seyd bettre if I hadde
had conninge. / For oure boke seith, ' al
that is writen is writen for oure doctrine' ;
and that is myn entente. / Wherfore
I biseke yow mekely for the mercy of
god, that ye preye for me, that Crist have
mercy on me and foryeve me my giltes : / (1010)
—and namely, of my translacions and
endytinges of worldly vanitees, the whiche
I revoke in my retracciouns : / as is the 1085
book of Troilus ; The book also of Fame ;
The book of the nynetene Ladies ; The
book of the Duchesse ; The book of seint
Valentynes day of the Parlement of
Briddes ; The tales of Caunterbury, thilke
that sounen in-to sinne ; / The book of
the Leoun ; and many another book, if
they were in my remembrance ; and
many a song and many a lecherous lay ;
that Crist for his grete mercy foryeve me
the sinne. / But of the translacion of
Boece de Consolacione, and othere bokes
of Legendes of seintes, and omelies, and
moralitee, and devocioun, / that thanke
I oure lord Jesu Crist and his blisful
moder, and alle the seintes of hevene ; /
bisekinge hem that they from hennes-
forth, un-to my lyves ende, sende me
grace to biwayle my giltes, and to studie
to the salvacioun of my soule :—and
graunte me grace of verray penitence,
confessioun and satisfaccioun to doon in
this present lyf ; / thurgh the benigne 1090
grace of him that is king of kinges and
preest over alle preestes, that boghte us
with the precious blood of his herte ; / so
that I may been oon of hem at the day of
dome that shulle be saved : *Qui cum*
*patre, &c.*                              1092

### Here is ended the book of the Tales of Caunterbury, compiled by Geffrey Chaucer,
### of whos soule Jesu Crist have mercy.   Amen.

# APPENDIX.

———•———

## VARIATIONS AND EMENDATIONS.

THE text of Chaucer is, in some places, corrupt, and in others can be much improved by some emendation, usually of a slight character.

The text of the best authorities, as improved by collation with other good authorities, is here given. Variations from these are denoted by an obelus (†) in the text, which may be considered as marking a reading as to which there is some doubt. These are most numerous in the Romaunt of the Rose, the Book of the Duchesse, and the House of Fame. There are very few doubtful readings in the Canterbury Tales, for which there are better authorities than in other cases. In the following Appendix all the doubtful readings and editorial emendations are accounted for. I do not, however, notice words which are placed between square brackets, such as the word 'a' on p. 1, l. 12. It will be understood, once for all, that all such words are *supplied*, and are *missing* in the originals, though often necessary for the sense or the metre, or for both.

## ROMAUNT OF THE ROSE.

The authorities are G. (the Glasgow MS.); and Th. (Thynne's edition of 1532). Also, from the nature of the case, F. (the original French text, here quoted from the edition by Méon, Paris, 1813). No other authorities exist. Many lines are wholly missing in G.; and when it is not cited, this must be understood. Thus, it has lost lines 1–44.

Page 1. 3. Th. sweuen; *but the plural is required.* 4. Th. that false ne bene. 25. Th. slepte; (sleep *is more usual*). 38. Th. hatte; *read* hote (be called).

Page 2. 66. G. Th. had; *read* hath. 102. G. Th. buskes (*not* Chaucer's *form*). 110. G. Th. gan I. 138. G. Th. Enclosed was; *see* l. 1652; F. *Tant clos.* 149. G. Th. mynoresse (!); F. *moverresse.*

Page 3. 196. G. Th. myscoueiting (!); F. *mesconter.* 220. G. Th. courtpy (*see* Cant. Tales, A 290). 248. *Both* peynted.

Page 4. 255. *Both* Upon any worthy man falle. 277. *Both* and so breketh. 324. *Both* rent.

Page 5. 382. *Both* may neuer. 442. *Both* ay (*giving no sense*); *read* shal. 444. *Both* grace (!), *for* face; F. *lor vis.*

Page 6. 485. G. laddris; Th. ladders; *see* l. 523. 492. G. yeer; Th. yere; *read* yerd; *see* l. 656. 501. *Both* wolde '*for* nolde; *by confusion*). 505. *Both* god kepe it fro care, *a false rime; clearly substituted for* god it kepe and were. *Were* is the E. spelling of the verb in the French text, which has *que Diex garisse.* 520. *Both* For; *read* Ful; (wo *is here an adjective* = sad). 536. G. ony; Th. any; *read* a.

Page 7. 564. *Some lines lost here*; 3 *lines of* F. *left untranslated.* 586. *Both* may; *read* mayden. 602. *Both* lande of Alexandryne; *but* Alexandryn *is an adjective.* 603. G. hidre be; Th. hyther be.

Page 8. 660. *Both* places. 668. *Both* That; *read* These. 720. Th. reuelrye; G. reuerye; F. *reverdie.*

Page 9. 761. *Both* made; *read* make. 791. *Both* bode (*no sense*); *read* Bede; Ne bede I = I would not offer.

Page 10. 859. G. seye; Th. sey. 860. G. pleye (!); Th. pley (!). 865. *Both* I wot not what of hir nose I shal descryve (*eleven syllables*). 866. *Two lines lost here.* 879. *Both* Love and as hym likith it be. 923. *Both* Turke bowes two ful wel deuysed had he (*too long*).

Page 11. 959. *Both* shoten; *see* l. 989. 984. *Both* on; *read* of. 1007. *Both* And an; *read* As was an; F. *Ainsinc cum.* 1017. *Both* wyntred; *but see* l. 1020. 1026. *Both* thought; *read* thinketh. 1031. *Both* Sore (!); F. *Sade.* 1034. *Both* And hight (!).

Page 12. 1037. *Both* in werk (!). 1058. Th. prill; G. prile; (*error for* prikke, *written so as to look like* prilke). 1080. Th. amyled; G. enameled. 1089. *Both* durst (!); *error for* thurfte, *more commonly* thurte. 1117. *Both* ragounces; F. *jagonces.*

Page 13. 1188. G. sarlynysh; Th. Sarlynysshe; F. *Sarrazinesche.* 1201. *Both* gousfaucoun (!); F. *gonfanon.* 1210. *Both* He caste. 1233. Th. hempe; G. hempe ne (= hempene). 1236. *Both* a; *read* oo (one).

Page 14. 1244. *Both* Bitokeneth. 1282. *Both* And she (!); *read* Youthe; F. *Jonesce*; *see* l. 1302. 1303. *Both* that; *read* thus; *see* l. 1310. 1313. G. loreyes (*error for* loreres); Th. Laurelles. 1315. Th. ended; G. eended (= y-ended). 1324. *Both* durst (*as in* l. 1089). 1332. *Both* she (*for second* he). 1334. *Both* hadde (*for* bad); *and* bent (*for* bende); *both omit* it. 1335. *Both* an (*for* on).

Page 15. 1341. G. hadde me shette; Th. had me shete (*but* shete *is not a pp.*). 1343. *Both* had me greued. 1348. *Both* hadde in all the gardyn be. 1366. *Both* gardin (*for* yerd). 1369. *Both* Parys (!); *for* paradys. 1397-8. Th. knytte, sytte.

Page 16. 1440. Th. dilectable. 1447. Th. garden; *read* yerde in; cf. 1348, 1366. 1448. Th. efters (!); F. *tout l'estre.* 1453. Th. shoten; *read* shete. Th. goodnesse (*for* good mes); cf. 3462. 1498. G. velaynesly; Th. vilaynously. 1527. *Both* musede so.

Page 17. 1591. *Both* entrees; F. *Tout l'estre.* 1593. *Both* ye (*for* he). 1594. *Both* Ye (*for* He). 1608. *Both* laughyng (!); *read* loving.

Page 18. 1641. *Both* sighed. 1644. *Both* strengthes. 1648. G. bitrisshed; Th. bytresshed. 1663. *Both* me; *read* be; F. *fusse.* 1666. G. wole; Th. wol. 1674. Th. ware; G. waxe; *both have* Rone. 1698. *Both* hath; *omit* wel? 1700. *Both* roses. 1713. *Both* For; *read* Ful.

Page 19. 1721. G. botheum; Th. bothum. 1732. *Both* Sithen. 1758. *Both* two (!). 1766. *Both* certis euenly; *read* certeinly. 1771. *Both* his; *read* a. 1814. *Both* lefte (!); *read* felte.

Page 20. 1848. *Both* mighte it. 1851. *Both* sene I hadde. 1853-4. *Both* thore, more; *see* l. 1857. 1860. G. Castith; Th. Casteth. 1913, 1914. *Transposed in* G., Th.

Page 21. 1924. *Both* softyng; *see* 1925. 1925. *Both* prikkith. 1965. *Both* loue; *read* louers. 2002. *Both* of; *read* to.

**Page 22.** 2038. *Both* queynt. 2044. *Both* taken; *read* tan; cf. 2068. 2046. *Both* disteyned; F. *Deceus.* 2067. *Both* susprised. 2068. *Both* taken; *read* tan; cf. 2044. 2076. G. disese; Th. desese; F. *dessaisir.* 2116. *Both* degree.

**Page 23.** 2154. *Both* bigynneth to amende. 2176. G. say; Th. saye. 2185. *Both* vnto; *for* to. 2195. *Both* in; *read* a.

**Page 24.** 2264. *Both* on; *read* upon. 2271. Th. aumere; G. awmere; *see* 2087. 2279. *Both* costneth; F. *couste.* 2285. *Both* Farce. 2294. G. Th. knowith (!); F. *rit* 2302. *Both* pleyneth; *read* pleyeth. 2327. *Both* menen.

**Page 25.** 2336. *Both* londes; *read* loues. 2341. *Both* this swifte; *read* swich yift; F. *si riche don.* 2365. *Both* and; *read* in. 2427. Th. sene; *read* sende; F. *envoier.* 2432. Th. gone and visyten.

**Page 26.** 2466. *Better omit* of. 2473. *Both* Thought; *read* That swete ? 2499. G. yitt; Th. yet; *read* yif.

**Page 27.** 2564. Th. forwerede; G. forweriede; *see* 3251. 2569. *Both* se; *read* seme. 2617. *Both* I wote not; *read* I noot. 2619. *Both* better. 2621. *Both* on hir I caste. 2622. *Both* That. 2628. *Both* liggen; *read* ly.

**Page 28.** 2650. *Both* whider (!). 2675. Th. whan; G. whanne; *read* wham *or* whom; F. *De qui tu ne pues avoir aise.* 2676. Corrupt. F. *Au departir la porte baise* (i. e. the lover is to kiss the door). 2709, 2710. *Both* more, fore. 2712. *Both* to gon; *omit* to.

**Page 29.** 2774. *Both* aftirward. 2796. G. Thenkyng; Th. Thynkyng; cf. 2804. 2824. *Both* not ben; F. *tu seroies.* 2833. *Both* me; *read* hem; cf. 2845.

**Page 30.** 2917. *Both* thou (*for* they). 2935. *Both* declared thee.

**Page 31.** 2992. *Both* warrans; F. *Ge vous i puis bien garantir.*

**Page 32.** 3052. *Both* Venus hath flemed. 3115. *Both* arise. 3125. *Both* And late (*or* lette) it growe (*too long*). 3136. Th. His eyes reed sparclyng as the fyre-glowe (*too long*); sparclyng *is a gloss on* reed.

**Page 33.** 3150. G. it; Th. he; *read* I; F. *ge.* 3207. *Both* For Nature; *I omit* For. 3209. *Both* but if the.

**Page 34.** 3264. *Both* seyne; feyne *seems better.* 3274. *Both* he be a; *I omit* a. 3301. *After* gete, Th. *inserts* the, *and* G. thee. 3319. *Both* thought; *read* taughte. 3331. *Both* Who that; *I omit* that. 3337. *Both* cherisaunce; F. *chevisance.*

**Page 35.** 3399. Th. forbode; G. forbede; *read* forbad. 3433. Th. suche; G. sichen; F. *puis qu'il me siet.*

**Page 36.** 3447. *Both* where that the; *I omit* that. 3490. *Both* That he had. 3491. G. Thanne; Th. Than; *read* That; F. *Qu' Amors.* 3522. *Both* ye (*for* he); F. *Que il.* 3525. *Both* it is.

**Page 37.** 3548. This (=This is); F. *C'est.* 3554. *Both* Vpon (*for* On). 3604. *Read* thar; Th. dare. 3626. Th. eftres. 3643. Th. the god of blesse; F. *Diex la beneie.*

**Page 38.** 3660. Th. That so; *omit* so. 3690. Th. grapes be ripe. 3694. *Both* Though. 3697. *Both* rennyng (!). 3698. *Both* come (*absurdly*); *see* l. 2700; *read* to me. 3710. G. herte is; Th. hert is; *read* hertis (=hertes). 3718. *Both* neithir (*for* nor). 3745. *Both* pleyne *or* playne. 3751. *Both* ye; *read* to.

**Page 39.** 3755. Th. with his hete. 3756. *Both insert* me *after* bad. 3774. G. it wille; Th. at wyl. 3851. *Both* verge; *see* 3234.

**Page 40.** 3880. *Both* lye. 3895. *Both* trechours. 3902. *Both* herte I crye. 3907. *Both* lowe; *read* loude. 3928. *Both* must; *read* mot; *supply* take. 3942. *Both* Do; *read* To. 3943. *Both* Thanne (*or* Than) close; F. *Qui les roses clorra entor.*

Page 41. 3994. Th. vilanously; G. vilaynesly. 4021. G. an high; Th. an hye. 4026. *Both* To make.

Page 42. 4089. *Both place* it *after* I.

Page 43. 4181. *Both* of; *read* as. 4188. *Both* Roses; F. *rosiers.* 4194. *Both* who (*for* whiche).

Page 44. 4272. *Both* walketh (!). 4285. *Both* Which (*for* Ther); *giving no sense.* 4291. *Both* except. 4322. *Both* wente aboute (!); *read* wende a bought (a = have); F. *Ges cuidoie avoir achetés* (I weened to have bought them). 4339. G. tiliers; Th. tyllers. 4352. *Both* wente best abouen to haue.

Page 45. 4363. *Both* but; *read* al. *Both* lust. 4365. *Both* is; *read* am. 4366. *Both* charge. 4372. G. wole; Th. wol; *read* wal. 4425. *Both* good.

Page 46. 4467. *Both* her (*for* his). 4476. *Both* preise. 4550. *Both* Loue; *read* lorde. 4556. Th. moche that it; G. mych that.

Page 47. 4561. *Both* yeue good wille; F. *se Diex plaist.* 4587. *Both* ne failid; *I omit* ne. 4617. *Both* not; *read* nist; cf. 4626. 4657. *Both* I; *read* han.

Page 48. 4705. *Both* And through the; *read* A trouthe. 4721. Th. lyke; G. like; *read* sike. 4722. G. trust; Th. truste; (thrust = thirst). *Both* and (*for* in). 4723. *Both* And. 4725. *Both* And. 4731. *Both* Sen.

Page 49. 4755. *Both* by (*for* be). 4764. *Both* That; *read* But. 4793. *Both* euer; *read* er (i.e. before). 4796. *Both* al by partuere. 4799. *Both* greven. 4807. *Both* diffyned here. 4811. G. kned; Th. knedde. 4812. *Both* With. 4823. *Both* engendrure; *see* 6114. 4837. *Both* han her lust. 4846. *Both* what; *for* who.

Page 50. 4858. *Both* their. 4892. G. perell; Th. parel; *but read* tyme (*see* 4891). 4921. *Both* But that if. 4933. *Both* this. 4935. *Both* youthes chambre(*or* chambere); F. *Jonesce sa chamberiere.* 4943. *Both* And mo of (!). 4945. *Both* remembreth. 4948. *Both* him.

Page 51. 4955. *Both* gan. 4960 *Both* neither preise. 5004. Th. stondeth; G. stondith. 5010. *Both* weped. 5021. *Both* he (*for* hir). 5028. *Both* list to loue.

Page 52. 5050. *Both* gouen. 5051. *Both* so; *read* sho (*or* she). 5059. *Both* loued. 5068. *Both* That; *read* But; cf. 4764. 5085. *Both* to; *read* they. 5107. G. herberest hem; Th. herborest. 5116. *Both* the; *read* thy; F. *ton.* 5117. *Both* by thought; F. *ta jonesce.* 5144. G. ay; Th. aye; *read* alway.

Page 53. 5155. *Both* That; F. *Lors.* 5162. *Perhaps* say = assay. 5201 (*rubric*). *Both* Aunsete; *error for* Amistie. 5229. *Both* oo state; *read* oon estate; *see* 5400.

Page 54. 5278. *Both* bothe the. 5283. *Both* this. 5285. *Both* vnyte (!). 5287. *Both* And; *read* A man. 5292. Th. causes; G. cause; *see* 5301, 5523. 5335. *Both* he; cf. 5337, 5341. 5341. *Both* hir; *read* the. 5345. *Both* Thurgh the; *I omit* the.

Page 55. 5360. *Both* greueth so groueth. 5379. *Both* him silf (*or* selfe). 5389. *Both* kepen ay his; *see* 5367. 5393. *I omit* alle *before* his. 5401. *Both* ought to be. 5404. *Both* hath. 5408. G. it; *read* in; Th. *omits.* 5419, 5420, 5425, 5427, 5436. *Both* hym (!); F. *les.* 5433. *Both* to (*for* so).

Page 56. 5452. Th. chere (*for* there); G. cheer (!). 5463. *Both* thus. 5478. *Both* For to shewe; *read* She sheweth. 5486. *Both* affect. 5491. *Both* For al that yeueth here out of drede. 5493. G. late; Th. lette. 5544. *Both* fablyng; F. *cheans* (i.e. falling). 5546. *Both* caste.

Page 57. 5555. *Both* in (*for* is). 5556. *Both* depe (*error for* doþe = doth). 5569. Th. haue you to haue; G. ha yow to ha. 5577. *Both* perceyueth. 5590. G. mavis; Th. mauys; F. *muis* (bushels). 5598. *Both* that (*for* it). 5617. *Both* berne. 5641. *Both* take.

Page 58. 5699. *Both* where ; F. *guerre.* 5701. *Both* shal thogh he hath geten (!), 5713. *Both* Thus is thurst. 5741. G. fy ; Th. fye ; *read* sy. (From *fy* to *sy* means from the first syllable of *fy-sy-cien* (phisician) to the second.)

Page 59. 5755. *Both* shewing. 5761–2. *Supply* it *in* 5761 ; *it occurs after* Himsilf *in* 5762. 5781. *Both* The ; F. *Trois.* 5788. *Both* vnto. 5821. *Both* nyl not.

Page 60. 5855. *Both* kepte ; F. *qui mestrie.* 5860. *Both* that ilke. 5883. *Both* As my nede is. 5900. *Both* That such toures ben ; *I omit* That *and* ben.

Page 61. 5942. *Both* folyly. 5959. *Both* beaute (!). 5960. *Both* That I ; *I omit* That. 5976, *Both* ful dere. 6002. *Both* grede ; *error for* gnede. 6006. *Both* beaute (*as in* 5959). 6009. Th. wol ; G. wole.

Page 62. 6064. *Both* hindreth.

Page 63. 6165. *Both* which ; F. *tex* (such). 6169. *Both* lette. 6174. *Both* nede ; F. *besoignes.* 6205. *I supply this line* ; went his wyle = turns aside his craft. 6206. Th. begylen ; G. bygylyng. 6237. Th. commen ; G. comyn.

Page 64. 6243. *Both* ful many ; *omit* ful. 6256. *Both* maketh the ; *omit* the. 6292. *Both* planten most. 6296. *Both* feyne ; F. *dire.* 6314. *Both insert* shal *before* never. 6317, 6318. Two half-lines lost ; words supplied by Kaluza.

Page 65. 6341. *Both* and reyned (!) ; *for* streyned ; *see* 7366. 6355. *Both* Ioly (!) ; *read* blynde. *I supply* ther. 6372. *A line lost* ; supplied as in Morris's edition ; F. *Si n'en sui mes si receus.* 6378. *Both* I (*for* me). 6407. *Both* not ; *read* yit.

Page 66. 6460. *Both* it is ; F. *Porquoi.* 6466. *Both* woth (!). 6481. *Both* seruest ; F. *sembles.* 6491. *Both* bettir. 6493. *Both* of a pore. 6500. *Both* me a dyne, 6515. *Both* not. 6522. *Both* Hath a soule. 6532. G. thrittene ; Th. thirtene (*wrongly*).

Page 67. 6539. G. beggith ; Th. beggeth. 6542. G. goddis ; Th. goddes. 6565. G. ther ; Th. their. 6569. *Doth* yaf. 6570. G. folkis ; Th. folkes. 6572. *Both* they ; *read* leye ; F. *gisoient.* 6606. *Both* Ben somtyme in ; *see* 6610.

Page 68. 6667. *Both* haue bidde ; *I omit* haue. 6688. Th. hondis ; G. *omits.* 6700. *Both* Yit. 6707. *Both* mendiciens (-ence).

Page 69. 6819. *Both* wrine ; *both* hem ; *both* at. 6823, 6824. *Both* robbyng, gilyng.

Page 70. 6880. Th. Ne wol ; G. Wol ; *read* Nil. 6902, 6907. *Both* burdons. 6911. *Both* burdons ; *but* borders *are meant.* 6925, 6926. *Both* him.

Page 71. 6974. *I omit* a *after* tymes. 7018. G. werrien ; Th. werryen. 7029. *Both* these (*for* thefe), *and* that (*for* or) ; F. *lerres ou.* 7038. *Both* them.

Page 72. 7041. G. cheffis ; Th. cheffes ; F. *fromages.* 7092. Th. We had ben tormented al and some ; (G. *different line, in late hand*) ; F. *Tout eust este tormente.* 7109. G. *has here* l. 7110, *followed by a blank line* ; Th. *has* That they [*read* he] ne might the booke by, *followed by a spurious line.* 7110. Th. To the copye, if hem.

Page 73. 7145. *Both* no. 7159. *Both* vpon. 7173, 7174. I supply these lines by conjecture ; F. *Par Pierre voil le Pape entendre.* 7180. *Both* That (*read* And) ; to (*read* that). 7221. *Both* worthy ; *see* 7104. *Both* mynystres ; *read* maistres.

Page 74. 7316. *Both* slayn ; F. *escorchiés.*

Page 75. 7368. G. gracche ; Th. gratche. 7389. Th. deuysed. 7392. Th. salowe ; *read* falowe. 7394. Th. to ; *read* tho. 7409. Th. And. 7429. Th. humbly. 7432. Th. remeued.

Page 76. 7473. Th. hath hadde the. 7488. Th. doughty (!) ; F. *poudreus.* 7533. Th. she nat herselfe (*wrongly*).

Page 78. 7653. G. wole ; Th. wol. 7662. *Both* wot ; F. *fait.* 7663. Th. we (*for* ye) ; G. *omits.*

# THE MINOR POEMS.

## I. AN A. B. C.

*The MSS. used to form this text are :* C. — MS. Ff. 5. 30 in the Camb. Univ. Library; Jo. = MS. G. 21, in St. John's College, Cambridge ; Gl. = Glasgow MS. Q. 2. 25 ; L. = MS. Laud 740, in the Bodleian Library ; Gg. = MS. Gg. 4. 27, in the Camb. Univ. Library ; F. = Fairfax 16, in the Bodleian ; B. = Bodley 638 ; Sion = Sion Coll. MS. *The text follows closely the first of these ; but is corrected by collation with the others.*

Page 81. 163. *All the MSS. insert* suffred *after* eek ; *probably caught from the line above. Or perhaps* his herte *was caught from the line below : in which case, read* And suffred eek, that Longius him pighte. *And note, that* pighte *should surely be* prighte, i. e. pricked, *as in* Cant. Tales, F 418. Pighte *properly means* pitched. *Hence read :* And suffred eek, that Longius him prighte.

## II. THE COMPLEYNTE UNTO PITE.

*The MSS. are :* Tn. (Tanner 346) ; F. (Fairfax 16) ; B. (Bodley 638) ; Sh. (Shirley's MS., Harl. 78) ; Ff. (Ff. 1. 6, in the Camb. Univ. Library) ; T., *here put for* Trin. (Trin. Coll. Camb. R. 3. 19) ; *also* Ha. (Harl. 7578). *The text follows* F. *mainly.*

Page 82. 21. MSS. was (*for* nas), *twice ; wrongly.* 77. MSS. is (*for* nis).

## III. THE BOOK OF THE DUCHESSE.

*The authorities are only* Th. (Thynne's edition, 1532) ; *and three MSS., viz.* F. (Fairfax 16) ; Tn. (Tanner 346) ; B. (Bodley 638). *I follow* F. *mainly.* B. *and* F. *are much alike.*

Page 83. 6. *All* take no kepe. 14. *All* sorwful (*badly*) ; *read* sory. 23. *All* this.

Page 84. 76. *Not in* Tn. B. ; Th. F. of Alcyone his wyfe. 80. *Not in* Tn. B. ; Th. F. began to yerne ; *read* gan to erme. 82. *Not in* Tn. B. ; Th. F. her thought so (*copied from* 81) ; *read* he dwelte so. 86. *Not in* Tn. B. ; Th. F. That she had this ; *I omit* she, *and supply* alas *from* 87, *where it occurs after* him, *and makes the line too long.* 101. *All* this lady ; *for* she. 107. *All* wepte ; *read* weep. 131. *All* right so (*but* right *belongs to* l. 132).

Page 85. 149. *All* speke right so (*but* right *belongs to* l. 150). 158, 159. *All* noght (*for* nothing). 175. Tn. slepte ; F. slept ; *see* 177. 185. *All* up and axed. 204. *All* am. 206. *I supply* look. 207. *All* for suche ; *read* at whiche. 212. *All* allas ; *read* A.

Page 86. 264. *All insert* quene *after* goddesse. 294. *All* And ; *read* I. 296. *All insert* my *before* slepe. 300. *All* ouer al ; *I omit* ouer. 328. *All* and of king. 329. *All repeat* of king *before* Lamedon. 330. *All insert* And eke *before* of Medea. 331. *All* and of (*for* and). 332. (*Marked by mistake ; so in* MSS.) 334. *All* And ; *read* Of. 342. *All insert* to *before* cold.

Page 87. 348. *All* And I ; *omit* And. 380. *All* and so at ; *omit* so. 443. *All insert* right *before* wonder.

Page 88. 454. *All but* B. *insert* right *before* yong. 473. *All insert* ful *before* wel. 479. *After this line,* Th. *inserts* And thus in sorowe lefte me alone ; *it is spurious.* [Hence there is no line 480.] 498. *All* for ther no ; *and* is (*for* was). 517. *All* had ygret ; *read* grettë ; *see* 503. 548. *Insert* good ; cf. 714, 721.

Page 89. 570. *All* with his ; *omit* his. 571. *All* may no ; *omit* no. 583. *All* so ful ;

*omit* ful. 584. *All* That; *read* Thógh. 586. *For the former* hit, *all have* him; *see* 585. 589. F. B. Thesiphus; Tn. Tesiphus; Th. Tesyphus (*miswritten for* Cesiphus = Sesiphus). 599. F. Th. sorowe (!); Tn. sorov (!); *read* song. 630. Th. Tn. floures; F. B. flourys; *read* flour is.

Page 90. 660. *All* in the; *omit* the. 681. *All* she my fers; *read* my fers she (Koch). 693. *All* For ther; *omit* For. 721. *All* yis parde; *omit* yis. 728. *All* also; *read* als. 732. *All* the quene; *omit* the. 740. *All* no man; *read* noon. 745. F. Tn. Loo she that may be; Th. Howe that may be; *here* she *is an error for* sir; *and* how that may be *for* how may that be; *the edition of* 1550 *has* Howe may that be.

Page 91. 751. *All insert* shalt *after* thou; *omit it* (Koch). 771. *All* I prayde; *omit* I. 779. *All* moste able; *omit* moste. 785. *All* ryght so; *omit* ryght. 802. *All* That tyme and; *omit* That tyme. 805. *All* on a day. 806. *All* ther that I; *omit* that. 823. *All* Than any other planete in heven. 828. *All* and of; *omit* of. 829. *All* and so; *omit* and. 840. *All* counseyl (*a gloss upon* reed, *the original word*). 844. *All* better.

Page 92. 895. *All* But which; *omit* But. 905. Was white; *omit* white (*reserved for* l. 948). 924. *All* swere wel; *omit* wel. 930. *All* never yet; *omit* yet. 942. *All* and pure flat; *omit* pure. 943. *All* or; *read* and.

Page 93. 959. *All* nere pure; *omit* pure. 971. *All* swere wel; *read* sweren. 994. *All* And therto; *omit* And. 997. *All* What harme was; *but* harm *is monosyllabic*. 1020. wolde not; *read* nolde. 1028. *All* into; *read* to. 1040. *All* and my goddesse (!); *read* and my lisse (i. e. consolation). 1051. *All* loked her; *omit* her.

Page 94. 1075. *All* nay trewly I; *omit* trewly. 1099. *All* coude tho; *read* tho coude. 1147. *All* hit not never; *omit* not.

Page 95. 1188. *All* am; *read* nam. 1189. *All* sey right; *omit* right. 1234. *All* to false; *omit* to. 1239. *All* ryght as; *omit* ryght.

Page 96. 1264. *All* thynges; *read* thing. 1322. *All* ther was; *omit* ther.

## IV. THE COMPLEYNT OF MARS.

*The authorities are:* F. (Fairfax 16); Tn. (Tanner 346); Ju. (Julian Notary's edition); Harl. (Harl. 7333); T. (Trin. Coll. Camb., R. 3. 20); Ar. (Arch. Selden B. 24, in the Bodleian Library); Th. (Thynne's edition, 1532). *I follow* F. *mainly*.

Page 98. 89. *All* nygh dreynt; *omit* nygh. 125. *All transpose* hir *and* don.

Page 99. 141. *All* god helpe; *read* helpe god; *and accent* sely *and* Venus *on the latter syllable*.

Page 100. 274. *Most* MSS. *have* to so; T. *omits* to.

## V. THE PARLEMENT OF FOULES.

*The authorities are:* F. (Fairfax 16); Gg. (Gg. 4. 27, Camb. Univ. Library); Trin. (Trin. Coll. Camb. R. 3. 19); Cx. (Caxton's edition); Harl. (Harleian 7333); O. (St. John's Coll., Oxford); Ff. (Ff. 1. 6, Camb. Univ. Library). *I have also consulted* Tn. (Tanner 346); D. (Digby 181); *and others. I follow* F. *mainly; chiefly corrected by* Gg.

Page 101. 39. *All* he; *read* hit; *see* 36, 43.

Page 106. 396. *All* have formed.

Page 109. 613. Gg. reufulles (!); Pepys, rowthfull; *rest* rewful (!).

## VI. A COMPLEINT TO HIS LADY.

*Only two MS. copies :* Sh. (Shirley's MS., Harl. 78); Ph. (Phillipps·9053, now Addit. 34360). *Also* Ed. (edition of 1561). *I follow* Sh. *mainly; but correct many bad spellings ; and supply many words, and even lines. Lines* 124–133 *are in* Ph. *only.*

Page 111. 14. *All* now doth; *I omit* now. 15. *This line is supplied, to rime with* l. 17. 19. Sh. and yit my; *I put* fro *for* yit. 24. *This line supplied ; to rime with* l. 22 ; cf. Compl. of Mars, 189. 25, 26. *Supplied* ; cf. Compl. to Pite, 22, 17 ; Anelida, 307. 33, *I omit* she *before* sleeth. 56. *A line lost* ; *supplied from* Anelida, 181.

Page 112. 59. *Supplied from* Anelida, 182. 68. Sh. euer do. 78. Sh. youre; *read* yow. 79. Sh. wist that were ; *I omit* that. Sh. your hyenesse *(repeated from* 76); *read* yow distresse. 82. *(The dagger should precede* is); Sh. thane is ; *omit* thane. 102. Sh. beon euer ; *read* ever been. 103. *Imperfect ; I supply* here. 104. Sh. But the ; *omit* But. 114. Sh. nought; *read* nothing. 120. Sh. no trewer so verrayly; Ed. no trewer verely *(false rime).* 127. Ph. For wele ; *om.* For. 129. *Not in* Sh. ; Ph. That yow myght offenden. 132. *Not in* Sh. ; Ph. no blisse ; *omit* no. 133. Ph. dwelle withyn.

## VII. ANELIDA AND ARCITE.

*Authorities :* Harl. (Harl. 7333); F. (Fairfax 16) ; Tn. (Tanner 346) ; D. (Digby 181); Cx. (Caxton's edition) ; B. (Bodley 638); Lt. (Longleat MS.) ; Th. (Thynne's edition, 1532). *I follow* F. *mainly.*

Page 114. 91. Th. Tn. Harl. trusteth ; *rest* trusted ; *read* trust (=trusteth). 129. *All* lenger she ; *omit* she.

Page 115. 174. *All* speketh she. 191. *All* un-to ; *read* to.

Page 116. 241. *All* be founde; *but* be *was copied in from* l. 240.

## VIII. CHAUCERS WORDES UNTO ADAM.

*From* T. (Trin. Coll. Camb., R. 3. 20). *Also in* Ed. (edition of 1561).

Page 118. 3. T. thy long lokkes ; *omit* long. 4. T. wryte more truwe ; *omit* more.

## IX. THE FORMER AGE.

*Two copies :* I. (Ii. 3. 21, Camb. Univ. Library); Hh. (Hh. 4. 12, in the same). *Chiefly from* I.

Page 118. 3. I. paied of the ; *omit* the. 11. I. gnodded ; Hh. knoddyd ; *correctly* gnĭden, *pt. pl. of* gnĭden.

Page 119. 23. *Both* No batails trompes ; *omit* batails. 34. I. No places wildnesse ; Hh. No place of wildnesse ; *omit* places, place of. 56. *A line lost ; I supply* it.

## X. FORTUNE.

*Authorities :* I. (Ii. 3. 21, Camb. Univ. Library); A. (Ashmole 59) ; T. (Trin. Coll. Camb.) ; F. (Fairfax 16) ; B. (Bodley 638); H. (Harl. 2251).

## XI. MERCILES BEAUTE.

*One copy :* P. (Pepys 2006). 36. P. this ; *read* ther.

## XII. TO ROSEMOUNDE.

*One copy :* MS. Rawl. Poet. 163 ; leaf 114.

Page 121. 11. semy *(sic)* ; *read* seemly. fynall *(for* final, *a misreading of* smal).

## XIII. TRUTH.

*Authorities:* At. (Addit. 10340); Gg. (Gg. 4. 27, Camb. Univ. Library); E. (Ellesmere MS.); Ct. (Cotton, Cleop. D. 7); T. (Trin. Coll. R. 3. 20); F. (Fairfax 16); *and others. Chiefly from E. The* Envoy *is in* At. *only.*

Page 122. 19. Know thy contree; Harl. F. T. Loke vp on hie. 20. Hold the hye wey; Harl. F. Weyve thy lust.

## XIV. GENTILESSE.

*Authorities:* A. (Ashmole 59); T. (Trin. Coll. R. 3. 20); Harl. (Harl. 7333); Ct. (Cotton, Cleop. D. 7); Ha. (Harl. 7578); Add. (Addit. 22139); Cx. (Caxton's edition). *I follow* Cx. *mainly.*

Page 123. 20. Cx. makes hem eyres, that can hem queme ; A. mathe his heyre him that wol him qweme ; Ct. That maketh his heires hem, &c.

## XV. LAK OF STEDFASTNESSE.

*Authorities:* Harl. (Harl. 7333); T. (Trin. Coll. R. 3. 20); Ct. (Cotton, Cleop. D. 7); F. (Fairfax 16); Add. (Addit. 22139); Bann. (Bannatyne); Th. (Thynne's edition, 1532); *and others. I follow* Ct. *mainly.*

## XVI. LENVOY A SCOGAN.

*Authorities:* Gg. (Gg. 4. 27, Camb. Univ. Library); F. (Fairfax 16); P. (Pepys 2006); Th. (Thynne's edition, 1532). *I follow* F. *mainly.*

## XVII. LENVOY A BUKTON.

*Authorities:* F. (Fairfax 16); Th. (Thynne's edition); Ju. (Julian Notary's edition). *I follow* F. *mainly.*

## XVIII. THE COMPLEYNT OF VENUS.

*Authorities:* T. (Trin. Coll. R. 3. 20); A. (Ashmole 59); Tn. (Tanner 346); F. (Fairfax 16); Ff. (Ff. 1. 6, Camb. Univ. Library); Ar. (Arch. Selden, P. 24); P. (Pepys 2006); Th. (Thynne's edition, 1532). *I follow* F. *mainly.*

N.B. Another authority is the set of three original French Ballades by Otes de Graunson, which Chaucer here imitates.

Page 125. 31. *All* Pley *or* Pleye; *read* Pleyne, *translation of original* French *Plaindre.*

## XIX. THE COMPLEINT TO HIS PURSE.

*Authorities:* F. (Fairfax 16); Harl. (Harl. 7333); Ff. (Ff. 1. 6, Camb. Univ. Library); P. (Pepys 2006); Add. (Addit. 22139); Cx. (Caxton's edition); Th. (Thynne's ed. 1532). *I follow* F. *mainly.*

## XX. PROVERBS.

*Authorities:* F. (Fairfax 16); Ha. (Harl. 7578); Ad. (Addit. 16165). *I follow* F. *mainly.*

Page 126. 1. *All insert* thus *after* these; *I omit* thus.

## XXI. AGAINST WOMEN UNCONSTANT.

*Authorities:* Ct. (Cotton, Cleop. D. 7); F. (Fairfax 16); Ha. (Harl. 3758); Ed. (Stowe's edition, 1561).

Page 127. 17. *All* stondeth; *read* stant.

## XXII. COMPLEINT DAMOURS.

*Authorities :* Harl. (Harl. 7333); F. (Fairfax 16); B. (Bodley 638).
Page 127. 4. *All* right thus ; *omit* right. 9. *All* Ne ; *read* For.
Page 128. 86. *I supply* ther *from* Parl. Foules, 310.

## XXIII. A BALADE OF COMPLEYNT.

*Sole copy :* MS. Addit. 16165, fol. 256, back.

## XXIV. WOMANLY NOBLESSE.

*Sole copy :* MS. Addit. 34360, fol. 21, back.
Page 129. 13. *This line is supplied by conjecture.* 18. MS. for to ; *I omit* for.
25. And thynkith be raison (*too long*). 26. for til do the ; *I omit* the, *and substitute* to
*for* til.

## TRANSLATION OF BOETHIUS.

*Authorities :* C. (Camb. Univ. Library, Ii. 3. 21); A. (Addit. 10340); Ed. (Thynne's
edition, 1532); Cx. (Caxton's edition); Ii. (Ii. 1. 38); &c. *I follow* C. *mainly.*
Page 131. Prose I. 74. Cx. Th. from ; MSS. *omit* from.
Page 133. Pr. III. 63. Cx. Th. Soranos (*as in* Latin text); C. A. Sorans. Met. IV.
12. Cx. Th. leyte ; Ii. leit ; C. A. light.
Page 134. Pr. IV. 97. *This Gloss is misplaced in the* MSS. ; *it comes in before* Textus
*in* l. 87.
Page 144. Pr. III. 66. *I omit* and *before* fulfuldest ; *it is worse than needless.*
Page 153. Pr. VIII. 28. C. A. windinge ; Cx. wyndy ; Lat. *uentosam.*
Page 156. Pr. II. 125. *I supply* nat, *for clearness* ; *it is implied in the following* ne.
Page 188. Pr. VI. 300. *All* the ; *read* that.
Page 190. Met. VI. 38. *Read* bretheth ; Ii. brethith ; A. bredith ; C. Ed. bereth;
Lat. *spirat.*
Page 196. Pr. III. 192. *All* of the whiche (*no sense*) ; *read* than whiche.

## TROILUS AND CRISEYDE.

*Authorities :* Cl. (Campsall MS.); Cp. (Corp. Chr. Coll. Cam. 61); H. (Harl. 2280);
H2. (Harl. 3943); Cm. (Gg. 4. 27, in Camb. Univ. Library); Ed. (edition by Thynne,
1532). *I follow* Cl. *and* Cp. *mainly, which are much alike.*
Page 247. 17. *All* hem ; *read* him ; *see* l. 19.
Page 249. 144. Cl. Cp. H. ben ay I-lyke ; Ed. to ben aye ylike ; H2. bene ylyke ;
Cm. ay ben I-lik ; *read* been y-like ay.
Page 255. 572. Cm. thourrste ; Cp. H. thruste ; Cl. dorste ; H2. Ed. durst; *read*
thurfte.
Page 279. 391. H. truste (*rightly*) ; *rest* trust. *All* to finden (*or* finde); *omit* to.
Page 314. 1109. *All* the est ; *read* th'est.
Page 321. 1586. *All* That she ; *omit* That. 1618. *All* Come *or* Com.

# THE HOUS OF FAME.

*Authorities:* F. (Fairfax 16); B. (Bodley 638); P. (Pepys 2006); Cx. (Caxton's edition) Th. (Thynne's edition, 1532). *I follow* F. *mainly.*

Page 326. 8. *All* why this; *omit* why. 11. why these; *omit* why. 20. *All* is more; *omit* is. 24. *All needlessly insert* the (*or* her) *before* brayn.

Page 327. 88. *All* pouerte; *read* povert; *or elide the final* e. 119. *All* slept, slepte; *read* sleep; *see* 438.

Page 329. 362. *All* But al; *omit* But.

Page 330. 366. *All* in-to; *read* in. 370. MSS. Allas (*or* alas !); *read* Eneas. (*However* Th. *has* him, alas.) 399. Cx. Th. Oenone (*which read as four syllables,* O-e-no-ne *as in* Troil. i. 654).

Page 331. 513. *All* sely; *read* selly (i. e. strange).

Page 332. 557. Cx. Th. P. agast so; *read* so agast. 603. *All* do; *read* done (*gerund*). 613. *All* herke; *read* herkne; *see* 725. 618. *Deficient; I supply* goddesse. 621. *All* lytel (litell) ; *read* lyte.

Page 333. 727. Cx. Th. P. a worthy; F. B. worthe a; *omit* a.

Page 334. 764. *All* herke; *see* 725. 827. F. And that sum place stide; B. Th. And that som styde; (*not in* Cx. P.); *read* And that the mansioun; *see* 754, 831. 830. *All* That; *read* Than.

Page 335. 896. Cx. Th. gan to; *rest* to; *read* gan. 911. *All* token (!); *read* toun; *see* 890.

Page 336. 1007. F. Cx. Th. B. Athalantes; P. athlanntres (cf. Atlante, Ovid, Fasti, v. 83).

Page 337. 1114. F. citee; P. cite (= site); *rest* cyte.

Page 338. 1177. *Supply* craft *from* l. 1178, *where it occurs, after* cast, *in* Cx. Th. P. 1189. B. Rabewynnes; P. Babeweuries; (*all corrupt*). 1210. F. Saten; B. Sate; Cx. Th. Sat; P. Sett; *read* Seten.

Page 339. 1259. Th. pleyeng; *rest* pley. 1271. *All* the (*put for* thee). 1303. F. hat; B. hate; Cx. Th. hackyng; *read* hatte.

Page 340. 1361. F. B. Sit; Cx. P. Sat; *read* Sitte. 1373. *All* wonderly; *see* 1327. 1415. *All* And thus; *omit* And.

Page 341. 1494. F. high the (*for* highthe); Cx. Th. heyght; *read* highte; *see* 744. 1527. *All* into; *read* in.

Page 342. 1570. *All* Upon; *read* Up.

Page 343. 1666. *All* werkes; *read* werk (*and so in* 1701, 1720). 1686. *All* of bawme; *omit* of. 1725. F. B. Th. Al so; *rest* And so; *read* So.

Page 344. 1765. F. B. now let se; *omit* now. 1813. *All* grete, gret; *read* gretest.

Page 345. 1853. F. Th. be noght for; Cx. B. be for; *read* be but for. 1887. *All* thinge, thing; *read* thinges. 1897. *All* wote; *read* wiste; *see* 1901. 1902. *All* dwelled *or* dwellyth. 1907. B. Whithen; *rest* Why than; *read* Whiche. 1940. F. Cx. B. hattes (!); Th. hutches; *read* hottes.

Page 346. 1961, 1962. *All* werres, restes; *read* werre, reste. 1967. *All* and eek of; *omit* and eek (cf. 1968). 1975. *All wrongly write* misgovernement *as one word.* 2009. *All* these; *read* swiche. 2017. F. frot (*for* froit = fruit); B. foot; Cx. Th. swote. 2021. *All* yaf in : *omit* in. 2026. F. B. here anoon (anon); Cx. Th. here; *read* anoon heer.

Page 347. 2049. *All* he (!) ; *read* the other. 2053. *All* And thus *(twice)*; *omit* And *(twice)*. 2061. F. B. forth ryght to ; Cx. forth unto ; Th. streyght to ; *read* forth to. 2076. F. B. Went every mouthe (!) ; Th. Cx. Wente euery tydyng ; *read* Wente every word. 2083. *All* and wente ; *read* hit wente. 2104. B. haue that oon ; F. han on ; Th. have one. *All omit* of.

Page 348. 2152. B. nose ; F. Th. noyse (!). F. an highen (!) ; Th. on hyghen (!) ; B. and yen ; *read* on hyghe *(or* on hye).

## THE LEGEND OF GOOD WOMEN.

*Authorities: for* Text A *(earlier version)* of the Prologue : *sole copy* C. (Gg. 4. 27, in Camb. Univ. Library). *For* Text B *(later version)* of the same, and all the rest : F. (Fairfax 16) ; Tn. (Tanner 346) ; T. (Trin. Coll. Cam. R. 3. 19) ; A. (Arch. Selden. B. 24) ; B. (Bodley 638) ; P. (Pepys 2006) ; Th. (Thynne's edition, 1532) ; *also* C. *(as above)*; Add. (Addit. 9832).

Page 353, col. 1. 135. C. *is here corrupt* ; *it has*—The honour and the humble obeysaunce. *I suggest* They dide honour and humble obeysaunces ; *or read* Yelding honour, &c. *(as in* col. 2). Col. 1 ; 137, 138 ; *imperfect* ; *I fill up the gaps.*

Page 370. 842. *All* renten (rente), *wrongly* ; *read* renden.

Page 374. 1126. *All* honourable ; *read* noble ; *see* 1143, 1210, 1222.

Page 375. 1217. C. bestys wilde ; T. A. P. wild bestys ; *rest* wilde hertes ; *read* hertes wilde. 1238. *All* and becom *(against metre)*; *read* to been.

Page 378. 1463. *All* yle of ; *omit* of.

Page 383. 1879. *All* himself *or* himselfe ; *read* himselve.

Page 387. 2138. *All* was performed ; *read* performed was.

Page 388. 2227. *All* quyte him ; *read* him quyte.

Page 393. 2592. Th. And what ; C. T. That what ; *read* What.

## TREATISE ON THE ASTROLABE.

*Authorities:* A. (Camb. Univ. Library, Dd. 3. 53) ; B. (Bodley, E. Museo 54) ; C. (Rawlinson 1370) ; D. (Ashmole 391) ; E. (Bodley 619) ; F. (Corpus 424) ; G. (Trin. Coll. Cam. R. 15. 18) ; H. (Sloane 314) ; I. (Sloane 291) ; K. (Rawlinson, Misc. 3) ; L. (Addit. 23002) ; M. (St. John's Coll. Cam.) ; N. (Digby 72) ; O. (Ashmole 360) ; P. (Camb. Univ. Library, Dd. 12. 51) ; Q. (Ashmole 393) ; R. (Egerton 2622) ; S. (Addit. 29250). *I follow* A. *mainly* ; *collated with* B. C. I. M. P. *The latter part (after* Part II. § 40) *from* L. M. N. O. P. R. S.

Part 399. § 12. 8, 9. MSS. wrongly transpose *umbra versa*, and *umbra recta* (= *umbra extensa*).

Page 402. § 3. 51, 53. *For* 18, *some* MSS. *have* 12.

Page 403. § 3. 62, 63. *Some* MSS. 8 *and* 2 ; *others*, 9 *and* 10. 64. *Some* 23 ; *others* 10. § 4. 12. C. P. for-seide same degree ; *omit* same. 25. *All* 15 ; *read* 25 ; Lat. text, *viginti quinque.*

Page 409. § 25. 45. Two sets of readings here ; the second set puts the Sun *in* 10 degrees of Leo, with an altitude of 56, and declination, 18 ; difference, 38.

Page 410. § 28. 37. *All* heed (heued) *for* ende, *absurdly* ; cf. 27, 31.

Page 414.  § 40.  8. *Read* for sothe ; *miswritten* for sonne *in* A. B. ; *others vary.*

Page 415.  § 40.  75. A. *omits* of *and* degrees ; *but retains* 3.  93. P. *supplies the last five words, which* A. B. C. E. *omit.*  § 42.  24, 25. *For* 2, M. *has* 6 ; *for* 3, M. *has* 4.

Page 416.  § 44.  20. N. wreten ; *read* wryte.  36. L. N. O. passid ; M. *omits* ; *read* lasse.

Page 417.  § 45.  10. L. I wold wyttyn ; N. Iwyton ; O. wrytoun.


# THE CANTERBURY TALES.

*Authorities :* E. (Ellesmere MS.) ; Hn. (Hengwrt MS.) ; Cm. (Gg. 4. 27, Camb. Univ. Library) ; Cp. (Corpus Chr. Coll. Oxford) ; Pt. (Petworth MS.) ; Ln. (Lansdowne 851) ; Hl. (Harl. 7334). *Also, occasionally,* Dd. (Dd. 4. 24, Camb. Univ. Library) ; Reg. (Reg. 17 D. XV.) ; Add. (Addit. 5140) ; Li. (Lichfield MS.) ; Sl. (Sloane, 1685).

Page 421.  179. Hl. cloysterlees (*see* 180) ; Cm. rekeles ; *rest* recchelees, recheles.

Page 422.  252 *b*, 252 *c* ; *from* Hn. ; *rest omit.*

Page 435.  1290. *All* moste, muste, most ; *read* mot.

Page 443.  1979. Hl. swymbul ; *rest* rumbel.

Page 449.  2420. *All insert* the (*or* thy) *before* victórie ; *it clogs the line.*

Page 458.  3155, 3156. *From* E. Cm. Hl. ; *rest omit.*

Page 462.  3451, 3457 ; astromye *is intentional.*

Page 465.  3721, 3722. *From* E. (*also in old editions*) ; *rest omit.*

Page 466.  3818. Nowélis *is an intentional error* ; *see* 3834.

Page 476.  47. Dd. But ; *rest* That (*wrongly*).

Page 484.  621. *A short line* ; *I insert* ful.

Page 486.  791. Hl. vn-to ; Pt. to ; *rest* til ; *read* un-til.

Page 492.  1163–1190. E. Hn. Cm. *omit* ; *mainly from* Cp.  1189. *Most MSS.* phislyas ; Sloane, phillyas ; Ln. fisleas ; *read* physices, i. e. physices liber.

Page 503.  1995. *Supplied from* MS. Reg. 17 D. xv ; *most MSS. omit this line.*

Page 509.  2252, 2253. *Not in the* MSS., *but necessary* ; *supplied from* 2274 *and* 2280, *which see.*

Page 519.  2623, 2624. *Not in the* MSS. ; *supplied by translating the* French text.

Page 525.  2854. *From* namore *to* god *is not in the* MSS. ; *but is necessary.*

Page 536.  3564. After this line most MSS. insert the stories from NERO to CRESUS (ll. 3653–3956) ; incorrectly.

Page 538.  3657. MSS. North ; *read* South.

Page 541.  3910. Hl. Valirien ; *rest* Valerius ; ed. 1561, Valerie (rightly).

Page 546.  4266. *All* MSS. *insert* herkneth *or* herken *after* But.

Page 582.  1294. After this line most MSS. insert ll. 1307, 1308 ; which are out of place here. MS. Hl. is right.  1307, 1308. Nearly all MSS. omit these lines, having inserted them after l. 1294 above. MS. Hl. is right.

Page 625.  2240. The MSS. omit the word *stories*, leaving sense and metre incomplete.

Page 628.  20. Most MSS. have *pitous*, which will not scan ; but Hn. has *piëtous*, which also occurs in Troilus.

Page 635.  620. *I supply* ne.

Page 653.  277. For ' Valerians,' the MSS. absurdly have 'Cecilies' ; but the Latin original has ' Valeriani.'

Page 664. 1171. E. terned; Cm. ternede; *rest* torned, *wrongly.* So also in l. 1274 below.

Page 674. 10. Chaucer has made a mistake; for *the mones* read *Saturnes.* Libra is the exaltation of Saturn, not of the Moon.

Page 687. 387. Hl. springers; Hn. sprynge; E. Pt. Ln. spryngen. Perhaps 'springes' would be better.

Page 689. 443. *All MSS. transpose* Laban *and* Pharao.

Page 696. 616. Some needful words are here supplied; MSS. omit 'god ... bitraysen.'

Page 707. 858. *Read* busshes; E. Seld. Ln. beautees (!); Cm. beauteis (!); Hl. beautes (!); Pt. bewtees (!).

Page 711. 955. E. Cm. Danyel; *rest* Dauid, *as in the* French *original.*

# GLOSSARIAL INDEX.

———◆———

THE references in this Index are given according to the following scheme.

Poems denoted by Arabic numerals are Minor Poems. Thus, under 'Abaved,' the reference '3. 614' means Minor Poem no. 3, line 614, or l. 614 of the Book of the Duchesse. The letter 'R.' refers to the Romaunt of the Rose, Fragment A, in pp. 1–18; the rest of the Poem, not being Chaucer's, is indexed separately. Thus 'R. 163' means l. 163 of the Romaunt.

The five books of Boethius are denoted by B 1, B 2, B 3, B 4, B 5, respectively; and the 'prose' and 'metrical' sections are denoted by 'p' and 'm.' Thus, under 'Abaissen,' the reference 'B 4. p 7. 81' means 'Boethius, bk. iv. prose 7, line 81.' The five books of Troilus are denoted by T. i., T. ii., T. iii., T. iv., and T. v. Thus 'T. iii. 1233' means 'Troilus, bk. iii., line 1233.'

The House of Fame and the Legend of Good Women are denoted by 'HF.' and 'L.' respectively. If, in the latter case, the italic letter 'a' follows the number of the line, the reference is to the earlier (or A-text) of the Prologue to the Legend. Thus 'HF. 865' means 'House of Fame, line 865.' Again, 'L. 2075' means 'Legend of Good Women, line 2075;' and 'L. 200 a' means 'Legend, &c., line 200 of the text in the left-hand column.'

The Prologue and the two books of the Treatise on the Astrolabe are denoted, respectively, by 'A. pr.,' 'A. i.,' and 'A. ii.' Thus the reference 'A. ii. 10. 8' means 'Astrolabe, bk. ii. § 10, line 8;' and 'A. pr. 10' means 'Astrolabe, prologue, line 10.'

References to the Canterbury Tales are known by the use of the letters A, B, C, D, E, F, G, H, and I, which are used to denote the various Groups into which the Tales are divided. In this case, 'A' is never followed by a full stop or by Roman numerals, as when the 'Astrolabe' is referred to; and such a reference as 'B 5,' meaning line 5 of Group B, is quite distinct from 'B 5. p 1. 1,' where 'B 5' means bk. v. of Boethius, and is invariably accompanied by the 'p' or 'm' denoting the 'prose' or 'metre.'

**Summary of the Minor Poems.** The Minor Poems are all numbered, viz. 1 (ABC.); 2 (Compleynte unto Pite); 3 (Book of the Duchesse); 4 (Mars); 5 (Parlement of Foules); 6 (Compleint to his Lady); 7 (Anelida); 8 (Wordes to Adam); 9 (Former Age); 10 (Fortune); 11 (Merciless Beauty); 12 (To Rosemounde); 13 (Truth); 14 (Gentilesse); 15 (Lak of Stedfastnesse); 16 (Envoy to Scogan); 17 (Envoy to Bukton); 18 (Venus); 19 (To his Purse); 20 (Proverbs); 21 (Against Women Unconstant); 22 (Amorous Complaint); 23 (Balade of Compleynt); 24 (Womanly Noblesse).

**Alphabetically,** the references are to A (Group A of Cant. Tales); A. (Astrolabe); B (Group B of C. T.); B 1 ... B 5 (Boethius, books 1 to 5); C, D, E, F, G, H, I (Groups C to I of C. T.); HF. (House of Fame); L. (Legend of Good Women); R. (Romaunt of the Rose); T. i. ... T. v (Troilus, books 1 to 5). The Minor Poems, numbered 1 to 24, are given above.

N.B. Words containing *ay, ey, oy, aw, ew, ow,* are sometimes entered as if spelt with *ai, ei, oi, au, eu, ow,* respectively.

**Abbreviations.** Besides *s.*, *adj.*, and *adv.*, for *substantive, adjective, adverb,* the following are used in a special sense :—*v.*, a verb in the infinitive mood ; *ger.*, gerund ; *pr. s.*, present tense, 3rd person singular ; *pr. pl.*, present tense, 3rd person plural. Other persons are denoted by the figures 1 or 2.

Fragments B and C of the 'Romaunt' are glossed in a separate Index.

## A.

**A,** the first letter of the alphabet, T. i. 171 ; the letter A, A 161.

**A,** *indef. art.* a, A 24, &c. ; *al a,* the whole of a, E 1165 ; one, D 1396 ; one and the same, 21. 5 ; about, some, L. 2075.

**A,** *prep.* on, on (the), in, for ; A-nighte, by night, B 3758 ; A-dayes, a-days, E 1164 ; A-morwe, on the morrow, A 822 ; A three, in three, A 2934 ; A goddes half, ' on God's side,' in God's name, D 50 ; A goddes name, in God's name, A 854.

**A !** *int.* ah ! 3. 213.

**A ! ha !** *interj.* aha ! T. i. 868.

**Abaissen,** *ger.* to be dismayed, B 4. p 7. 81 ; *pp.* amazed, spell-bound, abashed, cast down, disconcerted, E 317, 1108.

**Abak,** *adv.* backwards, A 3736 ; aback, back, L. 864.

**Abakward,** *adv.* backward, B 3. m 12. 66.

**Abandoune,** *v.* devote, I 713 ; *pr. s.* abandons, B 2767.

**Abasshen,** *v.* fear, be abashed, R. 1552 ; *pp.* abashed, confused, confounded, disconcerted, 5. 447 ; R. 805, &c.

**Abate,** *v.* lower, put down, B 3780 ; depreciate, R. 286 ; 2 *pr. s. subj.* subtract, A. ii. 10. 8 ; *pp.* enfeebled, B 3. p 5. 52 ; put down, I 191.

**Abaved,** *pp.* confounded, disconcerted, 3. 614.

**Abayst** ; see **Abaissen.**

**Abc.,** alphabet, A. i. 11. 3.

**A-bedde,** in bed, T. i. 915.

**Abegge,** *v.* pay for it, A 3938.   A Kentish form. See **Abeye, Abye.**

**A-begged,** a-begging, F 1580.

**Abet,** *s.* abetting, aid, T. ii. 357.

**Abeye,** *v.* pay for, C 100. See **Abye.**

**Abiden, Abit** ; see **Abyde.**

**Abite,** *s.* habit, dress, L. 146 *a.*

**A-blakeberied** ; see **Blakeberied.**

**Able,** *adj.* capable, 3. 786 ; fit, suitable, adapted, A 167 ; fit, L. 320 ; fit for, 3. 779 ; deemed deserving, 1. 184 ; fitting, R. 986.

**Ablinge,** *pr. pt.* enabling, lifting, B 3. m 9. 37 ; fitting, B 1. m 6. 19.

**Abodes,** *pl. of* Abood, *s.*

**Aboghte, Aboght** ; see **Abye.**

**Abood,** *s.* delay, A 965 ; tarrying, T. v.

1307 ; abiding, continuance, HF. 1963 ; *pl.* delays, T. iii. 854.

**Abood,** *pt. s. of* Abyde.

**Aboute,** *prep.* about, round, throughout, round about, near.

**Aboute,** *adv.* about, engaged in, T. v. 1645 ; in due order, in turn, A 890 ; around, here and there ; *been a.,* go about, endeavour, A 1142.

**Aboven,** *prep.* above.

**Abregge,** *ger.* to abridge, shorten, T. iii. 262 ; A. with thy peynes, to shorten thy pains with, T. iv. 426.

**Abregginge,** *s.* abridging, B 5. p 1. 57 ; diminishing, I 568.

**A-breyde,** *v.* awake, T. iii. 1113 ; come to my senses, HF. 559 ; Abrayd, *pt. s. (strong form),* woke up, started up, 3. 192 ; Abreyd, 1 *pt. s.* started from sleep, HF. 110 ; Abrayde, *pt. s. (weak form),* started, B 4198 ; Abreyde, awoke, T. i. 724.

**Abroche,** *v.* broach, D 177.

**Absénte,** 2 *pr. pl. subj.* absent yourself, 1. 43.

**Abusioun,** *s.* abuse, absurdity, T. iv. 990 ; deceit, B 214 ; a shameful thing, scandal, T. iv. 1060.

**Abyden,** *v.* abide, await, 1. 131 ; wait for, HF. 1086 ; be still, withdraw, F 1522 ; *pr. s.* awaits, B 2175 ; dwells, T. ii. 987 ; Abit, *pr. s.* waits for, T. i. 1091 ; abides, G 1175 ; *imp. s.* stay, wait, A 3129 ; *imp. pl.* B 1175 ; *pres. pt.* E 757 ; Abood, *pt. s.* awaited, T. iv. 156 ; stopped, HF. 1062 ; expected, 3. 247 ; Abiden, *pt. pl.* abode, T. i. 474 ; Abiden, *pp.* waited, B 3. p 9. 191.

**Abydinge,** *s.* expectation, B 2. p 3. 66.

**Abye,** *v.* pay for, A 4393 ; *pr. pl.* undergo, B 4. p 4. 86 ; Aboughte, *pt. s.* paid for, T. v. 1756 ; suffered for, A 2303 ; Aboght, *pp.* paid for, L. 2483 ; purchased, 18. 37 ; bought dearly, L. 1387 ; atoned for, A 3100. See **Abegge, Abeye.**

**A-caterwawed,** a-caterwauling, D 354.

**Accésse,** *s.* feverish attack, T. ii. 1315.

**Accident,** *s.* that which is accidental, T. iv. 1505 ; incident, T. iii. 918 ; accidental occurrence, HF. 1976 ; unusual appearance, E 607 ; outward appearance (see note), C 539.

**Accidie,** *s.* sloth, I 388.

**Accioun,** *s.* action, i. e. accusation, 1. 20.

Accomplice, v. accomplish, A 2864.

Accord, s. agreement, B 2988; harmony, B 4069; peace, I 992. See Acord.

Accordaunce, s. concord, harmony, R. 496.

Accordaunt, adj. suitable, B 4026.

Accorde, v. agree; pr. s. beseems, L. 2583. See Acorde.

Accuseth, pr. s. reveals, R. 1591.

Accusement, s. accusation (of her), T. iv. 556.

Accusour, s. revealer, T. iii. 1450.

Achát, s. buying, purchase, A 571.

Achátours, pl. buyers, caterers, A 568.

Ache, s. ache, T. iv. 728.

A-chekked, pp. checked, hindered, HF. 2093.

Acheve, v. achieve, L. 1614.

Achoken, v. choke, stifle; pp. L. 2008.

Acloyeth, pr. s. overburdens, 5. 517.

A-compas, adv. in a circle, L. 300.

Acomplisshe, pr. s. subj. fulfil, comprehend, B 3. p 10. 179.

Acord, s. agreement, 5. 371; concord, 5. 381, 668; accord, 3. 316; in a., in tune, 5. 197; al of oon a., in tune, 3. 305. See Accord.

Acordable, adj. harmonious, B 2. m 8. 23.

Acordaunce, s. concord, B 2. m 8. 14.

Acordaunt, adj. suitable, A 37, 3363; A. to, in harmony with, 5. 203.

Acorde, v. accord, grant, allow, agree, concern; pt. s. suited, A 244; pt. pl. agreed, L. 168; pres. part. agreeing, B 1737; pp. agreed, A 818.

Acorse, 1 pr. s. curse, T. iv. 839.

Acounte, v. consider, B 3591; pt. s. valued, cared, 3. 1237; 2 pt. s. didst reckon, B 2. p 5. 113.

Acountinge, s. reckoning, calculation.

Acoyede, pt. s. caressed, B 2. p 3. 73.

Acquitance, s. release, A 4411; deed of release, A 3327.

Acquyte, v. acquit, D 1599.

Acurse, v. curse, T. iii. 1072.

Acused, pt. s. blamed, T. ii. 1081.

Acustomaunce, s. system of habits, habitual method of life, HF. 28; had of a., was accustomed, B 3701.

Adamant, s. adamant, A 1990; loadstone, magnet, R. 1182.

Adawe, v. awake, recover, T. iii. 1120.

A-day, in the day, T. ii. 60.

Adding, s. (the) addition, A. ii. 41. 16.

Adjeccioun, s. addition, B 5. p 6. 212.

A-doun, adv. downwards, down, L. 178; down below, HF. 889; below, H 105; at the bottom, G 779.

Adrad, pp. afraid, A 605; Adred, 3. 1190.

Adressinge, s. directing, B 4. p 5. 101.

Adversarie, adj. hostile, I 697.

Advertence, s. attention, heed, T. iv. 698.

Advócacýes, pl. pleas, T. ii. 1469.

Advocats, pl. advocates (in which the t is mute), C 291.

Afer, adv. afar, HF. 1215.

A-fère, on fire, T. i. 229.

A-fered, pp. afraid, affrighted, T. i. 974; Aferd, A 628.

Affectis, pl. desires, T. iii. 1391.

Affermed, pp. agreed upon, L. 790; established, A 2349.

Affiance, s. trust, B 1330.

Afforced, pp. forced, I 974.

Affray, s. fray, quarrel, D 2156; terror, B 1137; fright, 4. 214; dread, 7. 334.

Affrayeth, pr. s. arouses, excites, R. 91; pp. frightened, afraid, B 563; scared, B 4468; roused, 3. 296.

Affyle, v. file, i. e. render smooth, A 712.

Afor-yeyn, prep. over against, T. ii. 1188.

Afounde, v. founder, perish, 12. 21.

Afrayed, adj. scared, distracted, R. 154.

Afright, pp. affrighted, B 4085.

After, prep. according to; in expectation of, for, B 467; to get, A 525; according as, L. 575; after, i. e. to fetch, L 1130; towards, A 136; in accordance with, 8. 4; by inheritance from, L. 1072; A. as, according as, 5. 216; A. oon, alike, A. 1781; A. me, according to my command, E 327; A. the yeer, according to the season of the year, F 47; A. that, according as, T. ii. 1347.

A-fyre, on fire, D 726; 1. 94; A-fère, T. i. 229.

Again, prep. when exposed to, L. 2426; Agayn, against, B 580; towards, A 2680; (so as) to meet, R. 785; opposite to, R. 1577; exposed to, H 110; contrary to, F 748; just before, B 4268; near, G 1279; to meet, B 391; in comparison with, L. 189; Ageyn, against, A 66; compared with, R. 1011; turned towards, L. 48.

Agains, prep. against, contrary to, in answer to, instead of, before, in presence of, to meet, near to; against, near; against, B 3754.

A-game, adv. in play, in jest, in mockery, in sport, 4. 277.

Agaste, ger. to terrify, T. ii. 901; pr. s. deters, frightens, B 4. p 6. 323; pt. s. frightened, L. 1221; pt. s. refl. was affrighted, A 2424; pp. scared, frightened, terrified, A 2931; aghast, B 4079; afraid, A 4267.

**Agayn-ward**, *adv.* backward, at the point of return, A. i. 17. 14 ; back again, B 441.

**Ages**, *pl.* times, periods, B 3177.

**Agilten**, *v.* do wrong, L. 436 ; *pt. s.* did offence, D 392 ; wrongly committed, L. 2385 ; I *pt. s.* wronged, HF. 329 ; offended, T. iii. 840 ; *pr. s. subj.* (if he) offend, I 150 ; *pp.* offended, I. 122 ; sinned, T. v. 1684.

**Agon**, *v.* to go away ; Ago, *pp.* gone away, T. v. 1054 ; gone, F 1204 ; passed away, A 2802 ; past, L. 1766 ; dead, L. 916 ; *to ben ago*, to be off, 5. 465 ; Agon, *pp.* departed, A 1276 ; gone away, C 810 ; past, C 246 ; *nat longe a. is*, it is not long ago, D 9 ; passed away, A 1782 ; dead, E 631 ; ago, B 1841.

**Agreable**, *adj.* pleasing, HF. 1097 : -es, *pl.* pleasant, B 3. m 2. 31.

**Agreablely**, *adv.* complacently, B 2. p 4. 140.

**Agreabletee**, *s.* equability, B 2. p 4. 127.

**A-greef**, in dudgeon, lit. ' in grief,' T. iii. 862 ; sadly, T. iv. 613 ; amiss, 5. 543 ; in dudgeon, B 4083.

**Agregge**, *v.* aggravate ; *pr. s.* I 960 ; *pr. pl.* I 892 ; *pt. pl.* aggravated, B 2209.

**Agreved**, *pp.* angry, A 2057 ; vexed, L. 345 ; aggrieved, E 500.

**Agrief** ; see **Agreef**.

**Agrisen**, **Agroos** ; see **Agrysen**.

**Agroted**, *pp.* surfeited, cloyed, L. 2454.

**Agrysen**, *v.* shudder, tremble, feel terror, B 1. p 3. 22 ; *v.* feel terror, H F. 210 ; 2 *pr. s.* dreadest, B 2. p 1. 71 ; *pr. s.* trembles, shivers, B 1. m 6. 11 ; Agròòs, *pt. s.* shuddered, was terrified, became frightened, T. ii. 930 ; A-grisen, *pp.* filled with dread, B 3. p 1. 18.

**Agu**, *s.* ague, B 4150.

**Aguiler**, *s.* needle-case, R. 98.

**A-heigh**, *adv.* aloft.

**Ajuged**, *pp.* ; *a. biforn*, prejudged, B 1. p 4. 109.

**Ake**, *v.* ache, T. ii. 549 ; *pr. pl.* B 2113.

**Aketoun**, *s.* a short sleeveless tunic, worn under the hauberk, B 2050.

**Akinge**, *s.* pain, T. i. 1088.

**Aknowe**, *pp.* conscious ; *am aknowe*, I acknowledge, B 1. p 4. 169.

**Akornes**, *s. pl.* fruits, B 4. m 3. 28.

**Al**, *adj.* all, A 10 ; Alle, *pl.* all, A 26, 53 ; Al, every, R. 1586 ; *as s.* everything, T. iii. 1764 ; *al a*, the whole of a, A 854 ; *and al*, and all, 3. 116 ; *at al*, in every respect, wholly, C 633 ; at all, D 1078 ; *al day*, all the day, 3. 1105 :—Al, *adv.* quite, entirely, altogether, 5. 540 ; all over, R. 840 ; *al on highte*, quite aloud, A 1784 ; *al by oon assent*, quite with one accord, 5. 557 :—Al, *conj.* although, HF. 1740 ; whether, G 839 ; *al be*, although, albeit, 4. 274 ; *al be that*, although, 5. 8 :—Al and som, the whole matter (collectively and severally), D 91 ; Al and somme, each and all, all, the whole, 7. 26 ; Al and som, 5. 650 ; Alle and some, one and all, A 3136 ; Al only, *adv.* merely, simply, 2. 62 ; Al so, so, E 1226 ; Al thing, everything, R. 53 ; Al thus, exactly thus, 5. 30. See Alle.

**Al**, *s.* awl, 13. 11. See **Oules**.

**Alambyk** (álambiik), *s.* alembic, T. iv. 520 ; *pl.* G 794.

**Alaunts**, *pl.* dogs of a huge size, A 2148.

**Alayes**, *s. pl.* alloy, E 1167.

**Al-be-it**, although, L. 1363.

**Albificacioun**, *s.* albefaction, whitening, G 805.

**Alday**, **Al-day**, *adv.* continually, A 1168 ; always, L. 1250 ; everyday, at any time, 4. 237.

**Alder**, *gen. pl.* of all ; *oure alder*, of us all, 1. 84. See **Aller**.

**Alder-best**, *adv.* best of all, 3. 87. See **Aller**.

**Alderbeste**, *adj.* best of all, 3. 246.

**Alderfaireste**, *adj. fem. def.* fairest of all, 3. 1050.

**Alderfirst**, *adv.* first of all, B 2393 ; in the first place, R. 1000 ; for the first time, B 1. p 3. 25.

**Alderfirste**, *adj.* first of all, T. iii. 97.

**Alderlast**, *adv.* lastly, R. 449.

**Alder-lest**, least of all, T. i. 604.

**Alderlevest**, dearest of all, T. iii. 239.

**Alderman**, *s.* the head of a guild, A 372.

**Aldermost**, *adv.* most of all, T. i. 152.

**Alder-next**, *adv.* nearest of all, next, 5. 244.

**Alderwysest**, *adj. pl.* the wisest of all, T. i. 247.

**Ale and breed**, drink and meat, B 2062.

**Alemandres**, *pl.* almond-trees, R. 1363.

**Alembykes**, *pl.* alembics, G 794.

**Alestake**, *s.* ale-stake, i. e. a horizontal stake or short pole projecting from an ale-house to support a sign or bush, A 667.

**Aley**, *s.* an alley, B 1758 ; *pl.* walks, E 2324.

**Aleys,** *s. pl.* service-berries, berries of the service-tree, R. 1377.

**Algate,** *adv.* always, A 571; at any rate, 3. 887; nevertheless, L. 238; in any case, T. ii. 964; all the same, D 588; at all hazards, HF. 943.

**Algates,** *adv.* in every way, 22. 43; by all means, D 1514; at any rate, in any case, 3. 1171; wholly, F 246; nevertheless, B 2222; all the same, B 520.

**Aliene,** *v.* alienate, B 1. p 6. 60.

**Al-if,** even if, T. iii. 398.

**Alkamistre,** *s.* alchemist, G 1204.

**Alle,** *dat. s. and pl. of* Al; *at alle,* in every case, 4. 36; *in alle,* in any case, 3. 141; Alle, *pl.* all (of you), T. ii. 402. See **Al, Aller.**

**Allegeaunce,** *s.* alleviation, 24. 22.

**Allegged,** *pp.* allayed, B 4. p 4. 12.

**Aller,** of all, *gen. pl. of* Al; *our aller,* of us all, A 823; *hir aller,* of them all, A 586.

**Alliaunce,** *s.* kindred, 1. 58; espousal, E 357.

**Allone,** *adj.* alone, 4. 141; *lat me a.,* let me alone, i. e. trust to me, T. iii. 413.

**Allow,** 1 *p. s. pr.* (I) approve, (I) applaud, F 676.

**Allye,** *s.* relative, B 3593.

**Allyen,** *ger.* to ally myself, E 1414; *pp.* allied, 2. 65; provided with friendly aid, B 3720.

**Almesse,** *s.* alms, B 168; *pl.* almsdoings, I 1030.

**Almicanteras,** *s. pl.* small circles of declination (in the celestial sphere), A. i. 18. 2, 8.

**Almury,** *s.* the 'denticle' or tooth-like point or pointer situate on the Rete near the 'head' of Capricorn, A. i. 23. 1.

**Aloes,** *pl.* aloe, *in comp.* ligne-aloes, T. iv. 1137. (*Aloes* is a pl., not a gen. case).

**A-lofte,** *adv.* on high, T. v. 259.

**A-londe,** *adv.* on land, ashore, L. 2166; *him were lever a-l.,* he would rather be on land, L. 2413.

**Along on,** along of, owing to, T. iii. 783.

**Al-only,** *adv.* solely, T. v. 1779.

**Aloon,** *adj.* alone; *her aloon,* all by herself, E. 2478.

**Alose,** *v.* commend, T. iv. 1473.

**Al-outerly,** *adv.* entirely, absolutely, 3. 1244; All-utterly, HF. 296.

**Alpes,** *pl.* bull-finches, R. 658.

**Also, Al-so,** *adv.* and *conj.* as, R. 212, 1122; *adv.* so, A 3104; Alswa, also (Northern), A 4085; A. many, as many, L. 528; A. muche as, as much as, D 2134; Als, also,

besides, 3. 728; as, B 2850; *frequently used in expressing a wish,* 4. 267.

**Altercacioun,** *s.* altercation, dispute, B 4427.

**Alther-fairest,** *adj. superl.* fairest of all, R. 625.

**Alther-fastest,** *adv. sup.* as fast as possible, HF. 2131.

**Altherfirst,** *adv,* first of all, at first, HF. 1368.

**Alther-firste,** *adj.* first of all, 3. 1173.

**Altitude,** *s.* the elevation of a celestial object above the horizon, measured along a vertical arc, A. pr. 60.

**Al-utterly;** see **Al-outerly.**

**Alwey,** *adv.* always, ceaselessly, all the while, A 185.

**Alyne,** *adv.* in an exact line, A. ii. 38. 27.

**Am,** am; *in phr.* it am I; it is I, B 1109.

**Amadrides,** *s. pl.* hamadryads, A 2928.

**Amalgaming.** *s.* the formation of an amalgam, G 771.

**A-mayed,** *pp.* dismayed, T. i. 648.

**Ambages,** *pl.* ambiguous words, T. v. 897.

**Ambel,** *s.* amble; *an a.,* in an amble, at an ambling pace, B 2075.

**Ambes as,** double aces, B 124.

**Amblere,** *s.* an ambling nag, A 469.

**Ameled,** *pp.* enamelled, R. 1080.

**Amenden,** *v.* make amends, A 3074; to surpass in demeanour, F 97; *pr. s. subj.* may (He) amend, D 1810; *pt. s.* improved, R. 1427; did good, 3. 1102; *pp.* improved, B 4048; remedied, D 1097; surpassed, B 3444.

**Amendement,** *s.* amends, A 4185.

**Amenuse,** *ger.* to lessen, 1496; *v.* diminish, I 360; *pr. s.* diminishes, I 359; becomes less, A. i. 21. 76.

**Amerciments,** *s. pl.* fines, exactions, I 752.

**Amesureth,** *pr. s.* measures, B 2. p 1. 95.

**Ameved,** *pt. s.* moved, changed; *nought a.,* changed not, altered not, E 498; Amoeved, *pp.* perturbed, I 670.

**Amiable,** *adj.* kind, B 2168; courteous, I 629; kindly, R. 1226.

**A-midde,** *adv.* in the midst, R. 147.

**Amidde,** *prep.* amid, in the midst of, F 409.

**Amiddes,** *adv.* in the midst, 5. 277.

**A-middes,** *prep.* in the midst of, A. i. 18. 4; in the middle, A 2009.

**Amis,** *adv.* amiss, 3. 1141; wrong, L. 1291; wrongly, B 3370; *seyde amis,* gave an unwelcome answer, 5. 446.

**Amoeve;** see **Ameve.**

Amonesteth, *pr. s.* admonishes, I 76; recommends, B 2484.

Amonestinge, *s.* admonition, I 518.

Among, *adv.* as well, T. iii. 1816; all the while, 3. 298.

Amonges, *adv.* sometimes, variously, B 2. p 1. 119.

Amonges, *prep.* amongst, A 759.

Amonicioun, *s.* pointing out, B 1. p 4. 10.

Amorettes, *pl.* love-knots, R. 892.

*Amor vincit omnia,* love conquers all, A 162.

Amorwe, A-morwe, on the morrow, A 822, 1621; in the morning, 3. 1103.

Amounteth, *pr. s.* means, A 2362; amounts to, F 108.

Amphibologyes, *pl.* ambiguities, T. iv. 1406.

Amy, *s.* friend, C 318.

An, a, A 575; An eighte busshels, a quantity equal to eight bushels, C 771.

An, *prep.* on; An heigh, on high, E 2326.

Ancille, *s.* handmaiden, 1. 109.

Ancre, *s.* anchor, 10. 38; Anker, L. 2501.

And, *conj.* if, 6. 112; L. 217.

Anes, *adv.* once (Northern), A 4074.

Angle, *s.* angle (a technical term in astrology), B 304; angular distance from the meridian, A. ii. 4. 48.

Angle-hook, *s.* fish-hook, 4. 238.

Angre, *s.* anguish, R. 320.

Anguissh, *s.* anxiety, B 3. p 3. 55.

Anguissheth, *pr. s.* wounds, pains, B 3. m 7. 1.

Anguissous, *adj.* distressed, R. 520; sorry, I 304; distressful, T. iii. 816.

Anhange, *ger.* to hang, C 259; *pp.* B 3945.

Anientissed, *pp.* brought to naught, B 2438.

A-night, in the night, A 1042; at night, D 1827.

A-nightes, *adv.* by night, R. 18.

Anlas, *s.* a short, two-edged knife or dagger, broad at the hilt and tapering to the point, formerly worn at the girdle, A 357.

Annexed, *pp.* tied, 2. 72; attached, C 482,

*Anni collecti,* collected years, A. ii. 44. 27. When a table contains quantities denoting the change in a planet's place during round periods of years, such as 20, 40, or 60 years, such a change is entered undered under the heading *Anni Collecti.*

*Anni expansi,* expanse years, A. ii. 44. 26. When a table contains quantities denoting the change in a planet's place

during only a few years, viz. from 1 to 19 years, such changes are entered separately under the headings 1, 2, 3, &c., years, which are designated the *expanse* (or separate) years.

*Annis collectis et expansis,* the collected years and expanse years, A. ii. 45. 18. See above.

Annueleer, *s.* a priest who received annual payments, a chaplain, G 1012.

Annunciat, *pp.* pre-announced, i. e. whose birth was foretold, B 3205.

Anon, *adv.* anon, immediately, at once, A 32, 748.

Anon-right, *adv.* immediately, L. 115, 1503.

Anon-rightes, *adv.* immediately, A 3480.

Anoy, *s.* vexation, T. iv. 845; trouble, B 1320; torture, B 3. m 12. 25; sadness, I 678, 680; *pl.* troubles, I 518.

Anoye, *v.* annoy, vex, T. iv. 1304; *pr. s.* annoys, vexes, B 2234; gives offence, 5. 518; does harm, F 875; *impers.* it vexes, G 1036; *pr. pl.* harm, B 2187; *imp. pl.* injure ye, B 494; *pp.* displeased, D 1848; wearied, I 726; peevish, I 1051.

Anoyful, *adj.* annoying, tiresome, B 2222.

Anoyous, *adj.* annoying, tedious, B 2433 : disagreeable, B 2235.

Answere, *v.* answer, D 1077; *a. of,* answer for, be responsible for, L. 2212; be suitable for, B 4. p 3. 69.

Answering, *s.* answer, E 512.

Autartik, *adj.* southern, A. ii. 25. 11.

Antem, *s.* anthem, B 1850.

Antiphoner, *s.* anthem-book, B 1709.

Antony, fyr of seint, erysipelas, I 427.

Anvelt, *s.* anvil, 3. 1165.

Any-thing, at all, in any degree, T. i. 848.

Aornement, *s.* adornment, I 432.

Apaire ; see Apeiren.

Apalled, *pp.* vapid, I 723; weakened, A 3053; pale, F 365; languid, B 1292.

Aparayles, *s. pl.* ornaments, B 2. p 4. 69. (Lat. *ornamentis.*)

Aparaile, *v.* apparel, D 343; prepare, L. 2473; Apparaillen, *v.* prepare, B 2532; *pr. s.* endues, I 462; *imp. s.* prepare, B 2534.

Aparailements, *s. pl.* ornaments, B 2. p. 5. 181.

Aparceyve ; see Aperceive.

Apassed, *pp.* passed away, B 2. p 5. 35.

Apaye, *v.* to satisfy; *pp.* satisfied, T. v. 1249; pleased, T. iii. 421; *yvel a.,* ill pleased, L. 80; E 1052.

Apayre; see Apeiren.

Apayse; see Apese.

Ape, *s.* ape, HF. 1212; dupe, A 3389; *pl.* dupes, T. i. 913.

Apeiren, *ger.* to injure, impair, A 3147; *v.* I 1079; grow worse, HF. 756; 1 *pr. pl.* perish, T. ii. 329; *pp.* impaired, B 1. p 5. 67; injured, T. i. 38.

Aperceive, *v.* perceive, E 600; Apárceyve, T. iv. 656; *pr. s.* discerns, I 294.

Aperceyvinges, *pl.* perceptions, observations, F 286.

Apert, *adj.* manifest, I 649.

Apert, *adv.* openly, F 531.

Apertenant, *adj.* belonging to, such as belongs to, 2. 70; suitable, E 1010.

Aperteneth, *pr. s. impers.* appertains, B 2171; *pr. pl.* I 83; *pres. pt.* belonging, G 785.

Apertly, *adv.* openly; clearly, I 294.

Apese, Apeise, *v.* appease, pacify; E 433; *imp. pl.* mitigate, 4. 10; *pr. s. refl.* is pacified, B 3051; 2 *pr. pl.* T. iii. 22; *pt. s.* B 2290; *pp.* appeased, T. i. 250.

Apeyre; see Apeiren.

Apeyse; see Apese.

Apose; see Appose.

Apotecarie, *s.* apothecary, B 4138; *pl.* preparers of medicines, A 425.

Appalled; see Apalle.

Apparaunte, *adj. pl.* apparent, manifest, R. 5.

Apparence, *s.* appearance, F 218; seeming, HF. 265; apparition, F 1602; false show, F 1157; *pl.* apparitions, F 1140.

Appese; see Apese.

Appetyt, *s.* desire, A 1680.

Appetyteth, *pr. s.* seeks to have, desires, L. 1582.

Applyen, *v.* be attached to, B 5. p 4. 14.

Apposed, *pt. s.* questioned, G 363; *pp.* opposed, alleged, B 1. p 5. 54.

Apprentys, *adj.* unskilled, as novices, R. 687.

Appreved, *pp.* approved, E 1349.

Appropred, *pp.* appropriated, made the property of, 14. 18.

Approwours, *pl.* approvers, informers, D 1343.

Aprochen, *v.* approach, T. v. 1.

Apurtenance, *s.* appurtenance; *pl.* I 793.

Apyked, *pp.* trimmed, adorned, A 365.

Aqueynte me, make myself acquainted, 3. 532; *pt. pl.* became acquainted, HF. 250; *pp.* acquainted, B 1219.

Aquyte. *imp. s.* requite, T. ii. 1200.

Arace, *v.* eradicate, uproot, T. v. 954; tear away, 6. 20; *pr. s. subj.* root out, eradicate, T. iii. 1015; *pp.* torn, borne along; torn away, B 3. p 11. 165.

Araise; see Areise.

Aray, *s.* array, dress, L. 1505; arrangement, T. iii. 536; state, dress, A 41, 73; attire, I 932; array of garments, L. 2607; order, E 262; ordinance, E 670; position, D 902; condition, A 934.

Arayed, *pp.* dressed, ready, T. iii. 423; clad, R. 472; adorned, T. ii. 1187; *wel a.,* well situated, T. ii. 680; equipped, A 2046; dressed, F 389; ordered, B 252; appointed, F 1187.

Arbitre, *s.* will, choice, B 5. p 3. 18.

Arches; see Ark.

Archaungel, *s.* titmouse, R. 915.

Archewyves, *s. pl.* archwives, ruling wives, E 1195.

Ardaunt, *adj.* ardent, B 3. m 12. 15; eager, B 4. p 3. 116.

Arede, *v.* explain, disclose, T ii. 1505; counsel, T. iv. 1112; interpret, 3. 289; *ger.* to divine, T. ii. 132.

Areise, *v.* raise; Areysen, *ger.* to levy, I 567; *pp.* praised, L. 1525; raised, A. ii. 2. 7.

Arest, *s.* rest (for a spear), A 2602.

Areste, *s.* arrest, B 4090; detention, A 1310; responsibility, E 1282; delay, L. 806; hesitation, L. 1929; deliberation, L. 397.

Areste, *v.* stop (a horse), A 827; Do a., cause to be stopped, B 4210.

Aretten, *v.* impute, B 2. p 4. 14; A. upon, *pr. s.* accuses, I 580; *pr. pl. subj.* ascribe, I 1082; *ye n'arette it not,* ye impute it not, consider it not, A 726; *pp.* imputed, A 2729.

A-rewe, *adv.* successively, lit. in a row, D 1254.

Areyse; see Areise.

Argoile, *s.* crude tartar, G 813.

Arguinge, *s.* argument, L. 475.

Argumented, *pt. s.* argued, T. i. 377.

Aright, *adv.* rightly, well, A 267; aright, G 1418; properly, F 694; wholly, A 189; exactly, T. v. 364; certainly, B 3135.

Arisen, Arist; see Aryse.

Ariste, *s.* arising, rising, A. ii. 12. 16.

Ark, *s.* arc, referring to the arc of the horizon extending from sunrise to sunset, B 2; daily course of the sun, E 1795; arc, the apparent angular distance passed over by the sun in a day and a night, A. ii. 7. 12; Arches, *pl.* arcs, A. ii. 7. 15.

**Armes,** *pl.* arms, weapons, 7. 1 ; coat-of-arms, A 1012.

**Arm-greet,** *adj.* thick as one's arm, A 2145.

**Arminge,** *s.* putting on of armour, B 2037.

**Armipotente,** *adj.* powerful in arms, A 1982.

**Armoniak,** *adj.* ammoniac ; applied to *bole*, G 790, and *sal*, G 798. It is a corruption of Lat. *armeniacum*, i. e. Armenian.

**Armonye,** *s.* harmony. 3. 313.

**Armure,** *s.* defensive armour, 4. 130 ; B 2009.

**Armurers,** *pl.* armourers, A 2507.

**Arn,** *pr. pl.* are, HF. 1008.

**Aroos ;** see **Aryse.**

**A-roume,** *adv.* at large, in an open space, HF. 540.

**A-rowe,** *adv.* in a row, HF. 1835.

**Arowe,** *s.* ; see **Arwe.**

**Arrace ;** see **Arace.**

**Array, Arraye ;** see **Aray, Arayed.**

**Arrerage,** *s.* arrears, A 602.

**Arrette ;** see **Aretten.**

**Arrivage,** *s.* coming to shore, HF. 223.

**Arryve,** *v.* arrive, come to land, 10. 38 ; *pr. s.* (it) arrives, L. 2309 ; *pt. s.* drove ashore, B 4. m 3. 1 ; *ycel-a.,* ill-fated, R. 1068.

**Ars-metrýke,** *s.* arithmetic, D 2222.

**Artelleries,** *s. pl.* engines for shooting, B 2523.

**Arten,** *ger.* to constrain, urge, T. i. 388.

**Artificial,** *adj.* A. ii. 7. *rub.* The *day artificial* is the length of the day, from the moment of sunrise to that of sunset.

**Artik,** northern, A. i. 14. 10.

**Artow,** art thou, A 1141 ; thou art, L. 986.

**Arwe,** *s.* arrow, T. ii. 641 ; Arowe, 7. 185 ; *pl.* arrows, A 107.

**Aryse,** *v.* arise, be raised, T. iv. 1480 ; *pr. s.* rises, I 971 ; Arist, *pr. s.* (*contr. from* ariseth) arises, B 265 ; Aròòs, *pt. s.* arose, 5. 575 ; stood up, L. 831 ; Arisen, *pt. pl.* arose, T. ii. 1598 ; Aryse, *pr. s. subj.* may arise ; Fro the sonne aryse, from the point where the sun rises.

**Arysing,** *s.* rising, rise, A. ii. 12. 1.

**Aryve,** *s.* lit. arrival ; landing, disembarkation of troops, A 60.

**Aryve ;** see **Arryve.**

**As,** so (in asseverations), 3. 838, 1235 ; an expletive, expressing a wish, commonly used with an imperative, e. g. *as lat,*

pray let, B 859 ; *as lene,* pray lend, A 3777, &c. ; As, like, B 1864 ; as that, F 1018 ; As after, according to, B 3555 ; As ferforth as, as far as, B 19 ; As in, i.e. for, B 3688 ; As now, at present, at this time, A 2264 ; on the present occasion, G 944 ; for the present, G 1019 ; As nouthe, as at this time, at present, A 462 ; As of, with respect to, 5. 26 ; As swythe, as soon as possible, at once, 7. 226 ; As that, as soon as, F 615 ; as though, 3. 1200 ; As ther, there, 4. 117 ; As to, with reference to, F 107 ; As to my wit, as it seems to me, 5. 547.

**As,** *s.* an ace, B 3851 ; Ambes as, *pl.* double aces, B 124.

**Asay ;** see **Assay.**

**Ascaunce,** as if, perhaps, G 838 ; in case that, L. 2203 ; Ascaunces, as if, D 1745 ; as if to say, T. i. 205, 292. Compounded of E. *as,* and O. F. *quanses,* as if.

**Ascencioun,** *s.* ascension, ascending degree, B 4045 ; rising up, G 778.

**Ascende,** *v.* ascend, rise (a term in astrology), I 11 ; *pres. part.* ascending, in the ascendant, i. e. near the eastern horizon, F 264.

**Ascendent,** *s.* ascendant, A 417 ; *pl.* HF. 1268. The 'ascendant' is that degree of the ecliptic which is rising above the horizon at a given moment.

**Asemble ;** see **Assemble.**

**Asëuraunce,** *s.* assurance, T. v. 1259.

**Ash ;** see **Asshe.**

**Ashamed,** *pp.* put to shame, A 2667 ; *for pure a.,* for very shame, T. ii. 656.

**Asketh,** *pr. s.* requires, T. i. 339.

**Asking,** *s.* question, L. 313.

**Aslake,** *v.* diminish, A 3553 ; *pp.* assuaged, A 1760.

**Asonder,** *adv.* asunder, apart, A 491.

**Asp,** *s.* aspen tree, A 2921 ; *collectively,* R. 1384. A. S. *æps.*

**Aspect,** *s.* an (astrological) aspect, A 1087. An 'aspect' is the angular distance between two planets. The principal aspects are *five,* viz. conjunction, sextile, quartile, trine, and opposition, corresponding to the angular distances 0°, 60°, 90°, 120°, and 180°, respectively.

**Aspen-leef,** *s.* leaf of an aspen tree, D 1667.

**Aspre,** *adj.* sharp, bitter, T. iv. 827 ; vexatious, B 3. p 8. 19 ; cruel, B 2. p 8. 39 ; fierce, hardy, 7. 23.

**Asprenesse,** *s.* asperity, B 4. p 4. 159.

**Aspye,** *s.* spy, C 755.

**Aspye**, v. spy, see, A 1420; Aspyen, v. behold, T. ii. 649.

**Assaut**, s. assault, A 989.

**Assay**, s. trial, D 290; *doon his a.*, make his attempt, L. 1594; A-say, test, L. 28 a.

**Assaye**, v. try, make trial of, B 3149; try, 3. 574; endeavour, F 1567; *ger.* to assail, T. i. 928; *pr. s.* experiences, B 3. m 2. 13; *pr. pl.* try, L. 487; *imp. pl.* try, E 1740; *pp.* proved, tested, tried, experienced, T. iii. 1220, 1447; A 1811.

**Assayle**; see Assaile.

**Assege**, s. siege, T. i. 464, ii. 107.

**Assege**, v. besiege; *pt. pl.* T. i. 60; *pp.* A 881.

**Assemble**, v.; come together, I 909; *ger.* to amass, B 3. p 8. 8; *pp.* A 717; united, G 50.

**Assemblinge**, s. union, I 904, 917.

**Assendent**; see Ascendent.

**Assente**, v. agree to, A 374; assent, A 3092; consent, B 3469; agree, E 11, 88, 129.

**Asshe** (1), s. ash-tree, 5. 176; *collectively*, ash-trees, R. 1384.

**Asshe** (2), s. ash (of something burnt); Asshen, *pl.* ashes, 7. 173; A 1302.

**Assoilen**, *ger.* to discharge, pay, B 5. p. 1. 15; *v.* loosen; *pr. s.* absolve, pardon, C 913; *pp.* explained, B 5. p 6. 311.

**Assoiling**, s. absolution, A 661.

**Assure**, s. assurance, protestation, 7. 331.

**Assure**, v. feel secure, trust, T. v. 870; rely, T. v. 1624; declare (to be) sure, 7. 90.

**Assyse**, s. assize, session, A 314; judgement, 1. 36; position, R. 900.

**Asterte**, v. escape, L. 1802; A 1595; escape from, L. 2338; D 968; get away, withdraw, 3. 1154; release, D 1314; *pt. s.* escaped, T. iii. 97; *pp.* escaped, B 437.

**Astonie**, v. astonish; *pr. s.* astonishes, HF. 1174; *pp.* astonished, T. i. 274, iii. 1089.

**Astonyinge**, s. astonishment, B 4. p 5. 33.

**Astore**, v. to store; *pp.* A 609.

**Astrolabie**, s. astrolabe, A. pr. 4.

**Astrologien**, s. astrologer, astronomer, D 324.

**Astrologye**, s. astrology, A 3192, 3514.

**Astromye** (*for* Astronomye), *an ignorant form*; see Atempre.

**Asure**, s. azure, R. 477.

**Asweve**, v.; *pp.* dazed, put to sleep, HF. 549.

**A-swown**, adv. (*from pp.*) in a swoon,

L. 2207; Aswowe, 7. 354; *hence* Aswowne, in a swoon, T. iii. 1092; A 3823.

**At**, prep. at, A 20, &c.; of, R. 378; as to, 6. 114; by, D 2095; in the presence of. T. ii. 984; with, beside, HF. 1593; to, HF. 1603; At me, with respect to me, B 1975; At erste, firste of all, HF. 512; At his large, free, free to speak or be silent, A 2288; At on, at one, agreed, A 4197; At shorte wordes, briefly, 5. 481; At regard, with regard, I 180; At yë, at (your) eye, with your own eyes, visibly, A 3016; *have at thee*, I attack thee, L. 1383.

**At-after**, prep. after, B 1445.

**Atake**, v. overtake, G 556, 585.

**Ataste**, 2 *pr. s. subj.* taste, B 2. p 1. 41.

**Ataynt**; see Atteine.

**Atazir**, s. evil influence, B 305.

**Atempraunce**, s. temperament, B 4. p 6. 214; adjustment, moderation, temperance, C 46.

**Atempre**, adj. temperate, mild, L. 128, 1483; moderate, T. i. 953; mild, 5. 204; R. 131; modest, I 932.

**Atempre**, v.; *pr. s.* attempers, B 1. m 2. 23; *refl.* controls himself, B 2704.

**Atemprely**, adv. temperately, I 861; moderately, B 2728.

**Atempringe**, s. controlling, B 5. p 4. 101.

**Ateyne**; see Atteine.

**Athamaunt**, s. adamant, A 1305.

**Athinken**, v. displease, T. v. 878; Athinketh, *pr. s. impers.* (it) repents, T. i. 1050.

**At-ones**, adv. at once, at one and the same time, B 670.

**Atoon**, adv. at one, E 437.

**At-rede**, v. surpass in counsel, T. iv. 1456; A 2449.

**At-renne**, v. surpass in running, T. iv. 1456; A 2449.

**Attamed**, *pp.* broached, B 4008.

**Attayne**; see Atteine.

**Atte**, *for* at the, D 404; Atte beste, in the best way, A 29, 749; Atte fan, at the fan, H 42; Atte fulle, at the full, completely, A 651; Atte gate, at the gate, B 1563; Atte hasard, at dice, C 608; Atte laste, at the last, B 506; Atte leste, at the least, at least, B 38; Atte Bowe, at Bow, A 125.

**Atteine**, v. attain, R. 1495; succeed in, 4. 161; *pp.* apprehended, B 3. p 3. 25.

**Attempre**; see Atempre.

**Attry**, adj. venomous, I 583.

**A-tweyn**, adv. in two, 3. 1193.

**A-twinne**, adv. apart, T. iii. 1666.

**Atwixe**, prep. betwixt, R. 854.

A-twixen, *prep.* between, T. v. 472.
A-two, in twain, 7. 94 ; L. 758.
A-tyr, *s.* attire, dress, T. i. 181.
Auctor ; see Auctour.
Auctoritee, *s.* authority, B 2355 ; recognised text, A 3000 ; statements of good authors, D 1.
Auctour, *s.* author, HF. 314 ; originator, H 359 ; creator, T. iii. 1765.
Audience, *s.* hearing, 5. 308 ; audience, B 3991 ; open assembly, D 1032.
Augrim, *s.* algorism, i.e. numeration, A. i. 7. 6 ; Arabic numerals, A. i. 8. 6.
Augrim-stones, *pl.* counters for calculating, A 3210.
Auncessour, *s.* ancestor ; *pl.* R. 391.
Auncestre, *s.* ancestor, 5. 41.
Auncetrye, *s.* ancestry, A 3982.
Aungel, *s.* angel, R. 916.
Aungellyk, *adj.* angelical, T. i. 102.
Aungellyke, *adv.* like an angel, L. 236.
Auntre it, *v.* risk it, A 4209 ; Auntred him, *pt. s.* adventured himself, A 4205.
Auntrous, *adj.* adventurous, B 2099.
Autentyke, *adj.* authentic, 3. 1086.
Auter, *s.* altar, 5. 249.
Avale, *v.* fall down, T. iii. 626 ; doff, take off, A 3122 ; Avalen, *pr. pl.* sink down.
Avantage, *s.* advantage, F 772 ; *to don his a.*, to suit his own interests, B 729 ; *as adj.* advantageous, B 146.
Avante ; see Avaunte.
Avaunce, *v.* promote, L. 2022 ; *ger.* T. i. 518 ; be profitable, A 246 ; cause to prosper, HF. 640 ; help, 10. 31.
Avaunt, *s.* vaunt, boast, A 227, E 1457.
Avaunte (her), *v. refl.* boast (herself), 7. 296 ; *ger.* to extol, HF. 1788 ; *v. refl.* boast, vaunt himself, D 1014.
Avaunting, *s.* boasting, A 3884.
Avauntour, *s.* boaster, 5. 430.
Avenaunt, *adj.* graceful, comely, R. 1263.
Aventayle, *s.* ventail, E 1204.
Aventure, *s.* chance, 4. 21 ; peril, B 1151 ; misfortune, L. 657 ; fortune, 18. 22 ; luck, T. ii. 288, 291 ; circumstance, L. 1907 ; *of a.*, by chance, HF. 2090 ; *on a.*, in case of mishap, T. v. 298 ; *in a.*, in the hands of fortune, T. i. 784 ; *per a.*, perchance, A. ii. 12. 6 ; *in a. and grace*, on luck and favour, 4. 60 ; *good a.*, good fortune, 5. 131, 7. 324 ; *pl.* adventures, A 795 ; accidents, C 934.
Aventurous, *adj.* random, B 1. p 6. 98 ; adventitious (Lat. *fortuitæ*), B 2. p 4. 17.
Avisee, *adj.* deliberate, L. 1521.
Avisioun, *s.* vision, R. 9 ; HF. 7.
Avouterye, *s.* adultery, 5. 361.

Avoutier, *s.* adulterer ; *pl.* I 841.
Avow, *s.* vow, A 2414, 2237.
Avowe, *v.* avow, own, proclaim, G 642 ; *pr. s.* vows, 7. 355.
Avoy, *interj.* fie ! B 4098.
Avys, *s.* advice, consideration, opinion, A 786, B 2442.
Avyse, *v.* consider, T. i. 364 ; contemplate, T. v. 1814 ; *refl.* consider, B 664 ; *imp. s.* take heed, A 4188 ; *imp. pl.* consider, deliberate, A 3185 ; *pp.* clearly seen, R. 475 ; with mind made up, T. iii. 1186 ; advised, careful, A 3584 ; deliberate, I 448 ; wary, A 4333 ; forewarned, B 2538 ; *well a.*, well advised, B 2514.
Avysely, *adv.* advisedly, B 2488 ; seriously, I 1024 ; carefully, A ii. 29. 29.
Avysement, *s.* consideration, B 2941 ; counsel, T. ii. 343 ; deliberation, B 86 ; determination, L. 1417.
Await, *s.* watch, D 1657 ; surveillance, H 149 ; waiting, T. iii. 579 ; watchfulness, T. iii. 457 ; Have hir in awayt, watch her, B 3915 ; *pl.* plots, B 3. p 8. 11.
Awaite, *v.* await ; *pr. s.* waits, 1. 111 ; watches, B 1776.
Awaiting, *s.* attendance, T. 250.
Awaitour, *s.* lier in wait, B 4. p 3. 122.
Awake, *v.* wake, awake ; Awook, 1 *pt. s.* aroused, 3. 1324 ; *pt. s.* awoke, F 367 ; Awaked, *pt. s.* awoke, A 2523.
Award, *s.* decision, I 483.
Awen, own (Northern), A 4239.
A-wepe, a-weeping, in tears, T. ii. 408.
A-werke, *adv.* at work, D 215.
Aweye, *adv.* out of the way, done with, T. ii. 123 ; gone, 7. 319 ; from home, B 593 ; astray, B 609.
Aweyward, *adv.* away, backwards, H 262.
Awhape, *v.* amaze ; *pp.* scared, L. 132 ; stupefied, 7. 215 ; confounded, T. i. 316.
Awook ; see Awake.
Awreke, *v.* avenge, 2. 11 ; *pr. s.* avenges, R. 278 ; *pp.* H 298 ; A 3752.
Awry, *adv.* on one side, R. 291.
Axen, *v.* ask, L. 835 ; Axe at, ask of, T. ii. 894 ; *pr. s.* requires, T. ii. 227.
Axing, *s.* question, L. 239 *a* ; request, A 1826.
Ay, *adv.* aye, ever, A 63, 233 ; Ay whyl that, all the while that, 4. 252.
Ay-dwellinge, *adj.* perpetual, everabiding, B 5. p 6. 97.
Ayein, *prep.* opposite to, T. ii. 920 ; against, T. i. 902.
Ayein, *adv.* again, back, 5. 100.

**Ayein-ledinge**, *adj.* returning, reconducting, B 3. m 9. 42.

**Ayeins**, *prep.* against, A 1787; towards, at the approach of, 5. 342.

**Ayeins**, *adv.* against, to, A 3155.

**Ayeinward**, *adv.* again, on the other hand, B 2. p 4. 126; back again, T. iii. 750, iv. 1581.

**Ayel**, *s.* grandfather, A 2477.

**Azimut**, *s.* azimuth, A. ii. 31. 22.

## B.

**Ba**, *v.* kiss, D 433; *imp. s.* A 3709.

**Babewinnes**, *pl.* (lit. baboons), grotesque figures in architecture, HF. 1189.

**Bachelere**, *s.* young knight, R. 918, 1469; an aspirant to knighthood, A 80.

**Bachelrye**, *s.* bachelor-hood, H 125; company of young men, E 270.

**Bad**; see **Bidde**.

**Badder**, *adj. comp.* worse, F 224.

**Bagge**, *v.*; *pr. s.* looks askant, 3. 623.

**Baggepype**, *s.* bagpipe, A 565.

**Baggingly**, *adv.* squintingly, R. 292.

**Baite**, *v.* bait; feed, B 466; *pp.* baited, tormented, R. 1612.

**Bak**, *s.* back, 3. 957; cloth for the back, coarse mantle, rough cloak, G 881.

**Bakbyter**, *s.* backbiter, I 495.

**Bake metes**, baked meats, meat pies, I 445.

**Bakhalf**, the back or flat side of the astrolabe, A. i. 4. 1.

**Bak-side**, *s.* the back of the astrolabe, A. i. 15. 3.

**Balaunce**, *s.* a balance, G 611; *in balaunce*, in jeopardy, G 611; in suspense, 3. 1021.

**Bale**, *s.* sorrow, 3. 535; *for bote ne bale*, for good nor for ill, 3. 227.

**Balke**, *s.* balk, beam, A 3920; *pl.* transverse beams beneath a roof, A 3626.

**Balled**, *adj.* bald, A 198, 2518.

**Bane**, *s.* death, L. 2159; destruction, HF. 408; cause of death, A 1097; slayer, T. iv. 333.

**Banes**, *pl.* bones (Northern), A 4073.

**Bar, Bare**; see **Bere**, *v.*

**Barbe**, *s.* barb (part of a woman's head-dress, still sometimes used by nuns, consisting of a piece of white plaited linen, passed over or under the chin, and reaching midway to the waist), T. ii. 110.

**Barbre**, *adj.* barbarian, B 281.

**Bareine**, *adj.* barren, B 68, D 372.

**Barel ale**, barrel of ale, B 3083.

**Bark**, *s.* (of a tree), T. iii. 727.

**Barm-clooth**, *s.* apron, A 3236.

**Barme**, *s.* (*dat.*) bosom, lap, B 3256, 3630.

**Baronage**, *s.* assembly of barons, A 3096.

**Barre**, *s.* bar, A 1075; **Barres**, *pl.* stripes across a girdle, A 329.

**Barred**, *pp.* furnished with 'bars,' A 3225.

**Barringe**, *s.* adorning with (heraldic) bars, I 417.

**Basilicok**, *s.* basilisk, I 853.

**Baste**, *v.* baste; *pres. part.* basting, tacking on, R. 104.

**Bataile**, *s.* battle, fight, L. 1647; troop, B 5. m 1. 4.

**Batailen**, *v.* fight, B 1. p 4. 251.

**Batailled**, *adj.* embattled, i. e. notched with indentations, B 4050.

**Batere**, *v.* batter; *pr. s.* strikes, I 556.

**Bathe**, both (Northern), A 4087.

**Bathe**, *ger.* to bathe, to bask, T. ii. 849; *refl.* to bask, B 4457.

**Bauderye**, *s.* bawdry, act of a pandar, T. iii. 397; mirth, A 1926.

**Baudrik**, *s.* baldric, belt worn transversely over one shoulder, A 116.

**Baudy**, *adj.* dirty, G 635.

**Baume**, *s.* balm, HF. 1686.

**Baundon**, *s.* power, disposal, R. 1163.

**Bay**, *adj.* bay-coloured, A 2157.

**Bayard**, a horse's name; a horse, A 4115.

**Be-**, *prefix*; see also **Bi-**.

**Beau**, *adj.* fair; *beau sir*, fair sir, HF. 643.

**Be-bled**, *pp.* bloodied, covered with blood, B 3. m 2. 14.

**Beblotte**, *imp. s.* blot, T. ii. 1027.

**Bechen**, *adj.* made of beech, G 1160.

**Become**, *v.* go to, L. 2214; *pp.* gone to, 7. 247.

**Bed.** *s.* L. 2211; station, B 3862; bed (of herbs), B 4411.

**Beddinge**, *s.* couch, A 1616.

**Bede**, *v.* offer, proffer, HF. 32; G 1065; 1 *pr. s.* proffer, 7. 304; Bedeth, *pr. s.* proffers, E 1784; Bede, 1 *pt. pl.* directed, told, I 65; Boden, *pp.* commanded, T. iii. 691; ordered, L. 266.

**Bede**, *pt. pl. and pp. of* Bidde.

**Beden**, *pt. pl. of* Bidde.

**Bedes**, *pl.* beads, A 159.

**Bedote**, *v.* befool, L. 1547.

**Bedrede**, *adj.* bedridden, D 1769.

**Beek**, *s.* beak, F 418.

**Beem**, *s.* balk, B 4362; Bemes, *pl.* beams, R. 1574.

**Been**, *pl.* bees, F 204.

**Beer**, bare; *pt. s. of* Bere.

**Beest**, *s.* beast, F 460; Beest roial = royal beast, i. e. Leo, F 264; brute, G 288; beast, quarry, R. 1452.

**Beet,** *pt. s. and imp. s. of* Bete.

**Beeth,** *imp. pl. of* Ben, to be.

**Beggestere,** *s.* beggar, properly a female beggar, A 242.

**Behette ; see Bihote.**

**Bekke,** 1 *pr. s.* (I) nod, C 396; *pt. s.* nodded to, T. ii. 1260.

**Bel amy,** i. e. good friend, fair friend, C 318; Bele, *adj. fem.* fair, beautiful, HF. 1796; Bele chere, excellent fare, B 1599; Bele chose, beautiful part, D 447.

**Belle,** *s.* bell, T. ii. 1615; (of a clock), 3. 1322; (sign of an inn), A 719; *bere the b.,* be the first, T. iii. 198.

**Belweth,** *pr. s.* roars, HF. 1803.

**Bely,** *s.* belly, B 2167.

**Bely,** *s.* a pair of bellows, I 351.

**Bely-naked,** *adj.* entirely naked, E 1326.

**Beme,** *s.* trumpet, HF. 1240; *pl.* B 4588.

**Bēn, Been,** *v.* be, 1. 182; 1 *pr. pl.* are, 3. 582; Ben, 2 *pr. pl.* B 122; consist, I 82; Beth, *pr. pl.* are, F 648; Be, *pr. s. subj.* exists, it should be, 4. 49; Be, 1 *pr. s. subj.* be, am, D 1245; Beth, *imp. pl.* be, C 683; Been, *pp.* 3. 530; A 199; Be, *pp.* been, R. 322; *I had be,* I should have been, 3. 222; Be as be may, be it as it may, however it be, L. 1852; Be what she be, be she who she may, T. i. 679; Lat be, let alone, D 1289.

**Bench,** *s.* bench, T. ii. 91; table, B 1548; bench (law court), 1. 159.

**Bend,** *s.* band, R. 1079.

**Bende,** *v.* bend, R. 1334; turn, T. ii. 1250; Bente, *pt. s.* bent, H 264; Bent, *pp.* 1. 29; arched, A 3246.

**Bendinge,** *s.* adorning with (heraldic) bends, I 417. A *bend,* in heraldry, is a broad diagonal band upon a shield.

**Bène,** *s.* bean, 11. 29.

*Benedicite,* bless ye (the Lord), A 1785; (pronounced *ben'cite*), T. i. 780, &c.

**Benisoun,** *s.* benison, blessing, B 2288.

**Bent,** *s.* grassy slope ; Bente, *dat.* A 1981.

**Berafte ; see Bireve.**

**Berd,** *s.* beard, A 270, 2173; *in the berd,* face to face, T. iv. 41; *make a berd,* deceive, A 4096; *make his berd,* delude him, D 361.

**Bère,** *s.* bear, L. 1214; the constellations Ursa Major and Ursa Minor, HF. 1004.

**Bère,** *s.* bier, 2. 105; 19. 5.

**Bere,** *v.* bear, carry, B 3564; transport, F 119; confer on, L. 2135; Bere yow, conduct yourself, D 1108; Beren on honde, accuse, D 393; Beren him on hond, assure him, D 232 (cf. 226); Bereth him, conducts himself, behaves, A 796;

Bereth hir, comports herself, T. ii. 401; Berth hir on hond, bears false witness against her, B 620; Bereth him on hond, accuses him, I 505; Sickly berth, take ill, dislike, E 625; Bore, *pr. pl.* 3. 894; Bere, 2 *pt. s.* barest, T iv. 763; Bar, *pt. s.* bare, carried, A 105; possessed, D 997; *pt. s. refl.* conducted himself, T. iii. 490; Bar on honde, made him believe, D 575; Bar her on honde, brought against her a charge which he feigned to believe, 7. 158; Baren us, 1 *pt. pl.* conducted ourselves, A 721; Baren me on hond, bore false witness against me, B. 1. p 4. 180; *pr. s. subj.* may pierce, A 2256; Ber, *imp. s.* carry, D 1139; Ber ayein, take back, T. ii. 1141; Boren, *pp.* born, D 1153; Bore, *pp.* born.

**Bere,** *s.* head-sheet, pillow-case, 3. 254.

**Berie,** *s.* berry, A 4368.

**Berie,** *v.* bury, C 884.

**Beringe,** *s.* behaviour, B 2022; carriage, E 1604.

**Berke,** *v.* bark; Borken, *pp.* shrieked (lit. barked), B 1. p 5. 1.

**Berm,** *s.* barm, i. e. yeast, G 813.

**Bern,** *s.* barn, B 3759.

**Beryle,** *s.* beryl, HF. 1184.

**Besaunt-wight,** *s.* weight of a besant, R. 1106. (*Besant,* a gold coin of Byzantium.)

**Bespreynt ; see Bisprenge.**

**Bestialitee,** *s.* animal condition, T. i. 735.

**Bet,** *adj. comp.* better, 10. 47; HF. 108.

**Bet,** *adv.* better, A 242; *go bet,* go faster, go as quickly as possible, 3. 136; *the bet,* the better, HF. 559; *bet and bet,* better and better, T. iii. 714.

**Béte,** *v.* remedy, heal, T. i. 665; amend, mend, assist, I 421; kindle, A 2253.

**Bète,** *ger.* to beat, flap, B 4512; to hammer out, C 17; Beet, *pt. s.* adjoined (lit. beat), R. 129; Beten, *pp.* beaten, B 1732; *as adj.* beaten, ornamented with the hammer, R. 837.

**Beth,** *pr. pl.* are, B 2350; *imp. pl.* be, 1. 134.

**Betraising,** *s.* betrayal, L. 2460.

**Bettre,** *adj.* better, A 256; *b. arm,* right arm, T. ii. 1650.

**Bever,** *adj.* made of beaver, A 272.

**Beye,** *ger.* to buy, T. v. 1843; *v.* B 1462. See **Bye.**

**Bibbe,** *v.* ; *pp.* imbibed, A 4162.

**Bible,** *s.* bible, A 438; book, HF. 1334.

**Bi-bledde,** *pp. pl.* covered with blood, A 2002.

**Bicched bones,** *s. pl.* dice, C 656.

**Bi-clappe,** *ger.* to catch (as in a trap), G 9.

**Bicome,** *ger.* to become, D 1644 ; Bicomth, *pr. s.* goes, T. ii. 795.

**Bidaffed,** *pp.* befooled, E 1191.

**Bidde,** *v.* ask (*confused with* Béde, *v.* command, bid) ; *ger.* to request, L. 838 ; 1 *pr. s.* pray, T. i. 1027 ; Bit, *pr. s.* bids, A 187 ; Bad, *pt. s.* prayed, begged, T. iii. 1249 ; besought, T. i. 112 ; requested, E 373 ; 1 *pt. s.* bade, F 1212 ; *pt. s.* bade, commanded, D 108 ; Beden, *pt. pl.* bade, B 2233 ; Bidde, *pp.* commanded, B 440 (where *han bidde* = have bidden) ; Bede, *pp.* bidden (*as if from* Bede), 3. 194 ; 1 *pt. s. subj.* would seek, R. 791 ; Bid, *imp. s.* pray, T. iii. 342 ; bid, 3. 144 ; Biddeth, *imp. pl.* pray, T. i. 36.

**Bidding,** *s.* request, L. 837.

**Bidelve,** *v.* ; Bidolven, *pp.* buried, B 5. p 1. 51.

**Biden,** *pp. of* Byde.

**Bifallinge,** *s.* coming to pass, T. iv. 1018.

**Biforen,** *prep.* before, B 3553 ; in front of, G 680.

**Biforen,** *adv.* in the front part (of his head), A 1376 ; beforehand, A 1148 ; in front, A 590 ; in a good position, A 572 ; of old time, F 551 ; first, E 446.

**Biforn,** *prep.* before.

**Bigete,** *v.* beget ; Begat, *pt. s.* L. 1562 ; Bigeten, *pp.* B 3138.

**Biginne,** *v.* begin, A 42 ; Bigonne, 2 *pt. s.* G 442 ; Began, 2 *pt. s.* (*false form for* Bigunne), L. 2230 ; Bigan, *pt. s.* A 44 ; Bigonne, *pt. pl.* F 1015 ; Bigonne, *pp.* T. ii. 779.

**Bigoon,** *pp.* ornamented, R. 943 ; *wel b.,* well contented, joyous, merry, 5. 171 ; fortunate, T. ii. 294 ; *wel bigo,* well content, R. 693 ; *wo b.,* distressed, L. 1487, 2497 ; *sorwfully b.,* distressed, T. i. 114 ; *wers b.,* more wretched, T. v. 1328.

**Bigyleres,** *pl.* beguilers, I 299.

**Bihalve,** *s. dat.* behalf, T. ii. 1458.

**Bihate,** *v.* hate ; *pp.* B 3. m 4. 6.

**Biheste,** *s.* promise, B 37 ; command, T. ii. 359 ; *pl.* promises, i. e. all that they profess to prove, A. pr. 26.

**Bihete,** 1 *pr. s.* promise, G 707 ; 2 *pr. s.* dost promise, B 4. p 2. 1 ; *pr. s.* promises, I 379. See Bihote.

**Bihetinge,** *s.* promising, B 2. p 8. 16.

**Bihewe,** *v.* ; Behewe, *pp.* carved, HF. 1306.

**Bihighte,** *pt. s.* promised, T. v. 1204 ;

Bihighte, *pt. pl.* T. iii. 319 ; Bihight, *pp.* T. v. 354. See Bihote.

**Biholde,** *v.* behold, A 2293 ; Behelde, *v.* behold, 7. 80 ; Behelde, *pt. s. subj.* should see, T. ii. 378 ; Biholde, *pp.* beheld, G 179.

**Bihote,** 1 *pr. s.* promise, A 1854 ; Behette, *pt. s.* 5. 436.

**Bihove,** *s. dat.* profit (lit. behoof), R. 1092.

**Bihove,** *v.* suit, 13. 5 ; *pr. s.* (it) behoves, T. iv. 1004 ; *pr. pl.* are necessary, I 83.

**Bihovely,** *adj.* helpful, T. ii. 261 ; needful, I 107.

**Bi-jape,** *v.* ; *pp.* jested at, tricked, T. i. 531.

**Biker,** *s.* quarrel, L. 2661.

**Biknowe,** *v.* acknowledge, B 886 ; Biknoweth, *pr. s.* I 481 ; Beknew, *pt. s.* confessed, L. 1058 ; I am bi-knowen = I acknowledge, B 3. p 10. 88.

**Bilde,** *ger.* to build, HF. 1133 ; Bilt, *pr. s.* HF. 1135 ; Bilt, *pp.* 1. 183. See Bulde.

**Bilder,** *s. as adj.* builder, used for building, 5. 176.

**Bileve,** *s.* faith, L. 2109 ; creed, A 3456.

**Bileve** (1), *v.* believe ; *imp. pl.* G 1047.

**Bileve** (2), *v.* to remain, stay behind, F 583.

**Bilinne,** *v.* cease, T. iii. 1365.

**Bille,** *s.* bill, petition, 1. 59, 110 ; letter, E 1937 ; writ, D 1586.

**Binde,** *v.* bind, enthral, 4. 249 ; Bynt (*for* Bint), *pr. s.* binds, 4. 47, 48 ; Bond, *pt. s.* bound, fastened, R. 241 ; Bounden, *pp.* bound, B 270 ; bound up, D 681.

**Binding,** *s.* constraint, A 1304.

**Binime,** *v.* take away, B 4. p 3. 36 ; Binemen, *pr. pl.* B 3. p 3. 65 ; Bi-nomen, *pp.* taken away, B 3. p 3. 69.

**Binne,** *s.* bin, chest, A 593.

**Biquethe,** *v.* bequeath, D 1121.

**Biraft, -e** ; see **Bireve**.

**Bireine,** *v.* ; Bireyned, *pp.* rained upon, T. iv. 1172.

**Bireve,** *v.* bereave, B 3359 ; restrain, T. i. 685 ; take away, G 482 ; *me wo bereve,* rob me of woe, 6. 12 ; Bireved, *pt. s.* bereft, D 2071 ; Birafte, *pt. s.* B 83 ; Biraft, *pp.* bereft, T. iv. 225 ; A 1361.

**Birthe,** *s.* birth, B 192.

**Biscorned,** *pp.* scorned, I 278.

**Bisege,** *v.* besiege ; *pr. s.* L. 1902 ; Bisegede, *pt. pl.* T. i. 149.

**Biséken,** *v.* beseech, pray, B 2306, 2910 ; By-séke, *v.* beseech, T. iv. 131 ; Biseken, 1 *pr. pl.* implore, A 918 ; Bisoughtest, 2 *pt. s.* didst beseech, T. v. 1734 ; Bisoghte, *pt. s.* B 2164.

**Bisemare**, *s.* contemptuous conduct, A 3965.

**Bisette**, *v.*; Besette, *v.* employ, L. 1069; bestow, 3. 772; Besette, disposed of, L. 2558; used up, D 1952; bestowed, A 3715; established, A 3012; fixed, I 366; Beset, *pp.* bestowed, T. i. 521.

**Biseye**, *pp.* beseen; *wel b.*, fair to see, good-looking, R. 821; well provided, 3. 829; *goodly b.*, fair to see, good in appearance, T. ii. 1262; *yvel b.*, ill-looking, E 965; *richely b.*, rich-looking, splendid, E 984.

**Bishende**, *v.*; Beshende, *v.* bring to ruin, L. 2696.

**Bishitte**, *v.*; Bishet, *pp.* shut up, T. iii. 602.

**Bishrewe**, 1 *pr. s.* beshrew, D 844.

**Bisie**, *v. refl.* take pains, B 3034; Bisie me, employ myself, G 758; *pt. pl.* occupied themselves, 5. 192.

**Bisily**, *adv.* diligently, A. ii. 38. 8; completely, T. iii. 1153; eagerly, F 1051; well, 2. 33.

**Bisinesse**, *s.* business, B 1415; busy endeavour, A 1007, G 24; diligence, 3. 1156; C 56; industry, G 5; labour, 5. 86; work, activity, T. i. 795; trouble, ado, 7. 99; careful attention, B 2979; attentiveness, 7. 250; care, A 520.

**Bi-smokede**, *adj. pl.* dirtied with smoke, B 1. p 1. 31.

**Bismotered**, *pp.* besmutted, marked with spots of rust, &c., A 76.

**Bispet**, *pp.* spit upon, I 276.

**Bisprenge**, *v.*; Bespreynt, *pp.* sprinkled, bedewed, 2. 10.

**Bistad**, *pp.* bestead, in trouble, R. 1227; *hard b.*, greatly imperilled, B 649.

**Bistryden**, *v.*; Bistrood, *pt. s.* bestrode, B 2093.

**Bisy, Besy**, *adj.* busy, industrious, R. 1052; active, L. 103; useful, I 474; attentive, F 509; anxious, 2. 2.

**Bisyde**, *prep.* beside; *ther b.*, beside that place, 3. 1316; *of b.*, from the neighbourhood of, A 445; *b. his leve*, without his leave, HF. 2105.

**Bisydes**, *prep.*; *him b.*, near him, A 402.

**Bisydes**, Besydes, *adv.* on one side, G 1416.

**Bit**, *pr. s. of* Bidde.

**Bitake**, 1 *pr. s.* commend, I 1043; commit, E 161; resign, A 3750; 1 *pr. s.* deliver, entrust, L. 2297; Bitook, *pt. s.* entrusted, G 541; Bitaken, *pp.* B 3. m 2. 47.

**Biteche**, 1 *pr. s.* commit (to), consign (to), B 2114.

**Bithinke**, *v.* imagine, think of, T. iii. 1694; Bethinke, *v.* 2. 107; *ger.* to reflect, HF. 1176; Bithoughte, 1 *pt. s. refl.* bethought myself, R. 521; I am bithought, I have thought (of), A 767; Bithought, *pp.* T. ii. 225.

**Bitid, Bitit**; see **Bityde**.

**Bitook**; see **Bitake**.

**Bitore**, *s.* bittern, D 972.

**Bitraise, Bitraisshe**, *v.* betray; Bitrayseth, *pr. s.* C 92; *pp.* betrayed, T. iv. 1648; I 269; Bitraisshed, R. 1648; Bitrasshed, R. 1520.

**Bitrenden**, *v.*; Bi-trent, *pr. s.* encircles, goes round, T. iv. 870; twines round, T. iii. 1231.

**Bitwixen**, *prep.* between, A 880; Betwixen, 5. 148; Bitwixe, A 277; Bitwix, L. 729.

**Bityde, Bityden**, *v.* happen, T. ii. 623; arrive, B 3730; *pr. s. subj.* E 306; Bityde what b., happen what may, T. v. 750; Bitit, *pr. s.* betides, happens, T. ii. 48, v. 345; Bitidde, *pt. s.* befell, T. v. 1641; Bitid, *pp.* T. iii. 288; Betid, HF. 384.

**Bitydinge**, *s.* an event, B 5. p 1. 37.

**Bitymes**, *adv.* betimes, soon, G 1008.

**Biware**, *v.*; Biwared, *pp.* spent, expended, laid out (as on wares), T. i. 636.

**Biwepe**, *ger.* to bemoan, T. i. 763; Biwopen, *pp.* bathed in tears, T. iv. 916.

**Biwreye**, *v.* make manifest, reveal, T. iii. 377; Biwreyest, 2 *pr. s.* revealest, B 773; Biwreyd, *pp.* betrayed (viz. by having your words revealed), H 352.

**Biwreying**, *s.* betraying, B 2330.

**Bi-wryen**, *v.* disclose, reveal, T. ii. 537; Bewrye, betray, 5. 348. (Wrongly used for Biwreye.)

**Blak**, *adj.* black, A 294; Blake, *pl.* A 557; Blakke, *def.* HF. 1801.

**Blak**, *s.* black clothing, 3. 445.

**Blake**, *s.* black writing, ink, T. ii. 1320.

**Blakeberied**, **a**, a-blackberrying, i. e. a-wandering at will, astray, C 406.

**Blaked**, *pp.* blackened, rendered black, B 3321.

**Blandishe**, *pr. s. subj.* fawn, I 376.

**Blankmanger**, *s.* a compound of minced capon, with cream, sugar, and flour, A 387. Named from its white colour.

**Blasen**, *ger.* to blow, HF. 1802.

**Blaspheme**, *s.* blaspheming, 16. 15.

**Blasphemóur**, *s.* blasphemer, C 898.

**Blast**, *s.* puff, T. ii. 1387.

**Blaste**, *ger.* to blow a trumpet, HF. 1866.

**Blaunche**, *adj. fem.* white (see **Fevere**), T. i. 916.

**Blaundisshinge**, *pret. pt. as adj.* bewitching, B 3. m 12. 23; Blaundissinge, flattering, B 2. p 1. 31.

Bleche, v.; pp. bleached, 9. 45.

Blede, v. bleed, L. 2696; Bledde, pt. s. bled, T. ii. 950.

Blemished, pp. injured, B 1. p 4. 312.

Blende, v. blind, T. iv. 648; ger. to deceive, T. iii. 207; to blind (or read toblende, v. blind utterly), T. ii. 1496; Blent, pr. s. blinds, 5. 600; Blente, pt. s. blinded, T. v. 1194; Blent, pp. 15. 18; deceived, E 2113.

Blere, v. blear, bedim; Blere hir yë, dim their eye, cajole them, A 4049; pp. deceived, G 730.

Blering, s. dimming; bl. of an yë, cajoling, A 3865.

Blesse, v. bless; Blesseth hir, pr. s. crosses herself, B 449.

Bleve, v. remain, T. iv. 1484; remain (at home), T. iii. 623; ger. to dwell, T. iv. 1357.

Blew, pt. s. of Blowe.

Blew, adj. blue, A 564; 3. 340; as s. blue clothing, 21. 7.

Bleyne, s. blain, blemish, R. 553.

Bleynte, pt. s. blenched, started back, A 1078; turned aside, T. iii. 1346. Pt. s. of Blenche, v.

Blinde, v.; Blynde with, ger. to blind (the priest) with, G 1151.

Blinne, v. leave off, cease, G 1171.

Blisful, adj. happy, 9. 1; conferring bliss, 1. 24; blessed, 3. 854; merry, R. 80; sainted, A 17.

Blisful, adv. joyously, 5. 689.

Blisfully, adv. happily, A 1236.

Blisfulnesse, s. happiness, B 2. p 4. 75.

Blisse, v. bless, E 553. Perhaps read blesse, kesse. See Blesse.

Blissed, pp. happy, 9. 43.

Blo, adj. blue, smoke-coloured, HF. 1647.

Blody, adj. causing bloodshed, A 2512.

Blondren; see Blundre.

Blood, s. lineage, 7. 65; offspring, E 632; kinswoman, T. ii. 594.

Blosme, s. blossom, A 3324.

Blosme, v. blossom; pr. s. E 1462; pp. covered with blossoms, R. 108.

Blosmy, adj. blossoming, T. ii. 821; full of buds, 5. 183.

Blowe, v. blow, A 565; Blew, pt. s. 3. 182; (it) blew, T. iii. 678; Blowen, pp. proclaimed by trumpets, A 2241.

Blundre, v.; pr. s. runs heedlessly, G 1414; 1 p. pl. pr. Blondren, we become mazed, G 670.

Blythly, adv. gladly, 3. 749, 755.

Blyve, adv. quickly, soon, L. 60; as bl.,

very soon, as soon as possible, T. i. 965; forthwith, R. 706, 992; also bl., as soon as possible, T. iv. 174.

Bobance, s. presumption, boast, D 569.

Boce, s. protuberance (boss), I 423.

Boch, s. botch, pustule, B 3. p 4. 14.

Bocher, s. butcher, A 2025.

Bocler, s. buckler, A 3266.

Bode (1), s. foreboding, omen, 5. 343.

Bode (2), s. abiding, delay, 7. 119.

Bode, v. proclaim; pr. s. heralds, B 4. m 6. 17.

Boden, pp. of Bede.

Body, s. person, F 1005; principal subject, E 42; corpse, 3. 142; B 1872; my b., myself, B 1185; pl. metallic bodies (metals), answering to celestial bodies (planets), G 820, 825.

Boef, s. beef, E 1420.

Boës, pr. s. (it) behoves, A 4026. (Northern.)

Boght, Boghte; see Bye.

Boist, s. box, C 307; pl. HF. 2129.

Boistous, adj. rude, plain, H 211.

Boistously, adv. loudly, E 791.

Bokel, s. buckle, R. 1086.

Bokeler, s. buckler, A 112. A small round shield usually carried by a handle at the back. See Bocler.

Bokelinge, pres. pt. buckling, A 2503.

Bokes, pl. books, A 294.

Boket, s. bucket, A 1533.

Bolas, pl. bullace-plums, bullaces, R. 1377.

Bolde, v. grow bold, 5. 144.

Bōle, s. bull, T. iii. 723, iv. 239.

Bōle armoniak, Armenian clay, G 790.

Bolle, s. a bowl, G 1210.

Bolt, s. crossbow-bolt, A 3264.

Bolt-upright, on (her) back, A 4266, B 1506.

Bomble, v.; pr. s. booms (as a bittern), D 972.

Bon, adj. good, HF. 1022.

Bond, s. bond, obligation, A 1604; band, fetter, T. iii. 1766; obligation (compelling the service of spirits), F 131.

Bonde, s. bondman, D 1660, I 149.

Bonde-folk, s. pl. bondmen, I 754.

Bonde-men, s. pl. bondmen, I 752.

Bóne, s. petition, boon, prayer, request, 3. 129, 835.

Bood, pt. s. of Byde.

Bōòn, s. bone, R. 1059; ivory, T. ii. 926; Bònes, pl. bones, A 546.

Bōòr, s. boar, A 2070; Bores, gen. sing. boar's, B 2060; Bores, pl. A 1658.

Bōòst, s. loud talk, A 4001; boast, L. 267; pride, B 3289; boasting, C 764; swelling, G 441.

Bòòt, *s.* boat, T. i. 416, ii. 3.

Bóót, *s.* help, remedy, T. iii. 1208.

Boot, *pt. s. of* Byte.

Boras, *s.* borax, A 630, G 790.

Bord, *s.* table, A 5², B 430; plank, 3. 74; board, i. e. meals, G 1017; *to b.*, to board, A 3188, D 528; *into shippes bord*, on board the ship, A 3585; *over-bord*, overboard, B 922.

Bòrdels, *s. pl.* brothels, I 885.

Bordel-women, *pl.* women of the brothel, I 976.

Bordure, *s.* border, raised rim on the front of an astrolabe, A. i. 4. 4.

Bore, *s.* bore, hole, T. iii. 1453.

Bore, Boren, *pp. of* Bere.

Borel, *s.* coarse woollen clothes, D 356; Borel men, laymen, B 3145. See Burel.

Bores; see Boor.

Borken, *pp. of* Berke.

Borne, *v.*; Borneth, *pr. s* burnishes, smoothes, T. i. 327.

Borwe, *s.* pledge, A 1622; *to b.*, in pledge, as a pledge, T. v. 1664; *leyd to b.*, laid in pledge, pawned, T. ii. 963; *to b.*, for surety, 4. 205; *Venus here to b.*, Venus being your pledge, T. ii. 1524.

Borwe, *v.* borrow, B 105.

Bos, *s.* boss, A 3266. See Boce.

Bost, *s.*; see Boost.

Bòste, *v.* boast; *pr. s.* D 1672.

Bóte, *s.* good, benefit, D 472; remedy, profit, 3. 38; advantage, T. i. 352; healing, T. i. 763; help, T. ii. 345; healer, 22. 45; relief, G 1481; salvation, B 1656; *doth b.*, gives the remedy for, 5. 276; *for b. ne bale*, for good nor for ill, 3. 227.

Botel, *s.* bottle (of hay), H 14.

Botelees, *adj.* without remedy, T. i. 782.

Boteler, *s.* butler, HF. 592.

Boterflye, *s.* butterfly, B 3980.

Botes, *pl.* boots, A 203, 273.

Bothe, both, A 540; *your bothes*, of both of you, 1. 83; *your bother*, of you both, T. iv. 168.

Botmelees, *adj.* bottomless, unreal, T. v. 1431.

Bough, *s.* bough, R. 1403; Bowes, *pl.* R. 108.

Bought, Boughte; see Bye.

Bouk, *s.* trunk of the body, A 2746.

Boun, *adj.* prepared, F 1503.

Bounde, *s.* bound; *pl.* bounds, limits, L. 546, 1673.

Bountee, *s.* goodness, kindness, 1. 9; good deed, I 393; delightfulness, R. 1444.

Bountevous, *adj.* bountiful, bounteous, T. i. 883; C 110.

Bour, *s.* bed-chamber, HF. 1186; B 1932; lady's chamber, R. 1014; inner room, B 4022.

Bourde, *s.* jest, H 81; *pl.* D 680.

Bourde, 1 *pr. s.* jest, C 778; *pp.* 5. 589.

Box (1), *s.* box-tree, A 2922; boxwood, L. 866; money-box, A 4390; box, C 869.

Box (2), *s.* blow, L. 1388.

Boydekin, *s.* dagger, A 3960.

Bracér, *s.* bracer, a guard for the arm in archery, A 111.

Bragot, *s.* a beverage made of honey and ale, A 3261.

Braid, *s.* quick movement; *at a b.*, in a moment, R. 1336; Brayd, a start, L. 1166.

Brak, *pt. s. of* Breke.

Brasil, *s.* dye made from a certain dye-wood, B 4649.

Brast, Braste; see Breste.

Braun, *s.* muscle, A 546; brawn (of the boar), F 1254.

Braunche, *s.* branch, T. v. 844.

Brayd, Brayde; see Breyde.

Brede (1), *s.* breadth, R. 825, 1124; space, T. i. 179; *on brede*, abroad, T. i. 530.

Brede (2), *s.* roast meat, HF. 1222.

Brede, *ger.* to breed, T. iii. 1546; grow, T. v. 1027; Breden, *ger.* to breed, arise, L. 1156 (cf. Vergil, Æn. iv. 2); Bred, *pp.* bred up, F 499.

Breech, *s.* breeches, B 2049, C 948.

Breem, *s.* bream, a fish, A 350.

Breke, *v.* break, A 551, C 936; *br. his day*, fail to pay on the day, G 1040; *ger.* to interrupt, B 2233; Brak, *pt. s.* 3. 71; Breke, *pr. s. subj.* 4. 242; Breke, 2 *pr. pl. subj.* break off, T. v. 1032; Breke, *pt. s. subj.* would break, B 4578; Broke, *pp.* broken, A 3571; Broken, *pp.* ship-wrecked, L. 1487.

Brekke, *s.* break, flaw, defect, 3. 940.

Bremble-flour, *s.* flower of the bramble, B 1936.

Breme, *adj.* furious, T. iv. 184.

Breme, *adv.* furiously, A 1699.

Bren, *s.* bran, A 4053.

Brenne, *v.* burn, 17. 18; to be burnt, T. i. 91; Brinne, *ger.* to burn, D 52; Brendest, 2 *pt. s.* didst burn, A 2384; Brende, *pt. s.* 1. 90; was burnt, HF. 163; was set on fire, HF. 537; Brenned, *pt. s.* was inflamed with anger, R. 297; Brende, *pt. pl.* caught fire, HF. 954; Brente, *pt. pl.* L. 731: Brent, *pp.* 7. 115;

Brend, *pp.* B 4555; *as adj.* bright, R. 1109.

Brenning, *s.* burning, 4. 133; greed of gold, R. 188.

Brenningly, *adv.* ardently, T. i. 607; fervently, A 1564.

Brere, *s.* briar, R. 858; Breres, *pl.* underwood, A 1532.

Brest, *s.* breast, A 115, 131.

Brest-boon, *s.* breast-bone, A 2710.

Breste, *v.* burst, T. v. 1008; afflict, T. iii. 1434; break, D 1103; Brest, *pr. s.* bursts, A 2610; breaks, T. i. 258; Brast, *pt. s.* burst out, T. v. 1078; burst, L. 1033; broke, 3. 1193; Brast, *pt. s.* burst (*or read* braste = would burst), T. v. 180; Braste, *pt. pl.* burst, T. ii. 326; Broste, *pt. pl.* B 671, C 234; Brosten, *pt. pl.* 4. 96; Braste, *pt. s. subj.* would burst, T. ii. 1108; Brosten, *pp.* burst, T. ii. 976; broken, L. 1300.

Bresting, *s.* bursting, F 973.

Bretful, *adj.* brimful, A 687, 2164.

Bretherhed, *s.* brotherhood, religious order, A 511.

Brew, *pt. s.* contrived, B 3575.

Breyde, *ger.* to start, T. iv. 230, 348; *v.* awake, F 477; Breyde, 1 *pr. s.* start, T. v. 1262; Breyde, 1 *pt. s.* awoke, D 799; Breyde, *pt. s.* started, T. v. 1243; went (out of his wits), B 3728; drew, B 837; Brayde, *pt. s.* took hastily, HF. 1678; Brayd, *pp.* started, gone suddenly, 7. 124.

Brid, *s.* bird, HF. 1003; young of birds, 5. 192.

Brige, *s.* contention, B 2873. F. *brigue.*

Brigge, *s.* bridge, A 3922.

Bright, *adj.* fair, R. 1009.

Brighte, *adj. as s.* brightness (after *for*), T. ii. 864.

Brike, *s.* a trap, snare, 'fix,' dilemma, B 3580.

Bringe, *v.* bring; Bringes, 2 *pr. s.* bringest, HF. 1908 (a Northern form); Broghten, *pt. pl.* B 2590; *made broght,* caused to be brought, HF. 155.

Brinne, *ger.* to burn, D 52. See Brenne.

Brocage, *s.* mediation, A 3375.

Broche, *s.* brooch, R. 1193; small ornament, bracelet, 4. 245.

Brode, *adv.* broadly, plainly, A 739; far and wide, HF. 1683; wide awake, G 1420.

Brodere, *adj.* larger, A. ii. 38. 1.

Brok, i. e. Badger, a horse's name, D 1543.

Broken; see Harm. And see Breke.

Brokkinge, *pres. pt.* using a quavering voice, A 3377.

Bromes, *pl.* broom (bushes so called), HF. 1226.

Brond, *s.* torch, L. 2252; firebrand, B 3224; Bronde, *dat.* piece of burning wood, B 2095.

Brood, *adj.* broad, A 155, 471; thick, large, F 82; Brode, *pl.* R. 939; expanded, R. 1681.

Broste, -en; see Breste.

Brotel, *adj.* brittle, frail, T. iii. 820; fickle, L. 1885; unsafe, insecure, E 1279; transitory, E 2061; Brutel, B 2. p 5. 6.

Brotelnesse, *s.* frailty, T. v. 1832; insecurity, E 1279; fickleness, 10. 63.

Brotherhede, *s.* brotherhood, D 1399.

Brouded, *pp.* embroidered, A 3238, B 3659.

Brouke, *v.* enjoy, use, B 4490; keep, E 2308; 1 *pr. s. subj.* (*optative*), may have the use of, HF. 273; Brouken, *pr. pl. subj.* (*opt.*), may (they) profit by, L. 194.

Browding, *s.* embroidery, A 2498.

Broyded, *pp.* braided, A 1049.

Brutel; see Brotel.

Brybe, *v.* steal, filch, A 4417; rob, D 1378.

Bryberyes, *pl.* ways of robbing, D 1367.

Brydale, *s.* wedding, A 4375.

Brydel, *s.* bridle, 7. 184.

Brydeleth, *pr. s.* controls, 4. 41.

Buffet, *s.* blow; Buffettes, *pl.* I 258.

Bugle-horn, *s.* drinking-horn made from the 'bugle' or ox, F 1253.

Buk, *s.* buck, 5. 195; Bukke, B 1946; Bukkes, *gen.* buck's, A 3387.

Bulde, *v.* build; Bulte, *pt. s.* built, A 1548.

Bulle, *s.* papal bull, C 909.

Bulte, *pt. s. of* Bulde.

Bulte, *v.* boult, sift, B 4430.

Burdoun, *s.* burden of a song, bass-accompaniment, A 673.

Burel, *adj.* rough, unlettered, F 716; lay (people), D 1872, 1874. The idea is that of a man dressed in *burel,* or coarse woollen cloth. See Borel.

Buriels, *s. pl.* burial-places, i. e. the catacombs, G 186.

Burne, *v.* burnish; *pp.* A 1983; polished, HF. 1387; lustrous, C 38. See Borne.

Burnet, *adj.* made of coarse brown cloth, R. 226.

Busk, *s.* bush, R. 54; *pl.* A 1579.

But, *conj.* except, unless, 2. 82; 3. 117.

But, *as s.* an exception, a 'but,' I 494.

But and, but if, L. 1790.

**But-if,** *conj.* unless, R. 250.

**Buxom,** *adj.* yielding, 6. 125; obedient, B 1287.

**Buxomly,** *adv.* obediently, E 186.

**Buxumnesse,** *s.* submission, 13. 15.

**By,** *prep.* by, A 25, &c.; as regards, with respect to, concerning, 6. 126; with reference to, 5. 4; for, on account of, R. 844; *by proces,* in process, B 2665; *by me,* beside me (*with accent on* by), T. ii. 991; *by the morwe,* in the morning, L. 49.

**By,** *adv.* beside; *faste by,* close at hand, R. 1274.

**By and by,** *adv.* one after another, in due order, in due place, L. 304, A 1011.

**Byde,** *v.* wait, T. i. 1067; A 1576; Bood, *pt. s.* waited, T. v. 29; Bïden, *pp.* stayed, E 1888.

**Bye,** *v.* buy, pay for (it), D 167; *go by,* let us go to buy, G 1294; Bye, *pr. pl. subj.* 18. 26; Boghte, *pt. s.* bought, A 2088; redeemed, E 1153; *b. agayn,* redeemed, C 776.

**Byhight,** *pp.* promised, T. v. 1104.

**Bying,** *s.* buying, A 569.

**By-japed,** *pp.* tricked, made a jest of, T. v. 1119.

**Bynt him,** binds himself, 4. 47; Bynt her, 4. 48.

**By-path,** *s.* by-way, T. iii. 1705.

**Byrde,** *s.* maiden, lady, R. 1014.

**By-seke,** *v.* beseech, T. iv. 131.

**Byte,** *v.* bite, T. iii. 737; cut deeply, F 158; burn, A 631; Bòòt, *pt. s.* bit, B 3791; Bïten, *pp.* bitten, L. 2318.

**Bytinge,** *s.* wound, B 3. m 7. 7.

**By-word,** *s.* proverb, T. iv. 769.

**By-wreye,** *v.* reveal, T. iii. 367.

### C.

**Caas,** *s.* circumstance, I 105; *sette caas* = suppose, A. ii. 42. 24; Caas, *pl.* cases of law, A 323.

**Cacche,** *v.* catch, G 11; lay hold of, 3. 969; come by, HF. 404; Caughte, *pt. s.* took, conceived, E 619; took, A 498; pulled, L. 1854; Caught, *pp.* obtained, E 1110; taken, F 740.

**Caitif,** *adj.* captive, miserable, wretched, A 1552.

**Caitif,** *s.* wretch, R. 340; *pl.* captives, A 924.

**Cake,** *s.* a round and rather flat loaf of bread (in the shape of a large bun), A 668, 4094, C 322.

**Calcening,** *s.* calcination, G 771.

**Calcinacioun,** *s.* calcination, G 804.

**Calcule,** *v.* calculate; Calculed, *pt. s.* F. 1284.

**Calculer,** *s.* the calculator or pointer, A i. 23. 2. See **Almury.**

**Calculinge,** *s.* calculation, T. i. 71.

**Calendes,** *pl.* kalends, introduction to a new time, T. ii. 7.

**Calle,** *s.* caul, a net used to confine women's hair, A. i. 19. 4; headdress, D 1018; to 'make a hood above a caul' = to befool, T. iii. 775.

**Camaille,** *s.* a camel, E 1196.

**Camuse,** *adj.* low and concave, A 3934, 3974.

**Can,** 1 *pr. s.* know, L. 1987; know how, am able, E 304, F 4; can, B 42; understand, F 1266; am able to say, 5. 14; *pr. s.* knows, 3. 673; has, E 2245; knows (of), A 1780; has skill, T. ii. 1197; *can on,* has knowledge of, F 786; *can hir good,* knows her own advantage, D 231; *can thank,* owes (them) thanks, A 1818; 2 *pr. pl.* know, B 1169.

**Canel-boon,** *s.* collar-bone (lit. channel-bone, with reference to the depression in the neck behind the collar-bone), 3. 943.

**Canelle,** *s.* cinnamon, R. 1370.

**Cankedort,** *s.* state of suspense, critical position, T. ii. 1752.

**Canon,** *s.* the 'Canon,' the title of a book by Avicenna, C 890; rule, explanation, A. pr. 105.

**Canstow,** 2 *p. s. pr.* knowest thou, A. pr. 20; canst thou, T. iv. 460.

**Cantel,** *s.* portion, A 3008.

**Cape,** *ger.* gape after, T. v. 1133. See **Gape.**

**Capel,** *s.* horse, nag, H 64; cart-horse, D 2150.

**Cappe,** *s.* cap, A 586; *set the wrightes cappe,* i. e. made a fool of him, A 3143.

**Carbouole,** *s.* carbuncle-stone, R. 1120.

**Cardiacle,** *s.* pain about the heart, C 313.

**Care,** *s.* anxiety, sorrow, grief, trouble, 7. 63; T. i. 505, 587; ill-luck, 5. 363; *pl.* miseries, T. i. 264.

**Care,** *v.* feel anxiety, E 1212; Care thee, *imp. s.* be anxious, A 3298.

**Careful,** *adj.* full of trouble, 6. 44, 133; sorrowful, A 1565.

**Careyne,** *s.* corpse, carcase, 5. 177.

**Carf,** cut; see **Kerve.**

**Cariage,** *s.* a carrying away; *upon c.,* in the way of carrying anything away, i. e. that I can carry away, D 1570; Cariages, *s. pl.* tolls due from the tenant to his feudal lord imposed by authority, I 752.

**Carl,** *s.* man, A 3469; rustic, countryman, A 545.

**Cárole,** *s.* a dance accompanied with singing, R. 744, 781, 793.

**Carole,** *v.* dance round singing, 3. 849; *pp.* danced, R. 810.

**Carpe,** *v.* talk, discourse, A 474.

**Carrik,** *s.* barge, D 1688.

**Cart,** *s.* chariot, HF. 943.

**Cartere,** *s.* charioteer, B 5. p 4. 100.

**Cart-hors,** *pl.* chariot-horses, HF. 944.

**Cas,** *s.* accident, chance, HF. 254, 1052; affair, L. 409; occasion, B 36; adventure, L. 1630; mischance, L. 1056; *in cas that,* in case, A. ii. 3. 2; *upon cas,* by chance, A 3661; *in cas if that,* in case that, T. ii. 758; *in no maner cas,* in no way, D 1831; *set a cas,* suppose that, T. ii. 729; *to deyen in the cas,* though death were the result, E 859.

**Cast,** *s.* occasion, turn, B 3477; contrivance, plan, HF. 1178.

**Caste,** *v.* cast (accounts), B 1406; Casten, *v.* throw, T. ii. 513; *c. with a spere,* throw with a spear, HF. 1048; fling, A 3330; contrive, HF. 1170; Caste, 1 *pr. s.* conjecture, A 2172; Casteth, *pr. s.* casts about, I 692; considers, G 1414; applies, B 2781; *refl.* devotes himself, G 738; Cast, *pr. s.* casts, R. 1574; Caste, 1 *pt. s.* threw, 5. 172; Casten, *pp.* thrown, B 1796; Cast, *pp.* overthrown, T. ii. 1389; contrived, B 3891; *c. biforn,* premeditated, I 543.

**Castelled,** *adj.* castellated, I 445.

**Castel-yate,** castle-gate, HF. 1294.

**Catapuce,** *s.* caper-spurge (*Euphorbia Lathyris*), B 4155.

**Catel,** *s.* property, wealth, possessions, goods, A 373, 540.

**Cause,** *s.* cause, 1. 26; A 419; reason, T. v. 527; plea, 2. 46; Cause causinge, first cause, T. iv. 829; *by the c. that,* because, A 2488; *by that c.,* because, T. iv. 99; Cause why, the reason why, T. iii. 795; the reason for it (was), A 4144.

**Causeles,** *adv.* without cause, F 825.

**Cave,** *s.* cave, HF. 70; used to translate the astrological term 'puteus,' 4. 119.

**Cavillacioun,** *s.* cavilling, D 2136.

**Celebrable,** *adj.* celebrated, B 4. m 7. 30.

**Celerer,** *s.* keeper of a cellar, B 3126.

**Celle,** *s.* cell, A 172, 1376.

**Centaure,** *s.* centaury, *Centaurea nigra,* B 4153.

**Centre,** *s.* a point on a *rete* representing a star, A i. 21. 12.

**Ceptre,** *s.* sceptre, B 3334, 3563.

**Cercle,** *s.* HF. 791; sphere, 16. 9.

**Cerclen,** *ger.* to encircle, T. iii. 1767; *pr. s.* R. 1619.

**Cered,** *pp. as adj.* waxed, G 808.

**Cerial,** *adj.* belonging to a species of oak, the *Quercus cerris,* A 2290.

**Ceriously,** *adv.* minutely, with full details, B 185. Ducange has 'Seriose,' fuse, minutatim, articulatim.' From Lat. *series,* order.

**Certein,** *adj.* sure; Certeins, *pl.* certain, B 5. p 5. 115; *c. gold,* a stated sum of money, B 242; *c. tresor,* a quantity of treasure, B 442; *c. yeres,* a certain number of years, B 3367; Certeyn, a certain sum, a fixed quantity, G. 776.

**Certein,** *adv.* certainly, indeed, assuredly, A 375.

**Certes,** *adv.* certainly, R. 374, 439.

**Ceruce,** *s.* white lead, A 630.

**Cese,** *v.* cause to cease, T. i. 445; put an end to, 4. 11. See **Cesse.**

**Cesse,** *v.* cease, B 1066; *c. cause,* when the cause ceases, T. ii. 483; *c. wind,* when the wind ceases, T. ii. 1388.

**Cetewale,** *s.* setwall, i.e. zedoary, A 3207, B 1951. O. F. *citoal.* A medicinal substance obtained in the East Indies, having a fragrant smell, and a warm, bitter, aromatic taste, used in medicine as a stimulant. (The name *setwall* was also given to valerian.)

**Ceynt,** *s.* cincture, girdle, A 3235.

**Chaffare,** *s.* bargaining, I 851; traffic, G 1421; trade, A 4389; merchandise, ware, B 1475, D 521; matter, subject, E 2438.

**Chaffáre,** *ger.* to trade, barter, deal, traffic, B 139.

**Chaires,** *s. pl.* thrones, B 4. m 2. 6.

**Chalánge,** *v.* ; *pr. s.* 1 *p.* claim, F 1324; Chalaunged, *pt. s.* arrogated, B 2. p 6. 36.

**Chalanging,** *s.* false claim, accusation, C 264.

**Chalaundre,** *s.* a species of lark (*Alauda calandra*), R. 914; *pl.* R. 663.

**Chalice,** *s.* cup, I 879.

**Chalk-stoon,** *s.* a piece of chalk, G 1207.

**Chalons,** *pl.* blankets or coverlets for a bed, A 4140. Cf. E. *shalloon.*

**Chamberere,** *s.* maidservant, lady's maid, D 300.

**Chambre-roof,** roof of my room, 3. 299.

**Champartye,** *s.* equality, participation in power, A 1949. F. *champ parti.*

**Chanon**, *s.* canon, G 573.

**Chapeleine**, *s.* chaplain, A 164.

**Chapelet**, *s.* fillet, circlet for the head, chaplet, R. 563, 845, 908.

**Chapitre**, *s.* chapter, D 1945.

**Chapman**, *s.* trader, merchant, A 397; Chapmen, *pl.* B 135.

**Chapmanhede**, *s.* bargaining, B 1428; trade, B 143.

**Char**, *s.* chariot, 7. 24, 39, 40.

**Charbocle**, *s.* carbuncle (a precious stone), B 2061.

**Charge**, *s.* load, burden, R. 1352; responsibility, 5. 507; consideration, A 1284; importance, 3. 894; care, A 733; particular note, D 321; a heavy thing, HF. 746; weight, L. 620; consequence, L. 2383; *of that no ch.*, for that no matter, it is of no importance, G 749.

**Charge**, *v.* load, L. 2151; command, L. 493; *pp.* burdened, I 92; bidden, L 940.

**Chargeant**, *adj.* burdensome, B 2433.

**Char-hors**, *pl.* chariot-horses, T. v. 1018.

**Charitáble**, *adj.* loving, L. 444; kind, A 143.

**Charitee**, *s.* charity, love, T. 1. 49; for seinte ch., i. e. *either* (1) for holy charity; *or* (2) for the sake of St. Charity, A 1721, B 4510, D 2119.

**Charmeresses**, *fem. pl.* workers with charms, HF. 1261.

**Chaste**, *v.* to chasten; *pp.* taught, F 491. O. F. *chastier.* See **Chastyse**.

**Chasteyn**, *s.* chestnut, A 2922. See **Chesteynes.**

**Chástisinge**, *s.* chastening, 1. 129.

**Chastyse**, *v.* to rebuke, restrain, B 3695; chasten, 1. 39. See **Chaste.**

**Chaunce**, *s.* chance, A 1752; incident, 3. 1285; destiny, 3. 1113; luck, G 593; 'chance,' a technical term in the game of hazard, C 653.

**Chaunging**, *s.* change, 21. 17.

**Chaunteth**, *pr. s.* sings, A 3367, E 1850.

**Chaunte-pleure**, title of a song upon grief following joy, 7. 320.

**Chaunterie**, *s.* an endowment for the payment of a priest to sing mass, agreeably to the appointment of the founder, A 510.

**Chayer**, *s.* chair, B 3803; throne, B 1. m 5. 3.

**Cheef**, *adj.* chief, 3. 910, 911.

**Cheef**, *s.* chief, head, L. 2109.

**Cheek**, *s.* cheek, i. e. cheekbone, B 3228.

**Cheep**, *s.* market, price; *to greet cheep,* too cheap, D 523; *as good chep,* as

cheaply, T. iii. 641; a time of cheapness. HF. 1974.

**Chees**; see **Chese.**

**Cheeste**, *s.* wrangling, I 556. A. S. *cēast.*

**Chek**, *s. as int.* check (at chess), 3. 659.

**Chekkere**, *s.* chess-board, 3. 660.

**Chekmat**, checkmate, T. ii. 754.

**Chelaundre**, R. 81; see **Chalaundre.**

**Chep, -e**; see **Cheep.**

**Chepe**, *ger.* to bargain (with her), D 268.

**Chere**, *s.* face, countenance, T. i. 14; look, mien, R. 1014; entertainment, A 747; favour, 7. 108; appearance, 19. 4; behaviour, A 139; look, glance, sign, T. i. 312; good cheer, mirth, A 4363; kindly greeting, 4. 146; show, B 2377; kindly expression, E 1112; *doth him chere,* makes him good cheer, L. 2452; *be of good ch.,* be of good cheer, T i. 879; *sory ch.,* mournful look, D 588; Cheres, *pl.* faces, R. 813; looks, T. ii. 1507.

**Cherl**, *s.* churl, boor, fellow, 5. 596; L. 136; slave, I 463; man (in the moon), T. i. 1024; *pl.* violent men, fierce men, R. 880.

**Chertée**, *s.* affection, B 1526.

**Cherubinnes**, *gen.* cherub's, A 624.

**Cheryse**, *pl.* cherries, R. 1376.

**Ches**, *s.* chess, 3. 619, 652, 664.

**Chése**, *v.* choose, 5. 399, 400; Cheest, *pr. s.* chooseth, 5. 623; Chees, 1 *pt. s.* chose, 3. 791; Chees, *pt. s.* chose, B 3706; Chees, *imp. s.* choose, L. 1449; Cheseth, *imp. pl.* D 1232; Chose, *pp.* chosen, 3. 1004.

**Chesinge**, *s.* choosing, choice, B 2305, E 162.

**Cheste**, *s.* chest, casket, T. v. 1368; box, trunk, L. 510; coffin, D 502.

**Chesteynes**, *pl.* chestnuts, R. 1375.

**Chevauchee**; see **Chivachee.**

**Cheve**, *v.*; *in phr.* yvel mote he cheve = ill may he end, *or* ill may he thrive, G 1225.

**Chevesaile**, *s.* (ornamented) collar or neckband of a gown, R. 1082.

**Chevisaunce**, *s.* borrowing, L. 2434; agreement to borrow, B 1519; dealing for profit, A 282.

**Chevise**, *v. refl.* accomplish (her) desire, 4. 289. O. F. *chevir.*

**Chideresse**, *s.* a scold, R. 150.

**Chieftayn**, *s.* captain, A 2555.

**Chiertee**, *s.* fondness, D 396; love, F 881.

**Chike**, *s.* chicken, R. 541.

**Chiknes**, *pl.* chickens, A 380.

**Child**, *s.* young man, A 3325; Childes

pley, child's play, E 1530 ; Childe, with, with child, L. 1323.

Childhede, *s.* childhood, R. 399.

Childly, *adj.* childlike, 3. 1095.

Chilindre, *s.* cylinder, portable sun-dial, B 1396.

Chimbe, *s.* rim of the barrel, A 3895.

Chimbe, *v.* chime (as a bell), A 3896.

Chimenee, *s.* fireplace, A 3776.

Chinche, *s.* niggard, miser, B 2793, 2809.

Chincherye, *s.* niggardliness, miserliness, B 2790.

Chirche, *s.* church, A 708, 2760.

Chirche-hawe, *s.* churchyard, I 964 ; *pl.* I 801.

Chirche-reves, *pl.* church - officers, churchwardens, D 1306.

Chirketh, *pr. s.* chirps, D 1804 ; *pres. pt.* rustling, B 1. m 6. 10.

Chirking, *s.* creaking, grating noises, A 2004, I 605; Chirkinges, *pl.* shriekings, cries, HF. 1943.

Chisels, *s.* scissors, I 418.

Chit, chides ; *pr. s. of* Chyde.

Chiteren, *v.* chatter, prattle, G 1397.

Chiteringe, *s.* chattering, chirping, T. ii. 68.

Chiváchee, *s.* feat of horsemanship, H 50; Chevauchee, swift course (lit. ride), 4. 144. O.F. *chevauchee*, an expedition on horseback.

Chívachýe, *s.* a military expedition, A 85.

Chivalrye, *s.* knighthood, the accomplishments of a knight, A 45; knightly conduct, valour, R. 1207 ; L. 608; troops of horse, cavalry, company of knights, A 878.

Chogh, *s.* chough, 5. 345.

Choppen, *v.* strike downwards, knock, HF. 1824.

Chose, *pp. of* Chese.

Chuk, *s.* cluck, 'chucking' noise, B 4364.

Chukketh, *pr. s.* clucks, B 4372.

Chyde, *v.* chide, T. iii. 1433 ; complain, F 650; reproach, T. v. 1093 ; Chit, *pr. s.* chides, scolds, G 921 ; Chidde, 1 *pt. s.* chid, D 223.

Chydester, *s.* (female) scold, E 1535.

Chydinges, *pl.* scoldings, HF. 1028.

Chyning, *adj.* gaping, yawning, B 1. p 6. 41. A.S. *cīnan*, to gape open.

Ciclatoun, *s.* a costly kind of thin cloth, B 1924.

Cinamome, *s.* cinnamon, as a term of endearment, sweet one, A 3699.

Cink, *num.* cinque, five, C 653.

Cipres, *s.* cypress, 5. 179; *(collectively)*, cypresses, R. 1381.

Circumscryve, *v.* enclose, comprehend, T. v. 1865.

Citole, *s.* kind of harp, a stringed instrument, A 1959.

Citrinacioun, *s.* citronising, the turning to the colour of citron, a process in alchemy, G 816.

Citryn, *adj.* citron-coloured, A 2167.

Clamb, *pt. s. of* Climben.

Clamour, *s.* A 995; outcry, D 889.

Claperes, *pl.* burrows (for rabbits), R. 1405.

Clappe, *s.* thunderclap, HF. 1040.

Clappe, *s.* prating, foolish talk, A 3144.

Clappe, *v.* clap ; *hence*, chatter, prattle, G 965 ; *pr. s.* knocks, D 1581, 1584 ; *pr. pl.* talk unceasingly, I 406 ; Clappeth, *imp. pl.* E 1200; Clapte, *pt. s.* shut quickly, A 3740.

Clapping, *s.* chatter, idle talk, E 999.

Clarioning, *s.* the music of the clarion, HF. 1242.

Clarioun, *s.* clarion, trumpet, HF. 1240, 1573, 1579.

Clarree, *s.* clarified wine, wine mixed with honey and spices, and afterwards strained till clear, A 1471, E 1807.

Clasped, *pp.* fastened, A 273.

Clatereth, *pr. s.* says noisily, B 2259 ; *pt. pl.* rattled, A 2423.

Clateringe, *s.* clanking, A 2492 ; clashing, D 1865.

Clause, *s.* sentence ; *also*, agreement, stipulation, T. ii. 728 ; *in a clause*, in a short sentence, briefly, 22. 38.

Clawe, *v.* rub, D 940; *ger.* to scratch, T. iv. 728 ; *pt. s.* stroked, A 4326 ; Clew, 1 *pt. s.* rubbed, HF. 1702.

Cleerly, *adv.* entirely, B 1566.

Cleernesse, *s.* glory, G 403.

Clefte, *pt. s. of* Cleve (1).

Clène, *adj.* clean, A 504 ; unmixed, B 1183.

Clène, *adv.* clean, entirely, wholly, R. 1380.

Clennesse, *s.* purity, A 506.

Clense, *v.* cleanse, A 631.

Clepen, *v.* call, name, A 643, 2730 ; call out, A 3577 ; *pr. s.* D 102 ; F 382 ; *men cl.*, people call, E 115 ; Clepe . . . ayein *(or again)*, *v.* recall, T. ii. 521 ; *pt. s.* called, F 374 ; Clepte, *pt. s.* called, R. 1331; summoned, B 2432 ; Clept, *pp.* named, G 863.

Clere, *adj.* clear, R. 681 ; bright, 3. 340 ; well-sounding, 3. 347 ; noble, pure, HF. 1575.

Clere, *adv.* clearly, A 170; L. 139.

Clere, *v.* grow clear, T. ii. 2, 806; *ger.* to grow bright, T. v. 519; to shine clearly, L. 773.

Clerer, *adj. comp.* brighter, 3. 822.

Clergeon, *s.* a chorister-boy, B 1693.

Clergial, *adj.* clerkly, learned, G 752.

Clergye, *s.* learning, D 1277.

Clerk, *s.* clerk, scholar, student, A 285; writer, D 689.

Clernesse, *s.* brightness, L. 84.

Cleve (1), *v.* cleave, cut, split, R. 859; L. 758; Clefte, *pt. s.* split, 3. 72; Cloven, *pp.* A 2934; Clove, *pp.* cleft, dimpled, R. 550.

Cleve (2), *v.* adhere; *pr. pl.* B 3. p 11. 112.

Clew, *s.* clew, L 2140.

Clew, *pt. s. of* Clawe.

Cley, *s.* clay, G 807.

Clifte, *s.* cleft, L. 740; chink, B 4. p 4. 296.

Cliket, *s.* latch-key, E 2046, 2117, 2121, 2123.

Climben, *v.* climb, F 106; Clamb, *pt. s.* B 1987; Clomb, 1 *pt. s.* climbed, HF. 1118; Clomben, *pt. pl.* climbed, A 3636; Clamben, *pt. pl.* climbed, HF. 2151; Cloumben, B 2590; Clomben, *pp.* T. i. 215; ascended, B 4388; Clombe, *pp.* risen, B 12; *were clombe*, hadst climbed, B 3592.

Clinking, *s.* tinkling, B 3984.

Clippe (1), 1 *pr. s.* embrace, T. iii. 1344.

Clippe (2), *v.* cut hair, A 3326.

Clipping, *s.* embracing, R. 342.

Clobbed, *adj.* clubbed, B 3088.

Cloisterer, *s.* resident in a cloister, A 259, 3661.

Cloisterlees, *adj.* outside of a cloister, A 179.

Cloke, *s.* cloak, T. iii. 738.

Clokke, *s.* clock, B 4044; *of the cl.*, by the clock, B 14.

Clom, *interj.* be silent, mum! A 3638.

Clombe, -n; see Climben.

Clôòs, *adj.* close, secret, T. ii. 1534; closed, B 4522; Clos, closed, R. 1675.

Clôòth, *s.* piece of clothing, D 1633; infants' clothing, T. iii. 733.

Clos, *s.* enclosure, B 4550.

Closet, *s.* small room, T. ii. 599, 1215.

Closing, *s.* enclosure, boundary, R. 527.

Closure, *s.* enclosure, I 870.

Clote-leef, *s.* a leaf of the burdock or clote-bur, G 577. A. S. *clâte*, a burdock.

Clôth, *s.* cloth, garment, D 238; clothes, D 1881.

Clothen, *v.* clothe, T. v. 1418; Cladde, *pt. s.* clad, T. iv. 1690; *refl.* clothed himself, 7. 145; Cledde, *pt. s.* T. iii. 1521; Clad, *pp.* R. 409; covered, A 294; furnished, 3. 352.

Clothered, *pp.* clotted, coagulated, A 2745. (Other MSS. *clotered, clotred.*)

Clothlees, *adj.* naked, I 343.

Cloud, *s.* sky, T. iii. 433.

Cloumben; see Climben.

Clout, *s.* bit of cloth, C 736; patch, R. 458; *pl.* fragments, E 1953; rags, C 348.

Clouted, *pp.* patched up, R. 223.

Cloven, *pp. of* Cleve (1).

Clowes, *pl.* claws, HF. 1785.

Clow-gelofre, *pp.* clove, the spice so called, R. 1368; Clowe-gilofre, B 1952. Fr. *clou de girofle.*

Clustred, *pp.* covered with clouds, B 1. m 3. 6. (Lat. *glomerantur.*)

Clymat, *s.* a belt or zone of the earth included between two given lines of latitude, A. ii. 39. 28; *pl.* zones of latitude, A. i. 3. 4; Clymates, sets of almicanteras calculated for various terrestial latitudes, A. i. 14. 4.

Clyven, *pr. pl.* cleave, keep, B 3. p 11. 115.

Clyves, *pl.* cliffs, L. 1470.

Coagulat, *pp.* clotted, G 811.

Cod, *s.* bag; used of the receptacle of the stomach, C 534.

Coempcioun, *s.* an imposition so called, lit. joint purchase, the buying up of the whole of any commodity in the market, B 1. p 4. 90.

Cofre, *s.* coffer, chest, L. 380; money-box, F 1571; coffin, 5. 177.

Cogge, *s.* cock-boat, L. 1481.

Coghe, *ger.* to cough, T. ii. 254.

Coillons, *pl.* testicles, C 952.

Cok, *s.* cock, 5. 350; *thridde c.*, third cock, A 4233.

Cok! cok! the noise made by a cock, B 4467.

Cokenay, *s.* cockney, effeminate creature, A 4208.

Cokewold, *s.* cuckold, A 3152.

Cokkel, *s.* cockle, i. e. the corn-cockle, *Agrostemma githago*, B 1183.

Cokkes, *corruption of* Goddes, H 9, I 29.

Cokkow, *s.* cuckoo, HF. 243.

Còl, *s.* coal, T. ii. 1332; Cole, A 2692.

Col-blak, *adj.* coal-black, A 2142.

Cold, *adj.* cold, A 420; chilling (often in phr. *cares colde*), T. iii. 1260; disastrous, B 4446.

Colde, *v.* grow cold, B 879, F 1023.

Coler, *s.* collar, T. v. 811; Colers, *pl.*

collars, A 2152 (or read *colerd*, provided with collars).

*Colera* (Lat.), choler, B 4118.

Colere, *s.* choler, B 4136.

Colerik, *adj.* choleric, A 587, B 4145.

Col-fox, *s.* coal-fox, fox with black marks, B 4405.

Collacioun, *s.* conference, E 325.

Collateral, *adj.* adventitious, subordinate, T. i. 262.

Collect, *pp.* collected in groups, F 1275.

Colóur, *s.* colour, 7. 173; complexion, hue, R. 213; outward appearance, 2. 66; pretence, 10. 21; excuse, D 399; *pl.* fine phrases, HF. 859; hues, pretences (a pun), F 511.

Colpons, *pl.* shreds, bundles, A 679; billets, A 2867.

Coltish, *adj.* like a colt, E 1847.

Columbyn, *adj.* dove-like, E 2141.

Colver, *s.* dove, L. 2319. A. S. *culfre.*

Combred, *pp.* encumbered, B 3. m 10. 9.

Combre-world, *s.* one who encumbers the world, who lives too long, T. iv. 279.

Combust, *pp.* burnt, G 811; quenched (as being too near the sun), T. iii. 717.

Come, *v.* come; *come thereby*, come by it, acquire it, G 1395; Come, *ger.* to come, future, 3. 708; Comestow, comest thou, L. 1887; Cometh, *pr. s. as fut.* shall come, 4. 11; Comth, *pr. s.* comes, B 407; Cam, *pt. s.* came, F 81; Cŏm, *pt. s.* 3. 134; Cŏmen, *pt. pl.* L. 1241; Cŏmen, *pp.* come, 4. 81; *ben comen*, are come, B 1130; Com of, i. e. seize the opportunity, be quick, T. ii. 1738; D 1602; Cometh, *imp. pl.* A 839.

Cŏme, *s.* coming, G 343. A. S. *cyme.*

Comédie, *s.* comedy, pleasant tale, one that ends happily, T. v. 1788.

Comeveden, 2 *pr. pl. as* 2 *pr. s.,* didst instigate, T. iii. 17. See Commeveth.

Comlily, *adv.* in a comely way, 3. 848.

Commeveth, *pr. s.* moves, induces, T. v. 1783; Commeve, *pr. s. subj.* move, T. v. 1386. See Commoeve, Comeveden.

Commoeve, *ger.* to move, influence, B 4. p 4. 275.

Commoevinge, *s.* moving, disturbing, B 1. m 4. 6.

Commune, *adj.* general, common, B 155; *in c.,* commonly, A 1261.

Commune, *s.* the commons, E 70; *pl.* commoners, A 2509.

Compaignable, *adj.* companionable, B 1194.

Companye, *s.* company, A 24; companionship, 4. 219.

Comparisoned, *pp.* compared, B 2. p 7. 118.

Compas, *s.* circuit, 4. 137; circlet, wreath, R. 900; circle, A 1889; a very large circle, HF. 798; circumference, 20. 5; enclosure, orb, world, as in *tryne compas,* the threefold world (earth, sea, and heaven), G 45; pair of compasses, A. ii. 40. 13; craft, contriving, HF. 462; *pl.* circles (*or, perhaps,* pairs of compasses), HF. 1302.

Compasment, *s.* plotting, contrivance, L. 1416.

Compasse, *v.* contrive, R. 194; planned, L. 1414; Compassed, *pp.* drawn with compasses, fashioned circularly, A. i. 18. 1; planned, L. 1543.

Compassing, *s.* dimension, R. 1350; contrivance, A 1996.

Compeer, *s.* gossip, close friend, A 670; comrade, A 4419.

Compilatour, *s.* compiler, A. pr. 70.

Cómpleynt, *s.* a 'complaint' or ballad, 2. 43; 3. 464.

Complexioun, *s.* complexion, A 333; temperament, I 585; the (four) temperaments, HF. 21.

Compline, *s.* evening service, A 4171.

Complisshen, *v.* accomplish, B 4. p 4. 24.

Comporte, *v.* bear, endure, T. v. 1397.

Composicioun, *s.* agreement, A 848, 2651.

Compotent, *adj.* all-powerful, B 5. p 6. 53.

Compouned, *pp.* composed, HF. 1029; tempered, L. 2585; mingled, HF. 2108; constructed, drawn, A. pr. 11.

Comprehende, *v.* take (it) in, T. iv. 891; take in (in the mind), F 223; *pr. s.* comprises, I 1043.

Comprende, *v.* comprehend, contain, T. iii. 1687.

Comunalitee, *s.* empire, B 4. p 6. 402.

Comune, *adj.* general, common to all, T. iii. 1415; accustomed to, 3. 812; Comun profit, the good of the country, 5. 47; 75.

Comune, *s.* a common share in a thing, E 1313.

Comyn, *s.* cummin, B 2045. 'A dwarf umbelliferous plant, somewhat resembling fennel, cultivated for its seeds.'—Webster.

Con, *imp. s.* grant; Con me thank, grant me thanks, thank me, A. pr. 62.

Conceite, *s.* conception, thought, L. 1764; idea, G 1214; notion, T. i. 996.

Conclude, *v.* draw a conclusion, B 14; include, put together, G 429; attain to success, G 773; *ger.* to summarize, A 1358; Concluded, *pp.* come to a conclusion, E 1607.

Conclusioun, *s.* decision, judgement, A 1845; result, successful end of an experiment, G 672; purpose, D 115; moral, L. 2723; reason, F 492; performance, F 1263; result, summary, A 1743; end (of life), HF. 103; fate, 22. 23; *as in c.*, after all, 4. 257; 15. 4; Conclusiouns, *pl.* mathematical propositions, theorems, A 3193.

Condys, *pl.* conduits, R. 1414.

Confedred, *pp.* rendered confederates, conjoined, 2. 42, 52.

Conferme, *v.* confirm, T. ii. 1526.

Confirme, *ger.* B 4. p 7. 90 (but an error for *conforme*; Lat. ' conformandae).'

Confiteor, ' I confess,' I 386.

Confiture, *s.* composition, C 862. Fr. *confiture*, a mixture, preserve.

Conforten, *v.* comfort, E 1918; *pr. s.* encourages, A 2716; *pr. pl.* strengthen, I 652.

Confounde, *v.* destroy, 1. 40; 12. 10; *pp.* put to confusion, 1. 5; overwhelmed, B 100; destroyed in soul, G 137.

Cónfus, *pp. as adj.* confused, T. iv. 356; convicted of folly, G 463; confounded, A 2230.

Congeyen, *v.* give us our congée, tell us to depart, T. v. 479.

Conjectest, *2 pr. s.* supposest, T. iv. 1026.

Conjectinges, *pl.* conjectures, B 2598.

Conjoininge, *s.* conjunction, G 95.

Conjuracioun, *s.* conjuring, I 603.

Conne, *v.* be able, L. 2044; know, T. iii. 83; have experience, T. i. 647; know how, T. iii. 377; con, learn, B 1730; Conne, 1 *pr. s.* can, T. ii. 49; *2 pr. s. subj.* canst, knowest how, T. ii. 1497; *pr. s. subj.* may, A 4396; 1 *pr. pl.* can, are able, B 483; know, HF. 335; Conne, 2 *pr. pl.* can, A 4123; can (do), T. i. 776; owe (me thanks), T. ii. 1466; Connen, *pr. pl.* know how to, E 2438; *al conne he*, whether he may know, G 846.

Conning, *s.* skill, knowledge, L. 68, 412; T. i. 83; experience, B 1671; learning, B 2929.

Conning, *adj.* skilful, B 3690.

Conningest, most skilful, T. i. 331.

Conningly, *adv.* skilfully, E 1017.

Consecrat, consecrated, B 3207.

Conseil, *s.* council, B 204; counsel, B 425; secret counsel, A 1141; secret, A 3504; advice, B 2211; counsellor, A 1147.

Conseile, *v.* counsel; *pt. pl.* B 2554.

Consentant, *adj.* consentient, consenting (to), C 276.

Consentrik, *adj.* having the same centre, A. i. 17. 5; tending to the same centre, A. i. 16. 9; at the same altitude, A. ii. 3 56.

Consequent, *s.* sequel, result, B 2577.

Conservatif, *adj.* preserving; *c. the soun*, preserving the sound, HF. 847.

Conserve, *v.* keep, preserve, T. iv. 1664.

Consistórie, *s.* council, T. iv. 65; court of justice, C 162.

Conspiracye, *s.* plot, B 3889, C 149.

Constable. *s.* governor, B 512.

Constáblesse, *s.* constable's wife, B 539.

Constaunce, *s.* constancy, I 737.

Constellacioun, *s.* influence of the stars, F 781.

Constreyneth, *pr. s.* constrains, E 800; *pt. s.* L. 105; *pt. s. refl.* contracted herself, B 1. p 1. 15; *pp.* constrained, compelled, E 527, F 764, 769.

Constreynte, *s.* distress, T. iv. 741.

Construe, *v.* divine, make out, T. iii. 33; *ger.* to translate, B 1718; *imp. pl.* interpret, L. 152.

Consulers, *s. pl.* consuls, B 2. p 6. 13.

Consumpte, *pp. pl.* consumed, B 2. m 7. 27.

Contagious, *adj.* contiguous, B 3. p 12. 5.

Contek, *s.* strife, contest, T. v. 1479; A 2003.

Contemplaunce, *s.* contemplation, D 1893.

Contenance, *s.* appearance, F 1485; show, B 2378; gesture, B 2227; demeanour, E 924; self-possession, E 1110; pretence, I 858; *fond his c.*, i. e. disposed himself, T. iii. 979; *pl.* modes of behaviour, R. 1001.

Contene, *v.* contain, T. iii. 502; *pt. s.* held together, B 3. p 12. 40.

Continued, *pp.* accompanied, eked out, I 1046.

Contract, *pp.* contracted, incurred, I 334.

Contraire, *adj.* contrary, R. 348; T. i. 212.

Contraire, *s.* the contrary, HF. 1540; adversary, 2. 64.

Contrárie, *adj.* contrary, B 3964; *in c.*, in contradiction, G 1477.

Cóntrarie, *s.* contrary, A 3057; contrary thing, HF. 808; opponent, A 1859; opposition, T. i. 418.

Contrárien, *v.* oppose, F 705; *pt. s.* gainsaid, D 1044.

Contrarious, *adj.* contrary, adverse, B 2249; *pl.* B 2311.

**Contrarioustee,** *s.* contrary state, I 1077.

**Contree,** country, R. 768 ; fatherland, home, B 2. p 4. 120.

**Contree-folk,** people of his country, L. 2161.

**Contree-houses,** *pl.* houses of his country, homes, 7. 25. Lat. *domos patrias.*

**Contree-ward, to his,** towards his country, L. 2176.

**Contubernial,** *adj.* familiar, at home with (lit. sharing the same tent with), I 760.

*Contumax, adj.* contumacious, I 402.

**Convenient,** *adj.* fitting, suitable, I 421 ; *pl.* suitable, F 1278.

**Convers ;** *in convers,* on the reverse side, T. v. 1810.

**Conversacioun,** *s.* conversation, i. e. manner of life, B 2501.

**Converte,** *v.* change, T. i. 308 ; swerve, C 212 ; *ger.* to change his ways, T. iv. 1412 ; to change her mind, T. ii. 903.

**Convertible,** *adj.* equivalent, A 4395.

**Conveyen,** *v.* introduce, E 55 ; *pr. s.* accompanies, L. 2305; *pt. pl.* conducted on their way, A 2737.

**Convict,** *pp.* overcome, 1. 86.

**Cony,** *s.* rabbit ; Conies, *pl.* R. 1404 ; Conyes, *pl.* 5. 193.

**Cook,** *s.* cook, A 351 ; Cokes, *pl.* C 538.

**Coomen,** *pt. pl.* came, B 1805.

**Cop,** *s.* top, A 554 ; summit, B 2. m 4. 6 ; hill-top, HF. 1166.

**Cope,** *s.* cope, A 260 ; cape, R. 408 ; cloak, T. iii. 724 ; vault, L. 1527.

**Coper,** *s.* copper, HF. 1487.

**Copie,** *s.* copy, T. ii. 1697.

**Coppe,** *s.* cup, A 134, F 942.

**Coráge, Córage,** *s.* heart, spirit, mind, disposition, mood, inclination, R. 257, 423, 849, 1302, 1614 ; A 22 ; courage, B 1970 ; will, desire, B 2713 ; impetuosity, I 655 ; attention, H 164 ; spite, R. 151 ; encouragement, R. 22; *of his c.,* in his disposition, F 22 ; Corages, *pl.* dispositions, natures, A 11.

**Corbets,** *pl.* corbels, HF. 1304.

**Cordeth,** *pr. s.* agrees, T. ii. 1043.

**Cordewane,** *s.* Cordovan leather, B 1922.

**Corfew-tyme,** *s.* curfew-time, about 8 p.m., A 3645.

**Corige,** *v.* correct ; *pr. s.* B 4. p 7. 39.

**Cormeraunt,** *s.* cormorant, 5. 362.

*Cor meum eructavit,* D 1934. See Ps. xlv. 1.

**Corn,** *s.* grain, A 562 ; chief portion, B 3144 ; Cornes, *pl.* crops of corn, B 3225 ; grains of corn, HF. 698.

**Cornemuse,** *s.* bagpipe, HF. 1218. Fr. *cornemuse.*

**Corniculere,** *s.* registrar, secretary, G 369. Lat. *cornicularius,* a registrar, clerk to a magistrate.

**Corny,** *adj.* applied to ale, strong of the corn or malt, C 315, 456.

**Corone,** *s.* crown, garland, E 381 ; Coroune, crown, garland, 2. 58 ; Córoun, crown, L. 216 ; the constellation called 'the Northern Crown,' L. 2224.

**Corosif,** *adj.* corrosive, G 853.

**Coroumpinge,** *s.* corruption, B 3. p 12. 82.

**Coróuned,** *pp.* crowned, B 3555.

*Corpus, s.* body, A 3743 ; *Corpus,* the body (e. g. of Christ), B 3096 ; *Corpus Dominus,* false Latin for *corpus Domini,* the body of the Lord, B 1625 ; Corpus Madrian, the body of St. Mathurin, B 3082 ; Corpus bones, *an intentionally nonsensical oath, composed of* 'corpus domini,' the Lord's body, and 'bones,' C 314.

**Correccioun,** *s.* fine, D 1617.

**Corrumpable,** *adj.* corruptible, A 3010.

**Corrumpeth,** *pr. s.* becomes corrupt, L. 2237 ; *pt. pl.* corrupted, I 819.

**Corrupcioun,** *s.* destroyer, 5. 614.

**Cors,** *s.* body, L. 676, 876 ; corpse, T. v. 742.

**Corse,** *pr. s. subj.* curse, E 1308.

**Corsednesse,** *s.* abomination, T. iv. 994.

**Corseynt,** *s.* a saint (*lit.* holy body) ; esp. a shrine, HF. 117. O.F. *cors seint.*

**Corumpe,** *v.* become corrupt, B 3. p 11. 58. See **Corrumpe.**

**Corve, -n ;** see **Kerve.**

**Cosin,** *s.* cousin, A 1131 ; *as adj.* akin, suitable to, A 742, H 210 ; Cosins germayns, cousins-german, first cousins, B 2558.

**Cosinage,** *s.* kinship, B 1226, 1329.

**Cost** (1), *s.* expense, A 192, 213.

**Cost** (2), *s.* choice, condition ; Nedes cost, of necessity (lit. by condition of necessity), L. 2697. Icel. *kostr,* choice, condition, state.

**Costage,** *s.* cost, expense, B 1235, 1562.

**Coste,** *s.* coast, B 1626 ; region, D 922 ; Costes, *pl.* parts of the sky, A. i. 19. 10.

**Costeying,** *pres. part.* coasting, R. 134.

**Costlewe,** *adj.* costly, I 415. Cf. Icel. *kostligr.*

**Costrel,** *s.* flask, kind of bottle, L. 2666.

**Cote,** *s.* cot, E 398 ; dungeon, A 2457.

**Cote,** *s.* coat, jacket (for a man), A 103, 328 ; skirt, petticoat, *or* gown (for a woman), R. 226; *pl.* coats, surcoats, or coats-of-arms (see below), HF. 1332.

Cote-armure, coat-armour, coat shewing the arms, coat-of-arms, T. v. 1651.

Couche, *v.* lay down, place; cower, E 1206; *pt. s.* laid in order, placed, 5. 216; G 1157; *pp.* set, placed, laid, A 2933, 3211; beset, begemmed, A 2161.

Couching, *s.* laying down, letting the astrolabe lie flat on the ground, A. ii. 29. 29.

Coude, 1 *pt. s.* could, was able, L. 116; knew how, 3. 517; *pt. s.* knew, 3. 667, 1012; understood, R. 179; *as aux.* could, R. 175; Coude her good, knew what was for Dido's advantage, L. 1182; Coude no good, knew no good, was untrained, 3. 390; Coud, *pp.* known, 3. 787; learnt, I 1041. See Can, Conne.

Counseil, *s.* advice, A 784; secrets, A 665: Counseyl, secret, 5. 348.

Counte, 1 *pr. s.* account, 11. 29; *pt. s.* 3. 718.

Countenaunce, *s.* appearance, show, A 1926; looks, appearance, G 1264; shewing favour, 3. 1022; demeanour, R. 814; pretext, A 4421; *pl.* looks, R. 1309.

Counting-bord, *s.* counting-house table, B 1273.

Countour (1), *s.* arithmetician, 3. 435; auditor, A 359.

Countour (2), *s.* abacus, counting-board, 3. 436; counting-house, B 1403.

Countour-hous, *s.* counting-house, B 1267.

Countrepeise, *v.* render equivalent, HF. 1750; countervail, T. iii. 1407.

Countrepleted, *pp.* made the subject of pleadings and counter-pleadings, argued against, L. 476.

Countretaille, *s.* lit. countertally, i. e. correspondence (of sound); *at the c.*, in reply, E 1190.

Countrewaite, *pr. s. subj.* keep watch over, I 1005; watch against, B 2509.

Coupable, *adj.* culpable, blameworthy, B 2731, I 414.

Coupe, *s.* cup, L. 1122.

Coured, *pt. s.* cowered, R. 465.

Cours, *s.* course, T. ii. 970; life on earth, G 387; orbit, A 2454.

Courser, *s.* horse, T. ii. 1011; *pl.* steeds, A 2501.

Court, *s.* court, A 140; manor-house, D 2162.

Courtepy, an upper short coat of a coarse material, R. 220; A 290, D 1382.

Court-man, *s.* courtier, E 1492.

Couthe, 1 *pt. s.* could, R. 513; knew, 3. 800; knew how, A 390; Couth, *pp.* known, T. iv. 61; Couthe, *pp. pl.* well-known, A 14.

Couthe, *adv.* in a known way, manifestly, HF. 757.

Coveityse, *s.* covetousness, A 3884, C 424; bodily craving, I 819; lust, I 336.

Covenable, *adj.* fit, proper, fitting, suitable, 18. 25; agreeable, B 4. p 6. 224; congruous, B 3. p 12. 179.

Covenably, *adv.* suitably, fitly, B 2423.

Covent, *s.* convent, conventual body, B 1827, D 1863.

Coverchief, *s.* kerchief worn on the head, D 590; *pl.* A 453.

Covercle, *s.* pot-lid, HF. 792.

Covered, *pp.* covered, A 354; recovered from, healed of, L. 762.

Covertly, *adv.* secretly, R. 19.

Coverture, *s.* disguise, R. 1588; Covertures, *pl.* coverings, I 198.

Covetour, *s.* one who covets, 4. 262.

Covyne, *s.* deceitfulness, A 604. ' *Covine*, a deceitful agreement between two or more to the prejudice of another;' Cowel, Law Dictionary.

Cow, *s.* chough, D 232. See Chogh.

Coward, *adj.* cowardly, 5. 349.

Cowardye, *s.* cowardice, A 2730.

Cowardyse, *s.* cowardice, T. iv. 602, v. 412.

Coy, *adj.* quiet, A 119; shy, L. 1548.

Coye, *v.* quiet, calm, cajole, T. ii. 801.

Coynes, *pl.* quinces, R. 1374. O. F. *coin*, quince.

Crabbed, *adj.* shrewish, cross, bitter, E 1203.

Cracching, *s.* scratching, A 2834.

Craft, *s.* cunning, C 84; skill, T. i. 665; art, R. 687; trade, occupation, 3. 791; A 692; secret, mystery, R. 1634; might, B 3258; contrivance, F 249.

Craftily, *adv.* artfully, in a studied manner, T. ii. 1026; skilfully, B 48.

Crafty, *adj.* skilful, clever, A 1897; sensible, 3. 439.

Craketh, *pr. s.* utters boldly, A 4001; sings in a grating tone (like a corn-crake), E 1850.

Crampissheth, *pr. s.* draws convulsively together, contracts, 7. 171. Cf. ' Deth *crampishing* into their hert gan crepe;' Lydgate, Falls of Princes, bk. i. c. 9. Cf. O.F. *crampir*, 'être tordu;' Godefroy.

Crased, *pp.* cracked, G 934.

Creant, *adj.*; *seith creant*, acknowledges himself beaten, I 698. Probably short for *recreant*.

**Creat,** *pp.* created, 16. 2 ; B 2293.

**Creaunce,** *s.* credence, belief, creed, B 915 ; object of faith, B 340.

**Creaunce,** *v.* borrow on credit, B 1479 ; *pr. s.* borrows, B 1493 ; *pp.* B 1556.

**Creep,** *pt. s. of* Crepe.

**Crekes,** *pl.* crooked devices, wiles, A 4051. See *Creek*; *s.* (1), § 7, in the New E. Dict.

**Crepe,** *v.* creep, 3. 144 ; Creep, *pt. s.* crept, A 4226 ; Crepten, *pt. pl.* D 1698 ; Cropen, *pp.* crept, T. iii. 1011.

**Crepul,** *s.* cripple, T. iv. 1459.

**Crepusculis,** *s. pl.* twilights, durations of twilight, A. ii. 6. *rubric.*

**Crevace,** *s.* crevice, crack, HF. 2086.

**Crinkled,** *pp.* full of turns or cranks, L. 2012.

**Crips,** *adj.* crisp, curly, HF. 1386 ; Crisp, R. 824.

**Cristen,** *adj.* Christian, B 222, 1679.

**Cristendom,** *s.* the Christian religion, B 351 ; Christianity, G 447.

**Cristenly,** *adv.* in a Christian manner, B 1122.

**Cristianitee,** *s.* company of Christians, B 544.

**Croce,** *s.* staff, stick, D 484. See *Crose*, § 2, in the New E. Dict.

**Crois,** *s.* cross, 1. 60.

**Croked,** *adj.* crooked, R. 926 ; crooked (things), 13. 8 ; 'tortuous,' A. ii. 28. 32.

**Crokes,** *pl.* crooks, hooks, L. 640.

**Crokke,** *s.* earthenware pot, 13. 12.

**Crommes,** *s. pl.* crumbs, G 60.

**Crone,** *s.* crone, hag, B 432.

**Cronique,** *s.* chronicle, B 4398.

**Croos-lyne,** *s.* cross-line, the line from right to left through the centre, A. i. 12. 7.

**Crop,** *s.* top, sprout, new twig, T. ii. 348 ; *crop and rote,* top and root, everything, T. v. 1245 ; Croppes, *pl.* tree-tops, ends of branches, R. 1396 ; new shoots, A 7.

**Cropen,** *pp. of* Crepe.

**Croper,** *s.* crupper, G 566.

**Cros,** *s.* cross, 1. 82 ; Crois, 1. 60.

**Croslet,** *s.* crucible, G 1147.

**Crouche,** 1 *pr. s.* mark with the cross (to defend from elves), A 3479 ; E 1707.

**Croude,** *v.* push, HF. 2095 ; *pr. s. 2 p.* dost press, dost push, B 296.

**Crouke,** *s.* pitcher, jug, A 4158.

**Croun,** *s.* crown (of the head), A 4041 ; (referring to the tonsure), B 1499.

**Crouned,** *pp.* crowned, R. 1266 ; supreme, F 526.

**Croupe,** *s.* crupper, D 1559.

**Crouperes,** *pl.* cruppers, I 433.

**Crowding,** *s.* pressure, motive power, B 299.

**Croys,** *s.* cross, A 699, 4286.

**Crul,** *adj.* curly, A 3314 ; *pl.* A 81. Friesic *krul,* curly.

**Crydestow,** didst thou cry out, A 1083 ; *pp.* proclaimed, HF. 2107.

**Cryinge,** *s.* outcry, A 906.

**Cryke,** *s.* creek, A 409.

**Cucúrbitès,** *s. pl.* cucurbites, G 794. ' *Cucurbite,* a chemical vessel, originally made in the shape of a gourd, but sometimes shallow, with a wide mouth, and used in distillation ; ' Webster.

*Culpa, mea,* i. e. I acknowledge my fault, T. ii. 525.

**Culpe,** *s.* guilt, blame, I 335.

**Culter,** *s.* coulter (of a plough), A 3763.

**Cunning,** *adj.* skilful, 2. 97.

**Cunning,** *s.* skill, 5. 167, 487.

**Cuppe,** *s.* a cup, F 616.

**Curacioun,** *s.* cure, healing, B 2463 ; mode of cure, T. i. 791.

**Curat,** *s.* parish-priest, vicar, A 219 (the words *vicar* and *curate* have now, practically, changed places).

**Cure,** *s.* cure, remedy, T. i. 469 ; charge, B 2. p 3. 32 ; diligence, A 1007 ; attention, A 303 ; heed, care, 2. 82 ; endeavour, B 188; careful purpose, HF. 1298 ; supervision, D 1333 ; *I do no cure,* I care not, L. 152 ; *lyth in his cure,* depends on his care for me, L. 1176 ; *did his besy cure,* was busily employed, 5. 369 ; *his lyves cure,* the object of his thoughts always, 4. 131 ; *honest cure,* care for honourable things, C 557 ; *in cure,* in her power, B 230.

**Curiositee,** *s.* curious workmanship, HF. 1178 ; intricacy, 18. 81.

**Curious,** *adj.* careful, attentive, B 1433; eager, R. 1052 ; skilful, A 577 ; delicately made, A 196 ; magical, F 1120.

**Currours,** *s. pl.* runners, couriers, HF. 2128.

**Cursednesse,** *s.* abominable sin, wickedness, C 276, 400 ; shrewishness, E 1239 ; malice, B 1821.

**Curteis,** *adj.* courteous, *hence,* compassionate, I 246 ; courteous, R. 538.

**Curteisye,** *s.* courtesy, A 46, 132.

**Custume,** *s.* custom, D 682 ; *pl.* payments, I 752 ; imports, I 567.

**Cut,** *s.* lot, A 835, 845, 854.

**Cutte,** *v.* cut, C 954 ; Cutted, *pp.* cut short, L. 973.

## D.

Daf, s. foolish person, A 4208.

Dagged, adj. tagged, cut into hanging peaks at the lower edge, I 421.

Dagginge, s. a cutting into tags, I 418.

Dagon, s. small piece, D 1751.

Dalf, pt. s. of Delve.

Daliaunce, s. gossip, A 211; playful demeanour, favour, 12. 8; pl. dalliance, toying, C 66.

Damageous, adj. injurious, I 438.

Dame, s. mother, C 684; dam, A 3260; madam, A 3956; goodwife, D 1797.

Damiselle, s. damsel, R. 1240; pl. R. 1622.

Dampnacioun, s. condemnation, C 500; curse, D 1067.

Dampne, pr. to condemn, L. 401; pp. A 1175, 1342; damned, I 191.

Dan, s. (for Dominus), lord, sir, a title of respect, HF. 161; B 3982; Daun, HF. 137.

Dappel-gray, adj. dapple-gray, B 2074.

Dar, 1 pr. s. dare, A 1151; Darst, 2 pr. s. darest, T. i. 768; B 860; Darstow, darest thou, L. 1450; Dorste, 1 pt. s. durst, might venture (to), L. 2054; pt. s. A 227; Dorstestow, wouldst thou dare, T. i. 767; 1 pt. s. subj. might dare, 2. 60. See Durre.

Dare, pr. pl. doze, B 1293.

Darketh, pr. s. lies hid, L. 816.

Darreyne, ger. to decide one's right to, A 1853; to decide, A 1631; to decide your claims (to), A 1609. O.F. deraisnier.

Dart, s. dart, 6. 40; (given as a prize in an athletic contest), D 75.

Daswen, pt. pl. dase, are dazzled, H 31; pp. confused, HF. 658. O.F. daser (Godefroy).

Date-tree, s. date-tree, R. 1364.

Daun; see Dan.

Daunce, s. dance, R. 808; play, T. iv. 1431; set, company, HF. 639; the newe d., the new dance, T. ii. 553; the olde d., the old game, the old way of love, A 476, C 79.

Dauncen, v. dance, A 2202.

Daunger, s. disdain, R. 1524; imperiousness, 7. 186; liability, A 1849; sparing, stint, R. 1147; power, control, R. 1470; Power to harm (personified), L. 160; in d., within his jurisdiction, under his control, A 663; in hir d., at her disposal, R. 1049; with d., sparingly, charily, D 521.

Daungerous, adj. forbidding, sparing, A 517; niggardly, D 1427; grudging, hard

to please, R. 1482, 1492; reluctant, D 514; inhospitable, R. 490.

Daunten, v. tame, subdue, R. 880; pr. s. T. ii. 399, iv. 1589; pp. frightened, D 463.

Dawe, v. dawn, B 3872, E 1832.

Daweninge, s. dawn, A 4234, B 4072.

Dawes, s. pl. days, F 1180.

Dawing, s. the Dawn (Aurora), T. iii. 1466.

Dawning, s. dawn, 3. 292.

Day, s. day, A 19; time, B 3374; appointed time for repaying money, G 1040; on a day, one day, some day, R. 1493; Dayes, pl. appointed days for payment, F 1568, 1575; lifetime, B 118; now a dayes, at this time, E 1164.

Dayerye, s. dairy, A 597; pl. D 871.

Dayesye, s. daisy, L. 182, 184, 218.

Debaat, s. strife, A 3230, B 2867; war, B 130; mental conflict, 3. 1192; quarrelling T. ii. 753.

Debate, v. fight, war, B 2058; quarrel, C 422.

Debonair, adj. calm, benign, gentle, I 658; Debonaire, fem. well-mannered, B 4061; gracious, courteous, R. 797; as s. kind person, 3. 624.

Debonairely, adv. meekly, I 660; graciously, 3. 851, 1284; with a good grace, HF. 2013; courteously, 3. 518; T. ii. 1259.

Debonairetee, s. gentleness, I 467; graciousness, 6. 108.

Deceivable, adj. deceitful, 15. 3; E 2058.

Declamed, pt. pl. discussed, T. ii. 1247.

Declinacioun, s. declination, angular distance N. or S. of the equator, E 2223, F 1033.

Declyneth, pr. s. turns aside, B 4. p 6. 195; pr. s. possesses declination, A ii. 19. 12.

Declyninge, adj. sloping, B 5. m 1. 19.

Decoped, pp. lit. 'cut down;' hence, pierced, cut in openwork patterns, R. 843.

Dède, dead; see Dèèd.

Dède, ger. to grow dead, become stupefied, HF. 552.

Deden, pt. pl. did, T. i. 82. See Doon.

Dedicat, pp. dedicated, I 964.

Deduyt, s. pleasure, A 2177.

Deed, s. deed, act; Dede, dat. 1. 45; B 1999; in dede, indeed, A 659, B 3511; with the dede, with the act thereof, D 70; Dede, pl. (A. S. dǣda), 5. 82.

Dèèd, adj. dead, R. 215; dead, livid (of hue), R. 441; for d., as dead, T. iv. 733;

Dede, *def.* L. 876; *d. slepe,* heavy sleep, 3. 127; Dede, *pl.* sluggish, 5. 187; *woundes dede,* deadly wounds, 3. 1211.

Dèèdly, *adj.* mortal, I 99; dying, L. 885; deathlike, 3. 162.

Dèèdly, *adv.* mortally, G 476.

Dèèf, *adj.* deaf, T. i. 753; Deve, *pl.* G 286.

Deel, *s.* part, R. 1074; *never a deel,* not at all, I 1007; not a bit, HF. 331; *every deel,* every whit, wholly, T. ii. 590; Deel, *pl.* times, 6. 35; Del, part, R. 28; share, 3. 1001; *every d.,* every whit, A 1825; *eche a d.,* every whit, T. iii. 694; *a greet del,* to a large extent, A 415; very often, 3. 1159; *no del,* no whit, T. i. 1089; *never a d.,* not a whit, 3. 543.

Deer, *s. pl.* animals, B 1926.

Dees, *pl.* dice, T. ii. 1347, iv. 1098.

Dees, *s.* daïs, HF. 1360, 1658.

Deeth, *s.* death, B 3567; pestilence, plague, T. i. 483; *the deeth,* the pestilence (with special references to the pestilences of 1349, 1361, and 1369), A 605.

Defame, *s.* dishonour, B 3788, C 612.

Defaute, *s.* fault, 22. 56; fault (as a hunting term), 3. 384 *(were on a defaute y-falle,* had a check); lack, defect, want, 3. 5, 25, 223; sin, B 3718, C 370.

Defence, *s.* resistance, L. 1931; hindrance, R. 1142; covering, 5. 273; prohibition, T. iii. 138; denial, D 467.

Defendaunt, *s.;* *in his d.,* in defending himself, in self-defence, I 572.

Defende, *ger.* to defend, B. 2631; to forbid, G 1470.

Defet, *pp.* exhausted, (lit. defeated), T. v. 618; cast down, T. v. 1219.

Deffendeth, *pr. s.* forbids, I 651; *pp.* I 600.

Defoulen, *v.* trample down, *hence,* defile, F 1418; *pp.* trampled down, I 191; defiled, T. v. 1339; disgraced, B 4. m 7. 47 (Lat. *turpatus*).

Defyne, I *pr. s.* pronounce, declare, T. iv. 390.

Degree, *s.* rank, 5. 453; condition, position, A 1841; step, R. 485; footstep, B 4. m 1. 42; horizontal stripes, B 1. p 1. 38; of the zodiac, F 386; *at lowe degree,* R. 883; *at alle degrees,* in every way, A 3724.

Degysè, *adj.* elaborate, I 417.

Degysinesse, *s.* elaborate style, I 414.

Degysinge, *s.* elaborate ornamentation, I 425.

Dekne, *s.* deacon, I 891.

Del; see Deel.

Delen, *ger.* to have dealing with, A 247;

Dele, *ger.* to have dealings, T. iii. 322; to deal, L. 1158; *v.* argue, T. ii. 1749; Deled, *pt. pl.* had intercourse, L. 1517; Deled, *pp.* apportioned, D 2249.

Deliberen, *v.* deliberate, consider, T. iv. 169; *pt. s.* deliberated, B 2916.

Delicacye, *s.* amusement, B 3669; wantonness, 9. 58. i

Delicat, *adj.* delicious, E 1646; delicate, E 682; dainty, I 432.

Delices, *s. pl.* delights, B 2602; tender feelings, B 2. p 4. 78; sinful pleasures, B 3. p 7. 1.

Delicious, *adj.* giving delight, T. v. 443.

Deliciously, *adv.* luxuriously, E 2025.

Delitable, *adj.* delightful, R. 1440; delicious, R. 1371; *pl.* delightful, F 899.

Delitably, *adv.* pleasingly, B 4. p 1. 2.

Delitous, *adj.* delicious, R. 489.

Deliver, *adj.* quick, active, A 84.

Delivere, *v.* set free, 13. 7; do away with, T. iii. 1012; *ger.* to set free (after a legal decision), 5. 508.

Deliverly, *adv.* nimbly, B 4606; quickly, T. ii. 1088.

Delivernesse, *s.* activity, B 2355.

Delphyn, *s.* the constellation Dolphin, HF. 1006.

Delte, *pt. s. of* Delen.

Delvo, *v.* dig, A 536; Dalf, I *pt. s.* dug, B 5. p 1. 99; Dolve, *pt. s. subj.* had digged, B 5. p 1. 87; Dolven, *pp.* buried, 3. 222. A. S. *delfan.*

Delyces, *s. pl.* delights, pleasures, C 547, G 3; favourites (Lat. *delicias*), B 2. p 3. 74.

Delyè, *adj.* delicate, fine, B 1. p 1. 23. O. F. *delié.*

Delyt, *s.* delight, joy, 3. 606; pleasing ornamentation, L. 1199.

Delytable, *adj.* delightful, L. 321.

Delyte, *v.* delight, please, 5. 27; *refl.* take pleasure, 5. 66; Delyte me, I *pr. s.* delight, L. 30.

Delytous, *adj.* delicious, R. 90.

Demaunde, *s.* question, T. iv. 1694, v. 859.

Deme, *v.* judge, 14. 6; decide, conclude, T. ii. 371; suppose, 4. 158; give a verdict, G 595; Demen, *v.* deem, judge, A 3161; decide, B 3045; I *pr. s.* condemn, D 2024; decree, C 199; suppose, E 753; Demeth, *imp. pl.* judge, decide, L. 453; suppose, A 3172.

Demeine, *v.* manage, HF. 959.

Demeyne, *s.* dominion, B 3855.

Demoniak, *s.* madman, D 2240.

Demonstracioun, *s.* proof, HF. 727.

**Demonstratif,** *adj.* demonstrable, D 2272.

**Denticle,** *s.* pointer, A. i. 23. 1. See **Almury.**

**Denye,** *v.* refuse, T. ii. 1489; **Deneyed,** *pp.* denied, B 3. p 10. 16.

**Depardieux,** *interj.* on the part of God, by God's help, T. ii. 1058, 1212.

**Departe,** *v.* separate, part, 7. 285; sever, T. ii. 531; divide, I 1006; *imp. s.* distinguish, T. iii. 404.

**Departinge,** *s.* dividing, I 425, 1008; departure, 5. 675; separation, 4. 25.

**Depe,** *adv.* deeply, 3. 165; 7. 8.

**Depeynted,** *pp.* depicted, L. 1025; painted, R. 478; stained, T. v. 1599.

**Depper,** *adv. comp.* deeper, T. ii. 485; B 630.

**Depraven,** *pr. pl.* calumniate, 4. 207.

**Depressioun,** *s.* the angular distance of the southern pole from the horizon, A. ii. 25. 10.

**Dere,** *adj.* dear, 1. 99; 4. 147.

**Dere,** *adv.* dearly, 1. 86; 18. 26.

**Dere,** *s. dat.* deer, R. 1453.

**Dère,** *v.* injure, harm, T. i. 651. A. S. *derian.*

**Dereling,** *s.* darling, A 3793.

**Derk,** *adj.* dark, R. 1009; inauspicious, 4. 120; *as s.* inauspicious position, 4. 122.

**Derke,** *s.* darkness, gloom, 3. 609.

**Derkest,** *adj. superl.* darkest, B 304.

**Derkly,** *adv.* darkly, HF. 51.

**Derknesse,** *s.* darkness, B 1451.

**Derne,** *adj.* secret, A 3200, 3278.

**Derre,** *adv. comp.* more dearly, T. i. 136, 174; A 1448.

**Derth,** *s.* dearth, HF. 1974.

**Deryveth,** *pr. s.* is derived, A 3006.

**Desceivaunce,** *s.* deception, B 3. p 8. 53.

**Descencioun,** *s.* descension, A. ii. 4. 55. The technical signification seems to be —the 'house' or portion of the sky just above the western horizon, so that a planet in his descension is about to set.

**Descensories,** *s. pl.* G 792. '*Descensories*, vessels used in chemistry for extracting oils *per descensum*;' Tyrwhitt.

**Descerne,** *v.* discern, T. iv. 200.

**Descharge,** *pr. s. subj.* disburden, I 360.

**Desclaundred,** *pp.* slandered, B 674.

**Descryve,** *v.* describe, R. 705; HF. 1105.

**Desdeyn,** *s.* disdain, contempt, A 789.

**Desert,** *s.* merit, 4. 31; *pl.* merits, T. iii. 1267.

**Deserte,** *adj.* lonely, HF. 417.

**Deservedest,** *2 pt. s.* didst deserve, C 216.

**Desespaired,** *pp.* in despair, 6. 7.

**Desespeir,** *s.* despair, T. i. 605, ii. 6.

**Desesperaunce,** *s.* hopelessness, T. ii. 530, 1307.

**Desherite,** *ger.* to disinherit, B 3025.

**Deshonestee,** *s.* unseemliness, I 833.

**Désiróus,** *adj.* ambitious, 9. 59; ardent, F 23.

**Deslavee,** *adj.* foul, I 629; inordinate, unrestrained, I 834. '*Deslavé,* pp. non lavé, crasseux, sale;' Godefroy.

**Desordeynee,** *adj.* unregulated, inordinate, I 818, 915.

**Desordinat,** *adj.* inórdinate, I 415.

**Despeired,** *pp.* sunk in despair, 2. 91; T. v. 713.

**Despence,** *s.* expense, D 1874; expenditure, money for expenses, B 105.

**Despende,** *v.* spend, T. iv. 921; *2 pr. s.* wastest, B 2121; *pp.* spent, A 3983.

**Despendours,** *pl.* spenders, B 2843.

**Despenses,** *pl.* expenditure, B 2842.

**Desperacioun,** *s.* despair, 1. 21.

**Déspitous,** *adj.* spiteful, R. 173; angry, jealous, D 761; merciless, A 516; scornful, A 1777, I 395.

**Despitously,** *adv.* scornfully, B 3785; angrily, A 4274; maliciously, B 605; cruelly, E 535.

**Desplayeth,** *pr. s.* spreads open, A 966.

**Desponeth,** *pr. s.* disposes, T. iv 964.

**Desport,** *s.* diversion, merriment. amusement, T. i. 592; B 2158.

**Desporte,** *v.* rejoice, T. v. 1398

**Despoyled,** *pp.* robbed, I 665.

**Despyt,** *s.* malice, spite, T. i. 207; contempt, disdain, D 1876; scorn, L. 372; malice, L. 1771; ill-humour, I 507; a deed expressing contempt, B 3738: *in d. of,* in contempt of, 5. 281; *in your d.,* in contempt of you, B 1753; *in his d.,* in scorn of him, L. 134.

**Desray,** *s.* confusion, I 927.

**Desseveraunce,** *s.* separation, T. iii. 1424.

**Destemperaunce,** *s.* inclemency, B 3. p 11. 130.

**Destempred,** *pp.* distempered, I 826.

**Destinal,** *adj.* fatal, B 4. p 6. 172; predestined, B 4. p 6. 110.

**Destourbe,** *ger.* to disturb; *d. of,* to disturb in, C 340; *pr. s.* hinders, I 576; interrupts, B 2167.

**Destourbing,** *s.* trouble, 18. 44.

**Destrat,** *pp.* distracted, B 3. p 8. 19.

**Destreyne,** *v.* distress, T. iii. 1528; *ger.* constrain, force, H 161.

**Destroubled,** *pp.* disturbed, 3. 524.

**Desyringe,** *adj.* desirous, B 2767.

**Determinat,** *adj.* determinate, exact, fixed, D 1459; properly placed (on the astrolabe), A. ii. 18 (rubric).

**Détermýne,** *v.* come to an end, T. iii. 379; Determined, *pp.* settled, B 5. p 4. 9.

**Dette,** *s.* debt, L. 541; A 280.

**Dettelees,** *adj.* free from debt, A 582.

**Dettour,** *s.* debtor, B 1587, D 155.

*Deus hic,* God (be) here, D 1770.

**Deve,** *pl. of* Deef, deaf.

**Devil,** *s.* L. 2493; *what the devil,* L. 2694; *how d.,* how the devil, T. i. 623; *a d. meye,* in the way to the devil, in the devil's name, A 3134; *a twenty devil way,* in the way of twenty devils, i. e. to utter destruction, L. 2177; an exclamation of petulance, A 3713, 4257.

**Devoir,** *s.* duty, T. iii. 1045; A 2598.

**Devyn,** *s.* astrologer, T. i. 66.

**Devyne,** *v.* guess, T. v. 288; *ger.* T. iii. 765; to prophesy (by), 5. 182; Devyne, *pr. pl.* suspect, T. ii. 1745; Devyne, *pr. s. subj.* let (him) guess, HF. 14.

**Devyneresse,** *s.* female diviner, T. v. 1522.

**Devys,** *s.* contrivance, R. 1413; supposition, R. 651; direction, A 816; *at his d.,* according to his own wish, R. 1326; *at point d.,* with great exactness *or* exactitude, R. 830; Devyses, *pl.* heraldic devices, badges, L. 1272.

**Devyse,** *v.* to relate, tell, describe, T. iii. 41; A 34; recommend, T. ii. 388; devise, suggest, ordain, L. 437; plan, L. 1453; *ger.* to tell, describe, 5. 398; to relate, A 994; to frame, E 739; to tell of, T. i. 277; *pr. s.* narrates, describes, 5. 317; *pr. pl.* imagine, discourse, F 261; *pp.* described to, told, R. 476.

**Devysing,** *s.* arrangement, A 2496.

**Dewe,** *adj.* due, I 867.

**Dexter,** *s.* a courser, war-horse, B 2103. Fr. *destrier,* a war-horse, Low Lat. *dextrarius.* The squire rode his own horse, and led his master's horse beside him, on his *right* hand.

**Deye,** *s.* dairywoman, B 4036. Icel. *deigja.*

**Deye,** *v.* die, 5. 469, 651; Deyde, *pt. s.* A 2846; Deyed, *pp.* R. 456; Deyde, *pt. s. subj.* should die, A 3427.

**Deyen,** *ger.* to dye, to dip, B 4. m 6. 14.

**Deyinge,** *s.* death, B 1850; *lay on deying,* lay a-dying, B 3906.

**Deyne,** *v.* deign, 7. 231; Deyneth him, *pr. s.* he deigns, 7. 181; L. 395; *him deyned,* he deigned, B 3324, 4371; *hir deyned,* she deigned, 4. 39.

**Deynous,** *adj.* scornful, A 3941.

**Deyntee,** *s.* worth, value, D 208; *took lesse d. for,* set less value on, 7. 143; a peculiar pleasure, B 139; pleasure, F 681, 1003; Deyntees, *pl.* dainties, A 346.

**Deyntee,** *s. as adj.* dainty, pleasant, rare, T. v. 438; good, A 168.

**Deyntevous,** *adj.* dainty, E 265.

**Deys,** *s.* daïs, platform, the high table in a dining-hall, A 370, 2200.

**Diademe,** *s.* diadem, crown of an emperor, 14. 7.

**Diápred,** *pp. as adj.* variegated, diversified with figures, A 2158.

**Dich,** *s.* ditch, A 3964.

**Dichen,** *v.* make a dyke round, L. 708; *pp.* provided with a moat, A 1888.

**Dide, Didest;** see **Doon.**

**Diete,** *s.* diet, daily food, A 435.

**Diffamacioun,** *s.* defamation, D 1304.

**Diffame,** *s.* ill report, E 540, 730.

**Diffame,** *ger.* to dishonour, HF. 1581; *v.* cry down, D 2212.

**Diffinicioun,** *s.* clear exposition, D 25.

**Diffinisshe,** *pr. s. subj.* define, B 5. p 1. 36.

**Diffinitif,** *adj.* definite, final, C 172.

**Diffusioun,** *s.* prolixity, T. iii. 296.

**Diffye,** 1 *pr. s.* defy, spurn, D 1928.

**Diffyne,** *ger.* define, state clearly, 5. 529; 2 *pr. pl.* conclude, HF. 344.

**Digestible,** *adj.* easy to be digested, A 437.

**Dighte,** *v.* prepare, L. 1288; prepare (himself), L. 1000; Dighte me, prepare myself to go, B 3104; ordain, place, T. iv. 1188; lie with, D 767; *pt. s. refl.* hastened, betook himself, T. ii. 948; lay with, D 398; Dight, *pp.* arrayed, equipped, T. iii. 1773; served, H 312; prepared, R. 941; prepared him to go, B 3719; Dighte, *pp. pl.* prepared, L. 2611. A. S. *dihtan;* from Lat. *dictare.*

**Digne,** *adj.* worthy, T. i. 429; honourable, noble, B 1175, C 695; suitable, B 778; proud, disdainful, A 517; scornful, repellent, A 3964.

**Dignely,** *adv.* scornfully, T. ii. 1024.

**Dignitee,** *s.* worth, dignity, C 701, 782; rank, E 470. Dignity, in astrology, signifies the advantages which a planet has when in a particular position in the zodiac, or in a particular position with regard to other planets (Bailey).

**Dilatacioun,** *s.* diffuseness, B 232.

**Diluge,** *s.* deluge, I 839.

**Dint,** *s.* stroke, HF. 534.

**Direct,** *adj.* directed, addressed, 18. 75;

*in directe*, in a line with, A. ii. 44. 26.
A planet's motion is direct when it
moves in the same direction as the
sun in the zodiac.

**Directe**, 1 *pr. s.* address, T. v. 1856.

**Disavaunce**, *v.* defeat, T. ii. 511.

**Disaventure**, *s.* misfortune, T. ii. 415.

**Disblameth**, *imp. pl.* free (me) from
blame, T. ii. 17.

**Disceyving**, *s.* deception, R. 1590.

**Dischevele**, *adj.* with (his) hair hanging
loosely down, A 683 ; with hair in dis-
order, L. 1315.

**Disciplyne**, *s.* bodily mortification, I
1052.

**Disclaundre**, *s.* reproach, T. iv. 564 ;
slander, I 623.

**Disconfiture**, *s.* defeat, A 1008 ; grief,
7. 326.

**Disconfort**, *s.* discouragement, discomfort, A 2010 ; grief, woe, T. iv. 311.

**Disconforten**, *v.* discourage, A 2704.

**Discordable**, discordant, T. iii. 1753.

**Discordances**, *s. pl.* discords, I 275.

**Discorden**, *pr. pl.* disagree, B 4. p 6.
208.

**Discordinge**, *adj.* different, B 3. p 2. 140.
(Lat. *dissidentes*.)

**Discovered**, *pp.* revealed, G 1468.

**Discovert**, *pp.* uncovered ; *at d.*, when
unprotected, I 714.

**Discryve**,*v.* describe, T. v. 267 ; Discreven,
*v.* T. iv. 802.

**Discure**, *v.* reveal, discover, 3. 549.

**Discussed**, *pp.* discussed, 5. 624 ; driven
away, B 1. m 3. 1.

**Disdeyn**, *s.* disdain, R. 296.

**Disencreseth**, *pr. s.* decreases, B 5. p
6. 85.

**Disese**, *s.* discomfort, grief, misery, 4.
216, 277 ; T. ii. 987 ; sorrow, 7. 226 ; displeasure, T. ii. 147 ; disease, ill, HF. 89 ;
inconvenience, I 609 ; distress, B 616 ;
unrest, F 1314.

**Disesen**, *ger.* to trouble, T. iii. 1468 ; *v.*
vex, T. iv. 1304 ; distress, T. i. 573.

**Disesperat**, *adj.* without hope, HF. 2015.

**Disfigurat**, *adj.* disguised, 5. 222.

**Disfigúre**, *s.* disfigurement, D 960.

**Disfigúre**, *v.* disguise, L. 2046 ; *pp.*
changed, A 1403.

**Disgressioun**, digression, T. i. 143.

**Disgyse**, *ger.* to disguise, T. v. 1577.

**Disherited**, *pp.* disinherited, deprived,
L. 1065.

**Dish-metes**, *pl.* spoon-meat, broth, I 455.

**Dishonest**, *adj.* unfaithful, H 214 ; Dishoneste, shameful, E 876.

**Disjoynt**, *s.* failure, A 2962 ; difficult
position, B 1601 ; *dat.* peril, T. iii. 496,
v. 1618.

**Dismal**, *s.* unlucky day, 3. 1206.

**Dismembred**, *pt. pl.* dismembered, I 591.

**Dismembringe**, *s.* dismembering, I 591.

**Disobeysaunt**, *adj.* disobedient, 5. 429.

**Disordenaunce**, *s.* violation of rules,
HF. 27.

**Disparage**, *s.* disgrace, E 908.

**Disparáge**, *v.* dishonour, A 4271 ; *pp.*
misallied, D 1069.

**Dispeire yow**, *imp. pl.* despair, E 1669.

**Dispence**, *s.* expenditure, expense, A
441 ; what I spend, D 1432 ; cost, B
1195 ; lavish help, HF. 260 ; Dispenses,
*pl.* expenses, R. 1144.

**Dispende**, *v.* spend, B 3500 ; *pp.* spent,
shared, B 2560.

**Dispeyred**, *adj.* despairing, F 1084.

**Dispítous**, *adj.* spiteful, R. 156 ; T. iii.
1458 ; grievous, sad, T. v. 199 ; Dís-
pitóusë, *voc.* pitiless, T. ii. 435 ; *def.
fem.* cruel, 3. 624.

**Dispítously**, *adv.* angrily, A 1124 ; spitefully, T. v. 1806 ; cruelly, HF. 161.

**Displesant**, *adj.* displeasing, I 544, 697.

**Displesaunce**, *s.* displeasure, T. iii. 480 ;
offence, C 74 ; Displesances, *pl.* annoy-
ances, C 420.

**Dispone**, *imp. s.* dispose, T. v. 300 ; *pr. s.*
disposes, orders, regulates, B 4. p 6. 60.

**Disport**, *s.* sport, pleasantry, A 137, 775 ;
amusement, diversioun, D 839 ; pleasure,
B 143 ; sport, 4. 177.

**Disporte**, *ger.* to amuse, HF. 571 ; to
exhilarate, T. ii. 1673 ; *v.* cheer, T. iii.
1133 ; *pr. pl.* sport, play, E 2040.

**Disposed**, *pt. s.* purposed, E 244 ; *pp.*
disposed, T. ii. 682 ; ready, T. iv. 230 ;
*wel d.*, in good health (the reverse of
*indisposed*), H 33.

**Disposicioun**, *s.* disposal, T. ii. 526, v. 2 ;
position, A 1087 ; frame of mind, B
2326.

**Dispoylinge**, *s.* spoil, B 4. m 7. 32.

**Dispreisen**, *ger.* to disparage, R. 1053 ;
*v.* blame, B 2261 ; *pres. pt.* depreciating,
B 2741.

**Dispreisinge**, *s.* blame, I 497 ; contempt,
B 2876.

**Disputisoun**, *s.* argument, E 1474 ; dispute, B 4428, F 890.

**Dispyt**, *s.* despite, scorn, L. 1822 ; disdain, HF. 1716 ; vexation, R. 1487 ; *in
d. of*, in spite of, HF. 1668.

**Disserveth**, *pr. s.* deserves, I 756.

**Dissever**, *v.* part, 2. 115 ; 17. 15 ; *ger.* to

part, G 875; *pp.* separated, B 4. p 3. 19.

Disseveraunce, *s.* severing, B 3. p 11. 64.

Disshevele, *adj.* with hair flowing down, 5. 235. See Dischevele.

Dissimulen, *v.* dissimulate, T. i. 322, iii. 434.

Dissimulinge, *s.* dissimulation, dissembling, T. v. 1613, G 1073.

Dissimulour, *s.* dissembler, B 4418.

Disslaundred, *pp.* defamed, L. 1031.

Dissolveth, *pr. s.* puts an end to, B 2. p 3. 92.

Distantz, *adj. pl.* distant; *evene distantz*, equidistant, A. i. 17. 52.

Distemperaunce, *s.* inclemency, I 421.

Distempre, *adj.* distempered, furious, B 4. p 3. 125.

Distempre, *v.* vex, B 2426; *imp. s.* be out of temper, D 2195.

Disteyne, *v.* stain, bedim, dull, L. 255.

Distingwed, *pp.* distinguished, B 2. p 5. 75.

Distourbe, *v.* disturb, T. iv. 563; (to) interfere with, T. iv. 934; prevent, T. iv. 1103. See Destourbe.

Distreyne, *v.* constrain, A 1816; get into his grasp, clutch, 20. 8; *imp. s.* constrain, T. v. 596; Distreyneth, *pr. s.* secures, clutches, grasps, 5. 337; afflicts, F 820; *pp.* misled, T. ii. 840; assessed, taxed, I 752.

Disturbed, *pp.* altered, T. ii. 622.

Disturne, *v.* turn aside, T. iii. 718.

Ditee, *s.* ditty, song, B 3. p 1. 2; *pl.* HF. 622. See Dyte.

Diurne, *adj.* diurnal, E 1795.

Divers, *adj.* diverse, various, 3. 653; *dat.* different, 2. 17.

Diversely, *adv.* in different ways, R. 1629.

Diversitee, *s.* variety, T. v. 1793.

Divinistre, *s.* theologian, A 2811.

Divisioun, *s.* distinction, A 1781; difference, 10. 33; *of my d.*, under my influence, 4. 273.

Divynailes, *pl.* divinations, I 605.

Divynen, *v.* guess, T. iii. 458; 1 *pr. s.* declare, 12. 19; *pres. pt.* guessing, A 2515.

Divyninge, *s.* opinion, A 2521.

Divynis, *pl.* theologians, A 1323.

Divynour, *s.* seer, soothsayer, B 5. p 3. 149.

Do; see Doon.

Doctour, *s.* doctor, A 411; (i.e. St. Augustine), C 117; theologian, I 85; *pl.* teachers, D 1648.

Dogerel, *adj.* doggrel, B 2115.

Dogge, *s.* dog, D 1369, E 2014.

Doghter, *s.* daughter, L. 114; B 151; Doghtren, *pl.* L. 1963; Doughtren, *pl.* T. iv. 22.

Doinges, *pl.* deeds, L. 1681.

Doke, *s.* duck, 5. 498, 589; A 3576.

Dokke, *s.* dock (plant), T. iv. 461.

Dokked, *pp.* cut short, A 590.

Dolve, Dolven; see Delve.

Domb, *adj.* dumb, HF. 656.

Domesday, *s.* doom's day, HF. 1284.

Domesman, *s.* judge, B 3680, I 594.

Dominacioun, *s.* power, A 2758; dominion, C 560; chief influence, F 352; supremacy, H 181.

*Dominus*; see *Corpus*.

*Domus Dedali*, the labyrinth of Daedalus, HF. 1920.

Don, *imp. s.* don, put on, T. ii. 954.

Don, Done; see Doon.

Dong-carte, *s.* dung-cart, B 4226.

Dongeoun, *s.* keep-tower, A 1057.

Donne, *adj. pl.* dun, dusky, T. ii. 908; dun-coloured, 5. 334.

Doom, *s.* judgement, F 928; opinion, P 3127; sentence, decision: *hir d.*, the decision passed on them, 5. 308; Dome, *dat.* opinion, T. i. 100; judgement, HF. 1905; C 637; *to my d.*, in my opinion, R. 901; *stonde to the d.*, abide by the decision, 5. 546; Domes, *pl.* judgements, A 323.

Doon, *v.* do, execute, A 960; do, 3. 194; act, B 90; cause, B 3618; *doon us honge*, cause us to be hung, C 790; *don her companye*, accompany her, 4. 125; *leet don cryen*, caused to be cried, F 46; Do, *v.* cause, T. iv. 1683; use, B 2204; fulfil, B 1653; make, 3. 145; *do werche*, cause to be built, G 545; Done, *ger.* to do, T. i. 1026; *what to done*, what is to be done, 3. 689; *for to done*, a fit thing to do, I 62; to be done, L. 1597; Doon, *ger.* to do, A 78, 768; to commit, I 90; to cause, R. 1178; to force, 5. 221; *to don*, from doing, B 4. p 6. 323; Do, *ger.* to make, 3. 1260; to cause, T. ii. 1022; to commit, I 129; Doost, 2 *pr. s.* makest, C 312; Dostow, doest thou, L. 315; Dooth, *pr. s.* causes, A 2396; Doth, *pr. s.* makes, 2. 7; causes, 6. 21; Doth forth, continues, E 1015; Doon, *pr. pl.* do, A 268; Do, *imp. s.* make, H 12; bring (it) about, A 2405; cause, G 32; *do hange*, cause me to be hung, G 1029; *do fecche*, cause to be fetched, B 662; *do wey*, put away, lay aside, G 487; take away, A 3287; *do stryken hir out*, cause her to be struck out, D 1364; *do come*, cause to come, B 2035; Dooth, *imp. pl.* do

ye, C 745, I 105; *as dooth*, pray do, F 458;
Didest, 2 *pt. s.* didst, T. iii. 363; Dide,
*pt. s.* did, 3. 373; caused, R. 607; put on,
B 2047; *dide hem drawe*, caused to be
drawn, B 1823; *dide don sleen*, caused to
be slain, caused (men) to have them
slain (*sleen*, like *don*, is in the infin.
mood), D 2042; *dide of*, took off, 3. 516;
Dide, *pt. s. subj.* should do, F 1404;
Diden, *pt. pl.* made, 22. 28; *pt. pl. subj.*
should do, L. 723; Doon, *pp.* done,
1. 54; past, ended, 3. 40; *doon to dethe*,
done to death, L. 889; *doon make*,
caused to be made, E 253; *hath doon
yow kept*, has caused you to be preserved, E 1098; *doon ther write*, caused
to be written (or described there), R.
413; *don to dye*, done to death, murdered,
R. 1063; Do, *pp.* done, L. 957; ended, E
2440.

Dore, *s.* door, R. 527, A 550; *out at d.*, out
of doors, T 1757, H 306.

Dormant; *table dormant*, a permanent
side-table, A 353.

Dorre, Dorring; see Durre, Durring.

Dorste; see Dar.

Dortour, *s.* dormitory, D 1855.

Doseyn, *s.* a dozen, A 578.

Dossers, *pl.* baskets to carry on the back,
HF. 1940.

Dostow, doest thou, D 239.

Dotard, *adj.* foolish, D 291.

Dote, *v.* dote, grow foolish, L. 261 *a*;
Doten, act foolishly, G 983.

Doth, *pr. s.* causes, R. 389; Doth ... carie,
causes to be carried, A 3410; makes, F
1257; *imp. pl.* do ye, B 2785. See Doon.

Double, *adj.* twofold, 4. 109; deceitful,
HF. 285.

Doublenesse, *s.* duplicity, 7. 159; 9. 63.

Doucet, *adj.* dulcet, i. e. dulcet (pipe),
sweet-sounding (pipe), HF. 1221.

Doughter, *s.* daughter, T. iii. 3; Doughtren, *pl.* T. iv. 22.

Doumb, *adj.* dumb, A 774.

Doun, *s.* down, soft feathers, 9. 45.

Doun, *adv.* down, F 323; *up and doun*, in
all directions, in all ways, B 53.

Doune, *dat.* down, hill, B 1986.

Dounere, *adv.* more downward, A. ii. 12.
22.

Doun-right, *adv.* at once, H 228.

Dounward, *adv.* outward, southward, A.
ii. 40. 63.

Doutance, *s.* doubt, T. iv. 963; *pl.* per-
plexities, T. i. 200.

Doute, *s.* doubt, 1. 25; fear, F 1096, I 91;
peril, L. 1613; suspense, E 1721; lack,

T. ii. 366; *out of doute*, doubtless, A 487;
*sans d.*, without doubt, D 1838; *with-
outen d.*, certainly, L. 383.

Doutelees, *adv.* without doubt, certainly,
T. ii. 494; A 1831.

Douten, *v.* fear, I 648; *pr. s.* fears, I 953;
Douteth, *imp. pl.* fear, T. i. 683.

Doutous, *adj.* doubtful, T. iv. 992.

D'outremere, *adj.* from beyond the seas,
foreign, imported, 3. 253.

Douve, *s.* dove, 5. 341; pigeon, C 397.

Dowaire, *s.* dower, E 848.

Dowe, 1 *pr. s.* grant, give, T. v. 230.

Dowve; see Douve.

Dradde; see Drede.

Draf, *s.* draff, refuse (of corn), chaff, I 35;
L. 312 *a*.

Draf-sek, *s.* sack full of 'draff,' A 4206.

Dragges, *pl.* digestive sweetmeats, A
426 (in MS. Harl. only; other MSS. have
*drogges*).

Dragoun, *s.* dragon, L. 1430, 1581; *tail of
the dr.*, the Dragon's tail, A. ii. 4. 36;
the point where a planet (esp. the moon)
passed from the northern to the southern
side of the ecliptic. (The opposite node
was called the Dragon's Head.)

Drasty, *adj.* filthy, worthless, B 2113, 2120.
Cf. A. S. *dresten*, *dœrstan*, dregs.

Drat, *pr. s. of* Drede.

Draught (of drink), L. 2667; move at
chess, 3. 682.

Drawe, *v.* draw, incline, E 314; *dr. him*,
withdraw himself, F 355; bring forward,
R. 6; *v.* attract, R. 1183; recall, A 2074;
*ger.* to draw, to carry, A 1416; to bring
back, I 239; Draweth along, *pr. s.* pro-
longs, B 1. m 1. 32 (Lat. *protrahit*); *pr.
pl. refl.* withdraw themselves, F 252;
Drough, *pt. s.* drew, A 4304; drew along,
T. v. 1558; *refl.* drew himself, approached,
B 1710; Drow, *pt. s.* drew, B 3292; drew
near, D 993; moved (as the sun), 5. 490;
hoisted, L. 1563; Drew, *pt. s.* attracted,
3. 864; *drowe to record*, didst bring to
witness, 16. 22; Drowe, *pt. pl.* drew, R.
1678; Drawe, *pp.* drawn, T. iii. 674;
*pres. part.* resorting, B 1217.

Drecche, *v.* be tedious, T. ii. 1264; *ger.* to
vex, T. ii. 1471; 2 *pr. pl.* tarry, T. iv.
1446; *pp.* vexed, troubled, B 4077.

Drecchinge, *s.* prolonging, I 1000;
Drecching, delay, T. iii. 853.

Drede, *s.* dread, fear, A 1998; uncertainty,
17. 28; doubt, 5. 52; *it is no drede*, without doubt, B 869, E 1155; *out of drede*,
without doubt, E 634; *pl.* fears, T. i.
463.

**Drede,** v. dread, fear, 1. 76; *refl.* dread, A 660; *ger.* to be dreaded, to be feared, B 4253; Drat, *pr. s.* dreadeth, dreads, T. iii. 328; Dredde, 1 *pt. s.* was afraid, T. ii. 482; Dradde, *pt. s.* feared, B 3402; Dradde him, was afraid, B 3918; Dradden, *pt. pl.* G 15; Drad, *pp.* E 69.

**Dredeles,** *adj.* fearless, B 3. m 12. 11.

**Dredeles,** *adv.* without doubt, certainly, 3. 764.

**Dredful,** *adj.* terrible, B 3558; fearful, timid, L. 109; cautious, A 1479.

**Dredfully,** *adv.* timidly, T. ii. 1128.

**Dreint, -e** ; see **Drenchen.**

**Dremed me,** *pt. s.* I dreamt, R. 51.

**Dreminges,** *pl.* dreams, B 4280.

**Drenchen,** (1) *ger.* to drown, A 3617; Drenche, v. drown, HF. 205; *do me drenche,* make (men) drown me, cause me to be drowned, E 2201 : Drenchen (2) v. be drowned, A 3521; be overwhelmed, L. 2919; *pr. s.* swamps, I 363; Dreinte, *pt. s.* (1) drowned, 3. 72; Dreynte, *pt. s.* drowned, I 839; Dreynte, *pt. s.* (2) was drowned, B 923; Dreynte, 2 *pt. pl.* were drowned, T. iv. 930; *pt. pl.* drowned, F 1378; Drenched, *pp.* drowned, L. 2178; Dreynt, *pp.* 3. 148; Dreynte, *pp. as def. adj.* drowned, B 69; *pp. pl.* HF. 233.

**Drenching,** *s.* drowning, A 2456, B 485.

**Drerinesse,** *s.* sadness, T. i. 701.

**Drery,** *adj.* sad, E 514; terrified, L. 810.

**Dresse,** v. direct, 14. 3; dispose, get ready, T. ii. 71; prepare, E 1049; set in order, A 106; v. *refl.* address oneself, E 1007; direct himself, go, A 3468; direct myself, R. 110; address himself, direct himself (*or perhaps,* mount), T. v. 37; Dresse her, settle herself, L. 804; Dresse, *ger.* to direct, B 2308; *ger. refl.* prepare himself, T. v. 279; prepare, 5. 88; *pt. s. refl.* raised himself, T. iii. 71; took up his station, A 3358; *pp.* arrayed, E 2361; prepared, 5. 665.

**Dreye,** *adj.* dry, A 3024; *as s.,* 5. 380.

**Dreyeth,** *pr. s.* dries up, drains, I 848.

**Dreynt, -e** ; see **Drenche.**

**Drogges,** *pl.* drugs, A 426.

**Drogh** ; see **Drawe,**

**Droghte,** *s.* drought, A 2, 595.

**Dronkelewe,** *adj.* addicted to drink, B 2383, C 495, D 2043.

**Drough,** *pt. s. of* Drawe.

**Droughte,** *s.* thirst (*siti*), B 2. p 7. 44.

**Drouped,** *pt. s.* were draggled, A 107.

**Drovy,** *adj.* dirty, muddy, I 816.

**Drow, -e** ; see **Drawe.**

**Druerye,** *s.* affection, R. 844.

**Drugge,** *ger.* to drudge, A 1416.

**Drunken,** *adj.* causing drunkenness, 5. 181.

**Drye,** *ger.* to endure, T. v. 42; v. suffer, endure, 4. 251.

**Dryve,** v. drive, F 183; hasten, D 1694; whirl round, 10. 46; pass away, T. v. 394; *dryve away,* pass away, C 628; Dryveth forth, *pr. s.* continues, goes on with, T. i. 1092; Dryfth, *pr. s.* impels, T. v. 1332; Dryven (the day), *pr. pl.* pass (the day), L. 2620; Dròòf, *pt. s.* drove, brought, T. v. 475; incited, T. iii. 994; Drīve, *pp.* driven, passed away, T. v. 389; completed, F 1230.

**Duetee,** *s.* duty, A 3060; debt, D 1391; sum due, D 1352.

**Dulcarnon,** *s.* an inexplicable dilemma, one's wit's end, T. iii. 931.

**Dulle,** *ger.* to feel dull, T. ii. 1035; makes dull, stupefies, G 1073, 1172; Dulled, *pp.* made of none effect, I 233.

**Dun,** *adj.* swarthy, R. 1213; Donne, *pl.* dusky, T. ii. 908; dun-coloured, 5. 334.

**Dun,** *s.* the dun horse, H 5. 'Dun is in the mire' is the name of an old rustic game.

**Dungeoun,** *s.* keep-tower, chief castle, L. 937.

**Dure,** v. last, endure, A 2770; remain, A 1236; live, T. iv. 765; continue, F 836.

**Duresse,** *s.* hardship, T. v. 399.

**Durre,** *ger.* to dare (to do), T. v. 840. See *Durren* in Stratmann; and see **Dar.**

**Durring,** *s.* daring, bravery; *d. don,* daring to do, courage to execute, T. v. 837.

**Durste** ; see **Dar.**

**Dusked,** *pt. pl.* grew dim, A 2806.

**Dwale,** *s.* soporific drink, A 4161.

**Dwelle,** v. remain, A 1661; tarry, stay, 3. 712; *ger.* to delay, HF. 252; Dwelled, *pp.* dwelt, A 1228; *imp. s.* remain, T. iv. 1449.

**Dwellinges,** *s. pl.* delays, B 1. m 1. 33 (Lat. *moras*).

**Dwyned,** *pp. as adj.* dwindled, R. 360.

**Dy,** say; *Je vous dy,* I tell you, D 1832, 1838.

**Dye,** v. die, 2. 7; *ger.* to die, B 114; Dyde, *pt. s.* died, HF. 106, 380; *pt. s. subj.* would die, D 965. See **Deye.**

**Dyen,** *ger.* to dye, B 4648.

**Dyere,** *s.* dyer, A 362.

**Dyinge,** *s.* death, B 3073.

**Dyke,** v. to make dikes or ditches, A 536.

**Dys,** *pl.* dice, A 1238. See **Dees.**

**Dyte,** *s.* ditty, 23. 16. See **Ditee.**

**Dyverseth,** *pr. s.* varies, T. iii. 1752.

## E.

**Ebbe,** *s.* low water, F 259.

**Ebben,** *v.* ebb, T. iv. 1145.

**Ecclesiaste,** *s.* minister, A 708.

**Ech,** *adj.* each, A 39, 369.

**Eche,** *v.* increase, augment, T. i. 887; iii. 1509; *ger.* enlarge, add to, HF. 2065.

**Echines,** *s. pl.* sea-urchins, B 3. m 8. 20 (Lat. *echinis*).

**Echoon,** each one, L. 290; A 2655; Echone, *pl.* (?), all, every one, C 113.

**Edified,** *pp.* built up, B 4. p 6. 284.

**Eek,** *adv.* also, eke, moreover, A 5, 41.

**Eem,** *s.* uncle, T. i. 1022. A. S. *ēam.*

**Eest,** *adv.* eastward, 3. 88.

**Eet, -e ;** see **Ete.**

**Effect,** *s.* deed, reality, T. i. 748; result, HF. 5; Theffect (*for* the effect), the sequel, L. 622; *in effect*, in fact, in reality, in practice, A 319.

**Eft,** *adv.* again, A 1669; another time, 3. 41.

**Eft-sone,** *adv.* soon after, G 1288; immediately afterwards, I 89; soon after this, H 65; hereafter, G 933; again, B 909; Eftsones, *adv.* very soon, L. 2322.

**Egal,** *adj.* equal, T. iii. 137.

**Egal,** *adv.* equally, T. iv. 660.

**Egalitee,** *s.* equality, I 949.

**Egaly,** *adv.* equably, B 2. p 4. 141; impartially, B 5. p 3. 142.

**Egge,** *s.* edge, sharp side, T. iv. 927; sword, 9. 19.

**Eggeth,** *pr. s.* incites, R. 182.

**Eggement,** *s.* instigation, incitement, B 842.

**Egging,** *s.* instigation, E 2135.

**Egle,** *s.* eagle, HF. 499.

**Egre,** *adj.* sharp, sour, R. 217; bitter, B 2367; keen, I 117.

**Egremoine,** *s.* agrimony, G 800.

**Egren,** *v.* incite (lit. make eager), B 4. p 6. 335.

**Eighte,** eighth, F 1280.

**Eightetene,** eighteen, A 3223.

**Eightetethe,** *ord. adj.* eighteenth, B 5.

**Eir,** *s.* air, A 1246, 3473.

**Eisel,** *s.* vinegar, R. 217.

**Ekko,** *s.* echo, E 1189.

**Elde,** *s.* old age, age, T ii. 393, 399; long lapse of time, 7. 12.

**Elde,** *v.* grow old, R. 396; *pr. s.* ages, makes old, R. 391.

**Elder,** *adj.* older, B 1720, 3450.

**Elder-fader,** *s.* grandfather, B 2. p 4. 50.

**Eldres,** *pl.* ancestors, B 3388.

**Eleccioun,** *s.* choice, 5. 409, 621; election (in astrology), B 312.

**Elenge,** *adj.* miserable, B 1412, D 1199.

**Elevat,** *pp.* elevated, A. ii. 23. 29.

**Elf-queen,** *s.* fairy-queen, B 1978, D 860.

**Ellebor,** *s.* hellebore, *Helleborus niger*, B 4154.

**Elles,** *adv.* else, otherwise, 3. 997; *elles god forbede*, God forbid it should be otherwise, G 1046.

**Elongacioun,** *s.* angular distance, A. ii. 25. 66.

**Elvish,** *adj.* elvish, i. e. absent in demeanour, B 1893; foolish, G 751, 842.

**Embassadrye,** *s.* embassy, negociation, B 233.

**Embaume,** *v.* embalm, L. 676; *pp.* covered with balm, R. 1663.

**Embelif,** *adj.* oblique, A. i. 20. 3; (as applied to angles) acute, A. ii. 26. 39. See the New E. Dict.

**Embelised,** *pp.* beautified, B 2. p 5. 75.

**Embosed,** *pp.* plunged deeply into the thicket, quite hidden, 3. 353.

**Embracinge,** *s.* embrace, I 944.

**Embrouded,** *pp.* embroidered, adorned, A 89.

**Embroudinge,** *s.* embroidery, I 417.

**Embusshements,** *pl.* ambuscades, B 2509.

**Emeraude,** *s.* emerald, B 1799.

**Emes,** *gen.* uncle's, T. ii. 466. See **Eem.**

**Emforth,** *prep.* as far as extends, to the extent of, A 2235. *Em-* is from A. S. *emn*, for *efen*, even.

**Emisperies,** *s. pl.* hemispheres, A. i. 18. 9.

**Empeireden,** *pt. pl.* made worse, B 2209.

**Emplastre,** 2 *pr. pl.* plaster over, bedaub, E 2207.

**Empoisoned,** *pp.* poisoned, B 2519, 3850.

**Empoisoning,** *s.* poisoning, C 891.

**Empoysoner,** *s.* poisoner, C 894.

**Emprenting,** *s.* impression, F 834.

**Emprinteth,** *imp. pl.* impress, E 1193; Emprented, *pp.* imprinted, F 831; taken an impression of, E 2117.

**Empryse,** *s.* enterprise, undertaking, L. 617, 1452.

**Empte,** *v.* empty, make empty, G 741; *pp. as adj.* exhausted, B 1. p 1. 10; worn out, shrunken (Lat. *effeto*), B 1. m 1. 20.

**Enbasshinge,** *s.* bewilderment, amazement, B 4. p 1. 43.

**Enbatailled,** *adj.* embattled, R. 139.

**Enbibing,** *s.* absorption, G 814.

**Enbrace,** *v.* embrace, hold firmly, 21. 11; Enbraced, *pp.* surrounded, T. v. 1816.

**Enbrouden,** *v.* embroider, L. 2351; *pp.* L. 119, 227.

Encens, s. incense, A 2429.

Encense, v. to offer incense, G 395, 413.

Enchantours, pl. wizards, I 603.

Enchaufeth, pr. s. burns, B 5. m 3. 19.

Enchaunten, v. enchant, T. iv. 1395.

Enchesoun, s. occasion, reason, B 2783; cause, T. i. 681.

Enclos, pp. enclosed, R. 138, 1652.

Enclyning, s. inclination, HF. 734.

Encomberous, adj. cumbersome, oppressive, burdensome, 18. 42; HF. 862.

Encombraunce, s. encumbrance, E 1960.

Encombre, v. encumber, L. 2006; pp. endangered, stuck fast, A 508; hampered, R. 889; hindered, I 687; embarrassed, weary, A 718.

Encorporing, s. incorporation, G 815.

Encrees, s. increase, A 2184.

Encrese, v. increase, 2. 103; Encressed, pp. E 408; enriched, B 1271.

Endamagen, v. harm, B 1. p 4. 91; pp. compromised, B 1. p 1. 73.

Ende, s. end, A 15; purpose, B 481; point, R. 973.

Ended, pp. finite, B 2. p 7. 113.

Endelees, adj. infinite, H 322.

Endelong, adv. all along, A 2678; lengthways, A 1991.

Endelong, prep. all along, F 992; along, L. 1498; down along, F 416.

Endentinge, s. indentation, I 417. Endented or Indented is an heraldic term, signifying notched with regular and equal indentations.

Endere, s. cause of the end, A 2776; i. e. who dost end, C 218.

Endetted, pp. indebted, G 734.

Ending-day, s. death-day, 18. 55.

Enditements, s. pl. indictments, I 800.

Endlang, adv. along, lengthways. See Endelong.

Endouted, pp. feared (with me), R. 1664.

Endyte, v. write, dictate, A 95, 325; endite, compose, write, L. 414, 2356; relate, G 80; tell, L. 1678; indict, B 3858; pp. related, B 3170.

Endyting, s. composing, 18. 77; pl. compositions, I 1085.

Enfamyned, pp. starved, A 2429.

Enfecteth, pr. s. infects, L. 2242.

Enforcen, ger. to enforce, B 2233; strengthen (your position), D 340; 1 pr. s. refl. insist, T. iv. 1016; Enforcen, pr. pl. gain strength, B 2355; imp. s. endeavour, B 2237.

Enformed, pp. informed, E 738, F 335; instructed, I 658.

Enfortúned, pt. s. endowed with powers, 4. 259.

Engendre, v. procreate, B 3148; produce, B 2582; v. beget, E 1272; pr. pl. are produced, B 4113.

Engendringe, s. product, B 2580.

Engendrure, s. procreation, B 3137; begetting, 5. 306; generation, D 128, 134; progeny, offspring, I 621; fraternity, I 375.

English, s. power of expression in English, L. 66.

Engreggen, pr. pl. burden, I 979.

Engyn, s. contrivance, T. iii. 274; device, R. 511; machine, F 184; skill, HF. 528.

Engyned, pp. tortured, racked, B 4250.

Enhabit, pp. devoted, T. iv. 443.

Enhauncen, v. raise, A 1434; ger. to exalt, I 614: Enhaunceth, pr. s. elevates, I 730; pt. s. raised, B 2291; pp. promoted, L. 1411.

Enhaused, pp. elevated, lifted above (the horizon), A. ii. 26. 37.

Enhausing, s. elevation, A. ii. 39. 26.

Enhorte, ger. to exhort, A 2851.

Enlaceth, pr. s. entangles, B 1. m 4. 23; pp. involved, made intricate, B 3. p 8. 6.

Enlumine, v. illumine, I 244; pt. s. E 33.

Enluting, s. securing with 'lute,' daubing with clay, &c., to exclude air, G 766

Enoynt, pp. anointed, A 2961.

Enpeiren, v. injure, B 4. p 3. 56.

Enpoysoninge, s. poisoning, B 1. p 3. 59.

Enprented, pp. imprinted, E 2178.

Enpresse, v. make an impression on, 21. 8.

Enquere, v. enquire, A 3166; search into, B 629.

Enqueringe, s. inquiry, B 888.

Ensample, s. example, A 496, 505; pattern, 3. 911; warning, R. 1539; instance, R. 1584; in e., to signify, A. i. 21. 41; pl. examples, F 1419; cases, A 2842.

Ensaumpler, s. prototype, B 3. m 9. 17.

Enseigne, s. ensign, standard, R. 1200.

Enseled, pp. sealed up, T. v. 151; fully granted, T. iv. 559.

Entaile, s. cutting, intaglio-work, R. 1081; Entayle, shape, description, R. 162.

Entaile, v. carve, R. 609; pp. R. 140.

Entalenten, pr. pl. stimulate, B 5. p 5. 6.

Entame, v. re-open (lit. cut into), 1. 79. O.F. entamer.

Enteccheth, pr. s. infects, B 4. p 3. 83; pp. endued with (good) qualities, T. v. 832. O. F. entechier, entachier.

Entencioun, s. intent, C 408 ; attention, T. i. 52 ; design, T. i. 211.

Entende, v. attend, T. iii. 414 ; give attention to, D 1478 ; dispose oneself, F 689 ; ger. to apply oneself, B 3498 ; to aim (after), incline (to), T. ii. 853 ; Entende, 1 pr. s. perceive, T. iv. 1649 ; attend, R. 597 ; pres. part. looking intently, B 1. p 2. 3.

Entendement, s. perception, HF. 983.

Entente, s. intention, intent, A 958, 1000 ; design, B 3835 ; wish, 18. 68 ; meaning, F 400, 959 ; attention, D 1374 ; endeavour, G 6 ; feeling, 5. 532, 580 ; mind, B 1740 ; plan, B 147, 206 ; do thyn e., give heed, 3. 752 ; as to comun e., in plain language, F 107.

Ententeden, pl. pt. gave their attention, L. 1155.

Ententif, Ententyf, adj. attentive, HF. 1120 ; B 2205 ; eager, R. 685 ; diligent, R. 436 ; devoted, R. 339 ; careful, E 1288.

Ententifly, adv. attentively, HF. 616.

Entermedled, pp. intermixed, R. 906.

Entraille, s. entrails, B 1763 ; inside, E 1188.

Entre, ger. to enter, 5. 147, 153. In A. ii. 44. s, entere hit = set down in writing.

Entrechaungeden, pt. pl. interchanged, exchanged, T. iii. 1369 ; pp. interchanged, T. iv. 1043.

Entrechaunginges, s. pl. mutations, B 1. m 5. 38 ; vicissitudes (Lat. uices), B 2. m 3. 20.

Entrecomunen, v. intercommunicate, T. iv. 1354.

Entrecomuninge, s. interchange, B 2. p 7. 63.

Entredited, pp. interdicted, I 965.

Entree, entry, entrance, R. 517, 530, 538 ; pl. entrances, HF. 1945.

Entrelaced, pp. intricate, B 3. p 12. 166.

Entremedled, pp. intermingled, HF 2124.

Entremes, s. intervening course, 5. 665. 'Entremets, certaine choice dishes served in between the courses of a feast ;' Cotgrave.

Entremette, v. refl. interfere, D 834 ; Entremeten (him), meddle with, 5. 515 ; imp. s. take part (in), meddle (with), T. i. 1026.

Entreparten, ger. to share, T. i. 592.

Entreteden, pt. pl. treated of, discussed, B 2466.

Entryketh, pr. s. holds fast in its subtle grasp, ensnares, 5. 403 ; Entryked, pp.

entrapped, R. 1642 ; 'Intriquer, to intricate, involve ;' Cotgrave.

Entune, v. intone, tune, T. iv. 4.

Entunes, s. pl. tunes, 3. 309.

Entysinge, s. allurement, I 353.

Enveniminge, s. poisonous effect, E 2060 ; poison, I 854.

Envenyme, v. infect, D 474 ; pp. B 3314.

Environinge, s. surface, B 5. m 4. 172 ; circumference, B 4. p 6. 85.

Enviroun, adv. roundabout, L. 300.

Enviroune, v. encompass, B 3. m 9. 45 ; pres. part. skirting, going round, R. 526.

Envóluped, pp. enveloped, involved, C 942.

Envýe, s. envy, B 3584 ; longing, R. 1653 ; to e., in rivalry, 3. 173.

Envye, v. vie, strive, 3. 406 ; vie (with), HF. 1231.

Envyned, pp. stored with wine, A 342.

Episicle, s. epicycle, A. ii. 35. 29. A small circle, the centre of which moves along the circumference of a larger one.

Equacion, s. equal partition, A. ii. 37. 24 ; Equacions, pl. equations, F 1279 ; Equaciouns, A. ii. 36 (rubric) ; calculations, A. i. 23. 5. By 'equations of houses' is meant the division of the sphere into twelve equal portions (or 'houses'), for astrological purposes.

Equales, adj. pl. of equal length ; houres equales, hours each containing sixty minutes, A. ii. 8. 3.

Equinoxial, s. equinoxial circle, B 4046.

Er, adv. before, formerly, A 3789.

Er, conj. before, A 1040, 1155 ; er that, before, A 36.

Er, prep. before, C 892 ; er tho, before then, L. 1062 ; er now, ere now, F 460.

Erbe, s. herb, L. 109 a.

Erbe yve, s. herb ive, ground ivy, Ajuga Chamaepitys, B 4156.

Erber, s. arbour, L. 97 a. See Herber.

Erchedeken, s. archdeacon, D 1300.

Ere (èèrə), s. ear, D 636 ; at ere, in (her) ear, T. i. 106.

Ere, s. ear (of corn), L. 76.

Ere (èrə), ger. to plough, A 886 ; pp. HF. 485. A.S. erian.

Erl, s. earl, B 3597, 3646.

Erme, v. feel sad, grieve, 3. 80 ; C 312. A.S. earmian, yrman.

Ernestful, adj. serious, T. ii. 1727 ; E 1175.

Erratik, adj. wandering, T. v. 1812.

Erraunt, adj. arrant, H 224 ; errant, stray (because near the middle of the chess-board), 3. 661.

**Errest**, *2 pr. s.* wanderest, T. iv. 302.

**Ers**, *s.* buttocks, A 3734. A. S. *ears.*

**Erst**, *adv.* first, at first, HF. 2075 ; A 776 ; before, 16. 21 ; aforetime, R. 692 ; *at e.*, first, for the first time, B 1884, G 151 ; at last, T. i. 842 ; *e. than*, before, A 1566 ; *long e. er*, long first before, C 662.

**Erthes**, *s. pl.* lands, countries, B 1. m 5. 61.

**Eschaufen**, *ger.* to burn ; *pr. s.* chafes, I 657 ; *pp.* heated, I 546.

**Eschaufinge**, *s.* heating, I 537 ; *pl.* enkindlings, I 916.

**Eschaunge**, *s.* exchange, A 278 ; *pl.* interchangings, HF. 697.

**Eschew**, *adj.* averse, I 971 ; Eschu, E 1812.

**Eschewe**, *v.* escape ; Eschue, *v.* avoid, T. ii. 696 ; A 3043 ; shun, G 4 ; *2 pr. pl.* eschew, avoid, T. i. 344 ; Eschewed, *pp.* B 4528 ; *imp. s.* T. ii. 1018.

**Ese**, *s.* ease, E 217, 434 ; amusement, delight, A 768, G 746 ; *do yow e.*, give you pleasure, 6. 78 ; *wel at e.*, fully at ease, T. ii. 750.

**Ese**, *v.* ease, 3. 556 ; relieve, L. 1704 ; give ease (te), R. 316 ; Esen, *ger.* to entertain, A 2194 ; *pp.* entertained, A 29.

**Esement**, *s.* benefit, A 4179, 4186.

**Espace**, *s.* space of time, B 2219.

**Especes**, *s. pl.* kinds, varieties (of sin), I 448.

**Espiaille**, *s.* sets of spies, B 2509, D 1323.

**Espye**, *s.* spy, T. ii. 1112.

**Espye**, *ger.* to observe, R. 795 ; *v.* perceive, HF. 706 ; enquire about, B 180 ; look about, L. 858.

**Essoyne**, *s.* excuse, I 164. Mod. E. *essoin.*

**Est**, *s.* east, B 297, 493, 3657.

**Estableth**, *pr. s.* settles, causes, B 4. p 4. 51.

**Estat**, *s.* state, condition, L. 125 ; rank, T. v. 1025 ; position, E 1969 ; Estaat, state, condition, rank, B 973, 3592, 3647; way, E 610 ; term of office, D 2018.

**Estatlich**, *adj.* stately, dignified, A 140 ; suitable to one's estate, B 3902.

**Estatuts**, *s.* ordinances, B 2. p 1. 48.

**Estraunge**, *adj.* strange, T. i. 1084.

**Estres**, *pl.* inward parts, recesses (of a building), L. 1715 ; A 1971 ; recesses, R. 1448 ; interior, A 4295.

**Esy**, *adj.* easy, A 223 ; moderate, A 441 ; gentle, 5. 382.

**Ete**, *v.* eat, A 947 ; Et, *pr. s.* eats, L. 1389 ; Eet, *pt. s.* ate, T. v. 1439 ; A 2048, 3421 ; Eete, *pt. pl.* ate, 9. 11 ; Ete, *pt. pl.* 3. 432 ; Eten, *pp.* eaten, A 4351.

**Eterne**, *adj.* eternal, A 1109, 1990 ; *s.* eternity, T. iv. 978.

**Ethe**, *adj.* easy, T. v. 850.

**Etik**, the Ethics of Aristotle, L. 166.

**Evangyle**, *s.* gospel, R. 445 ; *pl.* B 666.

**Even**, *adj.* even, equal, same, HF. 10 ; exact, R. 1350.

**Even**, *adv.* exactly, 3. 441 ; evenly, D 2249 ; regularly, R. 526 ; Evene joynant, closely adjoining, A 1060 ; *ful even*, actually, 3. 1329.

**Evene-cristene**, *s.* fellow-Christian, I 395, 805.

**Even-lyk**, *adj.* similar, B 5. p 2. 25.

**Ever**, *adv.* ever, always, A 50, &c. ; Ever in oon, always alike, continually, T. v. 451 ; incessantly, A 1771.

**Everich**, each, A 1186 ; every, A 241 ; each one, A 371 ; every one, E 1017 ; *e. of hem*, either of the two, B 1004 ; Everich other, each other, 7. 53.

**Everichoon**, every one, A 31, 747 ; each one, L. 2567 ; Everichone, *pl.* each one (of us), HF. 337 ; each of them all, all of them, T. iii. 412.

**Ever-mo**, *adv.* for ever, always, continually, L. 1239, 2035, 2634.

**Everydeel**, *adv.* every whit, A 368, D 162 ; altogether, A 3303.

**Evidently**, *adv.* by observation, A. ii. 23. *rubric.*

**Ew**, *s.* yew-tree, A 2923 ; *(collectively)* yew-trees, R. 1385.

**Exaltacioun**, *s.* (astrological) exaltation, D 702, E 2224.

**Exaltat**, *as pp.* exalted, D 704.

**Exametron**, *s.* a hexameter, B 3169.

**Excusascioun**, *s.* false excuse, I 680 ; plea, I 164.

**Excuse**, *s.* ; *for myn e.*, in my excuse, 7. 305.

**Executeth**, *pr. s.* performs, A 1664 ; Execut, *pp.* executed, T. iii. 622.

**Executour**, *s.* executant, D 2010.

**Executrice**, *s.* causer, T. iii. 617.

**Exercitacioun**, *s.* exercise, B 4. p 6. 298.

**Existence**, *s.* reality, HF. 266.

**Exorsisaciouns**, *pl.* exorcisms, spells to raise spirits, HF. 1263.

**Expans**, *adj.* (calculated) separately, F 1275. See *Anni expansi.*

**Expoune**, *v.* explain, B 3398, G 86 ; Expouned, *pt. s.* B 3346, 3399.

**Expres**, *adj.* expressed, made clear, D 1169.

**Expres**, *adv.* expressly, C 182, D 719.

**Expresse**, *ger.* to declare, 17. 5 ; *v.* relate, C 105.

**Expulsif,** *adj.* expellent, A 2749.

**Extenden,** *pr. pl.* are extended, B 461.

**Extree,** *s* axle-tree, A. i. 14. 2.

**Ey,** *s.* egg, B 4035, G 806.

**Ey,** *interj.* eh ! T. ii. 128; alas ! T. iv. 1087; what ! C 782.

**Eye,** *s.* eye ; *at eye,* evidently, L. 100 ; Eyen, *pl.* eyes, 1. 105 ; Eyen sight, eyesight, D 2060. See Yë.

**Eyed,** *adj.* endowed with eyes, T. iv. 1459.

**Eyle,** *v.* ail, A 3424.

**Eyr,** *s.* air, HF. 954 ; L. 1482 ; Eir, A 1246, 3473 ; Eyre, *dat.* air, gas, G 767.

**Eyr,** *s.* heir, L. 1598, 1819.

**Eyrish,** *adj.* of the air, aërial, HF. 932, 965.

**Eyse,** *s.* ease, D 2101. See Ese.

### F.

**Face,** *s.* face, A 199, 458; a technical term in astrology, signifying the third part of a sign (of the zodiac), ten degrees in extent, F 50, 1288.

**Facound,** *adj.* eloquent, 5. 521.

**Facounde,** *s.* eloquence, fluency, 3. 926 ; C 50.

**Facultee,** *s.* capacity, authority, *or* disposition, A 244 ; branch of study. HF. 248.

**Fade,** *adj.* faded, R. 311.

**Fader,** *s.* father, A 100 ; Fader, *gen.* A 781 ; *fader day,* father's time, B 3374 ; *fader kin,* father's race, ancestry, G 829 ; *pl.* ancestors, E 61 ; originators, B 129.

**Fadme,** *pl.* fathoms, A 2916.

**Fadres-in-lawe,** *pl.* parents-in-law. B 2. p 3. 42.

**Faile,** *s.* failure ; *withouten f.,* without fail, 2. 48 ; *sans faille,* B 501.

**Failen,** *v.* fail, grow dim, 5. 85 ; *pres. part.* failing, remote, A. ii. 4. 30.

**Fair,** *adj.* fine, D 2253 ; good, excellent, A 154 ; *a fair,* a good one, A 165 ; *as s.,* a fair thing, excellent thing (sarcastically), T. iii. 850 ; *voc.* O fair one ! HF. 518 ; *pl.* A 234 ; clean, R. 571 ; specious, R. 437.

**Faire,** *adv.* fairly, R. 774, 798 ; honestly, A 539 ; courteously, R. 592 ; clearly, D 1142 ; prosperously, L. 186, 277.

**Faire,** *s.* fair, market, B 1515.

**Faire Rewthelees,** Fair Unpitying One, *La Belle Dame sans Merci,* 6. 31.

**Fairnesse,** *s.* beauty, A 1098 ; honesty of life, A 519.

**Fair-Semblaunt,** Fair-show, R. 963.

**Falding,** *s.* a sort of coarse cloth, A 391, 3212.

**Fallen,** *v.* happen, T. iv. 976; light, E 126 ; suit, E 259 ; prosper, L. 186 ; *pr. s. subj.* may befall, R. 798 ; *impers.* may it befall, L. 277 ; *pr. s.* comes as by accident, 6. 4 ; comes, 3. 706 ; suffers depression (an astrological term), D 702, 705 ; Falles, *pr. s.* (Northern form), falls, A 4042 ; belongs, 3. 257 ; Fallen, *pr. pl.* happen, come to pass, R. 20 ; Fel, 1 *pt. s.* fell, 2. 15 ; Fil, *pt. s.* fell, A 845 ; happened, L. 589, 1162 ; was fitting, L. 2474 ; *fil on slepe,* fell asleep, HF. 114 ; *fil of his accord,* agreed with him, F 741 ; *as fer as reson fil,* as far as reason extended, F 570; Fille, 1 *pt. pl.* fell, became, D 812 ; Fillen, *pt. pl.* fell, B 3183, 3620; Fille, *pt. pl.* HF. 1659 ; *fille in speche =* fell to talking, F 964 ; Falle, *pp.* fallen, L. 1726, 1826; happened, A 324 ; accidentally placed, F 684 ; Falling, *pres. pt.* felling, causing to fall, T. ii. 1382.

**Fals,** *adj.* false, 3. 618 ; *false get,* cheating contrivance, G 1277 ; *voc.* B 4416.

**Falsen,** *v.* falsify, A 3175 ; deceive, L 1640 ; betray, T. v. 1845 ; False, *v.* be untrue to, 3. 1234 : *pp.* falsified, broken (faith), F 627.

**Falwe,** *adj.* fallow, yellowish, HF. 1936 ; A 1364.

**Falwes,** *pl.* fallow-ground, D 656.

**Fame,** *s.* notoriety, A 3148 ; rumour, L. 1242; good report, E 418 ; Fames, *pl.* rumours, HF. 1292.

**Familer,** *s.* familiar friend, B 4 p 6. 255.

**Famulier,** *adj.* familiar, at home, A 215, B 1221 ; of one's own household, E 1784 ; Famulere, affable, L. 1606.

**Fan,** *s.* vane, quintain, H 42.

**Fanne,** *s.* fan, A 3315.

**Fantastyk,** *adj.* belonging to the fancy, A 1376. Used with reference to the portion of the brain in the *front* of the head.

**Fantasye,** *s.* fancy, HF. 593 ; delight, A 3191 ; imagining, HF. 992 ; fancy, pleasure, D 190 ; imagination, A 3835, 3840 ; imaginary object, 9. 51; desire, will, B 3475 ; Fantasyes, *pl.* fancies, F 205 ; wishes, B 3465.

**Fantóme,** *s.* phantasm, delusion, B 1037.

**Farced,** *pp.* stuffed, L. 1373.

**Fare,** *s.* behaviour, conduct, A 1809, B 1453; condition, 2. 62 ; good speed, HF. 682 ; business, goings-on, T. iii. 1106 ; bustle, ado, HF. 1065 ; company, T. iii. 605 ; *evel fare,* ill hap, 2. 62.

**Faren,** *v.* behave, T. iv. 1087 ; *doth fare,* causes to behave or feel, T. i. 626; Fare, *ger.* to go, travel, T. v. 21, 279 ; to proceed, A 2435 ; Fare, 1 *pr. s.* go, G 733 ; it is with me (thus), 7. 320 ; am, B 1676 ; Farest, 2 *pr. s.* actest, 5. 599 ; art, HF. 887 ; Fareth, *pr. s.* acts, D 1088 ; is, 3. 113 ; happens, HF. 271 ; 1 *pr. pl.* live, G 662 ; 2 *pr. pl.* behave, D 852 ; *pr. pl.* seem, I 414 ; Fare, *pr. s. subj.* may fare, F 1579 ; Ferde, 1 *pt. s.* fared, T. ii. 1006 ; felt, 3. 99, 785 ; was placed, 5. 152 ; *pt. s.* behaved, A 1372 ; happened, T. i. 225 ; was, R. 876 ; seemed, R. 249 ; went on, HF. 1522 ; Ferden, *pt. pl.* behaved, A 1647 ; Ferde, *pt. s. subj.* should fare, R. 271 ; Faren, *pp.* fared, T. v. 466 ; D 1773 ; gone, B 4069 ; Fare, *pp.* fared, D 1782, gone, A 2436 ; walked, L. 2209 ; Ferd, *pp.* fared, T. iv. 1094 ; Faringe, *pres. pt. as adj.* ; *best f.*, best looking, fairest of behaviour, F 932 ; *f. aright*, prosper, T. i. 878 ; *far wel*, farewell, B 116 ; Fareth, *imp. pl.* fare, E 1688 ; *f. wel*, farewell, T. v. 1412.

**Fare-cart,** *s.* travelling cart, T. v. 1162.

**Fare-wel,** *interj.* it is all over ! F 1204, G 907 ; *go farewel*, be lost sight of, A. ii. 23. 12.

**Farsed,** *pp.* stuffed, A 233.

**Fasoun,** *s.* fashion, appearance, R. 708 ; shape, R. 551.

**Fast,** *s.* fasting, T. v. 370.

**Fast,** *adj.* firm, 7. 313.

**Faste,** *adv.* closely, R. 1346 ; close, near, A 1478 ; tight, R. 431 ; fast, quickly, T. i. 748 ; *as f.*, very quickly, G 1235 ; hard, soundly, 5. 94 ; intently, eagerly, R. 793 ; *faste by*, near to, A 1476 ; *faste by*, close at hand, 3. 369.

**Faster,** *adv.* closer, B 3722.

**Fatte,** *v.* fatten, D 1880.

**Faucon,** *s.* falcon, F 411, 424.

**Fauconers,** *s. pl.* falconers, F 1196.

**Fauned,** *pt. s.* fawned on, 3. 389.

**Faunes,** *pl.* Fauns, A 2928.

**Fawe,** *adj.* fain, glad, D 220.

**Fawe,** *adv.* fain, anxiously, T. iv. 887.

**Fay,** *s.* ; see **Fey.**

**Fayerye,** *s.* troop of fairies, E 2039 ; troops of fairies, D 859 ; enchantment, E 1743 ; Fairye, fairy-land, F 96 ; enchantment, F 201 ; *pl.* fairies, D 872.

**Fayn,** *adj.* glad, L. 130, 1137 ; fond, R. 1376.

**Fayn,** *adv.* gladly, A 766 ; *wolde f.*, would be glad to, E 696.

**Feblesse,** *s.* weakness, T. ii. 863 ; I 1074.

**Fecches,** *pl.* vetches, T. iii. 936.

**Fecchen,** *ger.* to fetch, T. v. 485 ; *ger.* to fetch, to be brought (i. e. absent), T. iii.

609 ; Fette, 2 *pt. s.* didst fetch, T. iii. 723 ; *pt. s.* fetched, L. 676 ; brought, T. v. 852 ; *pt. pl.* B 2041 ; Fet, *pp.* fetched, A 2527 ; brought, A 819 ; brought home, D 217.

**Fecching,** *s.* fetching, rape, T. v. 890.

**Fedde,** *pt. s.* fed, A 146.

**Fee,** *s.* reward, pay, 7. 193 ; Fee simple, an absolute fee or fief, not clogged with conditions, A 319.

**Feeld,** *s.* field, A 886, 3032 ; (in an heraldic sense), B 3573.

**Feendly,** *adj.* fiendlike, devilish, B 751, 783.

**Feet,** *s.* performance, E 429.  E. *feat.*

**Feffe,** *v.* enfeoff, endow, present, T. iii. 901 ; *ger.* to present, T. v. 1689 ; *pp.* enfeoffed, put in possession, endowed, E 1698.

**Fel,** *s.* skin, T. i. 91.

**Fel,** *adj.* dreadful, T. v. 50 ; cruel, A 2630 ; deadly, D 2002 ; terrible, B 2019 ; Felle, *voc.* cruel, A 1559 ; destructive, T. iv. 44.

**Felawe,** *s.* companion, comrade, A 395, 648.

**Felawshipe,** *s.* partnership, A 1626 ; companionship, B 2749 ; company, A 26.

**Felawshipeth,** *pr. s.* accompanies, B 4. m 1. 12.

**Feld,** *pp. of* Felle.

**Feldefare,** *s.* field-fare, 5. 364 ; T. iii. 861 ; *farewel f.*, i. e. farewell, and a good riddance ; because fieldfares depart when the warm weather comes.

**Felden,** *pt. pl. of* Felle.

**Fele,** *adj.* many, R. 189 ; E 917.

**Fele-folde,** *adj.* manifold, B 2. p 1. 16.

**Felen,** *v.* feel, experience, L. 692 ; Fele, understand by experiment, HF. 826 ; try to find out, T. ii. 387 ; Felte, 1 *pt. s.* 4. 217 ; Felede, *pt. s.* G 521 ; Feled, *pp.* perceived, T. iv. 984.

**Feling,** *s.* affection, 3. 1172.

**Felle,** *pl. and voc. s. of* Fel, *adj.*

**Felle,** *v.* fell, A 1702 ; Felden, *pt. pl.* caused to fall, R. 911 ; Feld, *pp.* cut down, A 2924.

**Feillen,** *pt. pl.* happened, T. i. 134.  See **Fallen.**

**Felliche,** *adj.* bitingly, severely, B 2. m 3. 13.

**Felnesse,** *s.* fierceness, B 1. m 6. 11.

**Felon,** *adj.* angry, T. v. 199.

**Felonous,** *adj.* fierce, wicked, B 1. m 4. 15 ; mischievous, I 438.

**Felonye,** *s.* injustice, B 4. p 6. 278 ; crime, A 1996 ; treachery, R. 165, 978 ; *pl.* iniquities, I 281.

**Femele,** *adj.* female, D 122, I 961.

**Femininitee,** *s.* feminine form, B 360.

**Fen,** *s.* chapter or subdivision of Avicenna's book called the Canon, C 890.

**Fenel,** *s.* fennel, R. 731.

**Fenix,** *s.* phoenix, 3. 982.

**Fer,** *adj.* far, A 388, 491; **Ferre,** *def.* A 3393.

**Fer,** *adv.* far, B 1781; Fer ne ner, neither later nor sooner, A 1850; *how f. so,* however far, 5. 440.

**Ferd,** *s. dat.* fear, T. iv. 607. (Always in phr. *for ferd,* or *for ferde.*)

**Ferd,** *pp. of* Fere, *v.*

**Ferd, -e** ; see **Faren,** *v.*

**Fere,** *s. dat.* fear, B 3369; panic, HF. 174.

**Fere,** *s.* companion, L. 969; mate, 5. 410, 416; wife, T. iv. 791; *pl.* companions, T. i. 224.

**Fere,** *s. dat.* fire, T. iii. 978.

**Fere,** *v.* frighten, T. iv. 1483; Fered, *pp.* afraid, G 924; Ferd, *pp.* afraid, T. ii. 124.

**Ferforth,** *adv.* far; *as f. as,* as far as, T. iv. 891; as long as, T. i. 121; *so f.,* to such a degree, 1. 170; *thus f.,* thus far, T. ii. 960.

**Ferforthly,** *adv.* thoroughly; *so f.,* to such an extent, A 960; so far, L. 682; *as f.,* as completely, D 1545.

**Ferfulleste,** most timid, T. ii. 450.

**Ferly,** *adj.* strange, A 4173.

**Fermacies,** *pl.* remedies, A 2713.

**Ferme,** *adj.* firm, E 663.

**Ferme,** *imp. s.* make firm, B 1. m 5. 61 (Lat. *firma*).

**Ferme,** *s.* rent, A 252 *b.*

**Fermely,** *adv.* firmly, T. iii. 1488.

**Fermerere,** *s.* friar in charge of an infirmary, D 1859.

**Fermour,** *s.* farmer of taxes, L. 378.

**Fern,** *adv.* long ago; *so fern =* so long ago, F 256.

**Fern-asshen,** *s. pl.* ashes produced by burning ferns, F 254.

**Ferne,** *pl. of* Ferren, distant, remote, A 14.

**Ferne** ; *f. yere,* last year, T. v. 1176.

**Ferre,** *adj. def.* distant, A 3393.

**Ferre,** *comp. adv.* farther, HF. 600; Ferrer, A 835.

**Ferreste,** *superl. pl.* farthest, A 494.

**Fers,** *s.* queen (at chess), 3. 654, 655; Ferses, *pl.* the pieces at chess, 3. 723.

**Fers,** *adj.* fierce, T. i. 225; *voc.* 7. 1.

**Fersly,** *adv.* fiercely, T. iii. 1760.

**Ferthe,** fourth, T. iv. 26, v. 476.

**Ferther,** *adj.* farther, B 1686, E. 2226.

**Ferther,** *adv.* further, 1. 148, 3. 1254.

**Ferther-over,** *conj.* moreover, A. ii. 26. 13.

**Ferthing,** *s.* farthing, D 1967; a very small portion, A 134.

**Fery,** *adj.* fiery, T. iii. 1600.

**Fest,** *s.* fist, A 4275, C 802.

**Feste,** *s.* feast, festival, A 883, B 418; *to f.,* to the feast, B 380; encouragement, T. ii. 361; merriment, T. ii. 421; Maketh feste, flatters, 3. 638; *pl.* tokens of pleasure, T. v. 1429.

**Festeth,** *pr. s.* feasts, A 2193.

**Festeyinge,** *pres. part.* feasting, entertaining, F 345.

**Festeyinge,** *s.* festivity, T. v. 455.

**Festlich,** *adj.* fond of feasts, F 281.

**Festne,** *ger.* to fasten, A 195.

**Fet** ; see **Fecchen.**

**Fete,** *dat. pl.* feet, 3. 199, 400, 502.

**Fether,** *s.* wing, A 2144.

**Fetis,** *adj.* neat, well-made, handsome, A 157; R. 776; splendid, R. 1133; graceful, C 478.

**Fetisly,** *adv.* elegantly, A 124, 273; neatly, trimly, A 3205, 3319; exquisitely, R. 837.

**Fette** ; see **Fecchen.**

**Fetys,** *adj.* well-made, R. 532; handsome, R. 821; splendid, R. 1133; graceful, C 478.

**Fetysly,** *adv.* exquisitely, neatly, R. 1235.

**Fey,** *s.* faith, A 1126, 3284; fidelity, L. 778.

**Feyn,** *adj.* glad, 7. 315.

**Feyne,** *v.* feign, pretend, A 736; speak falsely, 2. 4; *feyne us,* feign, pretend, B 351; Feigne, who-so f. may, let him, who can, pretend, B 3. p 10. 93.

**Feynest,** *adv.* most gladly, 5. 480.

**Feyning,** *s.* pretending, cajolery, F 556; pretence, feigning, L. 1556.

**Feynt,** *adj.* feigned, R. 433.

**Feyntest,** *2 pr. s.* enfeeblest, B 926.

**Ficchen,** *ger.* to fix, B 5. m 4. 18.

**Fiers,** *adj.* fierce, A 1508; proud, R. 1482.

**Fifte,** fifth, R. 962, 982; 16. 9.

**Figes,** *pl.* fig-trees, R. 1364.

**Fighten,** *v.* fight, L. 1096; Fight, *pr. s.* fights, 5. 103; Faught, *pt. s.* fought, A 399; Foughten, *pp.* A 62.

**Figure,** *s.* shape, 16. 27; form (as a man), B 3412; figure, 1. 94; figure (of speech), A 499; Figure, type, 1. 169; *pl.* figures (of speech), E 16; markings, A. pr. 75.

**Figuringe,** *s.* form, L. 298; figure, G 96.

**Fil,** *pt. s. of* Fallen.

**Fild,** *pp.* filled, 5. 610.

**Finch,** *s.* finch (bird), R. 915; *pulle a finch,* pluck a dupe, A 652.

**Finde,** v. find, 1. 72; A 648; invent, A 736; ger. to provide for, C 537; Fint, pr. s. finds, G 218; Fynt, pr. s. L. 1499; Fond, pt. s. discovered, A 2445; found out, T. i. 659; provided for, B 4019; Fonde, pt. s. subj. could find, 5. 374; pp. found, E 146; Founden, pp. found, B 612; provided, B 243.

**Finding,** s. provision, A 3220.

**Fint,** pr. s. finds, G 218.

**Firre,** s. fir-tree, A 2921.

**Firste,** adj. def. first, 3. 1166; my firste, my first narration, F 75; with the firste, very soon, T. iv. 63.

**Fish,** s. the sign Pisces, F 273.

**Fit,** s. a 'fyt' or 'passus,' a portion of a song, B 2078; bout, turn, A 4184.

**Fithele,** s. fiddle, A 296.

**Fixe,** pp. as adj. fixed, T. i. 298; solidified, G 779.

**Flambe,** s. flame, I 353.

**Flatour,** s. flatterer, B 4515.

**Flaumbe,** s. flame, HF. 769.

**Flayn,** pp. flayed, I 425.

**Fledde,** pt. s. fled, avoided, B 3445, 3874; Fledde herself, took refuge, L. 1225.

**Flee** (1), v. fly, F 503; leet flee, let fly, A 3806; Fleigh, pt. s. flew, HF. 921, 2087; Fley, pt. s. B 4362; Flowen, pt. pl. flew, B 4581; pp. flown, HF. 905.

**Fleen** (2), v. escape, A 1170; flee, L. 1307, 2020; Fleeth, imp. pl. 4. 6; Fleigh, pt. s. fled, B 3879.

**Fleen,** s. pl. fleas, H 17.

**Flees,** s. fleece, L. 1428, 1647.

**Fleet,** pr. s. floats, B 463.

**Flekked,** pp. spotted, E 1848, G 565.

**Flemen,** ger. to banish, T. ii. 852; pr. s. H 182; pp. banished, G 58.

**Flemer,** s. banisher, driver away, B 460.

**Fleminge,** s. banishment, flight, T. iii. 933.

**Flen,** pr. pl. fly, T. iv. 1356.

**Fleshly,** adv. carnally, B 1775.

**Flete,** v. float, bathe, T. iii. 1971; 1 pr. s. subj. may float, A 2397; Fleteth, pr. s. floats, B 901; flows, abounds (Lat. influat), B 1. m 2. 28; Fleet, pr. s. floats, B 463; pres. pt. floating, A 1956; Fletinge, pres. pt. flowing, B 1. p 3. 78 (Lat. limphante).

**Flex,** s. flax, A 676.

**Fley,** pt. s. flew, B 4362.

**Flikered,** pt. s. fluttered, T. iv. 1221; pres. pt. pl. fluttering, A 1062.

**Flitte,** v. pass away, I 368; pp. removed, T. v. 1544; pres. pt. unimportant, 3. 801.

**Flo,** s. arrow, H 264.

**Flokmele,** adv. in a flock, in a great number, E 86.

**Flood,** s. flood-tide, F 259; on a fl., in a state of flood, T. iii. 640.

**Florisshinges,** pl. florid ornaments, HF. 1301.

**Florouns,** s. pl. florets, L. 217, 220.

**Floteren,** pr. pl. fluctuate, waver, B 3. p 11. 227.

**Flotery,** adj. fluttering, wavy, A 2883.

**Flough,** 2 pt. s. didst fly, B 4421.

**Flour,** s. (1) flower, L. 48; of alle floures flour, flower of all flowers, 1. 4; flower, i.e. choice, A 4174; choice part, A 982; time of flourishing, A 3048: (2) flour, R. 356.

**Flour-de-lys,** s. fleur-de-lis, lily, A 238.

**Floureth,** pr. s. flourishes, T. iv. 1577; blooms, 7. 306.

**Flourettes,** s. pl. flowerets, buds, R. 891.

**Floury,** adj. flowery, 3. 398.

**Floute,** s. flute, HF. 1223.

**Floutours,** pl. flute-players, R. 763.

**Flowen,** pt. pl. and pp. of Flee (1).

**Floytinge,** pres. pt. playing on the flute, A 91.

**Fneseth,** pr. s. breathes heavily, puffs, snorts, H 62.

**Fo,** s. foe, enemy, B 1748; Foo, A 63; Foon, pl. B 3896; Foos, pl. B 2160.

**Fode,** s. food, D 1881, I 137.

**Foisoun,** s. plenty, abundance, R. 1359.

**Folde,** s. fold, sheepfold, A 512.

**Folden,** pp. folded, T. iv. 359, 1247.

**Foled,** pp. foaled, born, D 1545.

**Folily,** adv. foolishly, B 2639.

**Folk,** s. folk, people, A 12, 25; sort, company, 5. 524; pl. companies, 5. 278.

**Folowed wel,** followed as a matter of course, 3. 1012; Folweth, imp. pl. imitate, E 1189.

**Foly,** adv. foolishly, 3. 874.

**Folýe,** s. folly, foolishness, A 3045.

**Folyen,** pr. pl. act foolishly, B 3. p 2. 100.

**Fomen,** pl. foe-men, T. iv. 42.

**Fomy,** adj. foaming, covered with foam, A 2506.

**Fond;** pt. s. of Finde.

**Fonde,** v. endeavour, R. 1584; v. attempt, try, E 283; try to persuade, B 347.

**Fonde,** pt. s. subj. could find, 5. 374.

**Fonge,** v. receive, B 377.

**Fonne,** s. fool (Northern), A 4089.

**Font-ful water,** fontful of water, B 357.

**Fontstoon,** s. font, B 723.

**Foo;** see Fo.

**Foo,** s. foo', for foot, A 3781.

**Fool,** *adj.* foolish, silly, R. 1253.

**Fool,** *s.* fool, A 3005; jester, B 3271; *pl.* wicked persons, E 2278.

**Fool-large,** *adj.* foolishly liberal, B 2789, 2810.

**Fool-largesse,** *s.* foolish liberality, I 813.

**Foom,** *s.* foam, A 1659, G 564.

**Foo-men,** *s. pl.* foes, B 3255, 3507.

**Foon, Foos;** see **Fo.**

**Foot,** *as pl.* feet, A 4124.

**Foot-brede,** *s.* foot-breadth, HF. 2042.

**Foot-hot,** *adv.* instantly, on the spot, B 438.

**Foot-mantel,** *s.* foot-cloth, 'safeguard' to cover the skirt, A 472.

**For,** *prep.* for, A 486, &c.; in respect of, 5. 336; by reason of, R. 1564; for the sake of, B 4. p 6. 190; *for me,* by my means, T. ii. 134 ; *for which,* wherefore, F 1525; against, to prevent, in order to avoid, L. 231 ; *for fayling,* to prevent failure, T. i. 928; in spite of, C 129; *for al,* notwithstanding, A 2020 ; *for my dethe,* were I to die for it, 4. 186 ; *to have for excused,* to excuse, A. pr. 31.

**For,** *conj.* for, A 126, &c.; because, 3. 735, 789 ; in order that, B 478, F 102.

**For to,** *with infin.* in order to, to, A 13, 78, &c.

**Forage,** *s.* provision of fodder, E 1422; food, B 1973 ; winter-food, as hay, &c., A 3868.

**For-bede,** *v.* forbid, T. iii. 467; Forbedeth, *pr. s.* B 2774 ; Forbet, *for* Forbedeth, *pr. s.* forbids, T. ii. 717; *in phr.* god f., *or* Crist f. = God forbid, Christ forbid, T. ii. 113, 716; Forbad, *pt. s.* E 570 ; Forbode, *pp.* forbidden, E 2206.

**Forbere,** *v.* forbear (to mention), A 885 ; leave (him) alone, D 665; spare, A 3168 ; little consider, T. ii. 1660; Forbar, *pt. s.* forbare, T. i. 437; *imp. pl.* forgive, L. 80.

**For-blak,** *adj.* extremely black, A 2144.

**Forbode,** *s.* prohibition ; *goddes forbode,* it is God's prohibition (i. e. God forbid), L. 10 *a.*

**Forbrak,** 1 *pt. s.* broke off, interrupted, B 4. p 1. 7.

**For-brused,** *pp.* badly bruised, B 3804.

**Forby,** *adv.* by, past, L. 2539.

**Forbyse,** *ger.* to instruct by examples, T. ii. 1390. (A false form ; for *forbisne(n),* the former *n* being dropped by confusion with that in the suffix.)

**Force** ; see **Fors.**

**Forcracchen,** *ger.* to scratch excessively, R. 323.

**Forcutteth,** *pr. s.* cuts to pieces, H 340. .

**For-do,** *v.* destroy, 'do for,' T. i. 238, iv. 1681 ; For-dide, *pt. s.* slew, L. 2557 ; Fordoon, *pp.* overcome, vanquished, T. i. 525; ruined, T. v. 1687; destroyed, H 290; slain, L. 939.

**Fordriven,** *pp.* driven about, B 1. p 3. 71.

**For-dronken,** *pp.* extremely drunk, A 3120, 4150.

**Fordrye,** *adj.* very dry, withered up, F 409.

**Fordwyned,** *adj.* shrunken, R. 366.

**Fore,** *s.* path, trace of steps, D 110; course, track, D 1935. A. S. *for.*

**Foreyne,** *adj.* extraneous, B 3. p 3. 73.

**Foreyne,** *s.* outer chamber (*or* courtyard ?), L. 1962.

**Forfered,** *pp.* exceedingly afraid ; *forfered of* = very afraid for, F 527.

**Forfeted,** *pt. s.* did wrong, I 273.

**Forgaf,** *pt. s. of* Foryeve.

**Forgat,** *pt. s. of* Foryete.

**Forgift,** *s.* forgiveness, L. 1853.

**For-go,** *pp.* overwalked, exhausted with walking, HF. 115.

**Forgon,** *ger.* to give up, forego, (*better* forgo), T. iv. 195; lose, R. 1473; Forgoon, *pp.* lost, B 2183.

**Forheed,** *s.* forehead, R. 860 ; Forheved, B 1. p 4. 139.

**For-hoor,** *adj.* very hoary, R. 356.

**Forkerveth,** *pr. s.* hews in pieces, H 340.

**Forlaft,** *pp.* abandoned, C 83.

**Forleseth,** *pr. s.* loses, I 789. See **Forlorn.**

**For-leten,** *v.* abandon, give up, C 864 ; yield up, B 1848 ; Forlete, *pr. pl.* forsake, I 93 ; Forleten, *pp.* abandoned, given up, HF. 694.

**Forliven,** *v.* degenerate, B 3. p 6. 56 ; Forlived, *pp. as adj.* degenerate, ignoble, B 3. m 6. 13.

**Forlorn,** *pp.* utterly lost, L. 2663. See **Forlese.**

**Forlost,** *pp.* utterly lost, T. iii. 280.

**Forloyn,** *s.* note on a horn for recall, 3. 386.

**Forme,** *s.* form, A 305; form, lair (of a hare), B 1294.

**Forme-fader,** *s.* fore-father, first father, B 2293.

**Formel,** *s.* companion (said of birds), 5. 371, 373.

**Formely,** *adv.* formally, T. iv. 497.

**Former,** *s.* Creator, C 19.

**Former age,** the Golden Age of old, 9. 2.

**Formest,** *adj. sup.* foremost. 3. 890.

**Forn-cast,** *pp.* premeditated, B 4407.

Forneys, s. furnace, A 202, 559.

For-old, adj. extremely old, A 2124.

Forpampred, pp. exceedingly pampered, spoilt by pampering, 9. 5.

For-pyned, pp. wasted away (by torment or pine), A 205.

Fors, s. force, A 2723; no fors, no matter. no consequence, A 2723, B 285; no force, no matter, 18. 53; no fors is, it is no matter, T. iv. 322; no force of, no matter for, 10. 13; no fors of me, no matter about me, 4. 197; thereof no fors, never mind that, 3. 1170; make no fors, pay no heed, H 68; I do no fors, I care not, D 1254; I do no fors thereof, it is nothing to me, 3. 542; doth no fors, takes no account, I 711; what fors, what matter, T. ii. 378.

Forsake, v. deny, B 1. p 4. 164; leave, B 3431; Forsook, pt. s. forsook, R. 1538; Forsaken, pp. R. 1498; imp. pl. give up, C 286.

Forseid, pp. as adj. aforesaid, 5. 120.

Forseinge, s. prevision, T. iv. 989.

Forshapen, pp. metamorphosed, T. ii. 66.

For-shright, pp. exhausted with shrieking, T. iv. 1147.

For-sight, s. foresight, T. iv. 961.

For-sleuthen, v. waste in sloth, B 4286.

Forsleweth, pr. s. wastes idly, I 685.

Forsluggeth, pr. s. spoils, allows (goods) to spoil, I 685.

Forsongen, pp. tired out with singing, R. 664.

Forster, s. forester, A 117.

Forstraught, pp. distracted, B 1295.

Forswor him, pt. s. was forsworn, HF. 389; Forswore, pp. falsely sworn by, L. 2522; Forsworn, forsworn, L. 927.

Forth, adv. forth, on, further, onward, 5. 27; D 1569; F 604, 605, 964; forward, HF. 2061; out, 5. 352; continually, F 1081; away, T. i. 118; still, 4. 148; tho f., thenceforth, T. i. 1076; forth to love, i.e. they proceed to love, T. ii. 788.

Forther, adv. more forward, A 4222; Further, (go) further, A 4117.

Fortheren, ger. to further, T. v. 1707.

Forthering, s. furtherance, aid, L. 69 a.

Forther-moor, adv. further on, A 2069; Forthermore, moreover, C 357.

Forther-over, adv. moreover, C 648.

Forthest, adj. and adv. furthest, B 4. p 6. 136.

For-thinke, v. seem amiss, (or here) seem serious, T. ii. 1414; pr. s. impers. seems a pity (to me), E 1906; Forthoughte, pt. s. subj. should displease, R. 1671.

Forthren, ger. to further, help, assist, L. 71, 472, 1618; ger. to further, T. v. 1707.

Forth-right, adv. straightforwardly, straightforward, R. 295; F 1503.

Forthward, adv. forwards, B 263, F 1169.

For-thy, adv. therefore, on that account, A 1841, 4031.

Fortroden, pp. trodden under foot, I 190.

Fortuit, adj. fortuitous, B 5. p 1. 91.

Fortuna maior, a name for the auspicious planet Jupiter, T. iii. 1420. (Or else, a cluster of stars near the beginning of Pisces; cf. Dante, Purg. xix. 4).

Fortunel, adj. accidental, B 5. m 1. 16.

Fortunen, v. to give (good or bad) fortune to, A 417; Fortunest, 2 pr. s. renderest lucky or unlucky, A 2377; pt. pl. happened, chanced, 3. 288; pp. endowed by fortune, 4. 180.

Fortunous, adj. fortuitous, accidental, B 1. p 6. 9.

For-waked, pp. tired out with watching, 3. 126; B 596.

Forward, adv. foremost; first and f., first of all, B 2431.

Forward, s. agreement, covenant, A 33, 829.

Forwelked, adj. withered, wrinkled, deeply lined, R. 361.

Forweped, pp. weary, exhausted through weeping, 3. 126.

Forwered, pp. worn out, R. 235.

For-wery, adj. very tired, 5. 93.

Forwes, pl. furrows, 9. 12.

For-why, conj. for what reason, T. iii. 1009; wherefore, why, HF. 20; because, 3. 461, 793.

For-witer, s. foreknower, B 5. p 6. 329.

Forwiting, s. foreknowledge, B 4433.

For-wot, pr. s. foreknows, foresees, HF. 45.

Forwrapped, pp. wrapped up, C 718; concealed, I 320.

For-yede, pt. s. gave up, T. ii. 1330.

Foryelde, v. yield in return, requite, E 831.

Foryetelnesse, s. forgetfulness, I 827.

Foryeten, v. forget, T. iii. 55; pr. s. forgets, T. ii. 375; Forget, for Forgeteth, pr. s. forgets, R. 61; Forgat, 1 pt. s. forgot, C 919; For-yat, pt. s. T. v. 1535; For-yeten, pp. forgotten, A 2021; Forgeten, pp. B 2602.

Foryetful, adj. forgetful, E 472.

Foryetinge, s. forgetfulness, B 2. p 7. 98.

Foryeve, v. forgive, B 994; Foryaf, pt. s.

forgave, T. iii. 1129, 1577; Forgaf, *pt. s.* L. 162; Foryeve, *pt. pl.* L. 1848; Foryeven, *pp.* forgiven, T. ii. 595.

Foryifnesse, *s.* forgiveness, B 2963.

Fostreth, *pr. s.* cherishes, E 1387; Fostred, *pt. s.* nourished, fed, kept, E 222, H 131; *pp.* nurtured, nourished, C 219.

Fostring, *s.* nourishment, D 1845.

Fote, *s.* foot, short distance, F 1177; *dat.* L. 2711; *him to f.*, at his foot, L. 1314; *on f.*, on foot, F 390.

Fother, *s.* load, properly a cart-load, A 530; great quantity, A 1908.

Fot-hoot, *adv.* hastily, immediately, 3. 375.

Foudre, *s.* thunderbolt, HF. 535.

Foughten, *pp.* fought, A 62.

Foul, *s.* bird, F 149; *pl.* birds, L. 37, 130.

Foule, *adv.* vilely, D 1069; foully, 3. 623; 5. 517; evilly, A 4220; shamefully, L. 1307; hideously, D 1082; meanly, R. 1061.

Fouler, *adj. comp.* uglier, D 999.

Fouler, *s.* fowler, L. 132.

Founde (1), *ger.* to found, T. i. 1065.

Founde (2), *v.* seek after, 7. 241; 1 *pr. s.* try, endeavour, 7. 47.

Foundement, *s.* foundation, HF. 1132.

Foundred, *pt. s.* foundered, stumbled, A 2687.

Founes, *s. pl.* fawns, 3. 429; Fownes (*metaphorically*), young desires, T. i. 465.

Fourneys, *s.* furnace, B 3353.

Fourtenight, *s.* fourteen nights, a fortnight, T. iv. 1327.

Fowel, *s.* bird, A 190, 2437.

Foyne, *pr. s. imp.* let him thrust, A 2550; *pr. s.* A 2615; *pr. pl.* A 1654.

Foyson, *s.* abundance, plenty, A 3165.

Fraknes, *pl.* freckles, A 2169.

Frame, *ger.* to put together, build, T. iii. 530.

Franchyse, *s.* liberality, E 1987; nobleness, F 1524; privilege, I 452.

Frankeleyn, *s.* franklin, freeholder, A 331.

Frankes, *pl.* franks, B 1371, 1377.

Frape, *s.* company, pack, T. iii. 410. O.F. *frape*, troop.

Fraught, *pp.* freighted, B 171; *han doon fr.*, have caused to be freighted.

Frayneth, *pr. s.* prays, beseeches, B 1790.

Free, *adj.* liberal, generous, B 1366, 1854; bounteous, liberal, 3. 484; noble, beautiful, C 35; profuse, lavish, A 4387; *as s.* noble one, 6. 104.

Freedom, *s.* liberality, L. 1127.

Freele, *adj.* frail, fragile, I 1078.

Freend, *s.* friend, A 670.

Freendlich, *adj.* friendly, A 2680.

Freletee, *s.* frailty, C 78, D 92.

Fremede, *adj.* foreign; Fremed (*before a vowel*), strange, wild; *fremed and tame*, wild and tame, every one, T. iii. 529; Fremde, foreign, F 429. A. S. *fremede.*

Frenesye, *s.* madness, D 2209.

Frenetyk, *adj.* frantic, T. v. 206.

Frenges, *pl.* fringes, D 1383; borderings, HF. 1318.

Frere, *s.* friar, A 208, D 829.

Fresshe, *adv.* newly, L. 204.

Fresshe, *v.* refresh, R. 1513.

Fret, *s.* ornament, L. 215, 225, 228.

Freten, *v.* eat (governed by *saugh*), A 2019; *pr. s.* devours, R. 387; *pt. pl.* consumed, D 561; Freten, *pp.* eaten, devoured, A 2068; Frete, *pp.* B 475.

Fretted, *pp.* adorned, set, L. 1117.

Freyne, *v.* ask, question, T. v. 1227; *pt. s.* B 3022; *pp.* G 433.

Fro, *prep.* from, A 44; out of, 4. 254; *to and fro*, L. 2358, 2471.

Frogges, *pl.* frogs, R. 1410.

From, *prep.* from, A 128; apart from, T. iv. 766; from the time that, R. 850.

Frosty, *adj.* frosty, cold, A 268; which comes in the winter, 5. 364.

Frote, *ger.* to rub, T. iii. 1115; *pr. s.* A 3747.

Frothen, *pr. pl.* become covered with foam, A 1659.

Fro-this-forth, henceforward, T. iv. 314.

Frounced, *adj.* wrinkled, R. 365.

Frounceles, *adj.* unwrinkled, R. 860.

Frount, *s.* true countenance, B 2. p 8. 7.

Fructuous, *adj.* fruitful, I 73.

Fruit, *s.* fruit, 1. 38; result, F 74.

Fruytesteres, *s. pl. fem.* fruit-sellers, C 478.

Frye, *v.* fry, A 383, D 487.

Fugitif, *adj.* fleeing from (Lat. *profugus*), HF. 146.

Ful, *adj.* satiated, T. iii. 1661; *atte fulle*, at the full, completely, A 651.

Ful, *adv.* fully, F 1230; very, quite, B 3506, F 52; *f. many*, very many, F 128.

Fulfille, *v.* fulfil, 6. 17; Fulfelle (Kentish form), *ger.* T. iii. 510; Fulfuldest, *2 pt. s.* didst satisfy, B 2. p 3. 66; Fulfilled, *pp.* quite full, L. 54.

Fulsomnesse, *s.* copiousness, excess, F 405.

Fume, *s.* vapour, B 4114.

Fumetere, *s.* fumitory, *Fumaria officinalis*, B 4153.

Fumositee, *s.* fumes arising from drunkenness, C 567, F 358.

Fundement (1), *s.* foundation, D 2103; (2) fundament, C 950.

Funeral, *adj.* T. v. 302; funereal, A 2864, 2912.

Furial, *adj.* tormenting, furious, F 448.

Furie, *s.* monster, A 2684; rage, T. v. 212.

Furlongs, *pl.* furlongs, A 4166; Furlongwey, a short distance, B 557; Forlongwey, a brief time (lit. time of walking a furlong, 2½ minutes), T. iv. 1237.

Furre, *s.* fur, R. 228.

Furred, *pp.* furred, trimmed with fur, R. 227, 408.

Furringe, *s.* fur-trimming, I 418.

Further-over, moreover, 2. 85.

Furthre, *ger.* to help, HF. 2023; *pp.* advanced, 7. 273.

Fusible, *adj.* capable of being fused, G 856.

Fustian, *s.* fustian, A 75.

Futur, *adj.* future, T. v. 748.

Fyle, *v.* file, smoothe by filing, 5. 212; Fyled, *pp.* A 2152.

Fyn, *s.* end, R. 1558; death, T. ii. 527; result, B 3348, 3884; aim, E 2106; object, T. ii. 425, iii. 553; *for fyn,* finally, T. iv. 477.

Fyn, *adj.* fine, strong, A 1472; *of fyne force,* of very need, T. v. 421.

Fyne, *v.* finish, T. iv. 26; cease, end, T. ii. 1460.

Fynt, *pr. s.* finds, A 4071; Fint, G 218.

Fyr, *s.* fire, B 3734; Fyr of Seint Antony, erysipelas, I 427.

Fyr-makinge, *s.* making of the fire, A 2914.

Fysicien, *s.* physician, B 1. p 3. 4.


### G.

Gabbe, *ger.* to boast, prate, A 3510; 1 *pr. s.* lie, speak idly, 3. 1075; Gabbestow, liest thou, T. iv. 481.

Gabber, *s.* liar, idle talker, I 89.

Gable, *s.* gable-end, A 3571.

Gadeling, *s.* idle vagabond, gad-about, R. 938.

Gadereth, *pr. s.* gathers, A 1053.

Gaderinge, *s.* gathering, B 2765.

Gaillard, *adj.* joyous, merry, lively, A 4367.

Galantyne, *s.* a kind of sauce, galantine, 9. 16; 12. 17.

Galaxye, *s.* the Galaxy, Milky Way, 5. 56; HF. 936.

Gale, *v.* sing, cry out, D 852; *pr. s. subj.* exclaim, D 1336.

Galianes, *s. pl.* medicines, C 306. So named after Galen.

Galingale, *s.* sweet cyperus, A 381. (A spice was prepared from the root of the plant.)

Galle, *s.* sore place, D 940.

Galles, *pl.* feelings of envy, 9. 47.

Galoche, *s.* a shoe, F 555.

Galoun, *s.* gallon, H 24.

Galping, *pres. pl.* gaping, F 350.

Galwes, *s. pl.* gallows, B 3924.

Gamed, *pt. s. impers.* it pleased, A 534.

Gamen, *s.* game, sport, T. ii. 38, iii. 250; joke, jest, E 733; amusement, fun, merriment, A 2286, 4354.

Gan, *pt. s. of* Ginne.

Ganeth, *pr. s.* yawneth, H 35.

Gape, *v.* gape, gasp, B 3924; Gapeth, *pr. s.* opens his mouth, L. 2004; Gape (*also* Cape), *pr. pl.* gape, stare, A 3841.

Gapinges, *s. pl.* greedy wishes, B 2. m 2. 17 (Lat. *hiatus*).

Gappe, *s.* gap, A 1639, 1645.

Gardin-wal, *s.* garden-wall, A 1060.

Gardinward, *adv.* gardenward; *to the g.,* towards the garden, F 1505.

Gargat, *s.* throat, B 4524.

Garleek, *s.* garlick, A 634.

Garnement, *s.* garment, R. 896.

Garnere, *s.* garner, granary, R 1148.

Garnisoun, *s.* garrison, B 2217.

Gas, *pr. s.* goes (Northern), A 4037.

Gastly, *adv.* terrible, A 1984.

Gastnesse, *s.* terror, B 3. p 5. 29.

Gat, *pt. s. of* Geten.

Gat-tothed, *adj.* having the teeth far apart, A 468, D 603.

Gaude, *s.* gaud, toy, pretence, T. ii. 351; trick, C 389; *pl.* pranks, I 651.

Gaudè, *adj.* dyed with weld, A 2079. Fr. *gauder,* to dye with weld.

Gauded, *pp.* furnished with beads called *gauds,* A 159. (The bead or *gaud* was formerly called *gaudee,* from Lat. imp. pl. *gaudete.*)

Gaure, *v.* stare, T. ii. 1157; *ger.* to stare, gaze, A 3827.

Gay, *adj.* finely dressed, A 74, 111; joyous, R. 435; wanton, A 3769.

Gaylard, *adj.* lively, A 3336.

Gayler, *s.* gaoler, A 1064.

Gayneth, *pr. s.* avails, A 1176; *pt. s.* profited, T. i. 352.

Gaytres beryies, berries of the gay-tree or gait-tree (goat-tree), berries of the *Rhamnus catharticus,* or buckthorn, B

4155. Called *getbärs-trä*, goat-berry-tree. in Swedish dialects (Rietz).

**Geaunt**, *s.* giant, B 1997, 3298.

**Gebet**, *s.* gibbet, gallows, HF. 106.

**Geen**, *pp.* gone (Northern), A 4078.

**Geeth**, *pr. s.* goes, L. 2145.

**Generally**, *adv.* everywhere, T. i. 86.

**Gent**, *adj.* refined, exquisite, noble, B 1905; slim, A 3254; *fem.* graceful, R. 1032.

**Genterye**, s. nobility, magnanimity, L. 394; gentility, D 1146; gentle birth, I 452; rank, I 461; sign of good birth, I 601.

**Gentil**, *adj.* gentle, refined, A 72; gentle, worthy, B 1627; excellent, A 718; mild in manner, compassionate, A 647; well-bred, D 111; beautiful, R. 1081; charming, R. 1016.

**Gentillesse**, *s.* gentleness, noble kindness, courtesy, good breeding, L. 610, 1010, 1080; A 920; nobility, B 3854; gentility, D 1109; worth, E 96; kindness, G 1054; condescension, B 853; high birth, I 585; slenderness, symmetry, F 426; delicate nurture, E 593.

**Gentilleste**, *adj. sup.* noblest, E 72, 131.

**Gentilly**, *adv.* gently, honourably, A 3104; courteously, B 1093; frankly, F 674.

**Gentils**, *s. pl.* gentlefolk, A 3113.

**Geomancie**, *s.* divination by figures made on the earth, I 605.

**Geometriens**, *s. pl.* geometricians, B 3. p 10. 143.

**Gere**, *s.* gear, armour, A 2180; equipment, A 4016; property, B 800; utensils, A 352; apparel, A 365; *pl.* contrivances, F 1276.

**Gere**, *s.* changeful manner, A 1372; *pl.* changeful ways, A 1531.

**Gerful**, *adj.* changeable, T. iv. 286; A 1538. Cf. **Gery**.

**Gerland**, *s.* garland, R. 566.

**Gerner**, *s.* garner, A 593.

**Gery**, *adj.* changeable, A 1536.

**Gesse**, *v.* suppose, imagine, R. 1115; 1 *pr. s.* suppose, A 82, 117, B 3435, 3960.

**Gessinge**, *s.* opinion, B 1. p 4. 315.

**Gest**, *s.* guest, HF. 288.

**Geste**, *s.* romance, tale, story, T. ii. 83, iii. 450; *in geste*, in romance-form, like the common stock-stories, B 2123; *pl.* stories, D 642; occurrences, T. i. 145; exploits, affairs, T. ii. 1349; histories, history, B 1126; deeds, HF. 1434.

**Gestours**, *s. pl.* story-tellers, B 2036; Gestiours, HF. 1198.

**Get** (jet), *s.* contrivance, G 1277.

**Geten**, *v.* obtain, get, L. 2370; beget, E 1437; Get, *pr. s.* procures, I 828; Gete, 2 *pr. pl. as fut.* (ye) will get, 5. 651; Gat, *pt. s.* begat, B 715; got, 7. 206; procured for, A 703; Geten, *pp.* gotten, obtained, A 291; won, L. 1753; begotten, L. 1402; *han geten hem*, to have acquired for themselves, F 56.

**Gif**, *conj.* if (Northern), A 4181, 4190.

**Gigges**, *pl.* rapid movements, HF. 1942.

**Gigginge**, *pres. pt. pl.* fitting with straps, A 2504. From O.F. *guigue*, a handle of a shield.

**Gilden**, *adj.* golden, 3. 338.

**Gilt**, *s.* guilt, offence, F 757, 1039; *pl.* sins, B 3015.

**Giltelees**, *adj.* guiltless, innocent, A 1312.

**Giltif**, *adj.* guilty, T. iii. 1019.

**Gin**, *s.* contrivance, snare, G 1165; *pl.* traps, snares, R. 1620.

**Gingebreed**, *s.* gingerbread, B 2044.

**Gingere**, *s.* ginger, R. 1369.

**Ginglen**, *v.* jingle, A 170.

**Ginne**, *v.* begin, attempt, HF. 2004; Gan, 1 *pt. s.* began, T. i. 266; (*as auxiliary verb*), did, R. 734, 1129; Gonne, *pl.* did, E 1103; HF. 944, 1002; began, C 323; Gonnen, *pt. pl.* began, 5. 531; Gunne, *pt. pl.* began, HF. 1658; did, HF. 1384; Gunnen, *pt. pl.* did, T. ii. 150.

**Ginninge**, *s.* beginning, T. i. 377.

**Gipoun**, *s.* a short cassock or doublet, A 75, 2120.

**Gipser**, *s.* pouch, purse, A 357.

**Girdel**, *s.* girdle, A 358, 3250; central line, or great circle, A. i. 17. 49.

**Girden**, *ger.* to strike, B 3736. Properly to switch.

**Girdilstede**, *s.* waist, R. 826.

**Girles**, *pl.* young people, whether male or female, A 664.

**Girt**, *pr. s.* girds, L. 1775; *pp.* girded, A 329.

**Giser**, *s.* gizzard, liver, B 3. m 12. 47.

**Giterne**, *s.* kind of guitar, cittern, A 3333.

**Giterninge**, *s.* playing on the gittern, or cittern, A 3363.

**Glade**, *ger.* to gladden, cheer, E 1174; *ger.* to console, A 2837; to rejoice, 5. 687; Gladed, *pt. s.* cheered, T. i. 116; *imp. s.* 3 *p.* may he comfort, E 822; Gladeth, *imp. pl.* rejoice, 4. 1.

**Glader**, *s.* one that cheers, A 2223.

**Gladly**, *adv.* fitly, 887; willingly, F 224; by preference, L. 770; *that been gl. wyse*, that would be thought wise, F 372.

**Gladsom**, *adj.* pleasant, B 3968.

**Glareth**, *pr. s.* glistens, shines, HF. 272.

Glase, *ger.* to glaze, furnish with glass, T. v. 469. *To glaze one's hood* = to provide with a useless defence.

Glasing, *s.* glass-work, 3. 327.

Glede, *s.* burning coal, glowing coal or ashes, B 111; *coloured as the glede*, of a bright red, gules, B 3574; *pl.* glowing coals, L. 235. See Gleed.

Gledy, *adj.* glowing (as a coal), burning, L. 105.

Glee, *s.* music, T. ii. 1036; entertainment, B 2030; *pl.* musical instruments, HF. 1209.

Gleed, *s.* glowing coal, L. 735.

Glente, *pt. pl.* glanced, T. iv. 1223.

Glewe, *v.* fasten, glue, HF. 1761.

Gleyre, *s.* white (of an egg), G 806.

Gliden, *pp. of* Glyde.

Glimsing, *s.* imperfect sight, E 2383.

Gliteren, *pr. pl.* glitter, A 977.

Glood, *pt. s. of* Glyde.

Glose, *s.* glosing, comment, L. 328; F 166; explanation, D 1792; commentary, *hence* margin, 3. 333.

Glose, *ger.* to interpret, explain, T. iv. 1410; to flatter, B 3330; speak with circumlocution, E 2351; persuade cunningly, T. iv. 1471; cajole, D 509; comment on, B 1180.

Glosinge, *s.* explaining, D 1793.

Glyde, *v.* glide, A 1575; ascend, G 402; slip, T. iv. 1215; *up gl.*, rise up gradually, F 373; Glòòd, *pt. s.* went quickly, B 2094; Gliden, *pp.* glided, passed, E 1887.

Gniden, *pt. pl.* rubbed, 9. 11. From A.S. *gnīdan.*

Gnof, *s.* churl (lit. thief), A 3188. Mod.E. *gonoph.*

Gnow, *pt. s.* gnawed, B 3638.

Gobet, *s.* piece, morsel, fragment, A 696.

God, *s.* A 769; God be with you, farewell, C 748; Goddes, God's, Christ's, B 1166; (*pronounced* god's), D 1096; Goddes, *pl.* gods, false gods, 3. 1328.

Godhede, *s.* divinity, A 2381.

Godlihede, *s.* beauty, T. iii. 1730.

Godsib, *s.* sponsor, I 909.

Gold, *s.* made of gold, R. 1193.

Gold-bete, adorned with beaten gold, gilt, 7. 24. Cf. Y-bete.

Goldes, *pl.* marigolds, A 1929.

Gold-hewen, *pp.* hewn of gold, cut out of or made of gold, A 2500.

Goldlees, *adj.* moneyless, B 1480.

Goldsmithrie, *s.* goldsmiths' work, A 2498.

Golee, *s.* gabble (lit. mouthful), 5. 566. O.F. *golee.*

Golet, *s.* throat, gullet, C 543.

Goliardeys, *s.* buffoon, scurrilous talker, A 560.

Gomme, *s.* gum, L. 121.

Gon, *v.* go, proceed, F 200; walk, L. 1399; move, A 2510; *lete it goon*, let it go, G 1475; to walk, I 105; move, F 921; roam, L. 2066; Goost, 2 *pr. s.* goest, G 56; Goth, *pr. s.* goes, 1. 68; Gooth about, seeks for, T. i. 1091; Gooth, goes, B 385; Geeth, L. 2145; Gas (Northern), A 4037; Goon, *pr. pl.* proceed, go along, E 898; Goon, *pp.* gone, L. 792; B 17; Go, *pp.* gone, G 907; Geen (Northern), A 4078; Go, *pr. s. subj.* may walk, L. 2069; Go we, let us go, T. ii. 615; Goth, *imp. pl.* go, B 3384.

Gonfanoun, *s.* gonfanon, gonfalon, a sacred banner, R. 1201.

Gonge, *s.* privy, I 885.

Gonne, *s.* missile, L. 637; gun, cannon, HF. 1643.

Gonne, -n; see Ginne, *v.*

Good, *s.* property, goods, 5. 462; Gode, *dat.* benefit, HF. 1, 58; property, wealth, L. 2638; Godes, *pl.* goods, B 2605.

Goodlich, *adj.* kind, bountiful, G 1053.

Goodliheed, *s.* seemliness, T. ii. 842; goodly seeming, HF. 330; a goodly outside, HF. 274.

Goodly, *adj.* kindly, B 2921; excellent, L. 77; pleasing, right, B 3969; portly, B 4010.

Goodly, *adv.* patiently, T. iii. 1035; well, B 2420; kindly, HF. 565; reasonably, T. iii. 990; favourably, T. iii. 654; rightly, B 2860.

Good-man, *s.* master of the house, C 361; householder, L. 1391.

Goos, *s.* goose, 5. 358; Gees, *pl.* E 2275.

Goosish, *adj.* goose-like, foolish, T. iii. 584.

Goost, 2 *pr. s.* goest, B 2501.

Goot, *s.* goat, A 688, G 886.

Gore, *s.* 'gore' or gusset of a garment, B 1979; a triangular piece cut out, A 3237.

Goshauk, *s.* goshawk, B 1928.

Gossib, *s.* female companion, D 529; male (spiritual) relation, D 243; Godsib, sponsor, I 909.

Gossomer, *s.* gossamer, F 259.

Gōst, *s.* spirit, ghost, HF. 185; soul, 1. 56; mind, L. 103; ghost (ironically), H 55; the Holy Spirit, 1. 93; G 328; *yeldeth up the gost*, gives up the ghost, L. 886.

Gostly, Goostly, *adj.* spiritual, I 392.

Gostly, *adv.* spiritually, mystically, G 109; devoutly, truly, T. v. 1030.

Goter, s. gutter, channel for water, L. 2705.

Goune-clooth, s. cloth to make a gown, D 2247, 2252.

Governaille, s. mastery, E 1192; *pl.* rules, B 1. p 6. 32.

Governaunce, s. management, control, rule, HF. 945, 958; providence, T. ii. 467; dominion, B 3541; manner of action, F 311; self-control, T. ii. 1020; charge, care, C 73; demeanour, T. ii. 219.

Govérne, *v.* control, T. iii. 475; *imp. pl.* arrange, regulate, B 1451, E 322.

Govérneresse, s. *fem.* governor, ruler, mistress, 1. 141; 2. 80.

Governour, s. ruler, umpire, A 813; leader, L. 1060.

Grace, s. favour, 1. 46; mercy, F 999; pardon, B 647; good opinion, R. 1169; virtue, R. 1099; *hir grace*, her favour (i. e. that of the Virgin), B 980; *of grace*, out of favour, in kindness, F 161; *sory grace*, an ill favour, HF. 1790; disfavour, D 746; *harde grace*, displeasure, 5. 65; displeasure, disgust, D 2228; severity, HF. 1586; disfavour, misfortune, T. i. 713; ill luck (i. e. a curse upon him), G 665; Graces, *pl.* thanks, B 2994.

Gracelees, *adj.* unfavoured by God, G 1078; out of favour, T. i. 781.

Grame, s. anger, grief, harm, 7. 276.

Grange, s. barn, granary, A 3668.

Grant mercy, best thanks, G 1380.

Grapenel, s. grapnel, L. 640.

Gras (1), s. grass, R. 1419.

Gras (2), s. grace, B 2021.

Graspe, *v.* grope, T. v. 223.

Gras-tyme, s. time of eating grass, time of youth, A 3868.

Graunges, *pl.* granges, barns, granaries, HF. 698.

Graunt, s. grant, R. 851.

Graunt mercy, best thanks, G 1156.

Graunten, *v.* grant, R. 1483; fix, name, E 179; *pt. s.* assented to, L. 2665; *pt. pl.* consented to, A 786.

Grave, s. A 2778; pit, L. 680.

Graven, *v.* engrave, F 830; Grave, *v.* dig; *doth she gr.*, she causes to be dug, L. 678; bury, E 681; to engrave, C 17; Graven, *pp.* engraved, graven, HF. 193; buried, L. 785; Grave, *pp.* graven, HF. 157.

Grayn, s. dye; *in grayn*, in dye, i.e. dyed of a fast colour, B 1917.

Graythe, *ger.* to clothe, dress, R. 584.

Grece, s. grease, A 135.

Gredy, *adj.* greedy, ready, T. iii. 1758.

Gree (1), s. favour, good part, R. 42; good will, 18. 73; *in gree*, favourably, T. ii. 529.

Gree (2), s. degree, rank, L. 1313; superiority, A 2733.

Greef, s. grievance, D 2174.

Greet, *adj.* great, 3. 954; principal, B 1181; *voc.* B 1797; *pl.* L. 929; luxuriant, C 37; *a greet*, a great one, A 339; Grete, *def. adj. as s.*, the chief part, L. 574.

Grehoundes, s. *pl.* greyhounds, A 190.

Greithe, *v.* prepare, B 3784.

Gréne, *adj. as s.*, green colour, R. 573; A 103; green clothing (the colour of inconstancy), 21. 7; green place, green space, F 862.

Grenehede, *v.* greenness, wantonness, B 163.

Grenning, *pres. part.* grinning, R. 156.

Gres, s. grass, T. ii. 515; *pl.* grasses, HF. 1353.

Grete, *v.* greet; *imp. s.* L. 2299; Grette, 1 *pt. s.* L. 116.

Gretter, *adj. comp.* greater, A 197.

Grevaunce, s. grievance, trouble, hardship, B 2676; complaint (against us), 1. 63; discomfort, 5. 205; affliction, 10. 47; *pl.* distresses, T. i. 647.

Greve, s. grove, T. v. 1144; *pl.* A 1495; boughs, sprays, L. 227.

Greve, *ger.* to harm, R. 1042; feel vexed, grumble, T. i. 343; *pr. s.* grieves, harms, A 917; *impers.* it vexes, E 647.

Grevous, *adj.* grievous, painful, T. v. 1604.

Greyn, s. grain, corn, A 596; grain (dye), B 4649; *in greyn*, of a fast colour, F 511; Greyn de Paradys, grains of paradise, R. 1369; Greyn, grain (of paradise), cardamom, A 3690.

Greythen, *pr. pl.* prepare (themselves), get ready, A 4309; *ger.* to adorn, clothe, dress, R. 584. Icel. *greiða.*

Griffon, s. griffin, A 2133.

Grille, *adj. pl.* horrible, R. 73.

Grim, *adj.* angry, A 2042; fierce, A 2519.

Grimnesse, s. horror, I 864.

Grinte, *pt. s.* grinned, D 2161.

Grintinge, s. gnashing (of teeth), I 208.

Grisel, s. name given to an old man, whose hair is gray (lit. old horse), 16. 35.

Grisly, *adj.* horrible, terrible, awful, A 1363, 1971; very serious, T. ii. 1700.

Grobbe, *v.* dig, grub (up), 9. 29.

Grome, s. man; *gr. and wenche*, man and woman, HF. 206; *pl.* men, R. 200.

Gronte, *pt. s.* groaned, B 3899.

Grope, *v.* try, test, examine, A 644; *ger.* to search out, D 1817.

Grŏt, s. particle, atom, D 1292.

Grōte, s. groat, (Dutch) coin, C 945.

Grounded, pp. well instructed, A 414; founded, T. iv. 1672.

Groyn (1), s. (a swine's) snout, I 156.

Groyn (2), s. murmur, T. i. 349.

Groyning, s. murmuring, A 2460.

Grucche, v. murmur, T. iii. 643; ger. to grumble, D 443.

Grucching, s. grumbling, complaining, murmuring, D 406, I 499.

Gruf, adv. on their faces, grovellingly, in a grovelling posture, A 949, B 1865. Cf. Icel. ā grūfu, face downwards.

Grypen, ger. to grasp, R. 204.

Grys, adj. gray, G 559; pomely grys, i.e. dapple-gray.

Grys, s. a gray fur, A 194. ¶The fur of the gray squirrel.

Guerdon, s. recompense, meed, reward, R. 1526; him to g., as a reward for him, L. 2052.

Guerdone, v. reward, I 283; pp. B 2462.

Guerdoning, s. reward, 5. 455.

Gyde, s. guide, A 804; ruler, G 45; guide, wielder, 5. 136.

Gyde, ger. to direct, lead, T. i. 183; to guide, T. iii. 1811; pr. pl. conduct, T. ii. 1104.

Gyderesse, s. conductress, B 4. p 1. 9.

Gyding, s. guidance, T. v. 643.

Gye, v. guide, A 1950, E 1429; conduct (myself), L. 2045; govern, A 3046; rule, B 3587; instruct, control, B 1286; ger. to guide, T. v. 546; to regulate, I 13; as wisly he gye, so verily may he guide, 25. 8.

Gyle, s. deceit, A 2596; trick, T. iii. 777.

Gylour, s. beguiler, trickster, A 4321.

Gyse, s. guise, way, A 663; manner, R. 789, A 1208, 1789; custom, A 993; way, plan, T. iv. 1370.

Gyte, s. dress, perhaps skirt or mantle, A 3954; pl. D 559. Cf. gyde in Jamieson's Dict., where the sense is dress, skirt, or mantle. Gascoigne uses gite in the sense of dress in his Philomena, l. 117: 'A stately Nimph, a dame of heauenly kinde, Whose glittering gite so glimsed in mine eyes.'

## H.

Ha! ha! interj. B 4571.

Haberdassher, s. seller of hats, A 361.

Habergeoun, s. a hauberk or coat of mail, A 76, 2119.

Habitacle, s. habitable space, B 2. p 7. 59; Habitacles, pl. niches, HF. 1194.

Haboundaunt, pres. pt. abounding, B 3. p 2. 32.

Habounde, v. abound, B 3938, E 1286.

Habundant, adj. abundant, E 59.

Habundaunce, s. plenty, B 2322.

Habýten, pr. pl. inhabit, R. 660.

Hacches, pl. hatches, L. 648.

Hailes, pl. hail-storms, HF. 967.

Hainselins, s. pl. short jackets, I 422. O.F. hainselin, hamcellin, a sort of robe; cf. G. Hemd, shirt.

Haire, s. hair-shirt, R. 438.

Hakeney, s. old horse, R. 1137; G 559.

Halde, pp. held, esteemed (Northern), A 4208.

Hale, v. draw, attract, 5. 151; pr. s. draws back, 1. 68.

Half, s. side, HF. 1136; behalf, T. ii. 1734; Halfe, dat. 5. 125; on my halfe, from me, 3. 139; a goddes halfe, on God's side, in God's name, D 50; Halve, dat. side, part, T. iv. 945; pl. sides, A 3481.

Half-goddes, pl. demi-gods, L. 387.

Half-yeer age, of the age of half a year, A 3971.

Haliday, s. holiday, A 3309, 3340.

Halke, s. corner, R. 464; hiding-place, L. 1780; nook, F 1121; pl. G 311.

Halle, s. hall, A 353; dining-room, T. ii. 1170; parlour, B 4022.

Halp, pt. s. of Helpe.

Hals, s. neck, HF. 394; B 73; cut the hals, cut in the throat, L. 292 a.

Halse, 1 pr. s. I conjure, B 1835. The proper meaning of A.S. healsian is to clasp round the neck (A.S. heals), and thence to beseech, supplicate.

Halt, pr. s. of Holde and Halten.

Halten, ger. to limp, T. iv. 1457; Halt, pr. s. goes lame, 3. 622.

Halve goddes, pl. demigods, T. iv. 1545.

Halvendel, s. the half part (of), T. v. 335.

Halwen, ger. to hallow, I 919.

Halwes, pl. saints, B 1060; apostles, 3. 831; shrines of saints, A 14.

Haly-dayes, pl. holy-days, festivals, A 3952, I 667.

Ham, s. home (Northern), A 4032.

Hameled, pp. cut off, T. ii. 964. (It refers to the mutilation of dogs that were found to be pursuing game secretly. They were mutilated by cutting off a foot.) A.S. hamelian, to mutilate.

Hamer, s. hammer, A 2508.

**Hampred,** *pp.* hampered, burdened, R. 1493.

**Hand,** *s.* hand, A 108; *in his hande,* leading by his hand, L. 213.

**Handebrede,** *s.* hand's breadth, A 3811.

**Handwerk,** *s.* creatures, things created, D 1562.

**Hangeth,** *pr. s. as fut.* will hang, R. 193; **Heeng,** *pt. s.* hung, A 3250; **Heng,** *pt. s.* hung, R. 224, 240; (which) hung, E 1883; hung down, T. ii. 689; **Hanged,** *pp.* hung round, A 2568; hung, T. ii. 353.

**Hap,** *s.* chance, E 2057; luck, success, B 3928, G 1209; good fortune, 3. 1039; *h. other grace,* a mere chance or a special favour, 3. 810; *pl.* occurrences, 3. 1279.

**Happe,** *v.* happen, befall, A 585; *h. how h. may,* happen what may, T. v. 796.

**Happen,** *pr. s. subj.* (it) may happen, L. 78.

**Happy,** *adj.* lucky, T. ii. 621.

**Hard,** *adj.* hard, A 229; *of hard,* with difficulty, T. ii. 1236; *def.* cruel, 6. 106; F 499; *with h. grace,* with displeasure, severity (see **Grace**).

**Harde,** *adv.* tightly, A 3279.

**Hardely,** *adv.* boldly, R. 270; unhesitatingly, 6. 118; scarcely, R. 4; certainly, HF. 359.

**Hardiment,** *s.* boldness, T. iv. 533.

**Hardinesse,** *s.* boldness, A 1948, B 3210; fool-hardiness, B 2508; insolence, I 438.

**Harding,** *s.* hardening, tempering, F 243.

**Hardnésse,** *s.* cruelty, 4. 232; hardship, I 688.

**Hardy,** *adj.* bold, A 405; sturdy, F 19; rash, R. 1038.

**Harie,** *ger.* to drag, I 171; **Haried,** *pp.* pulled forcibly, A 2726.

**Harlot,** *s.* a person of low birth, servant-lad, D 1754; ribald, A 647; rogue, rascal, A 4268; **Harlotes,** *pl.* thieves, pick-pockets, R. 191. (Used of both sexes.)

**Harlotrye,** *s.* ribaldry, A 3145; wickedness, D 1328; evil conduct, E 2262; *pl.* ribald jests, A 561.

**Harm,** *s.* harm, 3. 492; A 385; *broken harm,* occasional injury, petty annoyance, E 1425.

**Harneised,** *pp.* equipped (lit. harnessed), A 114.

**Harneys,** *s.* armour, A 1006; gear, arrangement, I 974; fittings, A 2896; harness, I 433; provision, D 136.

**Harpe-stringes,** *pl.* harp-strings, HF. 777.

**Harping,** *s.* playing on the harp, A 266.

**Harpour,** *s.* harper, T. ii. 1030.

**Harre,** *s.* hinge, A 550. A.S. *heorra.*

**Harrow!** *interj.* help! A 3286. O.F. *haro.*

**Harwed,** *pt. s.* harried, despoiled, A 3512, D 2107. (Alluding to the harrying or harrowing of hell by Christ.) A.S. *hergian.*

**Hasard,** *s.* dice-play, C 465, 591.

**Hasardour,** *s.* gamester, C 596.

**Hasardrye,** *s.* gaming, playing at hazard, C 590.

**Hasel-wode,** *s.* hazel-wood, i.e. no news (see below), T. v. 505, 1174; *pl.* hazel-bushes, T. iii. 890. (Hazel-woods shake, i. e. that is no news, it is of no use to tell me that.)

**Haspe,** *s.* hasp, A 3470.

**Hast,** hast thou (so)? A 4268.

**Hast,** *s.* haste, T. iii. 1438.

**Hasteth,** *imp. pl.* make haste, I 72.

**Hastif,** *adj.* hasty, A 3545.

**Hastifnesse,** *s.* hastiness, B 2312.

**Hastow,** 2 *pr. s.* hast thou, A 3533.

**Hateful,** *adj.* hateful, D 366; odious (Lat. *odibile*), D 1195.

**Hateredes,** *s. pl.* hatreds, B 4. m 4. 2.

**Haubergeons,** *s. pl.* hauberks, I 1052, 1054.

**Hauberk,** *s.* coat of mail, A 2431, B 2053.

**Haunche-bon,** *s.* thigh-bone, A 3803; *pl.* haunch-bones, A 3279.

**Haunt,** *s.* abode, B 2001; 'limit,' usual resort, A 252 c; use, practice, skill, 447.

**Haunteth,** *pr.* habitually uses, T. v. 1556; is used to, A 4392; practises, C 547; *pr. pl.* resort to, I 885; practise, I 780, 847.

**Hauteyn,** *adj.* proud, stately, 5. 262; loud, C 330; **Hautein,** haughty, I 614.

**Haven,** *v.* have, T. iii. 1463; **Han,** *v.* F. 56; keep, retain, C 725; take away, C 727; obtain, G 234; possess (cf. 'to have and to hold'), B 208; **Hast,** 2 *pr. s.* hast thou so? A 4268; **Hath,** *pr. s.* has, L. 2700; **Han,** 1 *pr. pl.* have, L. 28; 2 *pr. pl.* A 849; **Han,** *pr. pl.* E 188, 381; possess, A. pr. 24; **Hadde,** 1 *pt. s.* possessed, 2. 34; **Hadde,** *pt. s.* had, L. 1859; had, possessed, E 438; took, E 303; **Hade** (used for the rime), *pt. s.* A 554, 617; **Hadden,** *pt. pl.* had, kept, E 201; **Hadde,** *pt. pl.* L. 1841; *I hadde lever,* I would rather, B 3083; **Have,** *imp. s.* take, F 759; **Have doon,** make an end, 5. 492.

**Havinge,** *s.* possession (*habendi*), B 2. m 5. 33.

**Hawe,** (1), *s.* haw, yard, enclosure, C 855.

**Hawe,** (2), *s.* haw (fruit of dog-rose), D 659; *with hawe bake*, with baked haws, i.e. with coarse fare, B 95.

**Hay,** *s.* hedge, R. 54.

**Hayl,** *interj.* hail! A 3579.

**Hayt,** *interj.* come up! D 1543.

**He,** *pron.* he, A 44, &c.; *used for* it, G 867, 868; *that he*, that man, HF. 2069; He ... he, this one ... that one, 5. 166; He and he, one man and another, T. ii. 1748; Him, *dat. and acc.* him, HF. or here, him or her, HF. 1003; *him semed*, it seemed to him, he appeared, B 3361; Hem, *pl. dat. and acc.* them, A 11; *hem seemed*, it seemed to them, they supposed, F 56.

**Hed,** *pp.* hidden, L. 208.

**Hede,** *s.* heed, A 303; *tak h.*, take care, 1. 47.

**Hede,** *v.* provide with a head, T. ii. 1042.

**Hèèd,** *s.* head, A 198, 293, 455; source, 16. 43; beginning, F 1282; *on his h.*, at the risk of his head, A 1725; *malgre hir hede*, in spite of all they can do, 4. 220; *maugree hir heed*, in spite of all she could do, D 887; *maugre thyn heed*, in spite of all thou canst do, B 104; Hedes, *pl.* heads, or first points of signs, A. i. 17. 20; Hevedes, heads, B 2032.

**Heef,** *pt. s. of* Heve.

**Heeld,** *pt. s. of* Holde.

**Heelp,** *pt. s. of* Helpe.

**Heeng,** *pt. s. of* Hange.

**Hèèp,** *s.* heap, i.e. crowd, host, A 575; great number, crowd, T. iv. 1281.

**Hèèr,** *s.* hair, R. 549; Hères, *pl.* HF. 1390.

**Hèèr,** *adv.* here, B 1177; Heer and ther, never long in one place, G 1174; *her and ther*, hither and thither, B 5. p 5. 33.

**Heer-agayns,** *prep.* against this, I 668.

**Heer-biforn,** *adv.* here-before, before this, F 1535.

**Heer-forth,** *adv.* in this direction, D 1001.

**Heer-mele,** *s.* the thickness of a hair, a hair's breadth, A ii. 38. 17.

**Heeste,** *s.* commandment, I 845.

**Heet,** *pt. s. of* Hote.

**Hegge,** *s.* hedge, T. v. 1144; *pl.* B 4408.

**Heigh,** *adj.* high, A 316, 522; great, A 1798; lofty, B 3192; learned, E 18; severe, B 795; Heighe, *def.* C 633; *in h. and lowe*, in both high and low things, i. e. wholly, A 817, B 993.

**Heighe,** *adv.* high up, T. iv. 996; high, B 4607; *an heigh*, on high, F 849.

**Heighly,** *adv.* strongly, T. ii. 1733.

**Helde,** *v.* hold, retain, D 272. See Holde (the usual form).

**Helde,** *pt. pl.* poured out, HF. 1686 (Better than 'held.') See Hielde.

**Hele,** *s.* health, L. 1159; recovery, well-being, 1. 80; prosperity, L. 296. A. S. *hǽlu.*

**Héle,** *dat.* heel, T. iv. 728.

**Hele,** *v.* conceal, B 2279; *pp.* hidden, B 4245. A.S. *helan.*

**Helelees,** *adj.* out of health, T. v. 1593.

**Helen,** *v.* heal, 11. 4; *pp.* A 2706.

**Helle,** *s.* hell, 4. 120; L. 2, 6.

**Helpe,** *s.* helper, assistant, L. 1616.

**Helpe,** *v.* help, A 258; H. of, cure of, A 632; Heelp, 1 *pt. s.* helped, A 4246; Heelp, *pt. s.* B 920; Halp, *pt. s.* A 1651; Helpeth, *imp. pl.* L. 68; Holpe, *pt. s. subj.* helped, R. 1230; Holpen, *pp.* helped, aided, F 666; healed, A 18.

**Helply,** *adj.* helpful, T. v. 128.

**Hem,** them; see He.

**Hemi-spere,** hemisphere, T. iii. 1439.

**Hem-self,** *pron. pl.* themselves, B 145; Hem-selven, F 1420.

**Hen,** *s.* hen, A 177; (as a thing of small value), D 1112.

**Hende,** *adj.* courteous, polite, gentle, A 3199, 3272, 3462.

**Henne,** *adv.* hence, T. i. 572.

**Hennes,** *adv.* hence, T. v. 402; now, HF. 1284.

**Hennes-forth,** *adv.* henceforth, R. 701.

**Hente,** *v.* catch, I 355; seize, A 3347; acquire, get, A 299; circumvent, T. iv. 1371; *dide her for to hente*, caused her to be seized, L. 2715; Hent, *pr. s.* seizes, catches, T. iv. 5; Hente, *pr. s. subj.* may seize, G 7; Hente, *pt. s.* caught, took, A 957; caught away, B 1144; seized, caught hold of, T. ii. 924; grasped, C 255; took forcibly, E 534; took in hunting, B 3449; lifted, G 205; *pt. pl.* seized, A 904; caught, R. 773; *pp.* caught, A 1581.

**Henteres,** *s. pl.* filchers, B 1. p 3. 89.

**Hépe,** *s.* hip, the fruit of the dog-rose, B 1937.

**Hepen,** *pr. pl.* augment, B 5. p 2. 46; *pp.* accumulated, T. iv. 236.

**Her, Hir,** *pron. poss.* their, B 136. A.S. *heora, hira,* of them; gen. pl. of *hē,* he.

**Heraud,** *s.* herald, A 2533.

**Heraude,** *ger.* to proclaim as a herald does, HF. 1576.

**Herber,** *s.* garden, T. ii. 1705; arbour, L. 203.

**Herbergage,** *s.* a lodging, abode, A 4329; B 4179.

**Herbergeours,** *s. pl.* harbingers, providers of lodgings, B 997.

**Herberwe,** *or* **Herberw,** *s.* harbour, A 403; inn, A 765; lodging, shelter, A 4119; dwelling, position, F 1035.

**Herberwe,** *ger.* to shelter, R. 491; **Herberweden,** *pt. pl.* lodged, B 2. p 6. 75.

**Herberwing,** *s.* lodging, sheltering, A 4332.

**Her-biforn,** *adj.* before this time, L. 73; a while ago, 3. 1136.

**Her-by,** *adv.* with respect to this matter, D 2204; hence, HF. 263.

**Herde,** *s.* shepherd, G 192; keeper of cattle, A 603.

**Herde-gromes,** *pl.* herdsmen, HF. 1225.

**Herdes,** *pl.* coarse flax, 'hards,' R. 1233.

**Herdesse,** *s.* shepherdess, T. i. 653.

**Here,** *pron.* her, R. 1260; &c.

**Here,** *poss. pron.* her, T. i. 285; &c.

**Here,** *adv.* here, in this place, on this spot, T. v. 478. (Dissyllabic.) See **Heer.**

**Here,** *v.* hear, A 169; **Heren,** *v.* HE. 879; **Herestow,** *2 pr. s.* hearest thou, A 3366; **Herth,** *pr. s.* hears, L. 327 *a*; **Herde,** *pt. s.* heard, A 221; **Herdestow, heardest thou,** A 4170; **Herd,** *pp.* heard, 3. 129.

**Here-agayns,** against this, A 3039; **Here-ayeins,** in reply to that, T. ii. 1380.

**Here and howne,** T. iv. 210; *perhaps* gentle and savage, i.e. one and all (doubtful). Cf. *here,* gentle, in Stratmann; and A.S. *Hūna,* a Hun.

**Herie,** *v.* praise, T. iii. 1672; **Heriest,** *2 pr. s.* worshippest, B 3419; *pr. s.* B 1155; *pt. pl.* worshipped, L. 786; *pp.* B 872. A.S. *herian.*

**Herke,** *imp. s.* hearken, E 1323; **Herketh,** *imp. pl.* D 1656.

**Herknen,** *v.* hearken, listen, I 81; *ger.* to listen to, 3. 752; **Herkne,** *v.* G 1006; *ger.* B 3159; *pt. s.* listened to, A 4173; **Herkned,** *pp.* listened, R. 630; *h. after,* expected, F 403.

**Herne,** *s.* corner, F 1121; *pl.* G 658.

**Herneys,** *s.* armour, A 2496; *pl.* sets of armour, A 1630.

**Heroner,** *s.* falcon for herons, T. iv. 413.

**Heronere,** *adj.* used for flying at herons, L. 1120. Said of a falcon.

**Heronsewes,** *s. pl.* hernshaws, young herons, F 68. *Heronsew* is derived, regularly, from A.F. *herouncel,* later *herounçeau;* a diminutive from *heroun,* like *lioncel* from *lion.*

**Herse,** *s.* hearse, 2. 15, 36.

**Hert,** *s.* hart, 3. 351; 5. 195.

**Herte,** *s.* heart, A 150, 229; dear one, T. ii. 1096; courage, 3. 1222; **Hertes,** *gen.* heart's, 1. 164; **Herte,** *gen.* T. ii. 445; **Herte rote,** root (bottom) of the heart, R. 1026; *myn hertes,* of my heart, 4. 57.

**Herte,** *pt. s.* hurt, 3. 883.

**Herte-blood,** heart's blood, A 2006, C 902.

**Hertelees,** *adj.* heartless, without heart, T. v. 1594; deficient in courage, B 4098.

**Hertely,** *adv.* heartily, A 762; thoroughly, L. 33; earnestly, 3. 1226; truly, 3. 85.

**Herte-rote,** *s.* root of the heart, depth of the heart, L. 1993.

**Herte-spoon,** *s.* 'the concave part of the breast, where the ribs unite to form the *cartilago ensiformis*' (Tyrwhitt), A 2606.

**Hert-hunting,** *s.* hunting of the hart, 3. 1313.

**Herth,** *pr. s.* heareth, L. 327 *a.*

**Hertly,** *adj.* heartfelt, honest, L. 2124; hearty, E 176, 502, F 5.

**Heryinge,** *s.* praising, I 682; praise, B 1649; glory, T. iii. 48.

**Heste,** *s.* command, commandment, behest, B 382; promise, F 1064; **Heeste,** commandment, I 845.

**Hète,** *s.* heat, R. 1508; passion, 4. 127; heat, *but put for* surge, B 1. m 7. 4.

**Hete,** *v.* promise, vow, 6. 77; *pr. s. subj.* promise, A 2398; *1 pr. s.* B 334; **Hette,** *pt. s.* 4. 185. See **Hote.**

**Heterly,** *adv.* fiercely, L. 638.

**Hèthen,** *adv.* hence (Northern), A 4033.

**Hethenesse,** *s.* heathen lands, A 49, B 1112.

**Hèthing,** *s.* contempt, A 4110. Icel. *hæðing.*

**Hette,** *pt. s.* heated, inflamed, 5. 145.

**Hette,** *pt. s.* promised, 4. 185. See **Hote.**

**Heve,** *v.* heave, lift, A 550; *ger.* to use exertion, labour, T. ii. 1289; *pr. s.* lifts up, B 5. m 5. 18; **Haf,** *pt. s.* heaved, A 3470; **Heef,** *pt. s.* lifted, B 1. p 1. 19.

**Heved,** *s.* head, HF. 550; beginning, A. ii. 16. 3; **Hevedes,** *pl.* B 2032.

**Heven,** *s.* heaven, A 519; the celestial sphere, B 3300; supreme delight, F 558; beautiful sight, T. ii. 637; **Hevene,** *gen.* heaven's, D 1181, G 542.

**Hevenish,** *adj.* heavenly, HF. 1395; of the spheres, 4. 30.

**Hevieth,** *pr. pl.* weigh down, B 5. m 5. 16.

**Hevy,** *adj.* heavy, R. 229; sad, 4. 12.

**Hewe,** (1) *s.* hue, colour, complexion, A 394, 1364; outward appearance, mien, D 1622; pretence, C 421.

Hewe, (2), *s.* (household)-servant, domestic, E 1785. A. S. *hīwa.*

Hewed, *adj.* coloured, R. 213.

Hey, *s.* hay, A 3262 ; grass, B 3407.

Hey ! *interj.* hey ! L. 1213.

Heye, *adj. def.* high, A. i. 16. 11.

Heyghte, *s.* height, A. ii. 22. 8.

Heyne, *s.* wretch, G 1319.

Heynous, *adj.* heinous, odious, T. ii. 1617.

Heyre, *adj.* hair, made of hair, C 736.

Heyre, *s.* hair-shirt, G 133.

Heysugge, *s.* hedge-sparrow, 5. 612.

Heyt, *interj.* come up, D 1561.

Hider, *adv.* hither, 4. 165.

Hidous, *adj.* hideous, A 3520; terrible, horrible, dreadful, A 1978, B 4583 ; ugly, R. 158.

Hidously, *adv.* terribly, A 1701.

Hielde, *pr. s. subj.* pour out, shed, B 2. m 2. 2 (Lat. *fundat*).

Hierdes, female guardian, protectress, T. iii. 619. See **Herdesse.**

Hight, Highte ; see **Hote.**

Highteth, *pr. s.* adorns, gladdens, B 1. m 2. 25.

Hild, *pt. s.* bent, inclined, 3. 393.

Hinde, *s.* hind, 3. 427.

Hindre, *v.* hinder, R. 1039.

Hindreste, *superl.* hindmost, A 622.

Hipes, *pl.* hips, A 472.

Hir, (1), *pers. pron. dat. and acc.,* to her, her, A 126, B 162, &c.

Hir, (2), *poss. pron.* her, A 120, B 164, &c.

Hir (3), *gen. pl.* of them ; Hir aller, of them all, A 586 ; Hir bothe, of both of them, B 221.

Hir, (4), *poss. pron.* their, A 11, B 140, &c. ; Her, B 3536, &c.

Hir thankes, with their good will, willingly, A 2114.

Hirës, hers, 5. 482, 588.

Hirnia, *s.* hernia, I 423.

His, *gen. masc.* his, A 47, 50, &c. ; *neut.* its, 1. 178 ; T. iii. 1088, v. 1379 ; *in phr.* Mars his = of Mars, L. 2593.

Histhankes, with his good will, willingly, A 2107.

Historial, *adj.* historical, C 156.

Hit, *pron.* it, 2. 117 ; Hit am I, it is I, 3. 186, L. 314 ; Hit weren, they were, HF. 1323.

Hit, *pr. s.* hides, F 512. *Hit* is a contracted form, equivalent to *hideth.*

Ho, *interj.* hold ! stop ! B 3957.

Ho, *s.* exclamation commanding silence, A 2533 ; stop, cessation, T. ii. 1083.

Hochepot, *s.* hotch-potch, mixture, B 2447.

Hoke, *dat. of* Hook.

Hoker, *s.* scorn, frowardness, A 3965. A. S. *hōcor.*

Hokerly, *adv.* scornfully, I 584.

Hold, *s.* possession, B 4064 ; grasp, F 167 ; keeping, D 599 ; fort, castle, B 507.

Holde, *v.* keep, preserve, D 1144 ; hold, keep, B 41 ; continue, go on with, T. ii. 965 ; restrain, 7. 309, 310 ; keep to (see Proces), F 658 ; Holden, *v.* hold, keep, F 763 ; keep, F 1163 ; think, consider, L. 857 ; *do than holde herto,* keep to it then, 3. 754 ; Holde up, hold up, 2. 24 ; Holde his pees, hold his peace, B 4625 ; Holde, 1 *pr. s.* consider, deem, G 739 ; Holdest, 2 *pr. s.* accountest, L. 326 ; Halt, *pr. s.* holds, 11. 16 ; T. v. 348 ; keeps, T. ii. 37 ; holds fast, T. iii. 1636 ; considers, G 921 ; esteems, D 1185 ; performs, 3. 621 ; remains firm, 10. 38 ; Holt, *pr. s.* holds, T. iii. 1374 ; Holden, 2 *pr. pl.* keep, L. 2500 ; Holde, 2 *pr. pl.* esteem, deem, T. v. 1339 ; Heeld, 1 *pt. s.* considered, E 818 ; Heeld, *pt. s.* held, A 175 ; took part, A 3847 ; esteemed, C 625 ; ruled, B 3518 ; Holden, *pp.* esteemed, held, A 141 ; considered, E 205 ; observed, F 1587 ; esteemed, L. 1709 ; bound, T. ii. 241 ; made to be, C 958 ; Holde, *pp.* esteemed, A 1307 ; *bet for thee have holde,* better for thee to have held, 5. 572 ; Hold up, *imp. pl.* hold up, A 783 ; Holdeth, *imp. pl.* keep, B 37 ; consider, A 1868.

Holdinge in hondes, cajolery, HF. 692.

Holly, *adv.* wholly, T. iii. 145.

Holm, *s.* evergreen oak, A 2921.

Holour, *s.* lecher, adulterer, D 254.

Holpe, -n ; see **Helpe.**

Holsom, *adj.* wholesome, T. i. 947 ; healing, 5. 206.

Holt, *s.* plantation, A 6.

Holt, *pr. s.* holds, T. iii. 1374.

Holwe, *adj.* hollow, G 1265.

Holwe, *adv.* hollow, A 289.

Hom, *adv.* homewards, F 635.

Homicyde (1), *s.* man-slayer, E 1994.

Homicyde (2), manslaughter, murder, C 644.

Hond, *s.* hand, A 193, 399 ; Beren him on h., make him believe, T. iv. 1404 ; Bere on h., accuse (of), D 226 ; Bar on h., made (them) believe, D 380 ; Bar him on h., assured him, T. iii. 1154 ; Holden in h., retain, cajole, T. ii. 477 ; Holde in h., T. iii. 773 ; delude with false hopes, 3. 1019.

Honest, *adj.* creditable, A 246 ; honourable, worthy, B 1751 ; seemly, decent, C 328 ; luxurious, E 2028.

Honestee, *s.* honour, L. 1673 ; goodness, B 3157 ; honourableness, 2. 40 ; womanly virtue, C 77.

Honestetee, *s.* honour, E 422 ; modesty, I 429 ; neatness, I 431.

Honestly, *adv.* honourably, B 1434 ; richly, E 2026.

Honge, *v.* hang, A 2410 ; be hung, C 790 ; *do me h.*, cause me to be hanged, T. i. 833 ; *2 pr. pl. subj.* hesitate, T. ii. 1242.

Hony, *s.* honey, A 2908 ; beloved one, A 3617.

Hony-comb, a term of endearment, sweet one, A 3698.

Hony-swete, sweet as honey, E 1396.

Hoodless, *adj.* without a hood, 3. 1028.

Hóók, *s.* hook, T. v. 777 ; sickle, B 3. m 1. 3 ; crosier, D 1317.

Hòòl, *adj.* whole, T. i. 961 ; sound, D 1370 ; unwounded, F 1111 ; perfect, G 111, 117 ; restored to health, L. 2468 ; entire, 3. 554.

Hòòl, *adj. as adv.* wholly, T. i. 1053 ; *al hool*, entirely, T. iii. 1013.

Hoolly, *adv.* wholly, R. 1163.

Hoolnesse, *s.* integrity, B 4. p 6. 202.

Hoolsome, *adj.* wholesome, B 2285.

Hoolsomnesse. *s.* health, B 2303.

Hòòm, *s. as adv.* home, homewards, L. 1619.

Hoomlinesse, *s.* domesticity, E 429 ; familiarity, B 2876.

Hoomly, *adj.* belonging to one's household, E 1785.

Hoomward, *adv.* homeward, T. iii. 621 ; Homward, A 2956.

Hòòr, *adj.* hoary, white-haired, grey-headed, A 3878.

Hoors, *adj.* ; see Hors.

Hoost, *s.* army, A 874.

Hòòt, *adj.* hot, L. 914 ; fervent, I 117 ; *as s.* 5. 380 ; Hote, *def.* hot, 5. 266 ; voracious, 5. 362 ; (as epithet of Aries, which induced heat of blood), F 51.

Hope, *s.* expectation, G 870.

Hope, 1 *pr. s.* fear, A 4029.

Hoper, *s.* hopper, A 4036, 4039.

Hoppe, *v.* dance, A 4375.

Hoppesteres, *pl.* dancers ; *used as adj.,* dancing, A 2017.

Hord, *s.* hoard, treasure, C 775 ; store (of apples), A 3262 ; treasure-house, I 821 ; avarice, 13. 3.

Hore, *pl. of* Hoor, *adj.*

Horn, *s.* horn, T. ii. 642 ; (musical instrument, used metaphorically), H 90 ; *pl.*

drinking-horns, A 2279 ; horns (of the moon), T. v. 652.

*Horoscopo* ; *in horoscopo*, within that part of the sky considered as the ascendent, A. ii. 4. 14.

Horowe, *adj. pl.* foul, scandalous, 4. 206. Cf. A. S. *horig*, filthy.

Hors, *s.* hors, A 168 ; the ' horse,' a name for the little wedge that passes through a hole in the end of the ' pyn,' A. i. 14. 7 (Arabic *alpheraz*, the horse) ; Hors, *pl.* A 74, 598.

Hors, *adj.* hoarse, 3. 347 ; Hoors, T. iv. 1147. A. S. *hás.*

Horsly, *adj.* like all that a horse should be, F 194.

Hose, *s.* hose, covering for the feet and legs, A 3933, G 726 ; Hosen, *pl.* A 456 ; Hoses, *pl.* A 3319.

Hospitaliers, *s. pl.* knights hospitallers, I 891.

Hoste, *s.* host (of an inn), keeper of a lodging, A 747. Often spelt *oste.*

Hostel, *s.* hostelry, HF. 1022.

Hostelrye, *s.* hostel, inn, A 23.

Hostiler, *s.* innkeeper, A 241 ; *pl.* servants at an inn, I 440.

Hote, *adj.* ; see Hoot.

Hote, *adv.* hotly, A 97, 1737.

Hote, *v.* command, promise ; *also,* be called, R. 38 ; Hoten, *v.* be called, D 144 ; Hote, 1 *pr. s.* command, HF. 1719 ; Hight, *pt. s. as pr. s.* is called, L. 417 ; Highten, *pt. pl. as pr. pl.* are called, L. 423 ; Hight, *pt. s.* was named, L. 725 ; Highte, *pt. s.* was called, was named, R. 588, 745 ; 1 *pt. s.* was called, A 4336 ; 1 *pt. s.* promised, 17. 5 ; Highte, *pt. s.* promised, T. v. 1636 ; *2 pt. pl.* promised, E 496 ; Hatte, *pt. s. as pr. s.* is called, is named, T. iii. 797 ; Hatte, *pt. pl.* were called, were named, HF. 1303 ; Hette, 1 *pt. s.* promised, 4. 185 ; Heet, *pt. s.* was named, HF. 1604 ; (who) was called, F 1388 ; Hetë (*for* Heet), 3. 200 ; Hoten, *pp.* called, A 3941 ; Hight, *pp.* promised, T. ii. 492 ; named, HF. 226. A. S. *hátan.* The parts of the verb show great confusion.

Hottes, *pl.* baskets carried on the back, HF. 1940. O.F. *hotte.*

Hound, *s.* dog, T. iii. 764.

Houndfish, *s.* dogfish, E 1825.

Houped, *pt. pl.* whooped, B 4590.

Hous, *s.* house, A 252, 343 ; *to hous,* to a reception by, L. 1546 ; Hous and hoom, house and home, H 229 ; Hous by hous, to each house in order, D 1765 ; a household, F 24 ; a 'mansion' of a planet (in astrology), F 672 ; a 'house' or portion of the sky (in astrology), B 304. The whole celestial sphere was divided into twelve equal portions, called *houses*, by six great circles passing through the north and south points of the horizon ; two of these circles being the meridian and the horizon. A *house*, when used for a 'mansion,' is a sign of the zodiac ; thus Aries was the mansion of Mars.

**Hóusbonde,** *s.* husband, B 2241.

**Housbondrye,** *s.* economy, A 4077 ; household goods, D 288.

**Housled,** *pp.* made a recipient of holy communion, I 1027.

**Hove,** *v.* hover, dwell, T. iii. 1427 ; *pr. pl.* wait in readiness, hover, L. 1196 ; *pt. s.* waited about, T. v. 33.

**How,** *interj.* ho! A 3437, 3577.

**Howne,** savage (?), T. iv. 210. See Here.

**Howve,** *s.* hood, T. iii. 775 ; Sette his howve, set (awry) his hood, make game of him, A 3911.

**Humanitee,** *s.* kindness, E 92.

**Humbely,** *adv.* humbly, T. v. 1354.

**Humblely,** *adv.* humbly, T. ii. 1719 ; L. 156.

**Humblesse,** *s.* meekness, A 1781, B 165.

**Humbling,** *s.* low growl (lit. humming), HF. 1039.

**Humme,** *ger.* to hum, T. ii. 1199.

**Hunte,** *s.* huntsman, A 2018, 2628.

**Hunter,** *s.* huntsman, A 1638.

**Hunteresse,** *s. fem.* female hunter, A 2347.

**Hurlest,** 2 *pr. s.* dost hurl, dost whirl round, B 297.

**Hurt,** *pr. s.* hurteth, hurts, T. v. 350.

**Hurtleth,** *pr. s.* pushes, A 2616 ; *pr. pl.* dash together, L. 638.

**Husht,** *pp.* hushed, silent, L. 2682 ; Hust, *as imp. s.* be silent, A 3722.

**Hy,** *adj.* high, A 306 ; Hye, *dat.* HF. 1133 ; great, E 135 ; Hye weye, *dat.* (the) high way, main road, A 897.

**Hyde,** *v.* hide, A 1477, 1481 ; lie concealed, F 141 ; Hydestow, hidest thou, D 308 : Hit, *pr. s.* hides, F 512 ; Hidde, 1 *pt. s.* hid, F 595 ; Hed, *pp.* hidden, L. 208 ; Hid, *pp.* hidden, R. 1598.

**Hye,** *adv.* high, aloft, HF. 905 ; L. 1200 ; loudly, 3. 305 ; proudly, T. ii. 401.

**Hye,** *v.* hasten, hie, A 2274, G 1151 ; *h. me,* make haste, G 1084 ; *ger.* to bring hastily, F 291 ; to hasten, HF. 1658 ; Hy thee, *imp. s. refl.* G 1295.

**Hye,** *s.* haste ; only in phr. *in hye,* in haste, T. ii. 88, 1712.

**Hyene,** *s.* hyæna, 10. 35.

**Hyër,** *adj.* higher, upper, HF. 1117.

**Hyne,** *s.* hind, servant, peasant, A 603, C 688. A. S. *hína.*

**Hyre,** *s.* hire, A 507 ; reward, 1. 103 ; payment, D 1008 ; ransom, T. iv. 506.

## I.

**I-,** *common prefix of past participles ;* see Y-.

**Icched,** *pp.* itched, A 3682.

**Ich,** *pron.* I, T. i. 678, iii. 1818.

**I-comen,** *pp.* come, T. iii. 1668.

**Idus,** *s. pl.* ides, F 47.

*Ignotum,* *s.* an unknown thing, G 1457. Lat. *ignotum,* an unknown thing ; comp. *ignotius,* a less known thing.

**I-graunted,** *pp.* granted, T. iv. 665.

**I-halowed,** *pp.* view-hallooed (of the hart), 3. 379.

**Ik,** I, A 3867, 3888.

**Il,** *adj.* evil, A 4174. (A Northern word.)

**Il-hayl,** bad luck (to you), A 4089. (A Northern form.)

**Ilke,** *adj.* same, very, A 64, 175 ; *that ilke,* that same, B 3663 ; *ilke same,* very same, L. 779.

**Imaginatyf,** *adj.* ; No-thing list him to been imaginatyf = it did not at all please him to imagine, he did not care to think, F 1094.

**Imagining,** *s.* plotting, A 1995 ; fancy, 18. 36.

**Imperie,** *s.* government, rank, B 2. p 6. 13.

**Impertinent,** *adj.* irrelevant, E 54.

**Impes,** *pl.* grafts, scions, B 3146. A.S. *imp.*

**Impetren,** *pr. pl.* impetrate, ask for, B 5. p 3. 225.

**Importáble,** *adj.* insufferable, B 3792, E 1144.

**Impossíble,** *adj.* impossible, T. i. 783 ; *as s.,* thing impossible, D 688.

**Impressen,** *v.* imprint, T. iii. 1543 ; imprint (themselves), find an impression, E 1578 ; *pr. pl.* make an impression (upon), G 1071.

**Impressioun,** *s.* remembrance, F 371 ; *pl.* notions, HF. 39.

**In,** *s.* dwelling, house, A 3547, 3622 ; inn, B 4216 ; lodging, B 1097.

**In,** *prep.* in, A 3, &c. ; into, B 119 ; = come within, 20. 6 ; on, I 105 ; against, I 695.

*In manus tuas,* into Thy hands (I commend my spirit), A 4287.

*In principio,* in the beginning, A 254, B 4353. Part of St. John, i. 1.

**Inde,** *adj.* indigo, dark blue, R. 67.
**Indeterminat,** *adj.* not marked upon the Astrolabe, A ii. 17. *rubric.*
**Indifferently,** *adv.* impartially, B 5. p 3. 142.
**Induracioun,** *s.* hardening, G 855.
**Inequal,** *adj.* unequal, A 2271 ; Inequales, *pl.* of varying length ; *houres inequales,* hours formed by dividing the *duration of daylight* by twelve, A. ii. 8. 1.
**Infect,** *adj.* of no effect, A 320 ; dimmed, B 4. m 5. 12.
**In-fere,** *adv.* together, B 328, D 924. Orig. *in fere,* in company.
**Infortunat,** *adj.* unfortunate, unlucky, inauspicious, B 302.
**Infortúne,** *s.* misfortune, ill fortune, T. iii. 1626, iv. 185.
**Infortúned,** *pp.* ill-starred, T. iv. 744.
**Infortuning,** *s.* unlucky condition, A. ii. 4. 43.
**Ingot,** *s.* a mould for pouring metal into, G 1206, 1209.
**Inhelde,** *imp. s.* pour in, infuse, T. iii. 44.
**Injure,** *s.* injury, T. iii. 1018.
**In-knette,** *pt. s.* knit up, drew in, T. iii. 1088.
**Inly,** *adv.* inwardly, intimately, extremely, greatly, T. i. 140 ; exquisitely, 3. 276.
**In-mid,** *prep.* amid, HF. 923.
**Inmortal,** *adj.* immortal, T. i. 103.
**Inne,** *dat. of* In, *s.*
**Inne,** *adv.* in, within, T. i. 387, 821.
**Inned,** *pp.* housed, lodged, A 2192.
**Inobedience,** *s.* disobedience, I 391.
**Inobedient,** *adj.* disobedient, I 392.
**Inordinate,** *adj.* unusual, I 414.
**Inpacience,** *s.* impatience, B 2734.
**Inpacient,** *adj.* impatient, B 2730.
**Inparfit,** *adj.* imperfect, B 3. p. 10. 18.
**Inplitable,** *adj.* intricate, impracticable, B 1. p 4. 90.
**Inpossible,** *s.* impossible thing, F 1009.
**Inset,** *pp.* implanted, B 2. p 3. 19.
**Inspired,** *pp.* quickened, A 6.
**Instable,** *adj.* unstable, F 2057.
**Instance,** *s.* suggestion, T. ii. 1441 ; urgent request, E 1611.
**Intendestow,** dost thou intend, T. v. 478.
**Intervalle,** *s.* interval, B 2724.
**In-til,** *prep.* unto, as far as, R. 624.
**Into,** *prep.* unto, B 2423.
**Intresse,** *s.* interest, 10. 71.
**In-with,** *prep.* within, in, B 1794, 2159, E 870, 1394, 1586, 1944.
**Ipocras,** a kind of cordial drink, E 1807. Named after Hippocrates.

**Ipocrite,** *s.* hypocrite, R. 414.
**Ire,** *s.* irritability, R. 314 ; quickness of temper, I 665 ; anger, A 1997.
**Irous,** *adj.* angry, B 2315, D 2014.
**Irreguler,** *adj.* a sinner against his orders, I 782.
**Is,** 1 *pr. s.* am (Northern), A 4031, 4045, 4202 ; 2 *pr. s.* art (Northern), A 4089.
**Issest,** 2 *pr. s.* issuest, B 3. p 12. 168.
**Issue,** *s.* outlet, vent, T. v. 205.
**It am I,** it is I, A 1736.
**I-wis,** *adv.* certainly, truly, verily, 6. 48.

## J.

**Jade,** *s.* a jade, i. e. miserable hack, B 4002.
**Jagounces,** *pl.* garnets (*or* rubies), R. 1117.
**Jalous,** *adj.* jealous, A 1329.
**Jalousye,** *s.* jealousy, A 3294.
**Jambeux,** *s. pl.* leggings, leg-armour, B 2065. From F. *jambe,* the leg.
**Jane,** *s.* a small coin of Genoa, B 1925, E 999.
**Jangle,** *v.* chatter, prate, T. ii. 666.
**Janglere,** *s.* story-teller, jester, babbler, A 560 ; talkative person, H 343.
**Jangleresse,** *s.* (female) chatterbox, prattler, D 638.
**Janglerye,** *s.* gossip, T. v. 755 ; talkativeness, B 2252.
**Jangles,** *s. pl.* idle pratings, HF. 1960 ; disputes, arguments, D 1407.
**Janglinge,** *s.* chattering, idle talking, I 649.
**Jape,** *s.* jest, trick, A 3390, 3799, 4201 ; jest, foolish conduct, D 1961 ; laughing-stock, HF. 414.
**Jape,** *v.* jest, T. i. 929 ; *ger.* to jest, L. 1699 ; H 4 ; Japedest, 2 *pt. s.* didst jest, T. i. 508, 924 ; *pp.* tricked, A 1729.
**Japere,** *s.* jester, T. ii. 340 ; mocker, I 89.
**Japerie,** *s.* buffoonery, I 651 ; jesting mood, E 1656.
**Jape-worthy,** *adj.* ridiculous, B 5. p 3. 148.
**Jargon,** *s.* talk, E 1848.
**Jargoning,** *s.* jargoning, chattering, R. 716.
**Jaunyce,** *s.* jaundice, R. 305.
**Jeet,** *s.* jet, B 4051.
**Jelous,** *adj.* jealous, suspicious, 4. 140.
**Jet,** *s.* fashion, mode, A 682.
**Jeupardyes,** *s. pl.* problems (at chess), 3. 666.
**Jewerye,** *s.* Jewry, Jews' quarter, B 1679.
**Jo,** *v.* take effect, come about, T. iii. 33. O.F. *joer* (F. *jouer*).

Jogelour, s. juggler, D 1467; pl. R. 764.

Jogelrye, s. jugglery, F 1265.

Jolif, adj. joyful, merry, R. 109, A 3355; in good spirits, B 4264; jovial, R. 435; frisky, A 4154; pretty, R. 610.

Jolily, adv. merrily, A 4370.

Jolitee, s. sport, amusement, merriment, A 1807; joviality, jollity, mirth, R. 616; enjoyment, F 344; comfort, A 680; excellence, H 197; happiness, HF. 682.

Joly, adj. full of merriment, D 456; jolly, joyous, R. 620; delightful, L. 176; festive, B 1185. See Jolif.

Jolyer, adj. comp. handsomer, F 927.

Jolyf; see Jolif.

Jolynesse, s. festivity, F 289; amusement, D 926.

Jolytee; see Jolitee.

Jompre, imp. s. jumble, T. ii. 1037.

Jordanes, pl. chamberpots, C 305.

Jossa, down here, A 4101. O.F. jos, down; ça, here.

Jouken, v. slumber, T. v. 409. O.F. joquier, jouquier, être en repos, jucher.

Journee, s. day's work, R. 579; day's march, A 2738; journey, E 783.

Jowes, s. pl. jaws, B 1. p 4. 107 (where the Latin text has faucibus); jaws, jowls, HF. 1786 (riming with clowes, claws).

Joynture, s. union, B 2. p 5. 51.

Jubbe, s. vessel for holding ale or wine, A 3628, B 1260. (It held 4 gallons.)

Judicial, adj. judicial, A. ii. 4. 59. Judicial astrology pretended to forecast the destinies of men and nations; natural astrology foretold natural events, such as the weather and seasons.

Juge, s. judge, A 814; umpire, A 1712, 1864.

Juge, s. judge; but an error for jug, a yoke, I 898. Belial is explained to mean 'absque iugo,' in the Vulgate.

Juge, 1 pr. s. judge, decide, 5. 629; pp. HF. 357.

Jugement, s. judgement, decision, A 778; opinion, B 1038; sentence, 5. 431.

Juggen, v. judge, T. ii. 21; deem, T. v. 1203; imp. pl. judge ye, T. iii. 1312.

Juparte, 2 pr. pl. jeopard, imperil, endanger, T. iv. 1566.

Jupartye, s. jeopardy, peril, hasard, T. ii. 465, 772. O.F. jeu parti (Lat. iocus partitus), a divided game.

Just, adj. just, exact, correct, D 2090.

Juste, v. joust, tourney, tilt, A 96, 2604.

Justes, s. pl. as sing. a jousting-match, A 2720.

Justing, s. jousting, L. 1115.

Justyse, s. judge, B 665, C 289.

Justyse, s. judgement, condemnation, 1. 142; administration of justice, C 587.

Juyse, s. justice, judgement, B 795; sentence, A 1739. O.F. juise.

## K.

Kalender, s. calendar, almanack, A. i. 11. 1; hence, a complete record of examples, L. 542; pl. 1. 73.

Kalendes, i.e. beginning, introduction, T. v. 1634. (Because the Kalends fall on the first of the month.)

Karf, pt. s. of Kerve.

Kaynard, s. dotard, D 235. O.F. caignard, cagnard, sluggard.

Kecche, v. catch, clutch, T. iii. 1375.

Kēchil, s. small cake, D 1747. O.E. coecil, small cake.

Keep, s. care, heed, notice (only in the phrase take keep); tak keep, take notice, D 431.

Keep, imp. s. take care! mind! A 4101.

Kek! interj. (represents the cackle of a goose), 5. 499.

Kembe, ger. to comb, R. 599; pr. s. E 2011; Kembde, pt. s. F 560; Kempte, pt. s. A 3374; Kembd, pp. combed, trimmed, A 2143.

Kempe, adj. pl. shaggy, rough, A 2134. Cf. Icel. kampr, beard, moustaches, whiskers of a cat; and see Camp, s. (4) in the New E. Dict.

Ken, s. kin, kindred, men, 3. 438. (A Kentish form.)

Kene, adj. keen, eager, 21. 6; cruel, 10. 27; bold, B 3439; sharp, A 2876.

Kene, adv. keenly, 6. 63; 11. 3.

Kenne, v. discern, HF. 498.

Kepe, v. take care (of), A 130; keep, preserve, L. 384; 1 pr. s. care, L. 1032; intend, T. i. 676; regard, reck, A 2238; I kepe han, I care to have, G 1368; pr. s. subj. may (He) keep, F 889; pt. s. E 223; retained, A 442; took care of, A 415, 512, B 269; imp. s. take care! A 4101; imp. pl. keep ye, B 764.

Kepe, s. heed (only in the phrase take kepe or take keep); I take kepe, 3. 6.

Keper, s. keeper, i.e. prior, A 172.

Kerchief, finely woven loose covering, 5. 272; kerchief, B 837.

Kers, s. cress; thing of small value, A 3756.

Kerve, v. carve, cut, T. ii. 325, F 158; Karf, pt. s. carved, A 100; cut, B 3647,

3791; Corven, *pp.* cut, A 2696; carved, HF. 1295; slashed, A 3318.

Kerver, *s.* carver, A 1899.

Kerving, *s.* carving, A 1925; cutting, crossing over, A 1. 19. 4.

Kerving-toles, *s. pl.* tools to cut with, T. i. 632.

Kesse, *v.* kiss, E 1057; Keste, *pt. s.* F 350. (A Kentish form.) See Kissen.

Kevere, *v.* to recover, T. i. 917; *pp.* covered, HF. 275, 352.

Keye, *s.* G 1219; key (*in place of* rudder), B 3. p 12. 80. Chaucer has translated *clauo* (rudder), as if it were *claue* (key).

Kichenes, *pl.* kitchens, D 869.

Kid, Kidde; see Kythen.

Kike, *v.* kick, D 941.

Kimelin, *s.* a large shallow tub, A 3548, 3621.

Kin, *s.* kindred, R. 268; *som kin*, of some kind, B 1137; *alles kinnes*, of every kind, HF. 1530.

Kinde, *s.* nature, R. 412, 1699; race, lineage, stock, D 1101; seed, I 965; the natural world, HF. 584; natural bent, F 608, 619; natural disposition, HF. 43; natural ordinance, 3. 494; kind, species, 5. 174; *of k.*, by nature, naturally, F 768; *pl.* sorts, HF. 204.

Kinde, *adj.* kind, A 647; natural, HF. 834, 836.

Kinde, *adv.* kindly, 7. 267.

Kindely, *adj.* natural, HF. 842.

Kindely, *adv.* by nature, D 402; naturally, HF. 832.

Kindenesse, *s.* kindness, 4. 298; love, devotion, L 665.

Kinges note, the name of a tune, A 3217.

Kinrede, *s.* kindred, B 2558; relations, A 1286; birth, A 2790; family, L. 2094.

Kirtel, *s.* kirtle, A 3321. A *kirtle* usually means a short skirt with a body.

Kissen, *v.* kiss, L. 761; Kiste, *pt. pl.* R. 788; *kist they been*, they have kissed each other, B 1074. See Kesse.

Kitte, *pt. s.* cut, B 600, 1761.

Knakkes, *s. pl.* tricks, I 652; contemptible ways, 3. 1033.

Knarre, *s.* a thickset fellow, sturdy churl, A 549.

Knarry, *adj.* gnarled, A 1977.

Knave, *s.* boy, servant-lad, page, R. 886; man-servant, servant, L. 1807; peasant, D 1190; Knave child, male child, B 715.

Knavish, *adj.* rude, H 205.

Knede, *v.* knead, A 4094; Kneden, *pp.* kneaded, R. 217.

Knet, Knette; see Knitte.

Knettinge, *s.* chain, B 5. p 1. 39.

Knightly, *adv.* bravely, L. 2085.

Knitte, *ger* to knit, I 47; 2 *pr. s. refl.* joinest (thyself), art in conjunction, B 307; Knit, *pp.* L. 89; conjoined, 5. 381; agreed, F 1230; wedded, F 986; joined in love, 4. 50; Knet, *pp.* R. 1397.

Knittinges, *pl.* connections, B 5. m 3. 18.

Knobbes, *pl.* large pimples, A 633.

Knoppe, *s.* bud, R. 1702.

Knotte, *s.* knot, gist of a tale, F 401, 407.

Knotteles, *adj.* without a knot, T. v. 769.

Knotty, *adj.* covered with knots, A 1977.

Knowe, *dat.* knee, T. ii. 1202.

Knowe, *v.* know, A 382; Knowestow, thou knowest, A 3156; Knewe, 2 *pt. s.* knewest, 10. 21; Knew, *pt. s.* A 240; Knewe, 1 *pt. s. subj.* could know, F 466; Knewe, *pt. pl.* D 1341; Knewe, *pt. s. subj.* were to know, R. 282; Knowen, *pp.* known, L. 421; shown, B 2702; Knowe, *pp.* known, L. 1382.

Knowing, *s.* knowledge, R. 1699; consciousness, 6. 114.

Knowinge, *adj.* conscious, B 3. p 11. 168; Knowinge with me, i. e. my witnesses, B 1. p 4. 50.

Knowlecheth, *pr. s.* acknowledges, B 2964.

Knowleching, *s.* knowing, knowledge, G 1432; cognition, B 5. p 5. 3.

Konning, *s.* cunning, skill, F 251.

Konninge, *adj.* skilful, T. i. 302.

Kukkow! *int.* cuckoo! 5. 499.

Kyken, *pr. pl.* peep, A 3841; *pp.* gazed, A 3445. Icel. *kikja*, Swed. *kika.*

Kyn, *pl.* kine, cows, B 4021.

Kyndely, *adj.* natural, 3. 761.

Kyndely, *adv.* naturally, by nature, 3. 778.

Kyte, *s.* kite (bird), A 1179.

Kythe, *v.* shew, shew plainly, display, F 748; declare to be, 7. 228; shew, 10. 63; *pr. s.* shews, L. 504; Kidde, *pt. s.* shewed, T. i. 208; Kid, *pp.* made known, L. 1028; known, 9. 46; Kythed, *pp.* shewn, G 1054; Kythe, *pr. s. subj.* may shew, B 636; Kyth, *imp. s.* shew, T. iv. 538; display, T. iv. 610; HF. 528; Kytheth, *imp. pl.* 4. 298.

## L.

Laas; see Las.

Labbe, *s.* blab, tell-tale, A 3509.

Labbing, *pres. part.* blabbing, babbling, E 2428.

Label, *s.* the narrow revolving rod or

rule on the front of the astrolabe, A. i. 22. 1.

Láborous, *adj.* laborious, D 1428.

Lacche, *s.* snare, springe, R. 1624.

Lace ; see Las.

Laced, *pp.* laced up, A 3267.

Lacerte, *s.* a fleshy muscle, A 2753.

Lache, *adj.* lazy, dull, B 4. p 3. 132.

Lachesse, *s.* laziness, I 720.

Lacinge, *s.* lacing ; *with layneres l.*, with the fastening up of straps, A 2504.

Lad, Ladde ; see Lede.

Lade, *ger.* to load, cover, T. ii. 1544.

Lady, *gen.* lady's, A 88, 695.

Laft, Lafte ; see Leve.

Lak, *s.* want, defect, lack, 3. 958 ; blame, dispraise, L. 298 *a ;* Lakke, *dat.* lack, want, 5. 87, 615 ; loss, F 430 ; *acc.* fault, E 2199.

Lake, *s.* a kind of fine white linen cloth, B 2048. The word probably was imported from the Low Countries, as *laken* is a common Dutch word for cloth or a sheet.

Lakken, *v.* find fault with, disparage, blame, R. 284 ; *pr. s.* lacks, B 1437; *pr. s. impers.* lacks ; *me lakketh,* I lack, 2. 105.

Lakking, *s.* lack, stint, R. 1147.

Lambish, *adj.* gentle as lambs, 9. 50.

Lampe, *s.* lamina, thin plate, G 764. F. *lame,* a thin plate, Lat. *lamina.*

Lange, *adj.* long (Northern), A 4175.

Langóur, *s.* weakness, 1. 7 ; slow starvation, R. 214 ; B 3597; languishing, R. 304 ; sickness, F 1101.

Languisshe, *v.* fail, HF. 2018.

Lapidaire, a treatise on precious stones, HF. 1352.

Lappe, *s.* fold, lappet, or edge of a garment, F 441, G 12 ; lap, A 686 ; a wrapper, E 585.

Lappeth, *pr. s.* enfolds, embraces, 4. 76.

Large, *adj.* large, A 472, 753 ; great, I 705 ; wide, broad, R. 1351 ; liberal, bounteous, R. 1168 ; *at his l.,* free (to speak or to be silent), A 2288 ; free to move, HF. 745 ; *at our l.,* free (to go anywhere), D 322.

Large, *adv.* liberally, 1. 174.

Largely, *adv.* fully, A 1908 ; in a wide sense, I 804.

Largenesse, *s.* liberality, I 1051.

Largesse, *s.* liberality, R. 1150; bounty, B 2465 ; liberal bestower, 1. 13.

Las, *s.* lace, snare, entanglement, L. 600 ; net, A 2389 ; Laas, lace, i. e. thick string, A 392 ; band, G 574 ; lace (i. e. laces), R. 843 ; Lace, snare, entanglement, 18. 50.

Lasse, *adj. comp.* less, R. 118 ; lesser,

A 1756; smaller, B 2262 ; less (time), A 3519 ; *lasse and more,* smaller and greater, i. e. all, E 67 ; *the lasse,* the lesser, R. 187.

Lasse, *adv.* less, 3. 927 ; *the las,* the less, 3. 675.

Last, *s. pl.* lasts, i. e. burdens, loads, B 1628. A.S. *hlæst,* a burden, load, a ship's freight.

Laste, *adj.* last, 10. 71 ; *atte l.,* at last, 3. 364 ; lastly, A 707.

Laste, *v.* endure, 4. 226 ; Last, *pr. s.* lasts, E 266 ; Laste, *pt. s.* lasted, B 1826 ; delayed, L. 791.

Late, *adj.* late ; *bet than never is late,* G 1410 ; *til now late,* till it was already late, 3. 45.

Late, -n, let ; see Lete.

Lathe, *s.* barn (Northern), HF. 2140 ; A 4088. Icel. *hlaða.*

Latis, *s.* lattice, T. ii. 615.

Latitude, *s.* (1) breadth, A. i. 21. 43 ; (2) the breadth of a climate, or a line along which such breadth is measured, A. ii. 39. 42 ; (3) *astronomical,* the angular distance of any body from the ecliptic, measured along a great circle at right angles to the ecliptic, A. pr. 110 ; (4) *terrestrial,* the distance of a place N. or S. of the equator, E 1797.

Latoun, *s.* latten, a compound metal, like pinchbeck, containing chiefly copper and zinc, A 699.

Latrede, *adj.* tardy, dawdling, I 718. A.S. *latræde.*

Latter, *adv.* more slowly, I 971.

Laude, *s.* praise, honour, HF. 1575 ; *pl.* lauds, a service held at 2 or 3 A.M., A 3655.

Laughe, *v.* laugh, A 474 ; Laugheth of, smiles on account of, A 1494; Lough, *strong pt. s.* laughed, R. 248 ; Laughede, *weak pt. pl.* R. 863.

Launce, *v.* rear, HF. 946.

Launcegay, *s.* a kind of lance, B 1942, 2011. Originally of Moorish origin.

Launcheth, *pr. s.* pushes, lets slide, D 2145.

Launde, *s.* a grassy clearing (called *dale* in 5. 327), 5. 302 ; glade, plain surrounded by trees, A 1691.

Laure, *s.* laurel-tree, HF. 1107.

Laureat, *adj.* crowned with laurel, B 3886, E 31.

Laurer, *s.* laurel-tree, 5. 182.

Laurer-crouned, laurel-crowned, 7. 43.

Lauriol, *s.* spurge-laurel, *Daphne Laureola,* B 4153.

**Laus,** *adj.* loose, B 4. p 6. 147.

**Laven,** *ger.* to exhaust, B 4. p 6. 14; **Laved,** *pp.* drawn up, B 3. m 12. 125. A. S. *lafian.*

**Lavender,** *s.* laundress, L. 358.

**Laverokkes,** *pl.* sky-larks, R. 662.

**Lavours,** *pt.* basins, D 287.

**Laxatif,** *adj. as s.* looseness, A 2736; *s.* laxative, B 4133.

**Lay** (1), *s.* song, lay, B 1959; **Layes,** *pl.* songs, F 710, 712, 947.

**Lay** (2), *s.* law; *hence* belief, faith, T. i. 340; creed, L. 336.

**Layneres,** *pl.* straps, thongs, A 2504. O.F. *laniere*; mod. E. *lanyard.*

**Layser,** *s.* leisure, T. ii. 227.

**Lazar,** *s.* leper, A 242.

**Leche,** *s.* physician, A 3904, C 916.

**Lechecraft,** *s.* art of medicine, T. iv. 436; skill of a physician, A 2745.

**Lecher,** *s.* healer, B 4. p 6. 238.

**Lechour,** *s.* lecher, B 1935.

**Lede,** *v.* lead, T. i. 259; carry, T. iv. 1514; lead, take, L. 2021; draw, R. 1608; govern, B 434; lead (his life), R. 1321; lead, R. 1129; Lede, *ger.* to lead, spend, F 744; to guide, R. 400; Let, *pr. s.* leads, T. ii. 882; Ladde, *pt. s.* led, R. 581; brought, 7. 39; carried, L. 114; conducted, B 3747; continued, R. 216; Ladden, *pt. pl.* led, R. 1310; Ledden, *pt. pl.* 9. 2; Ladde, *pt. pl.* B 3920; Lad, *pp.* led, L. 1108, 1948; brought, A 2620; conducted, A 4402; carried, L. 74.

**Leden,** *adj.* leaden, G 728.

**Ledene,** *s.* (*dat.*) language, talk, F 435, 478.

**Leed,** *s.* lead (metal), HF. 739, 1448, 1648; a copper, or caldron, A 202.

**Leef,** *adj.* lief, A 1837; dear, R. 103; precious, G 1467; lief, pleasing, T. v. 1738; pleasant, R. 1688; *yow so leef,* so desired by you, C 760; *that leef me were,* which I should like, HF. 1999; Leve, *def.* dear (one), A 3393; *vocative,* HF. 816; Lefe, *adj. fem. voc.* HF. 1827; Leve, *pl.* dear, T. iv. 82, v. 592.

**Leef,** *adj. as s.,* what is pleasant; *for l. ne looth,* for weal nor for woe, L. 1639; what is dear (to him), T. iv. 1585; beloved one, lover, lady-love, T. iii. 3.

**Leef,** *s.* leaf, L. 72; Leves, *pl.* leaves, R. 56; (of a book), D 790.

**Leefful;** see Leveful.

**Leefsel,** *s.* the 'bush' or leafy bundle (as a sign), at a tavern-door, I 411; Levesel, arbour of leaves, A 4060. Cf. Swed. *löfsal,* a hut made of green boughs.

**Leek,** *s.* leek, R. 212; a thing of no value, G 795.

**Leen,** *imp. s. of* Lene.

**Leep** (léép), *pt. s. of* Lèpe.

**Lees** (lèès), *s.* leash, G 19; snare, 7. 233.

**Lees,** *adj.* untrue, R. 8.

**Lees** (lèès), *s.* deceit, fraud; *a shrewed lees,* a wicked fraud, L. 1545; *vithouten lees,* without deceit, verily, HF. 1464.

**Lees,** *pt. s. of* Lese.

**Leeste,** *adj. sup.* least, B 2513; *atte l. weye,* at the very least, A 1121.

**Leet,** *pt. s. of* Lete.

**Lef,** *imp. s. of* Leve (leave).

**Lefe,** *adj. fem. voc.* dear, HF. 1827.

**Leful;** see Leveful.

**Legge, -n ;** see Leye, *v.*

**Leide,** 1 *pt. s. of* Leye.

**Leigh,** *pt. s. of* Lye (2).

**Lekes,** *pl.* leeks, A 634.

**Lemes,** *pl.* flames, B 4120. A.S. *lēoma.*

**Lemman,** *s. masc.* (male) lover, sweetheart, A 4240, 4247; *fem.* (female) lover, lady-love, A 3278, 3280; concubines, I 903.

**Lendes,** *pl.* loins, A 3237, 3304. A.S. *lenden,* pl. *lendenu.*

**Lene,** *adj.* lean, thin, R. 218, 444; weak, T. ii. 132.

**Lene,** *ger.* to lend, give, A 611; Lene, *imp. s.* lend, B 1376; Leen, *imp. s.* give, A 3082. A.S. *lǣnan.*

**Lene,** *v.* lean, incline, B 2638.

**Leng,** *adv.* longer; *ever l. the wers,* the worse, the longer it lasts, A 3872.

**Lenger,** *adj.* longer, L. 450, 2025.

**Lenger,** *adv.* longer, B 374, 2122, 3709; *ever the l.,* the longer, the more, 7. 129; *ever l. the more,* E 687.

**Lengest,** *adv. sup.* longest, 5. 549.

**Lente,** *s.* Lent-season, D 543.

**Lenvoy,** *s.* l'envoy, i. e. the epilogue or postscript addressed to the hearers or readers, E 1177 (*rubric*).

**Leonesse,** *s.* lioness, L. 805.

**Leonyn,** *adj.* lionlike, B 3836.

**Leos,** *s.* people, G 103, 106. Gk. λεώς.

**Leoun,** *s.* lion, L. 627, 829 : Léon. the sign Leo, F 265.

**Lepart,** *s.* leopard, A 2186; Libardes, *pl.* R. 894.

**Lepe,** *v.* run, A 4378; leap, L. 2008; Lepe up, *v.* leap up, HF. 2150; Léép, *pt. s.* leapt, A 2687.

**Lere,** *s.* flesh, skin, B 2047. Properly the muscles, especially the muscles of the thigh, which special sense is perfectly suitable here. A.S. *lira,* flesh, muscle.

**Lere,** *ger.* (1) to teach, 7. 98; *v.* teach, T. iv.

441; (2) to learn, T. v. 161; Lere, *ger.* to learn, find out, D 909; Lere, *pr. pl.* (1) teach, 5. 25; (2) learn, F 104; Lered, *pp.* (2) learnt, T. iii. 406.

**Lered,** *adj.* instructed, learned, C 283; A.S. *lǣred.*

**Lerne,** *v.* learn, A 308, D 994; Lerned of, taught by, G 748. (Chaucer here uses the word wrongly, as in mod. provincial English.)

**Lese,** *s. dat.* pasture, T. ii. 752; HF. 1768. A.S. *lǣs.*

**Lese,** *v.* lose, A 1215, 1290; Lese me, *v.* lose myself, be lost, 5. 147; Lees, *pt. s.* lost, L. 945; Leseth, *imp. pl.* B 19; Loren, *pp.* lost, L. 1048; Lorn, *pp.* lost, T. i. 373, iii. 1076, iv. 1613; forlorn, wasted, R. 366.

**Lesing,** *s.* falsehood, lie, HF. 2089; G 479; Lesinges, *pl.* lies, deceits, R. 2; lying reports, HF. 2123.

**Lesinge,** *s.* loss, I 1056; Lesing, A 1707; *for lesinge,* for fear of losing, B 3750.

**Lessoun,** *s.* lesson, lection, A 709.

**Lest,** *s.* pleasure, 3. 908; delight, A 132; desire, E 619; inclination, HF. 287; Lestes, *pl.* desires, HF. 1738. A Kentish form; for *lust.*

**Lest,** *pr. s. impers.* (it) pleases, L. 1703; (it) pleases (me), D 360; Thee lest, it pleases thee, 5. 114; Lesteth, (it) pleases, L. 480 *a*; Leste, *pt. s. impers.* (it) pleased, T. v. 517; *pers.* was pleased, T. iii. 452; Leste, *pr. s. subj.* (it) may please, L. 1338; As yow leste, as it may please you, L. 449; (it) would please, F 380; Her leste, it should please her, 5. 551. Kentish forms.

**Leste,** *adj. superl.* least, T. i. 281; *at the l.,* at least, 3. 973; *atte l.,* at least, B 38; Leste, *as s.,* the least one, 3. 283; *at the leeste weye,* at any rate, E 966.

**Let,** *pr. s. of* Lede.

**Lete,** *v.* let, B 3524; let, leave, A 1335; give up, let go, T. v. 1688; forsake, T. iv. 1199; let alone, leave, D 1276; quit, 1. 72; give up, lose, G 406; omit, depart from, 5. 391; Lete of, *ger.* to leave off, 18. 52; Leten, *v.* let, L. 2107; give up, R. 1690; forsake, T. iv. 1556; Leten, *ger.* to let go, T. i. 262; Late, *v.* let, T. iii. 693; Laten, *v.* let, A 3326; Lete, 1 *pr. s.* leave, 7. 45; Let, *pr. s.* lets go, repels, 5. 151; Lat, *pr. s.* lets, permits, T. iv. 200; Lete, 2 *pr. pl.* abandon, B 2505; Léét, *pt. s.* let, A 128; let go, A 1206; allowed, HF. 243; left off, A 3311; left, A 508; caused, permitted, B 373; caused, B 2194;

caused (to be), B 959; *leet . . . fecche,* commanded (men) to fetch, D 2064; *leet don cryen,* caused to be proclaimed, F 45; *leet make,* caused to be made, B 3349; *leet binde,* caused to be bound, B 1810; Let, *pt. s.* caused, L. 2624; *let calle,* caused to be called, L. 1684; let, 5. 279; Lete, *pt. pl.* let, B 3898; Lete, *pt. s. subj.* were to let, T. iii. 1762; Leet, *imp. s.* let, C 731; Lat, *imp. s.* let, 1. 79, 84; let alone, give up, T. ii. 1500; Lat be, let be, do away with, A 840; let me alone, A 3285; give up, HF. 992; Lat do, cause, C 173; Lat take, take, G 1254, H 175; Lat see, let us see, A 831; Lat goon, let slip (the dogs), L. 1213; Laten blood, *pp.* let blood, A 4346. A.S. *lǣtan.*

**Lette,** *s.* hindrance, T. i. 361; delay, T. iii. 235.

**Lette,** *v.* hinder, T. ii. 732; prevent, L. 732; oppose, stay, B 3306; cause delay, B 1117; wait, B 1440; tarry, B 4224; stop, desist, B 4279; cease, R. 279; Letten, *ger.* to put obstacles in the way (of), to decline (from), A 1317; Let, *pr. s.* prevents, B 3, p 10. 162; Lette, *pr. s. subj.; lette him no man, god forbede,* God forbid that any should hinder him, T. iii. 515; Letted, *pt. s.* hindered, A 1891; was hindered, B 2591; Letteth, *imp. pl.* hesitate, T. ii. 1136.

**Lette-game,** *s.* 'let-game,' one who hinders sport, T. iii. 527.

**Lettres,** *pl.* letters, (*also as sing.* a letter), B 736; 5. 19.

**Lettrure,** *s.* learning, B 3486; book-lore, B 3686.

**Letuarie,** *s.* electuary, remedy, C 307; *pl.* electuaries, A 426. Lat. *electuarium.*

**Leve,** dear; see **Leef.**

**Leve,** *s.* leave, B 1637, D 908; permission, L 2281; *bisyde hir leve,* without her leave, T. iii. 622.

**Leve** (1), *v.* leave, E 250; let alone, G 714; let go, 3. 1111; go away, 5. 153; leave alone, T. i. 688; *ger.* to leave off, T. i. 686; to forsake, G 287; Leve, 1 *pr. s.* leave, 2. 50; Leveth, *pr. s.* remains, 3. 701; Lafte, 1 *pt. s.* left, C 762; Lefte, left off, F 670; Laften, *pt. pl.* L. 168; Left, *pp.* omitted, I 231; Laft, *pp.* left, L. 1260; Leef, *imp. s.* leave, T. iv. 852; leave (it) alone, T. v. 1518; Lef, *imp. s.* forego, D 2089; Leve, *imp. s.* leave, A 1614; Leveth, *imp. pl.* leave, C 659. A.S. *lǣfan.*

**Leve** (2), *v.* believe, 5. 496; L. 10; *ger.* to be believed, HF. 708; Levestow, believest thou, G 212; Leveth, *imp. pl.* believe, 6. 88. A.S. *léfan, lýfan.*

**Leve** (3) *ger.* to allow, L. 2280; *god leve,* God grant, L. 2083, 2086. A. S. *léfan, lýfan.*

**Leveful,** *adj.* allowable, A 3912; permissible, D 37; Leefful, allowable, I 41, 917; Leful, permissible, T. iii. 1020.

**Levene,** *s.* flash of lightning, D 276.

**Lever,** *adj. comp.* liefer, rather; *me were lever,* I had rather, T. i. 1034, iii. 574; *me nis lever,* L. 191; *thee were l.,* thou hadst rather, B 2339; *him was l.,* A 293; *him were l.,* L. 2413; *have I l.,* I would rather, T. ii. 471; F 1360; *hadde I l.,* D 168; *hath l.,* F 692; *hadde l.,* L. 1536; *had hir l.,* she would rather, E 444; *him had be l.,* he would rather, A 3541.

**Levesel;** see Leefsel.

**Levest,** *sup.* dearest, most desirable, HF. 87.

**Lewed,** *adj.* ignorant, A 502, 574; unlearned, C 283; unskilled, rude, HF. 1096; wicked, foolish, F 1494; wanton, E 2129. A.S. *léwed.*

**Lewedly,** *adv.* simply, HF. 866; ignorantly, B 47; ill, G 430.

**Lewednesse,** *s.* ignorance, ignorant behaviour, D 1928.

**Ley,** lied; *pt. s. of* Lye.

**Leye,** *v.* lay, 4. 205; lay, cause to lie, T. iii. 659; lay a wager, HF. 674; pledge, T. iii. 1605; Leyn, *ger.* to lay up, to hoard, R. 184; Leggen, *ger.* to lay, A 3269; Legge, *v.* A 3937; Leyth, *pr. s.* A 4229; Leith, *pr. s.* D 2138; Leye, 1 *pr. pl.* lay out, expend, G 783; Leyn, *pr. pl.* lay, H 222; Leyde, *pt. s.* 3. 394; Leyde, 2 *pt. pl.* L. 2501; Leyden forth, *pt. pl.* brought forward, B 213; Leyd, *pp.* laid, A 3262; placed, R. 1184; overlaid, R. 1076; *I was leyd,* I had laid myself down, L. 208; Leyd, *pp.* laid, A 81; fixed, 3. 1146; set, 3. 1036; Ley on, lay on, A 2558.

**Leyser,** *s.* leisure, R. 462; A 1188; deliberation, B 2766; opportunity, A 3293.

**Leyt,** *s.* flame (of a candle), I 954. A.S. *léget, lýget,* M.E. *leit,* lightning.

**Libardes,** *pl.* leopards, R. 894.

**Libel,** *s.* written declaration, D 1595.

**Licentiat,** *adj.* one licensed by the pope to hear confessions, independently of the local ordinaries, A 220.

**Liche,** *adj.* like, R. 1073; similar, 7. 76; *it liche,* like it, F 62.

**Liche,** *adv.* alike, HF. 10.

**Liche-wake,** *s.* watch over a corpse, A 2958.

**Licorycë,** *s.* liquorice, R. 1368.

**Licóur,** *s.* moisture, A 3; liquor, T iv. 520; Licour, juice, C 452.

**Lief,** *adj.* dear, A 3501; Lief to, glad to, given to, A 3510; cherished, E 479; *goode leef my wyf,* my dear good wife, B 3084; *hadde as lief,* would as soon, D 1574; *as s.* dear one, B 4069.

**Lift,** *adj.* left (said of the left hand or side); R. 163.

**Lige,** *adj.* liege, C 337; Lige man, vassal, L. 379; Liges, *s. pl.* vassals, L. 382; *pl.* subjects, B 240. F. *lige,* from O.H.G. *ledic* (G. *ledig*), free. A *liege* lord was a *free* lord; in course of time his subjects were called *lieges,* from confusion with Lat. *ligare,* to bind.

**Ligeaunce,** *s.* allegiance, B 895.

**Liggen,** *v.* lie, B 2101; Ligginge, *pres. pt.* lying, T. iv. 29; Ligging, A 1011.

**Light,** *adj.* lightsome, joyous, R. 77; 3. 1175; active, nimble, R. 832; easy, 3. 526; wearing but few clothes (*also,* fickle), 21. 20; Lighte, *pl.* light (of weight), 5. 188; easy, A. pr. 36.

**Lighte,** *adv.* brilliantly, R. 1109.

**Lighte,** *ger.* (1) to make light, rejoice, T. v. 634; to render cheerful, T. i. 293; alleviate, T. iii. 1082; (2) *ger.* to feel light, to be glad, F 396, 914; Lighte, *pt. s.* lighted; *either in the sense* (1) lightened, made light, made happy, *or* (2) illuminated, B 1661.

**Lighte,** *v.* alight, descend, HF. 508; *pt. s.* alighted, B 786.

**Lighten,** *v.* shine, I 1037; Lighted, *pp.* brightened, 1.74; Light, *pp.* illuminated, L. 2506; Lighte, *imp. s.* illumine, G 71.

**Lightly,** *adv.* lightly, F 390; readily, 4. 205; quickly, I 534; easily, T. ii. 289; carelessly, I 1023; joyfully, A 1870.

**Lightned,** *pp.* enlightened, illuminated, F 1050.

**Lightnesse** (1), *s.* brightness, 5. 263.

**Lightnesse** (2), *s.* agility, A 3383.

**Lightsom.** *adj.* gay, R. 936.

**Ligne,** *s.* line, T. v. 1481.

**Ligne-aloes,** wood of the aloe, T. iv. 1137. (Properly a compound, i. e. *ligne-aloes*; where *aloes* is a plural form.)

**Likerous,** *adj.* lecherous, H 189; wanton, A 3244, 3345; E 214; gluttonous, C 540; greedy after indulgence, D 466; eager, F 1119; very vile (Lat. *nequissimi*), B 3. p 4. 31.

**Likerousnesse,** *s.* lecherousness, D 611; licentiousness, I 430; greediness, I 377; eagerness, I 741; appetite, C 84.

**Lilting-horne,** s. horn to be played for a lilt, HF. 1223.

**Limaille** ; see **Lymaille.**

**Lime,** s. limb, 3. 499 ; Limes, pl. R. 830.

**Limitacioun,** s. limit, D 877.

**Limitour,** s. limitor, a friar licensed to beg for alms within a certain limit, A 209, D 874.

**Linage,** s. lineage, race, A 1110 ; family, D 1135 ; noble family, R. 258 ; high birth, B 3441 ; kinsfolk, B 2192 ; kindred, B 999 ; consanguinity, L. 2602.

**Lind,** s. lime-tree, A 2922.

**Lipsed,** pt. s. lisped, A 264.

**Lisse,** s. comfort, T. v. 550 ; joy, T. iii. 343 ; assuaging, HF. 220 ; solace, 3. 1040 ; alleviation, F 1238. A.S. liss.

**Lissen,** v. alleviate, T. i. 702 ; soothe, 6. 6 ; Lissed, pp. relieved, F 1170. A.S. lissian.

**List** (1), s. pleasure, T. iii. 1303 ; will, D 633.

**List** (2), s. ear, D 634. A.S. hlyst.

**List,** pr. s. impers. it pleases (usually with dat.), A 1021, B 521 ; me list right evel, I was in no mind to, 3. 239 ; you list, it pleases you, 11. 77 ; List, pr. s. pers. is pleased, pleases, T. i. 518, 797 ; wishes, A 3176 ; Listeth, pr. s. impers. (it) pleases, T. ii. 700 ; pers. pleases, is pleased, HF. 511 ; likes, F 689 ; Listen, 2 pr. pl. are pleased, T. iii. 1810 ; Listen, pr. pl. list, choose, B 2234 ; Listen trete, choose to write, L. 575 ; Liste, pt. s. impers. (it pleased), L. 332 ; her liste, it pleased her, she cared, 7. 190 ; him liste, he wanted, 4. 92 ; hem liste, (it) pleased them, F 851. A.S. lystan.

**Listes,** pl. in sing. sense, lists, a place enclosed for tournaments, A 63.

**Listes,** s. pl. wiles ; in his l., by means of his wiles, 1. 85.

**Listeth,** imp. pl. listen ye, B 1902.

**Litarge,** s. litharge, ointment prepared from protoxide of lead, A 629 ; protoxide of lead, G 775.

**Litargie,** s. lethargy, B 1. p 2. 22.

**Lite,** adj. little, I 295 ; as s., a little, T. i. 291 ; adv. little, T. iv. 1330.

**Litestere,** s. dyer, 9. 17. Icel. lita, to dye.

**Lith,** s. limb (viz. of herself), B 4065. A.S. lið.

**Litherly,** adv. ill, A 3299. A.S. lyðer, evil.

**Livere** (1), s. liver, D 1839.

**Livere** (2), s. liver (one who lives), B 1024.

**Liveree,** s. livery, A 363.

**Livinge,** s. life-time, 7. 188 ; manner of life, C 107 ; state of life, G 322.

**Lixt,** liest ; see **Lye** (2).

**Lode,** s. load, A 2918.

**Lodemenage,** s. pilotage, A 403. Lodemanage is the hire of a pilot, for conducting a ship from one place to another.

**Lodesmen,** s. pl. pilots, L. 1488.

**Lode-sterre,** s. polar star, lodestar, A 2059.

**Lofte,** dat. upper room, L. 2709 ; on lofte, in the air, HF. 1727 ; aloft, B 277.

**Logge,** s. resting-place, B 4043.

**Logging,** s. lodging, B 4185.

**Loke,** v. (weak) lock up, D 317.

**Loken,** ger. to look, A 1783 ; v. behold, R. R. 812 ; Loked, pt. s. looked, A 289 ; Lokeden, pt. pl. L. 1972 ; imp. s. see, HF. 893 ; take heed, D 1587 ; Loke he, let him take heed, I 134 ; Loketh, imp. pl. behold, G 1329 ; search ye, C 578.

**Loken,** pp. of strong verb (Louken), locked up, B 4065.

**Loking,** s. look, gaze, 3. 870 ; countenance, B 2332 ; glance, L. 240 ; glance (of the eye), A 2171 ; aspect, 4. 51 ; examining, 5. 110 ; appearance, R. 290 ; looks, F 285.

**Lokkes,** pl. locks of hair, A 81, 677.

**Loller,** s. a loller, a lollard, B 1173. Loller (one who is sluggish) was confused with the name Lollard.

**Lomb,** s. lamb, L. 1798.

**Lond,** s. land, A 194, 400, 579 ; country, B 3548 ; upon lond, in the country, A 702.

**Lone,** s. dat. loan, B 1485 ; gift, grace, D 1861.

**Long,** prep. ; the phrase wher-on . . long = long on wher, along of what, G 930 ; Long on, along of, because of, G 922.

**Long,** adj. (before a vowel), tall, R. 817 ; pl. tall, high, R. 1384 ; long, A 93.

**Longe,** adv. long, A 286 ; for a long time, L. 2261.

**Longe** (1), v. desire, long for, L. 2260 ; yearn, T. ii. 546 ; Longen (2), v. belong, A 2278 ; pr. s. belongs, R. 754 ; (it) concerns, T. ii. 312 ; pr. pl. belong, F 1131 ; pt. s. befitted, R. 1222 ; Longing for, suitable for, F 39.

**Longes,** pl. lungs, A 2752.

**Longitude,** s. the distance between two given meridians, A. ii. 39. 19 ; the length or extent of a 'climate,' in a direction parallel to the equator, or rather a line along which to measure this length ; A. ii. 39. 28. The longitude of a star is measured along the zodiac ; that of a town, from a fixed meridian.

**Loos,** *s.* praise, renown, B 2834, 3036. O.F. *los.*

**Loos,** *adj.* loose, A 4064, 4138; Lous, free, HF. 1286.

**Looth** (lòòth), *adj.* loath, odious, A 486; hateful, A 3393; *me were l.,* it would displease me, B 91; *as s.,* what is hateful, misery, L. 1639.

**Loothly,** *adj.* hideous, D 1100.

**Loppe,** *s.* a spider, A. i. 3. 6.

**Loppewebbe,** *s.* cobweb, A. i. 21. 3.

**Lordeth,** *pr. s.,* rules over, 4. 166.

**Lordings,** *s. pl.* sirs, C 329, 573.

**Lore,** *s.* teaching, L. 2450; advice, T. i. 1090; lesson, T. i. 645, 754; instruction, B 342; learning, B 761; study, G 842; profit, 5. 15; doctrine, A 527. A.S. *lār.*

**Lore,** *pp. of* Lese.

**Lorel,** *s.* worthless man, abandoned wretch, D 273.

**Loren,** *pp. of* Lese.

**Lorer,** *s.* laurel, R. 1379.

**Lorn,** *pp. of* Lese.

**Los** (1), *s.* loss, A 2543; occasion of perdition, D 720.

**Los** (2), *s.* praise, renown, fame, L. 1514; report, L. 1424; *til her loses,* in praise of them, HF. 1688. O.F. *los.*

**Losengere,** *s.* flatterer, R. 1050; *pl.* R. 1056. O.F. *losengeur.*

**Losengerie,** *s.* flattery, I 613.

**Losenges,** *pl.* lozenges, HF. 1317; small diamond-shaped shields, R. 893.

**Lost,** *s.* loss, B 2. p 4. 185.

**Loth,** *adj.* loath, 3. 8; displeasing, R. 233.

**Lother,** *adj. comp.* more hateful, L. 191.

**Lothest,** *adj. superl.* most loath, F 1313.

**Lotinge,** *pres. part.* lurking, G 186. A.S. *lutian,* to lurk.

**Loude,** *adv.* loudly, A 171.

**Lough,** *pt. s. of* Laughe.

**Louke,** *s.* accomplice, A 4415.

**Loured,** *pp.* frowned, HF. 409.

**Lous,** *adj.* loose, free, HF. 1286.

**Lousy,** *adj.* full of lice, miserable, D 1467.

**Loute,** *v.* bow, do obeisance, T. iii. 683; *ger.* to bow down, B 3352; *1 pt. s.* stooped, bent, R. 1554.

**Love,** *s.* love, A 475; *fem.* lady-love, 4. 31; *voc.* O my love, A 672; *masc.* lover, L. 862.

**Lovedayes,** *pl.* days for settling disputes by arbitration, A 258; HF. 695.

**Love-drury,** *s.* affection, B 2085. The latter part of the word is O.F. *drurie, druerie,* love, passion.

**Loveknotte,** *s.* looped ornament, A 197.

**Loves,** *s. pl.* loaves, B 503.

**Lovyere,** *s.* lover, A 80.

**Lowenesse,** *s.* lowliness, I 1080.

**Lowly,** *adj.* humble, A 99.

**Luce,** *s.* luce, pike, A 350.

**Lucre,** *s.* lucre, gain, G 1402; *lucre of vilanye* = vile gain, B 1681.

**Lufsom,** *adj.* lovely, T. v. 911; lovable, T. v. 465.

**Lulleth,** *pr. s.* lulls, soothes, B 839.

**Luna,** *s.* the moon, G 826; a name for silver, G 1440.

**Lunárie,** *s.* lunary, moon-wort, G 800.

**Lure,** *s.* a hawk's lure, D 1340; *pl.* enticements, L. 1371.

**Lussheburghes,** *pl.* spurious coin, B 3152. Named from the town of *Luxembourg.*

**Lust,** *s.* desire, R. 1653; amusement, R. 1287; pleasure, R. 616; delight, 1. 106; will, desire, wish, B 188; interest in a story, F 402; *pl.* delights, 3. 581. A.S. *lust.*

**Lusteth,** *pr. s. impers.* (it) pleases, L. 996; Lust, *pr. s. pers.* pleases, E 1344; *impers.* (it) pleases, E 322; Luste, *pt. s. pers.* desired, G 1344; Luste, *pt. s. impers.* it pleased, G 1235.

**Lustier,** more joyous, G 1345.

**Lustihede,** *s.* cheerfulness, 3. 27; delight, H 274; enjoyment, F 288; vigour, L. 1530.

**Lustily,** *adv.* gaily, merrily, R. 1319.

**Lustinesse,** *s.* pleasure, jollity, A 1939; vigour, R. 1282.

**Lusty,** *adj.* pleasant, gay, A 80; jocund, F 272; lusty, H 41; joyous, R. 581; happy, R. 1303; joyful, A 1513; vigorous, L. 1038.

**Luxures,** *s. pl.* lusts, B 3. p 7. 12.

**Luxurie,** *s.* lechery, B 925, C 484.

**Lyard,** *adj.* grey, D 1563.

**Lycorys,** *s.* liquorice, A 3690.

**Lye** (1), *v.* lie, remain, 10. 52; Lye, *ger.* to lodge, D 1780; Lye . . by, *v.* lie beside, B 3470; Lye upright, lie on one's back, lie dead, R. 1604; Lystow, thou liest, H 276; Lyth, *pr. s.* lies, is, remains, R. 782; lies, 3. 146, 181; (he) lies, B 634; (that) lies, D 1829; remains, resides, B 3654; lies (dead), 3. 143; Lyth therto, belongs here, is needed, 3. 527; Lay, *1 pt. s.* lodged, A 20; was, A 538; Laye, *pt. s. subj.* would lie, T. iv. 1560; Ly, *imp. s.* T. ii. 953.

**Lye** (2), *v.* tell lies, lie, A 763; Lixt, *2 2 pr. s.* liest, D 1618, 1761; Ley, *strong pt. s.* lied, T. ii. 1077; Lyed, *weak pt. s.* lied, A 659. A.S. *lēogan.*

**Lye** (3), *v.* blaze, D 1142. A.S. *lȳge, s.* flame.

**Lyer,** *s.* liar, B 2256.

**Lyes,** *s. pl.* lees, dregs, HF. 2130.

**Lyes,** *pl.* (1) lees ; *or* (2) lies, D 302. Perhaps a double meaning is intended.

**Lyf,** *s.* life, A 71, 2776 ; Lyves, *gen.* life's, 6. 60 ; of my life, 3. 920 ; Our present worldes lyves space, the space of our present life in the world, 5. 53 ; Lyves day, lifetime, L. 1624 ; Lyve, *dat.* L. 59 ; On lyve, alive, L. 1792 ; in his time, D 43 ; Upon lyve, alive, T. ii. 1030 ; Of lyve, out of life, T. v. 1561 ; Bringe of lyve, cause to die, T. ii. 1608 ; My lyve, in my life, T. ii. 205 ; By thy lyf, during thy life, B 1621 ; Thy lyf, during thy lifetime, 17. 19 ; His lyve, in his life, L. 1099 ; Hir lyve, in their life, D 392 ; Lyves, *pl.* B 3284.

**Lyflode,** *s.* means of living, I 685. Mod.E. *livelihood.*

**Lyfly,** *adv.* in a lifelike way, A 2087.

**Lyke,** *v.* please, T. i. 431 ; *ger.* HF. 860 ; to be liked, R. 1357 ; Lyketh, *pr. s.* pleases, E 1031 ; *impers.* (it) pleases, E 311, 845 ; *us l. yow,* it pleases us with respect to you, E 106 ; Lyke, *pr. s. subj.* may please, D 1278 ; *thee l. nat,* it may not please you, L. 490 ; Lyked, *pt. s. impers.* pleased, R. 1312.

**Lyking,** *s.* pleasure, C 455; delight, B 3499.

**Lyking,** *adj.* pleasing, R. 868 ; pleasant, R. 1416 ; thriving, R. 1564.

**Lyklihed,** *s. dat.* likelihood, E 448.

**Lyklinesse,** *s.* probability, 22. 15.

**Lykly,** *adj.* likely, like, 16. 32.

**Lykne,** 1 *pr. s.* compare, 3. 636

**Lyknesse,** *s.* parable, A 2842.

**Lym,** *s.* lime, F 1149 ; quicklime, L. 649.

**Lymaille,** *s.* filings of any metal, G 1162 ; Lymail, G 1164 ; Limaille, G 853.

**Lyme,** *ger.* to cover with birdlime, T. i. 353.

**Lymere,** *s.* hound held in leash, 3. 365.

**Lymrod,** *s.* lime-twig, B 3574.

**Lyne,** *s.* line, T. i. 1068 ; fishing-line, 4. 242 ; line of descent, D 1135 ; *as lyne right,* straight as a line, T. iii. 228.

**Lyned,** *pp.* lined, A 440.

**Lyne-right,** *adj.* in an exact line, exactly in a line with, A. i. 21. 31.

**Lyoun,** *s.* lion, T. iii. 1780 ; v. 830 ; Lyouns, *pl.* R. 894. See Leoun.

**Lyst,** 2 *pr. s.* liest, reclinest, T. ii. 991 ; Lystow, liest thou, H 276.

**Lytargye,** *s.* lethargy, T. i. 730.

**Lyte,** *adj.* small, little, R. 532 ; slight, I 689 ; Lyte, *s.* a little, L. 29, 535 ; Lyte, *pl.* little, A 494.

**Lyte,** *adv.* little, 3. 884 ; a little, E 935 ; in a small degree, G 632, 699 ; *l. and l.,* by little and little, D 2235.

**Lythe,** *adj.* easy, soft, HF. 118.

**Lythe,** *ger.* to alleviate, cheer, T. iv. 754.

**Lyve** ; see **Lyf.**

**Lyvely,** *adv.* in a lively way, 3. 905.

**Lyves;** see **Lyf.**

**Lyves,** *adv.* in life ; hence, *as adj.* living, alive, T. iv. 252 ; *no lyves creature,* no living creature, T. iii. 13.

## M.

**M',** *sometimes put for* Me (before a vowel); *as in* masterte *for* me asterte.

**Ma fey,** my faith ! T. iii. 52.

**Maad;** *pp. of* Make.

**Maat,** *adj.* dejected, B 2. p 4. 42.

**Mad,** *pp.* made, L. 286. See **Make.**

**Madde,** *v.* go mad, 4. 253 ; *ger.* to be furious, T. i. 479.

**Mader,** *s.* madder, 9. 17.

**Magik,** *s.* magic, A 416.

**Magistrat,** *s.* magistracy, B 3. p 4. 26.

**Maheym,** *s.* maiming, I 625. Mod. E. *maim.*

**Maille,** *s.* mail, ringed armour, E 1202.

**Maister,** *s.* master, B 1627 ; doctor, D 2184 ; doctor (of divinity), D 1638 ; (as a term of address), 17. 1 ; one in authority, A 261.

**Maisterful,** *adj.* masterful, T. ii. 756.

**Maister-strete,** *s.* main street, L. 1965.

**Maister-temple,** *s.* chief temple, L. 1016.

**Maister-toun,** *s.* chief town, L. 1591.

**Maister-tour,** *s.* chief tower, F 226.

**Maistow,** mayest thou, HF. 699.

**Maistresse,** *s.* mistress, L. 88 ; governess, C 106.

**Maistrye,** *s.* mastery, great skill, A 3383 ; mastery, F 747, 764 ; control, B 3689, C 58 ; superiority ; *for the maistrye,* as regards authority, A 165 ; victory, B 3582 ; specimen of skill, HF. 1074 ; art, elegance, R. 842 ; a masterly operation (cf. F. *coup de maître*), G 1060.

**Majestee,** *s.* ; *his real majestee* = his royal majesty, i. e. high treason, B 1. p 4. 162.

**Make,** *s.* mate, D 270, H 186 ; equal, match, A 2556 ; wedded companion, wife, B 700; bride, E 1882 ; husband, D 85.

**Make,** *v.* make, A 184 ; compose, write, L. 69 ; *ger.* to compose, to write (about), R. 41 ; pretend to, counterfeit, T. ii. 1522 ; cause (it), T. ii. 959 ; Makestow,

2 *pr. s.* B 371 ; Maketh, *pr. s.* causes, A 3035 ; Maken, *pr. pl.* make, utter, A 9 ; Maked, *pt. s.* made, A 526 ; Makeden, *pt. pl.* T. iv. 121 ; Made, *pt. s. subj.* may have made, 4. 227 ; Made . . . broght, caused to be brought, HF. 155 ; Maked, *pp.* made, A 1247 ; composed, 5. 677 ; Maad, *pp.* made, A 394 ; Mad, *pp.* 3. 415.

**Makelees,** *adj.* peerless, T. i. 172.

**Making,** *s.* poetry, composition, L. 74, 413, 483.

**Malapert,** *adj.* forward, T. iii. 87.

**Male** (1), *s.* bag, wallet, A 694, 3115.

**Male** (2), *s.* male, D 122.

**Malefice,** *s.* evil contrivance, I 341.

**Maléncolyk,** *adj.* melancholy, A 1375.

**Malgre,** *prep.* in spite of, 4. 220.

**Malison,** *s.* curse, I 443 ; cursing, I 619.

**Malliable,** *adj.* malleable, such as can be worked by the hammer, G 1130.

**Malt,** *pt. s.* melted, HF. 922.

**Maltalent,** *s.* ill-will, ill-humour, resentment, R. 273, 330.

**Man,** *s.* A 167, 209, 223 ; (used indefinitely) one, B 43, D 2002 ; hero, B 3331 ; servant, I 772 ; Mannes, *gen.* of mankind, T. ii. 417 ; Men, *pl.* men, people, 18. 26 ; A 178 ; *sing. (unemphatic form of* man), one *(with sing. verb),* A 149, 232, C 675, G 392.

**Manace,** *ger.* to threaten, E 1752.

**Manasinge,** *s.* threatening, A 2035.

**Mandement,** *s.* summons, D 1346.

**Maner,** *s.* manor, place to dwell in, 3. 1004.

**Manere,** *s.* manner, A 858, D 1229 ; deportment, A 140 ; disposition, L. 251 ; manner, way, 3. 1130 ; ease of behaviour, 3. 1218 ; goodly courtesy of manner, 4. 294 ; *of manere,* in his behaviour, F 546 , Maner, way, 3. 433 ; manner, kind, sort *(used without* of *following), as in* maner doctrine, B 1689 ; *pl.* kinds, R. 1406.

**Manhede,** *s.* manliness, A 1285.

**Mannish,** *adj.* manlike, T. i. 284 ; human, B 2454 ; unwomanly, B 782.

**Mannish,** *adv.* like a man, boisterously, E 1536.

**Mansioun,** *s.* dwelling, A 1974 ; (a term in astrology), F 50 ; mansion (of the moon), F 1285 ; *pl.* daily positions or ' stations ' of the moon, F 1130. A mansion of a planet is the sign (or signs) of the zodiac in which the planet was thought to be peculiarly at home. A mansion of the moon refers to its position day by day in the sky.

**Mansuete,** *adj.* courteous, T. v. 194.

**Mansuetude,** *s.* meekness, I 654.

**Mantelet,** *s.* short mantle, A 2163.

**Manye,** *s.* mania, A 1374.

**Mappemounde,** map of the world, 12. 2.

**Mapul,** *s.* maple-tree, A 2923.

**Marble-stoon,** *s.* piece of marble, R. 1462.

**Marchal,** *s.* marshal, E 1930.

**Marchandyse,** *s.* barter, I 777.

**Marchant,** *s.* merchant, A 270.

**Marcial,** *adj.* warlike, T. iv. 1669.

**Marcien,** *adj.* devoted to Mars, D 610.

**Mareys,** *s.* marsh, D 970 ; Mareys, *pl.* marshes, B 2. p 7. 42.

**Marie,** *interj.* marry, i. e. by St. Mary, G 1062.

**Mark** (1), *s.* mark, fixed spot, L. 784 ; sex, race, D 696 ; sign, I 98.

**Mark** (2), *s.* a piece of money, of the value of 13*s.* 4*d.* in England, G 1026 ; *pl.* Mark, C 390.

**Market-beter,** *s.* swaggerer in a market, A 3936.

**Markis,** *s.* a marquis, E 64 ; *gen. sing.* marquis's, E 994.

**Markisesse,** *s.* a marchioness, E 283.

**Martyre,** *s.* martyrdom, T. iv. 818.

**Martyreth,** *pr. s.* torments, A 1562.

**Mary,** *s.* marrow, pith, C 542.

**Mary-bones,** *s. pl.* marrow-bones, A 380.

**Mase,** *s.* maze, labyrinth, L. 2014 ; bewilderment, T. v. 468 ; bewildering position, B 4283.

**Mased,** *adj.* bewildered, B 526 ; stunned with grief, 7. 322.

**Masednesse,** *s.* amaze, E 1061.

**Maselyn,** *s.* a bowl made of maplewood, B 2042.

**Massedayes,** *pl.* massdays, B 4041.

**Masse-peny,** *s.* penny for a mass, D 1749.

**Mast,** *s.* mast, i. e. the fruit of forest-trees, acorns and beech-nuts, 9. 7, 37.

**Masty,** *adj.* fattened, sluggish, HF. 1777. Lit. ' fattened on mast.'

**Mat,** *adj.* dejected, A 955 ; exhausted, T. iv. 342 ; dead, L. 126 ; defeated utterly, B 935.

**Mate,** *interj.* checkmate ! 3. 660 ; *adj.* exhausted, 7. 176.

**Materes,** *pl.* materials (of a solid character), G 779.

**Matrimoine,** *s.* matrimony, A 3095, E 1573.

**Maugre, Maugree,** in spite of ; as in *maugre al thy might,* A 1607 ; *maugree hir eyen two,* A 1796 ; *maugree thyne yën,* D 315 ; *m. her,* L. 1772 ; *m. Philistiens,* B 3238 ; *m. my heed,* in spite of all I can do, 3. 1201 ; *m. thyn heed,* B 104 ; *m. his heed,* A 1169 ; *m. her (hir) heed,* L. 2326,

D 887; *m. your heed*, in spite of all you can do, B 4602.

**Maumet**, *s.* idol, I 860.

**Maumetrye**, *s.* Mahometanism, idolatry, B 236. *Maumet* is a corruption of Mahomet or Muhammed; our ancestors wrongly held the Mahometans to be idolaters.

**Maunciple**, *s.* manciple, A 544. An officer who purchases victuals for an inn or college.

**Mavis**, *s.* song-thrush, R. 619.

**Mawe**, *s.* maw, stomach, B 486.

**May**, *s.* maiden, B 851.

**Mayde child**, girl, B 1285.

**Maydenheed**, *s.* maidenhood, virginity, D 888.

**Mayle**, *s.* mail-armour, T. v. 1559.

**Mayntene**, *v.* maintain, R. 1144; uphold, A 1778.

**Mayster-hunte**, *s.* chief huntsman, 3. 375.

**Maystres**, *s. pl.* masters, B 3. m 2. 12.

**Maystrie**, *s.* masterly act; No maystrie. an easy matter, L. 400.

**Maze**, 2 *pr. pl.* are in a state of bewilderment, E 2387.

**Mechel**, *adj.* much; *for as mechel*, for as much, A. pr. 6.

**Mede** (1), *s.* mead (drink), B 2042. See **Meeth**.

**Mede**, *s.* (2), mead, meadow, A 89.

**Medeleth**, *pr. s.* mingles, L. 874.

**Medeling**, *s.* admixture, B 1. p 4. 279.

**Medewe**, *s.* meadow, R. 128.

**Mediatours**, *s. pl.* go-betweens, I 967.

**Medle**, *v.* mingle, HF. 2102; meddle, take part in, G 1184; dye (*miscere*), B 2. m 5. 10; Medly, *v.* mingle, mix, B 2. m 5. 7; *imp. pl.* meddle, G 1424.

**Medlee**, *adj.* of a mixed colour, A 328.

**Meed**, *s.* reward, L. 1662; Méde, meed, reward, A 770; *to medes*, for my meed, for my reward, T. ii. 1201.

**Meel-tyd**, *s.* meal-time, T. ii. 1556.

**Meeth**, *s.* mead, A 3261, 3378; Meth, A 2279,

**Megre**, *adj.* thin, R. 218, 311.

**Meinee**; see **Meynee**.

**Meke**, 1 *pr. s.* humble, B 2874.

**Meke**, *adv.* meekly, 7. 267.

**Melancolious** (*accented* mélancólious), *adj.* melancholy, HF. 30.

**Meláncolýe**, *s.* melancholy, 3. 23.

**Mele**, *s.* meal (of flour), A 3995.

**Melle**, *s.* mill, A 3923, 4242.

**Melte**, *v.* melt, T. iv. 367; Malt, *pt. s.* HF. 922; Molte, *pp.* HF. 1145, 1149.

**Memorial**, *adj.* which serves to record events, 7. 18.

**Memórie**, *s.* memory, G 339; remembrance, A 3112, B 3164.

**Men**, *pl. of* Man; *also a weakened form of* Man, *in the sense* of 'one,' *or* 'some one'; used with a singular verb. See **Man**.

**Mendinants**, *pl.* mendicant friars, D 1907, 1912.

**Mene**, *adj.* middle, B 3. m 9. 28; *mene whyle*, mean while, G 1262; of middle size, T. v. 806; Mene, *adj. pl.* intermediate, 7. 286.

**Mene**, *s.* means, way, 11. 36; middle course, T. i. 689; instrument, E 1671; mediator, 1. 125; go-between, T. iii. 254; intermediary, I 990; the mean, L. 165; *pl.* means, instruments, D 1484.

**Meneliche**, *adj.* moderate, B 1. p 6. 111.

**Menen**, *ger.* to say, HF. 1104; to signify, B 3941; 1 *pr. s.* intend, A 793; Menestow, meanest thou, G 309; Mente, 1 *pt. s.* meant, intended, B 4614; purposed, 18. 50; declared, 7. 160; Ment, *pp.* intended, 5. 158.

**Mene-whyle**, mean time, D 1445.

**Mening**, *s.* intent, F 151.

**Menivere**, *s.* miniver, a fine fur, R. 227.

**Menstralcies**, pl. mintrelsies, HF. 1217.

**Mente**, *pt. t. of* Menen.

**Mentes**, *pl.* plants of mint, R. 731.

**Mercenarie**, *s.* hireling, A 514.

**Merciable**, *adj.* merciful, B 1878, 3013.

**Mercy**, *s.* 1. 7; (have) mercy, 1. 36; *graunt mercy*, much thanks, 10. 29.

**Mere**, *s.* mare, A 541; Mare, A 4055.

**Meridian**, *adj.* at the moment of southing, southern, A. pr. 93.

**Meridie**, *s.* midday, A. ii. 44. 48.

**Meridional**, *adj.* southern, F 263.

**Merier**, *adj.* pleasanter, sweeter, B 2024, 4041.

**Meritorie**, *adj.* meritorious, I 831.

**Merk**, *s.* image, F 880.

**Merken**, *v.* brand, B 1. p 4. 139.

**Merlion**, *s.* merlin, small hawk, 5. 339.

**Mermaydens**, sirens, R. 680, 682.

**Mersshy**, *adj.* marshy, D 1710.

**Merveille**, *s.* marvel, B 2736.

**Merveillous**, *adj.* marvellous, B 1643.

**Mery**, *adj.* merry, gay, R. 580; pleasant, A 235, 757; pleasant to hear, B 1186; Meriemen, followers, B 2029.

**Mes**; *at good mes*, at a favourable distance, so as to have a fair shot, R. 1453. O.F. *mes*.

**Meschaunce**, *s.* misfortune, A 2009; evil

occurrence, T. i. 92 ; a miserable condition, B 3204 ; unfortunate conduct, C 80 ; ill luck, B 4623 ; ill luck (to him), B 896 ; *with m.*, with a mischief, H 193.

Meschief, *s.* misfortune, A 493, B 3513 ; trouble, mishap, A 2551 ; tribulation, H 76.

Mesel, *s.* leper, I 624. O.F. *mesel.*

Meselrie, *s.* leprosy, I 625.

Messáge, *s.* (1), message, T. iii. 401 ; errand, B 1087 ; (2) messenger, B 144, 333.

Messager, *s.* messenger, A 1491.

Messagerye, *s.* a sending of messages (personified), 5. 228.

Messanger, *s.* messenger, HF. 1568.

Messe, *s.* mass, B 1413.

Messuage, *s.* dwelling-house, A 3979.

Meste, *pl.* most, i.e. highest in rank, greatest, E 131 ; *at the m.,* at most, T. v. 947.

Mester, *s.* service, office, occupation, A 1340. O.F. *mester* ; Lat. *ministerium.*

Mesurable, *adj.* moderate, A 435 ; modest, I 936.

Mesurably, *adv.* moderately, B 2795.

Mesure, *s.* moderation, 3. 881 ; measure, E 256 ; plan, 5. 305 ; *by m.,* not too much, 3. 872 ; moderately, R. 543 ; *over m.,* immeasurably, 5. 300 ; *out of m.,* immoderately, B 2607 ; *withoute m.,* beyond measure, 3. 632.

Mesuring, *s.* measure, R. 1349.

Met, *s.* measure of capacity, I 799.

Metamorphoseos, *gen. s.* (the book) of Metamorphosis ; it should be pl. *Metamorphoseon* ; B 93.

Mete, *adj.* meet, befitting, 3. 316 ; fit, L. 1043 ; *pl.* meet, A 2291.

Mete, *s.* equal, 3. 486.

Mete, *s.* meat, food, A 136, 1900 ; meat, L. 1108 ; repast, T. ii. 1462 ; eating, A 127.

Mete, *v.* meet, L. 148 ; find, 5. 698 ; to meet together, B 1873 ; Meteth, *pr. s.* meets (*men* being singular = *one*), A 1524 ; Mette, *pt. pl.* met, E 390 ; Metten, *pt. pl.* HF. 227 ; *wel met,* D 1443.

Mete, *v.* dream, T. iii. 1559, iv. 1396, v. 249 ; Met, *pr. s.* 5. 104, 105 ; Mette, 1 *pt. s.* 5. 95 ; Me mette, 1 *pt. s. refl.* I dreamt, R. 26 ; *pt. s. impers.* 3. 276 ; Met, *pp.* B 4445.

Mete, 1 *pr. s.* (I) measure, A. ii. 41. 8.

Metely, *adj.* well-proportioned, R. 822.

Meth, *s.* mead (drink), A 2279.

Meting (1), *s.* meeting, L. 784.

Meting, (2), *s.* dream, 3. 282.

Meve, *v.* move, stir, T. i. 472 ; *to him meved,* urged against him, L. 344.

Mewe, *s.* mew, i.e. coop wherein fowls were fattened, A 349 ; properly, a coop for hawks when moulting, F 643 ; hiding-place, T. iii. 602.

Mewet, *adj.* mute, T. v. 194.

Mexcuse, *for* Me excuse, excuse myself, 16. 36.

Meynee, *s.* household, B 1238 ; company, R. 1305 ; followers, suite, retinue, retainers, household-servants, R. 615, 634 ; household, menials, A 1258 ; army, troop, B 3532 ; assembly, HF. 933 ; Meinee, retinue, I 437 ; troop, A 4381 ; Meiny, crew, L. 2201. O.F. *meisnee, maisnee,* household.

Meyntenaunce, *s.* demeanour, 3. 834.

Michel, *adj.* much, A. ii. 23. 30.

Mid, *adj.* middle, 3. 660.

Middel, *s.* waist, R. 1032.

Midel, *adj.* neither tall nor short, 7. 79.

Mikel, *adj.* great, 7. 99 ; much, L. 1175.

Mile-wey, *s.* a space of 5°, which answers to twenty minutes of time, the average time for walking a mile ; hence the term, A. i. 7. 11.

Milksop, *s.* a piece of bread sopped in milk ; hence, a weak, effeminate man, B 3100.

Milne-stones, *pl.* mill-stones, T. ii. 1384.

Minde, *s.* remembrance, T. ii. 602 ; memory, B 527 ; *in m.,* in remembrance, F 109, 607.

Ministres, *pl.* officers, B 4233.

Ministreth, *pr. s.* administers, governs, B 3. m 6. 3.

Minne, *imp. s.* remember, mention, 16. 48.

Minstralcye, *s.* minstrelsy, E 1718 ; musical instrument, H 113 ; sound of music, F 268.

Mintinge, *pres. pt.* intending, B 1. m 2. 3.

Mirácle, *s.* wonder, A 2675 ; legend, B 1881 ; *pleyes of m.,* miracle-plays, D 558.

Mirour, *s.* mirror, R. 567, 1585.

Mirre, *s.* myrrh, A 2938.

Mirthe, *s.* pleasure, amusement, R. 601 ; Mirthe, Sir, Mirth (personified), R. 733.

Mirtheles, *adj.* sad, 5. 592.

Mis, *adj.* wrong, amiss, T. iv. 1348 ; bad, HF. 1975 ; blameworthy, G 999.

Mis, *s.* wrong, evil, L. 266 *a.*

Mis, *adv.* amiss, wrongly, T. i. 934.

Mis, 1 *pr. s.* lack, have not, 6. 47.

Misacounted, *pp.* miscounted, T. v. 1185.

Misaunter, *s.* misadventure, misfortune, T. 766.

Misaventure, *s.* misadventure, mishap, B 616; mischief, R. 422.

Misavyse, *pr. pl. refl.* act unadvisedly, D 230.

Misbileve, *s.* suspicion, G 1213.

Misbileved, infidels, 1. 146.

Misboden, *pp.* offered (to do you) evil, insulted, A 909.

Misborn, *pp.* misbehaved, B 3067 (lit. 'borne amiss').

Miscarie, *v.* go amiss, A 513.

Mischaunce, *s.* ill luck, R. 1548; mischance, R. 251; misfortune, L. 1826; *to mischaunce*, i.e. to the devil, T. ii. 222, v. 359; *how m.*, how the mischief, T. iv. 1362.

Mischeef, *s.* misfortune, L. 1278; danger, 4. 58; harm, R. 253.

Misconceyveth, *pr. s.* misunderstands, E 2410.

Miscounting, *s.* fraudulent reckoning, R. 196.

Misdemeth, *pr. s.* misjudges, E 2410.

Misdeparteth, *pr. s.* parts or divides amiss, B 107.

Misdooth, *pr. s.* ill-treats, B 3112.

Misdrawinges, *s. pl.* way of drawing aside, B 3. p 12. 107.

Misericorde, *s.* (there is) mercy, pity, T. iii. 1177; pity, B 2608.

Misérie, *s.* misery, B 3167.

Misese, *s.* trouble, I 806; discomfort, I 177; *pl.* injuries, B 1. p 4. 73.

Misesed, *pp.* vexed, I 806.

Misfille, *pt. s. subj.* it went amiss (with), A 2388.

Misforyaf, *pt. s.* misgave, T. iv. 1426.

Misgoon, *pp.* gone astray, I 80.

Misgovernaunce, *s.* misconduct, B 3202.

Misgyed, *pp.* misconducted, B 3723.

Mishap, *s.* ill luck, B 3435.

Mishappe, *v.* meet with misfortune, B 2886; *pr. s. subj.* (it) may happen ill for, A 1646.

Mishappy, *adj.* unhappy, B 2758.

Misknowinge, *s.* ignorance, B 3. m 11. 27.

Mislay, *pt. s.* lay in an uncomfortable position, A 3647.

Misledden, *pt. pl.* misconducted, T. iv. 48.

Misledinges, *pl.* misguiding ways, B 3. p 8. 2.

Mislyketh, *pr. s.* displeases, L. 1293.

Mislyved, *pp.* of ill life, treacherous, T. iv. 330.

Mismetre, *pr. s. subj.* scan amiss, T. v. 1796.

Mis-sat, *pt. s.* was not where it should be, 3. 941; misbecame, R. 1194.

Misse, *v.* fail, D 1416; draw to an end, 5. 40; *pt. s.* was wanting (to), T. iii. 445; *pp.* missing, T. iii. 537.

Mis-set, *pp.* misplaced, 3. 1210.

Misseye, 1 *pr. s.* speak amiss, 7. 317; *pr. s.* slanders, I 379; *missayd or do*, said or done wrong, 3. 528.

Misspeke, 1 *pr. s. subj.* speak wrongly, A 3139.

Mistaketh, 2 *pr. pl.* transgress, trespass, R. 1540.

Mister, *s.* trade, handicraft, occupation, A 613; need, R. 1426; Mester, occupation, A 1340; *what m. men*, men of what occupation, what sort of men, A 1710. See Mester.

Misterye, *s.* ministry, profession, I 895. From Lat. *ministerium*.

Mistihede, *s.* mystery, 4. 224.

Mis-torneth, *pr. pl.* turn aside, B 3. p 3. 9.

Mistyde, *v.* be unlucky, B 2886.

Miswanderinge, *adj.* straying (Lat. *deuius*), B 3. p 2. 27.

Miswent, *pp.* gone amiss, T. i. 633.

Mis-weyes, *s. pl.* by-paths, B 3. m 11. 3.

Miteyn, *s.* mitten, glove, C 372.

Mixen, *s.* dunghill, I 911.

Mo (mōō), *adj.* more, A. pr. 27; more (in number), A 576, 849; besides, L. 917; others, E 2113; another, E 1039; (others) besides, E 2263; many others besides, D 663; *tymes mo*, at other times, E 449; *othere mo*, others besides, G 1001; *na mo*, no more, none else, B 695.

Mo, *adv.* more, any longer, D 864; *never the mo, never mo*, never, D 691, 1099.

Mochel, *adj.* great, L. 1966; much, G 611.

Mochel, *adv.* much, B 3959.

Mochel, *s.* size, 3. 454, 861.

Moder, *s.* mother, B 276; the thickest plate forming the principal part of the astrolabe (Lat. *mater* or *rotula*), A. i. 3. 1; Modres, *gen.* B 1783; Modres, *pl.* C 93.

Moeble, *adj.* moveable, A. i. 21. 80.

Moeble, *s.* moveable goods, personal property, T. iv. 1380, 1460; *pl.* G 540.

Moedes, *s. pl.* moods, strains (of music), B 2. p 1. 50.

Moevable, *adj.* fickle, B 4. m 5. 32; *as s.* The firste m., the 'primum mobile,' A. i. 17. 50.

Moevabletee, *s.* mobility, B 4. p 6. 126.

Moeve, *ger.* to stir up, B 2218; *v.* move, I 133.

Moevere, *s.* mover, A 2987.

Moevinge, *s.* moving, motion, A. pr. 99;

Firste moeving, the 'primum mobile,'
A. i. 17. 45.

Moiste, *pl.* supple, A 457.

Moiste, *adj. as s.* moisture, R. 1564.

Mokereres, *s. pl.* misers, B 2. p 5. 18.

Mokre, *v.* hoard up, T. iii. 1375.

Molestie, *s.* trouble, B 3. p 9. 105.

Mollificacioun, *s.* softening, G 854.

Molte, *pp.*; see Melte.

Monche, *v.* munch, T. i. 914.

Mone, *s.* moon, A 2077; i.e. position or
'quarter' of the moon, A 403; Mone,
*gen.* B 2070; Mones, *gen.* F 1154.

Mone, *s.* moan, complaint, A 1366, F 920.

Mone, *v. refl.* to lament, T. i. 98.

Monstre, *s.* prodigy, F 1344; *pl.* B 3302.

Montaigne, *s.* mountain, B 24.

Mood, *s.* anger, A 1760; thought, C 126.

Moon, *s.* moan, lamentation, complaint,
L. 1169, 1799.

Moorne, 1 *pr. s.* mourn, A 3704.

Mooringe, *s.* mourning, plaint, A 3706.

Moot, *s. pl.* notes on a horn, 3. 376.

Moot, 1 *pr. s.* must, shall, B 1853; *pr. s.*
must, ought to, A 232; is to (go), B 294;
Mot, 1 *pr. s.* may, 4. 267; must, have
to, B 227; Most, 2 *pr. s.* B 104; Mot,
*pr. s.* must, has to, L. 388, 1945; Mote,
2 *pr. s. pl.* may, T. ii. 402; Moten, must,
L. 343; Mote (*or* Moot), *pr. s. subj.* may,
HF. 102; L. 843; is sure to, L. 1632;
Moot (*or* Mote) I goon, may I still go,
may I still retain the power to walk,
F 777; So moot (*or* mote) I thee, as
I may thrive, as I hope to thrive, C
309; As ever mote I, A 832; Foule
moot thee falle, ill may it befall thee,
H 40; Moot (*or* Mote) thou, mayst thou,
B 1626; Moste, 1 *pt. s.* must (go), B 282;
Moste, *pt. s.* must, 4. 250; had to, B
886; ought to (be), F 38; was made to,
B 3700; Mosten, *pt. pl.* should, L. 99;
Moste, *pt. s. subj.* might, L. 1573; *us
moste,* we must resolve to, G 946.

Moral, *adj.* excellent in character, T. iv.
1672.

Moralitee, *s.* moral tale, I 38; moral
writing, I 1088.

Mordre, *s.* murder, R. 1136; *m. wol out,*
B 4242.

Mordre, *ger.* to murder, kill, L. 1536.

Mordrer, *s.* murderer, 5. 353, 612.

Mordring, *s.* murdering, A 2001.

More, *adj.* greater, B 2396, E 1231; larger,
HF. 500; More and lesse, all alike,
every one, B 959; More and more, HF.
532; *with-outen more,* without further
trouble, T. iv. 133.

More, *adv.* more, A 219; in a greater
degree, B 3745.

More, *s.* root, T. v. 25. A.S. *moru.*

Mormal, *s.* sore, gangrene, A 386.

Morne, *s.* morning; *morne milk,* morning-
milk, A 358, 3236.

Morsel, *s.* morsel, bit, A 128; *m. breed,*
morsel of bread, B 3624.

Morter, *s.* mortar, 9. 15; a metal bowl for
holding wax, with a wick for burning,
T. iv. 1245.

Mortifye, *v.* kill; used of producing
change by chemical action, G 1431;
*pp.* deadened, I 233.

Mortreux, *pl.* thickened soups or pot-
tages, A 384. (Also spelt *mortrewes*;
thus *x* is for *s.*)

Morwen, *s.* morning, morrow, T. ii. 1555;
Morwe, L. 49, 108; fore part of a day,
T. iv. 1308; *by the morwe,* early in the
morning, A 334.

Morweninge, *s.* morning, A 1062; dawning, 4. 26.

Morwe-song, *s.* morning-song, A 830.

Morwe-tyde, *s.* morning-hour, E 2225;
*in the m.,* in the morning, B 4206.

Mosel, *s.* muzzle, A 2151.

Most, 2 *pt. s.* oughtest (to), 8. 3; Moste,
*pt. s.* must, ought (to), A 3088; must
(go), HF. 187; had to go, T. v. 5; was
obliged to, T. iii. 540; must, might, E
2102; *pt. s. subj.* might, L. 1594; Mosten,
*pt. pl.* must, might, T. ii. 1507; could,
HF. 2094.

Moste, *adj. sup.* greatest, F 199; chief,
D 1041; chiefest, F 361.

Mote (1), *s.* atom, T. iii. 1603; Motes, *pl.*
specks of dust, D 868.

Mote (2), *s.* motion (Lat. *motus*), A. ii. 44.
22. The 'mene mote' or *mean motion*
is the average motion of a planet during a given period.

Motre, *ger.* to mutter, T. ii. 541.

Mottelee, *s.* motley array, A 271.

Motthes, *s. pl.* moths, B 2187.

Motýf, *s.* motive; *hence* idea, notion, B
628, E 1491.

Moulen, *v.* grow mouldy, B 32; *pp.* A
3870.

Mountance, *s.* amount, value, quantity,
A 1570; amount (of time), L. 307; length,
T. ii. 1707; value, H 255.

Mourdaunt, *s.* chape, or metal tag, at
the end of a girdle, R. 1094. (Not 'the
tongue of a buckle.')

Moustre, *s.* pattern, 3. 912.

Moveresse, *s.* a fomentress of quarrels,
R. 149.

Mowe, *s.* grimace, T. iv. 7; *pl.* HF. 1806.

Mowen, *v.* be able; *mowen shewen*, become evident, B 5. p 4. 163; Mowen, *ger.* to have power, T. ii. 1594; May, 1 *pr. s.* may, B 89; can, B 231; Maystow, mayest thou, A 1918; Mowe, 1 *pr. pl.* can, B 2939; may, HF. 1735; Mowen, 2 *pr. pl.* can, 19. 25; Mowe, 2 *pr. pl.* may, L. 92; can, 3. 552; Mowen, *pr. pl.* are able to, D 1722; Mowe, *pr. pl.* may, can, A 2999; Mowe, 2 *pr. s. subj.* mayest, G 460; Mighte, *pt. s.* might, A 169, &c.; 1 *pt. s. subj.* could, E 638.

Mowinge, *s.* ability, B 4. p 4. 32.

Mowled, *pp.* decayed, A 3870.

Moysoun, *s.* crop, growth, R. 1677. O.F. *moison*; Lat. acc. *mensionem.*

Moyste, *adj.* fresh, new, B 1954, C 315.

Moysty, *adj.* new (applied to ale), H 60.

Muable, *adj.* changeable, T. iii. 822.

Muchel, *adj.* much, great, A 2352; a great deal of, F 349; *in 80 m.*, in so much, B 2644; many, G 673.

Muchel, *adv.* greatly, A 258; much, F 1129.

*Mulier est hominis confusio*, woman is man's confusion, B 4354.

Mullok, *s.* a heap of refuse, A 3873; confused heap of materials, G 938, 940.

Multiplicacioun, *s.* multiplying, i. e. the art of alchemy, G 849.

Multiplye, *v.* to make gold and silver by the arts of alchemy, G 669.

Murmuracion, *s.* murmuring, I 499.

Murmuringe, *s.* murmur, A 2432.

Murthe, *s.* mirth, joy, E 1123.

Murye, *adj.* merry, A 1386.

Muscle, *s.* mussel, D 2100.

Muse, *s.* muse, poetic faculty, 16. 38.

Muse, *ger.* to consider, T. iii. 563; *pr. s.* gazes into, R. 1592; *pp.* gazed, R. 1645.

Musice, Music, B 2. p 1. 49.

Musýke, music, 5. 62; Musik, B 4483.

Muwe, *s.* mew, pen (for hawks), cage, T. i. 381; *in muwe*, cooped up, T. iv. 496.

Muwe, *v.* change, T. ii. 1258.

Myle, *s.* mile, HF. 1038; *fyve m.*, five miles, G 555.

Mynde, *s. dat.* mind, recollection, 3. 15; *acc.* reason, 2. 34; 3. 511; *have minde upon*, remember, 19. 26.

Myne, *v.* undermine, T. iii. 767.

Mynour, *s.* one who mines, A 2465.

Myrie, *adj.* merry, A 1499.

Myrie, *adv.* merrily, A 3575.

Myrier, *adv. comp.* merrier, R. 876.

Mys, *pl.* mice, B 2. p 6. 37.

Myte (1), *s.* mite, thing of no value, A 1558.

Myte (2), mite, insect; *pl.* D 560.

## N.

N', *for* ne, not; as in *nacheveth* for *ne acheveth*, and the like.

Na, no (Northern), A 4175.

Na mo, i. e. no more, none else, B 695.

Nacheveth, *for* ne acheveth, achieves not, T. v. 784.

Nadde, *pt. s.* (*for* ne hadde), had not, R. 457.

Naddre, *s.* adder, E 1786.

Nadir, *s.* the point of the ecliptic exactly opposite to that in which the sun is situate, A. ii. 6. 1; see l. 12.

Nadstow, 2 *pt. s.* haddest thou not, didst thou not, A 4088.

Naille, *imp. s.* 3 *p.* let it nail, let it fasten, E 1184.

Naiteth, *pr. s.* refuses, B 1. m 1. 25.

Nake, 2 *pr. pl.* make naked, B 4. m 7. 70; Naked, *pp. as adj.* naked, A 1956, I 105; bare, HF. 133; destitute, void, weak, G 486; simple, plain, A. pr. 30.

Nakers, *pl.* kettle-drums, A 2511. From the Arabic.

Nale; *atte nale*, at the ale, at the ale-house, D 1349.

Nam, (*for* ne am), 1 *pr. s*, am not, A 1122, B 2710; *nam but deed*, am only a dead man, 3. 204.

Nam, *pt. s.* took, G 1297.

Name, *s.* good name, reputation, L. 1812; title, B 3. p 6. 36.

Namely, *adv.* especially, A 1268, 2709.

Namo, (*for* na mo), no more in number, A 101, 544; none other, no one else, D 957.

Namore, *adv.* no more, A 98.

Napoplexye, *for* Ne apoplexye, nor apoplexy, B 4031.

Nappeth, *pr. s.* naps, slumbers, nods, H 9.

Narette; see Arette.

Nart, (*for* ne art), art not, G 499.

Narwe, *adj.* small, B 4012; *pl.* A 625; close, closely drawn, D 1803.

Narwe, *adv.* narrowly, closely, A 3224; tightly, L. 600; carefully, E 1988.

Nas, (*for* ne was), was not, A 251, 288; *I nas but*, I was simply, 2. 21.

Nassayeth, *for* ne assayeth, attempts not, T. v. 784.

Nat, *adv.* not, A 74; Nat but, only, merely, L. 1899; quite, L. 2091.

Nat, (*for* ne at), nor at, B 290.

Nat forthy, *adv.* notwithstanding, B 2165.

Natal, *adj.* who presides over nativities, T. iii. 150.

Nath (*for* ne hath), *pr. s.* hath not, A 923.

Nathelees, nevertheless, A 35.

Nature, *s.* nature, A 11; kind, race, 5. 615; seed, I 577.

Naturel, *adj.* natural, A 416. A 'day natural' is a period of 24 hours.

Naught, *adv.* not, B 1701; not so, G 269.

Nave, *s.* nave (of a wheel), D 2266.

Naxe, ((*for* ne axe), ask not, T. v. 594.

Nay, *adv.* nay, no, G 1339; (*opposed to* yea), E 355; (answers a direct question), B 740; surely not! 3. 1309; *as s.* nay, untruth, 3. 147; It is no nay, there is no denying it, B 1956.

Nayte, *v.* withhold, deny, I 1013.

Ne, *adv. and conj.* not, A 70; nor, A 179, 526; *ne . . . ne*, neither . . . nor, A 603; (when used with a verb, a second negative is often added).

Nece, *s.* niece, B 1290.

Necesseden, *pt. pl.* compelled, B 3. m 9. 8.

Neddre, *s.* adder; *pl.* L. 699.

Nede, *s.* need, extremity, B 102, 658, 2360; extremity, difficult matter, B 2917; peril, B 3576; *at nede*, at need, 1. 112; *for nede*, if needful, R. 1123; *s. as adj.* needful, A 304; *pl.* matters of business, B 174, 1266; necessities, T. ii. 954; needs, G 178; *for nedes*, for very need, 3. 1201.

Nede, *adv.* necessarily, of necessity, R. 1441, 1473.

Nede, *v.* be necessary, B 871; Nedeth, *pr. s.* (it) is necessary, (it) needs, A 462; *what n.*, what is the need of, A 849; Nededè, *pt. s. impers.* (there) needed, A 4020, 4161; *us neded*, we should need, T. iv. 1344.

Nedely, *adv.* of necessity, necessarily, B 4435.

Nedes, *adv.* needs, necessarily, of necessity, L. 1298.

Nedes-cost, *adv.* of necessity, A 1477, L. 2697.

Needly, *adv.* necessarily, B 3. p 9. 87. See Nedely.

Neen, no (Northern), A 4185, 4187.

Neer, *adv. comp.* nearer, A 839, 968; *neer and neer*, A 4304; *as pos. adv.* near, A 1439; *fer or neer*, far or near, T. i. 451.

Neet, *pl.* neat, cattle, A 597.

Negardye, *s.* niggardliness, 10. 53.

Neghen, *v.* draw nigh, L. 318.

Neigh, *adj.* near, nigh, B 2558.

Neigh, *adv.* nearly, T. i. 60.

Neighebour, *s.* neighbour, A 535.

Neighen, *v.* draw near, T. ii. 1555.

Neither nother, (in) neither the one nor the other, B 5. m 3. 53.

Nekke-boon, *s.* neck-bone, B 1839; neck, D 906; nape of the neck, B 669.

Nel, 1 *pr. s.* will not, T. ii. 726.

Nempnen, *v.* name, B 507.

Nenvye, *for* ne envye, *imp. s.* envy not, T. v. 1789.

Ner, *adv. comp.* nearer, 3. 888; T. i. 448; Nere, 3. 38; *ner and ner*, B 1710; Ner the les, nevertheless, 4. 130.

Nercotikes, *pl.* narcotics, A 1472.

Nere (*for* ne were), 2 *pt. s.* wast not, 4. 112; *pt. pl.* were not, A 875, D 1944; 1 *pt. s. subj.* should not (I) be, T. ii. 409; Nere, *pt. s. subj.* would not be, should not be, A 1129; were not, B 3984; were it not, B 132; were it not (for), 1. 24, 180.

Nere, *adv.* nearer, R. 1454.

Nerf, *s.* nerve, i. e. sinew, T. ii. 642.

Nescapest (*for* Ne escapest), escapest not, L. 2643.

Nest, *s.* D 1691; *wikked nest*, i. e. *mau ni*, or Manny (referring to Sir Oliver Mauny), B 3573; *pl.* HF. 1516.

Net-herdes, *gen.* neat-herd's, B 2746.

Nether, *adj.* lower, A 3852.

Netherest, *adj. superl.* lowest, i.e. outermost, A. i. 18. 7.

Nevene, *v.* name, G 821; *herd hir name n.*, heard (him) name her name, T. i. 876; *pr. pl. subj.* may mention, G 1473.

Never, *adv.* never, A 70; *n. dide but*, never did aught that was not, 4. 297; *n. the neer*, none the nearer, G 721.

Neveradel, *adv.* not a bit, C 670.

Never-mo, *adv.* never oftener, never (with two exceptions), A. ii. 31. 5; never, 3. 1125.

Nevew, *s.* nephew, L. 1442; grandson, L. 2659.

Newe, *adv.* newly, freshly, afresh, A 365, 428; *of newe*, new, fresh, T. ii. 20; Newe and newe, again and again, T. iii. 116; continually, C 929.

Newed, *pt. s.* had something fresh in it, 3. 906; *pp.* renewed, B 3036.

Newefangel, *adj.* fond of novelty, F 618, H 193.

New-fangelnesse, *s.* fondness for novelty, L. 154; F 610.

Newe-thought, *s.* Inconstancy, R. 982.

**Nexte**, *adj. sup.* nearest, A 1413 ; easiest, T. i. 697.

**Ney**, *adj.* nigh, A. ii. 3. 78.

**Nigard**, *adj.* niggardly, R. 1172.

**Nigard**, *s.* miser, niggard, B 4105.

**Nigardye**, *s.* miserliness, B 1362.

**Nighte**, *ger.* to grow dark, become night, T. v. 515.

**Nighter-tale**, *s.* ; *by n.*, in the night-time, A 97. This expression seems to have resulted from a confusion of Icel. *ā nāttar-þeli*, in the dead of night, with Icel. *nāttar-tal*, a tale or number of nights.

**Night-spel**, *s.* night-spell, night-incantation, A 3480.

**Nigromanciens**, *s. pl.* necromancers, I 603.

**Nil**, 1 *pr. s.* will not, 3. 92, 1125 ; will (I) not, shall (I) not, T. v. 40, 43, 44 ; desire not, dislike, E 646 ; Nille, 1 *pr. s.* will not, G 1463 ; Nil, *pr. s.* will not, B 972 ; will not (have), 3. 586 ; will (she) not, 3. 1140 ; Nilt, 2 *pr. s.* wilt not, T. ii. 1024 ; Niltow, thou wilt not, T. i. 792.

**Nillinge**, *s.* refusing, B 5. p 2. 23.

**Nin**, *for* Ne in, nor in, E 1511, F 35.

**Nis**, for *ne is*, is not, 2. 77 ; Ther nis no more but, all that remains is that, L. 847.

**Niste**, 1 *pt. s.* knew not, F 502 ; *pt. s.* knew not, A 3414, 4225.

**Noble**, *s.* a gold coin, A 3256 ; *pl.* HF. 1315. (Worth 6s. 8d.)

**Nobledest**, *pt. s.* 2 *p.* ennobledest, didst ennoble, G 40. A translation of Dante's *nobilitasti.*

**Noblesse**, *s.* nobleness, R. 780 ; noble cheer, T. v. 439 ; nobility, D 1167 ; (title of respect), B 2956 ; magnificence, B 3438 ; high honour, B 3208 ; nobility, rank, R. 1034 ; worthy behaviour, B 185, 248.

**Nobley**, *s.* nobility, dignity, splendour, HF. 1416 ; noble rank, T. iv. 1670 ; assembly of nobles, G 449 ; state, F 77.

**Nof** (*for* Ne of ), nor of, D 571, 660.

**Noght**, *adv.* not, A 107 ; by no means, in no respect, A 1226 ; Noght but for, only because, D 645.

**Noght**, *s.* nothing, C 542 ; N. worth, worth nothing, H 200.

**Noisen**, 2 *pr. pl.* cry aloud, B 3. m 6. 10.

**Nokked**, *pp.* notched, R. 942.

**Nolde**, 1 *pt. s.* would not, did not want, 5. 90 ; (I) should not desire, G 1334 ; Noldest, 2 *pt. s.* wouldst not, 3. 482 ; Noldestow, if thou wouldst not, T. iii.

1264 ; Nolde, *pt. s.* would not, 1. 31 ; would not (have), A 1024.

**Nombre**, *s.* number, A 716 ; amount, sum, A. ii. 24. 5.

**Nombred**, *pp.* counted in, T. iii. 1269.

**Nomen**, *pp.* taken, T. v. 514 ; put, R. 408 ; Nome, *pp.* L. 822, 1018, 1777. Pp. of *nimen.*

**Nones, for the**, for the nonce, for the occasion, for this occasion, A 379, 523, 545, 879 ; on the spur of the moment, T. i. 561 ; for the time, T. ii. 1381 ; With the nones, on the condition, HF. 2099, L. 1540. Originally *for then anes*, for the once ; where *then* is the dat. of the def. article (A. S. ðām).

**Nonne**, *s.* nun, A 118 ; Nonnes Preest, Nun's Priest, B 4637.

**Nonnerye**, *s.* nunnery, A 3946.

**Noon**, none, no, A 318, 449 ; *or noon*, or not, or no, D 2069.

**Noot**, 1 *pr. s.* know not, L. 2660 ; Not, L. 193 ; Nost, knowest not, 3. 1137 ; Nostow, thou knowest not, HF. 1010 ; Noot, *pr. s.* knows not, C 284 ; Not, 4. 214. A. S. *nāt.*

**Norice**, *s.* nurse, B 4305.

**Norice**, *v.* nourish, foment, B 2204 ; *pp.* brought up, E 399.

**Norissing**, *s.* nutriment, A 437 ; growth, A 3017 ; Norishinge, bringing up, E 1040 ; *pl.* refections, B 4. p 6. 38 ; sustenance, B 1. p 6. 93 (Lat. *fomitem*).

**Noriture**, *s.* nourishment, T. iv. 768.

**Nortelrye**, *s.* education, A 3967.

**Northren**, northern, A 1987.

**Norture**, *s.* instruction, good manners, R. 179.

**Nory**, *s.* pupil (lit. foster-child), B 3. p 11. 233 ; Norry, B 1. p 3. 14.

**Nose-thirles**, *pl.* nostrils, A 557, I 209.

**Noskinnes**, *for* Noneskinnes, of no kind, HF. 1794. From *nones*, gen. of *noon*, none ; and *kinnes*, gen. of *kin.*

**Nost**, Nostow, Not ; see **Noot**.

**Not but**, only, 4. 121 ; T. iii. 1636.

*Nota*, i. e. observe, A. ii. 26. 33.

**Notabilitee**, *s.* notable fact, B 4399.

**Notáble**, *adj.* notorious, remarkable, B 1875.

**Notaries**, *s. pl.* scribes, I 797.

**Note**, *s.* (1) note (in music), A 235, B 1737 ; musical note, peal, HF. 1720 ; tune, 5. 677 ; *by n.*, according to musical notes, by note, R. 669 ; in concord, all at once, T. iv. 585.

**Note**, *s.* (2), employment, business, task, job, A 4068. A. S. *notu.*

**Noteful,** *adj.* useful, A. pr. 120.

**Notemuge,** *s.* nutmeg, B 1953.

**Notes,** *s. pl.* nuts, R. 1360.

**Not-heed,** *s.* crop-head, a head with hair cropped short, A 109.

**Nother,** neither, 7. 253; neither (of them), L. 192.

**Nothing,** *adv.* in no respect, in no degree, not at all, A 2505; *for n.,* by no means, D 1121.

**Notificacions,** *pl.* hints, B 5. m 3. 23.

**Notifie,** *pr. pl.* indicate, I 430; *pp.* proclaimed, B 256.

**Nouchis,** *s. pl.* jewelled ornaments, jewels (properly, setting for jewels), clasps, HF. 1350; Nowches, E 382. E. *ouch.*

**Nought,** *adv.* not, T. ii. 575, 673; not at all, 3. 3; B 2262.

**Noumbre,** *s.* number, 3. 440.

**Noumbre,** *v.* number, 3. 439; *pp.* counted in, T. iii. 1269.

**Noun-certeyn,** *s.* uncertainty, 18. 46; T. i. 337.

**Noun-power,** *s.* impotence, B 3. p 5. 22.

**Nouthe,** now, T. i. 985; *as nouthe,* at present, A 462.

**Novelrye,** *s.* novelty, T. ii. 756.

**Now,** *adv.* now, A 715; *for now,* for the present, 7. 343; *now and now,* from time to time, occasionally, F. 430.

**Nowches;** see **Nouchis.**

**Noyous,** *adj.* troublesome, HF. 574. Short for *anoyous.*

**Ny,** *adj.* near, B 2562; Nye, *def.* the one who is near, A 3392.

**Ny,** *adv.* nigh, nearly, B 2735; *as ny as,* as close to, A 588; *wel ny,* almost, A 1330.

**Ny,** *prep.* nigh, B 550.

**Nyce,** *adj.* foolish, B 3712, 4505; ignorant, R. 1257; foolish, weak, B 1083, G 493; ludicrous, A 3855; scrupulous, A 398.

**Nycely,** *adv.* foolishly, T. v. 1152.

**Nycetee,** *s.* folly, G 463; simplicity, A 4046; foolish behaviour, pleasure, D 412; scrupulousness, T. ii. 1288.

**Nye;** see **Ny.**

**Nyfles,** *pl.* mockeries, pretences, D 1760. Lit. 'sniffings'; O.F. *nifler,* to sniff.

## O.

**O** (òò), one, A 304, 363; a single, B 5. p 6. 158; one and the same, T. ii. 37; one continuous and uniform, HF. 1100. See **Oon.**

**Obeisant,** *adj.* obedient, E 66, I 264.

**Obeisaunce,** *s.* obedience, E 24, 502;

obedient act, E 230; obedient farewell, L. 2479; *in your o.,* in obedience to you, 2. 84; *unto her o.,* in obedience to her, L. 587; Obeisaunces, *pl.* acts of dutiful attention, L. 149; observances, L. 1268.

**Obeising,** *adj.* yielding, L. 1266.

**Objecte,** *adj.* presented, B 5. p 5. 5.

**Obligacioun,** *s.* bond, 15. 2; Obligaciouns, *pl.* sureties, B 3018.

**Oblige,** *v.; o. to you,* lay an obligation on you (to make me), T. iv. 1414.

**Obséquies,** *pl.* funeral rites, A 993.

**Observaunce,** *s.* respect, A 1045; homage, 7. 218; observance, L. 1608; ceremony, T. ii. 112; heed, I 747; *pl.* customary attentions, F 956; duties, L. 150.

**Observe,** *v.* favour, B 1821; *pr. s.* takes heed, I 303.

**Occasioun,** *s.* cause, L. 994.

**Occident,** *s.* west, B 297.

**Occidentale,** *adj.* western, A. i. 5. 9.

**Occupye,** *v.* take up, F 64; *pr. s.* follows close upon, T. iv. 836; dwells in, B 424; *imp. s.* hold to, B 4. p 7. 103.

**Octogamye,** *s.* marrying eight times, D 33.

**Of,** *prep.* of, A 2, &c.; by, R. 1260; concerning, about, F 1179; during, B 510; for, 13. 19; off, from, 3. 964; on account of, B 2208; as to, as regards, in respect of, F 425; as to, 3. 966; upon, 5. 555; over, B 2947; with, A 2055; some, A 146; *of a purpos,* on purpose, deliberately, B 2273; *of al my lif,* in all my life, 5. 484; *of grace,* by his favour, out of his favour, E 178; *fulfild of,* filled with, 7. 42.

**Of,** *adv.* off, away, 5. 494; (come) off, T. iv. 1106; off, A 2676; *com of,* be quick, have done, A 3728.

**Offensioun,** *s.* damage, A 2416.

**Offertorie,** *s.* offertory, A 710.

**Office,** *s.* office, employment of a secular character, A 292; employment, B 3446; duty, 5. 236; property, D 1144; place of office, D 1577; *with o.,* by the use of (Lat. *officio),* B 1. p 1. 3; *houses of o.,* servants' offices, E 264.

**Of-newe,** *adv.* newly, again, R. 1613; lately, E 938.

**Of-showve,** *v.* repel (lit. shove off), A 3912.

**Of-taken,** *pp.* taken away, B 1855.

**Ofte,** *adj. pl.* many; Ofte sythes, oftentimes, A 485; Ofte tyme, often, A 52; Tymes ofte, E 226.

**Ofter,** *adv. comp.* oftener, E. 215.

**Of that,** *conj.* because, L. 815.

Of-thowed, *pp.* thawed away, HF. 1143.

Oght, *s.* aught, anything, F 1469 ; anything of value, G 1333 ; *as adv.* ought, at all, B 1792.

Oghte ; see Owen.

Oke, Okes ; see Ook.

Olifaunts, *s. pl.* elephants, B 3. p 8. 29.

Oliveres, *s. pl.* olive-trees, R. 1314 ; olive-yards, B 3226.

Olyve, *s.* olive-tree, 5. 181.

Omelies, *s. pl.* homilies, I 1088.

On, *prep.* on, A 12 ; in, F 921 ; at, T. iii. 32 ; of, T. iii. 18 ; as regards, E 1424 ; against, T. ii. 865 ; towards, 4. 298 ; binding on, 10. 43 ; *hir on*, upon her, 3. 1217 ; *on eve*, in the evening, E 1214 ; *on reste*, at rest, F 379.

On, one ; see Oon.

Onde, *s.* envy, R. 148. A.S. *anda.*

Oneden, *pt. pl.* united, I 193 ; *pp.* united, complete, D 1968.

Ones, *adv.* once, B 588 ; united in design, C 696 ; *at ones*, at once, A 765.

On-lofte, *adv.* aloft, up in the air, in the sky, 5. 203, 683 ; above ground, F 229.

On-lyve, *adv.* alive, F 932. Lit. ' in life.'

Oo, one ; see Oon.

Ook, *s.* oak, A 1702 ; Oke, *dat.* 3. 447 ; (*collectively*), oaks, R. 1384.

Oon, one, R. 624 ; always the same, the same, one and the same, B 2142 ; united, agreed, T. ii. 1740 ; alone, unwedded, D 66 ; the same, i.e. of small consequence, 3. 1295 ; the same thing, alike, F 537 ; *oon the faireste*, one of the fairest, E 212 ; *in oon*, in the same state, unchangeably ; *ever in oon*, ever alike, always in the same manner, E 602 ; continually, D 209 ; *oon and oon*, one by one, A 679 ; *after oon*, equally good, A 341 ; *that oon*, one thing, T. iv. 1453 ; the one, C 666 ; *many oon*, many a one, A 317, E 775 ; *felle at oon*, came to one agreement, T. iii. 565 ; *many on*, many a one, D 680 ; *everich on*, every one, B 1164 ; Oo, one, G 207 ; a single, R. 1236 ; one and the same, 3. 1293.

Ooned, *pp.* united, B 4. p 6. 81.

Open-ers, *s.* fruit of the medlar, A 3871.

Open-heeded, with head uncovered, D 645.

Opie, *s.* opium, A 1472 ; Opies, *pl.* opiates, L. 2670.

Opned, *pp.* opened, T. iii. 469.

Opposen, *v.* oppose ; *o. me*, lay to my charge, D 1597.

Oppresse, *v.* suppress, 10. 60 ; violate, F 1411 ; *ger.* to put down, G 4.

Oppressioun, *s.* oppression, wrong, L 2592 ; tyranny, 10. 19 ; violation, L 1868.

Or, *conj.* ere, G 314.

Or, *prep.* before, R. 864.

Or, *conj.* or, A 91, &c. ; Or . . . or, either . . . or, R. 261.

Oratorie, *s.* closet for prayers, A 1905.

Ordal, *s.* ordeal, T. iii. 1046.

Orde, *dat.* point, L. 645. A.S. *ord.* And see Word.

Ordenee, *adj.* well-ordered, B 4. p 1. 46.

Ordenély, *adv.* conformably, in order, B 4. p 6. 313.

Ordenour, *s.* ruler, B 3. p 12. 102.

Ordeyned, *pp.* provided, A 2553 ; appointed, F 177 ; prepared, G 1277 ; ordered, I 336 ; ( = ordeynee), *pp.* regulated, T. i. 892.

Ordinaat, *adj.* orderly, E 1284.

Ordinatly, *adv.* methodically, I 1045.

Ordinaunce, *s.* arrangement, A 3012 ; provision, B 250 ; orderly arrangement, A 2567 ; consideration, 18. 38 ; order, B 2303 ; resolve, B 2258 ; command, 10. 44.

Ordred, *pp. as adj.* ordained, I 782.

Ordure, *s.* filthiness, I 841 ; rubbish, T. v. 385.

Ore, *s.* grace ; *thyn o.*, (I pray for) thy grace, A 3726. A.S. *ār.*

Ore, *s.* ore (of metal), D 1064. A.S. *ōr.*

Ores, *s. pl.* oars, L. 2308.

Orfrays, *s.* gold embroidery, gold braid, fringe with golden threads, R. 462, 869, 1076. A.F. *orfreis*, O.F. *orfrois.*

Organs, *s. pl.* 'organs,' the old equivalent of organ, G 134.

Orgon, *pl. as sing.* organ (Lat. *organa*), B 4041.

Orient, *s.* east, A 1494.

Oriental, *adj.* eastern ; (hence) of superior quality, L. 221.

Orisonte, *s.* horizon, T. v. 276.

Orisoun, *s.* prayer, A 2372.

*Orizon rectum*, or right horizon, A. ii. 26. 35. This means the horizon of any place situate on the equator, which could be represented by a *straight* line upon a disc of the astrolabe.

Orloge, *s.* clock, 5. 350 ; B 4044.

Orphelin, *adj.* orphaned, B 2. p 3. 33.

Orpiment, *s.* orpiment, G 759, 774, 823. '*Orpiment*, trisulphide of arsenic'; Webster.

*Oruscupum*, i. e. horoscope, A. ii. 3. *rubric.*

Osanne, i. e. Hosannah, B 642.

Ost, *s.* host, army, L. 1906.

**Ostelments,** *s. pl.* furniture, household goods, B 2. p 5. 135. (L. *supellectilis.*) Cf. F. *outil.*

**Ostesse,** *s.* hostess, B 4. m 3. 23.

**Otes,** *s. pl.* (of) oats, D 1963.

**Other,** *adj.* second, R. 953, 976; the other, A 427; *what o.,* what else, T. i. 799; *that o.,* the other, F 496; Other, *pl.* others, R. 1304; Othere, *pl.* other, A 794; others, HF. 2151; *gen. pl.* others', HF. 2153; Otheres, *gen. sing.* each other's (lit. of the other), C 476.

**Other,** *conj.* or, 3. 810; Other . . or, either . . or, G 1149.

**Other-whyle,** *adv.* sometimes, B 2. p 1. 120.

**Ouche,** *s.* nouch, clasp, D 743. See **Nouchis.**

**Ought,** *s.* anything, 3. 459; *as adv.* at all, T. ii. 268; *in ought that,* in as far as, T. iii. 1241.

**Oughtestow,** oughtest thou, L. 1957.

**Oule,** *s.* owl, D 1081.

**Oules,** *pl.* awls; spiked irons for tormenting men, D 1730. A.S. *awel.*

**Ounces,** *pl.* small portions, A 677; ounces, G 756.

**Ounded,** *pp.* wavy, T. iv. 736.

**Oundinge,** *s.* adornment with waved lines, I 417.

**Oundy,** *adj.* wavy, HF. 1386. F. *ondé.*

**Out,** *adv.* out, A 45, &c.; *used for* come out, HF. 2139; go out, T. iv. 210; fully, T. iii. 417; *mordre wil out,* murder will out, B 1766; Out and out, entirely, T. ii. 739.

**Out,** *interj.* alas! A 3825; Out! harrow! B 4570.

**Out of,** *prep.* without, C 157; out of, A 452.

**Out-breke,** *v.* break out, break silence, 2. 12.

**Out-breste,** *v.* burst out, T. iv. 237.

**Out-bringe,** *v.* utter, L. 1835.

**Outcast,** *pp.* cast out, T. v. 615.

**Out-caughte,** *pt. s.* drew out, B 1861.

**Out-drawe,** *pp.* drawn out, T. iv. 1226.

**Oute,** *adv.* away, T. v. 553; out, i. e. uttered, D 977.

**Outen,** *v.* put out, utter, exhibit, G 834; utter, E 2438; Oute, 1 *pr. s.* utter, offer, D 521. A.S. *ûtian.*

**Outereste,** *adj. superl.* uttermost, farthest, B 2. m 6. 17.

**Outerly,** *adv.* utterly, entirely, E 335.

**Outfleyinge,** *s.* flying out, HF. 1523.

**Out-hees,** *s.* outcry, hue and cry, alarm, A 2012.

**Outher,** *conj.* either, R. 250.

**Outherwhyle,** *adv.* sometimes, B 2733, 2857.

**Outlandish,** *adj.* foreign, 9. 22.

**Outrage,** *s.* excess (*luxu*), B 2. m 5. 5; cruelty, injustice, A 2012.

**Outrageous,** *adj.* excessive, B 2180; immoderate, I 743; violent, rampant, R. 174; excessively bold, R. 1257.

**Outrageously,** *adv.* excessively, A 3998.

**Outrance,** *s.* great hurt, excessive injury, 24. 26.

**Outraye,** *v.* lose temper, E 643. O. F. *outreer,* to surpass.

**Outrely,** *adj.* utterly, B 4419; entirely, B 2943, 3072; decidedly, B 2210.

**Out-ringe,** *v.* ring out, T. iii. 1237.

**Out-rood,** *pt. s.* rode out, T. v. 604.

**Out-rydere,** *s.* rider abroad, A 166. The name of a monk who rode to inspect granges, &c.

**Out-springe,** *v.* come to light, T. i. 745; Out-sprong, *pt. s.* spread abroad, C 111.

**Out-sterte,** *pt. pl.* started out, B 4237.

**Out-straughte,** *pt. s.* stretched out, R. 1515.

**Out-taken,** *pp.* excepted, B 277.

**Out-twyne,** 2 *pr. pl.* twist out, utter, 12. 11.

**Out-wende,** *v.* proceed, HF. 1645.

**Over,** *prep.* above, R. 1475; beyond, D 1661; besides, F 137; Over hir might, to excess, C 468.

**Over,** *adj.* upper, A 133; Overest, *superl.* uppermost, A 290.

**Over-al,** *adv.* everywhere, A 216, 249, 1207; in all directions, T. i. 928; on all sides, D 264; in every way, E 2129; throughout, E 1048; Over al and al, beyond every other, 3. 1003.

**Over-blowe,** *pp.* past, L. 1287.

**Overcaste,** *v.* overcast, sadden, A 1536.

**Overcomer,** *s.* conqueror, B 1. m 2. 15.

**Overdoon,** *pp.* carried to excess, G 645.

**Over-gilt,** *adj.* worked over with gold, R. 873.

**Over-goon,** *v.* pass away, T. i. 846; overspread, B 2. p 7. 42.

**Overkerveth,** *pr. s.* cuts across, crosses, A. i. 21. 90.

**Overlad,** *pp.* put upon, B 3101. Lit. *led over.*

**Overlade,** *v.* overload, L. 621.

**Overlight,** *adj.* too feeble, B 4. m 3. 34.

**Over-loked,** *pp.* perused, 3. 232.

**Overlyeth,** *pr. s.* lies upon, I 575.

**Over-passeth,** *pr. s.* surpasses, B 5. p 6. 117.

**Over-raughte**, *pt. s.* reached over, *hence,* urged on, T. v. 1018.

**Over-shake**, *pp.* shaken off, 5. 681.

**Overshote**, *pp.* ; *had overshote hem,* had over-run the scent, 3. 383.

**Over-skipte**, 1 *pt. s.* skipped over, omitted, 3. 1208.

**Oversloppe**, *s.* upper-garment, G 633. Cf. Icel. *yfirsloppr,* an upper garment. See **Sloppes**.

**Oversprede**, *v.* spread over, cover, E 1799 ; Over-sprat, *pr. s.* over-spreadeth, T. ii. 767 ; Overspradde, *pt. s.* covered, A 2871.

**Overspringe**, *pr. s. subj.* overpass, F 1060.

**Overtake**, *v.* overtake, attain to, G 682 ; Overtook, 1 *pt. s.* caught up, 3. 360.

**Overte**, *adj.* open, HF. 718.

**Overthrowe**, *v.* be overturned, be ruined, HF. 1640.

**Over-throwinge**, *adj.* overwhelming, B 1. m 2. 2 ; headlong (Lat. *praecipiti*), B 2. m 7. 1 ; headstrong (Lat. *praecipiti*), B 1. m 6. 25 ; revolving, B 3. m 12. 43.

**Overthrowinge**, *s.* falling down, B 2755 ; *pl.* destruction (Lat. *ruinis*), B 2. m 4. 17.

**Overthwart**, *adv.* across, A 1991 ; opposite, T. iii. 685 ; askance, R. 292.

**Overtymeliche**, *adv.* untimely, B 1. m 1. 18.

**Over-whelveth**, *pr. s.* overturns, turns over, agitates, B 2. m 3. 17.

**Owen**, *v.* owe, own, possess ; Oweth, *pr. s.* owns, possesses, C 361 ; Oweth, *pr. s. refl.* it is incumbent (on him), L. 360 *a* ; Oghte, 1 *pt. s.* ought, 4. 216 ; Oughtestow, 2 *pt. s.* oughtest thou, T. v. 545 ; L. 1957 ; Oghte, *pt. s. impers.* it were necessary, B 2188 ; *him oghte,* he ought, L. 377 ; it became him, B 1097 ; *hir oghte,* became her, E 1120 ; *us oghte,* it behoved us, we ought, 1. 119 ; *hem oghte,* they ought, G 1340 ; *us oghte* (subj.), it should behove us, we ought, E 1150 ; Oghte, *pt. s.* owed, L. 589 ; ought, A 505 ; Owed, *pp.* due, B 4. p 5. 18.

**Owene**, *adj. def.* own, C 834 : *myn owene woman,* independent, T. ii. 750 ; *his owne hand,* with his own hand, A 3624.

**Owh**, *interj.* alas, B 1. p 6. 25.

**Owher**, *adv.* anywhere, A 653.

**Oxe**, *s.* ox, C 354 ; Oxes, *gen.* E 207 ; Oxen, *pl.* A 887.

**Oxe-stalle**, *s.* ox-stall, E 398.

**Oynement**, *s.* ointment, unguent, A 631.

**Oynons**, *pl.* onions, A 634.

## P.

**Paas**, *s.* pace, step, L. 284 ; *goon a paas,* go at a footpace, C 866.

**Pace**, *v.* pass, go, A 1602 ; pass, T. i. 371 ; go away, 15. 9 ; pass away, A 175 ; surpass, go beyond, T. iii. 1272 ; walk, T. v. 1791 ; overstep, HF. 392 ; come, HF. 720 ; *p. of,* pass over, T. ii. 1568 ; *of this thing to p.,* to pass this over in review, HF. 239 ; *to pace of,* to pass from, B 205 ; 1 *pr. s.* pass over (it), go on, HF. 1355 ; proceed, go on, A 36 ; 1 *pr. s. subj.* depart, F 494 ; 2 *pr. s. subj.* go, D 911.

**Paillet**, *s.* pallet, T. iii. 229.

**Paire**, *s.* pair, A 473 ; set, A 159 ; *as pl.* pairs, 5. 238. (*Pair,* in the sense of 'set,' is applied to many things of the same kind and size.)

**Paisible**, *adj.* peaceable, 9. 1.

**Palasye**, *s.* palsy, R. 1098.

**Pale**, *s.* perpendicular stripe, HF. 1840.

**Palestral**, *adj.* athletic, pertaining to wrestling, T. v. 304.

**Paleth**, *pr. s.* renders pale, B 2. m 3. 3.

**Paleys**, *or* **Paleis - chaumbres**, *pl.* palace-chambers, 9. 41.

**Paleys-gardyn**, palace-garden, T. ii. 508.

**Paleys-ward, to,** toward the palace, T. ii. 1252.

**Paleys-yates**, *pl.* gates of the palace, 4. 82.

**Palinge**, *s.* adorning with (heraldic) pales, or upright stripes, I 417.

**Palis**, *s.* palisade, stockade, B 1. p 6. 41 ; paling, rampart, B 1. p 3. 86. O.F. *palis, paleis.*

**Palled**, *pp.* pale, languid, H 55.

**Pan**, *s.* brain-pan, skull, A 1165.

**Panade**, *s.* kind of knife, A 3929, 3960.

**Panier**, *s.* pannier, E 1568 ; *pl.* baskets for bread, HF. 1939.

**Panne**, *s.* pan, A 3944.

**Panter**, *s.* bag-net for birds, L. 131 ; *pl.* nets, R. 1621. O.F. *pantiere.*

**Papejay**, *s.* popinjay, B 1559, 1957, E 2332 ; applied in England to the green wood-pecker (*Gecinus viridis*).

**Paper**, *s.* account-book, A 4404.

**Paper-whyt**, *adj.* white as paper, L. 1198.

**Papingay**, *s.* popinjay, R. 81. See **Papejay**.

*Par amour* ; see **Paramour**.

*Par cas,* by chance, C 885.

*Par companye,* for company, A 3839, 4167.

**Paradys**, *s.* paradise, R. 443.

Paráge, *s.* kindred, birth, D 250; rank, D 1120.

Paraments, *pl.* mantles, splendid clothing, A 2501. See **Parements.**

Paramour, (for *par amour*), *adv.* for love, B 2033; longingly, B 1933; with devotion, A 1155; Paramours, passionately, T. v. 332; A 2112; with excessive devotion, L. 260 *a*; by way of passionate love, T. v. 158; *for p.*, for the sake of passion, E 1450; *for paramours*, for love's sake, A 3354.

Paramour, *s.* (1) concubine, wench, D 454; *pl.* A 3756; lovers, paramours, T. ii. 236; Paramour (2), love-making, A 4372.

Paraunter, perhaps, L. 362.

Paraventure, peradventure, perhaps, F 955.

Parcel, *s.* part, F 852; small part, 2. 106.

Parchemin, *s.* parchment, B 5. m 4. 14.

Pardee, (F. *par Dieu*), a common oath, A 563, 3084; Pardieux, T. i. 197.

Pardoner, *s.* seller of indulgences, A 543, C 318.

Paregal, *adj.* fully equal, T. v. 840.

Parements, *s. pl.* rich hangings or ornaments, (applied to a chamber), L. 1106; F 269. See **Parements.**

Parentele, *s.* kinship, I 908.

Parfey, by my faith, in faith, HF. 938.

Parfit, *adj.* perfect, A 72, 422.

Parfitly, *adv.* perfectly, R. 771; wholly, B 2381.

Parfourne, *v.* perform, B 2402; Parfourne, *ger.* to fulfil, B 3137; *p. up*, complete, D 2261.

Parfourninge, *s.* performance, I 807.

Parisshens, *pl.* parishioners, A 482.

Paritorie, *s.* pellitory, *Parietaria officinalis*, G 581.

Parlement, *s.* (1) deliberation, decision due to consultation, A 1306; (2) parliament, T. iv. 143; *p. of Briddes*, Parliament of Birds, I 1086.

Parodie, *s.* period, duration, T. v. 1548. (A curious confusion of *paródie* (so pronounced) with *period*.)

Parsoneres, *s. pl.* partners, partakers, B 5. p 5. 101.

Parten, *v.* share, T. i. 589; *ger.* To p. with, participate in, L. 465; 1 *pr. s.* part, depart, T. i. 5; Parteth, *pr. s.* departs, L. 359; Parted, *pp.* dispersed, T. i. 960; gone away, taken away, L. 1110.

Parteners, *s. pl.* partners, partakers, I 968.

Parting-felawes, *s. pl.* fellow-partakers, I 637.

Part-les, *adj.* without his share, B 4. p 3. 44.

Partrich, *s.* partridge, A 349.

Party, *adv.* partly, A 1053.

Partye, *s.* portion, A 3008; partial umpire, taker of a side, A 2657; portion, T. ii. 394.

Parvys, *s.* church-porch, A 310.

Pas, *s.* pace, B 399; step, D 2162; distance, R. 525; foot-pace, A 825; grade, degree, 4. 134; grade, I 532; passage, B 2635; *a pas*, at a footpace, T. ii. 627, v. 60; F 388; *pl.* paces, yards, A 1890; *thousand pas*, a mile, B 1. p 4. 270.

Passage, *s.* period, R. 406.

Passant, *pres. pt. as adj.* surpassing, A 2107.

Passen, *ger.* to surpass, exceed, conquer, A 3089; overcome, L. 162; outdo, G 857; *pr. s.* passes away, F 404; Paste, *pt. s.* passed, T. ii. 658; passed by, T. ii. 398; Passing, *pres. pt.* surpassing, A 2885; *pp.* past, spent, E 610; surpassed, 7. 82; passed by, 5. 81; overblown, gone off, R. 1682.

Passing, *adj.* excellent, F 929; extreme, E 1225.

Passioun, *s.* suffering, B 1175; passion, 1. 162; passive feeling, impression, B 5. m 4. 52.

Pastee, *s.* pasty, A 4346.

Patrimoine, *s.* patrimony, I 790.

Patroun, *s.* patron, 4. 275; protector, 7. 4; pattern, 3. 910.

Pawmes, *pl.* palms (of the hand), T. iii. 1114.

Pax, *s.* the 'osculatorium,' or 'paxbrede,' a disk of metal or other substance, used at Mass for the 'kiss of peace,' I 407.

Pay, *s.* pleasure, 5. 271; *more to pay*, so as to give more satisfaction, 5. 474.

Paye, *v.* pay, A 806; *pt. s.* A 539; *pp.* satisfied, pleased, 9. 3; *holde her payd*, think herself satisfied, 3. 269.

Payen, *adj.* pagan, A 2370.

Payens, *s. pl.* pagans, L. 786.

Payndemayn, *s.* bread of a peculiar whiteness, B 1915. Lat. *panis Dominicus*.

Payne, *s.* pain; *dide his payne*, took pains, F 730.

Payre, *s.* a pair, R. 1386; Paire, *pl.* pairs, R. 1698.

Pece, *s.* piece, 5. 149; *pl.* pieces. T. i. 833.

Peches, *pl.* peaches, R. 1374.

Pecok, *s.* peacock, 5. 356.

**Pecok-arwes,** *pl.* arrows with peacocks' feathers, A 104.

**Pecunial,** *adj.* pecuniary, D 1314.

**Pees,** *s.* peace, A 532, 1447; *in p.,* in silence, B 228.

**Pees,** peace! hush! be still! B 836.

**Pekke,** *s.* peck (quarter of a bushel), A 4010.

**Pekke,** *imp. s.* peck, pick, B 4157.

**Pel,** *s.* peel, small castle, HF. 1310. O.F. *pel;* from Lat. acc. *pālum.*

**Pelet,** *s.* pellet, stone cannon-ball, HF. 1643.

**Penaunt,** *s.* a penitent, one who does penance, B 3154.

**Pencel** (1), *s.* pencil, brush, A 2049.

**Pencel** (2), *s.* small banner, sleeve worn as a token, T. v. 1043. Short for *penoncel.*

**Pénible,** *adj.* painstaking, B 3490; Penible, careful to please, E 714; Penýble, inured, D 1846.

**Penitauncer,** *s.* confessor who assigns a penance, I 1008.

**Penitence,** *s.* penance, I 101, 126.

**Penne,** *s.* pen, quill, L. 2357.

**Penner,** *s.* pen-case, E 1879.

**Penoun,** *s.* pennon, ensign or small flag borne at the end of a lance, A 978.

**Pens;** see **Peny.**

**Peny,** *s.* penny, R. 451; money, A 4119; Penyes, *pl.* pence, R. 189; Pens, *pl.* pence, C 376.

*Per cas,* by chance, L. 1967.

*Per consequens,* consequently, D 2192.

**Peraventure,** *adv.* perhaps, HF. 304; C 935.

**Percen,** *v.* pierce, B 2014; *pr. s.* pierces with his gaze, 5. 331.

**Perche,** *s.* perch (for birds to rest on), A 2204; wooden bar, R. 225; a horizontal rod, A. ii. 23. 44. Lat. *pertica.*

**Percinge,** *s.;* for percinge = to prevent any piercing, B 2052.

**Perdurable,** *adj.* everlasting, eternal, B 2699; Perdurables, *adj. pl.* everlasting, I 811.

**Perdurablete̊,** *s.* immortality, B 2. p 7. 63, 103.

**Pere,** *s.* peer, equal, B 3244, F 678.

**Peregryn,** *adj.* peregrine, i.e. foreign, F 428.

**Pere-jonette,** *s.* a kind of early-ripe pear, A 3248.

**Peres,** *pl.* pears, R. 1375, E 2331.

**Perfit,** *adj.* complete, A. i. 18. 4.

**Perfitly,** *adv.* perfectly, A. pr. 21.

**Perfourne,** *ger.* to perform, B 2256; be equivalent to, A. ii. 10. 16.

**Peril,** *s.* B 2672; *in p.,* in danger, 4. 108; *upon my p.,* (I say it) at my peril, D 561.

**Perisse,** *v.* perish, I 254.

**Perle,** *s.* pearl, L. 221.

**Perled,** *pp.* fitted with pearl-like drops, A 3251.

**Perréé,** *s.* jewellery, precious stones, gems, B 3495, 3550.

**Perrýe,** *s.* jewellery, A 2936; Perrie, HF. 1393.

**Pers,** *adj.* of Persian dye, light-blue, R. 67.

**Pers,** *s.* stuff of a sky-blue colour, A 439, 617.

**Perséveraunce,** *s.* endurance, T. i. 44; constancy, 3. 1007.

**Persévere,** *v.* continue, D 148; *pr. s.* lasts, C 497.

**Perséveringe,** *s.* perseverance, G 117.

**Persly,** *s.* parsley, A 4350.

**Persóne,** *s.* person, figure, T. ii. 701; Pérsoun, parson, A 478.

**Pert,** *adj.* forward, frisky, A 3950. Short for *apert.*

**Pertinacie,** *s.* pertinaciousness, I 391.

**Pertinent,** *adj.* fitting, B 2204.

**Pertourbe,** *ger.* to perturb, T. iv. 561.

**Perturbacioun,** *s.* trouble, B 1. p 1. 98

**Perturbinge,** *s.* perturbation, D 2254.

**Pervenke,** *s.* periwinkle, R. 903; Pervinke. R. 1432.

**Pesen,** *pl.* peas, L. 648.

**Pesible,** *adj.* calm, B 1. p 5. 3.

**Pestilence,** *s.* the (great) pestilence, A 442, C 679; curse, B 4600, D 1264.

**Peter,** *interj.* by St. Peter, B 1404, G 665.

**Peyne,** *s.* pain of torture, A 1133; T. i. 674; *in the p.,* under torture, T. iii. 1502; care, F 509; toil, G 1398; penalty, B 3041; endeavour, R. 765; penance, B 2939; *upon p.,* under a penalty, E 586.

**Peyne,** *v. refl.* take pains, endeavour, B 4495; put (myself) to trouble, HF. 246; Peyne, 1 *pr. s. refl.* take pains, C 330, 395; Peyned hir, *pt. s. refl.* took pains, A 139, E 976; Peyned hem, *pt. pl. refl.* R. 107.

**Peynte,** *v.* paint, C 12; colour highly, HF. 246; smear, L. 875; *do p.,* cause to be painted, 3. 259; *pt. s.* F 560; Peynted, *pp.* painted, L. 1029; Peynt, *pp.* R. 248.

**Peyntour,** *s.* painter, T. ii. 1041.

**Peynture,** *s.* painting, C 33.

**Peyre,** *s.* pair, A 2121; a set (of similar things), D 1741.

**Peysible,** *adj.* tranquil, B 3. m 9. 51. (L. *tranquilla.*)

**Peytrel,** *s.* poitrel, breast-piece of a horse's harness; properly, the breast-plate of a horse in armour, G 564; *pl.* I 433. A. F. *peitrel*, Lat. *pectorale*.

**Phitonesses,** *pl.* pythonesses, witches, HF. 1261.

[**Physices,** *gen.* of physics, *or* natural philosophy, B 1189. Lat. *physices*, gen. of *physicē*, natural philosophy. (I propose this reading.)]

**Pich,** *s.* pitch, A 3731, I 854.

**Piëtee,** *s.* pity, T. iii. 1033, v. 1598.

**Piëtous,** *adj.* piteous, sad, T. iii. 1444; sorrowful, T. v. 451; merciful, F 20.

**Pigges-nye** (lit. pig's eye), a dear little thing, A 3268.

**Pighte,** *pt. s. refl.* pitched, fell, A 2689; *pt. s. subj.* should pierce, should stab, I. 163 (but this is almost certainly an error for *prighte*, pt. s. subj. of *prikke*).

**Piked,** *pt. s.* stole, L. 2467.

**Pikerel,** *s.* a young pike (fish), E 1419.

**Pilche,** *s.* a warm furred outer garment, 20. 4.

**Pile,** *ger.* to pillage, plunder, I 769; *v.* rob, despoil, D 1362.

**Piled,** *pp.* deprived of hair, very thin, A 627; bare, bald (lit. peeled), A 3935.

**Pileer,** *s.* pillar, HF. 1421.

**Pilled,** *pp.* robbed, L. 1262.

**Pilours,** *pl.* robbers, pillagers, A 1007, 1020.

**Pilwe,** *s.* pillow, E 2004.

**Pilwe-beer,** *s.* pillow-case, A 694.

**Piment,** *s.* sweetened wine, A 3378.

**Pin,** *s.* pin, small peg, F 127, 316; fastening, brooch, A 196; thin wire, A. ii. 38. 8; Hangeth on a joly pin, is merry, E 1516.

**Pinche,** *v.* find fault (with), pick a hole (in), A 326; Pinchest at, 2 *pr. s.* blamest, 10. 57; *pp.* closely pleated, A 151.

**Piper,** *s. as adj.* suitable for pipes or horns, 5. 178.

**Pissemyre,** *s.* pismire, ant, D 1825.

**Pistel,** *s.* epistle, E 1154; message, sentence, D 1021.

**Pit,** *pp.* put (Northern), A 4088.

**Pitaunce,** *s.* pittance, A 224.

**Pitee,** *s.* pity, 1. 68; Pite were, it would be a pity (if), 3. 1266.

**Pith,** *s.* strength, R. 401; D 475.

**Pitóus, Pítous,** *adj.* compassionate, A 143; merciful, C 226; pitiful, A 953; plaintive, R. 89, 497; mournful, R. 420; piteous, sad, sorrowful, A 955; pitiable, B 3673; Pitousë, *fem.* full of compassion, L. 2582.

**Pitously,** *adv.* piteously, B 1059; pitiably, B 3729; sadly, A 1117.

**Place,** *s.* place, A 623; manor-house (residence of a chief person in a small town or village), B 1910, D 1768.

*Placebo,* vespers of the dead, so called from the initial word of the antiphon to the first psalm of the office (see Ps. cxiv. 9 in the Vulgate version), I 617; a song of flattery, D 2075.

**Plages,** *s. pl.* regions, B 543; quarters of the compass, A. i. 5. 12.

**Plain,** *adj.*; see **Playn.**

**Plane,** *s.* plane-tree, A 2922.

**Planed,** *pt. s.* planed, made smooth, D 1758.

**Plante,** *s.* slip, cutting, D 763; piece of cut wood, R. 929.

**Plastres,** *s. pl.* plasters, F 636.

**Plat,** *adj.* flat, certain, A 1845; Platte, *dat.* flat (side of a sword), F 162, 164.

**Plat,** *adv.* flat, B 1865; plainly, B 886; fully, T. ii. 579.

**Plate,** *s.* plate-armour, 9. 49; stiff iron defence for a hauberk, B 2055; the ' sight' on the ' rewle,' A. i. 13. 2.

**Plated,** *pp.* covered with metal in plates, HF. 1345.

**Platly,** *adv.* flatly, plainly, T. iii. 786, 881.

**Plaunte,** *s.* plant, F 1032.

**Plaunte,** *imp. s.* plant, T. i. 964.

**Playen me,** *v. refl.* to amuse myself, R. 113.

**Playing,** *s.* sport, R. 112.

**Playn,** *adj.* smooth, even, R. 860; *in short and pl.*, in brief, plain terms, E 577; Plain, flat, H 229.

**Playn,** *s.* plain, B 24.

**Plede,** *ger.* to dispute, B 2559.

**Pleding,** *s.* pleading, 3. 615.

**Pledoures,** *pl.* pleaders, lawyers, R. 198.

**Plee,** *s.* plea, 5. 485; *pl.* suits, 5. 101.

**Plegges,** *s. pl.* pledges, B 3018.

**Pleinedest,** 2 *pt. s.* didst complain, B 4. p 4. 168.

**Pleinte,** *s.* complaint, lament, B 66.

**Plenére,** *adj.* plenary, full, L. 1607.

**Plentee,** *s.* plenitude, fulness, I 1080; abundance, R. 1434.

**Plentevous,** *adj.* plentiful, A 344.

**Plentevously,** *adv.* plenteously, B 2. p 2. 86.

**Plesaunce,** *s.* pleasure, C 219, D 408; delight, A 2409; pleasant thing, 3. 773; pleasure, will, A 1571; kindness, E 1111; pleasing behaviour, F 509; pleasantness, L. 1373; happiness, L. 1150; amusement, F 713; will, delight, B 149.

**Plesaunt,** *adj.* pleasant, satisfactory, pleasing, A 138, 222.

**Plesen,** *v.* please, A 610, F 707.

**Plesinges,** *adj. pl.* pleasing, B 711.

**Plesure,** *s.* pleasure, 6. 126.

**Plète,** *ger.* to plead, bring a law-suit, T. ii. 1468.

**Pletinges,** *pl.* law-suits, B 3. p 3. 67.

**Pley,** *s.* play, sport, A 1125; dalliance, 4. 178; jesting, I 539; delusion, 3. 648; *pl.* games, T. v. 304; plays, D 558; funeral games, T. v. 1499.

**Pleye,** *v.* amuse oneself, B 3524, 3666; *ger.* to play, be playful, be amused, A 772; to amuse (myself), B 3996; to amuse (ourselves), L. 1495; play (on an instrument), A 236; 1 *pr. s.* jest, B 3153; 1 *pr. pl.* play, B 1423; *pr. pl.* F 900; *pt. s.* played, rejoiced, T. i. 1013; was in play, 3. 875; Pleyd, *pp.* 3. 618.

**Pleyinge,** *s.* amusement, sport, A 1061.

**Pleyinge,** *adj.* playful, B 3. m 2. 27.

**Pleyn** (1), *adj.* full, A 2461; complete, A 315, 337.

**Pleyn** (2), *adj.* plain, clear, L. 328; honest, 5. 528; plain, i. e. open, A 987; *as s.* plain (fact), A 1091; *pl.* smooth, 5. 180.

**Pleyn** (1), *adv.* full, T. v. 1818; entirely, A 327.

**Pleyn** (2), *adv.* plainly, A 790; openly, E 637.

**Pleyne,** *v.* complain, lament, B 1067; *refl.* 6. 50; *v.* to whinny (as a horse), 7. 157; *pl. upon,* cry out against, L. 2525; 1 *pr. s.* make complaint, L. 2512; *pp.* said by way of complaint, L. 326 *a.*

**Pleyning,** *s.* complaining, lamenting, 3. 599.

**Pleynly,** *adv.* plainly, openly, (*or,* fully), A 1733.

**Pleynte,** *s.* plaint, complaint, 2. 47; Pl. of Kynde, Complaint of Nature, 5. 316.

**Plighte** (1), *pt. s.* plucked, drew, T. ii. 1120; pulled, B 15; *pp.* plucked, torn, D 790. The infin. would be *plicchen,* variant of *plukkien* or *plukken.*

**Plighte** (2), 1 *pr. s.* plight, pledge, F 1537; *pt. s.* L. 2466; *pp.* pledged, C 702.

**Plomet,** *s.* plummet, heavy weight, A. ii. 23. 42.

**Plom-rewle,** *s.* plummet-rule, A. ii. 38. 10.

**Plough-harneys,** *s.* harness for a plough, i. e. parts of a plough, as the share and coulter, A 3762.

**Ploumes,** *s. pl.* plums, R. 1375.

**Ploungen,** *ger.* to plunge, bathe, B 3. p 2. 48.

**Ploungy,** *adj.* stormy, rainy, B 1. m 3. 9.

**Plowman,** *s.* ploughman, E 799.

**Plukke,** *v.* pluck, pull, T. iv. 1403.

**Plye,** *v.* ply, mould, E 1430; bend, E 1169.

**Plyght,** *pp.* plighted, T. iii. 782.

**Plyt,** *s.* plight, T. ii. 712, 1731; condition, B 2338; position, T. ii. 74; Plyte, *dat.* mishap, wretched condition, 5. 294; plight, 23. 19; state, G 952.

**Plyte,** *ger.* to fold, T. ii. 1204; *pt. s.* turned backwards and forwards, T. ii. 697.

**Poeplish,** popular, T. iv. 1677.

**Poesye,** *s.* poetry, T. v. 1790.

**Poinant,** *adj.* poignant, I 130, 131.

**Point, Poynt,** *s.* point, A 114; position, I 921; *in point,* on the point of, about to, B 331, 910; *at point,* ready, T. iv. 1638; *in good p.,* in good case, A 200; *fro p. to p.,* from beginning to end, B 3652; *p. for p.,* in every detail, E 577.

**Point-devys;** *at p.,* with great neatness, exactly, carefully, HF. 917; A 3689, F 560.

**Pointel,** *s.* style, i. e. stylus, writing implement, B 1. p 1. 3.

**Poke,** *s.* bag, A 3780, 4278,

**Poked,** *pt. s.* incited, T. iii. 116; nudged, A 4169.

**Pokets,** *s. pl.* little bags, G 808.

**Pokkes,** *s. pl.* pocks, pustules, C 358.

**Pol** (1), *s.* pole, long stick; Pole, *dat.* L. 2202.

**Pol** (2), *s.* pole (of the heavens), A. i. 14. 9.

**Polax,** *s.* pole-axe, L. 642.

**Polcat,** *s.* polecat, C 855.

**Policye,** *s.* public business, C 600.

**Pollax,** *s.* pole-axe, A 2544.

**Polut,** *pp.* polluted, B 1. p 4. 281.

**Polýve,** *s.* pulley, F 184.

**Pomel,** *s.* round part, top, A 2689.

**Pomely,** *adj.* marked with round spots like an apple, dappled, A 616; Pomely-gris, dapple-gray, G 559.

**Pomgarnettes,** *s. pl.* pomegranates, R. 1356.

**Pompe,** *s.* pomp, A 525.

**Pool,** *s.* pole (of the heavens), A. i. 18. 20.

**Pope-Holy,** i. e. Hypocrisy, R. 415.

**Popelote,** *s.* poppet, darling, A 3254.

**Popet,** *s.* puppet, doll; spoken ironically, and really applied to a corpulent person, B 1891.

**Popinjay,** *s.* popinjay, R. 913.

**Poplér,** *s.* poplar-tree, A 2921; (collectively) poplar-trees, R. 1385.

**Popped,** *pt. s. refl.* tricked herself out, R. 1019.

**Popper,** *s.* small dagger, A 3931.

**Poraille,** *s.* poor people, A 247.

**Porche,** *s.* Porch, B 5. m 4. 1.

**Pore,** *adj.* poor, L. 388.

**Porisme,** *s.* corollary, B 3. p 10. 166.

**Porphúrie,** *s.* a slab of porphyry used as a mortar, G 775.

**Port** (1), *s.* port, carriage, behaviour, A 69 ; bearing, mien, L. 2453.

**Port** (2), *s.* haven, T. i. 526, 969.

**Portatif,** *adj.* portable, 3. 53.

**Porthors,** *s.* portesse, breviary, B 1321. From *porter*, to carry, *hors*, abroad.

**Portours,** *pl.* porters, T. v. 1139.

**Portreiture,** *s.* drawing, picture, R. 827 ; set of drawings, A 1968; picturing, HF. 131.

**Portreye,** *v.* pourtray, depict, 1. 81 ; Portrayed, *pp.* painted in fresco, R. 140 ; full of pictures, R. 1077.

**Portreying,** *s.* a picture, A 1938.

**Pose,** *s.* a cold in the head, A 4152, H 62. A.S. *ge-pose.*

**Pose,** 1 *pr. s.* put the case, (will) suppose, A 1162.

**Positif,** *adj* positive, fixed, A 1167.

**Positioun,** *s.* supposition, hypothesis, B 5. p 4. 48.

**Possessioners,** *s. pl.* men who are endowed, D 1722.

**Possessioun,** *s.* great possessions, wealth, F 686 ; endowments, D 1926.

**Posseth,** *pr. s.* pusheth, tosseth, I.. 2420.

**Post,** *s.* support, A 214 ; pillar, A 800.

**Postum,** *s.* imposthume, abscess, B 3. p 4. 14.

**Potáge,** *s.* broth, B 3623, C 368.

**Potente,** *s.* crutch, R. 368 ; staff, D 1776.

**Potestat,** *s.* potentate, D 2017.

**Pothecárie,** *s.* apothecary, C 852.

**Pouche,** *s.* pocket, A 3931 ; *pl.* money-bags, A 368.

**Poudre,** *s.* dust, HF. 536 ; powder, G 760 ; gunpowder, HF. 1644.

**Poudred,** *pp.* besprinkled, R. 1436.

**Poudre-marchaunt,** *s.* the name of a kind of spice, A 381.

**Pounage,** *s.* pannage, swine's food, 9. 7.

**Pound,** *pl.* pounds, A 454.

**Poune,** *s.* pawn at chess, 3. 661.

**Pounsoned,** *pp. as adj.* stamped, pierced, I 421.

**Pounsoninge,** *s.* punching of holes in garments, I 418.

**Pouped,** *pt. pl.* blew hard, puffed, B 4589 ; *pp.* blown, H 90.

**Poure,** *ger.* to pore, look closely, A 185 ; to pore over (it), R. 1640 ; 1 *pr. pl.* (we) pore, gaze steadily, G 670.

**Poured,** *pp.* poured, R. 1148.

**Pouring,** *s.* pouring (in), T. iii. 1460.

**Pous,** *s.* pulse, T. iii. 1114.

**Poustee,** *s.* power, B 4. p 5. 13.

**Povertee,** *s.* poverty, 3. 410 ; Povérte, *s.* poverty, T. iv. 1520 ; Póvert, poverty, R. 450 ; Povért, C 441.

**Povre,** *adj.* poor, R. 466, A 225.

**Povre,** *adj. as s.* poor, *hence* poverty, 10. 2.

**Povre,** *adv.* poorly, E 1043.

**Povreliche,** *adj.* poorly, in poverty, E 213, 1055.

**Povrely,** *adv.* in poor array, A 1412.

**Povrest,** *adj. superl.* poorest, C 449, E 205.

**Poynaunt,** *adj.* pungent, A 352, B 4024.

**Poynt,** *s.* sharp point, 7. 211 ; very object, aim, A 1501 ; point, bit (of it), part, R. 1236 ; a stop, G 1480 ; *up p.*, on the point, T. iv. 1153 ; *in p. is*, is on the point, is ready, 1. 48; *fro p. to p.*, in every point, 5. 461 ; *to the p.*, to the point, 5. 372 ; *at p. devys*, exact at all points, R. 830; to perfection, exquisitely, R. 1215 ; *pl.* tags, A 3322.

**Poynte,** *ger.* to describe, T. iii. 497 ; *pr. pl.* stab, R. 1058 ; *pp.* pointed, R. 944.

**Poyntel,** *s.* style for writing, D 1742.

**Practisour,** *s.* practitioner, A 422.

**Praktike,** *s.* practice, D 187.

**Praye,** *s.* prey, 1. 64.

**Praye,** *pr. pl.* petition, make suit, I 785.

**Praying,** *s.* request, prayer, R. 1484.

**Preamble,** *s.* D 831.

**Preambulacioun,** *s.* preambling, D 837.

**Precedent,** *adj.* preceding, A. ii. 32. 4.

**Preche,** *v.* preach, A 481, 712; Prechestow, thou preachest, D 366.

**Prechour,** *s.* preacher, D 165.

**Preciousnesse,** *s.* costliness, I 446.

**Predestinee,** *s.* predestination, T. iv. 966.

**Predicacioun,** *s.* preaching, sermon, B 1179.

**Preef,** *s.* proof, assertion, D 247 ; experience, L. 528 *a* ; test, proof, G 968 ; the test, H 75.

**Prees,** *s.* press, crowd, B 393, 646 ; the throng of courtiers, 13. 4 ; press of battle, 9. 33 ; *in p.*, in the crowd, 5. 603.

**Preesseth,** *pr. s.* throngs, A 2580.

**Prefectes,** *gen.* prefect's, G 369. Lit. 'an officer of the prefect's (officers).'

**Preferre,** *pr. s. subj.* precede, take precedence of, D 96.

**Preignant,** *pres. pt.* plain, convincing, T. iv. 1179.

**Preisen,** *ger.* to praise, (worthy) of being praised, R. 70 ; *v.* appraise, estimate, R. 1115; prize, esteem, R. 1693.

Preiseres, *s. pl.* praisers, B 2367.

Preisinge, *s.* honour, glory, I 949.

Prelát, *s.* prelate, A 204.

Premisses, *pl.* statements laid down, B 3. p 10. 121.

Prenostik, *s.* prognostic, prognostication, 10. 54.

Prente, *s.* print, D 604.

Prenten, *ger.* to imprint, T. ii. 900.

Préntis, *s.* apprentice, A 4365.

Prentishood, *s.* apprenticeship, A 4400.

Prescience, *s.* foreknowledge, A 1313.

Prese, *ger.* to press forward, T. i. 446; *v.* hasten, 2. 19.

Presénce, *s.* 1. 19; *in pr.*, in a large assembly, E 1207.

Present, *adv.* immediately, 5. 424.

Presentarie, *adj.* ever-present, B 5. p 6. 78.

Presented, *pp.* brought, L. 1297.

Presenting, *s.* offering, L. 1135.

Presently, *adv.* at the present moment, B 5. p 6. 123.

President, *s.* the one who presided in parliament, T. iv. 213.

Presoun, *s.* prison, T. iii. 380.

Press, *s.* throng, T. i. 173; Presse, *dat.* instrument exercising pressure, A 81; mould, A 263; *on presse*, under a press, in a suppressed state, down, T. i. 559; press, a cupboard with shelves (for linen, &c.), A 3212.

Prest, *s.* priest, B 1166.

Prest, *adj.* ready, prepared, prompt, 5. 307; *pl.* prompt, T. iv. 661.

Pretende, *v.* attempt to reach, seek (after), T. iv. 922.

Preterit, *s.* past time, B 5. p 6. 48.

Pretorie, *s.* the Roman imperial body-guard, the Pretorian cohort, B 1. p 4. 94.

Preve, *s.* proof, B 4173; experimental proof, A. ii. 23 *rubric*; *at p.*, (when it comes) to the proof, T. iii. 1002; *at p.*, in the proof, T. iv. 1659; *armes preve*, proof of fighting power, T. i. 470.

Preve, *v.* prove, C 169; bide the test, G 645; succeed when tested, G 1212; Preved, *pp.* proved to be so, T. i. 239; tested, G 1336; approved, E 28; exemplified, E 826; shewn, F 481.

Prevetee, *s.* secret place, recess, T. iv. 1111.

Prevey, *adj.* secret, B 4. p 3. 122.

Previdence, *s.* seeing beforehand, B 5. p 6. 131.

Prevy, *adj.* privy, unobserved, 3. 382; not confidential, HF. 285.

Preye, *ger.* to beseech, T. ii. 1369; to pray, 2. 20; Preyde, *pt. s.* B 391;

Preyeden, *pt. pl.* D 895; Preyed, *pp.* E 773.

Preys, *s.* praise, B 3837.

Pricasour, *s.* a hard rider, A 189.

Prighte, *pt. s.* pricked, F 418 (*inferior* MSS. *have* pighte). No doubt, the reading *pighte* in 1. 163 should also be *prighte*. See Priken.

Priken, *v.* incite, urge, T. iv. 633; Prik, 1 *pr. s.* spur, rouse, 5. 389; Priketh, *pr. s.* excites, A 11, 1043; spurs, D 656; pricks, aches, D 1594; Prighte, *pt. s.* F 418 (see above); Priked, *pt. s.* spurred, B 1964.

Priking, *s.* hard riding, A 191, A 2599.

Prikke, *s.* point, HF. 907; sting, I 468; a small mark, a peg, A. ii. 42. 4; a dot, A. ii. 5. 20; piercing stroke, A 2606; point, critical condition, B 119.

Principals, *adj. pl.* cardinal, A. ii. 31. 17.

*Principio, in*, in the beginning (St. John, i. 1), A 254.

Pris, *s.* prize, A 2241.

Privee, *adj.* secret, A 3295; private, I 102; intimate, R. 600; closely attendant, E 192; *privee man*, private individual, B 2. p 3. 77.

Privee, *adv.* secretly, F 531; Privee and apert, secretly and openly, D 1114; *pr. neap.*, neither secretly nor openly, D 1136.

Privee, *s.* privy, C 527, E 1954.

Prively, *adv.* secretly, A 652; unperceived, R. 784.

Privetee, *s.* privacy, R. 1294; secrecy, B 548; secrets, secret, D 531, 542, 1637; private affairs, A 1411; private apartment, A 4334; privy parts, B 3905.

Privy, *adj.* secret, L. 1267, 1780.

Proces, *s.* process, B 2665; proceeding, F 1345; process of time, F 829; argument, B 3. p 10. 62; matter, T. ii. 485; L. 1914; story, HF. 251; occurrence of events, B 3511; *dat.* course (of time), 3. 1331.

Procutour, *used for* Procurator, proctor, D 1596.

Proeve, *s.* proof, B 5. p 4. 83.

Proeve, 1 *pr. s.* approve, B 5. p 3. 28; *pr. s.* shews, B 2. m 1. 17.

Professioun, *s.* profession of religion, D 1925; oath of profession (as a monk), B 1345.

Proferestow, dost thou offer, T. iii. 1461.

Profre, *s.* offer, L. 2079.

Proheme, *s.* proem, prologue, E 43.

Prolaciouns, *s. pl.* utterances, B 2. p 1. 50.

Prolle, 2 *pr. pl.* prowl about, search widely, G 1412.

**Pronounced**, *pp.* announced, T. iv. 213.

**Proporcionables**, *adj. pl.* proportional, B 3. m 9. 20.

**Proporcioned**, *pp.* made in proportion, F 192.

**Proporcionels**, *s. pl.* proportional parts, F 1278.

**Propre**, *adj.* own, T. iv. 83; especial, B 2175; peculiar, D 103; well-grown, A 3972; well-made, A 3345; comely, A 4368; handsome, C 309; Propres, *pl.* own, B 1. m 6. 20; *of propre kinde*, by their own natural bent, F 610.

**Proprely**, *adv.* fitly, A 1549; literally, I 285; naturally, D 1191; appropriately, A 729.

**Propretee**, *s.* peculiarity, 10. 69; characteristic, B 2364; peculiar possession, T. iv. 392.

**Prose**, *v.* write in prose, 16. 41.

**Prospectyves**, *s. pl.* perspective-glasses, lenses, F 234. Chaucer here makes the usual distinction between reflecting mirrors and refracting lenses.

**Prospre**, *adj.* prosperous; *prospre fortunes*, well-being, B 1. p 4. 62.

**Protestacioun**, *s.* protest, A 3137.

**Prove**, *v.* test, A. ii. 23, *rubric*; Proveth, *pr. s.* proves, F 455.

**Proverbed**, *pp.* said in proverbs, T. iii. 293.

**Provost**, *s.* prefect, B 1. p 4. 64; chief magistrate, B 1806.

**Provostrie**, *s.* praetorship, B 3. p 4. 90.

**Prow**, *s.* profit, advantage, B 1598, 4140, C 300, G 609.

**Prowesse**, *s.* prowess, T. i. 438; excellence, D 1129; profit, B 4. p 3. 71.

**Proyneth**, *pr. s.* prunes, i.e. trims, makes (himself) neat, E 2011. O.F. *proigner*.

**Prydelees**, *adj.* without pride, 6. 29.

**Prye**, *ger.* to pry, peer, T. ii. 404; to gaze, A 3458; *v.* spy, T. ii. 1710.

**Pryme**, *s.* prime (of day), usually 9 A.M., A 2189, 2576, 3554; *fully pr.*, the end of the first period of the day (from 6 A.M. to 9 A.M.), B 2015; *pr. large*, past 9 o'clock, F 360; *passed pr.*, past 9 o'clock, D 1476; *half way pryme*, half way between 6 and 9 A.M., half-past seven, A 3906.

**Pryme face**, *s.* the first glance, T. iii. 919.

**Prymerole**, *s.* primrose, A 3268.

**Prys**, *s.* price, value, R. 1134; worth, excellence, F 911; praise, E 1026; esteem, F 934; glory, L. 2534; reputation, D 1152; renown, A 67, 237; prize, I 355.

**Pryse**, *ger.* to esteem, to be esteemed, R. 887.

**Pryved**, *pp.* deprived, exiled, 1. 146.

**Pryvee**, *adj.* secret, A 2460.

**Puffen**, *ger.* to blow hard, HF. 1866.

**Pulle**, *s.* a bout at wrestling, a throw, 5. 164.

**Pulle**, *v.* pluck, T. i. 210; to draw, T. ii. 657; *pulle a finche*, pluck a finch, cheat a novice, A 652; *a pulled hen*, a plucked hen, A 177.

**Pultrye**, *s.* poultry, A 598.

**Puplisshen**, *pr. pl. refl.* are propagated, B 3. p 11. 135.

**Purchacen**, *ger.* to procure, acquire, I 742, 1066; gain, I 1080; win, 21. 19; buy, A 608; *pr. pl.* promote, B 2870; *imp. s.* 3 *p.* may (He) provide, B 873; Purchace, *imp. pl.* provide (for yourself), T. ii. 1125.

**Purchas**, *s.* proceeds, gifts acquired, A 256; gain, D 1451, 1530.

**Purchasing**, *s.* conveyancing, A 320; acquisition of property, D 1449.

**Purchasour**, *s.* conveyancer, A 318.

**Pure**, *adj.* very (lit. pure), A 1279; utter, 3. 1209; *the p. deth*, death itself, 3. 583.

**Pure**, *adv.* purely, 3. 1010.

**Pured**, *pp. as adj.* pure, F 1560; very fine, D 143.

**Purfiled**, *pp.* ornamented at the edge, trimmed, A 193.

**Purgacioun**, *s.* discharge, D 120.

**Purgen**, *ger.* to purge, B 4143; *pt. s.* expiated, B 4. m 7. 4 (Lat. *piauit*); *pp.* cleansed (by baptism), G 181.

**Purpos**, *s.* purpose, R. 1140; design, A 1684; *to purpos*, to the subject, 5. 26; *it cam him to p.*, he purposed, F 606.

**Purposen**, *v.* purpose. I 87; *pr. pl.* propose, T. iv. 1350.

**Purpre**, *adj.* purple, T. iv. 869.

**Purpre**, *s.* purple, R. 1071; purple raiment, I 933.

**Purs**, *s.* purse, A 656.

**Pursevauntes**, *s. pl.* pursuivants, HF. 1321.

**Pursuit**, *s.* continuance, perseverance, T. ii. 959; continuance in pursuit, T. ii. 1744; appeal to prosecute, D 890.

**Purtreye**, *v.* draw, A 96; *pt. s.* E 1600.

**Purtreyour**, *s.* draughtsman, A 1899.

**Purveyable**, *adj.* with provident care, B 3. m 2. 5.

**Purveyaunce**, *s.* providence, A 1252, 1665; foresight, D 566, 570; equipment, B 247; provision, A 3566, F 904; pre-arrangement, T. iii. 533; *unto his p.*, to provide himself with necessaries, L. 1561.

**Purveyen**, *v.* provide, B 2532; *pr. s.* foresees, T. iv. 1066; *p. of*, provided with, D 591.

Purveyinge, *s.* providence, T. iv. 986.

Put, *s.* pit, T. iv. 1540.

Puterie, *s.* prostitution, I 886.

Putours, *s. pl.* pimps, procurers, I 886.

Putten, *v.* put, lay, 7. 344; *v.* suppose, B 2667; Put, *pr. s.* puts, I 142; Put him, puts himself, L. 652; Putte, *pt. s.* B 1630; set, L. 675; *p. up*, put away, 2. 54.

Pye, *s.* magpie, A 3950, B 1399.

Pye, *s.* pie, pasty, A 384.

Pyk, *s.* pike (fish), 12. 17.

Pyke, *v.* (1) peep, T. iii. 60; *ger.* (2) to pick at, T. ii. 1274; *pr. s.* (3) makes (himself) tidy or smooth, E 2011.

Pykepurs, *s.* pick-purse, A 1998.

Pyled, *pp.* peeled, bare, bald, A 4306.

Pyn, the pin which passes through the central hole in the Astrolabe and its plates, A. i. 14. 1.

Pyn, *s.* pine-tree, R. 1379.

Pyne, *s.* pain, torment, T. v. 6; hurt, 5. 335; toil, HF. 147; place of torment, HF. 1512; suffering, A 1324, 2382; woe, torment, B 3420; the passion, B 2126. A.S. *pīn*.

Pyne, *ger.* to torture, A 1746; *pr. s.* pines away, 7. 205; grieves, bemoans, I 85; *pp.* examined by torture, B 4249.

Pype, *s.* pipe, musical instrument, B 2005; *pl.* pipes, tubes, A 2752.

Pypen, *v.* pipe, whistle, A 1838; play on the bag-pipe, A 3927; Pype, make a piping noise, T. v. 1433; play upon a pipe, A 3876; *pp.* faintly uttered, HF. 785; *pres. pt.* piping (hot), hissing, A 3379.

Pyrie, *s.* pear-tree, E 2217, 2325. A.S. *pyrige*.

## Q.

Quaad, *adj.* evil (Flemish), A 4357; Quad, bad, B 1628. Du. *kwaad*.

Quaille, *s.* quail, E 1206.

Quake, *v.* tremble, shiver, R. 462; quake, A 3614; shake, T. iii. 542; Quook, *pt. s.* quaked, A 1576, 1762; Quaked, *pp.* B 3831; Quaketh, *imp. pl.* quake, fear, T. ii. 302.

Quaking, *s.* fear, 7. 214.

Quakke, *s.* a state of hoarseness, A 4152.

Qualm, *s.* pestilence, A 2014; evil, plague, R. 357; foreboding of death, T. v. 382.

Quappe, *v.* heave, toss (lit. shake, palpitate), L. 1767; beat repeatedly, L. 865; palpitate, T. iii. 57.

Quarter-night, the time when a fourth part of the night is gone, 9 P. M., A 3516.

Quayles, *gen. pl.* quails, 5. 339.

Queinte, *adj.* curious, B 1426.

Quek! *int.* quack! 5. 499, 594.

Quelle, *v.* kill, C 854; *pr. pl.* strike, T. iv 46.

Queme, *v.* please, T. 695; *pr. pl.* subserve, T. ii. 803.

Quenche, *v.* put a stop to, T. iii. 846; be quenched, I 341; Queynte, *pt. s.* was quenched, A 2334, 2337; Queynt, *pp.* extinguished, A 2321, 2336.

Quene, *s.* queen, R. 1266.

Querele, *s.* quarrel, I 618; *pl.* complaints, B 3. p 3. 67.

Quern, *s.* hand-mill, 9. 6; *dat.* B 3264.

Questemongeres, *s. pl.* questmen, jurymen, I 797.

*Questio, quid iuris*, the question is, how stands the law, A 647.

Questioun, *s.* dispute, A 2514; problem, D 2223.

Queynt, *adj.* strange, 3. 1330; curious, dainty, R. 65; adorned, R. 1435; welldevised, HF. 228; neat, R. 98; sly, A 3275; curiously contrived, HF. 126; F 234; hard to understand, 3. 531; graceful, R. 610.

Queynte, *adv.* artfully, HF. 245.

Queynte, *s.* pudendum, A 3276, D 332, 444.

Queynteliche, *adv.* curiously, cunningly, HF. 1923; daintily, R. 569; strangely, R. 783.

Queyntise, *s.* finery, I 932; art, I 733; ornament, R. 840.

*Qui cum patre*, D 1734, I 1092. The formula used at the end of a sermon.

*Qui la*, who's there? B 1404.

Quik, *adj.* alive, F 1336; lively, A 306; ready, I 658.

Quiken, *v.* quicken, revive, T. i. 443; *ger.* to grow, T. i. 295; to make alive, quicken, G 481; *ger.* to take life, burst forth, HF. 2078; *pt. s.* burst into flame, A 2335; *pp.* endowed with life, F 1050.

Quikkest, *adj. superl.* liveliest, busiest, F 1502.

Quiknesse, *s.* life, 3. 26.

Quinible, *s.* shrill treble, A 3332.

Quirboilly, *s.* boiled leather, B 2065.

Quisshin, *s.* cushion, T. ii. 1229.

Quistroun, *s.* scullion, kitchen-drudge, R. 886. O.F. *coistron*.

Quit, -te; see Quyte.

Quitly, *adv.* freely, wholly, A 1792.

Quod, *pt. s.* said, A 1234.

Quoniam, pudendum, D 608.

Quook, *pt. s. of* Quake.

**Quyte**, *v.* requite, reward, repay, recompense, give in return, R. 1542; 5. 112; 10. 75; HF. 670; free, ransom, A 1032; *ger.* to remove, free, 7. 263; *quyte with*, to requyte with, A 3119; *hir cost for to quyte*, to pay for her expenses, B 3564; *quyte hir whyle*, repay her time, i. e. her trouble, B 584; *pt. s.* repaid, R. 1526; *pt. pl.* released, T. iv. 205; Quit, *pp.* rewarded, requited, HF. 1614; set free, G 66; discharged, quit, F 1758; *as adj.* free, F 1534.

## R.

**Raa**, *s.* roe (Northern), A 4086.
**Raby**, Rabbi, D 2187.
**Rad**, **-de**; see **Rede**.
**Radevore**, *s.* piece of tapestry, L. 2352. From F. *ras de Vore*, serge from La Vaur.
**Rafles**, *s. pl.* raffles, I 793.
**Raft**, **-e**; see **Reve**.
**Rage**, *s.* passion, R. 1613; craving, R. 1657; madness, 3. 731; L. 599; violent grief, F 836; violent rush, fierce blast, A 1985.
**Rage**, *v.* romp, toy wantonly, A 257, 3273, 3958.
**Ragerye**, *s.* wantonness, E 1847; passion, D 455.
**Raked**, *pp.* raked, B 3323. Literally, the sentence is—'Amongst hot coals he hath raked himself'; the sense is, of course, 'he hath raked hot coals around himself.'
**Rakel**, *adj.* rash, T. i. 1067; hasty, T. iii. 1437.
**Rakelnesse**, *s.* rashness, H 283.
**Rake-stele**, *s.* handle of a rake, D 949. See **Stele**.
**Raket**, *s.* the game of rackets, T. iv. 460.
**Rakle**, *v.* behave rashly, T. iii. 1642.
**Ram**, *s.* ram, L. 1427; (as prize at a wrestling-match), A 548; Aries, the first sign in the zodiac, A 8.
**Rammish**, *adj.* ramlike, strong-scented, G 887.
**Rampeth**, *pr. s.* (lit. ramps, romps, rears, but here) rages, acts with violence, B 3094. We should now say—'She *flies* in my face.'
**Rancour**, *s.* ill-feeling, ill-will, malice, R. 1261.
**Ransaked**, *pt. s.* ransacked, came searching out, 4. 28.
**Rape**, *s.* haste, 8. 7. Icel. *hrap*.
**Rape**, *v.*; in phrase *rape and renne*, corrupted from an older phrase *repen* and *rīnen* (A. S. *hrepian and hrīnan*), i. e.

handle and touch, clutch and seize, G 1422.
**Rascaille**, *s.* mob, T. v. 1853.
**Rated**, *pp.* reproved, scolded, A 3463. Short for *arated*, variant of *aretted*; see **Arette**.
**Rathe**, *adv.* soon, HF. 2139; early, A 3768.
**Rather**, *adj. comp.* former, T. iii. 1337.
**Rather**, *adv.* sooner, 3. 562; more willingly, A 487; *the r.*, the sooner, 2. 82.
**Raughte**; see **Reche**.
**Raunson**, *s.* ransom, A 1024.
**Rave**, *2 pr. pl.* are mad, T. ii. 116.
**Raven**, *s.* the constellation Corvus, HF. 1004.
**Ravines**, *s. pl.* rapines, thefts, I 793.
**Ravinour**, *s.* plunderer, B 4. p 3. 117.
**Ravisshe**, *v.* snatch away, B 2. m 7. 32; *go r.*, go and ravish, T. iv. 530; *pp.* rapt, E 1750; overjoyed, F 547; *part. pres.* snatching away, B 4. m 6. 39.
**Ravisshing**, *adj.* swift, violent, B 1. m 5. 4; enchanting, 5. 198; destroying, B 1. m 5. 60 (Lat. *rapidos*).
**Ravyne**, *s.* ravening, greediness, 5. 336; ravin, prey, 5. 323; Ravines, thefts, I 793. O.F. *ravine*, L. *rapina*.
**Ravysedest**, *2 p. s. pt.* didst draw (down), B 1659.
**Rayed**, *pp.* striped, 3. 252.
**Rēal**, *adj.* royal, regal, T. iii. 1534; L. 214, 284, 1605.
**Rēaltee**, *s.* royalty, sovereign power, 10. 60.
**Rēaume**, *s.* realm, kingdom, L 2091.
**Rebekke**, *s.* old woman, dame, D 1573.
**Rebel**, *adj.* rebellious, A 833, 3046.
**Rebelling**, *s.* rebellion, A 2459.
**Rebounde**, *v.* return, T. iv. 1666.
**Rebuked**, *pp.* snubbed, I 444.
**Recche** (1), *v.* reck, care, heed, 5. 593; *is nought to r.*, no matter for, T. ii. 434; *pr. s.* recks, cares, A 2397; Recche of it, care for it, *pr. pl.* F 71; *it recche, pr. s. subj.* may care for it, T. iv. 630; Roghte, *pt. s.* recked, cared, regarded, 3. 887; *impers.* he cared, L. 605; Roughte, *pt. s.* recked, cared, T. i. 496.
**Recche** (2), *pr. s. subj.* interpret, expound, B 4086.
**Recchelees**, *adj.* careless, reckless, R. 340; regardless, HF. 668.
**Recchelesnesse**, *s.* recklessness, I 111, 611.
**Receit**, *s.* receipt, i. e. recipe for making a mixture, G 1353.
**Rechased**, *pp.* headed back, 3. 379.
**Reche**, *v.* reach, give, hand over, 3. 74;

Raughte, *pt. s.* reached, A 3696 ; reached up to, A 2915 ; reached (out, *or* forward), A 136 ; proceeded, T. ii. 446; Reighte, *pt. s.* reached, touched, HF. 1374.

Reclaiming, *s.* enticement, L. 1371.

Reclayme, *v.* reclaim (as a hawk by a lure), i. e. check, H 72.

Recomaunde, *v.* recommend, T. ii. 1070.

Recomende, *ger.* to commit, G 544.

Recomforte, *ger.* to comfort again, T. ii. 1672.

Recompensacioun, *s.* recompense, HF. 665.

Reconciled, *pp.* re-consecrated, I 965.

Reconforte, *v.* comfort again, A 2852, B 2168.

Record, *s.* report, D 2049 ; testimony, 3. 934.

Recorde, *v.* witness, bear in mind, A 1745 ; remember, T. v. 445 ; (to) record, recording, 5. 609 ; Recorde, 1 *pr. s.* bring (it) to your remembrance, A 829.

Recours, *s.* recourse, B 2632 ; resort, T. ii. 1352 ; *wol have my r.,* will return, F 75 ; *pl.* orbits, B 1. m 2. 14.

Recovere, *v.* regain, T. iv. 406.

Recoverer, *s.* recovery, 22. 3. O. F. *re-covrier, recoverer.*

Reddour, *s.* violence, vehemence, 10. 13.

Rede, *v.* read, A 709 ; advise, counsel, L. 2217 ; interpret, 3. 279 ; Ret, *pr. s.* advises, T. ii. 413 ; Redeth, *pr. s.* advises, T. iv. 573 ; Redde, *pt. s.* read, D 714, 721 ; interpreted, 3. 281 ; Radde, *pt. s.* read, T. ii. 1085 ; D 791 ; advised, 5. 579 ; Red, *pp.* read, 3. 224 ; Rad, *pp.* read, B 4311.

Rede, *dat.* counsel, T. iv. 679 ; see Reed.

Rede, *adj.* red ; see Reed.

Rede, *adj.* made of reed ; referring to a musical instrument in which the sound was produced by the vibration of a reed, HF. 1221.

Rede, *s.* red (i. e. gold), T. iii. 1384; the blood, B 356 ; red wine, C 526, 562.

Redelees, *adj.* without counsel ; not knowing which way to turn, 2. 27.

Redely, *adv.* soon, HF. 1392; readily, truly, HF. 1127.

Redoute, *v.* fear, B 1. p 3. 21.

Redoutinge, *s.* reverence, A 2050.

Redresseth, *pr. s.* amends, I 1039 ; *pr. pl. refl.* erect (themselves) again, rise again, T. ii. 969 ; Redressed, *pt. s.* reasserted, vindicated, F. 1436; Redresse, *imp. s.* reform, 1. 129 ; Redressed, *pp.* roused. B 4. p 2. 139.

Reducen, *v.* sum up, B 3. p 8. 61.

Redy, *adj.* ready, A 21, 352 ; dressed, F 387 ; at hand, 2. 104.

Reed, *s.* counsel, advice, plan, A 1216, 3527; profit, help, remedy, 3. 203 ; counsel, adviser, A 665 ; *I can no r.,* I know not what to do, 3. 1187 ; *without reed,* helpless, 3. 587 ; *to rede,* for a counsel ; *best to rede,* best for a counsel, best to do, T. iv. 679 (*not* a verb).

Reed, *adj.* red, A 153 ; (of the complexion), 3. 470 ; Rede, *adj. def.* red, A 957 ; *indef.* (*rare*), L. 2589 ; Rede, *pl.* 1. 89.

Reed, *s.* redness, L. 533.

Reed, *imp. s.* read, H 344.

Reednesse, *s.* redness, G 1097.

Rees, *s.* great haste, T. iv. 350.

Refect, *pp.* restored, B 4. p 6. 414.

Refere, *v.* return, T. i. 266 ; Referred, *pp.* brought back, B 3. p 10. 180.

Refiguringe, *pres. pt.* reproducing, T. v. 473.

Refreininge, *s.* refrain, burden, R. 749.

Refreyden, *v.* grow cold, T. v. 507; Refreyd, cooled down, 12. 21.

Refreyn, *s.* refrain, T. ii. 1571.

Refreyne, *v.* bridle, curb, I 385.

Refresshinge, *s.* renewing, I 78.

Reft, -e ; see Reve.

Refus, *pp. as adj.* refused, rejected, T. i. 570.

Refut, *s.* place of refuge, refuge, 1. 14 ; safety, 1. 33.

Regals, *pl.* royal attributes, L. 2128.

Regalye, *s.* rule, authority, 2. 65.

Regard ; *to the r. of,* in comparison with, B 2. p 7. 126; *at r. of,* 5. 58.

Registre, *s.* narrative, A 2812.

Regne, *s.* kingdom, dominion, realm, A 866 ; dominion, rule, A 1624.

Regnen, *pr. pl.* reign, 4. 50.

Reherce, *v.* rehearse, repeat with exactitude, A 732 ; *ger.* to enumerate, I 239 ; recount, B 89.

Rehersaille, *s.* enumeration, G 852.

Rehersing, *s.* rehearsal, A 1650 ; recital, L. 1185.

Reighte, *pt. s.* reached, touched, HF. 1374. Pt. t. of *reche.*

Reines, *s. pl.* rain-storms, HF. 967.

Rejoye, *v.* rejoice, T. v. 395.

Rejoyse, *ger.* to make rejoice, 1. 101 ; feel glad, T. v. 1165.

Rekene, *ger.* to reckon, A 401.

Rekening, *s.* reckoning, account, 3. 699; A 600.

Reketh, *pr. s.* reeks, smokes, L. 2612.

Rekever, 1 *pr. s.* (for *future*), (I) shall retrieve, do away, HF. 354.

**Rekke,** 1 *pr. s.* care, C 405, E 1090; *pr. s. impers.* (it) recks (him), he cares, L. 365; *yow r.*, you reck, 7. 303; *what r. me*, what do I care, D 53.

**Rekne,** *v.* reckon (*also* 1 *pr. s.*), A 1933.

**Relayes,** *s. pl.* fresh sets of hounds, reserve packs, 3. 362.

**Relees,** *s.* release, 1. 3; ceasing; *out of relees*, without ceasing, G 46.

**Relente,** *v.* melt, G 1278.

**Relesedest,** 2 *pt. s.* forgavest, I 309; Relessed, *pt. s.* forgave, B 3367.

**Relesing,** *s.* remission, I 1026.

**Releve,** *ger.* to raise up, relieve, T. v. 1042; *pp.* restored, I 945; Releved, *pp.* revived, L 128; recompensed, A 4182; made rich again, G 872.

**Relevinge,** *s.* remedy, I 804.

**Religioun,** *s.* religion, A 477; state of religion, life of a nun, R. 429; a religious order, B 3134; the religious orders, B 3144.

**Religious,** *adj.* belonging to a religious order, B 3150; devoted to a religious order, T. ii. 759; *as s.*, a monk or nun, I 891.

**Relik,** *s.* relic, L. 321.

**Reme,** *s.* realm, B 1306.

**Remede,** *s.* remedy, T. i. 661.

**Remedies,** *pl.* (Ovid's) Remedia Amoris, 3. 568.

**Remembre,** *v.* remember, I 135; *pr. pl.* remind, F 1243; *pr. s.* recurs to the mind, 4. 150; Remembringe him, calling to remembrance, T. ii. 72.

**Remenant,** *s.* remainder, rest, A 888.

**Remeve,** *v.* remove, T. i. 691.

**Remorde,** *pr. s. subj.* cause (you) remorse, T. iv. 1491; *pr. s.* vexes, plagues, troubles, B 4. p 6. 293.

**Remors,** *s.* remorse, T. i. 554.

**Remounted,** *pp.* comforted, B 3. p 1. 9.

**Remuable** (1), *adj.* changeable, variable, T. iv. 1682.

**Remuable** (2), *adj.* capable of motion (Lat. *mobilibus*), B 5. p 5. 37.

**Remuen,** *v.* remove, B 2. p 6. 55. (Lat. *amouebis.*)

**Ren,** *s.* run, A 4079.

**Renably,** *adv.* reasonably, D 1509.

**Rende,** *v.* rend, T. iv. 1493; Rent, *pr. s.* rends, tears, L. 646 *a*; Rente, *pt. s.* tore, A 990.

**Rending,** *s.* tearing, A 2834.

**Renegat,** *s.* renegade, apostate, B 932.

**Reneye,** *v.* deny, renounce, abjure, B 376, 3751.

**Reneyinge,** *s.* denying, I 793.

**Renged,** *pp.* ranged, placed in rows, R. 1380.

**Renges,** *pl.* ranks, A 2594.

**Renne** (1), *v.* run, I 721; *ger.* A 3890; *pr. s.* runs, D 76; is current, E 1986; approaches quickly, T. ii. 1754; goes easily, A. i. 2. 1; arises, L. 503; spreads, L. 1423; *renneth for*, runs in favour of, B 125; Ronnen, *pt. pl.* ran, A 2925, 3827; Ronnen, *pp.* advanced, lit. run, R. 320; *is r.*, has run, has found its way (into), HF. 1644.

**Renne** (2), *v.*; *only in the phrase*, rape and renne, G 1422. See **Rape.**

**Renomed,** *pp.* renowned, B 3. p 2. 124.

**Renomee,** *s.* renown, L. 1513.

**Renoun,** *s.* renown, fame, 2. 88.

**Renovelances,** *s. pl.* renewals, HF. 693.

**Renovelle,** *v.* renew, B 3035; are renewed, I 1027.

**Rente,** *s.* revenue, income, A 256; payment, tribute, 3. 765; *to r.*, as a tribute, T. ii. 830.

**Repair,** *s.* resort, repairing, B 1211, D 1224.

**Repaire,** *ger.* to go home, B 1516; to repair, find a home, T. iii. 5; to go back (to), HF. 755; *v.* return, F 589.

**Reparacioun,** *pl.* reparations, makings up, HF. 688.

**Repentaunce,** *s.* penitence, A 1776.

**Repentaunt,** *adj.* penitent, A 228.

**Répenting,** *s.* repentance, L. 147.

**Repeyre,** *v.* repair, return, T. v. 1571.

**Repleccioun,** *s.* repletion, B 4027.

**Repleet,** *adj.* replete, full, B 4147.

**Replenissed,** *pp.* filled, I 1079.

**Replicacioun,** *s.* reply, A 1846; involution, B 3. p 12. 170.

**Replye,** *v.* object, E 1609.

**Reporte,** *v.* relate, tell, C 438.

**Reportour,** *s.* reporter, A 814. (The host is so called because he receives and remembers the tales; they were all addressed to him in particular. Thus 'reporter' has here almost the sense of 'umpire.')

**Reprehencioun,** *s.* reproof, T. i. 684.

**Reprehende,** *v.* reproach, T. i. 510; *pr. pl.* blame, criticise, B 3. p 12. 134.

**Repressed,** *pp.* kept under, L. 2591.

**Répreváble,** *adj.* reprehensible, C 632; *r. to.*, likely to cast a slur on, 15. 24.

**Repreve,** *s.* reproof, B 2413; shame, C 595; reproach, E 2206.

**Repreve,** *v.* reproach, F 1537; reprove, H 70.

**Reproved,** *pp. as adj.* blamed, accused,

R. 1135; Reproeved, *pp.* stultified, B 2. p 5. 127.

Repugnen, *ger.* to be repugnant (to), B 5. p 3. 6.

Requerable, *adj.* desirable, B 2. p 6. 32.

Requeren, *v.* entreat, seek, B 2927; ask, D 1052; *pp.* necessitated, T. iii. 405.

Resalgar, *s.* realgar, G 814. ' *Realgar*, a combination of sulphur and arsenic, of a brilliant red colour as existing in nature; red orpiment'; Webster.

Resceived, *pp.* received; wel resceived, favourably situated with respect to other planets, &c.; A. ii. 4. 51.

Rescous, *s.* a rescue, help, T. iii. 1242; A 2643.

Rescowe, *v.* (to) rescue, save, T. iii. 857; rescue, T. v. 231.

Rescowinge, *s.* rescuing, I 805.

Rese, *ger.* to shake, A 1986.

Résembláble, *adj.* alike, R. 985.

Resolven, *pr. pl.* flow out, B 5. m 1. 1; Resolved, *pp.* dissolved, melted, B 2. p 7. 164.

Resonable, *adj.* talkative, 3. 534.

Resort, *s.* resource, T. iii. 134.

Resoun, *s.* reason, right, A 37, 847; argument, speech, sentence, T. i. 796.

Resóuneth, *pr. s.* resounds, A 1278.

Rosport, *s.* regard, T. iv. 86, 850.

Respyt, *s.* delay, B 948; respite, delay, reprieve, G 543; *withoute more respyt*, without delay, forthwith, R. 1488; *out of more respyt*, without any delay, without any hesitation, T. v. 137.

Respyte, *ger.* to hesitate, 7. 259.

Reste, *s.* rest, repose, F 355; *at reste*, at rest, fixed, T. ii. 760; *at his reste*, as in its home, 5. 376; *to reste*, (gone) to rest, A 30; Restes, *pl.* times of repose, T. ii. 1722.

Reste, *v.* remain (with), T. iii. 1435; rest, repose, T. ii. 1326.

Restelees, *adv.* restlessly, R. 370.

Resurreccioun, *s.* resurrection, i.e. re-opening (of the daisy), L. 110.

Ret, *for* Redeth, *pr. s.* advises, T. ii. 413.

Retenue, *s.* retinue, troop of retainers, suite, A 2502; E 270; *at his r.*, among those retained by him, D 1355.

Rethor, *s.* orator, B 4397, F 38.

Rethorien, *adj.* rhetorical, B 2. p 1. 46.

Rethorien (*written* Retorien), *s.* orator, B 2. p 3. 61.

Retorneth, *pr. s.* brings back, B 5. p 6. 301; *pres. pt.* revolving, T. v. 1023.

Retourninge, *s.* return, A 2095.

Retracciouns, *s. pl.* retractions, things which I withdraw, I 1085.

Retreteth, *pr. s.* reconsiders, B 5. m 3. 57.

Retrograd, *adj.* moving in a direction contrary to that of the sun's motion in the ecliptic, A. ii. 4. 53.

Reule, *s.* rule, A 173.

Reulen, *v.* rule, B 4234; Reule hir, guide her conduct, E 327.

Reuthe, *s.* ruth, 1. 127.

Reve, *s.* reeve, steward, bailiff, A 542, 3860.

Reve, *ger.* to rob (from), T. iv. 285; to take away, G 376; *to r. no man fro his lyf*, to take away no man's life, L. 2693; Reven, *ger.* to reave, plunder, I 758; to bereave, T. i. 188; Reveth, *pr. s.* forces away, 5. 86; Rafte, *pt. s.* bereft, D 888; reft, B 3288; Refte, *pt. s.* bereft, HF. 457; Raft, *pp.* torn, reft, T. v. 1258; taken from, L. 2590; bereaved, F 1017.

Revel, *s.* revelry, sport, A 2717; min-strelsy, A 4402.

Revelour, *s.* (the) Reveller, A 4371; a reveller, A 4391.

Revelous, *adj.* fond of revelry, B 1194.

Reverberacioun, *s.* vibration, D 2234.

Reverdye, *s.* rejoicing, R. 720. O.F. *reverdie*, ' feuillée, verdure; joie, allé-gresse '; Godefroy.

Reverence, *s.* respect, A 141; respectful manner, A 305; fear, I 294; *thy r.*, the respect shewn to thee, B 116.

Revers, *s.* reverse, contrary, 18. 32.

Revoken, *ger.* to recall, T. iii. 1118.

Revolucioun, *s.* revolving course (orbit), 4. 30.

Reward, *s.* regard, attention, T. ii. 1133, v. 1736; *having r. to*, considering, 5. 426; *take r. of*, have regard, I 151.

Rewde, *adj.* plain, unadorned, A. pr. 49.

Rewe, *s.* row, line, A 2866; *by rewe*, in order, D 506.

Rewe, *ger.* to have pity, A 2382; be sorry, T. ii. 455; do penance for, G 447; *pr. s. impers.* makes (me) sorry, I am sorry, A 3462, B 4287.

Rewel-boon, *s.* (probably) ivory made from the teeth of whales, B 2068.

Rewful, *adj.* lamentable, sad, L. 1838; sad (one), B 854.

Rewfulleste, *adj. sup.* most sorrowful, A 2886.

Rewfully, *adv.* sadly, T. iii. 65.

Rewle, *s.* the revolving long and narrow

plate or rod used for measuring and taking altitudes, A. i. 1. 6; it revolves at the *back* of the Astrolabe; *pl.* rules, A. pr. 44.

Rewledest, 2 *pr. s.* didst control, B 1. p 4. 238.

Rewliche, *adj.* pitiable, B 2. p 2. 67.

Rewme, *s.* realm, R. 495.

Rewthe, *s.* ruth, pity, E 579; a pitiful sight, E 562.

Rewthelees, *adj.* ruthless, unpitying, 5. 613; 6. 31.

Reye, *s.* rye, D 1746.

Reyes, *pl.* round dances, HF. 1236. Mid. Du. *reye*, 'a round daunce'; Hexham.

Reyn, *s.* rain, A 492; storm of rain, A 3517.

Reyne, *s.* rein, A 4083.

Reyne, *v.* rain down, T. v. 1336; rain, 4. 287. See Ron.

Reynes, *s. pl.* loins, I 863.

Reyse, *ger.* to build up, D 2102; *r. up*, to exact, 'realise,' D 1390.

Reysed, *pp.* gone on a military expedition, A 54. O.F. *reise*, 'expédition militaire, incursion sur une terre ennemie'; Godefroy.

Rhetorice, Rhetoric, B 2. p 1. 48.

Riban, *s. as pl.* ribbons, HF. 1318.

Ribaninges, *pl.* silk trimmings, borders, R. 1077.

Ribaudye, *s.* ribaldry, ribald jesting, A 3866, C 324.

Ribible, *s.* rebeck, lute with two strings, A 4396.

Ribybe, *s.* term of reproach for an old woman, D 1377.

Riche, *adj. pl.* rich people, A 248.

Richely, *adv.* richly, F 90.

Richesse, *s.* riches, wealth, D 1110, 1118; Richesses, *pl.* wealth, riches, B 2560.

Rideled, *pp.* plaited, gathered in (at the neck, or waist), R. 1235, 1243. '*Ridelé*, plisse'; Godefroy.

Riden, *pt. pl. and pp.* rode, ridden.

Riet, 'rete,' A. i. 3. 5. The 'rete' or 'net' is the circular plate with many openings which revolves within the 'mother.'

Right, *adj.* straight, upright, R. 1701; right, 1. 75; *voc.* own, F 1311.

Right, *adv.* just, exactly, A 257, 535; wholly, C 58; even, B 2173; Right that, that very thing, 3. 1307.

Right, *s.* 1. 21; *by right*, justly, B 44; *by alle r.*, in all justice, T. ii. 763; *at alle rightes*, in all respects, fully, A 1100.

Rightful, *adj.* perfect; *rightful age*, (in)

her prime, R. 405; just, 1. 31; righteous, 5. 55; lawful, I 744.

Rightwis, *adj.* righteous, just, L. 905.

Rightwisnesse, *s.* righteousness, C 637, D 1909; justice, 14. 8.

Rikne, *imp. s.* reckon, compute, A. ii. 27. 10. See Rekene.

Rinde, *s.* rind, bark, T. iv. 1139; hard skin, T. ii. 642.

Ring, *s.* ring, F 83; concourse, L. 1887; *lyk r.*, i.e. in ringlets, A 2165.

Ringe, *v.* make to resound, A 2431; ring, resound, T. ii. 233; Rong, *pt. s.* rang, 5. 492; Ronge, *pp.* T. ii. 805.

Riot, *s.* riotous conduct, gaming, A 4395, 4392.

Riote, *v.* riot, gamble, A 4414.

Risen, *pp. of* Ryse.

Risshe, *s.* rush, T. iii. 1161.

Rist, *pr. s. of* Ryse.

Rit, *pr. s. of* Ryde.

Riveer, *s.* river, B 1927.

Robbour, *s.* robber, B 3818.

Roche, *s.* rock, F 500; *pl.* HF. 1035.

Rode, *s.* complexion, A 3317, B 1917.

Rode, *s. nom.* rood, cross, HF. 57.

Rode-beem, *s.* rood-beam, D 496. (A beam across the entrance to the choir of a church, supporting a rood or cross.)

Rody, *adj.* ruddy, F 385, 394.

Roes, *pl. of* Roo.

Roggeth (ruggeth), *pr. s.* shakes, L. 2708. Icel. *rugga*.

Roket, *s.* rochet, tunic, R. 1240, 1242, 1243. An outer garment, usually of fine white linen.

Rokke, *s.* rock, L. 2195.

Rokken, *ger.* to rock, A 4157.

Rolle, *s.* roll, C 911.

Rollen, *ger.* to roll, revolve, T. ii. 659; *pt. s.* revolved, D 2217; *pp.* much talked of, T. v. 1061.

Romaunce, *s.* romance, T. iii. 980.

Rombled, *pt. s.* fumbled, moved about with his hands, groped about, G 1322.

Rombled, *pt. s.* buzzed, muttered, B 3725.

Romen, *v.* roam, wander, A 1099; Romed, *pt. s.* A 1065, 1069; *pp.* gone, L. 1589.

Ron, *pt. s.* rained, T. iii. 640, 677. A.S. *rān*, *pt. s.* rained.

Rond, *adj.* round, circular, A. ii. 38. 1.

Rong, -e; see Ringe.

Ronges, *pl.* rungs, rounds of a ladder, A 3625. A.S. *hrung*.

Ronne, -n; see Renne.

Roo, *s.* roe, 5. 195; Roes, *pl.* roes, R. 1401.

Rood, *pt. s. of* Ryde.

Roof, *pt. s. of* Ryve.

Roon, *s.* rose-bush, R. 1674. Halliwell gives *roan*, a clump of whins, as a Northumberland word; and we find the spelling *ranes* in the allit. Morte Arthure, 923.

Roos, *pt. s. of* Rysc.

Roost, *s.* roast meat, A 206.

Ropen, *pp.* reaped, L. 74.

Rore, *s.* uproar, T. v. 45.

Rore, *ger.* to roar, T. iv. 373; *pr. s.* resounds, A 2881.

Roring, *s.* loud lament, E 2364.

Rose, *s.* rose, R. 1700; *ger.* of the rose, A 1038.

Rose-leef, *s.* rose-leaf, R. 905.

Rose-garlond, *s.* garland of roses, HF. 135.

Rosen, *adj.* made of roses, R. 845; Rosene, *adj. def.* rosy, B 2. m 8. 6.

Roser, *s.* rose-bush, R. 1651, 1659; I 858.

Rosë-reed, *adj.* red as a rose, G 254.

Roste, *v.* roast, A 383; *pp.* A 147.

Rosy hewed, of rosy hue, T. ii. 1198.

Rote, *s.* (1) root, A 2, 423; the radix, fundamental principle, G 1461; source, B 358; i.e. foot, E 58; *on rote*, firmly rooted, T. ii. 1378; *herte rote*, bottom of the heart, D 471; (2) root, the tabulated number written opposite a given fixed date, A. ii. 44. 2; the 'epoch' of a nativity, B 314.

Rote, *s.* rote; *by rote*, by rote, by heart, A 327, B 1712.

Rote, *s.* a musical stringed instrument, a kind of fiddle, of Celtic origin; said to be a fiddle with three strings, A 236. O. F. *rote*, from O. H. G. *hrotta*, *rotta*, Low Lat. *chrotta*; of Celtic origin, from O. Irish *crot* (Gael. *cruit*, W. *crwth*); whence also E. *crowd*.

Rotelees, *adj.* rootless, T. iv. 770.

Roten, *adj.* rotten, A 3873; corrupt, filthy, I 139.

Roten-herted, *adj.* rotten-hearted, I 689.

Rotie, *pr. s. subj.* render rotten, A 4407.

Roughte; see Recche.

Rouketh, *pr. s.* cowers, crouches, is huddled up, A 1308.

Roule, *v.* gad (lit. roll), D 653.

Roum, *adj.* roomy, spacious, A 4126.

Roum, *s.* room, spare, L. 1999.

Roumer, *adj.* larger, A 4145.

Rouncy, *s.* a hackney, nag, A 390.

Rounde, *adv.* roundly, i.e. easily, with an easy (not jerky) motion, B 2076; melodiously, C 331.

Rounded, *pt. s.* stood out in a rounded form, A 263.

Roundel, *s.* roundel, roundelay, a kind of poem, A 1529; a small circle, HF. 791, 798.

Roundnesses, *pl.* orbs, orbits, B 4. m 6. 52.

Roune, *v.* whisper, B 2025; *ger.* D 1572; *pt. s.* HF. 2044. A. S. *rūnian.*

Route, *s.* company, rout, troop, band, train, A 622, 889, 2153; number, R. 1667; flock, R. 909; *pl.* T. ii. 620.

Route (1), *v.* roar, T. iii. 743; murmur, HF. 1038; *ger.* to snore, 3. 172; *pr. s.* snores, A 3647. A. S. *hrūtan.*

Route (2), *v.* assemble in a company, B 540.

Routhe, *s.* pity, ruth, compassion, mercy, F 1261, 1349; lamentation, L. 669; a pity, a sad thing, A 914.

Routhelees, *adj.* ruthless, pitiless, B 863.

Routing, *s.* snoring, A 4166, 4214; whizzing noise, HF. 1933.

Rowe, *s.* row, 3. 975; line, HF. 448; *by r.*, in a row, T. ii. 970; Rowes, *pl.* rays, beams (of light), 4. 2.

Rowe, *adv.* roughly, angrily, G 861.

Rowed, *pp.* rowed, T. i. 969.

Rowm, *adj.* roomy, large, wide, A. i. 2. 3.

Rowne, *ger.* to whisper, T. iii. 568.

Rowthe, *s.* ruth, pity, 3. 465; sorrow, 3. 97.

Royaltee, *s.* royalty, E 928.

Royleth, *pr. s.* meanders, wanders, B 1 m 7. 10.

Royne, *s.* roughness, R. 553.

Roynous, *adj.* rough, R. 988.

Rubbe, *v.* rub out, 8. 6.

Rubee, *s.* ruby, HF. 1362.

Rubible, *s.* ribibe, rebeck, A 3331.

Rubifying, *s.* rubefaction, reddening, G 797.

Rubriche, *s.* rubric, D 346.

Ruby, *s.* ruby, 12. 4. Rubies, *pl.* 4. 246.

Ruddok, *s.* redbreast, robin, 5. 349.

Rude, *adj.* harsh, R. 752; poor, E 916; inhospitable, H 170; of humble birth, D 1172.

Rudeliche, *adv.* rudely, A 734.

Rudenesse, *s.* boorishness, T. iv. 1677; rusticity, E 397.

Ruggy, *adj.* rough, A 2883.

Rule, *imp. pl.* regulate, order, I 592; *pp. as adj.* well-mannered, L. 163.

Rum, ram, ruf; nonsense words, to imitate alliteration, I 43.

Rumbel, *s.* rumbling noise, A 1979; rumour, E 997.

Rumbleth, *pr. s.* moves to and fro with an indistinct murmuring noise, HF. 1026.

Rumblinge, *s.* noise, D 2133.

Rused, *pt. s.* roused herself, rushed away, 3. 381.

Russhing, *pres. pt.* rushing, A 1641.

Ruste, *ger.* to rust, A 502; *pr. s. subj.* rust, A 500.

Rusty, *adj.* rusty, A 618; besmirched as with rust, R. 159.

Ryal, *adj.* royal, 1. 144; Rial, 2. 59.

Ryde, *v.* ride, A 27, 94, 102; ride at anchor, L. 968; Ryden, *ger.* (*with* out), to go on expeditions, A 45; Ryde, *ger.* (*with* out), to ride abroad to inspect, B 1255; (see **Outrydere**); Rydestow, ridest thou, D 1386; Rit, *pr. s.* rides, A 974; Ròòd, *pt. s.* rode, A 169; Rīden, 1 *pt. pl.* (we) rode, A 825; *pt. pl.* C 968; Rīden, *pp.* ridden, B 1990.

Ryding, *s.* jousting, *or* riding in procession, A 4377.

Rym, *s.* rime (usually mispelt rhyme), B 2115, 2118; Ryme, *dat.* HF. 623; a tale in verse, B 1899; verse, D 1127; *pl.* B 96. A. S. *rīm.*

Ryme, *v.* describe in verse, put into rime (*or* rhyme), A 1459, B 2122.

Rymeyed, *pp.* rimed, *or* rhymed, F 711; see above.

Ryming, *s.* riming, *or* rhyming, versemaking, B 2120; the art of riming, B 48.

Ryot, *s.* riotous living, C 465.

Ryotour, *s.* roysterer, C 692.

Rys, *s.* spray, branch, twig, R. 1015; A 3324. A. S. *hrīs.*

Ryse, *ger.* to rise, A 33; to get up, F 375; Rist, *pr. s.* rises, A 3688, 4193; arises, T. i. 944; Ròòs, 1 *pt. s.* rose, 2. 17; *pt. s.* A 823; Risen, *pp.* A 1065; Riseth, *imp. pl.* I 161.

Ryve, *ger.* to pierce, T. v. 1560; *v.* thrust, L. 1793; pierce, C 828; tear, E 1236; Ròòf, *pt. s.* rove, rived, pierced, L. 661, 1351. Icel. *rīfa.*

## S.

Sable, *s.* sable, black, 4. 284.

Sachels, *s. pl.* bags, B 1. p 3. 83.

Sacrement, *s.* the eucharist, I 582.

Sacrifye, *v.* do sacrifice, L. 1348.

Sacrifyse, *s.* sacrifice, L. 1310.

Sacrilege, *s.* I 801; sorcery, B 1. p. 4. 282.

Sad, *adj.* stable, firm, I 129, 310; staid, A 2985; sober, E 220, 237; fixed, constant, unmoved, settled, E 693, 754; sad, R. 211; devoted, 23. 9; trusty, H 275; serious, grave, 3. 918; calm, settled, G 397; staid, L. 1581, 1876; earnest, HF. 2089; Sadde, *pl.* grave, E 1002; steady, 3. 860; discreet, B 135; sure, H 258.

Sadel, *s.* saddle, L. 1199.

Sadel-bowe, *s.* saddle-bow, A 2691.

Sadly, *adv.* firmly, A 2602; discreetly, B 1266; steadfastly, I 124; carefully, D 2164; firmly, tightly, E 1100; unstintingly, B 743.

Sadnesse, *s.* soberness, staidness, E 1591; patience, E 452.

Saffron with, *ger.* to tinge with saffron, to colour, C 345.

Saffroun, *s.*; like saffron = of a bright yellowish colour, B 1920.

Sak, *s.* sack, R. 457; Sakkes, *pl.* bags, L. 1118.

Sakked, *pp.* put in a sack, A 4070.

Sal, *pr. s.* shall (Northern), A 4043.

Sal armoniak, *s.* sal ammoniac, G 798, 824. Lat. *sal armeniacum*, Armenian salt. *Sal ammoniac*, chloride of ammonium. The word *armoniac* certainly answers to the Lat. *Armeniacum* in the old treatises. Yet the right spelling is *ammoniac.*

Sal peter, *s.* saltpetre, G 808. Lat. *sal petræ*, rock-salt; nitrate of potassa;—called also nitre.

Sal preparat, *s.* prepared salt, G 810.

Sal tartre, *s.* salt of tartar, G 810. '*Salt of tartar*, carbonate of potash; . . . first prepared from cream of tartar'; Webster.

Salewe, *v.* salute, I 407; *pr. s.* B 1284; Salewed, *pp.* F 1310.

Salowe, *adj.* sallow, R. 355. (But read *falowe.*)

Salte, *adj. def.* salt, L. 1462.

Saluing, *s.* salutation, A 1649.

Saluwe, *ger.* to salute, T. iii. 1785; Salued, 1 *pt. s.* L. 315.

Salvacioun, *s.* salvation, 4. 213; security, B 2361.

Salve, *s.* salve, cure, T. iv. 944; *pl.* healing remedies, A 2712.

Salwes, *pl.* willow-twigs, osiers, D 655.

Samit, *s.* samite, a rich and glossy silk material, T. i. 109; robe made of samite, R. 836, 873.

Sang, *s.* song (Northern), A 4170.

Sangwin, *s.* stuff of a blood-red colour, A 439.

**Sangwyn,** *adj.* very ruddy, A 2168; blood-red, A 333.

**Sans,** *prep.* without, B 501.

**Saphires,** *s. pl.* sapphires, B 3658.

**Sapience,** wisdom, B 2184; *pl.* kinds of intelligence, G 338.

**Sarge,** *s.* serge, A 2568.

**Sarpulers,** *s. pl.* sacks made of coarse canvas, B 1. p 3. 82. Cf. F. *serpillière.*

**Sarsinesshe,** *adj.* Saracenic, R. 1188. If *sarsinesshe* can be taken as a sb., it may refer to *sarsnet.*

**Sat;** *pt. s. of* Sitte.

**Satin,** *s.* satin, 3. 253.

**Satisfaccioun,** *s.* penance, I 87; restitution, I 108.

**Sauf,** *adj.* safe, safely kept, G 950; in safety, 4. 197.

**Sauf,** *prep.* save, except, A 2180.

**Saufly,** *adv.* safely, with safety, B 2373, 4398.

**Saugh,** *pt. s. of* See.

**Saule,** *s.* soul (Northern), A 4187.

**Sauns,** *prep.* without; *sauns faille,* without fail, certainly, HF. 188, 429. See Sans.

**Sauter,** *s.* psalter, R. 431.

**Sautrye,** *s.* psaltery, a kind of harp, A 296, 3213, 3305, H 268.

**Savacioun,** *s.* salvation, T. ii. 381, 563; *withoute any savacioun,* without saving any, HF. 208.

**Save,** *s.* sage (the plant), A 2713.

**Save,** *prep. and conj.* save, except, A 683; Save your grace, by your leave, B 2260.

**Saven,** *ger.* to save, keep, 1. 117; *pr. s. subj.* may (He) save, A 3108; *pp.* kept inviolate, F 531.

**Save-garde,** *s.* safe-conduct, T. iv. 139.

**Saveour,** *s.* saviour, 19. 16.

**Saveren,** *pr. pl.* mind, care for, I 820.

**Savinge,** *prep.* except, A 2838.

**Savoringe,** *s.* taste, I 207.

**Savorous,** *adj.* pleasant, R. 84.

**Savory,** *adj.* pleasant, T. i. 405.

**Savour,** *s.* savour, D 2196; pleasantness, F 204; pleasure, 10. 20; smell, G 887; scent, R. 925; interest, T. ii. 269; *pl.* odours, 5. 274.

**Savoure,** *v.* taste, D 171; *pr. pl.* mind, care for, I 820; *imp. s.* have relish for, 13. 5.

**Savoured,** *adj.* perfumed, R. 547.

**Savouringe,** *s.* tasting, I 959.

**Savourly,** *adj.* enjoyably, A 3735.

**Sawcefleem,** *adj.* covered with pimples (due to an excess of humour called *salsa phlegma*), A 625.

**Sawe,** *s.* saying, speech, A 1163; word, B 2925; discourse, G 691.

**Sawe, Say;** see See.

**Sayde,** said; see Seye.

**Saylours,** *pl.* dancers (who leap in dancing), R. 770. '*Sailleor, Sailleur,* sauteur, danseur'; Godefroy.

**Scabbe,** *s.* scab, R. 553; a disease of sheep, C 358.

**Scalded,** *pp.* burnt, A 3853.

**Scale,** *s.* scale, or rather, double scale, for measuring both by *umbra recta* and *umbra versa,* A. i. 12. 3.

**Scalle,** *s.* scab, 8. 3.

**Scalled,** *pp.* having the scall, scabby, scurfy, A 627.

**Scantitee,** *s.* scantiness, I 431.

**Scantnesse,** *s.* scarcity, I 420.

**Scapen,** *v.* escape, T. v. 908.

**Scarlet-reed,** *adj.* scarlet-red, B 4351.

**Scarmishing,** *s.* skirmish, L. 1910.

**Scarmyche,** *s.* skirmish, T. v. 1508.

**Scars,** *adj.* parsimonious, B 2789.

**Scarsetee,** *s.* scarcity, B 2790.

**Scarsly,** *adv.* parsimoniously, A 583.

**Scatered,** *pp.* scattered, G 914.

**Scathe,** *s.* scathe, harm, misfortune, 'a pity,' A 446; *Polymites to &c.,* to the harm of P., T. v. 938.

**Scatheles,** *adv.* harmlessly, R. 1550.

**Science,** *s.* science, knowledge, 5. 25; learned writing, B 1666; wisdom, I 229.

**Sclat,** *s.* slate, 11. 34.

**Sclaundre,** *s.* slander, HF. 1580; ill-fame, disgrace, E 722; scandal, I 137.

**Sclave,** *s.* slave, T. iii. 391.

**Sclendre,** *adj.* slender, slight in make, A 587; thin, B 3147; poor, B 4023.

**Scochouns,** *pl.* escutcheons, painted shields, R. 893.

**Scole,** *s.* school, B 1685, 1694; manner, fashion, A 125, 3329; discipline, T. i. 634; 'the schools,' D 2186.

**Scole-matére,** *s.* subject for disputation in the schools, D 1272.

**Scoler,** *s.* scholar, A 260.

**Scolering,** *s.* young scholar, note to D 44; line 6.

**Scole-termes,** *pl.* school-terms, E 1569.

**Scoleward;** to scoleward = toward school, B 1739.

**Scoleye,** *ger.* to study, A 302.

**Scomes,** *s. pl.* foam, lather, B 4. m 7. 61. Lit. 'scums.'

**Score,** *imp. s.* notch, cut, mark, B 1606.

**Scorkleth,** *pr. s.* scorches, shrivels, B 2. m 6. 28.

**Scorned,** *pt. s.* 3. 927; jested at, B 4277.

Scorning, *s.* scorn, T. i. 105.

Scorpion, *s.* E 2058; sign of Scorpio, HF. 948.

Scot, a horse's name, A 616, D 1543.

Scourges, *s. pl.* whips, plagues, E 1157.

Scourging, *s.* correction, 4. 42.

Scrippe, *s.* scrip, bag, D 1737.

Scripture, *s.* writing, inscription, (on a ring), T. iii. 1369; passage of writing, L. 1144; *pl.* manuscripts, A 2044.

Scrit, *s.* writing, deed, E 1697; T. ii. 1130.

Scrivenish, *adv.* like a scrivener, T. ii. 1026.

Scriveyn, *s.* scribe, 8. 1.

Seche, *ger.* to seek, i.e. to be sought for (it was easily had), A 784; to seek out, D 909.

Secree, *adj.* secret, trusty, 5. 395; secret, B 2251; able to keep secrets, D 946.

Secree, *adv.* secretly, F 1109.

Secree, *s.* a secret, B 3211; Secree of secrees, secret of secrets, Lat. Secreta Secretorum (the name of a book), G 1447.

Secreenesse, *s.* secrecy, B 773.

Secrely, *adv.* secretly, E 763

Secte, *s.* sect, company, E 1171; religion, faith (lit. 'following'), F 17.

Seculer, *s.* a layman, B 4640.

Sede, *v.* bear seed, 7. 306.

See, *s.* sea, A 59; *fulle see,* high tide, A. ii. 46. 4.

See, *s.* seat, HF. 1361; seat of empire, B 3339; *pl.* seats HF. 1210.

See, *v.* see, L. 2560; *ger.* to see, look, F 366; to look (upon), 3. 1177; *as fut.* shall see, 4. 190; Seestow, seest thou, HF. 911; Say, 1 *pt. s.* saw, T. v. 992; Say, *pt. s.* saw, B 4304; Sey, *pt. s.* B 1, 7; Seigh, 1 *pt. s.* saw, A 193; Seigh, *pt. s.* A 1066, F 850; Saugh, 1 *pt. s.* saw, A 764; *pt. s.* A 850, 1400; Sy, *pt. s.* G 1381; Sawe, 2 *pt. s.* sawest, B 848; Saugh, 2 *pt. pl.* G 1106 (with *ye*); Sawe, *pt. pl.* B 218; Seye, *pt. pl.* saw, T. iv. 720; Seyen, *pt. pl.* G 110; Syen, *pt. pl.* B 2879, 4568; Sye, *pt. pl.* E 1804; *pr. s. subj.* may (he) behold or protect, B 156; Sawe, *pt. s. subj.* were to see, A 144; Seyn, *pp.* seen, B 1863; Seye, *pp.* D 552.

Seed-foul, *s.* birds living on seeds, 5. 512.

Seek, *adj.* sick, ill, L. 2409, 2436; *def.* A 424; Seke, *def. as s.* man in a fever, 5. 104; Seke, *pl.* A 18, 245.

Seel (1), *s.* bliss, A 4239. A.S. *sǽl.*

Seel (2), *s.* seal, B 882.

Seemlinesse, *s.* dignity of bearing, L. 1041.

Seemly, *adj.* delicate, pleasing, 12. 11; seemly, L. 2074.

Seestow, seest thou, HF. 911.

Seet, *pt. s.* sat (false form, due to pl. *sēten*), A 2075.

Seetes, *pl.* seats, A 2580.

Seeth, *pt. s.* seethed, boiled, E 227.

Sege, *s.* throne, B 1. p 4. 285; siege, L. 1696.

Seggen, 1 *pr. pl.* say, T. iv. 194.

Seigh, *pt. s. of* See.

Sein, *ger.*; That is to sein, that is to say, A. pr. 26.

Seinte, *adj. fem.* holy, D 1824.

Seintuarie, *s.* sanctuary, I 781; a consecrated object, C 953.

Seistow, sayest thou, A 1125.

Seith, *pr. s.* says, A 178.

Seke; see Seek, *adj.*

Seke, *v.* search through, B 60; seek, B 1633; *ger.* A 13, 510; to seek, i.e. a matter for search, G 874; Sekestow, seekest thou, T. iii. 1455; Seken to, 1 *pr. pl.* press towards, 2. 91; 2 *pr. pl.* search through, B 127; Soghte, 1 *pt. s.* sought, A. ii. 45. 11; *pt. s. subj.* were to examine, C 488.

Sekernes, *s.* security, 7. 345.

Sekirly, *adv.* certainly, L. 163 *a.*

Selde, *adj. pl.* few, E 146.

Selde, *adv.* seldom, A 1539, B 2343; Selden, B 2594; Seld, B 2343.

Seled, *pp.* sealed, B 736.

Seles, *pl.* seals, T. iii. 1462.

Selily, *adv.* happily, B 2. p 4. 96.

Selinesse, *s.* happiness, T. iii. 813.

Selle, *s. dat.* boarding, A 3822. A Kentish form; M.E. *sulle, sille*; A.S. *syll.* (*Flore* = ground beneath the boards.)

Selle, *v.* sell, F 1563; barter, A 278; *for to selle,* for sale, D 414; *to selle,* for sale, A 3821; Solde, *pt. s. subj.* were to sell, R. 452.

Selly, *adj.* wonderful (MSS. sely), HF. 513. A.S. *sellīc, seldlīc,* strange.

Sely, *adj.* happy, T. iv. 503; kind, 4. 89; good, B 1702; holy, B 682; innocent, simple, A 3404; poor, pitiable, T. i. 871; wretched, A 3896; hapless, L. 1254, 1336. A.S. *sǽlig.*

Semblable, *adj.* like, B 2294.

Semblaunce, *s.* likeness, R. 425; appearance, R. 145.

Semblaunt, *s.* appearance, semblance, look, E 928, F 516; *in hir s.,* apparently, R. 863.

**Seme,** v. appear, seem, F 102 ; ger. to seem (to), T. i. 747 ; pr. pl. F 869 ; pt. s. (there) seemed, A 2970 ; impers. (it) seemed, A 39, E 296 ; him semed, it seemed to them, they supposed, F 56 ; the peple semed = it seemed to the people, the people supposed, F 201.

**Semelihede,** s. seemliness, comeliness, R. 1130 ; gracefulness, R. 777.

**Semely,** adj. seemly, comely, A 751.

**Semely,** adv. becomingly, A 123.

**Semes,** s. pl. seams, I 622.

**Semicope,** s. half-cope, short cope, A 262.

**Seming,** s. appearance, 3. 944 ; to my s., as it appears to me, B 1838.

**Semisoun,** s. half-sound, i.e. suppressed sound, A 3697.

**Senatorie,** s. senatorial rank, B 3. p 4. 93.

**Senatour,** s. senator, L. 584.

**Sencer,** s. censer, A 3340.

**Sencinge,** pres. pt. censing, perfuming with incense, A 3341.

**Sendal,** s. a thin silk, A 440.

**Sende,** v. send, B 144 ; Sent, pr. s. E 1151 ; Sende, pt. s. sent, A 4136 ; Sente, pt. s. B 3927 ; Sendeth, imp. pl. send ye, C 614 ; Sente, pt. s. subj. would send, B 1091.

**Sene,** adj. visible, manifest, apparent, A 134, 924, F 645. A.S. gesēne, gesŷne, adj. evident, visible.

**Sene,** ger. to behold, to see, L. 1034 ; to look at, L. 2649 ; to look on, D 1245 ; to seem, L. 224 ; on to sene, to look on, L. 2425.

**Senge,** v. singe, D 349 ; Seynd, pp. broiled, B 4035.

**Sengle,** adj. single, unmarried, E 1667.

**Senith,** s. (1) the zenith, A. i. 18. 4, 22. 6 ; (2) the point where a given azimuth-circle meets the horizon, A. i. 19. 12 ; the point of sunrise, A. ii. 31. 13.

**Sensibilitees,** s. pl. perceptions, B 5. m 4. 8.

**Sensible,** adj. perceptible by the senses, B 5. p 4. 212.

**Sent, -e ;** see **Sende.**

**Sentement,** s. feeling, fancy, T. ii. 13 ; susceptibility, T. iii. 43 ; passion, L. 69.

**Sentence,** s. meaning, drift, E 2288 ; contents, C 190 ; subject, B 1753 ; opinion, B 113, 3992 ; 'decision, 5. 530 ; meaning, sentiment, instruction, A 306, 798 ; tenor, theme, HF. 1100 ; decision, speech, 5. 383 ; judgement, order, I 17 ; verdict, G 366 ; general meaning, I 58.

**Septemtrioun,** s. north, B 3657.

**Septentrional,** adj. northern, A. ii. 40. 50 ; Septentrionalis, pl. A. ii. 40. 36.

**Sepulcre,** s. tomb, D 498.

**Sepulture,** s. mode of burial, T. v. 299 ; burial, L. 2553 ; tomb, A 2854.

**Serchen,** v. search, B 2597 ; pr. pl. go about, haunt, D 867.

**Sereyns,** s. pl. sirens, R. 684.

**Sergeaunt of the Lawe,** sergeant-at-law, A 309.

**Serie,** s. process, argument, A 3067.

**Sermone,** ger. to preach, speak, C 879.

**Sermoning,** s. argument, A 3091 ; talk, A 3597.

**Sermoun,** s. discourse, L. 2025 ; T. ii. 965 ; tale, T. ii. 1115 ; pl. writings, B 87.

**Servage,** s. servitude, thraldom, A 1946, B 368.

**Servant,** s. lover, A 1814 ; servant, D 1501.

**Servisable,** adj. willing to serve, A 99 ; serviceable, E 1911 ; useful, E 979.

**Servitour,** s. servant, D 2185.

**Servitute,** s. servitude, E 798.

**Servÿse,** s. service, serving, A 250 ; religious service, T. i. 315 ; musical performance, 3. 302.

**Sese,** pr. s. subj. seize, 5. 481 ; pp. caught, 4. 240 ; seised, possessed, T. iii. 445.

**Sesoun,** s. season, F 1034 ; prime, R. 1678.

**Sestow,** seest thou, T. iii. 46.

**Sete,** s. seat, throne, B 3715, I 162.

**Sete, -n ;** see **Sitte.**

**Setewale,** s. zedoary, setwall. R. 1370. See **Cetewale.**

**Sethe,** v. seethe, boil, A 383.

**Sette,** ger. to set, place, L. 540 ; setten a myte, care a mite, T. iii. 900 ; Sette, 1 pr. s. suppose, T. ii. 367 ; B 2681 ; Sette cas, imagine the case, B 3041 ; 2 pr. pl. esteem, T. ii. 432 ; Sette, 1 pr. s. subj. set, A 3911 ; Set, pr. s. setteth, sets, 2. 101 ; D 1982 ; cares, T. iii. 832 ; puts, 3. 635 ; Sette, 1 pt. s. counted, regarded, D 659 ; Sette me, placed myself, L. 115 ; sette nat a kers, accounted not worth a cress, A 3756 ; Sette at nought, counted as nothing, F 821 ; Sette him, sat down, C 207 ; Sette hir, sat, B 329 ; Sette her on knees, knelt down, B 638 ; Sette hem, seated themselves, L. 301 ; C 775 ; Setten hem adoun, set themselves, G 396 ; Set, pp. placed, A 132, 2528 ; put, B 440 ; set, R. 846 ; appointed, 4. 52 ; E 774 ; wholly devoted, 6. 100 ; wel set, seemly, 3. 828 ; set the wrightes cappe = made a fool of him, A 3143 ; Set, imp. s. stake (as at dice), T. iv. 622.

**Seur,** adj. sure, B 2642, 2953.

**Seur,** adv. surely, T. iii. 1633.

**Seurly,** adv. surely, B 2913.

**Seurtee,** s. surety, A 1604, B 243.
**Sewe,** v. follow, 25. 12 ; ensue, B 2619, 2692 ; pt. s. pursued, B 4527.
**Sewes,** s. pl. lit. juices, gravies ; used here for seasoned dishes, delicacies, F 67.
**Sewing,** adj. conformable, in proportion, similar, 3. 959. Lit. ' following.'
**Sexte,** sixth, HF. 1727.
**Sexteyn,** s. sacristan, B 3216.
**Sey,** 1 pt. s. saw, 3. 1089 ; Seyn, pp. seen, B 172, 624. See See.
**Seye,** v. say, A 738 ; to be told, B 706 ; to seyn, A 284 ; for to seye, to say, A 468 ; this is to seyn, A 181 ; that is to seyn, A 797 ; Seistow, sayest thou, B 110 ; as who seyth, like one who says, i. e. so to speak, T. v. 883 ; Seggen, 1 pr. pl. say, T. iv. 194 ; Seydestow, saidest thou, G 334 ; Seyd, pp. B 49 ; Seyeth, imp. pl. say ye, A 1868.
**Seyl,** s. sail, A 696, 3532.
**Seyn,** pp. seen, B 1863, 4471.
**Seynd,** pp. singed, i. e. broiled, B 4035.
**Seynt,** s. saint, 3. 1319 ; Sëynt (dissyllabic), A 120, 509, 687, D 1564 ; Seynte, saint (or holy), A 1721.
**Seyst,** 2 pr. s. sayest, B 109 ; Seystow, 2 pr. s. sayest thou, A 3490.
**Shaar,** s. a plough-share, A 3763.
**Shad, -de** ; see **Shede.**
**Shadwe,** s. shadow, B 7, 10 ; shade, 3. 426 ; scene, B 2. p 3. 89 ; Shadowe, reflection, R. 1529.
**Shadwed,** pp. shadowed, shaded, A 607.
**Shaft,** s. wooden part of an arrow, A 1362 ; pl. shafts of spears, A 2605.
**Shal,** 1 pr. s. owe, T. iii. 1649 ; owe (to), T. iii. 791 ; shall (do so), F 688 ; must, A 853 ; am to be, 2. 53 ; am to (go), G 303 ; Shalt, 2 pr. s. must go, D 1636 ; Shaltow, 2 pr. s. shalt thou, A 3575 ; Shal, pr. s. shall be, T. v. 833 ; is to be, HF. 82 ; must, is to, A 187 ; must (come), T. iv. 1106 ; will, L. 1276 ; must (do so), R. 387 ; owes, F 750 ; Sholde, 1 pt. s. should, B 56 ; ought (to have done so), 3. 1200 ; Sholdestow, shouldst thou, 10. 60 ; wouldst thou, D 1944 ; Sholde, pt. s. should, A 184 ; ought to, B 44 ; had to, E 515 ; was to, B 3891 ; would, B 3627 ; Shul, 1 pr. pl. must, have to, B 351 ; must, B 1900 ; Shullen, 2 pr. pl. shall, B 4652 ; Shullen, pr. pl. must, A 3014.
**Shale,** s. shell, HF. 1281.
**Shalmyes,** pl. shawms, HF. 1218.
**Shame,** s. A 503 ; Shame of his degree, i. e. lest it should shame his condition (as husband), F 752 ; Shames deth, shameful death, B 819, E 2377.
**Shamen,** v. put to shame, F 1565 ; thee shameth, it shames thee, thou art ashamed, B 101.
**Shamfast,** adj. modest, shy, A 2055, C 55 ; shame-faced, ashamed, R. 467.
**Shamfastnesse,** s. modesty, A 840 ; sense of shame, I 985.
**Shap,** s. A 1889 ; privy member, I 423.
**Shapen,** v. plan, devise, A 3403 ; find means (to do), A 809 ; pr. s. intends, L. 1289 ; Shape, pr. pl. dispose, B 2989 ; Shapen hem, intend, F 214 ; Shóóp, pt. s. befel, T. ii. 61 ; devised, planned, T. i. 207 ; made, gave, L. 2569 ; prepared for, E 198 ; plotted, B 2543 ; created, E 903 ; contrived, E 946 ; Shoop me, 1 pt. s. refl. addressed myself, 2. 20 ; prepared myself, L. 180 ; Shoop him, pt. s. refl. got ready, L. 625 ; determined, F 809 ; Shopen, pt. pl. made ready, B 2995 ; Shapen, pp. determined, A 1108 ; destined, A 1392 ; shaped, L. 2014 ; planned, B 951 ; prepared, B 249 ; appointed, B 253 ; disposed (themselves), B 142 ; built, 7. 357 ; cut out, T. iii. 734 ; Shape, pp. destined, ordained, A 1225 ; allotted, T. ii. 282 ; created, B 3099 ; imp. pl. refl. dispose yourself, B 2307.
**Shaply,** adj. fit, A 372 ; likely, T. iv. 1452.
**Sharpe,** adv. sharply, B 2073.
**Shave,** v. shave, A 3326 ; Shaven, pp. cut smooth, R. 941 ; Shave, pp. shaven, A 588.
**Shaving,** s. a thin slice, G 1239.
**Shawe,** s. wood, A 4367, D 1386.
**She,** she, A 446 ; She . . . she, one woman and another, T. ii. 1747.
**She-ape,** s. female ape, I 424.
**Shedeth,** pr. s. sheds, I 577 ; Shedde, pt. s. shed, B 3447 ; Shadde, pt. s. poured, B 3921 ; Shad, pp. distributed, B 1. m 1. 18.
**Sheef,** s. sheaf, A 104 ; Sheves, pl. HF. 2140.
**Sheep,** s. a sheep, A 506 ; a meek person, D 432.
**Sheld,** s. shield, A 2122 ; pl. French crowns (coins worth 3s. 4d.), A 278 ; Sheeld, pl. B 1521.
**Shelde,** pr. s. subj. may he shield, HF. 88.
**Shende,** v. disgrace, T. iv. 1577 ; ruin, B 927 ; render contemptible, T. v. 893 ; reproach, T. v. 1060 ; destroy, HF. 1016 ; Shent, pr. s. ruins, I 848 ; defiles, I 854 ; Shente, pt. s. harmed, injured, B 4031 ; Shente, pt. s. subj. should destroy, T. ii. 357 ; Shent, pp. spoilt, T. ii. 37 ; defeated, L. 652 ; scolded, B 1731.

**Shendshipe**, *s.* shame, I 273.

**Shene**, *adj.* bright, A 115; glistening, R. 127; fair, E 2528; beautiful, B 692, F 1045. A.S. *scēne*, *scȳne*.

**Shene**, *adv.* brightly, 4. 87.

**Shepe**, *s.* hire, I 568. See **Shipe**.

**Shepne**, *s.* stable, shed, A 2000. A.S. *scypen*. See **Shipnes**.

**Shere**, *s.* pair of shears, A 2417.

**Shere**, *ger.* to shear, cut, B 3257.

**Shering-hokes**, *pl.* shearing-hooks, contrivances for severing ropes in a seafight, L. 641.

**Sherte**, *s.* shirt, A 1566; chemise, T. iv. 96.

**Shet**, *pp. of* Shette.

**Shete**, *s.* sheet, G 879; *pl.* A 4140.

**Sheten**, *v.* shoot, I 714; Sheteth, *pr. s.* shoots, R. 960.

**Sheter**, *s. as adj.* fit for shooting, (lit. shooter), 5. 180.

**Shethe**, *s.* sheath, R 2066.

**Shette**, *v.* shut, enclose, T. iii. 1549; shut, close, D 1141; Shette, *pt. s.* shut, A 3499; closed, fastened up, T. ii. 1090; Shetten, *pt. pl.* shut up, enclosed, T. i. 148; Shet, *pp.* shut, R. 529.

**Sheves**, *pl.* sheaves, HF. 2140.

**Sheweth**, *pr. s.* pretends, appears, B 2386; appears as, is shewn, A. i. 7. 9.

**Shifte**, *v.* provide, distribute, ordain, D 104; assign, G 278.

**Shilde**, *pr. s. subj.* shield, T. ii. 1019; defend, B 2098; forbid, A 3427.

**Shimering**, *s.* glimmer, A 4297.

**Shine**, *s.* shin, A 386.

**Shined**, *pt. s.* shone, L. 2194.

**Ship**, *s.* 1. 16; Shipe, *dat.* (into the) ship, (into the) ark, A 3540.

**Shipe**, *s.* hire, pay, reward, 7. 193; Shepe, hire, I 568. A.S. *scipe*, stipendium.

**Shipman**, *s.* sailor, skipper, A 388.

**Shipnes**, *pl.* stables, sheds, D 871. See **Shepne**.

**Shirreve**, *s.* sheriff, A 359. Lit. 'shire-reeve.'

**Shiten**, *pp.* defiled, dirty, A 504.

**Shitting**, *s.* shutting, R. 1598.

**Shivere**, *s.* thin slice, D 1840.

**Shiveren**, *pr. pl.* break, A 2605.

**Sho**, shoe, A 253.

**Shod**, *pp.* provided with shoes, HF. 98.

**Shode**, *s.* parting of the hair, A 3316; the temple of the head, A 2007.

**Shof**, *pt. s.* pushed, T. iii. 487.

**Shoken**, *pt. pl.* shook, R. 363.

**Sholder-bone**, *s.* shoulder-blade-bone, C 350.

**Shonde**, *s.* disgrace, HF. 88; B 2098.

**Shoo**, *s.* shoe, D 492; Shoos, *pl.* A 457; Shoon, *pl.* B 1922.

**Shoof**, *pt. s.* 1 *p.* shoved, pushed, R. 534; *pt. s.* drove, L. 2412.

**Shoon** (shóón), *pl. of* Shoo.

**Shoon** (shòòn), *pt. s. of* Shyne.

**Shorn**, *pp.* shaven, B 3142.

**Shorte**, *v.* shorten, D 1261; *to shorte with your weye*, to shorten your way with, A 791.

**Shortly**, *adv.* briefly, A 30.

**Short-sholdred**, *adj.* short in the upper arm, A 549.

**Shot**, *s.* a missile, B 4539; arrow, A 2544.

**Shot-windowe**, *s.* a window containing a square division which opens on a hinge, A 3358, 3695.

**Shour**, *s.* shower, T. iv. 751; onset, conflict, T. iv. 47; *pl.* assaults, T. i. 470. Cf. E. 'a *shower* of darts.'

**Showving**, *s.* shoving, pushing, H 53.

**Shredde**, *pt. s.* shred, cut, E 227.

**Shrewe**, *s.* scoundrel, accursed wretch, D 284; shrew, peevish woman, E 1222, 2428; planet having an evil influence, A. ii. 4. 54; evil one, G 917.

**Shrewe**, *adj.* evil, wicked, G 995.

**Shrewe**, 1 *pr. s.* beshrew, curse, B 4616.

**Shrewed**, *adj.* evil, wicked, bad, L 1545; accursed, D 54.

**Shrewedly**, *adv.* cursedly, D 2238.

**Shrewednesse**, *s.* wickedness, evil, B 2721; cursedness, D 734; *pl.* evil deeds, I 442.

**Shrifte-fadres**, *pl.* father-confessors, D 1442.

**Shrighte**, *pt. s.* shrieked, A 2817; *pp.* T. v. 320.

**Shrimpes**, *pl.* small creatures, dwarfs, B 3145.

**Shroud**, *s.* robe, R. 64.

**Shrouded**, *pp.* clad, R. 55.

**Shryked**, *pt. pl.* shrieked, B 4590.

**Shryking**, *s.* shrieking, T. v. 382.

**Shryned**, *pp.* enshrined, C 955; canonised (ironically), 21. 15.

**Shryve**, *ger.* to confess, I 129.

**Shulder-boon**, *s.* blade-bone, I 603.

**Shuldres**, *pl.* shoulders, R. 328.

**Shull, Shullen, Shulde**; see **Shal**.

**Shyne**, *ger.* to shine, 10. 62; Shòòn, *strong pt. s.* shone, A 198; Shynede, *weak pt. s.* shone, L. 1119; Shined, L. 2194.

**Sib**, *adj.* related, akin, B 2565.

**Sicamour**, *s.* sycamore, HF. 1278.

**Sicer**, *s.* strong drink, B 3245.

**Sigh**, 1 *pt. s.* saw, R. 818.

**Sighte,** *pt. s. of* Syke.

**Signet,** *s.* signet-ring, T. ii. 1087.

**Signifiaunce,** *s.* signification, R. 995; significance, HF. 17; prediction, R. 16.

*Significavit,* a writ of excommunication, A 662.

**Sik,** *adj.* sick, ill, A 1600.

**Siker,** *adj.* sure, A 3049, B 4353; safe, G 864; certain, G 1047; sure, steady, D 2069; in security, 17. 28.

**Siker,** *adv.* uninterruptedly, T. iii. 1237; surely, T. ii. 991.

**Sikered,** *pp.* assured, L. 2128.

**Sikerer,** *adj.* surer, more to be trusted, B 4043.

**Sikerly,** *adv.* certainly, surely, truly, A 137.

**Sikernesse,** *s.* security, safety, confidence, B 425; state of security, T. ii. 773.

**Sikly,** *adv.* ill, with ill will, E 625.

**Silver,** *s.* money, A 232, 713.

**Silver,** *adj.* silvery, A 1496.

**Similitude,** *s.* comparison; *hence,* proposition, statement, G 431; sympathy, likeness, F 480; one like himself, A 3228.

**Simphonye,** *s.* a kind of tabor, B 2005.

**Simple,** *adj.* modest, R. 1014; innocent, 3. 861.

**Simplesse,** *s.* Simplicity (personified), R. 954.

**Sin,** *conj. and adv.* since, 4. 273.

**Singe,** *v.* sing, A 236; Singestow, singest thou, H 244; Song, 1 *pt. s.* sang, 3. 1158; Songe, 2 *pt. s.* didst sing, H 294; Song, *pt. s.* A 1055; Songen, *pt. pl.* sang, F 55; Songe, *pt. s. subj.* were to sing, 3. 929; Songen, *pp.* sung, T. v. 645; Songe, *pp.* A 266; recited, T. v. 1797.

**Singularitees,** *s. pl.* separate parts, particulars, B 5. m 3. 45.

**Singuler,** *adj.* particular, B 2. p 7. 64; single, I 300; a single, G 997; private, B 2625; *singular profyte,* special advantage, HF. 310.

**Singulerly,** *adv.* singly, B 4. p 6. 77.

**Sinne,** *s.* sin, A 561.

**Sinwes,** *s. pl.* sinews, I 690.

**Sippe,** *v.* sip, taste, D 176.

**Sire,** sir, my master, A 355; Sires, *gen.* sire's, father's, i. e. Saturn's, E 2265.

**Sis cink,** i. e. six-five, a throw with two dice, B 125.

**Sisoures,** *pl.* scissors, HF. 690.

**Sit,** *pr. s.* sits; see **Sitte.**

**Site,** *s.* situation, HF. 1114; E 199.

**Sith,** *conj.* since, A 930; Sith that, since, F 930, H 120.

**Sith,** *adv.* afterwards, C 869; then, L. 302.

**Sithen,** *conj.* since, B 2947; Sithen that, since, A 2102.

**Sithen,** *adv.* since, ago, A 1521; since then, R. 1641; since, T. iii. 244; afterwards, A 2617; then, next, L. 304; *goon s. a greet whyl,* a great while ago, L. 427; *gon s. longe whyle,* long ago, T. i. 718.

**Sithes,** *pl.* times, A. ii. 42. 9.

**Sitte,** *v.* sit, A 94; Sit, *pr. s.* sits, dwells, A 1599, 3641; befits, suits, B 1353; is fitting, T. i. 246; *yvel it sit,* it is unbecoming, E 460; Sat, *pt. s.* sat, A 469; affected, T. iv. 231; suited, L. 1735; became, R. 750; *sat on knees,* knelt, 3. 106; *hit sat me sore,* it was very painful for me, 3. 1220; T. iii. 240; Seet, *pt. s.* sat (false form, due to pl. *sēten*), A 2075; Sēten, *pt. pl.* sat, A 2893; Sete, *pt. s. subj.* would befit, T. i. 985, ii. 117; were to sit, 3. 436; was sitting, 3. 501; Sēten, *pp.* sat, D 420; dwelt, A 1452; *wel sittinge,* well suited, R. 986.

**Sittingest,** *sup. adj.* most fitting, 5. 551.

**Sive,** *s.* sieve, G 940.

**Sixte,** sixth, D 45, F 906.

**Skant,** *adj.* scanty, sparing, niggardly, 1. 175.

**Skarmish,** *s.* skirmish, T. ii. 611.

**Skars,** *adj.* scarce, 9. 36.

**Skathe,** *s.* harm, T. iv. 207.

**Skile,** *s.* reason, cause, HF. 726; *gret sk.,* good reason, E 1152; reasonable claim, L. 1392; *pl.* reasons, arguments, HF. 867.

**Skilful,** *adj.* reasonable, L. 385; discerning, B 1038.

**Skilfully,** *adv.* reasonably, with reason, G 320; particularly, 4. 155.

**Skilinge,** *s.* reason, B 4. p 6. 155.

**Skinketh,** *pt. s.* pours out, E 1722.

**Skippe,** *ger.* to skip, jump, T. i. 218; *v.* dance, A 3259; leap, E 1672; pass over, L. 622; Skipte, *pt. s.* leapt, F 1402.

**Skulle,** *s.* skull, A 3935, 4306.

**Skye,** *s.* cloud, HF. 1600.

**Slake,** *v.* assuage, R. 317; slacken, abate, F 841; desist (from), E 705; cease, E 137; end, E 802; Slake of, omit, L. 619; Slake, *pr. s. subj.* grow slack, wane, T. ii. 291; Slakede, *pt. s. subj.* should relax, B 2. m 8. 18.

**Slakke,** *adj.* slow, A 2901; *def.* slack, E 1849.

**Slakker,** *adj. pl.* slacker, more tardy, B 1603.

**Sledes,** *s. pl.* sledges, vehicles, B 4. p 1. 78. Pl. of *sled.*

**Slee,** *v.* A 661 ; Sleen, *ger.* to slay, A 1222 ; Slee, 1 *pr. s. as fut.* shall slay, B 2002 ; Sleeth, *pr. s.* slays, A 1118 ; Slowe, 2 *pt. s.* didst slay, T. iv. 506 ; Slow, *pt. s.* slew, B 627 ; extinguished, B 3922 ; Slough, *pt. s.* 7. 56 ; Slawe, *pp.* slain, A 943 ; Slawen, *pp.* E 544 ; Slayn, *pp.* slain, A 63.

**Sleep,** *pt. s. of* Slepe.

**Sleere,** *s.* slayer, A 2005.

**Sleet,** *s.* sleet, L. 1220 ; F 1250.

**Sleigh,** *adj.* sly, artful, A 3201.

**Sleighly,** *adv.* cunningly, T. v. 83.

**Sleighte,** *s.* trickery, T. iv. 1459 ; trick, B 2386 ; sleight, T. ii. 1512 ; contrivance, E 1102 ; plan, E 2131 ; dexterity, A 1948 ; cunning, L. 1382 ; skill, G 867 ; *pl.* plans, T. iv. 1451 ; devices, tricks, E 2421.

**Slely,** *adv.* slily, i. e. skilfully, A. ii. 29. 20.

**Slepe,** *s.* sleep, F 347 ; *on slepe,* asleep, L. 209.

**Slepe,** *v.* sleep, 3. 3 ; Slepestow, sleepest thou, A 4169 ; Sleep, 1 *pt. s.* siept, HF. 119 ; Sleep, *pt. s.* A 98 ; Slepte, *weak pt. s.* E 224 ; Slepe, *pt. pl.* 3. 166, 177.

**Sleping,** *s.* sleep, B 4202.

**Sleping-tyme,** *s.* time to sleep, 6. 54.

**Slepy,** *adj.* sleep-bestowing, A 1387.

**Slowthe,** *s.* sloth, I 388.

**Sleye,** *pl.* sly, subtle, T. iv. 972.

**Sleyly,** *adv.* slily, T. ii. 1185 ; subtly, T. ii. 462.

**Slider,** *adj.* slippery, A 1264.

**Slighte,** *s.* sleight, cunning, C 131.

**Slike,** *adj.* sleek, R. 542.

**Slinge-stones,** *pl.* stones from a sling, T. ii. 941.

**Slinke,** *ger.* to slink, T. iii. 1535.

**Slippe,** *v.* slip, L. 623.

**Slit,** *pr. s. of* Slyde.

**Slitten,** *v.* pierce, F 1260.

**Slivere,** *s.* a slice, portion, T. iii. 1013.

**Slo,** *s.* sloe, R. 928 ; Sloo, A 3246.

**Slogardye,** *s.* sluggishness, sloth, laziness, A 1042.

**Slombrestow,** slumberest thou, T. i. 730.

**Slombry,** *adj.* sleepy, I 724.

**Slomeringe,** *s.* slumber, T. ii. 67.

**Slong,** *pt. s.* threw, flung, H 306. Pt. t. of *slingen.*

**Sloo,** *s.* sloe, A 3246 ; Slo, R. 928.

**Sloppes,** *s. pl.* loose garments, I 422.

**Slough,** *s.* slough, mire, H 64.

**Slough,** *pt. s.* slew, A 980 ; see Slee.

**Slouthe,** *s.* sloth, T. ii. 959.

**Slow,** *s.* slough, D 1565 ; Slough, H 64.

**Slow,** *pt. s. of* Slee.

**Slowh,** *pt. s.* slew, B 4. m 7. 43.

**Sluggy,** *adj.* sluggish, I 706.

**Sluttish,** *adj.* slovenly, G 636.

**Sly,** *adj.* L. 1369 ; sly (one), A 3940 ; Slye, *def.* cunning, crafty, 7. 48 ; skilful, F 672 ; *pl.* artfully contrived, F 230.

**Slyde,** *v.* slide, T. v. 351 ; pass, go away, E 82, F 924 ; Slit, *pr. s.* passes away, 5. 3 ; G 682 ; Slydinge, *pres. pt. as adj.* moving, i. e. unstable, T. v. 825.

**Slyk** (*for* Slyke?), *adj.* sleek, D 351.

**Slyk,** *adj.* such (Northern), A 4130, 4170.

**Slyly,** *adv.* sagaciously, A 1444.

**Smal,** *adj.* small, A 153 ; *a smal,* a little, 6. 113.

**Smal,** *adv.* little, D 592 ; *but smal,* but little, F 71 ; high (of musical notes), 12. 11.

**Smalish,** *adj.* smallish, R. 826.

**Smart,** *adj.* brisk (said of a fire), G 768.

**Smatre,** *pr. pl. refl.* taste slightly, I 857.

**Smert,** *adj.* smart, quick, R. 831 ; brisk, G 768 ; *pl.* painful, 3. 507.

**Smerte,** *s.* pain, smart, F 480, 856, 974 ; anguish, A 3813.

**Smerte,** *adv.* smartly, sharply, A 149 ; sorely, E 629.

**Smerte,** *ger.* to smart, L. 502 ; Smert, *pr. s.* pains (me), 1. 152 ; Smerte, *pr. s. subj.* (it) may pain, A 1394 ; Smerte, *pt. s.* felt pain, T. ii. 930 ; Smerte, *pt. s. subj. impers.* (it) might give pain to, A 230.

**Smit, -en ;** see Smyte.

**Smithed,** *pt. s.* forged, A 3762.

**Smitted,** *pp.* smutted, i. e. besmirched, sullied with dishonour, T. v. 1545.

**Smoking,** *pres. pt.* reeking with incense or perfume, A 2281.

**Smokless,** *adj.* without a smock, E 875.

**Smoky,** *adj.* smoke-like, T. iii. 628.

**Smoot,** *pt. s. of* Smyte.

**Smoterliche,** *adj.* smirched in reputation, A 3963.

**Smothe,** *adj.* smooth, A 690.

**Smothe,** *adv.* smoothly, A 676.

**Smyler,** *s.* smiler, flatterer, A 1999.

**Smyte,** *v.* strike, A 1220 ; Smyten of, smite off, L. 1817 ; Smyteth, *pr. s.* knocks, L. 393 ; Smit, *pr. s.* smites, E 122 ; Smòòt, *pt. s.* smote, struck, A 149 ; Smiten, *pp.* struck, T. ii. 1145.

**Snewed,** *pt. s.* abounded, A 345.

**Snibben,** *v.* reprove, chide, lit. 'snub,' A 523 ; *pp.* reprimanded, A 4401.

**Snorteth,** *pr. s.* snorts, A 4163 ; *pt. s.* was drawn together (as in sniffing), R. 157.

**Snow,** *s.* R. 558 ; argent (in heraldry),

white, B 3573; *pl.* snow-storms, HF. 967.

**Snowish**, *adj.* snowy, white, T. iii. 1250.

**So**, *adv.* so, A 102; such, B 2205; in such a way, such, T. iii. 1579; so, i.e. pray (with verb in subj. mood), T. iii. 1470; So as, as well as, as far as, 4. 161; *so have I Joye*, as I hope to have bliss, 3. 1065.

**So**, *conj.* provided that, L. 1319; So as, whereas, B 4. p 3. 40; So that, provided that, C 186.

**Sobrely**, *adv.* gravely, F 1585; Soberly, sadly, with a melancholy look, A 289.

**Sobrenesse**, *s.* sobriety, I 834.

**Socour**, succour, help, A 918, F 1357; *do yow s.*, help you, 4. 292.

**Socouren**, *v.* aid, T. iii. 1264.

**Socours**, *s.* help, L. 1341.

**Soden**, *pp.* sodden, boiled, I 900.

**Sodein**, *adj.* prompt, forward, T. v. 1024.

**Sodeinly**, *adv.* suddenly, F 1015.

**Softe**, *adj.* soft, A 153; gentle, slow, B 399; mild, D 1412.

**Softe**, *adv.* softly, A 2781; gently, C 252; tenderly, B 275; timidly, 3. 1212.

**Softely**, *adv.* softly, F 636; quietly, G 408; in a low tone, L. 2126.

**Softneth**, *pr. s.* assuages, L. 50.

**Sojourne**, *v.* dwell, T. v. 1350; tarry, R. 381; remain, D 987.

**Soken**, *s.* toll, A 3987. A. S. *sōcn.*

**Sokingly**, *adv.* gradually, B 2766. 'Sokyngly, *idem quod* esyly'; Prompt. Parv.

**Sol**, Sol (the sun), G 826.

**Solas**, *s.* amusement, A 798; solace, I 206; comfort, F 802; consolation, T. ii. 460; relief, B 1972; diversion, B 1904; pleasure, B 3964; playfulness, R. 844; joy, T. i. 31; ease, L. 1966.

**Solde**, *pt. s. of* Selle.

**Solempne**, *adj.* festive, grand, E 1125; cheerful, A 209; important, A 364; illustrious, B 387; superb, F 61; public, I 102.

**Solempnely**, *adv.* pompously, with pomp, A 274.

**Solempnitee**, *s.* pomp, A 870; outward show, C 244; due ceremony, E 1709.

**Soleyn**, *adj.* sole, solitary, 3. 982; unmated, 5. 607, 614.

**Solsticioun**, *s.* the solstice, or point of the ecliptic most remote from the equator, A. i. 17. 9.

**Som** (sum), *indef. pron.* some, A 640, B 1182; one, a certain man, G 922; one, 3. 305; another, 5. 476; *som shrewe is*, some one (at least) is wicked, G 995; Som ... som, one ... another, A 3031; Somme, *pl.* some, B 2139; some (of them), L. 1050.

**Somdel**, *adv.* somewhat, B 4011; a little, L. 1183; in some measure, A 3911.

**Somer**, *s.* summer, A 394; Someres game, summer-game, athletic exhibition, D 648.

**Somer-sesoun**, *s.* spring, early summer, B 3. p 8. 43.

**Somme**, *pl.* some, T. iv. 995; see **Som**.

**Somme**, *s.* sum, F 1220; chief point, upshot, L. 1559; *pl.* sums of money, B 1407, G 675.

**Somne**, *v.*; see **Sompne**.

**Somnour**, *s.* summoner, apparitor, an officer who summoned delinquents before the ecclesiastical courts, A 543.

**Somonce**, *s.* summons, D 1586.

**Sompne**, *v.* summon, D 1577; Somne, *v.* D 1347.

**Sompnolence**, *s.* somnolence, I 706.

**Somtyme**, *adv.* once, A 65, 85; sometimes, B 1667; some day, B 110.

**Sond**, *s.* sand, B 509, 4457.

**Sonde**, *s.* message, B 388, 1049; sending, I 625; gifts, B 1049; visitation, B 760, 826; trial, B 902; message (*or* messenger), G 525.

**Sonded**, *pp.* sanded, T. ii. 822.

**Sondry**, *adj.* various, A 14, 25.

**Sone** (sune), *s.* son, A 79, 336.

**Sone**, *adv.* soon, A 1022; speedily, D 1264.

**Sone-in-lawe**, *s.* son-in-law, E 315.

**Sonest**, *adv. superl.* soonest, B 3716.

**Song**, -e, -en; see **Singe**.

**Sonne**, *s.* sun, A 7, 30.

**Sonne-beem**, *s.* sunbeam, D 868.

**Sonnish**, *adj.* sun-like, golden, T. iv. 736, 816.

**Soor**, *s.* sore, wound, A 1454.

**Soor**, *adj.* wounded, grieved, A 2695; sore, F 1571; sad, T. v. 639.

**Soot**, *s.* soot, an emblem of bitterness, T. iii. 1194.

**Sooth**, *adj.* true, L. 14; *as adv.* truly, C 636.

**Sooth**, *s.* truth, A 284; Sothe, G 662; Sothe, *dat.* B 1939.

**Soothfastnesse**, *s.* truth, B 4518.

**Soothly**, *adv.* truly, A 117.

**Sooty**, *adj.* begrimed with soot, B 4022.

**Sop**, *s.* sop (of toasted bread), E 1843; Sop in wyn, wine with bread soaked in it, A 334.

**Soper**, *s.* supper, A 348; Sopeer, F 1189.

**Sophistrye**, *s.* evil cunning, L. 137.

**Sophyme**, *s.* a sophism, trick of logic, E 5 ; *pl.* deceits, F 554.

**Sore**, *adv.* sorely, A 148 ; *bar so sore*, bore so ill, E 85.

**Sore**, *ger.* to soar, HF. 531 ; to mount aloft, F 123.

**Sorer**, *adv.* more sorely, L. 502.

**Sorest**, *adv.* most sorely, 5. 404.

**Sormounte**, *ger.* to surpass, R. 667 ; *pr. s.* rises above, T. iii. 1038.

**Sort**, *s.* lot, T. ii. 1754 ; destiny, chance, A 844 ; kind, A 4381 ; divination, T. i. 76.

**Sorted**, *pt. s.* allotted, T. v. 1827.

**Sorwe**, *s.* sorrow, grief, A 951 ; mourning, B 2171 ; sympathy, compassion, F 422 ; *with sorwe*, with ill luck to you, D 308.

**Sorwestow**, thou sorrowest, B 1. p 6. 80 ; *pr. s.* I 85 ; *pr. pl.* A 2824.

**Sorweful**, *adj.* sorrowful, L. 1832.

**Sorwefulleste**, *adj.* most sorrowful, E 2098.

**Sorwefully**, *adv.* sadly, A 2978.

**Sorwing**, *s.* sorrow, 3. 606.

**Sory**, *adj.* sorrowful, mournful, A 2004, 2010 ; sad, B 2899 ; unlucky, B 1949 ; ill, C 876 ; miserable, H 55.

**Sory**, *adv.* sorely, B 2. p 4. 100.

**Soster**, *s.* sister, A 3486.

**Sote**, *adj.* sweet, A 1, B 2348.

**Sote**, *adv.* sweetly, L. 2612.

**Sotel**, *adj.* subtle, cunning, 18. 43.

**Soteltee**, subtlety, skill, 18. 77.

**Soth**, *adj.* true, B 169 ; North, L. 14

**Sothe**, *s.* truth, A 845. See **Sooth.**

**Sother**, *adj. comp.* truer, G 214.

**Sothfastnesse**, *s.* truth, B 2365 ; certainty, I 380.

**Sothly**, *adv.* verily, soothly, A. pr. 23.

**Soth-sawe**, *s.* true saying, truth, HF. 2089 ; *pl.* HF. 676.

**Sotil**, *adj.* subtle, cunning, L. 1556, 2559 ; subtly woven, A 1054 ; thin, A 2030.

**Sotilly**, *adv.* skilfully, R. 1119 ; cleverly, R. 772.

**Sotted**, *adj.* besotted, befooled, G 1341.

**Souded**, *pp.* confirmed, B 1769.

**Sought, -e** ; see **Seke.**

**Souke**, *ger.* to suck, A 4157 ; to embezzle, A 4416 ; *pp.* been at the breast, E 450.

**Soul**, *adj.* sole, single, E 2080.

**Soule**, *s.* soul, A 656, 781.

**Soulfre**, *s.* sulphur, HF. 1508.

**Soun**, *s.* sound, musical sound, A 674, E 271 ; vaunt, L. 267 ; *pl.* sounds, A 2512.

**Sound**, *adj.* unhurt, L. 1619 ; *pl.* in strong health, T. iii. 1526.

**Sounde**, *ger.* to heal, make sound, 7. 242 ; *v.* heal, R. 966.

**Soune**, *ger.* to sound, to utter, T. ii. 573 ; imitate in sound, speak alike, F 105 ; **Sounen**, *v.* sound, *hence*, tend, redound, T. i. 1036 ; **Souneth**, *pr. s.* tends (towards), relates, (to), T. iii. 1414 ; is consonant (with), B 3157 ; makes (for), H 195 ; **Sounen**, *pr. pl.* tend, I 1068 ; *pt. s.* inclined, T. iv. 1676 ; *pres. pt.* accordant with, in agreement with, A 275 ; **Souninge** in, tending to, A 307.

**Souned** ; *beste s.*, best-sounding, T. ii. 1031.

**Soupe**, *v.* sup, T. ii. 944.

**Souper**, *s.* supper, T. ii. 947.

**Souple**, *adj.* pliant, A 203.

**Sourdeth**, *pr. s.* arises, I 475.

**Soure**, *adj.* bitter, cruel, B 1. p 4. 88.

**Soure**, *adv.* sourly, bitterly, B 2012.

**Soures**, *s. pl.* sorrels, bucks of the third year, 3. 429.

**Sourmounteth**, *pr. s.* surmounts, rises above, T. iii. 1038.

**Sours**, *s.* source, origin, T. v. 1591 ; E 49 ; a springing aloft, HF. 544 ; swift upward flight, D 1938, 1941.

**Souter**, *s.* cobbler, A 3904.

**Soutiltee**, *s.* device, D 576.

**Souvenance**, *s.* remembrance, 24. 14.

**Sovoraynetee**, *s.* sovereignty, E 114, F 751 ; supremacy, D 818.

**Sovereyn**, *adj.* supreme, very high, A 67 ; chief, B 3339 ; sovereign, D 1048 ; superior, A ii. 28. 39 (a technical term, applied to the western signs of the zodiac) ; *as s.* lord, 1. 69 ; master, G 590 ; Sovereyne, *fem.* 5. 422 ; **Sovereyns**, *pl.* superiors, I 392, 402.

**Sovereynly**, *adv.* royally, B 2462 ; chiefly, B 4552.

**Sovereyntee**, *s.* supremacy, D 1038.

**Sowdan**, *s.* sultan, B 177.

**Sowdanesse**, *s.* sultaness, B 358.

**Sowe**, *v.* sew up, T. ii. 1201, 1204 ; *pp.* sewn, A 685.

**Sowen**, *v.* sow, B 1182 ; Sowen, *pp.* R. 1617 ; Sowe, *pp.* T. i. 385.

**Sowle**, *s.* soul, life, T. ii. 1734.

**Sowled**, *pp.* endued with a soul, G 329.

**Sowne**, *v.* sound, play upon, A 565 ; sound, T. iii. 189 ; Sowneth, *pr. s.* sounds, I 160 ; signifies, A. i. 21. 62 ; *pr. pl.* play, F 270 ; Sowneth, *pr. pl.* tend (to), are consonant (with), F 517 ; Souned, *pt. pl.* tended, B 3348. See **Soune.**

**Space**, *s.* room, T. i. 714 ; space of time, A 87 ; while, C 239 ; opportunity, spare time, A 35 ; course, A 176.

**Spak,** *pt. s.* spake, A 124 ; see **Speke.**

**Span,** *pt. s.* spun, L. 1762.

**Spanne,** *s.* span, A 155.

**Span-newe,** *adj.* span-new, T. iii. 1665. Lit. 'newly spun.'

**Spare,** *v.* spare, refrain, A 192 ; cease, 5. 699 ; *pp.* passed over, L. 2602.

**Sparhauk,** *s.* sparrow-hawk, B 1957.

**Sparinge,** *s.* moderation, I 835.

**Sparkle,** *s.* small spark, B 2095.

**Sparow,** *s.* sparrow, 5. 351.

**Sparre,** *s.* wooden beam, A 990, 1076.

**Sparth,** *s.* battle-axe, A 2520.

**Sparwe,** *s.* sparrow, A 626.

**Spaynel,** *s.* spaniel, D 267.

**Spece,** *s.* species, sort, I 407 ; *pl.* kinds, A 3013, I 865.

**Speche,** *s.* speech, L. 1084 ; discourse, A 307 ; talk, A 783, D 1020 ; address, 3. 1131 ; oratory, F 104.

**Special,** *adj.* special ; *in special,* especially, in particular, A 444, 1017.

**Spéctacle,** *s.* eye-glass, D 1203.

**Spede,** *ger.* to succeed, C 134 ; Spede me, *v.* be quick, 5. 385 ; Spede, *pr. s. subj.* speed, prosper, A 769 ; Spedde, *pt. s.* hastened, moved quickly, A 3649 ; made to prosper, B 3876 ; *pt. s. refl.* hasted, A 1217 ; 1 *pt. s. refl.* L. 200 ; *pp.* terminated, determined, 5. 101 ; accomplished, G 357.

**Speed,** *s.* help, T. ii. 9 ; success, T. i. 17 ; *for comune spede,* for the good of all, 5. 507.

**Speedful,** *adj.* advantageous, B 727.

**Speere,** *s.* sphere, F 1283.

**Speke,** *v.* speak, 3. 852 ; Spekestow, speakest thou, G 473 ; Spak, 1 *pt. s.* spake, L. 97 ; *pt. s.* 3. 503 ; Speken, *pt. pl.* 3. 350 ; Spaken (*better* Speken), *pt. pl.* spake, T. i. 565 ; Speke, *pt. s. subj.* might speak, T. ii. 1119 ; Spoken, *pm.* A 31.

**Speking,** *s.* speech-making, oratory, 5. 488 ; speaking, H 335.

**Spelle,** *s. dat.* a story, B 2083.

**Spence,** *s.* buttery, D 1931.

**Spending-silver,** *s.* silver to spend, money in hand, G 1018.

**Spere,** *s.* spear, A 114 ; *as nigh as men may casten with a spere,* a spear's cast, HF. 1048.

**Spere,** *s.* sphere, orbit, 4. 137 ; 16. 11.

**Sperhauk,** *s.* sparrowhawk, B 4647.

**Sperme,** *s.* seed, B 3199.

**Sperred,** *pp.* barred, T. v. 521.

**Spete,** *v.* spit, T. ii. 1617 ; Spetten, *pt. pl.* I 270.

**Spewe,** *v.* vomit, B 2607.

**Spewing,** *s.* vomit, I 138.

**Spicerye,** *s.* mixture of spices, B 2043.

**Spille,** *v.* spill, drop, T. v. 880 ; kill, L. 1574 ; destroy, ruin, E 503 ; perish, 6. 121 ; *ger.* to destroy, T. v. 588 ; *to sp. labour,* to lose labour, H 153 ; *doth me sp.,* causes me to die, 6. 14 ; Spillestow teres, lettest thou tears fall (Lat. *manas*), B 1. p 4. 4 ; *pp.* killed, B 857 ; lost, 1. 180 ; ruined, D 1611 ; confounded, D 388.

**Spirit,** *s.* A 2809 ; Spirites, the (four) spirits in alchemy (sulphur, sal ammoniac, quicksilver, arsenic), G 820 ; vital forces, 3. 489.

**Spitous,** *adj.* malicious, R. 979 ; inhospitable, 22. 13.

**Spitously,** *adv.* spitefully, D 223 ; vehemently, A 3476.

**Spoke,** *pp. of* Speke.

**Sponne,** 2 *pt. pl.* did spin, T. iii. 734.

**Spoon,** *s.* spoon, F 602 ; Spones, *pl.* C 908.

**Spore,** *s.* spur, A 2603 ; *pl.* A 473.

**Sporne,** *ger.* to spurn, kick, 13. 11 ; *pt. s.* spurns, treads, T. ii. 797 ; *pt. s.* tripped himself up, A 4280.

**Spot,** *s.* defect, E 2146.

**Spousaille,** *s.* espousal, wedding, E 115, 180.

**Spoused,** *pp.* wedded, E 3, 386.

**Spouted,** *pp.* vomited, B 487.

**Sprayned** ; see **Springen.**

**Sprede,** *v.* spread, open, 4. 4 ; *ger.* to expand, R 1679 ; Spradde, *pt. s.* spread, E 418, 722 ; covered, 7. 40 ; Sprad, *pp.* spread, A 2903 ; dispersed, 3. 874 ; Spradde, *pp. pl.* wide open, T. iv. 1422.

**Spreynd** ; see **Springen.**

**Spring,** *s.* dawn, A. ii. 6. 6 ; first growth, R. 834 ; *pt.* merry dances, HF. 1235.

**Springe,** *strong v.* spring up, grow, A 3018 : rise, B 4068 ; spread abroad, 7. 74 ; spring, be carried, L. 719 ; *ger.* to rise (as the sun), A 2522 ; to dawn, A 822 ; to arise, 1. 133 ; Sprang, *pt. s.* grew up, R. 1425 ; Sprong, *pt. s.* spread out, R. 1704 ; Spronge, *pp.* become famous, A 1437 ; grown, L. 1054 ; *spronge amis,* alighted in a wrong place, HF. 2079.

**Springen,** *weak v.* sprinkle, scatter, sow broadcast, B 1183 ; Spreynd, *pp.* sprinkled, B 422, 1830 ; Sprayned, *pp.* B 2. p 4. 132. A.S. *sprengan.*

**Springers,** *s. pl.* sources, origins, I 387.

**Springing,** *s.* source, E 49.

**Spurne,** *v.* spurn, kick, F 616.

**Spyce,** *s.* spice, R. 1367, 1371 ; *pl.* spicery, L. 1110 ; species, kinds, I 83, 102.

**Spyced,** *pp.* spiced, A 3378 ; scrupulous, A 526, D 435.

**Spycerye,** *s.* collection of spices, mixture of spices, A 2935, B 136.

**Spyr,** *s.* spire, shoot, T. ii. 1335.

**Squames,** *s. pl.* scales, G 759.

**Squaymous,** *adj.* squeamish, sparing (except rarely), A 3337.

**Squiereth,** *pr. s.* attends, accompanies, D 305.

**Squire,** *s.* a 'square,' a carpenter's instrument for measuring right angles, D 2090 ; *pl.* measuring-rules, A. i. 12. 3.

**Squyer,** *s.* squire, A 79.

**Stable,** *adj.* abiding, A 3004, 3009 ; firm, 3. 645 ; sure, E 1499 ; constant, 4. 281 ; steadfast, F 871.

**Stablissed,** *pp.* established, A 2995.

**Stadie,** *s.* race-course, B 4. p 3. 11.

**Staf,** *s.* staff, stick, L. 2000 ; (perhaps a bed-staff), A 4294, 4296 ; Staves, *gen.* of the shaft of a car, 7. 184.

**Staf-slinge,** *s.* a staff-sling, sling with a handle, B 2019.

**Stages,** *pl.* positions, HF. 122.

**Stak,** *pt. s.* stuck, T. iii. 1372 ; was fastened on, R. 458.

**Stakereth,** *pr. s.* staggers, L. 2687.

**Stal,** *pt. s. of* Stelen.

**Stalke,** *s.* stalk, A 1036 ; piece of straw, A 3919 ; Stalkes, *pl.* (Lat. *palmites*), B 1. m 6. 15 ; stems, T. ii. 968 ; uprights of a ladder, A 3625.

**Stalke,** *v.* creep up (to), T. ii. 519 ; move stealthily, L. 1781 ; *pr. s.* walks stealthily, A 1479 ; moves slowly, A 3648.

**Stalle,** *s. dat.* ox-stall, T. v. 1469.

**Stamin,** *s.* a coarse harsh cloth, tamine, tammy, L. 2360 ; I 1052. O.F. *estamine.*

**Stampe,** *pr. pl.* bray in a mortar, C 538.

**Stanched,** *pp.* staunched, B 2. p 2. 53.

**Stank,** *s.* lake, tank, pool, I 841. E. *tank.*

**Stant,** stands ; see **Stonde.**

**Stapen,** *pp.* advanced, B 4011, E 1514 (*in* MS. E.).

**Stare,** *s.* starling, 5. 348.

**Starf,** *pt. s. of* Sterve.

**Stark,** *adj.* strong, E 1458 ; severe, B 3560.

**Startling,** moving suddenly, L. 1204.

**Staunchen,** *v.* satisfy, B 3. m 3. 3.

**Stede,** *s.* place, HF. 731 ; *in stede of,* instead of, B 3308.

**Stede,** *s.* steed, A 2157.

**Stedfastnesse,** *s.* constancy, firmness, E 699 ; stability, 15. 7.

**Steer,** *s.* bullock, A 2149.

**Steked,** *pp.* stuck, L. 161 *a.*

**Stele,** *s.* lit. handle ; i. e. the (cool) end, A 3785.

**Stelen,** *v.* steal, A 562 ; Steleth, *pr. s.* steals away, B 21 ; Stal, *pt. s.* stole, L. 796 ; came (or went) cunningly, HF. 418 ; went stealthily, B 3763 ; *stal away,* stole away, 3. 381 ; Stole, *pp.* stolen, A 2627.

**Stellifye,** *v.* make into a constellation, HF. 586, 1002.

**Stemed,** *pt. s.* shone, glowed, A 202. A.S. *stēman.*

**Stenten,** *v.* leave off, A 903 ; *ger.* to stay, A 2442 ; *v.* cease, leave off, B 3925 ; Stente, 2 *pr. s. subj.* cease, 18. 61 ; Stente, *pt. s.* ceased, stopped, 3. 154 ; L. 1240 ; remained, L. 821 ; stayed, T. i. 273 ; Stente, *pt. pl.* ceased, T. i. 60 ; delayed, L. 633 ; *pp.* stopped, A 1368.

**Stepe,** *adj. pl.* glittering, bright, A 201, 753. A.S. *stēap.*

**Steppes,** *pl.* foot-tracks, L. 829, 2209.

**Stere,** *s.* helm, rudder, B 833 ; pilot, helmsman, guide, B 448 ; *in stere,* upon my rudder, T. v. 641.

**Stere,** *v.* steer, rule, T. iii. 910 ; 1 *pr. s.* steer, T. ii. 4 ; *pp.* controlled, L. 935.

**Stere,** *v.* stir, move, excite, T. i. 228 ; propose, T. iv. 1451 ; *pr. s.* stirs, HF. 817.

**Sterelees,** *adj.* rudderless, B 439.

**Steresman,** *s.* steersman, HF. 436.

**Steringe,** *s.* stirring, motion, HF. 800.

**Sterlinges,** *pl.* sterling coins, C 907.

**Sterne,** *adj.* stern, E 465 ; violent, T. iii. 743.

**Sterre,** *s.* star, 5. 68, 300 ; constellation, HF. 599.

**Stert,** *s.* start, T. v. 254 ; *at a stert,* in a moment, A 1705.

**Sterte,** *v.* start, go quickly, T. ii. 1634 ; move away, T. iii. 949 ; pass away, B 335 ; leap, skip, R. 344 ; Stert, *pr. s.* rouses, HF. 681 ; Sterte, 1 *pt. s.* departed, T. iv. 93 ; rushed, L. 811 ; leapt, A 952 ; went, T. ii. 1094 ; went at once, L. 660 ; Sterting, *pres. pt.* bursting suddenly, L. 1741.

**Sterve,** *v.* die, A 1249 ; die of famine, C 451 ; Starf, *pt. s.* L. 1691 ; A 933, B 283 ; Storven, *pt. pl.* C 888.

**Stevene,** *s.* voice, sound, language, A 2562 ; rumour, talk, T. iii. 1723 ; time, moment, esp. of an appointment, A 1524 ; sound, L. 1219 ; meeting by appointment, 4. 52 ; *sette st.,* made appointment, A 4383.

**Stewe,** *s.* a fish-pond, A 350 ; a small room, closet, T. iii. 601 ; brothel, HF. 26.

**Stewe-dore,** *s.* closet-door, T. iii. 698.

**Steyre,** *s.* degree (Lat. *gradus*), 4. 129; Steyres, *gen.* stair's, T. iii. 205.

**Stiborn,** *adj.* stubborn, D 456, 637.

**Stidefast,** *adj.* steadfast, B 2641.

**Stif,** *adj.* strong, A 673; bold, R. 1270; hard, D 2267.

**Stiken,** *ger.* to stick, T. i. 297; Stiked, *pt. s.* stuck, B 509; fixed, B 2007; Stikede, *pt. s.* pierced, B 3897; Stikked, fixed, L. 2202; *pp.* stabbed, B 430; *a stiked swyn,* a stuck pig, C 556.

**Stikinge,** *s.* sticking, setting, I 954.

**Stikkes,** *pl.* palings, B 4038.

**Stillatorie,** *s.* still, vessel used in distillation, G 580.

**Stille,** *adv.* quietly, L. 816; still, D 2200.

**Stille,** *ger.* to silence, T. ii. 230.

**Stingeth,** *pr. s.* pierces, L. 645.

**Stinte,** *v.* leave off, A 1334; cease, G 883; cause to cease, 1. 63; end, E 747; *ger.* to cease, B 2164; to stop, T. ii. 383; cease, I 720; restrain, R. 1441; stop, avert, L. 1647; Stinte, 1 *pr. s.* leave off telling, HF. 1417; *pr. pl.* cease, I 93; *pt. s. subj.* may cease, B 413; Stinte, *pt. s.* ceased, A 2421; was silent, 3. 1299; *pt. pl.* stopped (*or pr. pl.* stop), L. 294; Stinte, *pt. s. subj.* should cease, T. i. 848; *pp.* stopped, T. iii. 1016; *stint thy clappe,* hold your tongue, A 3144; Stinteth, *imp. pl.* stay, T. ii. 1729.

**Stintinge,** *s.* ceasing, end, B 2. m 7. 37.

**Stiren,** *v.* stir, excite, B 2696.

**Stiropes,** *s. pl.* stirrups, B 1163.

**Stirte,** *pt. s.* started, D 1046; rushed, H 303; went quickly, E 2153.

**Stith,** *s.* anvil, A 2026. Icel. *steði.*

**Stod, -e ;** see **Stonde.**

**Stok,** *s.* a block of wood, A. ii. 38. 6; source, 14. 1; race, A 1551; *pl.* stumps, A 2934; posts, T. iii. 589.

**Stoke,** *ger.* to stab, thrust, A 2546.

**Stokked,** *pp.* fastened in the stocks, T. iii. 380.

**Stole,** *s.* stool, frame for tapestry-work, L. 2352; *pl.* chairs, D 288.

**Stole,** *pp. of* Stelen.

**Stomak,** *s.* stomach, T. i. 787; appetite, D 1847; compassion, D 1441.

**Stomblen,** *pr. pl.* stumble, A 2613.

**Stonde,** *v.* stand, B 1050; be placed, A 745; be understood, be fixed, E 346; be set in view (as a prize at a game), B 1931; *fynt stonde,* finds standing, L. 1499; Stont, *pr. s.* stands, is, T. iii. 1562; Stant, *pr. s.* stands, B 618; consists, I 107, 1029; is, B 1304; Stood, *pt. s.* A 354;

stuck fast, D 1541; Stonden, *pp.* HF. 1928.

**Stongen,** *pp.* stung, A 1079.

**Stoon,** *s.* stone, A 774; precious stone, gem, R. 1086.

**Stoon-wal,** stone-wall, L. 713.

**Stoor,** *s.* store, stock (of a farm), A 598; store, D 2159; value, D 203.

**Stopen,** *pp.* advanced, E 1514 (MS. E. has *stapen*).

**Stoppen,** *v.* stop, T. ii. 804.

**Store,** *s.* store, value, B 4344; possession, L. 2337.

**Store,** *ger.* to store, B 1463.

**Store,** *adj. voc.* audacious, bold, E 2367. Icel. *störr.*

**Storial,** *adj.* historical, A 3179; Storial sooth, historical truth, L. 702.

**Storie,** *s.* history, legend of a saint (or the like), A 709; history, E 1366; tale, story, 7. 10; *pl.* books of history, T. v. 1044.

**Storven,** *pt. pl. of* Sterve, died, C 888.

**Stot,** *s.* a stallion, horse, cob, A 615; heifer (a term of abuse), D 1630.

**Stounde,** *s.* hour, time, while, A 1212, 4007; short time, B 1021; moment, L. 949; *in a stounde,* at a time, once, A 3992; *upon a stounde,* in one hour, T. iv. 625; *pl.* hours, seasons, T. iii. 1752.

**Stoundemele,** at various times, from time to time, T. v. 674.

**Stoupe,** *ger.* to stoop, G 1311.

**Stour,** *s.* battle, contest, R. 1270.

**Stout,** *adj.* strong, A 545.

**Straighter,** *adj.* more stretched out, more expanded, R. 119.

**Strake,** *v.* move, proceed, 3. 1312.

**Strange,** *adj.* strange, F 89; external, D 1161; not its own, A. ii. 19. 7. Every star has its *own* degrees (of longitude) in the equator and ecliptic.

**Strangenesse,** *s.* estrangement, B 1576.

**Stranglen,** *pr. pl.* strangle, worry, I 768.

**Strangling,** *s.* A 2458; *of str.,* caused by strangling, L. 807.

**Straught, -e ;** see **Strecche.**

**Straunge,** *adj.* strange, foreign, A 13; unwonted, 7. 202; difficult, hard to agree upon, F 1223; like a stranger, T. ii. 1660; unfriendly, estranged, R. 1065; distant, unbending, 5. 584; not well known, A. ii. 17. *rub.*; [a *strange* star is one that is not represented upon the Rete of the Astrolabe]; *pl.* strangers, T. ii. 411.

**Straungely,** *adv.* distantly, T. v. 955.

**Straw,** *s.* T. iii. 859; *as interj.* a straw! F 695.

Strawen, v. strew, L. 207; 2 pr. s. subj. F 613; pp. strewn, I 918.

Strayte, s. strait, B 464.

Strecche, v. stretch, B 4498; extend, T. ii. 341; reach, 7. 341; Streighte, pt. s. stretched, HF. 1373; Straughte, pt. pl. extended, A 2916; Straughten, pt. pl. stretched out, R. 1021; Streight, stretched out; long str., stretched at full length, T. iv. 1163; pp. as adv. straight, T. ii. 599.

Stree, s. straw, A 2918; pl. 3. 718.

Streem, s. river, current, L. 2508; stream, A 464; ray (of light), 2. 94.

Streen, s. strain, i. e. stock, progeny, race, E 157.

Streight, adj. straight, 3. 957.

Streight, adv. straight, straightway, A 671.

Streight, -e; see Strecche.

Streit, adj. narrow, A 1984; scanty, R. 457; B 4179; strict, A 174; pl. scanty, small, D 1426. A. F. estreit.

Streite, pp. as adj. def. drawn, B 4547. (It here represents Lat. strictus.)

Streite, adv. closely, T. iv. 1689; strictly, L. 723; tightly, A 457.

Streitnes, s. smallness, A. i. 21. 55.

Stremeden, pt. pl. streamed, T. iv. 247.

Streng, s. string, D 2067; pl. 5. 197.

Strenger, adj. comp. stronger, B 2410.

Strengest, strongest, T. i. 243.

Strengest-feythed, strongest in faith, T. i. 1007.

Strengthe, s. strength, A 84; force, 3. 351; pl. sources of strength, B 3248.

Strepen, v. strip, E 1958; do str. me, cause me to be stripped, E 2200.

Strete, s. street, T. ii. 612; dat. HF. 1049; street, road, way, 1. 70; B 1683.

Streyne, v. compress, T. iii. 1205; strain, press, E 1753; constrain, E 144; hold, confine, R. 1471; ger. to compress, T. iii. 1071; Streyne, pr. pl. strain (as through a sieve), C 538.

Streyt, adj. small, B 3. m 2. 26.

Strike, s. hank (of flax), A 676.

Strogelest; see Strugle.

Stroke, ger. to stroke, T. iii. 1249.

Strokes, pl. of Strook.

Strompetes, s. pl. strumpets, B 1. p 1. 54.

Stronde, dat. shore, L. 2189; Strondes, pl. shores, A 13.

Strong, adj. difficult, B 2635; pl. severe, A 1338, 2771.

Stronge, adv. securely, R. 241.

Stroof, pt. s. of Stryve.

Strook, s. stroke, A 1701; Strokes, pl. T. iii. 1067.

Strouted, pt. s. stuck out, A 3315.

Strowe, v. strew, L. 101 a.

Stroyer, destroyer, 5. 360.

Strugle, v. struggle, E 2374; Strogelest, 2 pr. s. C 829.

Stryf, s. quarrel, strife, A 1187, 2784; took stryf = 'took up the cudgels,' B 1. p 4. 93.

Stryk, s. stroke, mark, A. ii. 12. 19.

Stryke, v. strike; Stryken out, strike out, D 1364; Strȳke, pp. struck, 11. 35.

Stryve, v. strive, struggle, 10. 30; oppose, E 170; Stroof, pt. s. strove, vied, A 1038.

Stryvinge, s. striving, strife, B 2674.

Stubbel-goos, s. fatted goose, A 4351.

Stubbes, pl. stumps, A 1978.

Studie, s. study, A 303; state of meditation, A 1530; Study, library, F 1207, 1214; Studies, pl. endeavours, B 3. p 2. 93; desires, B 4. p 2. 56.

Studie, v. study, A 184; ger. give heed, I 1090; Studieth, pr. s. deliberates, E 1955.

Stuffed, pp. filled, E 264.

Sturdely, adv. boldly, 4. 82.

Sturdinesse, s. sternness, E 700.

Sturdy, adj. cruel, hard, harsh, stern, F 698, 1049; firm, T. ii. 1380; D 2162.

Sty, s. pig sty, D 1829.

Stye, ger. to mount up, B 4. p 6. 414.

Style (1), s. a stile, a means to get over a barrier by climbing, C 712, F 106.

Style (2), s. style, mode of writing, F 105.

Styves, pl. stews, D 1332.

Styward, s. steward, B 914.

Suasioun, s. persuasiveness, B 2. p 1. 45.

Subdekne, s. subdeacon, I 891.

Subgit, adj. subject, T. v. 1790; Subget, T. i. 231.

Subgit, s. subject, T. ii. 828; pl. servants, D 1990.

Subjeccion, s. (1), suggestion, (a thing subjected to the mind), I 351; (2), subjection, obedience, B 270; submission, 4. 32; subjection, governance, B 3656, 3742.

Sublymatories, s. pl. vessels for sublimation, G 793.

Sublymed, pp. sublimed, sublimated, G 774. 'Sublimate, to bring by heat into the state of vapour'; Webster.

Sublyming, s. sublimation, G 770.

Submitted, pp. subjected, B 5. p 1. 44; ye ben s., ye have submitted, B 35.

Subtil, adj. subtle, C 141; ingenious, A. pr. 60; skilful, L. 672; finely woven, 5. 272.

**Subtilitee,** *s.* subtlety, craft, secret knowledge, G 620; skill, craft, G 844; *pl.* tricks, E 2421.

**Subtilly,** *adv.* craftily, A 610; subtly, F 222.

**Subtiltee,** *s.* subtlety, F 140; specious reasoning, HF. 855; skill, B 4509; trick, D 1420.

**Succedent,** *sb.* a 'succedent' house, A. ii. 4. 48. The *succedent* houses are the *second, fifth, eighth,* and *eleventh,* as these are *about to follow* the most important houses, which are the *first, fourth, seventh,* and *tenth.*

**Sucre,** *s.* sugar, T. iii. 1194.

**Sucred,** *pp.* sugred, T. ii. 384.

**Suffisaunce,** *s.* sufficiency, A 490; sufficient food, D 1843; enough, a competence, 10. 15; contentment, B 4029; 3. 703.

**Suffisaunt,** *adj.* sufficient, good enough, A 1631; A. pr. 7; capable, L. 2524; well endowed, L. 1067.

**Suffisauntly,** *adv.* sufficiently, A. pr. 43; availably, B 2492.

**Suffrable,** *adj.* patient, D 442.

**Suffraunce,** *s.* longsuffering, B 2479; patience, E 1162; Suffrance, longsuffering, B 2654; permission, F 788.

**Suffraunt,** *pres. pt. as s.* patient man, T. iv. 1584; *as adj.* patient, tolerant, 3. 1010.

**Suffre,** *v.* suffer, permit, A 649; endure, 3. 412.

**Suffyse,** *v.* suffice, B 3648; Suffyseth, (it) suffices, 12. 15; Suffyce, *imp. s.* be content (spend frugally), 13. 2.

**Suggestioun,** *s.* a criminal charge, B 3607; hint, I 331.

**Sugre,** *s.* sugar, B 2046.

**Sukkenye,** *s.* short frock, tunic, R. 1232. O.F. *souquanie*; F. *souquenie* (Cotgrave).

**Summitted,** *pp.* submitted, B 3. p 10. 15; subjected, B 4. p 6. 145.

**Superfice,** *s.* surface, A. i. 21. 42; *in the s. of,* in the immediate neighbourhood of, A. i. 21. 32.

**Superfluitee,** *s.* superfluity, excess, A 436; over-abundance, A. pr. 50.

**Supplien,** *v.* supplicate, entreat, B 3. p 8. 11.

**Supportacioun,** *s.* support, B 2332.

**Supprysed,** *pp.* surprised, T. iii. 1184.

**Surcote,** *s.* upper coat, A 617.

**Surement,** *s.* pledge, F 1534.

**Suretee,** *s.* security, D 903; careless confidence, 7. 215.

**Surfeet,** *s.* surfeit, I 913.

**Surmounteth,** *pr. s.* surpasses, L. 123.

**Surplys,** *s.* surplice, A 3323, G 558.

**Surquidrie,** *s.* over-confidence, presumption, I 403; arrogance, T. i. 213. O.F. *surquiderie.*

**Sursanure,** *s.* a wound healed outwardly, but not inwardly, F 1113.

**Surveyaunce,** *s.* surveillance, C 95.

**Suspecioun,** *s.* suspicion, T. ii. 561.

**Suspecious,** *adj.* ominous of evil, E 540.

**Suspect,** *adj.* suspicious, ominous of evil, E 541.

**Suspect,** *s.* suspicion, B 2385.

**Sustenance,** *s.* support, living, E 202.

**Sustene,** *v.* sustain, support, F 861; maintain, 1. 22; endure, B 2654; uphold, preserve, B 160; hold up (herself), 7. 177.

**Suster,** *s.* sister, L. 592, 986; Her suster love, love for her sister, L. 2365; Sustren, *pl.* T. iii. 733; Sustres, *pl.* B 4057.

**Suwe,** *ger.* to follow, T. i. 379.

**Suyte,** *s.* suit, array (of like kind), A 2873; Sute, uniform pattern, 3. 261.

**Swa,** so (Northern), A 4040.

**Swal,** *pt. s. of* Swelle.

**Swalowe,** *v.* swallow, HF. 1036.

**Swalwe,** *s.* swallow, A 3258.

**Swappe,** *s.* a swoop, the striking of a bird of prey, HF. 543.

**Swappe,** *ger.* to swap, strike, E 586; Swapte, *pt. s.* dashed, T. iv. 256; fell suddenly, E 1099; Swap, *imp. s.* strike off, G 366.

**Swartish,** *adj. as adv.* dark, HF. 1647.

**Swatte,** *pt. s. of* Swete.

**Swayn,** *s.* servant-lad, young man, A 4027.

**Sweigh,** *s.* motion, sway, B 296.

**Swelleth,** *pr. s.* swells, A 2743; Swal, *pt. s.* D 967; *up swal,* was puffed up with anger, B 1750; Swollen, *pp.* proud, E 950.

**Swelte,** *v.* die, T. iii. 347; Swelt, *pr. s.* dies, 4. 128; *pt. s.* died, E 1776; languished, fainted, A 1356.

**Swelwe,** *v.* swallow, B 2808.

**Swerd,** *s.* sword, A 112.

**Swere,** *v.* swear, A 454; Swoor, 1 *pt. s.* E 2312; Swore, 2 *pt. s.* L. 1378; Swòòr, *pt. s.* swore, 7. 101; Sworen, *pt. pl.* swore, B 344; Sworn, *pp.* sworn (to the contrary), T. iv. 976; A 1089; sworn (to do it), G 681; bound by oath, F 18; sworn (it should not be so), D 640.

**Swering,** *s.* swearing, C 631.

**Swete,** *adj.* sweet, A 5, 2427; *as s.* sweet one, love, 3. 832.

**Swete,** *s.* sweetness, 5. 161.

**Swete,** *v.* sweat, G 579; Swatte, *pt. s.* sweated, B 1966.

**Swete herte,** sweetheart, T. iii. 69.

**Swete-Loking,** Sweet-Looking, R. 920.

**Swetnesse,** *s.* sweetness, 1. 51; nourishment, 3. 415.

**Swetter,** *adj.* comp. sweeter, R. 622, 768.

**Swety,** *adj.* sweaty, 9. 28.

**Sweven,** *s.* dream, R. 28; *pl.* dreams, R. 3.

**Swevening,** *s.* dream, R. 26; Sweveninges (*pron.* swev'níngez), R. 1.

**Sweynte,** *pp. as def. adj.* tired out, slothful, HF. 1783. Pp. of *swenchen.*

**Swich,** *adj.* such, A 3, 243, 313; such a thing, B 4626; Swich a, such a, B 3921; Swich ocn, such a one, F 231.

**Swimme,** *v.* swim, A 3550, L. 2450; Swommen, *pt. pl.* were filled with swimming things, 5. 188.

**Swink,** *s.* labour, toil, A 188, 540.

**Swinke,** *v.* toil, labour, T. v. 272; to cause to labour, HF. 16; *pr. pl.* work for, G 21; Swonken, *pp.* toiled, A 4235.

**Swinker,** *s.* labourer, toiler, A 531.

**Swire,** *s.* neck, throat, R. 325.

**Swogh,** *s.* (1) sough, low noise, 5. 247; murmur, HF. 1031; sigh, groan, A 3619; rustling noise, blast, A 1979; whizzing noise, HF. 1941; Swogh, (2), swoon, D 799; Swow, grief, 3. 215.

**Swollen,** *pp.* proud, E 950.

**Swolow,** *s.* gulf, L. 1104.

**Swolwe,** *v.* swallow, H 36.

**Swommen,** *pr. pl.* were filled with swimming things, 5. 188.

**Swonken,** *pp.* toiled, A 4235.

**Swoot,** *s.* sweat, G 578.

**Swote,** *adj.* sweet, A 2860, 3205; *pl.* R. 60. See Sote, Swete.

**Swote,** *adv.* sweetly, T. i. 158.

**Swough, Swow;** see Swogh.

**Swoune, Swowne,** *v.* swoon, faint, T. ii. 574; Swowned, *pt. s.* swooned, A 2943; *pp.* A 913.

**Swow,** *s.* swoon; hence, anguish, 3. 215.

**Swowne,** *s.* swoon, F 1080; Aswowne, in a swoon, C 245.

**Swowning,** *s.* swooning, C 246.

**Swyn,** *s.* swine, boar, F 1254; hog, D 460.

**Swynes-heed,** *s.* pig's head (a term of abuse), A 4262.

**Swythe,** *adv.* quickly, C 796; *as sw.,* as soon, T. v. 1384; as quickly as possible, immediately, B 637, G 936.

**Swyve,** *v.* lie with, A 4178; *pp.* dishonoured, A 3850.

**Sy,** saw; *pt. t. of* See.

**Sye,** *ger.* to sink down, T. v. 182.

**Sye, Syen,** saw; see See.

**Syk,** *adj.* sick, ill; *for syk,* on account of being sick, D 394; Syke, *def.* F 1100; *pl.* sick persons, T. iii. 61.

**Syk,** *s.* sigh, F 498.

**Syke,** *v.* sigh, T. iii. 1360; Syke, *ger.* to sigh (*but perhaps read* syte, i.e. to grieve, *for the rime*), T. ii. 884; Syketh, *pr. s.* sighs, 5. 404; 22. 62 (men sigh); Syked, *pt. s.* sighed, A 2985; Sighte, *pt. s.* sighed, B 1035.

**Sykliche,** *adj.* sickly, T. ii. 1528.

**Symonials,** *s. pl.* simoniacs, I 784.

**Symonye,** *s.* simony, D 1309.

**Syre,** *s.* master of the house, D 713; master, 5. 12.

**Sys,** *num.* six (at dice), B 3851.

[**Syte,** *v.* to grieve; *perhaps the right reading in* T. ii. 884.]

**Sythe,** *s.* time, R. 80; Sythe, *pl.* (orig. a gen. pl.), A 1878; *ofte sythe,* oftentimes, E 233, G 1031; Sythes, *pl.* times, A 485.

**Sythe,** *s.* scythe, L. 646.

## T.

**T',** *for* To, *frequently prefixed to verbs; as* tabyde, tamende, &c.

**Taa,** *v.* take (Northern), A 4129.

**Tabard,** *s.* a herald's coat-of-arms, hence, (1) the same, as an inn-sign, A 20; (2) a ploughman's loose frock, A 541.

**Tabernacles,** *pl.* shrines, HF. 123, 1190.

**Table,** *s.* table, A 100; *table dormaunt,* permanent side-table, A 353; tablet, writing-tablet, 3. 780; tablet, plate, HF. 142; table (of the law), C 639; one of the thin plates on which almicanteras are engraved, A. ii. 21. 6; *at table,* at board, i.e. entertained as a lodger, G 1015; Tables, *pl.* tables (for calculation), F 1273; dining-tables, B 1442; writing-tablets, D 1741; plates, A. i. 14. 3; the game of 'tables' or backgammon, F 900.

**Tabour,** *s.* small drum, D 2268.

**Tabouren,** *pr. pl.* drum, din, L. 354.

**Tabregge,** *for* To abregge, to abridge, shorten, T. iii. 295.

**Tabreyde,** *for* To abreyde, to awake, T. v. 520.

**Tabyde,** *for* To abyde, to abide, T. v. 33.

**Tache,** *s.* defect, 21. 18. See Tecches.

**Tacheve,** *for* To acheve, to achieve. L. 2111.

**Tacompte,** *for* To acompte, to reckon up, 22. 17.

**Tacord,** *for* To accord, i. e. to agreement, H 98.

**Tacorde,** *for* To acorde, to agree, 1. 27.

**Tacoyc,** *for* To acoyc, to decoy, T. v. 782.

**Taffata,** *s.* taffeta, A 440.

**Taffraye,** *for* To affraye, to frighten, E 455.

**Taillages,** *s. pl.* taxes, I 567.

**Taille,** *s.* tally, an account scored upon two similarly notched sticks, A 570, B 1606.

**Take,** *v.* seize, T. ii. 289 ; present, offer, G 223 ; *ger.* to take, A 34 ; Takestow, takest thou, G 435 ; Take me, 1 *pr. s.* betake myself, B 1985 ; Took, 1 *pt. s.* drew in, breathed in, B 1. p 3. 3 (Lat. *hausi*) ; hit, D 792 ; *pt. s.* handed over, gave, B 1484 ; had, B 192 ; Toke, 2 *pt. s.* tookest, 3. 483 ; Toke, *pt. pl.* took, F 1240 ; received, F 356 ; Take, *pp.* taken, A 3007 ; entrusted, I 880 ; brought, 1. 20 ; Tak, *imp. s.* receive, B 117 ; accept as a result, A. ii. 25. 57 ; *tak kepe*, take heed, observe, B 3757 ; *tak she*, let her take, 5. 462 ; Taketh, *imp. pl.* take, 4. 9.

**Takel,** *s.* tackle, archery-gear, arrows, A 106.

**Tald,** *pp.* told (Northern), A 4207.

**Tale,** *s.* tale, A 3126 ; story, A 36, 831 ; account, B 4308 ; enumeration, E 383 ; *I gan finde a tale to him,* I thought of something to say to him, 3. 536 ; *telle tale,* give an account of, A 330.

**Tale,** *v.* tell a tale, talk, speak, T. iii. 1235 ; Talen, *ger.* to tell tales, A 772 ; *pr. s. subj.* talk about, I 378.

**Talent,** *s.* inclination, wish, desire, B 2439 ; desire, appetite, C 540 ; longing, B 2. p 1. 12.

**Taling,** *s.* tale-telling, B 1624.

**Talighte,** *for* To alighte, i.e. to alight, E 909.

**Talle,** *adj.* docile, obsequious, 4. 38. (A rare sense.)

**Tamende,** *for* To amende, to redress, E 441.

**Tanoyen,** *for* To anoyen, to injure, B 492.

**Tanswere,** i. e. to answer, D 1589.

**Tapes,** *pl.* tapes, A 3241.

**Tapicer,** *s.* upholsterer, maker of carpets, A 362.

**Tapite,** *v.* cover with tapestry, 3. 260.

**Tappe,** *s.* tap, A 3890, 3892.

**Tappestere,** *s.* female tapster, barmaid, A 241, 3336.

*Tarditas,* *s.* slowness, I 718.

**Tare,** *s.* tare, kind of weed, A 1570.

**Tareste,** *for* To areste, to arrest, F 1370.

**Targe,** *s.* target, shield, A 471 ; defence, 1. 176.

**Tarien,** *v.* tarry, B 983 ; delay (used actively), F 73 ; 1 *pr. s.* tarry, T. iii. 1195 ; *pp.* delayed, T. ii. 1739.

**Tarraye,** *for* To arraye, to array, arrange, E 961.

**Tart,** *adj.* of sharp flavour, pungent, A 381.

**Tartre,** *s.* tartar, G 813 ; *oille of Tartre,* (probably) cream of tartar, or bitartrate of potassium, A 630.

**Taryinge,** *s.* tarrying, delay, A 821.

**Tas,** *s.* heap, A 1005, 1009, 1020. O.F. *tas.*

**Tassaille,** *for* To assaille, i. e. to assail, E 1180.

**Tassaye,** *for* To assaye, to test, prove, try, E 454, 1075.

**Tasseled,** *pp.* fringed, provided with tassels, R. 1079 ; A 3251.

**Tassemble,** *for* To assemble, to bring together, D 89.

**Tassoille,** *for* To assoile, i.e. to absolve, C 933.

**Tassure,** *for* To assure, B 1231.

**Tast,** *s.* taste, relish (for), 5. 160.

**Taste,** *v.* try, test, L. 1993 ; *pt. s.* experienced, T. i. 639 ; *imp. s.* feel, G 503.

**Taughte,** *pt. s. of* Teche.

**Taverner,** *s.* innkeeper, C 685.

**Tavyse,** *for* To avyse (me), to deliberate, B 1426.

**Tawayte,** *for* to awayte, to dwell, remain, 25. 7.

**Taylage,** *s.* taxation, 9. 54.

**Tecches,** *pl.* evil qualities, defects, T. iii. 935 ; characteristics, HF. 1778.

**Teche,** *v.* teach, instruct, A 308, *ger.* to show, R. 518 ; Techen, *v.* direct, B 4139 ; *ger.* to inform (him of), D 1326 ; Taughte, 1 *pt. s.* taught, told, D 1050.

*Te deum,* the anthem so called, D 1866.

**Teer,** *s.* tear, E 1104.

**Tehee,** *interj.* (denoting) laughter, hee-hee ! A 3740.

**Telle,** *v.* tell, recount, relate, A 38 ; compute, 3. 440 ; *ger.* to tell, to be told, F 447 ; 1 *pr. s.* account, B 4344 ; Telle no tale, set no store, 5. 326 ; Telles, *pr. s.* (Northern form), tells, 3. 73 ; HF. 426 ; Tolde, 1 *pt. s.* counted, HF. 1380 ; accounted, D 203, 208 ; *pt. pl.* esteemed, T. i. 131 ; *herd told,* heard (it) told, T. i. 197 ; Tolde, *pp. pl.* told, B 56.

Tembrace, *for* To embrace, T. v. 224;
E 1101.

Temen, *v.* bring; *temen us on bere*, bring
us on our bier, let us die, HF. 1744.

Temper, *s.* mood, R. 346.

Temperaunce, *s.* temperance, moderation, F 785.

Tempest, *s.* storm, A 406; tempest (alluding to a passage in Statius), A 884.

Tempest thee, *imp. s.* violently distress
thyself, 13. 8; *2 pr. s. subj.* vex, perturb,
B 2. p 4. 75.

Tempestous, *adj.* tempestuous, T. ii. 5.

Temple, *s.* inn of court, A 567.

Temprede, *pt. s.* modulated, B 3. m 12.
22; *pp.* tempered, G 926. (In alchemy,
to *temper* is to adjust or moderate heat.)

Temps, *s.* tense; *futur temps*, future
tense, time to come, G 875.

Temptour, *s.* tempter, D 1655.

Ten, ten, A 454; *ten so wood*, ten times
as mad, L. 735.

Tenbrace, to embrace, B 1891.

Tencresen, to increase, E 1808.

Tendure, to endure, E 756, 811.

Tendyte, *for* To endyte, to compose,
write, T. i. 6; to relate, A 1209.

Tene, *s.* vexation, A 3106; sorrow, grief,
T. v. 240; cross, trouble, T. ii. 61. A.S.
*tēona.*

Tenour, *s.* outline of the story, L. 929.

Tenquere, *for* To enquere, to ask, E 1543.

Tenspyre, *for* To enspyre, i. e. to inspire,
G 1470.

Tenthe, tenth, HF. 63, 111; Tenthe
some, company of ten, T. ii. 1249.
(Sometimes *tenthe some* means 'ten in
all.')

Tentifly, *adv.* attentively, carefully, E
334.

Tercel, *adj.* male (of an eagle), 5. 393,
449; *pl.* 5. 540; *as s.* male eagie, 5. 405.

Tercelet, *s.* male falcon, 5. 529, 533; F
504, 621; Tercelets, *pl.* male birds of
prey, 5. 659; male hawks, F 648.
'*Tiercelet*, m. the tassell, or male of
any kind of hawke, so tearmed, because he is, commonly, a third part
lesse then the female'; Cotgrave.

Tere, *s.* tear, B 3251.

Tere, *v.* tear, B 1326; scratch, R. 325;
Torn, *pp.* L. 2103.

Terins, *s. pl.* tarins, siskins, R. 665. F.
*tarin.*

Terme, *s.* set time, appointed time, T. v.
696; period, space of time, 'term,' a
portion of the zodiac, being one-third
of a 'sign,' or 10°, F 1288; (during the)

term, A 1029; *terme of his lyve*, while
he lives, G 1479; *in terme*, in set phrases,
C 311; *pl.* pedantic phrases, A 323; legal
jargon, R. 199; periods, A 3028; terms,
C 51, F 1266.

Terme-day, *s.* appointed day, 3. 730.

Termyne, *v.* determine, express in 'good
set terms,' 5. 530.

Terrestre, *adj.* earthly, E 1332.

Terve, *pr. s. subj.* flay, G 1274 (*so in* MS.
E.); Terved (*not* Terned), *pp.* skinned,
G 1171 (*so in* MS. E.). This is certainly
the right word; in G 1171, read *terved*
[not *torned*], and in G 1274, read *terve*
[not *torne*]. See my letter in the Athe-
naeum, Mar. 24, 1894. So in Havelok,
603, for *tirneden* read *tirueden = tirve-
den*, i. e. rolled back.

Tery, *adj.* tearful, T. iv. 821.

Tescape, to escape, F 1357.

Tespye, *for* To espye, to spy out, espy,
B 1989, 4478.

Testers, *pl.* head-pieces, A 2499.

Testes, *s. pl.* vessels for assaying metals
(Tyrwhitt), G 818.

Testif, *adj.* heady, headstrong, T. v. 802;
A 4004.

Tete, *s.* teat, A 3704.

Texpounden, to expound, B 1716.

Text, *s.* text, quotation from an author,
B 45; saying, A 177, 182; text (as opposed to a gloss), 3. 333.

Textuel, *adj.* well versed in texts, learned,
H 235; I 57.

Teyd, *pp.* tied, bound, E 2432.

Teyne, *s.* a thin plate of metal, G 1225,
1229. Lat. *tænia.*

Th', *for* The; *common, as in* thabsence,
*for* the absence.

Thabsence, the absence, A 1239.

Thadversitee, the adversity, E 756.

Thakketh, *pr. s.* strokes, pats, D 1559.
A. S. *þaccian.*

Thalighte, *for* Thee alighte; *in thee
alighte*, alighted in thee, B 1660.

Thank, *s.* expression of thanks, A 612;
thanks, E 2388; *can th.*, owes thanks,
A 1808; *his th.*, the thanks to him,
L. 452; *my thankes*, by my goodwill,
willingly, R. 1666; *his thankes*, of his
free will, willingly, A 1626; *hir thankes*,
of their own will, A 2114.

Thanke, 1 *pr. s.* thank, E 1088; Th. hit
thee, thank thee for it, 10. 51.

Thanne, *adv.* then, D 2004, I 104; Than,
then, A 12; next, 5. 324; *er than*, sooner
than, before, G 899.

Thar, *pr. s. impers.* (it) is necessary, is

needful; *thar ye*, it is needful that ye, B 2258; *thar thee*, it is needful for thee, you need, *or* thou needst, D 329, 336, 1365, H 352; *him thar*, it is needful for him, he needs, T. ii. 1661; he must, A 4320; Thurte, *pt. s.*; *th. him*, he needed, R. 1089, 1324; *yow thurfte*, you would need, you need, T. iii. 572.

**Tharivaile**, the arrival, the landing, HF. 451.

**Tharmes**, the arms, armorial bearings, HF. 1411.

**Tharray**, the array, A 716.

**Thascry**, *for* The ascry, the alarm, T. ii. 611.

**Thassay**, the assay, the endeavour, 5. 2.

**Thassege**, the siege, T. iv. 1480; the besieging force, T. iv. 62.

**Thassemblee**, the assembly, B 403.

**Thassemblinge**, the assembling, B 2431.

**That**, *rel. pron.* that which, whom, 3. 979; *that of*, from whom, 3. 964; That oon, the one, A 4013; That other, the other, A 4013; That, with reference to whom, G 236; *if that*, if, 3. 969, 971.

**Thaventayle**, *for* The aventayle, the mouthpiece of a helmet, T. v. 1558.

**Thavision**, *for* The avision, the vision, 3. 285.

**Thavys**, the advice, A 3076.

**The**, *def. art.* A 2, &c.

**The**; *as in* The bet, by so much the better, 3. 668; The las, by so much the less, 3. 675.

**The**, *for* Thee, *pers. pron.* F 676, &c.

**Théatre**, *s.* theatre, area for a tournament, A 1885.

**Thedom**, *s.* success, B 1595.

**Thee**, *v.* thrive, prosper, R. 1067; *never mot she thee*, may she never prosper, 5. 569; *mot he never thee*, may he never prosper, T. ii. 670; *lat him never thee*, let him never prosper, B 4622; *thou shalt never thee*, E 1388; *he shal never thee*, G 641; *also moot I thee*, as I may thrive, as I hope to prosper, D 1215, E 1226; *so moot I thee*, D 361; *as mote I thee*, T. i. 341; *so theech*, for *so thee ich*, as I may thrive, as I hope to prosper, C 947, G 929; *so theek*, for *so thee ik*, as I hope to prosper, A 3864.

**Theef**, *s.* thief, robber, D 1338.

**Theefly**, *adv.* like a thief, L. 1781.

**Theffect**, *for* The effect, the result, A 1189; the substance, pith, L. 1180, 2403; the matter, contents, 2. 56; the source, D 1451; the moral, B 2148; the sum (of the matter), A 2366.

**Thegle**, the eagle, B 3573.

**Their**, the air, D 1939.

**Thembassadours**, the ambassadors, T. iv. 140, 145.

**Theme**, *s.* text, thesis, C 333, 425.

**Themperour**, the emperor, 3. 368.

**Then**, *conj.* than, L. 1693, 2092.

**Thencens**, the incense, A 2277, 2938.

**Thenchauntements**, *pl.* the enchantments, A 1944.

**Thenche**, *v.* imagine, A 3253.

**Thencheson**, *for* The encheson, the reason, cause, T. v. 632.

**Thencrees**, the increase, A 275.

**Thende**, the end, B 423, 965, 3269.

**Thengendring**, the engendring, the process of production, HF. 968.

**Thengyn**, the (warlike) engine, HF. 1934.

**Thenke**, *v.* think of, 5. 311; *1 pr. s.* think, intend, E 641; Thenkestow, thinkest thou, T. iv. 849, 1088; Thoghte, *1 pt. s.* thought, 3. 448; Thenke on, think of, 16. 47.

**Thenne**, *adj.* thin, A 4066.

**Thenne**, *adv.* then, T. ii. 210.

**Thenne**, *adv.* thence, D 1141.

**Thennes**, *adv.* thence, i. e. away from that place, T. iv. 695; thence, R. 791; *as s.*, the place that, G 66.

**Thennes-forth**, *adv.* thenceforth, B 1755.

**Thentencioun**, the intention, G 1443.

**Thentente**, *for* The entente, the design, B 930; the purpose, end, G 1306; the meaning, T. v. 1630.

**Thentree**, the entrance, A 1983.

**Thenvyous**, *for* The envyous, the spiteful, malicious, 3. 642.

**Theologie**, *s.* theology, I 1043.

**Theorik**, *s.* theory, theoretical explanation, A. pr. 98.

**Ther**, *adv.* there, B 62, 1190, &c.; where, T. ii. 618; when, B 474; whither, at which, B 469; whereas, D 1213, G 724; wherefore, T. iii. 1437; wherever, D 128; as to which, T. ii. 588; wherefore (I pray that), D 1561.

**Ther-aboute**, *adv.* about it, D 1837; therein, G 832; round it, A 937.

**Therafter**, *adv.* afterwards, 3. 66.

**Ther-agayns**, *prep.* against that, I 665; in reply, T. ii. 369.

**Ther-as**, **Ther as**, there where, where, B 2384; there, I 162; whereas, D 1177; where that, A 34, 172; when that, L. 1277; Ther-as that, where, 1. 160: Ther that, where, F 267.

**Therbe**, the herb, HF. 290.

**Ther-bifore**, *adv.* before that time, D 631 ; beforehand, E 689, 729.

**Ther-biforn**, *adv.* beforehand, A 2034 ; previously, A 3997.

**Therby**, by it, to it, D 984 ; into possession of it, F 1115 ; beside it, R. 1184.

**Ther-fore**, *adv.* therefore, A 189 ; for that purpose, A 809 ; on that account, L. 1863 ; on that point, E 1141 ; for it, L. 1391.

**Therfro**, therefrom, from it, HF. 895.

**Ther-inne**, therein, in it, B 1945, 3573.

**Ther-of**, *adv.* with respect to that, E 644 ; concerning that, 3. 1132 ; A 462 ; from that, 3. 1166 ; thereby, I 314 ; of it, 20. 8.

**Ther-on**, *adv.* thereupon, A 160 ; thereof, F 3.

**Ther-oute**, *adv.* out there, out in the open air, B 3362 ; outside there, G 1136.

**Therthe**, the earth, R. 1423.

**Therto**, *adv.* besides, moreover, D 1251 ; to it, 2. 100 ; likewise, R. 1262.

**Ther-upon**, *adv.* immediately, A 819.

**Ther-whyles**, whilst, B 5. p 6. 250.

**Therwith**, *adv.* withal, for all that, 3. 954 ; moreover, F 931 ; thereupon, 3. 275 ; at the same time, B 3210.

**Ther-with-al**, thereupon, A 1078 ; therewith, with it, by means of it, A 566 ; beside it, besides, R. 226 ; at once, L. 148 ; thereat, L. 864.

**Theschaunge**, the exchange, T. iv. 146.

**Theschewing**, the avoiding (of anything), 5. 140.

**Thestat**, the estate, the rank, condition, A 716.

**Thewed**, *pp.* ; *wel thewed*, of good disposition, 4. 180.

**Thewes**, *s. pl.* habits, natural qualities, E 409, 1542 ; good qualities, virtues, G 101 ; customs, habits, manners, T. ii. 723 ; morals, HF. 1834.

**Thexcellent**, the excellent, B 150.

**Thexcuse**, thee excuse, D 1611.

**Thexecucion**, the execution, 10. 65.

**Thexpériénce**, the experience, E 2238.

**Thider**, *adv.* thither, A 1263.

**Thider-ward**, *adv.* thither, A 2530.

**Thikke**, *adj.* thick, A 549 ; stout, plump, A 3973.

**Thikke**, *adv.* thickly, R. 1396.

**Thikke-herd**, *adj.* thick-haired, A 2518.

**Thikke-sterred**, *adj.* thickly covered with stars, A. ii. 23. 2.

**Thilke**, that, R. 660, &c. ; such a, A 182 ; that same, A 1193 ; that sort of, I 50 ; *pl.* those, HF. 173.

**Thimage**, the image, L. 1760.

**Thing**, *s.* fact, C 156 ; property, wealth, R. 206 ; deed, legal document, A 325 ; *for any thing*, at any cost, A 276 ; Thing, *pl.* things, L. 11, 2140 ; Thinges, *pl.* things, A 175 ; matters of business, B 1407 ; poems, L. 364 ; pieces of music, F 78 ; services, prayers, B 1281.

**Thingot**, the ingot, G 1233.

**Thinke**, *v.* seem, T. i. 405 ; Thinketh, *pr. s. impers.* (it) seems, B 1901 ; *me th.*, it seems to me, A 37, 2207 ; *how th. yow*, how does it seem to you, D 2204 ; Thoghte, *pt. s. impers.* (it) seemed, L. 1697 ; *me thoughte*, it seemed to me, A 385 ; *him th.*, it seemed to him, A 682 ; *us th.*, it seemed to us, A 785 ; *hir th.*, it seemed to her, D 965, 967.

**Thinne**, *adj.* thin, A 679 ; poor, feeble, 9. 36 ; E 1682 ; scanty, limited, G 741.

**Thirleth**, *pr. s.* pierces, 7. 211 ; *pp.* A 2710.

**This**, A 175, &c. ; *contracted form of this is*, T. ii. 363, iii. 936, v. 151 ; This is, *pronounced* this, 5. 411, 620 ; A 1091, D 91 ; Thise (dhiiz), *pl.* (monosyllabic), A 701, B 59, &c.

**Tho**, *pl.* those, A 498, 1123, 2351, 3246.

**Tho**, *adv.* then, at that time, A 993, 3329, &c. ; still, 3. 1054.

**Thoccident**, the occident, the west, B 3864.

**Thoffice**, the office, the duty, B 2863.

**Thoght**, *s.* anxiety, B 1779, E 80.

**Thoghtful**, *adj.* moody, I 677.

**Tholde**, *pl.* the old, D 857.

**Tholed**, *pp.* suffered, D 1546. A.S. *þolian.*

**Thombe**, *s.* thumb, A 563.

**Thonder**, *s.* thunder, A 492.

**Thonder-dint**, *s.* stroke of lightning, D 276 ; -dent, thunder-clap, A 3807.

**Thonder-leyt**, *s.* thunder-bolt, B 1. m 4. 12 ; lightning, I 839.

**Thonke**, 1 *pr. s.* thank, E 380.

**Thonóur**, the honour, B 1767, E 1449.

**Thorgh**, *prep.* through, 5. 127, 129.

**Thorient**, the orient, the east, B 3871, 3883.

**Thoriginal**, the original, L. 1558.

**Thorisonte**, the horizon, E 1797, F 1017.

**Thorisoun**, the orison, the prayer, A 2261.

**Thorpes**, *pl.* villages, 5. 350.

**Thorugh-passen**, *pr. pl.* penetrate, B 4. m 3. 49.

**Thought**, *s.* anxiety, T. i. 579.

**Thoumbe**, *s.* thumb, A. i. 1. 2.

**Thourgh-girt**, *pp.* struck through, T. iv. 627. From M.E. *gurden*, to strike.

**Thral,** s. thrall, slave, subject, servant, B 3343, C 183, D 155.

**Thral,** adj. enthralled, A 1552, I 137; Thralle, pl. enthralled, B 2751; Thral, as pl., L. 1940.

**Thraldom,** s. slavery, B 286, 338.

**Thralle,** v. subject, T. i. 235; subjugate, R. 882.

**Thraste,** pt. s. thrust, T. ii. 1155.

**Threde,** v. thread, R. 99.

**Threed,** s. thread, A 2030; thread (of destiny), T. v. 7.

**Threpe,** 1 pr. pl. (we) call, assert to be, C. 826. A. S. prēapian.

**Threshfold,** s. threshold, A 3482.

**Threste,** v. thrust, push, A 2612; pt. pl. vexed, T. iv. 254.

**Threte,** v. threaten, L. 754.

**Threting,** s. menace, G 698.

**Thretty,** adj. thirty, F 1368.

**Thridde,** third, A 1463, 2271.

**Thrift,** s. success, welfare, T. ii. 847; profit, success, G 739, 1425; good thrift bad, prayed for the welfare (of), blessed, T. iii. 1249; by my thrift, if I succeed, T. ii. 1483.

**Thriftieste,** most successful, T. i. 1081; most thriving, T. ii. 737.

**Thriftily,** adv. carefully, A 105; profitably, A 3131; encouragingly, F 1174.

**Thrifty,** adj. profitable (to the buyer), B 138; serviceable, D 238; provident, 7. 197.

**Thringe,** v. press, T. iv. 66; Throng, pt. s. forced his way, 7. 55; thrust, E 2353.

**Thriste,** pt. s. thrust, T. iii. 1574.

**Thrittene,** thirteen, D 2259.

**Thritty,** thirty, E 1421.

**Throf,** pt. s. of Thryve.

**Throng,** pt. s. of Thringe.

**Throp,** s. thorp, small village, E 199, 208.

**Throstel,** s. throstle, song-thrush, 5. 364.

**Throte,** s. throat, 3. 945.

**Throte-bolle,** s. ball of the throat, 'the protuberance in the throat called Adam's apple,' A 4273.

**Through-out,** quite through, 11. 3.

**Throwe,** s. short space of time, while, period, B 953, 3326.

**Throwe,** ger. to throw, T. ii. 971; Threw, pt. s. T. iii. 184; Threwe, pt. pl. R. 786; Throwe, pp. thrown, L. 1960; Throwen, pp. cast, HF. 1325; twisted, turned, T. iv. 1159.

**Throwes,** pl. torments, T. v. 206; throes, T. v. 1201.

**Thrustel,** s. thrush, B 1963.

**Thrusteth,** pr. s. thirsts, yearns, L. 103.

**Thrustle-cok,** s. male thrush, B 1959.

**Thrye,** adv. thrice, T. ii. 89, 463.

**Thryes,** adv. thrice, A 63, 463.

**Thryve,** v. thrive, prosper, E 172; ger. G 1411; so thr. I, as I hope to thrive, D 1764; Throf, pt. s. flourished, B 3. m 4. 5.

**Thryvinge,** adj. vigorous, B 5. m 4. 24 (Lat. uigens).

**Thunworthiest,** the unworthiest, 22. 19.

**Thurfte,** pt. s. impers. (with yow), you would need, you need, T. iii. 572. See Thar.

**Thurgh,** prep. through, 1. 27; by means of, A 920.

**Thurgh-darted,** pp. transfixed with a dart, T. i. 325.

**Thurghfare,** s. thoroughfare, A 2847.

**Thurgh-girt,** pp. pierced through, A 1010.

**Thurghout,** prep. throughout, F 46; all through, B 256, 464; quite through, C 655.

**Thurgh-shoten,** pp. shot through, T. i. 325.

**Thurrok,** s. sink, the lowest internal part of a ship's hull, I 363, 715. A. S. þurruc.

**Thurst,** s. thirst, B 100.

**Thursteth,** pr. s. thirsts, T. v. 1406; pt. s. impers. he was thirsty, B 3229.

**Thurte;** see Thar.

**Thwitel,** s. large knife, whittle, A 3933.

**Thwyte,** pr. pl. whittle, cut up for, HF. 1938; Thwiten, pp. carved, whittled, R. 933.

**Tid,** pp. of Tyde.

**Tidifs,** s. pl. small birds, F 648. Cf. Eng. titmouse, titlark. See Tydif.

**Tikel,** adj. unstable, A 3428.

**Tikelnesse,** s. instability, 13. 3.

**Tikled,** pt. s. tickled, D 395.

**Til** (before a vowel), prep. to, A 180; as a Northern word (before a consonant), A 4110; Til and fra, to and fro (Northern), A 4039. Icel. til.

**Til,** conj. until, A 1760; til that, A 1490, F 360.

**Tilyere,** s. tiller, B 5. p 1. 86.

**Timber,** s. material, T. iii. 530.

**Timbestere,** s. female timbrel-player, tambourine-player, R. 769.

**Timbres,** s. pl. timbrels, tambourines, R. 772.

**Tipet,** s. tippet, cape, A 233.

**Tiptoon,** pl. tiptoes, B 4497.

**Tissew,** s. a band, T. ii. 639.

**Tit,** pr. s. betides, T. i. 333. See **Tyde.**

**Titering**, *s.* hesitation, vacillation, T. ii. 1744.

**Titlelees**, *adj.* without a title, usurping, H 223.

**To** (tòò), *s.* toe, A 2726; Toon, *pl.* B 4052; Toos, *pl.* B 4370.

**To** (tóó), *prep.* to, A 2; gone to, A 30; (used after its case), G 1449: for, 1. 184; as to, as for, L. 2096; *him to*, for him, 3. 771; *to that*, until, 4. 239.

**To**, *adv.* too, B 2129; moreover, beside, T. i. 540; overmuch, G 1423; *to badde*, too evil, very evil, L. 2597.

**To-** (1), *intensive prefix*, lit. in twain, asunder. A.S. *tō-*, G. *zer-*.

**To-** (2), *prepositional prefix*, *as in* To-forn. A.S. *tō-*, G. *zu-*.

**To-bete**, *v.* beat amain, T. v. 1762; beat severely, G 405.

**To-breke**, *v.* break in pieces; *pr. s.* (it) breaks in pieces, R. 277; breaks asunder, G 907; is violently broken, HF. 779; To-broken, *pp.* broken in pieces, destroyed, 16. 1; To-broke, *pp.* broken in half, D 277; severely bruised, A 4277.

**To-breste**, *v.* burst in twain, T. ii. 608; *pr. s. subj.* may (she) break in twain, T. iv. 1546; may be broken in twain, 1. 16; *pr. pl.* break in pieces, A 2611; To-brosten, *pp.* broken in twain, A 2691.

**To-cleve**, *v.* cleave in twain, T. v. 613.

**To-dasshte**, *pt. s.* dashed violently about, R. 337; *pp.* much bruised, T. ii. 640.

**Tode**, *s.* toad, I 636.

**To-drawen**, *pr. pl.* allure, B 4. m 3. 46; To-drowen, *pt. pl.* tore in pieces, B 1. p 3. 42; To-drawen, *pp.* distracted, B 1. p 5. 76.

**To-driven**, *pp.* scattered, L. 1280.

**To-forn**, *prep.* before, F 268; *god to-forn*, in God's sight, T. i. 1049.

**To-forn**, *adv.* in front, beforehand, B 5. p 6. 300.

**To-geder**, *adv.* together, 5. 555; To-gider, B 3222; To-gidre, A 824.

**Toght**, *adj.* taut, D 2267.

**To-go**, *pp.* dispersed, L. 653.

**To-greve**, *v.* grieve excessively, T. i. 1001.

**To-hangen**, *v.* put to death by hanging, HF. 1782.

**To-hepe**, *adv.* (lit. into a heap), together, T. iii. 1764; L. 2009.

**To-hewen**, *pr. pl.* hew in twain, A 2609; *pp.* cut through, T. ii. 638; To-hewe, *pp.* hewn in pieces, B 430.

**Toke**, 2 *pt. s.* tookest, 3. 483; *pt. pl.* took, F 1240; received, F 356.

**To-laugh**, *pr. s.* laughs out, laughs excessively, T. ii. 1108. (Short for *to-laugheth*.)

**Told, -e**; see **Telle**.

**Tollen** (1), *v.* take toll, A 562.

**Tollen** (2), *v.* attract, entice, B 2. p 7. 18.

**Tombesteres**, *s. pl. fem.* dancing girls, lit. female tumblers, C 477. A.S. *tumbian*, to tumble, dance.

**Tomblinge**, *pres. pt. as adj.* fleeting, transitory, B 2. m 3. 21 (Lat. *caducis*).

**To-melto**, *v.* melt utterly, T. iii. 348.

**Tonge**, *s.* tongue, 3. 930; A 265; *dat.* speech, language, 16. 21.

**Tonged**, *pp.* tongued, 3. 927.

**Tonges**, *s. pl.* tongs, I 555.

**Tonne**, *s.* tun, barrel, cask, A 3894.

**Tonne-greet**, *adj.* great as a tun, A 1994.

**Toon, Toos**, *pl. of* To, *s.*

**Tooth-ake**, *s.* toothache, R. 1098.

**Top**, *s.* top, A 2915; top (of the mast), main-top, L. 639; tuft of hair, C 255; top (of the head), A 590; crown (of the head), T. iv. 996; Top and tail, beginning and end, HF. 880.

**To-race**, *pr. pl. subj.* tear in pieces, E 572. Here *race* is probably short for *arace*, to tear up.

**Tord**, *s.* piece of dung, B 2120, C 955.

**To-rende**, *pr. pl. subj.* tear in pieces, T. ii. 790; To-rente, *pt. s.* distracted, T. iv. 341; rent asunder, B 3215; tore in pieces, L. 820; To-rent, *pp.* rent in pieces, C 102, E 1012.

**Torets**, *pl.* small rings on the collar of a dog, A 2152. See **Turet**.

**Tormentinge**, *s.* torture, E 1038.

**Tórmentóur**, *s.* tormentor, 10. 18; executioner, B 818.

**Tormentrye**, *s.* torture, D 251.

**Tormentyse**, *s.* torment, B 3707.

**Torn**, *s.* turn, C 815.

**Tornen**, *v.* turn, G 1403; return, A 1488.

**Torney**, *s.* tourney, T. iv. 1669.

**To-romblen**, *v.* rumble, crash, L. 1218.

**Tortuos**, *adj.* lit. tortuous, i. e. oblique, applied to the six signs of the zodiac (Capricorn to Gemini), which ascend most rapidly and obliquely; Tortuous, B 302.

**To-scatered**, *pp.* dispersed, D 1969.

**To-shake**, *pp.* shaken to pieces, L. 962; tossed about, L. 1765.

**To-shivered**, *pp.* been destroyed, 5. 493.

**To-shrede**, *pr. pl.* cut into shreds, A 2609.

**To-slitered**, *pp.* slashed with numerous cuts, R. 840.

To-sterte, v. start asunder, burst, T. ii. 980.

To-stoupe, v. stoop forwards, D 1560.

To-swinke, pr. pl. labour greatly, C 519.

To-tar, pt. s. tore in pieces, rent, B 3801.

Totelere, subst. as adj. tattling, tale-bearing, L. 353.

To-tere, pr. pl. rend, tear in pieces, C 474; To-tar, pt. s. rent, B 3801; To-tore, pp. G 635; To-torn, pp. much torn, 5. 110; defaced, T. iv. 358; dishevelled, R. 327.

Tother; the tother (for that other), the other, L. 325 a.

To-trede, v.; al to-trede, trample under foot, I 864.

Toty, adj. dizzy, A 4253. Spenser has totty; F. Q. vii. 7. 39.

Touchinge, s. touch, I 207.

Tough, adj. troublesome, pertinacious, in phr. make it tough, to behave in a troublesome, pertinacious, and forward manner, T. v. 101; made it tough, was captious, 3. 531; behaved pertinaciously, T. iii. 87.

Toumbling, adj. perishing, B 3. p 9. 168. See Tomblinge.

Toun, s. town, A 217; farm, B 4138; neighbourhood, R. 446.

Tour, s. tower, F 176; tower (of London), A 3256; mansion (in astrology), 4. 113. (In B 2096, the sense is that his crest was a miniature tower, with a lily above it.)

Touret, s. turret, A 1909.

Tourne, v. turn, T. ii. 688; return, D 988.

Tourneyinge, s. tournament, R. 1206.

Tourneyment, s. tournament, B 1906.

Tourning, s. turning round, R. 761.

Toute, s. buttocks, backside, A 3812, 3853.

Toverbyde, ger. to survive, D 1260.

Towayle, s. towel, cloth, R. 161; Towaille, B 3935, 3943.

Towne; out of t., away, T. iii. 570, 577, 1091.

To-wonde, pt. s. (with substitution of the weak for the strong form, as in abreyde), flew in pieces, became broken, 4. 102. The form towond, flew in pieces, occurs in Sir Ferumbras, 2568.

To-yere, adv. this year, HF. 84; D 168.

Trace, s. trace, steps, 14. 3; Traas, procession, L. 285.

Trace, 1 pr. pl. go, 5. 54.

Trad, pt. s. of Trede.

Tragedien, s. writer of tragedy, B 3. p 6. 3.

Traisoun, s. treason, B 4307.

Traitorye, treachery, B 781.

Traitour, s. traitor, HF. 267.

Translaten, ger. to translate, L. 370; pp. changed, dressed afresh, E 385.

Transmuwe, v. transform, T. iv. 467; pp. T. iv. 830.

Transporten, v. extend, B 1. p 4. 241.

Trappe, s. trap, snare, A 145; trap-door, entrance, T. iii. 741.

Trapped, pp. furnished with trappings, A 2890.

Trappe-dore, s. trap-door, T. iii. 759.

Trappures, pl. trappings for horses, A 2499.

Traunce, s. trance, A 1572; half-conscious state, B 3906; brown study, D 2216.

Traunce, ger. to tramp about, T. iii. 690.

Trave, s. wooden frame for holding unruly horses, A 3282. O. F. tref, from Lat. acc. trabem, beam.

Travers, s. 'traverse,' a curtain, screen, T. iii. 674; E 1817.

Trayed, pt. s. betrayed, HF. 390; L. 2486.

Trays, s. traces, T. i. 222; A 2139. O. F. trais, pl. of trait, a trace. The E. traces is a double plural.

Traysen, ger. to betray, T. iv. 438.

Trayteresse, s. fem. traitress, 3. 620, 813.

Traytour, s. traitor, A 1130; gen. pl. of traitors, hence traitorous, C 896.

Trecherye, s. treachery, trickery, B 4520.

Trechoures, pl. traitors, R. 197.

Trede, 1 pr. pl. tread, A 3022; Tret, pr. s. treads, D 2002; Trad, pt. s. trode, B 4368; Troden, pt. pl. HF. 2153; Troden, pp. stepped, C 712.

Trede-foul, s. treader of fowls, B 3135, 4641.

Tragédie, s. tragedy, sad story, T. v. 1786.

Tregetour, s. a juggler who used mechanical contrivances, HF. 1277; pl. F 1141.

Trench, s. a hollow walk, alley, F 392. F. trancher, to cut.

Trenchant, adj. cutting, sharp, A 3930.

Trenden, v. revolve, B 3. m 11. 4.

Trentals, pl. (sets of) thirty masses for the dead, D 1717, 1724.

Tresor, s. treasure, wealth, B 442, C 779.

Tresorere, s. treasurer, I. 107; 19. 18.

Tresorie, s. treasury, HF. 524.

Trespas, s. wrong, B 2547; transgression, L. 408, 463.

Trespassours, s. pl. offenders, B 2548.

Tresse, *s.* a (three-fold) plait (of hair), R. 779; HF. 230; A 1049.

Tresse, *ger.* to dress (my) hair, to plait, R. 599; *pp.* plaited, D 344.

Tressour, *s.* head-dress, R. 568. Probably a 'caul,' or net of gold thread.

Tret, *pr. s. of* Trede.

Tretable, *adj.* tractable, docile, I 658; yielding, L. 411; inclinable, 3. 923; inclined to talk, 3. 533.

Trete, *v.* treat, T. iv. 58; treat of, tell, 5. 34; *ger.* to speak, converse, C 64; *pp.* explained, B 5. p 1. 3.

Tretee, *s.* treaty, A 1288; discussion, F 1219; agreement, E 1892.

Tretis, *s.* treaty, B 233; account, T. ii. 1697; treatise, A. pr. 5; story, B 2147.

Tretys, *adj.* well-proportioned, long, A 152; well-fashioned, R. 1016; graceful, R. 932. O. F. *tretis.*

Trewe, *adj.* true, A 531; honest, L. 464; *pl.* the faithful, B 456.

Trewe, *adv.* correctly, 8. 4.

Trewe, *s.* truce, T. iii. 1779, iv. 58; Trewes, *pl.* the days of truce, T. v. 401.

Trewe love, *s.* true-love (probably a leaf of herb paris or some aromatic confection), A 3692.

Trewely, *adv.* truly, certainly, A 481.

Trewer, *adj.* truer, 6. 117.

Trewer, *adv.* more truly, 3. 927.

Treweste, *adj. superl.* truest, F 1539.

Treye, *num.* 'tray,' three, C 653.

Triacle, *s.* a sovereign remedy, B 479, C 314. O. F. *triacle.*

Trikled, *pt. pl.* trickled, B 1864.

Trille, *v.* turn, twirl, F 316. Cf. Swed. *trilla,* to turn round.

Trip, *s.* small piece, D 1747.

Trippe, *v.* dance, A 3328; *ger.* to trip, to move briskly with the feet, F 312.

Trist, *s.* trust, T. i. 154, iii. 403.

Triste, *s.* tryst, station, T. ii. 1534.

Triste, *v.* trust, L. 333; *ger.* to trust (to), L. 1885.

*Tristicia,* sadness, I 725.

Troden; see Trede.

Trogh, *s.* trough, A 3627.

Trompe, *s.* trumpet, L. 635.

Tromped, *pt. s.* sounded the trumpet, E 1719.

Trompes, *pl.* trumpeters, 7. 30; A 2671.

Tronchoun, *s.* broken shaft of a spear, A 2615. O. F. *tronchon.*

Trone, *s.* throne, A 2529; throne (of God), heaven, C 842.

Tropik, *s.* the turning-point, a name for the solstitial points, A. i. 17. 13.

Tropos, *s.* a turning; but interpreted by Chaucer to mean 'agaynward,' i. e. backward, A. i. 17. 13.

Trotteth, *pr. s.* trots, i. e. goes, is, E 1538.

Troublable, *adj.* disturbing, B 4. m 2. 12.

Trouble, *adj.* tempestuous, turbid, B 1. m 7. 3; dull, H 279; disturbed, I 537; anxious, E 465; vexed, 6. 133.

Troubly, *adj.* cloudy, obscure, B 4. m 5. 35.

Trouthe, *s.* truth, A 46; fidelity, L. 267; troth, promise, A 1610.

Trowen, *v.* believe, HF. 699; 1 *pr. s.* trow, believe, imagine, A 155; Trowestow, dost thou think, B 1. p 3. 24.

Troyewardes, to, towards Troy, T. i. 59.

Truâes, *s. pl.* trifles, I 715.

Trumpen, *v.* blow the trumpet, HF. 1243.

Trussed, *pp.* packed, A 681.

Truwe, *s.* truce, T. iv. 1312, 1314.

Tryce, *v.* pull, drag away, B 3715. Cf. E. *trice up* (nautical term).

Trye, *adj.* choice, excellent, B 2046.

Tryne compas, the threefold world, containing earth, sea, and heaven, G 45.

Tubbe, *s.* tub, A 3621.

Tuel, *s.* pipe, slender chimney, HF. 1649. O. F. *tuel,* F. *tuyau.*

Tukked, *pp.* tucked, A 621.

Tulle, *v.* entice, allure, A 4134.

Tunge, *s.* tongue, 1. 128.

Turet, *s.* the eye in which the ring of the astrolabe turned, A. i. 2. 1. Cotgrave has '*Touret,* the little ring by which a Hawkes *lune* or *leash* is fastened unto the Jesses.' See Torets.

Turment, *s.* torment, R. 274.

Turmente, *ger.* to vex, L. 871.

Turne, *ger.* to turn, A 2454; *v.* turn (in a lathe), A 3928; Turnen; *v.* return, L. 2619; *pp.* at an end, 3. 689.

Turneyinge, *s.* tournament, A 2557; mock tournament, R. 1407.

Turtel, *s.* turtle-dove, A 3706, E 2080.

Turves, *s. pl.* turf-plots, patches of turf, L. 204; E 2235.

Tusked, provided with tusks, F 1254.

Tuskes, *pl.* tusks, T. v. 1238.

Tuwel, *s.* hole, D 2148. See Tuel.

Twelf, twelve, C 30.

Twelfmonth, *s.* twelvemonth, year, A 651, D 909.

Twelfte, *adj.* twelfth, 4. 139.

Tweye, two, A 704, 792; Twey, B 2203; *tw. and tw.,* in pairs, A 898.

Tweyfold, *adj.* double, G 566.

Tweyne, twain, 2. 76; 4. 95.

**Twigges**, *s. pl.* twigs, HF. 1936.

**Twighte**, *pt. s.* twitched, drew quickly, T. iv. 1185; Twight, *pp.* distraught, (lit. twitched), T. iv. 572; pulled, D 1563. The infin. is *twicchen*.

**Twinkeling**, *s.* twinkling, 4. 222; momentary blinking, E 37.

**Twinkled**, *pt. pl.* twinkled, A 267; *pp.* winked, B 2. p 3. 79.

**Twinne**, *v.* sever, part, T. iv. 1197; *tw. from his wit*, lose his mind, 7. 102; depart, B 3195, F 577; *ger.* to separate, B 517; to depart (from), C 430.

**Twinninge**, *s.* separation, T. iv. 1303.

**Twiste**, *s.* (1) twist, tendril, T. iii. 1230; (2) twig, spray, E. 2349.

**Twiste**, *v.* wring, torment, F 566; 1 *pt. s.* tortured, D 494; *pt s.* wrung, E 2005; Twiste, *pt. s. subj.* would compel, constrain, T. iii. 1769; Twist, *pp.* twisted, HF. 775.

**Two so riche**, twice as rich, L. 2291. Cf. **Ten.**

**Twyes**, *adv.* twice, A 4348; Twye, A. i. 16. 13.

**Tyd**, *sb.* time, hour, T. ii. 1739; (*usually*) Tyde, R. 1452; season, F 142; Tydes, *pl.* tides, A 401.

**Tyden**, *v.* befall, happen, B 337; *pr. s.* comes (to), (a Northern form) A 4175; Tit, *pr. s.* betides, T. i. 333; Tid, *pp.* happened, T. i. 907.

**Tydif**, *s.* small bird, perhaps the titmouse, L. 154. See **Tidifs.**

**Tyme**, *s.* time, A 35, 44; *by tyme*, early, betimes, L. 452; *in good tyme*, 3. 370; Tymes, *pl.* hours, 5. 283; moments, R. 380; (*preceded by a number*) Tyme, *gen. pl.* times, T. i. 441.

**Tyne**, *s.* barrel, 12. 9. O. F. *tine.*

**Tyren**, *v.* tear, rend, B 3. m 12. 49; *pr. pl.* pull to pieces, T. i. 787.

**Tytled**, *pp.* dedicated, I 894.

## U.

*Umbra extensa*, or *recta*, the lower part of the 'skale'; *Umbra versa*, the upper part of the same, A. i. 12. 8.

**Umbreyde**, *pt. s.* upbraided, reproached, L. 1671.

**Unagreable**, *adj.* miserable, B 1. m 1. 32 (Lat. *ingratas*).

**Unbityde**, *v.* fail to happen, B 5. p 4. 39.

**Unbodie**, *v.* leave the body, T. v. 1550.

**Unbokele**, v. unbuckle, F 555.

**Unbrent**, *pp.* unburnt, B 1658.

**Unbroyden**, *pp.* unbraided, T. iv. 817.

**Unbuxumnesse**, *s.* unsubmissiveness, 24. 27.

**Uncircumscript**, *pp.* boundless, T. v. 1865.

**Unconning**, *adj.* unskilful, 6. 75.

**Unconninge**, *s.* ignorance, B 3066.

**Unconvenable**, *adj.* unsuitable, I 431.

**Uncouple**, *v.* to let loose, B 3692.

**Uncouth**, *adj.* curious, A 2497; strange, HF. 1279 (where the text has *uncouthe*, but read *uncouth*).

**Uncouthly**, *adv.* uncommonly, strikingly, R. 584.

**Uncovenable**, *adj.* unseemly, I 631; unfit (for good), B 4. p 6. 333.

**Uncunninge**, *adj.* ignorant, B 1. p 1. 68.

**Uncurteisly**, *adv.* rudely, E 2363.

**Undefouled**, undefiled, B 2. p 4. 24.

**Undepartable**, *adj.* inseparable, B 4. p 3. 62.

**Undergrowe**, *pp.* of short stature, A 156.

**Undermeles**, *pl.* undern-times, *perhaps* afternoons, D 875. See below.

**Undern**, *s.* B 4412, E 260, 981. A particular time in the morning is here implied, either about 9 a.m., or somewhat later. (Also applied to signify mid-afternoon.)

**Undernom**, *pt. s.* perceived, G 243; Undernome, *pp.* reproved, I 401.

**Underput**, *pp.* subjected, B 1. p 6. 97.

**Underpyghte**, *pt. s.* stuffed, filled underneath, B 789.

**Underspore**, *v.* thrust (the staff) under, push beneath, A 3465.

**Understonde**, *v.* understand, A 746; *pr. pl.* C 646; Understonde, *pt. s. subj.* should understand, T. i. 1035; Understonde, *pp.* understood, T. v. 1186.

**Undertake**, *v.* affirm, E 803; *ger.* to conduct an enterprise, A 405; warrant, R. 461; dare say, B 3516.

**Undevocioun**, *s.* lack of devotion, I 723.

**Undigne**, *adj.* unworthy, E 359.

**Undo**, *ger.* to unfold, reveal, 3. 899; *v.* unfasten, T. iii. 741; *pr. s.* opens, A 3727.

**Undoutous**, *adj.* undoubting, B 5. p 1. 32.

**Uneschewably**, *adv.* inevitably, B 5. p 3. 135.

**Uneschuable**, *adj.* inevitable, B 5. p 1. 105.

**Unethe**, *adv.* scarcely; *wel unethe*, scarcely at all, HF. 2041.

**Unethes**, *adv.* with difficulty, T. ii. 566.

**Unfamous**, *adj.* lost to fame, HF. 1146.

**Unfestlich**, *adj.* unfestive, jaded, F 366.

**Ungiltif**, *adj.* guiltless, T. iii. 1018.

Un-grobbed, *adj.* not digged round, 9. 14.

Unhap, *s.* ill luck, T. i. 552.

Unhappily, *adv.* unluckily, T. v. 937.

Unhardy, *adj.* cowardly, A 4210.

Unhele, *s.* misfortune, sickness, C 116.

Unholsom, *adj.* ailing, weak, T. iv. 330.

Universe ; *in universe*, universally, T. iii. 36.

Universitee, *s.* the universal, B 5. p 4. 187.

Unkinde, *adj.* unnatural, B 88 ; cruel, 5. 434.

Unkindely, *adv.* unnaturally, C 485.

Unkindenesse, *s.* unkindness, B 1057.

Unkonning, *adj.* unskilful, A 2393.

Unkorven, *adj.* uncut, unpruned, 9. 14.

Unkouth, *adj.* strange, T. ii. 151.

Unkunninge, *adj.* ignorant, R. 686.

Unlaced, *pp.* disentangled, B 3. p 12. 166.

Unleveful, *adj.* not permissible, I 593, 777.

Unloven, *ger.* to cease to love, T. v. 1698.

Unlust, *s.* disinclination, I 680.

Unlyklinesse, *s.* difficulty in pleasing, T. i. 16.

Unlykly, *adj.* unpleasing, E 2180.

Unmanhod, *s.* an unmanly act, T. i. 824.

Unmerie, *adj.* sad, HF. 74.

Unmighty, *adj.* unable, T. ii. 858.

Unneste, *imp. s.* leave thy nest, T. iv. 305.

Unnethe, *adv.* scarcely, hardly, with difficulty, A 3121, B 1050, 1816, 3611.

Unnethes, *adv.* scarcely, B 1675, D 2168.

Unordred, *adj.* not belonging to a religious order, I 961.

Unparigal, *adj.* unequal (Lat. *inparem*), B 3. p 1. 13.

Unpleyten, *v.* unplait, explain, unfold, B 2. p 8. 11.

Unpurveyed, *adj.* unprovided, uncared for, B 2. p 1. 22.

Unraced, *adj.* unbroken, untorn, B 4. p 1. 53.

Unremeved, *pp.* unremoved, without (its) being moved, A. ii. 46. 37.

Unreste, *s.* restlessness, D 1104.

Unright, *s.* wrong, T. iv. 550 ; injury, T. ii. 453.

Unrightful, *adj.* wicked, L. 1771.

Unsad, *adj.* unsettled, E 995.

Unsavory, *adj.* displeasing, I 510.

Unscience, *s.* unreal knowledge, no knowledge, B 5. p 3. 113.

Unselinesse, *s.* unhappiness, B 4. p 4. 38.

Unsely, *adj.* unhappy, B 2. p 4. 8.

Unset, *adj.* unappointed, A 1524.

Unshethe, 1 *pr. s.* unsheathe, remove, T. iv. 776.

Unshette, *pt. s.* unlocked, E 2047.

Unshette, *adj. pl.* not shut, HF. 1953.

Unshewed, *pp.* unconfessed, I 999.

Unsittinge, *adj.* unfit, T. ii. 307.

Unskilful, *adj.* foolish, T. i. 790.

Unskilfully, *adv.* unreasonably, B 1. p 4. 223.

Unslekked, *adj.* unslacked, G 806.

Unsofte, *adj.* harsh, E 1824.

Unsolempne, *adj.* uncelebrated, B 1. p 3. 64.

Unspeedful, *adj.* unprofitable, B 5. p 6. 337.

Unstaunchable, *adj.* inexhaustible, B 2. p 7. 126 (Lat. *inexhausta*).

Unstaunched, *adj.* insatiate, B 2. p 6. 115 (Lat. *inexpletam*).

Unstraunge, *adj.* well-known, A. ii. 17. *rubric.*

Unswelle, *v.* become less full, T. iv. 1146.

Unswete, *adj.* bitter, HF. 72.

Unthank, *s.* no thanks, want of thanks, T. v. 699 ; a curse, A 4081.

Unthrift, *s.* nonsense, T. iv. 431.

Unthriftily, *adv.* poorly, G 893.

Unthrifty, *adj.* profitless, T. iv. 1530.

Untold, *adj.* uncounted, A 3780.

Untressed, *adj.* with hair loose, 5. 268; unarranged, E 379 ; unplaited, A 1289.

Untretable, *adj.* inexorable, B 2. p 8. 2.

Untrewe, *adv.* untruly, A 735.

Untriste, *v.* distrust, T. iii. 839.

Untyme ; *in untyme*, out of season, I 1051.

Unwar, *adj.* unaware, T. i. 304 ; unexpected, B 427.

Unwar, *adv.* unexpectedly, unawares, T. i. 549.

Unwelde, *adj.* (unwieldy), too weak to support herself, R. 359; difficult to move, H 55 ; difficult to control, A 3886.

Unwemmed, *adj.* unspotted, spotless, B 924, G 137, 225.

Unwened, *adj.* unexpected, B 4. p 6. 260.

Unwist, *adj.* unknown, T. ii. 1294 ; *unwist of*, uninformed of, T. i. 93 ; unknown by, L. 1653.

Unwit, *s.* folly, 4. 271.

Unwot, *pr. s.* fails to know, B 5. p 6. 177.

Unwrye, *v.* reveal, T. i. 858.

Unyolden, *pp.* without having yielded, A 2642.

Up, *adv.* up ; open (outwards, not upwards), A 3801 ; *as v.* up with, HF. 1021 ; *up and down*, T. ii. 659 ; in all directions, A 977 ; backwards and forwards, A 1052.

Up, *prep.* on, upon, A 2543 ; *up peril*, on peril, D 2271 ; *up peyne*, under the penalty, D 1587; *up poynt*, on the point, ready, T. iv. 1153.

Up-bounde, *pp.* bound up, T. iii. 517.

Up-caste, *pt. s.* cast up, B 906.

Up-drow, *pt. s.* drew up, L. 1459.

Up-enbossed, *pp.* raised, L. 1200.

Up-haf, *pt. s.* uplifted, A 2428.

Upon, *prep.* upon, A 131; in, F 925; against, D 1313.

Upon, *used adverbially,* upon (him or her), on, D 559, 1382.

Uppe, *adv.* up, i. e. left open, F 615.

Up-plight, *pp.* plucked up, pulled up, B 3239.

Upright, *adv.* i. e. reversed, D 2266; *also,* lying on one's back (mostly of people asleep or dead); A 4194; B 1801.

Up-rist, *pr. s.* rises up, L. 1188; A 4249.

Up-riste, *s. dat.* up-rising, A 1051.

Upronne, *pp.* ascended, F 386.

Up-so-doun, *adv.* upside down, A 1377, G 625.

Upspringe, *v.* rise (as the sun), 4. 14.

Upsterte, *pt. s.* upstarted, arose, A 1080, 1299.

Up-yaf, *pt. s.* yielded up, gave, A 2427.

Up-yolden, *pp.* yielded up, A 3052.

Uságe, *s.* usage, habit, A 110; *hadde in uságe,* was accustomed, B 1696; *was in uságe,* B 1717.

Usaunce, *s.* custom, R. 683.

Usaunt, *pres. pl. as adj.* addicted, I 821; accustomed, A 3940.

Usen, *ger.* to accustom, I 245; *v.* use, B 44; Useth, *pr. s.* is accustomed, L. 364.

Us-selve, *pron.* ourselves, I 349.

Usshers, *s. pl.* ushers, F 293.

Usure, *s.* usury, B 1681.

Us-ward, to, towards us, B 2938.

Utter, *adj.* outward, G 498.

Uttereste, *adj. superl.* supreme, E 787.

## V.

Vache, *s.* cow, beast, 13. 22. The reference is to a quadruped that looks *down to the earth.*

Valance, *s.* (*possibly*) sign of zodiac opposite the mansion of a planet, 4. 145; if so, the reference here is to the sign of Aries.

Valóur, *s.* worth, R. 957.

Vane, *s.* a weather-cock, E 996.

Vanish, 1 *pr. s.* shrink up, waste away, C 732.

Variaunce, *s.* variation, T. iv. 985; Variance, difference, I 427.

Variaunt, *adj.* varying, G 1175.

Vassalage, *s.* prowess, L. 1667.

Vavassour, *s.* a sub-vassal, next in dignity to a baron, A 360.

Veine, *adj. fem.* vain, R. 447.

Veluët, *s.* velvet, R. 1420; Veluëttes, *pl.* F 644.

Venerian, *adj.* devoted to Venus, D 609.

Venerye, *s.* hunting, A 166, 2308.

Venge, *v.* revenge, B 2471.

Vengeresses, *s. pl.* avengeresses, avenging deities, B 3. m 12. 38.

Venim, *s.* venom, poison, R. 1089; malice, B 891, C 421; corruption, A 2751; dye (Lat. *ueneno*), B 2. m 5. 12.

Ventusinge, *s.* cupping (a surgical operation), A 2747.

Venus, venereal pleasure, D 464.

Ver, the spring, T. i. 157.

Veray, *adj.* very, true, real, L. 1068.

Verdegrees, *s.* verdigrease, G 791.

Verdit, *s.* verdict, A 787.

Vernáge, *s.* a wine of Italy, B 1261.

Vernicle, *s.* vernicle, A 685. A copy of the sacred handkerchief on which the impression of the Saviour's face was distinguishable.

Vernisshed, *pt. s.* varnished; hence (jocularly), lined in a lavish way, A 4149.

Verre, *s.* glass, T. ii. 867.

Verray, *adj.* very, true, A 72, 422; *v. force,* main force, B 3237.

Verrayly, *adv.* verily, truly, 2. 73.

Verrayment, *adv.* verily, B 1903.

Versiflour, *s.* poet, B 2783.

Vertu, *s.* virtue, A 307; quickening power, A 4; power, A 2249; valour, R. 1208; mental faculty, HF. 550; magic influence, F 146, 157; *v. plese,* satisfy virtue, be virtuous, E 216.

Vertuous, *adj.* virtuous, A 251; full of virtue, D 1113; full of healing power, R. 1097; holy, I 455.

Verye (a word used in a charm), A 3485. Perhaps for *weri,* an accursed creature; A.S. *wearg.*

Vese, *s.* rush (Lat. *impetus*), A 1985.

Vessel, *s.* (*collectively*), vessels, plate, B 3338.

Vestiment, *s.* clothing, F 59.

Veyne, *s.* vein, A 3.

Veyne-blood, *s.* bleeding at a vein, A 2747.

Viáge, *s.* voyage, travel, journey, T. ii. 75; expedition, attempt, T. iii. 732.

Vicaire, *s.* deputy, deputed ruler, 5. 379; Vicary, a vicar, I 22.

Victor, *s. as adj.* of victory, 5. 182.

**Vigile,** s. wake, T. v. 305.

**Vigilyes,** pl. vigils, A 377.

**Viker,** s. vicar, D 2008.

**Vileinous,** adj. evil, B 2693.

**Vileins, Vileyns,** adj. villainous, L. 1824; rude, D 1268; sinful, I 854, 914; evil, wicked, I 556.

**Vileinsly,** adv. evilly, I 154; Vilaynsly, shamefully, R. 1498.

**Vileinye,** s. vile conduct, B 2547; great harm, A 4191; despiteful language, reproach, D 34, 53; disgrace, A 942; unfit speech, A 70; servitude, I 143; discourtesy, rudeness, C 740; vileness, HF. 96; reproach, T. iv. 21; evil-doing, B 1681.

**Vinolent,** adj. full of wine, D 467, 1931.

**Violes,** s. pl. vials, phials, G 793.

**Virelayes,** s. pl. ballads with a particular return of rime, F 948; L. 423.

**Viritoot,** s. brisk movement, A 3770.

**Viritrate,** s. hag, D 1582.

**Viságe,** v. put a face (on it), disguise, E 2273.

**Visitaciouns,** s. pl. visits, D 555.

**Visýte,** ger. to visit, A 493, 1194.

**Vitaillo,** s. victuals, provisions, A 248, 569.

**Vitaille,** v. provide with victuals, L. 1093.

**Vitaillers,** pl. victuallers, A 4366.

**Vitremyte,** s. (probably) a woman's cap, an effeminate head-dress, B 3562.

**Voided,** pp. removed, F 1195; cleared, emptied, L. 2625.

**Vois,** s. voice, R. 751. See **Voys.**

**Volage,** adj. giddy, volatile, R. 1284; wanton, H 239.

**Volatyl,** s. as pl. fowls, B 1262.

**Voltor,** s. vulture, B 3. m 12. 46; pl. T. i. 788.

**Volupeer,** s. night-cap, A 4303; Voluper, woman's cap, A 3241.

**Vouche,** v.; only used with sauf, safe; Vouche sauf, v. to avouch as safe, call safe, vouchsafe, grant, deign, permit, A 812, B 1641, E 2341; 1 pr. s. am content, T. iv. 90; 2 pr. pl. vouchsafe, grant, deign, L. 2038; Voucheth sauf, imp. pl. vouchsafe, E 885, F 1043.

**Voyde** (voidéé), s. ' voidee,' a light dessert, with wine and spices, T. iii. 674.

**Voyden,** v. get rid of, expel, A 2751, E 910, F 188; imp. s. depart from, E 806; Voydeth, imp. pl. send away, G 1136.

**Voys,** s. voice, A 688, C 531; rumour, E 629; commendation, E 1592; report, T. iii. 1723.

**Vulgar,** adj. A. ii. 9. 5. The day vulgar is the length of the 'artificial' day,

with the durations of morning and evening twilight added to it.

**Vyce,** s. fault, error, T. i. 689; F 101; defect, D 955.

## W.

**Waast,** s. waist, B 1890.

**Waat,** pr. s. knows (Northern), A 4086.

**Wacche,** s. sentinel, B 2216.

**Wachet,** s. light blue colour, A 3321. Later E. watchet.

**Waden,** v. pass, E 1684; wade (through), D 2084; enter (into), T. ii. 150; go, descend, B 3684.

**Waf,** pt. s. wove, L. 2364.

**Wafereres,** s. pl. makers of gaufres or wafer-cakes, confectioners, C 479.

**Wages,** pl. A 1803; pay, recompense, 4. 244.

**Wagging,** s. shaking, T. ii. 1745.

**Waiten,** v. attend on, L. 1269; pr. s. watches, E 708; imp. s. observe, A. ii. 5. 18.

**Wake,** v. be awake, lie awake, 18. 27; Waken, v. act. awake, B 1187; pr. s. watches, F 819; Wook, 1 pt. s. awoke, 5. 695; remained awake, B 3809; Waked, pp. awaked, 3. 294; kept wake, caroused, 3. 977.

**Wake-pleyes,** pl. funeral games, A 2960.

**Waker,** adj. vigilant, 5. 358.

**Waking,** s. watching, being awake, 3. 611; period of wakefulness, B 22; pl. vigils, I 257.

**Wálet,** a wallet, A 686; Walét, A 681.

**Walked,** (for Walketh), s. walking; in phr. go walked, for go a-walketh, gone a-walking, 3. 387; D 1778.

**Walken,** ger. to walk, roam, A 2309; Welk, 1 pt. s. walked, T. ii. 517; is walked, is gone, went, A 2368.

**Walsh-note,** gen. sing. walnut's, HF. 1281.

**Walwe,** ger. to wallow, roll about, T. i. 699; pr. pl. wallow, tumble, A 4278; pr. s. tosses, L. 1166; rolls about, D 1085; pp. involved, immersed, 12. 17; Walwinge, pres. part. causing to roll, B 1. m 7. 4 (Lat. woluens).

**Wanges,** s. pl. molar teeth, A 4030.

**Wang-tooth,** s. molar tooth, B 3234.

**Wanhope,** s. despair, A 1249.

**Wanie,** v. wane, A 2078.

**Wante,** v. be wanting, be absent, L. 361; fail, be lacking, I 514; pr. s. is lacking, H 338.

**Wantownesse,** s. wantonness, B 31; mannerism (of speech), A 264.

**Wantrust**, *s.* distrust, T. i. 794; H 280.

**War**, *adj.* prudent, discreet, cautious, T. i. 203; aware, A 157, 896, 3604; *was I w.*, I observed, 5. 218, 298; *I was w.*, 3. 445; *ben w.*, beware, T. i. 635; *be w.*, beware, 13. 11; take warning, G 737; *be w. fro*, beware of, L. 473; beth *w.*, beware, T. iii. 1180; B 1629, 3281.

**War him**, let him beware, A 662; *war yow*, make way, B 1889.

**Warde**, *s. dat.* (?) keeping; *on w.*, into his keeping, 3. 248; *in our w.*, C 201; *under my w.*, I 880.

**Wardecors**, *s.* body-guard, D 359.

**Warderere**, *for* warde rere, look out behind, A 4101.

**Wardrobe**, *s.* privy, B 1762.

**Ware**, *adj.* aware, 3. 1030.

**Ware**, *s.* wares (for sale), merchandise, B 140, 1246.

**Ware**, *imp. pl.* beware, B 4416.

**Warente**, *ger.* to warrant, protect, C 338.

**Wariangles**, *pl.* shrikes, butcher-birds, D 1408.

**Warien**, *ger.* to curse, T. ii. 1619; 1 *pr. s.* B 372.

**Warisoun**, *s.* requital, R. 1537.

**Warisshe**, *v.* cure, I 998; recover, be cured, B 2172; *pp.* cured, B 2467.

**Warisshinge**, *s.* cure, B 2205.

**Warly**, *adv.* warily, carefully, T. iii. 454.

**Warne**, *v.* reject, refuse, 1. 11; 1 *pr. s.* warn, bid you take heed, B 16, 1184; invite, B 2652; 2 *pr. s. subj.* inform, HF. 893; *pp.* forewarned, L. 2658; given notice, B 1578.

**Warnestore**, *ger.* to fortify, defend, B 2487; to garrison, B 2521; *pp.* provisioned, B 1. p 3. 85.

**Warnestoring**, *s.* fortifying, B 2525.

**Waryce**, *v.* heal, cure, C 906.

**Waste**, *adj. pl.* wasted, partially destroyed, A 1331.

**Wastel-breed**, *s.* cake-bread, bread of the very best quality, A 147.

**Wastour**, *s.* waster, E 1535.

**Watering**, *s.* watering-place (for horses), A 826.

**Wawe**, *s.* wave, B 508, I 363.

**Waxen**, *pp.* become, T. v. 1014, 1374, 1376.

**Wayk**, *adj.* weak, L. 2428, 2713.

**Wayken**, *ger.* to grow weak, lessen, T. iv. 1144.

**Waymenten**, *ger.* to lament, I 230.

**Waymentinge**, *s.* lamenting, lamentation, A 995, 1921.

**Wayn**, *s.* car, B 4. m 1. 34.

**Wayten**, *ger.* to observe, T. i. 190; to

watch for, F 1263; to watch, F 444; *v.* to expect, B 467; *pr. s.* seeks occasion, A 1222.

**Webbe**, *s.* a weaver, A 362.

**Wedde**, *s. dat.*; *to w.*, as a pledge, in pledge, A 1218, B 1613.

**Wedde**, *ger.* to wed, T. v. 863.

**Wedding**, *s.* wedlock, 17. 24.

**Wede**, *s.* weed, robe, garment, A 1006, B 2107, E 863.

**Weder**, *s.* weather, D 2253, F 52; storm, T. ii. 2, iii. 657.

**Wedes**, *pl.* weeds, T. i. 946.

**Weel**, *adv.* well, A 926; well placed, luckily situated, B 308.

**Weeldinge**, *s.* power, control, B 2800.

**Weep**, *pt. s. of* Wepe.

**Weeply**, *adj.* tearful, sorrowful, B 1. p 1. 3.

**Weet**, *s.* wet, A 4107.

**Weex**, *pt. s.* waxed, grew, G 513.

**Wegge**, *s.* a wedge, A. i. 14. 6.

**Wehee**, *s.* a whinnying noise, A 4066.

**Weilawey**, alas! D 216.

**Wel**, *adv.* well, A 384, B 25; much, L. 1386; many, L. 11; certainly, L. 452; fully, A 29, 49; about (*used with numbers*), A 24; *wel royal*, very royal, F 26; *wel ny*, very nearly, B 3230; *wel the bet*, much better, T. ii. 92; *wel unethe*, scarcely at all, L. 33 *a*; *to be wel*, to be in favour, 3. 845; *wel is him*, it is well for him, T. i. 350; *well was him*, it was well for him, B 4066; *ful wel*, very well, A 122.

**Welawey**, *int.* alas! T. iii. 1695.

**Welde**, *s.* weld, *Reseda Luteola*, 9. 17.

**Welde**, *s.* power, control, R. 395.

**Welden**, *ger.* to have control over, to move with ease, D 1947; to control, D 271; to wield, L. 2000; **Welte**, *pt. s.* B 3200.

**Weldy**, *adj.* wieldy, active, T. ii. 636.

**Wele**, *s.* happiness, success, prosperity, well-being, good fortune, A 895, 3101, B 122.

**Weleful**, *adj.* prosperous, happy, B 2507; blessed, B 451.

**Welefulnesse**, *s.* happiness, B 1. p 3. 35.

**Welk**, *pt. s. of* Walken.

**Welked**, *pp. as adj.* withered, C 738, D 277.

**Welken**, *s.* heaven, sky, HF. 1601; Welkne, 10. 62.

**Welmeth**, *pr. s.* wells, gushes, R. 1561.

**Welte**, *pt. s.* wielded, i.e. lorded it over, possessed for use, B 3200.

**Wel-willy**, *adj.* benevolent, benign, beneficent, T. iii. 1257.

**Wem**, s. blemish, R. 930; hurt, F 121.

**Wemmelees**, adj. stainless, G 47.

**Wenden**, ger. to go, A 21, 2214; pass away, A 3025; go, pass, B 1683; Went, pr. s. goes, T. ii. 36, 812; Wente, pt. s. went, A 78, B 1739; Wente him, pt. s. went, G 110; Wentestow, 2 pr. s. hast thou gone, A 3486; Went, pp. gone, L. 1651; ben went, are gone, B 173; is went, is gone, G 534.

**Wending**, s. departure, T. iv. 1344, 1436.

**Wene**, s. supposition, doubt, T. iv. 1593; withouten wene, without doubt, R. 574, 732.

**Wenen**, v. ween, suppose, imagine, consider, L. 12; G 676; expect, A 4320; Wenestow, weenest thou, thinkest thou, D 311; Weneth, pr. s. imagines (with men = one), A 2195; Wende, 1 pt. s. imagined, T. v. 693; supposed, F 585; fancied, A 1269; Wendest, 2 pr. s. subj. shouldst ween, T. i. 1031; Wende, pt. s. subj. would have thought, C 782; Wend, pp. supposed, T. iv. 384; imagined, T. v. 1682.

**Wenged**, adj. winged, HF. 2118.

**Wenges**, pl. wings, L. 168 a.

**Weninge**, s. imagination, supposition, T. iv. 992.

**Went**, pr. s. and pp. of Wenden.

**Wente**, pt. s. of Wenden.

**Wente**, s. turn, T. ii. 63; path, passage, T. iii. 787; footpath, 18. 69.

**Wepe**, v. weep, A 144, 230; Weep, pt. s. wept, A 148, B 606, 4052; Wepte, pt. s. (weak form), B 267; Wepen, pp. T. i. 941; Wopen, pp. F 523.

**Wepen**, s. weapon, L. 1994.

**Werbul**, s. tune (warble), T. ii. 1033.

**Werche**, v. work, perform, B 566; Wroghtestow (for Wroghtest thou), thou didst cause, B 3583; Wroghte, pt. s. worked, A 497; contrived, B 1788; made, E 1152; Wroughte, 1 pt. s. acted, A. ii. 3. 46; did, R. 701; Wrought, pp. made, formed, R. 559; born, B 3619; created, G 326; composed, L. 372.

**Werde**, pt. s. of Were (wear).

**Werdes**, s. pl. fates, destinies, B 1. m 1. 14.

**Were**, s. weir, 5. 138; T. iii. 35.

**Were**, s. doubt, 3. 1295; HF. 979; mental struggle, L. 2686. Lowl. Sc. weir.

**Were**, 2 pt. s. wast, T. iv. 762; it were, they were, E 850; al were it, though it were, D 1172.

**Were** (wère), v. wear, 21. 7; Werede, pt. s. wore, A 1388, 3235; Werde, R. 875;

**Wered**, A 75; Wered upon, 1 pt. s. wore upon (me), D 559.

**Were**, ger. to defend, A 2550.

**Weringe**, s. wearing, I 1052.

**Werk**, s. work, A 479; act, L. 891.

**Werken**, v. act, A 3527; pr. s. acts, L. 1385.

**Werkers**, pl. doers, D 1937.

**Werkes**, pr. pl. ache, A 4030.

**Werking**, s. deed, H 210; mode of operation, G 1367.

**Werne**, ger. to refuse, T. iii. 149, iv. 111; v. refuse, R. 1485; warn off, R. 636; Werned, pp. forbidden, R. 442.

**Werning**, s. let, forbidding, R. 1142.

**Werre**, s. war, T. ii. 868; trouble, T. v. 1393; of werre, in war, T. i. 134; to w., in enmity, 1. 116.

**Werre**, adv. worse, 3. 616.

**Werreye**, ger. to make war, A 1484; v. war against, A 1544; pr. s. opposes, I 487.

**Werreyour**, s. warrior, L. 597.

**Wers**, adj. worse, A 3872.

**Werste**, adj. superl. worst, T. ii. 304.

**Werte**, s. wart, A 555.

**Wery**, adj. (being) weary, T. iv. 707; worn, R. 440, 664; beaten repeatedly, lit. weary, B 4. m 5. 17.

**Wesele**, s. weasel, A 3234.

**Wesh**, pt. s. of Wasshe.

**Weste**, v. turn to the west, L. 61, 197.

**Westren**, v. to go to the west, T. ii. 906.

**Wete**, s. perspiration, G 1187.

**Wete**, v. wet, HF. 1785.

**Wether**, s. sheep, T. iv. 1374.

**Weven**, v. weave, L. 2352; Waf, pt. s. wove, L. 2364.

**Wex**, s. wax, A 675, E 1430.

**Wexen**, v. wax, grow, become, B 2265, G 877; 1 pr. s. subj. may I become, G 1377; Wexe, 2 pr. pl. increase, grow (in applauding), E 998; Wex, pt. s. grew, became, A 1362; increased, L. 727; Woxe, pp. grown, R. 1460; become, HF. 1494.

**Wexede**, pt. s. coated with wax, A. ii. 40. 28.

**Wey**, s. way, A 34; path, R. 1345; the sun's apparent daily path, A. ii. 30. 5; the sun's apparent annual orbit, A. i. 21. 49; a furlong wey, a short time (lit. short distance), E 516; go wey, go thy way, T. i. 574; do wey, take away, A 3287.

**Weyen**, v. weigh, B 3776; oghte weyen, ought to weigh, L. 398.

**Weyere**, s. the 'weigher,' a translation

of the Lat. *equator*; because the days and nights, at the equinoxes, are equal; A. i. 17. 25.

**Weyk**, *adj.* weak, 7. 341.

**Weylaway**, *interj.* alas! A 938.

**Weymentinge**, *s.* lamenting, A 902; lament, T. ii. 65.

**Weynes**, *s. pl.* chariots, B 4. m 5. 6.

**Weyven**, *ger.* to turn aside, E 1483; *v.* waive, neglect, T. ii. 284; put aside, D 1176; forsake, G 276; abandon, B 2406.

**Whan**, when, A 5, 18, 179.

**What**, whatever, 4. 170; what sort of a, L. 1305; what with, B 21, 22; why, T. ii. 262, 292; what! how! L. 1800; What that, whatever, E 165; What man that, whoever, B 2645; What .. what, partly, . . partly, HF. 2058.

**Wheelen**, *ger.* to cause to revolve, T. i. 139.

**Whelkes**, *pl.* pimples, blotches, A 632.

**Whelp**, *s.* cub, A 2627.

**Whenne**, *adv.* whence, E 588.

**Whennes**, *adv.* whence, B 2400.

**Wher**, *adv.* where, B 1785, &c.; wherever, R. 1669; Wher as (*or* Wher-as), where that, where, B 647, 1311.

**Wher**, whether, (*a common contracted form of* whether), 3. 91.

**Wher-as**, *adv.* where that, where, T. iii. 516.

**Whereof**, *prep.* in what respect, R. 703; for what, R. 1552.

**Wherfore**, for any cause, C 216.

**Wher-on**; *long wher-on*, because of what, G 930.

**Wher-so**, whether, B 294; wherever, L. 439.

**Wher-through**, *adv.* by means of which, 3. 120.

**Wherto**, *adv.* for wherefore, T. i. 409.

**Whete**, *s.* wheat, C 375.

**Whether**, *adj.* which (of two), A 1856.

**Whette**, *pp. pl.* sharpened, T. v. 1760.

**Which**, *pron.* which, A 161; whom, A 568; what kind of, L. 1883; Which a, what kind of a, what a, L. 668, 869, &c.

**Whider**, whither, T. v. 428, 486.

**Whilk**, which (Northern), A 4078.

**Whilom**, *adv.* once, D 2017.

**Whippeltree** (*better* Wippeltree), cornel-tree, A 2923.

**Whirle**, *ger.* to rush, go swiftly, T. v. 1019; *v.* be whirled round, 5. 80.

**Who**, *interrog.* who, T. v. 371; D 692; *indef.* who (it might be), 3. 244; one who, 3. 559; whoever, who, T. v. 1115; Who was who, which was which, A 4300.

**Whyle**, *s.* time, A 3299; *worth the wh.*, worth while, T. v. 882.

**Whyl-er**, *adv.* formerly, G 1328.

**Whyles**, *gen. s. as adv.*; *the whyles*, whilst, 3. 151.

**Whylom**, *adv.* once, formerly, once on a time, R. 10. 362.

**Whyne**, *v.* whine, whinny, D 386.

**Whyt**, *adj.* white, A 238; *as sb.*, white wine, C 526, 562; *pl.* innocent, guileless, T. iii. 1567; specious, flattering, T. iii. 901.

**Whyte**, *s.* white (i. e. silver), T. iii. 1384.

**Widwe**, *s.* widow, A 253.

**Widwehode**, *s.* widowhood, I 916; Widwehed, L. 295 *a*.

**Wierdes**, *pl.* fates, T. iii. 617; Wirdes, L. 2580. A.S. *wyrd*.

**Wight**, *s.* a person, creature, man, living being, A 71, 280; whit, short while, A 4283; Wightes, *pl.* creatures, men, beings, A 3479.

**Wight**, *adj.* active, B 3457; fleet, A 4086.

**Wighte**, *s.* weight, HF. 739; A 2145, 2520.

**Wike**, *s.* week, C 362. See **Wyke**.

**Wiket**, *s.* wicket-gate, small gate, E 2045, 2118.

**Wikke**, *adj.* evil, wicked, bad, A 1087, 1580; false, B 2247; depraved, 10. 55; much alloyed, HF. 1346.

**Wikked**, *adj.* bad, wicked, L. 2395; *pl.* wicked, I 112. In B 3576, *wikked nest* is put for F. *mau ni*, i. e. Sir Oliver Mauny; see the note in the larger edition.

**Wikkednesse**, *s.* evil, 17. 7.

**Wil**, *s.* will, 6. 83. See **Wille**.

**Wil**, 1 *pr. s.* desire, wish, 7. 244; *pr. s.* desires, B 1843.

**Wilde**, *adj.* wild; Wilde fyr, wild fire, fire not easily put out, Greek fire, D 373; flaming spirits, I 445; a disease, erysipelas, A 4172, E 2252; Wilde, *pl.* A 2018.

**Wildnesse**, *s.* wilderness, 9. 34.

**Wilen**, *pr. pl.* will, R. 1683.

**Wilful**, *adj.* voluntary, B 3, p 11. 167.

**Wilful**, *as adv.* wilfully, willingly, 5. 429.

**Wilfulhed**, *s.* wilfulness, L. 355 *a*.

**Wilfully**, *adv.* willingly, voluntarily, of free will, by choice, B 4486, C 441.

**Wilfulnesse**, *s.* wish, B 2572.

**Wille**, *s.* own accord, will, 1. 45, 57; pleasure, desire, E 326, F 1, 8; Willes, *gen.* F 568; *as by his w.*, willingly, 17. 12.

**Wille**, *v.* will, desire, E 721.

**Willing**, *s.* desire, E 319.

**Willingly**, *adv.* of free will, E 362.

**Wilnen**, *v.* desire, A 2114; Wilnest, *2 pr.*

*s.* desirest, A 1609 ; Wilned, 1 *pt. s.* 3. 1262, 1267. A.S. *wilnian.*

**Wilninge,** *s.* willing, wishing, B 3. p 11. 88 ; *pl.* desires, B. 3. p 11. 175.

**Wilow,** *s.* willow-tree, A 2922.

**Wiltow,** 2 *pr. s.* wilt thou, A 1156 ; wishest thou, B 2116 ; wilt thou (go), D 1387.

**Wimpel,** *s.* wimple, a covering for the head, gathered round it, and pleated under the chin, A 151.

**Wimpleth,** *pr. s.* conceals (as with a wimple), B 2. p 1. 66.

**Windas,** *s.* windlass, F 184.

**Winde,** *ger.* to turn, T. iii. 1541 ; to revolve, T. ii. 601 ; to roam about, L. 818 ; Winde, *v.* wind, entwine, T. iii. 1232 ; intertwine, 5. 671 ; ply, bend, T. i. 257 ; bind with cloths, E 583 ; twist and turn, G 980 ; Winde, 2 *pr. s. subj.* mayst go, T. iii. 1440 ; Wond, *pt. s.* wound, went about, L. 2253.

**Windinge,** *s.* twisting, I 417.

**Wind-melle,** *s.* wind-mill, HF. 1280.

**Windre,** *ger.* to trim, R. 1020 ; *pp.* trimmed, R. 1018. Cf. O. F. *guignier.*

**Windy,** *adj.* unstable as wind, B 2. p 8. 28.

**Winged,** provided with wings, A 1385.

**Winke,** *v.* wink, B 4496 ; nod, F 348 ; remain awake, T. iii. 1537 ; Winke, 1 *pr. s.* am asleep, 5. 7.

**Winne,** *ger.* to win, gain, A 427 ; to conquer, F 214 ; to get gain, C 461 ; *w. fro,* to get away from, T. v. 1125 ; Wan, 1 *pt. s.* got, D 1477 ; won, gained, A 442, 989 ; *pt. s. used as pt. pl.* F 1401 ; Wonnen, *pp.* won, A 877, 3381.

**Winning,** *s.* gain, profit, A 275, D 416.

**Winsinge,** *pres. pt.* wincing, starting aside, i.e. skittish, A 3263.

**Winter,** *pl.* years, T. i. 811.

**Wirche,** *v.* work, A 3430 ; provide, E 1661 ; give relief, A 2759 ; *in passive sense,* to be made, HF. 474 ; *ger.* to perform, A 3308 ; Wirk, *imp. s.* do, E 1485.

**Wirdes,** *pl.* Fates, L. 2580 ; Wierdes, T. iii. 617.

**Wirk,** *imp. s.* work, do, E 1485.

**Wirkinge,** *s.* efficiency, B 3. p 11. 26 ; actions, D 698 ; calculation, F 1280.

**Wis,** *adv.* certainly, verily, surely, T. ii. 381, 474, 563 ; A 2786, D 621 ; *as wis,* as sure (as), T. iv. 1655 ; assuredly, F 1470. See **Ywis.**

**Wisly,** *adv.* certainly, truly, verily, A 1863, 3994, 4162.

**Wisse,** *v.* instruct, T. i. 622 ; inform, D 1415 ; show, tell, D 1008 ; 2 *pr. s. subj.*

teach, 5. 74 ; *imp. s.* direct, guide, 1. 155. A.S. *wissian.*

**Wissh,** 1 *pt. s.* washed, R. 96, 125,

**Wisshe,** *v.* wish, T. ii. 406.

**Wist, -e** ; see **Witen.**

**Wit,** *s.* reason, R. 1535 ; understanding, B 2702 ; judgement, A 279 ; mind, R. 1694 ; knowledge, mental power, R. 401 ; wisdom, T. iv. 1508 ; proof of intelligence, E 459 ; Wittes, *pl.* senses, B 202 ; wits, F 706 ; opinions, F 203.

**Witen,** *ger.* to know, to wit, T. v. 1324 ; Wite, *ger.* to know, 3. 493 ; to discover, D 1450 ; *do you wite,* make you know, inform you, T. ii. 1635 ; Woot, 1 *pr. s.* wot, know, A 389 ; *pr. s.* knows, 2. 30 ; Wot, 1 *pr. s.* L. 4 ; *pr. s.* knows, B 195 ; Woost, 2 *pr. s.* knowest, T. i. 633 ; Wost, 2 *pr. s.* L. 542 ; Wostow, thou knowest, A 2304 ; Witen, 1 *pr. pl.* wit, know, A 1260 ; Witen, 2 *pr. pl.* D 1890 ; know ye, H 1, 82 ; Woot (*wrongly used for* Wite), 2 *pr. pl.* know, A 740 ; Wiste, 1 *pt. s.* wist, knew, E 814 ; Wistest, 2 *pt. s.* knewest, A 1156 ; Wistestow, knewest thou, T. iii. 1644 ; Wiste, *pt. s.* knew, R. 1344 ; Wist, *pp.* known, B 1072 ; Witeth, *imp. pl.* know, T. i. 687. A.S. *witan* ; *pr. t. wāt, wāst, wāt,* pl. *witon* ; pt. t. *wiste.*

**With,** with, A 5, 10, &c. ; *to hele with your hurtes,* to heal your wounds with, F 471.

**With-drow,** 1 *pt. s.* subtracted, A. ii. 45. 12.

**Withholden,** *ger.* to retain, I 1041 ; Withholde, *pp.* retained, B 2202 ; detained, G 345 ; shut up, kept in confinement, A 511.

**Withinne-forth,** *adv.* within, B 5. p 5. 14.

**With-oute-forth,** *adv.* outwardly, I 172.

**Withouten,** *prep.* besides, as well as, A 461 ; excepting, T. ii. 236.

**Withseye,** *v.* contradict, gainsay, A 805 ; refuse, L. 367 ; renounce, G 457.

**Withstonde,** *v.* withstand, oppose, B 3110 ; Withstonde, *pp.* withstood, T. i. 253.

**Witing,** *s.* knowledge, cognizance, A 1611.

**Witingly,** *adv.* knowingly, I 401.

**Witnesfully,** *adv.* publicly, B 4. p 5. 11.

**Witterly,** *adv.* plainly, truly, L. 2606.

**Wivere,** *s.* wyvern, snake, T. iii. 1010. O. F. *wivre,* lit. viper.

**Wlatsom,** *adj.* disgusting, B 3814 ; heinous, B 4243.

**Wo,** *s.* woe, R. 319 ; *me is wo,* I am sorry,

L. 1985; *wo were us*, woe would be to us, E 139.

**Wo**, *adj.* unhappy, R. 312; sad, grieved, A 351.

**Wode**, *adj.*; see **Wood**.

**Wode-binde**, *s.* woodbine, honeysuckle, A 1508.

**Wodedowve**, *s.* wood-pigeon, B 1960.

**Wodewale**, *s.* the green woodpecker, *Gecinus viridis*, R. 914.

**Wodnesse**, *s.* madness, T. iii. 794.

**Wol**, 1 *pr. s.* (I) will, A 42; desire, E 646; Wole, 1 *pr. s.* am ready to, T. i. 589; Wolt, 2 *pr. s.* wilt, E 314; Woltow, wilt thou, A 1544; dost thou wish, D 840; Wol, *pr. s.* will, B 60; wills, desires, HF. 662; wishes for, T. ii. 396; wishes (to go), will go, L. 1191; permits, H 28; Wole, will go, D 353; *wol adoun*, is about to set, I 72; Wol ye so, if you so wish it, E 2264; Wil ye, wish ye, F 378; Woln, *pr. pl.* will, wish (to have), A 2121; Wollen, *pr. pl.* will, B 2561; Wolde, 1 *pt. s.* desired, 6. 48; should like, B 1637; Woldestow, if thou wouldst, L. 760; wouldst thou, B 4536; Wolde, *pt. s.* would, A 144; would like to, B 1182; wished, L. 952; required, F 577; would go, would turn, F 496; wished to, 4. 124; T. ii. 514; Wolde . . . unto, would go to, B 3786; *god wolde*, oh! that God would grant, 3. 665; *wolde god*, oh! that God would be pleased, D 1103; Wolde whoso nolde, i.e. whoever would or would not, T. i. 77; Wold, *pp.* desired, 18. 11; willed, B 2190, 2615.

**Wolde**, *s. dat.* possession, R. 451.

**Wolle**, *s.* wool, L. 1791.

**Woln, Woltow**; see **Wol**.

**Wombe**, *s.* belly, A 4290; womb, E 2414; the depression in the front of an astrolabe, A. i. 3. 3.

**Wombe-side**, the front of the astrolabe, A. i. 6. 10.

**Wommanhede**, *s.* womanhood, B 851.

**Wond**; *pt. s. of* Winde.

**Wonde**, *v.* desist, L. 1187.

**Wonder**, *adj.* wonderful, wondrous, strange, T. i. 419.

**Wonder**, *adv.* wondrously, R. 242.

**Wonderly**, *adv.* wondrously, A 84.

**Wonder-most**, *adj. sup.* most wonderful, HF. 2059.

**Wonders**, *adv.* wondrously, R. 27.

**Wone** (wunə), *s.* custom, usage, wont, T. ii. 318; HF. 76.

**Wone**, *v.* dwell, inhabit, G 332; Woneth, *pr. s.* dwells, lives, D 1573; Woneden,

*pt. pl.* dwelt, A 2927; Woned, *pp.* dwelt, T. i. 276; wont, accustomed, T. ii. 400, v. 277.

**Wones** (wòònez), *pl.* places of retreat, *hence*, range of buildings, D 2105. See **Woon**.

**Wonger**, *s.* pillow, B 2102.

**Woning**, *s.* habitation, house, A 606.

**Wonne, -n**; see **Winne**.

**Wood**, (wòòd), *s.* woad, 9. 17.

**Wood**, (wóód), *adj.* mad, A 184, 582, 636; mad with anger, D 313; *for wood*, as being mad, madly, furiously, L. 2420; *for pure wood*, for very rage, R. 276; *ten so wood*, ten times as fierce, L. 736; Wode, *def. adj.* mad, T. ii. 1355.

**Woodeth**, *pr. s.* rages, G 467.

**Woodly**, *adv.* madly, A 1301.

**Woodnesse**, *s.* madness, rage, A 2011, 3452.

**Woon** (wòòn), *s.* resource, T. iv. 1181; plenty, abundance, L. 1652; number, L. 2161; retreat, secure place, HF. 1166; *of sorwe woon*, abundance of sorrow, 3. 475; Wones, *pl.* places of retreat, range of buildings, D 2105.

**Woost, Woot**; see **Wite**.

**Wopen**, *pp. of* Wepe.

**Worcher**, *s.* worker, maker, 4. 261.

**Worcheth**, *pr. s.* works, 3. 815.

**Word**, *s.* word, A 304; *good word*, approval, T. v. 1081; *w. by w.*, word by word, D 2244; *at shorte wordes*, briefly, in a word, L. 2462; *hadde the wordes*, was spokesman, I 67.

**Word and ende** (*for* Ord and ende), beginning and end, T. ii. 1495, iii. 702, v. 1669; B 3911.

**Worm-foul**, *s.* birds which eat worms, 5. 505.

**Wort**, *s.* unfermented beer, wort, G 813.

**Wortes**, *pl.* herbs, B 4411, E 226.

**Worthen**, *v.* be, dwell, T. v. 329; to become, 4. 248; Worth, *pr. s.* is, (or, *as fut.*) shall be; (*hence*) Wo worth, it is woe to, it shall be woe to, it is ill for, it shall be ill for, T. ii. 344; Wel worth of dremes ay thise olde wyves, it is well for these old wives as regards dreams, i. e. dreams are all very well for old women, T. v. 379; Wel worth [*not* worthe] of this thing grete clerkes, it is well for great writers as regards this thing, i. e. this thing is all very well for great writers, HF. 53; Worth upon, gets upon, B 1941; Worth up, get up on, mount, T. ii. 1011.

**Wost, Wostow, Wot**; see **Wite**.

**Wouke,** s. week, T. iv. 1278, v. 492.

**Wounde,** s. wound, 1. 79; plague (Lat. *plaga*), I 593; Woundes of Egipte, *pl.* plagues of Egypt (unlucky days so called), 3. 1207.

**Wowe,** ger. to woo, T. v. 1091.

**Wowing,** s. wooing, L. 1553.

**Woxen,** pp. of Wexe.

**Wrak,** s. wreck, B 513.

**Wrak,** pt. s. avenged, T. v. 1468.

**Wrang,** adv. wrongly, amiss (Northern), A 4252.

**Wrastlen,** v. wrestle, B 3456.

**Wrathen,** ger. to render angry, T. iii. 174.

**Wraw,** adj. angry, H 46; Wrawe, peevish, fretful, I 677.

**Wrawnesse,** s. peevishness, fretfulness, I 680.

**Wrecche,** s. sorrowful creature, A 931; wretched man, T. i. 708.

**Wrecche,** adj. wretched, F 1020.

**Wrecchednesse,** s. misery, B 3540; mean act, F 1523; folly, I 34; miserable performance, F 1271; miserable fare, H 171.

**Wreche,** s. vengeance, T. v. 890, 896.

**Wreek,** imper. s. of Wreke.

**Ween,** v. cover, clothe, R. 56; Wreigh, pl. s. covered, hid, T. iii. 1056.

**Wreke,** (wrèkə), v. wreak, avenge, C 857; pr. s. subj. avenge, L. 2340; 2 pr. pl. F 454; Wrak, pt. s. T. v. 1468; Wreken, pp. revenged, F 784; Wroken, pp. T. i. 88.

**Wreker,** s. avenger, 5. 361.

**Wrenches,** s. pl. frauds, stratagems, tricks, G 1081.

**Wreste,** v. constrain, force, T. iv. 1427.

**Wreye,** v. bewray, reveal, A 3503.

**Wrighte,** s. workman, A 614.

**Wringe,** v. squeeze, force a way, HF. 2110; wring, HF. 299; Wrong, pt. s. wrung, pinched, D 492.

**Writ,** s. scripture, A 739.

**Writ, -e, -en;** see **Wryte.**

**Wroght, -e;** see **Werche.**

**Wroken,** pp. of Wreke.

**Wrong,** s.; had wrong, was wrong, 3. 1282.

**Wrong,** adv. astray, A 1267.

**Wrooth** (wròòth), adj. wroth, angry, 3. 513, 519.

**Wrot,** pt. s. wrote, T. i. 655.

**Wroteth,** pr. s. tears with the snout, buries the snout, pokes about, I 157.

**Wrye,** ger. to hide, T. iii. 1569; to disguise, T. i. 329; v. cover, E 887.

**Wrye,** v. reveal, discover, flood with light, 4. 91. Variant of **Wreye,** q. v. [It might be better to read *wreye,* and *deye* in l. 90.]

**Wryen,** v. turn aside, 3. 627; ger. to turn, go, T. ii. 906; pt. s. bent, A 3283.

**Wryte,** v. write, A 96; Writ, pr. s. writeth, writes, T. i. 394; Wroot, pt. s. B 725; Wrōt, T. i. 655; Wrĭten, pt. pl. wrote, HF. 1504; Write, 1 pt. s. subj. were to write, B 3843; Wrĭten, pp. written, 2. 43.

**Wrythe,** ger. to turn aside, T. iv. 9; to wriggle out, T. iv. 986; Wrytheth, pr. s. writhes out, throws forth wreaths of smoke (Lat. *torquet*), B 1. m 4. 10; Wryth, pr. s. writhes, wreathes, T. iii. 1231.

**Wyd,** adj. wide, A 491.

**Wyde,** adv. widely, far, T. i. 629.

**Wyde-where,** far and wide, everywhere, B 136.

**Wyf,** s. woman, C 71; wife, 3. 1082; mistress of a household, G 1015; to w., for wife, A 1860; Wyves, pl. women, wives, L. 484.

**Wyfhood,** s. womanhood, B 76.

**Wyflees,** adj. wifeless, E 1236.

**Wyfly,** adv. womanly, wife-like, L. 1737.

**Wyke,** s. week, T. ii. 430, 1273.

**Wyle,** s. wile, plot, T. iii. 1077; subtlety, 5. 215.

**Wyn,** s. wine, A 334; *wyn ape,* H 44; wine which made a man behave like an *ape* (so also *lion-wine, pig-wine, sheep-wine*).

**Wynt,** pr. s. turns, directs, L. 85; Wond, pt. s. wound, L. 2253.

**Wyr,** s. bit, L. 1205.

**Wys,** adj. wise, prudent, A 68; to make it wys, to make it a subject for deliberation, to hesitate, A 785.

**Wyse,** s. way, manner, L. 20.

**Wyser,** adj. wiser, one wiser than you, L. 2634.

**Wyte,** s. blame, reproach, G 953; *yow to wyte,* for a blame to you, i. e. laid to your charge, R. 1541.

**Wyte,** ger. to blame, T. i. 825 (understand *is* before *nought*); Wyten, v. accuse, I 1016.

## Y.

**Y-,** a prefix used especially with the pp., like the A. S. ge- and G. ge-. See below. It also occurs in the infinitive, as in *y-finde, y-here, y-knowe, y-see, y-thee.*

It also occurs in the adjective *y-sene*. For further information, see under the forms of the infinitive mood; e. g. for the infin. of *y-bake*, see **Bake**.

**Yaf**; *pt. s. of* Yeve, to give.

**Yald**, *pt. s. of* Yelden, to yield.

**Yare**, *adj.* ready, L. 2270.

**Yate**, *s.* gate, T. ii. 617.

**Yave**; see **Yeve**.

**Y-bake**, *pp.* baked, L. 709.

**Y-banisht**, *pp.* banished, L. 1863.

**Y-barred**, *pp.* barred, R. 480.

**Y-bathed**, *pp.* bathed, T. iv. 815.

**Y-bedded**, *pp.* put to bed, T. v. 346.

**Y-been**, *pp.* been, B 4487.

**Y-benched**, *pp.* furnished with benches, L. 98 *a.*

**Y-beten**, *pp.* beaten, T. i. 741; beaten, forged, A 2162; formed in beaten gold, A 979; struck, coined, L. 1122.

**Y-blent**, *pp.* blinded, R. 1610; A 3808; deceived, 3. 647.

**Y-blessed**, *pp.* blessed, B 4638.

**Y-bleynt**, *pp.* blenched, turned aside, A 3753.

**Y-blowe**, *pp.* blown, T. i. 384.

**Y-boren**, *pp.* born, C 704, E 626; Y-bore, born, E 158; borne, carried, T. v. 1650; moved, F 326.

**Y-bought**, *pp.* bought, T. i. 810.

**Y-bounden**, *pp.* bound, 5. 268.

**Y-bowed**, *pp.* diverted, B 4. p 6. 179.

**Y-brend**, *pp.* burnt, G 318; Y-brent, HF. 940.

**Y-broght**, *pp.* brought, L. 938.

**Y-brouded**, *pp.* embroidered, L. 159 *a*. Cf. A. S. *brogden*, pp. of *bregdan*.

**Y-caught**, *pp.* fixed, 3. 838.

**Y-chaped**, *pp.* furnished with chapes or metal caps (which were placed at the end of the sheath), A 366.

**Y-cheyned**, *pp.* chained, 17. 14.

**Y-clad**, *pp.* clad, clothed, R. 890.

**Y-clawed**, *pp.* clawed, torn, D 1731.

**Y-clenched**, *pp.* clinched, riveted, A 1991.

**Y-cleped**, *pp.* called, A 410, 867, G 129, H 2; invoked, T. iv. 504; summoned, B 2435; named, A 3313; Y-clept, called, A 376.

**Y-comen**, *pp.* come, HF. 1074; *ycome aboute*, come about, passed, B 3364.

**Y-córouned**, *pp.* crowned, L. 219.

**Y-corumped**, *pp.* corrupted, B 5. p 2. 28.

**Y-corven**, *pp.* cut, G 533; Y-corve, A 2013. See **Kerve**.

**Y-coupled**, *pp.* coupled, wedded, E 1219.

**Y-coyned**, *pp.* coined, C 770.

**Y-crased**, *pp.* cracked, broken, 3. 324.

**Y-cristned**, *pp.* baptized, B 240.

**Y-crowe**, *pp.* crowed, A 3357.

**Y-dampned**, *pp.* condemned, L. 2030.

**Y-darted**, *pp.* pierced with a dart, T. iv. 240.

**Ydel**, *adj.* idle, empty, vain, B 2778; *in ydel*, in vain, B 2494, F 867.

**Y-dight**, *pp.* decked, A 3205.

**Ydolastre**, *s.* idolater, B 3377.

**Ydole**, *s.* idol. 3. 626.

**Y-doon**, *pp.* done, B 4610; over, E 1894.

**Y-drad**, *pp.* dreaded, T. iii. 1775.

**Y-drawe**, *pp.* drawn, A 396, 944.

**Y-dressed**, *pp.* dressed, arranged, set, E 381.

**Y-dronke**, *pp.* drunk, B 2601.

**Y-dropped**, *pp.* bedropped, covered with drops, A 2884.

**Yë**, *s.* eye, R. 296; *at yë*, at eye, to sight, evidently, G 964, 1059; Saugh with yë, perceived, A 3415; Yën, *pl.* eyne, eyes, B 3260, 3392.

**Ye**, *adv.* yea, verily, T. i. 534.

**Yeddinges**, *pl.* songs, A 237.

**Yede**, *pt. s.* walked, went, G 1141, 1281. A. S. *ëode.*

**Yeer**, *s.* year, A 347; Yere (*in phr.* many a yere), B 132; Yeres ende, year's end, D 916; Yeer by yere, year after year, B 1688; Fro yeer to yere, 5. 321; Yeer, (*archaic*) *pl.* A 82; Yeres, (*new*) *pl.* B 463.

**Yef**, *imp. s.* give, T. v. 308.

**Yeftes**, *pl.* gifts, T. iv. 392.

**Yelden**, *ger.* to yield up, D 912; to yield to, pay, D 1811; Yelt, *pr. s.* yields, T. i. 385; Yelde, *pr. s. subj.* requite, D 1772, 2177; Yald, *pt. s.* afforded, B 4. m 7. 25; Yeld, *imp. s.* restore, C 189; Yolden, *pp.* yielded, T. i. 801; submissive, T. iii. 96; Yeldinge, *pres. pt.* giving, B 2994.

**Yeldhalle**, *s.* guild-hall, A 370.

**Yelding**, *s.* produce, lit. 'yielding,' A 596.

**Yelleden**, *pt. pl.* yelled, B 4579.

**Yelpe**, *ger.* to boast, A 2238; *pr. pl.* prate, T. iii. 307.

**Yelwe**, *adj.* yellow, R. 310.

**Yeman**, *s.* yeoman, A 101.

**Yemanly**, *adv.* in a yeomanlike manner, A 106.

**Yen** = Yën, *pl.* eyes; see **Yë.**

**Y-ended**, *pp.* ended, R. 1315.

**Yerd**, *s.* yard, garden, R. 492.

**Yerde**, *s.* rod, stick, T. i. 257, 740; switch,

A 149; rod, 'caduceus,' A 1387; yard (in length), A 1050; correction, E 22.

Yerne, *adj.* eager, brisk, lively, A 3257.

Yerne, *adv.* eagerly, soon, D 993; briskly, quickly, glibly, 5. 3; C 398; *as y.*, very soon, HF. 910.

Yerne, *ger.* to yearn for, to be longed for, T. iv. 198; *v.* desire, T. iii. 152.

Yeten (yéétən), *v.* pour, shed, B 1. m 7. 1. A.S. *gēotan.*

Yeve, *v.* give, A 232; Yevest, 2 *pr. s.* givest, F 1033; Yeveth, *pr. s.* E 93; Yeve, *pr. s. subj.* may (he) give, E 30; Yaf, 1 *pt. s.* gave, E 861; Yaven, *pt. pl.* G 415; Yeven, *pt. pl. subj.* would give, HF. 1708; Yeven, *pp.* given, A 1086; devoted, 7. 111.

Yeveres, *pl.* givers, I 791.

Yeving, *s.* giving, 18. 37; what one gives, 4. 230.

Yexeth, *pr. s.* hiccoughs, A 4151.

Y-fallen, *pp.* fallen, B 3166; happened, G 1043; having befallen, C 496.

Y-fare, *pp.* gone, T. iii. 577.

Y-felawshiped, *pp.* made companions, B 2. p 6. 91.

Y-fere, together, B 394, E 1113, G 380. Cf. Infere.

Y-fet, *pp.* fetched, F 174, G 1116.

Y-fetered, *pp.* fettered, A 1229.

Y-fethered, *pp.* feathered, R. 951.

Y-feyned, *pp.* feigned, invented, L. 327 *a*; evaded, E 529.

Y-ficched, *pp.* fixed, B 4. p 6. 125.

Y-finde, *v.* find, F 470; Y-founde, *pp.* L. 1668.

Y-flit, *pp.* moved, whirled along, B 1. m 2. 14.

Y-folowed, *pp.* followed, 3. 390.

Y-forged, *pp.* made, A 3256.

Y-formed, *pp.* created, HF. 490.

Y-fostred, *pp.* fostered, sustained, E 213; brought up, A 3946.

Y-founde, *pp.* found, A 1211, 3514.

Y-founded, *pp.* set on a foundation, 5. 231; based, 3. 922.

Y-freten, *pp.* eaten, devoured, L. 1951.

Y-frounced, *adj.* wrinkled, R. 155.

Y-fyned, *adj.* refined, delicately formed, R. 1696.

Y-fyred, *pp.* fired, L. 1013.

Y-gerdoned, *pp.* rewarded, B 5. p 3. 182.

Y-geten, *pp.* gotten, procured, A 3564.

Y-glased, *pp.* glazed, 3. 323.

Y-glewed, *pp.* fixed tight, F 182.

Y-glosed, *pp.* flattered, H 34.

Y-goon, *pp.* gone, L. 2206, 2213.

Y-graunted, *pp.* granted, C 388.

Y-grave, *pp.* dug up, cut, L. 204; dug out, 3. 164; engraved, graven, A 3796; buried, D 496.

Y-greved, *pp.* harmed, A 4181.

Y-grounde, *pp.* ground, A 3991; sharpened, pointed, A 2549.

Y-grounded, *pp.* grounded, 3. 921.

Y-growen, *pp.* grown, A 3973.

Y-halwed, *pp.* consecrated, L. 1871.

Y-harded, *pp.* hardened, F 245.

Y-hated, *pp.* hated, HF. 200.

Y-hent, *pp.* seized, caught, C 868.

Y-herd, *pp. as adj.* covered with hair, A 3738.

Y-here, *v.* hear, T. iv. 1313.

Y-heried, *pp.* praised, T. ii. 973.

Y-hevied, *pp.* weighed down, B 5. m 5. 26.

Y-hid, *pp.* hid, G 317.

Y-hight, *pp.* called, T. v. 541.

Y-holde, *pp.* esteemed to be, A 2374; celebrated, A 2958; considered, C 602; indebted, L. 1954; continued, E 1932; restrained, HF. 1286.

Y-hurt, *pp.* hurt, A 2709.

Y-japed, *pp.* jested, T. i. 318.

Yif, *conj.* if, L. 2059, 2312.

Yif, *imp. s.* give; *see* Yive.

Yift, *s.* gift, 3. 247, 695, 1270.

Yilden, *ger.* to repay, B 5. p 1. 14; Yildeth, *pr. s.* yields, produces, B 4. m 6. 31. See Yelden.

Y-joigned, *pp.* joined, B 2. p 6. 93.

Yis, yes, L. 517.

Yisterday, yesterday, R. 1040.

Yit, yet, L. 4, 106.

Yive, *ger.* to give, A 225; Yiveth, *pr. s.* gives, 18. 38; *pr. s. subj.* may (he) give, 3. 683; Yiven, *pp.* given, granted, 3. 765.

Yiver, *s.* giver, L. 2228.

Y-kempt, *pp.* combed, A 4369.

Y-kist, *pp.* kissed, T. iv. 1689.

Y-kneled, *pp.* kneeled, L. 1232.

Y-knet, *pp.* knotted, tightly bound, T. iii. 1734; Y-knit, joined, 6. 32.

Y-knowe, *v.* know, F 887; recognize, HF. 1336; discern, D 1370; *pp.* known, 3. 392.

Y-korven, *pp.* cut, B 1801.

Y-koud, *pp.* known well, 3. 666.

Y-lad, *pp.* carried (in a cart), A 530.

Y-laft, *pp.* left, A 2746; left behind, F 1128.

Y-laid, *pp.* laid, L. 2141.

Y-lain, *pp.* lain, remained, L. 2410.

Yle, *s.* isle, island, HF. 416, 440; region, province, L. 1425.

Y-lent, *pp.* lent, G 1406.
Y-lered, *pp.* educated, T. i. 976.
Y-let, *pp.* hindered, obstructed, B 5. p 4. 34.
Y-leten, *pp.* left, allowed, B 4. p 4. 308.
Y-leyd, *pp.* laid, A 3568.
Y-liche, *adj.* alike, similar, L. 389.
Y-liche, *adv.* alike, equally, A 2526.
Y-lissed, *pp.* eased, T. i. 1089.
Y-lived, *pp.* lived, T. v. 933.
Y-logged, *pp.* lodged, B 4181.
Y-loren; *pp.* lost, L. 26 ; Y-lorn, *pp.* lost, T. iv. 1250.
Y-lost, *pp.* lost, HF. 183.
Y-loved, *pp.* loved, T. i. 594.
Y-lyk, *adj.* like, A 592 ; alike, A 2734 ; Y-lyke, like, A 1539.
Y-lyke, *adv.* alike, equally, L. 55, 731.
Y-lymed, *pp.* caught (as birds with bird-lime), D 934.
Y-maad, *pp.* made, caused, HF. 691.
Ymagéries, *pl.* carved work, HF. 1190, 1304.
Ymagined, *pp.* considered, intentional, I 448.
Y-maked, *pp.* made, L. 122, 222.
Y-marked, *pp.* set down, marked out, planned, HF. 1103.
Y-masked, *pp.* enmeshed, T. iii. 1734.
Y-medled, *pp.* mingled, T. iii. 815.
Y-mel, *prep.* among (Northern), A 4171.
Y-ment, *pp.* intended, HF. 1742.
Y-met, *pp.* met, A 2624 ; Y-mette, *as pl. adj.* met, B 1115.
Y-meynd, *pp.* mixed, mingled, A 2170.
Y-moeved, *pp.* moved, B 4. m 6. 7.
Ympne, *s.* lyric poem (lit. hymn), L. 422.
Y-mused, *pp.* mused, reflected, HF. 1287.
Y-nempned, *pp.* named, I 598.
Y-nogh, *adj.* enough, sufficient, A 373, 3149 ; Y-now, G 1018 ; Y-nowe, *pl.* 5. 233.
Y-nogh, *adv.* enough, sufficiently, 6. 13 ; Y-nough, R. 247.
Y-nome, *pp.* caught, overcome, T. i. 242 ; taken, L. 2343.
Y-norisshed, *pp.* educated, T. v. 821.
Y-offred, *pp.* offered, dedicated, L. 932.
Yok, *s.* yoke, E 113, 1285.
Yolde, -n ; see Yelden.
Yolle, *pr. pl.* cry aloud, A 2672.
Yomanrye, *s.* yeomanry, A 3949.
Yon, *adj.* yon, A 4178.
Yond, *adv.* yonder, A 1099.
Yong, *adj.* young, A 79.

Yonghede, *s. dat.* youth, R. 351.
Yore, *adv.* formerly, of old, B 174, 272 ; for a long time, a long while, A 1813 ; long ago, long, 1. 150 ; *yore agon,* long ago, 5. 17 ; *yore ayo,* A 3437 ; *ful y.,* very long ago, 7. 243, 346 ; *of tyme y.,* of old time, F 963.
Youling, *s.* loud lamentation, A 1278.
Y-painted, *pp.* painted, R. 892.
Y-passed, *pp.* passed, R. 380 ; past, E 1892.
Y-payed, *pp.* paid, A 1802.
Y-piked, *pp.* picked over, G 941.
Y-plesed, *pp.* pleased, D 930.
Y-pleyned, *pp.* complained, T. iv. 1688.
Y-pleynted, *pp.* full of complaint, T. v. 1597.
Y-plounged, *pp.* plunged, sunk, B 3. p 11. 122.
Y-plyted, *pp.* pleated, gathered, B 1. p 2. 31.
Ypocras, Hippocrates ; *hence* a kind of cordial, C 306.
Ypocryte, *s.* hypocrite, F 514.
Y-portreyd, *pp.* covered with pictures, R. 897.
Y-porveyed, *pp.* foreseen, B 5. p 3. 45.
Y-prayed, *pp.* invited, E 269.
Y-preised, *pp.* praised, HF. 1577.
Y-preved, *pp.* proved (to be), A 485.
Y-pulled, *pp.* plucked, i. e. with super-fluous hairs plucked out, A 3245.
Y-purveyed, *pp.* foreseen, B 5. p 3. 88.
Y-queynt, *pp.* quenched, A 3754.
Y-quiked, *pp.* kindled, I 536.
Y-quit, *pp.* quit, acquitted, F 673.
Y-raft, *pp.* bereft, snatched away, A 2015 ; reft, robbed, L. 1572.
Yre, *s.* ire, anger, vexation, 1. 30.
Y-red, *pp.* read, T. iv. 799.
Y-reke, *pp.* raked together, A 3882.
Y-rekened, *pp.* accounted, D 367 ; taken into account, F 427.
Yren, *s.* iron, R. 1184.
Yren, *adj.* iron, G 759.
Y-rent, *pp.* taken, T. v. 1654 ; torn, B 844.
Y-ronge, *pp.* rung, told loudly, HF. 1655.
Y-ronne, *pp.* run, A 8, 3893 ; continued, L. 1943 ; run together, A 2693 ; inter-laced, R. 1396 ; clustered, A 2165.
Y-rouned, *pp.* whispered, HF. 2107.
Y-satled, *pp.* settled, E 2405.
Y-sayd, *pp.* said, 3. 270.
Y-scalded, *pp.* scalded, A 2020.
Y-schette, *pp. pl.* shut, B 560.
Yse, *s.* ice, HF. 1130.

**Y-see**, v. behold, T. ii. 354; *imp. s.* see, look, T. ii. 1253; **Y-seyn**, *pp.* seen, L. 2076.

**Y-sene**, *adj.* visible, A 592, F 996; manifest, T. iv. 1607; L. 1394. A.S. *gesēne, gesŷne.*

**Y-set**, *pp.* set, A 4337; placed, 5. 149; set down, F 173; seated, C 392; appointed, A 1635; planted, R. 604.

**Y-seye**, *pp.* seen, HF. 1367; **Y-seyn**, T. v. 448.

**Y-seyled**, *pp.* sailed, B 4289.

**Y-shad**, *pp.* scattered (Lat. *sparsas*), B 3. m 2. 33.

**Y-shaken**, *pp.* quivering, sparkling, B 1. m 3. 17.

**Y-shamed**, *pp.* put to shame, HF. 356.

**Y-shapen**, (*strong*) *pp.* shaped, prepared, B 3420; provided, A 4179; contrived, G 1080; **Y-shaped**, (*weak*) *pp.* prepared, T. iii. 1240.

**Y-shave**, *pp.* shaven, A 690.

**Y-shent**, *pp.* put to shame, severely blamed, D 1312.

**Y-shette**, *pp. pl.* shut, B 2159.

**Y-shewed**, *pp.* shown, T. v. 1251; made manifest, 4. 181.

**Y-shore**, *pp.* shorn, T. iv. 996.

**Y-shove**, *pp.* borne about, L. 726.

**Y-slayn**, *pp.* slain, HF. 159; **Y-slawe**, B 484.

**Y-smite**, *pp.* smitten, wounded, B 3. m 7. 7.

**Y-songe**, *pp.* sung, D 1726; **Y-songen**, L. 270.

**Y-sought**, *pp.* sought, T. iii. 1317.

**Y-sounded**, *pp.* sunk, T. ii. 535.

**Y-sowen**, *pp.* sown, HF. 1488.

**Y-sped**, *pp.* sped, A 4220.

**Y-spended**, *pp.* spent, B 5. p 4. 15.

**Y-sprad**, *pp.* spread, B 1644; **Y-spred**, A 4140.

**Y-spreynd**, *pp.* sprinkled, A 2169.

**Y-spronge**, *pp.* sprung, shot out, R. 718; divulged, HF. 2081.

**Y-stalled**, *pp.* installed, HF. 1364.

**Y-stiked**, *pp.* stuck, A 1565; stabbed, F 1476.

**Y-stint**, *pp.* stopped, D 390.

**Y-stonde**, *pp.* stood, been, T. v. 1612.

**Y-stonge**, *pp.* stung, C 355.

**Y-storve**, *pp.* dead, A 2014.

**Y-strawed**, *pp.* bestrewn, 3. 629.

**Y-strike**, *pp.* struck, 11. 34.

**Y-suffred**, *pp.* suffered, T. v. 415.

**Y-sweped**, *pp.* swept, G 938.

**Y-sworn**, *pp.* sworn, A 1132; sworn (to do it), T. v. 283.

**Y-swowned**, *pp.* swowned, L. 1342.

**Y-take**, *pp.* caught, B 3514; taken, L. 617.

**Y-thanked**, *pp.* thanked, D 2118.

**Y-thee**, v. thrive, T. iv. 439.

**Y-thewed**, *pp.* disposed; *wel y-thewed*, well-conducted, 5. 47; R. 1008.

**Y-thonked**, *pp.* thanked, T. iv. 2.

**Y-throngen**, *pp.* confined, B 2. p 7. 53.

**Y-throwe**, *pp.* thrown, T. iv. 6; cast out, 2. 89.

**Y-told**, *pp.* told, A 3109.

**Y-torned**, *pp.* turned, B 4. m 5. 1.

**Y-travailed**, *pp.* laboured, with difficulty, B 5. p 3. 45.

**Y-trespassed**, *pp.* sinned, B 2609.

**Y-tressed**, *pp.* plaited in tresses, T. v. 810.

**Y-treted**, *pp.* discussed, B 4. p 1. 70.

**Y-tukked**, *pp.* tucked up, L. 982.

**Y-turned**, *pp.* turned, A 1238, 2062.

**Y-twinned**, *pp.* parted, T. iv. 788.

**Yve**, B 4156; *see* Erbe.

**Yvel**, *adj.* ill, evil, T. ii. 1001.

**Yvel**, *adv.* ill, R. 213, 1067.

**Yveles**, *s. pl.* evils, B 2618.

**Yvory**, *s.* ivory, B 2066; **Yvoire**, 3. 946.

**Y-voyded**, *pp.* removed, F 1159.

**Y-war**, *adj.* aware, T. ii. 398.

**Y-warned**, *pp.* warned, B 4422.

**Y-waxen**, *pp.* grown, become, T. v. 275; **Y-waxe**, 3. 1275.

**Y-wedded**, *pp.* wedded, L. 1179.

**Y-went**, *pp.* gone, HF. 976.

**Y-went**, *pp.* weened, imagined, T. v. 444.

**Y-wet**, *pp.* wetted, A 4155.

**Y-whet**, *pp.* whetted, 7. 212.

**Y-wimpled**, *pp.* provided with a wimple, A 470; covered with a wimple, L. 797.

**Y-wis**, *adv.* certainly, truly, verily, R. 279, 350, 357.

**Y-wist**, *pp.* known, B 5. p 3. 36.

**Y-wonne**, *pp.* gained, T. iv. 1315; won, D 2293; arrived, L. 2427.

**Y-worthe**, *pp.* become, 3. 579.

**Y-wounde**, *pp.* wound, covered up, 12. 18.

**Y-woven**, *pp.* woven, completed, L. 2360.

**Y-woxen**, *pp.* grown, E 1462.

**Y-writen**, *pp.* written, 5. 124, 141.

**Y-writhen**, *pp.* wreathed, wrapped round, R. 160.

**Y-wroght**, *pp.* made, A 196, B 2054; shaped, L. 1173; depicted, 3. 327; ornamented, R. 897; Y-wroghte, *pp. pl.* fashioned, 5. 123.

Y-wroken, *pp.* avenged, 16. 26; Y-wroke, wreaked, T. v. 589.

Y-wronge, *pp.* forced, L. 2527.

Y-wryen, *pp.* hidden, T. iii. 1451; covered, A 2904.

Y-yeve, *pp.* given, T. iii. 1376; Y-yive, T. iii. 1611.

## Z.

Zeles, *pl.* zeal, T. v. 1859.

*Zodia, s. pl.* beasts, A. i. 21. 61.

Zodiac, *s.* zodiac, A. pr. 109. An imaginary belt in the heavens, of the breadth of 12°, along the middle of which runs the ecliptic. The Astrolabe only showed the *northern half* of this belt.

# GLOSSARY TO FRAGMENTS B AND C OF THE ROMAUNT OF THE ROSE.

FRAGMENT B = ll. 1706–5810.
FRAGMENT C = ll. 5811–7698.

THE following Glossary (which includes proper names) is separated from the preceding because Fragments B and C of the Romaunt are not by Chaucer.

Fragment B abounds in Northern words and forms. Words in Fragment C have 'C' prefixed to the number of the line.

——◆◆——

**A**, *v.* (to) have, 4322.
**Abandoun :** *in abandoun*, fully, without stint, 2342.
**Abawed**, *pp.* amazed, 3646; Abawid, 4041.
**Abaysshed**, *pp.* cast down, 3370.
**Abey**, *v.* (*for* Abeye), suffer (for it), pay (for it), C 6713. See **Abye**.
**Abiding**, *s.* delay, 2222.
**Abit**, *s.* habit, dress, religious dress, 4914.
**Abit, Abood;** see **Abyde**.
**Abood**, *s.* delay, C 7697.
**Aboven**, *adv.* in luck, 4352.
**Abraide**, *v.* start up, break forth, 5156; Abraid, 1 *pt. s.* awoke, 1806; Abreyde, *pt. s.* broke out, 3967.
**Abrede**, *adv.* abroad, 2563.
**Absente**, *pr. s. subj.* abstain, refrain, 4911.
**Abstinence-Streyned**, i.e. Constrained Abstinence (personified), C 6341, 7366.
**Abyde**, *ger.* to await, 4910; *v.* expect, 5329; watch for, 4913; Abit, *pr. s.* dwells, 4977, 4989; stays, 5012; Abood, 1 *pt. s.* endured, waited, 3694.
**Abye**, *v.* pay for, C 5888, 5976; Abyeth, *pr. s.* C 7642.
**Accord**, 1 *pr. s.* agree to, 2083; Accorded, *pt. pl.* agreed, C 5815; *pp.* reconciled, C 5846.

**A-cold**, *adj.* cold, chilly, 2658.
**Acoye**, *v.* quiet, allay, 3564.
**Acquyte**, *v.* defray the expense, pay for, C 6742.
**Ado** (*for* at do), to do, 5080.
**A-fere**, *adv.* on fire, 4073.
**Afered**, *pp.* afraid, 3604.
**Affray**, *s.* terror, 3866; fear, 2034.
**Affrayed**, *pp.* frightened, 3113.
**Affye**, *v.* trust, 3155.
**Aforn**, *adv.* formerly, 3952.
**Aftir**, *prep.* according to, 2255.
**Afyne**, *adv.* completely, 3690.
**Agast**, *adj.* afraid, C 6106.
**Ageyn-coming**, *s.* returning, 2518.
**Ageyns**, *prep.* in comparison with, 5536.
**Agilte**, *pr. s.* sinned against, offended, C 5833, 6784; Agiltest, 2 *pt. s.* C 7572.
**Ago**, *pp.* gone, 2932.
**A-gree**, *adv.* in good part, 4349.
**A-greef**, *adv.* in bad part; *take not agreef*, take it not amiss, C 7573.
**Aken**, *v.* ache, C 6908.
**Al**, *conj.* although, 1754.
**Al-day**, *adv.* continually, 2484.
**Alder**, *adj. gen. pl.* of (us) all, C 6948.
**Alderfirst**, *adv.* first of all, C 7505.
**Alegged**, *pt. pl.* alleviated, 1768. See **Allege**.
**Aleggement**, *s.* alleviation, 1890, 1923.

**Algate,** *adv.* alway, always, 5157, C 7477; at any rate, C 7152.
**Allege,** *v.* exempt (lit. alleviate), C 6626; Alleggith, *pr. s.* alleviates, 2588.
**Allegeaunce,** *s.* alleviation, 1871.
**Allowe,** *v.* approve of, value, 5186.
**Almesse,** *s.* alms, C 6624.
**Al-only,** *adv.* alone, C 5819.
**Alosed,** *pp.* noted, famed, 2354.
**Al-out,** *adv.* altogether, 2101, 2935.
**Al-outerly,** *adv.* utterly, C 6302, 7663.
**Alowe,** *v.* accept, approve of, 5175.
**Also,** *conj.* as, C 6767.
**Amende,** *v.* advance, succeed, C 5876.
**Among,** *adv.* sometimes, 2325, 3241, 3304.
**Amourettes,** *s. pl.* sweethearts, 4755.
**Amyas,** a curious error; for At Myas, i. e. at Meaux, 3826. F. text, *a Miaus.*
**And,** *conj.* if, 2051, 4441.
**Anger,** *s.* pain, anguish, 1877; Angres, *pl.* torments, 2554, 3789.
**Angerly,** *adv.* cruelly, 3511.
**Angre,** *ger.* to vex, 3526.
**Angry,** *adj.* cruel, 2628, 3265.
**Anguissous,** *adj.* anxious, 1755.
**Anker,** *s.* an anchoress, a female recluse shut up either in a cell attached to a church, or living under a religious rule in her own house, C 6348.
**Anon-right,** *adv.* straightway, 1778.
**Anoy,** *s.* discomfort, pain, vexation, 1919, 2099, 4404.
**Anoynt,** *pp.* anointed, 1888.
**Apaired,** *pt. s.* injured, C 7522.
**Apayed,** *pp.* satisfied, 2854, 5631.
**Aperceyved,** *pt. s.* perceived, C 6312.
**Aperceyving,** *s.* perception, C 6318.
**Apert,** *adj.* open, obvious, C 6621.
**Apostlis newe,** i. e. the preaching friars, C 6270.
**Apparence,** *s.* mere outward appearance, 5550; evidence, C 7660.
**Apparent,** *adj.* distinct, 2583.
**Appert,** *adj.* open, C 6150. See Apert.
**Appose,** *v.* oppose, C 6555, 7146. F. text, *oposer.*
**A-queynt,** *pp.* acquainted, 3080.
**Aqueyntable,** *adj.* affable, 2213.
**Arace,** *v.* pull out, 1752.
**Arblasters,** *s. pl.* men with crossbows, 4196.
**Aresóneth,** *pr. s.* reasons with, argues, C 6220.
**Arest,** *s.* rest (for a spear), C 7561.
**Arette,** *v.* impute, 3327.
**Areyse,** *v.* raise up, 4361; rouse, C 7159.
**A-rowe,** *adv.* in a row, C 7606.
**Ascape,** *v.* escape, get out of the difficulty, C 6515.

**Asker,** *s.* one who begs, C 6674.
**A-slope,** *adv.* aside, awry, 4464.
**Assay,** *s.* attempt, 3449; quality, temper, 4350.
**Assayed,** *pp.* tried, proved, 2688.
**Asseth,** a sufficiency, 5600.
**Assoile,** *v.* absolve, C 6364; *pp.* explained, C 6557.
**Assoiling,** *s.* absolving, C 6412.
**Assured,** *pp.* secured, 4309.
**Astat,** *s.* state, plight, 2416; Astate, condition, 4672, C 6856.
**Astoned,** *pp.* astonished, 3859.
**A-sundir,** *adv.* diversely, 4477.
**A-swone,** in a swoon, 1736.
**At,** *prep.* at the hands of, from, C 6870; At al, at all points, 5249; *at leeste way,* at least, C 5827; *at wordis fewe,* in a few words, briefly, 2129.
**Attendith,** *pr. s.* attaches itself, appertains, 5309.
**Attour,** *s.* array, 3718.
**Augustins,** *s. pl.* Austin Friars, C 7461.
**Aumenere,** *s.* purse for alms, 2271.
**Auntre,** *v. refl.* venture, 2495.
**Avale,** *v.* descend, 1803.
**Avaunced,** *pp.* promoted, C 6951; helped, 3468.
**Avaunt,** *adv.* in advance, forward, 3959, 4790.
**Avaunt,** *v. refl.* boast, 4788.
**Avauntage,** *s.* profit, 5808.
**Avenaunt,** *adj.* becoming, seemly, 2058; pleasant, 3679; condescending, 4622.
**Aventure,** *s.* chance, fortune, fate, 2118, 4376; case, C 7308.
**Avouterye,** *s.* adultery, 4954.
**Avysed,** 1 *pt. s. refl.*; Avysed me, applied myself, 1807.
**Awayte,** *s.* ambush, 4497.
**Awayted,** *pp.* watched; *awayted with,* watched by, 3066.
**Axe,** *v.* ask, C 6559.
**Ayeines,** *prep.* against, C 7178.

## B.

**Bachilere,** *s.* young knight, 2828.
**Bagge,** *s.* purse, C 6834.
**Baillye,** *s.* custody, jurisdiction, 4217; enclosure, C 7574.
**Balaunce,** *s.* suspense, 4667.
**Balis,** *s. pl.* troubles, sorrows, 4441.
**Bane,** *s.* death, 4491.
**Baren,** *pt. pl.* bare, C 6243.
**Baronage,** *s.* the assembly of barons, C 5812.
**Bataile,** *s.* host, C 5849; *pl.* battalions, C 7348.

Batayled, *pp.* battlemented, 4200.

Bate, *s.* strife, 4235.

Baud, *adj.* jolly (lit. bold), 5674.

Bayly, *s.* bailiff, C 6218.

Beau-sire, *s.* fair sir, C 6053.

Bede, *v.* stretch out (lit. proffer), 1710.

Bede, *pt. s. subj.* might pray, C 7374.

Bedels, *s. pl.* officers, C 6812.

Begger, *s.* Beguin, hence, mendicant, C 7282; Beggers, Beguins, C 7256.

Begyne, *s.* Beguine, C 7368.

Bemes, *s. pl.* trumpets, C 7605.

Berafte, *pt. pl. subj.* should deprive, C 6669.

Bern, *s.* barn, 5589.

Besaunt, *s.* bezant, 5592.

Besinesse, *s.* diligence, 3624.

Bestial, *adj.* stupid, C 6716.

Bete, *pr. s. subj.* cure, 4441.

Bialacoil, i. e. Bial Acoil, Fair Reception, 2984, 2999, 3011.

Bigoon, *adj.*; *wel bigoon*, well off, 5533.

Bigyns, *s. pl.* Béguines, C 6861.

Biheest, *s.* promise, 4446, 4474.

Bihote, *v.* promise, 4446.

Bihove, *s. dat.* behoof, 2964.

Bilefte, 1 *pt. s.* remained, 3360.

Bimene, *imp. s. refl.* bemoan thyself, 2667.

Biset, *pt. s.* employs, 5262.

Bishet, *pp.* shut up (in prison), 4488.

Bit, *pr. s.* abides, 5330.

Bitaught, *pt. s.* commended, 4438.

Bitrasshed, *pp.* betrayed, 3910.

Blake, *adj. pl.* black (monks), Benedictines, C 6695.

Blende, *ger.* to blind, to deceive, 3954; Blent, *pp.* deceived, C 6652.

Blered, *pp.* bleared, dimmed, deceived, 3912.

Blinne, *v.* desist from, C 6611.

Blyve, *adv.* quickly; *as bl.*, very quickly, 2799.

Boden, *pp.* commanded, 2721.

Boece, Boethius, 5661.

Book; *the book*, i. e. the Canon Law, C 6385; the Bible, C 6636.

[Borders, *s. pl.* C 6911. *Better reading; for* burdens.]

Bordillers, *s. pl.* brothel-keepers, C 7034.

Borowe, *s.* pledge, C 7331.

Bosarde, *s.* buzzard, 4033.

Bote, *s.* remedy, 1760.

Botes, *s. pl.* boots, 2265, C 7262.

Botoun, *s.* bud, 1721, 1761, 2960.

Bougerons, *s. pl.* sodomites, C 7022.

Bought, *pp.*; *a bought*, to have bought, 4322.

Bountee, *s.* kindness, 3147; goodness, C 6597.

Braide, *ger.* to bestir itself, wake up, C 7128.

Braste, *ger.* to burst, 3186.

Brede, *s.* breadth; *on br.*, abroad, 3635.

Breken, *v.* disobey, 3478.

Brenne, *v.* burn, 2475.

Brenning, *s.* burning, 2727.

Brere, *s.* briar, C 6191.

Brest, *v.* burst, 4107.

Breve, *adj.* short, 2350.

Brimme, *adj.* cruel, 1836.

Brocages, *s. pl.* contracts, C 6971.

Brond, *s.* fire-brand, 3765.

Burdens, *error for* Borders, C 6911.

Burdoun, *s.* staff, cudgel, 3401.

Burnettes, *s. pl.* dresses made of fine woollen cloth dyed brown, 4756.

But-if, *conj.* unless, 1962.

Buxom, *adj.* obedient, pliant, 4419.

By, *prep.* in, C 6616; beside, C 7032.

By and by, in order, 2345; precisely, 4581.

Bye, *v.* buy, pay for, 2052.

Bytinge, *pres. part.* cutting, C 7420.

## C.

Caas, *s.* case, plight, 3371; *pl.* cases, C 6759.

Caleweys, *s. pl.* soft, sweet pears (which came from Cailloux in Burgundy), C 7043.

Calle, *v.* recall, 3974.

Camelyne, *s.* camel's-hair stuff, C 7367.

Can, 1 *pr. s.* (I) know, 4796; *pr. s.* understands, C 5872; Can him no thank, offers him no thanks, 2112: Canst, 2 *pr. s.* feelest, 4399.

Caribdis, Charybdis, 4713.

Carmes, *s. pl.* Carmelites, White Friars, C 7462.

Cas, *s.* occasion, C 7481.

Caste, *v. refl.* apply himself, 2031; Cast, *pr. s.* casts, 4330; considers, 5620; Caste, *pt. s. refl.* set himself, 1860.

Castels in Spayne, castles in the air, 2573.

Casting, *s.* vomit, C 7288.

Catel, *s.* property, 5376.

Cause; *in cause*, to blame, 4525.

Caytif, *s.* poor wretch, 3554.

Chace, *v.* chase away; *do ch.*, caused to be chased away, C 7534.

Chafe, *v.* irritate, 3685.

Chamberere, *s.* chamber-maid, 4935.

Chanoun, *s.* canon, 3278.

**Chapitre,** *s.* chapter, C 6532.

**Chapman,** *s.* trader, 5591.

**Chargid,** *pt. s.* instructed, 2145.

**Chasteleyn,** *s.* castellan, governor of a castle, C 6327.

**Chasteleyne,** *s.* the wife of a chastelain or governor of a castle, 3740.

**Chastye,** 1 *pr. s.* reprove, C 6993.

**Chere,** *s.* countenance, favour, 3952; appearance, 5486, C 6474; delight, 3805.

**Cherete,** *s.* fondness, 3516.

**Chese,** *v.* choose, 4426; Chese . . . hem to, *pr. pl.* choose for themselves, C 6230.

**Chevered,** *pp.* shivered, 1732.

**Chevisaunce,** *s.* resource, remedy, 3337.

**Chevise,** *v.* occupy himself (for me), manage (for me), settle my cause, C 6425.

**Chiche,** *adj.* parsimonious, 5588.

**Chideresse,** *s.* scold, virago, 4266.

**Chinche,** *adj.* mean, avaricious, C 5998. Nasalised form of **Chiche.**

**Chinchy,** *adj.* mean, grudging, niggardly, C 6002.

**Ciergis,** *pl.* wax tapers, C 6248.

**Clarree,** *s.* a sweet liquor consisting of a mixture of wine, clarified honey and various spices, as pepper and ginger, &c., C 5967, 5971.

**Clepe,** *v.* call, C 5907.

**Clipsy,** *adj.* eclipsed, dim, 5349.

**Clomben,** *pp.* climbed up, C 6933.

**Cloos,** *adj.* close, discreet, C 6104.

**Close,** *v.* enclose, 4372.

**Closer,** *s.* enclosure, 4069.

**Cloth,** *s.* dress, C 6345.

**Colour,** *s.* way, manner, C 6282.

**Come,** *s.* coming, C 7628.

**Compas,** *s.* circuit, 1842; circumference, 4183; Compace, perfection, 3208.

**Compassen,** 1 *pr. pl.* study, observe closely, C 6932.

**Complisshen,** *v.* accomplish, 2132.

**Comprende,** *v.* consider, include (in my explanation), C 6633.

**Compte,** *s.* counting, account, 5026.

**Comunably,** *adv.* commonly, usually, C 7237.

**Comunely,** *adv.* publicly, 4801.

**Comuntee,** *s.* community, common possession, 5209.

**Concours,** *s.* course, result, 4360.

**Conestablerye,** *s.* a ward of a castle under the command of a constable, 4218.

**Coninges,** *s. pl.* conies, rabbits, C 7044.

**Conisaunce,** *s.* understanding, knowledge, 5465, 5559; acquaintance, 4668.

**Conjecte,** 1 *pr. pl.* conspire, C 6928.

**Conne,** 2 *pr. s. subj.* mayst be well instructed, 2315.

**Consequence,** *s.* result, C 6448.

**Consolacioun,** the 'Consolation of Philosophy,' 5661.

**Constreynaunce,** *s.* constraint, C 7438.

**Contene,** *v.* remain, 2641; *refl.* bear himself, 2248; Conteyne, *v.* contain (himself), 4923; Contene, *pr. pl. refl.* maintain themselves, C 6805.

**Contrarie,** *s.* perplexity, 4478.

**Contrarious,** *adj.* hostile, 3354.

**Controve,** *v.* compose songs, 4249; *ger.* to invent, C 7547.

**Contune,** *v.* continue, 4354, 5332.

**Convay,** *ger.* to accompany, 2428.

**Corage,** *s.* mood, temper, 4928.

**Cordileres,** *s. pl.* Franciscans, (so called from wearing a girdle of rope), C 7461.

**Cornewayle,** Cornouaille in Brittany, 4250.

**Corumpable,** *adj.* corruptible, 4856.

**Cos,** *s.* kiss, 3663.

**Cost,** *s.* coast, place, 3931; quarter, 2477.

**Cotidien,** *adj.* quotidian, daily; *as s.* a quotidian ague, 2401.

**Couchen,** *pr. pl.* impose, C 6903.

**Countesses,** *s. pl.* C 6860.

**Countours,** *s. pl.* accountants, C 6812.

**Coupe-gorge,** *s.* Cut-throat, C 7422.

**Couth,** *pp.* known, 2000; evident, 4213.

**Coveityse,** *s.* coveting, desire, 4129; covetousness, 5072.

**Covenable,** *adj.* seemly, fitting, suitable, C 6020, 6752; excellent, C 7181.

**Covent,** *s.* convent, 4904, C 7380.

**Coverchief,** *s.* kerchief, head-covering, C 7369.

**Covert,** *adj.* secret, hidden up, C 6149.

**Coverture,** *s.* concealment, 2172.

**Covyne,** *s.* intrigue, secret plan, 3799.

**Coy,** *adj.* quiet, hidden, 4297.

**Crece,** *s.* increase, progeny, 4875. (*Fortened* crece seems to mean destroyed progeny, i. e. abortion.) See crease ( = increase) in the New E. Dict.

**Croce,** *s.* crozier, C 6470.

**Crownet,** *s.* coronet, 3203.

**Cunne,** *v.* shew; *cunne him maugree,* shew him ill-will, 4559; 1 *pr. pl.* can, C 5879; *pr. pl.* know (how), C 6174; *pr. s. subj.* be able, C 5992.

**Cure,** *s.* charge, 1962, C 6562; care, 4222; cause of care, 2456; heed, C 7557; aid, C 6752; jurisdiction, 3540.

**Curious,** *adj.* diligent, zealous, C 6578, 6590.

Customere, *adj.* accustomed, 4936. F. text, *coustumiere.*

Cut, *pr. s.* cuts, C 6198.

## D.

Dagges, *s. pl.* loose tags or shreds of cloth, C 7260. (I can find no exact account of the fastening here referred to; I suppose that the *dagges*, or tape-like strips, had button-holes, through which the *knoppes* or buttons passed.)

Daliaunce, *s.* talk, 2850.

Dampning, *s.* damnation, C 6643.

Dar, *pr. s.* dare, 6049.

Daunce; *the olde d.,* the old game, 4300.

Daungere, *s.* resistance, 1932; reluctance, 2318; power, control, 2051.

Daungerous, *adj.* shy, reluctant, backward, 2312; hard to please, 2824; cruel, 3594, 3727.

Daunte, *v.* conquer, subdue, 3300.

Daunting, *s.* taming, 4032.

Dawed, *pt. s. subj.* would dawn, 2633.

Dawes, *s. pl.* days, 2838, C 6616.

Debonairly, *adv.* graciously, pleasantly, 2382.

Defaute, *s.* lack, 5789.

Defenced, *pp.* defended, 4310.

Defensable, *adj.* helping to defend, 4168.

Defoule, *v.* trample down, C 6000.

Defyle, *v.* bruise, C 7317.

Degree, *s.* rank, C 7214; manner, C 7442.

Deignous, *adj.* disdainful, 3593.

Del, *s.* deal; Dele, bit, least thing, 5139; *not . . a del,* not a whit, C 6897, 7433; *never a del,* not at all, C 6036; *every del,* every whit, C 6017.

Delectacioun, *s.* delight, 4821.

Deles (Northern form), *pr. s.* distributes, 5419.

Deliciously, *adv.* daintily, C 6729.

Deliverly, *adv.* quickly, 1927, 2283, 3005.

Delyces, *s. pl.* pleasures, C 7281.

Demeigne, *s.* possession, ownership, 5586; Demeyne, dominion, rule, 3310.

Demene, *v.* put up with, 5238.

Depart, *v.* divide, 2367, 5279.

Departing, *s.* division, 4613.

Dere, *v.* injure, destroy, 4336; *pp.* 2100.

Desert, *s.* deserving, 4269.

Desperaunce, *s.* desperation, 1872.

Desporte, *ger.* to cheer, to divert, 2014.

Despyt, *s.* aversion, C 5996.

Dever, *s.* endeavour, 5299.

Deviaunt, *adj.* divergent, turned away, 4789.

Devoid, *adj.* free, 4312.

Devoided, *pp.* removed, 2929.

Devyne, *v.* interpret, 3800.

Devys, *s.* disposal, 1974; will, 3621; *by devys,* to judge from her appearance (?), 3205. (F. text, *et a son vis.*)

Deyned, *pt. s. subj.*; *him deyned,* it appeared good to him, C 6950.

Deynous, *adj.* disdainful, 3728.

Deyntee, *s.* value, 2677.

Diffyne, *v.* define, 4807.

Dight, *v.* prepare, 4240.

Discomfit, *pp.* disconcerted, 4067.

Discordaunce, *s.* disagreement, 4715, 5208; discordant melody, 4251.

Discorde, *ger.* to disagree, 4716.

Discreven, 2 *pr. pl.* describe, 4803.

Disdeinous, *adj.* disdainful, C 7412.

Disese, *s.* uneasiness, 5244.

Disese, *ger.* to trouble, 3526.

Disgysen, *v.* apparel, 2250; Disgyse, 1 *pr. s.* disguise, C 6358.

Dishonest, *adj.* unfair, unreasonable, 3442; immodest, 4262.

Disordinat, *adj.* inordinate, 4816.

Dispendith, *pr. pl.* spend, 5681.

Dispitous, *adj.* unmerciful, spiteful, C 6162; malicious, froward, 2212, 3457.

Displesaunce, *s.* displeasure, 3436.

Disport, *s.* delight, 3468; happiness, 2894.

Disrewlily, *adv.* irregularly, 4900.

Disseise, *v.* dispossess, deprive, (F. *des-saisir*), 2076.

Disserve, *v.* deserve, 3093.

Disseyved, *pp.* deceived, C 6628.

Dissolucioun, *s.* dissoluteness, 4898.

Distincte, *v.* distinguish, C 6199.

Distoned, *adj.* out of tune, 4248.

Ditee, *s.* discourse, 5286, 5652.

Divyne, *s.* divinity, C 6488.

Do, *v.* cause; *do make,* cause to be made, 2080; *pr. s. subj.* accomplish, C 5869; Doand (Northern), *pres. part.* doing, 2708; Don, *pp.* put, placed, C 6564.

Dole, *s.* lamentation, mourning, 2956, 4317. O.F. *doel.*

Dolven, *pp.* buried, 4070.

Dom, *s.* dumb, 2220, 2409, 2492.

Dool, *s.* grief, 4480.

Dool, *s.* portion; *halfen dool,* half portion, halving (it), 2364.

Doth, *pr. s.* causes, 2772, 2786, 2790; brings, 5558; gives, 1984.

Double, *adj.* twofold, 1756.

Doublenesse, *s.* double-dealing, duplicity, 2366.

Doun, come down, C 5868.

Dout, *s.* fear, 2102.

Doutable, *adj.* doubtful, 5413; imperilled, unstable, C 6274.

Doute, v. fear, 2023 ; 1 pr. s. 2108 ; 2 pr. pl. 2079.

Douting, s. doubt, C 6074.

Draught, s. draught, bout, act, 4869. F. text, Car maint n'i trairoient ja trait.

Drede, s. doubt ; withouten dr., without doubt, 2199, 2251, C 6214 ; Dread (personified), 3958, 5861.

Drerihed, s. sorrow, 4728.

Dresse, v. prepare, 1773 ; pr. s. subj. refl. set himself, C 6535.

Dreye, adj. dry, 1743.

Drough, pt. s. drew, 1725.

Droune, ger. to be drowned, 4710, 5022.

Druery, s. loyal affection, 5064.

Drye, v. suffer, undergo, 4390 ; endure, 3105 ; ger. to fulfil, C 7484.

Dulle, 1 pr. s. become stupefied, 4792.

Dure, v. last, endure, C 6841.

Duresse, s. severity, 3547, 3570.

Dwelling, s. delay, 2440.

Dyamaunt, s. adamant, 4385.

Dyden, pt. pl. died, C 6245.

Dyne, v. as s. dinner, C 6500.


## E.

Eche, v. add, 1994 ; help, aid, 4618.

Effect, s. reality, 5486.

Eft, adv. again, 1783.

Eftsone, adv. soon afterwards, C 6094 ; Eftsones, C 6649.

Egre, adj. acid, 4179.

Egre, adv. sharply, 5474.

Elde, s. old age, 4885.

Elengenesse, s. solitariness ; hence, sadness, disquietude, C 7406. F. text, soussi.

Elis, s. pl. eels, C 7039.

Elles, adv. otherwise, in all other respects, 3429.

Empressid, pp. pressed, 3691.

Empryse, s. undertaking, care, 2147 ; doings, 3508 ; enterprise, C 5825 ; design, 1972 ; conduct, action, 2186 ; privilege, 2008 ; rule, 4905.

Enchesoun, s. occasion, 2504, 3982, 4242.

Enclyne, v. be subject (to), respect, bow down (to), C 6814.

Encombre, v. disturb, 5434 ; pr. s. importunes, teases, C 6675 ; pr. pl. perplex, 4482 ; pp. annoyed, C 7628.

Enfaunce, s. infancy, youth, 4288.

Enforce, v. compel, C 6407 ; pr. pl. refl. endeavour, C 6275 ; pp. augmented, 4499.

Engendrure, s. procreation, 4849.

Engreveth, pr. s. displeases, 3444.

Enhaunce, ger. to exalt, advance, C 7246.

Enlangoured, adj. faded with langour, pale, C 7399.

Enlumined, pp. illumined, 5344.

Enpryse, s. quickness of movement, 2636. See Empryse.

Enquestes, s. pl. legal inquisitions, C 6977.

Ensure, 1 pr. s. assure, 4850 ; pp. C 7212.

Entayle, s. figure, shape, 3711.

Entencioun, s. attention, 4701 ; intent, C 6258 ; diligence, 2027 ; of e., intentionally, 2976 ; pl. meaning, drift, C 7170.

Entende, v. pay attention, 2153.

Entendement, s. intention, 2188.

Entent, s. mind, 2187 ; purpose, 2488 ; disposition, 5696 ; endeavour, 3906 ; intention, design, C 5811, 5869.

Ententif, adj. diligent, careful, 2022 ; adv. 1720.

Entermete, v.refl. intermeddle, interfere, 2966 ; 1 pr. s. refl. busy (myself with), C 6971.

Entremees, s.pl. entremets, dainty meats, C 6841.

Entremete, v. interfere, C 6635, 7233 ; ger. C 6503 ; ger. refl. C 5946 ; 1 pr. s. intermeddle, interfere, C 6498, 6840 ; pr. s. C 5921.

Enviroun, adv. about, 3203, 4163 ; round about, 4203.

Enviroune, 1 pr. pl. go about, C 7017.

Equipolences, s. pl. equivocations, equivocal expressions, C 7076.

Erke, adj. weary, wearied, 4867.

Ernes, s. ardour, (of love), 4838.

Ernest, s. earnest, pledge, 3680.

Ers, s. posteriors (F. cul), C 7578.

Espleyten, v. perform, execute, C 6174.

Espye, s. spy, 3871.

Establisshing, s. decree, C 6369.

Estate, s. state of life, position, 4901.

Estres, s. pl. recesses, inner parts, 3626.

Existence, s. reality, 5549, C 7470.

Expowne, ger. to expound, C 7172.

Eyth, adj. easy, 3955. A.S. ēað.


## F.

Fable, s. deceitfulness, C 6602.

Fade, adj. pallid, faded, 2399.

Fadome, s. pl. fathoms, 4159.

Failed, pp. as adj. wanting, defective, C 7470.

Fainte, adj. feigned, C 7405.

Fairhede, s. fairness, beauty, 2484.

Fallaces, s. pl. deceits, C 7077.

**Fallith,** *pr. s. impers.* befits, 4025; belongs, C 6976.

**Falsen,** *pr. pl.* deceive, 4833.

**Fand,** *pt. pl.* found, 2707.

**Fard,** *imp. s.* paint, 2285.

**Fardels,** *s. pl.* loads, bundles, 5683.

**Fare,** *s.* welfare, condition, C 6498.

**Fare,** *v.* depart, vanish away, C 6045; *pr. pl.* go, 5564; journey, 5509; *pp.* gone, 2710.

**Faute,** *s.* fault, defect, 3837.

**Fawe,** *adj.* fain, blithe, C 6476.

**Fay,** *s.* faith, 2155, 5106.

**Fee,** *s.* property, fief, C 6044.

**Feers,** *adj.* fierce, 3372.

**Feeste,** *s.* encouragement, 5061.

**Fel,** *adj.* cruel, savage, 2211; harsh, 4028; stern, C 7342; Felle, *pl.* painful, 3789.

**Felde-fare,** *s.* field-fare, 5510.

**Fele,** *adj.* many, 4446, C 6038.

**Fele,** *v.* perceive (smell), 1844.

**Feller,** *adj. comp.* crueller, 4103.

**Felones,** *adj. pl.* evil, wicked, C 6711. *His f.* iangelinges, his evil pratings, his injurious talk. Suggested by F. *Maugre les felonesses jangles* ; where *felonesses* is a plural *adjective* ; see Godefroy.

**Feloun,** *adj.* cruel, C 5998.

**Fere,** *s.* fire, 2471, 5086.

**Fered,** *pp.* fired, inflamed, 5278.

**Fetisly,** *adv.* neatly, perfectly, 2267.

**Fetys,** *adj.* well-made, 2088.

**Feynte,** *adj.* feigned, 5563.

**Feyntyse,** *s.* deceit, guile, 2947, 2998, 3492; evasion, 1971.

**Fiaunce,** *s.* confidence, trust, 5481.

**Fil,** *pt. s.* fell, condescended, 3437; Fille, *pt. pl.* found themselves, C 5813.

**Fit,** *s.* mood, 5197.

**Flawme,** *s.* flame, 3707.

**Flawnes,** *s. pl.* flawns; a dish composed of new cheese, eggs, powdered sugar, coloured with saffron and baked in small tins called 'coffins'; C 4042.

**Flayn,** *pp.* flayed, C 7316. Miswritten *slayn.*

**Flemed,** *pt. s.* exiled, drove into exile, 3052, C 6781. A. S. *flýman.*

**Floytes,** *s. pl.* flutes, 4251.

**Foles,** *gen.* fool's, 5266.

**Foly,** *adj.* foolish, 4299, 5085.

**Fond,** *adj.* foolish, 5367.

**Fonde,** *v.* attempt, 5858.

**Foole,** *adj.* foolish, C 7539.

**Foon,** *pl.* foes, 5552, C 6940.

**Foote,** *v.* dance formally, 2323.

**Foot-hoot,** *adv.* instantly, 3827.

**For,** *prep.* to prevent, 4229; for fear of, 2365; on account of, 2190.

**Forboden,** *pp.* forbidden, C 6616.

**Force,** *s.* ; *I yeve no force,* I care not, 4602 ; *of f.,* necessarily, 1796.

**Fordone,** *pp.* undone, 4339.

**Fordrive,** *pp.* scattered, 3782.

**Forewardis,** forwards ; *hennes f.,* henceforward, C 7304.

**Forfare,** *v.* perish, 5388, 5778.

**For-ofte,** *adv.* very often, 4876.

**For-peyned,** *pp.* distressed, 3693.

**Forsake,** *v.* refuse, 2822; withstand, 1876.

**Forstere,** *s.* forester, C 6329.

**Fortened,** *pp.* destroyed, 4875. (Or perhaps 'obstructed'; cf. A. S. *fortýnan,* to shut up.) See Crece.

**Forthenke,** *v.* rue, repent, 3957, 4060.

**Forthy,** *conj.* because ; *not f.,* not on that account, (*perhaps*) nevertheless, 4509.

**Forwandred,** *pp.* spent with wandering, 3336.

**Forwardis,** *s. pl.* agreements, C 7303.

**Forwerreyd,** *pp.* utterly defeated, 2564.

**Forwery,** *adj.* tired out, 3336.

**For-why,** wherefore, 1743.

**Forwoundid,** *pp.* sorely wounded, 1830.

**Foryet,** *v.* forget, 3243 ; *pr. s.* C 6538.

**Foryeve,** *ger.* to abandon, give up, 3438.

**Fraunchyse,** *s.* liberty, 4906; nobility, 2007; generosity, 3003; Bounty, 3501; Freedom, C 5865.

**Frere,** *s.* friar, C 7377; Friar Wolf, C 6424.

**Freres Prechours,** *s. pl.* preaching friars, i.e. the Prechours, or Dominican friars, C 7458.

**Fret,** *pp.* fretted, adorned, 3204; set, 4705.

**Fretted,** *pp.* furnished, lit. ornamented, C 7259.

**Frouncen,** *pr. pl.* shew wrinkles, C 7261; Frounced, *pp.* wrinkled, 3137.

**Fyne,** *v.* cease, 1797 ; *pr. pl. subj.* end, depart, 5356.

## G.

**Gabbeth,** *pr. s.* speaks falsely, lies, C 6700.

**Gabbing,** *s.* lying, C 7602, 7612.

**Gadring,** *s.* accumulation, 5782.

**Garisoun,** *s.* healing, 3248 ; garrison, 4279.

**Garnement,** *s.* dress, 2256.

**Garnisoun,** *s.* fortress, 4204.

**Gate,** *s.* way, wise, 3332, 5167, 5230 (Northern).

**Gentilnesse,** *s.* kindness, 4605; good breeding, 2005; nobility, 5237.

**Gerner,** *s.* garner, C 5988.

**Gesse** ; *withoute gesse,* doubtless, 2817.

**Geten,** *pp.* gotten, 5701.

**Geting,** *s.* obtaining, attainment, 3284.

**Gibbe,** Gib (Gilbert), a cat, C 6204.

**Ginne,** *s.* warlike engine, 4176.

**Ginneth,** *pr. s.* begins, 2154.

**Gisarme,** *s.* a weapon bearing a scythe-like blade fixed on a shaft and provided also with a spear-point like a bayonet, C 5978.

**Giterne,** *ger.* to play on the guitar, 2321.

**Glose,** *v.* flatter, 5097; *pp.* explained, C 6890.

**Gloumbe,** *v.* frown, look glum, 4356.

**Gnede,** *s.* stingy person, C 6002. (Mis-written *grede.*)

**Go,** *pp.* gone, 2423; empty, C 6834.

**Gonfanoun,** *s.* gonfalon, banner, 2018.

**Gospel Perdurable,** The Everlasting Gospel, C 7102.

**Graithe,** *v.* dress, array, C 7368.

**Graunt mercy,** best thanks, C 7504.

**Gree,** (1) *s.* way (lit. grade); *in no maner gree,* in no kind of way, 5743.

**Gree,** (2) *s.* favour; *atte gree,* with favour, 4574; *take at gree,* accept with a good will, in *gree,* in good part, 2306.

**Grete,** 1 *pr. s.* weep, lament, 4116 (Northern).

**Greves,** *s. pl.* thickets, 3019.

**Groffe,** *adv.* face downward, 2561.

**Groine,** *pr. s. subj.* grumble, murmur, C 7049.

**Grucchen,** *pr. pl. subj.* grumble at, begrudge, C 6465.

**Grucching,** *s.* refusal, C 6439.

**Grype,** *v.* seize, C 5983.

**Guerdoning,** *s.* reward, 2380, C 5908.

**Gyler,** *s.* beguiler, 5759.

**Gype,** *s.* frock; perhaps a smock-frock (alluding to the numerous gathers in the front of it), C 7262.

## H.

**Ha,** *v.* have, 5569.

**Hade,** 2 *pt. s.* haddest, 2400.

**Halp,** *pt. s.* helped, 1911.

**Halt,** *pr. s. refl.* considers himself, 4901; keeps, C 7032.

**Hardement,** *s.* courage, 1827, 2487, 3392.

**Harlotes,** *s. pl.* rascals, ribalds, C 6068.

**Harneis,** *s.* armour, gear, C 7477.

**Harneys,** *v. refl.* dress, equip thyself, 2647.

**Hat,** *adj.* hot, 2398.

**Hatter,** *adj. comp.* hotter, more hotly, 2475.

**Haunt,** *v.* practise, 4868; *ger.* to haunt, frequent, C 6601; *pr. s. subj.* practise, C 7029.

**Haunting,** *s.* haunt, abode, C 6081.

**Hauteyn,** *adj.* haughty, C 6101; *fem.* 3739.

**Havoir,** *s.* having, 4720.

**Haye,** *s.* hedge, 2971, 2987.

**Hele,** *v.* conceal, 2858; *ger.* 2522; *pr. pl.* C 6882.

**Hele,** *s.* health, 4721.

**Hem,** *pron.* them, 2218.

**Hemmes,** *s. pl.* phylacteries, C 6912.

**Hend,** *adj.* ready, useful, 3345.

**Hente,** *ger.* to seize, 3364; *pt. s.* 1730, 4092; *pt. pl.* snatched, C 7136; *pp.* plucked, C 7644.

**Herber,** *imp. pl.* take up your abode, C 7586; 2 *pt. s.* didst harbour, 5107.

**Herbergere,** *s.* host, entertainer, C 7585; *pl.* 5000.

**Herberwe,** *s.* shelter, lodging, C 6201, 7495.

**Herberwe,** *v.* shelter, lodge, C 6145.

**Herde,** *s.* shepherd, C 6453; *pl.* C 6561.

**Herie,** *pr. pl.* honour, praise, C 6241. A.S. *herian.*

**Hertly,** *adj.* true-hearted, 5433.

**Het,** *pp.* heated, 3709.

**Heten,** *v.* promise, C 6299.

**Hight,** *pr. s.* is named, C 6341; *pp.* promised, 2803.

**Hoked,** *adj.* hooked, furnished with hooks, 1712; barbed, 1749.

**Hole,** *adj.* whole, complete, 5443.

**Holtes,** *s. pl.* plantations, C 6996.

**Homager,** *s.* vassal, 3288.

**Hoolly,** *adv.* wholly, 1970.

**Hoomly,** *adj.* homely, familiar, C 6320.

**Hoor,** *adj.* gray-haired, C 6335; Hore, *adj.* hoary, gray, 3196; *pl.* hoary (a frequent epithet of trees, perhaps with reference to trees of great age), C 6996.

**Hornpypes,** *s. pl.* musical instruments, formed of pipes made of horn, 4250.

**Hostilers,** *s. as adj. pl.* keeping an inn, C 7033.

**Hoteth,** *pr. s.* promises, 5422; *pr. pl.* 5444.

**Housel,** *v.* give the Host (to), C 6438.

**Hulstred,** *pp.* concealed, hidden, C 6146.

**Humanitee,** *s.* human nature, 5655.

**Hy,** *s.* haste; *in hy,* in haste, 2393, 3591.

## I.

**Ich,** *pron.* I, C 6787.

**If,** *conj.* if (i. e. if the matter be wisely inquired into), 4454.

**Imped,** *pp.* engrafted, 5137.

**Impes,** *s. pl.* grafts, C 6293.

**Importable,** *adj.* insufferable, C 6902.

In-fere, *adv.* together, 4827.
Isse, *v.* issue, 1992.

## J.

Jangleth, *pr. s.* prattles, C 7540.
Jangling, *s.* prating, chattering, C 5852 ;
  *pl.* idle words, C 6711.
Jape, *s.* jest, C 7519 ; *pl.* tricks, C 6835.
Jape, 1 *pr. s.* mock, scoff at, C 6471.
Jolily, *adv.* after a jolly sort, C 7031 ;
  pleasantly, 2248 ; nicely, neatly, 2284 ;
  deservedly, C 7664.
Joly, *adj.* fine, gay, C 7248.
Jolynesse, *s.* jolliness, joy, 2302.
Joweles, *s. pl.* jewels, 2092, 5420.
Joyne, 1 *pr. s.* enjoin, 2355.
Jupartye, *s.* jeopardy, 2666.

## K.

Kembe, *imp. s.* comb, 2284.
Kenne, *v.* show, teach, 2476.
Kepe, *s.* heed, 3475.
Kepe, *v.* keep ; *kepe forth*, perpetuate,
  4854 ; 1 *pr. s.* care, C 6440 ; keep, 3476 ;
  care, wish, C 6083 ; *pr. pl.* care, C 6093.
Kernels, *s. pl.* battlements, 4195.   F. text,
  *les creniaus.*
Kerving, *pres. pl. as adj.* cutting, 3813.
Kesse, *v.* kiss, 2006.
Kid, *pp.* made known, 2172 ; evident, 3132.
Kirked, *adj.* crooked (?), 3137.
Knet, *pp.* knit, fastened, 4700, 4811 ; *pp.
  pl.* fast bound, 2092.
Knewe, 1 *pt. s. subj.* disclosed, C 6090.
Knopped, *pp.* fastened, C 7260.   A *knoppe*
  is properly a button ; hence *knoppen*, to
  fasten with a button.

## L.

Laas, *s.* toils, snare, C 6029, 6648 ; Lace,
  cord, string, C 7373 ; net, 2792 ; snare,
  5093.
Laced, *pp.* entangled, caught, 3178.
Lakke, 2 *pr. pl.* blame, 4804.
Lambren, *s. pl.* lambs, C 7013.
Largesse, *s.* liberality, 2354 ; C 5853.
Las, *s.* net, 2790.   See Laas, Lace.
Late, *ger.* to let, permit, allow, 3145, C
  6676 ; *v.* let, 5574 ; Lat. *pr. s.* lets remain,
  5493.
Lauhwith, *pr. s.* laughs, 2294.
Lay, *s.* law, religious belief, C 6749.
Leef, *adj.* willing, 2335.
Lees, *s. pl.* lies ; *withouten lees*, truly,
  3904, 5728.

Leful, *adj.* allowable, permissible, 5195.
  Lit. 'leave-ful.'
Leggen, *ger.* ease, relieve, 5016.   (Short
  for *aleggen*.)
Lemes, *s. pl.* rays, 5346.
Lemman, *s.* sweetheart, C 6056, 6305.
Lene, *v.* lend, 3053, C 7026.
Lening ; *in lening*, as a loan, 2373.
Lepand, *pres. part.* running (with short
  jumps), 1928.
Lere, *ger.* to teach, 2143, 2149 ; *v.* teach,
  5152 ; learn, 2451, 4808.
Lered, *adj.* learned, C 6217.
Lese, *v.* lose, C 5915, 5924 ; *pr. s.* 2149.
Lesing, *s.* lie, falsehood, 2174, 4835.
Let, *pr. s.* leads (his life), C 6111.
Lete, *v.* cease, 2463 ; leave C 6457 ; let
  alone, C 6556 ; abandon, C 6169 ; allow,
  permit, 6458 ; 1 *pr. s.* leave, C 6354 ;
  abandon, C 6997 ; *pp.* let, 1791.
Lette, *s.* let, hindrance, 3756.
Letten, *v.* hinder, 3590 ; delay, 3940 ;
  stop, 1832 ; cease, 2807 ; desist, 1832.
Letting, *s.* hindrance, C 5931.
Lettrure, *s.* literature, writing, C 6751.
Leve, *v.* believe, 3303.
Leve, *v.* live, 2336.
Lever, *adv.* rather, C 6793 ; *me were lever*,
  I had rather, C 6168.
Lewd, *adj.* lay (folk), the ignorant, C
  6217.
Lewedist, *adj. superl.* most ignorant,
  4802.
Leye, *pt. pl.* lay, lived, C 6572.
Liche, *adv.* alike, equally, 4160.
Ligging, *pr. pt.* lying down, 4002.
Likerous, *adj.* licentious, 4264.
Likly, *adj.* similar, 4852.
Lisse, *v.* abate, 4128 ; *ger.* to be eased, to
  feel relief, 3758.
List, *s.* pleasure, will, 1957.
List, *pr. s.* wishes, C 6139.
Loigne, *s.* tether, 3382, C 7050.
Loke, *pp.* locked up, 2092.
Long ; *of long passed*, of old, 3377.
Longith, *pr. s.* befits, 2321.
Loos, *s.* renown, reputation, 2310, C 6103 ;
  ill fame, C 7081.
Lorn, *pp.* lost, 4327, 4502, 4508, C 5973.
Losengeours, *s. pl.* deceivers, 2693.
Loteby, *s.* paramour, C 6339.
Lough, *pt. s.* laughed, C 7295.
Loure, *pr. s. subj.* scowl, C 7049.
Loute, *v.* bow, 4384 ; bow down, C 7336 ;
  *pr. pl. subj.* bow down, C 6917.
Lowe, *ger.* to appraise, i.e. to be valued
  at, 4532.
Luce, *s.* pike (fish), C 7039.

**Lyflode,** *s.* livelihood, 5602, C 6663.
**Lyken,** *v.* please, 1854, C 6131.
**Lyte,** *adj.* little, small, 2279, 3557 ; *adv.* C 7551.
**Lythe,** *adj.* delicate, 3762.

## M.

**Maat,** *adj.* bewildered, overcome, 1739. See **Mate.**
**Maistryse,** *s.* strength, dominion, 4172.
**Make,** *ger.* to cause, C 5931 ; *pr. pl.* propound, C 6186.
**Male,** *s.* bag, wallet, 3263 ; money-bag, C 6376.
**Maltalent,** *s.* ill-humour, 3438.
**Mangonel,** *s.* a military engine on the principle of the sling-staff for casting stones, a catapult, C 6279.
**Mar,** *adj.* greater, 2215 ; *adv.* more, 1854.
**Marchandise,** *s.* barter, C 5902.
**Mare,** *adv.* more, 2709.
**Markes,** *pl.* marks (coins), C 5986.
**Marreth,** *pr. s.* disfigures, 4679.
**Mate,** *adj.* distracted, 5099 ; downcast, 4671 ; dispirited, 3167, 3190. See **Maat.**
**Maugree,** *s.* ill-will, 4399 ; reproach, 3144 ; *prep.* in spite of, C 6711 ; *maugre youres,* in spite of you, C 7645.
**Mayme,** *v.* maim, C 6620 ; *pr. s.* wounds, 5317. See **Meygned.**
**Maysondewe,** *s.* hospital, 5619.
**Medle,** *v.* interfere, 3788 ; **Medle,** *v. refl.* meddle ; *m. him of,* deal with, C 6050 ; *to medle,* for meddling, 4545.
**Meke,** *v.* mollify, 3394 ; have mercy, 3541 ; **Meked,** *pt. s. refl.* humbled himself, 3584.
**Mendience,** *s.* beggary, mendicancy, C 6657, 6707.
**Mene,** *s.* mean, middle state, C 6527.
**Mene,** *adj.* middle, mean, 4844.
**Mene,** 1 *pr. s.* bemoan, 2596.
**Menour,** Minorite, Franciscan friar, C 6338.
**Mes** ; *s. at good mes,* at a favourable opportunity, 3462. O. F. *mes.*
**Mete,** *adj.* meet, fitted, 1799.
**Mete,** *v.* meet, succeed, 4571.
**Mevable,** *adj.* moveable, 4736.
**Meve,** *v.* move, incite, 2327.
**Mewe,** *s.* coop, cage (a falconry term), 4778.
**Meygned,** *pp.* hurt, maimed, 3356. See **Mayme.**
**Meynee,** *s.* household, C 6870, 7156.
**Meynt,** *pp.* mingled, 1920 ; Meynd, 2296.
**Mich,** *adj.* many, 2258, 5555.
**Micher,** *s.* thief, C 6541.

**Miches,** *s. pl.* small loaves of finest wheaten flour, 5585.
**Mis,** *adj.* amiss, wrong, 3243.
**Mischeef,** *s.* misfortune, C 6731.
**Misericorde,** *s.* mercy, 3577.
**Misseying,** *s.* evil-speaking, 2207.
**Mister,** *s.* occupation, trade, C 6976 ; *whatever mister,* of every kind of occupation, C 6332.
**Mistere,** *s.* need, C 7409.
**Miswey,** *adv.* astray, 4764.
**Mixens,** *s. pl.* dunghills, C 6496.
**Mo,** *adj. pl.* others besides, 3023 ; more (in number), C 5990.
**Mochel,** *adj.* great, 3117 ; *to m.,* too much, 3442.
**Moeble,** *s.* moveable property, C 6045.
**Moeve,** *v.* move, i. e. prefer, make, C 6039.
**Moneste,** 1 *pr. s.* admonish, charge, 3579.
**Monyours,** *s. pl.* coiners, C 6811.
**Mot,** *pr. s.* must, 3784 ; *so mote I go,* as I hope to walk about, C 6591.
**Mowe,** *v.* be able, 2644.
**Musard,** *s.* muser, dreamer, C 7562 ; sluggard, 3256, 4034 ; dolt, C 7562.
**Muwis,** *s. pl.* bushels, 5590.

## N.

**Nathelesse,** nevertheless, C 6195.
**Ne,** *conj.* unless, 4858.
**Nede,** *adv.* necessarily, C 7633.
**Nedely,** *adv.* needs must, C 6117.
**Neden,** *v.* be necessary, C 5990.
**Nedes,** *s. pl.* necessities, C 6174.
**Nedes,** *adv.* of necessity, 1792.
**Neer,** *adv.* nearer, 1708. See **Nerre.**
**Neigh it nere,** *v.* approach it more nearly, 2003.
**Nempned,** *pp.* named, mentioned, C 6224.
**Nere,** were not, were it not for, 2778 ; were there not, 2778 ; had it not been for, C 7328.
**Nerre,** *adj. comp.* nearer, 5101.
**Neven,** *v.* name, C 5962 ; recount, C 7071.
**Nil,** *pr. s.* will not, C 5821, 6045.
**Nomen,** *pt. pl.* took, C 7423 ; *pp.* taken, 5404.
**Noncerteyne,** *adj.* uncertain, 5426.
**Nones,** for the, for the nonce, occasionally, C 7387.
**Nonne,** *s.* nun, C 6350.
**Noot,** 1 *pr. s.* know not, C 6367.
**Noriture,** *s.* bringing up, C 6728.
**Norys,** *s.* nurse, 5418.
**Not,** 1 *pr. s.* know not, 5191.
**Note-kernel,** *s.* nut-kernel, C 7117.
**Noye,** *s.* hurt, 3772.

**Noyen,** *ger.* to vex, 4416.
**Noyous,** *adj.* harmful, 3230, 4449.
**Noyse,** *s.* evil report, 3971.
**Nyce,** *adj.* foolish, silly, 4262, 4877, C 6944.
**Nycetee,** *s.* foolishness, 5525.
**Nyghe,** *v.* approach, 1775.


### O.

**Obeysshing,** *s.* submission, 3380.
**Of,** *prep.* out of, owing to, 3981; concerning (Lat. *de*), 4884; off, 5470; (some) of, (part) of, 1993. Or it may mean 'by,' 'on account of.'
**Offense,** *s.* discomfort, 5677.
**Of-newe,** *adv.* newly, afresh, 5169.
**Onlofte,** *prep.* aloft, on high, 5503.
**Oon,** *adj.* one, 4812; *in oon,* without change, 3779.
**Ostages,** *s. pl.* hostages, 2064, C 7311.
**Other-gate,** *adv.* otherwise, 2158.
**Ought,** *adv.* in any way, C 6096.
**Outake,** *prep.* except, 4474.
**Outerly,** *adv.* wholly, utterly, 3489, 3742.
**Outrage,** *s.* wrong, 2082, 2086; scandalous life, 4927; outrageous deeds, C 6024 (mistranslated).
**Outrageous,** *adj.* exceeding great, 2602; ill-behaved, 2192.
**Outslinge,** *v.* fling out, C 5987.
**Out-take,** *prep.* except, C 5819.
**Over-al,** *adv.* everywhere, 3050, 3914.
**Overgo,** *v.* pass away, 3784; *pr. pl.* trample on, C 6821.
**Overwhelme,** *v.* roll over, 3775.
**Ow,** 1 *pr. s.* ought, 4413.


### P.

**Palasyns,** *adj. pl.* belonging to the palace; *ladyes palasyns,* court ladies, C 6862.
**Papelard,** *s.* hypocrite, deceiver, C 7283.
**Papelardye,** *s.* hypocrisy, C 6796.
**Parage,** *s.* parentage, descent, 4759.
**Par-amour,** with devotion, 2830.
**Paramour,** *s.* paramour, lover, 5060.
**Paramours,** *adv.* with a lover's affection, 4657.
**Parceners,** *s. pl.* partners, C 6952.
**Parcuere,** *adv.* by heart, 4796.
**Pardee,** F. *pardieu,* 4433, C 5913.
**Parfay,** by my faith, C 6058.
**Part,** *s.* duty, 5032.
**Parte,** *v.* divide, 5283.
**Party,** *s.* part; *in party,* partially, 5338.
**Parvys,** *s.* room over a church-porch, C 7108.

**Pas;** *a pas,* apace, quickly, 3724.
**Passaunt,** *adj.* surpassing, 3110.
**Passe,** *v.* penetrate, 1751.
**Patre,** *v.* recite the paternoster, C 6794.
**Pay,** *s.* satisfaction, C 5938; liking, taste, 1721; *me to pay,* to my satisfaction, C 6985.
**Paye,** *ger.* to appease, 3599.
**Peire,** *v.* damage, C 6103.
**Peire of bedis,** *s.* rosary, C 7372.
**Pens,** *s. pl.* pence, C 5987.
**Pensel,** *s.* a standard, ensign, or banner, (particularly of bachelors-in-arms), a pennoncel, C 6280.
**Pepir,** *s.* pepper, (metaphorically) mischief, C 6028.
**Perauntre,** *adv.* peradventure, 5192.
**Percas,** *adv.* perchance, C 6647.
**Persaunt,** *adj.* piercing, 2809; sharp, 4179.
**Pese,** *ger.* to appease, 3397.
**Pesible,** *adj.* peaceable, gentle, C 7413.
**Peyne,** *s.* penalty, C 6626; pain, hardness, 2120; *up peyne,* on pain (of death), C 6617.
**Peyne,** *v. refl.* endeavour, C 7512; *pr. s. refl.* takes pains, C 6014.
**Piment,** *s.* spiced wine or ale, C 6027.
**Pitous,** *adj.* excusable, deserving pity, 4734; merciful, C 6161.
**Plat,** *adv.* flat, flatly, 1734, C 7526.
**Pleyne,** *v.* lament, complain, 2299, C 6405.
**Pleynt,** *s.* complaint, C 6012.
**Plight,** *pt. s.* plucked, 1745.
**Plongeth,** *pr. s.* plunges, 5472.
**Plyte,** *s.* affair, C 5827.
**Poeste,** *s.* power, virtue, 2095.
**Pole,** *s.* pool, C 5966.
**Port,** *s.* demeanour, manner, 2038, 2192; Porte, 4622.
**Porte-colys,** *s.* portcullis, 4168.
**Possed,** *pp.* pushed, tossed, 4479; *pp.* driven, 4625.
**Potente,** *s.* crutch, C 7417.
**Poustee,** *s.* power, influence, C 6533, 6957, 7679; dominion, C 6484.
**Povert,** *s.* poverty, C 6181.
**Prece,** *ger.* to press, 4198.
**Predicacioun,** *s.* preaching, 5763.
**Preise,** 1 *pr. s.* value, appraise, 4850.
**Prese,** *v.* press; *pr. s.* intrudes, C 7627; *pr. pl.* intrude, C 7629; *imp. s.* endeavour, 2899.
**Pressure,** *s.* wine-press, 3692.
**Preve,** *v.* prove, 4170.
**Preving,** *s.* proof, C 7543.
**Preyse,** 1 *pr. s.* value, esteem, 1983. F. *pris.*

Prike, *imp. s.* gallop, 2314.

Pris, *s.* esteem, 2310.

Privetee, *s.* secret, 5526, C 6878, 6882.

Procuratour, *s.* a collector of alms for hospitals or sick persons, C 6974.

Propre, *adj.* own, C 6565, 6592.

Provable, *adj.* capable of proof, 5414.

Provende, *s.* allowance, stipend, C 6931.

Prow, *s.* profit, gain, 5806, 1940.

Pryme temps, first beginning, 4534 ; the spring, 4747.

Prys, *s.* praise, 1972 ; price, C 5927.

Pugnaunt, *adj.* poignant, keen, 1879.

Pullaille, *s.* poultry, C 7043.

Pulle, *v.* pluck, strip, C 5984 ; *pr. pl.* flay, strip, C 6820.

Puple, *s.* people, rabblement, C 7159.

Purchas, *s.* acquisition, C 6838.

Purchasen, *ger.* to procure, C 6607.

Purpryse, *s.* park, enclosure, 3987, 4171.

Purveaunce, *s.* provision, C 7326.

Purveye, *ger.* to procure, 3339.

Put, *pr. s.* puts, 3556, 4444, C 5949.

Pyne, *s.* endeavour, 1798 ; misery, C 6499.

Pynen, *v.* torment, punish, 3511.

### Q.

Quarels, *s. pl.* square-headed crossbow-bolts, 1823.

Quarteyne, *adj. as s.* quartan fever or ague, 2401.

Queme, *ger.* to please, C 7270.

Quenche, *v.* be quenched, 5324.

Quene, *s.* quean, concubine, C 7032.

Querrour, *s.* quarry-man, hewer of stone, 4149.

Quethe ; *I quethe him quyte,* I cry him quit, C 6999.

Queynt, *adj.* elegant, 2251 ; curious, fanciful, C 6342 ; strange, 5199 ; pleased, 3079 ; shewing satisfaction, 2038.

Queyntly, *adv.* neatly, easily, 4322.

Queyntyse, *s.* elegance, 2250.

Quik, *adj.* alive, 3523, 4070, 5056.

Quitly, *adv.* quite, entirely, C 5843.

Quitte, *pl. s. reflex.* ; *quitte him,* acquitted himself, 3069 ; *pp.* requited, 3146, 6088 ; made amends for, 2599 ; rid, 1852.

Quook, 1 *pt. s.* quaked, 3163 ; *pt. pl.* 3966.

Quyte, *pp. as adj.* quit, C 5904 ; free, C 5910 ; entire, 2375.

Quyte, *v.* acquit, release, C 6032 ; fulfil, 5032 ; 1 *pr. s.* C 6412 ; *imp. s.* 2222, 1392.

### R.

Racyne, *s.* root, 4881.

Rage, *s.* rage, spite, 3809 ; malignity, venom, 1916 ; madness, 3292 ; *in r.,* mad, 4523.

Ramage, *adj.* wild, 5384.  O. F. *ramage.*

Rape, *s.* haste, 1929.

Rape, *adv.* quickly, C 6516.

Rathe, *adj.* early, C 6650.

Ravisable, *adj.* greedy for prey, C 7016.

Ravyne, *s.* plunder, C 6813.

Rebel, *adj.* rebellious, C 6400.

Recche ; *what recchith me,* what care I, 3447.

Recreaundyse, *s.* cowardice, 2107, 4038.

Recreaunte, *s.* coward, 4090.

Recured, *pp.* recovered, 4920, 5124.

Rede, *s.* good advice, 3859 ; Reed, C 7328.

Rede, 1 *pr. s.* advise, 1932 ; read, 1819.

Reed, *s.* advice, C 7328 ; Rede, 3859.

Refreyne, *ger.* to bridle, C 7511.

Reft, *s.* rift, 2661.

Refte, 2 *pt. pl.* deprived, 3562.

Refuyt, *s.* refuge, escape, 3840.

Rehete, *v.* cheer, console, C 6509.

Reisins, *s. pl.* fresh grapes, 3659.

Relees, *s.* relief, 2612 ; release, 4440.

Relesse, 1 *pr. s.* give up, C 6999.

Religioun, *s.* religious order, 3715; monastic life, C 6155.

Religious, *adj.* pious, C 6236 ; *as s.* a nun, C 6347 ; R. folk, monastics, C 6149.

Remued, *pt. s.* moved, C 7432.

Rendre, *v.* recite, 4800.

Reneyed, 1 *pt. s. subj.* should renounce, C 6787.

Repeire, *v.* return, 3573, 4131.

Repreef, *s.* reproach, 4974, C 7240.

Repreve, *s.* reproach, 5261 ; Reprove, upbraiding, 5525.

Requere, *pr. s. subj.* request, ask, 5233 ; *pp.* asked, 5277.

Rescous, *s.* service, endeavour to support, C 6749.

Resonables, *adj. pl.* reasonable, C 6760.

Resoun, *s.* correct manner, 2151.

Reveth, *pr. s.* takes away, C 6254 ; *pt. s.* bereaved, 4351.

Reverte, *v.* bring back, C 7188.

Revolucioun, *s.* revolution, turn (of fortune's wheel), 4366.

Reward, *s.* regard, consideration, 3832.

Rewe, *v.* rue, be sorry, 4060 ; *it wol me rewe,* I shall be sorry, 5170.

Reyne, *v.* rain down, fall as rain, 1822.

Reynes, Rennes (in Brittany), 3826.

Ribaned, *pp.* adorned with lace (of gold), 4752.

Ribaud, *s.* labourer, 5673; *pl.* ribalds, C 7302.

Ribaudye, *s.* ribaldry, 2224; riotous living, 4926.

Right, *adv.* just, exactly, 5347; quite, C 6398, 6411; *right nought*, not at all, 2071.

Rimpled, *adj.* wrinkled, 4495.

Riveling, *pres. part.* puckering, C 7262.

Rochet, *s.* linen garment, 4754.

Rode, *s. dat.* rood, cross, C 6564.

Rody, *adj.* ruddy, 3629.

Roignous, *adj.* scurvy, rotten, C 6190.

Roking, *pres. part.* rocking, quivering, trembling, 1906. Cf. Shak. *Lucr.* 262.

Ronne, *pp.* advanced, 4495.

Roser, *s.* rose-bush, 1789, 1826, 1833, 2967.

Rought, 1 *pt. s.* recked, heeded, 1873; 1 *pt. s. subj.* should not care, C 7061.

Rowe, *adj. pl.* rough, 1838.

Rude, *adj. as pl. s.* common people, 2268.

Ryve, *v.* pierce, C 7161; be torn, 5393; Ryveth, *pr. s.* is torn, 5718.

### S.

Sad, *adj.* serious, staid, composed, 4627; *pl.* grievous, C 6907.

Sadnesse, *s.* sobriety, discretion, 4940.

Sailen, *v.* assail, C 7338.

Sakked Freres, *Fratres de Sacco*, Friars of the Sack, C 7462.

Salowe, *adj.* sallow; *but read* falowe, i. e. fallow, C 7392.

Salue, *ger.* to salute, 2218; *pr. s. subj.* 2220.

Samons, *s. pl.* salmon, C 7039.

Sat, *pt. s. impers.* suited, 3810.

Sautere, *s.* psalter, C 7371.

Say, 1 *pt. s.* saw, 1722; Sawe, *pt. s. subj.* saw, 1719.

Say, (*for* Assay), *v.* essay, attempt, endeavour, 5162.

Saynt, *adj.* girded, girdled (?), C 7408.

Scantilone, *s.* pattern, C 7064.

Scole, *s.* scholarship, learning, 3274.

Score, *s.* crack (or hole) in a wall, 2660.

Scrippe, *s.* scrip, wallet, C 7405.

Secree, *adj.* secret, 5257.

Secree, *s.* secret, 5260.

Secte, *s.* class, category, 5745; *gen.* of (our) race, 4859.

Seden, *v.* bear seed, fructify, 4344.

See, *pr. s. subj.* see; *so god me see*, as (I hope) God may protect me, 5693.

Seer, *adj.* sere, dry, 4749.

Seignorye, *s.* dominion, 3213.

Seke, *adj.* sick, 5729, 5733; *pl.* 4829.

Semblable, *adj.* similar, C 5911.

Semblable, *adj. as s.* resemblance, one like himself, 4855; *pl.* like (cases), C 6759.

Semblant, *s.* appearance, disguise, C 6202; (his) hypocrisy, C 7449; seeming, 3205, 3957.

Sen, *conj.* since, 1984.

Sentence, *s.* meaning, C 7474; *pl.* opinions, C 5813.

Sermoneth, *pr. s.* sermonizes, preaches, C 6219.

Servage, *s.* servitude, 4382, 5807.

Serviable, *adj.* serviceable, C 6004.

Sette, *v.* fasten (an accusation), 3328; Set, *pr. s.* places, 4925, 4957; *pt. pl.* besieged, C 7344; *pp.* established, 2077.

Seure, *adj.* sure, 4304.

Seurere, *adj. comp.* surer, more secure, C 5958.

Seynt Amour, William St. Amour, C 6781. (He wrote against the friars who advocated the Eternal Gospel.)

Shende, *v.* shame, put to shame, 3116; *ger.* to injure, 2953; *pr. s.* ruins, 4776, 5310; *pp.* disgraced, ruined, 3479, 3933.

Shene, *adj.* fair, 3713.

Shere, *pr. s. subj.* can cut, shear, 4335; may shave, C 6196.

Shete, *ger.* to shoot, 1798; Shet, *pt. s.* shot, 1727, 1777.

Shette, *ger.* to shut, 4224; *v.* shut up, 2091; *pr. pl.* shut up, 5771; Shet, *pp.* shut, 4368.

Shewing, *s.* demeanour, 4041.

Shitteth, *pr. s.* shuts, 4100; Shit, *pp.* shut up, 2767.

Shoon, *s. pl.* shoes, 2265.

Shrewis, *s. pl.* knaves, C 6876.

Shrift-fader, *s.* confessor, C 6423.

Shryve, *v.* hear confessions, C 6364.

Sigh, 1 *pt. s.* saw, 1822.

Sight, 1 *pt. s.* sighed, 1746.

Sikerer, *adj. comp.* safer, C 7310.

Sikerest, *adj. superl.* securest, C 6147.

Sikernesse, *s.* certainty, 1935, 2365.

Sikirly, *adv.* certainly, C 6906.

Similacioun, *s.* dissimulation, C 7230.

Simplesse, *s.* Simplicity (the name of an arrow), 1774; simplicity, C 6381.

Sire, *s.* father; *sire ne dame*, neither father nor mother, C 5887.

Sith, *conj.* since, 1964, 4367, C 6266.

Sithen, *adv.* afterwards, 1999, C 7130.

Sitte, *pr. pl. subj.* sit, fit, 2267; Sittand, *pres. pt.* (Northern) fitting, 2263; Sitting, *pres. pt.* fitting, suitable, 3654; befitting, 2309, 4675.

Skaffaut, *s.* scaffold, a shed on wheels with a ridged roof, under cover of which the battering ram was used, 4176.

Skile, *s.* reason, 3120, 4543 ; avail, 1951.

Slake, *v.* abate, 3108.

Sleen, *ger.* to slay, C 7195 ; *pr. s.* 2590.

Sleighe, *adj.* sly, cunning, C 7257.

Sleightes, *s. pl.* missiles, C 7071 ; tricks, C 6371.

Slo, *v.* slay, 3150, 4592 ; *ger.* 5521 ; Sloo, *v.* 1953, 3523 ; Slo, *pr. s. subj.* 4992, 5643.

Slomrest, 2 *pr. s.* slumberest, 2567.

Slowe, *s.* moth, 4751. F. *taigne.*

Smete, *pp.* smitten, 3755.

Snibbe, *v.* snub, reproach, 4533.

Sojour, *s.* sojourn, 4282 ; dwelling, 5150.

Solempnely, *adv.* publicly, with due publicity, C 6766.

Soleyn, *adj.* sullen, 3896.

Sophyme, *s.* sophism, C 7471.

Sore, *adv.* closely, strictly, 2055 ; ardently, 2075.

Sote, *adj.* sweet, 4880.

Soth-sawe, *s.* truth-telling, C 6125, 6130, 7590.

Sotilly, *adv.* subtly, 4395.

Soudiours, *s. pl.* soldiers, 4234.

Spanishing, *s.* expanding, expansion, 3633. O.F. *espanir,* to expand.

Sparred, *pt. s.* locked, fastened, 3320.

Sparth, *s.* a battle-ax, C 5978.

Spered, *pp.* (*for* sperred), fastened, locked (F. *senti la clef*), 2099.

Sperhauke, *s.* sparrowhawk, 4033.

Spille, *v.* kill, 1953 ; destroy, 2162 ; *ger.* to surrender to destruction, 5441 ; *pt. s.* spoiled, 5136 ; *pp.* exhausted, 4786.

Spitel, *s.* hospital, C 6505.

Springe, *pr. pl.* grow, increase, C 5988 ; *pp.* advanced, C 6954.

Springoldes, *s. pl.* catapults, 4191.

Squared, *pp.* cut square, 4155.

Squierly, *adj.* like a squire, C 7415.

Squyre, *s.* square (carpenter's square), C 7064.

Stant, *pr. s.* stands, waits, 5004.

Stark, *adj.* downright, C 7292.

Stede, *s.* place, C 5898.

Stille or loude, silently or aloud, under all circumstances, C 7532.

Stinten, *v.* cease, C 6849 ; *pp.* stopped, C 6473.

Stonde forth, *ger.* to stand out, persist, 3547 ; Stont, *pr. s.* stands, consists, 5581 ; Stant, *pr. s.* waits, 5004.

Stounde, *s.* hour, time, 1733 ; *pl.* hours, 2639.

Stounde, *s.* ; (probably an error for *wounde,* wound), 4472.

Stoundemele, *adj.* momentary, 3784.

Stoundemele, *adv.* hourly, from one hour to another, 2304.

Stoutnesse, *s.* pride, obstinacy, 1936.

Streite, *adj.* close-fitting, 2271.

Strene, *s.* strain, breed, 4859. A.S. *strēona.*

Strepe, *v.* strip, fleece, C 6818.

Streyne, *v.* constrain, compel, C 6406 ; *pt. s.* urged, C 7631.

Streyned-Abstinence, Constrained Abstinence, C 7325.

Stuffen, *pr. pl.* provide with defenders, C 6290. F. text, *corent les murs garnir.*

Suen, *v.* pursue, seek, 4953.

Suffraunce, *s.* patience, submission, 3463.

Suspecious, *adj.* suspect, open to suspicion, C 6110.

Sustening, *s.* sustenance, C 6697.

Swelte, 2 *pr. s. subj.* die, 2480.

Swete, 2 *pr. s. subj.* sweat, feel heat, 2480.

Swink, *s.* toil, labour, C 6596.

Swinke, *v.* labour, C 6619 ; *ger.* to toil, 2151, 5685 ; *pr. s.* toils, 5675.

Swinker, *s.* toiler, C 6857.

Swinking, *s.* toiling, C 6703.

Swoning, *s.* swooning, swoon, 1737.

Sy, i. e. if (F. *si*), i. e. haphazard, 5741.

Sythes, *pl.* times, 2048, 4868 ; Many sythe, often, 2257.

## T.

Take, *v.* lay hold, 5351 ; take arms, 3529 ; hand over, C 7265 ; *v. refl.* surrender, 1947 ; *t. on hem,* apply to themselves, C 6107 (F. text, *sur eus riens n'en prendront*); *pr. s.* betakes, commits himself, C 6442 ; *pp.* taken ; *him take,* betaken himself, C 7280 ; Tan, *pp.* C 5894.

Takel, *s.* weapon, arrow, 1729, 1863.

Tale, *s.* reckoning ; *yeve I litel tale,* I pay little heed, C 6375.

Talent, *s.* good will, inclination, C 6134 ; fancy, C 7110 ; longing, 3472 ; desire, intent, 1716 ; spirit, disposition, C 7674.

Tan, *pp.* taken, C 5894. See Take.

Tapinage, *s.* hiding ; *in tapinage,* sneakingly, C 7363.

Tatarwagges, *s. pl.* fluttering tatters, C 7259.

Taylagiers, *s. pl.* tax-gatherers, C 6811.

Tecche, *s.* fault, bad habit, 5166 ; *pl.* C 6517.

Teched, *pt. s.* taught, C 6680.

Telle, *v.* account, 5053.

**Templers,** *s. pl.* Knights-Templars, C 6693.

**Temprure,** *s.* tempering, mixing, 4177.

**Temps,** *s.* time; *at prime temps,* at the first time, at first, 3373.

**Tene,** *s.* ruin, blight, 4750.

**Tespye,** *v.* to espye, 3156.

**Than,** *conj.* than if, 4328.

**Thank,** *s.* thanks, 4584; (F. text, *son gré deservir*); good will, 2698, 2700; *in thank,* with thanks, with good will, 2115, 4577; Thankes, *pl.* thanks, 2036; *thy thankis,* with thy good will, 2463.

**Thar,** *adv.* there, 1853, 1857.

**Thar,** *pr. s. impers.* needs; *you thar,* you need, 3604.

**Thee,** *v.* thrive; *so mote I thee,* as I hope to thrive, 3086, 4841, C 5899.

**Thempryse** (*for* The empryse), the custom, 2286.

**Ther-geyn,** *prep.* against this, C 6555.

**Thilke,** *pron.* that, 2106, C 5980.

**Thing,** *s. pl.* things, property, C 6670.

**Thinges,** *s. pl.* business, doings, C 6037.

**This,** *for* this is, C 6057, 6452.

**Thought,** *s.* the object of thought personified(?), 2473. (But a corrupt reading; read *That swete,* answering to *S'amie* in the F. text.)

**Threste,** 1 *pr. s.* thrust, C 6825.

**Thringe,** *ger.* to thrust, C 7419.

**Thritty,** *adj.* thirty, 4211.

**Throwe,** *s.* moment, 1771, 3867.

**Thrust,** *s:* thirst, 4722.

**Thurgh-sought,** *pp.* examined thoroughly, 4948.

**Til,** *prep.* to; *him til,* to him, 4594.

**Tilier,** *s.* tiller, husbandman, 4339.

**To-beten,** *pp.* belaboured, C 6126.

**Tobeye,** to obey, 3534.

**To-drawe,** *pp.* torn in pieces, C 6126.

**Toforn,** *prep.* before, 2969; God toforn, in the sight of God, C 7198.

**Token,** *pt. pl.* took (i. e. took Christ to witness, appealed to Christ), C 7122. (The translation is entirely wrong; hence the lack of sense.)

**Tolde,** *pp.* (*error for* Told), told, C 6598.

**To-me-ward,** towards me, 3354, 3803.

**To-moche-Yeving,** Giving too much, C 5837.

**Ton, the,** the one, 5217; *the toon,* 5559.

**To-quake,** *v.* quake greatly; *al to-quake,* tremble very much, 2527.

**To-shake,** *v.* shake to the foundations, ruin, C 5981.

**To-shar,** *pt. s.* lacerated, cut in twain, 1858.

**To-shent,** *pp.* undone; *al to-shent,* utterly undone, 1903.

**Touret,** *s.* turret, 4164.

**Tourn,** *s.* turn, 5470.

**Trace,** *v.* walk, go about, C 6745; *pr. pl.* walk, live, 5753.

**Transmewe,** *v.* transmute, be changed, 2526.

**Trasshed,** *pp.* betrayed, 3231.

**Trechour,** *s.* traitour, C 7216; cheat, C 6602.

**Tree,** *s.* wood, 1747, 1808, 2408, C 7061.

**Treget,** *s.* trap, snare, C 6312; trickery, guile, C 6267, 6825.

**Tregetours,** *s. pl.* tricksters, C 7587.

**Tregetrye,** *s.* trickery, C 6382; trick, C 6374.

**Trepeget,** *s.* a military engine made of wood, used for hurling large stones and other missiles, a trebuchet, C 6279.

**Trichour,** *adj.* treacherous, 6308.

**Trist,** *v.* trust, 4364; *pp.* 3929.

**Trouble,** *adj.* troubled, 1755.

**Troubler,** *adj. comp.* dimmer, less bright, C 7116.

**Trowandyse,** *s.* knavery, villany, 3954.

**Trowe,** *v.* believe, C 6873.

**Truaunding,** *s.* idling, shirking, C 6721.

**Truaundyse,** *s.* idleness, shirking, C 6664.

**Truaunt,** *s.* idler, loafer, C 6645.

**Tumble,** *v.* cause to tumble, cause to perform athletic feats, C 6836; *ger.* to tumble, 5469.

**Turves,** *s. pl.* sods of turf, C 7062.

**Twinne,** *v.* separate, go apart, 4813; part, 5077; depart, 4367.

## U.

**Unavysed,** *adj.* heedless, indiscreet, foolish, 4739.

**Unbond,** *pt. s.* released, C 6416; *pp.* unfastened, 4700; opened, 2226.

**Unclosed,** *pp.* untied, unfastened, 4698.

**Unclosid,** *pp.* unenclosed, 3921, 3925.

**Undirfongith,** *pr. s.* undertakes, 5709.

**Unese,** *s.* uneasiness, trouble, 3102; discomfort, 2596.

**Unhappe,** *s.* mishap, ill fortune, 5492.

**Unhyde,** *v.* unfold, reveal, 2168.

**Unlefulle,** *adj.* illicit, 4880.

**Unnethe,** *adv.* scarcely, i.e. it will scarcely be, C 6541; Unnethis, hardly, 5461.

**Unrelesed,** *adj.* unrelieved, 2729.

**Unsperd,** *pp.* unbolted, unbarred, 2656.

**Unthrift,** *s.* wastefulness, 4926.

**Unwelde,** *adj.* impotent, feeble, 4886.

Up-caste, *pt. s.* lifted up, C 7129.

Updresse, *v.* set up, prepare, C 7067.

Up-right, *adv.* on thy back, 2561.

Urchouns, *s. pl.* hedgehogs, 3135.

Utter, *adj.* outer, 4208.

## V.

Vailith, *pr. s.* avails, 5765.

Valour, *s.* worth, 5236, 5556; value, 5538.

Vassalage, *s.* prowess, courage, C 5871.

Vekke, *s.* old woman, hag, 4286, 4495.

Vendable, *adj.* venal, vendible, saleable, 5804.

Verger, *s.* orchard, 3234, 3618, 3831, 3851.

Vermayle, *adj.* vermilion, scarlet-red, 3645.

Vilaynsly, *adv.* disgracefully, 3994.

Vileyn, *s.* peasant, yokel, churl, 1990; Vilayns, *gen.* churl's, 1992.

Vitaille, *s.* victuals, delicacies, C 7044.

Voide, *v.* drive away, 5164; *pr. s.* removes, 2833, 2845; *imp. s.* remove, clear, 2283; *imp. pl.* put away, 3571.

Voluntee, *s.* will, desire, 5276.

Vouche, *pr. s.* 1 *per.* vouchsafe; For sauf of cherlis I ne vouche, for I do not vouchsafe, among churls, 2002. (Or read *to* for *of.*)

Vounde, *pp.* (?) well found, hence, excellent, C 7063.

## W.

Wacche, *s.* watching, lying awake, 4132.

Wade, *v.* wade, go about, 5022.

Walkyng, *s.* walking (?), 2682. (Perhaps read *talking*; F. text, *parlers*.)

Walowe, *v.* toss (*or* roll) about, 2362.

Wanhope, *s.* despair, 4432, 4453, 4708.

Wante, *v.* be lacking, 2530.

Ware, *s.* commodity, C 5926.

Warne, *v.* inform, C 7657; *pt. s.* refused, C 5840; *pp.* refused, denied, 2604, 3426, 5245, C 7502.

Wawe, *s.* wave, 4712.

Wayte, *ger.* to beset (me) with, to plot, 3938.

Weder, *s.* storm, 4336.

Weed, *s.* religious habit, C 6359.

Welfaring, *adj.* well-favoured, C 6866. F. text, *beles*.

Wel-Helinge, *s.* Good-concealment, C 5857.

Wene, *s.* expectation, 2046; *withouten wene*, doubtless, 2415, 2668, 2683, 4596.

Wene, *v.* suppose, 2761; (*read* mak'th [him] wene; F. text, *Qu'il se cuide*); *pr.*

*s. subj.* imagine, 5672; Wende, 1 *pt. s.* imagined, 4322.

Wening, *s.* imagination, 2766.

Went, *pp.* departed, turned away, C 6185.

[Went, *pr. s.* turns aside, C 6205.] Supplied by guess.

Were, *s.* distraction (F. *guerre*), 5699; *withouten were*, without doubt (a characteristic expletive phrase, common in Fragment B), 1776, 2568, 2740, 3351, 3452, 4468, 5485, 5657, 5692.

Were, *v.* wear away, devour, 4752; *ger.* to wear, i. e. to wear away (the shore), 4712; *pr. pl.* C 6215; *pt. pl.* C 6244.

Werne, *v.* deny, refuse, 3443, C 6673; *ger.* 3730. See **Warne**.

Werrey, *v.* war against, oppose, C 6926; *ger.* to make war upon, 3251; *pr. s.* wars against, 3699; 1 *pr. pl.* make war, C 7018; Werreyed, *pp.* warred against, 3917.

Wery, *v.* worry, strangle, C 6264.

Wethers, *s. gen.* wether's, sheep's, C 6259.

Weyked, *pp. as adj.* too weak, 4737.

Wher, *conj.* whether, 2617, 5191.

Whetted, *pp.* sharpened, C 6197.

Whitsonday, *s.* Whitsunday, 2278. Cf. 'Garlands, Whitsunday, iijd.'; Brand's Pop. Antiq. s. v. Whitsun-ale.

Whylom, *adv.* sometimes, 4355, 5350; formerly, 4123, C 7090.

Whyte monkes, *s. pl.* Cistercians, i.e. Reformed Benedictines, C 6695.

Wicked-Tonge (F. *Malebouche*), C 7424.

Wight, *s.* man, creature, C 5961.

Wight, *adj.* active, 4761.

Wilfully, *adv.* willingly, 4808, C 5941.

Willen, *v.* desire, 2482.

William, W. Seint Amour, C 6763, 6778.

Wimple, *s.* wimple, 3864. A band usually of linen which covered the neck, and was drawn up over the chin, strained up each side of the face, and generally fastened across the forehead; called also barbe, gorget, or chin-cloth.

Winde, *v.* turn about, 1810; escape, 2056.

Winke, *v.* sleep, 4568; 2 *pr. s. subj.* 2348.

Wis, *adv.* verily, C 6433.

Wite, *v.* know, C 6105, 6208, 6939; Wit, *v.* 3145, 5574; Wist, *pt. pl.* knew, C 5864; Wisten, *pt. pl. subj.* knew, C 6087.

Wone, 1 *pr. s.* dwell, C 6143.

Woning, *s.* dwelling-place, C 6082.

Woning-places, *s. pl.* dwelling-places, C 6119.

Wonnen, *pt. pl.* won, C 6252.

**Wood**, *adj.* mad, 3138, 3776, C 6263; raging, 1921.

**Wook**, 1 *pt. s.* kept awake, watched, 1877.

**Woot**, *pr. s.* knows, 5257.

**Worche**, *v.* work, cause, C 6052.

**Worche**, *v.* deal (with what they have to do), C 6037. MS. G. has *worthe*; *Lat ladies worthe* = let ladies alone. The passage is obscure.

**Worchinges**, *s. pl.* doings, C 6585.

**Worth**, *adj.* worthy, C 7104.

**Wost**, 2 *pr. s.* knowest (thou), 4977; Wostow, knowest thou, C 6075, 6373.

**Woxen**, *pp.* grown, C 7140.

**Wrapped**, *pt. s. subj.* should wrap, C 6260.

**Wratthed**, 1 *pt. s.* made angry, 4108; *pp.* enraged, 3097.

**Wreke**, *pp.* revenged, 3362.

**Wrenche**, *s.* turn, trick, 4292.

**Wreying**, *s.* betraying, disclosure, 5220.

**Writ**, *pr. s.* writes, C 6585.

**Wryen**, *ger.* to cover, C 6684; *v.* disguise, C 6795; cover up, clothe, C 6819 (F. text, *s'afublent*).

**Wrythe**, *v.* twist, 4359.

**Wurching**, *s.* machination, C 6123.

**Wyte**, *s.* blame; *to wyte,* a matter of reproach, 3558.

### Y.

**Yaf**, *pt. s.* gave, 2339, 4500.

**Yalt**, *pr. s. refl.* betakes himself, 4904. See **Yelde**.

**Yate**, *s.* gate, 4230.

**Yates**, *s. pl.* gates (*but miswritten for* gates, i. e. ways), 5722.

**Y-bake**, *pp.* baked, C 7048.

**Y-do**, *pp.* done; *have y-do,* have done! 1941.

**Yë**, *s.* eye, 4264.

**Yedest**, 2 *pt. s.* wentest, 3227; Yede, *pt. s.* went, 5151; has gone, 2585.

**Yeft**, *s.* gift, granting, 3664.

**Yelde**, *v.* yield, 1933; submit (thyself), C 6283; *imp. s.* yield, 1930.

**Yerne**, *adv.* readily, eagerly, C 6719.

**Yerning**, *s.* affection, C 5951.

**Yeten**, *pp.* poured out, 5702. Pp. from A.S. *gēotan.*

**Yeve**, 1 *pr. s.* care, regard, C 6464.

**Yeving**, *s.* giving, C 5907.

**Y-fere**, *adv.* together, in company, 3806.

**Y-holpe**, *pp.* helped, holpen, 5505.

**Ying**, *adj.* young, 2208. A Northern form.

**Y-let**, *pp.* hidden, 5335.

**Yliche**, *adv.* equally, alike, 3630.

**Yolden**, *pp.* requited, 4556. See **Yelde**.

**Yore**, *adv.* long ago, C 7599.

**Youth-hede**, *s.* youthhood, 4931.

**Ypocryte**, *s.* hypocrite, C 6482.

**Yre**, *s.* anger, 3174. F. text, *ire.*

**Y-sene**, *adj.* visible, C 6806.

**Yvel**, *adv.* ill, 5238.

**Y-wis**, *adv.* certainly, 2788, 5554, 579c; C 5825, 5896, 5915, 6879, 6932, 7400, 7564.

### THE END.

PRINTED IN GREAT BRITAIN AT THE UNIVERSITY PRESS, OXFORD
BY JOHN JOHNSON, PRINTER TO THE UNIVERSITY